KEY TO PRONUNCIATIONS

s	see, miss	z	zeal, lazy, those
sh	shoe, push	zh	vision, measure
t	ten, bit		
th	thin, path	ə	occurs only in unaccented syllables and indicates the sound of
ŧh	that, other		
ŭ	up, love		
ū	use, cute		
û	urge, burn		a *in* alone
			e *in* system
v	voice, live		i *in* easily
w	west, away		o *in* gallop
y	yes, young		u *in* circus

B.C.	
600	Ezekiel Babylonians sack Jerusalem Exile in Babylon
	Second Isaiah Cyrus begins Persian Empire Haggai and Zechariah
500	Second temple built
	Nehemiah rebuilds Jerusalem
400	The Law accepted as Scripture
	Alexander conquers East
300	Egypt rules Palestine
	The Prophets accepted as Scripture
200	Syria rules Palestine
	Maccabees Hasmonean rulers
100	
	Romans conquer Palestine
	Herod the Great
	Third temple built
A.D.	
	Jesus' ministry Paul's ministry, letters Gospel of Mark written Romans destroy Jerusalem Matthew, Luke-Acts written
100	The Writings close OT Canon
	Last NT books written

THE INTERPRETER'S DICTIONARY OF THE BIBLE

EDITORIAL BOARD

THE INTERPRETER'S DICTIONARY OF THE BIBLE

An Illustrated Encyclopedia

IDENTIFYING AND EXPLAINING ALL PROPER NAMES AND
SIGNIFICANT TERMS AND SUBJECTS IN
THE HOLY SCRIPTURES, INCLUDING THE APOCRYPHA
With Attention to Archaeological Discoveries and
Researches into the Life and Faith of Ancient Times

IN FOUR VOLUMES

מלאה הארץ דעה את־יהוה

The earth shall be full of the knowledge of the Lord—ISAIAH 11:9*c*

NEW YORK *Abingdon Press* NASHVILLE

Library of Congress Catalog Card Number: 62-9387

SET UP, PRINTED, AND BOUND BY THE PARTHENON PRESS, AT NASHVILLE, TENNESSEE, UNITED STATES OF AMERICA

ABBREVIATIONS

א — Codex Sinaiticus
A — Codex Alexandrinus
AA — *Alttestamentliche Abhandlungen*
AAA — *Annals of Archaeology and Anthropology*
AASOR — *Annual of the American Schools of Oriental Research*
Ab. — Aboth
Add. Esth. — Additions to Esther
AFO — *Archiv für Orientforschung*
AJA — *American Journal of Archaeology*
AJSL — *American Journal of Semitic Languages and Literatures*
AJT — *American Journal of Theology*
Akkad. — Akkadian
Amer. Trans. — *The Complete Bible, an American Translation* (Smith and Goodspeed)
ANEP — J. B. Pritchard, ed., *The Ancient Near East in Pictures*
ANET — J. B. Pritchard, ed., *Ancient Near Eastern Texts*
AO — *Der alte Orient*
APAW — *Abhandlungen der Preussichen Akademie der Wissenschaften*
Apoc. — Apocrypha
Apocal. Bar. — Apocalypse of Baruch
Aq. — Aquila
ʿAr. — ʿAruk
ARAB — D. D. Luckenbill, *Ancient Records of Assyria and Babylonia*
Arab. — Arabic
ʿArak. — ʿArakin
Aram. — Aramaic
ARE — J. H. Breasted, *Ancient Records of Egypt*
ARN — Aboth d'Rabbi Nathan
art. — article
ARW — *Archiv für Religionswissenschaft*
ASAE — *Annales du service des antiquités de l'Égypte*
Asmp. Moses — Assumption of Moses
ASV — American Standard Version (1901)
AT — *Altes* or *Ancien Testament*
ATR — *Anglican Theological Review*
ʿA.Z. — ʿAbodah Zarah

B — Codex Vaticanus
BA — *Biblical Archaeologist*
Bar. — Baruch
Barn. — The Epistle of Barnabas
BASOR — *Bulletin of the American Schools of Oriental Research*
B.B. — Baba Bathra
Bek. — Bekereth
Bel — Bel and the Dragon
Ber. — Berakoth
Bez. — Beẓah
B.K. — Baba Ḳamma
bk. — book
B.M. — Baba Meẓiʿa
Bibl. — *Biblica*
Bibl. Stud. — *Biblische Studien*
Bik. — Bikkurim
BS — *Bibliotheca Sacra*
BW — *Biblical World*
BWANT — *Beiträge zur Wissenschaft vom Alten und Neuen Testament*
BWAT — *Beiträge zur Wissenschaft vom Alten Testament*
BZ — *Biblische Zeitschrift*
BZAW — *Beihefte zur Zeitschrift für die alttestamentliche Wissenschaft*
BZF — *Biblische Zeitfragen*

C — Codex Ephraemi Syri
ca. — *circa* (about)
CDC — Cairo Genizah Document of the Damascus Covenanters (The Zadokite Documents)
cf. — *confer* (compare)
ch. — chapter
Chr. — Chronicles
Clem. — Clement (I and II)
Clem. Misc. — Clement of Alexandria *Miscellanies*
Col. — Colossians
col. — column
Cor. — Corinthians
CSEL — *Corpus Scriptorum Ecclesiasticorum Latinorum*
D — Codex Bezae; Codex Claromontanus; Deuteronomist source
Dan. — Daniel
Dem. — Demai
Deut. — Deuteronomy
Did. — The Didache
div. — division
DSS — Dead Sea Scrolls

E — east; Elohist source
EB — Early Bronze Age
EB — *Études bibliques*
Eccl. — Ecclesiastes
Ecclus. — Ecclesiasticus
ed. — edited, edition, editor
e.g. — *exempli gratia* (for example)
Egyp. — Egyptian
EH — *Exegetisches Handbuch zum Alten Testament*
EI — Early Iron Age
Eph. — Ephesians
ʿEr. — ʿErubin
ERV — English Revised Version (1881-85)
Esd. — Esdras
esp. — especially
Esth. — Esther
ET — *Expository Times*
Ethio. — Ethiopian
Euseb. Hist. — Eusebius *History of the Christian Church*
Euseb. Onom. — Eusebius *Onomasticon*
Exod. — Exodus
Exp. — *The Expositor*
Ezek. — Ezekiel

fem. — feminine
fig. — figure (illustration)
FRLANT — *Forschungen zur Religion und Literatur des Alten und Neuen Testaments*

G — Greek
Gal. — Galatians
Gen. — Genesis
Giṭ. — Giṭṭin
Gordon — C. H. Gordon, *Ugaritic Manual*
Gr. — Greek
GSAI — *Giornale della società asiatica italiana*

GTT — *Gereformeerd theologisch Tijdschrift*

H — Hebrew; Holiness Code
Hab. — Habakkuk
Hag. — Haggai
Ḥag. — Ḥagigah
Ḥal. — Ḥallah
HAT — *Handbuch zum Alten Testament*
HDB — James Hastings, ed., *A Dictionary of the Bible*
Heb. — Hebrew; the Letter to the Hebrews
HERE — James Hastings, ed., *Encyclopedia of Religion and Ethics*
Herm. Mand. — The Shepherd of Hermas, Mandates
Herm. Sim. — The Shepherd of Hermas, Similitudes
Herm. Vis. — The Shepherd of Hermas, Visions
Hitt. — Hittite
HKAT — *Handkommentar zum Alten Testament*
Hor. — Horayoth
Hos. — Hosea
HS — *Die heilige Schrift des Alten Testaments*
HTR — *Harvard Theological Review*
HUCA — *Hebrew Union College Annual*

ICC — International Critical Commentary
i.e. — *id est* (that is)
IEJ — *Israel Exploration Journal*
Ign. Eph. — The Epistle of Ignatius to the Ephesians
Ign. Magn. — The Epistle of Ignatius to the Magnesians
Ign. Phila. — The Epistle of Ignatius to the Philadelphians
Ign. Polyc. — The Epistle of Ignatius to Polycarp
Ign. Rom. — The Epistle of Ignatius to the Romans
Ign. Smyr. — The Epistle of Ignatius to the Smyrnaeans
Ign. Trall. — The Epistle of Ignatius to the Trallians
intro. — introduction
Iren. Her. — Irenaeus *Against Heresies*
Iron — Iron Age
Isa. — Isaiah

J — Yahwist source
JA — *Journal asiatique*
JAOS — *Journal of the American Oriental Society*
Jas. — James
JBL — *Journal of Biblical Literature and Exegesis*
JBR — *Journal of Bible and Religion*
JEA — *Journal of Egyptian Archaeology*
Jer. — Jeremiah
JJGL — *Jahrbuch für jüdische Geschichte und Literatur*
JNES — *Journal of Near Eastern Studies*
Jos. Antiq. — Josephus *The Antiquities of the Jews*
Jos. Apion — Josephus *Against Apion*
Jos. Life — Josephus *Life*
Jos. War — Josephus *The Jewish War*
Josh. — Joshua
JPOS — *Journal of the Palestine Oriental Society*
JQR — *Jewish Quarterly Review*
JR — *Journal of Religion*
JRAS — *Journal of the Royal Asiatic Society*
JSOR — *Journal of the Society of Oriental Research*
J.T. — Jerusalem Talmud
Jth. — Judith
JTS — *Journal of Theological Studies*
Jub. — Jubilees
Judg. — Judges
Just. Apol. — Justin Martyr *Apology*
Just. Dial. — Justin Martyr *Dialogue with Trypho*

KAT — *Kommentar zum Alten Testament*
Kel. — Kelim
Ker. — Kerithoth
Keth. — Kethuboth
KHC — *Kurzer Hand-Kommentar zum Alten Testament*
Ḳid. — Ḳiddushin
Kil. — Kil'ayim
KJV — King James Version
KUB — *Keilschrifturkunden aus Boghazköi*

L — Lukan source
Lam. — Lamentations
Lat. — Latin
LB — Late Bronze Age
Lev. — Leviticus
LXX — Septuagint

M — Matthean source
M. — Mishna
Ma'as. — Ma'asroth
Ma'as Sh. — Ma'aser Sheni
Macc. — Maccabees
Mak. — Makkoth
Maksh. — Makshirin
Mal. — Malachi
Mart. Polyc. — *The Martyrdom of Polycarp*
masc. — masculine
Matt. — Matthew
MB — Middle Bronze Age
Meg. — Megillah
Me'il. — Me'ilah
Mek. — Mekilta
Men. — Menaḥoth
mg. — margin
MGWJ — *Monatsschrift für Geschichte und Wissenschaft des Judentums*
Mic. — Micah
Miḳ. — Miḳwa'oth
M.Ḳ. — Mo'ed Ḳaṭan
MS, MSS — manuscript, manuscripts
MT — Masoretic Text
MVAG — *Mitteilungen der vorderasiatisch-aegyptischen Gesellschaft*

N — north
n. — note
Nah. — Nahum
Naz. — Nazir
NE — northeast
Ned. — Nedarim
Neg. — Nega'im
Neh. — Nehemiah
NF — Neue Folge
Nid. — Niddah
NKZ — *Neue kirchliche Zeitschrift*
NS — Nova series
NT — New Testament
NTS — *New Testament Studies*
NTSt — *Nieuwe theologische Studien*
NTT — *Nieuw theologisch Tijdschrift*
Num. — Numbers
NW — northwest

Obad. — Obadiah
Ohol. — Oholoth
OL — Old Latin
OLZ — *Orientalistische Literaturzeitung*
'Or. — 'Orlah
OT — Old Testament

P — Priestly source
p., pp. — page, pages
Par. — Parah
PEQ — *Palestine Exploration Quarterly* (*Palestine Exploration Quarterly Fund*)
Pers. — Persian
Pes. — Pesaḥim
Pesiḳ. dRK — Pesiḳta di Rab Kahana
Pesiḳ. R. — Pesiḳtha Rabbathi
Pet. — Peter
Phil. — Philippians
Philem. — Philemon
Phoen. — Phoenicia
Pir. R. El. — Pirke di Rabbi Eliezer
PJ — *Palästina Jahrbuch*
pl. — plate (herein, color illustration)
Pliny Nat. Hist. — Pliny *Natural History*

Polyc. Phil. — The Epistle of Polycarp to the Philippians
Prayer Man. — The Prayer of Manasseh
Prov. — Proverbs
Ps., Pss. — Psalm, Psalms
PSBA — *Proceedings of the Society of Biblical Archaeology*
Pseudep. — Pseudepigrapha
Pss. Sol. — Psalms of Solomon
pt. — part
PTR — *Princeton Theological Review*

Q — *Quelle* ("Sayings" source in the gospels)
1QH — Thanksgiving Hymns
1QIs[a] — Isaiah Scroll (published by the American Schools of Oriental Research)
1QIs[b] — Isaiah Scroll (published by E. L. Sukenik, Hebrew University, Jerusalem, Israel)
1QM — War Scroll
1QpHab — Habakkuk Commentary
1QS — Manual of Discipline
1QSa — Rule of the Congregation

RB — *Revue biblique*
REJ — *Revue des études juives*
Rev. — Revelation
rev. — revised, revision, reviser
R. H. — Rosh Hashanah
RHPR — *Revue d'histoire et de philosophie religieuses*
RHR — *Revue de l'histoire des religions*
Rom. — Romans
RR — *Ricerche religiose*
RS — *Revue sémitique*
RSR — *Recherches de science religieuse*
RSV — Revised Standard Version (1946-52)
RTP — *Revue de théologie et de philosophie*

S — south
Sam. — Samuel
Samar. — Samaritan recension
Sanh. — Sanhedrin
SE — southeast
sec. — section
Shab. — Shabbath
Sheb. — Shebi'ith
Shebu. — Shebu'oth
Sheḳ. — Sheḳalim
SL — *Series Latina*
Song of S. — Song of Songs
Song Thr. Ch. — Song of the Three Children (or Young Men)
Soṭ. — Soṭah
SPAW — *Sitzungsberichte der Preussischen Akademie der Wissenschaften*
STZ — *Schweizerische theologische Zeitschrift*
Suk. — Sukkah
Sumer. — Sumerian
Sus. — Susanna
SW — southwest
SWP — *Survey of Western Palestine*
Symm. — Symmachus
Syr. — Syriac

Ta'an. — Ta'anith
Tac. Ann. — Tacitus *Annals*
Tac. Hist. — Tacitus *Histories*
Tam. — Tamid
Tanḥ. — Tanḥuma
Targ. — Targum
T.B. — Babylonian Talmud
TdbK. — Tanna debe Eliyahu
Tem. — Temurah
Ter. — Terumoth
Tert. Apol. — Tertullian *Apology*
Tert. Marcion — Tertullian *Against Marcion*
Tert. Presc. Her. — Tertullian *Prescriptions Against the Heretics*
Test. Asher — Testament of Asher
Test. Benj. — Testament of Benjamin
Test. Dan — Testament of Dan
Test. Gad — Testament of Gad
Test. Iss. — Testament of Issachar
Test. Joseph — Testament of Joseph
Test. Judah — Testament of Judah
Test. Levi — Testament of Levi
Test. Naph. — Testament of Naphtali
Test. Reuben — Testament of Reuben
Test. Simeon — Testament of Simeon
Test. Zeb. — Testament of Zebulun
Theod. — Theodotion
Theol. — *Theology*
Theol. Rundschau — *Theologische Rundschau*
Thess. — Thessalonians
Tim. — Timothy
Tit. — Titus
TLZ — *Theologische Literaturzeitung*
Tob. — Tobit
Ṭoh. — Ṭohoroth
Tosaf. — Tosafoth
Tosef. — Tosefta
TQ — *Theologische Quartalschrift*
trans. — translated, translation, translator
Tristram *NHB* — H. B. Tristram, *The Natural History of the Bible*
TSBA — *Transactions of the Society of Biblical Archaeology*
TSK — *Theologische Studien und Kritiken*
TT — *Theologisch Tijdschrift*
TU — *Texte und Untersuchungen zur Geschichte der altchristlichen Literatur*
TWNT — *Theologisches Wörterbuch zum Neuen Testament*
Ṭ.Y. — Ṭebul Yom

Ugar. — Ugaritic
'Uḳ. — 'Uḳzin

vol. — volume
vs., vss. — verse, verses
VT — *Vetus Testamentum*
Vulg. — Vulgate

W — west
WC — Westminster Commentaries
Wisd. Sol. — Wisdom of Solomon
WZKM — *Wiener Zeitschrift für die Kunde des Morgenlandes*

Y — Yahweh
Yeb. — Yebamoth
Yom. — Yoma

ZA — *Zeitschrift für Assyriologie und verwandte Gebiete*
Zab. — Zabin
ZAW — *Zeitschrift für die alttestamentliche Wissenschaft*
ZDMG — *Zeitschrift der deutschen morgenländischen Gesellschaft*
ZDPV — *Zeitschrift des deutschen Palästina-Vereins*
Zeb. — Zebaḥim
Zech. — Zechariah
Zeph. — Zephaniah
ZNW — *Zeitschrift für die neutestamentliche Wissenschaft und die Kunde der älteren Kirche*
ZS — *Zeitschrift für Semitistik*
ZST — *Zeitschrift für systematische Theologie*
ZThK — *Zeitschrift für Theologie und Kirche*

E (ELOHIST) ĕl′ō hĭst, ĭ lō′—. One of the principal narrative sources or strata of the PENTATEUCH. The term is derived from a Hebrew word for "God" (אלהים, *Elohim; see* GOD, NAMES OF, § 3*c*), the use of which is characteristic of this source.

EAGLE [נשׁר; Aram. נשׁר (Dan. 4:33—Aram. 4:30; 7:4); ἀετός]. Alternately: VULTURE (Prov. 30:17; Lam. 4:19; Hos. 8:1). Any of several large diurnal birds of prey of the family Accipitridae of the genus Aquila.

The eagle, classified as unclean in Lev. 11:13; Deut. 14:12, was the largest flying bird to be found in Palestine. Probably in the biblical period, as in the nineteenth century, the two types of eagle commonly seen were the Golden Eagle (*Aquila chrysaëtos*) and the Imperial Eagle (*Aquila heliaca heliaca*). What impressed the OT writers most about the eagle was the sweep of its flight (Prov. 23:5; Isa. 40:31; Obad. 4) and the swiftness of its movement; the latter frequently served as a simile (Deut. 28:49; II Sam. 1: 23; Jer. 4:13; cf. Rev. 12:14; M. Ab. 5:20; for this use in Ugaritic, see *ANET* 131*a*, lines 14, 16, 21). Reference is also made to the eagle's swooping down on its prey (Job 9:26), to its nesting in inaccessible places (Job 39:27; Jer. 49:16), and to its solicitude for its young (Deut. 32:11). The allusion to the renewal of its youth (Ps. 103:5) doubtless indicates that these birds were known to lead very long lives.

It seems probable that the term נשׁר was also used for "vulture"; it would, in fact, be difficult to distinguish a vulture from an eagle when it was high in the sky, though the ancient naturalists were aware of the differences between the two birds (Aristotle *History of Animals* VI.5-6; Pliny Nat. Hist. X.3-4, 7). As most vultures are characterized by the head and neck being more or less bare, it has been suspected that the reference in Mic. 1:16 is to a vulture. The latter, moreover, is characteristically a carrion-eating bird, and is more gregarious than the eagle; hence the RSV translates נשׁר as "vulture" in Prov. 30:17 (a possible reference to the vulture's removal of the eyes of its victim); Lam. 4:19; Hos. 8:1; and the RSV mg. renders ἀετός as "vulture" in Matt. 24:28; Luke 17:37.

The eagle, doubtless because it was the monarch of the birds, furnished various figures to the prophets and apocalyptists. Each of Ezekiel's four-faced cherubim has the face of an eagle (Ezek. 1:10; 10: 14), and the same prophet uses two eagles in his allegory in ch. 17. In Dan. 7 the lion with eagle's wings (vs. 4) combines the noblest of the beasts and the noblest of the birds to represent the Babylonian kingdom (cf. the use of "gold" in 2:32). In Rev. 4:7 one of the four living creatures surrounding God's throne is said to be like a "flying eagle"; in 8:13 an eagle, possibly the creature mentioned in 4:7, utters a warning to those dwelling on earth (cf. eagles speaking in II Esd. 11:7-10; as a letter carrier in II Bar. 77:17-26). This association of eagles (or vultures) with deity was a very old one in the ancient world. In Akkadian art the eagle symbolizes, or is closely connected with, various deities, as, e.g., the god Ningirsu (*see bibliography*). In the *Iliad* Zeus selects an eagle to carry a fawn to the Achaeans (VIII.247-52; cf. XXIV.308-16).

See also FAUNA § B1.

Bibliography. E. Ebeling and B. Meissner, "Adler," *Reallexikon der Assyriologie* (1932), I, 37.

W. S. MCCULLOUGH

EAGLE, GIER. *See* VULTURE.

EANES. KJV Apoc. form of MAASEIAH 13.

EAR (HEARING) [אזן; οὖς]. The ear is frequently mentioned in the Bible in its literal, physical sense, but its figurative use as a symbol of the complete process of hearing and, by extension, of understanding and obedience is far more significant. The concrete term "ear" is often employed where our own modes of thought would lead us to use a more abstract word such as "hearing" or "attention." "To speak in the ears" (Deut. 5:1 KJV) means "to speak in the hearing" (so RSV); "to incline the ear" (Ps. 88:2) means "to give attention." The "ear" can also designate the whole faculty of understanding, as in Job 13:1; and because "hearing" in the full sense must include understanding, it is possible to say of people that they "have ears, but hear not" (Jer. 5: 21). In many passages the word "ear" might well be translated "mind," as in Job 33:16; cf. LXX.

For the apprehension of the divine word, the possession of physical ears is not enough; God must "open" the ears so that the word is received with comprehension and a spirit of willing obedience (Job 36:10; Ps. 40:6; Isa. 50:4-5). "Uncircumcised" ears are ears which have not been thus opened (Jer. 6:10; Acts 7:51). Ears may also be "heavy" (Isa. 6:10), and men who have physical ears may in fact be "deaf" (Isa. 43:8).

In the Bible, the key word for man's response to God is "hearing" rather than "seeing" (*see* EYE; SEEING). For the mystery religions the highest religious experience was that of "seeing" the god; but for the Bible, where the basic religious attitude is obedience to the divine word, the emphasis is on "hearing" his voice. The most important formula of Israel's religion begins characteristically: "Hear, O Israel." "He who is of God" is not the mystic who has seen a vision, but one who "hears the words of God" (John 8:47). R. C. DENTAN

EAR OF GRAIN. "Ear" in this sense usually translates שבלת or στάχυς (Gen. 41:5-7, 22-27; Ruth 2:2; Job 24:24 KJV [RSV HEAD]; Isa. 17:5; Mark 4:28), the individual head of grain. Other terms are: מלילה (Deut. 23:25—H 23:26), referring to rubbed ears of wheat; אביב (Lev. 2:14), ears which are ripe but soft, whose grains may be roasted and eaten; and כרמל (II Kings 4:42), newly ripened ears.

R. W. CORNEY

EARLY RAIN [יורה, מורה]. Alternately: AUTUMN RAIN; FIRST RAIN; KJV FORMER RAIN. The first rains of autumn beginning the rainy season. They were important as softening the ground for plowing, and were linked with the latter rain (*see* SPRING RAIN) as a token of divine goodness (Deut. 11:14; Ps. 84:6; Jer. 5:24; Joel 2:23).

See also PALESTINE, CLIMATE OF.

R. B. Y. SCOTT

EARNEST. KJV translation of ἀρ(ρ)αβών (II Cor. 1:22; 5:5; Eph. 1:14; RSV GUARANTEE). The word is of Semitic origin, but is found in classical Greek, probably having been brought into Greece by the Phoenicians. In the LXX it translates ערבון (e.g., in Gen. 38:17-18; Deut. 24:6; Job 24:3) and means anything used as a pledge. In Greek from the fourth century B.C. it commonly means "earnest money," and in the papyri it is frequent for a deposit or down payment in business transactions (e.g., BGU 446, 5). In the NT it is used figuratively of "the Spirit" as a guarantee of part payment of the believer's "inheritance" (Ephesians)—namely, immortality—as it is implied in the context of II Cor. 5:5. Cf. the figure in Rom. 8:23 ("the first fruits of the Spirit"). The pledge aspect is reflected in the equation of ἀρραβών with a "seal" in II Cor. 1:22; Eph. 1:14. As in other NT passages, the terminology thus specifically reflects the usage of contemporary documents regarding INHERITANCE and ADOPTION (cf. Rom. 8:15; Gal. 3:18; Heb. 9:15).

Bibliography. J. B. Lightfoot, *Notes on the Epistles of St. Paul* (1895), pp. 323-24; A. Plummer, *II Corinthians* (1915), pp. 41, 150; J. H. Moulton and G. Milligan, *The Vocabulary of the Greek NT* (1929), pp. 79, 346-47; B. Ahern, "The Indwelling Spirit, Pledge of Our Inheritance," *Catholic Biblical Quarterly*, 9 (1947), 178-89.

A. WIKGREN

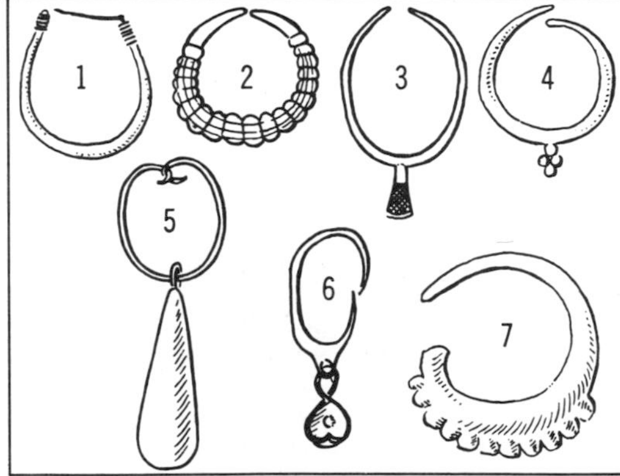

From Kurt Galling, *Biblisches Reallexikon* (Tübingen: J. C. B. Mohr)

1. Gold earrings: (1-5) from Tell el-'Ajjul; (6) from 'Athlit; (7) from Tell Jemmeh

EARRING. The translation of several words:

a) נזם (Exod. 35:22; Judg. 8:24-26; RING in Gen. 24:22, 30, 47; 35:4; Exod. 32:2-3; Job 42:11; Prov. 25:12; Hos. 2:15), a general term for "ring," referring to an earring when qualified by the phrase "in the ears" (Gen. 35:4; Exod. 32:2-3).

b) עגיל (Num. 31:50; Ezek. 16:12), a circular-shaped ornament—whether disc or ring is not clear.

c) לחש in Isa. 3:20 KJV (RSV AMULET).

d) Ἐνώτια (Jth. 10:4).

Fig. EAR 1.

See also PENDANT 3.

J. M. MYERS

EARTH. Biblical views about the earth in its physical aspect are to be found in the OT. The NT has no occasion to touch on the subject, while the intertestamental scriptures confine themselves (as in Ecclesiasticus) to vague praises of the beauties of cosmos, or (as in Enoch) to visionary fantasies.

1. Physical and geographical features
2. Fertility
3. God's earth and devil's earth
4. Mother earth
5. Creation and eschatology

Bibliography

1. Physical and geographical features. The Hebrews regarded the earth as a flat strip (cf. Isa. 42:5; 44:24, where the verb רקע, primarily "flatten out," describes its creation), suspended athwart the cosmic ocean (Pss. 24:2; 136:6) or in empty space (Job 26:7). It was supported on pillars (Job 9:6; Ps. 75:3—H 75:4), joists (Ps. 104:5), or props (מוסדות; II Sam. 22:16; Prov. 8:29; Isa. 24:18; Jer. 31:37; cf. Ugaritic *msdt arṣ,* II AB, i.40), the lower ends of which reached down to the nether world. To prevent its being submerged by the surrounding waters, it was hemmed in by a protective bound (חוג; Job 26:10; Prov. 8:29), probably conceived as a range of mountains, like the Qâaf of later Arabic folklore. *See bibliography* § 2.

The total surface of the earth was comprehended by the expression "the four edges" (ארבע כנפות הארץ, RSV "the four corners"; Isa. 11:12; Ezek. 7:2 [LXX πτέρυγες; Vulg. *plagae*]; cf. Job 37:3 [Vulg. *termini*])—an expression which recurs in Akkadian (*kippat irbitti*) and which also finds its counterpart in the early Aramaic inscriptions from Zenjirli (Pannamu 14: רבעת ארק; Bar Rekub 3-4: Tiglath-pileser, מרא רבעי ארקא = Akkad. *šar kibrat irbitti,* KB II, 2.8.34, etc.). In Job 38:13 the word for "edges" (כנפות) is taken in the literal sense of "skirts," and God is said to grasp them every morning and shake them out so as to rid them of the wicked, as if the latter were dust or vermin.

The ultima Thule of the earth was popularly identified with the wild regions lying to the N, or NE, of Syria (Jer. 6:22; 31:8; 50:41; etc.). This will explain why the ark of Noah, drifting to the end of the world, is said (Gen. 8:4) to have come to rest on the mountains of Ararat—i.e., Urartu-Armenia. In the same way, the Greeks spoke of Scythia as the "back of beyond" (e.g., Aeschylus *Prometheus Vinctus* 1-3), and the Hittites of the land of the Lullu, near Lake Urmiah.

In II Esd. 6:42 it is stated that six parts of the

earth are habitable, while a seventh is covered by water. This strange notion is without parallel in any other ancient writer, but it is of great interest to observe that precisely the opposite of it is attributed by Roger Bacon (*Opus majus* I, 290, ed. Bridges) to Ptolemy. Since, however, no such assertion is actually to be found in the latter's extant writings, and since it runs counter to what he elsewhere has to say about the surface of the earth, it is not improbable that his original statement in fact agreed with that of II Esdras but was misunderstood by Bacon or his source. *See bibliography* § 3.

2. Fertility. The fertility of the earth was thought to be dependent largely on the conduct of men—an idea which recurs in other cultures (cf., e.g., *Odyssey* XIX.109 ff; Hesiod *Works and Days* 225-27). Accordingly, misdeeds occasioned blight or drought. This belief, shared by several ancient and primitive peoples, stemmed originally from the notion that human misbehavior upset the balance and order of nature in general. In the Bible, however, the concept is expressed in theological terms: such actions offend the tutelary deity (*genius loci*) and cause him to withdraw his presence and providence (cf., e.g., Deut. 11:16-17; Joel 1). *See bibliography* § 4.

In Isa. 62:4 the barren but subsequently requickened earth is likened to a woman who is at first abandoned, or put away (עזובה), but eventually remarried (בעולה). This comparison of the soil to a woman, and of its rain-giving god to her impregnator, occurs already in the Tell el-Amarna Letters (74, rev. 7, Knudzton), and is, indeed, virtually ubiquitous in ancient literature (*see bibliography* § 5). Conversely, when the earth lies barren, this may be described in terms of sexual unchastity (חנף; Isa. 24: 5; Jer. 3:1; etc.).

The earth was considered to be polluted especially by bloodshed. Nothing would grow where innocent blood had been spilled (Gen. 4:11-12; Num. 35:33-34), and such soil would be bereft of rainfall (II Sam. 1:21). The idea is admirably illustrated by the Ugaritic *Poem of Aqhat,* where the murder of that youth is first revealed by a sudden failure of the crops, and where his father, Dan'el, invokes drought upon the blood-stained ground. Analogous notions obtained in classical antiquity (cf. Sophocles *Oedipus Rex* 22-30; Livy XLV.5). *See bibliography* § 6.

Hebrew law required that the earth lay fallow every seventh year (Exod. 23:10-12; Deut. 31:10). Although this came to be explained as a humane concession to the poor, it probably originated in the common ancient practice of measuring time in seven- or eight-year "leases" (*see bibliography* § 7). When a lease expired, an interval of "death" ensued until the next lease began. *See* JUBILEE, YEAR OF.

3. God's earth and devil's earth. The soil of any given area was regarded as the "estate" (נחלה) of the local deity (cf. II Sam. 20:19; Ps. 79:1; Jer. 2:7; 16: 18; etc.), who, as its landlord and "quickener," was entitled to a prime share (tithe) of its produce (*see bibliography* § 8). Waste land, on the other hand, was the domain of noxious spirits, the natural habitat of demons (cf. Isa. 13:21; 32:14; *see* DEMON § 1*e*). So, too, among the modern *fellaḥîn* of Palestine, stony soil is called "devil's land" (*arḍ Iblîs*). An interesting parallel may be adduced also from Sir Walter Scott's celebrated *Letters on Demonology and Witchcraft* (no. 3). In many parishes of Scotland, we are told, a certain portion of land, known as the "gudeman's croft," used to be left unplowed and uncultivated as the preserve of the Devil. *See bibliography* § 9.

4. Mother Earth. There is no evidence that even recalcitrant Israelites ever worshiped the earth. But that this was the case among their Semitic neighbors there can be no doubt. A deity named Erṣîtu—i.e., "Earth"— is mentioned in an early list of gods from Asshur; while in the mythological poems from Ras Shamra-Ugarit (II AB, i.16; I* AB, v.11; etc.), *A-r-ṣ-y*—i.e., "Lady Earth"—is one of the brides of Baal. It is probable, however, from the words of Job 1:21 ("Naked I came forth from my mother's womb, and naked shall I return thither" [where "thither," strangely omitted in the RSV, is *deictic,* the speaker pointing to the earth]), that the concept of Mother Earth was not unknown in Israel. *See bibliography* § 10.

5. Earth in cosmogony and eschatology. In the account of the Creation in Gen. 1 the earth is said to have been created on the third day of that process (vss. 9-10); while in the account preserved in Gen. 2 we are informed (vss. 5-6) that it was at first watered, not by rains, but by a subterranean flow (אד = Akkadian *edu*). The latter notion retrojects into cosmogony the climatic conditions that actually obtain every autumn at the beginning of the agricultural year. *See* COSMOGONY § A2*c*.

A renewal, even a prodigious increase, of the earth's fertility is a feature of the "new creation" which is to follow the collapse of the present world order. A special stream of living waters will be released (Zech. 14:8); the skies will rain oil and the wadies run with honey (Joel 31:18—H 4:18; Amos 9:13; Sibylline Oracles 3:774-77; II Enoch 8:5; etc.).

On "earth" as a euphemism for the nether world, *see* DEAD, ABODE OF THE.

Bibliography. 1. General: R. Patai, *'Adham we'adhamah* (*Man and Earth;* 1943; in Hebrew).

2. On the encircling mountain: A. J. Wensinck, *The Ideas of the Western Semites Concerning the Navel of the Earth* (1916), pp. 5-7.

3. On the statement in II Esd. 6:42 concerning the proportion of water to habitable land: S. Gandz, *Proceedings of the American Academy for Jewish Research,* XXII (1953), 25-32.

4. On fertility as dependent on human behavior: J. G. Frazer, *The Golden Bough,* I, ii, 111-17; M. Delcourt, *Stérilités mystérieuses et naissances maléfiques dans l'antiquité classique* (1938).

5. On the comparison of the earth to a woman: P. Haupt, *JAOS,* XXVI (1906), 417-20; E. S. Hartland, *Primitive Paternity* (1909), I, 309-10; M. Eliade, *Traité d'histoire des religions* (1949), pp. 224-25, 230-31.

6. On the infertility of the earth through bloodshed: T. H. Gaster, *Thespis* (1950), p. 296.

7. On seven-year leases: J. G. Frazer, *The Golden Bough,* IV, 68 ff; VII, 80 ff.

8. On the deity as a landlord to whom a tithe is given: W. Robertson Smith, *The Religion of the Semites* (3rd ed., by S. A. Cook; 1927), pp. 459, 554.

9. On "devil's land" in Arabic folklore: T. Canaan, *ZDMG,* LXX (1916), 168.

10. On the deification of the earth in a text from Asshur (VAT 10173, ii.4): O. Schroeder, *ZA,* XXXIII (1921), 130. On Mother Earth among the Semites: T. Nöldeke, *ARW,* VIII (1910), 161 ff; K. Briem, *ARW,* XXIV (1926), 179-95; M. Stein, *Tarbiz,* IX (1938), 257-77 (in Hebrew).

T. H. GASTER

EARTHENWARE. *See* POTTERY.

EARTHQUAKE [רעש, shaking, trembling; σεισμός, shaking, *as of a sieve*]. A trembling of the earth, caused sometimes by volcanic activity but more frequently by a displacement, often very slight, of the earth's crust (tectonic earthquake). When the wave of vibration is severe, it produces spectacular secondary effects, such as loud rumbling noises (Ezek. 3:12-13), avalanches (I Kings 19:11), fissures in the earth (Num. 16:32), and destructive fires (Rev. 8:5).

Palestine lies within the active earthquake zone bounded by the Alps, the Caucasus, and the Himalayas, in which some twenty per cent of recorded earthquakes occur. Although the incidence of earthquakes is greater in Syria to the N, Palestine experiences an average of one or two destructive earthquakes per century, and two to six light shocks each year. The geologically unstable Jordan Valley and the fault lines which run into it obliquely from both E and W create the conditions necessary for movements of the earth's surface. Principal centers of earthquake activity are in Upper Galilee, in the Samaritan territory near Nablus (biblical Shechem), and on the W edge of the Judean Mountains near Lydda, with secondary centers in the Jordan Valley at Jericho and Tiberias.

Classical and modern writers record at least seventeen major earthquakes in the Palestine area during the Christian era. An idea of the destructiveness of these tremors is provided by the earthquake of 1837, which did severe structural damage in twelve districts and took over four thousand lives.

The French archaeologist Claude Schaeffer uses destruction levels caused by earthquakes as a means of comparative dating of biblical sites, and finds evidence for a particularly heavy quake covering the whole region *ca.* 1365 B.C.—i.e., during the period of the sojourn in Egypt. A memorable earthquake from which Amos' prophecy is dated took place in the reign of Uzziah (786-744 B.C.; Amos 1:1; Zech. 14:5). Josephus describes a severe shock during the reign of Herod (Antiq. XV.v.2), evidence of which was found in the buildings of the Essene community at Qumran. Matthew mentions earthquakes in connection with the crucifixion and resurrection of Jesus (Matt. 27:54; 28:2), and Luke records a tremor which broke open the prison at Philippi where Paul and Silas were confined (Acts 16:26).

The earthquake is one mark of Yahweh's presence for revelation (Exod. 19:18) or for destructive judgment (Isa. 29:6). From the latter use it is only a step to the appearance of earthquakes among the catastrophic disasters of the last days (Matt. 24:7; Mark 13:8; Luke 21:11; Rev. 6:12; 8:5; 11:13, 19; 16:18).

Bibliography. G. A. Smith, *Jerusalem* (1908), vol. I, ch. 4. C. F. A. Schaeffer, *Stratigraphie Comparée* (1948), ch. 1. D. H. K. Amiran, "A Revised Earthquake-Catalogue of Palestine," *IEJ,* I (1950-51), 223 ff; II (1952), 48 ff.

L. E. TOOMBS

EAST. *See* ORIENTATION.

EAST, THE PEOPLE OF THE [בני קדם, *benê qedhem*]; KJV alternately: CHILDREN OF THE EAST; MEN OF THE EAST. A term used very broadly to indicate those nations who lived to the E of the Israelites. Thus, in Gen. 29:1, Jacob came to the lands of the people of the East in Paddan-aram. In Judg. 6-8 the term denotes Arab groups who accompanied the Midianites and the Amalekites in attacking Israel, and the same is true for Jer. 49:28; Ezek. 25:4, 10. On the other hand, in Isa. 11:14 the term seems to be equivalent to Edom and Moab, and in Job 1:3 seems to have been included under this designation. The Eastern peoples had a special reputation for wisdom (I Kings 4:30—H 5:10); this may have been the reason for introducing the wise men from the East in the story of the birth of Jesus (Matt. 2:1-12). S. COHEN

EAST COUNTRY [ארץ קדם, *'ereṣ qedhem*] (Gen. 25:6). The land to which Abraham sent the children of his concubines. The term is equivalent to that part of Arabia which lies SE of Palestine.

EAST GATE [שער המזרח]. A gate mentioned in Neh. 3:29, but not as one of the structures restored by Nehemiah; perhaps identical with the "eastern gate of the house of Yahweh" (Ezek. 10:19; 11:1). The term "east gate" is used erroneously for the POTSHERD GATE in Jer. 19:2 KJV. *See* JERUSALEM § 7*b*. G. A. BARROIS

EAST SEA, EASTERN SEA [ים הקדמוני]. A name employed in certain late prophetic passages (Ezek. 47:18; Joel 2:20; Zech. 14:8) for the lake called the Salt Sea in the Pentateuch and Joshua and at present known as the DEAD SEA. The designation is derived from the sea's position on the E boundary of the ancient land of Israel. W. H. MORTON

EAST WIND [רוח קדים, קדים]. Not merely a wind direction like "north wind" (Prov. 25:23), but the name of a wind with special characteristics, now known as the khamsin or sirocco. It is a hot, dry, dusty wind from the deserts to the S and SE of Palestine (Jer. 4:11; Hos. 13:15) which often blows for several days in the transitional months April-June and September-November. High temperatures and extremely low humidity, together with dust-filled air, make this weather trying to men and animals (Isa. 27:8; Jonah 4:8) and withering to vegetation (Gen. 41:6; Ezek. 17:10). The wind may become a gale or WHIRLWIND (Job 27:20-21), wreck seagoing vessels (Ps. 48:7—H 48:8; Ezek. 27:26), and drive back the shallow waters of the Reed Sea (Exod. 14:21).

See also PALESTINE, CLIMATE OF.

R. B. Y. SCOTT

EASTER. KJV translation (erroneous) of πάσχα (RSV PASSOVER) in Acts 12:4. *See* PASSOVER AND FEAST OF UNLEAVENED BREAD.

EATING. *See* MEALS.

EBAL ē'bəl [עיבל]. **1.** Ancestor of a Horite subclan in Edom; the third son of clan chief Shobal (Gen. 36:23; I Chr. 1:40).

2. Alternate form of OBAL.

EBAL, MOUNT. A mountain located N of and directly opposite Mount Gerizim, with which it forms the sides of an important E-W pass. SHECHEM lies at the E entrance and modern Nablus in the valley between the mountains. The modern name is Jebel Eslamiyeh. *See* GERIZIM, MOUNT; PALESTINE, GEOGRAPHY OF.

From *Atlas of the Bible* (Thomas Nelson & Sons Limited)

2. Mount Ebal is to the right, while Mount Gerizim stands to the left. The modern village of Balata, at the S edge of Tell Balata (ancient Shechem), lies near the pass between the two mountains.

The Hebrews, on entering Canaan after the time of Moses, were to confirm the covenant with Yahweh; this involved the setting of the blessing on Mount Gerizim and the curse on Mount Ebal (Deut. 11:29). It is not clear from this passage that the mountain itself was to be cursed, although this has become the tradition. From Deut. 27:13 we gather that the mountain was the place from which curses were pronounced by Reuben, Gad, Asher, Zebulun, Dan, and Naphtali upon any persons who would break the commandments. A degree of sanctity for Ebal is implied in Deut. 27:4 (Samaritan Pentateuch "Gerizim"), where the tradition is reported that stones inscribed with the law are to be placed on Mount Ebal. According to Josh. 8:30, 33, Joshua built an altar on Mount Ebal, and under his leadership the people engaged in a covenantal ceremony, with half of them in front of Ebal and the other half in front of Gerizim, and the ark of the covenant between them. Figs. EBA 2; JAC 7.

Bibliography. G. A. Smith, *The Historical Geography of the Holy Land* (1896), pp. 119-23; E. Nielsen, *Shechem* (1955): see index of OT passages cited above; D. Daly, *The Geography of the Bible* (1957), pp. 20, 36, 178, 180. W. L. REED

EBED ē'bĕd [עבד, *evidently a shortened form of* עבדאל, servant of God]. **1.** The father of Gaal, who led the rebellion against Abimelech at Shechem (Judg. 9:26-35).

2. One of those who returned to Palestine with Ezra (Ezra 8:6). The LXX and I Esd. 8:32 have ὤβεθ, so it is possible that his name is an abbreviation of עבדיה, "Servant of Yahu." M. NEWMAN

EBED-MELECH ē'bĭd mĕl'ĭk [עבד־מלך, servant of the king]. An Ethiopian EUNUCH in Zedekiah's court, who rescued Jeremiah from the cistern (Jer. 38:7-13). The oracle in Jer. 39:15-18 (sometimes considered a Deuteronomic addition) promised Ebed-melech that he would survive the destruction of the kingdom, as a reward for his deed.

The title *ebed* (lit., "slave") was adopted, apparently for the first time by David, from Akkadian practice, and was used in Edom and Ammon as well. It designated the class of court (often mercenary) officials, as distinguished from the older institution of tribal elders. In "Ebed-melech" it has become a proper name (known also in Assyrian and Nabatean). J. M. WARD

EBENEZER ĕb'ə nē'zər [אבן העזר, stone of help]. A place near APHEK where the Israelites had two battles with the Philistines, in the second of which the ark was captured (I Sam. 4:1-11; 5:1). The site may be Majdel Yaba, NE of Jaffa.

I Sam. 7:12 mentions another Ebenezer, a stone which was set up between Mizpah and Yeshanah (MT SHEN) to commemorate a victory over the Philistines. This passage comes from the later, unhistorical section of the book, and is apparently an attempt to give a more pleasant explanation of the name. S. COHEN

EBER ē'bər [עבר, *eponym from* עברי, HEBREW; *in 2-4 below a few* Heb. *MSS read* עבד (*'ébhedh*), servant; *in 2-5* LXX *tends to read* Ωβηδ *or* Αβεδ]. An eponym. Noth (*see bibliography*) reads *'ébhedh* ("servant") in all occurrences except Num. 24:24.

1. The eponymous ancestor of the Hebrews (Gen. 10:21, 24-25; 11:14-17; Num. 24:24 [*see bibliography*]; I Chr. 1:18-19, 25). J makes Eber an ancestor of all Semites (Gen. 10:21-25; *see* SHEM; JOKTAN), while P restricts the progeny of Eber to the Hebrews alone (Gen. 11:14-26). The Chronicler combines the two theories (I Chr. 1:17-27). In Num. 24:24, Eber should probably not be read as a proper name but as the word עבר for "region beyond" (here, beyond the Euphrates), which is the same as the name Eber in Hebrew.

2. A family of the tribe of Gad (I Chr. 5:13).

3. A family of the tribe of Benjamin (I Chr. 8:12).

4. Another family of the tribe of Benjamin (I Chr. 8:22).

5. A postexilic priest (Neh. 12:20).

Bibliography. M. Noth, *Die israelitischen Personennamen* (1928), p. 252; J. Skinner, *Genesis*, ICC (2nd ed., 1930), pp. 187 ff.
H. H. GUTHRIE, JR.

EBEZ ē'bĕz [אבץ] (Josh. 19:20); KJV ABEZ ā'bĕz. A town in Issachar. Its location is unknown. Possibly "Ebez" is an error for רבץ, "resting place," with the LXX B reading Ῥεβὲς.

Bibliography. W. F. Albright, "The Topography of the Tribe of Issachar," *ZAW* (1926), p. 231.
G. W. VAN BEEK

EBIASAPH. Alternate form of ABIASAPH.

EBIONITES, GOSPEL OF THE ē'bĭ ə nīts ['Εβιωναῖοι *or* -ῖται; אביונים, poor]. A gospel referred to and cited by Epiphanius alone under this title, but probably (although this is denied by many) to be identified with the Gospel According to the Hebrews. *See* HEBREWS, GOSPEL ACCORDING TO THE.

If, as many scholars still contend, this gospel is not to be identified with the Gospel According to the Hebrews, our sole knowledge of it depends upon Epiphanius, who vies with Jerome for the distinction of being the least to be trusted of the ancient fathers in such matters. His several references to and citations of this writing (*Heresies* XXX), while confusing, suggest that it is essentially the same as the Gospel According to the Hebrews, referred to by several of the early fathers and frequently confused with the Gospel of the Nazarenes (*see* NAZARENES, GOSPEL OF), which Jerome mistakenly claimed to have translated for the first time from Hebrew into Greek and Latin. Epiphanius' quotations which are to be considered in connection with the Ebionite Gospel According to the Hebrews list the twelve apostles with John in first place; replace the locusts which John the Baptist was said to have eaten with honey cakes (the Ebionites were, of course, vegetarians); mention John the Baptist's lineage; deny the supernatural birth of Jesus; quote Jesus' word in the form: "I came to destroy the sacrifices, and if ye cease not from sacrificing, the wrath of God will not cease from you"; and, again in line with their vegetarian scruples, alter Jesus' word about preparation for the Last Supper to a revealing question: "Have I desired with desire to eat this flesh of the Passover with you?"

Bibliography. E. Hennecke, *Handbuch zu den Neutestamentlichen Apokryphen* (1904); B. W. Bacon, *Studies in Matthew* (1930), especially pp. 478-95; J. Schoeps, *Theologie und Geschichte des Judenchristentums* (1950). Epiphanius' quotations have been conveniently collected in M. R. James, *The Apocryphal NT* (1924), pp. 8-10. M. S. ENSLIN

EBONY [הבנים, *hobhnîm, only plural, from* Egyp. *hbny;* ἔβενος]. The highly prized core wood of the tree *Diospyros ebenum* König (and other species), imported from S India and Ceylon (and perhaps Ethiopia). It is mentioned along with ivory tusks, which were a part of Tyre's trade with the "men of Rhodes" (Ezek. 27:15; the RSV follows the more plausible LXX and a few Hebrew MSS; KJV "Dedan"). The Egyptians, Phoenicians, Babylonians, Greeks, and Romans prized ebony and ivory for use in furniture (ebony inlaid with ivory is exceptionally beautiful), vessels, and turned objects. It was also used in the Near East for idols.

3. Ebony

Some scholars read the difficult שנהבים in I Kings 10:22 ("ivory") as שן והבנים, "ivory and ebony," thus finding another reference to ebony, an item of trade with Solomon; but *see* IVORY; FAUNA § A2*i*.

See also FLORA § A8*a;* RHODES; TRADE AND COMMERCE; TYRE.

Fig. EBO 3.

Bibliography. H. N. and A. L. Moldenke, *Plants of the Bible* (1952), p. 95. J. C. TREVER

EBRON ē'brən [עברון] (Josh. 19:28); KJV HEBRON hē'brən. A town in the territory allotted to Asher. "Ebron" is generally regarded as a mistake in the MT for ABDON.

EBRONAH. KJV form of ABRONAH.

ECANUS. KJV Apoc. form of ETHANUS.

ECBATANA ĕk băt'ə nə [Aram. אחמתא; Old Pers. *hagmatāna,* place of gathering(?); Pahlavi *'hm(t'n);* Elam. *ag-ma-da-na;* Akkad. *a-ga-ma-ta-nu;* 'Αγβάτανα, 'Αμαθά (II Esd. 6:2 LXX A), 'Εκβάτανα]; KJV ACHMETHA ăk'mə thə; KJV Apoc. ECBATANE ĕk băt'ə nē. A city located at the foot of the Elvend Mountain; now Hamadan.

According to Herodotus (I.96), the city was founded by the Median king Deioces (*see* MEDIA), while the story contained in Jth. 1:1-4 (*see* ARPACHSHAD) seems to have little historical value. Cyrus the Great captured Ecbatana in the middle of the sixth century, and it then became the favorite summer residence of the Achaemenian kings (Xenophon *Anabasis* III.5.15; *Cyropaedia* VIII.6.22). At Ecbatana during the reign of Darius I a copy of Cyrus' decree concerning the rebuilding of the Jerusalem temple was found, according to Ezra 6:2. *See* CYRUS.

The city's architectural outlay and lavish construction are described by the Greek authors. Despite the alleged destruction and looting by Alexander the Great, the city remained famous for its luxury and once more became a summer capital, this time of the Parthian rulers (Strabo XI.522; XVI.743). After a slight decline in its importance under the Sassanians the present town was built after the Islamic conquest of Iran, and it is frequently mentioned thereafter by the Islamic authors. It survived severe damage by the Mongol armies in 1220 and again in the next century by Tamerlane. Today it is one of the principal cities of Iran. Its location on the roads from Baghdad to Teheran and from Khorramshahr on the Persian Gulf to Teheran makes it a center of traffic and commerce, as it used to be under the Achaemenians and after, on the main route from Mesopotamia to Iran and farther E to India and Central Asia.

No thorough archaeological work has so far been undertaken at Ecbatana-Hamadan. The modern city is built on top of the ancient, and excavations would necessitate extensive demolition of existing buildings. Incidental discovery of silver and golden objects and of a number of Old Persian inscriptions, which mention *Ariyāramna* (Ariaramnes), the great-grandfather of Darius the Great, and his son *Aršāma* (Arsames), among others, are sufficient to show the great promise of the city as an archaeological site.

The alleged tomb of Esther and Mordecai which is to be found in Hamadan is, perhaps, the tomb of the wife of the Sassanian ruler Yazdegird (399-420/421).

Bibliography. C. A. Barbier de Meynard, *Dictionnaire géographique, historique et littéraire de la Perse* (1861), pp. 597 ff; E. Weissbach, "Ecbatana," in Pauly-Wissowa, *Realenzyclopädie der klassischen Altertumswissenschaft,* V (1905), 2155-58; E. Herzfeld, *Archaeological History of Iran* (1935). On the gold treasure, see: *The Illustrated London News* (July 17 and Aug. 21, 1948). On the inscriptions, see: R. G. Kent, *Old Persian* (1950), pp. 107, 111, 113-14, 116, 147, 153, 155.

M. J. DRESDEN

ECCLESIASTES ĭ klē′zĭ ăs′tēz ['Εκκλησιαστὴς, one who participates in a popular assembly]. Alternately: KOHELETH kō hĕl′əth (*properly* Qoheleth) [קהלת, preacher(?) *or* speaker before an assembly(?) *or* officer of the assembly(?)]. The pen name of the author (1:12) and the name of his book, the twenty-first book of the OT in the common English versions. The book, like Job, is a noble example of OT wisdom literature. Attributed by courtesy to King Solomon, it was probably written during the Greek period (*ca.* 250), and its author may have been a Jewish sage schooled in the wisdom tradition and affected by the spirit (rather than the particulars) of Greek philosophy. Though not wholly uncommitted, he explored life with an open mind and recorded his findings as to what is best for a man. His counsel of pleasure is modified by his unacknowledged standards of right and wrong and by his sense of pity for the human state.

1. Title. "Ecclesiastes" is the English spelling by way of the Vulg. of the Greek word ἐκκλησιαστὴς. This Greek noun is related to the more common word 'εκκλησία (the NT term for "church" or "congregation"). In the LXX the term appears in the title verse of the book: "The words of Ecclesiastes, the son of David, king of Israel in Jerusalem" (1:1; cf. 1:12). Read instead with the Hebrew term, the title verse reads: "The words of Koheleth, the son of David. . . ." "Koheleth" (or "Qoheleth") is the English spelling of קהלת, a name which is found seven times in Ecclesiastes and nowhere else in biblical literature. It appears to be a feminine active participle of the verb קהל, which means "to come together" (*niph'al*) or "to bring together" (*hiph'il*) and is not used in the *qal* except here. It is related to the masculine noun *qāhāl,* "assembly," which circumstance doubtless influenced the Greek translators. The meaning of the name, however, is not clear. The customary rendering, "the Preacher," is not satisfactory; this translation goes back to the Latin commentary of Jerome, who interprets the word as *concionator,* "speaker before an assembly," but "Preacher" is a poor translation, because whatever Koheleth may be doing in his book, he is not "preaching."

Though the form *qôhéleth* is feminine, it is construed (1:2; 12:8-10) with masculine verbs, and the feminine form of the Hebrew verb in 7:27—concealed in the English of the RSV—is probably an error: false word-division. The masculine intent of the word is beyond question, since Koheleth appears as a "son," not a daughter, of David (1:1) and as a "king," not a queen, in Jerusalem (1:12). It is customary to compare two names of similar form among "Solomon's servants" listed in Neh. 7:57, 59, which may be occupational titles. One of these, "Sophereth," which though feminine in form might mean "Scribe," is indeed very much like "Koheleth," which could by analogy mean "Officer of the Kahal (assembly)."

Whatever the meaning of the word—and it remains obscure—the author obviously employed it as a proper noun. It was his name: "I Koheleth have been king over Israel in Jerusalem" (1:12)—this despite its use twice with the article ("the Koheleth"), in 7:27 (with different word-division as in the RSV) and 12:8 (but cf. 1:2). The editor who supplied the title verse certainly understood the word as a name: "Koheleth, the son of David."

To be sure, no son of David, to our knowledge, bore the name Koheleth. Moreover, to our knowledge no son of David but Solomon was "king over Israel in Jerusalem." "Koheleth," then, substitutes for Solomon, and the author by design personates Solomon. For his purposes, to seem as one to whom no avenue was closed, able by reason of his superior mind and unlimited wealth and populous harem to gratify all earthly desires, the author made of himself a Solomon, since by his time that ancient king had in popular fancy achieved renown for wisdom and surpassing splendor (I Kings 10:23). Without himself adopting the name of Solomon, without even calling himself the son of David (not he but his editor wrote 1:1), he yet suggests Solomon in his words in 1:12: "I Koheleth have been king over Israel in Jerusalem."

By thus personating Solomon, the author of Ecclesiastes both employed and enhanced the tradition concerning Solomon—the tradition that said of him: "He also uttered three thousand proverbs; and his songs were a thousand and five" (I Kings 4:32—H 5:12); the tradition that made him the author also of Proverbs and the Song of Solomon and, eventually, of the Wisdom of Solomon and the Psalms of Solomon, and that made him likewise the beneficiary of an annual income starting with "six hundred and sixty-six talents of gold" (I Kings 10:14) and the proprietor of "seven hundred wives, princesses, and three hundred concubines" (I Kings 11:3). It was such a Solomon the author of Ecclesiastes would have a person think of as he listened to the tale of the author's own experiments at lavish living.

2. Canon. This evocation of Solomon, for the author's own, quite different purposes, perhaps also facilitated the admission of his book into the OT canon. At the close of the pre-Christian era the school of Hillel regarded Ecclesiastes as a book "which soils the hands" (is holy); not so the school of Shammai (M. 'Eduyot V.3). As late as the end of the first Christian century the academies were still considering whether the book is holy (M. Yadayim III.5; T. Shab. 30*b;* ARN I). It contains contradictions, some said; others suggested: it is not revealed wisdom, for it sets forth Solomon's private opinions

(T. Meg. 7*a*). If in one sense the book came too close to Solomon and was suspect just because, not God, but he seemed to be speaking in it, in another sense its attribution to Solomon of old may have saved it for the canon. The *Tosefta* suggests that books known to be recent products were not endorsed: "Ben Sira and books of later vintage are not sacred" (Tosef. Yadayim 2.13). But a book with Solomon's seal upon it could hardly be labeled modern. So Ecclesiastes was admitted to the CANON OF THE OT.

3. Position. In the LXX the three books attributed to Solomon (Proverbs, Ecclesiastes, and the Song of Solomon) follow on Psalms, attributed to the father of Solomon. The KJV and the RSV adopted this order, but the English version of the Jewish Publication Society includes Ecclesiastes with the Song of Solomon, Ruth, Lamentations, and Esther to make the Five Scrolls (*megilloth*), and these follow on the longer books Psalms, Proverbs, and Job among the Writings (*Kethubhim*) or Hagiographa. There is a rabbinic tradition which groups Proverbs, the Song of Solomon, and Ecclesiastes together as in the LXX, though with a different explanation: that King Hezekiah and his school preserved these three books (T. B.B. 14*b*-15*a*). Naturally, too, midrashic literature also groups together the "Solomonic" books; *Midrash Shir Hashirim Rabbah* to Song of S. 1:1 (section 10) suggests that Solomon wrote the Song of Solomon in his youth, when one sings, Proverbs when he attained maturity, and Ecclesiastes in his old age, because it is the way of old men to speak of life's illusions. There is a difference of opinion among the authorities in that midrashic passage, one suggesting that Solomon wrote Proverbs before the Song, another that he wrote all three books in a burst of inspiration near the end of his life—but all agree that old age had come upon him by the time he wrote Ecclesiastes.

The Solomonic tradition accounts for the grouping of Proverbs, the Song of Solomon, and Ecclesiastes, but another principle is involved in the clustering of the "five scrolls" characteristic, with rare exceptions, of Hebrew Bible MSS and editions. It was probably the custom of reading the scrolls in the synagogue on certain holy days that brought them together. There is no direct evidence from early times for the public reading of Ecclesiastes, but by the end of the eleventh century it was an established custom to read this scroll in the house of worship on the Feast of Tabernacles (*Machzor Vitry*, pp. 440-41), and the other four had since earlier times been assigned to appropriate occasions. In Bible MSS the five scrolls do not appear in a final, fixed order, though Ecclesiastes is usually in third or fourth place and in the company of the Song of Solomon.

4. Language, text, and versions. The association of Ecclesiastes with Solomon being no more than a literary device misunderstood, the date of the book is an open question. For determining the relative date the character of the Hebrew in which it is written is one fairly safe criterion. Style in this instance has more than usual significance. A hypothesis to the effect that the biblical book is a Hebrew translation of an Aramaic original, though warmly and ably defended, has not produced conviction. Such rhythmic lines as 7:15-20 are too good to be a translation from even a cognate language. The language of Ecclesiastes is better described as a stage in the development of the Hebrew itself. The book was written in the Hebrew of its author's day, and this was in transition to the Mishnaic idiom. The *waw* consecutive forms of the verb are all but totally lacking, and there is a relatively large proportion of participles; the relative pronoun ש appears about as often as אשר; a Persian word occurs—the word for PARK; and too many words and forms for chance suggest that the author and his public spoke Hebrew with an Aramaic accent. Such phenomena and others distinguish the language of Ecclesiastes from classical Hebrew and give it a pre-Mishnaic flavor. The bearing of this fact upon the question of the date of the book is obvious.

The text of Ecclesiastes is relatively clean. Some obscurities can be cleared up easily; little remains quite dark.

If the text of Ecclesiastes is fairly intact, the book had no very long history of textual transmission before it began to enjoy the loving care which preserved the whole Bible text almost unchanged throughout the Christian centuries. That there are no great differences between the Hebrew text and the early versions, including the quite literal Greek translation, apparently means that the recensions of the Hebrew text current in the age of the translators were fairly uniform; and this fact adds to the impression that the text of Ecclesiastes had no very long history before it became fixed. The probable date of the book points to the same conclusion.

5. The author and his times. Except that we know he was not Solomon, we know very little directly about the author of Ecclesiastes. Why, wishing to be associated with Solomon, he chose for himself the name Koheleth is not obvious. We can hardly suppose that he expected his readers to think automatically of Solomon's assembling of Israel in Jerusalem to dedicate his temple, even though the Hebrew word for "assemble" in I Kings 8:1 is from the same root as the name Koheleth. He may, instead, have meant to say something specific about himself, adopting a *nom de plume* that both concealed and suggested his identity. To us it suggests no more than that possibly he was a public figure connected with some "assembly." That, like Solomon whom he personates, he lived in Jerusalem, as he says in 1:12, 16, we have no reason to question. His urbanity and his cosmopolitanism, as well as his casual attitude toward temple affairs (5:1-5), suggest his residence in that center of cult and culture. His first-person narrative combines homiletic artistry with autobiography, invention with experience; and it is difficult to segregate the fact from the fiction. We could safely say that the author had the means himself to satisfy, to some extent at least, the desires to which in the person of Koheleth he gives full rein. He had wealth; he could indulge his appetites; he could entertain and travel; with his love of beauty and learning he could explore the arts and sciences. The author, like his personation, had experimented with life and could speak out of knowledge. It is probable too that, even as the Midrash surmised, he was advanced in years when he wrote and could speak feelingly of youth's advantage and the inconvenience of old age.

Both the author and his times went into the making of his book. The author played a dominant role; his book is a mirror of his personality, which united independence of judgment with a relaxed and charitable attitude and a grave and wistful disposition. This nature he brought to play upon his times, and their interaction produced the book. His times contributed as well.

The date of Ecclesiastes can be determined with some degree of assurance. Though, as it has seemed, the book was written late in the biblical period, it was certainly written before the Maccabean struggle, of which (unlike Daniel) it knows nothing; for, though the author Koheleth had an independent mind, he was not detached from realities, and the grim events of *ca.* 165 B.C. would not have passed him unnoticed. The total absence of apocalyptic thought is only partly explained by the fact that Koheleth has quite different concerns; his times apparently were not so desperate that men must escape into apocalypse.

This negative evidence finds positive support in ECCLESIASTICUS, a book which is readily datable (*ca.* 190 B.C.) and which appears to borrow thoughts and phrases from Ecclesiastes. If the similarities are genuine borrowings and not chance—and they seem too many for chance—Ecclesiastes was well known by 190 B.C. and must have been "published" sometime before 200, though not too long before. Thus, a date in the latter half of the third century is probable.

Other considerations add to the probability of this date. Although there are marked similarities (especially between Ecclesiastes and Epicureanism), no direct influence of Greek philosophers or philosophic systems—Stoics, Epicureans, Cynics, Cyrenaics—upon Ecclesiastes is demonstrable (Koheleth was indeed no philosopher, and Ecclesiastes is no "system"); and yet a Socratic spirit of untrammeled inquiry and of the autonomy of the human mind breathes through the lines of Koheleth—such a spirit as might well have been current in the mildly Hellenized Jerusalem of the century following the division of Alexander's empire.

More readily tangible for fixing the date of Koheleth than the suspicion of Greek influence on his way of thinking is the ideological position which his book occupies among the books of wisdom. This is best seen in the series Ezekiel, Proverbs, Job, Ecclesiastes. Schematically stated—with each step an oversimplification—this was the process: Answering to a human need among the recently exiled, Ezekiel established the principle that each man always receives from God what penalty his offense has warranted, what compensation his virtue has earned. Initially resisted, this principle gained favor until in the heyday of proverbial wisdom, when the bulk of Proverbs was being written, it had become axiomatic. A bold spirit, the author of Job, whose senses taught him otherwise, wrote an agonized doubt. The doctrine, now become an orthodoxy, is piously defended by Job's friends (and Elihu). It is, indeed, defended by Job himself, in desperate confusion, as he is painfully aware of flagrant injustice yet under compulsion to defend the principle of divine justice. Going beyond Job, the author of Ecclesiastes simply denies divine justice and acquiesces in the lack of it. Though an oversimplification, this description of the process is essentially right, and Koheleth, standing at the end of this line but before Ecclesiasticus and Daniel, may well belong to the third century—no earlier than this, since each of the stages starting with Ezekiel's statement of the principle involved a radical ideological readjustment. *See* WISDOM § 2*b-d*.

6. Unity of the book. The discussion of the author and his times has proceeded as though the book of Ecclesiastes were a unit, which is by no means certain. In fact, an editor, at least, and probably a glossator (one or more) had a hand in the book in addition to its author. The author identifies himself in first-person narrative style in 1:12 and continues with his confidential autobiography almost to the end of the book. But at the end (starting with 12:8), as at the beginning (1:1-2*a*) and once with a phrase in the heart of the book (7:27), Koheleth's "publisher" puts in a good, if not quite accurate, word for him. In 1:2*a;* 7:27 (with different word division in the Hebrew); and 12:8 this publisher merely adds the words "says Koheleth." He fashions his title page (1:1) after 1:12, 15, and so writes: "The words of Koheleth, the son of David, king in Jerusalem." The publisher's endorsement comes at the end: "Besides being wise, Koheleth also taught the people knowledge, weighing and studying and arranging proverbs with great care. Koheleth sought to find pleasing words, and uprightly he wrote words of truth" (12:9-10). The rest is similar; after Koheleth no more books need be written (12:11-12). And then, the "finis" line: "The end of the matter; all has been heard" (12:13*a*).

But after the end still some good counsel (13*b*-14): "Fear God, and keep his commandments; for this is the whole duty of man. For God will bring every deed into judgment, with every secret thing, whether good or evil." And this concluding advice, these maxims, introduce a new question. They mirror the orthodoxy of Job's friends. If they are original with Koheleth, then he has not abandoned the principle expressed in the discourses of those friends of Job and in these concluding verses of this book, that God treats each man according to his individual merit. But the body of Koheleth's work indeed denies this very principle. There are two possible ways to explain the contradiction. Conceivably the tension was within the author of Ecclesiastes, as seemingly it was within the author of Job. Alternatively, the tension was within the wisdom schools. And this latter explanation appears the more probable; Koheleth speaks with a single voice, but his colleagues have other views. If this explanation is correct, then the two maxims which now conclude the book and several more which now appear within the body of the work are the edifying contributions of a wisdom glossator who was moved by a spirit different from that of the author. And he probably speaks for others as well as himself—representing a normative view as against the heterodoxy of Koheleth, possibly even drawing upon a collection of proverbs already at hand.

That the book contains contradictions has long been recognized. The contradictions were offered as one reason for withholding it from the canon (*see* § 2 *above* and T. Shab. 30*a*, *b*). And recent opinion has held that the book was extensively glossed by one or more pious wisdom editors in an effort to blunt the edge of its dissidence. It is really only a question of how much.

In the somewhat disjointed latter half of the book, irrelevancy is hard to determine and therefore no very convincing test. The proverbs in 7:1-13 are a case in point. They deal with various matters and are strongly reminiscent of the book of Proverbs. And yet the recurrent ironical note and the grim humor: "The day of death [is better than] the day of birth"; "Say not, 'Why were the former days better than these?' " "Wisdom is good with an inheritance"; "Who can make straight what [God] has made crooked?" (vss. 1, 10, 11, 13); these may well mark the expressions as thoughts of Koheleth himself—his somewhat random musings, to be sure. The verse 7:26 is another example; but for its wry humor the latter part of the verse might even seem to go contrary to Koheleth's principles: "I found more bitter than death the woman whose heart is snares and nets, and whose hands are fetters; he who pleases God escapes her, but the sinner is taken by her."

Doctrine is a better test. If a proverb in Ecclesiastes gives conventional expression to a familiar and received doctrine which Koheleth is otherwise intent upon discrediting, this proverb is likely to be the work of the *fidei defensor*. Not that Koheleth demanded consistency—even consistency could be carried too far: "Do not make yourself overwise; why should you destroy yourself?" (7:16). Yet he took a position and was not given to casuistry. Doctrinally considered, the following passages, at odds with Koheleth's argument, appear to be glosses: "I said in my heart, God will judge the righteous and the wicked, for he has appointed a time for every matter, and for every work" (3:17 with a minor correction); "He who fears God shall come forth from them all" (7:18*b*); "He who obeys a command will meet no harm, and the mind of a wise man will know the time and way" (8:5); "Though a sinner does evil a hundred times and prolongs his life, yet I know that it will be well with those who fear God, because they fear before him; but it will not be well with the wicked, neither will he prolong his days like a shadow, because he does not fear before God" (8:12-13); "Know that for all these things God will bring you into judgment" (11:9*b*). Among the many scholars who suspect that Ecclesiastes contains "corrections" of this sort, it is these passages (along with 12:13*b*-14) on which the most will agree.

Now it is true that one is able to interpret away most of the difficulties in these (and other) probable glosses or explain away the apparent differences; but on the one hand the ingenuity involved in the explanation or the complexity of the interpretation raises the question whether any author could trust any reader to discover his meaning and logic without a commentary to supply the transitions, and on the other hand it would be stranger still if such a book as Ecclesiastes had been transmitted intact with never a reader's horrified "correction," when as a matter of course books with a far lower shocking potential were quite freely glossed. That someone glossed Koheleth's work in the interest of right thinking is more than probable (the author of Wisd. Sol. 2, quite a while later, was thoroughly incensed), but the glosses are fewer than some have supposed.

We do not obtain a synoptic view of the book even when we have reduced it by the few verses added editorially and tendentiously. What remains is no argument systematically unfolded; in large part it is musings loosely accumulated, and the associative links are at times not to be recovered. The book is a kind of philosopher's diary, pages from an artist's notebook, a thinking aloud, a gathering of literary fragments published without plan. The unity is of mood more than form.

7. Thought of Koheleth. Koheleth thinks of many things, but prominent in his speculation are the areas of wisdom (how we know), ethics (what is good), and religion (God's way with man).

a. Wisdom. Koheleth was making a study of human society. He set out to observe and take notes, and, because men are basically alike, himself to experiment (2:1) and to record his own findings (7:27). He was animated by a spirit of inquiry. He applied his mind "to seek and to search out by wisdom all that is done under heaven" (1:13), determined to "see what was good for the sons of men to do . . . during the few days of their life" (2:3*b*). To this end he undertook specific projects: "to know madness and folly" (1:17; cf. 2:12; 7:25), to know "how to cheer my body with wine" (2:3*a*), to learn what goes on "in the place of justice" (3:16), and to examine all things (8:9, 16; 9:1).

Having observed them by reason of his inquiring mind, he makes sorrowful record of sundry social phenomena: "oppressions . . . practiced under the sun" (4:1), "in the place of justice, . . . wickedness" (3:16), "riches . . . kept by their owner to his hurt" (5:13—H 5:12), "a man to whom God gives wealth, . . . and honor, . . . yet . . . does not give him power to enjoy them" (6:2), "folly . . . set in many high places, . . . slaves on horses, and princes walking on foot" (10:6-7). He relates more fully certain cases illustrative of the world's folly: the case of the lonely miser (4:7-8), the case of the fickle mob (4:13-16), the case of the forgotten man (9:13-16).

It is not, to be sure, an objective catalogue of social data which he compiles; his interpretation colors the record. He has seen that one fate comes to the wise man and the fool (2:14); he has "found more bitter than death the woman whose heart is snares, . . . and whose hands are fetters" (7:26). He has seen that "the race is not to the swift, . . . nor favor to the men of skill; but time and chance happen to them all" (9:11). His observations are many (7:15, 27; 8:9), and he opens his record with a sweeping conclusion; "I have seen everything that is done under the sun; and behold, all is vanity and a striving after wind" (1:14). This generalization he permits himself as a man of broad experience and great wisdom (1:16).

Not only does he have eyes in his head; this man is also given to introspection and reflection; "I said to myself" is his phrase (1:16; 2:1)—"I said to myself, 'What befalls the fool will befall me also; why then have I been so very wise?' And I said to myself that this also is vanity" (2:15). He ponders his evidence; when he sees injustice, he says "in his heart," or considers the possibility, that God is thus testing the sons of men (3:18; cf. vs. 17): "I saw," "I perceived," "I know" (1:17; 2:13; 3:14; 4:4; 8:16-17). The most significant of these conclusions is his repeated well-considered opinion that what is best for men is "to be happy and enjoy themselves as long as they live" (3:12, and often).

It is notable that Koheleth evokes no authority for his statements other than experience and the reasoned conclusions to which observed phenomena necessarily point. His book contains nothing of the prophetic "word of the Lord," nor any reference to Sinai—nothing even of things "that our fathers have told us" (Ps. 78:3). The author sets out to test all notions against the evidence of his own experience. He indeed claims no more than this for his book, and Rabbi Simeon ben Menasya was half right when he said that it is Solomon's private wisdom (T. Meg. 7*a*).

The spirit of free inquiry which breathes through the book of Koheleth is a remarkable feature of the book, one which it shares in part with Job, since Job, too, seeks truth—if need be, at the cost of received dogma (Job 13:7-12). There is hardly anything that Koheleth does not query.

Koheleth, wise with the wisdom of Solomon, admits his superiority: "I have acquired great wisdom . . . ; my mind has had great experience of wisdom and knowledge" (1:16; cf. 2:9). Although he says: "I have acquired," referring to his wisdom as to an earned degree, wisdom is not for him always something which a man obtains through his own efforts; it may resemble "native intelligence" and come as a gift from God to the man who pleases him (2:26; cf. 9:3). As such it is like the wisdom which came to Solomon as a divine favor, according to the narrative in I Kings 3:3-14. But the proverbialists regarded wisdom as an acquisition; in Prov. 4:5, 7, and throughout Prov. 1–9, they invite the youth to acquire wisdom, just as, according to Eccl. 1:16, Koheleth did for himself. In Koheleth wisdom is a synonym of "knowledge" and "skill" (1:18; 2:21; 7:12; 9:10).

It is because Koheleth has gained such great wisdom that he can undertake his study of human life (1:13; 2:3; and possibly 9:13, if we translate, not "example of," but "through" wisdom). He even turns wisdom on itself, through wisdom considering the virtue of wisdom—weighing it against folly (1:17; 2:12; cf. 2:3*b;* and especially 7:23-25).

Koheleth finds that it is a misfortune when fools bear rule (4:13; 10:5-6), and that intelligent leadership is more effective than an army (9:14-15*a,* 16*a,* 18). He finds one fortunate who is wise, for wisdom brings a man luck (10:2), preserves and protects him (7:12*b,* 19), and helps him both earn a living (10:10?) and advantageously use his acquired wealth (7:11-12*a;* cf. 2:18-19). A fool, he says repeatedly, is known by his chatter (5:3*b*—H 5:2*b;* 7:5; 10:12*b*-13, 14*a;* similarly 7:6, 9; 10:1, 3), but welcome and precious are the words of the wise (7:5; 9:17; 10:12*a*). For him wisdom is practically the same as virtue, folly the same as sin (7:16-17). God "has no pleasure in fools" (5:4—H 5:3), but joy comes along with wisdom as a gift of God (2:26; cf. 9:1). The wise man, indeed, may smile (8:1), for wisdom brightens his life (2:13-14*a*). Koheleth commends wisdom.

But in his attitude toward wisdom and folly, Koheleth is both conventional and undogmatic. He is healthy-minded enough to recognize and acknowledge the advantages of intelligence as against stupidity. But he refuses to be dogmatic even about these advantages and has to say: "The wise man dies just like the fool" (2:16; cf. vs. 14*b* and 6:8). "What befalls the fool will befall me also; why then have I been so very wise?" (2:15). Here, too, he commends moderation; as with righteousness and evildoing, so with wisdom and folly: "Be not righteous overmuch, and do not make yourself overwise. . . . Be not wicked overmuch, neither be a fool. . . . It is good that you should take hold of this, and from that withhold not your hand" (7:16-18*a*). One can go too far even in being wise:

> In much wisdom is much vexation,
> and he who increases knowledge increases sorrow
> (1:18).

In fact, his position proceeds from his skepticism. Though for knowledge he relies on nothing more than upon the conclusions which his own observations and experiments lead to, he is yet dubious that thus he can sound the depths of life. "All this," he says, "I have tested by wisdom; I said, 'I will be wise'; but it was far from me. That which is, is far off, and deep, very deep; who can find it out?" (7:23-24). "When I applied my mind to know wisdom, and to see the business that is done on earth, . . . then I saw all the work of God, that man cannot find out the work that is done under the sun. However much man may toil in seeking, he will not find it out; even though a wise man claims to know, he cannot find it out" (8:16-17).

b. Ethics. Without defining his terms, as though he means by them what everyone else means, Koheleth speaks of the "righteous man," צדיק, and the "wicked man," רשע (7:20; 8:10; 9:1; and together in 7:15-17; 8:14; 9:2); of "justice," משפט, or "righteousness," צדק, and "wickedness," רשע (5:8—H 5:7; 7:17, 25; and together in 3:16); of "sin," חטא (5:6—H 5:5; 7:20; and in 10:4 "offences"), and "sinners" (8:12; 9:2, 18). Like their English equivalents the Hebrew words for "good" and "evil," טוב and רע, sometimes have moral overtones, and frequently do not, connoting instead "good fortune" and "misfortune." Though Koheleth often employs these two words, he seldom uses "good" for "virtuous" and "evil" for "sinful"; yet he does, e.g., in 7:20; 9:2, 18 ("good"); and 5:1—H 4:17 (?); 7:15; 9:3 ("evil"). He probably means what the eighth-century prophets meant when he uses their vocabulary in 5:8—H 5:7: "If you see . . . the poor oppressed and justice and right violently taken away," or in 4:1: "I saw all the oppressions. . . . And behold, the tears of the oppressed. . . . On the side of their oppressors . . . power" (and cf. 7:7). Despite his questioning, Koheleth, when speaking of morals, thus employs conventional words in their conventional sense.

Koheleth, therefore, had his standards, knew between good and evil, and was not "above" or "beyond" them. No doubt his behavior was that of any honest, decent, and respectable citizen. If it be objected that he was a slaveholder (2:7), the objection is not valid—having slaves in his day was a mark of respectability.

He behaved himself, was neither immoral nor amoral. Only, he could not say (*a*) how he knew the morally good, nor (*b*) why he chose it, nor yet (*c*) how, indeed, he was able to choose at all. Though consideration of these three questions, fundamental to any ethics, was central to his purpose, he found no answers for them.

a) How does one know right from wrong? Koheleth does not undertake an answer in terms of the question. When he asks: "Who knows what is good for man while he lives the few days of his vain life?" (6:12), he is asking a related but different question, not what is morally right but what is empirically profitable—and, as he knew, the two need not be the same. So his rhetorical question is not a denial that man can know the good but skepticism about whether man knows even what is good for him.

Koheleth's way to knowledge is through observation, but his inquiries and experiments are also not a quest for knowledge of the absolute moral good; they are a search for the profitable course. He makes little use of ways to knowledge except the way of experience. There is a possible reference to revelation in the term "listen" in 5:1—H 4:17: "To draw near to listen is better than to offer the sacrifice of fools." But all in all, Koheleth holds, God conceals more than he communicates (8:17; 11:5; *see below*). It may be inferred that because he phrases many of his thoughts as proverbs, he stood under the influence of the schools and their wisdom. And it is probable that, since he uses conventional ethical terms often in a quite conventional sense, he was less unorthodox by nature than by profession, and for him, too, right and wrong were—more than he knew them to be—the mores of his society. He was no anarchist by nature.

There is this ambiguity about the ethics of Koheleth: that he never clearly suggests the source of man's knowledge of right and wrong, but also he does not deny the possibility of having such knowledge.

b) Why a man should choose the right, Koheleth really cannot say. There is no apparent advantage in it for a man. "There are righteous men to whom it happens according to the deeds of the wicked, and there are wicked men to whom it happens according to the deeds of the righteous" (8:14; cf. 7:15). And all alike must die: "One fate comes to all, to the righteous and the wicked" (9:2; cf. 2:15). If virtue goes unrewarded, sin unrequited, in this life, even less notice is taken of them in death (cf. 6:6*b;* 9:5). The dead rest forever in darkness; like an "untimely birth" which "comes into vanity and goes into darkness," where "it finds rest" (6:3-5; cf. 11:8), the dead are no longer sentient or desirous (9:6). "There is no work or thought or knowledge or wisdom in Sheol" (9:10). Since reward and punishment are not apparent either in life or in its sequel, why should one choose the right?

c) How, indeed, can man choose at all? Like many another in our theological tradition, in the matter of man's freedom to choose despite predestination and nature's endless repetitions (1:4-10) Koheleth abides in paradox. He can hold that "there is . . . a time for every matter" (3:1-8; cf. 3:14); he can say: "The righteous and the wise and their deeds are in the hand of God" (9:1), and ask: "Apart from him who can eat or who can have enjoyment?" (2:25 with a minor correction; cf. 7:13); he can speak thus of all that is foreordained, and he can then shift ground and for his ethics put upon man the responsibility: "God made man upright, but they have sought out many devices" (7:29); "also the hearts of men are full of evil" (9:3; cf. the gloss, 8:11). Whether God holds the reins loose or tight, man lives as though he is choosing his way.

Although, then, the author of Ecclesiastes develops no clear-cut system of ethics which contains answers to these basic questions, he yet proposes a way of life and a social attitude. They may be viewed as three admonitions.

Since absolute righteousness is beyond human reach ("Surely there is not a righteous man on earth who does good and never sins" [7:20]), a person should not demand of himself the impossible and suffer sure defeat, but neither should he let himself go completely, to his sure ruin: "Be not righteous overmuch, and do not make yourself overwise; why should you destroy yourself? Be not wicked overmuch, neither be a fool; why should you die before your time?" (7:16-17). This counsel of moderation has a timeless quality, from Aristotle's "mean" to current psychotherapy. It is the first admonition.

Koheleth's second admonition runs like a brightly colored cord through the loose fabric of his book. It is the charge to make the most of life—while it lasts. Seven times this is said: in 2:24-25; 3:12-13; 3:22; 5:18–6:2—H 5:17–6:2; 8:15; 9:9; 11:8-9—with some variety but with essential sameness: "There is nothing better for a man than that he should eat and drink, and find enjoyment in his toil" (which means "through his earnings"). When here (2:24-25) he first states the theme, Koheleth continues: "This also, I saw, is from the hand of God," which cannot mean "ordered by God" but can only mean "permitted" (cf. 3:13). Ignoring his theoretical determinism, Koheleth begs men to take advantage of this chance, their portion (5:18-19—H 5:17-18; 9:9). There is an urgency in his voice as, in 11:9, he turns to youth with a special word: "Rejoice, O young man, in your youth, and let your heart cheer you in the days of your youth; walk in the ways of your heart and the sight of your eyes." Such is his insistence that one may believe he regarded the pursuit of happiness as no less than a moral obligation and interference with another's right to life as a sin and a crime, an evil which "lies heavy upon men . . . , a sore affliction" (6:1-2).

This second admonition, like a refrain, seven times repeated, punctuates the discourse and seems to be its author's foremost thought. "I commend enjoyment," he says, "for man has no good thing under the sun but to eat, and drink, and enjoy himself" (8:15). But he has one further thing to say, and it is yet more striking.

The high point in the ethics of Ecclesiastes is found in 4:1-12. Koheleth has compared men to beasts; all are from the dust and share one destiny (3:19-21). Here, with compassion for the human victims of human rapacity, he speaks of the law of the jungle in the society of man: "I saw all the oppressions that are practiced under the sun. And behold, the tears of the oppressed, and they had no one to comfort them! On the side of their oppressors there was power, and there was no one to comfort them" (4:1). Ironically, this lawless law can be defended as the source of profit and progress: "I saw that all toil [i.e., profit] and all skill in work come from a man's envy of his neighbor" (4:4*a*)—competition is the life of trade.

But utter loneliness may be the exorbitant price of success; the victor may miss out on life and achieve no more than resplendent solitude, and "this also is vanity and an unhappy business" (4:7-8), and "woe to him who is alone when he falls and has not another to lift him up" (4:10).

Better then that men help one another—this is the third admonition. Let the herd unite for profit, and for comfort, and for survival: "Two are better than one, because they have a good reward for their toil"; moreover, "if two lie together, they are warm"; also, "a threefold cord is not quickly broken" (4:9-12).

This, then, is the positive side of Ecclesiastes' ethics: pity for the human state, leading to a plea for mutual aid.

c. Religion. The religion of Koheleth, like his ethics, displays a duality; herein a practical piety mingles with a theoretical heterodoxy.

Koheleth acknowledges God—no question there—and recognizes that God is the creator and the source of life (12:1, 7; cf. 7:29), and he assumes with less than proof some continuing divine activity in human society—even a kind of individual care and attention: "To the man who pleases him God gives wisdom and knowledge and joy; but to the sinner he gives the work of gathering and heaping, only to give to one who pleases God" (2:26; cf. 2:25; 7:26*b*). His ethics reveals in part (*see above*) how he supposes a man might "please" God, with conduct which includes elements of conventional morality. He also commends a modicum of religious practice, in the narrower sense of the term: Go to the house of God, but not so much to offer sacrifices and to multiply prayer as "to listen" (5:1-2—H 4:17–5:1), and "pay what you vow" (5:4-6—H 5:3-5). He does not protest—he lacks enthusiasm for the cult; nevertheless, he would have a man discharge his obligations; "fear God!" (5:7—H 5:6).

There are also less usual features in his religion, as the shape of his ethics indeed suggests. For one thing, his God is somewhat withdrawn and not very communicative.

Biblical religion locates God in heaven, but it rarely makes him inaccessible: one prays. Koheleth says: "Be not rash with your mouth, . . . for God is in heaven, and you upon earth" (5:2—H 5:1).

Biblical religion puts God in constant communication with man—through lawgiver, prophet, and priest, and directly—in response to prayer. Though once Koheleth suggests that in the house of God one "listen" (5:1—H 4:17), he otherwise emphasizes the inscrutable mystery of God: "Man cannot find out" (8:17; cf. 7:14). "As you do not know how the spirit comes to the bones in the womb of a woman with child, so you do not know the work of God who makes everything" (11:5, with a minor correction; cf. 9:1). This is reminiscent of God's challenge to Job and is no isolated expression otherwise, but it is not the commoner biblical view.

Not only is Koheleth's God remote and silent; he is inflexible. Biblical religion knows a God who listens to reason, and is influenced by man's repentance. The words of Koheleth's God are the "laws of the Medes and Persians."

> Consider the work of God;
> who can make straight what he has made crooked?
> (7:13);

and "Whatever God does endures for ever; nothing can be added to it, nor anything taken from it; God has made it so, in order that men should fear before him" (3:14). This is the description of a God who determines and changes not.

Biblical religion is dominated by the doctrine of the "two ways." The ethics of Koheleth (*see above*) ignores a deterministic element in his religious thinking (9:1; 2:25), and repeatedly urges man to "eat and drink and take pleasure," quite as though the choice is his. Ignoring the limitation, Koheleth is nearer biblical religion than he is in his determinism. Urging man to enjoy life because this "is God's gift to man" (3:13), he is probably not so much repudiating the determinism in his religious position as he is emphasizing the remoteness of God. God's essential unconcern gives man the chance (this is his "lot" or "portion") to make the most of his short life.

Bibliography. Introductions and commentaries: M. Jastrow, *A Gentle Cynic* (1919). P. Volz, "Hiob und Weisheit," *Schriften des AT* (1921). A. L. Williams, "Ecclesiastes," *Cambridge Bible* (1922). H. Odeberg, *Qohaelaeth* (1929). H. W. Hertzberg, *Der Prediger* (1932). K. Galling, "Die Fünf Megilloth," *HAT* (1940). V. Reichert and A. Cohen, "The Five Megilloth," *Soncino Books of the Bible* (1946), pp. 104-91. R. H. Pfeiffer, *Introduction to the OT* (1948), pp. 724-31. I. Bettan, *The Five Scrolls* (1950), pp. 123-91. A. Bentzen, *Introduction to the OT* (1952), II, 188-91. A. D. Power, *Ecclesiastes or The Preacher* (1952). R. Gordis, *Koheleth—The Man and His World* (1955). O. Eissfeldt, *Einleitung in das AT* (1956), pp. 605-17. O. S. Rankin, Introduction and Exegesis of Ecclesiastes, *IB*, V (1956), 3-88.

Special studies: G. G. Bradley, *Lectures on Ecclesiastes* (1898). D. B. Macdonald, *The Hebrew Literary Genius* (1933), pp. 197-215. H. L. Ginsberg, *Studies in Koheleth* (1950); "The Structure and Contents of the Book of Koheleth," *Supplements to VT*, III (1955), 138-49.

See also bibliography under WISDOM. S. H. BLANK

ECCLESIASTICUS ĭ klē'zĭ ăs'tə kəs [Lat., *from* ἐκκλησιαστικός, of (*i.e.*, to be read in) church]. The seventh book (and probably the earliest to be written) of the APOCRYPHA, ascribed to Jesus (Hebrew Joshua; Aramaic Jeshua) the son of Sirach, who appears to have taught in Jerusalem during the first quarter of the second century B.C. It is the most comprehensive sample of extant Jewish WISDOM literature and bears striking resemblances to the canonical book of Proverbs; although, unlike the latter, it is more obviously the work of one author, showing a general uniformity of style which makes it much more than a mere collection of maxims drawn from multifarious sources. The work has been widely respected in both Jewish and Christian circles.

1. Date
2. Text
3. Author

1. Date. A general consideration of Ben Sirach's thought and style suggests that his work was written sometime during the century immediately preceding the outbreak of the Maccabean Revolt in 168 B.C. But there are two passages which seem to supply more precise information.

a) From the Greek translator's preface we gather that he was a grandson of the author, that he arrived in Egypt in the thirty-eighth year of the reign of Euergetes, and that after living there for some time he started work on his translation from the Hebrew. There were two Ptolemaic kings who bore the title "Euergetes" (i.e., "Benefactor")—namely, Ptolemy III Euergetes I (247-221) and Ptolemy VII Euergetes II Physicon (170-117)—but as the former reigned for little more than twenty-five years, the latter must be the one to whom reference is made in the Prologue. Thus it may be inferred that the translator arrived in Egypt in 132 B.C., and that his grandfather, Ben Sirach, flourished in the early decades of the second century—before the persecution under Antiochus IV Epiphanes in 168 B.C., to which he makes no allusion.

b) Ben Sirach's eulogy of the high priest Simon son of Onias (50:1-24) gives the impression that he had only recently held office; the phrase "in his life" (vs. 1 G) seems to imply that his death has taken place, while in the concluding lines (vss. 23*b*-24 H) there is a prayer for peace among the sons of Simon so that the covenant with Phinehas (cf. 45:23; Num. 25:12-13), which restricted the high priesthood to the first-born descendants of ZADOK, might be maintained forever. Josephus mentions two high priests named Simon son of Onias: one of these, Simon I the Just, is assigned to a period *ca*. 300 B.C. (Antiq. XII. ii.5; iv.1); the other, Simon II, was in office *ca*. a century later (Antiq. XII.iv.10; v.1; cf. III Macc. 2: 1). Some scholars have identified Simon I with the Simon of Ben Sirach's eulogy, partly to allow time for the growth of legendary fame about his name. On the other hand, in view of the confused nature of the data, it is arguable that Simon I is really a fiction of the rabbinical imagination. In the Mishna (Ab. 1.2) he bridges a gap of over two centuries, mediating the tradition from the men of the Great Synagogue in the time of Ezra (*ca*. 400 B.C.) to Antigonus of Socho (*ca*. 180 B.C.); and Josephus apparently knows nothing of him, save that he was renowned for his piety and benevolence (Antiq. XII.ii.5). According to the Talmud, Simon I the Just received Alexander the Great in 332 B.C. (T.B. Yom. 69*a*), whereas Josephus reports that it was the high priest Jaddua, grandfather of Simon I, who received Alexander (Antiq. XI.viii.4-5). Moreover, while we learn from the Talmud that Onias son of Simon the Just built the temple for the worship of Yahweh in Egypt (T.B. Men. 109*b;* J.T. Yom. 6.3), Josephus contradicts himself by attributing the founding of the temple at Leontopolis to Onias III son of Simon (War VII.x.2-4) and to Onias IV son of Onias III (Antiq. XII.v.1; v.7; XIII.iii.1-3). But whether it was the son or the grandson of Simon who was responsible for the building of the temple in Egypt (*ca*. 163 B.C.), the reference is clearly not to Simon I the Just but to Simon II (Antiq. XII.iv.10), whose son Onias III (II Macc. 3–4) was removed from office early in the reign of Antiochus Epiphanes (175-164). Thus it is not impossible that Simon I the Just is a legendary figure originating in the rabbinical schools to cover the dark period between Ezra and Antigonus of Socho, and that Josephus sought to bridge the gap by utilizing an artificially constructed list of high priests.

Accordingly, the inference may reasonably be drawn that Ecclesiasticus was written between 195 (the approximate date of the death of Simon II) and 171, when Antiochus Epiphanes, having already deposed Onias III (the last legitimate high priest of Zadokite descent) in favor of his brother Jason, removed the latter and appointed Menelaus, a Benjamite, in his stead. Ben Sirach manifestly knew nothing of this flagrant violation of the covenant with Phinehas, although he seems to betray anxieties about possible future developments in certain passages (45: 26; 50:24 H).

2. Text. There are three principal extant recensions of the text of Ecclesiasticus—namely, the Greek of the LXX and its descendant versions, the Syriac of the Peshitta, and the Hebrew fragments with which are associated the rabbinic quotations. The Syriac MSS represent a uniform kind of text, the other two recensions mixed types; and in the case of the Greek MSS, but not in that of the Hebrew MSS, the evidence allows of a subdivision into two groups, Greek I and Greek II. The Hebrew recension used in the making of Greek II seems to have been based on that behind Greek I. On the other hand, the two later recensions, represented by the Syriac and the Hebrew MSS, are apparently on direct lines of descent from Ben Sirach's autograph. But they show signs of influence from the older recensions, the Syriac MSS having readings peculiar to Greek I and Greek II, and the Hebrew MSS having readings peculiar to Greek I, Greek II, and the Syriac. Not being canonical, the text was free from authoritative control; and as the work was popular, it was frequently copied over a prolonged period—hence the numerous textual changes and corruptions to which the MSS bear witness.

In 1896-1900 almost two thirds of Ecclesiasticus was recovered in Hebrew from four MSS, designated A, B, C, D, belonging to the eleventh and twelfth centuries, found in the Genizah (or synagogue repository for worn-out MSS) in Old Cairo. A fifth MS from the Genizah, MS Adler 3597, designated E in the textual criticism of Ecclesiasticus, was published in 1931, adding 34 distichs in Hebrew to the 1,056 provided by MSS A, B, C, D, out of the 1,616 represented in Greek. In 1956 it was reported that on two fragments from Cave 2 at Qumran scraps of verses from 6:20-31 had been identified, and in 1957 that the text was practically the same as that of the Hebrew MS A. For a thorough discussion of the relationship among the several witnesses to the text, *see* the work of M. H. Segal in the *bibliography*.

3. Author. Apart from the scanty information supplied by the Greek prologue and quotations in later writings, our knowledge of the author is based entirely upon internal evidence.

a. Name. Ecclesiasticus is the only book in the Apoc. to which the author attached his name; the others are either attributed to some outstanding individual in Hebrew history or allowed to appear anonymously. The extant texts, however, give the name in various ways. The Genizah text (B) in 50:27 has: "Simon, son of Jesus, son of Eleazar, son of Sira"; the colophon (after 51:30) has two renderings of the name, the first being "Simon, son of Jesus, who is called son of Sira," the second being as in 50:27; the Hebrew copy owned by Saadia Gaon in the tenth century evidently had the same name as the extant text in 50:27. The Syriac colophon has "Jesus, son of Simon, who is called son of Asira ['captive']" twice repeated (with minor variants). It is not improbable that the inclusion of "Simon" in the genealogy is a scribal error due to the occurrence of the name in 50:1, 24 H. The Greek text in 50:27 has "Jesus son of Sirach the Jerusalemite," but the best MSS (א, A, B) add "Eleazar" to "Simon." In his preface the Greek translator names the author "my grandfather Jesus," and the Greek title prefixed to 51:1 (doubtless an early scribal heading) reads: "Prayer of Jesus son of Sirach." *See* SIRACH, SON OF.

b. Interests. Ben Sirach was well versed in the Scriptures, particularly the books of Proverbs and Psalms and the Pentateuch; and, while remaining true to the religion of his fathers, he shows a relatively broad outlook. He had reflected long on life and its vicissitudes (cf. 51:13-22), and though he had a philosophical turn of mind, his wise sayings largely represent a form of prudentialism. His philosophy of life was practical and empirical, and he was skeptical of metaphysical speculations, holding that the ultimate mysteries of the world are beyond human comprehension (3:17-24).

Ben Sirach had traveled in foreign lands (34:11) and had frequently been in danger of death (34:12); he speaks of perils of all kinds from which God had delivered him, though here (51:1-12) he may be expatiating on a poetic theme and deliberately imitating the psalms of suffering. Perhaps like other wise men he had participated in diplomatic missions and had known what it was to appear before rulers (39:4).

Ben Sirach's counsel ranges over a wide area of human activity, and he deals with social and religious duties, the highest of which is the search for wisdom (14:20–15:8). But his utilitarianism is never far from his thoughts, and he does not forget to stress that the acquisition of wisdom, besides the spiritual values it brings, will eventually benefit with pecuniary rewards (51:28).

Ben Sirach is deeply mistrustful of women, thinking of them as enticers to wickedness (42:9-14); this view seems to be partly based on personal knowledge of unhappy marriages (25:16-26) and of the worries occasioned to fathers by the possession of highly sexed daughters (26:10-12), and partly on a metaphysical theory concerning the origin of evil (25:24); on the other hand, he does not think that a happy marriage is impossible (26:1-4), holding that the husband of a good wife is more blessed by far than a bachelor (36:18-26). He advocates strictness in the training of children (30:1-13).

He had considerable poetic talent, as is shown in the psalms of praise for the works of God in nature (42:15–43:33).

He defends the work of physicians against objections which may have been leveled against them from religious scruples (cf. II Chr. 16:12), arguing that healing skill comes from God (38:1-8). But it cannot be argued from this that Ben Sirach practiced medicine, nor can it be inferred from his respect for the priesthood (45:6-26) that he was a priest. The probability is that he was a scholar who conducted classes in Jerusalem, and in 51:23 he is evidently inviting young men to attend his academy (בית המדרש—the first occurrence in extant literature, but later used commonly of rabbinical schools). He had applied himself to the study of wisdom while he was still young, before his travels abroad (39:4). As a scholar and teacher he combined the functions of "sage" and "scribe"—i.e., he imparted general instruction for the conduct of life (the sort of teaching we find in the book of Proverbs) and at the same time taught the ordinances of the law of Moses. In his portrayal of the genuine scribe Ben Sirach may well be presenting an idealized picture of his own career (38:24–39:11): a man of culture with the means to devote his time to study, a man who has traveled abroad and who attains to eminence in public affairs.

c. Hellenism. In his counsels respecting banquets of wine accompanied by music and animated conversation (32:4-6—G 35:4-6), and in his suggestion that an intelligent man avoids consorting with loose women, just as the cultivated palate avoids inferior foods (36:18-24; cf. 9:4; 19:2), Ben Sirach reflects a way of life which seems to have been much affected by the diffusion of Greek civilization which followed on the conquests of Alexander the Great. Moreover, as he had traveled abroad and served in the courts of foreign princes (34:11-12—G 31:12-13), the likelihood is that he had come into still closer contact with Hellenistic culture. But we cannot definitely say that he had learned Greek, and the parallels which have been cited between certain of his aphorisms and pronouncements made by Greek authors, especially Euripides and Theognis, largely belong to the common stock of ideas to which ancient moralists gave expression. Like Plato, he can advocate temperance (31:12-30—G 34:12-30); like Euripides, he can show a deep mistrust of women (25:24); like Theognis, he can condemn false friendship (37:1-6)—but these similarities by no means prove that he had firsthand acquaintance with the works of the Greek writers in question. Perhaps more noteworthy is 11:28, where Ben Sirach declares that no one should be called happy before his death, for this is a point frequently made in Greek writings (cf. Herodotus I.32; Aeschylus *Agamemnon* 928-29; Sophocles *Oedipus Rex* 1528-30; Euripides *Troades* 509-10; etc.). In 13:2 a piece of advice to the effect that one should not associate with people who are richer and more powerful than oneself, is reinforced by what appears to be an allusion to Aesop's fable (329) of the pot and the kettle. Holding that God discloses his secrets to the humble, Ben Sirach asserts the vanity of all human endeavors to solve the ultimate problems of existence (3:17-25), and here he may be thinking specifically of the excessive confidence of certain Greek philosophers in the powers of human reason. Such repudiation of what is taken to be a form of intellectual arrogance comes to expression in earlier Hebrew writings (Job 9:10; 11:7; Isa. 40:13-14; 55:8-9), as well as in the works of certain Greek authors (Euripides *Helena* 1137-49; *Bacchae* 393-94; 427-31). Ben Sirach's conception of the scribe as a man of leisure (Ecclus. 38:24) may have been determined to some extent by Greek ideals concerning the scholarly philosopher or lover of wisdom (the word "scholar" is derived from σχολή, "leisure"), but it should be noticed that there are parallels elsewhere, as in the Egyptian *Instructions of Duauf,* e.g.; on this question Jewish tradition does not seem to have followed Ben Sirach's advice, for Jewish scribes or biblical scholars appear generally to have made a point of learning a trade, as in the well-known case of the apostle Paul, who was a tentmaker (Acts 18:3; cf. M. Ab. 2.2). Accordingly, while Hellenistic culture may have had some positive influence on Ben Sirach's thought, it cannot be said that such influence was either profound or extensive.

The fact is that the negative influence of Hellenism is much more pronounced than the positive, and this may help to account for the combination of particularism and universalism in Ben Sirach's thought—a paradox which is, however, to be found already in the writings of the prophets. Although Yahweh is the creator of all things (42:15–43:33), Israel is his chosen people who will ultimately be glorified (17:17; 44:21; 47:22); and although Wisdom is a divine quality that suffuses all created existence, yet she has her proper home in Zion in the midst of an honored people (24:8-12) and can even be identified with the law of Moses (24:23). Hence, in addition to the general principles of ethical prudentialism, such as largely make up the book of Proverbs, we have also something of the work of a scribe as this was later to be understood in Jewish circles—i.e., the expositions of a man who had made a special study of the Scriptures with a view to facilitating progress in living according to the declared will of God (cf. the first paragraph of the Greek prologue). The adoption of Hellenistic customs appears to have reached its height in 174-171 B.C. during the high priesthood of Jason (II Macc. 4:13) the second son of Simon II, who was appointed by Antiochus Epiphanes; but already when Ben Sirach was writing, Jewish society seems to have been seriously affected by the allurements of Greek civilization, and it is probably in the light of such a situation that his call for an uncompromising obedience to the words of the Lord is to be understood (cf. Ecclus. 2:15). Only the sinner tries to walk along two ways at the same time—i.e., presumably, tries to combine Judaism in religion with Hellenism in culture (2:12). Only misguided individuals argue (with Epicureanlike confidence) that man is too trivial a creature for his conduct to be an object of God's concern (16:17-23). The Lord, whose eyes are ten thousand times brighter than the sun (23:19), will punish those who lose their powers of endurance (2:14), and it is woe to those who forsake the law of the Most High God (41:8) and are ashamed of their divine heritage (42:2). No matter how lowly his circumstances, a man who fears the Lord ranks higher than noblemen, judges, and rulers (10:24). But Ben Sirach offers no argued critique of Hellenism; he presupposes that divine Wisdom is uniquely embodied in the Scriptures. This is a self-evident axiom, and other faiths are idolatrous, no more effective than the groans of a eunuch who embraces a maiden (cf. 30:18-20).

4. Contents. Ecclesiasticus may be largely based on lecture notes which Ben Sirach rewrote in verse for publication, but he evidently followed no definite scheme in the arrangement of his material. Although there are several passages concerning wisdom in the first forty-one chapters, which may have been intended to serve as introductions to the topics they precede, the fact remains that, apart from 42:15–50:26, the constituent sections are not clearly indicated. It is not surprising, therefore, that many different proposals have been made regarding the division of the book. One view is that the work falls into two principal parts, chs. 1–23; chs. 24–50, which were published separately; and two pieces of evidence have been cited in support. Firstly, the two parts begin with the book's longest poems in praise of wisdom (1:1-20; 24:1-29; cf. the opening disquisition on wisdom in Prov. 1–9). Secondly, in 24:30-34 Ben Sirach, writing metaphorically, declares that his canal, fed by the law of Moses, which is like a great fructifying stream that overflows its banks (vss. 23-29), became a river and his river a sea, and so he can again pour out his teaching like prophecy; this may be taken to mean that after the publication of his first volume he found that his material continued to grow, and consequently he soon had enough for the publication of a second. It is also to be observed that after 42:14, short moralizing essays fall away; the section 42:15–50:26 is made up of three relatively long poems, the first in praise of God for his works in nature (42:15–43:33), the second in praise of the fathers of old (chs. 44–49), the third in praise of Simon the high priest (50:1-26). Perhaps these poems had previously been published separately, and Ben Sirach decided to incorporate them into his larger work, rounding off the whole with a blessing and commendation (50:27-29). Subsequently he appended the fifty-first chapter, which ends with an acrostic poem telling how the author came to obtain wisdom (vss. 13-22; cf. the closing acrostic in Prov. 31:10-31), which he now offers to the untaught (vss. 23-30). The doxology and tailpiece, which appear only in Hebrew and (with variations) in Syriac, could have been added after Ben Sirach's death by an admirer and imitator. Thus, including the Greek prologue and the appendices, the work may be conveniently considered under five main heads. Certain NT parallels are indicated in parentheses.

a. The Greek prologue. The translator commends his grandfather's work and, in view of the difficulties, begs the reader to be indulgent of any imperfections in his translation from the Hebrew.

b. First main section (chs. 1-23). This section, perhaps the first published volume, is introduced with a poem celebrating wisdom: all wisdom is of divine origin and has its beginning in the fear of the Lord (1:1-20).

1:22–4:10: Hypocrisy and pride exclude the possibility of a man's acquiring wisdom. Acceptable men are tested in the furnace of humiliation. Filial piety and almsgiving atone for sin (cf. 3:3, 30, with Mark 12:33). The poor should be treated with kindness.

4:11–6:17: Despite her discipline, wisdom gives help and joy to those who seek her. Avoid sinful shame and false embarrassment, harshness and trust in wealth, insincerity and rashness in speech. Be quick in listening, slow in answering (5:11; cf. Jas. 1:19).

6:18–8:7: The search for wisdom should continue from youth to old age. Beware of political ambition and of mere formalism in religion (cf. Ecclus. 7:14 with Mark 11:25; Ecclus. 7:34 with Rom. 12:15; Ecclus. 8:5 with Rom. 3:23). One should be just and kind.

8:8–10:29: Wisdom is obtained from the sages and the aged. One should be prudent in one's personal associations, avoiding loans and pledges and lawsuits with judges and intimate conversation with strangers. Special care is needed in one's relations with women. New friends are like new wine (9:10; cf. Luke 5:39). Rulers should be wise and humble, for the Lord rules the earth.

10:30–14:19: The wisdom of a humble man will raise him to a position of authority. Avoid passing hasty judgments on people, and do not argue about a matter which does not concern you. Avoid dissipating your energy in many activities, for the busy man may find that death takes him before he has time to enjoy his accumulated wealth (11:19; cf. Luke 12:16-20). Be content with your profession, and call no one happy before his death. Avoid associating with people who are wealthier and more powerful than you. Riches should be used to make life pleasant for oneself and for others before death presents itself.

14:20–18:26: The happy man is he who meditates on wisdom. God created man free to choose between good and evil, but he is not responsible for human waywardness (cf. 15:11-12 with Jas. 1:13). It is better to die childless than to have impious children. Wickedness brings destruction upon a people. The Lord created an ordered universe and gave man dominion over lower creatures; he endowed man with the power to think, that he might praise the Creator. God is merciful as well as just, so resort to him for forgiveness; being aware of the transitoriness of men, he pours out mercy upon them. Kind words should accompany your gifts (cf. 18:15 with Jas. 1:5); in times of prosperity think of poverty and need.

18:27–20:26: The wise man guards against wrongdoing and shows understanding in his sayings. One should control one's appetites, for wine and women bring men to ruin. Avoid malicious gossip. A God-fearing fool is better than an intelligent sinner. Reproof should be timely and without violence. Appearances are not trustworthy, for a windfall may result in a loss.

20:27–23:27: Wisdom will bring a man to a position of authority. The way of sinners is smoothly paved with stones, but at its end is the pit of Sheol (21:10; cf. Matt. 7:13). Weep less bitterly for the dead than for the fool whose presence is a heavy burden. A friend should not be reviled, but should be assisted in his adversity. Avoid making a habit of swearing oaths, of uttering the name of the Holy One, and of using lewd and vulgar words. Nothing is hidden from the Lord, and he will duly punish those who commit sexual sins, thereby showing that obedience to the divine commandments surpasses all other goods.

c. Second main section (24:1–42:14). This section, which may have constituted the earlier part of a second publication, is introduced, like its predecessor, with a poem in celebration of Wisdom, though this time as a personified figure she speaks in the first person (24:1-22). Wisdom pervades all things, but in a special sense dwells in the beloved city of Jerusalem (24:1-12; cf. Prov. 8:22-31; also John 1:1-18, where the Logos enlightens every man, and yet in a distinctive way came to reside in Jesus). She can be identified with the law of Moses, from which Ben Sirach's own work has taken its rise and so grown that he can again make instruction shine forth for the benefit of future generations (Ecclus. 24:23-34).

25:1–26:27: A harmonious marriage is one of three beautiful things, and an adulterous old fool is one of three hateful types of men. A man with an intelligent wife is one of ten things pleasant to contemplate. Nothing is worse than an iniquitous wife, and the tongue-lashing of a woman who is jealous of a rival wife is the most frightening of four scourges of the tongue. Strict watch should be kept over a headstrong daughter. A modest wife adds charm to charm.

26:28–29:28: Three things are grievous to see: a warrior (Syriac "rich man") brought to poverty, an intelligent man treated contemptuously, a righteous man turning to sin. A merchant is especially likely to become dishonest. The character of a man can be discerned in his manner of reasoning. Among stupid people watch for a chance to leave, but among thoughtful people stay on. Do not betray a friend's confidences, or pretend friendship with evil designs, for he who digs a pit will fall into it (cf. 27:26 with Prov. 26:27; Eccl. 10:8). Practice forgiveness, and then your sins will be pardoned in prayer (Ecclus. 28:2; cf. Matt. 6:12). Avoid strife, which may lead to bloodshed, and slander, which brings destruction. The tongue can be worse than the sword, but the pious are protected against it. Lend when your neighbor is in need (cf. Ecclus. 29:10 with Jas. 5:3), despite the fact that you may not be repaid, and thereby you will gain spiritual treasure (Ecclus. 29:11; cf. Matt. 6:20). A simple life at home is better than sumptuous fare in another man's house.

30:1–32:13—G 30; 34:1–35:13: A father who loves his son will often whip him. There is no wealth better than health of body. A sick man can no more enjoy life than an idol can enjoy an offering of fruit, and so beware of anxiety over gold, which makes one prematurely old. At dinner parties do not be greedy, thereby avoiding sleeplessness, nausea, and colic; and be moderate in drinking wine, for in excess it destroys one's health and reputation. Leave in good time and do not linger at the end of a banquet.

32:14–33:18—G 35:14–36:16*a;* 30:25-27: A God-fearing man will find true understanding in the law, but a sinful man will adapt the law's meaning to suit his own convenience. Do nothing without forethought; and when you have acted, do not regret, for he who trusts the Lord will not suffer loss. God distinguished holy days from ordinary days, and likewise he distinguished among men and appointed their different ways, exalting some and abasing others; thus men are as clay in the hands of the potter. Ben Sirach is the last of a long series of teachers, and so he is like one who gleans after the grape gatherers; the Lord has blessed him, and so he can offer wisdom to the leaders of the people.

33:19–36:17—G 30:28–33:13*a;* 36:16*b*-22: The head of a family should retain his authority by not giving his property to relatives before his death. Indolent slaves should be dealt with strictly, and yet one should not be uncharitable. He who has traveled acquires much cleverness. Ritual acts without genuine piety are valueless. Ben Sirach prays the Lord to deliver his people from their Gentile oppressors and gather together the dispersed tribes of Israel according to the prophecies spoken in his name.

36:18–38:23—G 36:23–38:23: As foods vary in quality, so do women. Some friends are friends only in name. For advice one should consult a pious man and one's own heart, praying to God for his divine guidance. Resort to a physician when you are ill, for medical skill comes from God, and do not neglect to pray. In cases of bereavement mourn only for a day or two, not the customary seven (38:17; cf. 22:12), and do not give your heart to sorrow, as you do the dead no good and you injure yourself.

38:24–39:35: The wisdom of the scribe depends on the opportunity of leisure. Artisans do necessary work in the life of a community, but they are not qualified for leadership in its affairs. On the other hand, the scribe devotes himself to the study of the law, seeks out the wisdom of the ancients, is concerned with prophecies, and makes himself at home with the obscurities of parables (cf. 39:2-3 with Mark 4:10-13). He will give counsel to rulers; through his prayers he will acquire God-given wisdom, and his fame will never be blotted out. The pious should praise the Lord, who supplies every need.

40:1–42:14: Mental and physical suffering comes to all men, but more particularly to the wicked. The wealth of the unjust will dry up like a torrent, whereas righteousness endures forever. Death is God's decree for all flesh and should be accepted with equanimity. The days of a good life may be numbered, but a good name, unlike a bad one, endures forever. One should be ashamed of certain things, but not of others, such as the law of God and just dealing. A man's wickedness is better than a woman who does good.

d. Third main section (42:15–50:29). The three relatively long poems in 42:15–50:24 may have appeared on certain special occasions prior to their incorporation into the work as it now stands.

42:15–43:33: God's glory is reflected in the world he has created, and even his holy ones are unable to recount all the wonder of his works. God is omniscient and has so organized natural processes that they operate harmoniously together. Celestial luminaries, meteorological phenomena, and the ocean show forth the greatness of the Creator. He is the All and transcends all his works, many of which are hidden from us.

Chs. 44–49 (Hebrew title "Praise of the fathers of old"; Greek title "Hymn of the fathers"; cf. Heb. 11: 4–12:2): The great men of the past should be praised. They won fame during their lives; and though some of them have left no memorial, yet their righteous deeds have not been forgotten, and their prosperity will remain with their descendants. So the congregation proclaims the praise of Enoch, Noah, Abraham, Isaac, Jacob, Moses, Aaron, Phinehas, Joshua, Caleb, the judges, Samuel, and David. Solomon merits praise for his building of the temple and for his youthful wisdom, but he put a stain on his honor by giving way to sexual lust; Rehoboam and Jeroboam I sought out every sort of wickedness till vengeance came upon them. Glorious were Elijah, Elisha, Hezekiah, Isaiah, Josiah, Jeremiah, Ezekiel, Job (49:9 H; cf. Ezek. 14:14, 20), the twelve (minor) prophets, Zerubbabel, Jeshua, and Nehemiah. Enoch was translated to heaven, and the bones of Joseph were cared for; Shem and Seth were honored among men, and Adam above every living being in creation.

50:1-24: Simon II the high priest, son of Onias (cf. Jos. Antiq. XII.iii.3; iv.10), was the leader of his brethren and the pride of his people (so in the Hebrew and the Syriac; in the Greek this line is lacking, but cf. 49:15*b* G). In his days the temple was fortified, a large reservoir was built, and Jerusalem was strengthened. He made the court of the sanctuary glorious when, clothed in his official vestments and surrounded by priests, he performed sacred ministrations in the temple.

50:25-29: The Idumeans, the Philistines, and the Samaritans are especially detestable. Ben Sirach has written much instruction in this book, and he who lays it to heart will become wise; the light of the Lord will illuminate his path.

e. Appendices (ch. 51). These are not all to be found in the Greek MSS.

51:1-12: A psalm of thanksgiving praising God for delivering the author from various afflictions.

After 51:12:i-xvi: A liturgy preserved only in Hebrew (cf. Ps. 136). Perhaps it was omitted in the Greek translation because the sons of Zadok, who are praised in it (51:12:ix), were no longer high priests in 132 B.C. Or perhaps it was added by a later writer whose outlook was Pharisaic (though he does not mention the doctrine of the resurrection of the dead) and messianic (the words: "O give thanks to him who makes the horn of the house of David to bud," in 51:12:viii, express sentiments absent from 36:1-17; cf. 47:22, which may be a gloss).

51:13-30: An alphabetical acrostic poem recounting how Ben Sirach acquired wisdom through seeking it from the days of his youth, and inviting the untaught to attend his school (cf. vss. 23-27 with 6: 24-28; 24:19-22; Matt. 11:28-30).

After 51:30: An alphabetical acrostic canticle preserved only in Hebrew and (with variations) in Syriac.

5. Language and style. Although Hebrew continued to flourish as the language of the schools, Aramaic influence was making itself felt when Ben Sirach was writing, and so it is not surprising that numerous Aramaisms should appear in his work. To some extent his style is imitative and repetitive, but it would be an exaggeration to say that it is decadent; and a study of the language scarcely affords reasons for opposing the view that his book was written earlier than such canonical works as Daniel and Esther. While his composition bears the impress of the living language of his time, Ben Sirach is quite capable of writing classical Hebrew, and stylistically he is by no means inferior to the later psalmists and to the later authors of the book of Proverbs. Although he may never attain to the artistic level of the superb poetic constructions of the book of Job, he possesses considerable literary talent and can deftly relieve the monotony of moralizing verse by combining the lyrical with the didactic. Many of his epigrams compare well with the best in Proverbs (see especially Prov. 25–27), and his magnificent poem in praise of the works of God in nature (Ecclus. 42:15–43:33) compares not unfavorably with such hymns as Ps. 147 or even with passages in Job. In a general way Ben Sirach would seem to derive his literary inspiration from the books of Psalms and Proverbs, and correspondingly two main species of verse may be distinguished in his work—the didactic and the devotional or lyrical. Despite his identification of wisdom with the law of Moses, he never sets forth legal regulations in a juristic style.

a. Didactic verse. While the greater part of Proverbs consists of isolated aphorisms (e.g., Prov. 10:1–22:16 is made up of 375 epigrams, each comprising one independent distich), such couplets complete per se occur but rarely in Ecclesiasticus (e.g., 21:8), which is largely constituted by more sustained versified essays of varying length. Like the authors of Proverbs, Ben Sirach usually employs the normal Hebrew literary unit of verse, a distich or couplet of balanced lines or hemistichs in synonymous, antithetic, or synthetic parallelism, with four stress-accents on each (*see* POETRY, HEBREW). Popular aphorisms generally assumed this form (cf. Isa. 22:13*b;* Ezek. 18:2*b;* etc.); it was a unit of verse easy to imitate and in lengthy passages easy to omit—facts to which the variants in the MSS of Ecclesiasticus bear ample testimony. More prolonged numerical proverbs, which may have developed from the riddle (חידה; cf. Ecclus. 8:8; 47:17 H), are to be found in 23:16-17; 25:1-2, 7-11; 26:5-6, 28; 50:25-26 (cf. Prov. 30:15-31; Amos 1–2; etc.). Usually Ben Sirach does not leave his distichs in isolation but connects them with related verses to form continuous passages with a dominant theme, some of which have strophic divisions, although this is particularly noticeable in the lyrical sections.

b. Devotional verse. As in the book of Proverbs, so in Ecclesiasticus, the glories of personified wisdom are celebrated in psalmlike verse (1:1-21; 24:1-22; cf. Prov. 8:1-31; also Job 28:12-28). This is what we should expect, for Ben Sirach holds that the ideal sage, besides imparting moral instruction in wise sayings when inspired by God, also offers thanks to the Lord in prayer (39:6). From time to time he exhorts his readers to bless their Maker, who satisfies them with good things (e.g., 32:13); and he presents a personal song of thanksgiving in 51:1-12 (cf., e.g., Ps. 18). Ben Sirach shows great admiration for the liturgy of the temple, evidently with choir and congregation singing antiphonally (50:18-19), and he extols David for adorning divine worship with his liturgical compositions and choral arrangements (47:8-10). An example of Ben Sirach's liturgical writing—if it is genuine—is set forth in 51:12:i-xvi (preserved only in Hebrew), a canticle of thanksgiving apparently meant to be rendered antiphonally (cf. Pss. 118:1-4; 136:1-3). His panegyric upon the heroes of Israel's past (Ecclus. 44–49) bears a strong resemblance to such hymns as Ps. 105, with its laudatory celebrations of the Lord for his wonderful deeds wrought in ancient times on behalf of his chosen people. The eulogy of the high priest Simon (50:1-24) has an exalted conclusion in a psalmlike prayer (vss. 22-24; cf. 45:26). Lyrical strains suddenly appear in didactic passages (e.g., 23:19-20), and an elegiac note of regretfulness is struck in some of the poems, occasionally as prayers (14:17-19; 17:27-28; 18:8-10; 22:27). Perhaps the finest examples of Ben Sirach's lyrical talent are to be found in the hymns to the glory of God in 39:12-35; 42:15–43:33, both exemplifying strophic divisions; thus 43:6-26 (in the Hebrew) has six stanzas of four distichs each.

6. Doctrinal antinomies. Ben Sirach holds that the greatest good is wisdom, a divine quality to some extent present in all creation. It can be discerned in the world generally and in the law of Moses more particularly; by earnest endeavor men can increasingly assimilate wisdom, and Ben Sirach would shed light upon this highest of all human quests by offering his readers the results of his lifelong reflection on the basic conditions of human existence. His teaching is thus extremely comprehensive, and its many-sidedness may be brought out by a consideration of certain fundamental antinomies, contrary viewpoints which he does not succeed in harmonizing with one another. That Ben Sirach was aware in some measure of the presence of such antinomies in his work seems to be indicated by his emphasis on the limitations of the human understanding (3:23). They seem to be latent in all developed forms of biblical religion. *See* BIBLICAL THEOLOGY, HISTORY OF.

a. Predestination and freedom. Ben Sirach takes over the ethical monotheism implied in the teaching of Amos and his prophetic successors, and assumed in many of the Psalms and in the book of Proverbs. The Lord is the one and only God (Ecclus. 36:5). He is "the all" (43:27), an expression which is not, however, to be construed in terms of strict pantheism, for God transcends his works (43:28). He is almighty and all-seeing (15:18), and knows what will be, as well as what has been (42:19). He created the cosmos, all the parts of which are permanently adjusted to one another so as to operate in mutual harmony (42:23)—a conception which manifestly precludes the possibility of any veritable eschatology. Good and evil alike proceed from God (11:14; cf. Isa. 45:7), and human destiny is in his hands (Ecclus. 33:10-13—G 36:10-13), not in man's (11:10-13). The Lord rules with justice (35:12—G 32:14-15), requiting men according to their deserts (16:12) and controlling the course of events for the benefit of the righteous and the punishment of the wicked (39:22-31). Yet in his compassion he forgives sins and saves in time of affliction (2:11). Wisdom herself is of divine origin (1:1); God poured her out upon all his works (1:9) and supplied her to those who love him (1:10). On the other hand, man is a free being, and wisdom is acquired by human effort (6:18-37). He can choose between good and evil, and therefore the responsibility for sin must not be attributed to God (15:11-20). Ben Sirach is quite confident that man was left in the power of his own inclination (יצר) at the Creation (15:14); this doctrine may have stemmed from Jeremiah's conception of the human heart as the root of sin (cf. Jer. 17:9). Thus, although at times he may need divine help to overcome his evil propensities (Ecclus. 23:4-6), the finite individual alone is finally responsible for the way in which he works out his destiny. No one is without guilt, and all deserve punishment (8:5), and yet man possesses the inherent volitional power to amend his ways and turn to goodness (17:26; 21:1).

b. Pessimism and optimism. Man was created out of dust (33:10—G 36:10) and returns to dust (17:1; 40:11). His span of life is short (17:2; 18:9-10), inevitably terminating, though apparently with a few exceptions (48:9; 49:14), in the dismal existence of Sheol, where there is no luxury (14:16), no singing of praises (17:27), no inquiry (41:4). Nevertheless, even death, the gateway to Sheol, is welcome to those in need and whose strength is failing (41:2). The doctrine of Sheol is made less gloomy in Greek I in certain passages (e.g., 7:17), and some of the glosses in Greek II go so far as to affirm that there is eternal bliss for the obedient beyond the grave (e.g., 2:9; 19:19; cf. the glosses in the Latin version in 17:23, 27; 21:10; 24:32). Besides the fear of death, troubles of one sort or another are the common lot of rich and poor alike—nightmares, calamities, famines, afflictions, and plagues (40:1-11). There are moments of happiness, but these are always likely to come to a sudden end (18:25-26). All men are sinful (8:5), women especially so (42:14), and it was through the sin of Eve that human beings became mortal (25:24). On the other hand, good women do exist, and happy marriages are possible (26:1-4; 36:18-26—G 36:27-31). Man was made in the image of God and granted dominion over beasts and birds (17:3-4), being equipped with intelligence and skill (17:7; 38:6). All the works of the Lord are good, and he supplies every need (39:33); the world constitutes a magnificent unity in its rich variety (42:22-25). Whatever misfortunes may exist, they are due punishments for the wicked (27:25-29; 39:25-31) or blessings in disguise (20:9-11) or means of proving the genuineness of an individual's piety (2:5).

c. Retributive justice and factual truth. God is just or impartial in his treatment of his creatures (35:12—G 32:14-15), so that good things come to good people and evil things to sinners (39:25). Holding neither the Platonic doctrine of the immortality of the soul nor anything corresponding to the Pharisaic notion of the resurrection of the body (10:11), Ben Sirach teaches that just retribution operates wholly on this side of the grave, and he thinks it easy for the Lord to reward a man, even on the day of his death, according to his conduct (11:26). On the other hand, Ben Sirach is not unaware of the sort of objections that are raised against a theory of this kind, e.g., in the book of JOB. He evidently recognizes that the hard facts of common experience at least prima facie militate against it, and in this case he makes a deliberate attempt to overcome the antinomy by resorting to a distinction between appearance and reality. Things are not what they seem to be, and are not therefore to be taken at their face value. The Lord may be slow to anger (5:4), yet his wrath rests upon sinners (5:6), and the day of calamity will inevitably come (5:8), whereas the fear of the Lord brings gladness and long life (1:12). The prosperity of the wicked lacks permanence (40:13), but the afflictions of the righteous are sent to test them (2:5) or to discipline them for their moral improvement (18:13-14; 32:14-15—G 35:14-15), and good fortune may be concealed in adversity (20:9). Moreover, the spiritual rewards of piety are not to be overlooked; the righteous man finds true friends (6:16), wins a good name that outlives him (39:9-11), and realizes that the fear of the Lord is better than knowledge or intelligence (19:24) and better than riches and strength (40:26).

d. Ritualism and ethics. Ben Sirach greatly respects the priesthood and the ritualism of the temple. In one passage divine Wisdom is personified and represented as ministering before the Creator in the holy tabernacle (24:10). The Lord bestowed special privileges upon Aaron the first high priest (45:6-22), and he established a covenant of peace with Phinehas that he and his descendants should always enjoy the dignity of the priesthood (45:24; cf. Num. 25:10-13). Simon the high priest made the court of the sanctuary glorious when, arrayed in his official vestments, he went up to the holy altar while presiding over ceremonies in the temple—perhaps on the Day of Atonement (50:11). Ben Sirach therefore calls upon his readers to honor the priests and to pay the contributions due to them as ministers of the Lord (7:29-31), the festivals and sacrifices being divinely ordained (33:8—G 36:8; 35:4-5—G 32:6-7). On the other hand, in line with the tradition established by Amos, Ben Sirach so emphasizes the ineffectiveness of ritual performances per se, that in the last-cited passage the only justification he can give for the offering of sacrifices is that they are included among the requirements of the law. A man who robs the poor in order to make an oblation is no better than one who kills a son before his father's eyes (34:20—G 31:23). In themselves sacrifices do not atone for sin (7:8-9); God will not accept the offerings of the unrighteous (34:18-19—G 31:21-22), and a man who fasts for his sins without genuine repentance gains nothing by his formal self-humiliation (34:26—G 31:31). It is the offerings of the righteous that are acceptable to God, particularly when they are given generously (35:6-10—G 32:8-12), and it is the practice of justice and kindness—as in filial piety (3:3) and almsgiving (3:30)—that atones for sin.

e. Universalism and particularism. Following the teaching of prophets like Amos, with his stress on divine justice; Jeremiah, with his deep sense of personal responsibility; and Deutero-Isaiah, with his notion of a world-wide mission, Ben Sirach holds that there is one universal God, whose will is valid for all mankind. The Lord is the creator of the world who is everywhere present (16:26-30; 43:27), the ruler of the nations who requites all men according to their deserts (10:14-17; 16:11-14); and the conception of race can be construed entirely in terms of piety and morals (10:19). On the other hand, Israel is the Lord's own portion (Ecclus. 17:17; cf. Deut. 32:8), his first-born son (Ecclus. 36:12; cf. Exod. 4: 22) whose days are without number (Ecclus. 37:25), and Jerusalem is his beloved city and dwelling place (24:8-12; 36:13). So Ben Sirach can pray that God will crush the foreign nations opposed to Israel (36: 3-10—G 33:3-12) and vindicate the prophets by gathering together the scattered tribes of Jacob—his nearest approach to a belief in a messianic expectation (36:11-17—G 33:13*a;* 36:16*b*-22; such passages as 47:22; 51:12:viii may well have been added later). And in an outburst of vexation he gives expression to his detestation of the Idumeans, the Philistines, and especially the Samaritans (50:25-26).

f. Reason and revelation. Ben Sirach's ethics are evidently derived from a study of the writings of the sages, particularly the book of Proverbs, and from his own rational reflection upon his varied experiences of life. Much of his practical wisdom is sound enough, as when, e.g., he argues that gluttony should be avoided because of its deleterious effects on the health (31:20—G 34:20); but his moral generalizations are not always convincing, and his teaching is not always consistent. Thus he sometimes implies that women are inherently evil (25:24; 42:14) and at other times that this is not the case (25:1; 26:3). While these contradictions may be due to the fact that the counsels were given on various occasions and reflect different moods and circumstances, such inconsistencies seem to show that Ben Sirach's rationalistic prudentialism suffers from certain serious limitations. For one thing, he persistently refuses to try to see things from any other standpoint than that of a man who is a somewhat despotic head of a family. Thus when he condemns the sparing of the rod (30:1), he does not carefully scrutinize the pertinent evidence for his pronouncement, but simply jumps to the conclusion that a boy strictly brought up will turn out to be a son of whom his father can boast in the presence of his acquaintances (30:2-3). On the metaphysical plane Ben Sirach's intellectualistic aspirations are most easily discernible perhaps in his various attempts to demonstrate that his doctrine of God's retributive justice does not conflict with the facts of common experience. On the other hand, he freely owns to the limitations of the human understanding (3:17-24) and assumes as axiomatic that God has revealed his will for men in the law delivered to Moses (45:5), which fills the human mind with wisdom (24:25). So it is in terms of respect for the law rather than in terms of rationalistic prudentialism that he defines wisdom (19:20; 21:11); and just as wisdom is older than creation (24:9; cf. Prov. 8:22-31), so the law antedates Moses, as it was already known to Abraham (Ecclus. 44:20) and even to primordial humanity (17:11-14; cf. Siphre on Deut. section 37-f. 76*a-b*). With such an identification of wisdom with the law (24:23), the sum of moral truth comes to be found, not in any sort of rationalistically argued ethics, but simply in obedience to the will of God as revealed in the Scriptures. Nevertheless, Ben Sirach is far from regarding the Pentateuchal legislation as being all on the same level of importance; the ritualistic rulings are taken to be secondary to the ethical, and the requirements concerning diet, lustrations, and the sabbath are passed over in complete silence. Thus his moral rationalism and his religious faith in the revelation of God to Israel are not integrated in a consistent scheme of thought. He does not seek to justify his view concerning the primacy of the ethical in the law, any more than he tries to show that the counsels of his general prudentialism can be deduced from the Pentateuch by legitimate exegesis. It is true that he goes beyond the position represented in the book of Proverbs by emphasizing the identity of Wisdom and the law, and in certain passages he anticipates Talmudic developments, as when, e.g., he approaches a juristic distinction between intentional and unintentional wrong oath-taking (23:11). But the great difference between Ben Sirach's teaching and rabbinics remains; and it is perhaps significant that in his enumeration of the great men of the past (chs. 44-49), there is not so much as a passing allusion to Ezra, the man who in the Pharisaic and Talmudic tradition was destined to become the prototype and paragon of the genuine scholar.

Bibliography. I. Lévi, *L'Ecclésiastique* (Hebrew text, French trans. and commentary; 2 vols.; 1898-1901); "Sirach, the Wisdom of Jesus the Son of," *Jewish Encyclopedia,* XI (1905), 388-97. R. Smend, *Die Weisheit des Jesus Sirach,* I (Hebrew text and German trans.; 1906); II (commentary; 1906); III (Greek-Syriac-Hebrew index; 1907). G. H. Box and W. O. E. Oesterley, "The Book of Sirach" (English trans. with introduction and notes), in R. H. Charles, ed., *The Apoc. and Pseudep. of the OT* (1913), I, 268-517. R. H. Pfeiffer, "Ecclesiasticus by Sirach" (introduction), *History of NT Times* (1949), pp. 352-408.

For the argument that Simon I never existed, see: G. F. Moore, "Simon the Righteous," *Jewish Studies in Memory of Israel Abrahams* (1927), pp. 348-64. For the contrary view, cf.: H. Englander, *The Hebrew College Jubilee Volume* (1925), pp. 145-69; S. Zeitlin, *The Proceedings of the American Academy for Jewish Research,* III (1932), 145-46.

On the Genizah MS E, see: J. Marcus, ed., *The Newly Discovered Hebrew of Ben Sira* (1931). For the textual history, see: M. H. Segal, "The Evolution of the Hebrew Text of Ben Sira," *JQR,* N.S., XXV (1934-35), 91-149. For the view that the Genizah text is a translation, and for Ben Sirach's doctrine, cf.: A. Büchler, "Ben Sira's Conception of Sin and Atonement," *JQR,* N.S., XIII (1922-23), 303-35, 461-502; XIV (1923-24), 53-83. For the style, see: W. Baumgartner, "Die literarischen Gattungen in der Weisheit des Jesus Sirach," *ZAW,* XXXIV (1914), 161-98; cf. H. J. Cadbury, "The Grandson of Ben Sira," *HTR,* XLVIII (1955), 219-25.

For a parallel (with predestinarian tendencies) between Ecclus. 33:7-15—G 36:7-15 and 1QS 3:14-4:26, cf.: P. Winter, "Ben Sira and the Teaching of Two Ways," *Vetus Testamentum,* V (1955), 315-18.

For a reconstruction of the Hebrew text as a whole, see: M. S. Segal, *Sepher Ben Sira Ha-shalem* (1953).

On the Qumran fragments, see: J. T. Milik, *Ten Years of Discovery* (1959), p. 32. T. A. BURKILL

ECLIPSE. *See* SCIENCE, §§ A2*c,* B2*b*iii, C2*b*.

ECSTASY [ἔκστασις, from ἐξίστημι, to put out of place]. A mental condition in which consciousness is wholly or partly in suspension, thought and volition cease, and the subject is directed and controlled by the Spirit of God. The word "ecstasy" conveys the idea of the soul or spirit's temporarily leaving the body (the Greek view) and finding union with the divine; this idea is foreign to Hebrew thinking, where the personality in ecstasy is no longer himself but the agent of the spiritual power invading or possessing him. Ecstasy may be spontaneous or stimulated artificially by music, dancing, or contemplation of objects (I Sam. 9; II Kings 3:15), and is sometimes termed madness because of accompanying physical movements, incoherent speech, and frenzied behavior (II Kings 9:11; cf. I Cor. 14:23). Appearing with great diversity universally, it defies rigid definition, and is better viewed collectively to cover conditions of trance, dream, vision, audition, rapture, frenzy, exultation, and related states ranging from entire absence of consciousness to complete or partial awareness.

1. In the OT. In the OT we find the ecstasy of primitive prophecy, produced by group participation in song and dance, contagious, culminating in trance (I Sam. 10:5, 12; 19:20); of the elders, when Moses wishes that "all the LORD's people" were prophets (Num. 11:25-29); of Elijah, when he experienced wind, earthquake, fire, and voice (I Kings 19:11-18); of David dancing before the ark (II Sam. 6:12-23). Abraham's vision in "deep sleep," the vision and audition at the burning bush, the wrestling of Jacob at Penuel, all bear marks of ecstasy (Gen. 15:12; 32:24; Exod. 3:2-14).

Ecstasy does not cease with the development of classical prophecy. The ministries of Isaiah and Amos begin in states of ecstasy (Isa. 6; Amos 7–9). "I am like a drunken man," declares Jeremiah (23:9; cf. Acts 2:13-15). His vision of desolation—sky darkened, mountains quaking, hills moving, earth deserted—is clearly ecstatic (Jer. 4:23-26). Ezekiel, subject to trance and catalepsy, speaks of the Spirit's lifting him, falling upon him, transporting him, entering into him (2:2; 3:14, 23-27; 8:3; 11:1, 5; 37:1). Abnormal elements of ecstasy are, however, subservient to moral and spiritual ends in classical prophecy.

2. In the NT. Events surrounding the birth and ministry of Jesus show signs of ecstasy: the exultation of Elizabeth and Mary (Luke 1:41-55), and the inspired utterances of Zechariah, Simeon, and Anna (Luke 1:67-79; 2:25-39); the heavens opened, the dove, the voice, at his baptism (Mark 1:9-11); his temptation, resembling Ezekiel's being carried about by the Spirit (Luke 4:1-12; cf. Ezek. 8:3); his transfiguration, with the cloud (the "Shekinah"), the voice, the mystic trance induced by intense communion (Mark 9:2-8); his high-priestly prayer suggesting the highest state of spiritual union with the Father (John 17).

The church begins in ecstasy—the wind, the fire, the tongues, indicating exalted states of feeling following much prayer and intense messianic conviction (Acts 2:2-4). Peter's trance vision and audition, at prayer, is clearly ecstatic (Acts 10:9-16). Elements of ecstasy may also be present in Stephen's vision (Acts 7:55; cf. 6:15).

Ecstatic moods and speech (glossolalia) during worship threaten the welfare of the church at Corinth (I Cor. 12–14; cf. I Thess. 5:19-21). Paul speaks with tongues (I Cor. 14:6, 18); he hears divine voices (II Cor. 12:9; Acts 18:9; 22:17); his conversion experience indicates ecstasy (Acts 9; 22; 26); he is "caught up to the third heaven," hears unutterable things, not knowing whether "in the body or out of the body" (II Cor. 12:2-4). He places little weight upon such transports, urging Christians rather to seek the love of Christ which surpasses all knowledge credited to the ecstasies of pagan cults (Rom. 8:38-39; cf. Eph. 3:14-19). John, "in the Spirit on the Lord's Day," hearing a voice and seeing a vision, is doubtless in a state of ecstasy. For NT religion generally, however, being "in the Spirit" represents normal Christian living.

Bibliography. W. R. Inge, *Christian Mysticism* (1932); K. E. Kirk, *The Vision of God* (1932); A. Guillaume, *Prophecy and Divination* (1938); M. Barnett, *The Living Flame* (1953).

E. ANDREWS

ED ĕd [עֵד, witness]. The name given to the altar in Josh. 22:34 KJV (RSV WITNESS). The word is actually omitted in the MT, but is added on the basis of the Syr. and the context. *See* WITNESS, ALTAR OF.

EDAR. KJV form of EDER in Gen. 35:21. *See* EDER, TOWER OF.

EDDIAS. KJV Apoc. form of IZZIAH.

EDDINUS ĕd'ə nəs ['Εδδεινοῦς (B); 'Εδδινοῦς (A)]. Alternate name of JEDUTHUN 2.

EDEN ē'dən [עֵדֶן, delight]. **1.** A Levite in the reign of King Hezekiah, and one of those who cleansed the temple (II Chr. 29:12). It is unclear whether or not II Chr. 31:15 refers to the same individual.

2. *See* BETH-EDEN.

EDEN, GARDEN OF [גַּן־בְּעֵדֶן, גַּן־עֵדֶן, *see below*]. A garden of trees planted by Yahweh, in which Adam and Eve first dwelt.

1. Etymology
2. Usage
3. Site
4. Theological significance

Bibliography

1. Etymology. The root of the word "Eden," עֵדֶן, is uncertain in Hebrew. A connection with the Sumerian-Akkadian *edinu*, meaning "wilderness" or "flatland," is possible. The LXX derived the word from the Hebrew verb עדן, "to delight," and translated "garden of Eden" as "garden of delight," παράδεισος τῆς τρυφῆς. This led to the traditional identification of the Garden of Eden with PARADISE.

2. Usage. "Eden" occurs thirteen times in the singular, undetermined form to designate a location. In three cases (Gen. 2:8, 10; 4:16) it refers to a geographical land in which the garden is placed, גַּן־בְּעֵדֶן, "garden in Eden." A shift in meaning occurs in Gen. 2:15; 3:23-24, which speaks of the גַּן־עֵדֶן, "garden of Eden." In certain of the prophets the meaning diverges even further from that of simply a geographical land. Isa. 51:3 sets Eden parallel to the "garden of Yahweh." The highly mythical passage of Ezek. 28:13 places Eden in apposition to the "garden of God" (cf. also Ezek. 31:9, 16, 18; 36:35; Joel 2:3).

3. Site. It is generally agreed among scholars that the section Gen. 2:10-14 stems from a tradition which is at variance with the rest of Gen. 2. These verses interrupt the context and are written in a different style. According to this ancient tradition a river with its source in Eden issues from the garden as a single stream, and then divides into four branches. The third and fourth branches are well known. HIDDEKEL, חדקל, is certainly the Tigris, although the name occurs only once again in the OT (Dan. 10:4). It is more closely defined as flowing קדמת אשור, "east of Assyria." This presents something of a problem, since Assyria extends far to the E of the Tigris. Some have understood אשור as Asshur, the ancient capital of Assyria, but this interpretation seems improbable. The fourth river, the פרת, is unequivocally the Euphrates, derived from the Akkadian *Purattu.*

The identification of the first two rivers is very controversial, and no generally accepted conclusion has been reached by scholars. Pishon, פישון, is described as the "one which flows around the whole land of Havilah, where there is gold . . . . Bdellium and onyx stone are there." The name appears only once in the OT. It probably should be understood as an appellative from the root פוש, "to spring forth." HAVILAH, חוילה, appears as SW Arabia in Gen. 10:28, and again as the E frontier of the Ishmaelite Arabs, which would point instead to NE Arabia (25:18). Some connect Havilah with the word חול, "sand," and understand it as merely a general designation for the "land of sand." The mention of precious stones does not help in regard to location.

GIHON, גיחון, is described as the "one which flows around the whole land of Cush." The etymology is uncertain, but it may be an appellative from the root גוח, "burst forth." Although it occurs nowhere else in the OT as a river, the name does appear as the well-known spring E of Jerusalem. Jewish and Christian tradition identified Gihon with the Nile (cf. Jer. 2:18 LXX). Cush signifies almost always Ethiopia, but there are occasional exceptions (Gen. 10:8). Although the meaning in this passage remains uncertain, Ethiopia lends itself as the most probable interpretation.

In the light of this evidence, it should become clear that any reconstruction of the geography is based on a measure of hypothesis. Nevertheless, some reconstructions are more plausible than others. Earlier attempts have failed in trying to harmonize the biblical account with modern scientific geography by identifying two of the rivers of Eden with Babylonian canals. In such interpretations there is no understanding of the legendary-mythical nature of the material. Certainly the Tigris and Euphrates never had a common source!

A most attractive theory interprets this tradition as an ancient picture of the four world rivers encircling the entire earth. According to this hypothesis the Pishon is identified with the Indus, which was conceived of as encircling Arabia and flowing into the Nile. The Nile, in turn, rising with the Euphrates, crossed below the Persian Gulf and encircled Ethiopia. This presupposes that Africa and India were connected; this was the common concept in the antique world (cf. Arrian *Anabasis* VI.i). We know that down to the time of Alexander's Indian expedition the Indian Ocean was unknown, in spite of earlier explorations, and that the Arabian and Persian gulfs were considered to be lakes.

4. Theological significance. Although the concept of a primeval paradise appears well developed in many ethnic religions (Persian, Indian), it is found only sporadically in the Near East. The Sumerian "land of Dilmun" and the Babylonian "cedar forest of Irini" and "garden of Siduri" are only indirect parallels to the Garden of Eden. The failure of genuine parallels to the OT ultimately stems from a different concept of man's nature in the Near Eastern religions.

The writer of Gen. 2 has described the Garden of Eden in language arising out of the myth. Nevertheless, he has reworked the ancient material to make his own unique witness. The garden was planted after the creation of man; this repudiates the mythical idea that Yahweh lived there. Again, man was placed in the garden to work it, not just to enjoy its luxury. Man was driven from the garden on account of his disobedience, because Eden symbolized the state of unbroken fellowship between God and man.

Bibliography. Among the standard commentaries on Genesis, J. Skinner, *ICC* (1910), is superior. For a thorough discussion of the various interpretations up to 1937, see: T. C. Vriezen, *Onderzoek naar de Paradijsvoorstelling bij de oude semietische Volken* (1937), pp. 148 ff. Important among the older literature are: F. Delitzsch, *Wo lag das Paradies?* (1881); W. F. Albright, "The Location of the Garden of Eden," *AJSL,* 39 (1922), 15 ff. More recent interpretations are: G. Hölscher, *Drei Erdkarten* (1949), pp. 35 ff; L. Koehler, "Problems in the Study of the Language of the OT," *Journal of Semitic Studies,* I (1956), 8-9. J. Simons, *The Geographical and Topographical Texts of the OT* (1959). For an excellent discussion of the antique world picture, see: *Grosser Historischer Weltatlas,* herausgegeben vom Bayerischen Schulbuch-Verlag, I (1953), Tafel 8*c*, and the *Erläuterungen,* I (2 Aufl., 1954), pp. 58-59; E. G. Kraeling, *Bible Atlas* (1956), pp. 42 ff. B. S. CHILDS

EDEN, HOUSE OF. *See* BETH-EDEN.

EDER ē′dər [עדר, *probably* Aram. *form of* עזר, helper; LXX B Αἶδαθ (I Chr. 23:23), ʼΗλά (I Chr. 24:30); LXX A ʼΏδερ, LXX B ʼΏδηδ (I Chr. 8:15)]; KJV ADER ā′dər in I Chr. 8:15. **1.** A Levite (I Chr. 23:23; 24:30).

2. A Benjaminite family (I Chr. 8:15).

Bibliography. M. Noth, *Die israelitischen Personennamen* (1928), p. 63. H. H. GUTHRIE, JR.

3. A village of Judah in the Negeb province of Beer-sheba (Josh. 15:21; probably LXX ARAD is correct).

EDER, TOWER OF [מגדל עדר, tower of the flock] (Gen. 35:21). A place between Bethelehem and Hebron where Jacob camped after the death of Rachel. The term is used in its literal sense to designate Mount Zion in Mic. 4:8, where it is translated "tower of the flock."

EDES. KJV Apoc. of IDDO 8.

EDICT [דת, פתגם]. A public proclamation, written and sealed with the king's signet and publicly read (Ezra 6:11; Esth. 2:8; 9:1, 13). What distinguishes an edict from a decree is its written form and public pronouncement. Note that one of the words translated "edict" is כתב, "a writing" (Esth. 8:8-9; cf. 3:12).

The Bible emphasizes the irrevocability of Medo-Persian law (Ezra 6:11; Esth. 8:8-9; Dan. 6:8), but there is no extrabiblical evidence of this. Darius III is said to have ordered the execution of Charidemos and later acknowledged that he erred but could do nothing about it (Diod. Sic. 17.30). That this argues for the immutability of Persian law may be questioned, as execution had already taken place. It may simply mean he could not undo the deed. In Esther the royal edict to exterminate the Jews was counteracted by another permitting the Jews to take vengeance on their enemies (Esth. 8:8-13). Severe penalties were attached to the violation of Persian edicts (Ezra 6:11; *see* IMPALEMENT).

In the NT Moses' parents are listed as an example of faith in being unafraid to transgress the royal edict to slay all male babies (Heb. 11:23).

See also LAW; DECREE. V. H. KOOY

EDIFICATION [οἰκοδομή, building]. The Greek root of this word appears in several forms and compounds in the NT—"build," "build up," "builder," "building," "upbuilding," "edify," "edification," "encouraged" (I Cor. 8:10), and "structure" (Eph. 2:21). The word appears only as a verb in the Synoptic gospels, where it almost always has the literal meaning: "to build or construct."

Paul, who frequently uses the Greek word in both noun and verb forms, never uses it literally, in the sense of "erecting" a building. He uses it often metaphorically in the sense of "building" or "building up" the church, and of "building up" fellow believers. In one or two passages (the number depends on whether Paul wrote Ephesians) Paul describes the church as a building (I Cor. 3:9; Eph. 2:21). He also speaks of "building" the church on the foundation he has laid (I Cor. 3:10, 12, 14); and Eph. 2:20 speaks of the church as "built upon the foundation of the apostles and prophets."

But Paul uses the word more frequently to mean "edify" or "edification" in the sense of "strengthening, unifying, making for peace"—the opposite of "dissipating, disrupting, destroying, or causing dissension." To the Corinthians (I Cor. 14:26) he writes: "Let all things be done for edification"—i.e., for the upbuilding, strengthening, and uniting of the church. "Edification" does not have primarily an emotional connotation; it has the meaning of "making whole, harmonious, and one." And so, finally, Christians are to "build up" one another (I Thess. 5:11)—i.e., to strengthen and encourage one another. And it is primarily love which "builds up" (I Cor. 8:1).

B. H. THROCKMORTON, JR.

EDNA ĕd'nə [Ἔδνα = עדנה, delight; *cf.* Ἕδνα *or* Ἐέδνα, bride price *or* wedding gift]. The wife of Raguel, Tobit's kinsman; and the mother of Sarah, the bride of Tobias (Tob. 7:2, 14 ff; 8:11-12). The Vulg. and the OL give her name as Anna. Her farewell to her son-in-law is memorable (10:12).

J. C. SWAIM

EDOM ē'dəm [אדום, the red region]; EDOMITES ē'də mīts' [אדומים אדמיים]. A country and its people, neighbors of the Israelites to the E and the S. All the monuments and written records of the Edomites have perished, so what information can be obtained about them comes from the writings of their neighbors and enemies, the Israelites, Egyptians, Assyrians, and Babylonians, and from archaeological exploration. Both Edom and Edomites are mentioned frequently in the Bible; in addition, there are places where, because of the similarity between the letters ד (*d*) and ר (*r*), the text has wrongly read ארם, "Aram" (i.e., Syria), and ארמים, "Arameans" (i.e., Syrians), for אדם, "Edom," and אדמים, "Edomites," such as II Kings 16:6; II Chr. 20:2, where the KJV has followed the MT, but the RSV has followed an emended text.

1. The land
   a. Fortress Edom
   b. The outlying regions
   c. The hinterland
2. The people
3. History
4. Edom in biblical literature

Bibliography

1. The land. The territory of the Edomites falls into three distinct parts: Fortress Edom, the outlying regions, and the hinterland to the W.

a. Fortress Edom. This consisted of an irregular quadrilateral, *ca.* seventy miles from N to S and an average of fifteen miles E to W. The N boundary was the deep ravine of the Brook Zered (Wadi el-Ḥesa), which separated it from Moab; the E boundary faced the desert a few miles W of the modern railway line from Damascus to Mecca; the S boundary was the scarp of the Neqb esh-Shtar, overlooking the Hismeh Valley; and the W boundary was the line of hills that overlook the Arabah from the E. It was this territory that received the name of Edom, "the red region," from the red rocks and soil that abound everywhere through it; SEIR, "the wooded region," was the name specifically given to the slopes E of the Arabah, though in biblical literature "Edom" and "Seir" are sometimes used interchangeably.

Ca. twenty-five miles below the Brook Zered, the W wall is partly broken by the Punon (Feinan) embayment, which extends eastward for *ca.* nine miles of lower country and furnishes a crossroad from the Arabah into Edom. This divided the territory into two unequal parts—the N, which ranges from 5,000 to 5,300 feet above sea level, with its chief stronghold at Bozrah (modern Buseireh); the S, which is higher, ranging from 5,300 to nearly 5,700 feet, with its chief stronghold at Teman (modern ruins of Tawilan). Down through the middle of the stretch ran the Edomite part of the King's Highway, which, after crossing the Brook Zered at el-'Aineh in Moab, climbed up the Wadi Laban into the plateau and then followed a course that passed through or close to Tophel, Bozrah, Shobek, and Dana, until it descended into the Hismeh Valley.

The entire boundary of this Edom was dotted with a series of fortresses, especially on the E frontier, which was exposed to raids from the desert. These fortresses, which were set back some miles from the edge of the plateau and near enough to one another

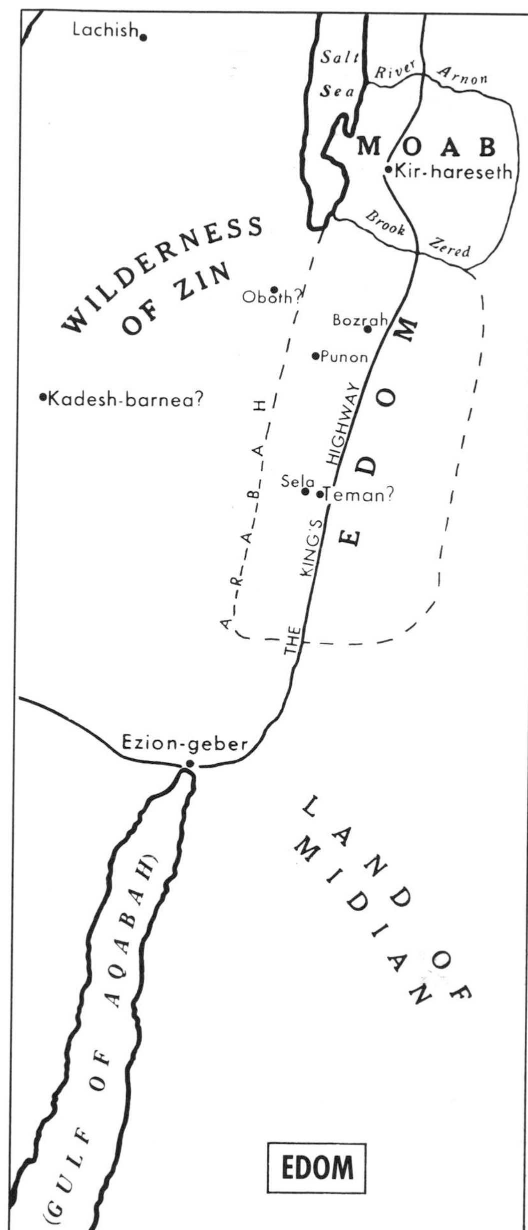

to communicate by fire signals, formed a formidable barrier against any attack on the country and indicate a well-organized military system under a strong central government.

b. The outlying regions. These consist of the ARABAH and the region S of the Neqb esh-Shtar as far as the Gulf of Aqabah. These parts were not settled by the Edomites, but because of their proximity to the Fortress Edom, they were essentially under Edomite control. They were important as trade routes which permitted an exchange of the products of Syria and Mesopotamia with those of Egypt and Arabia. The Arabah, in particular, possessed copper and iron mines which were worked by the Edomites and contributed greatly to their wealth. When the area was under the domination of the Hebrews, its mineral resources were exploited by them. *See* MINES; EZION-GEBER.

c. The hinterland. This was a stretch W of the Arabah which was never settled or even effectively controlled by the Edomites but was occupied by nomadic tribes which owed a nominal allegiance to Edom, and in some cases, such as those of the Kenizzites and Amalekites, were reckoned to be of Edomite origin (Gen. 36:11-12). When Moses wrote to the king of Edom, asking that the Israelites be permitted a passage through his land, and stating that they were at Kadesh, "a city on the edge of your territory" (Num. 20:16), he was speaking the language of diplomacy. Actually, when the king of Edom refused them passage, the Israelites had no difficulty in passing through the hinterland and the outlying regions, and only had to avoid Fortress Edom.

2. The people. The biblical narratives in Genesis, as well as allusions in the prophetic books, constantly emphasize the close racial relationship between the Israelites and the Edomites. It is probable, therefore, that like the former, the Edomites came originally from Aram. However, there are also reports that they intermarried with the Canaanites (Gen. 26:34, where "Hittites" is used in this meaning), Ishmaelites (Gen. 28:9), and the aboriginal Horites of Seir (Gen. 36:20-30, contradicting the statement in Deut. 2:12), so that they were a composite group.

While the Edomites practiced agriculture to some extent, their chief wealth came to them from their trade. The copper and iron which they mined from their hills could be exchanged for the products of Arabia, Egypt, Syria, and Babylonia; and the caravans that lumbered through the country not only paid toll, but also purchased food and lodging there.

It is probable that the Edomites spoke a dialect of Hebrew, as did all their neighbors, for there is no hint of a difference in language. Their religion seems to have been polytheistic; among the gods that can be traced from the names of their kings are Qos or Qosan (the Kose of Josephus), Hadad, and possibly Edom. Their government was monarchical long before that of Israel, and to judge from the list of kings that has been preserved, it was elective (Gen. 36:31-39).

3. History. Archaeological investigations have shown that from the twenty-third to the twentieth century B.C. there was a flourishing civilization in Edom, after which the land was uninhabited, save for roving bands of Bedouins, until the thirteenth century. The cause of this catastrophe must have been a foreign invasion, probably that of Chedorlaomer and his allies (Gen. 14), which swept through the length of the country along the King's Highway, destroying as it went. The Edomites of the Bible arrived in the thirteenth century and were well established in the country under a king by the time of the Exodus. Both Edom and Seir are mentioned by the pharaohs Mer-ne-Ptah (1225-1215) and Ramses III (1198-1167) as being subject to them, but it is uncertain how real these claims may be.

There was no contact between Edom and Israel during the period of the Conquest and of the judges, unless CUSHAN-RISHATHAIM was, as some hold, an Edomite chieftain. Saul is said to have defeated the Edomites (I Sam. 14:47), and David "won a name for himself" by being the first to subdue the country. He put garrisons throughout the country, and his general Joab made the defeat more crushing by a six-month campaign of extermination against the Edomite males (II Sam. 8:13-14; I Kings 11:15-17). This conquest was of exceeding importance for the prosperity of Israel in the reign of Solomon, for as a result of it the latter not only secured the rich trade from Arabia but also began to exploit the mines of Edom on a large scale. The guerrilla warfare of Hadad (I Kings 11:14-22) appears to have been more of an annoyance than a serious threat.

Despite the division of the kingdom which weakened the forces of Judah, Edom seems to have remained in subjection. The list of the cities plundered by Shishak (*ca.* 925 B.C.) includes some from Edom, indicating that it was still considered a part of Judah. In the time of Jehoshaphat, Edom was ruled by a governor (I Kings 22:47) for a time; but later a native ruler was apparently appointed, for a "king of Edom" is mentioned in the expedition against Moab (II Kings 3). This appointment proved unfortunate, for Edom successfully revolted under the next king of Judah, Joram (II Kings 8:20-22).

The independence of Edom lasted *ca.* fifty or sixty years until it was assailed by new attempts of Judah. Amaziah achieved a partial conquest as far S as Sela (II Kings 14:7), and his successor, Azariah (Uzziah), completed it by once more extending the limits of Judah to Elath (II Kings 14:22). In 735 B.C. Edom once more won back its freedom from the feeble Ahaz (II Kings 16:6), apparently in alliance with Aram and Israel. This league was broken up when the Assyrians came to the rescue of Judah, and in 732 Kaush-malaku, the king of Edom, paid homage and tribute to Tiglath-pileser III at Damascus (*ANET* 282). For the next hundred years Edom was a vassal of Assyria; in 711 and 701 it joined with the nearby states, with the backing of Babylon, but on each occasion the coalition was quickly broken up.

As a result of these wars and the necessity of paying heavy tributes, the prosperity of Edom, which had been at its height in the thirteenth–eighth centuries B.C., declined rapidly in the next two hundred years. The Edomites submitted quietly to the Babylonian yoke (604 B.C.). When Nebuchadrezzar besieged and captured Jerusalem in 586, the Edomites joined his forces and exulted at the destruction of their ancient enemies (Ps. 137:7; Lam. 4:21-22; Obad. 10-16). After the deportation of most of Judah to Babylon and the flight of the remainder after the assassination of Gedaliah, the Edomites moved northward into S Judah, with Hebron as their capital; this is the IDUMEA of the postexilic period. During the Persian period the NABATEANS began pressing into the Edomite territory from the S and E, and by the fourth century they had built up a territory of their own with Petra as their capital. Many Edomites migrated into Idumea, but many others seem to have stayed and assimilated with the Nabateans.

The history of the Idumeans is unknown until the time of the Maccabean Revolt, when the triumphant Judeans began to make headway against their neighbors. Judas Maccabeus defeated the Idumeans in the Akrabattene in 164 (I Macc. 5:1-5; Jos. Antiq. XII. viii.1), and John Hyrcanus *ca.* 120 overran all Idumea and forcibly converted its inhabitants to Judaism (Jos. Antiq. XIII.ix.1; XV.vii.9). The result of this eventually was that an Idumean, Antipater, became the governor of the country in 63 B.C., and his son, Herod, founded in 37 the last dynasty of the kings of Palestine, who were ruling in the period of the NT. In the last great struggle against Rome (A.D. 66-73) the descendants of those Edomites who had exulted over the fall of Jerusalem some six hundred years before were its most fanatic defenders.

4. Edom in biblical literature. Just as Jacob was identified with Israel, Esau was identified with Edom (Gen. 36:1). While the story of the two brothers has a plot of its own, many of its features are based on the fortunes of the two nations. The name of Edom is explained either from the ruddiness of Esau (Gen. 25:25) or from the redness of the lentil porridge for which he jestingly sold his birthright (Gen. 25:30). The S boundary of Israel was marked by Mount Halak, which faced the Edomite boundary of Seir (Josh. 11:17; 12:7); accordingly Jacob is described (Gen. 27:11) as being "smooth" (*ḥālāq*) and Esau as "hairy" (*śā'îr*). The blessing which Isaac gives to Esau (Gen. 27:39-40) foreshadows the historical fact that Edom was for a time subject to Judah and later regained its independence.

In view of the constant hostility between Edom and Judah in the time of the kings, it is not surprising that nearly all the Judean prophets are hostile toward the Edomites. Amos denounces them for their employment of slaves and their ferocity in war; he also mentions that the Moabites once burned the bones of a king of Edom to lime, in a border war of which there is no other record (Amos 1:6, 9, 11; 2:1). The entire little book of Obadiah is devoted to predicting the doom of Edom; and numerous similar passages are to be found (Ps. 137:7; Isa. 11:14; 34: 5-17; Jer. 49:7-22; Ezek. 35; Mal. 1:2-4). On the other hand, Zephaniah and Zechariah do not include Edom among the nations whose doom they predict; the law of Deuteronomy is fairly lenient in the admission of Edomites into the community (Deut. 23:8); and the author of Job, rising above national feelings, makes his hero and all the other characters of his story not Judeans, but Edomites.

Bibliography. F. Buhl, *Geschichte der Edomiter* (1893). N. Glueck, "Explorations in Eastern Palestine, II," *AASOR,* Vol. XV (1935); *The Other Side of the Jordan* (1940), pp. 114-34.

S. COHEN

EDREI ĕd'rĭ ī [אדרעי]. **1.** A residence city of Og, king of Bashan (Deut. 1:4). It was situated at the extreme S boundary of Bashan near the desert, and was apparently the place where the king watched for an enemy attack either from the S or from the E. Moses and the Israelites invaded Bashan from the desert and defeated Og in the plain before Edrei. The city and the district around it were assigned to the Machir clan of the tribe of Manasseh. The name and the site are retained by the modern city of Der'a near the Yarmuk River, *ca.* sixty miles due S of Damascus; it has many ruins and inscriptions and an ancient subterranean city.

2. A city in Naphtali (Josh. 19:37). It may be the same as *'tra,* No. 91 in the list of Thut-mose (*ANEP* 242).

S. COHEN

EDUCATION, OT. The OT shows a great concern for the education of the young, and some of its most important portions are seen to have been written by men who were evidently teachers of the people.

1. Technical terms
2. Ancient Near Eastern background
3. Regard for children in ancient Israel
4. The aims of education according to the OT
5. The history of education in ancient Israel according to the OT and rabbinic literature
6. Pedagogics in the OT
7. Literacy in ancient Israel

Bibliography

1. Technical terms. The technical term for "instruction," "teaching," or "direction" in the OT is תורה, and is derived from ירה, "to point out, show," hence "give direction, teach"—e.g., I Sam. 12:23: והוריתי אתכם בדרך הטובה והישרה, "I will instruct you in the good and the right way." Instruction, teachings, both human and divine, become synonymous in the OT with the proper way of life, or laws of conduct, both toward God and toward man, hence *Torah,* "teaching, the Law." The modern Hebrew word for "education," חנוך, is derived from the root חנך, "to train," and is found in the OT at a late period in the imperative verbal form in Prov. 22:6: חנך לנער על פי דרכו, "Train up a child in the way he should go."

The root of the verb "to learn" is למד; see מלמד, "oxgoad" (Judg. 3:31). The sense of training a bullock to the goad or the yoke (cf. Hos. 10:11) would be extended to "become/make accustomed to, (be) train(ed) in," as in Jer. 2:24: למד מדבר, "used to the wilderness." Further extension brings the meaning "learn/teach" in general. It is to be noted, however, that the root *lmd,* meaning "learn/teach," is found in Ugaritic (3 *Aqht*:rev. 29), and the root *lamâdu,* "learn," is found in Akkadian. In the *pi'el* the verb means "to teach"—e.g.: "that he might teach them war" (Judg. 3:2).

Another verb, used at a later period, is יסר, in the sense of "to discipline, correct, admonish," hence "to instruct," and in many cases implies a degree of severity—e.g.:

> He is instructed aright;
> his God teaches him
> (Isa. 28:26).

The noun is מוסר, "wisdom and instruction" (Prov. 1:2). In one instance the *hiph'il* of בין is used: "He said to the Levites who taught all Israel" (II Chr. 35:3). The object of knowledge is also referred to as בינה or תבונה, "insight, understanding":

> The fear of the Lord is the beginning of wisdom,
> and the knowledge of the Holy One is insight
> (Prov. 9:10);

> Yes, if you cry out for insight
> and raise your voice for understanding
> (Prov. 2:3).

Teachers are referred to as מורים and מלמדים, from the verbal roots mentioned above:

> I did not listen to the voice of my teachers
> or incline my ear to my instructors
> (Prov. 5:13).

The term חכם, "wise," is often used—e.g.: "The lips of the wise spread knowledge" (Prov. 15:7); "The teaching of the wise is a fountain of life" (Prov. 13:14). The plural word "wise" recalls the Greek σόφοι, who had their schools, pupils (בנים; *see* § 5 *below*), discipline (מוסר), principles, and collections of wisdom (דברי חכמים). Also, at a late period, מבין, "teacher," from the root בין, is also found: "teacher and pupil alike" (I Chr. 25:8).

Pupils are למודים, "those who are taught"—e.g.: "Seal the teaching among my disciples" (Isa. 8:16); "the tongue of those who are taught" (Isa. 50:4); תלמידים (I Chr. 25:8). Pupils are also called בנים, "sons":

> Come, O sons, listen to me,
> I will teach you the fear of the Lord
> (Ps. 34:11).

2. Ancient Near Eastern background. Education in ancient Israel fitted into the general framework of education in the ancient Near East.

A number of "school texts," dating from *ca.* 2500 to the first half of the second millennium B.C., show that numerous schools for future scribes flourished throughout ancient Sumer. Many tablets contain short texts set as copying exercises, together with the pupils' own copies (and their mistakes, with the teachers' corrections). We also gain information regarding school life and personnel from essays on the subject written by some of the teachers. It was at these scribal schools that the literary creations of the past were carefully copied and studied by the more mature pupils, and it is because of these assiduous students that many of these texts have come down to us at all.

The main purpose of the Sumerian schools was to train professional scribes for the multifarious needs of the temples, the palaces, the courts, and all the other administrative and economic needs of the life of the time. Accordingly, the complete cultural heritage of the cuneiform world passed through the hands of the scribes and was transmitted by them. Education was voluntary, and since it involved both time and cost, it is natural that we find, in the many cases in which scholars identified themselves, that they came from the higher social and economic strata of the urban communities.

Among the school personnel were the *ummia,* the "expert" or "professor," who was the head of the school, and the "assistant professor" or "big brother," who prepared the daily exercises for the pupils. It is interesting, in view of the fact that one term for "pupils" among the later Israelites was *bānîm,* "sons," that another term for the Sumerian *ummia* was "school father," and the pupil was called "school son." Other members of the faculty were teachers of drawing and Sumerian. There was also a system of monitors in charge of discipline. The teachers were all paid out of the tuition fees collected from the parents of the pupils.

Among the school texts which have come down to us, and from which we may gain a notion of the subject matter studied, are classified lists of words indicating a basic knowledge of the botanical, zoological, mineralogical, and geographical lore of the time; mathematical tables; mathematical problems with their solutions; and many grammatical and lexicographical texts. The myths and epic tales used for study and copying have already been mentioned. This assimilation of the corpus of the cultural heritage would have taken some years to accomplish, and we know from the texts that the pupil attended school from sunrise to sunset and was subject to strict discipline. The teachers were held in great respect by the parents of the pupils, as we learn from a text describing how a father goes to elaborate lengths in order to mollify with gifts the teacher of his son, who had not been doing too well. This system of scribal schools originated by the Sumerians prevailed throughout Western Asia, and even when Sumerian ceased to be a living language, it was studied in the schools and its texts copied, as many bilingual glossaries of Sumerian and Akkadian, which have come down to us from much later times, attest.

Following the Fertile Crescent, we come across more information from the upper Euphrates. In the palace of Mari two rooms were discovered which were quite evidently schoolrooms. They were equipped with rows of benches and desks made of clay, and a few tables scattered over the floor were evidence of their occupation by the pupil-scribes. Many small shells were also found scattered about, and these had doubtlessly served as counters in the study of arithmetic. An organized system of instruction prevailed, then, at least to provide the educated corps of palace scribes along the upper Euphrates during the first portion of the second millennium B.C., in accordance with the cultural tradition of Mesopotamia.

We have definite information regarding organized instruction in pre-Israelite Canaan in the form of a very interesting tablet from Shechem, described by Albright (*BASOR*, no. 86, pp. 28 ff) and dated by him *ca.* 1400 B.C. It is a letter to a notable in Shechem from his son's teacher: "From three years [ago] until now thou hast me paid—is there no grain nor oil nor wine which thou canst send? What is my offense that thou hast not paid [me]? The children who are with me continue to learn—their father and their mother every [day a]like am I." This teacher evidently conducted a regular class: although this parent stopped paying his son's tuition, the other children continued to learn, and the class went on. Classroom instruction, then, in the regular tradition of the ancient Near East, was also a feature of the cultural life of Canaan for some time before the Israelite conquest. Note especially the fact that the teacher regards his pupils as his sons, again within the same tradition, to be continued in biblical terminology, where a regular technical term for "pupils" is *bānîm.*

From Egypt, at the W end of the Fertile Crescent, we gain another clear notion of school life and methods. We have a number of New Kingdom papyri, writing boards, and ostraca which served as schoolboy exercise texts. These are, for the most part, didactic in nature, in the tradition of the wisdom literature of the ancient Near East. As in Mesopotamia, we see the teacher's corrections in the margins of the texts. Another type of copy exercise was the model letter, actual and fictitious, some addressed to teachers. The texts all indicate that the profession of scribe was most highly regarded in ancient Egypt, and was the gateway to all the preferred government positions of both emolument and honor. Horemheb, pharaoh of Egypt, who had been a general, is familiar to us from his statue, where he is represented as a seated scribe. Other professions and occupations are compared unfavorably with that of the scribe, and the sole method of achieving this exalted goal is that of diligence. The teacher beats the pupil often, but it is for the future scribe's own good: the model letters contain beautiful wishes and praises for teachers in gratitude for their severe regimen of instruction. The best method of attaining felicity and preferment is, as we would say, "to keep one's nose to the grindstone." Wine is to be shunned, and also idle music and girls—which reminds us of the exhortations against the "loose woman" of Proverbs.

The scribal school in Egypt was attached to the temple, and was called, significantly, the "house of life." The schoolboy learned writing, not the least important aspect of which was calligraphy, and studied the ancient literature, copying the many texts and absorbing the teachings of the letters and the didactic literature. At the end of this "elementary" course the student scribe was transferred to one of the government administrations, where he received further instruction and supervision from an older official. This higher education included—in addition to instruction in the complex duties of the office—composition, geography, and natural science. If the boy was destined for the priesthood, he would receive additional instruction in theology and medicine.

Against this general background of the educational system of the ancient Near East, we may place the picture of education in OT life, perhaps not on such an elaborate scale as that obtaining in the larger urban centers of Mesopotamia and Egypt, but surely within the same tradition.

3. Regard for children in ancient Israel. In the OT, children are among the most precious gifts of the Lord, and count among the chief blessings to be gained by those who have deserved them of him:

> Unless the LORD builds the house,
> those who build it labor in vain.
> . . . .
> Lo, sons are a heritage from the LORD,
> the fruit of the womb a reward.
> Like arrows in the hand of the warrior
> are the sons of one's youth.
> Happy is the man who has
> his quiver full of them!
> (Ps. 127:1, 3).

Blessed are all who fear the Lord and walk in his ways, for they shall be happy, and it shall be well with them:

> Your wife will be like a fruitful vine
> within your house;
> your children will be like olive shoots
> around your table.
> Lo, thus shall the man be blessed
> who fears the LORD
> (Ps. 128:3-4).

Among the blessings of security and plenty and old age, not the least are numerous offspring (Job 5:25). Thus, in the running theme of all earthly good to be earned as the result of righteousness, children are a most intimate and integral portion. They are also regarded as a reward for their own sake, and we find no trace in the OT of the ancient Mesopotamian view that they are to be acquired so that they may slake their dead parents' thirst in the underworld. It is simply that in the view of the OT the happiness of mankind is not to be understood without children. When the Lord returns to Zion and dwells in the midst of Jerusalem, two scenes of happiness will distinguish the event: old men and women will once again sit peacefully in the streets of the city, "and the streets of the city shall be full of boys and girls playing in its streets" (Zech. 8:5).

For children to figure so prominently among the chief blessings resulting from the fear of the Lord, and for children playing happily in the streets to signalize the Lord's return to Zion, the love of children must have been great indeed among the ancient Hebrews. Further, it was the Lord himself who was the prototype of the loving and merciful father; and conversely, the author of Ps. 103, in order to convey a powerful simile of the Lord's mercy, states that the Lord pities those who fear him, as a father pities his children (vs. 13).

It was natural that in a society in which children were held in such high regard, the careful upbringing and education of these children would be considered, as will be seen, one of the most important functions of parenthood, and that wisdom, which was the means of acquiring fear of the Lord and its consequent righteousness which would result in the Lord's earthly blessings for one's children, was held in the greatest esteem and regarded as the optimum of human attainment.

4. The aims of education according to the OT. The general aims of education in ancient Israel were twofold: (*a*) the transmission of the historical heritage of the Hebrew nation—the story of God's covenant with his people and the saga of the workings of that covenant in subsequent history—and (*b*) instruction in the ethical conduct of life—how one's life can be conducted for the purpose of attaining the utmost happiness on earth. According to the evidence of the OT, the first aim was stressed during the formative period of Israel's nationhood, in order that succeeding generations of the new nation might be nourished by the powerful historic memories of the period of its founding by means of the covenant with God, and thus be established upon a firm basis in the consciousness of the people. At a later period, when the nation was firmly established and the kingdom was organically functioning for a time, the second element, that of concrete ethical monotheism as leading to earthly good, was stressed and organized in the wisdom literature, notably the book of Proverbs. However, even in the earlier period, teachings regarding the ethical conduct of life were of major importance, as evidenced by certain portions of the Pentateuch in general, and, of course, by the Decalogue in particular.

The Hebrews are strongly enjoined to teach their children the powerful memories of the redemption of Israel from bondage in Egypt and its entry into Canaan, and by the most effective method—that of arousing the children's curiosity. After setting up the twelve stones taken from the Jordan, Joshua says to the people of Israel: "When your children ask their fathers in time to come, 'What do these stones mean?' then you shall let your children know, 'Israel passed over this Jordan on dry ground' " (Josh. 4:21-22). The Passover sacrifice and the eating of unleavened bread are to serve to prompt the children to ask why these things were done, and the Israelite father is commanded to teach his child their historic and religious symbolism (Exod. 12:26-27; 13:7-8, 14). These vivid memories of the redemption from Egypt and the great wonders that God showed to Israel in establishing and protecting its nationhood are used as prime educational factors through to the later period of the First Commonwealth. In various portions of Deuteronomy we find the same injunctions to remember the testimonies and ordinances connected with the Exodus and to teach them to the children (Deut. 4:9-10; 6:20-21; 7:17-19; 32:7).

The educational aim of transmitting the ethical heritage is already stated succinctly in Genesis: "I have chosen him [Abraham], that he may charge his children and his household after him to keep the way of the LORD by doing righteousness and justice; so that the LORD may bring to Abraham what he has promised him" (Gen. 18:19). Righteousness and justice are embodied in the Decalogue of Exod. 20:1-17, and are given religious sanction in Lev. 19:2: "You shall be holy; for I the LORD your God am holy." Immediately following this opening verse, and in the rest of the same chapter, there follow commandments regarding reverence for parents; providing gleanings for the poor and for the sojourner; and prohibitions of stealing, of false dealings, of lying and false oaths, and of oppression of neighbors, servants, and the physically handicapped. Included are injunctions for ethical dealing between man and man, and various other commandments which make for the good and just society, including respect for the aged (vs. 32) and love for the stranger (vs. 33). These ideas of social justice are intimately associated with and proceed from the holiness of God, and this fellowship in God's holiness and love for God is the key precept, along with God's unity, which is commanded to be taught by the Israelite to his children in Deut. 6:7. It is the following of these precepts of ethics and morality which constitutes the "fear of the LORD," which is considered "the beginning of knowledge" in Prov. 1:7; 9:10; and which will lead to the good life on earth.

The book of Proverbs, which is a manual of instruction in itself, from the later period, contains a third purpose of education, which has many parallels in the wisdom literature of the ancient Near East. This is instruction in the practical conduct of daily existence—how to get along with equals and superiors, and how to keep out of trouble. Many of the maxims and wise saws of Proverbs sound quite familiar in terms of the modern educational jargon of "adjustment." Proper manners and how-to-get-along-with-people teachings formed a major portion of Egyptian instruction (cf. the Teaching of Amen-em-Ope, Ptah-Hotep, and Ka-Gemni) and were, for practical considerations, incorporated also in ancient Israelite education. Instruction in sensible sex life was also not neglected (Prov. 5:3-21). As an organized textbook of education, Proverbs stresses the importance of instruction as of the utmost necessity for the good life. As a matter of fact, wisdom is equated with life itself. For wisdom, which includes knowledge both of those ethical principles leading to righteousness and of the practical skills of social adjustment, is the wellspring of existence, and healing to all human flesh (Prov. 4:10, 13, 20-23; 8:35; 10:16; 11:30; 12:28; 14:27). The purpose of education—that men may receive instruction in righteousness, justice, and equity, and in wise dealing, prudence, and discretion—is stated in the proem to the book itself (1:2-4). Continuity of learning—the fact that study is an ongoing, lifelong process—is also emphasized; the man of wisdom and understanding can always increase his learning and skill (1:5). Finally, at a later period, delight in study is an end in itself; happiness in learning *is* life, and true happiness consists in meditating on the law (instruction) of the Lord by day and by night (Ps. 1:2).

5. The history of education in ancient Israel according to the OT. According to the OT, it was incumbent primarily upon every father of a family to impart instruction to his children, at least during their early childhood. The early memories of the Exodus and the fear of the Lord are to be retold in the presence of children (Exod. 10:2; 12:26-27). Abraham is to instruct not only his children but his entire household in the way of the Lord (Gen. 18:19). The Shema (Deut. 6:4-9), the most important set of precepts in the Pentateuch after the Decalogue, commands each Israelite to teach the words of God diligently to his children. This duty of transmitting the heritage received from one's father on to one's children was recognized as of prime importance through to the later period of the First Commonwealth, and this principle of the continuity of the educational tradition, to receive the heritage and to pass it on to generations yet unborn, was crystallized as an educational doctrine commanded by God (Ps. 78:3-6). During the Second Commonwealth also, the very young child received his first instruction and his reverence for the sayings of the wise from his father (Prov. 4:3-4).

It would seem, however, that even at an early period it was customary to devote a child to the service of the deity, in which case he was brought to the sanctuary as soon as he was weaned, as exemplified by the case of Samuel. Samuel must needs have received not only general, but also specialized, instruction from Eli in order to perform his ministrations before the Lord. There is no reason to believe that Samuel was an isolated case, and since Samuel was not a Levite, but an Ephraimite, it is quite possible that it was a general practice to devote some children to the service of the sanctuary, in which case they would have received the most developed type of education that their milieu afforded, analogous possibly to the education received by the youngsters in the temple schools of Egypt.

At an early age, children were trained in the everyday duties of the family, such as the pasturing of sheep (e.g., I Sam. 16:11) and the work of the fields (II Kings 4:18). In at least some instances, artistic training was not neglected, as witness David's skill in playing the lyre while still a youth (I Sam. 16:15-18). Music and the dance were also taught, and evidently the Israelites of all periods had a lively taste for these arts (I Sam. 16:18; Judg. 21:21; Ps. 137; Jer. 31:13; Lam. 5:14). The graphic arts—specifically the arts of the celator, or worker in metals—were held in particularly high esteem. The skilled artist Bezalel receives his inspiration directly from God, who fills his mind with wisdom and knowledge of his craft, and, what is particularly important in this connection, inspires him also to teach his art to others.

Girls learned household crafts, such as baking (II Sam. 13:8), spinning, and weaving (Exod. 35:25-26). During the Second Commonwealth, when organized schools were already in existence, they were intended, of course, only for boys, and girls remained at home to learn the various household skills (Prov. 31:13-31). In cases where the household did not boast of any sons, the daughters would do the boys' work, such as pasturing and watering the sheep (Gen. 29:6; Exod. 2:16). Some women had received a relatively good education and hence became prophetesses, for which they had to have a good knowledge both of Israel's past history and of current happenings. An example of the early period is, of course, Deborah (Judg. 4:4 ff; 5). During the later period of the First Commonwealth we have the prophetess Huldah (II Kings 22:14-20). In the book of Proverbs, the mother is regarded as of equal importance with the father in imparting instruction (Prov. 1:8; 6:20). In the same remarkable book we have the compilation of the wisdom of Lemuel (ch. 31) which he had received from his mother (vs. 1). This would indicate that within Israel's orbit, at any rate, there existed women who were educated to such a degree that they played a role in wisdom tradition analagous to that of the *hakhamim*.

Among the higher classes, particularly the royal families, we have reference to nurses or guardians (*omnim*) who would have, in these cases, assumed the duties of instruction of their charges along with their other duties *in loco parentis* (Ruth 4:16; II Sam. 4:4; II Kings 10:5; Isa. 49:23).

The Gezer Calendar supplies some quite interesting details regarding instruction among the peasants of central Palestine during the period of the Early Monarchy. The tablet is dated by Albright (*BASOR*, no. 92, pp. 16 ff) on the basis of both external and internal evidence and supported by comparative epigraphy, to the second half of the tenth century. It was Albright also who pointed out that this small limestone plaque, just large enough to be held comfortably in the hand of a twelve-year-old-boy, was actually a schoolboy's writing tablet, as evidenced by signs on both sides of scraping to clear it for reuse. In addition, the text itself, which is a sort of "poetic ditty" concisely describing the months of the Palestinian agricultural year, is rhythmically mnemonic in nature. An adult farmer would have no need of such a device. The text on the plaque, then, would be the ancient Israelite boy's equivalent of: "Thirty days hath September . . . ." Albright indicates further that the boy was in all likelihood writing from dictation. The Gezer tablet is, accordingly, excellent archaeological evidence of the extent of literacy among even the peasants of the time of the early Israelite monarchy, of the use of a standard pedagogic device such as the mnemonic and of the use of dictation as one method in instruction.

Reference to bands or companies of prophets in

I Samuel (10:5, 10; 19:20) has led some authorities to infer that there were actually "schools of the prophets" with organized instruction. Such an inference cannot, of course, be proved one way or the other, but one can safely surmise that there was at least a certain body of knowledge and/or skills which was imparted to these youths, for prophecy seems to have been a definitely established "profession" at the very beginning of the history of the Israelite kingdom.

When the tradition of Yahwistic prophecy was established on a firm foundation during the period of the monarchy, the prophets may be safely assumed to have had groups of disciples whom they taught (Isa. 8:16). Isaiah uses the term למודים, which, as we have seen, is one of the technical terms used for pupils or disciples. Elijah's disciple and successor was Elisha (I Kings 19:16), and he was evidently one outstanding pupil of an outstanding prophet, for we have mention of a large group of "sons of the prophets" at Bethel (II Kings 2:3 ff). These "sons of the prophets" evidently regarded Elisha with a great deal of respect (cf. vs. 7), and after the translation of Elijah acknowledged Elisha as their master (vs. 15). "Sons" or בנים, as pointed out above (§ 1), is one technical term for "pupils." As master, Elisha was also responsible for the welfare of the widows and children of any of his pupils who died (II Kings 4:1-2 ff), and assumed the care of providing food for his disciples in time of famine (II Kings 4:38). It is interesting to note that among the body of science at the command of the prophets, and which they transmitted to their pupils, was a knowledge of poisonous herbs and their antidotes (II Kings 4:39-41). This was evidently a part of their general knowledge of the medical science of their day (II Kings 4:19, 32-35). These medical arts were part of the general science of the ancient Near East, and were taught by both priests and prophets to their pupils in ancient Israel, as in the temple schools of Egypt and Mesopotamia.

As the prophets taught their own small groups of disciples who trained for a highly technical profession, so the priests and Levites trained the members of their craft. However, upon the latter devolved also the duty of instructing the people at large in the precepts of the Israelite religion. In the blessing of Moses, the tribe of Levi is named as the preceptor of the people:

> They shall teach Jacob thy ordinances,
> and Israel thy law (Deut. 33:10).

In the Levitical Code, among the general duties of the sons of Aaron is the injunction to teach the people of Israel (Lev. 10:11). This function of the priesthood continued to be quite important to the final period of the First Commonwealth: Jehoshaphat sent learned priests and Levites to travel throughout all the cities of Judah and teach the people, using the Book of the Law of the Lord as a text (II Chr. 17:8-9). Under Josiah, the function of teaching the people was among the duties of the Levites (II Chr. 35:3), and during this period and later this Levitical function was recognized by the prophets (Mal. 2:6-7). The priesthood, however, was supposed to give instruction to the people free of charge, and acceptance of any emolument for this purpose was regarded as reprehensible (Mic. 3:11). The method of teaching was evidently to visit the various towns periodically and to gather all the inhabitants together, both Israelite and non-Israelite, and expound the Torah to them (Deut. 31:10-13; II Chr. 17:8-9). This pedagogical function of the Levites was continued after the Return (Neh. 8:7-9), and evidently they were skilled at exegesis and exposition (vs. 8). They were called מבינים (lit. "they who cause to understand"; Neh. 8:7, 9; Ezra 8:16).

During the Persian period, we know that there was current among the Jews of Elephantine, in Egypt, a manual of instruction analogous to the book of Proverbs—namely, the Words of Ahiqar. This work is in the old tradition of the wisdom literature of the ancient Near East, of which Proverbs is a part, and the presence of a wisdom literature would betoken teachers who instruct their disciples in their knowledge. At the beginning of the body of proverbs in Ahiqar, there is the statement: "What is stronger than the wine foaming in the press? The son who is trained and taught" (col. VI, ll. 79-80; Sachau, pl. 44; text in Cowley, *Aramaic Papyri of the Fifth Century B.C.*, p. 214; in translation, p. 222). It may be safe to assume that the "son" is the old technical term for "pupil," as in Proverbs, with the pupils learning their maxims with the aid of the rod, which must not be withheld.

In Israel itself, it is most likely that for some time after the Return the body of teachings (*torah*) continued to be the property and responsibility of the priesthood. We have seen that the exposition of the accumulated tradition to the people was one of the most important functions of priests and Levites, and this aspect of the sacred office would tend to become most important and have government sanction in the Second Commonwealth, which remained a theocracy, in fact and then in name, until the time of Herod the Great. The great revival of Israel, both nationally and culturally, was initiated by Ezra and Nehemiah. Ezra was himself a priest (Ezra 7:1-5; Neh. 8:2), and evidently a member of that section of the priesthood which specialized in knowledge of the Torah and its teaching (Ezra 7:6, 10). He took it upon himself to continue in the priestly tradition of teacher to the people, and brought with him from Babylon a copy of the Torah, which he expounded before the assembly of the returned exiles. This assembly included the teaching Levites who were termed, as mentioned above, מבינים (MT; RSV Neh. 8:3, 9), in order to refresh their knowledge also. He stood upon a "wooden pulpit" (Neh. 8:4) above the people and read to them, surrounded by his assistants, the teaching Levites (8:7, 9) who assisted him in his interpretation and exposition, which was done in a clear and detailed manner, so that all might understand. This was probably the same manner in which the Torah was expounded on Mondays and Thursdays throughout the ensuing days of the Second Commonwealth, when advantage was taken of the Monday and Thursday market days in the cities of Palestine to read and expound the law to the people congregating there. Later, a method was worked out whereby the Torah was read in consecutive sections, the cycle being completed every three years. Thus was initiated the first large-scale program of adult education in history.

In the subsequent period, with the growing involvement of the upper echelons of the priesthood in politics and the other priests and Levites in the intricacies and large-scale operations of the temple service, biblical exposition and scholarship tended to be concentrated in the hands of a group of men known as סופרים, "scribes." Their occupation dated from the early days of the First Commonwealth, where they are mentioned among the first officers of the kingdom, along with the generals of the army and the chief priests (II Sam. 8:17). Their chief functions were evidently secretarial, and they would have been responsible for the inditing of diplomatic correspondence and compiling the annals of the kingdom. Influence was apparently considerable in this respect from Egyptian government organization, where the occupation of scribe was very highly regarded, and where some of them became generals of the army, and in such cases as Hor-em-heb became kings themselves. Thus under King Uzziah, Jeiel the scribe is mentioned among the generals of the army, and the verse (II Chr. 26:11) might be interpreted to name Jeiel as a general himself. It is possible that many of the scribes were Levites, who would naturally combine both scribal and teaching duties, thus serving as ancestors of the definite institution of the scribes of the Second Commonwealth, who were the custodians of the Torah and its interpretation. Thus, in First Commonwealth annals, Shemaiah, a Levite, serves as a scribe under David (I Chr. 24:6), and a body of Levites who were scribes under Josiah is mentioned (II Chr. 34:13). In First Commonwealth times, too, scribes are already mentioned as having attributes of scholarship and wisdom. Jonathan, David's uncle, is a counselor, a "man of understanding" (מבין, one of the technical terms for "teacher" mentioned in § 1 *above*), and a scribe (I Chr. 27:32). Baruch, the secretary and disciple of Jeremiah, and thus one of the "sons of the prophets," is also a scribe (Jer. 36:26). In the last days of the First Commonwealth, the scribes are already recognized as a professional class, who presume to be learned custodians of the Torah (Jer. 8:8). It is from within the traditional framework of scribal priests, possessed of the intellectual heritage of Israel, that Ezra appeared. He is known as "Ezra the scribe" in later Jewish literature, and is described as a "scribe skilled in the law of Moses" (Ezra 7:6, 11; cf. Neh. 8:4, 9, 13). From the time of Ezra onward, the scribes became a specialized class of biblical scholars and exegetes, and as such were recognized as the official teachers and spiritual leaders of the people.

According to the traditions recorded in the Mishna, these scribes, who were the repositories of Israel's cultural heritage, were known, during the earlier period of the Second Commonwealth, as the "men of the Great Assembly" (אנשי כנסת הגדולה), possibly because of their connection and intellectual descent from Ezra and his scribes who expounded the Torah before the great assemblies of the people at the time of the Return. In Tractate Aboth of the Mishna, which is entirely didactic, the "men of the Great Assembly" (or "men of the Great Synagogue," translating כנסת according to its Greek equivalent, συναγωγή; actually, the synagogue as a house of worship had not yet come into being) were the direct descendants of the prophets as custodians of the Torah, and lived between the time of Ezra and Nehemiah and the time of Alexander the Great. It is, in all probability, these scribes who are "the wise" of Proverbs (*see* § 1 *above*), and it is most likely they who prepared and collated the wisdom literature of the OT, and their role as educators was strongly reflected in their work—e.g., Proverbs *passim,* where "wise" ="teacher" and "son"="pupil." The book is a compendium both of their methods of instruction and pedagogical attitudes and of a large portion of the content of the subject matter taught in their schools, again in the didactic tradition of the ancient Near East. They, in turn, were the predecessors of the series of doctors of the law who flourished roughly from the time of the Seleucids through the Maccabean and Roman periods up to the time of the completion of the Mishna, *ca.* A.D. 200. For about two centuries, then, the scribes who constituted the "men of the Great Assembly" slowly built up their method of biblical exegesis and interpretation and constant adaptation of the law to meet the exigencies of their times into the formidable structure of the Mishna. This naturally presupposes a system of instruction of Torah on a more or less formal scale, with generations of scholars handing down their body of knowledge to their disciples, who became scholars in turn. At the very beginning of the Tractate Aboth, the three most important maxims of the "men of the Great Assembly" are given. They are: "Be deliberate in judgment, raise up many disciples, and make a fence around the Law (Heb. *torah*)." Thus within this succinct summary of their activities, along with the injunctions of deep examination and interpretation for the purpose of applying the law to the everyday life of their times, is included the establishment of the means of educating disciples to transmit the heritage. Their successors were the series of scribes beginning with Simon the Just (*ca.* 280 B.C.; Jos. Antiq. XII.ii.5), whose maxims in Aboth are replete with the atmosphere of the house of study. The term "house of study" itself is found in the last chapter of Ecclesiasticus (*beth midrash;* Ecclus. 51:23), and is the first mention of the institution which later became one of the foundations of Judaism.

Josephus speaks of elementary education as a long-established institution. He derives the authority for the education of children from the Mosaic Law (Antiq. IV.viii.12; Apion II.xxv), and emphasizes the extreme solicitude of his people for the instruction of children (Apion I.xii). Education begins as soon as the child is capable of being sensible of anything (Apion II.xix). Philo states that Jews are instructed in knowledge of their laws from their earliest youth, and are taught, so to speak, from their very swaddling clothes (*Leg. ad Caium* 31). During the entire latter period of the Second Commonwealth, literacy was quite widespread, and books of the law were found in many houses of private individuals (I Macc. 1:56 ff). Hence education of the children in the school would have begun with the teaching of reading, and subsequently consisted of the study of the Torah from the texts themselves. Josephus does not hesitate to boast that by his fourteenth year he had such a profound knowledge of the law that even the high priest and the chief men of Jerusalem used to come to him for consultation on practices of interpretation (*Vita* 2).

The establishment of a mandatory system of schools was ascribed, in the rabbinic literature, to the Pharisees. The Pharisees, after their recall during the reign of Salome Alexandra (76-67 B.C.), enjoyed the broad popular support of the bulk of the urban population. Under the leadership of Simon ben Shetah, they understood the wisdom of spreading their teachings among the people in a systematic manner. It was Simon (Jer. Keth. VIII.11) who ordained that children (lit. "babes") should attend the elementary school (בית־הספר, "house of the Book"—i.e., the Torah), where the Torah was the text of instruction, supplemented by explanations and interpretations based upon the oral law, that vast body of homiletical and legal commentary upon the Torah which had been accumulating under the scribes during the Second Commonwealth, and which was the basis for Pharisaic teaching. The first of these Pharisaic schools were established in Jerusalem, and the system later spread to the urban centers of the other districts. A few years before the destruction of the temple, Joshua ben Gamala (B. B. 21*a*) enacted that teachers of children be appointed in every province and in every town, and that children be admitted to school at the age of six or seven years. The children's teacher was the חזן, who was evidently a factotum who combined the instruction of children in reading with duties of a more general nature (Sabb. I.3).

Secondary and higher education for adolescents and young men of promise was continued in the בית־המדרש, of which several were conducted by the great Pharisaic teachers themselves. Some of these acquired a wide reputation as instructors, and Hillel came from Babylonia to continue his education at the school of Shemaiah and Abtalion. The בית־המדרש was considered to have more sanctity than even the synagogue (Meg. 26*b*-27*a*). The young students discussed, under the leadership of the Pharisaic sages, the interpretation of the Torah, and the application of its precepts to the greatly changed life of Palestine in the Greco-Roman times. It was these discussions and "lecture notes" which grew into the Mishna, which in turn became the basis for normative Judaism. For the mass of the adult population, there was the regular system of "adult education" mentioned *above*, whereby the Torah was studied weekly. To Josephus this is already a well-established custom.

6. Pedagogics in the OT. The OT, as a collection of writings by prophets and scribes, who, as we have seen, became the teachers of Israel, would naturally tend to express theories of education and pedagogic viewpoints, whether conscious or implied. We can, therefore, form some impressions of both methods of education and the educator's view of his mission from an examination of the text.

To begin with, education itself was regarded as a mission commanded by God (e.g., Deut. 4:7). Further, the prototype of all teachers was the Lord himself, who, through Moses, is the divine teacher of Israel. Moses says: "And now, O Israel, give heed to the statutes and the ordinances which I teach you" (Deut. 4:1; the *pi'el* verb מלמד, "teach," is used, not "command"), and: "Behold, I have taught you statutes and ordinances, as the LORD my God commanded me" (vs. 5). The educational process has divine sanction and authority. The Lord himself is the teacher of Moses (Exod. 4:12). Even when the latter demurs at accepting his mission, God says to him: "I . . . will teach you what you shall do" (vs. 15). Likewise, when the Lord is angry with his people, it is only as a teacher is angry with his pupils, and even when he punishes them, he will still be close to them and guide them in the correct path: "Though the Lord give you the bread of adversity and the water of affliction, yet your Teacher will not hide himself any more, but your eyes shall see your Teacher" (Isa. 30:20). The same sentiment is found in Job 36:22:

> Behold, God is exalted in his power;
> who is a teacher like him?

Man begs God for instruction:

> When I told of my ways, thou didst answer me;
> teach me thy statutes!
> Make me understand the way of thy precepts,
> and I will meditate on thy wondrous works
> (Ps. 119:26-27).

The Lord is "he who teaches men knowledge" (Ps. 94:10). Furthermore, in days to come, when God will restore Zion, "All your sons shall be taught by the LORD" (Isa. 54:13)—the first expressed desire for universal education.

As to all teachers of the ancient Near East, chastisement is a necessary concomitant of instruction:

> He who chastens the nations, does he not chastise?
> He who teaches men knowledge.
> . . . .
> Blessed is the man whom thou dost chasten, O LORD,
> and whom thou dost teach out of thy law
> (Ps. 94:10, 12).

This parallelism of the roots יסר and למד possibly has its prototype in the Egyptian verbal root "teach, instruct, discipline," with the determinative of physical force, implying chastisement.

Despite the necessity for the use of the rod, teaching should be done with quiet restraint, for: "The words of the wise heard in quiet are better than the shouting of a ruler among fools" (Eccles. 9:17).

In addition, God, as divine Teacher, not only imparts knowledge to men, but also actually inspires them to teach in turn (Exod. 35:31-35). The office of teaching, then, would have been a sacred one indeed, and quite honorably regarded by all.

During both commonwealths, instruction of children began at a very early age, apparently soon after they were weaned (Isa. 28:9). According to the testimony of Josephus, in his time it was a very old tradition that children began their education at their first glimmerings of consciousness (*see* § 5 *above*). Actual teaching began quite early in the morning (Isa. 50:4; Jer. 32:33, reading literally with the MT and translating with previous English versions—e.g., Moulton —"rising up early and teaching them"). Note that in both these references it is God as exemplary teacher who imparts instruction at early morning. Both beginning the child's education as early as possible and utilizing the morning hours when the mind is fresh have been universally recognized as two of the basic foundations of pedagogy.

Also among the fundamental laws of education is the axiom of teaching the child a little at a time. Recognition of this pedagogic maxim, along with the previously mentioned one of beginning education at an early age, is found in Isaiah:

> For it is precept upon precept, precept upon precept,
> line upon line, line upon line,
> here a little, there a little (28:10).

The Hebrew for "precept upon precept, line upon line," *ṣaw laṣaw, qaw laqaw,* has also been interpreted to mean "letter by letter," *ṣaw* being taken as an old form of the letter צ and *qaw* as an old form of ק, using the analogy of ו. Pedagogically speaking, this would illustrate the method of teaching reading by teaching the individual letters of the alphabet first.

Most instruction was imparted orally:

> He awakens my ear
> to hear as those who are taught
> (Isa. 50:4; cf. Prov. 1:8 *et passim*).

Mnemonic devices for easier memorization were also used, as illustrated in Prov. 31:10-31, where the first letter in vs. 10 is א, and each successive verse begins with the consecutive letter of the alphabet, to vs. 31, which begins with ת.

Another teaching device was the parable (משל). This was a form of figurative expression in narrative, which usually took the form of an allegory or fable vividly illustrating the truth or application of a principle or argument by analogy. The term may have been used originally to denote a poetic oracle (e.g., in the Oracle of Balaam, Num. 23:7; RSV "discourse") and then a popular saying used to point up an analogy (I Sam. 10:12) or a story in the form of a riddle (Ezek. 17:2). The parables in the OT are used for moral instruction, and are shown to convey such a vivid import that those to whom the parables are directed grasp the lesson in spite of themselves (e.g., II Sam. 12:1 ff). It is interesting to note that the lesson thus skilfully directed to David was given by a prophet. Later, the term משל was used for the body of wisdom instruction (Prov. 1:1, the title of the book translated "The Proverbs of Solomon"). The scribes and doctors of the Second Commonwealth used them extensively; they are to be found all through the Talmudic literature of the period, and their widespread use in teaching is illustrated by the extensive recourse which was had to them in the NT—e.g., the various parables of Jesus.

7. Literacy in ancient Israel. Some of the earliest inscriptions indicating the transition from the cumbersome syllabic and ideographic script of Akkadian cuneiform and Egyptian hieroglyphic and hieratic (a combination of ideographic, syllabic, and alphabetic script) to the purely alphabetic script which was the ancestor of the convenient "Roman" script used throughout the civilized world of today have been found in what was ancient Canaan. It was possibly not accidental that a crude form of alphabetic cuneiform was in use at Ugarit down to the fourteenth century B.C. At any rate, the N Semitic script, which was the ancestor of our own, was in widespread use in the Israelite orbit by the time of the entry into Canaan. With such a simplified method of writing, literacy would tend to be rather common, as the N Semitic alphabet was easily learned and easily taught. The Gezer Calendar, described above, is an excellent case in point, illustrating the use of this alphabet in learning during the Early Monarchy.

According to the OT, literacy, while not universal (Isa. 29:11), was nevertheless quite widespread. In Joshua, mention is made of three men from each tribe who were to provide a written description of the land of Canaan (18:4, 8-9). Gideon catches at random a lad of Succoth, who is able to write down for him the names of the important men of the city (Judg. 8:14). Literacy seems to be a common phenomenon according to Deuteronomy. The children of Israel are commanded to write the words of God upon the doorposts of their houses and upon their gates (Deut. 6:9). Moses also commands that the words of the Torah be written upon stones smoothed over with plaster, and that the inscriptions be set up so that all may read (Deut. 27:2-8). In the coming days of the kingdom, the king himself is to write in a book a copy of the Torah, and is to read in it all his days (Deut. 17:18-19). According to Isaiah, any child could write down at least simple numbers or tallies (Isa. 10:19). The Siloam Inscription, with its exclusive interest in the purely technical details of the completion of the tunnel, was evidently written by one of the workmen, or possibly the engineer of the project. Literacy would have been quite common, then, in the days of Hezekiah. The Lachish Letters and the later Elephantine Papyri of the Persian period indicate not only the widespread use of writing in daily affairs; the development of the script into a rapid cursive is indicative also of the great broadening of its use by the masses of the people. I Macc. 1:56 shows that copies of the Torah were found in many private houses. The mass of Talmudic literature, which is a compilation and conflation, for the most part, of the notes of students taken down during the exposition and discussion of the Law by the masters, is an indication of the great degree of literacy during the later days of the Second Commonwealth.

Bibliography. J. Simon, *L'éducation et l'instruction des enfants chez les anciens Juifs* (1879). A. Klostermann, *Schulwesen im alten Israel* (1908). F. H. Swift, "Hebrew Education in the Family After the Exile," in *The Open Court,* vol. XXXII, no. 1 (Jan., 1918); *Education in Ancient Israel from Earliest Times to A.D. 70* (1919). J. A. Maynard, *A Survey of Hebrew Education* (1924). L. Dürr, *Die Erziehungswesen im Alten Testament und im antiken Orient* (1932). E. Ebner and S. Eliezer, *Elementary Education in Ancient Israel During the Tannaitic Period (10-220 C.E.)* (1956). H. Gese, *Lehre und Wirklichkeit in der alten Weisheit* (1958). W. Barclay, *Education Ideals in the Ancient World* (1959).

For the N Semitic inscriptions, see D. Diringer, *The Alphabet* (1949), pp. 195-247.

The Gezer Calendar is studied and commented upon by W. F. Albright in *BASOR,* no. 92 (Dec. 1943), pp. 16 ff.

For ancient Near Eastern background, see A. Erman, *The Literature of the Ancient Egyptians* (trans. A. M. Blackman; 1927), pp. 185-242. E. Chiera, *They Wrote on Clay* (1938), ch. 13. G. E. Mendenhall, *BA,* XI:1 (Feb., 1948; Mari). S. N. Kramer, *From the Tablets of Sumer* (1956), chs. 2-3.

J. KASTER

EDUCATION, NT.

1. Jewish education
   a. Jewish Dispersion
   b. Religious education
   c. Curriculum
   d. Translations
   e. Jewish schools
   f. Jewish teachers
2. Greek and Roman education
   a. Hellenistic culture
   b. The Greek schools

Bibliography

1. Jewish education. ***a. Jewish Dispersion.*** Adequate treatment of Jewish education in the NT period is complicated by the fact that at the time Jews were so widely dispersed, probably more of them living outside Palestine than within. The major Jewish communities in foreign lands were in Egypt and Mesopotamia, but substantial communities were also found in most of the cities of the Roman Empire, especially in Syria, Asia Minor, Greece, Italy, and North Africa. Because of the homogeneous character of Jewish culture, it might be presumed that Jewish education in the various regions of the Dispersion closely approximated that in the homeland, but this could not be assumed without question. Wherever Jews settled, in order to survive, they had to become bilingual, acquiring the vernacular speech in addition to their own mother tongue. Moreover, their livelihood was dependent on mastery of the trades, industries, and forms of commerce prevailing in the newly adopted area. In some way, whether in schools or not, they had to learn the languages and skills necessary to the production and distribution of goods and services. As a matter of course, Jews living outside Palestine acquired many new skills. At this distance we are not always able to say how this new learning was acquired.

b. Religious education. The most obvious generalization about Jewish education in the NT period is that it was primarily religious, which is true also of education in the OT period. God was the presupposition of all Jewish life and culture. To a considerable extent this was true of Greeks and Romans, but it was far more characteristic of the Jews. The idea of secular life and culture was foreign to Jewish thought, as it was to a large extent to all ancient cultures. When one considers the difference between the Hebrew and Greek theories of knowledge, this distinction becomes clear. The tendency of Greek thought, as of Roman after it, was to emphasize the human element in knowledge. Greeks and Romans believed that man's mind itself discovered truth; so they stressed the development of human reason; and this led to study of sciences and the abstract disciplines of philosophy. Hebrews, by contrast, believed that all truth comes from God; that God is the creator, judge, and redeemer of man; and that he reveals to man whatever knowledge is necessary for his welfare. Hebrew learning revolved about the concepts of God and man, yet not in a speculative sense; and so far as man was concerned, education had to do mainly with the moral and spiritual life. Man's health and prosperity depended on a satisfactory relationship with God.

Jewish education of that period is as notable for what it lacks as for what it contains. We find very little of a scientific character. Hebrew culture was prescientific, knowing nothing about physics, chemistry, biology, physiology, and other natural sciences. Hebrews knew many practical trades. They were familiar with skills necessary for construction of ordinary buildings; they understood the simple processes involved in mining and metallurgy, and different types of work with stone and wood. But even in these matters, as the OT shows, where expert skills were required, they had to seek aid from the Phoenicians. Yet in spite of Jewish mastery of practical skills, we hear of no schools to teach such things. There were no schools of music, architecture, sculpture, painting, arts of the theater, and the like. Indeed, most of these, especially the arts of painting, sculpture, and the theater, were associated with pagan religions. So Jewish culture never cultivated these arts, so characteristic of Greek and Roman life.

In a similar way, Jews and Christians of the NT period had no schools of philosophy. The very presuppositions of their culture made this impossible, philosophy being a humanistic enterprise. The nature of philosophical speculation tends to deny the concept of revelation on which all Jewish and early Christian education was based.

As there is no evidence of trade schools among Jews and Christians of the period, we may assume that carpenters, masons, engineers, smiths, potters, and the like learned their trades as apprentices. This may have been true also of musicians and singers of the temple choirs and orchestras, but the prominence and importance of these artists in the worship services suggest that there must have been professional schools for them.

c. Curriculum. The basic curriculum of Jewish education was the Bible itself, the theory being that God had inspired the Scriptures so that they were a perfect repository of truth, containing all that was necessary for the welfare and happiness of man both here and hereafter (*see* CANON OF THE OT). But there were other important books, not included in this collection, which in some way must have had a place in Jewish education. The best known of these is the group of some fourteen writings known as the OT APOCRYPHA. Some of these, such as the Wisdom of Solomon, the Wisdom of Sirach (Ecclesiasticus), and I Maccabees, are of excellent quality. Except for their late dates, they would probably have been accepted into the Jewish canon. There is another group of indefinite number usually referred to as the PSEUDEPIGRAPHA, late books, mostly without literary merit, but always reflecting religious beliefs held in popular circles of both Jews and Christians. It may be doubted that they found a place in formal schools of the time, yet they had a wide circulation.

Such ideas as the Jews had about the natural sciences were embedded in incidental ways in their Scriptures. Prescientific beliefs about the earth, light, sun, moon, and stars, and about both plant and animal life, are reflected in the creation stories of Genesis; also in numerous other places in the Bible. Hebrews had no books on government and political science as such, yet in the Pentateuch lies the constitution on which the Hebrew state was based; and the same is true of many other aspects of culture. In the ancient period there was no medicine as such; there were no physicians. These matters were in the hands of the priests, and what little we can find about them is scattered through various parts of the OT. No recognition of physicians appears until Ecclesiasticus (*ca.* 200 B.C.), wherein (38:1-12) there is high praise for both physician and pharmacist. This late recognition of healing arts may show a Greek influence on Hebrew culture.

More congenial to Hebrew and early Christian ideas of disease were beliefs about demon-possession and the mental aberrations resulting from it. Such books as Tobit and I Enoch, from the late Jewish literature, and the NT gospels show numerous examples of belief that demons invaded human beings and either temporarily or permanently deranged their minds. Both Jews and Christians dealt with such forms of mental illness by means of exorcism, in which there was an extensive traffic. This black art was surely not taught in the schools, yet in some way it was possible for interested persons to learn its secrets. These beliefs became so deeply intrenched in Western culture that they were not eradicated until the emergence of modern scientific medicine, which substituted concepts of neuroses and psychoses for demons.

d. Translations. Except for a few relatively short passages, notably in Ezra and Daniel, the original language of the canonical Jewish scriptures was Hebrew. The short passages just noted were in Aramaic; some of the apocryphal books were written in Greek. Hebrew continued to be the basis of the most scholarly interpretation of the biblical texts, but by the end of the OT period the vernacular speech of Palestinian Jews, and others to the E, was no longer Hebrew, but Aramaic. This meant that if the Scriptures were to be used by the Jews in schools and otherwise in a language the people could understand, translations into Aramaic were necessary; and such there were. They are known as Targums. *See* TARGUM.

In a similar way, during the last pre-Christian centuries those Jews who had settled in Egypt, Asia Minor, Greece, and Italy had adopted the Greek language. Thus they also became unable to read the Scriptures in Hebrew, and Greek translations became a necessity. There were several of these, the best known being the Septuagint supposed to have been produced in Egypt. The Greek translations not only made the Scriptures available to Greek-speaking Jews, but also enabled non-Jews to read the Jewish Bible. Many Gentiles thereby acquired an admiration for Judaism. The Greek translations therefore prepared the way for the spread of Christianity. Indeed, most early Christians used only Greek translations of the Hebrew scriptures, quotations in the NT itself being based on Greek texts. All the NT books were written in Greek, intended, of course, for the Greek-speaking churches, ranging all the way from Antioch to Rome. It needs to be kept in mind also that Greek was widely spoken even in Palestine, and that many Palestinians were bilingual. From the time of Herod the Great all coins of Palestine were inscribed in Greek. Greek was almost the universal language of the Roman Empire; so much so that when Paul wrote his letter to the church at Rome, without apologies he wrote it in Greek, assuming that Christians there could read and understand it. It is evident that the religious education of many Jews and most Christians in the Empire at the time was based on Greek translations of the Scriptures.

The use of Greek not only made the Jewish scriptures available to people almost everywhere, but—equally important—it made Greek culture accessible, first to Jews and then to Christians. Thus emerged a new understanding of religion by each new generation as it made use of the legacy of Greece as well as that of Palestine. Such Jewish writings as the Wisdom of Solomon and those of Philo of Alexandria illustrate this new synthesis from the Jewish side, and the use of the concept of the Logos in the Letter to the Hebrews and the Gospel of John indicates a beginning of the same process among Christians. In subsequent centuries the seeds thus sown bore rich fruit for both Jews and Christians.

e. Jewish schools. A Jewish view of the importance of education in the life of a young man is indicated in a saying of somewhat uncertain date in Pirke Aboth 5:27 to the effect that a child is ready to begin study of the Scriptures at five, the Mishna at ten, the commandments at thirteen, the Talmud at fifteen, and is ready for marriage at eighteen. If professional education was contemplated, it would follow the age of eighteen.

The first teachers of Hebrew children were their parents. Injunctions to this effect are numerous in the law books and Proverbs. It was probably the father's duty to teach his son how to read and write, and such practical skills and elements of history and tradition as would enable him to enter with some understanding into his cultural heritage.

There is no reference to elementary schools until the Maccabean period. At the time of Queen Alexandra (75 B.C.), Simon Ben-Shetach decreed that children should attend elementary school. This was after Greek influence had begun to penetrate Palestine, and probably shows that Jewish education was beginning to respond to it.

In a formal sense, the most fundamental Jewish educational institution was the SYNAGOGUE, which dates at least from the Babylonian exile. This institution grew up in response to the needs of Jews, now far from their homeland, for a means of maintaining their culture and faith. It was first of all a place of assembly in all matters of interest to the Jewish community. It also served as a place of worship. But above all it was a place of study. The school was conducted either in the synagogue proper or in rooms adjacent to it. Hundreds of synagogues came into existence, wherever Jewish communities were found. So important did they become that they were built in Palestine, even in Jerusalem. Their educational function was so important that synagogues were not even thought of as rivals of the temple. Yet in fact the synagogue had essentially replaced the temple in Jewish life even before its fall in A.D. 70. After the temple was gone, the synagogue was able to carry on Jewish culture without a serious break. Judaism had become more a matter of education than of temple rituals. The Essenes at Qumran organized themselves in eight-hour shifts and maintained a continuous study of the Scriptures day and night.

Above the synagogue was a more advanced study of a professional type. This goes back to Ezra, who returned from Babylon to Jerusalem *ca.* 458 B.C. to institute a renaissance of both education and religion in the destitute and discouraged Jewish homeland. During the succeeding generations there followed a series of great teachers like himself, constituting what was known as the Great Synagogue (actually not a synagogue in a technical sense; *see* SYNAGOGUE, THE GREAT). These outstanding teachers, each in his own time, were heads of a school in Palestine, one whose learning came to set the standard for Judaism the world over. The best known of these teachers from the NT period were Shammai and Hillel, at the time of Herod the Great, and Hillel's grandson Gamaliel, under whom Paul was a student near A.D. 30.

These great teachers began their work with the written law, but they also included the oral traditions, judgments, and interpretations of scholars prior to their time. This oral law was similar to decisions of courts in our time, both state and federal, which every court must take into consideration in reaching its decisions. At the time of Christ the traditions had to be passed along by memory; it was felt that only the Scriptures should be written down. In time the body of tradition became so large that it was necessary to reduce it to writing; this was done by Rabbi Judah *ca.* A.D. 200; and it became the MISHNA, the earliest part of the TALMUD.

In Jewish schools there was no formal recognition of alien cultures, not even by the study of foreign languages. At the end of his book *Antiquities of the Jews* (XX.xi.2), Josephus remarks for the benefit of Greek readers that he has taken great pains to obtain Greek learning, also to understand the elements of the Greek language, but that nevertheless he is still unable to pronounce it accurately; for, he remarks, "our nation does not encourage those who learn the languages of many nations. It looks upon this sort of accomplishment as common," emphasizing that true wisdom is obtained by study of the Jewish law. Josephus, Philo and Paul, and all other Jews with a good knowledge of Greek had to acquire it on their own initiative, probably in Greek schools.

f. Jewish teachers. Even before the founding of synagogues there had been teachers among the Hebrews. Moses was supposed to have been the greatest of OT teachers. But most of the Hebrew leaders after his time, including priests, were teachers, each in his own way. King Solomon had a reputation for scholarship. Some of the greatest of the teachers were prophets; but as prophecy began to decline, teachers of a new type emerged. The sages who produced the wisdom literature were the immediate successors of the prophets. These in turn appear to have been succeeded by the scribes. Ezra himself was a scribe (7:12, 21) as well as a priest; so his successors should be regarded as scribes. Sirach (Ecclus. 38:24), who mentioned the scribe with such high praise, must have considered himself one. The term "scribe" was finally replaced by "rabbi." We should not attempt to make a sharp differentiation in function between the teachers indicated by these various names. Jesus, the best known of all biblical teachers, was often critical of the scribes, yet in Matt. 13:52 he said: "Therefore every scribe who has been trained for the kingdom of heaven is like a householder who brings out of his treasure what is new and what is old." In this sense, Jesus himself was a scribe. As a teacher he fits into the category of sage or scribe better than that of prophet. Most of his sayings have a proverbial-epigrammatic quality. He spoke, not as a prophet, but on his own authority, like the sages.

2. Greek and Roman education. *a. Hellenistic culture.* The Greeks had a genius for scholarly and artistic attainments. First they achieved high standards of cultural excellence for themselves; then they became the teachers of the ancient world. During the classical period of Greek history the privileges of education were mainly enjoyed only by the aristocratic upper classes, but the achievements of that early period were never entirely forgotten by Greeks of later centuries. The ancient Greek ideal of education was to produce men like those portrayed in the poetry of Homer. They were outstanding in physical strength and courage, skilful with weapons but also in music, disciplined in all the rigors of war, and exhibiting at the same time the gentler graces of chivalry. Such were the qualities of a Greek gentleman.

The creative power of the classical era produced such poets as Aeschylus, Aristophanes, Euripides, and Sophocles; philosophers like Socrates, Plato, and Aristotle; as well as many artists of equal excellence in other fields.

The cultural vigor of that brilliant period began to wane along with the decline of the economic and political power of individual Greek states which ushered in the Hellenistic age. The spectacular career of Alexander the Great (336-323 B.C.) marked the beginning of that age, which was to last for some five centuries. The most notable political characteristic of the period was the rise of Western empires. With Alexander, domination of that world moved for the first time from the Orient to the Occident. *Ca.* two centuries of uncertainty followed Alexander. This period was characterized notably by the Hellenistic kingdoms of Syria and Egypt, which, in turn, were followed by Rome, the most completely Hellenized empire of antiquity. Romans were the true heirs of Greece. Yet they did not slavishly adopt Greek culture; they always knew how to adapt it to their own purposes, exploiting its practical elements, frequently adding barbaric touches of their own.

The Hellenistic age was thus a cultural, as well as a military and political, phenomenon. It was the time during which the culture of Greece was carried, either by the power of its inherent virtues or the far-ranging influence of Greek commerce, or by imposition of Greek military and political force, far beyond the frontiers of the Greek states, until it spread like a veneer over the cultures of most of the nations of the Mediterranean world. These less sophisticated peoples, under the Greek spell, to a considerable extent adopted the Greek language, religion, education, and philosophy. They wished to be Greeks; often they imagined they were. Yet not one of them was ever able to reproduce fully the excellence of the ancients they admired.

b. The Greek schools. Greek education was informed by the idea that every attribute of body, mind, and soul, properly disciplined, is inherently good and worthy of expression. There was hardly a negative element, almost no asceticism, in Greek culture as it sought to bring to maturity every incipient virtue of human personality. It was therefore humanistic in the best sense; not that it repudiated religion, but that the gods themselves were so conceived that they inspired the development and exercise of all of man's potential powers. Greek education required rigorous intellectual labor; no other society has seen more clearly the importance of prolonged application of intelligence to all the problems and wonders of both the natural world and the soul of man. Yet no other culture has ever given more place to athletic sports, music, dancing, and arts of the theater, presenting both the tragic and the comic elements of life, as well as a calendar of annual festivals in which a whole people joined in the worship of its gods.

The gymnasium was the educational institution in which preparation was made for this dynamic expression of the versatility of Greek genius. For the first seven years of his life a Greek boy was in the hands of his mother—a girl had no education outside the home. Then he was sent to school, where he was under the care of men. The elementary school, where he was taught the necessary practical rudiments of learning, occupied a boy's attention until he was about fifteen. Sons of families able to bear the expense were then sent to the gymnasium between the ages of sixteen and eighteen. The discipline was rigorous, the basic element being physical training. The name "gymnasium" is derived from *gymnos*, "naked," from the Greek custom of stripping off all clothing before engaging in athletics. "Music," a flexible term including poetry, dancing, and allied matters, was very important. A third area involved the study of literature, the sciences, and politics. The gymnasium was open to the public; visitors were usually present; and students could join in discussion of current topics with their elders.

The original purpose of the gymnasium was to prepare young men for citizenship. Hence the gymnasium was limited to the native-born. Gymnasium training was usually followed by two years of compulsory military service for those demonstrated to be eligible by birth or otherwise. This was called the *ephebia*. The first year was devoted to intensive military instruction at Piraeus, the second to campaign maneuvers and garrison duty at frontier posts. When this training was completed satisfactorily, the *ephebus* was admitted to full rights and responsibilities of citizenship.

The gymnasium was one of the most important agencies for the preservation of Greek culture; it served Greek culture as the synagogue did Jewish. Wherever Greeks planted colonies, and where native peoples were desirous of acquiring Greek culture, gymnasiums were established. From Italy to Babylon and Persia, more than a hundred cities had these centers of Greek learning. At the beginning of the Maccabean Rebellion in 167 B.C., one of the main causes of resentment felt by the fanatical nationalists was a Greek gymnasium some Jewish liberals had established in Jerusalem (I Macc. 1:14-15; II Macc. 4:9-15). The conservative residents of this ancient city were shocked to see their sons performing in this new sports center stripped naked and wearing the wide-brimmed Greek hats. It is probable that gymnasiums existed also in the Decapolis, where, since the time of Alexander, Greek colonists had developed a flourishing culture. Several of these cities, such as Scythopolis and Philadelphia, had excellent theaters; Gerasa had two. Herod built a theater in Jerusalem; also a theater and amphitheater at Caesarea, where he staged games and combats on the order of those at Rome.

As Athens and other Greek cities lost their political independence, the *ephebia* lost its original purpose; there was no longer a point in training young men for military service and citizenship for a country which had lost its autonomy. But as the military nature of the organization died out, the institution was transformed into something like a liberal-arts college patronized by sons of aristocratic families. Its training was somewhat like that of a university of our time. Athens, Tarsus, and Alexandria were famous. Yet the period of training at Athens was often not more than one year: at best it was superficial. Study was of two types, either philosophy or rhetoric; and the schools were now open to foreigners as well as natives. The education offered there did little more than equip a few wealthy and unoccupied young men to enjoy their leisure time.

Bibliography. H. L. Strack and P. Billerbeck, *Kommentar zum NT aus Talmud und Midrasch* (4 vols.; 1922-28); G. F. Moore, *Judaism* (3 vols.; 1927-30); H. L. Strack, *Einleitung in Talmud und Midrasch* (1930); H. Danby, *The Mishnah* (1933); W. Jaeger, *Paedeia* (3 vols.; 1939); S. V. McCasland, *By the Finger of God* (1951); M. Burrows, *The Dead Sea Scrolls* (1955); M. P. Nilson, *Die Hellenistische Schule* (1955); H. I. Marrou, *A History of Education in Antiquity* (1956); E. Würtwein, *The Text of the OT* (1957); M. Hadas, *Hellenistic Culture* (1959).

S. V. McCasland

EGG [ביצים, *plural only;* ᾠόν]. Eggs of the domesticated fowl did not become a common item of food in Palestine until *ca.* the fifth century B.C. or later. The eggs of small birds (e.g., pigeon, dove, partridge; cf. Deut. 22:6; Isa. 10:14) were gathered for food. In Luke 11:12, quite possibly the egg of the domesticated fowl is meant, as these were numerous in Palestine by that time. The reference in Isa. 59:5 to the eggs of a viper is figurative for the schemes of evil men. The ostrich's habit of leaving eggs in the sand to be warmed and hatched is mentioned in Job 39:14.

The obscure word חלמות, translated "white of an egg" in Job 6:6 KJV, may refer to the juice of the Purslane or the egg of a small game bird.

In Jewish ceremonial a roasted egg is included among the objects on the Seder table on the eve of Passover to represent the burnt offering. There is no reference to the method of cooking eggs in ancient times. According to the Mishna they were boiled (Shab. 9.15), broken and fried (Shab. 1.10), mixed with oil and fried (Shab. 8.5), or spread upon fish (Bez. 2.1).

Bibliography. A. R. S. Kennedy, "Fowl," *EB*, vol. II (1901) cols. 1559-60; J. Jacobs, "Eggs," *Jewish Encyclopedia* (1903), V, 54; G. E. Wright, *Biblical Archaeology* (1957), p. 184*a*.

V. H. Kooy

EGLAH ĕg'lə [עגלה, heifer]. A wife of David; the mother of Ithream (II Sam. 3:5; I Chr. 3:3).

EGLAIM ĕg'lĭ əm [אגלים] (Isa. 15:8). A town on the border of Moab. Its site is unknown. Eusebius mentions Agallim, eight miles S of Areopolis (Rabba). In that area today is Rujm el-Jilimeh, a pile of field stones flung into a heap by plowmen. Khirbet Jeljul, *ca.* 4½ miles farther S, is a Nabatean-Roman site.

Bibliography. N. Glueck, *Explorations in Eastern Palestine*, III, *AASOR*, XVIII-XIX (1937-39), 98, 100.

E. D. Grohman

EGLATH-SHELISHIYAH ĕg'lăth shĭ lĭsh'ə yə [עגלת שלשיה, the third Eglath]. A place in Moab mentioned in the oracles against Moab (Isa. 15:5; Jer. 48:34). The location is uncertain. Instead of a place name, the KJV translates "an heifer of three years old." E. D. Grohman

EGLON ĕg'lŏn [עגלון, young bull(?); Akkad. *Ig-la-nu*]. **1.** The obese king of Moab who invaded

W Jordan territory in the region of Jericho, held it subject for eighteen years, and was treacherously assassinated by EHUD (1), the second deliverer in the book of Judges (3:12-25).

Eglon's W Jordan campaign was carried on with the help of the neighboring Ammonite kingdom and the desert Bedouin called Amalekites. Since the "city of palms," JERICHO, had previously been destroyed, this early-twelfth-century-B.C. Moabite occupation was probably subjugation of the surrounding territory, including perhaps Bethel. The bringing of the annual tribute (cf. that required later by MESHA) provided Ehud with the occasion for his exploit on Eglon. According to late rabbinic tradition, the fat king's rising from his chair, out of respect for a divine word, was rewarded by his daughter Ruth's becoming ancestress of David, but in the original story his respect won only his own death and the loss of the territory of Benjamin and Ephraim W of the Jordan River.

Bibliography. K. Tallqvist, *Assyrian Personal Names* (1914), p. 95. *See also* the bibliography under EHUD.

C. F. KRAFT

2. A Canaanite royal city. Though Tell en-Nejileh, three miles to the SE, has been suggested, Tell el-Hesi seems the more likely modern location. It is seven miles SW of Lachish, at the very edge of the foothills which extend out into the coastal (Philistine) plain.

Eglon was one of the cities in the Amorite coalition led by Adonizedek of Jerusalem against the Gibeonite confederacy (Josh. 10:1 ff). Because of treaty commitments, Joshua, then encamped at Gilgal, agreed to help the Gibeonites. After a bitterly fought battle near Azekah, the coalition was routed. The leaders, including Debir king of Eglon, fled into a cave near MAKKEDAH, from which they were brought by Joshua's men and were executed. Their bodies were hung from trees until sundown and were then cut down and buried in the cave, after which the cave was sealed. After this victory, the Israelites occupied the cities of the coalition (Josh. 10:28 ff; cf. also 12:7 ff). Eglon was totally destroyed (laid to the *herem;* 10:35). Archaeological evidence indicates a destruction of Eglon in the late thirteenth century, about the same time as Lachish. Subsequently it became a part of the tribe of Judah, district of Lachish (15:39). V. R. GOLD

EGYPT ē'jĭpt [מצרים]; **EGYPTIAN** ē jĭp'shən [מצרי]. A land in NW Africa; in the narrowest sense the two banks of the Nile River from the First Cataract N to the region of modern Cairo (Upper and Middle Egypt) and the Delta (Lower Egypt). In this article Egypt includes both the comprehensive biblical name, Mizraim, and the term for Upper Egypt, Pathros.

Ancient Egypt was one of the earliest civilizations and for many centuries one of the most powerful nations. For much of her history she laid claim to the oases W of the Nile Valley, Nubia between the First and Second Cataracts, the Red Sea coast, and much of the Peninsula of Sinai. Shortly after 2000 B.C. she pushed an empire S of the Second Cataract and shortly after 1500 B.C. to the Fourth Cataract. Soon after 1500 B.C. she carved out an Asiatic empire, with claims running N to the Euphrates River, but with the most effective holdings in Palestine and Phoenicia. Fig. EGY 4.

The Egyptians called their country the "Two Lands [of Upper and Lower Egypt]" or the "Black Land," in contrast to the "red" desert, or simply "the land." The name Egypt is of late application and probably derives from an epithet for Memphis, *Hi-ku-Ptah,* the "House of the Spirit of [the god] Ptah." The name MIZRAIM was not used by the Egyptians, but Pathros came from the Egyptian, *pa-to-resi,* the "south land." An Egyptian counterpart for "Dan to Beer-sheba" in the Bible was "Migdol to Syene"—i.e., from a NE frontier fortress to Aswan at the First Cataract.

1. Geography.* The Greek writers pointed out that the land of Egypt is the gift of the Nile. NE Africa is a desert country, essentially rainless. Only the flow of the Nile and particularly its annual inundation make human life possible in that part of the world, and this has been true throughout historical times. Because of this, the Egyptian saw a decided contrast between his land and the neighboring countries and felt that this favorable contrast showed the solicitude of the gods for his land. Figs. EGY 5-6.

a. Physical. From the equatorial lakes of Africa, the White Nile starts a four-thousand-mile course northward to the Mediterranean. At Khartum in the Sudan it meets the Blue Nile, which originates in Abyssinia, and the two unite for the final nineteen-hundred-mile flow of the Nile proper. Through sandstone and limestone, this river has carved out a valley in which habitation is possible. Transverse barriers of harder stone cut across the course of the Nile, creating six cataracts, which have been natural frontiers. Some annual rainfall is effective in the latitude of the Fourth Cataract, which in the eighth century B.C. and following was the center of a kingdom the Bible calls Cush or Ethiopia. The region between the Third and First Cataracts is Nubia. N of the First Cataract lies Egypt in the narrower sense.

The Nile Valley is hemmed in by the Libyan and Red Sea hills, and the six-hundred-mile course from the First Cataract to Memphis (near modern Cairo)

From *When Egypt Ruled the East* (The University of Chicago Press)

4. Ancient Egyptian Empire (*ca.* 1500-1000 B.C.)

varies in width from one to twenty-four miles of arable land. From the Cairo region N the land fans out into the broad stretches of the Delta, with a maximum width at the N of *ca.* 125 miles. Today the Delta has two branches of the Nile; anciently it had at least five.

The equatorial and Abyssinian rains are seasonal and they combine to enlarge the Nile in an annual flooding. This inundation gives Egypt wide-spreading waters beginning in July and subsiding from September on. The prosperity of Egypt depends upon a good inundation and the planned retention of the flood waters for a maximum period. With a system of catch basins or canals, the waters may be held for as long as possible at some distance from the banks of the river. In the dry season lifting devices have been employed to bring up subsurface water. Before the modern system of dams was introduced, the inundation used to deposit an annual increment of fresh and fertile silt upon the land as a natural fertilizer. Irrigating waters, fertilizing silt, and a warm climate made Egypt one of the richest agricultural countries in the world. It could look upon neighboring lands as decidedly inferior.

In contrast to Canaan or to Mesopotamia, Egypt was relatively insulated against invasion from outside or even from major foreign influence. The long trough of Upper Egypt was fringed by the infertile Red Sea Desert and the formidable Libyan Desert. At the NW only a limited access was possible along the Libyan coast. At the NE the wilderness of Sinai dried out much of the contact from Asia. Only when the Egyptian state was weak or divided, could the HYKSOS, Assyrians, Babylonians, Persians, and Arabs penetrate Egypt successfully. Because of the screening effect of the Sinai wilderness, Egypt's successful hold on an Asiatic empire or an Asiatic power's successful hold on Egypt had to be supported by control of the seaways across the E Mediterranean.

The N half of the Delta was afflicted with salt

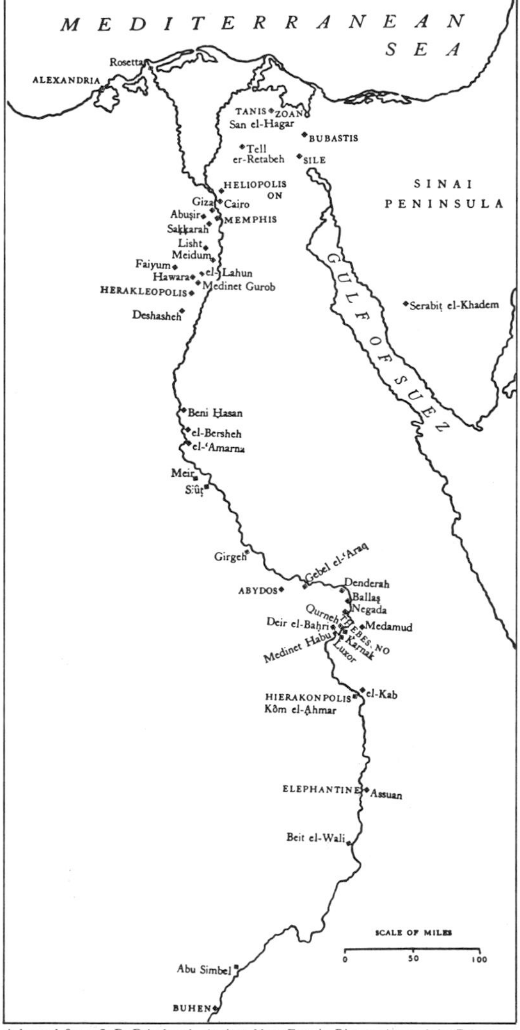

Adapted from J. B. Pritchard, *Ancient Near East in Pictures* (copyright Princeton University Press)

5. Egypt

Courtesy of the Oriental Institute, the University of Chicago

6. The Nile Valley at Thebes

marshes. The ancient cities lay twenty-five miles inland from the Mediterranean and were reached along one of the Nile arms. Until Alexander the Great founded Alexandria, there was no major city on the coast. Pelusium, which Ezek. 30:15 calls the "stronghold of Egypt," was probably more of a frontier fortress than a commercial metropolis. The chief cities of biblical interest were Zoan (Tanis) and/or Rameses in the commercial E Delta; On (Heliopolis) and Memphis at the apex of the Delta near modern Cairo; Thebes, the capital city in Upper Egypt; and Syene (Aswan) at the First Cataract. In addition, the agriculturally rich Middle Egypt always had a metropolis, such as Siut.

The N wind has always been the prevailing wind, bringing cool from the Mediterranean and permitting navigation southward against the current of the Nile. In the spring there may be many days of S wind from the desert, producing sandstorms which lay a "thick darkness" (Exod. 10:22-23) over the land.

b. Economic. Egypt's wealth and power rested upon an agricultural base.* Barley was the chief crop, with wheat and emmer less important. Flax made the linen of Egypt prized in the ancient world. There was a generous range of vegetables, and melons were widely raised. In other fruits Egyptian crops were marginal to the agricultural land; e.g., the grape was cultivated in the oases, the Faiyum, and the fringes of the Delta. For many centuries until the coming of paper, papyrus from the marshes was a valued export. Figs. EGY 7-8.

Only in good, firm wood for houses or ships was Egypt poor. From early historical times there was a brisk trade with Phoenicia for cedar, fir, and cypress. Cedar resin also became a desired import for the embalming process.

Livestock were important in the Egyptian economy. There was no such emphasis on sheep and wool as in Asia (Gen. 46:34). However, large cattle were abundant, and hides went into the export market. The camel was very rare until Persian times; the donkey was the earlier caravan animal. The horse was introduced *ca.* 1700 B.C., and the Egyptian horse market was flourishing some centuries later (I Kings 10:28-29). Fish, the goose, and the duck were abundant enough to be important in the Egyptian diet.

Egyptian hills are rich in building and sculpturing stone, from hard stones like granite and basalt to softer materials like limestone and alabaster. An essential contrast between Egypt and Mesopotamia was that Egypt could build colossal monuments out of stone, whereas Mesopotamia had to rely upon brick. Until the Iron Age, Egypt was also fortunate in the command of mineral deposits: copper in the Red Sea Hills but especially in W Sinai, gold in the Red Sea Hills and in Nubia. Copper for her bronze tools and weapons and gold for purchasing power were two of ancient Egypt's great assets. When the Iron Age came in before 1100 B.C., Egypt had to rely upon purchases from abroad, and her relative strength fell off.

The irrigated black soil was so precious that the Egyptian farmers lived in tightly built villages and went out to their fields. Legally there was no such thing as private property, since everything belonged to the god-king, but in practice, Egyptian commoners treated soil, houses, cattle, and chattels as their own. For economy's sake, the villages were regularly built in the same places, so that most of the ancient towns are now buried deep under the rising alluvial soil. Therefore, our knowledge of domestic life is rather limited. However, for burial there was always the sand of the nearby desert, so that tombs and mortuary temples have survived. Village houses and even royal palaces were of mud brick, whereas tombs and temples were of stone. Consequently, the accident of survival has made the Egyptian emphasis on life after death seem to us a preoccupation with death, which it was not.

The black soil was too valuable to be cut up by permanent roads, while the Nile or its branches were always near to serve as arteries of movement. Thus

Courtesy of the Cairo Museum; photo courtesy of the Metropolitan Museum of Art

7. An Egyptian wall painting, from tomb of Nakht at Thebes (fifteenth century B.C.). Upper section shows harvest scenes; middle section shows man chopping down tree, and a laborer breaking soil; lower section shows a laborer plowing, and a person watching laborers from a booth.

from prehistoric times on, the Egyptians were a river-faring people, and by the beginning of history they had taken their boats out onto the open sea. Trade with Phoenicia and the Aegean may have been as much in foreign ships as in Egyptian, but on the Red Sea the Egyptian vessel was dominant in the trade southward to the land of incense, myrrh, gums, and ivory, which the Egyptians called Punt.

The chief commercial-military road to Asia left Egypt near modern Kantarah, cut across N Sinai, and reached Palestine near modern Gaza. This was a useful road for caravans and moderately large flocks of sheep, but for large bodies like armies on the march and also for security it was necessary to police and fortify the water holes along the way. Perhaps because of these police and communications

From *When Egypt Ruled the East* (The University of Chicago Press)

8. Egyptian harvest scene

posts, Moses led the children of Israel "by way of the wilderness" rather than "by way of the land of the Philistines" (Exod. 13:17-18).

In most basic commodities ancient Egypt was self-sufficient. Construction wood, tin, silver, and iron had to be imported from N sources. Olive oil was an early import from Asia. Otherwise, her foreign trade was in luxury items: lapis lazuli, obsidian, marquetry, and metalwork from Asia; ivory, incenses, gums, and rare skins from Africa.

*c. **Racial.*** In physical type the ancient Egyptian belonged to the slight, brunet family which is called the Mediterranean race. He was relatively short, of slight frame, dark in hair and color of eyes, but not originally dark in skin color. Hair on face and body was light. He was physically like the Hamites and S Semites.* Even before historical times another type with a broader skull appeared, but in a minority which was soon absorbed by the dominant type. In early history the Negro was unknown to the Egyptian, and the Nubian and Sudanese peoples to his S were physically akin to him. By 2000 B.C. the Negro was visible at the Third Cataract, and by 1500 B.C. the Egyptian Empire, pushing S to the Fourth Cataract, was in constant contact with Negroes. However, Negro characteristics were not prominent in the Egypt with which the Hebrews had contact, except for such Ethiopian pharaohs as Tirhakah, and even they probably had mixed blood. The eunuch of the Candace of Ethiopia, whom Philip baptized (Acts 8:26-39), may have been a Negro. Fig. EGY 9.

Linguistically, ancient Egyptian was a composite of the Semitic and Hamitic branches of language. There was a sufficiently strong relation to Semitic so that many root words are the same in Egyptian and Semitic and borrowing by one side or the other was relatively easy. However, even though the structural formation of Egyptian and Semitic is akin, including an emphasis on a consonantal skeleton, with the vowels subject to grammatical change, the Egyptian language stands outside the Semitic family as normally analyzed and shows definite but imperfectly recorded ties to the Hamitic family. There were physical and linguistic reasons for the Egyptians to be conscious of difference from their Asiatic neighbors. The ancient Egyptians called neighboring peoples by geographical or racial names—"Nubians," "Libyans," or "Asiatics"—but until very late times they applied no ethnic term to themselves; they called themselves simply "the people."

In medieval and modern times, it has been possible to separate dialects within Egypt. There has been a major cleavage in dialect between Lower and Upper Egypt. The same distinction has not been possible for the times of the pharaohs, because the written language was much more under the standardizing control of priestly tradition. However, through a literary reference we do know that it was difficult for a man from the First Cataract to understand the speech of a man from the Delta marshes.

For the Egyptian of the Delta, most of his sacred shrines lay to the S. The temple of the sun-god Re was at On (Heliopolis). Near Memphis were the pyramid area and the ancient cemetery of Sakkarah. Herakleopolis (biblical Hanes) was an important town near the Faiyum. At Hermopolis in Middle

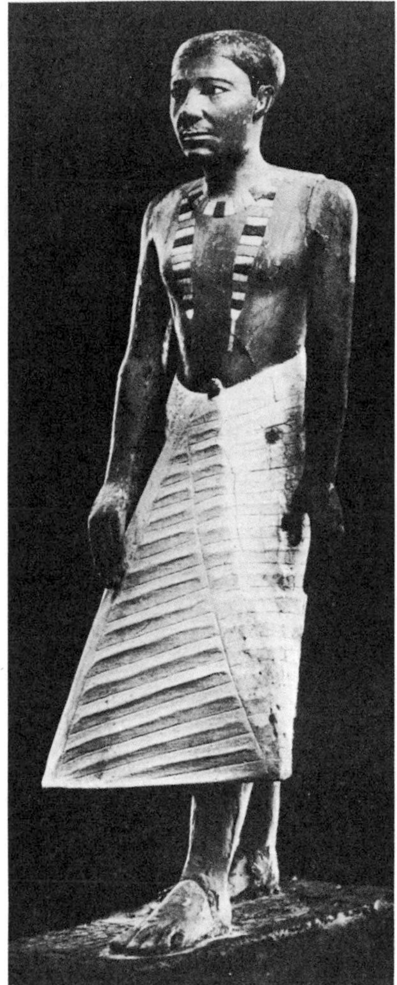

Courtesy of the Nelson Gallery—Atkins Museum (Nelson Fund), Kansas City, Missouri

9. Methethy, an Egyptian nobleman of the king's entourage, Fifth-Sixth Dynasty (*ca.* 2350 B.C.)

Egypt was the temple of Thoth, moon-god and god of wisdom. Farther S at Abydos lay a holy place of pilgrimage, the shrine of Osiris, god of the dead. Thebes, an effective capital from 2100 B.C. on, was an important provincial capital after 1300 B.C., because at Karnak lay the mighty temple of the imperial god, Amon-Re. Furthermore, the Nile, source of Egyptian life, came from the S. Perhaps this is why Ezek. 29:14 calls Pathros (Upper Egypt) the land of the origin of the Egyptians.

2. History. From Greek times, the history of the pharaohs has been divided into thirty dynasties, the first at the beginning of written history *ca.* 3000 B.C., the thirtieth ending with the conquest of Alexander the Great in 332 B.C. Then the dynasty of the Ptolemies ran from 306 to 30 B.C. Three political plateaus of older history were the Old Kingdom or pyramid age, Third through Sixth Dynasties (2700-2200 B.C.); the Middle Kingdom, chiefly the Twelfth Dynasty (2000-1800 B.C.); and the New Kingdom or Empire, Eighteenth through Twentieth Dynasties (1570-1090 B.C.). Subsequently there came the Ethiopian period, including the Twenty-fifth Dynasty (715-663 B.C.), the Saitic revival of the Twenty-sixth Dynasty (663-525 B.C.), and the Persian period (525-332 B.C., with interludes of Egyptian reassertion).

Scholars have not attained exact chronology for Egypt before 663 B.C. The farther back one goes, the greater the margin of disagreement becomes. For dates before 2000 B.C. there may be wide disagreement, with estimates for the beginning of the dynasties ranging from 3200 to 2830 B.C. Fortunately the disagreement among scholars on dates for most of the biblical period is not wide, falling usually within the stretch of a single generation.

a. Prehistoric and Old Kingdom (to 2200 B.C.). Archaeologists have traced a series of prehistoric cultures, although there is still an important gap at the time when man first settled down beside the Nile as a farmer. Flint implements have been found in geological context, from crude fist hatchets of the Old Stone Age down to rippled and polished knives in early historic times. The NE African plateau was once well watered. Gradually it dried up, and man, animals, and plants were driven down to the margin of the sole remaining water, the Nile River. Hunting in the uplands became an inadequate source of food; close association at the river bank of man and plant and animal foods promoted the process of domestication. Possibly at the same time as in the hills above the Mesopotamian plain, possibly somewhat later, NE African man ceased to be a Libyan hunter and became an Egyptian herdsman and farmer, living in a village on the margin of the land watered by the Nile. The basic social unit was no longer the family alone; it became the village community.

Very gradually certain amenities were introduced, such as houses with inner sectioning into rooms, doors and windows, granaries for storage, linen in place of hides, containers made of pottery, better tools, metal objects, jewelry, and cosmetics. Objects of foreign derivation show a modestly active trade. Worship of gods and a belief in survival after death are shown by amulets, figurines, and the materials placed in the grave for future life. The diet was enriched. Weapons and broken bones show the competition of one community against another for possession of territory.

As the population increased, it was not enough to herd a few animals down to the marshes which fringed the Nile, nor enough to tease a few marginal plants with a hoe and to depend upon the natural watering from the Nile. The marshes had to be cleared and drained for new fields. Irrigation was necessary to carry the water farther from the Nile and hold it for a longer time. The animal-drawn plow could cultivate wider fields than the hoe. These new activities took a long time and involved cooperation between different towns. The community enlarged from individual agricultural villages to provinces of common interests. Widespread irrigation and the use of the plow were probably the immediate preludes to history.

The motivating factors which carried the Egyptians from the barbarism of prehistory into the civilization of historical times will remain a matter of speculation. However, one factor can be detected.

Just before the beginning of the dynasties there appeared in Egypt elements which were borrowed from Mesopotamia. These certainly included the cylinder seal, a kind of brick architecture developed in Mesopotamia, and certain artistic motifs. They may have included also the idea of writing and its method of setting down objects and concepts in pictorially recognizable form. Since no comparable borrowings from Egypt have been found in Mesopotamian excavation, the priority of Mesopotamian civilization may be conceded. Fig. VES 15.

Ca. 3000 B.C. a family from Upper Egypt succeeded in conquering all of Egypt and founding the First Dynasty. Since this formation of the first state is generally coincident with the first written records, the earliest monumental sculpture and architecture, well-controlled metallurgy, governmental development of copper mines, and such amenities as tables, beds, and chairs, we call this period also the beginning of history and of civilization in Egypt. Fig. EGY 10.

In later tradition the founder of the First Dynasty was called Menes. Although the credit to a single individual remains uncertain, a family from Abydos in the S did form the First Dynasty and set up a capital at Memphis, near the point where Upper and Lower Egypt join. Probably the conquest and unification of Egypt had taken several generations before the formal institution of the new capital and required several generations after Menes to complete the conquest and to organize the new state. The first two dynasties, lasting two to four centuries, were occupied in working out the forms of the new nation.

Courtesy of the Cairo Museum

10. Stone palette from Hierkonopolis celebrating victory of King Nar-mer of the First Dynasty (*ca.* 3000 B.C.) of Egypt. Before the King are four standard-bearers and bound, headless corpses of his enemies.

By the beginning of the Third Dynasty, *ca.* 2700 B.C., Egypt was mature enough to express the forms of her new culture. The brilliant pyramid age began with the Stepped Pyramid of Djoser (or Zoser), the first large-scale monument constructed entirely of hewn stone. Credit for this architectural revolution is customarily given to Djoser's brilliant minister, Ii-em-hotep. If the credit is deserved, Ii-em-hotep was rightly esteemed as one of the wise men of Egyptian tradition. Under Djoser the bureaucracy was reorganized, to meet the problems of a more complex state. The government continued to be a theocracy, vested in the person of the king, who was a god; the king's sons continued to hold the most responsible offices; and there was no effective division between priestly and civil offices; but the assignment of authority to individuals to act in the name of the king was the first large step toward the building up of a secular bureaucracy. Egypt was markedly king-centered from the Third to the late Fifth Dynasty: the flat-topped tombs of the princes and nobles, tombs which archaeologists call mastabas, clustered close to the pyramid of the king, who was still the only one who was by definition as a god assured of eternal life. If he needed his court for eternal rule in the next world, then they might also have eternal life in his service.

The Fourth Dynasty (2650-2500 B.C.) was the peak of Egypt's material and artistic glory. It was the age of the three great pyramids of Gizeh:* the Great Pyramid, built as a tomb for Khufu* (or Cheops); the Second Pyramid for Khaf-Re (or Chephren); and the Third Pyramid for Men-kau-Re (or Mycerinus). The Great Pyramid was rightly one of the seven wonders of the world. Despite its tremendous mass and despite man's limited experience in massive architecture, the leveling of a stone surface for the pyramid, its trueness of angle and length, and the precise fitting of huge stones were carried out with the most meticulous accuracy. Legend of later times says that Khufu and Khaf-Re were hated by their own people, and there is some evidence to support this legend. If so, the unpopularity will have arisen more from the economic obligation to supply labor and materials for the largest monument ever erected for a single man than from the bitterness of laborers under a taskmaster's whip. Forced labor was always a regular obligation upon the ancient Egyptians. Figs. EGY 11-12; Pl. XXVI*c*.

By the Fourth Dynasty writing was competent to meet all normal needs of government and religion. Statuary, relief sculpture, and painting enjoyed the sophisticated ability to render beautifully organized scenes and the depiction of mortals in the serene expectation of immortality. Early in Egyptian history art was more successfully "Egyptian," in the blissful capture of eternity, than it was in the following 2,500 years. These were great accomplishments, effected within an extraordinarily short period of apprenticeship.

Of course, the extreme focus upon the divine person of the king was subject to challenge. The Fifth Dynasty (2500-2350 B.C.) saw the rise of two other gods. The sun-god Re of Heliopolis gained political power by the acknowledgment that he was the father of the ruling king. Osiris, the god who had died but yet lived on to rule in another realm, came into prominence as the god of the dead, and kings who had died thereby became Osiris (*see* § 3 *below*). Further, there was a centrifugal force at work within the state: the royal family and court had a lesser voice in government, whereas outlying officials, while claiming loyal service to the king, wielded greater authority. Nobles who no longer felt a need for clinging to the king's divine immortality began to build their tombs in their own home districts.

A warning should be issued about the precise historical value of Egyptian inscriptions. For the ancient Egyptian, truth lay in faithful conformance to the divine order. Within this divine order the king was a god, omniscient and infallible, and men faithful to this belief might be rewarded with eternal happiness. Thus the "portraits" of ancient Egyptians may show some element of personal features or character, but this element was overlaid by the serenely eternal type most acceptable to the gods. Similarly, every orthodox inscription shows the king bringing order and success to his nation by superhuman discretion and power. This was conformance to the truth of faith, rather than to objective observation. Texts which are written out of this psychology of devotion have to be tested against any other knowledge we may possess. It is disconcerting for the historian to note that the Fifth Dynasty king Sahu-Re recorded a victory over a certain Libyan family, that a century and a half later the Sixth Dynasty king Pepi II conquered the same family, and that seventeen centuries later the Ethiopian pharaoh Tirhakah again conquered the identical family. This was faithfulness to a favorite tradition, rather than fidelity to historical fact. The historian must accept his data at face value, unless there is clear reason for distrust; but he must be ready to modify his understanding as soon as new material puts the previous interpretation in a new light.

The decentralization of the state which had begun in the Fifth Dynasty continued in the Sixth (2350-2200 B.C.). Tomb autobiographies of provincial nobles show a self-confidence verging on arrogance. Egypt's foreign relations became more active. To the S there was an energetic penetration into the Sudan. From the First Cataract caravans were led by nobles, who had the tasks of promoting the flow of trade, securing favorable alliances with Nubian princes, and enlisting Nubian soldiers for the Egyptian army. A basic import from the S was cattle, but there was an eager interest in luxury goods: incense, gums, ivory, and leopard skins.

Relations with Palestine-Syria showed a double pattern. At GEBAL (Byblos) in Phoenicia there was a temple of strong Egyptian influence. For dedication in this temple the kings of Egypt sent a series of offerings. The trade in cedar from the Lebanon and the trans-shipping facilities of the port of Gebal were to the advantage of both Gebal and Egypt. In Palestine, however, the situation was not so friendly to the Egyptians. *Ca.* 2325 B.C., Egypt had to send

Courtesy of the Arab Information Center, New York

11. The sphinx and the pyramid of Khaf-Re at Gizeh, near Cairo

Trans World Airlines Photo

12. Aerial view of the pyramids of Khufu, Khaf-Re, and Men-kau-Re at Gizeh

five military expeditions against the "sand-dwellers," the people of S Palestine. When these campaigns failed to crush the hostility, a final expedition was mounted by water and penetrated farther N, probably N of the Carmel range. Although the Egyptian texts, as always, claimed a complete success, it was no more than a temporary victory. As the central government weakened at the end of the Old Kingdom and in the first intermediate period, the Asiatics took advantage of a slackened frontier to trickle into the Egyptian Delta.

b. First intermediate period, Middle Kingdom, second intermediate period (2200-1570 B.C.). The Old Kingdom showed structural weakness when ineffective kings were unable to check the growing independence of the nobles. Egypt suddenly disintegrated into fragments. There were at least three competing pretenders to wide rule, but many provincial nobles began to act independently and to claim for themselves the perquisites of kingship. Texts describing the period tell of governmental chaos, overturn of social classes, neglect and robbery of the tombs, the cutting short of foreign trade, and the infiltration of Asiatic Bedouins into the Delta. The human inclination to find a scapegoat moved the Egyptian to place blame upon these Asiatics for the time of troubles. But it was really the weakness of the state which left the borders unguarded, until a slow but steady influx of Bedouins amounted to a major problem.

From the standpoint of religion and thought, the first intermediate period is extraordinarily interesting, because Egypt suffered severely from the overturn of the old values of stability and prosperity. There were reactions of despair, hedonism, and cynicism. One social prophet even dared to point a finger of criticism at one of the kings of the time and blame him for failing to correct the situation. Out of the confusion and the varied reactions to confusion there emerged two constructive forces. The first of these was the realization that the confident materialism of the Old Kingdom had been inadequate for the desired goals of worldly success and eternal life. Men came to feel that a good life was also necessary, exhibited in pious service to the gods and in a concern for fellow men. After death a man was to be judged by the gods for good character, and not simply for position and wealth. The second force, related to the first, was a feeling for the common man. This new sense of social justice could only be real if it were felt that the peasant was also a man of worth. One of the proudest boasts of the inscriptions in this period was: "I was a good little man." A vigorous document insisted that a peasant had rights to justice from a royal official.

This scaling down of the social order and this belief that moral worth should win immortality were reflected in the politics of the first intermediate period, which showed decentralized feudalism, and in the new spread of the rights of immortality to a wider number. Those funeral ceremonies and those mortuary texts which had formerly been the exclusive prerogative of kings were now the rights of the nobility. Every "good man," if his character were judged righteous, would now become the god Osiris at death and enter into eternal happiness. Out of material and political chaos the Egyptians had discovered new values.

Ca. 2100 B.C. the competition for power in Egypt narrowed down to a contest between two city-states. Herakleopolis near the Faiyum felt herself to be the bearer of a tradition inherited from the Old Kingdom at Memphis. To the S there was an upstart city, Thebes, previously unknown to history. *Ca.* 2050 B.C., Thebes was victorious and reunited Egypt for the period which we call the Middle Kingdom. The rewards were peace, stability, the prosperity of an orderly Egypt, and a resumed foreign trade. The price which the new Theban rulers had to pay lay in the loose fealty of semi-independent feudal lords. Indeed, the newly organized state, after only two generations, saw this new ruling family swept aside by another Theban family, the Twelfth Dynasty (1990-1780 B.C.).

Later ages looked back at the Twelfth Dynasty as a golden classical age of Egyptian history. The new kings realized that they faced a difficult task in welding the separate forces of the state into a unity. They were strong and conscientious rulers. They won new agricultural land by large-scale irrigation works and an observation post S of the Second Cataract to estimate the volume of the annual inundation before it arrived. Nubia was conquered as empire, and a frontier fortress was set above the Second Cataract. A fortified trading house was maintained S of the Third Cataract. Trade was resumed with Phoenicia, and at least one military raid was undertaken into Palestine, as far as Shechem, to keep caravan routes open. The princes of Phoenicia and N Syria were cultivated with generous royal gifts. Palestine and Syria were under the cultural domination of Egypt, even though no political empire was attempted there.

Under the Old Kingdom it had not been necessary to assert the benign power of the king. His godlike qualities had been manifest. The Middle Kingdom was more loosely organized, and the new sentiment for the smaller man presented a challenge to kingship. Therefore, these new kings deliberately issued written publicity on their behalf. A document was published, ostensibly centuries old, in which a prophet foretold the anarchy of the first intermediate period and the messianic delivery of Egypt by the first king of the Twelfth Dynasty. For the use of the priestly schools other documents were prepared, telling of the unceasing constancy of the king, the rewards for loyalty to the throne, and the virtues of being a good Egyptian. These texts were given such momentum that they became Egyptian classics. The Prophecy of Neferti was copied for three centuries, while the Wisdom of Amen-em-het I, the Story of Si-nuhe, and the Satire on the Trades were still used in the government schools seven hundred years later.

The Twelfth Dynasty was particularly active in developing the copper mines of Sinai. Whereas the Old Kingdom had sent army units to Sinai, to mine the ore and to hold off the Bedouins, the Middle Kingdom relied more upon good relations with the Asiatic sheiks and brought them into the outer orbit of Egyptian culture. They were proud to be depicted on monuments at the Sinai mines, with their names and titles written in Egyptian hieroglyphic.

We can only guess at the forces which led to the disintegration of the Middle Kingdom. Despite the success of the Twelfth Dynasty kings in promoting the prosperity of the land and in winning the adherence of provincial nobles, there must have been a structural weakness in a state which still had a strongly decentralized character. Without strong kings, the fealty of the nobles would slacken. Both in Asia and in Africa there were movements of new foreign peoples, which may have cut down on the lucrative foreign trade. At any rate, the end of the Twelfth Dynasty and the beginning of the Thirteenth saw brief reigns and an obvious element of internal weakness.

A group of strange documents belongs to the century following 1850 B.C. These are the "execration texts," written magical formulas for the cursing and confusion of the king's enemies. Within a set formula, the name or the title of such a foe was inscribed upon a pottery bowl or upon the clay figurine of a bound captive. As this inscribed object was ceremonially smashed, so would perish every enemy of the king. Several Egyptians were so cursed, and from their names they seem to have been conspiring members of the royal family. Such magic averted evil thoughts, speeches, plots, and dreams. Actual and potential enemies among the Nubians and Libyans were so cursed. The most interesting group of names comes from Asia, cursing the named rulers of Ashkelon, Shechem, Laish, Beth-shemesh, Acre, Tyre, and so on. As it applied to Jerusalem, the full formula ran: "the Ruler of Jerusalem, Yaqar-'ammu, and all the retainers who are with him; the Ruler of Jerusalem, Sez-'anu, and all the retainers who are with him—who may rebel, who may plot, who may fight, who may talk of fighting, or who may talk of rebelling—in this entire land."

Clearly the execration texts reflect uneasiness on the part of the Egyptian king. At home he had very specific opponents, and he feared hostility abroad from many princes. If he could not win their good will, he could resort to magic to confound them. Insofar as the evidence can be understood, the towns of Palestine were ruled by Semitic princes, who felt no obligation of loyalty to the king of Egypt.

The second intermediate period, like the first, started with the disintegration of the state into parts, a weakened rule at Thebes and a competing dynasty in the Delta. As before, an enfeebled state did not maintain its frontiers, so that Asiatics penetrated the Delta before 1700 B.C. This time it was no trickle of Bedouins; the invaders entered with military force. Tradition calls them the HYKSOS, or, by an incorrect etymology, the Shepherd Kings. The word "Hyksos" has an Egyptian origin, which unfortunately is not very illuminating: *hiku-khasu,* "rulers of foreign countries." Their main locus in Egypt was a great encampment at Avaris in the NE Delta. Similar beaten-earth-fortification enclosures have been noted in the Delta, Palestine, and Syria. Avaris is to be found either at Tanis (Zoan) or a short distance S of Tanis.

An argument that the Hyksos located their power at Tanis somewhere *ca.* 1720 B.C. has been based upon an Egyptian monument found at Tanis, the "Stele of the Year Four Hundred." This was erected shortly before the Nineteenth Dynasty, to commemorate the four hundredth year of the rule of the god Seth. Seth, who is depicted upon the stele in the costume of an Asiatic god, was for the Egyptians the god of foreign countries. Thus the stele, ignoring the Hyksos, states that four hundred years before 1320 B.C. an Egyptian god of foreign lands began a sway at or near Tanis. Since this should be the general time at which the Hyksos began their domination of Egypt, it is proper to interpret the inscription as applying to their rule but avoiding reference to hated invaders.

The Hyksos introduced into Egypt and into Syria-Palestine certain new factors—the horse and chariot, the composite bow, a heavier sword, body armor, and their rectangular fortress of beaten earth. Because these elements seem exotic to the Near East, a home origin for the Hyksos has been sought beyond the Caucasus or even in Central Asia. We do not know the ultimate source of the new factors which they introduced. However, insofar as Egypt was concerned, the Hyksos were Asiatics, and they called them by the same terms which they applied to their immediate Asiatic neighbors, *'Aamu* and *Retenu.* Such Hyksos personal names as can be identified prove to be Semitic, like Jacob-har and Simeon. Even though the horse and chariot and other warlike elements may ultimately derive from a territory outside the Near East, these new means of attack and defense were seized upon by the people of Syria-Palestine for their own advantage. Some of this advantage lay in Canaan, but a definite triumph was to invade once-proud Egypt, conquer her, and set up dynasties of Semitic Hyksos kings as overlords.

The question whether the Hyksos age (1720-1570 B.C.) includes the time of Joseph and the beginning of the Israelite sojourn in Egypt has been debated since the time of Josephus. It has been argued that a Semitic king would more naturally appoint Joseph his first minister. Those who argue for a date *ca.* 1225 B.C. for the Exodus point to the 430 years of sojourn in Exod. 12:40-41 and reach a date of 1655 B.C. for the entry of the children of Israel into Egypt. These are valid arguments, but the problem is much more complex than can be treated here. Certainly the Hyksos as a whole cannot be equated with the children of Israel.

Although Egyptian inscriptions picture the Hyksos as arrogant and impious, this was no barbarian horde. The Hyksos adjusted to Egyptian ways and commissioned good Egyptian works of art. In particular, they seem to have been active merchants. They introduced in Egypt a new system of weights, a recently discovered stele tells of "hundreds" of Hyksos ships laden with rich cargo at an Egyptian port, and objects bearing the names of Hyksos kings have been found all over the Near East.

The Hyksos kings at Avaris tolerated the existence of weakened Theban rulers and were content with the firm possession of the Delta and tribute from Thebes. In the course of time the Egyptians at Thebes themselves acquired the new weapons of warfare. *Ca.* 1580 B.C. a Theban king named Ka-mose found the situation intolerable. His counselors urged him not to provoke a war. He stood in peaceful relations with the Asiatics to the N and the Nubians to the S; although the Egyptians could not claim sway N of Hermopolis in Middle Egypt, they were permitted to pasture their cattle in the Delta; war might endanger the advantages they held. Ka-mose brushed aside the counsel of his nobles and started a war of liberation.

c. Early New Kingdom (1570-1375 B.C.). Ka-mose succeeded in pushing the Hyksos back into the Delta, but it was reserved for the following king, Ah-mose I, to expel the Hyksos, reunite Egypt, and thus start the Eighteenth Dynasty (1570-1305 B.C.). After three campaigns, Ah-mose captured Avaris. The war then shifted to Palestine, where the town of Sharuhen was besieged for three years before it fell. The clear implication is that the Hyksos fell back upon their homeland in Asia. For a few generations the new dynasty was too busy with the political reorganization of Egypt to undertake more than occasional raids into Palestine-Syria.

The domination of Egypt by Asiatic rulers had made a real difference in the nationalistic spirit of the land. Previously there had been a lofty complacency about Egypt's clear superiority to the nomadic and seminomadic neighbors across her borders. The task of asserting this superiority by military, political, or commercial activity had been the responsibility of the king. For most Egyptians a deep love of home and a scorn for foreigners turned thoughts and interests inward into the land of the Nile. But the shock of foreign domination deeply affected the national psychology. This must never happen again. A feeling of imperialistic patriotism invaded the land. In the Egyptian texts it was, not the "army of his majesty," but "our army," that took the fields to seek Egypt's revenge.

To be sure, this did not happen immediately, nor did it happen without some conflict of opinion within Egypt. The Middle Kingdom had had an African empire, and this was re-established as far as the Third Cataract early in the Eighteenth Dynasty. But what should be the Egyptian attitude toward the enemies in Asia? *Ca.* 1490 B.C. there was a political controversy over this question.

The protagonists in the struggle were the young King Thut-mose III* and Queen Hat-shepsut. She and her nonmilitary policy had the first success. The youthful Thut-mose was thrust into obscurity and inactivity. Hat-shepsut seized power and proclaimed herself, not queen, but king, so that she might reign as a god. For eighteen years she ruled with vigor (1486-1468 B.C.). The Egyptian energies were devoted to reconstruction, building enterprises, and peaceful foreign trade. Her beautiful temple of Deir el-Bahri at Thebes devotes major space to the depiction of a commercial enterprise, the expedition down the Red Sea to the land of Punt, for incense, myrrh, ebony, apes, gold, and leopard skins. Her party was interested in re-establishing that cultural and economic dominance in foreign lands which the Old and Middle Kingdoms had enjoyed. The incense land of Punt probably lay both on the Somali African coast and on the Arabia Felix Asiatic coast at the S end of the Red Sea. If it is not precisely the biblical Ophir, it is a good counterpart thereof. Fig. EGY 13.

Hat-shepsut suddenly fell from power and disappeared from history. Within a few months, her young relative Thut-mose III (1490-1436 B.C.) set out on a military campaign into Palestine. The implication is clear that the warlike and imperialistic party had succeeded in overthrowing the party of peace and free trade.

Thut-mose III was a man of great military and administrative ability. He devoted seventeen campaigns to Asia, founded an Egyptian empire running up into N Syria, and introduced the military and civil controls to hold the area. His fame dominated Syria for a full century. In Egypt his throne name, Men-kheper-Re, gave magical authority to scarabs for a thousand years.

Thut-mose described his initial campaign into Asia as the punishment of a "rebellion," which is a self-righteous falsehood. He also called himself the "smiter of the rulers of foreign countries [*hiku-khasu* or Hyksos] who had attacked him." The continuing memory of the disgrace inflicted upon Egypt by the Hyksos was a powerful motive in the setting up of empire and the thrusting of Egypt's frontier back from Sinai to N Syria.

This "rebellion" of May, 1468 B.C., consisted of a coalition of 330 princes of Palestine and Syria, "each one of them having his own army." As the princes were rulers of little city-states, the entire confederacy need not have been very large. The presiding Asiatic leader was the prince of Kadesh on the Orontes. From the S had come such towns as Gezer, Joppa, Aijalon, and Beeroth; from the Plain of Sharon came Aphek and Soco; from the N seacoast of Palestine there were Acco and Achshaph; from the Valley of Jezreel appeared Megiddo, Dothan, and Beth-shan; from Transjordan there were Ashtaroth and Edrei; from Galilee appeared Merom and Hazor; and Syria was represented by such important towns as Damascus, Aleppo, and Carchemish. Major Phoenician

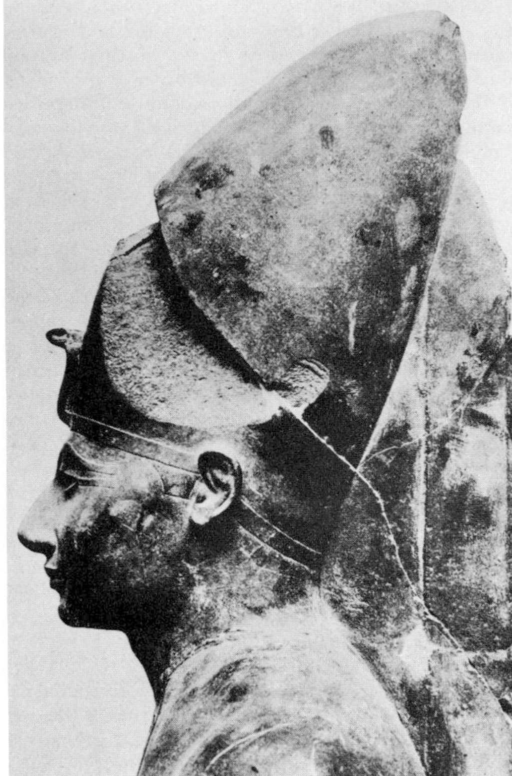

From *When Egypt Ruled the East* (The University of Chicago Press)

13. Thut-mose III, upper part of statue in the Cairo Museum, from Karnak

cities like Tyre and Gebal did not join the coalition, perhaps wishing to maintain their trade with Egypt.

The coalition assembled at Megiddo in the Valley of Jezreel, to gain the potential advantage of the shelter of the Carmel range against the advancing Egyptian army. Thut-mose moved with great energy and daring. Perhaps the Asiatic army relied too much upon the protection of the mountain range, because the pharaoh threw his forces successfully through the Megiddo Pass and emerged into the valley without loss. Then both armies encamped for the night. The battle the following day was a quick Egyptian victory. The demoralized Asiatics fled for safety within the walls of Megiddo, while the Egyptian soldiers were occupied in looting the rich tents of the enemy. The city was encircled with a moat and a wall of timbers and was subjected to a seven-month siege. The booty was great: more than two thousand horses, two thousand cattle, and twenty thousand sheep; abundant gold, silver, metal-work, and inlaid furniture. The victory had come just at the time of the Palestinian harvest, so that the Egyptian army was able to reap 450,000 bushels of wheat, "in addition to what was cut as forage by his majesty's army."

In December what was left of the starving enemy inside Megiddo surrendered and sued for pardon. Thut-mose was magnanimous. He stripped them of their possessions, he took away their fine horses and chariots, but he let them return to their homes after taking an oath of fealty to his person. Only as a mark of vassaldom they went home on donkeyback. Never again did a Syrian-Palestinian group of such wide composition unite to confront Egypt.

In the following nineteen years Thut-mose III conducted sixteen more campaigns in Asia. Some of them were mere parades of power, to keep the awe of the pharaoh alive in his new empire. Some involved actual fighting against Kadesh on the Orontes or the state of MITANNI in upper Mesopotamia. On the eighth campaign Thut-mose enjoyed the diversion of an elephant hunt in the marshes of Syria, and the herd was reported as numbering 120.

The newly won Egyptian territory was organized with resident garrisons, Egyptian high commissioners, and a courier service. The Mediterranean ports were seized and equipped for Egyptian use. The cedar groves of Lebanon were made an Egyptian preserve. The pharaoh wisely maintained local princes upon their thrones, but took their sons and brothers to be hostages in Egypt. The princelings were brought up at the Egyptian court, until their fathers died and they might succeed to the throne. In this way, with a combination of force and clemency, Thut-mose welded a strong empire, which was remarkably loyal to Egypt for the best part of a century.

Thut-mose III's son, Amen-hotep II (1439-1406 B.C.), demonstrated by two vigorous Syrian campaigns that there would be no lapse of Egyptian control. In the first of these he captured a knightly courier "of the Prince of Naharin, carrying a letter of clay at his throat," in the Plain of Sharon. That international correspondence on cuneiform clay tablets which is so well known from the Tell el-Amarna Letters was already a diplomatic factor in the region. The prince of Naharin or Mitanni may have been inciting the local rulers to rebellion against Egypt. In his second campaign Amen-hotep fought in the general vicinity of Soco. The pharaoh brought back to Egypt nearly 90,000 Asiatic prisoners. Among them were 3,600 *'Apiru*, which is the Egyptian writing for the term HABIRU in cuneiform. These were differentiated in the list from the settled inhabitants of Palestine-Syria and from the nomadic Bedouins, on the basis of either location or way of life. Thus this controversial group enters into the Egyptian records.

The newly won Asiatic empire made profound differences in Egyptian culture. Now many Egyptians resided abroad in towns of Palestine and Syria, while vast numbers of Asiatics, ranging from hostage princes to captive slave laborers, lived in Egypt. The luxury products and the works of art of Asia were found desirable in Egypt, and trade was active. It was no longer possible to believe that the gods cared only for Egypt, when Egypt so obviously desired to hold other lands. Shrines for gods of the Nile Valley were erected in Asia, but the Egyptians who lived abroad also set up offering steles to such Asiatic deities as Baal and Anath. Within Egypt there were priests of Baal and Ashtoreth. Other facets of Egyptian culture were incised by foreign influence. Literature was invaded by foreign words, such as *migdol* for a fortress or *markabah* for a chariot. Very soon parents would be naming their children with Asiatic names, such as Ben-Anath, "Son of Anath," or Pa-Khura, "the Horite."

As wealth flowed into Egypt, ostentation became a mark of cosmopolitan sophistication. Art was profoundly affected: it became livelier, more naturalistic, and softer in line; it became more interested in the immediate activities of life, at the cost of an emphasis on eternal bliss. In art the influences of Crete were stronger than those of Asia or Africa. Temple architecture showed the new imperial ostentation and the new wealth of the temples by an expansion toward the colossal. When Egypt's troubles with Mitanni were resolved, the pharaoh was graciously pleased to take a Mitannian princess as wife. Thus the august Egyptian palace was invaded at the top level; it had already been peopled at the lower level with slaves in the kitchen and weaving rooms. As the empire Egyptianized Asia to a marked degree, so also was Egypt Asiaticized.

Three generations of such triumph, power, and wealth brought the imperial magnificence of Amen-hotep III (1398-1361 B.C.), who saw Egypt's efforts crowned with apparently unassailable success. Syria and Palestine silently accepted the Egyptian peace; their vassal status had the compensations of orderly prosperity. Phoenicia and Crete were devoted to their commercial ties with Egypt. Mitanni, which was fading as a power, was in peaceful alliance with Egypt. The Hittites, Babylonians, and Assyrians were not yet ready to challenge Egypt in Syria; their kings exchanged royal gifts with the pharaoh. Amen-hotep and the commoner Tiy, whom he had made his chief queen, contented themselves with careless enjoyment of the fruits of conquest.

d. Amarna period (1375-1300 B.C.). An Egyptian peace imposed by conquest and administration had its obvious advantages, both to the Egyptians and to their Asiatic subjects. Equally obvious to those subjects were the possible rewards of independence. The period of international correspondence mirrored in the letters found at TELL EL-AMARNA opened with a few signs of dissatisfaction in the Asiatic empire. Even though each Syrian prince wrote to the pharaoh in a spirit of slavish devotion, he might take the opportunity to advise his liege lord that some other prince was acting treacherously. The prince of Gebal humbly fell "seven times and seven times beneath the feet of the king, my lord," and begged the pharaoh to stop the territorial aggrandizement of the prince of Amurru, who at the same time was writing to protest his doglike loyalty. When the Egyptian capital ignored these accusations as being local jealousies, the Asiatics who were experimenting in separatism were emboldened to continue.

Egypt was preoccupied with an internal contest for power. In earlier ages there had been no effective line between church and state. The same individual had been a high government official, an important priest, and a commander of the army. Now these different services had become so demanding that they had become professionalized and specialized. The needs of a large and widespread government had enlarged and emphasized the civil service, for which schools now trained boys to be clerks rather than priests. An army stationed abroad for an indefinite time and composed in part of foreign mercenaries required professional officers and soldiers. Further, the temples had changed radically. The national gods were the guarantors of victory; in return they received a lion's share of the booty. In particular, Amon-Re, the god of empire, came to possess huge lands, great bodies of workers, and a rich annual income. Thus three estates divided apart in Egypt and were set into competition. And the pharaoh himself saw the dissipation of his divine authority. There came into being a four-way contest for power, among the pharaoh, the civil service, the army command, and the priesthood.

In part it was this contest which precipitated the "Amarna Revolution," headed by the heretic pharaoh, Amen-hotep IV (1369-1353 B.C.), who later changed his name to AKH-EN-ATON.* The new trends in art, architecture, literature, and religion were already working their way into the expression of the state without visible opposition. The new social forces, through the rise of persons previously unknown to position, were necessary to the enlarged state. Foreigners were factors within the state, even in the palace. The daughter of obscure Egyptians had become the honored queen of Amen-hotep III. Even in religion there had already been trends toward a narrowed-down devotion to one god, which sounds essentially monotheistic. The Aton, the life-giving disk of the sun, had been worshiped two generations before Akh-en-Aton's reforms. Of course, new tendencies strain relations between conservatives and liberals, but Egypt had previously been able to compromise and accommodate. Now the pharaoh found himself increasingly the captive of the highest civil servants and the highest priests. To regain his former pre-eminence, he seized upon the new trends as materials for a revolution. Fig. AKH 8.

Since Amen-hotep III appointed his son as coregent, the two kings had a joint reign of perhaps nine years. The formal and open break came while the older king was still living, without apparent objection from him. Indeed, there is evidence that Amen-hotep III and Queen Tiy were in good relation to the revolutionary movement, even though they did not join their son in abandoning the old capital at Thebes. In the sixth year of his reign the younger Amen-hotep gave up the attempt to introduce a new religion in Thebes, which was dominated by the god Amon. The young heretic changed his name from Amen-hotep, "Amon is satisfied," to Akh-en-Aton, probably meaning: "It is well with the Aton." He moved his capital from Thebes to the new site Akhet-Aton, near modern Tell el-Amarna, some two hundred and more miles to the N, and he took a vow never to leave his new garden city. He began a vigorous movement to concentrate worship upon the life-giving power of the sun disk, the Aton, and he sent agents throughout Egypt and the empire to remove the names of gods, particularly the name Amon, from the inscriptions. The revolutionary break had been made. *See also* § 3 *below*.

Physically Akh-en-Aton was not strong or well. His ancestors, vigorously setting up empire, had emphasized physical strength, vigor, and endurance. He was not strong enough to follow this precedent, and he resorted to leadership in spiritual, artistic, and intellectual fields. The Amarna art exaggerated the naturalistic trends of the immediate past in sketchy and lively scenes which were almost caricatures of the older serene and poised art. As the pharaoh was long-jawed, sloping-shouldered, and potbellied, so also were his attendants depicted in imitative flattery. In an excess of candor, the formerly cloistered royal palace was opened up to public view, with scenes of the family in affectionate intimacy. Formerly, Egyptian art had been detached from the here and now, in order to achieve timeless and spaceless eternity. But Akh-en-Aton's artists delighted in scenes of the immediate present in the capital city, with a storytelling which was as lively as a Greek vase painting.

In the break with the past, Akh-en-Aton's administrators were new people, who repaid him for their suddenly advanced position by a servile loyalty. The old conservative families who had formerly administered state and temple were cut off from power. Thus there was no diplomatic experience in the problems of foreign affairs. The Asiatic empire went to pieces, and there is evidence that there was internal trouble in the control of the army and the collection of taxes.

The Tell el-Amarna Letters and the Hittite archives tell the story of the disaffection in Palestine and Syria. Not only did Syrian princes try to detach for themselves little states, but a new power, the Hittite Empire, moved out of Anatolia to seize Syrian territory. Those princes who remained loyal to Egypt lost their thrones when the pharaoh ignored their appeals for help. E.g., the prince of Gebal was forced to flee from his town and seek asylum farther S.

The princes in Palestine saw the decomposition of Egyptian power in Syria, and some of them, such as the prince of Shechem, intrigued for personal power, while still writing servile letters to the pharaoh. Mobile invaders, the HABIRU, penetrated the land for their own advantage. The loyal prince of Jerusalem pleaded for only fifty soldiers to hold the land for the pharaoh. The Egyptian capital was too preoccupied to send additional troops. The N part of the empire fell away to the Hittites; the S part was carved up into small independent states.

At Amarna there was trouble. Akh-en-Aton's ailment was apparently progressive. His beautiful queen, Nefert-iti, fell from favor and was exiled to a N suburb. Akh-en-Aton had no sons to aid him in rule. He married his eldest daughter to a youthful favorite, Smenkhkere, and made the young man his coregent. Smenkhkere (1355-1352 B.C.) returned to Thebes, and the worship of the god Amon was resumed. Although Akh-en-Aton would not leave his capital or desert his god, a compromise which was really a surrender was necessary to save his rule.

After Akh-en-Aton's death, Smenkhkere soon disappeared from view. Another son-in-law, Tut-ankh-Aton, changed his name to Tut-ankh-Amon (1352-1344 B.C.),* thus protesting his loyalty to the forces of reaction, abandoned the capital at Tell el-Amarna, and returned devotedly to the older forms in religion and government. He also died while young, and after a brief reign by an elderly relative of the Amarna family, Eye, rule left his family. The commander of the army, Hor-em-heb (1340-1303 B.C.), seized the throne in order to restore law and order to a confused and resentful state. Hor-em-heb vigorously put down rebellion and corruption. Later

Egyptian records make him the first legitimate pharaoh after Amen-hotep III, thus expunging the names of the Amarna family from history as heretics. Fig. TOM 69.

e. Late New Kingdom (1300-1100 B.C.). The Nineteenth Dynasty (1303-1202 B.C.) brought in a new family, with a new political orientation. The names of the Eighteenth Dynasty, Amen-hotep and Thut-mose, showed dedication to Amon of Thebes and to Thoth of Hermopolis in Middle Egypt. The names of the Nineteenth Dynasty, Ramses, Seti, and Mer-ne-Ptah,* expressed devotion to the gods of the N, Re of Heliopolis (On), Seth of the NE Delta and of foreign countries, and Ptah of Memphis.

Courtesy of the Cairo Museum; photo courtesy of the Metropolitan Museum of Art

14. King Mer-ne-Ptah, from Thebes

Within a generation the capital city would be Rameses in the NE Delta; Thebes would become a traditional, seasonal, and religious capital, although it continued to be a provincial seat of government. Egypt's concerns had moved N. Fig. EGY 14.

The military interests and the concern of the army to regain stability are shown by the succession of military pharaohs. General Hor-em-heb was succeeded by Ramses I (1303-1302 B.C.) and his son Seti I (1302-1290 B.C.), both of whom had had army careers. Seti I's determination to restore older glories appears in the term which he applied to the beginning of his reign—the "renaissance."

The reconstruction of the empire was the first concern of the new dynasty. Seti I in his first regnal year campaigned from the Suez frontier to the hills of Galilee, put down an attempt by Palestinian princes to unite, and seized the town of Beth-shan on the Jordan. Subsequently he defeated the *'Apiru* or Habiru of Mount Jarmuth near Beth-shan. He realized the importance of good communications and took care to maintain and police the caravan stations across N Sinai. With the land of Canaan again in control, Seti was able to face the major enemy and campaigned against the Hittites in Syria. Perhaps there was no conclusive engagement between the two powers, but the pharaoh was successful in taking Kadesh on the Orontes and setting up a triumphal stele in that town.

Fig. EGY 15.

Courtesy of the Metropolitan Museum of Art

15. Egyptian wall painting showing Apuy's house and garden, from Nineteenth Dynasty, Thebes

At home Seti I's energies were devoted to the continued problem of checking official abuses. At Thebes and Abydos he started major building operations, showing a more restrained taste in art and architecture than his son Ramses II. Fig. EGY 16.

In his fifth regnal year Ramses II (1290-1224 B.C.; *see* RAMSES 2) fought against the Hittite king Muwatallis at Kadesh on the Orontes.* As allies the Hittites brought such city-states of N Syria as Carchemish, Aleppo, and Ugarit, some of the older peoples of Asia Minor like Arzawa and Kizuwadna, and some of the new Sea Peoples of Asia Minor, such as the Dardanians and the Mysians. As mercenaries on his side Ramses had those Sea Peoples who were later to give their name to the island of Sardinia. The ethnic composition of the battle offers a chapter in the protohistory of the classical world. In the battle the Egyptians suffered an inconclusive setback. By 1270 B.C., Egypt and the Hittites had resolved their difficulties in a treaty of alliance and mutual assistance, and *ca.* 1257 B.C. the new peace was confirmed by Ramses II's marriage to the daughter of the Hittite king. Although the final thirty-three years of Ramses II's long reign were unmarked by major incident, the Sea Peoples were using the period to increase their aggressive strength against the Hittites and Egypt. Fig. RAM 4.

Ramses II was a great builder within Egypt, and he unscrupulously appropriated the monuments of his predecessors for himself. In the Delta the royal residence city of Rameses (*see* RAMESES) was named after him, so that serious attention must be given to his claim to be the Pharaoh of the Oppression, as the builder of the store cities of Pithom and Rameses. However, the Egyptian texts present no supporting evidence, specifically upon the enforced toil of the children of Israel or upon a major exodus in the reign of his successor.

Courtesy of Pan American World Airways

16. Statues of Ramses II and columns of the temple at Luxor

Ramses II's long reign produced a swarm of royal princes, many of whom died before their father. His thirteenth son, MER-NE-PTAH, must have been old when he succeeded to the throne (1224-1214 B.C.). His two great problems were keeping alive his hard-pressed Hittite ally with shipments of grain, because the pressure of the Sea Peoples was shaking the prosperity of Anatolia, and of repelling an invasion of Libyans and Sea Peoples at his W frontier in his fifth year. A poem of victory which commemorated this W victory ends with the only mention of Israel in Egyptian literature, and it has therefore been called the "Israel Stele":

> The princes are prostrate, saying: "Mercy!" . . .
> Desolation is for Libya; the Hittites are pacified;
> The Canaan is plundered with every evil;
> Ashkelon is carried off; Gezer is seized upon;
> Yanoam is made as if non-existent;
> Israel is laid waste, he has no offspring;
> The Horite land has become a widow for Egypt!

This is a poetic, nonhistorical outburst. However, it specifically makes the Israelites a people in or near Canaan. The hieroglyphic writing of the word "Israel" is determined with the signs for people rather than place, and this probably shows them to be nomadic or seminomadic, rather than settled. Thus an Israel existed in Asia by 1220 B.C., so that this date must be considered in relation to an exodus and a wandering. There may have been an exodus in the thirteenth century B.C., but the problem of forty years' wandering before the entry into Canaan makes it difficult to regard Mer-ne-Ptah as the pharaoh of the Exodus.

The Nineteenth Dynasty ran out its course with feeble kings succeeding one another rapidly. Then for a brief time, perhaps 1202-1197 B.C., there was an interregnum, in which a Syrian ("Horite") seized the throne of Egypt. Probably he had not invaded the land; perhaps one of the Asiatic chamberlains serving at the palace was able to take over power. E.g., at the court of Mer-ne-Ptah a chief herald had been a Semite named Ben-ozen. The account of this interregnum in a text written a generation later runs: "Afterwards other times came in empty years, and Irsu, a Syrian with them, made himself prince. He set the entire land as tributary before him. One man joined another that their property might not be plundered. They treated the gods like mortals, and no offerings were presented in the temples." There is some doubt about the reading of "Irsu" as a name, and nothing more is known of this episode.

A new dynasty, the Twentieth (1197-1090 B.C.), appeared to "cleanse the great throne of Egypt." Its only important figure was Ramses III (1195-1164 B.C.; *see* RAMSES 3).* At the end of his reign this pharaoh still held territory in Canaan, for his mortuary testament states that he guaranteed for Amon the nine Palestinian towns which he had given to that god. Within a generation after his death the Asiatic empire collapsed, the Sinai mines were abandoned, and Egypt withdrew into her shell. Fig. RAM 5.

Ramses III lost his life in a conspiracy which originated in his own harem. The court which was constituted to try the plotters was composed of palace officials, among them the Semitic butler Mahar-baal. When the accused of higher ranks were found guilty, they were permitted to take their own lives; the lesser criminals were executed.

In his mortuary testament, Ramses confirmed the Egyptian temples in their holdings. The detailed figures are difficult to relate to the total area and population of Egypt, but it seems possible that the various great temples held no less than ten per cent of the people and twelve per cent of the agricultural land, and that the temple of Amon-Re of Karnak alone owned one person out of every fifteen and one acre out of every ten. The vested power of the temples was certainly extraordinarily high.

The reigns of the later kings of the dynasty—all named Ramses—were weak and brief. There came inflation, famine, strikes by government laborers, plundering by soldiers, and official corruption. A series of tomb robberies began *ca.* 1225 B.C. and was unchecked for a full generation, resulting in the thorough looting of the royal and noble tombs at Thebes. The dynasty ended with the last of the kings named Ramses a feeble palace prisoner, controlled by the viziers of Upper and Lower Egypt, the high priest of Amon, and the army commander.

f. Postimperial period (1100-700 B.C.). After the empire Egypt never regained her former dominance in the E Mediterranean world. There might be forays into Palestine and Syria, and some of the pharaohs intrigued against the successive powers of Assyria, Babylonia, and Persia, but they never again attained widespread and long control in Asia. In large part this foreign weakness arose from domestic weakness. Egypt kept breaking up into smaller states, either Upper and Lower Egypt as a loosely co-operative duality, or a large number of locally independent states. The empire had manufactured armies of mercenary soldiers. To them were assigned the tasks of conquest and defense, so that there was less pressure upon the native Egyptians to serve the state. In the Delta a strong mercantile interest emphasized local, rather than national, advantage. Upper Egypt (Pathros) was the grain-producing land, and Thebes was a focal point for the nostalgic memory of past grandeur. From the time of Samuel to the fall of the kingdom of Israel, Egypt was normally in a state of divided weakness.

Ca. 1100 B.C. the high priest of Amon at Thebes sent an emissary, Wen-Amon, to Gebal in Phoenicia, to secure cedar for the sacred boat of the god. The document telling of Wen-Amon's misfortunes has no reference to the reigning pharaoh, because he was then of little account. The independent ruler of Tanis (Zoan) found a Syrian ship for the envoy, but appropriated his credentials. In the Palestinian harbor of Dor, then ruled by some of the Sea Peoples, Wen-Amon was robbed of his gold and silver. When he reached Gebal, the local prince brusquely refused to deal with him, except on the basis of prior payment. He brushed aside Wen-Amon's eloquence about the might of Egypt and the god Amon. Finally, after a year of insults and misadventures, Wen-Amon received new payment from Egypt and was given the cedar. This story is a vivid illustration of the low esteem into which Egypt had fallen in that very Phoenician town which had once been the Asiatic center of pro-Egyptian feeling.

The Twenty-first Dynasty (1090-940 B.C.) had two centers of gravity, Tanis and Thebes, working independently but co-operatively. A powerful family at Thebes used the army as a training ground, before young men moved into the high priesthood of Amon and finally onto the throne. The merchant dynasty at Tanis was based upon sea trade across the E Mediterranean. Solomon's Egyptian queen may have been a daughter of this family, and his trading in horses and chariots may well have been with the princes of Tanis.

The rulers at Thebes undertook the pious task of restoring a minimum of order and decency to the thoroughly robbed cemetery of Thebes. The pillaged mummies of the great pharaohs were rewrapped and consigned to a new hiding place. Other than this, the chief records of the dynasty show a marked reliance upon the oracle of a god for guidance. E.g., a rebellion at Thebes was put down, and the leading rebels were exiled to the oasis of Kharga. After some time, the high priest consulted the god Amon as oracle and received an order that the exiles should be allowed to return, that no such banishment should be imposed in the future, but that the punishment for murder should be capital punishment. We do not know just how such an oracle was articulated, but the priest reported it for public action.

The empire had brought Libyan mercenaries into Egypt, and many of them rose to local power in the Delta and the Faiyum, proudly retaining their hereditary title, "Great Prince of the Me" or Meshwesh. Out of such a family located at Herakleopolis (Hines) near the Faiyum came Sheshonk or SHISHAK, founder of the Twenty-second Dynasty (940-745 B.C.) with its capital at Bubastis (Pibeseth) in the Delta.* So little is known of his successors that the period has to be dismissed as weak and unimportant. Egyptology can offer no records to the question whether the thousand soldiers from Musri, who fought against Shalmaneser in 853 B.C. at Karkara in N Syria, were from Egypt or from another Musri. At the period Egyptian troops under the leadership of Hadadezer of Damascus seem unlikely, but of course this small number might have been committed to an opposition against the growing power of Assyria. Figs. SHI 53-54.

The Twenty-third Dynasty was of minor importance, and the Twenty-fourth was confined to a single pharaoh, Bek-en-ranef or Bocchoris (715-709 B.C.). Late tradition credits him with codifying the law of contract for Egypt. This is the earliest Egyptian reference to codified law. Even though older law on papyrus or parchment may have perished, there is still a striking contrast between our knowledge of Mesopotamian or Hebrew law on the one hand and Egyptian law on the other. To a great degree law and judgment in Egypt had been phrased as, first, the divine word of the king, and, later, the divine word of the god's oracle, and not impersonally written law.

g. Ethiopian and Saitic periods (700-525 B.C.). Sometime around the reign of Bocchoris, a new force entered Egyptian history. This was the rise of the Cushite or Ethiopian pharaohs. Their family seat was Napata near the Fourth Cataract, where a modest annual rainfall, African caravan routes, the breeding of cattle and horses, and nearby deposits of iron permitted local power. Their family background was a mixture of Hamitic, Libyan, Negro, and perhaps Egyptian strains. *Ca.* the middle of the eighth century B.C. they consolidated their power in Cush. They were then ready to move against weak Egypt.

Ca. 720 or 715 B.C. one of these Cushite rulers, Pi-ankhi, had achieved such power that he had some backing in Upper Egypt. An army of his was consolidating his holdings S of Thebes. Pi-ankhi learned that a prince of Lower Egypt was also enlarging his territory, had taken the W Delta, and was operating in Middle Egypt. Pi-ankhi then personally took the field against the Egyptians, captured a series of cities in Middle Egypt, and finally broke the back of resistance by taking Memphis. Sixteen N rulers were forced to submit and take an oath of allegiance to Pi-ankhi. Egypt had fallen under the power of the Ethiopians, even though a weakened local rule went on for a few years.

The inscription of Pi-ankhi is interesting as showing how a non-Egyptian was more devoutly Egyptian than the native rulers whom he conquered. He ordered his army to be properly pious in the holy city of Thebes, he himself participated in a Theban festival, and he made a pilgrimage to the shrine of the sun-god at Heliopolis (On). When the Egyptian rulers came to make submission to Pi-ankhi, three kings were not permitted to enter because "they were eaters of fish, which is an abomination to the palace"; only one might come in to surrender for all, "because he was pure and did not eat fish."

Before returning to the Fourth Cataract, Pi-ankhi achieved the double purpose of demonstrating his devotion to the Theban god Amon and of leaving a reliable agent in Egypt. At Thebes a woman had become the most powerful servant of the god, under the title "divine votaress of Amon." The existing votaress was the daughter of a Twenty-third Dynasty pharaoh. Pi-ankhi forced this princess to adopt his sister as her daughter and successor. Thus she was well placed to serve Ethiopian interests in Egypt, when the pharaoh was absent at his Fourth Cataract capital.

Now came the pressure upon Palestine and then upon Egypt from a succession of imperial conquerors —Assyrians, Babylonians, Macedonians, and Romans. Only occasionally did Egypt commit major military forces to the field; rather, she preferred to resort to diplomatic intrigue by inciting the little rulers of Palestine-Syria to resist the invaders. For the Twenty-fifth or Ethiopian Dynasty (*ca.* 710-663 B.C.), we know little about the reigns of the first two kings (*but see* SO). On the third pharaoh, *see* TIRHAKAH. In the reign of this Cushite pharaoh there was a formal Egyptianizing of temples in the region of the Third and Fourth Cataracts. Architects, artists, and temple gardeners were imported from Egypt itself, and the pharaoh even persuaded princesses of Lower Egypt to serve as priestesses in temples a thousand miles to the S. It is possible that the temple rituals of Egypt were as scrupulously observed in Cush as at home. At one and the same time Egypt was changing under foreign influences and was attempting to resist change by new formalism—sacerdotal emphasis on ritual, cults of sacred animals, reliance upon oracles, and syncretism of gods. Cush was less exposed to outside influence, and there in the S some of the older forms of the religion may have survived with greater vigor.

Meanwhile, foreign powers which were more united and more ambitious than Egypt were moving toward the domination of that land. The Assyrian conquerors were consolidating their position in Syria-Palestine before the attack upon Egypt across the difficult Sinai desert. TIGLATH-PILESER operated chiefly in Syria but penetrated as far S as Gaza. Sargon II (*see* SARGON 2) took Samaria, overthrew the kingdom of Israel, and defeated the Egyptians at Raphia. SENNACHERIB captured cities of Judah and besieged the Jerusalem of Hezekiah. His general assured the people of that city that their reliance upon the pharaoh of Egypt was a trust in a "broken reed," which could only injure him who leaned upon it (Isa. 36:6). Sennacherib defeated the Egyptian forces at Eltekeh in S Palestine in 700 B.C. It may have been in 688 that the Assyrian king moved up to Pelusium on the Egyptian frontier, where his successful advance was cut short by plague (Isa. 37:36). It was reserved for ESARHADDON in 671 B.C. to penetrate Egypt, capture Memphis, and send Tirhakah in flight to the S. The Ethiopian claim to the rule of all Egypt was denied; many small Delta dynasts were confirmed in their local rule, but as Assyrian vassals. Somewhat later Tirhakah's nephew Tanut-Amon (664-653 B.C.) came out of Cush, recaptured Memphis, and briefly defied the Assyrians. He was no match for ASHURBANIPAL, who not only won back Memphis but marched as far S as Thebes and subdued that mighty city. Thereafter the Ethiopians remained in their distant S province.

Esarhaddon had recognized certain small princes of Lower Egypt as legitimate rulers of city-states. Among them was a family at Saïs in the W central Delta. A later member of this family, Psamtik or Psammetichus I (663-609 B.C.), took advantage of the loose Assyrian sponsorship to enlarge his power and claim the rule of all Egypt. The Twenty-sixth Dynasty (663-525 B.C.) is also called the Saitic period, the Renaissance, or the Restoration, by modern scholars. A trend had already started in the preceding century, to study the past glories of Egypt and to attempt to reproduce them. Art reverted to the expressions of the Old and Middle Kingdoms; entire scenes were copied from ancient tombs to adorn the walls of contemporary tombs; old monuments were excavated, restored, and imitated; the classical literature was studied, with a conscientious attempt to reproduce it in form and spirit; and officials were clothed with a series of ancient and now meaningless titles. Where, toward the beginning, this archaism had the excitement of rediscovery and the hope of spiritual encouragement, it produced works of vigor and charm. Later it became sterile, as the ritualistic search for a past glory in an age that had little inner glory.

Another marked feature of the Saitic period was the strong influence of foreigners in Egypt. The commercial interest of the dynasty was strong. The Phoenician merchants were welcomed in the Delta. Clusters of political exiles from Asia were granted asylum in Egypt. In the old Egyptian cities sections were designated for Greek merchants and artisans, and in the W Delta an entire market city, Naucratis, was assigned to the Greeks. Furthermore, the power of this dynasty was maintained by foreign mercenaries. Around the person of the pharaoh himself these were Greeks—Ionian and Carian Greeks, for the most part. The loyalty of the native Egyptians to an upstart rule had become doubtful; the purchased support of foreign professional soldiers seemed to provide a solid base. This reliance upon foreign mercenaries continued throughout the dynasty, despite a mutiny and attempted desertion of the Greeks under Hophra.

At Thebes, always haughtily restless, the Saites continued the Ethiopian policy, and in 654 B.C. forced the divine votaress of Amon to adopt the daughter of Psammetichus I and thus secured a Saitic agent in the southland.

A revival of Egypt's ancient glory involved also a military effort to extend the state. Shortly after 600 B.C. the Greek mercenaries were sent S to the Second Cataract on a conquering expedition. But it was particularly in Asia that the dynasty attempted to regain power. According to Herodotus, Psammetichus I invaded Palestine and laid siege to Ashdod. His successor was even more vigorous (*see* NECO), campaigning ambitiously in Palestine and Syria, and by tradition was industrious in attempts to improve Egypt's waterways and sea trade. Neco's decisive defeat by the crown prince of Babylonia, Nebuchadrezzar, at Carchemish in 605 B.C., for a time quieted Egypt's ambitions in Asia. However, a generation later HOPHRA tried to stir up Judah in revolt against Babylon and thus was a major factor toward the fall of Jerusalem and the Babylonian captivity. The dynasty finally entered an internecine family struggle for power and laid Egypt open to the Persian conquest.

h. Persian, Ptolemaic, and Roman periods (525 B.C.-A.D. 70). The century following the collapse of the mighty Assyrian Empire and the fall of Nineveh was a period of readjustment. At first it seemed that Babylon might regain its ancient dominance through the vigor of Nebuchadrezzar, but the abrupt emergence of a new force, the Persians under Cyrus, shifted the center of power eastward. In 525 B.C., Egypt fell like an overripe fruit into the hands of the Persians under Cambyses; there is good evidence that the conqueror had Egyptian collaborators. Egyptian tradition insists that Cambyses was brutal and impious. Since he was a conquering invader, he himself may have been very rigorous, but his successors preferred to cultivate Egypt as a valued Persian satrapy. Darius I (522-486 B.C.) did his best to appear to the Egyptians as a legitimate pharaoh. Tradition says that he was cordial to the native priests; certainly he was responsible for the building of at least one new temple. Between the Nile and the Gulf of Suez he completed the canal which had been of interest to Pharaoh Neco; along its line in the Wadi Tumilat he erected five steles inscribed in cuneiform and hieroglyphic. Under his reign we first hear of the Jewish colony at the First Cataract (*see* ELEPHANTINE PAPYRI). Since this colony had existed before the time of Cambyses, it probably had been founded as a frontier garrison in the Twenty-sixth Dynasty. The Saites had not only had Greek mercenaries; there had also been Asiatics, including Jews.

Egypt was not grateful to the Persians for a mild policy. The death of Darius was the signal for a revolt, which Xerxes I put down with severity. But meanwhile the Greeks at Marathon and Salamis were demonstrating that, when the Persian armies reached the end of their long communication lines, they could be defeated, so that rebelliousness became a normal Egyptian attitude. Persian rule was effective from 525 to 404 B.C., then there came three brief native dynasties based on the Delta, and then Persian domination reasserted itself in 341 B.C. Of the Egyptian rulers only Nectanebo I (379-361) and Nectanebo II (359-341) were strong enough to weld Egypt into some temporary unity and to engage in large building enterprises. The Persian period is one of brief flashes of energy, with long stretches of smoldering inertia.

Two explosive forces burst upon the ancient oriental world—Hellenism as a culture of vigorous ideas, and the military genius Alexander of Macedon, who promoted this culture by his success on the field of battle. After Alexander the Great had defeated Darius III of Persia at Issus in Cilicia in 333 B.C., he decided to build a strong Western empire before advancing E against the Persian bases. Stubborn Tyre had to be subdued to secure the E Mediterranean, and then Alexander moved on Egypt. That country had been so blindly hostile to Persia that it welcomed a deliverer. The Persian satrap surrendered immediately, the Macedonian army entered Memphis, and Alexander paid his respects to the Egyptian gods in the autumn of 332 B.C. Then marching NW to the Mediterranean coast, he founded a new city, named Alexandria after himself. No important Egyptian city had ever been on the coast before, nor had ancient Egypt ever had so large and so cosmopolitan a metropolis. With great daring, Alexander marched through the formidable W desert to the oasis of Siwah to consult the oracle of the god Ammon. He was saluted as the god's son, and from this time forward he based his actions on the belief that he had a divine mission in life. The Egyptian concept that their king was a god (*see* PHARAOH) deeply affected the mystical young warrior.

From Egypt, Alexander set out to conquer the world, penetrating into India. When he died in 323 B.C., his half-brother and his still unborn son were the obvious heirs. The real power, however, lay in the control of Alexander's senior generals, even though they at first gave nominal service to the heirs. One of the generals, Ptolemy, son of Lagus, ruled Egypt as satrap. When in 306 B.C. the succession finally became an issue, the empire was carved up, Cassander taking Macedonia and the NW, Seleucus taking Syria and the E, with a capital at Antioch, and Ptolemy taking Egypt and the SW. When Alexander's son died, Ptolemy I Soter I emerged fully as pharaoh of Egypt and founder of the Ptolemaic Dynasty (305-30 B.C.).

The dynasty began with the devoted attention of the new rulers to the interests of Egypt. They gave respectful attention to the old Egyptian religion, and there was extensive building of new temples throughout the land. Alexandria became a famous center of intellectual life and a vigorous commercial city. The traditional political organization into provinces was retained for most of Egypt, but three cities, Alexandria and Naucratis in the Delta and Ptolemaïs in Upper Egypt, were granted self-government on the pattern of the Greek polis. The Ptolemies energetically promoted the agricultural productivity of Egypt, with new canals in the Delta and extensive land reclamation in the Faiyum. Even though the dynasty was foreign in origin, it presented a contrast to previous conquering regimes by living in Egypt and making efforts to appear natively devoted to that land.

The latter part of the Ptolemaic Dynasty, from *ca.* 220 B.C. on, showed a decided weakening in power and in character, through family feuds for the rule, through unwise military enterprises into the territory claimed by the Seleucids, through an attempt to secure the support of powerful Rome, and through sheer frivolity.

Under Ptolemy I (305-285 B.C.) there was set up in Alexandria a museum, a temple of the Muses, for study in the arts and sciences, with privileged resident scholars and an ambitious program for the acquisition of MSS. The great library of Alexandria came to accumulate half a million scrolls. Within this inviting intellectual climate, Alexandria became the exciting center for old and new ideas of the civilized world. The cataloguing of MSS and textual criticism were initiated; science, particularly geometry and astronomy, received great impetus. The research museum and the library reached an early height and were not maintained with the same enthusiasm. Then it was Caesar, for the glory of Rome, who began the looting of the MS treasures.

When finally in the seventh century A.D. the Muslim invaders entered Alexandria, there was only a withered stalk of the once magnificent plant left for their zealous burning. Meanwhile, despite this withering, the first Ptolemy had made Alexandria a capital for ideas and discussion, and so it remained for nearly a thousand years. Fig. PTO 74.

The new rulers were not content to hold Egypt alone, and Ptolemy III Euergetes I (246-221 B.C.) conquered land which was also claimed by the Seleucids in Palestine and Syria, thus initiating seventy years of struggle with the kings at Antioch.* Antiochus III (the Great) began to take back the Asiatic territory which Egypt had seized. Although the weak Ptolemy IV Philopator defeated Antiochus at Raphia in 217 B.C.,* Egypt was unable to reap advantage from this victory. Philopator mismanaged both the Egyptian economy and his relations with the native Egyptians, so that his power at home was weakened by local revolts, particularly at Thebes. The Seleucids of Antioch were consistently at the attack; the Ptolemies of Alexandria dissipated their energies by bitter family quarrels. When Egypt then summoned to her support the new Western power, Rome, she sacrificed some of her independence and increasingly became a client of Rome. In 170 B.C., Antiochus IV actually invaded Egypt and ruled there for two years, until Rome demanded his withdrawal. Shortly after this the Seleucids tried to control the high priesthood at Jerusalem, with the result that Onias IV fled to Egypt, was received by Ptolemy VI Philometor, and was permitted to build a Jewish temple at Leontopolis in the S Delta. Figs. PTO 71, 72, 74.

The sordid story of the family feuds and futile weaknesses of the later Ptolemies need not be told. The power of Rome became increasingly felt in Egypt. Finally a century of political intrigues produced one last member of the family who was able to use great diplomatic genius to try to preserve the independence of her land, Cleopatra. Her methods may have been devious and ignobly direct, but her patriotic purpose remained steadfast—the preservation of Egypt's sovereignty. First Caesar came to Egypt in 48 B.C.; from 41 B.C. on, it was Antony who dallied in Alexandria, while plotting his return to Rome. With each of them she pursued her single-minded goal. Yet she was no match for imperial Rome, and after the defeat of Antony and Cleopatra at Actium, she took her own life in 30 B.C., rather than become a vassal. Egypt became a vassal state for many centuries.

The Roman rule of Egypt was oppressive. The land had a reputation for rebelliousness, but, as one of the chief sources of grain to feed the empire, Egypt had to be kept in order. Augustus did not grant the customary pattern for Roman provinces, under which there was some local dignity although the Roman Senate made the essential decisions, but he initiated a tight control under the personal supervision of the emperor. The large force of three legions was garrisoned on the land, and Augustus not only had the appointment of the prefect but even exercised a veto control over senators' visits to Egypt. A very efficient government was introduced, and it was honest, but it had only an official and demanding relation to the Egyptians. Taxes were heavy, and, since the collection of taxes was farmed out, they became oppressively heavy upon the little man. A cold and rigorous system bled Egypt white. Roman taxation and the military control over their once proud spirits changed the Egyptians' outlook on life. As the weight of this world became too burdensome, they turned to the hope of another and better world. When Christian evangelists worked in Egypt in the second century A.D., they found a ready audience.

3. Religion. Ancient Egyptian religion was a polytheism, which, in the course of three thousand years, showed a high complexity. Certain generalities persisted throughout this long course, but no simple analysis will do justice to the changes appearing in the process of time.

The world of the ancient orientals was thoroughly saturated with the presence of the gods, so that every phenomenon and every process in man's life could be attributed to the agency of gods. There was no separation of life into the religious and the secular, with the partial exception of administrative and business life after the state became highly complex *ca.* 1500 B.C. There was no acceptance of natural law, with its impersonal chain of cause and effect, so that any phenomenon could be traced back to natural causes, but whatever happened was attributed to the agency of the gods. Since it was possible to deify a human being, to see the divine in plant or animal or forces of nature, and to personify qualities such as "truth" or "command" or "fate," the gods were indefinitely many and their agency widespread. Therefore, science could not work out a detached explanation of what occurred in climate or weather, plant and animal life, astronomy, or medicine. History was deeply concerned with its present generation, and had only an annalistic interest in the past. Not only were the gods always present and always ready to intervene in life; Egypt had its own national gods to apply themselves to the various aspects of life, and particularly one resident god, the king of Egypt, whose divine function was to apply his powers to the advantage of his land. One might fairly say that, for the really important phases of life, the miraculous was more real to the ancient Egyptian than the natural.

After the appearance of any phenomenon or after any event, the Egyptians would relate this to the activity of their gods by myth. Over the course of centuries such myths were elaborated to a high complexity. From our modern point of view they might seem to be self-contradictory, since everything was possible to the gods, so that different explanations of the same phenomenon were not to be questioned by mere man; they simply enlarged the range of the gods' powers by demonstrating a wide range of possibilities. E.g., the creation story was told in several different ways about a single god; it was even told to the glory of different gods in different terms. This variety of explanations of a single process was not felt to be inconsistent; rather, it strengthened the concept by making it broadly characteristic of divinity: creation is a continuing power of any great god, and the creative process is to be confidently accepted from any great god.

A religious state, which fervently believed that the gods might intervene at any time, never fully admitted that there was any distinction between the sacred and the secular, particularly when the head of the state was a god. In earlier Egypt there was no distinction between a priest and a layman—the high official, by virtue of his service to the state, was civil administrator, army commander, and priest of the temple. Art and literature were deeply rooted in religion. Only when the exacting demands of a large and complex state after 1500 B.C. made professionalism necessary, do we find full-time priests and full-time civil servants. Even then the dogma of a theocratic state and the myth-making mentality of the Egyptian refused to admit that there was or could be any final division between religious and secular.

The Egyptians lived in houses of mud brick on the fertile alluvial soil. Over the millenniums the slow accumulation of deposit has obliterated most of the evidence of the private life. However, the desert was always near at hand for the stone structures of eternal life—i.e., the temples and the tombs. The result is that we have a disproportionate amount of evidence surviving from this preservative setting in the desert. We are relatively well informed on official religion, as shown in the great state temples, and on mortuary religion, as shown in the tombs. It is more difficult to reach certainty on the correspondence of the state's official religion to the personal beliefs and private devotions of individuals and on the correspondence of life as shown in the tomb scenes and texts to the daily life of persons. The analysis of ancient Egyptian religion inevitably suffers from this incompleteness of survival.

a. Older official religion. For modern understanding, three types of ancient Egyptian gods may be identified. (*a*) There were divinities of place, such as Ptah of Memphis, Khnum of the First Cataract region, or the crocodile god Sobek of the Faiyum. (*b*) There were cosmic deities, such as Nut, goddess of the sky; Geb, the earth-god; Re, the sun-god; and eight divinities of pre-creation chaos. (*c*) There were gods responsible for some function or aspect of life, such as Ma'at, goddess of truth and justice, Bes, god of the household and childbirth, and Sekhmet, goddess of war and disease. By historical times these three categories appear as thoroughly blended, so that Thoth was god of Hermopolis, moon-god, and god of wisdom; Hat-Hor was goddess of Dendereh, sky-goddess, and goddess of love. Throughout Egyptian history and apparently back into prehistory, there was a process of syncretism, whereby recognition of similarity permitted blending. Various falcon gods all came to be Horus,* and similarity of status or purpose permitted mergers, such as Amon-Re or Atum Re-Har-akhti. Fig. FAL 1.

The gods of place have been called totems. This is valid, provided the term does not involve blood-relationship of the people of a community with their totem god. A single being—human form, animal, bird, serpent, tree, crossed arrows, scepter, etc.—was the divine force for a city or region and a totem in this sense. However, there never was any claim that the people of Siut were blood-brothers of the wolf-god Up-wawet of Siut, so that all wolves had to be sacred in that area. Rather, the god Up-wawet might function or make his appearance in a single wolf. Frequently a single animal or other symbol was maintained in a temple for such use of a god. Until Greco-Roman times there was no animal-worship in ancient Egypt, with a universal devotion to a sacred bull or other being. Before that time, only the one dedicated animal in the temple was sacred.

This regional god seems to have been African in origin and relationships. Such totemistic representation of a people or community can be seen in modern African survivals. In Asia the same psychology toward a god was not marked. The reverence for a single force as the divine promoter of a region led easily into the Egyptian concept that their king was a god, a belief which again has its reflection among African tribes, but which was intermittent and incomplete in Asia.

The cosmic gods were more clearly paralleled in

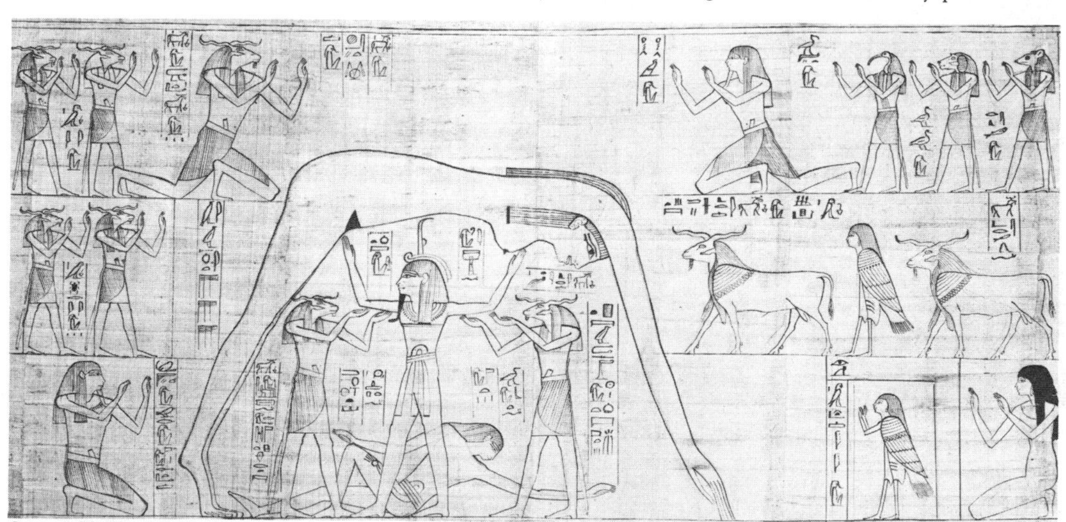

Courtesy of the Trustees of the British Museum

17. The sky-goddess Nut arched like the heavens, supported by the air-god Shu, while at Nut's feet is the earth-god Geb; from a papyrus at Deir el-Bahri

Asia, as were the cosmic myths, such as the creation myth or the myth of the destruction of mankind by an angry god. The theological system of Heliopolis had in itself a progressive myth of the creation of the universe. The god Atum, whose name means "the All," took his place upon a little mound of earth rising out of the waters of chaos and brought the elements of the cosmos into being. Just so, new life rises annually out of the flood waters of the Nile. Atum's own two children were Shu, god of air, and Tefnut, goddess of moisture. These two in turn produced Geb, the earth-god, and Nut,* the sky-goddess —the firmament below and the firmament above. Geb and Nut brought forth the pair Osiris and Isis* and the pair Seth and Nephthys. Osiris and his sister-wife, Isis, came to be the forces of life or regeneration, and Seth the force which destroyed life. The Ennead or "nine" gods just listed were treated as a corporation of supreme gods, most specifically in the theology of Heliopolis, but also generally in Egypt. The successive separations of phenomena in this myth show a broad general similarity to the creation story of Genesis. Figs. EGY 17-18.

Courtesy of the Trustees of the British Museum

18. Isis protecting Osiris with her wings

Another important myth lay in the Osiris saga, which showed many variations. If we select certain components from these versions, Osiris had been a ruler in this world: his brother Seth killed him by trickery. Seth then took over the rule of Osiris. Isis,* the sister-wife of Osiris, succeeded in reclaiming her husband's body and in giving it some measure of revival by her magic. Osiris, the ruler who had died but who lived on in death, thus became the ruler of the dead, and kings of Egypt at death became Osiris, to continue their rule in another realm. Isis also retreated into hiding in the marshes and there brought forth her son, Horus, who tried to avenge his father, Osiris, by combatting his uncle Seth for earthly rule. Ultimately Horus won this contest and became a principle of kingship; every king of Egypt while living was Horus.* Seth became a god of storm, of the desert, and of foreign lands. Figs. ISI 16; FAL 1.

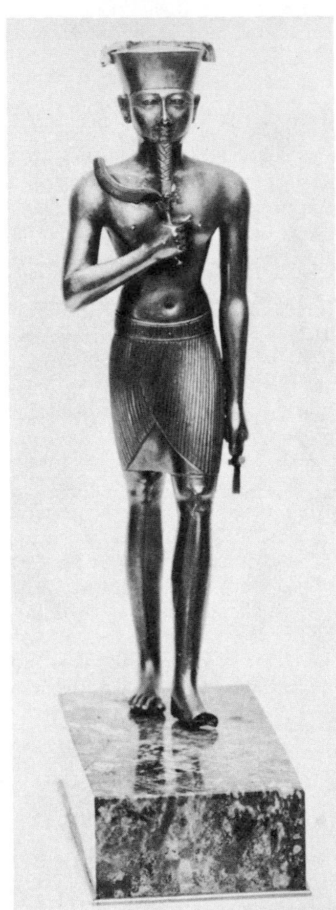

Courtesy of the Metropolitan Museum of Art; gift of Edward S. Harkness, 1926

19. Statuette of the god Amon in the precinct of the Great Temple of Amon at Karnak

The supple generosity of Egyptian mythology can be seen in the problem of defining the supreme god. Several deities were addressed as "father of the gods." Atum, as a creator, had clear title to priority. Re, the sun-god, was also dominant. Har-akhti, or Horus triumphant upon the horizon, was a victorious and ruling god. By the Eleventh Dynasty the god of a new capital city, Thebes, emerged as Amon* and was soon united with Re as Amon-Re, the imperial god. Such a merger of aspects of power produced Atum Re-Har-akhti, a composition of ruling forces. This syncretistic tendency was not monotheism; gods might blend for combinations of power, but were also distinct in specific function, as a spectrum is one but the colors are many. Fig. EGY 19.

Of the many other gods who might be listed, perhaps the most important was Ptah, earth-god, creator-god in his own independent myth, and patron of arts and crafts. His shrine was at Memphis, and, when this became a capital in the First Dynasty, Ptah's power rivaled that of Re at Heliopolis across the river.

From the beginning the king of Egypt was a god, the divine principle of rule upon earth. The earliest inscriptions call him Horus. At first perhaps only he was assured of happy eternal life, because he was a god. It is clear that lesser persons had some sort of continued life after death, because their graves were equipped with offerings for their maintenance, but this may have been shadowy and restricted, as it was with the Semites. However, the king was a god who did not die but who continued to rule in the next existence; he would therefore need his court and his officials and his servants over there. Thus his need of them could offer them eternal life in his service, in the same status they had achieved in life. From the First Dynasty we know of burials of kings, princesses, and nobles, where personal servants, with their tools of service, were buried at the same time as the master. This grisly custom soon died out in Egypt, although the juxtaposition of king's pyramid and nobles' tombs continued for several centuries. Through much of the Old Kingdom the mastaba tombs of the royalty and nobility clung closely to the pyramid of the king, asserting the retainers' hope of happy immortality through immediate relation to the ruler. Throughout Egyptian history the mortuary texts continued to assert that a proper burial was an "offering which the king gives," even though the individual himself might have undertaken the entire responsibility. Beginning in the Fifth Dynasty, there was a decentralizing tendency, and nobles began to seek their burials and their eternal happiness in their home districts. Although this shows that the former dependence upon the divine king was no longer necessary for immortality, the dogma continued to insist on devoted service to the ruler.

The Egyptian interest in life after death bulks large in our view, because their elaborate tombs have been preserved for us. Yet there was no morbid fear of death; on the contrary, there was a triumphant assertion of continued life. Tomb texts are almost arrogantly confident; tomb scenes are full of richness, gaiety, and even humor. From our first view *ca.* 3000 B.C. down to 1200 B.C., the prevailing psychology was: we Egyptians lead a full, abundant, and cherished life, and the gods will continue this richness after death. Only in the late period, after Egypt's glory had been threatened and life had become restricted, did the mortuary religion strike a more somber note, with paradise a release from this world or a reward for conformance and patience in this world.

The Egyptian faith that an abundant life might be eternal and that the future world reproduced the rich and rewarding aspects of this life offers a contrast to the dim and uncertain future life of the Babylonians and the Hebrews. The reason for this contrast is not clear, but must arise from security and assurance of good in Egypt. Usually the land was secure from major threat of invasion, and the normal Egyptian expectation was for warmth, adequate food, and a life with a small encouragement for man to better his status among men. To be sure, such a statement applies to kings and nobles, because the peasants and the slaves were inarticulate as far as we are concerned; they must have endured burdensome toil, with little prospect of release. But even the peasant on Egypt's rich fields could contrast himself favorably with the neighboring nomads, who had to seek a meager existence in the deserts or marginal lands. Even the peasant could feel that the gods had singularly blessed the Egyptians beyond other peoples and thus hope that his service to his master might be the means of gaining service in a future life and thus of denying obliteration through death.

The centrality of the god-king in the earlier Old Kingdom and the emphasis on his agency in procuring eternal happiness brought forth the pyramid age, in which the supreme energies of the state were concentrated on giving the ruler the mightiest and most enduring tomb possible. In a strictly productive sense, this work of building a monumental tomb was bad economy for the state. In a religious sense, the triumphant denial of death through an assertive and everlasting structure nourished the Egyptian's confidence in himself and in the destiny which the gods had wrought for him. This confidence contributed to Egypt's dominance in her early world.

The visible absolutism of earliest Egypt rests on the dogma that the king was a god. In contrast to Mesopotamia and the Hebrews, there could be no impersonal, written, and codified law, because the spoken word of the god-king was always available and always final. At first, rule was centered in the palace, the royal princes served as the highest ministers, and other members of the king's family filled as many offices as possible. From the Third Dynasty forward the bureaucracy was constructed and enlarged. The king's absolutism was diluted by the use of high officials who did not carry the divine blood and who had to exert personal authority at a distance from the palace. They continued to assure the king that their every act was in his divine service, but their authority continued to increase throughout the course of the later Old Kingdom, so that there was a progressive decentralization and a weakening of the effectiveness of the king.

From the beginning the king had been the god Horus. The Fifth Dynasty opened with a marked shift of emphasis. The king now became the "son of Re," from this time forward practically all the royal names which proclaimed the purposes of rule were constructed with the name of the sun-god Re, and sun-temples of Re were built near the royal pyramid and of relatively large size. Clearly the independence of the king had been limited by forcing upon him filial devotion to the sun-god. The priesthood at Heliopolis (On) must have emerged into political power, just as a millennium later the priesthood of Amon at Thebes was to become commandingly powerful.

Apart from the mortuary religion, we know little about temples and priests in the Old and Middle Kingdoms. Temples must have been modest, relative to the mighty structures which would appear in the New Kingdom. The priesthood was not yet a full-time service but was staffed from the high personnel of the state, nobles and officials, in conformance with the principle that a sacred state made no distinction between the secular and the ecclesiastical. Many of these lay priests served in rotating shifts.

Great resources of the state were, of course, employed to build the king's pyramid tomb and to give him mortuary service in perpetuity. The same diversion of resources and of time was available for the nobles. A man might live his life in house of mud brick, but his eternal home was a mastaba of stone, massively organized to last forever. Further, his survival depended in large measure upon eternal service on his behalf. Thus, as an "offering which the King gives," fields were set apart to provide income for goods and services. Barley and flax from these fields might be made into bread, beer, and linen for offering at the tomb, or they might be used to purchase other mortuary offerings and to secure the perpetual services of funerary priests, who would make these offerings and who would offer prayers for the dead. Such goods and services were in addition to the furnishings placed in the tomb at the time of burial and in addition to the elaborate funeral ceremony. The setting aside of large resources for the maintenance of the dead, carried on over several centuries, very seriously ate into the economy of Egypt. As long as the state was stable and prosperous, Egyptians could afford to pay this high price for the supreme boon of eternal life. In any period of breakdown, this disproportionate economy would become intolerable and would be swept aside to the advantage of the living.

Within the royal pyramids of the Fifth and Sixth Dynasties lengthy texts were inscribed, to promote and ensure the triumphant immortality of the god-king. These Pyramid Texts include a ritual for making offerings, magical charms to advance the king or to protect him from peril, hymns and prayers on his behalf, and fragments of mythology to identify him more securely with the other gods. Much of this was already very ancient, here written in permanent form for the first time. Every means was taken to guarantee the deceased king's welfare, from making him a humble servant of the sun-god to making him the ruthless conqueror of the world of the gods. The Pyramid Texts are a rich, if confusing, source of information on the royal mortuary beliefs and practices in the Old Kingdom.

A state in which the absolutism of the king was gradually diluted, which finally disintegrated into the feudal separatism and chaos of the first intermediate period, could not maintain the separate glory of the god-king. Already in the Old Kingdom the nobles had appropriated for themselves some of the funerary ceremonies of the kings; in the first intermediate period they seized also upon the Pyramid Texts, thereby making themselves gods after death. As this process was defined, each dead Egyptian might become the god Osiris, who had himself survived death. The Old Kingdom Pyramid Texts became the Middle Kingdom Coffin Texts, inscribed inside the wooden coffins of nobles and ladies. The New Kingdom versions of such texts were written on papyrus and are called the Book of the Dead.* This was no book in the sense of our Bible. Not only did each of these three stages present variants on old texts and completely new texts, but it is rare to find two MSS which have the same selection of "chapters" in the same reading. Out of the available religious and magical sources the priests selected and re-edited texts which they thought appropriate. Figs. EGY 20; WEI 13.

The opening up of divine immortality to Egyptian nobles has been called a democratization of the next world. Such a term has to be understood in the ancient Egyptian setting, without any modern concept of universal democracy. The nobles and high officials were affected, and this, in a society which had no fixed castes, might be theoretically universal. In practice the good man was the high-placed and highly regarded man, who alone could afford to purchase the elaborate services of mortuary religion. For the peasant and the slave, eternity was probably uncertain and dependent upon his master's need of him in the next world.

Parallel to the extension of paradise after the collapse of the Old Kingdom, there was a tendency toward wider good, both in the understanding of what is most highly regarded by the gods and in the extension of good to a wider number of persons. The formerly assumed values of position, wealth, and a heavy investment in the tomb and its services had broken down in the disorder of the first intermediate period. The kingship was divided among rival claimants and was no longer distinct from ordinary humanity. Rich had become poor, and poor had become rich. In the doubt and frustration of a time of disorder and social change, man looked for new answers to some of his old problems. There were despair and cynicism, there was an encouragement to mere earthly pleasure while ignoring the next world, and there was the longing for a saving messiah. One important answer lay in a search for social justice.

Throughout Egyptian history a word of highest quality was *ma'at,* which may be translated as "right" or "order" or "conformity," as "truth," as "justice," or sometimes as "righteousness." The Egyptian had no word which meant directly morally "good." *Ma'at* was the quality which man had to render to the king and which the king had to render to the gods. Sometimes this was simply the orderly seasons of the sun, moon, and inundation; sometimes it was the arbitrary order imposed by a centralized government; sometimes it was truth or veracity in speech. It was also just administration, and one epithet of the vizier was the "high priest of *ma'at.*"

When the prosperous order of the Old Kingdom went to ruins, the Egyptians sought for new values, and for *ca.* two hundred years they defined *ma'at* as social justice, the right of every man to the good things of life. Rich and poor alike had god-given rights to the use of the flood waters. The king had a weighty obligation to be sleeplessly vigilant on behalf of all his subjects. The poorest peasant had an innate right to impartial justice from the administrator. There were even a few brief claims that all men—i.e., all Egyptians—were equal in the sight of the creator god. The Middle Kingdom was a time of

Courtesy of the University Museum of the University of Pennsylvania

20. Egyptian papyrus; a section of the "Book of the Dead"

local sovereignty on the part of nobles, and the kings of the land found it to their advantage to combat this separatism by conscientious efforts toward the well-being of all Egyptians. The portraits of the period show the lines of this sense of duty engraved upon the faces of the king. This demand upon man for a life of social concern for his fellow man was reflected in the mortuary religion. Now the deceased had to stand before the gods, with the deeds of his life piled up as legal exhibits. If there was an excess of good, he would be admitted to eternal happiness.

It would be pleasing to assert that this change from material good to moral good was a gain which Egypt cherished and defended. But this insistence at the beginning of the Middle Kingdom that all men had equal rights and that the highest value was a life morally adjusted to men and gods was no longer firmly stated after the state again became prosperous. The conscientiousness of the kings had brought back wealth, power, and security. Worldly success as a recognized good came back again into the texts; concern for the little man faded; and magic and religion united to assure the orthodox worshiper that obedient conformity would win favor from the gods, including eternal life. Individual conscience was not so important as regularity within the system. To be sure, the gains were not entirely lost; the deceased continued to stand before the god Osiris and to deny in detail wrongdoing in his life. *Ma'at,* although essentially obedient acceptance of the system, continued to have a moral tone. But, after the early Middle Kingdom, later ages did not so clearly demand from man simple piety to the gods and humanity to fellow men.

In part, the retreat from equalitarianism and social justice was a product of the second intermediate period, when Egypt was invaded by Asiatics, the HYKSOS. Even after the Hyksos had been expelled and the New Kingdom set up, there was a sense of political insecurity; after 1700 B.C. there was always some threat to Egyptian sovereignty from foreigners. Under this sense of peril, the state could easily be organized in an authoritarian tone, with power and privilege concentrated in the hands of the ruling few. This ruling few included the more powerful priesthoods.

The Old Kingdom capital had been at Memphis in the pyramid area at the N. The Middle Kingdom rule had come from Thebes in the S. A god at Thebes was Amon, the "hidden one," an unseen and ever-present force. As Amon-Re he became the supreme national god and ultimately the imperial god. Important enterprises were started only after a favorable oracle from the god. Then, when the enterprise was successful, the god reaped his reward from a grateful king. Temples became larger, and priests became more prominent.

This process reached its climax in the New Kingdom, when Egyptian armies marched forth to conquer the world, under the sanction of the gods, returned with abundant booty, and thankfully enriched the temples with captive slaves and spoils. Then the priesthood became a full-time activity, and from 1400 B.C. on, the temples became colossal structures.

The three great priesthoods of the land came to be those of Re at Heliopolis (On), of Ptah at Memphis, and of Amon-Re at Thebes. In particular the high priest of Amon-Re of Karnak (Thebes) was a powerful official, with strong family ties into the civil bureaucracy, and a rival to the king in power. By 1200 B.C. the various temples of Egypt owned at least one eighth of the arable land and possibly as much as one tenth of the population, and the temple of Amon-Re held much more than half of this tremendous possession. In addition to the booty which came to Amon-Re as the result of his blessing foreign conquest, the god was a major beneficiary from the gold mines of Nubia, and the pharaoh made the god generous annual gifts.

In the Middle Kingdom the temple of Amon-Re at Karnak had been of modest dimensions. The great conquering pharaohs of the New Kingdom started it on its colossal career, until it became the soaring, sprawling complex which can be seen today. Thousands of serfs and captive slaves worked its great estates scattered throughout the land. In the late New Kingdom we read much more about the oracle of Amon-Re and how his divine sanction was necessary for every major activity of the state. Naturally this increase in wealth and power loomed as a threat to the kingship.

With the New Kingdom empire, two other rivals to the pharaoh appeared. The empire tried to hold lands as far S as the Fourth Cataract and as far N as the Euphrates River. Egypt became the prosperous focus of the world. The bureaucracy was enlarged and consolidated, and this civil service interlocked thoroughly with the priesthood for generation after generation, contributing the ruling personnel for Egypt from a few major families. The army could no longer be formed by a seasonal draft of civilians, since garrisons were now located in distant lands. The army became a standing force, and the commander of the army became a professional, who wielded the strongest police force of Egypt and thus could assume political power. The pharaoh, the priesthood, the civil service, and the army became overlapping rivals for the control of Egypt. In a time of great wealth and of imperial dominance the rewards of control were great.

b. Amarna reformation and reaction. Within a sacred state the tensions which have just been indicated were contributing forces toward a major break with the past, the so-called Amarna revolution. Among several other factors, the struggle for power was undoubtedly a cause of cleavage. The pharaoh, who in dogma was still the absolute god, saw his authority invaded by rival powers. The break was sharpest and most bitter between the heretic pharaoh AKH-EN-ATON and the older religion, particularly the priesthood of Amon. The civil service, which derived from the same families as the priesthood, stood on the conservative side with the older religion. The new force, the army, saw its advantage with the king.

However, the origins of the Amarna reformation are varied. So much has been written about the originality of the new movement, particularly its religion, that it must be stressed that all its elements were present in Egypt in some form before the time of the heretic king. This does not deny originality in the fresh ardor with which these elements were expressed. Politically the Amarna revolution was a reaction to recapture the former centrality of the king. In this vigorous combat, the exciting expressions in art and religion were not inventions but new assertions of already existing influences.

The far-flung empire was a century old. In art the excitation of the empire had already broken down the old rigidities, based upon the unemotional search for eternal life, and introduced a warm interest in the here and now, with more naturalism and a more flexible line for the human image. Some foreign influence is certain here, although the expression of Egypt's conquering vigor is an adequate explanation of the change. In language the old classical speech was already dead in everyday usage. It was only necessary to accept the currently spoken language as appropriate for purposes of the state and of religion. This was in line with Akh-en-Aton's emphasis on *ma'at,* which here was "truth" in the sense of naturalism or candor.

Akh-en-Aton's religion expressed the devotion to a single god, the Aton or sun-disk, as a life-giving power. The pharaoh referred to the Aton as the "sole god, like whom there is no other." This god was not restricted to Egypt, but was the universal nourisher of all mankind and all life everywhere, the creator and the sustainer. In this commitment to one god and in the violent break with the old religion, Akh-en-Aton had his followers hack out of the old inscriptions the name of the god Amon, frequently the names of other gods, and often the words "the gods" or "all the gods." For the king there was but one god. Fig. AKH 9.

Many of the elements of this new faith were old. Sun-worship in Egypt had existed from the beginnings. A worship of the Aton specifically as a god was two generations older than Akh-en-Aton. Syncretism, whereby two or more divine forces could be merged into one, was centuries old. Hymns addressing a deity as the "sole god," with both a flattering emphasis and an exclusive surrender on the part of the worshiper, had appeared centuries earlier. Universalism was a product of the century-old empire: when the Egyptians marched out to conquer and hold a larger world, they could no longer think of their gods as functional for Egypt alone, but they had to concede that the gods cherished other peoples also. Temples to Egyptian gods were built in Asia; such Semitic deities as Baal and Ashtoreth were worshiped in Egypt. It was only necessary for Akh-en-Aton to bring together some of these existing factors and to give them such emphasis that they seem to have been changed.

It is also clear that Akh-en-Aton made his break, changed his name, and moved his capital, while his father and coregent, Amen-hotep III, was still living. As far as we can see, the older king remained at Thebes and continued to serve the older system, including its polytheism. This is certainly a qualification to the violence of the break.

Thus *ca.* 1375 B.C. a young pharaoh changed his name from Amen-hotep (IV) to Akh-en-Aton, thus officially breaking with Amonism and embracing Atonism, moved his personal capital from Thebes to TELL EL-AMARNA, took a vow never to leave this new site or desert his new god, and gave himself up to new adventures in religion, art, literature, social organization, and town-planning. The temples of Amon and of other gods were bereft of annual royal gifts and of tribute from abroad; it is not clear whether the young king's fervor closed them completely, although this is to be inferred from his hacking gods' names out of inscriptions. The old governing families of the civil service and the priesthood were dropped, and administration was turned over to new persons, ardent followers of the new faith. Thus the heretic king tried to break the vested power of the old gods, who had become so great that they were remote from the people. In particular, he disavowed the god Amon, the "hidden one" in a mighty temple, and he worshiped the candid sun-disk out in the open air. This was *ma'at* or truth. Politically Akh-en-Aton reasserted his exclusive right to rule, over against the forces which had encroached upon this right.

Akh-en-Aton's beautiful hymn to the Aton gives the essence of the new faith. For all the world there was but one god, creator and sustainer of life, a god who cherished Egyptians and foreigners, plants and animals. Nighttime, when the sun-disk was absent, was like the "manner of death"; when the sun-disk arose again in the morning, all life rejoiced. The similarity of this hymn to the 104th psalm in thought and structure is very marked, even though it is impossible to assume a direct connection between the Egyptian and the Hebrew. Yet it must be stressed that Atonism was a fervent nature-worship and made no demand upon the worshiper beyond loving gratitude. There was little ethical content in the new faith. Atonism thus stands in striking contrast to Hebrew monotheism, with the latter's categorical demands upon man for an upright life.

Two gods were worshiped at Amarna. Akh-en-Aton and his queen, Nefert-iti, gave their sole adoration to the Aton. All of Akh-en-Aton's followers worshiped him as god-king. He became their soul source of good in this life, and, since the older mortuary gods had been eliminated, he was their sole reliance for good after death. It is true that there was a father-son relationship between the Aton and Akh-en-Aton, so that they might both be considered parts of the same godhead. But it must be emphasized that lesser people at Amarna did not practice Atonism; they only reverted to that fervent devotion to the god-king which had characterized Egypt in the earlier Old Kingdom. Atonism was certainly a very qualified monotheism.

Because Akh-en-Aton's exclusive adoration of one god was earlier than the monotheism ascribed to Moses, Atonistic monotheism has been claimed as the inspiration of the Hebrew faith. After all, Moses was educated as an Egyptian. This is a difficult problem, but a direct lineage seems almost impossible. The specific teaching of Atonism was on the high level of the pharaoh at the new capital in Middle Egypt. Even though we cannot date Moses precisely, the means whereby such a teaching could be transmitted are not clear. One assumes that Moses was at least a century later, after Atonism had long been proscribed as heretical, and was located hundreds of miles away to the N. Further, there is a real truth to the story that Moses fled from Egypt, discovered the true God in the wilderness, and returned to liberate his people from Egypt and all that was Egyptian. The new Hebrew faith was anti-Egyptian, and it was a cardinal principle that the Israelite God had defeated the pharaoh and pharaoh's reliance upon Egyptian gods. Disconnection, rather than connection, is clearly indicated.

If it is true that the factors of the Amarna faith had been present in Egypt before the time of Akh-en-Aton, it is also true that some of them persisted after his time: universalism and the tendency to simplify divinity down to a single god of adoration, humble gratitude, and a father-son relationship between god and man. When worship of the Aton became heresy, these factors, which had been present in Egypt with relation to other gods, were not cast out. Thus, if one desires to find connection between Mosaic religion and Egyptian religion, such ideas may have been current in N Egypt or in Egyptian temples in Asia at the time of Moses. However, it is also true that any cast of thought or expression borrowed from Egypt was thoroughly made over for the children of Israel, making an independent religion based on independent experience.

The Amarna revolution started with high enthusiasm, as an exciting assertion in all phases of life. It came to a tragic and dishonored end. Akh-en-Aton was a physical weakling and may have had an ailment which was progressively serious, while the whole movement depended upon his personal leadership. Since the troubles in the Asiatic empire were of little concern to the pharaoh, the Asiatic holdings fell away to the Hittites or to local princes. Within Egypt the loyalty of the provinces was probably withheld from the capital, so that taxes may have been in default. Compromise or surrender became inevitable. Akh-en-Aton took as his coregent a young son-in-law, Smenkhkere, and permitted this new king to return to Thebes, where he paid some homage to Amon. Akh-en-Aton was able to remain true to his vow never to leave Amarna. Time was running out, and *ca.* 1350 B.C. both Akh-en-Aton and Smenkhkere disappeared from the scene. Whether there was violence we do not know, but there is some evidence that burial had to be hasty and then was endangered by the enemies of the revolution.

A second son-in-law, Tut-ankh-Aton, made the full surrender. He made a formal disavowal of the Aton by changing his name to Tut-ankh-Amon, returned to Thebes, and paid the price of the victorious older gods by "doubling, tripling, and quadrupling" the property of the temples. There were brief reigns by Tut-ankh-Amon and Eye, an elderly member of the family, and then Hor-em-heb, a general of the army, took over the throne to restore order and confidence. The conservative forces had won, and Atonism became heresy. Later tradition dropped out the reigns of the four members of the Amarna family as illegitimate and pretended that General Hor-em-heb had succeeded Akhenaton's father, Amen-hotep III.

Egypt was never again the same. The old cohesive sense of high destiny and common purpose could not be recaptured. Sporadically the same struggle for power recurred among the same four contestants—the pharaoh, the priesthood, the civil service, and the army—and there were a few individual pharaohs of high ability; but, generally speaking, the pharaoh could not recapture his supreme authority. Increasingly he became the figurehead of the state and the captive of custom. The army wielded striking power and was more often the victor in the struggle than the priests or the bureaucrats. Out of army command emerged the Nineteenth, Twenty-first, and Twenty-second Dynasties.

It has been stated above that Atonism became heresy, but that aspects of the expression of the religion did continue. In other areas also, the Amarna break with the past had lasting effects. Art retained some of the lithe naturalism of the new movement and continued to tell specific stories about actual occurrences. Language and literature remained closer to reality, with writing permitted to use current forms and literature somewhat more secular. In religion itself, there were even some later hymns which have been called monotheistic, because god under several different names was addressed in the singular, as if various deities were all functional forms of a single god. Such hymns are monotheistic if the definition of this term is elastic enough to include them.

The powerful old gods who had withstood rebellion—Amon, Re, and Ptah—were now entrenched by victory. Their temples became larger, their estates became richer, and their priests became more powerful. This must have created new cleavages in the state. Like high officials, high gods were too busy to be bothered with small affairs. Only the powerful could seek out the powerful, so that ordinary men must have been cut off from access to the great gods. They would have to seek out gods who, like themselves, were not mighty and successful. This division of great and small gods and this clinging of little men to little gods were clear features of the later times.

c. Religion in late times. For two centuries the late New Kingdom tried to recapture an empire and reclaim Egypt's former glories and dominations. In the end it was unsuccessful. One might say that the gods of Egypt were too busy running their vast estates to take the field of battle. Or one might say that the gods of the Hittites and of the Sea Peoples were active in opposition. It is clear that the forces against Egypt were greater than before and that Egypt's answer was less the unison of religious patriotism and more the employment of paid professionals and foreign mercenaries. Egypt put up a bold front. Temples continued to be colossal and were inscribed with boastful claims of triumphant conquest and wide domination. Egyptian temples were erected in the African and Asiatic empires. Yet it was a losing struggle, and *ca.* 1150 B.C., Egypt withdrew from empire.

About the same time a succession of weak pharaohs began. They were unable to stem a tide of corruption in the Egyptian government and became the palace captives of the high officials and priests. Desperately hard times came upon the land. The proud spirit withered, and national ambition gave way to individual ambition.

After 1100 B.C., Egypt could not compete equally with Assyria or Babylonia or Persia or Macedonia or Rome as a world power. Internally she was normally divided, with mercantile states in the N and agricultural states in the S. When she temporarily achieved some semblance of union or dared to try for foreign conquest, it was with the help of hired mercenaries or with the backing of foreign powers. The former arrogant confidence and the old encouragement to individual or group initiative were gone. Increasingly the Egyptian became introspective and cautious; it was safer to cling blindly to careful conformance to ritual and regulation.

As early as the Nineteenth Dynasty a change appeared in the scenes of the nobles' tombs. In place of a vigorous and lusty emphasis upon the abundant things of this life, which would be richly extended into the next life, the scenes showed the mortuary services and charted the perils of the passage into the other world. The statement was no longer: this is a good life, and it will last forever. Now the emphasis had become: life itself is restricted, and the passage to the hereafter is not easy; only a rigorous conformance to the practices of the mortuary religion can win for man a continued life. The joy of living had disappeared, and it followed that the future itself had some uncertainty.

Personal religion also showed this new sobriety. Formerly a father had encouraged his son to a life of vigorous activity: be alert and well trained, and you will get ahead; the smart man can seize for himself the rewards of this world. Now abruptly the emphasis had become resignation to one's lot in life: entrust yourself to the arms of the god; he alone can remedy your woes and reward you for submissiveness. There was little room for individual initiative. The deities Fate and Fortune had become powerfully controlling. The good man was no longer the "knowing one"; he was now the "silent one."

This humble piety appeared particularly in two types of documents: dedicatory tablets set up by relatively modest people and the instructions which a father gave to his son. For the first time the Egyptian was aware of a sense of sin—not the ritualistic denial of wrongdoing, but a contrite admission of error. Little steles carried the confession that an individual had committed wrong and that the god had punished him; the god was right and just in this chastisement, and now the worshiper prayed to his god for mercy and healing. Success was for the god alone; man without god was doomed to failure. The normal state of man alone could only be wrongdoing, but the normal state of the god was to be merciful and to rescue man. This humble piety and the faith that the god was a punishing but loving father were, of course, most marked among poor people, but they were characteristic of the age, and even a high-placed official was at pains to insist that he was "truly silent"—i.e., humbly submissive.

The new obedience can be seen most clearly in a papyrus which gave the advice of the agricultural official Amen-em-Opet to his son. This must be dated after the tenth century B.C., possibly three centuries later. The essence of this instruction was that the "heated man" who strives for his own advantage is doomed to destruction, whereas the "silent man" is like a fruit tree growing in a garden. It is wrong to strive for riches and success; "poverty in the hand of the god is better than riches in a storehouse." He who is submissive upon earth will receive his reward in a contented hereafter: "How happy is he who reaches the next world, when he is safe in the hand of the god!" Sections of this text are extraordinarily like passages in the Hebrew book of Proverbs, and there is little doubt that the instruction of Amen-em-Opet is the original for Prov. 22:17-24:22.

If man might no longer be encouraged to individual initiative, religion offered him a sense of community in disciplined tasks. There were new emphases on exact ritual practice, on magic, and on oracles. There was now emerging that Egypt which Herodotus saw, when he described the Egyptians as the most religious of people because they were so scrupulous about specific ritual practices, such as ceremonial cleanliness. Formerly such temple symbols as the sacred animal had been simply one out of several means given to a god so that he might make his appearance. Now the sacred animal became the center of an elaborate cult, so detailed and so devoted that one may now speak of animal-worship. A sacred bull had formal processions and a costly expenditure for his divine burial. Cats and apes and crocodiles were mummified to maintain the sacred body. Cats came to dominate the city of Bubastis, where a cat-goddess had her temple, and dead apes and ibises were sent long distances to be given a reverent burial at Hermopolis. This was a shift from the former belief that a god may be ever present as he wishes and that man needs only a few focal points for the god's activity to the belief that the symbol provided for the god's presence was the god himself.

Egypt had always had recourse to magic, but magical texts and apparatus began to increase in the late New Kingdom. Thereafter the paraphernalia for the magical securing of advantage and warding off of evil became even more abundant. A man could purchase a papyrus or an elaborately carved image to protect himself from the bite of a snake or a scorpion, or he could seek out a magician who would chant an incantation over waxen images to place a hex on a man's enemies.

There was also an added emphasis upon guidance by the oracle of a god. When the sacred statue was carried in procession, a man might halt the god and place a yes-or-no question in the presence of witnesses; he expected to be answered by a visible sign from the god. The state itself posed to the god formal questions about the succession to the throne, the pardoning of political exiles, or even the ownership of a well. It was entirely consistent with Egyptian beliefs that Alexander the Great made a dangerous pilgrimage through the W desert to consult the oracle of Ammon at the oasis of Siwah.

Because of this ritualistic piety there was a dual process at work. The political capitals of Egypt moved easily to new cities for temporal or commercial advantage, but some of the older cities increased in sacred importance as seats of a god who might give oracular direction. Such a holy city was Thebes in the S. In late times the political capital was normally in the N, but Thebes was the home of the revered god Amon. The people of Thebes felt their importance, and the city became a focus of a resentfully rebellious spirit. The pharaohs had to control this separatism by placing a reliable agent in Thebes. A sister or daughter of the reigning pharaoh would be appointed the divine votaress of Amon, would speak on behalf of the king and also the god, and thus become the effective ruler of the Theban area.

The syncretistic process which had always had play in Egypt also received continued emphasis, so that it was possible to see identifications of different gods with one another. In contrast to the rigidity of ritual performance, there was a broad flexibility of divine being. The priests of Egypt might be solemnly mysterious about what they did, but they were eagerly accommodating in explaining the broad interests of their gods. Thus it was easy for the Greeks to identify Amon with their Zeus, Thoth with their Hermes, or Hat-Hor with their Aphrodite. Further, the new introspectiveness and the new emphasis upon ritual performance without any explanation for the reasons for performance meant that Egyptian religion became a "mystery," and thus it had its exotic and inexplicable appeal to Greeks and Romans as something which might have mystic power simply because it was strange.

To apply the term "fossilization" to Egyptian religion of late times may be too harsh. The nature of divine being continued to be flexible, sometimes appearing to be wildly polytheistic and sometimes convergently monotheistic. Egypt continued to be hospitable to deities and worshipers from other religions. E.g., Jewish soldiers at Elephantine might have their synagogue, or political exiles from Jerusalem might build a temple to Yahweh at Leontopolis in the Delta. However, a thousand years of political impotence and domination by foreigners did dry up Egyptian spiritual strength. Emphasis shifted from faith to works.

The Egyptians were going through hieratic gestures to avoid making personal decisions themselves and in the hope that the gods would direct destiny in every respect. Life no longer had its surplus of riches at home or from abroad or its clear sense of superiority over other peoples. When finally Roman taxation was so extreme as to set a penalty upon abundance within Egypt itself, the final attachment to the old faith was broken. Then Christianity entered with the message that the next world would be a release from and a reward for the acceptance of privation in this world, and the Egyptians went over to Christianity with ardor.

4. Egyptology. Biblical studies, ancient history, and field archaeology have been separate parts of a larger whole. The techniques of excavation and of the analysis of pottery were transferred from Egypt to Palestine *ca.* 1890, and Egyptology for a long time profited from a central curiosity about Egypt in the biblical account. It is appropriate, therefore, to give a brief statement about the standards, achievements, and shortcomings of Egyptology.

The study of ancient Egypt proceeds from history or the analysis of texts and from archaeology or the analysis of physical materials. Despite the persistence of the Coptic language in the liturgy of the Egyptian Christian church, the earlier stages of the Egyptian language and the understanding of the hieroglyphic, hieratic, and demotic writings had been lost to knowledge after the introduction of Christianity into the land. Hieroglyphic two centuries ago was assumed to be an involved, occult writing. There was little interest in field excavation before Schliemann's dramatic results at Troy. Before the nineteenth century, the Bible and the classical writings contributed all that we knew about ancient Egypt.

When Napoleon Bonaparte led a military expedition to Egypt in 1798, he brought with him a staff of historians and scientists. Their observations and recordings reopened an interest in ancient Egypt. Among the discoveries was the Rosetta Stone, containing the same text in Greek and in two Egyptian writings. This was to prove the critical element in Champollion's decipherment of hieroglyphic in 1822. Meanwhile, the opening up of Egypt to Western enterprise greatly enriched public and private museums in Europe with the products of Egyptian art and literature. In the first half of the nineteenth century industrious copying expeditions brought back to Europe a wealth of scenes and texts for scholarship to study. The materials were available so that Egypt might begin to tell her own independent story. As yet there was only looting rather than excavation, philology was only in its undisciplined infancy, and history was written chiefly in biblical and classical terms.

In 1850 a Frenchman, Auguste Mariette, began in Egypt a recorded series of clearances of major monuments and became the dominant figure in the land for thirty years, thus setting a pattern of Western control of Egyptian antiquities which lasted many decades. In the psychology of the time, the work continued to be interested in show pieces and in biblical connections, rather than in an Egyptian process itself.

In the 1880's three figures appeared who changed the study of ancient Egypt to a discipline of higher standards. The young Frenchman, Gaston Maspero, came to direct the antiquities service for a full generation. He was a historian of genius and was able to use the native Egyptian source materials to full advantage. A young German, Adolf Erman, brought order and recognized rules to the study of the ancient Egyptian language in its various periods. A young Englishman, Flinders Petrie, revolutionized field archaeology, not only for Egypt but also for Palestine and Mesopotamia, by his insistence upon respect for every bit of the excavated evidence and upon accurate recording and publication. Petrie made a neglected material, ordinary pottery, the critically decisive factor for excavations which were defective in inscriptions. Archaeology thus could become a science of respected standards. Petrie continued over an extraordinary career to excavate many of the richest sites in Egypt, Sinai, and Palestine. No other single figure has so richly contributed to our knowledge of the physical remains from Egypt or the sequence of cultures.

An inevitable result of the abundance of new material and new insights was that the focus of interest shifted from Egypt's connections with the Hebrews, the Greeks, and the Romans to the process of Egyptian culture in itself. Work in Egypt had produced regrettably little evidence to answer very specific questions about biblical relations. It is true that in recent years the balance has shifted a little: now excavations in Palestine or Phoenicia produce a good measure of evidence upon Egyptian influence abroad.

Ca. the beginning of the twentieth century Americans entered the scene and contributed two notable figures. George A. Reisner of Harvard advanced Petrie's techniques to new standards of precision and excavated with great success in the Sudan and in the pyramid area. James H. Breasted of the University of Chicago became America's most widely recognized ancient historian and produced books on Egyptian texts, history, and religion which still carry great weight.

It is impossible to claim that the ancient Egyptian language is as well known as Hebrew or Greek. Nor does excavation produce the same detailed analysis in a larger setting that it can achieve in Greek or Roman archaeology. Egyptology, however, has reached a firm understanding of careful methodology, has blocked in with success most of the succeeding ages of Egyptian history, and is now able to present a consistent and significant story.

Bibliography. J. H. Breasted, *A History of Egypt* (1905); *Development of Religion and Thought in Ancient Egypt* (1912). *Cambridge Ancient History,* vols. I-IX (1923-32). S. R. K. Glanville, ed., *The Legacy of Egypt* (1942). H. Frankfort, *Ancient Egyptian Religion* (1948). H. Frankfort *et al., The Intellectual Adventure of Ancient Man,* which was abridged by Penguin Books as *Before Philosophy* (1949). J. A. Wilson, *The Burden of Egypt* (1951), which is in a paperback ed., *The Culture of Ancient Egypt.* J. Černý, *Ancient Egyptian Religion* (1952). J. B. Pritchard, ed., *ANEP* (1954); *ANET* (2nd ed., 1955). G. Steindorff and K. C. Seele, *When Egypt Ruled the East* (2nd ed., 1957).

J. A. WILSON

EGYPT, BROOK OF [נחל מצרים; *in* Ezek. 47:19; 48:28 נחלה]; KJV RIVER *or* STREAM (Isa. 27:12) OF EGYPT. A stream marking the traditional SW boundary of Canaan (Num. 34:5; I Kings 8:65; II Kings 24:7; II Chr. 7:8; Isa. 27:12; Ezek. 47:19; 48:28) and of the tribe of Judah (Josh. 15:4, 47). It is paired with the "entrance of Hamath" (*see* HAMATH, ENTRANCE OF) as the other terminus, except in Isa. 27:12, where the N boundary is the Euphrates.

The Brook of Egypt is identified with the Wadi el-'Arish, which has its origin in the middle of the Sinai Peninsula and flows into the Mediterranean midway between Gaza and Pelusium. During the rainy season it is a rushing stream, into which the waters of numerous tributaries drain in its course to the sea; but in summer it dwindles to a dry bed. The Arabic name is derived from the village el-'Arish, located near its mouth.

In other passages the S boundary of the ideal territory of Israel is the "river of Egypt" (Gen. 15:18; cf. Jth. 1:9; *see* EGYPT, RIVER OF), the SHIHOR (Josh. 13:3; I Chr. 13:5), or the Brook of the Arabah (Amos 6:14; *see* ARABAH, BROOK OF). Some or all of these may possibly be designations for the Wadi el-'Arish.

The Assyrian records of Sargon I and Sennacherib refer several times to the Brook of Egypt (*naḥal* [*mat*]*Muṣri*), once with the added remark "and there is no river," evidently to distinguish it from the Nile (*ANET* 286, 290, 292).

Bibliography. E. H. Palmer, *The Desert of the Exodus* (1872), p. 233; A. Musil, *Arabia Petraea* (1907), vol. II, pt. 1, pp. 229 ff; A. Alt, *ZDPV*, LXVII (1945), 130 ff. J. L. MIHELIC

EGYPT, RIVER OF. 1. נהר מצרים. The S boundary of the territory promised to Abram's descendants in Gen. 15:18. Since the word נהר means a "large river," the reference must be to the Nile, but some would emend to נחל, "brook" (*see* EGYPT, BROOK OF). The phrase is used also in Jth. 1:9.

2. KJV form of "brook of Egypt." *See* EGYPT, BROOK OF. J. L. MIHELIC

EGYPTIAN, THE ē jĭp'shən [ὁ Αἰγύπτιος] (Acts 21:38). A person with whom Paul is said to have been mistakenly identified. The reference raises two questions: (*a*) Who was he? (*b*) What is Luke's intent in introducing the reference to him?

Since Luke nowhere else mentions the Egyptian, Luke's reply to the first question is simply that (*a*) he did not speak Greek, and was therefore an uncivilized barbarian, and that (*b*) as leader of the ASSYRIANS he had "recently" led four thousand of them in rebellion out into the desert. He is described from the standpoint of the tribune—namely, as a barbarian rebel, a disturber of the peace on the edge of the Empire. That a religious element was thought to be involved in this revolt may be implicit in the word "assassins"; in the motif of the desert, where it was commonly supposed the Messiah would appear; and analogously in the fact that Paul was involved in a religious dispute, although Luke does not make this explicit.

Interestingly enough, Josephus mentions an Egyptian, strikingly similar and likewise unnamed, in both War II.xiii.3-5 and Antiq. XX.viii.6 (written fifteen years later). In War II.xiii.3 the assassins (sicarii) are described as dagger men running wild in Jerusalem, murdering whom they will, even Jonathan the high priest. However, they are not associated with the desert. Then in II.xiii.4 "another body" of "more wicked" men laid waste the city. They pretended to divine inspiration and induced the multitudes to follow them into the wilderness, "pretending that God would there show them the signals of liberty." But Felix, anticipating a revolt, sent horsemen and footmen, "who destroyed a great number of them."

In War II.xiii.5 follows the Egyptian, described as a false prophet and as the most mischievous of all, "for he was a cheat, and pretended to be a prophet also." He led thirty thousand men from the wilderness to the Mount of Olives, hoping to enter Jerusalem by force, overwhelm the Roman garrison, and subdue the people. Again, Felix took the initiative and with his Roman soldiers assisted by the people, put the Egyptian to flight, destroyed or took alive most of the rest, and dispersed the others into hiding.

In describing the same events in Antiq. XX.viii, Josephus describes the same rebels as robbers, impostors, and deceivers; he does not here use the word "assassins." Contrary to War II.xiii.3-4, here it is the dagger men who persuaded the multitude to follow them into the wilderness to behold signs and wonders. Here, Felix "brought them back, and then punished them." In the *Antiquities* the man from Egypt came to Jerusalem. Nothing is said about the wilderness. Rather, he persuaded the "multitude of the common people" to go with him to the Mount of Olives. There he promised to show them how at his command the walls of Jerusalem would fall down and they could enter the city unhindered. Again, Felix came "with a great number of horsemen and footmen." He killed four hundred of them and took two hundred alive. "But the Egyptian himself escaped."

The three accounts, the brief statement of Acts 21:38 and the two longer ones of Josephus, obviously refer to the same Egyptian and at least to the same sort of event. All three mention the dagger men, either in connection with the Egyptian or in the context, the wilderness motif, and the revolt. And all affirm or imply that the Egyptian escaped. Yet the details vary greatly and cannot be harmonized. If Luke's four thousand cannot be harmonized with either the thirty thousand of the *War* or the four hundred killed and two hundred captured according to the *Antiquities*, neither can Josephus' two sets of numbers be made to fit each other. The four hundred or two hundred of the *Antiquities* are scarcely appropriate to the statement in the *War* to the effect that Felix destroyed or took alive most of the thirty thousand. In any case, all such numbers are likely to be fictitious. Luke's estimate of four thousand (one hundred times forty) may be meant simply to indicate a very large number.

The accounts in Josephus—and, indeed, historical probability—seem to require that the Egyptian be a Jew or at least a proselyte. Otherwise how could a non-Jew have led a Jewish rebellion? Critical as Josephus was of the rebellion, he can hardly have intended to suggest that the Jews stooped to uncovenanted leadership to win their liberty. Yet Paul's reply (Acts 21:39): "I am a Jew," seems to imply that the Egyptian was not.

Further, Josephus' description of the Egyptian as a prophet-pretender, as claiming to be an instrument of God to overthrow Rome, seems appropriate only to a Jew. And if the wilderness-assassins-Mount of Olives motifs do not have messianic connotations, they surely do have religious-political ones. This argues for the Jewishness of the Egyptian.

Probably both Luke and Josephus assumed that an "Egyptian" rebel leader and his "assassin" followers in and about Jerusalem would not have Greek as their common language, even if Greek was widely known in the great cities of Roman Egypt; and that this would be true whether or not the Egyptian was an Alexandrian Jew.

In answer to the second question, the intent of Luke in introducing the Egyptian into the narrative is to show that (*a*) Paul, who speaks excellent Greek, is a civilized citizen of the Roman Empire; (*b*) the tribune, who stands for Roman officialdom, proposes the identification of Paul with a barbarian anti-Roman rebel only to drop the charge, and by implication to vindicate Paul's loyalty to Rome; (*c*) Paul, being a city-man, should not be confused with the false prophets and false Christ of Matt. 24:24-26, who say: "Lo, he is in the wilderness"—i.e., with the political messianists; and (*d*) since Paul is an authentic Jew, addressing the people in the "Hebrew language" (Acts 21:40), and has been appointed by the "God of our fathers" to know his will (22:14), he is entitled to all the rights and privileges of Judaism as a legally recognized religion in the Empire.

Bibliography. F. J. Foakes-Jackson and K. Lake, *The Beginnings of Christianity*, I (1920), 356, 422-24; II (1922), 357; IV (1933), 276-77. E. Haenchen, *Die Apostelgeschichte* (1956), pp. 556-58. F. D. Gealy

EGYPTIAN VERSIONS. *See* Versions, Ancient, § 5.

EGYPTIANS, GOSPEL ACCORDING TO THE. A Greek gospel current in Egypt during the second century, with distinct doctrinal emphases. Clement refers to it at least six times, but all his quotations seem to be of one passage in which, in good Gnostic fashion, Jesus is engaged in a dialogue with Salome with regard to the propriety of marriage. In answer to her question: "How long shall death prevail?" (*Miscellanies* III.6.45) his answer is in essence: "So long as women bear children." But in reply to her further observation: "I have done well, then, in not bearing children," Jesus replies: "Every plant eat thou, but that which hath bitterness eat not" (III.9.66). Again, in referring to those who "set themselves against God's creation because of continence," Clement cites this gospel as carrying the word of Jesus: "I came to destroy the works of the female" (III.9.63). In another apparent reference to the same section he cites Cassian's quotation: "When Salome inquired when the things concerning which she asked should be known, the Lord said, 'When you have trampled on the garment of shame, and when the two become one and the male with the female is neither male nor female" (III.13.92), and comments: "In the first place we have not this saying in the four gospels which have been delivered to us, but in that according to the Egyptians."

A distinctly similar quotation is made in II Clem. 12.2: "For when the Lord himself was asked by some one when his kingdom would come, he said, 'When the two shall be one, and the outside as the inside, and the male with the female neither male nor female.' " In this writing the source is not mentioned, and the author makes the quotation without apology or qualification. A similar logion is found in the third-century Oxyrhynchus fragment (P 645): "His disciples say unto him, 'When wilt thou be manifest to us, and when shall we see thee?' He saith, 'When ye shall be stripped and not be ashamed.' "

Whether the Gospel According to the Egyptians is to be seen as the source from which these latter two quotations in paraphrase are taken, or whether they come from a parallel source, is debatable. The reference to Gen. 2:25 is especially clear in the form of the quotation in the Oxyrhynchus saying. If this particular passage is a fair sample, the Encratite tone of this apocryphon would not appear any marked advance beyond the reply of Jesus to the gibe of the Sadducees (Mark 12:25).

In his first homily on Luke, Origen names this gospel as one of those produced by men who, rashly and without the needful gifts of grace possessed by the writers of the four canonical gospels, attempted to produce gospels of their own. Hippolytus (*Heresies* V.7) remarks that the Naassenes support their doctrine of the "changes of the soul" by this work. Epiphanius (Her. LXII.2) reports its use by the Sabellians in their claim that the Father, Son, and Holy Spirit are one. The references are far too scanty to provide any very clear picture of its content or of its degree of variance from orthodox doctrine.

That the writing bearing the title *Book of the Great Invisible Spirit or Gospel of the Egyptians*, discovered at Chenoboskion in 1946 (*see* Apocrypha, NT), has any direct relation to this second-century apocryphon, would seem most improbable. M. S. Enslin

EHI ē′hī [אחי]. Listed as a son of Benjamin (Gen. 46:21); but the word is probably an erroneous fragment for Ahiram.

EHUD ē′hŭd [אהוד, אחוד (I Chr. 8:6)]. **1.** A left-handed hero, son of Gera ("Abihud," a personal name in I Chr. 8:3, may be an error for "father of Ehud"), and great-grandson of Benjamin. He delivered his countrymen from an eighteen-year Moabite oppression by treacherously assassinating King Eglon and cutting off the escape of the Moabite army of occupation, thus bringing "rest" to Israel for two generations (Judg. 3:12–4:1). *See* Eglon 1.

Some scholars see in the narrative two interwoven accounts (Judg. 3:17*a* logically follows vs. 15*b*, and vss. 18-19 seem an intrusion between 17*b* and 20). Whether or not the story is a unity, there is a genuine ancient folklore ring about the clever ruse by which Ehud repulsed Moab. Having publicly paid the accustomed tribute to the Moabite king and returned homeward to the Gilgal oracle, he recrossed the Jordan, secured private audience with the king, and left-handedly plunged his specially prepared thirteen-inch sword completely into the unsuspecting king's body. When Eglon's servants found the reason for which the private chamber was locked, Ehud was marshaling W Jordan Israelite troops to prevent ten thousand able-bodied Moabite soldiers from fleeing homeward across the Jordan.

While Ehud is not termed a judge, that he was regarded as a God-inspired deliverer is indicated, not only by the Deuteronomic introduction and conclusion to the story (Judg. 3:12-15*a*, 28-30; 4:1), but also by the probable significance of his association with the oracle and landmark, "sculptured stones," near Gilgal (vss. 19, 26).

2. Son of Bilhan, and great-grandson of Benjamin (I Chr. 7:10), or more likely of Zebulun. Apparently this genealogy was originally that of Zebulun (Benjamin's is I Chr. 8), but on account of an early error of "Benjamin" for "Zebulun" in 7:6, Benjaminite names have been introduced, including a brother of Ehud named Benjamin.

Bibliography. E. L. Curtis, *Chronicles,* ICC (1910), pp. 144-49, 156-59; L. Desnoyers, *Histoire du peuple hébreu* (1922), I, 133-37; T. J. Meek, "Some Emendations in the OT," *JBL,* XLVIII (1929), 163-64; E. G. Kraeling, "Difficulties in the Story of Ehud," *JBL,* LIV (1935), 205-10; C. A. Simpson, *Composition of the Book of Judges* (1957), pp. 9-12, 93, 107-8, 122.

C. F. KRAFT

EKER ē'kər [עקר, offspring(?)] (I Chr. 2:27). Part of the postexilic clan of JERAHMEEL 1.

Bibliography. M. Noth, *Die israelitischen Personennamen* (1928), p. 232.

EKREBEL. KJV form of ACRABA.

EKRON ĕk'rən [עקרון, barren place(?) *or* fertile place(?); Egyp. *'Angrun;* Akkad. *Amqarruna*]; PEOPLE OF (THOSE OF) EKRON, KJV EKRONITES [עקרנים, עקרוני]; Apoc. ACCARON ăk'ə rŏn ['Ακκαρών]. The northernmost of the five principal cities (pentapolis) of the Philistines (Josh. 13:3), *ca.* nine miles E of the Mediterranean, near the beginning of the Valley of Sorek leading to Jerusalem. Though not mentioned in the prebiblical Egyptian records, it was probably an old Canaanite town like other members of the pentapolis (note the Semitic character of the name and the reference to Canaanite territory in Josh. 13:3; cf. Jos. Antiq. V.iii.1). It was assigned to Judah (Josh. 15:11, 45-46) or to Dan (19:43), before that tribe migrated. There is a tradition that Judah captured it with other parts of Philistia (Judg. 1:18), but when it next appears, it is in the hands of the Philistines and the captured ark is brought there from Gath (I Sam. 5:10). The ark proved troublesome and was returned to the Israelites at Beth-shemesh (5:11-12; 6:9-18). The tradition that Ekron and Gath fell to Israel in the time of Samuel (7:14) is hardly correct, for the Philistines were able to retreat to these two places after defeat (17:52).

Ekron next appears in an inscribed list of places captured by SHISHAK in his invasion of *ca.* 918 B.C. (I Kings 14:25). Then we have the rather amazing information that Ahaziah, son of Ahab and king of Israel (*ca.* 850-849), being ill, preferred to consult BAAL-ZEBUB, the deity of Ekron, rather than the God of Israel (II Kings 1:2-16). Apparently the religion of Ekron was a form of Baalism, and was making inroads in Israel. Elijah denounced Ahaziah for seeking an oracle from Baal-zebub. Several later prophets denounced Ekron and her sister cities (Jer. 25:20; Amos 1:8; Zeph. 2:4; Zech. 9:5, 7).

From the inscriptions of SENNACHERIB we learn that Ekron played a part in the campaign of that king against rebellious Hezekiah of Judah (701 B.C.). Padi, king of Ekron, who was loyal to Assyria, had been seized by certain elements in his city and handed over to Hezekiah for imprisonment. Sennacherib took Ekron, although it had help from Egypt, and put the rebels to death. He then forced Hezekiah to release Padi, restoring the latter to control in Ekron. Padi also received territory taken from Judah. His successor, Ikausu, was not so fortunate, being laid under tribute, along with Manasseh of Judah, by both Esarhaddon and Ashurbanipal in their great campaigns against Syria and Egypt.

Apart from the prophetic passages (*see above*), the next information on Ekron is found in the Apoc. (I Macc. 10:89), where it is related that Alexander Balas gave the city to Jonathan Maccabeus as a reward for the latter's loyalty. In the fourth century A.D. it still had a Jewish population (Euseb. Onom. "Akkaron"). It is mentioned in connection with a march of Baldwin I during the Crusades (*ca.* A.D. 1100) and in a few other medieval sources, after which it drops from view.

Archaeologists are somewhat in disagreement with regard to the exact identification of the site, though there is no question about the general location. Two places are suggested: 'Aqir, bearing a semblance of the ancient name; and Qatra, three miles to the S. If Qatra is correct, the name has shifted, as has happened in a number of other places. More recently Khirbet el-Muqanna', farther to the S, has been suggested.

Bibliography. E. Robinson, *Biblical Researches in Palestine,* II (3rd ed., 1867), 226-29, the original identification with 'Aqir, useful references to medieval sources. E. Klostermann, *Das Onomastikon der Biblischen Ortsnamen,* Die gr. chr. Schriftsteller d. erst. drei Jahrhunderte, Eusebius Werke, vol. III, no. 1 (1904), pp. 22-23. W. F. Albright, "The Sites of Ekron, Gath, and Libnah," *AASOR,* II-III (1923), 1-7, strongly rejects 'Aqir, espouses Qatra. G. Beyer, "Ekron," *ZDPV,* LIV (1931), 159-70. A. Alt and G. von Rad, *Palästinajahrbuch,* XXIX (1933), 13, 32-41. J. Simons, *Handbook . . . of Egyptian Topographical Lists* (1937), pp. 186, 202. J. B. Pritchard, ed., *ANET* (2nd ed., 1955), pp. 287-88, 291, 294. G. Naveh, "Khirbet al-Muqanna'—Ekron," *IEJ,* VIII (1958), 87-100, 165-70.

W. F. STINESPRING

EL ĕl [אל]. The basic Semitic word for "God," probably derived from a root meaning "power." In ancient sources it could designate any supernatural power, and was applied especially to the high god El, father of all gods and lord of heaven and storm. *See also* GOD, NAMES OF, § C1.

B. W. ANDERSON

ELA ē'lə [אלא] (I Kings 4:18); KJV ELAH. The father of Shimei, who was the commissariat officer of Solomon in Benjamin.

ELADAH. KJV form of ELEADAH.

ELAH ē'lə [אלה, some kind of large tree, oak(?)]. **1.** A chief of EDOM (Gen. 36:41; I Chr. 1:52). The reference, however, is probably to a place rather than to a person. *See* ELATH.

2. King of Israel *ca.* 886-885 B.C.; son of BAASHA (I Kings 16:6, 8, 13-14; cf. Jos. Antiq. VIII.xii.4). Elah was killed by Zimri in the revolt that ultimately brought the Dynasty of OMRI to the throne.

3. The father of Hoshea, the last of the kings of Israel (II Kings 15:30; 17:1; 18:1, 9).

4. A family of the clan of CALEB (I Chr. 4:15). It may be that, as in 1 *above,* the reference is to a place (Elath?) rather than to a person.

5. A Benjaminite family dwelling in Jerusalem in postexilic times (I Chr. 9:8; missing from the parallel list in Neh. 11).

Bibliography. M. Noth, *Die israelitischen Personennamen* (1928), pp. 38, 90.

H. H. GUTHRIE, JR.

ELAH, VALLEY OF [עמק אלה, valley of the terebinth]. A valley in which Saul and the Israelites encamped prior to the battle with the Philistines which was won by Israel when David killed the Philistine champion, Goliath (I Sam. 17:2, 19; 21:9).

Courtesy of the Israel Office of Information, New York

21. The Valley of Elah

It is identified with the fertile, well-watered Wadi es-Sant ("Valley of the Acacia"), fourteen or fifteen miles W-SW of Bethlehem. The passage into the valley was protected by the fortress of AZEKAH (Tell ez-Zakariyeh), between which and Soco the Philistine forces pitched camp.

Fig. ELA 21; Pl. XII*a*. V. R. GOLD

ELAM ē'ləm [עֵילָם; Akkad. *elamtu,* highland]. **1.** A son of Shem (Gen. 10:22; I Chr. 1:17), and the eponymous ancestor of the Elamites. *See* ELAM (COUNTRY).

2. A Korahite in the time of David (I Chr. 26:3).

3. A priest at the dedication of the walls of Jerusalem in the time of Nehemiah (Neh. 12:42).

4. A descendant of Benjamin (I Chr. 8:24), probably related to 5 *below* (cf. I Chr. 8:24; Ezra 8:7).

5. The head of a family that returned to Palestine after the Exile (Ezra 2:7; Neh. 7:12; I Esd. 5:12). According to Ezra 2:31 (=Neh. 7:34), the family of "another Elam" returned too; but since both families numbered 1,254, they are possibly identical. A member of this family, Jeshaiah son of Athaliah, returned with Ezra (Ezra 8:7). Another, Shecaniah, urged Ezra to act against those who had married foreigners (Ezra 10:2), and six of its members separated from foreign wives (vs. 26). Elam is also said to have sealed Ezra's covenant (Neh. 10:14—H 10:15).

M. NEWMAN

ELAM (COUNTRY) [Heb.-Aram. עֵילָם; Elam. *haltamti;* Akkad. *elamtu;* 'Ελυμαΐς (*cf.* I Macc. 6:1; *see* ELYMAIS); Old Pers. *(h)ūja, (h)ūvja;* Middle Pers. *hužž;* Modern Pers. *Khuz(istan)*]; ELAMITES —īts. An area covering the territory of the Zagros Mountain range and of modern Luristan and Khuzistan; the capital was SUSA.

Gen. 10:22 lists Elam (עילם) as one of the children of Shem, together with Asshur, Arpachshad, Lud, and Aram; and Ezra 4:9 mentions the "men of Susa" (שושנכיא) and the Elamites (עלמיא) among the companions of Rehum and Shimshai. In Jer. 49:34-39 the destruction of Elam is foreseen (see also Isa. 21: 2). The Elamites ('Ελαμεῖται) are mentioned along with Parthians, Medes, and others among those present in Jerusalem on the day of Pentecost (Acts 2:9).

1. History. Ever since its earliest beginnings the history of Elam, a state occupying the slopes of the Iranian Plateau toward the lower Tigris Valley, has followed the pattern of alternating periods of invasions into that valley, resulting in more or less permanent possession of its regions and of temporary conquest of parts or all of its territory by Mesopotamian rulers. That long history, known through Mesopotamian as well as documents in the Elamite language (*see below*), most of which were recovered in Susa, may be conveniently arranged in three major periods: (*a*) earliest times to 1800; (*b*) 1800-1100; (*c*) 1100-645.

a. First period. Urban communities and settlements existed as early as the end of the fourth millennium. Contact between Sumer and Elam in the "heroic age" of Sumer is attested by the statement that En-men-barage-si, the twenty-first ruler of the Dynasty of Kish, "carried away as spoil the 'weapon' of Elam" (*ANET* 265). In their turn the Elamites may have invaded Babylonia during the "reigns" of Lugalbanda and Dumuzi, presumably kings of the First Dynasty of Uruk. Tradition has it that Eannatum, king of Lagash and Kish, conducted a successful campaign against Elam (after 2400). Sargon of Akkad (*ca.* 2150), then, conquered Elam, which is said to be "standing (in obedience) before Sargon, king of the country" (*ANET* 267). Judging from the statement: "From Elam came the Elamite(s), from Susa the Susian(s)" (*ANET* 268), for the purpose of lending assistance with the construction of a temple, it seems as if Gudea of Lagash wielded great influence in Elam. Shulgi, second king of the Third Dynasty of Ur (before 2000), erected a temple in Susa for Inshushinak, the god of that city. Ibbi-Sin, the last king of the same dynasty, was made prisoner by the Elamites. The destruction of Ur by the Elamites and Subarians is deplored in a lamentation text from *ca.* the middle of the second millennium (*ANET* 455-63).

b. Second period. In the first centuries of this period Elam was governed by a long series of *sukkalmah,* indigenous rulers who were considered the representatives of Inshushinak, the god of Susa. *Ca.* 1770 its power was apparently strong enough to install Elamite rulers (Warad-Sin, Rim-Sin) in Larsa for a period of some sixty years. By the end of the eighteenth century Hammurabi put a temporary end to Elam's expansionist aspirations. In the Kassite period Elam seems to have held the position of a province of Babylonia after having been conquered by Kurigalzu II (*ca.* 1350). This intermezzo, once more, was followed by one of revival, which culminated in the reign of Shutruk-Nahhunte (*ca.* 1200), who returned from a successful raid against Babylonia with, among other trophies, the famous law code of Hammurabi, which was rediscovered in 1902-3 at Susa. This upward swing continued under Shilhak-Inshushinak (*ca.* 1150). It came to an abrupt end *ca.* 1130, when Nebuchadnezzar I reduced Elam, once more, to the status of a Babylonian dependency, in which it stayed for some three centuries, as clearly testified by the almost complete silence of the Elamite sources.

c. Third period. Under Hubannugash, "king of Susa" (*ca.* 740), his grandson Shutruk-Nahhunte II, and their successors the policy of Elam was dominated by its alliance with Babylonia against Assyria. The struggle ended with the complete destruction of

Courtesy of Foto Marburg

22. Relief of the time of Ashurbanipal, showing Elamite prisoners eating; from Nineveh

the power of Elam at the hands of Ashurbanipal (*ca.* 645).* Before that time (*ca.* 680) the Persians seem to have succeeded in taking from Elam the part known as Anshan, as is shown, perhaps, by the title "king of the city of Anshan" assumed by Cyrus I. After the fall of Nineveh (612) the protectorate over Elam passed to the Median king Cyaxares. The success of the revolt of Cyrus II against Astyages brought Elam under Persian rule. Its name appears immediately after Media in the satrapy lists of the Achaemenian kings. Darius had to overcome several revolts in Elam in the beginning of his reign before he was able to settle down in Susa in 521. Fig. ELA 22.

Courtesy of Editions des Musées Nationaux, Paris

23. An Elamite archer with spear (fifth century), member of the Persian army; from Susa

2. Language. Several suggestions have been made as to the relationship of Elamite with other languages or language groups, such as Caucasian. None of these hypotheses has been generally accepted.

Several stages can be discerned in the language as it became known in documents from different periods: (*a*) from the middle of the third millennium, written in a largely figurative and only partially understood script; (*b*) from the sixteenth to the eighth century, written in cuneiform; and (*c*) from the fifth and fourth centuries, in the Elamite version of the inscriptions of the Achaemenian kings.

The Elamite language may well have been used for many centuries after Elam ceased to exist as an independent nation. As late as the middle of the tenth century A.D. the Muslim author Iṣṭaḫrī noticed that the inhabitants of Khuzistan spoke Khūzī, besides Arabic and Persian.

Fig. ELA 23.

Bibliography. F. W. König, *Geschichte Elams* (1931); G. G. Cameron, *History of Early Iran* (1936); C. Huart and L. Delaporte, *La Perse antique et la civilisation iranienne* (1943); R. Mayer, "Die Bedeutung Elams in der Geschichte des alten Orients," *Saeculum,* VII (1956), 198-220.

On the language, see: F. Bork, "Elam (Sprache)," *Reallexikon für Vorgeschichte,* III (1925), 70-83; R. Labat, *La structure de l'élamite, état présent de la question* (1951); H. H. Paper, *The Phonology and Morphology of Royal Achaemenid Elamite* (1955; with bibliography).

More than a hundred tablets from the treasury in Persepolis were published in G. G. Cameron, *Persepolis Treasury Tablets* (1948).

M. J. DRESDEN

ELASA ĕl'ə sə ['Ελασά] (I Macc. 9:5); KJV ELEASA ĕl'ĭ ā'sə. The place where JUDAS MACCABEUS was slain, in 161 B.C. Il'asa, near Beth-horon, may mark the place today.

N. TURNER

ELASAH ĕl'ə sə [אלעשה, God has made]. **1.** Son of Shaphan, and one of Zedekiah's emissaries to Nebuchadnezzar who bore Jeremiah's letter to the exiles in Babylon (Jer. 29:3).

2. Son of Pashhur the priest, and one of those with foreign wives (Ezra 10:22).

ELATH ē'lăth [אילת, אילות, אלות, grove of tall trees]. Alternately: ELOTH ē'lŏth. A city situated at the head of the Gulf of Aqabah, embarkation point of the navigation for Arabia. It is mentioned several times as being next to EZION-GEBER (Tell Kheleifeh); but Nelson Glueck, who excavated the site, found there was no room in the region for two cities, and concluded that Elath was a later name for Ezion-geber. The name Elath is probably of Edomite origin, since an Edomite dukedom of Elah is mentioned in Gen. 36:41 just before that of Pinon, which is apparently the same as Punon in the Arabah. For the earlier history of Elath, *see* EZION-GEBER.

The revolt of Edom in the time of Joram, the son of Jehoshaphat (II Kings 8:20-22), restored Ezion-geber–Elath to the Edomites. About sixty years later it was recaptured and rebuilt by Uzziah of Judah (II Kings 14:22). It remained in possession of Judah until the time of the weak Ahaz, when it was once more occupied by the Edomites *ca.* 735 B.C. (II Kings

16:6, where the RSV "Edom" is to be read throughout instead of "Syria"). From that time on, the city remained an Edomite possession but gradually decayed in importance. It was abandoned somewhere between the sixth and fourth centuries B.C., and the Nabateans, who had come to control the area, built a new city a little farther E, called Aila. Modern Aqabah, an Arab city, was built near the same site.

Bibliography. N. Glueck, *The Outer Side of the Jordan* (1940), pp. 89-113. S. COHEN

EL-BERITH ĕl bĭr′ĭth [אל ברית, covenant god] (Judg. 9:46). A god worshiped at Shechem. *See* BAAL-BERITH.

EL-BETHEL ĕl bĕth′əl [אל בית־אל, the god Bethel, *or* the god of Bethel] (Gen. 35:7). *See* GOD, NAMES OF, § C2*d*.

ELCIA. KJV form of ELKIAH.

ELDAAH ĕl dā′ə [אלדעה, *cf.* S Arabian *personal names Yada'-'il, Abiyada'*]. The last of Midian's five sons, from the line of Abraham and Keturah (Gen. 25:4; I Chr. 1:33).

ELDAD ĕl′dăd [אלדד, God loved(?); *cf.* Akkad. *Dadi-ilu,* Dadi is God] (Num. 11:26-27). An Israelite who prophesied in the wilderness camp. Eldad and a companion, Medad, were endowed by Yahweh in exceptional fashion with his spirit. At divine command, Moses had selected seventy elders of Israel to assist him in providing for the people, and a portion of the spirit which had empowered Moses was transferred by Yahweh to them. As a consequence of this endowment the seventy prophesied, although not permanently. Eldad and Medad were similarly empowered by the spirit to prophesy, without having been among the seventy chosen elders. Joshua's protest at such apparent irregularity was rejected by Moses with the wish that "all Yahweh's people were prophets."

The spirit of Yahweh appears in the narrative about the elders as the necessary endowment for the performance of a "political" function or office. Here an office could not be executed among the people without possession of the spirit, although it was evidently only Moses upon whom the spirit resided continuously. Nevertheless, the exceptional endowment of Eldad and Medad shows the independence of the spirit in relation to the particular office, and Moses' wish that the spirit of Yahweh would make all his people prophets indicates that the elders were not essentially, although they were functionally, different from the entire community.

Bibliography. K. L. Tallqvist, *Assyrian Personal Names* (1914), p. 67; M. Noth, *Die israelitischen Personennamen* (1928), p. 183. R. F. JOHNSON

ELDER IN THE OT [זקן; LXX πρεσβύτερο]. The common Hebrew word in Ezekiel, שיב, is derived from the root meaning "chin" or "beard," and so an elder is properly a man with a full beard. Elders are thus the grown-up men, powerful in themselves, by reason of personality, prowess, or stature, or influential as members of powerful families. They are local dignitaries or local rulers. There were elders in ancient Greece and Rome, and sheiks (elders) are characteristic of Arabia. Elders were known too in ancient Egypt (Gen. 50:7), and among the Moabites and Midianites (Num. 22:7).

1. Terminology. "Elder" (and KJV "ancient") translate a particular Hebrew word, but there are also a number of other terms denoting officials and officers among whom elders belong. There are also שרים (*see* PRINCE), who before the monarchy were identical with the elders (cf. Judg. 5:15; 8:6-16; Job 29:9), though in later days they became king's men, royal officials; חקקים: makers of statutes (Judg. 5:9, 14; cf. Isa. 10:1; 33:22); nobles (Num. 21:18; I Sam. 2:8; Job 12:21; etc.); men of valor (Judg. 11:1, etc.); or the "head" (Judg. 11:8; I Sam. 15:17; Job 29:25; etc.). Pedersen describes these persons as those who maintain or uphold the community. Isa. 3:2-3 gives another list of those who are the staff and stay of the community, and the elder is included among them. Incidentally Isaiah says that all these will fail and that boys, etc., will rule. There is thus implied a connection between the elderly, the elders, and the wise.

2. Origin and distribution. As parents wield authority in a family, so the elders wield authority in the life of the clan, tribe, or local community. This fact of age is undoubtedly the true origin of the authority of elders, and is the prerequisite of any official appointments that may be made (Exod. 12:21-22). There are three stories of such appointments. The first, in Exod. 18:13 ff (E), describes how Jethro, Moses' father-in-law, counseled Moses to spread the judicial burden among able men, who were to serve as rulers of thousands, hundreds, fifties, and tens. Here the plan of delegated authority is of Midianite origin and was given to Israel before they had even arrived at Horeb. In the parallel account in Deut. 1:13, Jethro is not mentioned, and the occasion is apparently subsequent to the departure from Horeb. In Exodus and Deuteronomy the word "ruler" is the word for "prince," and in Deut. 1:15 is further defined as "OFFICER." It is noticeable that in Exod. 18:12 the elders are already in existence as a recognized body before the princes and officers are appointed. Similarly the officers, *Shoṭerim,* are listed immediately after the elders in such passages as Num. 11:16; Deut. 29:10; 31:28; Josh. 8:33; 23:2; 24:1, and in association with the judges in Deut. 16:18; Josh. 8:33; 23:2; 24:1. It is clear, then, that the princes and officers were very similar and closely related to judges, and may have been in part, at least, recruited from the latter. Exodus and Deuteronomy contain the only references to captains of tens, but the other captains are military figures elsewhere in the OT. It has further been suggested that these early arrangements for the creation of subordinate officials may also conceal later arrangements, whereby the princes or officers represented the local officials of the country towns, and Moses the central authority of the king or the judge or priest at Jerusalem (Deut. 16:18; 17:8-13).

The third story, in Num. 11, is concerned with the selection of a group of seventy from the elders of Israel, who are officers in Israel. The criteria for their selection are not stated. Moses has so much of Yahweh's spirit that he can spare enough to give some to all those seventy to enable them to share with him in bearing the burden of Israel. These special elders were appointed and endowed at the tent of meeting when the theophanic cloud descended. Num. 11:17*b* suggests that the Numbers story is parallel to the stories in Exod. 18; Deut. 1. But even if the accounts are parallel, Num. 11 (also E) shows that the select group of elders is called for different purposes. Exod. 24:1-2, 9-11 (J), preserves a story of seventy elders in which they are religious functionaries, favored participants in theophany and sacred meal. From all these stories, whether parallel or not, it is clear that the elders and officers have a variety of functions. *See* § 3 *below*.

It is also clear that the elders exercised a continuing role in Israel's life. Family elders are mentioned in Gen. 50:7, and elders of Israel in the law books that follow, especially in Deuteronomy. They are often referred to in the books Joshua–II Kings. Their numbers depended, no doubt, on the size of the local community, but there were seventy-seven at Succoth (Judg. 8:14). There are few references to them in the pre-exilic prophets, though they are five times mentioned in Lamentations and four times in Ezekiel. There are references too in Ezra. Elders are thus represented as a constant feature of Israel's life from the days of Moses to those of Ezra, and they were as prominent under the monarchy as before it.

3. Functions. In general the elders and the officers may be said to have been leaders in war, judges in dispute, and givers of wise advice and witness in administration. The elders represent and maintain the community, and are thus the focal point of the community (Lev. 4:13-21; Deut. 21:1-9).Their judicial functions are specially prominent in Deuteronomy (cf. 19:2; 21:2-20; 22:15-18; 25:7-9). Such passages as Exod. 24:1-2, 9-11; Lev. 4:13-21 show them in cultic roles, and they are parties to the royal covenant with David (II Sam. 5:3). Elders of priests are mentioned (II Kings 19:2), and Schürer speaks of the elders of the synagogue. They are frequently mentioned after priests, especially in the NT.

Bibliography. H. Lietzmann, "Zur altchristlichen Verfassungsgeschichte," *Zeitschrift für wissenschaftliche Theologie,* LV (1914), 113-32; P. Volz, *Biblischen Altertümer* (1914), pp. 445-47, 463-68; A. Alt, "Älteste (Palästina-Syrien)," *Reallexikon der Vorgeschichte,* I (1924), 117-18; J. Pedersen, *Israel,* I-II (1926), Index under "elders," p. 558; A. C. Headlam and F. Gerke, "The Origin of the Christian Ministry," in R. Dunkerley, ed., *The Ministry and the Sacraments* (1937), pp. 326-67; L. Rost, "Die Vorstufen von Kirche und Synagoge im AT," *BWANT,* Vierte Folge, Heft 24 (1938), pp. 60-76, especially 61-64; J. Pedersen, *Israel,* III-IV (1940), 760; E. Lohse, *Die Ordination im Spätjudentum und im NT* (1951), pp. 21-27, 50-60; H. von Campenhausen, *Kirchliches Amt und geistliche Vollmacht in den ersten drei Jahrhunderten* (1953), especially pp. 82-134; W. Michaelis, *Das Ältestenamt* (1953); M. Weber, *Ancient Judaism* (trans. H. H. Gerth and D. Martindale; 1953), pp. 16-18; J. Jeremias, *Jerusalem zur Zeit Jesu,* (1958), pp. 88-100; M. Noth, *The History of Israel* (1958), pp. 107-8.

See also bibliography under MINISTER.

G. HENTON DAVIES

ELDER IN THE NT [πρεσβύτερος, *noun from adjective in comparative, lit.* older person, *hence* old man; *sometimes transliterated* presbyter]. The exact meaning of "elder" in the sense of "older person" is found in the parable of the prodigal son (Luke 15:25), with reference to the older of the two brothers, and in Acts 2:17 (Joel 2:28); I Tim. 5:1-2, where older men and women are contrasted with those who are younger. In Heb. 11:2 the word refers to famous men of past times, particularly the worthies of OT history. In the absolute sense, meaning "old man," especially one of wisdom and experience no less than of age, the term does not otherwise occur in the NT except in a technical sense of persons holding an office or position of special dignity and responsibility in the community, whether of Judaism or of the church.

The Christian office of elder stems, without question, from a similar institution of Judaism (*see* ELDER); but the title was also carried by officers of various Greek cult associations and by village magistrates in Egypt. Apart from the numerous references in both OT and NT, the duties of Jewish elders are known in considerable detail from the Mishnaic tractate Sanhedrin. In NT times each Jewish community had its council of elders or its presbytery (in the Diaspora, it was commonly called γερουσία, and the elders were termed "archons," ἄρχοντες). The most important of these, of course, was the council of seventy-one, the SANHEDRIN, of Jerusalem, which served as a kind of "supreme court" for all Jewry. These presbyteries had a general administrative oversight of the Jewish communities, and represented the Jews in relations with the Roman authorities. Their primary duty was judicial—interpreting the law and meting out punishment to offenders against it.

Similar arrangements for governance obtained in the Qumran covenant community. At the general sessions of the group the "elders" had places of second rank after the "priests" (1QS VI.9), and the community had a supreme council of twelve laymen and three priests who were "perfect in all that is revealed of the entire Law" and served as final interpreters and judges of it (VIII.1–IX.2).

Jewish elders were not responsible for worship in the synagogue, though they enjoyed seats of honor at the synagogue assemblies. Doubtless the synagogue rulers were frequently elected from among their number. The elders traced their descent of succession from Moses' appointment of the seventy elders in the wilderness (Num. 11:16 ff; cf. Josh. 24:31; Judg. 2:7; and especially M. Ab. I.1). They were selected by co-optation and ordained by prayer and the laying on of hands, after the pattern of Num. 27:18; Deut. 34:9. In the course of time the elders developed a vast body of precedents in interpretation of the law—the "traditions of the elders" mentioned in the gospels (cf. Mark 7:3-5; Matt. 15:2).

It was only natural that the church, once organized as a collective body, should adopt the institution, but the NT in no place provides an account of the first ordination of elders. We meet in Acts several references to elders in the Jerusalem church, associated with James and the apostles, and functioning among the Christian brethren in ways comparable to the Jewish Sanhedrin (11:30; 15:2, 4, 6, 22-23; 16:4; 21:18). We are told that Paul and Barnabas ordained elders for the mission churches they established in Asia Minor (14:23), and that Paul met with the elders of the church in Ephesus during his final journey to Jerusalem (20:17). In Paul's extant letters, however, elders as such are never mentioned; but they may be subsumed among the leaders who presided over the churches (προϊστάμενοι) in pastoral labor and admonition (Rom. 12:8; I Thess. 5:12-13). That Christian elders exercised pastoral duties may be inferred from the references in I Pet. 5:1-4; Jas. 5:14. Their seats of honor about the celebrant at the assemblies of worship—comparable to the place of Jewish elders in the synagogue—may be inferred from Rev. 4:4.

The most debated question concerning elders in the NT is the relation of this office to other ministries besides that of apostles. That they were closely associated with apostles in the councils and governing of the church is clear from the passages of Acts cited above. The writer of I Peter, whether actually the apostle or not, describes himself as a "fellow elder" in his exhortation to the elders (5:1). The enigmatic elder who wrote II and III John was accounted in church tradition as no other than the apostle John. A second-century bishop of Hierapolis, PAPIAS, was an avid collector of teachings and traditions stemming from the apostles by way of the elders, two of whom—Aristion and the Elder John—he associates with the apostles as "disciples" of the Lord (Euseb. Hist. III.39; cf. Iren. Her. V.33.3-4). Even Ignatius, who carefully distinguishes the elders from other ministers, compares the presbytery to the "council of the apostles" (Magn. 6.1; Smyr. 8.1). There is never, however, in any of the sources a confusion of apostles and elders, for the former were missionaries, the latter stationary leaders of local churches.

The case is different with regard to "prophets and teachers" and "bishops and deacons." Some critics believe, e.g., that the prophets and teachers who led the church in Antioch, according to Acts 13:1-3, were the elders of this church. There is nothing inherently impossible in this identification. An elder may very well have possessed the spiritual gift of prophecy or of teaching or both; and conversely, a person of such eminent charismata might be a most likely candidate for an office of leadership that was official and authorized by ordination. But there are no texts that make specifically such an equation between elders and charismatic ministers.

There are, on the other hand, a number of passages that appear to make the offices of elder and bishop synonymous. The classic theory of Lightfoot that the episcopate arose out of the presbyterate by a gradual process, whereby one of the elders of a local church was elevated to the position of monarchical bishop, has won many supporters. It is but a variant of this theory that supposes the early Christian communities to have been governed by a "college" of presbyter-bishops (*see* BISHOP). In Paul's farewell to the Ephesian elders, the author of Acts has him address them as ἐπίσκοποι (20:28). It has been much discussed whether the word is employed here in a technical sense of "bishops" or in a more general meaning of "overseers" (so KJV) or "guardians" (so RSV). A similarly puzzling passage is Tit. 1:5-7, where the qualifications for an elder and a bishop appear to overlap.

In view of the inconclusiveness of NT evidence, critics have centered attention upon the statements of the First Epistle of Clement (*see* CLEMENT, EPISTLE OF), a letter addressed by the church in Rome *ca.* A.D. 95 to the church in Corinth concerning the unwarranted deposition from the ministry of the Corinthians' bishops and deacons. According to the author of this letter, the apostles, foreseeing that there would be strife for the "title of bishop," made arrangements for a due succession of "tested men" to replace the bishops and deacons whom they had appointed. These men, whether appointed by the apostles or by "other men of repute" (ἐλλόγιμοι), should not, says the author, be removed from their office, if they have served blamelessly. "For our sin is not small if we eject from the episcopate those who have blamelessly and holily offered the gifts. Blessed are the elders who have finished their course before now . . . for they have no fear that anyone will remove them from their appointed office" (44.4-5).

Several questions arise from this testimony. Who were the "men of repute," the ἐλλόγιμοι, through whom the ministerial succession passed? In the three other instances where I Clement uses the term, it means persons enrolled among the elect—i.e., Christians of distinction and merit (57.2; 58.2; 62.3). There is no justification for Dom Gregory Dix's translation of it as "men accounted apostles" or "included in a list" of men accounted along with apostles. This is pressing the sense too far. The men of repute might have been bishops, prophets, or elders —any distinguished leaders of the church in the second generation of its history.

Likewise the term "elder" does not have a fixed meaning in I Clement. It is used seven times, other than in the passage cited: once of Jewish elders (55. 4); three times of "old men" in contrast to "younger men" (1.3; 3.3; 21.6); twice of those set over the Corinthian church, presumably as their ministers (54.2; 57.1); and once, where it is not clear whether it refers to the contemporary leaders or to those of past generations (47.6). It is, of course, a natural reading of ch. 44 to take "elders" as synonymous with the bishops who offer the gifts—i.e., the Eucharist. But it is equally natural to take the word in this context as a general description of the worthies of a bygone generation.

The theory that seems to fit best the meaning, not only of this text, but of all the slender evidence we possess from this period, is that some, though not necessarily all, of the elders were bishops. It has been suggested that the bishop was an "appointed elder"—i.e., one who was set to a special liturgical function. Thus all the bishops might be also accounted as elders, insofar as they functioned with the elders in ruling the churches. But not all the elders were bishops, but only those who presided over the Eucharistic assemblies.

It is first in Ignatius, and after him wherever the monarchical episcopate is firmly established, that the elders become clearly distinguished from the bishop, second after him in rank in the church's hierarchy. They continued to assist in governing the churches by serving the bishop as a council of advice; and, in his absence, they deputized for him as presiding ministers at the sacraments. Thus they came to take on "priestly" functions; but it is not until the middle of the third century that the word "priest" is applied to the elders as well as to the bishops.

Too little is known about the subject to say with any definiteness whether the elders were the ministers of ordination, after the apostles had passed from the scene. The single reference in I Tim. 4:14 suggests that they were, though it is not clear whether the "Timothy" to whom the Pastoral was addressed was a bishop or an elder. No further light is thrown on ordination in the early church until *ca.* 200, in the directives of Hippolytus' *Apostolic Tradition,* when the practices of conferring holy orders had become stabilized in ways that have continued ever since in Catholic and Orthodox churches. By this time, only bishops ordained bishops, and a bishop alone ordained a deacon. But the whole presbytery joined with the bishop in the laying on of hands at the ordination of an elder. Hippolytus remarks, however, that in this case the elder even so did not ordain, "but at the ordination of a presbyter he blesses while the bishop ordains" (IX.8).

Bibliography. For the older literature, *see bibliography* under MINISTRY, CHRISTIAN. H. Lietzmann, "Zur altchristlichen Verfassungsgeschichte," *Zeitschrift für wissenschaftliche Theologie,* LV (1913), 97-153; H. B. Swete, ed., *Essays on the Early History of the Church and the Ministry* (1921), especially pp. 57-214; O. Linton, *Das Problem der Urkirche in der neueren Forschung* (1932); R. Dunkerley, ed., *The Ministry and the Sacraments* (1937), pp. 326-87; K. E. Kirk, ed., *The Apostolic Ministry* (1946), pp. 113-303; B. S. Easton, *The Pastoral Epistles* (1947), especially pp. 188-97, 221-28; H. F. von Campenhausen, *Kirchliches Amt und geistliche Vollmacht inden ersten drei Jahrhunderten* (1953). *See also* commentaries listed under PASTORAL EPISTLES; CLEMENT, EPISTLE OF.

M. H. SHEPHERD, JR.

ELEAD ĕl′ĭ əd [אלעד, God has borne witness, *or* God has returned(?)]. A family of the tribe of Ephraim (I Chr. 7:21). Whether the tradition that Elead and his brother family Ezer were destroyed on a cattle raid in Gath (I Chr. 7:20-23) reflects some historical disaster or is an etiological explanation of the name of the clan of Beriah (I Chr. 7:23) is difficult to say.

Bibliography. M. Noth, *Die israelitischen Personennamen* (1928), p. 237.

H. H. GUTHRIE, JR.

ELEADAH ĕl′ĭ ā′də [אלעדה, God has adorned]; KJV ELADAH ĕl′ə də. A family of the tribe of Ephraim (I Chr. 7:20); not mentioned in the parallel list in Num. 26:35-37.

Bibliography. M. Noth, *Die israelitischen Personennamen* (1928), p. 182.

H. H. GUTHRIE, JR.

ELEALEH ĕl′ĭ ā′lə [אלעלה, אלעלא]. A city in Transjordan, rebuilt by the tribe of Reuben (Num. 32:3, 37) and later in the possession of Moab (Isa. 15:4; 16:9; Jer. 48:34). It is identified with modern el-ʿAl, *ca.* two miles N-NE of Heshbon.

E. D. GROHMAN

ELEASA. KJV form of ELASA.

ELEASAH ĕl′ĭ ā′sə [אלעשה, God has made; *same as* ELASAH]. **1.** A person or family of the clan of Jerahmeel of the tribe of Judah (I Chr. 2:39-40).

2. A member of the tribe of Benjamin, descended from Saul (I Chr. 8:37; 9:43).

Bibliography. M. Noth, *Die israelitischen Personennamen* (1928), p. 172.

H. H. GUTHRIE, JR.

ELEAZAR ĕl′ĭ ā′zər [אלעזר, God has helped; Ἐλεαζάρ]. **1.** The key figure through whom tradition traced the line of priestly descent from AARON. He was a N Israelite of considerable importance: his grace was memorialized in the land of Ephraim (Josh. 24:33; Simpson, however, regards the name here as part of late redaction). As the son of Aaron, he was invested by Moses as Aaron's successor (Num. 20:25-28; cf. Deut. 10:6), and he took the place of Aaron as Moses' helper (Num. 26:1, 3, 63; 27:2, 21). When Moses was about to die, he commissioned Joshua before Eleazar (27:18-23); Eleazar and Joshua, named in that order, distributed Canaan by lot among the tribes of Israel (32:28; 34:17; Josh. 14:1; 17:4; 19:51; 21:1). Eleazar became listed as the third of four sons of Aaron (Exod. 6:23), consecrated to the priestly office with Aaron and his brothers (Exod. 28:1; Num. 3:1-4). Nadab and Abihu were childless when destroyed by fire; the story of their rejection accentuated Eleazar and Ithamar as priests (Lev. 10). Sixteen courses of postexilic priests were assigned to Eleazar and eight to Ithamar (I Chr. 24). Eleazar was described as having been "chief over the leaders of the Levites" in the time of Moses (Num. 3:32; see also 4:16; cf. Aaron as the Levite par excellence). Eleazar was the father of Phinehas (Exod. 6:25; Josh. 24:33). Through Eleazar the descent of Zadok and of Ezra was traced to Aaron (I Chr. 6:3-15, 50-53; 24:3; Ezra 7:1-5).

See also PRIESTS AND LEVITES.

2. A son of Abinadab; consecrated to have charge of the Ark by the men of Kiriath-jearim who had brought it from Beth-shemesh and lodged it in the "house of Abinadab on the hill" (I Sam. 7:1).

3. Son of Dodo; one of the "three mighty men" whose individual exploits as David's warriors gained special fame (II Sam. 23:9-10; I Chr. 11:12-14; perhaps his name should be inserted in I Chr. 27:4).

4. A Levite; son of Mahli, of the family of Merari. He died without sons, and his daughters were married by kinsmen (I Chr. 23:21-22; 24:28; cf. Num. 36:6-9).

5. A priest, son of PHINEHAS 3. He assisted in the inventory of the temple treasure when it was returned to Jerusalem by Ezra (Ezra 8:33).

6. A son of Parosh, in a list of laymen who put away foreign wives and their children according to Ezra's reform banning foreign marriage (Ezra 10:25).

7. A Levite musician in the clockwise procession on the walls of Jerusalem during their dedication (Neh. 12:42).

8. "One of the principal scribes," martyred during the persecution of Antiochus IV Epiphanes (II Macc. 6:18-31).

9. The fourth son of Mattathias; surnamed Avaran; brother of Judas Maccabeus (I Macc. 2:5; cf. II Macc. 8:23). In the battle at Beth-zechariah between the army led by Judas and the Syrians, he fought his way through the ranks of the enemy to an elephant which appeared to bear Antiochus V Eupator, and was crushed as he killed it (I Macc. 6:43-46).

10. The father of JASON 2 (I Macc. 8:17).

11. An ancestor of Joseph the husband of Mary (Matt. 1:15).

Bibliography. Westphal, "Aaron und die Aaroniden," *ZAW,* XXVI (1906), 222-24; G. Berry, "Priests and Levites," *JBL,* XLII (1923), 235-36; M. Noth, *Die israelitischen Personen-*

namen (1928), pp. 20-21, 90, 175; K. Möhlenbrink, "Die levitischen Überlieferungen des ATs," *ZAW*, LII (1934), 214-18, 225; C. Simpson, *The Early Traditions of Israel* (1948), p. 322. T. M. MAUCH

ELEAZURUS. KJV Apoc. variant of ELIASHIB 3.

ELECT LADY [ἡ ἐκλέκτη κυρία]. A phrase used in II John 1:1 to designate the congregation to which the elder addresses his letter. Associated with this image of the local church as mother is the reference to its members as her children and to another congregation as her sister (vs. 13; cf. I Pet. 5:13). Blended in this phrase are two common ideas: that of the church as the elect and that of the messianic community as a woman bearing children (I Bar. 4–5; Gal. 4:25; Rev. 12). *See* ELECTION; CHURCH, IDEA OF.

Bibliography. A. E. Brooke, *Johannine Epistles* (1912), pp. 167-70; C. H. Dodd, *Johannine Epistles* (1946), pp. 143 ff; E. Stauffer, *NT Theology* (1955), p. 155; A. N. Wilder, Introduction and Exegesis of II John, *IB*, XII (1957), 209-16, 302-3. P. S. MINEAR

ELECTION. The religious conviction that God has chosen one out of a group of individuals, peoples, tribes, cities, or temples; established a unique and exclusive relationship with it; and imposed specific functions, obligations, or authority upon it. By far the most important usages have to do with (*a*) kings and priests, (*b*) the fathers of Israel, and (*c*) the city of Jerusalem. The first two usages are continued in the NT in the election of Jesus and of the Twelve, and of the church as a religious community.

1. Statement of the problem. There is no agreement among scholars concerning the precise definition of the term "election," or the range of religious convictions in biblical sources to which this term may properly be applied. The terminology involved in the concept of election includes primarily the Hebrew root בחר and its derivatives בחיר, בחור, and מבחר. There is no word in Hebrew which can be regarded as a synonym. In the NT similarly, the verb ἐκλέγομαι, "choose," and derived forms ἐκλεκτός, "chosen," and ἐκλογή, "election," are without true synonyms. The conclusion seems justified, that in both languages the terminology of "choice" with "God" as subject has become technical usage with a specific meaning not communicated by any other word.

None of the OT sources before Deuteronomy refers to Yahweh's choosing a people, yet on the other hand scholars have always acknowledged that the religion of ancient Israel was from the first based on a unique and exclusive relationship between Israel and Yahweh (as, indeed, in many other ancient religions). Radically differing conclusions have been obtained in scholarly investigations of the problem of election. Those who examine the actual occurrences and usages of the verb בחר, "choose," come inevitably to the conclusion that Yahweh's "choosing" Israel is a concept not demonstrably earlier than Deuteronomy. Other scholars, who start out with a definition of a chosen people as a "group separated from other nations and designated for a particular relation to God," see this conviction as a central feature of Israelite faith from Moses on. It is true that the study of a particular word cannot give reliable conclusions concerning the existence or nonexistence of a particular religious conviction; patterns of thought may very well exist without specific linguistic labels. Nevertheless, an innovation in linguistic terminology may actually result from a new function or meaning of a very old religious concept or conviction. The usage of the verb "choose" with "Yahweh" as subject and "Israel" as object may have resulted in an objectifying, an isolation, even a conventionalizing, of a conviction which previously had been latent or too closely bound up with other religious convictions to be isolated in a particular word.

In recent literature on the subject, three trends have appeared in scholarly opinion: (*a*) The continuation of older scholarly views, according to which the religion of early Israel was nationalistic, Yahweh being the symbol of national unity, and the concept of the "chosen people" a relatively late expression which conveyed a natural pride of nation and race as a religious conviction. (*b*) The assignment of this concept to the beginnings of Israel, implied in the religious narratives and interpretations of the dramatic events which took place in the time of Moses. Far from being an expression of a nationalistic pride, it is a part of the religious response to historic events which brought about the formation of a religious community that had not previously existed. (*c*) The view that there is a composite origin, one source stemming from the more nationalistic traditions connected with the patriarchal narratives, and the other coming from the Mosaic traditions. These two were merged by the Deuteronomist in the concept of God's choice of Israel.

Religious convictions frequently do not lend themselves to precise definition. There can hardly be any doubt that almost everything intended by the Deuteronomist is also specific or implied in the earlier religious traditions, yet we have no evidence that Israel was ever said to be "chosen" by Yahweh before *ca.* 623 B.C. The very rapid acceptance and popularity of the term can certainly be attributed to the fact that it gave clear expression to very old religious convictions precisely at a time when it was most needed as an assurance of the value of the religious faith and the community—i.e., following the destruction of the nation by Nebuchadnezzar in 587 B.C. It was a religious expression of the conviction that there was a permanent relation between Yahweh and Israel, in spite of the destruction of all the normal social, religious, and political institutions by which that community and faith had been preserved and perpetuated for some four or more centuries. It is no wonder that the expression "chosen people" has been a most important factor in the continuity of Jewish religion and culture. It is not surprising also that the secularization of the idea, its dissociation from the religious context in which it originated, has resulted in some of the least edifying episodes of human history, possibly inspiring, in part, racist theories of ethnic superiority.

2. Election as a human act. As in the case of most theological terms, election attributes to God an act which is familiar in human society and life—what might be called "anthropopraxy." For this reason alone, it is desirable to examine usages of the verb "choose" where human beings appear as subjects.

a. Pre-exilic sources. There are relatively few references to the choice of human beings by individuals. Gen. 6:4 tells of the "sons of God" choosing daughters of men, but this is unique. Nowhere else does the verb בחר refer to the taking of a bride, though in Akkadian the regular term for "spouse" is derived from a verb meaning "choose." In I Sam. 20:30, Saul upbraids Jonathan for having chosen David to his own hurt, but the text has been challenged here (see the commentaries). In I Sam. 8:18; 12:13 the king is the choice of the people, but elsewhere the king is the chosen of Yahweh (cf. Hos. 8:4). The king chooses men for the army (I Sam. 13:2; II Sam. 10:4; 17:1), and in P (Exod. 18:25) Moses chooses able men to be "heads" over the people. Joshua also chooses men for the army (Josh. 8:3). The very frequent use of this term in military context is perhaps reflected in the fact that בחור seems to be a technical term in many passages, perhaps meaning "elite troops."

Human choices frequently involve personal interests of the chooser. David is instructed to choose which of three punishments he shall suffer after the ill-advised census (II Sam. 24:12). He must choose a course of action when Absalom rebels (II Sam. 15:15); on the same occasion Barzillai, who had placed the king in his debt by services beyond the call of duty, suggests that the young man Chimham receive the royal reward due to Barzillai. David thereupon promises to do for the young man anything that Barzillai may choose. In the law of Deut. 23:16, the escaped slave is to dwell wherever he may choose.

Very rarely are choices in the early sources specifically associated with statements as to the superior characteristics of the object chosen. Sometimes this may be implied, as in the choice of men for the army (*see above*) and as in David's choice of stones for the battle with Goliath (I Sam. 17:40), or Elijah's offering first choice of bullocks to the prophets of Baal at Mount Carmel (I Kings 18:23, 25). Lot, on the other hand, chooses the Jordan Valley (Gen. 13:11), whose desirable characteristics are described in the preceding verse, but even here the interest of the narrator is rather to describe the character of Lot. Human choices are frequently, as here, involved with issues of religious or ethical nature, and the choice made is both an indication of character and the ground for subsequent well-being or punishment. Already in the Song of Deborah (Judg. 5:8) we find a correlation of "choosing new gods" and subsequent calamity, if the traditional interpretation is correct. Apart from this passage, only Josh. 24:15, 22; Judg. 10:14 speak of human beings' choosing a deity. In the former passage, the choice is grounded on the previous acts of the deity chosen, precisely the structure of the old covenant form. In Judg. 10:14 also, where Yahweh refuses to deliver Israel from oppression on the ground that they have chosen other gods, this choice is condemned on the grounds of Yahweh's previous acts on their behalf. Only in Isa. 41:24 do we have a possible late analogy to these three references to a human choice of a god. Contrast the account of Elijah on Mount Carmel, where the verb "choose" is not used. Only in the most archaic period of Israelite faith was there really a live option with regard to the religious community to which groups would belong: namely, the Canaanite city-states, the old familial religion of patriarchal times, or the Yahwistic community of Israel. All choices in subsequent times are entirely within the framework of the religious community of Israel, by definition worshipers of Yahweh.

Choice as a moral issue within the community is illustrated in Isa. 1:29, where the gardens are certainly associated with some pagan cult symbol; and 7:15-16, where ability to choose good and reject evil is the description of the morally responsible person. Finally, in Deut. 30:19 the two ways, life and death, blessing and curse, are set before the people for them to choose. Perhaps Jer. 8:3 should be included here: death is chosen by the wicked—who have chosen that which results in death.

b. Post-Deuteronomic sources. Almost all references to human choice are here religious alternatives between good and evil. Only in Isa. 40:20 is there an exception, in the craftsman's selection of wood which is appropriate for making an idol. In Job also there are some few choices which are not simply the preference of religious orthodoxy over against impiety. In 9:14, Job chooses words for his controversy with Yahweh; in 7:15, he is led by his nightmares to prefer death to life. In 29:25, he describes his former position, in which he chose "their way" for his contemporaries. His opponents, however, attribute to him evil choices: the "tongue of the crafty" (15:5); iniquity is his choice, according to Elihu (36:21), who exhorts: "Let us choose what is right."

Human choice is very frequently bound up with the proclamation of cause-and-effect relationships: in Isa. 66:3*b*-4*a*, Yahweh chooses affliction for those who choose their own ways and delight in their abominations. This is frequently emphasized in Proverbs also (1:29-33; 3:31). The righteous way is then not so much a matter of religious choice as simply common-sense preference of that which is objectively, intrinsically advantageous. Knowledge (Prov. 8:10), the fruit of wisdom (8:19), a good name (22:1), are all preferable (i.e., to be chosen) above gold, silver, and wealth.

Nevertheless, choice as an indication of human character is also illustrated in Pss. 84:11; 119:30, 173. It is difficult, however, to avoid a strong impression that in the postexilic sources human choice is, in general, limited to the question of accepting or being free from an increasingly rigid orthodoxy of actions; of adherence to or freedom from a well-defined tradition, which was regarded as objectively good and perfect; and in Proverbs especially, this choice was the means to all sorts of material ends.

c. NT usages. It is striking how little human choice appears in the NT, especially the sort of ethico-religious choice so emphasized in the postexilic OT sources. In view of the OT emphasis upon choosing the "way of life," Paul's uncertainty as to whether he should choose life or death (Phil. 1:22) is most interesting as an illustration of the redefinition of OT concepts. OT narratives are used as illustration in Heb. 11:25, where Moses chose ill-treatment with his people rather than the fleeting pleasures of sin. In Luke 10:42, Mary chose the better of two good alternatives. There are no other references in the NT to human choices involving religious issues.

Choices of individuals by human agency are also rare. The church chooses Stephen and six others for administrative functions (Acts 6:5), and Judas and Silas as messengers to Antioch (15:22-25). In neither case is there any indication that this is a divine choice; on the other hand, in both cases there is specific statement concerning the superior qualifications of those chosen, which contrasts sharply with the narratives of God's electing human beings.

In Luke 14:7 there is a unique example of choice based on nonreligious self-interest. Jesus observes those invited to a feast choosing places of honor, and commands the opposite procedure.

The silence of the NT concerning human choice of religious faith is the more striking in view of the fact that the Christian movement must have presented Jews and pagans alike with sharply defined alternatives.

3. God's election of individuals. ***a. Pre-Deuteronomic sources.*** There is no demonstrable reference to a divine choice of an individual in the premonarchic sources of the OT. This seems to come into Israelite tradition with the kingship, possibly from pagan sources, where kings had long been regarded as the chosen of the gods. Furthermore, the traditions treat the king as the chosen of both Yahweh and the people (I Sam. 10:24). Saul is the first of whom this term is used. David is chosen (I Sam. 16:8-10, 12). In II Sam. 6:21, David, speaking in the first person, claims to have been chosen by Yahweh above Saul and his house. Nowhere else in the OT do we have a similar first-person statement. Again, in II Sam. 16:18, Hushai's reply to Absalom presupposes that the king was chosen by Yahweh and the men of Israel. These are the only certain references to Yahweh's choice of individuals before the book of Deuteronomy, and all refer to the king. Some scholars believe that the prophetic oracle in I Sam. 2:28 is pre-Deuteronomic. If this is the case, we then have evidence that the originator of the priestly line of Eli (Aaron or Levi?) was chosen by Yahweh to function as priest. It is doubtful that this can be regarded as evidence for such a belief before the establishment of the monarchy.

b. Deuteronomy and related sources. It is surprising that this section of the OT refers so little to chosen individuals. In Deuteronomy itself, only Levi is called "chosen" for the specific function of service at the altar. In the Deuteronomic history, David is referred to as the chosen servant, with emphasis on the fact that he kept the commandments and statutes of Yahweh (I Kings 11:34), and it is for David's sake that Yahweh maintains a king at Jerusalem. For the Deuteronomist, the authority of the king is due only to the past promise of Yahweh.

c. Postexilic sources. The extension of the concept of chosen individuals to other personages of sacred traditions is characteristic in this period. In Second Isaiah, the terms "servant" and "chosen" seem nearly interchangeable as technical terms (*see* SERVANT), and are identified repeatedly with Jacob and Israel (Isa. 41:8-9; 44:1-2; cf. 14:1); Jacob/Israel is, in the first two passages cited, certainly the person of sacred tradition who is regarded as the ancestor of the Israelites. *See* § 4*b below.*

All references to chosen individuals involve persons of the remote past, with one exception. In Hag. 2:23, Zerubbabel is called both "servant" and "chosen," obviously in an attempt to revive the religious ideology of kingship associated with the Davidic monarchy, perhaps on the foundation of the prophetic oracle in Jer. 33:23-26, where Yahweh guarantees the permanence of the Davidic dynasty. This attempt in the postexilic community failed, and no one is called "chosen" again until NT times. As a matter of fact, Zerubbabel is the only identifiable, historic individual from Solomon to Jesus who is specifically called the chosen of Yahweh.

Other persons of sacred tradition regarded as chosen include Aaron (Num. 16:5, 7 P; 17:2); Moses (surprisingly for the first and last time in Ps. 106:23); David (Ps. 78:70); and finally Solomon, only in Chronicles (I Chr. 28:10; 29:1), where he is chosen to build the temple, and as a son of Yahweh (28:6). Last, but not least, Abraham is included among the chosen, only in Neh. 9:7.

d. NT literature. The limitation of the term in NT sources is important. First, Jesus himself is called "chosen" in the transfiguration narrative (Luke 9:35), by a voice from heaven (a variant reads: "My beloved"). In Luke 23:35 the term is used by scoffers mocking Jesus on the cross, and in I Pet. 2:4-6, an interpretation of Isa. 28:16 refers to Jesus as the "cornerstone chosen and precious," possibly following a different text from the Masoretic Hebrew.

All other references to chosen individuals in the NT have to do with the original Twelve plus Matthias. In Luke 6:13, Jesus calls and chooses the Twelve and names them "apostles," and they are then listed by name. In John 6:70, Jesus' choice of the Twelve, including Judas, is emphasized, as also in 13:18; 15:16. This latter passage is of particular interest in the specific denial that the Twelve had chosen Jesus, and in the emphasis placed on the function for which they were chosen. In 15:19, the separation from the world is also emphasized, with results which contrast greatly with those of postexilic wisdom literature, where human choice of the divinely approved way will result in all sorts of material and spiritual good. The choice of Matthias as a replacement for Judas contrasts sharply also with the choosing of Stephen and others (*see* § 2*c above*). Here, two men are proposed; prayer for the Lord's indication of his choice is offered; the lot is cast; and when it falls on Matthias, he is enrolled with the Eleven.

Peter, speaking in the first person (the only such case in the NT), states that God chose him from among the disciples to proclaim the gospel to the Gentiles (Acts 15:7). This is not an appointment to a peculiar status, which he already had, but is rather designation for a more specialized function. The important feature of this statement, for present purposes, is the fact that this must have been based on the events narrated in Acts 10: it is not a decision of the church, but a vision seen by an individual, on which this choice is grounded.

It is strange that Paul is never called "chosen." Acts 9:15 perhaps conveys the same idea when Paul, after his conversion, is called a "chosen instrument of mine." Again, the designation takes place by means of a vision to Ananias, but it is not the word ἐκλεκτός, "chosen"; rather, ἐκλογή, "election," is used here, as also in Rom. 9:11, where "God's purpose of election" is illustrated in the choice of Jacob before his birth, thus excluding any possibility that it is based on works.

To summarize all our evidence concerning individuals "chosen" by God, the following points are in order: (*a*) In the early sources of the OT every chosen individual occupies a definite office, first king and then priest. In the NT, Jesus is chosen, but the office is not defined; the Twelve are chosen and called apostles—whether this is an office analogous to that of priest and king depends upon the ecclesiastical presuppositions of the one who answers the question. (*b*) In every case in early OT sources the "chosen" individual is the first of a continuity in dynastic succession, his descendants occupying his office, except in the case of Saul, who was specifically rejected (and also the house of Eli). (*c*) In every case except Solomon (in the Chronicler only), the individual obtains his office by means other than regular, socially established, accepted conventions. (*d*) Postexilic OT sources seem to attribute the term to all great men of religious tradition (Moses, Abraham, Jacob), but not even at this late time is it ever used of the charismatic leaders, notably the judges and the prophets.

4. God's election of groups. ***a. Deuteronomy and related sources.*** Though the religious conviction that Israel was the peculiar possession of Yahweh certainly goes back to the very beginnings of Israel, the use of the term בחר as a theological expression of this conviction suddenly appears for the first time in Deuteronomy. Unless some of the psalms will in the future be successfully dated before Deuteronomy, no source knows the term in earlier times. It now seems doubtful to many scholars that the unknown author of Deuteronomy can be regarded as the inventor of this theological concept; rather, it seems likely that he fixed in writing an idea already current in some unknown circle, where it may have been very old indeed. It is quite likely that the root had some theological significance in pre-Mosaic times, as could be argued from the old Amorite (or East Canaanite) name Yabḫurum, which is linguistically equivalent to the later, Hebrew name Ibhar, known only as the name of one of David's sons (II Sam. 5:15). Since it is not likely that the old Amorite name had anything to do with kingship ideology, and since names of this type almost always referred to some activity or function of a deity, it is quite likely that this root, like a great number of Hebrew roots with equivalents in pre-Mosaic Amorite dialects, had an important religious significance in earliest Israel. Under the present circumstances, it is hardly consonant with scholarly caution to deny flatly that the term could have been known or used before Deuteronomy. Amos 3:2 is often cited as evidence that the concept, if not the term, existed in the middle of the eighth century. Amos 9:7-10 could also be interpreted easily as a prophetic polemic against a too-facile popular idea of a chosen people. The problem, however, is not that of the existence of a peculiar relationship between Yahweh and Israel; it is the origin of the term "chosen" (or the verb "to choose" with "God" as subject), and if it be a late term, whether or not it added anything new to the theology of the OT.

Religious concepts have a way of surviving by means of reinterpretation, of giving new meaning and function to very old terms—as also in law. It is difficult, therefore, to believe that the concept of the chosen people as it is found in Deuteronomy coincides exactly with an earlier use, if it did exist. Changes in culture inevitably bring along changes, often too subtle to define exactly, in the meaning of words. Particularly in a case such as this, when a term which we suspect was very old suddenly appears toward the end of an era, there is too great a contrast in the nature of the religious community itself to make it likely that the concept was exactly the same. The Deuteronomist was the heir of some six centuries of history and tradition; early Israel was certainly a rather loose federation of "tribes" of diverse origins, customs, and traditions, in which each man "did what was right in his own eyes," to the dismay of the Deuteronomist. That which is true of an ethnic group with its own history, language, and culture can hardly be true in all respects of a group which was just beginning to work out some sort of unity on the foundation of a common religious faith.

It seems, therefore, that if the term "chosen" was known before Deuteronomy, or, at any rate, if the relationship between Yahweh and Israel was one which grew not out of a so-called "tribal" religion in which kinship was the determining factor in membership in the religious community, but rather was a relationship established by some historical event at a given time and place, the religious meaning of God's "choosing" must be looked for within the framework of the religious bond which held early Israel together. This can only be the covenant tradition.

The Deuteronomic tradition fits very well into the structure of COVENANT forms of Mosaic times. Deut. 7:6-7 is the classical passage. Here the choice of Israel is grounded in Yahweh's initiative—his love (*see* LOVE IN THE OT)—and in the previously existing commitment to the forefathers—the covenant with Abraham. Very strong emphasis is here placed on the motif that the choice is determined by the nature of God, not by the characteristics or excellence of Israel. In some of the extrabiblical suzerainty treaties precisely the same motifs are presented. If

Yahweh's choosing the people is an early tradition, it seems much more likely that it referred originally to the choice of each individual, or the head of each family (cf. Acts 13:17)—granting a patriarchal form of social organization—which joined the Israelite religious community. It is difficult to see how it could have been a choice of a collective group which seems to have had only a rather loose organizational structure. With this hypothesis fits the fact that Deut. 7:6 is in the singular—only with vs. 7 does the plural form of address occur—though it must be admitted that this change of number is no very strong evidence. If this is actually a late recording of a very old tradition, it must be admitted that it is too far removed from the original social and theological context to enable us to reconstruct the original content of the religious conviction; at least we cannot do so with any assurance. It is perhaps worth pointing out here that the Decalogue is likewise presented in the second-person-singular form of the verbs involved.

More important for our present purpose is the fact that Yahweh's choice in Deuteronomy refers to the act which *initiated* that which has a continuity throughout the centuries. Exactly as in the case of the beginnings of the priesthood, the monarchy, and the temple, Yahweh chooses the one (or the many?) whose descendants enjoy the privileges and obligations conferred upon the one who founded the line which bears his name (viz., Aaron/Levi, David, Solomon, and at last Jacob, who is "chosen" for the first time in Deutero-Isaiah). The evidence is thus rather impressive for concluding that Yahweh's choice is closely bound up with ancient concepts of legitimacy. It is a religious conviction, even a part of ancient Israelite political theology, which establishes legitimacy and authority for those institutions of society and culture regarded as of crucial importance, the kingship and the priesthood. With the destruction of both in 587 (at least, the destruction of their functions), it could be seen that these were not, after all, of ultimate importance. The people themselves as a religious community could and did continue to exist in the absence of functioning king and priest. The old concept of Yahweh's choice was therefore transferred from Aaron and David to Jacob, the father (according to the normative religious traditions) of the twelve tribes. This conviction, which, as we have seen above, may have extremely old roots in the premonarchical period, established the religious right and will toward continuity in exile—or perhaps it would be more accurate to say that this term gave expression to that which was a deeply felt conviction. *See* KING; PRIESTS AND LEVITES.

In the Deuteronomic history there are very few references to a chosen people. God's choice of Israel at the beginning of its history furnishes for the Deuteronomic historian the grounds for Israel's existence, but the obligations of the covenant relationship were not accepted, and therefore it was difficult to identify the actual historical community of later times with the "chosen people." Solomon's prayer at Gibeon (I Kings 3:8) makes reference to "thy people" who are too numerous to be counted (contrast Deut. 7:7), but the term "chosen" is not used. That which is true at the beginning of God's creative activity in Israel cannot automatically be assumed true of the community in a much later time—the later community is only evidence that God has kept his promise.

Finally, in Jer. 33:23-26, which comes from some time shortly after the destruction of Jerusalem, we find the only prophetic usage before Ezekiel and Second Isaiah. This is a promise of the restoration of David's dynasty, and of divine mercy to the descendants of Jacob. This is particularly significant because it is in response to a popular cliché: "The LORD has rejected the two families which he chose." This seems to be the only passage (coming from popular, not prophetic, sources) which attributes the term to the N and S kingdoms (so some commentators). It would seem much better to identify the two families here as those of Jacob and David (vs. 26), since these two traditions of Yahweh's choice are those most emphasized in the exilic period.

b. Postexilic developments. Ezekiel refers to Yahweh's choice of Israel only in 20:5. It is not Jacob (Israel) but his seed in Egypt who seem to be the chosen, and the choice takes place accompanied by Yahweh's oath that he will deliver them from Egypt.

It is in Deutero-Isaiah that the concept of election reaches a culmination. Very characteristic of this prophet, and of a few other passages which seem to be closely related, is the double parallelism of Jacob=Israel and servant=chosen (Isa. 41:8-9; 44:1). These two religious symbols are brought together elsewhere only in Ps. 135:4; Isa. 14:1 (universally assigned to the postexilic period); and in prose, Ezek. 20:5, but without the reference to the servant. The formidable complexity of the chosen-servant problem in Second Isaiah makes any solution extremely tentative. Nevertheless, there are several passages in which Jacob=Israel seems to be definitely identified as the person of historical tradition (Isa. 41:8-10; 44:1-5), and elsewhere is identified with the collective community (so in Isa. 43:10-13 above all). The prophet is here engaged in an attempt to bridge the gap of centuries, and the gulf of discrepancy between the necessary characteristics of the chosen one and the actual nature of the people. In other words, he is cautiously identifying the chosen ancestor, Jacob, with his descendants, who may also be called chosen, at least in certain circumstances, in which the obligations attendant upon being chosen are very carefully emphasized. It must be emphasized that here, as elsewhere, it is the originator of the line of continuity to which the term originally and properly applies.

It is curious that the Chronicler never applies the term "chosen" to a corporate group other than the Levites except in the psalm of I Chr. 16:13 (=Ps. 105:6), where for the first and only time in OT literature we have the plural form of בחיר, "chosen one." The identification of the actual historical community with the chosen people is now complete, and being chosen is equated with being a descendant of Abraham/Jacob. Similarly, in I Chr. 15:2 it is no longer Levi who is chosen, but rather the Levites (cf. also II Chr. 29:11), but here Chronicles follows usage first found in Deut. 18:5.

c. NT literature. The most characteristic usage in the NT seems to be both a continuation and a modification of the OT concept.

In the teachings of Jesus, the elect are a group not closely defined, but seemingly a qualitative term perhaps analogous to the "righteous remnant" of OT prophecy. In Mark 13:20 (=Matt. 24:22), God will shorten the days for the sake of the elect; false prophets will almost lead even the elect astray; at the consummation, God will gather the elect from the four winds. Similarly, in Luke 18:7 (with which Rom. 8:33 may be compared), God will vindicate his elect. The term everywhere seems to convey a relationship to God which guarantees God's protection. If Judaism tended at least to identify the elect with the physical descendants of a chosen individual of the remote past, the identification of the elect in the NT went a different way. What this way was is a question which has never been agreed upon by scholars and theologians. First, it is necessary to point out the distinction between call and election. In Matt. 22:14: "Many are called, but few are chosen," the distinction is made, regardless of the particular interpretation of its connection with the context. This is not the only passage which makes such a distinction. Rev. 17:14 describes those who are with the Lamb, the Lord of lords and King of kings, as "called and chosen and faithful." Also, in II Pet. 1:10 there is an exhortation to "be the more zealous to confirm your call and election" as a necessary condition for entry into the eternal kingdom of Christ. Paul likewise (Col. 3:12) emphasizes the characteristics of the "chosen ones"—namely, compassion, kindness, lowliness, meekness, and patience—which are remarkably similar to the catalogue of fruits of the Spirit in Gal. 5:22. Finally, in I Pet. 1:2, the exiles of the Dispersion are addressed as "chosen and destined . . . and sanctified by the Spirit for obedience to Jesus Christ."

That the elect are identified with the Christian church in some way may be assumed. The only passage which clearly takes over OT terminology to apply it to the Christian community is I Pet. 2:9, where the LXX version of Exod. 23:22 (but cf. Exod. 19:6) is quoted, and followed by an indirect quotation of Hos. 2:23 with similar application to the Christians. An indirect use of OT terminology occurs also in Tit. 2:14, where the word περιούσιος, translated "people of his own," is the LXX rendering of the rare Hebrew word סגלה in Exod. 19:5; 23:22; Deut. 7:6; and elsewhere, which is closely connected with the concept of election. Other references in which the Christian community is identified with the elect are probably to be found in I Thess. 1:4; II Tim. 2:10; Tit. 1:1; II John 1:1, some of which are formulaic in nature, but the last is especially interesting in view of the fact that for Paul the election of the brethren of Thessalonica is known from its results.

The insistence of Deuteronomy that election is the result of God's initiative, not of the characteristics of man, is also taken up in the NT. The classical passage is I Cor. 1:27-28, where Paul describes in detail God's choice of the weak, foolish, despised, and lowly, in order to put to shame their opposites. Similarly, in Jas. 2:5, God chose the poor to become rich in faith. Both specifically deny any intrinsic superiority on the part of those chosen. Paul gives the reason: "that no human being might boast." The parable of the marriage feast in Jesus' teachings (Matt. 22:1-4) certainly seems to convey the same point, when the servants of the king gather all they found in the streets, good and bad.

In spite of the identification of the Christians as the elect, the OT emphasis upon Israel as the chosen could not be ignored. In Acts 13:17, Paul begins his sermon at Antioch in Pisidia with the statement: "The God of this people Israel chose our fathers . . . ," continuing with the message that the promises to the fathers are fulfilled in Jesus for the children (vss. 32-33). This is the theme also of Rom. 11. After denying that God has rejected Israel (11:2), he maintains that there is now, as in the days of Elijah, a remnant chosen by grace. These elect obtained what Israel sought, but the rest were hardened (11:7). Even here, it is impossible to regard election as something which is conferred by birth into an ethnic group. The apostle is trying to resolve a paradox, or escape a dilemma. First, there is the impossibility of rejecting the OT scripture, with its divine promises to Israel; but the Jewish rejection of Jesus, in whom these promises are fulfilled, made it impossible to regard all Israel as the elect. He follows the OT itself in the solution: "As regards the gospel they are enemies of God, . . . but as regards election they are beloved for the sake of their forefathers. For the gifts and the call of God are irrevocable." This would fit in with the OT emphasis upon the fact that the fathers are chosen, but not necessarily all descendants. They are called, they are beloved for the sake of the ancestors, but the elect are those who have responded in Christ, and are identified with the remnant in the prophetic teachings.

In the NT, then, election is an act of God, not based on any inherent superiority of those elected, but grounded in the love and grace of God and in his promises to the OT fathers. The election must be confirmed by the faithfulness, obedience, and personal characteristics of the elect; no historical continuity of biological descent, political or social institution, is relevant as a formal criterion by which the elect are to be identified (cf. John 1:13). "Election" is far from being a term expressing pride or claiming prestige and privilege of some social group; rather, it designates those who have responded to the call of God and consequently exhibit the characteristics of the elect. *See* CHURCH, IDEA OF.

5. God's election of inanimate objects. It is again Deuteronomy which emphasizes for the first time, and in some twenty-one passages, God's choice of a particular place for a specific function. In Deuteronomy itself it is only referred to as מקום, "place," since from the point of view of Moses' time the selection of Jerusalem is still in the future. The Deuteronomic history leaves no doubt that the "place" is Jerusalem. In I Kings 14:21, God has chosen the city to place his name there (cf. also I Kings 8:16, 44; 11:32-33; II Kings 21:7; 23:7). In the last cited passage there is a prophetic prediction of God's rejection of the city and temple which he chose. The Deuteronomic historian identifies the place as Jerusalem the city, and its importance is further defined as derived from the fact that God has chosen it as the place for the temple, in which he has placed his name. All this is, however, absent in the pre-exilic prophets. *See* TEMPLE, JERUSALEM.

God's choice of nonhuman objects occurs elsewhere. In Ps. 25:12, God chooses the "way" in which he will instruct the God-fearing man. In Isaiah there are references to the "doings" which God chooses (66:4), and the fasting which differs from that practiced by the prophet's contemporaries (58:5-6). After the Restoration, Zech. 3:2 again refers to Jerusalem as chosen. Mount Zion is chosen in Ps. 132:13. Chronicles continues the now well-established terminology with regard to Yahweh's choice of Jerusalem and the temple (II Chr. 6:6; 7:12; 33:7).

Of all this there is no hint in the terminology of divine choice in the NT. No city, place, temple, house, is referred to as chosen. In fact, the verb never has an inanimate object when "God" is subject. These symbols, which were so important to postexilic Judaism, were evidently disvalued in early Christianity from the beginning, and increasingly as the movement spread into the Gentile world. Jerusalem continues as a symbol, especially in Revelation, but it is the heavenly, not the earthly, city. Even more important for present purposes is the fact that this theological term was not transferred to some other locality or object, at least in NT times. All the significant religious uses of the term "choose" reversed the increasing tendency of Judaism to identify the relationship to God with any objective nation, ethnic group, place, temple, or group of cultural conventions. What God chose could be only human beings, whose personal characteristics exhibited those traits which were qualitatively in harmony with the divine will.

Bibliography. K. Galling, *Die Erwählungstraditionen Israels* (1928). H. H. Rowley, *The Biblical Doctrine of Election* (1953). K. Stendahl, "The Called and the Chosen," *The Root of the Vine* (1953), pp. 63-80. T. C. Vriezen, *Die Erwählung Israels nach dem AT* (1953). For a succinct statement of the older view, see J. M. P. Smith, "The Chosen People," *AJSL,* XLV (1928-29), 73 ff. Further discussion is to be found in various OT theologies, and in G. E. Wright, *The OT Against Its Environment* (1950), especially pp. 46-54.

G. E. MENDENHALL

EL-ELOHE-ISRAEL ĕl ĕl′ō hē ĭz′rĭ əl, ĕl′ĭ lō′hē— [אל אלהי־ישראל, God, the God of Israel] (Gen. 33:20). *See* GOD, NAMES OF, § C2*g*.

EL-ELYON ĕl′ĕl yōn′ [אל עליון, God the Exalted One, God Most High]. *See* GOD, NAMES OF, § C2*b*.

ELEMENT (ELEMENTAL SPIRIT) [στοιχεῖα, *from* στοῖχος, row, rank, series]. A term which has four basic meanings in the Greek:

a) Classical Greek relates the term to the spoken letters of the alphabet and to the fundamental principles or rudiments of any art, science, or discipline. This is the meaning in Heb. 5:12, where τα στοιχεῖα τῆς ἀρχῆς is translated as "the first principles."

b) The term is used to designate the basic components or constituents of the physical world—e.g., earth, fire, water, and air as the four basic elements. Such usage is found also in the noncanonical Jewish writings (Wisd. Sol. 7:17; 19:18; IV Macc. 12:13; Jos. Antiq. III.vii.7). It is this meaning that appears in II Pet. 3:10, 12, in relation to the destruction of the elements (στοιχεῖα).

c) The term came to include not only the physical elements but also the spirits behind them: the elemental spirits. In Hellenism the term had a double meaning, a philosophical and a mythical-religious. The philosophical sought after a unified understanding of the world (*see above*). However, the world could not be limited to nature; and thus cultural, psychological, and religious aspects stood side by side with the natural. The syncretistic movement in Hellenism kept both, but whereas the philosophical was kept alive almost only in astrological speculation, the mythical became strongly emphasized and provided a framework into which streamed the many oriental divine or half-divine beings, spirits, and angels (*see* ANGEL). The στοιχεῖα were personified and came to be understood as the final principles of life and all that is. They were the lords of the world; and being regarded as the supporting spirits of the elements from which man is created, they were considered worthy of man's worship. A similar emphasis is present in Jewish apocalyptic literature (Slavonic Enoch 19:1 ff; Ethiopian Enoch 60:11 ff; 69:22; Jub. 2:2; II Esd. 6:3; see also Rev. 7:1; 14:18; 16:5; 19:17).

It is this meaning that appears in Gal. 4:3, 9; Col. 2:8, 20. What the letters to the Galatians and the Colossians are attacking appears to have been a kind of religious syncretism of Hellenistic gnosis, Jewish ethical practice, and Persian mythology. The problem is that "beings that by nature are no gods" (Gal. 4:8) were involving the congregation in what amounted to polytheistic idolatry. Galatians associates the Jewish law and the "elemental spirits of the universe" (cf. Gal. 4:3, 5) and directly links the law to angels (3:19). Colossians associates the "elemental spirits of the universe" and angel-worship (cf. Col. 2:18, 20). *See* COLOSSIANS § 3.

The basic conflict is one of a self-culture with "human precepts and doctrines" (Col. 2:22-23) versus a "growth that is from God" (vs. 19); and the freedom in Christ versus slavery to the elemental spirits of the universe (Gal. 4:9). In both letters it is the question of a basically man-centered orientation versus a God-centered one in which also the problem of man finds its solution.

d) The term is used also with reference to stars and heavenly bodies. They were regarded as having spirits which affect the life and destiny of men. This astrological concern seems to appear in Gal. 2:10; Col. 2:16 (cf. Ethiopian Enoch 80:6) and indicates another factor in the syncretism confronting the congregations.

Bibliography. G. A. Deissmann, *Encyclopedia Biblica,* II (1901), 1258 ff; H. Schlier, *Der Brief an die Galater* (1951), pp. 133 ff. M. Dibelius, *An die Kolosser, Epheser, an Philemon* (1953), pp. 27 ff; E. Lohmeyer, *Der Brief an die Kolosser* (1954), pp. 4 ff, 103 ff.

P. L. HAMMER

ELEPH. KJV form of HA-ELEPH.

ELEPHANT [שנהבים, ivory, *from* שן, tooth, tusk, *and* הבים, *presumably plural of* הב, *possibly from* Egyp. *ꜣbw*, elephant (*cf., however, postbiblical* Heb. פיל, elephant; Syr. *pîl*); ἐλέφας (I Macc. 6:30; *etc.*)]. Any of certain large mammals of the suborder Proboscidea, of the family Elephantidae, their most striking external peculiarity being the long, flexible proboscis. Of the two living species, the Indian (*elephas indicus*) and the African (*elephas africanus*), the latter is the larger and

Courtesy of the Trustees of the British Museum

24. Black obelisk of Shalmaneser III, king of Assyria, which describes the events of his reign; showing elephant in middle section

the more active. Africa, however, has no long tradition of elephant-taming, so that domesticated elephants have been almost entirely of the Indian variety.

Elephants of the Indian species once roamed Western Asia. In the fifteenth century B.C. both Assyrian and Egyptian sources refer to elephant hunts in N Syria near Carchemish, and as late as the eighth century B.C. elephant hides and ivory are listed as gifts brought to Tiglath-pileser III at Arpad. It is evident, however, that as the cultivated area expanded and as the demand for IVORY increased, elephants decreased in numbers and eventually disappeared from the Assyrian domains, which would account for the absence of references to the elephant in the OT. Presumably the ivory inlays and the elephant hides, which Hezekiah of Judah sent to Sennacherib in 701 B.C., were imported from Ethiopia or Egypt (*ANET* 288).

Herodotus speaks of the elephant as a native of Africa (III.114), but Aristotle knows of the Indian species (*History of Animals* IX.1 [610*a*]). Fifteen of the latter variety were used by Darius III of Persia in 331 B.C. at the Battle of Gaugamela against Alexander of Macedon. The Hellenistic age took up this military use of elephants, employing animals imported from India, though it is claimed that the Seleucids bred and trained elephants at Apamea in Syria. That Lysias included thirty-two elephants in the force marshaled against the Palestinian Jews in 163 B.C. doubtless indicates that the Seleucids considered the situation a serious one (I Macc. 6:30). Fig. ELE 24.

W. S. McCULLOUGH

ELEPHANTINE PAPYRI ĕl′ə făn tī′nī, —tē′nī pə pī′rī. The Aramaic papyri of the fifth century B.C. found at Elephantine Island, opposite Assuan. The first body of material, composed of legal texts, was acquired from dealers and published by Archibald H. Sayce and Arthur E. Cowley in 1906. The second

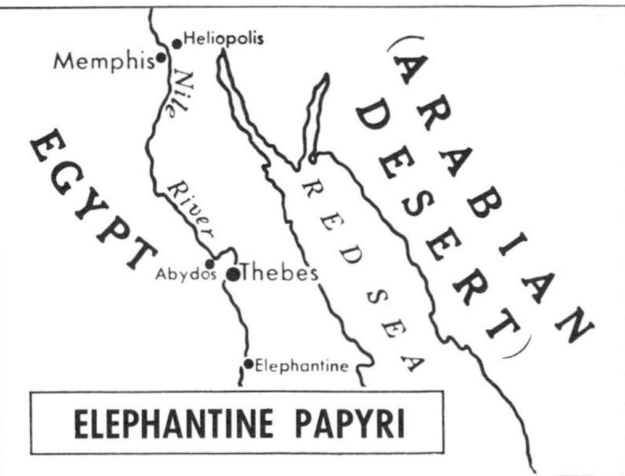

and most important lot was recovered by excavation carried on by the Berlin Museum and was published by Eduard Sachau in 1911. The third lot, much like the first in character, was actually the first to be found (1893), but came to light a considerable time after the other two, at the Brooklyn Museum; it was published by Emil G. Kraeling in 1953. Fig. ELE 25.

The papyri revealed that there was a colony of Hebrews on Elephantine Island (called *Yeb*) in the Persian era. They had a temple of their god, whose

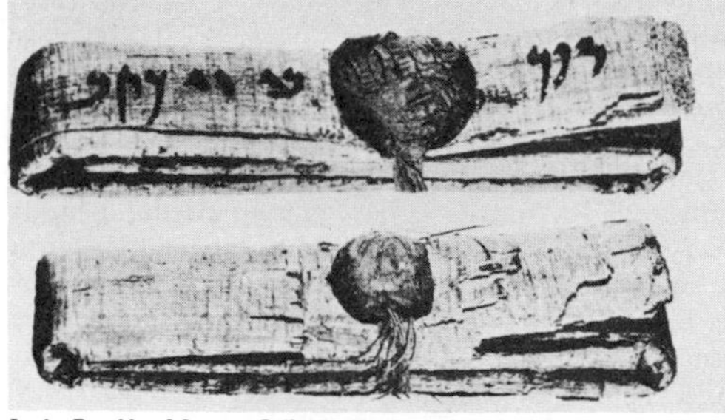

In the Brooklyn Museum Collection

25. Papyrus from Elephantine, containing a marriage contract in Aramaic, tied, rolled, and sealed

name is written *Yhw* (Yahu or Yaho). They sometimes refer to themselves as Arameans and apparently were living in an Aramaic-speaking environment and using the Aramaic language. As they claim that their temple existed before Cambyses' invasion of Egypt (525 B.C.), a sixth-century origin of the colony seems probable. A temple of a Semitic god can only have been imposed on the Egyptian community of Elephantine through the act of some Pharaoh who settled these people here (Amasis? 569-526 B.C.). Some regard the colony as of Israelite or of Syrian-Judean origin.

A great many of the Elephantine Papyri are legal texts. They reflect a variety of interesting situations in the lives of the colonists. There was considerable litigation. Often an oath by a god was imposed, and if a claimant refused to swear it, he lost his case. He then had to renounce his claim in a manner binding on his heirs. Sales of houses and conveyances, loans with harsh clauses protecting the creditor and requiring usurious interest, marriage contracts, documents of manumission and adoption, are all represented. These texts are largely derived from the archives of two families—in the Cairo texts that of Mahseiah bar Yedoniah and in the Brooklyn texts that of Ananiah bar Azariah, the *"lḥn* [cantor? temple servant?] of Yahu." This Ananiah married Tamut, handmaiden of Meshullam bar Zakkur, who was possessed of a boy named Palti. They had a daughter named Yehoyishma. Later Meshullam manumitted Tamut (whose name now appears as Tapimut, perhaps in consequence of her new status), but with the proviso that she and her daughter were to provide for him and his son Zakkur. When Yehoyishma wed, it was not Ananiah, but Zakkur, who acted on her behalf. Yehoyishma could become fully free only after the death of Zakkur.

There are also numerous letters among the Elephantine texts. All these except one—the Brooklyn letter—were recovered by the German excavations. Supreme among them is the one addressed to Bagoas, governor of Judea (*Yehud*), in which appeal is made for his intervention in their behalf to obtain restoration of the Yahu temple, which had been destroyed in 410 B.C. at the instigation of the priests of the Egyptian god Khnum (patron divinity of Elephantine) with the aid of the local Persian commander. The satrap Arsames, who has become more vivid through the publication of the Borchardt Aramaic Leather Documents by G. R. Driver in 1954, knew nothing of it and, in fact, was out of the country at the time. The Bagoas letter not only mentions this individual, about whom Josephus gives legendary report, but also Sanballat and the high priest Johanan (Neh. 12:22; cf. 13:28). The letter received no direct reply, but a memorandum was taken along by the Jewish messenger of what was to be said to Arsames on behalf of Bagoas and Delaiah, son of Sanballat. They recommended restoration of the temple and resumption of the cult, though without permission of bloody sacrifice. The Brooklyn papyri show that the temple must have been restored, and that Persian rule lasted longer in Upper Egypt than had been thought—to the time of the "Anabasis" of Cyrus the younger (401 B.C.). A letter reporting the accession of Nepherites (399 B.C.) shows that the colony still existed at that time, but it seems probable that this ruler removed the Jews from Elephantine.

The religion of these Jews tended toward syncretism. The great list of temple contributors shows that the treasurer had funds for the deities *Eshembethel* and *Anath-bethel,* as well as for Yahu. BETHEL, which appears as a god's name in Babylonian sources and probably also in some OT passages (cf. especially Jer. 48:13), may here be a mere equivalent of "God," just as El, the name of a divinity in the Ras Shamra Texts, has become in OT times. For the goddess Anath-bethel is also called Anath-yahu. The latter name must be rendered "the Anath of Yahu" and the others correspondingly. The salutations of the letters frequently refer to "the gods." In an ostracon a certain Jarcho invokes the Babylonian gods Bel, Nabu, Shamash, and Nergal; but he might, of course, be a non-Jew. The phrase "God of heaven" occurs several times, meaning Yahweh, as in Ezra-Nehemiah. An ostracon provides an instance of *Yhh ṣb't,* "Yahweh of hosts."

Of great interest is the order issued by authority of Darius II in 419 B.C. directing the colony to celebrate the Feast of Unleavened Bread. Whether the Passover was mentioned in the gap before the reference to the Mazzoth Festival is a moot question. It may be that this represents the introduction of Mazzoth into the Jewish festal calendar. The word *psḥ* occurs in an ostracon, though the translation "Passover" is not certain. There are also probable mentions of the "Day of Preparation" and of the Sabbath in the ostraca.

The Elephantine Papyri are of great importance for the question of the time of Ezra's coming and for the date of the Samaritan Schism. For a significant literary papyrus, *see* AHIKAR.

Bibliography. A. H. Sayce and A. E. Cowley, *Aramaic Papyri Discovered at Assuan* (1906). E. Sachau, *Aramäische Papyrus und Ostraka* (1911). A. Ungnad, *Aramäische Papyrus aus Elephantine* (1911), an independent treatment of Sachau's texts. W. Staerk, *Aramäische Urkunden zur Geschichte des Judentums* (1908); *Jüdisch-Aramäische Papyri aus Elephantine* (2nd ed., 1912; both this and the preceding are invaluable to the beginner, since texts are vocalized and annotated); *Alte und Neue Aramäische Papyri* (1912; translations and commentary)—all three in H. Lietzmann, ed., *Kleine Texte für Vorlesungen und Übungen*, nos. 22/23, 32, 94. E. Meyer, *Der Papyrusfund von Elephantine* (2nd ed., 1912). A. E. Cowley, *Aramaic Papyri of the Fifth Century B.C.* (1923), an invaluable handbook. H. Gressmann, *Altorientalische Texte zum AT* (2nd ed., 1926), pp. 450-51. A. Vincent, *La religion des Judéo-Araméens d'Élephantine* (1937). E. G. Kraeling, "New Light on the Elephantine Colony," *BA*, vol. XV (1952), no. 3; *The Brooklyn Museum Aramaic Papyri* (1953), pp. 3-119 (for a full account of the whole subject), 123-319 (for the new texts with translation and commentary). G. R. Driver, *Aramaic Documents of the Fifth Century B.C.* (1954). J. B. Pritchard, ed., *ANET* (2nd ed., 1955), pp. 222-23 (translations by H. L. Ginsberg).

E. G. KRAELING

ELEUTHERUS ĭ lo͞o′ thər əs [ἐλεύθερος, free]. A river in Syria rising at the base of Mount Lebanon and flowing to the sea; an important boundary line referred to in the exploits of Jonathan (I Macc. 11: 7; 12:30; cf. Strabo *Geography* 16.2.12); probably the modern Nahr el-Kebir. E. W. SAUNDERS

ELEVEN, THE [ἕνδεκα]. A term used in the resurrection narratives to designate the twelve disciples of Jesus minus the traitor Judas (Matt. 28:16; Mark 16: 14; Luke 24:9, 33; cf. Western text of I Cor. 15:5). Acts 1:26 records the selection of Matthias to replace Judas and his enrollment with the "eleven apostles" (but the Western text reads "twelve"). Note also the variant of Codex Bezae (D) in Acts 2:14, which reads "ten" instead of "eleven." *See also* APOSTLE; MINISTRY, CHRISTIAN; TWELVE, THE.

M. H. SHEPHERD, JR.

ELHANAN ĕl hā′nən [אלחנן, God is gracious]. **1.** A son of Jair. He slew a Philistinian giant at Gob (II Sam. 21:19; I Chr. 20:5). There are two diverse accounts of this exploit of Elhanan. In II Sam. 21:19 the text reads: "Elhanan the son of Jaareoregim, the Bethlehemite, slew Goliath"; while in I Chr. 20:5 the text is: "Elhanan the son of Jair slew Lahmi the brother of Goliath." It is generally agreed that the name Jaareoregim (יערי ארגים) is composed of a corrupted form of Jair and a transcriptional error that imported "oregim" (ארגים, "weavers") from the following line. Moreover, it is usually held that II Sam. 21:19, as emended above, represents the original text and that I Chr. 20:5 contains a harmonistic correction. Many scholars believe that the Philistine champion whom David slew was originally anonymous and that a later editor interpolated the name of Goliath, the giant actually slain by Elhanan, into the text of I Sam. 17; 21:9—H 21:10; 22:10. Older interpreters argued generally for the originality of I Chr. 20:5.

2. Son of Dodo the Bethlehemite; a member of the company of David's Mighty Men known as the "Thirty" (II Sam. 23:24; I Chr. 11:26).

Bibliography. A. R. S. Kennedy, "Samuel," *The Century Bible* (1904); J. Goettsberger, *Die Bücher der Chronik oder Paralipomenon*, HS (1939); W. Rudolph, *Chronikbücher*, HAT (1955); J. Bright, *A History of Israel* (1959), pp. 171 ff.

E. R. DALGLISH

ELI ē′lī [עלי, exalted; *an abbreviation of* Y is exalted]. The priest at Shiloh to whom the boy SAMUEL was brought to fulfil Hannah's vow (I Sam. 1:1–2:11). Associated with him in this priesthood were his two sons, Hophni and Phinehas (1:3). At this time the ark was kept at Shiloh (4:4), which may mean that this sanctuary was the central shrine of the Israelite amphictyony. It was the news of the capture of the ark by the Philistines and of the death of his two sons, who had accompanied it into battle, that caused Eli's death (4:11-18).

In I Sam. 2:27-36 we have a prophecy of the fall of the house of Eli, which seems to be an expansion of the oracle found in 3:11-14. The latter refers to an imminent catastrophe which will strike the house of Eli as a punishment for the sin of Eli's sons (2:12-17)—i.e., the capture of the ark and the destruction of Shiloh. The former shows a knowledge of the exile of Abiathar (I Kings 2:26-27) and of the problems of the priests dispossessed from the local sanctuaries mentioned in the account of Josiah's reform (II Kings 23:9).

I Sam. 2:27-36 also presupposes the accuracy of the genealogical references which connect Abiathar to the house of Eli. Abiathar is said to be "one of the sons of Ahimelech the son of Ahitub" (22:20; cf. II Sam. 8:17, where the correct reading is probably "Abiathar, the son of Ahimelech, the son of Ahitub"). I Sam. 14:3 describes Ahitub as "Ichabod's brother, son of Phinehas, son of Eli, the priest of the LORD in Shiloh," and gives the name of his son as Ahijah—the chaplain of Saul (vs. 18; *see* AHIMELECH 1). But vs. 3 seems spurious, for the genealogical clause is without syntax, and the mention of a brother's name in a genealogy is unusual. Nor does the genealogy serve any purpose in the ensuing account. Rather, the purpose of the verse is to connect both the Nob priesthood and Ahijah with the house of Eli and to include both in the condemnation of the Shiloh priesthood, so that it might appear that Yahweh had rejected all the priests mentioned in this period in favor of the Zadokites.

Eli's ancestry is nowhere given in the OT. One tradition assigns him to the Aaronide house of Ithamar (Jos. Antiq. V.xi.5; cf. I Chr. 24:3), another to the rival house of Eleazar (II Esd. 1:2-3; cf. Exod. 6:23, 25). Originally Eli's family was probably that of the ancient priesthood at Shiloh.

Bibliography. W. R. Arnold, *Ephod and Ark* (1917), pp. 14-15; M. Noth, *Die israelitischen Personennamen* (1928), p. 146. Contrast W. F. Albright, *Archaeology and the Religion of Israel* (1956), pp. 201-2. R. W. CORNEY

ELI, ELI, LAMA SABACHTHANI ē′lī, lä′mə, sə băk′thə nī [אלי אלי למה עזבתני; Aram. אלהי אלהי למה שבקתני, *see below;* ἠλὶ ἠλὶ λαμὰ σαβαχθανί]; ELOI, ELOI ē′lō ī— [ἐλωΐ] in Mark. The Hebrew-Aramaic expression cited in Matt. 27:46; Mark 15: 34 from Ps. 22:1 as an utterance of Jesus on the cross. The Markan form, with *Eloi*, is closer to the Aramaic, but much variation exists in the MS tradition of both Matthew and Mark, as the text was more or less conformed to the Hebrew or subject to the influence of the LXX. *Eloi* occurs for *Eli* in Matthew, and *Eli* for *Eloi* in Mark, in some good MS authorities. Assimilation of one gospel to the other, of course, accounts for some of this variation. *Lama* occurs as *lema* (the best attested reading in Matthew) and *lima,* both of which are closer to the Aramaic; the verb is variously transliterated, and in codices Vaticanus (B) and Bezae (D) in Mark and in D in Matthew a transliteration of the Hebrew is substituted. The evangelists accompany their quotation with a translation into Greek which is virtually identical but which differs from the LXX in the omission of πρόσχες μοι ("give heed to me"). The RSV renders both as: "My God, my God, why hast thou forsaken me?" Codex D and some OL MSS read ὠνείδισας, "reproach," for "forsake"—doubtless a softening of the statement, although a few scholars have regarded it as more primitive.

Opinion is divided in regard to the original language of the saying and as to whether Jesus himself would more naturally have used Hebrew or Aramaic. The texts themselves support an Aramaic or mixed form. Proponents of the Hebrew suggest that it would more easily explain the confusion of "my God" with "Elijah," and the reading "my Power" in the Gospel of Peter (5:10), a common metonym for "God" in this period. Cf. Aquila's translation here: ἰσχυρέ. While these points are debatable, the Murabba'at documents indicate that a form of Hebrew, somewhat influenced by Aramaic, may have been in use in Palestine in the first century A.D.

See also CRUCIFIXION; CHRIST.

Bibliography. E. König, *ET,* 11 (1900), 237-38, 334; E. Nestle, *ET,* 11 (1900), 287-88, 335-36; G. Dalman, *Die Worte Jesu* (2nd ed., 1930), pp. 42-44; V. Taylor, *Jesus and His Sacrifice* (1937), pp. 157-63; C. S. C. Williams, *Alterations to the Text of the Synoptic Gospels and Acts* (1951), pp. 38-40.
A. WIKGREN

ELIAB ĭ lī'əb [אֱלִיאָב, El is father]. **1.** A son of Helon; a leader of the tribe of Zebulun. He represented his tribe in the time of Moses in such concerns as the census and the dedicatory offerings for the tabernacle (Num. 1:9; 2:7; 7:24, 29; 10:16).

2. A Reubenite of the family of Pallu; the father of Dathan and Abiram, who were among the principals in the rebellion of Korah against the leadership of Moses and Aaron (Num. 16:1, 12; cf. Num. 26:8-9; Deut. 11:6).

3. One of the ancestors of the prophet Samuel; listed among the sons of Kohath (I Chr. 6:27—H 6:12). In the parallel genealogies his name is given as Elihu (I Sam. 1:1) and Eliel (I Chr. 6:34—H 6:19).

4. The eldest son of Jesse the Bethlehemite. His appearance and height thoroughly impressed Samuel as befitting a king, but he was passed over by the prophet in favor of David (I Sam. 16:6; I Chr. 2:13). Eliab was in the army of Saul when the Philistine giant defied them in the Valley of Elah, and became greatly incensed at his youngest brother, David, who had arrived at the scene of battle with provisions from home, because of his inquisitiveness regarding the rewards Saul had offered to the warrior that would slay the giant (I Sam. 17:13-28). Eliab's daughter Abihail appears to have been the mother of Mahalath, the wife of Rehoboam (II Chr. 11:18).

5. A Levitical musician who was among those who played harps set to *'alāmôth* (*see* MUSIC) in the sacred orchestra in the time of David (I Chr. 15:18, 20; 16:5).

6. One of the famed Gadite warriors who joined the proscribed band of David at Ziklag and who subsequently became officers in his army (I Chr. 12:9, 18—H 12:10, 19). E. R. DALGLISH

ELIADA ĭ lī'ə də [אֶלְיָדָע, God knows]; KJV ELIADAH in I Kings 11:23. **1.** One of the sons of David who was born at Jerusalem (II Sam. 5:16; I Chr. 3:8). In the parallel list he is called BEELIADA, which is a disguised form of Baaliada (I Chr. 14:6).

2. The father of REZON (I Kings 11:23).

3. A commander of a large force of Benjaminite bowmen in the royal military corps stationed at Jerusalem in the reign of Jehoshaphat (II Chr. 17:17).
E. R. DALGLISH

ELIADAS. KJV Apoc. form of ELIOENAI 5.

ELIADUN. KJV Apoc. form of ILIADUN.

ELIAH. KJV form of ELIJAH in I Chr. 8:27; Ezra 10:26.

ELIAHBA ĭ lī'ə bə [אֶלְיַחְבָּא, God hides]. A Shaalbonite or Shaalabbinnite; one of the company of the Davidic Mighty Men known as the "Thirty" (II Sam. 23:32; I Chr. 11:33).

ELIAKIM ĭ lī'ə kĭm [אֶלְיָקִים, God raises up; Ἐλιακείμ]. **1.** Son of Hilkiah, and royal chamberlain to Hezekiah (II Kings 18:18, 26, 37). This office (lit., "over-the-house") had increased in importance from Solomon's time (cf. I Kings 4:2-6) until it was second only to the king. Isaiah had prophesied (Isa. 22:15-25) that Eliakim would supersede Shebna; and we see in II Kings 18:18 that their ranks have been reversed.

2. The second son of Josiah; his name was changed to Jehoiakim by Pharaoh Neco when the latter made him the puppet king of Judah (II Kings 23:34). The name is given only here and in II Chr. 36:4. The significance of the new name was not in its intrinsic meaning ("Yahweh raises up" substituted for "God raises up"), but was simply in the fact that it was new. The Pharaoh had, in a sense, remade Jehoiakim, and the latter was his vassal. The "new person" was appropriately given a new name. The choice of name may have been satirical on Pharaoh's part, implying that Yahweh was on his side.

3. A priest at the dedication of the wall of Jerusalem after it had been rebuilt under Zerubbabel (Neh. 12:41).

4. Son of Abiud, named in the postexilic division of the genealogy of Jesus (Matt. 1:13).

5. Son of Melea, in Luke's genealogy of Jesus (Luke 3:30). J. M. WARD

ELIALIS ĭ lī'ə lĭs [Ἐδιαλείς (B), Ἐλιαλει (A)] (I Esd. 9:34); KJV ELIALI —lī. An Israelite who put away his foreign wife and children. The name is omitted in the parallel Ezra 10:38. C. T. FRITSCH

ELIAM ĭ lī′əm [אליעם, God is kinsman]. **1.** The father of Bathsheba (II Sam. 11:3); called Ammiel in I Chr. 3:5. The names are the same; the components are merely reversed.

2. Son of Ahithophel the Gilonite; one of the Mighty Men of David known as the "Thirty" (II Sam. 23:34). His name appears in a mutilated form in I Chr. 11:36*b* as Ahijah the Pelonite.

E. R. DALGLISH

ELIAONIAS. KJV form of ELIEHOENAI in I Esd. 8:31.

ELIAS. KJV NT form of ELIJAH.

ELIASAPH ĭ lī′ə săf [אליסף, God has added]. **1.** Leader of Gad; son of Deuel, or Reuel (Num. 1:14; 2:14; 7:42, 47; 10:20). He was one of twelve tribal leaders or deputies who assisted Moses in taking a census of Israel and in other tasks in the wilderness.

2. Leader of the Gershonites in the wilderness; son of Lael (Num. 3:24). The Gershonites were responsible for the care of the tabernacle and other appointments within the tent of meeting. *See* PRINCE.

Bibliography. M. Noth, *Die israelitischen Personennamen* (1928), pp. 70, 90, 173. R. F. JOHNSON

ELIASHIB ĭ lī′ə shĭb [אלישיב, God restores; *theophorous names with the element* restores *have been found in* Akkad., Aram., *and other Semitic languages;* Apoc. Ἐλιάσιβος]; KJV Apoc. ELEAZURUS ĕl′ĭ ə zōō′rəs (3 *below*); ELIASIB ĭ lī′ə sĭb (2 *below*); ELISIMUS ĭ lĭs′ĭ məs (4 *below*); ENASIBUS ĭ năs′ə bəs (5 *below*). **1.** A priest of the time of David (I Chr. 24:12).

2. High priest in the time of Nehemiah (Ezra 10:6; Neh. 3:1, 20-21; I Esd. 9:1). He directed the priests in the rebuilding of the Sheep Gate in the city wall (Neh. 3:1), and was subsequently guilty of defiling the temple by assigning space in it to Tobiah, the "Ammonite" opponent of Nehemiah (13:4, 7). The identification between this Eliashib and the high priest (e.g., 3:1) has sometimes been questioned, but without sufficient cause. *See* PRIESTS AND LEVITES.

3. A postexilic singer among those who had married foreign women (Ezra 10:24; I Esd. 9:24).

4. A layman; son of Zattu, in the same list as 3 *above* (Ezra 10:27; I Esd. 9:28).

5. A layman; son of Bani, in the same list as 3 *above* (Ezra 10:36; I Esd. 9:34).

6. A descendant of Zerubbabel and, remotely, of David (I Chr. 3:24). J. M. WARD

ELIASIS ĭ lī′ə sĭs [Ἐλιασείς (B)] (I Esd. 9:34). One of the Israelites, of the family of Bani, who put away his foreign wife and children in the time of Ezra. A clear parallel in Ezra 10:36-37 is not found.

C. T. FRITSCH

ELIATHAH ĭ lī′ə thə [אליאתה, God comes]. A temple musician, son of Heman (I Chr. 25:4, 27). Perhaps it is not a proper name, but part of a prayer which has been incorporated into this list of musicians. If so, we should read: *ēlî attā*, "Thou art my God." *See* GIDDALTI.

Bibliography. G. B. Gray, *Studies in Hebrew Proper Names* (1896), p. 220. R. W. CORNEY

ELIDAD ĭ lī′dăd [אלידד, God has loved] (Num. 34:21). A Benjaminite, son of Chislon. He was one of those appointed, under the oversight of Eleazar and Joshua, to superintend the distribution of the W Jordanian territory among the ten tribes to be settled in that area of Canaan. The meaning of the name Elidad and of other names in this account underscores Israel's dependence upon God for the new life in Canaan.

Bibliography. M. Noth, *Die israelitischen Personennamen* (1928), pp. 34, 183. R. F. JOHNSON

ELIEHOENAI ĭ lī′ə hō′ē nī [אליהועיני, my eyes are toward Yahu]; KJV ELIAONIAS —ō nī′əs [LXX Ἐλιαωνίας] in I Esd. 8:31; KJV ELIHOENAI ĕl′ə hō ē′nī in Ezra 8:4; KJV ELIOENAI ĕl′ĭ ō ē′nī in I Chr. 26:3. **1.** A gatekeeper of the Levitical family of Korah (I Chr. 26:3).

2. Head of a family who returned to Jerusalem with Ezra (Ezra 8:4; I Esd. 8:31).

Bibliography. M. Noth, *Die israelitischen Personennamen* (1928), pp. 32-33, 163, 216. H. H. GUTHRIE, JR.

ELIEL ĭ lī′əl [אליאל, El is my God(?)]. **1.** A chief or family of that part of the tribe of Manasseh which dwelt E of Jordan (I Chr. 5:24; not mentioned in the parallel family lists in Num. 26:28-34; Josh. 17:2 ff).

2. A Kohathite; one of the Levitical singers in the temple (I Chr. 6:34). This Eliel is apparently to be equated with the Eliab of I Chr. 6:27 and possibly with the Elihu of I Sam. 1:1.

3. Two chiefs or families of the tribe of Benjamin (I Chr. 8:20, 22; neither is mentioned in the parallel lists in Gen. 46:21; Num. 26:38-41).

4. Three(?) heroes among those in David's service (I Chr. 11:46, 47; 12:11). Whether the Eliel of I Chr. 12:11 is to be equated with one of the other two or not is impossible to say.

5. A Levite (*see* PRIESTS AND LEVITES) of the family of Hebron mentioned in connection with the bringing of the ARK OF THE COVENANT to Jerusalem (I Chr. 15:9, 11).

6. A Levite purportedly of the time of King Hezekiah (II Chr. 31:13).

Bibliography. M. Noth, *Die israelitischen Personennamen* (1928), p. 140. H. H. GUTHRIE, JR.

ELIENAI ĕl′ĭ ē′nī [אליעיני, *misspelling of* אליועיני, my eyes are toward Yahu]. A family of the tribe of Benjamin (I Chr. 8:20).

Bibliography. M. Noth, *Die israelitischen Personennamen* (1928), p. 237.

ELIEZER ĕl′ĭ ē′zər [אליעזר, my God is my help]; ELIEZAR in I Esd. 8:43; 9:19. **1.** The servant of Abraham who, in lieu of a son, would have been Abraham's heir (Gen. 15:2). The Hebrew text is difficult and probably corrupt (cf. commentaries *ad loc.*). Either Eliezer was from Damascus and the Hebrew rendered "heir" (KJV "steward") has been tampered with in order to play on "Damascus," or "Damascus" has been added to the text as a gloss on the word for "heir." It is presumably Eliezer who is sent to find a wife for Isaac (Gen. 24:2 ff).

2. Moses' second son (Exod. 18:4; I Chr. 23:15, 17; 26:25).

3. A person or family in a list wrongly assigned to Benjamin, actually of Zebulun (I Chr. 7:8).

4. A priest mentioned in connection with the bringing of the ARK OF THE COVENANT to Jerusalem (I Chr. 15:24).

5. A chief of the Reubenites (I Chr. 27:16).

6. A prophet in the time of Jehoshaphat (II Chr. 20:37).

7. A leader in the time of Ezra (Ezra 8:16; I Esd. 8:43).

8. A priest who put away his foreign wife (Ezra 10:18; I Esd. 9:19).

9. A Levite who put away his foreign wife (Ezra 10:23); called Jonah in I Esd. 9:23.

10. A member of the clan of Harim who put away his foreign wife (Ezra (10:31); apparently called Elionas in I Esd. 9:32.

11. A name in the Lukan genealogy of Jesus (Luke 3:29).

Bibliography. M. Noth, *Die israelitischen Personennamen* (1928), pp. 16, 18, 38, 70, 90, 154, 156.

H. H. GUTHRIE, JR.

ELIHOENAI. KJV form of ELIEHOENAI in Ezra 8:4.

ELIHOREPH ĕl'ə hôr'ĭf [אליחרף] (I Kings 4:3). Son of Shisha; one of the high officials in the Solomonic court. He shared with his brother Ahijah the position of royal secretary. However, J. A. Montgomery (*see bibliography*) considers this difficult name to be the office of an official known as "Over-the-Year" and, omitting the words "the priest" after Zadok (vs. 2), interprets the text to mean that Azariah ben Zadok held the office of "Over-the-Year"—i.e., the ranking officer (cf. Assyrian *līmu*).

Bibliography. J. A. Montgomery, *The Books of Kings*, ICC (1951).

E. R. DALGLISH

ELIHU ĭ lī'hū [אליהו *or* אליהוא, he (Yahu) is my God]. **1.** An ancestor of Samuel (I Sam. 1:1); called Eliel in I Chr. 6:34 and Eliab in I Chr. 6:27.

2. A chief of the tribe of Manasseh who deserted Saul to join David at Ziklag (I Chr. 12:20).

3. A Korahite gatekeeper (I Chr. 26:7).

4. One of David's brothers (I Chr. 27:18); but the name should be read "Eliab" with the LXX (cf. I Sam. 16:6; 17:13, 23; I Chr. 2:13; II Chr. 11:18).

5. The young man who speaks to Job when the three friends have failed to silence him (Job 32:2, 4-6; 34:1; 35:1; 36:1). Elihu's speeches are very probably an addition to the book. Represented as a BUZITE (cf. Gen. 22:21; Jer. 25:33) of the family of Ram (cf. Ruth 4:19; I Chr. 2:9-10), he would come from the same region as Job and the friends but be more closely connected with the Hebrews. His genealogy thus symbolizes the function the interpolater of Job 32–37 would have him fulfil—to raise the discussion to a more theological level.

See JOB, BOOK OF.

Bibliography. M. Noth, *Die israelitischen Personennamen* (1928), pp. 18, 70, 143.

H. H. GUTHRIE, JR.

ELIJAH ĭ lī'jə [אליה (II Kings 1:3), Y is God, *presents a wide variety of forms, as* אליהו (I Kings 17:1); אליה, LXX Ἠλίου (II Kings 1:3), Ἠλειά (I Chr. 8:27), Ἠλίας (Mal. 4:5—G 3:22), Ἐλιά (Ezra 10:21)]; KJV ELIAH ĭ lī'ə in I Chr. 8:27; Ezra 10:26; KJV NT ELIAS ĭ lī'əs (from Ἠλεῖας or Ἠλίας). **1.** *See* ELIJAH THE PROPHET.

2. A descendant of the patriarch Benjamin; a son of Jeroham. He was the head of a clan and dwelt in Jerusalem (I Chr. 8:27).

3. A priest who returned from the Exile in the time of Ezra. His father's name was Harim. Elijah, the priest, pledged to divorce the foreign wife whom he had married during the Exile (Ezra 10:21).

4. A returnee of Ezra's time; son of Elam. This layman divorced his wife of foreign origin whom he had brought back from the Exile (Ezra 10:26).

5. One of the ancestors of Judith; father of Ahitub (Jth. 8:1). His name is sometimes rendered as Elihu, because of the ambiguity of the Greek Ἠλίου, which represents both Elijah (II Kings 1:3) and Elihu (I Sam. 1:1).

S. SZIKSZAI

ELIJAH, APOCALYPSE OF. A brief, thoroughly Jewish apocalypse, written *ca.* A.D. 261. It has a conclusion very similar to that of Revelation: devastating wars of the Anti-Messiah (Gigit) conclude this present evil age; the Messiah (Winon?) establishes a forty-year kingdom of plenty, which the surviving saints enjoy; Gog and Magog war against Jerusalem, but are destroyed; a general resurrection and judgment usher in God's new and righteous age; the wicked are sent to a fiery pit, but the saints dwell with God in a combination of a glorious Jerusalem, seen descending from heaven to earth, and a new Garden of Eden.

Bibliography. M. Buttenwieser, *Die hebräische Elias-Apokalypse* (1897).

M. RIST

ELIJAH THE PROPHET. A prophet of the ninth century B.C. from Tishbe of Gilead in the Northern Kingdom; the master of Elisha. Elijah's faith in and zealous loyalty to the Lord predestined him to take leadership in the struggle against the encroaching forces of the Tyrian Baalism fostered by Jezebel. His acts and words were long remembered in the circle of disciples, and his fame grew to more than human dimensions until, finally, he was regarded as the harbinger of the eschatological age.

The reports on the acts of Elijah are dissimilar in nature, and they have to be measured separately for their historical value.

1. Miracles and miraculous elements
2. Struggle against Baalism
3. The prophet's denunciation of kings
4. Eschatological forerunner of the coming Day of the Lord

Bibliography

1. Miracles and miraculous elements. The thread of miracles repeatedly appears in the Elijah legends. At his first appearance in the biblical record, Elijah announced to Ahab the coming of a disastrous drought (I Kings 17:1) whose severity was also recounted in secular records (Jos. Antiq. VIII.xiii.2). During the drought, the prophet hid himself by the

Brook of Cherith and was fed by ravens. When the brook dried up, he went to Zarephath, a Phoenician town in the territory ruled by Sidon (I Kings 17:2-9). In Zarephath he stayed with a widow and her son. Their food was provided by the jar of meal and cruse of oil which remained miraculously unspent during the whole drought (vss. 10-16). One day the son of the widow became ill and died (or was close to death). But Elijah revived the child with the power of prayer and with the application of magico-medical techniques (vss. 17-24; cf. II Kings 4:34-35).

There emerges from Elijah's conversation with Obadiah (I Kings 18:1-16) the fact that the prophet was transported in a miraculous way by the Spirit of the Lord (vs. 12; cf. II Kings 2:16). There is a miraculous element in the fire descending from the sky and consuming the burnt offering in the scene of Mount Carmel (I Kings 18:20-46), but it is clear that the narrator did not lose sight of the main issue —the struggle of Yahwism against Baalism. In the same way, the miraculous feeding of Elijah by an angel on the road to Horeb (19:4-8) does not overshadow the central question of the encounter of the divine word and the prophet. The miracle of the fire, which descended from heaven on the prophet's word and consumed two of King Ahaziah's troops, each containing fifty men and a captain, who came to capture Elijah (II Kings 1:9-16), has a different character. The lack of ethical concern and the immoral thaumaturgical attitude is, on the whole, far removed from the spirit of the Elijah legends.

The narrative of the translation of Elijah (II Kings 2:1-12) dovetails with the Elisha legends, and serves to support the legitimacy of the prophetic succession of Elisha. This is the only account which places Elijah, otherwise always a solitary person, in the company of the prophetic guilds. Elijah and his disciple, Elisha, went from Gilgal to Bethel and from there to Jericho. Elijah repeatedly bade his disciple leave him alone, but Elisha followed his master in this peregrination. When they reached the Jordan, Elijah struck the water of the Jordan with his mantle, whereupon the water parted, and they crossed dry-shod (vss. 1-9).

Elisha, who was aware of the imminent translation of his master, asked Elijah for his share as the first-born (i.e., two thirds of the inheritance; cf. Deut. 21:17) from his spirit, which he apparently obtained (II Kings 2:15). Suddenly a chariot of fire and horses of fire separated the prophet and his disciple, and "Elijah went up by a whirlwind into heaven" (vs. 11). Some fifty men from the prophetic guilds sought him for three days in the mountains and valleys in vain (vss. 15-18), for they thought "it may be that the spirit of the LORD has caught him up and cast him upon some mountain or into some valley" (vs. 16; cf. I Kings 18:12).

2. Struggle against Baalism. During the reign of AHAB, who was politically one of the great monarchs of the Northern Kingdom, the very existence of Yahwism was endangered. Ahab's wife, Jezebel, daughter of Ethbaal, king of Tyre, brought, along with herself, the worship of the Tyrian Baal, erected a temple for the deity (I Kings 16:30-33), and supported a huge college of Baal and Asherah prophets (I Kings 18:19). Apparently "Ahab served Baal a little" (II Kings 10:18), but he did not completely abandon the faith of his fathers, as the names of his children, AHAZIAH; JEHORAM; ATHALIAH (all of them formed with the divine name Yahweh), indicate. But compromise, false tolerance, and syncretism were incompatible with the Lord's claim for exclusive allegiance. Probably the prophetic guilds' sharp criticism of the court's "limping with two different opinions" was the prelude to the general persecution of Yahwistic prophets (I Kings 18:13; 19:14). Against this dark background, the encounter of King Ahab and Elijah unfolds with dramatic force.

Elijah, himself, went to Ahab to announce the end of the drought (18:1). He was addressed by the king as "troubler of Israel," but he hurled the accusation back to Ahab, confronted him with his apostasy, and challenged the prophets of Baal to a contest (vss. 17-19), which would serve to decide whether the Lord or Baal was God. All Israel was summoned to witness the ordeal. Elijah stood alone against the 450 Baal prophets. The assembled people accepted as conditions of the contest that the sacrificial animals be placed upon the unkindled wood on the altars—one for Baal, another for the Lord—and that the prophets of Baal and Elijah were to ask for fire from the deity, with the provision that whichever deity answered with fire must be accepted as God (vss. 20-24). From morning until noon, the Baal prophets entreated their god, whirled around the altar in a grotesque, limping dance, and, in the final frenzy, cut themselves with lances and swords; but all these attempts were in vain; there was no divine answer (vss. 25-29). In contrast with the desperate, ecstatic frenzy of the Baal prophets, the dignity and serenity of Elijah were indicative of his profound trust in and reliance upon the only God. Upon Elijah's command, water was poured upon the sacrificial animal on the altar of the Lord, probably as a rain-making device in accord with ancient sympathetic magical practices (vss. 30-35). After this, Elijah prayed, and the fire of the Lord fell and consumed the burnt offering. In the presence of this miracle, the people confessed that the Lord was God, and, upon Elijah's command, massacred the prophets of Baal (vss. 36-40). The final scene of the contest of Mount Carmel is the coming of rain after the long drought and Ahab's and Elijah's return to the city of Jezreel (vss. 41-46). The details of the contest of Mount Carmel reveal the growth of the miraculous element in the tradition, but the essential historicity of the contest can hardly be denied.

The momentary victory of Elijah on Mount Carmel was of no avail, for in the next scene he fled from before the revenge of Jezebel. He went to Judah and from there on a pilgrimage to Mount Horeb. On the mount Elijah beheld the power of wind, earthquake, and fire, which phenomena belonged to the theophanic pattern (*see* THEOPHANY); but the Lord did not appear through these forces. Then a voice commanded Elijah to go and to anoint Hazael as king of Syria, Jehu as king of Israel, and Elisha as the successor to the prophet (19:1-17). In this command and in the divine promise to keep a remnant of seven thousand faithful to the true faith (vs. 18), the struggle of Baalism and Yahwism is the dominant theme. In a loosely connected story, Elijah called Elisha into his service (vss. 19-21); he did not anoint Hazael and Jehu, in spite of the divine commission, but later Elisha completed this mission (cf. II Kings 8–9).

The claim of Yahweh-worship to the exclusion of other deities reappears in the (most likely historical) incident of Elijah's condemnation of King Ahaziah, the son of Ahab, who sent messengers to inquire of the oracle of BAAL-ZEBUB, the god of Ekron, concerning his recovery from sickness (II Kings 1:1-8).

3. The prophet's denunciation of kings. Elijah courageously stood up against King Ahab and his son Ahaziah. He denounced these kings because of their syncretistic attitude which permitted the worship of foreign deities together with the worship of the Lord (I Kings 18:17-19; II Kings 1:1-8).

Besides these instances, the prophet raised his voice against the king in the case of Naboth's vineyard, where the ethical implications of Yahwism were at stake (I Kings 21). King Ahab ardently desired to acquire the vineyard of NABOTH, who refused to sell it. Jezebel instigated a trial in which Naboth was sentenced to death on a fabricated charge. After the execution of Naboth, Ahab took possession of the vineyard. Elijah's scornful words branded Ahab as a murderer and robber and foretold the doom of the royal house (I Kings 21:17-24).

The Chronicler reports of a letter of Elijah to Jehoram, king of Judah, proclaiming punishment for the king's apostasy and fratricide (II Chr. 21:12-15). The letter is generally recognized as a composition of the Chronicler.

4. Eschatological forerunner of the coming Day of the Lord. Elijah's memory was piously preserved in the circle of the prophetic guilds which claimed a spiritual kinship with Elijah through his beloved disciple Elisha. But he made a profound impression on the imagination of the people of Israel, too. Later ages remembered the mystery of Elijah's translation, and expected his return as the forerunner of the coming Day of the Lord (Mal. 4:5). He was expected to "turn the hearts of fathers to their children and the hearts of children to their fathers" (vs. 6), and to come forth from the heavenly chambers "to restore the tribes of Israel" (Ecclus. 48:10).

In the NT, the same role of the eschatological precursor is attributed to Elijah. Some of the contemporaries of Jesus thought that he was Elijah (Matt. 16:14; Luke 9:8). Others thought of John the Baptist as Elijah, but he disowned the role (John 1:21). Yet in the early church John, as the forerunner of Christ, was regarded either as an heir to the spirit and power of Elijah (Luke 1:17), or as Elijah redivivus (Matt. 11:14; 17:10-13). At the transfiguration of Jesus, Elijah appeared together with Moses (Matt. 17:3-4; Mark 9:4-5).

The "prophet" of the Dead Sea Manual of Discipline (IX. 11) is probably Elijah in the same role of messianic herald. He remained the expected harbinger of the age to come and of the Messiah, in the Mishnaic literature also (Sheḳ. 2.5; Soṭ. 9.15; B. M. 1.8; Eduyoth 8.7).

Bibliography. A. S. Peake, "Elijah and Jezebel. The Conflict with the Tyrian Baal," *BJRL,* XI (1927), 296-321; A. Alt, "Das Gottesurteil auf dem Karmel," *Beer-Festschrift* (1935), pp. 1-18; R. de Vaux, "Les prophètes de Baal sur le mont Carmel," *BMBeyrouth,* V (1941), 7-20; O. Eissfeldt, *Der Gott Karmel* (1953); K. Galling, "Der Gott Karmel und die Aechtung der fremden Götter," *Alt-Festschrift* (1953), pp. 105-25; *Elie le prophète selon les Ecritures et les traditions chrétiennes,* I (1956).

S. SZIKSZAI

ELIKA ĭ lī'kə [אליקא] (II Sam. 23:25). A Harodite whose name appears in the list of Davidic Mighty Men known as the "Thirty." He is omitted from the similar catalogue in I Chr. 11:27.

ELIM ē'lĭm [אילם, large trees]. The fourth stopping place after the Israelites crossed the Red Sea, and the first place where they found fresh water. It was marked by twelve springs of water and seventy palm trees (Exod. 15:27; 16:1; Num. 33:9-10).

Elim is commonly identified with Wadi Gharandel, where vegetation, palms, and abundant water are found. This site is *ca.* sixty-three miles from Suez, and travelers who make the journey to Sinai from Egypt usually camp there. Some scholars who would place Mount Sinai in Arabia have located Elim near Elath on the Gulf of Aqabah. It also has been suggested that the name Elim, dubiously interpreted as meaning "gods" (אלים), may refer to a cultic place located near the palm trees and water springs.

Bibliography. E. H. Palmer, *The Desert of the Exodus* (1872), p. 46.

J. L. MIHELIC

ELIMELECH ĭ lĭm'ə lĕk [אלימלך, God is king]. A Bethlehemite who, with his wife, Naomi, and his two sons, migrated to Moab in the days of the judges to escape the famine in Israel. After he and his two sons died, Naomi and Ruth, his daughter-in-law, returned to Bethlehem, where Ruth subsequently married his wealthy kinsman Boaz (Ruth 1:2-3; 2:1, 3; 4:3, 9).

E. R. DALGLISH

ELIOENAI ĕl'ĭ ō ē'nī [אליועיני, my eyes are toward my God]; KJV ELIONAS —ō'nəs ['Ελιωνας] in I Esd. 9:22, ELIADAS ĭ lī'ə dəs ['Ελιαδας] in I Esd. 9:28. **1.** A postexilic descendant of David (I Chr. 3:23-24).

2. A chief of the tribe of Simeon (I Chr. 4:36).

3. Listed as a Benjaminite family in what is actually a list of families of Zebulun (I Chr. 7:8).

4. A priest of the sons of Pashhur who put away his foreign wife (Ezra 10:22; I Esd. 9:22).

5. A son of Zattu who put away his foreign wife (Ezra 10:27; I Esd. 9:28).

6. A postexilic priest (Neh. 12:41).

Bibliography. M. Noth, *Die israelitischen Personennamen* (1928), pp. 32, 33, 163, 216.

H. H. GUTHRIE, JR.

ELIONAS ĕl'ĭ ō'nəs ['Ελιωνάς]. **1.** One of those who put away their foreign wives (I Esd. 9:32); apparently called Eliezer in Ezra 10:31.

2. KJV form of ELIOENAI (4) in I Esd. 9:22.

ELIPHAL ĭ lī'fəl [אליפל]. Son of Ur(?); a member of the Mighty Men of David known as the "Thirty" (I Chr. 11:35). However, in II Sam. 23:34 he is called Eliphelet (*see* ELIPHELET 2) the son of AHASBAI of Maacah, which the Chronicler rendered "Eliphal the son of Ur, Hepher the Mecherathite" (I Chr. 11:

35*b*-36*a*). Since the term "Mecherathite" is otherwise unknown, it appears reasonable to consider it a faulty reading of "Maacah," while "Ahasbai" was read by the Chronicler as "Ur Hepher." In these latter two readings is no doubt concealed the true name of the father of Eliphal. E. R. DALGLISH

ELIPHALAT. KJV Apoc. form of ELIPHELET 5.

ELIPHALET. KJV form of ELIPHELET in II Sam. 5:16; I Chr. 14:7; I Esd. 8:39.

ELIPHAZ ĕl′ə făz [אליפז, *possibly* God is fine gold *or* God crushes]. **1.** The eldest son of Esau and his Hittite wife Adah; husband of a Horite concubine Timna (Gen. 36:4, 10-11, 15; I Chr. 1:35-36). Thus the ancestor of several Edomite clan chiefs (אלופים; cf. Gen. 36:15).

2. The first and oldest of Job's three friends (Job 2:11; 4:1; 15:1; 22:1; 42:7, 9). Though the wisest, Eliphaz is presented throughout the dialogue as a dogmatician, holding to a "merely moralistic view of salvation." First Eliphaz exhorted Job to "despise not the chastening of the Almighty" (5:17) that he might enjoy prosperity, next accused him of "doing away with [religion]" (15:4) and turning against God, then finally charged him with numerous sins and concluded with an appeal for conversion that was still grounded on his dogma of retribution (ch. 22).

Since this Eliphaz is regularly called "the Temanite" (התימני), and TEMAN (תימן) designates both an Edomite district renowned for wisdom (cf. Jer. 49:7) and the eldest son of 1 *above* (Gen. 36:11), Eliphaz 2 may be seen as derived from Eliphaz 1.

See also JOB, BOOK OF. L. HICKS

ELIPHELEHU ĭ lĭf′ə lē′hū [אליפלהו, God, distinguish him!] (I Chr. 15:18, 21); KJV ELIPHELEH ĭ lĭf′ə lə. A Levite of the second rank appointed by David to be one of the "leaders with lyres." Names formed of vocative, verb in the imperative, and expressed object are rare in Hebrew, though not uncommon in other Semitic languages. The omission of this name from a similar list in I Chr. 16:5 may indicate that it is an addition to the original list.

Bibliography. G. B. Gray, *Studies in Hebrew Proper Names* (1896), pp. 220-22. R. W. CORNEY

ELIPHELET ĭ lĭf′ə lĕt [Heb. אליפלט, God is deliverance; Gr. Ἐλιφαλατος (I Esd. 8:39)]; KJV ELIPHALET in II Sam. 5:16; I Chr. 14:7; I Esd. 8:39. Alternately: ELIPHALAT —lăt [Ἐλιφαλατ] (I Esd. 9:33 KJV); ELPELET ĕl pē′lĭt, KJV ELPALET ĕl′pă lət [אלפלט, God is deliverance] (I Chr. 14:5). **1.** A son of David (II Sam. 5:16; I Chr. 3:6, 8; 14:5, 7). The repetition of the name in I Chr. 3; 14 must be due to a scribal error.

2. One of David's MIGHTY MEN (II Sam. 23:34); *cf.* ELIPHAL (I Chr. 11:35).

3. A Benjaminite, descendant of Saul and Jonathan (I Chr. 8:39).

4. One of those who returned from exile with Ezra (Ezra 8:13; I Esd. 8:39).

5. One of those who put away their foreign wives (Ezra 10:33; I Esd. 9:33).

Bibliography. M. Noth, *Die israelitischen Personennamen* (1928), pp. 16, 18, 34, 90, 156. H. H. GUTHRIE, JR.

ELISABETH. KJV form of ELIZABETH.

ELISEUS ĕl′ə sē′əs. Douay Version form of ELISHA.

ELISHA ĭ lī′shə [אלישע, God is salvation; Ἐλισαῖος]; KJV NT and Apoc. ELISEUS ĕl′ə sē′əs. A ninth-century-B.C. prophet of the N kingdom; the disciple and successor of ELIJAH. The biblical account of Elisha embraces a considerable part of the first thirteen chapters of II Kings.

1. His call and the dates of his ministry. Elisha, son of Shaphat, was a peasant of ABEL-MEHOLAH,* but that he was considerably rich is indicated by the fact that he was plowing with twelve yoke of oxen at the time that Elijah called him into his service (I Kings 19:19). The lavish farewell feast, consisting of the meat of the oxen, that he gave to the people before his departure with Elijah also supports the assumption that he was wealthy. Fig. ABE 2.

His name appears for the first time in a divine command given to Elijah, according to which Elijah had to anoint Elisha as his successor (I Kings 19:16-17). Apparently another thread of tradition reports the actual call, because there is no trace of anointment, but it is reported that Elijah cast his mantle upon Elisha (vss. 19-21). This act represented a real transfer of the prophetic power to Elisha, so he followed his new master. The same motif of the transfer of the prophetic commission and spirit to Elisha by means of Elijah's mantle appears in the scene where Elijah was transported, amid chariot and horses of fire, by a whirlwind into heaven (II Kings 2:13-15).

The beginning of Elisha's ministry coincides with the last years of Ahab's reign (I Kings 19:1-17) or the first years of Joram's reign (II Kings 2:15; cf. ch. 1), and bridges over half a century—to the first years of Joash' reign (II Kings 13:14-19). With approximate accuracy, his ministry can be dated between 850 and 800 B.C. His ministry and prophetic activity, reported by a reverential tradition which was transmitted in the circle of prophetic disciples, are shrouded by the veils of pious legends and miracle narratives.

2. His miracles. Elisha's first miracle was performed immediately after his master was taken up to heaven. He took Elijah's mantle, invoked the name of the Lord, and struck the water of the Jordan, which thereupon parted before him (II Kings 2:13-14). Thus he repeated the miracle performed by Elijah (vs. 8). The sons of the prophets (*see* PROPHET) of Gilgal, Bethel, and Jericho recognized him as their leader and the successor to Elijah (vs. 15).

Many of the miracle narratives are connected with these prophetic guilds and witness to a profound reverence and pious awe. Elisha healed the spring of Jericho by throwing salt from a new bowl into the spring (II Kings 2:19-22). By the miracle of the unspent jar of oil, he helped the widow of one of the sons of the prophets when a creditor wanted to take her two children as slaves in place of payment of her debts (4:1-7). Elisha repaid the hospitality of a wealthy Shunammite woman by promising a son to her, and years later he resuscitated the child when it died from sunstroke (vss. 8-37; cf. I Kings 17:8-24). Once, in a time of famine, one of the sons of the prophets put some wild gourds in the common meal of the prophetic monastery—unaware of their poisonous nature. When it was discovered that there was "death in the pot," the prophet made it harmless by putting some meal into the pottage (II Kings 4:38-41). Another time, he fed a hundred men with twenty loaves of barley and some fresh ears of grain (vss. 42-44). He healed Naaman, the commander of the Syrian army, who was afflicted with leprosy, and refused to accept the lavish presents of the grateful Syrian (5:1-19). When one of the prophetic disciples lost a borrowed axe head, Elisha caused it to float on the water (6:1-7); and then another time, he struck a Syrian raiding party with blindness and led them into Samaria, whereupon he caused their eyes to open. The king, following Elisha's magnanimous council, prepared a great feast for the captive Syrians and sent them away (vss. 8-23). Not even death could stop the miracles of the prophet, for when a dead man was put into the grave of Elisha, he was revived by the touch of the bones of the prophet (13:20-21).

The prophet appears in these narratives in a more than human role; he towers over the anonymous members of the prophetic guilds. Apparently these sons of the prophets preserved the memory of Elisha, but they embellished it with folkloristic and magical elements. The aim of the storyteller was, obviously, to enhance the fame of the prophet, even with such a repugnant story as that of the mocking children and the two she-bears (II Kings 2:23-25). The historical fact which emerges out of these miracle narratives is that Elisha was the beloved leader of the prophetic guilds; and his human greatness, piety, and willingness to help were lovingly remembered in the prophetic guilds.

3. His influence upon historical events. In the miracle narratives the historical person Elisha is hard to find, but there are some legends on the border between tales and historical narratives that help to shed light upon the historical role of Elisha. Some of these stories are overloaded with legendary elements, as are the reports on the healing of Naaman's leprosy (II Kings 5:1-19) and the miraculous capture of the Syrian raiding party (6:8-23). In others, the historical elements are dominant, as in the story of Elisha's oracle during the Israelite military campaign against the Moabites (3:4-27) and during the Syrian siege of Samaria (6:24–7:20).

Elisha's portrait as an actor on the scene of history is most markedly drawn in the happenings whereby he fulfils the legacy of his master, Elijah (I Kings 19:15-18), by preparing the revolutions of Hazael of Syria (II Kings 8:7-15) and Jehu of Israel (chs. 9–10). From all these semihistorical narratives, it becomes exceedingly clear that Elisha understood that his task was to direct the route of history. His friendly connections with the court after the Jehu revolution, and the high esteem in which he was held by King Joash, are convincingly mirrored in the deathbed scene of the prophet (13:14-19), where the weeping king cries: "My father, my father! The chariots of Israel and its horsemen!" (vs. 14). If modern scholarship does not pay the same lavish tribute to his greatness as his disciples did, his influence upon the history of Israel can hardly be questioned. He represents, in its initial state, the prophetic attitude which claimed the right to mold the nation's fate by proclaiming the Lord's will.

Bibliography. W. Erbt, *Elia, Elisa, Jona* (1907); J. Pedersen, *Israel, Its Life and Culture*, III-IV (1940), 108-20; A. Lods, *Israel from Its Beginnings to the Middle of the Eighth Century* (1953), pp. 420-23, 446-47. S. SZIKSZAI

ELISHAH ĭ lī'shə [אלישה]. The name of one of the descendants of Japheth in the "Table of Nations" (Gen. 10:4; I Chr. 1:7) and of a coastal area exporting purple and blue dye stuff to Tyre (Ezek. 27:7). Elishah is commonly associated with *Alashia,* occurring in cuneiform records found at Mari, Alalakh, Ugarit, Tell el-Amarna, and Khattushash, from the eighteenth to the thirteenth centuries B.C. This name is usually spelled *a-ra-sa* in Egyptian and occurs in the gentilic *alty* in an Ugaritic text. It is the opinion of most scholars that Elishah-Alashia refers to some part of Cyprus whence copper and other raw materials were exported. The use of this term in Ezek. 27 as distinct from *Kittim* ("Cyprus"; vs. 6) shows that at that period it referred to the non-Phoenecian part of the island.

Bibliography. G. F. Hill, *A History of Cyprus,* I (1940), 42-50; C. F. Schaeffer, *Enkomi-Alasia,* I (1952), 1-8.

J. C. GREENFIELD

ELISHAMA ĭ lĭsh'ə mə [אלישמע, God has heard].
1. The leader of the tribe of Ephraim at the census in the wilderness; the grandfather of Joshua (Num. 1:10; 2:18; 7:48, 53; 10:22; I Chr. 7:26). The name may be ancient, but the lists in which it appears are postexilic.

2. One of David's sons (II Sam. 5:16; I Chr. 3:6, 8; 14:7). In I Chr. 3:6 "Elishama" must be a scribal error, and "Elishua" should be read (cf. II Sam. 5:15).

3. A member of the royal family of Judah; grandfather of the Ishmael who slew Gedaliah (II Kings 25:25; Jer. 41:1).

4. Part of the tribe of Judah; descended from Sheshan the Jerahmeelite (I Chr. 2:41).

5. A priest, purportedly of the time of King Jehoshaphat (II Chr. 17:8).

6. A scribe at the court of Jehoiakim (Jer. 36:12, 20-21).

Bibliography. M. Noth, *Die israelitischen Personennamen* (1928), pp. 20, 21, 33, 90, 185; D. Diringer, *Le iscrizioni antico-ebraiche palestinesi* (1934), pp. 216, 232, 257.

H. H. GUTHRIE, JR.

ELISHAPHAT ĭ lĭsh'ə făt [אלישפט, God has judged] (II Chr. 23:1). One of the Judean commanders who aided Jehoiada the priest in securing the kingship for Joash against Athaliah.

ELISHEBA ĭ lĭsh'ə bə [אלישבע, my God is fortune *or* fulness] (Exod. 6:23). The daughter of Amminadab, and the wife of Aaron, to whom she bore four sons. The LXX erroneously transliterates 'Ελ(ε)ισάβεθ, "Elizabeth." The Hebrew name commonly occurs in ossuary inscriptions from the first two centuries A.D.

Bibliography. L. Koehler, "Hebräische Vokabeln II," *ZAW,* N.F. XIV (1937), 165-66 (on the meaning of the name).

J. F. Ross

ELISHUA ĕl'ə sho͞o'ə [אלישוע, God is salvation]. One of the sons of David who were born at Jerusalem (II Sam. 5:15; I Chr. 14:15). In I Chr. 3:6 he is called Elishama, which appears to be a transcriptional error imported from the following line.

ELISIMUS. KJV Apoc. variant of ELIASHIB 4.

ELIU ĭ lī'ū. **1.** Douay Version form of ELIHU.
2. KJV Apoc. form of ELIJAH.

ELIUD ĭ lī'əd ['Ελιούδ]. An ancestor of Jesus (Matt. 1:14-15; also Luke 3:23 ff in MS D).

ELIZABETH ĭ lĭz'ə bəth ['Ελισάβετ, 'Ελεισάβετ; *same as* אלישבע, ELISHEBA ĭ lĭsh'ə bə, God is an oath(?), God is good fortune(?)]; KJV ELISABETH. The wife of the priest Zechariah, and the mother of JOHN THE BAPTIST (Luke 1:5-66).

Elizabeth, who bore the name of Aaron's wife (Exod. 6:23; *see* ELISHEBA), was of priestly descent. From the standpoint of Jewish law and custom, which required priests to marry virgins of Israelitish birth but not necessarily of priestly families, her marriage to the priest ZECHARIAH (33) would have been considered ideal. In addition to pure lineage, both partners are described as possessing faultless characters (Luke 1:6). In them the highest form of OT piety was embodied.

But there was one limitation. Elizabeth, like Sarah and Hannah of old, was barren—to a Jewish woman a privation almost too great to be borne. The story in Luke records in language reminiscent of the pertinent OT narratives the wondrous deed of God by which her barrenness was overcome in her old age and a child of great promise—a way-preparer for the Messiah—was brought into the world.

Elizabeth is called by Luke a kinswoman or "relative" (συγγενίς) of Mary the mother of Jesus (1:36); the term is too broad to be of help in determining their precise relationship. It is possible that the passage suggests that Mary had priestly blood in her. *See* MARY THE MOTHER OF JESUS.

In certain OL MSS, in Irenaeus, and in Origen there is evidence that the Magnificat (Luke 1:46-55) in the original text of Luke may have been ascribed to Elizabeth rather than to Mary. This song, so like that of Hannah in I Sam. 2:1-10, in some respects is more appropriately ascribed to the former than to the latter.

Bibliography. H. L. Strack and P. Billerbeck, *Kommentar zum NT aus Talmud und Midrasch,* II (1924), 68 ff. E. Klostermann, *Das Lukasevangelium* (1929), pp. 5 ff. J. R. Harris, "Mary or Elizabeth?" *ET,* 41 (1929-30), 266-67; "Again the Magnificat," *ET,* 42 (1930-31), 188-90. L. Köhler, "Hebräische Vokabeln II," *ZAW,* 55 (1937), 165-66.

E. P. BLAIR

ELIZAPHAN ĕl'ə zā'făn [אליצפן, God has hidden—*i.e.,* protected]. Alternately: ELZAPHAN ĕl zā'făn [אלצפן] (Exod. 6:22; Lev. 10:4). **1.** A Kohathite Levite, son of UZZIEL 1 (Exod. 6:22). He was the head of the Kohathites in the wilderness (Num. 3:30). At Moses' direction he and Mishael, his brother, removed the bodies of Nadab and Abihu from the camp (Lev. 10:4). A father's house was derived from him (I Chr. 15:8; II Chr. 29:13).

2. Son of PAROSH; chosen from Zebulun as one of the ten tribal leaders who, with Eleazar and Joshua, were to divide the land of Canaan (Num. 34:25).

Bibliography. M. Noth, *Die israelitischen Personennamen* (1928), pp. 33-34, 178.

T. M. MAUCH

ELIZUR ĭ lī'zər [אליצור, God is a rock]. Leader of Reuben; son of Shedeur (Num. 1:5; 2:10; 7:30, 35; 10:18). He was one of twelve tribal leaders or deputies who assisted Moses in taking a census of Israel and in other tasks in the wilderness. *See* PRINCE.

Bibliography. M. Noth, *Die israelitischen Personennamen* (1928), p. 156.

R. F. JOHNSON

ELKANAH ĕl kā'nə [אלקנה, God has created *or* possessed]. **1.** A person or subdivision of the Levitical family of Korah (Exod. 6:24). The list in which it appears is postexilic. Elkanah was apparently a much-used name among the Levites, and whether this Elkanah is the same as one of the ones in 5-8 *below* is hard to say.

2. The father of Samuel (I Sam. 1:1, 4, 8, 19, 21, 23; 2:11, 20; I Chr. 6:27, 34). In I Samuel, Elkanah is an Ephraimite, but I Chronicles makes him, and so Samuel, a Levite (*see* PRIESTS AND LEVITES). The Chronicler may have made an honest mistake because of the profusion of Elkanahs in I Chr. 6 (*see* 5 and 6 *below*), but it is more likely that, in accord with his purpose, he consciously made the change. *See* CHRONICLES, I, II.

3. A Benjaminite warrior who deserted Saul to join David at Ziklag (I Chr. 12:6). The designation of this Elkanah as a Korahite must have to do with the town from which he came rather than with his being a member of the Levitical family (cf. I Chr. 2:43). Since I Chr. 12 is largely fictional exaggeration which is not borne out by I Sam. 27, the question is probably impossible to settle.

4. An official of the court of Ahaz, the mention of whose assassination appears in the Chronicler's rather fanciful account of Ahaz' reign (II Chr. 28:7).

5. A name in a list of Levites (I Chr. 6:23, 25, 36; *see* PRIESTS AND LEVITES).

6. A name in a list of Levites (I Chr. 6:26, 35; *see* PRIESTS AND LEVITES).

7. A name in a list of Levites (I Chr. 9:16; *see* PRIESTS AND LEVITES).

8. A Levitical GATEKEEPER of the ARK OF THE COVENANT (I Chr. 15:23).

Bibliography. M. Noth, *Die israelitischen Personennamen* (1928), pp. 20, 21, 172.

H. H. GUTHRIE, JR.

ELKIAH ĕl kī'ə ['Ελκεά; Vulg. *Elai*] (Jth. 8:1); KJV ELCIA. An ancestor of Judith; son of Ananias and father of Oziel.

J. C. SWAIM

ELKOSH ĕl'kŏsh [האלקשי] (Nah. 1:1); KJV THE ELKOSHITE —īt. The residence of the prophet Nahum.

Several traditions are extant concerning the location of the proposed site. Eastern medieval tradition located both the birth and the burial place of the prophet at Al-Qush, some fifty miles N of modern Mosul (near the ruins of ancient Nineveh). Such tradition does not antedate the sixteenth century, however, and the internal evidence of the book does not support an Assyrian location of the site.

In the prologue to his commentary on Nahum, Jerome speaks of his visit to the village of Hilkesei in Galilee, to which contemporary tradition pointed as the prophet's native home. Modern el-Kauzeh has been suggested as the site to which Jerome referred. A late Galilean tradition centers on Capernaum as probably meaning "the village of Nahum." Any Galilean location is rendered improbable, however, as a consequence of the fall of the N kingdom *ca.* one hundred years prior to the composition of the prophet's work.

Still another tradition, preserved by certain patristic writers, locates Elkosh in Simeonite territory—i.e., in S Judea. Pseudo-Epiphanius further localizes the site by specifying the vicinity of Begabar (Syrian *Bēt Gabrē*), the modern Beit Jibrin. Though the exact site remains undiscovered, the S Judean tradition seems more in keeping with the chronological and circumstantial setting of the prophet's work.

Bibliography. E. G. Kraeling, *Bible Atlas* (1956), p. 310; W. A. Maier, *The Book of Nahum* (1959), pp. 20-26.

W. H. MORTON

ELLASAR ĕl'ə sär [אלסר]. A country the king of which, Arioch, is mentioned in the Abraham traditions of Gen. 14. Neither Ellasar nor Arioch has so far been convincingly identified with countries or persons of known historicity. The old identifications with the S Babylonian kingdom of Larsa and its ruler Warad-Sin have been generally abandoned.

T. JACOBSEN

ELM. KJV translation of אלה (*'ēlâ*) in Hos. 4:13 (RSV TEREBINTH). The elm, *Ulmus campestris* L., is not a Palestinian tree.

ELMADAM ĕl mā'dəm ['Ελμαδάμ; 'Ελμωδάμ] (Luke 3:28); KJV ELMODAM ĕl mō'dăm. An ancestor of Jesus.

ELNAAM ĕl nā'əm [אלנעם, God is pleasantness] (I Chr. 11:46). The father of Jeribai and Joshaviah, both of whom are included in the sixteen additional names which the Chronicler adds to the catalogue of the "Thirty" as it is represented in II Sam. 23.

ELNATHAN ĕl nā'thən [אלנתן, God has given; 'Ελναθάν]; KJV Apoc. ALNATHAN ăl—. **1.** A Jerusalemite, father of Nehushta the mother of Jehoiachin (II Kings 24:8), and probably the son of Achbor; among the princes who took part in the episode of Baruch's reading of Jeremiah's scroll to Jehoiakim (Jer. 36:12). He led the party that fetched the fugitive prophet Uriah from Egypt and cut him down before Jehoiakim (Jer. 26:22-23). On Lachish Ostracon III (*see* LACHISH), which comes from this period, appears the following item: "The commander of the host, Coniah son of Elnathan, hath come down in order to go into Egypt." An identification between this Elnathan and that in the OT is possible though unlikely.

2. The MT of Ezra 8:16 lists two "chiefs" and one "man of insight" by this name among those returning from the Exile. According to I Esd. 8:44, there should be only two named here.

J. M. WARD

ELOAH ĕ lō'ə [אלוה]. A word for God found especially in the book of Job. *See* GOD, NAMES OF, § C4.

ELOHIM ĕl'ō hĭm, ĭ lō'hĭm (Heb. ĕl ō hēm') [אלהים]. The general term for "gods" or, when used in the plural of majesty, for "God" or "deity." *See* GOD, NAMES OF, § C3.

ELOHIST ĕl'ō hĭst, ĭ lō'hĭst. The author or compiler of the E source of the Pentateuch (*see* E), which is commonly associated with the N kingdom and dated to the eighth century B.C.

ELOI, ELOI, LAMA SABACHTHANI. *See* ELI, ELI, LAMA SABACHTHANI.

ELON ē'lŏn [אלון *or* אילון *or* אילן, oak *or* terebinth]; ELONITES ē'lə nīts. **1.** A son of Zebulun; probably an eponym (Gen. 46:14; Num. 26:26).

2. A Hittite (*see* HITTITES), the father of one of the wives of Esau (Gen. 26:34; 36:2). The name of the daughter is different in each case, probably because of differing traditions of Edomite genealogy (cf. Gen. 28:9; 36:9-14). In Gen. 26:34, LXX(A), Samar., and Syr. read "Elon the Hivite" (*see* HIVITES).

3. A minor JUDGE (Judg. 12:11-12). The name may merely be an etiological explanation of the name of the town AIJALON, where Elon is said to have been buried, since both are spelled the same in Hebrew.

Bibliography. M. Noth, *Die israelitischen Personennamen* (1928), pp. 7, 230. H. H. GUTHRIE, JR.

4. A village of Dan near Timnah (Josh. 19:43). The location may be 'Alein, W of Beit Mahsir, or Khirbet Wadi 'Alin between Deir Aban and 'Ain Shems (Beth-shemesh).

ELON-BETH-HANAN ē'lən bĕth hā'nən [אילון בית חנן, oak of the house of Hanan] (I Kings 4:9). A village of Dan in Solomon's second administrative district. It may be the same as Elon, or perhaps one should read with the LXX: "Aijalon (to) Beth Haran," or with another variant: "Aijalon and Beth Hanan" (cf. Josh. 19:42). V. R. GOLD

ELOTH. Alternate form of ELATH.

ELPAAL ĕl pā'əl [אלפעל, God of doing *or* creating(?)]. A Benjaminite clan or family (I Chr. 8:11-12, 18).

Bibliography. M. Noth, *Die israelitischen Personennamen* (1928), pp. 34, 172.

ELPALET. KJV form of ELPELET.

EL-PARAN ĕl pâr'ən [איל פארן, tree of Paran] (Gen. 14:6). The southernmost point reached by Chedorlaomer and his allies in their raid into Palestine, during the course of which Lot was taken captive. El-paran is probably the earlier name for Elath—Ezion-geber. V. R. GOLD

ELPELET. Alternate form of ELIPHELET.

EL SHADDAY ĕl shăd'ī [אֵל שַׁדַּי, God Almighty]. *See* SHADDAI; ALMIGHTY; GOD, NAMES OF, § C2*a*.

ELTEKEH ĕl'tə kə [אֶלְתְּקֵה, meeting place] (Josh. 19:44; KJV ELTEKE). Alternately: ELTEKE [אֶלְתְּקֵא] (Josh. 21:23). A Danite town assigned to the Levites; later it passed into Philistine hands, along with Timnah, the home of Samson's wife. In 701 B.C. a great battle was fought at Eltekeh between Sennacherib and the Egyptian-Ethiopian army, after which the victorious Sennacherib besieged and captured Eltekeh and Timnah, slew the rebellious leaders of Ekron, and then invaded Judah (cf. Assyrian *altaqū,* and the Hebrew variant reading *'altaqō* in Josh. 19:44). See the Sennacherib Prism, col. II, lines 79-83; col. III, lines 1 ff.

With the identification of Khirbet el-Muqanna as EKRON, the location of Eltekeh, which was N of Ekron and W of TIMNAH, is now uncertain.

Bibliography. Y. Aharoni, "The Northern Boundary of Judah," *PEQ* (1958), pp. 27-31. V. R. GOLD

ELTEKON ĕl'tə kŏn [אֶלְתְּקֹן] (Josh. 15:59). A village of Judah in the hill-country district of Beth-zur; probably to be identified with Khirbet ed-Deir, *ca.* two miles S of Hausan and *ca.* four miles W of Bethlehem.

ELTOLAD ĕl'tō'lăd [אֶלְתּוֹלַד, generation] (Josh. 15:30; 19:4). Alternately: TOLAD tō'lăd [תּוֹלָד] (I Chr. 4:29). A city of Simeon in the S of Judah, near Ezem and Hormah. The name seems to indicate that it was a shrine to which women would come to pray for children. The site has not yet been identified.

S. COHEN

ELUL ē'lŭl [אֱלוּל; Ελουλ]. The Hebrew form of Akkadian *ululu,* the sixth month of the year (August-September). *See* CALENDAR.

ELUZAI ĭ lōō'zī [אֶלְעוּזַי, God is my strength] (I Chr. 12:5—H 12:6). One of the disaffected Benjaminite warriors of the house of Saul, famous for their archery and ambidextrous slinging, who joined the outlaw band of David at Ziklag.

ELYMAIS ĕl'ə mā'əs [ἡ 'Ελυμαΐς] (Tob. 2:10; I Macc. 6:1; cf. Dan. 8:2). A city or province located, according to I Macc. 6:1, "in Persia."

In I Macc. 6:1 the minuscule MSS 64 236 534 and 19 62 93 542, dating from the ninth to the twelfth century and probably representing the LXX revision of Lucian (died A.D. 312), read: ὅτι ἐστὶν 'Ελυμαΐς ἐν τῇ Περσίδι πόλις, "that Elymais in Persia was a city"; while 728, which normally agrees with the first group above, has the variant λυμαεις. On the other hand, the so-called "q" group of minuscules and also 56 58 106 340, all dating from the eleventh to the fourteenth century, read: ἐν 'Ελυμαΐς, and are supported by Codex Alexandrinus, in which εν ελυμες would probably be pronounced about the same; while Codex Sinaiticus, Codex Venetus (eighth century), and 46 have εν λυμαις; 381 gives εν λυμαεις; and 55 and the corrector of 311 read πολις εν ελυμαις (the original of 311 is πολις ελυα). The evidence of these sources, especially "q" and A, makes it possible that the original statement was "that in Elymais in Persia there was a city" (so ERV).

Tob. 2:10 simply reads εἰς τὴν 'Ελυμαΐδα, "to Elymais" (RSV) or "into Elymais" (ERV), and there is nothing to indicate whether a city or a province is meant.

In his version of the incident in I Macc. 6:1, Josephus (Antiq. XII.ix.1) considers Elymais to be a city and adds that there was a temple of Artemis in it. Polybius (*Histories* XXXI.9 [11]) also mentions a sanctuary of Artemis in Elymais.

No such city is known, however, and Elymais is known as the name of a region or province. In Dan. 8:2 the text attributed to Theodotion and found in Codex Vaticanus reads ἐν Χώρᾳ Αἰλάμ, "in the province of Elam," but the LXX text preserved in the ninth-century cursive, Codex Chisianus (87), has ἐν 'Ελυμαΐδι Χώρᾳ, "in the province of Elymais." Thus Elymais and Elam are probably the same.

Strabo speaks of Elymais as the mountainous region N and E of Susis (XV.732, 744), the latter being the area between Babylonia and Persia, of which the most notable city was Susa (XV.727). Herodotus (III.91) identifies the same area as the eighth province of the Persian Empire. Ptolemy (*Geography* VI.3) says that the Elymaei dwell on the maritime coast of Susiana; Stephen of Byzantium (*De Urbibus*) describes their land as the part of Assyria which is toward Persia and near Susa. Since the differences in the foregoing references are relatively minor, it is probably to be recognized that Elymais, or Elam, and Susiana were essentially the same—namely, the region and the province between Babylonia and Persia, of which Susa was the chief city.

Bibliography. Weissbach, "Elymais," *Pauly-Wissowa,* vol. V (1903), cols. 2458-67; W. Kappler, ed., *Septuaginta,* IX, 1; in *Maccabaeorum liber,* vol. I (1936); F.-M. Abel, *Les livres des Maccabées* (1949), pp. 108-9. J. FINEGAN

ELYMAS ĕl'ə məs ['Ελύμας] (Acts 13:6-12). A Jewish magician (*see* MAGIC) and false prophet associated with Proconsul Sergius Paulus (*see* PAULUS, SERGIUS) at Paphos on Cyprus. He challenged Paul and Barnabas when they preached to the proconsul, and in turn Paul denounced him. Elymas was stricken blind temporarily.

Elymas is also called BAR-JESUS. Both the exact form of "Elymas" and its relation to "Bar-Jesus" are obscure. In vs. 8 the Greek has: "Elymas the magician (for that is the meaning of the name)." As the parenthesis follows "magician," it seems to say that the name means "magician." But this can hardly be, since in vs. 6, where the name is Bar-Jesus, he is also called a magician. In spite of the location of the explanatory statement, it probably intends to bring together the names Bar-Jesus and Elymas as equivalents. But in what way is not clear. There is no evident philological basis for saying that Greek "Elymas" is a translation of Aramaic "Bar-Jesus."

One group of scholars tries to solve the problem by referring the explanation to the word "Elymas." They hold that the author says: "Elymas means magician." They derive "Elymas" from the Aramaic *alīmā* ("strong"), or from the Arabic *'alim* ("wise"), both of which have a remote similarity in sound to "Elymas." So "Elymas" could be a transliteration meaning "magician."

Others apply the parenthesis to "Bar-Jesus" and make their approach through the Aramaic *Bar-Yeshua* and the verb *shawah.* They note that in D the reading is Ἕτοιμας, which represents Ἕτοιμος, meaning "prepared." Now since the *pi'el* of *shawah* may mean "to make ready," in this round-about way they attempt to equate "Bar-Jesus" with "magician."

But neither of these attempts is convincing. It is more probable that the parenthesis says only that the Greek name of this Jew is Elymas—an explanation in harmony with the Jewish practice of changing names when one moves from one culture into another. It is also stated here for the first time that Saul is also called Paul. Why the man chose the name Elymas is not indicated.

It is not impossible that the reading Ἕτοιμας is original. If so, we might identify him with Atomos, a magician who, according to Jos. Antiq. XX.vii.2, assisted the Procurator Felix in winning for his wife Drusilla, daughter of Agrippa I, who was already married to Aziz of Emesa. But this identification is only a remote possibility.

If Elymas was not Atomos, he was similar to him, as he was also to Simon Magus (Acts 8:9-24), whom Peter encountered at Samaria; and to Jewish exorcists met by Paul at Ephesus (19:13-17). Numerous Jews evidently became magicians by profession. Acts presents them only in opposition to Christians, so in an unfavorable light. That they were intimates of proconsuls and governors shows that they were men of recognized cultural attainments. Their profession was probably both a science and a faith; and it may be that they were conscientious in their opposition to Christianity.

Bibliography. On the attempt to equate "Bar-Jesus" with "magus," see R. J. Knowling, *Expositor's Greek Testament,* II (1917), 285-87; K. Lake and H. J. Cadbury, *Beginnings of Christianity,* IV (1933), 143-45; A. D. Nock, *Beginnings of Christianity,* V (1933), 164-88. S. V. McCASLAND

ELYON ĕl yōn' [עליון, the Exalted One, the Most High]. An ancient divine name associated with the El (God) of pre-Israelite Jerusalem (Gen. 14:18-24), and eventually applied to the God of Israel, Yahweh. *See* MOST HIGH; GOD, NAMES OF, § C2*b*.

ELZABAD ĕl zā'băd [אלזבד, God has given]. **1.** A Gadite warrior who joined David at Ziklag (I Chr. 12:12).

2. A Korahite GATEKEEPER (I Chr. 26:7).

Bibliography. K. Tallqvist, *Assyrian Personal Names* (1914), p. 100; M. Noth, *Die israelitischen Personennamen* (1928), pp. 21, 33, 34, 47, 77, 90. H. H. GUTHRIE, JR.

ELZAPHAN. Alternate form of ELIZAPHAN 1.

EMADABUN ĭ măd'ə bən ['Ημαδαβούν] (I Esd. 5:58); KJV MADIABUN mə dī'ə bŭn. A surname distinguishing a certain Jeshua from a Jeshua listed previously, among the returning Levites who rebuilt the temple. J. C. SWAIM

EMATH ē'măth. Douay Version form of HAMATH.

EMATHIS ĕm'ə thəs; KJV AMATHEIS ăm'ə thē'əs. Apoc. form of ATHLAI.

EMBALMING [חנטים, *from* חנט, to embalm]. The art of preserving dead bodies from decay, which had its origin in Egypt,* was not practiced among the Hebrews, as can be judged by the paucity of reference to it in the Scriptures and the condition of bodies discovered in thousands of tombs in Canaan. Fig. EMB 26.

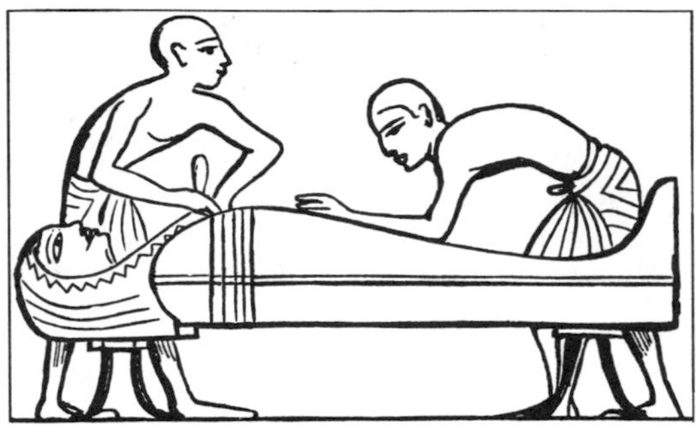

26. Embalming in Egypt

The only direct references in scripture to embalming are in Gen. 50:2-3, 26, where it is stated that Jacob (Israel) and Joseph were embalmed. This doubtless was done, and was mentioned, both to indicate that they were prominent figures in Egypt and to account for the preservation of their bodies until they could be buried in Canaan (Gen. 50:13; Exod. 13:19; Josh. 24:32, although the bones, rather than the body of Joseph, are mentioned). The use of spices (*see* SPICE) in connection with the bodies of Asa (II Chr. 16:14) and Jesus (John 19:39-40) was not embalming, and was probably motivated by a desire to purify ceremonially rather than to preserve.

The Hebrew term for "embalming" appears only in the passages in Genesis cited above and in Song of S. 2:13 in the expression: "The fig tree puts forth [חנטה] its figs," where the verb may be better rendered as "ripens," in the sense that the fruit becomes yellowish-whitish in color (cf. חטה, "wheat" or "grain," in Exod. 9:32; Deut. 8:8; etc.).

The description of the embalming of Israel indicates that the process required forty days (seventy days was common in Egypt, but see Herodotus and Diodorus Siculus, who describe the various steps of embalming), and that it was done by Joseph's servants, "the physicians" (רפאים, "healers" or "surgeons"). *See* PHYSICIAN; MEDICINE.

The fact that the Hebrews did not practice embalming is doubtless to be explained by their theological beliefs (*see* IMMORTALITY; RESURRECTION), as well as by their antipathy toward Egyptian religion, and the comparative poverty of Palestine, where the extreme expense of embalming made it prohibitive. W. L. REED

EMBASSY (Luke 14:32 [KJV AMBASSAGE]; 19:14 [KJV MESSAGE]). An abstract form for the concrete AMBASSADOR; either one or more ambassadors.

EMBROIDERY AND NEEDLEWORK. Interweaving materials of varied colors into a specific pattern was skilled work of the highest order and was the forerunner of brocading.

Materials for the tabernacle and the girdle for Aaron and possibly for his sons were embroidered work. There are a number of terms which relate to embroidery and needlework. רקם, "to weave colored fabrics, to embroider," in the expression מעשה רקם (lit., "work of the weaver in colored fabrics"; RSV "embroidered with needlework"; KJV "wrought with needlework" or "needlework"), is found in Exod. 26:36; 27:16; 28:39; 36:37; 38:18; 39:29. Oholiab a Danite was said to have been especially adept as an embroiderer in blue and purple and scarlet stuff and fine twined linen; he was called to perform his service for the tent of meeting (Exod. 35:35; 38:18, 23).

The word for "embroidered work" is רקמה. In Judg. 5:30 it is used to describe the desired handwork which Sisera was expected to bring home as booty in his battle with Israel. It is used figuratively of Jerusalem in the early days when the Lord clothed her with embroidered cloth (Ezek. 16:10, 13, 18). It is used of the robes of princes (Ezek. 26:16; "embroidered garments") and of the eagle (Nebuchadrezzar) rich in plumage "of many colors" (Ezek. 17:3). It was among the coveted articles of trade (Ezek. 27:16, 24), and it describes the linen sails of the ships of Tyre procured from Egypt (Ezek. 27:7). The bride in Ps. 45:14—H 45:15 was attired in "many-colored robes" (KJV "raiment of needlework"). In I Chr. 29:2 the term is applied to varied colored stones. A verbal form appears in Ps. 139:15 (רקמתי; "I was . . . intricately wrought"), used of the human embryo.

Another series of words also relates to weaving in patterns. Aaron's coat was to be woven (שבץ; cf. Akkadian *sabsinnu,* "weaver of patterns" [?]) in checker work of fine linen (Exod. 28:39; "weave"; KJV "embroider"). In Exod. 28:20 the rows of gems on the breastplate of Aaron are to be "set [משבצים] in gold filigree"; cf. also the "settings" (משבצות) of gems in Exod. 28:11, 13-14, 25; 39:6, 13, 16, 18. The "gold-woven robes" (משבצות זהב; RSV mg. "gold embroidery"; KJV "wrought gold") of the bride appear in Ps. 45:13—H 45:14. The high priest was to wear a "coat of checker work" (כתנת תשבץ; KJV "broidered coat"; Exod. 28:4). This type of work was produced by cutting the model of the garment from two different colors of material, to make an inner and outer portion of the garment, which were then sewed together in accordance with the desired pattern so as to produce a sparkling effect, like a gem.

Such embroidered and woven materials were the work of "one who is skilled" (מעשה חשב). Cherubim were "skilfully worked" on the curtains of the tabernacle (Exod. 26:1; 36:8), on the veil (Exod. 26:31; 36:35); the ephod was also made of varied colored materials "skilfully worked" (Exod. 28:6; 39:3); the breastpiece of judgment too was of "skilled work" (Exod. 28:15; 39:8; KJV "cunning work"; cf. Jer. 10:3; Hos. 13:2). The work referred to in these terms is more of the designer type than of the weaver or the embroiderer.

Bibliography. J. Macdonald, "Palestinian Dress," *PEQ* (Jan.-Apr., 1951), pp. 55-68. J. M. Myers

EMEK-KEZIZ ĕ'mĭk kē'zĭz [עמק קציץ, a valley cut off] (Josh. 18:21); KJV VALLEY OF KEZIZ. One of the cities of Benjamin, apparently related to a valley of like name near the SE boundary of the tribe's territory, and seemingly situated in the Jordan Plain in the vicinity of Jericho and Beth-hoglah. The exact location is unknown. W. H. Morton

EMENDATIONS OF THE SCRIBES [תקוני הסופרים]. A list of eighteen words authoritatively emended in the MT to avoid anthropomorphism. The list, which varies somewhat in number, is given in Masoroth to major MSS (*see* Text, OT, § 1*ci*), and in rabbinic works—e.g., Mekilta, Siphre, Yalkut Shimeon, Tanchuma to Exod. 15:7.

Bibliography. C. D. Ginsburg, *The Massorah* (1880-97), letter ת, vol. 11, p. 710, section 206; *Introduction to the Massoretico-Critical Edition of the Hebrew Bible* (1897), pp. 347-62. P. Kahle in H. Bauer and P. Leander, *Historische Grammatik die Hebräischen Sprache* (1922), pp. 76-77. B. J. Roberts

EMERALD. A variety of beryl of rich green color. Many of the stones commonly called "emerald" in Egyptian jewelry are really green feldspar. "Emerald" is used in the Bible to translate the following words:

a) ברקת (Ezek. 28:13), one of the stones on the covering of the King of Tyre.

b) נפך (*nōphekh*), a stone in the breastpiece of judgment (Exod. 28:18; 39:11); also noted with purple, embroidered work and fine linen, etc., as an article of trade between Edom and Tyre (Ezek. 27:16). In Ezek. 28:13 the word is translated "Carbuncle" (LXX ἄνθραξ; Vulg. *carbunculus*). Cf. the Egyptian *mfkt,* which is probably turquoise and so green in color.

c) Σμαράγδινος, an adjectival form of σμάραγδος. The former is used in the description of the one seated on the throne in Rev. 4:3; the latter denotes the fourth jewel in the foundation of the wall of the New Jerusalem (21:19).

See also Jewels and Precious Stones § 2.

W. E. Staples

EMERODS ĕm'ə rŏdz. KJV translation of טחרים and עפלים (RSV Tumors); an archaic form of "hemorrhoids."

EMIM, THE ē'mĭm [האימים (אמים), the terrible *or* frightful ones]. Ancient, presumably gigantic inhabitants of Transjordan, mentioned specifically as dwelling in Shaveh-kiriathaim (Gen. 14:5). Elsewhere called "Rephaim," they were called the "Emim" by the Moabites who dispossessed them (Deut. 2:10-11).

See also Anakim; Rephaim; Giant. L. Hicks

EMISSION. *See* Clean and Unclean.

EMMANUEL. *See* Immanuel.

EMMAUS ĕ mā'əs ['Εμμαούς; חמת, warm wells; *the Talmud uses the forms* אמאוס *and* עימאוס]. A Judean town now of uncertain identification, which was the destination of two travelers to whom Jesus appeared after his crucifixion. Fig. EMM 27.

Copyright: The Matson Photo Service

27. The modern village of El-Qubeibeh, one of the traditional locations of Emmaus

The name appears only once in the Bible, in Luke 24:13. In a postresurrection episode Jesus encountered Cleopas and a companion on the road to Emmaus, conversed with them the remainder of the journey, and accepted their invitation to eat—before he vanished as mysteriously as he had first appeared. For the identification of this town (Κώμη), the only clue given by Luke is that it was 7½ miles from Jerusalem. All external evidence and all tradition direct the attention westward from Jerusalem; nevertheless, there are no fewer than four modern towns proposed as NT Emmaus, ranging from 4 miles to 20 miles from Jerusalem:

a) Qaloniyeh (Colonia) is over 4 miles W of Jerusalem on the main road to Jaffa (Joppa). Josephus reported (War VII.vi.6) that Vespasian in A.D. 75 settled eight hundred veterans at "a place called Emmaus thirty stadia [under 4 miles] from Jerusalem"; this is half the distance stated by Luke. This town is probably the Mozah of Josh. 18:26.

b) El-Qubeibeh is 7 miles W of Jerusalem, but on a more northerly Roman road, passing by Nebi Samwil. Its connection with NT Emmaus is a very old tradition, since Crusaders in 1099 found near there an old Roman fort named Castellum Emmaus. When the guardian Franciscans erected the Church of Saint Cleophas in 1878, they unearthed the remains of a basilica judged to be Crusader or even Byzantine.

c) Abu Ghosh (named after a nineteenth-century brigand) is *ca.* 9 miles W of Jerusalem on the main road. It is known also as Kiryat el-'Enab, and has been identified with OT Kiriath-jearim. Its Crusader church stands over a Roman fort with an inscription stating that some of the Tenth Legion was stationed here. But the Emmaus colony of Josephus (War VII.vi.6) was much closer to Jerusalem. The guardian French Benedictines maintain here the Convent of Our Lady.

d) Amwas (Nicopolis, since the third century) is 20 miles W of Jerusalem on the road to Jaffa, in the Valley of Ajalon. It preserves the name, has two "warm wells," and in addition has the earliest attestation. The Bordeaux Pilgrim (*ca.* 333) and the Holy Paula (*ca.* 386) accepted this site, which the former placed at 22 Roman miles from Jerusalem. Jerome (cf. *On Daniel* 8:14) in the *Onomasticon* follows Eusebius in finding Emmaus here. It is identified with the Emmaus of Judas Maccabeus (I Macc. 3:40, 57), who there defeated the Syrian Gorgias (4:1-15). Josephus reports that it was the seat of a toparchy (War III.iii.5), which raises the objection that it was much more than a village (Κώμη). Emmaus had been burned by Varus before Josephus' generation (Antiq. XVII.x.9); and not until the third century was it rebuilt by Julius Africanus and then named Nicopolis. The Crusaders accepted this as NT Emmaus, and one finds there complex Byzantine-Crusader church ruins. The principal objection to its being the NT Emmaus is the distance of 20 miles, or 160 stadia, from Jerusalem. It is true that some good MSS read "160" instead of "60," but the best text is the traditional "60."

Bibliography. E. Robinson, *Biblical Researches in Palestine* (1867), II, 254; III, 146-50. L. H. Vincent and F.-M. Abel, *Emmaüs, sa basilique et son histoire* (1932). G. Dalman, *Sacred Sites and Ways* (1935), 226-32. R. deVaux and A. Steve, *Fouilles à Qaryet el-'Enab Abu Ghosh* (1950).

K. W. CLARK

EMMER. KJV Apoc. form of IMMER.

EMMOR. KJV NT form of HAMOR.

EMPEROR [βασιλεύς (I Pet. 2:13, 17; KJV *lit.* KING); σεβαστός=Lat. *title* AUGUSTUS (*so* KJV; Acts 25:21, 25)]. A title of the ruler of the Roman Empire (*cf.* CAESAR), derived from the Latin *imperator,* which was originally given to honor a general after a victory and retained only temporarily. Julius Caesar, however, used the title permanently, and because of his example it came to refer to supreme military authority. In this sense it was used by Augustus and his successors. In later times, when an army hailed a general as *imperator* he was recognized as its candidate for imperial office.

In theory the emperor ruled, not as *imperator,* but as *princeps,* "chief of state" (cf. the later *Duce* and *Führer*). Tiberius made this distinction by saying, "I am *dominus* [master] of my slaves, *imperator* of my troops, and *princeps* of the rest"—i.e., of the free civilian population (Dio Cassius *History* LVII.8.2). The older usage was continued, however; after military victories the emperor was hailed as *imperator,* and such events were noted in his official title and given publicity on the coinage. R. M. GRANT

EMPEROR-WORSHIP. Reverence paid to a Roman emperor, whether living or dead, as a divine being. Generally speaking, unofficial enthusiasm could recognize deity, or a germ of deity, in a living ruler, but officially (by vote of the SENATE) deity could be recognized only after the ruler's death. In the first two centuries those emperors who believed that they themselves were divine were all murdered or had to commit suicide (Caligula, Nero, Domitian, Commodus). "Consecration" was effected by a vote of the Senate after an emperor's death, as was the alternative, *memoria damnata* (though Nero was declared an enemy of the state in his lifetime). The good emperors, in the eyes of the Senate and of senatorial historians, were those who rejected the adulation of courtiers or of the populace.

The worship of kings had precedents both oriental and Greek, because of the narrow dividing line between gods and heroes and the general feeling that a great benefactor was in some sense divine; such worship was fairly common in the Hellenistic age, and was later more widespread in the East than in the

West. Thus in the East, Julius Caesar (*see* CAESAR, JULIUS) was praised as "a god manifest and the savior of the whole human race." At Rome, however, it took two years after his death, and a great deal of political pressure, before the Senate voted his deification. The appearance of a comet facilitated the process. AUGUSTUS was worshiped as a god in the provinces, but he officially permitted his worship even there only when it was combined with that of Rome. It was after his death that he was officially consecrated, when a praetor testified under oath that he had seen the wax image of the dead emperor ascending into heaven (Suetonius *Augustus* C.4). According to a later account (Dio Cassius *History* LVI.42), an eagle soared upward "as if" bearing the emperor's soul into heaven. The Empress Livia rewarded the praetor with 25,000 denarii (LVI.46). It has been argued that Augustus was officially recognized as divine in his lifetime, since he tells us (*Res gestae* II.10) that "by decree of the Senate my name was included in the Salian hymns, and it was enacted by law that my person should be sacred in perpetuity." Dio Cassius (LI.20) explains the first point by stating that in 29 B.C. the emperor's name was "included in their hymns equally with the gods." Yet this inclusion does not necessarily mean that in Roman eyes Augustus was a god. His successor, TIBERIUS, insisted upon divine honors for Augustus but refused them for himself and his family, permitting them only in the East for himself and his mother, and insisting that the Senate be given equal recognition.

CALIGULA asked the Senate to deify Tiberius, but because of the strained relations between the Senate and Tiberius in his last years the request was denied. Caligula himself was able to have his deceased sister Drusilla deified, with the assistance of a senator who swore he had witnessed her ascension. He gradually came to believe in his own deity, and required ritual abasement on the part of his courtiers. In the year 40 a temple to him was erected at Rome, and he required oaths to be taken by his genius ("familiar spirit"). After he was murdered, only the intervention of his successor, CLAUDIUS, prevented the Senate from declaring him an enemy of the state.

Claudius wrote an official letter to the Alexandrians in the year 41, refusing the establishment of a chief priest and temples dedicated to himself; he stated that such observances were suitable "only for the gods." The difference between official Roman policy and popular provincial practice is seen in the Egyptian prefect's edict in which the letter was published; it speaks of the "greatness of our god Caesar." In Britain a temple of the Divine Claudius was actually erected, after a Roman victory there. The worship of Drusilla was terminated, but she was replaced by Julia Augusta (Livia), the wife of Augustus.

NERO had Claudius deified, presumably in order to provide proof of his own rather dubious filial piety. He himself appeared on coins as Apollo the Lyre-Player, but when in 65 one of the consuls proposed the building of a temple to the Divine Nero, he rejected the suggestion as ill-omened; only dead emperors were really divine. A king of Armenia hailed him as a god, but before his death he had been condemned by the Senate and was never consecrated. His successor, VESPASIAN, refused divine honors, though he erected a temple to the Divine Claudius in an effort to recall happier days. On his deathbed he said ironically, "I fear I am becoming a god." Vespasian's son Titus had him consecrated, and in turn was consecrated after his death by Domitian.

As early as the year 89, DOMITIAN was addressed by his courtiers as Master and God, and soon oaths were required by his genius, though his name followed that of Jupiter. He was often called Master and God in the East, and it may well be that popular, or even local official, pressure upon Jews and Christians led to some local persecution in Asia, where it may be reflected in the book of REVELATION. After his death, however, he was declared an enemy of the state, and many of his executive decisions were rescinded by his successor, Nerva. His name was erased from many inscriptions.

Trajan (98-117) had Nerva consecrated, while rejecting divine honors for himself. In the year 112 his legate in Pontus and Bithynia was investigating the Christians and, as a test of their loyalty, required them to offer incense and wine before statues of the gods and of the emperor (Pliny *Epistle* X.96). This innovation, described in a report to the emperor, was not approved in Trajan's reply (97), and does not occur in later tests of Christians. Sacrifice to the gods can be required; a living emperor is not officially a god. Even though Pliny in his Panegyric on Trajan speaks of him as *deus,* this was not the emperor's official or private view of himself.

With the exceptions discussed above, the official Roman view recognized the difference between the gods and the living emperor. In a speech to the Senate ascribed to Tiberius by Tacitus (Ann. IV.38) the emperor states that he is only mortal, but adds that his temples are in the Senators' minds; he hopes for their approval after his death. Here Tiberius reiterates the views of Augustus as recorded in a letter addressed to his successor (Suetonius *Augustus* LXXI): "My goodness will transport me in celestial glory." This is to say that the approval of the Roman people, expressed through the Senate, will recognize a divinity already half-inherent in the emperor during his lifetime. When Augustus' "mind" had ascended to heaven, prayer could be addressed to it (cf. Tac. Ann. I.43).

On the other hand, outside Rome worship of a living emperor, theoretically spontaneous, was never discouraged by local authorities, who saw in it a vital symbol of solidarity, especially valuable in times of crisis. Those who rejected it were likely to be suspected of disloyalty, even though in theory it could not be required of civilians as a test (except in the one instance where Pliny appears to have gone too far). Christians repeatedly stated that while they could, and did, pray *for* the emperor, they could not possibly pray *to* him.

Bibliography. E. Bickermann, "Die römische Kaiserapotheose," *ARW,* XXVII (1929), 1-34; L. R. Taylor, *The Divinity of the Roman Emperor* (1931); K. Scott, *The Imperial Cult Under the Flavians* (1936); F. Vittinghoff, *Der Staatsfeind in der römische Kaiserzeit* (1936); M. P. Charlesworth, "The Refusal of Divine Honours, an Augustan Formula," *Papers of the*

British School at Rome, XV (1939), 1-10; R. M. Grant, *The Sword and the Cross* (1955); E. Stauffer, *Christ and the Caesars* (trans. R. G. Smith; 1955). R. M. GRANT

EMPTIED [ἐκένωσεν]. The crucial christological passage in the NT containing this word is Phil. 2:7; Paul says that Christ Jesus was "in the form of God, . . . but emptied himself, taking the form of a servant." There are three major interpretations of this "emptying":

a) Paul has been taken to mean that Christ emptied himself of the outer form of God and took on an outer form of a man. According to this view he appeared on earth in a disguise and was not really man.

b) Another view holds that Christ emptied himself of his divine attributes (omniscience, omnipotence, etc.)—of the "insignia of majesty"—and that what remained of him was born as a man. According to this view, however, not all of the divine in him was given up, for the love of God is still seen in him; hence he gave up some, or most, but not all, of the characteristics which he had when he was in the "form of God."

c) There is a third possible interpretation—viz., that no genitive of contents should be supplied with the word "emptied." Paul said, not that Christ Jesus emptied himself *of* anything, but that he emptied *himself.* Thus Paul is saying that rather than trying to grasp equality with God, Christ emptied himself of his life, not of some of its characteristics or of its outer form. The word translated "emptied" may also be translated "poured out": Christ poured out his life "unto death" (Phil. 2:8). Lying behind this picture is Isa. 53:12: "He poured out his life, his being [נפש; RSV 'SOUL'], to death." Cf. II Cor. 8:9. *See* CHRIST.
B. H. THROCKMORTON, JR.

ENAC ē'năk. Douay Version form of ANAK.

ENAIM ĭ nā'əm [עינים, two springs] (Gen. 38:14, 21). A place between Adullam and Timnah; possibly the same as ENAM. The present location is unknown.

ENAM ē'nəm [עינם] (Josh. 15:34). A village of Judah in the Shephelah district of Zorah-Azekah; probably same as ENAIM.

ENAN ē'nən [עינן, little(?) spring]. The father of Ahira, who was the leader of Naphtali in the wilderness (Num. 1:15; 2:29; 7:78, 83; 10:27). The name is apparently preserved in the place name HAZAR-ENAN.

Bibliography. M. Noth, *Die israelitischen Personennamen* (1928), pp. 38, 224. R. F. JOHNSON

ENASIBUS. KJV Apoc. form of ELIASHIB 5.

ENCAMPMENT. *See* CAMP.

ENCHANTER, ENCHANTMENTS. The OT uses several terms to designate an enchanter—i.e., a sorcerer who employs spells, charms, or omens in his occult practice. Because enchanters are generally listed together with other practitioners of the magic art, and the technique of the enchanter is nowhere stated, the English versions differ in their translations. Words translated "enchanter" are:

a) אשף (Dan. 1:20; 2:2, 10, 27; 4:7—H 4:4; 5:7, 11, 15; KJV ASTROLOGER), clearly a loan word from Akkadian *ašipu*, a class of conjuration priest.

b) חבר (Ps. 58:5—H 58:6; alternately CHARMER). The basic meaning of חבר (Akkadian *ḫabāru*) is "to be noisy"; hence חבר חברים is "one who mutters sounds," "a mutterer." *Cf. bibliography.*

c) KJV נחש (Deut. 18:10; RSV AUGUR).

d) KJV ענן (Jer. 27:9; RSV SOOTHSAYER).

The practice of the enchanter, like any other form of magic, was forbidden by law (Lev. 19:26; Deut. 18:10).

See also DIVINATION.

Bibliography. J. J. Finkelstein, *JBL,* 75 (1956), 328-31.
I. MENDELSOHN

END, THE [τὸ τέλος]. A term used in various general or common senses, but especially to designate the end of the present age—as, e.g., in Matt. 24:13-14; Mark 13:7; I Cor. 15:24; I Pet. 4:7. *See* ESCHATOLOGY OF THE NT. M. RIST

EN-DOR ĕn'dôr [עין דר, עין דור, עין דאר, spring of *dor*]. A city in Manasseh best remembered as the place where there resided a medium (KJV "witch") who was consulted by Saul king of Israel (I Sam. 28:7). At the time of the conquest of Canaan, the tribe of Manasseh was not able to drive out the Canaanites from En-dor (Josh. 17:11). En-dor is plausibly located at modern Endor on the N side of Little Hermon (Nebi Dahi), *ca.* four miles from Mount Tabor.

The text of Ps. 83:10—H 83:11, where En-dor is mentioned as the place at which Sisera and Jabin were destroyed, presents a problem, because the book of Judges makes no mention of En-dor. In the preceding verse there is a reference to Midian, which has led some scholars to propose that "En-harod" (cf. Judg. 7:1) should be read in vs. 10 rather than "En-dor." However, it is possible that the Hebrew text of the psalm is correct at this point, and that the psalmist knew of the proximity of En-dor to Mount Tabor and decided on the former merely to indicate the general locality of the destruction of Sisera and Jabin. W. L. REED

ENDURANCE. The translation of ὑπομονή in Luke 21:19; Rom. 5:3-4; II Cor. 6:4; Col. 1:11; Heb. 10:36; Rev. 1:9; 2:2, 19; 3:10; 13:10; 14:12 (KJV "patience" in all these passages). The RSV translates this word elsewhere by "PATIENCE"; "STEADFASTNESS"; and "perseverance." These other translations, to which one could add "fortitude," reveal the variety of connotations which the Greek word includes. It is used to describe a sword's power to sustain blows.
B. H. THROCKMORTON, JR.

EN-EGLAIM ĕn ĕg'lĭ əm [עין עגלים, spring of two calves] (Ezek. 47:10). A place on the shores of the Dead Sea; from here to En-gedi fishermen will cast their nets, according to Ezekiel's vision of Israel's restoration. Though 'Ain Hajlah (Beth Hoglah) has been suggested with reason, the more probable location is 'Ain Feshkha, *ca.* 1½ miles S of Khirbet Qumran. V. R. GOLD

ENEMESSAR ĕn′ə mĕs′ər. KJV translation of Ἐνεμεσσάρος. The book of Tobit is dated with reference to the captivity that took place "in the time of Enemessar king of the Assyrians" (Tob. 1:2 KJV). The Vulg. here has "Salmanasar"; and the RSV reads: "In the days of SHALMANESER, king of the Assyrians." Enemessar, an otherwise unknown name, is thought to be an inversion of the two parts of the Assyrian compound *SARRU-KINU,* meaning "the legitimate king," epithet of Sargon, the general who, on the death of Shalmaneser IV, seized the crown. At Tob. 1:15 the text reads: "When Shalmaneser died, Sennacherib his son reigned in his place." Since Sennacherib was the son of Sargon, there seems further evidence of the confusion between Enemessar and Shalmaneser.

J. C. SWAIM

ENEMY [איב; צר; צרר; שנא; ער; שרר; שור; קים; Aram. ער; ἐχθρός]. Alternately: ADVERSARY; FOE; HATER. One who dislikes or hates another and seeks to do him harm; an opponent or adversary; a hostile force, nation, or army.

While "enemy" in the OT refers usually to the national enemies of Israel (Josh. 24:11, etc.), it is also used to mean one's personal enemies (Exod. 23:4; Judg. 16:23; I Sam. 18:29; Esth. 7:6; etc.), especially in the Psalter (Ps. 3:7 *et passim*). Similarly, while "enemy" in the NT refers most often to personal enemies (Matt. 13:25; Gal. 4:16; etc.), it also is used to mean a foreign people (Luke 1:71; 19:43; cf. 21:20).

God is often spoken of in the OT as an enemy. He is an enemy to Israel's enemies (Exod. 23:22; Judg. 5:31; II Chr. 20:29; Ps. 68:1; etc.). Such a view was the basis of the early national traditions which viewed God as a warrior championing his people's welfare, bringing them out of Egypt, guiding them through the desert, and giving them Canaan as a promised land. This is the view expressed, not only in the traditions, but also by the prophets (Amos 2:9-10; Mic. 6:4-5; etc.). The prophets spoke also of God's abandoning his people to their enemies for judgment (Judg. 2:14; II Chr. 25:8; Jer. 12:7; cf. Hos. 5:15–6:1; Luke 19:41-44). They thus could call God in his judgments Israel's enemy (Isa. 1:24; Lam. 2:5). Even so the prophets insisted that in his role as enemy to Israel, God's love for them was the dominant factor (Isa. 54:7-8; Jer. 30:14; 31:2-3; Hos. 2:14). Job feels that he is God's enemy (13:24; 19:11; 33:10; cf. 40:1).

Man is God's enemy or, literally, hates him when he disobeys the divine commandments (Exod. 20:5; Deut. 5:8-10; 7:9-10). Paul speaks of sinners as enemies of God (Rom. 5:8; cf. Phil. 3:18), and elsewhere in the NT it is said that a friend of the world is an enemy of God (Jas. 4:4). The devil (*see* SATAN) is the enemy par excellence (Matt. 13:39; Luke 10:19; cf. Acts 13:10) and death the last enemy (I Cor. 15:26) to succumb to the reign of Christ (cf. Heb. 10:13).

The contrast drawn in the Sermon on the Mount (Matt. 5:43-44) between hating one's enemies and loving one's enemies is wrongly interpreted as a difference between OT and NT personal ethics. While there is no categorical commandment in the OT to love one's enemies, there is certainly none to hate one's enemies. Hatred of national enemies and persecutors pervades such OT works as Nahum, Obadiah, and Esther (cf. Ps. 137:7-9; Isa. 47; 49:22-26), and in the NT the book of Revelation. But a spirit of international good will under the universal sovereignty of God is the very basis of such thinking as is found in Ruth; Isa. 19:19-25; 40–55; Jonah (cf. I Kings 20:31; II Kings 5:20-23). The theme of the biblical doctrine of ELECTION from the early chapters of Genesis is that through Israel the rest of the world may be blessed (Gen. 12:1-3; cf. Jer. 4:1-2). Jeremiah in his letter to the exiles in Babylonia bids them pray for the peace and welfare of their enemies and captors (Jer. 29:7).

It is only in the NT, however, that the categorical imperative is made that a man should love his enemies (Matt. 5:43-44). Nonetheless, if this imperative were spelled out in terms of ethical conduct in given situations, the OT would afford the particulars. Exod. 23:4-5 directs the man who finds his enemy's ox or ass lost to return it to him. Saul defines righteousness in terms of repaying good for evil (I Sam. 24:17-19). Job claims, in defense of his righteous integrity, never to have rejoiced over the misfortune of an enemy (Job. 31:29). The book of Proverbs puts Job's claim in the form of a commandment: "Do not rejoice when your enemy falls" (Prov. 24:17). Paul, in fact, does spell out the meaning of love of one's enemy and in so doing quotes Prov. 25:21-22 to make his point (Rom. 12:14-21): "If your enemy is hungry, feed him; if he is thirsty, give him drink; for by so doing you will heap burning coals upon his head."

See also NATIONS; SIN, SINNERS; WRATH.

J. A. SANDERS

ENENIUS. KJV Apoc. form of BIGVAI.

ENGADDI. KJV Apoc. form of EN-GEDI.

EN-GANNIM ĕn găn′ĭm [עין גנים, spring of gardens]. **1.** A town in Judah (Josh. 15:34). It is perhaps to be identified with the Shephelah town Beit Jemal, approximately two miles S of Beth-shemesh, to the E of which is the spring ʿAin Fatir.

2. A town in Issachar (Josh. 19:21), assigned to the Gershonites as a Levitical city (21:29). The list in I Chronicles (6:73—H 6:58) at this point reads "Anem," but this is considered to be a textual error. It is generally identified with modern Jenin, located near a spring on the S side of the Plain of Esdraelon, where the chief route from Jerusalem and Samaria enters the plain. It has also been suggested that En-gannim probably replaces the original name En-ʿonam, and that the latter should be identified with modern ʿOlam. This site fulfils the topographical requirements of the limits of the territory of Issachar (Josh. 19:17-23) better than Jenin.

Bibliography. W. F. Albright, "The Topography of the Tribe of Issachar," *ZAW* (1926), pp. 231-32; A. Saarisalo, *The Boundary Between Issachar and Naphtali* (1927), pp. 62-63, 129; F.-M. Abel, *Géographie de la Palestine*, II (1938), 24, 62, 317.

G. W. VAN BEEK

EN-GEDI ĕn gĕd′ī [עין גדי, spring of the kid]; KJV Apoc. ENGADDI ĕn găd′ī. An important oasis at about the middle of the W side of the Dead Sea, *ca.* thirty-five miles SE of Jerusalem. The oasis is fed by a hot-water spring located three or four hundred feet above the base of a large cliff. The depression of the Dead Sea made it possible for the oasis to produce semitropical vegetation and to become noted for its palms, vineyards, and balsam (Song of S. 1:14; Ecclus. 24:14; Jos. Antiq. IX.i.2). The ancient site of En-gedi is SE of the oasis at Tell ej-Jurn, near the modern settlement of 'Ain Jidi. There are remains of a Byzantine aqueduct leading from the spring, and recently the walls of a Judahite fortress (from the period 900-600 B.C.) were discovered at Tell ej-Jurn. En-gedi was occupied by Amorites who were subjugated by Chedorlaomer and his allies in Abraham's day (Gen. 14:7, where Hazazon-tamar is En-gedi). Later the village was assigned to the wilderness district of Judah (Josh. 15:62).

Courtesy of the Israel Office of Information, New York

28. En-gedi on the shore of the Dead Sea

David sought refuge from Saul in the rugged terrain around En-gedi (I Sam. 23:29—H 24:1), and in a cave in the vicinity the incident occurred in which David cut off Saul's skirt but did not take his life (I Sam. 24). During the reign of Jehoshaphat (*ca.* 873-849) Hazazon-tamar (En-gedi) was a staging area for the Ammonites, Moabites, and Meunites prior to the battle at the Ascent of Ziz (II Chr. 20:2).

In Ezekiel's vision of Israel's restoration, fishermen will catch fish in the Dead Sea from En-gedi to En-eglaim (Ezek. 47:10).

Pls. IX*b;* XII*f;* Fig. ENG 28. V. R. GOLD

ENGINE [חשבון (II Chr. 26:15), *lit.* device, invention, *from* חשב, think, devise; מחי קבל (Ezek. 26:9 KJV), *lit.* the blow of an attacking object, *from* מחה, to strike, *and* קבל, *qᵉbhōl, cf.* Arab. *qubl*, front part, Akkad. *qablu*, battle, engagement]. Alternately: RSV BATTERING RAMS; KJV ENGINES OF WAR (Ezek. 26:9). A skilful mechanical device for using energy to do work, in this instance for military purposes.

1. History. Engines of war seem to have been developed in Western Asia first by the Assyrians, who employed wheeled towers in siege operations, either as vantage points for archers or to house battering rams. Large catapults for hurling stones, arrows, etc., appeared rather late in the Greek world, and here the name of Dionysius tyrant of Syracuse (430-367 B.C.) is important. Such artillery was used by Alexander the Great (356-323 B.C.), and thereafter it was part of the standard equipment of most Hellenistic armies, and later of the Roman legions. For references to these machines in the Maccabean period see I Macc. 6:51-52; 13:43. *See also* WEAPONS AND IMPLEMENTS OF WAR.

2. In the OT. ***a. Battering rams.*** For devices employed to batter down walls and gates, *see* BATTERING RAM. It is probable that the unusual phrase in Ezek. 26:9 (מחי קבל) should be translated "battering rams" (RSV) rather than "engines of war" (KJV).

b. Catapults, etc. In II Chr. 26:15 it is said that Uzziah of Judah (eighth century B.C.) set up engines on Jerusalem's defenses to shoot arrows and great stones. While it is impossible to disprove this statement, the fact remains that elsewhere in the Mediterranean area catapults and the like did not come into general use until considerably later than Uzziah's age. As the present form of I and II Chronicles is thought to come from *ca.* 300 B.C., some look upon this reference in II Chr. 26:15 as an anachronism.

Bibliography. For Roman engines at the siege of Jotapata in Galilee in A.D. 67, see Jos. War III.ix.166-70. For an account of ballistic machines down to the Roman age, see C. Singer, E. J. Holmyard, A. R. Hall, and T. I. Williams, eds., *A History of Technology*, II (1956), 698-720.

W. S. MCCULLOUGH

ENGLISH BIBLE. The first complete English translantion of the Bible was by John Wyclif in 1382. Before his day there had been translations of Psalms, the gospels, and other popular sections, but not of the Bible as a whole. After Wyclif, Tyndale (1525) translated the NT, and before his death in 1536 portions of the OT. His work opened the way for a constant stream of English Bibles that included the new AUTHORIZED VERSIONS down through the official revisions, including the RSV (1946-52). The Roman Catholic Church has produced several English Bibles and independent translations. *See also* VERSIONS, ENGLISH. J. R. BRANTON

ENGRAVING [פתוח, engraving, *from* פתח, engrave; Akkad. *pataḫu*, bore; *cf.* ἐντυπόω, carved (KJV ENGRAVEN)]. Forms of ancient engraving include: (*a*) Gems cut and inscribed, as on the BREASTPIECE OF THE HIGH PRIEST. The jeweler's art is the usual context of biblical engraving (Exod. 28:9, 11, 21, 35; 31:5; 39:6, 14; *see* JEWELS AND PRECIOUS STONES). (*b*) IVORY carving and inlaying, well illustrated by Palestinian archaeology. (*c*) Metal, as, metaphorically, an inscription engraved on a metal tablet (Jer. 17:1). (*d*) For engraving on seals and scarabs, *see* SEALS AND SCARABS; SIGNET (*see* II Tim. 2:19). (*e*) WRITING engraved on STONE (Deut. 5:8, 22; II Cor. 3:7; *see also* OSSUARIES; INSCRIPTIONS). (*f*) Wood carving, as on the Holy Place wainscoting of Solomon's temple (I Kings 6:18, 29; Ezek. 41:17-20). *See* TEMPLE, JERUSALEM.

The copper-bronze "graving tool" (chisel; Exod. 32:4) was one of a variety developed by the Akkadians. The jeweler's wheel was widely used by *ca.* 1500 B.C. Uncertain Hebrew words following a list of precious stones in Ezek. 28:13 may designate the ordinary tools of the gem-engraver, the polishing drum and drill.

Bibliography. J. H. Middleton, *Engraved Gems of Classical Times* (1891), p. 110, concerning Ezek. 28:13; P. L. Garber, "Reconstructing Solomon's Temple," *BA,* XIV (1951), 2-24; J. B. Pritchard, ed., *ANEP* (1954), pp. 21-70, for illustrations of various kinds of engraving; C. Singer *et al.*, eds., *A History of Technology,* I (1954), 612, 648-49, 663, 679.

P. L. GARBER

EN-HADDAH ĕn hăd'ə [עין חדה] (Josh. 19:21). A town in Issachar. It is probably located at el-Hadetheh, *ca.* six miles E of Mount Tabor.

EN-HAKKORE ĕn hăk'ə rĭ [עין הקורא, spring of the partridge *or* spring of the caller] (Judg. 15:19). A spring at LEHI, from which Samson drank. A word-play is made on the second meaning: Samson "called" on the Lord in his thirst, whereupon this spring was miraculously provided (vs. 18). Both meanings are equally good etymologically.

W. F. STINESPRING

EN-HAZOR ĕn hā'zôr [עין חצור, spring of Hazor] (Josh. 19:37). A fortified town in the territory of Naphtali. It is generally identified with Khirbet Hazireh, a site near Hazzur, in the hills of N Galilee.

Bibliography. F.-M. Abel, *Géographie de la Palestine,* II (1938), 65, 318. G. W. VAN BEEK

ENLIL ĕn'lĭl [lord of the wind]. The chief god of Nippur; king of the earth and lower atmosphere; the "master" (BEL) who overcame the chaotic waters and established Cosmos. His functions and title were later transferred to MARDUK, the god of Babylon.

Bibliography. M. Jastrow, *The Religion of Babylonia and Assyria* (1898), pp. 52-55; E. Ebeling and B. Meissner, *Reallexikon der Assyriologie,* II (1938), 382-90; E. Dhorme, *Les religions de Babylonie et d'Assyrie* (1945), pp. 26-31, 48-50. J. GRAY

EN-MISHPAT. *See* KADESH.

ENNOM ĕn'əm. Douay Version form of HINNOM. *See* HINNOM, VALLEY OF.

ENOCH ē'nək [חנוך, *possibly* retainer, follower (*cf.* חניכים *in* Gen. 14:14); Ενωχ]; KJV HENOCH hē'nək in I Chr. 1:3. **1.** Son of Cain, and the father of Irad (Gen. 4:17*a,* 18*a*).

2. Son of Jared, in the Sethite genealogy; the father of Methuselah (Gen. 5:17-24; I Chr. 1:3; Luke 3:37). Enoch lived in such intimate association with God (ויתהלך את־האלים; Gen. 5:22, 24; cf. 6:9; 17:1 [with לפני]) that "he was not, for God took him" (5: 24*b;* cf. Ecclus. 44:16; 49:14; Heb. 11:5). Enoch's translation (μετάθεσις) produced a large growth of later legend (Wisd. Sol. 4:10; Jude 14; *see* ENOCH, BOOK OF).

Bibliography. W. F. Albright, "The Predeuteronomic Primeval History (JE) in Gen. 1-11," *JBL,* LVIII (1939), 96.

3. A city built by Cain and named after his son Enoch (Gen. 14:17*b*). L. HICKS

ENOCH, BOOK OF. Alternately: I ENOCH; ETHIOPIC ENOCH. One of several pseudepigraphic writings ascribed to ENOCH 2. Gen. 5:18-24 gave rise to the belief that Enoch had been translated to heaven, where the secrets of the heavenly regions and the course of human events predetermined in heaven were disclosed to him. Consequently, it was in order that a book dealing with these subjects should carry his name as its author.

1. Text
2. Influence
3. Date
4. Contents
   a. Introduction
   b. Book I, Angels and Universe
   c. Book II, Parables of Similitudes
   d. Book III, The Heavenly Luminaries
   e. Book IV, The Dream Visions
   f. Book V, The Admonitions to Righteousness
   g. Conclusion

Bibliography

1. Text. This lengthy composite work of 108 chapters of quite uneven length was originally written in Hebrew or Aramaic, or, like DANIEL, in both these languages. It was translated into Greek at some early date, and from Greek into Ethiopic (*ca.* A.D. 500) and also into Latin. The original Semitic text has disappeared. The Greek text has been preserved in part: 1:1–32:6 is found in two eighth-century or later MSS discovered in 1886-87 in a Christian grave at Akhmim, Egypt; 6:1–10:14; 15:8–16:1 are cited in Syncellus (*ca.* A.D. 800); 89:42-49 is in a Vatican MS; and chs. 97–104; 106–108 are found in Egyptian papyri published by Bonner in 1937. 106:1-18 and some brief quotations are extant for the Latin. Fortunately, the entire work (presumably) is preserved in Ethiopic. In 1773 Bruce discovered three Ethiopic MSS containing Enoch in Abyssinia. Since then a score and more of similar MSS have come to light. Unfortunately, they are all quite late; the earliest, it is said, is sixteenth century. The first complete translation into a modern language was that made by Laurence in 1821. Since then, numerous publications of or about the book have testified to its value.

The book itself was probably composed in the first century B.C. Dates suggested are 95, 63, and during Herod's reign (37-4). It is not an original composition; rather, it is a compilation of disparate, in part inconsistent if not contradictory, sources of differing types by different writers of different times. It has been stated that certain DEAD SEA SCROLLS contain texts of sources used in Enoch, but as yet the evidence has not been thoroughly evaluated.

The extent to which the compiler reworked his sources cannot be determined. He certainly made little effort to harmonize them, for he has retained the differing views of the various sources in his book. To some extent he interwove his sources. Thus, a supposed Noachic source (*see* NOAH, APOCALYPSE OF) may be in 6–11; 54:1–55:2; 60; 65:1–69:25; 106–107. More typically, however, one source is followed by another, with little attention to chronological or logical sequence, or to consistency in thought.

The text, quite understandably, is quite corrupt. The textual problem is complicated by the consideration that the only source for much of the book is the Ethiopic text, which itself is a translation of the Greek translation. As Charles first noted and shows by his translation, many passages were originally in poetic form. This feature has been an aid in determining whether in the course of transmission lines have been omitted, added, lengthened, or shortened. Despite the condition of the text, in most instances the original thought seems to have been preserved.

2. Influence. The book of Enoch was well known to the Jews and later to Christians. Apparently it was used by the writers of the Testaments of the Twelve Patriarchs, the Assumption of Moses, the Apocalypse of Baruch, and IV Ezra. However, from the second century A.D. on, it is rarely mentioned in Jewish sources. As for its currency among the early Christians, Charles overstates the case when he says that nearly all the writers of the NT books were acquainted with it, and influenced by it, and that with the earlier fathers and apologists it had all the weight of a canonical book. Even so, concepts found in Enoch are found in various NT books, including the Gospels and Revelation, and Jude 14-15 cites it explicitly. It is quoted as scripture in Barnabas, and some of its verbiage may be reflected in the Apocalypse of Peter. A number of the earlier apologists did make use of it, and Tertullian, for one, might have welcomed it in the OT canon. However, by the fourth century it fell into disfavor in the West, being stigmatized by Jerome as apocryphal. The finding of Greek texts as late as A.D. 800 in a Christian grave in Egypt indicates a somewhat longer popularity of the book in the East. Its survival as a complete work, as noted before, is due to its use by the Ethiopian Christians, who included it with other apocryphal writings in the OT.

3. Date. The compiler of the book of Enoch arranged his work in five books corresponding, in part, to his major sources, with an introduction and a conclusion. Scholars are by no means in agreement concerning the dates of the various sources. The dating is in part determined by the presence or absence of reflections of historical events and persons, such as the Maccabean Revolt, Antiochus Epiphanes, the Hasmonean period, the reign of Alexander Janneus (103-70 B.C.), the beginning of the Roman period (63 B.C.), and the like.

With these uncertainties in mind, the divisions of Enoch with the suggested dates, as given by Pfeiffer, are as follows: Introduction, chs. 1-5 (*ca.* 150-100 B.C.); Book I, Angels and Universe, chs. 6–36 (*ca.* 100 B.C., though Charles and others assign it to the pre-Maccabean period); Book II, Parables or Similitudes, chs. 37-71 (100-80 B.C.); Book III, The Heavenly Luminaries, chs. 72–82 (150-100 B.C.); Book IV, The Dream Visions, chs. 83–90 (163-130 B.C.); Book V, The Admonitions to Righteousness, chs. 91–105 (100-80 B.C., save for the Apocalypse of Weeks [93:1-10; 91:12-17], 163 B.C.; Charles, however, places this fragment in the pre-Maccabean period); Conclusion, chs. 106–108 (100-80 B.C.; however, chs. 106–107, which are from the Noachic source, may be considerably earlier than the conclusion itself).

4. Contents. The book of Enoch is usually termed an apocalypse. This term applies, however, to only a small portion of the work, for much of it is nonapocalyptic. Still, it is replete with materials that came to be associated with apocalypses: purported visions, symbolism, angelology, demonology, resurrection, judgment, cosmology, the Messiah, the messianic reign, astralism, dualism, eschatology, heavenly tablets (books of life), the New Jerusalem, the tree of life, punishments for the wicked, rewards for the righteous, and the like. Revelation (*see* REVELATION, BOOK OF) alone compares with Enoch in the richness of its varied concepts. A summation of the important features of each division of the book will reveal its importance for both Jewish and Christian thinking.

***a. Introduction* (*chs. 1-5*).** The theme that recurs in the book of the coming punishments of the wicked and the rewards for the righteous is introduced. The end of the world is predicted, with the final judgment, the destruction of the wicked, and the resurrection of the righteous to an endless and sinless age.

***b. Book I, Angels and Universe* (*chs. 6-36*).** Chs. 6-11 (from the book of NOAH) attribute the fallen angels to the intercourse between the sons of God and the daughters of men (related in Gen. 6:1 ff). They, in turn, have corrupted mankind through their instructions in the arts and crafts of civilization. Enoch interceded for the fallen angels ("watchers"), but was instructed to predict their final doom (chs. 12–16). He then was conducted by angels of light on various journeys, throughout the earth, to Sheol, to the place of final punishment of the fallen angels, to the tree of life, to Jerusalem, and to the Garden of Righteousness.

***c. Book II, Parables or Similitudes* (*chs. 37–71*).** Strictly speaking, these are not parables in the rabbinic or gospel meaning of the term. Their basic message is the coming destruction of wickedness and the triumph of righteousness. The first parable (chs. 38–44) deals with the coming judgment of the wicked and the reward of the righteous, and with angels, archangels, and heavenly secrets of meteorology and astronomy. The second (chs. 45–57) depicts the Messiah, the Elect One, also called the SON OF MAN, sitting on his throne of judgment. The Son of man in Enoch is not a human being, but a pre-existent, heavenly, resplendent, majestic being who possesses all dominion and pronounces judgment upon all men and angels. The final triumph of the righteous, the resurrection and judgment, and the punishment of the wicked are depicted. The third parable (58–71) promises rewards for the righteous; reveals still further heavenly secrets; and depicts the measuring of Paradise, the judgment by the Elect One, the Son of man on his throne, the resurrection of the righteous with their garments of glory, and the punishment of the fallen angels.

***d. Book III, The Heavenly Luminaries* (*chs. 72–82*).** In Jewish legend Enoch was honored as the inventor of writing, mathematics, and astronomy. This astronomical treatise is concerned that time should be reckoned by the sun, not the moon. However, the writer's solar year is 364 days, even though he is aware of the 365¼-day year. This insistence upon a solar year may have been in opposition to the Pharisaic use of the lunar CALENDAR. An astrological motif appears in 80:2-8, where we learn that the last evil days will be marked (if not predetermined) by grave disorders among the heavenly bodies, sun, moon, and stars, as well as upon the earth. The heavenly tablets containing all the deeds of men of the future generations strike a strongly deterministic note not unrelated to astralism.

*e. **Book IV, The Dream Visions** (**chs. 83-90**).* The two visions comprising this section predict the future history of Israel. The first (chs. 83-84) predicts the Flood as a punishment upon the world because of sin, which is traced to the fallen angels. The second, after recounting the period from Adam to Enoch, predicts the future up to the time of the Maccabean period (thus indicating its date). Symbolic imagery is used: oxen symbolize the patriarchs; sheep, the faithful Israelites; beasts and birds of prey, the heathen oppressors; a sheep (with a great horn, which the birds of prey could not overcome), a Jewish leader, possibly Judas Maccabeus; and a white bull with great horns, the Messiah. There are also seventy shepherds, who may have been angelic guardians of Israel. In the final period the heathen will assault the Jews, but will be repulsed and swallowed up by the earth. Fallen and faithless angels and apostate Jews will be judged. The New Jerusalem will be established, the surviving Gentiles will submit and become converted, the righteous dead will be resurrected, the messianic kingdom will be founded, and the Messiah will appear.

*f. **Book V, The Admonitions to Righteousness** (**chs. 91-105**).* Enoch predicts the judgment of the wicked and the blessed resurrection of the righteous. This introduces the Apocalypse of Weeks, 93:1-10; 91:12-17 (163 B.C.). Beginning with Enoch's own time, the future is divided into ten unequal weeks, each marked by some special event. The second week is characterized by Noah; next in order are those of Abraham, Moses, the temple, and Elijah, with the seventh a week of degeneration, possibly the tragic period that precipitated the Maccabean Revolt. The eighth week will be marked by the victory of the righteous (the Maccabees) over their oppressors, followed by the rule of righteousness. All the works of the wicked will be brought to an end, and in the ninth week the world will be made ready for destruction. In the tenth week, which will be endless, a new heaven will replace the old. Possibly a resurrection and final judgment were in the original of this ancient source. The book continues with exhortations of the righteous and condemnations of the wicked, which some relate to the difficult days of Alexander Janneus (103-76 B.C.). The terrors of the Judgment are portrayed. In the hereafter the wicked will be punished, eternally, in Sheol, whereas the righteous will enjoy the bliss of heaven.

*g. **Conclusion** (**chs. 106-108**).* Chs. 106-107 from the earlier book of Noah relate the birth of Noah and predict the increase of sin following the Flood until the messianic reign is established. The final chapter reverts to the theme of dire punishments that await the wicked and the rewards assured to the righteous.

It is quite obvious that Enoch is a complex book, lacking unity of treatment and of concepts. Consequently, it is exceedingly difficult, if not impossible, to state the actual views of the compiler. But the summation of its contents reveals the indebtedness of early Christianity to this book, or to writings and traditions of a similar character.

Bibliography. G. Beer, "Das Buch Henoch," in E. Kautzsch, *Die Apokryphen und Pseudepigraphen des Alten Testaments* (1900), II, 217-310. R. H. Charles, *The Book of Enoch* (1912; reprinted 1921 with an Introduction by W. O. E. Oesterley); "Book of Enoch" in *The Apoc. and Pseudep. of the OT* (1913), II, 163-281. C. Bonner, *The Last Chapters of Enoch in Greek* (1937). H. H. Rowley, *The Relevance of Apocalyptic* (2nd ed., 1946), pp. 54-60, 77-84. R. H. Pfeiffer, *History of NT Times* (1949), pp. 75-79.

M. Rist

ENOSH ē'nŏsh [אנוש, man, mankind; *cf.* אדם (Pss. 8:4—H 5; 144:3)]. Alternately: ENOS ē'nəs. Son of Seth; the father of Kenan (Gen. 4:26; 5:6-11; I Chr. 1:1; Luke 3:38). J records the tradition that in some form Yahweh-worship began in Enosh' time (Gen. 4:26).

EN-RIMMON ĕn rĭm'ən [עין־רמון, spring of the pomegranate] (Josh. 19:7; Neh. 11:29). Alternately: AIN, RIMMON ān, rĭm'ən (Josh. 15:32; I Chr. 4:32; *see below*). A city assigned to Simeon (Josh. 19:7; I Chr. 4:32), and later to Judah's Negeb district of Hormah (Josh. 15:32). Returnees from the Exile resettled at En-rimmon (Neh. 11:29). It is usually identified with Khirbet Umm er-Ramamin, nine miles N-NE of Beer-sheba.

"Ain and Rimmon" in Josh. 15:32; I Chr. 4:32 should probably be "Ain-rimmon"—i.e., "En-rimmon."

V. R. Gold

EN-ROGEL ĕn rō'gəl [עין רגל, spring of the fuller, *or* wanderer, *or* spy]. A spring near Jerusalem, in the valley of the Kidron. It marked the limit between

29. En-rogel, modern Bir Ayyub ("well of Job"), below the village of Silwan

the tribes of Benjamin and Judah (Josh. 15:7; 18:16). When David had to flee from Jerusalem in the days of Absalom's rebellion, two of his men remained near En-rogel to gather intelligence concerning the progress of the revolt in the capital city (II Sam. 17:17). The clandestine coronation of Adonijah took place by the Serpent's Stone, near the spring (I Kings 1:9). En-rogel is commonly identified with the so-called Bir Ayyub, "Job's Well," on the left bank of the Wadi en-Nar (the Kidron), shortly after its junction with the Wadi er-Rababi (Valley of Hinnom).* The well is sunk deep into the rock and reaches an underground stream of water which gushes to the surface and flows down the valley after abundant winter rainfalls. The gradual filling of the valley has made it necessary to line the upper parts of the well with stone masonries which in their oldest stage may go back to Roman times. The constructions seen over the well are modern. *See* map under JERUSALEM. *See also* JERUSALEM § 5*b*. Fig. ENR 29.

Bibliography. G. A. Smith, *Jerusalem,* I (1907), 108-11; H. Vincent, *Jérusalem Antique* (1912), pp. 134-38; G. Dalman, *Jerusalem und sein Gelände* (1930), pp. 163-67; A. S. Marmardji, *Textes Géographiques Arabes sur la Palestine* (1951), p. 14; J. Simons, *Jerusalem in the OT* (1952), pp. 158-62; H. Vincent, *Jérusalem de l'Ancient Testament,* I (1954), 284-88.

G. A. BARROIS

ENROLLMENT [התיחש, enrolling; ἀπογραφή, registration]. A listing of people in a public register according to family, position, and tribe. Such genealogical lists may have been kept at a number of villages. Enrollments were customary for conscripting soldiers (cf. Num. 1:2-3; II Sam. 24:1-9; I Chr. 7:40; 21:1-5; II Chr. 25:5). Solomon, and evidently David before him, enrolled aliens to conscript them for work (II Chr. 2:17). Priests kept family registers to prove their right to priestly service and support (I Chr. 23:3; Ezra 2:61-63; cf. Neh. 7:61-65). Family registers were probably also kept. In the NT reference is made to Roman imperial policy to enroll people for purposes of taxation (Luke 2:2; Acts 5:37). *See also* CENSUS.

1. In the OT. Periodic enrollments seem to have been customary in Israel prior to the monarchy in raising armies (Num. 1:2-3; I Chr. 7:40), and even afterward when a king desired to go to war (cf. II Sam. 24:1-9; I Chr. 21:1-5; II Chr. 25:5). By means of his standing army the king more particularly protected himself and his claim to the throne.

Besides political enrollments, it is quite likely that family and tribal genealogical registers were kept (cf. Ezek. 13:9), with great stress on their preservation. The emphasis on family and ancestry, inheritance, tribal solidarity, and the pride and significance of being a true son of Abraham, and heir to the promises of God, make this all the more probable. The Chronicler tells us there was a genealogical register compiled in the time of Jotham and Jeroboam II. When and how often such enrollments were made is uncertain. Josephus states that the genealogy of his family was set down in public records (Life I) and claims that in his day the high priestly family record went back two thousand years. The Priestly writer and the Chronicler seem to have used such lists in their histories. How reliable these lists are is uncertain. *See also* GENEALOGY.

2. In the NT. Luke states that there was an enrollment of the Jews according to families, in their native city, for purposes of taxation when Augustus was emperor of Rome and Quirinius governor of Syria (Luke 2:2). This he terms the first enrollment, indicating there were others, another of which he records as taking place in the days of Judas the Galilean (Acts 5:37; cf. Jos. Antiq. XVIII.i.1; War VII.i.2). From Egyptian papyri it appears a periodic census by households every fourteen years was a feature of the imperial administration of Egypt. It is probable that such a policy was also normal in Syria. Periodic enrollment by households is emphasized in the edict of G. Vibrius Maximus (A.D. 104), which notifies the people that the time is near and that all who are outside their nomes are to go to their "domestic hearths" for this purpose.

There is some question as to the accuracy of Luke's date for the initial enrollment. Extrabiblical sources are silent as to a world-wide imperial census at the time of Jesus' birth. Moreover, while QUIRINIUS was governor of Syria at the time of the census of A.D. 6, Sentius Saturnius was governor in 8/6 B.C. (cf. Tert. Marcion 4.19). If the word "governor" is used somewhat loosely, it is possible it may apply to Quirinius, who may have held some military position in Syria at that time. But he appears not to have been the official legate.

Bibliography. W. R. Ramsay, *Was Christ Born at Bethlehem?* (1898), pp. 117-96; W. R. Harvey-Jellie, *Chronicles,* New Century Bible (1906), p. 36; W. R. Ramsay, *The Bearing of Recent Discoveries on the Trustworthiness of the NT* (1915), pp. 238-300; A. Deissmann, *Light from the Ancient East* (trans. L. R. M. Strachan; 1927), pp. 270-71.

V. H. KOOY

EN-SHEMESH ĕn shĕm'ĭsh [עין שמש, spring of the sun]. A place on the N boundary of Judah (Josh. 15:7) and the S boundary of Benjamin (18:17); identified with 'Ain el-Hod, 2¾ miles E of Jerusalem and just E of Bethany, the last spring on the road between Jerusalem and the Jordan Valley. Since the fifteenth century it has been called the "Spring of the Apostles."

V. R. GOLD

ENSIGN. *See* BANNER.

EN-TAPPUAH ĕn tăp'yōō ə [עין תפוח, spring of Tappuah] (Josh. 17:7). A place of uncertain location at the S border of Manasseh; probably to be associated with the Ephraimite city of the same name (*see* TAPPUAH 2) SW of Shechem.

ENTHRONEMENT OF YAHWEH. *See* KING.

ENTRY, TRIUMPHAL. *See* TRIUMPHAL ENTRY.

ENVOY. *See* MESSENGER.

ENVY. 1. In the OT. In the OT "envy" usually translates קנאה, which also connotes "jealousy," "ardor," "zeal," and "rivalry." Perhaps it has the connotation of "rivalry" in Eccl. 4:4; 9:6. The jealousy (also קנאה) of God is often referred to (cf. Exod. 20:5), punishing those who are evil. In Exod. 34:14 God's jealousy will not permit Israel to worship another god (cf. Deut. 4:24; 6:15; Josh. 24:19); and

God, being jealous, is avenging (Nah. 1:2). But the OT forbids man to be envious of violence (Prov. 3: 31) or of sinners (Prov. 23:17; cf. Ezek. 35:11).

2. In the NT. In the NT envy (φθόνος) is also forbidden, usually appearing in lists of vices (Rom. 1:29; Gal. 5:21; I Tim. 6:4; Tit. 3:3; I Pet. 2:1; in Mark 7:22 ὀφθαλμὸς πονηρός is translated "envy"). Matthew says that Pilate knew that it was "out of envy" that the Jews had delivered Jesus up (27:18). This seems a strange reason. Perhaps the hatred of the Jews was a perversion of a hidden yearning. According to Mark, it was the chief priests who had handed Jesus over "out of envy" (15:10). They were jealous of Jesus and wanted him out of the way.

Paul bids the Galatians not to envy one another (5:26), for envy estranges and love builds up. He tells the Philippians that some are preaching Christ "from envy" (1:15). They are envious of the response made to Paul's preaching, and they are trying to persuade his followers to accept a different gospel.

With the OT idea (*see* § 1 *above*) that God is a "jealous" God, cf. Jas. 4:5, where it is said that God yearns jealously ("jealously" translates a phrase including φθόνος). Some suggest this text has been corrupted. *See* JEALOUSY. B. H. THROCKMORTON, JR.

EPAENETUS ĭ pē′nə təs [᾿Επαίνετος, praised] (Rom. 16:5). A Christian greeted as the first believer in the province of Asia. The natural inference is that Epaenetus is still in Asia, and this strongly indicates the Ephesian destination of Rom. 16. The reading "Achaia" (᾿Αχαίας) in some texts of Rom. 16:5 is poorly attested and clearly mistaken, being derived from I Cor. 16:15. Epaenetus is greeted by Paul almost at the very beginning of the long list of persons mentioned by name, and is greeted as especially beloved. Aside from this passage there are no data concerning Epaenetus. J. M. NORRIS

EPAPHRAS ĕp′ə frăs, ĭ păf′rəs [᾿Επαφρᾶς, *a familiar form of* ᾿Επαφρόδιτος, charming] (Col. 1:7; 4:12; Philem. 23). A native of Colossae (Col. 4:12); a Christian preacher through whom the Colossians had come to know the gospel (1:7). He is not to be confused with Epaphroditus (Phil. 2:25; 4:18), who was a native of Philippi.

Epaphras was, at the time of the writing of Colossians and Philemon, a fellow prisoner with Paul (Philem. 23), but at a previous time he had evangelized Colossae and the neighboring towns of Laodicea and Hierapolis (Col. 4:12-13) under the direction of Paul—reading "on our behalf" in Col. 1:7, which is better attested than "on your behalf"—probably during Paul's long period of work in Ephesus (Acts 19:10). It was through Epaphras that Paul had come to know the situation of the Colossian church to which he addressed himself in Colossians. Paul speaks of Epaphras in terms of warmest commendation as his "fellow servant" (Col. 1:7) and even refers to him as a "servant of Christ Jesus" (4: 12)—a designation that Paul applies even to Timothy only once (Phil. 1:1). Paul praises Epaphras for his unstinting devotion to the well-being and progress of the Christian communities in Colossae, Laodicea, and Hierapolis. J. M. NORRIS

EPAPHRODITUS ĭ păf′rə dī′təs [᾿Επαφρόδιτος, handsome, charming] (Phil. 2:25). A friend and co-worker of Paul who served as messenger and bearer of a gift from the church at Philippi to Paul in prison. He had been a leader in the Philippian church who came not only to bring the gift which that church had collected for Paul, but also to stay and help him. In this service he had fallen ill—seriously so, for Paul reports that he was "near to death." Reiterating this point, Paul says: "He nearly died for the work of Christ, risking his life to complete your service to me" (Phil. 2:30). Now recovered, Epaphroditus was about to return to Philippi, to relieve the anxiety there about him and also Paul's anxiety. Paul asks that the church receive him "in the Lord with all joy."

Although Epaphras is a shortened form of Epaphroditus, we can hardly identify the Epaphras of Philem. 23; Col. 4:12 with the Epaphroditus of Philippians. The former leader had had significant leadership in three churches—Colossae, Laodicea, and Hierapolis (Col. 4:12-13)—and is designated in the Colossian letter as "one of yourselves." One person could hardly have had so close an identification with the interests of the Philippian church if he had also had as much leadership responsibility in the three other churches as the letter to the Colossians implies. The name was a common one in both forms in the first century. M. E. LYMAN

EPHAH ē′fə [עֵיפָה, darkness]. **1.** A son of Midian; eponym of an Arabian tribe (Gen. 25:4; I Chr. 1:33; cf. Isa. 60:6).

2. A concubine of Caleb; an eponym (I Chr. 2:46).

3. A Calebite family (I Chr. 2:47).

Bibliography. K. Tallqvist, *Assyrian Personal Names* (1914), p. 75. H. H. GUTHRIE, JR.

EPHAH (WEIGHT) [אֵיפָה, אֵפָה]. A dry measure equal to a tenth of a homer (Ezek. 45:11), estimated as 1.52 to 2.42 pecks or three eighths to two thirds of a bushel; mentioned extensively in the OT. In Zech. 5:5-11, which presents some textual problems, there is the vision of a woman in an ephah. It would seem that here the term means a container larger than the standard.

See also WEIGHTS AND MEASURES § C4*d*.

O. R. SELLERS

EPHAI ē′fī [*Kethibh* עוֹפַי, *Qere* עֵיפַי, *perhaps* bird, *from* עוּף, to fly] (Jer. 40:8). A Netophathite whose sons were among the captains in the open country that joined Gedaliah at Mizpah. The parallel passage in II Kings 25:23, however, omits the phrase "the sons of Ephai" and thus makes Tanhumeth "the Netophathite." M. NEWMAN

EPHER ē′fər [עֵפֶר, young deer *or* gazelle]. **1.** A clan of the tribe of Midian (Gen. 25:4; I Chr. 1:33). Some have connected this name with the *Apparu* of the inscriptions of Ashurbanipal, others with modern 'Ofr in Arabia. The fact that the name occurs in lists of tribes of the Hebrews nearest Midian (*cf.* 2-3 *below*) could indicate the incorporation of Midianite clans into Israel.

2. A family or clan of the tribe of Judah (I Chr. 4:17).

3. A family or clan of the part of the tribe of Manasseh which dwelt E of Jordan (I Chr. 5:24). *Cf.* HEPHER 1 (Num. 26:32).

Bibliography. M. Noth, *Die israelitischen Personennamen* (1928), p. 230.

H. H. GUTHRIE, JR.

EPHES-DAMMIM ē′fĭz dăm′ĭm [אפס דמים, end or border of Dammim (blood)] (I Sam. 17:1). Alternately: PAS-DAMMIM păs dăm′ĭm [פס דמים] (I Chr. 11:13). A staging area between Socoh and Azekah for the Philistine armies before the battle which was concluded by David's killing Goliath, the Philistine hero (I Sam. 17:1). Pas-dammim is probably the same as Ephes-dammim. Some scholars would add Pas-dammim to the parallel account in II Sam. 23:9.

Ephes-dammim is possibly to be identified with Damun, *ca.* four miles NE of Socoh. V. R. GOLD

EPHESIANS, LETTER TO THE ĭ fē′zhənz [᾽Εφεσίοι, *see* EPHESUS]. The tenth book in the NT canon; purporting to be a letter from the apostle Paul to the Christians at Ephesus. The RSV, however, follows the best ancient evidence in relegating to the margin the words "who are at Ephesus and" (1:1). As yet no completely satisfactory solution to the problems of destination, authorship, and purpose has been proposed. Remarkably few British scholars have abandoned the authenticity of Ephesians, but the majority of liberal scholars in America and Europe have done so. Ephesians is widely acclaimed as the greatest ecumenical document in the NT and as standing squarely in the Pauline tradition. Its use of liturgical texts (e.g., 1:3-14; 5:14) has recently been emphasized afresh, perhaps without sufficient caution, because Ephesians may have been a source for the second-century liturgies.

1. Authorship. The case for authenticity seems very strong at first. It claims to be by Paul (1:1; 3:1; cf. 4:1); its occasion (6:21-22) is identical with that of Col. 4:7-8; Philem. 1, 10, 23-24; and the magnificent hymn at 1:3-14 (if this is what it is) recalls similar poems in I Cor. 13; Phil. 2; Col. 1. The fervor and depth of Ephesians demand Paul as the author, it is said. If one shows close connections between Ephesians and Acts or I Peter or Revelation, the priority can be asserted for Ephesians. The letter was known almost certainly to Clement of Rome, Ignatius, Hermas, Polycarp, and the author of the Pastoral letters—i.e., from *ca.* A.D. 95. The earliest collected edition of the Pauline letters contained Ephesians; Marcion (*ca.* A.D. 140) accepted it, although he called it Laodiceans; and by the end of the second century it was canonical and assumed to be Paul's for Irenaeus, the (Roman) Muratorian Canon, and Clement of Alexandria. This unanimous tradition has strength; it was unchallenged until 1792. Obviously the onus of proof is on anyone who denies the ascription to Paul.

The defense will admit that the vocabulary and style are often unusual, and that certain thoughts mark an advance on Pauline teaching as found in Galatians, I and II Corinthians, and Romans. For Ephesians is the manifesto of a mighty controversialist at the end of his days, "all passion spent." As the place of non-Jews in God's new commonwealth was at last assured, Paul was free to write in positive, irenic vein; he lets his mind roam in spacious regions of heavenly truth (cf. II Cor. 12:1-4; I Cor. 2:6 ff); and the result is this profound contribution in which he expounds the meaning of Christ and his church. What other spiritual giant could possibly have produced Ephesians?

Since the address of 1:1 is so uncertain, it may be that Marcion's title, "To the Laodiceans," is correct, for Marcion must have relied on earlier tradition. A more popular suggestion among the conservatives (and some liberals) is, however, Archbishop Ussher's (1654)—that Paul wrote an encyclical to the Gentile Christians (2:11; 3:1). A space was left blank for the bearer (Tychicus) to insert place names as required. Intimate connections with Colossians are inevitable, since the two letters were composed at the same time, but Colossians dealt with Christology and the dangers of a specific heresy. Echoes of other Pauline letters must be due to the apostle's own memory.

Strong as it seems, this case is nevertheless very much weaker than its defenders allow.

The people addressed cannot be Paul's beloved Ephesian converts (Acts 19). They were unknown to the writer, who must "assume" that they understood about his status as the Apostle to the Gentiles and that they had been rightly instructed concerning Jesus the Messiah (1:15; 2:11; 3:2-6; 4:21). Paul could hardly be indulging in mere irony here; but how else can we understand such assumptions in a letter by him to a familiar church? Moreover, Ephesians lacks the truly personal elements we expect in a letter to one congregation or to the churches of a definite area. It will not do, therefore, to describe Ephesians as a circular to Asia Minor, including Ephesus, Colossae, and Laodicea. PHILEMON may be a letter to Laodicea (cf. Col. 4:16); we possess a genuine letter to the COLOSSIANS; and Rom. 16:1-23 has a much better claim to be considered a letter to the Ephesians (*see* ROMANS). Paul in his prison had no duplicators, and we must not ascribe modern practice to him. Galatians and I Peter show how a general letter might have been addressed. The "whole structure" (Eph. 2:21) does not mean, as has been suggested, "each single church" among the several to whom an encyclical was sent. Again, why did no copy survive except one containing "in Ephesus"? And why do the best and earliest MSS (Chester-Beatty papyrus 46, Vaticanus, Sinaiticus, 1739), as well as Marcion, Origen, and Basil, fail to retain these words, "in Ephesus"? Masson suggests that a disciple of Paul, inspired by Col. 4:15, addressed a letter in his master's name to the Laodiceans. Copyists at Ephesus, the capital of Asia Minor, removed the words "in Laodicea." What more natural at a later time than to substitute "in Ephesus" in order to make sense of the text (for it hardly makes sense without something like "in" followed by a place name)? Marcion's evidence, wherever it came from, would be discounted by the catholics as that of a heretic. Masson adds that the author of Ephesians interpolated 4:16 into Colossians, to recommend his own composition! This is too ingenious.

Scholars on both sides of the controversy pile conjecture on conjecture. Could not Marcion have derived his own "Laodiceans" from an authentic Col. 4:16, and his opponents offered "Ephesians" as a riposte? *See* § 2 *below*.

Linguistic considerations alone are not decisive; yet note that Ephesians has almost a hundred non-Pauline words, of which some forty are unique in the NT. The influence of Gnosticism and the mystery cults has been found in the use of "the aeon of this world" (2:2), "height" and "depth," and the group: "mystery" (not quite in the same sense as we find elsewhere in Paul), "knowledge," "wisdom," "mature." Some of these are borrowed from Colossians and other Pauline letters, so that Gnostic sources are unnecessary. The word "devil" is post-Pauline (cf. Matt. 4:1; Acts 13:10), and its employment instead of "Satan," "Belial," or "Tempter" is not explained by saying that it expresses the idea of an attacking demon. Unusual too is the phrase "in the heavenly places," used variously of Christ enthroned, of demonic powers, and even of Christians exalted with their Lord. This last idea cannot be taken literally, and the Pauline doctrine of the final dwelling of believers with Christ is better put at II Tim. 2:11-12. (Observe, however, that at Rom. 6:5 ff the idea is more eschatological than in Ephesians. If it be replied that Colossians equally stresses this concept, note Col. 3:4: "When Christ . . . appears." Ephesians is far less eschatological in tone.) Masson solves the problem of "the heavenly places" by showing that the term (ἐπουρανίοις) was required in the hymn of 1:3-14 for its sonority and the number of its syllables. Again, why does Eph. 6:12 reverse the normal order with "blood and flesh"? (So the Greek; both KJV and RSV change to the usual order.) Because, says Percy, Paul wanted to avoid misunderstanding or to prevent two Greek sigmas coming together. Yet Paul is willing to leave two sigmas together in Eph. 5:31; I Cor. 6:16!

The Greek style has perplexed conservatives and radicals alike, with the following features: the inordinate length of the sentences (e.g., 3:1-7; 4:11-16); many relatives and participles; clauses introduced by ἵνα; indirect questions; infinitives; tautological genitives; abstract forms; etc. Moffatt thought this was enough to disprove Paul's authorship; but Percy proves in detail that it is not. He takes each feature separately and has little difficulty in most cases in demonstrating that the style has parallels in the genuine Pauline letters. However, Percy fails to take account of the cumulative effect of the vocabulary; the style; the thought; and, above all, these added to the evidence that Ephesians betrays knowledge and use of every extant, canonical Pauline letter. If, indeed, Ephesians is a mosaic built up from the corpus of the genuine letters, how could the style fail to be Pauline on the whole, assuming that the author did his work with some skill? Moreover, Eph. 1–3 in Greek has no equal in Paul for sustained slow sonority. Compared with II Thessalonians, Galatians, Romans, or II Corinthians, Ephesians is a lifeless composition! No wonder it is said by some defenders of authenticity that Paul was a poor old soul, a weary apostle, or that he had taken off on mystic wing into the sublime empyrean!

Whatever may be thought of the situation existing between the Jewish-Christian and Gentile-Christian groups in the church before or after A.D. 70, it is certainly not Pauline to define Christ's mission as primarily to reconcile Jews and Gentiles (Eph. 2:15-16; 3:5 contradicts 3:3). Is not the "very least of all the saints" (3:8) a spurious humility? Does the teaching on marriage (5:22 ff) agree with Paul's in I Cor. 7? Would the apostle have moved so far in his attitude in such a short space of time? In spite of 1:10, 14, 18, 21; 4:4, 30; 5:5-6, pressed to their limit, does Ephesians display even as much eschatological adventism as Col. 3:4; Phil. 1:6, 10; 3:20-21, which probably belong to the same period as a genuine Ephesians would? Does not Eph. 2:1-5 ("dead through the trespasses and sins") fail to bring out Paul's doctrine of baptism as a sacramental death and rising again in union with Christ (Rom. 6:3 ff; Col. 2:12, 20; 3:1-4)?

The catholicity of the church in Ephesians is, of course, true to Paul's view (I Cor. 10:32; 11:22; 15:9 must not be underestimated; cf. I Cor. 10:18: "Israel *according to the Spirit*" is implied, and the Israel is the total entity within which local congregations belong). On the other hand, Paul did not speak of the apostles and prophets as the foundation of the church (Eph. 2:20; cf. I Cor. 3:11) nor of the "holy" apostles (Eph. 3:5). The collocation in short compass (Eph. 1–5) of so many diverse themes as the body, the bride, the temple, the Israel, and the new Adam, has no parallel in Paul.

But "only Paul could have written so excellently!" Did Socrates write the *Republic* and *Phaedo* of Plato, the *Nicomachean Ethics* and the *Poetics* of Aristotle? Did the eighth century B.C. produce few or many men of genius across the world? Was Shakespeare quite without peers, or must we waste our time trying to prove that only Lord Bacon could have composed Shakespeare's plays and lyrics? Not at all! Then a supremely creative age like the first Christian century was bound to produce more than a Paul, and it is all gain to know that the authors of Hebrews, Ephesians, I Peter, and John's gospel and letters, and John the Seer, are great minds not unworthy to set alongside Paul himself.

These objections to the conservative case are staggering, and they become decisive when added to two other major considerations—the intimate relationship between Ephesians and Colossians; and the use in Ephesians of phrases from the canonical Paulines (Hebrews, I and II Timothy, and Titus excepted, of course). Holtzmann first showed the way; Goodspeed followed with an important contribution; and Mitton has refined and improved the theory. *See bibliography*.

One third of the words in Colossians are found in Ephesians; and one quarter of the words in Ephesians appear in Colossians. The dependence can hardly be that of the same author on his own memory, because words and phrases from different parts of Colossians are conflated in Ephesians. By the same token Colossians (in its present form, too) is clearly the prior letter (as *ab* must be later than *a* or *b*) and must have been known intimately by the author of Ephesians. Yet the borrower seems often to quote from memory, for the run of consecutive words from Colossians seldom exceeds five (Eph. 6:21-22 = Col. 4:7-8 is the longest continuous passage). Assuming that 6:21-22 is part of the original text of Ephesians, we may suppose that a copy of Colossians was available to the writer of Ephesians. (Why he did not use it more often is a question that remains.)

The situation in both Colossians and Ephesians shows that, if both are authentic, they must have been sent from the same prison cell within days, perhaps even hours, of each other. How then can we explain the use of certain words with radically different meanings in the two documents? Οἰκονομία ("economy") is especially difficult. In I Cor. 9:17 and Col. 1:25 it means task or stewardship entrusted to a human agent; in Eph. 1:10; 3:2, 9, it means a plan or effective management, and is used of God's purpose for the consummation of the times. Cullmann's translation, "the plan of salvation," is not accurate. Similarly, "MYSTERY," which in Paul means a revealed secret (I Cor. 2:7, 13; cf. Mark 4:11), is defined in Col. 1:26-27; 2:2; 4:3 as "Christ in you, the hope of glory"; but in Eph. 1:9; 3:4, 9, the secret is the divine purpose to unite all things in Christ and to reconcile the Jews with the Gentiles. If Ephesians is non-Pauline, the word "mystery" may have the flavor of an esoteric doctrine rather than a revelation (for this idea cf. the use of *raz* in the Qumran literature—e.g., 1Q 27, "The Book of Secrets").

Percy would get round the difficulty by dismissing the different usage as merely a matter of emphasis. Masson too finds the meaning identical in both letters, but he insists that the Colossians references have been interpolated into Colossians by the author of Ephesians. A third word differently employed is "fulness" (*see* PLEROMA). At Col. 1:19 it applies to God's dwelling in Christ, by inference from 2:9 (RSV "of God" in 1:19 is absent from the Greek). Then in Eph. 1:23; 3:19; 4:13 "pleroma" is applied to the church as the body of Christ: "which is his body, the [pleroma] of him who fills all in all." "Pleroma" means complement, supplement, or full content (Rom. 11:12, 25; 13:10; 15:29; I Cor. 10:26; Gal. 4:4; and so in Eph. 1:10). It was also a technical term for the realm of the aeons in Gnostic speculation, from which, certain scholars assert, the author of Ephesians derived it. The genuine Pauline antecedents, and those behind such passages as Mark 1:15 (e.g., Lam. 4:18; Dan 2:20-23, 28), make it unnecessary to look to the Gnostics for the meaning here. According to some scholars Ephesians presents Christ as filling the church with his living reality; on the opposite side a large array of students (e.g., Chrysostom, Calvin, and Leenhardt) understands "pleroma" as supplement: the church as his body completes Christ, the head who is enthroned in heaven. The church would then be necessary to Christ. (The language is pictorial and not quite exact.) It remains strange, nonetheless, that Paul would use "pleroma" of Christ's relation to God and immediately after, contrary to his own teaching, of the church's relation to Christ. Dibelius would add to this list the word "soma" ("body")—in Colossians it is used of the universe, but of the church in Ephesians.

As an example of the way Colossians is adapted in its sister letter we may cite Col. 3:16-17 = Eph. 5:19-20. The phrase "in the name of the Lord Jesus" is connected in Colossians with the verb "do." In Ephesians the author has joined it rather to the next words, "giving thanks." This is the sort of memory trick that can be illustrated from many of our own prayers, especially pulpit prayers.

Perhaps the most significant argument against Paul's authorship, and the one that gives pungency to all these other considerations, is the exhibit of dependence on the remaining eight canonical Paulines. The following parallels are adequate to present a good case for the Goodspeed-Mitton thesis of dependence ("P" indicates purple passages of special interest):

	Romans		**Ephesians**
	1:21		4:17-18
	1:24		4:18-19
	2:11		6:9
	4:2		2:9
	5:1-2		2:18; 3:11-12
	5:15		3:7; 4:7
	8:16-17		1:14; 3:6
P	8:28		1:11
P	8:29		1:4-5
	11:33		3:8
	12:1		4:1
	12:2		5:10, 17
	12:3		3:7; 4:7
	12:5		4:25
	13:12		5:11

(*Other possible parallels in Eph.* 2:7, 9; 3:16; 4:27; 1:10)

	I Corinthians		**Ephesians**
	3:12, 6, 9, 16		2:20-21
P	4:12		4:28
	4:14, 16		5:1
P	6:9-10		5:5
	6:15-16		5:30-31
P	11:3		5:23
P	12:28		4:11
P	15:9-10		3:8

(*Other possible parallels in Eph.* 2:9; 4:6; 1:11; 4:4-5)

	II Corinthians		**Ephesians**
	1:1-2		1:1-2
	1:3		1:3
P	1:22		1:13; 4:30
	5:20		6:20
	1:12	(possibly)	2:3

	Galatians		**Ephesians**
	1:10		6:6
P	2:20		5:2, 25
P	4:4		1:10
	2:16	(possibly)	2:8-9
P	3:14	(possibly)	1:13

Philippians		Ephesians
4:18		5:2, 10
4:6	(possibly)	6:18

I Thessalonians		Ephesians
2:2		6:20
3:10		3:20
4:13		2:3, 12
5:9		1:14
2:12	(possibly)	4:1
5:8	(possibly)	6:14-16

II Thessalonians		Ephesians
2:14	(περιποίησις)	1:14
1:9	(possibly)	6:10 (Col. 1:11 conflated)
1:11	(possibly)	4:1 (I Thess. 2:12 conflated)

Mitton takes περιποίησις in Ephesians, with its use in I Peter, in a passive sense; but in I and II Thessalonians in an active. This is dubious. He allows no significant parallels to II Thessalonians.

Philemon	Ephesians
1	3:1
9	6:20

When this evidence is examined objectively in its total impact and significance, the case for the dependence of the author of Ephesians on an existing Pauline collection is unanswerable. Mitton (*see bibliography*) does a real service by his careful comparisons of Philippians with the other letters, and he finds that "the parallels in Ephesians are twice the number of those in Philippians even when full allowance is made for the greater length of Ephesians." He also proposes certain tests for an imitator's borrowing of existing letters: (*a*) he would show more correspondences; (*b*) he would reproduce the striking phrase; and (*c*) he would be inclined to borrow from the "purple passages." Accordingly, many sustained parallels are exhibited (e.g., Rom. 1:21-24; 12:1-5); see also the verses marked "P" above (e.g., Gal. 2:20). A similar comparison in the case of Philippians shows that there are four or five such groups, and all, with one exception, are insignificant. In Ephesians, however, out of twenty-five groups twenty are significant, Mitton finds.

Percy's view is that Colossians was indeed the model and that the variations are due simply to Paul. He fails to show why, in two letters issued simultaneously for the same general area (he accepts the encyclical theory), Paul should give only in Ephesians the teaching about Christ and the church in terms of the marriage relationship (the "great mystery"; 5:22-33); or why Eph. 6:4 (on children's upbringing) is more detailed than Col. 3:21; or why the meaning of the phrase "buying up the time" is altered in Eph. 5:15-16 from Col. 4:5.

When he comes to the dependence of Ephesians on other Pauline letters, Percy admits the "use" of Gal. 2:20; 3:14; 4:4; I Cor. 6:9-10; 12:28; 15:9; II Cor. 1:22; Rom. 1:21; 8:28-29. However, Paul probably had no collected edition of his own letters! When the complete list of Pauline parallels is examined, one can see that the problem involves more than a few uses of single verses. The point is that we can show how Ephesians is made up of phrases from the nine letters of Paul which have survived as part of the NT canon! Without necessarily committing oneself to every deduction and speculation offered by Goodspeed and Mitton, one must recognize that their evidence is overwhelmingly adequate to provide the desirable onus of proof against authenticity.

For all these reasons together—language, style, theological conceptions, the intimate relation to and use made of Colossians, and the intricate borrowings from the corpus of the canonical Paulines—we are bound to conclude that Ephesians is not from the hand of Paul. It is not even a letter, since the epistolary beginning and end are taken over for effect.

2. Origin, purpose, and value. The usual view—on the basis of authenticity—is that at the same time Paul wrote Colossians and Philemon from Rome, he wrote either to Ephesus or to the province of Asia a general letter summarizing his gospel and defending his mission. The scholars who have advocated Ephesus as the place of writing for the Imprisonment letters have not convincingly made out their case, except possibly for Philippians (*see* COLOSSIANS; EPHESUS).

N. A. Dahl, looking to the baptismal language in 1:13-14; 4:5, 30; 5:8, 26, suggests that Ephesians was written to newly settled congregations in order to teach them more fully, and with the authority of Paul the apostle, what they had received through baptism. This new version of the encyclical theory certainly draws attention to an important element, although at the cost of exaggeration. If Paul wrote to give post-initiation instruction, why did he lay the emphasis on Jewish-Gentile reconciliation? Why did he not deal with the everyday problems of Gentile Christians eating in Jewish Christian homes, or vice versa? Why did he say so much on baptism and nothing at all about the Lord's Supper, the sacrament of the Cross and the new covenant—especially if Jews and Gentiles were to eat together at the Lord's Table? In the ecumenical document par excellence of the NT canon this absence of teaching about the Eucharist is almost inexplicable (note 4:4); and even the supporters of the Goodspeed hypothesis are hard put to explain why a true Paulinist, with I Cor. 10–11 before him, should have thus neglected this topic. It does not seem probable that, as some hold, the silence is due to an absence of dispute in the primitive church over the Lord's Supper. Gal. 2:12 has little point if it has no bearing on the sacrament. (Eph. 5:20 carries no such sacramental reference.)

Similar objections apply to the theory that Ephesians is a revised edition of Colossians, designed for use as a baptismal homily by the primitive church. Ephesians does not read like a sermon at all, but like an imitation of a Pauline letter! Eph. 1:3; I Pet. 1:3 may be considered the typical opening of a homily, but this is to ignore the dependence of both on II Cor. 1:3, which can be proved in the case of Ephesians by all the arguments and synoptic parallels cited above. It is the fashion in some quarters to discount literary relationships in favor of a widespread catechetical tradition; but the evidence from Qumran helps to demonstrate that there was considerable use of documents and scribes, including the copying of

MSS, during the first century A.D. It will not do to use this to draw a picture of Paul and his assistants writing out circulars at Rome, but it may throw light on the practice of the church after A.D. 70 when the "holy apostles and prophets" were dead and being venerated, when the adventist hope was somewhat fading, and when apostolic tradition had to be preserved by literary means.

Goodspeed's view is that someone, probably Onesimus, the converted slave of Philemon, was stimulated by the publication of the Acts of the Apostles *ca.* A.D. 85 to search for Paul's letters to other churches. Onesimus, now bishop of Ephesus (cf. Ignatius *To the Ephesians*), collected and published those that he found, along with Colossians and Philemon, which he had long known intimately. Then, in order to commend the Pauline gospel and honor his master, he composed Ephesians and placed it at the head of the corpus. It was, as John Knox holds (*see* GALATIANS § 6), "a general letter to the churches serving as a preface to the particular church letters which followed and as a symbol that they too had something to say to the whole church." Knox thinks that Marcion replaced Ephesians by Galatians as the first letter in the canon, and that the Pastorals were added later; the date of the original collection he would place about A.D. 90-100 (*see bibliography*).

It is a weakness in Goodspeed's theory that dependence of Ephesians on Acts is doubtful (*see bibliography*), and that Ephesians is not quite a summary of the Pauline message. Did Onesimus, of all people, really need to read Acts before discovering where Paul may have written letters? C. L. Mitton, accepting this theory of Goodspeed in principle, declines to name an author but emphasizes the liturgical interest of this document. Acts 20 influenced the author, who wrote for Christians in the Ephesian area. How did it originate? According to Mitton, as follows: Tychicus as an old man was living near Ephesus, and to him the author, a devout disciple of Paul, revealed his desire to compose a letter in Paul's name. From Eph. 6:21-22 we should deduce that Tychicus approved the completed product. We can date this writing within five years, A.D. 87-92, Mitton says, because the authors of Revelation, I Clement, and the Pastorals seem to know Ephesians, and it must be a little later than 85, the estimated date of Acts. This speculation is quite fanciful. Moreover, 85 for the publication of Acts is far from being established.

The following points seem very probable: (*a*) the author of Ephesians knew Colossians intimately, and modeled his composition on it. (*b*) He knew the Paulines as a collection, which had been in existence for some time; and he revered Paul as a holy apostle, the greatest of the Christian missionaries to the Roman world and one of the foundation stones in the catholic church. (*c*) His primary theme is the unity of the church and its obligation to grow in the love and power of Christ. (*d*) "At Ephesus" (1:1) is probably the earliest guess about the supposed recipients, but the original text was based on Col. 1:1-2 with certain omissions: "Paul, an apostle of Christ Jesus by the will of God . . . , to the saints and faithful brethren[?] in Christ." (*e*) The writer cannot be identified. It might have been Onesimus. The use of Paul's name, so far from indicating that the apostle had been neglected and ignored, shows how influential and authoritative he was for the author and the circle of Christians with whom he had to do. (*f*) The date is later than A.D. 70, but the upward limit is uncertain. If Ephesians is known to I Clement, and if the latter should be dated *ca.* A.D. 95 (it could be nearer A.D. 115), then we should perhaps date Ephesians *ca.* A.D. 90. (*g*) Ephesians is an original and, indeed, brilliant composition in the Pauline manner, and many would not disagree with the estimate that if it is the work of a Pauline disciple, he must be the supreme interpreter of the apostle before Martin Luther. He is filled with the spirit of adoring praise and love expressed by Paul himself in Gal. 2:20; Rom. 5:5, 8; I Cor. 13, and he has real insight into the meaning of salvation by grace. The idea of recapitulation at 1:10 appears to be an original contribution and one that bore fruit in the theology of Irenaeus. On 1:3-14, which Lohmeyer divided into strophes, the careful commentary of Masson (*see bibliography*) may be consulted: "The structure of the hymn is ruled by parallelism, parallelism of the number of the syllables, and assonance of the initial and final syllables. The verses are grouped into six strophes of two stanzas each, representing as many unities of sense." He believes that vs. 13 was altered to suit the writer's purpose and that originally it ran as follows: "In whom we also were sealed after we had heard the word of truth, the gospel of salvation, by the holy spirit of promise." By metrical rules it is necessary to take the words "in love" with "he destined us" of vs. 5, as the RSV does; but the RSV wrongly adds "his" to "purpose" in vs. 9. Such an interpretation of these magnificent verses is most attractive.

Many scholars seem loath to abandon the Pauline authorship because to do so lessens the value of Ephesians perhaps. One must admit that there is some reduction in value; on the other hand, it is surely pure gain that the document should win its authority, not from its supposed authorship or even its place in holy scripture alone (Wordsworth wrote some banal poetry, and scripture contains Esther—some would add, Revelation!), but from its own qualities and in particular its capacity to be a vehicle for the living Spirit of truth, the truth as it is in Jesus. By this test Ephesians maintains an honored place in the affection of the church, and at a time of quickening in ecumenical affairs it stands in no danger of neglect.

3. Contents. Ephesians may be analyzed briefly as follows:

I. The salutation, 1:1-2

II. A. The *Jubilate* or *Benediction*, 1:3-14
 B. Paul's prayer for the recipients, 1:15-23

III. A. The redemption of the Gentiles by divine grace into the one church, the Israel of God, ch. 2
 B. Paul's apostolic commission, 3:1-13
 C. Paul's prayer renewed, ending in a doxology, 3:14-21

IV. Ethical admonitions
 A. Church unity, 4:1-16
 B. Christian goodness, 4:17–5:20

C. Family duties, 5:21–6:9
D. The Christian warfare, 6:10-20
V. The visit of Tychicus, 6:21-22
VI. Closing benedictions, 6:23-24

a. Theology. Before all time God the Creator predestined a salvation that should win men by his love and fashion a universe agreeable to his will (1:5), and now that Christ has inaugurated the age of redemption, we Christians adore God as the all-glorious Father, gracious and loving, the Father of Jesus the Messiah. God is eternal, holy, provident, and above all a redeemer. It was in the death of Christ that God won his victory of love, and through Christ he will fulfill his purpose (1:7; 5:2; cf. Mark 10:45). Eventually God will integrate his people, his angelic subjects, and everything that exists; in this way the judgment of his wrath will be set aside (2:3; 5:6). The Father wills that men and women should belong to his family, and the ultimate goal of a saint is to be filled "with all the fulness of God" (3:19)—a vague phrase that reminds one of Ignatius' ambition to "attain unto God" (Ign. *Trall.* 12:2); presumably it means the enjoyment of the fullest possible fellowship with God in the life eternal (cf. 4:18). The idea of God militant against the powers of darkness may be derived from Jesus' teaching and also Isaiah and the Wisdom of Solomon (6:10 ff; cf. too the apocalyptic Qumran document known as "The War Between the Children of Light and the Children of Darkness"). The language of Ephesians is trinitarian, but the Father remains the supreme God (1:17; 4:30; 5:20).

The Christology is basically Pauline. Observe that "Son of God" appears only once (4:13); the "BELOVED" is used as a messianic title (1:6; cf. Matt. 12: 8; Isa. 42:1, of Israel); and Christ is the Savior of the body, his church, rather than of the world of mankind (5:23; cf. I John 4:14). Ephesians has no missionary interest, for it is concerned with unity and maturity. In the light of 1:4; 2:3; 4:17 ff; 5:6, 11-12, which display no gracious solicitude for the disobedient, we must discount somewhat 1:13; 3:9; 6:19-20. 6:19-20 is a borrowed plume, to lend verisimilitude to the Pauline name. Christ is not only the church's head, as the chief cornerstone of the new temple of God (2:20; cf. Isa. 28:16); he is also head over the whole creation (1:22). As exalted to the right hand of God (1:20) he is the source of ministerial gifts (4: 11) and of light to the dead (5:14: death may mean here death "through the trespasses and sins" [2:1]; 5:14 may be a quotation from a baptismal hymn; and cf. 1:18 for "enlightenment," a word applied to baptism by Justin Martyr). Pre-existence may be seen in 1:4; but note too the human Jesus in the language of 1:15 and 4:21. The stress on Christ's authority over the created universe is notable.

In view of the dualism of the Qumran scrolls (e.g., 1 QS 3:13 ff), it is interesting to see the references to the devil, "prince of the power of the air," probably the same Belial or Beelzebul known to us from Jewish, Iranian, and Christian literature of this period (2:2; 4:27; 6:11). Some scholars would demythologize the concept of evil spirits, perhaps in psychological terms of wills that are self-centered, or in terms of spirit in inevitable conflict with matter (the flesh); others insist that the demonic expresses a reality in the universe, and that it is essential to any understanding of the problem of evil.

The captain of the divine forces is either Christ or the Holy Spirit (4:30; 6:17-18). The Spirit is given at baptism (1:13; the seal may be the sign of the cross marked with water; no reference to later "confirmation" is to be found in Ephesians). Hence are derived wisdom, revelation, and inward spiritual resource (1:17; 3:5, 16). The Spirit is also the earnest of the heavenly inheritance for which Christians hope (1:14, 18; 4:4; an eschatological element). Believers are to be servants of the Spirit, by whom they have access to the Father (2:18); are constituted one body (4:4); and are becoming God's dwelling place or temple (2:21-22, a process going on; cf. 1QS 8:5-6). The word (*rhema,* not *logos*) of God is the sword of the Spirit (6:17; cf. Heb. 4:12-13); i.e., the weapon employed by the Spirit (in scripture or in preaching?) is the gospel or a particular word from God (to a prophet or to the Savior). As man lives by every word that proceeds from the mouth of God, so is the Christian to fight by that word, and thus wage war in the power of God's Spirit. Similarly, he is to pray "in the Spirit" constantly, asking that he may receive, and interceding for all the saints (6:18; the teaching of Jesus on prayer may underlie this verse). Ephesians adds little to Paul's teaching on the Spirit; the author probably thought of the Holy Spirit as in some sense personal (just as the evil spirits are personal wills); but he has no clearly articulated doctrine of the Trinity. This is characteristic of Christian theology up to Irenaeus and Tertullian.

The church is the body of Christ; the bride of Christ (5:22 ff); and the temple of the Spirit (2:19-22). It is not legitimate to take the bride passage to mean that the church is a second Eve because Christ is the second Adam (a favorite Catholic deduction). Christ and the church together constitute the Adam (4:22-24, RSV "your old nature" should be "the old man"; 2:15, to "create in himself one new man"). For the church is the pleroma of Christ, the full measure of his being as the last Adam (1:23; 2:16, where the body may be the body that was crucified; 4:15-16, growing up into Christ; 5:30, we are members of his body, bone of his bone and flesh of his flesh!). There may be here a side glance at the words of Jesus at the Last Supper, if indeed Jesus then said (in Aramaic), "This is my flesh" (J. Jeremias, *The Eucharistic Words of Jesus;* cf. John 6:51 ff). Christ therefore cherishes his own flesh when he cares for the church; the body idea in this passage is just as important as the bride idea. One day the church will inherit the kingdom (5:5). Ephesians stands in the genuine Pauline tradition, in contrast with I Clement and other writings of subsequent times. It has been said that in Ephesians, Christ the head is in heaven, his body the church is on earth; hence the body is a mere rump. This is to press too far the dynamic picture language of the NT.

The church is catholic (to use the second-century word), because it is one, universal, holy, loyal to the one faith, and apostolic. The classic passage is 4:1-16; cf. 2:15, 21-22; 3:6; 5:6, 17. Faith in the sense of "doctrine" is Pauline (e.g., II Thess. 2:10, 13; Gal. 1:23; II Cor. 11:4; Rom. 10:9). The church is, however, an incomplete organism; it has to grow (2:21;

3:18-19; 4:12 ff). Love must be its primary characteristic as the redeemed community, the new Israel of God (1:5; 2:4; 4:15-16; 5:2, 25, 29; 6:23-24; *see* LOVE). It is also blessed with ministerial gifts from the risen Christ—apostles, prophets, evangelists, pastors, and teachers (contrast I Cor. 12:28, where some of the gifts are "impersonal" and where the evangelists and pastors do not appear). It is possible that 2:20 means us to understand that the apostles are the Twelve, the foundation stones of the temple (cf. Rev. 21:14; but contrast I Cor. 3:5 ff). Following Percy, translate 4:12: "for the equipment of the saints for rendering service to the building up of the body of Christ." This represents a high doctrine of the ministry and a certain stress on the institutional aspect.

The sacrament of baptism, as we have seen, is prominent in Ephesians; this agrees with the general picture of primitive Christianity and is important in the light of the sectarian baptist movements of contemporary Judaism. We must look to Col. 2:11-13, 20; 3:1-5 as the immediate source for Ephesians. But why is the Lord's Supper omitted? (*a*) Because there was no division over it? We have rejected this idea. (*b*) Because it was not in fact a focus for unity—at least in the author's own mind? (*c*) Because the writer was not interested in it? (*d*) Or, quite simply, because the Lord's Supper is missing from Colossians, his model letter! This last reason is probably the solution to the problem.

b. Ethics. The ethical teaching may be dealt with very briefly. The self-sacrificial offering of the Lord Jesus Christ is the pattern of that love which should exist between the saints. If salvation is by grace (2:5), there are, however, "good works" prepared beforehand for the saved to perform, as men risen from the dead (2:1, 5, 10; the predestination theme of 1:4-5 reappears here in rather strange guise). Christians are to live in a way befitting their high calling (4:1), and so in patience and mutual forgiveness (4:2). We note again the contrast, now in a strictly ethical application, between light and darkness, with ultimate reference to Christ as ruler of the church and the light of sinners (5:8-14). Light exposes and therefore is the instrument of judgment (cf. the same themes in the Gospel of John).

In the familiar list of household duties, the section on slaves has approximately the same length as that in Colossians, without the same personal poignancy; but that on wives is much extended, presumably to allow the writer to include his teaching about the "great mystery." Tit. 3:5 should be compared with Eph. 5:26. Christ acts as the high priest, perhaps, in the offering of his bride in spotless purity; but this thought takes second place to that of the bridegroom. It is worth pondering how a wife may be truly united to a husband and yet be subjected to him; no more than in Colossians is the wife told to love her husband, even as she loves her own body (see also I Cor. 7:4*b*). RSV "respects" in 5:33 should be either "revere" or "fear." The ethic is defective in the light of our Lord's teaching.

The need for prayer is summarily stated; and the concluding advice on Christian fortitude in the warfare from which there is no discharge has always appealed as being in the grand manner (6:10-20).

4. Text. The text of Ephesians is good, and at few places other than 1:1 is there serious divergence. Occasionally there has been harmonization with the parallel text of Colossians. At 1:15 the RSV retains "your love" despite its omission from some important authorities (Chester-Beatty Papyrus 46, Vaticanus, and Alexandrinus). At 2:5 insert "in" and omit "with" before "Christ." The RSV rightly omits "of our Lord Jesus Christ" after "the Father" in 3:14. Some authorities in 4:6 leave out "and Father of us all." After "descended" in 4:9 perhaps insert "first" (but this text need not refer to the descent into hell; earth itself may be the lower parts mentioned). "The fruit of light" is a difficult reading in 5:9, but for this reason it is preferable to "the fruit of the Spirit," which is read by Papyrus 46.

Bibliography. Introductions by Goodspeed; McNeile (2nd ed., rev. C. S. C. Williams); and Moffatt. A. Richardson, ed., *A Theological Word Book of the Bible* (London, 1950; New York, 1951). G. B. Caird, *The Apostolic Age* (1955).

Commentaries: T. K. Abbott (1897). J. A. Robinson (1903). J. F. Salmond (1906). M. Dibelius (1927). E. F. Scott (1935). C. Masson (1951). F. W. Beare, Introduction and Exegesis of Ephesians, *IB*, X (1953), 597-749—the best recent exposition; it accepts Goodspeed's thesis with reservations.

Special studies: E. J. Goodspeed, *The Meaning of Ephesians* (1933); *The Key to Ephesians* (1956)—for readers of the English text. The ground for Goodspeed's suggestion of Onesimus as the collector of the Pauline letters and the writer of Ephesians is laid in J. Knox, *Philemon Among the Letters of Paul* (1935; rev. ed., 1959). On the weakness of Goodspeed's theory, see G. Johnston, *The Doctrine of the Church in the NT* (1943). For further treatment of Knox's theory of the origin and purpose of Ephesians, see J. Knox, *Marcion and the NT* (1942). E. Percy, *Die Probleme der Kolosser-und Epheserbriefe* (1946)—the best defense of the Pauline authorship. L. Cerfaux, *La Théologie de L'Église suivant Saint Paul* (1948). S. Hanson, *The Unity of the Church in the NT: Colossians and Ephesians* (1950). L. Cerfaux, *Le Christ dans la Théologie de Saint Paul* (1951). C. L. Mitton, *The Epistle to the Ephesians* (1951). E. Best, *One Body in Christ* (1955). R. Bultmann, *Theology of the NT* (1955). F. Mussner, *Christus, Das All und Die Kirche* (1955). F. L. Cross, ed., *Studies in Ephesians* (1956).

G. JOHNSTON

EPHESUS ĕf'ə səs [ἡ Ἔφεσος] (Acts 18:19, 21, 24; 19:1, 17, 26, 35; 20:16, 17; I Cor. 15:32; 16:8; I Tim. 1:3; II Tim. 1:18; 4:12; Rev. 1:11; 2:1); EPHESIANS ĭ fē'zhənz. A large seaport city in the Roman province of Asia; a commercial and religious center, where the apostle Paul worked for an extended period (Acts 19:8, 10 states that he taught in the synagogue for three months and after that in the hall of Tyrannus for two years, while Acts 20:31 gives a round figure of three years for his total time there). The name Ephesus also appears in Eph. 1:1 in A D G and the later MSS of the Koine or Byzantine text family, but is not found in P[46] B ℵ(S); it is printed in the KJV but placed in the margin in the RSV. Ephesus and the Ephesians (οἱ Ἐφέσιοι) are mentioned in Acts 18:27 in D and the margin of the Harklean Syr.; the Ephesians are referred to in Acts 19:28, 34, 35, and Trophimus the Ephesian is spoken of in Acts 21:29.

On the deeply indented W coast of Asia Minor a number of river valleys descend to the sea and provide natural channels of travel and favorable locations of great cities. In the N is the valley of the Caicus River, where PERGAMUM was located. Far-

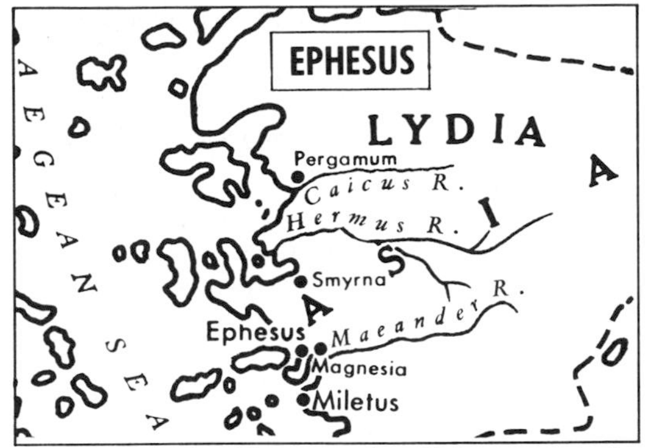

ther S are the Hermus, the Caÿster, and the Maeander. SMYRNA was near the mouth of the Hermus, MILETUS at the mouth of the Maeander. Although the Caÿster was smaller than the rivers on either side, it emptied into a good harbor and also gave excellent access to the valleys of both the Hermus and the Maeander. Therefore, the city located here had the most favorable situation of all and became the first of all the cities of the province of Asia. This was Ephesus.

In ancient times a gulf of the Aegean Sea evidently extended inward to where the city was, since, speaking of Ephesus and its famous sanctuary, Pliny (*Nat. Hist.* II.201) tells how "once the sea used to wash up to the temple of Diana." The natural harbor which was thus provided was gradually filled up, however, with the silt of the Caÿster. According to Strabo (XIV.641), the Pergamenian king Attalus Philadelphus (*ca.* 159-*ca.* 138 B.C.) thought that the harbor would be deepened if its entrance were made narrower; but when a mole was built for this purpose, the actual result was the opposite, and the whole harbor was made more shallow by the increased deposition of silt. In spite of these difficulties and because of its advantageous situation in other respects, Strabo reports that in his time Ephesus was growing daily and was the "largest emporium in Asia this side the Taurus." The silting up of the harbor and river mouth continued, nevertheless, and today the ruins of the ancient city lie in a swampy plain four or five miles inland from the sea.

According to Strabo (XIV.632, 640), the first inhabitants of the place were Carians and Leleges, but they were driven out by Androclus, son of the king of Athens, who led the Ionian colonization in this region and was later regarded as the founder of Ephesus. The immigration of the Ionians probably took place soon after the beginning of the first millennium B.C., but already long before their coming there existed at Ephesus the cult of a goddess whom the Greeks identified with Artemis (Pausanias VII.ii.6).

The first temple of Artemis was built, according to Strabo (XIV.640), by the architect Chersiphron. When Croesus came to the throne of Lydia (*ca.* 560 B.C.) and began his conquest of virtually all the nations W of the Halys River, the first Greeks he attacked were the Ephesians. As Herodotus (I.26) tells us, in the extremity of the siege they dedicated their city to Artemis and signified this by attaching a rope to the city wall from the temple, which stood seven stadia away from the ancient city. Afterward Croesus himself contributed to the temple not only oxen of gold but also the greater part of its pillars (Herodotus I.92).

In 546 B.C., Cyrus defeated Croesus, and after that, Harpagus, general of the Persian king, systematically overcame the Ionian cities (Herodotus I.162), doubtless including Ephesus. In 356 B.C., Alexander was born, and on the very day of his birth, according to the tradition reported by Plutarch (*Alexander* III.3), the temple of Artemis at Ephesus was burned. The fire was set by a certain Herostratus (Strabo XIV.640), and provided spectacular evidence of the behavior of flame and wind which Aristotle discussed soon afterward in his *Meteorologica* (III.1[371*a,* 32-34]).

In 334 B.C., Alexander the Great conquered the Persians at the Granicus River and Ephesus came under the Macedonian power. The citizens of the city had now begun to rebuild their famous temple with Dinocrates as architect, the man who later built Alexandria and proposed to carve Mount Athos into a statue of Alexander. At this juncture Alexander himself offered to pay all the expenses, provided that he might have the credit in an inscription, but the Ephesians declined the assistance, one of them putting it flatteringly that it was inappropriate for a god—namely, Alexander—to dedicate offerings to gods (Strabo XIV.641).

Of the successors of Alexander it was his general Lysimachus who obtained the greater part of Asia Minor and with it the city of Ephesus. Pausanias (I.ix.7) considered Lysimachus the founder of the "modern city of Ephesus," and tells how he brought additional settlers there from the cities of Lebedos and Colophon, which he had taken. Strabo (XIV.640) relates that Lysimachus "built a wall round the present city," and when the people were reluctant to move to the area thus marked out, he waited for a downpour of rain, blocked the sewers, and flooded the old city, whereupon the inhabitants were glad to make the change. As this indicates, the city was moved at this time to higher ground, and today the ruined walls and towers of the fortification of Lysimachus are found running along the top of the two chief hills at Ephesus, Panajir Dagh and Bülbül Dagh. At what was then the seashore at the N foot of the latter hill he also established a new harbor. To the city which he thus improved Lysimachus gave the name Ἀρσινόη in honor of his wife, Arsinoë, daughter of Ptolemy I, but the designation endured little longer than the lifetime of the king.

Lysimachus was defeated and slain by Seleucus I in 281 B.C., and the latter in turn entrusted to his son Antiochus I what had been the entire Asian empire of Lysimachus; thus Ephesus came under the sway of the Seleucids (Pausanias I.xvi.2). In 190 B.C. the Seleucid king Antiochus III the Great was defeated by the Romans at Magnesia near Sipylus, and the cities of Asia fell under the dominion of Rome (Livy XXXVII.xxxvii-xlv). In the Battle of Magnesia the Romans were assisted by King Eumenes II (197-159 B.C.) of Pergamum, and afterward they gave him much of the holdings of Antiochus in Asia Minor, including the city of Ephesus (Polybius XXI.xlv.10). When the last ruler of Pergamum,

Attalus III Philometor, died in 133 B.C., he bequeathed his kingdom to the Romans, and thereby Ephesus came again under their rule (Appian *Mithridatic Wars* 62; *Civil Wars* V.4). In 88 B.C. the Ephesians joined Mithradates VI Eupator of Pontus in acts of violence against the Romans, but this insurrection was soon put down by Sulla, while the victories of Pompey and the death of Mithradates in 64 B.C. marked the complete establishment of Roman control in the whole E Mediterranean. Under the reign of Caesar Augustus the benefits of general peace were enjoyed, and in 29 B.C. the Ephesians dedicated a sacred precinct to Rome and to Caesar (Dio LI.xx.6). As Cassius Dio in the passage just cited explicitly states, Ephesus had now attained the chief place in Asia, and in the next century or two it enjoyed that great glory to which its ruins still bear witness.

The first archaeological excavation at Ephesus was undertaken by J. T. Wood with the support of the British Museum and with the chief purpose of finding the famous ancient temple of Artemis. Beginning the search on May 2, 1863, Wood worked with the utmost persistence until on May 2, 1869, the wall of the temple was finally found. The clue to the discovery was a Roman inscription of the time of Trajan. This was uncovered in the theater and told how images of Artemis (cf. Acts 19:24) were carried from the temple to the theater for the birthday anniversary of the goddess, and how the city was entered by the Magnesian Gate and left by the Coressian Gate. Wood was able to locate these gates and then follow the road from the Magnesian Gate until he came upon the site of the temple. He continued his work until 1874, and in 1904-5 David G. Hogarth excavated further for the British Museum, studying in particular the earlier history of the sanctuary. In addition to this the Austrian Archaeological Institute conducted thorough excavations relating to the entire ancient city in 1898-1913, 1926-35, and again since 1954. Fig. EPH 30.

The railroad station at Ephesus is at the village of Ayasoluk, and nearby is the site of the Artemision, as the sanctuary of Artemis may be called. Here in the oldest period there was an enclosed area which contained a stone platform about ten by fourteen feet in size on which the cult image of the goddess may have stood, and a lower platform on which an altar may have rested. Next, the two platforms were combined into one, and after that an actual temple was built on them with an inner chamber (cella) and a hall in front of it, and perhaps a hall of columns around it.

In the middle of the sixth century B.C. the great marble temple was built, whose architect was Chersiphron and to which Croesus contributed the pillars. According to the relatively scanty remains, this must have been a structure *ca.* 180 by 360 feet in size, with the shrine of the cult image directly over the place of the oldest sanctuary. In the rebuilding after the fire of Herostratus and in the time of Alexander, the temple was raised on a large terrace nearly nine feet higher than before; but the finding of a pillar base directly above one of the Croesus temple suggests that the plan was otherwise essentially the same. This was the temple which was accounted one of the seven wonders of the ancient world, but which its adherents feared might come to "count for nothing" (Acts 19:27) through the preaching of the apostle Paul. It diminished in importance with the advance of Christianity, was burned by the Goths in A.D. 262, and thereafter was so despoiled that but little remained for the spade of the archaeologist.

From the Artemision an ancient street led approximately one mile W and somewhat S to the Coressian city gate. Immediately adjacent was the stadium. This was so placed at the NW foot of the Panajir Dagh that its seats on the S side were supported

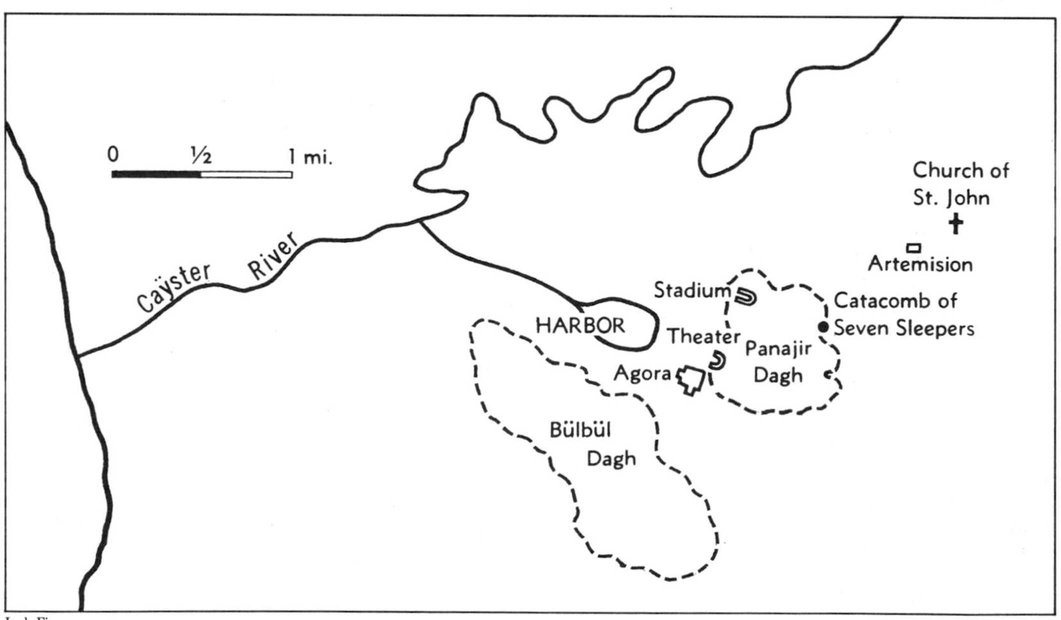

Jack Finegan

30. City plan of Ephesus

upon the rocks of this hill. It evidently served for athletic events and races of all sorts, while a round area was marked off at the E end which probably provided, in lieu of any other amphitheater, for gladiatorial combats and contests with wild animals. If Paul's words about fighting with beasts at Ephesus (I Cor. 15:32) are to be taken literally, this might have been the place of the struggle. As a matter of fact, the stadium was a focus of special interest in Ephesus about the time Paul was there, for an inscription shows that it was rebuilt under Nero (A.D. 54-68).

Less than half a mile S of the stadium was the great theater of Ephesus.* It was set into a hollow in the W declivity of the Panajir Dagh, and faced directly toward the harbor about half a mile away to the W. The general plan was probably the same from Hellenistic times on; rebuilding was carried on from Claudius (41-54) to Trajan (98-117). The marble seats for the audience were curved in somewhat more than a semicircle within the hollow of the hill; arranged in three ranks of twenty-two rows each, they provided for 24,000 spectators. The players appeared at first in the orchestra; in Roman times there was an elevated stage. The Hellenistic stagehouse was also rebuilt in Roman times, and the side which faced the viewers was elaborately decorated in three stories with pillars, niches, and statuary. Only the first two stories of this façade were completed

Courtesy of Theresa Goell

31. Theater and road to the harbor at Ephesus

under Domitian (81-96), and the third probably under Septimus Severus (193-211). It will, of course, be remembered that it was in the theater that the riot took place which was instigated by Demetrius in protest against the results of the preaching of Paul (Acts 19:23-41). Fig. EPH 31.

The main and most magnificent street of Ephesus ran in a straight line from the theater to the harbor.* With a monumental gateway at each end, this thoroughfare was about thirty-five feet wide, and was flanked on either side with colonnades over fifteen feet deep, back of which were buildings and shops. The street was rebuilt in the time of the Emperor Arcadius (395-408) and in his honor was then renamed Arkadiane. Along the N side of the street and in the very heart of the city was a series of buildings, the general layout of which must date from the time of Lysimachus, which were intended for the physical and intellectual development of the people—namely, baths, gymnasiums, and other buildings. Fig. EPH 32.

Courtesy of Ahmet Dönmez

32. Marble street at Ephesus

In the region S of the Arkadiane and SW of the theater was the agora. Here the present ruins date for the most part from a rebuilding in the first part of the third century A.D., in which, however, a great deal of earlier material was used. An open rectangular area, 360 feet on each side, was surrounded by pillared halls, back of which were shops and rooms. In the middle of the open area was a horologium—i.e., a sun and water clock. On the E side was an especially fine hall, dating from the time of Nero, so thoroughly destroyed as to suggest the work of an earthquake. Of the gateways which gave access to the agora, the best preserved is that on the S side, which has an inscription indicating that it was built by the freedmen Mazaeus and Mithridates in 4/3 B.C. in honor of Augustus and members of his family. In addition to architectural inscriptions there were also many inscriptions found on the bases of statues of illustrious persons, which were erected in great profusion in the agora as well as in other public places throughout the city. Other buildings not far from the agora were a library* and a temple (the latter perhaps dedicated to the Egyptian god Serapis),

Courtesy of Theresa Goell

33. The library of Celsus at Ephesus

both probably of the second century A.D. A little farther away on the slope of the Bülbül Dagh was another temple; and the finding of broken pieces of a colossal marble statue of Domitian (81-96) showed that this was the temple otherwise known to have been erected at Ephesus by the province of Asia for the worship of the emperor whom the Christians so long remembered as their archenemy. Fig. EPH 33.

As is well known, Christian tradition from the second century onward connects John the apostle and evangelist with Ephesus. As a matter of fact, the name Ayasoluk, which attaches to the village and also the hill in the vicinity of the Artemision, is derived from *Agios Theologos* ("Αγιος Θεολόγος), the title given to John in the Eastern church. From this hill he is supposed to have viewed the idolatrous worship in the Artemision, and on it at last to have been buried. Over the grave there arose a mausoleum and then a church. The excavation of the site showed that there were subterranean grave chambers here over which, probably early in the fourth century A.D., a quadrangular structure was erected which was later made into a large cross-shaped basilica by the addition of an apse in the E, a long three-aisled building in the W, a three-aisled transept projecting on either side, and finally a five-aisled E part, all roofed with wood. This church was in turn rebuilt on a yet more magnificent scale under the Byzantine emperor Justinian (527-65). It now attained a length of over 425 feet and had six large domes rising above its central portions. Such was the Church of Saint John the Theologian in Ephesus.

Between the stadium and the harbor are the ruins of another large church. It was built on the foundations of a pagan building more than 800 feet long, perhaps a school, and itself seems to have consisted of two churches arranged one behind the other, hence is commonly called a double church. The date of its erection was probably in the fourth century A.D., and an inscription of the time of Justinian found in the narthex shows that it was the famous Church of the Virgin Mary, in which the Council of Ephesus met in 431.

On the NE slope of the Panajir Dagh is yet another place of interest in Christian tradition. This is the Catacomb of the Seven Sleepers. In the persecution of Decius (A.D. 250), the legend runs, seven young men were sealed in a cave, fell asleep, and only awoke under Theodosius II (408-50) to testify again to their Christian faith. Upon their subsequent death they were buried in the cave, and a church was built over it, while the graves of many other saints were put in the same vicinity. At the place above indicated, with which the tradition just related was connected, the removal of great amounts of earth gave access to a catacomb containing hundreds of burial places. In the very midst of the area there was a church with ten burial chambers beneath it, on the walls of which were scratched and painted words of invocation to the seven youths and signatures of pilgrims from many lands dating down into the fifteenth century A.D.

It was perhaps in the fifth century A.D., and thus at about the same time that the seven youths were supposed to have been giving their final testimony, that an inscription was written which was found in the ruins of a gateway near the agora, and which also bears witness to the victory of Christianity at Ephesus. It was on a rectangular stone which had evidently served as the base for an idol of Artemis and on which a Christian had put up instead a cross. Referring to the cross, the inscription says: "Demeas has removed the deceitful image of the demon Artemis and in its place put this sign which drives away the idols, to the praise of God and of the cross, the victorious, imperishable symbol of Christ."

Bibliography. J. T. Wood, *Modern Discoveries on the Site of Ancient Ephesus* (1890). Bürchner, "Ephesos," *Pauly-Wissowa,* V (1903), cols. 2773-2822. D. G. Hogarth, *Excavations at Ephesus, The Archaic Artemisia* (1908); *Forschungen in Ephesos, veröffentlicht vom österreichischen archäologischen Institute* (5 vols.; 1906-44). J. Keil, *Ephesos, Ein Führer durch die Ruinenstätte und ihre Geschichte* (3rd ed., 1955).

J. FINEGAN

EPHLAL ĕf'lăl [אפלל, nicked(?)]. A Jerahmeelite family or person (I Chr. 2:37).

Bibliography. M. Noth, *Die israelitischen Personennamen* (1928), p. 228.

EPHOD ēfŏd [אפד] (Num. 34:23). The father of the Manassite leader Hanniel, who was selected to help superintend the distribution of W Jordanian Canaan among the tribes to occupy that territory.

Bibliography. M. Noth, *Die israelitischen Personennamen* (1928), p. 232.

R. F. JOHNSON

EPHOD (OBJECT) [אפוד]. An OT term the derivation and meaning of which are not clear, though one meaning of the word is reasonably certain.

The ephod is a priestly garment of some kind (I Sam. 22:18). In I Sam. 2:18, Samuel was girded with a linen ephod, as was David when the ark was brought to Jerusalem (II Sam. 6:14). It has been suggested that the words for "ephod of linen" or "white stuff" here mean "covering for nakedness" and that Samuel and David were wearing brief loincloths. The Priestly document prescribes an ephod for the high priest (see Exod. 28:28-29; 35:27; 39). It was a costly shoulder garment of gold, blue, purple, and scarlet, part of the ceremonial dress to which was attached the oracle pouch containing Urim and Thummim. There seems to be little doubt that the ephod was a garment and possibly a sleeveless, close-fitting garment put on priests and possibly on idols.

There are a number of passages where the meaning is uncertain. In Judg. 8:27, Gideon is said to make a golden ephod for Ophrah, and it ensnared Israel. This could be (*a*) a golden image representing Yahweh (cf. I Sam. 21:9); (*b*) the garment of the image of the deity with pockets for the oracles. This is suggested by Isa. 30:22: "Your gold-plated molten images," where the feminine noun of "ephod" describes the sheathing of images; and by II Kings 23:7, which speaks of the tunics woven by the women for the Asherah. But there is no reference to the ephod in this context. (*c*) Yet others have thought of a connection between the ark and the ephod. Thus in I Sam. 14:18 the Hebrew "ark of God" is read in the LXX as the ephod. This has led to the view that ephod and ark are closely related; that it is probable that there were many arks; and that ephod is a synonym for the ark, which itself was a miniature temple. It has thus been thought that the ephod too was some kind of miniature temple.

However, one may explain those passages which do not imply that the ephod was a garment. It is clear that there is a very close connection between ephod and teraphim, even if the relation between these two remains obscure (Judg. 17:5; 18:14, 17-18, 20; Hos. 3:4). Further, it is also clear that the ephod was a means of consulting the oracle—a portable object used by the priest in seeking divine direction. I Sam. 14:3, 18-19; 23:9; I Kings 2:26 show this clearly, for there the ephod is carried and consulted.

To the writer it would appear conclusive that the ark and ephod could not be identified or compared, for the biblical ark was not an instrument of divination. These passages would show that the ephod could be carried about, and that in turn could mean that the ephod was a garment, sometimes of very costly materials, as in the case of Gideon's; sometimes located in a shrine and perhaps too big to be carried about (Judg. 17:5; 18:14, etc.; I Sam. 19:13); sometimes carried about during military operations. In this latter case it was doubtless put on by the priest during manipulation of the oracle. Just as a crucifix or cross may be a large object on the wall of a church, or a small object carried on the body, so ephods may have been of different sizes and weights. Since a garment is assumed for some uses of the word, it is the feasible explanation of all references, except that when placed in the shrine it may have been thought of as a sacral covering.

Bibliography. T. C. Foote, "The Ephod," *JBL,* XXI (1902), 1-47. E. Sellin, "Das israelitische Ephod," *Nöldekefestschrift,* II (1906), 699-717. H. J. Elhorst, "Das Ephod," *JBL,* XXX (1910), 254-76. W. R. Arnold, *Ephod and Ark* (1917). H. Thiersch, *Ependytes und Ephod* (1936). E. Sellin, "Noch einmal der alttestamentliche Efod," *JPOS,* XVII (1937), 236-51; "Zu Efod und Terafim," *ZAW,* LV (1937), 296-98. R. de Vaux, Review of *Ependytes und Ephod* by H. Thiersch, *RB,* XLVII (1938), 108-11. H. G. May, "Ephod and Ariel," *AJSL,* LVI (1939), 44-69. J. Morgenstern, *The Ark, the Ephod and the "Tent of Meeting"* (1945). G. B. Caird, Introduction to I and II Samuel, *IB,* II (1953), 872-75.

See also the bibliographies under ARK OF THE COVENANT; TABERNACLE; TERAPHIM. G. HENTON DAVIES

EPHPHATHA ĕf'ə thə [ἐφφαθά, ἐφφεθά; Aram. אפתח *or, properly,* אתפתח, *Ethpeel of* פתח, to open] (Mark 7:34). An Aramaic expression attributed to Jesus in his healing of a deaf mute. Mark translates the word by διανοίχθητι, "be opened," and follows this with the statement that the man's ears "were opened" and that "[the bond of] his tongue was loosed." As elsewhere in Mark (*cf.* TALITHA CUMI), the retention of the Aramaic may be attributed to the desire of preserving actual expressions of Jesus and of enhancing the feeling of supernatural power in the act of healing. There is no evidence of the use of a formula, as in paganism, regarded as magically effective in and of itself. The same may be said of the unique use of a medium, here saliva. Both may be regarded as a means to reinforcement of the patient's faith. The combination, however, was used in an early baptismal rite as practiced in Milan and Rome.

See also HEALING; MIRACLE.

Bibliography. G. Dalman, *Jesus-Jeshua* (1929), pp. 11-12; L. J. McGinley, *Form-Criticism of the Synoptic Healing Narratives* (1944); V. Taylor, *The Gospel According to St. Mark* (1952), pp. 353-56. A. WIKGREN

EPHRAIM ē'frĭ əm [אפרים, *originally a region, perhaps from* פרה (to be fruitful; Judaic-Aramaic אפר[א], pasture land), *with the place name ending ayim*]; EPHRAIMITE —ə mīt [אפרתי]. **1.** The younger son of Joseph, and the eponymous ancestor of one of the twelve tribes; later a designation for Israel. He was born of Asenath, daughter of the high priest of On (Gen. 41:52; 46:20), and was adopted by Jacob along with Manasseh and treated as the first-born (48:1 ff). Consequently, in 50:23, Ephraim appears in the first position, ahead of Manasseh. His name was originally a geographical name and later became the name of a tribe.

The tribe of Ephraim belongs to that group (Joseph or Rachel) which apparently did not immigrate until a later stage in the process of the Israelites' occupation of the land (*Landnahme*)—a process stretching over decades and perhaps centuries, in the "empty space" which resulted in central Palestine from the evacuation to which Simeon and Levi were forced (Gen. 34; 49:5-7). For the general course of the settlement and the development of this group, *see* MANASSEH). Like Manasseh, and unlike Benjamin, the third partner, Ephraim first developed as a separate tribe in the cultivated area. The character of the landscape settled by Ephraim undoubtedly contributed its share to this end. The S third of the land separated its people sharply from the N by its numerous deeply cut transverse valleys and probably also by its denser forestation. The name of this mountainous region, which to a certain degree actually left its imprint on their character, was then also taken over as their tribal name by the group settling here. The designation "hill country of Ephraim" does not coincide exactly, to be sure, with the territory in which the tribe settled, but occasionally extends beyond it; essentially, however, the hill country of Ephraim was identical with the territory of the tribe of Ephraim. This is shown beyond question by the system of boundary descriptions dating from the pre-statehood period in the book of Joshua, where the S boundary runs approximately along the line Beth-horon–Bethel, the N boundary running along the general line of the Wadi Qanah, bending out to the N, E of the principal watershed, up to near Shechem (Josh. 16:6; 17:7).

In the course of time Ephraim outstripped its larger brother tribe Manasseh in importance (Gen. 48). This development is evident even at an early date. So Joshua was Ephraimite; his grave was pointed out in Timnath-serah (Khirbet Tibneh) in the hill country of Ephraim (Josh. 24:30; Judg. 2:9), where the family had its hereditary possession (Josh. 19:50). He was the victorious leader of the Ephraimite levy. Neither the heroic song nor the saga which forms the basis for Josh. 10 mentions Israel as a whole; the battle between Gibeon and Aijalon shows Ephraim already in the period of its expansion (Judg. 1:35). However, more than local significance belongs to Joshua as arbiter of the territorial claims of the tribes (Josh. 17:14) and especially in his role in Josh. 24 (surely amphictyonic now), where he organizes Israel around a new Yahweh sanctuary in the heart of the land and sets Israel upon her firm historical foundation. "As for me and my house" (vs. 15; cf. I Kings 15:27: the house of Issachar) might mean the whole tribe of Ephraim as champion for Yahweh. In other respects the tradition in Josh. 17:14 ff, which is but slightly touched up, seems to reveal that Ephraim invaded his later dwelling place from the N; the forest, which the Josephites are to clear, is precisely the hill country of Ephraim. Josh. 10 shows then how Ephraim pushed forward along the base of the Benjaminite wedge further toward the SW; Beth-Horon (Beit 'Ur el-Foqa) was already Ephraimite at the time of the establishment of the series of fixed boundary points (16:5). Ephraim, too, did not yet get down into the plain for a long time (Josh. 16:10; Judg. 1:29); not until the beginning of the period of the kings did the battles at Gibbethon (Tell el-Melat?) concern the securing of Gezer as a N Israelite possession. On the other side, Ephraim expanded toward the N; in Josh. 17:8 it is specifically stated that the town of Tappuah, with whose fields the Manassites had contented themselves, finally fell into the hands of the Ephraimites. Pirathon (Fer'ata), the home of the Ephraimite minor judge Abdon (Judg. 12:15), probably was also such an Ephraimite town in theoretically Manassite territory—but not Shechem, as the Chronicler believes (I Chr. 7:28). Ephraimites are mentioned relatively often in the early period. In the levy of the amphictyony they served under Gideon, when they were successful in catching two Midianite princes at the fords of the Jordan (Judg. 7:24; 8:1-2), and under Jephthah, when they again complained about not having been called to participate in the war with the Ammonites (leadership pretensions?), resulting in a warlike altercation with the Gileadites (12:1-6). From the latter tradition it is apparent that Ephraimites also took part in the colonization E of the Jordan (*see* MANASSEH), since they even allowed themselves to be branded as deserters (RSV "fugitives") by their countrymen (vs. 4). The passage of the Danites into their new home naturally led through Ephraimite territory (17:1, 8; 18:2, 13). The Levite whose evil experience on his journey set the judgment of the amphictyony in motion against Benjamin (19:1, 16, 18) came, like his host, from Ephraim; but both may be merely literary figures.

It appears that at times Ephraim played a special role in the twelve-tribe confederacy. Not only were the Levite and his host in the typically amphictyonic tradition just mentioned probably not domiciled there by chance, but also the minor judge Tola, who held an amphictyonic office, lived at Shamir in the hill country of Ephraim (Judg. 10:1-2), although he was appointed by the tribe of Issachar. In the Song of Deborah, too, where Zebulun and Naphtali clearly carried the main burden of the battle (Judg. 5:18), the place of honor at the head of the list of the members of the amphictyony is, nevertheless, granted to Ephraim (vs. 14). Similarly, Ephraim ranks ahead of Manasseh (Deut. 33:17) in the Joseph section of the Blessing of Moses. Should not all this be connected with the shifting of the center of the amphictyony from Shechem to Shiloh, to Ephraimite soil? Does it not thereby in turn show how Ephraim advanced into the forefront at the expense of Manasseh? Thus the tomb of Eleazar, the son of Aaron, could also be located in the hill country of Ephraim (Josh. 24:33). Shiloh is the scene of the story of Samuel's youth; and Samuel, the great initiator of the Israelite kingdom, was an Ephraimite (I Sam. 1:1). In the royal period Ephraim was among the few tribes which recognized Ish-baal (Ish-bosheth) at once as Saul's successor (II Sam. 2:9). Among David's "Thirty" there were two Ephraimites (II Sam. 23:30; cf. Josh. 24:30; Judg. 12:15). Under Solomon the central district around which the remaining eleven districts are arranged in a circle and which also includes the territory of Manasseh is, significantly, designated the hill country of Ephraim (I Kings 4:8). From Ephraim came Jeroboam, who represented the rights of the common freemen against the absolutist Solomon and who finally, by taking over the kingdom, completed the separation of the N tribes from the Davidic dynasty (11:26).

In the later literature the older importance of Ephraim can still be recognized in the fact that Ephraim is almost always given precedence over Manasseh. (To see how this appears in the lists and also in the Psalms and the narrative literature, *see* MANASSEH.) The corresponding passages for Ephraim are: lists in P, Num. 1:10, 32-33; 2:18-24; 7:48; 10:22; 13:8 (or 26:28, 35-37; 34:24); the Levite cities, Josh. 21:5-20=I Chr. 6:46-51; the lists of Chronicles, I Chr. 12:31; 27:20 (or 7:20-28). Ephraim ranks after Manasseh in the OT only in Num. 26:28, 35; 34:24; Josh. 14:4; 16:4; I Chr. 7:20; II Chr. 34:9; Ezek. 48:5 (where it is required by the form of the context). What the Chronicler has to say about Ephraim otherwise is to be found in the same passages as for MANASSEH; only I Chr. 12:20 is an exception. But the Chronicler gives equally strange special Ephraimite material: in I Chr. 27:10, 14, two of the commanders of the monthly divisions were Ephraimites (at least one of these is identical with one of David's thirty heroes; cf. II Sam. 23:30, but also vs. 26); in II Chr. 15:8; 17:2, Asa is said to have conquered Ephraimite cities; in 19:4, Jehoshaphat converts the people in the hill country of Ephraim; in 25:7, 9-15, Amaziah eliminates the Ephraimite volunteers from his holy army; in 28:7, 12, strange details from the Syro-Ephraimite War are related.

For the territory of Ephraim, *see* TRIBES, TERRITORIES OF, § 3*a*.

The basis for the use of "Ephraim" to designate Israel was provided by the unfortunate outcome of the Syro-Ephraimite War (734-732), in which the N kingdom of Israel saw itself robbed of its peripheral territories, which were turned into the Assyrian provinces of Dor, Megiddo, and Gilead; and Israel was reduced to its central territory, the old settlement area of the tribes of Manasseh and Ephraim. Since Ephraim had long since overshadowed Manasseh in its importance (*see above*), the designation of the rump state as Ephraim suggested itself automatically and endured, too, when this remnant was made into the Assyrian province of Samaria ten years later.

The designation is found first of all in the prophets who also experienced the catastrophe, most frequently in Hosea. The situation is clear when he uses "Ephraim" as an alternate expression for "Israel" (Hos. 4:17 [cf. vs. 16]; 5:3, 5; 6:10; 8:9 [cf. vs. 8], 11 [cf. vs. 14]; 9:8 [cf. vs. 7], 11, 13, 16 [cf. vs. 10]; 10:6; 11:3 [cf. vs. 1], 8-9; 12:1-2) and when he makes Ephraim parallel Samaria (7:1), Jacob (10:11), or the S kingdom of Judah (5:12-14; 6:4), or has Ephraim appear among the peoples, especially in connection with Assyria and Egypt (7:8, 11; 9:3). Not otherwise are Hos. 12:8, 14—H 12:9, 15; 13:1, 12, to be interpreted. Only in the case of 5:1, 11, can the meaning be the old, more restricted one, if one—along with

Alt—derives the oracle from the beginning of the Syro-Ephraimite War. Isaiah is the other contemporary of the catastrophe. He is surely still cognizant of the older usage when he divides "all the people" into "Ephraim and the inhabitants of Samaria" and in the same oracle has Manasseh devour Ephraim "and Ephraim Manasseh" (Isa. 9:9, 21—H 9:8, 20). But as early as 17:3 he mentions Ephraim alone as an ally of Damascus, and sometime later Samaria is for him the capital of Ephraim—i.e., of the remnant state of Israel (28:1, 3). In this period also 7:2 [cf. vs. 5], 8-9, was written. In the secondary portions the broader usage is clear (7:17; 11:13); here "Ephraim" already refers to the Israelite N in general. This meaning is found in common usage also in Jeremiah (7:15; 31:9, 18, 20) and Ezekiel (37:16, 19); in Ps. 78:9, 67; Zech. 9:10, 13; 10:7; perhaps also in Obad. 19 (if "Samaria" is an addition). Even the Deuteronomic historian, who otherwise knew well how to differentiate, makes a concession once to the linguistic usage of his time in that he combines the N part of the land W of the Jordan as the "house of Ephraim" in addition to Judah and Benjamin (Judg. 10:9).

See the bibliography under ASHER. K. ELLIGER

2. A town in the vicinity of Bethel (II Sam. 13:23). II Chr. 13:19 is probably concerned with the same geographical area in mentioning "Bethel with its villages and Jeshanah with its villages and Ephron with its villages." "EPHRON" (עפרון) may be the Chronicler's reading for "Ephraim."

In the NT the same city is probably mentioned in John 11:54; it is reported that Jesus went "to the country near the wilderness, to a town called Ephraim." In the time of the Maccabees a city by the name of Aphairema (Αφαιρεμα) was in the territory of Samaria that was added to the territory of Judah (I Macc. 11:34). Josephus (War IV.ix.9) doubtless has reference to the same place in his description of Vespasian's march against Jerusalem, during which he captured "Bethel and Ephraim, two small cities."

Et-Taiyibeh, *ca.* four miles NE of Bethel, and Samieh, in the same area but closer to the Jordan Valley, have been proposed as possible locations.

Bibliography. W. F. Albright, "Ophrah and Ephraim," *AASOR*, IV (1922-23), 125-33. W. L. REED

EPHRAIM, FOREST OF [יער אפרים]. A wooded stretch E of the Jordan into which the forces of David under Joab chased and slaughtered the army of the rebellious Absalom, who was caught by a tree in his flight and later slain by Joab there (II Sam. 18:6-17). The circumstance that a part of Manasseh was named after a tribe to the W of the Jordan can be explained by the supposition that the territory of Ephraim once extended farther to the E. This stretch of land, of a wooded nature, was lost by the tribe after its defeat by Jephthah near Zaphon, E of the Jordan (Judg. 12). Later interpreters, such as the Lucian LXX, who believed that the tribal territories were fixed in the time of Joshua, amended the text to "forest of Mahanaim"; but this is unlikely, as the battle seems to have been fought at some distance from Mahanaim. S. COHEN

EPHRAIM GATE [שער אפרים]; KJV GATE OF EPHRAIM. A gate of the first (oldest) rampart of Jerusalem, four hundred cubits E of the CORNER GATE (II Kings 14:13; II Chr. 25:23). The name was transferred to the corresponding gate in the second wall, restored by Nehemiah (Neh. 12:39). *See* map under NEHEMIAH. *See also* JERUSALEM § 6*b*.

G. A. BARROIS

EPHRAEMI SYRI, CODEX ĕf′rĭ ē′mī sĭ′rī. An early-fifth-century palimpsest Greek uncial codex MS of the Bible (symbol "C"). It is an important witness to the text of the LXX and the NT. *See* VERSIONS, ANCIENT; TEXT, NT. Fig. EPH 34.

34. Codex Ephraemi (fifth century A.D.)

Originally the MS contained the entire Bible. Only parts of Job, Proverbs, Ecclesiastes, Wisdom of Solomon, Ecclesiasticus, and Song of Songs are now extant from the OT. Portions of every NT book except II Thessalonians and II John are extant. It contains 209 leaves (64 in the OT; 145 in the NT) measuring 12¼ by 9½ inches. There is one column of writing, containing 40-46 lines per page. The upper writing contains a twelfth-century Greek translation of some writings of Ephraem Syrus.

The codex probably was brought to Florence from the East by John Lascar in the time of Lorenzo de' Medici. It came into the possession of the infamous Catherine de' Medici, who took it to France when she became the wife of Henry II. The codex became a part of the Royal Library and later a part of the MS collection of the Bibliothèque Nationale in Paris.

Bibliography. F. H. A. Scrivener, *Plain Introduction to the Criticism of the NT* (4th ed., rev. E. Miller; 1894), I, 121-24; C. R. Gregory, *Canon and Text of the NT* (1907), pp. 348-50; W. H. P. Hatch, *Principal Uncial MSS of the NT* (1939), plate XX; F. G. Kenyon, *Our Bible and the Ancient Mss* (5th ed., rev. A. W. Adams; 1958), pp. 121-22, 206-7.

M. M. PARVIS

EPHRAIMITE ē′frĭ ə mīt [אפרתי] (Judg. 12:5; I Sam. 1:1; I Kings 11:26); KJV EPHRATHITE ĕf′rə thīt in I Sam. 1:1; I Kings 11:26. A member of the tribe of Ephraim.

EPHRAIN. KJV form of EPHRON 2.

EPHRATHAH ĕf′rə thə [אפרתה]; KJV EPHRATAH ĕf′rə tä. Alternately: EPHRATH ĕf′rəth (Gen. 35:16, 19; 48:7; אפרת in I Chr. 2:19). **1.** The second wife of Caleb, and the mother of Hur and Ashhur (I Chr. 2:19, 24, 50; 4:4). The marriage preserves a memory of the northward movement of the Calebites, since Ephrathah is another name for Bethlehem.

J. F. ROSS

2. A city in Judah; identified with BETHLEHEM. Since, however, there is a significant denotation of the family of David as Ephrathites (Ruth 1:2; I Sam. 17:12), the two cities were evidently not identical, but Ephrathah was an older settlement which became absorbed into Bethlehem. It was still separate in the time of the patriarchs, for Rachel died on the way there (Gen. 35:19; *see* RACHEL'S TOMB). In one passage the names are combined as Bethlehem Ephrathah (Mic. 5:2—H 5:1).

3. A district in Palestine; apparently the same as the old tribal unit of Ephraim (Ps. 132:6).

S. COHEN

EPHRATHITE ĕf′rə thīt [אפרתי]. **1.** Gentilic of EPHRATHAH 2.

2. KJV form of EPHRAIMITE in I Sam. 1:1; I Kings 11:26. *See* EPHRAIM 1.

EPHRON ē′frŏn [עפרון, עפרן, *from* עפר, gazelle; Ἐφρών]; KJV EPHRAIN ē′frĭ ən in II Chr. 13:19. **1.** Son of Zohar; the Hittite from whom Abraham purchased the field containing the cave of MACHPELAH, to the E of MAMRE, for four hundred shekels' weight of silver (Gen. 23:8-17; 25:9; 49:29-30; 50:13).

L. HICKS

2. Mount Ephron, a district whose cities were on the border of Judah (Josh. 15:9). In Josh. 18:15, where the S boundary of Benjamin is traced, many scholars emend to insert "to Ephron" (so RSV), for the S boundary of Benjamin corresponds to part of the N boundary of Judah. The district cannot be located with certainty, although the ridge of mountains W of Bethlehem has been proposed.

3. A city in the vicinity of Bethel which Abijah took from Jeroboam I (II Chr. 13:19). The CT has עפרון—i.e., Ephron (RSV); the Masoretic pointing indicates עפרין—i.e., Ephrain (KJV). The place is probably to be identified with OPHRAH, a city of Benjamin (Josh. 18:23). Et-Taiyibeh, *ca.* four miles NE of Bethel, is generally accepted as the location of Ephron-Ophrah.

4. A strongly fortified city between Karnaim and Beth-shean (Scythopolis) in the Maccabean period. It tried to prevent the passage of Judas and the Israelites with him, but Judas assaulted the city and took it, slaying all its male inhabitants and taking spoil (I Macc. 5:46-52; II Macc. 12:27-29; see also Jos. Antiq. XII.viii.5).

Bibliography. W. F. Albright, "Ophrah and Ephraim," *AASOR*, IV (1922-23), 125-33.

W. L. REED

EPICUREANS ĕp′ə kyo͞o rē′ənz [Ἐπικούρειοι]. Adherents of a school of philosophy founded by Epicurus, who was born of Athenian parents in a colony on the island of Samos in 341 B.C. and died at Athens in 270. In 322, shortly after he had completed his prescribed year of military service at Athens, he and his family were forced to leave Samos and to take up life as poverty-stricken refugees at Colophon. Here he developed his philosophy, primarily a doctrine of deliverance from fear of gods and men, pain and death; and of a way to happiness or pleasure (ἡδονή; lit., "sweetness"), in spite of all the real and fancied ills of life. In 310 he opened his first school at Mytilene, but shortly thereafter moved to Lampsacus on the Sea of Marmora, where he attracted a devoted band of disciples, some of whom remained with him as long as they lived. In 306 his friends and followers clubbed together to buy him a house and garden at Athens, and there he lived and taught for the rest of his life. The Garden (κῆπος) became the center of a community which offered a haven of friendship and simplicity of life to all sorts and conditions of men and women, slave and free, of high repute and of ill repute; and from it, disciples of Epicurus carried his doctrine—to them a veritable gospel of liberation—to all parts of the Greek world, and beyond; indeed, his system receives its noblest exposition in the stately hexameters of the Roman Lucretius (99-55 B.C.).

The philosophy of Epicurus was primarily a system of ethics. The epistemology is puerile—a doctrine of the validity of sense impressions. Political theory held no interest for him whatever; and his doctrine of atoms is simply the explanation of a world in which the activity of gods is unnecessary. For gods, angels and demons, worship and sacrifices, mystery initiations, oracles and magic, astralism, fears and hopes of a life to come—in short, the whole apparatus of religion—have no place in his system. Religion is the great enemy, the begetter of monstrous deeds and the breeder of needless terrors. Gods indeed exist, living a life of endless bliss in ethereal realms far removed from the world of men; but they have no concern for man, desiring not his service, neither inflicting nor threatening evil, and imparting no blessing. Their undisturbed tranquillity (ἀταραξία) is the full realization of the life to which men should seek to attain; but the gods cannot help him to attain it. Moreover, it must be attained in this life, for the soul is dissolved at death into the atoms which compose it and has no future existence to dread or to desire.

Epicurus held that the one end of life is happiness, and the first prerequisite to its attainment is deliverance from the fear of the gods. This fear is forever removed in the man who has a true perception of the nature of things; this perception is itself supreme blessedness, and the great poem of Lucretius shows what profound delight his doctrine of nature could bring to men. His theory of atoms originated a century earlier, with Democritus, but he developed it along his own lines by combining it with a kind of hylozoism. The atoms are in constant movement and have the power to swerve in their courses, thus giving rise to the manifold forms of living things—plants, animals, and men—and leaving scope for free will. No divine assistance is needed to bring forth such a world, and no purpose or design, unconscious or deliberate, governs it; the future is in no sense fixed, and men are not in any degree the puppets of a will or power beyond their own control. The soul, like the body, is a composite of atoms, of material though refined substance, penetrating the spaces between the grosser atoms of which the body is composed, and dissolving with the dissolution of the body in death. It follows that all doctrines of a life to come, whether they promise bliss or threaten torments, are absurdities. The Epicureans who listened to Paul at Athens would certainly scoff when he spoke of the resurrection of the dead, and would not be among those who said: "We will hear you again about this" (Acts 17:32).

The happiness which Epicurus set as the end of human life was no ignoble self-indulgence. He and his community of the Garden lived chastely and frugally, abstaining from flesh and wine and holding that the physical union of the sexes is productive of far more harm than good. The ideal of life, the true happiness, was found in ataraxia, a tranquillity incapable of being shaken by terror, pain, destitution, the ruin of state and home, or any conceivable disaster. Even the worst of pains can be endured without the loss of happiness. "The wise man," said Epicurus, "will be happy even upon the rack." Unendurable pain quickly brings death, and in death there is nothing to fear; and in moments of intense agony the wise man will draw upon memory to recall blissful experiences of other days, and will live in the sweetness of the past, not in the distress of the moment. The great unfailing spring of happiness is friendship (φιλία), which in Epicureanism comes closer to the Christian virtue of love (ἀγάπη) than anything else in antiquity.

The philosophy of Epicurus has no history. The teachings of the master were treated as unalterable dogma, and were perpetuated through the centuries without any attempt at inquiry or advance.

Bibliography. Primary sources: H. Usener, *Epicurea* (1887), is the fundamental collection. "Epicurus" in Diogenes Laërtius, *Lives of Eminent Philosophers,* vol. II, bk. 10 (text with English trans. by R. D. Hicks; 1925). C. Bailey, *Epicurus, the Extant Remains* (1926). A. Vogliano, *Epicuri et Epicureorum Scripta in Herculanensibus Papyris Servata* (1928). For later Epicureans, see especially: Philodemus *Concerning Piety* in T. Gomperz, ed., *Herculanische Studien,* vol. II (1866). J. Winter, ed., *Diogenes of Oenoanda* (1907). H. Diels, ed., *Concerning the Gods,* Berlin *Sitzungsberichte* (1916-17). Lucretius *De Rerum Natura* (ed. C. Bailey; 3 vols.; 1947).

Articles and monographs: P. Shorey, *Plato, Lucretius, and Epicurus,* Harvard Studies in Classical Philosophy (1901). R. D. Hicks, "Epicureans," in J. Hastings, ed., *Encyclopedia of Religion and Ethics,* V (1912), 324-30. N. W. DeWitt, *Epicurus and His Philosophy* (1954). A. J. Festugière, *Epicurus and His Gods* (trans. C. W. Chilton; 1955). See also the commentaries on Lucretius; the histories of Greek philosophy, especially those of E. Zeller and T. Gomperz. F. W. Beare

EPIGRAPHY ĭ pĭg'rə fĭ. *See* Alphabet; Inscriptions; Writing and Writing Materials.

EPILEPSY (Matt. 4:24; 17:14-18; Mark 9:14-27; Luke 9:37-42). A distressing disorder of the central nervous system, marked by the occurrence of unconsciousness or convulsive fits, or both. It was known in earlier ages as the "falling sickness" from its Greek designation, and its aetiology is still far from clear. The attacks frequently begin in childhood or at puberty, and are associated with abnormal rhythms in the cerebral cortex.

Idiopathic or typical epilepsy is often preceded by an aura, a peculiar sensation which may be auditory, olfactory, gustatory, or visual in nature, and perhaps accompanied by loss of sensation in an extremity. Minor seizures (petit mal) may involve momentary loss of consciousness (*morbus caducens*), without any convulsions. Major attacks (grand mal) invariably produce unconsciousness, muscular flexion, arching of the back (opisthotonos), and cyanosis in the tonic phase, while severe muscular contractions, convulsions, and enuresis characterize the clonic phase. Several different forms of epilepsy have been described.

The epileptic boy whom Christ healed (Matt. 17:14-18; Mark 9:14-27; Luke 9:37-42) was probably a low-grade moron. Mark furnishes an accurate picture of idiopathic epilepsy, while Luke employs technical medical terms occurring in Hippocrates and elsewhere. Matthew uses σεληνιάζομαι ("to be moonstruck") in his description, reflecting the ancient belief in a connection between epilepsy and the lunar phases. Jesus also healed other epileptics (Matt. 4:24). R. K. Harrison

EPIPHANES ĭ pĭf'ə nēz ['Επιφανής, the Manifest (God)]. A title or surname assumed by the Syrian tyrant Antiochus IV, when he came to the throne, and later on by Antiochus VI after his coronation (*see* Antiochus 4, 6). It was the general practice for the Seleucid kings to take to themselves a second name. In scorn for his outrageous deeds, some of the subjects of Antiochus IV later altered the name to the nickname Epimanes, which means "mad"!

N. Turner

EPIPHI ĕp'ĭ fĭ [Επιφι]. The eleventh month of the Egyptian year, from June 25 to July 24, mentioned in III Macc. 6:38. According to this Hellenistic Jewish legend, Egyptian Jews were registered during a forty-day period from the twenty-fifth of Pachon to the fourth of Epiphi at Schedia outside Alexandria, preparatory to their execution by order of Ptolemy IV (221-203 B.C.); but they were miraculously delivered from their fate. *See* Time.

E. W. Saunders

EPISTLE ĭ pĭs'əl. *See* Letter.

EPISTLE OF THE APOSTLES. *See* Apostles, Epistle of the.

EPISTLES, APOCRYPHAL ə pŏk'rə fəl. A form of composition suggested by the letters in the NT, both those of Paul and those incorporated in the canonical Acts. They are comparatively few in number and for the most part trivial in content, although several attained wide circulation. The most significant is the Epistle of the Apostles (which is actually only superficially an epistle), although the correspondence between Abgarus and Jesus and several letters ascribed to Paul hovered for many years on the fringes of the canon in some circles (*see* Apostles, Epistle of the). There are also several letters ascribed to Pilate and purporting to record his reports regarding the trial of Jesus. For a list of the epistles treated separately, *see* Apocrypha, NT. M. S. Enslin

ER ûr [ער, watcher *or* watchful; *cf.* Heb. *personal names* ערי, יעיר (יעור); Ἤρ]. **1.** The first-born son of Judah and the Canaanite daughter of Shua. Although he was married to Tamar, he died childless, Yahweh having slain him as punishment for wickedness (Gen. 38:3-7; 46:12; Num. 26:19; I Chr. 2:3).

2. Grandson of Judah, and the father of Lecah (I Chr. 4:21).

3. The father of Elmadam in the Lukan genealogy of Jesus (Luke 3:28). L. Hicks

ERAN ĭr'ăn [ערן; LXX, Samar., Syr., עדן, delight]; **ERANITES** ĭr'ə nīts. Son of Shuthelah, and grandson of Ephraim; ancestor of the Eranites (Num. 26:36). In the Ephraimite genealogy of I Chr. 7:20, Eleadah occupies the position held by Eran in Num. 26:36, giving support to the LXX, Samar., and Syr. reading in the latter verse. R. F. Johnson

ERASTUS ĭ răs'təs [Ἔραστος, beloved]. **1.** City treasurer (οἰκονόμος, Latin *arcarius* [*rei publicae*]) of Corinth, who sends greetings to his fellow Christians in Rom. 16:23. Such officials were usually slaves or of servile origin, though often wealthy. A Latin inscription dating A.D. 50-100, found at Corinth by the American School of Classical Studies (*see bibliography*), names an Erastus who probably was an aedile and who paved a street. It is improbable, though not impossible, that he was the Erastus of Romans.

Bibliography. H. J. Cadbury, *JBL,* 50 (1931), 42-58, contains the inscription which mentions Erastus. W. Miller, *BS,* 88 (1931), 342-46.

2. A companion of Paul (Acts 19:22; II Tim. 4:20). It seems unlikely that he was identical with 1 *above.* F. W. Gingrich

ERECH ĭr'ĕk [ארך; Sumer. *Unug;* Akkad. *Uruk*]; **MEN OF ERECH** [ארכויא] (Ezra 4:9); KJV ARCHEVITES är'kə vīts in Ezra 4:9. One of the largest and most important cities of Sumer, located at modern Warka, *ca.* 160 miles S of Baghdad. It appears in Gen. 10:10 as a city of the kingdom of Nimrod in the land of Shinar. According to Ezra 4:9-10, the men of Erech and others were settled in the cities of Samaria and other parts of the province Beyond the River by Osnappar (probably Ashurbanipal).

The original village, Kullab, was founded by the "Ubaid" people (*see* Sumer) *ca.* 4000 B.C. The city called Erech, of which Kullab became a part, was built by Meskiaggasher, the founder of Erech's First Dynasty, who lived early in the third millennium. Meskiaggasher's successors were the "heroes" Enmerkar, Lugalbanda, and Gilgamesh. Between Lugalbanda and Gilgamesh, tradition placed Dumuzi (biblical Tammuz), the prototype of the god who died and was bitterly mourned. Among the more important later rulers of Erech were Lugalzaggesi, Utuhegal (*see* Sumer), and Sinkashid (*ca.* 1800 B.C.), noted for his building activities and for a prosperous reign during which the cost of living was extraordinarily low. From the time of Hammurabi, Erech became part of Babylonia and shared its fortunes and misfortunes until the fall of the Parthian Empire, when it was abandoned altogether.

Erech's chief deity was An, who in earliest days was the king of the Sumerian pantheon. But Erech's most beloved and celebrated deity was the ambitious and aggressive goddess of love, Inanna. According to the Sumerian mythographers, it was Inanna who brought the "divine laws," the *me*'s, from Eridu to Erech, to make it Sumer's leading city; it was with Inanna's help that Enmerkar subjugated distant Aratta and saved Erech from the W Bedu known as Martu. Inanna, according to the theologians, married King Dumuzi, to ensure the fertility and prosperity of Sumer, and a number of the later Sumerian kings were therefore identified symbolically with Dumuzi.

Excavations in Erech were conducted by German expeditions in 1912-13, 1928-39, and 1954-59. These laid bare the city walls, six miles in circumference; two ziggurats; and several temples from the late fourth and early third millenniums. From the same general period came hundreds of pictographic tablets; many seals and seal impressions; an extraordinary alabaster vase with what may be a "Dumuzi-Inanna" scene; and a remarkably expressive life-size head of a woman. From a much later date came a Seleucid tablet archive inscribed with Babylonian astronomical texts.

Bibliography. A. Falkenstein, *Archaische Texte aus Uruk* (1936). H. W. Eliot, *Excavations in Mesopotamia and Western Iran* (1950), exhibits 3-9. *AFO,* vol. 17 (1954-56), pt. 1, pp. 198-201; pt. 2, pp. 421-24; vol. 18 (1958), pt. 2, pp. 445-53.
S. N. Kramer

ERI ĭr'ī [ערי, watchful, vigilant]; **ERITES** ĭr'īts. Son of Gad; ancestral head of the "family of the Erites" (Gen. 46:16; Num. 26:16). *See* Shuni.

ERUPTION [ספחת, מספחת]; KJV SCAB. Any cutaneous redness, rash, spotting, or sore. It is one of the symptoms of Leprosy. Nonleprous swellings or rashes were diagnosed as such after the patient had been isolated for fourteen days.

See also Itch; Scab; Scall; Scurvy.
R. K. Harrison

ESAIAS. KJV NT form of Isaiah.

ESARHADDON ē'sər hăd'ən [אסר־חדן; Akkad. *Aššur-aḫ-iddin,* Ashur has given a brother (for a lost son)]. King of Assyria and Babylonia (681-669 B.C.); son of Sennacherib, and father of Ashurbanipal.

Esarhaddon had to fight for his throne when his father, Sennacherib, was murdered under circumstances of which we know but little, and through references that are difficult to harmonize. Esarhaddon, who had previously been designated crown prince and whose succession had been assured by oaths taken by his brothers and high officials, was in hiding—so at least, he asserts—when Sennacherib met his fate; but he was able to gain enough support to defeat his brothers in a battle at Hanigalbat and to move into Arbela, Asshur, and Nineveh, and thus to terminate the civil war very quickly. Since Esarhaddon was clearly pro-Babylonian, he did not encounter many difficulties in Babylonia, especially since Elam (apart from one incident) was not inclined to support any rebels at that time. He made a son of Merodach-baladan governor of Bīt-Yakīn, and this governor remained loyal to his lord. Esarhaddon's military planning was mainly directed toward subduing Egypt, which was continually inciting Palestine and Syria to rebellion. Energetic measures against Sidon and Kundi (677), as well as effective control of the Arabs (676), primarily by diplomatic means, preceded the first attack upon Egypt (675). Esarhaddon passed, on his way to Egypt, through the city of HARAN, where he received encouraging omens from the moon-god, Sin. Although his army met an initial defeat in Egypt, it continued to fight in the Delta region, and his general Ša-Nabû-šû eventually defeated Pharaoh Taharqa, forcing him to retreat toward Upper Egypt. Memphis was conquered in a quick advance, and Esarhaddon tried to rule the country by means of native rulers and Assyrian "advisers." The Assyrian domination was soon threatened by rebellion, and Esarhaddon found it necessary to embark in 669 on a new campaign. On the way to Egypt, however, he fell sick and died. On the essential frontier toward the N and the W, where the pressure of migrating Cimmerians and Medes was by no means diminishing, Esarhaddon was luckier in his military and diplomatic moves. In 679 the Cimmerians suffered a defeat, and in 673 sharp attacks had been mounted against the Medes, with incursions penetrating deep into Iran. An alliance with the SCYTHIANS, directed against the Medes, to be cemented by the marriage of a daughter of Esarhaddon to a barbarian ruler, and a group of treaties with the Medes—recently found in CALAH—demonstrate Esarhaddon's awareness of the potential dangers from these enemies. He was likewise rather fortunate in his arrangements for the succession to the throne. His younger son, Ashurbanipal, was made crown prince and assumed an important share of administrative duties to be discharged in the palace of the crown prince (*bīt ridûti*), while his elder brother, Šamaššum-ukīn, was made king of Babylon. In 672 the high officials of the country had to take an oath to assure the succession of Ashurbanipal; and, although a minor rebellion of discontented officials had to be put down in 670, this arrangement proved a success, inasmuch as Ashurbanipal became king without any difficulty.

Courtesy of the Trustees of the British Museum

35. Baked clay prism containing the annals of Esarhaddon

Esarhaddon dedicated much effort to the rebuilding of Babylon and other cities of the S and was much less interested than any other Assyrian king in the embellishment of his capital, Nineveh.

Figs. ESA 35; ASS 98.

Bibliography. R. Borger, *Die Inschriften Asarhaddons, Königs von Assyrien* (1956).

A. L. OPPENHEIM

ESAU ē′sô [עֵשָׂו, *see* § 1 *below;* Ησαυ]. Son of Isaac and Rebekah; elder twin brother of Jacob (Gen. 25:24-26; 27:1, 32, 42; I Chr. 1:34); traditional ancestor of the Edomites (Gen. 36; Mal. 1:2-3). *See* EDOM.

1. Etymology
2. The birth of Esau
3. Esau's birthright
4. The loss of the patriarchal blessing
5. The reconciliation

Bibliography

1. Etymology. Two etymologies are associated with this patriarch. The name of the patriarch's son is connected with שער, "hairy": "All his body [was] like a hairy mantle [כאדרת שער]; so they called his name Esau" (Gen. 25:25; cf. 27:11, 21-23). However, the two words are only slightly similar in appearance and sound. The "popular etymology" is obviously better suited to SEIR (שעיר), a name roughly designating Edom. Its association with Esau seems secondary.

The patronymic name is twice connected with the verb אדם, "to be ruddy or reddish-brown." Gen. 25:25 says that "the first [twin] came forth red" (אדמוני, "ruddy"); at vs. 30 he desired some of Jacob's pottage (אדם), "therefore his name was called Edom" (אדום).

2. The birth of Esau (Gen. 25:19-26). When barren Rebekah conceived, two children "struggled together within her," and she gave birth to twin boys. The first, being red and hairy, was named Esau (*see* § 1 *above*); the second, having grabbed his brother's heel, was called JACOB (*see* § 1).

The oracle embedded in this birth narrative (vs. 23) is an ethnic etiology, describing the relation of the Israelites (the sons of Jacob) to the Edomites (the sons of Esau; Deut. 2:4). Although Esau was the first-born (vs. 25), Jacob would be master over him—a "prophecy" reiterated by other Jacob-Esau traditions (*see below;* cf. Jer. 49:8; Obad. 6; Rom. 9:10-13).

3. Esau's birthright (Gen. 25:27-34). In contrast to the seminomadic shepherd Jacob, Esau became "a skilful hunter, a man of the field," of whose game Isaac loved to eat. When he returned famished from an unsuccessful hunt, Esau impetuously bargained away his birthright for bread and some of the pottage Jacob was brewing (cf. Heb. 12:16). *See* JACOB (ISRAEL) §C1*b*.

4. The loss of the patriarchal blessing (Gen. 27). For a third, and climactic, time the older brother was supplanted by the younger. When Esau brought in the savory food to obtain his father's deathbed blessing, he received instead a curse. Esau was not to share in the fertile land of Palestine

> (Behold, away from the fatness of the earth shall your dwelling be,
> and away from the dew of heaven on high),

but was to live by the sword and serve his younger twin. After a time, however, he would break free (vss. 39-40).

Edom's relations with Israel in the tenth and ninth centuries offer a parallel. The Edomites were conquered by David (II Sam. 8:12-14; I Chr. 18:13; cf. Num. 24:18) and remained subject to Judah until the reign of Joram (II Kings 8:20-22; II Chr. 21:8-10). *See* EDOM § 3.

As a result of this deceit Esau hated Jacob; and his plans to kill him were thwarted only by Rebekah's prompt intervention (Gen. 27:41-45).

5. The reconciliation (Gen. 33:1-16). When Jacob returned to Palestine twenty years later, he made careful preparation both to appease Esau and to protect himself against his brother's wrath (32:3-21; 33:1-3; *see* JACOB [ISRAEL] § C3*b*). But Jacob's preparations were unnecessary. Esau met his guilty brother and received him back without malice or recrimination (33:4-16).

In the final characterization the shortsighted selfishness and impetuosity which Esau exhibits as a young man must be balanced by the generosity and forgiveness which distinguish this reconciliation. In the early episodes Jacob gained from him by craft material rights; here Esau graciously grants him the priceless gift of forgiveness.

Bibliography. F. M. T. Böhl, "Wortspiele im AT," *Opera Minora* (1953), pp. 18-19, 25; V. Maag, "Jacob—Esau—Edom," *Theologische Zeitschrift* (1957), pp. 418-29.

L. HICKS

ESCAPE, ROCK OF [סלע המחלקות] (I Sam. 23:28); KJV SELA-HAMMAHLEKOTH sē'lə hə mä'lə-kŏth. A place, perhaps a cliff, in the wilderness of Maon to which David fled from Saul. Since this could be a cliff separated from another cliff by a narrow ravine across which one could easily see but not reach the opposite side without a detour of several miles, the suggestion of a place at the Wadi el-Malaqi, *ca.* eight miles E-NE of Maon, is a tempting possibility. The narrative would seem to indicate, however, that if a detour was necessary, it was nearly completed, since Saul appears to have been rather close on David's heels before the pursuit was ended by the report to Saul of a Philistine raid.

Bibliography. G. E. Wright and F. Filson, *Westminster Historical Atlas to the Bible* (2nd ed., 1956), p. 127.

V. R. GOLD

ESCHATOLOGY OF THE OT [ἔσχατον, the last thing]. The term "eschatology" has been in use only since the nineteenth century; it signifies the doctrine of the last things. One can distinguish an individual and a general eschatology, depending on whether the final fate of the individual is concerned or the future of the chosen people (national eschatology) or of the whole world (universal eschatology). Individual eschatology does not yet come into view very much in the OT; in any case, it is only very slightly marked by belief in Yahweh (*see* LIFE; DEATH; IMMORTALITY; RESURRECTION; SHEOL). Much more significant in the OT are the national and universal eschatological expectations, which are often merged with one another. In order to avoid misconceptions, one must understand clearly that the term "eschatology" is used in very diverse ways in OT research—above all, in a narrower and a broader sense. "Eschatology" in the narrower sense means: the (dogmatically firmly established) doctrine of the (dramatically conceived) end of history and of the course of the universe and the beginning of the time of eternal salvation. Prerequisite for this is the abrupt cleavage between this world and the transcendental world of God, as it became more and more firmly established in the post-exilic period and especially in the apocalyptic period (*see* APOCALYPTICISM). "Eschatology" in the broader sense refers to a future in which the circumstances of history are changed to such an extent that one can speak of a new, entirely different, state of things, without, in so doing, necessarily leaving the framework of history. If one defines "eschatology" in the narrower sense (as, e.g., Hölscher, Mowinckel, Frost; *see bibliography*), the OT contains eschatological concepts only at the very fringes. However, if one uses the term in the broader sense, as is now, with good reason, the custom (cf., e.g., Lindblom, Vriezen), then eschatology is a significant component of the OT faith.

1. Bases of the OT eschatology. Eschatological expectations are found among many peoples and in many religions. The common factor in all of them, despite all diversity, is the association of the ideas with occurrences which can be observed in nature. Following the pattern of all sorts of natural catastrophes, they infer a future destruction of the world (world conflagration, flood). As life on the earth, the world itself also grows old and dies—and rises again renewed. The natural-cyclical thinking (*see* TIME § 2*b*) speculates on the eternal rhythm of the ages of the world in analogy to the natural year. In contrast to all this, the eschatology of the OT and also the belief in Yahweh in general is primarily oriented to the history of God (in dealing) with his people. It is, therefore, not strange that the eschatological view of the OT finds no real parallels in nonbiblical religions, even if it has absorbed and elaborated on all kinds of foreign motifs. This is also true with regard to the Iranian eschatology, in which ethical postulates (retribution, ultimate victory of good over evil) have decidedly covered up its natural basis.

a. Eschatology and the history of salvation. The OT is the record of God (in dealing) with his chosen people. God manifests himself in leading the Israelites out of Egypt, in the granting of the Promised Land, in the victories over their enemies—in short, in the entire history of Israel—as Lord and Director of history and the world. On the basis of this experience of faith, they concluded that Yahweh created the world. Here, too, is the starting point of the eschatological expectation of the future: Yahweh keeps on influencing history and completes it by definitely establishing his dominion and granting his people complete fellowship with himself. The course of history is determined by the word of promise which God, in sovereign freedom, gives and fulfils from time to time. Eschatology is the part of the history of salvation which is still in prospect and which presses for realization. At the same time, it is not a question of a rectilinear further development of existing conditions, with which man could even assist or which he could at least calculate. Yahweh's dominion prevails victoriously and miraculously against opposition. The present state of affairs must make room for a new, different state of affairs in all kinds of catastrophes. The catastrophes, however, are not the primary and essential matter, although they furnish the most vivid colors for the picture of the future. The present state of affairs in the world must perish *because* Yahweh is coming and will create everything new, not vice versa. The coming of Yahweh is the central idea of OT eschatology. Because the same God, who will reveal himself victoriously in the future, has already manifested himself in history from time to time and still does, it is, for the present, not possible to make a complete separation between history and eschatology. Only when God becomes completely transcendental (so that secular history is also no longer regarded as history of salvation), only then, at the end of the OT period, does eschatology acquire its complete qualitative distinction from history. The classical prophets characteristically depict the final act of Yahweh as analogous to his earlier acts of salvation (deliverance out of Egypt: Isa. 10:24-27; 11:15-16; 43:16 ff; 51:10-11; 52:11-12; march through the desert: Isa. 48:21; Hos. 2:14-15—H 2:16-17; conclusion of the covenant on Mount Sinai: Jer. 31:31-34; Ezek. 37:26; victory over the Midianites: Isa. 9:3; 10:26; covenant with David: Isa. 55:3).

According to all that has been said, eschatology is not an accidental appendage, but, from the start, an essential and integrating constituent of the OT faith in God. But it does not have the same importance at all times and in all OT witnesses. In the case of the historical writings, which look back upon the past history of salvation, eschatological hopes can, in most cases, be only indirectly inferred. In peaceful years of abundance the expectation is of less importance than in times of crisis. The thinking of the priests, which is directed toward the legal aspect of the God-given orders, is much less eschatological than that of the prophets, who know themselves to be advance messengers of the Lord, who is coming to his people.

b. Judgment and salvation. Yahweh is the merciful Lord who saves, but also the holy Lord who will punish sin (Exod. 20:5-6; Isa. 6:3, 5). The two characteristic features constitute an indissoluble, paradoxical unit (*see* GOD, OT; LOVE IN THE OT; WRATH OF GOD). Accordingly Yahweh's eschatological acts comprise, with regard to content, both judgment and salvation. These two and a few basic concepts of the eschatological message of the prophets which are associated with them will now be briefly developed and presented in their relationship with one another, but without special attention to their historical appearance or any degree of completeness in the examples. In this connection the expression "judgment" is not used in the narrower sense as forensic action, but in a more general sense as the punishing and destroying intervention of God. For the term "judgment" in the narrower sense, *see* DAY OF JUDGMENT.

The attainment of the dominion of God demands victory over the enemies of Yahweh by those faithful to him, not only in the cosmic (Isa. 27:1) but also in the historical realms (Isa. 10:24-27). Yahweh sits in judgment over all that is ungodly, not in blind wrath, but to destroy sin: over the foreign gods (Zeph. 2:11), over the heathen nations (Jer. 25:15 ff; Ezek. 25–32), but also over the sins of his own people (Hos. 4:1-2; Mic. 6:1 ff) and some of its representatives (Jer. 11:21-23; 20:1-6). Various forces for punishment—from nature and from history—are available to God in doing this: the sword, hunger, and pestilence (Jer. 14:12; Ezek. 6:11-12); fire (Amos 1:4 ff); earthquakes (Amos 2:13); etc. Less specific threats of the peril of war (Amos 5:3), of deportation (5:5; 6:7), of a nation from afar (Isa. 5:26 ff; Jer. 5:15-17), may, in accordance with the course of history, be actualized in the historically hostile powers, the Assyrians (Isaiah) or the Babylonians (Jeremiah). Judgment is carried out according to the law of the talion (Isa. 33:1; Jer. 50:29). The oracle of judgment arises, not out of reflection on the moral conditions of the people, but primarily out of confrontation with the holy God who will appear, whom the people must meet (Amos 4:12). Many threats of judgment, therefore, are not provided at all with an ethical basis by words of reprimand. Nor is the apprehension of political catastrophes the decisive factor. In Amos and Hosea, in the early teaching of Isaiah and Jeremiah, the connection of a threat of judgment with the actual political situation is not at all prominent. That Yahweh himself and not some neutral fate is at the center of the prophecy of judgment, can also be seen by the prominent place occupied by the talk of the "DAY OF THE LORD" or of "that day," all the way from the earliest to the most recent time.

But right here it can be shown that the proclamations of judgment and of salvation belong together, by their very nature. Pure prophecy of calamity or pure prophecy of salvation is an abstraction. The Day of the Lord signifies at the same time the destruction of all ungodly powers and the deliverance of those who are loyal to Yahweh, of the REMNANT. While the people of Israel in the days of Amos regard themselves confidently as the remnant to whom salvation will be allotted on the Day of the Lord, the prophet also includes in his sermon of judgment the chosen people who have become apostate (Amos 3: 2). That Yahweh may, nevertheless, permit a remnant to survive the judgment rests entirely within his free jurisdiction (5:15: "may be"); but it is assured for the prophet for himself and his followers, and also probably for a renewed kingdom of Judah (9:11). The paradoxical union of love and holiness of God is reflected thus in the polaric tension between proclamation of doom and proclamation of salvation in most of the biblical prophets. The preponderance of the one or the other type depends upon the people addressed and the state of affairs at the moment. Before the great judgment in exile the proclamation of doom predominates; there is only slight mention of a salvation that shines through after it (Isa. 1:25-26; 2:1-5; 9:1-6; 11:1-9; Hos. 2:16 ff; Amos 9:11; Mic. 5: 1 ff). But as soon as the judgment has taken place, there is the change back to the prophecy of salvation (Deutero-Isaiah; Ezekiel); the prophecy of disaster is at the edge, but is not entirely lacking (Joel 3:4-5; Mal. 3:5).

The salvation to which Yahweh raised his people, from death in exile to new life, is, as previously, the judgment of God, a voluntary sovereign act. It cannot be traced back ethically as reward for better behavior or conversion of the people (Isa. 43:22 ff). The political situation of the world is also drawn into the promise of salvation only secondarily. In Deutero-Isaiah, King Cyrus of Persia is mentioned only in the polemic limitation against the objections of the heathen or of the exiles weak in faith, not in the primary prophecies of salvation. As to its content the great "change" (Hos. 6:11; Joel 3:1—H 4:1; Amos 9:14; Zeph. 2:7; the expression was applied to the return from exile only subsequently), salvation, which basically again consists of the coming of Yahweh (Isa. 40:9), is expressed in very diverse ways and with the aid of the most varied concepts and traditions. The expectation of a return to the conditions in PARADISE (Isa. 51:3; Hos. 2:20)—abundance of the blessings of the cultivated land (Joel 3:18—4:18; Amos 9:13), long life (Isa. 65:20), PEACE among animals (Isa. 11: 6-8), etc.—probably had its origin in myths of nature. Still more often, however, salvation is depicted as an even more glorious return of the good old days of the people of God under Moses or David (for examples *see* § 1*a above; see* RESTORATION). Yahweh himself is Shepherd and King (Isa. 40:11; 52:7; *see* SHEEP; KING). The messianic king, usually represented as David or a David redivivus, is considered by many, but not by all of the prophets to be a gift, among others, of the time of salvation (*see* MESSIAH, JEWISH). The role which the city of JERUSALEM is to play in the final drama should also be mentioned.

2. Pre-exilic eschatology. As soon as faith observes God's continual activity in history, there arises a sort (probably still very simple) of eschatology: God's intervention in the past comes to be expected—even more glorious—for the future. Eschatology is as old as the belief that God has chosen his people and is guiding them at present. Our sources enable us to recognize the eschatological expectations more fully only beginning with the biblical prophets; however, they are already present in the earlier period too and are tangible in traces.

a. Preprophetic expectations. Among the nomads in the time of the patriarchs the promise of a land of plenty made by the ancestral gods, who operated in the historical sphere, plays an important role (Gen. 15:7, 18). In the present connection, however, only their fulfilment is still recalled. After the annexation of the land and in the days of the early kings hopes for national salvation are found in the prophecies of Balaam (Num. 23–24), in the Blessing of Jacob (Gen. 49), and in the Blessing of Moses (Deut. 33). Their themes are Israel's victory over enemies (Num. 24:8; Deut. 33:17) and the happiness of paradise (Gen. 49: 11-12, 22; Num. 24:6-7; Deut. 33:13 ff). Here we already find, too, a forerunner of the belief in a Messiah (Gen. 49:10; Num. 24:17; *see* MESSIAH, JEWISH). It is a question only of the greatness of Israel, but scarcely of the fate of the nations. However, this is different in the programmatic outline of the story of salvation which the author of the Yahweh document has sketched (probably tenth century B.C.) in Gen. 12: 1-3. After the Fall the world is under God's curse. In the midst of this account of calamity (Gen. 3–11) Yahweh, by the choosing of Abraham, now begins his story of salvation, which has as its ultimate goal the salvation of all mankind, brought about through Israel. Finally, we can gather a few more ideas concerning the hopes for the future handed down among the people from the words of the biblical prophets. Amos, in his prophecy, starts from popularly held eschatological expectations (Amos 5:18). *See* DAY OF THE LORD.

b. Amos. In the eschatology of the first literary prophet the prophecy of doom is preponderant. In a series of visions (7:1-8; 8:1-2; 9:1) Amos became convinced that Yahweh would send misfortune upon Israel. To be sure, he proclaims judgment upon the hostile neighbor nations (1:3–2:3) in the style of the national prophecy of salvation which was rooted in their cult and familiar to his hearers, but the words of judgment attached to it strike the Israelites (who at first approve) all the more severely (2:6-16; vss. 4-5 are probably a later addition by which the sermon of punishment was to be made to apply actually to the kingdom of Judah). The proclamation of doom is summed up in the threat of the "Day of the LORD," which is "darkness, and not light" (5:18-20; 8:9: "that day"). The kingdom of the N, together with its dynasty, is to be destroyed (7:9, 11; 9:8); war (3: 11; 5:3; 6:14) and deportation (5:27; 6:7; 7:11), earthquakes (2:13; 6:11) and mass death (5:16-17; 6:9-10; 8:3), come upon the people. However, deliverance is not impossible for those who seek Yahweh and his will (5:4, 6, 14):

> It may be that the LORD, the God of hosts,
> will be gracious to the remnant of Joseph (5:15).

Positive prophecies of salvation are found only in 9: 11-15: the kingdom of David will arise again in its old greatness (vss. 11-12); and with that a new time of salvation begins after the judgment (vss. 13-15). The expectations in this message, still definitely bearing the imprint of the prophetic experience and the direct charge of proclamation, have not yet been expanded into a system of ultimate events. Israel is very much in the foreground, even when the calamity sent by Yahweh concerns her neighbors. The concepts of a last judgment, the end of the world, or a renewal of the world are still entirely lacking.

c. Hosea. Hosea, too, has the obligation of proclaiming calamity over Israel. As punishment for its sins (4:1 ff), especially for its defection to Baal of Canaan (2:13—H 2:15; 9:10), enemies will come upon Israel (5:8-9; 10:14-15; 13:16—H 14:1). Kingdom and cult will cease (3:4; 9:4; 10:2, 8); the people must go into exile (9:3, 6, 17; 11:5). The prophet is not concerned with a political forecast: Assyria and Egypt, paradoxically, stand side by side as the goal of the Exile. Rather, he is greatly concerned that it is Yahweh who sends the disaster (5:12, 14). Just because the relation between Yahweh and Israel—and not political foresight or a rigid doctrine of retribution—is the central point, promises of salvation can appear with the prophet, even more strongly than with Amos and more organically tied in with the judgment sermon. For Yahweh, in spite of everything, remains true to his love for Israel (3:1; 11:1 ff, 8-9). The goal, which he seeks to attain by pedagogic punishments (2:6-7—H 2:8-9; 3:4-5), is the restoration of their first love (2:14—H 2:16) in a wonderful, new, eternal relationship which includes the return of Israel (2:19 ff—H 2:21 ff; 3:5; 14:1 ff—H 14:2 ff). The glance at the nations of the world is missing in Hosea, likewise the messianic expectation (the words "and David their king" in 3:5 are probably a later, Judaic addition to the prophecy of the N Israelite).

d. Isaiah. We can single out only a few especially characteristic or new aspects of the diverse eschatological prophecy of Isaiah in the various periods of his activity. We find here for the first time, in addition to the prophecy which concerns only Israel or individual foreign nations, an eschatology with universal features. A general last judgment falls upon the pride and idolatry which oppose the claim of supremacy of the majestic God of the universe (2:10-21). The prophecy against the world power Assyria (14:24-27) closes with the announcement that Yahweh will lay his hand upon the whole earth and all the nations (vss. 26-27). The same is true also of the proclamation of salvation: all nations will someday make a pilgrimage to Mount Zion and establish a kingdom of peace under the rule of Yahweh (2:2-4).

Furthermore, Isaiah is the first prophet with whom there appears a well-developed conception of a plan of God (5:19; 14:24, 26-27; 28:29; 30:1). The ultimate goal of this plan, the establishment of the holiness and glory of Yahweh among his people and in the whole world, is already anticipated in the hymn of praise of the seraphim, which Isaiah hears when he is called (6:3). The realization of Yahweh's claim to sovereign authority means, first of all, judgment upon his people and their leaders (3:1 ff, 16 ff; 5:8 ff; etc.), and also upon the insubordinate foreign nations (10:5 ff; 14:24 ff; 17:1 ff). However, in addition to this radical judgment, which the prophet himself has to call forth by his sermons which dull the understanding of the people (6:9 ff), Isaiah proclaims a refining judgment (1:24-28) which permits a restoration of the former righteous state of affairs (vs. 26). Yahweh's plan of judgment against his people is also strange and wonderful to the prophet (28:21, 29; 29:14). It crosses the self-willed plans of Israel (29:15; 30:1), but also those of the other nations (7: 5-7; 8:9-10; 10:5 ff). This plan does not signify a rigid program; Yahweh's freedom to act one way or another continues to be preserved (28:23 ff).

But we cannot stop with this negative side of the establishment of Yahweh's claim of sovereign authority. Even if the term "plan" is not used for God's impending act of salvation, God's plan of salvation is nevertheless outlined in the background of the judgment, a plan which Isaiah, in ranges of ideas not always completely consistent, may first have presented only to a smaller group of followers. As in Amos, the idea of a REMNANT also appears in Isaiah (1:8-9; 7:3). It indicates the existence of a preceding judgment; and at the same time, it limits the scope of that judgment, since it forms a bridge between calamity and salvation. The remnant is personified in the first-born son of the prophet with the symbolic name SHEAR-JASHUB, "A remnant shall repent" (7: 3). The prophet himself, whose sins were forgiven in his experience of being called (6:5-7), together with his children and disciples, constitutes for the coming community the pledge of salvation (8:16-18; 14:32). Out of the tradition of the Songs of Zion (Pss. 46; 48; 76) are drawn the promises in which Mount Zion occupies the central position (Isa. 10:12; 14:32; 31: 4-5). On Mount Zion, Yahweh will lay a precious cornerstone, the foundation for the new structure of the time of salvation, which is founded on faith (28: 16). Beyond Israel, Mount Zion, as center of Yahweh's kingdom of peace, acquires significance for all nations (2:2-4). Alongside the idea of the remnant and the promise of the preservation of Zion there is, finally, also the messianic hope of Isaiah (7:10 ff[?]; *see* IMMANUEL; 9:2-7—H 9:1-6; 11:1-9; *see* MESSIAH, JEWISH). The connection with the actual political situation and with the threat of calamity is especially clear in the case of the Immanuel prophecy. The faithless dynasty in Jerusalem will be redeemed by the Messiah, who will establish a kingdom of peace and justice.

Isaiah probably always expects the arrival of the eschatological events in the near future, without, however, assigning definite dates, which might encroach upon God's freedom. The intimate and tense relation between eschatology and history in the case of Isaiah is revealed also in the fact that several times in the pursuit of his commission to put into effect Yahweh's desire for dominion among his people, he dared to express specific prophecies, which were directly political and, in part, limited as to time. In the war with Syria and Ephraim (734/33) he foretold the failure of the hostile attack, without removing thereby the basic threat to Judah (7:5-7, 16; 8:4). During the uprising of Ashdod (713-711) he symbolized the impending defeat of the ally of Egypt (ch. 20). In the siege of Jerusalem by Sennacherib (701) he proclaimed the collapse of the hostile efforts (37: 33-35). These political prophecies, of which ch. 20

was not literally fulfilled, must not be mistaken for the real eschatological prophecy of the judgment and deliverance of Yahweh, although they can be understood only in connection with it.

*e. **Micah.*** The eschatological prophecy in the parts of the book originating with Micah reminds us, in many respects, of that of his predecessor and contemporary Isaiah. Zion and Jerusalem are, however, also not excepted from the judgment which is to be expected (3:12; cf. Jer. 26:18). Micah expects the true ruler from Bethlehem (Mic. 5:2-6—H 5:1-5). He will deliver Israel from Assyria and establish a kingdom of peace to the ends of the earth.

*f. **Zephaniah.*** For Zephaniah a close association of the national eschatology with a marked universal expectation is characteristic. The judgment of the idolatrous and faithless Judah and Jerusalem (1:4 ff) is introduced by the announcement of a last judgment, which will sweep away everything (1:2-3). The earth is to be consumed by the fire of the wrath of Yahweh (3:8). Correspondingly, judgment is passed in more traditional forms on neighbor nations, specified individually, who in their pride boasted in the face of the people of the Lord of Hosts (2:10). The main theme of the prophecy of judgment in Zephaniah, however, is the proclamation of the great and terrible Day of the LORD (1:7 ff, 14-18; 2:2-3; 3:8), in which destruction is coming upon the whole world and all its inhabitants (1:18; 3:8). Evident here too is the truly prophetic imminent expectation of the catastrophe:

> The great day of the LORD is near,
> near and hastening fast
> (1:14; cf. vs. 7).

But the announcement of judgment is not the final word. As in the case of Amos, there exists in the warning of Zephaniah also the possibility that the remnant which seeks the right, justice, and humility (cf. Mic. 6:8) will be spared on the day of judgment. For this remnant there first come into question the "poor in the land," those who cannot depend upon their own resources. The "perhaps" leaves room for the free action of God. The remnant is also mentioned in the words against the foreign nations and in the promises of salvation. The remnant will triumph over its enemies (2:9). A purified humble and lowly people will seek refuge in the name of the Lord (3:11-13). Unless we are dealing here with later additions to his proclamation, the nations will also have a share in the salutary change (2:11; 3:9-10).

*g. **Jeremiah.*** While Nahum's and Habakkuk's prophecies of national salvation yield but little for our topic, the eschatology of Jeremiah shows a few new features—in addition to many already known. In his case, too, the preaching of judgment does not stem from his knowledge of the threatening political situation, although the political events have influenced the form of the threats of judgment more than in the case of any other prophet. The reason for the divine judgment of wrath is the disloyalty of the chosen people (ch. 2). In several passages it is Yahweh himself who brings destruction upon Judah and Jerusalem (9:9—H 9:10; 10:18; 13:26; 16:16-17; 18:17; 21:4 ff). Moreover, the execution of the judgment is pictured throughout the book in the most varied pictures of desolation and distress caused by enemies. The "enemy from the north" who plays a prominent role here (chs. 4–6) is at first simply a mysterious image, probably taken from tradition (cf. Isa. 5:27 ff). At the time of the approach of the Babylonians under King Nebuchadnezzar, this threat acquires historic clarity. That in this case it is not merely a matter of a purely historical prophecy, but rather of actualization of the old eschatological threat of judgment by taking political events into consideration, is shown by the remarkable juxtaposition of nonhistorical prophecies and others which can be understood only as purely historical (e.g., Jer. 21:7-9 alongside vs. 10). In contradistinction to earlier prophets, the calamity here is no longer only viewed primarily as visionary—for the future—but is actually experienced by Jeremiah in the catastrophe of Jerusalem. Given this close relationship of history and eschatological judgment, we can speak of the development of an actualizing eschatology (of disaster). On the other hand, the change to salvation in Jeremiah is still expected entirely in the prevailing form—for the future; for salvation is meant only for those against whom divine punishment has been carried out. A promise of salvation is first granted to the exiles from the kingdom of the N (3:12-13; 30–31). It is relatively modest, almost without marvelous features; but it brings, nevertheless, new, permanent conditions unknown until then (31:22, 31-34, 35-37). Then Yahweh takes pity on those who were deported with Jehoiakim in 597 (24:5-7; 29:10-14) and finally on the remnant in Judah who survived the catastrophe (23:4-6; 32:15 ff; 33:4 ff). Some of the exiles return (3:14; 24:6; 29:10) and live happily under good government (23:4); Jerusalem is rebuilt (33:4 ff). The messianic hope does not play an important role (23:5-6). The total inner renewal (24:7) should be emphasized, as it is powerfully expressed, above all in the prophecy of the new COVENANT (31:31-34). A universal eschatology is scarcely present in Jeremiah. To be sure, the foreign nations around Judah also fall under the judgment of Yahweh (25:15 ff; 27:3 ff; 46–49; cf. also 1:5; 36:2); but (except in additions to the prophecy of Jeremiah) we hear neither of their final destruction nor of any hope of a salvation intended for them.

3. Exilic and postexilic eschatology. *a. **Ezekiel.*** Ezekiel, who has much in common with Jeremiah, still belongs in the period of transition. Here, too, eschatology is concentrated entirely upon the people of Israel. To be sure, Ezekiel, in the traditional manner, turns against the neighbor nations (ch. 25); but he, too, has no knowledge of a really universal eschatology. Like Jeremiah, Ezekiel is concerned not only with outward, but also with inner, rebirth of the nation (11:19-20; 36:26-27). On the other hand, more emphasis now falls upon individual retribution, without thereby giving up the hope for the completion of the reign of God in favor of a purely individual eschatology. Between the catastrophe of 587 and the deliverance is inserted a judgment of purification (20:33-38). While Ezekiel, up until the fall of Jerusalem, untiringly proclaims the unavoidable, absolute judgment (chs. 4–24; the idea of a remnant, as in the case of Jeremiah, is not used), there appears subsequently the change to a message of hope (chs. 36–37; 40–48). For the sake of the honor of his name,

Yahweh will permit the people to rise again from the death of exile and lead them back to their own country (37:1-14), which will be like a Garden of Eden (36:35). God will turn completely to his people once more (36:28; 37:27-28; 48:35) and let them be ruled by his shepherd David (34:23; 37:24). A new temple (chs. 40–46), from which flows a life-giving stream (47:1-12), rounds out the picture of salvation, which is distinguished from that of Jeremiah by its marvelous heavenly colors, as well as by a certain formal arrangement qualified by penetrating reflection.

b. Deutero-Isaiah. The anonymous prophet in Isa. 40–55 represents a pure eschatology of salvation. The judgment has already taken place (40:1-2; 51:17-20); the time of salvation is immediately ahead (40:3 ff; 51:21-23). God comes with might for the deliverance of his people (40:10), not to reward them for their merit (43:22-25), but solely on the basis of his will to choose them (41:8-10) and of his mercy (54:7-8). Deutero-Isaiah awaits the return of Israel into its own country as a second wonderful exodus (43:14-21; 48:20-21; 51:10-11; 52:11-12; 55:12). Jerusalem and its temple shall be rebuilt (44:28). Yahweh reigns as King of Zion (52:7-8) in a kingdom of security and salvation (51:3; 54:13-14). But the enemies of Israel will be destroyed (47; 51:23). Faithful to the promise of mercy given to David, Yahweh makes an eternal covenant with Israel (55:3). Alongside this eschatology of national salvation we also find evident in Deutero-Isaiah a universal hope of salvation (previously to be probably found only in Isa. 2:2-4). The servant of Yahweh (*see* SERVANT OF THE LORD) has a divine commission to bring justice, light, and deliverance to the nations (42:1-4, 6-7), and thereby to extend the covenant of God to the entire world (vs. 6). His mission for the world is described explicitly in 49:6:

> It is too light a thing that you should be my servant
> to raise up the tribes of Jacob
> and to restore the preserved of Israel;
> I will give you as a light to the nations,
> that my salvation may reach to the end of the earth.

Also outside the songs of the Servant of the Lord the prophet expects the turn of the heathen to the God of Israel (45:23; 51:4-5; 55:4-5). In contradistinction to the eschatology of salvation of the earlier prophets, the coming of the Lord and the exaltation of Israel are not merely foretold for the future, but are described as already being in process of accomplishment. Here, even more distinctly than in Jeremiah's prophecy of doom, we have an actualizing eschatology. In form this eschatological expectation, which no longer merely proclaims in advance, but actually experiences a present reality, is distinguished by the fact that it no longer employs the customary type of promise, but uses that of the oracle of salvation and restoration. In content it shows itself in the fact that, without further ado, it fits the historic person of CYRUS, king of the Persians, into the eschatological events as the instrument of God (beside the servant of God; 41:2-3, 25; 44:28; 45:1, 13; 46:11; 48:14). The extravagant pictures of the prophecy of Deutero-Isaiah, which include all of nature in what takes place (40:4; 44:23; 55:12), do not allow us to infer a doctrine of cosmic catastrophes of the type of the later apocalyptic expectations (50:2-3; 51:6; 54:10). Hitherto existing conditions and future conditions are not separated by the end of the world, but run over directly into each other. The fact that a genuine eschatology is present is shown by Deutero-Isaiah's preference for the concept of salvation as a new creation (41:20; 45:8; 48:7), a *new* in contrast to the *old* (42:9; 43:18-19; 48:6-8). *See* NEW.

c. Haggai and Zechariah. In Haggai and Zechariah, in a period of eschatological high tension, we encounter once more a strongly actualizing eschatology. The time of salvation (Hag. 2:15-19) begins with the beginning of the construction of the temple. The visions by night of Zech. 1–6 depict God's measures for the establishment of his kingdom in Jerusalem. From the shaking of the world and the nations, the Persian governor ZERUBBABEL emerges as the messianic ruler (Hag. 2:20-23; Zech. 6:9-14). The imminent expectation of the end of time receives a point of crystallization in a historical figure. The arrangement of the text in Zech. 6:9-14 shows how the messianic expectation was later severed from its contemporary historical connection and put off into the future.

d. Anonymous postexilic eschatology. In postexilic times the prophetic charisma is gradually obliterated. With the exception of Joel, not one of the numerous authors of the minor prophetic writings or of the additions to the older prophetic writings is known by name (Obadiah is probably exilic; MALACHI was originally not a proper name). As to its content, the prophetic inheritance is handed down extensively, also actualized (cf. Isa. 16:13-14; 24:16-17), explained, and defended against objections. An accurate dating of the individual passages is, in most cases, no longer possible.

The influence of Deutero-Isaiah's prophecy of salvation appears in many passages in Isa. 56–66 (the so-called Trito-Isaiah), especially in 57:14-19; 60–62; 65:15-25; 66:5-24 (cf. also Pss. 96; 98). The creation of a new heaven and a new earth (Isa. 65:17; 66:22) is aimed at first only at the wonderful transformation of the present conditions at the time of salvation (cf. 65:18 ff), not, as yet, at the cosmologically anchored apocalyptic doctrine of the destruction of the old world and the coming of the new aeon (Enoch 91:16-17; Jub. 1:29; cf. Rev. 21:1). In the exultant description of the period of salvation, universalistic features are also not lacking:

> My house shall be called a house of prayer
> for all peoples (Isa. 56:7; cf. 66:23),

although Israel always occupies the central position. Further postexilic passages that speak of a turning of the nations to Yahweh or Jerusalem are found in the additions to the book of Isaiah (11:10; 17:7-8; 18:7; 19:18-25), to Jeremiah (3:17; 12:15-16; 16:19), and to Zechariah (2:11—H 2:15; 8:20-23; 14:16).

Naturally, the descriptions of a universal judgment are more frequent than the prophecies of a universal salvation. A powerful representation of the Day of the Lord is found within a threat against Babylon in Isa. 13:5-16. In Isa. 34–35 a judgment of the nations of cosmic proportion (34:2-4) introduces the judgment upon Edom (34:5-17). This is followed by the deliverance of Zion, depicted in a style completely dependent on Deutero-Isaiah (ch. 35). The reference to an older document of revelation (34:16) is characteristic of the late eschatology and apocalyptic writing, which can be understood as an exegesis of the words of the prophets. In the supplement to the book of Obadiah the "day of the LORD . . . upon all the nations" (vs. 15*a*) likewise introduces the triumph of Israel and the judgment upon Edom (vss. 16-21).

A universal judgment is expected also by Malachi and Joel. In Malachi the Day of the Lord comes burning like an oven upon all the arrogant and evildoers (4:1-3—H 3:19-21). The announcement: "Behold, I send my messenger to prepare the way before me" (3:1), by which the prophet himself was probably meant, is new. A subsequent explanation of it points to the returning prophet ELIJAH as this forerunner (4:5-6—H 3:23-24); this fact had a strong influence in the apocalypses of the NT period. Joel 1–2 interprets a plague of grasshoppers and drought as signs of the nearness of the Day of the Lord (1:15; 2:1-11). To this prophecy of real importance for that particular time are joined discussions of individual features of the approaching end of time, which, in part, already show an apocalyptic interest: outpouring of the Spirit (2:28-29—H 3:1-2), portents of the Day of the Lord in the heavens and on earth (2:30-31—H 3:3-4), announcement, preparation and execution of the judgment against the nations in the Valley of Jehoshaphat (3:1-3, 9-12, 13-17—H 4:1-3, 9-12, 13-17; *see* JEHOSHAPHAT, VALLEY OF), the time of Judah's prosperity (3:18-21—H 4:18-21). The conception of the judgment of the nations before Jerusalem may be derived from passages such as Isa. 14:25; 30:27 ff. In similar fashion the expectation of the "enemy from the north" (Jer. 3–6; 10:22; 50:9, 41-42) and his defeat (Joel 2:20) was described in more detail in the Gog prophecy of Ezek. 38:1–39:22 (*see* GOG AND MAGOG). The occupation of the scribes with earlier prophecies is revealed clearly in Ezek. 38:17; 39:8. It is not a question of an impending eschatological event, but of a happening "after many days . . . in the latter years" (38:8) and "in the latter days" (38:16), after Israel has long since returned to its land and lives there in security (38:8, 11-12, 14). The combination of exegesis of the prophetic tradition and the arrangement of the final events into separate acts of a drama, as well as the pseudonym behind which the author conceals himself, show that the transition to apocalyptic writing is under way.

Signs of the late eschatology based on the older prophetic literature show also in the pictures of the future in Zech. 12–14. The author or authors occupy themselves not only with the familiar ideas of the annihilation of the nations, the purification and exaltation of Israel, etc., but also with noteworthy individual features—e.g., with topographical details of the splitting of the Mount of Olives when Yahweh fights against the nations (14:4-5), or with physical changes of the landscape of Judah (vss. 8, 10). The cold of winter and the darkness of night will cease (vs. 6).

The so-called Isaiah apocalypse in Isa. 24–27 is not a genuine apocalypse, but probably a rather late composition of prophecies and songs with grandiose eschatological imagery. It begins with the threat of devastation of the whole world (24:1 ff). After the punishment of heavenly and earthly enemies Yahweh will reign as King of Zion (24:21-23). The heathen, too, will take part in a feast on Mount Zion; death will be destroyed forever, tears will be wiped away (25:6-9). The exiled will return to Jerusalem (27:12-13). With the ideas of the punishment of heavenly powers (24:21), which occur as yet incidentally, and of resurrection of the dead (26:19), the passage approaches the themes of the late Jewish apocalypticism.

4. Apocalyptic eschatology. While individual characteristic ideas and formal signs of late Jewish apocalyptic literature appear here and there, as we have seen, already in postexilic times, a fully developed apocalypticism is present in the OT only in the book of Daniel (for its content, *cf.* DANIEL; APOCALYPTICISM). Here we must note the essential differences between prophetic and apocalyptic eschatology. In content the new form of eschatology has many things in common with the earlier eschatology. Here, as well as there, it is a matter of the coming of the reign of God, in which the salvation of Israel is completely established. But the path is long from the epigrammatic sayings of an Amos to the pseudonymous, learned revelations of the book of Daniel. Between them lies the transition to a marked transcendentalization of God, which resulted in part from foreign influence. The gulf between the earthly and the heavenly world draws in its wake the development of a doctrine of angels (*see* ANGEL). Instead of the direct intervention of God in the history of this world, one now expects the destruction of this secularized world and the coming of the new aeon. The direct connection between the present and God's impending act of salvation is broken down. The more impatiently and confusedly they long for the end, the more it becomes the object of speculation and calculation by the scribes, expressed in the style of revealed esoteric doctrine (not as yet in Dan. 2; cf., on the other hand, 7:25; 8:14; 9:27; 12:7, 11-12). Old prophecies of the future are reinterpreted and fitted into a system of period theories and number symbolism (cf. Jer. 29:10; 25:11-12; Dan. 9:2). In this strange form, however, the basis of the OT eschatology, faith in the Lord of history and the world, who will soon establish his kingdom for the salvation of those who acknowledge him, is still vigorously expressed.

Bibliography. H. Gressmann, *Der Ursprung der israelitisch-jüdischen Eschatologie* (1905). E. Sellin, "Alter, Wesen und Ursprung der alttestamentlichen Eschatologie," *Der alttestamentliche Prophetismus* (1912), pp. 103-93. W. Cossmann, "Die Entwicklung des Gerichtsgedankens bei den alttestamentlichen Propheten," *Beihefte zur ZAW,* vol. XXIX (1915). S. Mowinckel, "Das Thronbesteigungsfest Jahwes und der Ursprung der Eschatologie," *Psalmenstudien,* vol. II (1922). G. Hölscher, *Die Ursprünge der jüdischen Eschatologie* (1925). N. Micklem, *Prophecy and Eschatology* (1926). O. Procksch, "Eschatologie," *RGG,* II (2nd ed., 1928), 329-39. H. Gressmann, *Der Messias* (1929). R. Volz, "Der eschatologische Glaube im AT," *Festschrift G. Beer* (1935), pp. 72-87. E. Sellin, "Die Lehre des AT vom göttlichen Gericht und vom göttlichen Heil," *Theologie des AT,* II (2nd ed., 1936), 77-142. J. Begrich, "Studien zu Deuterojesaja," *BWANT,* Vierte Folge, Heft 25 (1938). W. E. Müller, *Die Vorstellung vom Rest im AT* (1939). G. Pidoux, *Le Dieu qui vient* (1947). L. Černý, *The Day of Yahweh and Some Relevant Problems* (1948). W. Eichrodt, "Bundesbruch und Gericht," and "Die Vollendung des Bundes," *Theologie des AT,* I (5th ed., 1957), 309-49. W. Zimmerli, "Gericht und

Heil im alttestamentlichen Prophetenwort," *Der Anfang, Zehlendorfer Vorträge* (1949), pp. 21-46. C. Steuernagel, "Die Strukturlinien der Entwicklung der jüdischen Eschatologie," *Festschrift für Alfred Bertholet* (1950), pp. 479-87. J. Fichtner, "Jahves Plan in der Botschaft des Jesaja," *ZAW*, LXIII (1951), 16-33. G. A. F. Knight, "Eschatology in the OT," *Scottish Journal of Theology*, IV (1951), 355 ff. H.-J. Kraus, "Die Königsherrschaft Gottes im AT," *Beiträge zur historischen Theologie*, vol. XIII (1951). S. B. Frost, "Eschatology and Myth," *Vetus Testamentum*, II (1952), 70-80; *OT Apocalyptic* (1952). E. Würthwein, "Der Ursprung der prophetischen Gerichtsrede im Kult," *ZThK*, XLIX (1952), 1-16. W. Zimmerli, "Verheissung und Erfüllung," *Evangelische Theologie*, XII (1952), 34-59. F. Hesse, "Wurzelt die prophetische Gerichtsrede im israelitischen Kult?" *ZAW*, LXV (1953), 45-53. L. Köhler, "Heil durch Gericht," and "Heil durch Erlösung," *Theologie des AT* (3rd ed., 1953), pp. 208-30. J. Lindblom, "Gibt es eine Eschatologie bei den alttestamentlichen Propheten?" *Studia Theologica*, VI (1953), 79-114; "Historia och eskatologi hos de gammaltestamentliga profeterna," *Talenta quinque* (1953), pp. 13-24. T. C. Vriezen, "Prophecy and Eschatology," *Supplements to Vetus Testamentum*, I (1953), 199-229. E. Jenni, "Die Rolle des Kyros bei Deuterojesaja," *Theologische Zeitschrift*, X (1954), 241-56. E. Jacob, "L'achèvement," *Théologie de l'AT* (1955), pp. 254-75. S. Mowinckel, *He That Cometh* (trans. G. W. Anderson; 1955). E. Jenni, "Die politischen Voraussagen der Propheten," *Abhandlungen zur Theologie des Alten und Neuen Testaments*, vol. XXIX (1956). M. Noth, "Das Geschichtsverständnis der alttestamentlichen Apokalyptik," *Gesammelte Studien zum AT* (1957), pp. 248-73. E. Rohland, *Die Bedeutung der Erwählungstraditionen Israels für die Eschatologie der alttestamentlichen Propheten* (1956). T. C. Vriezen, "Das Königreich Gottes in der Zukunftserwartung," *Theologie des AT in Grundzügen* (1957), pp. 302-22. E. JENNI

ESCHATOLOGY OF APOC. AND PSEUDEP.

The extra-canonical books known in modern times as the APOCRYPHA and the PSEUDEPIGRAPHA were written, for the most part, between the beginning of the second century B.C. and the close of the first century A.D.; hence they are also known as the intertestamental literature. A number of these writings, especially those of the Apoc., contain little or no eschatology, but in others the subjects of the end of this world and of life beyond the grave are given a considerable amount of attention. There is, of course, no uniformity of belief among these books; indeed, because of their composite character, differing, even conflicting, eschatological concepts may be present in a single work. In all probability popular beliefs not found in the OT form the basis of these concepts; and Babylonian, Persian, and even Greek influence can be detected. Certain early Christian eschatological beliefs depend immediately upon ideas found in these writings.

1. General character
2. Sheol
3. Resurrection
4. The Judgment
5. Hellenistic Jewish views

Bibliography

1. General character. This intertestamental eschatology is based, first of all, upon a three-tiered conception of the universe, with this earth as the normal home of man; with heaven (or a series of heavens) above the earth, where God himself dwells; and with a lower world, which may be designated as Sheol (Hades), the place of the departed spirits, or as Gehenna (Hell, Tartarus), the place of punishment of the wicked. At times, and somewhat confusingly, the place of punishment is called Sheol.

Along with this went the belief in the composite nature of man as having two mutually dependent parts, body and soul—both necessary and good, since both had been created by God. The soul is separated from the body at death; beliefs concerning what happened to it following this separation varied. Under certain Hellenistic influences in Dispersion Judaism, some Jews accepted the idea that the soul was immortal, but that the body was unnecessary, if not evil. This idea led to a somewhat different type of eschatological thinking.

The greater number of the intertestamental writings express belief in but one age, this present age of human history, with no expectation that it will ever end. This age, however, was not considered to be static. Instead, in keeping with the nationalistic hopes of the Jews, it was seen as moving toward the establishment of God's theocracy on earth, his reign or kingdom, or, if a messiah were involved, toward a messianic kingdom. The advent of the kingdom would be marked by the punishment of the heathen nations; by the return of the exiles; and by peace, prosperity, and blessedness for Israel. Belief in the resurrection of the dead and in a final judgment often belonged to this expectation.

A basically different view, APOCALYPTICISM, also came into favor. It was characterized by a dualistic cosmic eschatology involving belief in two completely separate and distinct ages: the present, evil, temporal age under Satan's control; and the future, righteous, eternal age under God's immediate dominion. This belief, even more than that of the kingdom of God or of the messianic kingdom, usually provided for a resurrection and a last forensic judgment.

2. Sheol. Within these various frameworks of belief there was a considerable amount of speculation concerning the immediate fate of the soul when it was separated from the body at the time of death. The earlier teaching, in keeping with OT doctrines, was that the souls of both the righteous and the wicked went directly to Sheol at death, there to remain forever as disembodied spirits, or, perhaps, as spirits with shadowy bodies. Sheol was conceived of as a dark, dreary, dismal place under the earth, where no real life was possible. Life in Sheol was a mere existence, shadowy and aimless, sometimes compared to a deep, lasting sleep. Normally it was a place neither of punishment nor of reward; all, both the good and the evil, dwelt there (cf. Ecclus. 14:16; 22:11; 28:21; 30:17; 41:4; Bar. 2:17; 3:3; Tob. 3:6; 14:10).

This basic OT concept of Sheol began to change in the postexilic period. Instead of being the permanent home, Sheol came to be considered as an intermediate place for the departed spirits. In some instances it was the intermediate abode of the righteous only, who in time would leave it for the resurrection (Pss. Sol. 14:6-7; II Macc. 7:9; 14:46). The belief in a particular resurrection of the righteous alone presupposed that the wicked would remain in Sheol, which might then be thought of as a place of punishment. An interesting variation is presented in Enoch 22, where it is stated that Sheol is divided into three separate places. One, with a spring of water, is for the righteous, who eventually will be resurrected. The second is for those among the wicked who died without suffering retribution while on earth; they will be resurrected that they may be punished for their sins. The third will be the final dwelling of those among the wicked who have been adequately punished while living. The doctrine of a general resurrection of the good and bad alike, we should note, assumed that Sheol was an intermediate abode for the souls of all the dead.

For the most part, there was no connection between God and Sheol; indeed, it was taught that there was no knowledge of God in Sheol. An exceptional teaching is given in II Macc. 12:43-45, where Judas Maccabeus made prayers and propitiations to God for his followers who had fallen in battle, that they might be released from their sins to prepare them for the resurrection. This has been used as a proof text for the Roman Catholic doctrine of prayers for the dead in Purgatory, even though Sheol and Purgatory are two quite different conceptions.

Not all the dead, however, went to Sheol. According to the Apocalypse of Moses 33:4, when Adam died, his soul was taken up to Paradise, the third of seven heavens. We read in the Testament of Job that Elihu, who was an evil son of darkness, was cast down to the lower world when he died, but that Job, at his death, was taken by angels up to heaven by the throne of glory, where his children had preceded him. Similarly, there was the belief that the souls of the righteous go to heavenly "treasuries" (or heavenly chambers) at death to await the resurrection, whereas the souls of the wicked descend to Sheol (II Bar. 21:23 ff; 30:2; IV Ezra 7:95). According to IV Ezra, these chambers are guarded by angels, and the righteous who are in them enjoy rest and profound quiet as they wait to be resurrected.

A curious deviation is given in a brief poetic section of Jubilees (23:23-31). Times will gradually get better, God's law will be studied and obeyed, righteousness will become established, men will live to be a thousand years old, and the enemies of Israel will be vanquished. The souls of the righteous dead are in some undefined place, possibly heaven, while their bones rest upon the earth. When they see the kingdom of God established on earth, they are thankful and rejoice, and their bones are at rest. Presumably, but not definitely, the souls of the wicked who have died are in Sheol. There seemingly is no provision in this brief source for a resurrection or a final judgment.

A somewhat similar pattern is presented in the brief apocalyptic poem in Asmp. Moses 10. When the forces of evil that rule this age are overcome, and this age is brought to an end, Israel as a nation will rise to the stars where God dwells and will look down upon her enemy (Rome) on earth, or in Gehenna. Seemingly there is no expectation that the dead will be raised. Likewise, in the Apocalypse of Abraham, when this age of ungodliness under Azazel is ended and God's age of righteousness is inaugurated, the righteous who are alive will enjoy the fruits of Paradise, whereas the wicked will descend to the abyss.

3. Resurrection. It was but just that the righteous dead share in the joys of God's reign or of the messianic kingdom, whether it was thought of as coming in this present age or in the age to come. Likewise, it was only just that the wicked dead be punished. For the most part, the resurrection was to be physical, with the soul coming from Sheol or some other intermediate place to be reunited with the body, which had been buried here on the earth.

In some of the sources the resurrection is to be general—i.e., of both the good and the bad. In the Apocalypse of Moses, all descendants of Adam will be resurrected (41:3). We read in Test. Benj. 10:6-8 that all will be raised, first the patriarchs and heroes of Israel, and then the rest of the righteous and the wicked together. According to Enoch 51, there will be a general resurrection of all from Sheol. The physical nature of the resurrected body is evident in Sibylline Oracles IV.179 ff, for God shall fashion again the bodies of men and raise them up as they were in life. II Bar. 50 states that all the dead will be raised, and at first will be exactly as they were in this life so that they may recognize one another. A somewhat different sequence of events is given in IV Ezra. This present evil age will be followed by an interim of four hundred years, which will be for the Messiah and the righteous who are alive at the end of this age. When the messianic interval is ended, the Messiah and his companions will all die. However, when the new age is inaugurated, there will be a general physical resurrection of everyone (7:32, 37).

In several passages in Enoch, however, only the righteous will be raised (5:8; 61:5; 62:15-16; 90:32-36; 91:10). Contradicting the prediction in Test. Benj. 10:6-8 of a general resurrection, Test. Zeb. 10; Test. Judah 25:4 affirm that the godly alone will be raised, and, according to Judah, the martyrs especially, as seems to be the situation in II Macc. 7:9. Pss. Sol. 3:16 promises that those who fear the Lord will be raised to life eternal. A general resurrection was promised in II Bar. 50; but in ch. 30 of this same book, after the close of the messianic kingdom, when the Messiah is to return to heaven, the souls of the righteous who have been in the heavenly "treasuries" will be resurrected; but apparently the souls of the wicked will remain in Sheol, where they will waste away, knowing that their torment has come.

Not a great deal is said concerning the actual nature of the resurrection body. As noted before, according to Sibylline Oracles IV.179, the resurrected body will be just like the body that was buried. The martyrs in II Macc. 7:11; 14:46 expected to have their maimed and broken bodies restored in the resurrection. Enoch 62:15-16 relates that the bodies of the righteous who are resurrected will be clad in eternal garments of glory. The most detailed account, however, is given in II Bar. 50. At first the resurrected bodies of all who are raised in the general resurrection will be precisely as they were during life. However, they will undergo changes. The bodies of the righteous will, first of all, be glorified until they have the splendor of angels, and then they will be equal to the stars and more glorious than the angels. On the other hand, as the wicked see the glorious transformation of the bodies of the righteous, their own bodies will waste away.

4. The Judgment. Along with the belief in the resurrection went the expectation of a final or eschatological judgment, usually in connection with apocalyptic hope, but also as a part of the establishment of the theocracy in this age. As has been previously indicated, this is a forensic judgment different from the conflict in which the nations are vanquished prior to the establishment of the kingdom or before the end of this age. The pattern for this kind of judgment was probably set in Dan. 7:9-10 (cf. 12:1), with the "ancient of days" seated on his throne as the books are opened, prepared to give judgment. This probably inspired the similar scene in Enoch 47:3, showing the "Head of Days" seated on his throne to pronounce judgment from the opened books of the living that were before him. Similar descriptions are given in Enoch 90:2-27; IV Ezra 7:33 (cf. 6:20). In much the same manner, in the nonapocalyptic passage in II Bar. 24 the books will be opened and the Most High will judge. Actually, the final judgment is perfunctory, almost automatic, for people are judged by what they have done, as their deeds are inscribed in the heavenly books. Other references to the final judgment are less colorful. In Test. Benj. 10:6-8 it is merely stated that there will be a judgment, of the Israelites first and then of the Gentiles. Jth. 16:17 simply warns that there will be a day of judgment. A curious feature in some sources is that fallen angels, as well as human beings, will be judged (Jub. 5:10 ff; Enoch 10:6; 16:1; 19:1; 90:20-27).

God is usually the judge, as might be expected. However, contrary to other passages in Enoch, according to 45:3; 69:27-29 the heavenly Messiah, the Elect One or SON OF MAN, instead of God, will sit on a throne and pronounce judgment.

For the most part, the eschatological punishments of the wicked and rewards for the righteous have been indicated. As a rule the ungodly (usually Gentiles, at times apostate Jews) will be consigned to Gehenna or some other place of eternal punishment, usually in the lower world, where they will be continually tortured by fire and at times be eaten by worms. The righteous, on the other hand, will be rewarded in Paradise, in heaven, or on earth. If the last, they may live in a renewed earth, one that is marvelously productive, perhaps (cf. II Bar. 29). Or they may live in the heavenly Jerusalem or in the heavenly Garden of Eden come down to earth. The tree of life is another promise of reward. There will be a surcease of all sin, sickness, toil, oppression, persecution, and even death. Furthermore, the righteous will be in the presence of God, or, in messianic kingdoms, in the presence of the Messiah.

5. Hellenistic Jewish views. Finally, the eschatological views of Hellenistic Jewish sources deserve attention. Philo the Alexandrian philosopher probably represents an extreme view. For him the soul, which was pre-existent in heaven, was good, but the body of matter was evil, was indeed the prison house of the soul. At death each soul would leave its body-prison permanently; the souls of those who had lived good lives would return to heaven to an eternity of blessedness, but the souls of those who had lived evil lives would go to Tartarus to an eternity of punishment. The resurrection of the body was unthinkable; there would be no final judgment as in the sources that have been considered.

The Wisdom of Solomon, while retaining the more traditional view of a theocratic kingdom of indefinite duration in which the Jews who are alive at the time will judge the nations (3:7-8), in general holds to quite a different view, which resembles Philo's. The soul, pre-existent in heaven (8:20), is imprisoned in the body of matter temporarily (9:15). When he dies, each individual is judged personally; the wicked are sentenced to eternal punishment, but the righteous are rewarded with an eternity of blessedness and joy with God and his angels (ch. 5).

IV Maccabees is a martyrological treatise, with Stoic overtones, on the supremacy of reason over the passions, thus encouraging the persecuted to endure torture and death impassively. The wicked are not only punished in this life, but in addition at the time of their death their souls will enter upon an eternity of punishment by fire (9:9; 12:12). As for the righteous, the martyrs, when they are put to death, their souls will ascend to heaven, where Abraham, Isaac, and Jacob will receive them (13:17). Their glorious life throughout eternity will be in direct contrast both to their sufferings on earth and to the everlasting torments inflicted upon their persecutors (10:15).

Bibliography. E. Kautzsch, *Die Apokryphen und Pseudepigraphen des Alten Testaments* (2 vols.; 1900). R. H. Charles, *The Apoc. and Pseudep. of the OT* (2 vols.; 1913); *A Critical History of the Doctrine of a Future Life in Israel, in Judaism, and in Christianity* (1913). H. H. Rowley, *The Relevance of Apocalyptic* (rev. ed., 1946). *See also* the bibliographies under APOCRYPHA; PSEUDEPIGRAPHA.

M. RIST

ESCHATOLOGY OF THE NT. The spiritual climate in which the eschatology of the NT arose was thoroughly Hebraic-Jewish. This was true even of such writings as those of Paul, the Fourth Gospel, II Peter, and Revelation, all of which, there is every reason to believe, were either written on Greek soil or intended in large part for Gentile readers. The Greek culture made no direct contribution in this area save for a few verbal substitutions for Semitic equivalents (e.g., ᾅδης, "Hades," for *Sheol;* χριστός, "Christ," for *Messiah;* διάβολος, "devil," for Satanas; αἰών, "aeon," for *'ôlām,* and the like)—substitutes which persisted even in translation from the Greek. Moreover, such contributions as other pagan cultures, such as Egyptian and Iranian, had to make in the field of eschatology—and they were by no means inconsiderable—had already been absorbed into the stream of Jewish apocalypticism before the beginning of the Christian era. In consequence, it was through this latter medium alone that such elements were mediated to the Christian church.

1. The Jewish ethos. Behind the Jewish culture and forming the matrix out of which it arose was the teaching of the Hebrew prophets. In eschatology, as in every other area of theological teaching, the prophets were pioneers. The differentia by which their eschatological teaching was distinguished was a wholesome sanity coupled with the courageous faith that God would eventually vindicate his righteous rule within history. Beginning with Amos, these prophets foresaw the coming of the "day of the LORD" (5:18), when he would save and judge men on a universal scale (*see* ESCHATOLOGY OF THE OT). In the Jewish milieu contemporary with the rise of the Christian movement and even centuries earlier, various groups drew upon this common prophetic eschatological deposit, each group interpreting it after its own predilections and in line with its own interests.

The scribal movement which arose out of the harrowing experiences of the Exile, taking its lead from such prophets as Ezekiel and Haggai and spurred on by the ardent nationalism of leaders like Ezra and Nehemiah, compressed the eschatology they took over into a particularistic (nationalistic) mold such as has characterized Judaism ever since. Its normative statement is found in the rabbinic dictum: "All Israelites have a share in the world to come" (M. Sanh. 10.1). The pharisaic doctrine of the resurrection also could find some support in two or three passages of doubtful interpretation in the OT, though its materialistic elaboration (repugnant alike to Sadducee and church) was a scribal contribution without foundation in the Prophets.

From its contacts with Iranian thought during the Exile, Judaism also developed its peculiar brand of apocalyptic eschatology. Thence came the doctrines of the two kingdoms (of God and Satan), with their multitudes of denizens (men, good and bad, and angels and demons, respectively), the two aeons of Time and Eternity, the arranging and dating of the events of the "last times" in a determined series with definite dates, and the teaching regarding the Son of man—a heavenly figure coming "on the clouds of heaven" to judge the world. This apocalyptic eschatology was characterized also by a fantastic elaboration of genuine elements to be found in the Prophets, such as the nature of the viands served up at God's banquet table to his people; but the realization of the divine salvation and the divine "wrath" against man's sin was pushed forward into the eternal order beyond history. *See* ESCHATOLOGY OF THE APOCRYPHA AND PSEUDEPIGRAPHA.

The nationalistic party within the contemporary Judaism of the first Christian century—the Zealots with the sicarii or "dagger-men"—turned the particularism of both Pharisees and apocalyptists to good purpose. For them the Messiah who was to come would be a "Son of David" who would lead his forces into victorious battle against the enemies of Jewry and set up the throne and kingdom of his ancestor David. It was their self-appointed task, moreover, to discover this Messiah by recognizable "signs" and to aid him in his every activity by armed force. *See* ZEALOT.

2. Jesus' eschatological teaching. Jesus' eschatological teaching was given largely in Galilee and so usually in the context of the popular Jewish apocalyptic hope. Moreover, after his day it was communicated by preachers and teachers influenced by popular Jewish Christian interpretations of what he had taught, and when the time came for his teachings to be preserved in writing, this again was done by evangelists who had been subjected to the same influences. In consequence, to unravel his teachings from the interpretations put upon them is not an easy task. We cannot always be certain that it is the voice of Jesus to which we are listening and not that of his early interpreters.

a. Diversity of modern interpretations. As a result of what has just been said, very diverse points of view have developed among modern NT scholars relative to what Jesus actually taught on the subject of eschatology; and in all fairness to the student, one cannot elaborate one's own conclusions without placing them in the context of the conclusions of others.

The "old liberal" school held that the eschatological teaching ascribed to Jesus, particularly that found in the Synoptic gospels, was in its entirety that of the Jewish apocalyptic church. Jesus himself, on this view, was the promulgator merely of a simple ethic not unlike that of the rabbinic teaching of his day.

The school of "consistent eschatology"—represented by J. Weiss and Albert Schweitzer—swinging to the opposite extreme, saw in Jesus a full-fledged apocalyptist who conceived himself to be the "Son of man" about to come on the clouds of heaven, with a view to setting up the kingdom of God on earth.

"Form criticism" in the hands of a protagonist like Rudolf Bultmann has done little to support the claims of either of these older schools. For Bultmann, Jesus was nothing more than the "herald" of the kingdom's coming, who called all men to prepare for it by repentance and faith. The kingdom did not come in Jesus' lifetime, nor would it ever come through any human instrumentality (including that of Jesus himself), but only vertically at the hand of God to each person in his "existential" situation.

Nearly opposite to Bultmann's views was the "realized eschatology" of C. H. Dodd. For Dodd consistently held that for Jesus the prophetic eschatological teaching received fulfilment in his incarnate life and ministry; the "day of the Lord" of Amos had arrived; the future had begun to be realized in the present; the kingdom of God had come in Jesus' own person and work.

It is obvious that all these positions and mediating ones which fall between them cannot be right. To an extent they serve, indeed, to cancel one another out. Perhaps the best service they perform is the sharpening of our understanding of the nature of the problems involved in any approach to Jesus' teaching.

b. The phrase "kingdom of God." The sources of the Synoptic gospels appear to agree that Jesus began his ministry in the spirit of the "herald" of Isa. 52:7, announcing that the day had come for God to begin his reign, that his kingdom was about to be realized among men (Mark 1:14-15; Luke 7:22 [Q]; Luke 4:18 ff [L]; Matt. 4:23 [M]). This could only mean that the *eschaton* of the Hebrew prophets was near at hand and that in some as yet undefined way its coming was associated with the person and work of Jesus himself. Jesus, however, went beyond the somewhat indefinite proclamation to be expected from a mere herald: he also announced that the kingdom had actually arrived and that its power was at work among his hearers. Jesus' casting out of the demons, on his declaration, attested this fact (Luke 11:20=Matt. 12:28 [Q]), as did his binding of the "strong man" (Satan; Mark 3:27), a phenomenon which Jewish teaching anticipated as happening in the *eschaton* upon the arrival of God's reign. Further, Jesus distinguished between the prophetic era ending with John the Baptist and that which opened with his own activity (Luke 16:16=Matt. 11:12 [Q]), declaring that in the latter epoch the "good news of the kingdom of God" was being preached and that "every one" was entering it with violence—admittedly an enigmatic saying difficult of exact interpretation, but one at all events allowing of no doubt that to his mind the kingdom was already present. The saying at Luke 17:21 ("The kingdom of God is in the midst of you"; possibly from Q) is also perhaps to be understood as representing that the kingdom was present and functioning in his day.

T. W. Manson may be right in suggesting that the change in Jesus' teaching from a mere "herald's" announcement of the kingdom's nearness to the proclamation of its arrival occurred as a result of Peter's confession at Caesarea Philippi (Mark 8:27-30), the implication being that Jesus saw in a disciple's declaration of his messiahship the realization of God's *de facto* lordship in that disciple's life. At all events, it seems clear that Jesus did claim that the kingdom of God had come in his lifetime and that in consequence one may speak of his conviction that the *eschaton* had at last arrived. It appears equally certain, however, that for Jesus there remained a phase of kingdom experience not fully realized in his time. For he spoke on more than one occasion of a "day" yet to come (Mark 13:32; Luke 10:12=Matt. 10:15 [Q]), a day on which would occur the judgment of all men (Luke 10:13-15=Matt. 11:21-23 [Q]; Luke 17:26-27=Matt. 24:37-39 [Q]; Mark 8:38). Accordingly, he admonished his hearers to prepare for the coming of the kingdom in this consummated sense (Mark 13:33-37; Luke 12:42-46=Matt. 24:45-51 [Q]; Luke 12:35-40 [L/Q]; Matt. 25:1-12 [M]). For Jesus, therefore, the kingdom of God was at once a present reality and a future expectation: God's power was already at work among men; his judgment of their lives and persons was still to come.

c. Jesus' relation to the kingdom's coming. It appears reasonably certain—from Jesus' actions as well as from the nature of his teaching—that he considered himself as having a leading role in bringing into being both the present and future aspects of God's kingdom. The view has been advanced that Jesus, like the Hebrew prophets, thought of the kingdom of God in terms of a direct relationship between God and man, requiring no mediation on the part of a Messiah or other intermediary. Hence, it is argued, Jesus could have found no place for himself as "Messiah," "Suffering Servant," or "Son of man" to mediate the kingdom to his disciples. This view appears at once to misrepresent the teaching of the Hebrew prophets, to lay undue stress on the individualistic character of the kingdom experience, and to overlook the evidence of what Jesus actually thought of his relation to the coming of the kingdom. It is rather generally agreed that in the older account the appointment of Saul as king through anointing by Samuel was done at the express command of Yahweh (I Sam. 9:1–10:16)—an act of the prophet resulting in the creation of a contemporary messiah ("anointed one") to serve as Yahweh's viceroy among his people. The coronation psalms, moreover, employed in the ritual of the New Year's Festival (Pss. 2, 110; etc.) were intended to memorialize the office of the reigning king and his duties as God's vicegerent. Further, numerous passages in the prophetic literature of the Hebraic tradition looked for the coming of a great leader who should mediate the kingdom among God's people (e.g., Isa. 11:1-10; 49; 53; Jer. 23:1-8; Mic. 5:2 ff). In all these and similar prophetic passages the kingdom of God is a corporate experience mediated to God's people through his anointed representative. In some of them this representative is identified with the "remnant" of the people itself, in others with the contemporary or a shortly-to-arrive "anointed one," in still others with an ideal figure still far off but represented as very real to the prophet's inspired imagination.

It is generally agreed that the "voice" which spoke to Jesus at his baptism quotes from Ps. 2:7; Isa. 42:1—passages relating respectively to the coronation of the contemporary messiah and to the call or ordination of the (suffering) servant of the Lord. If this voice be thought to reflect the awareness of mission on Jesus' part—a view that will accord with the nature of his temptations in which two conceptions of messiahship (Satan's or the popular nationalistic type, and God's—that of a messiah who must win his way through suffering to moral leadership) appear to be struggling for Jesus' acceptance—then it will appear to be clear that from the beginning of his ministry Jesus conceived of himself as the (suffering) Servant-messiah called upon to inaugurate God's kingdom in the world. Jesus' later sayings regarding his "cross," his "baptism," his "cup"—sayings spoken in the context of the kingdom-of-God idea—will also accord with his sense of a mediatorial mission such as that for which the terms "Suffering Servant" and "Messiah" stand (cf. Mark 8:31-33; 10:35-45; etc.). And it will become intelligible that in times of strategic crisis Jesus endeavored to elicit from his disciples (Mark 8:27-30), from the multitudes (Mark 8:34 ff), from the high priest (Mark 14:62; note Matt. 26:64 and the probability that Jesus said, "Am I?" or "Do you say so?"), and from Pilate (Mark 15:2, where again a question may be intended—"Do you say so?"), an expression of faith in himself as God's accredited viceroy.

Jesus' actions confirm the impression gained from his words that he considered himself to be the mediator of the kingdom to God's people. For early in his ministry he began to surround himself with a small band of well-chosen disciples, twelve in all, to serve as a loyal nucleus at a time when opposition was increasing against him—opposition which in the end excluded him from the congregation of the Jewish community (Mark 6:1 ff). Such appointing of one's disciple-band was as exceptional in the Hebrew-Jewish ethos as it would be in our own. Neither prophet nor rabbi chose his own followers—Moses and Elijah by express divine command were exceptions to this rule (Deut. 34:9; I Kings 19:16). Jesus' choice of the Twelve was matched by his declaration that they should "sit on (twelve) thrones, judging the twelve tribes of Israel" (Matt. 19:28 = Luke 22:30 [Q]). The conclusion appears irresistible that the band of twelve was to form the nucleus of the prophetic "remnant" (the new Israel)—a sort of acted parable representing the new people of God, which, wherever they went with Jesus as their messianic leader at their head, would tell their own story that God's kingdom had at last come in the person and work of his accredited viceroy. The events of passion week—the so-called "triumphal entry" (Mark 11:1-10), the cleansing of the temple (vss. 15-17), and the Last Supper (14:22-25) more particularly—also constitute a series of acted parables in which Jesus, by means of object lessons after the fashion of many of the Hebrew prophets, rather clearly appears to wish to teach his generation that there is in their midst one who is Lord of city and temple, and host at the banquet table of God's kingdom (cf. also the feeding of the four thousand and the five thousand [Mark 6:35-44; 8:1-10]).

The term employed by Jesus to designate his function as mediator of the kingdom was "SON OF MAN," a phrase with a long history behind it. There appears to be a growing conviction among NT scholars that, as used by Jesus, it was intended to have several denotations, including the usual Aramaic usage for "I" or "one," the corporate sense of the "people of God" as in Dan. 7:13, and the titular meaning roughly equivalent to messiah. The originality of our Lord's usage of the term lies, not in his attaching an exaltation motif to it (this it already had in Dan. 7:13; I Enoch 37-71), but rather in the humiliation or suffering motif which he associated with it and which he probably took over from the figure of the Suffering Servant of Yahweh from Deutero-Isaiah and the Psalms (cf. Isa. 53; Pss. 22; 69).

If the above interpretation is correct, then we may conceive of Jesus as seeing the kingdom of God as having arrived in and through his own person and work. As "Son of man" he conceives himself to be God's Messiah or viceroy, who leads forth the "remnant," each member of which with himself bears aloft his cross (Mark 8:34; Luke 14:27), and thus shares in the redemptive task of the "Suffering Servant"; as corporate "Son of man" he believes also that he and his followers will share in the final consummation of the kingdom and God's judgment upon his world and mankind at the end of the age (Mark 13:24-27; Matt. 25:31-46 [M]).

d. Time and "signs" of the consummation. This subject gave the Jewish apocalyptists of Jesus' day much concern. They looked for numerous precursory events—such as the "woes of the Messiah," earthquakes, wars, cosmic catastrophes, etc.—which should herald the end of the age.

There is good evidence to the effect that Jesus neither concerned himself with times or seasons (Acts 1:7), nor taught that there would be "signs" of the consummation of the kingdom at the end of history (Mark 13:32-37; Luke 12:39-40 = Matt. 24:43-44 [Q]; Luke 21:34-36). The end would come suddenly and without warning—a suggestion which on its face appears reasonable; it seems inconceivable that the breaking of eternity into time should, so to speak, "cast its shadow before it"! If, then, Jesus uttered the so-called "Little Apocalypse" at Mark 13:1-31, it is likely that he meant thereby to refute the expectations of those looking for "signs" of the end. For he says repeatedly that his disciples are not to account this or that a "sign" (cf. vss. 5-8, 21-23); rather, the end of history and the appearance of the Son of man may be expected to come together "after the tribulation" of human experience, and of that "day" and "hour" only the Father has information (vss. 24-27, 32-37).

There is a large body of scholarly opinion, however, committed to the view that at some time in his ministry Jesus specified that the consummation would occur during the lifetime of some of his contemporaries (cf. Mark 9:1; 13:26; 14:62). While this opinion is to be respected, the passages on which it depends are capable of contrary interpretations which are more conformable to his teaching generally. It seems to make nonsense of Jesus' strenuous efforts to create of the Twelve the prophetic remnant which should form the nucleus of a new people of God pledged to an expanding program that would eventually, after the prophetic teaching and hope, extend its redemptive efforts to embrace the whole of mankind.

3. Popular Jewish Christian beliefs. The early Jewish church had inherited the popular eschatological teaching briefly outlined in § 1 *above.* Jesus' disciples had been Galileans—for the most part, at least—and it was in Galilee that the Zealot movement found its strongest support. Simon the Cananean (or Zealot) and probably also Judas Iscariot (probably Semitic for "sicarius") were from the band of superpatriots. There can be little doubt also that the literalism of the apocalyptic eschatology had a vogue among the Galileans from among whom Jesus' "fringe disciples" were drawn.

The Qumran sect was distributed throughout the Jewish world in small communities or "camps" (CDC 7.6; 12.22; etc.; cf. Jos. War II.viii.4), and it is now established that it considered itself an eschatological community, living in the "last times" and concerned to disseminate apocalyptic writings. That the early Jewish branch of the church saw in itself an eschatological community of much the same type is clear from a comparison of Acts with the Dead Sea Scrolls: both considered themselves the object of special enlightenment (Acts 2:17 ff; 1QS 1.9; 3.13, 24; 1QM); both practiced a common meal (Acts 2:42; 1QS 6.13-23) and community of goods (of free choice in Acts 4:32–5:11; by rule of the order in 1QS 1.1-15); both adhered to the old Jewish particularism (Acts 11:2, 19; Gal. 2:12-21 with Acts 15:1-35; 1QS 1.16 ff; 5.7-20); both looked for "times of refreshing" at the end of the age (Acts 3:19-21; 1QS 4.25; 1QH 11.13-14; 13.11-13; etc.) and for accompanying judgment of the wicked (Acts 3:23-24; 1QS 3.18; 4.20); both communities considered themselves to be the "sons of the covenant" which God had made with his people (Acts 3:25; CDC 6.11 ff).

The poverty of the Jewish church may have been —in part, at any rate—a result of its apocalypticism, which led to communal practices and perhaps to giving up of worldly occupations, as occurred at a later date during Paul's ministry (I Thess. 5:14; II Thess.

3:6-12; cf. Rom. 15:25; Acts 24:17). After the destruction of Jerusalem this Jewish branch of the church became known as "Ebionites" (Hebrew for "poor"). In the end this popular Jewish Christian apocalypticism was bound to issue in a kind of cynical despair, as with the passing of the years its "hope" of a literal fulfilment of the promise of the end of the age and the parousia of the Son of man during the first generation failed to materialize (II Pet. 3:3-4).

4. The teaching of the church's scriptures. By and large, the scriptures of the church were written outside the context of—though in the case of some of Paul's letters, flatly in opposition to—popular Jewish Christian beliefs. In the Synoptic gospels, Matthew's "special source" (M) has at times been held to reflect such beliefs and, as suggested under § 2*d above,* some would attribute the Little Apocalypse of Mark 13 to the same influence in the church. II Pet. 3:5-13 sounds like an answer to the cynical despair in which the early popular apocalypticism had issued (*cf.* § 3 *above*). On the whole, however, the church's scriptures were written for a community which had become conscious of itself as a people of God transcending racial or cultural boundaries and which by reason of its Hellenistic ethos was prepared to listen to a type of eschatological teaching as ecumenical as that of the Hebrew prophets from the day of Amos onward and as vitally realistic as that of Jesus himself. It will be convenient to treat of the eschatological teaching of these scriptures under four heads:

a. Fulfilment of OT hope. It was the joint witness of the prophetic spirits who wrote the Christian scriptures that the eschatological hope of the Hebrew prophets had been fulfilled in the incarnate life and work of Jesus and in the gift of his Spirit to the church. Jesus was the fulfilment of the "promises" relative to a redeemer who should redeem Israel and, through Israel, all mankind (Luke 1:54-55; 2: 29-32; Rom. 1:1-6; Eph. 2:11-22; Heb. 9:11-22). In like manner the gift of Jesus' Spirit to his church at Pentecost was a fulfilment of God's promise to pour out his Spirit upon all flesh (Acts 2:17-36; I Cor. 2: 6-13). Indeed, the church itself is the new people of God, the prophetic "remnant," God's own "building" or "temple" (Rom. 9:22-33; I Cor. 3:9, 16-17; Eph. 2:19-22; I Pet. 2:4-10). This factor of fulfilment imparts to the church's scriptures, as well as to its life, an atmosphere that is unmistakable. They are eschatological scriptures in the sense that their authors are convinced that the new day has dawned, the "last times" foretold by the prophets have begun, and the "day of the Lord" or alternatively the "parousia" of the Messiah is just at hand (Rom. 13: 11-14; Phil. 4:5; Heb. 1:2; 9:26; 10:25, 37-38; Jas. 5: 7-9; I Pet. 1:5, 20; 4:7; I John 2:18, 22; 4:3; Jude 18; Rev. 22:10, 12, 20).

John's Gospel is really no exception at this point, as the Johannine Jesus speaks of the "last day" on which salvation and judgment will finally be meted out (John 12:47-48), though the emphasis here is on the thought that eternal "life" is the present possession of Jesus' disciples (John 3:36; 5:24), that it is possible to be "sons of light" now (John 12:36), that oneness of spirit with the Father may be realized in the present age (John 17:20-21). Practically, such teaching meant that the church conceived the prophetic *eschaton* to have been split in two: the first half began within history with the Incarnation; the second half would await the Parousia and would extend into the beyond-history.

b. Kingdom of God and church. The half of the prophetic *eschaton* already in process of realization is the period of the church's life on earth. The church is, so to speak, the territory of the kingdom of God, the delimited area of his reign; the far-flung boundaries of the church's activities are the horizons of the kingdom. Beginning with Pentecost, church and Spirit go together in an indissoluble union (Eph. 4: 4). And the gift of the Spirit to the church means that Christ has begun his reign, having assumed authority as he sits at God's right hand (Acts 2:33-34; Phil. 2:9), and is already granting kingdom powers to his disciples (Eph. 4:8 ff), who have been transferred into his kingdom (I Thess. 2:12; Col. 1:13), and are, therefore, already at work in it (I Cor. 3:9-17; 12:4-31).

The church's ethical teaching finds its source at this point. Its ethic is an eschatological ethic in the sense that it is one whose requirements are capable of fulfilment only in the power of the Spirit given to the church in these "last times." It is one rooted in and assured by Christ's rule as God's viceroy through his Spirit granted to his church.

c. Parousia, judgment, end of the age. If the *terminus a quo* of the kingdom's presence in the world is the Incarnation, its *terminus ad quem* is equally clearly the parousia of the church's Lord at the end of history. It is striking that the church never adopted Jesus' terminology nor spoke of the parousia of the "Son of man" (Matt. 24:27; Mark 13:26; 14:62)! It spoke rather of the parousia of "Christ" (I Cor. 15: 23), of "our Lord Jesus" (I Thess. 2:19), of "our Lord Jesus Christ" (I Thess. 5:23; II Thess. 2:1; II Pet. 1:16), of "the Lord" (Jas. 5:7-8), even of "the day of God" (II Pet. 3:12), etc. Moreover, there is no slightest evidence of the waning in the church of this eschatological hope of the coming again of her Lord; whatever dates be assigned to the writings of the NT, they are first and last full of the assurance that the Lord is just "at hand" (Phil. 4:5; Jas. 5:3, 7-9; *cf.* further § 4*a above*). Accordingly, the Lord himself cries out: "Surely I am coming soon," and the church replies: "Amen. Come, Lord Jesus!" (Rev. 22:20). The latter, indeed, appears to have been a cry already employed by the Jewish church in Aramaic (*Maranatha;* I Cor. 16:22), and continued in a Greek form, at least to the end of the century. Clearly, in the church's teaching the Lord is present by his Spirit in his church at all times; equally at all times his parousia is "drawing nigh." Similarly, the church is living in the "last days"; yet the end has not yet come but is near at hand.

As for "judgment," the Johannine Jesus remarks: "He who rejects me . . . has a judge; the word that I have spoken will be his judge on the last day" (John 12:48). This is a poetic way of saying that men judge themselves by their attitude toward Jesus and that their estimate of themselves will pass current at face value in God's eternal order. It is possible to interpret the famous judgment scene in Rev. 20:4, 12-15, along similar lines (*see* REVELATION, BOOK OF, § E4).

In any case, the church believed in God's final judgment of all men, living and dead (Heb. 9:27; I John 4:17; Jude 6).

d. Resurrection and future life. There is good reason to believe that Jesus thought of eternal life as an experience of fellowship with God, to be had both within and without history without distinction. In the Synoptic gospels he is generally reported as having employed the term "kingdom of God" to denote the temporal aspect of such fellowship (*cf.* § 2*b above*), though a saying like that at Matt. 7:13-14 employs the word "life" to convey the same idea, as usually in John's Gospel (John 3:15; 5:24). That he believed in the resurrection, there is also good reason to believe, though there is no record that he inquired intimately into its nature (Mark 12:18-27). The terms "heaven," "hell," and the like, he employed in the manner current in his day (Mark 10:21; Luke 6:23 = Matt. 5:12 [Q]; Mark 9:43; Luke 12:5 = Matt. 10:28 [Q]). But Jesus' language in all such cases is the language of metaphor and parable, and it is quite impossible to reduce it to the level of scientific categories.

The church's scriptures agreed in all essential respects with Jesus' recorded teachings at these points, in only two particulars going beyond them. The first of these concerns the fact that eternal life (whether present or future) was now said to be God's gift through Jesus (Rom. 6:4; Col. 3:3-4; Jas. 1:12; I Pet. 3:7), or alternatively through his Spirit (Rom. 8:2; Gal. 6:8), and that in like manner the believer's resurrection is a gift of God in Christ (Acts 4:2; I Cor. 15:12-23). The second concerns the nature of the resurrection "body," in which, as Paul showed, there is both continuity and discontinuity with the temporal body (I Cor. 15:35-50).

Bibliography. In addition to the standard works on NT theology, such as those of Feine, Stauffer, and Bultmann, important special studies to be consulted include: C. A. A. Scott, *Christianity According to St. Paul* (1927); T. W. Manson, *The Teaching of Jesus* (2nd ed., 1935); R. Otto, *The Kingdom of God and the Son of Man* (1938); O. Cullmann, *Die Hoffnung der Kirche auf die Wiederkunft Christi* (1942); J. W. Bowman, *The Intention of Jesus* (1943); W. Manson, *Jesus the Messiah* (1943); G. S. Duncan, *Jesus, Son of Man* (1948); A. N. Wilder, *Eschatology and Ethics in the Teaching of Jesus* (1950); S. Mowinckel, *He That Cometh* (1955); W. G. Kümmel, *Verheissung und Erfüllung* (3rd ed., 1956; English trans., 1957).

J. W. BOWMAN

ESDRAELON ĕz′drĭ ē′lən [᾿Εσδρηλών]. The Greek name, derived from the Hebrew word "Jezreel," for the W portion of the Valley of Jezreel, including the Valley of Megiddon. *See* JEZREEL 4; MEGIDDON, VALLEY OF. Fig. JEZ 22.

ESDRAS, BOOKS OF ĕz′drəs [῎Εσδρας, *from* עזרא, Ezra]. The first two books in the APOCRYPHA. I Esdras, which is ῎Εσδρας α in the SEPTUAGINT, mainly covers the same ground as the OT book of Ezra and parts of Nehemiah (*see* EZRA AND NEHEMIAH, BOOKS OF) and II Chronicles; it is a freer Greek translation of the original Hebrew than the LXX version (῎Εσδρας β) of the latter books, and has been thought to be part of the true LXX version of Ezra-Nehemiah, while ῎Εσδρας β is the translation by THEODOTION of the same books. II Esdras, the second book in the Apoc., is a composite apocalyptic work (*see* APOCALYPSES) originally written in Greek —though some think there was a Hebrew original for much of it—but now existing only in Latin (three verses in ch. 15 have been found in a Greek papyrus, P Oxy. 1010) and in other versions made from the Greek. II Esdras is appended to the VULGATE.

1. The titles. The various titles of the books of Esdras are confusing; the data are largely given in the following table. The books with which this article is concerned are represented by the fourth and fifth columns; the second and third columns represent the OT Ezra-Nehemiah. *See* p. 141.

The first of our books has been known as both I and III Esdras, and for the sake of clarity as the "Greek Ezra." The second has been known as II or IV Esdras, or as the "Ezra Apocalypse."

2. I Esdras. ***a. Acceptance in the church.*** Although it is absent from codex SINAITICUS, I Esdras is in codices VATICANUS and ALEXANDRINUS. There are Old Latin versions (*see* LATIN VERSIONS, OLD) with a good text, and a useful Syr. version (*see* VERSIONS, ANCIENT). I Esdras occupied a place of equal importance with the Hebrew Ezra. It was in Origen's Hexapla. Augustine could find in it a prophecy of Christ. But Jerome (*see* VULGATE) was scornful, and since his day it has never been considered canonical. Later editions of the Vulg. relegated it to a subordinate position—in an appendix to the NT! *See* CANON OF THE OT.

b. Contents. Except in one section, I Esdras covers the same ground as the close of II Chronicles, the book of Ezra, and part of Nehemiah, but not in the same order. It plunges straight into the description of Josiah's Passover (II Chr. 35) and continues until Cyrus' decree after the Exile, permitting the return of the Jews and the rebuilding of the temple (to Ezra 1:11). But the narrative then follows Ezra 4:7-24, the Samaritan opposition in the reign of Artaxerxes. After this there is a section (I Esd. 3:1–5:6) which does not correspond with anything in the OT; it is mainly the story of a competition between three Jewish pages at Darius' court, to say whereof true wisdom consists, a competition which is won by Zerubbabel, who claims as his prize the king's permission for the Jews to return and rebuild Jerusalem. The narrative then reverts to that of Ezra 2, with a list of returning exiles under Zerubbabel, and an account of the Samaritan opposition to the building. The rest of the canonical Ezra, except for that part of ch. 4 mentioned above, which is out of place in Ezra, is now followed, dealing with the building of the temple in the reign of Darius, and with Ezra's visit and work in Jerusalem in the reign of Artaxerxes. Our book

	OT Ezra	OT Nehemiah	Paraphrase of II Chr. 35–36; Ezra; Neh. 8; with an original story.	A Latin pseudepigraph (apocalyptic)
LXX	Ἔσδρας β		Ἔσδρας α	
Vulg.	I Esdras	II Esdras	III Esdras	IV Esdras
Many later Latin MSS	I Esdras Esdras		III Esdras	II Esdras (=1–2) IV Esdras (=3–14) V Esdras (=15–16)
English Great Bible, 1539	I Esdras	II Esdras	III Esdras	IV Esdras
39 Articles VI, 1562	I Esdras	II Esdras	III Esdras	IV Esdras
Geneva Bible, 1560	Ezra	Nehemiah	I Esdras	II Esdras
KJV, 1611	Ezra	Nehemiah	I Esdras	II Esdras

ends with the account of Ezra reading the Law, as in Neh. 7–8. It has a sudden ending as well as an abrupt beginning.

c. Origin. What is the relationship with the Hebrew Ezra-Nehemiah, which it closely resembles, and the LXX Ἔσδρας β? If Ἔσδρας α and β are independent Greek translations of the same canonical work, Ezra-Nehemiah, then β is a painfully literal translation and α is more than ordinarily free. Some scholars think that α must be based on a very different Hebrew text from the MT which we possess (*see* MASORA), and thus provide valuable evidence for an ancient and rival OT text. However, we cannot be sure that I Esdras is not merely a loose compilation, based perhaps upon a previous Greek translation, or compiled from the Hebrew directly; and not all agree that the deviations in I Esdras are due to a different Hebrew text. There must have been more than one Greek version of many OT books, and we need not suppose that Ἔσδρας β was the only Greek version of Ezra-Nehemiah which existed in its own day.

I Esdras is an unsatisfactory piece of writing historically, as a glance at the summary of the contents will reveal; it passes from the reign of Cyrus to that of Artaxerxes, back to that of Darius, and on to that of Artaxerxes again. At the same time, whereas it usually differs from Ἔσδρας β and Ezra-Nehemiah, there are several instances where α and β agree in differing from the Hebrew. Some scholars, therefore, have suggested that behind Ἔσδρας β lay the MT, while behind Ἔσδρας α lay some older Hebrew text. From this older text a Greek translation was made, of which Ἔσδρας α is a redaction. Ἔσδρας β is a new translation from the revised Hebrew (the MT) but very much influenced by the translation of the older Hebrew text. The theory seeks to explain three things: the resemblances between Ἔσδρας α and β (because the "parent" of α was used in making β), the differences between them (they are based on different Hebrew texts), and the redactional traces in Ἔσδρας α. But it would satisfy the evidence merely to say that, whether or not there were two Hebrew originals, the author of Ἔσδρας β felt the unsatisfactory nature of Ἔσδρας α and improved matters by producing a very literal rendering of Ezra-Nehemiah. Nothing is gained by inventing a Greek prototype of I Esdras, of which no trace has survived.

Evidence for the earlier date of I Esdras is its position before Ἔσδρας β in the important MSS and the evidence of Josephus, who follows I Esdras closely in the Antiquities in preference to both the Hebrew book and Ἔσδρας β.

I Esdras, then, is the work of a compiler; he used some form of Chronicles-Ezra-Nehemiah, and added a story from an unknown source. Moreover, either he did not finish his work or some of it has been lost, for it begins and ends abruptly.

d. Purpose and value. The introduction of the Greek story makes the book self-contradictory, for King Darius sent Zerubbabel to rebuild Jerusalem and the temple, whereas according to 6:23 he does not know that Zerubbabel has any authority. There are many errors. As we have seen, the Persian kings are in the wrong order. The compiler's aim was to glorify Ezra, the Law, and the worship of God, especially in the temple, regardless of historical accuracy. On the other hand, some parts appear to be more historical than the canonical work—e.g., by ignoring Neh. 1:1–7:72, I Esdras avoids a gap of fourteen years and presents the story of Ezra logically; and Ezra 4:7-24 is put in its right place (*see* § 2*b* *above*), though "Artaxerxes" is an anachronism.

Probably there was little consistency in the original Hebrew accounts of the return from exile; I Esdras represents one tradition, the MT another. They are equally valuable to the historian of the period.

e. Date and place. The Greek story resembles ARISTEAS and may thus date from *ca.* 150 B.C. The final compilation must have been before A.D. 100 (it is used by Josephus). One is impressed by the agreements between I Esdras and the LXX of Esther and Daniel, which may suggest that all three were translated by the same hand. The date might then be 150-100 B.C., and the original Hebrew pre-Maccabean. It can hardly be later than 50 B.C. It seems to have been translated for the Jews of Alexandria.

3. II Esdras. ***a. Importance.*** Our second book is important chiefly because of its close resemblance in parts to the NT. Its popularity in the church is proved by the number of versions into which it has been rendered (Latin, Syriac, Ethiopic, etc.), and by quotations in the fathers beginning with Clement of Alexandria, *ca.* A.D. 200. The phrases *requiem aeternitatis* and *lux perpetua* (2:34-35) have obviously exerted a powerful influence on the Christian liturgy. Still, Jerome regarded the book unfavorably.

In the ERV and subsequent versions will be found a long section of seventy verses between 7:35 and 36 which is not in the KJV. This is because these verses were cut out of a MS of A.D. 822 (Codex Sangermanensis), probably for doctrinal reasons, and they were not generally accepted (*see* B. M. Metzger *bibliography*) until R. L. Bensly in 1874 found a Latin MS which contained the whole text. The excised passage denies the efficacy of prayers on behalf of those who are in the intermediate state after death (vs. 105).

b. Analysis and dates. The book is composite. Chs. 1-2 are an anti-Jewish addition to the original Jewish apocalypse (chs. 3-14). The addition was probably made by a Jewish Christian. The language often resembles that of the gospels.

The Ezra Apocalypse (chs. 3-14) may be divided into four sections: (*a*) the Salathiel Apocalypse (chs. 3-10), which is four visions, dealing with the problem of evil; in accordance with Pharisaic teaching, a solution is suggested in the life to come, rather than in this evil world, about which the Seer is pessimistic (*ca.* A.D. 100); (*b*) the Eagle Vision (11:1-12:39), concerned with the Roman Empire and the coming of Messiah (*ca.* A.D. 96); (*c*) the Vision of the Man rising from the sea (ch. 13), the Messiah, containing much older material (*ca.* A.D. 69); and (*d*) legend (ch. 14), telling how Ezra rewrote the sacred literature, both canonical and apocalyptic (*ca.* A.D. 100).

Chs. 15-16, the most recent and least valuable part of the book, are thought to be as late as A.D. 270; they contain verbal echoes of the NT. This section is not apocalyptic, but intended only as an appendix to the Ezra Apocalypse.

Neither the final form, then, nor the parts from which it has been compiled are pre-Christian, but much of the traditional Jewish material used in the first two parts (chs. 1-14) is pre-Christian. Probably these parts were issued as a book *ca.* A.D. 96, with the fall of Jerusalem very much in mind. The place of publication is more likely to have been Palestine than either Alexandria or Rome.

Bibliography. I Esdras: Articles in *Academy* (1893); *Proceedings of the Society of Biblical Archaeology* (1901-2), pp. 1,488-94. Greek text in the Cambridge editions of the LXX and in O. F. Fritsche, *Libri Apocryphi VT graece* (1871). German text by H. Guthe in Kautzsch, *Die Apokryphen . . . des AT,* I (1898). English text by E. C. Bissell (1880); J. H. Lupton in *Speaker's Commentary* (1888); C. J. Ball in *Variorum Apoc.* (1892); S. A. Cook in the Oxford Apoc. (1913). Introductions in histories of Schürer and Ewald; C. C. Torrey, *Ezra Studies* (1910); W. O. E. Oesterley, *The Books of the Apoc.* (1914); C. C. Torrey, *The Apocryphal Literature* (1945); R. H. Pfeiffer, *History of NT Times* (1949), pp. 233-57, and bibliography on p. 534; B. M. Metzger, *An Introduction to the Apoc.* (1957), pp. 11-19.

II Esdras: Articles in *Bibl. Stud.,* XX (1922; J. Keulers); *ZAW* (1929), pp. 222-49 (W. Mundle); *MGWJ* (1932-33; A. Kaminka), pp. 76-77. Latin text in "Texts and Studies," III.2 (1895); Violet, *Die Ezra-Apokalypse,* II (1924). German text by Gunkel in Kautzsch (*see above*), II. English text by Lupton (*see above*); Ball (*see above*); Box in Oxford Pseudep. and in *The Ezra Apocalypse* (1912); Oesterley in WC (1933). Introductions in C. C. Torrey, *The Apocryphal Literature* (1945), pp. 116-23; Pfeiffer (*see above*), pp. 81-86, and bibliography on pp. 86, 534; Metzger (*see above*), pp. 21-30, 231-38. Special studies: R. L. Bensly, *The Missing Fragment of the Fourth Book of Ezra* (1875); B. M. Metzger, "The 'Lost' Section of II Esdras (=IV Ezra)," *JBL,* 76 (1957), pp. 153-56.

N. TURNER

ESDRIS ĕz'drĭz [Ἔσδρις] (II Macc. 12:36); KJV GORGIAS. A leader of the troops of Gorgias in a battle with Judas Maccabeus. J. C. SWAIM

ESEBON. KJV Apoc. form of HESHBON.

ESEBRIAS. KJV Apoc. form of SHEREBIAH.

ESEK ē'sĕk [עשק, contention] (Gen. 26:20). A well dug by the servants of Isaac, which received this name because the herdsmen of Gerar contended for it and forced the patriarch to abandon it. The site is unknown, but it must have been near Gerar, probably in the Wadi esh-Sheri'ah. S. COHEN

ESHAN ē'shən [אשען, support] (Josh. 15:52); KJV ESHEAN ĕsh'ĭ ən. A village of Judah in the hill-country district of Hebron. The location is uncertain. The LXX has Σομα ("Soma"); Eshan may thus possibly be identifiable with Khirbet Sam'a, W of Domeh (Dumah) and *ca.* ten miles SW of Hebron. V. R. GOLD

ESHBAAL. *See* ISHBAAL.

ESHBAN ĕsh'băn [אשבן]. The second son of clan chief Dishon; ancestor of a native Horite subclan in Edom (Gen. 36:26; I Chr. 1:41).

ESHCOL ĕsh'kōl [אשכל, *usually* (grape-) cluster]. **1.** Brother of Aner and Mamre the Amorite, who were allies of Abram (בעלי ברית־אברם) in the defeat of Chedorlaomer (Gen. 14:13-24). *See* 2 *below.*

2. A valley near Hebron (probably to the N) from which Israelite spies brought back a cluster of grapes so large it had to be carried on a pole between two of them (Num. 13:23-24; Deut. 1:24). It is possibly to be identified with the wadi which arises just N of Ramet el-'Amleh, in an area noted for its vineyards. The wadi is dominated by Burj Haskeh, which may be a corruption of "Eshcol."

ESHEAN. KJV form of ESHAN.

ESHEK ē'shĕk [עשק]. A Benjaminite person or family descended from Saul (I Chr. 8:39). The verse, however, could be in the wrong context (cf. I Chr. 9:35-44).

Bibliography. M. Noth, *Die israelitischen Personennamen* (1928), p. 254.

ESHKALONITES. *See* ASHKELON.

ESHTAOL ĕsh'tĭ əl [אשתאול]; ESHTAOLITES —ə līts; KJV ESHTAULITES. A town first assigned to Dan (Josh. 19:41) and then incorporated in the Judahite district of Zorah-Azekah (15:33); possibly to be identified with Eshwa', N of Artuf. Its juxtaposition with Zorah is continued in Judges (13:25; 16:31; 18:2, 8, 11; cf. also I Chr. 2:53). Samson first responded to the Spirit of God between Zorah and Eshtaol and after his death was buried there. Zorah and Eshtaol were Danite centers from which the raiding party set out to capture Laish during the initial stages of the Danite migration northward (Judg. 18). V. R. GOLD

ESHTEMOA ĕsh'tə mō'ə [אשתמוע, listening post]. Alternately: ESHTEMOH ĕsh'tə mō [אשתמה] (Josh. 15:50). **1.** Son of Ishbah; a descendant of Caleb (I Chr. 4:17).

2. A Maacathite, son of Hodiah (I Chr. 4:19).

3. A city of Judah assigned to the Levites and named as a city of refuge (Josh. 21:14; I Chr. 6:57—H 6:42); later assigned to the highland province of Goshen (Josh. 15:50). It is identified with es-Semu'a, *ca.* nine miles S of Hebron.

According to I Sam. 30:28, it was one of the cities to which David sent some of the booty from his recapture of Ziklag from the Amalekites for services rendered him and his men during his flights from Saul. V. R. GOLD

ESHTON ĕsh'tən [אשתון, effeminate *or* uxorious(?)]. A family or clan of the tribe of Judah; probably a Calebite (I Chr. 4:11-12).

ESLI ĕs'lī ['Εσλί] (Luke 3:25). An ancestor of Jesus.

ESORA. KJV form of AESORA.

ESPOUSAL. KJV translation of חתנה (Song of S. 3:11; RSV WEDDING) and כלולה (Jer. 2:2; RSV BRIDE). "Espoused" is used by the KJV (RSV BETROTHED) to translate ארש (II Sam. 3:14), ἁρμόζειν (II Cor. 11:2), and μνηστεύειν (Matt. 1:18; Luke 1:27; 2:5). *See* MARRIAGE.

ESRIL. KJV Apoc. form of AZAREL.

ESROM. KJV NT form of HEZRON.

ESSENES ĕs'ēnz ['Εσσηνόι, 'Εσσαῖοι, *see* § 1 *below*]. An important Jewish community which was flourishing in Palestine during the lifetime of Jesus. Their teachings and practice were well known for centuries through the writings of Philo and Josephus. A remarkable series of discoveries in the wilderness of Judea, beginning in the year 1947, produced a major part of the community's literature as well as the ruined remains of the headquarters of the sect. This new evidence aroused widespread interest in the Essenes, with whom some scholars had long associated Jesus without winning general approval of their views. *See* DEAD SEA SCROLLS.

1. Etymology of the name. The name Essene has been derived from numerous Greek and Hebrew words: ὅσιος, "holy"; ἴσος, "egalitarian"; חסיד, "pious"; סחא, "to bathe"; צנוע, "modest"; עשין, "powerful"; אסיא, "a physician"; חזיא, "a seer"; עשה, "to do," whence "the observers of the law"; חזן, "watcher" or "worshiper"; חשאים, "the silent ones." The East Aramaic *hasên, hasayyâ,* "pious," has also been suggested. These and other derivations represent efforts of varying success to find linguistically plausible names in view of the known traits of the Essenes. There is no scholarly consensus on the etymology of the name Essene, which seems to have been a mystery as early as Philo, and probably never was used by the sect as a term of self-designation. The name Essene does not occur in the Dead Sea Scrolls.

2. Sources. *a. Philo.* The Essenes are described in two of Philo's works—*Hypothetica* 11.1-18; and *Every Good Man Is Free* 12–13. A comparison of these accounts indicates that they are based upon a common literary source or sources freely used by Philo (cf. *Hypothetica* 11.1 with *Every Good Man* 12.76*a; Hypothetica* 11.8-9 with *Every Good Man* 12.76*b, Hypothetica* 11.4 with *Every Good Man* 12.79; *Hypothetica* 11.10-13 with *Every Good Man* 12.86-87). These works were probably composed in Egypt before A.D. 50, and the source or sources upon which they were dependent presumably had been circulating there some years previously. In passages where both of Philo's accounts give the same factual descriptions, we are in touch with what may be presumed to be valuable information about Palestinian Essenism of the early decades of the Christian era.

A third work by Philo, *On the Contemplative Life,* is largely devoted to a lengthy account of the Therapeutae, an Essene-like community in Egypt. The significant differences between the Essenes and the Therapeutae can be accounted for on the basis of socio-economic and climatic factors plus a period of separate historical development of not more than one hundred years. The Palestinian Essenes may have been more rigorously activistic than their contemplative brethren in Egypt because of the necessities of economic survival. Egyptian climate and society were very conducive to the easy life of the Therapeutae, and it is altogether possible that they repre-ent a later development of a pre-Christian Palestinian Jewish sect which was also the parent body of the Essenes. It is equally possible that they are quite independent in origin. However, the hymns and liturgical material of the Dead Sea Scrolls seem to find a natural setting in the liturgical practices of the Therapeutae. Though not a direct source on Palestinian Essenism, Philo's description of the Therapeutae should be taken into account by the reader interested in the Essenes.

b. Josephus. *The Jewish War* (A.D. 75-79) contains a lengthy and detailed account of the Essenes (II. viii.2-13). A much briefer account in the *Antiquities* contains valuable additional information (XVIII.i.5). In this account the number of Essenes is given as "about four thousand." The same expression (ὑπὲρ τετρακισχίλιοι) is used by Philo (*Every Good Man* 12.75), whose works were presumably available to Josephus, though there is no evidence of literary dependence. A comparison of the complete accounts of the Essenes in the writings of Philo and Josephus indicates that both writers were dependent upon written sources which have been freely used.

In his autobiography (*ca.* A.D. 100) Josephus writes that at about the age sixteen, having made unusual progress in his studies of Jewish law, he resolved to acquaint himself with the various parties of his nation. There were the Pharisees, the Sadducees, and the Essenes. His intention was to select the best after thorough investigation of all three. Therefore, disciplining himself and working hard, he completed a study of all three. But, following this initial investigation, he was still not ready to make his selection. So he went down into the wilderness and zealously attached himself to a man named Bannus, with whom he lived for three years. At the end of this time, at the age of nineteen, his investigations having been thoroughly accomplished, he returned to Jerusalem and joined the Pharisees. The three years spent with Bannus would have covered most of the period between the beginning and the end of his investigations—namely, his sixteenth and nineteenth years. Therefore, the initial stage of his investigations, during which time he acquainted himself with all three sects, must have been a comparatively brief but highly concentrated course of study, most likely undertaken in Jerusalem. We may believe that Josephus had ample opportunity in Jerusalem or with Bannus to become acquainted with Essene teaching and practice. But that he ever became a member of an Essene community, or even a probationary member, is highly unlikely, as will become clear when the rules for admission are considered (*see* § 4*c below*). Thus Josephus' accounts cannot be regarded as coming directly from the hand of one who knew the Essene community from the inside. On the other hand, there are indications that certain parts of his description of the Essenes ultimately rest upon eyewitness accounts of just such authority (Jos. War II.viii.5).

There are five further references to the Essenes in the histories of Josephus: *Judas the Essene and Antigonus* (died 37 B.C.; Antiq. XIII.xi.2; War I.iii.5); *Herod and the Essenes* (Antiq. XV.x.4-5); *Essenes Interpret Dreams* (Antiq. XVII.xiii.3; War II.vi.3); *John the Essene General* (died A.D. 66; War II.xx.4; III.ii. 1-2); *Gate of the Essenes* (War V.iv.2).

c. Pliny. Pliny the Elder was a fellow soldier of Vespasian and probably had been in Palestine, possibly in company with the Tenth Legion as it marched down the Jordan Valley in May, A.D. 68. In his *Natural History* (5.15.73), completed in 77, Pliny includes a topographical description of Judea. In his description of the region along the W side of the Dead Sea, he begins with Jericho in the N and moves southward to the Essenes amid their palm trees, then on to fertile En-gedi, and finally reaches the mountain fortress Masada, which guarded the S border of Judea. There are only two oases between Jericho and Masada which are capable of sustaining community life on an agrarian basis such as is prescribed for the Essenes by the testimony of Pliny, Josephus, and Philo. These are 'Ain Feshkha (probably biblical EN-EGLAIM), located S of Jericho, and 'Ain Jidi (biblical EN-GEDI), which lies some distance N of Masada. In the light of these geographical and topographical facts, it seems quite likely that when Pliny mentions the Essenes amidst their palm trees, he is referring to a religious community which must have lived in or near the area of the 'Ain Feshkha oasis.

Scholars had long known that at the N end of the 'Ain Feshkha oasis on a plateau overlooking the Wadi Qumran were some ruins of ancient buildings. Subsequent to the discovery of the Dead Sea Scrolls, archaeologists, between the years 1951-56, excavated these ruins, which proved to be the headquarters of a closely knit community. By numismatic evidence it was conclusively established that this community was indeed occupying the oasis in the first century. Within the community buildings archaeologists found agricultural implements including pruning hooks, and large quantities of date seeds plus the charred remains of palm tree trunks which had been used as ceiling beams. Though the oasis is badly overgrown with reeds now and is marginal land at best, there is no doubt that its agricultural potentialities are sufficient to respond to determined efforts at cultivation. Ancient retaining walls and small agricultural stations indicate that in the past a considerable amount of land was once brought under cultivation. This land was probably systematically irrigated by water from the numerous springs in the area. A consideration of these matters further strengthens the ties which connect Pliny's celibate Essenes, who had "only palm trees for company," with the tightly knit community which in the first century inhabited the 'Ain Feshkha oasis and occupied the nearby community buildings. History knows of no other community but Pliny's Essenes existing in this general area in the first century. Furthermore, a careful surface exploration of the entire region, made subsequently to the excavation of the community headquarters, turned up no other possible sites with which Pliny's Essenes could be identified. Thus it is to be concluded, on the basis of topographical and archaeological considerations, that the Essenes of Pliny are to be identified with those who occupied the community buildings of the 'Ain Feshkha oasis in the first century. We may assume that the Essenes of Pliny are the Essenes of Philo and

Josephus, and that while their larger membership was scattered throughout the villages and towns of Judea, the headquarters of their community was in the wilderness near the Dead Sea.

d. Dead Sea Scrolls. The above considerations are of the greatest importance for an evaluation of the significance of the Dead Sea Scrolls for understanding the Essenes. It is impossible to separate these scrolls from the community which inhabited the area of the 'Ain Feshkha oasis in the first century. Fragments of over three hundred MSS were found in a single cave (Cave IV), located only a stone's throw from the scriptorium of the community.

With the scrolls from this Essene library in hand, it is possible to gain an interior point of view of the community, and to correct many misconceptions of the sect which might otherwise come from the tendency of a Philo or a Josephus to conform their portraits of the Essenes to the image of some Greek philosophical school. The scrolls also supplement our knowledge of Essene organization, teaching, and practice, and provide valuable material for the reconstruction of the history of the community. But above all, the scrolls make possible an understanding of the eschatological nature of this Jewish sect (*see* § 4 *below*).

e. Hippolytus. A lengthy description of the Essenes is found in a work believed to be by the third-century bishop Hippolytus, *Philosophumena* 9.4 (18*b*-28*a*). This description of the Essenes seems to show so much indebtedness to Josephus that it has often been thought to be without additional value. However, Kaufman Kohler held that Hippolytus had access to another source as well, because of the important respects in which his portrait of the Essenes differed from that of Josephus. There are two significant variations: (*a*) Hippolytus considered the Zealots (*see* ZEALOT) and the sicarii (*see* ASSASSINS) to be subordinate groups of Essenes; and (*b*) he omitted all references to sun worship as a practice of the Essenes. Morton Smith has shown that part of the account by Hippolytus was taken from a source which also (perhaps as an independent translation from a Semitic original) lay behind Josephus' account. Therefore, Josephus' account is not automatically to take precedence over that of Hippolytus. When these authorities differ, care must be taken to ascertain whether Hippolytus' account may not sometimes be nearer the original.

3. History of the Essenes. Any reconstruction of Essene history must be largely conjectural, since the amount of information is scanty and often difficult to interpret. What follows is more in the nature of a single historical synthesis than a scholarly consensus.

The Essenes seem to have had their origins among the HASIDEANS. Following the success of the Maccabean revolution and the achievement of national sovereignty, the Jewish nation entered a new phase of statehood in which the revolutionary families and parties began to vie with one another in a struggle for power in the affairs of the newborn state. The house of Simon the Hasmonean finally emerged as the dominant party, with a firm grasp on the high priesthood and eventually the kingship. But in the course of this post-revolutionary power struggle three major theocratic parties emerged: the SADDUCEES; the PHARISEES; and the Essenes. All these followed the revolutionary party line of separatism—i.e., strict observance of Mosaic law entailing a national existence for Israel separate from the Gentiles. The Pharisees and Essenes each developed out of rival wings of the earlier revolutionary Hasideans. Thus the many similarities between these two parties is to be explained by their common origin.

Jewish tradition pictures the Essenes active in Jerusalem up to the reign of Aristobulus I (*ca.* 105-104 B.C.; Jos. War. I.iii.5; Antiq. XIII.xi.2). But by the end of the reign of Alexander Janneus (*ca.* 76 B.C.), the Essenes had made a complete break with the Hasmoneans and were sharply critical of the compromising policies of all other parties (cf. *Nahum Commentary*). As the archaeological evidence indicates, it was at some time during, if not prior to, the reign of Janneus, that the Essenes moved their headquarters to Qumran (*see* DEAD SEA SCROLLS), where they remained until the HERODIANS brought the final downfall of the Hasmoneans in 36 B.C. Archaeological evidence indicates that at that time they abandoned Qumran, and it seems likely that they returned to Jerusalem and occupied a quarter in the S part of the city.

The major political problem with which Herod the Great (*see* HEROD [FAMILY]) had to contend was the opposition of the great mass of people who refused to acknowledge the legitimacy of his claims to the throne, and the ever-present threat that some royal claimant of the Hasmonean house would be able to overthrow him. Herod's solution to this problem was, on the one hand, to rely heavily on the military power with which Rome backed its puppet princes, and on the other hand to weaken the relative influence and power of the Hasmoneans among the people by conciliating and granting concessions to parties which had grievances against the Hasmoneans. In this respect the anti-Hasmonean Essenes would have been very useful to Herod. Herod excused the Essenes (and many of the Pharisees) from the loyalty oaths which he made the Jews take in the early years of his reign. This means that some kind of concordat had been reached between Herod and the Essenes, under which the Essenes could have returned to Jerusalem without fear of the kind of repressive or restrictive measures or the offensive temple practices which had forced them to leave the city in the days of the despised Hasmoneans.

It was probably in this period of unrestricted religious freedom that the Essenes carried out their intensive missionary campaigns which resulted in the founding of Essene communities in all the villages and towns of Judea.

When they moved their headquarters back to Qumran after Herod's death—and archaeological evidence makes it clear that it was at this time that they did return to Qumran—they left behind them in Jerusalem, as the only trace of their presence in the city, their name as a legacy for an entrance through the S wall, called the "gate of the Essenes" (Jos. War. V.iv.2). To gain control of the temple mount was the chief objective of every military campaign to capture Jerusalem. With the attack from the E blocked by the steep declivities of the Cedron Valley, it was necessary only to protect the N, W, and S flanks. Therefore, Herod strengthened the fortifications in the N and W sectors of the city, and it would have suited his purposes very well to have had a strict Jewish community in which anti-Hasmonean sentiment ran strong occupy a quarter in the S sector.

Herod's quick move to bring an obscure but legitimate priest from Babylon to Jerusalem as high priest was, no doubt, in part motivated by a shrewd design to conciliate all parties which rejected Hasmonean claims to the high priesthood, without risking the alienation of any one of these parties which might object to the elevation of a rival party's candidate to the office. If the Essenes did return to Jerusalem under the concordat they had with Herod, it is altogether likely that they had effective assurances that the new high priest would pay due regard to the peculiar legal interpretations of the sect. And even later, when under political pressure it became necessary for Herod for a short period to allow a captive member of the Hasmonean family to function as high priest, it is still quite likely that Herod did not permit the legal views of the Essenes to be flouted.

The friendly relations which Herod had with the Essenes had become legendary in Jewish tradition by the time of Josephus (Jos. Antiq. XV.x.5). Nevertheless, it is altogether probable that the Essenes would have had strong sympathies with those who near the end of Herod's life tore down the golden eagle which he had erected above the gate of the temple. Hippolytus tells us that the Essenes would not go through an entrance which had an image above it (*Philosophumena* 9.4 [26*a*]). When after Herod's death the multitudes demanded of Archelaus the punishment of those who had been instrumental in burning alive the men who had instigated the cleansing of the temple, the Essenes may well have lent their support to the popular clamor (Jos. War II.i.2). In the succeeding course of events three thousand worshipers were slain during the Passover festival. If this did not provide an occasion for the Essenes once more to abandon Jerusalem, then perhaps we should look to the later crucifixion of two thousand Jews by Gentile troops which had been sent down by the governor of Syria to restore order in the city (Jos. War II.i.1–v.2; Antiq. XVII.ix.1–x.10). All this was reminiscent of the days of Janneus, when the community had been led down into the wilderness in obedience to the words of Isaiah: "In the wilderness prepare the way of the Lord" (Isa. 40:3; 1QS 8.13-14). There is evidence that at least one Essene was still lending his services to the Herodian court as late as the period immediately following Herod's death (Jos. Antiq. XVII.xiii.3). But archaeological evidence makes it clear that about this time the headquarters of the community was shifted back to Qumran.

Two generations later, at the outbreak of war with Rome in 66, one of the Jewish generals was an Essene named John. What part the community as a whole played in this war is not known. But Josephus records that the Essenes distinguished themselves as faithful martyrs at the hands of their Roman captors (Jos. War II.viii.10). Their headquarters at Qumran were burned during this war, and the fate of their postwar membership is problematical. Some may have participated in the sporadic but continued resistance to Rome which did not end till Hadrian's crushing of the Bar Cocheba's revolt of 132-135. Toombs has shown that Bar Cocheba himself may have been an Essene. Ultimately the Essenes were probably assimilated by the Jewish Christian community and other Jewish groups which survived the prolonged struggle with Rome.

4. Description of the Essenes. A most important period of Essene history falls between the death of Herod and the outbreak of war in 66. In this period two new Jewish communities were born, Baptist and Christian. Wholly apart from the difficult question whether John the Baptist and Jesus may have been Essenes, an understanding of the teachings, practices, and organization of the Essene community in this period of Palestinian Judaism inevitably increases understanding of the contemporary Baptist and Christian movements, as well as of the Pharisees and the Zealots. Fortunately our sources of information on the Essenes for this period are very rich. We have happily recovered a considerable portion of the literature which was being read by the Essenes in the first century. We also have an abundance of data which has been gathered by archaeologists through a study of their community headquarters. Finally, we have the accounts of Philo and Josephus, who describe in great detail the Essenes as they were known in this period. The description which follows draws upon all these sources of information and provides a picture of the Essene community at that stage of its development which it had reached by the middle of the first century. This is the stage of Essene development which is of greatest interest to NT students. (On the use of the word "Baptist," *see* JOHN THE BAPTIST.)

The Essenes believed themselves to be the people of the New Covenant. They understood this "New Covenant" to be at once the "renewed old covenant" and the "eternal covenant" to be established at the end of days. Thus they were, like the primitive Palestinian church, a Jewish eschatological community. Philo and Josephus agree that the total membership of the Essenes was *ca.* four thousand (*Every Good Man* 12.75; Jos. Antiq. XVIII.i.15). This total membership could have gathered at Qumran on special occasions, as, e.g., at Pentecost, when they seem to have celebrated annually the renewing of the covenant. There was ample camping space for this large number in the environs of the community headquarters. But probably not more than a few hundred Essenes lived at the wilderness retreat regularly. The great majority of their membership was scattered about the villages and towns of Judea (*Hypothetica* 11.1; Jos. War II.viii.4).

Because of their strict adherence to the Levitical purity laws the Essenes were scrupulous in their avoidance of all ceremonial uncleanness. Since the larger cities were contaminated by the presence of Gentiles and by the nonobservance of the purity laws, the Essenes tended to avoid them (cf. *Every Good Man* 12.76).

a. Communal life. The Essenes practiced a communal ownership of property. There was no abject poverty nor inordinate wealth among their membership (Jos. War II.viii.3; cf. Antiq. XVIII.i.5; Philo *Every Good Man* 12.86; *Hypothetica* 11.10-13). Philo writes: "No one's house is his own in the sense that it is not shared by all, for besides the fact that they dwell together in communities, the door is open to visitors from elsewhere who share their convictions" (*Every Good Man* 12.85).[1] Josephus confirms and elaborates on the remarkable hospitality Essenes showed other members of their brotherhood: "On the arrival of any of the sect from elsewhere, all the resources of the community are put at their disposal, just as if they were their own; and they enter the houses of men whom they have never seen before as though they were their most intimate friends. Consequently they carry nothing whatever with them on their journeys, except arms as a protection against brigands. In every community there is one of the order expressly appointed to attend to visiting members from other communities, who provides them with raiment and other necessities" (War II.viii.4).[2]

Josephus writes that the Essenes "entirely addict themselves to husbandry" (Antiq. XVIII.i.5). Philo's more detailed statement somewhat qualifies this: "Some of them labor on the land skilled in sowing and planting, some as herdsmen taking charge of every kind of cattle and some superintend the swarms of bees. Others work at the handicrafts . . . and shrink from no innocent way of getting a livelihood. Each branch when it has received the wages of these different occupations gives it to one person who has been appointed as treasurer. He takes it and at once buys what is necessary and provides food in abundance and anything else which human life requires" (*Hypothetica* 11.8-10).[3]

Josephus refers to these communal treasurers as "stewards" and records that they were "good men and priests" (Antiq. XVIII.i.5; cf. 1QS 6.19-20).

Philo continues his account: "Thus having each day a common life and a common table [cf. 1QS 6.2-3] they are content with the same conditions, lovers of frugality who shun expensive luxury as a disease of both body and soul. And not only is their table in common but their clothing also. For in winter they have a stock of closely woven woolen cloaks ready and in summer inexpensive vests, so that he who wishes may easily take any garment he likes, since what one has is held to belong to all and conversely what all have one has. Again if any one is sick he is nursed at the common expense and tended with care and thoughtfulness by all. The old men too, even if they are childless, are treated as parents of a not merely numerous but very filial family and regularly close their lives with an exceedingly prosperous and comfortable old age; so many are those who give them precedence and honor as their due and minister to them as a duty voluntarily and deliberately accepted rather than enforced by nature" (*Hypothetica* 11.11-13; cf. *Every Good Man* 12.86-87).[3] Josephus writes in a similar vein: "There is no buying or selling among themselves, but each gives what he has to any in need and receives from him in exchange something useful to himself; they are, moreover, freely permitted to take anything from any of their brothers without making any return" (War II.viii.4; cf. *Every Good Man* 12.79).[2]

[1] Reprinted by permission of the publishers and The Loeb Classical Library from Loeb Classical Library Volume: Philo *Every Good Man Is Free* (Cambridge, Mass.: Harvard University Press, 1941).
[2] Reprinted by permission of the publishers and The Loeb Classical Library from Loeb Classical Library Volume: Josephus *Jewish Wars* (Cambridge, Mass.: Harvard University Press, 1927, 1956).
[3] Reprinted by permission of the publishers and The Loeb Classical Library from Loeb Classical Library Volume: Philo *Hypothetica* (Cambridge, Mass.: Harvard University Press, 1941).

Every Essene was subject to the authority of his superiors, and his daily life was almost entirely governed by orders from above. Only two things were left to individual discretion, assistance to one in need and compassion. "Members may on their own initiative help the deserving, when in need, and supply food to the destitute; but presents to relatives are prohibited, without leave from the stewards" (Jos. War II.viii.6).[2]

b. Marriage. Philo writes that the Essenes eschew marriage "because they clearly discern it to be the sole or the principal danger to the maintenance of the communal life, as well as because they particularly practice continence" (*Hypothetica* 11.14).[3] Essene celibacy, however, as we know from the Dead Sea Scrolls, was a vocational celibacy (cf. 1QM 7.5-7). Each Essene was a volunteer for the Lord and subject to the disciplinary demands of the holy-war legislation of the Torah. A very strict interpretation of the regulations for the army of Israel made it advisable for long-term enlistees to avoid marriage (cf. Deut. 23:9-14). After copulation with his wife, an Israelite was unclean until evening (Lev. 15:18). During his period of uncleanness he could not enter the camp of Israel, because unless the camp were free from impurity at all times, the angelic hosts upon whom victory depended would not remain. Because the Essenes believed they were the true Israel (the Children of Light encamped ready for the advent of the final war against Belial and the Children of Darkness), they practiced a kind of eschatological holy-war continence. As the decades passed, this eschatological continence seems to have changed into a kind of vocational celibacy with possible ascetic overtones. Certainly the wilderness headquarters near the Dead Sea was not conducive to marriage and family life. This probably explains why relatively few female skeletons were found in the Essene cemetery at Qumran.

Josephus admits that the Essenes did not condemn marriage on principle, though in practice they avoided it. These nonmarrying Essenes "adopt other men's children, while yet pliable and docile, and regard them as their kin and mold them in accordance with their own principles" (War II.viii.2).[2] At another place he writes: "There is yet another order of Essenes, which, while at one with the rest in its mode of life, customs, and regulations, differs from them in its views on marriage. They think that those who decline to marry cut off the chief function of life, the propagation of the race, and, what is more, that, were all to adopt the same view, the whole race would very quickly die out. They give their wives, however, a three-years' probation, and only marry them after they have by three periods of purification given proof of fecundity. They have no intercourse with them during pregnancy, thus showing that their motive in marrying is not self-indulgence but the procreation of children. In the bath the women wear a dress, the men, a loincloth" (War II.viii.13).[2] This is definite proof that not all Essenes were celibate, and that those in the first century who were declining to marry were being criticized by Essenes who apparently believed that some more realistic adjustment to the circumstances consequent to the delay of the holy war was necessary.

There can be no doubt that Essene practice should be interpreted against the background of the holy-war legislation in the Torah. E.g., each initiant upon admission was presented with a small mattock which he always carried about with him and with which he obediently dug a trench when he went outside the camp to relieve himself, and with which he afterward replaced the excavated soil (Jos. War. II.viii.7, 9). This mattock and this precise practice are prescribed for the Israelite warrior in Deut. 23:12-13.

c. Admission requirements. It was not easy to become an Essene. Josephus writes: "A candidate anxious to join their sect is not immediately admitted. For one year, during which he remains outside the fraternity, they prescribe for him their own rule of life, presenting him with a small mattock, the loincloth already mentioned, and white raiment. Having given proof of his temperance during this probationary period, he is brought into closer touch with the rule and is allowed to share the purer kind of holy water, but is not yet received into the meetings of the community. For after this exhibition of endurance, his character is tested for two years more, and only then, if found worthy, is he enrolled in the society. But before he may touch the common food, he is made to swear tremendous oaths: first of all that he will practice piety toward God, next that he will observe justice toward men; that he will wrong none whether of his own will or under another's orders; that he will forever keep faith with all men, especially with the powers that be, since no ruler attains office save by the will of God; that should he himself bear rule, he will never abuse his authority nor, either in dress or by other outward marks of superiority, outshine his subjects; to be forever a lover of truth and to expose liars; to keep his hands from stealing and his soul pure from unholy gain; to conceal nothing from the members of the sect and to report none of their secrets to others, even though tortured to death. He swears, moreover, to transmit their rules exactly as he himself received them; to abstain from robbery; and in like manner carefully to preserve the books of the sect and the names of the angels. Such are the oaths by which they secure their proselytes" (War II.viii.7; cf. 1QS 6.14-23).[2]

d. Discipline. The discipline of the Essene community was very strict. Josephus continues his account: "Those who are convicted of serious crimes they expel from the order; and the ejected individual often comes to a most miserable end. For, being bound by their oaths and usages, he is not at liberty to partake of other men's food, and so falls to eating grass and wastes away and dies of starvation. This has led them in compassion to receive many back in the last stage of exhaustion, deeming that torments which have brought them to the verge of death are sufficient penalty for their misdoings. They are just and scrupulously careful in their trial of cases, never passing sentence in a court of less than a hundred members; the decision thus reached is irrevocable. After God they hold most in awe the name of their lawgiver [probably Moses, but possibly their founder, known in the scrolls as the Teacher of Righteousness], any blasphemer of whom is punished with death. It is a point of honor with them to obey their elders, and a majority; for instance, if ten sit together, one will not speak if the nine desire silence. They are careful not to spit into the midst of the company or to the right, and are stricter than all Jews in abstaining from work on the seventh day; for not only do they prepare food on the day before, to avoid kindling a fire on that one, but they do not venture to remove any vessel or even to retire to ease themselves. . . . They are divided, according to the duration of their discipline, into four grades; and so far are the junior members inferior to the seniors, that a senior if but touched by a junior, must take a bath, as after contact with one outside the community" (War II.viii.8-10; cf. 1QS, col. 6, l. 24; col. 7, l. 25).[2]

e. The temple. The Essenes participated in the Jerusalem temple cult worship by sending what they had dedicated to God "into the temple." But the special conditions of purity which they observed were so strict that they could not themselves enter the "common court of the temple." Thus it was necessary for them to offer sacrifices within the purity of their own community, which otherwise they would have offered in the Jerusalem temple (Jos. Antiq. XVIII.i.5). Bones of sheep and goats which had been carefully buried in bowls were uncovered by archaeologists within the Essene community headquarters near the Dead Sea. The scrolls indicate that the Qumran community considered itself a "holy of holies" (1QS 8.13–9.11). Thus archaeological and literary evidence suggests that the Essenes did continue to observe certain sacrificial rites, even though they did not do so in the Jerusalem temple. The eschatology of the sect indicates that its members looked forward to a day when the temple in Jerusalem would be wrested from the hands of wicked priests and restored to their own community of righteous priests. The Essenes seem to have observed their festivals according to a different calendar from that in use in Jerusalem.

f. Daily worship. There are indications that Josephus may have thought that the Essenes engaged in sun worship (War II.viii.5, 9). If so, he was probably mistaken, since neither Philo nor Hippolytus makes reference to this extraordinary practice. Neither do the Dead Sea Scrolls support such a view. These scrolls do suggest that the time of sunrise was the occasion for special prayers for the community (1 QS 10.1, 10). In fact, fragments of a papyrus MS found in Cave IV contain set prayers for the sunrise services. From the Essenes' practice of praying daily at sunrise may have arisen the notion that they worshiped the sun. With this exception, the account which follows seems quite reliable: "Before the sun is up they utter no word on mundane matters, but offer to him certain prayers which have been handed down from their forefathers, as though entreating him to arise [it is possible that in Josephus' source the prayers offered were offered to God, and the entreaties were daily petitions for the coming of his kingdom]. They are then dismissed by their superiors to the various crafts in which they are severally proficient and strenuously employed until the fifth hour, when they again assemble in one place and, after girding their loins with linen cloths, bathe their bodies

[2] Reprinted by permission of the publishers and The Loeb Classical Library from Loeb Classical Library Volume: Josephus *Jewish Wars* (Cambridge, Mass.: Harvard University Press, 1927, 1956).

in cold water. After this purification, they assemble in a private apartment which none of the uninitiated is permitted to enter; pure now themselves, they repair to the refectory, as to some sacred shrine. When they have taken their seats in silence, the baker serves out the loaves to them in order, and the cook sets before each one plate with a single course. Before the meal begins, the priest says a grace, and none may partake until after the prayer. When breakfast is ended, he pronounces a further grace; thus at the beginning and at the close they do homage to God as the bountiful giver of life. Then laying aside their raiment, as holy vestments, they again betake themselves to their labors until evening. On their return they sup in like manner, and any guests who may have arrived sit down with them. No clamor or disturbance ever pollutes their dwelling; they speak in an orderly manner, each deferring to the other. To persons outside, the silence of those within appears like some awful mystery" (War II.viii.5).[2]

In the Essene community headquarters near the Dead Sea, archaeologists uncovered cisterns, some of which were appropriately designed to be used by the Essenes when they took their baths for purification. Also uncovered was a large room capable of seating two hundred persons. This room was adjoined by a smaller room in which were found over one thousand pieces of pottery, including plates and bowls, serving dishes, water decanters, wine flasks, and drinking cups. This building complex was presumably the refectory and its pantry which served the community as the sacred place where the Essenes at Qumran gathered to eat in silence and with thankful hearts. There are indications in the Dead Sea Scrolls that the priest blessed separately the bread and the wine and that at least some of the Essene meals had an eschatological reference and were held in anticipation of the messianic banquet (1QS 6.5-6, 20-21; 1QSa 2.11-22).

9. Study of scriptures. The Essenes gave great importance to the study of their sacred scriptures (Jos. War II.viii.6; 1QS 6.6-8). Though they studied their scriptures every day, Philo relates that they particularly devoted the sabbath to this activity. He writes: "For that day has been set apart to be kept holy and on it they abstain from all other work and proceed to sacred spots which they call synagogues. There, arranged in rows according to their ages, the younger below the elder, they sit decorously, as befits the occasion, with attentive ears. Then one selects one of the sacred rolls and reads aloud and another of especial proficiency comes forward and expounds what is not understood. For each roll is studied by them for the symbolic meaning of their emulated traditions" (*Every Good Man* 12.81-82).[1] This enigmatic statement by Philo about Essenes' studying their scriptures for symbolic meaning is clarified by the Dead Sea Scrolls. The Essenes believed that the promises of God foretold by the prophets were actually being fulfilled in the history of their own community. Therefore, they studied their scriptures to understand better what was happening to them and what would happen in the future. Josephus writes: "There are some among them who profess to foretell the future, being versed from their early years in holy books, various forms of purification and discourses of prophets; and seldom, if ever, do they err in their predictions" (War II.viii.12).[2]

There are a number of commentaries or *peshers* among Essene writings. In these *peshers* the author comments upon the text of a particular prophetic book, and interprets what is written to apply to his own time. A careful study of these Essene comments yields valuable, though often obscure, information on the history of the sect during the living memory of the author. For a complete list of the writings in the Essene library, *see* DEAD SEA SCROLLS.

Bibliography. For the nineteenth-century literature on the Essenes, see the essay on the Essenes in J. B. Lightfoot, *Dissertations on the Apostolic Age* (1892). For the best pre-Qumran study of the Essenes, see K. Kohler's article "Essenes" in the *Jewish Encyclopedia.* For an authoritative study of the Essenes in the light of the Dea Sea Scrolls, and for important literature on this subject, see F. M. Cross, Jr., *The Ancient Library of Qumran and Modern Biblical Studies* (1958). M. Smith, "Josephus and Hippolytus," *HUCA* (1958). L. Toombs's views on Bar Cocheba as an Essene are in "Barcosiba and Qumran," *NTS* (Oct., 1957), pp. 65-71. *See also* bibliography under DEAD SEA SCROLLS.

W. R. FARMER

ESTHER, BOOK OF ĕs'tər [אסתר; Akkad. *Ishtar* (*the Babylonian goddess*) *or* Pers. *stara,* star]. The OT book which tells the story of the deliverance of the Jews won by Esther under the Persians and gives the reason for the institution of Purim; a symbol of heroic resistance against persecution. In the book Esther has two names: (*a*) Esther, used when she is given her official Persian title as queen; (*b*) Hadassah (Hebrew "Myrtle"), which seems to be regarded as her Jewish name (Esth. 2:7).

Esther, a beautiful Jewish maiden living in Susa, capital of the Persian Empire, was selected for the king's harem, and so delighted King Ahasuerus (Xerxes) that he made her his queen. Then Haman, the prime minister, influenced the king to issue an edict authorizing the annihilation of all Jews in the Empire. In this emergency Esther was able to persuade Ahasuerus to proclaim a second edict reversing the situation, thus saving the lives of her people, and accomplishing the annihilation of their enemies. The rejoicing following this victory, the two days of feasting and gladness on the fourteenth and fifteenth of Adar, was then fixed by Queen Esther as an annual celebration, the festival of Purim (9:17-32).

1. Contents
2. Purpose
3. Historicity
4. Date
5. Place in the canon

Bibliography

1. Contents. The great Persian king Ahasuerus, angered by the disobedience of his queen Vashti, banished her from his presence. Among the beautiful maidens selected to fill her place was Esther, a Jewish girl, who so pleased Ahasuerus that she was made queen. Then Esther's cousin and former guardian, Mordecai, aroused the enmity of Haman, the newly appointed prime minister. Haman incited

[1] Reprinted by permission of the publishers and The Loeb Classical Library from Loeb Classical Library Volume: Philo *Every Good Man Is Free* (Cambridge, Mass.: Harvard University Press, 1941).
[2] Reprinted by permission of the publishers and The Loeb Classical Library from Loeb Classical Library Volume: Josephus *Jewish Wars* (Cambridge, Mass.: Harvard University Press, 1927, 1956).

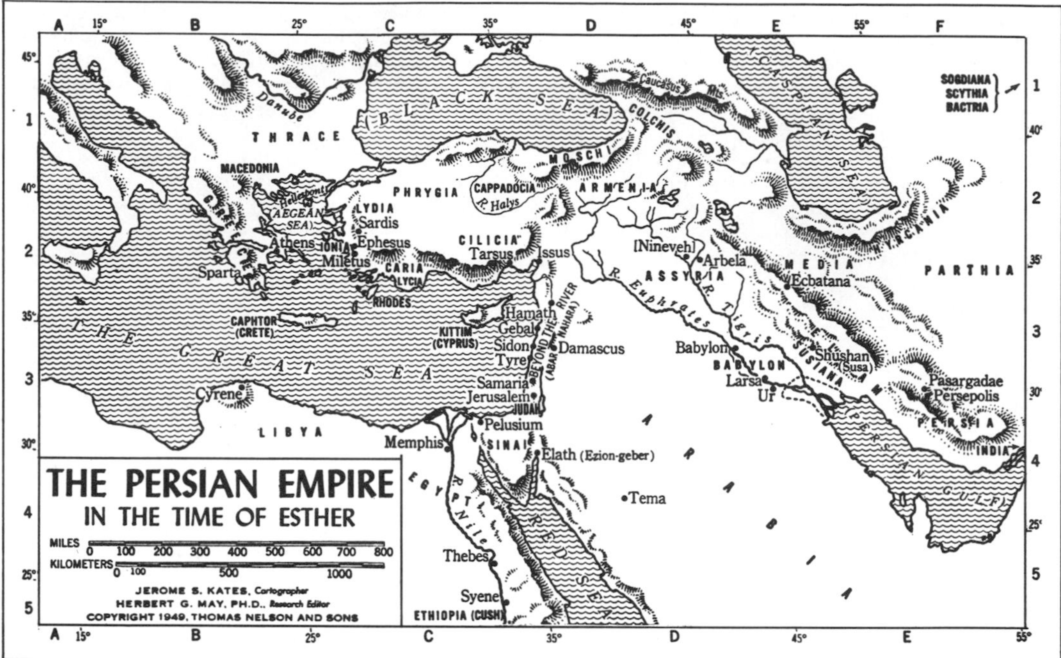

the king to authorize the destruction of all Jews in the Empire, on the pretext that their laws were "different from those of every other people" so that they did not "keep the king's laws" (3:8). When Mordecai heard of this, he informed Esther, urged her to appeal to the king, and overcame her hesitancy to risk her life by arousing the king's displeasure (4:14). Esther approached the king, told him that the edict would mean the destruction of her and her people, and persuaded him to issue a new edict permitting the Jews to take vengeance on their enemies. Haman was executed on the gallows he had prepared for Mordecai, the Jews annihilated their enemies, and Mordecai became the new prime minister. Then Mordecai and Esther instituted the annual celebration of Purim to commemorate those days when the Jews won deliverance from their enemies (9:17-32).

2. Purpose. The book of Esther is unique among the books of the Bible in the way it deals with religious issues. The underlying question of the book, the question of destruction or survival for Jews under persecution, is certainly a matter of religious concern. Awareness of divine purpose in securing this survival seems to be the basis for Mordecai's conviction that the Jews will be delivered even if Esther does not act (4:14; see also his challenging question to Esther in the same verse: "Who knows whether you have not come to the kingdom for such a time as this?"), and for the opportune sleeplessness of the king just at the time when it was necessary (6:1). Josephus, commenting on the fact that Haman suffered the death he had planned for Mordecai, says that he "cannot forbear to admire God, and to learn hence his wisdom and his justice" (Antiq. XI.vi.11). The book of Esther itself, however, seems deliberately to avoid specific references to God or to religious practice. God is not mentioned in the book, even when the sense seems to demand it, as when Mordecai suggests that deliverance for the Jews may arise "from another quarter" if not from Esther herself (4:14). Prayer does not accompany fasting in Esther's preparation for putting her request before the king (4:16). Victory seems to depend, not so much on loyalty to Judaism (cf. the book of Daniel), as on the use of political maneuver and appeal to self-interest. The spirit of vengeance is considerably more prominent than the spirit of devotion. It is going too far to say that Esther "has no religious content and can arouse no pious thoughts" (Schauss [*see bibliography*]), but certainly piety in its usual sense receives little emphasis in this book.

One consistent purpose of the book, however, is to explain the celebration of a traditional observance of Judaism, the festival of Purim (*see* PURIM for a discussion of the nature and origin of this festival). The omission of reference to God is understandable in a book intended to be read at a festival of merry-making, noise, and conviviality. The major theme of the book, persecution returning on the head of those who initiate it, leads through all the details of the story to the final victory which Purim celebrates. From the first mention of Haman's patiently casting "Pur, that is the lot," day after day until he could find a day propitious for attempting the destruction of the Jews (3:7-11), until the final hanging of Haman "on the gallows which he had prepared for Mordecai" (7:10), and the Jews' celebration of their days of rejoicing—i.e., the days called Purim (9:26)—the story seems to move inevitably toward the institution of the festival of deliverance. Purim is a festival, beloved in the Jewish tradition, which is not mentioned in the Law. To explain the historical reason for the observance of this festival is the important function of the book of Esther.

It is this function which gives unity to the book as a whole. One section of the book which many critics have regarded as a separate unit is 9:20–10:3. This section differs to some extent in style and language from the rest of the book, and presents certain discrepancies, such as the celebration of one or two days of festival (cf. 9:19; 9:20-22; see Paton, *Esther,* pp. 57-60). The differences in style, however, accompany a change in subject matter. The reference to "Pur" in 3:7 requires the concluding reference to Purim in 9:26. One purpose of the book may well be to reconcile actual diversity in the celebration of Purim in different localities (cf. the reference to one day in II Macc. 15:36, and to both days in Jos. Antiq. XI.vi.13, and in M. Meg. 1.1-2). In this case the variation in practice can probably explain the variation in the text of Esther. It is possible that the author may have used a separate source in 9:20–10:1, but in view of the consistent purpose of the book, to provide the historical background for the celebration of Purim, the variations do not seem significant enough to deny the unity.

3. Historicity. The external form of the book of Esther supports the claim to historicity. The author employs the customary formula for the beginning of an historical account (ויהי; cf. Joshua, Judges, Samuel), and ends with the typical reference to the complete chronicle (Esth. 10:2; cf. I Kings 14:19, 29; 15:23). His references to Persian customs show considerable accurate knowledge (the king's council in 1:14, regard for propitious days in 3:7, the way of honoring a hero in 6:8). It is now generally accepted that Ahasuerus (*'Aḥashwērôsh*) is the Hebrew rendering of the Persian *Khshayarsha,* a name more familiar in its Greek form, *Xerxes* (cf. Paton, *Esther,* p. 53). More recently cuneiform evidence has been found to show that there was a Persian official named *Mardukâ* (Mordecai) in Susa at the end of the reign of Darius I or the beginning of the reign of Xerxes (cf. A. Ungnad, *ZAW,* LVIII [1940-41], 240-44; LIX [1942-43], 219). *See* XERXES 1. Fig. AHA 5.

Other details in the book of Esther are not supported by historical evidence, however. Xerxes' queen was neither Vashti nor Esther, but Amestris. Many of the details are improbable. If Mordecai was among those who went into exile in 597 B.C. (2:6), he must have been at least 122 years old when he became prime minister in the twelfth year of Xerxes (474), and he would have had as his cousin a beautiful maiden, presumably *ca.* 100 years younger than he was (2:7). The edict of Xerxes permitting the Jews to kill 75,000 of his subjects (9:16) seems unlikely. Other elements seem to have literary, rather than historical, justification. The repeated delay of Esther in telling the king her request provides the occasion for the pride, and then the fall, of Haman. The banquet lasting 180 days (1:4), the twelve-month beauty treatment (2:12), the gallows eighty-three feet tall (7:9), the complete reversal of the fortunes of Haman and Mordecai—the number of elements of this nature gives a strong impression of fiction to the story. Some of the main themes—the heroine who saves her people by her beauty, the Jew who becomes the trusted official of a great king, or the king who tries a new maiden each night—appear in other writings also (cf. Judith, Daniel, *The Arabian Nights*). Whether the author invented a wholly fictional account together with the festival of Purim which it purports to explain, whether he was putting in Jewish form a Babylonian festival which originated in mythical adventures of the divine cousins Marduk and Ishtar, or whether he based his romance on some incident involving the historical Xerxes and *Mardukâ* (cf. Anderson, *IB,* vol. III, pp. 826-27), is difficult to tell. In any case, it seems probable that the book of Esther is primarily romance, not history.

4. Date. The book of Esther may be dated in the late Persian or Greek period, and probably the latter. The language suggests the Hellenistic period. Ben Sirach, writing *ca.* 180 B.C., does not mention Esther or Mordecai in his list of the heroes of Israel (Ecclus. 44–50). The earliest witness to the existence of the book of Esther is probably the LXX translation (at the end of the second century B.C.?). Then II Macc. 15:36, dating probably from the first century B.C., makes reference to "Mordecai's day." The dispersion of the Jews is taken for granted in the book (3:8), as is the practice of conversion to Judaism (9:27). The book reflects a period of great bitterness against Gentiles, directed more toward concern with political than with religious survival. The reign of John Hyrcanus—i.e., *ca.* 125 B.C.—at the height of the political ambitions of the Hasmoneans, makes a probable setting for the book.

5. Place in the canon. Esther is the last of the five *Meghilloth* or Scrolls, which are found in the *Kethubhim* or Writings, the third division of the Hebrew canon. These five scrolls, the Song of Songs, Ruth, Lamentations, Ecclesiastes, and Esther, are read on special occasions during the year. Esther is the reading appointed for Purim.

Both Jews and Christians were slow to admit Esther to the canon. The early Jewish comments on the text show their concern to make the religious aspect of the book more apparent. They add references to God's purpose, and prayers by Mordecai and Esther (see the Additions to the Book of Esther, now included in the Apoc., or First Targum on Esth. 3:4; 4:2). The delay of Esther in 5:4 is attributed by the Second Targum to her desire to remove hatred from the heart of Haman, and change the hearts of the Jews.

For later Judaism, Esther has become the symbol of deliverance, while Haman represents the force of cruelty and prejudice from which Jews have suffered throughout their history. The downfall of Haman, brought about by his futile attempt to annihilate the Jews, is a triumphant reminder of the continuing life of Israel in the face of persecution. The vindictiveness of the book is certainly one element in it, but the power of the book as a symbol of hope in a history of suffering is equally clear.

Bibliography. L. B. Paton, *The Book of Esther,* ICC (1916); H. Schauss, *The Jewish Festivals* (1938), pp. 237-64; S. Goldman, "Esther," in A. Cohen, ed., *The Five Megilloth* (1946); I. Bettan, *The Five Scrolls* (1950), pp. 195-247; B. W. Anderson, Introduction and Exegesis of Esther, *IB,* III (1954), 823-74.

D. HARVEY

ESTHER (APOCRYPHAL). Six passages, consisting of 105 verses not found in the Hebrew text of the book of Esther but interspersed through the Greek translation in the LXX; gathered together as a separate book, the Additions to the Book of Esther, in the Apoc. This expanded edition of the canonical book was probably prepared *ca.* 100 B.C. by an Egyptian Jew who injected a religious note into this popular story and heightened its anti-Gentile character.

1. The Additions. Besides minor textual variants, the enlarged edition includes the following narratives: Addition A (11:2–12:6), the dream of Mordecai; Addition B (13:1-7), the edict of Artaxerxes against the Jews; Addition C (13:8–14:19), prayers of Mordecai and Esther; Addition D (15:1-16), Esther's appearance before the king; Addition E (16:1-24), decree of Artaxerxes in behalf of the Jews; Addition F (10:4–11:1), the interpretation of Mordecai's dream. These additions may be reintegrated with the canonical text thus: A, preceding 1:1; B, after 3:13; C and D, after 4:17; E, after 8:12; F, after 10:3.

Jerome first removed them from their context because he did not find them in the Hebrew text which he translated, and grouped them in an appendix to Esther in the order of F, A, B, C, D, E, attaching explanatory notes to each passage. In the course of transmission these notes were omitted, resulting in the traditional printing of these passages numbered from 10:4–16:24 in an incoherent sequence which purports to be a unified book. The RSV text is designed to assist the reader to reconstruct easily the original LXX form.

2. Relationship to canonical Esther. The popularity of the story of Esther and its quasi-canonical status is attested by a number of widely different recensions in addition to the MT translated in English versions of the OT. Besides the Greek text, which is known in five variant forms, two Aramaic targums and a number of homiletic commentaries on Esther survive. Although there is a considerable division of critical opinion on the authenticity of the Additions and the relation of the Greek to the Hebrew text, it may be said that most scholars believe that Greek Esther represents a second- or first-century B.C. translation from the Hebrew with the Additions composed in Greek by the translator for an Alexandrian Jewish audience. Roman Catholic scholars generally accept the priority of the Greek form of the tale as representing the original Hebrew or Aramaic story, from which the canonical Hebrew text was later abridged. A few Protestant scholars maintain that the original Aramaic story is best represented by the Greek versions, excluding only Additions A and F. Subsequently A and F were added to the story. According to the colophon in 11:1 of the LXX, a certain Lysimachus, who was "one of the residents of Jerusalem," translated the Semitic text in 114-113 B.C., at which time B and E may have been added.

A number of contradictions between the Greek and Hebrew texts have been noted—e.g., Haman is called a Macedonian in 16:10, 14 (cf. Esth. 3:1); the date fixed for the massacre of the Jews is the fourteenth of Adar rather than the thirteenth (13:6; 10:13; cf. Esth. 3:13; but also Add. Esth. 16:20).

3. Character. It is generally recognized that the canonical book of Esther is distinguished from other OT literature in its absence of reference to the God of Israel and to Jewish religious rites and practices. The Additions, however, are marked by a frank expression of prayer and devotion. If the prayers of Addition C are original, then the canonical book may represent a deliberate expunging of sacred references, perhaps to permit the story a more secular use at the Festival of Purim. But the spirit of prayer is sadly defaced by the assertion of a dark hostility between Gentiles and Jews (10:10; 13:4-5); indeed, it has been conjectured that the book may have been prepared as an anti-Gentile tract. Like the Wisdom of Solomon, it reflects the widespread anti-Semitism of the time, which found its counterpart in Jewish polemic against all heathen religions and in renewed devotion to the ancestral faith.

Bibliography. L. Ginzberg, *Legends of the Jews,* IV (1913), 365-448, for the story of Esther based on all known texts; J. A. F. Gregg in R. H. Charles, *Apoc. and Pseudep. of the OT* (1913), I, 665-71; C. C. Torrey, "The Older Book of Esther," *HTR,* XXXVII (1944), 1-40; R. H. Pfeiffer, *History of NT Times* (1949), pp. 304-12; B. M. Metzger, *An Introduction to the Apoc.* (1957), pp. 55-63. E. W. Saunders

ETAM ē'təm [עֵיטָם, place of birds of prey(?)]. **1.** A village in Simeon (I Chr. 4:32; it should probably be supplied before Ain-rimmon in Josh. 15:32, in the Negeb district of Beer-sheba; cf. also Josh. 19:7). The site is unknown.

2. A city of Judah in the hill-country district of Bethlehem (Josh. 15:59*a* LXX, which at this point adds a list of eleven cities of a district centered around Bethlehem, including Tekoa, Peor, Etam, Kerem, and others; cf. also I Chr. 4:3). Etam is probably to be identified with Khirbet el-Khokh, *ca.* two miles SW of Bethlehem, near Artas. To the W it overlooks 'Ain 'Atan, a spring supplementing 'Ain Salih, the chief source for the three Hellenistic-

Courtesy of Herbert G. May

36. One of Solomon's pools near Etam

Roman reservoirs now called the "pools of Solomon,"* and the S terminus for the aqueduct mentioned below. Fig. ETA 36.

After the secession of the N kingdom, Rehoboam fortified Etam (II Chr. 11:6), probably to secure his position in the S kingdom (cf. vss. 12 ff) as well as to serve as further protection against assault, possibly from the SE.

Josephus (Antiq. VIII.vii.3) describes Etan (Etam) as a favorite rural retreat of Solomon, who enjoyed taking the eight-mile journey from Jerusalem early in the morning in his chariot.

According to Josephus, Pontius Pilate used sacred funds (*qorban*) to build a great aqueduct two hundred stadia long (*ca.* twenty-three miles; Antiq. XVIII.iii.2; cf. War II.ix.4, where the length is said to be four hundred stadia). An earlier aqueduct, possibly built by Herod the Great to serve the Herodium leading from 'Ain 'Atan, was incorporated in Pilate's project.

Several passages in the Talmud note that the temple received water from an aqueduct leading from the spring of Etam, said to be *ca.* a hundred feet higher than the ground level of the temple. Today Bethlehem receives water by a pipe line from 'Ain 'Atan.

Bibliography. H.-J. Kraus, "Chirbet el-chōch," *ZDPV,* 72 (1956), 152-62. V. R. Gold

ETAM, ROCK OF [סלע עיטם] (Judg. 15:8, 11). A cave to which Samson resorted after burning the Philistines' crops, and from which the citizens of Judah took him to be handed over to the enraged Philistines. It is possibly to be identified with 'Araq Isma'in, 2½ miles E-SE of Zorah. The platform at the mouth of the cave affords an excellent view of the hills of the Shephelah. V. R. Gold

ETERNAL LIFE. *See* Life; Immortality.

ETERNITY. Endless span of time; dominion over time (as an attribute of God). *See* Time.

ETHAM ē'thəm [אתם]. The first stopping place of the Israelites after they left Succoth. Both Exod. 13:20; Num. 33:6-8 locate it "on the edge of the wilderness." The name is also given to a part of the Wilderness of Shur (Num. 33:8). Presumably the site was an Egyptian fortress on the E border of Egypt. It was probably located N of Lake Timsah at the edge of the Wadi Tumilat, by which Israel hoped to escape into the wilderness. Finding their way blocked by border fortifications, they were forced to turn back and camp in front of Pi-hahiroth between Migdol and the sea, in front of Baal-zephon.

See also Exodus, Route of. J. L. Mihelic

ETHAN ē'thən [איתן, long-lived, *given to a child as a good omen; cf. the adjective* איתן, permanent, ever-flowing]. The OT references to Ethan seem to point to four different people. Most of the pertinent material is so obscure or confusing as to produce legitimate questions about this listing. Several different lists have been proposed, ranging from one Ethan to four. Although no single reconstruction is without difficulties, several factors might justify identifying Ethan 1 in the following list with Ethan 2; Ethan 3 with the Joah (2) of I Chr. 6:21—H 6:6; and Ethan 4 with the Jeduthun (1) of I Chr. 16:41; 25:1-2; II Chr. 5:12; 35:15.

1. A son of Zerah, Judah's son by Tamar; the father of Azariah (I Chr. 2:6, 8).

2. A noted wise man called "the Ezrahite" (האזרחי), earlier than, though possibly contemporary with, Solomon (I Kings 4:31—H 5:11; cf. Ps. 89 title—H 89:1).

3. A Gershomite ancestor of Asaph (I Chr. 6:42—H 6:27).

4. A Merarite, son of Kish (I Chr. 6:44—H 6:29; 15:17, 19).

Bibliography. M. Noth, *Die israelitischen Personennamen* (1928), p. 224. L. Hicks

ETHANIM ĕth'ə nĭm [אתנים, ever-flowing streams]. The pre-exilic name for the seventh Hebrew month (September-October), of Canaanite origin. It was so called because during this month only permanent streams still contained water, this being the end of the dry season. Later this month was called Tishri. *See* Calendar. S. J. De Vries

ETHANUS ĭ thā'nəs [Vulg. *Echanus*] (II Esd. 14:24); KJV ECANUS ĭ kā'nəs. A scribe listed as one of five who were "trained to write rapidly."

J. C. Swaim

ETHBAAL ĕth'bāl [אתבעל, with him is Baal, *or* man of Baal; Ιθώβαλος (Jos. Antiq. VIII.xiii.1)]. King of the Sidonians whose daughter Jezebel married Ahab of Israel (I Kings 16:31). A priest of Astarte, he gained the throne by murdering the last of the descendants of Hiram I (Jos. Apion I.xviii). He continued the commercial expansion of the Phoenicians, founding the colony of Auza in Lybia (Jos. Antiq. VIII.xiii.2). The erection of a stele to the Tyrian deity Melcart by Ben-hadad shows that Ethbaal had made an alliance with Damascus as well as Israel. The purpose of these alliances was doubtless to protect Phoenician trade with the hinterland and to ensure against landward attacks. A year-long drought occurred during his reign (Jos. Antiq. VIII.xiii.2; cf. I Kings 17).

Bibliography. J. B. Pritchard, ed., *ANET* (2nd ed., 1955), p. 501. R. W. Corney

ETHER ē'thər [עתר, perfume(?)]. **1.** A village of Judah in the Shephelah in the Libnah-Mareshah district (Josh. 15:42); probably to be identified with Khirbet el-'Ater, *ca.* a mile NW of Eleutheropolis (Beit Jibrin).

2. A village in Simeon (Josh. 19:7; probably to be supplied after Ain-rimmon in 15:32). The parallel list in I Chr. 4:32 reads "Tochen"; "Athach" in I Sam. 30:30 is possibly also a faulty reading for "Ether" (cf. LXX B for Josh. 15:42: Ιτακ). The site is probably Khirbet 'Attir, *ca.* fifteen miles NE of Beer-sheba. V. R. Gold

ETHICS IN THE OT. The ethics of the OT is based, not on a philosophical or theoretical system, but on the traditions of both Israel and Canaan, on the sociological necessities of the people, and on the personal religious experiences of the leaders of the congregation.

- A. The roots of OT ethics
  1. The traditions
     - *a.* The seminomad cattle-breeders
     - *b.* The peasants
     - *c.* The city dwellers
  2. The sociology of Israel
     - *a.* The tribes
     - *b.* The decline of collectivism
     - *c.* The decline of objectivism
  3. Personal experiences
     - *a.* The sages and the prophets
     - *b.* Job and Ecclesiastes
     - *c.* The Yahwistic writer of the Pentateuch
- B. The Yahwistic character of OT ethics
  1. The covenant
     - *a.* The historical character of OT ethics
     - *b.* The religious basis of OT sexual ethics

c. The limitations of OT ethics
2. "You shall be holy, for I am holy"
a. Yahweh's selection of Israel, and his mercy
b. Yahweh's might
c. Yahweh's representatives
Bibliography

A. *THE ROOTS OF OT ETHICS.* **1. The traditions.** The traditions of Israel were not those of the camel-riding nomads in the desert who, in the first century after the occupation of Canaan, were the enemies plundering the harvest and the herds (Judg. 6:3; 7:12). The camel, which was for Israel an unclean animal (Num. 11:4; Deut. 14:7), was never the main basis of their wealth. But it may be that the strong sense of liberty and democracy which characterizes the political attitude of Israel before and during the monarchy was influenced by some reminiscences from the free life in the desert.

a. The seminomad cattle-breeders. The main trend of Israelite tradition derives from the cattle-breeding seminomads who lived on the borders of the cultivated land. They depended on the possibility of watering their flocks in due time and having grass for them during the whole year. For this they were obliged to conclude treaties between their own groups and with the owners of the cultivated grounds concerning the springs and wells or the allowance of gleanings after the ingathering and in the years of fallow. The sacredness of covenants (ברית) was essential for their life, including the covenant with their God, who might increase or stop the fertility of their animals, retain or give rain, multiply or diminish the wild beasts or the serpents, and protect the people from demons or human enemies who were frequently swifter and better armed. After the invasion of Canaan they preserved the feeling that they had not got it by their own strength (Deut. 6:10; 8:11 ff) but that they had depended on their mighty God in the past and depended on him in the present time and in the future. In contrast to the peasant, the cattle-breeder was for them the man whom Yahweh liked (Gen. 4:3-5), and some groups among them tried to retain these inherited forms of life even in Palestine until the sixth century B.C. (Jer. 35). The social differences among them were small, the dangers of life being nearly the same for every member of a group. Compared with the peasant, they were poor; compared with the Bedouins, generally peaceful—e.g., Abraham (cf. Gen. 13:8), with exception in Gen. 14. Since they were obliged to stay together, their ethics had to be an ethics of brotherhood and of dependence upon a God who protected faithfully (e.g., Exod. 34:6) the poor (e.g., Ps. 118:6 ff) and asked faithfulness toward himself and among the members of his covenant (e.g., Hos. 4:1). They might sacrifice the first-born animal of their flocks, and the question arose early if there was a possibility of saving the life of the first-born son (Exod. 13:15; 34:20) and of the first-born of the most important animal in their wanderings, the ass (Exod. 13:13; 34:20). They did not need holy places for their cult but might sacrifice anywhere they liked and wherever their God wandering with them ordered (Exod. 20:24).

b. The peasants. The attitude of the peasant was quite another one. He stayed on the ground he had inherited from his fathers, who had freed the field from stones, planted the fruitful trees, built the house, and dug the well or the cistern. They were buried in the neighborhood or even under the house. As their heir he had the right and the duty to defend his substance against all who wanted to detract from it, even against his own king who offered a good exchange (I Kings 21:2-3). The connection with the fathers—in the later formulations of the law understood as the commandment of Yahweh, who gave the estate to them—had to be preserved, even when it was sold for economic reasons. In every fiftieth year, the "Jubilee" (*see* JUBILEE, YEAR OF), the ground in the open country (not in the walled cities!) went back to the family of its former owner (Lev. 25:8 ff). The peasant's life, of course, was endangered by lack of rain, by locusts, and by human enemies, but not in the same degree as that of the seminomads. From time immemorial his field was under the protection of its Baal, who secured its fertility (cf. Hos. 2:15), and the peasant did well to give him his tribute from the crops and to honor him and his Astarte by the ancient rites, including the "holy wedding" in the High Place. The tradition in which the Israelite peasant lived was to a high degree formed by pre-Israelite customs. The peasant was a traditionalist who wanted to deliver his ancestors' heritage to his son by teaching him to do as his fathers had done (Exod. 13:14 ff).

c. The city dwellers. The third group is the city dweller in the former Canaanite cities occupied by the Israelites mostly under David (Jerusalem [II Sam. 5:6 ff]) and Solomon (e.g., Gezer [I Kings 9:16-17]), built (Samaria [I Kings 16:24]) or rebuilt (e.g., Jericho [I Kings 16:34]) by them. The Canaanite population became amalgamated with the Israelite overlords, and these themselves incorporated in the economic and social system of city life. As centers of handicraft, of primitive industries, and of international commerce (I Kings 20:34), the towns were centers of higher artistic culture in the temples, the kings' strongholds (cf. I Kings 22:39), and the houses of the wealthier people (cf. Amos 3:15; 6:4). They were too the intermediaries with the literature and the thinking ("wisdom") of foreign countries. As every "capitalist," the city dweller loaned money to the poorer—e.g., the peasant in a year without rain—or to widows and orphans in actual need, and asked for a pledge consisting, in the case of the poorest, of their garment (Exod. 22:25-26), their children (Exod. 21:7), or their personal freedom (Deut. 15:12 ff). The use of such financial superiority without pity was in perpetual conflict with the Israelite ethics of COVENANT and under the curse of the covenant God (e.g., Isa. 5:8 ff; Mic. 2:1 ff), the rich becoming the godless and the poor the godly. So the ethical traditions in the OT are not uniform or homogeneous but derive from different sources according to the manifold national and social groups forming the "Israelite" people.

2. The sociology of Israel. ***a. The tribes.*** The influence of the sociology of Israel upon the ethics of the OT went even deeper as the social structure of the whole life of the people underwent essential changes. At the beginning there was the confederation of tribes united by the veneration of Yahweh as their common God. His ordinances were destined primarily to preserve peace in their midst by securing life, wife, possession, and honor of every member (Exod. 20:13-16), especially of father and mother (Exod. 21:15-17), against bad words, bad acts, and even all covetousness (Exod. 20:17). After the occupation of Canaan these leading principles of the "moral" decalogue (*see* TEN COMMANDMENTS) and the Book of the Covenant (Exod. 20–23) were adapted to the new necessities. They tried to protect the house (Exod. 20:17) and the field's frontier (Deut. 19:14; 27:17), to lower the hardships of an economic system based on slave labor—especially for a male or female "Hebrew" slave (Exod. 21:1 ff)—and to avoid abuses of pledges (Exod. 22:24 ff). But this social system proved unsatisfactory in the Philistine crisis which obliged Israel to install a KING in the interest of national self-preservation. Now some political duties arose: the loyalty to Yahweh's anointed (I Sam. 24:7; II Sam. 1:14), the payment of taxes, and the acknowledgment of some rights limiting the personal freedom and the power of the family's head over his children (I Sam. 8:11 ff). But the influence of the kings on the ethics remained so restrained that only one rule is said to have been instituted by David (I Sam. 30:24). The Israelite ethics did not become a political one, for the monarchy was only an episode in Israel's history, and the division into two states after only two generations lowered the influence of the kings. The Persian authorities, when reconstituting the congregation by Artaxerxes' order, did so on the basis of the older law of the God of heavens who dwells in Jerusalem (Ezra 7:12 ff) and did not ask, in the political field, for more than the prayer for the king (Ezra 6:10). The sociological form of Israel's life was from the fifth century again the congregation, but now its members were no more tribes but single men.

b. The decline of collectivism. This was, indeed, the deepest change in the ethical, as in the religious, field: the decline of collectivism. Of course, there had been a certain individualism in Israel before II Kings 14:6; Deut. 24:16; Ezek. 18. There were early personal responsibilities—e.g., the Levirate marriage to be contracted by the surviving brother under specialized regulations (Gen. 38:8). The formulation of the *lex talionis* in Exod. 21:23 may be ambiguous, "you" being either (as clearly in Lev. 24:19) the offender or his social group who may be hurt in any of its members, but in Exod. 21:28 ff the lord of the ox is alone responsible and is alone to be punished. But the main ethical subject in the older times was, without question, the collective unit—the wider FAMILY embracing all generations of common blood living together (cf. even Ps. 133:1), later the matriarchal or (since David only) the patriarchal family embracing parents and their children, the tribe, the congregation, the nation. The "you" of the Decalogue is clearly "Israel," to whom Yahweh gave the Promised Land. The unit as ethical subject had to put out of its midst all transgressors of the fundamental statutes (e.g., Deut. 13:6) or to punish the minor "sinners" according to the rules given by custom or by law. The unit had to search for any guilt among its members, by testimonies of witnesses or by oracle, and to watch over equal right for the rich and for the poor (Exod. 23:1 ff) without partiality and bribes (Deut. 1:17; 16: 19). The responsibility for the unit lay with its representatives—the father, the elders, the kings, and the priests—in the double sense that the unit was punished for their sins (II Sam. 24:15) and that they themselves had to bear the transgressions of their unit (cf. Isa. 53:5). Besides this the guilt of any member of the unit might be the cause of a catastrophe for the whole group (cf. Josh. 7:11). The responsibility thus put on every action brought forth the great earnestness of OT ethics.

This collectivism soon was felt to be an injustice. It was thought to be better that ten righteous save the wicked town than that they perish with it (Gen. 18:32). As such individualistic criticism was older in the higher cultures of Egypt and Mesopotamia than the existence of Israel, the decline of collectivism was stronger in a milieu with early foreign influences, especially in the WISDOM literature. The wise men taught a personal ethical attitude, among younger people, in the sexual life, in behavior toward older men in higher social position, and in a prudent respect before God. So long as the unit was the ethical subject, every misfortune was explicable by the sin of the fathers (Exod. 20:5) or an unknown member to be discovered by lot or by other methods of inquiry (Josh. 7:14; I Sam. 14:40 ff). The individualistic outlook, with its personal responsibility, led to the ethical crisis we see in the life of Jeremiah (cf. 15:15 ff; 20:7 ff), in Ps. 73, in Job and Ecclesiastes accusing God of injustice in his deeds. "Justice" meant now: to give to the individual life or death according to his personal attitude. But in spite of all declarations of Ezekiel, the fate of every member was so interwoven with the life and death of his unit that a separation according to his righteousness or wickedness remained a dogmatic dream in this world. Only faith in a compensation in the world to come (cf. Dan. 12:2-3) might hinder the development of an ethical skepticism, which was inevitably connected with an individualistic outlook combining good deeds and good life, piety and fortune.

c. The decline of objectivism. This decline of collectivism went hand in hand with the decline of an objectivism for which "sin" might exist without knowledge and intention of the acting person. For an old but long-surviving attitude, to be "guilty" did not depend on the will to violate a commandment. The Babylonian surgeon was punished severely when his patient died (Code of Hammurabi § 215), and an Assyrian adulterer even when he did not know that the woman with whom he had had intercourse was married (Assyrian Law § 22). This is exactly the case in the Yahwistic writer's version of Pharaoh and Sarah's situation, and Gen. 12:18 shows clearly his criticism of the tradition he had to tell. The same criticism is highly enforced by the Elohistic version in Gen. 20:1 ff, and is to be seen in some regulations starting already with the Book of the Covenant (*see* COVENANT, BOOK OF THE). The owner of a goring ox that killed a man was free from guilt if he had not been told that this beast was accustomed to gore (Exod. 21:28-29). In the same way, a man who struck another without having lain in wait for him might flee to an asylum ordered by God (Exod. 21:13). For the other old oriental laws too, objectivism declined, and guilt became connected only with will and knowledge. This development influenced deeply the ethical consciousness: to be a sinner was no more a question of fate but of man's decision.

3. Personal experiences. ***a. The sages and the prophets.*** In the different groups among the people the right ethical attitude was taught by different men: in the family by the father (and the mother), in the cultic organization by the priest (*see* PRIESTS AND LEVITES) or the cultic prophet who gave advice about the sacrifices and the conditions for the admission to the holy place. In the tribe the elders had the same duty, and in the congregation of the tribes the "Speaker" (נשיא), who proclaimed in the great assembly of the seventh year the duties toward God and fellow men. The sages taught the sons of the wealthier families and received as compensation a certain amount. They taught what they had learned from their predecessors (Job 8:8 ff), and their authority was based on the conformity of their sayings with experiences had and to be had again in practical life with the king, the great or the poor, the good or the bad wife (Prov. 16:10 ff; 19:6 ff; 23:29 ff). They believed that the rules according to which Yahweh rewarded deeds were to be seen in the realities of life, that they might be taught, and that in this way the fear of him was the beginning of knowledge (Prov. 1:8). It was considered better to learn what the sages had experienced in the civil and the religious field (Eccl. 7:5; 9:17-18), and in their optimism they thought that everybody who learned the right way would be able to do what he was taught (cf. Deut. 30:15 ff).

But there was another group of "teachers" who were in connection with the tradition but depended to a much higher degree on their own experiences—the prophets (*see* PROPHET). They shared the tradition that Yahweh was the only God of the covenant, demanding brotherhood, punishing his people for all transgressions (Amos 3:2). In the soul of the prophet Yahweh's demands for pity upon the poor, his warnings against all luxury (e.g., Amos 6:1 ff) and the abuse of wealth (cf. Amos 2:6 ff), were so overwhelming that the cult became worthless in their eyes (e.g., Isa. 1:10 ff; Amos 5:21 ff) and the greatest sacrifices (e.g., Mic. 6:6 ff) an offense to the God of justice and mercy. They heard Yahweh's words proclaiming his own faithfulness and the nation's faithlessness with such tremendous power that they were convinced: his holiness obliged him now to make an end. As messenger of God the prophet had to announce in his own words the terrible things he had heard, and this obedience against his own desires was the prophet's ethics. The single demands he had to proclaim were not original. The protection of widows and orphans belonged, like care for the needy, to the deeds of the true king in the Egyptian or the Mesopotamian ideology, as well as of the Ugaritic Danel. That "God" preferred righteousness to sacrifice was recognized long before I Sam. 15:22 by an old Egyptian sage. Original is the strength with which social justice and brotherhood was confessed to be the central, and sometimes even the only, demand of Yahweh; the preponderant, and sometimes even the exclusive, characteristic of ethics in his will. Such earnestness destroyed all optimistic outlook in Jeremiah's experiences (13:23). For him and for Ezekiel the right ethical attitude was not made possible by teaching, but only by a miracle of their God in changing the heart of stone into a heart of flesh and giving his spirit of obedience and good will (Jer. 31:33-34; 36:26 ff).

b. Job and Ecclesiastes. In spite of the fact that the sages were generally more bound to tradition, there were among them men whose belief in the truth of what they had learned was corroborated—or, on the contrary, destroyed—by personal experiences. Both types are to be found in the book of Job (*see* JOB, BOOK OF). The common dogma of the just reward of men's deeds by God is reinforced for Elihu by a personal revelation (Job 4:16 ff), but the sage speaking through Job himself has learned by his sufferings that this teaching is wrong—again, dogmatic dream. There is no interdependence of fate and justice (e.g., 9:19-23). Only a personal vision of God's majesty and the greatness of his creative power is able, not to solve the intellectual problem, but to teach the sufferer that he has no right at all to question God's actions. Such a critical attitude also has its precursors in the oriental literature starting with the so-called "Sumerian Job." But what we find in the biblical book of Job does not depend on the reading of such texts or the hearing about them. This crisis comes with inner necessity in an ethical attitude which tries to calculate and is pious not "for nought" (Job 1:9).

Similar things are to be said of ECCLESIASTES. Here too we are in the presence of personal experiences (e.g., 1:12 ff; 2:1 ff, 12-16, 20 ff) which destroyed the traditional outlook so completely that the only ethical counsel to be given in this world of "vanity of vanities" is the use of the occasions to rejoice which God gives and to fear him—i.e., not to provoke his punishments. This skepticism has its parallels in the Greek philosophical literature but its roots in the personal thinking of a sage poet who felt with sorrow the differences between dogma and life.

c. The Yahwistic writer of the Pentateuch. Such personal experiences of life's injustice made by a sage even in the beginning of Israelite wisdom are reflected as early as in the work of the Yahwistic writer (J) in the Pentateuch. He does not criticize the collectivism of God's punishments in its totality. In the beginnings of men's history the disobedience of the first couple was the reason for all sufferings, including death of the whole of mankind. Such dogma may be preached where no momentary practical question is to be answered. But when in the wars between Israel and their neighbors cities were destroyed with all the cruelties of that time (cf. I Sam. 11:2; 27:9), doubts arose about the justice of the results of such warfare methods. Such doubts are living already in Tablet XI of the Gilgamesh Epic, whose content is surely much older than the only preserved Ninevite Text: The Deluge, says Ea, was "unreasoning," because it did not impose the consequences of sin (only) to the sinners (*ANET* 95). Far be it from God to slay the righteous with the wicked (Gen. 18:25; cf. Job 9:22; Eccl. 8:14). "History," as he had experienced it and feared that he would have to experience it again, became for J a problem whose riddle was not to be solved by human thinking. The attitude of Pharaoh during the Egyptian plagues was understandable only by the fact that Yahweh hardened his heart (Exod. 7:3). His justice thus becomes a formal one: he punishes sins whose ultimate cause he is himself (cf. Ezek. 20:25-26; Rom. 1:24 ff). In spite of such riddles man has to believe in God's promises. Confidence in Yahweh's words, beginning with the promise given to Abraham, and obedience toward his demands even when they are not understandable, is the only right ethical attitude for the Israelite pious. Its model is the Yahwistic (and later the Elohistic) picture of Abraham himself leaving his country (and sacrificing his son), the contrary the lack of faith in Yahweh's guidance through Moses shown by the generation in the wilderness.

B. *THE YAHWISTIC CHARACTER OF OT ETHICS.* 1. The covenant. *a. The historical character of OT ethics.* In view of pre-Israelite traditions and extra-Israelite influences upon the ethics of the OT, the fact has to be underlined that they underwent very deep changes, not only by the development of the nation's life and culture but to an even higher degree by the deciding force of the faith in Yahweh the God of the COVENANT. This alliance is considered after the model of the suzerainty treaties of the ancient Near East which were contracted between a mightier king (e.g., the Hittite Great King) and his vassals. The former ordained the conditions under which his partners might live in peace and friendship with him. The mightier was free to make or not to make the covenant, but if he made it, he too was bound to fulfil what he promised. The obligations of both sides might greatly differ, but the sanctity of the covenant was the same for them under the guarantee of the gods. By establishing the covenant Yahweh limited his own freedom, and he did so in complete liberty without any preceding obligation or rational motive. His love for Israel and the fathers (cf., e.g., Deut. 4:36; 7:8) was as inexplicable as every true love in the world. This covenant was for the Israelite faith a historical fact connected in all traditions with Moses and the liberation from Egyptian bondage, and its stipulations contained from the beginning religious and ethical norms. Consequently, the OT ethics took on a strong "historical" character, at least so far as it was governed by the prescriptions of the law. The sages (*see* § A3*a above*) might give rational warnings against visiting a harlot, drunkenness, or friendship with a gossip (Prov. 5: 3 ff; 20:1; 29:20). The Law (*see* LAW IN THE OT) gives its orders in Yahweh's name without any reasoning why he demands such or such an attitude. It is probable that in a prehistoric time some hygienic experiences had provoked CIRCUMCISION or the prohibition of pork, which is not easily digestible under high temperatures. Cases of illness for such reasons may have been—as all such experiences—interpreted as signs of anger of a god or a demon. In the OT we find no trace at all of reflections of this kind. The reason, known perhaps a millennium or more before Abraham and Moses, had been completely forgotten. Yahweh stipulated as conditions of his covenant what he liked. For this the cultic and the ethical commandments were, for the law, on the same level of importance. The Decalogue forbids the making of images and labor on the sabbath with the same earnestness as murder, adultery, and theft. In the "apodictic" utterances of the Book of the Covenant the strikes and curses against father and mother and the boiling of a kid in his mother's milk (Exod. 21: 15, 17; 23:19) are both sins against the God of the covenant. Where reasons are given for a statute, they are not rational but historical. Why is the male firstling of the cattle to be set apart to the Lord? Because Yahweh slew the first-born in the land of Egypt (Exod. 13:14)! Why is it forbidden to make an IMAGE of Yahweh? Because Israel heard the sound of his words out of the midst of the fire but saw no form on that day (Deut. 4:12, 15). Why shall a manservant and a maidservant rest on the SABBATH? There are two explanations, both historical: because of God's rest on the seventh day (Exod. 20:11) or because Israel was a slave himself in Egypt (Deut. 5: 15). When through the incorporation of Canaanite sanctuaries into the Israelite cult their prescriptions became adapted to it, they too were considered as given by Yahweh in the legislation on Sinai or in the land of Moab. They were observed "because they are ordered and belong to all works of the Most-High" (Ecclus. 33:7; 35:7 ff).

Behind all sayings of Yahweh there is the same authority of his tremendous power, shown first of all in the liberation from Egypt, and of his anger, shown in his punishing the people in the wilderness. From this authority the two main motives of Israel's ethics gained their historical and not at all dogmatic reason: to fear and to love him. The God of the covenant had the right to bless or to curse his people according to their deeds, because the tradition knew that Israel had accepted the stipulations of the covenant (Exod. 19:8; 24:3; Josh. 24:21 ff) voluntarily and had been instructed about its risk, and there was no other god able to protect the nation against Yahweh's wrath. Of course, human nature misled Israel frequently to misunderstand such a covenant with the mighty God to be an unconditioned guarantee, to consider Yahweh's self-binding as an absolute obligation for him to help in any case, to forget what was told about the fiery serpents or the plague of Shittim (Num. 21:6; 25:1). Corroborating such elements in the writings of J and E in the Pentateuch, the Deuteronomists stylized the whole history of Israel from Egypt until the catastrophe of 587 as history of sin, and preached Yahweh's vengeance against all unfaithfulness. This earnestness of Yahweh's demands for deeds was based on what they had to tell about his deeds, and the people's confidence in his truth had its basis in the experiences of his grace in the past. The tension between fear and love in the Israelite ethics, as in Israelite piety, the irrationalism of the law, and the great earnestness with which obedience and faith were asked for have the same root: the historical character of the covenant. Consequently, the prophetic polemics against the cult's endangering the right ethical attitude by its "heathenish" methods and rites had to be historical: Yahweh did not speak to the fathers concerning burnt offerings and sacrifices (Jer. 7:22; cf. Amos 5:25). What is said to men is not a list of offerings, but to do justice and to love kindness and to walk humbly with God (Mic. 6:8).

b. The religious basis of OT sexual ethics. This influence of the covenant ideology was not only a formal one but also decided, to a certain degree, the contents of the Israelite ethics. First of all, the fact has to be taken into account that there is only *one* God of the covenant. Other nations might have other gods and goddesses—the question at what time the last theoretical consequences were drawn of Israel's "monotheism" is not to be solved here—but the congregation that had entered into the covenant had to worship no other god and to trust in no help of any other "divine" being (departed spirit, demon). This uniqueness was reinforced by Yahweh's jealousy. He wanted his uniqueness to be recognized by facts and deeds and not by theories. No other god should partake of his glory. Not to adore other gods or an image even of Yahweh himself meant to exclude from his service, e.g., the manners and rites connected in the religions of the ancient Near East with the sexual differentiation of the pantheon: the imitation of the "holy wedding" between gods and goddesses in the form of the so-called holy prostitution in the sanctuaries. No sacred harlot (קדשה, "a holy one") should be in Israel (Deut. 23:17). There existed in Israel, as even in Christian countries of the present age, harlots (זונות) who seduced the youngsters (Prov. 7:10 ff), but to have intercourse with them was a secular (and bad), not a sacred, act. The priests were forbidden to marry one of them (Lev. 21:14), and what they earned should not be brought to the temple in payment of any vow (Deut. 23:18). Every father had the duty of preventing his daughter's going that way, to avoid bad example (Lev. 19:29). A priest's daughter or a widow committing harlotry was to be killed (Gen. 38:24; Lev. 21:9), as an adulterous couple (Lev. 20:10).

By these ordinances much license in the sexual field was prohibited (at least in theory) and the whole matter of love brought into close connection with Yahweh and his will. This fact is of high importance for OT ethics, because the regulations of betrothal and marriage in the old oriental civil laws, including those of the Israelites, had been primarily dominated by economic and financial, not by ethical, reasons. The bride price (מהר) was to be paid to the father of the girl either in labor (Gen. 29:18, 27), in money, or in other goods (Exod. 22:16). A boy who would try to avoid such duty by seducing a girl and so lowering her value risked having to pay the מהר without getting her. Later, he had to deliver to the father fifty shekels—i.e., five times the valuation for a girl of the same age in the case of a special vow of persons (Lev. 27:3) and nearly twice the price of a slave (Exod. 21:32), and he lost the right of divorce (Deut. 22:29). Intercourse with a betrothed girl who was already in the possession of her future husband was equal to adultery and consequently punished by the death of both, except when the girl cried for help (Deut. 22:22 ff).

But these economic regulations were combined with another system, for which sexuality was primarily under a taboo which nobody could break without the most serious consequences. To offend the rules of the taboo meant to commit something evil and to work folly (נבלה; cf. I Sam. 25:25). Who did so became himself unclean, and his impurity infected the community in which he lived and which tolerated him as its member. In Israel this system was incorporated in the Yahwistic law. It was Yahweh's command that the sexual sinner was to be purged from the midst of Israel (Deut. 22:21) exactly as, e.g., the seducer to the service of foreign gods (Deut. 13:9; 17:7), the false witness, or a man's abductor (Deut. 19:19; 24:7). It was Yahweh who regulated the מהר. For him a harlot's hire or the marriage of a man with his own divorced wife who had belonged in the meantime to another husband was an abomination (תעבה; cf. Deut. 23:17; 24:4) which defiled the land. So adultery became a great sin and wickedness against God, a despite of Yahweh's word, and evil in his sight (II Sam. 12:9). Even to look upon a virgin (Job 31:1) was forbidden for a man who wanted to be just. Of course, in Israel, as everywhere in the world, young lovers did not ask too much about what was allowed, as the Song of Solomon shows. They had their pleasures where they might find them. If the theory that the Song of Solomon was originally a sacred play showing the holy wedding of Tammuz and Ishtar is right, this book would testify to the importance of the fact that these rites were forbidden in Israel. But the regulation of the sexual life within the covenant with Yahweh did not mean asceticism. All irregularities such as homosexuality or intercourse with an animal or with certain members of the family were an abomination for Yahweh (Lev. 20:11-17), but not the regular use of the vital forces. In the beginning he ordered the man and his wife to be fruitful and multiply, and this command was a part of his first blessing (Gen. 1:28). The joy of the bridegroom leaving his chamber is a poetical image of the rising sun (Ps. 19:5). Children were Yahweh's gift (Ps. 127:3), and a son born in his father's old age was a real source of pride for him (Gen. 44:20). It was Yahweh's promise to multiply Abraham's descendants as the stars of heaven and as the sand on the seashore (Gen. 22:17). To be childless was a hard fate and a severe punishment for a wife, and she asked her god to take it away from her (I Sam. 1:10 ff). To cause a miscarriage, even unwillingly, was an act to be fined (Exod. 21:22 ff). While there was no monastic ideal in Israel before the Essenes, the OT ethics in the sexual field was dominated, not by an asceticism which would go against the Creator's intentions, but by a feeling of shame (Gen. 3:2) which detested all behavior opposite to the monastic ideal (Deut. 25:11-12) and had very strong anti-Canaanite roots. The fear of nakedness, especially in the cult (Exod. 20:26; cf. 28:42; 39:28), may have had its origin in the prehistoric belief in the god dwelling in the stone, but the combination of this fear with the first disobedience in Gen. 3:7, 10, shows a deeper feeling. It is in the strictest contrast with the representations of the old oriental goddess (e.g., the Syrian Qadesh in Egyptian reliefs) in her complete nakedness, frequently with exaggerated demonstration of her sexuality. *See* SEX.

c. The limitations of OT ethics. The covenant ideology was, finally, the reason for some limitations within OT ethics. A deep gorge existed between the duties toward a member of the covenant's congregation, including the sojourners who were in a legal contract with an Israelite family or tribe (as a "ger"), and all members of a foreign nation. Even the prohibition to bear false witness is limited in some commands by the words "against your neighbor" (Exod. 20:16), not taken in a local sense but designating the member of a smaller or larger community to which both belong. Jeremiah did not hesitate to tell a lie to save the king's life (Jer. 38:25-27), and the storytellers accepted the legend that Yahweh counseled Samuel to feign a sacrifice in order to hide the conspiracy with David before Saul (I Sam. 16:2), or in the story of Elisha's provoking Hazael to give a wrong oracle to Ben-hadad (II Kings 8:10). Good deeds, even of a foreigner, might constitute a community within which a lie should not be told (Gen. 12:16 ff; 20:9). Hospitality protected the foreigner from all danger, but the killing of the king of the enemies might nevertheless be celebrated (Judg. 5: 24 ff).

How a foreigner could become a SOJOURNER is not mentioned in the OT. There was a great variety of political or economic reasons which would oblige a man to leave his homeland and go to worship foreign gods—e.g., Ruth's following her husband's mother (Ruth 1:16; cf. I Sam. 26:19). Once recognized as a sojourner, he was to be protected by all tribes forming the covenant, even against the tribe whose guest he was (Judg. 20:3 ff); this regulation favored the Levites living without their own tribal inheritance as sojourners in the midst of the other tribes.

The sojourner had to observe some ethical, as well as cultic, laws—e.g., the laws regulating sexual behavior (Lev. 18:26). He was forbidden to work on the sabbath (Exod. 20:10; Deut. 5:14), to curse Yahweh (Lev. 24:16), to worship Molech (Lev. 20: 2), or to sacrifice in the wrong place (Lev. 17:8 ff). He was under the *jus talionis* (Lev. 24:22), as he benefited by the asylum, the water for impurity, and the offerings for error (Num. 15:26; 19:10 ff; 35:15). Generally he was among the poor, always facing the risk of being obliged to sell himself (Lev. 25:45), and for this he was admitted to the poor's privileges: the daily payment of his hire, the tithe of the third year, the gleanings and the fallen grapes especially in the seventh year (Lev. 19:9-10; 25:6; Deut. 24:14; 14:28; cf. Deut. 24:19). Yahweh liked these sojourners and did not want Israel to forget that they themselves had been sojourners in Egypt (e.g., Exod. 22:21; Deut. 10:17 ff). But this love of Yahweh for them did not involve the possibility of changing the economic status. When a sojourner became rich and was able to lend to an Israelite, such a situation was considered as Yahweh's curse against Israel (Deut. 28:43).

That the treatment of the sojourners was primarily based, not on a humanitarian feeling, but on their legal status as partial partakers in the covenant is seen by the fact that toward all other foreigners there was no humanitarian feeling at all. The cruelties of David against the Geshurites, the Girzites, and the Amalekites are reported without any pity or criticism (I Sam. 27:8), which is lacking too in the ordinances to destroy utterly all nations dwelling in Palestine, from the Hittites to the Jebusites (Deut. 20:17). Such regulation is reported to have been executed in the cases of Jericho (with the exception of Rahab's family [Josh. 6:23 ff]) and Ai (Josh. 8:25), but not in the cases of Jerusalem (cf. Ezek. 16:3) and Gibeon (Josh. 9:3). The cruelties of old oriental warfare were excused in later times by the covenant ideology. Foreign nations dwelling in the midst of Israel could become a danger for the exclusiveness of Yahweh's worship (Deut. 20:19). Economic reasons were in opposition to such fervor. It was better that the inhabitants of a foreign town do forced labor for Israel, the women together with the children and the cattle be taken as booty, alive or fruitful trees give their fruits to the Israelite conqueror instead of being killed or cut (Deut. 20:10 ff), but all these milder regulations were limited to the cities far away and not endangering the covenant. In the same way the "humanitarian" interdiction of being a hard creditor or of taking interest was limited to "any of my people" (Exod. 22:25). It was permissible to loan upon interest to a foreigner (Deut. 23:19 ff) who too did not benefit from the release in the seventh year like a slave bought from a foreign country (Deut. 15:3; Lev. 25:6). And the lawgiver knew that even within the covenant there was much hardness of human heart, giving to humanitarian regulations the opposite effect. The POOR from whom one was forbidden to take interest might be unable to get money or victuals he needed in an actual famine; but the Deuteronomist fights against such base considerations by the utopian promise that there shall be no poor in the land and by the fear that Yahweh will listen when the poor cries to him (Deut. 15:4, 9, 11).

2. "You shall be holy, for I am holy." ***a. Yahweh's selection of Israel, and his mercy.*** Yahweh himself acted in a different way toward Israel and toward the foreign nations. He selected Israel to be his people—or, according to a tradition nearly forgotten in the actual text of the OT, the Most High gave him Israel as his people (Deut. 32:8-9)—and this selection included duties not only for Israel but also for Yahweh himself. He had to protect it from enemies, from famine, lack of rain, locusts, earthquake, and all other dangers connected with Palestinian life. His care for Israel included too the obligation to give them a cult and a ritual by which to cleanse them from all physical and spiritual impurity, to teach them the right way leading to life and blessing (Deut. 30:19). The old oriental gods were believed to be at the same time terrible and friendly, givers of death and sustainers of life, punishing and forgiving sins. The only question was which moment was stronger in every one of them, as the dispute between Ea and En-lil, who produced the great flood in the Gilgamesh Epic, shows for the Babylonian religion. Yahweh was among the terrifying when he appeared accompanied by pestilence and plague (Hab. 3:5), and Israel's sins might oblige him to bring all his terrors over them. The imagery of his curses, especially in Deut. 28, shows a perversion of feeling exceeding the terrors in the curses in the abovementioned treaties between old oriental states. But when Israel observed his statutes, it would enjoy all his goodness. In the old oriental picture of the ideal god and the ideal king, their goodness included their care for widows, orphans, and the poor whose protector the king had to be. He was not allowed to take the vineyard he liked by killing the possessor (I Kings 21:1 ff). Yahweh treated his people as the "poor." He refrained from using his kingly, terrifying power against Israel. In the same manner he desired that in the midst of his people the rich, the mighty, and first of all the king refrain from using their economic or political power against their poorer brethren and even against slaves. The slave (*see* SLAVERY) too, if he was an Israelite or belonged to the privileged class of the Habiru, was free from working on the sabbath and was to be released at the end of the seventh year if he liked and he had to be provided with some food for the first days of his liberty (Exod. 20:10; 21:1 ff; Deut. 15:12 ff), in remembrance that Israel had been a slave in Egypt (Exod. 20:2). To rule over one of his brethren with harshness was forbidden for every Israelite (Lev. 25:46). The old feeling for liberty and democracy, which may have been inherited from the sojourn in the desert, was integrated into the religious faith in Yahweh's mercy for his people and its members.

To be holy meant for God not to be overwhelmed by his anger like a man's losing self-control (Hos. 11:8-9). And it was the duty of every Israelite to be holy like him—compassionate and merciful. This "humanitarian" feeling toward the members of the covenant did not include Yahweh's general humanization. His anger against his and his people's enemies remained as terrible as ever until the latest testimonies in the OT—e.g., the picture of the glorious one coming from Edom in crimsoned garments (Isa. 63:1) or of the undying worm in the last verse of the book of Isaiah (66:24). In the same way none of Yahweh's enemies had to be pitied or spared, even by his own father or mother (Deut. 13:8). The covenant with Yahweh prevailed over the family! Antagonism against the breakers of the covenant limited the "humanism" both of Yahweh and of the Israelites. Loving God was combined with the commandment to love one's NEIGHBOR, but the neighbor was limited by the "sons of your own people" in the same verse, Lev. 19:18. It was only against the neighbor in this sense that the Israelites were not to have any hate or desire for vengeance. The injunction alluded to in Matt. 5:43 ("You shall . . . hate your enemy") is not to be found in the OT and reflects its spirit only when understood of the enemy, not in the private, but in the public sphere, the enemy being the member of a community outside the covenant, a community with which there was no "peace." In private life the commandment of Lev. 19:17-18 is interpreted by the wisdom literature as including giving aid to the enemy when he was hungry or thirsty, and Yahweh would reward the Israelite who did so (Prov. 25:21-22)—Paul does not cite this promise when he combines Lev. 19:18 with Deut. 32:35 in Rom. 12:19.

b. Yahweh's might. Within the covenant the ethics of the OT was governed by faith in the power of Yahweh in the creation of the world and no less in the history of Israel, as well by help as by punishments. This power was greater than any human faculty. Before Yahweh all men were nothing, fading flowers when his breath blew upon them (Isa. 40:7). There was no exception for anyone—not for the great king of the world empire nor for the prophet who remained always man and never became a deified being. To recognize the difference between God and man, never to forget the distance existing between them, is the main point in OT ethics. Man shall be like God in his life's conduct according to God's love and truth within the covenant. But he is not allowed to become like God in the sphere of power and knowledge. Both belong together. Yahweh had power because of his knowledge of all that existed, of the good deeds and thoughts as well as of the bad ones. Without knowledge, power is blind and justice impossible, and without power knowledge is useless. By the Spirit of Yahweh the Messiah would have them both (Isa. 11:2). Because the "knowledge of good and evil" embraces the creative power producing life (*see* GOOD), this was the first temptation: to want to be like God exactly by knowing good and evil, to "know" by sexual intercourse (Gen. 3:5). What is for the priestly writer Yahweh's greatest blessing for men he created in his image, is for the Yahwist obtained by disobedience and for this reason under the curse: to be fruitful, and by this not to "die" but to survive in offspring. The desire to "live" is attested by the whole old oriental literature. But to try to live against God's commandment and the limitations set by him is the first and greatest sin destroying the possibilities of "life." Man has the right to be proud—God made him little less than himself (Ps. 8:5)—but he has to acknowledge precisely this "little less" by word and deed. This is what Job has to learn by the speeches of God in the storm, through the majestic questions about the origin of cosmic phenomena. And this is the background of the prohibition to produce images. Whoever fabricates an image is its lord, since he has the right even of destroying it. The artist would have a magic power even over the god whose figure he made, and for this the feeling of the distance between Yahweh and all men hindered the development of any religious art and, on account of the primary importance of religion in all ancient art, the development of any art. It became an ethical duty not to be an artist. Even in the expression that man is fashioned in the image of God, the same feeling of distance is at work. It testifies at the same time to the democratic feeling of Israel—man and not the king, as in Assyria, is god's image!—and to God's superiority. Man is his work and not his son, nor does he partake of God's *physis* as in Babylonian speculations telling that Marduk gave his blood to create the first man. The magical power the artist possesses over his work was transformed into God's ethical power to command, which had as its counterpart the ethical duty for men to fulfil these commandments. The sphere of interrelation between Yahweh and men was the ethical sphere, both for him and for men. God's ethics was the self-control of his truth, man's ethics not to abuse this self-control but to refrain from all overestimation of his position to be God's image and partner of his covenant.

c. Yahweh's representatives. The same is true of Yahweh's representatives—the king, the priest, and the prophet. The king, limited in relations with his people by the covenant made with the eldest, was his god's servant who was obliged to obey. Saul was rejected for the sparing of Agag in spite of the regulations of the ban (I Sam. 15:18 ff), and Nathan announced to David the punishment for Uriah's murder (II Sam. 12:1 ff). The law of Deuteronomy obliges the king to read daily in this book that he may learn to fear Yahweh, to live without luxury, many wives, or horses (Deut. 17:16 ff). The king to come was to be humble and ride on an ass, not on a horse (Zech. 9:9). Aaron, the first and greatest of all priests, and even Moses, the greatest of all prophets, had to die, and they were not allowed to enter the Promised Land, because they did not obey the word of their God (Num. 20:24). Nobody knows Moses' tomb (Deut. 34:6)—thus Israel avoided making him the object of a cult. Isaiah had to be cleansed before his vocation by one of the seraphim (Isa. 6:6), and only a late legend tells of Jeremiah's living in the other world and praying for his people (II Macc. 15:14). In contrast to the poet, the prophet was not allowed to produce or to change or to suppress any word said to him. He had to obey without fear and without questioning:

> To all to whom I send you you shall go,
> and whatever I command you you shall speak (Jer. 1:7).

The prophet's ethics was none other than his people's religious ethics: to obey his God, believing that the God of the election and the covenant was the only God superior to all men, loving truly his people as he had loved the fathers, giving them laws by which they might live, and leading him the right way to an end he knew, an end which would be peace.

Bibliography. J. Hempel, *Das Ethos des Alten Testaments* (1938); G. E. Wright, *The OT Against Its Environment* (1950); F. Michaelis, *Dieu à l'image de l'homme* (1950); N. North, *Sociology of the Biblical Jubilee* (1954); G. E. Mendenhall, *Law and Covenant in Israel and the Ancient Near East* (1955); H. H. Rowley, *The Faith of Israel* (1956); P. van Imschoot, *Théologie de l'AT*, II (1956), 83 ff, 278 ff; T. C. Vriezen, *Theologie des Alten Testaments in Grundzügen* (1956), pp. 271 ff; E. Jacob, *Théologie de l'AT* (1957); G. von Rad, *Theologie des Alten Testaments*, I (1957).

J. HEMPEL

ETHICS IN NONCANONICAL JEWISH WRITINGS. Though the Mishna (the oldest stratum of the Talmud), as well as the writings of Philo and Josephus, could be included among the noncanonical Jewish writings, it is with the Apoc. and the Pseudep. that this article chiefly deals.

Biblical precedents and rabbinic parallels suggest themselves almost constantly throughout the noncanonical writings. Works such as Phocylides and Menander and large parts of Ecclesiasticus consist almost exclusively of ethical maxims and amount essentially to ethical codes.

A. *REWARDS AND PUNISHMENTS.* Except in Test. Asher 2:5-6, 8; 4:2-3, and possibly in Ecclus. 31:31, where dividing lines become blurred, these writings envisage a clear-cut distinction between right and wrong. Ethical precepts are regarded as emanating from on high, although exceptions do occur. This happens where human actions are viewed in the light of their natural consequences, as often in Ecclesiasticus and as in Aristeas 205-6.

> A pleasant voice multiplies friends,
> and a gracious tongue multiplies courtesies.
> (Ecclus. 6:5.)

> Do not shrink from visiting the sick,
> because for such deeds you will be loved.
> (Ecclus. 7:35.)

> The indolent may be compared to a filthy stone,
> and everyone hisses at his disgrace.
> (Ecclus. 22:1.)

Many are such passages which, while they deal with ethics, contemplate no supernatural intervention.

1. Otherworldly consequences. Except for some concern, now and then, about the prosperity of the wicked and the tribulations of the righteous (Syr. Apocal. Bar. 14:2-7; IV Esd. 1[or 3]:29-36), the noncanonical writings accept, without challenge, the doctrine of divine rewards and punishments. But these rewards and punishments are not limited to this world—either as it is (Apocal. Moses 8; Ecclus. 16:13; 21:9; 35:18-19; 39:29-30) or as it is to be "at the end of days" (Syr. Apocal. Bar. 30:4-5; 40:1-30; 51:1-6; Apocal. Elijah 21:1 ff). The noncanonical literature sees divine punishment in a world beyond. The entirety of the pseudepigraphic work known as the Vision of Esdras, in its depiction of specific punishments for specific sins, resembles the *Inferno* of Dante. Other writings that expatiate upon the penalties awaiting in the hereafter are the Apocalypses of Abraham, Baruch (64:8), Esdras, and Sophonias, and the Testament of Isaac (6:6). The

Apocalypse of Sophonias (II, 15:5, 8) perceives, in hell, bribers chained hand and foot and with their hands tied to their necks, and usurers wrapped in fiery mats. Abraham has a vision of the infernal punishments in store respectively for murder, unchastity, theft, and avarice (Apocal. Abraham 24:5-10). The rewards of the virtuous are corresponding, both "at the end of days" (Syr. Apocal. Bar. 51:3; II Esd. 2:24) and in the world beyond (Apocal. Esd. 1:12; Apocal. Shadrach 16:5; Ecclus. 34:13). At the predicted last judgment, according to Apocal. Elijah 41:2, the wicked will have to look upon the grace enjoyed by the righteous, while the righteous behold the torments of the damned.

2. "Manner for manner." The concept known in the Talmud as "manner for manner"—the manner of reward or punishment resembling that of the merit or the sin—is recurrent (II Esd. 2:23; II Enoch 50:5; 51:1; Test. Zeb. 6:6-7; 8:1; Tob. 4:11). "God does to you as you do to others" (Test. Zeb. 5:3). "Do not turn your face away from any poor man, and the face of God will not be turned away from you" (Tob. 4:7). Ecclus. 28:1 warns that one who seeks revenge will meet with divine revenge. Particularly does II Maccabees exploit this theme. Antiochus is seized with a "pain in his bowels for which there was no relief . . . and that very justly, for he had tortured the bowels of others with many and strange inflictions" (9:5-6). Not only Nicanor's head, but also his hand, is struck off, that hand which "had been boastfully stretched out against the holy house of the Almighty" (15:30, 32; cf. I Macc. 7:47). Menelaus was put to death at a tower filled with ashes; properly so, because of the sin which he had committed against the altar where the ashes are holy (13:8). When Vis. Esdras 40:41 sees in hell those who have misguided wayfarers, and notices how the eyes of these deceivers are beaten with thorny switches, we are again reminded of "manner for manner."

3. Retribution without responsibility. The noncanonical writings occasionally revert to the doctrine that Jer. 31:29; Ezek. 18:2 assail when they reject the maxim: "The fathers have eaten sour grapes, and the children's teeth are set on edge." IV Esd. 5(or 7):118 declares that, for the sin of Adam, punishment pursues all of Adam's descendants. Somewhat akin is the view in Syr. Apocal. Bar. 77:10 that, for the sin of Israel, devastation had come upon Israel's innocent soil. This detachment of retribution from responsibility creates, for some of the writers, a quandary. While Ecclus. 33:13, like the OT (Exod. 4:21; 7:3; 14:4, 8; Josh. 11:20; I Kings 12:15; Isa. 6:10), accepts the conclusion that people are punished for their sins even when divinely constrained to commit those sins, Apocal. Abraham 23:12-13; 26; 27 finds this bewildering. Not far removed is the thought in Apocal. Shadrach 5:5, which pleads for divine leniency toward sinful man on the ground that, like smoke, the devil enters the human heart and teaches every evil. Ecclesiasticus, while recognizing the problem, abdicates all attempts at explanation (15:11-12).

B. *MORAL EXCELLENCES*. 1. Kindness and sympathy. Among the qualities rated as admirable are kindness and graciousness. Test. Benj. dwells upon the desirability of kindness to rich and poor alike. Also among the virtues is courtesy, exemplars of which, according to Aristeas 122, were the translators of the Law, attentive in conversation as they were thorough at investigation. Allied with kindness and graciousness are sympathy and mercy (Ecclus. 16:12; 35:20; 40:17; 45:1; Add. Esth. 13:2; I Macc. 2:57; Test. Iss. 5:2; Test. Zeb. 5:3; Tob. 14:9). Ecclus. 7:34 urges:

> Do not fail those who weep,
> but mourn with those who mourn.

Similar is the thought in Test. Iss. 7:5. Aristeas 188 voices the persuasion that, if the punishment we inflict is less than deserved, we win people from their badness. In the Apocalypse of Sophonias (II, 17:1, 3), Abraham, Isaac, and Jacob, among the redeemed, supplicate God in behalf of the damned. Nor is there lack of encomium on love. Issachar professes to have loved every person as he did his own children (Test. Iss. 7:6).

2. Benevolence. All of this well comports with the emphasis laid, in many passages, upon benevolence. Sibylline Oracles admire, as a paragon, that race, the Jews, among whom the wealthy send portions of their harvest to the destitute (3:244). Giving to the poor should not be deferred (Ecclus. 4:3). It should be abundant, if one's means allow; it should not be omitted entirely even if one's means are scant (Tob. 4:8). A typical giver was Job, who, according to Test. Job (10:1-6), had farms the product of which was at the disposal of the needy. To supply his tables for the poor, Job assigned ten of his fifty ovens. Other paragons of benevolence were Issachar (Test. Iss. 7:5), Tobit (Tob. 1:13, 16-17; 2:2; 14:2), King Ptolemy (Aristeas 290), and Simon the Maccabee (I Macc. 14:14). Zebulon, of an earlier age, would compassionately share his catch of fish with every stranger (Test. Zeb. 6:4-5).

a. Rewards of benevolence. Almsgiving carries a deep religious import (Ecclus. 4:10; 17:22; 35:2; Tob. 4:11; 12:8). Aristeas holds that, when people of devout mind undertake something in behalf of benevolence, Almighty God directs their deeds and their decisions (18). Following the tendency to express commendation by predicting heavenly rewards, the rewards anticipated for benevolence are extraordinary. One of these rewards is escape from affliction (Ecclus. 29:12-13; 40:24; Tob. 4:9; 14:11). Another is preservation of one's wealth (Ecclus. 31:11). Another is remission of sins (Ecclus. 3:30; II Enoch 63:1-2; Tob. 12:9; Zadokite Fragment 18:3, 8). According to Ecclus. 17:22, a man's alms procure forgiveness even for his sons and daughters. Another reward is deliverance from death (Ecclus. 40:24; Tob. 4:10; 12:9). Then there are the rewards of the hereafter (Ecclus. 4:10; II Enoch 9:1; 50:5; 51:1; Tob. 14:10). Vision of Esdras finds the almsgiver untouched by the flames of hell (7:26). Promised likewise are spiritual rewards:

> You will then be like a son of the Most High,
> and he will love you more than does your mother
> (Ecclus. 4:10).

b. Forms of benevolence. Benevolence takes a variety of forms. One is that of providing the needy with food (Ahikar 8:15; II Enoch 9:1; 42:9; 63:1; Test. Iss. 7:5; Tob. 4:16). Another is that of furnishing clothes (II Enoch 9:1; 42:8 Version B; 63:1; II [or V]

Esd. 2:20; Vis. Esd. 7; Tob. 1:17). Zebulun, when he saw a poor person unclothed in winter, would secretly obtain a garment from his home and supply the lack (Test. Zeb. 7:1). Another form of benevolence consists in lending, even if repayment is uncertain (Ecclus. 29:1-3, 8-10, 16). Job is reputed to have had 3,500 excellent plow oxen available to anyone who needed them (Test. Job 10:1-6). Likewise figuring here are hospitality (Ethiopic Ahikar 8; Tob. 2:2; cf. Philo *Questions and Solutions on Genesis* IV.10); burial of the dead (II [or V] Esd. 2:20, 23; Tob. 1: 17-18; 2:3-4, 7; 12:13); visiting the sick (Arabic Ahikar 2:57; Ecclus. 7:35; Test. Zeb. 6:4-5); and speaking words of consolation (Ecclus. 7:34; IV Esd. 14:13; Test. Iss. 5:2).

c. Objects of benevolence. Singled out as objects of benevolence are widows and the fatherless (Bar. 6:38; Ecclus. 4:10; 14:10; 35:14; III Sibylline Oracles 242), the stranger (Zadokite Fragment 8:17), the homeless, the captive, the aged, the unmarried woman in need of a dowry (Zadokite Fragment 18:5), the broken, the weak, the blind (II Esd. 2:21). II Macc. 3:10 quotes the high priest as telling the obtrusive Heliodorus that there was money laid up in the temple "belonging to widows and orphans." Job is represented as having twelve tables reserved for widows and thirty for strangers (Test. Job 10:1-6). The poor, the widows, and the cripples are reported to have mourned Job's passing (Test. Job 56:1).

d. Spirit of benevolence. Of no little moment is the spirit in which the giving is to be done (Ecclus. 10: 23; 18:16-17; II Enoch 63:1-2).

> Incline your ear to the poor,
> and answer him politely and humbly.
> (Ecclus. 4:8.)

Similar thoughts arise in Ecclus. 35:9; Tob. 4:16-17; Test. Iss. 5:2. Test. Zeb. 7:4 reports that once, when Zebulun found nothing on the spur of the moment to give to a poor person, he, with lamentations of sympathy, accompanied the poor person for seven stadia.

e. Organization of benevolence. Zadokite Fragment 18:2-3 sketches a form of communal charity organization. Every month each person was to pay his income of two days to a certain public official who was to spend these funds for charitable aid. Tob. 1:8 mentions, with enthusiasm, the allocation of the third tithe ordained in Deut. 14:28.

3. Social justice. Related to benevolence is that type of concern for the underprivileged which we today call social justice (Ecclus. 4:9; 32:13; II Esd. 2:21; Aristeas 190; III Sibylline Oracles 234-47; Test. Iss. 5:2). Judith (9:11) prays: "Thou art God of the lowly, helper of the oppressed, upholder of the weak, protector of the forlorn, savior of those without hope." The widow, the fatherless, and the stranger are again singled out for special solicitude (Ecclus. 35: 14-15; II [or V] Esd. 2:20; II Enoch 42:9 Version B; 50:5; III Sibylline Oracles 242; Zadokite Fragment 8:13), likewise servants and slaves (Syr. Ahikar 3:2; 4:5; Ecclus. 7:20-21; 10:25; Jub. 50:7; Aristeas 20-22). "If you have a servant, let him be as yourself . . . . Treat him as a brother" (Ecclus. 33:30-31). The release of slaves and of captives is spoken of several times (Jth. 16:23; Aristeas 22, 24; I Macc. 10:33). Considerable is said about aiding the underprivileged in the law court (Ahikar 2:57; Ecclus. 4:9; II Enoch 2:20-21; Zadokite Fragment 16:3). Aristeas 188, 208, 290, favors clemency for law violators. The scruple about the prompt payment of wages is pronounced in a number of passages (Ecclus. 4:1; Aristeas 258; Test. Job 12:4; Tob. 4:14; 5:14-15; 12:1).

4. Wisdom. As in the wisdom literature of the OT, wisdom is also in the noncanonical writings the subject of boundless adoration. Encomiums on wisdom occupy long stretches (Ecclus. 14:20–15:8; 24:1–25:2; Wisd. Sol. 9), where wisdom is extolled in many a fine metaphor and turn of phrase. In Ecclus. 24:1–25:2, as in the biblical book of Proverbs, Wisdom personified proclaims her advantages. Wisd. Sol. 4:8-9 declares that old age is honorable only by virtue of the wisdom that attends it. Allied with wisdom are understanding (Ecclus. 5:10; 25:8), knowledge (Ecclus. 11:5), temperance and prudence (Ecclus. 25:9; Wisd. Sol. 8:7, 9), and willingness to accept advice (Ecclus. 32:19; Tob. 4:18). Commended also is the study by which knowledge is acquired (Ecclus. 6:18, 35; 8:8; 39:1; 51:28). Wisdom is linked with godliness (Ecclus. 27:11) and with that widely applauded trait, the "fear of the Lord" (Ecclus. 7:31; 19:20). The interbraiding of wisdom with the "fear of the Lord" occupies the entire opening chapter of Ecclesiasticus. Nurtured by wisdom is reverent and peace-conserving speech (Ecclus. 19:6; 21:26; 22:27), likewise the readiness to keep silent (Ecclus. 20:1, 5-6); although when Ecclus. 4:23 advises:

> Do not refrain from speaking at the crucial time,
> and do not hide your wisdom,

we come upon somewhat divergent counsel.

Invoking, like Philo (*On Abraham* 92; *On Genesis* III.10, 46-50, 52, 61; *Who Is the Heir of Divine Things* 268-70), the language of the Greek philosophers, IV Macc. 1:1-6 acclaims "reason," which is credited with power over impulses like excitement, pain, and fear—impulses which hinder justice, will power, discretion, and moderation. As in Philo (*On Abraham* 245-61), moderation is stressed likewise in Aristobul, Second Piece (66). Aristeas 122, in like spirit, lauds the translators of the Law for observing the golden mean.

5. Thrift, truthfulness, honesty, faithfulness, courage. Other traits deemed worthy are thrift (Ecclus. 18:25; 19:1; III Sibylline Oracles 239) and hard work (Arabic Ahikar 8:18; Syr. Ahikar 8:20; Tob. 2:11-12), with special commendation of agriculture (Ecclus. 7:15; Aristeas 108-11; Test. Iss. 5:3; 8:18), notwithstanding the fact that elsewhere Ecclesiasticus (38:25-26) dwells on the plowman's limitations and handicaps.

There is abounding admiration for truthfulness and for honesty (Ecclus. 5:10; 46:19), which includes scruple about the correctness of weights and measures (Ecclus. 42:4), and for fairness (Ecclus. 11:2). To this group belongs also faithfulness (Ecclus. 22:23; 27:17; 29:3; II Esd. 6:28; III Sibylline Oracles 376-77), with particular reference to the person who has gone one's surety.

> Do not forget the favor of your surety,
> for he has given his life for you.
> (Ecclus. 29:15.)

Ecclus. 3:21; 25:2 emphasize the virtue of requiting a good turn. Like Philo (*On Abraham* 217-44), this literature applauds courage and fortitude (Ecclus. 46:1; Wisd. Sol. 8:7). Jub. 17:15-18 lauds Abraham for having proved trustful amid all tribulations, while Ecclus. 4:9 urges: "Do not be faint-hearted in judging a case."

6. Rituals. The religious rituals and the merit of their observance are occasionally considered (Syr. Apocal. Bar. 66:4; Apocal. Sophonias II, 11:5; Ecclus. 7:31; 14:11; 18:22; 35:9; 38:11; 47:9-10; Jub. 21; 36:6-9; I Macc. 14:15), although I Macc. 2:41 reports, with approval, the decision to fight the Syrian foe on the sabbath. The rituals are sometimes spiritualized (Tob. 12:8). Aristeas 169 maintains that the distinction between clean and unclean animals, in the Jewish dietary, has the purpose of teaching just and right conduct. The cloven hoof and the cud chewing of the permitted animals typify the moral implications of memory (153-54). The teaching of kindness is the reason behind the permitting of gentle birds and the forbidding of ferocious ones (145-48). The hand washing required before prayer is a symbol of innocence (306). As for the usages of the temple:

> He who keeps the law makes many offerings;
> he who heeds the commandments sacrifices a peace offering.
> He who returns a kindness offers fine flour,
> and he who gives alms sacrifices a thank offering
> (Ecclus. 35:1-2).

7. Nonritualistic religion. The nonritualistic side of religion obtains equally clear recognition, with its concern about love toward God (Test. Iss. 5:2; 7:6), simplicity (Test. Iss. 4:2, 4, 6; Test. Reuben 4:5), patience (Ecclus. 1:23; 2:4), and humility (Ecclus. 3:17, 23; 4:7; 7:17; 18:21; 32:10; Aristeas 122, 257, 282; Test. Gad 5:3; Test. Joseph 17:8; 18:3). "The greater you are, humble yourself the more" (Ecclus. 3:18). Thoughts of poverty (Ecclus. 18:25) and of death (Ecclus. 10:9-11; 14:12) are suggested as a means by which humility can be fostered. Penitence (Ecclus. 18:21; 20:3) is also urged.

8. Marriage. Not a little stress is laid upon marriage. "Where there is no wife, a man will wander about and sigh" (Ecclus. 36:25). Ecclus. 42:9-10 dwells upon a father's fears lest his daughter fail to marry or, being married, "lest she be hated" and "lest she be barren." There is insistence upon endogamy (Tob. 4:12-13), and Tob. 6:12 cites, with deference, the ancient law of the kinship obligation in the choice of a spouse. Along with this there are ponderings on what constitutes wifely excellence (Ecclus. 25:8; 26:1-4, 13-21, 26). Ecclus. 25:26 acclaims the woman who honors her husband. Nor is Ecclesiasticus (7:25-26) indifferent to reciprocal obligations on the part of the man. 36:22 notes that

> A woman's beauty gladdens the countenance,
> and surpasses every desire of man.

Nonetheless, at that beauty, one should not stumble (25:21). Aristeas 250 advises that, to get along with his wife and to avoid marital quarrels, a man should bear in mind that women are irrational and flighty.

9. Persons to be revered. Considerable attention is bestowed upon the duty of honoring one's parents (Ecclus. 3:3-4; 7:27; 23:14; Tob. 4:3). Ecclus. 3:12-13 admonishes: "Help your father in his old age, and . . . even if he is lacking in understanding, have patience." Ecclus. 8:6 extends the application to all who are of advanced years. Further laid to heart are the honoring and compensating of priests (Ecclus. 7:31), the respecting and the employing of physicians (Ecclus. 38:1-5), and the reverencing of any great person (4:7).

10. Political virtues. Among the things receiving approbation are good government (Ecclus. 10:1-3; 14:4, 8-9, 12, 14; Add. Esth. 13:2; Aristeas 291; III Sibylline Oracles 373), justice (III Esd. 4:39; IV Esd. 5:114; Aristeas 18, 169, 291; III Sibylline Oracles 234, 374; Wisd. Sol. 8:7; Tob. 14:9), patriotism (Jth. 12:8), and obedience to the law (Syr. Apocal. Bar. 46:5; Ecclus. 46:7).

11. Universalism. From time to time this literature sounds a note of universalism (Bar. 1:11-12; 2:21; I Macc. 8:17, 24-27; 10:25-45; 11:32; 12:1; 13:36 ff; 14:16-18, 20; 15:1, 16). I Macc. 6:12-13 describes how King Antiochus, when dying, repents of the spoliations and atrocities he has committed against the Jews and how he yearns to make amends. The entirety of the Letter of Aristeas presupposes cordial relations between Judea and Egypt. Graciousness toward non-Jews is a frequent attitude. This characterizes especially the Testaments of the Twelve Patriarchs. Test. Levi 5:7 holds that the righteous among the Gentiles are to share in the boons awaiting the righteous of Israel. In the messianic future, the heathen as well as Israel are to enter upon the divine redemption (Test. Asher 7:3; Test. Benj. 9:2; 10:5; Test. Simeon 6:5). But it is anticipated that the Gentiles will come eventually to accept the Jewish outlook (Test. Dan 6:7; Test. Judah 25:5; Test. Levi 8:14; 18:9; Test. Naph. 8:3).

C. *MORAL DEFECTS.* Which now are the traits that are evil? Certain qualities are viewed from the angle of psychology. Thus IV Esd. 1:20-21 contends that, despite the giving of the law, the bad heart remains the root of all the world's troubles. Ecclus. 7:16; 18:31; 23:2; Apocal. Shadrach 5:5 contain similar reflections. The whole of IV Maccabees is an ethicopsychological disquisition, not unlike the deliverances of Philo concerning the subjection of the intellect to the sway of passion and the contrast between reason and sensuality (*Who Is the Heir of Divine Things* 268-70; *On Abraham* 4.20-21).

1. Folly. As wisdom is extensively lauded, its opposite is vigorously rebuked (Bar. 3:28). There are frequent and often witty allusions to the fool in Ecclesiasticus.

> He gives little and upbraids much.
>
> . . . .
>
> A fool will say, "I have no friend,
> and there is no gratitude for my good deeds;
> those who eat my bread speak unkindly."
> (Ecclus. 20:15-16.)

The unwise are characterized by an imperviousness to the instruction, the counsel, or the reproof by which their defect might be corrected (Ecclus. 3:26; 6:20-21; 21:6, 12, 18-20; 22:7; Tob. 4:18).

2. Reprehensible speech. As a person's speech can manifest his wisdom, it can also betray his folly

(Ecclus. 9:18; 14:1; 20:18; 21:26; 22:27; 25:8; 27:7). Ecclus. 28:17-18 says:

> The blow of a whip raises a welt,
> but a blow of the tongue crushes the bones.
> Many have fallen by the edge of the sword,
> and yet not as many as have fallen because of the tongue.

Particularly objectionable is the babbler (Ecclus. 19: 6; 20:5, 7). Yes, talk in sheer abundance is distasteful (Ecclus. 20:8; 23:1-9). "Speak concisely, say much in few words" (Ecclus. 32:8). Also deprecated are talebearing and calumny (Greek Apocal. Bar. 8:5; 13:4; Ecclus. 5:14; 19:7; 41:23; Aristeas 162-66). Especially deplored are the "double tongue" (Ecclus. 6:1; 19:26; 27:23; Test. Benj. 6:4-6) and dissimulation (I Macc. 11:53; 13:19; Pss. Sol. 4:10; Wisd. Sol. 14:25). The violation of confidences (Ecclus. 19:7; 27:16, 18; 41:23) is also reprehensible. Scolding is among the traits branded as detestable in a woman (Ecclus. 26:27); but it is no less repellent in a man (Ecclus. 41:22). The "wicked woman" is the theme of not a few passages (Ecclus. 25:16-26; 26:6-12, 23-27). Another flaw relating to speech is that of interrupting the speech of others (Ecclus. 11:8). Likewise deprecated are backbiting (Ecclus. 28:14), slander (Test. Isaac 5:12), excessive swearing (Ecclus. 23:9, 13; 27:14), and, of course, perjury (Greek Apocal. Bar. 4:17; Pss. Sol. 4:4; Wisd. Sol. 14:25, 29). Connected with talebearing is a person's willingness to believe everything he hears (I Macc. 10:61). Ecclus. 19:13 advises:

> Question a friend, perhaps he did not do it;
> but if he did anything, so that he may do it no more.

3. Unfaithfulness and deceit. Another despicable trait is unfaithfulness (Ecclus. 9:10; 12:9; I Esd. 1:48; Wisd. Sol. 14:25). Opprobrium in the extreme is also heaped upon treachery, falsehood, and deceit (Ecclus. 7:12; 10:8; 25:2; 37:1; Add. Esth. 16:6; I Macc. 7: 16, 27-30; 11:53; 15:27-36; II Macc. 3:4; 4:24, 34; 12:4; Pss. Sol. 4:4; Sus. 1:55, 59). Bel and the Dragon describes the imposture perpetrated by the priests of Bel and their exposure by Daniel. Apocal. Esd. 3:12 foresees, with alarm, how "brother will betray brother, children rise up against their parents, friend against friend, servant against master."

4. Lack of love. As love ranks high among the virtues, hate holds a corresponding place among the obliquities (Test. Gad 4:5-6); similarly uncharitableness and stinginess (Bar. 6:28; Ecclus. 4:5-6; 12:3; 14:3, 10; 31:8, 24; Wisd. Sol. 19:14-15), and charity that is harsh (Ecclus. 18:15) and grudging (II Enoch 62:1-2). Sinful likewise is failure to visit the sick, the widow, and the orphan (Apocal. Sophonias II, 11:4-5). As bringing comfort is a virtue, its opposite is a transgression (Ecclus. 4:1-3).

5. Lack of social justice. As consideration for the underprivileged is a merit, its opposite is in many passages pronounced an iniquity. There is a discernible tendency to idealize the poor (Ecclus. 3:19 [or 20]; 4:6; 10:30-31; 11:1; 13:18; 31:4; 32:16 [or 17 or 20]; 35:13-14, 16-17; IV Esd. 14:13; Pss. Sol. 5:2, 13-14; 10:7; 15:2; Test. Gad 7:6; Zadokite Fragment 9:10), to disparage the wealthy (I Enoch 94:8-9; 96:4, 6, 8; 97:8; 99:12-13, 15), and to dwell upon the possible juncture of wealth with moral shortcoming (Arabic Ahikar 2:52; Ecclus. 10:23; 13:3; 14:3; 20:21; 25:2; 30:14; Ascens. Moses 7:5-6). Among the derelictions specified is the delaying or withholding of wages (Tob. 4:14), dismissal from employment (Aristeas 258-59), and the removal of the landmark (III Sibylline Oracles 240; Zadokite Fragment 1:11; 8:1; 9:13, 49). Apocal. Elijah (3:2-3) charges that the Israelites, returning from captivity, "seize houses, rob farms, slay widows and orphans in the streets"; yet curiously the text proceeds to anticipate that these oppressors will obtain pardon if they repent. Ascens. Moses 7:6 scorns the exploiters and oppressors who claim their doings are acts of righteousness.

6. Injustice, censoriousness, anger. Another evil is injustice, be the victim rich or poor (Ecclus. 40:2; 41:18); likewise unfairness, such as judging a person by his outward appearance or circumstances (Ecclus. 11:2; 22:23).

> Do not find fault before you investigate;
> first consider, and then reprove
> (Ecclus. 11:7).

Other evils are impatience (Ecclus. 2:14), censoriousness (Ecclus. 8:5; 21:12; 22:20; 31:31; Test. Abraham 6:4), lack of sympathy (Ecclus. 4:3; 7:11, 34; II [or V] Esd. 2:21), enmity (Ecclus. 6:1; 25:14), and anger (Ecclus. 1:22; 4:29-30; 10:18; 23:16; 29:23; 30: 24; Test. Isaac 5:11; Test. Reuben 4:8). It is better to rebuke openly than to be secretly enraged (Ecclus. 20:2).

7. Vindictiveness, covetousness, avarice. Further qualities pronounced objectionable are vindictiveness (Ecclus. 8:7; 28:1; Test. Benj. 8:1; Test. Dan 1:4; Test. Isaac 5:12; Test. Iss. 4:5), covetousness (Ecclus. 5:8; 10:9; 14:9; 30:14-17; III Sibylline Oracles 236; Tob. 5:18), and avarice (Apocal. Abraham 24:10; Ecclus. 29:23; 30:14-17; 31:6, 11: Test. Judah 19:1; Tob. 5:19). Not far removed from avarice is the conduct of one concerning whom Ecclus. 20:15 says: "Today he lends and tomorrow he asks it back." The aversion to lending on interest is reflected in Apocal. Sophonias 15:8, which sees those who lend on interest punished in hell.

8. Theft, dishonesty, bribery. Also excoriated are theft (Apocal. Abraham 24:8; Greek Apocal. Bar. 4:17; 8:5; 13:4; Ecclus. 14:4; 41:19, 21; III Sibylline Oracles 239, 380; Wisd. Sol. 14:25; Tob. 2:13) and dishonesty (Ecclus. 4:31; 22:4; III Sibylline Oracles 237), including the use of false measures (I Enoch 99:2). In this regard, certain occupations come under suspicion. Sin sticks "close between buying and selling" (Ecclus. 27:2). "A merchant shall hardly keep himself from doing wrong; and a huckster shall not be freed from sin" (Ecclus. 26:29). Bribery also stands on the sinister list (Apocal. Sophonias II, 15: 5; Ecclus. 40:12; Ascens. Moses 5:5). Likewise viewed askance is mendicancy (Ahikar 2:52-53; Greek Ahikar 26:10; Ecclus. 29:22-28; 40:28-30). Castigation alights upon sloth (Armenian Ahikar 2: 35; Ecclus. 4:29; 10:27; 22:1; Test. Reuben 3:7), notwithstanding the divergent thought that

> Good and bad, life and death,
> poverty and wealth, come from the Lord
> (Ecclus. 11:14; cf. Ecclus. 11:17; 31:4).

9. Drunkenness, gluttony. Drunkenness is likewise pilloried (Greek Apocal. Bar. 4:16-17; 8:5; 13:4;

Ecclus. 19:1-2; 26:8; 31:25-31; Tob. 4:15). Greek Apocal. Bar. 4:8; Apocal. Abraham 23:5-6 identify the vine with the forbidden fruit of Gen. 2:17; 3:1. Also frowned upon are gluttony (Ecclus. 23:6; 30:25; 31:17, 20; 37:29-31; Heroclitus of Ephesus VII, 5:1; Test. Benj. 6:2) and sybaritic excesses (Ascens. Isaiah 2:9-11; Ecclus. 19:5; Her. VII, 5:1; Test. Iss. 4:2-3), and thoughtless extravagance (Ecclus. 18:33). Nonetheless, it is admitted that there can be excesses of the other extreme, such as inordinate mourning (Ecclus. 38:17).

10. Violence and war. Vehemently reprobated are violence and strife (Greek Apocal. Bar. 8:5; 13:4; Ecclus. 20:4; 27:14; 28:8; I Macc. 1:24; Wisd. Sol. 14:25). Reproof is leveled not only at violence but also at incitement to violence (Apocal. Abraham 17: 12; Wisd. Sol. 14:25-26). Murder is consummately abhorred (Apocal. Abraham 24:5-6; Greek Apocal. Bar. 8:5; 13:4; III Sibylline Oracles 235; IV Sibylline Oracles 163-64; Test. Benj. 7:1-2: Test. Judah 22:1). And notable are the arraignments of war (Syr. Apocal. Bar. 48:37; I Enoch 8:1; 52:6, 8-9; 69:6; Heraclitus of Ephesus 6:1-3; 7:1-2; Jub. 11:2; 23:19-20; Pss. Sol. 17:33 [or 37]; III Sibylline Oracles 235, 367, 751, 753, 755-56, 780-81; IV Sibylline Oracles 163-64; V Sibylline Oracles 253, 381-83; Test. Benj. 7:1-2; Test. Isaac 5:11; Test. Judah 22:1). Echoing the biblical Jeremiah, Baruch quotes God as saying, "Bend your shoulders and serve the king of Babylon, and you will remain in the land which I gave to your fathers" (2:21). Other striking expressions of a pacifist tenor can be found in Jos. Antiq. XIV.ii.1; Jos. War II.xvi.351; and among the rabbis (Gittin 56A; Abot de R. Nathan IV). The extreme of wickedness is, of course, persecution such as that perpetrated by King Antiochus (I Macc. 1:1 ff; II Macc. 5–7).

11. Sins of sex. There are frequent disparaging references to the improprieties of sex. Adultery is attributed to drunkenness (Greek Apocal. Bar. 4:17), music (Pseudo-Philo 2:8), feminine song (Ecclus. 9: 4), dancing (Test. Judah 23:2), masculine gazing (Ecclus. 9:5, 7-8; 41:21; Pss. Sol. 4:4: Test. Benj. 8: 2-3; Test. Isaac 5:13; Test. Reuben 3:10), and dalliance and lingering in the proximity of women (Ecclus. 9:9; 23:5-6; 41:22-23; 42:12-13; Test. Reuben 3:10). Ezra, in Vis. Esd. 17, sees tortured in hell the wives who adorned themselves not for their husbands but for others. Ecclus. 42:14 says that "better is the wickedness of a man than a woman who does good."

Among the evils connected with sex is jealousy (Greek Apocal. Bar. 8:5; 13:4; Ecclus. 9:1; 26:6; Wisd. Sol. 1:10; Test. Reuben 4:5). Cognizant of marital tensions, Ecclus. 25:22 meanwhile observes that

> There is wrath and effrontery and great disgrace
> when a wife supports her husband.

Stigmatized also are perversions such as homosexuality (Apocal. Abraham 24:9; Her. VII, 5:1; Wisd. Sol. 14:26). Ezra perceives, among those undergoing tortures in hell, those who have committed incest with their mothers (Vis. Esd. 21). Enoch (I Enoch 15:2-4) beholds the angels rebuked for consorting with human females as reported in Gen. 6:2.

12. Pride, vanity, envy. Also among the failings upon which this literature dwells are pride and envy (Syr. Apocal. Bar. 83:13-16; Ecclus. 6:2; 11:4, 6, 30; 13:1; Test. Isaac 5:12; Test. Reuben 3:5) and ambition (Ecclus. 7:4; II Macc. 4:7) and too much inquisitiveness (Ecclus. 3:21, 23).

> Better is a man who works and has an abundance of
> everything,
> than one who goes about boasting, but lacks bread.
> (Ecclus. 10:27.)

Ecclus. 11:19 points out the indiscretion of one

> When he says, "I have found rest,
> and now I shall enjoy my goods!"
> He does not know when his time will come;
> he will leave them to others and die.

Suggestive of Philo, Test. Benj. 6:2, 4-5 asserts that a person of right mind is not passionately concerned about the transitory. He is indifferent to honor or dishonor, poverty or wealth. Likewise upbraided are envy (Syr. Apocal. Bar. 48:37; Ecclus. 9:11; 30:24; Test. Gad 7:2, 6; Test. Iss. 4:5; Test. Reuben 4:5; Wisd. Sol. 6:23) and recklessness (Ecclus. 3:26). Another sin is that of being stiff-necked (Ecclus. 16: 11). But there is also a drawback in bashfulness (Ecclus. 20:22-23). Among the traits to be avoided, mention is likewise made of indecorum (Ecclus. 41: 17-23) and of irreverence toward the aged (Wisd. Sol. 2:10).

13. Idolatry. In matters of ritual, the worst of sins is idolatry (Greek Apocal. Bar. 8:5; 13:4; II Esd. 1:6; Jub. 20:1-9; Aristeas 140; I Macc. 1:47; Pseudo-Philo 2:8-9; Test. Judah 23:1; Wisd. Sol. 14:6, 23, 25, 27, 29). Idolatry is ridiculed in the manner of Isa. 44:9-19; 46:6 (Apocal. Abraham 1–6; 23–25; Bar. 6:4; 8:58; Wisd. Sol. 13:11-19; 14:1; 15:5-19). No little irony ensues from the report concerning the soldiers in II Macc. 12:40 that "under the tunic of every one of the dead they found sacred tokens of the idols of Jamnia, which the law forbids the Jews to wear." This same army had, a short time before, been battling valiantly against idolatrous practices. The text goes on to state that, for this slump into idolatry, sacrifices of propitiation were offered in the temple at Jerusalem. For resistance to idolatry, praise is bestowed upon Abraham (Jub. 12:1, 6), King Josiah (Ecclus. 49:1-4), Daniel (Bel 1:22), Mattathias (I Macc. 2:45), Judas Maccabeus (I Macc. 5:68), and Simon the Maccabee (I Macc. 13:47). Jth. 8:18-19 recounts, with satisfaction, how idolatry was uprooted in Israel through God's annihilation of those that preached it. Also denounced is apostasy (I Macc. 1:14, 43).

14. Superstition. A number of passages expatiate upon the banefulness of superstition, such as belief in dreams, divinations, soothsayings, witchcraft, ventriloquism, and such as addiction to strange rites and ceremonies (Greek Apocal. Bar. 8:5; 13:4; Ecclus. 34:2-7; Test. Judah 23:1; Wisd. Sol. 12:3-5; 14:23). Abhorrence of child sacrifice comes to expression in Wisd. Sol. 12:5; while unbelief is objurgated in Ecclus. 2:13 and blasphemy in I Macc. 7:38. Finally, Vis. Esd. 45:46 beholds in hell, lying on the ground and overpoured with glowing lead and iron, those who taught, but did not practice, the divine word.

D. *DIVERGENCES.* We have examined the moral judgments to be found in the noncanonical Jewish writings. But the picture, as we have seen, does not prevail uniformly. We have noted some minor deviations. There remain to be noted some major deviations.

1. Chauvinism. Commingled with the universalism already noted, there are strains of chauvinism (Apocal. Abraham 22:6; 29:19; 30:4; Ecclus. 26:2-3; 36:7; IV Esd. 4:56, 58; V Esd. 1:11; Aristeas 139; II Macc. 6:14; Wisd. Sol. 12:22; Test. Levi 4:4). IV Esd. 4:59; 5:11 hold that the world was created for the sake of Israel. The book of Judith is furiously belligerent toward Israel's foes even though Holofernes, whom Judith eventually decapitates, is made to speak as if he believed in Israel's God (11:22). Related to this are the strictures against exogamy (I Esd. 8:70, 93; 9:7-36; Jub. 20:4). The aversion to war has its antithesis in many a passage in which war is glorified (Ecclus. 47:4, 7; Eupolemos 3:5; I Macc. 3:4, 21, 58; 5:68; 10:46; 14:7, 9-10; II Macc. 15:21). When I Macc. 11:47 reports, with satisfaction, that at Antioch "the king called the Jews to his aid, and they all rallied about him and then spread out through the city; and they killed on that day as many as a hundred thousand men," the scruple against the taking of human life is obviously in abeyance.

2. Revenge and severity favored. When it comes to international conflict, revenge no longer meets with disapproval (Ecclus. 35:18; 48:8; Add. Esth. 16: 18; Jth. 9:2; I Macc. 2:67; 13:6; II Macc. 1:17; 12: 6). Even outside of international conflict vindictiveness is sometimes sanctioned (Ecclus. 25:7; 30:6). Ecclus. 39:28-30 sees the inimical forces of nature as instruments of revenge on the part of God. When treachery is inflicted upon a national enemy, it becomes a virtue (Jth. 10:12; 11:5; 13:8; 15:9; 16), and cruelty becomes an excellence (Jos. Antiq. I.x.176; I Macc. 5:15; 10:36; II Macc. 1:16; 8:19-20, 24; 12: 6, 16; Philo *On Abraham* 233). Nor are the cruelties praised except as they are inflicted on foreign foes (Syr. Apocal. Bar. 66:3-4; Ecclus. 16:12; Jub. 20:4; I Macc. 2:24-25; 9:73). A species of militancy, of course, is the pleasure felt at the furious suppression of nonconformist cults (Syr. Apocal. Bar. 66:4; Jub. 12:12; I Macc. 2:45; 5:68).

3. Lawlessness and harshness condoned. Nor are these writings unanimous as regards loyalty to the state. The books of the Maccabees anticipate the American maxim, "Resistance to tyrants is obedience to God" (esp. I Macc. 2:19). At one point there is even admiration for a mass uprising (II Macc. 4:39). An offset to the above-mentioned approbations of kindness are passages which urge the rigid disciplining of servants (Ecclus. 33:24-28; 42:5), of children (Ecclus. 7:23-24; 30:1, 7, 10; 42:5) and even of one's wife (Ecclus. 25:26).

4. As to accepting advice, as to honesty, as to benevolence. The admonition about accepting advice has its opposite in Ecclus. 37:13, which counsels thinking for oneself. The teaching about leniency toward one's foes is counterbalanced by words of caution against trusting one's foes (Ecclus. 12:1-18). The insistences upon honesty have their antithesis when Ezekiel the tragedian (163-65) admires the departing Hebrews for their spoliation of the Egyptians (Exod. 11:2; 12:35-36). An offset to the copious praises of almsgiving appears when Ecclus. 12:1, 4-5, 7, exhorts:

> Give to the godly man, but do not help the sinner.
> Do good to the humble, but do not give to the godless.
> . . . .
> Give to the good man.

A similar thought is that of II Enoch 51:1. Ecclus. 11:34 (cf. 11:29) warns:

> Receive a stranger into your home and he will upset you with commotion,
> and estrange you from your family.

Ecclus. 29:20 apprehends the possibility of one's becoming impoverished if he gives too liberally.

5. As regards humaneness. By contrast with Apocal. Sophonias II, 17:5, which tells how the righteous in heaven pray for the damned, Elijah 9:2 reports that God keeps the righteous from hearing the wails of the damned so as to prevent this intercession. According to Apocal. Abraham 31:6, the destruction of idolaters should cause the elect to jubilate. Contrasting with the generous humanitarianism of some noncanonical passages, Phocylides 95 charges that the masses are volatile and that the rabble cannot be trusted.

The commentators dwell upon the political and the cultural factors which have, within the domain of ethical teaching, brought about the transition from the biblical to the noncanonical. Even a superficial reading makes one conscious of the difference, notwithstanding the abundance of doctrine and of phraseology common to both sets of writings.

Bibliography. E. Kautsch, *Die Apokryphen und Pseudepigraphen des Alten Testaments* (1900); R. H. Charles, *The Apoc. and Pseudep. of the OT* (1913); P. Riessler, *Altjuedisches Schrifttum Ausserhalb der Bibel* (1928).

ABRAHAM CRONBACH

ETHICS IN THE NT. Fundamental is the recognition that in the NT morality finds its setting in religion. Nowhere is the gospel set forth without a moral demand, and nowhere is morality (illumined from whatever sources, Hebraic or Hellenistic) understood apart from the gospel.

A. *THE TEACHING OF JESUS.* 1. Its setting. The above indissoluble connection between ethics and religion is preserved in the summary of the proclamation of Jesus given in Mark 1:15: "The time is fulfilled, and the kingdom of God is at hand; repent, and believe in the gospel." This verse is, therefore, highly pertinent to the understanding of the ethics of Jesus.

a. The reaffirmation of ethical monotheism. There is the reference to a time fulfilled (Gal. 4:4). This is to be understood, as is made evident in the rest of the NT, in the light of the expectations expressed in the OT, and in Judaism, that, at some future date, God would act for the salvation of his people. The ministry of Jesus is the fulfilment of these expectations (e.g., Isa. 10:22; 35:4; 43:3; 45:17-22; 60:16; Joel 2:28 ff; etc. [*see* ESCHATOLOGY OF THE OT, APOCRYPHA AND PSEUDEPIGRAPHA]). But, as fulfilment, implicitly here and explicitly elsewhere, the coming of the kingdom of God does not ignore the moral content of these expectations: the ethical aspirations of the OT and Judaism, the Law and the Prophets, are not annulled; they are fulfilled (Matt. 5:17-18). This means that Jesus consciously accepted the ethical tradition of his people. This was what he had been nurtured on, and it is the source of much of his moral insight. E.g., it has been possible to claim that in the figure of the Suffering Servant (Isa. 53) Jesus could have found the most profound emphases of his ethical teaching. No iconoclast, Jesus affirmed the tradition of ethical monotheism in Judaism, and he assumed and constantly appealed to, the scriptures of his people (Mark 12:28-37; Matt. 4:4, 6-7, etc.). But Jesus passed, nevertheless, beyond his nurture. Nor was it only his own zeal for the doing of God's will that enabled him to do this. Rather, we must couple with this the next item in Mark 1:15.

b. The ethics of the kingdom of God. The ethical teaching of Jesus is not only a reaffirmation of the ethical tradition of Judaism, but is also the concomitant of his overwhelming conviction that the kingdom of God was "at hand." We may go further. As the parables and other sayings show, Jesus preached that the active rule of God was not only approaching, but, in a real sense, already present or in process of realization in his ministry (*see* ESCHATOLOGY OF THE NT). From the most insignificant beginnings, its growth was assured (Matt. 13:39; Mark 4:3-8, 26-29, 30-32; Luke 13:18-19, 20-21). Similarly, the hour of salvation is declared to have struck (Matt. 11:5; Luke 4:18-19; 7:22). In the symbols of the wedding (John 2:9), of the harvest (Matt. 3:12; 9:37-38; 13: 28-29), of the garment (Mark 2:21-22), and of the new wine (Mark 2:21-22), this is implicit, as it is also in the temptation narratives, and in the presentation of Jesus as the shepherd (Matt. 15:24; Luke 19:10), the physician (Mark 2:17), and as victor over Satan (Matt. 12:28; Luke 10:18). Jesus proclaimed the active and imminent rule of God (the term "KINGDOM OF GOD" refers primarily, not to any geographic or communal entity, but to God's rule, as here indicated). It is in the light of this that he understands the demands of God—i.e., in the light of God's "availability" in meeting them. The ethic of Jesus is an ethic of the kingdom of God, of the "end" when God's rule is to be established. And this meant, in accordance with Jewish expectation, that it was the ethics of a new creation, of a new heart and spirit, of a new covenant, of a new people—a new Israel that had responded to Jesus' call to repentance and received the rule of God (Isa. 4:2-4; 44:3-5; Jer. 24:6-7; 31: 33-34; 32:38-40; 33:8; 50:20; Ezek. 11:19-20; Zech. 5:5-11; 13:1-2; Jub. 1:29; II Bar. 32:6; 17:2; Ezek. 7:75).

But—and this it is essential to grasp—the coming near of the kingdom of God in the ministry of Jesus is an act of sheer grace. It is of God's good pleasure alone that it is in process: it has not waited upon any worthiness in Israel by way of repentance or otherwise, as was the expectation in Judaism (Pesiḳ. dRK 163-64; Joma 86*b;* Sanh. 97*b*). And, as it was a free gift, so did the rule of God bring with it a gift, that of the forgiveness of sins. The gospels thrill with this. This is so even though the word "grace," with this connotation—i.e., in the sense of "God's active love"—does not occur in the Synoptics. Salvation has come to the poor, the sinful, and the outcast (Matt. 18:12-14; 21:28-31; Mark 2:16; Luke 15:4-7, 8-10; 18:9). Particularly is this expressed in Luke 15:16-17 in the parable of the prodigal son, which reveals the Father's boundless love.

2. Its standards. These two aspects of the kingdom or rule of God proclaimed by Jesus—its presence and imminence and its character as "grace" —have profound significance for his ethical teaching.

a. The ethics of grace. Because the rule of God is an expression of grace, the moral demands of Jesus are the counterpart of God's grace. The grace of God in action, in exorcism, healing, forgiveness, and "power," which is the coming of the kingdom, imposes demands consonant with itself. The very acceptance of grace, because of the very nature of grace, lays upon the recipient a demand corresponding to it. Grace imposes its own terms—i.e., the demand to love. It is therefore no accident that in the SERMON ON THE MOUNT, the Beatitudes, which are the expression of God's grace, precede the statement of the demands of Jesus, which are thus deliberately set in the context of grace. This is reinforced if, as is possible, the Beatitudes (as, indeed, all the sermon) are a commentary on the prophetic vision of redemption found in Isa. 61, the ethic being thus rooted in redemption. And it is in this light that we are to understand the emphasis in the teaching of Jesus on love.

Not only in the sermon does this appear, but elsewhere, especially in Mark 12:28, where the two commandments of love to God and to the neighbor are declared respectively to be the first and second of the commandments. Not only the occurrence of the Golden Rule (Matt. 7:12) as a climactic summary of the Sermon on the Mount, but also the prominent place given to love in the rest of the NT (John 3:16; Rom. 13:8-10; I Cor. 8:1; 13; Col. 3:14), justifies the conclusion that love (*agape*) was of the essence of Jesus' ethical teaching. The significance of the emphasis in Jesus, however, on love to God and neighbor has been questioned. In Mark 12:28-34 he has merely combined two verses from the OT, and in Judaism itself distinctions between heavy and light commandments were recognized. Akiba (A.D. 135) summarized the law in the love of neighbor (Lev. 19:18; Sifra 89.4), and the GOLDEN RULE is used by Hillel and in the Letter of Artiseas, though in its negative form. As for love to God, this belongs to the Shema (Deut. 6:5), which was taken earnestly by all pious Jews (T.B. Ber. 61*b*). Nevertheless, three things are noteworthy:

a) The explicit combination of the love of God and the love of neighbor is only made by Jesus. This must not be taken to mean that the two are identical: this would be to empty the love of God of its numinous quality and the God, whom Jesus loves, is the Lord of heaven and earth; though God is love, love is not God. But, on the other hand, the love of neighbor is not, for Jesus, merely a means to the love of God. Love to God and love to the neighbor are not identical. This is expressed beautifully in the parable of the good Samaritan. To love the neighbor is to be neighbor to him. The same parable suggests the second intensification of the concept of love by Jesus.

b) It includes not only the national kinsman or neighbor but even the enemy. Love is here universalized (Matt. 5:38 ff).

c) Despite the passages in Jewish sources, where the law is summed up in a single precept, like Lev. 19:18, as by Akiba, there is no real parallel to the elevation of love to pre-eminence by Jesus. When Hillel quoted the Golden Rule, as the quintessence of the law, he thereby had no intention of invalidating the rest of the law (*see* LAW IN FIRST-CENTURY JUDAISM). Jesus, on the other hand, gave absolute priority to love.

But the nature of love has to be further described. The term "love" (*agape*) is used of love to God, as we have seen, but, outside Mark 12:28-29, the Synoptics do not refer to love to God, although this is implied in other passages dealing with the love of neighbor (Matt. 5:23-24; 6:12; Mark 12:28 ff). This is significant: it indicates that the essence of love to God is no emotional or mystical relationship, but obedience in the service of the neighbor. This, which is the imitation of God (Matt. 5:48; 18:23-35), extends to the humblest material service, which is demanded by Jesus of all men (Matt. 25:31-46) to all men (Luke 10:30-37). "Religious" acts as such are not condemned; they are assumed (e.g., prayer, fasting [Matt. 6:1 ff]), but they can have no priority over, nor be divorced from, the love of the neighbor (Matt. 5:22-23), and this is rooted in the love of God himself. This last must not be taken to mean, however, that the love (*agape*) of which Jesus speaks is to be absolutely differentiated from all human affection (*eros*). For Jesus, as for the OT, there is a real affinity between the affection which man feels for man, and the love of God. At least, human affection is not annulled in the love of God and neighbor. As in the OT the love of God for his people is expressed in human terms (Isa. 65:2), and the love of husband and wife becomes a type of God's love for Israel (Hosea), so the same word is used by Jesus of loving a friend and loving an enemy—i.e., for human affection, and the love which transcends the natural affections, and has its source in God. The conclusion is inevitable that both have their source in him (Matt. 5:46). The love of the Father is to be repeated in the love of his sons—i.e., of those who take upon themselves the yoke of his rule (Matt. 5:45).

This radicalizing of the ethical demand in the teaching of Jesus is not confined to his understanding of love. Other demands of the rule of God are proclaimed with the same utter nakedness, in their absolute state. As compared with the ethical teaching of the rabbis, who were concerned to "hedge" the naked commandments of God with the art of a "kind of compromise," that of Jesus, almost throughout, strikes a note of absolute radicalism (*see* LAW IN THE NT). Not only murder, but anger, is condemned (Matt. 5:21 ff); not only adultery, but the lustful glance (Matt. 5:27 ff). There is demanded, not an eye for an eye, but boundless, uncalculating love; the uttermost moral absolutism is proclaimed; an impossible is set before us. Considerations of prudence become at best secondary; the light of the rule of God in Jesus has illumined all God's demands with terrible clarity, because with gracious clarity. This it is that explains the utter radicalism with which Jesus proclaimed his ethics: he places men immediately under the gracious and demanding will of God, relentless and uncompromising, untouched by the relativities and contingencies of "the world," as it is unlimited by human sin. The ethics of Jesus then is the ethics of grace, of God's rule, as known by him.

b. Ethics and the end. At this point we have to ask whether considerations, not only of the presence of the rule of God, but of its imminent inbreaking, have influenced the ethical teaching of Jesus.

Some scholars (especially Schweitzer) have termed the absolute ethics of Jesus an ethic of the interim, designed merely for that very brief period of history which was left before the final end of history, which the Messiah was soon to inaugurate: this it is that explains the "impracticability" and "absoluteness" with which Jesus proclaimed the demands of God. Our attitude toward this understanding of Jesus' ethic depends partly on our interpretation of Jesus' attitude toward the "future." If, with some scholars, we regard the imminence of the end as merely formal, a dramatization of spiritual realities in which there is no real temporal imminence contemplated by Jesus, then that imminence cannot have been a considerable factor in his teaching. But even if we accept the view of perhaps the majority of scholars, that Jesus did expect the near "end of the world," there are factors which make it difficult to think of his ethics as merely an *Interimsethik*.

The early church clearly did not so understand the teaching, because it retained this when the hope of an immediate end of the existing order had waned.

Moreover, the way in which the commandments are given does not suggest "emergency orders" for an interim only. Nowhere in the Synoptics is an appeal made to the "end of the world" as a ground for ethical conduct, as is the case probably in Paul in I Cor. 7:26. It is best to see in the absolute demands of Jesus the obverse side of the absolute succor made available in the coming of the kingdom of God: they presuppose the latter and express the demands of grace in essential, if not formal, independence of the imminent incidence of "the end."

c. The ethics and the person of Jesus. Not only so, but there is another consideration that illumines much in the absolutism of many of Jesus' demands. The coming of the kingdom of God was closely associated with the person of Jesus himself (*see* KINGDOM OF GOD; JESUS CHRIST). The call to repentance came to be understood as a call to follow after Jesus (אחרי הלך). To judge from Mark 1:16 ff, the conception of the Christian life as a call to follow Jesus, or to discipleship to Jesus (this is not, at this point, to be confused with the imitation of Christ, but regarded as entry upon his way of life), emerged very early in his ministry, but it probably received more emphasis in the later stages of it, when Jesus set his face to go to Jerusalem, when the imperative need to support him became clear. But to be associated with Jesus was to be open to the extraordinary tensions of the crisis in which he was involved, which meant readiness for unusual sacrifices and special duties (Matt. 12:30; Mark 9:38-40; Luke 11:23). The "way" of the Christian becomes the "way" of confession (Matt. 10:18, 22, 24, 39; Mark 8:34-37; 10: 29-30), and of loyalty (Matt. 8:18-22; 19:16-22; Mark 6:8-9; Luke 10:2). Much of the absolutism demanded in these passages is not for general or universal application, but directed to the specific historical crisis of the ministry of Jesus, which laid upon his followers special renunciations, as they were severally able. Jesus demanded both the sanctification of natural conditions—e.g., marriage (Mark 10:2 ff)—and, when necessary, their transcendence. The point is that ethics in the context of the "warfare" of his ministry could not but at times be "totalitarian."

d. Misconceptions. At this juncture it would be well to remove a Roman Catholic misconception. Already in the third century, Origen (Commentary on Rom. 3:3) and Tertullian (*To His Wife* 2.1) distinguished between the "advice" and the "requirements" of the gospel. The latter are binding on all Christians; the "advice" is for those who would live the holier life. On two main phases of conduct was there "advice"—riches (Matt. 19:21; Mark 6:7-9; 10:21) and sex (Matt. 19:12; 22:30). Poverty and celibacy, while impossible of fulfilment by all Christians, conferred special merit on those who practiced them. But it is best to see in such absolutes the recognition, not of two standards of morality, but of different aptitudes and of different demands in the setting of the ministry. On the other hand, the view familiar to Protestants, that the intention of the absolute demands of Jesus is to produce penitence and despair, and thus to prepare the way for the acceptance of Christ, finds little, if any, support in the gospels. These absolutes are set, as we saw, in a context of grace: in the gospels it is not so much that the demands lead us to grace, as that the encounter with the grace of Christ, or of the kingdom, reveals the incalculable nature of the demands of God. This, it is true, leads again and again to repentance, but only because there has been a "prevenient grace," which is the "coming of the kingdom." This simultaneously creates repentance and reveals demand; and the more it is appropriated, the more it intensifies both the repentance and the demand without limit (Matt. 18:21). This is why to do all the demand is still to be "unworthy servants" (Luke 17:10).

e. Ethics applied. The above discussion might create the impression that the ethical teaching of Jesus dealt only in absolutes. But, before this conclusion is drawn, two considerations should be examined:

a) The tradition of his teaching in the Synoptics, in addition to containing ethical principles, which are of universal application—e.g., that of love and self-denial—contains practical injunctions (e.g., Matt. 18:15 ff). It is possible that, with FORM CRITICISM, we should relegate such passages to the invention of the early church. However, it should not be overlooked that Jesus was not only prophet and Messiah, but also a teacher of "wisdom" (Matt. 5:14-15; 6:27, 34). It has, indeed, been possible to appeal to the essential rationality of his ethical demands, despite their absolute character (Bultmann). These made, it has been argued (over against the Jewish law, which requires a blind obedience to what is therein set forth, reasonable or otherwise), only demands which are self-evidently good; i.e., insight into the right conduct to be followed in any given situation is furnished by that situation itself. In this view the demands of Jesus are eminently self-authenticating. This is to go too far. The words of Jesus are proclaimed by him as authoritative: for him, it is not their self-authenticating character that is significant but their source in God's will. As the demand of God, the teachings of Jesus could not be derived from the essential requirement of any given situation. Precisely the ability, or insight, to define this requirement, as the essential will of God, was the role of Jesus as teacher. Nevertheless, that Jesus' demands could have been defined as rational, should warn us against absolutizing them too severely. The possibility is not to be ruled out that Jesus himself, despite his vivid apprehension of the absolutes, was also aware of the necessity of compromise. Much as he was a universalist in principle, but a particularist in practice, who confined his ministry to Israel (Matt. 10:5-6, 23), so he may have been absolutist in his ethical principles, and yet prepared to issue injunctions of compromise. This suggestion is made hesitatingly, because it is impossible not to recognize that the hand of the church is to be traced in ethical teaching, as in the parables, and that what was originally absolute often became parenetic.

b) In two passages Jesus deals with specific issues, divorce (Mark 10:2-9) and the payment of taxes to Caesar (Mark 12:13-17). In Mark 10:2-9, Jesus describes the Mosaic permission of divorce (Deut. 24:1) as a concession to the hardness of men's hearts —i.e., to their mental and moral petrifaction. Against this permission, he appeals to the aboriginal will of God in creation, which he finds revealed in the story of the creation of man in Gen. 1:27; 2:24. (There can be little doubt that the exceptive phrase introduced, forbidding divorce "except on the ground of unchastity," in Matt. 5:32; 19:9, is an "ecclesiastical" modification.) In the light of God's purpose in creation, Jesus refuses to contemplate divorce at all. The created order here becomes a guide to the moral. And elsewhere, by implication, Jesus finds a congruity between the natural order and the moral order (although he never uses terms such as these). Thus the parables employ natural phenomena for moral and spiritual edification (e.g., Mark 4:1 ff). Jesus finds no mere analogy, but an inward affinity, between the natural and the spiritual order. The kingdom of God is intrinsically like the processes of nature (Matt. 6:26-30; Luke 12:24-28). In Matt. 5: 44-48 the imitation of God in his work in creation is the guide to conduct (cf. Matt. 6:19-20; 7:24; 10:

29; 13:24 ff, 28; 24:27 ff; Mark 4:3 ff, 26 ff; Luke 12:55; 16:21).

The other passage, Mark 12:13-17, where Jesus deals with a specific moral issue is, perhaps, also to be understood in the light of this evaluation of the ethical significance of the created order. Jesus answers: "Render to Caesar the things that are Caesar's, and to God the things that are God's." This is not ironical, as if Jesus implied that Caesar is after all merely a straw puppet; nor does it mean that the world of politics and the world of religion are two distinct spheres, each governed by its own principles (Luther). Jesus recognizes the claims of the state. At the same time he requires that all that is God's due should be given to God; and the claims of God are all-embracing, although the state has its rightful claims. The saying, on this view, is essentially concerned with the problem of the state. But another possibility is open. The question, earnestly asked by the opponents of Jesus, is, by his answer, relegated to a secondary place. "Your real concern," he might have said, "should be to give to God what is his. Your coins belong to Caesar, but you yourselves to God." A further thought is probably present. The coins bearing the image of Caesar belong to him, but men, through their creation, bear the image of God and so belong to him. Jesus is not essentially concerned with the state, but with the claims of the inbreaking rule of God. Elsewhere also he is completely realistic in his estimate of the state and its powers (Luke 14:31-32; 16:1-7; 18:1-5), but he conceives his mission, not in terms of political power and reform, but of redemption from sin (Matt. 4:3-10; Mark 2:17; 10:45; Luke 4:3-12; 19:10). This does not mean flight from the world, however, as with the Essenes, but entry into it to proclaim God's rule (Matt. 10:16). Mark 10:42, despite its ruthless realism, bespeaks no rejection of the world, but only a recognition of the fascination and danger of power. In the same way, the attitude of Jesus toward wealth is determined by his concern for obedience to the rule of God. Jesus was open to the realities of the economic and social order of his day (Matt. 13:47-50; 20:1-15; Mark 4:3 ff; Luke 12:37 ff; 17:7-10). His eschatological message did not lead him to belittle the work of every day. But he was not concerned with the distribution of wealth as such, although fully aware of human inequalities (Mark 14:7). His woes against the wealthy, which are emphasized in Luke (6:24), but are not peculiar to that gospel (cf. Matt. 6:24), are due, not to any zeal for economic reform as such, but to his awareness of the "demonic" character of wealth, as of power (Mark 10:27), its tendency to come between man and God. This is not to be weakened to a demand by Jesus for "inner" or "spiritual" detachment from wealth: wealth in its actuality is suspect (Matt. 6:19-20; Mark 10:23-27; Luke 12:16-21). Poverty, as such, is neither condemned nor praised by Jesus (Matt. 5:3 correctly interprets Luke 6:20). He faced economic inequality realistically, while he uncovered, equally realistically, the dangers of riches. Throughout, his concern was that men should seek first the rule of God (Matt. 6:33).

What, however, concerns us particularly is the fact that in his discussion, both of divorce and of taxes to Caesar, Jesus makes an explicit and implicit appeal to the order of creation. Are we to conclude that there is an antinomy in his ethical teaching? Does he, on the one hand, proclaim absolute demands, which radically cut across the "natural" inclinations and affections of men, and, on the other, declare his demands to be truly "natural"? On this, two comments are pertinent: The OT, as we saw, drew no sharp distinction between nature and grace (or *agape* and *eros;* Pss. 8; 19), so that Jesus has precedents. But to this it may be objected that the OT does not, at least as explicitly, demand the absolutes as does Jesus. We must, therefore, look deeper. When Jesus finds "nature" pointing to his absolute demands, the "nature" which he sees is "the nature" intended by God, not "nature" as it actually is, itself corrupted by the Fall. I.e., the insight which enabled Jesus to penetrate to the primordial purpose of God for man in the moral realm enabled him also to discover anew "nature" in its primordial intention. Like some poets, in their childhood but not in their adulthood (cf. Dylan Thomas, "Fern Hill"; Wordsworth, "Intimations of Immortality"), Jesus saw "nature" as it came from God, before it, too, had become involved in the fall from "grace." He saw it renewed by grace, and so saw in it a confirmation of the moral demands of grace. It is no antinomy, therefore, that we find in Jesus, but the triumph of grace over nature and sin, and thus the rediscovery of the unity of both creation and redemption.

3. Its sanctions. No systematized statement of the motives for the good life is to be expected. Not that of a moral philosopher, Jesus' speech was poetic, parabolic, and hyperbolic, not "scientific"; his concern, not academic definition and precision, but practical and prophetic. He, therefore, offers no analysis of virtue after the manner of a Greek philosopher, no discussion of virtue for virtue's sake. Essentially he appeals to two sanctions:

a) He urges repentance, the final repentance before the kingdom of God (Mal. 4:4-6), and does so in a context of rewards and punishments related to that kingdom. In the tradition, as we now have it, the punishments threatened, perhaps, preponderate over the promises of grace. Jesus points to the terrors of the Day of Judgment (Matt. 5:22; 10:15; 11:22; 12:38-42; Luke 10:13-15) or of the Day of the Son of man (Matt. 10:32-33; 25:31-46; Mark 8:38). Punishment is also loss of the life of the age to come (Matt. 10:38-39; Mark 8:35); the command to watch implies danger (Matt. 24–25). On the other hand, entry into the kingdom of God is the supreme good. Thus the aim of the demands of the Sermon on the Mount is to enable men to enter the kingdom (Matt. 5:3-10, 20; Luke 22:28-30). The rewards of the kingdom seem to include, not only the blessings of the age to come, but tangible things in this age (Matt. 19:23 ff; Luke 6:38; nor should it be forgotten that the Beatitudes imply present blessedness, as well as eschatological), except that for Jesus this age is already under the seal of the age to come. While Jesus occasionally appeals to motives of a rationalistic and utilitarian kind (in Luke 16:16-20 he warns against folly, and in 16:1-17 demands prudence), the possession of or entry into the kingdom of God remains the chief motive. Put in this way, the kingdom of God has itself become a reward, so that the concept of reward is in a dominating position in the ethical teaching of Jesus, which, as we saw, is an ethic of the kingdom. But certain facts are cautionary. Jesus himself warns explicitly against certain rewards and asks for the direction of life toward God himself (Matt. 6:1 ff); to him, after we have done all, we are still unworthy servants (Luke 17:10); real "reward" we cannot gain. So too, in the Beatitudes, the blessings given are not conditioned by obedience but given by grace. It would, therefore, seem that the concept of reward cannot have been a fundamental one for Jesus.

b) Then, what are the fundamental sanctions for him? His ethic, we have seen, is determined by the kingdom of God. To emphasize the words "of God" is to discover wherein Jesus finds the sanction for his ethic. It is the imitation of God, the God who took the initiative in giving the kingdom, that constitutes the motive for the good life in Matt. 5:38-41; Luke 6:31, 36—this without any eschatological reference (cf. Matt. 10:8*b*). The new understanding of God gives to Jesus the absolutism of his demands, and reverence for and obedience to God, the hallowing of his name, his motives for the good life (Matt. 5:16, 34-35; 23:20-22).

We can now evaluate the sanctions used by Jesus. He employed the appeal to scripture, to the rewards and punishments traditional in the furniture of apocalyptic, and in this he was, naturally, governed by motives of pedagogy in dealing with his contemporaries. These sanctions, however, are not the fundamental ones; to make reward for Jesus the fundamental motive is to misunderstand the nature of the rule of God, to which he asks for submission. This rule man can only accept in humility. Since its demand is that of love, submission to it, by this very token, cannot be motivated by any selfish concern. "To love God and to love man," which the receiving of the kingdom implies, by its very nature, excludes religious egoism and eudaemonism. The reward that the acceptance of the kingdom gives in abounding measure (Matt. 25:21, 23; Luke 6:38) is that of grace, which means that those are rewarded who seek no reward. In response to God's grace the Christian enters into a personal relationship of sonship with God the Father; and the Christian moral life arises out of this relationship without concern for reward. The good life is the acceptance of God's gift; its reward lies in the acceptance itself, just as punishment lies in the act of rejection—i.e., in lack of love before love made manifest. In the rule of God, announced by Jesus, man encounters a love measureless in grace, the acceptance or rejection of which brings measureless reward and measureless loss (Matt. 25: 21, 33; Luke 6:38; 12). It is a grace that puts to shame all thought of reward and punishment.

Are we then to conclude that the sanctions of reward and punishment at the Judgment Day are merely formal? Some have drawn this conclusion. It may be that Jesus has, in his pictures of that day, dramatized the inevitable consequences, for good or ill, of the rejection of his appeal. But, whatever the degree of literalness or symbolism we apply to such imagery of reward and punishment as he used, this is not to be isolated from his preaching of the kingdom of God—i.e., from the grace of God. This is the essential reference of all the ethic of Jesus.

It is insufficient to define the ethic of Jesus as one of love (Harnack, Niebuhr), since it is the ethic of God, who, while he is love, is also Lord of heaven and earth: it is also insufficient to define it as radical obedience, "which exists only when a man inwardly assents to what is required of him, when the thing commanded is seen as intrinsically God's command" (Bultmann), because this empties obedience of the richness of the ethical tradition of Judaism and of the meaning of "God" to Jesus as creator and redeemer. The ethics of Jesus is best thought of as the demands which are placed upon those who have accepted God's rule, as Jesus proclaimed and lived it. By its very nature, as the demand of the kingdom of God which is at work, the ethics of Jesus is at once an ethic of grace and forgiveness, gratitude and obedience, and, because it is inextricably bound up with his person and those who have responded to him, it is the ethics of a new community of God, which he called into being, the new Israel, his body. Does this imply that Jesus is a new Moses? In the sense that he issued a set code, the answer to this is in the negative. In the sense that he revealed the will of God, the quality and direction of the good life demanded by him, it is in the affirmative. That Jesus thought of his ministry in terms of that of a new Moses is likely in view of the Last Supper, when he instituted a new Israel "in his blood." *See bibliography.*

B. *THE EARLY CHURCH.* The gospels, from which the above account of the ethical teaching of Jesus is drawn, were the products of the early church, and the motifs already emphasized by Jesus reemerge, with inevitable modifications, in its ethical teaching. But the point of departure for the understanding of this is not only the ministry of Jesus, but also the Resurrection. As this was the ground for the emergence of the primitive community, as a well-knit and self-conscious group, so the Resurrection was also the immediate inspiration of its ethic. Because the Resurrection was not only a triumph of life over death; it was also a triumph of forgiveness over sin. The Resurrection was an expression, perhaps even *the* expression, of God's grace in Christ, because the risen Christ came back to those who had all forsaken him and fled, who had slept during his agony. The Resurrection, as forgiveness, emerges clearly in Paul. The grace of Christ in appearing to a persecutor of the church was marvelous to him (I Cor. 15:8-9). If Luke 5:1-11 is a resurrection scene transferred to the ministry, as many think, the same thing is true of Peter (cf. John 21), and that Jesus first appeared to him, who had thrice denied him, is significant. Thus the Resurrection, which reassembled the scattered disciples to constitute the church, was founded in the grace of Christ and of God in Christ. It was of a piece with the whole ministry of Jesus, and the ethic of the community, like the ethic of Jesus, was to be an ethic of grace—i.e., for those who knew the Resurrection as forgiveness, for the new Israel of God, which the forgiven came to constitute. From this can be seen the main emphases in early Christian ethical teaching.

1. Koinonia ethics: vertical. The ethic of the earliest Christians was an ethic of community or fellowship (κοινωνία). This, however, has to be carefully assessed. Its essential reference is not to the human fellowship which the members of the community enjoyed with one another, although this is most certainly not to be excluded from the connotation of the term. Primarily the emphasis is on the common sharing in the grace of the risen Lord. The participation of the various members in the forgiving experience of the Resurrection lent to them a common grace wherein they stood. This fellowship, in grace, could not but create a warm human relationship: the members became brethren for whom Christ had died; their ethic was the expression of their fellowship, which was, at one and the same time, a fellowship with one another and "in Christ."

2. The imitation of Christ. This reference to Christ shows again that the fellowship was rooted in a particular event—immediately in the Resurrection and, behind this, in the life and death of Jesus, with which, as an expression of grace, the Resurrection was wholly congruous. Thus the ethic of the community is linked to the understanding of an event —the life, death, and resurrection of Jesus. In this the church came to see the act of God himself in history, and the appropriation of this event became the dynamic of the good life—i.e., much in the ethic of the early church is the imitation of God "in Christ." The sign of this appropriation and, therefore, of this ethic, became BAPTISM, which is traced back by Acts to Pentecost; and, although it was not universal (Acts 1:14-15; 19:1-7), it is possible that most Christians were baptized (Rom. 6:3; I Cor. 12:13; Gal. 3:27). Since Jesus had figuratively connected his own baptism with his coming passion (Mark 10:38), it is also possible that this had come to be combined with the rite of baptism in the minds of the Twelve also, so that the germ of later Pauline teaching on baptism as dying and rising with Christ was present from the first.

In any case, for Paul ethics is inseparable from the life, death, and resurrection of Jesus. He divided his own life clearly into two parts: first, his life under the law when he was a Jew, and secondly, his life "in Christ." The two parts were distinctly separated by his experience on the road to Damascus. The act by which a Christian acknowledged his faith, and really began to live "in Christ," was baptism. This act symbolized a death to the old life under the law, and a rising to newness of life "in Christ," or in "the Spirit." By baptism, the Christian, through faith, had died, risen, been justified: he was a new creation. All that was now necessary for him was to become what he was. His ethical life is rooted in what he is. For Paul, ethics thus is indicative in character. This motif—the appeal to God's act in Christ—is not confined to baptismal contexts; see II Cor.8:9; 12:1; Phil. 2:5-8. The imitation of God in Christ is also Johannine: "We love [him], because [and as] he first loved us" (I John 4:19).

But the imitation of Christ, as the imitation of God's act in redemption, does not exhaust this motif. The figure of the historical Jesus, as such, played a real part in the moral development of the early church. There can be little doubt that part of the reason for the preservation of stories about the life of Jesus, such as we have in the gospels, was the desire to imitate Jesus in his acts. During the actual ministry the call which went out, that men should follow him, meant, under the circumstance, readiness to enter upon his way of suffering—i.e., to take up the cross literally (Mark 8:34, etc.). In the life of the early church, while persecution, and, therefore, violent death—walking the way of the cross literally—was always a possibility, more often Christians were called upon to imitate their Lord in virtues of the daily round, less spectacular, but no less arduous perhaps, than readiness to die—in love, forbearance, patience, mercy, etc. The degree to which the imitation of Christ, in this sense, played a part in the lives of Christians has been variously assessed. If, as some form critics assert (*see* FORM CRITICISM), early Christians, including Paul, were largely uninterested in that life, then the imitation of Christ cannot have been significant. But this position the whole of our previous discussion, with its emphasis on the rootage of Christian ethics in the "event," will have, by implication, invalidated.

Again, it has been urged that where Paul mentions the "imitation of Christ" in I Cor. 11:1; I Thess. 1:6, the reference is not to the details of the character and conduct of Jesus, but to the central act of his self-giving. Paul would have agreed, we are to assume, with Kierkegaard that: "If the contemporary generation had left behind them nothing but the words, 'We have believed that in such and such a year God appeared among us in the humble figure of a servant, that he lived and taught in our community, and finally died,' it would have been enough." But this is invalidated by the fact that Christ is an object of imitation in the same sense as Paul is (I Cor. 11:1); the apostle holds up certain qualities of the historic Jesus which were to be imitated; he points to Jesus, who pleased not himself (Rom. 15:3), to his meekness and gentleness (II Cor. 10:1); he commands liberality through a reminder of him who was rich and became poor (II Cor. 8:8-9; cf. Phil. 2:5-6). The description of "love" in I Cor. 13 is probably based on the life of Jesus—is, in short, a sort of character sketch of the Lord. There can be little question that for Paul every Christian is pledged to an attempted ethical conformity to Christ. So also is it with John (John 13) and I Peter (2:21). Thus, both as an act of God and as "human," the life of Jesus is the paradigm of the Christian life.

3. The divine purpose and the Holy Spirit. The ethic of the church, since it is directed to and by Jesus of Nazareth, as the Messiah, has throughout an eschatological reference; it is related to the purpose of God in salvation revealed in Jesus. This comes out most clearly in Paul's understanding of his call to be an apostle. This meant for him that he was taken up by God's grace to share in the redemptive activity of God now at work in the church. True, the apostolic consciousness of Paul was more intense than that of most Christians, and his calling, in a sense, unique as the apostle to the Gentiles. But the whole community also was "called"—i.e., caught up into the large counsel of God. This shines through the literature of the NT (*see* CHURCH, IDEA OF). Christians are, therefore, delivered from futility: they share in the work of salvation (including their own) inaugurated by Jesus, and ethical decisions are to be made in this light.

Another way of saying the same thing is to claim that the Christian life is life in the Spirit, because the Spirit is the eschatological gift, which warrants the community's consciousness of itself as the community of the end. This is the meaning of Acts 2. Attempts to maintain that the Spirit, in the earliest days of the church, had no ethical significance must be rejected. The character that the Spirit had already acquired in the OT makes it impossible to interpret him at any time in the church as merely a wonder-working power, mysterious and non-ethical. It was the Spirit that had inspired the prophets, who had discerned between the precious and the vile, that would create a new heart in the new Israel of Ezekiel's vision, and inspire the messianic times with counsel, wisdom, and righteousness. Above all else, for Judaism, the Holy Spirit was the inspirer of the Scriptures; but this, in itself, implied the "ethicization" of the Spirit, because it was through these that Israel knew the moral demands made upon it.

Thus for Acts, Paul, and the rest of the NT, the Spirit was essentially creative and life-giving, not only in the ecstatic aspects of life, but also in the moral. The coming of the Spirit should never be separated from the Resurrection as grace: like the Resurrection, the Spirit is an "energy of forgiveness." Thus for Paul the Spirit becomes the source of Christian morality. Love, joy, peace, righteousness, and "every victory won" in the moral sphere are the fruit of the Spirit (Gal. 5:22-23). The connection of the Spirit with morality in the Fourth Gospel is different. Here the primary function of the Spirit is the illumination of the church (John 14:26; 16:3, 14), the unfolding to it of what Jesus during his lifetime could not reveal, because the disciples could not bear it (16:12). It would seem to be only given on condition of a response to moral obedience (14:15). But the close relationship between the Holy Spirit and the risen Lord in John should again warn us against any de-ethicization of it (John 14:26 includes a reference probably to the ethical teaching of Jesus). Nevertheless, it is in Paul that the Spirit, as the dynamic of the good life, comes to his own. Moreover, it was Paul who isolated the moral aspect of the activity of the Spirit, and thus brought order into the confusion of popular Christian thinking in this field and made "love" the criterion of the Spirit's activity and presence (I Cor. 13).

4. Koinonia ethics: horizontal. The ethics of the NT is not only indicative, pointing to the fellowship (*koinonia*) of the church "in Christ," to the historic Jesus and the act of God in him, to the divine purpose and the presence of the Spirit; it also contains a "horizontal" imperative. The church did not luxuriate in "grace," but took practical steps to give expression to grace. The chief gift of grace, and fruit of the Spirit, was love (*agape*). This it was that led to the experiment usually referred to as the communism of Acts (2:42-45). Not indifference to this world's good, engendered by belief in its approaching end, nor the presence among believers of elements related to the communal sect at Qumran (although such "communism" as we find in Acts would be natural in a milieu influenced by the latter), nor any conscious reflection on the indivisibility of the spiritual and material—none of these primarily led to this. Rather, the experiment was the natural, spontaneous expression of life in the Spirit, with which the neglect of the poor was incompatible. This appears from the naïveté of the experiment. Owners sold their property and handed over the proceeds to the apostles, who administered a common fund from which the needs of the poor were met, presumably in the form of common meals. The contributions to the common pool were voluntary (Acts 5:1-11). Living on capital eventually led to economic distress (Acts 11:29; 24:17; I Cor. 16:1; II Cor. 8:1 ff; Gal. 2:10). The experiment failed, not to be repeated in this form, but it witnesses to the "fellowship" ethic of the primitive community in its realism. It lived in the absolutes, not only because the end was at hand, but also because of the intensity of its experience of forgiveness.

This emphasis on the communal nature of the Christian way persisted throughout the NT. It is ultimately rooted in the teaching of Jesus, who not only gathered the Twelve as the representatives of the new Israel to follow him, but attached them in a kind of organic union with himself. Those who accept the disciples whom he sent accept him (Matt. 10:40); those who refuse them refuse him (Matt. 10: 14-15); to give to one of the least of the brethren of Christ is to give to him (Matt. 25:31-45); the followers of Christ can suffer with him and represent him (Matt. 5:11-12); to receive a child in his name is to receive him (Matt. 18:5-6). From this background, Paul's Christ mysticism developed, his concept of the solidarity of Christians with their Lord; his understanding of the church, as the new Israel, the body of Christ, is rooted in the ministry of Jesus himself. How this is developed ethically is seen in I Corinthians. One of the criteria for the proper conduct is the upbuilding of the body (I Corinthians, *passim*). Similarly, in the Fourth Gospel the concept of the disciples, the church, as branches of a vine (John 15), or, in I Peter, of Christians, as constituting living stones in the temple of God (I Pet. 2:4-5), expresses the same truth—that the ethical life of Christians is a life in community, because they share in the one Lord. Thus Christian ethics in the NT is never atomistic. No individual lives to himself. On the other hand, he is not at the mercy of the community, even of the church itself, because the body itself is subordinated to the Head, Christ. The lordship of Christ is a safeguard against both a spurious individualism and a totalitarian collectivism. *See* CHURCH, IDEA OF.

5. "Casuistry" and the words of Jesus. The same impulse which led to the experiment in communism, the awareness of the "horizontal" significance of the *koinonia* in grace, in part at least, led to other developments:

a) At first, in the awareness of its resources in grace, the church attempted to live in the light of the absolutes. For certain elements the commandments of Jesus in their absolute form were for long guides to conduct. But, under the inevitable compromises, it became necessary for the church to apply these absolutes to life. First, there began that process which tended to transform the absolutes into practical rules of conduct. The classic example is the way in which the prohibition of divorce was made practicable by the addition of the exceptive clause: "except on the ground of unchastity" (Matt. 5:31 ff). Because it is Matthew that reveals this best, it has been claimed that the words of Jesus as such played a significant part in the ethical development of the church only in Jewish Christian circles. But this is not so. The Pauline letters also appeal to the words of Jesus as authoritative. These words were an important source for Paul's ethical teaching. The extent to which the Pauline letters are reminiscent of the Synoptic gospels has been insufficiently recognized. There are very many such reminiscences. Two factors emerge:

Paul interweaves words of Jesus "unconsciously" into his exhortations, which suggests that these words were bone of his bone (see, e.g., Rom. 12:14 [Matt. 5:44]; 12:17 [Matt. 5:39 ff]; 12:21 [Matt. 5:38 ff]; 13:7 [Matt. 22:15-22; Mark 12:13-17; Luke 20:20-26]; 13:8-10 [Matt. 22:34-40; Mark 12:28-34; Luke 10:25-28]; 14:10 [Matt. 7:1; Luke 6:37]; 14:13 [Matt. 18:7; Mark 9:42; Luke 17:1-2]; 14:14 [Matt. 15:11; Mark 7:15]; I Thess. 4:8 [Luke 10:16]; 5:2-3 [Matt. 24:43; Luke 12:39]; 5:6 [Matt. 24:42; Mark 13:37; Luke 21:34, 36]).

Also, there is clear evidence that there was a collection of sayings of the Lord to which Paul appealed (e.g., Acts 20:35; I Cor. 7:10; 9:14; 11:23 ff; 14:37; I Thess. 4:15-16; see especially I Cor. 7:25). Not only in matters of a legislative character does Paul find guidance in the words of Jesus, but also in more personal matters (Rom. 7), where possibly his discovery of the supreme importance of motive goes back to Jesus. In I Cor. 7:25 he refers to a word of Christ as a commandment (ἐπιταγή); in two places he uses the very words "the law of Christ" where the reference is, in part at least, to the teaching of Jesus. This is no declension on Paul's part to a primitive legalism, but the recognition of the fact that his exalted Lord was never, in his mind, divorced from Jesus the rabbi, that the Spirit is never divorced from the historic teaching of Jesus. And, although in the Fourth Gospel the ethical teaching of Jesus, as such, plays little part, the function of the Spirit is to recall the words of Jesus. The same emphasis appears in I John, where there is constant appeal to the commandments of the Lord, and frequent echoes of them. *See bibliography.*

Nevertheless, there is a difference of emphasis (but only of emphasis) in Matthew and Paul, as over against the Johannine literature. The words of Jesus appear in the former two over their wide range. But even there they are summed up in one word, "love" (ἀγάπη). Thus the climax of the Sermon on the Mount at Matt. 7:12 is the Golden Rule. Paul and John, like the Synoptics, emphasize the centrality of "love" (Rom. 13:8-10; I Cor. 8:1; 13; Col. 3:14; I John 3:1; 2:7-10; 4:7-16). The meaning of "love" has again to be carefully noted (*see* § B4 *above*). Partaking more of active good will than of emotion, it can be commanded, as emotions cannot. In I John it is used in a "down-to-earth" manner as involving willingness to share one's goods (I John 3:17). For Paul it is the fulfilment of the law and the principle of cohesion in the Christian community. The expression of love is multiple (I Cor. 13), but its essential nature is revealed in Christ's dying for men. It is this kind of act that is demanded of those who "love."

b) The necessity which led to the application of the absolutes of Jesus to life led the church to take over for its own use codal material whether from Hellenism or from Judaism or both. Most of the letters reveal a twofold structure: a first part, dealing with "doctrine," is followed by a second, dealing with ethics. Romans is typical. Chs. 1–11 deal with doctrine; 12:1 ff deals with ethics, and it is causally connected with chs. 1–11. The ethical sections of the various letters reveal a common tradition of catechesis, which may have been used in the instruction of converts, especially at baptism (*see bibliography*). Cf. Rom. 12:1; Eph. 4:20-6:19; Col. 3:8-4:12; Heb. 12: 1-2; Jas. 1:1-4:10; I Pet. 1:1-4:11; 4:12-5:14. This common tradition must not be regarded as having a fixed pattern, but the similarity in the order and contents of the material in the above sections is too marked to be accidental. The presence in them of the imperative participle (e.g., at Rom. 12:9-19), a form not common in Hellenistic Greek but familiar in Hebrew legal documents, suggests that Paul, and other early Christian writers, drew upon rabbinic code material, such as is found in the Dead Sea Scrolls (Manual of Discipline 1:18 ff actually has the imperative participle), Mishna Demai and Derek Eretz Rabba and Zuta. There are also parallels to the tradition in Hellenistic sources. The church probably took over much pagan ethical convention from the Jewish Diaspora. Whatever the exact source of the material, the church found it necessary to borrow from non-Christian sources.

6. NT ethics and "the world." What, finally, is the relation of ethics in the NT to "the world"? That non-Christian ethical forms could be taken up into the Christian tradition, without incongruity, means that there was a point of affinity between them and Christian forms. This point lies in the relation of the ethics demanded by the NT to creation. For Jesus, we saw, there was an affinity between the natural and the ethical. Thus he found human relations, at one level, a clue to the will of God (Matt. 7:11; *see* § B5 *above*). The created order, and man as part of this order, bears the "image of God." Thus it is natural that the ethical tradition of mankind, in this case of Hellenism and Judaism, should be of use to the church, whose ethic not only can transcend the natural but also can confirm it. Thus Paul can refer to what nature itself teaches (I Cor. 11:14) and make use of the rough rabbinic equivalent of the Stoic "law of nature" (Rom. 1; 2): he speaks of what is fitting (τὰ καθήκοντα; e.g., Rom. 1:28) like a Stoic, and makes appeal to CONSCIENCE. Probably the "apostolic decree" of Acts 15 makes use of the Noachian commandments also—i.e., of laws that were reckoned as binding upon every living soul, which had been given to Noah, the father of mankind, before the revelation on Sinai. Still more important is it that the Christ, who is the redeemer in the NT, and the revealer of God's moral purpose, is also the agent of creation (John 1; Col. 1; Heb. 1), so that the ethics of the NT, rooted as it is in the gospel, is not only of relevance to the church, but also to the world, insofar as this ethics affirms and confirms what is truly natural for all men in virtue of their creation.

Can we go further in relating the Christian ethic to the world? Indirectly, the life of the church, insofar as it really is the community of grace, can convict the world of sin and reveal to it life of a new quality and direction. Does the NT reveal more—an ethic directly relevant to politics and society, etc.? Although there was evident in the church a Christian-ization of personal relations (see Philemon), within the existing order, the church, partly under the impact of the expectation of the Parousia, was apparently not concerned to change the social structures of the time, evil as many of them were. The preaching of Jesus on the kingdom of God had political repercussions in the ministry: He attracted Zealots (*see* ZEALOT) for a time, but, rejecting their methods, ultimately disappointed them. When Paul discovered that the term "kingdom of God" was being misunderstood politically, he dropped it almost entirely (Acts 17:7-8). Either submission to the powers that be is advised (Rom. 13:1); or an abortive hatred that can only lead, not to their redemption, but to their destruction (Apoc.); or there is care not to offend (I Peter), although the limits of the claims of Caesar are also recognized (*see bibliography*).

From all this, are we to conclude that NT ethics are primarily designed to cultivate the garden of the church, the fragrance of which is to sweeten the surrounding wilderness, which, however, is to sustain no frontal attack? To many the answer to this must be in the affirmative. Even in I Cor. 6:1-11, it is claimed, Paul gives no rules for an institutional reform, even in the church, but demands merely that at each point there should be radical obedience to love. This, it is urged, seems to be the case everywhere. Neither Jesus nor Paul reflects on the social consequences of his actions (Rom. 12:2: be *not* conformed to this world). This is to go too far. As stated above, Jesus may have left instructions for the discipline of the disciples, and Paul was a catechist and an organizer. Moreover, recently the attempt has been made to find a basis for a "kerygmatic social ethic and an aggressive social action" in Paul's view of the conflict between God, Christ, and the church, and the evil, unseen powers of evil, the demonic principalities and powers, the "rulers of this world" (see Colossians, Ephesians, etc.). These last represent the structural elements of unregenerate society, the false authorities of culture. The struggle of Christ against these powers goes on until the Parousia: in this, Christians share and thus engage in social action. They are thus governed by a lively HOPE. This theory preserves the profound truth that the coming of the kingdom of God is never merely a gift, but also a demand to confront the brute realities of the universe: it is in tension. Little examined, the theory, however, faces one difficulty in the NT itself—namely, that while the "unseen powers" in Paul may be mythological expressions of social, political, and economic realities, it is difficult to give them this significance in the Synoptics, which belong largely to the same milieu. And the question must be asked whether it is legitimate to demythologize the "principalities and powers" (as does Wilder). In any case, the real justification for a struggle against social evils lies in the very nature of the grace which created the church and to which it responds; this needs no recourse to "demythologization." Chronological preoccupation with the Parousia, and its own social weakness, made this less clear to the early church than it need be to us.

NT ethics is dominated by the fact of Christ. We have seen an indicative pointing to what he did in his life, death, and resurrection, by the appropriation of which the Christian has died to sin and risen to newness of life; and an imperative derived mainly from his words, but also drawing upon Jewish and Hellenistic ethical traditions. In short, the work and words of Jesus, and these in indissoluble unity, constitute the ethics of the NT, of the new Israel. We might say that it differs from the ethics of the old Israel mainly in this, that while in Judaism, within the complex of the event which redeemed Israel from Egypt—i.e., the Exodus—it is the law of the covenant rather than the agent of the covenant, Moses, that is emphasized; in Christianity, the new exodus, it is the opposite that is true: here the person of Jesus, the agent of the new covenant, achieves preeminence, rather than his word of demand. Christ has taken the place of the law and has become the "new Torah."

Bibliography. On the tradition of catechesis in the early church, see P. Carrington, *The Primitive Christian Catechism* (1940); E. G. Selwyn, ed., *The First Epistle of St. Peter* (1946). On the appeal to Jesus' commandments in I John, see C. H. Dodd, *The Johannine Epistles* (1946), pp. xxxviii ff. On Jesus as a new Moses, see W. D. Davies, *Torah in the Messianic Age and/or the Age to Come* (1952). On the NT attitude toward the claims of the state, see O. Cullmann, *The State in the NT* (1956). See also: T. W. Manson, *The Teaching of Jesus* (1931); R. Bultmann, *Jesus and the Word* (1934); A. N. Wilder, *Eschatology and Ethics in the Teaching of Jesus* (2nd ed., 1939); T. W. Manson, *Jesus the Messiah* (1943); O. Cullmann, *Christ and Time* (1950); C. H. Dodd, *Gospel and Law* (1950); R. Schnackenburg, *Die Sittliche Botschaft des NT* (1954); A. Schweitzer, *The Quest of the Historical Jesus* (3rd ed., 1954); W. D. Davies, *Paul and Rabbinic Judaism* (1955), pp. 111-46; A. N. Wilder, "Kerygma, Eschatology and Social Ethics," in *The Background of the NT and Its Eschatology* (Studies in Honour of C. H. Dodd; eds. Davies and Daube; 1956), pp. 509-36.

W. D. DAVIES

ETHIOPIA ē'thĭ ō'pĭ ə [כּוּשׁ; CUSH ko͞osh in Gen. 2:13; 10:6; I Chr. 1:8; Ezek. 38:5; ETHIOPIANS —ənz. The ancient name of the territory S of Egypt, corresponding roughly to the present Sudan.

1. Name. Much confusion has arisen between the terms "Ethiopia" and "Cush," which for the biblical period may be taken as more or less synonymous. The MT has only one word: כּוּשׁ (*Kûš*). The LXX transcribes the name as Χους in the ethnographic lists (Gen. 10:6-8; I Chr. 1:8-10), where Cush is represented as a son of Ham (*see* CUSH 1); but the name is elsewhere rendered by Αιθιοπια ("Ethiopia"), the Greek name for this same area during classical antiquity, beginning with the Homeric

Imprimerie de l'Institut Français d'Archéologie Orientale

37. A model showing Ethiopians carrying bows and arrows; from the Middle Kingdom (2050-1800 B.C.)

poems. The KJV follows the LXX division between "Cush" and "Ethiopia," with the exception of Isa. 11:11, where the LXX has Αἰθιοπία but the KJV has "Cush." The RSV likewise follows the LXX, with the exception of Gen. 2:13, where "Cush" is found for the LXX Αἰθιοπία. The gentilic כּוּשִׁי (*Kûšî;* plural *Kûšîm*), "Cushite," is translated Αἰθίοψ, "Ethiopian," by the LXX with the exception of II Sam. 18:21-23, 31-32, where it is merely transliterated Χουσι. The KJV has "Ethiopian(s)" everywhere but in the II Samuel passages, where "Cushi" is taken as a personal name. The RSV employs "Cushite" for the II Samuel passages and in Num. 12:1 (against the LXX and the KJV) but follows the LXX elsewhere with "Ethiopian(s)." Hebrew *Kûš* is borrowed from Egyptian *kꜣš;* cuneiform attestations include *kāš-* (from Tell el-Amarna) and *kūs-* (Late Assyrian). Fig. ETH 37.

2. Extent. The name Cush appears in Egyptian sources for the first time in the reign of Sesostris I (1971-1930 B.C.) and seems to have been employed during the Middle Kingdom as the name of a relatively small area between the Second and Third Cataracts, separated from Egypt itself by the land of Wawat, which extended southward from Syene (Assuan) to the Second Cataract. During the New Kingdom the name Cush took on a much wider meaning but was for some time used in both the narrow and the wider senses; there is no evidence that the biblical use of the term reflects anything but the prevailing designation of all known (or legendary) territory S of Egypt. It is of interest to note that the Egyptian name for an inhabitant of this region was *nḥsy,* which is preserved in the originally Egyptian names Tahpanhes and Phineas.

3. Political significance. Nubia, as this general area is more commonly called, broke away from Egyptian domination soon after the year 1000 B.C. and became an independent kingdom, with its capital at Napata, near present-day Jebel Barkal. Thanks to the work of the brilliant American archaeologist G. A. Reisner at the royal cemetries of El Khurru and Nuri, both near Napata, an unbroken sequence of rulers has been established reaching down into the third century B.C., at which time Napata was abandoned and a new capital founded farther to the S at Meroe. This Meroitic branch of the Nubian Kingdom continued until the fourth century A.D., when it was overwhelmed by an invasion from the Axumite kingdom of Abyssinia.

The period during which the rulers of Napata exercised sovereignty over Egyptian territory proper coincides roughly with the Twenty-fifth, or Ethiopian, Dynasty of the Manethonian tradition, and is assigned the years 715-663 B.C. In actual fact, however, Kashta, the first Napatan king of whom we know, took advantage of the weak hold that the Saïte ruler Tefnakht (Twenty-fourth Dynasty) exercised over Upper Egypt and conquered that territory, with its chief city, Thebes, *ca.* 750 B.C. His son Piankhi led a campaign northward to the Mediterranean *ca.* 725 and succeeded in uniting all Egypt under Nubian rule. The details of this march are known from the remarkable stela set up by Piankhi at Napata and now exhibited in the Cairo Museum. The political situation must have been highly unstable, for we know that Tefnakht was still ruling in the Delta *ca.* 720. It was not until a further successful campaign of Shabaka, the successor of Piankhi, that the Saïte Dynasty (Twenty-fourth) was brought to an end and Nubian rule firmly established.

Shabaka is thus reckoned as the first ruler of the Twenty-fifth Dynasty; he was succeeded by Shabataka (701-690), Taharka (690-664), and Tanutamun (664-663). Taharka (Hebrew *Tirhāqāh*) is mentioned, both in Isa. 37:9 and in the Assyrian records, as an ally of Hezekiah in his rebellion against the Assyrian ruler Sennacherib, specifically in connection with the second invasion, which must have taken place between 689 and 686 B.C. According to the biblical account, Sennacherib returned to Nineveh after his army was decimated by an angel of the Lord (presumably by a pestilence, as in Herodotus II.141). Sennacherib's successor, Esarhaddon (681-669), invaded Egypt in 670 and reduced it to a province of the Assyrian Empire. Tanutamun, who still ruled at Napata, attempted to regain Egypt from the Assyrians, but his campaign ended in defeat with the destruction of Thebes in 663 by Ashurbanipal. Retiring to Napata, Tanutamun continued to rule the Nubian Kingdom, while in Egypt proper Psamtik I, first ruler of the Twenty-sixth Dynasty, assumed the throne under the aegis of Ashurbanipal.

Bibliography. G. Reisner, "The Meroitic Kingdom of Ethiopia," *JEA*, 9 (1923), 34-77. C. C. Rossini, *Storia d'Etiopia*, Africa Italiana, III (1928). T. Säve-Söderbergh, *Ägypten und Nubien* (1941). D. Dunham, *The Royal Cemeteries of Kush*, vol. I: *El Khurru* (1950); vol. II: *Nuri* (1955). G. Posener, "Pour une localisation du pays Koush au Moyen Empire," *Kush*, VI (1958), 39-68.

T. O. LAMBDIN

ETHIOPIAN EUNUCH (Acts 8:27-40). A minister of CANDACE, queen of ETHIOPIA, who was converted to Christianity through Philip the evangelist (*see* PHILIP 7). Two interrelated questions are here involved: Who was the Ethiopian eunuch? What is the significance of this event in the plan of Acts?

As a geographical or ethnic term, Ethiopia (כּוּשׁ; Αἰθιοπία; Latin *Aethiopia*) has had an extended history and varied meaning. It has been used to refer to Africa S of Egypt, to Arabia, and even to India. At times it simply appears to have been a useful word to give vague designation to all peoples far distant from the Mediterranean basin living in the far S and E. In Homer, the Ethiopians are the farthest of mankind: the sun sets there. In Amos 9:7, the implication is somewhat the same. Likewise, the term has covered a wide variety of racial groups. The word itself was sometimes said to mean "burnt-faced" or "swarthy-faced," and thus taken to refer to any dark-skinned person. E.g., Herodotus (III.17-23; VII.69-70) distinguishes between woolly-haired Ethiopians (Negroes) and straight-haired ones (primitive Indians).

By late biblical times, however, the geographical meaning of the term had come to be well limited to the lands S of Egypt, to the part of later Anglo-Egyptian Sudan between Assuan and Khartoum, and especially to the kingdom of Meroe, at the confluence of the Nile and the Astaboras (today, Tacassi), a district sometimes spoken of as an island by ancient geographers.

As a fertile region, abounding in gold, copper, iron,

precious stones, ivory, ebony, cereals, dates, aromatics, the kingdom of Meroe (with its earlier capital, Napata) was a caravan center and the seat of some extended economic, political, and cultural activity (Isa. 45:14). Important contacts with the Egyptians, Arabians, Greeks, Phoenicians, and Jews obtained. There is evidence of some variety of racial features in the sculptures of various periods.

While the Ethiopian kings in Napata (*ca.* 700-300 B.C.), and afterward in Meroe, used the Egyptian language in hieroglyphic writing for formal inscriptions, from the first century B.C. to the end of the third century of the Christian era, a native language and script called Meroitic is common. From the time of Ptolemy II (308-246 B.C.) the kingdom became partly Hellenized. Greeks had visited there since 665 B.C. (Strabo XVI.773-74, 785-87). That a high officer in the queen's court—indeed, the treasurer of her kingdom—should be able to read the Greek roll of Isaiah is not a problem. How he had the roll, if he was neither a Jew nor a proselyte, may be a problem; yet a court official could find a way.

The narrative in Acts seems to emphasize two things: the man was an Ethiopian, and he was a eunuch. His name is not given. Instead, he is introduced into the dialogue five times as "a" or "the" eunuch, but without comment as to whether he was a Jew or a Gentile, a proselyte or a "God-fearer," and without concern to identify him ethnically.

Was the "Ethiopian eunuch" a Jew, whether by birth or as a proselyte? Those who say he was either have to deny that he was properly a eunuch or to maintain that Isa. 56:3-5 is to be taken as evidence that the legislation of Lev. 21:20; Deut. 23:1 was no longer (on occasion) enforced. But the probabilities support neither position. Luke's fivefold use of "eunuch," unqualified, suggests that he means it as such, and does not simply think of it as a synonym for "minister" without any implication of mutilation. That the eunuch should have been properly such fits the pattern both of the Greek idea of non-Greek civilizations and of court officials and keepers of harems (Esth. 2:14) when such existed or where the rulers were queens, as in Meroe.

If a eunuch, then, he was most probably not a born Jew, and only less probably a Gentile proselyte.

Perhaps the most that can be said is that the Ethiopian eunuch best fits the type of half-believer in Judaism, the "God-fearer," and as seems to have been the case with many such Gentiles, was ready for the Christian reading of the OT. That Cornelius later figures so importantly in Acts as the first Gentile convert does not prove that the eunuch was a Jew or that Luke thought he was.

In this narrative, then, Luke will show that (*a*) the gospel addresses itself to the peoples who dwell on the outermost fringes of the inhabited world; (*b*) as an "Ethiopian" the eunuch is an outlander (his ethnic origin is strictly undetermined) who comes to the light, and as a high official he is a king who comes to the brightness of its rising; and (*c*) as a eunuch, he serves as an example of one by nature "not-my-people" becoming "my people." The church now sees the response prayed for in Ps. 68:31: "Let Ethiopia hasten to stretch out her hands to God" (see also Isa. 11:11).

Bibliography. W. K. L. Clarke in F. J. Foakes-Jackson and K. Lake, *Beginnings of Christianity*, II (1922), 101-3; J. Garstang, *Meroe, the City of the Ethiopians* (1911); C. J. Cadbury, *The Book of Acts in History* (1955), pp. 15-18.

F. D. GEALY

ETHIOPIC VERSION ē'thĭ ŏp'ĭk. Made *ca.* the fourth or fifth century A.D., this translation of the Bible is represented today only by late copies, dating from the thirteenth and succeeding centuries. *See* VERSIONS, ANCIENT, § 9.

B. M. METZGER

ETH-KAZIN ĕth kā'zĭn [עתה קצין] (Josh. 19:13); KJV ITTAH-KAZIN ĭt'ə kā'zĭn. A town on the border of Zebulun. Its location is unknown, but according to the context, it should be in the vicinity of Gath-hepher, possibly at Kefr Kenna.

Bibliography. F.-M. Abel, *Géographie de la Palestine*, II (1938), 63, 351.

G. W. VAN BEEK

ETHMA. KJV Apoc. form of NEBO.

ETHNAN ĕth'nən [אתנן, gift *or* hire]. Listed as a family of the tribe of Judah (I Chr. 4:7); he could be identified with ITHNAN, a town of S Judah (cf. Josh. 15:23).

Bibliography. M. Noth, *Die israelitischen Personennamen* (1928), p. 171.

H. H. GUTHRIE, JR.

ETHNARCH ĕth'närk [ἐθνάρχης]. A title with an original meaning of "ruler of the people"; often rendered "governor." Used over a period of centuries, the term can well have changed meanings from time to time, so that obscurity and variation combine to make it an uncertain term.

"Ethnarch" was apparently a title of royalty granted to a dependent monarch. It was higher than "TETRARCH" but lower than "king." SIMON MACCABEUS (I Macc. 14:47) is called "commander and ethnarch"; HYRCANUS II was both the ethnarch and the high priest (Jos. Antiq. XIV.viii.5; x.2), though he was denied the crown (XX.x.4). ARCHELAUS, son of Herod, was not deemed worthy of the title "king," and was named "ethnarch" instead (Jos. Antiq. XVII.xi.4; War II.vi.3; Matt. 2:22 and Jos. Antiq. XVIII.iv.3 allude either loosely or incorrectly to Archelaus as "king"). Much later, Origen (*Letter to Julius Africanus* 14) described the chief of the Jews in Palestine as "ethnarch," adding that the ethnarch is "in no way different from a king of the people."

The preceding definition supposes a use of the title in a situation in which a people resident in its own land was governed by a ruler who was subject to the Roman authority. Respecting Jews, however, there were situations in which a community was located outside Judea, as in Alexandria in Egypt, and was there subject to Roman rule. Could the term "ethnarch" apply to the Jewish "ruler" in such a situation? Apparently so, for Josephus quotes Strabo (Antiq. XIV.vii.2) as follows: "An ethnarch of their own has been installed, who governs the people and adjudicates suits and supervises contracts and ordinances, just as if he were the head of a sovereign state" (see also XIX.v.2). Philo of Alexandria, however, seems not to have used the term "ethnarch," but rather "genarch" (γενάρχης; *Against Flaccus* X). Another term was used for the head of the Alexandrian Jewish community, "alabarch" (ἀλαβάρχης); neither the connotation nor the etymology of this term is known.

The only use of the term in the NT is in II Cor. 11:32: "At Damascus, the ethnarch [RSV governor] under King Aretas guarded the city of Damascus in order to seize me." Commentators divide as to whether this ethnarch was the appointed representative of the Nabatean king Aretas (9 B.C.-A.D. 39), who controlled Damascus; or whether Damascus at the time was under Roman control and the ethnarch a Nabatean with functions somewhat like those of the Jewish ethnarch in Jerusalem. It is uncertain whether or not DAMASCUS remained unbrokenly under Roman rule after its seizure by Pompey (*ca.* 65 B.C.); hence there exists this division among the commentators.

Bibliography. In addition to the standard commentators on II Corinthians, see J. Juster, *Les juifs dans l'empire Romain* (1914), 1, 391-400. E. Schürer, *A History of the Jewish People in the Time of Jesus Christ* (English trans., 1891), I; II, 280, n. 201; II, 357-58; *TSK*, XCIX (1899), 95 ff. S. SANDMEL

ETHNI ĕth'nī [אתני, gift *or* hire]. An ancestor of ASAPH in a genealogy of Levitical SINGERS (I Chr. 6:41). The list is postexilic and, to a great extent, artificial, representing an attempt to trace Levitical pedigrees back to the time of David. Jeatherai appears in place of Ethni in I Chr. 6:21, possibly because of a scribal error.

Bibliography. M. Noth, *Die israelitischen Personennamen* (1928), p. 171. H. H. GUTHRIE, JR.

ETHNOGRAPHY AND ETHNOLOGY. *See* MAN, ETHNIC DIVISIONS OF.

EUBULUS ū bū'ləs [Εὔβουλος, well advised]. A Christian man whose greetings are conveyed in II Tim. 4:21. The name is often found in papyri and inscriptions. F. W. GINGRICH

EUCHARIST ū'kə rĭst [εὐχαριστία, thanksgiving]. The name commonly used by Christians of the post-apostolic and later periods for the rite of the LORD'S SUPPER. There is no indisputable use of the word in this technical sense in the NT; though I Cor. 14:16 possibly contains an allusion to the "thanksgiving" over the elements of the Supper, and I Tim. 4:3-4 applies it to the giving of thanks over ordinary food. The references to thanksgiving in Christian worship in Eph. 5:20; Phil. 4:6; Col. 3:17; I Tim. 2:1 are of a more general character.

The verb form, εὐχαριστεῖν, is found in the accounts of Jesus' feeding of the multitude (Matt. 15:36; Mark 8:6; John 6:11) and of the Last Supper (Matt. 26:27; Mark 14:23; Luke 22:17, 19; I Cor. 11:24). It is synonymous with εὐλογεῖν, "bless," the term more generally employed to translate the Hebrew root ברך for blessings over food (cf. Mark 6:41; 8:7; 14:22 and parallels; and the noun form in I Cor. 10:16). Elsewhere in the NT, the verb is used of giving thanks over ordinary food (Acts 27:35; Rom. 14:6; I Cor. 10:30). M. H. SHEPHERD, JR.

EUERGETES ū ûr'jə tēz [εὐεργέτης, benefactor]. A title bestowed by ancient states upon those famed for notable deeds of benevolence who in modern days would receive a distinguished service award (cf. Luke 22:25). The author of Ecclesiasticus dates his work with reference to his coming "to Egypt in the thirty-eighth year of the reign of Euergetes" (Ptolemy VII). J. C. SWAIM

EUGNOSTOS, LETTER OF ūg nŏs'təs. A Gnostic writing in Coptic found at Chenoboskion in 1946 (*see* APOCRYPHA, NT). In this writing Sophia Pangeneteira is the feminine counterpart of Soter, the bisexual creator of all things. They produce six bisexual spirits, the sixth of which is Archigeneter (masculine)-Pistis Sophia (feminine). In the WISDOM OF JESUS (*see* JESUS, WISDOM OF), which is based upon this epistle, Pistis Sophia is one of the aeons. This suggests that the term "Pistis Sophia" may well have been drawn from Gnosticism of the type represented in this newly discovered library.

M. S. ENSLIN

EUMENES ū'mə nēz [Εὐμενής, well-disposed]. Mentioned in I Macc. 8:8 as a king to whom the Romans had given much Syrian territory. He was Eumenes II, king of Pergamum (197-158 B.C.), who had helped the Romans during their war with the Seleucid Antiochus the Great. *See* ANTIOCHUS 3.

N. TURNER

EUNATAN ū nā'tən. KJV Apoc. form of ELNATHAN.

EUNICE ū'nĭs [Εὐνίκη, good victory]. Daughter of LOIS (II Tim. 1:5); wife of a Gentile (Acts 16:1); and mother of TIMOTHY. She is commended by the author of II Timothy for her faith. Coming from Derbe or Lystra in Galatia, she was a Jewess (perhaps a widow) who had been converted to Christianity.

Her faith and that of her mother, Lois, are referred to in II Tim. 1:5 to make the point that Timothy, though young (cf. I Tim. 4:12; II Tim. 2:22), stands in a tradition of Christian experience which compensates for his lack of years.

B. H. THROCKMORTON, JR.

EUNUCH [סרים; LXX σπάδων, NT εὐνοῦχος, *from* to emasculate]. Alternately: OFFICER; CAPTAIN. A CHAMBERLAIN for the women's quarters in the royal household; usually a castrated male person. There are married eunuchs (Gen. 39:1), but Potiphar may not be literally a eunuch, as the word may indicate his office only. However, if he were a eunuch, his anger against Joseph would have more force. Usually the word implied sterility (I Sam. 8:15; Isa. 56:3) in Israel (cf. in Babylon [Dan. 1:3]; in Persia [Esth. 2:3]; in Ethiopia [Jer. 38:7; Acts 8:27]).

These men could be high officials (Gen. 39:1; Acts 8:27). But in Israel they were excluded from the covenant congregation, as were all impaired and defective persons (Lev. 22:24; Deut. 23:1). This made the threat of exile calamitous (Isa. 39:7). There is no certainty that this prophecy was carried out, or that Daniel was a eunuch (II Kings 20:17-18), although Herodotus suggests that captives were commonly made eunuchs. The Tyrian Jezebel used eunuchs (I Kings 22:9; cf. II Kings 8:6; 9:32). David had such officers (I Sam. 8:15; I Chr. 28:1). The last kings of

Judah knew them (II Kings 24:15; 25:19; Jer. 41:16). Herod the Great used a eunuch for cupbearer (Jos. Antiq. XV.viii.4; XVI.viii.1). The law-abiding eunuch is praised (Wisd. Sol. 3:14); and in the messianic kingdom, despite Deuteronomy, these castrated outcasts will rank before the unfaithful of Israel (Isa. 56:3-5).

The expression to be a eunuch for Christ's sake (cf. Matt. 19:12) probably refers to those who are voluntarily giving up the use of their reproductive powers to serve better in the kingdom. The verb is perhaps used metaphysically and may not involve surgery. Some think Jesus here refers to John the Baptist or himself. In Ecclesiasticus the opposite idea is conveyed, as eunuchs are figured as powerless men (Ecclus. 20:3; 30:21).

See also OFFICER. C. U. WOLF

EUODIA ū ō'dĭ ə [Εὐοδία, good journey, success]; KJV EUODIAS —əs (masculine, now considered incorrect). A Christian woman in the church at Philippi, in which congregation women were prominent from the beginning (Acts 16:12-15). She and Syntyche (Συντύχη, "coincidence," "success") are advised by Paul in Phil. 4:2 to compose their differences and live in harmony with each other. We have no way of knowing whether their quarrel was of a personal or a doctrinal nature.

In vs. 3 Paul calls upon his "true yokefellow" (σύζυγος) to help these women. This may have been a reference to Epaphroditus (2:25, etc.), though there are other possibilities. The proposal to take it as a proper name, Sy(n)zygus (so Westcott-Hort mg.), is rendered improbable by the fact that we do not yet have any examples of the word used as a proper name elsewhere. F. W. GINGRICH

EUPATOR ū'pə tôr [Εὐπάτωρ, of a noble father]. A surname or title assumed by the Seleucid king Antiochus V (*see* ANTIOCHUS 5), presumably because he was the son of Antiochus Epiphanes.

EUPHEMISM ū'fə mĭz'əm. *See* LITERATURE.

EUPHRATES ū frā'tēz [פרת, *from* Assyro-Babylonian *Purattu,* from Sumer. *Puranun; also from* Assyro. Babylonian *Purattu der ives, via* Old Pers. *Ufratu;* Εὐφράτης]. The largest river in Western Asia. According to biblical tradition the Euphrates was one of the four branches into which the river issuing from the Garden of Eden divided. It formed the upper, N boundary of the territories promised by Yahweh to Israel (Gen. 15:18; Deut. 1:7; 11:24; Josh. 1:4) and was reached by the Hebrew monarchy at its peak (II Sam. 8:3; 10:16; I Kings 4:24). The Euphrates is sometimes designated "the River" (Num. 22:5; Deut. 11:24; Josh. 24:3, 14; etc.; see also "the great river" in Josh. 1:4). It is also thus found in the name of the province "BEYOND THE RIVER."

1. The Upper Euphrates.* The Euphrates originates in Armenia and is formed by the confluence of two separate branches. The westernmost of these, Kara Su, is usually considered the actual beginnings of the Euphrates; it flows out of a circular pond in the region N of Erzerum and takes a westerly course. The E branch, Murat Suyu, originates in the region E of Erzerum and follows a course westward roughly parallel to that of Kara Su. The two join N of Malatiya to form the Euphrates proper. Flowing first SE, then SW, from Malatia, the Euphrates enters the Syrian Plain at Samsat, ancient Samosata, which lies on the right bank of the river and marks an important ford. Ancient Samosata was the capital of the Hellenistic kingdom of Commagene, the Assyrian Kummukh. Fig. EUP 38.

2. The Middle Euphrates. Farther S the river passes Jerablus, the site of ancient Carchemish, also on the right bank. Originally the center of a small city-state, Carchemish became an important provincial capital of the kingdom of Mitanni, of the Hittite Empire, and later of the Assyrian Empire. On the Euphrates at Carchemish, Nebuchadnezzar II of Babylon won his decisive victory over Neco of Egypt in 605 (cf. II Kings 24:7; Jer. 46). S of Carchemish the Euphrates receives the Sajur (Assyrian Sagur), which flows into it from the W; and as the

Courtesy of William Sanford La Sor

38. The Euphrates River near its source in the Armenian highlands

Euphrates continues in southeasterly direction, it is joined first by the Belikh (Assyrian Balikhu), later by the Khabur.* Both these rivers flow into the Euphrates from the N. Continuing SE, the river passes Salehiya, classical Dura-Europos, and Albu Kemal near the site of ancient Mari. Flowing E to Ana and again SE, the river reaches Hit, ancient Itu, famous as a major source of bitumen in antiquity. Fig. HAB 1.

3. The Lower Euphrates. From Hit the modern Euphrates flows to Felluja and S to Museyyib, where it divides into two branches. The main branch, the Hindiya branch, flows past Hindiya, through Bahr Shinafiye, and on to Samawa. The lesser of the two branches, the Hilla branch, flows past Hilla and ancient Babylon to reach Diwaniya, and then S to join the Hindiye branch S of Samawa. From Samawa the course leads SE past Nasiriye, through Lake Hammar, and on to juncture with the Tigris shortly before Basra. As Shatt-el-Arab the two rivers flow united past Basra and on into the Persian Gulf.

4. The Lower Euphrates in antiquity. In antiquity the course of the Euphrates seems, in its lower parts, to have been rather different from what it is today. In the region around Felluja the ancient course veered rather more to the E than does the present-day course and passed by the city of the sun-god,

Sippar, famous to late classical times as a seat of Chaldean learning. From Sippar the river ran southward to Kish, seat of the legendary First Dynasty of Mesopotamia. From Kish it passed to Nippur, the city of the storm-god Enlil and the major religious center of Sumer. Passing Nippur, it touched on Shuruppak (modern Fara), where the Sumerian Noah, Ziusudra, built his ark; then S to Erech (Uruk, modern Warka), famous as the city of Ishtar and of the epic hero Gilgamesh. From Erech the Euphrates continued to Ur, birthplace of Abraham in biblical tradition; S of this city it flowed through extensive marshes, eventually reaching the Persian Gulf. Besides this its main course the Euphrates sent off a W branch which took off in the neighborhood of Sippar and flowed through Babylon. This branch, called the Arachtu, became, *ca.* the beginning of the first millennium B.C., the main course of the river, and was known from then on as the Euphrates. It was clearly this course that Jeremiah referred to when he instructed Seraiah to read his book of prophecies when he came to Babylon and then to bind a stone to the book and cast it into the middle of the Euphrates as a sign of the coming destruction of that city (Jer. 51:60-64). T. JACOBSEN

EUPOLEMUS ū pŏl′ə məs [Εὐπόλεμος, skilful in war]. A Jewish ambassador. He was sent by Judas Maccabeus, after the victory over Nicanor, to Rome to make an alliance, in 161 B.C. (I Macc. 8:17; II Macc. 4:11). There was a Jewish historian named Eupolemus who wrote a history of the Jews in Greek about this time. It is possible that he is the same person as the statesman. N. TURNER

EUROCLYDON. *See* NORTHEASTER.

EUTYCHUS ū′tə kəs [Εὔτυχος, fortunate, lucky]. A youth of Troas who sat one evening in a window of an upper chamber while Paul talked. Overcome by sleep, Eutychus fell out and was taken up dead; but Paul declared him alive (Acts 20:7-12).

In this narrative in a "we section" of Acts, the author as an eyewitness implies that Paul could restore the dead. This traditional viewpoint is weakened by ambiguity in the story. The boy was "taken up dead" (ἤρθη νεκρός), not "as though dead" (ὡς νεκρός; Rev. 1:17; cf. Mark 9:26), yet Paul found life in him. Most commentators think that Paul's action, embracing the lad, is patterned upon prophetic restorations (I Kings 17:21; II Kings 4:34); some doubt that the youth was dead. The window of the upper room (ὑπερῷον; Acts 1:13; 9:37, 39, not the same word as in Luke 22:11-12) was on the third story, counting the ground floor as the first; hence the third is second in American usage. The distance does not necessarily imply a fatal fall. Probably Eutychus was unconscious and thought dead, though the story stresses the revival of his life by Paul (Acts 20:10) and its continuance (vs. 12). Though the story gives notable details which illuminate early Christianity, there is no report about prayer, faith, or thanks to God. D. M. BECK

EVANGELIST ē văn′jə lĭst [εὐαγγελιστής; Lat. *evangelizator* (Tertullian), *evangelista* (Vulg.); *from the verb* εὐαγγελίζεσθαι, to announce good news]. A title, not of an office, but of an activity, of early Christian missionaries and preachers of the gospel. The word is rare outside Christian literature. It occurs in an inscription of Rhodes (CIG XII.1.675) of a pagan announcer of oracles. In the NT the term is employed three times: (*a*) Acts 21:8, of Philip, one of the SEVEN; (*b*) Eph. 4:11, where it follows "apostles" and "prophets" in a list of Christian ministries endowed by the ascended Lord with spiritual gifts for the nurture and increase of the church (*see* MINISTRY, CHRISTIAN); and (*c*) II Tim. 4:5, of the ministry of Timothy, probably a reminiscence of I Thess. 3:2, in which Paul describes Timothy as "God's servant [in some MSS "fellow worker"] in the gospel of Christ."

In the earliest times, no doubt, the activity of the apostles was not rigidly distinguished from that of evangelists (cf. Gal. 1:8; I Clem. 42; Barn. 8.3). Later Christian usage viewed the evangelists as disciples of the apostles, or as imitators of their example (so Euseb. Hist. II.3.1; III.37.2—and V.10.2-3, where Pantaenus, the founder of the Catechetical School at Alexandria in the second century, is counted as an evangelist). It is probably in this sense that one should understand the reference to a wandering apostle in Did. 11.4-6.

A more restrictive use of "evangelist" to denote the authors of the canonical gospels first appears in third-century writers. The transition may be noted in Hippolytus *On Antichrist* 56, with reference to Luke, and in Tertullian *Against Praxeas* 21, 23, and in Dionysius of Alexandria (as quoted in Euseb. Hist. VII.25.8), with respect to John. But the association of the four canonical gospels with the four living creatures of Rev. 4:7 goes back to Iren. Her. III.11.8: the lion=John, the ox=Luke, the man=Matthew, and the eagle=Mark. The use of these symbols in Christian art, however, cannot be traced prior to the fifth century, by which time the symbols of John and Mark, as given in Irenaeus, have been exchanged.

Another specialized use of "evangelists" occurs in later church orders and liturgies. The *Apostolic Church Order* 19, composed in Egypt *ca.* A.D. 300, reminds the reader of the lections at the liturgy that "he carries out the office of an evangelist." In the Liturgy of Chrysostom, the deacon, prior to his chanting of the gospel lection, describes himself as the "evangelist of the holy apostle and evangelist."

Bibliography. H. Leclercq, "Evangélistes (Symboles des)," *Dictionnaire d'archéologie chrétienne et de liturgie*, V (1922), 845-52. M. H. SHEPHERD, JR.

EVE ēv [חוה; Εὕα; *see below*]. The first WOMAN; wife of Adam; designated as the mother of the human race.

1. Etymology. The derivation of the name חוה is very controversial. The popular etymology in Gen. 3:20 connects it with the root "to live," which in Hebrew is חיה, not חוה. Rabbinical exegesis joined the name to the Aramaic חויא, "serpent." This theory has been revived in modern times as the scientific etymology, without winning general support. *See bibliography.*

2. In the Genesis narratives. The reference to Eve in 3:20 does not fit well in its present context. It is generally assumed that this verse stems from a different recension of the story. It is a parallel to the more usual appellative form, "the woman" (האשה), linked in the wordplay of 2:23 to "the man" (איש).

According to Gen. 1:27 (P), mankind was created in two sexes, male and female. According to Gen. 2:18 ff (J), the male was created first. When Yahweh recognized man's loneliness in the company of mere animals, he formed woman from one of his ribs. The woman was tempted by the serpent into eating the forbidden fruit and causing her husband also to eat. Her punishment took the form of pain at childbirth and subordination to the man. Eve gave birth successively to Cain, Abel, Seth, and other children (Gen. 4:1-2, 25-26; 5:1-5).

The ancient age of this material is indicated by the many etiological motifs which are woven into the narrative. Woman was formed from a rib (2:21); man and wife "belong" together (2:24-25); pain at childbirth is a curse (3:16 ff). However, the attempt to reconstruct an earlier stage of the story in which Eve appears as a mythical figure, does not commend itself.

3. In the NT. Eve is mentioned twice in the NT. In I Tim. 2:11-15 the NT writer argues that the woman's place in the church should be one of silence and submissiveness. He refers to the Genesis story to establish the creative order and to prove woman's vulnerability. The exegesis rests most probably on a current rabbinical interpretation (*see bibliography*). Paul uses Eve in II Cor. 11:3 as an illustration of how easily one can be led astray.

Bibliography. OT etymology: L. Köhler and W. Baumgartner, *Lexicon in Veteris Testamenti* (1953), give nine possible derivations. A thorough discussion of the Punic text published by M. Lidzbarski in *Ephemeris für semitische Epigraphik,* I (1902), 26-27, as a suggested parallel to Eve, is given in: T. C. Vriezen, *Onderzoek naar de Paradijsvoorstelling bij de oude semietische Volken* (1937), pp. 192-93; L. Köhler, *OT Theology* (English trans., 1957), p. 246, note 102. In addition to the standard Commentaries on Genesis, see: H. Gressmann, "Mythische Reste in der Paradieserzählung," *ARW,* 10 (1907), 358 ff; B. Reinach, "La Naissance d'Eve," *RHR,* 78 (1918), 185 ff; H. Tuerck, *Pandora und Eva* (1931). For the rabbinical exegesis, see "Eva" in the Index of H. L. Strack and P. Billerbeck, *Kommentar zum NT,* IV (1928), 1225.

B. S. Childs

EVENING. *See* Day.

EVENING SACRIFICE. *See* Sacrifice and Offerings § A2*b*i.

EVERLASTING. *See* Time.

EVI ē'vī [אוי, desire(?)]. One of the five Midianite kings killed in battle by the Israelites under Moses (Num. 31:8; Josh. 13:21). In Num. 31 the battle is apparently to be set against the background of the religious apostasy into which Israel had fallen under Midianite enticements (ch. 25). In Josh. 13, however, the five Midianite leaders, called princes of Sihon, are said to have fallen in the same battle in which Moses defeated Sihon the Amorite king.

R. F. Johnson

EVIDENCE. An occasional translation of the following words (*a*) עד (Exod. 22:13—H 22:12; KJV and alternately RSV WITNESS); (*b*) μάρτυς (Matt. 18:16; II Cor. 13:1; I Tim. 5:19; KJV and alternately RSV WITNESS); (*c*) μαρτύριον (Jas. 5:3; KJV WITNESS). The word is also used to translate the following phrases: (*a*) לפי עדים, "on the evidence of witnesses" (Num. 35:30; KJV "by the mouth of witnesses"; cf. Deut. 17:6 19:15); (*b*) יגיד צדק, "gives honest evidence" (Prov. 12:17; KJV "sheweth forth righteousness").

The term is used chiefly in a legal sense—i.e., as "ground for belief," as "testimony," whether personal, in the language of documents, or in the form of material objects, which tends to prove or disprove a conclusion or establish a fact. Evidence therefore consists in statements or proofs admissible as testimony in a legal inquiry or a court of law. More generally, the word is used with reference to appearances from which inferences may be drawn.

Paul's counsel that any charge must be sustained by the evidence of two or three witnesses (II Cor. 13:1; cf. I Tim. 5:19) was based on a venerable legal tradition in Israel (Num. 35:30; Deut. 19:15), of which Jesus was aware (Matt. 18:16). The giving of evidence was regarded as a religious duty and was basic to the administration of justice in Israel (Deut. 17). Such evidence was admissible even in cases involving capital punishment (Num. 35:30; Deut. 17:2-7); according to Deut. 17:2-7 witnesses were expected to cast the first stones at a defendant who had been found guilty of apostasy.

The importance of giving honest evidence is frequently emphasized in the OT (Exod. 20:16; 23:1 ff; Proverbs *passim*). In cases where witness is borne falsely, the accuser is to receive the punishment which he had intended for the falsely accused (Deut. 19:15-21).

See also Justice; Court of Law.

H. F. Beck

EVIL [רע, רעה, bad, *from the verb* רעע, to be bad; κακός, κακία, *and* πονηρός, πονηρία, bad; φαυλός, mean, *hence* bad]. Both in Hebrew and in Greek usage "evil" has primarily a pragmatic and qualitative sense. As judged by its appearance or effects, something is evil when it is worthless and corrupt (II Kings 2:19; Prov. 20:14; 25:19; Jer. 24:2; Matt. 6:23; 7:17); displeasing, ugly, and sad (Gen. 21:11-12; 28:8; 41:19-20; Neh. 2:3; Eccl. 7:3); or painful and injurious (Gen. 26:29; 31:7; Deut. 26:6; 28:35; I Sam. 18:10; II Sam. 12:18; Prov. 11:15; Rev. 16:2).

As an extension of the latter, "evil" means the "trouble," "distress," and "calamity" which mankind, and particularly Israel, must endure (Gen. 19:19; 47:9; Ps. 90:15; Matt. 6:34; Eph. 5:16). Evil in this sense is often spoken of as a punishment or chastisement sent from God (Deut. 31:17; I Kings 14:10; II Kings 21:12; Jer. 26:19; Amos 9:4). Because under his providential control God uses it for his wise though severe purposes, he is spoken of as the author of evil (Job 2:10; Isa. 45:7; Amos 3:6). Israel's struggle with the theological meaning of suffering constitutes one of the leading problems of the OT. *See* Suffering and Evil.

Often in the OT, and predominantly in the NT, "evil" has a moral and spiritual connotation. Thus it indicates the wrong that men do to one another

(Gen. 19:7; 44:5; Deut. 26:6; Judg. 11:27; 19:23; Jas. 3:8; etc.). It also indicates the moral badness, maliciousness, and perversity of the sinful heart (*see* SIN). The "doers of evil" are therefore the wicked (Job 8:20; Ps. 26:5; Prov. 17:4; Isa. 1:4; Jer. 20:13; etc.). The expression "good and evil" covers the whole range of moral or spiritual possibilities, with their necessary consequences, in such passages as Gen. 2:9; 3:5; II Sam. 14:17 (cf. Job 1:1; Ps. 34:14—H 34:15; Amos 5:14-15; Mic. 3:2), although elsewhere (e.g., Gen. 31:24; Deut. 30:15) it appears in a more pragmatic sense. S. J. DE VRIES

EVIL ONE, THE [ὁ πονηρός]. A way of referring to SATAN. The term occurs several times in the NT (Matt. 13:19; John 17:15; Eph. 6:16; I John 2:13-14; 5:18-19). There is no OT equivalent, although the adjective רע ("in poor condition," "sick," "evil," "vicious") occurs often. The NT meaning is especially obvious in Matt. 13:19. In the parallels ὁ ζατανᾶς ("Satan") appears in Mark 4:15, ὁ διάβολος ("the devil") in Luke 8:12.

Questionable passages are Matt. 5:37; 6:13; Luke 11:4 (in MSS CDΘ, etc.); II Thess. 3:3, where the genitive form τοῦ πονηροῦ may be derived either from the masculine (*see above*) or the neuter, τὸ πονηρόν. The question is primarily discussed with regard to the last petition of the LORD'S PRAYER in Matt. 6:13. The RSV gives "the evil one" in a footnote. In the early church the Eastern writers followed a masculine interpretation; the Western fathers, with the exception of Tertullian, a neuter understanding. Present-day exegesis in general follows the neuter interpretation—i.e., the evil of the present and of the last days to come. E. DINKLER

EVIL SPIRIT. *See* DEMON.

EVIL-MERODACH ē'vəl mĕr'ə dăk [אויל מרדך; Akkad. *Amēl-Marduk,* man of Marduk]. King of Babylon (562-560 B.C.); son of NEBUCHADREZZAR.

Of the two years during which this king ruled we know nothing, since no fragment of the Babylonian Chronicle happens to cover that period. His brother-in-law followed him on the throne (as Neriglissar) in a rebellion that has all the appearances of an interdynastic struggle. It should be noted that Nabonidus mentions as his predecessors and models Nebuchadrezzar and Neriglissar, and passes over Evil-merodach in silence. A. L. OPPENHEIM

EVODIUS, HOMILY OF ĭ vō'dĭ əs [Εὐοδίος]. A Coptic (Bohairic) writing containing a version of the ASSUMPTION OF THE VIRGIN. In this account Evodius, traditional first bishop of Antioch, is represented as Peter's successor in the see of Rome, one of the seventy-two disciples, and an eyewitness of the death and assumption of Mary. M. S. ENSLIN

EWE. *See* SHEEP; SHEPHERD.

EXACTOR OF TRIBUTE [נוגש, exactor] (Dan. 11:20; KJV RAISER OF TAXES). Alternately: TASKMASTER (Exod. 3:7; 5:6, 10, 13-14; Isa. 60:17 [KJV EXACTOR]). Usually a government officer who levied or collected tribute, taxes, or customs; also one whose duty it was to enforce the performance of work; a taskmaster. The Hebrew term was used derisively of one who, under the protection of official appointment and status, made illegal exactions or laid claim to something as a matter of right, often with the added idea of excess. The term is often used as though it were a synonym for "oppressor" or "extortioner."

As used in Dan. 11:20, the term is usually taken as a reference to the mission of Heliodorus, the finance minister of Seleucus IV Philopator (187-175 B.C.), to Jerusalem. This exactor was sent to see whether great wealth was being stored in the Jerusalem temple as rumored. He meant to claim such wealth for the Syrian treasury. Seleucus' preoccupation with finances arose from the obligation which he had to pay off an indemnity the Romans had levied against his father, Antiochus III, because Antiochus had affronted the Roman authority by invading Greece and parts of Asia Minor (see Polybius *Histories* XXI.14.7; Livy XXXVII.45.14; Justin *History of the World* XXXII.2; Diodorus Siculus XXIX.15).

Such an exactor might have visited Jerusalem at specified intervals. I Macc. 1:29 indicates that Antiochus Epiphanes (175-164 B.C.) had such an officer. H. F. BECK

EXCAVATION. *See* ARCHAEOLOGY.

EXCELLENT. The translation of the following words: (*a*) גדל (Isa. 28:29), "great"; (*b*) יתר (Dan. 5:12, 14), "abundant"; (*c*) καλός (Tit. 3:8; KJV GOOD), "morally good" or "praiseworthy." The word is used also in several phrases in the NT:

In Luke-Acts, Theophilus (Luke 1:3), Felix (Acts 24:2), and Festus (Acts 26:25) are addressed by the term "most excellent." The adjective κράτιστος used in these passages is based on a root meaning "strength," "power," or "sovereignty." The expression "most excellent" or "most noble" was commonly used to address one who held a higher official or social position than the speaker. In Acts 23:26 the word is translated "his EXCELLENCY."

In Rom. 2:18; Phil. 1:10 the word "excellent" appears in the phrase "approve what is excellent" (τὰ διαφέροντα), meaning the superior things, the things that really matter.

The sentence in I Cor. 12:31 in which "excellent" occurs is somewhat awkward. The phrase translated "more excellent," καθ' ὑπερβολήν, is usually used adverbially, meaning "to an extraordinary degree." Here it is used adjectivally. Perhaps we may translate: "a way still more extraordinary."

The author of Hebrews uses a word related to τὰ διαφέροντα. In 1:4 he speaks of the "name" of Jesus (i.e., his dignity and superiority, primarily as Son) as διαφορώτερος, "more excellent," than that of angels; and in 8:6 the ministry of Christ is "more excellent" than the Levitical cultus.

B. H. THROCKMORTON, JR.

EXCOMMUNICATION [Lat. *excommunicatio*]. Punishment of a church member, for error in doctrine or morals, by temporary or permanent exclusion from the sacraments or from membership. The Latin word is late; it is not found in the Vulg. The procedures which were developed in the later church derived only in part from the practices of the NT church.

Temporary exclusion from the services of the sanctuary for violation of ritual taboo was an integral part of Israelite-Jewish ceremonial law (*see* CLEAN AND UNCLEAN). For serious ritual offenses, such as eating leaven during the Passover season (Exod. 12:15, 19), failure to bring a slaughtered animal to the door of the tent of meeting (Lev. 17:4, 9) or to cleanse oneself from ritual impurity (Num. 19: 20), the prescribed penalty was to be cut off from (the congregation of) Israel, from the people, or from the assembly.

The first instance of the use of the threat of excommunication against recalcitrant members of the religious community was that of Ezra in his campaign against mixed marriages; failure to respond to Ezra's summons to a meeting in Jerusalem was to be punished by the confiscation of all the offender's property and expulsion from the congregation of the exiles (Ezra 10:8). This was a mitigated form of the ancient *ḥērem* (חרם), which involved death for the person and destruction for his property (Lev. 27:28-29).

In NT times the regular penalty for serious religious or moral offenses was exclusion from the synagogue. A mild form of exclusion, נדוי, which cut off the victim from conversation for a period of thirty days, could be inflicted by a single person. The more severe formal ban, *ḥērem,* which deprived the victim of all religious privileges for an indefinite period, could be imposed by not fewer than ten persons. A third degree of exclusion, שמתא, involving complete and final expulsion, is questioned by some scholars.

The use of three different terms in Luke 6:22 has been seen as reflecting the different grades of Jewish excommunication, but the terms are probably used synonymously. In the Qumran community members were punished for varying periods for different offenses. The nature of the punishment is not always specified. One form of punishment was exclusion for varying periods from the "purity"—i.e., the sacred food—of the "masters," or full members of the community. For cursing, or for gossip against the "masters," a member was excluded and not allowed to return. Two years' probation was required of a backsliding member before he could be restored to his former position in the community. A member of ten years' standing who backslid was dismissed permanently, and anyone who shared with him the sacred food or communal goods was likewise dismissed. The NT references to the contemporary Jewish procedure of excluding those who confessed Jesus to be the Christ use the term ἀποσυνάγωγος γίνεσθαι, "to be put out of the synagogue" (John 9:22; 12:42; 16:2). The exclusion here could hardly be from a single synagogue, but rather refers to the banishment of the victim from all social and religious fellowship with the Jewish community at large.

The early Christian communities naturally patterned their communal life after that of the parent religion and adopted its familiar terminology. The threefold admonition of the offending brother, first privately, then in the presence of two or three witnesses, and finally before the church (Matt. 18:15-17), is similar to the Jewish practice (Talmud 'Arak. 16*b;* M. Maṣṣoth I.10) and corresponds exactly to the rules of the Qumran sect (1QS 5.26–6.1). This probably reflects the practice of the Jewish Christian circles for which the Gospel of Matthew appears to have been composed.

The origin of Christian excommunication has been seen in the allusion to binding and loosing in Matt. 16:19; 18:18 (cf. John 20:23). The saying, however, probably has reference to the church's spiritual authority and not to any formal procedure of exclusion.

Paul, in dealing with disciplinary problems in the churches, had to resort to exclusion, or the threat of it, in order to maintain or restore order. In less serious cases he employed milder forms of moral suasion and economic and social pressures. For the Thessalonians who refused to work, he prescribed cutting off their food (II Thess. 3:10). This mode of punishment was systematized in the Qumran community where the ration of the offender was reduced in varying proportions and for varying periods, depending on the gravity of the offense. For the disobedient, Paul recommended a brotherly warning and the time-honored and effective sanction of social boycott: "Have nothing to do with him, that he may be ashamed" (II Thess. 3:14-15). But for serious moral offenses his blunt directive was: "Drive out the wicked person from among you" (I Cor. 5:13). A member of the church at Corinth who was living with his father's wife, Paul ordered to be excluded and delivered "to Satan for the destruction of the flesh, that his spirit may be saved in the day of the Lord Jesus" (I Cor. 5:1-5). It is not clear whether the "destruction of the flesh" of the culprit means physical death or the purging of the lusts of the flesh, but, at any rate, the drastic treatment was intended for the good of the offender and for the salvation of his spirit. Whether the offender in question is the one for whom Paul in his second letter recommends forgiveness (II Cor. 2:6-11) is not certain. The punishment had been imposed by the "majority" ὑπὸ τῶν πλειονῶν (vs. 11), which term corresponds to the רבים of the Qumran sect's Manual of Discipline. It would seem that the offender had been thoroughly chastened and had undergone a radical repentance, which, in Paul's opinion, had earned him the right to be reinstated in the community. Some of the members of the church still wished to exclude him, but Paul felt that the punishment should be ended and that the members should forgive and comfort him, so as not to defeat the purpose of the punishment and lead to ruin rather than rehabilitation, thus giving Satan advantage.

The Corinthian and Thessalonian letters reflect a rather loose disciplinary organization, without rigid rules, modifiable in accordance with circumstances. The Pastoral letters exhibit a less flexible attitude toward discipline, especially in regard to doctrinal matters. The man who is heretical or factious in matters of doctrine is to be warned in the same way as a moral offender, and then shunned (Tit. 3:10). Dissemination of false doctrine is grounds for exclusion from the fellowship (I Tim. 1:20; 6:3; II John 10). Excommunication was not simply a matter of discipline, or of consigning the offender to Satan, but its main purpose was to keep the church from corruption by amputation of the diseased member. According to rabbinic tradition (Talmud, Sanh. 107*b*), Jesus was excommunicated, put under the ban (*ḥērem*). The Greek rendering of the Hebrew term *ḥērem* is ἀνάθεμα, and it may be that when Paul says (I Cor. 12:3) that no one speaking by the spirit of God ever says "Jesus is Anathema," he is replying to the charge that Jesus had been excommunicated, by asserting that the action could not have been in accord with God's spirit. Paul himself expressed willingness to become anathema, accursed and cut off from Christ, if it could mean the winning of his fellow Jews to Christ (Rom. 9:3). Paul felt that anyone who preached a gospel contrary to his (Gal. 1:8) or who had no love for the Lord (I Cor. 16:22) should be anathema, or excommunicated. The question of authority, or who may excommunicate whom, arose inevitably with heresy and schism, when ambitious leaders, like Diotrephes (III John 9-10), undertook to exercise the power.

The NT reflects only the beginnings of what was to develop into an elaborate procedure. The young church was still flexible. Its gradual transformation into a vast and powerful organization led to the development of a complex legal structure.

See ANATHEMA; CHURCH, LIFE AND ORGANIZATION OF; DEVOTED; HERESY. M. H. POPE

EXECRATION. An occasional translation (Num. 5:21, 27; Jer. 42:18; 44:12) of אלה, which is more commonly rendered "OATH" and "CURSE." The term refers to the curse itself and to the victim of the curse.

Execration is, in a sense, the antithesis of blessing and consecration. Blessing and consecration involve making someone or something holy or setting him or it aside for a holy use; execration, cursing, especially when pronounced by a person with spiritual authority, renders the person or thing unholy and useless.

Jeremiah warned his exilic compatriots that God would pour his wrath out on those who fled from Judah to Egypt, so that they would become an "execration, a horror, a curse, and a taunt" (42:18). A similar warning was addressed to the Jews in Egypt because they had fled and because they were willing to participate in the heathen rites of the Egyptians (44:12). An oath of purgation, involving a conditional curse as part of a trial by ordeal of jealousy, was used in Israel as a Levitical device for determining the guilt or innocence of a woman suspected of adultery, when there was no evidence to support the suspicion (Num. 5:11-31). A comprehensive summary of the curses which would befall an Israelite if he and his nation were disloyal to God is presented in Deut. 28:15-68. Generally in the OT those who persist in their sinfulness run the risk of being cursed by God.

Curses, threats, and magical cursing were used extensively in the ancient Middle East and especially in Egypt. Our earliest Egyptian examples of execration texts date from the twenty-fifth century B.C. and are contained in the pyramid and other tomb texts from Sakkarah. Such texts were designed to serve various purposes—e.g., to protect the honor of a king lest any should speak evil against his name after his death or to ward off tomb-robbers by reminding them of the fate which would befall them in this and the afterlife should they disturb the peace of the dead. Egyptian royal decrees often included the threat of dispossession and capital punishment for subjects who would not comply with the law. In instances where supposed violators of a law could not be indicted, for want of conclusive evidence, the king would invoke divine vengeance against the supposed offenders. In the Middle Kingdom of Egypt the magical cursing of supposed and actual enemies of the state was a common practice. The names and designations of such enemies were inscribed on pottery bowls or written on papyrus and placed in glass bottles; the bowls and bottles were then smashed, either underfoot or with stones. Presumably the power of the enemy was thereby weakened, if not utterly destroyed. Among those so exorcised in the texts we have from the Middle Kingdom were Asiatic princes, Nubians, Libyans, rebellious Egyptians, and all evil forces. Magical cursing of a conditional kind for the protection of children and other persons was also used extensively in ancient Egypt.

See also SIN.

Bibliography. For examples of Egyptian execration texts, together with references to literature on the subject, see: J. B. Pritchard, ed., *ANET* (2nd ed., 1955), pp. 326-29. W. F. Albright, *JPOS* (1928), pp. 223 ff; *BASOR,* 81 (Feb., 1941), 16 ff; 83 (Oct., 1941), 30 ff.

See also: W. R. Smith, "On the Forms of Divination and Magic Enumerated in Deut. 18:10, 11," *Journal of Philology,* 13 (1884), 113-28; 14 (1885), 273-87. R. C. Thompson, *Semitic Magic* (1908). A. Guillaume, *Prophecy and Divination* (1938). J. Pedersen, *Israel, Its Life and Culture* (4 vols. in 2; 1926-40), pp. 411-52. G. E. Wright, *The OT Against Its Environment* (1950), pp. 78-93. H. F. BECK

EXECUTIONER [פקדה, punishment (Ezek. 9:1; KJV THEM THAT HAVE CHARGE); KJV σπεκουλάτωρ (Mark 6:27; RSV SOLDIER OF THE GUARD)]. One who puts another to death, usually in carrying out a legal sentence of capital punishment. In Ezek. 9:1 the term refers to an OFFICER in charge of a city. Potiphar was captain of the guard (Gen. 37:36; 40:3 [שר הטבח]; cf. Jer. 39:9; Dan. 2:14; etc.). He was one of the bodyguard of the king. This captain of guard might act as executioner (I Kings 2:25, 34). But the OT has no special word for those who carried out the sentence of capital punishment.

The Roman administration in NT Palestine reserved exclusive jurisdiction over capital crimes. The term "executioner" was probably attached to the bodyguard of the king or proconsul, since the Greek σπεκουλάτωρ originally meant "scout" or "SPY." Soldiers were the executioners of Jesus (Luke 23:47; John 19:23). C. U. WOLF

EXHORTATION. A translation of παράκλησις (alternately ENCOURAGEMENT; APPEAL; COMFORT; CONSOLATION). It is often difficult to determine just which meaning an author intended, especially as between "exhortation," "encouragement," and "comfort."

In Rom. 12:8, "he who exhorts, in his exhortation," could also be translated: "he who encourages (or comforts), in his encouragement (or comforting)." Phil. 2:1 may mean "Christian exhortation" rather than "encouragement in Christ" (RSV). In II Cor. 8:17 "appeal" (RSV) could be translated "exhortation." In Rom. 15:4 "encouragement" (RSV) could be translated "consolation," etc.

The expression "word of exhortation" occurs in Acts 13:15, where Paul is asked if he has such a word for his hearers; and in Heb. 13:22 the writer asks his readers to bear with his "word of exhortation." And in many other passages believers are exhorted or admonished or commanded.

B. H. Throckmorton, Jr.

EXILE. The period in biblical history when the Babylonians forced most of the inhabitants of Judah and Jerusalem to migrate from their native homes to Babylonia. The period dates from either the first deportation in 598 B.C. (Esth. 2:6; Matt. 1:11) or, more commonly, the second in 587, to the edict of Cyrus in 538 or the completion of the new temple in 515. The word may also refer to the general state of forced absence from one's native habitat (Amos 1:15; I Pet. 1:17), with or without reference to the Babylonian exile (*see* Dispersion). Or it may be used of an individual banished from his home (II Sam. 15:19; Amos 7:17; Acts 7:29; Jer. 20:3 LXX). It may refer in the abstract sense to the condition of being exiled or collectively to the people who are in exile (*see* § 1*a below*). In the NT "exile" may be used figuratively to mean life on earth (Heb. 11:13).

1. Terminology for "exile" in the Bible. ***a. In OT Hebrew and Aramaic.*** The most common Hebrew term for "exile" is the noun גולה (II Kings 24:15). Occurring less frequently, though with precisely the same meaning, is גלות (II Kings 25:27). They are used interchangeably (Amos 1:6, 15) as synonyms in either the abstract sense (Ezek. 1:2; 12:11) or the collective, meaning "exiles" (Jer. 29:20, 22). Their use is contemporaneous, indicating that no priority is indicated in the history of Hebrew literary style. In exilic and postexilic OT literature the reference is almost invariably to the Assyrian and Babylonian exiles (Obad. 20) and subsequent Dispersion; however, גולה is used in an apocalyptic sense at least once (Zech. 14:2). In pre-exilic literature the reference may be to forced migrations other than those effected by Assyria and Babylonia (Amos 1:6, 9). The word is by no means limited in OT usage to the fate of Israel and Judah (Isa. 20:4; Nah. 3:10; Jer. 46:19; 48:7, 11; 49:3).

The Aramaic noun for "exile" is גלו, used only in the phrase בני גלותא, meaning "sons of the exile" or "exiles," replacing the collective sense of the Hebrew cognate (Ezra 6:16; Dan. 2:25; 5:13; 6:13—H 6:14).

The verb גלה is used in making historical reference to the Assyrian deportation of the N ten tribes (II Kings 15:29; 17:11; I Chr. 5:26) and to the Babylonian exile of Judah (II Kings 24:14; II Chr. 36:20; Ezra 2:1; Lam. 1:3); only once does it refer to the fate of a foreign nation (Amos 1:5). The prophets freely use the verb, as well as the noun, in pronouncing divine judgment on the people (Isa. 5:13; Jer. 13:19; Amos 5:27; Mic. 1:16; cf. Hos. 10:5). The Aramaic verb הגלי occurs twice in the OT meaning "take into exile" (Ezra 4:10; 5:12).

A synonym for גלה in Hebrew is שבה, "take captive," frequently used in reference to the Exile (Ezek. 6:9). The nouns שבי and שבית, meaning "captivity" or "captives" (in the collective sense), are used as synonyms of גולה (Deut. 32:42; Ezra 2:1; Neh. 7:6; Ezek. 12:11; Nah. 3:10). It should be carefully noted that שבה and its cognates are general in meaning and refer frequently to events other than the Exile.

The words צעה, "bow down" (Isa. 51:14), and בלע, "swallow up" (Isa. 49:19), are among the poetic synonyms of גלה.

b. In LXX Greek. The Greek nouns used to translate גולה and גלות are αἰχμαλωσία, "captivity" or "prisoners of war" (II Kings 24:14), and μετοικεσία, "deportation," "captivity," "exile" (II Kings 24:16). The cognate verbs αἰχμαλωτεύειν, αἰχμαλωτίζειν, and μετοικίζειν translate גלה. Μέτοικος, "exile," is used in mistranslation of מגור, "terror" (Jer. 20:3). Παροικία, "exile," translates גולה (I Esd. 5:7; Ezra 8:35).

c. In NT Greek. In the NT, μετοικίζειν means "take into exile" (Acts 7:43; cf. Amos 5:27), and μετοικεσία means "deportation" or "exile" (Matt. 1: 11-12, 17). Αἰχμαλωσία means "captivity" (Rev. 13: 10; Jer. 15:2 LXX), and παροικία "exile" (I Pet. 1:17). πάροικος (Acts 7:29; I Pet. 2:11) and παρεπίδημος (I Pet. 1:1; 2:11; Heb. 11:13) mean "exile" or "alien." Αἰχμαλωτίζειν means "scattered as captives" (in Luke 21:24). Διασπορά (John 7:35; Jas. 1: 1; I Pet. 1:1) means "Dispersion." Matt. 1:11-12, 17, contain the only direct historical references in the NT to the Exile of the OT.

2. History of the Exile. Throughout their history the people of Israel and Judah were forced to play the role of political buffer between Egypt to the SW and the governments in Mesopotamia to the NE. While Egypt was the most dominant power to be dealt with during the early periods of biblical history, it was the rise of a powerful Assyrian government in the eighth century B.C. and an even more powerful Neo-Babylonian renaissance in the seventh century which brought about the total eclipse of the N tribes and the utter prostration of Benjamin and Judah.

After the split of the United Monarchy into the kingdoms of Israel to the N and Judah in the S (*see* Israel, History of), each government independently reached the zenith of its power and prestige in the eighth century B.C. Israel attained its summit during the reign of Jeroboam II (*ca.* 786-746) and Judah under the rule of Uzziah (Azariah; *ca.* 783-742). However, it was during this period that Assyria began seriously and ruthlessly to build its empire. Tiglath-pileser III (745-727) captured the cities of Naphtali (II Kings 15:29) and carried the inhabitants of the tribes of Naphtali, Reuben, Gad, and the half-tribe of Manasseh (I Chr. 5:26) captive to Assyria (733). After Tiglath-pileser had taken Damascus, capital of Syria (732), he appointed for N Israel her last king, Hoshea. Hoshea rebelled, however, *ca.* 724, depending on an ineffective Egyptian government for help, and was taken prisoner by the Assyrians. Samaria, capital of Israel, held out until early in 721, the siege having been laid by Shalmaneser V (727-722) and the fall of the city effected by Sargon II (722-705). This marked the end of the ten tribes: "None was left but the tribe of Judah only" (II Kings 17:18). According to the biblical account the Assyrians exiled the Israelites to Assyria, in Halah (cf. Obad. 20), on the Habor, the river of

Gozan, and in the cities of the Medes (II Kings 17:6; 18:11); on the other hand, they brought people from Babylon, Cuthah, Avva, Hamath, and Sephar-vaim to the cities of Samaria (II Kings 17:24; cf. Ezra 4: 10).

This displacement of populations was, it seems, complete so far as the identity of the N ten tribes is concerned; for they eventually assimilated beyond the point of return to any historical continuum with their Israelite origins. Sargon II in his inscriptions boasts proudly of his conquest of the "land of Beth-Omri" (Samaria) and records that 27,290 Israelites were deported.

For the history of Judah in the following century, *see* ISRAEL, HISTORY OF.

Just as Amos and Hosea had announced divine judgment of destruction and exile on Israel, so Isaiah, Micah, Zephaniah, Jeremiah, Habakkuk, and Ezekiel were in agreement on the fate of Judah under that same judgment.

Ashurbanipal was the last great king of Assyria (died *ca.* 630), and his passing marked the end of effective Assyrian dominance of Judah. Though the Neo-Babylonian Empire (626-539) was soon to fill the power vacuum, both Judah and Egypt tried to take advantage of the respite. Judah's aspirations were effectively checked at the battle of Megiddo Pass when Josiah, king of Judah (640-609), was killed. With him went any hope of reuniting and strengthening Israel under a Davidic monarch. Egypt enjoyed a further moment of dominance of the little buffer state. Although Nebuchadnezzar decisively defeated Egypt at Carchemish (May-June, 605) the Babylonian Chronicle itself records a defeat at the hand of Egypt *ca.* 601.

One of Josiah's sons, Jehoahaz, ruled for three months (609) before he was deported to Egypt, where he died (II Kings 23:31-34; II Chr. 36:1-4; Jer. 22:10-12). Eliakim, a second son, whose name Pharaoh Neco changed to Jehoiakim, reigned eleven years (609-598) before the Babylonians under Nebuchadnezzar (605-562) laid siege to Jerusalem (II Kings 23:34–24:6; II Chr. 36:4-8). Jehoiakim died during the siege, and his son, Jehoiachin, after reigning three months (December, 598–March, 597), was exiled to Babylon (II Kings 24:6-8; II Chr. 36:9-10; cf. Jer. 22:24-30; Esth. 2:6; Matt. 1:11). A third son of Josiah, Mattaniah, whose name was changed to Zedekiah by Nebuchadnezzar, then ruled the vassal state of Judah for eleven regnal years (March, 597–July, 587) until the fall of Jerusalem, when he was blinded and taken exile to Babylon (II Kings 24:17–25:7; II Chr. 36:10-21; Jer. 39:1-7; 52:1-11; Ezek. 12:12-13; 17:5-10, 13-21). Jer. 52:11 adds that Zedekiah was there imprisoned until he died. Hence, three of Judah's kings, Jehoahaz, Jehoiachin, and Zedekiah, suffered personal exile.

There were three deportations of Jews to Babylonia. The description of the first (598) is vividly given in II Kings 24:12-16, where, along with the young King Jehoiachin, his mother, his palace retinue, and the temple and palace treasures, it is said that 10,000 captives were taken and "none remained, except the poorest people of the land" (vs. 14). Jer. 52:28-30, seemingly an extract from some official document of the Exile, gives the total number for the three deportations as 4,600 persons, with 3,023 having been taken in 598 and the remainder in 587 and 582.

The discovery of the Lachish Ostraca (*see* LACHISH) and the excavations of such contemporary fortress towns as Debir, Lachish, and Bethshemesh give graphic evidence of the defeat Judah suffered in 598-597 and testify to the pitiable estate to which she succumbed in the years between 597 and 587. Only the new evidence of the real strength of Egypt and Nebuchadnezzar's annual trips back to Babylon for the New Year festivals, and not Judah's own position, can possibly explain how Zedekiah and his nobles (Jer. 27–29; 34; 37–39; cf. Ezek. 12:12-13; 17:5-21) could rebel against the Babylonian yoke. This rebellion led to the second deportation.

The second deportation is described in II Kings 25:8-21; Jer. 39:8-10; 40:7; 52:12-34 (aside from the references to the fate of Zedekiah). The temple, the palace, and private homes were burned, the walls of the city destroyed, the temple treasures further confiscated, and more people deported (August, 587).

Gedaliah, the former mayor of the palace, was appointed governor of Judah by the Babylonians. He held office in the village of Mizpah until he was assassinated. Many of the remaining Jews fled to Egypt, forcing Jeremiah to join them (II Kings 25: 22-26; Jer. 40–44; *see* DISPERSION).

Yet a third deportation of men of rank and skill, a Babylonian reprisal for the assassination of Gedaliah, took place in 582.

Supported by Nebuchadnezzar's own royal archives is the account given of the favorable treatment in Babylonia of Jehoiachin (II Kings 25:27-30; Jer. 52: 31-34), who had been deported in 598. In 561, after the death of Nebuchadnezzar and on the accession of EVIL-MERODACH, Jehoiachin was freed from prison to sit among the kings who were also in exile in Babylon. The last great king of the Neo-Babylonian Empire was NABONIDUS (555-539), whose cultural and religious policies and frequent absences from the capital led to Babylonia's defeat at the hand of Cyrus of Persia.

The Edict of Cyrus (II Chr. 36:22-23; Ezra 1:1-4), to release the Jews in exile to return home to rebuild the temple in Jerusalem, is supported by archaeology and in keeping with the known policies of the new Persian Empire. How many people returned to Judah at this time or later under Cambyses and Darius I is not certain. Conditions in Palestine were by no means attractive, while the comparatively lenient Babylonian policies toward their captives detained many Jewish families permanently. They had communities of their own at TEL-ABIB on the Chebar Canal (Ezek. 1:1; 3:15) near NIPPUR. Some of the people had their own houses (Jer. 29:5; Ezek. 8:1; 12:1-7), married (Jer. 29:6; Ezek. 24:18), and engaged in profitable livelihood (Neh. 1:11; Isa. 55:1-2; Zech. 6:9-11). Egyptian papyri and Babylonian contract tablets dating from the early postexilic period give evidence of a comfortable existence in the Dispersion. It appears that such comfort may have resulted from the understandable expediency of many Jews to defect from their own faith and ancient customs to take up worship of the Babylonian deities (Isa. 46:1, 12; 50:11; cf. Jer. 44). On the other hand, there is ample evidence that many Jews (the faithful?) did not fare so well (Ps. 137:1-6; Isa. 14:3; 42:22; 47:6; 51:7, 22-23).

Nonetheless, following 538, a number of Jews did return, among them the Davidic scion ZERUBBABEL and the high priest Joshua. The prophecies of Haggai and Zechariah, which date from August, 520, to February, 519, argue for the speedy rebuilding of the temple in Jerusalem. The temple was completed in March, 515, which usually marks the end of the period commonly called the Babylonian exile.

3. Importance of the Exile. The Exile was a period remarkable for its prophetic and literary activity. Jeremiah, located in Jerusalem until his deportation to Egypt, and Ezekiel and Deutero-Isaiah, located in Babylonia, were in remarkable theological agreement on the importance for Judah of its experience and interpretation of divine activity in the calamity of defeat and exile. Not only was this event to be understood as divine retribution, but more significantly as God's judgment, which, if accepted by faith, would be a revelation of God's love and commitment forever (Isa. 54:9-10; Jer. 31:2-3). Out of the experience would issue a new covenant (Jer. 31:31-34) born of divine judgment to bind the people to God (Ezek. 36:26) in the role of servant and witness to the world (Isa. 43:10; *see* SERVANT OF THE LORD) of his universal sovereignty.

Habakkuk (1:12–2:4) offered his interpretation of trust and faith for the early exile, while a successor arose to deride the last days of Babylonian dominance (Hab. 2:7-19). In this period many scattered oracles and poems were penned (Deut. 32; Ps. 137:1-6; Isa. 13–14; 21; 63; Lamentations) to interpret the suffering and encourage the exiles.

Priestly literary activity in Babylonia produced an agonizing reappraisal of the Yahwistic cultus (Lev. 17–26; Ezek. 40–48) to rid it of any element which might have evoked the divine judgment of the Exile (*see* EZEKIEL; HOLINESS). Out of the Exile, JUDAISM was born.

The Exile is at the heart of the biblical understanding of divine judgment and revelation. It was the crucible of Israel's faith. It is the foundation stone of any biblical understanding of the Cross.

See also ISRAEL, HISTORY OF.

Bibliography. W. F. Albright, "The Biblical Period," in L. Finkelstein, ed., *The Jews,* I (1949), 3-69; J. B. Pritchard, ed., *ANET* (1955), pp. 282-317, 321-22; W. F. Albright, "The Nebuchadnezzar and Neriglissar Chronicles," *BASOR,* no. 143 (1956), pp. 28-33; D. N. Freedman, "The Babylonian Chronicle," *BA,* vol. XIX, no. 3 (1956), pp. 50-60; J. P. Hyatt, "New Light on Nebuchadnezzar and Judean History," *JBL,* LXXV (1956), 277-84; E. R. Thiele, "New Evidence on the Chronology of the Last Kings of Judah," *BASOR,* no. 143 (1956), pp. 22-27; D. J. Wiseman, *Chronicles of Chaldaean Kings (626-556 B.C.) in the British Museum* (1956).

J. A. SANDERS

EXODUS, BOOK OF ĕk'sə dəs [ואלה שמות, and these are the names (Exod. 1:1), *or simply* שמות; LXX Ἔξοδος, a going out]. The second book of the OT, which receives its name from the LXX designation of the chief event recorded in it—namely, Israel's "going out" of Egypt. In the Jewish canon it is the second book of the Law (Torah, contained in the Pentateuch). In Christian exegesis the events of deliverance from slavery and the covenant at Sinai

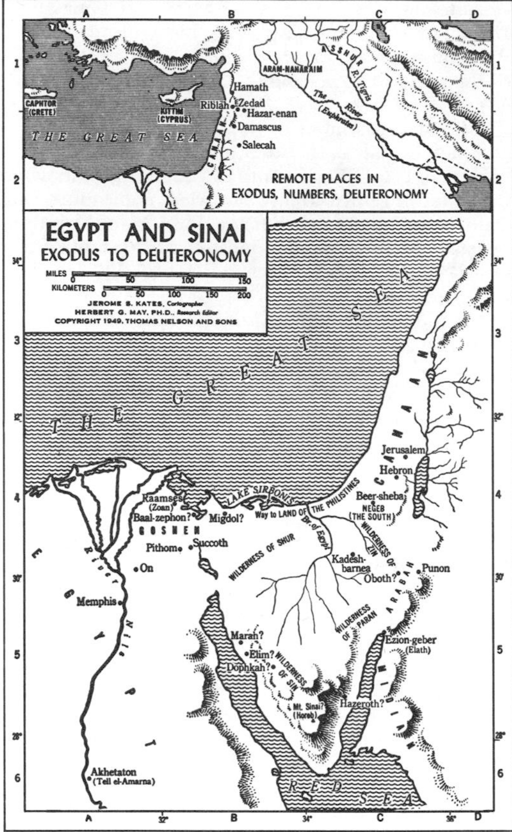

have received more attention than the law contained in the book, particularly because they have provided a language for comprehending the Atonement (God's "deliverance" in Christ) and the New Covenant. For Israel the events recorded in the book were a testimony to the work of God in fulfilment of promise whereby she became the "people of Yahweh," saved from Egyptian slavery, bound together in covenant with her Lord, and provided with a cultic center (tabernacle and ark of the covenant) which gave assurance of God's "tabernacling" presence in her midst (*see* §§ 1*c*, 4*c*, *below*).

1. Contents
    a. The deliverance
    b. The covenant, its breach and renewal
    c. The tabernacle and its furnishings
2. Historical background
3. Composition
4. Significance
    a. God's deliverance from Egyptian slavery
    b. The Sinai covenant
    c. The tabernacle

Bibliography

1. Contents. The diverse contents of the book are set within a geographical outline which may be quickly summarized as follows: (*a*) 1–19:2, Israel's deliverance from Egyptian slavery and journey to Mount Sinai; (*b*) 19:3-40:38, Israel at the holy mount. A more adequate summary, however, may be given under the following headings: (*a*) the deliverance (1:1–19:2); (*b*) the covenant (19:3–24:18), its breach and renewal (chs. 32–34); (*c*) the tabernacle and its furnishings: Moses instructed concerning them (chs. 25–31); Moses directs their construction (chs. 35-40).

a. The deliverance. The introduction to this section in ch. 1 succinctly describes the situation with which the subsequent events deal: a new government in Egypt which "did not know Joseph" and which made the Hebrews state slaves, forced to work on public projects, while cruel methods were used to cut down their numbers. In the first main section (2:1–6:27) we are told how God raised Moses to deliver his people and sent him with his brother Aaron to the Egyptian pharaoh. Though reared in the Egyptian court, Moses received his call at "Horeb, the mountain of God" (3:1), in the area to which he had fled. His objections and feeling of inadequacy were overcome in God's commissioning (chs. 3–4), and his message to his people was to include the good news that the "God of the Fathers," who now was come to them under a new name, "Yahweh" (3:13-15; 6:2-3), had "seen their affliction" (4:31) and would save them.

In 6:28–10:29 the contest of God with Pharaoh is described through a series of nine plagues (*see* Plagues in Exodus), in which the central theme is expressed in the words: "The Egyptians shall know that I am Yahweh" (7:5; cf. 8:22; 9:14, 16; 10:1-2). Balanced with this is the statement reiterated after every plague, concerning the hardness of Pharaoh's heart, which God uses for his own purpose, and which serves to create a gradually increased sense of tension, leading to the climax (note 7:13, 22; 8:15, 19, 32; 9:7, 12, 35; 10:20, 27). A minor theme concerns the Egyptian magicians, who by the use of their occult arts are at first able to duplicate the feats of Moses before they are bested and forced to retire from the scene (7:11, 22; 8:7, 18; 9:11).

The double climax of the story is given in 11:1–15:21, when after the killing of the Egyptian first-born, Pharaoh allows Israel to depart (12:29-36), only to face a new crisis before the Red Sea, through which God leads the people safely while destroying the Egyptian pursuers (14:19-31). The colorful narrative in this section is interrupted at two points by the insertion of relevant material. The first interruption (chs. 12–13) concerns the detailed regulations for the observances of the Passover and the redemption of the first-born, as these were observed in later Israel. As is usual in the OT, the instructions for such important cultic rites have been inserted in the narrative with the event they commemorate. The second insertion is the great hymn of praise, triumph, and thanksgiving, placed at the conclusion of the section in 15:1-18—a hymn perhaps once used in the Passover liturgy. No tradition of authorship is preserved. According to vs. 1 Moses and Israel sang it, while another tradition (vs. 21) relates it to Miriam, Moses' sister. In the latter case it is cited only by its Incipit (the first line quoted as a title).

The final portion of this section of the book depicts Israel's journey to Sinai (Horeb; *see* Sinai, Mount), and the trouble encountered along the way (15:22–19:2). The main theme here is the people's murmuring and rebellion against God and against Moses. In vivid contrast to the triumph and wonder of God's unparalleled acts of salvation is the sudden introduction of the people's faithless response when difficulty is encountered. Yet the faithfulness of God is emphasized in his gracious provision of sustenance, notably Manna. The important narrative regarding the judicial procedures introduced for the adjudication of disputes (ch. 18) seems out of place in this section, since its scene is the encampment at the sacred mount (cf. 18:5 with 19:1-2).

b. The covenant (19:3–24:18), its breach and renewal (32–34). At the sacred mountain before which Moses received his call and commission (3:1), Moses now becomes the mediator of the covenant relation between God and people. Through him God first offers the covenant, and the people accept (19:3-8). They then prepare for the great theophany, which is described in terms taken from a mountain storm (19:16-19), a language common to theophany in the OT. Then out of the thundering and the cloud God identifies himself and gives the stipulations of the covenant (20:1-17; the Ten Commandments). There follows a code of specific law, which scholars have named the "Book of the Covenant" from 24:7; this is contained in 20:23–23:33 and is introduced (20:18-22) by the people's request of Moses to be the mediator between God and themselves. Thus a distinction is drawn between the Decalogue, as God's covenant revelation, and the specific laws of the code. The former is designated the "words" of God (דברים; 20:1; 24:3; cf. Deut. 4:13; 5:4-5, 22), while the latter are the "ordinances" (משפטים; 21:1)—i.e., the specific legal procedures which the community is to employ.

The ceremony whereby the covenant was sealed is described in ch. 24. The reading of the covenant's stipulations and their formal acceptance by the people was accompanied by a sacrificial ceremony in which the blood of slain animals was partly thrown upon the altar and partly sprinkled upon the participants after the formal vows had been taken (cf. I Cor. 11:25: "the new covenant in my blood").

Precisely what Moses read and what the people promised to obey is not entirely clear in the text. 24:3 says that Moses "told the people all the words of Yahweh and all the ordinances," meaning in the context both the Decalogue and the code in 20:23–23:33, and the people promised to "do" them. Vs. 4 then says that Moses wrote only the "words" (presumably meaning the Decalogue). He then prepared the altar and the blood (vss. 5-6), and read the people the "book of the covenant," to which they replied: "All that Yahweh has spoken we will do" (vs. 7). If Moses read what vs. 4 says that he wrote, then we must presume that the title "book of the covenant" refers to the Decalogue and not to the code of "ordinances." In this case, the formal covenant vows of Israel would be understood to have been taken only on the basis of the "words" (i.e., Exod. 20:1-17), which with their prologue would be called the "book of the covenant" (24:7) or simply the "covenant" (Deut. 4:13; and cf. the setting of the Deuteronomic edition of the Decalogue in 5:3-5, 22).

In chs. 32–34 the story continues with Aaron's making of a golden bull, which is taken as a major offense against the covenant, with Moses' anxious intercession to allay the Lord's anger, and with his breaking of the two tablets on which the "testimony" (i.e., the Decalogue; cf. 25:21; 31:18) was engraved, meaning that the covenant had been breached. Following repentance on the part of the people (33:4-6), Yahweh does not allow Moses to see his "glory" (vs. 22), but he reveals his name as signifying a gracious, patient, loving, and forgiving personality. Here an old cultic confession is employed which is frequently quoted in part elsewhere in the OT and which is the only such confession composed of a selection of divine attributes (34:6-7; cf. 33:19). Moses is then told to make two stone tablets like the first, which had been broken, signifying the reconstitution of the covenant. There follows in 34:10 God's formal declaration of the covenant, and in 34:27-28 Moses is told to write the ten words (Decalogue) on the two tablets. In between (vss. 11:26), we thus would expect to find the stipulations of the covenant (the Decalogue) repeated. Instead, vss. 18-26 preserve cultic instructions, specifying the chief religious festivals of Israel. Many scholars have interpreted these as another series of ten commandments, a "ritual decalogue." Because of the type of injunction herein contained and especially because of the great difficulty in discovering or in reconstructing precisely ten laws from the text as preserved, another view seems preferable. Vss. 11-17 are a hortatory warning against the dangers of idolatry in Canaan. In this section a variant and very archaic form of the first two commandments is preserved: "You shall worship no other god" (vs. 14), and "you shall make for yourself no molten gods" (vs. 17). We should expect to find, in what follows, the other eight commandments. Instead, we encounter a festival calendar which in a variant form also appears in 23:12-19. In other words, for a reason which is now difficult to discover, a section which originally contained a form of the Decalogue has been displaced, and another type of material has been inserted, perhaps to avoid repetition.

c. The tabernacle and its furnishings. While Moses "was on the mountain forty days and forty nights" (24:18), he received from God the instructions concerning the religious cultus (chs. 25–31), which are subsequently carried out (chs. 35–40). The formal setting of each of these sections in the second half of Exodus thus differs one from the other, while the essential content, with minor differences, is the same. In the first, Yahweh instructs Moses: "Speak to the people of Israel" (25:1-2); i.e., the cultus is received by indirect or mediated revelation, like the laws of the so-called "Covenant Code" (20:23–23:33). In chs. 35–39, on the other hand, Moses reports what he has received to the assembled people (35:1), who carry out the instructions, while in ch. 40 Yahweh gives Moses fresh orders regarding the final stage of the work, the actual erection of the tabernacle, and the consecration of its objects and its priesthood (vss. 1-15); and these are faithfully followed (vss. 16-33).

In the first section there are two parts, chs. 25–29 and chs. 30–31, the latter apparently being a miscellaneous collection of items supplementing the former. God's instructions begin with a direction that the people be asked to contribute the needed material as a freewill offering (25:1-9). Directions for the items in the sanctuary then follow: the ark with its lid or "mercy seat" (*see* ARK OF THE COVENANT), within which the "testimony" (Decalogue) was to be placed (25:10-22), the offering table with its vessels (vss. 23-30), and the lampstand for seven lamps (vss. 31-40). There follows the description of the two-roomed tent shrine with its easily dismantled wooden frames over which fine leather covering was thrown (ch. 26), the court and its altar (ch. 27), the dress and consecration of the priests and altar (28:1–29:37), and the daily burnt offering (29:38-42). In a fitting conclusion to this section Yahweh promises to meet the people at the sanctuary that there they may be hallowed by his glory, to consecrate the tent, altar, and priesthood, and "to tabernacle" with his people and be their God (29:43-46).

In chs. 30–31 the altar of incense within the main cult room is depicted (30:1-10); a sanctuary tax is imposed as an atonement offering (vss. 11-16); the cultic laver, anointing oil, and formula for incense are described (vss. 17-38); Bezalel and Oholiab are selected as craftsmen and artists (31:1-11); and the observance of the sabbath is designated as the sign of the Mosaic covenant (vss. 12-17).

In the second main section Moses begins by announcing the freewill offering, which is brought (35:1-29). Then God's appointment of Bezalel and Oholiab is announced (35:30–36:1), and with the assistance of the able men they make: the parts for the tabernacle (36:2-38); the ark, table, lampstand, altar of incense, altar of burnt offering, the laver, the court curtains, and the priests' vestments (chs. 37–39). In 40:1-33 everything is put in its proper place and consecrated, after which the final climax of the book is recounted, when "the glory of Yahweh filled the tabernacle" (vss. 34-38).

2. Historical background. In itself the book of Exodus contains few references by which the events it describes can be fitted into their precise historical background in ancient history. The first mention of Israel outside the Bible is by the Egyptian pharaoh Mer-ne-ptah, who on a stele set up in the fifth year of his reign (*ca.* 1220 B.C.) published a hymn of victory in which he described a triumphant raid in Palestine. Among certain Palestinian city-states which he claims to have conquered (Ashkelon, Gezer, Yanoam) he lists the "people of Israel" as desolate and without offspring (*ANET* 378). It could be inferred from this that Israel was by that time in possession of at least the central and S portions of the Palestinian hill country, while the cities mentioned were in or near coastal and Galilean areas which Israel did not control. Archaeological evidence from the sites of Bethel, Lachish, Debir, and probably Hazor suggests a thirteenth-century date for the Israelite conquest of Canaan and may be taken to be in accord with the information of Mer-ne-ptah's stele (*see* JOSHUA, BOOK OF). The important reference in Exod. 1:11 to the effect that Israel in Egypt "built for Pharaoh store cities, Pithom and Raamses" (probably *Tell er-Retabeh* and *San el-Hagar* in the E Delta) seems to point to the same century for the period of the Exodus. This is inferred from the fact that the Egyptian kings of the Eighteenth Dynasty (*ca.* 1570-1310) maintained their capital at Thebes in Upper Egypt and did little, if any, building in the Nile Delta. On the other hand, the pharaohs of the Nineteenth Dynasty (*ca.* 1310-1200) shifted their base of operations to the Delta and erected many new structures there, particularly at the site of Ramses, their capital in the Delta, in order to reconquer and control their Syro-Palestinian empire. Such information leads to the supposition that the Exodus took place during the first half of the thirteenth century, with Ramses II (*ca.* 1290-1224) as pharaoh at the time.

This chronology of the Exodus, first proposed by W. F. Albright (*see bibliography*), though subject to future revision in detail, now appears to accord better with archaeological information than the older views which dated the Exodus either about the time of Mer-ne-ptah or during the mid-fifteenth century B.C. The former is too late a period to account for the archaeological data, while the latter appears to have little support except from two biblical passages: I Kings 6:1; Judg. 11:26. The first of these states that Solomon began to build the temple 480 years after the exodus from Egypt, which then would have occurred *ca.* 1440. This figure, however, is a round number which may easily have been computed by multiplying the twelve generations known to exist between the Exodus and Solomon (I Chr. 6:4-10, 50-52) by the forty years usually reckoned as the length of a generation. The passage in Judges is more difficult; in it Jephthah informs the Ammonite king that Israel has possessed her territory in Transjordan for 300 years. This would date the Mosaic conquest of that land in the fourteenth century, if we are to date Jephthah in the eleventh. Here again, however, the figure in question is a round number, which may well reflect the editorial chronology of the book of Judges. There the editor has reckoned the judges and oppressions as successive, one following the other, instead of being in part contemporary, so that a three-century period has artificially been computed.

Since from Egyptian sources we know that it was customary for Bedouins and Asiatics to be admitted into Egypt in time of famine, we may infer that the Israelites were a part of the shifting population of seminomadic shepherds and cattle-breeders who resided in the Nile Delta. They were thus a convenient source of labor for the pharaohs of the Nineteenth Dynasty, who not only needed the labor but perhaps also feared for the stability of their NE border while engaged in their Asiatic conquests. Furthermore, it is not unlikely that Israel would have been a part of the group of people whom the pharaohs, and many others in Asia, called *'Apiru,* a term with which "HEBREW" is somehow related. It is improbable, however, that the name indicated a nationality during the second millennium B.C. Instead, it was probably used for landless aliens who were not citizens of the particular legal community in which they resided. This conforms with the use of the term "Hebrew" in the early historical traditions of the OT, where it is used for the most part in relation to foreigners who needed a designation which they understood and for whom the term "Israel" would have had no meaning. The biblical tradition speaks of a "mixed multitude" or "rabble" (Num. 11:4), composed of such Hebrews, of whom Israel was the dominant part, which Moses was able to release from their bondage at a time when Egypt was severely shaken by a series of plagues. These and other factors were understood to be a demonstration of the power of Yahweh and the means by which he humbled the Egyptian pharaoh.

Whether all twelve of the Israelite tribes—or, if not, precisely which ones—were involved in the exodus under Moses, is a debated problem which at this time cannot be satisfactorily solved. Since the biblical tradition and archaeological investigation combine to suggest that the invading Israelites under Joshua did not conquer the Shechem area of N central Palestine, we must surely infer that the covenant ceremony reported there (Josh. 24) brought into the tribal league elements which had not left Egypt under Moses. Indeed, one might argue, with Martin Noth (*see bibliography*), that the twelve-tribe league, as it was known in the period of the judges, first came into being in the Shechem ceremony. When he further specifies, however, that the six "Leah tribes," for whom Shechem was the amphictyonic center, were at that time made a part of the larger amphictyony, we must assume that these groups had not been involved in the Exodus. Yet the dominance of the figure of Joseph in the tradition of the N tribes makes such a supposition difficult. All scholars are agreed that the one tribe most closely connected with Egypt is the tribe of Levi, because of the Egyptian names preserved within it (e.g., Moses, Phinehas, Hophni, Pashhur, and perhaps Hur and Merari). Beyond this, however, there is no agreement on the tribal groups involved, and because of the complexity of the biblical tradition it seems improbable that the problem can be solved. Indeed, it is possible that before the period of the judges the composition and even the names of the tribal groups may have been somewhat different from those which later existed, but even this cannot be proved.

The traditions of Israel as preserved in historical, legal, prophetic, and cultic materials, however, all point to the exodus and wilderness periods of the nation's life for the foundations of the faith. All tribal groups of later Israel thus came to accept the traditions of this period as normative. The origins of Yahwism are traced to the Mosaic era, which in some sense must be reckoned as Israel's creative period. While in itself this period is difficult to reconstruct historically, it is even more difficult to depict the pre-Mosaic background of Israel's faith. Perhaps the most elaborate attempt to set the Mosaic era within the cultural and religious atmosphere of the Late Bronze Age is W. F. Albright's *From the Stone Age to Christianity*. In this book he attempts to show both the continuity and the discontinuity of Mosaic faith with its background, while defining that faith as monotheism. This view was presented with the aid of the new horizons of history now available, which necessitate a revision of older views that interpreted monotheism as a gradual development, an achievement of the evolutionary process. While there is still considerable disagreement over the point, the context of the debate has changed considerably. It is widely agreed that Israel did have an early creative period in which there was a radical devaluation of the world's spiritual powers and the exclusive worship of Yahweh demanded. While a development and refinement of conceptions took place in the centuries which followed, these were within the context of the exclusive holiness and "jealousy" of Yahweh. As a result, the debate has become, in no small measure, one between the proper choice and definition of the terms employed to describe Israel's faith in its early stages —whether "monotheism," "monolatry," or some other related term.

One of the most common views regarding the origin of Yahwism is the assumption that Yahweh was the God of one of the tribal groups which later composed the confederacy. From Exod. 18 it is argued that Jethro, Moses' father-in-law, was a Yahweh priest of the Midianite tribe of the Kenites. The Kenite hypothesis, thought first to have been proposed by Ghillany in 1862, rests, however, on an exceedingly tenuous basis. In any event, it cannot be regarded as particularly illuminating, because it does little more than attempt to explain one unknown by another. Whether Moses was originally influenced by the Kenites, or by the monotheism of Akh-en-Aton in Egypt, or by whatever unknown sources, it must still be supposed that he so transformed all that he borrowed that little actual resemblance to the original remained. Yet even this generalization is conjectural, because we as yet do not have sufficient evidence on which to base a firmly grounded hypothesis. The identification of Yahweh with the God of the fathers (Exod. 3:13-15; 6:2-3) presupposes both continuity and discontinuity, but little more can be said with confidence.

On the other hand, formal elements in the early legal and cultic institutions of Israel have been considerably illuminated in archaeological research. By way of illustration, two matters alone will be mentioned here which bear directly upon the exodus traditions. The first is the work on Israelite law, in particular the proof that the so-called "Covenant Code" in Exod. 20:23–23:33 contains a legal tradition derived from ancient Near Eastern common law, as illustrated by the Eshnunna, Hammurabi, Assyrian, and Hittite codes. The social conditions reflected in these codes differ markedly, and it is clear that Israelite law represented an adaptation for the cultural environment of the worshipers of Yahweh in Palestine.

Albrecht Alt in his *Die Urprünge des israelitischen Rechts* (1934) gave the discussion of this question a fresh orientation by distinguishing two legal traditions in Israel, which he termed the "casuistic" and the "apodictic." The first has arisen in judicial decisions, like English common law, which become legal precedents. In formulation the type contains a conditional clause, beginning with "if" (כִּי), which defines the case, and then concludes with the penalty. In form and content it is closely related to the other Near Eastern codes. The apodictic type of law, on the other hand, seems a characteristically Israelite formulation, in which God addresses his people directly (e.g., the Decalogue), and in which no distinction is made between the sacred and the secular. While in the Covenant Code the two types of law are mixed together, such an application of form criticism is able to isolate the forms and to suggest that each has had its separate origin and history, before reaching the present accommodation of one to the other.

A second investigation of importance for the historical background of the Exodus concerns the setting of the conception of a covenant between God and Israel. This covenant is a legal form, comprising a compact between two parties sealed by an oath. It must therefore have been adapted for theological purposes from ancient law. Yet the precise legal background has been difficult to discover.

The basic work on this subject, Johannes Pedersen's *Israel, Its Life and Culture,* I–II (1926), pointed to a setting in nomadic life where, in the absence of a strong central government, covenants, sealed by the gods of the respective parties, were a fundamental source of social cohesion and peace. The nomadic covenant, illustrated particularly by modern Bedouin life, is not a completely satisfactory background for the Israelite covenant between God and people, however, because the latter seems based upon a political background wherein God appears as sovereign and the people as his subjects or "servants."

G. E. Mendenhall (*see bibliography*) has pointed to a different type of background in which the parallels to the Mosaic covenant are most striking. This is the suzerainty treaty between a suzerain and a vassal, as known particularly from Hittite sources in the Late Bronze Age. In this type of covenant the suzerain identified himself and in the first person related the benevolent acts which his dynasty had performed in the vassal's behalf, that the latter might keep the treaty on a personal, rather than on a legal or enforced, basis. Then followed the treaty's stipulations, which defined the suzerain's interests while leaving the vassal free to order his own internal relations within the framework they provided. The detailed comparisons between the suzerainty and Mosaic covenants cannot here be described. Suffice it to say that in this view the Decalogue, with its preamble (Exod. 20:1-17), constitutes the covenant document, as the biblical setting appears to suggest (*see* § 1*b above*), while the code which follows in Exod. 20:23–23:33 is to be understood, not in the sense of constitutional law binding on the judges (for this there is no early Near Eastern parallel), but as legal tactics and procedures, as distinct from the legal policies of the Decalogue, which were subsequently collected for the guidance of people and judges.

3. Composition. Literary critical work on the book of Exodus has found within it the same documents or literary strata as were discovered in the book of Genesis, though admittedly the analysis has been considered more difficult (*see* PENTATEUCH). The supplementation of the older JE materials by the Jerusalem priesthood (P) is most clearly observed in the third main section of the book, which is concerned with the cultic center of the community's worship (chs. 25–31; 35–40). In the first two sections, while there has been considerable difference of opinion concerning individual passages, the basic division of the material is as in Table 1 (from J. E. Carpenter and G. Harford, *The Composition of the Hexateuch* [1902]). *See* pp. 193-94.

There are few literary critics today who would care to support this complex analysis in every detail, particularly in the precise separation of J and E, though there is still wide agreement regarding its main contentions. Chs. 20–23 are considered, e.g., as basically drawn from the E source, which here appears to have displaced J. Only a part of the latter's treatment of the same subject is preserved in

Table 1

Source	Verses
J	6 8-12 14a 20b 22 11-23a
E	1 15-20a 21 2 1-10 23b-25
P	1-5 7 13 14b
J	2-4a 5 7-9a *14 16-18 1-16
E	3 4b 6 9b-13 15 *19-21: 4 17·
P	1
J	19-20a 21-26 29-31 3 5-23 1
E	20b 27 5 1· 4 6
P	2-30
J	14 16-17a 18 21a 24: 1-4
E	7 15 17b 20b 23 8
P	1-13 19-20a 21b-22
J	8-15a 20-32 1-7 13-17· 23b 24b
E'	9 *19-23a 24a
P	5-7 15b-19 8-12
J	25b-30 33· 1-11 13b 14b-15a 15c-19
E	25a 31· 35R 10 12-13a 14a 15b
P	
J	24-26 28· 4-8 21-23 25-27
E	20-23 27 11 1-3 12
P	*9 1-20 24 28
J	29-34 37-39 3a 4-7· 10-13 21·
E	*35· 13 **3b **9 **14-19
P	*40-51 1· 20
J	5· 10a 11-14 19b 20b 21b
E	14 7 9a 10b 15a 16a 19a 20a
P	1-4 8 9bR 15b 16b-18 21a 21c-23
J	24a 25 27b 28b 30 1 22-25a 27
E	24b *31 15 *2-18 20· 25b-*26
P	26-27a 28a *29 *19
J	3 2b 7a 7c *2-4 7
E	16 4 17 1b-2a 4-6 7b 8-16 18 1R 5 8
P	1-3 *5-36 1a
J	9-11 *3b-6 11b-13 18
E	12-27 19 2b-3a 7-11a 14-17 19
P	2a 1
J	20-22 24· **2 **4b-6 **7b **9· **12b **17b
E	*23 20 1 3-4a 7a 8 12a 13-17a 18-26
P	11
J	*21b-22 *24 *13 *15b
E	21 1-36 22 1-21a *23 25-31 23 1-12 14-15a
P	

Table 1 (*continued*)

J		*17		*19		*23-25*a*		*27		31*b*-33		1·		9-11
E	16		18		20-22		25*b*-26		28-31*a*		24		3-8	
P														

J						*7-14				25-29		
E	12-15*a*		18*b*	32	1-6		15*a*		16-24		30-35	33
P		15*b*-18*a*						*15*b*				

J	1		3-4		12-23		1-23		25-28	
E		**2		*5-11		34		**24		
P										29-34

ch. 34, where it is used to describe the covenant's reconstitution. How much can be said about the editing of the E material in this section, however, is problematical. In chs. 22–23 evidence of the JE redactor is observed (designated in Table 1 by an asterisk before a verse), while in ch. 20 a number of verses are credited to the Deuteronomic redactor (designated in Table 1 by two asterisks before a verse). There are so many unknown factors in the transition of material, however, that it is now considered difficult to be precise about such editorial work. The close relation existing between the Deuteronomic school and the N Israelite schools represented by E and Hosea make it difficult, e.g., to specify Deuteronomic-like material in Exodus as being manifestly from later redaction and not a part of the original N Israelite source (E). The direction of influence, whether backward from D or forward from E to D, is in this instance more likely the latter than the former.

Wilhelm Rudolph (*see bibliography*) attempted to eliminate E entirely. He has so focused attention upon the importance of the J stratum as to emphasize the role of its unknown author-compiler in the creation of the Hexateuchal story in the form in which we have it. We do not know E as a complete source but mainly as a supplementation of J, and Frank M. Cross, Jr., has argued persuasively that P can no longer be proved to be anything more than an editing and supplementing of JE.

The most important attempts to break up the J stratum of material in Exodus, and by adding other elements to create a new document, are Otto Eissfeldt's Lay source (L) and Julian Morgenstern's Kenite source (K). The latter is reconstructed as a Mosaic history, beginning with the birth of the great leader and culminating with the covenant based upon the assumed decalogue in Exod. 34. The former is projected as centering in the ideals of nomadic life, a layman's work with interests very different from those in the priestly community. Eissfeldt ascribes to his L the following passages in Exodus: portions of chs. 1–2; 3:21-22; 4:1-9, 19-26, 30*b*-31*a;* 7:15*b,* part of 17, 20; 12:21-27, 33-39; 13:3-16 in part, 20; part of ch. 14; 15:20-27; part of ch. 16; 17:1*a,* 8-16; part of 19:2-25; 24:1-2, 9-11, 13*a,* 14-15*a;* 32:17-18, 25-29; 33:3*b*-4 (from *Einleitung in das AT* [2nd ed., 1956], p. 231).

The complexity of the priestly materials has long been observed, and literary criticism has sought to solve the question by the assumption of a complex redaction and supplementation. Gerhard von Rad (*see bibliography*) has attempted to divide P into two basic sources of approximately the same length (P^A and P^B). Yet the time is past when the continued further breakdown of the biblical text into different documents may gain wide acceptance. The reason is the vigorous attack upon the methodology of literary criticism, led particularly by Scandinavian scholars, and the growing awareness that a book like Exodus reached final written form only after a long transmission in both oral and written form. Hence one can no longer assume that purely literary analysis can solve the complex problems it presents, because the unknown factor is the history and psychology of oral tradition, of which the written form is simply a stage in its fixation. If, e.g., P represents a collection of materials, both oral and written, assembled from the fragmentary older sources available to the priests of the exilic and early postexilic periods, then we must assume that each item of its content must be examined on its own merits, and further that the methods used by literary criticism for its analysis are adequate only in part. We can no longer be sure that unevenness and even discrepancy within a particular "document" betray the work of a supplementer or redactor, when the problem may have presented itself to an original compiler of the material from the variety within the oral tradition with which he was dealing.

Furthermore, the liturgical movement within biblical studies has called attention to the cultic setting of much of the material transmitted. The liturgical element must, therefore, receive serious consideration as a warning to purely documentary analysis before the latter proceeds too far. An important case in point is Johannes Pedersen's study of Exod. 1–15. To him these chapters constitute the central core of the Pentateuch and are taken from cultic ceremony. They are a "cult legend forming a separate whole and which has not been formed by the mechanical combination of independent parallel expositions." They reflect the "annual re-living of historical events, as it took shape down through the ages," and the inequalities of the text cannot be explained satisfactorily by a presumption of separate "sources." The narrative is not a simple history, compiled for history's sake, but a "cultic glorification," a celebration of God's great victory by the worshiping people in the paschal festival. Its object is not to report ordinary events but to describe events of a different character, exploits in which God is glorified and a people made great. Unevenness in the report must be explained by accretions accumulated in cultic usage, rather than by purely literary criteria.

This viewpoint, which Pedersen would extend also to the Sinai covenant sections of Exodus, makes an important emphasis: namely, that a large part of the OT material was used in worship and was transmitted and refracted by this usage. Questions arise, however, regarding the implications of Pedersen's views on Exod. 1–15. Did the cultus originate the epic, or did it simply use and refract it? The question can be argued both ways, but it seems very doubtful whether liturgy creates an epic which has not already been in existence. Furthermore, the question arises as to whether the cultic emphasis actually eliminates the necessity of positing literary fixing of the oral tradition by different circles of the people at different times. It is questionable whether the documentary hypothesis in some form can be completely dismissed by the liturgical and oral-tradition movements; indeed, in their detailed work they seem unable to do away with it completely. The "documents" remain as collections of material, even though it is held that they do not admit of being arranged in an evolutionary scheme.

The same questions arise regarding the liturgical interpretation of the covenant section in chs. 20–24. Gerhard von Rad, e.g. (in *Das formgeschichtliche Problem des Hexateuchs* [1938]), interprets the whole Sinai tradition as a cultic legend, the *Sitz im Leben* of which was a cultic festival in which the following liturgical acts can be reconstructed: (*a*) exhortation (Exod. 19:4-6), with historical presentation of the Sinai events; (*b*) recitation of the law (Decalogue and Book of the Covenant); (*c*) the promise of blessing (23:20 ff); and (*d*) the concluding of the covenant (ch. 24). That these chapters were so used liturgically is most probable. Consequently, literary criticism in itself cannot be expected to solve the basic questions regarding their present form. Yet the problem again arises as to whether the cultic festival has created the tradition or even the material it has used. The cultus transmits, refracts, and combines historical tradition for liturgical purposes in community life, but one cannot assume without question that the tradition, even in all of its written form, was created in and by the cultic ceremonies and their officiants.

Finally, the method of studying such materials as are contained in the historical books of the OT, termed the "history of tradition," may be mentioned. For Martin Noth (*see bibliography*) the Pentateuchal traditions are to be understood in the first instance as the sacred traditions of the twelve-tribe league on the soil of Palestine during the period of the judges. To penetrate their meaning and history, one must pursue a careful literary analysis to separate the documentary strata of the tradition. Noth's conclusions here are fairly orthodox, though he agrees that J provides the basic literary material, while P gives the framework, and E, though once an independent source, cannot be reconstructed as a continuous document, since it has been used as a supplement to J. Both J and E, however, are derived from a common source, which already contained the basic orientation of the whole within the tribal covenant. Behind this, however, lies the history of the traditions contained in the documents. Five major themes can be isolated, Noth believes, from the various traditions. These are: the Exodus, the entrance into the Promised Land, the promise to the patriarchs, the wilderness wandering, and the revelation on Mount Sinai. The first, fifth, and part of the fourth of these themes are contained in Exodus, and the remaining material, which serves to join them together, is later and artificially contrived to give the whole a unity which the original did not possess. Noth maintains that not even the figure of Moses was originally what connected the themes. Moses was once only a minor tribal sheik, whose grave was encountered by some group on its way into the land, and was only gradually drawn into the traditions.

The question arises, however, as to the proper use of the methodology of form criticism and the history of tradition. One can, indeed, separate the themes or traditions and to a certain extent trace their history within the cultus. But is it possible, without some external checks, to use internal criteria of this sort for historical reconstruction? In cultic practice, e.g., it is true that the exodus and the Sinai themes were separate, because the two seem not to appear together in confessions. Yet what is the proper inference from this fact? Does cultic separation of themes in liturgy mean original historical separation, so that the group involved in the Exodus was not the same as that related to the Sinai experience? In Christian practice a liturgy for Good Friday or Easter may not mention the other events in the church's kerygma, but one cannot infer from such cultic separation of themes that historically they were originally separated.

This is not to say that no historical inferences may be drawn from literary, form-critical, and tradition-history research. Yet the historical tradition lying within and behind the present form of the traditions cannot be reconstructed solely from presuppositions drawn from or imposed upon these methodologies without the use of all factual data and perspectives which archaeology supplies. Only with the latter always in the foreground can hypotheses safely be formulated.

4. Significance. The events recorded in the book of Exodus lie at the very center of Israelite faith and life. The theological significance of these events may be succinctly summarized under the three main headings which constitute the book's content (*see* § 1 *above*).

a. God's deliverance from Egyptian slavery. While we cannot be certain as to which tribal groups were involved in the Exodus, we can be quite sure that the tradition was accepted as normative by all members of the twelve-tribe league, and that very early in the nation's life the spring nature festival was "historicized" as the Passover, a celebration of God's act of deliverance. At an early period also the fall olive festival was likewise "historicized" as the Feast of Tabernacles or Booths, the latter symbolizing the life in the wilderness wanderings.

The first thing to observe, then, about the exodus event is that it formed the center of the Israelite confessions of faith and cultic worship. The knowledge of God was communicated in the people's worship, by means of a narrative, wherein historical happenings were related as the great deeds of God, who had brought a people into existence. The Hebrew mind was trained by this manner of communication to view the historical scene as the arena of God's primary self-disclosure, whereas by contrast the polytheist looked to the mythical happenings behind the natural order, in the cultic celebration of which he experienced his religious exaltation. The exodus event ultimately meant for Israel a radical demythologizing of nature as it was interpreted in contemporary polytheism.

Furthermore, the Exodus gave rise to a language which in the Bible as a whole remained central: e.g., "deliver," "redeem," "salvation," "bring out," "lead forth," "mighty acts," "signs and wonders," etc. The event thus became in OT theology a nucleus around which a variety of terms and meanings adhered. In both prophecy and cultic life, therefore, it could be referred to in variant situations, and different meanings could be deduced: e.g., praise of God's majesty and power (Ps. 66); praise of his merciful and gracious nature (Pss. 103:6 ff; 135–36); meditation upon God's love and by contrast Israel's lack of loving obedience (Hos. 11; and note the great narrative hymns in Pss. 78; 106); individual supplication for deliverance from trouble, grounded in the mighty deeds of old (Ps. 77); the first exodus as the basis of hope for the proclamation of a second exodus, this time from Babylonian captivity (Isa. 51:9-11).

A second thing to observe is the manner in which the Exodus determined the people's understanding of the RIGHTEOUSNESS of God. This righteousness was ultimate power acting to save or deliver the weak, the oppressed, the poor, the enslaved. It was not primarily justice distributed according to social status, but redemptive action according to need. Israelite economic life reflected this understanding profoundly, even in the earliest preserved laws. As God is righteous, so Israelites were to be righteous; and this meant economically that weakness and poverty were not to be made into a source of profit by the strong (cf. Exod. 22:25-27), whether the weakness was that of a fellow Israelite or of a stranger ("sojourner") in a status comparable to Israel's in Egypt (22:21).

Finally, it may be recalled that the Israelite conception of ELECTION, of God's choice of Israel to be his "own possession among all peoples, . . . a kingdom of priests and a holy nation" (19:5-6), arose as a primary inference from God's act of deliverance from Egypt. In the OT there is a double tradition of this special election, the Genesis narratives fixing God's choice in the call of Abraham, while other references, particularly in the Prophets, refer it to the exodus period. Yet there can be no doubt that historically the conception of Israel as the chosen people of Yahweh arose in the latter period, though it probably drew on early traditions subsequently interpreted and presented as the time of promise which was partly fulfilled in the Exodus (*see bibliography*). Furthermore, the exodus event provided the setting in which the relationship between God and people was comprehended. The primary act which called the people into being was by God's gracious initiative, one which Israel could not explain on grounds of merit or requirement. Having been the recipients of this unmerited act of grace, the people were called upon to respond with love and fidelity, while sin took on overtones of faithless infidelity and inhuman betrayal of love. The grace of God and the people's response in this type of relationship appear to be what is involved in that basic word in the Hebrew theological vocabulary, *ḥésedh,* translated "steadfast love" in the RSV.

b. The Sinai covenant. The election of Israel was given form in the conception of COVENANT—a fact to be inferred, not only from the Sinai traditions, but also from the theological vocabulary, in which legal terms play such a large role. "Covenant" was a pact or treaty between two parties sealed by an oath. Yet there were different kinds of covenants known in Israelite life and in the contemporary world. The simplest were those between two different seminomadic groups, the purpose of which was to prevent intertribal strife (e.g., Gen. 21:27; 26:28; 31:44). The covenant between two individuals is illustrated by the pact of undying friendship between Jonathan and David (I Sam. 18:3; 20:16-17; 23:18). In international politics there were two types of covenant, the parity treaty between equals and the suzerainty treaty between an emperor or suzerain and a vassal.

In Israel the basic terminological pattern revolves around the picture of a divine ruler who reveals his will to a people who as his "servants" are expected to "hearken" (שמע) and to "obey"—i.e., to "serve" (עבד). I.e., the basic symbol used for God is a political one, and the language expressive of the relation between God and people takes form around this symbol. An objection to this view has been that the term "king" for God is rarely, if ever, used in Israel's earliest literature. This is to be explained, however, by the fact that "king" (מלך) in Syria-Palestine referred primarily to the princeling of a city-state, one among many. Yahweh as Ruler, on the other hand, was not one among many; hence the symbolism depicting his "kingship" would be expected to be derived from the emperor figure, the "king of kings," who is not one among many.

On this basis, the one type of ancient covenant that fits Israel's understanding of the relation of God and people is the suzerainty treaty. Indeed, the parallelism between this treaty form and the OT traditions regarding the Mosaic covenant are so remarkable that it is difficult to believe that they are accidental. In this view the covenant document (Exod. 20:1-17; i.e., the "words" [*see* § 1*b above*]) presents the stipulations of the ruler, defines his interests, and thus becomes the legal policy of the community. Legal tactics, on the other hand, by which the community attempts to carry out the policy, are to be found in the positive law, the "ordinances" (משפטים), which have the position, not of direct, but of mediated, revelation in Israel. The situation in the original covenant differs, however, from that in Judaism, wherein the mass of detailed positive law is considered as a constitution to enforce action. Yet the earlier legal codes in Israel (e.g., Exod. 20:23–23:19) were not constitutional law; like the earlier codes among other peoples, they were compiled for the instruction of the people, and perhaps to unify legal practice. No judge ever decided a case on the basis of the "constitution"; the mentality did not exist at that time for this type of action.

Interpreted in this background, the Mosaic covenant, as the legal form in which self-understanding was provided for Israel, takes on fresh meaning and significance. It explains, e.g., the freedom involved in the early tribal league which led to a resistance of the monarchy. It also provides the setting for legal language to become theological language, and as well for historians and prophets to interpret the history of Israel in the Promised Land in terms of God's controversy with his people. Furthermore, the suzerainty treaty is the only known type of covenant which would have enabled Israel to join "gospel" and "law" together in such close association. This type of treaty, which began with a personal narration of the benevolent acts of the monarch toward the vassal, had as its purpose the binding of ruler and vassal together in a relationship which led the latter to respond from a sense of gratitude, rather than from purely legal necessity. Hence the prologue to the Decalogue binds the Exodus and the covenant together, so that legal obligation in Israel was set within the context of the grace of God, who had redeemed a people from slavery and had become their Lord, Protector, and Guide.

c. The tabernacle. The editor of the older JE material from the circles of the Jerusalem priesthood (P) has appended to the exodus and Sinai covenant narratives a detailed description of the Israelite cultus —i.e., of the place of worship (chs. 25-31; 35-40), the services of worship, the priesthood, and related matters (in Leviticus and Numbers). One of the main reasons for the desire to preserve the TABERNACLE traditions from the nation's earliest times lay in the priestly conception of the meaning of Israel's central sanctuary. This conception is given clear expression in Exod. 29:43-45: "There I will meet with the people of Israel, and it shall be sanctified by my glory. . . . And I will dwell among the people of Israel, and will be their God."

To the Jerusalem priesthood, the holy PRESENCE in the people's midst was what made Israel a people. The tabernacle was the sign and seal of the divine presence, and the place where he could be met and worshiped. The key words for P's theology in the passage quoted above are: "meet," "glory," "dwell." The tabernacle, or "tent of meeting," is interpreted by P as the place where God will meet his people and hallow them. His presence is marked by his "glory," the envelope of brilliance that surrounded him, or a cloud that hid this brilliance from the human eye. By this conception P can affirm the real presence of the Lord in the people's midst, without encountering the danger believed to exist in too intimate a personal encounter. It thus expresses both the hiddenness of God and the knowledge of his "tabernacling" presence in the people's midst. The term "dwell" in priestly theology is for this circle a technical theological expression. It is not the common term used of human "dwelling" in an earthly abode (ישב); the latter is used of God only in relation to his heavenly temple. Because of the problem of expressing the immanence of the transcendent God in an earthly structure, the priests adopted an archaic term that meant "to tent" (שכן). Yahweh does not "dwell" on earth as a human being does; but he has graciously consented to "tent" ("tabernacle") in his people's midst (cf. John 1:14, where the Greek uses the same expression for the Word become flesh).

This richly sacramental conception of Israel's central sanctuary represents an adaptation of the polytheistic conception of the temple as the divine palace on earth, but without the almost materialistic, unspiritualized idea of divine immanence so characteristic of polytheism. Even this adaptation, however, appears to have been unacceptable to the Deuteronomic school, for whom the sanctuary was to be understood as the place which Yahweh chose to have his name "tabernacle," and thus as a symbol of God's accommodation to human need in providing a place to which prayer could be directed (note especially I Kings 8:27 ff). For the priests of Jerusalem, however, the tabernacle tradition represented Yahweh's revelation of himself as the "tabernacling" God, who in the sanctuary could be met and who there would sanctify his people as they worshiped him.

Bibliography. Commentaries: H. Holzinger, *KHC* (1900). B. Baentsch, *HKAT* (1903). A. H. McNeile, *WC* (1908). S. R. Driver, Cambridge Bible (1911). G. Beer and K. Galling, *HAT* (1939). J. C. Rylaarsdam, *IB*, vol. I (1952).

Among Introductions to the OT, see especially: O. Eissfeldt (2nd ed.). S. R. Driver. R. H. Pfeiffer. A. Weiser. A. Bentzen. J. E. Carpenter and G. Harford, *The Composition of the Hexateuch* (1902).

Other works: J. Pedersen, *Israel, Its Life and Culture,* I-II (1926); III-IV (1940). K. Galling, *Die Erwählungstraditionen Israels* (1928), on the conception of Israel as the chosen people of Yahweh. M. Noth, *Das System der zwölf Stämme Israels* (1930), pp. 65-86. G. von Rad, *Die Priesterschrift im Hexateuch* (1934). W. F. Albright, *BASOR,* LVIII (1935), 10-18, proposes a chronology of the Exodus. W. Rudolph, *Der "Elohist" von Exodus bis Josua* (1938). F. M. Cross, *BA*, X (1947), 65-68. M. Noth, *Überlieferungsgeschichte des Pentateuch* (1948)—a most important study of the history of traditions of the book of Exodus. T. J. Meek, *Hebrew Origins* (rev. ed., 1950). M. Noth, *Geschichte Israels* (2nd ed., 1954). G. E. Mendenhall, *Law and Covenant in Israel and the Ancient Near East* (1955). W. F. Albright, *From the Stone Age to Christianity* (2nd ed., 1957). G. E. Wright, *Biblical Archaeology* (1957).

G. E. WRIGHT

EXODUS, ROUTE OF. A discussion of the route followed by the people of Israel on their departure from Egypt involves an attempt to comprehend the geographical indications in the books of Exodus, Numbers, and Deuteronomy concerning Israel in the Nile Delta and in the wilderness. It must be confessed at the outset that the biblical record and our knowledge of ancient geography are at many points too imprecise to permit us to construct anything more than reasonable hypotheses.

1. Israel in the Nile Delta. According to the literary critical division of the sources, the first definite geographical notation concerning the Exodus in the older collections of JE is Exod. 13:17-18. Here we are told that God led the people, not by the "land of the Philistines route," though that was near, but by the "Reed Sea [*yam sûph; see* RED SEA] wilderness route," in order that they might not have to face immediate war. The former is an apparent reference to the main military route along the Sinai coast to Palestine, called by the Egyptians the "Ways of Horus" and defended by a series of fortifications described by Pharaoh Seti I (*ca.* 1308-1290 B.C.) in his Karnak inscription. It began at the frontier fortress of Zilu, near modern Qantarah, and continued to

Raphia in S Palestine. The second route cannot be determined, unless we can fix the location of the "Reed Sea." An Egyptian text mentions two bodies of water near the city of Rameses (Tanis) in the E Delta. One is the "water of Horus" (the Shihor of Isa. 23:3); the other is the "Papyrus Marsh," which recalls the biblical "Reed Sea."

The other geographical notations are those contributed by P, who provided a detailed itinerary as an outline for the older Exodus materials (12:37; 14:1-2; cf. Num. 33:5-8). According to this information Israel started out from Rameses, journeyed to Succoth, and thence (Exod. 13:20; Num. 33:6) to Etham, on the edge of the wilderness. Once there, the people were commanded to turn back and "encamp in front of Pi-ha-hiroth, between Migdol and the sea, in front of Baal-zephon; you shall encamp over against it, by the sea" (cf. the placement in Num. 33:7: "They set out from Etham, and turned back to Pi-ha-hiroth, which is east of Baal-zephon; and they encamped before Migdol").

With the identification of Rameses with Tanis, as a result of the excavations there of P. Montet since 1929, and of Succoth with Tell el-Mashkutah, the first stage of the journey in this itinerary is clear. Israel went S from Tanis to the Wadi Tumilat, intending to cross the border into the Sinai wilderness by the inland route to Beer-sheba. (If, with a few scholars, Rameses is identified with Qantir, a short distance SW of Tanis, the general meaning and direction of the route remains the same.) Presumably encountering difficulty in breaking through the frontier fortresses (Etham?), they turned back northward the way they had come. The remaining three sites, which, if located, would place exactly the point where the Reed Sea was crossed, are all mentioned in Egyptian inscriptions. A papyrus letter mentioning the god "Baal-zephon and all the gods of Tahpanhes" suggests that a temple of Baal-zephon existed at Tahpanhes (Daphne, modern Tell Defneh), and that this is the location of the exodus site. Pi-ha-hiroth cannot be identified, except that in Exod. 14:2 it would appear to have been E or NE of Daphne. If so, then the crossing of the Reed Sea would have been in the area of, probably to the N of, modern Qantarah (the approximate location of Zilu, the frontier fortress on the "land of the Philistines route"), along the S extension of modern Lake Manzala. Migdol is usually identified with Tell el-Heir, near Pelusium, NW of Qantarah in Sinai, though it is the implication of Exod. 14:2 that it was W, not E, of the sea.

These data suggest that Israel was unable to cross into Sinai by the common routes because of the Egyptian fortresses. To presume that they continued southward to cross near Suez on the Red Sea ignores the implication of the biblical account that they turned back the way they had come after reaching the Wadi Tumilat, and as well the location of Baal-zephon at Daphne. We are thus led to the assumption that the only available way into Sinai was across the shallow waters in the S extension of Lake Manzala. The fact that this was done successfully by remarkable circumstance was celebrated in later Israel as God's greatest act of salvation. That the Reed Sea could not have been a N extension of the Red Sea, has been proved by the recent discovery that the level of the Red Sea has not changed markedly within historical times.

2. Israel in the wilderness. The route through the Sinai wilderness depends, of course, upon the location of the sacred mountain to which Israel journeyed (*see* SINAI, MOUNT). If it is located in the traditional area among the granite peaks at the S end of the Sinai Peninsula, then Israel would have traveled along the W shore of the Red Sea to the area of Ras Abu Zeneimeh, where the headquarters of modern manganese mining operations are today located, and then have turned inland by a series of valleys to the area of Jebel Musa (Figs. SIN 62-63). While none of the stations of the biblical record can be identified along this route with certainty, the following appear to be the most likely:

The bitter waters of Marah (Exod. 15:22-25; Num. 33:8-9) are usually identified with 'Ain Hawarah, some forty-five to fifty miles S of the tip of the Gulf of Suez, though this source is hard to interpret as being three days' journey from the Reed Sea (Exod. 15:22). Perhaps 'Ain Musa or an unknown spring near the Bitter Lakes, as has been suggested, would be a more fitting location. Elim (Exod. 15:27; Num. 33:9), with its many springs and trees, is probably to be identified with the Wadi Gharandel; the encampment by the Red Sea (Num. 33:10), perhaps at the site of the fifteenth-century Egyptian port of Merkhah, five miles S of Ras Abu Zeneimeh; the Wilderness of Sin (Exod. 16:1; Num. 33:11), a plain along the edge of the Sinai Plateau, Debbet er-Ramleh; Dophkah (Num. 33:12), the Egyptian mining center of Serabit el-Khadim; Rephidim (Exod. 17:1; Num. 33:14), Wadi Rafayid; the encampment in the wilderness of Sinai before the sacred mountain (Exod. 19:1-2; Num. 33:15), the small plain of er-Raha at the foot of that series of peaks of which Jebel Musa is the highest.

The route from Mount Sinai or Horeb to Kadesh-barnea is designated by Deut. 1:19 as "that great and terrible wilderness." It would have followed a series of valleys, between the main Sinai plateau and the coastal chain of mountains of Ezion-geber on the N tip of the Gulf of Aqabah (Num. 33:35), and thence inland, up and over the high ridges lining the Wadi 'Arabah to the area of 'Ain Qedeis and 'Ain Qudeirat in the Judean Negeb. According to Deut. 1:2, this was a journey of eleven days, a distance which closely corresponds to that of Edward Robinson and Eli Smith in 1838 (*see bibliography*). None of the stations listed in Num. 33:17-35 can be identified with any certainty, unless it be Hazeroth at 'Ain Khadra, a spring some eighteen hours' journey from Sinai according to Abel (*see bibliography*).

Two general terms are applied in the tradition to the area through which the route passes: the Wilderness of PARAN, encountered after Israel left Sinai (Num. 10:12; 12:16); and the Wilderness of Zin (*see* ZIN, WILDERNESS OF), in which Kadesh was located (Num. 13:21; 20:1; 33:36). It would appear, however, that the two are not always sharply distinguished, for Kadesh is also said to have been in the Wilderness of Paran (Num. 13:3, 26; Num. 33:36 LXX). Indeed, the latter may have been a much more general term, judging from its application even to the area of Maon and Carmel, NE of Beer-sheba, in I Sam. 25:1.

If the sacred mountain is not to be located in the traditional area at the apex of the Sinai Peninsula, the route of the wilderness wanderings would depend upon its location. If because of its association with the Midianites (Exod. 2:15-16; 3:1) and because of assumed volcanic data behind Exod. 19, Mount Sinai is to be located in Arabia, E of the Gulf of Aqabah, then the route followed from Egypt would have been across the old Mohammedan pilgrim route to Aqabah. If, on the other hand, Sinai is located near Kadesh because of the association of these two in the tradition, then one would presume that the route would have followed the inland road to Beer-sheba. Both roads across Sinai begin at the E end of the Wadi Tumilat by the modern Lake Timsah. In neither case, however, can any of the stations in the biblical route be identified with any known sites along these two routes, at least with any degree of confidence.

Bibliography. E. Robinson, *Biblical Researches,* I (11th ed., 1856), 60-172. C. W. Wilson and H. S. Palmer, *Ordnance Survey of the Peninsula of Sinai* (1869-72). W. M. F. Petrie, *Researches in Sinai* (1906). A. H. Gardiner, *Journal of Egyptian Archaeology,* vol. 5 (1918), pp. 127-38, 179-200, 242-71; vol. 10 (1924), pp. 87-96; vol. 19 (1933), pp. 122-28. C. S. Jarvis, *Yesterday and Today in Sinai* (1931). F.-M. Abel, *Géographie de la Palestine,* II (1938), 208-16. W. F. Albright, *BASOR,* no. 109 (Feb., 1948), pp. 15-16. E. G. Kraeling, *Rand McNally Bible Atlas* (1956), pp. 100-118. G. E. Wright

EXORCISM [ἐξόρκωσις, *from* ἐξορκίζω, to bind with an oath, to conjure]; EXORCIST [ἐξορκιστής] (Acts 19:13). The practice of expelling evil spirits from persons or places by means of incantations and the performance of certain occult acts. In the early stages of the Sumero-Akkadian religion evil spirits were considered a separate entity, unrelated to the gods; later, however, they were assumed to be the direct offspring of the cosmic deities, particularly of the sky-god Anu. The evil spirits were believed to be the cause of all kinds of calamities occurring in nature and the bearers of diseases and mental aberrations among men. Once such a spirit took possession of a man, it was the task of the conjuration priest (Akkadian *āšipu* or *kalû*), who acted as a messenger of one or several gods, to cast it out of the afflicted body.

The methods employed in exorcising evil spirits were primarily based on sympathetic or imitative magic. The priest would fashion a likeness of the demon (or of the sorcerer who had bewitched the person) in clay, wax, or any other material, and then, after the recitation of certain formulas, destroy it; the principle was that what had happened to the image would also happen to the demon or sorcerer himself. Another technique was to form a likeness of the patient in some plastic material and then induce the evil spirit to leave the sufferer's body and enter into its counterpart. In some cases the priest would also apply medication in the treatment of the possessed person. The following is an excerpt from an Assyrian incantation recited by the sufferer himself.

Incantation. Be off! Be off! Depart! Depart!
Your wickedness like smoke rises heavenward!
By the life of Shamash [the sun-god], the Mighty, verily be ye exorcised!
By the life of Asaruludu [i.e., Marduk], the incantation-priest of the gods, verily be ye exorcised!
By the life of Gira [the fire-god], who consumes you, verily be ye exorcised!
From my body verily may ye separate![1]

Considering the widely held belief in the existence of evil spirits and also in the efficacy of the magicians to dispose of them, it is surprising that the OT maintains complete silence about this branch of magical practice. The only allusion to an "evil spirit" (רוח רעה, always in the singular!) which took possession of a man and "tormented" (בעת) his mind is found in the story of Saul (I Sam. 16:14-16; 18:10; 19:9). However, the melancholy king was relieved from his mental depressions by the skilful playing of the lyre by young David—a performance hardly to be considered an act of exorcism in the classical style. The absence of any direct reference to exorcism in the OT is particularly remarkable, since the postbiblical literature relates the activities of the exorcists as a matter of incontestable fact. The angel Raphael instructed Tobit (6:7, 16-17; 8:3) to ban the evil spirit from the marriage chamber by making a fire and placing on the embers the heart and liver of a fish, and "then the demon will smell it and flee away, and will never again return." Josephus (Antiq. VIII.ii.5) reports: "God granted him [Solomon] knowledge of the art used against demons for the benefit and healing of men. He also composed incantations by which illnesses are relieved, and left behind forms of exorcism with which those possessed by demons drive them out never to return. And this kind of cure is of very great power among us to this day, for I have seen a certain Eleazar, a countryman of mine, in the presence of Vespasian . . . free men possessed by demons." Rabbi Johanan ben Zakkai, a contemporary of Josephus, once prescribed the following technique to expell demons: "Take roots of herbs, burn them under him [the possessed person], and surround him with water, whereupon the spirit will flee" (Pesik. dRK 40*b*).

In the NT evil and unclean spirits are reported to have been exorcised by Jesus and the disciples without recourse to incantations or occult performances. Jesus cast out demons by the "Spirit of God" (Matt. 12:28), and by his own word (Matt. 8:16; Mark 1:25; 5:8; 9:25; etc.). This power to drive out spirits was bestowed by Jesus upon his disciples (Matt. 10:1; Mark 6:7), and they accomplished the charge by invoking his name (Mark 16:17; Acts 16:18; etc.). According to Acts 19:13-14 there were professional Jewish exorcists at Ephesus who tried to expel evil spirits in the name of the Lord Jesus, saying: "I adjure you by the Jesus whom Paul preaches" (see also Mark 9:38).

Like the ancient Babylonian exorcists who invoked the names of the great cosmic deities in their incantations, Babylonian magicians of the first centuries of the Christian era invoked the names of pagan gods (and those of Jewish origin the name of Yahweh) in their attempts to drive out evil spirits (cf. J. A. Montgomery, *Aramaic Incantation Texts from Nippur,* nos. 9, 26, and particularly 36, which is a close parallel to the Tobit charm).

[1] I. Mendelsohn, ed., *Religions of the Ancient Near East* (New York: The Liberal Arts Press, Inc.).

Bibliography. G. Meier, *Die assyrische Beschwörungssammlung Maqlu* (1937); E. Reiner, *Šurpu. A Collection of Sumerian and Akkadian Incantations* (1958). I. MENDELSOHN

EXPIATION [כפרים, כפרת, כפר; ἱλασμός, ἐξιλασμός, ἐξίλασις, ἱλαστήριον, ἱλάσκεσθαι, ἐξιλάσκεσθαι]; KJV PROPITIATION (*see* § 1 *below*). An atoning action which obliterates sin from God's sight and so restores to holiness and the divine favor.

1. Terminology. The word "expiation" occurs only once in the KJV (Num. 35:33 mg.), as does also the verb "expiate" (Isa. 47:11 mg.). In the ERV-ASV "expiation" appears twice in the text (Num. 35:33; Deut. 32:43) and "expiated" four times in the margin (I Sam. 3:14; Isa. 6:7; 22:14; 27:9). Two of these (I Sam. 3:14; Isa. 27:9), in addition to Num. 35:33; Deut. 32:43, are brought into the text of the RSV, in which also "expiation" replaces "propitiation" in Rom. 3:25; Heb. 2:17; I John 2:2; 4:10.

a. In biblical Hebrew. The idea of expiation or ATONEMENT is expressed by the Hebrew verb כפר and its corresponding substantives כפרים and כפרת. The root meaning of כפר, which occurs only in the *Pi'el* and derivative forms, is uncertain. Some maintain that it means "to cover," like the cognate Arabic word *kaphara*. The frequent use of כפר as a parallel to the verb כסה, "to cover," gives support to this view (e.g., Pss. 32:1; 85:2; cf. Neh. 4:5; Job 31:33; Prov. 17:9). Others hold that the etymological meaning of כפר is preserved in the Syriac cognate *kephar* (*Pa'el kappar*), "to wipe" or "to wipe away," and cite the parallel usage of כפר and מחה, "to blot out" or "to wipe away" (e.g., Jer. 18:23; cf. Ps. 51:1, 9—H 51:3, 11; Isa. 43:25; 44:22). The same meaning is suggested by the Akkadian cognate *kuppuru*, "to wash away" or "to erase," although it has been maintained that the root meaning of *kuppuru* includes also the idea of "to cover." It is probable that both meanings are present in כפר. Common to both is the idea of annulling or obliterating sin, and it is in this figurative sense that כפר is used.

b. In LXX Greek. The translators of the LXX usually render כפר by the verb ἱλάσκεσθαι and (more frequently) its intensive compound ἐξιλάσκεσθαι, and the corresponding nouns כפרים and כפרת by ἱλασμός, ἐξιλασμός, ἐξίλασις, and ἱλαστήριον. When translating כפר and its derivatives, these words of the ἱλάσκεσθαι class do not usually have their primary classical meaning of "propitiation" but convey the sense of "expiation," which is only secondary in their classical and Hellenistic use (cf. Plato *Laws* 862*c*).

c. In NT Greek. In the NT the terms used for "expiation" are the verb ἱλάσκεσθαι and the nouns ἱλασμός and ἱλαστήριον. They always bear the meaning of their LXX, and never of their classical, usage.

2. In the OT. A peculiarity of the Hebrew verb כפר is that "God" is never its object—i.e., it does not, as some have maintained, signify an atoning action directed toward God. Only with reference to a human object, and with a human agent, does it have the meaning of "propitiation." In its general sense of "making atonement" it signifies an action which is directed toward sin or ceremonial uncleanness (e.g., Pss. 65:3; 78:38; Isa. 6:7; Jer. 18:23). The action may take place before or in the presence of God (Lev. 6:7—H 5:26; 14:18, 29, 31; 15:30; 19:22; Num. 31:50), but it is never directed toward him.

a. Extraritual expiation. When expiation is not linked with the cultus, it is usually a direct act of God—he is the subject who expiates or atones—and the object of the act of expiation is the sin or offense, which is thus "covered" or "erased" by God himself from his own sight (cf. Pss. 32:1; 51:9; Isa. 43:25; 44:22; Jer. 18:23). The verb כפר has then the sense of "to treat as covered (or wiped away)" and hence "to forgive" (e.g., Pss. 65:3; 78:38; 79:9; 85:2—H 85:3; Jer. 18:23; Ezek. 16:63; cf. Isa. 6:7). This expresses clearly the realization that only God can remove man's sin, and that God's forgiveness is not conditional upon any human act of propitiation but springs from his own initiative and has its source in his own mercy and grace (cf. Pss. 78:38; 79:9; Mic. 7:18).

There are a few instances where extraritual expiation is effected through the intervention of a human agent who is identified with his people and yet is particularly zealous toward God. After the breach of the covenant through the worship of the golden calf, the divine wrath is expressed in slaughter and plague, but expiation is brought about through the prayer of Moses (Exod. 32:30-34). It is not his intercession which of itself expiates; rather, through his identification with the people Moses expresses their penitence, so that God can now put away their sin (cf. Gen. 18:23-33; Num. 14:11-20; Amos 7:4-6). An example of a different kind occurs in Num. 25:6-13, where Phinehas makes expiation for Israel's participation in the sensual worship of Baal-peor by killing an Israelitish man and a Midianitish woman engaged in ritual prostitution. Expiation is made possible because by his zeal Phinehas has expressed the divine revulsion against sin. Again, expiation is effected through the execution by the Gibeonites of seven sons of Saul, because this tragic act expresses God's justice in the land (II Sam. 21:1-14; cf. Num. 35:32-33; Aaron's burning of incense, by which the plague was stayed [Num. 16:46-48], is really an example of ritual expiation).

These instances set forth the principle that God does not, in forgiving sin, condone it. Expiation may involve an expression of the divine wrath and a participation on the part of some representative man in God's righteous anger. Repentance and trust in the divine mercy are required of those whose sin is expiated.

b. Expiation and the cultus. In the later literature of the OT expiation is closely associated with cultic rites. In such cases the subject who makes expiation is the divinely appointed priest or high priest (e.g., Lev. 4:20, 26, 31, 35; 5:10, 13, 16, 18; 6:7; 7:7; 16:6,

11, 16-18, 24, 32-33; I Chr. 6:49; II Chr. 29:24; Neh. 10:33; Ezek. 43:20, 26). When an offering only is mentioned (Exod. 30:15-16; Lev. 1:4; 17:11; Num. 31:50; 35:33), it is still by implication the priest who is the subject. The sin or offense is no longer the direct object, but expiation is made for or on behalf of (על or בעד) the individual or the community; or the verb is used absolutely as a technical term, "to make expiation," the object being unexpressed. It is only construed with a direct object when applied to something material—e.g., the altar of incense (Exod. 30: 10), the altar of burnt offering (Exod. 29:36-37; Lev. 8:15; 16:18, 20, 33; Ezek. 43:20, 26), the sanctuary (Lev. 16:16, 20, 33; Ezek. 45:20). In such cases it has the sense of cleansing or purifying (cf. the LXX rendering of καθαρίζειν for כפר in Exod. 29:37; 30:10, and of καθαρισμός for כפרים in Exod. 29:36; 30:10).

The common ritual means by which expiation is made is sacrifice (*see* SACRIFICE AND OFFERINGS), which is to be understood, not in terms of propitiation, but in terms of sacrament. God himself provides the means of expiation, through which his forgiveness is made real and appropriated (Lev. 17:11).

3. In the NT. The work of Christ is referred to in terms of expiation four times in the NT (Rom. 3:25; Heb. 2:17; I John 2:2; 4:10). On each occasion the word used is one of the ἱλάσκεσθαι class, by which the LXX renders the Hebrew word כפר and its derivatives, and these Greek words are to be understood in terms of their LXX use. The work of Christ is therefore represented, not as the propitiation by the Son of the Father's wrath, but as the divine act of "covering" or "blotting out" sin, since "God was in Christ reconciling the world to himself" (II Cor. 5: 19).

a. The place of expiation. In Rom. 3:25 Paul says that God has put forward Christ "as an expiation by his blood" (ὃν προέθετο ὁ θεὸς ἱλαστήριον . . . ἐν τῷ αὐτοῦ αἵματι). Grammatically ἱλαστήριον could be either an adjective in the singular masculine or a neuter noun. In the LXX, however, it regularly translates the Hebrew substantive כפרת, the lid of the ark or MERCY SEAT (Exod. 25:17-22; Lev. 16:14-15; cf. Heb. 9:5). This was the place of expiation on which the blood was sprinkled by the high priest on the Day of Atonement (*see* ATONEMENT, DAY OF). Thus the cross of Christ is represented by Paul as the place where God's forgiving mercy is manifested in the annulling of sin.

b. The act of expiation. The writer of the Letter to the Hebrews portrays Christ as the great High Priest whose work is "to make expiation for the sins of the people" (εἰς τὸ ἱλάσκεσθαι τὰς ἁμαρτίας τοῦ λαοῦ; Heb. 2:17). This is a rendering of the Hebrew term לכפר. Christ is therefore represented as performing an atoning act by which man's sin is "covered" or "blotted out."

c. The sacrifice of expiation. The word ἱλασμός occurs twice in I John. Christ is said to be the "expiation for our sins" (ἱλασμός περὶ τῶν ἁμαρτιῶν ἡμῶν; I John 2:2; 4:10). Although the Johannine letters are not influenced by LXX usage to the same extent as Romans and Hebrews, it is noteworthy that both the noun ἱλασμός and the phrase τὸ περὶ ἁμαρτίας are used in the LXX to translate the Hebrew substantive חטאת, "sin offering." This is clearly the meaning of ἱλασμός here. It is supported by the earlier reference to the blood of Jesus cleansing from all sin (I John 1:7), since in the LXX καθαρίζειν twice renders כפר (Exod. 29:37; 30:10) and appears as a synonym for ἱλάσκεσθαι. Christ is thus portrayed as a "sin offering," which is the divinely ordained sacrifice most closely related to the expiation of sin.

In this way Christ "fulfils" the OT conception of expiation. He is both Priest and sacrificial Victim, and at his cross atonement is made for the sin of the world.

Bibliography. E. Riehm, *Der Begriff der Sühne im AT* (1877); H. Schultz, "Sacred Ceremonies," *OT Theology,* I (English trans., 1892), 397-400; W. R. Smith, "The Deuteronomic Code and the Levitical Law," *The OT in the Jewish Church* (1892), pp. 380-81; A. B. Davidson, "The Word 'Atone' in Extra-ritual Literature," *Exp.,* Fifth Series, vol. X (1899), pp. 92-103, a valuable discussion reproduced with some slight alterations in "Atonement and Forgiveness," *The Theology of the OT* (1904), pp. 315-56; S. R. Driver, "Expiation and Atonement (Hebrew)," in J. Hastings, ed., *Encyclopedia of Religion and Ethics,* V (1908), 653-59; G. B. Gray, "Sacrifice, Propitiation, and Expiation," *Sacrifice in the OT* (1925), pp. 55-95; C. H. Dodd, "Atonement," *The Bible and the Greeks* (1935), pp. 82-95, by far the most important and exhaustive study of the use of words of the ἱλάσκεσθαι class in the LXX; V. Taylor, "Sacrifice," *Jesus and His Sacrifice* (1937), pp. 49-53; A. G. Hebert, "Atone, Atonement," in A. Richardson, ed., *A Theological Word Book of the Bible* (1950), pp. 25-26; R. Abba, "Sacrifice," *The Nature and Authority of the Bible* (1958), pp. 230-37; E. Jacob, "Sin and Redemption," *Theology of the OT* (English trans., 1958), pp. 293-94; T. C. Vriezen, "The Cult," *An Outline of OT Theology* (English trans., 1958), pp. 286-301.

R. ABBA

EXTORTION [עשק (Ps. 62:10—H 62:11; Ezek. 22: 7, 12; EXTORTED PRACTICE; EXTORTION *in* Ezek. 18:18; 22:29); ἁρπαγή (KJV RAVENING *in* Matt. 23:25; Luke 11:39]; EXTORTIONER [ἅρπαξ (Luke 18:11; *alternately* ROBBER)]. A psalmist who may have been a person of some position warns against confidence in the methods of extortion and robbery; power thus gained will give rise to delusive hopes (62:10—H 62:11). Confidence in such methods is the antithesis to trust in God, who can bring worthy aims to fruition (62:1 ff). The way of extortion and rapacity cannot be depended on for salvation (49:5-15). Extortion is one of the crimes listed by Ezekiel in conjunction with his exposition of the doctrine that God deals justly and retributively with every individual (18:18); in other references he suggests that extortion was a common crime among his contemporaries (22:7, 12, 29). Similar charges of extortion, rapacity, and wickedness were leveled against the Pharisees by Jesus (Matt. 23:25; Luke 11: 39; cf. 18:11).

H. F. BECK

EYE [עין; ὄμμα, ὀφθαλμός]. The eye has far less theological significance in the Bible than the EAR. Like the ear, the eye may occasionally be used to represent the whole process of cognition and understanding, as in Jer. 5:21. It is frequently used in the sense of "judgment" or "opinion" (Prov. 3:7; Jer. 7:11). On rare occasions it may "see" God, as in Isa. 6:5, although this privilege is usually accorded to it in an eschatological context (Isa. 33:17; Ezek. 38:23; cf. Rev. 1:7).

More frequently the eye is merely the ordinary, physical eye, represented either as seeing or as expressing mental attitudes or emotion, especially sorrow. The expression of sorrow is a natural activity of the eye, since, next to the faculty of vision, the production of tears is its most characteristic function (Ps. 119:136; Jer. 9:1). Brightness of the eyes is a sign of physical and emotional well-being (I Sam. 14:27; Ps. 38:10), as dimness is a symptom of its opposite (Job 17:7). The eyes can express arrogance (Prov. 6:17), humility (Ps. 123:2), pity (Ezek. 16:5), and mockery (Prov. 30:17). The term "eye" is often used in such a way as to be almost synonymous with "desire" or "lust" (Prov. 17:24; Eccl. 4:8; II Pet. 2:14).

The phrase "evil eye" does not refer to magical practices, but to the eye which expresses the stingy or envious disposition of its owner (Prov. 23:6 KJV; Mark 7:22 KJV).

See also SEEING. R. C. DENTAN

EYE PAINT. Painting around the eye was common in ancient Egypt and Babylonia, but among the Hebrews it is mentioned chiefly in connection with women of ill repute.

1. Biblical references
2. Materials
3. Receptacles
4. Application
5. Purpose

Bibliography

1. Biblical references. The word פוך with the meaning "black eye paint" is used three times in the Bible: II Kings 9:30 says that Jezebel (the Sidonian princess who married Ahab) "painted [lit., 'applied eye paint to'] her eyes" (not KJV "face"), in her effort to be attractive to Jehu. In Jer. 4:30 Jerusalem, personified as a harlot, is said to "enlarge" her "eyes [not KJV 'face'] with paint." One of Job's daughters is called Keren-happuch, meaning "horn of eye paint" (Job 42:14).

In Ezek. 23:40 the harlot Oholibah, representing unfaithful Jerusalem, paints her eyes. The verb here used is כחל, and from the same root is the Arabic *kuḥl,* meaning "eye paint."

It will be noted that most of these references associate eye-painting among the Hebrews with women of evil character. Prov. 6:25; Isa. 3:16 refer to wanton glances, not to eye-painting.

2. Materials. In ancient Egypt the commonest materials were malachite (a green ore of copper), used especially in the early period, and later galena (a dark gray ore of lead, sulphide of lead, PbS), which became the more common. An Egyptian name for the latter, *sdemet,* was borrowed by the Greeks in the form στίμμι and by the Romans in the form *stibium* (which refers, however, to antimony trisulphide; *see below*). As early as the Neolithic period in Egypt individuals prepared their own powder by grinding the ore on palettes, usually of slate. Later the powder was evidently prepared commercially. In Babylonia the eye paint *gukhlu,* related to Arabic *kuḥl,* was usually stibnite, antimony trisulphide (Sb_2S_3). This is listed as part of the tribute of King Hezekiah to Sennacherib in the latter's annals. In Egypt today eye paint is made not only from lead ore but also from burned frankincense, almond shells, or safflower. The biblical references above are probably to a powdered mineral, either galena or stibnite.

3. Receptacles. The name of Job's daughter, Keren-happuch (Job 42:14; *see* § 1 *above*) indicates that eye paint could be kept in a horn. In ancient Egypt the dry powder was kept in reeds, reedlike tubes of stone or metal, and especially in small jars of alabaster. Sometimes the powder was made into paste and kept in a shell, both in Egypt and in Babylonia. For Palestinian cosmetic bowls or palettes, *see* COSMETICS § 5.

4. Application. In ancient Egypt a little rod made of wood, ivory, or metal was first moistened in water (perhaps scented, as at present) and then dipped into the powder. The resulting paste adhering to the rod was drawn around the eye, prolonging the outer corner, and over the eyebrow. Sometimes green malachite was used under the eye and black for the rest. Metal and ivory applicators ("kohl sticks") are found in Palestine excavations. Fig. EYE 39.

Courtesy of the Oriental Institute, the University of Chicago

39. Queen Nefert-iti, cast of a sculptor's model from Tell el-Amarna, showing use of eye paint

5. Purpose. The cosmetic purpose of eye paint was to emphasize the eye and to make it appear larger and more almond-shaped. It was also thought to protect the eyes from glare and disease.

Bibliography. S. Hille, "Ueber den Gebrauch und Zusamensetzung der orientalischen Augenschminke," *ZDMG,* V (1851), 236-42. E. W. Lane, *An Account of the Manners and Customs of the Modern Egyptians* (5th ed., 1871), I, 45-46. S. Krauss, *Talmudische Archäologie,* I (1910), 238-40. B. Meissner, "Das Antinomgebirge," *OLZ,* XVII (1914), 52-55; *Babylonien und Assyrien,* I (1920), 244, 347. A. Erman and H. Ranke, *Aegypten und aegyptisches Leben im Altertum* (1923), pp. 257-58, 312, 349, 605, 610, 612. G. Dalman, *Arbeit und Sitte,* V (1937), 343, 351. L. Koehler, "Alttestamentliche Wortforschung.

Pūk," *Theologische Zeitschrift,* III (1947), 314-18. A. Lucas, *Ancient Egyptian Materials and Industries* (3rd ed., 1948), pp. 99-103. R. J. Forbes, *Studies in Ancient Technology,* III (1955), 17-20, 39-40. J. A. Thompson

EYELIDS OF THE MORNING [עפעפי־שחר] (Job 3:9); KJV DAWNING OF THE DAY. Alternately: EYELIDS OF THE DAWN (Job 41:18—H 41:10). A term usually taken poetically as a figure referring to the first streaks of light which herald the rising sun. The term is used in the OT only in conjunction with references to Leviathan, a marine monster, different versions of which figured prominently in ancient Egyptian and Semitic mythology. Men were powerless before this monster, which they could neither capture nor control and whose extraordinary strength, gnashing teeth, and gleaming eyes terrorized them (Job 41:1 ff; cf. Ps. 74:14).

Leviathan was one of the several symbols of the forces of the primeval chaos (Job 26:12; Pss. 74:13-14; Enoch 60:7-9; II Esd. 6:49-52; cf. Ps. 104:26). According to many ancient traditions this dragon or monster was capable of causing eclipses by swallowing the sun and moon or by surrounding them with his coils, perhaps even of controlling the day and the night. Among the ancient Egyptians, Sukhos, the crocodile which was the incarnation of the god Sebak, was pictured riding on the back of the rising sun; in later tradition he was regarded as the darkness of the night, which triumphed over the sun. In Egyptian hieroglyphics the eye of the crocodile represents the dawn, and Egyptian records mention that the reddish eyes of the crocodile are seen under the water before the animal comes to the surface.

OT writers, perhaps without believing in the existence of these living monsters, used them as poetic images with which to express more forcefully the idea of God's control over the forces of nature.

H. F. Beck

EZAR. KJV form of Ezer 1 in I Chr. 1:38.

EZBAI ĕz'bī [אזבי] (I Chr. 11:37). The father of Naarai, who was one of the Mighty Men of David known as the "Thirty." However, in II Sam. 23:35*b* Naarai the son of Ezbai is called Paarai the Arbite. It would seem that "the son of Ezbai" (I Chr. 11:37) is a corruption of "the Arbite" (II Sam. 23:35*b*) and that the original name in the list was Naarai the Arbite.

Bibliography. J. W. Rothstein, "Das erste Buch der Chronik," *KAT* (1927); W. Rudolph, "Chronikbücher," *HAT* (1955). E. R. Dalglish

EZBON ĕz'bŏn [אצבן *or* אצבון]. **1.** Eponym of a family of the tribe of Gad (Gen. 46:16); called Ozni in Num. 26:16.

2. According to the text, a Benjaminite family (I Chr. 7:7); but I Chr. 7:6-11 is, most likely, a genealogy of Zebulun assigned to Benjamin by error.

H. H. Guthrie, Jr.

EZECHIAS ĕz'ē kī'əs. Douay Version form of Hezekiah.

EZECHIEL ĭ zē'kyəl. Douay Version form of Ezekiel.

EZECIAS. KJV Apoc. form of Hezekiah.

EZEKIEL ĭ zē'kyəl [יחזקאל, God strengthens; Ιεζέκιηλ]. A prophet of the Babylonian exile; son of the priest Buzi (1:3). The book appears after Jeremiah in the Hebrew canon and after Lamentations in the versions.

A. *AUTHOR.* Traditionally the author of the book entitled Ezekiel has been thought to be none other than Ezekiel himself, who was a part of that company of Jews carried captive in 598 B.C. by Nebuchadrezzar. This young man, who grew up in the environs of the Jerusalem temple, was the son of a Zadokite priest, Buzi, and in all probability was himself being trained for the priesthood or possibly had already taken the robes of office. In any event, when Jehoiachin surrendered to the armies of Nebuchadrezzar (II Kings 24:10-17) in 598 B.C., Ezekiel was among that unhappy band who made the torturous trek to Mesopotamia. Some of the captives who survived the march were settled by the Canal Chebar at a place called Tel-Abib (*til-abûbû,* "hill of the storm god"), where the Jewish community eked out a bare existence. Exactly what the future prophet did during the early years of captivity is not known. Unlike his contemporary, Jeremiah, he was married, but little else of his personal life is a matter of record.

In the year 593 somewhere in Mesopotamia, during a thunderstorm, Ezekiel saw his wondrous vision of God and received the call to be a prophet to Israel. The natural setting for the vision was a great cloud from the N (1:4); the living creatures were like a "flash of lightning" (1:14); the noise of heavenly beings was similar to the noise of "many waters" (1:24), while the throne of God had the appearance of a "bow that is in the cloud" (1:28). Obviously the

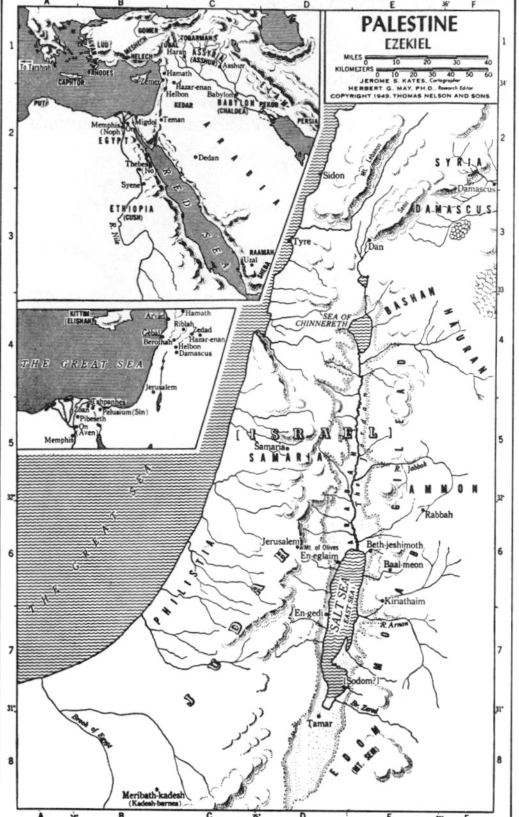

conscious and subconscious had an inevitable interplay which created a great vision of the chariot of God moving where it would. Ezekiel's vision of wheels within wheels, far from being only a grotesque image with little meaning, symbolized the profound insight that God was not imprisoned or immobilized but could move where he wished. Prophet and people undoubtedly had assumed that God was native to Palestine and that his home was the temple, but Ezekiel perceived that the divine presence recognized no terrestrial boundary or barrier. Undoubtedly the four faces of a man, a lion, an ox, and an eagle symbolically dramatize God's reign over every area of human and animal life. The vision rightly understood represents a high point in divine revelation and human insight.

Having seen a vision, the son of Buzi then received his call to service as a prophet to the people. Whether he was called to prophesy to the inhabitants who remained in Jerusalem or to the people who were his immediate congregation in Tel-Abib has become a major area of difficulty for students of the book. Some scholars maintain that the prophet returned to Jerusalem after his call and actually lived in that doomed city during the time of his prophesying to the inhabitants of it. The traditional view, however, has always held that Ezekiel was in Babylonia for the entire time of his prophetic ministry. Whether his residence was Tel-Abib or Jerusalem, there can be no doubt that his prophecies were largely directed to the inhabitants of Jerusalem until the fall of that city in 587.

Ezekiel was reluctant to be a prophet. The symbolic scroll which he had to eat was at first bitter but in time became sweet (cf. ch. 2). Words he was reluctant to speak for God became delectable. He was appointed a watchman for the house of Israel, being made responsible for her spiritual survival. However, the call meant that whether the people would hear or not was of no major consequence: they would know that a prophet had been among them. This would guarantee their chance to repent and justify God's judgment upon the unrepentant.

Apparently the prophet was subject to visionary trances when for a long time he would remain motionless and uncommunicative. It is possible that he was silent for long periods of time, but the evidence is not strong enough for such an unequivocal conclusion (cf. 3:26-27; 33:21-22). During the years of prophetic activity a great personal sorrow came into the life of Ezekiel on the occasion of his wife's death, but with stoic self-control he used the tragedy to drive home a major spiritual message to the people (cf. 24:15-24). In the period that followed the destruction of Jerusalem, when the tone of his message changed from judgment to restoration, this pastor of the exiled congregation became much appreciated as a most excellent preacher whose message was a "love song" and whose voice was "beautiful" (cf. 33:32). Having spoken doom, he looked to the future with great hope, because God's spirit could blow on death to bring life, and because in the restored land "God was there."

In Ezekiel the man there is a strange hybridization of the priest and the prophet, a fact which has often been noticed in studies of this spiritual leader. Yet the priestly and prophetic facets of his make-up were not antithetical, as has sometimes been supposed. True, the priestly element can be clearly detected in many places where liturgical exactitude is reflected, but the prophetic fire always remains in this man as one who had seen a vision of God's chariot. Of more importance than the elements of priest and prophet which mingled in one personality is the fact that he was a man of transition between pre-exilic faith and postexilic religion. He was the product of a faith which was rooted in the soil of Palestine; at the same time he was compelled to worship God without temple or priesthood, and to affirm the existence of a holy people without a land. This conflict is the key to the personality of the man and the measure of his greatness.

Literarily Ezekiel rose to tremendous heights of poetic beauty but quickly reverted to the most prosaic style. His figures of speech and his use of stories are unequaled elsewhere in the OT. Symbolism and reality meet in his creative mind and mingle to make him a literary giant and to label his work an artistic masterpiece. But, as is true of all men of genius, his personality was often enigmatic and his work was not simple.

B. *HISTORICAL BACKGROUND.* One major aim of the Josianic reform (621 B.C.) was to centralize worship in the temple at Jerusalem. As a result, priests like Jeremiah of Anathoth, who issued from Abiathar, lost their status overnight. On the contrary, the Zadokite family, to which Buzi the father of Ezekiel belonged, now constituted the recognized priesthood, in charge of true worship at Jerusalem, without competitive interference from provincial shrines. However, Josiah's reform did not last. In 609 the king died at Megiddo, and the reform movement died with him. After 605 Jehoiakim supported the Chaldean regime for a few years but finally revolted. Jehoiachin, his successor, after a three-month reign, had to surrender the city of Jerusalem to the armies of Nebuchadrezzar (598). It was in the exile which followed that Ezekiel went to Babylonia. Zedekiah (Mattaniah) became king in the land (598-587), but after *ca.* eight years he also revolted. His rebellion was summarily crushed, and Jerusalem was utterly destroyed in 587.

Ezekiel's early youth witnessed a quick revival of "pure religion" following the discovery of some portions of DEUTERONOMY. However, the military failure of Josiah brought syncretism back into vogue; society was corrupted from within and from without. As had been the case for centuries, Palestine was a pawn between two large empires. Geographically the land was a bridge linking the two great population centers of Mesopotamia and Egypt. There were pro-Egyptian and pro-Chaldean parties active in Jerusalem in the days of Zedekiah and before. The population always seemed to feel that one great power would counterbalance the other, or when one dominated, it was anticipated that the other would deliver. The multitudes of ordinary citizenry thus looked in hope for deliverance from sources which could not deliver, and false security prevented moral and religious response to the prophetic voice.

C. *LOCALE.* The problem of setting for the Ezekiel prophetic ministry is not an easy one to solve; this fact is evidenced by an increasingly wide diversity of opinion. Traditionally the prophet has been understood as a member of the exile community at Tel-Abib, where his visions were seen and his oracles were uttered. Yet the major part of his message in chs. 1–24 is admittedly directed to the people in Jerusalem, which he calls a "bloody city." Indeed, he was called to prophesy to the "rebellious house"—in all likelihood the people in Palestine who were ruled over by Zedekiah and who remained in Judah. His prophecies seem to have little relevance to the Tel-Abib community. Having Ezekiel speak his word in Babylonia but direct it to an audience which neither sees nor hears him is out of keeping with the concept of a prophet's standing immediately before those to whom he is speaking. Furthermore, the fact that the exilic prophet possessed such intimate knowledge of events and people in the Holy City makes acceptance of a Babylonian locale quite difficult. The prophet seems to walk in Jerusalem (cf. ch. 8), and his words apparently have immediate effect on the inhabitants of the doomed city (11:13-14). Finally, his symbolic actions would have had little meaning in any place but Palestine. These facts bulk large as one seeks to understand how the traditional view of Babylonian locale could stand under careful scrutiny.

As a result of the above consideration, a number of alternative views present themselves: (*a*) Quite a large and distinguished number of scholars declare that Ezekiel was called to prophesy in Palestine and that his entire prophetic ministry was fulfilled in the Holy Land. These feel that the Babylonian locale was created out of imagination by a "Babylonian editor." Likewise, some students consider Ezekiel's figure to have been fictitious, while others maintain that he lived in Palestine at a much earlier or later date, but all identify the locale as Palestine whether the prophet's personality is historical or not. (*b*) A second group solves the problem by putting Ezekiel first in Mesopotamia, then back in Palestine, and finally again in exile. Ezekiel thus is understood as having received the first vision in Mesopotamia (ch. 1), but his call to speak to a rebellious house (ch. 2) and to be a watchman (ch. 3) led him to return to Palestine. So he went back and remained there until the destruction of Jerusalem in 587. (*c*) A number of competent scholars, perhaps a majority, still hold that Babylonia is the correct locale for the prophetic ministry, though they deny him any such power as clairvoyance.

There are many Babylonian elements in the text which can hardly be excised. The inaugural vision is among the exiles, and Ezekiel sits overwhelmed among them. When he is said to go to Jerusalem (e.g., 8:3), does he actually visit there, or is he experiencing a spiritual transport? Much of the material in the book is clearly visionary, and as such would be just as relevant at Tel-Abib as at Jerusalem. The initial call belongs to this type (1:4–3:15), as also the grotesque description of the siege and fall of Jerusalem (chs. 8–11). The vision of the Valley of Dry Bones (37:1-14) and the vision of the temple restored (chs. 40–48) do not require Ezekiel's physical presence in either place. There is nothing unusual about an exile's walking in the spirit through the familiar streets of his home city, witnessing those forces in action which he remembers well and news of which he receives regularly from travelers.

Ezekiel did receive a call in Babylonia and did fulfil his mission among the exiles. To the prophet there was but one Israel, to whom he spoke whether present or far away, and it was a matter of no importance that some of the chosen people were living in Palestine and some in Babylonia. In fact, the exiles were no less a rebellious house than were those who still lived at home, for both groups had refused to obey God. Though his prophecies of doom had reference to the city of Jerusalem and its inhabitants, still there was a real relevance to the exile community. At Tel-Abib many people kept alive the hope that they would soon return to their homeland, but Ezekiel's words and symbolic actions put an end to any such illusion. Moreover, there were lines of communication open between Palestine and Tel-Abib (see Jer. 29): both the words and the actions of Ezekiel could reach the ears of the Jerusalem community.

Small bits of evidence serve, not to demonstrate, but to strengthen the case for a Babylonian locale. In Babylonia, not in Palestine, it was normative to draw city maps on clay tablets as the prophet does in ch. 4. Moreover, the wall through which the prophet dug (12:1-6) was undoubtedly a mud-brick wall native to Mesopotamia, not a stone wall common in the hill country of Palestine.

Mullo-Weir (*see bibliography*) points out that בקעה is the word used for "valley," not נחל or עמק as one might expect for Palestine, and that this usage also represents strong evidence for a Babylonian locale. The same term refers to the wide valley or plain of Shinar in Gen. 11:2, where the Mesopotamian atmosphere is unmistakable. Actually the positing of a Palestinian locale raises the problem of the Babylonian atmosphere, which all but saturates the book from the imagery in ch. 1 onward.

Finally, there is little reason to doubt the traditional view since the Jews would have been very reluctant to have a genuine prophet speak outside the land, if in fact there were not overpowering evidence for such a conclusion. All sorts of rationalizations were devised to explain how God appeared to a prophet in a pagan land. Ezekiel was transported to Jerusalem by the Spirit of God, but he was always physically present in Tel-Abib, while his detailed knowledge of the city which was home and the center of faith permitted him exact visions of the events going on in the city. Such details as are found in chs. 8; 11 probably were drawn from memory, since close scrutiny reveals round numbers and generalizations. The problem of Pelatiah's death (11:1-13) looms large, for in this case, at least, there was an actual death brought on by the denunciation of Ezekiel. The ancient Hebrews' ideas of cause and effect were somewhat different from ours. Who can say whether Pelatiah was in Jerusalem or Tel-Abib?

There is a strange fluidity between the visionary and the real in this prophecy. The Spirit of Yahweh is said to have transported Ezekiel to the E gate of the temple, where he saw twenty-five men, one of whom was Pelatiah the son of Benaiah (11:1-2). It is possible that Pelatiah, though seen in vision by the E gate, actually lived at Tel-Abib. The wicked counsel given coincides with that of the false prophet in Jer. 28, and the warning of Ezekiel is similar to that of Jeremiah's letter to the exiles (Jer. 29). Indeed, if Ezekiel called the city a caldron (Ezek. 24:6; RSV "pot"), then why is the same expression considered evil counsel when spoken by another? Ezek. 11:3 should be rendered: "The building of houses is not near. This is the caldron, and we are the flesh." Reference here is to the exile community and to the easy optimism which predicted a quick return home, obviating the need to build houses. Jerusalem, however, according to Ezekiel, will not stand but will be utterly decimated. Hearing this, Pelatiah falls dead in Tel-Abib, where his evil counsel has been devised. This hypothetical approach, properly developed, might not only answer the Pelatiah problem but also help ch. 11 make sense.

The conclusion which must be reached, on the basis of cumulative evidence, is that Ezekiel, as tradition maintains, was a prophet among the exiles in Babylonia, and there he was called to be the spokesman of God, both to his immediate company and to the Judeans who remained in the land of Palestine.

D. *DATE AND COMPOSITION.* 1. Date of writing. A number of dates have been proposed for the composition of this prophetic work. Of course, not all students or scholars agree that the book is in any degree a single effort of one person, for a considerable number understand it to be a composite from several sources.

For this group the segments of the work are variously dated. C. C. Torrey seriously proposed in his *Pseudo-Ezekiel and the Original Prophecy* that the book is a pseudepigraphon based on II Kings 21:2-16, written in 230 B.C. with a Palestinian setting. However, this historical novel was edited before 200 B.C. and given a Babylonian locale. Thus to Torrey the entire work is non-historical, as is its chief character, Ezekiel himself. This is part and parcel of the Torrey view on the whole exilic period, which he sees as a ripple, not a wave, in history. James Smith, a Scottish scholar, holds that the prophet really spoke to the N kingdom of Israel in the time of King Manasseh, and not to Judah or to the Exile at all. Others, especially Nils Messel, date the prophecy in the time of Ezra-Nehemiah, while Lawrence E. Browne has suggested Alexander the Great as the figure around which history was moving when these words were uttered and recorded.

The modified traditional view is that Ezekiel the book is the product directly or indirectly of Ezekiel the man. For some time certain scholars who otherwise recognize the integrity of the prophecy have called in question the Ezekielian authorship of chs. 38–39, the so-called Gog-Magog passages, and chs. 40-48, which picture in vision the land restored. There is, as we shall have occasion to see, real reason for such a conclusion, but evidence is still strong that these passages belong to the Ezekiel cycle of thought.

A number of arguments usually presented as evidence prove to be nothing more than assumptions. E.g., it has been long understood that the Aramaisms of this prophecy indicated a late date. Moreover, most writers were content to accept the unqualified assertion that the book was linguistically saturated with Aramaic influence. Upon investigation, one quickly discovers that Aramaic was the lingua franca of the Assyrian Empire from the last half of the eighth century onward. Its presence in any composition cannot, therefore, be taken as evidence for a fourth-century date. On the contrary, some Aramaic influence could be expected in both the seventh and the sixth centuries. The grand assumption thus falls to the ground. More interesting is the extent of Aramaic in Ezekiel. So far as actual vocabulary is concerned, only nine definite Aramaic roots appear, two of which, סגן and פחה, were drawn from earlier Aramaic lingua franca. Nine other words may be related to Aramaic, but are more probably to be understood as products of a general Semitic vocabulary. Morphologically, the influence is stronger, as is evidenced in verb forms, noun endings, and pronominal alterations. This is what one would expect to find in a bilingual situation where an Aramaic-using scribe, writing Hebrew, would inadvertently make a considerable number of formal mistakes. In syntax the Aramaic influence is negligible if it exists at all. Thus the extent of Aramaic influence amounts to what one would expect among the exiles in the first half of the sixth century. In no case can its presence or extent be mustered as evidence for a late date.

In reading Ezek. 40:5 ff one discerns that this vision is actually a subconscious reflection of a real temple drawn from memory. The E gate of the temple when reconstructed proves to be of the same general Solomonic type as that unearthed by Nelson Glueck and others at Megiddo. Actually this type of construction was not found after the early ninth century

B.C. Therefore, this memory must have arisen from one who knew the temple of Solomon in detail. Such a person lived in Jerusalem before that temple was destroyed in 587 B.C. That person in all probability was Ezekiel himself.

This book, unlike any other, specifically dates several of its sections. Albright and others are right in accepting the correctness of these dates and in understanding them as reckoned from the time of Jehoiachin's captivity, which would also coincide with the year of his reign (cf. 1:2; 8:1; 20:1; 24:1; 26:1; 29:1, 17; 30:20; 31:1; 32:1, 17; 33:21; 40:1). The thirtieth year mentioned in 1:1 refers to the thirtieth year of Jehoiachin, who was still considered the rightful ruler of the exile nation, and it was in this thirtieth year that Ezekiel or some editor "published his book." The "twelfth year" in Ezek. 32:1; 33:21 should be read the "eleventh year." Otherwise the dates are substantially correct; however, all the material appearing between two dates should not be understood as being in proper chronological sequence.

The general date for Ezekiel must therefore remain the first half of the sixth century until such time as new evidence is discovered.

2. Editing. The book of Ezekiel is not a composite work like that of Isaiah, nor is it a conglomerate piece like that of Jeremiah. Although this view is generally accepted, there are many who would decidedly demur. In 1925 Hölscher (in *Ezechiel, Der Dichter und das Buch*) ferreted out 170 verses of poetry which he identified as genuine prophetic utterance largely because it was poetic in nature. Hölscher contributed very much to the study of poetry, but failed to recognize the fact that poets also write prose. Volkmar Herntrich, I. G. Matthews, and others have been less radical in their analyses of the book.

In 1943 Irwin (*see bibliography*) recovered by inductive method some 251 verses which he felt belonged to the prophet, and recognized also the possibility that some other material was genuine. For him, the poetic center of ch. 15 (i.e., vss. 2-5) is authentic, while the remainder (i.e., vss. 6-8) is a commentary by a later redactor or editor. He assumed that the nature of the fire is the important fact, not the value of the wood (as a confused editor erroneously thought). Having thus discovered a key, Irwin proceeded to analyze the book on the basis of the literary quality of material thus "discovered." Later (*see bibliography*) he vigorously defended his own views. H. H. Rowley (*see bibliography*) rejected them and concluded tentatively that the major part of the material in the present book goes back to either the prophet or his disciples. A later editor fashioned the prophecy in its present form. G. Fohrer (*see bibliography*) also viewed the book as a work composed primarily of original material; indeed, he preserved more of the text than did Rowley. Mullo-Weir (*see bibliography*) added his support to the general view that the main source of the book of Ezekiel is the prophet himself.

Herbert May (*see bibliography*), though not so radical as either Hölscher or Irwin, contended that at least forty per cent of the book is definitely not original and that many other passages are highly questionable. May worked on the assumption that there are vast quantities of non-Ezekielian material and is definitely disposed to support this assumption in his discussion.

What constitutes a genuine oracle? Needless to say, few if any of the prophetic utterances manifest the accuracy of a stenographic transcription. Probably some material was written by the prophet; how much, nobody can accurately say. Certainly he drew from earlier sources (possibly some of the poetry predates the prophet). Admittedly editors who were disciples left their mark on the text. However, if we are narrowly to maintain that Ezekiel material is only that which preserves the exact words the prophet said or wrote, then there is very little we could claim for him. On the other hand, if we are willing to credit the author with that part of the book which preserves in essence what he said or wrote, whether he composed it as it now stands or not, then the major part of the prophecy must be understood as having originated with him. The spirit and the mind of Ezekiel are clearly felt throughout the whole work, even in those sections which are generally recognized as editorial. Except for those portions which predate Ezekiel (e.g., early poetry), the great preponderance of the prophecy originated directly or indirectly with him.

The full answer to the composition of Ezekiel has not been reached. In all probability, the editing was finished within the sixth century and the book drawn from the writings and sayings of Ezekiel was completed soon after the return from exile (*ca.* 539-520 B.C.). Ezekiel himself may have begun the process of compilation in the thirtieth year of the Captivity (cf. 1:1), and his disciples finished it subsequent to his death.

3. Present arrangement. It is obvious, even after the most cursory reading of Ezekiel, that the work changes motif at the end of ch. 24. Chronologically this marks the end of Jerusalem, and prophetically the emphasis is changed from doom to resurrection. Hope replaces despair. The denunciations of sin are replaced by exhortations to have faith. However, this shift of emphasis is not immediately felt until the foreign nations have come in for divine judgment (cf. chs. 25–32).

The key to the present arrangement of Ezekiel is to be found in Ezek. 24:27; 33:21-22, which historically belong together, having reference to the same event. Ch. 33 is a carefully devised suture, designed to bind several independent pieces together. It consists of three doublets (33:1-9 = 3:19-21; 33:10-19 = ch. 18; 33:23-29 = 11:14-21), together with a personal note about the prophet (33:30-33). The aforesaid historical allusion (33:21-22) completes the chapter. Thus the compiler, whoever he was, took the oracles of judgment in chs. 1–24, which had probably been recorded together with the foreign-nations chapters (25–32), and added them to chs. 34–37, which were independent, detached prophecies from Ezekiel, as were chs. 38–39. To this point (chs. 1–39) the book was completed with the promise that evil forces would be destroyed. That this portion of the book was finished during the lifetime of Ezekiel is probable.

4. Chs. 40–48. Quite early in the course of modern Ezekielian research some scholars began to demur so far as crediting the last nine chapters of the book to the prophet himself. Although there is reason for thinking that these nine chapters did circulate as a single piece for a time, it is possible that some of the parts came from other sources than Ezekiel. The survey of the general arrangements of the temple (chs. 40–42; 46:19, 24) and the instructions concerning the altar (43:6-27) are certainly from Ezekiel directly or indirectly. It would seem that the introduction of the passage on the glory of Yahweh (43:1-5) is little more than a literary device used in order to tie this section to the rest of the book. There is reason to doubt the Ezekielian origin of the sections on the allotment of the land (45:1-9; 47:13–48:35) and the regulations and measures (45:10–46:18). However, description of proper priesthood is what one might expect from a Zadokite priest (ch. 44), as also the vision of a life-giving stream issuing from beneath the temple (47:1-12).

A final conclusion on the authorship of chs. 40–48 is not possible at this juncture. Much of the material did originate with the prophet, and yet all of it is either a reflection or a refraction of his point of view. In all probability an editor has been more at work here than in any other part of the book. On the face of it, these chapters as they now stand must be attributed to the editor who also lived before the Zerubbabel-Joshua restoration of the temple.

E. *GENERAL CONTENT.* 1. Outline.

I. Prophecies of doom (before the fall of Jerusalem, chs. 1–24
  A. Vision and call, 1:1–3:21
    1. Introduction, 1:1-3
    2. Vision, 1:4-28
    3. Call of God, 2:1–3:3
    4. Detailed instructions, 3:4-21
      a. Speak to Israel, vss. 4-11
      b. Prophet's personal reaction, vss. 12-15
      c. "Be a watchman," vss. 16-21
  B. Prophecies and visions of judgment, 3:22–7:27
    1. Consequences to the prophet, 3:22-27
    2. Symbolic siege of city, ch. 4
    3. Extent of desolation, ch. 5
    4. Idolatry denounced, ch. 6
    5. Punishment for sin, ch. 7
  C. Visions, chs. 8–11
    1. Abominations in Jerusalem seen, ch. 8
      a. Baal image, vss. 1-6
      b. Hidden idols, vss. 7-13
      c. Fertility worship, vss. 14-15
      d. Sun worship, etc., vss. 16-18
    2. Vision of complete destruction, ch. 9
    3. Vision of God reappears, ch. 10
    4. Denunciation and hope, ch. 11
      a. Leaders rebuked, vss. 1-12
      b. Pelatiah dies, vs. 13
      c. Promise of renewal, vss. 14-21
      d. God's spirit is withdrawn, vss. 22-25
  D. Oracles concerning Jerusalem, chs. 12–19
    1. Captivity predicted, ch. 12
      a. Prince's escape enacted, vss. 1-7
      b. Captivity and distress, vss. 8-20
      c. Popular proverbs, vss. 21-28
    2. False prophets, ch. 13
    3. Elders denounced, 14:1-11
    4. No hope in present situation, 14:12-20
    5. Future remnant, 14:21-23
    6. Useless vine, ch. 15
    7. Story of unfaithful lover, ch. 16
    8. Parable of the two eagles, ch. 17
    9. Discourse on individual responsibility, ch. 18
    10. Parable of the lioness and cubs, ch. 19
  E. Oracles of judgment against the Lord, chs. 20–24
    1. Review of checkered history, 20:1-44
    2. Judgment, 20:45–21:32
      a. Against Judah and Jerusalem, 20:45–21:7
      b. Song of the consuming sword, 21:8-17
      c. Prediction of Chaldean attack, 21:18-27
      d. Ammon to be conquered, 21:28-32
    3. Catalogue of Jerusalem's sins, ch. 22
    4. Story of two sisters, ch. 23
    5. Last days, ch. 24
      a. The city a caldron, vss. 1-14
      b. Death of the prophet's wife, vss. 15-24
      c. Concluding section, vss. 25-27

II. Foreign-nations prophecies, chs. 25–32
  A. Immediate neighbors of Israel, ch. 25
    1. Ammon, vss. 1-7
    2. Moab, vss. 8-11
    3. Edom, vss. 12-14
    4. Philistia, vss. 15-17
  B. Tyre, 26:1–28:24
    1. Destruction foretold, 26:1-14
    2. Effect on other nations, 26:15-18
    3. No memory of great city, 26:19-21
    4. Lament, ch. 27
    5. Overthrow of proud king, 28:1-10
    6. Lament over Tyre, 28:11-19
    7. Against Sidon, 28:20-24
  C. Interlude about Israel's restoration, 28:25-26
  D. Egypt, chs. 29–32
    1. Prophecy against Egypt, 29:1-13
    2. A base kingdom re-established, 29:14-16
    3. Egypt for Nebuchadrezzar, not Tyre, 29:17-21
    4. Babylon will conquer, ch. 30
    5. Pharaoh warned about Assyria's fate, ch. 31
    6. Final lament for Egypt, ch. 32

III. Prophecies of restoration and hope (after the fall of Jerusalem), chs. 33–37
  A. Review of former oracles, ch. 33
  B. Future promise, chs. 34–37
    1. Discussion of shepherds: past and future, ch. 34
    2. Oracle against Edom, ch. 35
    3. Explanation of destruction and promise of restoration, ch. 36
    4. The Valley of Dry Bones, ch. 37
  C. Gog and Magog, chs. 38–39

IV. The temple and city of God, chs. 40–48
  A. Measurement for the house, chs. 40–42

B. The appearance of the glory of Yahweh, 43:1-12
C. Regulations for temple and service, 43:13-46:24
   1. Altar, 43:13-27
   2. Personnel, 44:1-45:8
   3. Instruction about sacrifices, etc., 45:9-46:24
D. Healing waters, 47:1-12
E. Divisions of restored land, 47:13-48:35

The prophecy of Ezekiel is concerned from the outset with a prophet whose first commission was to express God's judgment upon Judah for its breach of covenant faith. Ezekiel carefully made a case for the rightness of God's condemnation, demonstrating that historically the fault was with a faithless people, not a capricious deity. It was to a rebellious house he was called as a watchman to warn against impending doom. His first visions consisted of a symbolic siege and a graphic description of complete desolation. Idolatry is excoriated in ch. 6, and national sin is labeled for dire punishment in ch. 7. The visions of Ezek. 8-11 alternate between the reason for and the description of doom. Jerusalem's sorry record is detailed in chs. 12-19, where all phases of life from leadership to people are brought under the withering scrutiny of prophetic insight. In the series of oracles are the parable of the vine (ch. 15), the story of the waif (ch. 16), the parable of the eagles (ch. 17), and the account of the lioness and her cubs (ch. 19). Literary skill is used to clinch the indictment which God had against Judah and Jerusalem. Oracles of judgment again are the crux of chs. 20-24.

In chs. 25-32 the universal God stands in judgment over other nations than the Hebrews. Hope rises triumphant in chs. 33-37, and 38-39; 40-48 give a fitting climax with the destruction of evil and the promise of a new society where God would dwell. From judgment in chs. 1-24; 25-32, the prophet moves quite naturally to hope which will rise out of the ashes of destruction. The problem of utter desolation is met head on in the Valley of Dry Bones passage, while the fact of rampant evil is effectively dealt with in Gog and Magog (chs. 38-39). After this, the future glory of God's people and God's land can be described with confidence (chs. 40-48).

2. Major themes. Several themes have been developed in the book beyond their development in previous prophets. One needs to understand the circumstance of Judah and the situation in life for the average Hebrew to appreciate fully the contribution of Ezekiel.

The popular theological notion of the day was that Jerusalem, being God's dwelling place, was inviolate against attack. This concept had been fostered by the defeat of Sennacherib in 701 B.C. and the prophecies of Isaiah ben Amoz in connection therewith. Yahweh's city was Jerusalem, and the temple was his house which no enemy could ever conquer or profane. When, therefore, the temple was destroyed and Jerusalem was reduced to rubble, the popular faith of Israel was dealt a blow from which the people would not have recovered had it not been for the prophetic voice and word. To the average Hebrew, God had been defeated, his land conquered, and his people scattered. The foundation of faith had thus been shattered almost beyond repair.

a. Consequences of the absence of God from life. The absence of God from life signals the beginning of destruction. People had wantonly forsaken God and had in the truest sense become a "rebellious house" (cf. 2:1 ff). Jerusalem was a bloody city (22:2), and her elders were men who had secret places of idolatry (8:7-13). Her prophets were false (13:1-16), and her people worshiped other gods, openly bowing also before the forces of nature (8:14-17). A history of disloyalty was the story of this people, who were like an unfaithful wife (ch. 16) or a younger sister more scarlet than the older (ch. 23) or a useless vine (ch. 17). This constituted a sorry moral situation, where the requirements of God had not even been attempted.

The requirement for God's presence in life is obedience to his will and the keeping of his law, which must be expressed in quality of life, not in ritual alone. When rebellion became the dominant attitude and life was immoral in quality, Yahweh could no longer lend his support to the life of the people. Ezekiel met the popular theology of the day with a vision wherein the כבוד יהוה, "Yahweh's Glory," withdrew from the city (11:22-23). As soon as the Spirit of God absented himself, Jerusalem was doomed to destruction. While the well-being and continuance of any city or region was dependent upon obedience to the Almighty, in no sense was God dependent upon Judah or Jerusalem, but they were alive at his sufferance.

The God who was not a welcome part of living became immediately the judge of life and executor of judgment. Yahweh, according to the prophetic view, would make Jerusalem a desolation (cf. ch. 6); his servant marked its people for destruction (ch. 9); he would destroy the illusion which false prophets had erected (ch. 13); his hand would punish his beloved who had been unfaithful (ch. 16); his sword would go forth to destroy the wicked people (ch. 21); and his vengeance would be felt on the idolatrous nation (ch. 23). God who was not allowed to give life to his people gave them in full measure death, destruction, and exile. God who was not redeemer became the judge.

That God did not desire this destruction is made plain by the prophet. With anguished cry Ezekiel says in the name of Yahweh: "Why will you die, O house of Israel?" The covenant had been broken. God had been faithful and they had been unfaithful; therefore, destruction was a necessity.

b. God as the key to life. Easily the most searching doctrine of the OT is developed by the exilic prophet. He plumbed the depths of the spiritual nature of man when he recorded the positive side of the lesson which history was seeking to teach a people. In the Genesis account of Creation man was a lifeless, inert being until the breath or spirit of God was breathed into him; then he became a living soul. The difference between life and death, according to the prophet, was to be found in the presence of God's spirit in individual or corporate life.

Three passages in the prophecy relate to this great theme. The vision of the Valley of Dry Bones (37:1-14), the river proceeding from the temple (47:1-12), and the name of the city which God would create: Yahweh Shamah.

In the Valley of Dry Bones vision (ch. 37), the concept that God makes the difference between life and death is graphically described. There are three phases to the oracle: (*a*) the prophet saw a vision of a valley filled with dry, bleached bones, presumably a battlefield where the fallen warriors of the defeated were never buried. In all probability such desolate regions had been known by exiled Ezekiel, who had seen his own land reduced to death. The Almighty asks the question: "Can these bones live?" Hope had been all but extinguished among the exiles. Was there any reason for hope? God then answered with action. Ezekiel would prophesy, and the spirit of God would breathe or blow upon the death-filled valley and in doing so would raise the fallen army once more to be a mighty host.

The second part of the vision (vss. 7-12) describes the obedience of God's prophet and the result. A noise was heard; an earthquake was felt. Bones were brought together and sinews grew, after which the human form was finished, except for the breath of life. Then the breath of God was breathed into these soldiers, and they stood up as a very great army. Doubtless Ezekiel utilized the ancient idea that the E wind was the *rûaḥ* of Yahweh, but whatever the expression, the spirit or breath of God spelled the difference between life and death. The same creative force which had brought life to man, making him a living soul, could revive a dead people and make them live again.

The prophet left nothing to the imagination of his reader, pointing out that the vision meant that God would restore his people Israel, who were now as dead, and make them live again. The secret of such restoration is summed up in the words: "I will put my Spirit within you, and you shall live." Just as the removal of that spirit had meant death and judgment, so now its return signaled life and strength.

Perhaps the most arresting picture in the entire prophecy is the life-giving stream which issued from beneath the temple where God dwelt (47:1-12). Here was the river of life, which later became so much a part of the future hope for Christendom. A great river was formed by the waters which proceeded from under the altar of the temple, and as it moved toward the Dead Sea, a remarkable miracle occurred. The small stream became so great that it could not be crossed. When it reached the Dead Sea, the brackish waters of that body of water were purified, and fish were caught there at En-gedi and En-eglaim. Although the salt marshes were not reclaimed, on the banks of the river where the desert had formerly prevented growth, there were food trees which bore fruit monthly. The difference between a salt sea and a fresh-water lake, the difference between desert and a flourishing land, was the life-giving water of God proceeding from his throne or altar.

The great triumphant theme of Ezekiel is struck in the last two words of the prophecy: *Yahweh Shamah* (יהוה־שמה), "Yahweh is there." This shall be the name of the New Jerusalem in the midst of a restored land. It is the most important message Ezekiel had for his people—namely, that any society must be sure that "the Lord is there," since the difference between life and death, hope and despair, was the presence of God. For man is dead until he is made alive by the indwelling spirit of God; society is doomed, however virile at the moment, if it is abandoned by God, but even hopeless death becomes life when the breath of God is felt. So the great prophet gave to posterity a lasting insight into the ways of God with the spiritual life of man.

c. God as ruler of history. In no sense was the exilic prophet first with the concept that God was sovereign of history. From the time of Moses onward, the great leaders in Hebrew faith had known that God's dominion went far beyond the confines of the Promised Land and his rule was over all. Yet the popular notion persisted that somehow Yahweh was a national god who would protect his own. His dwelling was specifically located at Jerusalem in the temple. Ezekiel did much to dispel once for all this false notion, although it was left for Second Isaiah to describe the universal greatness of God in all its true grandeur.

The God whom Ezekiel knew appeared riding in a heavenly chariot which was possessed by his invisible spirit. This chariot was equipped with wheels so that the chariot could move in any direction, to any place where the Spirit might direct. The God whom Ezekiel beheld was mobile and was in no sense to be understood as dwelling in Jerusalem alone. Indeed, the prophet's vision was not in Palestine at all, nor in the temple or a temple; it was seen in heaven above the earth and in a cloud out of the N.

He not only directed the former destinies of his people, moving kings like pawns on the checkerboard of history; the Almighty at the moment was directing the armies of the mighty Chaldeans in their attack against Judah and Jerusalem. But, having used the forces of Chaldea to do his bidding, he could stand in judgment, not only upon his own people, but on all people. Egypt and Tyre were under his rule and therefore under his judgment. God was the Lord of men and nations; history was under his final control.

d. Individual responsibility. Ezekiel was not the originator of the idea of individual responsibility as has been claimed, but he gave a greater impetus to the idea, which was old as the Hebrew heritage of faith. Individual responsibility within the life of the community had long been recognized, though often overshadowed by corporate responsibility of the covenant community. So long as there was an actual physical land and people of God, this would continue. The prophets spoke of the nation and people as a corporate personality, using individuals to demonstrate the general condition. The prophet devotes one entire chapter (18) to the very difficult problem of inherited guilt. The subject is oversimplified with the ringing answer: "The soul that sins shall die," and no reference is made to acknowledged cumulative guilt of the fathers.

The prophet does not solve this knotty problem but concludes that the individual is responsible before God. In the circumstances this had become rather obvious, since the visible covenant community had disintegrated or was in process of disintegrating. The main unit remaining was the individual who might or might not be in a position to share corporate responsibility. That the individual, however bad his forebears had been, might escape punishment by a good life was plainly understood. Furthermore, as a sort of prelude to the gospel, the prophet makes it plain that there is no such condition or possession as inherited righteousness. It is God's will that every individual should now fulfil in himself the covenant requirements and avoid the destruction of judgment. To do so was an individual's responsibility. Other great themes are most surely found in Ezekiel, but these four are dominant.

e. History as a vindication of God's character. More than any other of the writers of the OT, this prophet explains the actions of the Almighty as derived from a desire to vindicate himself in history and before the world. The expression "You shall know that I am the LORD," or a variation of it, is used dozens of times. All actions spring from the desire that men may know what sort of God Yahweh is. Some scholars and theologians have expressed regret at this prophetic emphasis, calling it crude in expression and cold in outlook, but this is most surely not the case.

The prophet, having accepted the fact that God is a holy and righteous God, simply takes the next logical step. The Almighty's actions are a proof that he is such a god. Whether by his absolute destruction of hypocrisy as in ch. 8 or his loving concern expressed in ch. 34, the net effect is that the nations may know what sort of God Yahweh is. Who can quarrel with the fact that history is the arena for the revelation of God's meaning in the life of man? Admittedly a piece like ch. 20 does not represent the manner in which a twentieth-century theologian would express this doctrine. God is here depicted as freeing Israel from Egyptian bondage, withholding judgment in the wilderness and in the settled land for his "name's sake." Because he had sworn to free Israel and to lead them to a promised land, he did so, even though they had not fulfilled their covenant. To have failed might have been misunderstood as weakness among the nations and would have done irreparable harm to the honor of God. Certainly such failure would have been interpreted as proof of the weakness of God, not the sin of man. But now God, having been long-suffering far beyond the deserving of this people, would destroy them, and the surrounding nations would know why. God thus used an unworthy nation to vindicate his true nature and reveal himself to the world. The theme of a God not caught up in the maelstrom of history but ever demonstrating his nature through events constitutes a great contribution to religious thought.

f. The inner quality of true religion. This is in no sense an exclusive emphasis for Ezekiel, but it cannot be overlooked as a major contribution. Proud pretense by prophets and people is likened to a whitewashed wall which will fall in rain or storm. True religion is not a veneer but an inner strength (cf. 13:1-16). External show is no substitute for heartfelt loyalty, as the prophet made so very clear in denouncing the elders for worship in rooms of imagery (8:7-13). The need of people is not for a superficial change but for an alteration at the center of living. God promises that the new day will come because in his people he will put a new heart and a new spirit (cf. 11:19; 18:31; 36:26). Only by such inner change of being can men be acceptable before God. Yet it is God who gives man the new heart and new spirit.

3. Place in the development of the Hebrew faith. Since an increasing number of students and scholars have accepted the date of early sixth century B.C. for Ezekiel, and since a large proportion feel his influence in most of the book, it is possible briefly to understand the place of the prophecy in the development of the Hebrew faith. The book stands at the great divide between pre-exilic religion of a land with a covenant people and postexilic religion of a legal community without a land. Ezekiel draws from the background of one and makes large contribution to the other. He manages to recover from the ashes of destruction the precious faith of the past and with it to give people the new hope of a more profound faith. The continuance of the Jewish faith as a factor in history is proof enough that the prophet did his job very well indeed.

4. Relationships to the rise of Judaism. It has long been recognized that Ezra was, in fact, the father of Judaism, as he instituted the legal concept of a religious community. However, Ezekiel laid the groundwork of the exclusiveness that characterized Judaism and took the first steps toward a legalistic attitude. The corruption by the heathen had been one cause for the downfall of Jerusalem; hence the future must have safeguards against such intrusion of outside influence. It was the worship of foreign gods and the popularity of cults other than Jewish which brought dissolution of the social order. The fence of law, which was made to protect the chosen people against such influence, is implied in Ezekiel, as one might expect, and the seeds of Judaism were here; but in no sense did the prophet foresee what ends his ideas would reach.

5. Influence on NT thought. The vision of God (1:22-28) is felt quite strongly in all the visions of Revelation. The voice of Christ in Revelation was "like the sound of many waters" (Rev. 1:15; 19:6); his feet were burnished bronze (1:15), while his throne was like jasper stone and carnelian; and there was a rainbow about the throne, like an emerald to look upon (4:3). Lightning came from the throne, and there were four living creatures "full of eyes in front and behind" (4:6). The author of Revelation apparently borrowed from the prophetic word, and the borrowed material was shaped for a new usage.

In addition to the vision of God the biblical idea of a holy city, a new Jerusalem, originated from Ezekiel and Second Isaiah. Once more the key to the existence of this new city was the presence of the living God, who would no longer require a temple, its use having been made unnecessary by Jesus Christ. However, in Revelation as in Ezekiel the city is carefully measured, and its dimensions are given (Rev. 21:15-27). Even though the idea of this city proceeding from God is native to Second Isaiah, the concept must find its more original source with Ezekiel.

That remarkable figure of a river of living water proceeding from beneath the throne of God, transforming the land through which it moves, was also borrowed by the writer of Revelation. The trees along the bank yield their fruits monthly in exactly the way described by the prophet.

The concept of a good shepherd, by which so many have come to think of Jesus, came also from this rich prophetic source. Ezekiel saw the Messiah in terms of a shepherd who would do for the people what all their rulers had failed to accomplish. God promised to set up a single shepherd, even his servant David, who would feed the sheep of Israel; but more specifically God himself promised to be the shepherd of his people. This shepherd theme was beautifully adapted by Jesus to his own time. He was the good shepherd, and all others were hirelings to whom the sheep did not belong. Jesus had read and had understood Ezekiel quite well before he spoke the words recorded in John 10:1-39.

Another passage in the Gospel According to John is adapted from the thought of the prophet—i.e., John 15, which is an adaptation of Ezek. 15. The vine which bears no fruit and thus is useless served as a common base for both discourses.

Gog and Magog are definitely original to Ezek. 38–39, as is the emergent notion of an Armageddon. Of course, to Ezekiel, Gog was a person and Magog was a land, while in Revelation they are represented as two persons. In both cases the idea represented evil in full array against God, with such rebellion facing inevitable defeat.

The Gospel of John and the Revelation are most directly akin to the prophet, bearing in themselves the definite imprint of literary kinship. Jesus was well acquainted with the book of Ezekiel, from which he drew expressions to frame the new picture of Christian faith. Indeed, he used the title "Son of man" very frequently in the sense that it was used by the prophet. The NT bears a close kinship to the prophecy of Ezekiel and is furnished much background ideology and prophetic insight from that source.

6. Literary figures. Few authors in OT literature have experimented with new forms of literary expression as much as Ezekiel did. We mention but a few: the prophet as a responsible watchman (3:16-21); irresponsible religion likened to whitewash on a wall about to collapse (13:8-16); the story of a waif in the woods (ch. 16); the city of Jerusalem a caldron (24:6 ff); the story of two sisters (ch. 23); the song of the sword (21:8-17); Egypt a primeval monster (ch. 29); Tyre as a proud mistress fallen (ch. 26). These and other figures mentioned above, such as the useless vine, the good shepherd, the life-giving stream, the holy city, the throne of God, and others, demonstrate how rich is this literary style and the contribution to biblical expression.

F. *APOCALYPTIC AND CLAIRVOYANT ELEMENTS.* **1. Reason for apocalyptic.** Once the Jewish state was destroyed and Jerusalem was no longer existent, the future fulfilment of God's great purposes was raised from an altogether earthly setting in history above history. God had previously worked in the vortex of history through a chosen people and in a land of promise. Now, however, that people had become no people and that land no promised place. Many dreams of restoration were not fulfilled as expected, so the fulfilment of God was lifted above the realm of normal event. Thus the book of Ezekiel became a prologue to apocalyptic, which glimpsed the glorious future in secretive terminology and symbolic language. The Gog-Magog cycle, the Valley of Dry Bones, and the division of the land are certainly in the best apocalyptic style. In fact, ch. 9 is what one might call classically apocalyptic in conception and execution. However, the true apocalypse of God's bringing history to a climax had still to develop, and Ezekiel was little more than an initiator—in expression rather than in idea.

2. Abnormal personality. The claim that Ezekiel was an abnormal personality should be readily admitted, for it is deviation from the norm which frequently is the measure of true greatness. No "normal person" would have been sensitive enough to experience the presence of God or sensible enough to give expression to that experience. However, attempts to psychoanalyze the prophet seem bound to failure. The twentieth century is too far removed from that era, and there is such a paucity of information about "the patient" that no accurate analysis could be expected. Actually there are in all people enough slight deviations from the norm that any future investigator might conceivably make a case for any kind of abnormality for a given individual. That symbols and meanings change with altering cultures has been demonstrated.

The prophet was a sensitive soul given to a semi-mystical type of daydream by which he was able to live in scenes familiar to conscious experience. He was not gifted with clairvoyance—if, in fact, there be such a gift. A troubled spirit himself, he moved from doom to resurrection and expressed this for his people in a superb book.

G. *CANONICITY.* It was only after certain safeguards had been established that the Jewish community admitted this prophecy to their canon of scripture. The delay in acceptance was partially explained by the fact that Ezekiel's vision of God occurred outside the Holy Land and partially because chs. 1; 10 were considered dangerous in the hands of the wrong people. Apparently with the growing dispersion of Jews the first objection became *de facto* void because God's people were in many lands. The first chapter, with its marvelous vision and mysterious chariot, was forbidden to all who were under thirty years of age, nor was it ever read at synagogue services, lest it give rise to "theosophical speculations." After burning three hundred jars of oil, Hananiah ben Hezekiah was able to justify the admission of the exilic work to the canon of Jewish scripture, even though its legal sections had not been completely harmonized with the Pentateuch.

By NT times, when the heritage of apocalyptic had come to the fore in biblical books of Zechariah and Daniel, as well as in countless intertestamental works, Ezekiel—especially ch. 1—was most acceptable. Its influence on the writings of the NT and in the training of Jesus has already been assessed. For Christians it is accepted as the work of a major prophet and is read as that which is the Word of God, in whatever sense this concept is meant by the group using the book.

H. *TEXT.* A long discussion of the text would not be in place here, even though a restudy of it is overdue. Hölscher and Irwin have reduced the text by means of a preconceived key to the true Ezekielian material. Hölscher succeeds in isolating the poetic material, for which scholars are in his debt. However, few agree, nor does Hölscher insist, that only poetry is genuine.

The text is corrupt at many places and has suffered much at the hands of editors and copyists. LXX and Syr. are helpful in attempting to find the original, but every clumsiness in style does not necessarily indicate a nonoriginal expression. The Hebrew leaves much to be desired, but with the help of the versions it is possible to get a fair translation.

Cooke offers an excellent analysis of the MT as compared with the Greek. *See bibliography.*

Bibliography. C. C. Torrey, *Pseudo-Ezekiel and the Original Prophecy* (1930); J. B. Harford, *Studies in the Book of Ezekiel* (1935); G. A. Cooke, *A Critical and Exegetical Commentary on Ezekiel,* ICC (1937); I. G. Matthews, *Ezekiel,* An American Commentary on the OT (1939); W. A. Irwin, *The Problem of Ezekiel* (1943); C. G. Howie, *The Date and Composition of Ezekiel* (1950); G. Fohrer, *Die Hauptprobleme des Buches Ezechiel* (1952); C. J. Mullo-Weir, "Aspects of the Book of Ezekiel," *Vetus Testamentum,* II (1952), 97-112; W. A. Irwin, "Ezekiel Research Since 1943," *Vetus Testamentum,* III (1953), 54-66; H. H. Rowley, *The Book of Ezekiel in Modern Study* (1953); G. R. Driver, "Linguistic and Textual Problems of Ezekiel," *Bibl.,* vol. 35 (1954); H. G. May, Introduction and Exegesis of Ezekiel, *IB,* VI (1956), 41-338. C. G. Howie

EZEL ē'zəl [אזל] (I Sam. 20:19 KJV). A stone at which David made an appointment with Jonathan. The RSV, following the LXX, emends the passage to אצל הארגב, "beside yonder stone heap."

EZEM ē'zəm [עצם]; KJV twice AZEM ā'zəm. A city of Simeon in the Negeb of Judah (Josh. 15:29; 19:3; I Chr. 4:29). The KJV, following the pausal form of the Hebrew name, renders it as Azem in the first two passages. Its location is uncertain; a possible site is Umm el-'Azem, two low knolls on the NE side of the road that leads from Boweidah to er-Remthah, about 2½ miles N of Beer-sheba.

S. Cohen

EZER ē'zər [אצר (*in* 1 *below*), *from* lay up, store up; עזר (*in* 2-6 *below*), *from* help, succor; *cf. proper names* אביעזר, אחיעזר, אליעזר, יועזר]. **1.** The sixth son of Seir; a clan chief of the native Horite inhabitants of Edom (Gen. 36:21, 27, 30; I Chr. 1:38, 42).

2. A Judahite, father of Hushah (I Chr. 4:4).

3. An Ephraimite slain by the men of Gath (I Chr. 7:21).

4. A Gadite warrior who went over to David (I Chr. 12:9—H 12:10).

5. A Levite, son of Jeshua, who repaired a section of the wall of Jerusalem under Nehemiah's direction (Neh. 3:19).

6. A priest who participated in the dedication of the wall (Neh. 12:42). L. Hicks

EZERIAS. KJV Apoc. form of Azariah.

EZIAS. KJV Apoc. form of Uzzi.

EZION-GEBER ĕ'zĭ ən gē'bər, —gā'bər [עציון גבר, *from* gadyan bush *plus* giant(?)]; KJV often EZION-GABER —gā'bər. An important port and foundry city situated at the head of the Gulf of Aqabah. The biblical references to Ezion-geber are confined to the fact that it was a station on the journey of the Israelites on their way to the Plains of Moab (Num. 33:35-36; Deut. 2:8) and that it was a port from which ships sailed to Ophir, bringing back gold, almug wood, silver, ivory, and apes (I Kings 9:26-28; 10:11, 22). The greater part of our knowledge of the city comes from archaeological investigation.

1. Location. The biblical references cited above make it clear that Ezion-geber was located somewhere in the Wadi el-'Arabah and that, being a seaport, it must obviously have been on a part of the Red Sea—i.e., its W arm, the Gulf of Aqabah. Various sites were proposed for its location, some far up in the Arabah, on the mistaken supposition that the gulf extended farther N in biblical times. It was not until 1934 that Fritz Frank, in his explorations of the region, reported the discovery of a place at

Courtesy of Nelson Glueck

40. Looking S through the excavated gateway of Ezion-geber (Tell el-Kheleifeh) toward the Gulf of Aqabah

Tell el-Kheleifeh, *ca.* two miles W-NW of the modern city of Aqabah, which contained pottery from the Early Iron Age (1200-900 B.C.), and which he believed to be the proper site. This opinion was agreed to by Nelson Glueck when he visited the tell in 1936 and was completely confirmed with the excavations that he made from 1938 on, under the auspices of the American Schools of Oriental Research. Figs. EZI 40; JOT 31.

Glueck found the remains of four towns on top of one another, all of which had been destroyed by fire. The first and lowest of these towns had been set on virgin soil and showed evidences of having been built all at one time, indicating a carefully worked-out plan. The style of the buildings and the city wall are very close to those that are identified with the building operations of Solomon at Megiddo and other sites in Palestine. The chief feature of the town was a series of structures with flues and air

From "The Epic of Man," *Life* (copyright 1957 by Time Inc.); painting by Carroll N. Jones, Jr.

41. Copper refinery foundry operated by Phoenician metallurgists by the Red Sea for King Solomon

channels that traversed the walls and the floors; the bricks of the walls had become kiln-baked by reason of an intense heat within, and bore traces of sulphur and of metals. This was evidently a foundry which was used for the final process of refining the ingots of copper and iron that had been worked up in crude form near the mines in the Arabah.* The presence of this foundry explained why the town was located in this spot, which was not ideal for a port, being about three hundred feet from the water, nor for a place of residence, since it was exposed to the sun and the wind-blown sand. It was precisely at the farthest point W where sweet water could be obtained and yet where advantage could be taken of the strong winds that swept down the Arabah. It became obvious that this city must have been built by Solomon, the only king of Israel of the period who possessed the freedom from war, the resources, and the assistance of Phoenician planners to build up such a foundry and port city. Figs. EZI 41; MET 43.

Glueck further noted that there was not enough room in this location for two separate cities and concluded that Ezion-geber and Elath, at least in the book of Kings, were but different names for the same place. The change from the former name to the latter took place between the time of Jehoshaphat (876-851 B.C.) and Amaziah (796-767). The successive destructions of the four cities by fire were evidence of the successive captures and recaptures of the place, some of which are recorded in the Scriptures.

2. History. At the time when the Israelites under Moses passed through the region, Ezion-geber and Elath were only miserable collections of mud huts without significance except that they gave their names to the future city. The Israelites, being denied a direct passage through Edom itself, were forced to make a long circuit down the Wadi el-'Arabah to the head of the gulf, and then around the S and E boundaries of Edom (Deut. 2:8). The Edomites made no attempt to develop the location, and it was not until David had conquered the whole region and Solomon embarked on his career of industrial and commercial expansion that Ezion-geber was built and acquired its importance. The elaborate foundry supplied copper and iron both for the vessels of the temple and for trade; a navy, manned by Phoenician sailors, made trips to Ophir in Arabia (I Kings 9:26-28); and it was no doubt at the same port that the Queen of Sheba arrived on her journey to Jerusalem (I Kings 10:1-13).

After the division of the kingdom, Ezion-geber fell to the kingdom of Judah. The first city was sacked and destroyed, undoubtedly by Shishak in his invasion of Palestine (*ca.* 925 B.C.), which included a number of places in Edom. A second city was built on the ruins of the first, and the fortifications were strengthened; the place continued to flourish as an industrial center, but there is no further mention of the fleet, which may have been wrecked or else destroyed by the Egyptian attack. Jehoshaphat, another king who enjoyed a prosperous reign, attempted to renew navigation from Ezion-geber; but his ships were wrecked in the gulf, and he declined any further ventures in such a dangerous element (I Kings 22:47-49).

For the subsequent history of the city, *see* ELATH.

Bibliography. N. Glueck, *The Other Side of the Jordan* (1940), pp. 89-113. S. COHEN

EZNITE, THE ĕz'nīt [עֶצְנִי]. *See* ADINO.

EZORA ĭ zôr'ə ['Εζωρά] (I Esd. 9:34). Head of a family of Israelites who put away their foreign wives and children. The name is not found in the parallel Ezra 10:39-40, where it appears to be replaced by Adaiah and Machnadebai. C. T. FRITSCH

EZRA ĕz'rə [עֶזְרָא, *possibly from* עֲזַרְיָה, Yahweh helps; Εσρας, Εσδρας, Εζδρας]; EZRAH [עֶזְרָה, help; Εσρ(ε)ι, Εζρι, Ιεζραα] in I Chr. 4:17. **1.** One of the priests who came from Babylonia to Jerusalem with Zerubbabel (Neh. 12:1, 13; Azariah in Neh. 10:2).

2. A priest living in Nehemiah's time (Neh. 12:33).

3. The supposed author of his own memoirs in the books of EZRA AND NEHEMIAH (Ezra 7–10; Neh. 8–10). According to these records Ezra, whose genealogy is given in Ezra 7:1-5, led a caravan of Babylonian exiles to Jerusalem in 458 B.C. (if the seventh year of Artaxerxes I is meant in 7:8) or in 397, if Artaxerxes II is meant (vss. 6-10). Great authority was given him in an Aramaic royal decree (vss. 11-26), for which he thanked the Lord (vss. 27-28). A list of the exiles who returned with Ezra and of the temple vessels which they brought is given in ch. 8. In Jerusalem, Ezra was horrified by the toleration of marriages of Jews to heathen women (ch. 9). The congregation repented, the marriages were ordered dissolved, and a census of the mixed marriages was taken (ch. 10). The Book of the Law was read (Neh. 7:73*b*–8:12); the Feast of Tabernacles was celebrated; and a day of penance, followed by a general confession of sins, was observed (8:13–9:37). The leaders signed a ratification of the law as it was read (9:38–10:39—H 10:40), pledging themselves to oppose mixed marriages, to observe the sabbath and the sabbatical year, to pay the temple tax, and to supply the temple with the wood and the legal sacrifices and offerings.

This is all we know of Ezra from the Bible; even though he is called a priest and a scribe, even though he is said to have come from Babylonia with God's law in his hand, it is difficult to explain why he was regarded as a second Moses who revived Judaism. Most of his autobiography, if not all, was written by the Chronicler long after his death—assuming that he is a historical figure. One Jewish tradition identified him with the prophet Malachi (Meg. 15*a;* Targ. to Mal. 1:1); it is said that the whole record of Jewish literature was restored by him (Justinian *de cultu feminarum* I.3; cf. II Esd. 14); and, indeed, that "If Moses had not anticipated him, Ezra would have received the Torah" (Tosef. Sanh. 4.7). Long before, the Chronicler had regarded him as the founder of the guild of the scribes.

Bibliography. *See* the bibliography under EZRA AND NEHEMIAH, BOOKS OF. R. H. PFEIFFER

EZRA AND NEHEMIAH, BOOKS OF. A single volume in the Hebrew Bible and in the original LXX, until the two parts were separated in a Hebrew MS dated 1448 and in most printed editions, following the Vulg.; but Origen (died 254) and Jerome (died 420) knew this material as two books in Greek. They are the sequel of I-II Chronicles (Ezra 1:1-3*a* repeats II Chr. 36:22-23) and were written by the Chronicler (*see* CHRONICLES, I AND II), except when he quotes earlier sources. They relate the history of the Jews from 536 to 432 B.C.

1. Outline of contents
2. Canonicity
3. Historical problems
   a. The edict of Cyrus
   b. Interruption in the building of the temple
   c. The building of the temple in 520-516
   d. The work of Ezra
   e. "The words of Nehemiah"
   f. Opposition to the rebuilding of the walls of Jerusalem
   g. Supplements to the memoirs of Nehemiah
4. Literary problems
5. Authorship and date

Bibliography

1. Outline of contents.

I. The return of the exiles (538 B.C.) and the rebuilding of the temple (520-516 B.C.), Ezra 1–6
   A. Shesh-bazzar leads the Babylonian exiles to Jerusalem, chs. 1–2
      1. The edict of Cyrus, 1:1-4
      2. Return of the exiles bringing the temple vessels, 1:5-11
      3. List of the returning exiles, 2:1-67
      4. Contributions to the temple, 2:68-70
   B. Rebuilding of the altar in Zion and celebration of Tabernacles, 3:1-6
   C. Rebuilding of the temple, 3:7–6:22
      1. The beginning of the work, 3:7-13
      2. Opposition of the Samaritans, ch. 4
         a. Rejection of Samaritan assistance, 4:1-5
         b. Accusations against Jerusalem under Xerxes I (485-465) and Artaxerxes I (465-424), 4:6-16 (vss. 8-16 in Aramaic)
         c. Reply of Artaxerxes forbidding the fortification of Jerusalem, 4:17-23 (in Aramaic)
         d. Interruption of the work, 4:24 (in Aramaic)
         e. Completion of the reconstruction of the temple under Darius I (521-485) in 516, 5:1–6:18 (in Aramaic)
         f. Celebration of the Passover, 6:19-22

II. The work of Ezra, Ezra 7–10 (concluded in Neh. 7:73*b*–10:39—H 10:40)
   A. Introduction, 7:1-10
      1. Ezra's ancestry, vss. 1-5
      2. Ezra's trip to Jerusalem, vss. 6-10
   B. Decree of Artaxerxes I (465-424), 7:11-26 (vss. 12-26 in Aramaic)
   C. Ezra's doxology, 7:27-28
   D. List of exiles who returned with Ezra, 8:1-20
      1. Genealogical list, vss. 1-14
      2. Additional Levites, vss. 15-20
   E. The safe journey, with the holy vessels, 8:21-36
   F. The mixed marriages, chs. 9–10
      1. Ezra's horror at the toleration of mixed marriages, 9:1-5
      2. Ezra's confession of sins in a prayer, 9:6-15
      3. The repentance of the congregation, 10:1-5
      4. The calling of a national assembly, 10:6-8
      5. The mixed marriages ordered dissolved, 10:9-17
      6. List of the men with foreign wives, 10:18-44

III. Nehemiah's administration of Judea, Neh. 1–12
   A. Nehemiah allowed to go to Jerusalem, 1:1–2:8
      1. Nehemiah informed of Jerusalem's misery, 1:1-3
      2. His sadness and prayer, 1:4-11
      3. Nehemiah sent to Jerusalem, 2:1-8
   B. Nehemiah's decision to rebuild the city walls, 2:9-20
      1. His arrival in Jerusalem, vss. 9-11
      2. His secret inspection of the walls, vss. 12-16
      3. His decision to rebuild the walls evokes

the scorn of Sanballat and Tobiah, vss. 17-20

C. The building of the walls, chs. 3–4
   1. List of the wall builders, ch. 3
   2. Opposition of the enemies, ch. 4

D. Economic hardships, ch. 5
   1. Nehemiah's remedies for the hardships, 5:1-13
   2. His serving unselfishly twelve years as governor, 5:14-19

E. Plots of the enemies and completion of the walls, 6:1–7:5*a*
   1. Invitation to a conference, 6:1-4
   2. Slanderous accusations, 6:5-9
   3. False report of a planned assassination, 6:10-14
   4. The completion of the walls, 6:15
   5. The reaction of the enemies, 6:16-19
   6. Defensive measures, 7:1-3
   7. The small population of Jerusalem, 7:4-5*a* (continued in 11:1-2)

F. List of the returned exiles, 7:5*b*-73*a* (cf. Ezra 2)

G. The reading of the law, 7:73*b*–9:37 (perhaps to follow Ezra 10)
   1. Ezra's reading of the law, 7:73*b*–8:12
   2. Celebration of the Feast of Tabernacles, 8:13-18
   3. A day of penance, followed by a confession of sins in a long prayer, 9:1-37

H. The covenant ratifying the law, 9:38–10:39—H 10:40
   1. List of the signers, 9:38–10:27—H 10:28
   2. Pledges made, 10:28-39—H 10:29-40
      a. To avoid mixed marriages, 10:28-30—H 10:29-31
      b. To observe the sabbath and the sabbatical year, 10:31—H 10:32
      c. To pay the temple tax, 10:32—H 10:33
      d. To supply wood and offerings for the services, 10:33-34—H 10:34-35
      e. To supply the first fruits, firstlings, tithes, and other contributions to the temple, 10:35-39—H 10:36-40

I. Rearrangement of the population of Judea, ch. 11
   1. One in ten Jews to live in Jerusalem, vss. 1-2 (the sequel of 7:4-5*a*)
   2. Leaders living in Jerusalem, vss. 3-24
   3. Judean and Benjaminite villages, vss. 25-36

J. Priests and Levites who returned with Zerubbabel (538) and other lists, 12:1-26
   1. Priests, vss. 1-7
   2. Levites, vss. 8-9
   3. High priests from Joshua (538) to Jaddua (331), vss. 10-11
   4. Priests in the time of Joiakim son of Jeshua, vss. 12-21
   5. Levites in the days of Joiakim and Nehemiah, vss. 22-26

K. Dedication of the walls of Jerusalem, 12:27–13:3
   1. Gathering of the Levites and musicians, 12:27-29
   2. Purification of clergy and people, 12:30
   3. List of civil and religious authorities, 12:31-43
   4. Collectors of offering for the clergy, 12:44-47
   5. Exclusion of heathen from Jerusalem, 13:1-3 (cf. Deut. 23:3-7)

L. Nehemiah's second visit to Jerusalem, 13:4-31
   1. Nehemiah expels Tobiah, vss. 4-9
   2. Nehemiah collects the payments due the Levites, vss. 10-14
   3. Nehemiah enforces the sabbath observance, vss. 15-22
   4. Nehemiah's measures against mixed marriages, vss. 23-29
   5. Concluding summary, vss. 30-31

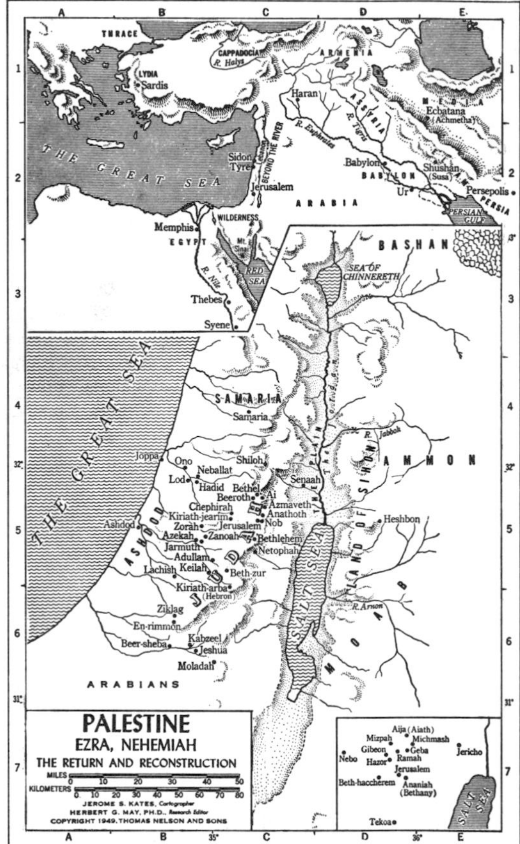

2. Canonicity. Since Ezra-Nehemiah reported historical information not available elsewhere and I–II Chronicles related the history told in Samuel and Kings (with additions), apparently Ezra-Nehemiah was canonized before I–II Chronicles. This seems to explain the incongruous order of the books in the Hebrew Bible, in which I–II Chronicles is the last book of the OT, as already in the Talmud (Baraita B. B. 14*b*). These books were all omitted from the biblical canon of the Syriac Christian Church and of Theodore of Mopsuestia (died *ca.* 428), as well as that of Nestorius (died *ca.* 451) and his followers.

3. Historical problems. All our historical information for the history of the Jews in the century 538-432 B.C., except for the rebuilding of the temple in Jerusalem (520-515 B.C.) reported in the books of Haggai and Zechariah, is contained in Ezra-Nehemiah; Josephus adds nothing but legends. Nothing is known of the century 432-331 B.C. The separate sources contained in Ezra-Nehemiah must be examined separately.

a. The edict of Cyrus. This famous edict (538 B.C.), allowing the exiles in Babylonia to go back to Jerusalem and rebuild the temple, is extant in II Chr. 36:22-23; Ezra 1:1-4; I Esd. 2:1-7 (cf. Ezra 6:3-5; I Esd. 6:24-26; Jos. Antiq. XI.i). The return of the Jews is reported in Ezra 1:5-11; I Esd. 2:8-15 (cf. Ezra 5:13-16; I Esd. 6:17-20). The returning exiles are listed in Ezra 2:1-67; Neh. 7:6-69; I Esd. 5:7-43 (cf. Jos. Antiq. XI.iii.10), and their contributions to the temple and settlement in Judea in Ezra 2:68-70; Neh. 7:70-73*a;* I Esd. 5:44-46.

The edict of Cyrus is extant in Hebrew (Ezra 1 and, partially, in II Chr. 36) and in Aramaic (Ezra 6:3-5; cf. 5:13-15). According to the Hebrew version, Cyrus declares that Jehovah had ordered him to build the temple, and all exiles are allowed to go to Jerusalem, bringing gifts from their heathen neighbors. According to the Aramaic version, Cyrus gave exact specifications for the new temple, to be built at the expense of the government, and ordered the return of the temple vessels. Both, if they are complete decrees, as they seem to be, can hardly be authentic. The first is generally regarded as spurious; but the second, while conceivably real, is historically a dead letter. For we know from Haggai and Zechariah that eighteen years later (520 B.C.) nothing was known of such a decree, which had never been enforced. Either Cyrus issued a decree to which no one paid any attention, or both versions of the decree are Jewish forgeries based on the dreams of Second Isaiah about a return of the exiles, and of Ezekiel about an imminent rebuilding of the temple.

The report of the Shesh-bazzar's caravan of exiles (Ezra 1:5-6) bearing to Jerusalem 5,469 temple vessels (2,499 is the actual total of those listed) in Ezra 1:7-11 (cf. 5:13-15) is manifestly a product of the Chronicler's vivid imagination. As for the list of those who had been exiled by Nebuchadnezzar in 586 B.C. and returned with Shesh-bazzar in 538, fifty-two years later (Ezra 2), it is said elsewhere to be a list of the inhabitants of Judea in the time of Nehemiah a century later (Neh. 7). Only an editor entirely unaware of the length of the Persian period (538-331) could have used this list, which may be an official record of a census of unknown date, for naming people alive from 586 to 444, at least 142 years. The historical value of the list, which may not be a concoction of the Chronicler, is unknown. In any case it is difficult to believe that the exiles in three deportations (597, 586, 581 B.C.; Jer. 52:28-30), numbering 4,600 men, could have become 42,360 descendants returning to Jerusalem fifty years later (Ezra 2:64), while many others stayed in Babylonia (Jos. Antiq. XI.i,iii); Neh. 1:3 knows nothing of any exiles that had returned. It seems that for the events of 538 the Chronicler had no genuine information.

b. Interruption in the building of the temple. Apparently in the seventh month of 538 (Ezra 3:1-7) the sacrificial worship was resumed in Zion (but see Neh. 7:73*b*); but the Chronicler's ignorance of facts unfortunately continues from 538 to 520, a period for which reliable sources may not have been accessible to him. For he assumes that the regular morning and evening burnt offering was offered before the temple was rebuilt and that the Levites began their service at twenty years of age (3:8, in contrast with Num. 4:3; 8:24). And he attributes the stopping of the work on the temple (allegedly begun in 536 B.C.) to Samaritan opposition (4:1-5, 24), long before the Samaritan Schism (in 432 or 332 B.C.), and adduces as evidence of this hostility a much later letter to Artaxerxes opposing the building of the walls (Ezra 4:6-23). None of the information for the period from 538 to the beginning of the building of the temple in 520, except perhaps some proper names, is historically credible.

c. The building of the temple in 520-516. For the inception of the work, the Chronicler in Ezra 5:1-2 could use the genuine information contained in Hag. 1:12, 14-15; Zech. 4:9; 8:9. But for its completion he lacked all sources and relied on his imagination (Ezra 6:14-22). Apparently unaware of the inconsistency, the Chronicler reports that the work began in 536 (Ezra 3:8-13; 5:16), for which there is no reliable evidence, and in 520 (4:24; 5:1-2), as was actually the case.

In 5:3-6:16 the Chronicler reproduces in Aramaic a letter to Darius I (5:6-17) and the king's reply (6:3-12), giving the text of the decree of Cyrus (6:3-5) and allowing the building of the temple. The authenticity of these documents has been defended by Eduard Meyer and seriously questioned by C. C. Torrey: critical opinion will probably remain divided on this question, although the presence of the decree of Cyrus (which had never been enforced for eighteen years; cf. Hag. 1:2; 2:15) militates against the historicity of this correspondence, which contains the incredible permission to the Jews to draw from the royal treasury in Syria unlimited funds for the building of the temple (6:8) and for the costs of the temple rituals (6:9-10). If such had been the case, the building would not have looked "as nothing" to those who remembered Solomon's temple (Hag. 2:3). These official documents and the narratives surrounding them were written obviously by a Jew—if not by the Chronicler, by an earlier writer of kindred spirit.

d. The work of Ezra (Ezra 7-10; Neh. 7:73*b*-10:39—H 10:40). The events of Ezra 7-10 are dated in the seventh year of Artaxerxes (7:7-8), and those in Neh. 8-10 in the twentieth year (1:1; 2:1). If Artaxerxes I Longimanus (465-424) is meant, the years in question would be 458 and 444; if Artaxerxes II Mnemon (404-358), they would be 397 and 384. Unfortunately critics have defended these various possibilities, and no unanimity of opinion seems possible: did Ezra's activity precede or follow Nehemiah's? Has the story of Ezra any basis in fact? Is Ezra, as W. F. Albright asserted, the Chronicler himself? Each part of the memoirs of Ezra should be tested separately for its historicity.

The genealogy of Ezra going back to Aaron (7:1-5) is obviously a concoction of the Chronicler: it is the Chronicler's line of high priests (I Chr. 6:3-14—H 5:29-40; cf. 6:50-53—H 6:35-38), which is at least in part unhistorical.

In his Aramaic decree, Artaxerxes (7:11-26) sent to Jerusalem Ezra "the priest, the scribe of the law of the God of heaven" (vs. 12), and gave to him unlimited authority—including the spending of funds from the royal treasury for the support of the temple (vss. 20-22), and forbidding the taxation of the Jewish clergy (vs. 24). The terminology of this decree is Jewish rather than Persian (see 7:15-17, 24-26; the Jewish law is identified with wisdom in vs. 25). S. R. Driver explains this as due to a Jewish revision, and R. Kittel as due to Ezra's or other Jews' participation in the redaction; the reproduction in the decree of the wording of Ezra's petition would also account for the Jewish style (E. Meyer). Other guesses are possible, but the authenticity of the decree can never be proved. Since Ezra was not a Persian official (as Nehemiah was), his powers are inconceivable. If the decree is questionable, the genuineness of Ezra's memoirs, of which it is part (7:27-28), is accordingly doubtful.

Ezra speaks in the first person only in 7:27–9:15 (except 8:35-36): he reports his journey from Babylonia to Jerusalem, and lists the laymen and the Levites who accompanied him, as well as the priests in charge of the gold, silver, and precious vessels (ch. 8). In Jerusalem he was shocked to hear that many Jews had married heathen wives (ch. 9). The story continues in the third person: the congregation was troubled, a popular assembly was called, and a census revealed that 113 Jews had married alien women (ch. 10). Unless a glorious end of Ezra's memoirs has been mysteriously lost, Ezra, though empowered to enforce the Jewish law by an edict of Artaxerxes, accomplished nothing except lamenting foreign marriages and taking a census. If nothing is lost, Ezra never had any royal authority whatsoever, and never was assured of the co-operation of the Persian authorities in Syria (Ezra 8:36). Whatever date we assign to Ezra's mission in Jerusalem, before or after Nehemiah's coming, nothing that is reported about him is unquestionably historical.

The attribution of Neh. 8–10 to Ezra's memoirs does not dispel the fog surrounding the work and personality of Ezra, who was regarded by the rabbis as a second Moses. If Ezra came from Babylonia in 458 (Ezra 7:7) with God's law in his hand (7:6, 14, 25), why did he wait until 444 (Neh. 1:1), when Nehemiah was allegedly present (Neh. 8:9; 10:1), to have it ratified? And why did he not sign the ratification with the others? The historicity of Neh. 8–10, much as we would like to assume it as basic for the canonization of the Pentateuch, remains questionable. If Ezra read the law in 458 (according to H. H. Schaeder), why did Nehemiah not enforce it until 432 (Neh. 13:4-31)? In conclusion, the extant information about Ezra is unreliable: he may well have been a historical character whose life was told by the Chronicler as romantically as that of David; or (as G. Hölscher claims) he may have been a purely legendary person unknown to Sirach (Ecclus. 49:11-13). So we must conclude with R. A. Bowman (*IB*, vol. III, p. 564): "The questions that divide scholars here are whether the Chronicler's function was that of an editor, compiling and arranging his sources, . . . or whether he was predominantly an author, using few sources . . . , but, on the other hand, writing from his own imagination great stretches of material."

e. "The words of Nehemiah" (Neh. 1:1–7:73*a*; 13:4-31). Although according to Neh. 5:14, Nehemiah was Persian governor of Judea from 444 to 432 (if Artaxerxes I is meant), a second visit in 432 is mentioned in 13:6. Nevertheless, the autobiography written by Nehemiah in 1:1–7:73*a* (and probably in 13:4-31) has always been regarded as substantially genuine and therefore the best historical source for Jewish history from 520 to 175 B.C.—in fact, one of the basic historical documents in the Bible. Only the conclusion in 13:4-31 has been questioned by critics (notably C. C. Torrey); there is no impelling reason for denying its historicity.

f. Opposition to the rebuilding of the walls of Jerusalem (Ezra 4:6-23). The accusation against the Jews in the time of Xerxes I (485-465) is not reproduced in Ezra 4:6, but the one under Artaxerxes I (465-424) in vss. 7-10 is given in full (vss. 11-16), as well as the royal answer (vss. 17-22); 4:8-24 is in Aramaic. The Chronicler in vs. 24 confused the objections to the building of the fortifications of Jerusalem (vss. 7-23) with alleged objections to the building of the temple (which presumably no one objected to). This misunderstanding does not necessarily mean that these documents are not historical; on the contrary, it is proof that the Chronicler did not write them. These are the least suspect of all the Aramaic documents, but may nevertheless be Jewish forgeries.

g. Supplements to the memoirs of Nehemiah (Neh. 11:1–13:3). C. C. Torrey regards them as written by the Chronicler, while others consider them quoted from "the Book of the Chronicles" (Neh. 12:23). It is questionable whether any historical information about Nehemiah may be gleaned from these passages, although they may shed a little light on the days of the Chronicler.

4. Literary problems. In spite of rare dissenting voices it is now certain that the Chronicler, who wrote I–II Chronicles, is the author or editor of Ezra-Nehemiah; the only question is what sources he incorporated into his work. The autobiography of Nehemiah (Neh. 1:1–7:73*a;* and perhaps 13:4-31) has never been seriously questioned as a genuine earlier source, but the authenticity of the memoirs of Ezra is by no means above suspicion, as has been seen above. And critics who have concluded that Ezra's memoirs are authentic have reached widely differing conclusions about what they included, since only in 7:27–9:6 does Ezra speak in the first person. In fact, all attempts to determine the original contents of the Ezra memoirs (if, indeed, there was such a document) must forever remain conjectural. The style and contents of the Ezra narratives are so similar to those of the Chronicler that they have plausibly been ascribed to him and, as has been seen above, furnish no genuine historical information. If the Chronicler is not the author of the Ezra memoirs, as seems likely, they must have been written by a kindred spirit in the fourth century or by an imaginative editor who freely expanded a brief account about Ezra. But if the Chronicler really used some Ezra source, it had been so rewritten before him or by him that it is hopeless to attempt to identify it. Even the dossier of Aramaic official documents in 4:8–6:18; 7:12-26 is thoroughly Jewish in character and much later than the Persian kings to whom the decrees and the letters are attributed. Unless the Chronicler freely compiled the whole collection, the most likely view is that the Chronicler found this dossier in a Jewish work composed shortly before his time; but 7:12-26 seems to be entirely from his hand, as the Ezra memoirs in general. This does not, however, mean that Ezra was a purely fictitious character. He may well have been a Jerusalem Jew in the time of Nehemiah, remembered for his learning and piety, and selected by the Chronicler, who was wont to date Jewish institutions considerably earlier than their true origin (as temple music in the time of David), as the first of the scribes (סופרים; γραμματεῖς, νομικοί) or students of the law (Ezra 7:10-11). There were, however, no scribes before the canonization of the Pentateuch *ca.* 400 B.C. Scribes and teachers were probably familiar in the time of the Chronicler, although the first one known to us is Ben Sirach, the author of Ecclesiasticus (*ca.* 180 B.C.), in which he gives us samples (in poetry) of his classroom lectures and of his biblical learning.

Although the memoirs of Nehemiah are the only genuine source used by the Chronicler in Ezra-Nehemiah, their actual extent is disputed. Presumably they are contained in Neh. 1–7; 12:27-43; 13:4-31, which may include some additions and revisions. E.g., the statement in Neh. 5:14, according to which Nehemiah remained in Jerusalem 444-432, is out of harmony with the obvious briefness of his first visit (2:6; 6:15), the reported events of which lasted less than a year. The prayer in 1:5-11 resembles the national confessions of sin in Ezra 9:6-15; Dan. 9:4-19, which are for the most part echoes of Deuteronomy. The hand of the Chronicler appears in 4:2; 5:13; 7:1-3, and elsewhere; the list of the wall builders (3:1-32) may not have been an original part of the memoirs. The unquestionably genuine parts from the pen of Nehemiah are 1-2; 4:1–6:19 (with some revisions); and presumably the kernel of 7:1-5*a;* 11:1-2; 12:31, 37-40; in spite of the traces of the Chronicler's work, evident in 13:1-3, the account of Nehemiah's second visit in 432 (notably in 13:14-27, 29, 31) sounds like an authentic expression of Nehemiah.

In contrast with the pale and ineffective personality of Ezra, Nehemiah stands forth as a vigorous and successful man of action. Through his energy, self-denial, and shrewdness he brought new life to the helpless and pathetic Jewish community in Jerusalem, and may have saved it from extinction. He stood at the end of an era: the Hebrew language was giving way to Aramaic as the vernacular (Neh. 13:23-24), and the heroic period of Judah was becoming the pious age of the Jewish congregation, obedient to the law of Moses.

5. Authorship and date. Seldom and with dubious arguments has it been denied that the same author wrote, and in part edited, I–II Chronicles and Ezra-Nehemiah, as seems obvious from the style, interest in the ritual and in the Levites, and sacrifice of historical reality to the glorification of Judaism. Curiously, A. C. Welch and W. A. L. Elmslie regard the identity of the end of II Chronicles and the beginning of Ezra as a proof that these books were written by different authors. (For the characteristic views of the Chronicler, who is generally considered the author of Chronicles-Ezra-Nehemiah, *see* CHRONICLES, I AND II.) The view that the Chronicler is Ezra (cf. the early rabbis, church fathers, and commentators) has been revived by W. F. Albright.

The Chronicler presumably wrote between 350 and 250. The list of David's descendants comes down to at least 350, and the latest high priest, Jaddua (Neh. 12:11, 22), was a contemporary of Alexander (died 323), according to Jos. Antiq. XI.vii.2; viii.7. Most likely the Chronicler wrote a few years before 250. Of course, those who regard these two passages as later additions date the Chronicler *ca.* 400; by emending Ezra 7:8 and supposing that Ezra followed Nehemiah under Artaxerxes II (404-358), R. A. Bowman concludes that the Chronicler was active "no earlier than about 365-350 B.C." (*IB,* III, 554).

Bibliography. Commentaries: C. Siegfried in W. Nowack, ed., *Handkommentar* (1901). A. Bertholet in K. Marti, ed., *KHC* (1902). L. W. Batten, ICC (1913). W. Rudolph in O. Eissfeldt, ed., *HAT* (1949). M. Rehm in F. Nötscher, ed., *Echter Bibel* (1950). J. J. Slotki, *Soncino Books of the Bible* (1951). R. A. Bowman, Introduction and Exegesis of Ezra and Nehemiah, *IB,* III (1954), 551-819.

Special studies: C. C. Torrey, *Ezra Studies* (1910). J. Meinhold, "Ezra der Schriftgelehrte?" in K. Marti Festschrift, *BZAW,* vol. 41 (1915). S. Mowinckel, *Ezra den Skriftlärde* (1916); *Statholderen Nehemia* (1916). J. A. Bewer, "The gap between Ezra Chapters 1 and 2," *AJSL,* 36 (1919), 18-26. M. Kegel, *Die Kultusreformation des Ezra* (1921). W. F. Albright, "The Date and Personality of the Chronicler," *JBL,* 40 (1921), 104-24. A. van Hoonacker, "La succession chronologique Néhémie-Esdras," *RB,* 32 (1923), 481-94; 33 (1924), 33-64. H. H. Schaeder, *Esra, der Schreiber* (1930). M. Burrows, "Nehemiah 3:1-32 as a Source for the Topography of Ancient Jerusalem," *BASOR,* 14 (1934), 115-40. A. C. Welch, *Post-exilic Judaism* (1935). R. de Vaux, "Les décrets de Cyrus et de Darius sur la reconstruction du Temple," *RB,* 46 (1937), 29-57. M. Noth, *Überlieferungsgeschichtliche Studien,* I (1943), 110-80. A. S. Kapelrud, *The Question of Authorship in the Ezra Narrative* (1944). A. Bentzen, "Ezras Persönlichkeit," *Studia Theologica,* 2 (1948), 95-98. H. H. Rowley, "The Chronological Order of Ezra and Nehemiah," *Ignace Goldzieher Memorial Volume* (1948). A. Bentzen, "Sirach, der Chronist und Nehemiah," *Studia Theologica,* 3 (1949), 158-61. K. Galling, "The 'Gōlā-List' according to Ezra 2 = Nehemiah 7," *JBL,* 70 (1951), 149-58. I. Arana, "Sobre la colocación original de Neh. 10," *Estudios Bíblicos* (1951), pp. 379-402. N. H. Snaith in H. H. Rowley, *The OT and Modern Study* (1951), pp. 107-14; "The Date of Ezra's Arrival in Jerusalem," *ZAW,* 63 (1952), 53-66. H. H. Rowley, *The Servant of the Lord* (1952), pp. 131-59. A. Jepsen, "Nehemiah 10," *ZAW,* 66 (1954), 87-106. M. Avi Yonah, "The Walls of Nehemiah," *IEJ,* 4 (1954), 239-48. H. H. Rowley, "Nehemiah's Mission and Its Backgrounds," *Bulletin of the Johns Rylands Library,* 37 (1954-55), 528-61; "Sanballat and the Samaritan Temple," *Bulletin of the Johns Rylands Library,* 38 (1955-56), 166-98. H. Cazelles, "La mission d'Esdras," *Vetus Testamentum,* 4 (1954), 113-40.

See also bibliography under CHRONICLES, I AND II.

R. H. PFEIFFER

EZRAHITE ĕz′rə hīt [אזרחי; LXX Ἰσραηλείτης]. The family or clan of Ethan and Heman, legendary wise men and poets (I Kings 4:31; Pss. 88:1; 89:1). The word is probably a gentilic form of "Zerah," since I Chr. 2:6 designates Ethan and Heman as sons of Zerah. H. H. GUTHRIE, JR.

EZRI ĕz′rī [עזרי, my help] (I Chr. 27:26). Son of Chelub; the steward in charge of the agriculture of the crown lands in the time of David.

FABLE. A form of didactic narrative in which plants or animals think, speak, and behave as people do. The fable is related to the ALLEGORY and the PARABLE; in all three types the actors and what they do resemble, but remain distinct from, the characters, who are the narrator's real concern, and their actions. The reader or hearer knows the difference, draws the parallel, and discerns the moral. What distinguishes the fable from the other forms is the human behavior in it of trees and beasts and inanimate nature.

The Hebrew Bible contains two prime examples of the fable. Both are political. The longer one is spoken to the lords of Shechem by Jotham, sole survivor among the sons of Jerubbaal after Abimelech's coup (Judg. 9:8-15). The trees, seeking a king, appeal in vain to the olive tree, the fig tree, and the vine; the bramble alone is willing—but promises tyranny. In the second, shorter fable (II Kings 14:9), Jehoash of Israel rebuffs King Amaziah with an insult: A thistle acted presumptuously against a cedar, and a wild beast came and trampled the thistle. The first biblical fable (above) warns the people of Shechem against the violent Abimelech; the second suggests to Amaziah that he is courting disaster. What is told in a fable does not, of course, really happen, and this the hearer well knows; the story is recounted and heard for the sake of the "moral" only.

What is said of Solomon in I Kings 4:33—H 5:13 about his speaking "of trees" and "of beasts" may mean that he was reputed as a fabulist.

S. H. BLANK

FACE [אַף, nose (Gen. 3:19); עַיִן, eye (Exod. 10:5); פנים; πρόσωπον]. In many instances "face" refers simply to the human or animal face, but it is also used analogically in such figurative expressions as "face of the deep" or "face of the waters" (Gen. 1: 2), "face of the ground" (Gen. 2:6), or "face of the sky" (Matt. 16:3 KJV).

The face is the part of the body through which a man's attitudes are most clearly expressed. Therefore, "to avert or hide the face" from a person is to express displeasure (Ps. 102:2; Ezek. 39:23); "to set the face against" is to express hostility (Jer. 21:10); "to make the face to shine upon" is an indication of friendly acceptance (Num. 6:25); and "to set the face to" expresses determination (Jer. 42:17; Luke 9:51).

Since a man's "face" reflects his personality and character, the word can be used to mean "PERSON" and is frequently so translated. Thus, in the English phrase "to respect or regard persons" the word for "persons" in the original is literally "faces" (Deut. 1:17 KJV; Matt. 22:16 KJV). In some cases it is used in a weakened sense in which it is merely the equivalent of a personal pronoun (Jer. 1:8; cf. KJV with RSV). In other instances it has the more precise sense of "PRESENCE" and is so rendered in the English versions (Exod. 10:11; Acts 5:41).

From this last idiom is derived the most important theological use of the term "face," for it occurs repeatedly with regard to the presence of God. Sometimes the Hebrew or Greek word for "face" is simply translated "presence" (Gen. 4:16; II Thess. 1:9); in many other places the concrete word "face" is allowed to stand, but will be better understood when regarded as a metaphor for the more abstract word "presence" (Ps. 27:8; Matt. 18:10). In a few places the "face (or presence) of the Lord" seems almost a hypostasis (like ANGEL; NAME; GLORY)—the term is used to designate a local manifestation of Yahweh where motives of reverence have led the writer to avoid the unqualified use of the divine name or a pronoun referring to divinity; the clearest example is Exod. 33:14-15. The phrase "BREAD OF THE PRESENCE" (Exod. 25:30; KJV "shewbread") is to be interpreted in the light of this conception.

Bibliography. A. R. Johnson, "Aspects of the Use of the Term פנים in the OT," in H. J. Fück, ed., *Festschrift Otto Eissfeldt* (1947), pp. 155-59.

R. C. DENTAN

FACETS [עינים, eyes] (Zech. 3:9); KJV EYES. The flat surfaces of a cut gem. A stone with seven facets on which inscriptions were to be placed was given to the postexilic priest Joshua. *See* JEWELS AND PRECIOUS STONES.

L. E. TOOMBS

FAIENCE. The term applied to a type of glazed siliceous ware used in Egypt from predynastic times for the manufacture of tiles, vessels, small figures of animals and human beings, and ornamental jewelry. The material consists of two or three layers: (*a*) an inner core of comparatively coarse grains of quartz, (*b*) a second layer (often not present) of finely ground quartz, usually white, to enhance the (*c*) external layer, a glass glaze with various chemically obtained colors.

Bibliography. A. Lucas, *Ancient Egyptian Materials and Industries* (2nd ed., 1934), pp. 101-15.

T. O. LAMBDIN

FAIR HAVENS [οἱ Καλοὶ Λιμένες] (Acts 27:8). A harbor on the S side of Crete.

The harbor is doubtless to be identified with a bay E of Cape Littinos which is still known as Kalous Limionas. This anchorage opens to the E and SE and is partially protected by a few small islands. In 1853 Captain T. A. B. Spratt found the ruins of a chapel dedicated to Paul (*Hagios Paulos*) on a hill overlooking the haven. This naval officer considered that the harbor would be inconvenient and unsafe in winter on account of E and SE winds blowing directly into the bay; this accords with the opinion expressed in Acts 27:12. *See also* LASEA.

Bibliography. T. A. B. Spratt, *Travels and Researches in Crete* (1865), II, 1-6; H. Balmer, *Die Romfahrt des Apostels Paulus und die Seefahrtskunde im römischen Kaiserzeitalter* (1905), pp. 315-18; M. N. Elliadi, *Crete, Past and Present* (1933), p. 139.

J. FINEGAN

FAITH, FAITHFULNESS. Faith is belief in something or trust in some person. In theology it properly describes man's apprehension of the absolute or transcendent. It is response to revelation as contrasted with discovery of new knowledge. KNOWLEDGE is correlative with facts or information or truth, and belongs to the sphere of epistemology. Faith is the more distinctively religious term. There is a necessary distinction here, though it is misleading to differentiate too sharply. For faith may be described as a kind of knowledge, and certainly reason is involved in the act of faith ("blind" faith being a psychological impossibility). In relation both to faith and to knowledge, certitude is predicable.

For the Bible the object of faith is God, and the highest personalization is reached in the NT proclamation that God has revealed himself in a human life, and may be addressed as "Father of our Lord Jesus Christ." In this usage faith is primarily trust rather than belief, a matter of personal relationship rather than of abstract knowledge.

Faith is the indispensable preliminary without which true religious experience cannot develop. It is man's initial awareness of God and also a continuing attitude of personal trust in God. God's movement toward man is primary; the initiative is with God. But there must be the corresponding movement on the human side, and this is basically what is meant by faith. For this reason the importance of faith cannot be overemphasized. Religious and moral attainment is impossible without it. The NT affirms that "all things are possible to him who believes" (Mark 9:23); right standing with God is by faith alone (Rom. 1:17; 5:1; Gal. 2:16; etc.); "without faith it is impossible to please him" (Heb. 11:6).

Whether this is defined as an act of the reason or of the will, or whether it is viewed as pure passivity, may be disputed. The main thing to note is that it is man's acceptance of God, and response to God's offer of himself; man's receiving of God's gift, rather than his own gift, effort, or achievement. God has spoken his WORD (and the Bible mediates this word [Heb. 1:1-2]). Man can say Yes or No to it. Faith is man's Yes to the Word of God. And when the Word comes to a focus in Christ, faith also may be said to center on this focus.

- A. Terminology
  - 1. Hebrew
  - 2. Greek
  - 3. In the NT
    - *a.* The Synoptic gospels
    - *b.* The Pauline writings
    - *c.* The Johannine writings
    - *d.* The adjective
- B. Conception of faith in the OT
  - 1. Recognition of God as the living One
  - 2. A moral response
  - 3. In relation to the covenant
  - 4. A corporate experience
  - 5. Signs
  - 6. Fear of the Lord
  - 7. An exclusive demand
  - 8. The keeping of the law
- C. Conception of faith in Judaism
- D. Conception of faith in the NT
  - 1. The Jewish heritage
  - 2. The teaching of Jesus
  - 3. Primitive Christianity
  - 4. The distinctive Pauline connotation
    - *a.* Relationship with God
    - *b.* The new creation
    - *c.* Freedom
    - *d.* Sonship
    - *e.* The content of the Christian faith
    - *f.* Love
    - *g.* Conviction
  - 5. The distinctive Johannine connotation
    - *a.* Basic ideas
    - *b.* The significance of "witness," μαρτυρία
    - *c.* Acceptance of testimony
    - *d.* How faith arises
    - *e.* Jesus the object of faith
  - 6. Definition of faith in Hebrews
  - 7. Other NT connotations of faith
- Bibliography

A. *TERMINOLOGY.* 1. Hebrew. The most important of the Hebrew terms for faith is the root אמן, which signifies "firmness," "stability." The verb is used in the *Hiph'il* in the sense "believe," "trust," "say Amen to" anyone or anything. It is not a strictly causative meaning, as is usual with the *Hiph'il* form of the verb, but declaratory. The verb is constructed absolutely, or with the prepositions ב and ל (trust *in* a person or thing), and occasionally with כי ("that" —i.e., an object clause). A relationship is implied, and ultimately a personal one, for behind the object which is the basis of trust there is a person. The outstanding usage is that in which God is the object, and this is implied even when there is no preposition (e.g., Ps. 78:32). The precise meaning is "hold God" (נאמן; *Niph'al* participle)—i.e., "trustworthy," the fundamental reality; nothing is so sure, permanent, or reliable as God.

The LXX renders האמין by πιστεύειν 45 times and 6 times by a compound of πιστεύειν, by πείθεσθαι once, mostly followed by the dative corresponding to ב or ל.

For the absolute use, see Exod. 4:31; Ps. 116:10; Isa. 7:9; 28:16. The basically religious meaning passes into the moral one of "resolution," especially in face of danger. This is contrasted with the timidity of Ahaz (Isa. 7:4) and the frantic opportunism of other rulers in Jerusalem in Isaiah's time (Isa. 28:15).

For the use with ב: (*a*) of belief in God, see Gen. 15:6; Exod. 14:31; Num. 14:11; Deut. 1:32; II Chr. 20:20; Ps. 78:22; (*b*) of trust in men, see Exod. 19:9; II Chr. 20:20; Job 4:18; Jer. 12:6; (*c*) of belief in things, see Pss. 106:12, 24 (words); 119:66 (commandments); 78:32 (miracles—RSV *"despite* his wonders" is unnecessary).

For the usage with ל, see Gen. 45:26; Exod. 4:1, 8; Exod. 4:8-9 (belief in "signs"); Isa. 43:10 (in Yahweh); 53:1. No distinction of meaning can be derived from the use of these two Hebrew prepositions.

Two nouns from the same root, אמת (107 occurrences) and אמונה (47 occurrences), occur fairly frequently in the sense of "firmness," "faithfulness." They have often been translated "truth" in English versions, and in the LXX they are rendered ἀλήθεια, "truth," rather than πίστις (ἀλήθεια 119 times; πίστις 26 times). This is probably because they correspond to the *Niph'al* form of the verb, which has a more passive meaning, and because the *Hiph'il* form (which becomes πιστεύω in the LXX) did not get its proper cognate noun until the Aramaic stage of development of the Hebrew language. These two nouns are used with reference to God and men alike. They are often associated with חסד, "grace," "steadfast love," and צדק, "right."

These words tend to become comprehensive terms for true religion—e.g., אמת in Pss. 25:5; 26:3; 86:11; Dan. 8:12; 9:13; 10:21; אמונה in II Chr. 19:9; Jer. 7:28; Hab. 2:4. The same tendency is observable with the verb.

Five other verbs fall to be considered in this connection: first, בטח (LXX πεποιθέναι, ἐλπίζειν), "feel oneself secure," is used 57 times in a religious reference, 60 times in a secular sense. The basis of trust may be God or man. If a distinction is to be made between it and האמין, it will be that בטח implies a state rather than a relationship of response or mutuality. But often the words are used interchangeably, as in Ps. 78:22. בטח is a general term like האמין for the attitude of the true believer. Cf. Pss. 32:10; 37:3; 125:1; Prov. 16:20; 28:25; 29:25; Jer. 39:18; Zeph. 3:2.

Another verb, חסה (LXX ἐλπίζειν 20 times, πεποιθέναι 9 times, and other verbs in 7 other places), "seek refuge," "hide oneself," especially in God, as in Ps. 25:20, is used only 5 times in a secular sense, as against 34 times in a religious sense.

There are three other verbs of waiting or hoping, capable of a secular sense as well as a religious one: קוה, יחל, and חכה. The most prominent LXX renderings are ἐλπίζειν and (ὑπο)μένειν. We need not differentiate between them, and it is sufficient to refer for illustration of their usage to Pss. 33:20-22; 37:9; 42:5; 130:5-7; Isa. 8:17; 40:31. There are times when faith can show itself only as hoping against hope; the Lord seems to be hiding his face (Isa. 8:17) or disregarding man's right (Isa. 40:27). But even then faith which still "waits for the Lord" is distinguishable from mere resignation. The first of the two verbs in Isa. 8:17 is חכה, which seems to carry an aura of secrecy or mystery (cf. Dan. 12:12; Hos. 6:9). *See* WAIT; HOPE.

2. Greek. In classical Greek usage the verb meant "trust," "have confidence in," whether of persons or of things (expressed normally by the simple dative), or "believe," in the sense of "be confident that" (followed by the infinitive or an ὅτι clause). The noun πίστις signified "trust," "confidence," or more objectively "trustworthiness," often in the concrete sense of "pledge," "guarantee," "proof." The word could be used with reference to things divine, but for religious belief in a general sense—e.g., in the existence of God—a Greek would probably use a different verb—e.g., νομίζω. A specifically religious sense for πιστέυω was not developed until the Hellenistic period; the older usage, of course, continued. Of authors who might be quoted from the period prior to and contemporary with the NT, we must be content to refer to two only, the Hermetic writer(s) and Philo.

The Hermetic tracts are difficult to date but are roughly contemporary with primitive Christianity. They show affinity both with Philo and with Gnosticism, and set forth a philosophic mysticism. Their place of origin is probably Alexandria, and Hebrew influence is not out of the question. The word πιστεύω has here come to mean "receive revelation" —i.e., "be on the way to attain salvation and immortality." This is due to reason—not simply to the intellective faculty in man, but to divine illumination. God himself is conceived as Mind (νοῦς). Faith is thus identified with the higher knowledge, which is the way of salvation. An enlightened member of these sects can say: "I believe [πιστεύω] and bear testimony; I enter upon life and light" (*Corpus Hermeticum* I.32). Philo's voluminous pages show most of the Greek meanings for πίστις and πιστεύω, as well as some coloring from the more personal, Hebraic sense, when he speaks of "faith toward God" (ἡ πρὸς θεὸν πίστις). But he can also use the words in a mystic-philosophic sense—e.g., when he defines πίστις as ἀφανοῦς ὑπόληψις, "apprehension of the unseen." The meaning "revelation" perhaps lies behind Ignatius' reference to Christ as the "perfect faith," ἡ τέλεια πίστις (Ign. Smyrn. 10.2).

See also the notion of "truth" in the Dead Sea Scrolls (*see* § C *below*).

3. In the NT. The linguistic usage of the NT (πιστεύω, "I believe"; πίστις, "faith") may be examined in a threefold classification: (*a*) the Synoptic gospels, representing (roughly) primitive Jewish Christianity, based on the teaching of the Lord himself; together with Acts, James, the Pastoral letters, Hebrews, and Revelation, representing non-Pauline Christianity; (*b*) the Pauline writings; (*c*) the Johannine writings.

a. The Synoptic gospels. The most common of the usages to be noted here is the absolute use of the verb in the sense of belief in God (Christ) as almighty, as self-revealing, and as beneficent in his attitude toward mankind, particularly toward his worshipers (Matt. 8:13; 21:22; Mark 5:36; 9:23; 15:32; Luke 8:12-13, 50; Acts 4:4; 5:14; 8:13, 37; 11:21; 13:12, 39, 48; 14:1; 15:7; 17:12, 34; 18:8; 19:2). The participles of this verb are used with the article as a term for Christians—e.g., Matt. 18:6; Acts 22:19; I Pet. 2:7 (present participle); Mark 16:16-17; Acts 4:32; 11:21; Heb. 4:3 (aorist participle); Acts 15:5; 18:27; 19:18; 21:20, 25; Tit. 3:8 (perfect participle).

Among less frequent uses there is the meaning "trust," "give credence to," with the dative case of the person or thing (e.g., Matt. 21:25, 32; Mark 16:13-14; Luke 1:20; Acts 8:12; 16:34; 24:14; 26:27; 27:25; II Tim. 1:12; Jas. 2:23). Three other cases, without a following dative, are in this category of meaning: Matt. 24:23, 26; Luke 22:67. In Acts 18:8 the simple sense of "trust" has given way to the more specific sense of "conversion," "faith."

Sometimes the object of the verb is expressed by a "that" (ὅτι) clause (Matt. 9:28; Mark 11:23-24; Luke 1:45; Acts 9:26; Heb. 11:6; Jas. 2:19). This repeats the LXX rendering כי after האמין. Twice the object is stated by an accusative and infinitive (Acts 8:37; 15:11).

In a few cases the object of faith is indicated by the use of a preposition: by εἰς and the accusative (Matt. 18:6; Acts 10:43; 14:23; 19:4; I Pet. 1:8); by ἐπί with the accusative (Matt. 27:42; Acts 9:42; 11:17; 16:31; 22:19); by ἐπί with the dative (Luke 24:25; I Pet. 2:6; I Tim. 1:16); by ἐν with the dative (Mark 1:15). No distinction of meaning can safely be drawn. It is better to regard these prepositional constructions simply as influenced by the Hebrew usage of האמין followed by ב or ל.

As for the use of the noun, πίστις, in the Synoptic gospels, it mostly carries the meaning of confidence in God and trust in his power to heal and save. Jesus urges his hearers to have this faith in God (Mark 11:22), or he pronounces after a cure: "Your faith has made you well" (Mark 5:34 etc.). This is a straightforward usage, and this meaning must be maintained in two passages of some obscurity (Luke 18:8; 22:32). Similarly in Acts (see especially 14:9). Three times in Pauline speeches (Acts 20:21; 24:24; 26:18) the specific reference of faith to Christ is brought out by the use of εἰς with the accusative following the noun, a usage already noted in connection with the verb.

b. The Pauline writings. The Pauline letters do not exhibit any real development of usage, as compared with the foregoing, but it is justifiable to treat them as a separate class because of their extent and because of the significant place which Paul's theology assigns to faith. This will be noted here, more particularly in the case of the noun πίστις; for a full exposition, *see* § D4 *below*.

It is the participial use in which Paul shows the largest accord with the writings of our first classification. It looms even more prominently in his total usage, as the following references indicate: Rom. 1:16; 3:22; 4:11; 10:4, 11; I Cor. 1:21; 14:22; Gal. 3:22; Eph. 1:19; I Thess. 1:7; 2:10, 13. These are present participles, mostly in the plural, with the article: "the believing ones," as a synonym for Christians or church members. In two instances (II Thess. 1:10; 2:12) Paul uses the aorist participle similarly, referring more specifically to the time when those concerned attained their faith. In Gal. 3:8-9 as an alternative to "believers" he coins the phrase "those who depend on faith" (οἱ ἐκ πίστεως). There are further instances of the absolute use of the verb in Rom. 4:18; 10:9-10; 13:11; 15:13; I Cor. 3:5; 15:2, 11; II Cor. 4:13.

Each of the syntactical forms already noted recurs in Paul, but none is prominent. There is no additional construction either with the verb or with the noun. The verb is found with the dative 4 times; with ἐπί and the accusative twice, ἐπί and the dative once; with εἰς 3 times; with ἐν once; with the accusative of direct object once; with the accusative and infinitive once; with a ὅτι clause twice.

The noun πίστις in Paul carries deeper and more theological significance than the usage we have considered in the first classification. This arises to a large extent from his more rabbinical treatment of the OT, particularly in his connection of it with δικαιοσύνη (justification) and νόμος (law). He is closer to Synoptic usage when he gives πίστις the sense of utter dependence on God and belief in his power, as in Rom. 4:16-20; Col. 2:12. But in these it is clear that it is a theologian rather than a historian of the church who is writing. One occurrence with θεοῦ as subjective genitive is noteworthy (Rom. 3:3): this is God's faith in the sense of trustworthiness, a familiar OT conception of God, which is not normally expressed in the NT by the noun πίστις, but by the adjective πιστός. The objective genitive Ἰησοῦ or its equivalent—faith centered on Jesus (Christ)—occurs several times (Rom. 3:26; Gal. 2:16, 20; 3:22; Eph. 3:12). Once the noun is coupled with ἐν χριστῷ (Col. 1:4; cf. Eph. 1:15), once with εἰς χριστόν (Col. 2:5), in Christ.

c. The Johannine writings. The Johannine usage is very distinctive. It is clearly rooted in the primitive usage of the church, as is seen from the reappearance of the use of the verb followed by the dative, with a ὅτι clause, and from the absolute use. There are also two cases of a noun in the accusative as direct object of the verb (John 11:26; I John 4:16).

The absolute πιστεύειν is very frequent (John 1:7, 50; 3:12, 15; 4:41-42, 48, 53; 5:44; 6:47, 64; 10:25; 11:15, 40; 12:39; 14:29; 16:31; 19:35; 20:8, 25, 29).

The usage with the dative, in the meaning "give credence to," whether of persons or of things, is somewhat more frequent than in earlier NT writers (2:22; 4:21, 50; 5:24, 38, 46-47; 8:45-46; 10:37-38; 14:11 [combined with a ὅτι clause]; I John 3:23; 4:1; 5:10). There seems to be no difference of meaning between this and the usage with εἰς, which we are about to consider (cf. John 6:29-30; 8:30-31; I John 5:10).

We now come to the more characteristic Johannine development. The usage with ἐν is not found (with the possible exception of 3:15, where, however, the participle πιστεύων is taken absolutely by some commentators). In 20:31 the phrase "in his name" belongs to "may have life" rather than to "believing." The usage with ἐπί also is absent from John. The use of the ὅτι clause after πιστεύω, on the other hand, is much more frequent in John than in other NT writers. It gives the content of the thing believed and thus constitutes a more intellectual sense than the moral sense of reliance implied by the dative usage; it means, not trust in Christ, but belief that he is Messiah or was sent by the Father, or the like. Thus πιστεύω is approximating to γινώσκω, "I know." The references are: 8:24; 11:27, 42; 13:19; 14:10-11; 16:27, 30; 17:8, 21; 20:31; I John 5:1, 5. *See* KNOWLEDGE.

On John's identification of believing with knowing, see John 4:42; 6:69; 16:30; 17:3, 8, 20-25; I John 4:16*a*. Some scholars distinguish πιστεύω as the beginning of the right attitude (to Jesus; to ἀλήθεια, "truth") from γινώσκω as the riper development (cf. John 4:42; 6:69; 8:31-32; 10:38). For the connection with truth, see John 8:45-46; 18:37; 19:35; I John 5:20; II John 1-4; III John 3-4. From I John 2:21-23 we see how knowing the truth is synonymous with knowing Christ, because the opposite is denying Christ, the nadir of unbelief. Here, as in I John 3:1-6; 5:1-5—and elsewhere—John can write almost indiscriminately of knowing and believing in Christ. Finally, there is the usage with εἰς in John 2:11; 3:16; 4:39; 7:38-39; 9:35-36; 11:45, 48; 12:36-37, 44, 46;

14:1, 12; I John 5:10. This usage is as prominent in John as it is rare elsewhere in the NT, and seems to have no parallel in the LXX or nonbiblical Greek. Some see no distinction between this usage and that with the dative, and certainly in some places they are merely alternatives—e.g., John 14:11-12. But if εἰς is more than an equivalent for the Hebrew ל or ב after האמין, it may be intended to point definitely to Christ as the basis or true center of faith. (In that case it approximates to the usage with ὅτι, believing something *about* Jesus—e.g., his messiahship or sonship [20:31; cf. Rom. 10:9; I Thess. 4:14, his resurrection]). This is even clearer in the more elaborate construction εἰς τὸ ὄνομα πιστεύειν (John 1:12; 2:23; 3:18; I John 5:13; to which we may add I John 3:23 [τῷ ὀνόματι]). "To believe *into* the name of Christ" means to receive Christ. The use of "name" recalls the baptismal formula and was perhaps chosen because of baptismal practice, with its implication that the baptized convert passed into Christ's lordship like a slave entering the possession of a new owner. Alternatively, believing on the name might mean, in accordance with OT conceptions, believing or accepting or appreciating fully the *character* or authority of Jesus (cf. "name" in John 10:25; 17:6). *See also* NAME.

The noun πίστις, "faith," does not occur in John except in I John 5:4. This is probably not accidental, but parallel with the (deliberate) avoidance of the noun γνῶσις, "knowledge."

d. The adjective. Πιστός carries on the ordinary Greek sense, both active and passive, whether of persons or of things: "trustful," "trustworthy"; cf. Luke 16:10-12; I Thess. 5:24; I Cor. 1:9; I Tim. 1:15; II Tim. 2:11, 13. In the LXX it is used of persons, like Abraham, Samuel, David; Abraham in particular is often called ὁ πιστός, "the faithful one" (Num. 12:7; I Macc. 2:52; II Macc. 1:2; Ecclus. 44:20; cf. Gal. 3:9). Also it is used of things—e.g., the covenant (Ps. 88[89]:28); commandments (Ps. 110[111]:7); water (Isa. 33:16). For its use in reference to God, see Deut. 7:9; 32:4; Isa. 49:7. The NT develops a new meaning which makes πιστός synonymous with πιστεύων, the present participle of the verb—i.e., "a believer," "a Christian"; sometimes τῷ κυρίῳ, "to (or in) the Lord," is added (John 20:27; Acts 16:1, 15; I Cor. 4:17; Eph. 1:1; Col. 1:2; I Tim. 4:10; I Pet. 1:21). The antithesis is ἄπιστος, which moves away from the meaning "untrustworthy" to that of "unbelieving" (Mark 9:19; Luke 12:46; I Cor. 6:6; 7:12-15; 14:22-24; II Cor. 6:15). Similarly the noun ἀπιστία (Mark 6:6; 9:24; Rom. 11:20, 23; I Tim. 1:13; Heb. 3:19).

From the positive sense is derived the Christian coinage ὀλιγόπιστος (Matt. 6:30; 8:26; 14:31; 16:8).

B. *CONCEPTION OF FAITH IN THE OT.* In the light of the linguistic usage catalogued above, and with reference to the teaching of the OT as a whole about God and man's relationship with him, we may set out the OT conception of faith under the following eight heads:

1. Recognition of God as the living One. The foundation stone of OT faith is that God is the One to whom the world and every living thing owe their existence and on whom they depend for their survival and well-being (Gen. 1-2; Exod. 3; 20:2-3; Deut. 4:39; Isa. 43:10-11; cf. Rom. 4:17*b;* I Cor. 8:6*a*). This is axiomatic for biblical authors. The skeptical effusion Ecclesiastes was not accepted into the canon of the OT until orthodox insertions had been made which conformed to this axiom.

The objective reference to the ground of faith is typical of Hebrew thought. The subjective factor of man's feeling about God is not much considered. Man must accept the fact of God and his own dependence, and this is faith. The worthiness of the object is stressed; the attitude of the subject is not analyzed.

Man's status before God is that of a creature in relation to its creator, a finite being in relation to the infinite (Gen. 1-2). A distinction is made between man and all other creatures, in that he is affirmed to bear the image and likeness of God (Gen. 1:26-27); but the gulf created by his failure to conform to the Creator's intention is also emphasized (Gen. 3:22).

This is embryonic in Gen. 3, and reiterated in Deuteronomy, with its frequent calls to observe the divine statutes (4:40; 6:25; etc.) and equally frequent warnings of the consequences of refusal (1:43; 30:15-20), and also in the prophetic exposure of the people's sins. *See* SIN.

Thus it appears that penitence and obedience, rather than faith, are the key words; or faith as a moral quality—i.e., faithfulness (as in Hab. 2:4; Matt. 23:23; Gal. 5:22)—rather than as a primarily religious quality, directed to God rather than to men.

Consider how obedience is stressed in the case of Noah (Gen. 6:9, 22; 7:5); Abraham (Gen. 22:1-18—an example of faith being put to the test; cf. Heb. 11:8, 17); Joshua (Josh. 1:7-8; 24:22-31); Samuel (I Sam. 15:17-33). *See* OBEDIENCE.

2. A moral response. Faith in the OT is thus a moral response, not the acceptance of ideas or dogmas about God. It concerns will rather than intellect or emotions. It is trust rather than belief. This corresponds to the nature of Yahweh and his revelation. *See* GOD, OT; REVELATION.

The personal character of God is not fully known until he can be called, as in the NT, the "Father of our Lord Jesus Christ."

3. In relation to the covenant. The meaning of faith must be seen in relation to the covenant, not simply in relation to creation. It is trust in the God who within his general providence has brought Israel into a special relationship with himself; Yahweh "chose" Israel (Deut. 7:6-7). The covenant implied a mutuality of obligation (Deut. 26:16-19). Yahweh can be relied on to keep his part of the contract, to "keep the covenant and the steadfast love" (Deut. 7:9); this is his "faith" or faithfulness (האל הנאמן). Faith on the side of his earthly partner is to be shown in keeping the "commandment and the statutes and the ordinances" (6:17; 7:11). The book Deuteronomy is very significant in demonstrating the significance of the COVENANT, which is central in Hebrew religion. Man's faith is based on God's trustworthiness as evidenced in blessings received.

In addition to this obligation to keep the commandments, the following key words of Deuteronomy may be noted: man is to heed (lit., "hear") the statutes (4:1; 7:12); to cleave or hold fast to Yahweh (4:4; 10:20); to seek and turn to him (4:29-30); to turn, in the sense of "repent," after apostasy (30:2-10); to obey his voice (4:30); to love him "with all your heart," etc. (6:5); to fear him (6:2, 13; 10:20); to remember him (7:18-19; 8:2-3, 18-20; 9:7). As noted above, faith and duty are closely allied; for the Hebrew the moral aspect of faith took precedence over the intellectual and emotional. The other main emphasis in Deuteronomy is on undivided loyalty to Yahweh and full concentration on his service. This faith clearly includes a sense of election and membership of a specially favored people. Josh. 4:24 makes a contrast between Israel, who are to fear Yahweh, and the rest of mankind, who are to recognize his power. It is not denied that other nations may have some knowledge of God. Their worship is often mocked at, but the maturer thought of the OT allows that Yahweh is the God of the whole earth and has concern for all nations (e.g., Ps. 33:8-22). But Israel is drawn into a special relationship (Ps. 33:12). For her, therefore, faith is a heightened kind of awe, trust, and hope, insofar as Israel experiences Yahweh's "steadfast love" (חסד), the characteristic term for Yahweh's concern for his covenant people (Ps. 33: 18-22).

This development of faith depended on being born an Israelite, a "son of Abraham." Abraham's own faith and experience are thus exemplary for his descendants, and the references to them must be considered.

The earliest statement of the promise to Abraham is Gen. 12:1-3. In the work of the priestly school this is related to the foundation of the covenant between Israel and Yahweh (Gen. 17:1-8, 19-21; Exod. 6:4-8; Deuteronomy, *passim*). The promise is repeated in Gen. 15:1-6, where we have specific mention of Abraham's faith in vs. 6*a:* "and he believed (in) Yahweh." The meaning clearly is "confidence in Yahweh's promise." The distinctive verb which is used (האמין ב) implies the dependability of the one to whom the faith is directed, and is cognate with the important noun inadequately rendered "truth" in many English versions (e.g., 24:27; 32:10).

Paul's exegesis of this passage (Rom. 4:17-21) is correct. The faith in question apprehends God as one who brings into being things which do not exist (vs. 17*b*).

In contrast to this Pauline emphasis on faith Gen. 12:4 points to Abraham's obedience (cf. 26:5; 22:18). This is why Jewish exegetes could refer to Abraham as an exemplar of righteousness rather than faith; even 15:6 makes a connection between faith and righteousness, and the Pauline argument of Rom. 4 revolves around righteousness as well as faith.

The promise to Abraham is fundamental in these narratives of the patriarchs (Gen. 17:1-8, 19-21; 26: 3-5, 24-29; 28:13-15; 35:11-12; 48:4 [cf. Exod. 32:13; Deut. 34:4; Josh. 21:43-45; 24:1-13]). God guarantees it, and this is his "truth" (אמת), or faithfulness. On man's side, faith is simply believing that God is of such a character, even when the evidence seems to point the other way (see Gen. 17:17-18). *See* ABRAHAM.

It remained for Christian development to point out that it was possible to be a son of Abraham without being a member of the true people of God—in Pauline phraseology, to have descent from Abraham "according to the flesh," but not "according to the spirit" (Matt. 3:7-10; 7:21; 8:11-12; Luke 16:24-25; John 8:33-47; Gal. 3:26-29; Rom. 4).

In the Christian proclamation there was a new center of loyalty, Christ, taking the place of Abraham and Moses; a new covenant replacing the old. The old faith, which could have been described as faith in the name of Abraham, is sublimated into faith in the name of Jesus Christ.

4. A corporate experience. The religion of Israel was a corporate rather than an individual experience. This must be kept in mind when we are considering faith. The individualized conception of faith implied in modern usage, especially among Protestants, is not to the fore in the OT.

To some extent the Psalms, with their many expressions of individual piety, provide an exception to this. The tendency of scholars to assign larger numbers of Psalms to a pre-exilic date emphasizes at the same time their corporate usage (*see* PSALMS, BOOK OF). In this discussion it is easy to erect false antitheses. It must be remembered that an originally private confession or prayer may become the expression of a whole congregation's devotion, as any hymnbook shows.

As used in the organized worship of Israel, particularly the greater temple festivals, the Psalms are unique expressions of Israel's faith. We note the following:

a) Many Psalms give evidence of intense personal trust in God, even though the specific terms for faith or hope, etc., are not used (e.g., 42; 46; 51; 63; 84; 96; 102–3; 116; 118; 121; 139; 145).

b) Yahweh's faithfulness—i.e., the ground of man's faith—is often referred to (e.g., 36:5-7; 89 *passim;* 92: 1-2; 94:18; 98:1-3; 100:5 [cf. Isa. 26:1-4]).

c) Trust in Yahweh is most frequently expressed as thankfulness and joy over some deliverance (e.g., 5:11; 9:10; 13:5; 18:1-3; 22:1-5; 27:14; 62:1, 5-8; 141:8). Sometimes this deliverance is from "enemies" or "the wicked" (e.g., 7:1; 11:1; 17:7; 25:1-2; 31; 56; 86; 143).

d) Faith appears sometimes as undivided concentration on Yahweh (16:1, 8; 37:1-9; 62).

5. Signs. Distinctive of Hebrew religion was the sense of the need for a "sign" (אות). The underlying thought is that whoever, God or man, is worthy of trust must be able to give evidence of it: a primitive, but not ignoble idea; for the sign means the presence of God, and his readiness to save, as in John's Gospel 2:11, etc.). The following passages refer to signs in connection with the classic deliverance from Egypt: Exod. 4:1-9, 30-31; 7:3; 14:31; Num. 14:11; Deut. 4:34; 7:19. For signs of the saving presence of God at other times of crisis, see Judg. 6:36-40; Isa. 7:10-17; Dan. 4:2-3. *See also* SIGNS AND WONDERS.

6. Fear of the Lord. The Hebrew's trust in God could contain within itself the fear of God. These two basic attitudes were not incompatible. This again is typical of Hebrew religion (cf. Ps. 40:3; 56:3). Fear of Yahweh is paralleled with hope in his love (Ps. 147:11). In Dan. 6:26-27 true religion is defined as fear of the living God and belief in his power to deliver his faithful servants from danger. (See also Gen. 22:12; Exod. 14:31; Lev. 19:14, 32; 25:17; Isa. 8:13.)

The fear of the Lord is allied to knowledge and wisdom (Isa. 11:2). It is the "beginning" of wisdom (Ps. 111:10; Prov. 1:7); i.e., it is the primary requisite for one who would be wise. The Hebrews were on the side of those who say, "I believe in order to understand." The only reasoning that mattered for them was that which started from the presuppositions of faith—a faith, moreover, which trembled in reverence before God.

If a man fear Yahweh, what else need he fear? asks a psalmist (Ps. 27:1)—i.e., the fear of Yahweh brings a sense of security, and thus is related to trust or confidence (cf. Job 4:6, where Eliphaz says to Job: "Is not your fear of God your confidence?").

The full exposition of this language would set it in the context of the conception of God as King and Father, and of the divine holiness. *See* FEAR.

7. An exclusive demand. Hebrew religion made a total demand upon its adherents (cf. Deut. 6:5; 18:13; I Kings 8:61; 11:4; Isa. 38:3). The ideal of unwavering confidence in Yahweh is expressed in David's utterance before Goliath (I Sam. 17:37, 45-47). The twin ideal is undivided allegiance. "You shall have no other gods before me" (Exod. 20:3 = Deut. 5:7). Idolatry is regularly ridiculed and condemned, and apostasy is the sin of sins. Faith in Yahweh is thus an exclusive faith, corresponding to the jealousy of Yahweh, who will not give his glory to another (Isa. 42:8). *See also* JEALOUSY.

There is linguistic support for this in the fact that האמין, the master verb in the vocabulary of believing, is never used of devotion to false gods (though בטח and חסה are). It is the absolute use of האמין which is significant. Two passages of Isaiah come up for consideration here, and perhaps justify the claim that Isaiah saw more deeply into the significance of faith than any other OT author. The passages in question are 7:9; 28:16. Isaiah condemned the behavior of Jerusalem's rulers at two times of crisis: in 734, when a confederation of Israel and Syria was threatening Judah; and in 701, when an Assyrian army was approaching. In his judgment their action was at best political opportunism, at worst sheer panic. He in the strength of his faith in God could detach himself from the immediate danger and survey it objectively in its true proportions. He was sure of God's presence ("Immanuel," "God is with us," seems to have been a favorite word of his during the earlier crisis: 7:14; 8:8, 10). They, on the other hand, took no account of God at all. Their fear prompted only resort to superstition (8:19). Isaiah's utterances seem to mean that Israel needs real principles for her statecraft, and these can be derived only from her religion; no political or any other security is possible without faith:

> If you will not believe,
> surely you shall not be established
> (7:9).

The verbs in both clauses here are from the same Hebrew root, אמן, but this wordplay cannot be reproduced in English. Again, "He who believes [*Hiph'il* participle used absolutely] will not be in haste" (28:16): the man of faith has a stability that saves him from joining in a general panic (cf. 30:15-18).

This is faith which expresses the whole man, a fundamental attitude determining the whole of a man's conduct, a total dedication of the self to God (8:13), resulting in peace of mind, freedom of action, and true strength (30:15, where גבורה, "strength," signifies basically the strength of the male as contrasted with the female, then the valor of a warrior). Isaiah describes it as the foundation stone of the true religious community (28:16; cf. I Pet. 2:6, where this verse is applied with some aptitude to the Christian church).

8. The keeping of the law. In the postexilic period faithfulness to the law was the increasingly dominant expression of faith. Torah was, in the words of S. Schechter, "both an institution and a faith." The faithful are presented as ideals of law-observing righteousness—e.g., Daniel and Judith (Dan. 1:8; 6:10; Jth. 8:5-6; 11:17); the Maccabees and their supporters (I Macc. 2:29-38, 49-68). In Bar. 4:1-2 the Torah is:

> the book of the commandments of God,
> and the law that endures for ever.
> All who hold her fast will live,
> and those who forsake her will die.

In the wisdom literature the law is not prominent, except in Ecclesiasticus, where it is identified with wisdom, and we read:

> All wisdom is the fear of the Lord,
> and in all wisdom there is the fulfilment
> of the law (19:20; cf. vs. 24).

In Jubilees the law is the revelation of eternal and absolute truth and right, every detail is of perpetual relevance, and no further revelation is necessary. Aristeas 158, 168, speaks of it as divine oracles (λόγια) and even calls it "the Scripture" (ἡ γραφή): "Its purpose is to enable us throughout our whole life and in all our actions to practise righteousness before all men, being mindful of Almighty God." In IV Maccabees the martyr Eleasar in his defense before Antiochus declares: "We do not believe any stronger necessity is laid upon us than that of obedience to the Law" (5:16). On the other hand, the author of the apocalyptic work known as IV Ezra, brooding over the problem of sin and destiny, finds this superficial and not sufficiently related to hard experience. For him the law is indeed glorious and eternal, but its acceptance by Israel as God's gift has not enabled them to keep it and become perfect; evil could still triumph over good in men's hearts (3:20-22). Thus the law cannot redeem; only God in his mercy can do that. The rabbis would argue that the law does have this power, and that its study is a sufficient antidote against evil. II Baruch also is more optimistic about what the law can do:

> In Thee do we trust, for lo! Thy law is with us,
> and we know that we shall not fall so long as
> we keep Thy statutes (48:22).

But for IV Ezra man's trust cannot rest on possession of the law, but only on God himself.

C. *CONCEPTION OF FAITH IN JUDAISM.* Judaism as reflected in the APOCRYPHA and the PSEUDEPIGRAPHA (*ca.* 200 B.C.–A.D. 100) understood faith in the same sense in which the OT speaks of it. The difference is that it contains a larger element of loyalty to Hebrew traditions, and centers more closely round observance of the law, and, in Palestine itself, the services of the temple. Increasing acquaintance with Gentile ways inspired fresh denunciations of idolatry (e.g., the later chapters of Wisdom and the verses of the Jewish Sibyllists), and confirmation of the monotheism of the Shema ("The LORD our God is one LORD" [Deut. 6:4]), and of the conviction that Israel is God's covenant people, distinguished by divine election from all other peoples. Emphasis on the sovereignty and transcendence of God was deepened. He is the God of the whole earth, and will ultimately vindicate Israel—the latter theme belongs particularly to the apocalyptic writers. A generous attitude toward Gentiles (e.g.:

> The compassion of the Lord is for all living beings.
> He rebukes and trains and teaches them,
> and turns them back, as a shepherd his flock
> [Ecclus. 18:13];

cf. also the Testaments of the Twelve Patriarchs) alternates with a less generous one (Jubilees and IV Ezra). Certain special doctrines are developed, if not actually introduced. The chief of these concerns life after death; teaching about angels and demons was much developed. In some writers (e.g., Tobit, the Prayer of Manasses) we find a deep belief in the power of prayer and an intense, if simple, piety. But on the nature of faith itself, as an attitude of the soul or as communion with God, nothing significantly new appeared. The best that can be quoted is perhaps the passage in IV Maccabees (15:1–17:2), concerning the martyrdom of the seven sons of Eleasar at the hand of Antiochus' torturers, and the fortitude with which their mother encourages them to endure. This the author regards as due not only to reason inspired by the Jewish law (one of his main themes), but also to the "nobleness of faith."

This Judaism was essentially practical, concerned with carrying out in daily conduct the precepts of the law. The Shema and the Ten Commandments were its only creed, and its aim was orthopraxis rather than orthodoxy. "I believe in thy commandments," cries a late psalmist (Ps. 119:66; similarly Ecclus. 33[36]:3). It would, however, give a wrong impression to speak of Jews' believing in the law. Fundamentally they believed in God, apart from whom nothing was conceivable, and the law called forth their highest energies because it was his greatest gift to them.

In the Diaspora some development of the conception of faith is to be noted. The Jews had to see their religion in contrast with polytheism. This resulted in a new appreciation of the excellence of monotheism. Also, as a consequence of proselytism, a conception of faith grew up as acceptance of a truer religion, which a man deliberately chooses for himself as distinct from what he has been born and brought up in. The distinction between believers and unbelievers begins to be seen as not coterminous with that between Jew and Gentile. National boundaries are irrelevant here. The "fool" of Ps. 53:1 is not necessarily a Gentile! Physical descent is not the only claim to a share in the inheritance of Abraham. This is a very significant development in religion. It is a movement toward a more intellectual understanding of faith (i.e., belief) and away from the understanding of faith as personal trust or fidelity (see Wisd. Sol. 11:26–12:2; 13:1-9; 15:1-6; IV Macc. 15:24; 16:18-23; 17:2).

It must be admitted that it is often impossible to dogmatize about the precise meaning of faith in writings of this category, because some are available only in translations of the original.

In Philo of Alexandria (20 B.C.–A.D. 49) the biblical basis is clear, though Philo drank deeply of the Greek spirit. He frequently contrasts reliance on the outward world and the things of sense (φαινόμενα) with trust in God; for him faith is essentially a turning away from the world to concentrate on God. This is not entirely negative, for Philo is convinced that he has a positive apprehension of reality. The unseen world is real to him; faith is a kind of certainty (βέβαια ὑπόληψις). He has learned this from Plato, but he has also learned from the OT more than Plato could teach him about the oneness, the creative sovereignty and providence, of God, the supreme reality. He believes, moreover, that the mind which is constantly striving to apprehend God may be granted a more immediate vision in the experience of ecstasy (ἔκστασις). His conception of faith, therefore, has more in common with the mystic's search for ultimate reality than with that personal trust in God as revealed, which is the hallmark of the Bible's pioneers of faith. Moreover, he retains enough of Jewish moralism to speak of faith as "queen of the virtues"; in a sense, he sees faith as one's duty to God.

For rabbinic Judaism faith meant confidence in God, the simple acceptance of God's existence and his good intention toward Israel. As with the OT, it was hardly at all speculative; and the answer, if people found faith difficult to maintain in the face of life's hardships, was Rabbi Akiba's dictum: "A man should habitually say all that the Merciful [i.e., God] does is for the best." This confidence was based on God's acts of deliverance in Israel's history, more particularly the deliverance of the Red Sea.

This faith moves over into the sense of loyalty, faithfulness, as in Hab. 2:4, or as in the case of Abraham. The rabbis, like Philo, often cite Abraham as an outstanding example of faith, quoting Gen. 15:6 but expounding it, with other passages—e.g., Gen. 22—to show that Abraham fully conformed to God's will. This is the overriding connotation to faith for the rabbis: obedience to the law in every detail.

This implies that for the rabbis, as for Judaism of the last two centuries B.C., a subtle shift of emphasis has taken place in the conception of God and incidentally of faith as well. For whereas in the OT faith is centered on God's saving acts in history and human experience, now the basis of faith is a written record. This means a kind of petrifaction of history, for canonized tradition instead of the events of history has become the vehicle of the divine revelation; God is a voice or a pen rather than a person. These are the seeds of the controversy which we meet in the writings of Paul concerning faith and works. There was need of a new prophet to rescue the concept of faith as personal response to God, and as the precondition of moral obedience rather than as identifiable with moral obedience.

The Qumran brotherhood, as revealed in the hymns of the Dead Sea Scrolls, had a conception of God's "deep truth" and of themselves as its children or inheritors. It is not clear whether this is simply the late Jewish veneration for the Torah, or whether it has the more mystic sense of revelation. This community may be contemporary with the NT, but the date is disputed. *See* DEAD SEA SCROLLS.

D. *CONCEPTION OF FAITH IN THE NT.* **1. The Jewish heritage.** The basic belief in God is always presupposed (Mark 11:22; Acts 16:34; 27:25; I Thess. 1:8; Heb. 6:1).

For the sense of belief in the word(s) of God or the written word of scripture, see: Luke 1:20; 24:25, John 2:22; 5:46-47; Acts 24:14; 26:27.

For faith as trust in God (the dominant meaning in the teaching of Jesus), see: Mark 2:5; 5:34, 36, etc.; II Cor. 5:7. More particularly, as trust in God's *power,* see: Mark 4:40; 9:23; 11:22-23; Luke 17:6; Acts 14:9; Rom. 4:17-20; I Cor. 12:9; 13:2; Heb. 11 *passim*; Jas. 1:6; 5:15.

For the meaning "obedience," see: Rom. 1:5; 6:17; 10:16; 15:18; 16:26.

For the close connection between faith and hope, see: I Thess. 1:3; Rom. 4:18; I Cor. 13:13; I Pet. 1:9, 21; Heb. 11:1.

For the meaning "faithfulness," see: Matt. 23:23; Gal. 5:22; I Pet. 1:7; 5:9; II Tim. 4:7; Heb. 11:7; Jas. 1:3.

2. The teaching of Jesus. For Jesus himself, faith was essentially trust in God. God is King and Father, and is lovingly present to heal and help man in his need and sin. Jesus' sense of the presence of God must be pronounced unique. His faith was, indeed, communion with God to which human experience offers no parallel, and the Christian doctrine of his divinity and unique sonship was later formulated to express this. The basis for this doctrine is his own teaching as recorded in the gospels. Critical treatment of the gospels must attempt to measure how much can reliably be attributed to the Master himself, and how much is the belief of the early church or the opinion of the evangelist. But in this matter of Christ's divine sonship—i.e., his unique relationship to God such as could be attributed to no other man—sane criticism can hardly reject as unauthentic three basic passages where Christ refers to God as Father in a sense which puts him alone in the category of Son: Mark 12:1-9 (this makes his sonship as unique and unrepeatable as Calvary); 13:32*b;* Matt. 11:27 (=Luke 10:22). *See also* SON OF GOD; FORM CRITICISM.

It is presumptuous to attempt to reconstruct the inner consciousness of Jesus. But it may be affirmed that his sense of his special relationship to God as Father is behind all his utterances about faith. God's fatherly presence is nearer than men conceive; miracles can be done, if only men would expect miracles (Mark 11:20-24). God is waiting to shower his gifts upon men, but men are so loath to receive them (Luke 11:9-13; 14:16-24; 18:1-8). Divine power is available to heal men's sicknesses, just as divine mercy longs to forgive men's sins (Mark 2:5-12; note the dialogue, and the contrast between the faith of the few [vs. 5] and the amazement of the majority [vs. 12] and the objections of an ecclesiastical vested interest [vs. 7]; cf. 3:1-6). It appears that Jesus was surprised at people's obtuseness and unwillingness to count on God's goodness and power to save (Mark 5:34, 36). On the other hand, he expressed appreciation when he found genuine faith (Luke 7:9) or penitence (Luke 7:50).

The opposite of faith is worry, so typical of mankind. The animal and plant creation simply relies on divine providence: if only men could follow that example, instead of being "of little faith," chary of trusting God! The secret is to give priority to God and his kingdom (Luke 12:22-32). Something like irritation seems to be attributed to Jesus over the fact that one distracted parent was too anxious to expect healing for an epileptic boy, and that the disciples whom he had trained had lost the power to put that father in touch with divine healing (Mark 9:17-24, 28-29). Similarly he rebukes the disciples after a storm (Mark 4:40), not simply for cowardice, but for losing faith—i.e., forgetting that God is near and his providence real. This incident throws light on the distinction between Jesus and his most intimate followers: no storm or crisis could shake his faith (cf. Matt. 14:31). The lack of faith of his fellow countrymen surprised him (Mark 6:6): how was it that people through small-mindedness could doubt the power of God, and refuse to recognize the prophetic word and wisdom bestowed upon him? On the assumption of Jesus' real humanity, there need be no doubt about the genuineness of his surprise on these occasions (it may be detected also in Luke 17:5-6, 17-18). Reflection on it may have led him to compare his own experience of human obtuseness with that of Isaiah, and to formulate the theory that lies behind Mark 4:11-12. Many scholars, however, regard this theory as due to the disappointment of some early Christian missionaries over the response to their preaching. However this may be, we may take his surprise as a further indication of the intimacy of his own communion with God, or of the depth of his own faith, as compared with that of his audiences.

God is King as well as Father; the kingship or kingdom of God is the other twin focus round which the teaching of Jesus moves. And faith in God's kingship meant for Jesus belief that through his ministry in Palestine, God was dynamically present as never before in Israel's history; in fact, his kingdom was then entering into human experience, was "at hand" (Mark 1:15; 9:1), or even "has come" (Luke 11:20= Matt. 12:28; Luke 16:16=Matt. 11:12; Luke 17:21 [cf. Luke 4:17-21]; *see also* KINGDOM OF GOD).

The teaching of Jesus is the laws of this kingdom. His "I say unto you" outdates the ancient laws to the same extent to which the presence of God's kingly rule outdates the prophecy and promise of it (Matt. 5:1-11, 17-48). His power to heal is the liberating power of God; his victorious attack on the evil that plagues human life (demons) is the overthrow of Satan's kingdom in order that God's kingdom may be established (Luke 10:1-11, 16-20; 11:14-23). His presence constitutes the kingdom, and his disciples are its citizens, for their response to his invitation is entry into the kingdom (Matt. 18:3-4; Mark 10:15; 12:34; Luke 14:21-23). It is the greatest of privileges (Luke 10:23-24). It may also be called the culmination of faith, or faith being transformed into sight—in fact, the vision of God (Luke 10:21-22). *See also* TEACHING OF JESUS.

3. Primitive Christianity. The teaching and ministry of Christ culminated in his death and resurrection, and the total impact of all this on the minds of his disciples generated the Christian faith. In its specifically Christian meaning "faith" is faith in God's decisive activity through Christ for man's redemption

(Acts 2:22-24, 32-33; 4:10-12; 10:37-43; 13:26-39; Rom. 4:24-25; I Pet. 1:20-21).

It was not a general belief in God, nor even in the saving activity of God as proclaimed in the OT; but in God as finally revealed in and through Christ. (The usage of the Greek verb with the prepositions εἰς and ἐπί—i.e., belief directed *into* or *upon* Christ—aptly expresses this.) For the NT, Christ is the new focus of faith.

It should not be forgotten, however, that although Jesus himself, as we have seen, spoke of faith mainly as faith in God as Father and King, he also called men to believe in himself. The focusing of faith on Christ was an element in his own ministry, and not merely a product of the Resurrection. In this point it is more than ever necessary to scrutinize the gospel records so that what was really the later conviction of the church is not wrongly attributed to him. But when every caution is taken, it must be allowed that many utterances of Christ did so direct men's attention and loyalty to himself that they constitute the nucleus or embryo of the fuller apprehension which the Resurrection made possible. The following verses may be so interpreted: Mark 8:34-38 (cf. Matt. 10:37-38); 9:37 (cf. Matt. 10:40); 10:29-30, 32*b*, 38, 45; 11:9-10, 29-33; 12:1-11, 35-37; 13:6*a* ("in my name"), 9*b* ("for my sake"; cf. Matt. 10:18), 13*a* ("for my name's sake"), 31-32; 14:17-25; Matt. 9:28 (where note "I am able," not "God is able"; this use of the first-person pronoun may, however, be due to the evangelist); 10:24-25, 32-33; 11:27-30; 16:17-19; 19:28.

In primitive Christianity faith meant, in the first place, acceptance of the gospel message (Acts 8:13-14; Rom. 10:17; I Thess. 2:13; John 20:31). The core of this message was that God's redemptive actions culminated in Jesus of Nazareth, whose divinely controlled ministry terminated in martyrdom, but who was authenticated as Messiah and Lord by his resurrection from the dead (Acts 2:36-38). On faith as acceptance of Christ's lordship (i.e., absolute, divinely given authority), and its relation to his resurrection, see Rom. 1:3-6; 10:9; and on faith in the Resurrection as faith in the activity (ἐνέργεια) of God, see Eph. 1:19-20. Faith was normally accompanied by baptism as the sign of repentance and guarantee of forgiveness and renewal by the Holy Spirit (Acts 2:38; 10:43; 18:8; 20:21). Faith "in the name of Jesus," or "through him," releases divine power to heal (Acts 3:16; 4:10; 9:34). He is the Servant of God, the Prophet of Deut. 18, the fulfiller of all God's promises (Acts 3:25), the Son of God (Acts 9:20), the only mediator of salvation (Acts 4:12).

Those united in these new convictions can be described as "the believers" (Acts 4:32; 11:21, where the aorist participle implies reference to the point in the past when the belief was attained—i.e., conversion; more commonly the perfect participle is used, implying the continuing attitude of faith [cf. Acts 15:5; 16:34; 18:27; 19:18; 21:20, 25]). The noun "the faith" is summarily used for these convictions—i.e., the fundamental kerygma (Acts 6:7; 13:8; 14:22; 16:5).

Gentiles also were included, for the "door of faith" (Acts 14:27) was opened to them as well as to Jews. What this meant for a typical non-Jewish community is illustrated in I Thess. 1-3. Their faith produced results ("work"; 1:3; 2:13); they lived a "life worthy of God" (2:12). It meant, basically, abandoning idolatry for the one true God, and trust in Jesus as their future deliverer (1:9-10). They could rely on the faithfulness of God (5:24; cf. II Thess. 3:3).

This faith, as evidenced at the earliest stage of the church's existence, may be summarized as follows:

a) Break from the past, from other religious allegiances (I Cor. 8:6; I Thess. 1:9*b*), from sin (Acts 3:19; Rom. 6:12-23). It meant repentance (Mark 1:15; Acts 2:38; 20:21; Heb. 6:1).

b) It is still belief in God's word, but that word has been personalized in Christ (Acts 11:17; 14:23; 16:31). A personal relationship to Christ is implied, even though the adequate expression of this had to wait for such moving reflections of Paul's experience as Gal. 2:16, 20; Phil. 1:21; 3:8-12; 4:13; II Cor. 1:20; 4:4-6 (cf. I Pet. 1:8).

c) Faith is not only the subjective attitude, but also the content of what is believed (Acts 6:7; Jude 3, 20; Eph. 4:5; I Tim. 1:19; 3:9; 4:6). This aspect is seen even in Paul (Rom. 1:5; 4:14 [where faith is parallel to law]; 10:8; Gal. 1:23; possibly also Gal. 3:23, 25). The meaning of faith in I Cor. 15:14, 17, combines both senses mentioned above.

d) The meaning of the verb πιστεύειν, "to believe," ranges from "attain faith"—i.e., be converted (especially in the aorist; Acts 4:4; 8:13; 9:42; etc.)—to "exercise faith" and "have faith"—i.e., not the activity but the state of being a Christian, not a Jew or a pagan.

e) It is the conviction that God has not only acted in the past history of Israel but also is acting now decisively and finally (Acts 2:17-21; 3:18-21; I Cor. 10:11*b;* Heb. 1:1-2).

4. The distinctive Pauline connotation. In Paul we find a new emphasis on the indispensability of faith. Only when a man has faith is he in a right relation with God, able to understand himself and to act rightly. Faith is not, as with Philo, the goal of man's religious development, but its beginning. "You stand fast only through faith" (Rom. 11:20). "Whatever does not proceed from faith is sin" (Rom. 14:23).

a. Relationship with God. Faith as means of right status with God ("reconciliation," καταλλαγή), as endowment with righteousness (δικαιοσύνη), is the sense in Acts 13:39; Rom. 1:16-17; 3:21-22; Gal. 2:16 (here "justified" is the verb cognate with the noun "righteousness"). *See also* RECONCILIATION; RIGHTEOUSNESS (NT).

The basic human problem is: How can a man be good, realize his ideals, attain righteousness? This may be treated, as in ancient Greece and by modern humanism, as a problem of independent ethics. For the Hebrews there was no ethics apart from religion, and so this problem was essentially a religious problem: man's goodness was formulated as conformity with God's will. It was not a problem of knowing what God's will is (cf. Socrates' thesis that virtue is knowledge, and that if people know what the good is, they will naturally do it; this visualizes the problem differently, and by religious standards superficially). God's will had been revealed for Israel in the law of Moses; all that was necessary was for every

Israelite to hear and obey. The inspiration to do so was the sense of gratitude to God for the gift of the law, and for all his other bounties. It rested with the free will of man, and there was no reason why man should not keep all the commandments. God had done his part, so to speak; for man the way was clear, and, though not always easy, not impossible.

To Paul this problem presents itself as more complex than this. The observable fact of human inability to achieve goodness required a deeper diagnosis. Paul is prepared to admit that all peoples have their laws, and individuals their sense of right and wrong, to guide them in their moral endeavor. What the Jews had was a particularly high and developed moral code (see Rom. 2). The baffling fact was that these codes have not actually resulted in high moral achievement. This was the argument from experience, not a theological dogma. Paul's doctrine of sin rests upon it (*see* SIN), and his conception of the gospel has its roots here too. For his Christian understanding enables him to regard the moral degradation of man (which he so powerfully argues in Rom. 1:18–3:20), not as an impasse or a *reductio ad absurdum* of human experience, but as the occasion of God's supreme saving activity. He would have agreed with that Jewish contemporary of his who put into one of the hymns of the Dead Sea Scrolls the sentiment: "No man can be righteous without Thy help."

But he would not have agreed with that earnest brotherhood that the old endowment of God's law and "deep truth" availed, even with the aid of a new exposition ("Teacher of Righteousness," or correct expositor). The "power for salvation" which Paul proclaims as good news (Rom. 1:16*a*) is the fact that God has taken upon himself responsibility for the desperate plight of the human race, and is offering his own righteousness to fill the gap left by man's manifest inability to achieve righteousness by his own endeavors. Man does not deserve this, and cannot earn it. It depends solely on the mercy of God and his compassion over man and concern that man shall be brought to perfection as his ultimate destiny (Rom. 9:15-16; 11:29-36).

To become aware of this, after recognition of the moral need (the knowledge of sin [Rom. 3:20]; the sinfulness of sin [Rom. 7:13*b*]), is what Paul means by faith. It is the only response men can make to God's superlative offer. But on the basis of this response everything in the way of religious and moral development becomes possible: "He who through faith is righteous shall live" (Rom. 1:17*b*); "peace with God" (Rom. 4:22–5:1); moral attainment, for the righteous, which begins as a divinely bestowed status or potentiality, is progressively actualized in moral growth (Rom. 5:17-21; 6:12-19; I Cor. 1:30).

II Cor. 5:17-21 is another main passage about this new life of reconciliation made possible by God's offer and Christ's humiliation to the sinful level (vs. 21*a*). Christian preaching is the announcement of this, with urgent appeal (vs. 20). For the same thought in the words of a later imitator, see Eph. 2:13-16; and for the final reconciliation, see Eph. 1:10.

In Phil. 3:5-9 Paul devaluates the privileged status of the Jew, and his own high merit according to Jewish standards, by rigorous self-discipline, etc. (which he does not here, as in Galatians and Romans, call "works," but "confidence in the flesh"), in comparison with that acceptance with God which comes from faith. We note the contrast between "my own righteousness" (i.e., self-made salvation, which by reference to the law could be estimated as of the very highest value, "blameless" [vs. 6]) and God's righteousness. Faith creates an entirely new perspective and standard of values. What before seemed right and of supreme worth now seems valueless (vs. 7). This transvaluation is "because of Christ." Knowing Christ and taking a new status of utter dependence on God (=faith [vs. 9*b*]) is now of "surpassing worth." It means sharing a new life and prospect, which is God's gift and a kind of resurrection (vss. 10-11).

Rom. 3:3-7 contrasts the divine faithfulness (πίστις) and truthfulness with human unbelief and falsity. The argument is inconclusive in its total context of Rom. 2–3, but it makes clear that God is the sure ground of man's faith. The Jews have not attained righteousness, and many things in the world and in human experience have gone wrong; but the fact of divine revelation (vs. 2) remains, and with it the privileged position of the Jews. They have misinterpreted it and their own privilege, but the true meaning of that revelation waits to be drawn out, and Paul proceeds to do this. He first establishes his argument about universal sinfulness (3:19-20, 23). Then he affirms the opportunity of righteousness for mankind by God's special provision. God's own righteous character has been manifested (vs. 21) in the experience of men—viz., in the life of Christ, more particularly his death (vs. 25*a*). This is already a historic event, but it is also divine activity. Moreover, it is not merely a past spectacle, but a continuing process ("is being revealed" [1:17], the present tense of this verb being significant) of communication of the quality of righteousness from its originator to his creatures. The means of receiving it on the human side is faith, and only faith (3:22, 25*a*, 26*b*, 28; cf. 1:16-17; 9:30-33; 10:4-9). It cannot be earned, even by those who have the law to guide them (3:20*a*); it is a free gift, the offer of divine grace (3:24; 4:16; 5:15-17). The law's function, Paul argues elsewhere, was not to inspire good conduct, but the negative one of revealing bad conduct in its true colors (3:20; 5:20; 7:7-13; Gal. 3:19-24).

This is the new insight Paul has contributed on the nature of faith, and it is his chief self-differentiation from Judaism. The importance of faith in his sense cannot be overstated. For it is the inauguration of the condition which means more than anything else to man: freedom from sin, and harmony with God. Man cannot cope with his major need apart from divine enabling; all he can do is to have what Paul calls faith. Wishes and prayers and effort ("works," whether moral or ritual) are of no avail; even the moral law does not convey moral power. Man must simply confess his helplessness and make himself open to the divine grace. This fundamental humility and willingness to depend on God, abandoning self-sufficiency and the effort to make oneself worthy, is faith in the Pauline sense. Eph. 2:8-9 succinctly states the essentials. There is a place for moral endeavor, the law has to be fulfilled, faith has to be energized by love; but Paul is concerned with a precondition, without which none of these other things is possible. To reject this is the unbelief exemplified in Israel (Rom. 9:27–10:4), and in all who choose to live their lives their own way—in Paul's terms, who prefer their own righteousness to God's. In the last resort man's fate depends on God (Rom. 9:16); but how loath human dignity is to admit this! As Paul himself admits, not all have faith (II Thess. 3:2).

b. The new creation. Faith then is basic in Christian experience. Christians are "the believers" indeed (I Cor. 1:21), but in a deeper sense now. In virtue of faith they are a new creation, a new society (II Cor. 5:17). They are incorporated "in Christ." This is what believing "in" or "into" Christ becomes in the Pauline interpretation (Phil. 3:9-10). In this new corporate reality conventional and inherited distinctions cease to matter (Gal. 3:26-28). It is the true posterity of Abraham, the realization of the final unity of mankind (Gal. 3:6-9, 14, 29).

Alternatively to men of faith being in Christ, Christ may be said to be in them (II Cor. 13:5; Gal. 4:19).

Again, the experience of being in Christ may be described as being in the Spirit (Rom. 8:1-4, 9-17; I Cor. 12:13; II Cor. 3:17-18; Gal. 3:2-5, 14). The Spirit means moral power—power even to carry out the commands of the law (Rom. 8:4; Gal. 5:16-18, 22-25). "In Christ" is a sphere in which righteousness is actually attainable (II Cor. 5:21*b*).

In more individual reference, it is ineffable communion with the risen Lord. Of his own intimate sense of Christ's personal control, Paul can write II Cor. 12:9; Gal. 2:20; Phil. 1:21. Of the possibility of all believers' realizing this intimacy, he writes Col. 2:6-7 (cf. Eph. 3:16-19). The life of faith is a Christ-possessed life, not one of striving for personal ideals, realizing ego capacities, etc. These latter attitudes toward life are mere boasting (Rom. 3:27; 4:2) or confidence in the flesh—i.e., human capacity (Phil. 3:3-4); they stultify the grace of God and the sacrifice of Christ (Gal. 2:21).

Paul sees in the sacrament of baptism, with its features of total immersion and re-emergence from the water, an apt symbol of the end of the old life and the beginning of the new (Rom. 6:3-11; Col. 2:12-13).

c. Freedom. Faith means freedom (Gal. 4:1–5:13) —freedom from wickedness ("former lusts"; Rom. 6:12-19; Eph. 2:1-5; Col. 3:5-10; I Thess. 4:3-9) and from other authorities which mankind acknowledges —e.g., moral law (Rom. 7:4-6; Gal. 3:23–4:7; for fuller explanation of the antithesis between faith and law, *see* LAW IN THE NT), natural law, fate, the power of the stars, etc. (Gal. 4:3, 8-9; Col. 2:20; *see also* ELEMENT).

d. Sonship. The new society of faith, inaugurated by God through Christ and empowered by the divine Spirit, is a divine society, not explicable by purely human considerations. Its members are sons of God, sharing the sonship of Christ (Rom. 8:14-17; Gal. 3:26; 4:4-7). *See* SONS OF GOD.

e. The content of the Christian faith. What was the content of the faith of these believers? A crucified Messiah, says Paul, in whom paradoxically the power and wisdom of God are made known (I Cor. 1:21-24; 2:5). From the secular point of view this is folly; it is not what men expect or can easily reconcile with their *Weltanschauung*. But it is the redeeming activity of God. God was in Christ reconciling the world to himself (II Cor. 5:19; Col. 1:12-20); lifting men out of the consequences of their sins (II Cor. 5:21*a;* Gal. 1:4; 2:20*b;* 3:13); making possible resurrection for men—i.e., new possibilities of life—as an ultimate consequence of Christ's resurrection (Rom. 1:1-4; 4:25; I Cor. 15:3-11; Phil. 3:10-11). These are the implications of the simpler statement that the object of faith is the lordship of Christ (II Cor. 4:5-6; Phil. 2:5-11).

f. Love. The moral effects of faith can be expressed in terms of love (ἀγάπη). Paul never argues this point; he assumes it. In a nutshell the connection is stated in Gal. 5:6: faith becomes active "through love." The preposition is somewhat ambiguous here; it may mean "by means of"—love, as it were, prompting every expression of faith; or it might signify the attendant circumstances. Love is the chief product of the Spirit in human lives (I Cor. 13; Gal. 5:22); and in this sense has more eternal significance than faith (I Cor. 13:13). Love can be described as the "fulfilling of the law" (Rom. 13:10*b*), which is also the work of the Spirit (Rom. 8:4). For the general connection of faith and love, see Eph. 1:15; 3:17; 6:23; I Thess. 1:3; 3:6; II Thess. 1:3; Philem. 5. *See also* LOVE IN THE NT.

g. Conviction. Paul can use "faith" in the sense of "conviction" (Rom. 14:1, 22-23). In this chapter weakness in faith means overscrupulous anxiety, the opposite of confidence (vs. 5*b*). Elsewhere in a similar discussion (I Cor. 8:7 ff; 10:29) Paul uses the term "conscience." The fact that he can use πίστις, "faith," in such a context indicates how fundamental faith was for him. It affected the whole of a man's behavior, and anything which has nothing to do with a man's faith is sin for him (Rom. 14:23).

5. The distinctive Johannine connotation. The Fourth Gospel has a distinctive conception of faith, parallel to the Pauline, but deviating from it through closer association with knowledge. For the Johannine writer, believing in Christ is tantamount to knowing Christ or knowing God (the noun is avoided, and the verb is used exclusively).

a. Basic ideas. The Prologue introduces the thought of bearing witness to Christ (vss. 7, 15), beholding Christ (vs. 14). Christ is veritably God in his self-communication to mankind. He is the Word of God and the Son of God, bringer of life and light, grace and truth—in other words, knowledge of God —of which he is the unique purveyor (vs. 18). The response of men to this witness is described as receiving Christ (vss. 11-12, 16), beholding (vs. 14), knowing (vss. 10, 18; cf. 3:11, and *see below*). The ultimate outcome of such response is sonship (vs. 12). But a negative response is also possible (vss. 10-11); the fact of human rejection of Christ is much emphasized in this gospel, which through its middle chapters traces a kind of parallel development of faith and unbelief, a judgment process set in motion by the impact of Christ upon human society, those who accept him electing themselves to true (eternal) life, and those who reject him in fact condemning themselves, though they do not realize it. See 3:16-21; 5:24-29; 6:35-40, 64-66; 7:40-52; 8:42-47; 10:26-28; 12:35-43 (cf. Mark 4:10-12; and *see* JUDGMENT).

The actual verb πιστεύειν, "to believe," is not prominent in the Prologue, but in vs. 7 it means acceptance of the message about the incarnation of the Word, which was a presentation of the knowledge of God hitherto unavailable, a revelation of God's glory, an impartation of divine grace and truth which surpassed even the giving of the law through Moses.

b. The significance of "witness," μαρτυρία. The God who willed his own revelation and the salvation of men ordained also the necessary attestation of his saving action. "There was a man sent from God, whose name was John. He came for testimony, to bear witness to the light, that all might believe through him" (1:6-7).

John the Baptist was the first witness, and due space is allotted him in the opening chapter, apart from the Prologue (1:29-35). Here the content of the Christian faith is summarily stated as the divine sonship of Christ, his endowment with the Holy Spirit and ability to impart it, and his efficacy as bearer or remover of the world's sin. The earliest disciples of Christ immediately are under constraint to bear witness that he is Messiah, King, Prophet, and Son of God (1:41, 45, 49). More general references to the witness are found in 3:11; 12:17; 19:35; 21:24 (cf. I John 1:2; 4:14), sometimes with simple assertion of its truth, sometimes with an indication of its effectiveness. From the episode of the woman of Samaria we learn how the honest expression even of hesitant and groping faith may cause faith in many (John 4:28-29, 39-42).

This vital witness is not purely human advocacy, even though men are its mouthpiece. It is ultimately divine (5:32-37), and deposited in scripture—i.e., the OT (5:39)—more particularly the words of Jesus (not yet regarded as scripture in the sense of the OT; 5:47). The assertion that God himself is the guarantor of the witness is made again in I John 5:7-12. Christian preaching is no less than God's calling attention to his own gift of eternal life for men, made available through his Son alone. When the Spirit is said to be the confirming power, as in this passage (vss. 7:8); I John 4:13-14; and in John's Gospel (15: 26-27); or when Christ so speaks of his own witness, the primary witness of God is implied.

It is not convincing to every hearer, but Christian preaching cannot give up this conviction (John 8:13-18). The effects of faith in men's lives may also be said to bear witness, apart from any spoken word, as when Jesus patiently claims that his "works" attest his Father's presence and saving power (John 10:25*b*, 38*b;* 14:10-11) and adds that those who believe will actually perform similar works to the glory of God (14:12-14).

c. Acceptance of the testimony—i.e., faith—in the main narrative of John's Gospel. It is worth while to set out first the Johannine conception of witness, because it is the objective factor to which faith is the corresponding subjective. Faith is the acceptance of the witness.

Nothing is more important than that the testimony should be heard and responded to. The urgency of *hearing* is underlined in this gospel (e.g., 4:41-43; 5: 24; 8:43; 14:23-24; 17:6-8). Failure to respond is also frankly recognized.

The first narrative of Jesus at work shows the disciples finding, seeing, and believing in him (1:35-51). The last (20:19-29; assuming that ch. 21 was the later work of a redactor) reaffirms this privilege of seeing and believing, and points forward to a faith which has no physical seeing as its basis. True faith is independent of material aids, as future generations of believers will exemplify (20:29, 31; cf. 17:20-21). To incipient faith is given a promise of heavenly vision and realization of the pre-eminence of the Son of Man (i.e., Christ as Redeemer), and unlimited spiritual power (1:50-51; 11:40; 14:12).

d. How faith arises. Faith results from witnessing a "sign" (σημεῖον; 2:11, 23). A sign in this gospel means what the other gospels call a "power" or "mighty work" (Mark 6:3-5, etc.). But it is more than a miracle in the sense of an abnormal or unprecedented event; it means something done or said by Jesus which makes people aware of the power of God operating through him; it is a particular manifestation of the divine glory which is the meaning of his incarnation (1:14). A sign occasions faith in those who witness it, though not in all (4:50-54; 8:30; 10: 42; 11:45-47; 12:9-11).

There is disparity between John and the other gospels here, insofar as in John signs are performed to evoke faith (or faith is evoked after a sign) whereas in the Synoptics miracles are performed only in response to faith. *See* MIRACLE; SIGNS IN THE NT.

For a description of how faith arises in the believer, note 17:6-8, though in place of psychological analysis we have an aspect of the determinism of this gospel: only those will attain faith who are "given" to Christ by the Father (cf. 6:37-40, 44). But we may say that, following an initial receptiveness, faith consists of keeping the teaching of Christ, which is the word or words of God. It is a much deeper thing than dependence on human opinions (5:44). Clearly John is not interested in how faith is produced so much as in its content. This is described as the "word" of Jesus in 2:22, where that word is an interpretation of a passage of scripture, or has some connection with a passage of scripture (Ps. 69:9). For scripture as the object of faith, see 5:39.

In these passages the Greek verb has the noun in the dative case, and the meaning is "place reliance on," a simple colloquial sense. But there seems to be also a movement toward a more intellectualized meaning, as in passages where "believe" is followed by an object clause or by the preposition "in," specifying the content of the belief. The logical end of this development is when "believe," πιστέυειν, is not distinguishable from "know," γινώσκειν. Thus the evangelist's comment in 2:22 refers to new meaning which could be discerned in scripture in the light of Christ's resurrection, and confirmation of belief in the authority by which he cleansed the Jerusalem temple and spoke of himself as an adequate substitute for it (cf. 4:21-26).

e. Jesus the object of faith. The meaning which stands out as of greatest significance is belief *in* Jesus, of which he is the object and which is specifically directed *into* him, an anomaly by comparison with normal Greek prepositional usage being used to bring out what is distinctive of Christian faith. 3:15-18 illustrates this well. This faith, which is the gateway to eternal life, is centered upon the Son of God (who is also the Son of man; vs. 14), whose earthly activity owes its origin to the divine love. It is also connected with the energy of the Spirit of God (vss. 5-8). It causes a new birth in the believer (vss. 3-8), and creates that life which in this gospel is called eternal, and is the comprehensive term for the sum of God's gifts and for the highest level to which man can attain (cf. 5:24; 6:47; 7:38; 20:31; I John 1:1-2).

We now have the main definition of the content or object of faith. This is illustrated many times, nowhere perhaps more movingly than in the discourse with the woman of Samaria, who is led away from her irreligious arguments and way of life to an understanding of true worship and true religion and to confession that the coming Messiah, the center of true religion, has in fact come and is revealing himself to her (John 4:26). Faith is experience of the climax of revelation. The object of faith is Jesus, who is Messiah of both Jews and Samaritans, but not confined in his significance to them. For the Samaritans here represent the whole non-Jewish section of mankind, and he is "Savior of the world" (vs. 42; cf. 9:35-37; 11:25-27).

But Jesus declares his conformity with his Father. All that he says and does is as the Father directs. Belief in him, therefore, is belief in his Father, God (5:19-27; 12:44, 49; 14:1, 6-11; 16:27-30; I John 2:23). Similarly, knowing is knowing both the Father and the Son (John 17:3; II John 9*b*).

The verb "believe" is used also in an absolute sense (cf. John 1:7, 50; 4:42, 53; 6:47; 11:15, 40; 14:29; 16:31; 19:35; 20:8, 25, 31*c*). This is often in passages where there is reference to seeing (e.g., 6:36; 11:40; 20:25-31), and in the judgment of some scholars faith is a form of vision. On the importance of seeing, see 12:45; 19:35; 20:8, 29. This sense of faith with no reference to its object is set in relief in the central chapters by contrast with the half-belief (7:12, 26, 35; 12:42-43), mere opinion (7:24; 8:50), or outright unbelief (7:47-52; 9:40-41; 11:45-53), of others.

Faith is the primary privilege and obligation (6:29, 35-40; 12:36 [cf. I John 5:4-5]). Conversely, not to believe is the greatest tragedy; in fact, it is sin (John 1:10-11; 16:9), and as such carries dire consequences (3:18, 36; 8:24). How much it costeth not to follow (believe in) Christ!

6. Definition of faith in Hebrews. In Heb. 11:1 we have a concise definition of faith: it is the solid reality of hope, conviction about the invisible world (the word ὑπόστασις, "solid reality," has the philosophic sense of "being, nature," as in 1:3: "the very stamp of his nature"; but the meaning in 11:1 may be the more concrete one: "title-deed" as Moulton-Milligan's Vocabulary suggests). This is somewhat Platonic, but the subsequent illustrations are in the manner of Hellenistic Judaism, which added to its fundamental belief in Yahweh's goodness to his worshipers (vs. 6*b*) the more philosophic notion of his existence in the noumenal world, the antithesis of the phenomenal world (vs. 3*b*). Faith means such awareness of God (vs. 27*b*) and that ideal world as enables men to endure all kinds of tribulations (vss. 25, 32-38; 12:2-3) and to live in detachment from the things of time and sense, even pronouncing judgment on them (11:7*b*), realizing that eternal salvation involves quite different conditions. It means the conviction that one is an heir of the eternal city (vss. 10, 14-16), taking God's promises seriously.

There is nothing distinctively Christian in this, but in 12:2 it is related to the main theme of Hebrews by the description of Christ as "pioneer and perfecter of our faith."

Obviously this conception of faith has a large element of hope in it, as in I Peter (cf. I Pet. 1:3, 7-9, 21).

7. Other NT connotations of faith. The well-known passage in the Letter of James (2:14-22) disparages faith as mere belief, a nominal monotheism which neither affects behavior nor calls forth personal trust; even devils may be said to have faith in this sense (vs. 19)! It hardly needs pointing out that this is far from the Pauline conception. It has been argued that James is controverting Paul here; on the other hand, the view is being revived that James's letter was earlier than those of Paul. James magnifies conduct at the expense of faith, and vss. 2:21*a*, 24, explicitly contradict Rom. 4; so that Paul's teaching on faith and works seems to be presupposed. Possibly the situation James was addressing was one in which antinomianism was a danger because the strong moral interest of Paul had been misunderstood. The moralism of James represents the continuing influence in the church of the ethics of Hellenistic Judaism.

The Pastoral letters, Jude, and Revelation reflect conditions of the second or third generation, when the term "faith" can be used to denote the basic doctrine of churches that are now becoming conscious of themselves in a nonbelieving environment. The new society must build itself upon this foundation; it is a precious trust for which they must be prepared to struggle (Jude 3, 20). It is a divine secret (mystery) imparted to them (I Tim. 3:9). It must be preserved (II Tim. 4:7; Rev. 14:12). Some have given it up (I Tim. 5:8, 12; Rev. 2:13). The ethical interest appears in the linking of faith with a good conscience, or with love (I Tim. 1:14, 19; 2:15; 3:9; 6:11). How different from the way in which the creative teacher of an earlier generation had brought out the moral implications of faith (Rom. 6)! In these writings the noun "faith" is more prominent than the verb "to believe." But the use of the verb also is affected by this second-generation atmosphere, for it is twice used in the passive in the sense of being entrusted with the gospel (I Tim. 1:11; Tit. 1:3). The same or a very similar tendency is to be noted in the usage of the noun in Acts, where it is often hard to say whether faith is the believer's attitude toward Christ, or the doctrine of the churches (e.g., Acts 13:8; 14:22; 16:5). It is something to be *obeyed* (6:7).

Bibliography. A. Schlatter, *Der Glaube im NT* (3rd ed., 1905)—still the fundamental treatment; W. H. P. Hatch, *The Pauline Idea of Faith,* Harvard Theological Studies, II (1917); Bousset-Gressmann, *Die Religion des Judentums* (3rd ed., 1926); J. Pedersen, *Israel, Its Life and Culture,* I (1926), 336-48; Strack-Billerbeck, *Kommentar zum NT* (1928), on Rom. 4:2-3; G. F. Moore, *Judaism* (1927-30); C. H. Dodd, *The Bible and the Greeks* (1935), pp. 42-75; H. A. Wolfson, *Philo* (1947); C. H. Dodd, *The Interpretation of the Fourth Gospel* (1953), pp. 151-86. E. C. BLACKMAN

FALCON [איה, *'ayyâ, cf.* Akkad. *ayau, unidentified bird;* Arab. *yu'yu'*, hawk; LXX ἰκτῖνος, kite (Lev. 11:

Courtesy of James B. Pritchard

1. Egyptian stone relief showing a falcon, a form of Horus, standing above a frame in which is a three-towered palace and a serpent which represents the Horus name of the king (*ca.* 3000 B.C.)

14 *and probably* Deut. 14:13); γύψ, vulture (Job 28:7); Vulg. *vultur*, vulture; Targ. (Onq.) טרפיתא, hawk]. Alternately: KITE (Lev. 11:14 KJV; Deut. 14:13); VULTURE (Job 28:7 KJV). A small or medium-sized bird of prey of the family Falconidae, of the genus Falco, of which several species have been observed in Palestine (*Falco biarmicus feldeggii* and *tanypterus, Falco peregrinus, Falco tinnunculus, Falco subbuteo subbuteo*). It is only a surmise, though a reasonable one, that איה refers to these birds (cf. "according to its kind" in Lev. 11:14). In Job 28:7 their keen sight is alluded to, which is, in fact, a characteristic of the falcons.

Fig. FAL 1. W. S. McCullough

FALL, THE. The Bible speaks of the "fall" of individuals into sin, a continuing occurrence (I Cor. 10:12; I Tim. 3:6-7; 6:9; Heb. 4:11; Jas. 5:12). It also knows of the fall of the wicked angels (II Pet. 2:4; Jude 6; cf. Slavonic Enoch 29:4-5), which was connected in the intertestamental literature with the myth of the marriage of these angels with women (cf. Gen. 6:2, 4). But in Christian theology "the Fall" signifies the transgression of Adam and Eve recorded in Gen. 3. The word itself does not occur in this sense in the canonical scriptures (but cf. II Esd. 7:118). Although the story of the Garden appears to have had little effect upon OT thought, it dominates the NT doctrine of the origin of sin (cf. Rom. 5:12-19; for details, *see* Sin §§ 1*c*, 2*b*, 3*c*). A discussion of the Fall must therefore concern itself primarily with the Paradise account, which needs to be considered from several points of view.

It has long been apparent to critical scholarship that the background of the Genesis narrative is to be found in mythological elements common to the traditions of various ancient Near Eastern peoples. The biblical account itself furnishes the strongest evidence that this was the case. It contains conceptions which are entirely strange to the standpoint of Yahwism. E.g., Gen. 3:22 describes God as being fearful of man's "equality"; vs. 8 speaks in gross anthropomorphism of Yahweh's walking in the Garden; the speaking (and walking!) serpent is entirely foreign to the Hebrew conception of nature; the name Eve appears to be ultimately derived, despite the folk etymology of vs. 20, from the name of a Semitic serpent-goddess. Moreover, Hebrew religion located the abode of Yahweh in Canaan or on Mount Sinai, not in a garden in the East. The motifs of a garden of the gods (*see* Eden, Garden of; Paradise), with its mysterious trees, are common in ancient mythologies, and the Tree of Life appears in various pictorial representations.

There can be little doubt that the Hebrews knew the cosmological legends of the ancient Near East. Some of the Babylonian and Sumerian myths offer interesting parallels to the biblical account. It may be that the Akkadians knew a temptation tradition similar to that of Genesis, if we may judge by a cylinder seal in the British Museum which depicts a man and a woman (god and goddess?) seated before a palm tree and reaching out for its fruit, with a standing serpent coiled behind the woman as if whispering in her ear. This interpretation has, however, been challenged. More certain parallels are to be found in the Gilgamesh Epic and in the Myth of Adapa.

The theme of the Gilgamesh Epic is the search for immortality. Such a hero as Gilgamesh may possess great strength and wisdom, being half divine himself, but he is never allowed to forget that the gods have reserved immortality for themselves. The story comes to a climax in Tablet XI, which tells of his being given two chances to obtain immortality but losing them both, first through weakness and second by a cruel accident in which a serpent steals a life-giving plant from him.

In the Adapa story the god Ea, who is motivated by jealousy, deliberately misleads his devotee Adapa (which may mean "man") into refusing the gift of immortality when it is offered to him by Anu, the chief of the gods.

It should be obvious that none of these traditions parallels the biblical story of the Fall closely enough to be considered a direct antecedent. As a matter of fact, the differences are almost as striking as the similarities. Probably the most important difference is the entirely distinct morality of the Genesis story, which attributes man's failure to his own sin, and not to his weakness or to fate or to the envy of the gods (except in the secondary material). Another striking difference is that the basic Genesis material is concerned with the obtaining of knowledge instead of the obtaining of life. In the Sumero-Akkadian mythology man could have wisdom equal to that of the gods (cf. the Atrahasis Myth), but he was denied life; in the biblical story he might have obtained life, but he was denied a "divine" knowledge.

It seems very likely that the Hebrews were familiar with a polytheistic legend current in Palestine in which jealous deities were struggling to keep man from stealing their prerogatives, and in which a SERPENT god or demon, at odds with them, introduced man to the secret of a forbidden tree, through which he was enabled to become like them.

Nothing is more evident than the fact that the Yahwistic writer of the basic fall story in Gen. 3 rejected almost the entire polytheistic background of his material in order to transform it into an account that was in keeping with the high moral and spiritual insights of his religion. The serpent appears (without explanation of where he comes from or who he is; he is certainly not SATAN—a late interpretation) as the insidious enemy of both man and God, who are not at odds but live in perfect harmony until he intervenes. The Yahwist omits mention of the Tree of Life. He is concerned solely with the TREE OF KNOWLEDGE. This may have appeared in polytheistic mythology as a magic tree, imparting a kind of occult knowledge, but in the biblical tradition it was divested of magical associations and became nothing more than the object by which man's obedience to God was tested.

Critical scholarship agrees that the third chapter of Genesis, like the rest of the Paradise story, has undergone a long literary development, and that the text has suffered a degree of corruption. Without attempting to delineate the details of literary analysis (see the Commentaries), one ought at least to make clear what the basic Yahwistic account contained and what elements came from a variant tradition which perhaps existed in a parallel recension and was added by a redactor.

The Yahwistic writer himself was responsible for most of Gen. 3:1-19, 23, with perhaps minor glosses from a later hand. He depicts the approach of the serpent, Eve's naïve rejoinder to his query, the serpent's deliberate lie, the woman's fascination with the fruit, her sin and that of her husband, the resulting shame and attempt to hide from Yahweh. He adds the details of the ensuing inquest and the sentence passed upon the culprits for their misdeeds. The etiological motivation of this account is striking. It attempts to answer many basic questions: Why are people ashamed of their nakedness? Why does the serpent creep in the dust, and why does mankind hate him? Why do women suffer when they bear children? Why are they dominated by their husbands? Why does a man have to toil so hard for his bread?

Although some scholars have denied it, the fall story also answers the questions of the origin of sin and the origin of death. The former is especially evident from the succeeding chapters, which show plainly that in the Yahwist's mind man had contracted a fatal tendency toward spiritual corruption. The origin of death appears in the condemnation of man to return to the dust from which he was taken (vs. 19). It is true that the story does not suggest that man was created immortal; immortality was perhaps to have been the reward of obedience. But even so, man's disobedience brought the penalty of death that had been threatened (2:17; 3:3), despite the serpent's assurance to the contrary. The threat of immediate death was not carried out, but in the end the result was the same, as God left sinful mankind to return to its natural end.

The redactor evidently felt that this statement of the reason for human mortality was not sufficiently explicit. Making use of a tree-of-life tradition (cf. 2:9), he pictured Yahweh in 3:22, 24, as being envious of man, who actually had obtained divine knowledge. Determined to ward off this threat of equality, Yahweh now deprives man of immortality by barring him from the Tree of Life. These verses are in glaring conflict with the purer view of Yahweh's character in the original account. It may be, as later exegetes have suggested, that in the finished form of the story the redactor intended the reference to man's equality to be understood ironically. This is doubtless an interpretation that is valid for biblical theology as a whole.

The story of the Fall must also be appreciated for its psychological perceptiveness and theological profundity. It is superbly simple and effective. No human being who has himself sinned can escape from discerning that Eve and Adam's sin is his own. The story has pedagogical effectiveness because every reader, however unsophisticated he may be, instinctively knows that the ambitious self-assertion, the delusion of injured prerogative, the morbid curiosity for something undiscovered and forbidden, the reckless decision against unresisting obedience, the overpowering shame that comes over the sinners as their brazen courage leaves them, are things that he too could experience. He knows that he too would hide in the trees of the Garden, would tell Yahweh half-truths to disguise his guilt, and would blame others for his sin.

Even though they reject the traditional view of the Fall as a historical event, modern theologians are able to turn to the Genesis story for an insight into the real paradox of human existence. In Gen. 2–3 Adam appears as generic man, האדם (*see* ADAM). He thus represents human nature as created in the divine image—i.e., as related to nature and yet rising above it through the free spirit which his Creator gave him. He also represents mankind as owing unquestioning allegiance to God, as finding the meaning of his existence in harmony with his Creator and not in an independent self-sufficiency. Further, Adam's temptation to snatch a knowledge which as a mere creature he could never have, born of anxiety and distrust, is typical of the temptation in which every man stands at every moment of his existence. Finally, the crumbling of the rebel's bravado as he is summoned before God symbolizes the hollowness of every human pretense over against his Maker.

Thus, quite apart from the theory of a hereditary transmission of the effects of Adam's fall, it should be apparent that Adam's real theological importance is his representation of all mankind in its defiance of God's will. Paul, while affirming a historical connection in Rom. 5:12-19, puts the emphasis on Adam's representative and symbolic function as the counterpart of Christ. As the Apocalypse of Baruch puts it, "Each of us has been the Adam of his own soul" (54:19).

The Paradise narrative helps us to understand the real nature of sin. Sin is possible only because man has been created in God's image. He has a freedom of self-assertion which is his divine endowment. Sin comes when man uses this freedom to measure himself against God, trying to be independent of his control. Immediately man discovers his terrible mistake. He learns that his freedom is only a finite freedom, and he can never really be as God. He has obtained a practical knowledge of the possibilities of good and of evil (*see* TREE OF KNOWLEDGE), but in a way that his Creator never intended, through a life of pain and spiritual bondage which is ever a continual frustration of the true greatness for which God has made him.

Bibliography. In addition to the relevant sections in the commentaries and books on biblical theology, there are valuable monographs on the subject of Paradise and the Fall. One of the most valuable of these is P. Humbert, *Études sur le récit du paradis et de la chute dans la Genèse* (1940). Other important titles are: H. T. Obbink, *Het bijbelsch Paradijsverhaal en de Babylonische bronnen* (1917); N. P. Williams, *The Ideas of the Fall and of Original Sin* (1927); J. Begrich, "Die Paradieserzählung," *ZAW,* L (1932) 93 ff; K. Budde, *Die biblische Paradiesgeschichte* (1932); T. C. Vriezen, *Onderzoek naar de paradijsvoorstelling bij de oude Semietische volken* (1937); J. Coppens, *La connaissance du bien et mal et la péché du Paradis* (1948).

S. J. DE VRIES

FALLOW DEER. KJV translation of יחמור (RSV ROEBUCK) in Deut. 14:5; I Kings 4:23—H 5:3.

The context in Deut. 14:5 points to a ruminant, and probably to a member of the DEER family. Bodenheimer holds it to be the Fallow Deer (*see* FAUNA § A2*e*iv), a smaller deer than the Red Deer (*ca.* thirty-six inches high at the withers), of yellowish-brown color, found originally in the Mediterranean area and in Persia; two species, *dama dama* and *dama mesopotamica,* are recognized. But C. R. Conder contended, on the basis of bones found at Carmel, that it was the Roe, *capreolus capreolus.*

W. S. MCCULLOUGH

FALLOW GROUND [ניר] (Jer. 4:3; Hos. 10:12, where the absolute form of the noun is used as an accusative of cognate meaning with the verb נירו; the construct form is used only in Prov. 13:23, where the Hebrew text is meaningless as it stands). Fallow ground is usually broken up with plow and harrow, but it is left unseeded for the purpose of destroying weeds and insects and allowing the fertility of the soil to be restored.

The custom of letting land lie fallow was common among primitive people, and the practice was regarded as serving a religious function. The religious law of Israel required that the cultivated land should lie idle every seventh year (Exod. 23:11). There is no evidence that a fallow year was observed during any considerable part of Israelitic history. Lev. 26:34-35 would seem to imply that it was not.

H. F. BECK

FALSE APOSTLES [ψευδαπόστολοι]. Persons who came to Corinth (II Cor. 11:13) claiming to be "servants of Christ" (vs. 23); Paul denounces them as servants of Satan disguising themselves as servants of righteousness (vss. 13-15). They evidently boasted of their Jewish origin (vs. 22). They came with letters of recommendation from other churches; when they left, they seem to have asked for such letters (II Cor. 3:1; for this custom, see Acts 18:27). It is not clear that they were either Judaizers or antinomians in principle, but Paul says bluntly that they preach "another Jesus" and a "different gospel" and live in a "different spirit," and he implies that their motives were selfish and the moral results of their influence bad (II Cor. 11:4, 6, 18-20; 12:20-21). They were largely responsible for the rebellion against Paul in the church at Corinth.

F. V. FILSON

FALSE CHRISTS. Persons who will imitate Jesus Christ, and who by their pretensions and miracles, and presumably by their false teachings as well, will deceive people and lead them astray (Mark 13:22; Matt. 24:24; cf. Luke 21:8). In some respects the second beast of Rev. 13:11 ff is a false (or pseudo-) Christ. However, false Christs should be differentiated from the satanic Antichrist, who is to be the personal adversary of Jesus Christ at his second advent. But *see* ANTICHRIST.

M. RIST

FALSE PROPHET. *See* PROPHET.

FALSE WITNESS. *See* WITNESS.

FAMILIAR SPIRIT. Divination by means of communication with the spirit of the dead (necromancy) was known and practiced in the ancient Near East (cf. the Gilgamesh Epic, Tablet XII, where Gilgamesh conjured up the spirit of Enkidu in order to inquire about the state of the dead in the nether world). The OT employs two technical terms, אוב and ידעני, and one descriptive term, דרש אל המתים, to denote "necromancy." The exact meanings of the first two words (used as a hendiadys eleven times against the use of אוב in only four passages) are not definitely known. While both the KJV and the RSV render ידעני with "wizard," the former translates אוב as "familiar spirit," and the latter as "medium" (but "spirit" in I Sam. 28:8 and "ghost" in Isa. 29:4). The third term (lit., "one who consults the dead") is found only twice in the OT (Deut. 18:11; Isa. 8:19), and in both cases in conjunction with אוב and ידעני.

The technique used by the necromancers (male and female) is nowhere described in detail. In the story of the witch of Endor (I Sam. 28), Saul asked his servants to seek out for him a "woman who is a medium" (lit., a "woman who possesses an אוב"). When Saul arrived at Endor, he said to the woman: "Divine for me by an אוב [RSV 'a spirit'], and bring up for me whomever I shall name to you." The witch conjured up the spirit of Samuel, and when she saw it, she exclaimed: "I see an אלהים [RSV 'a god'] coming up out of the earth" (the word *ilu,* "god," is used in Akkadian in reference to the spirits of the departed; *see bibliography*). In the story of Endor the spirit of Samuel is depicted as conversing with Saul in a clear voice, but Isa. 8:19; 29:4 characterize the utterances of the spirits as coming up from the ground in a chirping, muttering, or whispering sound.

The art of necromancy is prohibited in the OT

(Lev. 19:31; Deut. 18:11; cf. Isa. 8:19), and its practitioners, as well as those who seek guidance from them, are liable to the death penalty (Lev. 20:6, 27; cf. I Chr. 10:13). The kings who drove the necromancers out of the land are praised (cf. I Sam. 28:3, 9; II Kings 23:24), and those who tolerated them are severely condemned (cf. II Kings 21:6; II Chr. 33:6).

See also DIVINATION.

Bibliography. On the Akkadian word *ilu,* see A. L. Oppenheim, *The Interpretation of Dreams in the Ancient Near East* (1956), p. 223. Cf. the Ugaritic expression *'ilm arṣ,* "ghosts in the nether world," in C. H. Gordon, *Ugaritic Handbook* (1947), I Aqhat 112, 141. I. MENDELSOHN

FAMILY. Since marriage was patriarchal—i.e., father-centered—among the people of the Bible, the family was a community of persons, related by ties of marriage and kinship, and ruled by the authority of the father. The biblical family, especially when marriage was polygamous, was large. It included the father, mother(s), sons, daughters, brothers, sisters (until their marriage), grandparents, other kinsmen, as well as servants, concubines, and sojourners (aliens). The Israelites were encouraged to have large families, for economic as well as religious reasons. The family grew both by birth and by covenants made with other groups and individuals. The solidarity of the family was maintained by its organization around the father figure and by the application of the principle of retributive justice in terms of corporate (family) responsibility.

The family functioned as a religious community, preserving past traditions and passing them on through instruction and worship. Forces that threatened the integrity and security of the family, such as economic change and the influence of alien cultures and religions, were vigorously opposed by many of the biblical writers. The importance of the family is to be seen in the projection of this concept beyond the boundaries of the family as such. It then refers to Hebrew tribes, the nations of Israel and Judah, foreign nations, and to all of Israel, viewed as a community of faith rather than a nation. In the NT it identifies the Christian community as well. The family was endangered in this period by the conflict between paganism and the Christian faith. The origin of the Christian church is associated with worship among the families and in the homes of the first Christians.

1. Terminology. The Bible uses several terms to express the idea of family. The most common is בית (lit., "house"); in the NT related words are οἰκία ("family") and οἰκιακός ("relatives"—i.e., members of the family group). The OT uses a second term with the meaning "clan" or "family": משפחה. The Greek word πατριά signifies "family," "clan," "kinship." In several of these we may observe that the idea of "house" or "household" stands out. The first named, בית, may indicate at times "house" as a place, "house" as the occupants of the home—i.e., "family." So we read of Abram's trained men, "born in his house" (Gen. 14:14; cf. 17:12-13). In Exod. 1:21 the word refers to "families" which God "gave" to the Egyptian midwives. In one instance the word refers to a family of linen workers (I Chr. 4:21). The meaning of "family of descendants" appears quite often. The "house of David" is one illustration of this use (I Kings 12:19).

The word οἰκία, "household, family," appears in Matt. 12:25; 13:57; Mark 3:25; 6:4. "Those of his household" translates the word οἰκιακός, "relatives," while members of the household (family) are identified in Isa. 58:7 LXX; Gal. 6:10; Eph. 2:19; I Tim. 5:8, the second and third of these referring to members of God's family (*see* § 5*c below*). The word משפחה, "clan" or "family," suggests the larger family group in Gen. 24:38—the house of Abraham's father and kindred in the city of Nahor. It simply means the various families of the Israelite elders in Exod. 12:21; and in Lev. 20:5 it designates any family which is implicated in the practice of human sacrifice. The Greek word πατριά may also be considered here. Joseph is said to be of the lineage (πατριά) of David (Luke 2:4); and "every family in heaven and on earth" receives its name from the Father (Eph. 3:15). In the book of Tobit the term simply means "kinsman" (5:12), and similarly Judith's ancestry is said to be the same as that of her husband—i.e., the same tribe and family (Jth. 8:2).

2. The extent of the family. The Hebrew family was an inclusive community, consisting not only of immediate members closely related by ties of blood or marriage. It included also slaves, concubines, foreigners, and hired servants. Abraham circumcised every male of his house, slaves born of slave parents or bought in the market from a foreigner, as well as his son Ishmael (Gen. 17:23, 27). Jacob's family is described as including his sons, their little ones, their wives, his sons' sons, his daughters, and his sons' daughters, "all his offspring" (46:5-7), "sixty-six persons in all," not counting his sons' wives (vs. 26). A family could also have foster fathers and nursing mothers (Isa. 49:23).

a. Emphasis upon many children. CHILDREN, especially sons, were extraordinarily important in the biblical family. This emphasis is especially conspicuous in the patriarchal period of Hebrew history, as far as numbers are concerned. The Hebrew people were commanded to be fruitful and multiply, as was the first human couple (Gen. 1:28; 9:1). The size of families would vary greatly, especially when we recall the variation in the number of wives a man might marry. King Ahab is said to have had seventy sons (II Kings 10:1) in Samaria. The evidence indicates that the families of biblical people were by no means small. They grew by procreation, through one or more marriages.

b. Other forms of growth. Marriage is actually a covenant between two families. This covenant unites them and, by the process of merging, produces a larger kin group. Thus growth may occur in this way. The affair of the sons of Jacob and Shechem involved an alliance between two families of different ethnic groups (Israelite and Hivite) through marriage (Gen. 34:8-22). The family grew also by the purchase of slaves, the birth of slaves to slaves already owned, and doubtless the exercise of protective care over various sojourners and impoverished people who sought help. Marriages with more than one wife in effect created families within families, in that the children of one mother would live in her quarters and be set apart from those of another woman with the same husband (*see* MARRIAGE § 1*c*). While the control of the father prevailed over all subfamilies whose children he had begotten, these mother-centered communities would tend to stand apart from one another. Each such group would add slaves and servants to serve its own needs. An instance of the inclusion into the family group of the whole clan of a mother's family shows how enlargement could occur (Judg. 9:1-2).

3. Status and role of family members. In the family community the functions and relationships of its various members are defined by custom and, to a degree, enforced by codes of law. Central, of course, is the role of the father in the patriarchal family. By no means negligible, the mother's relation to this community is characterized by special tasks and responsibilities. Sons are of supreme importance in carrying on the family's name. Their sisters play a subordinate role until their marriage, when they join the family of their husband. Other family members and kinfolk play a part which is not always clearly identified.

a. The father. The authority of the father stands out in the pages of scripture. The "father" may be a grandfather or a great-grandfather. A father has the right to offer his son as a sacrifice (Gen. 22); he must teach his sons (Prov. 1:8); he can destroy members of his family if they entice him from his allegiance to his God (Deut. 13:6-10); and his compassion for his children is used to describe the divine mercy (Ps. 103:13; see also Luke 16:24: "Father Abraham"; John 4:53). The father begets, instructs, disciplines, and loves his children. For further details, *see* FATHER.

b. The mother. The word for "mother" in the OT is אם, probably derived from the root אמם, "be wide, roomy," from *ummu,* "womb." The mother, although having the primary function of producing children, has considerable authority over the family's life. E.g., Sarah directed Abraham to cast out Hagar (Gen. 21:10), and he complied, although reluctantly. Rebekah advised and abetted her son in his theft of the birthright from his brother Esau (27:11-17). The mother of Micah directed the manufacture of an image to be put in a shrine in her son's house (Judg. 17:2-6). The mother exhibits love and care for members of her family also. The prophet speaks of the comfort that a mother gives as indicative of the compassion of Israel's God (Isa. 66:13); while the psalmist emphasizes a mother's care by declaring that if it ceases, the Lord will provide what he lacks (Ps. 27:10).

Respect and obedience were also demanded toward the mother (see Prov. 1:8; 6:20; 10:1; 15:20; Ezek. 22:7, where respect for one's mother is enjoined or disrespect is condemned). Laws which demand such respect and obedience are to be seen in Exod. 20:12; Lev. 19:3; Deut. 22:15. Disrespect and disobedience are prohibited in Exod. 21:15, 17; Lev. 20:9; Deut. 21:18; 27:16. The love which is displayed toward a mother may be detected also.

Thus the mother, the essential bearer of children, and the wife, who satisfies the sexual desires of her husband, is also the object of love and honor. She possesses authority over her family which appears to be second only to that of the father. She loves her children and instructs them even as she disciplines them. She is concerned for their code of behavior and for their relation to God. If she is the mother of a king, she may well seriously influence religious affairs of the state.

c. Sons. Second in importance only to the father in the Hebrew family are sons. Descent is reckoned through the male—i.e., through a man's sons (see, e.g., genealogies in Ezra 10:18 ff). They determine the perpetuation of his name and personality. The longing for sons is therefore understandable. Sons are to be disciplined and carefully trained in the traditions of the community and in the meaning of wisdom (Deut. 8:5; Prov. 3:12; 13:24; 19:18; 29:17). A son is told:

> With all your heart honor your father,
> and do not forget the birth pangs of your mother.
> Remember that through your parents you were born;
> and what can you give back to them that equals their gift to you? (Ecclus. 7:27-28).

Besides designating the male offspring of a particular father and mother, the word "son" (בן) signifies descendants or membership in a particular tribe or nation (Gen. 10:21; 19:38; I Chr. 5:23; II Chr. 29:13; Ezra 1:3-7; titles of Pss. 42–49; 84–85; 87–88; etc.). "Sons of God" occurs to show a close, nonphysical relation (Deut. 14:1; Ps. 29:1 ["heavenly beings"]; Isa. 43:6; III Macc. 6:28; Matt. 5:45). It refers also to membership in a guild or order, such as the prophetic order (I Kings 20:35; II Kings 2:3, etc.; 6:1; 9:1; Amos 7:14), and to a person possessing a certain quality or trait, such as power, as "mighty man" (lit., "son of power"; I Sam. 14:52; I Kings 1:52). It has another figurative use also, when it occurs to indicate the age of a person, a "son of five hundred years" (Gen. 5:32; cf. Gen. 7:6; 50:26; Num. 32:11; Josh. 14:7, 10; etc.). But as a word to identify a particular member of the family, it involves the obligation of respect, obedience, the willingness to accept the task of continuing the family line, and in the case of the first-born son (*see* INHERITANCE; BIRTHRIGHT) the duty of training for leadership as the prospective head of the family. *See* SON OF GOD; SON OF MAN.

d. Daughters. This term, בת, is employed to identify the female child born of a woman (Gen. 30:21) and is often parallel to "son" in the OT (Gen. 5:4, 7). In Gen. 34:17 a girl is called by this name by her brothers, as well as her father. The book of Ruth uses it in referring to "daughter-in-law" (1:11-13, etc.). It may name women of a particular city or land, such as "daughters of Zion" (Isa. 3:16; cf. Num. 25:1; Josh. 17:6; Isa. 49:22; Lam. 3:51; etc.). For an account of the place of women (and daughters) in the Hebrew community, *see* WOMAN.

e. Other categories. The Bible notes the relation of brother and sister and has terms to express each. The word used for "brother" is אח, and for "sister," אחות. In a polygamous family the former also identified a half brother and a nephew, "son of a brother." It may describe membership in the same tribe (Num. 16:10; 18:2, 6; II Sam. 19:13), or membership in the same national group (Exod. 2:11; 4:18; Deut. 15:12; Neh. 5:1, 5, 8; Isa. 66:20). The term for "sister" singles out in some instances the female child of the same father but a different mother (Gen. 24:30; Lev. 18:11; Ezek. 22:11). It is parallel to "bride" in Song of S. 5:1-2 (cf. Gen. 20:12). With respect to each other, members of the family in either classification have no special functions or obligations that are not imposed upon them because of their sex in a patriarchal family. Other members of the family are not specifically identified. Kinsmen are mentioned, although their precise relationship to the family in the limited sense is usually not defined. The word used is עם, "people" (Gen. 49:29; Num. 27:13; Judg. 5:14), where being gathered to one's people is expressed. "Uncle" and "aunt" occur also, in the words דוד and דדה, derived from the root meaning "beloved" (see Isa. 5:1). The use of these two words does not reveal any special function in the family community. Other classes represented in the Hebrew family, perhaps especially in those which were wealthy, include aliens, slaves, servants, and the needy, who may or may not have been kinsmen.

4. Solidarity of the family. The family was held together by the central, dominant father figure, supported by the influence of the mother and wife in many cases. During the early pastoral period of biblical history the large, patriarchal family was able to flourish, checked only by famine and disease. With the development in Canaan (Palestine) of an agricultural, urbanized culture, the Hebrew family, as every other facet of the social order, was required to make adaptations to new conditions. This threatened a breakdown of cherished ways of living. To meet this, ancient customs were reaffirmed and the ancient faith was used to undergird them.

a. Authority of the father figure. The function of the father has previously been briefly indicated. He symbolized tradition, the family ancestry, its cult, its power of survival, and its hope for the future. He came under bitter attack when he failed in this function (Ps. 78:8; Amos 2:7). The father as the ancestor of the family or clan became the center of preserved and recited tradition, so that his piety and devotion to God could be made an example for his descendants. So the stories of Abraham, Isaac, and Jacob (Gen. 12 ff) embodied recitals of the mighty acts of God and of the heroic deeds of paternal ancestors. The father as the visible symbol of the greatness of Israel's (and each family's) past helped to preserve the family from radical modification.

b. Concept of corporate solidarity. Corporate (family) responsibility to protect the family's honor and name through the practice of blood revenge was an effective instrument in biblical times (II Sam. 3:27; 16:8; II Kings 9:26; etc.; *see* AVENGER OF BLOOD). Each member of a family was urged to fight for the defense of his brethren, sons, daughters, wives, and homes (Neh. 4:14). And each member was obligated to protect the entire family by the uprightness and correctness of his own conduct. In a time of economic distress an entire family might be sold for debt (Matt. 18:25). On the positive side, whole families may enjoy the experience of redemption (Acts 11:14; 16:33).

c. The function of religion. In ancient Israel, religion played a positive role in the determination of family solidarity, as noted above with respect to the function of the father. Under the impact of Canaanite culture, Israel's faith, through the consolidation of family ties, sought to survive in terms of the old pastoral ideal. But the infiltration of concepts and behavior patterns sanctified by the flourishing fertility cult of Canaan worked against such a survival. Intermarriage wth alien peoples also affected this effort to preserve the ancient ways. Drastic steps were taken to eliminate the danger from this source by the enforcement of wholesale divorces (Ezra 9:2; 10:3, 16-17; Neh. 13:23-30), with a resulting destruction of many families for the sake of the purity of the faith. A similar problem confronted the families which were involved in the Christian movement of the first century A.D. This movement caused dissension in many families. By forsaking his own family for the sake of Christ, a man will have eternal life (Matt. 19:29). Hatred of members of one's family is demanded (Luke 14:26). Luke adds that the faithful will be delivered up (betrayed) by parents, brothers, kinsmen (21:16). These words point to a radical disruption of family life, calling for reconstruction on a new basis. In a period of transition, religion becomes a divisive, not a cohesive, force.

5. Wider use of the concept of family. So meaningful was the biblical experience of the family that its use was extended to make it apply to the Hebrew tribes, to the nations of Israel and Judah, to foreign nations, and to Israel viewed as a covenant community under God. It was applied to the Christian people as well.

The importance of the family in biblical society and its function as the center of religious instruction account for the application of the term to Israel and to the community of Christ as the family of God. In the chapter that contains the essence of the so-called New Covenant the prophet writes of the time when Yahweh will be the God "of all the families of Israel, and they shall be [his] people" (Jer. 31:1). Early Christian writers continue the use of this figure by speaking of the Christians as comprising "God's family" (I Tim. 3:15; I Pet. 4:17).

6. The family of Jesus. The allusions to the family of Jesus are sometimes colored by the purpose of his teachings and the motive of the compilers of the gospels which contain them. Jesus' mother and brothers are referred to (Matt. 12:46); but in this context he declares that his family is whoever does the will of God (vs. 50). The next chapter of Matthew refers to his mother and brothers and to his sisters as well (13:55-56). The names of Jesus' brothers are given, but his sisters are not mentioned by name (Mark 6:3). The Gospel of John declares that Jesus' brothers did not believe him (7:5).

7. The family and the early church. It is probable that the first churches were house-churches—i.e., they were communities of Christians who shared the Lord's Supper, sang hymns, read scripture, and prayed in various homes. The place of women in the history of this period in the church's life is significant (*see* WOMAN). Meetings in house-churches, or at least in homes, are reported (Rom. 16:5). Paul lived and worked in the home of Aquila and Priscilla at Corinth. He writes to them and refers to the church in their house (I Cor. 16:19). Christians are urged to demonstrate their faith by providing for their own families. One who fails to do this is worse than an unbeliever (I Tim. 5:8). All believers are members of the household of God (Eph. 2:19), which is the household (family) of faith (Gal. 6:10). Marriage and the family are important in the life of the early church, especially so because of the pagan forces that threatened them. The language of family relations is transferred to the vocabulary of religion to describe God and man's relation to him. We may note such terms in this context as "Father," "children," "sons," "brothers."

See also GOD, OT; GOD, NT; MARRIAGE; SEX; WOMAN; CHILD; WIDOW; DIVORCE; FATHER.

Bibliography. T. G. Soares, *The Social Institutions and Ideals of the Bible* (1915); E. B. Cross, *The Hebrew Family* (1927); D. Jacobson, *The Social Background of the OT* (1942). *See also* the bibliographies under MARRIAGE; WOMAN; SEX.

O. J. BAAB

FAMINE [כפן, רעב, רעבון (*alternately* HUNGER; KJV *alternately* DEARTH); λιμός (*alternately* HUNGER; KJV *alternately* DEARTH, FASTING); *cf.* νηστεία, fasting]. The word is used to express varying degrees of the general condition of scarcity of food:

a) A time of general famine (Job 5:20).

b) A particular famine, due to DROUGHT, in the

Courtesy of the Metropolitan Museum of Art

2. An Egyptian wall painting showing an emaciated desert herdsman leading three oxen in an offering of gifts to Ukh-hotep (*ca.* 1971-1928 B.C.)

Courtesy of the Service des Antiquités, Cairo

3. Egyptian relief, showing starving people; from Saqqarah, Fifth Dynasty (*ca.* 2500-2350 B.C.)

time of Abram (Gen. 12:10), of Isaac (26:1), of Joseph in Egypt (seven years in 41:27; universal in 41:54), of Ruth (1:1), of David (three years in II Sam. 21:1; seven [LXX three] years threatened in 24:13), of Elijah (I Kings 18:2), of Elisha (II Kings 4:38; seven years in 8:1), of Claudius (universal; Acts 11:28).

c) Famine in a besieged city: Samaria (II Kings 6:25; 7:4); Jerusalem (II Kings 25:3; Lam. 4:8-10).

Famine is listed among punishments sent by God (Isa. 51:19; Jer. 14:13-18; Amos 4:6) and among apocalyptic woes to come (Mark 13:8).

Since rainfall in Palestine is marginal and irregular, crop failure through drought (Hag. 1:10-11), blight, or locusts (Amos 4:9); loss of cattle and herds (I Kings 18:5); and the ravaging of the land in warfare (Isa. 1:7; 3:1, 7) quickly led to starvation. Cannibalism was not unheard of in the extremities of a siege (II Kings 6:28; Lam. 4:10).

Figs. FAM 2-3. R. B. Y. SCOTT

FAN. *See* FORK.

FARE. The translation of שכר in Jonah 1:3. The term (elsewhere WAGES; HIRE; REWARD for service and faithfulness) is used here in connection with the purchase by Jonah of passage on a ship bound for Tarshish.

FARMER [γεωργός, soil-worker]; KJV HUSBANDMAN. Alternately: TENANT (Matt. 21:33 ff and parallels); VINEDRESSER (John 15:1). A tiller of the soil. The word is used in general of one who raises crops (II Tim. 2:6; Jas. 5:7), and in the parable of the wicked tenants (Matt. 21:33 ff; Mark 12:1 ff; Luke 20:9 ff) and the allegory of the vine and its branches (John 15:1 ff; cf. I Cor. 3:6-9) of those who produce grapes.

See also AGRICULTURE; VINE.

FARTHING. *See* MONEY § 3*c*.

FAST, FASTING. The origins of fasting as a moral and religious discipline are obscure. Its widespread connection with rites of mourning caused Herbert Spencer to seek its origins in the custom of the leaving of food and drink with the dead that they, instead of the living, might make use of them. Another scholar sought the origin of fasting in the discovery of primitive man that abstinence from food and drink would induce a state of susceptibility to visions and dreams in which direct access to the realities of the spiritual world could be found. Fasting has also been said to be nothing more than preparation for the sacramental eating of holy flesh in a ritual meal. No clue to the origin or original purpose of fasting is to be found in the biblical literature, and it is probably best simply to describe its usage on the basis of the biblical references to it. For the Bible, where, in accordance with the prevailing oriental custom, it must denote complete abstinence from food, fasting can be an expression of any strong emotion or grief. It is connected with mourning, repentance, calamity, and urgent supplication. It can be a spontaneous public or private observance, though, beginning with the postexilic period, Judaism developed set fasts at regular times of the year. Fasting as a private, individual act of devotion also became extremely popular in postexilic times, and, though neither Jesus nor the early church laid down rules for fasting, it was taken for granted as a religious discipline by them.

1. Terminology
   a. In biblical Hebrew
   b. In NT Greek
2. Fasting before the Exile
   a. Fasting by individuals
   b. Public fasts
3. Fasting after the Exile
   a. Public fasts
   b. Private fasting as a work of merit
   c. The Prophets on fasting
4. Fasting in the NT
   a. Jesus' teaching on fasting
   b. Fasting in the early church

Bibliography

1. Terminology. While most of the references to fasting in the OT employ one verbal root and its derivative noun, other words or phrases may also be used to convey the idea of fasting. In the NT one root, in either its verbal or its nominal form, is used.

a. In biblical Hebrew. The Hebrew word used most frequently to denote fasting is the noun צום (Neh. 9:1), which is derived from the verb צום (II Sam. 12: 21, 23). The noun and the verb, in typical Semitic fashion, may be used together—"to fast a fast" (II Sam. 12:16). The uses of the root in other Semitic languages, as well as in Hebrew, indicate that its primary meaning has to do with complete abstinence from food. It is this root which predominates in the pre-exilic narrative literature, in the prophetic books, and in the Psalms. Parallel words or phrases, used infrequently, are לא אכל לחם, "not eat bread (I Sam. 28:20); לא ברה לחם, "not eat bread" (II Sam. 12:17); and כנע, "afflict oneself" (I Kings 21:29). The most frequently used synonym is ענה נפש, "to afflict one's soul" (Lev. 16:29). This phrase is the technical one for fasting in the Priestly Code, and tends to become standard thereafter. Once a noun, תענית, from the root "to afflict," is used in the OT, and this noun came to be used widely in postbiblical Hebrew (Ezra 9:5). The Aramaic adverb טות, "fastingly, hungrily," is also used once in the OT (Dan. 6:18—H 6:19).

b. In NT Greek. The verb "to fast" in both the LXX and the NT is νηστεύω (Matt. 9:15; Luke 5: 33). It always denotes fasting as a religious practice. The noun for "fasting" is νηστεία (Matt. 17:21), and it almost always denotes fasting as a pious discipline. Paul, however, uses the noun in two instances simply to denote hunger brought about by necessity (II Cor. 6:5; 11:27). The latter indicates that the basic meaning of the root is "to do without food," and this is supported by the use of the noun νῆστις, from the same root, which simply means "hungry" or "not eating" (Matt. 15:32; Mark 8:3). The noun ἀσιτία (Acts 27:21) and the adjective ἄσιτος seem to bear no religious connotation. The verb απέχομαι, "to abstain, to hold off from," seems to be used of abstinence from certain kinds of foods rather than of fasting as such (Acts 15:29; I Tim. 4:3). Its use is not, however, restricted to abstinence from foods (I Thess. 5:22; I Pet. 2:11).

2. Fasting before the Exile. Though fasting was undoubtedly practiced from the earliest times in Israel, references to it in literature that can with certainty be dated before the Exile are not numerous. Many of the references to it in stories of events of the period before the Exile are in sources which, as written documents, must be dated later. Fasting must simply have been taken for granted in the earlier period, and the greater number of references to it in the later literature indicates a growing conviction of its meritoriousness as a pious practice.

a. Fasting by individuals. There is no indication that fasting, in itself, was considered, in the period before the Exile, to be a meritorious pious practice. The mention of fasting by individuals is always connected with some particular occasion, and fasting is usually accompanied by other expressions of self-humiliation, particularly by the wearing of sackcloth. The purpose of such fasting seems to have been to excite the pity and compassion of God, whether in moments of distress or in moments of penitence. This is true, certainly, of the narrative in which fasting is most frequently mentioned, the account of David's distress at the illness of the child conceived by Bathsheba as a result of his illicit affair with her (II Sam. 12:16-23). The surprise of David's retainers at the king's behavior after the child's death indicates that fasting was a normal mourning custom. The motive of exciting the divine compassion also lies behind the penitential fast of Ahab after Elijah's indictment of him and Jezebel for their behavior in the incident of Naboth's vineyard (I Kings 21:27).

Fasting must also, from very ancient times, have been employed as a preparation for the attempt to receive communications from God in dreams and visions and by other such means. Saul, e.g., fasted in connection with the attempts to receive such a communication which culminated with his visit to the woman necromancer at Endor (I Sam. 28:20). While the motive behind them is probably primarily that of legendary exaltation of the miraculous powers of saintly men, the references to the fasting of Moses and Elijah in connection with their encounters with God indicate that fasting was one of the means by which men prepared themselves for the receiving of divine communications (Exod. 34:28; I Kings 19:8).

b. Public fasts. It is not until after the Exile that any record of set fasts for the whole community is found. This is not, however, to be taken to mean that there were necessarily no such fasts. The question, e.g., of whether or not the Day of Atonement, the occasion of a set, public fast (*see* ATONEMENT, DAY OF), was observed prior to the Exile, is one which cannot be answered on the basis of the available evidence. It is not likely that such an observance was artificially invented by the circles responsible for the Priestly Code.

Nevertheless, the fact remains that the only public fasts mentioned as having taken place in the pre-exilic period are spontaneous ones, arising out of the specific needs of specific occasions. It was undoubtedly the custom to fast at times of mourning, and we hear of such fasting in connection with the deaths of Saul and Jonathan (I Sam. 31:13; II Sam. 1:12). Public fasts, like the fasts of individuals, could also be means of urgent supplication of divine aid and compassion, particularly before war or after calamity in battle (Judg. 20:26; I Sam. 14:24; II Chr. 20:3). Fasting could, for the group as well as for the individual, also be the means of expressing repentance (I Sam. 7:6). Though part of the plot of Jezebel against Naboth and therefore hypocritically proclaimed, the fast mentioned in I Kings 21:9, 12, shows that fasting was an expression of penitence by the community for wrongdoing in its midst. The only fast of pre-exilic times which could be interpreted as a definitely set occasion of the year is the one mentioned in connection with Baruch's reading of Jeremiah's scroll (Jer. 36:6, 9). The passing reference to it does not, however, provide sufficient evidence for a definite decision. Moreover, the reference to this fast may very well be part of material added to an originally simpler narrative in line with a tendency to magnify the solemnity and importance of the occasion upon which Jeremiah's words were read to the king.

These pre-exilic public fasts could be either spontaneous group expressions of deep emotion (I Sam. 31:13) or officially proclaimed by the king (I Chr. 20:3). Custom apparently determined the length of a fast, which might last for a week (I Sam. 31:13) or, as is still the custom among the Muslims on the days of the holy month of fasting, be discontinued at sundown (II Sam. 1:12). As in the case of individual fasts, public fasts from food might be accompanied by other expressions of grief or remorse (Judg. 20:26; I Sam. 7:6; II Sam. 1:11).

3. Fasting after the Exile. It was in the postexilic period that the stated public fasts of later Judaism came to be observed and that private fasting came to be a popular expression of piety.

a. Public fasts. Spontaneous fasts on occasions of distress or mourning continued in later times. Such fasts could be means of earnest supplication proclaimed by a leader in the community (Ezra 8:21-23; I Macc. 3:47; II Macc. 13:12). They could also, as is reflected in the late story in Jonah, be expressions of repentance (Jonah 3:5), and undoubtedly continued also to be a means by which the community besought the divine compassion at times of calamity (Esth. 4:3, 16). The prophetic book of Joel reflects the way in which a disaster such as a plague of locusts could provide the occasion for a solemn fast, which was not only an expression of supplication at a time of dire need but also a repentant pleading for mercy in the day of God's visitation of his people (Joel 1:14; 2:12, 15). Fasts such as these continued to be accompanied by such other means of self-affliction as weeping and the wearing of sackcloth and ashes.

The postexilic movement that resulted in the welding of the Jews into a unified, worshiping community centered around the temple in Jerusalem was responsible for the establishment of set days of fasting in the calendar. It may be that such days originated and were observed in earlier times, but their universal and established observance among the Jews was the result of the movement toward a normative Judaism that followed the Exile. Four such stated fasts are mentioned in the book of the prophet Zechariah (Zech. 8:19; cf. 7:3, 5). The conclusion of the book of Esther refers to the fast in preparation for PURIM, which, it is claimed, originated in the events recounted in that book (Esth. 9:31; cf. 4:3, 16).

It was the Day of Atonement (*see* ATONEMENT, DAY OF) which, though it may well have been less widely observed earlier, became the most prominent occasion of fasting in postexilic Judaism (Lev. 16:29, 31; 23:27, 29, 32; Num. 29:7). It was on this day that fasting was an expression of penitence accompanying Israel's solemn confession of her sins and the ritual through which atonement was sought. In the provisions laid down for the Day of Atonement in the Priestly Code, fasting is referred to as "afflicting the soul." Though it is dated at a different time from that of the Day of Atonement, the fast mentioned in Neh. 9:1 would appear to be a similar stated occasion upon which the community corporately expressed penitence for its sins.

b. Private fasting as a work of merit. Fasting by individuals continued, in later times, to be a means by which mourning, penitence, urgent supplication, and other such moods could find expression (Ezra 10:6; Neh. 1:4; Dan. 9:3). Fasting was also still thought of as an effective preparation for the reception of divine communications in visions (Dan. 10:3). As time went on, however, fasting came to be a formalized expression of piety in Judaism, and, with or without some specific occasion of distress, was an accepted act of devotion (cf. Pss. 35:13; 69:10). It was the custom of the pious to fast on the second and fifth days of the week (Ta'an. 12*a;* Luke 18:12; Did. 8:1), and the especially devout might fast even more (Jth. 8:6). The value of the discipline of fasting is pointed out in the apocryphal and pseudepigraphal Jewish literature (Tob. 12:8; Test. Reuben 1:10; Test. Simeon 3:4; Test. Judah 15:4; Test. Iss. 7:3; Test. Joseph 3:4; 9:2), and the NT reflects the way in which fasting had come to play so large a part in the piety of Jewish groups such as the Pharisees and the disciples of John the Baptist (Matt. 6:16; Mark 2:18). The Manual of Discipline of the Qumran community also illustrates how special groups within Judaism were given to the practice of fasting. Indeed, in the early years of the Christian era fasting came to be so much identified with the Jews that the Emperor Augustus is said to have boasted that he fasted more than a Jew (Tac. Hist. V.4). The emphasis on fasting in Judaism sprang more from a desire for meritorious living in line with the ethical emphasis of the OT than it did from the ascetical emphasis which came into Christianity from Greek dualism. The latter motive was not, however, entirely absent from Hellenistic Judaism, especially in Alexandria.

c. The Prophets on fasting. The only reference to fasting that could at all be ascribed to one of the great pre-exilic prophets is found in Jer. 14:12. The absence of other pre-exilic prophetic pronouncements on the subject must be due to the fact that fasting did not occupy the prominent place it did in later Judaism. The other references to fasting in prophetic books, aside from Joel (*see* § 3*a above*) are from the period of disillusionment and strife which followed early postexilic attempts to re-establish Israel in her homeland (Isa. 58:3-4; Zech. 7:5). As might be expected, given the general tone of prophetic teaching, the prophets did not condemn fasting as such, but inveighed against the insincerity with which it was being practiced (cf. Joel 2:12-13).

4. Fasting in the NT. The NT both provides evidence of Jesus' attitude toward fasting and shows how he and the earliest Christians, against the background of first-century Judaism, took it for granted as a pious practice.

a. Jesus' teaching on fasting. The two dominical sayings in which fasting is mentioned indicate that Jesus' attitude was in accord with the prophetic insistence on sincerity in religious observances and also that his conviction of the close connection between his own mission and the coming of the kingdom of God left no time for attention to the lesser details of pious practice.

Jesus maintained, in the same vein as Isa. 58:3-4, that fasting, like any other expression of devotion, is something done to the glory of God, not a means by which the admiration of men is to be sought (Matt. 6:16-18; cf. Luke 18:9-14). It is to be noted that fasting is not, in itself, condemned. The emphasis is one that is consonant both with prophetic teaching and with Jesus' own sayings on other subjects: God looks, not upon outward actions, but upon the disposition of the heart. The worth of fasting, as of any other act, lies in the devotion of which it is the expression. Without such devotion it is, of itself, meaningless.

The second saying of Jesus on fasting carries a different emphasis. Just as the Lord's Prayer was the result of a request that he, like other religious teachers, give his disciples direction in prayer, this saying resulted from a request that he, like other teachers, give his disciples some rule on fasting (Matt. 9:14-15; Mark 2:18-20; Luke 5:33-35). In line with the note struck in the saying now preserved in the Matthean Sermon on the Mount, Jesus refused to lay down any specific regulation on the nature or frequency of fasting for his disciples. The reason given for this is that the way in which the kingdom of God is breaking through into human history in his presence and ministry leaves room only for joy and thankfulness. There is no time for concentration on lesser things. Though the latter part of this saying, the assertion that the time for fasting will come when the bridegroom is gone, may have been added under the influence of Jesus' death, its presence in the gospels was undoubtedly influential in the rise of the tradition of a pre-Easter fast in the Christian community.

Given the fact that he and his disciples seem to have been faithful in their observance of the rites and customs of Judaism, it is probable that Jesus did keep such fasts as the one connected with the Day of Atonement. Indeed, however the Matthean account of his temptation may have been expanded in the course of its transmission, it could be recounted of him that he did fast at times of spiritual crisis (Matt. 4:2; cf. Mark 1:13). But his teaching on the subject was in line with the prophetic tradition and with his own eschatological outlook.

b. Fasting in the early church. The only clear references in the NT to fasting as a religious act in the early Christian community associate it with times of solemn prayer, particularly with the setting apart of officers in the church (Acts 13:2-3; 14:23). The occurrences of the word in the Pauline letters seem simply to denote going without food at times when there was none to be had (II Cor. 6:5; 11:27). There can, however, be no doubt that fasting did soon come to be regarded by the Christians as a commendable pious practice. Evidence of this is found in the tendency to add references to it to the text of the NT, the Textus Receptus containing allusions to fasting which are absent from the earliest MSS (Matt. 17:21; Mark 9:29; Acts 10:30; I Cor. 7:5). Literature of the subapostolic age indicates that the pre-Easter and prebaptismal fasts came early to be widely practiced, and Christians could be exhorted, like Jews, to fast twice in the week—on Wednesdays and Fridays, however, instead of Tuesdays and Thursdays (Did. 8.1).

Bibliography. E. B. Tylor, *Primitive Culture,* I (1871), 277, 402; H. Spencer, *Principles of Sociology,* I (1876), 170, 284-85; W. R. Smith, *Religion of the Semites* (2nd ed., 1901), p. 434; J. A. MacCulloch in J. Hastings and J. A. Selbie, eds., *Encyclopedia of Religion and Ethics,* V (1912), 759-65; I. Abrahams, *Studies in Pharisaism and the Gospels: First Series* (1917), pp. 121-28; G. F. Moore, *Judaism,* II (1927), 55 ff, 257 ff; H. L. Strack and P. Billerbeck, *Kommentar zum NT aus Talmud und Midrasch,* IV (1928), 77-114. M. S. Freiberger, *Die Fasten im alten Israel* (1929). J. A. Montgomery, "Ascetic Strains in Early Judaism," *JBL,* LI (1932), 183-213.

H. H. GUTHRIE, JR.

FASTS AND FEASTS. *See* FEASTS AND FASTS.

FAT. *See* SACRIFICE AND OFFERINGS § A2*a*.

FATE [דרך (KJV WAY), מקרה (KJV THAT WHICH BEFALLETH *in* Eccl. 3:19; EVENT *in* Eccl. 2:14; 9:2-3), מוה (KJV HABITATION *in* Jer. 49:20; 50:45), עת (KJV TIME), פקדה (KJV VISITATION)]. That which is one's lot or fortune in life. In the Bible "fate" usually has reference to the inevitable fact of death, which comes alike to the wise and the foolish, the rich and the poor, the righteous and the wicked, the pious and the irreverent (Ps. 49:13; Eccl. 2:14; 3:19; 9:2-3). Man is counseled to live his life in the face of it (Eccl. 2:24; 3:12-13).

For the biblical writer fate is directly related to the sovereign will of God. There is no fatalistic concept, such as the Greek μοῖρα or the Muslim *kismet.* God rules the world, personally and directly, determining the fate of all things (cf. Isa. 45:1-8; Amos 3:6; Matt. 10:29-30; Luke 12:24-28). Man's life is in God's hands. (Among the later rabbis it was common belief that man's life and fortune were determined from year to year by judicial procedure in the supreme court above.) While the Jews believed in foreordination, as Josephus avers (Jos. Antiq. XIII.v.9), it was always maintained so as to leave man ultimately responsible for his destiny. God, in his providence, determines what shall befall a man, but not whether he shall be righteous or wicked.

The mystery of the divine rule was ever a problem. A theory of theodicy was developed—blessing for the righteous, adversity for the wicked—but the Hebrew discovered theodicy did not accord with experience. Job and Ecclesiastes appeared as a protest against such a view. Apocalyptic sought a solution to the inequities of life in future judgment and the eschaton. The biblical author ultimately solved the problem by faith. Life could not be explained in terms of rewards and punishments, but God was found to be sufficient for every need (cf. Job 19:25-27; Ps. 73:23-26; Rom. 8:35-39; II Cor. 9:8-10), and the rewards of the spirit found to be infinitely greater than any physical misfortune (cf. II Cor. 4:7-11). Calamity became a summons to repentance (Luke 13:1-5), and death became the gateway to life (I Cor. 15:51-57; Phil. 1:21-23).

Bibliography. G. F. Moore, *Judaism in the First Centuries of the Christian Era,* I (1927), 408 (note 1), 454-58; J. Hempel, *Gott und Mensch* (2nd ed., 1936), pp. 199-233; D. B. MacDonald, *The Hebrew Philosophical Genius* (1936), pp. 85-93.

V. H. Kooy

FATHER [אב, *cf.* Assyrian *abhu,* decides; πατήρ].

1. The immediate male ancestor
2. A more remote ancestor
3. "Gathered to the fathers"
4. An honorary title or term of respect
5. The originator or prototype of a class or condition
6. A name for God

1. The immediate male ancestor. The father of the family demanded honor and obedience, and his authority could not be questioned. When Abraham was directed to sacrifice his son Isaac, the son did not demur (Gen. 22; cf. II Kings 3:27). The law enjoins children to honor their father and their mother (Exod. 20:12; Deut. 5:16; Ecclus. 3:1-16). Death may be the penalty for cursing a father or for striking him (Exod. 21:15, 17). The father could sell his daughter as a slave (vs. 7). A father might destroy members of his own family if they enticed him from his faith (Deut. 13:6-10). He was responsible for the conduct of the required religious observances and ceremonies, such as circumcision (Gen. 17:27). He gave religious nurture to his children and provided for their physical safety (Deut. 1:31; Job 1:5; Hos. 11:1-3). He was the teacher of his sons and their glory (Prov. 1:8; 17:6), and he must therefore be respected and heard (19:26; 30:11). The father loves his children and rejoices over their uprightness (Ps. 103:13; Prov. 23:25; Jer. 47:3). The father grieves over his dead son (II Sam. 18:33), because he knows he cannot leave the son behind to carry on his name (Ecclus. 30:4).

2. A more remote ancestor. "Father" may refer to the forefathers of an individual or a community, as well as to the immediate father (Gen. 28:13; 32:9; I Kings 15:11; 19:4; II Kings 19:12; etc.). The term is commonly applied to ancestors of the entire community of Israel. Abram was told that he would be the "father of a multitude of nations" (Gen. 17:4); the God of Israel's fathers promised the land of Canaan to their descendants (Deut. 27:3). Those who heralded the entrance of Jesus into Jerusalem used the words: "Blessed be the kingdom of our father David that is coming!" (Mark 11:10; see also Luke 3:8; 16:24; John 6:58; 7:22; Rom. 4:1; I Cor. 10:1; Jas. 2:21).

3. "Gathered to the fathers." To signify death as well as some kind of continuation of the family after death in the underworld, the phrase "slept with the fathers" or "gathered to the fathers" is encountered. "David slept with his fathers" (I Kings 2:10; cf. Deut. 31:16; II Kings 22:20).

4. An honorary title or term of respect. Micah said to the Levite: "Be to me a father and a priest" (Judg. 17:10; cf. 18:19). Elisha the disciple addressed Elijah the teacher prophet: "My father" (II Kings 2:12). Similarly, the king of Israel so addressed Elisha (II Kings 6:21; 13:14); and David called Saul his "father" (I Sam. 24:11; cf. II Kings 5:13; Isa. 22:21). "Fathers" is a title applied to older members of the Christian community, equivalent to "elders" (I John 2:13). This honorary title should be reserved for God, one writer declares (Matt. 23:9*a*).

5. The originator or prototype of a class or condition. Spokesmen for the Rechabite group named Rechab as their father in the sense of "founder" (Jer. 35:6); and Jabal was the "father" of tent-dwellers and cattle-raisers (Gen. 4:20). Jubal was the "father" of the musicians "who play the lyre and pipe" (Gen. 4:21). Phinehas is named as the father of the priestly class (I Macc. 2:54), and Abraham is said to be the "father" of all who believe (Rom. 4:11, 16-17). John 8:44 names "your father the devil" and the "father of lies"—i.e., the source of evil and hypocrisy. "Father" may signify compassion also (Job 29:16; 31:18; Ps. 103:13) and thus characterize all who display this virtue.

6. A name for God. For the theological significance of this term in the Bible, *see* God, OT; God, NT. The word occurs in both parts of the Bible in relation to the nature of God. It appears often as an element in proper names revealing some attribute of the divine being. E.g., Abiel may be translated "El is (my) father" (I Sam. 9:1). Various names may be found with meanings such as "My father is judge," "My father knew," "My father is majesty," "My father is goodness," etc.

For bibliography, *see* Children; Family; Marriage.

O. J. Baab

FATHERLESS [יתום, orphan, *probably from* be alone, bereaved; ὀρφανός (Jas. 1:27; RSV ORPHANS)]. Although this word may be equated with "orphan," in no instance of the use of יתום in the Bible is it clear that both parents are dead. Hebrew law carefully provided for fatherless children with special tithes at the end of every three-year period and the requirement that gleanings be left in the fields for them (Deut. 14:29; 24:19-21; 26:12; 27:19). The plea to care for the fatherless is frequent (Exod. 22:22; Deut. 10:18; 24:17; Isa. 1:17; 10:2; Jer. 22:3; Zech. 7:10; Ecclus. 4:10; Jas. 1:27). The fatherless child is often associated with the Widow in the biblical pleas that compassion be shown for the needy. Responding to the demands of their God to show mercy to the needy, the Jews after their victory over Nicanor gave some of the spoil to the orphans and widows in the community (II Macc. 8:28).

Perhaps in some instances the fatherless was a daughter rather than a son, although this cannot be proved. The daughter inherited from her father only in the absence of sons (Num. 27:7-11). Thus the fatherless daughters required special consideration in the Israelite community.

It has been suggested that the "fatherless" were the female children of sacred prostitutes, who obviously had no identifiable father. Their life was integrated with the sanctuary or temple and would have been seriously disrupted by the Josianic reform in 621. These cult children were sometimes adopted by barren women who thus reduced the surplus of children of the gods at the shrine (see Hos. 1 for symbolic names).

O. J. Baab

FATHERS, APOSTOLIC. *See* Apostolic Fathers.

FATHER'S HOUSE [בית־אב; οἰκία]. In the OT the expression may be noted when Joseph speaks to his brothers and to his "father's household" (Gen. 46:31; 50:22). The term בית means, not only "house" in a physical sense, but the Family or household of a man in a social-psychological sense. In this passage Joseph addresses the inclusive family community, consisting of his brothers, their families, and the herdsmen who serve them. A similar usage occurs in Judg. 11:2, where Jephthah's brothers by another woman thrust him out so that he cannot inherit "in our father's house"—i.e., family. In the sense of clans and families, especially in connection with taking a census, the phrase appears frequently in the plural, "fathers' houses" (see especially Num. 1:2, etc.; I Chr. 4:38; 5:13 ff; 7:2, 7; 23:11; Ezra 2:59; 10:16; Neh. 7:61; etc.).

In the NT the words identify the temple of the Lord in Jerusalem: "You shall not make my Father's house a house of trade" (John 2:16; cf. Acts 7:47, 49). When sought by his parents, Jesus said: "Did you not know that I must be in my Father's house?" (Luke 2:49)—i.e., the temple. In the Fourth Gospel the expression signifies heaven as the dwelling place of God (John 14:2). The Greek word οἰκία is used instead of the parallel term οἶκος.

See also Father; Heaven.

Bibliography. For a discussion of heaven as God's dwelling place, see O. Schaefer, *ZNW,* 32 (1933), 210-17.

O. J. Baab

FATHOM [ὀργυιά] (Acts 27:28). A unit of measurement based on the length from the tip of one hand to the tip of the other when the arms are outstretched —i.e., four cubits or *ca.* six feet. *See* Weights and Measures § D4*f.*

FATLING [מריא, מח, משנה; σιτιστός]. A domestic animal, bovine, important for its use in Israel's sacrificial practices. *See* Sacrifice and Offerings.

A product of Israel's agricultural milieu, the fatling figured prominently among those animals worthy to be used for cultic offerings. The name is concerned primarily, not with the species, but with the quality of the animal. Only the most desirable, the choice, could be offered to the Lord. It is the well-cared-for, well-fed animal which is worthy. A variety of terms appear in the MT, often rendered FAT CATTLE in the KJV.

Most important of the terms is מריא, used for cattle which are raised and fed for meat. When used in sacrifice, what was offered up was the choicest product of Israel's agriculture. In Isa. 1:11, it is modified by חלב, "the fat one"—i.e., the prime quality. The term in many places is related to sacrifice: it is offered in the sacrifice of slaughter (זבח; II Sam. 6:13; I Kings 1:9, 19, 25; Ezek. 39:18), in burnt offering (עלה; Isa. 1:11), and related to peace offering (שלם; Amos 5:22). It was not the only animal offered but is listed often with other sacrificial animals: ox (II Sam. 6:13; I Kings 1:19, 25), rams (Isa. 1:11), sheep (I Kings 1:9, 19, 25), and oxen (I Kings 1:9). In Ezek. 39:18 "fatling" is treated as a term of classification for all the animals being sacrificed. While the term applies specifically to cattle in a technical sense, it is also an inclusive term for animals worthy of sacrifice. In only one instance is the term used in a nonsacrificial context (Isa. 11:6).

A less used term, מח, more directly stresses the quality of choiceness or fatness. It is derived from the noun for "marrow," thus does not refer to a kind of animal but to the quality. It is mentioned in a noncultic context (Isa. 5:17), and is also related to burnt offering (עלה) along with rams, bulls, and goats (Ps. 66:15).

Among the animals spared by Saul (I Sam. 15:9) is משנה. The term refers to the fact that what is spared is the best. It is suggested that the term is rightly שמן, "the fat ones"; more probably it means the "second offspring," שנה, which is superior to the firstlings. In either case, it is an animal of agricultural life along with sheep, oxen, and lambs. In Matt. 22:4, a σιτιστὰ was prepared for a feast, along with oxen. This feast had no relation to cultic activity. Thus cattle especially fed for meat were used both for cultic and noncultic activity. The fatling, as a sacrificial animal, is not unique, other than that it represented the best Israel could take from its life with which to come before its God.

W. Brueggemann

FATTED. A participial adjective used to render the following Hebrew and Greek terms:

a) אבוס (Prov. 15:17, of an ox; I Kings 4:23—H 5: 3, in the plural, of fowl).

b) מרבק (lit., "stall," whence "calf" of a stall—i.e., a stall-fed or fatted calf; I Sam. 28:24; Jer. 46:21).

c) Σιτευτός (Luke 15:23, 27, 30).

In Amos 5:22 the plural of מריא, "fatling," is rendered "fatted beasts."

H. F. Beck

FAUCHION fô'chən. KJV translation of ἀκινάκης (RSV SWORD) in Jth. 13:6; 16:9. *See* Weapons and Implements of War.

FAUNA. Every translation and every commentary of the Bible has had to deal with words which indicated names of animals. Almost none of these translators or commentators has had any knowledge of animals, and most of them still less of the animals of the Holy Land. Linnaeus was quite right when he said in one of his seminaries (*ca.* 1750) that the natural history of the Holy Land is less well known than that of the most distant provinces of India.

The most compendious study on the animals of the Bible is the voluminous folio *Hierozoicon* (1663), written by Samuel Bochartus of Caen. This study is a compilation of all the earlier traditions, translations, and commentaries, with comparative study of the meaning of each word in the other Semitic languages and of pure etymology.

Frederick Hasselquist of Uppsala, a student of Linnaeus, visited the Holy Land in 1752, but died soon afterward at Smyrna. In his posthumous *Iter Palaestinum* (Stockholm, 1757), he began with the interpretation of biblical names. But he assumed that no changes had occurred in the fauna of the land since the days of the Bible. Thus, he denied the presence of the lion in those historical times, merely because lions no longer were found in the eighteenth century in Palestine. As sand grouse (*Pterocles*) were very common in the Jordan Valley during his visit, he was certain to have the שלו of Exod. 16:13; Num. 11:31-32; Ps. 105:40 before him; it, however, is identified with the quail. Even the marvelous *Fauna and Flora of Palestine* (London, 1884) of Canon Henry Baker Tristram of Durham, the father of the natural history of Palestine, and his successors were unable to identify a very great number of the animals mentioned in the Bible. The knowledge of the actual fauna of the country, of animals extinct in historical times or since the Pleistocene Age, was, of course, of the greatest importance for the interpretation of the animal names of the Bible. But it left still many questions open. If we should briefly summarize the present state of our knowledge in this respect, we should have first to confess that a very great part of these names are *nomina nuda,* names the true interpretation of which we are still unable to give, and probably will always be unable to give. The reason is usually that the name appears only once or twice and is not connected with a special habit or habitat or character. In these cases neither etymology nor comparison with related languages is able to solve the problem. Pure etymology has long since been abandoned as a method of identifying an animal when no further indications help to support the etymological solution. Still less reliable is the conclusion from related languages. Thus צב ("lizard") means "tortoise" in Hebrew (Lev. 11:29), but the equivalent *dhab* in Arabic means the big lizard *Uromastyx.* In addition, we know that animal names change their identification in time and in space—i.e., during the centuries and in various areas of the language. In Jewish tradition we have an excellent illustration of such changes in the word צבי, doubtless the "gazelle" of the Bible, but unanimously interpreted by European Jewry of latter centuries as "deer," merely because the red deer was well known to them, while no gazelles populate Europe. This may also be correct for the interpretation of the צב. In other Hebrew literature it was alternatingly used for a big lizard or for a tortoise. The former interpretation fits well the big *Uromastyx* lizard, the *dhab* of the Arabs, which is a recognized delicacy of the Bedouins. This is much more likely to have been mentioned under the forbidden animals than the tortoise *Testudo,* which is rare in the desert and offers little meat for food.

In certain cases the interpretation became clear, once the fauna of Palestine was known. The שפן of the Bible (Lev. 11:5; Deut. 14:7; Ps. 104:18; Prov. 30:26; "badger") cannot refer to the rabbit, as Luther presumed in his translation, but it is the coney (*Procavia capensis*), well characterized by habitat and behavior in the biblical data. It cannot be the rabbit, as this animal does not, and did not, occur in Palestine. For this lack of zoogeographical consideration these early interpreters should not be reproached, as such zoogeographical differences were generally unknown in their days.

The modern Hebrew language has made use of a number of *nomina nuda* or even of definitely wrong identifications. As long as the reader is well aware that these modern names make no pretense of identifying the biblical name, but merely make use of an available ancient Hebrew word without meaning, everything is in order. But we must beware of assuming that such names are authentic interpretations of the biblical name. Thus, it is now clear that the ברברים אבוסים on King Solomon's table (I Kings 4:23; "fatted fowl") were geese, and not swans. We cannot know for what reason early interpreters identified this bird with a swan; perhaps their imagination suggested to them that this royal animal must have a wonderful taste. Anyhow, nearly contemporaneous ivory carvings from Megiddo show a row of peasants bringing fattened geese into town. But the goose has a well-accepted modern name, אוז, and it was quite properly decided to retain the modern name for "swan," as no other old name is available for this bird and as a long tradition has correlated "swan" with ברבור; but it is understood that the swan of King Solomon is a goose.

A. Mammalia
- 1. Domestic
  - *a.* Equidae
    - i. Horse
    - ii. Ass
    - iii. Mule
  - *b.* Suidae
  - *c.* Camelidae
  - *d.* Bovidae
    - i. Cattle
    - ii. Buffalo
    - iii. Goat
    - iv. Sheep
  - *e.* Carnivora
    - i. Dog
    - ii. Cat
- 2. Wild
  - *a.* Chiroptera
  - *b.* Insectivora
  - *c.* Carnivora
    - i. Wolf
    - ii. Jackal and fox
    - iii. Bear
    - iv. Hyena
    - v. Lion
    - vi. Leopard
  - *d.* Hyracoidea
  - *e.* Perissodactyla

- i. Onager
- ii. Artiodactyla
- iii. Wild Boar
- iv. Deer

f. Bovidae
- i. Wild Ox
- ii. Gazelle
- iii. Ibex
- iv. Antelope
- v. Varia

g. Lagomorpha

h. Rodentia
- i. Mole rat
- ii. Mouse

i. Proboscidea

j. Varia

k. Primates

l. Cetacea

B. Aves
1. Falconidae
2. Strigidae
3. Struthionidae
4. Passerine birds
5. Herons and related birds
6. Doves and gallinaceous birds
   - *a.* Dove
   - *b.* Goose
   - *c.* Domestic fowl
   - *d.* Partridge
   - *e.* Quail
   - *f.* Varia

C. Reptilia and amphibia

D. Pisces

E. Insecta
1. Siphonaptera
2. Orthoptera
3. Rhynchota
4. Hymenoptera
   - *a.* Ant
   - *b.* Wasp
   - *c.* Bee
5. Lepidoptera
6. Aphaniptera
7. Diptera
   - *a.* Fly
   - *b.* Gnat
   - *c.* Insect larvae

F. Invertebrata other than insects
1. Mollusca
2. Vermes
3. Arachnoidea
   - *a.* Scorpion
   - *b.* Spider
4. Anthozoa
5. Addendum

Bibliography

A. *MAMMALIA.* The animal names in the NT are almost all clearly identified. Those of the OT, however—apart from those of domestic animals, most big carnivores, and a few other mammals—are mere *nomina nuda*, the identification of which is impossible.

1. Domestic. *a. Equidae.* i. Horse. The horse is believed to have been introduced into the Middle East from Persia by the Hyksos, invading Egypt early in the second millennium B.C. But recently bones of horses (domesticated) have been discovered in a settlement of the Negeb in the Chalcolithic period. What was interpreted as evidence of horse sacrifices was discovered in Tell el-Ajjul (Beth-eglaim). In the Bible horses in Egypt are mentioned as early as Gen. 47:17 (see also Exod. 14:9-28, etc.), but not until the times of David and Solomon was the horse in common use by the Hebrews and did horsemen (פרושים) form part of the army. The horse stables of King Solomon are well known; it is even probable that he was the center of an important trade of horses in the Middle East (*see* STABLE; MEGIDDO; HORSE). The local horse is a light horse, similar to the type of the Arabian horse. It should be added that the origin of domestication of the horse is by no means clear. It had obviously been introduced, already domesticated, into the Middle East from the N or the NE. Some even assume an independent domestication in the land of the Hittites. The discovery of bones in the Negeb has made the horse's early history in the Middle East very uncertain. רכש designates a team of horses in I Kings 4:28—H 5:8; Mic. 1:13, and post horses in Esth. 8:10, 14.

ii. Ass. This classification includes the ass (חמור), the she-ass (אתון), the young ass (עיר): *Equus asinus*. The local ass is clearly a descendant of the wild Nubian ass, recognizable by its black shoulder and back stripes. Before the camel came into its full symbiosis with the Bedouins of the desert, the ass was a very efficient "ship of the desert." It has been shown that until the beginning of the twentieth century ass caravans annually crossed the Sahara from Morocco to the Red Sea and back. Asses were common since the days of Abraham. In later times big white asses were highly appreciated. *See also* ASS. Fig. ASS 94.

iii. Mule. The mule (פרדה, פרד) is mentioned beginning with the time of King David, and was highly appreciated for riding (II Sam. 13:29, etc.). It was, of course, forbidden to breed mules in Israel, as was every hybridization (cf. the law of diverse kinds [כלאים; Lev. 19:19]). The mules had hence to be brought from beyond the country. Fig. MUL 78.

b. Suidae. The swine (חזיר) belonged to the unclean animals, but they were kept by the Canaanite pagans. Isaiah (65:4; 66:17) expresses abomination of the flesh of swine and of mice. On the other hand, we find the proper name Hezir (חזיר; I Chr. 24:15; Neh. 10:20), in one instance a priest's name. This fact deserves a closer study than it has had so far. Also in the NT swine are unclean animals. *See also* SWINE.

c. Camelidae. The one-humped camel or dromedary (גמל; *Camelus dromedaries* L.) is mentioned in the days of the patriarchs (Gen. 32:15, etc.), but the Midianites in the days of the judges (twelfth century B.C.) are the first illustration of any raid of camel Bedouins into the settled land (Judg. 7:12). The conclusion has been drawn from this fact, as well as from the rarity of camel documentations in the art of ancient Mesopotamia (until the seventh century) and in Egypt (until the Ptolemies), that the camel of the patriarchs is an anachronism. The documentation of and on camels is, to be sure, very scanty but continuous in ancient Egypt and Mesopotamia. Some kind of taboo may have prevented its earlier illustration in art. What appear to be domestic camels, judging from the tightly full hump, appear already *ca.* 7000 B.C. on the rock carvings of Kilwa in the extreme E of Transjordan. The explanation is obvious. The domestication of the wild dromedary began with keeping, with utilization of wool and milk; then it passed slowly to the use of light burdens, and it ended in the fully established symbiosis between camels and Bedouins, finding its expression in the famous camel raids of the Midianites. This long way from semidomestication to a highly integrated domestication took thousand of years, of which we have witness from the Bible and biblical archaeology. בכרה, בכר (Isa. 60:6; Jer. 2:23; "young camels"), as well as כרכרות (Isa. 66:20; "dromedaries"), are young camels. *See also* CAMEL.

d. Bovidae. **i. Cattle.** The cattle (בקר; *Bos primigenius*) of the Bible have many names: שור, "ox"; פר, "bull"; פרה, "cow"; עגל, עגלה, "calf." אבירים (Judg. 5:22; Ps. 22:13; Isa. 10:13; etc.) are animals or men of big stature. This important wealth of ancient Israel was not used for milk or for meat production; cattle were the usual animals for drawing the plow. It was a small cattle like the present Beiruti race. It is very remarkable, however, that all the mosaic pavements and wall paintings from the Hellenistic to the Byzantine periods represent only a zeboid cattle. The crossing of both has apparently resulted in the modern Damascus cattle. While one archaeologist has found one race of cattle through all the layers of the excavations of Megiddo (apparently our Beiruti cattle), another describes five different races of cattle from as many different strata at Gezer. The history of cattle in Bible times needs much intensified study. מקנה may designate possessions of cattle or livestock (e.g., Gen. 4:20; 30:29). Fig. COW 51.

ii. Buffalo. The domestic buffalo (called מרי today; *Bos bubalis* L.) appears in Palestine for the first time on an Arabic sculpture of the seventh century. Shortly later on, it is mentioned by Saint Willibald in the swamps of Huleh. There is no indication that it was present in Palestine in biblical times.

iii. Goat. The goat was common and has many names. The general name is עז. Many names refer to the he-goat (i.e., צפיר, שעיר, עתוד, תיש). גדי is the young goat. The race is the Syrian or Mamber goat (*Capra hircus mambrica*), which is characterized by its long, pending ears and its backward-curved horns. Since oldest times goats have helped in causing extreme erosion in the hill country. Among our oldest animal drawings are goats feeding upon trees. The goat is so much more dangerous to the vegetation than the sheep, as the former tears the plant out of the soil while the latter cuts it above the soil.

iv. Sheep. Sheep, giving wool and milk and meat, were the greatest wealth of the patriarchs. The *Ovis orientalies vignei* Blyth always has a fat tail. While this has a flat hump at the end of it, we find a long, fatty tail on all illustrations from Hellenistic to Byzantine times. The general name is צאן (also including goats) and שה. The ram is איל, the ewe רחל. כבש is a sheep older than one year, עלה a suckling lamb, כר a young lamb in pasture. *See also* SHEEP.

e. Carnivora. **i. Dog.** The dog (כלב; *Canis familiaris* L.) was common in ancient Palestine. It was, of course, the semidomestic Paria dog, which is affiliated to man as scavenger, serving man as a watchdog, announcing the approach of any stranger by its loud and continued barking. No personal relations existed between man and dog, but a flock of dogs was impersonally affiliated to a settlement. As scavenger, the dog was despised. It is probable, but not proved, that the Sel̄uki greyhounds of the Bedouins of the desert already existed in Bible times. But the hunting dogs of the Hellenistic to Byzantine art were not imported before the Hellenistic period, certainly not into Jewish Palestine. *See also* DOG.

ii. Cat. The domestic cat (חתול; καττος; *Felvis silverstris catusil*) is not mentioned in the Bible before the apocryphal Letter of Jeremiah 6:22 (*ca.* 300 B.C. or later). It was certainly much older in Palestine. In the Egyptian fortresses from Beisan to Gaza were temples to the goddess Baste, whose sacred animal was the domestic cat. The Egyptians domesticated it first in their temples.* As a pagan idol it was a taboo to the Jews; hence it is not mentioned, while cat amulets are not rarely found in these ancient Egyptian temples. Figs. CAT 18-19.

2. Wild. ***a. Chiroptera.*** The designation עטלף (Lev. 11:19; Deut. 14:18; Isa. 2:20) is the common name for all the many species of local bats, none of which is denominated specifically, but generally as inhabiting caves and ruins. The identification of עטלף has, so far, not been doubted.

b. Insectivora. Certainly no shrews (*Soricidae*) are mentioned in the Bible. No certain identification of the hedgehogs, three species of which occur and are common in Palestine, can be made from the Bible. The recent name is קפוד, which occurs in Isa. 14:23 ("hedgehog"); 34:11 ("porcupine"); Zeph. 2:14 ("hedgehog"), but cannot be interpreted with certainty as "hedgehog."

c. Carnivora. **i. Wolf.** The wolf (זאב; *Canis lupus* L.) was common in the times of the Bible all over Palestine. It was a danger to sheep and shepherds.

ii. Jackal and fox. The jackal (*Canis aureus syriacus* H.E.) is one of the most common and most conspicuous mammals of the country still today. Its nightly wailing makes it impossible to overlook it. It is also the carrion-feeder, which was the שועל mentioned in the Bible ("jackals" in Ps. 63:10—H 63:11; Lam. 5:18, but elsewhere "foxes"); but the fox is not a carrion-feeder. There is not the slightest doubt that the many references to this animal in the Bible refer to the jackal. It is not so certain that the שועלים קטנים of Song of S. 2:15 are "little foxes." The איים and the ציים (Isa. 34:14, etc.) appear to refer to the wailing of the jackals. The תנים, which are often mentioned in the wilderness (Isa. 13:22; 43:20; etc.), are dragons. It is often but unauthentically interpreted as the jackal. This would leave us with the possible exception of שועלים קטנים in Song of S. 2:15, without any name for the fox, which actually is quite possible. We should, however, not assume that both these species have been understood under one name. The fox (*Vulpes vulpes palaestinae* Thos.) is fairly common in Palestine, but by far not so conspicuous and not so noisy as are the jackals.

iii. Bear. The bear (דב; *Ursus arotus syriacus* H.E.) was fairly common in Bible times all over the settled and the hilly country. It was a danger to fruit trees and to herds (II Sam. 17:8, etc.). The color of the Syrian bear ranges from dark red-brown to the rare light specimens. The last bear was killed in Upper Galilee just before World War I. The still fairly common bear of the S and central Lebanon and Hermon was exterminated there by the hunting expeditions of the armies. But it still survives in N Syria, NW Persia, and S Turkey.

iv. Hyena. The striped hyena (צבוע; *Hyaenahyana* L.) is not mentioned in the Bible except as a geographical name: the Valley of Zeboim (i.e., Valley of Hyenas; I Sam. 13:18; cf. also the town Zeboim [Neh. 11:34]). There is no dissent about the identity of the name.

v. Lion. The lion (*Panthera leo persica* Mey.) has many names in the Bible, where it is mentioned 130 times. ארי אריה is the general name; כפיר is a young lion; לביא, לביאה (Ps. 57:4—H 57:5; Ezek. 19:2; Nah. 2:13), refer to an old lion and lioness respectively; ליש (Job 4:11; Prov. 30:30; Isa. 30:6) is a poetic name for a full-grown lion. The last lion was killed in Palestine at Ledja near Megiddo in the thirteenth century. From the twelfth century we have vivid descriptions of lion hunts on the Orontes in Syria in the Memoirs of Usamah ibn-Munquidh. In the thickets of the Euphrates and of the Tigris, the lion disappeared only during the nineteenth century. Various travelers, from Hasselquist to Roth, have pointed out that no lion bones have been found and that no lions occurred in Palestine in the memory of the living, and that the leopard was probably meant in the biblical references. There is, however, not the slightest reason, either from the zoological or from the philological point of view, to doubt the common occurrence of the real lion in Bible times. We should not forget that in historical times lions still occurred in Greece. The local lion was the Persian race, which is by no means so short-maned as some descriptions pretend. Its bones have recently been found at Megiddo.

vi. Leopard. The leopard (נמר; *Panthera pardus tulliana* Val.) is now almost extinct in Palestine, apart from temporary invasions in summer of a few individuals from the Lebanon and Hermon. Yet just before the First World War five leopards were killed around Jerusalem, and just after World War II one was shot near Beer-sheba. Tristram points out correctly that the sentence: "Their horses are swifter than leopards" in Hab. 1:8 refers to the cheetah or hunting leopard (*Acynonyx jubatus venaticus* Geoff.; נמר הצעיד). This animal can be readily distinguished from the leopard, with its ringed spots, by the solid spots of the cheetah, as well as by its forelegs' being conspicuously higher than its hindlegs. Its use for hunting is old, and a Byzantine sculpture of a cheetah with collar has been found in Palestine.

No other carnivore is reliably reported in the Bible.

d. Hyracoidea. There can be no doubt that the שפן (Lev. 11:5; Deut. 14:7; Ps. 104:18; Prov. 30:26; "badger") is the Syrian coney (*Procavia capensis syriacus* Schreb.), which lives among rocks from the Dead Sea Valley to the Hermon. Many European translators who were unfamiliar with this animal held it to be a rabbit. Fig. FAU 4.

***e. Perissodactyla.* i. Onager.** The Syrian onager (*Equus hemionus hemihippus*) of the Syrian Desert is the only onager which lived in Bible times in Palestine (mainly see Job, Isaiah, and Jeremiah). It has

4. Coney (*Hyrax Syriacus*)

With the kind permission of Mossad Bialik

5. Onager

been mentioned above that the Hebrew פרא (Job 6:5; Isa. 32:14; Jer. 14:6; etc.; "wild ass") and the Aramaic ערד (Dan. 5:21) are synonyms for the same animal. As only one type of onager has lived in historical times in the area, we have to stop looking for two kinds of onagers. It has been extinct for *ca.* a hundred years in the Syrian Desert (Isa. 32:14; Dan. 5:21). Fig. FAU 5.

ii. Artiodactyla. We have, to begin with, a very ancient misidentification. The name Behemoth (בהמות) in Job 40:15-24 is not the hippo (*Hippopotamus amphibius* L.) but has the same meaning as in all other places of the Bible—namely, "beast" or "wild beast." Tur-Sinai has definitely cleared the jungle of prejudices grown around this misinterpretation (see his Job Commentary).

iii. Wild Boar. The wild boar (חזיר; *Sus scrofa*[*?*] *screfa* L.) is still common in swamps, but has disappeared from the rest of the country. Its survival was made possible because neither Jews nor Muslims, nor many of the native Christians, eat it, and hence they do not regard it as game.

iv. Deer. Rather complicated is the interpretation of the deer of Palestine. Three species lived there, all still surviving in the N part of the Middle East, but none any longer in Palestine. Throughout the Middle

East these three species disappeared in the following sequence:

a) Red Deer (*Cervus elaphus*[*?*] *maral* Gray)

b) Fallow Deer (*Dama mesopotamica* Brooke)

c) Roe Deer (*Capreolus capreolus capreolus* L.)

Their Hebrew names are very uncertain: איל is apparently the general name for "deer." The red deer was certainly present in the country in Bible times. A splendid wall-drawing was recently discovered in a sepulchral cave of the Hasmonean period in Jerusalem, but we are unable to associate any of the quotations of the Bible with this species. Its present-day name is אילה, איל, and we are inclined to regard this important game as the deer on King Solomon's table (I Kings 4:23—H 5:3). The two other species were certainly common in that time. The יחמור (Deut. 14:5; I Kings 4:23—H 5:3; "roebuck") seems to be the fallow deer; yet it must be noted that when Conder discovered the Carmel roe *ca.* 1880, he found it called *yaḥmûr* by the Arabs. Anyhow, we remain without any biblical name for the common roe deer, as the interpretation of אילה שלוחה (Gen. 49:21; "hind let loose") as "roe deer" certainly is a misunderstanding, meaning "the deer has been sent." The roe deer thus makes necessary a new name, אילן. It does not seem to be mentioned in the Bible.

f. Bovidae. **i. Wild Ox.** Among the Bovidae we have first to note the *Auerochs* (*Bos primigenius* L.). It was Tristram who first identified ראם with this animal instead of the traditional unicorn (Num. 23:22; Ps. 22:21—H 22:22; etc.; "wild ox"; KJV "unicorn"). This does not mean that in biblical times the *Auerochs* still lived in Palestine, but it was certainly plentiful in the Gezireh of Aram-naharaim. In the Assyrian language *rīmu* certainly was *Bos primigenius.*

ii. Gazelle. The symbol of beauty is throughout the Bible the gazelle (צבי, צליה), which is in the country represented commonly by *Gazella gazella gazella* Pall., the mountain gazelle, and by *G. dorcas saudiya* C. a. S., the dorcas gazelle. Fig. GAZ 12.

iii. Ibex. As the last of the identifiable species of this group must be mentioned the Nubian ibex (יעל [Ps. 104:18; "wild goats"]; יעלה [Prov. 5:19; "doe"];

6. Ibex (*Capra Beden*)

יעלה סלע [Job 39:1; "mountain goat"]; cf. I Sam. 24:2 ["Wild-goats' Rocks"]; *Capra ibex nubiana* F. Cuv.). Fig. FAU 6.

iv. Antelope. דישון (Deut. 14:5; "ibex"), in a list of unclean animals, is apparently identical with Akkadian *da-as-su,* and in this event it will mean (with all reservations, but very probably, as this is the biggest antelope of Iraq) the Arabian Oryx (*Oryx leucoryx*).

v. Varia. We have to exclude a few species which, since Tristram and Aharoni, have been interpreted as belonging to animals of this group. No satisfactory evidence exists for the former Asiatic occurrence of the addax (*Addax nasomaculatus* Balinv.) and of the *Bubale Hartebeest* (*Alcelaphus buselaphus buselaphus* Pall.). It must be added that the barbarian wild sheep (*Ammotrages lervia* Pall.) may have occurred in ancient times in the mountains of S and SE Palestine, but no definite proof is available.

Absolutely unidentifiable but apparently belonging to this group are: אקו (Deut. 14:5; "wild goat"), now used for *Capra hircus aegagrus* L.; תאו, תוא (Deut. 14: 5; Isa. 51:20; "antelope"), now used for *Alcelaphus buselaphus* Pall. and for the European Bison (*Bison bonasus* L.). With regard to אנקה (Lev. 11:30; "gecko"), it is doubtful whether it is a small mammal or a lizard. זמר (Deut. 14:5; "mountain-sheep") is unidentifiable; the word is now used for the Arabian Oryx (*Oryx leucoryx* Pall.).

g. Lagomorpha. The common hare of the country (ארנבת; Lev. 11:6; Deut. 14:7) is the Palestine hare (*Lepus europaeus judaeus* Gray). Very much rarer are still little-known forms of *Lepus capensis* and of *Lepus arabicus.*

h. Rodentia. **i. Mole rat.** A very characteristic animal in the landscape of the Mediterranean part of the country is the Syrian mole rat (*Spalax ehrenbergi ehrenbergi* Nhrg.), whose hills are very conspicuous in winter and spring, especially in the terra rossa. Three Hebrew names are connected with it: the Aramaic אשות appears in the Talmudic literature only. חפר פרות (Isa. 2:20; "moles") are mentioned, together with bats, as inhabitants of ruins and dark refuges. The root חפר, meaning "to burrow," would suit excellently the mole rat, but it is doubtful if פרות belongs to the name. The third word is practically unidentifiable: חלד (Lev. 11:29; "weasel"). It is mentioned together with "mouse" and צב ("great lizard"; but *see above*). Some think that it is the same word as the Arabic *ḫuld,* "mole rat." Anyhow it is used in the Mishna, as well as in modern Hebrew, in this sense. The biblical interpretation of חלד remains open. It should be added that no mole (*Talpa Insectivora!*) occurs in Palestine.

ii. Mouse. עכבר (Lev. 11:29; I Sam. 6:4 ff; Isa. 66:17; "mouse") is the general word for all small rodents. It refers, of course, also to the Levant house mouse (*Mu musculus praetextus* Brants). In I Sam. 6 it refers to the Levant vole (*Microtus guentheri* D. a A.), where it appears first as an agricultural pest. But the often-assumed connection with the Philistine epidemic, which may have been the true plague, is by no means certain. שך (Jer. 5:26; taken as a verb) is probably a collective word for "mice" or "rodents." Tur-Sinai regards it as the equivalent of the Akkadian *šikkû.*

*i. **Proboscidea.*** The elephant is, of course, no native of Palestine. Yet still *ca.* 1500 B.C. the Indian elephant (*Elephas maximus indicus* L.) lived in the Orontes Valley, where it was hunted by Thutmose III. In the time of the Maccabeans (I Macc. 6:30, 34, 37) elephants were used in the armies of the Diadoches as tank units are used in modern armies. IVORY has been used for artistic work at least since the second millennium in the country. But this ivory was introduced from the African elephant (*Loxodon sp.*). The word שנהב (I Kings 10:22; II Chr. 9:21; "ivory") means "tooth of the elephant," הב being derived from the Egyptian *ꜣbw,* "elephant."

*j. **Varia.*** The תחש of the tabernacle (Exod. 26:14; 35:7; etc.; "goatskins"; KJV "badgers' skins") is variously interpreted. Tur-Sinai interprets it as the skins of black goats, in contrast to the white goatskins. The sandals of Ezek. 16:10 may well refer to the marine Dugong (*Dugong dugon* Mull.), as its thick skin is widely used by the Bedouins of the Sinai for sandals. The interpretation "badgers' skins" makes no sense. While we must leave open the question what the תחש of Exod. 25:5 really is, there is little doubt that the תחש of Ezek. 16:10 ("shod you with תחש [leather]") refers to the skin of the Dugong (*Dugong dugon* Mull.). Many travelers in the Sinai have described sandals from the skin of this animal on the feet of the Bedouins as late as the nineteenth century.

*k. **Primates.*** The קופים and תכיים of I Kings 10:22; II Chr. 9:21 have been regarded as apes and parrots. Both the KJV and the RSV translate "apes and peacocks." Albright has pointed out (1921) that the latter word must be Egyptian *kyw,* mentioned with *gfw* (whence Hebrew קופים, *qôphîm*) as monkeys of a related species. Tur-Sinai rejects this view and holds that the words refer to precious stones (the LXX renders them by "carved and hewn stones"). In a letter Albright has written: "I welcome the chance to clarify my position on *tukkîyîm* (perhaps to be pronounced *tekîyîm*). The Egyptian word which occurs with *gfw,* 'monkeys,' in the Middle Egyptian story of the Shipwrecked Sailor is *kyw* (plural). The same word appears later in the feminine form *kyt* (for references to *kyw* and *kyt* see Erman-Grapow, *Worterbuch der ägyptischen Sprache,* V, 110, and *Belegstellen,* V, 17). The word appears in syllabic spelling in the New Kingdom as *ka-y(a),* applied to a monkey and to an animal from Nubia which could be taught to dance; it is construed both with the masculine article *p* and with the feminine *t* (*Worterbuch der ägyptischen Sprache,* V, 116). Hebrew *tukkîyîm* (or *tekîyîm*), with the Egyptian feminine article and the Hebrew masculine plural, is on a par with Arabic *timsâḥ,* "crocodile," from the late Egyptian feminine *te-msáḥ* (the masculine was *pe-msáḥ*). See my discussions of the word in *AJSL,* XXXVII, 144 (1921), and *Archaeology and the Religion of Israel,* p. 212, n. 16. For the Egyptian and Hebrew words for "crocodile" see T. O. Lambdin in *JNES,* XII (1953), 284 ff, where a full discussion of the linguistic problems will be found.

*l. **Cetacea.*** It has already been pointed out that the Leviathan (לויתן) is an old mythological creature, certainly not specifically referring to "whale," for which it is used today.

B. ***AVES.*** **1. Falconidae.** For big birds of prey the general words are: עיט (Isa. 18:6; 46:11; Jer. 12:9; etc.; "bird of prey"), today used for *Aquila,* "eagle"; נשר ("eagle" in Exod. 19:4; Deut. 28:49; 32:11; II Sam. 1:23; etc.; "vulture" in Lam. 4:19; Hos. 8:1), today "vulture." According to Tur-Sinai, טחות ("clouds"; KJV "inward parts") and שכוי ("mists"; KJV "heart") of Job 38:36 are also general names for birds of prey. All the smaller diurnal birds of prey are designated as נץ (Lev. 11:16; Deut. 14:15; Job 39:26; "hawk"), a name used today for *Accipiter,* the "sparrow hawks." In the expression העיט צבוע (Jer. 12:9; "speckled bird"), the word צבוע is certainly not "hyena." Nor does it mean "speckled," for in the OT it is used only for prey. The meaning thus is "bird of prey."

The following specific determinations are possibly correct, even if this is only more or less probable: פרס ("ossifrage" in Lev. 11:13; "vulture" in Deut. 14:12) is the Lammergeier (*Gypaëtus barbatus* L.). נשר, apart from its general meaning, may be referred to as *Gyps fulvus* L., the Griffon Vulture, which is called *naśr* in Arabic. רחם (Lev. 11:18; Deut. 14:17; "vulture") may be *Neophron percnopterus* L., the Egyptian eagle, the *raḫam* of the Arabs. דאה (Lev. 11:14; "kite"), איה ("falcon" in Lev. 11:14; Job 28:7; "kite" in Deut. 14:13), ראה (Deut. 14:13; "buzzard"), דיות (Isa. 34:15; "kites"), perhaps the variants only scribal errors for דאה, are all probably kites (*Milvus*), of which three species occur in the country. עזניה (Lev. 11:13; Deut. 14:12; "osprey") means today the Black Vulture (*Aegypius monachus* L.). The biblical meaning remains uncertain.

2. Strigidae. The owls of the Bible are still more difficult to identify. Thus קפוז (Isa. 34:15; "owl") and לילית (Isa. 34:14; "night hag") are probably owls, in addition to the latter's meaning of "night ghost." לילית serves today for *Strix,* the tawny owl. In the lists of Lev. 11; Deut. 14 we find as birds, probably belonging to the owls, תחמס ("nighthawk" in Lev. 11:16; "hawk" in Deut. 14:15), according to Tristram and M. Dor the goatsucker, *Caprimulgus sp.* ינשוף ("ibis" in Lev. 11:17; "great owl" in Deut. 14:16; "owl" in Isa. 34:11), perhaps a great owl, is used today for *Otus,* the eared owl. כוס ("owl" in Lev. 11:17; Ps. 102:6—H 102:7; "little owl" in Deut. 14:16) is used for the little owl (*Athene noctua*). תנשמת (Lev. 11:18; Deut. 14:16; "water hen") is used for the barn owl (*Tyto alba* Scop.). To all these names of uncertain meaning we have to add the most difficult problem of יען, יענה, or בת היענה (Lev. 11:16; Deut. 14:15; Isa. 13:21; Mic. 1:8; etc.), translated "owl" in the KJV and "ostrich" in the RSV. *See* § B3 *below.*

3. Struthionidae. The uncertain יען, יענה, or בת היענה (Lev. 11:16; Deut. 14:15; Isa. 13:21; Mic. 1:8; etc.; "ostrich") may refer to the ostrich.* בת היענה means "daughter of the desert," and it would seem that the ostrich is suitably named the daughter of the desert. It is also quite natural that this giant bird should be mentioned in the Bible at a time when it was by no means rare. The present use of the word is to designate the ostrich (*Struthio camelus* L.), but in some passages (Mic. 1:8, etc.) it may have been used for owls. Fig. OST 16.

4. Passerine birds. צפור is a general word for "birds," perhaps mainly for the passerine birds. In other Semitic languages it was the name for what today are birds (צפורים or עוף). If דרור (Ps. 84:3—H 84:4; Prov. 26:2; "swallow") was used in the same sense for small birds, or applied to any species in the Bible, we are unable to decide. In medieval Hebrew דרור meant "swallow"; today it is "sparrow."

סוס, סיס (Isa. 38:14; Jer. 8:7; "swallow"), is used today for "swifts" (*Apus*), and quite possibly this was already the biblical meaning. עורב (Gen. 8:7; I Kings 17:4, 6; etc.) is the general name for ravens (*Corvidae*), and we have no reason to doubt its authenticity.

5. Herons and related birds. אנפה (Lev. 11:19; Deut. 14:18) was probably the general name for the heron family (*Ardeidae*), as it is today. חסידה (Lev. 11:19; Deut. 14:18; Jer. 8:7; etc.; "stork") has for very long been used for "stork" (*Ciconia alba.*), a very common passing migrant in spring, so that it may quite well be a continuous tradition, provided that the stork bred in Bible times in Palestine. קאת ("pelican"* in Lev. 11:18; Deut. 14:17; "hawk" in Isa. 34:11; "vulture" in Ps. 102:6—H 102:7; Zeph. 2:14), the "vomiter," is a night bird. שלך (Lev. 11:17; Deut. 14:17) is undeterminable, but usually translated as "cormorant." עגור (Isa. 38:14; Jer. 8:7) is usually and probably correctly translated as "crane" (*Grus grus* L.), in which sense it is also used today. But it has also been translated as "swallow." Its migration is not so conspicuous as that of the swallow, and the crane has a croaking cry while on migration. These facts would make "swallow" more probable, if we had any other positive hint for this solution. The last of the water birds is שחף (Lev. 11:16; Deut. 14:15; "sea gull"), absolutely undeterminable, today being used for "gull" (*Larus*) from an onomatopoetic interpretation of the name. Fig. PEL 24.

6. Doves and gallinaceous birds. ***a. Dove.*** The two names for doves are: יונה for the "rock pigeon" (*Columbia livia* L.), both wild and domestic, and תור (Gen. 15:9; Lev. 1:14; 5:7; etc.; "turtledove"), which comprises all species of turtledoves (*Streptopelia*).

b. Goose. The ברברים אבוסים (I Kings 4:23; "fatted fowl") of King Solomon's table are, without doubt, fatted geese. Peasants carrying geese in their arms to the market are seen on ivory carvings from Megiddo from the tenth century B.C. The term is traditionally translated as "swan," but no swan is common in Palestine and none is regarded as food. As we have now a Hebrew name (of Eastern origin) for "goose," אוז, we continue to use ברבר for "swan."

c. Domestic fowl. We now come to the difficulties concerning the domestic fowl (*Gallus gallus* L.). The Sumerian name *tarnegol* is not found in the Bible. The NT used the Greek ἀλέκτωρ (COCK). But two Hebrew seals from Palestine with the rooster depicted on them make the presence of the species a certainty in the first millennium B.C.

d. Partridge. קורא (I Sam. 26:20; Jer. 17:11) is usually understood to be the Greek "partridge" (*Alectoris graeca* L.) or, probably incorrectly, *Ammoperdix heyi*. Yet Tur-Sinai remarks that these places do not refer to any bird but to a verb form "calling." The connection with דגר in Jer. 17:11 ("gathers a brood") means nothing, as this word occurs twice only and cannot be interpreted with any certainty as "breeding"—the present-day use of the verb. Tur-Sinai understands it as an onomatopoetic word for "cooing"—which actually suits very well. Thus, he thinks, these places may equally well refer to the domestic fowl, without giving it a specific name. Many modern interpreters who insist that the word דגר means "breedings" add that the female of the rock partridge lays two batches of eggs, and while laying the second batch the hen leaves the rooster sitting on the first batch. Both arguments stand on rather weak legs, but Tur-Sinai gives the more convincing reasoning. He also interprets with the LXX זרזיר מתנים (Prov. 30:31; "strutting cock"), usually translated and used for "greyhound," as "lewd cock."

e. Quail. This is a bird whose identity is little doubted. שלו (Exod. 16:13; Num. 11:31-32; Ps. 105:40; "quail") was tentatively assumed to be a sand grouse (*Pterocles*) by Hasselquist and others before

With the kind permission of Mossad Bialik

7. Quail

the bird migrations were known. Today there is unanimity that it refers to the quail (*Coturnix coturnix* L.).* Also the reference to an occasional disease caused by the eating of quails has found medico-historical support. Fig. FAU 7.

f. Varia. It has been mentioned above that if the word תוכיים (I Kings 10:22; II Chr. 9:21; "peacocks") refers to an animal, it is a species of monkey, but neither peacock nor parrot. Tur-Sinai thinks it means a precious stone.

קפוד ("hedgehog" in Isa. 14:23; Zeph. 2:14; "porcupine" in Isa. 34:11) has often been thought to indicate a bittern (*Botaurus stellaris* L.). This translation has no support whatsoever.

רננים (Job 39:13; "ostrich") is in an adjectival relationship to "wing" and is no bird.

C. *REPTILIA AND AMPHIBIA.* There is very little that can be done about the final identification of most of the reptiles.

The LEVIATHAN, לויתן (Job 3:8; Pss. 74:14; 104:26; Isa. 27:1), is the primordial dragon; it is known by this name (*ltn*) in Canaanite mythology. While being today used for "whale," there is no such indication in the Bible.

תנין, *tannîn* ("sea monster" in Gen. 1:21; Ps. 148:7; "dragon" in Isa. 27:1; 51:9; etc.; *see* DRAGON), is both a mythological creature appearing as *tnn* ("dragon") in Canaanite texts and every big animal of the waters, sea as well as rivers. As the latter the crocodile (*Crocodilus niloticus* L.) is included. The word is today applied to the crocodile only.

לטאה (Lev. 11:30; "lizard") is certainly a general name for lizards, including agamas, skinks, etc. It occurs but once, mentioned together with אנקה ("gecko"), כח ("land crocodile"), חמט ("sand lizard"), and תנשמת ("chameleon"). All these are absolutely unidentifiable. They probably all belong to the lizards. תנשמת (Lev. 11:18; Deut. 14:16; "water hen") again appears as a name of a bird. Today the words in usage are: לטאה as "lizard" (*Lacerta*), חמט as "skink" (*Scincidae*), כח for the giant lizards *Varanus griseus* Daud. and *Varanus niloticus* Geoffr.

שממית (Prov. 30:28; "lizard"), which lives in palaces it built for itself, is a spider. From the context it is clear that שממית builds its own palace and not that it lives in the palaces of the great. Today the name is used for the geckoes (*Geckonidae*). The צפרדע (Exod. 8:2-13—H 7:27-8:9; Pss. 78:45; 105:30; "frog") of the second Egyptian plague has never been doubted to be a frog.

The usual identifications of the biblical snakes seem all to be wrong. נחש (Gen. 3:1 ff; Deut. 8:15; etc.) is obviously a general name for snakes, and as such it is still used today. פתן ("asp" in Deut. 32:33; Job 20:14, 16; Isa. 11:8; "adder" in Pss. 58:4—H 58:5; 91:13), always identified with the Egyptian asp *Naja haje,* which apparently does not occur in Palestine but is common in Egypt, is, according to Tur-Sinai, *bašmu* in Akkadian, *bṯn* in Ugaritic and Arabic, every big snake. Anyhow, its biblical identification is absolutely unknown. The same is true of שפיפון (Gen. 49:17; "viper"; KJV "adder"), which today is used for the *Cerastes* vipers (*Cerastes cerastes* L., *Cerastes vipera* L., *Pseudocerastes fieldi* Schm.) צפעני (Prov. 23:32; Isa. 11:8; 59:5; Jer. 8:17; "adder") may well be the common Palestine viper* (*Vipera palaestinae* Wern.), the cause of almost all accidents in the settled area of Palestine. It is used today in this sense, but its biblical identification is uncertain. The אפעה (Job 20:16; Isa. 30:6; 59:5; "viper") has always been identified with the Arabic *'afʿā,* which is the Carpet Viper (*Echis colorata* Gunt.). It has probably referred to that common poisonous snake of the Jericho Plain, which was feared throughout the Middle Ages and became, under the name of Tyr, Tyre, the monopoly of the Sultan of Egypt as the most important and valuable ingredient of theriaca, that famous antidote for the bite of all poisonous snakes. It is used today in this sense, and the identification may also be the biblical one. This *Echis* may also be meant by שרף, *śārāph,* or "fiery serpent" (Num. 21:6, 8; Deut. 8:15) and the fiery flying serpent of Isa. 14:29; 30:6, because just the same legends were told in the Middle Ages about this serpent as in the Bible. From a zoological point of view they are, of course, entirely indeterminable. Fig. FAU 8.

With the kind permission of Mossad Bialik

8. A Palestinian viper

עכשוב of Ps. 140:3—H 140:4 ("viper"), translated as ἀσπίς ("asp") in Rom. 3:13, is, according to Tur-Sinai, the same word as עכביש (Job 8:14; Isa. 59:5; "spider").

D. *PISCES.* דג is, of course, the general name for fishes. There is not one specific fish name in the Bible. We may mention only that the great fish which served as model for the legend of Jonah was apparently not a whale but a great shark. Great sharks are known to have swallowed men entirely without any external wounds. *See also* FISH.

E. *INSECTA.* 1. Siphonaptera. There is no reasonable doubt that כנים (Exod. 8:16-18—H 8:12-14; Ps. 105:31; Isa. 51:6; "gnats") refers to lice in general and especially to *Pediculus humanus* L., the human body louse. There is little doubt that the third of the Egyptian plagues (Exod. 8:16-17; Ps. 105:31) referred to the latter, as lice were held a great abomination in Egypt.

2. Orthoptera. Of all the many names for locusts and eventually grasshoppers and other Orthoptera, only the name ארבה (Exod. 10:4-19, etc.; "locust") is certain, belonging to the Desert Locust (*Schistocerca gregaria* Forsk.), on which a number of excellent ecological observations are given (Nahum on heliothermy, Exodus on wind directions and locust flights, etc.). It seems most probable that גזם ("cutting locust"), ילק ("hopping locust"), חסיל ("destroying locust"), of Joel 1:4 were only various stages of the Desert Locust. סלעם ("bald locust"), חרגל ("cricket"), and חגב ("grasshopper"), mentioned as clean food in Lev. 11:22, may be also references to various stages of the locust,* but may equally refer to other groups of the order. Today the following names are used: חגב for short-horned (*Acrididae*),* חרגל for long-horned grasshoppers (*Tettigoniidae*)—this, of course, without any prejudice to the biblical identity of these names. Locusts were served as food to John the Baptist in Matt. 3:4; this is not now regarded as exceptional. Figs. LOC 33; GRA 38.

3. Rhynchota. תולעת שני (Exod. 25:4; 26:1; etc.; "scarlet stuff") and כרמיל (II Chr. 2:7, 14; 3:14; "crimson fabrics") refer to the crimson scales,* *Kermes nahalali* Bdhmr., *Kermes biblicus* Bdhmr., *Kermes greeni* Bdhmr., which are abundant in N Palestine on various oaks. The females mature in March-April, when they reach pea-size. They are either globular or have a deep median furrow. They are of various shades of brown, but after death they all are black-brown. The eggs are taken from the broken body of the mother and carefully rubbed into balls, from which the crimson dye is extracted. Fig. FAU 9.

The "manna" (מן) of Exod. 16:31 ff; Num. 11:6, 9; etc.,* is the sweet excretion of two scale insects living on the twigs of the manna-tamarisk (*Tamariscus mannifer*); this phenomenon is still occurring every early summer in the wadis of the Sinai mountains.

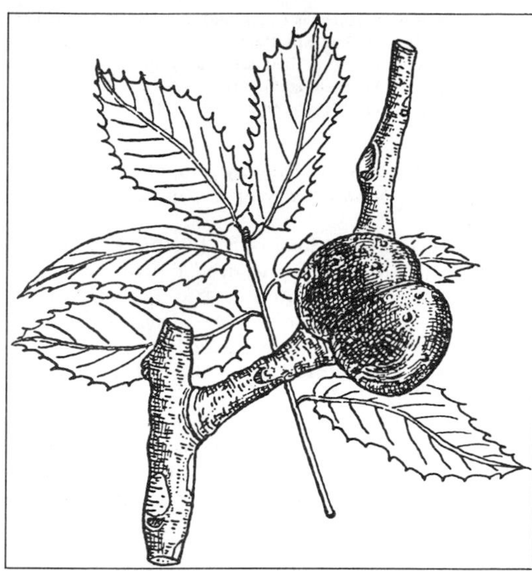
With the kind permission of Mossad Bialik
9. Crimson scale

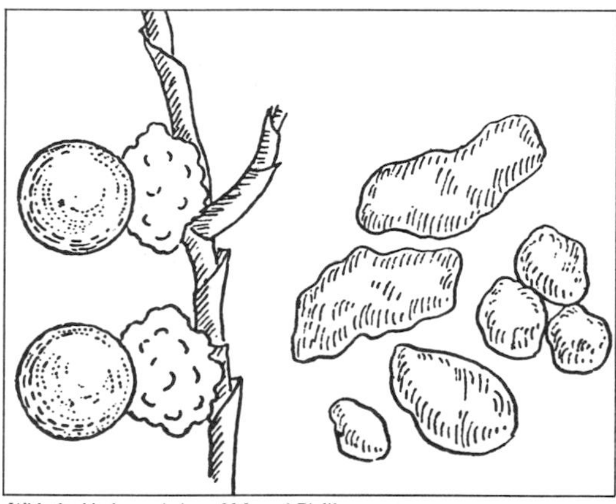
With the kind permission of Mossad Bialik
10. Manna

The names of the scale insects are: *Trabutina mannipara* Ehr. and *Najacoccus serpentinus minor* Green. For a full discussion of the manna problem, *see bibliography*. Fig. FAU 10.

4. Hymenoptera. ***a. Ant.*** The word נמלה (Prov. 6:6; 30:25) refers to ants in general, but especially to the Harvester Ant (*Messor semirufus* And.), which harvests grain within its nests. Fig. ANT 28. *See also* ANT.

b. Wasp. צרעה (Exod. 23:28; Deut. 7:20; Josh. 24:12; "hornet"), used today for wasps (*Vespidae*) in general, is in the Bible doubtless the hornet (*Vespa orientalis* F.), which was in Egypt regarded as one of the symbols of military might. In the same sense it is used in the books of the Bible.

c. Bee. The honeybee (דבורה; Deut. 1:44; Judg. 14:8; Ps. 118:12; Isa. 7:18), *Apis mellifica syriaca* B.R., is not a crossing of the Italian and the Egyptian bee, but a dark southern form of *Apis mellifica* L., while the Egyptian bee belongs to the African species (*Apis unicolor* Latr.). There is no reference in the Bible to beekeeping. All references indicate the hunting of wild honey (*see bibliography*). The rapid re-creating and strengthening quality of honey is well described in I Sam. 14:27. Beekeeping was common in Palestine at the time of the Mishna, when also bee laws were well established. The hives were horizontal tubes made from mud and straw (see Ohaloth).

5. Lepidoptera. עש (Job 4:19; Isa. 50:9; 51:8; etc.; "moth") is the cloth moth (*Tineola pellionella* L.). In Job 27:18 we find an allusion to the cylindrical tubes which the larva webs as its house. In Isa. 51:8 סס ("worm") is the larva of the moth. The general reference is more to the larva, the massive destroyer of woolen clothing, than to the adult moth.

6. Aphaniptera. The flea (פרעש; *Pulex irritans* L.) is only twice mentioned in the Bible—i.e., by David to Saul (I Sam. 24:14—H 24:15; cf. 26:20) as a simile for the most insignificant creature. In latter times the king of the fleas was said to court at Tiberias.

7. Diptera. ***a. Fly.*** זבוב (Eccl. 10:1; Isa. 7:18) is a general word for flies, of which many species live in Palestine in the vicinity of human habitats. The common housefly is *Musca vicina* Macq. BAAL-ZEBUB (בעל זבוב) may mean "Lord of Flies" (II Kings 1:2 ff).

רמה ("worms" in Exod. 16:24; Job 7:5; 17:14; 21: 26; etc.; "maggot" in Job 25:6; Isa. 14:11) are the maggots of flies from corpses.

b. Gnat. ערב (Exod. 8:21-31—H 8:17-27; Pss. 78: 45; 105:31; "fly"), in one of the Egyptian plagues, is usually translated as "mosquito" or "gnat." The name cannot be identified. It may be identical with the Harvester Gnat, the *barghaš* of the Arabs, *Trichotanypus tiberiae* Kieff. and related species. It is a small midge (*Chironomidae*) which enters the eyes, ears, nose, etc., of the field workers in the early morning during the harvest season.

c. Insect larvae. תולעה (Exod. 16:20; Isa. 14:11; 41: 14; "worm") is used like the Arabic *dûd*, mainly referring to insect larvae.

F. *INVERTEBRATA OTHER THAN INSECTA.*
1. Mollusca. שבלול (Ps. 58:8—H 58:9; "snail"), which occurs only once in the Bible, is used today for "snail"; but the word has no relation to any animal, according to Tur-Sinai. The interpretation as "snail" appeared in the Middle Ages only, when Ibn Esra identified it also with a medusa.

The precious dyes of purple, ארגמן (Exod. 25:4–39:29; Num. 4:13; Jer. 10:9; etc.; "purple") and תכלת (Exod. 25:4–39:31; Num. 4:6; Jer. 10:9; etc.; "blue" or "violet"), products of Phoenicia which are mentioned at 2000 B.C. already as brought to Aram-naharaim, were prepared on the Phoenician coasts from Ugarit to Dor, with Tyre as the famous center. They were produced from three mollusks: *Murex brandaris* L., *Murex trunculus* L., and *Purpura haemastoma* L. Only recently could Pfister by chemical methods identify the true purple color as black-violet. We assume that תכלת is a secondary extract which was considerably lighter in color. Others assume, without any factual foundation, that תכלת was the dye from another marine snail (*Yanthina*) or of a cuttlefish (*Sepia*). In recent times the number of those who assume both names to be two colors prepared from the same animals is on the increase, especially as it is claimed that תכלת is not the same word as that used now for "sky-blue." The first conclusion seems acceptable, while no valid basis for the second thesis can be given. תכלת is obviously a very light violet dye as contrasted to the black-violet dye of ארגמן.

2. Vermes. There is no dissension on עלוקה (Prov. 30:15) as "leech" (*Hirudinea*), of which *Limnatis nilotica* Sav. is the common local giant species.

3. Arachnoidea. ***a. Scorpion.*** There is also no disagreement about "scorpions," which are understood to come under the name עקרבים (Deut. 8:15; I Kings 12:11, 14; II Chr. 10:11, 14; Ezek. 2:6), *Scorpiones,* of which about a dozen species occur in Palestine. There is the geographical name "Ascent of AKRABBIM"—i.e., "Ascent of Scorpions"—in Num. 34:4; Josh. 15:3; Judg. 1:36. Fig. SCO 32.

b. Spider. There is no doubt that עכביש (Job 8:14; Isa. 59:5) is a general name for "spider." We must add to this name עכשוב (Ps. 140:3—H 140:4; "vipers"), which, according to Tur-Sinai, is the same word as עכביש. In this place it may refer either to an actually poisonous spider or to a general popular belief that all or many spiders are poisonous.* According to the reading of the text by some scholars to the effect that the שממית (Prov. 30:28; "lizard"), today a name for "gecko," lives in palaces like those of kings, which it has itself built, also belongs to the spiders (*see* § C *above*). The reasons why some authors refer to the אנקה (Lev. 11:30; "gecko") also as a spider are not convincing. Fig. SPI 75.

4. Anthozoa. The present name for corals is אלמוג, which is mentioned in I Kings 10:11-12; II Chr. 2:8; 9:10-11 ("almug/algum wood"). It is, however, now generally agreed that this name refers to a very precious wood which was imported by King Solomon through Tyre. ראמות ("coral" in Job 28:18; Ezek. 27:16; "high" in Prov. 24:7) has nothing to do with corals.

5. Addendum. גביש (Job 28:18; "crystal"; KJV "pearls") is often translated "pearls." According to the competent information of Tur-Sinai, it is a precious stone, a crystal, but has nothing to do with pearls. Μαργαρίτης (Matt. 7:6; Rev. 18:12; etc.) doubtless refers to pearls.

Bibliography. S. Bochartius, *Hierozoicon* (1662). F. Hasselquist, *Iter Palaestinum* (1757). H. B. Tristram, "The Survey of Western Palestine," *Fauna and Flora of Palestine* (1884); *The Natural History of the Bible* (1898). E. W. G. Masterman, *Studies in Galilee* (1909), ch. 2: "The Inland Fisheries of Galilee." E. Schmitz, *Eine Baerenjagd in Palastina* (1912), pp. 174-76. P. K. Hitti, *An Arab Syrian Gentleman and Warrior* (*Usamah ibn Munqidh;* 1929). F. S. Bodenheimer, *Animal Life in Palestine* (1935). D. M. A. Bate, "Palaeontology: The Fossil Fauna of the Wadi el-Mughara Caves," in D. A. E. Garrod and D. M. A. Bate, *The Stone Age Man of Mount Carmel,* vol. I (1937); "Animal Remains," in P. L. O. Guy, *Megiddo Tombs* (1938), pp. 209 ff. W. F. Albright, *From the Stone Age to Christianity* (1940), p. 196. J. P. Free, "Abraham's Camels," *JNES* (1944), pp. 187-93. F. Harper, *Extinct and Vanishing Mammals of the Old World* (1945). R. Pfister and L. Bellinger, *The Excavations of Dura-Europos: Final Report,* 4, pt. 2: "The Textiles" (1945). J. R. Ellermann and T. C. S. Morrison-Scott, *Checklist of Palaearctic and Indian Mammals* (1951). F. S. Bodenheimer, *Insects as Human Food* (1953). H. Tur-Sinai, *Lashon ve-Sepher* (1955). F. S. Bodenheimer, *Ha-Hai be-Artsot ha-Mikrah,* vols. I-II (1951; 1956); *Animal and Man in Bible Lands* (1960).

On manna, see: F. S. Bodenheimer, *Ergebnisse der Sinai Expedition 1927* (1929), pp. 45-88; "The Manna of Sinai," *BA,* X (1947), 2-6.

The opinion that references to honey in the Bible indicate the hunting of wild honey is explained in F. S. Bodenheimer, "The Honeybee in Ancient Palestine," *The Bee World,* 15 (1934), 123, where also is discussed the opposite opinion of A. Armbruster, *Die Bienenzucht im Alten Orient, Archiv für Bienenkunde,* XIII (1932; rev. ed., 1952), 1-43.

F. S. BODENHEIMER

FAWN [עֹפֶר; *cf.* Arab. *ghufr,* young chamois, young antelope; *see below*]. A young animal, usually a young deer.

עֹפֶר occurs only in Song of S. 2:9, 17; 4:5; 7:3—H 7:4; 8:14, in all cases being used figuratively. The RSV employs "fawn" only in 4:5; 7:3—H 7:4 (cf. KJV YOUNG ROE); elsewhere it treats the word as "YOUNG ONE" and translates the phrase "young one of the stags" as "YOUNG STAG" (cf. KJV YOUNG HART).

In Gen. 49:21 the RSV attempts to clear up a puzzling text ("words of beauty," hence KJV "goodly words") by emending the MT "words of" to "fawns of" (*'imrê* to *'immᵉrê,* lit., "lambs of"), thus obtaining "comely fawns." W. S. MCCULLOUGH

FEAR. The concept of fear in the Bible is related to a wide range of emotions, extending from simple apprehensiveness to utter terror or dread, caused by the suspicion of an impending peril, known or unknown. It appears in theological as well as secular contexts, the former illustrated in such expressions as "the fear of Yahweh" or "the fear of God." In such cases the reference is to an emotional experience of a complex nature which is connected with the perception or the awareness of the holy (*see* HOLINESS), and which produces the concomitant reactions of repulsion, attraction, fascination, awe, reverence, love, trust, faith, worship, and adoration. The commingling of these impulses or feelings—some of which are mutually exclusive—appears not only in the Bible but also in the nonbiblical literatures of the ancient Near East (*see bibliography*).

1. Terminology of fear in the Bible. The word "fear" and its synonyms (reverence, awe, dismay, dread, distress, trouble, terror, horror, etc.) occur several hundred times in the English versions of the OT and more than a hundred times in those of the NT. They are used to render into English more than a score of Hebrew words and their derivatives, and at least three Greek words and their derivatives.

a. Fear in biblical Hebrew. The most common Hebrew term for "fear" is the noun יראה (Jonah 1:10; Prov. 1:7) and its cognate מורא (Ps. 19:9—H 19:10), both derived from the verb ירא (Ps. 130:4). The noun פחד is translated "dread" (Job 13:11) and usually indicates an intense emotion. The chief synonyms, with various degrees of strength, are אימה, "dread" (Gen. 15:12); בעתה, "terror" (Jer. 8:15); מגור, also rendered "terror" (Jer. 6:25); while חת, חתה, חתת, חתית, and מחתה indicate a shattering dismay (as in Gen. 35:5). The respective strength of each of these words depends to no small extent upon the context in which it appears. Many other Hebrew or Aramaic words designate the emotion of fear by implication. Using a typically Semitic mode of expression, biblical writers are prone to suggest an inward disturbance by depicting its outward manifestations. Fear, distress, and dismay are thus suggested by many different words which mean trembling, quaking, shaking, quivering, shuddering, staggering, reeling, hair-bristling, palpitating, writhing, twirling, whirling, etc.

b. Fear in LXX Greek. The LXX translators usually rendered the common Hebrew word יראה by the Greek εὐσέβεια, "reverence," "respect," "piety" (Isa. 11:2), although they sometimes used φόβος, which is the most common Grek word for "fear" (Prov. 1:7*a*). They also employed the same word to translate פחד (Job 13:11) and אימה (Gen. 15:12). Occasionally they selected δειλία, "fearfulness," "timidity," "cowardice," for the same Hebrew word אימה (Ps. 54:4—H 55:5).

c. Fear in NT Greek. In the NT the verb φοβοῦμαι, "to be afraid," "to bc struck with fear," "to be seized with alarm," occurs several times (Matt. 10:31; etc.). Likewise, the noun φόβος means ordinarily "fear" or "awe" (Mark 4:41) and occasionally "reverence" or "respect" (Rom. 13:7). The terms δέος, "awe" (Heb. 12:28), and δειλία, "timidity" (II Tim. 1:7), appear only once in the NT, and so does the verb δειλιάω (John 14:27). The word εὐσέβεια, "reverence," "respect," "piety," "godliness," appears in some passages (Acts 3:12; I Tim. 2:2; 4:7, 8; 6:5 ff; II Tim. 3:5; II Pet. 1:3, 6 ff), and so does its cognate verb εὐσεβέω, "to act reverently" (I Tim. 5:4), or "to worship" (Acts 17:23). The word εὐλάβεια means "reverence" (Heb. 12:28) or "godly fear" (Heb. 5:7). Both εὐλαβής (Luke 2:25; Acts 2:5; 8:2; 22:12) and εὐσεβής (Acts 10:2, 7; II Pet. 2:9) are used to designate "the pious" (חסיד, צדיק, and possibly נדיב).

It will be noted that the idea of anxiety in the Bible seems to be rather sharply distinguished from that of fear. Both Hebrew words דאג, "to be anxious" (Ps. 38:18—H 38:19), and רגז, "to be disturbed" (II Sam. 7:10), are sometimes rendered by the LXX as μεριμνάω, "to be troubled with cares," and the same verb is used by the NT writers in a similar sense (Matt. 6:27, 31; 10:19; cf. Luke 12:22, 25; I Cor. 7:32 ff; Phil. 4:6; cf. I Cor. 12:25; Phil. 2:20).

2. Fear in the OT. In its secular sense, the emotion of fear seizes animals when they react in the presence of the superior power of men (Gen. 9:2), although some are described as fearless (Job 39:16; 41:33). Even the world of nature experiences fear (Ps. 76:8). Men generally fear catastrophes of a cosmic character (Ps. 46:2).

a. Worldly fear. Man is afraid whenever a threat arises against his security and especially his life. Cain, because he is a vagabond upon the face of the earth, knows that anyone who finds him may slay him (Gen. 4:14). Jacob fears the avenging of Esau, his brother (Gen. 32:7), and later is afraid of emigrating to an unknown country (Gen. 46:3). The Hebrews are dismayed by the strength of the Canaanites (Num. 14:9; etc.). A shepherd is afraid at the roaring of the lion (Amos 3:8). The witch of Endor shrieks when she sees the ghost of Samuel (I Sam. 28:12), and Eliphaz of Teman experiences fear at the vision of a nocturnal spirit (Job 4:14). Job is tortured by physical and mental pains which defy explanation and fears the proximity of premature death (Job 3:25; 21:6; 22:10; etc.). There are hundreds of examples of secular fear in the OT.

b. Fear and sin. Man fears God, but such an emotion is ambiguous, for it may both repel and attract. In the first sense the fear of God may result from a sense of sin and therefore correspond more or less to the expectation of a destructive or chastising retribution. Thus man is afraid in the garden after his act of disobedience (Gen. 3:10). Sarah is afraid because she laughed at the word of Yahweh, and her fear prompts her to deny her manifestations of skepticism (Gen. 18:15). Abimelech and his servants are sore afraid when they become aware of the offensive character of their behavior (Gen. 20:8 ff). Moses is afraid of God's anger and hot displeasure caused by the people's worship of the golden calf (Deut. 9:19). The psalmists are aware of the terror which seizes sinners at the expectation of punishment (Pss. 76:8 ff; 78:33; etc.). At least in one instance man's fear of death coalesces with the sense of his iniquity (Ps. 90:7-11; *see* DEATH; SIN).

Occasionally suffering men are terrified because they find in God the author of their misery; and yet they are unwilling or unable to explain the hostility of the Deity against them as a result of their sinfulness, of which they are unaware (Job 23:15; Pss. 22:1 ff; 88:1 ff).

Consonant with an interpretation of the sinful condition of man, Hebrew eschatology develops a fearful expectation of the day of Yahweh (*see* DAY OF THE LORD) when men will be paralyzed by terror before judgment (Deut. 32:25; Ps. 48:5 ff; Isa. 2:6-22; 13:6-8; 31:7; Ezek. 27:35 ff; Joel 2:1; Amos 5:18; Hab. 3:2; Zech. 9:5; Mal. 3:2-3; etc.).

c. Fear and revelation. More often, the OT refers to fear in the context of divine revelation. One of the typical features of the theophanies is the formula which is again and again addressed to man by Yahweh or his representative throughout the OT: "Fear not!" (Gen. 15:1; Exod. 14:13; Judg. 6:23; Isa. 41:10; etc.). All the traditions of the self-disclosure of God to men suggest in one way or in another the element of *mysterium tremendum.* There is a mystery in divine holiness which produces in man a sense of terror (see the expression "the Fear of Isaac" in Gen. 31:42; cf. vs. 53).

But this kind of dread is not merely negative. It

accompanies the perception of God's glory and may generate an emotion of exultation and joy at the discovery of God's intense concern and love for man (Ps. 18; Hab. 3; cf. vss. 16 and 18). This kind of fear is the result not only of the knowledge that Yahweh is a holy God, but also of the apprehension of his saving grace. The concept of the "numinous" is to be seriously qualified whenever it is applied to Hebrew modes of theological thinking, for the God of Israel, from the time of Moses, at least, is not an impersonal "numen" but a personal Being who intervenes in the affairs of men and whose self-disclosure is ultimately a gracious uncovering of active will, saving intent, and creative purpose.

For instance, Jacob is seized by terror and exclaims at the vision of the heavenly ladder, "How awesome is this place!" But he adds in the same breath, with a sense of certainty and expectation, "This is none other than the house of God, and this is the gate of heaven!" (Gen. 28:17.) His experience of dread is inseparable from the reaffirmed sense of his destiny and the acceptance of a "tremendous" promise of land and posterity, whose goal is the establishment of peace and harmony for the whole of mankind (Gen. 28:13-14).

Likewise Moses at the burning bush is afraid to look upon God (Exod. 3:6), but this negative fear is compounded with a positive emotion at the disclosure of the name of Yahweh and of the divine purpose in history (cf. the fear of the divine name in Pss. 99:3; 111:9; etc.). To be sure, in at least one theophanic story, the people's reactions to the manifestation of divine presence are those of blind terror and trembling (Exod. 19:16; 20:18 [LXX], 20*b;* Deut. 5:4-5), but the whole tradition is embedded in the theological concept of Israel's inability or unwillingness to fulfil her mission, and this kind of fear is therefore related to the motif of sin and revolt as described above (*see* § 2*b; see also* THEOPHANY; PRESENCE).

By extension, men who have come into direct and immediate relation with God may produce an emotion of fear in the common people. "When Aaron and all the people of Israel saw Moses, behold, the skin of his face shone, and they were afraid to come near him" (Exod. 34:30; cf. Josh. 4:14; I Sam. 12:18; 18:12). The stories of the ark (I Sam. 5–6; II Sam. 6) and the temple ritual of holiness (Leviticus) derive from a similar complex of fear at the physical contact with the divine (cf. Ps. 5:7; etc.; *see* HOLINESS).

d. Fear and worship. The attraction-producing fear which arises from theophanic encounters is carried over into the cultic context of worship, and it is also transferred to the psychological experience of the immediate presence of God. The OT repeatedly associates the emotion of fear with the complex of faith, trust, love, and communion; and it is perhaps at this juncture that the biblical mode of thinking is most startling to the modern Western mind. For the ancient Hebrew, a member of the holy people, covenanted with a holy God for a unique purpose in history, there is no paradox in the liturgical command, "Serve Yahweh with fear, and rejoice with trembling!" (Ps. 2:11.)

Israel worships the covenant God, and the sacramental memory of the Exodus becomes for her the ground of hope against all odds that God will triumph over evil and will fulfil his purpose in creation. Thus the Yahweh of the Exodus is adored through the centuries of biblical history, "majestic in holiness, terrible in glorious deeds" (Exod. 15:11). The eschatological hope transcends the fear of enemies here and now or the terror of judgment at the moment of the advent of God. At the same time trust in the saving power of the Deity does not do away with fear of him. On the contrary, the acceptance of salvation produces a kind of awe which is only compatible with the humility, the brokenness, the utter contrition of the saved. This fear is not the result of God's destroying wrath or condemning judgment. It arises from the perception of his very love, unmerited, gratuitous, unearned. At the promise of God's decision not to execute the fierceness of his anger—for he is God and not man, the Holy One in the midst of Israel—the people "shall go after the LORD, he will roar like a lion; yea, he will roar, and his sons shall come trembling from the west; they shall come eagerly like birds from Egypt, and like doves from the land of Assyria" (Hos. 11:9-11*a*). And as if to prevent any misunderstanding of the true intention of God, and to dispel any ambiguity in the emphasis on "trembling," the oracle concludes with the promise, "I will return them to their homes, says the LORD" (Hos. 11:11*b; see* JEALOUSY; LOVE).

It is because there is a kind of fear which is not incompatible with faith that the psalmist is able to exclaim, "But there is forgiveness with thee, that thou mayest be feared" (Ps. 130:4). Faith in Yahweh delivers from worldly fears (Ps. 23:4) because faith involves a true fear of a totally different quality which is based on the recognition of God's holiness. "Do not fear what they fear [the fear of men], nor be in dread. But the LORD of hosts, him you shall regard as holy; let him be your fear, and let him be your dread" (Isa. 8:12*b*-13; cf. Deut. 1:17; *see* WORSHIP IN THE OT).

e. The fear of the Lord. Hence, the expression "the fear of the LORD" (*yir'ath Yahweh*) becomes the familiar way of describing the religion of biblical Judaism in the postexilic period (see Proverbs and Ecclesiastes). It would be a grave error, however, to soften the meaning of the expression and to ignore its central element of *mysterium tremendum.* Although many commentators and historians have fallen into this error during the past hundred years, the fear of the Lord is not merely to be equated with reverence, piety, or religion because it is impossible today to revaluate and again charge these terms with their ancient—but now largely lost—connotation of awesomeness. It is true that biblical religion is summed up in the law to love God absolutely and exclusively (Deut. 6:4-5), but this love, precisely because it is absolute and exclusive, imposes upon man a demand which is never devoid of fearful dimensions. Thus the love of God in the *Shema'* (Deut. 6:4-5) is never separated from the fear of God (cf. Deut. 6:2, 13; 10:20; 28:58 with 11:1, 13, 22; 19:9; 30:6, 16; etc.; see also

Jer. 32:39 ff), because absolute love means total surrender.

It is in the exacting and inclusive sense of an absolute love that the fear of the Lord becomes the principle of human behavior and the beginning of wisdom (Job 28:28; Ps. 111:10; Prov. 1:7; *see* WISDOM). The true love of man for God creates a sense of anguish at the very thought of moral evil, revolt, rebellion, or compromise (Ps. 51:6-15). At the end of all other attributes, the messianic figure will receive the spirit of the fear of the Lord (Isa. 11:2).

3. Fear in the Apoc. and Pseudep. The literature of the Apoc. and Pseudep. appears to be little concerned explicitly with the idea of fear, either in its secular or in its theological sense. Nevertheless, the author of IV Esdras experiences "dismay" over Israel's trials, and he thinks that before the "inconceivable glory" of the Lord, the hosts of heaven "stand trembling" (8:21). The influence of the Greek mind is revealed when "fear" is described as "nothing but surrender of the helps that come from reason"—προδοσία τῶν ἀπὸ λογισμοῦ βοηθημάτων (Wisd. Sol. 17:12—G 17:11). Even the expression "the fear of God" or "the fear of the Lord" receives scant attention (Ecclus. 1:11-20; 2:7-11; 21:11; II Esd. 8:28). In one passage the fear of sin is made the prerequisite of wisdom (Pirke Aboth 3:12; cf. 2:6). In other places "to fear the Lord" becomes the practical equivalent of "to love God" (Ecclus. 2:15-17; cf. 40: 25-27; Aristeas 159, 189; Test. Benj. 3:3, 4*b*).

Yet some rabbis established a distinction between the love and fear of God. Simeon ben Eleazar said, "Greater is he who acts from love than he who acts from fear" (Soṭ. 31*a;* cf. Sifre Deut. 6:5). Others debated the question whether fear or love of God was the motivation of Job's piety (M. Soṭ. 5:5).

4. Fear in the NT. While the concept of fear in the NT does not occupy a central place, the use of the word and its synonyms offers a remarkable parallel to that in the OT.

a. Worldly fear. The emotion of fear in a nontheological context is frequently referred to. For example, Joseph is afraid to return to Judea when he hears that Archelaus reigns there in the place of Herod (Matt. 2:22). The authorities, on several occasions, are afraid of the people (Matt. 14:5; 21:26, 46; Mark 11:18; Acts 5:26).

It is a similar kind of worldly fear, timidity, cowardice, the dread of dangers, demons, enemies, death, which is in the mind of the NT writers when they extol the fruits of the new life and maintain that God in Christ delivers from secular fear. Thus the spirit of slavery would allow the brethren to fall back into fear, but the spirit of sonship makes them cry, "Abba! Father!" (Rom. 8:15). Love of man for God which is the reflection of God's love for man dispels all fears of disease, oppression, persecution, and death. In this sense, there is no fear in love (I John 4:17-18). Christians experience no longer the spirit of timidity or cowardice (δειλία) but a spirit of power and love and self-control (II Tim. 1:7; *see* LOVE).

b. Fear and Christ. Another brand of fear is created among men by the witness of the deed of God in Christ. The coming of Jesus is described in terms which are reminiscent of the self-disclosure of God in the OT. The theophanic formula "Fear not!" is used in the narratives of the birth of John the Baptist and Jesus (Luke 1:13, 30; 2:10), and the Synoptic and more particularly the Lukan traditions place it not infrequently in the mouth of Jesus (Luke 5:10; 8:50; 12:7, 32). The Fourth Gospel quotes the same formula in a christological epiphany (John 12:15). The episode of the Transfiguration (Matt. 17:6-7; Luke 9:34) and the stories of the Cross and of the Resurrection (Matt. 27:54; 28:4) are told in terms which likewise echo the manifestations of God at the time of the Exodus. Fear is still a self-centered emotion, which reveals sinful man's unwillingness to accept the implications of his divine calling (Mark 10:32).

c. Fear and joy. An altogether different fear seizes the disciples when they confront holiness in the person of Jesus. The worldly fear of danger in a storm is soothed but a sacred awe takes its place as the disciples discern the power of their Lord (Mark 4:37-41; cf. Matt. 9:8; 14:26-27; Mark 5:15, 33). When Jesus heals or raises from the dead, the bystanders glorify God, and they are at the same time filled with awe (Luke 5:26), for they become conscious of the intervention of God himself in their own history. They claim jubilantly that "God has visited his people," but this very awareness thrust them into fear (Luke 7:16).

As in the OT, this feeling is not incompatible with elation, trust, and certainty. And thus the women at the empty tomb, aware of the victory of Christ over death, "departed quickly . . . with fear and great joy" (Matt. 28:8; cf. Mark 16:8). The growth of the church in Jerusalem yields a similar consequence (Acts 2:43). There is no contradiction, among the early Christians, between the experience of joy and the sense of theological fear.

d. Those who fear the Lord. Like the Hebrew expression "fear of Yahweh," which implies complete reliance on the promise of the covenant God, the NT expression "those who fear God" is employed to describe the faithful (Luke 1:50; cf. 18:2, 4). Quite clearly, however, men who are thus designated do not represent the average religionists of their time. They are inspired by an intense hope and a personal dedication to the will of God, whatever it may be and wherever it may lead them. The same expression designates also in the NT some pagans who had been converted to the Jewish faith (Acts 10:2, 22, 35; cf. 13:43 [σεβόμενος, "worshiper"]; 16:14; 17:4, 17; 18:7; *see* PROSELYTE).

e. Fear and sanctification. The new man in Christ is delivered from worldly fears, but he is constantly reminded that he has to fear evil in all its forms (Matt. 10:28; Rom. 11:20). The sanctification of the Christian individual as well as that of the church is the fruit of the fear of the Lord (II Cor. 5:10-11; 7:1; cf. Col. 3:22; Heb. 10:31; etc.; *see* SANCTIFICATION; HOLY SPIRIT). It is thus a grave error to maintain, with many moderns, that Christianity, as opposed to Hebraism, has replaced the fear of God by the love of God. The NT, as well as the OT, understands so profoundly the tragic dimensions of love and knows so acutely the awesomeness of the divine presence that it proposes to man no other prospect than the service of God "with fear and trembling" (Phil. 2:12).

The church is built up and multiplies, "walking in the fear of the Lord and in the comfort of the Holy Spirit" (Acts 9:31). To worship and to adore the Savior is to glorify and to fear the name of the Lord, creator of heaven and earth, who alone is holy (Rev. 14:6-7; 15:3-4).

Bibliography. B. J. Bamberger, "Fear and Love of God in the OT," *HUCA*, VI (1929), 39-53. J. Hänel, "Die Ehrfurcht vor Gott," *Die Religion der Heiligkeit* (1931), pp. 106-34. W. Eichrodt, "Die Gottesfurcht," *Theologie des ATs,* III (1935), 18-33. R. Sander, "Furcht und Liebe im palästinischen Judentum," *BWANT,* Vierte Folge, Heft 16 (1935). J. Hempel, "Die Furcht vor Jahve," *Gott und Mensch im AT* (1936), pp. 4-33. G. Nagel, "Crainte et amour de Dieu dans l'AT," *Revue de Théologie et de Philosophie, XXXII* (1944), 175-86. R. Otto, *The Idea of the Holy* (trans. J. W. Harvey; 10th ed., 1946). R. H. Pfeiffer, "The Fear of God," *IEJ,* V (1955), 41-48 (includes a valuable survey of the idea of religious fear in the nonbiblical literatures of the ancient Near East).

S. Terrien

FEAR OF ISAAC [פחד יצחק]. An ancient divine name which stems out of the pre-Mosaic cult of the "God of the fathers" (Gen. 31:42, 53), as do also the names "God of Abraham" (perhaps "Shield of Abraham" [Gen. 15:1]) and "Mighty One of Jacob" (Gen. 49:24). In the case at hand, the deity was known within the circles of Isaac by the name of the patriarch who received the revelation and established the cult. Frequently פחד is translated "fear, dread" (LXX φόβος)—i.e., the deity is the One who aroused fear on the part of Isaac, even as Jacob was overcome by dread in a holy place (Gen. 28:17; *see further* Fear; Holiness). On the other hand, the linguistic relation of פחד to Aramaic and Arabic *paḫiḏ faḫiḏ* ("thigh, loins, hip"; cf. Job 40:17), Ugaritic *pḫd* ("flock"), and later Palmyrenian *paḥdâ* ("family, clan, tribe") lends support to the view that originally it meant "kindred, kinsman." The archaic meaning, "Kinsman of Isaac," would accord well with the cult of the fathers, which was based upon the relationship between a family or clan and the god who revealed himself in a special way to the patriarchal leader.

As in the case of other pre-Mosaic divine names, this one was later appropriated by Israel as a title for Yahweh. Thus in the present revision of Pentateuchal traditions Yahweh is the "God of the fathers" who, in the time before Moses, manifested himself in various ways to Abraham, Isaac, and Jacob. *See further* God, Names of.

Bibliography. A. Alt, *Der Gott der Väter* (1929); H. G. May, "The God of My Father: A Study of Patriarchal Religion," *JBL* (1941), pp. 155 ff; W. F. Albright, *From the Stone Age to Christianity* (2nd ed., 1957), pp. 248-49.

B. W. Anderson

FEASTS AND FASTS [חגים; צומות]. The seasonal occasions of national and religious celebration in Israel. The feasts were marked by thanksgiving, and often by joyous feasting; and, in direct contrast (cf. Zech. 8:19), the fasts were seasonal recollections of national disaster and times of communal penitence.

A. Feasting
B. Fasting
C. The festal observances
  1. Canonical
    a. The sabbath
    b. The New Moon
    c. The seventh New Moon
    d. The seventh year
    e. The pentecostal year
  2. Pilgrim
    a. Passover and Feast of Unleavened Bread
    b. Weeks
    c. Booths
  3. Noncanonical
    a. The Feast of Dedication
    b. Purim
    c. *Simḥath Torah*
D. The fasts
  1. Canonical
  2. Noncanonical
Bibliography

A. *FEASTING.* In a broad sense the term "feast" can be used with reference to all set times of communal observance in Israel. The RSV recognizes this by frequently translating מועדים ("times," "seasons") by the phrase "appointed feasts" (e.g., Lev. 23:2, 4, 44; Isa. 1:14; Ezek. 36:38; 44:24; 45:17; Hos. 2:11). Thus, in Lev. 23 this phrase even includes the Day of Atonement in a list of mandatory observances, though it is, properly speaking, a fast rather than a feast. In Ezek. 45:17 the Hebrew term for "appointed feasts" includes the new moons and the sabbaths (cf. Hos. 2:11), though in 44:24 the latter are mentioned separately; and in 36:38 the term probably refers only to the pilgrim feasts.

In contrast to the general reference of "appointed feasts," the word "feast," based on the Hebrew חג, is used almost exclusively of the three great annual pilgrim festivals: Unleavened Bread, Weeks, and Booths. The verb from which the noun issues means "to make pilgrimage." Pilgrimages included processions, dances, feasting, and, sometimes, drunkenness. In Ps. 107:27 the verb is translated "reeled," to describe the staggering gait of sailors aboard ship in a storm. It seems probable, however, that connotations such as reeling, dancing, and feasting are derivative from the basic idea of pilgrimage.

The term "feast" is used of the celebrations Israel made in honor of the idolatrous golden calf (Exod. 32:5-6, 17-19). While this was not strictly a pilgrim feast, the account gives a vivid picture of the expansive demonstrations of popular excitement characteristic of these feasts. It also serves as a reminder that all feasts were high religious occasions. A few general references to the great feasts of Israel (Isa. 29:1; 30:29; Amos 5:21; 8:10; Nah. 1:15—H 2:1) also hint at the exuberance characteristic of these occasions. While present in all, it was especially characteristic of Booths (*see* Booths, Feast of). In connection with this feast the term חג occurs in a special sense in Ps. 118:27, which, as part of the Hallel, was sung at Booths. The psalmist calls on the celebrants to bind the חג to the horns of the altar with branches. In all probability the term here does not refer to the sacrifice, as was formerly supposed, but to the procession itself. As part of its circumambulation of the altar the procession attaches itself to its horns.

In Exod. 34:25 there occurs the single explicit reference to the Passover as a feast; it may also be implied in Exod. 23:18; Ps. 81:3—H 81:4; and, perhaps, in Ezek. 45:21. It is a striking fact, however, that the term should be used so sparingly of Passover though occurring with great frequency to describe the intimately related observance of Unleavened Bread (Exod. 12:14; 23:15; 34:18; Lev. 23:6; Deut. 16:16; II Chr. 8:13; 30:13, 21; 35:17; Ezra 6:22; Ezek. 45: 23). Sometimes the word is associated more strictly with the special days of SOLEMN ASSEMBLY in this feast, whether the first (Num. 28:17) or the last (Exod. 13:6). Many historians of the Israelite cultus hold that originally Booths was the only pilgrim festival. In this connection they point out that at its observance, in connection with the dedication of Solomon's temple, it is referred to simply as "the feast" (החג; I Kings 8:2, 65; cf. II Chr. 5:3; 7:9), as though it was the only one. The fact that the month of the feast is mentioned in two of these instances perhaps qualifies this singularity somewhat. However, it is also designated as "the feast of the Lord" (Lev. 23:39). In any case, the term is applied very frequently to Booths as one of the three great pilgrimages (Exod. 23:16; 34: 22; Lev. 23:34; Deut. 16:13, 16; 31:10; II Chr. 8:13; Ezra 3:4; Zech. 14:16, 18-19). It also occurs in relation to the less prominent festival of Weeks (Exod. 23:16; 34:22; Deut. 16:10, 16; II Chr. 8:13).

At the center of the great pilgrim feasts were the festal sacrifices. These sacrifices were mainly communal meals, eaten with great joy. The eating of meat, a relatively rare occurrence in ancient Israel, and originally always having a religious significance, coupled with the drinking of wine, gave to a feast both its festal and its sacral character. In contrast to others, the festal sacrifice was known as a זבח, "slaughter." It was eaten at the sites of ancestral altars (Gen. 46:1) or at the designated centers of worship as a common meal "before God" (Exod. 18: 12). God himself was assumed to participate symbolically by receiving the choice portions of fat which were burned on the altar. He also shared the wine through the libations that were offered at a later stage of the cultus. As has been emphasized in recent scholarship, the great feasts were occasions of "covenant renewal" at which the bonds that held Israel together as the people of God were reknit.

The whole range of festal observances, both the pilgrim feasts and the "appointed times" of a festal nature, will be surveyed in outline below. In the meantime a presentation of the general data on fasting and fasts is in order.

B. *FASTING.* As the word צום indicates, abstinence from food is the basic form of a fast. There are, however, many elaborations of this. There is also a wide range of occasions for fasts.

As in the case of the great feasts, communal fasts were held at the site of a central shrine. Following defeat in their war with Benjamin, the Israelites came to fast and weep "before the LORD" in Bethel, where the ark was (Judg. 20:26-27). Samuel is said to have summoned all Israel to a convocation of penitence and fasting at Mizpah, his own seat as priest-judge (I Sam. 7:5-6); much later, in the days of the Maccabees, Judas and his brothers, lacking access to Jerusalem, summoned their followers to Mizpah for a fast day because of its ancient reputation as a site of worship (I Macc. 3:42-54). Jeremiah sent Baruch to read his book to the people at the temple on a fast day, when people from the towns would have come to Jerusalem (Jer. 36:4-6). The great public fasts, not regularly scheduled but called for reasons of dire emergency, had their natural center in the temple at Jerusalem; and the king, the prophets, and the priests played leading roles (II Kings 19:1-7). A sample litany is given in Joel 2:17; some of the penitential psalms were very probably the outcome of the public liturgical ceremonies of the fast days.

The public summons to a fast seems to have been an accepted custom in time of crisis (Jer. 36:9; Joel 2:15). In I Kings 21:9 ff, we learn that, as a trap for Naboth, Queen Jezebel forged letters in Ahab's name calling the nobles and judges, asking them to proclaim a fast. Naboth was to be brought to trial on the false charge of having cursed God and the king (I Kings 21:5-16). The fast must in this case probably be understood as a means of counteracting the power of the curse. At the preaching of Jonah the repentant king of Nineveh "proclaimed a fast" for his city that involved the abstinence from both food and water by animals as well as men (Jonah 3:5, 7-8). Esther sent instructions to Mordecai to gather all the Jews in Susa to a fast in her behalf (Esth. 4:15-16) under circumstances that gave it the significance of a service of intercession.

A typical fast was for a single day (Judg. 20:26; I Sam. 7:6), with the abstinence lasting until sunset; the great official fast of the Day of Atonement conformed to this pattern. Abstinence from wine and water (I Sam. 7:6; Dan. 10:3; Jonah 3:5, 7-8), as well as from food, was practiced. Garments were rent or exchanged for sackcloth; people sat on the ground and threw dust and ashes on their heads. Whether sitting or in ceremonial procession, there was weeping. The hair was left undressed and the body unwashed (II Sam. 12:16; I Macc. 3:47). There are occasional criticisms of these external forms (Isa. 58: 1-5; Joel 2:12-13); but this summons to "rend your hearts and not your garments" must not be interpreted as an attempt to abolish fasts, but to give them meaning as expressions of genuine penitence or sorrow. The prophet Zechariah (7:1-7) counseled those who made inquiry to lift the fasts of the fifth and seventh months (*see below*), commemorating the destruction of the temple and of the Judean state respectively. The issue was raised, in all probability, because these had in his day been restored. His counsel, which did not prevail, was not based only on the fact that the restoration had taken place, however; he was troubled by the fact that as a sacrifice, all fasting, like all feasting, though done before the Lord, has an inescapable ambiguity about it: it is both a form of self-dedication and of self-preservation.

Along with forms of abstinence, sacrifice in some form was a characteristic of all communal fasts. At Mizpah, Samuel "poured [water] out before the LORD" (I Sam. 7:6; cf. II Sam. 23:16-17); this was a primitive form of sacrifice which indicates that, while the codification of fasting practices occurred late in OT history, fasts had been observed all along. The ordinance for the Day of Atonement (Lev. 16) indicates that the sin offering was the most typical sacrifice offered on a fast day; but burnt offerings and peace offerings are also mentioned (Judg. 20:26).

Some fasts, both individual and public, were acts

of repentance to avert threatening disaster. The response of Ahab to the word of Elijah (I Kings 21:27) and of Nineveh to the preaching of Jonah (Jonah 3:5-8) are of this type (cf. also Neh. 9:1; Esth. 4:16; Jer. 14:12). So was David's fast (I Sam. 12:16-20), the course of which amazed his courtiers. Other fasts, perhaps even more common, in view of the surprise caused by David's rejection of this type, were really acts of mourning, with confessions of guilt following the occurrence of disaster. The mourning over the fall of the city, illustrated by the book of Lamentations and many psalms, belongs to this group. Mourning rites at the time of death constitute a special instance of the observance of the fast (cf. I Sam. 31:13). In external form the observances of the two types of fast were very similar, though the motivation is fundamentally different.

In the late OT period the fast, notably the private fast, seems to have become increasingly prevalent. The two motivations cited above became combined: i.e., a fast might at the same time be an act of mourning for the disaster that had already struck and an act of repentance that might avert further disaster. But in addition to this, the fast seems to have acquired a new function as a means of personal spiritual cleansing and illumination. Daniel "was mourning for three weeks" (10:2 ff). The account of his behavior conforms to the description of a fast. At the end of this period he receives a vision which he alone is capable of enduring (vs. 7).

C. *THE FESTAL OBSERVANCES.* The distinction between the pilgrim feasts of Israel and other "appointed" times of celebration was ultimately superseded by a more significant one—i.e., that between those that were provided for in the law and were, therefore, canonical; and those that rested simply on custom.

1. Canonical. The wide range of feasts provided for in the Pentateuchal legislation falls into two main groups: (*a*) the sabbath, and other "appointed" times related to it; and (*b*) the great pilgrim feasts.

a. The sabbath. The wide range of legal material that serves as a basis for the observance of the SABBATH (שבת, "rest") includes the following: Exod. 16: 22-30; 20:8-11; 23:12; 31:12-16; 34:21; 35:2-3; Lev. 19:3; 23:3; 26:2; Num. 15:32-36; 28:9-10; Deut. 5:12-15. The great bulk of this material belongs to the priestly strand of the Pentateuch. While sabbaths were undoubtedly a feature of Israelite observance from the beginning, the legislation about the sabbath proper and its central role as a sign of Israel's relation to the Lord, was probably a much later development. Originally sabbaths were very probably lunar observances, marking important phases of the moon. In Israel, however, the sabbath no longer depends on this natural cycle; it occurs every seventh day, cutting across and gradually superseding in importance such lunar observances as the new moons. The sabbath commemorates both creation (Exod. 20:8-11; cf. Gen. 2:1-3) and Israel's release from slavery (Deut. 5:12-15; cf. Exod. 23:12). It is a sign of Israel's state of holiness, because of its election by God and its relation to him in the covenant. This relationship is to be set forth in the holiness or "separation" of Israel on the sabbath: from all work and ordinary occupation (Exod. 35:2-3), and from contact with the secular world outside the house (Lev. 23:3). And on the positive side it was exemplified in the sanctification of the home; in light and joy that replaced mourning; and in appearing "before the LORD," whether in a holy convocation at the temple (Lev. 26:2) or in the study of the law. The tractate in the Mishna stands as a monument to the care with which the consecration of the sabbath was defined. The breaking of the sabbath constituted apostasy from the covenant and was punishable by death (Num. 15:32-36). In the order of temple sacrifices the festal character of the sabbath was noted by doubling the sacrifices offered on an ordinary day (Num. 28:1-10).

b. The New Moon. The feast of the NEW MOON (חדש, "new moon," "month") was probably the original form of the sabbath, before the latter was separated from the lunar cycle. The canonical requirement of the observance of the new moons is not so much legally prescribed as presupposed; this is indicated by the fact that the law specifies the amount and manner of the sacrifices (Num. 10:10; 28:11-15). It is to be noted that these are greater than those for the sabbath (Num. 28:1-10) and that their offering was accompanied by the blowing of trumpets as a mark of the festal character of the occasion. The tabernacle had reputedly been set up on the first new moon of the year (Exod. 40:2, 17). Though the Feast of the New Moon had its roots in a native cultus, it had been fully assimilated by Israelite faith and was a sign of the eternal character of the covenant and of the faithfulness of the Lord who instituted it (Ps. 104:19; Ecclus. 43:6-8). The persistence of the Feast of the New Moon contributed to Israel's adherence to a lunar calendar in governing its religious and communal life, with subsequent results for the Christian Year.

c. The seventh New Moon. In contrast to the new moon in general there is a specific prescription in the Law (Lev. 23:24-25) for the festal observance of that of the seventh month. Further, the sacrifices are greater than for other new moons (Num. 29:16). The seventh month is Tishri, in which both the Day of Atonement (*see* ATONEMENT, DAY OF) and the Feast of Booths (*see* BOOTHS, FEAST OF) occur. The traditional explanation for the special observance of the new moon of this month is built on the principle of the sacredness of the number seven. The force of this argument is impressive. It can point to the fact that, beginning with the sabbath on the seventh day, the entire cycle of feasts related to it (*see* § C1*a above*) is arranged on the basis of multiples of seven: the seventh day, the seventh month, the seventh year, and the forty-ninth year (seven times seven), to introduce the Year of Jubilee. The same sabbatical principle is operative elsewhere, notably in the computation of the Feast of Weeks. Since Wellhausen, the attempt has been made to interpret the special observance of the first of the seventh month as a form of New Year's observance. Israel's year originally ended in the autumn, but more probably at the close of Tishri, since Booths seems to have been the last feast of the annual cycle. Since the Jewish New Year currently occurs on the first of Tishri, some of those who consider the Feast of the Seventh New Moon a new year's observance have proposed that the change was made by the Jews in the Babylonian exile to offset the festivities of the Babylonian New Year on the first of Nisan; but evidence for a satisfactory solution of the problem is wanting.

d. The seventh year. Every seventh year (שבת שבתון לארץ, "sabbath of rest for the land") was a festal year. It was a celebration of Israel's faith that the land was a gift of God to his people. The land, like the people, was holy: this feast was for the sake of the land, so that it might rest (Exod. 23:11), and like the people, keep "a sabbath of solemn rest . . . to the LORD" (Lev. 25:4). As a double portion of manna appeared on the sixth day (Exod. 16:5), so the command to observe the rest of the land was coupled with the promise that in the sixth year the land would bear fruit for three years (Lev. 25:21). The sabbatical year was also for the sake of the people. It was the year when all Israelite slaves were to be set free (Exod. 21:2-6), in which the poor and animals might eat freely of what the land produced by itself (Exod. 23:10-11; Lev. 25:6), and in which all creditors would be released from debt (Deut. 15: 1-6). The festal year fortified the sabbatical principle, which was a sign that Israel's existence and its land were a gift and an inheritance. Jeremiah notes that the requirement of the festal year was frequently ignored or observed opportunistically (34:8 ff); and the Exile is interpreted as God's punishment for this disobedience and as his vindication of the right of the land to observe its sabbath (Lev. 26:32-35).

e. The pentecostal year. The fiftieth year (דרור, "freedom"), or the year of Jubilee, followed the completion of a series of seven sabbatical years. It is apparent that the plan is modeled upon the observance of Weeks on the fiftieth day following the waving of the barley sheaf at the Feast of Unleavened Bread (Lev. 23:15-16), after the completion of seven sabbaths. This special festal year is provided for only in the priestly legislation (Lev. 25:8-55; 27:17-24); and since its requirements were virtually identical with those of the sabbatical year, including the restoration of property to its ancestral owners and the release of slaves (Lev. 25:10, 13), there are real grounds to question whether the institution was ever much more than an idealistic "plan." It may be significant that the characteristic term, "freedom," "liberty" (Lev. 25:10), is used of the seventh year by Jeremiah (34:8, 15, 17). While the year of Jubilee may have had a slight role in social history it eventually became a very influential Christian eschatological metaphor (Isa. 61:1-2; cf. Luke 4:18-19). *See* JUBILEE, YEAR OF; WEEKS, FEAST OF; PASSOVER AND FEAST OF UNLEAVENED BREAD.

2. Pilgrim. ***a. Passover and Feast of Unleavened Bread.*** This feast, kept for seven days, Nisan 14-21, and marked by two holy convocations (*see* CONVOCATION, HOLY), combined two originally separate observances. The basic canonical ordinances for it are the following: Exod. 12:1–13:16; 23:15; 34:18-20, 25; Lev. 23:4-14; Num. 28:16-25; Deut. 16:1-8. For a description of the rites of the feast, and of their history and meaning, *see* PASSOVER AND FEAST OF UNLEAVENED BREAD.

b. Weeks. This one-day festival was kept early in the third month, on the fiftieth day after the offering of the barley sheaf at the Feast of Unleavened Bread. It marked the end of the grain harvest and the beginning of the season for the offering of first fruits. The basic Pentateuchal texts are: Exod. 23:16; 34:22; Lev. 23:15-21; Num. 28:26-31; Deut. 16:9-12. For a full discussion, *see* WEEKS, FEAST OF.

c. Booths. This feast was kept for seven days, beginning on the fifteenth of the seventh month. It represented Israel's assimilation of an ancient vintage festival and commemorated the wandering in the wilderness. The legal provisions relating to it are: Exod. 23:16; 34:22; Lev. 23:33-36, 39-43; Num. 29: 12-32; Deut. 16:13-16. For an account of the rites, *see* BOOTHS, FEAST OF.

3. Noncanonical. ***a. The Feast of Dedication.*** This eight-day festival (חנכה, *hanukkah:* "dedication"), also known as Lights, commemorates the victories of Judas Maccabeus and the purification and rededication of the temple under his leadership. He is credited with the institution of the annual observance (I Macc. 4:52-59), beginning on the twenty-fifth of the ninth month.

b. Purim. This feast (פורים, "lots") is a carnival-like celebration of one (or two) days, the fourteenth of the twelfth month, to celebrate the deliverance of the Jews from Haman by Esther and Mordecai. The institution of the feast is related in the book of Esther (9:24 ff). The Feast of Nicanor (I Macc. 7:49), celebrating a Maccabean victory on the thirteenth of the same month, was apparently absorbed by PURIM.

c. Simḥath Torah. This festal observance in honor of the Law (שמחת תורה, "Joy of the Law") is now an appendix of Booths (*see* BOOTHS, FEAST OF) and falls on the ninth day of that festival. The Ezra tradition (Neh. 8:9; I Esd. 9:50) locates a very similar observance on the first day of the seventh month.

D. *THE FASTS.* 1. Canonical. The Mosaic law provides for only one communal fast, the Day of Atonement (יום הכפורים, "the day of coverings"). This most solemn fast occurred on the tenth day of the seventh month. The Mosaic prescriptions for the observances are: Exod. 30:10; Lev. 16; 23:26-32; 25:9; Num. 29:7-11. In its complex rites, indebted to a great variety of antecedent sources, the Day was both an act of repentance and expiation to ward off disaster and a means of making available the effectiveness of divine power. Though as an institution it was of postexilic origin, the Day of Atonement incorporated many ancient Israelite practices and meanings in its forms. *See* ATONEMENT, DAY OF.

2. Noncanonical. The fairly common practice of proclaiming communal fasts in Israel has been discussed above. These were generally occasional in nature, rather than institutional. Two, however, had become annual events among the exiles in Babylon. Both were fasts of mourning. The one commemorated the burning of the temple on the ninth day of the fifth month (cf. II Kings 25:8 with Jer. 52:12), and the other the murder of Gedaliah on the second of the seventh month (Jer. 41). Despite the counsel of Zechariah (7:3-5), the former of these has survived as an annual institution. Its title is תשעת באב, "the ninth of Ab." In contemporary Jewish Orthodoxy this fast, though not Mosaic, has been practiced with utmost seriousness.

Bibliography. I. Elbogen, *Der jüdische Gottesdienst* (2nd ed., 1924). G. B. Gray, *Sacrifice in the OT* (1925). H. Schauss, *The Jewish Festivals* (1938). H. Frankfort, *The Problem of Similarity in Ancient Near Eastern Religions* (1951). E. Auerbach, "Die Babylonische Datierung . . . ," *Vetus Testamentum,* II (1952), 334-42. H.-J. Kraus, *Gottesdienst in Israel* (1954). J. Wellhausen, *Prolegomena to the History of Ancient Israel* (1957), pp. 17-164. E. Auerbach, "Die Feste im alten Israel," *Vetus Testamentum,* VIII (1958), 1-18; "Neujahrs und Versöhnungs-Fest . . . ," *Vetus Testamentum,* VIII (1958), 337-43. H.-J. Kraus, "Zur Geschichte des Passah-Massot-Festes . . . ," *Evangelische Theologie,* 18 (1958), 47-67.

J. C. RYLAARSDAM

FELIX, ANTONIUS ăn tō′nĭ əs fē′lĭks [Φῆλιξ]. PROCURATOR of Judea from 52 to 60 and successor to Cumanus. According to Acts 23:24–24:27, Felix was procurator at the time of Paul's last visit to Jerusalem and his arrest there. When Felix was recalled by Nero, Paul was turned over to the new procurator, FESTUS.

1. In Josephus. Felix, according to Josephus (Antiq. XX.vii.1), was the brother of an influential Roman named Pallas. In 52 (or 53) Felix was named procurator. Some two years later, Felix was busy putting down uprisings by "robbers and impostors" who "were a multitude not to be enumerated" (War II.xiii.2-3). By treachery Felix seized one such leader, Eleazar the son of Deneas, after giving him an assurance of no harm. He utilized the services of these robbers (identified as Sicarii) in the murder of the high priest Jonathan (Antiq. XX.viii.5). A Jew out of Egypt (see Acts 21:38), who led a large number of Jews, was attacked by Festus; the leader escaped, never to be heard from again, but four hundred of his followers were slain (Antiq. XX.viii.6; see War II.xiv.6).

Felix was recalled to Rome. A deputation of Jews went to Rome to accuse Felix, but the influence and intervention of Pallas saved him from punishment (Antiq. XX.viii.9).

Felix married DRUSILLA, a sister of Agrippa II, after persuading her to leave her husband, Azizus king of Emesa (Antiq. XX.vii.2); she bore him a son, Agrippa. Felix was married two other times.

2. In Roman sources. Scattered notices about Felix appear in the works of the Roman historians Suetonius and Tacitus. A conflict exists in the data provided by Josephus (Antiq. XX.vi.3–vii.1; War II.xii.8) and Tacitus (Ann. XII.54). The latter supposes that Felix was procurator of Samaria and Judea while Cumanus was procurator of Galilee, whereas Josephus relates that Felix succeeded Cumanus as procurator of Judea. Most scholars prefer Josephus on this point.

Suetonius (*Claudius* 28) reports that Felix had been married to three royal women (*reginarum*). One was Drusilla; another was the granddaughter of Mark Antony and Cleopatra; the third is unknown (see Tac. Hist. V.9).

Tacitus (Ann. XII.54) reports that Felix believed that he could commit all kinds of evil with impunity. The influence of his brother was undoubtedly a spur to his arbitrariness. Tacitus comments that his actions only provoked further difficulties. Some six years after Felix' recall, the Jewish War broke out; Josephus is the source of the credible contention that Felix' term, with its cruelties and oppressions, provided the cause of the war; neither Festus nor his successors (Albinus, 62-64; Florus, 64-66) would have been able to avert the disaster, had they been minded to, and they were not. Felix is a prime example of colonial mismanagement.

Apparently he was a freedman, deriving his name Antonius from Antonia, the mother of the Emperor Claudius. (A scribal error in Suidas is the basis of a wrong contention that Felix bore the name Claudius.)

3. In Acts. Acts relates that the Roman tribune Claudius Lysias sent Paul from Jerusalem to Felix in Caesarea; five days later the high priest Ananias and one Tertullus laid before Felix the case against Paul. Tertullus is portrayed as speaking of the peace enjoyed under and the reforms introduced by Felix. Paul's speech begins: "Realizing that for many years you have been judge over this nation, I cheerfully make my defense." After Paul's speech, Felix, to whom is attributed a "rather accurate knowledge of the way," postponed the decision; he kept Paul in custody, but gave him "some liberty." A few days later, Felix and his Jewish wife, Drusilla, sent for Paul "and heard him speak upon faith in Christ Jesus." Felix was alarmed when Paul "argued about justice and self-control and future judgment." Felix said: "Go away for the present; when I have an opportunity I will summon you." Felix hoped "that money would be given him by Paul. So he sent for him often and conversed with him." When Festus became the new procurator, Felix, "desiring to do the Jews a favor," kept Paul in prison (Acts 23:24–24:27).

The reliability of Acts is a general problem (see G. H. C. MacGregor, *IB,* IX [1954], 12-14, for a brief summary), in which the incident of Felix constitutes but a detail. While MacGregor (p. 307) states that "there is nothing in Luke's narrative that is either improbable or inconsistent," he concedes that "some radical critics have questioned the historicity of Paul's 'trial' before Felix."

Neither Josephus nor Paul's letters relate or allude to any connection between Paul and Felix.

Bibliography. "Antonius," Pauly-Wissowa, *Real-Encyclopadie der classischen Altertumswissenschaft,* vol. I (1804), cols. 2616 ff; E. Schürer, *A History of the Jewish People in the Time of Jesus Christ* (English trans.; 1891), div. 2, vol. II, pp. 174-82.

S. SANDMEL

FELLOE fĕl′ō. KJV translation of גב (RSV RIM), a part of the wheels used for the stands of bronze in Solomon's temple, in I Kings 7:33; Ezek. 1:18.

FELLOWSHIP. *See* COMMUNION.

FENCE [גדר (Ps. 62:3—H 62:4), גדרה (Nah. 3:17; KJV HEDGE)]. A stone wall enclosing a field, town, etc. In Ps. 62:3—H 62:4 a man beset by enemies is described as a "tottering fence" (lit., a "pushed-in wall")—a wall whose stones are out of line and whose fall is imminent.

FENCED (CITY). KJV translation of some derivatives of בצר, "enclose," and צור, "confine" (RSV FORTIFIED). *See* CITY § B2*b*.

FERRET. KJV translation of אנקה (RSV GECKO).

FERTILITY CULTS. The oldest common feature of the religions of the ancient Near East was the worship of a great mother-goddess, the personification of fertility. Associated with her, usually as a consort, was a young god who died and came to life again, like the vegetation which quickly withers but blooms again. The manner of the young god's demise was variously conceived in the myths: he was slain by another god, by wild animals, by reapers, by self-emasculation, by burning, by drowning. In some variations of the theme, he simply absconded. His absence produced infertility of the earth, of man, and of beast. His consort mourned and searched for him. His return brought renewed fertility and rejoicing.

In Mesopotamia the divine couple appear as Ishtar and Tammuz, in Egypt as Isis and Osiris. Later in Asia Minor, the Magna Mater is Cybele and her young lover is Attis. In Syria in the second millennium B.C., as seen in the Ugaritic myths, the dying and rising god is Baal-Hadad, who is slain by Mot (Death) and mourned and avenged by his sister-consort, the violent virgin Anath. In the Ugaritic myths there is some confusion in the roles of the goddesses. The great mother-goddess Asherah, the wife of the senescent chief god El, seems on the way to becoming the consort of the rising young god Baal, with whom we find her associated in the OT. Ashtarte also appears in the Ugaritic myths, but she has a minor and undistinguished role.

The OT furnishes abundant evidence as to the character of the religion of the land into which the Israelites came. Fertility rites were practiced at the numerous shrines which dotted the land, as well as at the major sanctuaries. The Israelites absorbed the Canaanite ways and learned to identify their god with Baal, whose rains brought fertility to the land. A characteristic feature of the fertility cult was sacral sexual intercourse by priests and priestesses and other specially consecrated persons, sacred prostitutes of both sexes, intended to emulate and stimulate the deities who bestowed fertility. The agricultural cult stressed the sacrifice or common meal in which the gods, priests, and people partook. Wine was consumed in great quantity in thanksgiving to Baal for the fertility of the vineyards. The wine also helped induce ecstatic frenzy, which was climaxed by self-laceration, and sometimes even by self-emasculation. Child-sacrifice was also a feature of the rites. It was not simply a cult of wine, women, and song, but a matter of life and death in which the dearest things of life, and life itself, were offered to ensure the ongoing of life.

See also ANATH; ASHERAH; ASHTORETH; BAAL; DAGON; GOD, OT VIEW OF; HIGH PLACE; PROSTITUTION; SACRIFICE AND OFFERINGS; TAMMUZ; UGARIT.

Bibliography. E. G. Kraeling, "The Real Religion of Ancient Israel," *JBL,* 47 (1928), 133-59. H. G. May, "The Fertility Cult in Hosea," *AJSL,* 48 (1932), 73-98. W. C. Graham and H. G. May, *Culture and Conscience* (1936). W. F. Albright, *Archaeology and the Religion of Israel* (1942). G. Östborn, *Yahweh and Baal: Studies in the Book of Hosea and Related Documents,* Lunds Universitets Arsskrift 51, no. 6 (1956). J. Gray, "Cultic Affinities Between Israel and Ras Shamra," *ZAW,* 62 (1949/50), 1-4; reprinted in *The Legacy of Canaan* (1957), pp. 207-20. M. H. POPE

FESTAL GARMENT [חליפות שמלת, חליפות בגדים]; KJV CHANGE OF RAIMENT or GARMENTS. An outfit worn on gala occasions (Gen. 45:22; Judg. 14:12-13, 19; II Kings 5:5, 22-23). The word חליפה, "change," when used of clothing, acquires the meaning of a special garment for other than everyday use.

FESTAL ROBE [מחלצה; *cf.* Akkad. *ḫalṣu,* clean; Arab. *ḫalaṣa,* to be clean, pure, white] (Isa. 3:22); KJV CHANGEABLE SUIT OF APPAREL. Alternately: RICH APPAREL (Zech. 3:4); KJV CHANGE OF RAIMENT. In the Isaiah passage it is a part of the finery of the daughters of Zion, and may refer to extra fine, white robes. In the Zechariah passage the allusion is to the garments which replaced the filthy garments in which Joshua the high priest was brought before the heavenly courts. In this instance the term might refer to priestly robes or, more probably, to clean garments which symbolized Joshua's innocence of the charges brought against him. Such a change of garment may reflect a court rite. H. G. MAY

FESTIVAL. *See* FEASTS AND FASTS.

FESTUS, PORCIUS pôr'shəs fĕs'təs [Φῆστος]. PROCURATOR of Judea probably from 60 to 62. He is known only from the NT and Josephus. Problems of chronology, debated for decades, focus on Festus.

1. In Josephus. Festus followed FELIX as procurator, and preceded Albinus. What Josephus relates about him (Antiq. XX.viii.9-11) can be summarized briefly (War II.xiv.1 is scarcely more than a mention).

At Caesarea (by the Sea) under Felix, bloody conflicts between Jews and pagans had arisen; pagans denied Jews a share in the administration of the city. The Jews appealed to Nero, but in vain. The conflicts thereupon became worse.

The Sicarii (wielders of small swords, *sicae*) were regarded by Festus as bandits. A certain impostor had persuaded the Sicarii that his leadership would bring them deliverance and freedom. The forces of Festus destroyed both the leader and his follower.

A dispute arose between Agrippa II and the priests over the erection of a wall designed to blot out Agrippa's view of the temple from the portico on which the king ate and, with Festus' consent, slept. Festus sided with Agrippa. The priests appealed to Rome, with the result that the wall was permitted to stand. Most writers believe, as is probable, that Festus died before this decision was announced.

2. In Acts. Acts 24:27 relates that when Felix was succeeded by Festus, Paul, in prison already for two years, came under Festus' jurisdiction. Chs. 25–26 relate that Festus visited Jerusalem, inviting the Jewish authorities to come to Caesarea to give testimony against Paul. Paul was offered the opportunity of going to Jerusalem to be tried there; in reply Paul "appealed to Caesar."

When Agrippa II and his sister Bernice visited Caesarea, Felix put Paul's case before the king, so that Agrippa expressed a wish to hear Paul. On the next day Paul was brought in before them and given permission to speak. After his speech (which Festus thought proved Paul a madman) Agrippa told Festus that Paul could have been set free, had he not appealed to Caesar.

MacGregor (*see bibliography*) expresses the judgment that the "vivid piece of drama is securely founded on fact"; he cites, however, respectable opinion—e.g., Goguel, who regards the narrative as "frankly incredible." Goguel's opinion is to be preferred.

Josephus lacks completely any mention of Paul, so that this incident naturally is not found in Josephus.

3. The chronological problem. On the supposition that the incident is based on fact, the age-old (and gratuitous) problem of its chronology can be stated as follows. Eusebius (*Chronicle*) declares that Festus became procurator in the second year of Nero's reign (56) and Albinus in the sixth or seventh year (61 or 62). This would have Festus' term last five or six years; but Josephus' account seems to suppose a very short term. That Albinus became procurator in 62 seems to be confirmed by Josephus. If the date of Albinus' becoming procurator is fixed as 62, and if Festus served but for two years, then Eusebius and Jerome err in setting Festus' entrance into the procuratorship as early as 56.

But on the preferable supposition that the incident of Paul and Festus is not based on fact, it is unnecessary to attempt to construct a consistent and persuasive chronology. Virtually all that the NT relates about the Herodian period is absent from Josephus. *See* HEROD (FAMILY). Krenkel (*Lukas und Josephus*) argues with some persuasiveness that the history which Luke reproduces is derived from Josephus. A telling argument against Krenkel, however, is the absence from Josephus of most of what Luke relates. If Josephus was indeed a source utilized by Luke, then he used it with the freedom and imagination of an artist, and not with the discipline of a modern historical researcher.

Bibliography. G. H. C. MacGregor, Exegesis of Acts, *IB*, IX (1954), 318-19. An immense literature exists in support of both a long term (56-62) and a short term (60-62) for Festus. K. Lake, *The Beginnings of Christianity,* V (1933), 466-67, favors the date 56, but a short term. F.-M. Abel, *Histoire de la Palestine depuis la Conquête d'Alexandre jusqu'à l'invasion Arabe,* I (1952), 468-69, prefers the dates 60-62. On older literature, see E. Schürer, *The History of the Jewish People in the Time of Jesus Christ,* div. 1, vol. II (1891), p. 182, note 38.

S. SANDMEL

FETTER. The translation of words which have the general meaning "anything that restricts or restrains" (נחשת, אסור, and δεσμός), as well as those which bear the specific meaning "shackle for the foot" (כבל[?] and πέδη). Fetters were made from wood, bronze (called נחשת, "bronze," just as in English shackles are frequently called "irons") or iron (Ps. 149:8). A captive's hands could be inserted in a manacle which would then be suspended from his neck by a rope. His feet might be bound with shackles, which were joined by a chain or rope so that the hobbled prisoner could take only short steps (Ps. 105:18; Mark 5:4). In Eccl. 7:26 the hands of a woman "more bitter than death" are metaphorically described as "fetters."

See also CHAIN.

Bibliography. J. B. Pritchard, ed., *ANEP* (1954), figs. 10, 49-51, 55, 57, 325-26.
R. W. CORNEY

FEVER [חרחר, דלקת, קדחת, שחפת; LXX πυρετός, δυσεντέριον]. While it is not always easy to identify the diseases mentioned in the Bible, the incidence of febrile conditions is generally described in terms which permit reasonably consistent interpretation.

חרחר (Deut. 28:22 [LXX ἐρεθισμός; RSV "fiery heat"; KJV "extreme burning"]) is probably a description of undulant (Malta) fever, or of erysipelas.

דלקת, "inflammation" (Deut. 28:22 [LXX ῥῖγος, "ague"]), probably describes malarial fever.

קדחת (Lev. 26:16 [LXX ἴκτερος; KJV "burning ague"]; Deut. 28:22 [LXX πυρετός]) may describe two different stages of the same general febrile condition, the former referring to the incidence of jaundice (icterus) with malarial fever, and the latter indicating the fever itself.

שחפת (Lev. 26:16; Deut. 28:22 [LXX ἀπορία]), translated "CONSUMPTION" in the English versions, is a wasting disease accompanied by fever. Phthisis is not common in Syria. The disease implied is more probably undulant fever, which is frequently accompanied by anemia, febrile paroxysms, and emaciation.

Πυρετός is generally used to describe malaria, a disease of frequent incidence and severe mortality in ancient Palestine. Peter's wife's mother (Matt. 8:14; Mark 1:30; Luke 4:38) and possibly the nobleman's son at Capernaum (John 4:52) were thus afflicted.

Δυσεντέριον (Acts 28:8 [RSV DYSENTERY; KJV "bloody flux") is dysentery accompanied by fever (πυρετός), perhaps relapsing malarial fever. But the condition described may be acute gangrenous dysentery, which is normally fatal. R. K. HARRISON

FIELD. A tract of ground used for farming (*see* AGRICULTURE) or for grazing (*see* PASTURE LANDS), varying in size and fertility according to the economic status of the owners and the geographical location of the territory involved.

The Hebrew word שדה is the one most commonly translated "field," and is often used in a context where it is impossible to determine its size or purpose (Gen. 2:5, 19; 4:8; Exod. 1:14; 22:5; Deut. 5:21; etc.). The word was sometimes used to designate a larger area than would be owned by one person (שדה מואב, "country of Moab"; KJV "field of Moab" in Gen. 36:35). The same word was used to designate an uncultivated region where game could be hunted (Gen. 27:5), a cultivated area where crops could be grown (Ruth 2:2, etc.; Job 24:6; Ps. 107:37), and a pasture where herds could graze (Gen. 34:5; Exod. 9:21; Num. 22:4). Details concerning the purchase of a field at Anathoth by Jeremiah are reported in Jer. 32:7 ff.

Other Hebrew words used to designate a cultivated field are: שרמות (Jer. 31:40); יגבים (Jer. 39:10); שדמה (Isa. 16:8); שדי (Deut. 32:13); חלקה (II Sam. 14:30); חוץ (Job 5:10). Aramaic בר in Dan. 2:38, etc., refers to a field in the open country.

Three Greek words rendered "field," ἀγρός, χώρα, and χωρίον, may refer either to areas limited in size or to the open country (Matt. 6:30; Luke 15:25; John 4:35; Acts 1:18).

See also FULLER'S FIELD; POTTER'S FIELD.

W. L. REED

FIELD OF BLOOD. *See* AKELDAMA.

FIERY SERPENT [שרף, *śārāph*] (Num. 21:6, 8; Deut. 8:15; in KJV also Isa. 14:29; 30:6). The serpents sent among the Israelites in the wilderness of wandering, which caused the death of many of the Israelites (Num. 21:6, 8; Deut. 8:15); the reference may be in part to the fiery inflammation caused by the bite of the serpent (see Hebrew *sāraph,* "to burn"). The flying (fiery) serpents of Isa. 14:29; 30: 6 are apparently legendary in character. In the context of the latter is a reference to the mythological serpent-dragon, Rahab.

See also SERPENT; SERPENT, BRONZE; SERAPHIM.

H. G. MAY

FIG TREE, FIG [תאנה, *te'ēnâ;* תאנים *te'ēnîm;* Akkad. *tittu;* Arab. *tîn;* συκῆ, σῦκον]. A tree and its fruit, *Ficus caricus* L., referred to more than sixty times in the Bible. תאנה (Gen. 3:7, etc.) and συκῆ (Matt. 21: 19, etc.) usually refer to the tree, while תאנים (Num. 13:23, etc.) and σῦκον (Matt. 7:16, etc.) refer to the fruit. Other words are used for the fruit to indicate its various stages of development; בכורה *bikkûrâ* (Isa. 28:4, etc.), refers to the early fruit, which usually ripens in June; and פגה, *paggâ* (Song of S. 2:13), and the Greek ὄλυνθος (Song of S. 2:13 LXX; Rev. 6: 13[?]; cf. Isa. 34:4) refer to the early spring green fruit, which emerges before the leaves from the branches of the previous season. דבלה, *debhēlâ* (I Sam. 30:12, etc.) and the Greek παλάθη (I Kings 25:18 LXX, etc.) refer to a cake of pressed figs, which was also used medicinally as a fig poultice (II Kings 20: 7 = Isa. 38:21).

The large, palmate leaves of the tree provided the "aprons" for Adam and Eve (Gen. 3:7), and shade from the sun (John 1:48, 50). The fruit was a feature of attraction for the Hebrews approaching Palestine (Num. 13:23; Deut. 8:8; cf. Num. 20:5). Almost all the references to the fruit of the fig tree are indications of its great importance to the life of ancient times, as it continues to be in the Holy Land today.

The majority of the references to the fig are metaphorical. It appears often as an illustration in stories and parables: in Jotham's fable of the trees (Judg. 9:10-11); in Jeremiah's parable concerning the exiles (the "good figs"; Jer. 24; cf. 29:17); as a symbol of peace and prosperity (I Kings 4:25; II Kings 18:31 = Isa. 36:16; Joel 2:22; Mic. 4:4; Hag. 2:19; Zech. 3:10); and frequently in prophecies of impending national distress (Jer. 5:17; 8:13; Hos. 2: 12; Joel 1:7, 12; Amos 4:9).

The most difficult passage to interpret is the story of Jesus' cursing the fig tree (Mark 11:13-14, 20-21; and its parallel in Matt. 21:18-21), which seems so out of character. Many explanations have been offered, but without any permanent solution. That it may have been a dramatic illustration of the parable in Luke 13:6-9, pointing to the tragic end of those who produce no fruit from their lives, seems possible. The absence of the early spring green figs (Song of S. 2:13), which normally precede the leaves and indicate that the tree would bear fruit that season, may have been the basis of the story, though it would not explain the impulsive action of Jesus. Perhaps the story was originally intended as an apocalyptic symbol. That the original context and meaning of the story have been obscured or lost is clear. The

Trans World Airlines Photo

11. Fig tree in the foreground, with Nazareth on the hillside in the background

fact that Luke omits the story is indicative of an early recognition of the difficulties. *See bibliography.*

Ezek. 27:17 refers to the products which were exported from Judah and Israel, including the obscure "wheat of Minnith, and Pannag" (KJV). By slight emendation it becomes "wheat, olives and early figs" (RSV), one of several suggestions which attempt to solve the textual problem. Three Hebrew MSS read ופגג for ופנג, in support of this emendation. If the fig were meant by the writer, however, it seems strange that he did not use the usual word for the fruit in such a context. Another suggested reading is דנג, "wax" (Amer. Trans.).

Another species of fig, *Ficus sycomorus* L., is common in the Holy Land. *See* SYCAMORE.

See also FLORA § A2*c;* AGRICULTURE; FOOD; PANNAG.

Fig. FIG 11; Pl. XII*b*.

Bibliography. I. Löw, *Die Flora der Juden,* I:1 (1926), 224-54; I. J. Condit, *The Fig* (1947); H. N. and A. L. Moldenke, *Plants of the Bible* (1952), pp. 103-6. For summary of the problem of Jesus' cursing the fig tree, see D. M. Beck, *Through the Gospels to Jesus* (1954), pp. 272-73.

J. C. TREVER

FIGURED STONE [משכית, אבן משכית]. Probably religious scenes painted or carved on stone, depicting some kind of ritual offensive to the Hebrews. At any rate, they were forbidden to set up such stones (Lev. 26:1; KJV IMAGE OF STONE) and enjoined to remove them from the land (Num. 33:52; KJV PICTURES).

In Ezek. 8:12, where the prophet speaks of a room or rooms of these objects maintained by the elders of Israel, the RSV translates "pictures" (KJV "imagery"). The word is found elsewhere in variant meanings (Ps. 73:7; Prov. 18:11; 25:11).

Cf. the stone reliefs or orthostats found in the excavations, such as the basalt orthostat with a lion carving from the thirteenth-century Canaanite temple at Hazor. Fig. ART 65.

Bibliography. W. F. Albright, *Archaeology and the Religion of Israel* (1942), pp. 165 ff; Y. Yadin, *BA,* XIX (Feb., 1956), p. 10 and Fig. 1.

J. M. MYERS

FIGUREHEAD [παράσημος] (Acts 28:11); KJV SIGN. The word used for the emblem on the prow of the Alexandrian ship on which Paul sailed from Malta, ultimately to Rome. It was of the TWIN BROTHERS, Castor and Pollux, twin sons of Zeus and Leda. The Greek text, Παρασήμῳ Διοσκούροις is literally "marked by the Dioscuri [or Twin Brothers]." They were considered to bring good luck to the ship because the sight of the constellation in bad weather was a good omen. B. H. THROCKMORTON, JR.

FILIGREE [משבצות, משבצים, *lit.*, interwoven work, *from* שבץ, to weave in a checker pattern]; KJV OUCHES (i.e., settings for precious stones). Ornamental work in fine gold wire, used in making clasps and settings for jewels.

The two onyx stones on the ephod (Exod. 28:11; 39:6) and the twelve jewels of the breastplate (Exod. 28:20; 39:13) were set in filigree, and filigree clasps held the breastplate to the shoulders of the ephod (Exod. 28:13, 25; 39:16, 18; *see* BREASTPLATE; EPHOD [OBJECT]). The design was probably a rosette or simple floral pattern similar to those seen on Palestinian ivories. *See* IVORY.

See also JEWELS AND PRECIOUS STONES; METALLURGY. L. E. TOOMBS

FILLET. 1. חשוק. A band or collar of metal binding the tops of the pillars of the court and of the door of the TABERNACLE, probably just below the capitals. Those of the door pillars were of gold (Exod. 36:28), while those of the pillars of the court were of silver (38:10-12, 17, 19). Some scholars have understood them to be rods joining the tops of the pillars, with the curtains attached to them. However, this interpretation raises problems at several points in the description of the tabernacle:

a) The verbal form "were filleted" (Exod. 27:17; 38:17, 28). The Aramaic root means "to bind," and the LXX translates it "cased (covered) with silver."

b) The absence of any reference to such rods in the instructions in Num. 4 for the transportation of the tabernacle.

c) The clear inference of Exod. 26:32, 37, that the veil and the screen of the tent hung by hooks from the pillars themselves rather than from rods.

Therefore, it seems best to consider the fillets as bands, in which were probably fixed the hooks by which the curtains were hung from the pillars.

2. KJV translation of חוט in Jer. 52:21 (RSV CIRCUMFERENCE), indicating a thread or measuring line used to measure the circumference of the pillars in front of the temple.

Bibliography. A. H. McNeile, *Exodus*, WC (1908), *addenda*.
S. V. FAWCETT

FINE. *See* CRIMES AND PUNISHMENTS.

FINE FLOUR. Flour ground from only the inner kernels of the wheat. *See* FLOUR.

FINE LINEN. *See* LINEN.

FINERY [תפארת, splendor, beauty, ornament] (Isa. 3:18); KJV BRAVERY. A term referring to the luxuriousness of the anklets worn by the society women of Jerusalem.

FINGER OF GOD [כאצבע אלהים]. A figurative expression for the power of God. The finger is viewed as the instrument of work; this is especially true with reference to God. Not infrequently the finger is understood to be the equivalent of the hand, which also represents the divine power. Thus it was the finger of God that brought forth the plagues which confounded the Egyptian pharaoh and his magicians (Exod. 8:19—H 8:15). The Law was written on tables of stone by the finger of God (Exod. 31:18; Deut. 9:10). The creation of the heavens was the work of God's fingers (Ps. 8:3). Jesus leaves us free to infer that he cast out demons by the finger of God—i.e., that he possessed divine power over evil spirits (Luke 11:20).

By contrast, the hands and fingers of men are often given over to the fabrication of idols (Isa. 2:8), and other worthless activities (17:8). In times of adversity the faithful should not conclude that the Lord's hand has been "shortened" (59:1), but rather that they have been separated from God because their own hands have been defiled with blood and their fingers with iniquity (59:3). H. F. BECK

FINING POT. The KJV translation of מצרף in Prov. 17:3; 27:21. This Old English is replaced by CRUCIBLE in the RSV.

FIR TREE [תדהר, *tiḏhār* (Isa. 41:19; 60:13); ברוש, *b*ᵉ*rôš* (Ps. 104:17; Ezek. 27:5; 31:8; RSV *elsewhere* CYPRESS), Aram. *b*ᵉ*rôṯ* (Song of S. 1:17 KJV; RSV PINE)]. Although the true fir, *Abies cilicica* Carr., which grows best in high alpine regions like the cedars of Lebanon, would suit the associations of ברוש in the OT, most botanists and biblical scholars have abandoned this translation, because of the sparsity of the tree in the Lebanons, in favor of the pine, cypress, or juniper; but its choice for the rare word תדהר seems reasonable in the contexts in which it appears. תדהר is the tree associated with the "glory of Lebanon." Many translations of the word have been offered, including "savin," "plane" (*see* PLANE TREE), "pine," "elm" (Douay and modern Hebrew), etc. Any translation is gratuitous, for there are no cognates to assist identification.

See also FLORA § A9*f*. J. C. TREVER

FIRE. Fire is used as a motif of theophany and of divine punishment and purification. Fire is, of course, also an important part of domestic life (*see* COOKING AND COOKING UTENSILS), and it was a frequent implement of war in OT times (*see* WAR, METHODS OF). Since these facts are self-evident, we may concentrate on the symbolic aspects of fire.

1. Vocabulary
2. Fire and theophany
3. Fire and worship
4. Fire and the divine action
   a. Fire and punishing destruction
   b. Fire as purification

Bibliography

1. Vocabulary. A large number of words are used to express various kinds of fire (for further vocabulary, *see* BURNING). Most important of these in Hebrew is אש (probably onomatopoetic; Gen. 22:6;

Lev. 2:14; Deut. 13:16; etc.); variants: אשה (Jer. 6:29); *'ish,* "flame" (Nah. 2:3); Aramaic אשא, "flame" (Dan. 7:11). אור (Isa. 24:15 KJV) is properly "LIGHT." בערה (from בער) is "that which burns." The cognates להב (Judg. 13:20, etc.), להבה, להבת (Ps. 29:7; Isa. 47:14; etc.; לבה [Exod. 3:2] is probably a contraction), and probably שלהבת (Job 15:30; Song of S. 8:6), all mean "flame." משאת (from נשא, "to lift") is a fire signal (Judg. 20:38, 40; Jer. 6:1 KJV; RSV SIGNAL). זקים (Prov. 26:18) and לפיד (Judg. 15:4) may be translated "firebrand" (RSV "torch"), as is אוד (Isa. 7:4; Amos 4:11; Zech. 3:2). שרפים (Num. 21:6, 8; Deut. 8:15; etc.) is sometimes rendered "fiery serpents" (*see* SERAPHIM). כליל ("flame" in Judg. 20:40 KJV) is rightly translated "whole." Principal verbs are: יצת (II Sam. 14:31), "to set afire"; שרף (Exod. 29:14, etc.), "to burn"; להט (Deut. 32:22, etc.), "to set afire"; בער (Exod. 3:2, etc.), "to burn." Aramaic words are נור (Dan. 3:22; 7:9-10), "fire"; שביב (Dan. 7:9), "flame."

The main Greek word for "fire" in the NT is πῦρ (Matt. 3:10; Acts 2:3; I Cor. 3:13; etc.), with its cognates: πυρά, "fire" (Acts 28:2-3); πύρινος, "the color of fire" (Rev. 9:17); πύρωσις, "fiery ordeal" (I Pet. 4:12); πυρόω, "to be set on fire" (Eph. 6:16; Rev. 3:18). Φλόξ, "flame" (Luke 16:24; II Thess. 1:7), and φλογίζω, "to set aflame" (Jas. 3:6), occur several times. In addition, φῶς, properly "light," is translated "fire" in Mark 14:54 and in Luke 22:56 KJV.

2. Fire and theophany. Fire is a consistent element of the description of THEOPHANY throughout biblical literature. The appearance for covenant with Abraham (Gen. 15:17), the appearance in the burning bush (Exod. 3:2; cf. Acts 7:30), Yahweh's leading Israel in the pillar of fire by night (Exod. 13:21-22; 14:24; Num. 9:15-16; 14:14; Deut. 1:33; Neh. 9:12, 19; Pss. 78:14; 105:39; Isa. 4:5; *see also* GLORY), his appearance in fire on Mount Sinai (Exod. 19:18; 24:17; Deut. 4:11-36; 5:4-26; 9:10, 15; 18:16; cf. I Kings 18:24; Heb. 12:18), are of the central elements in Israel's faith (*see* SINAI, MOUNT). Indeed, it may be argued that the Sinai experience is the foundation of OT fire imagery. Some of the elements of the Sinai theophany seem to suggest that it was a volcano, whereas others indicate a thunderstorm. Certainly Yahweh is frequently described under the figure of a storm (II Sam. 22:9, 13; Pss. 18:8—H 18:9;18:12-13—H 18:13-14; 29:7; 50:3; 105:32; Ezek. 1:4, 13; 10:2, 6-7). Other fiery theophanies, however, do not have stormy surroundings (cf. I Kings 18:24, 38; I Chr. 21:26; II Chr. 7:1, 3). Christ's appearance in the vision of John (Rev. 1:14; 2:18) is with "eyes of fire," and the descent of the Holy Spirit (Acts 2:3) is accompanied by "tongues of fire." The fire persists in visions of eschatological theophanies (cf. Isa. 4:5; 64:2—H 64:1; 66:15; Dan. 7:9-10; Joel 2:30—H 3:3; Mic. 1:4; Zech. 2:5—H 2:9; Mal. 3:2; Enoch 14:12-22; Acts 2:19; Rev. 15:2; 19:12). Fire is a symbol of HOLINESS and in some cases of protection (cf. especially Zech. 2:5—H 2:9). The fire motif in theophanies is evocative of the divine presence.

3. Fire and worship. The use of fire in Israel's worship mirrors the principal meanings of the symbol. The ever-burning fire on the ALTAR (Lev. 6:12-13) shows the continual presence of God. The practice of burning offerings in fire mirrors the use of fire as symbolic both of the divine judgment on sin and of purification of the sinner (*see* SACRIFICE AND OFFERINGS). Therefore Nadab and Abihu are punished for offering "strange fire" to Yahweh (Lev. 10:1; RSV "unholy fire"). The pagan custom of burning children in fire as sacrifice is also condemned (Deut. 12:31; 18:10; II Kings 16:3; 17:17, 31; 21:6; 23:10; Jer. 7:31 [*see* HINNOM, VALLEY OF THE SONS OF]; 19:5), partly because it was sacrifice to pagan deities (*see* MOLECH) and partly because it was human sacrifice.

4. Fire and the divine action. In most cases fire represents the divine action on earth. "Our God is a consuming fire" (Heb. 12:29; cf. Deut. 4:24). Fire is his servant (Ps. 104:4; Heb. 1:7), and his word is like fire (Jer. 23:29; cf. 5:14; 20:9).

a. Fire as punishing destruction. By far the majority of instances have this as their intention. Fire is a symbol of destruction because of its power to consume. In the extension to the idea of holiness, fire becomes further a symbol of destruction. Since wickedness is sometimes compared to fire (cf. Isa. 65:5; Hos. 7:6; Jas. 3:5-6), its punishment is consumption by fire (cf. Gen. 19:24; Lev. 10:2; Josh. 7:15). Thence the image receives the force of the WRATH OF GOD (cf. Ps. 89:46—H 89:47; Jer. 4:4; 15:14; 21:12; Lam. 1:13; 2:3; Ezek. 22:31) and of JEALOUSY (cf. Deut. 4:24; Ps. 79:5; Ezek. 36:5 KJV; 38:19 KJV; Zeph. 3:8). As time went on, fire more and more took its place in the eschatological judgment. Beginnings can be seen in the cosmic destroying fire of Deut. 32:22; Job 28:5; Amos 7:4. In later prophecy, punishing fire has a definitely eschatological flavor (cf. Isa. 33:11; 50:11; 66:24; Ezek. 38:22; 39:6; Zeph. 1:18). In apocalyptic, particularly of the Pseudep., we have almost a theology of fiery judgment (cf. the abyss of fire [Enoch 18:11; 90:23-26; *see* GEHENNA]; fire of judgment [Dan. 7:11; Enoch 10:6; 21:7; 67:13; 91:9; 100:9; 102:1; 108:3; III Bar. 4:16; II Bar. 48:39, 43; Jth. 16:17; Test. Judah 25:3; cf. Sibylline Oracles 4:43; IV Macc. 9:9; 12:12]). Likewise the NT frequently cites fire as an element of judgment (cf. Matt. 3:10, 12; 5:22; 13:40; 18:8-9; 25:41; Mark 9:43-48; Luke 17:29; II Pet. 3:7; Jude 23; Rev. 8:7; 9:18; 11:5; 14:10; 19:20; 20:9-15; 21:8). Whether this is dependent on Persian influence cannot finally be determined. *See* DAY OF JUDGMENT; DAY OF THE LORD; ESCHATOLOGY.

b. Fire as purification. Just as the fire of altar and sacrifice denotes purification of sin, so the fire metaphor has this meaning. The experience of history is sometimes seen as purification by fire, particularly in the Babylonian exile (Ps. 66:12; Isa. 43:2), but this purification may be in vain (Jer. 6:29; Ezek. 22:20-21; 24:12). Certainly the Day of Yahweh will purify Israel (Zech. 13:9; Mal. 3:2; 4:1—H 3:19). This motif finds more expression in the NT (cf. I Cor. 3:13, 15; I Pet. 1:7; Rev. 3:18), and the references to "baptism by fire" (Matt. 3:11; Luke 3:16; 12:49) would appear to have the same thrust (*see* REFINING; BAPTISM). Fire, as the metaphor of God's holiness, may destroy or it may purge. It does not leave man comfortably alone.

Bibliography. C. M. Edsman, *Le baptême de feu* (1946); *Ignus Divinis: le feu comme moyen de rajeunissement et d'immortalité; contes, légendes, mythes et rites* (1949).

E. M. GOOD

FIREBRAND [אוד (1 *below*); זקים, brands *or* sparks (2 *below*)]. **1.** A word used metaphorically by Isaiah: two angry kings are derisively described as "smoldering stumps of firebrands" (Isa. 7:4). "Brand" is the translation in Amos 4:11; Zech. 3:2: Israel is a "brand plucked out of the burning."

2. An object thrown by a madman (Prov. 26:18; cf. Isa. 50:11).

3. KJV form of TORCH in Judg. 15:4.

F. T. SCHUMACHER

FIREPAN [מחתה, *from* חתה, to rake together]. A pan for raking and carrying live coals to and from the altar; made of bronze (Exod. 27:3; 38:3) or, less probably, of pure gold (I Kings 7:50=II Chr. 4:22). It was a part of the altar equipment and was used in connection with the sacrifices (Num. 4:14; II Kings 25:15=Jer. 52:19). When incense was dropped on the live coals, the pan became a CENSER (Lev. 10:1; 16:12; Num. 16:6, 17-18, 37-39). It was also used with the SNUFFERS of the lampstand, evidently to serve as a "tray" (KJV "snuffdish") for disposing of burned portions of the wicks (Exod. 25:38; 37:23; Num. 4:9).

J. L. MIHELIC

FIRKIN fûr'kĭn. KJV translation of μετρητής (RSV converts into gallons) in John 2:6. A measure of *ca.* ten gallons. *See* WEIGHTS AND MEASURES § C4*o*.

FIRMAMENT. The traditional English rendering, following the LXX στερέωμα and the Vulg. *firmamentum,* of the term רקיע, used in Gen. 1:6-7 and elsewhere to denote the expanse stretched across the sky in order to separate the upper and lower waters.

The Hebrew term means properly a "strip of beaten metal" (cf. Exod. 39:3; Num. 17:3; Jer. 10:9; Sheḳ. 9*b;* Phoen. CIS I, 90) and harks back to the conception of the sky as a mirrorlike surface—a conception which recurs in Job 37:18, and which finds a classical counterpart in the common Homeric expression "brazen heaven" (*Iliad* V.504; XVII.425; *Odyssey* III.2; Pindar *Pythian Odes* X.22, *Nemean Odes* VI.3). The picture is elaborated in Job 26:23, where the movement of winds across the sky is represented as God's breathing on its surface in order to polish it.

See also HEAVEN. T. H. GASTER

FIRST AND LAST [ראשון ואחרון]. A title used by Second Isaiah (Isa. 41:4; 44:6; 48:12; cf. 40:28; 43:10-11) to express Yahweh's eternal majesty and power. The prophet of the Exile does not think of Eternity in abstract and nonhistorical terms, but presses temporal language to its utter limits by saying concretely:

> Before me no god was formed,
> nor shall there be any after me
> (Isa. 43:10).

The title ὁ πρῶτον καὶ ὁ ἔσχατον appears in Rev. 1:17; 2:8; 22:13; cf. 1:11.

See also GOD, NAMES OF, § D4*c*.

B. W. ANDERSON

FIRST FRUITS [בכורים; ἀπαρχή]. The sacrifice offered by the Hebrews for the redemption of the annual crop. Early Semitic peoples held that, inasmuch as the Deity was the creator of all living things, vegetable, animal, and human, they belonged primarily to him, and therefore were endowed with the quality of sanctity, were "holy" (קדוש). Accordingly, use of them by men for any purpose was tantamount to violation of the Deity's prior rights in them and would entail divine retribution. Yet, as these things were indispensable to the existence of men, a way had to be found to make possible the termination of this state of sanctity or taboo and the transfer to the condition of profane existence and use of these various forms of life: the use of grain, vegetables, and fruits, and also of the flesh of animals, as food; and likewise the admission of children, at the proper age, into clan or tribe membership, activities, and obligations. The principle prevailed that the sacrifice to the Deity, the giving back to him, of a part, and particularly the first, and presumably therefore the best, part, of the tabooed object "redeemed" (פדה) the remainder, nullified the Deity's prior property rights to it, and rendered it "profane" (חול), free for ordinary use by men and for participation in the normal activities of the clan or tribe. Such redemption sacrifices of the annual crop were known as "first fruits," of animals as "firstlings," and of human beings as "first-born."

First fruits were regularly offered in ancient Israel at the annual Festival of Weeks (Exod. 34:22; Lev. 23:15-22; Num. 28:26; Deut. 16:9-12; *see* WEEKS, FEAST OF), known originally as the Festival of the Harvest (Exod. 23:16). It was celebrated originally upon the day following the completion of the seventh week—i.e., upon the fiftieth day, after the cutting of the first sheaf of the new crop, at the close of the grain harvest. Originally this day of cutting the first sheaf followed immediately the seventh and final day of the Unleavened Bread Festival and, in the earliest calendar current in ancient Israel was celebrated as the NEW YEAR. In the latest calendar of Bible times these fifty days were reckoned from the second day of the PASSOVER AND FEAST OF UNLEAVENED BREAD, and so the festival fell upon the sixth of the month Sivan. Such is the dating of this festival in the official Jewish calendar today.

In the NT the term "first fruits" is used figuratively (Rom. 8:23; 11:16; 16:5; I Cor. 15:20, 23; 16:15; Jas. 1:18; Rev. 14:4).

J. MORGENSTERN

FIRST-BORN [בכור, בכורה, בכירה; LXX *and* NT πρωτότοκος, *cf.* ἀπαρχή]. That which first opens the womb (פטר רחם). The ancient Semites believed the first-born belonged to the deity and were to be sacrificed to him. The Hebrews related this offering to the exodus event. Within the family and tribal spheres a certain preferential status, preciousness, sanctity, authority, sovereignty, responsibility, and right of succession accrued to the first-born. In a figurative sense the term was applied to Israel, the king, the Messiah, and in the NT to Jesus.

1. Right of the first-born
2. Offering of firstlings
3. Human sacrifice
4. Figurative meaning
5. Jesus as first-born

Bibliography

1. Right of the first-born. The term "first-born" (בכור) is used predominantly in the OT to designate the eldest son (e.g., Gen. 10:15; 22:21; Exod. 6:14; Num. 3:2; cf. גדול, "eldest," in Gen. 44:12; I Sam. 17:28). While the prerogatives of the first-born are basically those of sanctity, the emphasis on ancestry, family, and inheritance among the Hebrews gave a special distinction to the first-born son. As the first strength of the father, he became the next head of the family (or clan or tribe), and embodied the soul and character of the social group, becoming responsible for its continuance and welfare. As such he acted with a certain authority, felt a greater responsibility (cf. Reuben; Gen. 37:22), and received a preferential treatment (cf. Gen. 43:33). As his BIRTHRIGHT he had claims on the family BLESSING (cf. Gen. 27:1-4, 35-37) and received a double portion of the family inheritance (Deut. 21:17; cf. *ANET* 185, 220, for a similar allotment in the Middle Assyrian Laws, Tablet B, no. 1, and the Nuzi-Akkadian Laws, no. 3). In the Code of Hammurabi, while all sons seem to share equally, the first-born is at times given a special present (*ANET* 173, no. 165) or a preferential share (*ANET* 173, no. 170); note that Elisha asks to be Elijah's successor by laying claim to this right (II Kings 2:9). It was perhaps a father's privilege to pass by the first-born for a younger son (e.g., Isaac [Gen. 17:19-21]; Ephraim [Gen. 48:13-20]; Solomon as king [I Kings 1:32-37; cf. II Sam. 3:3; II Chr. 21:3]; Shimri as clan chief [I Chr. 26:10]), but custom frowned on the procedure, and later Deuteronomic law banished the practice (Deut. 21:15-17).

In the case of Levirate MARRIAGE the first-born was considered heir of the deceased brother.

With regard to daughters, the term "first-born" (בכירה) refers simply to the elder (Gen. 19:31, 33, 37; I Sam. 14:49). Laban gives it as a Mesopotamian custom that the eldest daughter is to be married first (cf. Gen. 29:26).

2. Offering of firstlings. From pre-Canaanite days, Israel acknowledged the first-born to belong to God (Exod. 22:29*b*-30 E; 34:19-20 J; cf. 13:1-2 P), as Head of the Tribe or Giver of Fertility—later, no doubt, as Lord (בעל) of the Land (cf. Pss. 24:1; 50: 10, 12). The firstlings of domestic animals were offered to the deity at the spring pastoral festival (at the yeaning period) by a sacrifice and communal meal (*see* SACRIFICE AND OFFERINGS). The first-born possessed a peculiar sanctity and efficacy, and, when offered to the deity, guaranteed the fertility and continuity of the flock or herd, and released the remainder from taboo so they could be appropriated. There is possibly a relationship between this spring festival and the wilderness sacrifice of the Exodus account (Exod. 3:18; 5:3; 8:27; cf. 10:25), as well as the later Passover celebration (Exod. 34:18-20, 25-26; *see also* FIRST FRUITS). Subsequently the offering of firstlings was given new meaning in the context of the exodus faith (Exod. 13:14-15 J; Deut. 15:19-20 D).

In the early days of Palestinian existence the firstlings of flock and herd were sacrificed at the local sanctuary (the eighth day; Exod. 22:29*b*-30 E), and the worshiper partook of the meal. The firstling of an ass was to be redeemed with a lamb or have its neck broken (i.e., blood was not to be shed as taboo; Exod. 13:11-13; 34:19*b*, 20, J). In the Deuteronomic regulations the sacrifice was to be an unblemished animal (not previously worked or shorn, since sacred), offered perhaps yearly at the central sanctuary, with the meal eaten by the owner and his household. The blemished were not to be sacrificed, but eaten in the towns (Deut. 15:19-23). In the Priestly Code the sacrifices became the property of the priest. Unclean animals were redeemed when a month old at five shekels (Num. 18:15-18), or at valuation plus a fifth; if not redeemed, they were to be sold by the priest at valuation (Lev. 27:26). When the Levites took the place of the first-born of Israel (Num. 3:12; 8:16), possibly all firstling domestic animals were to be redeemed for a price (cf. Num. 3:41). At this period the offering became a virtual tax or tribute, and not only the first-born, but also a tithe of herd and flock, were considered to belong to Yahweh (Lev. 27:32; cf. Tob. 5:13) and consequently to the priests.

3. Human sacrifice. How the first-born of man was offered to Yahweh is not certain—on occasion, perhaps, as a sacrifice. Human sacrifice does not seem to have been unknown, or especially revolting, to Israel in the early days (Gen. 22:2-3; Judg. 11: 34-39; II Sam. 21:9; cf. Ezek. 20:26). But the practice does not seem to have been widespread and was soon abandoned (cf. Gen. 22, which vindicates the substitution of a ram for human first-born; see also Exod. 13:13, 15; 34:20, J). It is quite possible many first-born sons were devoted to the Lord for service as priests, before there was an ordered priesthood (cf. I Sam. 1:11, 22).

In the law codes of Israel, first-born sons were to be redeemed—originally, perhaps, by a ram (cf. Gen. 22:9-13), and later for five shekels (Num. 3:47; 18: 16, P). When the Levites became the Lord's instead of the first-born (Num. 3:46-47; 18:15-18), all first-born were perhaps to be redeemed. Here sanctity disappeared and tribute became exacted.

There was a revival of human sacrifice in the time of Ahaz (II Kings 16:3; cf. II Chr. 28:3) and Manasseh (II Chr. 33:6), with piacular significance (cf. II Kings 17:31; Ezek. 16:21; Mic. 6:7). A high place (Tophet) in the Valley of Hinnom (*cf.* GEHENNA) became the scene of infant sacrifices to Molech prior to the Exile (II Chr. 28:3; Jer. 7:31; 19:5-6; cf. Isa. 30: 33[?]). How much of this pertained to the first-born is uncertain; some, probably. One notes that in the days of Ahab, Mesha the Moabite king offered his first-born as a burnt offering on the wall in order to rid his country of Israelites (II Kings 3:27). Much has been made of infant remains found at Gezer and Taanach as evidence of first-born sacrifice, but the evidence is inconclusive. Foundation and wall sacrifices of human beings were certainly known. At times these involved the first-born (II Kings 3:27; cf. I Kings 16:34[?]).

The prophets spoke out against this revival in no uncertain terms (cf. Jer. 7:30-34; 19:4-9; 44:6-10; Ezek. 16:20, 27), emphasizing that it had no expiatory value in the sight of God (Mic. 6:7) and was instrumental in bringing about the downfall of the nation (Jer. 44:6, 22).

4. Figurative meaning. In a figurative sense the word "first-born" is used to designate a special quality or strength, the first of a thing being the strongest (cf. "first-born of death" [Job 18:13], a deadly disease; "first-born of the poor" [Isa. 14:30], the poorest).

The term also implies a special close relationship, affection, authority, and sovereignty as the preferential heir. In this sense Israel is called Yahweh's first-born (Exod. 4:22; Pss. Sol. 18:4; II Esd. 6:58); the seed of David, the highest of kings (Ps. 89:27), interpreted by the rabbis as referring to the Messiah.

5. Jesus as first-born. In the NT the term is applied chiefly to Jesus, who is called the first-born of Mary (Matt. 1:25; Luke 2:7), with the emphasis probably more on previous virginity than on later childbearing.

When the word is figuratively applied to Jesus, it implies a certain preferential status and closeness to God, even as Israel in the OT (Heb. 1:6: God's first-born); a certain priority over, and oneness with, men, in inaugurating the new life (Col. 1:18; Rev. 1:5: "first-born of the dead"; cf. I Cor. 15:20: "the first fruits [ἀπαρχή] of those who have fallen asleep"; Rom. 8:29: "the first-born among many brethren"); a certain dignity and sovereignty as heir and destined ruler of all (Col. 1:15: "first-born of all creation"). This uniqueness in relation to God and oneness with men is expressed also by the use of "Son" (υἱός; John 1:34, 49, etc.) and "only Son" (μονογενής; John 1:14, 18; 3:16, 18) in the Fourth Gospel.

In one instance in the NT the term has a historical reference to the exodus event (Heb. 11:28). The phrase "assembly of the first-born" (12:23) refers to the departed faithful, who stand in a peculiar and special relation to God as though first-born sons. Such is the blessing of salvation; it makes one fellow heir with Christ, who is the first-born of God.

Bibliography. J. Wellhausen, *Prolegomena to the History of Israel* (trans. J. S. Black and A. Menzies; 1885), pp. 83-92, 102. R. A. S. Macalister, "Excavation of Gezer," *PEQ* (1903). J. B. Lightfoot, *St. Paul's Epistles to the Colossians and Philemon* (1912), pp. 140-56. G. B. Gray, *Sacrifice in the OT* (1925), pp. 33-36, 86-93. W. R. Smith, *The Religion of the Semites* (3rd ed., 1927), pp. 458-65, 688-92. J. Pedersen, *Israel,* I-II (1926), 193, 258-59; III-IV (1947). I. Mendelsohn, "On the Preferential Status of the Eldest Son," *BASOR,* no. 156 (Dec., 1959), pp. 38-39.

V. H. KOOY

FIRSTLING. *See* SACRIFICE AND OFFERINGS.

FIRST-RIPE [בכור, בכורה, ראשית] (Num. 13:20; 18:13; Isa. 28:4 [KJV HASTY]; Jer. 24:2; Mic. 7:1; Nah. 3:12). An adjective describing the fruits, vegetables, and grains which ripen first and are a token of the coming harvest. The first-ripe fruits, like the FIRST-BORN (usually of men, though sometimes of animals) and the FIRSTLINGS (always of animals), were to be offered to God, the Creator of all life. The offering of the first-ripe fruits figured prominently in the corporate worship of Israel (Lev. 23:9-21) and in individual worship (Exod. 23:19; Deut. 26:1-11). The term "first-ripe" or "FIRST FRUITS" (ἀπαρχή) was used metaphorically by several NT writers and came to have popular theological connotations (Rom. 8:23; 11:16; 16:15; I Cor. 15:20, 23; 16:15; Jas. 1:18; Rev. 14:4).

See also SACRIFICE AND OFFERINGS; WORSHIP IN THE OT.

H. F. BECK

FISH [דג (דאג *in* Neh. 13:16); דגה, *cf.* Ugar. *dg;* נפש, *wrongly rendered "fish" in* Isa. 19:10 KJV; ἰχθῦς, ἰχθύς; ἰχθύδιον (Matt. 15:34; Mark 8:7), *diminutive of the preceding;* ὀψάριον (*only in* John), *diminutive of* ὄψον, cooked food, relish, fish]. The Bible makes no distinction among the many species of fish in the Mediterranean and in the fresh waters of Palestine. They were all "fish" (דג or דגה) to the ancient Hebrews.

A. Kinds of fish
   1. *Cichlidae*
   2. *Cyprinidae*
   3. *Siluridae*
B. Literary allusions and symbolism
   1. In the Bible
   2. In the Mishna
   3. In ancient symbolism
      a. Pagan
      b. Jewish
      c. Early Christian
Bibliography

A. *KINDS OF FISH.* Since the NT makes reference to fishing on the Sea of Galilee, it is of interest to mention the main species of fish which are to be found there.

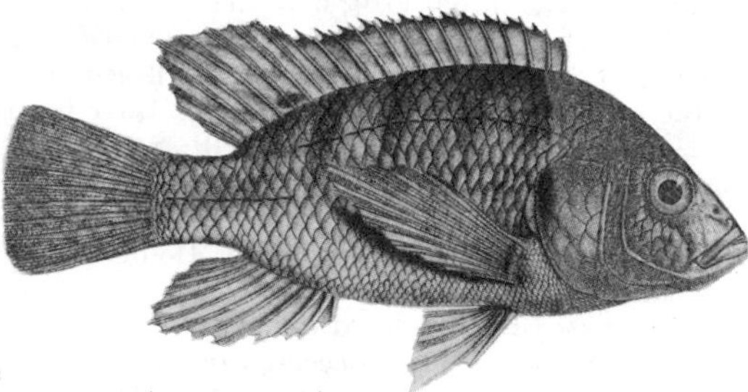

12. Tilapia (*Chronis Simonis*)

13. Clarias (*Cabites Insignis*)

1. *Cichlidae.* This is the *musht* of the Arabs, a family of mouth-breeding fishes of Ethiopic origin. Here belong *Tilapia galilaea* Art., *Tilapia nilotoca* L., *Tristramella sacra* Gthr., etc. Fig. FIS 12.

2. *Cyprinidae.* Among these are the bigger species of the carp family which belong to the barbels (*Barbus*), with two common species (*B. canis* C. V., *B. longiceps* C. V.), and a number of *Varicorhinus* species, as well as the small *Acanthrobrama terrae-sanctae* H. St., called "sardines."

3. *Siluridae.* This is the catfish, *Clarias lazera** C. V. It may reach large size. It is this fish that Josephus recognized as present also in the Nile, and so he presumed a subterranean connection with the Nile. Fig. FIS 13.

All fish with fins and scales were regarded as clean, but those without them were regarded unclean (Lev. 11:9-12). Among the unclean fish in the Sea of Galilee is the catfish, in the coastal waters the eel, and in the Mediterranean probably sharks, rays, and lampreys.

The fish brought from Tyre and Sidon were, of course, preserved by being salted, dried, or pickled.

Thus we find on Lake Tiberias (Sea of Galilee) in the days of Herod a town Tarichaea, whose name indicates it was a center for the preservation of fish, and there was naturally a big fish industry there (cf. ταριχεία, "pickling," "seasoning," and τάριχος, "fish" dried, pickled, or salted).

Among the gates of Jerusalem there was a fish gate. *See* JERUSALEM § 7*b*. *See also* FISHER.

F. S. BODENHEIMER

B. *LITERARY ALLUSIONS AND SYMBOLISM.* Fish, which were found in great variety in the waters of the Holy Land, figured in many ways in the life and thought of its people.

1. In the Bible. Fish, whose flesh Paul recognized as different from that of other creatures (I Cor. 15:39), were created by God (Gen. 1:20-22) and are subject to his will (Isa. 50:2; Ezek. 38:20; Zeph. 1:3). They are often grouped with birds, cattle, and creeping things, to constitute the fauna of the OT (Gen. 1:26; Job 12:7-8; etc.), and as such they were one of the subjects of Solomon's discourses (I Kings 4:33). Over the fish, as over all other subhuman life, man is to exercise dominion (Gen. 1:28; Ps. 8:6-8—H 8:7-9). In the general prohibition of graven images in Deut. 4:15-18, the "likeness of any fish" is included.

The fish of Egypt (Ezek. 29:4-5) are also mentioned in the OT, (*a*) as eaten by the Hebrews during their sojourn in the land (Num. 11:5), and (*b*) as victims of the first plague in Moses' time (Exod. 7:18, 21; Ps. 105:29).

In Ezekiel's picture of the Lord's glorious future for Israel, the life-giving river flowing from the temple is to sweeten the waters of the Dead Sea so that fish will abound there (Ezek. 47:7-10).

There are three literary fish in the Scriptures: the great fish of the book of Jonah; the fish that met Tobit at the Tigris River, and whose internal organs served Tobit so well (Tob. 6:1-5, etc.); the fish that paid the temple tax for Jesus and Peter (Matt. 17:27).

The Bible makes very slight use of fish as a figure of speech. In Eccl. 9:12; Hab. 1:14 man's helplessness in the world is compared to that of fish taken in a net. In Matt. 13:47-48 the variety of fish which a large net will bring to shore serves to characterize the kingdom of heaven.

2. In the Mishna. Clean fish (unclean fish caught in fishing may be sold [Sheb. 7.4]) may be cooked in milk and served with cheese (Hull. 8.1), and they may also be cooked with leeks (M. Sh. 2.1) and eaten with eggs (Bez. 2.1). Some fish were salted (Ned. 6.3), and others were evidently pickled, for fish brine is referred to (Ter. 11.1; Ned. 6.4; A.Z. 2.6). Some cured or pickled fish were seemingly imported from both Egypt and Spain (Maksh. 6.3). One variety of brine (*muryês* or *muryîs*), to which wine was sometimes added, was used as a sauce and as a preservative (cf. A.Z. 2.4). Fish oil could be put in lamps (Shab. 2.2), and the skins of some fish were used for various domestic purposes (Kel. 10.1; 16.1; 24.11).

3. In ancient symbolism. *a. Pagan.* Fish are frequently introduced into ancient art to give a realistic touch to water scenes. Often, however, a fish appears in a composition without any obvious appropriateness, and in such cases it would seem to have symbolic significance, possibly to represent deity, power, fecundity, etc.

In the dynastic period of Egypt, several kinds of fish appear to have been worshiped or venerated—e.g., at Oxyrrhynchus, Seth was worshiped in the form of a sharp-nosed fish; the *ʾbdw* fish occurs in a number of mythological and magical texas.

The fish appears in designs on painted pottery found in the excavations of Canaanite cities, especially *ca.* 1500 B.C., along with dove, snake, stag, goat, palm-tree, and other motifs. Pl. XX.

In Assyrian religion, Ea was sometimes represented by a fabulous monster with the body of a fish, and the exorcist-priest wore on occasion a garment like a fish skin.

A ninth-eighth-century Babylonian seal shows a large fish upright between two men (*see bibliography*).

In the Persian age, Xenophon refers to the sacred fish of the Chalus River in Syria (*Anabasis* I.4). Some centuries later, Lucian's account of the goddess Derceto (half woman, half fish), and of certain sacred fish, at least testifies to the perpetuation in Syria of this old veneration of the fish (*The Syrian Goddess* 14).

b. Jewish. Jewish artists and craftsmen made a limited use of the fish (*see bibliography*). Doubtless, in some cases the fish was employed as a conventional decorative detail; in others, the past association of fish with various cultic practices may have established it popularly as a kind of talisman.

c. Early Christian. It is probable that the considerations mentioned in § 3*b above* account in part for the appearance of the fish in the art of the oldest Christian catacombs. How early the Greek word for "fish" (ἰχθύς) came to be interpreted as a cipher for "Jesus Christ, Son of God, Savior" (Ἰησοῦς Χριστός Θεοῦ Υἱός Σωτήρ), we do not know; but once this identification was made, the fish became a standard Christian symbol. Fig. ACR 3. *See bibliography.*

Bibliography. On pagan symbolism: A. Moortgat, *Vorderasiatische Rollsiegel* (1940), no. 687; cf. E. D. Van Buren, *The Fauna of Ancient Mesopotamia as Represented in Art* (1939), pp. 104-8.

On Jewish symbolism: E. R. Goodenough, *Jewish Symbols in the Greco-Roman Period* (1953), especially vol. II, nos. 11, 84, 261, 371, 380, 545, 635, 897, 900, 914.

On early Christian symbolism: J. Finegan, *Light from the Ancient Past* (1946), pp. 382-83.

W. S. McCULLOUGH

FISH GATE [שער הדגים]. A gate of Jerusalem mentioned in connection with the Mishneh or SECOND QUARTER (Zeph. 1:10) and the fortifications of Manasseh (II Chr. 33:14). The Fish Gate was restored by Nehemiah (Neh. 3:3; 12:39). *See* map under NEHEMIAH.

See also JERUSALEM § 7*b*.

G. A. BARROIS

FISHHOOK. The translation of two words:

a) חכה (Aram. חכתא; KJV HOOK) in Job 41:1—H 40:25 (HOOK in Isa. 19:8; Hab. 1:15; KJV ANGLE).

b) סיר דוגה (Amos 4:2).

FISHING. This work may be for pleasure, profit, or provision. The kings of Egypt engaged in fishing for sport. In the early days of Israel the Phoenicians were the fishers. Again after the Babylonian exile, Tyrians monopolized the fishing industry (Neh. 13:

16). The Philistines called their god Dagon, perhaps reflecting in this name their interest in fishing (I Sam. 5:4).

There is no evidence that the Israelites engaged in fishing for pleasure or sport. To them it was hard work. The job, in addition to catching the fish, included salting and peddling the fish, as well as mending nets and sails and keeping the boats in repair (Ezek. 26:5; Matt. 4:21). Fishermen brought the fish to market in baskets. There was a fish gate and possibly a fish market in Jerusalem (II Chr. 33:14). The fish brought as far as Jerusalem were probably dried and salted. There were similar markets in other large cities such as Athens. The fishermen often worked together in bands or guilds (Job 41:6; Luke 5:10). They sometimes worked at night (Luke 5:5; John 21:3). Fishing was done in the Nile (Isa. 19:8), the Mediterranean (Neh. 13:16), the Sea of Galilee (Matt. 4:18), the Jordan, Lake Huleh, the Orontes, the Tigris and Euphrates, and the Aegean Sea.

Several methods of fishing are noted in the Bible (Hab. 1:15). Fishhooks (חכה) have been used from prehistoric times in Palestine and Egypt. Bone fishhooks were found in Natufian settlements. Iron fishhooks occur in the time of Solomon at Ezion-geber. Hooks were still in use in NT times (ἄγκιστρον; Matt. 17:27). The mythical beast LEVIATHAN could not be caught by hooks (Job 41:1-7). This passage and Amos 4:2 suggest that originally a thorn (סיר) was the fishhook. The hook and line are noted in Isa. 19:8. There is no mention of a fishing rod. There were two types of fish nets. One was thrown by hand (Eccl. 9:12), usually while the fisherman was standing on the shore (Ezek. 47:10). Perhaps Peter and Andrew used this method, while the sons of Zebedee used the dragnet (Matt. 4:18, 21; ἀμφίβληστρον δίκτυον). A larger net was used from the boats (Luke 5:4-7) and was operated like a sieve from a circle of boats closing in to one another or to the shore (σαγήνη; Matt. 13:47). The spear (צלצל) or the barbed harpoon (שכה) was used from prehistoric times (Job 41:7, 26).

Courtesy of the Trustees of the British Museum

14. Assyrian fishing with a line, from a monument of Nineveh, from the time of Sennacherib (704-681 B.C.)

Courtesy of Staatliche Museen, Berlin

15. Three fishermen pull lines of net, from a tomb relief of Ra-hotep, Fourth Dynasty (2650-2500 B.C.).

Metaphorically the symbol of fishing is used for captive Israel (Eccl. 9:12; Ezek. 29:4; Hab. 1:14). The judgment of God against Israel is as if many fishermen and hunters have been sent out to catch the rebellious people (Jer. 16:16; Ezek. 47:10). The LXX in the Jeremiah passage uses "avengers" for fishers.

Jesus performed miracles of fishing (Luke 5:1 ff; John 21:1 ff), not to mention the feeding of the five thousand (John 6:1 ff). In the NT many of the disciples were fishermen (Matt. 4:18, 21; Mark 1:16; Luke 5:2). By a metaphor the entire NT mission is a fishing operation. The disciples and all succeeding them are called by Jesus to be "fishers of men" (Matt. 4:19; Mark 1:17; Luke 5:10; cf. Jer. 16:16). These men accepted Jesus' call and apparently gave up all their investment in equipment and customary fishing rights. The Christian anagram ἰχθύς forms a confession based on "Jesus Christ, God's only Son," and the symbol of the fish is consonant with this Christian commission to be fishers of men.

Figs. FIS 14-15. C. U. WOLF

FITCHES. KJV translation of כסמים (RSV SPELT) in Ezek. 4:9 and of קצח (RSV DILL) in Isa. 28:25, 27. "Fitch" is an archaic form for the common "vetch," a leguminous plant of the Vicia genus, of which many species are found in Bible lands. *Vicia ervilia* L., called in Arabic *kirsannah,* is identified by some botanists as the *kussemet* of the OT. It is a vetch used today for camel fodder, but hardly suits the biblical references. It is doubtful if vetch was present in Bible times.

See also FLORA § A6*c;* SPICE.

Bibliography. H. N. and A. L. Moldenke, *Plants of the Bible* (1952), pp. 152-53. J. C. TREVER

FLAG. KJV translation of אחו (RSV REED) in Job 8:11 and of סוף (RSV REED) in Exod. 2:3, 5; Isa. 19:6. Both these words refer to a kind of REED or grass which grows by rivers and lakes.

אחו (*'āḥû,*) appears also in Gen. 41:2, 18 (KJV MEADOW), and probably in Hos. 13:15 (*'āḥîm;* KJV BRETHREN). Zohary (*see* FLORA § A11) favors the translation "meadow" for *'āḥû,* but in Job 8:11 the parallelism with *gōmê* (*see* PAPYRUS) indicates that a marsh reed or grass is meant. The LXX translates *'āḥû* here with βούτομον, which perhaps led Moldenke and Post to suggest the *Butomus umbellatus* L., the flowering RUSH (cf. Liddell, Scott, and Jones, *A Greek-English Lexicon,* where βούτομον is identified with *Carex riparia* Curt., a sedge). But in Gen. 41:2, 18, the LXX transliterates the Hebrew, apparently intending the more general "reed grass." "Marsh grass" or "reed grass" would probably be better for all these passages.

סוף (*sûph*) in the OT usually occurs in the phrase *yam sûph,* "Sea of Reeds," which the LXX translated *thálassa 'eruthrá* (RED SEA; Exod. 10:19; etc.); but in Exod. 2:3, 5; Isa. 19:6, *sûph* alone seems to mean "reed" or "rush" (cf. Jonah 2:5—H 2:6; *see* WEEDS 3). The general meaning seems to be intended rather than a particular species, but probably includes the cattail, *Typha angustata* Bery et Choub.

J. C. TREVER

FLAGON. A large wine pitcher. In the KJV of Isa. 22:24, "flagons" is a good translation of נבלים. In other KJV passages, however, the word translated "flagons" (אשישה) is now known to be a "cake of raisins," as in the RSV (II Sam. 6:19; I Chr. 16:3; Song of S. 2:5; Hos. 3:1). Where the RSV uses "flagon" (Exod. 25:29; 37:16; Num. 4:7; Isa. 22:24), the term is a good translation. J. L. KELSO

FLAGSTAFF. The translation of תרן in Isa. 30:17 (KJV BEACON). Elsewhere the word is translated "MAST" (Isa. 33:23; Ezek. 27:5).

FLASK. A term used in the RSV to refer to four different vessels. In the story of the wise and foolish virgins, it was a small-sized oil juglet (ἀγγεῖον; Matt. 25:4; KJV "vessel"). In the anointing of Jehu (II Kings 9:1-3), it was a small perfume juglet (פך; KJV "box"). In Jer. 19:1 the flask (בקבק; KJV "bottle") was a water decanter used on the tables of better-class homes. Its narrow neck made it impossible to mend the vessel. In Luke 7:37 the term is ἀλάβαστρον, "alabaster flask" (KJV "alabaster box"); it contained ointment with which the woman anointed Jesus.

Alabaster juglets were used for thousands of years as containers for the more expensive perfumes. By NT times glass was just coming in to replace alabaster. For pottery flasks, *see* Pls. XX-XXI. Fig. OIN 5.

J. L. KELSO

FLAX [פשתה, *pištâ;* פשתים, *pištîm;* Akkad. *pištu;* Punic *phoist;* λίνον]. A cultivated plant, *Linum usitatissimum* L., and some products made from it. The plant is referred to only in Exod. 9:31 (the flax crop of Egypt destroyed by hail); Josh. 2:6 (Rahab hid the spies under stalks of flax which were drying on the roof). Judg. 15:14 may refer to burning stalks of flax.

Elsewhere *pištîm* seems to refer to the combed fibers or spun thread already prepared for weaving, or finished linen cloth (Jer. 13:1; Ezek. 44:17-18; etc.; *see* LINEN). Samson snapped the new ropes by which he was bound, as though they were burned flax ropes (or stalks? Judg. 15:14). The good wife is one who gathers her wool and flax "and works with willing hands" (Prov. 31:13). Isaiah predicted the workers in combed flax would be in despair (Isa. 19:9). Ezekiel saw a man with a "line of flax and a measuring reed" (Ezek. 40:3). The harlot mother (Israel) received her wool and her flax from her

Courtesy of Winifred Walker

16. Flax

lovers, and God would take them away (Hos. 2:5-9—H 2:7-11).

A lamp wick made from flax seems to be intended in Isa. 42:3 ("dimly burning wick"; KJV "smoking flax"; cf. Matt. 12:20). Armies and warriors "are extinguished, quenched like a wick" (Isa. 43:17) by the Lord.

The stalks of the flax plants are pulled when the seeds are ripe, dried, deseeded, then soaked ("retted") until the outer fibers are loosened. Again they are dried, after which the fibers are separated from the inner core by "hackling," then combed in preparation for spinning into thread. The short, tangled fibers which are left over from the combing are the "tow" (נערת) referred to in Judg. 16:9; Isa. 1:31. The tow makes a coarse yarn. Fig. HAR 7.

In the tenth-century-B.C. Gezer Calendar, the month of the harvest of flax is mentioned ("His month is pulling[?] of flax; *see* CALENDAR).

See also CLOTH; FLORA § A4; LINEN.

Fig. FLA 16.

Bibliography. I. Löw, *Die Flora der Juden,* II (1924), 210-16; H. N. and A. L. Moldenke, *Plants of the Bible* (1952), pp. 129-33.

J. C. TREVER

FLEA [פרעש; Akkad. *parša'u, paršu'u;* Arab. *barghût,* flea, *cf. barghash,* mosquito] (I Sam. 24:14—H 24:15; 26:20 KJV [RSV LIFE, with LXX]). An insect (order Siphonaptera), wingless, but a powerful leaper. Many species are found in Palestine, including *Pulex irritans,* on man. David symbolically uses it to indicate his insignificance.

See also FAUNA § E1.

Bibliography. *See* bibliography under ANT.

W. W. FRERICHS

FLEET [אני] (I Kings 9:26-27; 10:11, 22); KJV NAVY OF SHIPS. *See* SHIPS AND SAILING; EZION-GEBER.

FLESH IN THE OT. The word used to translate two Hebrew words in the OT—viz., בשר and שאר, the latter being of rare occurrence compared with the former (LXX σάρξ, sometimes σῶμα). The word בשר is probably connected with the Arabic *bathar* ("skin") and the Akkadian *bišru* ("flesh and blood," "blood relationship"), and may originally have meant the flesh next to the skin. The term שאר is connected with the Arabic *tha'r* ("blood," "blood revenge") and the Akkadian *šîru* ("flesh"), and may originally have meant the inner flesh which was full of blood.

1. Literal use. The word בשר (less often שאר) designates the soft, muscular part of the body of both men and animals. The flesh is thought of as dust which has been made alive (cf. Gen. 2:7; 7:22), but it is still called flesh, even when dead, until it returns as dust to the earth (Eccl. 12:7). Flesh can be used as food (Gen. 9:4; 40:19; II Kings 9:36).

2. Use by synecdoche. "Flesh" is the word Hebrew normally uses when reference has to be made to the body (Num. 19:7 KJV; I Kings 21:27; II Kings 4:34), though the phrase "flesh and bones" also occurs. Inasmuch as flesh is the outward manifestation of soul (נפש), it can have psychic functions, and the word can be used in the same way as "soul" or "heart" or "bones" of the whole person (e.g., "flesh faints" [Ps. 63:1—H 63:2]; "heart and flesh sing for joy" [Ps. 84:2—H 84:3]). By a further extension of usage, the phrase "all flesh" can denote living creatures, both animal and human, the nuance doubtless intended being their creaturely weakness (see Gen. 6:17; 7:16, 21; Ps. 136:25, of animals; Gen. 6:12; Ps. 145:21; Isa. 40:5-7; 49:26*b;* 66:23; Joel 2:28—H 3:1, of men). "Flesh" can be used euphemistically (Lev. 15:2-3, 7, 19 KJV; possibly also Ezek. 16:26 KJV; 23:20 KJV; 44:7, 9).

3. Use by metonymy. The word "flesh" can be used in connections where natural relationship is being spoken of. Adam says of the woman: "This at last is bone of my bones and flesh of my flesh" (Gen. 2:23). The unit of relationship may be the family (Gen. 2:24; 29:14), the township (Judg. 9:2), the people (II Sam. 5:1). Flesh almost stands for corporate personality.

4. Theological significance. The fact that "flesh," as just explained, was used to indicate different degrees of kinship, and, indeed, that "all flesh" could mean "humanity," could suggest that man was essentially a social being. This, of course, would not have been a sufficient basis for ethical conduct unless the individual was roused to a sense of his responsibility in relation to the group. Yet it did provide a natural basis for the recognition by the individual, constituted as such by God, that his obligation to obey God was inclusive of the obligation to serve his brother.

A number of passages make it plain that "flesh" to the Hebrew mind suggested "weakness," "frailty." In Gen. 6:3 the implication is that, because man is flesh, he is mortal (cf. Job 34:15). In Ps. 78:39, God excuses sin on the ground that men are flesh (cf. Ps. 103:12-16). In II Chr. 32:8, the arm of flesh of the king of Assyria—i.e., his weakness—is contrasted with God, who is all-powerful (cf. Job 10:4; Ps. 56:4; Jer. 17:5). In Isa. 31:3, flesh is contrasted with spirit as weakness with strength. Yet, while flesh in the OT is regarded as weak, it is not regarded, as in the NT, as also sinful. The nearest we get in the OT to the NT idea is in Ps. 78:39. Actually, the promise is made (Ezek. 11:19-20; 36:26-27) that men will receive a new spirit and a heart of flesh to replace their heart of stone so that they may obey God.

Bibliography. H. W. Robinson, *The Christian Doctrine of Man* (1911); E. de W. Burton, *Spirit, Soul, and Flesh* (1918), pp. 66-72; J. Pedersen, *Israel, Its Life and Culture,* I-II (1926), pp. 578 *et passim;* A. R. Johnson, *The Vitality of the Individual in the Thought of Ancient Israel* (1949), pp. 39-41; C. Ryder Smith, *The Bible Doctrine of Man* (1951), pp. 24-25; J. A. T. Robinson, *The Body* (1952), pp. 11-16. N. W. PORTEOUS

FLESH IN THE NT [σάρξ, κρέας]. The elementary meaning of "flesh" is the substance covering the bones of animals or man, but the word has numerous figurative meanings, as will be seen. Κρέας occurs only in Rom. 14:21; I Cor. 8:13, where it refers to flesh of sacrificed animals. But σάρξ is also often used in this sense, and it is the usual word for "flesh" in the NT. It is the ordinary translation of Hebrew words for "flesh" in the SEPTUAGINT.

1. To denote kinship. Flesh enters into a common idiom in the OT to express blood kinship. One encounters it, e.g., in Gen. 2:23; Judg. 9:2; II Sam. 5:1; etc.; but the idiom was still used in the NT period, as indicated by Rom. 1:3; 9:3; 11:14.

2. As a metonym for "man." One of the most frequent uses of "flesh" was as a metonym for "man," especially when man was thought of as a frail being in contrast with God. The word occurs in the OT in such passages as Gen. 6:12; II Chr. 32:8; Isa. 40:5; Jer. 17:5; but it is equally familiar in the NT, as in Matt. 24:22; Mark 13:20; I Pet. 1:24. But the most famous example is John 1:14: "The Word became flesh," which means that the divine Logos became a human being.

3. "Flesh and bones." On the other hand, the essential differentiation between a man and a bodiless spirit was seen in the concept of flesh and bones. In Luke 24:36-43 the risen Christ challenges his doubting disciples: "Handle me, and see; for a spirit has not flesh and bones."

"Flesh and bones" was also an idiom in the OT to express kinship. One finds this, e.g., in Gen. 2:23; Judg. 9:2; II Sam. 19:12; but the idea occurs also in the NT period. The critical reading of Eph. 5:30 is: "We are members of his body," but a rejected reading adds: ". . . of his flesh and of his bones." This reading has enough age to be in the Syr. and Vulg. versions. It shows a survival of the Hebrew notion that the essence of a man is in his flesh and bones.

4. "Flesh and blood." "Flesh and blood" is also used in the NT, both as a metonym for "man" and to express kinship. This idiom does not appear in the OT. Apparently the first occurrences of it are Ecclus. 14:18; 17:31. It may be that this poet originated the expression. At any rate, it is frequent in later rabbinic writings and was to find extensive use in the NT.

We come upon the phrase as a metonym for "man" first in the famous words of Jesus in Matt. 16:17: "Blessed are you, Simon Bar-Jona! For flesh and blood has not revealed this to you." But if we keep in mind the date when Matthew was written, rather than the time when Jesus spoke the words, we have to say that they occur first in Paul, who also had a gift for colorful language. In Gal. 1:16, Paul says: "I did not confer with flesh and blood." In Eph. 6:12 he remarks: "We are not contending against flesh and blood." These passages from Paul use "flesh and blood" as a metonym for "human being." But in I Cor. 15:50 ("Flesh and blood cannot inherit the kingdom of God") and Heb. 2:14, the idiom is a metonym for the "physical body."

"Flesh and blood" is used to express the idea of kinship in the NT interpretation of the Lord's Supper, although this is along spiritual lines. Either symbolically or really, the bread and wine are believed to become the flesh and blood of Christ. As Jesus says in John 6:53: "Unless you eat the flesh of the Son of man and drink his blood, you have no life in you." The idea appears to be that the very essence of the life of Christ is found in his flesh and blood, and that the disciple is able to participate in this divine life by means of the sacrament. So flesh and blood have become the basis of kinship in the new spiritual family of faith, and the elements which were before only a simple but colorful metonym have now acquired a transcendental, theological meaning.

5. In Paul's vocabulary. Paul provides one of the most interesting developments in the meaning of "flesh" in his triangular analysis of the INNER MAN in Rom. 7:7-25. This is one of the most picturesque and significant phases of the NT doctrine of man (*see* MAN, NATURE OF [NT]). Paul views the self as having three elements: reason, which is the seat of God's law; the flesh, out of which lawless desire rises; and the ego or "I" in control of the will, which must choose between the law of God and the lawless desires of the flesh. He elaborates the concept of the flesh as the seat of desire again in Gal. 5:16-24. His thinking about personality is reflected in the school of depth psychology associated with Sigmund Freud and his followers. According to Paul, man is in bondage to the flesh, from which he can be delivered only by the grace of God through Christ. Freud analyzed the self into a trinity of the ego, superego, and id, to the latter of which he said man is enslaved.

Paul's view has slight affinity with anything in the OT. Its kinship is closer to that of Philo (*On the Giants* 29), who speaks of the flesh as the chief cause of ignorance; and of Epicurus, who, according to Plutarch (*Morals* 135C), regards the flesh as the bearer of sinful feelings and desires—a view with which Plutarch himself appears to be in sympathy. The philosophical thought deriving from Plato, Orphism, and various Gnostic systems, as well as from later Manicheism and other ascetic ideas based on a distrust of the flesh, shows the mood to which Paul in his own way was giving expression. The sense of sin and desire for redemption were unique marks of the Hellenistic age in which he lived.

6. As a euphemism. "Flesh" is used as a euphemism for the male sex member in references to the rite of circumcision, both in the OT (Gen. 17:11, 14, 23-25) and in the Pauline language of Rom. 2:28; Eph. 2:11; Col. 2:13.

Bibliography. F. Brown, S. R. Driver, and C. A. Briggs, *Hebrew-English Lexicon* (1907); E. D. Burton, *Commentary on Galatians* (1921), pp. 492-95; M. Burrows, *Outline of Biblical Theology* (1946); J. Knox, Exegesis of Romans, *IB*, IX (1954), 491-504; W. Bauer, *Greek-English Lexicon of the NT* (1957).

S. V. MCCASLAND

FLESH POT [סיר הבשר]. Literally, a kettle (full) of meat. The Israelites in the wilderness spoke of sitting by the flesh pots and eating bread to the full while they were in Egypt (Exod. 16:3). This is a striking statement, for the Israelites are claiming that they had plenty of meat, as well as bread, to eat in Egypt! Meat, however, was not the poor man's diet.

J. L. KELSO

FLESH-HOOK. KJV translation of מזלג (RSV FORK).

FLINT [חלמיש (Ps. 114:8; Isa. 50:7; *elsewhere usually* FLINTY ROCK; *cf.* Akkad. *elmēšu,* diamond); צר *ṣōr* (*cf.* Akkad. *ṣurru,* flint; *ṣurtu,* flint knife; Arab. *ẓarra,* to cut)]. An impure variety of quartz. It breaks with a conchoidal fracture and is very hard. Flint artifacts were among mankind's earliest implements, and prehistoric cultures may be distinguished by flint types which can be stratigraphically dated. Flint in-

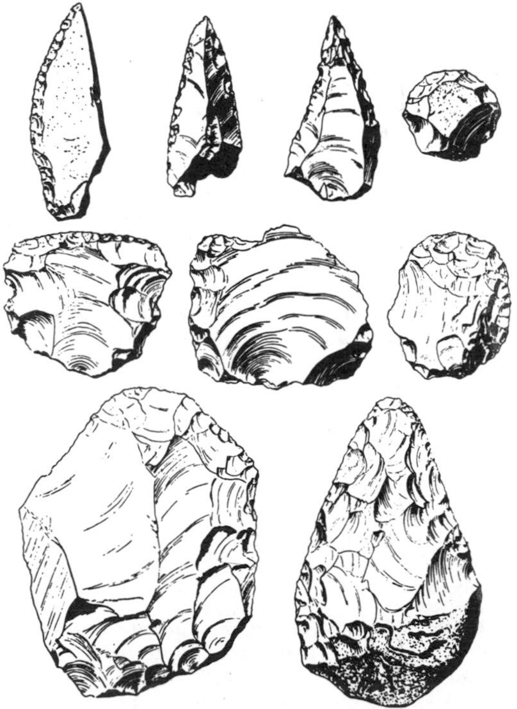

From Garrod and Bate, *The Stone Age of Mount Carmel* (Oxford: Clarendon Press)

17. Lower Paleolithic flint instruments from Wadi el-Mugharah

struments continued to be used after the introduction of metals.* They were used for many purposes—as scrapers, axes, knives, weapons, sickle blades, picks, awls, etc. (Fig. FLI 17.) *See also* PREHISTORY; WEAPONS AND IMPLEMENTS OF WAR; CIRCUMCISION. Fig. SIC 56.

The *ṣōr* in Exod. 4:25 (RSV mg. KNIFE; KJV SHARP STONE) is Zipporah's instrument for circumcising her son. "Knives of flint" (חרבות צרים) in Josh. 5:2-3 designate the flint instruments used by Joshua in circumcising the Israelites at Gilgal. In Isa. 5:28 (reading *ṣōr* for *ṣar*) the horses' hoofs are counted as flint. In Ezek. 3:9 ADAMANT is harder than flint. The Lord turns flint into a spring of water (Ps. 114:8)—an allusion to the exodus miracle (Deut. 8:15; cf. Exod. 17:6; Num. 20:8-11; Deut. 32:13). Flint symbolizes the determination of the Servant of the Lord in Isa. 50:7. W. E. STAPLES

FLOAT. KJV translation of דברה (I Kings 5:9—H 5:23) and רפסדה (II Chr. 2:16—H 2:15; RSV RAFT).

FLOCK. *See* SHEEP.

FLOGGING [מהלמות (KJV STROKES *in* Prov. 18:6; KJV STRIPES *in* Prov. 19:29), strokes, stripes, blows]; FLOG [נכה (Prov. 17:26; KJV STRIKE), smite, strike, attack (and destroy); μαστιγόω (Matt. 10:17; KJV SCOURGE), *alternately* CHASTISE, SCOURGE]. The practice or system of punishment by repeated lashes or blows, usually with a rod or whip; or an instance of such punishment.

Beating is recognized as a legitimate form of punishment in Deut. 25:1-3. According to Proverbs, hasty and poor judgments, like careless talk, often lead to strife; the settling of strife involves punishment for those who have been wrong, and it should be recognized that flogging is "for the backs of fools" (Prov. 19:29; cf. 18:6; 20:3). It is permissible to beat a child and so to correct him (23:13-14).

Elsewhere in the OT it is recognized that even the innocent may sometimes be smitten and crushed by evil individuals and cliques (Isa. 52:13–53:12, especially 53:5). The suffering of the innocent, often at the hands of evildoers, is a common theme in the Psalms (13; 22; 28; 31:9-24; 35; 38; 41; 69; 71; 86; 102; 109).

Jesus warned certain of his disciples that they would be beaten in the synagogues if they continued to preach the gospel (Mark 13:9). According to Acts 5:40, the apostles were beaten by representatives of the Sanhedrin and charged not to speak in the name of Jesus, but only after Gamaliel had pleaded with his fellow members not to put the defendants to death (vss. 33-39). Paul, who himself had beaten and imprisoned many Christians (Acts 22:19-20), was flogged with rods three times (II Cor. 11:25; see, e.g., Acts 16:11-24, where both Paul and Silas were involved). H. F. BECK

FLOOD. The translation of a number of words, which may be divided according to three distinct connotations:

a) A stream overflowing: מים בלהות (Job. 27:20); פרץ מים (II Sam. 5:20); שבלת (Ps. 69:2—H 69:3); שטף (Dan. 9:26); שפעה (Job 22:11); πλήμμυρα (Luke 6:48).

b) The primeval flood, "heavenly ocean": מבול (Gen. 6:17; Ps. 29:10); נהרות (Ps. 93:3); נזלים (Exod. 15:8); תהמת (Exod. 15:5); κατακλυσμός (Luke 17:27).

c) The "waters of Noah," the Deluge: מבול (Gen. 9:28); κατακλυσμός (Matt. 24:38). *See* FLOOD (GENESIS).

The imagery of *a* is taken from the sudden rush of water in a wadi or ravine following heavy rains in the vicinity. The primeval-flood imagery (*b*) reflects the cosmological myth of Yahweh's victory at Creation over the dragon of chaotic waters (Job 26:12; Ps. 74:13-14—H 74:12-13), and the belief that waters from the cosmic sea poured down through the lattice windows of heaven and gushed up from beneath the earth (Gen. 7:11). Hence the Deluge (*c*) showed the destructive power of the מבול, or primeval flood, when Yahweh released it from its bonds, and was also a symbolic event in the myths of beginnings which Israel inherited from Mesopotamia. R. B. Y. SCOTT

FLOOD (GENESIS) [מבול; LXX κατακλυσμός, *see* § 2*b below*]. The catastrophic deluge recounted in Gen. 6–9 as divine judgment on the corrupt world, from which only NOAH and those with him in the ARK OF NOAH were saved. Similar sagas of a great flood in the (prehistoric) past, many of which relate as their cause the sin of mankind, exist throughout the world. Their relation to one another and to the biblical account is not always clear. The origin of these legends is generally considered to be folk recollection of actual inundations, but the legends seem also to be incorporated into some scheme of cosmic cycles, independent of historical traditions of a flood, in which the flood catastrophe ends one epoch and begins a new age with new men. The biblical story accepts the cyclical tradition for the past but expressly denies it for the future (Gen. 9:15).

1. The OT account. Since the wickedness of man was very great on the earth, God repented of his creation and determined to destroy both men and beasts (Gen. 6:5-13); only the righteous Noah and his family would be spared (vss. 8-9). God therefore announced to Noah his intention to destroy the earth (6:13, 17; 7:4) and ordered him to build an ark according to definite plan and dimension (6:14-16). Into the ark Noah was to take all his family (6:18; 7:1), members of every species of animal (6:19-20; 7:2-3) "to keep their kind alive upon the face of all the earth" (7:3), and provisions for the duration of the floodwaters (6:21). Noah followed the divine command (6:22; 7:5, 7-9, 13-16), and when the ark was finished, he entered with all his family and every species of animal into the ark, and God "shut him in" (7:16). Then the heavens were opened and rain descended, and "all the fountains of the great deep burst forth," bringing a great flood upon the earth (7:11). Everything on earth was flooded, "and all flesh died." "Every living thing that was upon the face of the ground . . . [was] blotted out from the earth" (7:21-23*a*) by waters which eventually rose fifteen cubits above the highest mountains (7:17-20).

Finally, after the water had subsided, the ark landed "upon the mountains of Ararat" (8:4), and Noah sent out first a raven and then a dove (8:6-12) to determine whether the land was dry. When he knew the ground was dry (8:13-14), Noah and all who were with him went forth from the ark (8:15-19), and Noah sacrificed to God (8:20). Whereupon God was pleased and determined never again to destroy man as he had done (8:21-22) by a flood (9:8-11). Then God blessed Noah and his family (9:1-7) and gave the rainbow as the sign of his covenant with the earth that "the waters shall never again become a flood to destroy all flesh" (9:12-17).

2. The literary character of the biblical story. ***a. The sources.*** Even though the story appears simple and homogeneous, the existence within it of two independent and partially inconsistent parallel flood stories, the earlier Yahwistic (J) and the postexilic Priestly (P), can easily be demonstrated. Aside from observing the distinctive use of the divine name (Yahweh, RSV LORD [Gen. 6:5-8; 7:1, 5, 16*b;* 8:20-21]; God [Gen. 6:9-13, 22; 7:16*a;* 8:1-15; 9:1, 6, 8, 12, 16-17]) and certain differences in usage (cf. 7:2: "the male and his mate" [J] with 6:19; 7:9, 16: "male and female" [P]), one can distinguish duplicate representations of nearly every phase of the narrative: God sees the wickedness of man (J 6:5-7; P 6:11-13) and commands to enter the ark (J 7:1-3; P 6:18-20); Noah enters the ark (J 7:7-9; P 7:13-16). The Flood comes (J 7:10; P 7:11); the waters increase (J 7:17*b;* P 7:18-20). All flesh is destroyed (J 7:22-23; P 7:21). God decides against a future destruction (J 8:21-23; P 9:9-11). In addition to these parallels, there are also several contradictions: In J the ark is already present; in P (6:14-16) it has to be built. In J, Noah takes into the ark seven pairs of every clean animal and one pair of every unclean, while in P he takes one pair of every kind, without distinction. Further, P, which contains precise dates, gives the time of the increase of waters as 150 days and the entire duration of the Flood as one year, while J gives it as 40 days (7:4, 12, 17; 8:6). For J the Flood is caused by rainfall (7:4) which begins seven days after Noah and his family enter the ark (7:10), while for P the catastrophe is brought on by rainfall and the eruption of underground waters (7:11; 8:2).

When one separates the two strands of the story, one discovers two series of passages, each of which forms an all-but-continuous narrative. The J story includes the passages 6:5-8; 7:1-5, 7, (8-9), 10, 12, 16*b*, 17*b*, 22-23; 8:2*b*, 3*a*, 6-12, 13*b*, 20-22; while the P narrative includes the others: 6:9-22; 7:6, 11, 13-16*a*, 17*a*, 18-21, 24; 8:1-2*a*, 3*b*-5, 13*a*, 14-19; 9:1-17. The differences in style and literary power between the narratives of J and P are apparent. The J story is an imaginative, charming tale, containing the picturesque incident of sending out the raven and the dove, while the P narrative is "formal, precise, and calculated." The existing conflate biblical account skilfully preserves the information contained in both sources.

The thesis that only two sources are to be found in the flood narrative is not quite satisfactory in explaining all the diversity present in the existing biblical account. Scholars claim to have discovered still a third, independent strand within the existing narrative, variously labeled J^1, L, S, E. The evidence they have adduced to prove the point cannot easily be controverted and serves to emphasize both the complexity of the historical growth of the flood story and the hypothetical nature of any theories brought forward to describe or explain the origin of the existing biblical account.

The presence of separate strands in the biblical story is apparent, but any theory to explain the phenomenon completely is necessarily only a working hypothesis. It has been argued, e.g., that the material cannot "be resolved into its constituent elements with any degree of certainty" and that the "alleged remnants of each supposed document" do not necessarily all together constitute the whole original document. If we possessed the original documents in their entirety "(assuming, for the sake of argument, that such documents ever existed), we might see at once that there were no discrepancies at all between the two" (Heidel; *see bibliography*). Arguments like these rightly call attention to the existing biblical story, which at some point must be considered as it now exists, but they detract in no way from the generally accepted source analysis and contribute nothing to a satisfactory explanation for the present state of the biblical narrative. They do, however, remind one that the theories of the composition of the Pentateuch are not conclusively proven facts but only plausible and cogent hypotheses. *See* PENTATEUCH.

b.* מבול *(mabbûl). The Hebrew term for the catastrophe is המבול, occurring everywhere in the story with the definite article (Gen. 6:17; 7:6-7, 10, 17; 9:11, 28; 10:1, 32; 11:10) except in 9:11, 15. This usage suggests that for the Hebrews the מבול was a well-known entity to which water belonged (Gen. 6:17; 7:7). Its only occurrence elsewhere in the OT is Ps. 29:10.

The word was often derived from the Akkadian *abūbu* by way of a supposed *wabūbu,* "cyclone," which is used in the Babylonian flood narrative in a way corresponding to the use of מבול in the Hebrew narrative. But this derivation is highly improbable, for (*a*) the dissimilation from "b" to "l" is unknown in Semitic grammar, and (*b*) the doubled consonant in the Hebrew word remains unexplained if *abūbu* be the prototype, to say nothing of (*c*) the problem of the shift from "a" to "m" at the beginning. Some scholars suggested the Akkadian *bubbulu, biblu, bibbulu,* "inundation," as the prototype of the Hebrew מבול. While this derivation is linguistically possible, it seems nevertheless improbable, because the word used in the Akkadian story is not *bibbulu* but rather *abūbu.* Another suggestion is to derive מבול from the Akkadian root *nbl,* "to destroy." This etymology also has linguistic difficulties, but in addition it makes of the Hebrew word an abstraction, "destruction," which scarcely fits the usage in Genesis. The theory that מבול goes back to an Akkadian original has generally been given up.

It has been shown that מבול with the meaning "deluge" occurs only in P and the texts dependent on P (Gen. 9:11, 15, 28; 10:1, 32; 11:10), while, e.g., Isaiah (54:9) when referring to the story avoids the word altogether and speaks simply of the "waters of Noah." That מבול originally cannot have denoted "deluge," however, is clear from its usage elsewhere in the flood story. At its first occurrence in P, God announces to Noah his intention to bring *the* מבול of waters upon the earth (6:17). The new thing for Noah obviously is not the well-known מבול, but the announcement of its being brought upon the earth. In J, Noah learns, to begin with (7:4), only God's intention to destroy the earth with water; the מבול is mentioned first in 7:10. Further, whenever the Flood itself is mentioned throughout the story, it is referred to as "the water" (Gen. 7:18-20, 24; 8:1, 3, 5, 8-9, 11, 13) as in Isa. 54:9. The word מבול, on the other hand, occurs only in connection with the inception of the catastrophe. In J the Flood is never spoken of as the מבול, but only as the "waters of the מבול." Thus, "after seven days the waters of the מבול came upon the earth" (7:10; cf. 6:17; 7:6, 17). Moreover, the sequence 7:10, 12 (J): "After seven days the waters of the flood came upon the earth, . . . and rain fell upon the earth forty days and nights," makes it clear that the מבול is not a terrestrial object but is located in heaven. In the light of these considerations Ps. 29:10 makes clear that the מבול "is an ancient designation for the heavenly ocean" which "lies directly at Yahweh's feet" (Begrich; *see bibliography*).

The use by P of מבול with the meaning "the Flood" indicates the firm place the term had in the flood tradition, as well as the gradual fading from memory of its original meaning in the course of Israel's development. This change in meaning occurred probably in two stages: (*a*) The idea that the מבול itself, instead of simply the waters of the מבול as in J, came upon the earth was a natural conclusion if it were once supposed that the מבול actually emptied itself at the time of the Deluge (which is not stated in the story). Then the notion would be that just as God in Gen. 1 separated the waters of the primeval world, giving each its place above or beneath the firmament, so he allowed them, according to P, to flow together again in the flood story to form a new chaos. (*b*) Once the מבול had been closely connected with the idea of the waters of the Flood spread over the entire earth, the shift in its meaning from heavenly ocean to the world-wide Flood is a matter of course.

Finally, the derivation of מבול is to be sought either from the Hebrew יבל, "to flow," "to stream," or from נבל, "waterskin" (cf. Job 38:37). If the latter derivation is correct, then מבול is the technical term for the "heavenly ocean" or the "heavenly store of water jars."

3. The literary dependence of the biblical story. That many flood legends exist throughout the world is a long-known and well-attested fact. At one time this widespread distribution of a flood tradition was considered proof of the historicity of the biblical account, which with some expected modification had been spread throughout the world as people migrated from their original homeland in the Near East. This notion has necessarily been given up. We know, e.g., that numerous peoples have no flood legend in their literature. Flood stories are almost entirely lacking in Africa, occur only occasionally in Europe, and are absent in many parts of Asia. They are widespread in America, Australia, and the islands of the Pacific. In addition, many of the known flood legends differ radically from the biblical story and stand independent of it and of one another. Many do not know a world-wide flood at all, but only a local inundation; not all relate the rescue of a man or a family who "found favor in the eyes of the LORD." Often the heroes save themselves in boats or by scaling mountains, without intervention of the gods. Further, only a few of the flood stories give the wickedness of man as the cause for the Flood. In many instances nothing is said about either the characteristics of the Flood or the means of its origin. Often storms cause an inundation, sometimes rains and ocean tidal waves, occasionally earthquake. The saved may be a single person (man or woman), a couple, an entire family, a definite or an indefinite number of people. Only in a few sagas are seeds and representatives of various species of animals taken into the vessel of deliverance. The duration of the Flood, if given, varies from a few days to many years. Facts of this kind disprove the claim that the biblical account is the parent of all flood stories.

There is, however, one flood tradition which bears such striking resemblance to the biblical story that it must be directly related to it. This is the cuneiform (Sumerian, Babylonian, Assyrian) tradition. Since before the Christian era, the existence of a Babylonian flood story, resembling in many respects the biblical story, has been known. Berossus, a Babylonian priest, compiled a history of Babylonia, containing a flood story, which he published in Greek *ca.* 275 B.C. Unfortunately, his work has been lost, but extracts from it were collected by Greek historians and so transmitted to us (*see* § 3*c below*). Berossus' account of the Flood was commonly believed to have been adapted from the biblical story. But the discovery and publication in 1873 by George Smith of the British Museum of the "Chaldaean Account of the Deluge" proved conclusively that the Babylonian story was markedly older than the Hebrew version and had, in fact, been written down about the beginning of the second millennium B.C., long before the Hebrew migrations into Palestine. The documents published by Smith came from the library of Ashurbanipal (668-626?), who had collected at his palace in Nineveh copies of the great works of Mesopotamian literature. The tablets identified by Smith were fragments of the Gilgamesh Epic (there are twelve tablets in all), of which the Flood constitutes a single episode of three hundred lines, recorded on Tablet XI. Fig. FLO 18.

a. The Gilgamesh Epic. Gilgamesh, mourning the death of his friend Enkidu and increasingly obsessed with the fear of death, decides to go to his ancestor Utnapishtim (variant of Atrahasis); Old Babylonian Utanapishtim; Sumerian Ziusudra; Greek Xisouthros), the Babylonian Noah, to learn from him the secret of eternal life. After great difficulty and hardship Gilgamesh finds Utnapishtim, who tells him that he and his wife won immortality by surviving a flood, the details of which he recounts vividly. When the gods determined to destroy the world, Ea, contrary to the plan of En-lil, in a dream commanded

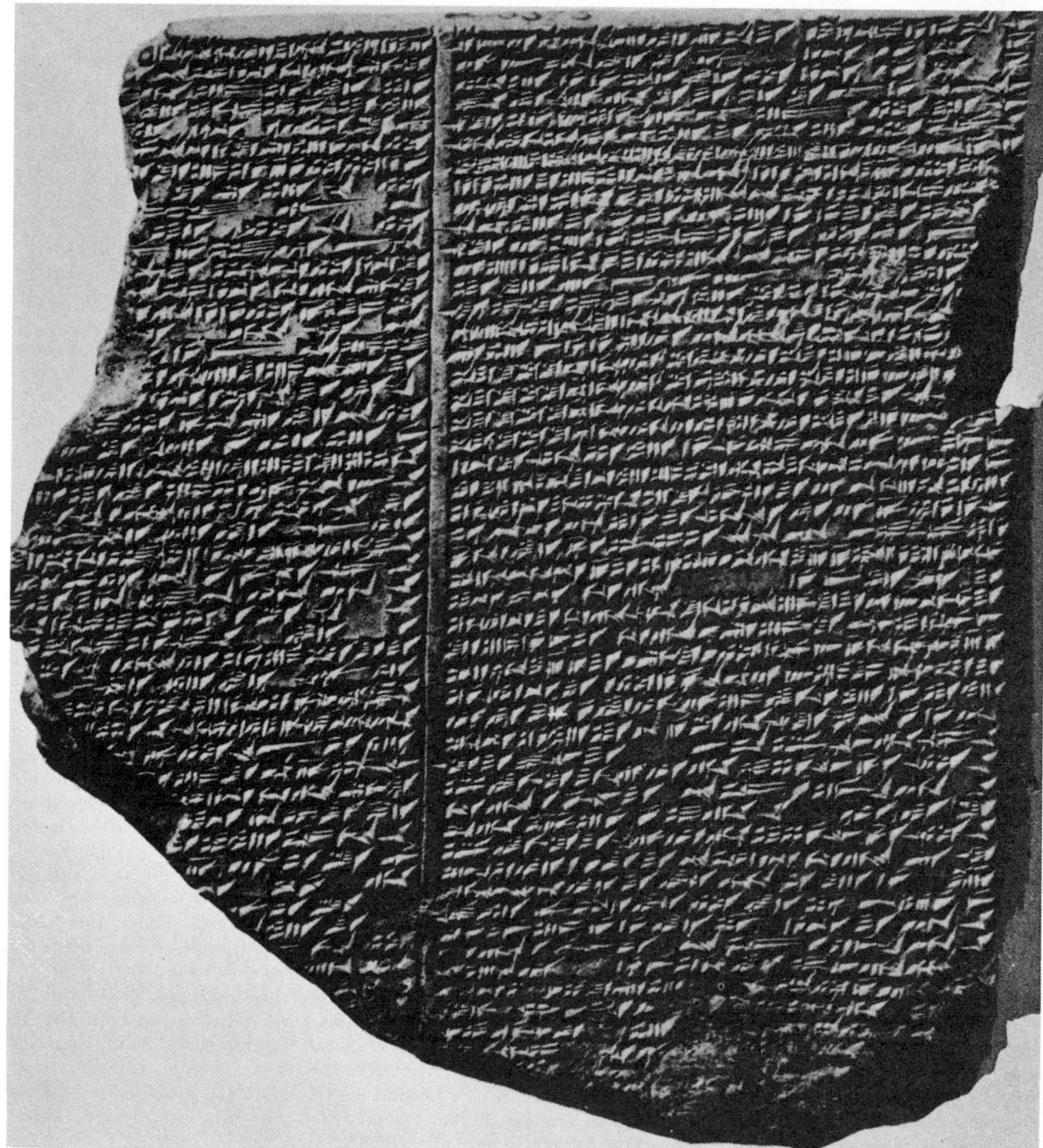

Courtesy of the Trustees of the British Museum

18. Fragment of the Babylonian account of the Flood, from Nineveh (Quyunjiq); Tablet XI of the Gilgamesh Epic

Utnapishtim, who was living in Shuruppak (modern Fara), to tear down his house and build a ship with the shape of an exact cube measuring two hundred feet per side, in which he would save himself and the "seed of all living things." Utnapishtim was not to tell his fellow citizens the reason for his action, but when they asked him where he was going, he was only to answer them with an ambiguous statement about a visit to the gods, which to them would be a promise of prosperity but to Utnapishtim would designate the impending Deluge.

When Utnapishtim awoke, he began work on the ship, and within five days had "laid her framework." The vessel had six decks (i.e., seven stories), and each story was divided into nine sections, providing in all a ship with sixty-three compartments. After calking the boat with pitch and treating it with oil, on the seventh day he had it ready for launching. Then he loaded the boat with silver and gold, "whatever he had of all the living beings," all his family and kin, the beast and wild creatures of the field, "all the craftsmen," and the boatmen.

After Utnapishtim himself had entered and shut the door, the skies grew black with clouds, thunder rumbled, lightning flashed, the rivers rose, breaking dams and dikes, and the tempest swept over the land. It was so dark that a man could not recognize his fellow. So bad was the Deluge that even the gods "cowered like dogs (and) crouched against the outer wall." Six days and nights the wind blew, while downpour, tempest, and flood overwhelmed the land. "When the seventh day arrived, the flood(-carrying) south-storm subsided . . . the sea grew quiet, the tempest was still, the flood ceased." Utnapishtim looked out upon the sea: "Stillness had set in, and all of mankind had returned to clay."

After an unspecified time the ship came to rest upon Mount Nisir (modern Pir Omar Gudrun, NE of Kirkuk), where it remained motionless for six days. On the seventh day Utnapishtim released a dove, which, finding no resting place, returned to the ship. Then he set free a swallow, which also returned. Finally he released a raven, which "went forth and, seeing that the waters had diminished, he eats, circles, caws, and turns not round." At this sign, Utnapishtim opened the door of the ship for every creature to go forth, while he offered sacrifice to the gods. The gods "smelled the sweet savor" and "crowded like flies about the sacrifice."

When En-lil arrived, he was angry to find that someone had escaped the Deluge, but he submitted to Ea's reproach that the Flood had been too severe and rewarded Utnapishtim and his wife with immortality. In the words of the narrative, he said: "Hitherto Utnapishtim has been but human. Henceforth Utnapishtim and his wife shall be like unto us gods. Utnapishtim shall reside far away, at the mouth of the rivers!"

b. Cuneiform recensions. The oldest account of the Flood is the Sumerian version found at Nippur. It was inscribed in six columns on a tablet, only the lower one third of which has been preserved. In this story Ziusudra learns of the gods' decision to send a flood "to destroy the seed of mankind." The instructions to Ziusudra which must originally have been included in the story are missing, because the text is broken at this point. When the text resumes, the Flood has already raged upon the earth seven days and nights and "the huge boat had been tossed about by the windstorms on the great waters." Then Utu, the sun-god, came forth, and Ziusudra sacrificed to him and the rest of the gods. Finally "Anu (and) En-lil cherished Ziusudra, life like (that of) a god they give him, breath eternal like (that of) a god they bring down for him. Then, Ziusudra the king . . . in the land of Dilmun, the place where the sun rises, they caused to dwell."

In addition to the Sumerian tablet, a second fragment of a flood story, written in Old Babylonian, was excavated at Nippur. Only a few lines of the tablet are preserved. The text seems to relate the decision of a god to destroy the earth with a flood. A great ship is to be built bearing the name "Preserver of Life." A strong roof is to be constructed, and into the ship are to go "beasts of the field and fowl of the heavens."

The Atrahasis (Old Babylonian "Atramhasis") epic containing a flood narrative is known to us only from four small fragments from three original tablets, which contained a total of 1,245 lines. Two fragments are from the Old Babylonian recension, the other two from an Assyrian version. The Assyrian tablets were found in the library of Ashurbanipal, while the Babylonian are about a thousand years older, going back to the time of King Ammizaduga (first Babylonian dynasty). According to this story the Flood was preceded by severe plagues, sent in vain by En-lil to restrain the "oppressive . . . clamor of mankind." When everything else failed, En-lil determined to send the Deluge. Ea warned Atrahasis in a dream, in words strikingly like those of the Gilgamesh story, and Atrahasis built his ship according to the design given him by Ea. After the Flood subsided, the earth was repopulated from "fourteen wombs." The narrative of the earth's repopulation, though present at the end of the Assyrian version of the Atrahasis myth, appears originally to have been part of a creation story and to have no integral relation to the flood account.

Other allusions to a flood exist in cuneiform literature, but to date no further extended story has been discovered. Cf. A. Jeremias (*see bibliography*), pp. 136-37.

c. The account of Berossus. The youngest known Babylonian flood version is that of Berossus (*see above*). Extracts from this work were made by Alexander Polyhistor of Miletus (second-third century A.D.) and by Eusebius (A.D. 260?-340?) in his Chronicle. The Chronicle of Eusebius, which unfortunately exists only in fragments, was quoted at length by Georgius Syncellus (died sometime after 810) in his *Chronography* (53.19-56) of events from Creation to Diocletian, and is also contained in a complete Armenian recension. Only the high lights of the Chronicle are given in Jerome's translation of Eusebius. According to Berossus' account, a deluge occurred during the reign of Xisouthros or Sisithros (same as Ziusudra). Cronos (corresponding to Ea) revealed to him in a dream the imminent destruction of the world by a deluge and commanded him to write a history and bury it in Sippar, to build a boat, stock it with provisions, take into it all species of animals, and set sail. He was to answer those who asked him whither he was sailing: "To the gods, in order to plead with them for the good of mankind." Xisouthros obeyed the command and survived the Flood. After the storm abated, Xisouthros released "some birds," which returned to the boat; after some days he released them again, only to have them return with mud on their feet. When they were released the third time, however, the birds did not return. Then Xisouthros made an opening in the vessel and, seeing that the ship rested on a mountainside, disembarked with his family and the pilot. When he had sacrificed to the gods, he and those who had disembarked with him disappeared. Those remaining on the ship then came out to look for Xisouthros; but they could only hear his voice, telling them to honor the gods, and that they should return to Babylon, recover the records hidden in Sippar, and make them known to all men. The voice finally informed them that they were then in Armenia. So they returned and rebuilt Babylon, but the vessel remained in the mountains of Armenia, where, according to the story, people still scrape off pitch from it to make amulets.

d. The problem of dependence. The points of contact between the Hebrew and the Mesopotamian flood stories are numerous. In both traditions the hero is a pious man, divinely warned of the coming catastrophe and saved from destruction because of his fear of god. In both traditions careful attention is given to the size of the boat; both take care for the repopulation of the earth; for both the Flood is world wide, involving great masses of water (in Gen. 7:19 the water rises fifteen cubits above the mountains).

The duration of the storm is variously given. The effect of the Flood is total destruction. The boat comes to rest on a mountain. Birds are released so that the hero may secure information about the decrease of the waters. (The biblical order—raven, then dove—is more sensible than the Babylonian; for the raven could alight on floating carrion and live, while the dove required growing trees in the valley. The raven's failure to return to the ship would have told Utnapishtim nothing, whereas the dove's failure to return gave Noah the information he sought.) Noah disembarked only at the command of God, but the Mesopotamian hero left the vessel at his own discretion. Both traditions relate several acts of worship after the hero's escape from the Flood, and both traditions recount divine blessings on the survivors, with an indication (in Gilgamesh) and a promise (in Genesis) that a similar catastrophic deluge will never again occur.

In the Gilgamesh Epic, Utnapishtim received eternal life. The biblical story may preserve an allusion to a similar translation of Noah in 6:9*b:* "Noah walked with God." The possibility of this allusion is suggested by 5:24: "Enoch walked with God; and he was not, for God took him" (J), which appears perhaps to have been misunderstood by P in 5:22: "Enoch walked with God after the birth of Methuselah three hundred years, and had other sons and daughters." If this supposition is correct, both the dependence of the Hebrew tradition on the Babylonian and its revision and reworking by the Hebrews become even clearer. A further allusion to the Babylonian story may be found in Gen. 11:2: "As men migrated in the east, they found a plain in the land of Shinar." This passage, which does not follow logically from 11:1, does make sense when considered as a sequel to the flood narrative (J), which assumes that the ark landed at a point W of Babylon. Such a conclusion to the flood narrative is reminiscent of the conclusion to the flood story given by Berossus (*see* § 3*c above*). Further, in Berossus' version the flood survivors have to be told where they are; a similar allusion to being "lost" may perhaps be inferred from Gen. 11:2.

The historical relation between the actual biblical and Mesopotamian flood stories cannot be determined precisely. The main outline of the Hebrew account obviously stems from the Babylonian flood tradition. That the Hebrew story is derived from the Babylonian cannot be doubted, but the differences in details and in spirit between the two narratives are so great that a literary dependence of the biblical upon the Babylonian cannot be proved and is, in fact, improbable. The Babylonian flood tradition was, in all likelihood, not transmitted directly to the Hebrews but rather was mediated to them through the Amorites and proto-Arameans, and the Hebrews adapted the story to fit their theological presuppositions. Instead of the Babylonian gods, who lie to one another, cheat and deceive both one another and mankind, who cower in terror before the flood-storm and then flock like flies to the sacrifice after the Deluge, we find in the biblical account the righteous, omnipotent, merciful God, "majestic in holiness, terrible in glorious deeds, doing wonders" (Exod. 15:11). In Genesis the Flood is interpreted unmistakably as divine judgment on a corrupt world, and the story is so well told that it has even today the same power to stir the conscience, for which purpose the biblical writers told it.

4. Historicity of the Flood. In Genesis the flood story is incorporated into the history of mankind, so that all the then known peoples of the earth are said to be descended from Noah's three sons and CANAAN. This corresponds to the earlier Mesopotamians' attempt to incorporate the Deluge into their history (cf. the Sumerian King List, *ANET* 264). Attempts like these at historical documentation of the flood narrative naturally raise a question about the historicity of the Flood. Was there an actual inundation which forms the historical core of this Near Eastern flood tradition?

The belief in a deluge covering the whole earth and destroying all men and animals except those preserved in an ark has been largely given up. Aside from the great variety in substance and detail which exists in the flood myths of the world, making their reference to a single historical event impossible, and apart from the advances of anthropology which show that early civilization could not have been interrupted by a flood within millenniums of the time assigned to it by biblical chronology, the obvious difficulties of the biblical narrative itself preclude reference to an inundation of the whole world as we know it. The ark could never have weathered a storm such as Genesis describes, nor could it possibly have contained a pair of every existing species of animal and creeping thing, to say nothing of providing proper subsistence conditions for such a menagerie. Neither would the eight members of Noah's family have been able to care for a zoo of such proportions, even assuming they really had been able to collect one pair of every species of life.

That the deluge story is a reminiscence of some one of those prehistoric catastrophes reported by geologists is unthinkable. The biblical account is scarcely a report of that occurrence, as at least one writer maintains, which separated the Tertiary period from the Quaternary, recalling events of at least thirty thousand years ago. It is psychologically and physically impossible that men could remember prehistoric catastrophic events of the kind known to geologists, even assuming, for the sake of argument, that Homo sapiens was on earth at that time.

If there is historical substance to the flood tradition, it must be found in some local Mesopotamian disaster of special magnitude, which could be confirmed by archaeological evidence. For a flood of the proportions described in the Babylonian and biblical accounts would leave an alluvial deposit, above and below which could be found traces of human activity, but within which would be found none. Two archaeologists of repute have claimed to have discovered proof of the Flood: Sir Leonard Woolley at Ur and Stephen Langdon at Kish. The two alluvial layers, however, cannot be dated contemporaneously and must refer to two separate inundations, one at Ur and the other at Kish. Alluvial layers similar to those at Ur and Kish have been found at Uruk, Fara (ancient Shuruppak), Telloh (ancient Lagash), and Nineveh.* These findings seem to indicate that these Mesopotamian cities did at various times experience severe flooding by either the Tigris or the Euphrates River, or by both. Some such violent

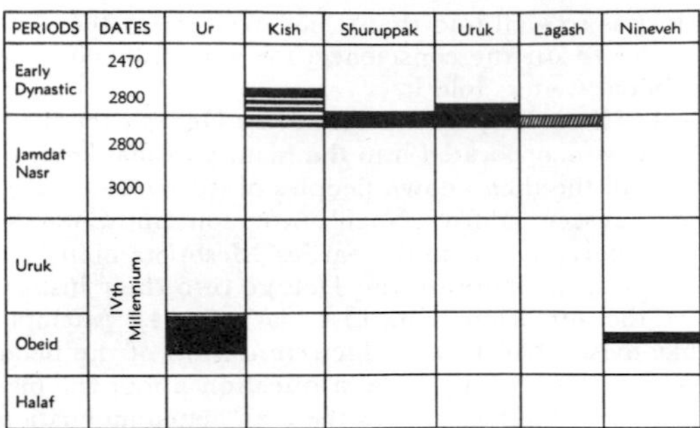

PERIODS	DATES	Ur	Kish	Shuruppak	Uruk	Lagash	Nineveh
Early Dynastic	2470 2800						
Jamdat Nasr	2800 3000						
Uruk	IVth Millennium						
Obeid							
Halaf							

From Parrot, *The Flood and Noah's Ark* (Neuchâtel: Delachaux & Niestlé)

19. Mesopotamian sites showing flood deposits

flooding, accompanied by heavy rains and perhaps earthquake, may form the basis for the flood tradition in cuneiform literature on which the Genesis account depends. Fig. FLO 19.

Bibliography. Commentaries: H. Gunkel, *HKAT* (5th ed., 1922). J. Skinner, ICC (2nd ed., 1930)—comprehensive.

Etymological studies: J. Begrich, "Mabbūl, Eine exegetisch-lexikalische Studie," *ZS,* 6 (1928), 135-53—the standard work. W. F. Albright, "The Babylonian Matter in the Pre-Deuteronomic Primeval History," *JBL,* 58 (1939), 91-103.

Flood traditions: R. Andree, *Die Flutsagen ethnographisch betrachtet* (1891). H. Usener, *Die Sintfluthsagen* (Religionsgeschichtliche Untersuchungen III; 1899). M. Winternitz, "Die Flutsagen des Alterthums und der Natürvölker," *Mitteilungen der anthropologischen Gesellschaft in Wien,* 31 (1901), 305-33—excellent survey of the material. J. G. Frazer, *Folklore in the OT,* vol. I (1918). E. G. Kraeling, "The Earliest Hebrew Flood Story," *JBL,* 66 (1947), 279-93.

The Gilgamesh Epic: G. Smith, "The Chaldaean Account of the Deluge," *TSBA,* II (1873), 213-34. A. Jeremias, *Das At im Lichte des alten Orients* (4th ed., 1930). A. Heidel, *The Gilgamesh Epic and OT Parallels* (2nd ed., 1949). J. B. Pritchard, *ANET* (2nd ed., 1955).

Berossus: A. Schoene, ed., *Eusebi chronicorum libri primer* (1875); the Armenian version ed. by J. B. Ancher [2 vols.; 1818]); *Die Weltchronik des Eusebius in ihrer Bearbeitung durch Hieronymus* (1900).

Historicity of the Flood: J. Riem, *Weltenwerden* (1924). H. Peake, *The Flood, New Light on an Old Story* (1930). J. Boehmer, "Tellurische Trümmerstücken im Flutbericht der Genesis," *ZAW,* 50 (1932), 117-24. A. Parrot, *The Flood and Noah's Ark* (1953), contains a useful introduction. L. Woolley, *Excavations at Ur* (1954). M. Eliade, *Patterns in Comparative Religion* (1958).

J. H. Marks

FLOOR. 1. קרקע, the floor of a building. Solomon's temple is described as having a floor covered with boards of cypress (I Kings 6:15) and overlaid with gold (vs. 30). The dust of the earthen floor of the tabernacle was regarded as possessing special qualities (Num. 5:17). The word is used of the BOTTOM of the sea in Amos 9:3.

See also Architecture; House.

2. גרן, a threshing floor; an open space of rock or pounded earth exposed to the wind and used for Threshing and Winnowing grain.

FLORA.

A. Classification of biblical plants
  1. Cereals and legumes
    a. Wheat
    b. Emmer
    c. Barley
    d. Millet
    e. Beans
    f. Lentils
  2. Fruit trees
    a. Almond
    b. Apple
    c. Fig
    d. Husks
    e. Mulberry tree
    f. Nuts
    g. Olive tree
    h. Palm tree
    i. Pomegranate
    j. Sycomore
    k. Vine
  3. Vegetables and gourds
    a. Onion
    b. Garlic
    c. Leek
    d. Melon
    e. Cucumber
  4. Flax
  5. Cotton
  6. Flavors and condiments
    a. Anise
    b. Coriander
    c. Fitches
    d. Cummin
    e. Mint
    f. Mustard
    g. Saffron
  7. Balms, drugs, and incense
    a. Aloes
    b. Balm
    c. Bdellium
    d. Henna
    e. Cane, calamus, sweet cane, sweet calamus
    f. Cassia
    g. Cinnamon
    h. Galbanum
    i. Incense, frankincense
    j. Myrrh
    k. Spikenard, nard
    l. Spices
  8. Costly timbers
    a. Ebony
    b. Gopher wood
    c. Algum, almug timber
  9. Forest trees and shrubs
    a. Acacia tree, acacia wood
    b. Bay tree
    c. Bush, thornbush
    d. Cedar
    e. Cypress
    f. Fir, fir tree
    g. Heath
    h. Juniper
    i. Laurel
    j. Hyssop
    k. Mallow
    l. Myrtle
    m. Oil tree, wild olive
    n. Oak
    o. Plane tree
    p. Storax tree
    q. Tamarisk

r. Terebinth, turpentine tree
s. Thick tree
t. Willow
10. Lilies and roses
11. Reeds and rushes
a. Reeds
b. Rush, papyrus, bulrushes
c. Cattail
d. Rush, bulrush, hook, caldron
e. Flag, meadow, reeds
12. Thorns and thistles
a. Thorn
b. Brier
c. Thistle
13. Weeds and nettles
a. Nettle
b. Wheel, rolling thing, whirling dust
c. Cockle
d. Tares
14. Wormwoods and poisons
a. Gall, hemlock
b. Wormwood
c. Bitter herbs
d. Wild gourds
15. Hedges and fences
a. Brambles, thorns
b. Thorns
16. Other plants
a. Gourd
b. Capper
c. Mandrake
d. Manna
B. The vegetal landscape
1. History of the flora
2. Vegetation units
a. The Aleppo pine forest
b. Evergreen oak maquis and forest
c. Deciduous broad-leaved oak forest
d. Evergreen park woods
e. Evergreen Mediterranean dwarf shrub formation
f. Deciduous steppe forest
g. Tamarisk woods
h. The riparian forest
i. The Saxaul forest
j. Sagebrush steppes
k. Succulent shrub desert
l. Swamps and marshes
m. Sand-dune vegetation
n. Vegetation of tropical oases
C. Man and plants
1. Man and trees
2. Native plants in everyday life
a. Industrial plants
b. Medicinal plants
c. Pasture and forest plants
3. Wild ancestors of cultivated plants
4. Man and weeds
5. Agriculture through the ages
Bibliography

A. *CLASSIFICATION OF BIBLICAL PLANTS.* It may seem surprising that the number of plant names mentioned in the Bible is not much over 100, while the flora of the land of the Bible comprises *ca.* 2,300 species. It should be remembered that the Bible as a historical, legislatorial, and literary work can by no means fully reflect the relations between the people and their plant environment. It is therefore quite understandable that many very common or even useful plants, including many forest trees and shrubs, ornamental plants, and edible herbs, find no mention in the Scriptures.

But it is not the number of plants which is important in this biblical florula. Notwithstanding its limitations, it provides a deep insight into many aspects of life associated with the plant world. Not only agriculture is involved in or illuminated by this flora, but also religion, customs and practices, law, commerce, manufacturing, architecture, medicine, sanitation, cosmetics, and even love.

The frequency of the mention of the names of plants in the Bible is not always in proportion to their use and distribution. E.g., the cedar, which has never been native in Palestine, appears seventy times in the Bible, while the wheat plant is mentioned only thirty-two times. Foreign drugs and balms are much more frequently mentioned than many native useful trees and herbs.

The identification of plant names is a difficult and responsible task, which unfortunately has not always been successfully done. There are three types of plant names in this respect: (*a*) those indubitably and unanimously identifiable, (*b*) those which need further study and research before identification can be made, and (*c*) those for which there seems to be no hope that accurate identification can be made. The last group is quite considerable in number, and comprises those names about which there is much confusion, inconsistency, and controversy among biblical scholars. The reason for this is that there are many plants which are very poorly described, or which are mentioned in association with an environment or use which would suit scores of various species. Here we could include plants like thistles, reeds, and rushes. Most of such names have a collective or general meaning, and do not denote specific plants. There are also plant names embodied in ancient proverbs and phrases which passed down from generation to generation, the detailed connotation of which has been lost through the ages.

Besides linguistic methods of research, the plant lore of the Bible requires also a geographical and ecological approach, and an adequate knowledge of the local flora. The latter can be of great help in avoiding many mistranslations and absurdities met with in current literature, and in excluding from the biblical flora such items as rye, heath, box trees, cockles, tares, teil trees, chestnuts, which have never been native to or grown in Palestine.

In the following short discussions of the biblical plants their uses and descriptions are given. For the sake of brevity the reasons for the identification are given only where it has seemed necessary. For further study, *see bibliography*.

1. Cereals and legumes. ***a. Wheat*** (חטה; σῖτος). One of the most important field crops of Palestine since the Early Bronze Age (3300-2000) and probably earlier is wheat (*Triticum durum,* Host). Its general area of cultivation extends throughout the warm temperate and subtropical regions. Its centers of origin are Anterior and Central Asia. Wheat is an annual grass with two-ranked leaves. The ears are rather thick and compact with three-flowered to five-flowered spikelets, each subtended by two glumes and producing two to three grains. The hard grains contain, among other substances, a high percentage of gluten, which renders the flour most suitable for baking and pastry. Wheat is sown with the first winter rains or before, and is harvested in June or July. Special varieties of this wheat species are grown in various parts of the country. In biblical times, as at present, wheat was consumed not only in the form of bread, cakes, and wafers, but also as "parched grain" (קלי; I Sam. 25:18, etc.) and as green or fresh ears of grain (כרמל; Lev. 2:14; 23:14; II Kings 4:42). It was also brought as a cereal offering (KJV "meal offering"). Wheat and barley were the only cereals included within the "seven kinds" with which the land was blessed (Deut. 8:8). A wild-growing wheat, *Triticum dicoccoides* (Koern.) Schulz, is supposed to be the wild ancestor of certain cultivated wheats. For wheat in the NT, *see* WHEAT.

b. Emmer. This is a translation of כסמת, כסמים, mentioned in Exod. 9:32; Isa. 28:25; Ezek. 4:9. This plant (RSV SPELT; KJV "rie," "fitches") is *Triticum dicoccum* Schrank. There is no evidence that rye, fitches, and spelt were grown in biblical times in Palestine, but emmer has been found in old Egyptian tombs, and its cultivation in the Near Eastern countries in biblical times is almost certain. Emmer is a kind of wheat, with very dense ears and a brittle rachis. The spikelets are usually two-flowered, and their glumes are prominently keeled. The slender red grains are acute at each end and remain in chaff after threshing. Emmer is much inferior to durum wheat (*see* § A1*a above*). Its growth requirements are more modest than those of wheat.

c. Barley (שעורה, שערים). One of the most ancient cereals, known to have been grown in Palestine and elsewhere since the Early Bronze Age (3300-2000) and probably earlier, is barley (*Hardeum vulgare* L.; Exod. 9:31; Num. 5:15; Job 31:40; etc.). Its countries of origin are supposed to be Anterior and Central Asia. It is an annual grass, growing up to three feet high. Its leaves are broader than those of wheat. The ears are composed of clusters, each consisting of three one-flowered spikelets. According to the variety, all or only the central flowers of the spikelets produce grains. The grains are attached to the chaff, which is furnished with a long awn. Barley is extensively cultivated in Palestine as a winter crop. It is harvested in May. It is less demanding than wheat and thrives well under drier conditions. *See also* BARLEY.

d. Millet (דחן). This is an annual grass (*Panicum miliaceum* L.; Ezek. 4:9), attaining a height of three feet or so. The flowers are borne on much-branching and spreading panicles. The minute, almost globular grains are an excellent forage, but are also eaten by men as porridge or bread. Millet has been known since ancient times in Persia and is probably indigenous in the East Indies. The Arabic name *dukhn* refers also to some varieties of sorghum, so that it is not improbable that *sorghum annuum,* the *durra* of the Arabs, is also involved here. *Durra* is of African origin and is known from Egypt at *ca.* 1000 B.C. *See also* MILLET.

e. Beans (פול). This plant, referred to in II Sam. 17:28; Ezek. 4:9, is the common broad bean (*Vicia faba* L.), grown in gardens and in fields of Palestine and elsewhere. It has been known since the Bronze Age (3300-2000) and is used as a pulse eaten roasted or boiled; it is also grown as a green manure plant. It is two to three feet high. The leaves consist of two or three pairs of broad leaflets. The flowers are borne in axillary clusters; their color is white, marked with a purple spot. The large pods contain several seeds. The origin is not certain. *See also* BEANS.

f. Lentils (עדשים). Identification of the lentil (*Lens esculenta* Moench; Gen. 25:34; II Sam. 17:27-29) is certain. The Arabic name is *'adas.* This is an annual plant, with a slender stem and pinnate leaves; the flowers are whitish and violet-striped; the pods are small and contain single seeds; the shape of the seed is biconvex-lenticular. Lentils have been grown as a field crop in Palestine and adjacent countries since very ancient times. They are mainly cooked as pottage and are especially popular with the poor. *See also* LENTILS. Fig. LEN 26.

On "spelt," *see* §A1*b above.*

2. Fruit trees. *a. Almond* (לוז, שקד). Identification of this tree (*Amygdalus communis* L.; Gen. 43:11; Jer. 1:11; etc.) is certain. The almond tree is eight to twenty feet tall and sheds its leaves in winter. The leaves are oblong-elliptical. The flowers are large and handsome; their color is white to pink. The fruit is a drupe, of which the large seed is eaten. The seed contains a high percentage of fat. The almond tree grows wild in Palestine, Syria, and other countries of the Near East. Several varieties have been cultivated in Palestine since ancient times. The recent discovery of the almond tree in the Negeb suggests its occurrence also in the Sinai Mountains, and this may explain the adoption by the Israelites of almond branches as a model of the lampstand (Exod. 25:33-36). The Arabic name for the almond tree is *lawz.* It is not improbable that the geographical name Luz (Bethel) is due to the occurrence in the past of almond trees in this locality. *See also* ALMOND. Fig. ALM 16.

b. Apple (תפוח). Among the various identifications suggested for this name, mentioned in Prov. 25:11; Song of S. 7:8; etc., none is more plausible than that of the apricot, *Prunus armeniaca* L. It fits the context completely. The apricot tree is twelve to twenty feet tall, its spreading branches and its dense foliage affording much shade; its leaves are ovate and heart-shaped at the base. It blossoms in spring, producing white-pinkish flowers in profusion. The fruit, not unlike a plum, is very aromatic and delicious in taste. The apricot is a very common fruit tree in Anterior Asia, but there are no clear evidences as to its existence in Palestine during biblical times. *See also* APPLE.

c. Fig (תאנה, תאנים; συκῆ, σῦκον). The fig tree (*Ficus carica* L.; Num. 13:23; 20:5; Matt. 7:16; etc.) is one of the most popular fruit trees, which together with the vine typified freedom and prosperity at the time of the Bible. It is a deciduous tree, ten to twenty feet tall, very irregularly branching; the branches are often curved. The large leaves are palmately lobed. The minute flowers are aggregated within a pearlike or a globular fleshy receptacle called syconium (פגה, "fig fruit"; Song of S. 2:13; RSV "figs"; KJV "green figs"), which has a small opening at the broad end. The fig tree has been cultivated since ancient times in the Mediterranean and Anterior Asian countries. It is of high esteem, because of its delicious fruit and heavy shade. It often escapes cultivation and inhabits old walls and river banks. It produces two crops: the winter figs, occurring on leafless twigs, are small, hard, and not edible; the summer figs, which ripen from the middle to the end of the summer, are the only usable crop. They are eaten fresh or dried and pressed into cakes (דבלה; Isa. 38:21). There is a wild variety of fig named the caprifig (*Ficus carica* L. var. *silvestris* Nees), which, unlike the true fig, produces in its syconia also male flowerets. Although its fruits are inedible, it has been largely planted for pollination of certain varieties of the true fig tree. In Palestine the wild fig tree is no more used, as the local fig varieties produce fruits without pollination. *See also* FIG. Fig. FIG 11; Pl. XV*b*.

d. Husks. This is the KJV translation of κεράτια (Luke 15:16; RSV PODS). It is generally believed that the husks are the pods of the carob tree (*Ceratonia siliqua* L., the חרוב of the Mishna). It is an evergreen dioecious tree, ten to twenty feet high, with a hemispheric crown. Its leaves are composed of a few pairs of leathery, glossy leaflets. It flowers mainly in late summer; its flowerets are yellowish-green and borne on branches of the previous year. The fruits, which ripen *ca.* ten months after flowering, are dark brown fleshy pods, four to eight inches long. They have a dry, fleshy, sweet pulp and many small, stony seeds. The pods are collected and widely used as fodder for cattle and sheep; they are also eaten fresh by man. A sirup and a kind of honey are prepared from the pulp by the Arabs. Some authorities believe that the "honey" in some passages of the OT refers to the husks of the carob tree. *Ceratonia siliqua* is one of the most common forest trees native to Palestine.

e. Mulberry tree. The translation "mulberry" for the Hebrew בכאים in II Sam. 5:23-24; I Chr. 14:14-15; Ps. 84:6 (BACA) is an unfounded identification. Still less certain and controversial to the context, at least ecologically, is *Populus euphratica,* or "balsam trees" (so RSV), brought forward by Moldenke and others. There is no evidence to believe that this name refers to any plant. The sycamine tree in Luke 17:6 is more likely to be a mulberry tree, at least because of its Greek name. Of the mulberry species, the black and the white, the former (*Morus nigra* L.) was probably the more popular. *Morus nigra* is a deciduous and dioecious tree, ten to twenty feet high, with a broad crown and large and often lobed leaves. Its small green flowerets are aggregated in catkins or heads. The female entire head ripens to a fleshy, sweet fruit, which is eaten fresh or cooked. Its origin is supposedly Persian. *See also* MULBERRY TREES;* SYCAMINE. Fig. MUL 77.

f. Nuts. This is the translation of בטנים in Gen. 43:11, as well as of אגוז in Song of S. 6:11. The first-mentioned refers to the genus *Pistacia*. Some authorities believe that בטנים are the fruits of *Pistacia vera,* which is cultivated for its almondlike nuts. But there is strong evidence that this name refers either to the fruits of *Pistacia palaestina* or to *Pistacia atlantica,* the fruits of which, though much smaller and less tasteful than those of *Pistacia vera,* are commonly eaten fresh or roasted, and even offered for sale, by Arab villagers. This is in full agreement with the Greek translation (*Terebinthos*) and the Douay Version ("turpentine"). It also agrees with the Arabic name *buṭm* in the whole Near East, and with the geographical indication of the context. The Hebrew name for the trees is אלה (*see* TEREBINTH). The nut in Song of S. 6:11 is the walnut, *Juglans regia* L. It is a handsome dioecious tree with a broad, hemispherical crown. Its leaves are composed of two to six pairs of ovate to elliptical, entire, glabrous, and fragrant leaflets. The numerous male flowerets are arranged in long catkins, while the few female ones are borne in the axils of the upper leaves. The fruit has a fleshy outer skin containing a tannin substance, while the inner stone contains a single folded seed, which is very nutritive because of its high percentage of fat. The timber is very much appreciated in the manufacture of costly furniture. According to Josephus, walnuts have been widely cultivated in the past. At present, the tree is less common in Palestine. The countries of its origin are probably Persia and Transcaucasia. *See also* NUTS. Fig. NUT 23.

g. Olive tree (זיתים, זית). The olive tree (*Olea europaea* L.) was the most important fruit and oil tree of Palestine in biblical times and prior to that period. This is attested by the findings of olive kernels in Meggido from the Bronze Age (3200-2000). The olive tree is an evergreen tree, fifteen to twenty feet high, with a thick, gnarled, and often twisted trunk, and a broad, ovate, much-branched crown. It reaches an age of several hundred years, and some trees are estimated to be over a thousand years old. The leaves are leathery, lanceolate to oblong, green and glabrous above, and white and scurfy beneath. The small, white flowers are arranged in loose racemes and appear generally in May. The fruit is a fleshy drupe varying in size according to variety; it ripens five or six months after flowering. At full maturity the green color of the fruit turns black. The fleshy pulp of the fruit contains, among other substances, about fifty per cent oil. The fruits are eaten, green and black, fresh or conserved in salt water or in acid. Oil extracting was very common in the past, as it is at present. Ancient oil presses are found abundantly even among natural forests. Apart from serving the everyday diet, oil was widely used as fuel for lamps, in medicine, in sacrificial offering, perfumery, and probably also in soap manufacture. The fruits are removed from the tree by beating the branches with long sticks. The hard wood of this tree is hardly workable and, thus, scarcely used for building and manufacture. The olive tree was a symbol of superiority and divine blessing (Judg. 9:8-9), fertility (Ps. 128:3), beauty and freshness (Jer. 11:16), and peace (Gen. 8:11; Neh. 8:15). Because of its very ancient cultivation, the origin of the olive tree is still unknown. Yet many authorities believe that the wild olive tree (*Olea europaea* L. var. *oleaster*), native to Palestine and other Mediterranean countries, is the wild ancestor of the cultivated species. For the cultivated olive (καλλιέλαιος) and wild olive (ἀγριέλαιος) in Paul's metaphor, see Rom. 11:17, 24. *See also* OLIVE TREE; WILD OLIVE. Fig. OLI 7.

h. Palm tree (תמר). This is the date palm (*Phoenix dactylifera* L.), a dioecious tree, generally forty to sixty feet tall. The trunk is simple, unbranched, and the pinnate leaves reach a length of four to six feet. They are arranged in a terminal cluster, from which the flowering shoots arise. The flowers are white and arranged in much-branched panicles enclosed in a spathe, which splits into two boatlike valves. The male flowers produce abundant pollen, borne by the wind to the female flowers. In order to secure efficient pollination, palm growers used to climb up to the top of the tree and put branches of male flowers near the female ones, or spray pollen on the female flowers. The fruit is a one-seeded berry *ca.* two inches long; it contains a high amount of sugar and is very nutritive. There are Bedouins in desert oases whose main diet consists of dates and camels' milk. The origin of the date palm is as yet not adequately known. Its cultivation dates back to early prehistoric time. Its present range of cultivation embraces the entire tropical and subtropical zones of the globe. Its main centers of cultivation and varietal diversity are Iraq, Iran, and some North African countries. In Palestine date growing was centered in the Coastal Plain and in the Jordan Valley. Jericho, En-gedi, Zoar, and Elath were once famous for their date-palm groves. Because of its manifold use, the date palm once played an important part in agriculture. Apart from the fruits, which were eaten fresh, dried, and in the form of cakes, other parts of the tree were also used: The leaves were applied to cover roofs; the trunk supplied timber, the young flowering shoots yielded a sort of wine, and from the fibers of the leaves robes were woven. The palm was respected by the ancients as a tree of pride and grace. Many localities and men bore the name of the palm. *See also* PALM TREE. Pl. XII*d*.

i. Pomegranate (רמון). The Arabic name is *rumman*. This is a small deciduous tree up to twelve feet tall (*Punica granatum* L.; Num. 20:5; Deut. 8:8; etc.). The leaves are oblong to lanceolate, entire and reddish when young. The large, showy red-scarlet flowers appear in summer; they are subtended by several large, leathery calyx lobes. The fruit is as large as an orange; it has a leathery, yellow-to-purple rind and is crowned by the persistent calyx. The pink or red seeds are juicy and have an acid, agreeable taste. The tree has been widely cultivated in Palestine since ancient times. The origin of the pomegranate is referred by some scholars to the East Indies. In addition to the common use of the fruit, a wine is also prepared from the juice, and the rind of the fruit is used in dyeing and leather tanning. The fruit was a symbol of profusion and a pattern in painting and sculpturing. *See also* POMEGRANATE. Pl. XI*c-e*.

j. Sycomore (שקמים, שקמה; συκομορέα). This species *Ficus sycomorus* L.; I Kings 10:27; I Chr. 27:28; Amos 7:14; etc.; RSV "sycamore") has nothing in common with the North American sycamore tree. The sycomore of the Bible is a strong tree, reaching a height of thirty feet or more and an age of several hundred years. It has a round or oval, much-branched crown. The rather large leaves are unlobed, and the figs are arranged in dense clusters on the older branches. They are more or less globular in shape, much smaller and inferior in taste and sugar content than those of the fig tree. Yet they are collected and eaten by the population of the Coastal Plain, where the sycomore has been widely cultivated in the past as a fruit tree. The Hebrew word *bôlēs* in Amos 7:14, associated with sycomores, is now commonly believed to mean "piercing" or "puncturing" the premature fruit with a nail or another sharp implement in order to accelerate ripening. This is said to have been a practice with Egyptian sycomore growers. The wood of the sycomore is known for its durability, and mummy coffins made of this wood have been found in old Egyptian tombs. It is also used sometimes for furniture and building. The sycomore tree is native to tropical Africa. It has also been cultivated in the Jordan Valley. *See also* SYCAMORE. Fig. SYC 93.

k. Vine (גפן, גפנים; ἄμπελος). The grapevine (*Vitis vinifera* L.) is one of the most ancient cultivated plants. Its cultivation dates back in Palestine to the Early Bronze Age (3200-2000 B.C.). In biblical times the grapevine was one of the most important plants in economical and cultural life. The rich botanical and agrotechnical vocabulary associated in the Bible with the vine testifies to the high level of viticulture at that period. The grapevine is a trailing or climbing shrub with very long branches. The leaves are rounded in outline, heart-shaped at base, and generally five-lobed. The threadlike tendrils borne on the branches are organs which enable the vine to climb up to house roofs and treetops. The vine blossoms in the spring; the flowers are small, greenish, and arranged in compound panicles. They have a sweet smell. The fruits are berries containing a few seeds. In certain varieties of the cultivated vine, the berries are seedless. There are hundreds of varieties of the cultivated vine, differing from one another by shape, taste, sugar content, color of the fruit, and other characteristics of the plant. The range of vine cultivation is world wide and embraces all the warm temperate and subtropical regions. In Palestine, the vine was and is still cultivated in most climatic zones, with special varieties for each zone. Vintage is spread over the entire summer season from July to October. The grapes are eaten fresh or dried (raisins), but more often they are pressed to juice and wine. For the latter, stone presses were and are still in use. The vine was a symbol of peace, fertility, and prosperity, and also an emblem of the nation. It was later widely used in painting and sculpture. Many localities and men bore the name of the vine, or names associated with it. Anterior Asia is believed to be the region of origin of *Vitis vinifera*. *See also* VINE; WINE AND STRONG DRINK.

3. Vegetables and gourds. *a. Onion* (בצלים). The Hebrew name is preserved in the Mishna and the Talmud and also in Arabic. The common onion (*Allium cepa* L.; Num. 11:5) is a member of the lily family. It is a perennial herb, with a large underground bulb, composed of several fleshy coats. The leaves are hollow, and so is also the long stalk terminating with a dense, globular umbel of pink to white flowers. The fruits are small capsules with a few seeds in each. It is cultivated in most regions of the earth. In Palestine it has been introduced from Egypt, where it is known from very ancient times, and where special varieties have been developed. Onions are used as a vegetable and a culinary seasoning. *See also* ONION.

b. Garlic (שומים). The Hebrew name is still preserved in the Talmud and among the Arabs. Garlic (*Allium sativum* L.; Num. 11:5) is a perennial herb of the lily family, with a subterranean bulb composed of several membranous tunics, each bearing a number of bulbils (cloves). The stem is tall and bears long, flat, linear leaves and an umbel of white or pinkish flowers. The fruit is a small capsule containing a few seeds. All parts of the plant have a pungent odor. The garlic is grown everywhere in gardens, mainly as a culinary seasoning. It has been known since ancient times in the countries of Anterior Asia, where it was no doubt first brought into cultivation. One of its closest wild relatives is *Allium ampeloprasum* L., which grows as a weed in Palestine and adjacent countries. The garlic is rather popular with the people of the Near East, who use it cooked or eat it raw with bread. *See also* GARLIC.

c. Leek (חציר). Leek (*Allium porrum* L.; Num. 11:5) is a tall herb resembling garlic, but with a more elongated bulb and much longer leaves. As in garlic, all parts of the plant have an acrid taste. Its bulb and leaves are widely used in cookery, as a flavor and as a vegetable. They are also eaten raw. In Egypt leeks have been grown since prehistoric times, and up to the present the leek is common in markets in all countries of the Near East. The Hebrew name חציר is also applied in the Bible to grass, hay, and green herbs in general. In this meaning it is mentioned twenty-seven times in the Bible. It may be synonymous with דשא (Isa. 40:7-8, etc.) and with עשב (Gen. 1:30, etc.). *See also* LEEKS. Fig. LEE 25.

d. Melon (אבטחים). This is the plant commonly named watermelon (*Citrullus vulgaris* L.; Num. 11:5). The Arab name for it is *baṭîḫ*. It is an annual plant grown in summer. The trailing stems and branches bear large leaves, deeply lobed. The large yellow flowers are separated into male and female ones. The fruit is a globular or elliptic berry ten inches or more in width. The fleshy, juicy pulp is aromatic and refreshing, and is widely served in Palestine and elsewhere. It has been grown in the Near Eastern countries since time immemorial, and has its origin in tropical Africa.

e. Cucumber (קשואים). It is generally believed that the Hebrew name denotes the common cucumber, *Cucumis sativus* L., but there is no evidence that this species was grown in biblical times in Egypt. What is clear is that ancient Egypt grew, apart from the watermelon mentioned above, three other gourd species—viz., *Cucumis melo* L. (the muskmelon), *Lagenaria leucantha* (Duch.) Rusby, and *Cucumis chate* L. Only the first of these three is so delicious and tasteful that the Israelites could have longed for it while in the desert (Num. 11:5). It is almost certain that *Lagenaria* was already in biblical times named דלעת, as it was later named in the Mishna and the Talmud. A locality name, Dilean (דלען; Josh. 15:38), may be associated with this name of gourd. The collective name (מקשה; Isa. 1:8) is a melon field and not a cucumber garden, as translated by the RSV and the KJV, since lodges are put in melon fields and not in cucumber gardens. It seems, thus, more likely that the Hebrew קשואים denotes the muskmelon, grown in Egypt since prehistoric times and native to tropical Africa. *See also* CUCUMBER.

4. Flax (פשתה; λίνον). The identification of this plant (*Linum usitatissimum* L.; Exod. 9:31; Isa. 42:3; 43:17) is certain. Flax is the most ancient textile plant of the Near Eastern countries. The manufacture of linen from flax was known long before biblical times. Although flax is at present scarcely cultivated in Palestine, it was an important field crop in the period of the Talmud, when a rich agrotechnical vocabulary was associated with this plant. Flax is a tender annual plant, two or three feet high, with narrow leaves and blue or whitish flowers. The fruit is a capsule containing several oleiferous seeds. The oil is used as food and in the paint industry. The material remaining after oil extraction is made into cakes and used as cattle feed. There are two groups of flax varieties: one is grown for oil, the other for fibers. The origin of flax is referred to Anterior Asia. Native to Palestine is a wild flax species, *Linum angustifolium* L., which is closely related to the cultivated species, and believed by some to be the ancestor of the latter. *See also* FLAX. Fig. FLA 16.

5. Cotton (כרפס). The rendering "cotton" for this plant (*Gossypium herbaceum* L.; Esth. 1:6) is not in contradiction with botanical facts. The oriental cotton seems to have been a very ancient crop in Persia, India, and perhaps other countries of Anterior Asia, but its cultivation in Palestine during biblical times may be doubted. Cotton is an annual or perennial plant with large three-to-seven-lobed leaves, and showy flowers, subtended by a cup-shaped involucre. The fruit is a capsule containing several seeds, beset with a dense cover of long white hairs—the cotton fibers. At present cotton grows easily in various parts of the country and yields heavy crops. *See also* COTTON.

6. Flavors and condiments. ***a. Anise.*** Some commentators are right in rendering "dill" (*Anethum graveolens* L.) for the KJV "anise" (ἄνηθον; Matt. 23:23),* but not for קצח (Isa. 28:25, 27). Indeed, dill is cultivated among the Arabs of Palestine, while the true anise is not. Dill was also grown in ancient times, and its name in the Talmud is שבת. It is an annual plant, *ca.* two feet high, with leaves dissected into capillary lobes and with large umbels of yellow flowers. The fruits are flattened with marginal wings. It is chiefly used for flavoring pickles, but it also yields an ethereal oil used in medicine. *See also* ANISE; DILL. Fig. ANI 27.

b. Coriander (גד). This is an annual plant one or two feet high (*Coriandrum sativum* L.; Exod. 16:31; Num. 11:7). It has strongly dissected leaves and umbels of white flowers. The fruits are globular, *ca.* 1½ lines across, gray to black. The whole plant has a heavy, unpleasant odor, but the fruits are used as a condiment and are sown by the Arabs in the vegetable gardens, often together with dill. It also occurs in Palestine and Syria as a weed. In the Talmud it is called כסבר. It is also known as a medicinal plant, at present rather obsolete. Its likening to manna should be restricted only to the size and shape of the seeds. *See also* CORIANDER. Fig. COR 41.

c. Fitches. "Fitches" are mentioned twice by the KJV, once for קצח (Isa. 28:25, 27) and once for כסמים (Ezek. 4:9). Both are mistranslations. The latter is to be identified with emmer (*see* § A1*b above*), and the former is undoubtedly *Nigella sativa* L., which is the nutmeg flower or the black coriander. This is in full agreement with the text as regards its threshing and its comparison with cummin. The Arabic name for *Nigella sativa* is *qazḥa*. It is an annual plant *ca.* a foot high with dissected leaves and handsome white to blue flowers. The fruit is a capsule containing many small, black, strongly pungent seeds. The seeds are used in some oriental and East European countries along with cummin as a condiment for dishes, and especially are they sprinkled on bread. At present it is only sparsely cultivated in Palestine vegetable gardens. *See also* FITCHES.

d. Cummin (כמן; κύμινον). This is an annual plant one to two feet tall (*Cuminum cyminum* L.; Isa. 28:25, 27; Matt. 23:23). Its leaves are much dissected into long, linear lobes. The small flowers are pink to white and arranged in umbels. The fruits are small, linear to elliptical, and strongly aromatic. Cummin is widely cultivated for the seeds, used as a flavor for liquors, cakes, and bread. In Palestine it is scarcely grown at present. *See also* CUMMIN. Fig. CUM 54.

e. Mint (ἡδύσμον). This plant (Matt. 23:23; Luke 11:42) is presumably a kind of *Mentha,* which was probably grown for flavoring because of the strongly aromatic odor of the leaves and flowers. Three species of *Mentha* are native to Palestine, and none of them is cultivated. *See also* MINT. Fig. MIN 52.

f. Mustard (σίναπι). The identification *Brassica nigra* (L.) Koch does not fully agree with the context (Matt. 13:31-32, etc.). This annual plant is known to have been once cultivated for oil secured from the seeds. In Palestine it is at present one of the common weeds, exceeding in height all others and projecting far above the level of grainfields by its flowering branches. Its leaves are large, and lyrate in shape, and its flowers are yellow. Its small, linear pods contain small, blackish seeds. *See also* MUSTARD. Fig. MUS 93.

g. Saffron (כרכום). Whether this name (Song of S. 4:14) is identical with the tropical *Curcuma zedoaria* or with *Crocus sativus* cannot be readily decided. For "crocus" is the Greek and Arabic name; against it is its listing along with foreign spices. *Crocus sativus* L. is a small, bulbous plant with narrow leaves and a stalk bearing a few showy flowers. The commercial product is the aromatic style and threadlike stigmas of the flower, which are picked out, dried, and pounded into small cakes. It is mainly used as a vegetable dye for coloring food and liquors. *Crocus sativus* is neither native nor grown in Palestine at the present time, but it might have been once cultivated there for the above purpose, as it is still grown in other countries. Saffron is also used in medicine, as a flavoring, and in perfumes. *See also* SAFFRON.

7. Balms, drugs, and incense. ***a. Aloes*** (אהלות, אהלים; ἀλόν). The identification *Aquilaria agallocha* Roxb. is given by most of the modern commentators. It refers, however, only to the passages in Ps. 45:8; Prov. 7:17; Song of S. 4:14; John 19:39; and not to Num. 24:6, in which this name should perhaps be substituted by "oaks," as suggested by Moffatt. *Aquilaria,* or the eaglewood, is a tropical tree native to Southern Asia. It has oblong to lanceolate entire leaves and small flowers arranged in clusters. It has a fragrant wood and is used as an incense and also in medicine and perfumery. *See also* ALOES. Fig. MAS 16.

b. Balm (צרי). Some authorities identify this name with *Balanites aegyptiaca* (L.) Del. This is a tropical tree rather common in the oases of the Dead Sea surroundings and the Lower Jordan Valley. It has thorny branches bearing pairs of obovate-elliptical leaflets and clusters of small, greenish flowers. The fruit resembles a small plum and contains oil, which is used by the Arabs for healing various kinds of illness. This identification does not fit the text (Gen. 37:25; 43:11; etc.), insofar as this tree also occurs in Egypt and was not needed to be sent there as a gift. The identification of צרי with *Pistacia lentiscus* is an absurdity, as the latter does not occur at all in Gilead, as required in Gen. 37:25. *See also* BALM.

c. Bdellium (בדולח). According to Smith (1898) this is a gum resin secured from certain species of *Commiphora* native to tropical Arabia. But there is no valid argument for this identification (Gen. 2:12; Num. 11:7). Moffatt denies its identity with plants altogether, translating "bedolach-pearls."

d. Henna (כפר). This word is used in Song of S. 1:14; 4:13 (KJV "camphire"). Loew and others identify this name with *Lawsonia inermis* L., the henna tree of the Arabs, grown in many Arabic countries for its sweet-scented, white flowers and for its "henna." The latter is a yellow, orange, or red dye prepared in the form of a paste from the crushed leaves mixed with water. This dye is commonly used by Arab women in cosmetics, mainly for coloring the tips and nails of fingers and toes, as well as other parts of the body. Colored nails have been observed on some Egyptian mummies. How far "henna" was used as a cosmetic among the Hebrews is unknown, although cosmetics in general seem to have been rather common during biblical times. That *Lawsonia* might have been a common garden plant in Jericho and En-gedi in biblical times is ascertained from the fact that it has been observed in Jericho, as well as in Arab gardens of the Coastal Plain. *Lawsonia inermis* is a small tree with opposite elliptical-lanceolate leaves and with richly branching, flowering panicles. Its fruits are capsules. It is probably native to the East Indies. *See also* HENNA. Fig. HEN 14.

e. Cane, calamus, sweet cane, sweet calamus. These translations seem to refer to one or a few plant species of the genus *Cymbopogon*. The Hebrew קנה, which generally means "reed," is here associated with the epithet הטוב, meaning "sweet" or "sweet-scented" (Jer. 6:20, etc.). Sometimes the epithet בשם is added (Exod. 30:23), and in some phrases the epithet has been dropped (Song of S. 4:14, etc.). It is mostly listed along with other spices and drugs. The conventional name of the cane is *Cymbopogon martini* (Roxb.) Stapf (*Andropogon aromaticus* Royle). It is a perennial grass, which yields the familiar ginger-grass oil. This species is only one out of a whole group of species yielding sweet-scented, volatile oils (among them ginger-grass oil, citronella oil, lemon-grass oil) known as "Indian grass oils." Another commercially important species is *Cymbopogon nardus* (L.) Rendle, known for its highly aromatic citronella oil, widely used for perfumes in India and adjacent countries. It is also noteworthy that *Cymbopogon schoenanthus* (L.) Spreng., found in old Egyptian tombs, is considered by Loret as a source for one of the ingredients of the "sacred perfume" of the ancient Egyptians. It is seen from the above that a few allied species may be involved in the name קנה. *See also* SWEET CANE.

*f. **Cassia.*** There are two Hebrew words rendered "cassia": קדה (Exod. 30:23-24, etc.) and קציעות (Ps. 45:8). For the former *Cinnamomum cassia* Blume has been suggested by some authorities. Although there is no sound evidence for this identification, it does not disagree with the context of the phrases. *Cinnamomum cassia* is a tree very like *Cinnamomum zeylanicum.* It is native to India, Ceylon, and Malaya. The product is the dried bark, peeled off from the branches and stems of the tree in the form of hollow tubes. Its quality is said to be inferior to the true cinnamon. It could have been imported to Palestine via S Arabia, a famous trade center of drugs, incenses, and spices during biblical times. More dubious is the identification of קציעות, suggested by some commentators to be *Saussurea lappa* (Dec.) Clarke, the Indian orris. This is a perennial plant with large leaves and a tall, thistlelike stem bearing purple flower heads. The roots of this plant possess very fragrant substances used for perfumes and incense and also in medicine. It is native in the Himalaya Mountains, from which it is exported to other countries. *See also* CASSIA.

*g. **Cinnamon*** (קנמון). This is an evergreen tree, twenty to thirty feet high (*Cinnamomum zeylanicum* Nees; Exod. 30:23; Prov. 7:17; Song of S. 4:14). Its bark is ash-colored, its leaves lanceolate and glossy, and its flowers white and arranged in clusters. It is native to Ceylon and Malaya, but is rather widely cultivated in other tropical countries for its valuable bark, which is peeled off from the younger branches and brought to commerce as hollow bark tubes. Another product is the fragrant oil extracted from the fruits and the bark. The use of cinnamon at the time of the Bible was threefold: as a delicious flavor for food, as a perfume, and as an ingredient of the "holy oil." Like many other spices, it was imported to Palestine via S Arabia or via Tyre by the Phoenicians. *See also* CINNAMON.

*h. **Galbanum*** (חלבנה). The plant referred to is a member of the carrot family (*Ferula galbaniflua* Boiss. et Buhse [or an allied species]; Exod. 30:34). It is a high perennial herb, with a strong taproot and finely dissected leaves. The yellow or yellowish-green flowers are arranged in umbels. The stem and root contain a yellow or brown gum, which looks like amber. This gum is strongly fragrant when burned. It has been used both in medicine and as an incense in Asian countries. Persia is believed to be the country of origin of galbanum. In biblical days it was used as an ingredient of the incense in the tabernacle. *See also* GALBANUM.

*i. **Incense, frankincense*** (לבונה, לבנה). It is generally agreed that the Hebrew name (Exod. 30:34) is identical with certain species of *Boswellia.* These are low trees or shrubs with pinnate leaves and small white or green flowers.* They grow in E tropical Africa, in tropical Arabia, and in India. The branches exude a gum in the form of glittering drops, which when burned or heated give off a strong balsam odor. By making incisions in the bark of the branches, the amount is considerably increased. This gum was imported from Arabia, chiefly for the use of sacrificial services. Some authorities maintain that the incense used in the service was not a pure substance but a mixture of several ingredients. It is now known that the incense was also used by the Egyptians and others for embalming and fumigating. "Frankincense" (λίβανος) appears in the NT in Matt. 2:11; Rev. 18:13. *See also* FRANKINCENSE. Fig. STA 76.

*j. **Myrrh.*** This name occurs as a translation of both לט (Gen. 37:25) and מר, מור (Song of S. 5:13). The identification of the former is very obvious. It is generally believed that לט is a fragrant gum known as "labdanum" or "ladanum" or "laudanum," which is exuded from a species of *Cistus.* The assumption that this is *Cistus creticus* is not consistent with the pertaining text, as this species does not occur in Gilead. The other two suggested species, *Cistus salvifolius* and *Cistus villosus,* are much more common in W Palestine than in Gilead. Moreover, it is doubtful that these plants ever secrete gum. It is therefore not improbable that the Greek rendition στακτή for לט and נטף (Exod. 30:34) is right, and both names may refer to a species of *Commiphora* (*opobalsamum*), as suggested by the ASV mg., or to another gum-bearing plant. The Hebrew מור is generally identified with *Commiphora myrrha* (Nees) Engl. or with an allied species. *Commiphora myrrha** is native to Arabia, Abyssinia, and Somaliland. It is a thorny shrub or a small tree with leaves composed of three leaflets; the flowers are small, and the fruits are plumlike drupes. A fragrant, slightly bitter and pungent resin is exuded from the branches and stems. By making incisions in the bark, larger amounts of this gum can be obtained. The gum was once highly esteemed as a drug, a perfume, and an embalming substance. It was also an ingredient of the holy oil, along with other aromatic substances. "Myrrh" (σμύρνα) appears in the NT in Mark 15:23; John 19:39. *See also* MYRRH. Fig. MYR 94.

*k. **Spikenard, nard*** (נרד). This is a perennial herb of the *valerian* family, with strongly aromatic root-stocks (*Nardostachys jatamansi* [Wall.] DC.; Song of S. 1:12). The stem is one to twenty-one inches high; the leaves are oblong to ovate. The flowers are arranged in heads. The fruits are small and hairy. It is native to the Himalaya Mountains and is used as a perfume in India and other Asian countries. It is also known in commerce. For "nard" in the NT (νάρδος; Mark 14:3; John 12:3), *see* NARD. Fig. NAR 6.

*l. **Spices*** (בשם). These are mentioned in Exod. 25:6; 30:23; 35:8; I Kings 10:10; etc., and are also referred wrongly sometimes to צרי (e.g., Ezek. 27:17; "balm"). The Hebrew בשם, בשמים, has been variously translated. It includes such spices as balm, balsam. The Hebrew name, although not always denoting a specific plant or its products, refers mostly to *Commiphora opobalsamum* (L.) Engl. or to its products. *Commiphora opobalsamum* is a tropical deciduous shrub growing in SW Arabia. It has trifoliate leaves and white flowers. It contains a deliciously fragrant resin, which exudes from the branches in the form of yellow drops, not unlike honey drops. When hardening, the resin turns dark. The yield may be increased by making incisions in the stem and branches. In Arabia the resin is highly esteemed in medicine. In the days of the Bible it was used as an ingredient of holy oil and incense, as well as for a perfume, and probably also as a medicinal substance. According to various sources this plant has been grown since the time of Solomon and thereafter in Jericho, and probably also in En-gedi, Zoar, etc. These localities present tropical sites in the Jordan Valley and in the Dead Sea surroundings. It may also have been grown in the lowlands of Gilead near the outlets of the rivers Nimrim and Jabbok, which are also tropical; hence the name "balm of Gilead." It is highly probable that, along with the latter species, other species of *Commiphora,* such as *Commiphora myrrha,* were cultivated in this tropical zone of Palestine. It is also highly probable that these "balm gardens" were partially, at least, planted from seeds brought by the Queen of Sheba. They lasted long after the conquest of Judea by Titus; and there are records on the existence of the "balm shrub" in Palestine from the first centuries of the Christian era. For NT references to "spices" (ἄρωμα; Mark 16:1; Luke 23:56; 24:1; John 19:40), *see* SPICE.

8. Costly timbers. ***a. Ebony*** (הבנים). The identification of this tree (Ezek. 27:15) as *Diospyros ebenum* Koenig seems to be correct. The name is of Egyptian origin. Ebony wood was well known in Egypt, and pieces of it, as well as some of its manufactures, were found in old Egyptian tombs. The wood of this tropical tree is highly praised, and is listed along with ivory and gold. It is a black or dark brown wood, hard, heavy, and most durable. It is used for costly furniture, instruments, and ornaments. It is a tall tree, indigenous in Ceylon, with simple leaves and bell-shaped flowers. It is also probable that some other species of the genus *Diospyros* are involved in the name "ebony." *See also* EBONY.

b. Gopher wood (גפר). All the attempts to identify gopher (Gen. 6:14) with trees like pine, cypress, plane tree, etc., are unacceptable. *See also* GOPHER WOOD.

c. Algum, almug timber (אלמגים, אלגומים). The identity of this tree (I Kings 10:11-12; II Chr. 2:8; 9:10-12) is uncertain. *See also* ALMUG.

9. Forest trees and shrubs. ***a. Acacia tree, acacia wood*** (שטים, שטה). This tree (Exod. 25:5-38; Deut. 10:3; etc.) is the *Acacia raddiana* Savi. The Egyptian name *šndt,* from which the Hebrew name is derived, is still preserved by the Arabs for *Acacia albida* Del. But this species does not occur in Sinai. Of the three species native to Sinai, *Acacia raddiana* is the most common and most suitable for building purposes. It is an evergreen tree, ten to eighteen feet tall, with a thick trunk and a spreading crown. The branches bear strong spines which are the stipules of the small, bipinnate leaves. The small, yellow flowers are aggregated in globular heads. The pods are spirally curved and bear many seeds. The wood is hard and durable. The locality Shittim in the Jordan Valley was called so because of the abundance of acacia trees in the surrounding territory. *See also* ACACIA. Pl. XII*e-f.*

b. Bay tree. This is the KJV translation of אזרח in Ps. 37:35 (RSV CEDAR). For discussion of the bay tree (*Laurus nobilis*), *see* BAY TREE.

c. Bush, thornbush (סנה). The identification *Rubus sanctus* Schreb. for this plant (Exod. 3:2-4) is recorded here after Loew (Fl. d. Juden 3:178). The bush is common in moist soils and near river banks throughout Palestine and Syria. It is a shrub *ca.* three feet high, with spiny branches and leaves composed of three oblong or roundish leaflets. The white or pink flowers are arranged in clusters, and the fruit is an edible berry. Neither this identification nor that which renders "acacia" has any satisfactory base. *Rubus* was not observed in Sinai, while the true name for "acacia" is *shiṭṭa.*

d. Cedar (ארז). This is the *Cedrus libani* Barrel. The cedar of Lebanon is one of the most famous trees of the plant world. It is a mighty, beautiful, and long-living tree of the pine family. It reaches a height of a hundred feet or so, and its trunk may attain a width of six to nine feet. In the cedar forests of the Lebanon there are specimens a thousand years old or older. Its crown is very broad and its branches horizontally spread. Its green-gray needles are borne in clusters. The male flowers are arranged in linear, oblong cones and the female in ovate, globular ones. The mature female cones are ovate, *ca.* three inches long. The seed-bearing scales of the cone detach from one another at maturity. The cedar is rather common in middle and N Lebanon, where it is confined to an altitude between 4,500 and 5,700 feet above sea level. There are indications that in the past it also occurred in S Lebanon, but it never grew in Palestine. Apart from Lebanon, this species of cedar also occurs in the Taurus Mountains, and a particular variety of it grows in Cyprus. Since ancient times, Lebanon cedars were cut and exported to Egypt, Assyria, and Palestine. Its timber was used for construction of temples and royal palaces, as well as for shipbuilding. At the time of David and Solomon, as well as thereafter, large amounts of cedar timber were imported into Palestine for the construction of the temple and other houses. The cedar was a symbol of grandeur and might (Ps. 92:12—H 92:13, etc.), pride and majesty (II Kings 14:9, etc.). It is mentioned seventy times in the Bible, but some of the references, at least those associated with purification of the lepers and of infested houses, are certainly to be referred to other conifers, such as *Pinus halepensis** or *Juniperus phoenicea* (*see* §§ 9*g, m, below*). *See also* CEDAR. Fig. PIN 57.

e. Cypress (תאשור). The identification *Cupressus sempervirens* L. var. *horizontalis* (Mill.) Gord. refers only to those cases where "cypress" is rendered for תאשור, as in Isa. 41:19; 60:13; Ezek. 27:6 (RSV PINE). One of the most absurd translations of תאשור is the box or box tree (*Buxus* sp.), a tree neither native to nor ever grown in Palestine. Smith, Moffatt, and Loew are right in rendering "cypress" for תאשור, for geographical and linguistic reasons. The cypress is native to Palestine and has recently been found growing wild in Gilead and Edom. It is also commonly cultivated all over Palestine. It is thirty to fifty feet high, with an erect trunk and spreading branches (the pyramidal form is a cultivated variety of this species). The leaves are minute, scalelike, and appressed to the branches. The seed-bearing cones are globular, an inch or so across; the seeds are narrowly winged. The cypress is native mainly to the E Mediterranean countries. It is used as an ornamental and as a windbreak tree, but also in building. Its wood is known for its durability. *See also* CYPRESS.

f. Fir, fir tree. There is much confusion among the translators and commentators in the identification of the Hebrew names of trees and shrubs; and the fir tree is just one example. It has been rendered for the Hebrew אזרח, תאשור, בראש, etc. Most authorities, however, render "fir" for ברוש, ברות. This refers to one of the juniper species growing along with the cedar in the Lebanon, most probably to *Juniperus excelsa* Bieb. It is a high and robust tree with spreading branches, much resembling the cedar in structure. It is strongly fragrant; its leaves are small and scale-shaped, and its female cones are fleshy, small, globular bodies less than half an inch across. Its timber is highly valued in building because of its durability. That neither the *Cupressus sempervirens* nor the *Pinus halepensis* should be referred to this name is evident from the fact that both these trees are native to Palestine and would not have been imported from the Lebanon. *See also* FIR; PINE.

g. ***Heath.*** This name is rendered in some translations for ערוער, ערער, in Jer. 17:6; 48:6. This translation is erroneous, as there are no heath trees in deserts. More plausible is the identification with *Juniperus,* as given by some commentators. The Arabic name *ʿarʿār* is still preserved for *Juniperus phoenicea* L., of which single trees and small groups of trees are met with in Sinai and in the S outskirts of Mount Seir facing the Desert of Edom. *Juniperus phoenicea* is a shrub or a small tree with an ovate oblong crown and with small, scalelike leaves. The cones are small and globular. It is common throughout the Mediterranean countries. *See also* JUNIPER.

h. ***Juniper.*** This is the KJV translation of רתם (I Kings 19:5, etc.; RSV BROOM), which is *Retama raetam* (Forsk.) Webb. The Arabic *ratam* is still applied to this plant. It is a broomlike, much-branched shrub three to six feet high. It bears small, oblong-lanceolate leaves in winter and has handsome white flowers arranged in small clusters. The fruit is a one- or two-seeded pod. It is most characteristic of the deserts and sand dunes and is used by the Bedouins for fuel.

i. ***Laurel*** (ארן). It is now well established that this name, mentioned only once in the Bible (Isa. 44:14), is not an "ash," as translated by the KJV, but the laurel (*Laurus nobilis* L.; RSV CEDAR). This is linguistically well argued by Loew. The laurel is an evergreen, dioecious tree, reaching fifteen feet in height. It has leathery, ovate or elliptical leaves and white-cream flower clusters. The fruit is a black berry, somewhat smaller than the olive fruit. All parts of the plants contain fragrant ethereal oil, well known in medicine as the laurel oil. The leaves and the fruits are used for flavoring pickles. The laurel is native to Palestine and to other Mediterranean countries. It is a member of the forests and maquis and blossoms in spring. In modern Hebrew ארן is applied to *Pinus halepensis,* and *Laurus* is called after its Aramaic name, ערא.

j. ***Hyssop*** (אזוב; ὕσσωπος). A large body of literature has been accumulated on the biblical hyssop (*Majorana syriaca* [L.] Feinb.; Exod. 12:22; Lev. 14:4; etc.). Perhaps no plant name has been so controversially and inconsistently interpreted as the hyssop. But it is now almost agreed and validly based that the hyssop is identical with *Majorana syriaca* (*Origanum maru* L.). It is in full agreement with the context of all the phrases in the Bible in which it is mentioned, including I Kings 4:33, as it also grows between rocks and cliffs. One of the most convincing evidences for this identification is that the plant is still in use with the Samaritans, who apply its branches as a brush for the sprinkling of the blood of the Passover sacrifice. This is a perennial herbaceous white, hairy shrub, one to two feet high, with slender branches and small ovate, opposite and woolly-hairy leaves. The minute, white flowers are arranged in small, dense heads or spikes. The whole plant is strongly aromatic, reminiscent of mint; and, like the latter, it is used for extraction of an ethereal oil. Its slender branches can be easily cut, made into bunches, and used as sprinklers. In the Bible it was a symbol of humbleness as against the grandeur of the cedar (I Kings 4:33). It was used for sprinkling the doorposts of the Israelites in Egypt, for purification of lepers and infested houses, and also in the sacrifice of the red heifer. In the NT it was used to administer vinegar to Jesus, according to John 19:29. *See also* HYSSOP. Fig. HYS 38.

k. ***Mallow*** (מלוח). This species of *Atriplex* (*Atriplex halimus* L.; Job 30:4) is the most common in the saltlands of Palestine. The leaves are often eaten by hungry shepherds of the desert. Thus it fits well the context in Job. *Atriplex halimus* is a shrub up to four feet high. Its ovate, obtuse leaves are covered with vesicular hairs. Its small, green flowers are arranged in spikelike bodies, and its small fruits bear single seeds. *See also* MALLOW.

l. ***Myrtle*** (הדס). The myrtle (*Myrtus communis* L.; Neh. 8:15; Isa. 41:19; 55:13; Zech. 1:8, 10-11) is an evergreen, much-branched shrub, two to four feet high. The leaves are glabrous, ovate to lanceolate, opposite or arranged in whorls of threes. The flowers are white and arranged in clusters. The fruits are blue-blackish berries. Almost all the parts of the plant contain a fragrant aromatic oil used in perfumeries. The fruits are edible. It is native to Palestine and other Mediterranean countries. At present it is met with in Mount Carmel and Galilee, but it has been found in Samaria and near Jerusalem. It thus fits geographically the context in Nehemiah. While the myrtle played an important part in classical mythology and was a symbol of heroism and immortality, it has typified peace and thanksgiving with the Hebrews. It has continuously remained, together with the ethrog, the palm leaf, and the willow branches, one of the "four kinds" used by the Jews in the tabernacle feast. *See also* MYRTLE.

m. ***Oil tree, wild olive*** (עץ השמן). This is probably the *Pinus halepensis* Mill. (Neh. 8:15; Isa. 41:19; etc.). Not all the interpretations of the Hebrew name are acceptable. They are in conflict with the contexts in which the name is mentioned, both for geographical and for botanical reasons. It is certainly not identical with the olive tree, which has a name of its own so commonly used in everyday life. This name has not been changed in the Talmud nor by the Arabs and other Semitic peoples. Olive-tree wood is very little used in carpentry, and among the thirty-eight occurrences of זית in the Bible there is not a single one associated with building or wood manufacture. In Nehemiah the true olive tree is listed along with the oil tree. This is sufficient to show that "oil tree" and "olive tree" are different trees. The translation "wild olive" (RSV), which is a low, thorny bush, for the oil tree is even more improbable, because one can neither build from its wood nor fetch branches of it, as the phrase in Nehemiah demands. That the oil tree is not a species of *Elaeagnus,* as misunderstood by some students, follows from the fact that the latter is an introduced plant, rather rare in Palestine. It is also very doubtful whether it was grown in Palestine at the time of the Bible. *Pinus halepensis* is most likely the plant to fit the context, at least in most of the phrases in which עץ השמן is mentioned. It was one of the most common evergreen trees of Palestine, occurring all over the mountain range from the Lebanon in the N to Hebron in the S. There are evidences that the surroundings of Jerusalem were once densely inhabited by this tree. It has a soft, workable wood and is largely used in building and carpentry. The most convincing support for this assumption is the fact that this tree (or *Pinus bruttia,* which is very close to it) is up to the present day named by Kurdish Jews עץ השמן. These Jews are undoubtedly descendants of old Babylonian Jewish communities with which the true Hebrew name of the pine has been preserved. It is called "oil tree" because tar and turpentine are secured from it. *Pinus halepensis,* the Aleppo pine, or the Jerusalem pine, is thirty to fifty feet high. It has an ovate or round crown. The needles are arranged in pairs; the male flowers are borne on the lower branches, while the ovate, *ca.*-three-inch-long female cones are confined to the upper branches. *Pinus halepensis* is now widely used in afforestation.

n. Oak (אלון, אלונים). There is no question that אלה and אלון—namely, terebinth and oak respectively—represent different trees (*Quercus calliprinos* Webb, *Quercus ithaburensis* Decne). This is obvious from Isa. 6:13; Hos. 4:13; etc. Specific identification of אלה and אלון is difficult. This does not exclude the possibility that all these names may also have been applied to big trees in general. There are three species of oaks in Palestine, but only the two mentioned above are involved in the biblical name. *Quercus calliprinos* is an evergreen tree which may attain a height of fifty feet. The leaves are leathery and often spiny-margined, 1-1½ inches long. The flowers are inconspicuous, and the fruit is an acorn. It is the most common tree in the Mediterranean parts of Palestine and also in other E Mediterranean countries. *Quercus ithaburensis* is a broad-leaved, deciduous tree, confined to lower altitudes and less common than the former. Both are leading plants of forests and maquis (bushy lands); aged trees of both species are found as "sacred trees" or "sacred woods." The oak symbolized might and grandeur (Amos 2:9) and long life (Isa. 6:13). It was also connected with sacrificial offering (Hos. 4:13), and under the shade of the oak the dead of the beloved were buried (Gen. 35:8). *See also* OAK.

o. Plane tree (ערמון). The plane tree (*Platanus orientalis* L.; Gen. 30:37; Ezek. 31:8; KJV CHESTNUT TREE) is a deciduous tree, thirty to fifty feet high, with a broad, ovate crown and large, hairy, deeply lobed (three to five lobes) leaves. The flowers are green and inconspicuous, and are arranged in globular heads pending on long stalks. It grows on river banks, mainly in the N part of Palestine. *See also* PLANE TREE.

p. Storax tree (לבנה; Gen. 30:37; Hos. 4:13; RSV POPLAR). It is surprising how far some interpreters went in putting along with the native oak and terebinth, growing on dry hillsides, an introduced tree which requires deep soil and heavy irrigation such as the poplar. If this is because the Hebrew name requires a white plant, there is a white tree growing naturally among the oaks and terebinths, known as the storax tree (*Styrax officinalis* L.). This is called by the Arabs *'abhar*, meaning "bright," and they also call it *lubnā*. *Styrax officinalis* is certainly not that tree supplying the costly drug which is known in pharmacopeias under "storax" and which comes from *Liquidambar* spp. or from *Styrax benzoin.* This gum has been considered, without valid reasons, to represent the Hebrew נטף, rendered "stacte" in the Greek and other translations. There is also no evidence whatever for the identification of נטף with *Liquidambar orientalis* Mill., as maintained by others. *Styrax officinalis* is a small tree or a high shrub with ovate leaves, green above and woolly white beneath. It has long, flexible twigs, and blossoms in spring. Its white, showy flowers remind one of those of the orange tree. The fruit is a green, velvety drupe in the size of a hazelnut. It is common all over the E Mediterranean countries. *See also* STACTE.

q. Tamarisk (אשל). Identification of this tree (*Tamarix aphylla* [L.] Karst., *Tamarix gallica* L.; Gen. 21:33; I Sam. 22:6; etc.) is certain. The Arabic name, *'athl,* is still preserved for one of the above species. Tamarisks grow abundantly in deserts, on dunes, in salt marshes, and on river banks. All mentions of אשל in the Bible fit perfectly *Tamarix,* both botanically and geographically. *Tamarix aphylla* is a leafless tree with green, jointed branches and a wide-spreading crown. It flowers in late summer; its small, white flowers are arranged in short racemes. The fruits are capsules with minute, feathery seeds. It is one of the fast-growing trees of Palestine. *See also* TAMARISK. Pl. XVI*b*.

r. Terebinth, turpentine tree (אלה). The identification is sure (*Pistacia palaestina* Boiss., *Pistacia atlantica* Desf.; Isa. 6:13; Hos. 4:13; etc.), with the exception of some mention in the form of אלה and אלון (*see* § 9*n above*). The renditions of "teil tree" and "elm" for the above Hebrew name by some translations are to be rejected, for the following reasons: the teil has only recently been introduced into Palestine; the elm has been recently found and is exceedingly rare. Both can by no means replace the common terebinth tree. The Palestine terebinth is a dioecious and deciduous tree, sometimes reaching a height of thirty feet. Its leaves are compounded of three to five pairs of lanceolate-elliptical leaflets, one to two inches long. The flowers are inconspicuous; the female ones develop small, globular stone fruits which have an acrid odor of turpentine. They are often roasted and eaten as nuts. While this is an E Mediterranean species, *Pistacia atlantica* is a semidesert tree characteristic of the E and S border of the Mediterranean zone. It is very similar in habit to the former, but it often grows to a higher tree with a broad and dense crown. As with oaks, there are many high and aged trees left of the once-flourishing steppe forests of the atlantic terebinth. Among them are also some "sacred trees" and small "sacred woods." *See also* TEREBINTH; NUT. Fig. TER 51.

s. Thick tree (עץ עבות). All the identifications as yet suggested for this name (Lev. 23:40; Neh. 8:15;

RSV "leafy tree"), with the probable exception of myrtle, are unacceptable.

t. Willow (ערבים). This may be identified both as *Salix* spp. and as *Populus euphratica* Oliv. (Lev. 23:40; Ps. 137:2). The willows of Ps. 137 are most certainly Euphrates poplars, for the following reasons: (*a*) *Populus euphratica* is so common on the banks of the "waters of Babylon" that no other tree may fit better the context than it. It is true that there are also some *Salix* species, but they are comparatively rare. (*b*) The Euphrates poplar is well known by producing narrow lanceolate or linear willow leaves on its younger shoots and branches, and this makes the tree very similar to a willow. (*c*) The Arabic name *gharab*, still preserved for the Euphrates poplar, is identical with the Hebrew ערב. The name in Lev. 23:40 means true willows, since the poplar is confined in Palestine to the Jordan Valley only, while willows occur near rivers, also in the mountain region. *Populus euphratica* is a high tree with two forms of leaves: broad rhomboid to ovate deltoid leaves and linear-lanceolate or oblong ones. The small flowers are arranged in catkins, and the fruits are capsules containing numerous minute seeds furnished with a bunch of hairs. On the banks of the Jordan River this tree forms, along with the Jordan tamarisk, dense thickets. Of the willows of Palestine the most common is *Salix acmophylla* Boiss. Willows differ from the poplars by their narrow leaves and by some details in the floral structure. They never attain the size of poplars. *See also* WILLOW TREE.

On "ash," *see* § A9*i above*. On "box tree" *see* § A9*e above*. On "chestnut tree," *see* § A9*o above*. On "elm," *see* § A9*r above*. On "pine," *see* § A9*m above*. On "poplar," *see* §§ A9*p*, *t*, *above;* MULBERRY TREES. On "stacte," *see* §§ A7*j*, 9*p*, *above*. On "teil," *see* §A9*r above*.

10. Lilies and roses. Lilies and roses, anemones, hyacinths, tulips, daffodils, irises, and many other showy plants have been suggested by various translators and commentators to represent the two names שושנים, שושן, שושנה, and חבצלת. A tremendous body of literature dealing with this subject has been accumulated (*see* the works of Loew and Moldenke in the *bibliography*). It is probable that all the suggestions presented in the current literature for identification of these Hebrew names are devoid of any scientific or otherwise convincing bases. Reference to "lilies" illustrates this point:

The expression "lilies of the field" (κρίνον; Matt. 6:28; cf. Luke 12:27) probably refers merely to the "flowers of the field." The reasons for this opinion are:

a) The Hebrew name שושנה, שושנים, in Song of S. 2:1-2, 16; 4:5; 6:2-4, is not identical with *Lilium candidum* L., as many authors incline to believe, or take for granted. *Lilium candidum,* the only lily native in Palestine, grows neither in the valleys nor among thorns or "brambles." It is an extremely rare plant, and from its ecological behavior it is evident that it must have been so also in the past. It has been found only in two localities: in Upper Galilee and on Mount Carmel. In both, it is hidden in shady holes or among cliffs, within dense woodland. Thus, there is no pasturing (feeding) among lilies, as suggested in the Song of Songs. But there are amazing quantities of most beautiful flowers forming variegated carpets in the plains, and there are handsome and attractive flowers among pastures and thorns of the hills. Mention may be made of only a few of over two scores of genera comprising most attractive flowers, such as *Ranunculus, Anemone, Cyclamen, Arum, Colchicum, Allium, Fritillaria, Tulipa, Hyacinthus, Sternbergia, Narcissus, Pancratium, Ixiolirion,* crocus, iris, and orchids. Each of them, because of its beauty, has its right to represent the "lily."

b) There is reason to believe that the name שושן, *shûshan,* is not specific and that it may denote the blossom of a plant or any plant with showy flowers. E.g., there is a phrase in the Talmud: שושנה של ורד (*shôshannâ shel wered*), the "blossom of the rose." According to one authority, the Arabic cognate *sûsan* denotes in some countries any brilliantly colored flower. In Palestine the Arabs call various attractive flowers *ward,* a name also specific for the rose plant. This may lead to the assumption that the name *sûsan* and its variants may have primarily denoted a particular plant species, and even *Lilium candidum* itself, but in time—and this may have happened very early in history—the name became generalized and abstract, denoting a certain group of flowers similar in some qualities to the original subject. The choice of "narcissus" to represent the חבצלת in Isa. 35:1 lacks any basis. There are more showy flowers to symbolize the gladness and blossoming of the desert. It seems that a good part of the literature about this subject is unproductive guesswork on nonidentifiable items. *See also* LILY.

Pls. XI*b;* XII*c*.

11. Reeds and rushes. This is a group of plants which possess many specific characteristics, such as the "reedy" habit and the confinement to swampy and aquatic habitats. As a group, these plants are easily recognizable. But it is rather difficult to distinguish between individual species and genera within this group. Ordinarily people are thus satisfied with a general name, such as "reed" or "rush." There is no reason to believe that botanical items were more accurately known by the people of the Bible than by people of today. Thus, confusion and uncertainty in naming and identification are quite natural. The names involved in this group are: קנה, סוף, גמא, אגמון, אחו, and אגם. They have been variously translated and even inconsistently rendered by the same authority. The renditions in English translations are "reed," "rush," "papyrus," "bulrush," "hook," "caldron," "flag," "meadow." In many cases the names denote the whole group, although originally they may have been specific. The following is a short presentation of the most plausible identifications suggested:

a. Reeds (קנה). There are at least five species of reeds in the flora of Palestine to which this name can be applied (II Kings 18:21; Job 40:21; Isa. 19:6; etc.). Among them, *Phragmites communis* Trin. is the most common and thus fits best the context of some phrases. It occurs along river banks all over Palestine. It is 4-10 feet high and ½-1 inch thick. It has a fluffy panicle of flowers, 1-1½ feet long. It very often grows together with *Typha angustata,* the cattail (*see* § A11*c below*). It must, however, be remarked that in some phrases (Job 40:21; Isa. 19:6;

35:7) this name has a more collective sense, comprising reed vegetation in general. *See also* REED; SWEET CANE. Pl. IX*c*.

b. Rush, papyrus, bulrushes (גמא). This Hebrew name has not always been uniformly translated (Exod. 2:3; Job 8:11; Isa. 18:2; 35:7). In Job it may well be a collective name, but in the remaining passages it fits well *Cyperus papyrus* L., which is very outstanding in its appearance and could not have been ignored. The papyrus plant is a perennial rush, ten to fifteen feet high and one to three inches thick. The green culm terminates in a compound umbel of long, flower-bearing rays. The flowers and fruits are inconspicuous. The culm is made of a soft white pith provided with air chambers. It is a tropical plant reaching in Palestine its N range of distribution. This is the famous papyrus plant of the ancients, from which papyrus rolls were prepared. Apart from the above use, the papyrus was one of the most important sources for various wickerwork, manufacture of mats, rods, and also small canoes. In Palestine it is very abundant in the Hule Valley, but also occurs in the Coastal Plain. In Egypt, where this plant was also used in ornaments, it disappeared from the banks of the Lower Nile. *See also* BULRUSH; PAPYRUS.

c. Cattail (סוף). This is the *Typha angustata* Bory et Chaub. It is mentioned several times in the Bible (Exod. 2:3, 5; Isa. 19:6; Jonah 2:5; RSV REED, WEED) and sometimes with קנה. From its occurring together with *Phragmites*, as well as from its Egyptian name (*twfy*), from which סוף was probably derived, the above identification gains some support. But this does not exclude the fact that this name was also applied as a group name. *Typha angustata* is a tall, grasslike perennial with very long, striplike, erect leaves and a cylindrical stem, bearing at the upper part separate male and female inflorescences of very minute flowers and fruits. It is used in various wickerworks. *See also* REED.

d. Rush, bulrush, hook, caldron (אגמון). This word is rendered "rush," "bulrush," and also "hook," "caldron," etc., in various translations. To restrict the meaning of this name more specifically, certain members of the genus *Scirpus* would fit best the content of the relevant phrases in the Bible. As lacustral plants they agree with the Hebrew name, which is derived from אגם, "lake." The flowering heads of the plants are bent down (Isa. 58:5). They are lower than the common reed (Isa. 9:14; 19:15). The culms are flexible and used in wickerwork. As far as this name in Job 41:2—H 40:26 refers to plants, the plants under discussion are not contrary to the context. The Hebrew name אגם in Jer. 51:32 probably means "swamp vegetation" and not "lake." Burning of the swamp plants in order to accelerate their growth is common practice with the inhabitants of the swamp areas. *See also* RUSH; REED.

e. Flag, meadow, reeds (אחו). Mentioned in Gen. 41:2; Job 8:11, this is a loan word from Egyptian *iyḥ* and *iḥy*. Most of the translations rendering "meadow" for אחו seem to be right. In the vicinity of water bodies there is a vegetation of grasses and low rushes fed by underground water or by floods. These are excellent grazing areas. *See also* FLAG.

12. Thorns and thistles. The number of Palestinian plants which belong to the category of thorns and thistles is much over a hundred. The biblical names, generally conceived as thorny or spiny plants, do not exceed fifteen. These are: אטד, ברקן, דרדר, חוח, חדק, נעצוץ, נהלול, סרפד, סלון, סירים, קוץ, קמוש, שמיר, שית. The English names used in various translations are "thorn," "thistle," "bramble," and "brier."

There are great difficulties, not only in the identification of these names with existing plants, but also in finding English names for them. Thus, it is no wonder that the above names have been so variously and inconsistently translated. Ordinary observers, and even some in touch with the native vegetation, are seldom able to distinguish between the various kinds of thistles and produce specific names for them. As in the case of lilies and roses, many names of thistles, which have been primarily specific, became later generalized. It seems that such phrases as קוץ ודרדר (Gen. 3:18, etc.; "thorns and thistles"), שמיר ושית (Isa. 5:6, etc.; "briers and thorns"), etc., sometimes repeatedly mentioned, became with time devoid of a specific meaning. There are, however, some particular plants in this group which for some reason deserve consideration.

a. Thorn. The thorn (Matt. 27:29; John 19:2), of which the "crown" of Jesus was made, was much discussed in literature, and the opinion is now held that this was *Zizyphus spina-christi* (L.)* or *Paliurus spina-christi* Mill. Neither Linné nor Miller, who named these species, was acquainted with the vegetation around Jerusalem. *Zizyphus spina-christi* does not occur naturally in the Judean Mountains, and there was no reason why the people of the Bible should have grown it there. A few trees have quite recently been planted in the vicinity of Gethsemane. This is a tropical tree which is rather common in the plains and valleys of Palestine, up to an altitude of a thousand feet or so. *Paliurus spina-christi* is a very rare shrub, confined to N Palestine, and has not been found S of Mount Tabor. But there are several spiny plants common in the vicinity of the place supposed to be Golgotha. Among them *Poterium spinosum* L., the סירים of the Bible (*see* § A15 *below*), is the most common. This is a low shrub of the rose family, with inconspicuous flowers, with small, compound leaves and thorny branches, of which the thorny wreath of Jesus might have been made. *See also* THORNS, CROWN OF; THISTLES. Fig. THI 59.

b. Brier (חדק). The only support for the identification of this plant (Mic. 7:4) as *Solanum incanum* L. is the Arabic name *ḥadaq,* still preserved for this plant. *Solanum incanum* is a perennial shrub, three to five feet high. The whole plant is beset with dense, woolly hairs. The branches and the leaves bear curved spines. The leaves are rather large with wavy margins. The flowers are pink or blue, and the fruit is a large yellow, nonedible berry containing several seeds. The plant is native to Dead Sea surroundings, and to the Lower Jordan Valley. *See also* BRIER.

c. Thistle. This name has been rendered in the translations for several Hebrew names of spiny plants. Only two of these names may be considered here: (*a*) דרדר (Gen. 3:18; Hos. 10:8), identified as *Centaurea* sp.; (*b*) חוח (Job 31:40; Isa. 34:13), identified as *Scolymus* sp. The identification of the former is based on the Arabic name *shawk ed-dardār,* which is applied to one or more species of *Centaurea* ("star thistle"), the most common of which are *Centaurea iberica* Trev. and *Centaurea hyalolepis* Boiss.* These are annual or biennial plants, in which most of the leaves are arranged in a rosette. The stem is much-branched and bears flowering heads surrounded by spiny scales. The flowers are mostly yellow. The leaves are gathered in winter by villagers and Bedouins, and are used as salads. *See* § A14*c below.* Fig. THI 58; Pl. XIV*b*.

Of *Scolymus* there are two species, and that which corresponds best to the context in Job is *Scolymus maculatus* L. This is a noxious weed abundant in the grain fields. It is three to four feet high. The stem is provided with spiny wings, and its green leaves have white patches and veins. The yellow flowers are arranged in spiny heads. On fallow ground it occupies large stretches. The same Hebrew name in Isa. 34:13 may well correspond to *Scolymus hispanicus* L. In II Kings 14:9 the חוח may well be identified with *Prunus ursina* Ky., a thorny shrub of the rose family, which bears small apricot fruits and which is quite common in the Lebanon.

13. Weeds and nettles. The number of weeds in Palestine fields is amazingly large. The names mentioned in the OT and commonly regarded as weeds are: חרול, גלגל, באשה. The names in English are "nettle," "wheel," "cockle," respectively. "Tare" is mentioned in the NT only.

a. Nettle (חרול). Many commentators agree that this name (Job 30:7; Zeph. 2:9; etc.) is identical with plants of the genus *Urtica*. In Palestine four species are involved, all of them being annuals with opposite broad, dentate leaves. The flowers and fruits are green and inconspicuous. The whole plant is beset with stinging hairs, which excrete an irritating liquid when touched. Some of these species grow on damp places, refuse heaps, or roadsides. *See also* NETTLE.

b. Wheel, rolling thing, whirling dust (גלגל). This name (Ps. 83:13; Isa. 17:13) has been variously translated. The most plausible translation is that of Goodspeed: "tumble weed." But this is surely not *Anastatica hisrochuntica,* as maintained by Moldenke and others, because this plant never rolls over the surface, but sticks to the ground for years. Besides, it is a very rare and tiny plant confined to the environs of the Dead Sea and the Arava Valley. In the flora of Palestine there are at least thirty species which are most typical tumble weeds. These are mostly much-branching annuals or perennials, the main stem of which breaks near its base after seed ripening, and rolls with the wind over plains and valleys. They look mostly like globular bodies. Sometimes a few of them meet together to form larger bodies which may frighten animals. The most common tumble weeds are *Gundelia tournefortii, Cachrys goniocarpa, Aellenia autrani, Salsola kali.*

c. Cockle (באשה). This is a mistranslation in Job 31:40 KJV. Cockle (*Agrostemma githago* L.) is exceedingly rare in Palestine and probably a newcomer. This word seems to be a collective name for "weeds" (so RSV). Similarly the word באושים in Isa. 5:2, 4, means grapes of wild or inferior vines.

d. Tares (ζιζάνιον). This is the KJV form of WEEDS in Matt. 13:24-30. It is now generally agreed that the word refers to the darnel, or *Lolium temulentum* L., an annual grass two to four feet high. The leaves are like those of wheat, but the ears are narrow and composed of many-flowered spikelets. The grains are equal in size and shape to those of certain varieties of wheat. They pass the screen meshes with the wheat grains and are therefore sown together with them, or ground with them into flour. Because of a fungus growing under the seed coat of the darnel grains, flour containing much of the darnel has a bitter taste and is even believed to be poisonous. The darnel is therefore one of the most noxious weeds of the grain crops. *See also* TARES.

14. Wormwoods and poisons. *a. Gall, hemlock.* These words are used by the KJV to translate ראש and רוש in Deut. 29:18; Jer. 23:15; etc. Some authorities claim that in most passages the Hebrew *rôsh* is a poisonous plant or one with a bitter root. In Hos. 10:4 *rôsh* is translated "hemlock" in the KJV. This is *Conium maculatum* L., which is rather common in waste places throughout Palestine. It is a much-branched perennial herb, three to four feet high with cut leaves like the carrot plant; it has large white-flowered umbels and small, ellipsoid fruits. It is supposed to be the plant whose poisonous juice was given to Socrates to drink. This is not contrary to the context of the pertaining passages in the Bible in which *rôsh* is mentioned with "wormwood" (לענה). It should, however, be remarked that other "bitter" plants native to Palestine are not excluded from consideration in the identification of this name. *See also* HEMLOCK; POISON; GALL. Fig. WOR 26.

b. Wormwood (לענה). This plant, mentioned in Deut. 29:18; Jer. 23:15; etc., is identified as *Artemisia herba-alba* Asso. This is the most widespread species of *Artemisia* in the deserts of Palestine and the adjacent countries. It is a dwarf, grayish-hairy, strongly aromatic, much-branched shrub. Its leaves are cut, and its flowers are arranged in minute heads. It has a bitter taste and is used in folk medicine. *See also* WORMWOOD.

c. Bitter herbs (מרורים). The plant which best fits the text (Exod. 12:8; Num. 9:11) is *Centaurea*. Indeed, several species of *Centaurea* grow in the desert; their leaves are arranged in rosettes and are gathered by the Bedouins of the desert and eaten as salad, despite their bitter taste. The Arabs name them *murar, murir, yamrur,* and *Yamrir.* The flowers of these plants are small and arranged in spiny heads. One of these species, also called *durdar* by the Arabs, is presumably the Hebrew דרדר (*see* § A12*c above*). *See also* BITTER HERBS.

d. Wild gourds (פקועות שדה). The identification of this plant as *Citrullus colocynthis* (L.) Schrad. is in full agreement with the context (II Kings 4:39), from both the geographical and the botanical viewpoint. It is a relative of the cultivated melon, and by its long, trailing branches, its palmately lobed leaves, and its tendrils, it is strongly reminiscent of a vine, or "wild vine" (גפן שדה), associated with the gourds in the above passage. Since this plant is not uncommon in the Jordan Valley and also in the Dead Sea surroundings, it also agrees with the geography of the Elisha story and with the "vine of Sodom" (גפן סדום) in Deut. 32:32. The fruits of this plant are globular, of the size of an orange fruit, with a hard yellow rind and a spongy pulp with numerous seeds. The pulp is widely used medicinally, mainly as a purgative. It has a strong, bitter taste and is presumably poisonous. The Hebrew name פקועה denotes, among others, a globular body. This name is still preserved by the Arabs for a kind of Tuber (mushroom) with a globular shape; it also denotes globular bodies in postbiblical literature. *Cucumis prophetarum* L., which also occurs in the Dead Sea region, is a rare plant with small, spiny fruits and has no resemblance to a vine. *Ecballium elaterium* L., another member of the same family, suggested by some authors, does not altogether fit the text. *See also* GOURDS, WILD. Fig. GOU 36.

On "vine of Sodom" and "wild vine," *see* GOURDS, WILD.

15. Hedges and fences. Hedges and fences have their own story to tell in Palestine. The Hebrew משוכה (Isa. 5:5, etc.) is a hedge built mostly of thorny plants, while גדר is a fence built of stones or stones and plants. Various plants have since biblical times been used as hedges. In the Coastal Plain hedges have been built for protecting vineyards and orchards against animals and theft. Since ancient times, *Lycium europaeum* L., the boxthorn, has been planted for this purpose, and only since *ca.* the seventeenth century has it been replaced by the American prickly pear, *Opuntia ficus-indica,* which has quite recently been replaced by *Acacia farnesiana.* All three types of hedges are still to be found in the Coastal Plain. In the stony mountain region three other types of hedges prevail. In one, there are bushes and shrubs of natural vegetation which were left around the cultivated plots and used both as a landmark and as a hedge. In the other, bushes of boxthorn were planted; and in the third type a stone fence generally not exceeding two to three feet in height is built, and to it a layer of dead shrubs of *Poterium spinosum* is added. Sometimes combinations of the three types are found.

a. Brambles, thorns (אטד). This word, translated "brambles" in Judg. 9:14-15 and "thorns" in Ps. 58:9, is *Lycium europaeum* L. The Arabic name is *'auśaj,* although this name is sometimes given also to *Rhammus* and the Greek translation of אטד is ῥάμνος, it is *Lycium* which fits the context. *Lycium* is a shrub three to six feet high. It has oblong, cuneate leaves and spiny branches; its flowers are pink to violet, and its fruits are edible berries. *See also* BRAMBLE.

b. Thorns (סירים). These "thorns" (Isa. 34:13; Hos. 2:6; etc.) refer to *Poterium spinosum* L., a much-branched shrub one to two feet tall. The branches are slender and spiny; the leaves are composed of a few dentate leaflets; the flowers are green and inconspicuous; the fruits are dry berries with two to three seeds. This plant is the most common shrub of Palestine; it is widely used by the Arabs for fuel and fencing. The passage in Ps. 58:9 is perhaps better understood when the relation between סירה and אטד as hedge plants is considered (*see also* § A12*a above*). This plant is called by the Arabs *netesh* or *billan,* but a plant similar to it but growing in the desert areas bears the Arabic name *sirr,* and this is *Noea mucronata.* Pl. XIV*c.*

16. Other plants. ***a. Gourd*** (קיקיון). According to Smith, Loew, and others, this word in Jonah 4:6-7 (RSV PLANT) is not a gourd but the castor bean plant, *Ricinus communis* L. This is a fast-growing perennial which may attain the height of ten feet. Its large leaves are palmately divided into several lobes. Its flowers are arranged in spikelike clusters, the male beneath the female ones. The fruit is a capsule containing three large seeds. The oil extracted from the seeds is used in medicine and as a lubricant in machinery. The castor plant grows wild in Palestine, but was probably introduced earlier from tropical countries. It is known from Egypt in ancient times under the name *kiki;* it is not improbable that the Yonas plant may have been *Ricinus.*

b. Capper. This is a translation of אביונה in Eccl. 12:5 (RSV-KJV DESIRE). The Greek and the Vulg. render κάππαρις, *capparis.* This name is also mentioned in the Mishna and the Talmud. *Capparis spinosa,* or its local varieties, is a plant two to three feet tall. It has round or nearly round leaves and spiny stipules. Its large white flowers are open for one night only; its fruits are many-seeded, fleshy berries. The flower buds are conserved in acid and used as a condiment. In the past both the buds and the young fruits were used as an aphrodisiac.

c. Mandrake (דודאים). The identification of this plant, mentioned in Gen. 30:14-16; Song of S. 7:13, as *Mandragora officinarum* L. is certain. It is a stemless perennial herb, with thick, branched roots and with large, ovate or oblong, wrinkled leaves, arranged in a rosette. The bluish, bell-shaped flowers are borne on long stalks, and the plumlike, yellowish-red fruits have a delicious fragrance. They are edible, but are said to be narcotic, purgative, and emetic. The mandrake has ever since been a plant of many superstitious tales and unbased beliefs. Because of the shape of its roots and root branches, which may sometimes resemble a human body, and especially its lower parts, it has long been, and still is, in use with some primitive people as an aphrodisiac. In Palestine it is common in fields and waste places of the Mediterranean zone. It flowers early in winter and gives its fruits in spring. *See also* MANDRAKE. Fig. MAN 7.

d. Manna (מן). The literature hitherto accumulated on "heaven bread" is tremendous. As yet there is no adequate scientific explanation of the manna represented in the Bible (Exod. 16:31-35, etc.). Some authorities attempt to identify the manna with certain lichens or with a substance exuded from tamarisk trees, or with an excrement of certain scale insects living on tamarisk trees. However, although these identifications are based on substantial findings, the substances involved are quantitatively by far insufficient to have supported the heavy population wandering in the desert. *See also* MANNA.

B. *THE VEGETAL LANDSCAPE.* 1. History of the flora. Paleobotanical and paleogeographical evidences have clearly shown that the recent Palestine flora and vegetation have been successively built up by various stocks, which reached this country in various geological periods and through different migration routes. During the Oligocene and Miocene periods, the Palestine-Syrian part of the E Mediterranean region was detached from the N part of this region by a wide arm of the ancient Mediterranean Sea, deeply extending into Asia. Palestine, then connected with Africa, was governed by a tropical climate and inhabited by a tropical flora and vegetation of the African stock.

With the advent of the Pliocene period, the tropical flora became strongly decimated, and only remnants of it were pushed down to the hot enclaves of the Jordan Valley, where they are preserved up to the present. At that period the Mediterranean Sea lost its E branch, and an open land connection was established between Palestine and the N countries, wherefrom Palestine received its Mediterranean and its Irano-Turanian elements. Together with this migration wave, Palestine was open to the influx of Saharian desert plants which inhabited the driest parts of the country. From that period on, and during the entire Pleistocene period, Palestine was subjected only to minor climatic oscillations, so that the make-up of its flora and vegetation did not change considerably. The three plant geographical territories—namely, the Mediterranean, the Irano-Turanian, and the Saharo-Sindian—had already been in existence since the Pliocene period.

2. Vegetation units. When man first appeared in Palestine, there was already a diversity of vegetation units there, which were due then, as today, to the differences in climate and soils in the various parts of the country. The following types of vegetation existed then as today: (*a*) pine forest, (*b*) hard-leaved evergreen oak maquis and forest, (*c*) deciduous broad-leaved oak forest, (*d*) evergreen park woods, (*e*) evergreen Mediterranean dwarf shrub formations, (*f*) deciduous steppe woods, (*g*) tamarisk woods, (*h*) riparian forests, (*i*) saxaul forests, (*j*) sagebrush steppes, (*k*) succulent shrub deserts, (*l*) swamp and marsh vegetation, (*m*) sand-dune vegetation, and (*n*) vegetation of tropical oases.

a. The Aleppo pine forest. This is one of the southernmost pine forests of the Northern Hemisphere. The dominating tree is *Pinus halepensis.* It is accompanied by other trees and shrubs, such as *Pistacia lentiscus, Arbutus andrachne, Phillyrea media, Cistus villosus, Cistus salvifolius,* and others. This forest type is confined to highly calcareous soil of the mountain region. At present it covers considerable areas on Mount Carmel, in Samaria, and in Gilead, while remnants of it are preserved in Galilee and Judea. The reason for the devastation of the pine forest lies primarily in the fact that the soil occupied by this forest is most easily reclaimed for cultivation in the mountains. Besides, it is the best timber tree and is most susceptible to fire.

b. Evergreen oak maquis and forest. The following variants may be distinguished:

The maquis comprises mainly low woods of the oak-terebinth (*Quercus calliprinos–Pistacia palaestina*) community, which is the most common wood formation in Palestine. The two dominating trees are the oak and the terebinth, and they are generally accompanied by other low trees and shrubs, such as: *Arbutus andrachne, Styrax officinalis, Cercis siliquastrum, Phillyrea media, Laurus nobilis, Crataegus azarolus, Rhammus alaternus.* A few low shrubs and a number of vines are characteristic of this community. Also there are a great many shade-demanding herbs and bulbous plants which are confined to the maquis. This wood community is widely distributed all over the E Mediterranean region. In Palestine it occurs in all the Mediterranean mountain ranges on both sides of the Jordan. It demands relatively low winter temperatures and accordingly does not occur at an altitude lower than 900 feet. It is best developed on red soils.

Remnants of a true evergreen oak forest, with almost exclusive dominance of the oak as a high tree, are found in various places throughout Mediterranean Palestine. They occur mostly as "sacred forests" or "holy trees."

A particular variant of the evergreen oak community is that met with in Edom at an altitude of 3,000-4,500 feet. Here the oak is mostly accompanied by the red juniper (*Juniperus phoenicea*).

c. Deciduous broad-leaved oak forest. This type is dominated by the Tabor oak (*Quercus ithaburensis*). It is much more limited in distribution than the former types. It has three centers in Palestine: (*a*) The Sharon forest. Only small remnants of this forest, once flourishing between the Yarkon River and the S slopes of Mount Carmel, have been left. It was supposedly a pure forest and was confined here to sandy clay soil. According to some travelers of the nineteenth century, it was one of the largest and most beautiful forests of the region. (*b*) The Samarian-Galilean type is the most widespread. The oak is accompanied here by other trees such as *Styrax officinalis* and occasionally also by *Pistacia palaestina, Crataegus azarolus, Cercis siliquastrum.* It is common on the SW slopes of Lower Galilee, and its remnants are met with in the Ephraim Hills. (*c*) The Bashan forest. This E variant is well characterized by *Pistacia atlantica,* which accompanies the oak in the W slopes of Bashan, Golan, and Gilead. One of its remnants is the "sacred forest" of the Dan Valley, which testifies to the beauty of this forest type in the past. From a look at these mighty oaks and terebinths, it is readily understood why these trees have been so proverbially admired in the Bible. The Tabor oak forests are less restricted in their soil requirements, but are confined to lower altitudes, not exceeding 1,500 feet above sea level. The Tabor oak is a shallow-rooting tree which regenerates easily after logging. It may attain a height of sixty feet and a very great age.

d. Evergreen park woods. This comprises a wood community, the leading plants of which are composed of *Pistacia lentiscus,* forming a green shrubby carpet, and of *Ceratonia siliqua,* a tree *ca.* twelve to twenty feet high, scattered among the shrubs. This community occupies large stretches on the W side of the Jordan, along the W foothill region, on consolidated sand dunes, on calcareous sandstones of the Coastal Plain, and also on the E slopes of Galilee and Samaria. It is confined to lower altitudes only and tolerates various soils.

e. Evergreen Mediterranean dwarf shrub formation. Where forest and maquis are destroyed, a series of plant communities, consisting of low shrubs, permanently or temporarily occupy the area. The leading plants of these communities are *Poterium spinosum, Cistus salvifolius, Cistus villosus, Calycotome villosa, Salvia triloba, Phlomis viscosa, Satureja thymbra,* and others. It is only on the E and S borders of the Mediterranean territory that these communities are final stages in the vegetal development. Elsewhere in this territory they are only temporary stages which, when not disturbed by man, are sooner or later replaced by woody vegetation which formerly inhabited the area.

But, as often happened, these communities have been largely destroyed by man during centuries to supply fuel, and this brought about extreme denudation of the hillsides in the midst of the Mediterranean territory.

f. Deciduous steppe forest. This type is characterized by its remotely scattered trees and by the semidesert shrubs or herbs filling the interspaces between the trees. *Pistacia atlantica* forms such forests in the Syrian Desert and elsewhere. In E Gilead this forest type, made up of mighty and aged trees of *Pistacia atlantica,* is still in existence. In the Hule Plains only remnants of this type occur.

g. Tamarisk woods. There are many species of tamarisk in Palestine. But only a few of them form woods. The most important habitat for this type are the salines near the Dead Sea, where certain varieties of *Tamarix gallica, Tamarix deserti,* and others form almost pure stands.

h. The riparian forest. This consists of a few plant communities such as that dominated by *Platanus orientalis* in the N part of the country. The banks of the Yarkon and other rivers are adorned by willows and *Populus euphratica* trees which form thickets on the banks of the Jordan River.

i. The Saxaul forest. This unit, which is common in the Aralo-Caspian region and in Persia, has its SW representative in the Arabah Valley. Here *Haloxylon persicum* is the dominant tree. It reaches a height of ten to twelve feet and grows on sand dunes, derived from igneous rocks or sandstones.

j. Sagebrush steppes. These are represented by several Irano-Turanian plant communities in the Judean Desert, the Negeb, and Transjordan. One of the most typical plant communities is dominated by *Artemisia herba-alba,* which is a low, strongly fragrant, gray shrub.

k. Succulent shrub desert. This comprises a series of plant communities dominated by dwarf shrubs, with fleshy leaves or stems. They form the vegetation in the extreme deserts of Palestine. The leading plants of these communities include *Zygophyllum dumosum, Anabasis articulata, Suaeda asphaltica,* and *Chenolea arabica.* Large portions of the Palestine deserts are almost plantless. Most of the soils are stony, salty, and dry.

l. Swamps and marshes. There are two main hydrographic centers in Palestine: the Jordan Valley and the Coastal Plain. In both a fairly rich hydrophytic vegetation occurs. The Hule marshes in the Upper Jordan Valley abound with various plant communities, the leading plants of which are: *Cyperus papyrus, Phragmites communis, Polygonum acuminatum, Iris pseud-acorus, Typha angustata,* and *Sparganium neglectum.* On river banks of the Coastal Plain, most of the plants mentioned, as well as various species of *Cyperus, Scirpus, Polygonum, Juncus acutus, Inula viscosa, Rubus sanctus,* and *Lythrum salicaria,* dominate.

m. Sand-dune vegetation. Among the plant communities of the coastal sand dunes, the most conspicuous ones are those dominated by *Ammophila arenaria, Artemisia monosperma, Ratama roetam,* and *Polygonum equisetiforme.* They are all evergreen, deep-rooting shrubs or grasses, which withstand salt spray brought from the sea, as also the moving of sand by the wind.

n. Vegetation of tropical oases. At the outlet regions of the permanent water currents in the Lower Jordan Valley, the Dead Sea shore, and the Arava Valley, there are small enclaves of tropical vegetation comprising, among others: *Acacia raddiana, Acacia tortilis, Salvadora persica, Zizyphus spina-christi, Balanites aegyptiaca,* and *Moringa aptera.* These are tropical trees of the African flora, which at an earlier geological period dominated in Palestine.

The major vegetation types listed above are units which existed in Palestine since very ancient times, including the biblical era. Climate, topography, and soils, which determine this diversity of vegetation, have not changed considerably since biblical times. Man's influence on vegetation, despite its large extent and duration, affected vegetation rather quantitatively than qualitatively, so the over-all pattern of the vegetal landscape and its diversity have been preserved almost in their entirety during the millenniums of human history in Palestine.

C. ***MAN AND PLANTS.*** The relations between man and the plant world around him were intimate from the very appearance of man on the earth. Man found his food, clothes, and shelter in this world of plants, and also his admiration of beauty and divinity. These relations grew closer as means and ways were invented toward a more efficient utilization of plants. The manifestations of these relations are so diverse that only a few aspects of them can be mentioned here.

1. Man and trees. In biblical times and thereafter, trees have played a primary role in man's daily and spiritual life. Adoration of trees, symbolizing trees with might and godliness, repeatedly occurs in the Bible. It was under the shade of trees that the judges of old gathered to dispense justice, that services were held, incense was burned, beloved and admired persons were buried. "Holy trees" and "sacred forests" abound not only in Palestine, but also in adjacent countries.

In contrast with this great respect for trees is the widespread destruction of forests wrought by man. Damage to forests was made through cutting trees for industry and fuel, through grazing by goats and sheep, through clearing and fires. Wood was widely used for timber for manufacture of implements, utensils, and ornaments. For millenniums, forests were the sole source of fuel for cooking, heating, and lime kilns. Timber was also exported to neighboring countries devoid of natural forests. The harbor of Dor (Tantura) at the foot of Mount Carmel was known as an export city of wood destined for Egypt. The fact that the country borders on deserts has always made the forests liable to heavy damage by the Bedouins. Continuous browsing of goats damaged the bud-bearing branches and deformed the tree habit into a shrub form. This is, no doubt, one of the main factors which, under Mediterranean conditions, has converted high forests into shrubby maquis. Reclamation of forest land for agriculture had the most devastating effect. There are a variety of methods by which this work has been done since the remote past. Not always has man been able to surmount the obstacles involved in removing trees from their natural habitat. In areas with deep soils, forests have been tracelessly exterminated; while in areas with rocky ground, large expanses of woods have been left, despite man's effort of destruction.

2. Native plants in everyday life. The use of native plants by man for food and other daily requirements, common everywhere in the present, was much commoner in older days. There are still desert tribes in the vicinity of Palestine who are entirely unacquainted with plant cultivation, and who obtain their vegetable food from the "herbs of the field." Hundreds of native species are used by the natives for food and other purposes. These were certainly more numerous in biblical times. Some of the food plants collected by the tribes and villagers are often offered for sale. Some of them are eaten as salads and greens, whereby leaves, stems, flower heads, and roots are used. Some of them are eaten raw, others after roasting or boiling. A considerable number are used as spices and condiments, while from others edible fruits are collected. Pulses are gathered from wild leguminous plants, which are richly represented in the flora of Palestine. Most interesting is the occurrence of a *Mesembryanthemum,* growing in the area of the Dead Sea, which is reportedly used in the Arabian Desert for preparing "wild bread." Grains of some wild cereals are also known to be collected for the same purpose.

a. Industrial plants. A number of plants belonging to the reeds and rushes, growing in moist habitats, have been used since ancient times up to the present day as fiber and wicker plants. Native markets, as well as those of the neighboring countries, abound with homemade wickerware such as mats, baskets, and trays, all manufactured from native plants such as *Juncus, Scirpus, Cyperus, Typha,* and *Salix.*

Among a number of wild plants, known for their yield of oil, are *Sinapis alba, Sinapis arvensis, Brassica nigra, Calepina irregularis, Eruca sativa,* and *Ricinus communis.* Some of them are no longer in use in Palestine but have certainly been used in the past. There are also many tannin and dye plants which have been widely used in the past. Especially interesting are the soap plants, used up to the present as sources for potassium. These plants mainly include species of *Haloxylon, Anabasis,* and *Salsola.* They are also sold in the markets of Cairo, Damascus, and Baghdad.

b. Medicinal plants. A large number of wild plants are used in folk medicine by the Arab population. A part of them are well known in the drug markets of the greater cities; others are widely used but have no commercial value. Some of them are known as "panaceas," others are specific. While the Bible does not mention much about these plants, postbiblical literature abounds with medicinal herbs. A few of them, at present widely used by the Arabs, are: *Majorana syriaca, Teucrium polium, Bongardia chrysogonum, Ruta bracteosa, Peganum harmala, Althaea officinalis, Citrullus Colocynthis, Achillea fragrantissima, Alkanna strigosa,* and *Matricaria chamomilla.*

c. Pasture plants. Mention should also be made of the numerous pasture plants native to the Palestine flora. Some of them are of wide repute and have been introduced in many countries. Similar is the abundance of honey plants, which enable heavy honey yields in two or three seasons of the year. A series of native plants are now grown in various countries as ornamental plants. Among native forest plants at present used in afforestation are *Pinus halepensis, Cupressus sempervirens, Ceratonia siliqua, Pistacia atlantica,* and *Tamarix* spp. Some of these plants were undoubtedly planted in biblical times.

3. Wild ancestors of cultivated plants. The flora of Palestine includes a number of species identical with, or close to, varieties of some most important cultivated plants. Among the plants in question, the following should be mentioned: *Amygdalus communis, Ceratonia siliqua, Olea europaea* var. *oleaster, Triticum dicoccoides, Hordeum spontaneum, Trifolium Alexandrinum, Lupinus luteus, Vicia sativa, Vicia narbonensis, Pisum elatius, Linum angustifolium, Daucus maximus,* and *Allium ampeloprasum.* The occurrence of these plants in Palestine points to the assumption that the local ancient population might have contributed to the formation of some cultivated plants, which is the highest achievement of civilization.

4. Man and weeds. Weeds are always associated with human activity in the cultivation of plants. There are *ca.* 450 species of weeds occurring among cultivated crops in Palestine. A part of them have been unintentionally imported along with crop seeds. Another part penetrated here from the neighboring steppes, while the majority of them are native plants which grew here in open sites similar to those of cultivated lands.

The richness of this weed flora is, no doubt, the result of the antiquity of agriculture. Indeed, weed seeds have been found in excavations belonging to the Bronze Age (3000-2000 B.C.). A geographical analysis of the weeds may perhaps disclose the history of agricultural lines of contact. Weed control during the ages has been so unsuccessful that man has always been largely troubled by weeds. He has looked upon weeds as a plague of God; and, being helpless to remove them from his fields by primitive means, he was sometimes compelled to harvest the weeds instead of the sown crop. Indeed, some of the cultivated plants have had their origin from weeds, such as rye, oats, etc.

5. Agriculture through the ages. The origin of cultivated plants is one of the most interesting chapters of human civilization, but also one of the most obscure. The first buds of plant cultivation are as yet unknown, both as to when and where. What is certain is that cultivation was preceded by a long period of collecting and storing of wild-growing plants. The transition from this stage to the stage of sowing was slow and not exclusive, as is the case with present-day agriculture in some regions where sowing and collecting exist side by side. While man easily learned sowing from nature, he had to invest much of his intellectual effort to convert wild plants into cultivated crop plants through selection and breeding. Palestine was, no doubt, part of this arena in which some important cultivated plants originated, and where agriculture might have had one of its first sprouts. This may be supported by the fact that some ancestors of cultivated plants are still growing wild here, and that, according to Vavilov, Palestine lies between two great centers where cultivated plants originated—viz., the Mediterranean and the Anterior Asian centers.

The earliest data on Palestinian agriculture come to us from the Mesolithic or Middle Stone Age (*ca.*

8000 B.C.). It was the so-called "Natufian" culture, in which sickles and hoes, used to break the soil before sowing, were found among other artifacts. In the Neolithic-Chalcolithic period (5000-3000) Palestine's agriculture was, according to some sources, rather developed and partly based on irrigation. From the Early Bronze Period (*ca.* 3000-2000) many findings of seeds and kernels in the Upper Jordan Valley, in Gezer, and in the Negeb testify to the existence of a comparatively high level of agriculture. Mention may be made, among other plants, of wheat, barley, lentils, broad beans, pomegranates, figs, vine, and olives.

For the Middle and Late Bronze period (2000-1200), as well as for the Early Iron period (1200-586), one needs no better source on agriculture than that of the Bible. At those periods Palestine had had already a variegated agriculture. Dry farming, as well as irrigation crops, was well known. Along with wheat, emmer, and barley, the main field crops, lentils, broad beans, and flax were also grown. As summer crops, millet or sorghum, or both of them, were grown. The gourd crops may have consisted of watermelons, muskmelons, and *Lagenaria*. The vegetable garden was rather poor in plants. Onions, leeks, and garlics were certainly grown as plants introduced from Egypt. Among the spices and condiments were cummin, coriander, dill, and nutmeg flower. Fruit-tree orchards and vineyards were highly developed. Among them were the vine, olive, fig, sycomore, date, almond, pomegranate, and probably also the apricot and the mulberry. A novelty was the introduction of the balm shrub (*Commiphora opobalsamum*) and probably also other balm species, as well as the henna (*Lawsonia inermis*), grown in the gardens of Jericho and En-gedi in the Jordan Valley.

The Late Iron period (600-300) and the subsequent Hellenistic period was an era in which agricultural development reached a standard considerably higher than in the following Roman-Byzantian and Arabic periods. A comparatively high level of agrotechnique in the agricultural industry and a very rich inventory of cultivated species characterize this era. Open to the influence of both the NE countries and Egypt, Palestine developed and improved its grain crops, its fodder plants, its vegetable gardens, and its orchards. New introductions for summer crops were rice, sesame, and probably cowpeas. Fodder plants included alfalfa, vetches, lupines, fenugreek, and clover. Carrots, beets, cabbages, radishes, artichokes, and some spices not adequately identified were added to the vegetable garden. New orchard plants were pears, quinces, pistachio, ethrog (*Citrus medica*), celtis (*Celtis australis*), and other varieties not defined. The Mishna, although compiled in the Roman period, clearly reflects the period under review, and is an inexhaustible source for learning about the history of agriculture of that period. It is not improbable that many of these novelties already existed prior to that time, but were not mentioned.

During the Arabic period very little was added to the agricultural technique and to the inventory of the cultivated plants. The banana, the sugar cane, and probably some new vegetables were introduced in this period. But agriculture, in general, was at its decline. Large stretches of mountain terraces, built during earlier centuries, were neglected and left to denudation. Many flourishing villages of the past turned into "tells" (ruin mounds), bearing the ancient name of the sites.

Under the Turkish rule, there is nothing to add except that of citriculture, which probably began in the sixteenth century. Long after the discovery of America, new plants came into the fields and gardens of Palestine. With the beginning of Jewish immigration a stream of new plants in each branch of agriculture flowed into Palestine. In agricultural technique, modern methods have been introduced. This ever-increasing trend toward modernization and rationalization of agriculture is now about to overshadow older achievements and to eliminate ancient crops from the country.

Bibliography. J. Smith, *Bible Plants, Their History* (1878). G. Dalman, *Arbeit und Sitte in Palaestina* (2 vols.; 1928). G. E. Post, *Flora of Syria, Palestine and Sinai* (2nd ed.), vol. I (1932); vol. II (1933). I. Loew, *Die Flora der Juden,* vol. I (1928); vols. II-III (1924); vol. IV (1934). H. N. and A. L. Moldenke, *Plants of the Bible* (1952). M. Zohary, *Geobotany* (1955; Hebrew).

M. ZOHARY

FLOUR [סלת (*alternately* FINE FLOUR; FINE MEAL); σεμίδαλις]. Flour is to be distinguished from MEAL (GROUND GRAIN) in that flour was ground from only the inner kernels of the wheat, whereas meal was ground from the whole kernels and the bran. Thus the grain from which flour was prepared was called the "finest of the wheat" (Deut. 32:14 [KJV "fat of kidneys of wheat"]; Pss. 81:16—H 81:17; 147:14). Accordingly it was a luxury (II Kings 7:1; Ezek. 16:13; Rev. 18:13). Nevertheless it was used by ordinary people: Sarah made cakes from it for the three strangers (Gen. 18:6). By far its most extensive use, however, was in CEREAL OFFERINGS (Exod. 29:2; Lev. 2; 7; Num. 15; 28–29; etc.), in which the flour was mixed with OIL (*see* § 2*c*).

See also CEREALS; THRESHING; WHEAT.

Bibliography. G. Dalman, "Die Mehlarten im AT," *BWAT,* XIII (1913), 64.

J. F. ROSS

FLOWERS (PLANTS) [ציץ; פרח; נצן, נץ, נצה; גבעל; ἄνθος]. The blossom, or reproductive part, of trees, shrubs, and other flora.

Among the hundreds of species of flowers believed to have grown in Palestine since ancient times, barely a dozen (including tree blossoms) are mentioned specifically. That flowers were noticed and appreciated is indicated by the above group of general Hebrew words which apply to them. Flowers of the fields appear as a symbol of the springtime (Song of S. 2:12). Frequently they were a symbol of the transitory nature of man's life (Job 14:2; Ps. 103:15; Isa. 5:24; 40:6-8; cf. Jas. 1:10-11; I Pet. 1:24). Woe is proclaimed against the fading flower of Ephraim's glorious beauty (Isa. 28:1, 4). The bloom of Lebanon fades before the power of God (Nah. 1:4). Blooms would provide the fragrance of the garden (Song of S. 4:16). The familiar "lilies of the fields" (Matt. 6:28; Luke 12:27) quite possibly refer to many flowers. *See* LILY.

Of the nearly one hundred different flora species mentioned in the Bible the following are the only flowers or tree blossoms specified, and the identification of several of these must be questioned:

a) ALMOND (לוז, שקד, *lûz, šāqēdh=Amygdalus communis* L.; Exod. 25:33-34; 37:19-20; Num. 17:8—H 17:23; Eccl. 12:5).

b) Colchicum (?; חבצלת, *ḥᵃbhaṣṣéleth=Colchicum autumnale* L.; Song of S. 2:1 [RSV ROSE]; Isa. 35:1 [RSV CROCUS]).

c) CROCUS (?; חבצלת, *ḥᵃbhaṣṣéleth*=several possible species; Song of S. 2:1 [RSV ROSE]; Isa. 35:1; *cf.* SAFFRON in Song of S. 4:14).

d) FIG (פגה, *paggâ=Ficus caricus* L.; Song of S. 2:13; cf. Hab. 3:17, a negative reference to its flowers, which are enclosed within a fleshy bract appearing as an unripe fig).

e) FLAX (פשתה, *pištâ=Linum usitatissimum* L.; "in bud," גבעל, in Exod. 9:31).

f) HENNA (כפר, *kôpher=Lawsonia inermis* L.; Song of S. 1:14; 7:11—H 7:12[?]; *see* HENNA).

g) LILY (שושן, *šôšan=Nymphaea lotus* L.[?] in I Kings 7:19, 22, 26; flowers in general in Song of S. 2:1-2, 16; 4:5; 6:2-3, 11; κρίνον=*Anemone coronaria* L., *Ranunculus asiaticus* L., *Papaver rhoeas* L., or flowers in general in Matt. 6:28; Luke 12:27; *Lilium candidum* L. [?] in Ecclus. 39:14; 50:8).

h) LOTUS (צאלים[?], *ṣe'ᵉlîm=Nymphaea lotus* L., in Job 40:21-22; שושן[?], *šôšan* [RSV LILY] in I Kings 7:19, 22, 26).

i) MALLOW (מלוח[?], *mallûᵃḥ=Malva sylvestris* L.; Job 24:24).

j) Narcissus (?; חבצלת, *ḥᵃbhaṣṣéleth=Narcissus tazetta* L., thought by some scholars to be the "rose" or "crocus" of Song of S. 2:1; Isa. 35:1; *see* ROSE).

k) Oleander (?; ῥόδον=*Nerium oleander* L.; Ecclus. 24:14; 39:13; cf. Ecclus. 50:8; Enoch 82:6; 106:2, 10; III Macc. 7:17; RSV ROSE).

l) OLIVE (זית, *záyith=Olea europaea* L.; Job 15: 33).

m) POMEGRANATE (רמון, *rimmōn=Punica granatum* L.; Song of S. 6:11; 7:12—H 7:13).

n) ROSE (ῥόδον=*Rosa phoenicia* L.; II Esd. 2:19; Wisd. Sol. 2:8).

o) VINE (i.e., grapevine; סמדר, *sᵉmādhar=Vitis vinifera* L.; Song of S. 2:13, 15; 6:11; 7:12—H 7:13; cf. Gen. 40:10; Isa. 18:5; Hos. 14:7—H 14:8).

The springtime traveler to the Holy Land today is impressed by the great masses of yellow flowers, most of which are chrysanthemums (primarily *Chrysanthemum coronarium* L.). They dominate hillsides and valleys and cover almost every ancient tell.

See also FLORA § A10.

Bibliography. A. A. Temple, *Flowers and Trees of Palestine* (1929); H. N. and A. L. Moldenke, *Plants of the Bible* (1952), Index; W. Walker, *All the Plants of the Bible* (1957).

J. C. TREVER

FLUTE. *See* MUSICAL INSTRUMENTS.

FLUX, BLOODY. KJV form of DYSENTERY.

FLY. The translation of two Hebrew words:

a) זבוב (*zᵉbhubh*), "moving to and fro"(?), a sound-imitating word like "buzz" (cf. Akkadian *zumbu;* Arabic *dhubâb,* "fly" or "bee"; Syriac *zebaba;* Amharic *zemb;* Mehri *ḏebbēt;* Eccl. 10:1; Isa. 7:18).

b) ערוב, from ערב, therefore "mixed insects, a swarm" (cf. Syriac *'arûba,* "mix"; Exod. 8:21-22, 24, 29, 31—H 8:17-18, 20, 25, 27; Pss. 78:45; 105:31).

Both are dipterous (two-winged) insects. Generally זבוב is understood as the common housefly, *Musca domestica.* The ruining of ointment by falling into it (Eccl. 10:1) is entirely in keeping with its habits. But, vexing as this species is in the Orient, a more aggressive one would more likely be used metaphorically of Egypt's invading army (Isa. 7:18). The wasp-sized horsefly, *Tabanus arenivagus,* which attacks horses, cattle, and even persons while traveling in automobiles, is the more likely species. The inhabitants of Ekron worshiped the god of flies, BAALZEBUB, to avert the evil done by flies (II Kings 1:2-3).

The ערוב is the stinging fly sent by God as the fourth of the PLAGUES IN EXODUS. It is translated uniformly as "swarms of flies" in both Exodus and Psalms (KJV "divers sorts of flies" in the Psalms). Various species could be referred to: the housefly (*Musca domestica*), the bluebottle fly (*Calliphora erythrocephala*), the dog fly (LXX), the Barghaš midge, or a Tabanid fly (*Stomoxys calcitrans*). The Barghaš enters the eyes, ears, and nose of fieldworkers during harvest. The *Stomoxys calcitrans* bites the legs of man and beast.

The maggot (רמה; Job 25:6; Isa. 14:11; etc.) and the WORM (Exod. 16:24; Deut. 28:39; Job 7:5; 17: 14; etc.) are the larvae of flies.

See also FAUNA § E7*a*.

Bibliography. G. Hort, "The Plagues of Egypt," *ZAW,* 69 (1957), 84-103; 70 (1958), 49-59. *See also* the bibliography under ANT.

W. W. FRERICHS

FODDER [בליל, בלל, mix, mingle]. Food for animals consisting of a mixture of grains (Job 6:5; 24:6). In Isa. 30:24 (cf. Judg. 19:21) the same word is translated "PROVENDER," and the food was salted, probably to make it more palatable as well as to satisfy the animals' need for salt. On the basis of the Arabic *balla,* "moisten," some scholars believe that בליל may have been brought to a preliminary stage of fermentation by soaking in water. H. N. RICHARDSON

FOLD. *See* SHEEPFOLD.

FOLLY. The translation of several uncomplimentary terms often used in the Bible and particularly in the wisdom literature to describe persons lacking wisdom and the senseless behavior of such persons. Folly is opposed to WISDOM (*see* § 2*b*), and a fool is the reverse of a wise man. Folly is a sort of behavior which is self-defeating or unprofitable; also, in the Bible, immoral, wanton, impious.

The more common Hebrew terms for "fool" are אויל, בער, כסיל, נבל, סכל, פתי, and חסר לב, and the related terms for "folly" are אולת, כסילות, נבלה, סכלות. While "folly" is the common denominator of all these nouns, certain ones among them have special connotations. The בער inclines to a subhuman mentality (brutishness); the פתי is simple, largely through want of experience; the נבל is less innocent than the merely foolish. Similarly, נבלה often appears to be an understatement for outright sinfulness.

Most of these terms are favored by the wisdom writers. Outside the books of Proverbs, Job, and Ecclesiastes, only בער, נבל, נבלה, and סכל occur with relative frequency.

Folly is often known by its opposite; it is contrasted

with wisdom in the wisdom literature quite as, in Deuteronomy, death and life, evil and good, curse and blessing are opposed (e.g., Deut. 30:15, 19). Not that folly is merely the negation of wisdom. Folly appears as a principle in human affairs—a power by its own right—which offers its wares to the unsuspecting young. The "foolish woman" of Prov. 9:13 is properly a personification of folly (cf. Prov. 14:1), conceived as the rival of the woman wisdom, who, in the parallel first section of the chapter (Prov. 9:1-6), entices the same youth (cf. Ecclus. 6:18-21). Koheleth the questioner examines with philosophic detachment the way of wisdom and the way of folly, to discern which indeed has the advantage (Eccl. 2:3), and he arrives at two answers: "Wisdom excels folly as light excels darkness" (2:13), but also: "The wise man . . . , the fool . . . ; one fate comes to all" (2: 14). This latter answer is colored by the special hues of Koheleth's thought. Otherwise, biblical man remained by the former view, the recognition of the superiority of wisdom.

The literature contains a number of clues also as to the specific nature of folly and the behavior of fools:

A fool is neither provident nor prudent. He "folds his hands" (Eccl. 4:5), follows worthless pursuits; and his fields and vineyards go to ruin (Prov. 12:11; 24:30-31); he "believes everything" and goes surety for his neighbor (Prov. 14:15; 17:18).

A fool is hot-tempered (Prov. 14:17, 29; Eccl. 7:9) and quarrelsome (Prov. 20:3), giving full vent to his anger (12:16; 29:11).

A fool talks loosely and too much. A proverb in his mouth is lame (Prov. 26:7; Ecclus. 20:20). Whereas if he kept his mouth shut he might be thought intelligent (Prov. 17:28), he talks without listening (18:13), babbles, and "flaunts his folly" (10: 14; 13:16; Ecclus. 20:13; 21:16, 25-26; 27:13). He speaks slander, gossip, and spite (Prov. 10:18; 11:12; 20:19), and stirs up strife (18:6).

A fool may be merely simple and uninstructed, young and susceptible (Prov. 1:4; 7:7; 9:4, 16; 14:15; Ecclus. 19:23-24). But he may also be wilfully perverse, ill-natured like Nabal or like Saul in their behavior toward David (I Sam. 25:25; 26:21), or a prey to cupidity like Achan (Josh. 7:15; Ecclus. 20: 14-17), and hating knowledge or reproof (Prov. 1:22; 12:1; 13:19), his way being "right in his own eyes" (12:15).

At its best, folly is a kind of epicureanism, dedication to a life of pleasure; for when Koheleth makes trial of "folly," what he does is to accumulate all the "good things" of the earth (Eccl. 2:1-11). At its worst, a fool's folly is rank immorality, rape, fornication, incest, adultery (Gen. 34:7; Deut. 22:21; Judg. 19:23-24; 20:6, 10; II Sam. 13:12-13; Prov. 6:32; Jer. 29:23), but also lesser wrongs (Ps. 69:5—H 69:6; Prov. 10:23).

Folly is the rejecting of God's will, for "the fear of the LORD is the beginning of knowledge" (Prov. 1: 7); but "the fool says in his heart, 'There is no God' " (Ps. 14:1), speaks falsehood of God (Job 42: 8; 2:10), and refuses him obedience (I Sam. 13:13; II Sam. 24:10; II Chr. 16:9).

So a fool learns the hard way, through the "rod of discipline" (Prov. 10:13; 16:22; 19:29; 22:15) if at all (cf. Prov. 17:16, 24; 18:2; 23:9; Ecclus. 22:7-15; 33:5), and goes to meet a bitter fate (II Sam. 3:33: "Should Abner die as a fool dies?"; cf. Job 5:2-5; Prov. 22:3; Eccl. 7:17; 10:12).

Both wisdom and folly are personal philosophies, different ways of looking upon life. Wisdom is the way of the religious man, and it leads to victory; folly is the way of the impious, and its end is defeat.

S. H. BLANK

FOOD. Although food was, of course, one of the necessities of life in biblical times (cf. Ecclus. 39:26), the Hebrews and early Christians did not enjoy as extensive a variety of foodstuffs as their modern descendants. Furthermore, the danger of famine due to crop failure and natural disasters (*see* § 2*d below; see also* FAMINE) was much greater in ancient times. These difficulties were enhanced by the lack of a well-developed system of trade whereby needy areas could be relieved by the food surpluses of other districts; in a time of famine Jacob and his sons were forced to procure grain from Egypt (Gen. 42:1-2). For these reasons the simple gathering and preparation of food occupied a major part of man's life; the alternative was death by starvation.

1. Varieties of food in the Bible
   a. Meat
   b. Fruit
   c. Vegetables
   d. Cereals
2. The significance of food in daily life
   a. As a bond of fellowship
   b. Gifts of food
   c. Foreign trade
   d. The danger of famine
3. The significance of food in the religious life
   a. As the gift of God
   b. In the eschatological age
   c. The devaluation of food

Bibliography

1. Varieties of food in the Bible. Of course, the Bible is not an encyclopedia of manners and customs, and it must not be assumed that all the foodstuffs consumed in biblical times are specifically mentioned in its pages. The main categories can, however, be determined with some degree of accuracy, although many of the details are missing.

a. Meat. In biblical times meat was not a regular part of the diet. It is missing in Sirach's list of the necessities of life, which otherwise includes salt, wheat, milk, honey, wine, and oil (Ecclus. 39:26). According to the priestly writer (*see* PENTATEUCH § A5), the reluctance to eat meat can be traced back to the Creation. When God created man, he gave him for food "every plant yielding seed which is upon the face of all the earth, and every tree with seed in its fruit" (Gen. 1:29); only after the Flood was man permitted to eat animal food (Gen. 9:3). The narrative preserves the tradition that in the golden age of the past there was perfect harmony among all creatures, human and animal. God does not command his creatures to kill one another. Even when permitting animal food, God prohibits the consumption of blood, for that is "its life" (Gen. 9:4; cf. Lev. 17:11, 14; Deut. 12:23). *See* CLEAN AND UNCLEAN.

Apart from religious scruples, the chief reason for abstaining from meat was simply the scarcity of domestic cattle in biblical times. One could secure meat by hunting wild GAME (*see also* HUNTING), but it was uneconomical to slaughter animals which could provide other necessities (*see* CHEESE; CURDS; MILK). Consequently meat was usually eaten only on the occasion of a SACRIFICE. There were exceptions, of course. An honored guest was entertained with a meal which included meat; Abraham took a calf from the herd when the three strangers arrived (Gen. 18:7). Naturally the return of a long-lost son was also an occasion for the eating of meat; the father commands the servants to "bring the fatted calf and kill it, and let us eat and make merry" (Luke 15:23). Oxen and fat calves are also mentioned in Jesus' parable of the marriage feast (Matt. 22:4).

These restrictions did not apply to the wealthy. We are told that Solomon's provisions for one day included "ten fat oxen, and twenty pasture-fed cattle, a hundred sheep, besides harts, gazelles, roebucks, and fatted fowl" (I Kings 4:23—H 5:3). Amos denounces the wealthy who

> eat lambs from the flock,
> and calves from the midst of the stall
> (6:4).

Roasting and boiling were the usual methods of preparing meat. The Passover lamb is to be roasted, not boiled (Exod. 12:8-9; cf. II Chr. 35:13), and a similar distinction was made at the Shiloh temple (I Sam. 2:15). Ezekiel, however, threatens Jerusalem with an "allegory":

> Set on the pot, set it on,
> pour in water also;
> put in it the pieces of flesh,
> all the good pieces, the thigh and the shoulder;
> fill it with choice bones.
> Take the choicest one of the flock,
> pile the logs under it;
> boil its pieces,
> seethe also its bones in it
> (Ezek. 24:3-5).

See COOKING.

Meat was also obtained from FOWL; quails were sent from heaven to the Israelites in the wilderness (Exod. 16:13), and pigeons and turtledoves are mentioned elsewhere. Eggs from wild birds were eaten in OT times (cf. Deut. 22:6; Isa. 10:14), but it is probable that the chicken was unknown in pre-exilic Palestine. However, the "egg" in Luke 11:12 is very probably the hen's egg. Similarly the eating of fish was rare in OT times, since the Hebrews controlled the Mediterranean coast only at infrequent intervals and were thus reduced to the Sea of Galilee for fishing. Thus in the wilderness the Israelites looked back with longing to the fish they had eaten in Egypt (Num. 11:5). But fish was a common food in NT times; the disciples had only five loaves and two fish in a "lonely place" (Mark 6:38 and parallels; cf. Matt. 15:34). At least four of the disciples (Peter, Andrew, James, and John) were fishermen (Matt. 4:18, 21; Mark 1:16, 19; cf. Luke 5:1-11).

b. Fruit. Olives and grapes were the most important fruits in biblical times, but they were generally made into OIL (*see also* OLIVE TREE) and WINE (*see also* HONEY; VINE). Of the fruits consumed in their natural state figs were the most popular. The early figs (בכרות, lit. "first-born") were regarded as special delicacies because of their sweetness:

> When a man sees it, he eats it up
> as soon as it is in his hand
> (Isa. 28:4; cf. Mic. 7:1).

Thus Hosea compares the Israelites in Egypt to the "first fruit on the fig tree" (Hos. 9:10), and Jeremiah claims that those who have gone into exile are "first-ripe figs," while those who remain in the land are "very bad figs, so bad that they could not be eaten" (Jer. 24:1-10). Cakes of dried figs (דבלים) were prepared for journeys (I Sam. 25:18; 30:12; I Chr. 12:40—H 12:41; cf. Jth. 10:5); they were even used to heal boils (II Kings 20:7; Isa. 38:21). *See bibliography.*

Since there are two towns and one person named TAPPUAH, the Hebrew word for "apple," it may be assumed that apples were eaten in OT times. Actual references are few, however; Joel reports that the apple tree is among the victims of the locust plague (Joel 1:12), and the loved one in the Song of Solomon asks to be refreshed with apples (2:5; cf. 7:8—H 7:9; 8:5). The actual identification is difficult, however; perhaps the citron or the quince is meant.

Other fruits included the pomegranate (Num. 13:23; 20:5; Deut. 8:8; etc.), the date (not mentioned by name, although there are references to the palm), and the sycamore fig (Amos was a "dresser of sycamore trees" [7:14]). *See* FRUIT (PRODUCTS).

c. Vegetables. The climate of Palestine is not suited for the growing of a wide variety of vegetables. In the wilderness the Israelites longed for the "cucumbers, . . . the leeks, the onions, and the garlic" they had enjoyed in Egypt (Num. 11:5); of these the cucumber is elsewhere mentioned only twice (Isa. 1:8; Jer. 10:5) and the others not at all. It should not be assumed, however, that the lack of specific references means that these vegetables were not known. Indeed, on the basis of modern parallels it is likely that at least onions and leeks were rather widely cultivated. More important, however, were beans and lentils. They could be boiled into POTTAGE, eaten in their natural state, or mixed with flour to increase the yield of BREAD (§ 1*a*). In addition to these the husks of the carob tree, although usually used as fodder for animals, served as emergency food (Luke 15:16). *See* VEGETABLES.

d. Cereals. In view of the above-mentioned reluctance to eat meat at everyday meals and the relative scarcity of fruits and vegetables, it is natural that cereal foods should make up a large part of the diet in biblical times. The Egyptian envoy Sinuhe reported that barley and emmer (a primitive form of wheat) were plentiful in Palestine-Syria. These two grains were by far the most important. BREAD was made from both wheat flour and barley meal, and was eaten at every meal. In a time of need, however, millet and spelt (KJV "fitches") could also be used in bread (Ezek. 4:9); spelt was usually used as a border for a field (Isa. 28:25). But these grains could also be eaten in other forms. It was customary to rub off the husks in one's hands and eat the fresh kernels. One of Elisha's friends brought the prophet and his friends bread and "fresh ears of grain"; the company proceeded to eat the uncooked grain (II Kings 4:42-44). Furthermore, the heads of grain could be roasted in a pan or merely held in the fire; this "parched grain" (KJV "parched corn") was appropriate at a harvest meal (Ruth 2:14), but was also eaten by the king himself (I Sam. 25:18; II Sam. 17:28). *See* NUT.

2. The significance of food in daily life. Food was not merely a means for sustaining life in biblical times; it had wide significance in the social and the economic life generally.

a. As a bond of fellowship. In OT times almost every pact or covenant was sealed with a common meal; the food consumed by both parties made them, so to speak, members of the same family or clan. In spite of the mutual suspicion between Jacob and Laban, they concluded their boundary treaty with a meal which lasted all night (Gen. 31:54). Such an agreement was not always made between two equal parties, however. Joshua and his men were convinced by the Gibeonites that they were "from a far country" and therefore needed the protection of a covenant; as a sign of agreement the Israelites ate of the provisions which the strangers had brought with them (Josh. 9:3-15). The bond thus created was so strong that it could not be broken even when it was discovered that the Gibeonites were actually from a nearby district (vss. 16-27). Similarly Mephibosheth, who described himself as a "dead dog," was adopted by David and thus was allowed to eat at the king's table, like one of his sons (II Sam. 9:7, 10-11).

Conversely, the refusal to eat food with someone was a mark of anger and a symbol of the rupture of fellowship; when Jonathan learned that Saul was determined to kill David, he "rose from the table in fierce anger and ate no food . . . , for he was grieved for David, because his father had disgraced him" (I Sam. 20:34).

This significance of food as a bond of fellowship may even be preserved in the Hebrew word for "covenant," ברית, which is often held to be derived from the root ברה, "to eat." However this may be, the phrase "covenant of salt" means a "permanent covenant," since eating salt with one's companions means to be bound to them in loyalty (Num. 18:19; II Chr. 13:5; cf. Ezra 4:14). Similarly Jesus' injunction: "Have salt in yourselves" (Mark 9:50; cf. Col. 4:6), is an encouragement to mutual loyalty among the disciples. *See* COVENANT; SALT.

b. Gifts of food. Because of the function of food in sealing personal and communal relationships, gifts of food were not merely a matter of form. The recipient, if he accepted the gift, was put under an obligation, and the giver was well aware of this. When it became necessary to make a second trip to Egypt in order to get food during a time of famine, Jacob and his sons were somewhat concerned about the good will of "the man" (Joseph) who had previously given them grain; the patriarch thus advised his sons to "take some of the choice fruits of the land in your bags, and carry down to the man a present, a little balm and a little honey, gum, myrrh, pistachio nuts, and almonds" (Gen. 43:1-11). Jacob had already had experience in such affairs. He had naturally worried about his reception at the hand of his disinherited brother, Esau, and had sent on ahead a gift of goats, sheep, cows, bulls, and asses (Gen. 32:3-21).

It was even more necessary to placate a political leader. When David was on the point of becoming king of all Israel, the people of Hebron, his former capital, made adequate provision for a feast lasting three days, and Israelites from as far as Issachar, Zebulun, and Naphtali "came bringing food on asses and on camels and on mules and on oxen, abundant provisions of meal, cakes of figs, clusters of raisins, and wine and oil, oxen and sheep, for there was joy in Israel" (I Chr. 12:38-40—H 12:39-41). Even when he was later forced to flee on the occasion of Absalom's revolt, David was brought food by his loyal subjects (II Sam. 16:1; 17:27-29); presumably they hoped that he would again rise to power and reward them accordingly.

The earlier prophets were also given gifts of food, either as payment for services rendered or as a sign of good faith. When Saul and his servant were looking for lost asses, they decided to consult the seer Samuel; Saul, however, was concerned because their bread was gone and they had no present to bring (I Sam. 9:6-7). On the occasion of his son's illness Jeroboam sent Ahijah a gift of loaves, cakes, and honey in hopes that the seer would predict a favorable outcome (I Kings 14:1-3). Ahijah was apparently not impressed, however; he announced the destruction of the house of Jeroboam, and the child died (vss. 6-18). Nevertheless, the custom of presenting gifts to prophets apparently survived. Amaziah could thus say to Amos: "O seer, go, flee away to the land of Judah, and eat bread there, and prophesy there" (Amos 7:12). Micah is scathing in his criticism:

> Thus says the LORD concerning the prophets
>   who lead my people astray,
> who cry "Peace"
>   when they have something to eat,
> but declare war against him
>   who puts nothing into their mouths
> (3:5).

c. Foreign trade. In spite of the unreliability of food supplies in Palestine itself, foodstuffs were the most important items of foreign trade in biblical times. Just as presents of food were made to private persons to insure their good favor, so relationships between Israel and her neighbors were improved by mutual gifts. Hosea complains that the people of Israel

> make a bargain with Assyria,
> and oil is carried to Egypt
> (12:1).

Naturally food was also given in exchange for foreign aid in one form or another. Hiram, king of Tyre, offered to supply cedar and cypress timber for the building of the temple on the condition that "[Solomon] shall meet my wishes by providing food for my household"; accordingly, large quantities of wheat and oil were sent from Israel to Tyre each year (I Kings 5:9-11—H 5:23-25). The same trade was effected four and a half centuries later when Zerubbabel and his associates sent "food, drink, and oil" to Tyre and Sidon in return for the cedar required for the rebuilding of the temple (Ezra 3:7).

Tyre became very rich as a result of such commerce; Ezekiel lists the many nations which had traded with her, among which were Judah and Israel, who "exchanged for your merchandise wheat, olives and early figs, honey, oil, and balm" (Ezek. 27:17).

d. The danger of famine. Perhaps the best-known famines in biblical times are those described in the story of Joseph (Gen. 41:54; 43:1; 47:13, 15) and in the Elijah narratives (I Kings 17:1, 7, 12; 18:2, 5). Although lack of rain was the chief cause of such crop failures, other natural disasters also played their part. Amos graphically describes the catastrophes sent by Yahweh: (*a*) he withheld the rain when the harvest was three months off; (*b*) he sent blight and mildew; (*c*) he caused the locust to devour fig and olive trees; and (*d*) he created a pestilence, probably affecting both men and animals (Amos 4:6-10; cf. Deut. 28:22; I Kings 8:37). To these may be added hail (Hag. 2:17), which is particularly damaging to cereal crops.

The only way to ward off the consequences of such a famine was to build up reserves of food in plentiful times. Having been warned by Pharaoh's dream that a famine was coming, Joseph suggested that one fifth of the food grown in the seven normal years be stored up against the approaching lean years (Gen. 41:34-36; cf. 47:24). The alternative to such a wise policy was simply malnutrition, if not death. Thus Jeremiah receives a "word of the LORD . . . concerning the drought":

> Because of the ground which is dismayed,
> since there is no rain on the land,
> the farmers are ashamed,
> they cover their heads.
> Even the hind in the field forsakes her new-born calf
> because there is no grass.
> The wild asses stand on the bare heights,
> they pant for air like jackals;
> their eyes fail
> because there is no herbage (Jer. 14:1, 4-6).

It is no wonder that people would

> trade their treasures for food
> to revive their strength
> (Lam. 1:11).

3. The significance of food in the religious life. In biblical times scarcely any secular activity failed to have a counterpart in the religious life of the people, and the production and consumption of food are no exception.

a. As the gift of God. Since God is the creator and sustainer of life, it is natural that biblical man should regard food as a divine gift. The Lord God planted the garden of Eden, put man in it, and "made to grow every tree that is pleasant to the sight and good for food" (Gen. 2:9). But man is not left to his own devices. God even teaches the principles of agriculture—how to level the surface of the ground, when to sow various seeds, and the way of putting wheat and barley in rows (Isa. 28:24-26). Ben Sirach thus urges his "son" not to hate "farm work, which [was] created by the Most High" (Ecclus. 7:15). The gift of food was renewed at the Conquest; Yahweh gave the wandering Israelites a "land of wheat and barley, of vines and fig trees and pomegranates, a land of olive trees and honey, a land in which you will eat bread without scarcity, in which you will lack nothing" (Deut. 8:7-9; cf. Josh. 24:13). Men and beasts have nothing which they have created for themselves; in praising God the psalmist says:

> These all look to thee,
> to give them their food in due season.
> When thou givest to them, they gather it up;
> when thou openest thy hand, they are filled with good things
> (Ps. 104:27-28; cf. 145:15-16).

A similar attribution of food to God is found in the Egyptian "Hymn to the Aton." *See bibliography.*

One must not presume upon God's gifts, however. The Israelites in the desert decided to test God by demanding food, thinking that it would be impossible to "spread a table in the wilderness"; in spite of his anger God gave them manna, the "bread of the angels," and "winged birds like the sand of the seas." After the people had eaten, however, God slew the strongest of the men because of their presumption (Ps. 78:18-31).

Since food is a bond between man and man (*see* § 2*a above*), it is even more natural that it should find a place in the expression of the relationship between man and God. Thus on Mount Sinai, Moses and the elders "beheld God, and ate and drank" (Exod. 24:11). Similarly one of the most important motifs in SACRIFICE AND OFFERINGS is the consumption of food. In the early days of Israel, food offerings were probably thought to be eaten by Yahweh, although in the name of God the psalmist asks:

> Do I eat the flesh of bulls,
> or drink the blood of goats?
> (Ps. 50:13).

Offerings of food continued to be made as long as the temple stood, however, and the pious Israelite undoubtedly felt that he had come closer to God when he had returned to him a part of his gifts. A similar motive lies behind the requirement that the FIRST FRUITS and a TITHE of all produce be brought to the sanctuary.

b. In the eschatological age. Since God created a fruitful garden at the beginning of his work, he will naturally bestow an abundance of food upon his faithful people in the days to come. Many of the prophetic books contain descriptions of the material blessedness of the New Age. Hosea looks forward to a time when Israel will be "allured" by Yahweh and given vineyards; "in that day" the heavens, the earth, the grain, the wine, and the oil will say "Jezreel"—i.e., "God sows" (Hos. 2:14-15, 21-22—H 2:16-17, 23-24). Similarly Amos predicts that at the time of Israel's restoration, men

> shall plant vineyards and drink their wine,
> and they shall make gardens and eat their fruit
> (9:14).

The imagery used by Joel (3:18—H 4:18; cf. Amos 9:13) is even more expressive:

> And in that day
> the mountains shall drip sweet wine,
> and the hills shall flow with milk.

Ezekiel even foresees the day when the waters of the Dead Sea will become fresh and thus able to support "very many fish"; on its banks "all kinds of trees for food" will grow (Ezek. 47:6-12). Later apocalyptic books also give descriptions of a messianic banquet to be held in heaven after this earth passes away; the NT contains several allusions to this coming event. *See* MEALS § 4*b*.

c. The devaluation of food. Important as food naturally was in both secular and religious affairs, it was never regarded as the sole source or end of man's life. The Deuteronomist knows that "man does not live by bread alone, but . . . by everything that proceeds out of the mouth of the LORD" (Deut. 8:3; cf. Jesus' reply to the tempter [Matt. 4:4; Luke 4:4]). And the author of the psalm of Habakkuk can say:

> Though the fig tree do not blossom,
>   nor fruit be on the vines,
> the produce of the olive fail
>   and the fields yield no food,
> the flock be cut off from the fold
>   and there be no herd in the stalls,
> yet I will rejoice in the LORD,
>   I will joy in the God of my salvation
>   (Hab. 3:17-18).

The clearest insight into the ultimate importance of food is to be found in the NT, however. In the Sermon on the Mount, Jesus says to his listeners: "Do not be anxious about your life, what you shall eat or what you shall drink, nor about your body, what you shall put on." Rather, "life [is] more than food, and the body more than clothing"; God knows that his children need these things (Matt. 6:25, 32; Luke 12:22, 30). On another occasion Jesus calls himself the "bread which comes down from heaven"; if any man eats it, he will never be hungry again. Ordinary food, symbolized by the manna, does not have this power (John 6:31-35, 48-59).

The author of Hebrews may have had such sayings of Jesus in mind when he admonished his readers: "It is well that the heart be strengthened by grace, not by foods, which have not benefited their adherents" (Heb. 13:9). Paul, however, has the final word when he quotes a slogan of his opponents: "Food is meant for the stomach and the stomach for food," and concludes: "God will destroy both one and the other" (I Cor. 6:13). *See also* AGRICULTURE; DRINK.

Bibliography. J. Benziger, *Hebräische Archäologie* (1927), pp. 62-72; W. R. Smith, *Lectures on the Religion of the Semites* (3rd ed., 1927), pp. 217-23; C. H. Gordon, *Ugaritic Literature* (1949), p. 129, on the use of fig cakes in healing; A. C. Bouquet, *Everyday Life in NT Times* (1954), pp. 69-79; R. J. Forbes, *Studies in Ancient Technology*, III (1955), 50-59, 84-104; J. B. Pritchard, ed., *ANET* (2nd ed., 1955), pp. 19 (the story of Sinuhe), 370 (Hymn to the Aton); E. W. Heaton, *Everyday Life in OT Times* (1956), pp. 81-115. *See also* the commentaries on Matt. 4; Luke 12; John 6. J. F. ROSS

FOODS, CLEAN AND UNCLEAN. Those foods permitted and prohibited to the Jews; the most important lists appear in Lev. 11; Deut. 14. *See* CLEAN AND UNCLEAN § 3*b*.

FOOL. *See* FOLLY.

FOOT [רגל; πούς]. In the Bible this word normally has its ordinary physical sense. The word is used metaphorically only in certain instances where it is a picturesque equivalent of "person" (I Sam. 2:9) or a personal pronoun (Pss. 40:2; 66:9; Rom. 3:15), and in the phrase "foot of arrogance" (Ps. 36:11). The expression "to put under the feet" (Ps. 8:6) is a symbol of conquest and dominion recalling the actual practice of conquerors in ancient times (Josh. 10:24); to sit "at the feet" (Luke 10:39; Acts 22:3) is a symbol of discipleship, recalling the practice of the schools. With the metaphors should also be included the euphemistic use of the term "feet" for the *pudenda* (Judg. 3:24 KJV; II Kings 18:27 Qere; Isa. 6:2; Ezek. 16:25 KJV).

Because of the dusty roads of the ancient world, feet quickly became dirty in traveling (Mark 6:11), and provision for the washing of a guest's feet was an ordinary act of hospitality (Gen. 18:4; Luke 7:44; John 13:5). The removal of the shoes in a holy place was necessary because of their previous defilement by contact with the profane earth (Exod. 3:5). Because of the lowliness of the feet and perhaps also because, as mentioned above, they symbolize subjection and discipleship, the most natural gesture of humility and self-abasement was to "fall at the feet" (I Sam. 25:24; Mark 5:22). A common method of punishment in ancient Israel was to bind the feet in the STOCKS (Job 13:27; Jer. 20:2). The reference in Deut. 11:10 to watering "with the foot" is evidently to some kind of irrigation machine. R. C. DENTAN

FOOT WASHING. A hospitable amenity in Palestine, extended to guests upon arrival at the home of their host. It was usually performed by a servant, or by the wife of the host, while the guests were reclining at table (Luke 7:44; cf. Mark 1:7 and parallels). The Fourth Evangelist relates that Jesus performed this menial service to his disciples at the Last Supper (John 13:4 ff), as an example of the humble ministry they must ever be ready to perform one for another. The incident is an acted parable of his teaching: "Whoever would be great among you must be your servant, and whoever would be first among you must be slave of all" (Mark 10:43-44 and parallels). The Fourth Evangelist undoubtedly intended the narrative to convey deeper meaning than a lesson in humility. It was a sign of the entirely selfless love of Jesus himself that took him to the humiliation of the Cross (cf. 13:1). Many commentators also believe the Evangelist considered the foot washing to be symbolic of the sacraments of baptism and the Eucharist, by which Christians are cleansed of the defilement of sin and nurtured in a communion of love with their Lord and with one another.

The service of foot washing of the "saints" is mentioned in I Tim. 5:10 among the qualifications of the order of widows (*see* WIDOW). The ceremonial washing of feet in the church's liturgy is first attested *ca.* 400 by Augustine (*Letters* LV.33), in connection with the Easter baptisms in certain churches. The earliest trace of the ceremony on Maundy Thursday—a custom continued in many churches to the present day—is in the seventh-century liturgy of the church in Spain.

Bibliography. O. Cullmann, *Early Christian Worship* (1953), pp. 105-10. M. H. SHEPHERD, JR.

FOOTMAN [רגלי (II Kings 13:7; *usually* FOOT SOLDIER); KJV רץ (I Sam. 22:17; RSV GUARD; *alternately* COURIER), *from* רוץ, to run]. A soldier in the infantry.

FOOTSTOOL [הדם רגל; כבשׁ, *see below;* ὑποπόδιον]. A word usually used metaphorically. According to II Chr. 9:18, Solomon's throne had a "footstool of gold." The word is כֶּבֶשׁ, which is probably a deliberate alteration of כֶּבֶשׂ, "lamb," which in turn is probably a scribal alteration for עגל, "calf." (Cf. I Kings 10:19, which has עגול לכסה—i.e., the "top of the throne," or "The throne had a rounded top behind" [so Syr., Vulg., etc.]. But Greek texts have the equivalent of "heads of calves"—i.e., "calves" for "rounded top" [עגל for עגול]—now generally accepted. The RSV translates: "At the back of the throne was a calf's head.") If the Chronicles text is correct, however, this text uses a later Hebrew word for "footstool," though the root from which it is derived expresses "dominion."

In Pss. 99:5 (cf. vs. 9); 132:7; Lam. 2:1, "footstool" is a metaphor for Zion, if not for the temple itself (see also "place of my feet," etc., in Isa. 60:13; Ezek. 43:7). In I Chr. 28:2 it is generally referred to the mercy seat, the lid of the ark. In these four references the word is metaphorical of obeisance in worship. In Isa. 66:1 (so Matt. 5:35; Acts 7:49) it is a metaphor of the earth, as contrasted with the heavens as the Lord's throne, and with the temple as an alternative footstool to the temple. In Ps. 110:1 it is a metaphor of Davidic dominion.

Ps. 110:1 is quoted by Jesus in his argument with the scribes and Pharisees (Matt. 22:44; Mark 12:36; Luke 20:43). Peter applies the verse to Jesus as proof of his dominion and ascension (Acts 2:35), and this is precisely re-echoed in Heb. 1:13; 10:13. In Jas. 2:3, Christians are warned not to give the best seats to the wealthy and show the poor to a standing or a lowly place ("footstool").

The place at God's feet—no doubt originally the ark (I Chr. 28:2), then the temple, then the earth—is the place where the enemies demonstrate the divine dominion through obeisance. The NT applies this idea of the footstool to the Ascension.

Figs. BAN 19; DAR 4. G. Henton Davies

FORBEARANCE. The English verb "forbear" has two connotations: (*a*) "desist, abstain, refrain from"; (*b*) "endure, bear, bear with." These are related, since to desist or refrain from positive action indicates a willingness to abide by the result.

In the KJV of the OT there are a number of examples of the first connotation in the translation of three separate Hebrew verbs: דמם, חדל, חשך, all of which are variously rendered in the LXX. The RSV has retained "forbear" in only four instances (I Kings 22:6, 15; II Chr. 18:5; Job 16:6); in other places it uses "refrain," "cease," "refuse," etc.

The only appearance of the second connotation is in Neh. 9:30 KJV: "Many years didst thou forbear them" (RSV "Many years thou didst bear with them"). The Hebrew original here means literally: "Thou didst stretch out upon them many years," and this is taken over word for word into the Greek of the LXX. Although the exact wording does not occur elsewhere in the OT, the idea that God patiently endures for a time the sinfulness and rebellion of his people appears a number of times (cf., e.g., Isa. 43:1-7; Jer. 31:1-3; Hos. 11:8-9). For the expression of this idea by other words, *see* Love; Longsuffering.

In the LXX there is found a number of times the verb ἀνέχομαι, which means literally "to hold oneself up" and which has the same two connotations found in the English "forbear," although it is never used to translate a Hebrew verb that is so rendered in English (cf., e.g., Gen. 43:31; Isa. 63:15; Amos 4:7, for the sense of "restrain," "withhold"; and Job 6:11, for the meaning "endure"). The cognate noun, ἀνοχή, is found only once in the LXX (I Macc. 12:25), where it seems to have the technical meaning of "truce."

In the NT "forbear" occurs in the KJV in both senses. In both the KJV and the RSV of Eph. 6:9 it is used to translate ἀνίημι, which in secular Greek meant "let go," "unloose," "relax"; and in this passage it clearly means "refrain from." In II Cor. 12:6 for the Greek φείδομαι (lit., "spare") the KJV has "forbear" and the RSV "refrain." The same is true of I Cor. 9:6, where the words represent merely the negative particle (lit., "not to work"). The other meaning of "forbear" is found in I Thess. 3:1, 5, where the Greek has στέγω, which means in the first place "cover," hence "protect," and then "endure" because one is protected. Here the KJV has "forbear" and the RSV "bear."

The verb, however, which in Greek best represents the English "forbear" is ἀνέχομαι. It occurs fourteen times, but is translated by "forbear" only in Eph. 4:2; Col. 3:13. Elsewhere it is translated in the KJV by "suffer" (Mark 9:19 and parallels; I Cor. 4:12; II Cor. 11:19-20; Heb. 13:22); "bear with" (Acts 18:14; II Cor. 11:1); "endure" (II Thess. 1:4; II Tim. 4:3). The RSV has "bear," "bear with," "endure," "submit to." In all these cases it means "put up with," "endure," "bear up under provocation"—sometimes in a bad sense, as in II Cor. 11:19: "For you gladly bear with fools"—and sometimes in a good, as in I Cor. 4:12: "When persecuted, we endure." In Eph. 4:2 a more strongly positive meaning is indicated; "forbearing one another in love" must mean more than "put up with," since there is nothing negative about Christian Love. This is reinforced by the concluding phrase of the series: "eager to maintain the unity of the Spirit in the bond of peace." Col. 3:13 uses "forbear" in the same positive way.

Mark 9:19 and parallels form a transition to the use of the word as applied to God. Here Jesus, when presented with the failure of his disciples to heal the epileptic boy, says: "O faithless generation, how long am I to bear with you?" From the point of view of the writer of the gospel this cannot be an expression of mere human impatience, especially in view of the story of the Transfiguration which has just been recounted. Jesus, as Son of God, is acting as God does. Jesus says: "O faithless generation," and then proceeds to heal the boy. The implication is that God acts in the same fashion. In spite of his Mercy the people of Israel have a long record of faithlessness, sinfulness, and rebellion. Such conduct merits punishment; and punishment must be meted out, if God is to be regarded as a God of justice. Since, however, he is also a God of mercy, he stays his hand in the hope that repentance will take place (cf., e.g., Neh. 9:26-38).

This gives us the key to the meaning of ἀνοχή, the cognate noun, as used in Rom. 2:4; 3:25, the only occurrences in the NT and translated "forbearance" in both KJV and RSV. In secular Greek the word meant "holding back," "stopping" (especially hostilities), and is therefore used most frequently for an "armistice" or "truce." The thought in Rom. 2:4 is that God, because of his kindness, delays "to inflict wrath" (3:5), in the hope that the sinner will repent. The thought is best understood if the passage is considered as a reply to one who might say that, if man is as bad as Paul paints him, then a just God would at once visit punishment upon him. Paul replies that the delay in inflicting the punishment is due to God's "forbearance" and is meant both to give opportunity for, and to lead the sinner to, repentance. Only repentance can prevent the application of the wrath on the "day of wrath" (Rom. 2:5). In Rom. 3:25 the reference is to the past. God had not inflicted to the full the penalty merited by sin—i.e., the complete destruction of the sinner—but in "his divine forbearance" he had passed over former sins because the "redemption which is in Christ Jesus" (vs. 24) had not yet been revealed. This "forbearance" is part of God's righteousness.

Bibliography. On the passages where the word occurs in Romans, see the Commentaries: W. Sanday and A. Headlam, ICC (1896); C. H. Dodd, *Moffatt NT Commentary* (1932); J. Knox, *IB,* IX (1954).

Special studies: O. J. Baab, *Theology of the OT* (1949), pp. 126-30; A. Richardson, "Forbear, Forbearance," *Theological Word Book of the Bible* (1950).

E. J. Cook

FORD [עברה, מעבר, מעברה, *all from* עבר, pass over, through]. A place where a river or other body of water can be crossed by wading.

1. Palestine. It was the Romans who built the first bridges in Palestine, in the early Christian centuries. This explains why the word "bridge" occurs nowhere in the Bible. In order to cross rivers in biblical times, other means had to be used; the commonest was a ford. The chief river to be thus crossed was the Jordan, whose fords are referred to in Josh. 2:7; Judg. 3:28; 12:5-6; I Sam. 13:7 (emending MT); II Sam. 15:28; 17:16 (with some Hebrew MSS; KJV "plains"); 19:18—H 19:19. In I Macc. 9:48, Jonathan and his men are said to have swum the Jordan, but they may only have waded it. In Gen. 32:22—H 32:23 the ford of the Jabbok (Wadi Zerqa) appears, and in Isa. 16:2 the fords of the Arnon (Wadi Mojib). The location of none of these crossings is known for certain, though the "fords of the wilderness" (II Sam. 15:28; 17:16) have been identified with two Jordan fords a few miles N of the Dead Sea, Mahadat el-Hajlah and Mahadat el-Henu. Presumably the fords associated with Jericho (Josh. 2:7) and Moab (Judg. 3:28) cannot have been too far from the Jordan's mouth.

The Jordan between the Sea of Galilee and the Dead Sea flows strongly, following a serpentine course of about two hundred miles—though the geographical distance is only sixty-five miles—with a depth of from three to ten feet and a width of about ninety. There have always been numerous spots at which it can be forded, though these change with changes in the river bed. It remains a moot question how heavy wheeled vehicles, both civilian and military, were transported in the biblical period across such muddy fords (*see* RAFTS). For an account of fording the Jordan *ca.* 1903 at El 'Abadiyeh, a little S of the Sea of Galilee, see W. Libbey and F. E. Hoskins, *The Jordan Valley and Petra* (1905), I, 138-41.

2. Babylonia. In Jer. 51:32 the "fords" of Babylon are referred to. These must be the crossings over the Euphrates and its numerous canals.

W. S. McCullough

FOREHEAD [מצח; μέτωπον]. The word is used in its literal sense as the spot where the golden plate on Aaron's turban was to be situated (Exod. 28:38) and where the insigne of a harlot was apparently worn (Jer. 3:3 [BROW]; Rev. 17:5). The marks which were to distinguish the men of God (Ezek. 9:4; Rev. 9:4) and the men of "the beast" (Rev. 13:16) were also to be placed there. Metaphorically, the hard forehead is a symbol of stubbornness (Ezek. 3:7-8).

R. C. Dentan

FOREIGNER [זר (*alternately* STRANGER; ALIEN), נכרי (*alternately* STRANGER; ALIEN); LXX *and* NT ἀλλότριος, ἀλλογενής (*alternately* STRANGER; ALIEN)]. As distinct from the גר, SOJOURNER, who makes Israel his home, the foreigner comes into temporary contact with Israel as trader, traveler, or soldier, without cutting ties with his original home.

The Hebrew words are used in four different ways. They describe:

a) The enemies who invade and threaten to overthrow the established order of Israel: (both terms in parallel), Prov. 5:10; Obad. 11; (נכרי alone), II Sam. 22:45-46; Pss. 18:44-45—H 18:45-46; 144:7; Eccl. 6:2; Isa. 60:10; 62:8; (זר alone), Job 15:19; Ps. 109:11; Isa. 1:7; 25:2, 5; Jer. 30:8; 51:51; Ezek. 7:21; 11:9; 28:7, 10; 31:12; Hos. 7:9; 8:7). *See* NATIONS.

b) The gods of the foreign nations which are temptations for Israel (both terms in parallel: Ps. 81:9—H 81:10; Jer. 5:19; נכרי alone: Gen. 35:2; Deut. 31:16; 32:12; Josh. 24:20, 23; Judg. 10:16; I Sam. 7:3; II Chr. 14:3—H 14:2; 33:15; Jer. 8:19; Mal. 2:11; זר alone: Deut. 32:16; Ps. 44:20—H 44:21; Isa. 17:10; 43:12; Jer. 2:25; 3:13; Ezek. 16:32).

c) The non-Israelites who came into ordinary contacts with the Israelites. Special legislation was necessary with regard to financial dealings (Exod. 21:8; Deut. 14:21; 15:3; 23:20—H 23:21), and proverbs warned against giving surety for strangers (Prov. 11:15; 20:16; 27:13) or being enticed by an אשה זרה or a נכריה (ADVENTURESS; Prov. 2:16; 5:3, 20; 6:24; 7:5; 23:27).

d) Those barred from the cult. Foreigners—either freemen (Exod. 12:43; Neh. 9:2; 13:30; Ezek. 44:7, 9) or slaves of Israelites (Gen. 17:12, 27)—were not allowed to participate in the cult, and even their animals were not suitable for sacrificial use (Lev. 22:25). In priestly legislation the זרים who are barred from contact with the holy objects include all who are not hereditary priests (Exod. 29:33; 30:33; Lev. 22:10, 12-13; Num. 1:51; 3:10, 38; 16:40—H 17:5; 18:4, 7). The more positive attitude toward foreigners in the worship of Israel in the pre-exilic period is seen in I Kings 8:41-43, while the postexilic horror of defilement is illustrated by Joel 3:17—H 4:17.

In the NT "foreigner" is used, rarely, to refer to non-Jews: Egyptians (Acts 7:6), Canaanites (Heb.

11:9, 34; ἀλλότριοι), and the Samaritan who shamed the Jewish lepers by giving thanks (Luke 17:18; ἀλλογενής). The reason for this rare use of the term as compared with the OT is that foreigners who were sojourners (πάροικοι) or strangers (ξένοι) could now become full members of the household of God, since the separating wall between Jew and Gentile was broken down (Eph. 2:11-19). With the disappearance of the Jewish political base for the life of God's people, Christians consider themselves as "aliens" (πάροικοι) on the earth, like the patriarchs (Acts 7:6, 29; Heb. 11:13; I Pet. 2:11), and their highest service is to care for strangers (ξένοι) as for Jesus himself (Matt. 25:35-44; III John 5).

Bibliography. A. Bertholet, *Die Stellung der Israeliten und der Juden zu den Fremden* (1896); M. Guttman, "The Term 'Foreigner' Historically Considered," *HUCA*, 3 (1926), 1-20; P. Humbert, "Les adjectifs 'Zar' et 'Nokri' et la 'femme étrangère' des proverbes bibliques," *Mélanges syriens offerts à M. Dussaud* (1939), pp. 259-66; L. Snijders, "The Meaning of זר in the OT," *Oudtestamentische Studien*, 10 (1954), 1-154.

E. J. Hamlin

FOREKNOW, FOREKNOWLEDGE [προγινώσκω; πρόγνωσις]. These words occur several times in the NT (Acts 2:23; 26:5; Rom. 8:29; 11:2; I Pet. 1:2, 20; II Pet. 3:17). The idea they represent, however, is much more pervasive throughout the Bible than might appear from the infrequent appearance of these terms, for it is inseparably related to such kindred conceptions as Election; Predestination or foreordination; Providence.

Basically the verb προγινώσκω means "to know in advance," and in this sense it is well attested in Greek sources (e.g., Thucydides II.64.8; Plato *Republic* IV.426*c;* Aristotle *Nicomachean Ethics* 6.2; Philo *On Dreams* I.2; Jos. War. VI.viii). Since the time of Hipprocrates the noun πρόγνωσις has been a special medical term, referring to a prediction or prognosis made on the basis of diagnosis. In the biblical tradition, however, God's foreknowledge is of a different kind from human foresight of future developments. The biblical usage is qualified by the recognition that God alone is the Lord of the times and that his purpose encompasses all events from the beginning to the consummation of history. In the biblical understanding, he alone has foreknowledge, although this trait is ascribed to pre-existent Wisdom in the Wisdom of Solomon (8:8). In a passage which is consonant with the biblical witness God's sovereignty over history is grounded in the fact that he has created all nations and Israel, his people: "He hath foreseen them and us from the beginning of the creation unto the end of the age, and nothing has been neglected by him even to the least thing" (Asmp. Moses 12:4).

1. God's knowledge. Lest divine foreknowledge, and the associated term "predestination," be misunderstood to mean historical fatalism or predeterminism, it is appropriate to begin with an understanding of biblical words for "know" (ידע; γινώσκω, ειδέναι) and "knowledge" (דעת; γνῶσις). Modern epistemology tends to assume that man is a thinker who stands over against the objects to be known, whether timeless realities or the objective world of persons, things, facts, etc. So viewed, God's knowledge is that of a divine mind which knows what eternally is or which comprehends encyclopedically all the facts that are knowable. But in the Bible knowledge comes, not so much through an intellectual vision of timeless reality or through the perception of objective facts, but in the context of personal relationship; and this is true above all with respect to God's knowledge of man and man's knowledge of God (*see* Knowledge). The man of faith confesses that he is known by God (Ps. 139:1; Jer. 1:5; I Cor. 8:3; 13:12; Gal. 4:9), in which case it is not meant that God knows facts about him but rather that God enters into relation with him, visiting, demanding, judging, and blessing. Thus God's knowing, being the expression of his personal will, is also an act of election (Gen. 18:19; Hos. 13:5; Amos 3:2; II Tim. 2:19), as indicated in the words: "I know you by name" (Exod. 33:12; cf. Isa. 43:1; 45:3-4; 49:1). Standing in a personal relationship to God, the biblical man affirms that his whole life, from beginning to end, is known by God, and from the same standpoint he perceives that all of human history is encompassed within the divine purpose.

From the experience of being known by God comes also the confession that God is omniscient, a central tenet of biblical faith despite passages, found in old folk tradition, which suggest that Yahweh acts to ascertain something he does not know (Gen. 3:9; 11:5; 18:21). God's knowledge is all-inclusive in the sense that nothing or no one can slip beyond the range of his personal lordship. The religious implication of divine omniscience is that God is inescapable: nothing is hidden from his view. Only the fool supposes that his deeds can be done in the dark without God's knowing (Job 21:27; Pss. 10:4, 11; 11:4-6; 33:13-15; 51:6; 138:6; Isa. 29:15-16). And if

> Sheol and Abaddon lie open before the Lord,
> how much more the hearts of men!
> (Prov. 15:11; cf. Job 26:6).

He knows man's thoughts (Ps. 94:11), his mortal weakness (Ps. 103:14); and therefore there is no hiding place in which the creature can escape from the God who knows him completely (Ps. 139:1-6).

> The eyes of the Lord
> are ten thousand times brighter than the sun;
> they look upon all the ways of men,
> and perceive even the hidden places;

this affirmation about the inescapable judgment of God is underscored by reference to divine foreknowledge:

> Before the universe was created, it was known to him;
> so it was also after it was finished
> (Ecclus. 23:19-20).

In the NT it is affirmed that nothing falls beyond the range of God's concern (Matt. 10:29-31). Moreover, it is said that the word of the Lord, sharper than any two-edged sword, pierces to the innermost center of man's life; for "before him no creature is hidden, but all are open and laid bare to the eyes of him with whom we have to do" (Heb. 4:12-13).

Thus the personal lordship of God means that nothing is hidden from him. And just as his searching eye scans the present scene, seeing "everything under the heavens," so the past and future are open before him. From the standpoint of faith, God's knowledge is also foreknowledge.

2. Foreknowledge of events. According to the ancient view, the gods are distinguished from men by virtue of their superior knowledge, as well as their immortality (cf. Gen. 3:22). Man's knowledge, particularly his knowledge of the future, is severely limited, and therefore he must seek divine direction if he is to have any inkling of his destiny. Various techniques of divination were developed to enable man to know and control the future, and these practices are often mentioned in the OT: interpretation of dreams (Gen. 41), necromancy (I Sam. 28), decision by the sacred lot (I Sam. 30:7-8), and prophetic oracle (I Kings 22:1-36; note the three main practices mentioned in I Sam. 28:6, 15). Although Hebrew prophecy rose far above its humble origins in soothsaying (I Sam. 9–10; note 9:9 and *see* PROPHET, PROPHETISM), it never surrendered its predictive reference to the future. To be sure, prophecy at its best was not an inquisitive prying into divine secrets for the purpose of enabling man to control his destiny. Nevertheless, the great prophets spoke as those who had heard Yahweh's decree in his heavenly council (Jer. 23:18, 22; cf. Isa. 6:8; 40:6; Amos 3:7), and their message to the present contained the announcement of what Yahweh was about to do in the accomplishment of his purpose. Divine foreknowledge, then, is the presupposition of the prophetic message about things to come, both in the OT and in the NT.

When the theme of foreknowledge is abstracted from faith's experience of the historical sovereignty of God, it is quickly converted into a doctrine which, to the reflective mind, apparently devaluates human freedom and historical creativity. However, divine foreknowledge has nothing to do with fatalism or determinism. It does not mean that history is written in advance, that it follows a chronological timetable drawn up by God. Nor does it mean that man's will is causally determined, whether by impersonal fate or by an impersonal system of laws. Rather, the affirmation about divine foreknowledge springs out of the experience of man's relation to a personal Lord whose personal will governs man's life from beginning to end. From the perspective of faith, nothing happens by chance or caprice, for God's will enfolds all happenings, even the evil that befalls a city (Amos 3:6). Again and again the prophets emphasize Yahweh's sovereign purpose:

> As I have planned,
> so shall it be,
> and as I have purposed,
> so shall it stand
> (Isa. 14:24-27; cf. 5:19; 19:17; 28:29; Jer. 50:45; Amos 3:7; Mic. 4:12).

In any given situation, the man of faith is conscious of the priority of God's purpose, and this may be expressed in temporal terms by saying that the event was previously planned, and therefore known, by God. It is not just that God can make the best of an unexpected situation and pull it into the orbit of his activity; rather the situation, viewed from the angle of faith, belongs intrinsically to God's prevenient purpose (cf. Gen. 45:4-8; Ps. 50:20; Prov. 16:4; II Pet. 3:9).

The priority of God's purpose is one of the fundamental themes of the prophecy of Second Isaiah. The gods of the nations cannot announce the things to come, for they are caught within the temporal process and are subject to the same weakness and limitation of vision as man. Yahweh, on the other hand, is the eternal God, the First and the Last (*see* GOD, NAMES OF, § D4*b*), whose purpose spans history from beginning to end. According to this prophet, Yahweh's unique and exclusive deity is attested by his foreknowledge: he alone can declare the things to come. History is the unfolding of his purpose, a movement of events from promise toward fulfilment.

> Who declared it from the beginning, that we might know,
> and beforetime, that we might say, "He is right"?
> (Isa. 41:26 and all of vss. 21-29; cf. 43:8-13; 44:6-8; 46:8-11; 48:3-8).

Moreover, Yahweh fulfils his purpose by doing something new in history, by performing a new act of creation (*see* CREATION § 3*b*).

> Behold, the former things have come to pass,
> and new things I now declare;
> before they spring forth
> I tell you of them (42:9; cf. 43:18-19).

Thus the new era, heralded by the rise of Cyrus and the imminent release of exiles, does not represent a change in the divine will, but only the fruition of Yahweh's saving purpose announced beforehand.

The book of DANIEL gives the impression that divine foreknowledge, communicated through prophetic vision, involves advance knowledge of historical details. Admittedly, apocalyptic writers tended to think of foreknowledge in this way (*see* APOCALYPTICISM). Some of the theological problems of the Daniel apocalypse vanish, however, when it is realized that it was written in the Maccabean period and that the prophetic "predictions" are, for the most part, a retrospective narration of historical events, a narration which becomes more accurate as the writer approaches his own period. The book bears witness to the experience of God's lordship over history. In retrospect it is discerned that history is not governed by caprice or by the powerful ambitions of nations, but solely by the prevenient purpose of God. Far from paralyzing human action, this sense of the overruling sovereignty of God provided the spring for action and the support for faith during the Maccabean trials, when overwhelming odds were arraigned against the Jewish people (cf. Dan. 11:32). Similarly in the story of Judith, the heroine acts in the confidence that God has designed the things that have come to pass as well as those that are to come, "for all thy ways are prepared in advance, and thy judgment is with foreknowledge" (Jth. 9:5-6). The prophetic knowledge of things to come is mentioned in other passages, such as Jth. 11:19; Jos. Antiq. VIII. viii.5; xv.6 (cf. Wisd. Sol. 18:6; II Pet. 3:17).

Since the NT is dominated by the announcement that God's promises have been fulfilled, the theme of divine foreknowledge is expressed in various ways. Paul proclaims the gospel of God "which he promised beforehand [προεπηγγείλατο] through his prophets in the holy scriptures" (Rom. 1:2). Frequently the gospel writers comment that events in the story of the Messiah occurred that what was spoken by the prophets might be fulfilled (Matt. 1: 22-23; 2:5-6, 15, 17; etc.). Although OT passages are often used with considerable freedom, these citations nevertheless express the conviction that the prior purpose of God was disclosed in the life, death, and resurrection of Jesus Christ. Jesus himself, according to the gospel portraits, believed that his task was to carry out the foreordained divine plan. At least in part, this accounts for the statements that "the Son of man must suffer" (Mark 8:31), that he "goes as it has been determined" (Luke 22:22), and that his appointed "hour" or "time" (*kairos*) has come (Matt. 26:45; Luke 12:40, 46; John 7:30; 12:27; 17:1). According to the kerygma of the primitive church, Jesus was betrayed and crucified "according to the definite plan and foreknowledge of God" (Acts 2:23; cf. 4: 28). It is wrong to deduce from these and similar NT statements that Jesus' career was mapped out in advance and that he submitted himself to a prearranged fate. Rather, the NT writers, viewing Jesus' career from the standpoint of faith, discern in these events the prevenient purpose of God. The event of the Messiah's coming was no divine afterthought, no casual and unexpected occurrence in history, but an essential part of God's redemptive purpose, announced in advance through his prophetic spokesmen. Moreover, just as it could be said that Moses was chosen from the time of Creation (Asmp. Moses 1:14; 12:4-7), so also the NT affirms that the Elect One (Luke 9:35; 23:35; cf. I Pet. 2:4) was purposed from the beginning: He was "destined [προεγνωσμένου] before the foundation of the world but was made manifest at the end of the times for your sake" (I Pet. 1:20; cf. John 17:24). Thus the saving activity of God, as manifested in Jesus Christ, is the expression of his eternal purpose, not a mere accommodation to historical circumstance. It should be emphasized that the language of foreknowledge and predestination belongs within the experience of God's lordship through Jesus Christ and therefore speaks "from faith to faith." When translated out of the situation of faith into abstract, logical categories, its meaning is inevitably diluted or falsified.

3. Foreknowledge and election. As indicated above, divine foreknowledge and divine election are intimately related. Indeed, the language of foreknowledge arises confessionally out of the awareness of God's call, whether that call is directed toward an individual or a people. This is clear, e.g., in the vocation of a prophet or an apostle. God's call not only summons a man to perform a task within the divine plan but also discloses the prevenience of the divine purpose in his personal history. Jeremiah doubtless came to his decision and responded to Yahweh's call out of an intense inner struggle. Nevertheless, from the vantage point of faith he perceived that Yahweh had meant for him to be a prophet all along. While he was still in his mother's womb, Yahweh knew him and appointed him for his task (Jer. 1:5). Similarly, Paul says, looking back from the time after his conversion, that he was set apart before he was born, called through divine grace (Gal. 1:15). In these instances the divine call prompts the awareness that the initiative is on God's side, that his purpose underlies every moment of one's life right from the beginning. Thus a psalmist confesses that Yahweh's eyes beheld him in his prenatal state, and that the days of his life were written in Yahweh's book even before they unfolded (Ps. 139:16).

God's people, too, share a common calling. Israel's election was grounded primarily in God's deliverance of his people from Egypt (Exod. 19:3-6; Jer. 2:2-7; Hos. 2:14-15—H 2:16-17; 11:1; Amos 3:1-2; 9:7; Mic. 6:4); but the traditions of the book of Genesis, in their present form, emphasize that even in advance of the Exodus and the Sinai revelation Yahweh was calling a people into existence and manifesting his prior purpose in the lives of the patriarchs. According to Second Isaiah, Yahweh's creation of Israel and his calling his people by name express the divine initiative and grace which lie behind and within Israel's history (Isa. 43:1). Furthermore, the Servant testifies:

> Yahweh called me from the womb,
> from the body of my mother he named my name
> (Isa. 49:1; cf. Jer. 1:5).

In the NT, Paul says of Israel, the "remnant, chosen by grace," that "God has not rejected his people whom he foreknew [προέγνω]" (Rom. 11:2; cf. vs. 5), and the prevenience of God's purpose is underscored by tracing his act of election back to the time when Jacob and Esau were still in the mother's womb (9:6-18).

In a special sense, however, the church is bound together by a divine calling. "Those whom he foreknew [προέγνω] he also predestined [προώρισεν] to be conformed to the image of his Son," writes Paul (Rom. 8:29). In this context (vss. 18-39) Paul expounds the doctrine of divine Providence in the most practical terms, at a time when Christians were facing difficult circumstances. Those "who are called according to his purpose" confess that in everything God works for good. Faith, therefore, is grounded solely upon God's initiative and grace, not upon changing human fortunes or the character of the world's response to the gospel. In this milieu of thought belong other NT affirmations: that the scattered exiles of the Christian dispersion are "chosen and destined by God" (κατὰ πρόγνωσιν Θεοῦ; I Pet. 1:2); that he "chose you from the beginning to be saved" (II Thess. 2:13); that God "chose us in [Christ] before the foundation of the world" and "destined [προορίσας] us in love to be his sons through Jesus Christ, according to the purpose of his will" (Eph. 1:4-5); that, although men of the Old Covenant lived by faith, "God had foreseen [προβλεψαμένου] something better for us" (Heb. 11: 40); and that the names of the faithful have been inscribed on the book of life from the foundation of the world (Rev. 17:8).

These statements about foreknowledge and predestination are not intended as expressions of pride or exclusiveness. On the contrary, they testify to God's initiative which precedes man's response, to the divine purpose which has priority over everything else. "What have you that you did not receive? If then you received it, why do you boast as if it were not a gift?" (I Cor. 4:7.) Thus salvation is traced back beyond anything human and temporal to the eternal purpose of God, which spans history from beginning to end and which has its center in Jesus Christ. Nor do these statements intend to destroy human freedom. On the contrary, the certainty that man's salvation is in God's hand frees the believer from worldly anxieties and enables him to affirm that "in all these things we are more than conquerors through him who loved us" (Rom. 8:37).

Bibliography. R. Bultmann in *TWNT,* I (1933), 688-719, especially 715-17; P. Minear, *Eyes of Faith* (1946), pp. 33-37; W. Eichrodt, *Theologie des Alten Testaments,* II (1948), 87-97; H. H. Rowley, *The Biblical Doctrine of Election* (1950); E. Stauffer, *NT Theology* (1955), pp. 51-55.

B. W. Anderson

FORERUNNER [πρόδρομος] (Wisd. Sol. 12:8; Heb. 6:20). A scout sent in advance of troops.

The word πρόδρομος is a technical military term in classical Greek for light-armed soldiers sent out as advance scouts. In Herodotus the term is used to designate the Scythian cavalry sent in advance of the regular army (IV.121-22, but simply as κήρυξ in I.60). In Alexander's army οἱ πρόδρομοι were a special corps of mounted guides (Arrian 1.12.7; Diodorus Siculus XVII.17).

The word can thus be understood in one of two senses: (*a*) as precursor or herald; (*b*) as scout—i.e., one who prepares the way. In the Wisdom passage the first meaning is clearly intended ("wasps as forerunners of [God's] army"), whereas in the Hebrews passage Christ is the forerunner who has entered heaven before us—i.e., the one who prepares the way (cf. John 14:2).

The OT notion of preparing the way for the one coming (Isa. 40:3-11; Mal. 3:1) is applied in the gospels to John the Baptist as forerunner of Jesus, though the term itself is never used (Matt. 11:10; Mark 1:2-8; Luke 7:27-28).

Bibliography. J. Kromayer and G. Veith, *Heerwesen und Kriegführung der Griechen und Römer* (*Handbuch der Altertumswissenschaft* IV, 3.2; 1928), pp. 53, 100.

J. W. Wevers

FORESAIL [ἀρτέμων, *apparently borrowed from* Lat. *artemon*] (Acts 27:40). A small sail above the mainsail; a topsail. *See* Ships and Sailing.

FORESKIN. *See* Circumcision.

FOREST. There are numerous OT references to forests which included shrubs, thickets, and trees, and the reports of travelers in Palestine during the period of Turkish control of the land and earlier indicate that trees were more common in Canaan in ancient times than at the present. *See also* Trees; Flora; Wood; House of the Forest of Lebanon.

The Hebrew word commonly rendered "forest" is יער (I Sam. 22:5; II Kings 19:23; Ps. 50:10; etc.). There is no way of determining with certainty the number of trees or the extent of such forests, but it is probable that they were much smaller and the wood less precious than that of the famous Cedars of Lebanon (I Kings 7:2; 10:17, 21; etc.). The same word is used in Isa. 21:13 to designate the "thickets in Arabia" (יער בערב; KJV "forest in Arabia"), on the supposition that there were no forests in Arabia. In Mic. 3:12 (cf. Jer. 26:19) the expression במות יער is to be understood as referring to a "wooded height" rather than to the "high places of the forest" (KJV), in view of the desolation which is predicted for Zion in the passage. יער is rendered "forest" (KJV "wood") in the following passages, where the context implies the presence of a number of trees; Deut. 19:5; Josh. 17:15, 18; I Sam. 14:25-26; II Sam. 18:6; Ps. 80:13; etc.

Other terms for collections of trees include חרש (II Chr. 27:4 KJV "forests"; RSV "wooded hills"; cf. I Sam. 23:15, where the KJV has "wood" and the RSV a proper name Horesh) and פרדס (Neh. 2:8), where a reference to the king's forest may indicate a royal preserve. The only NT reference to a "forest" occurs in Jas. 3:5, where the word ὕλη (KJV "matter"; mg. "wood") is used in a figure of speech that implies a recognition of the danger of forest fires (cf. Ps. 83:14—H 83:15).

Although forests in ancient Palestine were not extensive, the OT mentions them as being located in the hill country of Ephraim (Josh. 17:15, 18; II Sam. 18:6) and in the Negeb (Ezek. 20:46-47). It is probable that there were forests in Gilead, where trees are still numerous. Although there must have been trees on Mount Carmel in OT times, as there are today, the phrase יער כרמלו (II Kings 19:23; "its densest forest"; KJV "the forest of his Carmel"; cf. Isa. 37:24) is to be understood as referring to the thick forests of Lebanon (cf. reference to Lebanon in same vs.). Wild animals inhabited the forests (Ps. 80:13; Jer. 5:6; Amos 3:4; etc.) and made them places that were feared (II Sam. 18:8). According to I Sam. 22:5, David took refuge in the forest of Horeth (KJV "Hareth"), which has not been located with certainty, although the scene of David's activities as reported would indicate an area near the Philistine Plain.

W. L. Reed

FOREST OF LEBANON. *See* House of the Forest of Lebanon.

FORGE. *See* Furnace.

FORGETFULNESS, LAND OF [ארץ נשיה] (Ps. 88:12—H 88:13). A poetic term for Sheol which suggests that God (Ps. 88:5), perhaps like humanity (Ps. 31:12; Eccl. 9:5-6), forgets those who have died, and that the dead pass into utter oblivion. Contrast Job 14:21-22, in which the dead, however oblivious to the fortune of their descendants, retain some sort of psychological consciousness and experience great anguish about their own fate.

A plain of forgetfulness in the Greek Hades is mentioned by Plato (*Republic* X.621).

H. F. Beck

FORGIVENESS. In the Bible forgiveness is primarily the act of God by which he graciously takes away the obstacles or barriers which separate man from his presence, thus opening the way to reconciliation and fellowship. It is secondarily man's forgiveness of his neighbor, an aspect which becomes especially prominent in the teaching of Jesus.

A. Terminology
  1. In biblical Hebrew
  2. In LXX Greek
  3. In NT Greek

- B. In the OT
  - 1. God forgives
  - 2. The need of forgiveness
  - 3. The way of forgiveness
    - *a*. The covenant
    - *b*. The sacrificial cultus
    - *c*. Repentance
  - 4. The meaning of forgiveness
- C. In the NT
  - 1. John the Baptist
  - 2. The teaching of Jesus
    - *a*. Repentance and faith
    - *b*. Forgiveness in the new age
    - *c*. The centrality of the person of Jesus
  - 3. The apostolic church
  - 4. The meaning of forgiveness
- Bibliography

A. ***TERMINOLOGY.*** The idea of "forgiveness" is expressed by a number of different metaphors in Hebrew and Greek.

1. In biblical Hebrew. The metaphors of "sending away," "covering," "removing," and "wiping away" are used in Hebrew to express the notion of "forgiveness." The commonest term is the verb סלח, "to send away" (Lev. 4:20, 26; I Kings 8:30, 34; Pss. 86:5; 103:3). The verb כפר, "to cover," is especially frequent in the priestly tradition and expresses the idea of "atonement" or "propitiation" (Exod. 29:36; 30:10; Lev. 8:15; 16:20; Ezek. 43:20; 45:20). Other expressions are: the verbs פחה, "to wipe away" (Ps. 51:1, 7; Isa. 43:25; 44:22); נשא, "to lift away, remove" (Gen. 50:17; Ps. 32:5); and כסה, "to cover" (Neh. 4:5; Pss. 32:1; 85:2). The noun סליחה uses the picture of "removal" to express "forgiveness" (Ps. 130:4; Dan. 9:9).

2. In LXX Greek. The commonest term for "forgiveness" in the LXX is ἀφίημι, "to send away," which is used to translate כפר, נשא, and סלח. כפר is also rendered by ἱλάσομαι, "to be merciful." Εὐιλατεύω, "to be merciful," translates both נשא and סלח. סלח is also translated by ἵλεως. כסה is rendered by καλύπτω and ἐπικαλύπτω, both meaning "to cover," and by κρύπτω, "to conceal." Ἐξαλείφω, "to wipe away," translates מחה; and the noun ἱλασμός, "atonement," is used to translate סליחה.

3. In NT Greek. The commonest words for "forgiveness" in the NT are the verb ἀφίημι, "to send away" (Matt. 6:12, 14-15; 9:2; 12:31; etc.), and the noun ἄφεσις, "sending away" (Mark 3:29; Luke 3:3; 24:47; Acts 2:38), used both of God's forgiveness of sin and of man's forgiveness of his neighbor's offenses. The verb ἀπολύω, "to loose away," is used twice in Luke 6:37. The verb χαρίζομαι, "to be gracious to" (Luke 7:43; II Cor. 2:7, 10; Col. 2:13), stresses the generosity and graciousness of forgiveness. The noun πάρεσις, "a passing over," is used of "forgiveness" in Rom. 3:25. Ἐπικαλύπτω (Rom. 4:7) and καλύπτω (Jas. 5:20; I Pet. 4:8) both mean "to cover."

B. ***IN THE OT.*** Forgiveness is an expression of the religious relationship between God and man. God is Creator, Sustainer, and Judge of all the earth. Man is his creature, lives by his bounty, but is separated from him by his sin, and thus needs forgiveness, for he cannot live under God's wrath. When sins are forgiven, reconciliation is possible and man may experience again the blessings of fellowship with God.

1. God forgives. Israel has encountered a God of power. He is Lord of all the earth, and all that exists is the result of his creative will. He sends rain and harvest, grants strength and health to his creatures, and assigns the conditions of their existence (II Sam. 22:32-42; Job 26:6-14; Ps. 65:6-8). But where sin separates man from God, man does not experience God's blessing. Even though God's gifts sustain him, he does not have peace and fulness of life until through forgiveness God's blessing can rest on him (Ps. 32:3-4).

The God of Israel is the Holy One. He cannot endure evil or impurity. He is a jealous God and will not tolerate violation of his law (Lev. 11:44-45; 20:7; Deut. 7:6). But holiness is necessary for harmonious human life, and man thus needs the holiness of God in his life. Man cannot live without God, and as sinner he cannot approach God. Only the removal of sin can enable man to have a life of integrity and wholeness.

But Israel's God is also merciful (I Kings 8:23; Ps. 13:5; Isa. 60:10). He has no pleasure in the death of a sinner. Through the covenant he offers mercy to his people, granting the assurance of his favor through the cultus he has established. In spite of man's backsliding and unfaithfulness the covenant mediates the mercy of God, because it is based, not on the achievements of man, but upon the righteousness and reliability of God (I Kings 8:30; Ps. 130:3-4; Jer. 31:34).

2. The need of forgiveness. Living in confrontation with a holy God, man knows himself as a sinner. SIN is a fundamental distortion of human personality; its repercussions in human life are manifold and devastating. The OT has several words for "sin," expressing different aspects of man's separation from God. Sin is disobedience, straying from the will of God (Pss. 32:1, 5; 51:2); it is trespass or wickedness, an informed and deliberate violation of the law (Isa. 53:8; 59:20; Mic. 3:8); it is perversity, the petulant rebelliousness of the human spirit; it is iniquity or vanity, the pathetic emptiness of the creature trying to wage war with his Creator (Pss. 90:8; 103:3; Isa. 43:24; Amos 3:2); it is bondage:

> Their deeds do not permit them
> to return to their God.
> For the spirit of harlotry is within them,
> and they know not the LORD
> (Hos. 5:4).

As a consequence of sin man has lost fellowship with God. He is cut off from the source of life; his soul is crippled, the powers and effectiveness of the human person reduced. He lives under God's wrath, filled with anxieties and fears and out of harmony with nature and with his fellow men. Whereas God created him for a life of peace and harmony, he now lives in frustration.

Forgiveness is the removal of the barriers between God and man. Sin is covered, expiated; it is sent away, removed, wiped away; God has cast it behind his back (Isa. 38:17), or into the depths of the sea (Mic. 7:19). Forgiveness renews fellowship with God, who is the source of all holiness and life. His mercy and favor replace his wrath and judgment, so that the entire environment of human life has new possibilities. The created world is sanctified to man again, and new relationships become possible in community and family. Terror of conscience and dread of judgment give way to peace. Man's soul is healed, the powers of his personality restored and strengthened.

3. The way of forgiveness. ***a. The covenant.*** Israel's assurance that sin can be forgiven rests ultimately upon its COVENANT relationship to God. Yahweh has made himself known as the one, the unique, God. Unlike the gods of the nations, Yahweh the Creator is Lord of nature, Lord of history, the God who reveals his will and the God who manifests his love in choosing for himself a people. Israel's awareness of its election gradually transforms its religion and theology, as the implications of the covenant relationship are worked out. Israel's history is the struggle between the naturalistic and prophetic understanding of religion. The naïve and naturalistic relationship between God and people prevalent in ancient Semitic religion gives way before the knowledge of Yahweh as the transcendent One. He cannot be identified with his people, nor is his fate linked with that of his people. As Lord of the world he deals with Israel, not because he needs them, but because it is his nature to be merciful and gracious. Forgiveness is not something men gain by punctilious performance of the proper rituals; it is the free and sovereign gift of the loving God.

b. The sacrificial cultus. The chief instrument for the realization of forgiveness is the sacrificial cultus. As in all the religions of the ancient world, sacrifice (*see* SACRIFICE AND OFFERINGS) is a part of the common life of the OT world. But Israel's understanding of sacrifice gradually changes as it becomes aware of the implications of the covenant. This understanding is won through conflict, a constant battle on shifting fronts between prophetic religion and the various attempts to assimilate the religion of Israel to that of surrounding nations.

Participation in sacrifice was a dramatic-liturgical expression of the worship of God. The various actions of the ritual and ceremony enabled the worshiper to express his movement toward God and experience the gracious action of God toward him. His approach to the altar was an expression of his awareness of need, his sense of guilt and unworthiness, and his realization that his life could achieve wholeness only in the presence of God. As he placed his hands upon his sacrifice, he symbolized his identification with his gift, which, at least in the early days of Israel's history, was a product of his own care and toil. This was the acknowledging that God's claim involved his total being and that in offering his gift he was offering himself. The killing of the sacrifice and the sprinkling of the blood were the offering up of life, and, by previous identification, the life of the worshiper. The insistence on an unblemished sacrifice emphasized that worship is the offering of the best and most precious, life itself, to God. The burning of a portion of the offering symbolized the transformation of the gift and its acceptance by God. This emphasized the fact that sacrifice is not a barter transaction in which God forgives for a consideration, but that sacrifice is effectual because God in his mercy chooses to accept the offering as the offering of the worshiper's life. Sacrifice is not the purchase of forgiveness but the claiming of God's promise of mercy. The sacrificial meal expresses the restoration of fellowship between God and man. Man shares in the most intimate expression of friendship, the fellowship meal. At this climax of the ritual act the guilt-burdened worshiper is assured of pardon and experiences the restoration of wholeness to life. Admission once again to God's presence is the reintegration of man in the fellowship of the elect nation, the sanctification of the natural world created by God, and the resultant recovery of soundness of life.

The OT itself makes it clear that the prophetic understanding of the covenant religion did not always prevail in Israel. Nevertheless the Israelite, living as he did in an environment permeated with the atmosphere of sacrifice, would find it more significant than can we in our attempts to understand it from without by historical and theological analysis. Religious realities can be communicated by other than verbal symbols, and the sacrificial cultus was a significant agent in the tradition of the religion of Israel. *See* REDEMPTION.

c. Repentance. The third element in the realization of forgiveness is REPENTANCE. Yahweh reveals himself as Person and deals with his people as persons. The relation to God cannot be merely objective or impersonal. The prophetic movement ceaselessly emphasizes the demand for genuine repentance and amendment of life. The prophets protest vehemently against the mechanical and formalistic performance of sacrifice:

> For I desire steadfast love and not sacrifice,
> the knowledge of God, rather than burnt offerings
> (Hos. 6:6).

The cultus is not a device to purchase from God a license to continue a self-centered existence; it is the divinely given means for the sanctification of his people. "You shall . . . be holy, for I am holy" (Lev. 11:44-45). The purpose of sacrifice is not to acquire peace of mind inexpensively, but to provide the means for Israel's self-giving to Yahweh and dedication to his purposes. The prophetic insistence on repentance is not so much concerned with sorrow and contrition as with amendment of life, restitution, and righteousness:

> "Rend your hearts and not your garments."
> Return to the LORD, your God
> (Joel 2:13);

> Is not this the fast that I choose:
> to loose the bonds of wickedness,
> to undo the thongs of the yoke?
> . . . .
> Is it not to share your bread with the hungry,
> and bring the homeless poor into your house?
> (Isa. 58:6-7).

3. The meaning of forgiveness. The focus of forgiveness in the OT is the renewal of HOLINESS. This is a comprehensive notion with several aspects. It is, first, the removal of that which separates man from God, the source of holiness. Forgiveness is the taking away of barriers of sin and guilt in order that man may again enter the divine presence and experience God's blessing in his life.

Secondly, it is the restoration of divine favor and the overcoming of God's wrath. Man has been made to live in God and in community with his fellow man. Sin destroys both relationships. Forgiveness restores fellowship and makes possible harmonious relationships with the fellow man.

Thirdly, holiness is the healing of the soul, the recovery of strength and power in human life. The energies perverted or rendered powerless by sin can again be put to productive uses:

When I declared not my sin, my body wasted away.
. . . .
My strength was dried up as by the heat of summer
(Ps. 32:3-4).

But forgiveness restores strength:

No inhabitant will say, "I am sick";
the people who dwell there will be forgiven their iniquity
(Isa. 33:24).

A fourth emphasis comes to the fore in the exilic and postexilic periods: the stress on forgiveness as opening the way to holiness. With the temple in ruins and the people in exile, the Torah becomes more prominent and leads to a discipline in individual and personal holiness in which the ethical element is very prominent. There is an increased stress upon the holiness and transcendence of God, and a corresponding deepening of the sense of human sin and guilt. During this period the sense of forgiveness as restoration of integrity weakens, the ethical and juridical elements become more prominent, and forgiveness is seen more narrowly as the removal of guilt.

C. *IN THE NT.* Rabbinic Judaism was zealous to hold the prophetic faith of Israel as it had come down in the tradition of the elders. There was deep reverence for God and great concern for the proper exposition of his will as revealed in the Torah. An earnest seeking for holiness accompanied strenuous religious discipline. The temple was venerated as the abode of the divine name, the emblem of God's presence in Israel, and the ground for assurance of his favor to the covenant people. For communities outside Jerusalem the synagogue became the center of religious life, increasing the prominence of the Torah for the pious and strengthening the tendency to think of forgiveness in primarily ethical and legal terms.

Another potent influence in the religious life of NT times was APOCALYPTICISM. The long-frustrated yearning for the re-establishment of the Davidic kingdom found an outlet in hopes for the intervention of God in a dramatic or even catastrophic manner. Ordinary historical and political developments offered little hope for the establishment of the kingdom; eyes were raised to heaven in hopes of the action of God himself. The effect of apocalyptic thought was to lessen confidence in human powers; even genuine repentance is beyond human abilities. Man's only hope is that God will grant him the possibility of repentance as well as forgiveness.

1. John the Baptist. The work of John the Baptist introduced new elements into the religious situation. He proclaimed a BAPTISM of repentance unto remission of sins, and pointed to one to come who should bring the baptism of the Holy Spirit (Mark 1:4, 8). John's preaching and baptism aroused great interest, first because the voice of prophecy (*see* PROPHET) was heard in Israel again after centuries of silence. The spontaneity and unpredictability of the prophetic came to disturb the well-regulated system of Torah, tradition, and cultus. Secondly, his baptism was a striking innovation, combining the old prophetic call to repentance with the promise of forgiveness of sins through baptism. Its implied challenge to the cultus of the temple at Jerusalem was not lost upon the priestly authorities, who demanded that John present his credentials (John 1:19-27). If he were not the Messiah, or Elijah, or the prophet, by what authority did he baptize people and promise them forgiveness? Thirdly, John pointed to the imminent fulfilment of age-old messianic hopes, asserting that God's anointed one was in their midst and that the kingdom was at hand. His baptism was a preparation for the Messiah, a part of the purification of Israel promised before the great and terrible Day of the Lord (Matt. 3:11-12; Luke 3:15-17). John's imprisonment and death put an end to his public activity, but his connection of forgiveness with repentance and baptism continued to be significant in the work of Jesus of Nazareth.

2. The teaching of Jesus. After baptism at the hands of John, Jesus went about as a teacher and was accepted by many of his contemporaries as rabbi and prophet. His teaching very soon burst out of rabbinic and prophetic categories, however, and aroused strong opposition, especially among the religious authorities.

a. Repentance and faith. John the Baptist gave his demand for repentance a strongly ethical content with his insistence on fruits worthy of repentance, his exhortations to honesty and generosity, and his counsel that soldiers eschew robbery and extortion (Luke 3:10-14). Jesus began his ministry with words strikingly similar to John's preaching: "The time is fulfilled, and the kingdom of God is at hand; repent, and believe in the gospel" (Mark 1:15). There is the same emphasis on repentance, on eschatological fulfilment and the kingly rule of God; new is the coupling of repentance and belief in the gospel.

Jesus deepens the prophetic demand for repentance. He whets the cutting edge of the law by his insistence on inner purity and sincerity. The angry word and the lustful glance put man under judgment. The law of God requires not only outward conformity, but also a deep and complete correspondence to God's holy will. By his stress on the necessity of a forgiving spirit, he insists that repentance go beyond sorrow for sin and issue in a radical reorientation of personality. He repeatedly asserts that man cannot be forgiven if he will not forgive (Matt. 6:14; Mark 11:25; Luke 11:4; 17:3). The parable of the unmerciful servant ends on a disquieting note as the unforgiving servant is delivered over to torture: "So also my heavenly Father will do to every one of you, if you do not forgive your brother from your heart" (Matt. 18:23-35).

b. Forgiveness in the new age. Jesus also broadens the meaning of repentance. The prophets were aware that the repentance demanded by God lay beyond human powers, and therefore looked forward to the day when God would give his Spirit to men (Jer. 31; Ezek. 18; 37). Jesus announced that the significant time was fulfilled and God's royal rule was at hand. His miracles are signs of the powers of the messianic age at work in him (Mark 3:27; Luke 11:20-22). The parallel passage in Matthew makes the reference to the Spirit explicit: "If it is by the Spirit of God that I cast out demons, then the kingdom of God has come upon you" (Matt. 12:28). Repentance has been broadened to include faith, which is man's response to the manifestation of God's kingly rule. He who responds to the preaching of Jesus: "Repent, and believe in the gospel," lives in the new age, in which the rule of Satan is overcome and the reign of God established. Jesus' teaching concerning forgiveness must be seen in relation to the eschatological kingdom. In the new age the sinner not only is forgiven; he also shares in the life and power of God and is able to forgive others. One of the distinctive elements in the teaching of Jesus is his stress on the forgiveness of the brother. In the new age forgiveness of sin is conditional not only upon repentance and faith, but also upon forgiveness of others. This finds expression in the Lord's Prayer, the parable of the unmerciful servant, and other sayings, and in the example of Jesus in the prayer of forgiveness from the cross (Luke 23:34). It is carried a step further in response to Peter's question about frequency of forgiveness. Peter suggests the rabbinic figure: "As many as seven times?" But Jesus replies: "I do not say to you seven times, but seventy times seven" (Matt. 18:21-22; cf. Luke 17:3).

In the teaching of Jesus the meaning of the word "forgiveness" retains its OT content: the removal of barriers between man and God or man and man. But he relates the term to new and richer contexts—to a broader and deeper conception of repentance, to the fact of the messianic kingdom, and to a new ethics, the ethics of the new age. To do justice to his teaching, the word "forgiveness" must take on a heavier cargo of meaning, as it has done in theology since the Reformation, or new vocabularies must be prepared to express the new content, as was done in the apostolic church. The fact that "forgiveness" does not occur in the parables of the prodigal son (Luke 15) or the Pharisee and the tax collector (Luke 18:10-14) suggests that Jesus himself found the term in its rabbinic meaning too narrow for his purposes.

c. The centrality of the person of Jesus. However creative Jesus was as teacher of repentance and a new ethics, or as prophet of the new age, his most significant contribution comes through his relation of forgiveness to his own person and mission. Rabbinic theology, with its devotion to Torah and tradition, could probably have made room for the deepened understanding of repentance and ethics, but the preaching of the new age and its attendant interpretation of the OT proved shocking and offensive. Jesus' polemical attitude toward the tradition of the elders was offensive enough, but his interpretation of the OT with himself as the center of it seemed not merely shocking, but blasphemous.

For Jewish theology it was quite clear that God alone could forgive sins, and that he did so through the covenant, with its Torah and cultus. When a paralytic was carried to him, Jesus healed him, asserting that he had authority on earth to forgive sins. In giving a theological diagnosis to what seems primarily a medical problem, Jesus reasserted an interpretation of forgiveness which is prominent in the OT and identified it with his own career. Forgiveness removes the barriers caused by sin and thus opens the way to recovery of wholeness of personality, of health and integrity. Thus Jesus made the claim of authority to forgive, a claim which sounded presumptuous to his pious contemporaries, and backed up his claim with an act of the messianic age which showed before their eyes the restoration of soundness and health.

Another example of Jesus' radical reinterpretation of the OT is his relation to the temple. As the symbol of the abiding presence of God, it had an exalted place in Jewish religion. Jesus dared to put himself above the temple: "I tell you, something greater than the temple is here" (Matt. 12:6). In cleansing the temple Jesus either acted in disregard of law or asserted propietary authority. How he himself understood it is suggested by his quotation of the prophetic statement: "It is written, 'My house shall be called a house of prayer'; but you make it a den of robbers" (Matt. 21:13). At his trial it was charged: "We heard him say, 'I will destroy this temple that is made with hands, and in three days I will build another, not made with hands' " (Mark 14:58). The Fourth Evangelist regarded this as a true saying of Jesus and interprets it as a reference to his death and resurrection (John 2:21).

Another aspect of Jesus' reinterpretation of the OT is his identification of his life and death with the sacrificial cultus. At the Last Supper he interpreted his death as the "blood of the covenant, which is poured out for many for the forgiveness of sins" (Matt. 26: 28). Even if the last phrase is an editorial addition by the evangelist, the words "covenant" and "blood" indicate the use of sacrificial language. His death could be interpreted as the unfortunate result of several accidental factors such as Jewish malice, Pilate's cowardice, the uncertain temper of a festival crowd. It is here understood as an act of God similar to his dealings with Israel at the Exodus, the establishment of a new covenant sealed by a sacrifice offered not by men but by God.

That Jesus understood his work as the act of God is shown also by his words: "Whoever blasphemes against the Holy Spirit never has forgiveness, but is guilty of an eternal sin" (Mark 3:29). The words are his response to the scribes who asserted that his exorcism of demons was a manifestation of Satanic power. The sin is unforgivable, not because it is too shocking or heinous for God to forgive, but because it labels as diabolical the deeds by which God acts in his anointed servant. This is a perilous misuse of theology: in the name of piety to reject the approach of the merciful God. On Jesus' conception of his own nature and work, *see also* JESUS § F5.

3. The apostolic church. Jesus' interpretation of the OT is the starting point of the religious thought of the early church. The centrality of Jesus is seen in the use of the theology of the name of God with reference to the Messiah. As the summary term for God's self-manifestation to Israel, the word "name" emphasizes that the holy and transcendent God has revealed himself in the covenant. The apostles boldly use this language of Jesus: "There is no other name under heaven given among men by which we must be saved" (Acts 4:12; cf. 2:38; 10:43). He who cannot dwell in temples made by man makes his abode among men in Jesus of Nazareth.

Forgiveness of sins is still spoken of in the language of sacrifice, but the cultus has given way to the offering of Christ. His death is the sacrifice which removes sin: "Through this man forgiveness of sins is proclaimed to you" (Acts 13:38). "We are now justified by his blood" (Rom. 5:9), "whom God put forward as an expiation in his blood" (3:25). We have been ransomed "with the precious blood of Christ" (I Pet. 1:19). The sacrificial cultus is now seen in perspective, not as an end in itself but as a prophetic foreshadowing of the great offering made by God in Jesus Christ.

Repentance and faith remain conditions of forgiveness. They are related to the covenant, the new covenant established by the Messiah. But where Jesus uses the language of forgiveness even though he seems to find it inadequate, the apostolic church coins new vocabulary to expound the meaning of the new covenant. Paul speaks seldom of forgiveness of sins but often of being ἐν χριστῷ. The man of the new age is in Christ through baptism, which unites him to Christ in his death and his resurrection (Rom. 6:3-4). He prefers the verb χαρίζομαι, "to be gracious," perhaps because it stresses the generous and personal character of God's action and avoids the juridical associations of ἀφίημι. "Membership in the body of Christ," the "new man" or "new humanity," "RECONCILIATION," and "JUSTIFICATION" are other metaphors expressing the new state of things issuing from forgiveness of sins.

The Johannine writings similarly seldom use the word "forgiveness" (there is but one occurrence of the word in the Fourth Gospel), although allusions to temple and sacrifice are frequent. The meaning of discipleship is expressed rather by the term "abiding in Christ" or images such as the vine and the branches, which stress the intimacy of the relationship and the complete dependence of disciple upon the Lord.

4. The meaning of forgiveness. Although the NT has a variety of "theologies," it presents basically the same understanding of forgiveness as the OT. It is the covering or removal of sins, transgressions, iniquity, or impiety, thus making reconciliation possible. The richness and range of the OT understanding were narrowed and attenuated in the postexilic and rabbinic developments, where forgiveness was thought of in primarily ethical and juridical terms. But in the teaching of Jesus the horizons broaden again through the prophetic realism of his teaching on sin and repentance, the union of repentance with faith in the Messiah, and the relating of the whole question of forgiveness to the fulfilment of the messianic kingdom. While the term "forgiveness" retains lexically its first-century rabbinic value, it is put in richer contexts, and given new theological referents in its use.

Sin has multiple consequences in human life, involving rebellion against God, guilt, and bondage in sin. Forgiveness of sins has also various aspects, and the NT writers differ in their choice of emphasis. The Synoptic gospels lay most stress on Christ's conflict with the powers holding mankind in thrall. Jesus is the mighty one who despoils Satan's household, liberating the captives, healing the sick, cleansing lepers, restoring sight to the blind, and even giving life to the dead. Forgiveness appears here in the context of wholeness of life; to the paralytic, e.g., it meant recovery of ability to walk, to be fully a human being again. What he experienced through the power working in Jesus will be the eschatological gift of God to all men who accept his reign. This element is also prominent in the Fourth Gospel and the writings of Paul (Rom. 6; Eph. 1:7; Col. 1:14).

Where sin as guilt is stressed, forgiveness appears in the context of atonement or expiation. Here it is seen as release from guilt, deliverance from anxiety and a burdened conscience, and recovery of peace with God. This is the chief thrust of the Letter to the Hebrews, and is found also in the letters of Paul, I Peter, and the Johannine letters. The language of sacrifice is present not only in such expressions as "Lamb of God," "expiation," and "blood," but also less directly in allusions to Christ's death "for us" and "for the ungodly."

Where sin is thought of as rebellion, forgiveness is given the context of reconciliation, and expresses the removal of enmity between man and God. Man's proud and rebellious spirit has turned him away from God, and only through acquiring a new heart and spirit can he find his way back to the source of life. What is impossible for man is possible to God, who offers his Son and sends his Spirit. Forgiveness makes possible the sinner's adoption as son, the renewal of fellowship with the Father, access to the renewing powers of the new age.

Bibliography. W. Eichrodt, *Theologie des ATs,* III (1935), 81-148; E. B. Redlich, *The Forgiveness of Sins* (1937); J. Pedersen, *Israel,* IV (1940), 299-375; V. Taylor, *Forgiveness and Reconciliation* (1941), pp. 1-28; A. Richardson, *An Introduction to the Theology of the NT* (1958), pp. 348-50. W. A. QUANBECK

FORK. A translation of:

a) מזלג (I Sam. 2:13-14; KJV FLESHHOOK), a three-pronged sacrificial instrument; מזלגה (Exod. 27:3; 38:3; Num. 4:14; I Chr. 28:17; II Chr. 4:16; KJV FLESHHOOK), a sacrificial implement belonging to the altar in the tabernacle and to the temple.

b) מזרה (Isa. 30:24; figuratively in Jer. 15:7; KJV FAN), a pitchfork, probably with six prongs, used in winnowing.

c) Πτύον (Matt. 3:12 = Luke 3:17; KJV FAN), winnowing fork.

The translation "fork" is used in the KJV of I Sam. 13:21, but the Hebrew of this verse is obscure and has been the subject of various interpretations.

Forks were among the implements belonging to the altar of the tabernacle (Exod. 27:3; 38:3; Num. 4:14); these and other implements were made of bronze by Bezalel (Exod. 38:3; cf. vs. 23). Forks were also used by the priests at Shiloh in taking their portions from the pot in which the sacrifice was boiled (I Sam. 2:13-14). Similar sacrificial implements, to be made of gold, were ordered by David for the proposed Jerusalem temple (I Chr. 28:17). According to II Chr. 4:16, HURAM-ABI made them of burnished bronze. *See* SACRIFICE AND OFFERINGS.

WINNOWING with a fork (Isa. 30:24) is referred to figuratively in Jer. 15:7; Matt. 3:12 (=Luke 3:17) to suggest the judgment and chastisement of people.

H. F. BECK

FORM CRITICISM. Form criticism, also known as form history (*Formgeschichte*), as category criticism (*Gattungsgeschichte*), and as tradition analysis, is a method of dealing with folk material, whether written down or not, which for some part of its existence was oral tradition. While patches of such material quite often occur within works properly called "literary," this method intrinsically applies to subliterary "small literature," "folk literature."

1. The method in general
2. The method as applied to the Bible
3. Dibelius' "forms"
4. Dibelius and Bultmann

1. The method in general. The fundamental insight underlying this method is the recognition that folk memory—the vehicle of tradition—operates with small units, often no larger than a single couplet of poetry. Delimitation of these irreducible units of primitive tradition is the first task. But it soon becomes apparent, no matter what "folk's" tradition be under scrutiny, that similar units reappear—similar not so much in content as in structure, length, and tendency. In other words, a given folk at a given time is likely to use a limited number of types of unit, into one or another of which by an instinctive mnemonic economy it pours the content of each particular tradition. These several types are the "forms" or "categories" from which form criticism gets its name.

But such unit types grow out of the everyday life of their particular community: funerals, weddings, victories, defeats, worship and its liturgical acts, instruction, missionary propaganda, etc. These and the like are the "seat in life" of each kind of tradition unit. Tradition is never preserved for its own sake with conscious antiquarian intent, but only because some need or interest of the community presses it into service. In such service it stays alive as oral tradition as long as that practical interest remains alive.

The forms not only were the expression of the interests that kept specific traditions alive but also are the best available key for isolating and defining the specific interest in a given case. For many examples of a single form may be studied side by side until they disclose the relatively pure form among less pure variants, hybrid forms, and sometimes pseudo forms (epigonic imitations of the once living forms). That is to say, there is a kind of literary history here. Not, of course, in the sense of author-fathered literature, for the irrecoverable "author" of a specific tradition performed his function precisely by effacing himself and acting only as spokesman of the group in pouring their material into a living mold—one of the group-created, familiar, life-related "forms." But the forms themselves, apart from their content, have a history which in broad outline can be discerned—a preliterary literary history. This is the justification for speaking of "form *history*."

2. The method as applied to the Bible. Up to this point the Bible has been intentionally unmentioned. Insofar as the Bible contains tradition that once was oral (e.g., Proverbs, Genesis, the Synoptics, James), it invites treatment by this method; indeed, the name of the method was evolved within the biblical wing of its wide field—but only after it had been practiced nearly a century in secular folklore (a name which also was invented long after [1846] a new science had begun to study it). Jakob and Wilhelm Grimm were the scientific pioneers (from *ca.* 1812 onward). They already recognized and defined the differences between folk tale, myth, saga, and legend; they have had a host of successors in many lands. The method could and should be applied to many other fields—e.g., nursery rhymes, political jingles, and college cheers.

The scholar who most fertilely applied form criticism to the Bible was Hermann Gunkel (1862-1932; *see* BIBLICAL CRITICISM). He acknowledges a great debt to the genius of Herder and recognizes predecessors in Wellhausen and Norden, but it was Gunkel himself who conceived and named almost all the technical concepts which in English are better known through the works of his NT pupils. His essay on "Grundprobleme der israelitischen Literaturgeschichte" in *Deutsche Literaturzeitung,* XXVII (1906), cols. 1797-1800, 1861-66 (also in his *Reden und Aufsätze,* 1913), is a veritable mine in this respect.

After the wide acceptance of the two-source theory (*ca.* 1890) the literary investigation of the Synoptics was at a stalemate (*see* SYNOPTIC PROBLEM). The real problem was oral tradition. But how could one deal intellectually in any valid way with the oral tradition lying behind the accepted sources? A remarkably unanimous answer was proposed by three nearly independent and almost simultaneous works in the years 1919-21: Apply the folkloristic methods already so fruitfully used by Gunkel on the OT to the Synoptic tradition. Karl Ludwig Schmidt, developing then unpublished insights of his teacher, Martin Dibelius, showed (*Rahmen der Geschichte Jesu,* 1919) how casual and arbitrary the order of pericopes is in Mark, the oldest connected narrative source. A few months earlier in the same year Dibelius had published *Die Formgeschichte des Evangeliums,* giving the method its permanent name. In this small programmatic brochure Dibelius dealt only with such tradition units (pericopes) as seemed to him to fall particularly clearly into his five "forms": paradigm, *Novelle,* legend, parenesis, and myth.

3. Dibelius' "forms." Of these the paradigm turned out to be the most important—those concise, self-contained, and edifying (not "worldly") stories concentrated about a striking saying or deed of Jesus. The motive power which kept them alive and bore them along in tradition, he believed, was their continued use in Christian preaching. It is in stories of this form that we must seek for our surest information about Jesus of Nazareth. Next in importance are the exhortatory words preserved in the form he called parenesis; these owe their survival to the need of the Christian community for words of practical guidance in personal ethics and community self-discipline. But here tradition was so sensitive to the current need of the community that there is no guarantee that all the parenetic tradition goes back to Jesus himself. The *novelle,* typically relating some wonder and offering details that satisfy "worldly" curiosity, is much more

Hellenistic; and while some examples may contain historical reminiscence, they also contain floating stories transferred to Jesus (e.g., the Gerasene demoniac [Mark 5 and parallels]). The essence of legend (e.g., the twelve-year-old Jesus in the temple [Luke 2]) is not its unhistoricity (it can contain sound history), but its tendency to cast its religious hero into a rather stereotyped mold of the man of piety, whether the historical person fitted that mold or not. Even myth need not be devoid of history, but its interest is never in history but in the theological idea which it clothes with narrative form.

4. Dibelius and Bultmann. The most ambitious and controversial of the three works mentioned is Rudolf Bultmann's *Geschichte der synoptischen Tradition* (1921), which systematically sorts the entire material of all the Synoptics into a many-branched classification whose classes often overlap. Two of Bultmann's categories, apothegm and wonder tale, are closely analogous to Dibelius' paradigm and *novelle,* and the two very largely agree in assigning the passages selected by Dibelius to corresponding categories. But Bultmann is particularly interested in distinguishing between Palestinian and Hellenistic tradition, recognizing that only within the former can probable historical information about Jesus be found. The fact, however, that Bultmann declines on principle to treat "legend" and "historical narrative" separately (because they are so closely related and their mutual boundaries so little marked) leads many to regard Bultmann as almost totally skeptical about our present ability to know the historical Jesus. This is not an adequate impression. His *Jesus and the Word* and *NT Theology* indicate that he is willing to find more of historical fact within legendary material than was indicated in the 1921 book.

Whoever takes form criticism seriously finds that he can still write and teach on "deeds and words of Jesus" but not on "life and teaching of Jesus," for the latter would demand a knowledge of connection and development which had already been lost before Mark was ever written. In the eyes of the form critics and their disciples, those who continue to write "Lives" of Jesus are only adding to the already crowded shelf of the "Jesus novel." K. GROBEL

FORNICATION [זנונים, זנות; πορνεία; *etc.*]. The practice of sexual immorality and harlotry; hence a symbol for idolatry. In the OT it is equivalent to "playing the harlot" (Gen. 38:24; Deut. 22:21; etc.; *see* PROSTITUTION). In the NT the words for "fornication," "to practice fornication," etc., refer to every kind of sexual intercourse outside marriage.

See also ADULTERY. O. J. BAAB

FORT. KJV translation of words which the RSV translates "siegework," "siege wall," "fortress," "stronghold," "hill/high fortifications." *See* FORTRESS; FORTIFICATION; WAR, METHODS OF.

FORTIFICATION. The erection of artificial defense works around a city or camp. These at first merely improve the natural strength of the location, but become more complex in response to improved siege methods. The basic fortification is an encircling wall or walls, strengthened by towers and defended externally by a dry moat or a beaten-earth rampart.

Courtesy of William L. Reed

20. Fortifications of ancient Jericho on the W side of the city, as viewed from the W

Potential weak spots, such as gateways, pose special problems, as does the frequent necessity of bringing in a water supply from outside the city. Government buildings, situated on the highest part of the site, were usually guarded by secondary, inner defenses.

See also CITY; WALL; GATE; TOWER; WATER WORKS; WEAPONS AND IMPLEMENTS OF WAR; WAR, METHODS OF. Fig. FOR 20. L. E. TOOMBS

FORTRESS [מבצר, מצורה, משגב, מעוז, בירה, בירניה]. Alternately: STRONGHOLD; CITADEL; PALACE; DEFENSE; CASTLE; FORT; FORCE. A fortified city, a fortified place, a secure height or refuge, a stronghold, a citadel. In Pss. 59:9, 16-17; 62:2; 94:22 ("stronghold"); Isa. 33:16 (משגב; KJV "defense"), the fortress is symbolic of God as a protection and refuge. For the fortified city, *see* CITY § 2*b*.

The phrase "god of fortresses" (אלה מעזים) in Dan. 11:38 is ambiguous. The common explanation is that it means the Roman god Jupiter Capitolinus, for whom Antiochus IV promised to build a magnificent temple in Antioch (Livy XLI.20). Possibly, however, in the context of Dan. 11:36-39 it refers satirically to Antiochus himself, whose assumed title, "Epiphanes," means "god manifest," and whose rapid military successes made him a dread enemy to any besieged fortress (Dan. 11:24, 31, 39; I Macc. 1:19, 33; Jos. Antiq. XII.viii.3-4; ix.1). J. A. SANDERS

FORTUNATUS fôr'chə nā'təs [Φορτουνᾶτος; Lat. *Fortunatus; found in papyri and inscriptions in both* Greek *and* Latin *forms*]. A prominent member of the earliest Christian church at Corinth, mentioned in I Cor. 16:17 (in some MSS 16:15) as being with Paul in Ephesus when he wrote this letter; STEPHANAS and ACHAICUS were other Corinthians with him. The subscription to I Corinthians in the Textus Receptus names these three men as the bearers of the letter to Corinth; it is also conceivable that they brought to Paul the letter mentioned in I Cor. 5:9. The Fortunatus named in I Clem. 65:1 could hardly be identical with the one in Corinth, not only because of the lapse of five or six decades between the two works, but also since the Fortunatus of I Clement was from Rome, where this name was very common. F. W. GINGRICH

FORTUNE. *See* DESTINY.

FORTY. *See* NUMBER.

FORUM [φόρον, *from* Lat. *forum*]. The open place or market of a town, or the settlement itself.

FORUM OF APPIUS ăp'ĭ əs [τὸ 'Αππίου Φόρον] (Acts 28:15). A station on the Appian Way through which Paul passed as he was going to Rome.

The Forum of Appius was forty-three miles from Rome. Horace (*Satires* I.v.3-6) says that travelers covered the distance in one day, although on a journey thither from Rome he himself "lazily" preferred to take two days. The Forum of Appius was also at the head of a canal which ran through the Pontine Marshes to Feronia, a canal on which there was travel by boat. Horace had no high opinion of the Forum of Appius and described it as "crammed with boatmen and stingy tavern keepers." The Roman milestone at the Forum of Appius was marked "XLIII," and not far away was a carved stone of the Emperor Nerva with the words *ad Forum Appi* (*Corpus Inscriptionum Latinarum* X.6824-25).

Bibliography. C. Hülsen, "Appi Forum," *Pauly-Wissowa*, vol. II (1896), col. 242. J. FINEGAN

FOUNDATION. The translation of a number of words in the Bible. In the OT various forms derived from the stem יסד are translated "foundation" or "foundations" and used both literally and metaphorically. The foundation of Solomon's temple was of costly stones (I Kings 7:10). In Ezekiel's temple the foundations of the side chambers measured a reed of six cubits (Ezek. 41:8). From other stems are שתות (Ps. 11:3, a figurative reference); אשיות (Jer. 50:15), "foundations" (i.e., of Babylon) in the KJV, "BULWARKS" in the RSV; and Aramaic אשין (Ezra 4:12, of Jerusalem; 5:16, of the temple; 6:3 KJV [RSV "BURNT OFFERINGS," from a different root]). אמות (Isa. 6:4) is "foundations" in the RSV, "POSTS" in the KJV. In the NT both θεμέλιος and καταβολή are used extensively for both literal and metaphorical "foundation."

Courtesy of the American Schools of Oriental Research

21. Excavations at Tell Beit Mirsim, showing hall of a house (*b*) before and (*a*) after removal of foundations in June and July, 1930

Laying the foundation of a city or a temple was an elaborate ceremony in the ancient Middle East. At times it was accompanied by human sacrifice (Josh. 6:26; I Kings 16:34). Inscribed cylinders were placed in some Babylonian foundations. In excavations frequently remains of foundations show ground plans where the superstructure has been destroyed. Fig. FOU 21.

See also ARCHITECTURE; HOUSE; POST.

O. R. SELLERS

FOUNDATION, GATE OF THE [שער היסוד]. A gate in Jerusalem, possibly leading from the king's palace to the temple, mentioned in the narrative of the murder of Athaliah (II Chr. 23:5). The parallel passage (II Kings 11:6), the original Hebrew of which is probably corrupt, reads instead: "the gate SUR" or "gate of Sur" (שער סור).

See also ATHALIAH; JEHOASH; TEMPLE, JERUSALEM.

G. A. BARROIS

FOUNTAIN. A spring of water flowing from an opening in a hillside or valley; to be distinguished from a WELL or CISTERN. The limestone rock of Palestine is conducive to the formation of fountains, which are numerous. Fountains are also mentioned in the OT in a figurative sense in referring to the Lord or to wisdom as the source of life (*see below*).

In Hebrew a number of words are used to designate fountains which are rendered in English as "fountain" and "spring" without distinction between the two. Among the Hebrew words most commonly used are: עין (I Sam. 29:1), מעינת (Gen. 7:11), and מקור (Prov. 5:18). The following are used less frequently: ביר (Jer. 6:7; RSV "well"; KJV "fountain"), מבוע (Eccl. 12:6), אשדת (Deut. 4:49; RSV "slopes"; KJV "springs"), גל (Song of S. 4:12; RSV "garden" with some MSS and most versions; KJV "spring" with the MT), גלת (Josh. 15:19), מים חיים (Gen. 26:19; "springing water"), מוצא (II Kings 2:21), מעינים (Ps. 104:10), and תהמת (Deut. 8:7).

In the NT, where fountains or springs are mentioned infrequently, the Greek word is πηγή (II Pet. 2:17; Rev. 7:17; "springs").

The land of Canaan was to the ancient Israelite "a good land, a land of brooks of water, of fountains [עינת] and springs [תהמת], flowing forth in valleys and hills" (Deut. 8:7).

Although considerable skill was developed in conserving water in pools and cisterns, fountains were important as a source of water supply, and their presence often determined the location of a village. This importance is indicated by the use of the prefix "En" (fountain) in a number of place names (*see* EN-DOR; EN-EGLAIM; EN-GANNIM; EN-GEDI; EN-

RIMMON; EN-ROGEL; EN-SHEMESH; EN-TAPPUAH). One of the gates in the city wall of Jerusalem was called the Fountain Gate, probably because it was used by persons bringing water from En-rogel (Neh. 2:14; 3:15; 12:37). Among the famous springs mentioned in the OT were the one in the city of Nahor where Abraham's servant met Rebekah (Gen. 24:16), the one at Harod where Gideon encamped (Judg. 7:1), and the one near Jericho which was purified by Elisha (II Kings 2:21).

Primitive peoples believed that springs were inhabited by spirits. To the Hebrew patriarchs springs were not only important sources of water but also places of theophany (Gen. 16:7; 24:42). In later times fountains were mentioned as symbols of the Lord's power to give life and refreshment. The Lord is referred to as Israel's fountain (Ps. 68:26—H 68:27), and reverence for the Lord is spoken of as a fountain of life (Prov. 14:27). The Lord is also called the fountain of living water (Jer. 17:13), and the teaching of the wise man is described as a fountain of life (Prov. 13:14).

Among the fountains which are still sources of water for modern biblical villages may be mentioned the ones at Solomon's pools S of Bethlehem, in the Kidron Valley at Jerusalem, at Tell es-Sultan near Jericho, and the Virgin's Fountain in Nazareth. Thermal springs are located near the Sea of Galilee and E of the Dead Sea. Their warm, sulphurous waters are thought to have healing properties, and many persons suffering from various forms of rheumatism bathe in the springs (cf. Gen. 36:24: הימם במדבר, "hot springs in the wilderness").

W. L. REED

FOUNTAIN GATE [שער העין]; KJV GATE OF THE FOUNTAIN. A city gate in the SE section of Jerusalem, restored by Nehemiah (Neh. 2:14; 3:15; 12:37). Perhaps identical with the "gate between the two walls" (II Kings 25:4; Jer. 39:4; 52:7). *See* map under NEHEMIAH. *See also* JERUSALEM § 7*b*.

G. A. BARROIS

FOWL [ברברים, *see* FAUNA § C6*b;* LXX ὀρνίθων ἐκλεκτῶν, choice birds; *for* עוף (Aram. עוף), עיט, צפור (Aram. צפר), ὄρνεον, πετεινόν, *see* BIRD; BIRD OF PREY]. Any feathered vertebrate animal; usually in modern use restricted to domestic poultry.

It is agreed that the domestic fowl comes from the Indian jungle fowl (*Gallus gallus gallus*), but the time of its introduction into Western Asia is debatable. The NT (Matt. 23:37; 26:34; etc.) and the Mishna (e.g., Shab. 24.3) indicate that domestic fowl were well known to the Jews by the opening of the Christian era, but it is uncertain when they first came into Israel's life. The fact that the Mishnaic terms for "cock" (תרנגול; cf. Akkadian *ṭarlugallu*) and "goose" (אווז) are not in the OT, suggests that these birds were unknown to the Hebrews at least in the days of the monarchy. We must note, however: (*a*) a Hebrew seal, depicting a fighting cock and thought to date *ca.* 600 B.C., has been found at Tell en-Naṣbeh (Fig. JAA 1); (*b*) two potsherds, possibly as early as 600 B.C., with fowl incised on them, were unearthed at el-Jib (Gibeon) in 1956-57; (*c*) two cylinder seals from the Neo-Babylonian period have cocks on them.

The Greek word for "cock" (ἀλέκτωρ), appearing as a proper name in Homer *Odyssey* IV.10, is used as a common noun in the fifth century B.C. by Pindar (*Olym.* XII.14) and by Aristophanes (*Birds* 483-85); the latter reference, in which the cock is termed the "Persian bird," points to a connection between the cock and Persia, which suggests that Persia was the source from which the Greeks derived this bird. The Persians, or the somewhat earlier Medes, may in turn have obtained it from India.

In view of the above considerations, it is unlikely that domestic fowl were on Solomon's table; if any birds appeared there, they were probably game. The "fowls" (צפרים) prepared for Nehemiah (Neh. 5:18) may have been game, pigeons, or domestic fowl.

W. S. MCCULLOUGH

FOWLER [יקוש] (Pss. 91:3; 124:7; Prov. 6:5; Jer 5:26; Hos. 9:8). One who traps birds by sling, bait, lure, or snare for sport or for food. The verb is always metaphorical in the Bible. The snare is wickedness, evil, or idolatry (Pss. 91:3; 124:7; 141:9; Jer. 5:26-27). Perhaps decoy birds were tied in the traps (Ecclus. 11:32). False prophets are likened to fowlers (Hos. 9:8), yet God snares the wicked (Job 18:9-10; Hos. 7:12). Jesus also uses the metaphor of the snare (Luke 21:35). Business is a snare (Prov. 6:5). Besides the various kinds of nets the fowler also used throwing sticks and sling stones (Judg. 20:16).

Courtesy of the Service des Antiquités, Cairo

22. Birds being caught in a net cage by a fowler; from a tomb of Ka-gemni at Saqqarah; beginning of the Sixth Dynasty (*ca.* 2350-2200 B.C.)

See also BIRDS. Fig. FOW 22.

C. U. WOLF

FOX [שועל] (JACKAL *in* Ps. 63:10—H 63:12; Lam. 5:18), *cf.* Akkad. *šellebu, šēlabu;* Arab. *tha'lab;* Syr. *ta'lā;* ἀλώπηξ]. Any of certain widely distributed carnivorous mammals of the genus Vulpes, of the family Canidae, smaller than the wolves, having a long, bushy tail, and noted for speed, cunning, and resource. The fox is normally a solitary animal, mostly nocturnal; it feeds upon smaller animals, as well as insects and fruit. We do not know whether the two varieties of fox which Tristram found in Palestine in the nineteenth century (*NHB* 85-88) existed in the biblical period. *See* FAUNA § A2*c*ii.

The fox usually excavates its own burrow (cf. Matt. 8:20; Luke 9:58). Its proverbial slyness explains Jesus' allusion to Herod Antipas in Luke 13:32, though in Jewish usage "fox" may also suggest insignificance. The latter meaning may lie behind Tobiah's reference to Nehemiah's wall as being so flimsy as to break under the tread of even a fox (Neh. 4:3—H 3:35). The other OT references to foxes may, in fact, be to jackals, for only the latter hunt in packs, and, unlike the fox, they tend to be scavengers and therefore might be represented as prowling over ruins (Judg. 15:4-5; Ps. 63:10—H 63:11; Song of S. 2:15; Lam. 5:18; Ezek. 13:4). In Ezek. 13:4 "foxes" serves as an appropriate term for false prophets; the latter, amid Israel's misfortunes, seek only their own interest. "Foxes" and "little foxes" in Song of S. 2:15 are used symbolically, but the precise meaning of this verse depends upon the interpretation given to Song of Songs as a whole. W. S. McCullough

FRACTURE [שבר] (Lev. 24:20); KJV BREACH. The act of breaking a bone or cartilage or the result of such a break (cf. Lev. 21:19). The "breach" of Gen. 38:29 refers to perineal rupture or laceration. R. K. Harrison

FRAGRANCE. *See* Odor; Perfume.

FRAME. 1. מוט (KJV BAR), a receptacle for carrying the lamps and utensils of the tabernacle (Num. 4:10, 12).

2. מסגרת (lit., "enclosure"; KJV BORDER). This word has two uses:

a) A brace for the legs of the table of the presence (Exod. 25:25, 27; 37:12, 14; *see* Table; Tabernacle). *Ca.* three inches wide, it ran around the legs about halfway down, judging from the picture on the Arch of Titus. The rings for the carrying poles were in the legs near this frame.

b) A side panel (KJV BORDER) of the stands for the lavers in the temple (I Kings 7:28-36; II Kings 16:17; *see* Laver). *See also* 4 *below.*

3. קרש (KJV BOARD), a section of the skeletal structure of the Tabernacle, over which the curtains were spread (Exod. 26:15-29; 35:11; 36:30-34; 37:12, 14; 39:33; 40:18; Num. 3:36; 4:31). The earlier view that these frames were solid planks raised insuperable difficulties. Instead, they were formed of two up-

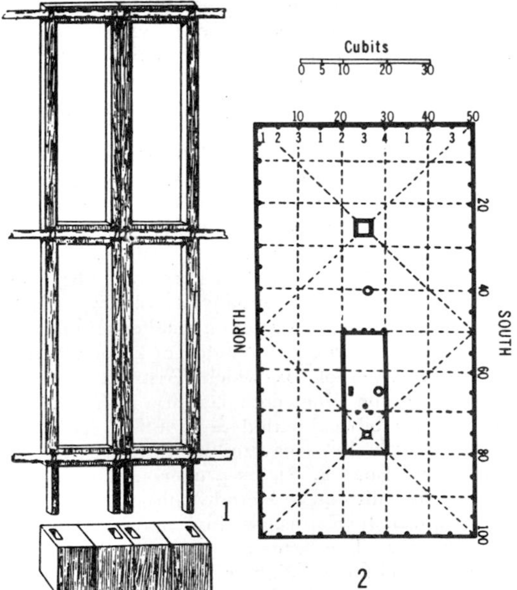

Reproduced from McNeile, *Book of Exodus,* by permission of the publishers, Methuen & Co. Ltd.

23. The tabernacle: (1) two *kerashim* (beams) with bars, rings, and bases; (2) plan of the court of the dwelling

rights of light wood, joined at the top, middle, and base by crossbars. Two legs were set in silver sockets on the ground. Each frame was 10 cubits high, 1½ cubits wide, and of no specified thickness. Figs. FRA 23; TAB 1.

4. שלב (I Kings 7:28-29; KJV LEDGE), a horizontal brace of the stands for the lavers of the temple. *See* Laver. *See also* 2 *above.*

5. שקף (I Kings 6:4; 7:4-5), שחיף (Ezek. 41:16), the casing of windows and doors. *See* Window; Temple, Jerusalem.

6. The human form. Three words have this meaning:

a) יצר (Ps. 103:14).

b) עצם ("bone, substance"; Ps. 139:15; KJV SUBSTANCE).

c) ערך ("order, symmetry"; Job 41:12—H 41:4; KJV PROPORTION).

7. A verb meaning "to plan or devise." צמד ("combine, join"; Ps. 50:19) is so translated, as is יצר ("form, fashion"; Ps. 94:20; Jer. 18:11 KJV [RSV SHAPE]); and in the KJV, תן ("give, permit"; Judg. 12:6, which refers to framing the lips to make a certain sound; Hos. 5:4; cf. RSV in both these instances).

Bibliography. A. H. McNeile, *Exodus,* WC (1908), pp. lxxiii-lxxvi; S. R. Driver, *Exodus,* Cambridge Bible (1911), pp. 272 ff; J. A. Montgomery and H. S. Gehman, *Kings,* ICC (1951), pp. 175-77. S. V. Fawcett

FRANKINCENSE [לבנה (Exod. 30:34; Lev. 2:1-2, 15-16; *etc.;* I Chr. 9:29; KJV *alternately* INCENSE—e.g., Isa. 43:23; 60:6; Jer. 6:20); λίβανος]. A fragrant gum resin consisting of small, white chunks and beads which are easily ground into a powder; this powder emits a balsamlike odor when burned.

Frankincense, technically called *libanum* (Medieval Latin, from the Arabic *al-luban*), is yielded in the form of a milky exudation by trees belonging to certain species of the genus *Boswellia* (for an account of the process by which the gum was obtained in his time, see Pliny *Nat. Hist.* 12.14 ff).The gum resin was imported into Palestine from Arabia, where it was probably produced in the central district of Hadramaut (Isa. 60:6; Jer. 6:20). The Arabic and Hebrew names were suggested by the fact that the gum resin is white.

According to the Levitical regulations frankincense was one of the major ingredients of the Incense which was holy unto the Lord (Exod. 30:34-38). The use of this incense for purposes other than those specified in the priestly legislation was forbidden. Incense compounded according to any other recipe could neither be offered to deity nor displayed in the holy place (vs. 9).

Frankincense was set before the holy of holies with the Bread of the Presence (Lev. 24:7); Josephus suggests that two golden cups filled with frankincense were set on top of the rows of holy bread (Antiq. III.vi.6). Frankincense and oil were added to the cereal offerings (Lev. 2:1-2, 14-16; 6:14-18), and the frankincense was subsequently burned (cf. Isa. 43:23; 66:3; Jer. 17:26; 41:5). The addition of frankincense to a sin offering (Lev. 5:11), or to a cereal offering of jealousy (Num. 5:15), was forbidden.

Stores of frankincense were kept in the Jerusalem

temple (I Chr. 9:29; Neh. 13:5, 9). Voluntary offerings of it are mentioned (Jer. 17:26). It was one of the gifts offered to the infant Jesus by the Wise Men (Matt. 2:11). The only other NT use of the word occurs in Rev. 18:13 (in both instances the Greek term is simply a transliteration from the Hebrew).

See also SACRIFICE AND OFFERINGS; INCENSE ALTAR; WORSHIP IN THE OT.

Bibliography. G. W. Van Beek, "Frankincense and Myrrh," *BA*, XXIII (1960), 70-94. H. F. BECK

FREEDMEN, SYNAGOGUE OF THE [συναγωγή τῶν Λιβερτίνων]; KJV SYNAGOGUE OF THE LIBERTINES. One of a number of synagogues at Jerusalem, conducted for Jews who spoke Greek rather than Aramaic, the latter being the native language of Palestinian Jews. This synagogue is mentioned in the NT only at Acts 6:9. The same passage refers to synagogues of the Cyrenians, Alexandrians, Cilicians, and Asiatics, but it is not certain that five separate groups are meant. E.g., "Cyrenians and Alexandrians" might be one congregation; or "those from Cilicia and Asia" might describe the Freedmen themselves. *See* ALEXANDRIA; CYRENE.

Some have conjectured, on the basis of the Armenian Version, that for Λιβερτίνων we should read Λιβυστίνων, "of the Libyans," which would match "of the Cyrenians." Assuming the correctness of the standard text, these Freedmen were former captives at Rome, or else children of former captives, who had been set free and had returned to Jerusalem. The Roman historian Tacitus indicates that freed Jewish captives were a special problem for the government (Ann. II.85).

Evidently the young church found it necessary to debate its faith with these Greek-speaking people. STEPHEN was assigned the task, which he performed with "wisdom" and "the Spirit" (Acts 6:10). He was one of seven men who had been ordained to minister particularly to Greek-speaking converts (vss. 1-6). Most of the other six bore Greek names, and it is likely that all seven were, like the Freedmen, immigrants from other lands. *See* SEVEN, THE.

PIERSON PARKER

FREEDOM. *See* LIBERTY.

FREEWILL OFFERING. *See* SACRIFICE AND OFFERINGS § A1*e*.

FRIEND, FRIENDSHIP. Usually the understanding that binds one man to another or (less commonly in the Bible) one woman to another (Judg. 11:37-38; Ps. 45:15—H 45:14), as distinct from love and from the affection uniting members of a family.

The word "friend" renders Hebrew nouns derived from the roots רעה II and אהב. One of these nouns, *rēaʿ*, serves a double purpose, frequently having the neutral meaning "another person," "neighbor," as in: "You shall love your neighbor as yourself" (Lev. 19:18). As "friend" the word suggests close companionship; after "your brother . . . , or your son, or your daughter, or the wife of your bosom," Deut. 13:6—H 13:7 next lists "your friend who is as your own soul." A proverb even says: "There is a friend who sticks closer than a brother" (Prov. 18:24). A high point in the ethics of wisdom is Koheleth's endorsement of friendship (Eccl. 4:9-12; *see* ECCLESIASTES § 7*b*). Notable examples of friendship in the Bible are the love between David and Jonathan (I Sam. 18:1; II Sam. 1:23) and the devotion of Barzillai to David (II Sam. 19:31-39—H 19:32-40). Though awkward, Job's friends were well-meaning (Job 2:11; 19:21; cf. 6:14-23) and stayed with him in time of trouble, thus controverting occasional cynical reservations as to friendship in proverbial wisdom (Prov. 14:20; 19:4, 7; Ecclus. 9:10). In Isa. 41:8 God refers to Abraham as "my friend." Such expressions of God's friendship for his people as those in Isa. 5:1-7; Jer. 12:7 facilitated the allegorical interpretation of the SONG OF SONGS. S. H. BLANK

FRIEND OF THE KING. A high court officer, intimate counselor, and companion of kings. Abimelech had such an officer in Ahuzzath (Gen. 26:26). Zabud and Hushai are so called in I Kings 4:5; I Chr. 27:33. In Maccabean times a special privileged class was composed of these persons (I Macc. 2:18; 3:38; 6:10; 10:65).

See also FRIEND. C. U. WOLF

FRINGE [κράσπεδον (Matt. 9:20; 14:36; 23:5; Mark 6:56; Luke 8:44; KJV HEM, BORDER); KJV ציצת (Num. 15:38-39; *see* TASSEL), גדל (Deut. 22:12; *see* TASSEL; WREATH]. A cord or thread which ended in a kind of tassel, sewn on at the four corners of the outer garment. The oldest of the passages dealing with fringes is that of Deut. 22:12: "You shall make yourself tassels on the four corners of your cloak with which you cover yourself." The cloak (כסות) was the square outer garment which was also used as a cover at night. According to the Numbers prescription, the cord was to be blue. Later on, white was permitted, probably because of the difficulty and costliness of the dye required. The threads had to be spun, and the fringes could not be made from the overhanging threads of the warp and woof of the garment itself. They could, however, be made from a sewn tuft. Talmudic practice required that they be made of eight white wool threads twisted a specified number of times with five double knots tied at prescribed intervals. A minimum length was prescribed, but not a maximum.

Both Numbers and Deuteronomy indicate that the tassels were to be attached to the outer garment, where they were quite conspicuous and would thus serve their prescribed purpose most effectively. Later, when the Jews were forced out of their land and were dispersed in foreign lands, such outward marks became especially noticeable and served to attract undue attention on the part of their persecutors. Hence the custom of wearing the fringes or tassels on a square woolen cloth carried under the outer garment, and from this developed the practice of the prayer shawl (טלית) worn on the head during prayer.

There were three tokens of remembrance prescribed for every Jew: the ציצת ("tassels," "fringes"); the מזוזה, the small cylinder with parchment scroll attached to the doorpost (Deut. 6:9; 11:20); and the טוטפות, arm and head bands or phylacteries (Exod. 13:9, 16; Deut. 6:8; 11:18). The purpose of the fringe or tassel was "to look upon and remember all the commandments of the LORD, to do them, not to follow after your own heart and your own eyes, which you are inclined to go after wantonly" (Num. 15:39). The origin of the wearing of fringes is obscure, but it was doubtless connected with magic or taboo of some kind, which was now sublimated by a high and exalted purpose.

The term "fringe(s)" occurs in the NT in connection with the woman who had an issue of blood and who touched the fringe of Jesus' garment (Matt. 9:20=Luke 8:44), and with those who brought their sick that they might do the same (Matt. 14:36=Mark 6:56). Matt. 23:5 records Jesus' severe condemnation of the scribes and Pharisees who, to be seen by men, made their fringes long. All the references are manifestly to the four fringes worn on the garments of all Jews for purposes noted above.

Figs. AHA 5; ASS 97; HUN 34. Monuments from the Near East illustrate many types of tassels and fringes (*ANET* 45, 52, 64, 351-54, 436, 441, 460, etc.).

Bibliography. E. Schürer, *History of the Jewish People,* div. 2, vol. II (1891), pp. 111-12; H. Strack and P. Billerbeck, *Kommentar zum NT aus Talmud und Midrash,* IV (1928), 276-92; F. J. Stephens, "The Ancient Significance of Sisith," *JBL,* 50 (1931), pp. 59-70. J. M. MYERS

FROG [צפרדע (Exod. 8:2-13—H 7:27–8:9; Pss. 78: 45; 105:30), *cf.* Arab. *ḍafda'*, *ḍifdi';* Jewish Aram. עורדענא; βάτραχος (Wisd. Sol. 19:10; Rev. 16:13)]. Any of various genera (especially at the genus *Rana*) of tailless leaping amphibians of the order *Ecaudata*.

All the references to frog in the OT and the Apoc. are to the frogs of the second plague in the Exodus story. The description in Rev. 16:13 of the three frog-like demons, which come as a result of the sixth angel's pouring out his bowl, doubtless reflects the unclean status of the frog among the Jews (cf. Lev. 11:10, 41); this status may have been further lowered by the traditional association of the frog (or toad) with the Egyptian goddess Heqt, who assisted women in childbirth. W. S. MCCULLOUGH

FRONTLETS [טוטפת, *from* נטף, to drop, drip?] (Exod. 13:16; Deut. 6:8; 11:18). Objects worn on the forehead between the eyes, just below the hairline, at prayer times. They were doubtless for more than memorial purposes and were regarded as effective against certain kinds of evil. In later times the PHYLACTERIES, which consisted of small cubical cases into which were inserted parchments inscribed with the words of Exod. 13:1-10, 11-16; Deut. 6:4-9; 11:13-21, served the same purpose.

The redemption of the first-born is "as a mark on your hand or frontlets between your eyes" (Exod. 13:16). The injunction to bind the words of God as a sign on the hands and that they should be as frontlets between the eyes was probably intended to be taken literally, since the reference was to the commands of God (cf. Exod. 13:9).

Bibliography. E. Schürer, *History of the Jewish People* (1891), div. 2, vol. II, pp. 113 ff; A. S. Yehuda and H. Grimme, *OLZ*, vol. 41 (1938), cols. 148 ff. J. M. MYERS

FROST. *See* SNOW; PALESTINE, CLIMATE OF.

FRUIT (PRODUCTS) [פרי; καρπός]. The edible pulp which surrounds the seed (or seeds) of many plants and trees, including nuts. פרי appears more than one hundred times in the OT and καρπός more than sixty in the NT, but the majority of these are symbolical rather than specific. The biblical peoples, being so close to the soil throughout their history, used these terms as an integral part of their vocabulary.

The most basic fruits of the ancient economy were, first, the OLIVE, then the FIG and the grape (*see* VINE), as illustrated by Jotham's parable (Judg. 9:7-15). Other fruits of the Bible include ALMOND; APPLE (more likely apricot or quince); DATES; MELON; mulberries (*see* MULBERRY TREES); pistachio NUT; POMEGRANATE; and SYCAMORE figs. The MANDRAKE and the carob bean (*see* HUSKS) were occasionally eaten.

Several Hebrew words in the OT in addition to the general word פרי, *pᵉrî*, specify certain types of fruit products:

a) אשישה (*'ᵃšîšâ*), "raisin cake" (II Sam. 6:19=I Chr. 16:3; Song of S. 2:5; Isa. 16:7; Hos. 3:1). *See* VINE.

b) בכורה (*bikkûrâ*), "first-ripe [June] fig" (Isa. 28:4; Jer. 24:2; Hos. 9:10; Mic. 7:1). *See* FIG.

c) דבלה (*dᵉbhēlâ*), "cake of [pressed] figs" (I Sam. 25:18; 30:12; II Kings 20:7=Isa. 38:21; I Chr. 12:40; cf. Ugaritic *dblt,* 55:28; 56:33). *See* FIG.

d) צמוק (*ṣimmûq*), "cluster of raisins" (I Sam. 25: 18; 30:12; II Sam. 16:1; I Chr. 12:40—H 12:41; cf. Ugaritic *ṣmqm*, 12+97:5, 17; 55:28; 56:34). *See* VINE.

e) קיץ (*qáyiṣ*), "summer fruit" (probably the ripe fig and other perishable fruits; II Sam. 16:1-2; Isa. 16:9; Jer. 40:10, 12; 48:32; Amos 8:1-2; cf. Ugaritic *qẓ,* 77:2, 24; 1 Aqht:18, 41).

f) תנובה (*tᵉnûbhâ*), fruit of the fig (also general produce; "good fruit" in Judg. 9:11).

Fruit from a newly planted tree could not be eaten until the fifth year (Lev. 19:23-25). The fourth year's crop was dedicated to the Lord, and any fruit of the first three years was considered forbidden.

See also FLORA § B; FRUIT (SYMBOL).

J. C. TREVER

FRUIT (SYMBOL) [פרי; καρπός; ἡ ὀπωρία (Rev. 18:14)]. Alternately: DESCENDANTS (Acts 2:30); RETURN (Rom. 6:21-22); HARVEST (Rom. 1:13; Jas. 3:18). There are several ways in which the word "fruit" is used symbolically in the Bible:

a) Children are sometimes referred to as the "fruit of the womb" (Gen. 30:2; Ps. 127:3; Isa. 13:18; cf. Luke 1:42), or praise described as the "fruit of the lips" (Isa. 57:18—KJV 57:19; cf. Heb. 13:15).

b) More often "fruit" denotes the rewards meted out by God (Jer. 17:10). The fruit of righteousness is the benefit bestowed for right action (Prov. 12:14; 31: 31; Isa. 3:10; Hos. 10:12; Amos 6:12; John 4:36; Phil. 4:17; Heb. 12:11), while the fruit of wickedness is the judgment it incurs (Prov. 1:31; Jer. 6:19; 21:14; Hos. 10:13; Mic. 7:13).

c) Most frequently "fruit" is the total result that issues from any specific action or disposition. The fruit produced may be evil (Matt. 3:10; 7:15-20; 12: 33; Luke 6:43-44*a;* Rom. 7:5), but is more often good

(Ps. 104:13; Matt. 3:8; 21:43; Rom. 7:4; Eph. 5:9; Phil. 1:11; Jas. 3:17). Paul describes his mission generally in these terms (Rom. 1:13; 15:28; Phil. 1:22; Col. 1:6), and beyond gifts given by the Spirit makes a special place for the "fruit of the Spirit" (Gal. 5:22). Seed (John 12:24), tree (Rev. 22:2), and vine (John 15:1-16) illustrate how God produces life among men. In like fashion disciples are urged to "bear fruit," καρποφορέω (Mark 4:20; Col. 1:10), and are criticized for being "unfruitful," ἄκαρπος (Mark 4:19; Eph. 5:11; Tit. 3:14; II Pet. 1:8; cf. I Cor. 14:14; Jude 12). I. W. Batdorf

FRYING PAN. KJV translation of מרחשת (RSV PAN), the vessel in which the cereal offering was cooked (Lev. 2:7; 7:9). It is more accurately identified as a kettle for deep-fat frying. *See* Pottery.

J. L. Kelso

FUEL [אכלה לאש, food for fire; בער (*in* Second Isaiah), to burn, consume]. In ancient Israel many different substances were used for burning: wood, vine branches, thornbushes, withered grass, dung, charcoal, chaff. A great variety of wood may be assumed, ranging from logs or faggots (Isa. 44:14-16) to sticks or twigs (I Kings 17:12). According to numerous references, the thorn was a very common fuel. This, as well as other shrubs, gave out a very intense heat, especially when reduced to charcoal. The Hebrews were, no doubt, aware of the advantages of reducing wood to charcoal; and references to the brazier, by means of which the houses of the upper classes were kept warm, indicate its use in this way (Jer. 36:22). Charcoal apparently was also piled up without a container (John 21:9). Chaff and straw were used but burned quickly, while dung burned slowly with low heat and much smoke. H. N. Richardson

FULFIL. This term, as well as such closely related terms as "fill" and "fill up," can be understood only in the light of an examination of a rather wide range of biblical words: מלא and of ἀνακεφαλαίοω, πίμπλημι, (ἀντανα-, ἀνα-, ἐκ-, συμ-)πληρόω, πληροφορέω πλήρης, πλήρωμα, τελειόω, (συν-)τελέω, τέλος. For τελειόω and (ἐπι-, συν-)τελέω, and a certain overlap in all these words, *see also* Ordination; Perfection. For πλήρωμα, *see* Pleroma. But it is to be noted here that πληροφορέω is clearly synonymous with πληρόω in II Tim. 4:5 (cf. Col. 4:17), 17 (cf. Rom. 15:19); possibly also in Luke 1:1 (but see Commentaries here); while "fulfil" is used for τελέω in Luke 22:37 (cf. 18:31: "accomplish"), and for τελειόω in Rev. 10:7; 17:17 (cf. Acts 20:24: "accomplish"; II Tim. 4:7: "finish"; Jas. 2:22: "complete"), and τέλος is rendered "fulfilment" in Luke 22:37.

1. Nontheological uses, literal or metaphorical. The uses in which the words under consideration mean "fill" or "complete" (whether of concrete things or of abstract matters) in a straightforward or "nontheological" sense (whether literal or metaphorical) require little discussion here.

a. In the OT. In the OT the only uses calling for attention under this heading are idiomatic ones, concealed in the Greek and English versions by nonliteral renderings.

The first is "to fill the hand," meaning "to ordain to the priesthood" (e.g., Exod. 28:41; 29:9; "ordain"). That the verb is here used literally, seems to be suggested by the ceremony as described in Exod. 29:24—a filling of the hands of the ordinand with offerings as part of the ritual. But the phrase "to fill the hand" became so regular a synonym for "ordain" that in Ezek. 43:26 it is applied to an inanimate object, the altar (RSV "consecrate," as though it were קדש); while in Exod. 32:29 there may, it has been suggested, be a grim *double entendre:* "You have ordained yourselves" (lit., "you have filled your hand") may mean, You have taken weapons in your hands (to slay your renegade brothers, and so "ordain" yourselves to the service of purity of worship).

At any rate, secondly, the same verb is used in the Hebrew, and still, probably, in an ultimately literal sense, in II Kings 9:24, where Jehu "filled his hand with the bow"—i.e., drew the bow to its full extent, or (so RSV) drew it "with his full strength"; and in Zech. 9:13 the metaphor seems to be taken from the same action (lit., "I have trodden Judah for myself"—the regular technical term for stringing a bow was to "tread" it): "I have filled the bow Ephraim"—i.e., "I have bent Judah as my bow; I have made Ephraim its arrow" (so RSV).

b. In the NT. In the NT there are entirely straightforward uses (literal or metaphorical) such as the following (*see also* Pleroma): Matt. 13:48 (fill a net with fish); Luke 2:40 (the child Jesus filled with wisdom); Luke 3:5 (fill up a valley so as to level it); John 12:3 (fill the house with fragrance); John 16:6 (grief filling the heart); Acts 5:28 (of the apostles' filling Jerusalem with their teaching). And just as the Spirit of God may be said to fill a person (Acts 6:3; Eph. 5:18), so may also Satan (Acts 5:3—so the best reading) or wickedness (Rom. 1:29). In this same straightforward sense it is perhaps right to interpret the verb used with a secondary accusative, as in Phil. 1:11 ("filled with the fruits of righteousness"); Col. 1:9 ("filled with the knowledge"), though these might mean "brought to maturity *in respect of.*"

2. Theological or ethical uses. Theologically or ethically the most important use is probably in connection with "fulfilling" prophecy, etc. But first, there are also the following:

a) In Matt. 23:32 the religious authorities are ironically bidden to fill up the measure of their fathers—i.e., to come up to their forefathers' standard of wickedness, or, perhaps, to complete the tale of wickedness begun by them. Similarly, in I Thess. 2:16 the Jews are spoken of as opposing the gospel, "so as always to fill up the measure of their sins" (ἀναπληρῶσαι)—a phrase reminiscent of Gen. 15:16, and implying a fixed amount destined to be achieved before the penalty falls (cf. Rev. 6:11).

b) In Num. 32:11-12 (cf. Num. 14:24; Deut. 1:36; Josh. 14:8-9, 14; I Kings 11:6), Caleb and Joshua, in contrast to the disobedient Israelites, are described as having "filled after" God (מלאו אחרי יהוה; LXX συνεπηκολούθησαν)—i.e., "wholly followed" him (so RSV). If this is the meaning, it is partly paralleled in the NT by Rev. 3:2: "I have not found your works perfect [lit., 'filled'] in the sight of my God" (cf. the use of τελειόω, in connection with implementing by action, in Jas. 2:22; I John 2:5; 4:12, 17-18).

So in Col. 4:17, Archippus is bidden: "See that you fulfil the ministry"—i.e., carry it through to completion, do it thoroughly (cf. Rom. 15:19: "I have fully preached the gospel," and so Col. 1:25; and Acts 12:25; 13:25; 14:26; but in Acts 19:21 the phrase merely means when this was finished—i.e., "after these events"). So, too, in II Thess. 1:11 the prayer is that God may "fulfil every good resolve"—i.e., enable them to put their good resolves into effect (cf. II Cor. 10:6, of obedience). "Completing by action," "implementing," and so "doing wholeheartedly" seem to be the connotations of such uses.

On the other hand, it is just possible that in the passages cited above, Num. 32:11-12, etc., the Hebrew phrase "fill after" means "corroborate." This may be suggested by I Kings 1:14, where Nathan instructs Bathsheba to speak to David, and then, says Nathan: "I will come in after you and will fill your words"—i.e., "confirm your words" (so RSV). But it is to be noted that "I will come in after you and fill" is not strictly analogous to "they filled after God," and it may be that the two idioms are distinct. Possibly the meaning here may even be "tell the whole story."

c) Very important is the famous passage Col. 1:24: "Now I rejoice in my sufferings for your sake, and in my flesh I complete [ἀνταναπληρῶ] what is lacking [τὰ ὑστερήματα] in Christ's afflictions for the sake of his body, that is, the church." For details of the long debate over these words, see the Commentaries.

For the present purpose it is sufficient to note that it is possible that one of the ideas entering into the word "complete" may be that which appears under *a* above viz., of a destined tale of sufferings to be entered into by those who are persecuted, just as a destined tale of sins is ironically allotted to the persecutors. In any case, it is clear that the message of the NT as a whole keeps inviolate the completeness and efficacy of the cross of Christ, while at the same time closely associating the apostles, and the whole church, with the implementing and the entering into what God has thus done in Christ. In a sense, but only in this qualified sense, the work of Christ is "incomplete" until thus "completed." For the idea of Christians' being brought to completeness (Eph. 3:19; Col. 2:10), *see* PLEROMA.

d) The verb is used to describe God as "filling" heaven and earth, in Jer. 23:24 (cf. Isa. 6:3[?]; Wisd. Sol. 1:7: "The Spirit of the Lord has filled the world"; and in Eph. 4:10 "that he might fill all things" is said of Christ). For the relation of this thought to the idea of the divine immanence and to Greek philosophic concepts, and for its relevance to the interpretation of "Pleroma," *see* PLEROMA.

But it is most obviously in relation to the "fulfilment" of the Old Dispensation in the New that the verb calls for notice in the NT.

Here it may make for clarity if certain aspects of the meaning and use of "fulfil" are defined, before the data are examined.

a) "Fulfil" can be related, both in Greek and in Semitic languages, to the Law and to the Prophets alike. It can signify the observing or meeting of the full requirements of the law (cf., of human requirements, Phil. 4:19: "My God will supply [lit., 'fill'] every need of yours"; and *see b above*); and it can also signify the bringing about of something which had been predicted (in which sense it is not far from the sense "confirm," "corroborate," discussed above). Note that τελεῖν and τελειοῦν, as well as πληροῦν, are used in both these senses (e.g., John 4:34; 19:28).

It will at once be evident that Jesus marks the confluence of these two senses. Insofar as the Law bears witness to the will of God as an ideal yet to be achieved, and the Prophets hold out hope of a time coming when it shall be fulfilled, one who perfectly fulfils the will of God confirms also the predictions of prophecy.

b) Sentences in the NT containing the verb range from the simple indicative statement (Matt. 2:17: "then was fulfilled what was spoken by the prophet") to the apparently predestinarian phrases such as: "All this took place to fulfil what the Lord had spoken by the prophet" (Matt. 1:22).

The Semitic mind is notoriously prone to blur the distinction (which to the Western mind seems to exist) between final and consecutive clauses. It would be rash, in reading the NT, always to press a Greek final clause to mean what it might mean if it were unaffected by Semitic thought. But it is probably something more than idiom or way of thought that is involved here. In the last resort, a phrase like "all this took place to fulfil" bears witness to the paradox that the Incarnation is the meeting place of free will and predestination. That "the Son of man must [δεῖ] suffer" is not contradicted, but rather complemented, by the declaration: "I lay down my life . . . . No one takes it from me, but I lay it down of my own accord" (John 10:17-18). In negative form, Acts 13:27 (if the sentence is not corrupt) expresses the tragic irony of the religious authorities' failing to recognize either who Jesus was or what the Prophets meant, and thus fulfilling the Prophets by condemning Jesus. All this, however, is not to deny that one side of the paradox is more clearly visible in some passages and the other in others: the balance is not always evenly held.

With these preliminary observations, the data may be examined more closely.

a) Matt. 5:17 ff may be an instance of the convergence of the two senses of "fulfilment," as applied respectively to Law and Prophets: "Think not that I have come to abolish the law and the prophets; I have come not to abolish them but to fulfil them. For truly, I say to you, till heaven and earth pass away, not an iota, not a dot, will pass from the law until all is accomplished." On the face of it, the saying appears to be at the extreme "legalistic" end of the traditions about Jesus. If some traditions show him to have been a revolutionary, challenging the Mosaic law in the name of a higher authority, this saying, by contrast, seems to place an almost rabbinic emphasis on the importance of the meticulous observance of the law. "Whoever then," it continues, "relaxes one of the least of these commandments and teaches men so, shall be called least in the kingdom of heaven; but he who does them and teaches them shall be called great in the kingdom of heaven. For I tell you, unless your righteousness exceeds that of the scribes and Pharisees, you will never enter the kingdom of heaven." It seems plausible, certainly, to attribute such words to the distorting influence of a strongly Judaic type of Christian community, traces of which are to be found elsewhere also. On this showing, it is simply a biased form of some saying of Jesus, the original form of which is lost. On the other hand, is it not conceivable that it represents fairly faithfully an "extreme" saying of the Lord himself, designed in so emphatic a form precisely in order to correct a misapprehension that the way of life he taught and showed was morally less exacting than that of the rabbis? On this showing, it would mean that Jesus' way of life—even if in detail it proved to involve breaches of the letter of the law (such as sabbath rules)—would in essence prove to be an "establishing" or "corroborating" of the law. And (as has already been said) if it was by "fulfilling" the prophecies of the coming of the kingdom of God that Jesus thus, in a new and deeper sense, "fulfilled" also the law, it is possible to recognize here a widely inclusive saying, combining the two senses of "fulfil"—namely, that of accomplishing a command and that of bringing true a prediction.

This leads on to "until all is accomplished" (vs. 18). Does this mean that all the requirements of the law (every dot of an "i," every cross of a "t") are going to be "fulfilled" (in literal obedience to every smallest item)? Or does it mean that the Mosaic law will remain in force until all Christ's ministry is accomplished, and will then be superseded and rendered obsolete (cf. Heb. 10:9-10, where στήσῃ, "establish," is similar to πληροῦν)? The former seems by far the more natural sense (and cf. vs. 19). But, if so, must it not be interpreted to mean that Christ's new "law" fulfils the old law by for the first time fully accepting and performing God's will, rather than by literally carrying out its detailed observances? At any rate, to be considered side by side with this saying is Matt. 3:15 (Christ to the Baptist, who demurs to baptizing him): "Let it be so now; for thus it is fitting for us to fulfil all righteousness." Christ's obedience in humbly accepting baptism is a way of fulfilling all God's just requirements—again, perfect obedience is seen as including within it all that was expressed in the minutiae of the law. For illustration of this description of total obedience in terms of the fulfilling of the (spirit and intention of the) Mosaic law, cf. Rom. 8:4 ("in order that the just requirement of the law might be fulfilled in us, who walk not according to the flesh but according to the Spirit"); 13:8 ("he who loves his neighbor has fulfilled the law"; cf. vss. 9-10; and *see* PLEROMA); Gal. 5:14 ("The whole law is fulfilled in one word, 'You shall love your neighbor as yourself' ").

b) Extreme instances of the "predestinarian" presentation of the fulfilment of prophecy include the already cited Matt. 1:22 ("to fulfil")—a recurrent formula in Matthew (see 2:15, 23; 4:14; 8:17; 12:17; 13:35; 21:4; cf. 26:56)—and John 19:24 ("This was to fulfil the scripture"), 28 ("Jesus, knowing that all was now finished, said [to fulfil the scripture], 'I thirst' "). Also, the theme of the blindness of unbelievers is viewed as the fulfilment of what was predicted and had to be (Mark 4:11-12; John 12:37-43). In the above instances, and in others like them, the level at which the fulfilment of the OT is seen varies considerably, from the superficial and merely verbal (e.g., Matt. 13:35, a play by the evangelist on the word "parable") to the profoundest principles of the relation of one personality to another (Matt. 12:17 ff).

But this "predestinarian" presentation is (as has been shown) balanced by a clear stress on the freedom of Christ's own will and the responsibility of his hearers; and an impressive pointer to the truth underlying both extremes is to be found in such a phrase as "his departure [ἔξοδος], which he was to accomplish [πληροῦν] at Jerusalem" (Luke 9:31). Here is the new Moses, who, by "departing" from this life voluntarily, in the pursuit of God's will, was to achieve the Exodus, the destined rescue of the people of God, of which the exodus of the old Moses was a foreshadowing. So in Luke 22:16 he looks forward to the fruition of the real Passover, when the kingdom of God has been fully brought into being.

In short, the essence of prophecy is the interpretation of the will of God. And when he comes who perfectly, and not only by external conformity but also with his whole soul, achieves that will, he necessarily acts in such a way as to fulfil the predictions on their deepest level. Jesus, and the Cross and the Resurrection, are "about Isa. 53" even more than Isa. 53 is "about Jesus"; for the Crucifixion is the achievement of God's will in that redemptive suffering which the prophet had been granted to adumbrate. Accordingly, the two formulas "Then was fulfilled" and "All this took place to fulfil" coincide here, and here supremely. "The testimony of Jesus is the spirit of prophecy" (Rev. 19:10).

c) The fulfilment of time is viewed in the NT in the light of the Incarnation as an aspect of the fulfilling of the Old Dispensation in the New. When Jesus first appeared publicly at the beginning of his ministry, his message was: "The time is fulfilled, and the kingdom of God is at hand" (Mark 1:15; cf. Gal. 4:4; Eph. 1:10). Thus, within the ministry itself, Jesus is shown in the Fourth Gospel as working to a divine plan, and refusing to act until the right moment has come (John 2:4; 7:30; 13:1). Further, beyond the ministry there is also seen a "divine timetable," related always to the Incarnation as the central point of history, and working itself out in terms of the fulfilling of God's purposes: there is a certain period for the Gentile domination, a destined quota of messianic woes, and a proper time for the ultimate consummation (Luke 21:24; Eph. 1:10; II Thess. 2:6; I Tim. 6:15; I Pet. 1:5; Rev. 6:11; 10:7; 11:18; 15:1, 8; 20:3; 22:10); cf. Col. 1:24 above. One of the most pregnant phrases in this connection is in Eph. 1:9-10, relating the Incarnation both to the full time and to the inclusive fulfilment of all God's purposes in Christ: "For he has made known to us in all wisdom and insight the mystery of his will, according to his purpose which he set forth in Christ as a plan for the fulness of time, to unite [ἀνακεφαλαιώσασθαι] all things in him, things in heaven and things on earth." See the Commentaries, especially on ἀνακεφαλαιώσασθαι. *See also* SEASONS; TIME. For the meaning of the phrase ἐν τῷ συμπληροῦσθαι τὰς ἡμέρας (τὴν ἡμέραν), in Luke 9:51: "When the days drew near," and in Acts 2:1: "When the day . . . had come," see the Commentaries.

Bibliography. J. Dupont, *Gnosis* (1949), ch. 7; H. Ljungman, *Das Gesetz erfüllen* (1954); W. D. Davies, *Mélanges bibliques* (in honor of A. Robert; 1957); G. le Grelle, S.J., *Nouvelle Revue Théologique*, 81.3 (Mar., 1959), pp. 232 ff.

C. F. D. MOULE

FULLER [כובס; LXX *and* NT γναφεύς, *from root* to card]. One who thickens and shrinks newly shorn wool and newly woven cloth, after cleansing it of natural oils. The word is sometimes used also for one who cleans or dyes the cloth or the garment. Perhaps he also traded in textiles.

The Hebrew כבס (Akkadian *kabašu*), "to tread," indicates the basic method of washing cloth (Exod. 19:10; II Sam. 19:24; etc.). The cloth was also beaten for cleansing purposes. Bleaching by the sun was the final stage. Such was the use of the fuller's field (II Kings 18:17). In Roman times the fuller was also the cleaner. There was a tax on his work. In Pompeii there is mention of a fullers' guild.

Soap was not used in OT times, but borith or the ashes of borith were used as an alkaline cleanser, just as among Assyrians and Hittites (Mal. 3:2). Water was necessary, so the fuller located his plant near a water supply (Isa. 36:2, etc.). Because of its unwelcome odors the fuller's plant was usually outside the city gates.

In OT times the concept of a fuller's cleansing is used metaphorically of persons who are cleansed of evil (Ps. 51:7; Jer. 2:22; 4:14). White garments were used for religious festivals, and they required special cleansing (Zech. 3:3; Rev. 4:4; etc.). The Messenger of the Lord is a refiner or a fuller (Mal. 3:2). In the NT the garments of the transfigured Christ are whiter than any fuller could make them (Mark 9:3; cf. Matt. 17:2).

See also DYEING; LYE.

C. U. WOLF

FULLER'S FIELD [שדה כובס]. In suburban Jerusalem, a place accessible by means of a road which passed near the canal of the Upper Pool. It is mentioned in connection with the interview of Isaiah and Ahaz (Isa. 7:3), and the meeting of the officers of Hezekiah with the commander of Sennacherib's army (II Kings 18:17; Isa. 36:2). The location of the Fuller's Field is linked with that of the Upper Pool, which was part of the network of canals and reservoirs drawing their water from Gihon (*see* GIHON [SPRING]; POOL; SILOAM). Accordingly, the Fuller's Field has been tentatively identified with the area adjoining the Bir Ayyub (*see* EN-ROGEL), or with an area below the S end of the city of David, close to an ancient fuller's plant (*see* FULLER). Josephus' "Monument of the Fuller" (War V.147) might suggest for the Fuller's Field a location outside the N wall of Jerusalem under the monarchy, which is improbable for contextual reasons. *See* JERUSALEM § 6*c*.

Bibliography. G. A. Smith, *Jerusalem*, I (1907), 105; II (1908), 127. J. Simons, *Jerusalem in the OT* (1952), pp. 334 ff. H. Vincent, *Jérusalem de l'Ancien Testament*, II (1956), 645.

G. A. BARROIS

FULNESS. *See* PLEROMA.

FULNESS OF TIME. A phrase used to translate πλήρωμα τῶν καιρῶν in Eph. 1:10, and πλήρωμα τοῦ χρόνου in Gal. 4:4 KJV. In both passages reference is being made to the final fruition of God's purposes for men and history. The RSV translates the phrase in Gal. 4:4: "When the time had fully come" (i.e., the time appointed by God for the fulfilment of his purposes).

See also ESCHATOLOGY OF THE NT; PLEROMA.

J. KNOX

FUNERAL. This is not a biblical term. For discussion of customs and beliefs relating to last rites, *see* BIER; BURIAL; EMBALMING; IMMORTALITY; MOURNING; RESURRECTION; DEAD, ABODE OF THE; TOMBS.

FURLONG. The measure of distance used consistently in the KJV to translate στάδιον (II Macc. 12:9-10; Luke 24:13; John 6:19; 11:18; Rev. 14:20; 21:16). In II Maccabees and Revelation, the RSV has the plural "stadia." Elsewhere it interprets in terms of miles. A stadion was 215.5 yards; a furlong is 220 yards. *See* WEIGHTS AND MEASURES § D4*e*.

O. R. SELLERS

FURNACE. Furnaces in the biblical period were made of brick or stone and varied considerably in size and plan, from the small types used in domestic industries to large commercial smelters such as those of Solomon at Ezion-geber (*see* § 3 *below*).* The necessary parts of a furnace are a fire box or chamber, flue (for natural or forced draft), area or chambers for the material to be fired, and an opening to give access to the interior. The primary uses of the furnace were: (*a*) smelting or reducing ore (*see* REFINER); (*b*) melting ore for casting or heating it for forging (*see* METALLURGY); (*c*) firing pottery and other ceramic objects (*see* POTTERY); (*d*) firing bricks (*see* BRICKKILN; BRICK); (*e*) making LIME. Fig. MET 43.

1. Terminology. While absolute distinctions are difficult to make, a clarification of biblical terminology will be helpful. The smelting and the melting or heating furnace seem to be indicated by the Hebrew word כור (Deut. 4:20; I Kings 8:51; Prov. 17:3; 27:21; Isa. 48:10; Jer. 11:4; Ezek. 22:18, 20, 22); kilns are indicated by כבשן (Gen. 19:28; Exod. 9:8, 10; 19:18) or possibly מלבן (*see* BRICKKILN). The Aramaic אתון (Dan. 3:6-26—G 3:6-93) probably corresponds to כור. All these terms are embraced by the Greek word κάμινος, which always translates them in the LXX except in I Kings 8:51, where כור is rendered by a special term χωνευτήριον, a furnace for smelting metal.

To be distinguished from the preceding class is the תנור (κλίβανος, an OVEN made of pottery which was used in BAKING. תנור is translated by "furnace" four times in the KJV (Gen. 15:17; Neh. 3:11; 12:38; Isa. 31:9); in the RSV it is changed to "fire pot" in Gen. 15:17 and "oven" in Neh. 3:11; 12:38, but elsewhere left as "furnace." In Neh. 3:11; 12:38 one of the designated towers of Jerusalem's walls is designated מגדל תנורים, "Tower of the Ovens." *See* OVENS, TOWER OF THE.

Also translated by "furnace" is עליל (Ps. 12:6—H 12:7), the meaning of which is uncertain. The translation "furnace" for מוקד (Ps. 102:3—H 102:4) is arbitrary (cf. Isa. 33:14, where it is rendered "burnings").

The distinction between κάμινος, "furnace" (Matt. 13:42, 50; Rev. 1:15; 9:2), and κλίβανος, "oven"

(Matt. 6:30; Luke 12:28), is preserved in the NT.

2. The figurative sense. "Furnace" and related figures such as "crucible," "refining," along with various metals and combustible materials and "fire," appear in a variety of contexts meaning generally "to prove, try, test." The Egyptian captivity is spoken of as an "iron furnace" (Deut. 4:20; I Kings 8:51; cf. Jer. 11:4), "iron" here referring to the quality of the ordeal. Yahweh refines his people in the "furnace of affliction"—i.e., in the Captivity (Isa. 48:10; cf. Prov. 17:3; 27:21; Ecclus. 2:5). The figure is developed at length in Jer. 6:27-30. Ezekiel depicts the wrath of God as the hot blast of the smelter's furnace (22:17-22). The testing of the smith's products consists in tempering and forging them (Ecclus. 31:26 Amer. Trans.; cf. 38:28) and the proving of the potter's vessels in their firing (27:5). On the other hand, the promises of Yahweh are sure because they are refined like silver (Ps. 12:6—H 12:7).

The persecutions of Maccabean times are symbolized in the fiery ordeal of the three young men in Dan. 3:8-30 (cf. IV Macc. 16:21; Jos. Antiq. X.x.5; I Clem. 45:7), which has its Christian counterpart in the martyrdom of Polycarp (Martyrdom of Polycarp 15:2). This figure is readily applied to the trial which prepares for life after death (Wisd. Sol. 3:6; Jas. 1:12; I Pet. 1:7) or eschatological judgment (Matt. 13:42, 50; cf. I Cor. 3:10-15; Rev. 14:10-11; 16:8-9).

3. Archaeological evidence. The discovery of the huge smelters of King Solomon at Tell el-Kheleifeh (Ezion-geber) and smaller refineries to the N in the Wadi Arabah provide good patterns for the type of industrial furnace in use in the Iron Age. A smaller furnace was found at Tell Qasile near Tell Aviv. For a description of the Arabah, Ezion-geber, and Tell Qasile furnaces, *see* METALLURGY §§ 4-6.

Three wishbone-shaped kilns were discovered at Megiddo. The draft in this case entered under the door, blew through both arms of the furnace, and escaped in a double flue at the rear. Pottery was found stacked in two of these kilns as though packed for firing. In size the Megiddo kilns are nearly ten by eight feet over-all. Kilns have also been found at Gaza and Tell en-Nasbeh (Mizpah?) which differ slightly in plan from those mentioned above.

It is entirely possible that furnaces such as those at Tell Qasile, Megiddo, and Tell en-Nasbeh were used for both metalwork and firing ceramics and brick. Lime kilns were less elaborate, to judge from one found at Beth-zur; it still contained a mound of calcined rocks.

Bibliography. F. Petrie, *Ancient Gaza,* vol. I (1931), p. 6, pls. 6:5, 52:1. P. L. O. Guy, *Megiddo Tombs* (1938), pp. 75-78, figs. 84, 89. N. Glueck, *The Other Side of the Jordan* (1940), chs. 3-4. W. F. Albright, *Tell Beit Mirsim,* vol. II (*AASOR,* vol. XVII [1936-37], pl. 40:7-8 (cf. pl. 31:7); III (*AASOR,* vols. XXI-XXII [1941-43]), 110. C. C. McCown, *Tell en-Nasbeh* (1947), p. 258, pl. 100, figs. 52B, 60. C. Singer *et al.*, eds. *A History of Technology* (1954), pp. 391-97, 577. G. E. Wright, *Biblical Archaeology* (1957), pp. 132-35.

R. W. FUNK

FURNACES, TOWER OF THE. *See* OVENS, TOWER OF THE.

FURNITURE. 1. כלי, "utensil, implement." This term refers to the total of the furnishings of the tabernacle (Exod. 25:9; 40:9), the tent of meeting (Exod. 31:7 KJV [RSV FURNISHINGS]; 39:33 KJV [RSV UTENSILS]; I Chr. 9:29 [KJV VESSELS]), or a house (Neh. 13:8; KJV STUFF). The KJV translates the term as "furniture" also (RSV UTENSILS) when it refers to the utensils of the table in the tabernacle (Exod. 31:8), of the lampstand (31:8; 35:14), and of the altar of burnt offering (31:9). The phrase כלי חמדה (Nah. 2:9—H 2:10), "precious thing," is translated "pleasant furniture" by the KJV.

2. KJV translation of כר (RSV SADDLE) in Gen. 31:34.

E. M. GOOD

FURROW. The translation of גדוד (Ps. 65:10—H 65:11), מענה (I Sam. 14:14; Ps. 129:3), and תלם (Job 31:38; 39:10; Hos. 12:11). Two words are incorrectly translated "furrow" in the KJV: עונה (Hos. 10:10) is better "iniquity" (so RSV), and ערוגה (Ezek. 17:7, 10) is better "branch" or "bed" (so RSV). *See* ACRE; PLOW.

O. R. SELLERS

GAAL gā′əl [געל]. Son of Ebed (Obed?). He incited the city of Shechem to revolt against its king Abimelech in premonarchical Israel (Judg. 9:26-41). Abimelech, son of Jerubbaal (Gideon) and a Shechemite woman, slew his seventy brothers in a bold *coup d'état* and established himself as king of Shechem, installing Zebul as his resident prefect, while he himself dwelt at Arumah. When Gaal and his kinsmen, who appear to have been Canaanites, moved to Shechem, Gaal incited the citizens to overthrow the half-Israelite Abimelech and to restore a native Canaanite ruler. Informed by Zebul of the plot and instructed how best to marshal his forces, Abimelech ambushed the city during the night and routed Gaal and his followers in an encounter the next morning. Gaal fled for safety within the walls of Shechem, but he and his clansmen were promptly expelled by Zebul. E. R. DALGLISH

GAASH gā′ăsh [געש]. **1.** Mount Gaash (Josh. 24:30). The tomb of Joshua was at TIMNATH-SERAH in the hill country of Ephraim and N of Mount Gaash. From its association with Timnath-serah Mount Gaash is to be sought *ca.* twenty miles SW of Shechem.

2. The brooks of Gaash (נחלי געש), the home of one of David's warriors (II Sam. 23:30; I Chr. 11:32). Probably the reference is to a region of valleys in the vicinity of Mount Gaash. W. L. REED

GABA. KJV alternate form of GEBA.

GABAEL găb′ĭ əl [Γαβαήλ; Vulg. *Gabelus*]. **1.** One of the ancestors of Tobit (Tob. 1:1).

2. The brother or son of Gabrias, and the man with whom Tobias had left the deposit of money which Tobias set out to recover (Tob. 1:14; 4:20; 10:2). Invited by Raphael, he brought the money bags, with their seals unbroken, to the marriage feast of Tobias and Sarah (9:2-6). J. C. SWAIM

GABAON găb′ĭ ən. Douay Version form of GIBEON.

GABATHA găb′ə thə [Γαβαθα] (Add. Esth. 12:1). One of two eunuchs of Ahasuerus whose conspiracy against him was discovered and revealed by Mordecai. *See* BIGTHAN.

GABBAI găb′ī [גבי] (Neh. 11:8). A Benjaminite dwelling in Jerusalem after the Exile. The text, however, is probably corrupt and possibly should be emended in accordance with vs. 14 to read גברי חיל, "mighty men of valor." M. NEWMAN

GABBATHA găb′ə thə [Γαββαθά *or* (TR) Γαββαθᾶ, *indeclinable; transliteration of uncertain* Aramaic *term, perhaps* גבתתא, open space, *or* גבתא, height; *given as the* "Hebrew" (*i.e.,* Aramaic) *of* λιθόστρωτον, paved area, *which in the* LXX *translated* רצף *or* רצפה]. The paved court before the palace of Herod in Jerusalem, where the governor held court seated upon the high bema.

The term appears only once in the Bible, in John 19:13, although its Greek equivalent appears a few times. In the gospel, Gabbatha is the setting for the public trial of Jesus before the Roman procurator Pontius Pilate. It obviously lay outside the governor's residence (*praetorium*), the site of which has not been certainly identified. Since the Middle Ages some have held that Gabbatha is to be located near the present citadel where Herod the Great had built a castle, inside the W wall. No paved court has yet been discovered there. The site now favored is that adjacent to Herod's Tower of ANTONIA, called by Theodosius (A.D. 530) the "house of Pilate." This identification is all the more inviting because of the ancient pavement to be seen in the basement of the Convent of Our Lady of Zion. An extensive *lithostroton,* or paved court, whose central area measures about 2,500 square yards, has been excavated here.* Each paving stone is more than a yard square and a foot thick; some are marked for gaming and others are cut for drainage. The court extends eastward, beneath the Convent of the Flagellation. In the time of Jesus this paved court lay outside the N city wall. The later walls of Herod Agrippa I and Hadrian enclosed this pavement NW of the Antonia. It may have been in the latter reign also that a triple triumphal arch was built in this "Gabbatha" area, now known anachronistically as the Ecce Homo Arch (cf. John 19:5). Its large central arch now spans the traditional Via Dolorosa. Its N arch forms the choir of the Ecce Homo Church built about 1870 in the Convent of Our Lady of Zion. It is necessary to gain admission to this convent in order to see the *lithostroton,* plausibly the Gabbatha of John 19:13. Fig. ANT 36.

Bibliography. M. Burrows, *BA,* I (1938), 17-19; C. C. Torrey, *ZAW,* 65 (1953), 232-33; L. H. Vincent, *Jérusalem de l'AT* (1954), pp. 216-21. K. W. CLARK

GABDES. KJV Apoc. form of GEBA.

GABRIAS gā′brĭ əs [Γαβρίας=גבריא]. Brother (Tob. 1:14) or father (4:20) of Gabael, with whom Tobit had left the money Tobias went to recover. J. C. SWAIM

GABRIEL gā′brĭ əl [גבריאל, *from* גבר, man or strong, *plus* אל, God, *hence* man of God, *or* God has shown himself mighty; Γαβριήλ]. A celestial being, first appearing in a vision as a man (אדם; Dan. 8:16) and called "the man [האיש] Gabriel" (9:21; *see* ANGEL). He functions to reveal that which is to come in the Day of Judgment, to make known a vision (8:17), and to give understanding (שׂכל) and wisdom (בין; 9:22).

In the pseudepigraphical literature he receives great attention. His title and position become more explicit. He is one of the four presences (I Enoch 40: 3) who look down from heaven (9:1). He is one of the Lord's glorious ones (II Enoch 21:3), one of the holy angels (I Enoch 20:7). He sits at the left hand of God (II Enoch 24:1) and is set over all powers (I Enoch 40:9).

His function is also defined. He is no longer only the revealer, as in Daniel, but is the primary intercessor (I Enoch 9:1; 40:6; II Enoch 21:3). His work is of a less partisan nature than that of MICHAEL; but his work includes an element of severity: He must destroy the wicked (I Enoch 9:9-10) and cast the wicked into the furnace that God may be avenged (54:6).

The NT references show him to be both revealer and bringer of reassurance. In Luke 1:11-20 he appears to announce the birth of John (cf. Judg. 13:3). In Luke 1:26-38 he announces the birth of a son to Mary. He is one who stands in the presence of God (1:19), and can therefore reassure: "Do not be afraid, . . . for your prayer is heard" (vs. 13); "Do not be afraid, Mary, for you have found favor with God" (vs. 30). An allusion is made to Gabriel in Rev. 8:2, though not by name, as one of those who stand before God.

The Targ. magnifies the importance of Gabriel; he is introduced into narratives of a much earlier period. He leads Joseph to his brothers (Gen. 37:15), with Michael he participates in the burial of Moses (Deut. 34:6), and he is sent by the Lord to destroy the armies of Sennacherib (II Chr. 32:21).

In a characteristically Hebraic sense, where the messenger is, there God is fully present. Gabriel acts as a messenger (מלאך) before he is understood as an angel, revealing the graciousness and powerful purpose of the One who sends him.

W. BRUEGGEMANN

GAD găd [גד, to penetrate; *actually the name of a deity of fortune* (*cf.* Isa. 65:11); *according to others, originally the name of a person, a shortened verbal form* (*perfect tense*)]; GADITE găd'īt [גדי]. The seventh son of Jacob, and the *heros eponymos* of the tribe of Gad. Born of Leah's personal maid Zilpah (Gen. 30:11), Gad was the older full brother of Asher; this fact is always evident in the enumeration of the sons together, wherein the precedence is given to Gad (Gen. 35:26; 46:16; Exod. 1:4; I Chr. 2:2).

Gad is occasionally confused with the geographical name Gilead, which is itself ambiguous. Why the tribe was considered of inferior rank is beyond our cognizance; perhaps the situation of the colonial land compelled it to make all kinds of concessions to the native population. The connection with the Leah group, indicated in the descent from Zilpah, is attested by the joint settlement with Reuben. Like Reuben, Gad crossed over the Jordan from the W (for the general proof for this theory of colonization, *see* MANASSEH). That Gad originally attempted at one time to gain a foothold in the land W of the Jordan is probably indicated by the Judean place name Migdal-gad in the district of Lachish (Josh. 15:37)—an additional indication, moreover, of the genetic relationship with the Leah group. Gad crossed the Jordan with the remnants of Reuben, perhaps, if the latter did not follow later. In any case, it is noteworthy that Num. 32 grants precedence to the Gadites ahead of the Reubenites almost throughout, while Josh. 13 re-establishes the traditional sequence; however, the sequence may be geographically or numerically determined. Of more significance is the observation that the lists presented in the two chapters (twice, indeed, in Num. 32: vs. 3 and vss. 34-38) divide the places differently between the two tribes. In so doing the greater originality belongs once more to Num. 32, since Josh. 13 divides the settlement territory of the two tribes quite schematically into a S half for Reuben and a N for Gad. That this is an artificial division is shown by the designation of Dibon (Dhiban) as Dibon-gad in Num. 33:45 ff. This designation agrees best with the information in 32:34, according to which the Gadites rebuilt Dibon, and also Aroer, which, since it is not more specifically designated, everyone must have identified with the well-known place on the Arnon. The redactor of Josh. 13:25 only secondarily has made Aroer a place "across from" or even "east of" Rabbah (=Rabbath-ammon, 'Amman). So also Gadite Ataroth, mentioned between Dibon and Aroer in Num. 32:34, is unanimously identified with Khirbet 'Attarus, nine miles S of Baal-meon (Ma'in), the most southerly Reubenite village. Actually the settlements of Gad and Reuben are manifestly to be thought of as mingled together, and even the arrangement in Num. 32 may be only approximately correct. In any case, the old description of the Gad border, dating from the period before the kings and preserved in Josh. 13:16, 26-27*b*, along with the more recent list of places (town list), appears also to outline only a single territory which, presumably, was designated as Gad, *a potiori*. Substantiating this point of view is the fact that in the time of Omri and Ahab, King Mesha of Moab (see Mesha Inscription, line 10) knew nothing else than that "since primitive times the people of Gad resided in the land of Ataroth." He does not mention Reuben at all; the Israelites E of the Dead Sea are simply Gadites to him. As a matter of fact, according to the list of places in Num. 32:34-36, the territory of Gad extends from Dibon and Aroer in the S to Jogbehah (Khirbet Jubeihah) in the NE and Beth-nimrah (Tell Bleibil) in the NW and thus includes the Reubenite sites of vss. 37-38.

There can scarcely be any doubt that Gad's original possession turned out poorly. Obviously it involved, at first, only the W edge of the land E of the Jordan, the wooded slope of the plateau of Belka, in which there were few cities which might be able to halt them. The slope did, however, afford sufficient opportunities for the cattle herders coming up out of the valley of the Jordan. The task which Gad set for itself, as well as for Reuben, whose fate was bound up with its own in the later course of its history, was to gain a place also on the Moabite-

Ammonite plateau. At first the conditions of living were rather meager. The Jephthah tradition throws a significant light on it. Jephthah had to earn his living abroad. His fellow tribesmen called him back from there when they could use him in their oppression by the little Ammonite people. Jephthah came from "Gilead" (Judg. 12:7), which might, in a narrower sense, mean the region around present-day Khirbet Jel'ad, S of the Jabbok, if the name is not, as in the Song of Deborah, a direct alternate for the tribal name Gad. The region belonged to the greater Gadite territory, and the altercation with the Ammonites shows that the latter were not inclined to permit their property rights on the plateau proper to be reduced by the intruders. The oldest poetry further clarifies the situation. The Song of Deborah uses the name Gilead at a spot where Gad is to be expected and reproves the tribe for quietly staying on the other side of the Jordan; Gad had other troubles at this time which caused both it and Reuben to neglect the interests of the amphictyony, although the tribe could not have refused its assistance otherwise, when, e.g., Gideon with the army of the amphictyony was able to pursue the Midianites into the region of Nobah and Jogbehah (Judg. 8:11). In the Blessing of Moses the statement about Gad (Deut. 33:20) begins with praise for him "who enlarges Gad." In spite of everything said about the military excellence of Gad, it becomes clear that the tribe needed space. At the end Gad's intervention for the amphictyony is praised. In the Blessing of Jacob the purport is similar, perhaps somewhat more confident:

> Raiders shall raid [lit., "Raiders raid"] Gad,
> but he shall raid [lit., "raids"] at their heels
> (Gen. 49:19).

Thus Gad finds itself in a contested situation, but masters it; the story of Jephthah provides an example of this.

The song in Num. 21:27*b*-30 probably leads into the period when the tribes Gad and Reuben fought for the extension of their settlement out into the Moabite Plateau. However, it can no longer be determined whether the song should be dated before or after the rise of the Israelite kingdom. That precisely David's time gave impetus to the advance of Israelite settlement is to be accepted. We hear previously that at the time of Saul many Israelites sought refuge from the Philistines in the "land of Gad and Gilead" (I Sam. 13:7). Even early in the time of David the Gadite Bani, who was subsequently reckoned among the "Thirty," found his way to him (II Sam. 23:36). David's census began at Aroer on the Arnon with the enrollment of the tribe of Gad, to whose territory Jazer (cf. Num. 32:35), probably in the headwaters of the Wadi Kefrein, is surely to be reckoned, but, apparently, no longer "Gilead," which then, in a broader sense, signified also the country N of the Jabbok (II Sam. 24:5-6). Under Solomon the same territory belonged to the "district of Gad" (I Kings 4:19 LXX), while Mahanaim (Tell Hejjaj, immediately to the S of the Jabbok) was already the residence of the governor of the neighboring district to the N (I Kings 4:14). That, later on, the Gadite property rights especially on the plateau E of the Dead Sea varied greatly, according to the weakness or the strength of the government of Israel, is shown by the Mesha Inscription. According to line 7, Omri had taken possession of the land of Medeba, which, according to the boundary description in Josh. 13:16, once had been Israelite (if the boundary was not merely an ideal at that time). Dibon, Mesha's royal city, had been lost to Gad a long time. Now Mesha reconquered Medeba, likewise Baal-meon and Ataroth (where, according to line 10, "the people of Gad had resided since primitive times"). These were all places on the plateau, but he retook also Nebo (Khirbet el-Mekhaiyet) close to the edge of the plateau and even Kiriathon, which was, according to Eusebius, ten Roman miles westward from Medeba, and therefore on the slope to the Valley of the Jordan. In effect, Mesha extended his kingdom to the latitude of the N end of the Dead Sea; the Gadites had to flee or submit to his rule. That the remnant of the Gadites had to suffer under Hazael's invasion soon thereafter and came under the dominion of Damascus is not to be doubted, even if the name of Gad, in a traditional enumeration (with the out-of-date territorial designation "from Aroer on"), came into the account only secondarily (II Kings 10:33). Jeroboam II re-established the holdings as far as the "Sea of the Arabah" (or should, in II Kings 14:25, we read "Brook of the Willows" [Wadi el-Hesa], as in Isa. 15:7?), and thus apparently was forced to respect the Moabite border at the N end of the Dead Sea. Constant troubles caused by the neighbors made the Israelites, who lived in the land E of the Jordan, politically active in the last years of the existence of the N Israelite state. After Shallum of Jabesh in N Gilead the Gadite Menahem (גדי, RSV "Gadi," is not a proper name) mounted the throne for a decade (II Kings 15:14, 17). Scarcely a decade later the remaining territory of his tribe belonged to the Assyrian province of Gilead. The final report on the story of the sufferings of this remnant is to be found in Jer. 49:1-6, which probably dates from the period of the Exile. According to this, Milcom succeeded Gad, and his people—i.e., the Ammonites—established themselves in his cities.

The later literature mentions the tribe of Gad in lists, for the most part. In so doing the Priestly Code generally moves Gad away from Asher and into proximity with Reuben (Num. 1:24-25; 26:15-18; also 2:14; 7:42; 10:20); in the list of the scouts Gad stands at the end, separated from Asher by Naphtali (13:15); only in the list of the heads of tribes does Gad stand with Asher—but after him (1:14); in the commission for the distribution of the W land Gad is missing, but is mentioned before that along with Reuben and the half-tribe of Manasseh (34:14). In the Deuteronomic historical work Gad appears—outside the sources—always in contexts which concern the three E Jordanian tribes, usually after Reuben as the first (Deut. 3:12, 16; 4:43; 29:7; Josh. 1:12; 4:12; 12:6; 13:8, 24, 28; 20:8; 22:1). In Deut. 27:13, Gad is between Reuben and Asher among those who speak the curse. In the lists of the Levite cities Gad's place is along with Reuben in the last group of three, once ahead of and once after Zebulun (Josh. 21:7; I Chr. 6:63—H 6:48; and Josh. 21:36; I Chr. 6:80—H 6:65 respectively). In Ezek. 48:27, Gad receives the last, most southerly strip of the land W of the Jordan, if one compares the situation of Reuben between Ephraim and Judah, a late confirmation of the fact that, not Reuben's, but Gad's territory in the E once extended to the most southerly point on the Arnon; in Ezek. 48:34 the first W gate is named for Gad—ahead of Asher. In the lists of Chronicles, Gad appears once with Reuben and the half-tribe of Manasseh in the traditional sequence among the E Jordanian followers (I Chr. 12:37—H 12:38); the next time Gad is missing completely (27:16 ff), as is Asher. What the Chronicler produces about Gad otherwise is—except for the usual genealogy (5:11-17), which ranks Gad in the traditional sequence between Reuben and the half-tribe of Manasseh, but after Judah and Simeon—unverifiable reports concerning Gadites who went over to David (12:8, 14—H 12:9, 15), concerning an appointment of Levite officials (26:32), concerning an abduction by Tiglath-pileser (5:26) and above all a report put in the time of Saul, on a war of the three E Jordanian tribes with the Hagrites in which an altercation of a later period with the Arab Bedouins who were pressing forward from the E is presumably reflected (5:18-22; cf. vs. 10).

In the NT, Gad appears with Asher after Judah and Reuben in the list of the sealed (Rev. 7:5).

For the territory of Gad, *see* TRIBES, TERRITORIES OF, § D8*a*. *See* the bibliography under ASHER.

K. ELLIGER

GAD (DEITY). A deity or genius of good luck worshiped by Jewish apostates, probably in the postexilic period, together with "Destiny" (מני, MENI; Isa. 65:11). The nature of the deity is clear from an Aramaic-Greek bilingual inscription from Palmyra, where he is identified with τύχη, "Fortune." His cult was particularly popular in the Hauran. The reference in Isaiah may be connected with Edomite or Arab penetration of Palestine after the Exile.

Bibliography. G. A. Cooke, *A Textbook of North Semitic Inscriptions* (1903), pp. 267-69.

J. GRAY

GAD (SEER) [גד, *a divine name; cf.* Phoen. גדעזיז, fortunate]. A seer associated with David. To him is attributed a history of David's reign. His name may indicate an association with the tribe of Gad (cf. I Chr. 12:8). He called upon the fugitive David to depart from the land of Moab (I Sam. 22:3-5) and was Yahweh's spokesman in the account of David's census of the people. At his command David purchased the threshing floor of Araunah the Jebusite (II Sam. 24; I Chr. 21), the site of Solomon's temple (I Chr. 22:1). Gad is said to have had a share in the origin of the temple Levites (II Chr. 29:25).

The "Chronicles of Gad the seer" (I Chr. 29:29) appear to have been part of the "Commentary on the Book of Kings" (II Chr. 24:27), utilized by the Chronicler in compiling his history (cf. 20:34). Perhaps collections of stories concerning the words and deeds of the prophets were compiled by scribal civil servants connected with the court at Jerusalem.

Bibliography. M. Noth, *Die israelitischen Personennamen* (1928), pp. 126-27; S. Yeiven, "Social, Religious and Cultural Trends in Jerusalem Under the Davidic Dynasty," *VT,* III (1953), 149-65; W. O. E. Oesterley and T. H. Robinson, *Introduction to the Books of the OT* (1958), p. 114.

R. W. CORNEY

GAD, VALLEY TOWARD [הנחל הגד]. A place connected with the beginning of David's census (II Sam. 24:5). The RSV translates: "from the city that is in the middle of the valley, toward Gad . . . ," probably meaning the Arnon Valley. The KJV phrases differently and translates "the river of Gad."

E. D. GROHMAN

GADARA găd'ə rə [Γαδαρά]; **GADARENES** —rēnz. A city of the DECAPOLIS. The only biblical references are in the gospel accounts of the healing of the demoniac. The Gadarenes are mentioned in Matt. 8:28 in the RSV and the best MSS and in Mark 5:1; Luke 8:26, 37, in the RSV mg. and inferior MSS. In all these passages variant readings are "Gerasenes" and "Gergesenes," indicating the confused condition of the text. *See* GERASA.

Although Gadara was *ca.* five miles SE of the Sea of Galilee, its territory included the hot springs of el Hamme, N of the Yarmuk. Moreover, coins indicate its shipping interests, so that the "country of the

1. Country of the Gadarenes as viewed from the Sea of Galilee

Gadarenes" may well have extended to the shore of the lake. Fig. GAD 1.

Ancient Gadara is the modern Um Qeis, built on a headland along the E edge of the Jordan Valley. The site has not been excavated, but the visible remains indicate that it was a city two miles in circumference. It was predominantly Greek in population (Jos. Antiq. XVII.xi.4; War II.vi.3) and was equipped with structures typical of a Greek city, including two theaters, a basilica, a colonnaded street, and baths.

Bibliography. F.-M. Abel, *Géographie de la Palestine,* II (1938), 145, 176, 323; E. G. Kraeling, *Bible Atlas* (1956), pp. 382-83; D. Baly, *Geography of the Bible* (1957), pp. 198, 229, 230.

D. C. PELLETT

GADDI găd'ī [גדי, fortune(?); Vulg. *Gaddis;* Apoc. Γαδδι]; KJV Apoc. CADDIS kăd'ĭs. **1.** One of the spies sent by Moses to spy out the land of Canaan; son of Susi, from the tribe of Manasseh (Num. 13:11).

2. The name of John (KJV Johanan), eldest brother of Judas Maccabeus, leader of the struggle for Jewish independence in the second century B.C. (I Macc. 2:2).

GADDIEL găd'ĭ əl [גדיאל, Gad is God(?), *or* God is my fortune(?)] (Num. 13:10). A member of the tribe of Zebulun sent to spy out the land of Canaan; son of Sodi. His name is probably the full form of the name GAD.

Bibliography. M. Noth, *Die israelitischen Personennamen* (1928), pp. 126-27, 140. R. F. JOHNSON

GADFLY [קרץ, nipper; Akkad. *qarasu,* nip off; Arab. *qāriṣ,* mosquito, *from qaraṣa,* pinch; Ethio. *qērṣe;* Ugar. *qrṣ*] (Jer. 46:20); KJV DESTRUCTION. A nipping or stinging insect. Both horseflies (*Tabanidae*) and botflies (*Oestridae*) are called gadflies. Jeremiah uses the term figuratively of Nebuchadrezzar, who invaded Egypt (568-567 B.C.). Gadflies approach with a loud hum and inflict painful wounds. The fleeing of the heifer in Jer. 46:20 suggests a more formidable foe than the mosquito.

See bibliography under ANT. W. W. FRERICHS

GADI gā'dī [גדי, my fortune, *perhaps an abbreviation of* גדיאל (GADDIEL), God is my fortune] (II Kings 15:14). The father of King Menahem.

GADITES găd'īts [גדי]. Members of the tribe of Gad.

GAHAM gā'hăm [גחם, flame, *or* burning brightly] (Gen. 22:24). The second son of Nahor and his concubine Reumah.

GAHAR gā'här [גחר]. Head of a family of temple servants who returned from the Exile with Zerubbabel (Ezra 2:47; Neh. 7:49). *See* NETHINIM.

GAI gī, gā'ī [גיא, valley]. A locality in Philistia near Ekron, according to I Sam. 17:52 MT (RSV mg.). The KJV translation, "the valley," is improbable, since the MT lacks the article. The LXX (Codex Vaticanus) reads "Gath," and this is followed by the ASV mg., the RSV text, and most modern interpreters. W. F. STINESPRING

GAIUS gā'yəs [Γάϊος; Lat. *Gaius*] **1.** A Christian man at Corinth, mentioned in I Cor. 1:14 as one of the two men in that church who were baptized by Paul himself. He is almost certainly the same as the Gaius of Rom. 16:23, which letter was written at Corinth. In the latter passage he appears as a man who was prominent enough to be host to Paul while he was writing the letter, and also to the whole church. He has been identified with the Titius Justus of Acts 18:7 (*see bibliography*).

2. A Macedonian Christian, traveling companion of Paul, one of the two who were seized with him at Ephesus in the disturbance caused by Demetrius the silversmith (Acts 19:29).

3. A Christian of Derbe, who accompanied Paul on a journey from Ephesus to Macedonia (Acts 20:4). It is possible that Gaius § 2 and § 3, who are mentioned within a short space of each other, both times in connection with Aristarchus, may be the same man. The variant Δουβήριος in MS D would make him a Macedonian from the town of Doberus.

4. The Christian leader to whom III John is addressed (III John 1).

Bibliography. J. Chapman, *JTS,* 5 (1904), 366; E. J. Goodspeed, "Gaius Titius Justus," *JBL,* 69 (1950), 382-83, in which 1 *above* is identified with the Titius Justus of Acts 18:7. F. W. GINGRICH

GALAAD găl'ĭ əd. KJV Apoc. and Douay Version form of GILEAD.

GALAL gā'lăl [גלל, *perhaps* tortoise; *cf.* Syr. גללא *and* NH גל]. **1.** Son of Jeduthun, and an ancestor of one of those who returned from Babylon (I Chr. 9:16; Neh. 11:17).

2. A Levite among those returned from Babylon (I Chr. 9:15).

Bibliography. M. Noth, *Die israelitischen Personennamen* (1928), p. 230. B. T. DAHLBERG

GALATIA gə lā'shə [Γαλατία]. A region and Roman province in Central Asia Minor, named after the Celtic tribe of the Galatians (Acts 16:6; 18:23; I Cor. 16:1; Gal. 1:2; II Tim. 4:10; I Pet. 1:1).

1. The people of Galatia
2. Hellenistic Galatia
3. Roman Galatia
4. The archaeology of Galatia
5. The N and S Galatian theories

Bibliography

1. The people of Galatia. The inhabitants after whom Galatia was called, the Γαλάται, were a branch of the Indo-European tribe of the Celts or Galli (Gauls). The group which settled in Asia Minor came to be referred to as Galatians rather than Celts, although etymologically the names are identical.

The wanderings of the Celts in Europe in the first millennium B.C. took one group to the Danubian region and into Greece, where they raided Delphi in 279 B.C. A branch of this movement was invited to cross the Bosporus by King Nicomedes I of BITHYNIA, who was in need of auxiliaries in a war against his brother (278). The Bithynian king thus officially encouraged an invasion which proved disastrous to Asia Minor. *Ca.* twenty thousand Galatians, including warriors and their families, are reported to have crossed the Bosporus. Larger numbers followed, and when the more immediate purpose of Nicomedes had been achieved, the Galatians began to raid in Western Asia Minor on their own.

Their tactics were to lay siege to cities and to terrorize the countryside, plundering farms and sanctuaries. The danger was first countered by the Seleucid king Antiochus I, who defeated the Galatians in battle, with the aid of elephants (*ca.* 275 B.C.). Perhaps as a result of an arrangement by Antiochus, the Galatians were assigned a territory in the interior of Western Asia Minor which was to become known as Galatia.

The pattern of invasion and raids by Indo-European hordes had been an ancient one in Anatolia, but the Galatians are the first group to appear in the clear light of history. Three different tribes were involved: the Tolistobogii, who raided Aeolis and Ionia; the Trocmi, who raided in the region of the Hellespont; and the Tectosages, whose raids were in Central Asia Minor. Their tribal organization is described by Strabo, presumably in an accurate rendering of institutions in existence before his time (XII.567). Each of the three tribes was divided into four clans called "tetrarchies" by the Greeks, each tetrarchy having its separate tetrarch, judge, war leader, and two lieutenants. The twelve tetrarchies had one council of three hundred members, which met at a place called Drynemetum.

The military prowess of the Galatian tribesmen made them desirable as mercenaries, but a continuous menace as potential enemies of the Hellenistic powers in Asia Minor.

2. Hellenistic Galatia. The land occupied by the Galatians after their initial defeat by Antiochus was part of the central plateau of Asia Minor around the upper Sangarius and the middle course of the Halys River, bounded on the N by the kingdoms of Bithynia and Pontus. The new Galatia was a region which

Courtesy of F. K. Doerner

2. The plain of Ancyra (modern Ankara), capital of ancient Galatia, as viewed from the citadel

had become Phrygian after the downfall of the Hittite Empire. Even under Persian rule the Phrygian element had remained predominant. Greek colonization had not penetrated beyond the coastal regions, and Greek cultural influence was weak. The leading Phrygian cities were Pessinus, the ancient cult center of the Mother of the Gods; Gordium, the old Phrygian capital; and Ancyra.* These cities managed to maintain their Phrygian character in the Hellenistic period, especially Pessinus, which was still under its own dynasty of priests in the first century B.C. The Galatians did not become urbanized and lived in open sites, retreating to mountain fortresses in time of military danger. The men of the tribes were far from sedentary. Bands of warriors were constantly out raiding neighboring territory and made it a practice to exact ransom from their intended victims. Fig. GAL 2.

The threat was especially felt at Pergamum, whose kings became the champions of the Greeks in Asia Minor against the barbarian Galatians. A celebrated victory was gained by Attalus I *ca.* 240 B.C., but his successors often found the Galatians siding with their enemies. In one of the major battles for the division of power in Asia Minor, Galatian infantry and cavalry fought for Antiochus III against Rome and its allies Pergamum and Rhodes (190 B.C., at Magnesia). This prompted the Romans to send Consul Manlius Vulso on a military campaign into Galatia in 189. The Galatians were thoroughly defeated and plundered by the Roman army, but continued to menace the Attalids. The Romans failed to punish the Galatians again and instead granted them independence (166).

Galatian relations with the kings of Pontus were better than those with Pergamum, until Mithradates V in his first war against Rome massacred several of the Galatian leaders and their families (86 B.C.). This was meant to facilitate the reorganization of Galatia, but the remnants of the Galatian princes revolted and supported the Roman cause, especially the leader of the Tolistobogii, Deiotarus.

After the defeat of Mithradates, Pompey reduced the number of Galatian tetrarchs from twelve to three. Deiotarus was given the title of king of Galatia and made ruler over a larger area than his ancestors had controlled. A stretch of the Pontic coast and regions to the S and the E, including a part of Lesser Armenia, were added to his domains. After many vicissitudes in the civil war Deiotarus emerged as king of all Galatia in 42 B.C., but he died soon afterward (40). His secretary Amyntas in 37-36 received the kingdom of Galatia and several other possessions in Southern Asia Minor. Augustus confirmed his rule. Amyntas was killed in an expedition against the tribes of the Pisidian Mountains in 25. This meant the end of the kingdom of Galatia.

3. Roman Galatia. After the death of Amyntas the Romans created the Galatian province. This included Galatia proper (the region from Pessinus in the W to Tavium in the E) with major extensions: Lycaonia, Isauria, and Pisidia, including such cities as ICONIUM; LYSTRA; DERBE; and in Pisidia, Apollonia; ANTIOCH; Sagalassus; and Selge. This irregularly shaped territory bordered on the kingdom of Cappadocia in the E, was enclosed by the Paphlagonian Mountains to the N and the Taurus to the S, and had the more civilized province of Asia as its W neighbor. A variety of native peoples, partly Hellenized and Romanized, were thus added to the Galatian tribes living in the core of the province.

The Galatian city of Ancyra was selected as the capital of the new administrative unit. A cult of Roma and Augustus was established in this city and a temple constructed in the Hellenistic building tradition of Asia Minor. The Greek and Latin versions of Augustus' inscription of his deeds (the Monumentum Ancyranum) were carved on its walls.

Ancyra, originally the center of the tribe of the Tectosages, thus developed into the chief city of Galatia. It lay on important roads which probably continued pre-Galatian communication systems. Its Galatian counterparts remained Tavium to the E, chief town of the Trocmi, and Pessinus to the W; both were sites of prominent sanctuaries and now developing into market towns for the countryside.

Even this large new province was to be extended soon by new annexations. In 6-5 B.C. E Paphlagonia and some land E of the Halys were added to Galatia, and three years later Amasia in Pontus followed. Pontus proper was annexed under Nero in A.D. 64, extending the Galatian province as far as Trapezus. Vespasian added Cappadocia and Lesser Armenia in A.D. 72, thus enlarging the province of Galatia to a size and a geographical importance approaching that of the former Hittite Empire.

This "greater Galatia" soon began to be subdivided again. Trajan separated the provinces of

Galatia and Cappadocia, leaving Galatia approximately the size it had after 25 B.C.: the core of original Galatia with S Paphlagonia, Lycaonia, and N Pisidia.

All these changes in the size of the Roman province did not abolish the difference between the land originally held by the three Galatian tribes and the peripheral districts. Linguistically the difference must have been obvious, in spite of Hellenization and Romanization. The descendants of the Galatian invaders maintained their Celtic language, as is attested by Jerome and other sources, until the end of the fifth century. In Lycaonia the peasants spoke their own Lycaonian language (Acts 14:11), while the Phrygians retained their idiom; and various other Anatolian dialects must have continued in use in the secluded areas of the mountains.

The peculiar tribal organization of the Galatians, although gradually turning into political designations accompanied by imperial titles, was kept alive, and is referred to on coins until at least the end of the second century A.D.

4. The archaeology of Galatia. Explorations of the district of the Galatians have mostly been concerned with collections of surface material, inscriptions, and the tracing of Roman roads. The location of the three chief cities is known. Pessinus, modern Balhissar, is a badly plundered site which has furnished much building material to the modern town of Sivrihissar, ten miles to the N. Apart from the *cavea* of the theater and tombstones in the necropolis, little can be seen of ancient Pessinus.

Gordium, once capital of the Phrygians, never became prominent as a Galatian site. After Manlius' campaign of 189 B.C. it seems to have survived as an unimportant settlement. Its successor, Ancyra (now Ankara, the capital of modern Turkey), has been extensively rebuilt. It has considerable Phrygian remains, but its major monuments date from Roman times: the temple of Augustus and Roma, Roman baths, a column of Julian, and numerous architectural fragments built into the citadel.

Tavium has been identified in the ruins of Büyük Nefezköy, some twenty miles W of Yozgat. The settlement here too is pre-Galatian and goes back at least to the third millennium B.C. No excavation has taken place here, but recent discoveries of Roman milestones have helped to prove the identification of the site and to furnish evidence of the Roman roads which crossed at Tavium.

In general it is difficult as yet to identify material remains of this district as Galatian. The Phrygian cast of much of the Hellenistic and Roman material is unmistakable, and the Galatian way of living was hardly conducive to the establishment of a characteristic style in major or minor arts.

5. The N and S Galatian theories. Since no archaeological evidence is available for the history of early churches in Galatia, the churches in I Cor. 16:1; Gal. 1:2 can only tentatively be interpreted as belonging to Galatia proper or to the enlarged province of Galatia. A strictly historical point of view would be slightly in favor of the N Galatian theory, especially in the interpretation of Gal. 3:1: "O foolish Galatians." The name of Galatians would hardly be an appropriate designation for all inhabitants of the Roman province, but rather would evoke special memories of the history of the tribe. The use of "Galatia" in a wider sense in I Pet. 1:1 does not solve the difficulties of the NT Galatians.

Bibliography. A. H. M. Jones, *The Cities of the Eastern Roman Empire* (1937), pp. 111-23; K. Bittel, *Kleinasiatische Studien* (1942), pp. 1-38; D. Magie, *Roman Rule in Asia Minor* (1950), pp. 453-67, 1303-29; I. W. MacPherson, "Roman Roads and Milestones in Galatia," *Anatolian Studies,* IV (1954), 111-20; K. Bittel, "Funde im östlichen Galatien," *Istanbuler Mitteilungen,* VI (1955), 22-41.

M. J. MELLINK

GALATIANS, LETTER TO THE gə lā'shənz [Γαλάται, *see* GALATIA]. A letter written by the apostle Paul to "the churches of Galatia" and now found as the ninth book of the NT canon. In it he defends his gospel of salvation by faith rather than by works of the law. It is one of the most significant of early Christian documents, not only because of the light it throws upon Paul and the primitive churches, but also because of the influence it has exerted in subsequent history. Although a short letter, it has always ranked with the much longer Roman and Corinthian epistles in importance. A polemical document itself, it has figured prominently in every struggle of the church to maintain freedom of the Spirit against legalism of any kind.

1. Authorship
2. Purpose
   a. The main issue
   b. The other extreme
   c. Synthesis
3. Contents
   a. Personal section
   b. Doctrinal section
   c. Ethical section
4. Destination
5. Date
6. Canonicity
7. Text

Bibliography

1. Authorship. There can be no serious question about the authorship of this letter. The testimony of the ancient church uniformly ascribes it to Paul with no hint of doubt or difference of opinion. Possible reminiscences of its language can be found in Christian writing even before the end of the first century, and it was unmistakably known and used as Paul's by the end of the second (as by Irenaeus, Clement of Alexandria, Tertullian, and the Muratorian Canon). The letter itself not only claims Paul as its author but contains nothing which is in the slightest degree inconsistent with that claim. The style and vocabulary, the views expressed, the personal characteristics manifested, are in all significant respects those found in Romans, I and II Corinthians, and other letters. If Paul wrote any of these letters, he undoubtedly wrote this one too. During the entire history of criticism this has very rarely been denied and today is universally acknowledged.

2. Purpose. At first sight, at least, the purpose of the letter seems equally clear. Paul had during the course of his missionary labors established a number of churches in the province of Galatia (as to just where, *see below* § 4). At some later time (*see* § 5) word

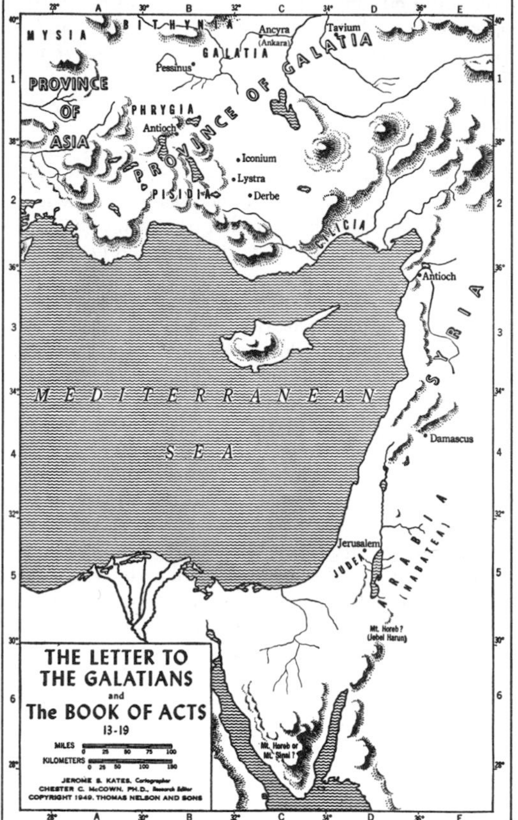

reached him that his Galatian churches were in grave danger of falling away from the truth of Christ as Paul understood it and as his converts had first learned it, and of embracing a "different gospel"—which from Paul's point of view was not a gospel at all. The preachers of the "new" gospel in Galatia, who were presumably visiting teachers, were also seeking to cast doubt on the authenticity of Paul's own apostleship and the authority of his teaching, insisting apparently upon the higher authority of certain apostles at Jerusalem. Paul wrote this letter in the first flush of his indignation and distress at hearing this news.

a. The main issue. We are left in no doubt whatever as to the main issue between Paul and his critics. It was the same issue as threatened to divide, and in a measure *did* divide, the whole church at the middle of the first century—the issue of the relation of the Christian to the Jewish law (*see* LAW; *also*, for further detail of Paul's view, *see* JUSTIFICATION; FAITH). Although it may be argued that Paul was not always consistent, it was certainly his characteristic position that to be in Christ meant being free from the legal requirements of Judaism. The believer is justified by faith alone. Non-Jews, therefore, might become full members of the body of Christ on the sole basis of faith in Christ, without assuming any of the obligations imposed by the legal code. Paul's opponents denied that any such freedom was possible. They held that the gospel fulfilled, but did not displace, the law. The Christian, as well as the Jew, was subject to its provisions.

These "Judaizing" teachers, as they are usually called, have been referred to above as "visiting teachers," and this seems likely in view of the way Paul distinguishes between them and the congregations he is addressing (e.g., in 1:9; 4:17; 5:10, 12; 6:13). It is well to remember, however, that he nowhere identifies them as "outsiders" and that there is no overruling reason why we should not think of them as being Galatians themselves. Nor can we be absolutely sure they were Jews. One would naturally assume they were, and the great majority of scholars have always so regarded them. Others, however, point to the present tense of the participle in 6:13—"Even those who receive circumsion [i.e., are being circumcised] do not themselves keep the law, but they desire to have you circumcised that they may glory in your flesh"—and urge that these Judaizers were Gentile Christians who had accepted circumcision and all that it involved and were now seeking to bring Paul's Galatian converts to the same position.

Although it is clear that the threat of large-scale apostasy is very real and Paul feels he is fighting for the very life of his churches in Galatia, one gathers he does not despair of countering the efforts of his opponents and of winning back to his "gospel" and to himself as an apostle of Christ the loyalty of his troubled and wavering congregations. Both his alarm and his hope appear in the vigorous defense of the integrity and independence of his own apostleship, in the impassioned argument for his position that salvation depends on faith alone (not on works of the law), and in the repeated and equally passionate allusions to the close personal and affectionate relations in which he has stood to the Galatians.

b. The other extreme. The issue raised by the Judaizers was, all agree, the principal occasion for the letter. Some scholars have urged, however, that it is not the sole occasion—or a sufficient occasion for this particular letter. They point to the section beginning with 5:13 and running almost to the end—a section primarily concerned with saying, "You were called to freedom, brethren; only do not use your freedom as an opportunity for the flesh. . . . If we live by the Spirit, let us also walk by the Spirit"—and urge that there were two distinctive parties in the Galatian churches. Over against the Judaizing party stood another, also hostile to Paul, which advocated, or at least allowed, moral license. Paul was, it is argued, defending his position on two fronts—against legalists who accused him of being too radical and against antinomians who called him too conservative.

As further evidence of the existence of such an antinomian party these scholars refer to 5:11: "If I, brethren, still preach circumcision, why am I still persecuted?"—a statement exceedingly perplexing and difficult on any view, but which is held to imply, at the very least, that Paul was being charged in Galatia with preaching circumcision. But who would have brought such an accusation? Certainly not the Judaizers. Such a charge could have been brought only by enemies at the opposite extreme.

These scholars also point to a certain ambiguity in the first two chapters of the letter, where Paul is describing and defending his own apostleship. On the one hand he seems to want to assert his independence of the older apostles at Jerusalem, to whom presumably the Judaizers are appealing; but on the other he seems equally eager to establish the fact that he not only consulted with them, but also sought and secured their approval of his message and his work among the Gentiles. In affirming his independence of the Jerusalem apostles, it may be argued, he is answering charges of obsequiousness made by the antinomians; in emphasizing their approval of his work he is denying the contentions of the Judaizers that he was an unaccredited "apostle" without the support of the pillars of the church.

c. Synthesis. The presence of these somewhat contradictory data cannot be denied, but most scholars would say that they do not need to be interpreted as implying an antinomian "party" in Galatia—although it must be conceded that they will prevent our defining Paul's purpose as simply as we might otherwise do. As for the admonitions against the misuse of freedom in which chs. 5 and 6 abound, they may very naturally be understood as a kind of corollary of Paul's vigorous insistence on the freedom itself. He stands for freedom from the law, but he wants to make clear that he does not stand for moral license. Obviously he would recognize that his position needed to be guarded against this misinterpretation, and he may have had some reason for believing that some of his supporters in Galatia were actually understanding him in this mistaken way. But one does not need to assume a hostile "party." Indeed, Paul appears to be dealing with a *moral* failure, or a possible moral failure, rather than with a theological error; and, as a matter of fact, it is more probable that he is trying to correct those who think of themselves as advocates of his own position than that he is seeking to refute the arguments of opponents.

As for the other evidences of ambiguity, again one can acknowledge them without having to resort to the theory of two hostile parties. For one thing, we may recognize that Paul was concerned, not only with the freedom of the Gentiles from the requirements of the Jewish law, but also with the unity of the church. The freedom of the Gentiles must be maintained, but it must not divide the body of Christ. This concern for unity will perhaps help explain the ambivalences in Paul's discussion of his relations with the apostles at Jerusalem; he wants to establish both his independence of them and the fact of their cordial support of his work.

It may also be suggested, by way of further explanation of some of the contradictory data, that Paul may be facing two kinds of Judaizers. Some of them, truly understanding Paul at the vital point, recognized him as an enemy; other Judaizers, misunderstanding him, were claiming him as a friend. Some truly recognized that Paul was preaching freedom from the law and denied that he had any authority to do so. Others, seeking to defend him from the Judaizers' own point of view, denied that he took so radical a position and pointed to his close relations with the apostles at Jerusalem. It would be to Judaizers of this latter kind that Paul says, "If I am still preaching circumcision. . . ." He would be as much opposed to his "friends" as to his "enemies"; and the fact that he must answer both would explain some of the peculiar ambiguities of the letter.

If it is contended that Paul's position on this issue of the law could hardly have been so misunderstood by his friends as this last suggestion implies, the answer is that we have in the book of Acts, which is certainly friendly to Paul, a document which actually misunderstands him in much the same way. Although Acts itself belongs to a later generation, it rests upon older sources, and it is not improbable that some, at least, of these older sources represented Paul as much less radical than his own letters show him to have been. These sources, like Acts later, must have been defenders of Paul, but defenders on grounds which Paul would vigorously repudiate. It is because Paul is, in this sense, "fighting on two fronts" that in this letter he seems as eager to establish that he does actually and consistently preach freedom from the law as to justify his position in doing so.

This complexity of the polemical situation and the necessity of answering contradictory claims and charges will help explain a certain frustration which one cannot help sensing in Paul's attitude. As he says, he hardly knows which way to turn (4:20). He is being attacked and being defended by persons who only partly understand him, and in certain respects deeply misunderstand him. His own conceptions of the meaning of the gospel and of his own apostleship are being misrepresented by some and rejected by others. He turns now in one direction, trying to make clear his position against those who are claiming him as a legalist, and now in the other, defending his position against those who are attacking him as a radical. But all are legalists or are in danger of becoming such, and one does not need to postulate a radical or antinomian "party." Paul is appealing with desperate, almost frantic, earnestness to the body of the Galatian Christians against legalists who, as he sees it, either unfairly attack or falsely defend him and, even more important, are tempting the church to reject the truth of Christ.

3. Contents. The letter may be summarily outlined as follows:

I. Salutation and introduction, 1:1-5
II. Personal defense, 1:6–2:21
III. Defense of the gospel, 3:1–4:31
IV. Ethical implications of the gospel, 5:1–6:10
V. Conclusion, 6:11-18

It begins very abruptly, the salutation itself containing both a defense of Paul's apostleship and a statement of his gospel: "Paul an apostle—not from men nor through man, but through Jesus Christ and God the Father, who raised him from the dead—and all the brethren who are with me, to the churches of Galatia: Grace to you and peace from God the Father and our Lord Jesus Christ, who gave himself for our sins to deliver us from the present evil age, according to the will of our God and Father; to whom be the glory for ever and ever. Amen." Paul's eagerness and haste to get to the business of the letter also appear in the omission of the paragraph of thanksgiving and felicitation which in every other letter immediately follows the salutation. As a matter of fact, Paul was in this moment not in the mood for compliment or thanksgiving, preoccupied as he was with the distressing news of the threat of apostasy in Galatia, which, we may assume, has just reached him. His letter reflects the first shock of his surprise and disappointment, and his immediate impulse to fight back.

a. Personal section. Paul is astonished, he declares, at hearing that the Galatians are so quickly turning away from the gospel which he had preached to them to accept "a different gospel," which is not a gospel at all. He refers to the way he had received the gospel message which he had brought to them. It was not a human affair, but had come to him through a revelation of Christ. He reminds them of his previous zeal as a Jew and of his opposition to the church. Far from learning anything from other Christians in this period, he had been fanatically persecuting them. It was God who had revealed his Son to him—suddenly and without previous preparation—that Paul might be Christ's apostle to the Gentiles.

Even after this transforming experience, he did not go to Jerusalem to see those who were already apostles, but remained in the neighborhood of Damascus, where the revelation had occurred. Apparently his enemies (or "friends") were saying that he had left Damascus for Jerusalem. Paul acknowledges leaving Damascus but insists that it was for the purpose of a visit to Arabia (the territory just to the east of Damascus), and that when his business there was completed he returned directly to Damascus. He did not go to Jerusalem until three years (or perhaps in the third year) afterward, and then he saw only Peter and James. (His oath to the truth of this statement suggests that it was being said that he saw others, perhaps some official council such as we read about in Acts 15.) Fourteen years later he went up to the city again—this time to lay before the leaders there (James, Peter, and John) the gospel (involving freedom from the law) which he was preaching to the Gentiles. These "pillars," after listening to him and his associate Barnabas, gave him the right hand of fellowship, the understanding being that he would work among the Gentiles and they among the Jews. The only stipulation was that the Gentile Christians should contribute to "the poor" of the Jerusalem church. This condition Paul readily accepted.

After describing (2:11-14) an incident in Antioch which revealed that although James and others, representing the more conservative "Jewish" point of view, had been willing for Paul to release the Gentiles from the requirement of circumcision, they were not willing to admit them to full fellowship in the church, Paul moves gradually into the more doctrinal middle section of the letter, which is well under way at the beginning of the third chapter.

b. Doctrinal section. This section does not exhibit a systematic or even an altogether coherent structure. Paul is now defending not so much himself as the soundness of his position, and he makes his points as they occur to him in the heat of discussion. His arguments tumble over one another.

He begins by appealing to the experience of the Galatians. Had they not received the Spirit simply upon believing the gospel, and without works of the law of any kind? He then appeals to the example of Abraham, who, we may suppose, figured largely in the arguments of his opponents. Abraham, Paul affirms, was a man of faith, receiving the promise of God's blessing centuries before the law was given. The later law cannot be thought of as abrogating God's original promise. Its purpose was the temporary one of revealing man's plight as the slave of sin in order that, in despair of himself, he might be moved to throw himself upon God's mercy in Christ, who had taken the law's "curse" upon himself and opened to us the possibility of freedom both from the penalty of the law and from the law itself. A child until he becomes of age is under the care of guardians or trustees, but at the appropriate time he becomes free—no longer a slave subject to the regulation of others, but a son. Christ has thus set us free. We have become sons and heirs of God. How, then, can the Galatians bear to think of turning back to slavery again?

Paul finds a final argument in the scriptural story of Sarah and Hagar, which he understands allegorically—Hagar standing for the present Jerusalem and the law system and bearing children who are slaves, and Sarah standing for the order of grace and for the "Jerusalem above" whose children are free.

c. Ethical section. The last section, constituting roughly the fifth and sixth chapters of the letter, begins with a strong appeal that the readers stand firm in the freedom with which Christ has set them free. They must resist and repudiate those who are unsettling them. But it is just as important that they not make their freedom an excuse for licentiousness or for pride. If they live by the Spirit, they should walk by the Spirit. And the fruit of the Spirit is never immorality, quarreling, party spirit, and the like, but rather "love, joy, peace, patience, kindness, goodness, faithfulness, gentleness, self-control." The letter closes with a personal appeal: "Far be it from me to glory except in the cross of our Lord Jesus Christ, by whom the world has been crucified to me, and I to the world. For neither circumcision counts for anything, nor uncircumcision, but a new creation. . . . Henceforth let no man trouble me; for I bear on my body the marks of Jesus."

4. Destination. Reference has already been made to some uncertainty as to the location of the churches to which Paul is writing. The uncertainty arises out of the ambiguity of the place name "Galatia." As is explained elsewhere (*see* GALATIA), in Paul's period this name belonged to a large province of the Roman Empire, but had been given the province only because of its earlier use to designate a region in the northern part of the province inhabited by an ethnic group who were still known as Galatians in a special, and more precise, sense. Are Paul's readers Galatians in that sense, or may the churches he is addressing be thought of as Galatian in the broader meaning of the term? This question cannot be answered with certainty, since Paul does not identify the churches more exactly; but the fact that he seems generally to have used geographical terms in the

Roman sense creates the strong presumption that by "the churches of Galatia" he means churches which might have been located anywhere in the province. Certainly when he mentions "the churches of Asia" (I Cor. 16:19) he is speaking in provincial terms. In the same way he alludes to "the churches of Macedonia" (II Cor. 8:1), and similarly to "Achaia" (II Cor. 9:2).

This question has had a certain interest because the book of Acts describes an evangelistic tour of Paul's through the southern part of the province in the course of which churches were established in Lystra, Derbe, Iconium, and Pisidian Antioch; and if "Galatia" can be interpreted in the more inclusive sense, it is possible to suppose that it is these churches to which Paul is writing. This is the "South Galatia" theory. If the narrower sense is correct—the "North Galatia" hypothesis—we must locate the churches in the northern region where the race of Galatians lived, and can only guess where the churches were or how they came to be established. Acts does not describe any visit of Paul into that region, although the possibility of such a visit is certainly not ruled out. Indeed, many scholars understand Acts 16:6 to refer to "North Galatia."

The fact that Paul probably used the term "Galatia" in the wider sense must not be taken to imply that the churches addressed were necessarily the churches of which we happen to hear in Acts. Those churches may have been located anywhere in a large region, north or south. Still, the Acts account of Paul's activities in the southern part of the province gives a certain weight to the "South Galatia" hypothesis. This whole issue, for the time being at least, is of minor importance because, even if we could surely identify the churches with those in South Galatia, we know so little about these churches from Acts or other sources that the information would be of negligible value in the interpretation of the letter itself.

5. Date. The question of the date of the epistle is both more controversial and more significant. It is also one of the most complicated problems in NT introduction (*see* CHRONOLOGY OF THE NT; PAUL). According to one view, Galatians is the earliest of Paul's letters and was written from Antioch in Syria after his return from the "first missionary journey" recorded in Acts 13–14 and before his departure for the "apostolic council" described in Acts 15 (*see* COUNCIL OF JERUSALEM). The principal argument for this view runs somewhat as follows: When Paul wrote Galatians, he had made two visits to Jerusalem since his conversion at Damascus, and only two. We can be sure of this because he speaks of only two visits in Gal. 1:18–2:10; and the nature of the argument he is making there would require that he mention other visits if they had occurred. The "council" visit in Acts 15 is the *third* visit of Paul to Jerusalem of which Acts tells us. Therefore the letter must have been written before it. But the letter presupposes the existence of Galatian churches; and, according to Acts, these churches were established just before the "council" (Acts 13–14). Therefore the letter was written between the events of Acts 14 and 15, or just after Paul's return from his first visit to Galatia and just before his third, the "council," visit to Jerusalem. This dating of the letter is supported by various minor considerations—e.g., Paul's saying in 1:6, "I am astonished that you are so quickly deserting . . . ." But the really decisive argument is the chronological one.

If we could trust entirely the accuracy of the Acts account of Paul's visits to Jerusalem, the case for the early dating would be unassailable. The great majority of scholars, however, do not find this case convincing. The major obstacle in the way of dating Galatians before the "apostolic council" of Acts 15 is the fact that in Gal. 2:1-10 Paul seems to be describing that same incident in retrospect. Acts 15 tells of a conference in Jerusalem participated in by James, Peter, Paul, Barnabas, and others and concerned with the problem of the status of Gentiles in the church. Paul in Gal. 2 tells of a conference involving the same principals and concerned with the same issue. To be sure, there are some striking differences—notably the more formal or official character of the Acts conference—but the differences can for the most part be explained by the development of the tradition and by the special interests of the author of Acts.

Those who date Galatians early must maintain that there were two conferences on the Jewish issue. The one described by Paul in Galatians took place on the occasion of Paul's visit to Jerusalem as recorded in Acts 11:29-30, which was made primarily for another purpose. The author of Acts, it is argued, does not mention this conference in this connection because he did not know of it; Paul himself tells us that it was a private affair (Gal. 2:2). The formal council described in Acts 15 was another and quite a different conference, held later and as a result of just such developments in the missionary field as the Letter to the Galatians exhibits.

But plausible as such contentions can be made, the majority of scholars are unconvinced. They are inclined to regard the Galatians and Acts narratives as accounts of the same conference, which means that the letter must have been written after the events of Acts 15. Various ways are resorted to of explaining the Acts error in calling this visit of Paul to Jerusalem the third visit rather than the second. The most popular of these is that an actual visit with two purposes was understood by the writer of Acts to be two visits. But such theories lie outside the scope of the present article. *See* CHRONOLOGY OF THE NT.

Once Acts 15 ceases to establish the latest possible date for Galatians, there is no reason why the letter should not be placed as late as the period of Romans and the Corinthian letters, with which it has close affinities in content; and it is usually so dated. It has been variously placed before Corinthians, between I and II Corinthians, and between II Corinthians and Romans—in any case, during the last few years of Paul's active career.

Yet a third possible date needs to be considered. It is usually taken for granted that this letter was written during a period when Paul was at liberty, but the possibility that it is one of the "imprisonment epistles" cannot be excluded. It is true that in Galatians Paul does not refer to his "bonds" as he does in the other letters of this category, but in view of the passionate earnestness of this particular letter and its intense preoccupation with its subject this silence cannot be regarded as significant. Moreover, if it is true that he nowhere refers to his imprisonment, it can also be said that he nowhere speaks of any prospective travel. One might have expected some reference to a later visit when Paul would personally confront his opponents (cf. II Cor. 10:2; 12:14; 13:10; etc.). Indeed, in view of the desperate importance of the issue in Galatia, one cannot help wondering why Paul is not going instead of writing. He says, "I could wish to be present with you now" (4:20). Why can he not be? One might expect him at least to promise, or threaten, a visit. It may also be pointed out that the words in the salutation, "all the brethren who are with me," may be considered strange if Paul was settled in or near one of his churches. Of course he may have been on a journey —but it is also possible that he was in prison.

If Galatians was written from prison, it was almost certainly written after Romans and was one of Paul's latest letters. This dating of Galatians after Romans, rather than shortly before it, has the advantage of making more intelligible Paul's being able to say with such complacency in Rom. 15:23: "Now, since I no longer have any room for work in these regions," etc. Such a remark is hard to understand almost immediately after the serious situation which the Letter to the Galatians reveals. But in view of how little we know about Paul's life, an argument of this kind cannot be pressed. It has been often argued that a comparison of parallel sections of Galatians and Romans (there are a number of striking examples) indicates the priority of Galatians. But this is far from certain. Despite the authority of some great names to the contrary, it is not clear that the Galatians parallels do not represent reminiscences, rather than anticipations, of the language of the longer letter. Romans was written in a relatively quiet and reflective mood; Galatians, in the heat of battle. The longer, more careful, statement does not need to be the later.

6. Canonicity. The Letter to the Galatians has a very interesting and important place in the early history of the CANON OF THE NT. The first definite event in that history was undoubtedly the collection of Paul's letters. This collection was made, probably at Ephesus and even more probably during the last decade of the first century, and was the work of some individual or church, or of some group of individuals or churches, who knew some of Paul's letters, knew of or suspected the existence of others, and believed that what he had written deserved to be much more widely known. The letters were sought out, assembled, and published as a single work for the use of the churches.

There is good reason to believe that the several letters were arranged in order of length, the Corinthian and the Thessalonian letters being taken together in each case, and Philemon being closely associated with Colossians. Whether this is true or not, however, the letter which we know as Ephesians, but which at first had no local address (*see* EPHESIANS), stood almost certainly at the opening of the book as the first epistle—a general letter to the churches serving as a preface to the particular church letters which followed and as a symbol that they too had something to say to the whole church. This collection of letters (identical with the Pauline corpus in our canon with the exception of the letters to Timothy and Titus, which were later added) was known apparently to the author of I Clement, Ignatius, and Polycarp, and may be supposed to have been widely distributed among the churches in the opening years of the second century.

It became even more important, however, when the heretical teacher MARCION at some time before the middle of that century adopted (and adapted) the collection as a major part of a new "Bible" for his followers. The Marcionites rejected the Jewish scriptures (which up to this time had been and for a while continued to be the sole scriptures for "orthodox" Christians) and put in their place the "Gospel and Apostle"—the "Gospel" being a document, shorter than, but very similar to, our Luke, and the "Apostle" being the collected letters of Paul. Apparently, however, Marcion did not leave the latter in their original order but replaced Ephesians in first place with Galatians. His reasons for giving Galatians the place of honor are clear enough. The emphasis with which Paul in this letter set gospel against law must have commended it especially to Marcion, who saw in it a great manifesto of that freedom of Christianity from Judaism, the new from the old, which he was most concerned to declare. This early issue between Ephesians and Galatians as regards their order in the Pauline letter corpus is perhaps reflected in the fact that even now the only exception to the order of length among the letters of Paul involves these two letters.

7. Text. The text of the letter is as surely established as that of any NT document. At many points of detail there must be some uncertainty since the MS evidence is ambiguous. But they are not important points, and even at most of these the agreement of the better witnesses establishes the text with reasonable probability. There is no evidence that the text of the letter has suffered any major derangement or revision in the course of its transmission.

Bibliography. Commentaries: J. B. Lightfoot (1892); E. D. Burton, ICC (1920), much the most adequate; H. Lietzmann, Handbuch zum NT (2nd ed., 1923); G. S. Duncan, Moffatt NT Commentary (1934); R. T. Stamm, *IB*, vol. X (1953). See also introductions to literature of the NT by Goodspeed, Moffatt, Jülicher, Barnett, etc.

Important special studies, especially regarding purpose: J. H. Ropes, *The Singular Problem of the Epistle to the Galatians* (1929); J. Munck, *Paulus und die Heilsgeschichte* (1954), ch. IV.

J. KNOX

GALBANUM găl'bə nəm [חֶלְבְּנָה, *ḥelbᵉnâ;* χαλβάνη]. The aromatic, resinous gum from a plant, probably *Ferula galbaniflua* Boiss. and Buhse or related species of giant fennel, imported from Persia or India. Identification of the ancient source of galbanum is still somewhat uncertain. According to Exod. 30:34, it was a "sweet spice" used as an ingredient of the holy incense burned in the tabernacle. In Ecclus. 24:15 the same list of spices appears in a metaphor in praise of Wisdom.

See also FLORA § A7*h;* INCENSE; SPICE.

Bibliography. H. N. and A. L. Moldenke, *Plants of the Bible* (1952), p. 102. J. C. TREVER

GALEED găl'ĭ əd [גלעד, witness heap]. A pile of stones heaped up by Laban and Jacob as a sign of their covenant and a boundary mark for their respective countries (Gen. 31:46-54). It is intended to furnish an etymology for the name Gilead; for the other name given the heap, *see* MIZPAH. A similar explanation is given in Josh. 22:10-34, where in the original story the altar built by the E tribes to symbolize their unity with the other Israelites must have been called Galeed, or possibly Ed (vs. 34); but the words were deleted by harmonistic editors. *See* WITNESS. S. COHEN

GALGAL găl'găl. Douay Version form of GILGAL.

GALGALA. KJV Apoc. form of GILGAL.

GALILEANS, THE. Inhabitants of GALILEE, including Jews, pagans, and, from the first century A.D., Christians. The Galileans may have been distinctive in their religious views.

1. Question of a Jewish party. The second-century Christian writers Hegesippus (quoted in Euseb. Hist. IV.22.7) and Justin Martyr (Dial. 80:4) mention Galileans among the religious parties of Judaism along with Pharisees, Sadducees, Essenes, and some more obscure groups. There is rabbinic evidence that in the first century A.D. customs prevailed in Galilee which were not current in other parts of Palestine. E.g., in Galilee a newly married pair were permitted to be alone on their wedding night; there were differences in the rights of a widow and with regard to the Day of Atonement; in Galilee no work was done on the day before Passover, and the festival may actually have been observed a day earlier; the Pharisees considered Galilean olive oil ritually impure; and the Galileans refused to accept the Pharisaic rule (an extension of Exod. 23:19; Deut. 14:21) that meat might not be eaten with dairy products. The Pharisees considered the men of Galilee as boorish, uncultivated, and pugnacious. It is not quite certain, however, that they constituted a self-conscious religious party or sect comparable to the Pharisees or Essenes. The variations in custom might be accounted for by their being *'ammê hā-'âreṣ*—i.e., unlettered, conservative agrarians who followed none of the parties then existing, and who were perhaps not deeply religious. On the other hand, some of the Galilean customs suggest the more conservative Pharisaic school of Shammai, in contrast to the school of Hillel, whose rulings later became dominant. Perhaps within Galilee itself more than one type of thought influenced local custom. There is no evidence that Jesus adhered to a Galilean religious party.

2. Galilean Christianity. Attempts have been made to analyze the type of Christianity current in Galilee in the first two centuries A.D. Of all the gospel material, that contained in Mark seems closest to the Galilean background. Most of Jesus' ministry is laid in this region. Mark includes two separate cycles of teaching material, one dealing with the kingdom of God and the other with the Son of man, both of which may be Galilean and which have counterparts in Q. The kingdom-of-God sayings are all placed in the setting of the Galilean ministry. Mark is the gospel which, of all four, has fewest parallels to the teaching of the Qumran Scrolls, which come from S Judea. The ending of the gospel looks forward to the Resurrection (or perhaps the manifestation of the Son of man) in Galilee, and in this Matthew follows Mark. By contrast, Luke and John show a greater interest in Jesus' activity in Samaria and Judea.

The later history of Galilean Christianity is obscure. James the brother of the Lord must have come from Galilee, but Acts and other sources picture him as head of the church of Jerusalem, and he may represent the type of Christian faith current there. Hegesippus (in Euseb. Hist. III.20.1-5) knows of grandsons of Jude the brother of the Lord who in Domitian's time lived in Palestine and owned their own farm. After they were questioned by the emperor and released, they "ruled the churches"; but, while this was probably in Galilee, it is not certain. Other members of Jesus' family such as Symeon the son of Clopas, seem to have been bishops in Palestine after the First Jewish Revolt. It is sometimes thought that the letters of James and Jude exemplify Galilean Christianity, but this rests principally on the names traditionally attached to these documents. James may, of course, reflect the thought of a conservative Jewish Christian church somewhere in Palestine.

Bibliography. E. Lohmeyer, *Galiläa und Jerusalem* (1936); L. Finkelstein, *The Pharisees* (1938), I, 43-60; R. H. Lightfoot, *Locality and Doctrine in the Gospels* (1938); L. E. Elliott-Binns, *Galilean Christianity* (1956); S. E. Johnson, *Jesus in His Homeland* (1957), pp. 7-9, 17-22. S. E. JOHNSON

GALILEE găl'ə lē [Γαλιλαία, Γαλειλαία; גליל, גלילה, *also* Aram. גלילא; *lit.* ring, circle, *and so* district, region; *referred to as* of the Gentiles, foreigners, τῶν ἐθνῶν (Isa. 9:1 *in* Matt. 4:15) *and* τῶν ἀλλοφύλων (I Macc. 5:15), הגוים]. A small region in N Palestine, earlier of vague and variable boundary; later a fixed administrative area under the Romans.

1. The region. After the separation of Solomon's kingdom (936 B.C.), the region later to be known as Galilee was the most northerly part of the N kingdom of ISRAEL. In 734 it was absorbed in the Assyrian Empire by TIGLATH-PILESER, and the record in II Kings 15:29 refers to that conquered area of Naphtali as the *galil.* Through the next six centuries the region passed in turn to Babylonia, Persia, Macedonia, Egypt, and Syria, while constantly experiencing infiltration and migration. The genuine Israelite population in the Persian period was but a minority among the dominant Gentiles, and when Judea issued a summons (attributed to Hezekiah) to gather at Jerusalem for worship in the temple, the response from the *galil* was meager (II Chr. 30:10-11). As late as Maccabean times the Jewish element was small, and was reduced still further when Simon's expedition to the N resulted in the defeat of the Gentile forces of Galilee and the evacuation of many Jews to Judea, for security (I Macc. 5:21-23). The region was not governed by Jews any time after 734 B.C. until 80 B.C., when Alexander Janneus subdued this

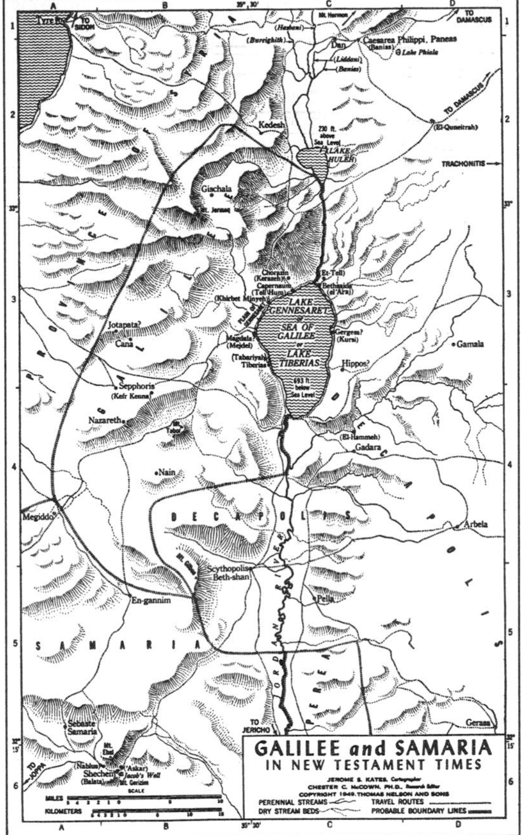

Gentile region and attempted to Judaize the population.

In 63 B.C. the whole of Palestine came under Roman rule, although a large degree of autonomy was granted the Jewish government, whether established in Jerusalem, Sepphoris, or Tiberias. When the kingdom of Herod the Great was split into three parts in 4 B.C., Sepphoris became the capital of Galilee until replaced by Tiberias *ca.* A.D. 25. In A.D. 44, Herod Agrippa I, the last Jewish ruler of Palestine, died after a six-year reign over Galilee, and all Palestine was then formed into a province and governed by procurators. The revolts of A.D. 66-73 and 132-35 brought death to thousands of Jews and destruction to the Jewish state, and after the fall of Jerusalem surviving Palestinian Jews converged upon Galilee. The cities of Tiberias and Sepphoris became Jewish, and the Diaspora came to look upon Galilee as its center. Tiberias became the chief school of Jewish learning in the West, where the Palestinian Talmud and the Tiberian system of vowel pointing were developed. In the meantime, Christianity in the fourth century was established as the dominant religion in the Empire, and in A.D. 451 the Council of Chalcedon set up the Patriarchate of Jerusalem for the governing of the church in Palestine. Galilee was placed in diocese II, under the patriarch Juvenal. In the seventh century Muslim rule over Galilee began, to be broken only by the twelfth-century interlude of the Crusades and the World War of 1918. The modern state of Israel, established in 1948, has included all of Galilee.

The term "Galilee of the Gentiles" or "of the nations" first occurs in the prophecy of Isaiah (*ca.* 705 B.C.), referring to the territory of Zebulun and Naphtali as occupied by a mixed population. Other contemporary references apply the name to the neighboring territory of Asher (I Kings 9:10-13), or of Issachar, or of Naphtali almost alone (II Kings 15:29). The name reflects a popular reputation for racial variety and mixture in and around these N frontier districts, rather than any formal political unit of administration.

In the Maccabean era Galilee assumed more definite boundaries, as later described by Josephus (War III.iii.1). Between it and Samaria to the S, the

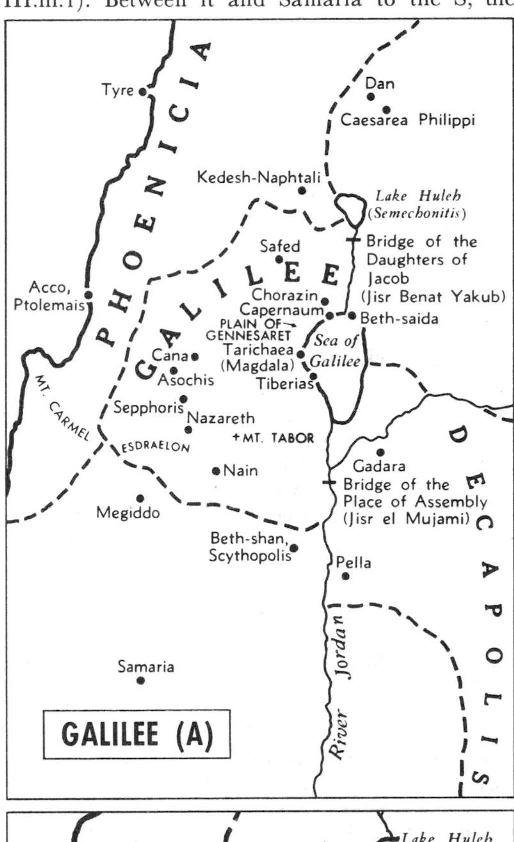

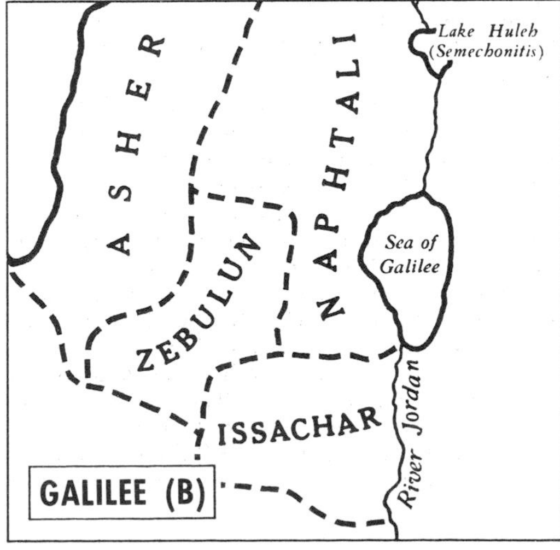

"Great Plain" Esdraelon (Plain of Megiddo, Valley of Jezreel) provided a natural boundary from Mount Carmel to Beth-shan (later Scythopolis). Bordering on Tyre to the N, Galilee reached to Lake Huleh, about fifteen miles S of Dan, which marks the more ancient border along the gorge of the River Litani. The Jordan rift made a natural E boundary, but the W boundary remains uncertain except that it bordered upon Syrian Phoenicia. Roman Galilee extended about twenty-five miles E and W, and about thirty-five miles N and S (about one sixth of the area of W Palestine). Galilee was itself divided into Upper and Lower by the Plain of Ramah on a line between Capernaum and Ptolemaïs. In altitude Lower Galilee ranged from 696 feet below sea level at the Sea of Galilee to *ca.* 500 feet above sea level, except for mountains in the SE reaching up to Mount Tabor (1,843 feet). Upper Galilee included the S ranges of the Lebanon Mountains, true "hill country" from *ca.* 1,500 to 3,963 feet high (Mount Jermak, the highest peak in Palestine).

The basic rock is limestone, in which natural caves abound. There is also volcanic rock, especially to the E and bordering upon the Jordan rift, where a lava cap still covers the limestone in places. The Horns of Hattin are a double volcanic peak 2,000 feet high, standing between Nazareth and the Sea of Galilee. The disintegration of this basaltic rock has produced a rich alluvial soil in the plains and valleys and terraces. Although the craters have long been extinct, there are many hot springs such as have made Tiberias a popular spa even to modern times. This area has left a record of many earthquakes in its archaeological ruins. The most striking natural phenomenon is the great Ghor, the deep cut of the Jordan Valley all along the E boundary. In the ten miles between Lake Huleh and the Sea of Galilee the river descends 926 feet in a rapid and ceaseless flow.

At intervals there were fords, later bridges, for E-W traffic across the Jordan, which led to the natural roadways through valley and plain. The "way of the sea" from Damascus (cf. Isa. 9:1) may have crossed the Bridge of the Daughters of Jacob (Jisr Benat Yakub), two miles below Lake Huleh, whence a road continued either W over the mountains via Safed or S through the Plain of Hazor to Capernaum and across the Plain of Gennesaret; then W through the Valley of Asochis (N of Sepphoris).

Once out on the open Plain of Esdraelon, caravans might deploy, some to nearby coastal destinations such as the port at Acco (Ptolemaïs) and others to far-off Egypt via a pass over the Carmel range, N of Megiddo. A shorter route to Egypt struck SW from the Plain of Gennesaret and passed N of Mount Tabor and near Nazareth, thence across the Plain of Esdraelon to Megiddo and down the coastal road. Another E-W road farther N passed through the Plain of Ramah, another passed by way of Sepphoris, and still another from Tiberias to Cana and near Nazareth via the Plain of Tor'an. Travelers on this route may have entered Galilee from the Decapolis at the Bridge of the Place of Assembly (Jisr el Mujami), about seven miles S of the Sea of Galilee. As far again to the S was another crossing, now known as the Bridge of Sheikh Hussein, between Pella and Beth-shan (Scythopolis), bringing travelers from the Decapolis (perhaps from Arabia) into the Plain of Esdraelon and to Acco. All these routes were more than local roads; rather, they were international highways which brought "Galilee of the Gentiles" into relationship with world trade and culture.

2. Its life. Life in Galilee was determined chiefly by the Lebanon Mountains, which gathered the beneficent moisture in the form of dew and snow and springs and literally poured it over the land. From as far as Mount Hermon, streams converged in the gorge of the Jordan, to the benefit of crops and cattle and the fishing industry around the Sea of Galilee. Terraced farms and orchards dotted even the N mountains, and grain and grass were abundant in the plains. With normal rainfall, crops were especially luxuriant in the valleys and plains of Lower Galilee, most of all in the Plain of Esdraelon. Simple but substantial industries developed, in processing the chief product such as olives and grapes and cattle. Oil, wine, fish, and grain were common exports. Another important source of income was the toll collected on the international trade routes. The taxes of Herodian Galilee supported an extensive building program under Herod the Great and Herod Antipas. Impressive public buildings were erected reflecting Hellenistic culture—such as baths, gymnasiums, theaters, and hippodromes, as well as entire new cities. The data on population are fragmentary and intricate, but a reasonable estimate for the first century would find about 350,000 Galileans, including a large slave element and about 100,000 Jews largely Hellenized. The primary language at this time was the universal Greek Koine, although many Jews spoke Aramaic, some with a local accent (Matt. 26:73). Herodian coins were inscribed solely in Greek.

The chief city of the old Galilee district was KEDESH-NAPHTALI, NW of Lake Huleh. It was often the scene of international conflict on the N border. The Persian conqueror designated it the capital of the satrapy of Galilee; Jonathan Maccabeus here won a battle against Demetrius of Syria; yet in the first century it fell to Tyre as the boundary of Galilee was pushed farther S to exclude it. Sepphoris was originally an influential agricultural town, situated almost in the middle of Galilee. In 55 B.C. the proconsul Gabinius of Syria chose it as administrative center for the district. Here the tetrarch Herod Antipas built up his capital after 4 B.C. In the revolt of A.D. 6 upon the death of the ethnarch Archelaus in Judea, Sepphoris was destroyed by Varus, proconsul of Syria, but was promptly rebuilt by Antipas and became the largest city of Galilee, with perhaps forty thousand residents. It lay only four miles N of Nazareth, and near a major E-W trade route. Safed was the highest town of importance in Galilee, standing 2,750 feet high in the NE mountains as they rise to the peak at Mount Jermak. However, it was not isolated, for one road from the Bridge of the Daughters of Jacob to Acco passed this way. The town was really part of the Galilee lake region and received daily supplies of fish in abundance. The moisture of the mountains permitted luxuriant vineyards and citrus groves. It later became one of the four largest cities, and one of the two sacred Jewish cities, in Galilee. It is not reported that Jesus ever visited this territory, nor is the city named in the Bible.

Some of Galilee's most important cities were around the shore of the Sea of Galilee, the NW quadrant of which was more Jewish. CAPERNAUM, at the N end, W of the Jordan mouth, was a lively and prosperous fishing town as well as a Roman military post. CHINNEROTH (3) was one of the oldest towns and lay on the NW coast on the edge of the Plain of Chinneroth, through which several streams flowed into the Sea of Galilee. This small and rich valley was known also as the Land of Gennesaret (modern el-Ghuweir). Tarichaea (MAGDALA), at the W-center of the lake, was a busy center for the processing of fish for export. TIBERIAS was a new city on the W shore, built *ca.* A.D. 25 by Herod Antipas as his capital to replace Sepphoris, and named to honor the emperor. Although this city was at first avoided by Jews because of a necropolis on the site, it later became the chief center of rabbinic learning and leadership, and one of two sacred cities in Galilee. The names Chinneroth, Gennesaret, and Tiberias, all were applied to the great lake also. Although the E half lay outside Galilee, it was often referred to as a part of Galilean life.

The religious worship in this northerly Gentile region was related to the many popular cults which had spread around the Mediterranean. Archaeological remains attest to the presence of these cults in Samaria, Phoenicia, Syria, and Transjordan. Shrines to numerous deities must have existed in the larger cities of Gentile Galilee, especially in a Roman town like Tiberias, and would have been found even in the more Jewish towns. They represented the normal and traditional worship of the Gentile majority in Galilee. The difficulties encountered in the religious relationship between Gentiles and Jews may be symbolized by one requirement—that Jews refrain from business dealings with Gentiles for three days before a Gentile religious festival. Synagogues likewise were to be found throughout Galilee, not only in towns primarily Jewish, like Capernaum, but also in towns primarily Gentile, like Sepphoris. A score of ancient synagogue structures have been discovered in Galilean towns, built *ca.* A.D. 200-600. The most impressive among these is the white limestone synagogue at Capernaum which was erected near the lake in the third century.

3. Jesus of Nazareth. In the light of history, Galilee's most significant period was the thirty-year span of the life of Jesus of Nazareth, and especially the short "active ministry" during which he proclaimed his gospel of salvation. This remarkable event has had far greater effect upon mankind than the concentration of national conflicts in this little "*galil* of the nations." Almost the entire career of Jesus of Nazareth lay within the borders of this tiny region. It is reported that he traveled once with his disciples to Caesarea Philippi, E of the Jordan and about thirty miles N from his home in Capernaum (Matt. 16:13; Mark 8:27). The same evangelists report another journey of about the same distance to the "border of Tyre" (Mark 7:24, Nestle), or to the "district of Tyre and Sidon" (Matt. 15:21), where he met the Syrophoenician woman whose daughter he cured. Upon occasion, Jesus entered the Greek territory E of the Jordan (Mark 7:31; 5:1 and parallels), especially the fishing town of Bethsaida (Mark 6:45; 8:22; Luke 9:10). He may have traveled to Jerusalem through the E district of Perea, although such a journey through Samaria is much more certain.

The gospel record does not encourage a conclusion that Jesus regularly attended the major festivals in Jerusalem. Galilean Jews were lax in the matter of personal attendance at the temple—this attitude was symbolic of the modified orthodoxy of Jews in the *galil* of the Gentiles. Much of the teaching of Jesus was not acceptable to orthodox interpreters; indeed, he gained a reputation for unusual and controversial interpretation. Although he was aware of the traditional and habitual understanding of the Torah, which pressed for acceptance more especially in Judea, he manifested a freshness and independence of mind as to the meaning and application of the Law, consonant with the religious spirit of the *galil.*

After his baptism by John, Jesus apparently withdrew from his family in Nazareth and adopted Capernaum as his home, quite possibly staying, when in town, at the home of Peter. Here on the shore of the lake he secured his first disciples, from among the fishermen. All the Galilean episodes recorded in the gospels are related to the Sea of Galilee, with but few exceptions. He may have made one later visit to Nazareth, where he appeared in the synagogue (Matt. 13:54; Mark 6:1-2). There is reported an episode in the town of Nain, six miles S of Nazareth (Luke 7:11); also, the wedding in Cana, NE from Nazareth (John 2:1). Mention has been made of a visit to Caesarea Philippi. All the rest of the gospel account, prior to the passion narrative, is in the setting of the Sea of Galilee. Even here, not many different towns are visited. Jesus preached mainly at the N end of the lake, most of all near Capernaum and repeatedly in Bethsaida. He speaks of his activity in Chorazin also and deplores the poor response in all three of these cities (Matt. 11:21-23; Luke 10:13-15). There is no gospel report of his going farther S, to Magdala or Tiberias.

He seems to have shared neither the revolutionary spirit of his fellows in Sepphoris nor the pro-Roman attitude of the residents of Tiberias. He preached the gospel of salvation mainly to the Jews, but also to Samaritans and Gentiles (including Romans). He would have encountered Pharisees and scribes in Galilean cities, but rarely a Sadducee or a priest. The controversies reported in the gospels in the Galilean setting deal with interpretation of the law and its obeservance, rather than with the ritual or conduct of temple worship. Although Jesus held many debates with scribes in Galilee, it was his defiance of the hierarchy in Jerusalem that resulted in his crucifixion.

Bibliography. E. Robinson, *Biblical Researches in Palestine,* II (1867), 330-449; E. W. G. Masterman, *Studies in Galilee* (1909); W. F. Albright, "Among the Canaanite Mounds of Eastern Galilee," *BASOR,* no. 29 (Feb., 1928), pp. 1-8; N. Glueck, *The River Jordan* (1946).

K. W. CLARK

GALILEE, SEA OF [ἡ θάλασσα τῆς Γαλιλαίας]. The larger lake in N Palestine, the chief feature of the Jordan waterway and of Galilean life.

1. Name. This ancient basin has been called by several names during the period of Hebrew history. The earliest of these was Chinnereth (*see* CHINNEROTH 1), from as early as the fifteenth century B.C. This was the name of a walled town referred to in Josh. 11:2; 19:35, identified with modern Tell el 'Oreimeh on the NW coast of the lake (*see bibliography*). The name may mean "harp," and the observation has been made that the tell is so shaped. The name has been applied to the adjacent hill, to the plain (I Kings 15:20), and to the lake (Num. 34:11; Deut. 3:17; Josh. 12:3; 13:27). Some have described the lake as harp-shaped, but the logic of this connection would lead to the conclusion that the name was first assigned to the lake. This is a priori less likely, and it is furthermore to be doubted that the earth-bound ancients would have recognized the silhouette of the lake, even from the surrounding heights. A later name for the lake was Gennesar (*see* GENNESARET), used in Maccabean and NT times (I Macc. 11:67; Luke 5:1). This name also is understood to belong to the town called Chinnereth and to the district of the plain (Matt. 14:34; Mark 6:53).

In the second century the lake was called Tiberias (John 6:1; 21:1), clearly derived from the city built by Antipas. It is this name that persists in the modern Arabic name, Tabariyeh. At about the same time, Pliny writes that the Lake of Gennesaret is by some called Tarichaea, from the name of the town (Nat. Hist. V.15.71). But the name by which the lake is best known is GALILEE, an old name for the region to the W. Although the name means "ring, circle," it is not likely that this is the reason it was applied to the lake; it is more plausible that the name was first given to the district, in recognition of the circle of Gentile nations which had infiltrated the region. In fact, the name as applied to the lake does not appear until the gospels use it.

The Greek name in the gospels was originally translated into English as "sea of Galilee," although this body of water is actually a fresh-water inland lake. The explanation for this is quite simple: the NT term θάλασσα is in the Greek ambiguous and may mean (in our usage) either a sea or a large lake. This is true also of the underlying Semitic term, ים. Wyclif and Tyndale chose the word "sea," which has been retained in most other translations. Luke, however, wrote λίμνη, and so also did his contemporary Josephus. Pliny chose the term *lacus*. These latter terms are properly translated as "lake" (so the RSV in Luke 5:1; 8:22, 33). In I Macc. 11:67 the simple term ὕδωρ is properly translated "water" of Gennesaret.

2. Formation. The shape of the Lake of Galilee is most like a great heart (more so than like a harp or a pear, as some have suggested). It is *ca.* thirteen miles long (N-S) and at its greatest width *ca.* eight miles, between el-Mejdel (Tarichaea) and Khersa (Gergesa). Its waters vary from green to blue, encircled by a ring of yellow or green—depending upon the season. The high mountains around it fall off sharply, especially on the E side, and thus indicate a conformation which reaches a considerable depth—around two hundred feet below the surface, which is itself almost seven hundred feet below sea level. Almost surrounded by mountains of considerable height, the lake is a vast bowl with an extended lip on the NW (the Plain of Gennesaret) and open at the N and S ends. As a natural phenomenon, the lake and the Jordan rift are of great age, the result of volcanic activity in the Cenozoic era. Around the lake, the action of basaltic intrusions and cappings have modified the limestone mass of the mountains.

On the E the cliffs of the Jaulan Plateau present a steep face to the lake, overhanging a plain less than a mile wide. On this side may be identified the ancient Gergesa (modern Gerga or Khersa), the setting for the stampede of swine that rushed down the cliff and were drowned (Mark 5:1 and parallels; although the texts have differing names, the episode requires a lakeside locale). On the W side of the lake the mountains form an amphitheater, leaving a narrow plain along the lake on which several important towns were situated. Toward the S, sulphuric hot springs are found which heat up at times, even creating hot streams under water. Directly W of the lake the distinctive Horns of Hattin rise to two thousand feet, capped by the flow of an extinct volcano. The highest neighboring mountains, although at a greater distance, lie to the NW where the town of Safed looks down from 2,750 feet over the lake.

The Galilee waters drain from as far N as Mount Hermon, and at one time formed a single long lake throughout the entire course to the Dead Sea. The lake has long been restricted to its present area, and the streams from the N first collect in a large, reedy marsh 230 feet above sea level, now called Lake Huleh (Semechonitis in Jos. War III.x.7; IV.i.1). The lake itself is *ca.* 3½ miles long and 3 miles wide, and teems with fish and birds. A notable patch of papyrus grows here, extending for miles across the lake and marsh. From Lake Huleh the waters rush rapidly down through a single narrow gorge of 10 miles to pour into the greater lake at the N end 930 feet lower. Nearing the lake, the land opens out eastward into a marsh where numerous additional but shorter streams flow directly into the lake. Moving around to the NW, one finds another open plain (el-Ghuweir) bordering for *ca.* 3 miles along the lake and reaching back into the hills for *ca.* 2 miles. This is the fertile Plain of Gennesaret (Chinnereth), the most productive and populous area along the coast. Through it several streams flow into the lake, chief of which is the "waters of Merom" (Josh. 11:5). The outlet of the lake is at the SW point in the area of hot springs, and there the lowland fans out to the E in a triangle between the Jordan and Yarmuk rivers.

3. Settlements. The lake was an active center of Galilean life, and to it or near it most of the roads of Galilee passed. Although the E cliffs did not invite traffic, travelers from the E crossed the Jordan rift both above and below the lake, which might then be approached along the N and W coast. Other roads fanned out from the lake, westward to Acco (Ptolemaïs), southwestward to Caesarea and along the coast, and southward to Judea. Local roads to

Kedesh, Ramah, and Sepphoris followed the plains. Travelers and merchants converged about the lake in the course of their activities. Fish from the lake region were transported in all directions locally, as well as to Damascus, to Jerusalem, and even to Spain.

Jesus of Nazareth, an artisan from a small town in the highlands, made a major change when he took up life in the city of CAPERNAUM in a center of the fishing industry and in the subtropical climate of the lake (Matt. 4:13; Mark 2:1). This city stood at the N end of the lake, three miles W of the Jordan and on the N edge of the Plain of Gennesaret. It was chiefly Jewish but a cosmopolitan center to which Galileans gravitated, like Nathanael from Cana, and Mary from Magdala, and Philip and the brothers Andrew and Peter from Bethsaida on the other side of the Jordan. Among the early acquaintances of Jesus in Capernaum were the associates in a large fishing partnership, including Zebedee and his sons (James and John) with the brothers Simon and Andrew (Mark 1:16; Luke 5:2-10), besides their employed assistants. This group owned at least two fishing boats; and it was they who had the marvelous catch, on the occasion when Jesus first encountered them (Luke 5:2-7). The Roman centurion whose servant Jesus healed (Matt. 8:5; Luke 7:2) is a reminder that Capernaum was a Roman military and customs post on the international highway. This Gentile official had contributed to the building of the synagogue in which Jesus taught.

Next to Capernaum, BETHSAIDA, meaning "the fishing place," drew the attention of Jesus. Three of his followers had been born there, and occasional trips across the lake were made to it (Mark 6:45; 8:22). It lay at the N end of the lake, in the delta E of the mouth of the Jordan, not far from Capernaum. It was in the Hellenistic territory ruled by the tetrarch Philip, who built it up to the grandeur of a city *ca.* 3 B.C., and named it Julias for the daughter of Augustus (Jos. Antiq. XVIII.ii.1). It is reported that Jesus retreated here from the Galilean authority of Antipas (Matt. 14:13; Luke 9:10). Some distance from Bethsaida, in an isolated place, was the setting for the episode of feeding a crowd that gathered to hear Jesus teach (Matt. 14:13; Mark 6:32). This was a boat journey away from Bethsaida (Mark 6: 45), probably on the E shore and a considerable distance from Bethsaida (Matt. 14:24; Mark 6:48). This was one of the occasions when a characteristic squall struck the lake (Matt. 14:24; John 6:18); another occasion was the longer sail to the E side at Gergesa (Mark 5:1 and parallels). Galilean fishermen have held respect and caution for these treacherous storms (especially after noontime), caused by cold winds from the W, or from Mount Hermon channeled down the gorge, which create a sudden tempest in the warm air covering the low-lying waters.

Another lake town of importance was CHORAZIN, lying away from the shore *ca.* two miles N of Capernaum and on the international highway. The gospels record no episode here, although it is stated that Chorazin and Bethsaida and Capernaum have failed to respond to the extensive activity of Jesus in all these cities. Once in the gospels, following the feeding of the crowd, it is mentioned that Jesus and his disciples landed on the shore of the Plain of Gennesaret, where at once people gathered about him to be healed. It is not at once clear whence these people might have come, for there is not known to be any town nearer than Capernaum and Magdala. The ancient town of Chinnereth, once so important, had long since fallen into ruin. The N part of the lake constituted the entire gospel setting for the activity of Jesus, from Capernaum around to Bethsaida—adding the single visit to Gergesa, where Jesus met only the demoniac. No preaching is recorded S of the Plain of Gennesaret, an area known to be Gentile.

On the S edge of this plain was the town of MAGDALA, which Pliny and Josephus call Tarichaea (Nat. Hist. V.15; Antiq. XX.viii.4; War II.xiii.2; III.x.1). Tarichaea is a late Greek name which means "preserving," and it describes the chief industry of the town, whose exports of salted fish were sent throughout the Roman world. Along with Tiberias, it was a focus of revolt and one of the last places in Galilee to yield to Vespasian. Probably the most important city on the lake was Antipas' capital, TIBERIAS. In the time of Jesus the city had no Jewish residents to whom he might have preached, because Jews deliberately avoided ritual contamination from the necropolis there. It was wholly a Gentile city, with Hellenistic architecture and customs and religion—in the heart of Roman Galilee. Although the coastal plain was narrow at this point, the city was crowned with a guardian acropolis on the dark basaltic rock where Antipas located his palace above the town. Its greatest attraction was its medicinal springs, which even won over the Jews in later years when Jerusalem gave way to the pagan Aelia Capitolina. The Sanhedrin was moved from Sepphoris to Tiberias, where was developed the chief center of Jewish learning in the West. Fig. TIB 62.

There are several lesser towns around the S portion of the lake, none of which is mentioned in the NT. A mile S of Tiberias is Hammam (*see* HAMMATH 2), characterized by its many splendid bath-

Courtesy of the Israel Office of Information, New York

3. Hills surrounding the Sea of Galilee

Courtesy of the Israel Office of Information, New York

4. The Sea of Galilee, with modern Tiberias in the foreground

houses, for here is the central area of the medicinal springs. It was suburban to the capital and attracted visitors in large numbers. Sennabris, Philoteria, and Semakh lie closer to the outlet of the lake, the last being E of that point. Hippos stands back on the E cliff, and farther N on the coast lies Gamala.

Excavations around the Lake of Galilee have uncovered the synagogues in some of its cities. Most famous is the white limestone structure of Capernaum, built *ca.* A.D. 200. In contrast stands the black basalt synagogue of Chorazin, which was perhaps a hundred years old when the town was destroyed *ca.* 350. The synagogue discovered in Arbela (two miles SW of Magdala-Tarichaea) may have been built in the second century by R. Nitai, while the one in Hammath (SE near Gadara) was built *ca.* 400 and destroyed by fire *ca.* 550. The last Jewish king to rule over any part of Galilee (or, in history) was Agrippa II (A.D. 56-100). His puppet kingdom was actually E of the Jordan, while Galilee proper was ruled by a Roman procurator. But Nero gave to Agrippa the Galilean lakeside cities of Tiberias and Magdala-Tarichaea, as well as Bethsaida-Julias with fourteen surrounding villages. When Agrippa died, these were all incorporated into the Roman province of Syria.

Figs. GAL 3-4.

Bibliography. E. W. G. Masterman, *Studies in Galilee* (1909); E. Huntington, *Palestine and Its Transformation* (1911), pp. 180-98; W. F. Albright, "Among the Canaanite Mounds of Eastern Galilee," *BASOR,* no. 29 (Feb., 1928), pp. 1-8; G. A. Smith, *Historical Geography of the Holy Land* (1931), pp. 439-63; N. Glueck, *The Jordan River* (1946), pp. 1-59.

K. W. CLARK

GALL (HERB) [ראש, *rôš;* χολή]. A bitter and poisonous herb; its juice, perhaps *Conium maculatum* L., is commonly thought to be the "hemlock" poison which Socrates drank. ראש is usually mentioned with WORMWOOD (Deut. 29:18—H 29:17; Jer. 9:15 KJV; 23:15 KJV; Lam. 3:19; "hemlock" in Amos 6:12 KJV), implying bitterness and tragedy. The KJV uses "gall" in these places and also in Ps. 69:21—H 69:22; Jer. 8:14; Lam. 3:5. The RSV translates ראש as "gall" only in Lam. 3:19. Elsewhere, in the light of the context, it translates more generally as "POISON" or as something poisonous—i.e., "POISONOUS FRUIT" (Deut. 29:18), "POISONED WATER" (Jer. 8:14; 9:15; 23:15; lit., "water of poison"), "POISONOUS WEEDS" (Hos. 10:4), "POISON" (Deut. 32:32; Ps. 69:21; Amos 6:12); also "BITTERNESS" (Lam. 3:5).

"Wine . . . mingled with gall" (χολή) was offered to Jesus on the Cross (Matt. 27:34; cf. Ps. 69:21; Mark 15:23). The word has a symbolic meaning in Acts 8:23.

See also FLORA § A14*a*.

Bibliography. H. N. and A. L. Moldenke, *Plants of the Bible* (1952), pp. 78-80.

J. C. TREVER

GALL (OF LIVER) [מררה, *from* מרר, to be bitter]. This word represented originally simply the abstract concept "bitterness" (Job 13:26: "bitter things"). It then came to be applied specifically to the gall bladder (Job 20:25) and, in a slightly different grammatical form, to the bile (16:13). In Tob. 6:8 there is mention of the use of the gall of a fish for medicinal purposes.

R. C. DENTAN

GALLERY. 1. תא (from Akkadian *ta'u;* alternately WALL), a side chamber in a gateway to a city or a temple. Galleries were probably designed partly for architectural reasons, but also the pedestrian, being caught in a gateway by a passing vehicle, might step into the safety of a side chamber or gallery. *See* TEMPLE, JERUSALEM.

2. "Galleries" is the KJV translation of רהט in Song of S. 7:5 (RSV TRESSES). The meaning of this word is unknown.

C. G. HOWIE

GALLEY [אני, *'onî,* ship; *cf.* Akkad. *anâtu, anûtu, etc.,* implements, furniture, tackle] (Isa. 33:21). A low and rather narrow seagoing vessel, propelled mainly by oars and used principally as a warship.

In Isa. 33:21 the phrase אני שיט, "ship of rowing," is translated "galley with oars" (KJV-RSV). If, as some maintain, Isa. 33 is of late date, the author may be thinking of the war navies of the Hellenistic kings. The only other allusions in the OT to rowed ships are to Tyrian vessels (Ezek. 27:6, 8, 26, 29). *See* SHIPS AND SAILING.

Bibliography. On the development of the galley in ancient times, see C. Singer, E. J. Holmyard, and A. R. Hall, eds., *A History of Technology,* I (1954), 741-43; II (1956; C. Singer, E. J. Holmyard, A. R. Hall, and T. I. Williams, eds.), 563-73.

W. S. MCCULLOUGH

GALLIM găl'ĭm [גלים, heaps]. **1.** The native city of Palti son of Laish, to whom Saul gave his daughter Michal as wife after his quarrel with her husband, David (I Sam. 25:44); possibly the same as 2 *below.*

2. A town of Benjamin on the route which Isaiah describes the Assyrian army as taking on its march to Jerusalem (Isa. 10:30). Albright, rearranging this passage on a metrical basis, places Gallim after Gibeah of Saul and locates it at Khirbet Kakul, half a mile W of Anata.

S. COHEN

GALLIO găl'ĭ ō. L. Junius Gallio Annaeus, mentioned in Acts 18:12-17 as PROCONSUL of Achaea, with headquarters at Corinth. He was son of the rhetorician M. Annaeus Seneca, and brother of Seneca the philosopher, millionaire, and tutor of Nero. He assumed the name Gallio when adopted by a wealthy friend and introduced to a political career. An inscription from Delphi clearly shows that he was proconsul of Achaea after the twenty-sixth acclamation of Claudius as *imperator* (*see* EMPEROR); this acclamation was given within a year after January 25, A.D. 52. Therefore Gallio was almost certainly proconsul either in 51-52 or in 52-53. This point is very important for the chronology of Paul's journeys.

While Gallio was in office, Jews at Corinth brought Paul before his judgment seat (which has been found in recent times) on the charge that the religion he advocated was contrary to law (Acts 18:13). Gallio refused to let Paul defend himself, and he dismissed the case on the ground that it involved Jewish law; in such matters he was unwilling to be a judge (vss. 15-16). Presumably his accusers were aware that Paul was protected by Roman law in a Roman COLONY and hoped for an administrative decision from the proconsul.

According to Gallio's own diagnosis, the climate of Achaea made him ill (Seneca *Epistle* CIV.1), and he was probably glad to return to Rome, where he became *consul suffectus* early in Nero's reign (Pliny Nat. Hist. XXXI.62). Involved in the conspiracy against Nero in which his brother lost his life, he won a temporary pardon but finally had to commit suicide (Dio Cassius *History* LXII.25; Suetonius *Rhetoric*).

Bibliography. F. J. Foakes-Jackson and H. J. Cadbury, *The Beginnings of Christianity*, IV (1933), 226-27; V (1933), 460-64 (K. Lake). H. J. Cadbury, *The Book of Acts in History* (1955), p. 44, with note 25. R. M. GRANT

GALLON. In John 2:6, μετρητάς δύο ἢ τρεῖς is translated "twenty or thirty gallons." (The KJV translates "two or three firkins." A firkin contains a little less than nine gallons.) *See* WEIGHTS AND MEASURES § C4*o*.

GALLOWS. *See* HANGING.

GAMAD, MEN OF gā'măd [גמדים] (Ezek. 27:11); KJV GAMMADIMS găm'ə dĭmz. Men from a place in Syria (a seaside town near Arvad?), possibly to be identified with *Kumidi,* mentioned in the Tell el-Amarna Letters. Some scholars read "Gomerim," and equate it with Ugaritic *gmrm*. Men of Gamad were in the army of Tyre, according to Ezekiel's oracle against that city. H. G. MAY

GAMAEL găm'ĭ əl. Apoc. alternate name for DANIEL.

GAMALIEL gə mā'lĭ əl [Γαμαλιήλ=גמליאל, recompense of God]. **1.** An honored Pharisaic member of the Sanhedrin, who counseled moderation in the treatment of Peter and other apostles (Acts 5:34-39) and is said to have been Paul's teacher (Acts 22:3).

This Gamaliel (I, "the Elder") was the grandson of the famous Rabbi Hillel and the grandfather of Gamaliel II. He was the first to bear the title "Rabban" ("our Master, our Great One"), rather than the ordinary "Rabbi" ("my Master"). During the second third of the first century his learning and generous spirit greatly enhanced the prestige of liberal Pharisaism and effected its dominance after the destruction of the temple in A.D. 70. His general outlook is indicated by his liberalizing the amount of movement permitted certain groups on the sabbath (R.H. 2.5), and his forbidding husbands to annul divorce proceedings without their wives' knowledge (Git. 4.2).

Jewish tradition erroneously regarded him as president of the Sanhedrin (a position held by the high priest while the temple was standing), and expressed his importance by saying, "When Rabban Gamaliel the Elder died, the glory of the Law ceased and purity and abstinence died" (Soṭ. 9.15).

His caution concerning extreme measures against the apostles may have been due (*a*) to his characteristically tolerant and generous spirit, (*b*) to a wish to protect Pharisaic Judaism—in so many respects at one with the teaching of the apostles (e.g., on the resurrection of the dead)—from the mounting hostility of the Sadducean hierarchy, and (*c*) to a true piety which divined in the events he had witnessed the purpose and power of God at work.

The reference in Gamaliel's speech to Theudas as prior to Judas the Galilean (Acts 5:36-37) and the assertion that Paul was Gamaliel's pupil (22:3) have caused scholars much difficulty. The only Theudas known to us, an insurrectionist of the time of the procurator Fadus (A.D. 44 ff), was beheaded by the Romans (Jos. Antiq. XX.v.1 ff). Judas' rebellion occurred in A.D. 6. Was there an earlier Theudas? Is Gamaliel's speech a confused construction by the author of Acts, possibly based on an inaccurate reading of Josephus or of one of his sources? Should the incident be placed later in the Acts sequence, perhaps in Acts 12, where a persecution of the church is described?

Was Gamaliel actually Paul's teacher? Why then the persecuting activities of the pupil, the lack of mention of Gamaliel in Paul's letters, the seemingly nonrabbinic (nonhalachic) character of Paul's exegesis, and the completely different attitude toward the law? Answers have been given, but not wholly satisfactory ones.

2. The leader of the tribe of Manasseh (Num. 1:10; 2:20; 7:54, 59; 10:23).

Bibliography. H. L. Strack and P. Billerbeck, *Kommentar zum NT aus Talmud und Midrasch,* II (1924), 636-40; M. S. Enslin, "Paul and Gamaliel," *JR,* 7 (1927), 360-75; J. W. Swain, "Gamaliel's Speech and Caligula's Statue," *HTR,* 37 (1944), 341-49; J. Knox, *Chapters in a Life of Paul* (1950), pp. 34-40; F. F. Bruce, *The Acts of the Apostles* (2nd ed., 1952), 146-49, 400. E. P. BLAIR

GAME [ציד, צידה]; KJV VENISON. Game in biblical times consisted chiefly of "harts, gazelles, roebucks, and fatted fowl" (I Kings 4:23—H 5:3, in the list of Solomon's provisions). ESAU was Isaac's favorite because he provided him with game (Gen. 25:28); Jacob was thus able to disguise himself as his brother by bringing the same (ch. 27).

See also COOKING AND COOKING UTENSILS; FOOD § 1*a;* HUNTING. J. F. ROSS

GAMES, OT. Of games and play the OT gives only scattered indications. But undoubtedly the Hebrew people had their games, for on occasion they were lighthearted; they had a sense of humor and enjoyed song and dance. *See* MUSIC; DANCE.

A contest was associated with the seven-day wedding feast in Judg. 14:12; Samson propounded a riddle involving a forfeit to be paid to the winner of the guessing contest.

Another contest is described in II Sam. 2:12-17. In this instance while waiting for the battle to be joined, twelve men were chosen from each side to engage in a contest of skill. It may have been boxing or WRESTLING,* for both are depicted in the art of the Near East. But it was more likely similar to fencing, since the result was fatal for both sides. Fig. WRE 27.

In Zech. 8:5 the prophet envisages the inhabitants of the restored city, the aged enjoying days of leisure and the boys and girls playing in the streets. Of the nature of their games there is no hint, but perhaps a suggestion is to be found in reliefs from Egypt which show girls dancing or playing a singing game and boys playing tug-of-war* and other games. Some archaeologists suggest that some of the molded clay figures may have been children's dolls. Job (21:11-12) also makes reference to carefree children engaged in singing and dancing. Fig. GAM 5.

Courtesy of the Oriental Institute, the University of Chicago

5. Relief from a Sixth Dynasty tomb of Mereru-ka at Saqqarah, showing boys playing games (including a tug of war, on the top panel); Sixth Dynasty (*ca.* 2350-2200 B.C.)

In the Hellenistic period the Jews readily adopted the Greek games, and the gymnasium and the theater became popular, much to the disgust of the orthodox. Wrestling, discus throwing, chariot racing, and the more brutal contests of men and beasts in the arena are specifically mentioned (II Macc. 4:7-17; Jos. Antiq. XV.viii.1).

Archaeology has added much to our knowledge of games in OT times. Most interesting among the

Courtesy of the Trustees of the British Museum

6. Inlaid game board, from Ur; Early Dynasty III (*ca.* 2500 B.C.)

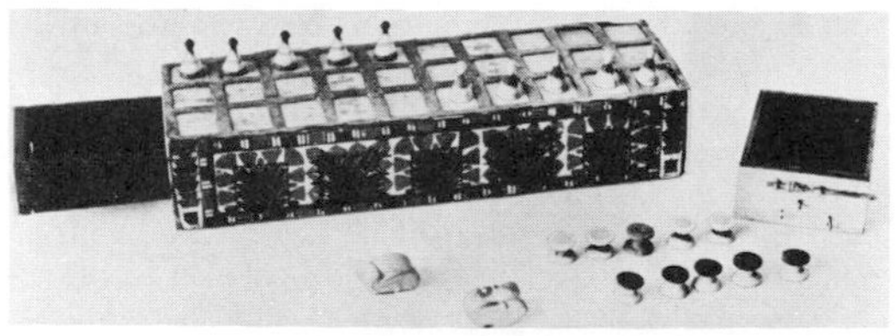

7. An Egyptian wooden gaming box, from the time of Tut-ankh-Amon (1361-1352 B.C.)

discoveries are the game boards and their accompanying playing pieces. In Palestine itself these have been found in a number of sites, among them Kiriath-sepher, Tell el-ʿAjjul, Beth-shemesh, and Gezer. They were apparently introduced from Mesopotamia, where they were used as early as the twenty-sixth century B.C., and found in the Royal cemetery of Ur.* They were also common in Egypt.* The Palestinian game boards date from the sixteenth century B.C. in the Middle Bronze Age. Figs. GAM 6-7.

In craftsmanship the boards are often quite elaborate and ornate, some being inlaid with ivory, ebony, shell, gold, and blue paste. In shape the boards vary, but the most common is rectangular, divided into twenty or thirty squares (*ca.* 4/5 inch to the side) on which the playing pieces were moved. Some boards have a series of holes, and the playing pieces are pegs, similar to a cribbage board and pegs. One such game board from Megiddo has fifty-eight holes (Fig. GAM 8). At the promontory of Umm el-Biyara, a strategic lookout post and stronghold

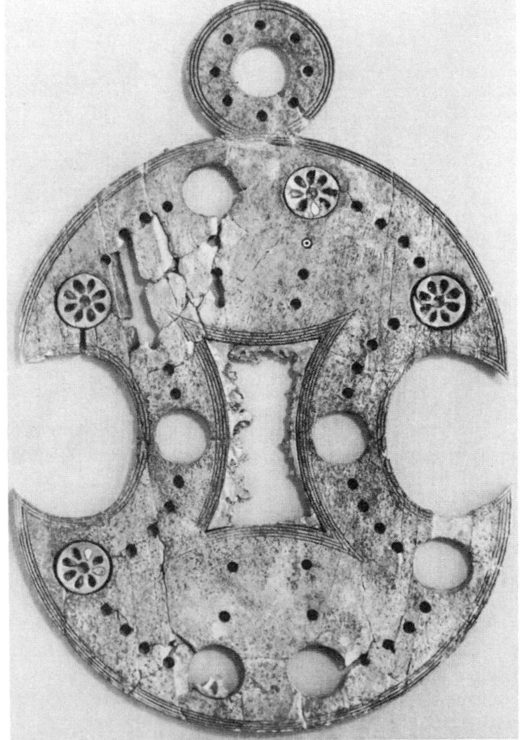

Courtesy of the Oriental Institute, the University of Chicago

8. An ivory game board for the game of fifty-eight holes; from Megiddo (*ca.* 1350-1150 B.C.)

guarding the city of Petra (Nabatean period), game boards, as at Mizpah, were carved in the living rock. The boards consist of three boxlike outlines, roughly rectangular in shape, within which are to be found double parallel rows of nine, ten, and eleven small rectangles respectively. In modern times the mancala game board is still etched on the rock or sand.

Playing pieces took various forms. One set, associated with a Twelfth Dynasty Egyptian game board, consisted of ten pegs of ivory, five with heads of dogs, five with heads of jackals, so that the game has been referred to as "hounds and jackals."* An

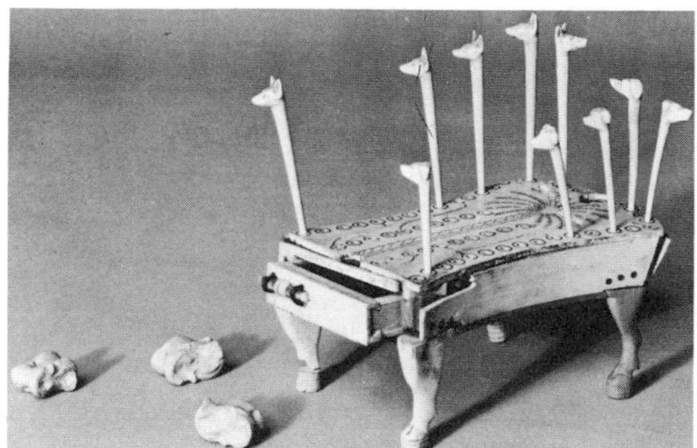

Courtesy of the Metropolitan Museum of Art; gift of Edward S. Harkness, 1926

9. Game of "Hounds and Jackals," played with ivory pieces on a board of ivory and veneer; to the left are three astragali (knuckle-bones); from the tomb of Renseneb, Thebes; Twelfth Dynasty (*ca.* 1990-1780 B.C.)

Courtesy of the Palestine Archaeological Museum, Jerusalem, Jordan

10. A limestone game board, with ten faïence playing pieces; in the lower right an ivory teetotum; from Debir (Tell Beit Mirsim), *ca.* 1800-1550 B.C.

earlier Egyptian set of playing pieces, fourteen in number, are roundels, seven of black shale inlaid with five white shell spots, seven of shell inlaid with five lapis spots. A set of ten pieces from Kiriath-sepher (Tell Beit Mirsim) is of blue faïence; five pieces are cone-shaped, five tetrahedrons. Figs. GAM 9-10.

With this latter set there was also an ivory teetotum, similar to a die, but in the form of a truncated pyramid. This was "pierced on four sides with varying numbers of holes, ranging from one to four." The movement of the players was thus determined by the cast or spin of the teetotum. In the game of "hounds and jackals" the movement of the pegs was determined by the cast of knucklebones.

Unfortunately we have no knowledge of the rules of play for these games. But there is ample evidence from archaeology that games were common.

Pl. XXIV.

Bibliography. W. F. Albright, "A Set of Egyptian Playing Pieces and Dice from Palestine," *Mizraim,* vol. I (1933), pp. 130-34, pl. XIV; J. D. Whiting "Petra, Ancient Caravan Stronghold," *National Geographic Magazine,* LXVII (1935), 139; W. F. Albright, *The Excavation of Tell Beit Mirsim,* vol. II: *The Bronze Age, AASOR,* vol. XVII (1936-37), pp. 48-49, pls. 21, 37; J. B. Pritchard, ed., *ANEP* (1954), figs. 212-19; E. W. Heaton, *Everyday Life in OT Times* (1956), pp. 91-92; W. H. Morton, "Umm el-Biyara," *BA,* XIX (1956), 33-34.

R. F. Schnell

GAMES, NT. The word "game" is not found in the NT, but there are many references to various kinds of games and sports. *See* Games, OT.

Jesus referred to the games of the children, as they played weddings and funerals (Matt. 11:17; Luke 7:32). The soldiers cast lots for the garments of Jesus, probably using dice of some form (Matt. 27:35). The Greeks and Romans were great lovers of games and sports, and through their influence the Jews became acquainted with them. In I Macc. 1:14; II Macc. 4:9 we see Greek games introduced to the Jews as a part of the Hellenizing program of the Seleucids. Josephus often mentions the efforts of the Herodian family to force the Greco-Roman games upon the Jews. Many of the more pious Jews resisted these games for various reasons. They came from Gentile, pagan sources. They were often connected with the worship of pagan deities. Athletes would often appear completely naked. And often there were much brutality and bloodshed, especially in the gladiatorial games of the Romans.

The most important of the Greek games were the Olympic at Olympia, the Pythian at Delphi, the Nemean at Argos, and the Isthmian on the Isthmus of Corinth. Competitions were held in foot races of various distances, chariot races, horse races, boxing, wrestling, hurling the discus and javelin, etc. The competitors went through a long, severe period of training under very specific rules. The rules of the games themselves were carefully observed. Those who were winners were given only crowns of leaves, olive, pine, laurel, or parsley, but they were held in very high honor by their fellow citizens.

It is easy to see how lessons could be drawn from these games. In I Cor. 9:24-27, Paul urges the Corinthians to play the game so as to win the prize, to keep themselves fit by exercising self-control, and to fight with a definite purpose rather than beating the air. Heb. 12:1-2 urges the running of a good race in the presence of the great crowd of heroes of former days, and of Jesus himself, the greatest of them all. Gal. 2:2 speaks of running a race in vain; 5:7, of running well. In Phil. 2:16, Paul speaks again of running in vain; and in 3:14 he uses the figure of pressing toward the goal to win the prize. In II Tim. 2:5 the young minister is urged to faithfulness in living up to the rules of the Christian life, as he is reminded that athletes do not win their prizes unless they compete in accordance with the rules of their games. Other, briefer references are made to games throughout the NT. S. A. CARTLEDGE

GAMMADIMS. KJV form of "men of Gamad." *See* GAMAD, MEN OF.

GAMUL gā'məl [גמול, *possibly* weaned *or* benefited] (I Chr. 24:17). A chief of the Levites.

GANGRENE. *See* CANKER.

GAR. KJV form of GAS.

GARDEN [גן, גנה, enclosure; גנן, surround, defend; κῆπος]. A fenced plot of ground used for various purposes. The fence might be a stone or mud brick wall or a hedge. *See* ORCHARD; EDEN, GARDEN OF.

In some parts of the Near East the garden might be extensive, adjoining the residence of some wealthy and influential person. It was often irrigated (Isa. 58:11) and might have a shelter built in it. The king's residence probably included an elaborate garden or private park (II Kings 25:4).

Gardens were used in many different ways. With trees planted in them, they were valuable for shade, and one might go walking or hold a banquet in his garden. With a pool installed, the garden might be used for bathing (Sus. 1:5-7). In addition to such recreational uses, gardens were places where flowers, herbs, or vegetables were cultivated (Song of S. 5:1; 6:2). Fruit and olive trees, as well as grape vines, were planted in gardens, and in the latter two cases there might be a press (*see* GARDEN OF GETHSEMANE). Gardens may have been used for worship (Matt. 26:36) and for observing idolatrous rites (Isa. 65:3). They were also used as burial places (II Kings 21:18; John 19:41) H. N. RICHARDSON

GAREB gâr'ĕb [גרב]. **1.** An Ithrite or, more probably, a Jattirite, who was one of the mighty men of David known as the "Thirty" (II Sam. 23:38; I Chr. 11:40). If one follows the reading of the MT, Gareb will then be an Ithrite—i.e., a member of the Ithrite family from Kiriath-jearim (I Chr. 2:53); but if the text is repointed on the basis of sound textual evidence (LXX: B[ab], A; Syr.), Gareb will then be from the city of Jattir, located SW of Hebron.

E. R. DALGLISH

2. A quarter of Jerusalem, presumably located on the SW hill; mentioned in the prophecy of Jer. 31:39 on the restoration of the city.

GARIZIM. KJV Apoc. form of GERIZIM.

GARLAND. The translation of three words:

a) לויה (Prov. 1:9; 4:9; with emendation, 14:24; KJV ORNAMENT OF GRACE), "something twisted, a wreath."

b) פאר (Isa. 61:3, 10; KJV BEAUTY; ORNAMENTS), an object worn as a sign of joy—e.g., by a bridegroom. *See* HEADDRESS; TURBAN 1.

c) Στέμμα (Acts 14:13), a wreath or chaplet wound around a priest's staff or worn on his head. Garlands were among the offerings for sacrifice brought by the priest of Zeus in honor of Paul and Barnabas at Lystra. *See* CROWN; HEADBAND; HEADDRESS.

J. M. MYERS

GARLIC [שומים, *šûmîm;* Aram. תומא, *tûmâ;* Arab. *thûm;* Akkad. *šûmu*]. A bulbous vegetable of the lily family, *Allium sativum* L., noted for its pungent odor. The Hebrews in the wilderness at Taberah (i.e., "burning") craved garlic and other foods they had had in Egypt (Num. 11:5). Herodotus (II.125) tells of an inscription on the great Pyramid of Cheops which listed garlic as one of the vegetables supplied in great quantities to the builders.

See also AGRICULTURE; FLORA § A3*b;* FOOD.

Bibliography. H. N. and A. L. Moldenke, *Plants of the Bible* (1952), p. 32. J. C. TREVER

GARMENT. *See* DRESS AND ORNAMENTS; FESTAL GARMENT; LINEN GARMENT.

GARMITE gär'mīt [גרמי, *gentilic of* גרם, Gerem (bone)] (I Chr. 4:19). Designation of Keilah in the list of Judah.

GARNER. GRANARY, a barn, a store. The noun "garner" is now nearly obsolete, and "granary" is commonly used instead, except, perhaps, in rhetorical language. "Garners" is the translation of מזו in Ps. 144:13. The KJV uses "garner(s)" also to translate אוצרות in Joel 1:17 (RSV STOREHOUSES; elsewhere אוצר=TREASURE; TREASURY; STORE; STOREHOUSE) and ἀποθήκη in Matt. 3:12; Luke 3:17 (RSV GRANARY; elsewhere KJV-RSV BARN).

In Isa. 62:9 a participial form of the verb "gather" or "remove" (אסף) is rendered "those who garner" (KJV "they that have gathered"). In this sense the verb means "to store" crops, in a granary—i.e., to gather them for preservation. H. F. BECK

GARRISON [מצב; מצבה, *maṣṣābhâ;* נציב; KJV מצבה, *maṣṣēbhâ* (Ezek. 26:11; RSV *correctly* PILLAR); *all from* נצב, to take a stand, be stationed]. A body of troops stationed for defense, usually on a frontier post.

In the tenth century B.C. the Philistines had garrisons placed deep in Judean territory: at Gibeath-elohim (I Sam. 10:5; *see* GIBEAH), at GEBA (I Sam. 13:3), and at Bethlehem (II Sam. 23:14; I Chr. 11:16). After their subjugation by David, the latter extended his own kingdom in turn and was able to place Israelite garrisons in Aram of Damascus (II Sam. 8:6) and in Edom (II Sam. 8:14; I Chr. 18:13). According to the Chronicler (II Chr. 17:2), Jehoshaphat placed garrisons not only in Judah but also in certain cities of Ephraim which his father, Asa, had taken from Baasha. Elsewhere, however, Asa is portrayed as more or less at the mercy of the N kingdom (cf. I Kings 15:16-24). J. W. WEVERS

GAS găs [Γάς] (I Esd. 5:34); KJV GAR gär. Ancestor of some among the sons of Solomon's servants. The name is omitted in the parallel Ezra 2:57.
C. T. Fritsch

GASH [גדד]; KJV CUT. To inflict incisions on the person as a sign of mourning or in the ecstatic worship of pagan deities (Jer. 41:5; 47:5; 48:37; cf. Hos. 7:14, where the RSV follows the LXX in reading גדד in place of גרר).
See also Mutilation.

GASHMU. *See* Geshem.

GASPAR găs'pər. In late tradition a king of India and one of the three Magi. *See* Melkon.

GATAM gā'təm [געתן]. An Edomite clan chief (אלוף געתם, perhaps "clan chief of Gatam"]; son of Eliphaz 1 (Gen. 36:11, 16; I Chr. 1:36).

GATE [שער, cleft, opening; πύλη, πυλών, θύρα]. The doors (דלת), beams (קורה), bolts (מנעול), and bars (בריח) are often mentioned (cf. Neh. 3:3, 14). The leaves (דלת), the opening (פתח, "entrance"), often by synecdoche stand for it and are translated "gate."

The gate of the city served for defense and as a "civic center." In II Sam. 18–19 details of a doubtlessly typical gate appear. There were two gates (two sets of piers?), a chamber above the gate over the double piers, and a roof above that which served as a lookout. The gate was the news center; David had but to appear there for the army and his supporters to recover their morale, which had been shattered by rumors of his grief over Absalom.

Courtesy of the Arab Information Center, New York

11. Damascus Gate, the principal gateway to the old walled city of Jerusalem

"Within your gates" may mean "within your towns" (so RSV; Deut. 12:12, 15, 17, 21, etc.). The gate (i.e., the space inside the gate) might be the place of market (II Kings 7:1, 18) or the place where the elders and judges or king might sit officially (Deut. 21:19; 22:15; Ruth 4:1, 11; II Sam. 18:24; Isa. 29:21), and so might be synonymous with the court or place of judgment (Amos 5:12, 15). For the gates of the Jerusalem temple, see especially Ezek. 40–47. Cf. also the gates of the tabernacle (Exod. 27:16; 35:17; etc.).

See also City; Temple, Jerusalem, §§ B2*b-c*. Fig. GAT 11.
C. C. McCown

GATE BETWEEN THE TWO WALLS [שער בין החמתים]; KJV GATE BETWIXT THE TWO WALLS in Jer. 39:4. A city gate to the SE of Jerusalem (II Kings 25:4; Jer. 39:4; 52:7); perhaps identical with the Fountain Gate.

GATH găth [גת, wine press; Akkad. *Gimtu, Ginti*]; GITTITE gĭt'īt. One of the five principal cities of the Philistines. It lay inland considerably S of Ekron, being farther E and nearer to Judah than any of its sister cities. Because of its position it changed hands from time to time, now and again coming under the control of Judah. Hence it is mentioned some forty times in the OT, though in a few instances other places of similar name may have been intended (*see below*).

Like other Philistine cities, Gath was considered by the Israelites an old city of Canaanite times, once inhabited by the Anakim, a race of giants (Josh. 11:22; *see* Anak). A reference in the Amarna Letters (*see* Tell el-Amarna) confirms its antiquity (No. 290, line 9: *Gimti*). There are traces of early conflict with the tribes of Ephraim and Benjamin (I Chr. 7:21; 8:13, possibly referring to another place farther N). Joshua did not take it, and it became Philistine (Josh. 11:22; 13:3). When the captured ark (*see* Ark of the Covenant) proved troublesome in Ashdod, it was then taken to Gath, where it again proved troublesome and was sent on to Ekron (I Sam. 5:6-10; 6:17). A late tradition implies that Gath and Ekron were taken by Israel in the time of Samuel (see Commentaries on I Sam. 7:14). However, these places remained Philistine at this time. Goliath, the huge Philistine champion, was a Gittite—i.e., a man from Gath (I Sam. 17:4, 23; II Sam. 21:19)—carrying on the tradition of the Anakim as to size. Other giant Philistine warriors also came from Gath (II Sam. 21:20-22; I Chr. 20:5-8). When the Philistines were defeated by Israel, they were able to flee for safety to Gath and Ekron, their two nearest cities (I Sam. 17:52).

David, in flight from Saul, attempted to take refuge with Achish, king of Gath, but was not well received, according to one tradition (I Sam. 21:10-15; Ps. 56:1). According to another tradition, David was welcomed, and actually entered the service of Achish, being willing to fight against the Israelites if necessary (I Sam. 27:1–28:2; 29). In his lament over Saul and Jonathan, the Philistine character of the city is made obvious (II Sam. 1:20). When David wished to delay bringing the ark to Jerusalem, he entrusted it for safekeeping to "Obed-edom the Gittite" for three months (II Sam. 6:10-11; I Chr. 13:13). It is not certain that this man came from the Philistine Gath (*see* Obed-edom 1). I Chr. 18:1 states that David took Gath in his final wars with the Philistines, but the parallel in II Sam. 8:1 reads Methegh-ammah. In any case, whether through conquest or through friendships formed during his service under Achish, David was able throughout his later career to command the services of a Philistine bodyguard, a band of most loyal supporters, under the command of Ittai the Gittite, who finally rose to be one of David's three top commanders (II Sam. 15:18-22; 18:2, 5).

During the time of Solomon there seems to have been easy communication between Jerusalem and Gath, either because of friendship or because of political control by Solomon. The Gittite king was still Achish by name, possibly the same man who had befriended David long before (I Kings 2:39-42). According to II Chr. 11:8-10, Rehoboam fortified Gath, it being considered one of the cities of Judah (*ca.* 922 B.C.). Perhaps this explains why Hazael of Aram (Syria) felt it necessary to take Gath in a campaign against Jerusalem in the time of Jehoash of Judah (*ca.* 837-800 B.C.—II Kings 12:17, if the Philistine Gath is meant; again, a place farther N would seem more fitting). At this time the city apparently reverted to the Philistines, for shortly thereafter Uzziah of Judah (*ca.* 783-742) attacked it in a campaign against the Philistines and partially destroyed it (II Chr. 26:6). Sargon II speaks of conquering and despoiling Gath and other rebellious cities of the area in connection with his campaign of 711 B.C. Thereafter it seems to disappear from history. Amos 6:2 probably refers to it as an example of a destroyed city. "Tell it not in Gath" (II Sam. 1:20; Mic. 1:10) had perhaps become proverbial as a phrase of disaster; it is also just possible that Micah was actually warning of the impending invasion of 711 (see *IB* on Mic. 1:10-16). Lists of Philistine cities in the prophetic writings noticeably omit Gath (Amos 1:6-8; Zeph. 2:4; Jer. 25:20; Zech. 9:5; cf. Josh. 13:3; I Sam. 6:17). It does not appear in the Apoc., the NT, or in Josephus in relation to events after 750 B.C. It is mentioned briefly in Euseb. Onom. and in Jerome's commentary on Mic. 1:10.

Because of the obscurity of the place since the eighth century B.C., it is not strange that a number of sites have been proposed from time to time as the location of Gath. The two best proposals seem to be Tell es-Safi, *ca.* twelve miles E of Ashdod, and Tell Sheikh Ahmed el-'Areini, near 'Araq el-Menshiyeh, *ca.* fifteen miles E of Ashkelon and some seven miles S of Tell es-Safi. Those who accept the latter identification generally place Libnah at Tell es-Safi.

Wine presses were common in ancient Palestine; hence there were various places named Gath, usually with some qualification. *See* GATH-HEPHER; GATH-RIMMON; MORESHETH-GATH; GITTAIM.

Bibliography. F. J. Bliss and R. A. S. Macalister, *Excavations in Palestine During the Years 1898-1900* (1902), pp. 63-66, favors Tell es-Safi. W. F. Albright, "The Sites of Ekron, Gath, and Libnah," *AASOR,* II-III (1923), 7-12, strongly favors Tell Sheikh Ahmed el-'Areini. See also: G. Beyer, "Gath," *ZDPV,* LIV (1931), 135-45. K. Elliger, "Die Lage von Gath," *ZDPV,* LVII (1934), 148-52. F.-M. Abel, *Géographie de la Palestine,* II (1938), 325-26. J. B. Pritchard, ed., *ANET* (2nd ed., 1955), pp. 286, 425, 489. B. Mazar (Maisler), "Gath and Gittaim," *IEJ,* IV (1954), 227-35, equates several references with Gittaim, to the N, near Lod; "Tell Gath," *IEJ,* VI (1956), 258-59, is a brief report on excavations at Tell Sheikh el-'Areini.

W. F. STINESPRING

GATH-HEPHER găth hē'fər [גת החפר]; KJV GITTAH-HEPHER gĭt'ə hē'fər [גתה חפר] in Josh. 19:13. A border town in the territory of Zebulun (Josh. 19:13); the home of the prophet Jonah, a contemporary of Jeroboam II of Israel (II Kings 14:25). It is probably to be identified with Khirbet ez-Zurra', a fairly extensive site located *ca.* three miles NE of Nazareth. Surface explorations have shown that it was occupied in Iron I and II (i.e., *ca.* 1200-600), and so in the period of Jonah, and probably in the Late Bronze period (*ca.* 1550-1200) also. A short distance to the N of the remains is the village Meshhed, the traditional site of the tomb of Jonah.

Bibliography. W. F. Albright, "New Israelite and Pre-Israelite Sites: The Spring Trip of 1929," *BASOR,* 35 (1929), 8.

G. W. VAN BEEK

GATH-RIMMON găth rĭm'ən [גת רמון, Gath (wine press) by the pomegranate]. **1.** A Danite city (Josh. 19:45) assigned to the Kohathite clan of the Levites (Josh. 21:24; I Chr. 6:69—H 6:54); probably to be identified with Tell ej-Jerisheh on the S bank of the River Yarkon (Nahr el-'Auja) near the mouth of the Wadi Musrara. It may also be the Gath (*k n t*), no. 63 of the list of Thut-mose III (1490-1436). Typical early Hyksos fortifications were found at Tell ej-Jerisheh.

2. A Levitical city in Manasseh (Josh. 21:25); one should probably read "Ibleam" (BILEAM) here with I Chr. 6:70—H 6:55 and the LXX.

Bibliography. B. Maisler, "The Excavations at Tell Qasile," *IEJ,* no. 1 (1950), p. 63, note 4, and the references noted there; Y. Yadin, "Hyksos Fortifications and the Battering Ram," *BASOR,* 137 (1955), 26.

V. R. GOLD

GAULANITIS gôl'ə nī'tĭs [גולן, *see below;* Γαυλανῖτις]. That portion of the Transjordan Plateau immediately E of Galilee.

Gaulanitis extended from the cliffs which rise steeply along the Jordan Valley to an indefinite boundary on the E with TRACHONITIS and Batanea. On the S the border was the Yarmuk, and on the N the districts of Ulatha and Paneas.

Although not mentioned in the Bible, Gaulanitis was apparently named for a city in the OT, "Golan [גולן] in Bashan" (Deut. 4:43; Josh. 20:8). The city was still in existence in the time of Josephus (War I.iv.4, 8). As part of the kingdom of Herod the Great, he willed Gaulanitis to his son Philip in 4 B.C. (Jos. Antiq. XVII.viii.1). After Philip's death in A.D. 34 it was added to the Roman province of Syria (Jos. Antiq. XVIII.iv.6), but later it was given to Herod Agrippa I by the Emperor Caligula (Jos. Antiq. XVIII.vi.10). It formed part of the kingdom of Herod Agrippa II when it took part in the Jewish revolt against Rome in A.D. 66-70 (Jos. War IV.i.1; Life 37).

Like the BASHAN of the OT, Gaulanitis was famed in NT times for its rich crops. Apparently it was more thickly populated then than it is now, although it is still fertile. The modern name for the same territory is Jaulan, which still preserves a form of the "Golan" of the OT, for which it was named.

Bibliography. G. Schumacher, *The Jaulan* (1888); F.-M. Abel, *Géographie de la Palestine,* II (1933), 155, 158.

D. C. PELLETT

GAULS gôlz [Γαλάται, *see* GALATIA]. A people, often called Celts by ancient writers, who were found chiefly in what is now France and North Italy; but they invaded Macedonia, Achaia, Thrace, and even

Asia Minor, where many settled and became known as Galatians. I Macc. 8:2 reports that the Romans had defeated the Gauls, perhaps in Asia Minor but probably in Western Europe (so RSV). II Macc. 8:20 tells of the (unauthenticated) defeat of Gallic mercenaries (from Asia Minor?) by a determined army of Jewish soldiers. Possibly Crescens went to Gaul for missionary work (II Tim. 4:10); the reading εἰς Γαλλίαν, fairly well attested, would certainly mean "to Gaul"; the somewhat better attested reading, εἰς Γαλατίαν, could refer to Gaul as "Galatia" but more probably means "to Galatia" in Asia Minor.

Bibliography. W. M. Ramsay, *A Historical Commentary on St. Paul's Epistle to the Galatians* (1900), pp. 45-52; W. Lock, *The Pastoral Epistles* (1924), p. 117; A. H. M. Jones, *The Cities of the Eastern Roman Provinces* (1937), ch. 4. F. V. FILSON

GAUZE, GARMENTS OF [גִּלְיֹנִים]; KJV GLASSES. An item of finery of the daughters of Zion (Isa. 3:23). Besides filmy shawls (from the root meaning "uncover" or "reveal") and mirrors, the word has also been interpreted as referring to glittering little plates of metal. The same word is used in Isa. 8:1 of something to write on (*see* TABLET). H. G. MAY

GAZA gā′zə, gä′zə [עַזָּה, *'azzâ;* Egyp. *Gadatu, Gedjet;* Akkad. *Ḫazzatu, Azzati;* Γάζα; *modern* Arab. *Ghazzeh*]; KJV AZZAH ăz′ə in Deut. 2:23; I Kings 4:24; Jer. 25:20; GAZITES gā′zīts; KJV GAZATHITES gā′zə thīts. A city in SW Palestine, best known from the Bible as the southernmost of the five principal cities (pentapolis) of the PHILISTINES; located *ca.* three miles from the seacoast, on the road to Egypt.

The first pronunciation given above is the standard English pronunciation of the biblical place name; the second is applied to the modern city by travelers, diplomats, commentators, etc., under the influence of the Arabic form of the name.

The city had a long history and was usually regarded as a place of importance, being mentioned about twenty times in the Bible and often in other literature. It was not a seaport (the nearby coast afforded no safe harbor), but rather was the land gateway between Egypt and Asia for caravan and military traffic. There is even evidence for trade with S Arabia.

Biblical tradition regards Gaza as ancient, going back into Canaanite times (Gen. 10:19; Deut. 2:23). This is borne out by the earliest Egyptian reference (Annals of Thut-mose III), mentioning Gaza as an important Egyptian-held town at which Thut-mose stopped near the beginning of his first campaign into Asia, *ca.* the year 1468 B.C. (see also Taanach Letter No. 6, *BASOR,* XCIV [1944], 24-27). The TELL EL-AMARNA Letters show the town still loyal to Egypt but in grave danger, like the rest of Palestine, from the incoming HABIRU (late Eighteenth Dynasty, *ca.* 1360 B.C.). The Nineteenth Dynasty restored Egyptian power; later Egypt weakened again (*ca.* 1200 B.C.). The Israelites were at first able to get a foothold in the region (Josh. 10:41; 11:22; 15:47; Judg. 1:18; 6:4), but the incoming Philistines soon took over the S coastal territory, and Gaza became identified with them (Deut. 2:23; Josh. 13:3; Judg. 16:1-2, 21; I Sam. 6:17). The territory of Solomon reached near Gaza but did not include it (I Kings 4:24).

Amos 1:6-7 condemns the city for its slave trade with Edom. This attests very active business enterprise, not always of the most ethical kind. We may compare the Minean (S Arabian) inscription telling of the importation of a female temple slave from Gaza. The prophetic oracle, if actually from Amos, would be dated about the middle of the eighth century B.C. Shortly after this, Tiglath-Pileser III (744-727), in his campaign against Damascus and Israel (733-732), also attacked and captured Gaza. Its king, Hanno, perhaps a leader in the anti-Assyrian conspiracy, fled to Egypt. However, he was soon able to return and resume his plotting, for *ca.* 721-720 his forces, in alliance with the Egyptians, fought a battle with Sargon II S of Gaza. This time he was captured and deported to Assyria, to be heard of no more. The city was now loyal to Assyria, so that Hezekiah, king of Judah, attacked it in his anti-Assyrian revolt (II Kings 18:8). This eventually brought down Sennacherib, who took away considerable territory from Judah, dividing it between Sillibel, the new pro-Assyrian king of Gaza, and other Philistine rulers (701). A king of the same name (the same man or a successor) paid tribute to Esarhaddon (680-669), the conqueror of Egypt, and to Ashurbanipal (668-633), the last strong king of Assyria. It is perhaps to this period, when the Philistines were holding Judean territory with the help of Assyria, that we can assign the bitter oracle against Gaza and the Philistines found in Zeph. 2 (note vss. 4-7, 13-14).

When Pharaoh Neco went N *ca.* 609 to support crumbling Assyria against the rising Chaldeans, he probably took Gaza into protective custody (Jer. 47:1; Herodotus *History* II.159). Jeremiah predicted that the Chaldeans would overwhelm Gaza, along with Judah, the rest of Philistia, and other surrounding nations (25:20; 47:5). Inscriptions of Nebuchadnezzar (605-562) show us the kings of Gaza, Judah, and other nearby principalities in captivity at Babylon.

Gaza and the Philistines continued into postexilic times, still being disliked by the Jews (Zech. 9:5). The city was incorporated into the Persian Empire at the time of Cambyses (525), though it remained virtually independent. It resisted Alexander for two months (332). The Philistines had disappeared by this time, and the population was made up of Persians and Arabs. Many of these were massacred, and the city was badly damaged. It was restored and became a center of Hellenism. In Maccabean times it yielded to Jonathan (I Macc. 11:61-62), but later plotted against the Jews and was virtually destroyed by Alexander Janneus (96 B.C.), so that certain Greek writers referred to it as ἔρημος, "desert(ed)." It was ordered rebuilt by the Roman general Gabinius (57 B.C.)—according to some, on a new site a short distance away—so that for a while there were two Gazas, though the original site eventually reasserted itself. This may have a bearing on the exegetical problem in connection with the last biblical reference to Gaza, Acts 8:26. Authorities are sharply divided as to whether the word ἔρημος, "desert," in this verse refers to the road or to the old, nearly abandoned city (see the Commentaries).

In Roman times Gaza was a flourishing seat of pagan culture, and Christianity was established only after a long and sometimes bloody struggle (*ca.* A.D.

400). It was taken *ca.* 635 by the Muslims, and, except for a brief interlude during the Crusades, has remained strongly Muslim to the present day.

The reference in I Chr. 7:28 KJV should read AYYAH. In I Macc. 13:43 GAZARA should be read. Because of the presence of the modern city on the old site, and other difficulties, no significant archaeological work has been undertaken here. The excavated site of Tell el-'Ajjul can hardly be considered one of the former locations of Gaza; it is rather to be identified as BETH-EGLAIM. During Hellenistic and Roman times there was a small seaport on the coast, bearing the name Maioumas, later changed to Constantia when it went over to Christianity. Another similar place just to the N was called Anthedon or Agrippias. The suggested derivation of the word "gauze" from Gaza is uncertain (cf. "damask" from Damascus, which is certain).

Bibliography. In addition to dictionaries and encyclopedias in English, consult F. Vigouroux, ed., *Dictionnaire de la Bible,* III (1903), 118-23, the best treatment of the classical and patristic sources. M. A. Meyer, *History of the City of Gaza* (1907), a dissertation, with good bibliographies. W. J. Phythian-Adams, "Reports on Soundings at Gaza, Etc.," *PEQ* (1923), pp. 11-36. J. B. Pritchard, ed., *ANET* (2nd ed., 1955), Index of Names, pp. 529, 543. E. G. Kraeling, *Rand-McNally Bible Atlas* (1956), pp. 417-18, the latest attempt to deal with the exegetical problem in Acts 8:26.

Among the more interesting Greek sources are: Arrian *Anabasis of Alexander* II.25-27; Plutarch *Lives, Alexander* XXV; Polybius *Histories* XVI.22*a;* Jos. Antiq. XIII.xii-xiii.

W. F. STINESPRING

GAZARA. Apoc. form of GEZER.

GAZATHITES. *See* GAZA.

GAZELLE [צבי; *feminine* צביה *in* Song of S. 4:5; 7:3—H 7:4, *plural* צבאים *in* I Chr. 12:8—H 12:9; צבאות (Song of S. 2:7; 3:5); *cf.* Akkad. *ṣabītu,* gazelle; Arab. *ẓaby,* gazelle; δορκάς (*a proper name,* Dorcas, *in* Acts 9:36, 39), *probably* the clear-eyed one, *from* δέρκομαι, to see clearly]; KJV ROE, ROEBUCK. A species of small ANTELOPE, with recurved horns (the subfamily Antilopinae among the Bovidae contains the gazelles), and one of the most graceful members of the antelope group. Two varieties may have been known in biblical Palestine: *gazella dorcas,* pale fawn in color, height at the withers twenty-one to twenty-two inches; and *gazella arabica,* dark smoky fawn in color, height *ca.* twenty-four to twenty-five inches (for Bodenheimer's views, *see* FAUNA § A2*f*ii). In biblical times the gazelle was probably the most abundant of the larger game animals (Tristram *NHB* 127-31).

Although not used for sacrificial purposes, the gazelle was a clean animal and could be eaten as food (Deut. 12:15, 22; 14:5; 15:22), and it is said to have graced Solomon's table (I Kings 4:23—H 5:3). Gazelles had to be hunted (which gives the author of Isa. 13:14 a figure for the fugitive Babylonians; cf. Prov. 6:5), but they were not easy to bag, for their speed of movement was proverbial (II Sam. 2:18; I Chr. 12:8—H 12:9). Their simple beauty and elegant form explain the gazelle similes applied both to the beloved and to the maiden in Song of S. 2:9, 17; 4:5; 7:3—H 7:4; 8:14. The oath in Song of S. 2:7; 3:5 ("by the gazelles or hinds of the field") is more difficult to understand. Possibly it was felt that the name of God should be left out of an adjuration concerned with human love, and there may have been some popular association of the gazelle and the hind with love-making which encouraged their use in this context. *See bibliography.*

Courtesy of the Cairo Museum; photo courtesy of the Metropolitan Museum of Art

12. Tut-ankh-Amon (*ca.* 1361-1352 B.C.) shooting gazelles with a bow; from an Egyptian wall painting in Thebes

Fig. GAZ 12.

Bibliography. R. Gordis, *The Song of Songs* (1954), pp. 26-28.

W. S. MCCULLOUGH

GAZER. KJV alternate form of GEZER.

GAZEZ gā'zĭz [גזז, sheep shearing(?)]. Apparently a Calebite family (I Chr. 2:46). The name is mentioned twice, both as a son and as a brother of Haran, but the verse is obscure and probably an addition.

Bibliography. M. Noth, *Die israelitischen Personennamen* (1928), p. 240.

H. H. GUTHRIE, JR.

GAZITES. *See* GAZA.

GAZZAM găz'əm [גזם, some kind of bird or insect] (Ezra 2:48; Neh. 7:51). Alternately: GAZZAN găz'ən [Γαζηρα] (I Esd. 5:31); KJV GAZERA gə zē'rə. A family of NETHINIM.

Bibliography. M. Noth, *Die israelitischen Personennamen* (1928), p. 230.

GEAR [σκεῦος, vessel, implement, thing] (Acts 27:17); KJV SAIL. Equipment or apparatus.

The context of Acts 27:17 indicates that this word is a nautical term, but the precise meaning is uncertain. Among the possibilities are: (*a*) "sail"; the phrase would then mean either "they lowered the sail" (cf. KJV) or "they shortened the sail"; this interpretation is supported by some minor MSS (including the Syr.) which read: τὰ ἱστία ("the sails"); (*b*) "ship's gear" (cf. RSV), such as ropes, sails, yards, pulleys; on being lowered they would be made fast on deck or stowed below; (*c*) "anchor," which would be let out to retard the progress of the vessel. *See* SHIPS AND SAILING.

W. S. MCCULLOUGH

GEBA gē'bə [גבע, hill, height]; KJV GABA gā'bə in Josh. 18:24; Ezra 2:26; Neh. 7:30; KJV Apoc. GABOES gā'bōz. One of the cities given to the Levites (Josh. 21:17; I Chr. 6:60) out of the inheritance allotted to the tribe of Benjamin (Josh. 18:24; I Chr. 8:6). This site represented the traditional N limits of the kingdom of Judah (II Kings 23:8; Zech. 14:10; cf. Neh. 11:31) and was the S guardian of the head of the Michmash Pass. It was situated E of Ramah and six miles N-NE of Jerusalem; both the ancient name and the site are preserved in the modern village of Jeba.

Because of its strategic situation, the site played an important role in the battles of Saul, Jonathan, and David with the Philistines (I Sam. 13:3, 16; 14:5; II Sam. 5:25; cf. I Chr. 14:16). In these and in related passages care must be exercised to distinguish the site from Gibeah and Gibeon, both of which are situated nearby and which are, at times, apparently confused with Geba in the Hebrew text (e.g., cf. II Sam. 5:25; I Chr. 14:16). Because of its strategic position, also, Geba was fortified by Asa with stones removed from Ramah (I Kings 15:22; II Chr. 16:6) and is listed by Isaiah as an important station in his visionary portrayal of the advance of a hostile army on Jerusalem from the N (Isa. 10:29). Subsequent to the Exile the site and its surroundings were repopulated by returnees from Babylon—many of whom were of Benjaminite extraction (Ezra 2:26; Neh. 7:30; 11:31; 12:29). W. H. Morton

GEBAL gē'bəl [גבל; Ugar. *Gbl;* Egyp. *Kubni;* Akkad. *Gublu;* Amarna *Gubla;* Βυβλος]; GEBALITES —īts; KJV GIBLITES gĭb'līts. **1.** A Phoenician city between Tripolis and Beirut; modern Jebeil. Figs. GEB 13-14.

The ancient Gebal was situated on a slope on the Phoenician coast, N of Berytus (Beirut). It was a center of trade and shipbuilding. The famous cedars of Lebanon, unsurpassed as material for shipbuilders, were found in the neighborhood and made Gebal an important city for all nations and kings who needed ships. It was situated sufficiently far from the Egyptian, Amorite, and Assyrian centers to evade complete domination by the great powers, but at the same time it was a convenient meeting place for trade and culture.

Gebal is one of the most ancient cities in the Near East, and its history can be traced far back. At the

Courtesy of Herbert G. May

13. Excavations at Gebal showing Roman columns and Middle Bronze Age foundations

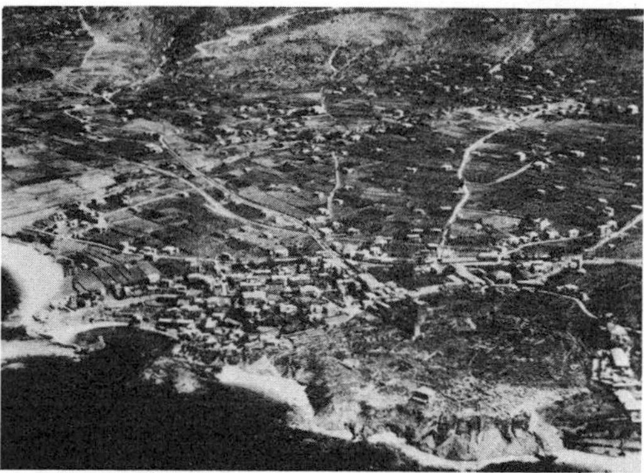

From *Atlas of the Bible* (Thomas Nelson & Sons Limited)

14. Aerial view of Gebal

bottom of the tell, close to virgin soil, objects have been found together with human bones, indicating that a Mediterranean race was living in Gebal in Neolithic times. Members of this race were rather small and delicately built. They lived in circular huts or in houses with rounded angles. Their dead were buried in large earthen pots. What language they spoke is not known. Toward the end of the fourth millennium B.C., however, this civilization vanished rather suddenly.

At the same time traces of a new civilization are found, not only in Byblos, but in all Phoenicia and Canaan.* They represent an urban form of life, and in Byblos a new style of architecture was used. Temples and houses were built, and the new city was guarded by a wall. New technical inventions are found—i.e., the wheel, sailing ships, the potter's wheel. Above all a new metal, bronze, was important. It was introduced by people coming into Phoenicia from the N. They were not the only ones to invade the country; Semites had also mixed with the former population. These different peoples mixed to form a new people, called Phoenicians by the Greeks, and one of their most important cities at the end of the fourth millennium was Gebal. Fig. PHO 53.

Objects which have been dug out in the ruins of the temples in Gebal are witnesses that the Egyptian influence in this Phoenician city was very great at a time which goes far back in history. A cylinder from the Thinite epoch (*ca.* 3000 B.C.) has been found, and also vases with the names of different Pharaohs, Mycerinus (twenty-seventh century B.C.), Unis and Pepi (twenty-fifth and twenty-fourth centuries B.C.), and others.

The Egyptian interest in Gebal was certainly not only of a religious character. Gebal exported jars with oil, spices, wine, leather, and other products. The Egyptians also needed ships, and to build ships they must have cedars and spruce from Lebanon. In the annals of Snefru (Fourth Dynasty, twenty-sixth century B.C.) there is an account of "bringing 40 ships filled with cedar logs" from Gebal.

At the end of the third millennium B.C., Gebal was destroyed and burned. A new city was built, and the names of the kings in the nineteenth and eighteenth centuries B.C. indicate that the rulers were Semites and most probably Amorites. But even if the leading classes were Amorites, the population was still mixed, now also with Hittites and Hurrians (Horites), who brought their bronze weapons and their ceramics from the N. There was also a certain cultural influence from the Aegean islands.

Toward the middle of the second millennium B.C., Hurrians, Hittites, and Mitannians for a short time ruled in Gebal, but then the names of the kings were again Semitic, now with the Aramaeans as the dominating element. The TELL EL-AMARNA Letters reveal that in the fourteenth century B.C., King Rib-Addi of Gebal was one of the few kings in these countries who remained faithful to the Egyptian Pharaoh. In the following centuries this situation changed. While Si-nuhe in his tale from the twentieth century B.C. tells that he was magnificently received in Phoenicia, Wen-Amon must report *ca.* 1100 B.C., that he met difficulties in Gebal and other Phoenician cities when he ordered lumber for Egypt.

Inscriptions written in a linear alphabetic system have been found, dating from around this time. The most important one is the Ahiram sarcophagus inscription from *ca.* 1000 B.C., found in Byblos in 1923.

Figs. GEB 15; MOU 72.

Courtesy of the National Museum, Beirut

15. Stone sarcophagus of Ahiram, king of Gebal (Byblos), with dedicatory inscription on the lid; relief on this side shows Ahiram on a "cherub" throne before an offering table and faced by seven figures (*ca.* 1000 B.C.)

In these centuries Gebal also took part in the great Phoenician expansion in trade and shipping. In the Bible the men from Gebal (Byblos) are mentioned as able seamen and master builders (I Kings 5:18—H 5:32; Ezek. 27:9; in Josh. 13:5 the land of the Gebalites is mentioned as not conquered).

Gebal shared the fate of the rest of Phoenicia, being conquered by the Assyrians, the Babylonians, the Persians, the Greeks, the Romans. Today the dominating ruins are from Greek and Roman times, together with the great castle built by the Crusaders in the eleventh century A.D.

Bibliography. M. Dunand, *Fouilles de Byblos,* vol. 1 (1937-39); M. Dunand, *Byblia grammata* (1945); W. F. Albright, *The Archaeology of Palestine* (1949), pp. 188-94.

2. A territory in the mountains S of the Dead Sea, near Petra; called Γεβαλήνη by the Greeks; today Gibal. It is mentioned in Ps. 83:7—H 83:8 along with other places in the S. A. S. KAPELRUD

GEBER gē′bər [גֶּבֶר, (vigorous) man]. Son of Uri; one of the twelve commissariat prefects of Solomon. He had as his district the land of Gilead (I Kings 4:19). *See* BEN-GEBER.

GEBIM gē′bĭm [גֵּבִים, trenches]. A city of Benjamin, located on the route taken by the Assyrian army, according to Isaiah, in its march on Jerusalem (Isa. 10:31). On a metrical analysis of the passage Gebim is placed after Ai and Michmash; hence it was probably near the latter places, although the exact site cannot be identified. S. COHEN

GECKO gĕk′ō [אֲנָקָה (Lev. 11:30), *possibly* groan *or* groaner, *from* אנק, to cry, groan; LXX μυγαλῆ, shrewmouse; Syr. *'omaqtā,* lizard; Targ. ילא, hedgehog]; KJV FERRET. A small, four-legged reptile of the family Geckonidae, of which there are *ca.* forty-nine genera. The ferret (KJV identification) is a member of the weasel family, allied to the polecat, bred chiefly for rabbit- and rat-hunting.

As the ancient versions indicate, the meaning of אנקה (*'ănāqâ*) is uncertain, though its place in Lev. 11 points to a reptile, as the Syr. surmised. If its name is derived from a characteristic cry, the gecko suggests itself, for it utters a rapid chirping or clucking sound, and several varieties are found in Palestine (Tristram *NHB* 265-66). *See bibliography.*

See also FAUNA § A2*fv*.

Bibliography. In support of the translation "gecko," see I. Aharoni, *RB,* 48 (1939), 554-56. W. S. MCCULLOUGH

GEDALIAH gĕd′ə lī′ə [גְּדַלְיָה, Yahu is great]. **1.** A musician, supposedly of David's time, to whom one of the postexilic Levitical families traced its line (I Chr. 25:3, 9).

2. Grandson of Hezekiah (perhaps thought by the writer to be the king of that name), and grandfather of the prophet Zephaniah (Zeph. 1:1).

3. Son of Pashur; one of the Jerusalemite princes that counseled Jeremiah's death (Jer. 38:1-6).

4. Exilic governor of Judah under Nebuchadnezzar (II Kings 25:22-26; Jer. 40:6–41:18). The contemporary seal of "Gedaliah who is over the house" was discovered at LACHISH. Gedaliah's father had protected Jeremiah (Jer. 26:24), and the son probably shared the prophet's moderate political views, thus winning Nebuchadnezzar's confidence. Jewish nationalist fanatics, led by Ishmael of the exiled royal house, murdered him while they were guests in his official residence in Mizpah. Figs. GED 16; SEA 35, no. 24.

By permission of the Trustees of the late Sir Henry S. Wellcome

16. Seal of Gedaliah with the inscription: "(belonging) to Gedaliah, who is over the house"

5. One of the priests who put away their alien wives (Ezra 10:18). J. M. WARD

GEDDUR. KJV Apoc. form of GAHAR.

GEDEON gĕd′ĭ ən. Douay Version form of GIDEON; also KJV form in Heb. 11:32; Jth. 8:1.

GEDER gē′dər [גדר, fence] (Josh. 12:13); GEDERITE —īt (I Chr. 27:28). A city of the Canaanites, conquered by Joshua. Since it is mentioned next to Debir, it was probably in the lowland (Shephelah) of Judah. It is not mentioned in the list of the cities of that tribe, and may have been abandoned; perhaps, however, it is the same as BETH-GADER.

S. COHEN

GEDERAH gĭ dĭr′ə [גדרה, wall, enclosure]. **1.** One of the towns of the Shephelah in the allotment to Judah (Josh. 15:36). Certain descendants of Judah, engaged in the service of the king, are listed as dwelling here and in the city of Netaim (I Chr. 4:23). Probably Gederah is to be identified with modern Jedireh, *ca.* ten miles SE of Lod.

2. A city of Benjamin from which came Jozabad, one of David's Mighty Men, skilful in warfare, who joined his band at Ziklag (I Chr. 12:4). Perhaps it is to be identified with a Jedireh near Gibeon.

W. H. MORTON

GEDEROTH gĭ dĭr′ōth [גדרות, sheepfolds]. A city of Judah in the Shephelah district of Lachish (Josh. 15:41); possibly to be located in the region of el-Mansurah. During the reign of Ahaz (*ca.* 735-715) the Philistines detached Gederoth from Ahaz' realm (II Chr. 28:18).

It has been identified with KEDRON (Κεδρών), fortified by Cendebeus and scene of the latter's defeat by John son of Simon Maccabeus (I Macc. 15:39; 16:9).

V. R. GOLD

GEDEROTHAIM gĭ dĭr′ə thā′ĭm [גדרתים, two sheepfolds]. A village of Judah in the Shephelah district of Zorah-Azekah (Josh. 15:36). The site is unknown.

It is the general consensus of scholarly opinion that וגדרתים ("and Gederothaim") should be read וגדרתיה ("and her sheepfolds") with the LXX (καὶ αἱ ἐπαύλεις αὐτῆς). This correction of what is probably a scribal error would also reduce the number of places listed for this province from fifteen to fourteen, as the MT total (vs. 36) suggests.

V. R. GOLD

GEDOR gē′dôr [גדור, wall(?), *or* pock-marked גדר; הגדור; *cf.* Arab. *gadara*]. **1.** A person or family of Benjamin (I Chr. 8:31; 9:37).

Bibliography. M. Noth, *Die israelitischen Personennamen* (1928), p. 228.

H. H. GUTHRIE, JR.

2. A city of Judah, mentioned after Beth-zur (Josh. 15:58). The mention of Penuel as the father of Gedor (I Chr. 4:4) may mean that he was its founder.

3. A Calebite city in Judah, mentioned with Soco and Zanoah; the founder was Jered (I Chr. 4:18). Two of David's followers, Joelah and Zebadiah, came from a Gedor (I Chr. 12:7), but it is not certain which city is meant.

4. A city mentioned as the limit of the conquests of the Simeonites (I Chr. 4:39); this should be emended to GERAR.

S. COHEN

GE-HARASHIM gĭ hăr′ə shĭm [גיא חרשים, valley of craftsmen] (I Chr. 4:14); KJV VALLEY OF CHARASHIM kə rā′shĭm. Alternately: VALLEY OF CRAFTSMEN [גי החרשים] (Neh. 11:35). A community of craftsmen named from a valley in the vicinity of Lod and Ono, on the S border of the Plain of Sharon. It is perhaps the modern Wadi esh-Shellal, the broad valley between Lod and Ono, on the main road between Joppa and Jerusalem. Alternately, the Sarafand el-Kharab, in a valley slightly farther to the SW, has been suggested.

Joab of Judah and of the lineage of Kenaz is represented as the "father" or founder of this community of craftsmen (I Chr. 4:14). Following the restoration from exile, the Valley of Craftsmen was resettled by Benjaminites (Neh. 11:35).

The origin of the name is uncertain, but it may preserve a memory of a Philistine iron monopoly when Israel's lack of smiths required the services of Philistine craftsmen for the sharpening of their various implements (I Sam. 13:19-20).

W. H. MORTON

GEHAZI gĭ hā′zī [גיחזי, גחזי, valley of vision(?)]. The servant (lit., "boy") of the prophet Elisha (II Kings 4:12; 5:20; 8:4). In the story of the Shunammite woman (4:8-37) Gehazi suggested to Elisha the gift of a son to the childless woman and her husband as a reward for her extended hospitality to them. He later bore the prophet's life-giving staff to the body of the boy when he had died of a head ailment (vs. 31). In the sequel (8:1-6) Gehazi is relating Elisha's wonders to the king when the Shunammite appears to ask, successfully, a boon of the latter. Gehazi is primarily known, however, for his dispassionate rudeness to the woman on the occasion of her appeal to Elisha on behalf of her dead son (4:27) and for the greedy cunning by which he attempted to claim for himself the reward which Elisha had refused from Naaman the Syrian, whom the prophet had cured of leprosy (5:19-27). Upon discovery of his servant's treachery Elisha cursed him with the disease of which Naaman had been cured.

J. M. WARD

GEHENNA gĭ hĕn′ə [γέεννα]. Fiery hell. Gehenna is the Greek and Latin form of גיא הנם, "Valley of Hinnom" (*see* HINNOM, VALLEY OF), the name of a ravine S of Jerusalem, which, during the days of the monarchy, was the scene of an idolatrous cult involving the passing of children through fire (II Kings 23:10; II Chr. 28:3; 33:6; Jer. 7:31; 32:35; *see* MOLECH; TOPHET). In the first century B.C., this name came to be used in a metaphorical sense, to denote the place of fiery torment believed to be reserved for the wicked either immediately after death or ultimately after the Last Judgment.

The general idea of a punitive conflagration appears, to be sure, in earlier portions of the OT (e.g., Deut. 32:22; Isa. 33:14), but it is only in the Greco-Roman period of Jewish history that the quite distinct concept of a blazing hell—a lake, or abyss, of fire—begins to emerge (cf. Dan. 7:10; Enoch 18:11-16; 27:1-3; 90:26; Jth. 16:17; II Esd. 7:36; Asmp. Moses 10:10; 1QS III.4, 13; 1QH III.29; etc.). The concept was doubtless influenced by the infiltration of Iranian ideas, for the articulation of it is clearly patterned on the Avestan doctrine of the ultimate judgment of the wicked in a stream of molten metal (*aya khšusta;* cf. Yasna 31.3; 51.9; etc.). Nowhere in the Apoc., however (except in the very late passage II Esd. 2:39), is this place actually called Gehenna. The application to it of the ancient biblical toponym —inspired, no doubt, by Jeremiah's dire prophecy against the notorious valley (19:2-10)—first appears in the NT (Matt. 5:22, 29-30; 10:28; 18:9; 23:15, 33; Mark 9:43, 45, 47; Luke 12:5; Jas 3:6), though a foregleam of it may be recognized in Enoch 27:2-3, where reference is made to "the accursed *valley*" of the eternally damned.

Gehenna is clearly conceived by the NT writers as identical with the "lake of fire" into which Hades (i.e., Sheol, the general abode of the dead) will itself ultimately be cast (Rev. 20:14). The conception seems, however, to have been somewhat fluid, for sundry rabbinic statements dating from the first and second centuries A.D. declare that Jews, by and large, will be delivered from it, and that none of them will remain there permanently except certain historic reprobates, the adulterer, and he who shames or vilifies his fellow man (R.H. 16*b*-17*a;* B.M. 58*b*). Moreover, while Rabbi Akiba affirms expressly that the torment of Gehenna lasts only for twelve months (M. 'Edūyôth 2.10), Philo states just as explicitly that wicked Jews will indeed be condemned to Tartarus (*On Execrations* 6) and that their punishment will be eternal (*On Cherubim* 1); and in the pseudepigraphic Ascension of Isaiah (3:13–4:32) the fiery depths are the final abode of the vanquished Beliar (i.e., Belial). Lastly, the association with the Valley of Hinnom is by no means constant, the flaming hell being alternatively located (Ascension of Isaiah 4:14; II Enoch 40:12; 41:2) in the third heaven!

The typological use of the name Gehenna reflects a tendency, which developed during the Hellenistic period, to gear visions of the last days to the names of persons and places mentioned in the OT. Analogous are the use of Armageddon, in Rev. 16:16, to denote the site of the final battle against evil (cf. Zech. 12:11); of "the wilderness of Damascus," in the Dead Sea Scrolls, to designate the place whither the faithful would go into exile before the coming of the Messiah (cf. Amos 5:27); and of the terms "the new Jerusalem" and "Tophet" in eschatological contexts. Comparable, too, is the antithetical use of "Garden of Eden" (גן עדן) to signify the celestial paradise (cf. especially II Esd. 7:36: "The furnace [i.e., *tôpheth?*] of Gehenna shall be disclosed, and opposite it the paradise of delight [i.e., גן עדן]"). This tendency, which helped at the same time to Judaize ideas adopted from foreign sources, has not yet received the attention which it deserves, but it is cardinal for an understanding of Jewish and Christian apocalyptic literature and, in general, of how the Scriptures were popularly interpreted during the crucial intertestamental period.

Gehinnom (the Hebrew form) is likewise employed in an extended, metaphorical sense in several passages of the Mishnah (Ḳid. 4.14; 'Edūyôth 2.10; Ab. 1.5; 5.19-20); and this usage passed subsequently into common Hebrew parlance, and is also to be found in the Koran (e.g., Sura 19.69). It may be added that the opprobrious expression "child of Gehenna [RSV 'hell']," applied in Matt. 23:15 to the scribes and Pharisees, is likewise applied in the Talmud (R.H. 17*a;* Keth. 65*a*) to the dissolute inhabitants of Mahoza, on the Tigris.

See also DEAD, ABODE OF THE.

Bibliography. On the general fluidity of the concept of a fiery hell, see I. Lévi, "Les morts et l'avènement de l'ère messianique," *REJ,* LXIX (1919), 125-26.

T. H. GASTER

GELBOE gĕl bō'ə. Douay Version form of GILBOA.

GELILOTH gĭ lī'lŏth [גלילות] (Josh. 18:17). *See* GILGAL 5.

GEM. *See* JEWELS AND PRECIOUS STONES.

GEMALLI gĭ măl'ī [גמלי, camel owner(?)] (Num. 13:12). The father of Ammiel, who was sent from the tribe of Dan to spy out the land of Canaan. The name Gemalli may originally have derived from גמל, "to finish" or "to do someone good."

Bibliography. M. Noth, *Die israelitischen Personennamen* (1928), p. 182.

R. F. JOHNSON

GEMARA gə mä'rə [גמרא]. The specific term for the discussions carried on in the rabbinic academies in ancient Palestine and Babylon on the Mishna, and which together with the Mishna constitute the TALMUD. The term is derived either (*a*) from an Aramaic root meaning "to repeat" and referring to that intellectual activity characteristic of the rabbinic schools of old which expressed itself in learning for learning's sake; or (*b*) from a Hebrew root meaning "to complete," for insofar as the discussion embodied in the Gemara take the form of a running commentary on the Mishna, they serve to supplement the Mishna and complete it. The Gemara also contains a vast amount of material which has little direct connection with the Mishna: legal reports, ethical maxims, homilies, historical information, and legendary lore. There are two Gemaras: the Palestinian, which originated mainly in Tiberias, in the third and fourth centuries; and the Babylonian, which grew out of Babylonian academies of Sura, Pumbeditha, and Nehardea during the period extending from the beginning of the third to the end of the fifth century.

I. EPSTEIN

GEMARIAH gĕm'ə rī'ə [גמריהו, Yahu has accomplished]. **1.** An emissary from Zedekiah to Nebuchadnezzar who carried Jeremiah's letter to the exiles in Babylon (Jer. 29:3). His father, Hilkiah, was probably neither Josiah's chief priest (II Kings 22:4) nor Jeremiah's father (Jer. 1:1).

2. Son of Shaphan the secretary, in whose temple chamber Baruch read Jeremiah's scroll (Jer. 36:10-12, 25). His son Micaiah heard, and reported to the palace. When, upon having the scroll read to him, Jehoiakim wished to destroy it, Gemariah was one of the princes who opposed.

3. Lachish Ostracon I (*see* LACHISH) mentions a "Gemariah son of Hissilyahu" (*ca.* 589 B.C.).

J. M. WARD

GENEALOGY. A biblical genealogy is an orderly list of names purporting to record either the pedigrees of individuals or the assumed relationships of such groups as families, clans, tribes, or nations. Lineage is traced through the male, with females mentioned only in comparatively rare instances—chiefly where they are of historical significance (Gen. 11:29; 22: 23; Num. 26:33; 27:1-11). Arrangement of genealogies may be either by ascending scale (individual to ancestor; e.g., Ezra 7:1-5) or by descending scale (ancestor to individual; e.g., Ruth 4:18-23).

1. Hebrew terms. The noun "generations" (תולדות), often used to introduce the late lists, signifies descent by birth and family relationship. Sometimes it is generalized to indicate simply "origin," as in the reference to the "generations of the heavens and the earth" (Gen. 2:4). Later Hebrew and Aramaic derive a verb "to register by families" (cf. I Chr. 4:33; 5:1, 7; etc.) from a noun "family register" (יחש; Neh. 7:5). The basic implication of the latter is legitimacy or nobility of birth.

2. Motives for compilation. Among the motives responsible for the compilation of the genealogies are: (*a*) individual identification for such legal purposes as inheritance, etc.; (*b*) establishment of rights to such social positions as nobility, kinship, and priesthood and to the rights and privileges thereto pertaining (cf. Ezra 2:59-63); (*c*) proof of racial purity; (*d*) prideful demonstration of relationship to an eminent worthy of the past; (*e*) strengthening of position or authority by tracing its origin back to an important ancestral appointment to that post.

Scarcely any personal genealogical data are found in the historical books Judges, Samuel, and Kings, nor any trace of officials responsible for assembling or preserving such records. In agreement with general Near Eastern usage, including that of the Arab Bedouins, whose kinsmen are reckoned only to the third generation with but a vague knowledge or complete ignorance of earlier kinsmen, early Hebrew family records (cf. Exod. 35:30) reach only to the "third and the fourth generation" (Exod. 20:5). As late as the Persian period, only once in the Jewish Aramaic papyri does identification of a witness reach the fourth generation.

3. Nonpersonal genealogies. Hebrew history is traced back to Adam, the ancestor of all (Gen. 5:1 ff), and even the early pre-exilic narratives contain "genealogical" lists going back to Adam. But the "genealogies" found in the earliest documents of the Pentateuch (J and E) are not individual pedigrees. Rather, they are supposed origins and recognized relationships of nations, cities, and people known to the author, set into the *form* of personal genealogical tables. While the early Hebrews may have believed the names represented individual progenitors of the groups named, the device of genealogical table, used also by the Greeks, Romans, and others for recording early "history" in a compact form, is a valuable didactic and mnemonic aid.

The antediluvian lists (Gen. 4:17-26; 5:3-31) are probably dependent upon Babylonian traditions. The descendants of Noah, set into the pre-exilic narrative (Gen. 10:8-19, 21, 24-30) and expanded by the priestly writer in the postexilic period, contain, not personal names, but those of peoples or tribes (Sheba, Dedan); countries (Media [Madai], Egypt [Miṣraim]); and even cities (Sidon). Sometimes the name form is gentilic (Jebusite, Hivite, Amorite) and even plural (Ludim). Since neither Elam nor Lydia is Semitic in origin nor are Hittites descendants of Canaanites, it is clear that the basis of relationship is not that of blood but is cultural and historical. The postdiluvian link between Shem and Abraham (Gen. 11:12-24) has likewise been shown to be geographical, representing place names in NW Mesopotamia, in the region associated with Abraham and his kinsmen.

Near kinsmen of the Hebrews are introduced into the historical narrative as tiny genealogical bits reflecting independent traditions. Moab and Ammon (Gen. 19:37-38) are related to Abraham through his nephew Lot. Of the Aramean kinsmen of Abraham (Gen. 22:20-24), at least Uz, Buz, Hazo, and Chesed are found elsewhere as place names, homes of Arameans in the Syrian desert (Job 1:1; 32:2, 6; Jer. 25:20, 23). Tebah and Maacah, less directly related to the Hebrews, appear as place names in the Bible (II Sam. 10:6, 8; cf. I Chr. 19:6-7). The Arabs (Gen. 25:1-4), introduced as descendants of Abraham, include such familiar place names as Midian, Sheba, and Dedan.

Thus the early "genealogies" are largely geographical and ethnic lists rather than individual pedigrees. A still unresolved problem is the point at which the genealogies become personal and individual. Some scholars believe that the lists have group significance through the whole tribal period, that the names that appear as persons are actually but eponyms, that concubines in contrast to wives indicate subordinate or mixed groups, that marriages represent consolidation of groups, etc. Others are inclined to recognize personal genealogies from the time of Abraham onward.

4. Personal genealogies. Extended personal genealogies do not develop until late. Most of them are incorporated in the work of the postexilic priestly writers and in that of the Chronicler. Not until the acceptance of the Deuteronomic law stressing the purity of the congregation (Deut. 23:2-8) was need felt for complete family records. Possible references to such data are found in Jer. 22:30; Ezek. 13:9. When the Deuteronomic reforms gave prestige to the Levites, they had a motive for constructing genealogies that showed their relationship to the great priests and religious leaders of the past. When there was danger that Hebrew minorities in exile might lose their identity, stress on racial purity increased, and individual and family pedigrees were constructed. From Babylon came Nehemiah and Ezra, insisting on racial purity and the purging of their people (Ezra 2:59-63; 10:9-44; Neh. 13:23-28). Then written proof of purity of descent was essential, and the construction of pedigrees increased.

5. Reconstruction of genealogies. The assembling of genealogies extending back from the Persian period (sixth-fourth centuries B.C.) to the patriarchal age (*ca.* 1900 B.C.), from the vague traditions and fragmentary family records which may have survived was a difficult task. The situation was analogous to that of the time of Caliph 'Omar I (A.D. 634-44), when the prescription that spoil taken from "infidels" was to be distributed among pensioners on the basis of kinship with Mohammed and participation in his early struggles, stimulated the interest in genealogy that was already current in pre-Islamic times. Men sought to prove the essential relationships. The late Arab pedigrees then assembled greatly resemble those of the Bible, and the means of their construction seem to have been quite similar. Earlier scant and incomplete family records and traditions were supplemented by additional names, often sheer inventions, to fill the embarrassing gaps.

a. Determination of interval. Before the proper number of generations can be assembled, a genealogist must have some estimation of the interval to be covered by the list and of the average extent of a generation. It is impossible to determine exactly the duration of a generation, since the figure varied from period to period, from a hundred years (Gen. 15:13, 16; Exod. 12:40) to as little as ten years (Bar. 6 [Letter of Jeremiah]:3). A generation should be from thirty to forty years (cf. Job 42:16). The term is once used for an actual thirty-eight years (Deut. 1:35; 2:14), for which the figure 40 would be used in ready calculation, and this figure seems to be the base used in genealogical calculation (cf. Ps. 95:10).

Some Jewish writers were ingenious, if not accurate, in producing chronological schemes which, by their symmetrical patterns, can be recognized as artificial. The interval between the Exodus and the founding of Solomon's temple was determined as 480 years (I Kings 6:1), and that between the founding of Solomon's temple and the founding of Zerubbabel's temple was believed to be equal to it. The genealogies of Christ in the gospels exhibit similar schemes, for the intervals involved are all based on multiples of seven names. Matt. 1:1-17 estimates the interval between Abraham and Jesus as forty-two generations symmetrically divided into three groups of fourteen generations each, even though some names must be used more than once to achieve such a result. Luke 3:23-38 has four series of names in multiples of seven, usually twenty-one to the series. For the period of David to the Exile, Matthew has fourteen generations (two times seven), while Luke gives twenty-one (three times seven), and similar figures are found for the period of the Exile to Jesus. Thus for the interval of David to Jesus, Matthew has twenty-eight generations, while Luke has forty-two —too great a difference to be reconciled. Not all the chronological schemes in the genealogies are as apparent as those in the gospels.

b. Traditions. Within the interval to be covered, approximately the correct number of names must be placed. Such data are of diverse origins. Some traditions about tribal affiliations persisted long after that tribalism was abandoned (cf. Luke 2:36; Rom. 11:1); and some brief, early lists (cf. Num. 26:58; Ezra 2:40; 3:9; Neh. 9:4) and possibly even some longer ones (cf. I Chr. 8:33-38) certainly were available. The Chronicler himself had some authentic extrabiblical information about earlier times. But, although the Chronicler insists that "all Israel was enrolled by genealogies; and these are written in the Book of the Kings of Israel" (I Chr. 9:1), it is doubtful that much genealogical data had survived in written form. Many old bits had never been recorded and were forgotten. Patriarchal tribal structure was lost in the monarchy, and war and exile doubtless took their toll on such family records as once existed. More complete and trustworthy are the postexilic records contemporary with the genealogists. Great gaps in pedigrees confronted the students of genealogy. Although they made sincere efforts to place the data, some of their sources were faulty, conflicting, and even spurious. Limited human judgment and copyist errors contributed to error in the result.

c. Supplementary names. Additional names, needed to fill the gaps in the genealogies, could be drawn from other lists of names, whether or not they were genealogies. Thus sixteen of the twenty-four priests and Levites assigned temple tasks by David (I Chr. 24) bear names characteristic in the postexilic period. Familiar Benjaminite names (Kish, Shimei, etc.) are introduced into the pedigree of Mordecai (Esth. 2:5), and even Machir and Mephibosheth are added in the Second Targum of Esther. At other times names in the same list are repeated, as in I Chr. 6:34-35*a* (cf. vs. 25); I Chr. 6:36-37 (cf. vs. 23). Clan and geographical names are often personified as "fathers" and "sons" (cf. I Chr. 2:18-24; 42-54). Some proper names are but corruptions of Hebrew words. Shuppim (I Chr. 26:16) is a distortion of "storehouses" (אספים; cf. I Chr. 26:15), and ישבי לחם (I Chr. 4:22 mg.) is a corrupt transcription of "they returned (to Beth)lehem." The very unusual "names" of the sons of Heman (I Chr. 25:4) are the Hebrew words of a fragment of a psalm: "Be gracious unto me, O Lord! Be gracious unto me! Thou art my God."

Differences in origin are responsible for many conflicts and discrepancies. Er appears as both brother (Gen. 46:12; Num. 26:19-20) and son (I Chr. 4:21) of Shelah. Sheshan had no son (I Chr. 2:34), but Ahlai is credited to him (I Chr. 2:31). Zerubbabel's father is Pedaiah (I Chr. 3:19) or the latter's brother, Shealtiel (Ezra 5:2; Hag. 2:2; Matt. 1:12; Luke 3:27).

6. Postexilic genealogies. Theoretically it should have been possible in the postexilic period for any Hebrew to prove his origin by tracing his line to his remote tribal connections. Actually, this was impossible, because only a few lines are fully developed, and collateral lines are dropped. By a process of gradual narrowing of interest, attention is drawn to the lines of important ancestors. The Chronicler, who gives the most complete lists, omits any genealogy for Dan, and he shows special interest in the tribes of Levi, Judah, and Benjamin, which contributed the bulk of the postexilic community. These tribes contain the pedigrees of the religious leaders, as well as those of the royal houses of Saul and David, to which many Jews proudly traced their ancestry.

7. Difficulties in use of genealogies. Frustrating difficulties confront the student of biblical genealogies: (*a*) Family terms ("father," "son," etc.) may be used in a wider sense than that of blood relationship. "Son" can mean "apprentice" or "guild member," with no reference to family connection. Treaties make men "brothers" even without a common ancestor (e.g., Israel and Tyre [Amos 1:9]). Even when kinship is involved, "son" is sometimes best rendered as "descendant." Similar diversity is found with "father," "daughter," etc. (*b*) Lack of surname intensifies the importance of the father's name. Fashions in Hebrew names existed, but some common names cause confusion when paternity is not given. It is then virtually impossible to determine whether duplicate names refer to the same person. (*c*) Repetition of names in the same list may be natural, since in some later periods a name may be a family tradition, often shared by grandfather and grandson (cf. Ecclus. Prologue, vs. 1) or father and son (Luke 1:59). Repetition of names, however, is also a means for padding a list to extend it (I Chr. 6). (*d*) The same person may be known by several names (e.g., Elihu/Eliab/Eliel [I Sam. 1:1; I Chr. 6:27, 34]; Tohu/Nahath/Toah [I Sam. 1:1; I Chr. 6:26, 34]). As king, Mattaniah became Zedekiah (II Kings 24:17). For religious reasons Merib-baal (I Chr. 8:34) was altered to Mephibosheth (II Sam. 4:4). (*e*) Personal names and geographical or group names are mingled in some genealogies. This may sometimes occur because of supplementing lists with names drawn from other lists not recognized as geographical. At other times a group may be designated by its location or personalized under the name of its chieftain or leader. (*f*) Omissions can be demonstrated in some genealogies. Some may be due to faulty copying, but others are deliberate. A father's name may be dropped and the individual related to a more remote ancestor (e.g., Zechariah [Zech. 1:1; cf. Ezra 5:1]; Achan [Josh. 7:1, 24]), or an important group may be dropped to make the names conform to a symmetrical pattern (e.g., three generations of kings of Judah are omitted in Matt. 1:7-11). Irregular numbers of generations frequently occur. Apparently the important element was the indication of general connections rather than intermediate steps. (*g*) Because of the possibility of the omission of necessary links and uncertainty about the length of the generation, genealogies offer comparatively little certain chronological assistance. The interest of the genealogist is historical and biographical rather than chronological. (*h*) There are other means than birth for relationship to a group. Non-Israelite Calebites and Jerahmeelites are incorporated in the tribe of Judah (cf. I Chr. 2:9, 25 ff, 36-42) because of service to the tribe (Num. 13:30; Josh. 14:6-14) or loyalty to David (I Sam. 27:10; 30:29). Genealogical connections must then be invented. (*i*) It cannot always be determined whether "personal" names refer to individuals or to groups. While the historical or sociological interpretation of genealogies lacks confirmation, it seems plausible in many instances, and it has analogies in Arab usage. (*j*) Lists of names suffer greatly in transmission, since it is a matter of copying with no means of checking connections. We should not be surprised to find many divergences in spelling, variation in order, or omissions.

Valuable and authentic bits of genealogical data are doubtless incorporated in the biblical genealogies, but they can be recovered only with great difficulty and with little certainty. The Talmud indicates that the study of the genealogies in Chronicles-Ezra-Nehemiah was thought to be particularly difficult. The enormous number of different interpretations led Mar Zutra to proclaim that there were four hundred camel loads of exegetical interpretations of the material between the name Azel in I Chr. 8:38 and the Azel in I Chr. 9:44 (*Pes.* 62*b*). One must be cautious about being dogmatic regarding solutions to genealogical problems.

Bibliography. W. R. Smith, *Kinship and Marriage in Early Arabia* (1885), pp. 6 ff, 10-12. G. B. Gray, *Studies in Hebrew Proper Names* (1896), pp. 2 ff. E. Kraeling, *Aram and Israel* (1918), pp. 18, 41, 44-45. W. F. Albright, *JBL,* XLIII (1924), 385-93. J. Pedersen, *Israel, Its Life and Culture* (1926), I, 257. W. O. Oesterley and T. H. Robinson, *A History of Israel* (1932), I, 51-52, 58 ff. S. Mowinckel, *The Two Sources of the Predeuteronomic Primeval History (JE) in Genesis 1-11* (1937). W. F. Albright, *JBL,* LVII (1938), 230-31; LVIII (1939), 95-97. L. Waterman, "Some Repercussions from Late Levitical Genealogical Accretions in P and the Chronicler," *AJSL,* LVIII (1941), 50. W. F. Albright, *Recent Discoveries in Bible Lands* (1955), pp. 76-77. B. Maisler, "The Campaign of Pharaoh Shishak to Palestine," *Vetus Testamentum,* Supplement IV (1957), p. 66.

R. A. BOWMAN

GENEALOGY (CHRIST). The genealogy of Christ is found in Matt. 1:1-16; Luke 3:23-38. As the two lists are somewhat different, they will first be considered separately.

1. Matthew. In Matthew, Jesus' genealogy is traced back through the kings of Judah, through David to Abraham. It is made clear in advance, in vs. 1, that the high points in the genealogy are David and Abraham. It was a common, though not universal, belief of the Jews that the Messiah would be a descendant of David (cf. Pss. Sol. 17:23); and the promises were made "to Abraham and to his offspring" (Gal. 3:16; cf. Gen. 12:7; 22:18).

Matthew begins his genealogy with Abraham, and his list of names may be divided into three groups, the first two containing fourteen names each and the third having thirteen, making forty-one names in all. The divisions are: (*a*) Abraham to David; (*b*) Solomon to Jechoniah and the Exile; (*c*) Shealtiel to Jesus. The number fourteen represents seven times two. It may also be a symbol for David (דוד), as the Hebrew *daleth* (ד) has the value of four and the *vau* (ו) of six.

The names from Perez to David (Matt. 1:3-6*a*) are taken almost verbatim from the LXX of Ruth 4:18-22, and agree with I Chr. 2:5-15. The list from Solomon to Jechoniah agrees with I Chr. 3:10-15 except that Matthew has omitted Ahaziah, Joash, and Amaziah between Joram and Uzziah (Azariah); and he has Jechoniah (Jehoiachin) for Jehoiakim. In the third division Zerubbabel is called the son of Shealtiel, as in Luke 3:27; Ezra; Nehemiah; Haggai; but in I Chr. 3:19 he is a son of Pedaiah and nephew of Shealtiel. Several of the names among these last thirteen occur only here in the Bible, and a period of almost five hundred years is covered by ten names from Zerubbabel to Joseph. It is clear that these are not enough names for the years they represent, and that some names have dropped out or been eliminated. The name of Jesus' grandfather is given as Jacob.

2. Luke. Luke traces his genealogy, not down to Jesus from Abraham, but backward from Jesus, all the way to Adam—and past Adam to God. Luke lists seventy-seven names (seventy-eight including God), in contrast to Matthew's forty-one. Seventeen names occur in both genealogies. Luke's list (reading from the end of the list back to the beginning) from Adam to Abraham is the same as that in Gen. 5; 11:10-27; I Chr. 1:1-4, 24-26, with the exception of the addition of Cainan as the son of Arphaxad (as in the LXX of Gen. 10:24; 11:12, and A of I Chr. 1:18). The list from Abraham to David is the same as Matthew's except for the addition in Luke of Arni and Admin; and the textual variations in connection with these names are numerous. The only other names appearing in both genealogies are Shealtiel, Zerubbabel, and Joseph. It is possible, however, that Matthat (Luke 3:24) is the same as Matthan (Matt. 1:15) and that Joda (Luke 3:26) represents a shortened form of Abiud (Matt. 1:13). Rhesa, whom Luke names as son of Zerubbabel, may not have been a person at all, but may have been a title, meaning "prince," which belonged to Zerubbabel. Thus "Zerubbabel Rhesa" meaning "Zerubbabel the Prince" became "Zerubbabel [begat] Rhesa." Finally, Luke's Joanan (Ἰωανάν)—listed as son of Rhesa—may be the Hananiah (Ἀνανιά) of I Chr. 3:19, who is listed there as a son of Zerubbabel. If Rhesa was originally a title, then originally in the genealogy used by Luke, Joanan appeared as Zerubbabel's son.

The dissimilarity in the genealogies of Matthew and Luke from David on is due to the fact that Matthew traces Jesus' lineage through Solomon, while Luke traces it through Nathan, another of David's sons also born of Bathsheba (II Sam. 5:14; I Chr. 3:5; 14:4). The men referred to in Luke's list between Nathan and Shealtiel and between Zerubbabel and Joseph (thirty-seven in all) are all unknown. It may be that Luke's genealogy was influenced by Jeremiah's curse on Jehoiakim and his son Jehoiachin (Jechoniah). Cf. Jer. 22:18-19, 28, 30; 36:30-31. In Matthew's genealogy Shealtiel is listed as the son of Jechoniah (as in I Chr. 3:17); but Luke lists Shealtiel as the son of Neri.

Luke's list, as has been noted, includes seventy-seven names (seven times eleven) from Jesus to Adam. As in Matthew, these names may be subdivided; but here they fall into four groups: (*a*) from Jesus to Zerubbabel, twenty-one names (seven times three); (*b*) from Shealtiel to Nathan, twenty-one names; (*c*) from David to Isaac, fourteen names (seven times two); and (*d*) from Abraham to Adam, twenty-one names. Zerubbabel, David, and Abraham are the crucial names in the genealogy.

3. Explanations of discrepancies. The differences between the genealogies in Matthew and Luke have caused difficulties from early days. From a letter written by Julius Africanus (*ca.* A.D. 220) to a certain Aristides, we learn that some considered the genealogies to be symbolic in character—that Matthew's represented Christ's royal character (the genealogy being traced through the kings of Judah) and that Luke's represented Christ's priestly role. Africanus himself (Euseb. Hist. I.7; VI.31) believed that the law of Levirate marriage explained the major discrepancy in the genealogies from David to Joseph. According to this law a widow, if she had no son, was to marry her deceased husband's brother; and if she had a son by him, he was to take the name of his mother's deceased, first husband, "that his name may not be blotted out of Israel" (Deut. 25:5 ff). Thus, it was said, Joseph was really the son of Heli (as in Luke), but he took the name of Heli's deceased brother (Mary's first husband) Jacob (as in Matthew). Heli and Jacob were, therefore, brothers; but they were uterine brothers, born of the same mother but of different fathers. Heli traced his ancestry back through his father to David, through Nathan (Luke); and Jacob traced his ancestry back also to David, but through Solomon (Matthew). This is an ingenious explanation, but perhaps a bit too neat.

Annius of Viterbo (*ca.* 1490) suggested that Matthew gave Joseph's genealogy, and Luke Mary's; and Lagrange shows that this interpretation of Luke's genealogy goes back to the fifth century. In more recent times B. Weiss defended this view.

In conclusion it may be said that the genealogies were probably drawn up independently, quite early, by different Jewish Christians in the interest, primarily, of substantiating Jesus' messiahship. On the questions of the text of Matt. 1:16, and of the relation of these genealogies to the doctrine of the Virgin Birth, *see* VIRGIN BIRTH.

B. H. THROCKMORTON, JR.

GENERAL [שר צבא; χιλίαρχος στρατηγός (I Macc. 10:65; KJV DUKE)]. An army rank belonging to Sisera (Judg. 4:7) and Joab (I Chr. 27:34 KJV; RSV COMMANDER) and mentioned in the NT in a list of persons of very high rank (Rev. 6:15; KJV and elsewhere RSV CAPTAIN). *See* ARMY § 3*f*.

J. A. SANDERS

GENERATION. 1. Frequently in the OT, a circle (דור, "circle" or "assemblage"; Aramaic דר; cf. Ugaritic) of life—i.e., the period from a man's birth to that of his son—and collectively the people who live in that period (Pss. 14:5 [=53:6]; 24:6; 49:20; 73:15; 84:11; 112:2; Jer. 2:31). In the NT, γενεά generally corresponds to this meaning.

2. In the plural, a list of successive births of family history (תולדות; Gen. 2:4; 5:1; generally FAMILIES; DESCENDANTS; GENEALOGIES). The word γένεσις has this meaning and is translated "generation" in Matt. 1:1 KJV (RSV rightly GENEALOGY).

3. KJV translation of γέννημα in Matt. 3:7; 12:34; 23:33; Luke 3:7 (RSV BROOD).

4. KJV translation of γένος in I Pet. 2:9 (RSV RACE).

Bibliography. F. J. Neuberg, "An Unrecognized Meaning of Hebrew DÔR," *JNES*, 9 (1950), 215-17.

S. J. DE VRIES

GENESIS jĕn'ə sĭs [בראשית; γένεσις]. The first of the five books of Moses. The development of Genesis, which is followed by Exodus, Leviticus, Numbers, and Deuteronomy, coincides in large measure with that of the larger unit to which it belongs—namely,

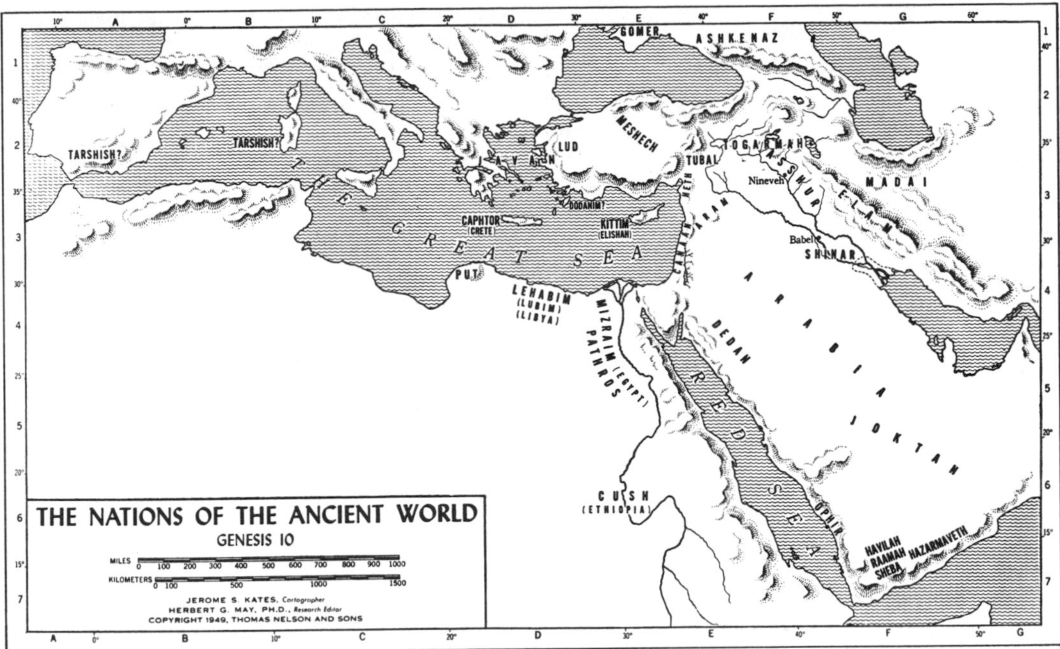

the Pentateuch. Thus the treatment of Genesis must also consider the Pentateuch as a whole from time to time. On the other hand, Genesis exhibits, in contrast to the remaining books of the Pentateuch, a greatness of a special type, which justifies its separate treatment. Since the manifold difficult questions which are occasioned by the Pentateuch can, for the most part, be more easily answered in the case of Genesis than in the case of Exodus, Leviticus, Numbers, and Deuteronomy, it is advisable to discuss the Genesis problems by themselves and, in so doing, to consider the other books of the Pentateuch only insofar as is absolutely required. Moreover, one can disregard completely here the fifth book of Moses, Deuteronomy, which presents a code of law mounted in a relatively meager narrative framework, continues the narrative from Genesis to Numbers only at the end (in parts of chs. 31–34), and can, therefore, in no case be considered to be as important as the threads J, E, and P or L, JE, and P (*see* §§ B1*c-f* *below*), which are basic to the narrative. In discussing attempts to explain Genesis and the Pentateuch in general as a compilation, be it of three or of four parallel narrative threads, and in the use of the concepts "three-source theory" and "four-source theory" in this connection, it should be remembered that Deuteronomy is not taken into consideration and is not included in this treatment.

A. Name, division, and content
B. Composition
  1. Literary analysis
    a. Fragment, completion, and documentary hypotheses
    b. Three-source theory and its difficulties
    c. Four-source theory
    d. Narrative thread L
    e. Narrative thread P
    f. Narrative threads J and E
  2. Time of origin
    a. *Terminus a quo*
    b. L
    c. J and E
    d. P
  3. Place of origin
    a. Difficulties
    b. L, J, and E
    c. P
  4. Compilation
    a. Reason for the rise of new narrative threads
    b. Decisive motives for blending
C. Prehistory of narrative threads
  1. Scope and type of the materials
  2. Literary genres
    a. Lists
    b. Songs and proverbs
    c. Cosmological-anthropological myths
    d. Legends connected with foreign lands
    e. Local legends of Canaan
    f. Cult legends
    g. Folk-historical notes within saga narratives
    h. Fairy tales and *novelle*
D. Historicity
  1. Transhistorical materials
  2. Secular history
  3. Religious history
E. Religious-ethical significance
Bibliography

A. *NAME, DIVISION, AND CONTENT.* The first of the five books of Moses is named by the Jews after its first word, בראשית, "in the beginning"; by the ancient church after the inscription in the LXX translation, which reads: Αὕτη ἡ βίβλος γενέσεως οὐρανοῦ καὶ γῆς, ὅτε ἐγένετο under 1:1–2:3: γένεσις κόσμου, "genesis of the world," or simply γένεσις,

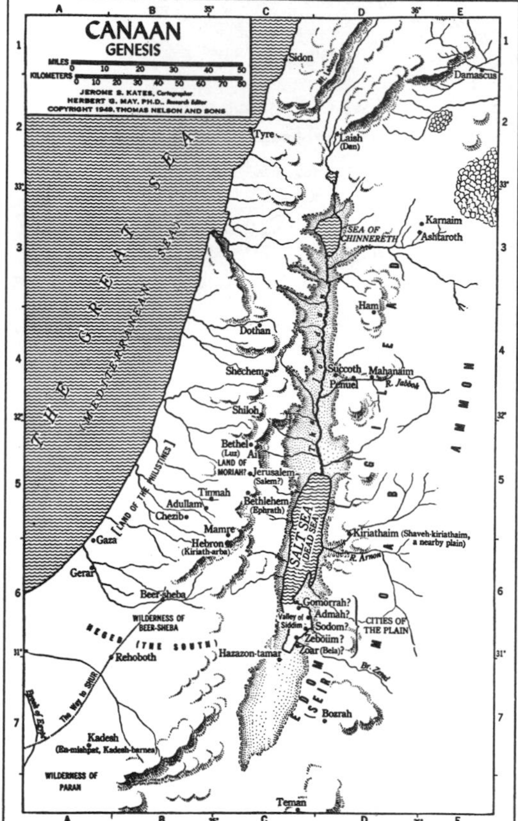

"genesis." Like other books of the OT, Genesis was also divided from early times into "sections" (*parashoth*). As the MSS from the first or second centuries B.C. which have been discovered in the desert of Judah show, the *parashoth* arrangement of the Hebraic books of the OT was already customary at that time. However, this division does not coincide with the chapter numbering to which we are accustomed. The division of the books of the OT into chapters occurs rather for the first time in its Latin translation, in the Vulg., and passed from it into the Hebraic MSS during the fourteenth century A.D.

The first unit of the fifty chapters of Genesis is the primitive history 1:1–11:9, which extends from the creation of the world to the cessation of the building of the tower and the dispersion of mankind, which had until that time formed a unit. The remaining units (11:10–50:26) contain the story of Abraham, Isaac, and Jacob, as well as of Jacob's sons, among whom Joseph plays an especially important role. Without being able to draw sharp boundaries, one may subdivide 11:10–50:26 thus: 11:10–25:11 (Abraham); 25:12–26:35 (Isaac); chs. 27–36 (Jacob and Esau, Jacob and Laban, the twelve sons of Jacob); chs. 37–50 (Joseph and his brothers).

In the form in which these fifty chapters are known to us they afford a continuous narrative of happenings extending over *ca.* 2,400 years, from the Creation, reckoned as the year 1, until 1656—according to 5:3, 6, 9, 12, 15, 18, 21, 28, 32; 7:6—the year of the Flood, and until the death of Jacob (47:28) and of Joseph (50:22). But the fifty chapters do not represent a complete whole meaningfully fashioned according to a unified plan. On the contrary, the marks of several hands and the signs of various times are to be observed everywhere. Thus the view, attested by the OT and the NT and sanctioned by Jewish and Christian tradition, that the Pentateuch and with it also Genesis were written by Moses, cannot in any case be true, and there can only be argument as to how the origin of the Pentateuch, in general, and of Genesis, in particular, can then actually be explained.

B. *COMPOSITION.* 1. Literary analysis. *a. Fragment, completion, and documentary hypotheses.* In attempting to determine the actual development of Genesis it is expedient to disregard, for the time being, the question of the age of the individual component parts which show up in the analysis and to confine oneself to a formal literary examination of the facts, to seek an explanation for the manifold literary obstacles and inequalities which the book presents: repetitions, contradictions, gaps, and seams, as they strike the eye of every even partially observant reader and have been observed again and again for more than a millennium and a half and have led to the most varied attempts at explanation. *See* BIBLICAL CRITICISM, HISTORY OF.

If these are combined in groups, disregarding variations in details, these three main groups may be formed: the fragment hypothesis, the completion hypothesis, and the documentary hypothesis. The fragment hypothesis reckons with a greater or lesser number of independent literary units—narratives,

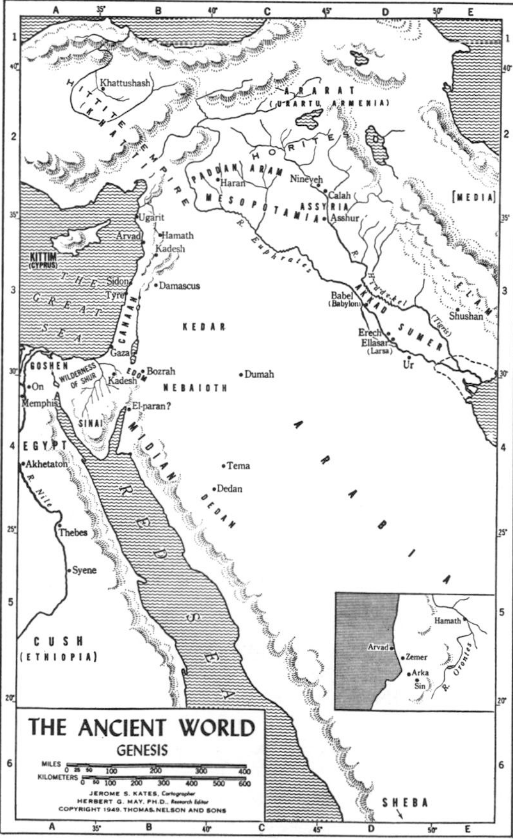

lists, maxims, poems, and the like—which were compiled later by an editor, perhaps by Ezra, but which until that time had had no connection of any kind. The completion hypothesis assumes that our Genesis is based on a continuous narrative thread and that this was completed by means of previously disconnected fragments of many varieties. According to the documentary hypothesis, on the other hand, the form of Genesis which we know is to be explained as the compilation of several parallel narrative threads. Of these three hypotheses the last, which originated with Jean Astruc (died 1766) and Johann Gottfried Eichhorn (died 1827) and has remained authoritative in the two centuries since that time, in spite of all the modifications and reverses which it has encountered, can, without doubt, most easily claim the most plausible explanation of the manifold literary problems of Genesis such as the change in the name of God—Elohim to Yahweh—the appearance of the same stories more than once, the lack of unity and the overcrowding of the narratives, and the like. However, this hypothesis is, to be sure, no panacea. On the contrary, Genesis exhibits many phenomena which are to be explained more easily according to the completion hypothesis or the fragment theory. Thus ch. 14, the campaign of the four kings from the East against five kings of Canaanite cities, is with good reason generally considered to be a secondary fragment attached to the otherwise complete Genesis; and the confusion of the lists in ch. 36, which are about Esau-Edom and are hard to unravel, may most plausibly be understood as an editorial compilation of several elements which until then had been isolated—i.e., of "fragments."

b. Three-source theory and its difficulties. The form of the documentary theory which, insofar as Genesis comes into consideration, can claim the widest circulation and acceptance is the three-source theory—i.e., the conception of Genesis as a compilation of three parallel narrative threads. One of these uses the name "Yahweh" for God and is therefore designated as Yahwist (J), while both the others say "Elohim" instead. Therefore one of them has been given the name "Elohist" (E) and the other, to differentiate it and out of consideration for its predilection for priesthood and ritual, the designation "Priestly Code" (P). Of these three narrative threads, J and P begin with the Creation (P, 1:1–2:4*a;* J, 2:4*b*–3:24). E, on the other hand, begins only in ch. 15 with Abraham and has thus no prehistory. Chs. 1–13 are, accordingly, subdivided by the three-source theory into J and P, in that 2:4*b*-3:24; 5:29; 6:1-4; 9:18-27; 11:1-9, 28-30; 12:1-4*a,* 6–13:5, 7-11*a*, 12*b,* 18, are assigned to J, and 1:1–2:4*a;* 5:1-28, 30-33; 9:28-29; 12:4*b*-5; 13:6, 11*b*-12*ab*, to P. 6:5–9:17, as well as 10; 11:10-32, however, are considered compilations from J and P, while the Cain and Abel story (4:2-16) and the boastful speech of Lamech (4:23-24) represent, perhaps, secondary additions to the J content and, therefore, are not to be regarded as belonging to any narrative thread originally.

This division of chs. 1–13 into three threads is not satisfying, because many a fragment must be ascribed to J which disturbs the course of its narrative and looks more like a secondary addition than a part which belonged originally. Such fragments are: (*a*) the genealogy of Cain (4:1, 19-24), which is impossible alongside the complete Seth genealogy of 5:1-28, 30-33 (certainly derived from P), and also alongside the remnants of a second Seth genealogy preserved in 4:25; 5:29 and ascribed to J and which, moreover, is not compatible with the J narrative of the Flood because it derives cattle raisers, musicians, and smiths who exist on earth in the presence of the narrator from Jabal, Jubal, and Tubal(-cain), and thus, obviously, does not recognize an interruption in the line descended from these three such as the Flood would have signified; (*b*) the incomplete story of the marriages of the sons of God with the daughters of men and the giants resulting from this union (6:1-4), which, since it presupposes the existence of the race of giants until the time of the narrator, likewise does not agree with the J narrative of the Flood; (*c*) the story of the blessing of his two elder sons, Shem and Japheth, and the cursing of his youngest son, Canaan, by Noah (9:20-27), which knows, not Shem, Japheth, and Ham as the sons of Noah, as does the J portion of the genealogy of ch. 10, but rather Shem, Japheth, and Canaan, and, moreover, obviously exhibits a substantially narrower geographical-political horizon than the genealogy (*see* § B2*b below*); (*d*) the story of the building of the tower (11:1-9), which produces an explanation for the diversity of peoples and languages quite different from J in ch. 10; (*e*) the story of the parting of Abraham and Lot (12:4*b*, 6-9; 13:2, 5-18), which does not belong to P and which manifestly conflicts with the story of the endangering of Sarai in Egypt (12:10–13:1), which is inserted in the middle of it.

Indeed, the phenomenon that the material allotted by the three-source theory to J is inconsistent in itself and contains fragments which are actually impossible alongside one another, is by no means restricted to chs. 1–13, but may also be observed further on in Genesis. Thus the story of the valid sale of his birthright by Esau to Jacob (25:29-34) can scarcely be brought into harmony with the story of the betrayal of Esau by Jacob (25:27-28; 27:1-45), which is admittedly compiled from J and E; and the assignment of the story of the endangering of Rebekah (26:7-11) to J would require the surely difficult assumption that the same author—namely, J—had presented the theme of the endangering of the ancestress twice, once about Sarai (12:10-13) and the second time about Rebekah (26:7-11). All kinds of inequalities are also exhibited by the stories assigned to J from chs. 29–33 about Jacob's wives and children, about his flight from Laban and his encounter with Esau. But it is admittedly particularly clear in the J material from chs. 34–50, in that here the main narrative is interrupted by fragments which, on the one hand, are differentiated from it by form and content and, on the other hand, appear to be connected among themselves. These are the stories of Simeon and Levi's violent measures against Shechem (ch. 34), of Reuben's relations with Bilhah (35:21-22*a*), of Judah's intercourse with his daughter-in-law, Tamar, and the twins resulting from this union (ch. 38), as well as the beginning of the so-called blessing of Jacob, obviously referring to 34; 35:21-22*a,* which at first (49:3-7) conveys, not blessings, but curses—that is to say, proclaims the punishment for that which

Reuben, as well as Simeon and Levi, has done, according to 34; 35:21-22*a*.

These fragments cannot in any case be derived from the same narrator as their surroundings—i.e., the Joseph story of chs. 37; 39–48; 50. Thus they have been declared to be "erratic blocks," which have got into their present context more or less by chance. Upon closer inspection, however, one soon recognizes that here it is by no means a question of blocks standing isolated; rather, these fragments form a continuity—i.e., they are to demonstrate how it happened that the oldest sons of Jacob—Reuben, Simeon, Levi, and Judah—lost their birthright and it had to fall to the next oldest, to Joseph: Reuben, Simeon, and Levi were expressly denied the birthright by their father; the fourth lost it through his own folly in that he, as is narrated in ch. 38, gave up the association with his brothers; and it can well be that originally a decree followed 49:3-7 which explicitly stated this. The negative declarations of Jacob concerning Reuben, Simeon, Levi, and Judah must have a positive one as counterpart, and this cannot have been anything but the awarding of the birthright to Joseph. 34; 35:21-22*a;* 38; 49:3-7; and the judgments on Judah and Joseph which originally followed 49:3-7 but were broken away or reshaped (*cf.* § C2*b below*) in the expansion of the last words of Jacob—originally restricted to Reuben, Simeon, Levi, Judah, and Joseph—to a series of decrees including all his sons, represent, thus, a parallel to the Joseph story contained in chs. 37; 39–48; 50 and attempt, like it, to explain Joseph's surpassing his brothers.

c. Four-source theory. The same fact which can be observed in 34; 35:21-22*a;* 38; 49:3-7—namely, that these fragments which interrupt the main J narrative form a continuity among themselves—is also true elsewhere in Genesis, especially clearly in the prehistory—i.e., in 1:1–11:9. Here the fragments which were spoken of above as interrupting the main narrative of J—one of the two stories of paradise which are combined in 2:4*b*–3:24; the Cain genealogy (4:1, 19-24); the marriages of the sons of God (6:1-4); Noah as the father of Shem, Japheth, and Canaan (9:20-27); and the building of the tower (11:1-9)—are bound together into a meaningful whole for which a consciously shaping author must be postulated. Under these circumstances one must give up the conception of the stories which do not fit properly into the main J narrative as isolated fragments which had, for no longer obvious reasons, been included in it, in favor of the assumption that they constitute, on the contrary, components of an independent narrative thread which runs parallel to the J material and which remains after these fragments have been withdrawn; that is to say, one must replace the three-source theory by a four-source theory. The newly established narrative thread must then, however, also be designated by a special symbol. The symbols J^1 and J^2, which were probably suggested for what are now taken to be two J threads, are not suitable, because it is customary to designate the secondary amplifications of the source in question by an exponent added to the source symbol—to use P^1, P^2, P^3, etc., e.g., for the succession of amplifications of the original material of P. Thus only those signs come into consideration for the two Yahwist threads which are similar in type to E and P—namely, which represent Roman capital letters. Under these circumstances J is appropriately reserved for the narrator to whom belongs the main block of the stories in Genesis which use the divine name Yahweh. The thread which encompasses the remaining Yahwist fragments, however, may be designated as the "lay source" (L) out of consideration for the fact that it—by its outspokenness for the world of the profane, the world of the "laity"—forms a sort of counterpole to P's preference for ritual and priesthood.

d. Narrative thread L. The main mass of the material in Genesis which is to be assigned to L has already been pointed out. Among the particularly characteristic elements chs. 18–19 (the story of Sodom); 25:21-26 (the story of the birth of Esau and Jacob); 32:24-33 (the story of the wrestling match between Jacob and El) should probably be added.

e. Narrative thread P. Although observations of many kinds suggest that the Genesis narratives which use Yahweh as the designation for God be divided into two parallel threads, the resulting four-source theory has not, at least at the present time, succeeded in establishing itself. If, therefore, no unanimity prevails among the experts in the analysis of the Yahwist content of Genesis, such unanimity is all the greater in the case of the designation of the material belonging to P, in that these pieces are very generally considered as P: the creation of heaven and earth, extending into the consecration of the sabbath (1:1–2:4*a*); the descendants of Seth up to Noah and his sons (5:1-28, 30-32); the story of the Flood (6:9–9:19), including the directions to Noah and closing with the establishment of the rainbow as a covenant; one of the two genealogies combined in ch. 10; the list of the descendants of Shem up to Terah and his sons, Abraham, Nahor, and Haran (11:20-26); Terah's move from Ur-Kasdim to Haran (11:27, 31-32); the departure of Abraham, Sarai his wife, and his nephew Lot for Canaan, the departure of Lot into the Plain of Jordan, and his rescue from the catastrophe which occurred there (12:4*b*-5; 13:6, 11*b*, 12*a;* 19:29); the birth of Ishmael (16:1*a*, 3, 15-16); the circumcision of Abraham, Ishmael, and the men of his house (ch. 17); the birth and circumcision of Isaac (21:2*b*-5); Sarah's burial in the cave of Mach-pelah acquired by Abraham (ch. 23); Abraham's burial in the cave of Mach-pelah (25:7-10); the descendants of Ishmael (25:12-17); Isaac's marriage to Rebekah (25:19-20); the birth of Esau and Jacob (25:26*b*); Esau's marriage to the Hittite women (26:34-35); Isaac's charge to Jacob to take a wife from Paddan-aram (27:46–28:9); Jacob's wives (29:24, 28*b*-29; 30:4*a*-9*b*); Jacob's departure from Paddan-aram and arrival in Canaan (31:18*b;* 33:18*a*); the revelation of God to Jacob in Bethel (35:6*a*, 9-13, 15); Jacob's sons (35:22*b*-26); the death of Isaac (35:27-29); Esau's departure to Mount Seir (36:1-2*a*, 6-8); Jacob's dwelling in Canaan (37:1); the removal of Joseph, as well as of his father and his brothers, to Egypt (37:2; 41:46*a;* 46:6-7; 47:5-11); the adoption of Ephraim and Manasseh by Jacob (47:27-28; 48:3-6); Jacob's blessing of his sons, Jacob's directions concerning his death and his burial (49:1*a*, 28*b*-33); the burial of Jacob in the Mach-pelah cave (50:12-13).

P becomes more detailed, then, only where the story turns to ritual and legal observances, as in the case of the Creation, the Flood, and the acquisition of the Mach-pelah cave. Otherwise P contents itself with the presentation of brief genealogical notes. Since, as we have seen, quite a number of chronological dates are to be found among them, P still retains, in spite of its brevity, the character of a connected narrative thread, which in addition derives its special stamp from the fact that the points at which the presentation forsakes the broader sphere treated previously and turns to a more restricted one, to conclude finally in the most restricted sphere, the history of the people of Israel, are all set off by the heading "These are the generations of . . .": 2:4*a* (inscription under 1:1–2:3); 5:1 ("This is the book of the generations of Adam"); 6:9; 10:1; 11:10, 27; 25:12, 19; 36:1 (9); 37:2.

f. Narrative threads J and E. What remains after the separation of the L material, specified in § B1*d above,* and the P content, which has just been presented, belongs to J and E—with the exception of the comparatively few secondary separate additions which are present in Genesis—and therefore need not be analyzed more closely. This would be difficult, too, or even impossible, because—apart from the remarkable discrepancy that J begins its statement with the creation of man and beast, while E does not begin until Abraham—the two threads are so similar that they may, indeed, be recognized without difficulty wherever the stories common to both have been placed side by side untouched by editing; but in the numerous cases where they have been compiled, they can be sorted out of the compilation only here and there with any certainty. One must then in these cases be satisfied with the designation of the material as JE content. Bound by such limitations, the singling out of J and E or JE from Genesis looks like this: the endangering of Sarai (12:10–13:1, in Egypt by the Pharaoh [J]; ch. 20, in Gerar by Abimelech, king of the Philistines [E]); the promise of land and descendants to Abraham (ch. 15 [JE]); the expulsion of Hagar (16:1-14, of the pregnant Hagar, who gives birth to Ishmael at Beer-lahai-roi [J]; 21:8-21, of Hagar and her son Ishmael born in Abraham's house [E]); the birth of Isaac (21:1-2, 6-7 [JE]); the covenant of Abraham with Abimelech in Beer-sheba (21:22-34 [JE]); the sacrifice of Isaac (22: 1-19 [JE]); the wooing of Rebekah (ch. 24 [JE]); the stealing of the birthright by Jacob (25:27-28; 27:1-45 [JE]); the revelation of God to Jacob in Bethel (28: 10-22 [JE]); Jacob's wives and children (chs. 29–30 [JE]); Jacob's flight from Laban, and the treaty between them (31:1–32:1 [JE]); the encounter of Jacob and Esau (32:2-24; 33:1-16 [JE]); the building of the altar in Bethel by Jacob (35:1-4, 6*b*-7 [E]); the death and burial of Deborah (35:8, 14 [E]); the birth of Benjamin, and the death and burial of Rachel (35:16-20 [E]); Joseph in Egypt (chs. 37; 39–41 [JE]); the first and second encounters of Joseph with his brothers in Egypt (chs. 42–43 [JE]); the hidden cup (ch. 44 [J]); Joseph's revelation of himself to his brothers (ch. 45 [JE]); the move of Jacob and his family to Egypt (46:1-5, 28-34; 47:1-6, 12 [JE]); Joseph's acquisition of the fields of Egypt for the Pharaoh (47:13-26 [J]); Jacob's stipulations about his burial, his blessing of Ephraim and Manasseh or of Joseph (47:27-31; 48:1-2, 8-22 [JE]); Jacob's death and burial, Joseph's magnanimous behavior toward his brothers, his stipulations concerning his burial, and his death (50:1-11, 14-26 [JE]).

2. Time of origin. ***a. Terminus a quo.*** Now it is a question of fixing the four parallel threads which have just been sifted from Genesis as it is available to us in terms of time. This is made extraordinarily difficult by the fact that unequivocal references to events which can be precisely determined chronologically do not exist in any of the threads and that one is almost exclusively dependent here on literary, cultural, intellectual, and religious historical criteria which are to a considerable extent ambiguous and, therefore, scarcely permit an entirely clear decision. Nevertheless, it is clear that all threads presuppose the conclusion of the seizure of the land of Canaan and its settlement from the time of the judges and the kings—namely, from *ca.* 1200 B.C. This territory had Edom and the Ishmaelite Bedouin tribes as S neighbors, Moab and Ammon and the Arameans as E neighbors, and the Philistines and Phoenicians as W neighbors. This means that they can scarcely have originated in their present form before the formation of the Israelite empire by David—in any case, not before the twelfth century B.C. Furthermore, the stories of Jacob and Esau, which appear in all four threads, obviously all look back on the subjugation of Edom by David; and if the blessing which Isaac can finally still give to his elder son, Esau, who has been robbed of his birthright, includes—along with the hardly comforting assertion that Esau will have to serve his brother—a suggestion of the possibility of shaking off this yoke (27:39-40 [E]); then, in all probability, this presupposes at least the first attempt of Edom to free itself from the rule of Israel (I Kings 11:14-22), and is therefore scarcely conceivable before the middle of the tenth century B.C. The date thus established may be considered the *terminus a quo* for all four Genesis narrative threads. None of them is older, and the only question is how much later they originated and how they are related to one another with respect to age.

b. L. In many respects the elements allotted to L make an especially archaic impression. First of all, it is clear that in the case of the L stories—such as those of the expulsion of the sons of Keturah by Abraham (25:1-6), or of the misdeeds of Reuben (35: 21-22*a*) and Simeon and Levi (ch. 34) and Jacob's curses punishing them (49:3-7), or of the peculiar fate of Judah (ch. 38)—it is a question of poetic, sagalike novelistic clothing of the events of tribal history, which permits these events to stand out quite clearly as such, which is itself quite thin, and which includes only as many motifs as are absolutely essential to make possible a story intended as a family-type proceeding. To recognize the enormous difference, one need only compare the Keturah story with the two Hagar stories of J (16:4-14) and E (21:8-21), and the stories concerning Reuben, Simeon and Levi, and also Judah (34; 35:21-23*a;* 38; 49:3-7), with the Joseph story (chs. 37; 39–48; 50). There the tribal background remains discernible, and the lines of the narrative serve only to make it understandable. Here the story, as such, is not only unusually expanded; but this expansion has almost completely concealed the tribal-history content and gives rise to the impression that one is concerned, not with tribes and peoples limited by time and space, but rather with human beings in general—as they appear in all times and in all places: with a mother who finds herself in the distress of pregnancy or is fearing her child's death of thirst; with a father who has been all too indulgent toward his youngest or next-to-youngest son; with a nestling son who has grown overconfident because of such favoritism and with brothers who hate him because of it and want to kill him.

It is obvious that these detailed narratives, which turn the specifically Israelitic into the universally human, are younger than those accounts of situations in tribal history which have been clothed in a scanty novelistic garb (*see* § B2*d below*). Furthermore, the story of Noah's blessing of his two elder sons, Shem and Japheth, and his cursing of his youngest son, Canaan (9:20-27), is in all probability older than the genealogical table (ch. 10: *cf.* § B1*b above*). For there, where Shem probably represents the Israelites, Japheth the Philistines, and Canaan the Canaanites subjected by the Israelites and the Philistines, the geographic-political horizon is narrower and more archaic than in the genealogical table, where under Shem, Japheth, and Ham all the people of the then known world are to be understood. Finally, many of the stories belonging to L, particularly its portion of the story of paradise and the Fall (2:4*b*–3:24), the story of the union of the sons of God with the daughters of men and the giants which resulted from this union (6:1-4), and the story of the building of the tower (11:1-9), bear witness to the nature of Yahweh as jealously guarding his divinity and determinedly warding off all attempts by human creatures to appropriate any of it, and thus manifest a very ancient conception of God, unknown to the other threads. According to all this, no serious obstacle stands in the way of establishing L in the reign of David or Solomon.

c. J and E. Of the remaining three narrative threads, J and E are so similar in their structure (*cf.* § B1*f above*) that it stands to reason that they belong to approximately the same period. However, there is no lack of phenomena which at least permit the conclusion that E must be younger than J. First of all, the conception of God represented by J is more anthropomorphic than that manifested in the case of E; and this difference is especially noticeable in a few of the stories which are retained entirely or almost entirely by J and E and which, although they resemble each other otherwise, go their own ways in this respect. In the Hagar story of J (16:4-14) Yahweh or Yahweh's messenger stands on earth and talks with Hagar; while the Hagar story of E has God or the messenger of God make his disclosures to her from heaven. The situation is similar in the two stories of Yahweh's or God's revelation to Jacob in Bethel, which are combined in 28:10-22 but can be clearly distinguished from each other. According to J, Yahweh stands before Jacob on the ground and talks to him; according to E, a ladder, on which the messengers of God climb up and down, serves as a connection between Jacob's resting place and heaven. If the conception of God is less anthropomorphic here than in J, then the E version of the endangering of Sarah (ch. 20) shows a refinement of ethical feeling as opposed to the J version of it (12:10–13:1), insofar as it attempts to soften the untrue statement of Abraham that Sarah is his sister by making Sarah his half sister. That the assumption that E was younger than J would make such differences between the two understandable is obvious. But the variation could also be caused by the fact that J and E stem from different contemporary groups; and, in any case, even though one were to believe in a lapse of time between J and E, it still remains uncertain how great one should imagine it to be.

For the absolute chronological dating of J and E, the criterion has often been considered decisive that the influence of the Prophets was to be felt in both, and indeed, in E even more strongly than in J, and that since such effects of propheticism would be unlikely before Amos and Hosea—i.e., before the middle of the eighth century B.C.—approximately that period must be regarded as the *terminus a quo* for both. Thus J has often been dated approximately 750 B.C.; and E, approximately 700 B.C. In so doing, a decisive argument for the dating of E approximately 700 B.C., an argument which lies beyond the framework of Genesis but which cannot be overlooked here, was the assumption that the story of the making and destruction of the golden calf in Exod. 32, which was assigned to E, looks back to the downfall —in the year 722 B.C.—of the N state of Israel, which had indulged in the worship of the golden calf, and was thus a *vaticinium ex eventu*. In reality, the gloomy threat with which Exod. 32 closes: "In the day when I visit, I will visit their sin upon them," can be and probably is a threat uttered before the catastrophe, as, indeed, the prophet Hosea, in any case, hurled his embittered threats against the cult of the golden calf decades before the decline of the N state and found a reason for them in the practice of this cult. Also unnecessary and improbable is the assumption that one cannot reckon with the effects of prophecy on the writing of Israelite history before *ca.* 750 B.C. and that wherever such exist in Genesis or in the Pentateuch in general, the sections in question could not have been dated before this period. The proclamation of the prophetic literature, which begins for us with Amos and Hosea, really represents nothing entirely new, but takes up ideas that are centuries older and develops them. Thus the dating of J at *ca.* the middle of the ninth century and of E at *ca.* 800 or 750 B.C. can be completely justified.

d. P. The fourth of the Pentateuchal narrative threads, the Priestly Code (P), which up until the middle of the nineteenth century was quite generally regarded as the oldest and was on this account also designated as the "basic text," is now practically unanimously considered the most recent source and believed to be derived from the exilic or the post-exilic period—i.e., from the sixth or the fifth century B.C. This dating is probably also correct. The decisive arguments for it are, to be sure, scarcely or only indirectly taken from the P material which belongs to Genesis, but are supported particularly by the P portion of the books from Exodus to Numbers—i.e., by the ritual regulations which are presented here by P.

The older histories—i.e., the books from Joshua to Kings—do not yet take these into consideration, while the more recent historical work, which originated in the fourth century B.C. and comprises Chronicles, as well as Ezra and Nehemiah, presents the history as though the law of P had been valid since Moses and thereby clearly presupposes the existence of P. This necessitates the assumption that P originated *ca.* 500 B.C. This conclusion, drawn from the nature of the P material in other books of the Pentateuch, is now substantiated by the P portion of Genesis insofar as this represents to a considerable extent an anticipation of the proclamation of the ritual laws which took place later on Sinai. This is true particularly of the account of the Creation (1:1–2:4*a*), which contains precise directions as to the food suitable for men and animals according to God's own will—that is to say, wants only vegetables included as such—and which ends with the institution of the sabbath; and also of the story of the Flood (6:5–9:17), which brings a change in the commandments about food given at the time of the Creation—namely, permits men and animals the enjoyment of meat and thereby grants to both the right to destroy life, limiting this, to be sure, so that the life of human beings is to remain inviolable under all circumstances and man is forbidden to eat flesh with the blood; and it is also true of the directions for circumcision, bound up with the promise of descendants and land property, as they were given to Abraham by God in ch. 17.

If observations of this type place the dating of P in the sixth or fifth century B.C. on a rather sound foundation, then the widely held opinion that his genealogical tables, which seem to be compendium-like summaries of detailed stories told by the older narratives are a sure sign of a late period, proves false. Genealogical tables clothed in scanty novelistic garb like those of the lists of the descendants of Nahor (22:20-24) or the enumeration of the sons born to Abraham by Keturah (25:1-5) are obviously very old, as we have already seen (§ B2*b above; cf.* § C2*f below*), in part even older than the J and E narratives which developed from them. If—and this is probably actually the case—P has further shortened the older Genesis narratives then known to bare genealogical tables, it has accomplished nothing new in so doing, but has carried on an old literary type. One might express it thus: In this respect P returns to L; but what was naïve in the case of L has now become "considered."

3. Place of origin. ***a. Difficulties.*** While the time of origin of the four narrative threads combined in Genesis can be decided with at least some certainty, it is impossible to get much beyond conjecture with regard to their place of origin. It is, to be sure, an established fact that we are indebted for the preservation of the parts of the OT which originated in the N state of Israel and dated from the period before its downfall in the year 722 B.C., to the S state of Judah, which existed for another century and a half, as well as to those who inherited the country and stayed on in it or to the Judeans exiled to Babylon. But the separation of this material which, in the last analysis, stems from the N state from the complete composite of the OT is very difficult; and, thus, also in the case of the narrative threads of the Pentateuch one can hardly give a completely definite answer to the question as to whether some of them are native to the N state. The possibility that this is the case surely exists, according to the aforesaid. Thus, of itself, there would be no objection to the widely supported assumption of the adherents to the three-source theory that, of the two older sources, J originated in the S state and E in the N state, and that J and E were then ambiguous and might be interpreted, not only as "Yahwist" and "Elohist," but also as "Judaic" and "Ephraimistic"—even more so, since the reason marshaled for it, the favoring of Judaic figures and interests in the case of J and of Israelitic-Ephraimistic in the case of E, already has some claim to consideration.

But these arguments are still not unequivocal and decisive. Disregarding entirely the fact that substitution of the four-source theory for the three-source theory—hence the division of the Yahwistic material into two parallel threads, L and J—severely distorts the basic analysis of the derivation of J from Judah and of E from Israel, it is very questionable whether the actual or apparent preponderance of Judaic elements in J and of Israelitic elements in E really permits a conclusion as to the home of the two threads or whether we have not rather to reckon with a national-religious and literary tradition common to both states in spite of their political separation, a tradition concerning the prehistory of Israel long before the separation of the kingdoms, which is, to be sure, taken into consideration only by Genesis. Thus, if, indeed, the accounts of the death and burial of Deborah and Rachel (35:8, 14, 16-20), which are conveyed by E but not by J, are connected with places in the N state, they can, nevertheless, have originated with some Judaic storyteller who was above the state boundaries in this respect.

Similarly, the fact that in the Joseph story of J it is Judah who attempts to rescue Joseph (37:26) and later charges his father (43:3) with the necessity for sending Benjamin along with the brothers who were going to Egypt for the second time, while according to E it is Reuben who goes into action both times, does not necessitate the assumption that the "singling out" of Judah could be expected only from a Judaic writer, while the mention of Reuben must be ascribed to an Israelite author, who probably consciously substituted Reuben for Judah, or who, if no controversy against J or a narrative similar to its Joseph story is to be assumed, of his own accord, by overlooking Judah, made the oldest of the sons of Jacob—Reuben—the spokesman for his brothers. On the contrary, E, without any consideration of possible relationship to the N or the S state, may simply have entrusted this role to Reuben as the oldest of the sons of Jacob; likewise, conversely too, the mention of Judah in J need not be political, but may be explained by the recollection, attested to 34; 35:21-22*a;* 49:3-7, that Reuben, Simeon, and Levi moved into the background fairly early and thereby made room for the next oldest brother, Judah.

b. L, J, and E. Thus there is a possibility, probably, that one of the three older threads of the Pentateuch—namely, E—had as its home the N state, but in view of the fact that the border between N and S obviously did not exist for the intellectual traditions of Israel and that they were cherished with the same zeal and the same love on both sides of the border, it also does not matter much where L, J, and E originated, whether in the S or the N state.

c. P. If, in the light of the above, the answer to the question as to the home of L, J, and E must remain undecided, and if it can be said with only some degree of probability that L and J stem from Judah and E originates in N Israel, then only two spots come into consideration as the home of P: either the exile community residing in Babylon and remaining here also after the repatriation of large numbers, or the land of Judah, which was by no means entirely depopulated during the Exile. There is probably more to support the first possibility than the second; first of all, P, at least in many respects, is similar to Ezekiel's vision (chs. 40–48) of the new temple, and like it seeks to provide a working plan for the re-establishment of the Jewish national and religious community hoped for in the future.

4. Compilation. ***a. Reason for the rise of new narrative threads.*** The four narrative threads L, J, E, and P exist for us in Genesis, as in the Pentateuch in general, as a compilation, similar to the way in which Tatian's Diatessaron has been built up out of the four gospels. But in contrast to this work, where it is well established that the compilation of the individual gospels to form the gospel harmony took place in one redactional act, it is impossible to make definite statements as to the manner in which the four narrative threads of the Pentateuch were combined, and it can only be conjectured. In all probability, however, there can be no serious consideration of redaction in one act—i.e., of the possibility that the narrative threads, which had existed independently up until that time—the time of the origin of the most recent thread of P—were combined by *one* redactor, such as Ezra, of whom many have thought. On the contrary, one must think of a series of redactions, must picture the course of events as if, first of all, the second-oldest thread had been combined with the oldest; and then the third oldest; and, finally, the most recent had been combined with the compilation of the three older threads. It must remain uncertain, however, whether the course of events was really so uniform and whether, perhaps, J and E, which we have seen are very closely related, were not already combined before they were combined with L.

b. Decisive motives for blending. The motives which, on the one hand, led to the creation of new narrative threads and, on the other, to the blending of the new creations with the older works are more clearly recognizable. The changes in outward circumstances and in intellectual conceptions brought about by the course of events caused the older presentation of the prehistory of Israel to seem out of date sometime after its composition and made a new draft necessary. Insofar as the new thread was mindful of the old one, which it was to replace, it was, on the one hand, dependent upon it; on the other, in opposition to it. But the observation of this at the same time positive and negative relationship of the new to the old thread is not sufficient for the understanding of its nature. On the contrary, the new draft exhibits, in spite of all dependence on its predecessor, an independent quality, in that it, as is also true of the most recent thread P, produces new materials, which have not been considered by the older threads, and in addition presents a literary creation of an individual quality. The fact, in itself very remarkable, that in each instance the new creation failed to achieve its goal of taking the place of the respective older work and equalling it—that, on the contrary, the more recent were always blended with the older and insofar contributed to their preservation—is explained by the continuity of the course of history to which all these creations belong and to which they are dedicated. In each instance the older presentation was just too solidly rooted in the consciousness of the Israelitic-Jewish national and religious community to be supplanted completely. To be sure, the new creation is always considered authoritative, as is naturally understandable; and thus the old which had been retained and combined with the new moved automatically into the light of the new, so that, finally, the whole thing was understood from the point of view of P. Basically this is the same process which repeated itself half a millennium later in the coalescence of the NT with the OT. The possibility, in itself natural and even to be expected, that pre-Christendom would reject the sacred book of Judaism, which, after all, was hostile to it, did not come to pass. Rather, the NT was combined with the OT, and, indeed, in such a manner that the old book was understood in the light of the new.

C. ***PREHISTORY OF NARRATIVE THREADS.*** **1. Scope and type of the materials.** It is obvious that the Pentateuchal narrative threads all have a history and presuppose materials of various types, already fixed in writing or merely transmitted orally. Beyond that, the possibility of even taking into consideration the existence of a thread still earlier than the oldest of the threads preserved for us deserves at least to be weighed. Proceeding from the three-source theory, and thus operating in Genesis with only J, E, and P, one was tempted to assume a common "groundwork," G, for J and E in view of their great similarity (*see* § B1*c above*). If the four-source theory is correct, then the assumption of a groundwork existing before J and E and used by them in common, which would have to be considered the oldest Pentateuchal thread, falls to pieces or could only be retained in a form in which between L, on the one hand, and J and E, on the other, one shoved in still another thread not preserved for us, which served J and E as a model. But this is not necessary or even merely plausible. On the contrary, L probably represents, in reality, the first attempt to write a history of Israel connected with the creation of the world and the history of the first human beings and extending up to the occupation of Canaan or perhaps even further. However, if L represents to this extent a new beginning, there can be no doubt that the materials it worked over are, to a great extent, older and much older than it is and, in large measure, actually go back to the time about which they want to tell. Moreover, these materials certainly existed for L, in part, at least, as separate stories; but, at the same time, there were probably also already collections of stories in small and middle-sized units, "cycles of sagas," perhaps the stories revolving around Jacob and Esau, on the one hand, and those dealing with Jacob and Laban on the other, which are not yet reconciled with each other in L—as they are in J and E —but form independent "cycles." Nothing more exact can any longer be determined concerning the prehistory of the materials used in the narrative threads of Genesis. One can scarcely go beyond a characterization of the materials found by the authors of these threads.

2. Literary genres. ***a. Lists.*** Along with the genealogical notes which give Genesis its essential character and which—as has already been mentioned (§§ B2*b, d, above*) and is later to be more precisely explained (§ C2*g below*)—were at first provided with only scanty narrative features but were later enlarged to detailed stories, the four narrative threads and the secondary passages added to them include many different kinds of material. Thus there are occasional real lists, mere enumerations of nations, tribes, or men, devoid of every narrative motif, like the list of the "kings who reigned in the land of Edom, before any king reigned over the Israelites" (36:31-39), which—no matter to whom it is to be ascribed, to one of the narrative threads or to the hand of the author of a supplement—must, in any case, be regarded as old and reliable and probably derived from the first half of the tenth century B.C.

b. Songs and proverbs. In addition, songs and maxims are to be found here and there in Genesis, many of which, at least, represent, not creations of the source authors, but something found by them and incorporated into their narrative. Even if a definite separation between the two groups is, unfortunately, not possible, they can, nevertheless, be separated with some probability. The oracle issued to Rebekah concerning the fruit of her womb (25:23), the benedictions which Isaac gives to his sons Esau and Jacob (27:27-29, 39-40), and the curses which Jacob pronounces upon Reuben, Simeon, and Levi (49:3-7) are so interlaced with their narrative context and exhibit so little independence that one must derive them from the authors of the narrative threads to which they belong. The situation is different in the case of the boastful speech of Lamech (4:23-24), of the solemn utterance concerning the atonement for the shedding of human blood (9:6), and of the blessings of Judah, Zebulun, Issachar, Dan, Gad, Naphtali, Joseph, and Benjamin (49:8-27). In contrast to 49:3-7, they have no close connection with the narrative context in which they are now inserted and probably owe their present position only to the desire to fashion the utterances concerning Reuben, Simeon, and Levi—which originally must have been followed, as we saw in § B1*b above,* by still other utterances concerning Judah and Joseph but not by the existing ones of 49:8-12, 22-25—into a complete series of utterances taking all of Jacob's sons into consideration.

c. Cosmological-anthropological myths. Among the narratives a special group is formed by those which are not, as are most of the sagas of Genesis, concerned with Israel and its neighbors, but are rather of a cosmological-anthropological nature; thus, the two or—since 2:4*b*-3:24, after all, probably represents a compilation of two parallel narratives—the three stories of the Creation (1:1-2:4*a;* 2:4*b*-3:24), the torsolike story of the marriage of the sons of God with the daughters of men and the resulting giants (6:1-4), and the two stories of the Flood combined in 6:5-19. These narratives also have the following in common: that they are of a mythological nature, that they show a strong resemblance to Sumerian-Akkadian writings or motifs, and that—and this is true, in any case, of the first story of the Creation and of the two flood stories—they are probably directly dependent on Sumerian-Akkadian prototypes, either in that these were already spread abroad in the Canaan of the second millennium B.C. and thus must have become known at once to the Israelites who invaded here or that the ancestors of the Israelites, who according to our tradition came from Mesopotamia to Canaan, brought these materials along.

The two series of "fathers," which, on the one hand, connect Noah with the Creation and, on the other hand, connect Terah or Abraham with Noah (4:17*b*, 25-26; 5; 11:10-32), are probably also copied from a Babylonian prototype. The Babylonian tradition starts the long list of kings with kings before the Flood, on the one hand, and kings after the Flood, on the other; and it would certainly be conceivable that Israel, where the monarchical principle arose rather late, transformed the kings of the Babylonian tradition into forefathers and the unbelievably long reigns of those kings into less high figures for years of life, which, nevertheless, far surpass the usual span. Since, however, the list of the descendants of Cain (4:1, 17-22), which ends in three parts with Jabal, the father of the nomadic or seminomadic cattle owners, Jubal, the father of the musicians, and Tubal(-Cain), the father of the smiths, apparently seeks to explain thereby the formation of the social groups existing in the nomadic or seminomadic society of that time, the possibility may well be considered that such lists of fathers arose of their own accord in Israel or with Israel's ancestors, as such things are to be found everywhere in the world, and especially the mention of the three ancestors at the end is particularly widespread.

d. Legends connected with foreign lands. To be distinguished from these materials, which, at least for the most part, are borrowed from abroad and have a mythological character, are those which, to be sure, also have foreign—especially, Babylonian and Egyptian—events as their subject but tend to tell about curious institutions and customs of foreign countries rather than to explain cosmological-anthropological phenomena mythologically. The story of the failure of the tower-building project has, of course, mythological vestiges, takes place in Babylon, and wants to show the reason for the fact—felt to be extraordinary—that mankind does not form a united community speaking the same language, but, rather, falls apart into many peoples speaking different languages. However, it differs from the stories of the Creation and the Flood in that it begins with the historic city of Babylon, with its unfinished temple tower and the confusion of languages unintelligible to the strangers entering it; and to this extent it may be compared with what Herodotus can tell his readers about the great and mysterious city of Babylon. The comparison with Herodotus' tales of foreign lands and peoples is still more justified in the case of the one portion of the narrative constituting the Joseph story, about how Joseph made the Egyptians with their fields slaves of the Pharaoh (47:13-26), a story, which, without being able to grasp clearly and definitely establish the basic socio-economic phenomenon, surely had in mind a historical phenomenon shocking to non-Egyptians.

The stories of Ishmael and of Jacob and Esau, which, to a great extent, play in the steppes stretching out in front of the land of the Palestinian culture to the E and S and in Mesopotamia, convey the local color of their setting outside Palestine; and, finally, the portions of the Joseph story which relate the experiences of Joseph, his brothers, and his father in Egypt—namely, chs. 39–48; 50—reproduce Egyptian conditions in a manner true to fact. However, the non-Israelitic element here is made subservient throughout to the narrative centering around Israel and its ancestors and thus incorporated into the Israelitic tribal tradition.

e. Local legends of Canaan. Not a few of the Genesis stories are connected with the land of Canaan and seek to explain peculiarities to be found there. Nature stories—i.e., such stories as are connected with natural occurrences—play a rather slight role among them. Disregarding individual etiological features such as explanations of geographical names —of Galeed, perhaps, as "witness heap" (31:46-48) or of Penuel as "the face of El" (32:31) or of Succoth as "booths" (33:17)—actually only the story of the downfall of Sodom (19:1-27) can be called a nature story. It is immaterial whether it refers to actual occurrences or represents an independent creative attempt to explain the bleak state of things which the Dead Sea and its environs cause and caused four millenniums ago; it is immaterial, too, whether it attempts to say that the Dead Sea did not exist before the catastrophe but originated only because of it; or whether it imagines that divine judgment touched only the—up until that time—fruitful surroundings of the sea: it is certain that we are concerned here with a saga connected with that region, taken over by Israel with its capture of the land, and woven into its own primitive history. A motif referring to a remarkable phenomenon which existed in the neighborhood of the Dead Sea is also to be found in the strange story, to be evaluated somewhat more precisely later (*see* § D1 *below*), of the campaign of the four Eastern kings against the five petty kings who resided in that region (ch. 14)—namely, the motif of the two of these Canaanite kings, the king of Sodom and the king of Gomorrha, who fell into bitumen pits while fleeing.

f. Cult legends. In contrast to the scarcity of nature stories, there is in Genesis a rather great abundance of cult legends—i.e., of legends which seek to give the origin of certain places and customs of worship. Like the nature stories, these cult legends are certainly also, at least in a great measure, originally Canaanite and were probably taken over then by the Israelites in their conquest of the land, along with the places and practices to which they refer. Nevertheless, this in no wise means, as must be more precisely shown (*see* § D3 *below*), that our tradition which speaks of a connection of the patriarchs with these religious places before Israel's capture of the land did not at the same time hold fast to pertinent memories. If one disregards the shorter references of cult-legend-like nature, as well as the P narratives which have already been considered (§§ B1*e*, 2*d*, *above*), which lead to the establishment of ritual-religious observances, one finds in Genesis these cult legends: Abraham's meeting with Melchizedek, king of Salem and priest of El Eljon, and the acknowledgment of this god by him (14:18-24); the revelation of El Roi to Hagar in Beer-lahai-roi (ch. 16) from J and the story from E which is parallel to it (21:8-21), which, although its scene of action is not named, probably is to be thought of as taking place there; the command of God to Abraham to sacrifice Isaac at a certain spot—no longer to be surely identified—and the accomplishment of a substitute sacrifice (22:1-19); God's revelation to Jacob in Bethel (28; 35:9-13, 15); the wrestling of Jacob with the El of Penuel and his blessing by him (32:24-32); the burial of the images of unknown gods by Jacob in Shechem and the building of an altar by him in Bethel (35:1-4, 6*b*-7).

Although detailed legends about them are not extant, the cults of Beer-sheba and Hebron have, nevertheless, left such clear marks on our narratives that one must surely trace the latter back to more detailed traditions about them which were once available. Even what is related (21:22-32; 26:12-33) about Beer-sheba as the scene of a covenant between Abraham or Isaac, on the one side, and Abimelech, the king of Gerar, on the other, gives an inkling of the religious significance of Beer-sheba. This stands out more clearly in the fact that the blessing bestowed on Abraham is ceremoniously repeated in Beer-sheba for Isaac (26:3*b*-5, 24-25*a*) and also for Jacob (46:1-4). This repetition—attached to Beer-sheba—of the blessing of Abraham suggests the assumption that the story of God's covenant with Abraham and the great promise made to him in it (ch. 15), which is now set in no definite location, took place in Beer-sheba, and the statement that Abraham "planted a tamarisk tree in Beer-sheba, and called there on the name of the LORD, the Everlasting God," which scarcely fits in its present location 21:33, originally stood at the end of ch. 15 and strongly emphasized here the significance of the preceding action and the dignity of its setting.

The religious significance of certain locations in or near Hebron, which surely extends back into the pre-Israelitic period, is attested, indeed, even by the story in ch. 18, according to which three heavenly beings were entertained there under a tree by Abraham. Even more clearly is this shown afterward by the fact—not expressly proved, but to be inferred with confidence—that the instructions for and the performance of the circumcision, about which ch. 17 tells, certainly took place in Hebron and that God on this occasion for the first time solemnly made known his name "El Shadday"—that, in other words, El Shadday was established in Hebron as El Olam was in Beer-sheba (*see* GOD, NAMES OF). Finally, it does not happen by chance, but is rather to be explained by the sacred character of the region, that, according to ch. 23, Abraham acquires a burial place here for Sarah, a tomb, in which, at least according to P, also he himself, as well as Isaac and Jacob, found a resting place (25:9-10; 35:27-29; 50:12-13). All these cult legends, however, just like the portions of other literary genres taken over into Genesis, have been coupled with the history of the ancestors of Israel or, more correctly, the history of the leading of these ancestors of Israel by their God, the Creator of heaven and of earth; and, to this extent, they are made subservient to the tribal and national sagas, which, indeed, form the real essence of Genesis.

g. Folk-historical notes within saga narratives. These tribal and folk sagas, which, as has been mentioned several times (*see* § B2*d above*), have their roots in genealogical lists of nations, tribes, and races—as well as other societies related by blood only in imagination—proceed from the assumption, or perhaps even from the fiction, that each of these groups is descended from its own forefather and give these fathers wives, who then bear the members of the groups regarded as their sons. In doing this, special attention is paid to the seniority of the sons, and the first-born is set off by name, in order thus to underline and explain the differences in the importance of the individual groups. The establishment of the differences in rank inside a group going back to the same ancestor can also be undertaken in the following manner: the father is given two wives, one fully authorized, the other recognized to a lesser degree; and, accordingly, the sons born by the first take precedence over their half brothers.

Examples of such genealogical lists animated by the mere introduction of a woman as mother of the sons of the ancestral father are given in 22:20-24, where the twelve sons of Nahor are divided between two women, a head wife and a concubine, as the first bears eight, the second four; and in 25:1-6, where six sons born to Abraham by his concubine Keturah are enumerated and the additional comment made that Abraham made his son Isaac, born by the head wife Sarah, his real heir and also gave portions to the descendants of Keturah, but still sent them "away from his son Isaac, eastward to the east country"—i.e., guaranteed the possession of the land of Canaan for Isaac. What appears in 22:20-24; 25:1-6 as a thin, skeletonlike sketch has been expanded in the story of Jacob's marriages and the birth of his children, on the other hand, and in the two Hagar stories, on the other, into full, exciting stories. The sentence which stands at the end of the note about the Keturah descendants, that Abraham sent them away, has undergone so thorough a revision in the two Hagar stories, that the tribal-historical motif—similar to 25:1-6—which is also basic to them, is almost hidden; and the same is true of the stories about Jacob's wives and children in chs. 29–30, in which the substitution of two head wives and two concubines for the single head wife and the single concubine in the simple arrangement of 22:20-24 made possible an exciting action quite impossible there.

Somewhat more detailed than 22:20-24; 25:1-6 are the stories of Jacob's vain attempt to precede his twin brother at birth (25:21-26) and of the similar, but successful, undertaking of Perez, the son of Judah and his daughter-in-law Tamar (38:27-30), although the fundamental basis of folk or tribal history remains clearly recognizable here. This foundation is more obscured, to be sure, in the story of the sale of his birthright by Esau to Jacob (25:29-34), inasmuch as the impression is given here that it is a question of the contrast of two brothers of very different types, of the good-natured, stupid older brother and the sly, capable younger brother. The same is true of the Cain and Abel story (4:2-16), which until well into the nineteenth century was quite generally understood to deal with the first murder in the history of mankind, a fratricide, and to describe the wickedness of human beings which even surpassed the Fall of ch. 3 and brought on the judgment of the Flood—and is frequently thus understood, even today; while the tribal-history content, as described below, was first recognized in the last third of the nineteenth century. The motif of the amazing outstripping of the elder brother or elder brothers by the younger experienced its most imaginative development—a development associated with almost complete dissipation of the background of tribal history, however—in the stories of the crafty usurpation of the birthright by Jacob (25:27-28; 27) and of Joseph's advance over his brothers (chs. 37; 39–48; 50).

The obscuring of the tribal and folk-historical background has, to be sure, not reached the same stage—by far—in the story of the rape of Dinah by Shechem, the son of Hamor, and the terrible judgment carried out by Dinah's brothers Simeon and Levi against Shechem and his companions (ch. 34), that it reached in the Joseph stories; on the contrary, it allows the historical events, which gave the impetus for its creation—namely, the conclusion of a treaty for trade and friendship between two groups of peoples and then its breaking with bloodshed—to be clearly recognized. But, on the other hand, Shechem, who is in love with Dinah; the brothers Simeon and Levi, who are shocked by the disgrace of their sister and thus of themselves; and their father, Jacob, who fears evil consequences, are so realistically depicted as men of flesh and blood that, at least at first, one has the impression that it is really a question here of the fates of individual men and not of friendly negotiations and bloody disputes between two tribal groups.

***h. Fairy tales and* novelle.** Contributing substantially to the obscuring of the tribal and folk-historical background is the fact that in the shaping of the Joseph story and other stories, numerous and varied literary motifs have been utilized. Thus the Joseph story has been expanded by novelistic and fictitious materials—in addition to the very loosely attached report of the pledging of the Egyptian landed properties, which has already been discussed (§ C2*d above*)—materials which probably had their home in Egypt or, in any case, came to our narrator from there—e.g., by the account of the temptation and defamation of Joseph by the wife of his Egyptian master (ch. 39) or that of the dreams of Pharaoh and Joseph's advancement (ch. 41). The marriage notice, very short in the case of Abraham and Nahor (11:29), has been replaced, in the case of Isaac and Jacob, by stories of courtship which are detailed and full of feeling, in that there the wooing of Rebekah (ch. 24), entrusted by Abraham to his major-domo, and here the meeting of Jacob with Rachel and his services rendered for many years to Laban willingly for her sake, are movingly and excitingly depicted (ch. 29). Also the material from 22:1-19, which we have seen (§ C2*f above*) was originally of a cult-legendary nature, is made subservient to a literary and at the same time religious goal—namely, to introduce a moment, exciting and retarding the suspense of the hearers and readers as much as possible and tying in with it a religious motif moving them as deeply as possible, since the story in its present form and in its present context seeks to show two things: first, that God's promise can, to be sure, at least apparently, be questioned but never made invalid, and then, that Abraham withstood with exemplary obedience the unbelievably difficult test of faith imposed on him by his God. In the case of the motif of the endangering of the ancestress, which appears three times, twice applied to Sarah (12:10–13:1; 20) and once to Rebekah (26:6-11), some have considered a folk- or tribal-historical interpretation; i.e., they have sought to relate these stories, or at least the first two of them, which have as their subject the menacing of and the protection of Sarah in Egypt, to the oppression of the Israelites and their deliverance from this distress, to consider them, consequently, as a parallel to Exod. 1–15. It is more probably a question here of a purely narrative motif, in that the danger threatening the wife of the one who received the promise, by whom the birth of the next bearer of the promise is to be expected, seems to call into question the promise itself; and here, bound up once more with the poetic motif, is a religious theological concern—namely, to show that God, in spite of all reverses, is still able to attain his goal.

D. *HISTORICITY.* 1. Transhistorical materials. The cosmological-anthropological-mythological narratives of 1:1–2:4*a;* 2:4*b*–3:24; 6:1-4; 6:5–9:19, may be withdrawn at once from the series of narratives which give cause and reason to the attempt to determine their historical content. For, great as the religious content of the stories of the Creation and the Flood is, they are, by their very nature, no more able to give information about the origin of the world than about the time and extent of the flood catastrophe, which—probably to be thought of as limited to S Babylonia—may have given rise to our narratives of the Flood, which have cosmic proportions. The same is true of the Sodom story (ch. 19). Furthermore, it is obvious that the stories which are purely poetic shapings of tribal- and folk-historical elements, like that of the wooing of Rebekah (ch. 24), likewise have little to offer the historian. Ch. 14 is a case of a very special type. The story told here of the victory of Abraham over the four Eastern kings under the leadership of Chedorlaomer of Elam—they were drawn up against the kings of five SE Canaanite city states who had become rebellious toward them—and of his meeting with Melchizedek, the king of Salem (i.e., probably Jerusalem), gives a very divided impression, of course. On the one hand, there are in it, so it seems, recollections of figures who played a role in the Near East around the middle of the second millennium B.C., even though in very distorted form; on the other hand, with the introduction of Canaanite kings of cities, which, at least in part, never existed but belonged entirely to legend, it enters upon the way of fanciful combinations, such as are characteristic of the late Jewish midrash. One may rather, as will be shown (§ D3 *below*), give credence to what the narrative can say about Abraham's relations with the El Elyon of Jerusalem.

2. Secular history. Historically valuable content is preserved, really in only two kinds of narratives contained in Genesis: the tribal- or folk-historical accounts and the cult legends. In the case of the former, which (*see* § D3 *below*) imagines all societies to be derived from one ancestral father, the names of the "fathers" and the "sons" are, in general, historical to the extent that these great men once actually existed—for the most part, to be sure, not as individuals, but as groups. Caution is in order in many cases with regard to the dating which has been imposed upon these great people. Thus, there is no kind of guarantee given that the fathers named in the Cain and Seth genealogical trees of chs. 4–5 (*see* § C2*g above*), who, at least for the most part, represented historically authenticated peoples or tribes, really belong in the early period in which they now appear. The same is true of the Cain and Abel story (4:2-16) and of the Noah-Canaan story (9:20-27). The first reflects, in all probability, the amazement, combined with a kind of horror, of Israel, having become settled in Canaan, that the tribe of Cain, which was, after all, related and closely connected, had not also established itself in Canaan, but had clung to the nomadic life (*cf.* § C2*g above*); and the second, in which, as has been observed (§§ B1*b*, 2*b*, *above*), under Shem the Israelites, under Japheth the Philistines, and under Canaan the Canaanites conquered by the Israelites and the Philistines, are to be understood, also assumes Israel's settlement in Canaan. The correct place for the two narratives, as far as time is concerned, is thus really not Genesis but the book of Joshua. That they are to be found in Genesis, and, indeed, quite early in it, can be explained by the fact that the forefathers assumed that the historical communities belong to a period having an almost mythical character; they are thus, to this extent, timeless, and can be put into any period desired. The time sequence of the Genesis stories is, in view of all this, not to be trusted without further ado.

A further curtailment of the historical value of the Genesis narratives is indicated by the fact—in part related to what has just been mentioned—that, in spots, they reflect very clearly conditions of the period of the judges or even of the kings and represent, thus, to this extent "retrojections" of later conditions into the time in which they claim to take place. This is true, as has been shown (§ B2*a above*), of Isaac's blessings on Jacob and Esau and, likewise, of Jacob's blessings on Judah, Zebulun, Issachar, Dan, Gad, Asher, Naphtali, Joseph, and Benjamin, which clearly assume that the tribes represented by these sons of Jacob have their residence in the places known to us from the time of judges and kings (*see* §§ B1*b*, C2*b*, *above*). These phenomena make it understandable that the narratives under consideration here have frequently been interpreted as mere reflection of later conditions and have been thought to yield nothing for the time about which they claim to speak, consequently nothing for the time before Moses. However, such mistrust overshoots the mark by far.

The features coinciding with the time of judges and kings, such as are very obviously exhibited by many a Genesis narrative, are not actually projected on an imaginary screen, but have been blended with traditions which have clung to reliable memories of figures, conditions, and events of the segment of history or prehistory of Israel before Moses. Thus it proves true—to proceed at once to the main point—that before the time when Egypt, Midian, and the desert of Sinai had become important for Israel or for certain ancestors of groups which were later absorbed by Israel, other, older ancestors of this people had had connections with Mesopotamia. The tradition that Abraham came from Haran to Canaan in the period before Moses is, thus, probably correct; and even the report—in other respects very questionable—that Abraham's father had sojourned in Ur-Kasdim could have preserved correctly the recollection that for a time this place or its surrounding territory was the home of groups of nomads or seminomads related to Abraham.

To go much further is, to be sure, scarcely permissible. Thus, in the case of Abraham it probably is actually a question of a single individual, a nomadic or seminomadic sheik with many followers. However, it is very questionable whether this is also true for Isaac and Jacob and whether these names should not rather be interpreted as personifications of tribes. The genealogical association into which our tradition brought the three, in that it made Isaac the son of Abraham and Jacob the son of Isaac, is probably just as definitely nonhistorical as the derivation of the twelve tribes of Israel from the twelve sons of Jacob having the same names. On the other hand, the occurrence reflected in the story of the assault on Shechem by Simeon and Levi (ch. 34) can and probably does actually belong to the pre-Mosaic period (*cf.* § C2*g above*), since the reports relative to the final conquest of the land of Israel, as they are given in the last chapters of Numbers, in Joshua, and in Judg. 1-2, no longer give any indication of a temporary sojourn by Simeon and Levi in central Palestine. Consequently, ch. 34 is correctly placed in Genesis. The exact date of the events related there, of course, remains undefinable.

In a similar way the stories of Abraham, Isaac, and Jacob make it plausible, indeed, that in pre-Mosaic times the former spent some time as a guest in S Palestine and the other two, probably not single individuals like Abraham, but tribes, dwelt in Canaan in the same capacity, Isaac in the extreme S of the country, Jacob in the land E of the Jordan and in central Palestine; but they do not permit a more exact placing of these figures as far as time is concerned. Under these circumstances it is justified and understandable that people have repeatedly examined the non-OT accounts which are at our disposal for the history of Palestine and of the Near East in general from the centuries of the second millennium B.C. which are being considered here: the Egyptian proscription texts belonging to the beginning of this millennium; the accounts of the Hyksos episode of the seventeenth and sixteenth centuries B.C.; the Mari Texts, which are roughly contemporary with them; and the Amarna Tablets, which are about three centuries younger, to see whether it would not be possible to establish some connection between one or another of the statements to be found here and this or that Genesis story, and in this manner to fix in time the figures or events appearing in the story in question. However, such investigations have not led to results in any way guaranteed or even probable.

The situation is similar in the case of the Joseph stories. The attempts to determine their historical content and the time of the persons and places here mentioned more exactly by comparison with accounts outside the OT—in this case, primarily the Amarna Letters—have also been unsuccessful in this instance. If, however, one probes our Joseph story itself for the historical elements it contains, one might discover from it that perhaps one or two centuries before the conquest of the land of Israel, ancestors of parts of the later Israel, apparently of Joseph and Levi, had gone to Egypt out of concern for food and had stayed there for several decades at least.

3. Religious history. If the tradition that ancestors of later Israel came to Canaan from Mesopotamia and later other groups of them, after a temporary residence in Egypt, penetrated across the Peninsula of Sinai into the land of Canaan is to be trusted at least in its general outlines, this is completely true of the reports at our disposal concerning the forms of worship of these two movements. In spite of the obliteration of the historical facts of the case caused by the conception of their God's absolutism, which was a matter of course for the authors of our Pentateuch threads, it remains clearly to be seen that the groups which penetrated Canaan from the S in the Mosaic period worshiped another god, different from the one worshiped by Abraham, Isaac, and Jacob. The former brought along the Yahweh cult: for the latter El was the authoritative God, the El about which sources newly accessible to us, above all the Ugaritic texts which belong to the fourteenth century B.C., have shown that he enjoyed the greatest respect among the Canaanites of that time and occupied an almost monarchical position in their pantheon. It is told of all three patriarchs—of Abraham, of Isaac, and of Jacob—that they worshiped this god. And the names appearing in the respective narratives—El Elyon (14:18-24), El 'Olam (15?; 21:33; 26:3-5, 24-25; 46:2-5), El Roi (16:13), El Shadday (17:1; 35:11; 43:14; 48:3; 49:25), El Bethel (28:10-22; 31:13; 35:1-7), and El of Penuel (32:24-32)—signify this *one* El; that is to say, they are to be understood as hypostases of him. That the patriarchs, or at least their followers, also worshiped other, apparently lower gods, brought along to Canaan from abroad, is not concealed by our tradition (31:53; 35:1-4; cf. Josh. 24:2); but, at the same time, it permits no doubt to arise about the fact that El and El alone is the god to whom respect is due. We may believe these accounts and consider it a historical fact that the ancestors of later Israel who came to Canaan as guests in the pre-Mosaic period were worshipers of El. This is also confirmed by the fact that the names of people and places formed with "Yahweh" as the theophoric element were preceded by other names which contained "El." *See* GOD, NAMES OF.

E. *RELIGIOUS-ETHICAL SIGNIFICANCE.* As an account of the prehistory of the people of Israel beginning with the creation of heaven and earth and the destiny of primitive mankind, Genesis contains a whole series of features which are of a national rather than a religious nature, or—since at that time the national and the religious formed a unit—are at least so judged by us. Among these, e.g., are the stories of the outwitting of Esau and Laban by Jacob. Also the blessings given by the patriarchs to their departing sons by no means have in view only the religious welfare but are aimed at the same time, often even principally, at the possession of economic and political power. This is true even of the blessing which, according to 12:1-4, God gives to Abraham as he departs on his travels abroad. For, just as surely as it aims at religious salvation, just so clear it is, at the same time, that the saying: "By you all the families of the earth will bless themselves" at least aims primarily, or surely in addition, at the earthly success of Abraham and his descendants, therefore of the people of Israel, and represents this as sought after and desired by the other peoples. One should, without hesitation, admit that those portions of Genesis which give more or less strong expression to national sentiments in this manner possess their own characters and, as a matter of principle, desist from the attempt to understand them as expressions of pure religiosity or even to put into them Christian values. Genesis is rich enough in purely religious values, even so.

To begin with, the stories of the Creation which are at the beginning of Genesis give powerful expression to the joyous certainty with which Luther begins his explanation of the first Christian article of faith: "I believe, that God created me and all creatures." The stories of the Fall and the Flood have this to say about it then, that, because of man's guilt, man and the world did not remain as God had desired them and created them. But even so, the world and man are not forsaken by God. On the contrary, God seeks out a man who, bound to him in inviolable religious communion, is to become the father of a people who are blessed and who are destined to be a blessing for mankind. Even if obstacles appear again and again in his way and that of the bearers of the promise who follow him, obstacles which threaten the fulfilment of the promise, God can overcome them all and bring the story to the conclusion he intended and wants to have. Joseph replies to his brothers when they express concern to him after the death of their father, lest he might take revenge on them now for that which they had once done to him: "You meant evil against me; but God meant it for good, to bring it about that many people should be kept alive, as they are today" (50:20). The view of the world and of history which is expressed here stands at the very pinnacle of Christianity.

Just as the religious content of Genesis has lasting meaning, so, too, does the ethical content. This is true, above all, of the stories considered in § C2*g* *above,* which, representing expansions of tribal- or folk-historical notes, have lifted the figures of their prototypes, which were bound to time or place, into the eternal (or supratemporal) and universally human and now cause human beings to appear before our eyes as members of families—father, mother, children, brothers—as they have always existed and always will. These figures are presented without any embellishment; but precisely because this is the case, they make an irresistible impression on hearers and readers all over the world—particularly on the children among them—even today, and radiate to them educational forces such as can scarcely be found elsewhere.

Bibliography. Commentaries: H. Gunkel, *Genesis, HKAT* (3rd ed., 1910); O. Procksch, *Genesis, KAT* (2nd-3rd eds., 1924); J. Skinner, ICC (3rd ed., 1930); S. R. Driver, *Genesis,* WC (15th ed., 1948); G. von Rad, "Der Erste Buch Mose," *Das AT Deutsch* (1949-53); C. A. Simpson and W. R. Bowie, "Genesis," *IB* (1952); R. de Vaux, *La Genèse,* La Bible de Jérusalem (2nd ed., 1956).

Studies on Genesis in general: E. Meyer, *Die Israeliten und ihre Nachbarstämme* (1906); A. Alt, *Der Gott der Väter, BWANT,* III, 12 (1929); C. A. Simpson, *The Early Traditions of Israel* (1944); O Eissfeldt, "Die ältesten Traditionen Israels," *BZAW,* vol. 71 (1950); A. Alt, *Kleine Schriften I* (1953), pp. 1-78; J. Steinmann, *Les plus anciennes traditions du Pentateuque* (1954); O. Eissfeldt, "El and Yahweh," *Journal of Semitic Studies,* 1 (1956), 25-37; B. Gemser *et al., Studies on the Book of Genesis,* Oudtestamentische Studien, 12 (1958).

On Gen. 1-11: S. Mowinckel and W. F. Albright, "The Babylonian Matter in the Predeuteronomic Primeval History (JE) in Gen. 1-11," *JBL,* 58 (1939), 87-103; W. Zimmerli, *"1. Mose 1-11," Die Urgeschichte* (1947), pp. 116-37; S. Kramer, *Biblical Parallels from Sumerian Literature* (1954); V. Maag, "Alttestamentliche Anthropologie in ihrem Verhältnis zur altorientalischen Mythologie, Asiatische Studien," *Études Asiatiques,* I-IV (1955), 15-44; S. Kramer, *From the Tablets of Sumer* (1956); G. Castellino, "Les origines de la civilisation selon les textes bibliques et les textes cunéiformes," *Vetus Testamentum,* Supplement IV (1957), pp. 116-37.

On Gen. 12-26: P. Dhorme, "Abraham das le cadre de l'histoire," *RB,* 37 (1928), 367-85, 481-511; 40 (1931), 364-74, 503-18; J. H. Kroeze, *Genesis Veertien, een exegetisch-historische Studie* (1937); R. de Vaux, "Les Patriarches Hébreux et les découvertes modernes," *RB,* 53 (1946), 321-48; 55 (1948), 321-47; 56 (1949), 5-36; P. Dhorme, *Recueil Ed. Dhorme* (1951), pp. 191-272.

On Gen. 27-36: H. Gressmann, "Sage und Geschichte in den Patriarchenerzählungen," *ZAW,* 30 (1910), 1-34; H. Gunkel, "Jakob," *Preussische Jahrbücher,* Band 176 (1919), pp. 339-62; O. Eissfeldt, "Stammessage und Novelle von Jakob und von seinen Söhnen," *Eucharisterion Hermann Gunkel,* I (1923), 56-77; H. Eising, *Formgeschichtliche Untersuchung zur Jakobserzählung der Genesis* (1940).

On Gen. 37-50: H. Gunkel, "Die Komposition der Joseph-Geschichten," *ZDMG,* 76 (1922), 55-71; H. Gressmann, "Ursprung und Entwicklung der Joseph-Sage," *Eucharisterion Hermann Gunkel,* I (1923), 1-55; G. von Rad, "Josephsgeschichte und ältere Chokma," *Vetus Testamentum,* Supplement I (1953), pp. 120-27; C. T. Fritsch, "God Was with Him," *Interpretation,* 9 (1955), 21-34: a theological study of the Joseph narrative; J. M. A. Janssen, "Egyptological Remarks on the Story of Joseph in Genesis," *Jaarbericht Ex Oriente Lux,* 14 (1955-56), 63-72; G. von Rad, *Die Josephsgeschichte* (1956); J. Vergote, *Joseph en Egypte,* Orientalia et Biblica Lovanensia III (1959).

O. EISSFELDT

GENEVA BIBLE jə nē′və. An English translation produced at Geneva. The NT was published in 1557, the OT in 1560. Edited by William Whittingham, it combined a thoroughgoing revision of the OT on the basis of the Hebrew text and essentially Tyndale's version of the NT. It was divided into chapters, with Robert Estienne's verse divisions, and made use of chapter summaries and marginal notes. It was very popular and the best translation available in its day. *See* VERSIONS, ENGLISH § 4*b*.

J. R. BRANTON

GENIZAH gə nēt′sə [גניזה, a storeroom, *from* Heb.-Aram. גנז, hide, store up]. A place, usually an unused room in a synagogue, to which Jews consigned sacred texts no longer fit for use, or heretical texts. These writings, handwritten or printed—indeed, anything that contained the name of God—were thus preserved from profanation.

The most famous of all genizahs is the one in Cairo, from which at the end of the nineteenth century there were brought forth about a quarter of a million biblical, liturgical, rabbinic, exegetical, and other fragments, chiefly in Hebrew, Aramaic, Arabic, Samaritan, and Greek.

Bibliography. E. Adler, *Jewish Encyclopedia,* V (1907), 612-13; S. Schechter, *Studies in Judaism,* Second Series (1908), pp. 1-30; A. Marx, *Universal Jewish Encyclopedia,* IV (1941), 531-33; P. E. Kahle, *The Cairo Geniza* (1947), pp. 1 ff; A. I. Katsh, *Ginze Russiyah* (1958), Introduction, pp. iv-xi (contains facsimiles of Genizah MSS). H. M. ORLINSKY

GENNAEUS gə nē′əs [Γενναίος; Vulg. *Gennaei*] (II Macc. 12:2); KJV GENNEUS. Father of Apollonius, who was governor (στρατηγός) of a district in Palestine in the time of Antiochus V. J. C. SWAIM

GENNESARET gĕ nĕs′ə rət [Γεννησαρέτ, LXX Γεννησάρ; Targ. גנסר]; KJV Apoc. GENNESAR gĕ nē′sär. **1.** An early name for the Sea of Galilee (*see* GALILEE, SEA OF), employed with ὕδωρ ("water of") or λίμνη ("lake of").

2. The well-watered and fruitful valley NW of the Sea of Galilee. *See* GALILEE, SEA OF. Fig. MAG 4.

K. W. CLARK

GENNEUS. KJV form of GENNAEUS.

GENTILES gĕn′tīlz. *See* NATIONS.

GENTILES, COURT OF THE. A designation of the outer portion of the temple area in the time of Herod, the part which—as has been inferred from the warning slab at the middle wall of partition—was accessible to non-Jews. There is no evidence of the expression itself in the sources, but the scene in Mark 11:15 ff is set in the Court of the Gentiles.

K. GALLING

GENUBATH gĭ nōō′băth [גנבת] (I Kings 11:20). The son of Hadad, the exiled scion of the royal house of Edom, and the sister of Tahpenes, the Egyptian queen. Genubath appears to have been adopted (Hebrew "weaned" seems preferable to LXX "reared") by Tahpenes as one of the royal sons. E. R. DALGLISH

GEOGRAPHY. *See* by countries or areas—e.g., ARABIA; ASIA MINOR; ASSYRIA AND BABYLONIA; CANAAN; EGYPT; MESOPOTAMIA; SUMER; SYRIA (ARAM). *See especially* PALESTINE, GEOGRAPHY OF.

GEOLOGY. *See* by countries or areas. *See especially* PALESTINE, GEOLOGY OF.

GEON. KJV Apoc. form of GIHON.

GEORGIAN VERSION. A translation of the Bible prepared for Christians in Caucasian Georgia, dating from *ca.* the fourth century A.D. *See* VERSIONS, ANCIENT, § 8.

GER gûr [גר, sojourner; Arab. *jār,* one who turns aside]. A person living in mutually responsible association with a community not originally his own, or in a place not inherently his own. The further meanings *gēr* acquires extend this basic connotation. *See* SOJOURNER.

GERA gĭr′ə [גרא, *shortened form of a compound word based* on גר, sojourner(?)]. **1.** A son of Benjamin; actually the eponym of a Benjaminite clan (Gen. 46:21). Though called a grandson of Benjamin, the Gera of 2 *below* must be the same clan, and the LXX brings Gen. 46:21 into agreement with I Chr. 8:3, 5. 3 and 4 *below* probably refer to this same Benjaminite clan.

2. A grandson of Benjamin (I Chr. 8:3, 5; *see* 1 *above*). Gera is listed as a son of Ehud in I Chr. 8:7, probably because of dittography from 8:5, where in turn, because of a corrupt text, the name is unnecessarily repeated from 8:3.

3. The father of Ehud (Judg. 3:15). *See* 1 *above.*

4. The father of the Shimei, who cursed David as he fled Jerusalem at Absalom's revolt (II Sam. 16:5; 19:16, 18; I Kings 2:8). *See* 1 *above.*

Bibliography. M. Noth, *Die israelitischen Personennamen* (1928), p. 148; W. F. Albright, *The Vocalization of the Egyptian Syllabic Orthography* (1934), p. 14. H. H. GUTHRIE, JR.

GERAH gĭr′ə [גרה]. A twentieth of a shekel. *See* WEIGHTS AND MEASURES § B4*g*.

GERAR gĭr′är [גרר; Apoc. τῶν Γερρηνῶν, A. Γεννηρῶν]; KJV Apoc. GERRHENIANS gə rē′nĭ ənz. An important city and district near the Mediterranean Sea S and SW of the S border of Canaan. It was ruled by a king with whom, after some difficulties, both Abraham and Isaac made a treaty of friendship (Gen. 20; 26); in both cases this king is named Abimelech, and if he is not the same man, this may be a royal title. The use of the term "Philistine" in reference to the people of Gerar is anachronistic, as it was not until some centuries later that the Philistines occupied the territory. Gerar is not mentioned in any of the Egyptian records, so the city was evidently not close to the seacoast route which the Egyptians followed in their campaigns. The only other mention of Gerar in the Bible is in II Chr. 14:13-14, where it is given as the limit of Asa's pursuit of the defeated Ethiopians. However, it is probable that the LXX reading Gerar for MT Gedor in I Chr. 4:39-40 is correct, as the statements that the region was a former residence of the sons of Ham (cf. Gen. 10:19) and that it was a fertile pasture land apply well to this territory.

During the Israelite period Gerar came under the dominion of the Philistines and later of Judah, and in postexilic times there was a considerable Greek settlement in the area. It is spoken of as Gerarike in the Talmud and as Geraritike or Geraritikon Salton in Christian sources. Later on, Orda in that region became the site of a bishopric; it is located on the Medeba map as a large city, on a straight line between Seana (Khirbet Sihan) and Photis (Khirbet

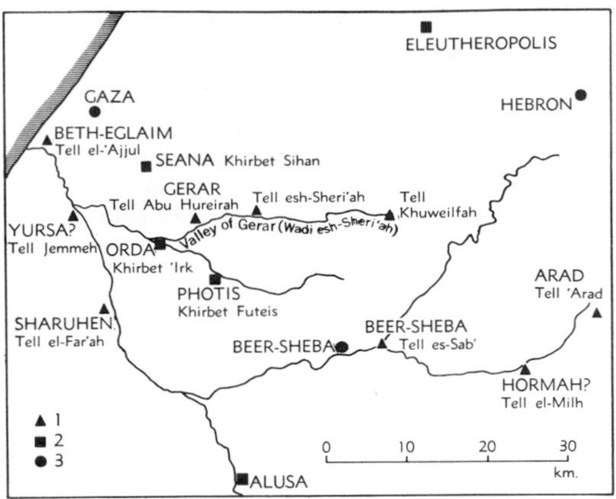

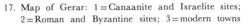

Courtesy of the Hebrew University, Jerusalem, Israel

17. Map of Gerar: 1 = Canaanite and Israelite sites; 2 = Roman and Byzantine sites; 3 = modern towns

Futeis), while Gerar is indicated as a small city to the N of Orda and W of Beer-sheba.

From these sources the site of Gerar can be identified as Tell Abu Hureirah on the N side of the Wadi esh-Sheri'ah, *ca.* fifteen miles NW of Beer-sheba. Excavations there have revealed a long period of settlement, beginning at least as early as the Chalcolithic period, the sherds being especially numerous from the latter half of the Middle Bronze period (1800-1600), which includes the age of the patriarchs.* The top of the tell seems to have been surrounded by a wall of rammed earth, which was precisely the construction favored at the time, and the actual city extended far southward and eastward toward the wadi, having the unusually large area of approximately 150,000 square meters. Tell Jemmeh, formerly a favored location for Gerar, is too near the coast and is probably the Yursa of the Egyptian lists and the Tell el-Amarna Letters. Fig. SIC 56.

Fig. GER 17.

Bibliography. Y. Aharoni, "The Land of Gerar," *Israel Exploration Journal,* VI (1956), 26-32. Contrast F. Petrie, *Gerar* (1928).

S. Cohen

GERASA gĕr'ə sə [Γερασηνοί, Γεργεσηνοί]; GERASENES gĕr'ə sēnz; KJV GERGESENES gûr'gə sēnz'. These names refer to two different cities: the Roman Gerasa (Jerash), twenty-six miles N of Amman in Jordan, and an unnamed Greek town on the E coast of the Sea of Galilee.

1. Identification. The name Gerasa does not appear in the Bible, although such a city name may be implied in Luke 8:26-27. The terms "Gerasenes" (KJV "Gergesenes") and "Gadarenes" (Gadara does not appear in the Bible) appear interchangeably in the same gospel episode of an exorcism by Jesus (Matt. 8:28; Mark 5:1; Luke 8:26, 37). In this story the scribes have confused these three names, as is seen by the fact that, from the fourth century on, MSS attest to all three terms for each of the three gospels. The KJV recorded Mark and Luke as referring to Gadarenes, and Matthew as referring to Gergesenes. But superior MS witness is now reflected in the RSV, which sets forth that Mark and Luke originally wrote "Gerasenes," and Matthew originally wrote "Gadarenes."

This reduces the problem to a simple inquiry as to the proper terms for the people involved. The gospels clearly locate the story somewhere on the E coast of Galilee. There the modern ruins of Khersa and Gerga suggest that either Gerasa or Gergesa could be an original form (unless the Arabic names merely reflect Christian tradition). In the early third century, Origen preferred Gergesa, not only because of the ruined cliff town with a similar name, but also because he knew of a Gadara and a Gerasa which might have caused confusion, both lying at some distance from the lake.

However, the locale of the story is the general area to which the people named belonged. Gerasa was forty miles SE, and Gadara was thirteen miles S, of the approximate gospel site, whereas the ruins of Gerga and Khersa suggest an ancient city on the E coast of the lake. "The city" (Luke 8:27) from which the demoniac emerged may have been Gergesa or another Gerasa, in Gadara, and within the larger district of Gerasa of the Decapolis. In conclusion, it may be said that archaeology offers two ruined towns on the coast whose people might have been Gerasenes or Gergesenes. But the gospels speak only of the *country* district rather than of a city, which fact favors the terms "Gadarenes" and "Gerasenes." Finally, the MS evidence indicates that originally Mark (followed by Luke) referred to the "country of the Gerasenes," while Matthew independently called it the "country of the Gadarenes."

The gospel story is the only source which refers to this lakeside city (πόλις). It does not name the city, nor is it said that the people were in this instance being called by the name of the particular city. Yet the existence of modern ruins called Gerga and Khersa suggests that "Gergesenes" or "Gerasenes" might have been so derived. The gospel episode is explicitly located at some point on the E coast. Luke states that when the disciples and Jesus disembarked upon the beach, they were met by a demoniac "from the city"—which must have stood upon the cliff. All three gospels say that the demoniac was accustomed to live in the caves (in the cliff side, probably). The Matthean account, which shows independence in several points, reports *two* demoniacs, who nevertheless speak and act as one. Of course, the presence of a herd of swine is a clear indication that this E district is Gentile. The herd stampede down a steep bank into the sea and are drowned. This describes a spot at least partially elevated above the beach, and at a point where the rock reaches out to the shore. At the end, the cured man reports the event in the city (Luke 8:39), or in the Decapolis (Mark 5:20). Now the Decapolis lay SE of the lake and included both Gadara and Gerasa (*see* § 2 *below*).

2. Gerasa (Jerash). Although this city is not mentioned in the Bible, we are dealing with a known site whose splendid ruins have never disappeared from view.* The silent city stands 2,000 feet high on the Transjordan plateau, *ca.* twenty miles E of the Jordan and twenty-six miles N of Amman. It lies in the valley of the Chrysorrhoas, a N tributary of the Jabbok River, and at the E base of a majestic peak

Courtesy of Herbert G. May

18. General view of Gerasa (Jerash), the street of the columns leading to the forum, and Hadrian's arch, the temple of Zeus, and the theater beyond

of 3,930 feet. Its origins go back to the Early Iron Age, when it must have been a simple Ammonite village. The Ptolemies of Egypt possessed it in the third century, after which Antiochus IV of Syria refounded it and honored it with the name of Antioch on the Chrysorrhoas. When the Maccabean kingdom of the Jews adopted an expansionist policy, Alexander Janneus seized Gerasa *ca.* 82 B.C. (Jos. War I.iv.8). Finally, it was taken by the Romans in 63 B.C. in the campaign of Pompey, and was one of the cities organized as the Decapolis. It was really a city-state, for its authority extended over a larger district: westward *ca.* fifteen miles, almost to the Jordan; southward *ca.* five miles to the Jabbok; and an uncertain distance into the E desert. To the N, it may have extended *ca.* fifteen miles, on a line with Scythopolis; or so it did, at least, in Byzantine times. The city's sphere of influence may have reached to the Sea of Galilee (Mark 5:1; Luke 8:26). Fig. GER 18.

Under the Pax Romana the increase of trade with distant Petra and Palmyra and even the Orient brought new wealth to Gerasa. When the Nabatean kingdom was conquered by Trajan (98-117), the Decapolis region was merged with it to form the province of Arabia, and Gerasa became one of its three chief cities. Its prosperity and importance are attested by the visit of the Emperor Hadrian in 129, which was commemorated by the erection of a great triumphal arch (which still stands).* Gerasa reached its zenith in the second century, toward the end of which there was constructed in the heart of the city the magnificent temple of Artemis. Fig. GER 19.

Courtesy of the Arab Information Center, New York

19. The Triumphal Arch, built at Gerasa in A.D. 129 to celebrate the visit of Emperor Hadrian

Gerasa had become a strong Christian center by the fourth century, when worship in the pagan temples had ceased. But not long after, the Muslim conquest engulfed Gerasa (635). Its fading glory was completely ended by a disastrous earthquake, perhaps in 746. Gerasa became a ghost city, and yet its buildings and monuments survived so well that nineteenth-century travelers readily perceived its former splendor; so that after a thousand years of neglect, its ruins have now received the attention of the archaeologist. Fig. GER 20.

Courtesy of the Arab Information Center, New York

20. The street of columns at Gerasa runs the entire length of the city from the forum to the N gate.

A decade of excavation began in 1925, and the work has clearly demonstrated that Gerasa must be considered, along with Baalbek and Palmyra, among the most magnificent of ancient cities.* The ten-foot-thick walls of imperial Gerasa roughly described a two-mile circle, with a diameter of 3,500 feet. Indeed, its transverse diameters were clearly marked by the N-S Via Antoniniana and an E-W street, whose intersection was arched by a monumental tetrapylon. Just E of the Via Antoniniana, and almost parallel, flowed the spring-fed Chrysorrhoas, for the city straddled the river, and its walls followed the slopes on E and W. The approach from the S

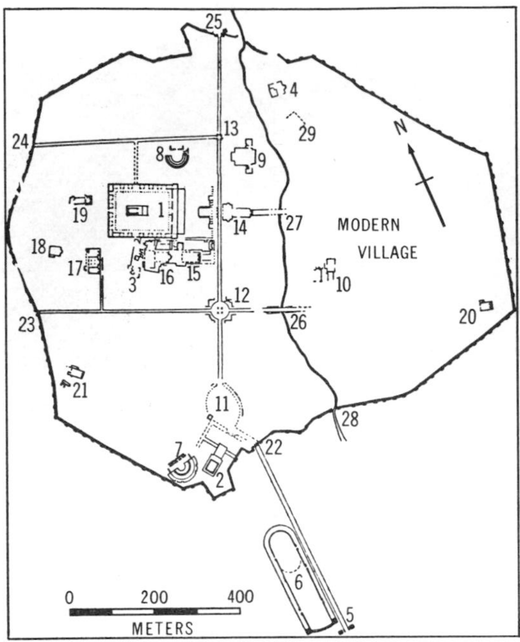

From Chester C. McCown, *The Ladder of Progress in Palestine*

21. Plan of the city of Gerasa: (1) temple of Artemis; (2) temple of Zeus; (3) temple "C"; (4) temple replaced by Church of the Prophets, Apostles, and Martyrs; (5) arch of Hadrian; (6) hippodrome; (7) S theater; (8) N theater; (9) W baths; (10) E baths; (11) forum; (12) S tetrapylon; (13) N tetrapylon; (14) propylaea plaza replaced by church; (15) temple replaced by church (Marianos); (16) Church of St. Theodore; (17) churches of Sts. Cosmas, John, and George; (18) Church of Genesius; (19) synagogue replaced by church; (20) Church of Procopius; (21) Church of Sts. Peter and Paul; (22) S gate; (23) SW gate; (24) NW gate; (25) N gate; (26-27) bridges; (28) waterfall; (29) 'Ain Kerawan

was through the great triumphal arch (*see above*) and along the length of the hippodrome (holding fifteen thousand spectators). Fig. GER 21.

Inside the triple south gate, on a hill to the W stood the temple of Zeus and beside it a theater seating three thousand patrons.* Continuing from the forum northward along the columned Via, and through the central tetrapylon, one arrives at the temple of Artemis (cf. Acts 19:34) situated in the NW quadrant. Artemis was the protectress of the city, and her glorious temple extended for fifteen hundred feet E and W, including its approaches. The worshiper would approach by a broad avenue E of the river, cross the wide bridge, pass through a triple gateway and along a porticoed street, into the court of the propylaea. He must cross the colonnaded boulevard, and again mount majestic steps sixty-five feet wide, pass under the high-columned portico, and through the door into the central court. This area is *ca.* 300 by 425 feet, and near its center is the sacred shrine, with steps and porticoed forecourt and ultimately the holy place of the goddess. Several temples to other deities, and additional theaters and baths, make up the public buildings of this magnificent E outpost. But the most delightful area of

Courtesy of the Arab Information Center, New York

22. The forum at Gerasa, enclosed within fifty-six towering columns

the city is the circular first-century forum,* many of whose columns have remained in place throughout the centuries. Figs. DEC 23; GER 22.

Though there is evidence that Christians were found here by the end of the second century, the Gerasene churches were all built in the period between the fourth and the sixth century. The pagan cults were then superseded, and their temples were adapted or replaced for Christian worship. Eleven Gerasene churches have been discovered, the most impressive being those just S of the temple of Artemis—the Cathedral of Saint Marianos and the Basilica of Saint Theodore. Of great interest is the synagogue-church, a Christian adaptation *ca.* A.D. 530 of a Jewish synagogue constructed *ca.* 300.* This was the only synagogue discovered in the city, and its location at the rear of the temple of Artemis suggests that the Jewish minority occupied an inconspicuous place in the city. Fig. GER 23.

From Sukenik, *Ancient Synagogues in Palestine and Greece* (The British Academy, Schweich Lectures, 1930); courtesy of the Hebrew University, Jerusalem, Israel

23. Mosaic floor in the vestibule of the Gerasa synagogue

Bibliography. J. W. Crowfoot, *Churches at Jerash* (1931); R. Fink, "Jerash in the First Century A.D.," *Journal of Roman Studies* (1933), pp. 109-24; C. H. Kraeling, *Gerasa, City of the Decapolis* (1938); C. C. McCown, *The Ladder of Progress in Palestine* (1943), pp. 309-25. K. W. CLARK

GERIZIM, MOUNT gĕr′ə zĭm [גרזים]. A mountain (modern Jebel et-Tor) directly S of Mount Ebal, with which it forms the sides of an important E-W pass. Shechem lies at the E entrance and modern Nablus in the narrow valley between the two mountains. Mount Gerizim stands *ca.* 2,900 feet above the Mediterranean and *ca.* 700 feet above the narrow valley between it and Mount Ebal;* it is formed of Eocene limestone, which gives it a somewhat gray and forbidding appearance on its upper slopes. From a military and commercial viewpoint it had a location of strategic importance. The only important E-W highway through the mountains of Ephraim in this region passed through the valley at its base. An important N-S highway from Jerusalem to the Galilee area crosses the other highway at the E entrance to the valley in the vicinity of Shechem. The mountains, standing like two sentinels, could be fortified and assure control of the roads in the vicinity. These factors, plus the presence of a reliable supply of water (cf. Jacob's well; John 4:6), combined to attract people to the area from a very early period. Fig. EBA 2.

Although Gerizim was very early in history a well-known religious site and remains so to the small community of Samaritans who celebrate the Passover on its summit, there are only four references to it by name in the Hebrew OT (Deut. 11:29; 27:12; Josh. 8:33; Judg. 9:7); it is referred to only as "this mountain" in the NT (John 4:20-21). In view of the fact that the area was visited by Abraham (Gen. 12:6), by Jacob (Gen. 33:18-20), and by Joshua (Josh. 8:33), a religious ceremony being reported in each case, it is surprising that Gerizim is mentioned so infrequently. The probable explanation is that its early place of importance was lost when David established the capital in Jerusalem. It has been suggested that the Judean writers and editors intentionally minimized the importance of Gerizim by failing to mention its name in connection with the patriarchs and in later history.

Moses charged the people to stand upon Mount Gerizim to pronounce the blessing (Deut. 27:12 names six tribes: Simeon, Levi, Judah, Issachar, Joseph, and Benjamin; the other six tribes were to stand opposite them on Mount Ebal for the curse). Preparation for the same ceremony is referred to in Deut. 11:29; and its completion is reported in Josh. 8:30-35, where half the people, including both sojourner and home-born, stood in front of Mount Gerizim and half of them in front of Mount Ebal, with the ark of the covenant between them. According to Josh. 8:30 (cf. Deut. 27:4, where the Samaritan Pentateuch reads "Gerizim" instead of "Ebal"), Mount Ebal, rather than Mount Gerizim, was the place where Joshua erected an altar and wrote a copy of the law on stones. Whether or not a temple was erected on either of the mountains in this early period is uncertain, although according to Samaritan tradition the sanctuary of the Lord, mentioned in connection with Joshua's final oration and covenant (Josh. 24:26), had reference to a temple on Gerizim. Except for the statement that Jotham's parable was spoken from the top of Mount Gerizim (probably from its slopes) to the men of Shechem (Judg. 9:7), a veil of silence drops over the place.

A temple was built on Gerizim by Sanballat, according to Josephus (Antiq. XI.viii.2, 4), at the time of the schism between the Jews and the Samaritans. Josephus places the event in the period of Alexander the Great; it probably should be dated more than a century earlier, in the time of Nehemiah. Josephus is also the source of the tradition that the Samaritan temple was destroyed by John Hyrcanus (Antiq.

24. Mount Gerizim, with the traditional tomb of Joseph in the foreground

XIII.ix.1; War I.ii.6). During a period of intense rivalry between the Samaritans and the Christians in the fifth and six centuries A.D. a church was constructed on Mount Gerizim by Zeno and one later by Justinian.

The archaeological picture is incomplete, although a Canaanite villa from *ca.* 1600 B.C. has been reported at the foot of the mountain, and the extensive remains on the summit are attributed to the time of Justinian.

See also EBAL, MOUNT; SAMARITANS; SHECHEM; PALESTINE, GEOGRAPHY OF.

Fig. GER 24.

Bibliography. E. Robinson, *Biblical Researches in Palestine,* II (1856), 275-80; M. Gaster, *The Samaritans, The Schweich Lectures, 1923* (1925; see Index); W. F. Albright, *Archaeology of Palestine* (1954), p. 92; D. Baly, *The Geography of the Bible* (1957), pp. 20, 178, 180.

W. L. REED

GERON gĭr′ŏn. RSV mg. translation in II Macc. 6:1. The text interprets γέροντα as "an Athenian senator," but transliteration as a personal name, Γέρων ("old man"), is possible; it appears in Greek inscriptions as a name. *See* SENATOR.

J. C. SWAIM

GERRHENIANS. *See* GERAR.

GERSHOM gûr′shəm [גרשם, גרשום, sojourner (גר) there (שם), *according to the popular etymology in* Exod. 2:22; 18:3(?); bell, *according to* Arab. *ğarasun*(?); Apoc. Γηρσών]; KJV Apoc. GERSON gûr′sŏn (I Esd. 8:29); GERSHOMITES —mīts. **1.** The elder son of Moses and Zipporah; born in Midian (Exod. 2:22; 18:3). He is named as the father of Jonathan, who officiated as priest to the Danites, as did his descendants until the Captivity (Judg. 18:30; the MT reads "Gershom, son of Manasseh"; Möhlenbrink favors "Gershom, son of Levi"; *see* the work of G. F. Moore in the *bibliography*). In ascription to David of arrangements existing in the postexilic time, fathers' houses derived from him and other sons of Moses are reckoned among the Levites in contradistinction to the Aaronites who were priests (I Chr. 23:13-16). A postexilic Levitical functionary of the house of Gershom was Shebuel, "chief officer in charge of the treasuries" (I Chr. 23:16; 26:24).

2. Same as GERSHON; a son of Levi (I Chr. 6:1, 16-17, 20, 43; 23:6-7). His descendants are called Gershomites, or the "sons of Gershom," in I Chr. 6:62, 71; 15:7.

3. A descendant of Phinehas (the priest, grandson of Aaron). He was the head of a father's house which returned with Ezra from Babylonia (Ezra 8:2; I Esd. 8:29).

Bibliography. G. F. Moore, *Judges,* ICC (1903), pp. 400-402; M. Noth, *Die israelitischen Personennamen* (1928), pp. 38, 223; K. Möhlenbrink, "Die levitischen Überlieferungen des ATs," *ZAW,* LII (1934), 223. T. M. MAUCH

GERSHON gûr'shən [גרשון, bell *according to* Arab. *ǧarasun*(?)]; GERSHONITES —shə nīts [הגרשני (Num. 3:21, 23-24; 4:24, 27-28; 26:57; Josh. 21:33; II Chr. 29:12); הגרשני, the Gershonite (I Chr. 26:21; 29:8); בני גרשון, the sons of Gershon (Num. 3:25; Josh. 21:6, 27); בני הגרשני, the sons of the Gershonites (I Chr. 26:21)]. Alternately: GERSHOM 2. One of the three sons of Levi (Exod. 6:16; Num. 3:17; I Chr. 6:1, 16, 43; 23:6), born before Jacob and his family migrated to Egypt (Gen. 46:11). Gershon had two sons, Libni (Ladan in I Chr. 23:7; 26:21) and Shimei (Exod. 6:17; Num. 3:18; I Chr. 6:17, 20).

The data concerning Gershon and those reckoned as descended from him (Gershonites) appear in P, Chronicles, and revision in P and Chronicles. The data show variations occurring in the arrangement of Levitical groups to one another and in the alignment of Levites vis-à-vis priests (*see* PRIESTS AND LEVITES). Three variations may be noted in the way the Gershonites were regarded:

a) In a tenth-century list of the allotment of Levitical cities (a list incorporated by P and expanded), the Kohathites, the Gershonites, and the Merarites were the three great groups of Levites; they are presented, not as concentrated around a sanctuary, but as separated by geographical location. Thirteen cities and their pasture lands in the extreme N and NE tribes of Palestine were assigned to the Gershonites (Josh. 21:6, 27-33; see I Chr. 6:62, 71-76).

b) Some texts in P and Chronicles indicate that the Gershonites at some time were the dominant group among the functionally interrelated Levitical groups. Gershon, Kohath, and Merari are named in that order (Gen. 46:11; Exod. 6:16; Num. 3:17; 26:57; I Chr. 6:1, 16; 23:6). Gershonites are mentioned first in a census notation (Num. 26:57) and named first in postexilic lists of singers (I Chr. 6:16-30) and Levitical functionaries in the temple (23:7-11). Significant persons and groups were reckoned in the Gershonite line: the musical guild Asaph (6:39, 43), the administrators of temple treasuries Ladan (23:7-9; 26:21) and Jehiel (29:8).

c) Some texts in P and in the revision in Chronicles show, not the Gershonites, but the Kohathites (the Levitical family to which Aaron belonged; *see* KOHATH) as the dominant Levitical group. Both the incorporated original text and the expansion in Josh. 21 list the Gershonites second and peripherally located, and the Kohathites as descendants of Aaron first and centrally located. In the wilderness encampment the location assigned the Gershonites (subdivided into the families of the Libnites and the Shimeites; Num. 3:21) was "behind the tabernacle on the west" (vs. 23); they were to care for and transport the external properties of the tabernacle (vss. 25-26; 4:24-26; 10:17); in this they were supervised by Aaron and his sons (4:27; Ithamar in vs. 28); for this task they were assigned two wagons and four oxen (7:7); they numbered 7,500 (3:22). In all these respects the Kohathites were pre-eminent. In a census of the Levites the Gershonites were numbered second (4:34-49). The Chronicler's account of the bringing of the ARK OF THE COVENANT to Jerusalem by David listed the Gershonites third and the Kohathites first, and later revision distinguished between the Aaronites and the Kohathites (I Chr. 15:4-7). The reviser in Chronicles used genealogies of Levi for the classification of the ordinary Levites but does not mention the Gershonites (ch. 24). In an account of the cleansing of the temple by Hezekiah, the Gershonites are mentioned last (II Chr. 29:12). They do not appear in accounts of temple repairs by Josiah (34:12) and a victory by Jehoshaphat (20:19).

Bibliography. M. Noth, *Die israelitischen Personennamen* (1928), pp. 38, 223; K. Möhlenbrink, "Die levitischen Überlieferungen des ATs," *ZAW,* LII (1934), 184-231; A. Welch, *The Work of the Chronicler* (1939), pp. 65 n., 82-85, 89, 95; J. Bright, Exegesis of Joshua, *IB,* II (1953), 651. T. M. MAUCH

GERSON. KJV Apoc. form of GERSHOM 3.

GERUTH CHIMHAM gĭr'o͝oth kĭm'hăm [גרות כמוהם, lodging place of Chimham] (Jer. 41:17); KJV HABITATION OF CHIMHAM. An unidentified place near Bethlehem, perhaps a khan, at which Ishmael and his fellow assassins stopped during their flight to Egypt. *See* CHIMHAM.

GESEM. KJV Apoc. form of GOSHEN 3.

GESHAN gĕsh'ən [גישן] (I Chr. 2:47); KJV GESHAM gē'shəm. Listed as a descendant of Caleb; otherwise unknown.

GESHEM gĕsh'əm [גשם, rain]. Alternately: GASHMU găsh'mū [גשמו] (Neh. 6:6 KJV; RSV mg.). An "Arab" who joined with Sanballat the Horonite and Tobiah the Ammonite in opposing the reconstruction of the walls of Jerusalem under Nehemiah. Their opposition consisted of ridicule (Neh. 2:19-20), an attempted plot to trap Nehemiah (6:1-3), and the threat to send a letter to the Persian king charging him with sedition (vss. 5-9), all of which failed. His title "the Arab" was an administrative term which indicates that he was the highest official of the province to the S of Judah, formerly Edom. Some think that he can be identified with an official of the same name on a Lihyanite Arabian inscription. Fig. KED 2.

Bibliography. F. W. Winnett, *A Study of the Lihyanite and Thamudic Inscriptions* (1937), pp. 14, 16, 50-51; H. Grimme, "Beziehungen zwischen dem Staate der Lihjān und dem Archämenidenreiche," *Orientalische Literaturzeitung,* XLIV (1941), 343. M. NEWMAN

GESHUR gĕsh′ər [גשור]; GESHURITES —ə rīts. A small kingdom located to the N of Bashan and S of Syria. It served as a buffer state between Israel and Aram. David was on friendly terms with it when he was still king of Judah only and sealed the alliance by marrying Maacah, the daughter of its king, Talmai; she became the mother of Absalom (II Sam. 3:3). The latter fled to his grandfather after the assassination of his half brother Amnon and remained three years until it was safe to return (II Sam. 13:37–14:24). Subsequently Geshur must have been a vassal state of Israel, but after the division of the kingdom it joined in alliance with Aram and raided Bashan (I Chr. 2:23). Eventually it seems to have been incorporated into the expanding kingdom of Damascus and to have shared the fate of the latter.

S. Cohen

GESHURITES gĕsh′ə rīts [גשורים]. **1.** The inhabitants of Geshur, a kingdom in the NE of Palestine (Deut. 3:14; Josh. 12:5; 13:11, 13).

2. A people dwelling in the Negeb, near the territory of the Philistines (Josh. 13:2). They are mentioned as one of the peoples against whom David made raids while he was at Ziklag (I Sam. 27:8), and they were probably wiped out as the tribes of Judah and Simeon pushed farther S in the time of the kings (cf. I Chr. 4:39-43).

S. Cohen

GESSEN gĕs′ən. Douay Version form of Goshen 3.

GESTAS gĕs′təs. A name given the unrepentant thief in the stories prompted by Luke 23:39-43. Among other forms of the name are Gistas, Gesmas, Stegmas, Dumachus. He is regularly contrasted with Dysmas.

GETHER gē′thər [גתר]. According to Gen. 10:23, one of the sons of Aram (cf. I Chr. 1:17); hence an Aramean town and kingdom.

GETHSEMANE gĕth sĕm′ə nĭ [Γεθσημανεί, *indeclinable;* Aram. גת שמני, oil vat; *a variant form,* Gesamani, Γησαμανεί, *was explained by Jerome as derived from* גיא שמני, fat valleys (Isa. 28:1), *but this form is more plausibly explained as a Greek corruption of the original name, into* γῆ σαμανεί, oil plot]. The site on the Mount of Olives where Jesus agonized in prayer before his betrayal there by Judas.

The story is told in each of the four gospels, although only Mark and Matthew report the site as Gethsemane. They speak of it as "a field" (χωρίον), and only its name, the "oil vat," suggests a grove of olive trees (Matt. 26:36; Mark 14:32). Luke calls it simply "the place," somewhere on the Mount of Olives—an accustomed region with Jesus (Luke 22:39-40). John locates it "across the winter stream [χειμάρρου] of the Kidron," and calls it a κῆπος or "garden," and from this citation alone is derived the traditional name, Garden of Gethsemane (John 18:1).

To ascertain the site of this episode seems impossible today, both because the gospels afford scant data and because the ancient olive groves were destroyed when Titus besieged Jerusalem in A.D. 70. Clearly it was not far from the city gate, and lay E of the Kidron and somewhere upon the Mount of Olives. One early tradition placed it outside the E gate and E of the valley floor (E of the modern paved road, where the Tomb of the Virgin is now located). Here as early as the fifth century a shrine was built, and the seventh-century pilgrim Arculf describes a rock here with the imprint of the knees of Jesus. On this site today the Franciscans maintain the Grotto of the Agony.

Another early identification, sometimes attributed to the fourth century, located Gethsemane higher on the slope. The Armenian, Greek, Latin (Franciscan), and Russian churches possess adjacent properties here, lying between the Russian Church of Magdalene and the Franciscan Basilica of the Agony (the Church of All Nations), both modern structures. The latter is built over fourth-century ruins, and within is a traditional Rock of the Agony. E of this church lies an olive grove walled in by the Franciscans, with gnarled trees up to nine hundred years old. An adjacent enclosure is that of the Greeks.

Courtesy of the Arab Information Center, New York

25. Within the Garden of Gethsemane, showing the ancient olive trees

From the language of John, some have deduced that Gethsemane was walled in, because Jesus "entered" and "went out"; further, that it was restricted private property whose owner granted Jesus access to it. However, the two verbs do not require or support such conjectures. Without doubt the olive grove was privately owned, for the production of oil was a chief industry. This grove may well have had its olive vat, like many another. The term "vat" does not indicate how the oil was extracted, whether by treading, pounding, pressing, or grinding, although the first of these was primitive and by the first century antiquated. Luke's reference to the "custom" of Jesus might mean no more than that each day he traveled past this grove between Jerusalem and Bethany. But the statement in John is more explicit —that Judas knew this grove from the disciples' repeatedly gathering here with Jesus. The Synoptic accounts (Matthew, Mark, and Luke) suggest that it was an extensive area within which members of the party could separate at a distance from one another.

Figs. GET 25; OLI 9; Pl. XIII*b*.

Bibliography. E. Robinson, *Biblical Researches in Palestine,* I (1867), 233-35; E. Kraeling, *Bible Atlas* (1956), p. 404.

K. W. Clark

GEUEL gū'əl [גאואל, majesty of God(?); *cf.* LXX Γουδιηλ, *probably for* גאול־אל, ransomed by God(?)] (Num. 13:15). A member of the tribe of Gad sent to spy out the land of Canaan; son of Machi.

Bibliography. M. Noth, *Die israelitischen Personennamen* (1928), p. 240.

R. F. JOHNSON

GEZER gē'zər [גזר]; KJV GAZER gā'zər in II Sam. 5:25; I Chr. 14:16. Alternately: GAZARA gə zā'rə [Γάζηρα, Γάζαρα] (I Macc. 4:15; 13:43; etc.; Jos. Antiq. XIII.ix.2; etc.); KJV GAZERA gə zē'rə in I Macc. 4:15; KJV GAZA gā'zə in I Macc. 13:43. A city in the plain of Palestine midway between Jerusalem and Joppa.

1. Name and identification. The name of Gezer can be recognized in hieroglyphic and Akkadian renderings (spelled respectively *Qdr* and *Gazri*), as well as in the Hebrew and Greek forms given above. The identity of these ancient names with that of the mound called in Arabic Tell el-Jazar (or Tell el-Jazari), near the village of Abu Shusheh, was first noted in 1871 by Clermont-Ganneau, who clinched the identification of the site in 1874 by finding the first of a series of engraved rock inscriptions, in which the words "boundary of Gezer" in Hebrew letters were combined with the Greek name Alkias. The inscriptions traced a rough arc encircling Tell el-Jazar at distances between one half and one mile on the S and E sides.

2. Exploration and history. Tell el-Jazar was partly excavated by R. A. S. Macalister on behalf of the Palestine Exploration Fund in 1902-5 and 1907-9, and again in 1934 by A. Rowe; those excavations have enabled the history of Gezer to be extended in time considerably beyond the range of literary records.

The site lay at the inner edge of the coastal plain at a spot well supplied with water from different springs, of which the nearest is 'Ain el-Yerdeh. It commanded the plain to the N and the W, where it overlooked both the coastal road approaching Lydda and Aphek (Tell Ras el-'Ain) from Gaza, and also the route which descended from Jerusalem. A watch-tower, half an hour's distance to the SE, gave the Gezerites a view of the road to Egypt for many miles southward. Gezer was settled by Lower Chalcolithic times, *ca.* 4000 B.C. The first inhabitants mostly lived in natural caves which they roughly adapted. Such caves, pitting the native limestone rock, continued to serve as dwellings or as cisterns for as long as Gezer remained an inhabited place. Subsequent domestic architecture was of the usual Palestinian village standard, using walls of small rubble with mud mortar. Three defensive walls were built at different times round the city, enclosing a narrow oblong, with two summits, lying E and W. Stratigraphic evidence is lacking for dating the defenses; but Macalister recorded some facts which prove that the second wall had already fallen into disrepair by the reign of Amen-hotep III; that wall might have been built in the Middle Bronze Age. It contained two gates, one on the N and one on the S side of the city. The latest wall, which is also the outermost, and which could be traced almost continuously round the tell, is presumably that which existed in the Maccabean Wars; it had been reinforced with towers and revetments at least twice in its history, and its first construction must go back many centuries. *See below.*

At all times of Egyptian imperial expansion Gezer was sure to attract the notice of the Pharaohs, and its first historical appearance in Egyptian monuments, a granite statuette found on the site and inscribed in hieroglyphics by one Heqab, is from not later than the Twelfth Dynasty. A fragment of an inscribed funerary statue has been attributed to the Thirteenth Dynasty. Commercial relations with Egypt under the Eighteenth and Nineteenth Dynasties are revealed by many imported objects, especially alabaster vases.

Perhaps stimulated by such contacts, Canaanite townsmen had in the meantime been working out a more convenient script than hieroglyphics for writing their own language; and a possible trace of their earliest essay has survived in a stray potsherd of the late Middle Bronze Age on which three probably alphabetic signs have been scratched in the clay before firing. Fig. GEZ 26.

Courtesy of the Harvard University Press

26. Inscribed potsherd from Gezer with early alphabetic inscription

Thut-mose III included Gezer among the captured Canaanite cities enumerated on the walls of the temple at Karnak after his Megiddo campaign (*ca.* 1468 B.C.). At least nine of the Tell el-Amarna Letters refer to Gezer, four of them written by the "Man of Gezer" himself. An obsequious servant of the king, Yapahu, writes to seek help for Gezer against the menace of the *SA-GAZ* and *Sutu*. Nevertheless, the "Handmaid of the King" was plundered and had to buy off the raiders with gifts of food and oil.

No signs of these troubles appear in the excavations, nor of Mer-ne-Ptah, the "Binder of Gezer," who boasted: "Ashkelon is taken; Gezer is captured; Yanoam is made as that which does not exist" (Israel Stela, *ca.* 1230 B.C.). Macalister, however, found an ivory pectoral engraved with Mer-ne-Ptah's cartouches and with a scene of adoration to Thoth.

The Canaanites were early concerned with safeguarding their water supply, and their most impressive monument was a rock-cut shaft and passage which descended by steps from a point in the W half of the city to a subterranean cavern containing a spring (*see* WATER WORKS). At a later date, probably, a great reservoir was excavated near the center of the city, presumably to store rain water. Neither of these works can be exactly dated; but the tunnel went out of use toward the end of the Bronze Age (1400-1200 B.C.). The reservoir might have been dug then to replace it, or possibly in the Solomonic age. It remained open long enough for the debris which filled it to contain Maccabean pottery.

Another impressive relic of Canaanite Gezer was a row of eight standing monoliths, which were found aligned N and S at a point inside the N wall of the city, about halfway along it. The tallest of the monoliths stood over ten feet high, and the shortest over five. Their majestic size and careful alignment strongly suggested a religious purpose; and Macalister found confirmation of this in the discovery of ten infant burials, in jars of Middle Bronze Age form, in the close vicinity. A massive stone pedestal socket, cup marks in the rock, a rock cavern with two interconnected chambers, two paved circular enclosures, and a cistern containing human and animal bones—all these grouped together led Macalister to interpret the assemblage as a Canaanite high place. However, since no sacrificial altar was found, no platform of offerings, and no traces of burning, the identification is open to question. W. F. Albright has suggested that the monoliths are to be explained as funeral stelae.

Mer-ne-Ptah cannot have destroyed Gezer, for the Israelites, who were active at about the same time and are mentioned in the same stela, failed to capture the town (Judg. 1:29), although they defeated and killed King Horam of Gezer (Josh. 10:33; 12: 12). In the partition of Canaan, Gezer lay on the boundary of Ephraim between Lower Beth-Horon and the sea (Josh. 16:3). Allotted to the Levitical tribe of Kohath (21:21), it remained a Canaanite city (Judg. 1:29), having presumably maintained itself equally against the Philistines, whose territory it confronted toward the S.

Pharaoh Shishak (*ca.* 945-924 B.C.) took Gezer from the Canaanites and gave it as a dowry to Solomon's Egyptian wife (I Kings 9:16). Whether the Canaanites were all evicted at that time may be doubted; but Solomon fortified the city, and it must be assumed that Israelites formed the garrison. To Solomon may probably be attributed a series of towers of mixed ashlar and rubble construction which Macalister found inserted secondarily in the outer city way. The build of these towers and the build and planning of a gateway in the S side of the same wall are closely paralleled by structures which have been discovered and ascribed to King Solomon at Megiddo and Hazor, two cities fortified by him simultaneously with Gezer (I Kings 9:15). This outer wall line was initially of poor and hasty construction. We can only guess that it was laid out at some time in the Late Bronze or Early Iron Age before Shishak's invasion.

To the earliest Israelite period belongs the "Gezer Calendar," a doggerel list of agricultural operations for twelve months, inscribed in early Hebrew characters on a clay pendant. *See* CALENDAR.

Tiglath-pileser III of Assyria left an inscribed relief in Calah showing an Assyrian army storming the town of *Gazru* (cf. II Kings 15:29; 16:7); and when Sargon destroyed the N kingdom (721 B.C.), Gezer must have passed under Assyrian control. Two clay tablets bearing contracts for land transactions in Assyrian cuneiform are relics of this period. Nothing more is heard of Gezer until the Wars of the Maccabees, when its situation within sight of Modin gave it importance to the Greeks. On two occasions (I Macc. 4:15; 7:45) it marked the end of Judas' victorious pursuit of the enemy—once in flight from Nicopolis, once from Adasa. It was fortified in 161 B.C. by Bacchides, and vexed the Jews (I Macc. 9: 50-52) until, in 143 B.C., Simon besieged and captured it (13:43-48). The town was then settled with Jews (14:34), and Simon himself built a residence there.

A barely legible graffito in Greek letters on a building stone found near the gate of the town has been read as follows: Πάμπρα(ς) Σίμωνος κατοπάζῃ πῦρ βασίλειον—a mock-epic hexameter which may be translated: "(Says) Pampras, to blazes with Simon's palace." It was at Gazara that Jonathan the son of Simon resided when his father put him in command of his forces (I Macc. 13:53). The rock-cut boundary inscriptions imply some allocation of land at about this period, Alkias being the presiding official.

Bibliography. R. A. Macalister, *The Excavation of Gezer, 1902-5 and 1907-9,* vols. I-III (1912); A. Rowe, *PEQ* (1935), pp. 19-33; Y. Yadin, *IEJ,* VIII (1958), 80-86 (on the Solomonic gate).

R. W. HAMILTON

GEZRITES. KJV form of GIRZITES.

GHOST [אוֹב (Isa. 29:4; KJV FAMILIAR SPIRIT); φάντασμα (Matt. 14:26; KJV SPIRIT)]. The apparition of a deceased person. *See* SHADES.

GHOST, HOLY. *See* HOLY SPIRIT.

GIAH gī'ə [גִּיחַ, bubble *or* burst forth as a bubbling spring(?)] (II Sam. 2:24). An unidentified site along Abner's path of flight from Gibeon toward the wilderness descent to the Arabah. The text of II Sam. 2:24 is probably corrupt; both the LXX and the Vulg. read as though based upon the Hebrew word for "ravine," and "Gibeon" can be associated with no identifiable wilderness. In place of "Gibeon," the similar "Geba" should perhaps be read, which was, indeed, on the threshold of the wilderness descent to the Jordan.

W. H. MORTON

GIANT. In common with other peoples the early Hebrews believed in a race of giants. Neither archaeology nor paleontology gives supporting evidence to the existence of a race or tribe of giant stock. Biologists accept the position that giants are deviates from the norm, as are dwarfs. Like dwarfs, giants are usually sterile.

Two circumstances undoubtedly led to belief in giants. First, the Hebrews knew of the existence of individuals of giant proportions. Several are listed in the Bible, most famous of whom is Goliath, the Philistine champion slain by David (I Sam. 17:23-

54). Note also the Philistine giants (רפא, רפה) in II Sam. 21:16-22; I Chr. 20:4, 6, 8. Job accuses God of attacking him like a "warrior" (גבור, KJV "giant"; Job 16:14). Second, the Hebrews found in Palestine many Megolithic structures for whose erection they assumed the strength of giants.

Giants had two major classifications. First, there were those thought to be the result of a union of a divine father and a human mother. Such a story appears in Gen. 6:1-4 (נפילים; RSV NEPHILIM). Second, there were human giants associated with certain tribes and nations. There is no evidence that the Hebrews believed that all giants were originally of divine-human origin. It should be observed that physical size, as well as length of years, was thought to have spiritual significance.

The KJV translates רפאים (a people inhabiting early Canaan) as "giants" in Deut. 2:11, 20; 3:11, 13; Josh. 12:4; 13:12; 17:15 (RSV REPHAIM). For the KJV "Valley of the Giants," *see* REPHAIM, VALLEY OF.

W. G. WILLIAMS

GIANTS, VALLEY OF THE. *See* REPHAIM, VALLEY OF.

GIBBAR gĭb'är [Aram. גבר, mighty man] (Ezra 2:20). The head of a family that returned to Palestine after the Exile. In the corresponding list of Nehemiah (7:25) the place name Gibeon (גבעון) appears. This and the fact that place names occur in Ezra 2:21 ff suggest that "Gibbar" might be a corruption of "Gibeon."

M. NEWMAN

GIBBETHON gĭb'ə thŏn [גבתון, mound *or* height(?)]. A town in W central Palestine assigned to the tribe of Dan (Josh. 19:44) before that tribe migrated to the N. It was also supposed to be a Levitical city of the clan of Kohath (21:23). In actual fact, it fell into the hands of the Philistines. At least two kings of Israel attempted to recapture it, but apparently without success (I Kings 15:27; 16:15, 17).

The site is tentatively identified with Tell el-Melat, a few miles W of Gezer.

Bibliography. G. von Rad, "Das Reich Israel und die Philister," *Palästinajahrbuch* (1933), pp. 30-42; W. Caspari, "Agbatana-Gibbeton," *ZDPV,* LVIII (1935), 160-84 (an exhaustive topographical study); E. G. Kraeling, *Rand-McNally Bible Atlas* (1956), pp. 272-73.

W. F. STINESPRING

GIBEA gĭb'ĭ ə [גבעא, a hill] (I Chr. 2:49). A grandson of Caleb, in the lineage of Judah. The geographical associations of Judah's descendants through Caleb, however, suggest a town in the hill country S of Hebron (cf. Josh. 15:57).

W. H. MORTON

GIBEAH gĭb'ĭ ə [גבעה, hill]; KJV GIBEATH gĭb'ĭ əth in Josh. 18:28. The Hebrew word commonly designates a hill or "height," as distinguished from a mountain. In several instances in the OT, however, it is employed as a place name.

1. A city in the hill country of Judah (Josh. 15:57; cf. I Chr. 2:49). Modern el-Jebaʿ, 7½ miles SW of Bethlehem, has been suggested as a possible identification. However, the site is listed in company with a group of cities belonging to a geographical district of Judah situated SE of Hebron. It should probably be sought, therefore, on the pastoral plateau of which Ziph, Carmel, and Maon are a part.

2. A city of Benjamin variously designated as "Gibeah, which [or 'that'] belongs to Benjamin" (Judg. 19:14; 20:4), "Gibeah of Benjamin" (Judg. 20:10; I Sam. 13:2, 15; 14:16), "Gibeah of the Benjaminites" (II Sam. 23:29; I Chr. 11:31), "Gibeah of Saul" (I Sam. 11:4; 15:34; Isa. 10:29. ["Gabath Saul" in NT times]), "Gibeath" (Josh. 18:28 KJV), and "Gibeath-elohim" (I Sam. 10:5; KJV "hill of God").

The city first enters upon the scene of Hebrew history for its inhospitable treatment of a journeying Ephraimite and the fatal ravishing of his concubine. Since both the city and the tribe identified themselves with the crime by refusing to deliver the culprits to justice, Gibeah became the focal point of Israel's punitive war against Benjamin, resulting in the destruction of the city and the near annihilation of the tribe (Judg. 19–20). Gibeah was the home of Saul (I Sam. 10:26); here he prophesied with a band of prophets, according to the prediction of Samuel, and therein received a third authenticating sign of his divine selection as the first king of Israel (vss. 1, 5, 10). It remained his home and became his provincial capital after he was acclaimed king at Mizpah (10:26; 15:34; 22:6; 23:19). As such, it played an important role in his struggles with the Philistines (13:2; 14:2, 16). Here came messengers from the beleaguered city of JABESH-GILEAD seeking aid against the oppressing Ammonites (11:4), and from here Saul issued his unique summons that Israel go to their relief (vs. 7). Here, also, he received a company of Ziphites seeking to betray the whereabouts of David (23:19; cf. 26:1). From Gibeah came three Mighty Men of David who helped him in war: Ittai son of Ribai (II Sam. 23:29; cf. I Chr. 11:31), and two sons of Shemaah, Ahiezer and Joash (I Chr. 12:2-3). From here, also, came Micaiah, mother of Abijah, king of Judah (II Chr. 13:2).

The city occupied a place of prominence in eighth-century-B.C. prophetic thinking, for Isaiah envisions it standing in the fearful path of an Assyrian advance on Jerusalem from the N (Isa. 10:29), and to Hosea its early history symbolized the continuing waywardness of Israel in his own day (Hos. 9:9; 10:9; cf. 5:8).

From the OT it is clear that Gibeah lay N of Jerusalem, between Jerusalem and Ramah, and near the main N-S road through the central hill country of Benjamin (Judg. 19:11-15; cf. Isa. 10:28-32). Josephus contributes the further knowledge that it was about thirty furlongs distant from Jerusalem (Jos. War V.ii.1). The site upon which this information comes to focus is Tell el-Ful (the "mound of beans") *ca.* 3½ miles N of Jerusalem and occupying one of the most elevated positions on the central mountain ridge. Its location commanded a fine outlook in all directions, making it an important watchtower over the hill towns of S Benjamin (cf. I Sam. 14:16).

Excavations conducted at Tell el-Ful in 1922-23 and again in 1933 by the American School of Oriental Research indicated a happy correlation between the archaeology of the site and the history of Gibeah of Saul. The first Hebrew settlement on the site, a small pleasant village of the twelfth century B.C., was found to have been destroyed by fire—possibly in the internecine struggle described in Judg. 19–20. The village which followed had a late-eleventh-century fortress of massive, rough-hewn masonry, whose surviving corner tower and casemate wall are thought to represent the citadel of Saul and to constitute the oldest datable Israelite fortification of the Early Iron Age.* This rustic "palace" of Israel's first king seems to have had a second story. The unpretentiousness of its structure and the simplicity of its furnishings, however, are suggested by the smallness of its rooms and the common quality of its artifacts. *Ca.* 1000 B.C. a second fortress of less massive masonry quickly rose on the destruction of the first, only to be abandoned after Jerusalem was made capital of the kingdom. Thereafter the site served as sentinel and outpost for Jerusalem on the N, experiencing intermittent periods of prosperity and decline. Scarcely a challenge could now be found to its identity with the Gibeah of Saul. Fig. GIB 27.

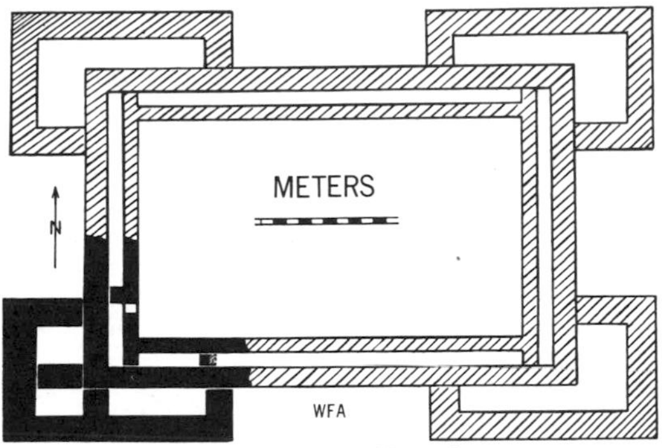

Courtesy of the American Schools of Oriental Research

27. Plan of Saul's citadel at Gibeah

3. A town in the hill country of Ephraim which had been given to Phinehas, son of Eleazar and grandson of Aaron, and which was the burial place of Eleazar (Josh. 24:33; Jos. Antiq. V.i.29). Here, too, according to an addition in the LXX, Phinehas himself was subsequently buried with his father. The OT makes no mention of the specific location of the site, and its identification remains uncertain. Eusebius perhaps offers a clue by referring to a Geba five miles N of Gophna (modern Jifna) which, in view of the similarity and frequent confusion of the names Geba and Gibeah, could possibly be identical with the town of Phinehas. Suggested modern identifications include Jibia, 4 miles NW of Jifna; Nebi Saleh, 2½ miles farther in the same direction; and et-Tell, NE of Jifna and to the S of Sinjil. Late Samaritan tradition locates the tombs of Eleazar and Phinehas at Awertah, 4 miles SE of Nablus.

4. A hill at Kiriath-jearim where the ark of the Lord was lodged in the house of Abinadab from the time of its return by the Philistines until David's first attempt to take it into Jerusalem (II Sam. 6:3-4 KJV; cf. I Sam. 7:1-2). The term should not be translated here as a place name, but, with the RSV (and I Sam. 7:1 KJV), simply "hill."

Bibliography. W. F. Albright, *AASOR,* IV (1924), 1-89; *BASOR,* 52 (1933), 6-12. C. C. McCown, *The Ladder of Progress in Palestine* (1943), pp. 205-9. W. F. Albright, *The Archaeology of Palestine* (1949), pp. 120-22. E. G. Kraeling, *Bible Atlas* (1956), pp. 143, 178. D. Baly, *The Geography of the Bible* (1957), p. 164.

W. H. MORTON

GIBEATH-ELOHIM gĭb'ĭ ăth ĕl'ō hĭm, —ĭ lō'hĭm [גבעת האלהים, hill of God; Gibeah of God] (I Sam. 10:5); KJV HILL OF GOD. A site where Saul, in accordance with the prediction of Samuel, prophesied with a band of prophets and therein experienced the third authenticating sign of his divine selection as king of Israel.

The site, called simply GIBEAH (2) in I Sam. 10:10, was distinguished as the one having both a high place and a symbol of Philistine hegemony; whether this symbol was in the nature of a garrison, a pillar, or a prefect is difficult to determine, with the last of the three possibilities perhaps to be preferred. In any case, the presence of this symbol would seem to equate Gibeath-elohim with the Gibeah of I Sam. 13:2-3 ("Geba" in vs. 3 should be "Gibeah," as in vs. 2), which is there identified as Gibeah of Benjamin—i.e., Saul's own city. The same conclusion is suggested both by the itinerary of Saul (10:2-5) and by the recognition of him among the inhabitants of the city (vss. 11-16). The site is to be located, therefore, at modern Tell el-Ful, three miles N of Jerusalem.

Bibliography. S. R. Driver, *Notes on the Hebrew Text and the Topography of the Books of Samuel* (1913), p. 80; E. G. Kraeling, *Bible Atlas* (1956), pp. 178-80.

W. H. MORTON

GIBEATH-HA-ARALOTH gĭb'ĭ ăth hā ăr'ə lŏth [גבעת הערלות, the hill of the foreskins] (Josh. 5:3); KJV HILL OF THE FORESKINS. A location in the vicinity of Gilgal, between Jericho and the Jordan, commemorating the circumcision of the Israelites following their entry into Canaan.

GIBEON gĭb'ĭ ən [גבעון, *from* גבע, hill]; GIBEONITES —ə nīts. A city of the tribe of Benjamin, now identified with the town of el-Jib, six miles NW of Jerusalem. Archaeological excavations were made at the site in 1956-57.

Fig. GIB 28.

Courtesy of Herbert G. May

28. Gibeon: the modern village (el-Jib) at the right, and the ancient tell at the left

1. Biblical history. The earliest occurrence of the name of Gibeon is in connection with the conquest of central Palestine by Joshua (Josh. 9). After the destruction of the cities of Jericho and Ai, the men of Gibeon, fearing that their town also might be attacked by Joshua, secured through a ruse a covenant of peace, which the Israelites felt obliged to keep even after the discovery of the misrepresentation of the Gibeonites. Five Amorite kings in the S, on hearing of the collaboration of the strong warriors of Gibeon with the invaders, besieged the town until

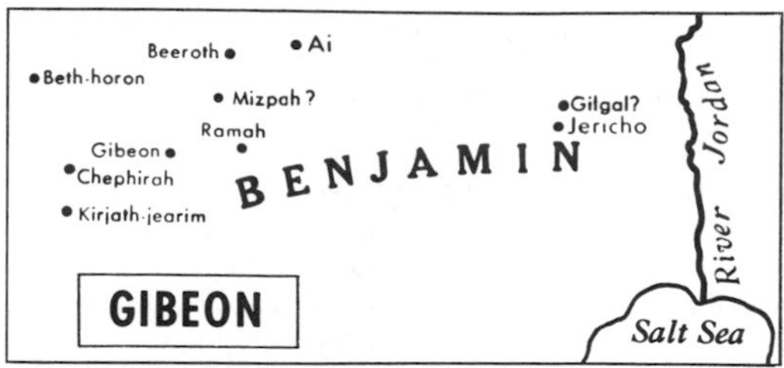

they were routed by Joshua, who in a surprise attack after an all-night march from Gilgal put to flight the Amorite confederacy (Josh. 10:1-11). This was the occasion on which the sun is said to have stood still for a day and stones from the sky to have fallen on the fleeing Amorites.

Gibeon is mentioned in Josh. 9:17 along with three other cities, Chephirah, Beeroth, and Kiriath-jearim, and its people are spoken of as Hivites in Josh. 9:7; 11:19. Mizpeh and Ramah, as well as Chephirah and Beeroth, are listed with Gibeon in Josh. 18:25-26, which consists of a list of the cities of Benjamin.

For a century and a half after the Conquest, Gibeon does not figure in events. At *ca.* 1000 B.C. the site is the setting for a spectacular contest between the forces of David and those of the rival house of Saul. David's captain Joab met with Abner, captain for Saul's son Ishbosheth, at the pool of Gibeon (II Sam. 2:12-17), where twelve men from each side transfixed their twelve opponents with swords. The place of this gruesome contest was named HELKATH-HAZZURIM, or the "field of sword-edges" (see RSV mg.). Another bloody episode, the slaughter of Amasa by Joab, is credited to have taken place at the "great stone which is in Gibeon" (II Sam. 20:8).

A tradition preserved in II Sam. 21:1-9 attributes the hanging of the seven sons of Saul to the Gibeonites; this was a privilege afforded them by David in order that they might have revenge on the house of Saul for an earlier attack which Saul is said to have made on Gibeon. At the beginning of the reign of Solomon, David's successor, Gibeon was the place of sacrifice, equipped with a great high place and an altar (I Kings 3:4), and it was here that Solomon had his famous dream (I Kings 3:4-15).

After four centuries the name of Gibeon comes to the fore in an account of the events of the year 586 B.C., in connection with the remnant from Jerusalem after the attack and destruction by Nebuchadnezzar. The false prophet Hananiah, who opposed Jeremiah, was from Gibeon (Jer. 28:1). Jer. 41:12 KJV mentions a place at the "great waters that are in Gibeon" (RSV "great pool"). The men of Gibeon were among those who helped rebuild the wall of Jerusalem in the fifth century B.C. (Neh. 3:7).

2. Extrabiblical references. In a list of the Egyptian king Sheshonk I (biblical SHISHAK), Gibeon is mentioned as one of the cities he either visited or took (*ANET* 242). According to Josephus, during October of A.D. 66 Cestius, "ascending through Beth-horon, pitched his camp at a place called Gabao [OT Gibeon], fifty furlongs distant from Jerusalem" (Jos. War II.xix.1).

3. Results of excavations. The site of el-Jib was excavated in 1956 and 1957 by the University Museum of the University of Pennsylvania and the Church Divinity School of the Pacific under the direction of J. B. Pritchard. El-Jib was suggested as the site of ancient Gibeon as early as 1838 by Edward Robinson, who saw in the Arabic *Jib* the remnant of the ancient Hebrew *Gibeon.* Although his judgment has prevailed generally since, it has been challenged by A. Alt (*see bibliography*) and others.

The hill on which el-Jib stands rises some two hundred feet above the plain and is watered by eight springs which flow from the base. One of these is the spring of the village, the principal water supply today. Leading up from the spring into the hill is a rock-cut tunnel which was partly entered as early as 1889. The area of the top of the south hill, the site of the ancient settlement, is approximately sixteen acres.

a. Periods of occupation. As a result of soundings made to bedrock on three different areas of the site, the occupational history of el-Jib was tentatively established. The earliest settlement was in the Early Bronze Period (*ca.* 2800 B.C.), from which there was abundant evidence of pottery jars and brick walls. In the Middle Bronze Period (*ca.* 1800 B.C.) the NW portion of the tell was inhabited. At the time of the Hebrew monarchy (Iron I Period) buildings covered the NW part of the mound. The major and most extensive settlement appears to have been during the Iron II Period (900-600 B.C.), when a city wall *ca.* ten feet thick, enlarged to a width of twenty-six feet in places, surrounded the entire area of the top of the hill. In the first century B.C. (a stratum dated by coins from the time of Alexander Janneus) there was an extensive settlement, evidenced by houses and plastered, stepped cisterns.

b. Water system. At the N side of the site was a round, rock-cut pool, which measured thirty-seven feet in diameter.* It was equipped with a circular stairway which leads downward around the edge of the pool. Seventy-nine rock-cut steps were uncovered. The pool is eighty-two feet deep. This pool

Courtesy of James B. Pritchard

29. The pool at Gibeon, showing part of the seventy-nine rock-cut steps

may well have been the distinguishing mark, the "pool of Gibeon," * mentioned in II Sam. 2:13. A tunnel, which extends from inside the Iron II Age city wall for a distance of 167 feet through solid rock to the spring of the village below, was used as a means of reaching the vital water supply of the city when it was under siege by an enemy. This tunnel, with its ninety-three steps, is similar in purpose to those found in Jerusalem, Gezer, Megiddo, and Ibleam. *See* WATER WORKS. Figs. WAT 8; GIB 29; STA 77.

c. Identification. In the debris which had washed down into the rock-cut pool from the hill to the S there were found fifty-six jar handles, many of them inscribed with the name Gibeon.* In addition to *gb'n,* there appeared the word *gdr,* possibly "the walled vineyard of," and the names Hananiah, Azariah, and Amariah. The finding of the name Gibeon at a site which, because of the Arabic name of the present-day settlement and the general geographical situation, had long been thought to be Gibeon, seems to make certain the identification. Fig. GIB 30.

Courtesy of James B. Pritchard

30. Jar handle with inscription *gb'n* (Gibeon) *gdr,* found in the debris of the "pool" at Gibeon

Courtesy of James B. Pritchard

31. Entrances to wine vats (x) at Gibeon (*ca.* 900-600 B.C.)

d. Winery. The excavations of 1959 and 1960 have disclosed sixty-six bell-shaped vats, cut from the solid rock of the hill, which had been used in the Iron II period as wine cellars. Fermenting vats, wine presses, and channels were found cut in the rock of the winery area. After the wine was pressed from the grapes, it was placed in large jars and lowered into the cellars, where a constant temperature of 65° could be maintained. Fig. GIB 31.

e. Necropolis. Twelve shaft tombs were discovered on the W side of the hill during the 1960 season. Although the tombs had been cut during the Middle Bronze period, two of them had been reused in the Late Bronze period. The pottery from these two Late Bronze tombs provides the first evidence for occupation of Gibeon during the period immediately before the time of Joshua.

Bibliography. A. Alt, *ZDPV,* LXIX (1953), 1 ff. *ILN* (Oct. 27, 1956), pp. 695-97. J. B. Pritchard, "The Water System at Gibeon," *BA,* XIX (Dec., 1956), 66-75; "Discovery of the Biblical Gibeon," *Bulletin of the University Museum* (Mar., 1957). *ILN* (Mar. 29, 1958), pp. 505-7; (Sept. 10, 1960), pp. 433-35; (Sept. 24, 1960), pp. 518-19. J. B. Pritchard, *Hebrew Inscriptions and Stamps from Gibeon, University Museum Monographs* (1959). J. B. PRITCHARD

GIBLITES. KJV form of GEBALITES. *See* GEBAL.

GIDDALTI gĭ dăl'tī [גִּדַּלְתִּי, *see below*] (I Chr. 25:4, 29). A son of Heman; one of those designated by King David to prophesy with music in the sanctuary. By itself the name would appear to mean "I have magnified [God]," but the name is part of a list that has long been recognized as a liturgical prayer in its origin.

Bibliography. For various interpretations of the name list in I Chr. 25:4, see W. R. Smith, *The OT in the Jewish Church* (rev. ed., 1892), p. 143; E. L. Curtis, *Chronicles,* ICC (1910), p. 278; W. A. L. Elmslie, I Chronicles, *IB,* III (1954), 426. Cf. R. Kittel, ed., *Biblia Hebraica.* B. T. DAHLBERG

GIDDEL gĭd'əl [גִּדֵּל, *perhaps for* גִּדּוֹל, big; *see bibliography;* Ἰσδαήλ]; KJV Apoc. ISDAEL ĭz'dĭ əl. **1.** Ancestor of one of the families of temple servants among the returned exiles (Ezra 2:47; Neh. 7:49). The name is lacking in I Esd. 5:30, where CATHUA stands in its stead.

2. Ancestor of one of the families of the "sons of Solomon's servants" among the returned exiles (Ezra 2:56; Neh. 7:58; I Esd. 5:33).

Bibliography. R. A. Bowman, Exegesis of Ezra, *IB,* III (1954), 584-85. B. T. DAHLBERG

GIDEON gĭd'ĭ ən [גִּדְעוֹן, hewer, slasher, (one who) cuts off (the hand); Γεδεών (Heb. 11:32; Jth. 8:1; KJV GEDEON)]; also JERUBBAAL. Son of Joash of the clan of Abiezer of the tribe of Manasseh; one of the chief "judges"—although the term "judge" is not specifically used of him—he was distinguished by unusual signs from Yahweh and by his completely delivering Israel from annual Midianite raids (Judg. 6:11–8:35).

The circumstances calling forth Gideon's heroic adventures were the regular forays of Bedouin bands from across the Jordan at harvesttime, seizing the hard-earned products of the W Jordan Israelites' labor (Judg. 6:2-6). Before these invaders, whose coming was like a plague of locusts (6:5; 7:12)—a stock Near Eastern simile for "overwhelming multitudes"—the harassed farmers fled into caves and mountain hideouts. The desperate situation was illustrated by Gideon's threshing his wheat, not as customarily with oxen on an open hilltop, but by hand in the cramped quarters and secrecy of a wine press (Judg. 6:11).

This perennial problem of the settled farmer adjacent to the desert was made in this case peculiarly terrifying because these were the first raids of camel riders known to Near Eastern history. By the use of camels the Midianite raiders could come from their home two hundred miles away to the SE and return again unscathed (*see* MIDIAN). Apparently they crossed the Jordan to harass both the region of the Valley of Jezreel, where at the edge of the territory of Manasseh Gideon's community of OPHRAH was probably located, and, farther S, the territory of Ephraim opposite the mouth of the River Jabbok. But while Manasseh and Ephraim were thus the tribes directly involved, the Midianites are said to have penetrated even to the southernmost coastal city of Gaza. Gideon's ridding the land of these invaders may be associated with the war with Midian in perhaps the second quarter of the eleventh century B.C., fought by Edomite King HADAD (Gen. 36:35).

The story of Gideon is clearly a composite of at least two sources, the earlier of which may have been an extension of the J source of the Hexateuch, and the later an extension of E, although there is no scholarly agreement on the details of their literary analysis.

The call of Gideon to his task came when, according to the earlier narrative in perhaps its original form (Judg. 6:11-24), like Abraham (Gen. 18) he entertained God or his angel unawares. Gideon's mood changed when the huge meal became a sacrifice, as the messenger who had sat under the sacred tree suddenly brought divine fire from the rock (cf. Elijah in I Kings 18). Unlike the similar story of an angelic appearance to the parents of SAMSON (Judg. 13), this narrative accounts for the name of a commemorative altar promising welfare: "Yahweh (is) peace," still standing in the writer's day and regarded as belonging to Gideon's community and his clan.

In the second, and probably later, story of Gideon's call (6:25-32, 36-40) his loyalty to Yahweh was shown by his breaking down his family's and community's Baal altar and its sacred pole or ASHERAH and thus receiving the name Jerubbaal; and his call was verified by the sign of the wet and dry fleece. The name JERUBBAAL and its relation to Gideon have received divergent interpretations:

a) The name came from the earlier period of cultural syncretism when "baal," meaning "lord" or "master," was a title given to Yahweh. Therefore Jerubbaal was the name given Gideon at birth by his father, himself a Yahweh-worshiper as indicated by his own name, JOASH (*cf.* ISHBAAL; MERIBAAL). The name Gideon was perhaps an honorific title meaning "hewer" or "grim warrior." The view that Jerubbaal was Gideon's real name may be corroborated by the fact that it, not Gideon, is used in the later story of his son Abimelech (Judg. 9:1-2, 5, 16, 19, 24, 28, 57). In the genealogy of the apocryphal heroine Judith, whose husband is named Manasseh, she is the seventh-generation descendant from a Gideon, son of Raphaim and grandson of Elijah, of the line of Israel (Jth. 8:1). Since this genealogy is probably fictitious (and Gideon is omitted in Codex Vaticanus), it throws light only on the tenacity of the name Gideon in tradition.

b) Jerubbaal and Gideon were actually two different heroes, their identification being the deliberate purpose of this narrative (6:25-32). This view is somewhat supported by the fact that the two names are independently used successively in 8:29-30, 32, and that in 7:1; 8:35 the editor finds it necessary to explain that Jerubbaal is Gideon.

c) Whatever the validity of either of the above two views, the point of the story is the reality of the conflict between Yahwism and Baalism. The clever answer of Gideon's father—that if Baal were really a god, he could fight his own battles—suggested the popular meaning for the name Jerubbaal: "Let Baal contend against him." For the root meaning of the name, *see* JERUBBAAL.

Gideon's sign of the fleece remaining dry while the hard threshing floor was wet—the more miraculous of the alternatives—is a test which may be compared with the cloth vanishing and reappearing at the word of Marduk in Tablet IV, lines 20-28, of the Babylonian Epic of Creation.

The story of Gideon's rout of the Midianite camp by a surprise attack just after the change of the guard at perhaps 10 P.M. is apparently a composite of both early and late narratives whose intertwined details can now scarcely be unraveled (7:1-23). Apparently in the early story the Midianites were aroused to self-slaughter by the sudden torchlight and the sounds of breaking pitchers and shouts of victory. In the later account the fear already in the Midianites' hearts, as revealed in the dream overheard by Gideon and his servant, turned to panic at the sound of trumpets and the sight of flashing swords.

That Gideon's own Abiezrite clansmen, some three hundred in number, were the fighting force both here and in the E Jordan pursuit (8:4) is emphasized to show the marvelous deeds of God-empowered men. Explanations of the water-drinking test by which the three hundred were selected have varied from that of God's deliberately choosing the least fit, suggested by Josephus, to its having no meaning or some veiled reference to the tribe of Caleb, "doglike." Perhaps the essential point was the attitude of alertness; at least the question of psychological fitness for battle had lain back of previously excusing the 22,000. The excellence of Gideon's strategy in planning, reconnaisance, timing, and use of personnel has been praised by military tacticians.

Stung by their defeat at the foot of Mount Gilboa at the edge of the Plain of Jezreel (6:33; 7:1), the Midianite fugitives headed for the highlands beyond the Jordan. Two traditions record Gideon's pursuit. According to the earlier (8:4-27), with his 300, although failing to get help from E Jordan kinsmen, Gideon valiantly pursued the 15,000 survivors of the one-time 135,000 Midianite raiders to their camp at Karkor many miles E of the Dead Sea, captured and later killed their two kings Zebah and Zalmunna, and out of the jewelry these raiders and their camels were wearing he made an EPHOD, perhaps an image overlaid with gold, as permanent memorial for his community. For further interpretation of this story, *see* ZEBAH AND ZALMUNNA.

According to the probably later account of the outcome (7:24–8:3), the leaders of the Midianite fugitives were not two kings, Zebah and Zalmunna, but two princes, Oreb ("Raven") and Zeeb ("Wolf"; *see* OREB AND ZEEB). These two princes, apparently bearing the names of their totem animals, fled, not E across the Jordan, but S into Ephraimite territory, where, at sites known to the writer as commemorating the deed, they were beheaded by the Ephraimites. Jealous of their prerogatives as proud masters of central Palestine, the Ephraimites were incensed at not having been called into the fray sooner than simply guarding the Jordan River fords against fleeing Midianites (cf. their attitude toward JEPHTHAH in Judg. 12:1). Gideon appeased them by praise and clever quotation of an old proverb modestly disparaging his own clan's significance (8:2). *See also* HAROD; MOREH 2; BETH-SHITTAH; ZERERAH; ABEL-MEHOLAH; TABBATH; BETH-BARAH; SUCCOTH 1; PENUEL 3; NOBAH 2; JOGBEHAH; TABOR.

Historically very significant was Gideon's ridding the Israelites, apparently permanently, of the Midianite camel raids. In fact, the "day of Midian" became a phrase designating true Israelite victory (Isa. 9:4—H 9:3; cf. Ps. 83:11—H 83:12; Isa. 10:26).

Politically and religiously significant was Gideon's refusal to inaugurate a hereditary monarchy (Judg. 8:22-23). Although he was wealthy enough to have a large harem and was doubtless a local potentate over his own clan, he refused the offer of kingship made by the people to their hero in the true Hebrew tradition of primitive popular democracy. Not only would he not be king over tribes, but at his death his own authority over his clan would be dissipated among his numerous sons. This was the complaint of his half-Canaanite son Abimelech which persuaded the citizens of Shechem to refuse to "deal well with Jerubbaal and his house." The language of Gideon's refusal—Israel is a theocracy; God alone is ruler—is that of the eighth-century or later antimonarchic strand in I Samuel, inspired perhaps by Hosea (cf. I Sam. 8:7; 10:19; 12:12; Hos. 9:9; 10:9; 13:10); but its reflection of Gideon's own self-effacing position is genuine. For further discussion of the role of kingship in this period, *see* ABIMELECH; JOTHAM.

Religiously significant was the charismatic nature of Gideon's judgeship. In the quaint language of Judg. 6:34: "The Spirit of the LORD clothed itself with [RSV 'took possession of'] Gideon." He was peculiarly Yahweh's man, favored with special divine revelations and unusual power; hence his success against impossible odds—300 against 135,000! According probably to the Deuteronomic editor of the Gideon stories, during his own day Gideon gave the land rest for a full generation. It was only after his death that his ephod, a true Yahweh symbol for him, "became a snare"—probably a religious explanation of Abimelech's unfortunate career—and the people "made Baal-berith their god" and "did not show kindness to [Gideon's] family."

Thus in unchronological order Gideon appears as the first of the heroes of faith whom the author of the Letter to the Hebrews would have told about if time had permitted his going on to discuss the conquest of Palestine (Heb. 11:32).

Bibliography. L. Desnoyers, *Histoire du peuple hébreu* (1922), I, 153-71; S. Tolkowsky, "Gideon's 300," *JPOS,* V (1925), 69-74; M. Noth, *Die israelitischen Personennamen* (1928), pp. 227-28; J. Garstang, *The Foundations of Bible History: Joshua, Judges* (1931), pp. 316-25; W. A. Irwin, *The OT: Keystone of Human Culture* (1952), pp. 212-15; F. Zimmermann, "Reconstructions in Judg. 7:25–8:25," *JBL,* LXXI (1952), 111-14; A. Malamat, "The War of Gideon and Midian: A Military Approach," *PEQ* (1953), pp. 61-65; E. Kutsch, "Gideons Berufung und Altarbau Jdc 6:11-24," *TLZ,* LXXXI (1956), 75-84; C. A. Simpson, *Composition of the Book of Judges* (1957), pp. 25-44, 96-99, 106-11, 125-28, 141-44, 147; C. F. Whitley, "The Sources of the Gideon Stories," *Vetus Testamentum,* VII (1957), 157-64.

C. F. KRAFT

GIDEONI gĭd'ĭ ō'nī [גדעוני, feller (of trees), *or* with wounded hand(?)]. The father of Abidan, who was the leader of Benjamin in the wilderness (Num. 1:11; 2:22; 7:60, 65; 10:24).

Bibliography. M. Noth, *Die israelitischen Personennamen* (1928), pp. 227-28.

R. F. JOHNSON

GIDOM gī'dəm [גדעם, a cutting off, desolation] (Judg. 20:45). A site in Benjamin, near the Rock Rimmon in the wilderness E of Gibeah, which marks the terminus of Israel's pursuit of Benjamin in the decisive engagement of their civil war.

GIER EAGLE jĭr ē'gəl. KJV translation of רחם (Lev. 11:18; RSV VULTURE) and רחמה (Deut. 14:17; RSV CARRION VULTURE).

GIEZI gī ē'zī. Douay Version form of GEHAZI.

GIFT, GIVING [נתן, מתן, מנחה, תרומה; δίδωμι, δόμα, δόσις; δωρέω, δῶρον, δώρημα; χάρισμα]. There are three types of gifts in the Bible.

1. From men to men. A "gift" may be a euphemism for "tribute," as in Judg. 3:15 ff; II Sam. 8:2, 6 (מנחה); II Kings 18:31 = Isa. 36:16 (ברכה, "blessing"); for "bribes," as in Prov. 18:16 (מתן); or for "extortion," as in Prov. 29:4 (תרומה). Some gifts from men to men are also gifts from God, like the "spiritual gift" which Paul desired to impart to the Roman Christians (Rom. 1:11), or to God, like the gift which the Philippian Christians sent to Paul, a "sacrifice acceptable and pleasing to God" (Phil. 4:18).

2. From God to men. "Every good endowment [δόσις] and every perfect gift [δώρημα] is from above" (Jas. 1:17)—this sentence incorporates an almost complete hexameter verse. God's crowning gift to men is his Son (John 3:16; Rom. 8:32; II Cor. 9:15). Among things called "gifts of God" are the satisfaction gained from honest labor (Eccl. 3:13; 5:19), salvation (Rom. 5:15, 17; Eph. 2:8), eternal life (John 4:10; Rom. 6:23), and the Holy Spirit (Acts 2:38; 8:20; 10:45; 11:17; cf. also Matt. 7:11 = Luke 11:13). In Eph. 4:8, "He gave gifts [δόματα] to men" is a quotation from Ps. 68:18 in a version conforming neither to the MT nor to the LXX (which speak of "receiving gifts among men") but to one represented in the Syr. and the Targ., followed here for its suitability to the picture of the triumphant Christ bestowing largess on his people in the form of SPIRITUAL GIFTS.

3. From men to God. Various sacrificial offerings are called "gifts" (e.g., Matt. 5:23-24, on offering one's gift at the altar; cf. Matt. 23:18-19). The gift to be presented by the healed leper in Matt. 8:4 (cf. Mark 1:44) is prescribed in Lev. 14:10 ff. The gifts of Luke 21:1-4 are freewill offerings for the temple treasury. The "offerings" (ἀναθήματα) of vs. 5 are votive. Abel's "gifts" (Heb. 11:4) were his offering (מנחה) of Gen. 4:4 (cf. Heb. 5:1; 8:3-4; 9:9).

For the gift of Matt. 15:5 = Mark 7:11, *see* CORBAN. *See also* SACRIFICE AND OFFERINGS. F. F. BRUCE

GIFTS, SPIRITUAL. *See* SPIRITUAL GIFTS.

GIHON (RIVER) gī'hŏn [גיחון]. One of the four rivers of Paradise (Gen. 2:13). *See* EDEN.

GIHON (SPRING) [גיחון, גחון, *from* גיח, to gush forth]. A spring in the Kidron (*see* KIDRON, BROOK), beneath the City of David. Its identification with the spring of Umm ed-daradj, inappropriately called Fountain of the Virgin, is certain. It is mentioned in connection with the anointing of Solomon (I Kings 1:33, 38, 45) and with Hezekiah's program of defense, when he diverted its waters to the W side of the City of David (II Chr. 32:30). Manasseh, Hezekiah's successor, completed the fortifications of the city by building an outer wall W of Gihon—i.e., between the former outlet of the spring and the rampart on the crest of the hill (II Chr. 33:14).

The spring gushes forth intermittently from a natural cave, once or twice a day at the end of the dry season, four to five times a day after a rainy winter. The etymology of "Gihon" may refer to this phenomenon. The pre-Israelite inhabitants of Jerusalem had dug an underground passage which permitted them to draw the water of Gihon without being exposed to an eventual enemy in case of a siege (*see* WATERWORKS). After the conquest by David, this passage went out of use, and the water was collected in a reservoir, from which an aqueduct with lateral openings ensured a more efficient irrigation of the valley. The surplus flowed into a second pool toward the junction of the Tyropoeon with the Kidron. The Assyrian threat prompted Hezekiah to block the spring and the aqueduct, and to make a tunnel which branched off from the cave and led the water to new reservoirs in the Tyropoeon, within the fortified perimeter of the city (*see* POOL; SHELAH, POOL OF; SILOAM). Whereas the tunnel is still in use, the gradual filling of the Kidron Valley has altered the surroundings of the spring, which is now reached from outside by two successive flights of steps. *See* map under SILOAM. *See also* JERUSALEM § 6*c*.

Fig. GIH 32.

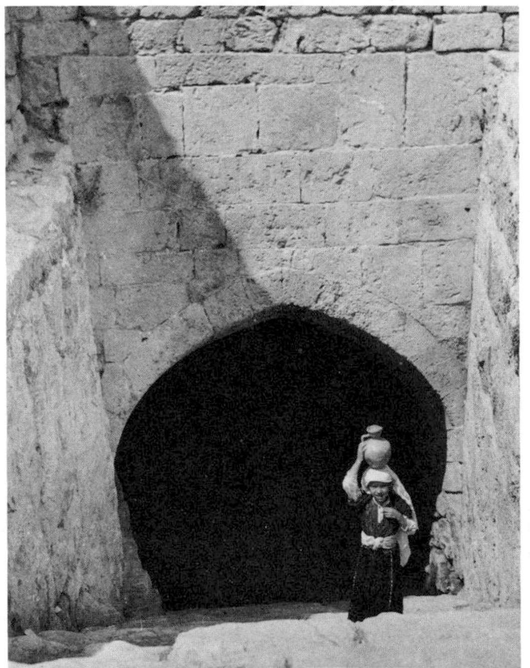

32. The Spring Gihon in the Kidron Valley

Bibliography. G. A. Smith, *Jerusalem,* I (1907), 87-91; H. Vincent, *Jérusalem Antique* (1912), pp. 135-36; G. Dalman, *Jerusalem und sein Gelände* (1930), pp. 168-73; J. Simons, *Jerusalem in the OT* (1952), pp. 163-64; H. Vincent, *Jérusalem de l'Ancien Testament,* I (1954), 260-64. G. A. BARROIS

GILALAI gĭ lā'lī [גללי] (Neh. 12:36). A musician who took part in the great procession at the dedication of the rebuilt wall of Jerusalem in the sixth century B.C.

GILBOA, MOUNT gĭl bō'ə [גלבע]. Modern Jebel Fuquʻah, a ridge of limestone hills reaching an elevation of 1,737 feet above the Mediterranean and located S of the Hill of Moreh at the E end of the Valley of Jezreel *ca.* six miles W of Beth-shean. The name of the modern village of Jelbun on the S slope preserves the ancient name.

Gilboa is best known as the place where Saul was slain in a battle with the Philistines. Because of its location near one of the two valleys leading into the Plain of Jezreel from the Jordan Valley, it was frequently the scene of military strife. Although not mentioned by name, it was probably the place of Gideon's camp when the Midianites were located on the N side of the valley (Judg. 7:1).

In I Sam. 28:4; II Sam. 21:12, "Gilboa" appears without the word "mount"; this may indicate that there was a village nearby from which the mountain took its name.

In choosing to defend Gilboa against the Philistines, Saul was taking advantage of the heights offered by the mountain where the superior equipment of the enemy would be less effective. Saul and his sons, including Jonathan, were slain on Mount Gilboa (I Sam. 31:1, 8). One tradition credits a young Amalekite with having been at the scene of battle and having killed the wounded Saul (II Sam. 1:6, 8).

The famous lament of David over Saul and Jonathan seems to contain a curse on the scene of their death:

> Ye mountains of Gilboa,
> let there be no dew or rain upon you,
> nor upsurging of the deep!
> (II Sam. 1:21).

The poetic parallelism of the verse and a similar

Courtesy of the Israel Office of Information, New York

33. The Valley of Jezreel, with Mount Gilboa in the background

phrase found in one of the Ras Shamra Tablets (*The Tale of Aqhat* C, i, 47) favor the RSV emendation "upsurging of the deep" for the MT "fields of offering."

Fig. GIL 33. W. L. REED

GILEAD gĭl'ĭ əd [גִּלְעָד, monument of stones(?)]; GILEADITES —ə dīts. **1.** Son of Machir and grandson of Manasseh; eponym of the tribe or territory of Gilead (Num. 26:29-30; 27:1; 36:1; Josh. 17:1, 3; Judg. 5:17; I Chr. 2:21, 23; 7:14, 17). It is often difficult to tell whether a given occurrence of the name refers to a person, a tribe, or a place. In 2 and 3 below it is probably actually this eponym which is being used. *See* 4 *below*.

2. The father of Jephthah (Judg. 11:1-2). *See* 1 *above*.

3. A clan or family of the territory of Gad (I Chr. 5:14), in Gilead. *See* 1 *above*. H. H. GUTHRIE, JR.

4. The name of a territory, a tribe, and possibly a city situated in the region to the E of the Jordan. The name is explained in the Bible as coming from GALEED, but this is folk etymology, and the true meaning of "Gilead" is probably "rugged country," in contrast to the fertile plain of Bashan, adjacent to it.

Gilead is mentioned as a "city of evildoers" (Hos. 6:8); but as the prophets and poets occasionally shortened names for the sake of rhythm (cf. Shittim for Abel-shittim in Mic. 6:5), it may stand for such a city as Jabesh-gilead or Ramoth-gilead. The same may be the case in Judg. 10:17, for elsewhere in the same story "Gilead" is always used in a wider significance. In the Song of Deborah (Judg. 5:17), however, Gilead is evidently a tribe, parallel to Reuben and Dan and equivalent to Gad. Elsewhere in the Bible and the Apoc. (which has the Greek form Galaad), Gilead is always used for a stretch of territory, and its inhabitants, which may be of more than one tribe, as Gileadites.

a. Description. The term "Gilead" is used somewhat loosely in the Bible. In its narrowest sense it refers to the area bounded by the Arnon on the S, the Jordan Valley on the W, the S-N part of the Jabbok and the desert to the E, and the limit of Bashan, a few miles S of the Yarmuk, on the N. In a broader sense, it extended farther N into Bashan and even beyond the Yarmuk. As a result of this vagueness the territory of Manasseh is sometimes mentioned as overlapping into Gilead, and in others it is only the tribes of Reuben and Gad who were settled there. The principal cities of the area were Ramoth-gilead, Jabesh-gilead, Mahanaim, Mizpah, and Succoth, and the later Greek cities of Pella and Gerasa.

Gilead is in general a highland region, rising from the valley of the Jordan, at least 700 feet below sea level, to heights of more than 3,300 feet, which are intersected by valleys and particularly by the river Jabbok (Nahr ez-Zerqa), which flows from E to W across its entire width. There is no single "Mount Gilead," as one might suppose from the KJV translation of the Hebrew הר הגלעד (Gen. 31:21, 23, 25; the occurrence in the MT of Judg. 7:3 is a textual error); the RSV rendering "hill country" is more exact. These hills and valleys were well watered, making the region a well-forested one, with good facilities for growing grapes and olives, while the "balm of Gilead" was proverbial (Jer. 8:22; 46:11).

b. History. The N part of Gilead, like Bashan, had a permanent settlement from the twenty-third century B.C.; but the S part, below the Jabbok, had the same period of relative lack of population from the twentieth to the thirteenth century as is found in the regions to the S. Not long before the entrance of the Israelites it was occupied by the Amorites and the Moabites; and Sihon, the Amorite king, extended his sway over Moabite territory as far S as the river Arnon. The Israelites under Moses dispossessed the Amorites, and the region was given to the E tribes of Reuben, Gad, and Manasseh (Num. 21). After the conquest of Canaan, the tribes E of the Jordan remained in comparative security and even refused to come to the help of their compatriots in the W who fought against Sisera (Judg. 5:16-17). Soon, however, they in turn were assailed by enemies from the E. The Midianites, with their Amalekite allies, overran the entire country; and it was only by the martial progress of Gideon, from W Manasseh, that the invaders were driven back (Judg. 6–7). About half a century later, the Ammonites took possession of the area, and the elders of Gilead had to summon Jephthah from his banishment to deliver them from this oppressive rule (Judg. 10–11).

Despite the victory of Jephthah, the Ammonites remained a constant menace. The first exploit of Saul after he was made king was to rescue the city of JABESH-GILEAD from Nahash, king of the Ammonites (I Sam. 11); this brought Gilead a measure of security, so that, after Saul was decisively defeated and slain by the Philistines, Abner could set up a kingdom for Ishbaal in Gilead (II Sam. 2:8-9), from which, as the Philistines withdrew from the territories that they occupied, he could extend his reign over the greater part of Palestine. David, who succeeded to the kingdom, had to fight once more against the Ammonites (II Sam. 8:12; 10:1-17); Gilead again became a place of refuge for him when he was fleeing from the rebellion of Absalom, and it was in Gilead that the decisive battle was fought that restored him to the throne (II Sam. 15–19).

During the ninth and eighth centuries B.C. a new menace arose in the Syrian (Aramean) kingdom of Damascus, which "threshed Gilead with threshing sledges of iron" (Amos 1:3). The territory became the scene of battles in which first Syria and then Israel prevailed. Ramoth-gilead was fiercely contested for; under the dynasty of Jehu the entire region was overrun by the Syrians and later recovered by Jehoash and Jeroboam II. As a result of this devastation and because of the rising power of Assyria, a faction seems to have arisen in Gilead which preferred an alliance with Syria to fight against the empire of the E. Shallum, the son of Jabesh (i.e., an inhabitant of Jabesh-gilead), overthrew the dynasty of Jehu, but after a month was in turn slain by the pro-Assyrian Menahem (II Kings 15:10-14). A more serious contender was Pekah, the son of Remaliah. The twenty years assigned to his reign (II Kings 15:27) cannot be fitted in any chronological scheme and can only be explained by the supposition that as early as *ca.* 750 B.C., in the latter part of the reign of Jeroboam II, he set up an independent kingdom in Gilead, where he ruled until 735, when he killed his predecessor with the aid of his Gileadites (II Kings 15:25) and attempted to unite all the surrounding regions against Assyria. The result was that the Assyrians carried away all the Israelite population of Gilead (II Kings 15:29) and that from that time on it was no longer part of the kingdom. During the postexilic period there were so few Jews in Gilead that Judas Maccabeus had to rescue them from the attacks of the Greeks and the Ammonites (I Macc. 5:9-54).

For the subsequent history of the region, *see* PERAEA.

Bibliography. D. Baly, *Geography of the Bible* (1957), pp. 226-31; N. Glueck, "Exploration in Eastern Palestine, III, IV," *AASOR*, XVIII-XIX (1939), XXV-XXVIII (1951).

S. COHEN

GILEAD, BALM OF. An aromatic resin reputed in antiquity for its medicinal properties. It probably received its name by being exported from Gilead to Egypt and Phoenicia (Gen. 37:25; Ezek. 27:17), since it is not native to Gilead. An antiseptic, counterirritant, and general medicament, it is variously identified with *Balsamodendron opobalsamum, Pistacia lentiscus,* and *Balanites aegyptiaca(l)* Delile. *See* BALM.

R. K. HARRISON

GILGAL gĭl′găl [גלגל; Γαλγαλ (*singular*), Γαλγαλα (*plural*)]. The word means "circle of stones"; such "circles" are still to be found in E Palestine. The name was applied to many towns, but always with the article (הגלגל) except in Josh. 5:9; 12:23. At least three such localities may be recognized in the OT.

1. Gilgal near Jericho (Josh. 4:19-20; 5:9-10; 9:6; 10:6-7, 9, 15, 43; 14:6; Judg. 2:1; 3:19; I Sam. 7:16; 10:8; 11:14-15; 13:4, 7-8, 12, 15; 15:12, 21, 33; II Sam. 19:15, 40—H 19:16, 41; Hos. 4:15; 9:15; 12:11—H 12:12; Amos 4:4; 5:5; Mic. 6:5). This was a city of the tribe of Benjamin, of special importance in the period of the Conquest and the Early Monarchy as a political, military, and religious center.

The chief contender for the locale of Gilgal has been Khirbet en-Nitleh, *ca.* 2 1/3 miles to the E of modern Jericho. The identification has been supported by the majority of scholars. The terrain about the famous tamarisk, Shejeret en-Nitleh, is strewn with Byzantine remains, and some have therefore concluded that Byzantine Galgala may have been located there. More recently, especially since 1931, Khirbet Mefjir, a mound *ca.* 1 1/4 miles from ancient Jericho (Tell es-Sultan) and bearing the magnificent remains of the palace of the Umayyad caliph Hisham (A.D. 724-43), has received the support of some scholars. The clearest topographical reference in the OT is Josh. 4:19, where Gilgal is said to be "on the east border of Jericho" (בקצה מזרח יריחו). Josephus (Antiq. V.vi.4) gives the distance from the place where the Israelites crossed the Jordan to Gilgal as 50 stadia (5 8/10 miles) and from Gilgal to Jericho as 10 stadia. In the *Onomasticon* Eusebius locates Gilgal "at about the second milestone from Jericho." These measurements suit Khirbet Mefjir much more precisely than Khirbet en-Nitleh. Moreover, an examination of the records of pilgrims supports this conclusion. A small sounding in the spring of 1954 in the region immediately to the N of Khirbet Mefjir unearthed remains from the Early Iron and Middle Iron periods (*ca.* 1200-600 B.C.); this is also the period of Gilgal's *floruit.* It seems probable, therefore, that Gilgal lay in this region.

The first encampment after the crossing of the Jordan was at Gilgal (Josh. 3-4; Mic. 6:5). There the Israelites erected the twelve memorial stones taken from the bed of the Jordan (Josh. 4:20-24). Gilgal was thus the first foothold on Palestinian soil, and it became the base for military operations, as well as a great sanctuary, originally, perhaps, only for the tribe of Benjamin. The earliest stories, in the main sanctuary reports, tell of the circumcision of the people—an etiological narrative explaining the origin of Gilgal from the verb "to roll away" (גלל); the celebration of the Passover; and the extraordinary theophany to Joshua (5:2-9, 10-12, 13-15). At Gilgal, too, Joshua made a treaty with the Gibeonites (9:3-15) and launched his campaign against the five Amorite kings (10:6-43). In Judg. 21:5, as in the early strata of Josh. 1-9, the rallying point for Israel is Gilgal, and with this the early traditions of Saul connect very well. It is clear that Gilgal was an amphictyonic center; the tradition of the twelve memorial stones doubtless dates from this period. Gilgal was one of the towns the prophet Samuel visited on his yearly circuit (I Sam. 7:16). It was there that Saul was made king (11:14-15), but there too that he was rejected (13:4-15*a;* 15:17-31). It was notably a place for sacrificial offering (10:8; 11:15*b;* 13:8-10; 15:21). It is probably to this Gilgal that we must assign the references in the eighth-century prophets; there the sanctuary and its sacrificial cult are bitterly denounced, as is the institution of the kingdom (Hos. 4:15; 9:15; 12:11; Amos 4:4; 5:5). But in the great controversy of Mic. 6:1-8 Yahweh reminds Israel of "what happened from Shittim to Gilgal" (vs. 5; cf. Josh. 4-5).

2. Gilgal of Elijah and Elisha (II Kings 2:1; 4:38). The *Onomasticon* (67.6) describes the location as follows: *Sed et iuxta Bethel quidam aliam Galgalam suspicantur.* In the biblical account of Elijah's translation into heaven, Elijah and Elisha are proceeding from Gilgal to Bethel to Jericho. While some have supposed that the reference is to Gilgal near Jericho, the majority of scholars have identified the place with Jiljulieh, situated on the top of a high hill of the central range, some seven miles N of Bethel, not far from Tell 'Alyata. It was from here that the prophets went their way to the Jordan River, where Elijah was taken up to heaven. The miracle of the healing of the unsavory pottage by Elisha is also associated with this Gilgal.

3. The MT contains a reference to a Gilgal in the list of Canaanite kings in Josh. 12:23: גוים לגלגל מלך, "king of the nations at Gilgal" (RSV "king of Goiim in Galilee"). This may be compared with the Harosheth-ha-goiim of Judg. 4:2, with which it is sometimes identified. Noth places it in the mountains of Samaria; Abel five kilometers N of Ras el-'Ain on the border of the Plain of Sharon; F. J. Bliss at the modern village of Jiljulieh, thirty miles S-SE of Tantura, which he identifies with ancient Dor. But the text may be corrupt. The LXX reads βασιλεία Γεὶ τῆς Γαλιλαίας (cf. RSV).

4. The reference to Gilgal in Deut. 11:30 is difficult: "Are they not beyond the Jordan, west of the road, toward the going down of the sun, in the land of the Canaanites who live in the Arabah, over against Gilgal, beside the oak of Moreh?" The context would lead us to expect a reference to Gilgal near Jericho, but the language seems to suggest a region near Shechem, between Gerizim and Ebal. See *IB,* II, 408.

5. In the description of the boundary line of Judah in Josh. 15:7 there is still another reference to Gilgal, "which is opposite the ascent of Adummim" (Tal'at ed-Damm, on the road from Jericho to Jerusalem). But in the parallel passage of Josh. 18:17 we read for Gilgal "Geliloth," which has some versional support (B Γαλιαωθ; A Αγαλλιλωθ; Syr. Geliloth).

Bibliography. Brief comments will be given in the atlases of G. E. Wright and F. V. Filson (Westminster), E. G. Kraeling, and L. H. Grollenberg. Many valuable articles are to be found in *PJ, BASOR,* and *ZDPV.* F.-M. Abel, *Géographie de la Palestine* (1933), gives a succinct statement of the various Gilgals. The following represent some of the more recent treatments: A. M. Schneider, "Das byzantinische Gilgal (chirbet mefjir)," *ZDPV,* 54 (1931), 50-59; A. Alt, "Josua," *Werden und Wesen des alten Testaments* (1935), pp. 13-20; K. Galling, *ZDPV,* 36 (1945), 34-43; J. Kraus, "Gilgal: Ein Beitrag zur Kulturgeschichte Israels," *Vetus Testamentum,* I (1951), 181-91; M. Noth, *Josua, HAT,* 7 (1953), *passim;* J. Muilenburg, "The Site of Ancient Gilgal," *BASOR,* 140 (Dec., 1955), 11-27.

J. MUILENBURG

GILOH gī'lō [גלה] (Josh. 15:51); GILO in II Sam. 23:34; GILONITE —nīt. A village of Judah in the hill-country district of Debir; usually identified with Khirbet Jala, five miles N-NW of Hebron. If correct, geographically Giloh would be more properly a part of the district of Beth-zur (Josh. 15:58 ff).

V. R. GOLD

GIMEL gĭm'əl [ג, *g*]. The third letter of the Hebrew ALPHABET as placed in the KJV at the head of the third section of the acrostic psalm, Ps. 119, where each verse of this section of the psalm begins with this letter.

GIMZO gĭm'zō [גמזו, abounding in sycamores(?)] (II Chr. 28:18). A city of Judah in the Shephelah; identified with modern Jimzu, *ca.* three miles SE of Lod (Lydda) and *ca.* four miles E of er-Ramleh. Gimzo, with its dependent villages, was captured by the Philistines during the reign of Ahaz (*ca.* 735-715) and was the home of a noted rabbi named Nahum.

V. R. GOLD

GIN. KJV translation of מוקש (RSV SNARE in Pss. 140:5—H 140:6; 141:9; TRAP in Amos 3:5) and פח (RSV TRAP; Job 18:9; Isa. 8:14). The word is a contracted form of "engine," now obsolete but formerly used of a mechanical device employed as a trap.

GINATH gī'năth [גינת] (I Kings 16:21-22). The father of Tibni the pretender to the Israelite throne.

GINNETHOI gĭn'ə thoi [גנתוי] (Neh. 12:4); KJV GINNETHO —thō. A corruption of GINNETHON.

GINNETHON gĭn'ə thŏn [גנתון]. **1.** A priest who witnessed the covenant renewal under Ezra (Neh. 10:6).

2. Head of a family of priests in the period of Joiakim (Neh. 12:16). If the names in the lists of Neh. 10; 12 are ancestral rather than individual, as is frequently supposed, there may be only one Ginnethon.

3. *See* GINNETHOI.

J. M. WARD

GIRDLE. The translation of the following words:

a) אבנט (from Egyptian *bnd;* Exod. 28:4, 39-40; 29:9; 39:29; Lev. 8:7, 13; 16:4; Isa. 22:21), the linen sash of a priest or official.

b) חגור, חגורה (I Sam. 18:4; II Sam. 18:11; 20:8; I Kings 2:5; Prov. 31:24; Isa. 3:24; APRON in Gen. 3:7; ARMOR in II Kings 3:21), usually an article of clothing, though frequently with the specialized meaning of a soldier's belt (I Sam. 18:4; II Sam. 18:11; 20:8; II Kings 3:21). Fig. DRE 38.

c) Ζώνη (Matt. 3:4; Mark 1:6; Acts 21:11; Rev. 1:13; 15:6; alternately BELT 5), originally the lower of two girdles worn by women; in the NT, somtimes an article of clothing worn by men, as by John the Baptist.

d) KJV and alternately RSV אזור. *See* WAISTCLOTH; BELT 1.

e) KJV חשב (RSV BAND).

J. M. MYERS

GIRGASHITE gûr'gə shīt [גרגשי]. A Canaanite tribe named seven times (Gen. 10:16; 15:21; Deut. 7:1; Josh. 3:10; 24:11; Neh. 9:8; I Chr. 1:14) in OT lists of peoples dispossessed by the Israelites, without indication of locality. They have been identified with the *Qaraqisha* of Hittite records. It is suggested that the name is theophorous, meaning "client of Gesh," a Sumerian god of light introduced to Palestine and Phoenicia *ca.* 2000 B.C.

In the NT (Matt. 8:28; Mark 5:1; Luke 8:26) what may be the same name appears as "Gerasenes," "Gadarenes," or "Gergesenes." *See* GERASA.

Bibliography. B. Maisler, "Zur Götterwelt des alten Palästina," *ZAW,* L (1932), 86-87; F.-M. Abel, *Géographie de la Palestine,* I (1933), 325; W. F. Albright, review of Abel's *Géographie de la Palestine, JPOS,* XV (1935), 189.

R. F. SCHNELL

GIRZITES gûr'zīts [*Kethibh* גרזי, *Qere* גזרי] (I Sam. 27:8); KJV GEZRITES gĕz'rīts; KJV mg. GERZITES gûr'zīts. An otherwise unknown people probably living between the Philistines and Egypt. They, like the Geshurites (Josh. 13:2; I Sam. 27:8) and the Amalekites, were the victims of raids by David during his sojourn at Ziklag. The LXX may support the omission of "Girzites" as a doublet of "Geshurites." The LXX reads only the one name Gezrites (and this is the *Qere* reading in the MT), which would mean the inhabitants of Gezer, but Gezer is too far N to fit the context. R. F. SCHNELL

GISHPA gĭsh'pə [גשפא] (Neh. 11:21); KJV GISPA gĭs'pə. One of the NETHINIM. The name may be a corruption of Hasupha (cf. Ezra 2:43).

GITTAH-HEPHER. KJV form of GATH-HEPHER in Josh. 19:13.

GITTAIM gĭt'ĭ əm [גתים, two wine presses]. The village to which the Amorite inhabitants of Beeroth fled for refuge, perhaps from the cruel persecution of an overly zealous Saul (II Sam. 4:3; cf. Josh. 9:17). Subsequent to the Exile, returning Benjaminites settled at the site (Neh. 11:33).

A location in the vicinity of modern Ramleh is most probable. Suggested identifications include *Qdtm* of the Shishak List (no. 25) and *Gamteti* of the Tell el-Amarna Letters. W. H. MORTON

GITTITE. *See* GATH.

GITTITH gĭt'ĭth. *See* MUSIC.

GIZONITE gī'zə nīt [גזוני]. A gentilic name predicated of HASHEM, whose name appears in the catalogue of the Mighty Men of David known as the "Thirty" (I Chr. 11:34). Since Gizon/Gizo is elsewhere unknown, some scholars have read with some support from the Greek, "the Gunite" (cf. I Chr. 5:15; 7:13); others emend to read "from Gimzo" (cf. II Chr. 28:18). E. R. DALGLISH

GLAD TIDINGS. The phrase "to show, declare, or bring glad tidings" occurs in the KJV four times (Luke 1:19; 8:1; Acts 13:32; Rom. 10:15), in all instances rendering the Greek verb εὐαγγελίζεσθαι, which in other passages in both the OT and the NT is rendered "to bring good tidings." No distinction is made between religious and secular usage. The phrase was introduced into the English Bible by Tyndale, who had it in Luke 1:19; Rom. 10:15, whereas Wyclif consistently used "to preach," "to evangelize," or "to shew." The phrase obviously gained currency with the early Protestants, for the KJV adopted it without precedent for Luke 8:1; Acts 13:32. The ERV-ASV added I Thess. 3:6. The RSV, however, replaced "tidings" with "news" in all the NT passages, while retaining "tidings" in II Sam. 18:27; Isa. 40:9; 41:27; 52:7; 61:1; and throughout the adjective "good" was substituted for "glad." Tyndale's usage indicates that in the Middle Ages the term "good news" was the common, popular designation of the GOSPEL. The usage still survives in our "noel," which originally designated the chant on Christmas Eve, in which the message of the angels (Luke 2:10) is repeated. (The derivation of "noel" from *natalis* is untenable, for etymological and historical reasons. Rather, it is the French *nouvelle,* still preserved in the *bonne nouvelle*—i.e., "gospel"—in the French Bible.) To English Protestants the term "glad tidings" appeared to be the most appropriate expression for the whole Christian message, characterizing it as coming from God and being destined to exhilarate man and to drive out anxiety and despair (cf. Luke 2:10 KJV: "good tidings of great joy"). According to the church fathers, the glad tidings were announced first to Eve in the so-called *protevangelion* (Gen. 3:14-15) and were continued in the divine promises scattered over the whole OT. O. A. PIPER

GLASS. 1. The well-known transparent or translucent substance (זכוכית; ὕαλος; KJV CRYSTAL in Job 28:17). Glass was considered by the Hebrews as a precious substance, and is mentioned chiefly in poetic similitudes (Job 28:17; Rev. 4:6; 15:2; 21:18, 21).

Because of defective industrial processes no sizable glass containers, such as bottles or decanters, were manufactured prior to the Roman period. Pieces of glass sticks of various colors, reheated and welded together, were fashioned as pearls and elements of necklaces or other trinkets. These are commonly found in tombs together with miscellaneous jewelry. Small vases for perfumes and unguents were obtained by welding sticks of glass around a core of sand and clay built around a bar of metal; core and bar were subsequently removed. Such vessels, often of many colors, are always opaque. The above technique was common in ancient Egypt. Greek traditions, however, locate the origin of glass industry in Phoenicia, where, indeed, numerous objects showing a similar technique were found, together with articles of transparent glass which have often become iridescent because of oxidation. The latter seldom antedate the Hellenistic era.

The glass beads and vases found in Palestine cannot be distinguished from Egyptian and Phoenician articles. They are probably imports; at any rate, there is no evidence of a local glass industry in biblical Palestine. Some of the smallest vials discovered in tombs have been designated as lachrymatories. In the measure in which this term refers, not to the shape of the vials, but to tear water being actually collected into them, it is wholly unfounded.

See also GLAZING.

Bibliography. G. Contenau, *La Civilisation Phénicienne* (1925), pp. 217-19; K. Galling, *Biblisches Reallexikon* (1937), cols. 198-200; G. A. Barrois, *Manuel d'Archéologie Biblique,* I (1939), 456-58.

2. KJV form of MIRROR. This translation is an archaeological anachronism. Ancient mirrors were made of polished metal, and glass mirrors were not invented until late Roman times.

The translation of the Hebrew גלינים in Isa. 3:23 KJV by "glasses," in the sense of "mirrors," is also to be rejected. This term may refer to trinkets of glassware. The RSV, however, interprets it "garments of gauze," which is highly hypothetical. The etymology suggests something shiny or transparent, without further precision. G. A. BARROIS

GLAZING. The potter's glazing (τὸ χρῖσμα), mentioned in Ecclus. 38:30, probably refers to the process of smearing with paint, after which the smeared vessel was polished. In the light of evidence from the Ugaritic texts, the RSV renders the first two Hebrew words of Prov. 26:23 (כסף סיגים) "like the glaze." The Hebrew means, literally, "silver of dross," and is mistranslated "silver dross" by the KJV; but the Ugaritic texts justify combining these two Hebrew words and translating them "like the glaze."

B. H. Throckmorton, Jr.

GLEANING [לקט; Arab. *laqaṭa,* pick up]. The practice of gathering or picking up what was left in the field after reaping. It also applied to grapes left under the vine or olives in the orchard. Technically, "gleaning" also applied to reaping what was left standing in the corners of the field. Hebrew law prohibited an owner from cleaning up his own field, vineyard, or orchard, so that there would be provision for the poor, the orphan, the widow, and the alien resident (Lev. 19:9 ff; 23:22; Deut. 24:19-21; cf. Judg. 8:2; Ruth 2:2 ff).

H. N. Richardson

GLEDE glēd. KJV translation of ראה (Deut. 14:13; RSV Buzzard). The term "glede" or "glead" is properly applied only to the red Kite (*Milvus milvus*).

GLORY. No fewer than twenty-five Hebrew words are rendered by δόξα in the LXX, though the four most important are כבוד, תפארת, הוד, and הדר. The English "glory" likewise renders many Hebrew words, but principally the same four, plus the Aramaic יקרא. The verb "glory" renders התהלל, "boast," and verbal forms of כבד and פאר lie behind "glorify" or "be glorified." Even for the RSV the linguistic equivalents are too complicated and too inconsistent to be set forth in detail, and the concordances and commentaries must be consulted.

1. In the OT
   a. Human glory
   b. Divine glory
   c. Eschatological glory
2. In the NT
   a. In the Synoptic gospels
   b. In the Fourth Gospel
   c. In Acts
   d. In the Pauline letters
   e. In Hebrews
   f. In the Petrine letters
   g. In Revelation

Bibliography

1. In the OT. ***a. Human glory.*** The word כבוד means basically "weight, importance, consideration," and the things that display men as possessing glory. This glory is seen in riches (Ps. 49:16; Isa. 61:6; Hag. 2:7 KJV), in the army of Assyria (Isa. 8:7; 17:3-4; 21:16), in the trees of Lebanon (Isa. 60:13; cf. 10:18), in royal figures alive (Esth. 1:4; Ps. 45:3; Dan. 11:20) or dead (Isa. 14:18). It is manifest also in reputation (Job 29:20; Pss. 4:2 KJV; 49:17), in spiritual status (Ps. 8:5), in priestly garments (Exod. 28:2, 40; cf. Ps. 45:13) in the first (I Chr. 22:5) and in the second temple (Hag. 2:3). The glory of Israel is the king (Mic. 1:15, unless nobility is meant), the ark (I Sam. 4:22), or Yahweh himself (Ps. 106:20; Jer. 2:11; Hos. 4:7[?]; cf. Pss. 3:3; 62:7). The Hebrew word also probably describes the self (Pss. 16:9; 108:1; etc.), unless "liver" is the right reading (cf. Gen. 49:6 LXX). Though clearly "glory" often expresses an external manifestation, it is also indicative of inner qualities and of the spiritual endowment of man's inner nature. This is clearly shown in the translation of the word in such passages as Gen. 49:6 ("spirit"); Pss. 7:5—H 7:6 ("soul"); 16:9 ("soul"); 30:12—H 30:13 ("soul"); 57:8 ("soul").

b. Divine glory. Much is made of the accounts of the divine glory in Isaiah, Ezekiel, the P document, and the Psalms, and theories of the development of the conception have arisen out of the chronological order of the material. Thus early conceptions of the glory descriptive of Yahweh's acts and might achieved deeper significance in Isaiah, and later a more physical interpretation in the visions of Ezekiel, from whom P developed the visible, fiery glory so characteristic of his writings. But, as so often, this chronological account ignores the significance and influence of the cult in the development of the conception. The association of glory with the Ark of the Covenant is clear and belongs to the days of the Early Monarchy (I Sam. 4:21-22; Pss. 24:7-10; 63:2; 78:61). It is generally acknowledged that Ps. 29 is a very early poem, perhaps with a Canaanite base, and in it "glory" appears as an ascription of praise (vss. 2-3; cf. I Chr. 16:28; 29:9, 11; Pss. 66:2; 96:8; 115:1). Perhaps the word referred to the character of the Deity as it was manifested in the storm (Ps. 29:3; cf. 19:1), or it may have pointed to some liturgical act performed in the temple cultus, such as the appearance of the ark or of the king or of some cultic official (29:9; cf. Exod. 19:16-24). The two occurrences of the "glory" in Isaiah (3:8; 6:3) are also connected with the temple, and suggest underlying cultic conceptions. The question thus arises whether the accounts of the glory in Ezekiel and P are not also derived from the same source. Ezekiel sees in vision the divine glory as the appearance of brightness, Fire, and rainbow in audible motion (Ezek. 1:28; 9:3; 10:4, 18-19), both moving from Jerusalem (11:23) and returning to it (43:2 ff; cf. Isa. 40:3-11). The visions of Ezekiel and the poems of the Second Isaiah may allude to the processional exit and entry of the ark in the Davidic cultus.

In the priestly writings the glory appears as a fiery presence associated with Sinai (Exod. 14:4, 17-18; 24:16-18; 34:29-35). Almost always, the glory in P is associated with the Tabernacle (Exod. 16:7, 10; 29:43; 40:34-35; Lev. 9:6, 23; Num. 14:10; 16:19, 42; 20:6), sometimes as a manifestation of favor, but more frequently as a sign of divine wrath. The association of "glory" with the cloud on the tabernacle shows the connection with the cultus (cf. I Kings 8:11=II Chr. 5:14; 7:1, 3). The verb שכן, "to dwell," is sometimes used in connection with the glory and the tabernacle (Exod. 24:16; Ps. 26:8); the glory is said to fill the tabernacle (Exod. 40:34-35) or temple (I Kings 8:11, etc.) and the whole earth (Ps. 72:19; Isa. 6:3; cf. Ps. 57:5=108:5; 113:4; etc.). Cultic glory may have its roots in the Canaanite worship of El Elyon (Deut. 32:8), and was perhaps adopted in Jerusalem at the time of David (Pss. 72 [cf. vs. 19]; 89:17; etc.). But it can also be the justification of God by the admission of guilt (Num. 14:21; Josh. 7:19; I Sam. 6:5), and such occasions belong in part to the altar or shrine.

Since the idea of glory is closely connected with the cultus, it also belongs to the revelation of God in history and in nature (Ps. 148:13), which in turn is symbolized in various elements of the temple institutions (cf. Num. 14:22; I Chr. 16:24; Ps. 96:3). It is from the glory of the tabernacling PRESENCE that the various emphases of Isaiah, of the P document, and of Ezekiel are probably derived. How close is the connection glory-Presence-God is shown in the fact that "glory" and "God" occasionally become synonymous (cf. Exod. 33:22 ["my glory"="I"]; Lev. 9:4, 6, 23; Ps. 113:4; Zech. 8:2; etc.).

c. Eschatological glory. The same features are repeated in the various descriptions of the eschatological glory. The glory that belongs to Lebanon shall become the possession of desert areas (Isa. 35:2), and of the temple to which the glory (i.e., wealth) of the nations shall come (Isa. 60:13; 66:12; cf. 60:11). The New Jerusalem will possess an abundant glory (66: 11; Zech. 12:7), which will be seen and proclaimed among the peoples of the world (Isa. 66:18-19). This glory (40:5) will be universally feared (59:19) and known (Hab. 2:14), and will be manifested in Israel (Isa. 24:23), where it is, in fact, the self-disclosure of God himself (4:5; 43:7; 58:8; 60:1-2, 19; Zech. 2:5). Thus Israel will become Yahweh's glory (Isa. 4:2; 46:13). From these passages it will be seen that the glory is understood as national-cultic as relating to Jerusalem, and personal as relating to Israel and to God himself.

2. In the NT. ***a. In the Synoptic gospels.*** The first three gospels use δόξα in a variety of ways. The word means Solomon's glory (Matt. 6:29, etc.) and the glory of the world's kingdoms seen in the temptation story (4:8, etc.). It is a description of the divine presence as a luminous manifestation (Luke 2:9; cf. Matt. 16:27; Mark 8:38), and an ascription of praise (Matt. 5:16 [verb]; 6:13 RSV mg.; Luke 2:14; 19:38; etc.). The word is also applied to the specific quality of the appearance of Jesus in his transfiguration (Luke 9:31-32), and to his second coming (Matt. 25: 31; Mark 13:26; Luke 21:27; 24:26). Noteworthy in Simeon's benediction is the identification of God's salvation, a "light of revelation to the Gentiles, and for glory to thy people Israel," with the infant Jesus (Luke 2:29-32).

b. In the Fourth Gospel. The glory of God's Word was uniquely manifested in Jesus (John 1:14), and it is a saving and ethical glory. It is demonstrated in his miracles (2:11; 11:4, 40); and so this glory, not sought by Jesus for himself (8:50, 54), as men seek glory for themselves (5:41, 44), is that glory which belonged to Jesus before the creation of the world (17:5), and to which he is to return (17:22, 24). This glory thus belongs to him because he seeks God's glory (5:41; 7:18). Indeed, God seeks his Son's glory (8:50), and glorifies him (8:54 [verb]). This glory is God's glory, once seen by Isaiah (John 12:41) and now manifested in Jesus (1:15). Of peculiar significance is John 13:31-38, where the theme of Jesus' glorification is prominent. His glorification is seen in his complete obedience, contrasted with the impending denial of Peter, which issues in his death and departure. The theme is further emphasized by the title "Son of man," which before the NT was a title of glory (e.g., Dan. 7:13; Enoch). His departure issues in the Resurrection, Ascension, and appearance at the end of the world (13:32). The "glory" terminology does not appear in the Johannine letters.

c. In Acts. Twice in Stephen's speech (Acts 7:2, 55) the expression "God of glory" is a pious formula possibly reminiscent of the Psalms (24:8 ff). In Acts 12:23 not to give God his glory is not to confess one's sins, a usage parallel to that mentioned above in the OT passages.

d. In the Pauline letters. The RSV still uses the word "glory" in certain passages where "boast" or the like would have better represented the sense of the Greek (e.g., Gal. 6:13-14; Phil. 1:26; 3:3; but cf. "glory" in 3:19). The cosmic sense of the word "glory" appears in such references as I Cor. 15:40-41, where the glory of the celestial is distinguished from the glory of the terrestrial, and where the glory of the sun is contrasted with the glory of the moon and that of the stars. Then again the word appears in the sense of a man's glory, his fame, honor, and reputation. Thus Paul claims he did not seek glory—i.e., the recognition of his position or rights—from the Thessalonians (I Thess. 2:6); rather, it is ever his aim to promote the glory of God (Rom. 15:6-7; I Cor. 10:31; II Cor. 4:15; 8:19). He uses the concept of glory to describe and define human relationships. He begins, as always, theocentrically, with the thought that a man is the image and glory of God, and then it follows that woman is the glory of man (I Cor. 11:7), and the word "for" in the next verse shows that Paul means that woman is to promote the glory of man, and that a man is to promote the glory of God. Hence certain directions about veiling. In the same way the Christians at Thessalonica are Paul's joy and glory (I Thess. 2:20), and the cause of his praise. The churches, too, are the glory of Christ, for they both reflect and promote the glory of their Lord (II Cor. 8:23). Paul's sufferings are an honor to the churches for whose sake he is suffering (Eph. 3:13).

It is therefore inevitable that "glory" should also appear in Paul many times as an ascription of praise (Rom. 4:20; II Cor. 1:20; Phil. 1:11; 2:11). Glory to God is, of course, particularly prominent in the doxologies (Rom. 11:36; 16:27; Gal. 1:5; Eph. 3:21; Phil. 4:20; I Tim. 1:17). Even as some of these passages either suggest or show, glory is for Paul something that properly belongs to God, even if the idea can be employed to illumine human relationships. God is the Source and Lord of glory, for glory belongs to him (Eph. 3:16) and is proper to him, as the doxologies show. He is the Father of glory (Eph. 1:17), and Jesus is the Lord of glory (I Cor. 2:8; cf. II Cor. 4:4). In II Cor. 4:4 the glory of God is given in the face of Jesus Christ, so that God's glory has become visible in a person and on that person's face (cf. Phil. 4:19). As God's glory used to be manifest in Israel in the tabernacling Presence (Rom. 4:9), so now it is manifest in Christ (II Cor. 4:6). In Eph. 1:12, 14, "praise of his glory" is a Christian circumlocution for "God," and elsewhere "glory" is a description for the manifest perfection of God in all his complete goodness and saving grace (Rom. 1:23; 3:7, 23; etc.) or power (Rom. 6:4; cf. John 11:40).

There is glory in God in Christ and in Christians, and the glory in Christians is Christ in them, and this in turn is the hope of glory (Col. 1:27). Christ's glory is given and will be fully given at the end of the world. Glory is thus in Paul an eschatological experience—i.e., it is a partly fulfilled reality, although it is also a future expectation, into which we enter by degrees (II Cor. 3:18; cf. Rom. 9:23; II Thess. 2: 14). There are many passages which speak of the heavenly estate in terms of "glory" (Rom. 5:2; 8:18; II Cor. 4:17; Col. 3:4; I Thess. 2:12; II Thess. 1:9; cf. I Tim. 3:16; Tit. 2:13).

All these references show that for Paul "glory" is an attribute of nature, of men and women in their natural and Christian estate, of the churches, and especially of God and Christ in their activity in the world and in the church, and in the Second Advent and in heaven.

e. In Hebrews. The word appears in several meanings. It describes man's glory in a quotation from Ps. 8. Men, though lower than the divine nature, are crowned with glory and honor, where glory is the essential dignity and honor, the outward manifestation reflecting the old Hebrew phrase "for glory and for beauty" (e.g., Exod. 28:2). In the same way Jesus, who also for a time condescended to be lower than the angels, is now himself crowned with glory and honor (Heb. 2:9). He has thus become the object of praise (3:3; 13:21), for Christ reflects, or is the revelation or effulgence of, the divine glory (1:3). The theocentric aspect of the word is also seen in 9:5, where the cherubim of glory are not simply glorious cherubim, but as flanking the Presence are part of the media of the revealed glory. The eschatological reference is seen in 2:10.

f. In the Petrine letters. In a quotation from Isa. 40, I Pet. 1:24 speaks of the fading glory or beauty of mortal flesh, but otherwise the references are eschatological and theocentric. Present trials will receive the reward of glory (I Pet. 1:7), an "unfading crown of glory" (5:4). God is the source and giver of glory, for he is the "Majestic Glory" (II Pet. 1:17; cf. Jude 25), who gave glory to the transfigured Jesus (II Pet. 1:17) and to the resurrected Jesus (I Pet. 1: 21; cf. vs. 11). God's eternal glory is in Christ (I Pet. 5:10). Likewise Christians will receive a revelation of the glory (I Pet. 4:13; 5:1), but this, indeed, already rests upon them (4:14). As in glory then and expecting glory, they are to ascribe glory to the God of glory (I Pet. 4:11; II Pet. 3:18; cf. Jude 25).

g. In Revelation. In 18:1 "splendor" translates the Greek "glory" of an angel illumining the earth. There are also some references to "giving glory to God" in the OT sense of justifying God and recognizing his right in the circumstances of the first woe (11:13; 14: 7; cf. 16:9 [refusing to do so]). The remaining references are theocentric and relative to worship. Doxologies to Christ (1:6) or to the Lamb (5:12-13) are given, and there are ascriptions of glory to God. The four beasts around the throne lead the heavenly worship (4:9) and are followed by the twenty-four elders (4:11). The angels share in the ascription of glory (7:12), and so does the great company of heaven (19:1), in recognition of God's judgment, and then for the marriage of the Lamb (19:7). God is thus the glorious center of heaven and attracts glory from all classes of the assembled company. There is a unity of worship to match the central glory, which actually filled the heavenly temple with smoke (15:8), so that no one could enter. But the heavenly glory is also gracious, for it is the center not only of heaven but also of the New Jerusalem. In that holy city which descended from heaven, the glory of God is its sun, its light (21:23), for the distinction of that city is the tabernacling glory of God (21:11; cf. vs. 3). By the light of that city the nations shall walk, and through the ever open gates of that city the wealth and honor of the nations shall be brought (21:24, 26). In Revelation, as in the rest of the NT, the fact of the Incarnation has given an irrevocable stamp to the image of the glory of God.

Bibliography. A. von Gall, *Die Herrlichkeit Gottes* (1900). J. Morgenstern, "Biblical Theophanies," *ZA,* XXV (1911), 139-93; XXVIII (1914), 15-60. I. Abrahams, *The Glory of God* (1925). A. H. Forster, "The Meaning of δόξα in the Greek Bible," *ATR,* XII (1929/30), 311-16. G. Kittel, *Die Religionsgeschichte und das Urchristentum* (1931), pp. 82-85. J. Schneider, *Doxa, eine bedeutungsgeschichtliche Studie* (1932). H. Kittel, *Die Herrlichkeit Gottes* (1934). G. R. Berry, "The Glory of Jahweh and the Temple," *JBL,* LVI (1937), 115-17. H. G. May, "The Departure of the Glory of Yahweh," *JBL,* LVI (1937), 309-21. B. Stein, *Der Begriff Kebod Yahweh und seine Bedeutung für die alttestamentliche Gotteserkenntnis* (1939). L. H. Brockington, "The Presence of God, a Study of the Use of the Term 'Glory of Yahweh,' " *ET,* LVII (Oct., 1945), 21-25. A. M. Ramsey, *The Glory of God and the Transfiguration of Christ* (1949). J. Duplacy, "L'espérance de la gloire de Dieu dans l'AT," *Bible et Vie Chrétienne,* VIII (1954). N. Hugedé, *La métaphore du miroir dans les Épîtres de saint Paul aux Corinthiens* (1957). E. Jacob, *Theology of the OT* (1958), pp. 79-82. A Richardson, *An Introduction to the Theology of the NT* (1958), pp. 64-67, 182-84. G. HENTON DAVIES

GLOSSOLALIA. *See* TONGUES, GIFT OF.

GLUTTONY. Though the word "gluttony" is not used in the RSV, "glutton" is the translation of the following: זולל, active participle of זלל, "to be light, worthless" (Deut. 21:20; Prov. 23:21; 28:7); φάγος (Matt. 11:19; Luke 7:34; cf. Tit. 1:12).

In NT usage the word is intended as a term of general opprobrium. A glutton may therefore be one who is voracious or one who proves to be a rascal or a scoundrel because of an inordinate fondness for some specified object or pursuit. The term was probably used in both senses in attempts to vilify Jesus (Matt. 11:19; Luke 7:34). The rich man, Dives, is portrayed in the Vulg. as a glutton (Luke 16:19-31; *dives epulo,* in the Vulg. heading). H. F. BECK

GNASHING. *See* TOOTH.

GNAT [כן, *plural* כנים, *abstract plural* כנם (KJV LICE; *cf.* Isa. 51:6 KJV); κώνωψ]. It is uncertain whether the gnat, the mosquito, or yet another insect is meant. Perhaps it is: (*a*) the Harvester Gnat, the *Barghaš* of the Arabs, a small midge (Chironomidae) which enters eyes, ears, and nose of fieldworkers during harvest (*see* FLY [ערוב]); (*b*) the Anopheles Mosquito, the transmitter of malaria; (*c*) the sand fly (Psychodidae), carrier of dengue fever and intruder into sleeping rooms of Egypt. Any of these three would satisfy the conditions of the third of the PLAGUES OF EGYPT (Exod. 8; Ps. 105).

כן (Isa. 51:6), elsewhere "thus," might here be the singular of כנים, "gnats," since כמו alone means "in like manner."

"Strain at" (Matt. 23:24 KJV) is a typographical error for "strain out." Straining out a gnat, the smallest unclean animal, is compared to the meticulous observance of self-imposed ceremonial trifles. Neglecting one's chief duties is compared to swallowing a CAMEL.

See also FAUNA § F7*b*.

See bibliography under FLY. W. W. FRERICHS

GNOSTICISM nŏs′tə sĭz əm. A modern term used to indicate a constellation of religious phenomena found during the second century and later. These phenomena include beliefs in the innate immortality of a divine spark, differentiated from both body and soul; the necessity for the escape of this element to its source, an unknown god; the control of the visible universe by evil spirits; and the bringing of knowledge (*gnosis*) about the unknown god and the divine element by a redeemer who descends to earth and returns above, having effected redemption by providing this knowledge to those who "by origin" are related to him. Some Gnostics also had rites which prepared the living or the dying for their ascent to the realms above.

The earliest testimonies we possess for the existence of Gnosticism as thus defined come from the second century, and from heretical groups rather loosely related to the Christian church. These groups made use of the Pauline letters and of the Gospel of John, and for this reason it is difficult (if not impossible) to determine whether Gnostic terminology is used by Paul and John. Many scholars, especially in Germany, have claimed that Gnostic ideas are to be found in both, in Paul's case especially in Colossians and Ephesians, the authenticity of which they often doubt. On the other hand, British and American scholars have usually claimed that Gnosticism is a second-century phenomenon, strongly influenced both by heterodox Judaism and by Christianity. The discovery of a kind of proto-Gnostic dualism in the DEAD SEA SCROLLS, as in APOCALYPTICISM generally, shows that there was an environment out of which certain Pauline and Johannine doctrines could have arisen apart from Gnosticism. And recent finds of Gnostic documents at Nag-Hammadi in Egypt reveal the presence of a kind of Jewish speculation within Gnostic thought itself.

1. Approach and method. The problem of the approach to Gnosticism has aroused considerable discussion. Some scholars have argued that the starting point should be sought by taking late systems in which various elements are combined, working out the interrelations of various themes, and then showing that aspects of these themes are to be found earlier. This method disregards chronology, but it has the advantage of presenting what early Gnostics may well have thought. At the opposite extreme stand those scholars who insist upon a fairly rigid chronological analysis and refuse to admit that later developments can explain what earlier writers had in mind. They argue that there was a development within Gnostic thought comparable to that within Christian theology, and that just as one cannot use Origen to explain the apostolic fathers, so one cannot use seventh-century Mandaeism (the religion of a baptist sect in Persia) to illustrate the thought of Gnostics five centuries earlier. It seems likely that both methods will continue to be employed.

Other controversies have concerned the sources of Gnostic thought, which have been found in Iranian and Egyptian religion, in Judaism, in Christianity, and in Hellenistic philosophy and astrology. In view of the extremely synthetic nature of Gnosticism, it is likely that all these elements contributed to it, although some of them (especially Judaism and Christianity) were more important than others.

A further question arises in relation to the role of mythology in Gnosticism. Did their myths arise before philosophical interpretations were given them? Or were the myths simply poetic ways of expressing philosophical or theological doctrines? This question is hard to answer on the basis of available materials, but it seems probable that different systems arose in different ways. Most Gnostics thought of themselves, not as Gnostics, but as Simonians, Valentinians, Sethians, Ophites, etc.

In dealing with Gnosticism it is therefore necessary to examine the various systems which flourished in the second century, a time when a real threat was presented to the Christian church and when many theologians, beginning with Justin and Irenaeus and later including Tertullian, Hippolytus, and Epiphanius, wrote refutations of Gnostic doctrines. The earliest detailed discussion of these systems is provided by Irenaeus, who wrote *Against Heresies ca.* 180, relying in part on a lost work of Justin (*ca.* 150) and in part on oral and written testimony from the Gnostics themselves, including a work called the *Apocryphon of John*, known from several Coptic versions of the fourth and fifth centuries.

2. Gnostic systems. ***a. Syrian Gnosis.*** The first system Irenaeus describes is that ascribed to SIMON MAGUS. We need not discuss this system in any detail, except to suggest that at least in the form in which Irenaeus knew it, it was clearly related to Christian doctrine. Simon is said to have regarded himself as Father, Son, and Holy Spirit; and his followers were saved by his grace, not by works of law (presumably an allusion to Eph. 2:8-9). Simon's descent from above through several heavens is related (as source, offshoot, or parallel) to what many second-century Christians believed about Jesus. A disciple of Simon, Menander, soon produced his own doctrine, believing that he himself was the Savior who had been sent from above and adding a magical(?) baptism which would provide perpetual youth (Irenaeus may have misunderstood this point). The passage of time proved that Menander was wrong. He may well have been providing an alternative to Christian doctrine known to him at Antioch, where Ignatius was bishop at this time.

Another Antiochene system is quite different. This

is the doctrine of Saturninus, who held like Menander that the supreme deity was completely unknown, but who spoke of Christ rather than himself as the Savior. The supreme power made spiritual beings, who made the world. They saw a "luminous image" which came from above, and they tried to copy it (an explanation of Gen. 1:26). Their attempt was only partly successful until a "spark of life" came down to animate their product. This spark, present in good men, is the element which is saved. Christ came to destroy all the spiritual beings, and men, hostile to the supreme being. Since ordinary human life, including marriage, procreation, and eating meat, is evil, he merely seemed to be a man (he may have been the luminous image which had appeared before). As in the Simonian system, the law was given by the inferior spiritual beings; Saturninus added that the prophets also were inspired by them, and included among these beings both Satan and the God of the Jews.

In the systems of Simon and Menander there is a female principle, the Thought of God, perhaps derived from the Wisdom of such books as Proverbs and Ecclesiasticus. The ethical ideas of these systems are antinomian and libertarian. On the other hand, for Saturninus there is no female principle, and he advocates extreme asceticism. He doubtless agreed with the apocryphal Gospel of the Egyptians that the Savior "came to destroy the works of the female."

In these two classes of Syrian Gnosis we find foreshadowed most of the later Gnostic developments. There is a supreme and unknown god revealed either by himself (Simonianism) or by a redeemer who has come to liberate men from the bondage of a wicked world. Redemption is produced by knowledge of this liberation rather than by ordinary moral behavior; the followers of Simon live in freedom *in* the world, while those of Saturninus live in freedom *from* the world. Both kinds of systems hold that the world and worldly morality are the products of hostile powers and that victory is to come by means of escape.

b. Marcion. The notion that the supreme god was completely unknown apart from his revelation in Jesus, and that the prophets were inspired by an inferior being, was taken over and developed by the famous heretic Marcion (*see* MARCION, GOSPEL OF), who was a member of the Roman church between 137 and 144. In his view there were two gods, one the good Father of Jesus, the other the Creator known through the OT. The gospel of Jesus and Paul was corrupted by those apostles who could recognize only the Creator. It looks as if Marcion was attempting to free Roman Christianity of its Jewish heritage (*see* HERMAS, SHEPHERD OF) at a time just after the disastrous Jewish revolt of 132-35. He himself was expelled by the Roman church.

c. Valentinus. *Ca.* the same time another Gnostic teacher, Valentinus, came to Rome and set forth a doctrine revealed to us in 1956 with the publication of his *Gospel of Truth,* discovered at Nag-Hammadi. This book is so much simpler, poetic, Jewish, and Christian than what Irenaeus tells us of his doctrine that scholars have argued that it represents an earlier stage of his teaching. There is little emphasis on the heavenly "aeons," and the supreme God is not separated from the Creator. But it can also be argued that this gospel represents Valentinus' teaching in a form intended to appeal to Jewish Christian readers. It could be either early or late. In Irenaeus we find a complicated mythological picture of the emanation of the "aeons" from the supreme being. The twelfth and lowest of these "aeons" was the female Sophia. Her instability led her to fall into the outer darkness, where she conceived spontaneously and brought forth a premature infant who was the creator of the universe we know. He used materials which were the solidification of her emotions; thus her grief resulted in tears, hence water. This creator, called Ialdabaoth (a parody of Yahweh Elohe Sabaoth?) in similar systems, regarded himself as the only god there was; he constantly struggled with his mother, Sophia, for control over mankind, since she had inserted a divine spark or spirit into men. In order to redeem both her and mankind, Jesus was sent down to collect the scattered spiritual seeds and to restore them to the "pleroma" (cf. Col. 1:19, etc.; *see* PLEROMA) of spiritual being, the "aeons" above. For Valentinians, human marriage was a symbolic imitation of the unions in the spiritual world, and we are not surprised to learn that for some of them a sacred marriage formed part of their ritual.

The Valentinian system is dualistic, but it is less dualistic than that of Saturninus or the *Apocryphon of John,* with which it has points of contact. In the *Apocryphon* there is a fuller description of the struggle between Ialdabaoth and Christ. Ialdabaoth made paradise and gave man a wife in order to chain him to the material world; Christ, however, persuaded man to eat from the tree of knowledge (*gnosis*). In the course of this struggle Christ came again and gave his true teaching (the content of the myth) to his disciple John—hence the title, the "secret doctrine" of John. The emphasis on John in this document and on the Gospel of John among the Valentinians is significant. It suggests that Gnostics recognized proto-Gnostic ideas in the traditional portrait of John's thought and developed these to suit themselves.

In the Valentinian group there was considerable variety. Ptolemaeus was their greatest systematizer, and we also know his *Letter to Flora,* perhaps addressed to the Roman church, in which he presented his doctrine in a manner intended to win the confidence of unsuspecting but orthodox Christians. The letter explains that there are different levels of law in the OT and, in a veiled way, relates these levels to the three classes of men which the Valentinians recognized (material or fleshly—pagans; animate or psychic—Christians; spiritual—themselves).

In order to deal with the spiritual nature of revelation the Valentinians had to provide allegorical exegesis, not only of the parables of Jesus (where three different items could often be found), but also of events in his life. Ptolemeus wrote an allegorical explanation of the opening verses of John, claiming that the "aeons" were symbolized there. Another Valentinian, Heracleon, prepared exegetical notes on at least the first eight chapters of John; these were later used by Origen in his Commentary.

d. Basilides. Quite a different type of Gnostic thought is represented by an older contemporary of Valentinus, Basilides. He taught that originally there was absolutely nothing. A nonexistent god then produced a nonexistent seed out of nothing, and from this seed there proceeded various kinds of existent things, including a "threefold Sonship" whose goal was to return to the nonexistent god. This return is also the goal of history. When the spiritual elements have all gone back above, oblivion will come over the earth, and there will be no further salvation. Perhaps because of his nihilistic emphasis, Basilides did not attract so many followers as Valentinus did; indeed, the church fathers tell us of only one, his son Isidore, who wrote treatises on ethics and on the allegorical interpretation of Greek and oriental literature.

e. Later systems. Later Gnostic systems essentially represent permutations and combinations of the elements found earlier. In the third and fourth centuries Gnostics made efforts to find their systems prefigured in Greek and oriental religious history, philosophy, and mythology, but much early Gnosticism was supplanted by the rise of the more radically dualistic MANICHEISM, which spread from Persia to the Roman Empire, in spite of official condemnation and Christian opposition. The church father Augustine was at one time a Manichee.

Christians felt threatened by both Gnosticism and Manicheism partly because both were mythological. These opponents knew an elaborate mythological cosmology toward which Christianity was either agnostic or openly hostile. Again, the Gnostic, like the Manichee, knew that he was essentially a part of God, a divine spark, and that nothing he did in the evil world made much difference. Moreover, Gnostic use of the allegorical method meant that Gnostics could claim to have the true explanations of difficult passages in the Christians' Bible. Only when Christian theology had developed to the point where it was able to beat the Gnostics on their own speculative ground did the threat come to an end. Suppression of Gnosticism by the state was a very effective factor.

3. Future study. What has been said above about Gnosticism is subject to some revision as the rest of the forty-four Gnostic works found in the large jar at Nag-Hammadi are published, but what has already appeared does not greatly alter the picture already available from the writings of the church fathers. It encourages a fairly conservative attitude toward their truthfulness. Proto-Gnostic influence on NT writings remains fairly probable, but it has never been shown that before the second century there was a figure of a Gnostic redeemer. The closest one might come would be by working backward from Simonianism, with what seems to be a revised version of Jesus, to the apocalyptic personages of late Judaism. It is likely, however, that the crystallization of Gnostic doctrine is due to the influence of Christian interpretations of Jesus, in cosmic terms different from those employed by Christians.

Finally, it is fairly clear that much of the debate over the question whether Gnosticism is to be found in the NT is a matter of definition. In itself, the term *gnosis* (found, e.g., in I Cor. 8:1, 7) means nothing more than "knowledge." While Paul prefers to speak of being known by God rather than knowing him (Gal. 4:9), the Fourth Evangelist is willing to say that "this is eternal life, that they know thee the only true God, and Jesus Christ whom thou hast sent" (John 17:3). Is such an expression Gnostic, proto-Gnostic, or neither? While on the one hand the Dead Sea Scrolls have suggested that there was a form of sectarian Judaism out of which such a doctrinal framework as that of John could arise, on the other hand the discovery of the *Gospel of Truth* makes equally clear the development of Valentinian Gnosticism out of heterodox Judaism. The Gospel of John is close to both.

It seems likely that the study of Gnosticism will be concerned with the ways in which it developed out of the wreckage of apocalyptic Judaism (in which Iranian elements were already present) and will trace the manner in which the failure of the apocalyptic hope, already faced to some extent in such writings as II Esdras and II Baruch, may have led to a transfer of the hope from this world to a realm of pure spirit. Gnosticism seems to have arisen in an environment where men had abandoned an expectation of God's immediate action on their behalf. The Gnostics almost universally rejected the OT as an authentic interpretation of human existence; instead, they held that it contained a secret revelation of a god who had not created the world. And it is significant that we seem to encounter two waves of Gnostic teaching, the first after the fall of Jerusalem in the year 70, the second after the bloody defeat of the Jews in 135. Gnosticism may be a reaction from apocalyptic Judaism, which led its proponents toward their almost universal hostility toward the God of the Jews. In this sense some Christian writers could be described as at least proto-Gnostic, even though they would certainly have rejected the full implications of the Gnostic world view.

Bibliography. W. Bousset, *Hauptprobleme der Gnosis* (1907); H. Leisegang, *Die Gnosis* (1924); F. C. Burkitt, *Church and Gnosis* (1932); W. Till, *Die gnostischen Schriften des koptischen Papyrus Berolinensis 8502* (1955); M. Malinine, H. C. Puech, and G. Quispel, *Evangelium Veritatis* (1956); H. Jonas, *Gnosis und spätantiker Geist* (1934-54; English ed., 1958); R. M. Grant, *Reader in Gnosticism* (1961). On Manicheism, see H. C. Puech, *Le manichéisme* (1949). R. M. GRANT

GOAD [מלמד, *from* למד, to learn; דרבנה (Eccl. 12:11); κέντρον (Acts 26:14; KJV PRICKS)]. A pointed stick used for driving or guiding cattle, especially oxen when plowing. Sometimes it was tipped with iron (I Sam. 13:21). It was used incidentally to clean mud and clay from the plowshare. Shamgar slew six hundred Philistines with the oxgoad (Judg. 3:31). Yet the Philistines held the monopoly on iron until the time of David.

"Goad" is also used metaphorically: The words of the wise are as goads urging men on to better works (Eccl. 12:11). Paul finds it useless to kick against the goads, the urging which God gives to his recalcitrant creatures (Acts 26:14).

Fig. MET 44, no. 21. C. U. WOLF

GOAH gō'ə [געה]; KJV GOATH gō'ăth. A quarter, or suburb, of Jerusalem, mentioned after the hill of GAREB, presumably to the E or SE of it, in the prophecy of Jer. 31:39 on the restoration of the city.

GOAL. *See* GAMES, NT.

GOAT [עז, female goat, *cf.* Akkad. *enzu,* she-goat, Arab. *'anz,* she-goat, *and 'anaza,* to turn aside; עתוד, male goat, *cf.* Akkad. *atûdu,* he-goat; צפיר, male goat, *from* Aram. צפיר (Ezra 6:17), *cf.* Syr. *ṣiphrayâ,* kid; שעיר, male goat, hairy one; שעירה; תיש, male goat, *cf.* Arab. *tais,* he-goat, Akkad. *daššu,* buck of gazelle; ἔριφος, kid; ἐρίφιον, *diminutive of* ἔριφος; τράγος, male goat, *probably* chewer]. A hollow-horned ruminant mammal allied to the sheep but of lighter build. Long before Israel's story began, possibly as early as the Neolithic Age, the goat, like the sheep, had been tamed; this was one of man's earliest successes in the domestication of animals. The goat of biblical Palestine was probably the Syrian or Mamber variety (*Capra hircus mambrica*), commonly black in color. *See* FAUNA § B1*c*.

1. Secular use. Goats were the principal source of the milk used in Israel (Deut. 32:14; Prov. 27:27); their flesh served as meat (Lev. 7:23; Deut. 14:4), their hair as raw material for a fabric used for tents and various domestic purposes (Exod. 25:4; 26:7; 36:14; I Sam. 19:13, 16), their tanned skins as leather (the word translated "goatskin" in Num. 4:6, etc., is uncertain; cf. Heb. 11:37), and their whole hides as skin bottles (cf. Gen. 21:14; Josh. 9:4; I Sam. 1:24; Matt. 9:17; etc.). Goats were a recognized form of wealth, and the size of the flocks, which consisted of sheep and goats, indicated the owner's status in the community (cf. Gen. 30:32, 43; I Sam. 25:2). Like the other domestic animals, goats were subject to the law of firstlings (Num. 18:15-17). For the he-goat as leader of the flock, see Jer. 50:8; for his stately gait, see Prov. 30:31. A gift of 7,700 he-goats to Jehoshaphat is recorded in II Chr. 17:11. According to Ezek. 27:21, much of Tyre's trade with Arabia was in sheep and goats.

2. As a sacrificial animal. A goat had to be at least eight days old before it could be offered to Yahweh (Lev. 22:27). A year-old male is specified for the Passover in Exod. 12:5, and a three-year-old female in God's covenant with Abram in Gen. 15:9. The use of goats as sacrifices (without further qualification) is referred to in Pss. 50:9, 13; 66:15; Isa. 1:11.

Most allusions to goats as offerings relate to specific kinds of sacrifice or to particular occasions, and in the majority of cases a male goat is required: as a burnt offering (Lev. 1:10; 22:19); as a peace offering (Lev. 3:6, 12; 17:3; Num. 7:17; etc.); as a guilt offering (Lev. 5:18); as a sin offering (Lev. 4:23; Num. 7:16; II Chr. 29:21; Ezek. 43:22, 25; 45:23), though in Lev. 4:28; 5:6 a she-goat is prescribed. The most striking use of goats in the Jerusalem cultus was on the Day of Atonement (Lev. 16; *see* AZAZEL). An early Christian view of these sin-offering procedures is expressed in Heb. 9:12-13, 19; 10:4.

3. In figurative and symbolic usage. A flock of goats serves as a simile for a woman's hair in Song of S. 4:1; 6:5, and for the relatively small size of Israel's army in I Kings 20:27. The he-goat typifies various human leaders in Isa. 14:9; Ezek. 34:17; Zech. 10:3, and the king of Greece (Alexander the Great) in Dan. 8:5-8. In Matt. 25:31-46, sheep and "kids" represent the righteous and the wicked (vss. 32-33; cf. Ezek. 34:17-22). W. S. MCCULLOUGH

GOATH. KJV form of GOAH.

GOATSKIN [תחש (KJV BADGERS' SKIN[S]), *see below;* αἴγειον δέρμα (Heb. 11:37), *from* αἴγειος, of a goat, *from* αἴξ, goat, *plus* δέρμα, skin, *from* δέρω, to skin]. Alternately: LEATHER (Ezek. 16:10). The skin of a goat, presumably tanned.

1. In the OT. In Ezek. 16:10 תחש is a leather from which a woman's shoes are made. Elsewhere (except Num. 4:25) it is preceded by עור or עורות, "skin" ("skins"); and the phrase "skin(s) of תחש" appears to mean a kind of leather, used as a covering for the tabernacle (Exod. 26:14; 36:19; 39:34) and for the ark and various other sacred objects (Num. 4:6-14). We may therefore infer that תחש is an animal.

There is no satisfactory etymology for תחש. Whatever meaning the word may once have had, it was unknown to the LXX (e.g., "hyacinth-colored skins" in Exod. 25:5), to Josephus (Antiq. III.vi.1), and to the Talmudic tradition. Arabic *tuḫas* (or *duḫs*), "dolphin," has often been cited as a possible cognate. This Arabic term may conceivably refer also to the dugong, found in the Red Sea. It seems unlikely, however, that either a dolphin or a dugong would be considered "clean" for the sacred purposes described in Exodus and Numbers, or that their leather would be readily available in a small inland community, as Exod. 25:5; 26:14; 35:7, 23, seem to presuppose. To take תחש as "badger" (KJV) appears to be insupportable: there is no philological justification for it; the "rock badger" (שפן; Lev. 11:5) is an unclean animal; it is doubtful if badger skin was ever as plentiful in Israel as the biblical references to תחש demand.

2. In the NT. As part of the destitution which the saintly men and women of the past endured, the author of Hebrews cites (11:37) their wearing of sheep and goat skins. W. S. MCCULLOUGH

GOB gŏb [גוב; *cf.* גב, Aram. גובא, pit, cistern] (II Sam. 21:18-19). A place of unknown location at which two battles were fought with the Philistines by David (presumably) and his men. In the parallel story (I Chr. 20:4), Gezer, rather than Gob, is given as the locale of the battle. The text of II Samuel may be corrupt at this point. V. R. GOLD

GOBLETS [כלים, vessels] (Esth. 1:7); KJV VESSELS. At the banquet of Ahasuerus drinks were served in golden goblets (vessels) of different kinds.

GOD, CHILDREN OF. *See* CHILDREN OF GOD.

GOD, NAMES OF. The name (שם; ὄνομα) of God is the key to understanding the biblical doctrine of God. In biblical terms the religious question is not: Does God exist? but: Who is our God? Just as an introduction to a person involves a disclosure of his personal name, so God's self-revelation in history is accompanied by the giving of his personal name, by which his people may worship and address him as "Thou." Thus God's name signifies the personal relation between God and people, which is the supreme characteristic of biblical faith (*see* GOD, OT VIEW OF). For Israel, God's personal name is Yahweh (*see* JEHOVAH). Other divine appellations that now appear in the OT, many of them borrowed from ancient religious usage, have been redefined in the light of Yahweh's historical revelation.

A. ***THE RELATION OF THE NAME TO THE PERSON.*** In the episode of the "burning bush" (Exod. 3) Moses hesitated to accept the commission from the "God of the fathers," for back in Egypt his countrymen would ask: "What is his name?" and he would have to identify the God who had spoken to him. This story presupposes a popular background of polytheism. In the ancient world, where man's life was surrounded by many divine powers, it was important to know what kind of god men were dealing with. For unless the god's name were known, it was impossible to enter into relationship with him and invoke him in worship. As late as the prophetic period it was believed that each people walks and acts in the name of its god, just as Israel walks in the name of its God (Mic. 4:5).

But more is involved here than polytheism. To understand Moses' question, we must consider the psychological significance of a personal name in antiquity (*see* NAME, PROPER). In modern usage, names are convenient labels by which we differentiate one thing from another, one person from another. But in the ancient world Shakespeare's question: "What's in a name?" would have been taken very seriously. For a person's self was expressed and contained in his name. Of Nabal (lit., "fool") it was said sarcastically: "As his name is, so is he" (I Sam. 25:25), but it could also be said soberly of anyone that his name *is* his very self. Thus when a radical change in a person's character took place so that he became a new man, he was given a new name. Abram's name was changed to Abraham when the blessing was given to him (Gen. 17), and Jacob's name was changed to Israel after his struggle with the divine being at the Jabbok (Gen. 32).

Analogously, God's self, his real person, is concentrated in his name. When the promise was given that a guardian angel would lead Israel in its journey, this was given special force by Yahweh's assurance that "my name is in him" (Exod. 23:20-21)—i.e., Yahweh himself would go with them (*see* GOD, OT VIEW OF, § C2*b*). The statement that Yahweh's name is Jealous (Exod. 34:14) indicates that Israel's God is jealous by nature (*see* GOD, OT VIEW OF, § D2). Moses' request for a theophany was granted when Yahweh appeared to him and "proclaimed the name of Yahweh" (Exod. 34:5; cf. 33:19)—i.e., the personal character of God was revealed (cf. vss. 6-7).

Because the divine name discloses God's nature, it is laden with the authority, power, and holiness of God himself. This accounts for the great reverence for the name which is one of the distinctive features of Israel's faith. According to the Decalogue, Yahweh's name must not be taken in vain (Exod. 20:7; Deut. 5:11). Prophets are inspired with divine authority when they speak in his name (Deut. 18:19; Jer. 26:20; 44:16), blessings and curses given in his name are potent (Num. 23–24), oaths taken in his name are binding (Deut. 6:13), and battles in his name are victorious (Pss. 20:7—H 20:8; 44:5—H 44:6). In the cultus men "call on the name of Yahweh" (Gen. 12:8; I Kings 18:24; etc.), confident that his name is the basis of the most personal access to God (Ps. 27:4) and his nearness and saving power (Ps. 54:1—H 54:3). The priest, in giving the Aaronic benediction (Num. 6:24-26), is to "put [Yahweh's] name upon the people of Israel" (vs. 27). The people are warned against defiling or blaspheming the name (Lev. 18:21; 24:11; etc.) and are exhorted to praise and sanctify the holy name of God (cf. the Lord's Prayer).

God's name, being filled with his very self, is active and powerful, for it is the sign of his real presence in the midst of his people (*see* GOD, OT VIEW OF, § C2*e*). Other peoples, it is said, will fear Israel, not because it is a powerful nation, but because it is called by Yahweh's name (Deut. 28:10). He delivers "for his name's sake" (Pss. 23:3; 25:11; 143:11; etc.), and his name is mighty among the nations (Jer. 10:6-7). Indeed, Yahweh's name is glorious in all the earth (Pss. 8:1—H 8:2; 48:10—H 48:11), not just in the sense of his world-renown, but in the deeper sense that he is sovereign.

The disclosure of God's name, then, is the index to understanding biblical faith. Israel's view of God does not find expression in a vague God-consciousness or in metaphysical abstraction, but in God's revelation in person. Those who "know the name of God" (Pss. 9:10—H 9:11; 91:14) know his identity and personal character and therefore, in contrast to the heathen (Ps. 79:6; Jer. 10:25), trust and hope in him. The Christian faith stands in line with this historical revelation, for it affirms that God's name—his real person—was manifested pre-eminently in Jesus Christ (*see* INCARNATION). Thus when Jesus is represented as saying: "I have manifested thy name" (John 17:6, 26), the meaning is that his mission was to reveal the very character and purpose of God.

B. ***THE COVENANT NAME, YAHWEH.*** The disclosure of God's name is inseparable from the historical experiences in which the divine presence and purpose were revealed to Israel. According to the tradition, the personal name, Yahweh, was introduced by Moses at the time of the Exodus. Through this decisive event Israel knows who God is: he is the One who rescued his people from Egyptian bondage (Exod. 20:2; Hos. 11:1; 12:9—H 12:10; 13:4; cf. Ezek. 20:5; Amos 2:10; 3:1-2). The new religious perspective which was mediated by Moses to his people cannot be adequately explained on the basis of a genetic development out of previously held religious views. Israel's faith represented a radically new kind of response to divine reality, a response which found expression in a unique covenant community with its distinctive worship, historical understanding, and sense of ethical responsibility. It is therefore highly significant that God's new revelation was tied closely to the disclosure of a new name, Yahweh, the full form of which came to be Yahweh, God of Hosts. *See* LORD OF HOSTS.

1. Pentateuchal traditions. The decisive new beginning in the Mosaic period is obscured by the present Pentateuchal narratives, which have been revised in the light of the exodus faith. The Yahwist narrative (*see* PENTATEUCH) traces the worship of Yahweh far back beyond the period of Moses and affirms that in the time of Enosh, the grandson of Adam, men first began to invoke the name of Yahweh (Gen. 4:26). This narrator's consistent use of the name from the story of Creation onward represents a theological attempt to view the whole of human history in the light of the covenant faith and to demonstrate that Yahweh is not just the God of Israel but of all mankind (Enosh means "man"). However, the latest Pentateuchal tradition, the priestly writing (P), gives a completely different view in Exod. 6:2-3: "And God said to Moses, 'I am Yahweh. I appeared to Abraham, to Isaac, and to Jacob, as God Almighty [El Shaddāy], but by my name Yahweh I did not make myself known to them' " (cf. Gen. 17:1; 28:3; 35:11; 43:14; 48:3; 49:25). Since it would have accorded with P's schematic plan to use the cultic name from the very first, it seems that in this instance P is bound by an old and reliable tradition. This conjecture is confirmed by a third Pentateuchal tradition, E, which avoids using Yahweh in the book of Genesis and affirms that the sacred name was first disclosed in the time of Moses (Exod. 3:1, 4*b*, 6, 9-14). All these traditions agree that Moses was not introduced to a new god. Yahweh was not born in the Mosaic period. The God who spoke to Moses was none other than the God who had led the patriarchs in their wanderings (the "God of the fathers"), the God who had been known previously as El Shaddāy or by some other name (*see* § C2 *below*). But the E and P traditions are undoubtedly correct in stressing the break between the patriarchal and Mosaic periods—a break signified by the disclosure of the name by which Israel was to worship God thenceforth. As indicated above, the knowledge of God, signified by this name, was based on Moses' prophetic interpretation of the meaning of the Exodus.

2. The origin of the name. Although the name was given new currency in Mosaic circles, the J account (Gen. 4:26) may preserve a dim recollection that it was known in the pre-Mosaic period. Thus the question of its original meaning is of some historical interest, although this type of investigation throws little light on OT theology.

In the earliest Hebrew the sacred name appeared as a four-letter word or tetragrammaton: YHWH (יהוה), without any vowel signs. Since the vowels were added very late, at the time of the fixing of the MT (*see* JEHOVAH), the OT itself gives no clue to its original pronunciation. Some help, however, is given by the early church fathers. Theodoret of Cyrus (fourth century A.D.) testifies that the Samaritans, who shared the Pentateuchal scripture with the Jews, pronounced the name 'Ιαβέ, and Clement of Alexandria (early third century A.D.) transliterated the "name of four letters" as 'Ιαουέ. Moreover, Egyptian Magic Papyri from the end of the third century A.D. attest to the patristic spelling, especially that of Theodoret. Following these hints, modern scholars believe the approximate pronunciation was "Yahweh."

It is not certain, however, that "Yahweh" was the oldest form of the name. A short form, "Yah" (יה), appears 25 times in the OT (e.g., Exod. 15:2; and the cultic cry "hallelu-yah"="praise Yah"). Sometimes the short form appears as "Yahu" (יהו) or "Yo" (יו), as in proper names like Joel ("Yo is God") or Isaiah ("Yah [or Yahu] is salvation"). The short form is found on jar-handle inscriptions of the post-exilic period and in the Elephantine Papyri of the fifth century B.C. Some scholars believe that "Yahu" is the more original form. But since the four-letter word is found in some of the oldest OT texts (e.g., the Song of Deborah [Judg. 5]), as well as extra-biblical documents like the Moabite Stone (ninth century) or the Lachish Letters (*ca.* 589 B.C.), it is probable that the original cultic form of the name was "Yahweh" (occurs *ca.* 6,800 times in the OT) and that the other forms are abbreviations.

It is not impossible that the sacred name was known before the time of Moses, but so far attempts to demonstrate this (e.g., on the basis of Akkadian personal names like *Yaum-ilu* or the alleged occurrence of "Yo" [*yw*] in the Ras Shamra Texts of the fourteenth century B.C.) have not yielded conclusive results. More persuasive is the Kenite hypothesis, according to which Moses became acquainted with the name through his association with the family of Jethro (also called Hobab), the priest of Midian. Fleeing from Egypt, Moses married Jethro's daughter (Exod. 2:15-22) and allegedly was initiated into the Midianite cult of the god Yahweh. Sinai (or Horeb) was a sacred spot in Midianite territory, and it was while Moses was tending Jethro's flocks in the vicinity of this mountain that Yahweh was revealed to him (Exod. 3). To this "holy ground" Moses led the Hebrews after the Exodus, and Yahweh's theophany was thenceforth connected in a special way with Sinai, as in the Song of Deborah (Judg. 5:4) or the Elijah narrative (I Kings 19:8-18). Advocates of this hypothesis draw attention to the fact that Jethro, rather than Moses, officiated at a sacrifice to Yahweh (Exod. 18:10-12) and suggested to Moses how he could facilitate the burden of his religious office (vss. 13-26). The supposition that the Kenites (a Midianite clan) and the Mosaic Hebrews (later known as Israelites) were bound by common devotion to Yahweh helps to explain why the former were allies of Israel during the invasion of Canaan (Judg. 1:16; cf. 4:11; 5:24). Although this hypothesis has much in its favor, it is based on a series of inferences from the biblical text and at best gives only a possible explanation of the source from which Moses drew the sacred name.

In any case, whether the name is traced to Midianites or to the region of Syria or Mesopotamia, the important question is the new content which the name acquired through Moses' interpretation.

3. Definition. Since, with the exception of Exod. 3:14, the OT itself makes no attempt to explain the meaning of the Tetragrammaton, it is not surprising that scholars have been unable to reach agreement on its linguistic meaning (*see bibliography*). Of the various hypotheses, the following may be mentioned.

According to one view, the effort to ascertain the basic meaning of the word is fruitless, because originally the name, perhaps in the short form "Yah" or "Yahu," was only an emotional ejaculation or solemn cultic cry. One scholar proposes, e.g., that the original form of the interjection was *yâ hûwâ,* meaning "O He, O That One." The majority view, however, is that we are dealing with a word, patterned according to the imperfect of a finite verb, which once described the God of Israel. Differences arise over two major questions: Is the stem of the verb simple (*Qal*) or causative (*Hiph'il*)? And what is the basic meaning of the root הוה (or היה)?

Some commentators who advocate the imperfect of the simple stem find in this usage of the verb "to be" the conception of Israel's God as "the One who is" —namely, the absolute and unchangeable God. Recent interpreters, however, have sought to do greater justice to the dynamic, activistic character of Israel's historical faith. It has been proposed, e.g., that the Tetragrammaton is derived from Arabic HWY in its allegedly basic meaning of showing passionate love (*hawā,* "passion") and therefore that it means "he who acts passionately, the Passionate." According to another view, the name comes from a verb "to speak" (Ugaritic HWT, from HWY, "word"), thus meaning "he who speaks," a view which has the merit of stressing the revelatory function of Israel's God.

Many scholars, however, defend the causative interpretation, though disagreeing on the basic meaning of the verb. One theory is that the verb means "cause to fall, fell," referring either to rain or lightning or to the destruction of foes. More persuasively, it is argued that the derivation is from Arabic HWY, "to blow," thus indicating that Yahweh was originally a storm-god. The Arabic origin of "Yahweh," it is held, accords with OT traditions which link him with the Negeb and with S sanctuaries like Sinai-Horeb and Kadesh. An unusual variation of the causative interpretation appears in the hypothesis that YHWH is a causative participle, after the analogy of a form appearing in the recently discovered Phoenician inscription from Karapte in S Anatolia. As an epithet for the God of Israel, it is alleged to mean "Sustainer, Maintainer, Establisher."

The theory which perhaps has aroused the greatest interest is one which derives the Tetragrammaton from הוה (later form היה) in the sense of "come to pass, come into being, be" (*see below*). Yahweh is the one who causes to be what comes to pass. It is held that the name echoes old liturgical formulas, found especially in Egypt, in which the deity was recognized as the one who continually brings about all that is—namely, the Creator and Sustainer of all. Having become acquainted with this idea while in Egypt, Moses rallied his people to follow and worship this God who revealed himself uniquely to him.

The divine name is explained on the basis of the Hebrew verb היה in Exod. 3:14, but the etymology is rather opaque. When Moses asked the name of the deity who had commissioned him, he received the strange answer: "I am who [or what] I am" (אהיה אשר אהיה). After the manner of popular etymologies found elsewhere in the Pentateuch (cf. Gen. 17:5; 27:36; 29:31-35), the divine name is interpreted on the basis of a wordplay on the verb הוה or היה, an alliteration which is more obvious in Hebrew than in English (YHWH [יהוה]: 'eHYeH [אהיה]). Two interpretations of this etymology have been advanced.

a. The present meaning. One interpretation takes the verb in the simple (*Qal*) stem. "I am" means that "I am here, really present, ready to help." Thus Yahweh's being is not passive and abstract, but is his being present. The second half of the statement ("that I am," אשר אהיה), according to this view, means that Yahweh makes himself present as he wills. He acts according to his sovereign freedom (cf. Exod. 33:19). The Tetragrammaton, then, means: "He is present."

b. The causative meaning. Another interpretation, which has much to commend it, takes the verb in the causative (*Hiph'il*) stem, which is precisely the grammatical form of the word "Yahweh." On this view, instead of "I am" we should read "I cause to be." When the whole enigmatic formula is changed into the causative, it means: "I cause to be what comes into existence." It is conjectured that behind this was an older formulation in the third person: "He causes to be what comes into existence" (*Yahweh 'asher yihweh*)—i.e., He is the Creator of all. This interpretation has the merit of putting the accent on Yahweh's dynamic lordship: He is the One who causes to be what is (or what happens)—i.e., historical events and natural happenings have their origin in his sovereign will.

In either case, Exod. 3:14 does not give a philosophical definition of God in terms of eternal, changeless, passive Being, as implied in the LXX translation εἰμί ὁ ὤν. Such metaphysical speculation would have been foreign to Israel's faith. The context of the passage sets forth the conviction that Yahweh is the active God, whose lordship is manifest in historical affairs (3:7-10). Having summoned Moses to be his agent, he overrules his protest about his inadequacy with the promise: "I will be with you" (vs. 12), and he sends him to Egypt to assure the Hebrews that the God of the fathers is powerful to deliver. Here divine reality is experienced in the voluntaristic terms of leadership and lordship. Yahweh is the God who manifests himself as Israel's redeemer, whose power humiliates the mightiest ruler of the day, and who calls the forces of nature into the service of his historical purpose.

It is rather striking, however, that the Yahweh etymology is not mentioned again in the exodus story, nor is it referred to explicitly anywhere else in the OT. It gives the impression of being an aside to Moses only. Moses was not instructed to give the explanation of the name to his countrymen in Egypt, but was merely to say that "Yahweh the God of your fathers . . . has sent me to you" (vs. 15). The narrative is concerned primarily with Yahweh's action and Moses' task. Hence some scholars have argued, not convincingly, that vss. 13-14 represent a parenthetical etymology added later to the tradition. Others, however, argue more plausibly that the passage is intentionally evasive and cryptic, and that it can best be understood in the light of the intimate relation between the name and the person of the bearer (*see* § A *above*). Knowledge of the name, it was feared, would give men power over the deity, because his person was contained in his name. Thus Jacob's request of the divine being at the Jabbok (Gen. 32:22-32): "Tell me, I pray, your name," was met with refusal, probably because such knowledge would give him magical power over his assailant. Similarly Manoah sought in vain to know the name of the angelic visitor who came to foretell the birth of Samson (Judg. 13:17-18). The same kind of reticence may be reflected in the indirect and evasive answer to Moses' query. He had asked to know the divine name in the belief that such knowledge would enable him to exercise influence over the deity. Instead, he was rebuked with a cryptic reply, summoned to serve the God who is free to act as he will, and promised that he would know who God is by the mighty acts that he would perform on behalf of his people.

The important feature of the name is not its linguistic value, but its historical associations. Whatever it meant once, it acquired concrete content through the historical experiences of Israel, beginning with the Exodus. Probably the Israelites soon forgot, if they ever knew, the literal meaning of the name. But Israel did not forget the connotation of the name which was given in the Mosaic period: "I am Yahweh who brought you up out of the land of Egypt." The witness of Israel's faith is not based on the cryptic etymology of Exod. 3:14 but on the historical evidence that Yahweh reveals his name (i.e., his personal character) through his mighty deeds.

C. *APPELLATIONS APPROPRIATED BY ISRAEL.* That the Sinai revelation marked a new beginning under the aegis of a special divine name is indicated by evidence concerning theophorous names —i.e., personal names compounded with "Yahweh." While these names began to appear from the time of Moses on, the biblical tradition indicates that they were lacking in the pre-Mosaic period.

It is difficult to reconstruct the religion of the patriarchal period, for the traditions have been reworked in the light of the Yahweh faith. The religion designated by the expression "the God of the fathers" (cf. Exod. 3:6) was undoubtedly polytheistic, as Josh. 24:2 explicitly states, and in many respects was part and parcel of the El-worship of the ancient Semites (*see below*). This is implied by P's statement that in the pre-Mosaic period Yahweh made himself known as El Shaddāy, and perhaps also by the E practice of using the Semitic name Elohim (*see* § C3 *below*) in the narratives covering the period from Abraham through Joseph (Gen. 12-50). Probably the religion of the fathers provided a special preparation for the Sinai revelation. But the ancestors of Israel also transmitted general Semitic divine names which once had polytheistic associations and which later were reinterpreted by being identified with the one name, Yahweh.

1. El (אל). This is the generic Semitic name for "God" or "deity." It appears in Akkadian in the form *ilu,* and is found likewise in other Semitic languages, such as Phoenician and South Arabic. Although the derivation of the word is uncertain, apparently its root meaning is "power," a meaning which is preserved in idiomatic expressions like "the mountains of El" (i.e., "mighty mountains"; cf. Ps. 36:6 KJV—H 36:7), "the cedars of El" ("mighty cedars"; cf. Ps. 80:10—H 80:11), or "the El of my hand" (usually translated "the power of my hand"; Gen. 31:29; Deut. 28:32). Basically the word designates the numinous divine power that fills men with awe and dread. An echo of this meaning is preserved in the story of Jacob, who awoke from a dream and, realizing that he had been sleeping in a sacred place, was filled with great dread (Gen. 28:17). In the present form of the story the El is identified with Yahweh (vs. 16); this is an indication of how the old Canaanite tradition associated with the Bethel sanctuary has been reworked by Israel.

It must not be supposed, however, that El religion moved at the level of primitive animism—i.e., the impersonal supernatural power known as mana. Admittedly there were animistic holdovers from ancient times, but during the patriarchal period (middle of second millennium B.C.) El was worshiped as a high God. In the Ras Shamra literature he is extolled as the chief god of the Canaanite pantheon, the father of the gods and the lord of heaven. The element "El" is found in biblical names such as Me-thusha-el (Gen. 4:18) and Ishmael (the ancestor of the Arabs; Gen. 16:11), and probably was once compounded with Jacob, Isaac, and Joseph (e.g., the form *Ya'qōbh-'el,* "May El Protect," appears in extrabiblical documents of the second millennium). The fact that the preponderance of theophorous names in the book of Genesis contain the element "El," and none the element "Yahweh," is strong evidence of the dependence of Israel's faith upon a Semitic heritage as transmitted through Canaanite cult centers.

After the time of Moses, the name El continued in use within Israelite circles, especially in poetic literature which preserves ancient linguistic usage. The use of the name in the book of Job probably reflects the sage's concern for God's relation to man as man, rather than for the particular historical revelation associated with the name Yahweh. There are other instances, too (e.g., Ps. 104:21), where the more general term for "deity" may have been intentionally employed. But for the most part, "El" is used as a synonym for "Yahweh." In the present form of the oracles of Balaam, El is none other than Yahweh who brought his people out of Egypt (Num. 23:8, 19, 22-23; 24:4, 8, 16, 23), and there are numerous other instances where "El" is used in parallelism with "Yahweh" (Ps. 85:8—H 85:9; Isa. 42:5) or clearly has the same meaning (Pss. 16:1; 17:6; Isa. 40:18).

2. Combinations of El. In the early tradition "El" does not always refer to the Canaanite father of the gods, but may refer indefinitely to deity. In this sense, it often appears in combinations which identify the god.

a. El Shaddāy (אל שדי). This probably meant "God, the one of the mountain(s)" (KJV-RSV "God Almighty"). As noted in § B1 *above,* El Shaddāy was worshiped in the patriarchal period, according to the P tradition. This tradition is probably authentic, as attested in old personal names containing the element "Shaddāy" (Zuri-shaddāy [Num. 1:6]; Ammi-shaddāy [vs. 12]; cf. Shedeur [vs. 5]), as well as occurrences of the divine name in ancient poetry (Gen. 49:25; Num. 24:4, 16). The chief El of the patriarchs was Shaddāy, probably the "god of the mountain(s)." The name apparently refers to this El's localization in a mountainous region or to his theophany in mountain storm (cf. the "earthquake, wind, and fire" associated with the Sinai theophany [Exod. 19; I Kings 19]). In the time of Abraham the deity was identified with the heavenly storm-god, Hadad, who was often known as Baal among the Canaanites. Thus the name attests to the NW Mesopotamian (Amorite) background of the patriarchs.

However, the nature religion implied in the worship of the mountain god was modified in the cult of the "God of the fathers." Patriarchal religion was based on a close personal, contractual relationship between the leader of a family and the God (El) who manifested himself in a special theophany. Tradition mentions the "God of Abraham" (Gen. 31:53), the "Kinsman [RSV 'fear'] of Isaac" (31:42), and the "Mighty One of Jacob" (49:24; cf. Isa. 1:24). The patriarchal god was not bound to a holy place, but to a family whose leader had chosen him in response to a special visitation. The god manifested his power, not in the sphere of nature primarily, but by protecting the family, upholding its social life, and guiding its historical pilgrimage. Undoubtedly this conception of the "God of the wanderers" provided the background and preparation for the Mosaic revelation, as the exodus story testifies.

After the patriarchal period, the original meaning of "Shaddāy" was eclipsed, and the name occasionally was used as a synonym for "Yahweh" (Ruth 1:20-21; Pss. 68:14—H 68:15; 91:1; Ezek. 1:24; 10:5). Excluding the book of Genesis and Exod. 6:2-3, the name occurs elsewhere in the OT thirty-five times, twenty-nine of which are in the book of Job. The author of Job favored this name, for evidently to him it was free from the specifically Israelite connotations of "Yahweh" and expressed the majesty and omnipotence of deity. The LXX renders "Shaddāy" in the book of Job as κύριος ("Lord") or παντοκράτωρ ("Almighty"), the latter influencing subsequent translations (so KJV and RSV). Aside from the quotation in II Cor. 6:18, παντοκράτωρ occurs only in the book of Revelation (e.g., 1:8; 4:8; 21:22).

b. El Elyon (אל עליון). This name, or simply Elyon (עליון, "Exalted One," "Most High"), in Canaanite usage was a title for the Exalted One, the highest god of the pantheon, El. The Canaanite background of the title is illustrated by the story in Gen. 14 which reflects the Jerusalem cultus in pre-Israelite times. Melchizedek, priest of El Elyon, blesses Abr(ah)am in the name of this God, whom he praises as "maker [or possessor] of heaven and earth" (vss. 18-20). The polytheistic associations of the name have been refined from the biblical story, for Abraham hastens to identify El Elyon with Yahweh (vs. 22). Likewise in the oracles of Balaam three Canaanite words for "deity"—"El," "Shaddāy," and "Elyon"—are grouped together (Num. 24:16). In these and other instances "Elyon" changed its meaning by becoming a synonym for "Yahweh" (Deut. 32:8-9; II Sam. 22:14; Pss. 7:17—H 7:18; 9:2—H 9:3; 21:7—H 21:8; 46:4—H 46:5; 91:1, 9; etc.). At times there seems to be a faint echo of the old polytheistic meaning (cf. Ps. 97:9), but in Israel's faith this language referred to the heavenly council, within which Yahweh rules over the divine beings (the בני־אלהים; cf. Pss. 29:1; 82:1, 6; 89:6—H 89:7) who serve him. *See* HOSTS.

During the major part of the OT period, however, the name Elyon fell into disuse, surviving only in the poetic and liturgical passages referred to above. But in the late postexilic period, when there was a strong tendency to stress the exalted and transcendent majesty of God, it enjoyed new favor. In its Aramaic form (אלהא עליא) it appears a number of times in the Aramaic section of Daniel (e.g., Dan. 3:26; 4:2—A 3:32; 4:24, 32, 34—A 4:21, 29, 31). It occurs frequently in the apocryphal books I Esdras and the Wisdom of Sirach, and quite often in the pseudepigraphical books Enoch, Jubilees, and IV Ezra. In the Greek form ὕψιστος it appears a few times in the NT (Mark 5:7 = Luke 8:28; Acts 7:48; 16:17; Heb. 7:1).

c. El Olam (אל עולם). This means "God the Everlasting One," "God of Eternity." As Elyon was associated originally with pre-Israelite Jerusalem, so El Olam was connected with the ancient Canaanite sanctuary of Beer-sheba (Gen. 21:33). The word עולם means "everlasting time," "time whose boundaries are hidden from view." As applied to El, presumably the meaning is that his sovereignty continues through the ages, unaffected by the passing of time.

When the Beer-sheba shrine was taken over by Israel, the title El Olam was applied to Yahweh, who was known as the "Living God" (*see* § D4 *below*). Yahweh's exaltation over the course of the ages is based on the proclamation that he is the "everlasting God" (אלהי עולם; Isa. 40:28), as expressed in the psalmist's affirmation: "From everlasting to everlasting thou art God" (Ps. 90:1-2; cf. 93:2; Isa. 26:4).

d. El Bethel (אל בית־אל). On the analogy of El Shaddāy, El Olam, and El Elyon, perhaps the word "Bethel" is a name of God (Gen. 35:7), as suggested in Gen. 31:13, where the definite article is used—viz., "the El Bethel" (האל בית־אל). Support for this view is found in the Elephantine Papyri of the fifth century B.C., where the God Bethel is definitely mentioned. On the other hand, some versions of Gen. 35:7 (Samar., LXX, Vulg.) interpret the words to mean the "El of Bethel"—i.e., the God revealed in the shrine named Bethel.

e. El Roi (אל ראי). This expression, perhaps meaning the "God who sees me," occurs in Gen. 16:13 as the name of the deity of the spring Beer-lahai-roi, who protected Hagar in the desert. It has been suggested that the name may mean "God of Vision or

Divining," in which case this God would have a special relationship to the diviner or seer (ראה).

f. El Berith (אל ברית). This name, "God of the Covenant," appears in Judg. 9:46, and alternatively in the form "Baal-berith" (Judg. 8:33; 9:4), as the God of the Shechem covenant alliance. The remains of the ancient Canaanite temple to this deity (9:4), excavated by archaeologists, can be seen to this day. Presumably the Shechem covenant tradition antedates the covenant alliance which Joshua made at the place (Josh. 24), and goes back at least to the Amarna period (end of fifteenth and first two thirds of fourteenth century B.C.), when Lab'ayu, Canaanite ruler of the city, made a league with the 'Apiru (*see* ISRAEL, HISTORY OF). The tradition is attested, not only by the name of the El or Baal who watched over the covenant, but also by the ascendancy of the "men of Hamor" (Judg. 9:28; cf. Gen. 33:19; 34), for the word חמור (lit., "ass") reflects the ancient practice of making a covenant by the ritual slaughter of an ass, as known from the Mari Letters. The Shechem tradition, then, is eloquent witness to the incorporation of earlier Canaanite religious conceptions into the Israelite faith at the time of the formation of the Israelite covenant confederacy.

g. El Elohe-Israel (אל אלהי ישראל). This name, "El the God of Israel," is also connected with the Shechem covenant tradition. According to Gen. 33:19-20, Jacob purchased a plot of land by the city of Shechem and there built an altar to the El (God) identified as the "God of Israel." The expression seems to indicate that the Jacob tradition has been revised in the light of later experiences, for Israel as a people came into being with the formation of the twelve-tribe confederacy in the time of Joshua. The full title of the God of the confederacy was "El the God of Israel," and from the time of Joshua on, El was identified with Yahweh (cf. Josh. 8:30).

In summary, these El names were originally pre-Israelite in their meaning. With the exception of El Shaddāy, they generally appear in connection with particular Canaanite shrines and reflect ancient Semitic religion. When the Israelites came into Canaan, they took over these shrines, together with the religious traditions associated with them, and rededicated them to the worship of Yahweh. The religious revolution brought about by this reinterpretation can be seen clearly from Joshua's demand that Israel must put away the "gods which your fathers served [in the region] beyond the River [Euphrates], . . . or the gods of the Amorites [Canaanites] in whose land you dwell" (Josh. 24:14-15), for Yahweh is a "jealous El" (vs. 19) who will not tolerate the worship of other gods. *See* GOD, OT VIEW OF, § D2.

3. Elohim (אלהים). This word appears frequently in the OT as a name for deity ("God," "gods"). Being plural in form, it echoes ancient polytheism, like the name El, to which it is closely related. In a few instances the plural sense is clearly expressed, as in Jotham's fable (Judg. 9:13) or Jethro's declaration that Yahweh is greater than the other אלהים (Exod. 18:11; cf. Exod. 12:12; 20:3; Deut. 10:17; I Sam. 4:8; II Sam. 7:23; Ps. 86:8).

In the great majority of instances, however, "Elohim" is used in a singular sense, even when, as a concession to the plural form of the word, the accompanying verb is in the plural (e.g., Gen. 1:26; 20:13; 35:7; Exod. 22:9—H 22:8). This use is often called the "plural of majesty" or *pluralis amplitudinis*—i.e., Elohim includes all gods; the fulness of deity is comprehended in him. Thus the word is equivalent to "deity" or "Godhead." In this sense it is used in the priestly account of Creation: "Then Elohim said, 'Let us make man in our image, after our likeness' " (Gen. 1:26). The passage presupposes the conception of the heavenly council (*see* HOSTS) ruled over by God (I Kings 22:19; Job 1:6; Pss. 82:1; 89:7; Isa. 6:8). This circle of heavenly beings or "sons of God" (בני אלהים) is referred to in the plural verb "let us" and the pronoun "our." Despite this court imagery, the priestly view is clearly monotheistic, for Elohim embraces the divine plurality in unity, and elsewhere in the priestly account the divine name is accompanied by verbs in the singular.

The "plural of majesty" did not arise first in Israelite tradition as a result of the identification of Elohim with Yahweh or the gradual development from polytheism to monotheism. On the contrary, this is an ancient pre-Israelite expression which was employed in Babylonia and Canaan even with a singular verb. Thus in Akkadian the plural word *ilanu* ("gods") could be used in homage to a particular god, like the moon-god Sin, to express the worshiper's view that he is the highest God, in whom the whole pantheon is represented. In the Amarna Letters, Canaanite vassals addressed the deified pharaoh as *ilania* ("my gods"), thus saying that the fulness of deity is concentrated in him.

In the singular sense "Elohim" is sometimes applied in the OT to the god of another people, as to Chemosh the god of the Ammonites (Judg. 11:24), Ashtoreth (Ishtar) goddess of Sidon (I Kings 11:5), or Baal-zebub of Ekron (II Kings 1:2). But in the majority of cases "Elohim" refers to the God known and worshiped in Israel. For Israel, Yahweh is not one El among many; he is God absolutely, the Lord of history and nature, who demands the exclusive homage of his people. This comes to emphatic expression in the challenge presented by Elijah (whose name means "My El is Yahweh") to the people in the time when the worship of the Phoenician Baal Melkart was being advocated: "If Yahweh is God [האלהים], follow him; but if Baal, then follow him" (I Kings 18:21; cf. vss. 37, 39). Elijah mocks the claim of the Baal to be God (vs. 27) and demonstrates dramatically that only Yahweh has the power that belongs to deity (*see* GOD, OT VIEW OF, § D6). The conviction that Yahweh is Elohim, God in the absolute sense, is emphasized in the Elohistic (E) narratives of the Pentateuch, so designated because the narrator prefers to use the divine name Elohim, especially for the period before the Mosaic revelation.

The use of Elohim in the priestly creation story, as noted above, is explained not only by the writer's avoidance of the special name Yahweh before the Mosaic period (Exod. 6:2-3), but especially by the attempt to avoid any taint of polytheism, such as was characteristic of ancient mythologies of CREATION. The name Elohim stresses the fact that God, the Creator, is the absolute Lord over his creation and the sovereign of history. Since the priestly scheme articulates history into several dispensations (Creation to Noah, Noah to Abraham, Abraham to Moses), each having its special blessing and commandment, and all leading up to the climactic revelation of Sinai, it is apparent that in Gen. 1 Elohim is none other than the God whose personal name, Yahweh, was later disclosed. Thus the priestly redactors of the Pentateuch in Gen. 2-3 placed Elohim in apposition to Yahweh in the expression "Yahweh Elohim" ("the LORD God"; e.g., 2:4*b*, 5, 7), the intention being to affirm that Yahweh is Elohim, the God of all times.

In the LXX the usual practice is to translate "El," "Elohim," and "Eloah" (*see below*) with θεός and to render "Yahweh" with κύριος. The word θεός, of course, had its own history and associations in Greek culture. In the NT, however, where this word is used as the basic word for "God," its meaning is not defined primarily out of the Greek thought-world but out of the sacred history of which the OT is the witness (Heb. 1:2).

4. Eloah (אלוה). This is thought by some to be a singular vocative form related to the plural form "Elohim." It occurs forty-two times in the book of Job and only fifteen times elsewhere (e.g., Deut. 32: 15, 17; Ps. 18:31—H 18:32; Prov. 30:5; Isa. 44:8; Hab. 1:11). In the latter cases it is usually synonymous in meaning with "Elohim" (Ps. 50:22-23) or with "Yahweh" (Ps. 139:19; cf. 114:7). The name is apparently favored in Job because it is not necessarily laden with the historical connotations of the "God of Israel." The word seems to appear with greatest frequency in the exilic and postexilic periods, as shown by some of the above citations, as well as II Chr. 32:15; Neh. 9:17; Dan. 11:37-39.

5. Baal (בעל). Although this word, meaning "lord, owner," could be used of human leaders (Num. 21: 28; Judg. 9:6; Isa. 16:8) or of the owner of cattle (Isa. 1:3), it is primarily a designation of the Canaanite god of storm and fertility (*see* BAAL). In ancient religious usage, the names Baal and El could be used alternatively, as at Shechem, where men invoked the covenant God as either El-berith or Baal-berith (Judg. 8:33; 9:4, 46). This fact leads one to expect that Baal, like El, would have been appropriated by Israel and identified with Yahweh. Undeniably, there were tendencies in this direction, as illustrated by the fact that in the early period of the settlement parents named children after the land-god Baal, apparently with no thought of abandoning Yahweh. Two ardent devotees of Yahweh, Saul and David, named children in this manner—e.g., Saul's son Ish-baal (II Sam. 4:1, 5; I Chr. 8:33) and grandson Mephibaal (II Sam. 4:4) or Merib-baal (I Chr. 8:34), and David's daughter Beeliada (I Chr. 14:7). However, the worship of Baal was based on a religious outlook basically incompatible with the Yahweh faith, and the rise of the prophetic movement, especially with Elijah, brought the issue to an either-or decision. The prophet Hosea, who emphasized the folly and sin of Israel's resorting to the Canaanite nature religion, declared that the time would come when Israelites no longer would call Yahweh "my Baal" (Jer. 2:8; 7:9; Hos. 2:16—H 2:18; cf. 2:8, 13, 17—H 2:10, 15, 19; etc.). So deep was the revulsion toward the name Baal, as a result of the victorious prophetic struggle, that later editors substituted for it the word בשת, "shame," in the proper names of the books of Samuel and Kings (e.g., Ish-bosheth, Mephibosheth).

6. Adon (אדון). This title ("lord"; Greek Adonis) is closely related in meaning to "Baal" and is also of foreign origin, as indicated by its appearance in Canaanite names like Adoni-zedek (Josh. 10:3). But while "Baal" is primarily a divine name, "Adon" is basically an honorific title. In ordinary speech etiquette, it was customarily used as a title of courtesy and respect in addressing a superior, just as we would say "sir," "your honor," "my lord." It was appropriately used by a subject when speaking to the king (I Sam. 24:8—H 24:9; 26:17; Jer. 22:18; cf. Gen. 44:18), by a wife to her husband (Gen. 18: 12), by a daughter or son to the father (Gen. 31:35), by a slave to his master (Gen. 24:12; Exod. 21:5; cf. Mal. 1:6), or by a subordinate to his leader (Num. 11:28). Thus the title refers to one's position of authority and prestige (Gen. 23:6; 45:8), and in this sense could be used as a title in addressing God, to whom, in the highest sense, honor and dominion belong.

In Israel's faith the title belongs pre-eminently to Yahweh, for he alone is the "Lord of all the earth" (Josh. 3:11, 13; Ps. 97:5; Mic. 4:13; Zech. 4:14; 6:5). Therefore the title is frequently used in apposition to Yahweh (Exod. 23:17; 34:23; Isa. 1:24; 3:15; 10: 16; Amos 8:1; and frequently in Ezekiel) or as a substitute (Pss. 90:1; 114:7; Isa. 6:1, 8, 11; Mal. 3:1).

In the postexilic period increasing reverence for the name of God made it expedient to safeguard the religious use of "Adon," lest men should address God as they would human superiors. Therefore, the title, when used in apposition to or in place of "Yahweh," was written in a distinctive way. First of all, the sacred title was spelled with the pronominal suffix ending (אדון+י). This ending "my" (י), however, merely became a part of the word, as in the case of "rabbi" (lit., "my great one") or "milady." In the second place, the divine title Adonai was vocalized in a slightly different manner from the similar form אדני, the secular word meaning "my lords" (Gen. 19:2) or, plural of "majesty," "my lordship." The difference was very slight—the short "a" in the diphthong (*ai*) of the latter word was merely lengthened to a long "a"; but the small difference was sufficient to mark *Adonai* as a distinctively religious term.

Fear of profaning the name of God led LXX translators to translate YHWH as κύριος ("Lord") and Masoretes to vocalize the Tetragrammaton with the vowels of *Adonai* (*see* JEHOVAH). The reflex of this reverence was also felt in certain parts of the OT, especially the prophetic books, where *Adonai* was often substituted for Yahweh. A probable example is Isa. 6:1, which now reads: "I saw אדני sitting upon a throne" (in vss. 1, 8, many MSS read יהוה). Textual changes of this kind were undoubtedly dictated by the attempt to avoid the divine name in a context where it seemed irreverent to use it (cf. Gen. 18:3, 27, 31, where *Adonai* is also used). Thus in the late postexilic period, when Jewish religion emphasized the transcendence and holiness of God, *Adonai* came to be, not just a title of honor and respect, but an expression of God's absolute lordship. *See* LORD.

D. *OTHER APPELLATIONS.* Israel also drew from the cultural milieu and from her own historical experience a number of epithets and metaphors in order to express faith in Yahweh.

1. Rock (Zur, צור). The meaning of this term is "rock." It has been suggested that, as it sometimes appears in parallel with סלע ("cliff," "crag"), the word was a figure of speech drawn from Palestinian scenery to portray divine strength and permanence. No doubt these local associations favored the continued usage of the word (cf. Isa. 32:2), but it is quite probable that the primary meaning was given in the pre-Mosaic period when the patriarchal deity, Shaddāy, was invested with mountain imagery (*see* § C2*a above*). In Akkadian prayers the deity was often addressed as "great mountain," and throughout the West men worshiped the great storm-god, Hadad, usually known as Baal among the Canaanites. Thus the mountain or rock imagery suggested by צור has its source in the NW Mesopotamian locale with which the patriarchs are connected. Support for this view is found in some of the early personal names like Elizur ("My God is a Rock"), who was the son of Shedeur or, probably more accurately spelled, *Shaddāy-'ôr* ("The Mountain One Shines [shows favor on me?]"; Num. 1:5). Another early name was Pedahzur ("May the Rock Redeem"; Num. 1:10).

Israel affirmed that Yahweh is the Rock of Israel (Isa. 30:29; cf. Gen. 49:24). The name often appears in poetic literature (e.g., Pss. 18:2—H 18:3; parallel with סלע: 18:31—H 18:32; 18:46—H 18:47; 19:14—H 19:15; 28:1; 78:35; 89:26—H 89:27; Isa. 17:10; 44:8; Hab. 1:12). An important passage in this connection is the so-called Song of Moses (Deut. 32), where it is affirmed that Yahweh is the Rock who has given birth to his people (vs. 18) and whose stability and steadfastness are their sole refuge (vss. 4, 15, 30-31). In Isa. 26:4 Yahweh is called an "everlasting rock." The KJV marginal translation "Rock of Ages" became the basis of A. M. Toplady's famous hymn by this title.

The reference to Yahweh as the "Rock of Israel" provided the basis for the rabbinic haggadah that the Rock followed the people during their wilderness wanderings, and this in turn prompted Paul to say that the Rock (πέτρα) of Israel was none other than Christ (I Cor. 10:4). In the NT, God is not called "Rock," perhaps because the LXX had rendered צור by "God" or some other term, although the associations of constancy, strength, unvarying mercy, etc., were carried over into the vocabulary of the Christian revelation.

2. Father, Brother, Kinsman. A cluster of names, such as אב, "father"; אח, "brother"; עם, "kinsman," were used in antiquity to express the very close family relation between the deity and his worshipers. We have already noticed that patriarchal religion was of this type, as illustrated in the divine name "Kinsman [פחד] of Isaac" (RSV "fear of Isaac"; *see* § C2*a above*). The conception of family kinship with the deity is reflected in personal names like Eliab, "My God is Father" (Num. 1:9; I Sam. 16:6); Ahiezer, "My [divine] Brother is help" (Num. 1:12); or Ammishaddai, "[The god of] my Kindred is Shaddāy" (Num. 1:12). The ancient Semitic background of these divine names is the view that the god was actually a blood relative of the clan or family, whose members were by the same token sons, brothers, and kinsmen of the god.

In this connection it is noteworthy that the conception of God as Father is much older than the NT or rabbinic period. It is found in the hymns of ancient Babylonia in which worshipers addressed the deity as "Father of the Land" and in the Canaanite worship of El as the all-father. It is also reflected in numerous names in the OT which contain the element אב, such as Abraham, Abimelech, Abishua, Absalom, and Abijah. However, during the period of the monarchy father-son imagery was avoided, evidently because it suggested the pagan notion of an actual physical or natural relationship between the god and his people (Jer. 2:27; cf. 3:19). When used, it was redefined to mean sonship by adoption, as in Yahweh's gracious election of Israel (Exod. 4:22-23; Hos. 11:1-4), or his adoption of the king as his son (II Sam. 7:14-15; Ps. 2:7). After the idea of divine fatherhood was freed from its pagan associations, the term אב was used with increasing frequency (cf. Isa. 63:16; 64:8—H 64:7; Mal. 1:6) in the Jewish and Christian vocabulary of worship. *See* GOD, NT.

3. King, Judge, Shepherd. Out of a political ideology came the related terms מלך, "king"; שפט, "judge"; רעה, "shepherd." In the ancient Semitic world it was a widespread practice to address the deity as King, as indicated by the many personal names containing the element מלך (e.g., Abimelech). This political anthropomorphism provided metaphorical language to express the relation between Yahweh, the Lord who had manifested his beneficence to his enslaved people, and Israel, whose responsibility within the covenant was that of servants who obey their sovereign (*see* COVENANT). Early attempts to make Israel a monarchy "like the nations" were resisted under the conviction that Yahweh alone is Israel's King (Judg. 8:23; I Sam. 8). Some scholars believe that during the monarchy an annual throne-ascension ceremony was held at the turn of the year, when the reigning king participated in rituals which dramatized Yahweh's ascension to his throne, his victory over all enemies, and his sovereign control of his people's destiny. However this may be, Yahweh was praised by the worshiping community as the "King of glory" (Ps. 24), and the idea of divine kingship appears frequently in the Psalms (5:2—H 5:3; 29:10; 44:4—H 44:5; 47:6-8—H 47:7-9; 48:2—H 48:3; 68:24—H 68:25; 74:12; 84:3—H 84:4; 95:3; 97:1; 99:4; 146:10). In his inaugural vision Isaiah beheld Yahweh as the King par excellence (Isa. 6:1, 5), and this theme is emphasized especially in the message of Second Isaiah, who announces that Yahweh, Israel's King (Isa. 41:21; 43:15; 44:6; 52:7) and the King of the world (52:10), is coming to inaugurate his eschatological kingdom. Thus the title provides the key to the understanding of the OT doctrine of the KINGDOM OF GOD.

The title "Judge," like "King," refers to the function of the ruler. In a passage from the fourteenth-century Ras Shamra Tablets the two terms are used of the deity in poetic parallelism: "Our king is Triumphant Baal, our judge, above whom there is no one!" Moreover, the word "judge" was used for the early leaders of the Israelite confederacy, whose task was not just to arbitrate legal disputes (as in our restricted meaning of the term), but to get justice for Israel by acting in military crises when the confederacy was threatened (see the book of Judges). In the highest sense, Yahweh is Judge (Gen. 18:25), for his actions in history set things right (*see* GOD, OT VIEW OF, § D5; RIGHTEOUSNESS IN THE OT), by humbling the oppressor and exalting the oppressed. Thus Israel could say:

> Yahweh is our judge, Yahweh is our ruler,
> Yahweh is our king; he will save us
> (Isa. 33:22).

The psalmist appeals to Yahweh to judge him (Ps. 7:8—H 7:9) or to come to judge the earth (Ps. 96:13).

The title "Shepherd" is also related to the office of kingship. In the ancient Orient the king was often styled as the shepherd of his people, as, e.g., in the prologue to the Code of Hammurabi, and the court language was also applied to deities whose role was to lead and protect the people. Divested of its ancient polytheistic associations, the term was applied to Yahweh throughout the OT period, and was particularly appropriate for expressing the personal relation between God and his people in the covenant. Israel is Yahweh's "flock" or the "sheep of his pasture" (Pss. 79:13; 95:7; 100:3), and Yahweh is the Shepherd (Gen. 49:24; Ps. 80:1—H 80:2) who leads (lit., "shepherds") and enfolds his people with goodness and concern, as expressed classically in the Twenty-third Psalm. The notion of Yahweh as King and Shepherd is illustrated beautifully in Isa. 40:11 (cf. Ezek. 34). In the NT the same thought appears in the parable of the shepherd (Luke 15:4-7) or the Johannine portrayal of Christ as the Good Shepherd (John 10:1-18).

4. Descriptive expressions. Besides the titles and epithets used along with the special name Yahweh, there are a number of descriptive expressions which point up particular traits of God as known within the covenant. Some of these, like the affirmation that Yahweh "sits enthroned upon the cherubim" (Ps. 99:1), reflect mythological motifs known throughout the ancient Near East. A particularly interesting example is "Cloud Rider," an expression that was once applied to Baal in the Ras Shamra literature and which was appropriated to express Yahweh's eternal sovereignty (Deut. 33:26; Ps. 68:4, 33—H 68:5, 34; cf. Isa. 19:1).

a. The living God (אלהים חיים, אלהים חי, אל חי). This is a characteristic description of Yahweh. It implies a contrast between Yahweh and other gods, who are powerless to save (I Sam. 17:26, 36; II Kings 19:4, 16; Jer. 10:10; cf. I Thess. 1:9), but in a more positive sense it expresses the life-giving power and directing presence of Yahweh in Israel's historical experience. Unlike the gods whose existence is bound up with the pattern of life and death in nature, Yahweh is the living Lord of history and nature, who made himself known at Sinai (Deut. 5:26), led his people triumphantly into the Promised Land (Josh. 3:10), spoke by the true prophet (Jer. 23:36), and made himself accessible to his worshiping people (Pss. 42:2—H 42:3; 84:2—H 84:3; cf. Matt. 26:63; Heb. 3:12; 9:14; 10:31; 12:22). At the time of the fulfilment of covenant history, Israel will be known as "sons of the living God" (Hos. 1:10—H 2:1; cf. Matt. 16:16). The same implication of Yahweh's inexhaustible vitality and life-giving power is expressed in the frequently employed oath formula, used either by a human being ("As Yahweh lives") or by God himself ("As I live, says Yahweh"). Indeed, because Yahweh lives, men may expect to receive from him the life which is equivalent to welfare and salvation (cf. Deut. 30:20). So the psalmist prays:

> Yahweh lives; and blessed be my rock,
> and exalted be the God of my salvation
> (Ps. 18:46—H 18:47).

In a metaphorical sense Yahweh is called the "fountain of living waters" (Jer. 2:13; 17:13; cf. John 4:14) or the "fountain of life" (Ps. 36:9—H 36:10). *See* §§ 4*b-c below; see also* LIFE.

b. The First and the Last. This is an expression used by Second Isaiah to convey the idea of Yahweh's eternal sovereignty over the whole sweep of time from beginning to end (Isa. 44:6; 48:12; cf. 41:4). The prophet does not speak of eternity in abstract and nonhistorical terms, but presses temporal language to its utter limits by saying concretely:

> Before me no god was formed,
> nor shall there be any after me
> (43:10).

The word עולם, "everlasting" (*see* § C2*c above*), which this prophet applies to Yahweh (40:28), does not imply any devaluation of time and history, as in the philosophies and mysticisms of Greece and India. It means a long duration of time, whether extending remotely into the past (antiquity) or indefinitely into the future (futurity), and thus suggests everlasting time, time whose boundaries are hidden from man's view (*see* TIME). Yahweh's everlasting sovereignty, then, is hidden within the shadow of the first and the last. The prophet is not concerned with metaphysical speculations, but with historical meaning. The sense of eternity is occasioned by the realization that Yahweh, unlike the idols, is not bounded by the limitations of man's finite life or by the changing cycles of nature. He is the everlasting God who acts within history to accomplish his purpose, and therefore men may rely upon him in faith, confident that his power does not fail. Thus the expression "the First and the Last" is a vivid way of saying that the whole sweep of human history from beginning to end is under the sway of the God who is Creator and Lord, and whose directing presence is known in history (46:10; cf. 45:21). This same note is accented in the NT under the conviction that God's sovereign lordship is manifest in Jesus Christ, the Alpha and the Omega (Rev. 1:8, 17; 2:8; 22:13).

c. The Ancient of Days. A similar idea is vividly expressed in the apocalyptic picture of "one that was ancient of days," whose appearance was that of an old man who had lived many years (Dan. 7:9, 13, 22; cf. Enoch 46:1-2; 47:3). Since the chapter is filled with symbolic imagery, it is clear that the writer does not suggest a literal portrait of God, for such anthropomorphic touches have another function in the theological syntax of biblical language (*see* GOD, OT VIEW OF, § C4; ANCIENT OF DAYS). The language is reminiscent of Ras Shamra texts in which El is called "king, father of years." The author of Daniel affirms that Israel's God is the living God—i.e., he "lives for ever" (Dan. 12:7), and his kingdom is everlasting (6:26—A 6:27; cf. Jer. 10:10). His sovereignty extends over all the ages, and before the Lord of history men and nations must stand for final judgment. The greatness of God is beyond man's comprehension, for, says the author of Job, "the number of his years is unsearchable" (Job. 36:26).

Thus the OT refines and deepens the theological implications of the expression "the living God." Unlike other ancient religions and philosophies, which either saw eternity and time in mutual opposition or affirmed that the gods were bound within the processes of nature, Israel affirmed that Yahweh, the everlasting God, is dynamically active in the temporal sphere, giving to history its meaning and direction. His eternity includes and transcends all the years of man's earthly experience, and Hebraic language finally presses to its very limits in the affirmation that "from everlasting to everlasting" he is God (Ps. 90:2; cf. 93:2; 145:13). *See* GOD, OT VIEW OF, § C2.

Bibliography. On the meaning of the divine name: J. Pedersen, *Israel: Its Life and Culture,* I–II (1926), 248 ff. O. Grether, *Name und Wort Gottes im AT, BZAW,* LXIV (1934), especially 1-58. G. von Rad, *Theologie des Alten Testaments* (1957), pp. 181-88.

On Yahweh: W. F. Albright, "The Name Yahweh," *JBL,* XLIII (1924), 370-78; XLIV (1925), 158-62; XLVI (1927), 175-78; LXVII (1948), 379-80. G. R. Driver, "The Original Form of the Name Yahweh: Evidences and Conclusions," *ZAW,* XLVI (1928), 7-25. O. Eissfeldt, "Neue Zeugnisse für die Aussprache des Tetragamms als Jahwe," *ZAW,* LIII (1935), 59-76. R. A. Bowman, "Yahweh the Speaker," *Journal of Near Eastern Studies,* III (1944), 1-8. N. Walker, *The Tetragrammaton* (1948). J. Obermann, "The Divine Name YHWH in the Light of Recent Discoveries," *JBL,* LXVIII (1949), 301-23. T. C. Vriezen, "Ehyeh asher ehyeh," *Festschrift A. Bertholet* (1950), pp. 498-512. A. M. Dubarle, "La signification du nom de Yahweh," *Revue des sciences philosophiques et théologiques,* XXXV (1951), 3-21. A. Murtonen, *A Philological and Literary Treatise on the OT Divine Names* (1952): includes Murtonen's essay "The Appearance of the Name YHWH Outside Israel," from *Studia Orientalia,* vol. XVI, no. 3 (1951). E. Dhorme, "Le nom du Dieu d'Israel," *RHR,* CXLI (1952), 1-18. E. Auerbach, *Moses* (1953), pp. 44-49. J. Gray, "The God YW in the Religion of Canaan," *Journal of Near Eastern Studies,* XII (1953), 278-83. G. R. Driver, "The Interpretation of YHWH as a Participle Form," *JBL,* LXXIII (1954), 125-31. E. Schild, "On Exodus iii 14: 'I am that I am,'" *Vetus Testamentum,* IV (1954), 296-302. S. D. Goitein, "YHWH the Passionate: The Monotheistic Meaning and Origin of the Name YHWH," *Vetus Testamentum,* VI (1956), 1-9. W. F. Albright, *From the Stone Age to Christianity* (2nd ed., 1957), pp. 258-61. R. Mayer, "Der Gottesname Jahwe im Lichte der neuesten Forschung," *BZ,* N.F., Jahrgang 2, Heft 1 (1958), pp. 26-53.

Other divine names and titles: O. Eissfeldt, "Jahwe als König," *ZAW,* XLVI (1928), 81-105. A. Alt, *Der Gott der Väter* (1929). W. F. Albright, "The Names Shaddai and Abram," *JBL,* LIV (1935), 173-204. E. Leslie, *OT Religion in the Light of Its Canaanite Background* (1936), pp. 54-69. O. Eissfeldt, "Baalshamem und Yahwe," *ZAW,* LVII (1939), 1-31. H. G. May, "The Patriarchal Idea of God," *JBL,* LX (1941), 113-28; "The God of My Father—A Study of Patriarchal Religion," *JBR,* IX (1941), 155-58. G. L. Della Vida, "El Elyon in Genesis 14:18-20," *JBL,* LXIII (1944), 1-29. W. Eichrodt, *Theologie des Alten Testaments,* I (1948), 81-96. O. Eissfeldt, *El im ugaritischen Pantheon* (1950). T. J. Meek, *Hebrew Origins* (rev. ed., 1950), pp. 82-118. J. P. Hyatt, "YHWH as the God of My Father," *Vetus Testamentum* (1955), pp. 130-36. M. H. Pope, *El in the Ugaritic Texts* (1955). W. F. Albright, *From the Stone Age to Christianity* (2nd ed., 1957), pp. 209-36, 243-49. E. Jacob, *Theology of the OT* (1958), pp. 43-64.

B. W. ANDERSON

GOD, OT VIEW OF. The God of the OT is not the object of man's thought but is the Subject, the living God, who wills to be the Lord of all man's thinking and living. Therefore, in a peculiar manner practically all of the OT is theology—i.e., thinking in relation to the God who has revealed himself in dramatic deeds of history and has entered into relationship with his people. It is only by abstraction that the subject of God can be singled out as one to be studied alongside many others. Israel's historians knew that to write history is to proclaim the deeds of God rather than to write the chronicles of men. In the OT the world is not regarded as a sphere which operates according to its own rational or moral laws, but as the creation of God in which everything serves his purpose. Man is not an autonomous being, but a creature whose very manhood rests on the fact that God visits him and cares for him. Ethics is not based on a scheme of moral principles or human values, but upon obedience to him whose deeds of justice and mercy have shown men what is good. Thus to explore the subject of theology in the OT is to enter a dynamic realm of life where all things and relationships find their meaning in the God who has chosen to reveal himself through the historical experiences of Israel, beginning with the call of Abraham and, in the Christian view, culminating in the career of Jesus Christ.

A. *ISRAEL'S KNOWLEDGE OF GOD.* In the OT the reality of God is the unquestioned presupposition of experience and thought. The question: Does God exist? is not only nonbiblical, but would not have made sense in the ancient world, where polytheism, rather than atheism, was the human concern. The biblical question is, rather: Who is our God?—i.e., What is his name? (*See* GOD, NAMES OF, § A). OT faith finds expression in the testimony that the Lord of history and creation revealed himself personally to Israel in the concrete episodes of their history and laid his covenant claim upon them. Within the community of faith there was ample room for religious doubt. The patriarchs were subjected to the despairing experiences that God would not, or could not, fulfil his promises. During the wilderness testing, the Israelites cried out: "Is the LORD among us or not?" (Exod. 17:7). Jeremiah likened God to a deceitful wadi whose waters fail in the dry season (Jer. 15:18). Job was tormented by the remoteness and absence of God and longed for some reconciliation with the Sovereign of the universe. Doubts of this kind were intense at times precisely because they were based upon a sense of the sovereignty of God. Only the "fool" says in his heart that there is no God (Pss. 10:4; 14:1; 53:1—H 53:2). This, however, is the practical atheism of the person who supposes that he can live as though God does not have to be reckoned with, who supposes in his heart that

> God has forgotten,
> he has hidden his face, he will never see it
> (Ps. 10:11; cf. Jer. 5:12).

The OT has no systematic doctrine of God, for God is not an idea to be incorporated into a logical system or into a spiritual thought-world. It is therefore wrong to expect an answer to the question of the nature of God, if this means an abstract analysis of what God is in himself—i.e., the attributes of his being. Just as persons are known in the context of relationship, so God's self is revealed in his historical relations with his people. He is the God of Abraham, Isaac, and Jacob, not the God of speculative thought. He is known by what he has done, is doing, and will do—i.e., in the events of history. As the psalmist affirms:

> He made known his ways to Moses,
> his acts to the people of Israel
> (Ps. 103:7).

OT theology, then, is fundamentally historical theology. It is profoundly and radically historical, for it rests upon the witness that God's revelation takes the form of a history. Just as the power of poetry is lost when translated into prose, so the vitality of Israel's faith is lost when the dramatic story of God's actions and men's responses is converted into abstractions.

The faith of Israel stands in contrast, not only to speculative thought, but also to the nature religions of antiquity. Although these religions took varying forms in the Fertile Crescent, they were all based upon a numinous awareness of divine powers operative in nature. Men believed that their lives were existentially dependent upon these powers for the successful cultivation of the soil, fertility of womb and flock, and the blessings of long life and well-being. In modern scientific culture these powers have been demythologized—i.e., emptied of divinity and reduced to impersonal forces or processes; but in antiquity nature's powers were personified as male and female deities and organized into a hierarchy or pantheon, within which each deity and his female counterpart performed an assigned function. Since the seasonal cycles of nature did not move by natural law but by the actions of the nature gods, man's religious task was to swing into the natural rhythm, thereby finding harmony, security, and salvation. He felt in the wrong if he was at odds with the natural powers, and he felt right if, through the practices of the cultus, he was integrated into the natural harmony and could even ensure that the balance of powers would not be upset. The seductive temptation of this type of religion is evidenced by Israel's history from the moment the people set foot on the soil of Canaan, where BAAL and his female counterpart (Ashtart) were worshiped by farmers.

The incompatibility of this religious outlook with Israel's historical faith is indicated by the vehement protest against Baalism, a protest which made it impossible for the divine name Baal to be accepted as a synonym for Israel's God (*see* GOD, NAMES OF, § C5). Israel dared to affirm, in disagreement with all her cultural neighbors, that divine reality is not encountered in the sphere of nature but in the sphere of historical experience. To be sure, the God of Israel was also the Lord of nature, for nothing lay outside the range of his sovereignty; Israel should look to him, not to the Baal, for the gifts of agriculture (Hos. 2:8-9—H 2:10-11). But first and foremost Israel's God was the Lord of history—the God who rescued Israel from Egyptian bondage, led his people through the wilderness and on to the Land of the Promise, raised up David as king and the prophets as his spokesmen, and acted in the great international crises to accomplish his sovereign purpose. Thus, in contrast to nature religion's emphasis upon the harmonious integration of man's life into the rhythms of nature, Israel's faith is characterized by a strong voluntarism: God makes known his will in historical events and lays his claim upon his people's will, calling them to decision, faithfulness, and responsible action. It is highly significant that the central motif of the OT is the COVENANT, a relational term that was drawn from the historical experience of jurisprudence and politics.

The OT, with its great diversity, is a literary deposit of Israel's historical experiences during a period of more than a millennium. This history, however, is not secular history, like that of any other nation, although it is obviously enmeshed with historical developments of the Fertile Crescent. In its inward dimension, Israel's history is theological history (*Heilsgeschichte* or sacred history)—a history of God in action to lead his people toward the fulfilment of his purpose for them and all mankind. From time to time history was narrated with new accents—e.g., by the Yahwist, the Deuteronomist, the Chronicler—but always for the sake of declaring God's dealings with his people. A succession of prophets arose to interpret the meaning of their contemporary situation in the light of what God had done, was doing, and would do. Ethical appeals were set within the remembrance of the "saving acts of the LORD" (Mic. 6:5). Israel's worship, as reflected in the book of Psalms, was an elevated praise of God for his majestic power to deliver, protect, and lead his people. And even where the historical emphasis seems to be most absent, as in the books of Job and Ecclesiastes, the religious questions are precisely those which were evoked by man's cry to understand the ways of God.

The presence of so much history in the OT is not to be explained as only a context for the emergence of theological ideas. Rather, this history is essentially theological in character, for it is the medium of God's self-revelation. For Israel to remember, to write, to recite, and to live history was a confession of faith.

B. *THE REVELATION OF GOD.* That God reveals himself is the consistent theme of the Bible from Gen. 1:1 on. The OT does not purport to be the record of human initiative in seeking for and discovering God, for—as the author of Job realized—God would elude men's search completely unless God on his own initiative were to reveal himself and speak his word. Men are enjoined to "seek the LORD" only because in his grace he has drawn near (Isa. 55:6-7). Very often the prophets give the impression that men are more disposed to turn away from God and hide from him than to seek him with their whole heart. Insofar as "revelation" means God's disclosure of himself, rather than data which men may discover by investigation, it testifies to God's overture, God's initiative. Often revelation takes men completely by surprise and arouses the deepest sense of dread. Moreover, in the book of Deuteronomy curious probing into what is hidden is condemned as presumptuous, for God has revealed in his Torah all that is needful for man's salvation (Deut. 29:29—H 29:28).

1. The hiddenness of God. The presupposition of REVELATION is that God is hidden from man's sight. Revelation, therefore, is God's unveiling or uncovering of himself and his purposes, as the verb גלה indicates (Deut. 29:29—H 29:28; I Sam. 3:21; Isa. 22:14; 40:5; 53:1).

In part, the hiddenness of God is the expression of his transcendence. God is prior to and exalted above man's world and the whole universe. In the OT divine transcendence is often expressed in terms of the ancient cosmological view of the universe: God's true dwelling place is not on earth but in heaven (Eccl. 5:2—H 5:1). From his lofty and remote dwelling place, he "comes down" to visit men and to take part in historical affairs (Gen. 11:7; Exod. 3:8; 19:11; 24:9-10; etc.). He sits "above the circle of the earth," as Second Isaiah puts it (Isa. 40:22), but nevertheless advances along a royal highway to rescue his people (40:3). Thus by using cosmological imagery in a religious rather than a scientific sense, Israel affirms that God is not a phenomenon of man's historical world, to be observed in the same way we see human beings or objects, or to be used for the service of human interests. God is invisible to man. This conviction is underscored by the Mosaic prohibition against making an image of him (Exod. 20:4) or by the ancient belief that ordinarily no man could behold him directly and live (Exod. 33:20; cf. Gen. 32:30—H 32:31; Exod. 19:21; 24:11; Judg. 6:22-23; Isa. 6:5). He is the exalted One, who dwells in the high and lofty place (Isa. 57:15; cf. 33:5). The OT is aware of the great contrast between the deity of God and the humanity of man, a contrast that is sensed even when boldly anthropomorphic language is used (*see* § C4 *below*). The great theophany of Job (chs. 38–41) conveys an overwhelming sense of the transcendent majesty and power of God the Creator.

The hiddenness of God, however, is not just due to God's exaltation far above man's world; it is also a characteristic of his presence in the world. The paradise story (Gen. 2–3) portrays God in a visible, human form dealing directly with man, but this story pertains to prehistory, not to the ordinary historical situation which prevails as a result of "paradise lost." In other parts of the OT it is said that God "appears" directly to individuals, or "lets himself be seen" (as the reflexive of the verb ראה suggests), but usually with a divine reserve or holding back. He appears in a dream (Gen. 28), in the form of an angel (ch. 18), or in a radiant envelope of glory (*see* § C4 *below*). This divine reserve is expressed in a passage which tells of Moses' request to be shown God's ways (Exod. 33:12-23). Protected in a cave from the blinding glory, Moses was enabled to see the Lord's back and not his face (vss. 22-23). Although the passage is highly anthropomorphic, it indicates that even in God's self-disclosure he remains partially hidden from human sight.

Prophetic teaching deepened the notion of God's hiddenness by connecting it with the blindness of sin. Though God is actually near, he is remote when his people forsake him and break his covenant. Having a rebellious heart, man hears but does not understand, sees but does not perceive (Isa. 6:9). Therefore, in a faithless generation God "hides his face," leaving men in despair about his absence from their world (Deut. 31:16-18) or about the "strange work" of judgment which he performs (Isa. 28:21). In the circle of faith men wait and hope for the time when he will show his face again to Israel (Isa. 8:17; 40:27; Jer. 14:7-9). It is perhaps against this background that we should understand the eschatological promise that the "pure in heart" shall see God (Matt. 5:8).

2. The unknown Lord of mankind. In the OT no limitations are placed on the sovereignty of the God of Israel. With increasing clarity and profundity men came to realize that the God who had revealed himself in their historical experience was actually the Creator and Lord of all mankind. His name is glorious in all the earth (Ps. 8:1—H 8:2), and powerful among the nations (Jer. 10:6-7). The question arises, then, as to whether the OT provides a basis for a conception of general revelation as distinct from God's special revelation to Israel.

The OT does not face this question as directly as does the NT (cf. John 1:1-18; Rom. 1:18-25). Although the J and P stories found in Gen. 1–11 testify that man as man (rather than man as an Israelite) may know God, the central concern of these narrators is to testify out of Israel's historical experience how God has chosen to reveal himself in order that all men may know him. These passages are written in the light of God's personal revelation to Israel, and they are firmly anchored to Israel's sacred history as a kind of historical prologue to the call of Abraham and the later revelation in the Mosaic period.

Nature, like the handiwork of an artist, proclaims the power and majesty of God and the creaturely status of man (Job 12:7-9; 38–41; Pss. 8; 19:1-6; 29;

104; Jer. 5:22). But it is doubtful whether the so-called nature psalms mean to say that nature reveals God clearly to all reasonable men. Addison's well-known hymn derives from the Nineteenth Psalm the notion that "reason's ear" can hear the music of the spheres, and that the order and beauty of nature testify to the hand of the divine Maker. But this interpretation is possible only when the psalmist's testimony is taken out of its true context. Israel knew that "nature" does not in itself clearly and unambiguously reveal God but deludes men into worshiping the nature gods of storm and fertility (cf. Rom. 1:21-25). The God of Israel spoke in the accents of historical events and demonstrated his power to use the forces of nature to bless or judge his people and to accomplish his historical purpose (*see* SIGNS AND WONDERS). Only from the standpoint of this historical revelation could Israel affirm that the Lord of Israel's history is actually the Creator of the ends of the earth and that to the ear of faith the heavens sing an inaudible anthem of praise to God.

If, then, God's primary sphere of revelation, according to the OT, is history rather than nature, the question arises as to whether he reveals himself in the histories of other peoples. At first Israel's faith was not primarily concerned with the broad question of the place of the nations in the divine purpose (*see* § E3 *below*), but rested upon the confessional recital of what God had done for Israel (see the old cultic credo in Deut. 26:5-10). Only with the broadening of Israel's historical horizons was it realized that the God of Israel is the Sovereign and Savior of the nations. The Yahwist, writing in the time of the early monarchy, understands the call of Israel (Gen. 12:1-3) within the context of an all-embracing divine sovereignty (*see* J). Amos insists that Israel's God had not only brought up Israel from Egypt, but also the Philistines and the Syrians from their places of origin (Amos 9:7). But although this prophet insists that God's activity was not confined to Israel, it is doubtful whether he meant to say that God (Yahweh) had actually made himself known to these nations in their historical experience. Instead, he insists strongly that Yahweh had known (i.e., entered into personal relationship with) Israel only (3:2; cf. 2:9-11), and that, since Israel could not plead ignorance of his historical revelation, as could other nations, a great burden of responsibility was placed upon this people. Second Isaiah perceived in the events of his time the activity of God, who was leading Israel back to her homeland and revealing his glory to all flesh (Isa. 40:5). But even this prophet, whose historical horizons are most spacious, understands that divine revelation is mediated to the nations through Israel. In 45:15 the nations apparently confess that the God who hides himself from them in a veil of mystery has revealed himself in what he is doing for Israel and that the meaning of all human history is bound up with Israel's unique history. Other OT passages indicate that God reveals himself to the nations primarily through his dealings with Israel (Exod. 7:5; Deut. 4:6-8; 29:22-28—H 29:21-27; Isa. 52:7-10; Jer. 33:9; Ezek. 37:27-28; 38:16, 23). The goal of history, it is said, will be realized when the nations go up to Jerusalem in order that they may learn the Torah of the God of Israel, and thus know him as he has revealed himself to Israel (Isa. 2:2-4; Mic. 4:1-4). Then they will know his name—i.e., they will know who is truly God (Ps. 79:6; Jer. 10:25).

3. The God of Israel. Thus the OT testifies that the revelation of God is bound up inextricably with a special history—the history of the people Israel. This conviction is underscored by the theological significance of the special name of God, Yahweh, the introduction of which in the Mosaic period marked a radically new beginning. From the pre-Mosaic period Israel inherited many religious conceptions which once belonged in the context of polytheistic nature religion. But these views were purged and transformed by being brought into the context of Israel's historical faith. Ancient divine names were given a new meaning by being identified with the one special name, Yahweh. *See* GOD, NAMES OF.

The name of God signifies the personal relationship between God and his people. Yahweh is the God of Israel, and Israel is the people of God. This twofold affirmation, which is expressed in the oldest poem of any length in the OT, the Song of Deborah (Judg. 5:3, 5, 11, 13), is the persistent motif of Israel's faith. The God whose sovereignty is hidden in nature and in general human experience had graciously revealed himself personally and concretely to one people, binding them to himself in a special relationship. The covenant formula: "I will be your God, and you shall be my people" (cf. Exod. 6:7; Jer. 31:33; Ezek. 37:27; Hos. 2:23—H 2:25; cf. Isa. 40:1: "my people . . . your God"), is the axis of Israel's life and thought.

In a profound sense, the doctrine of Israel's ELECTION lies at the heart of Israel's faith. Admittedly, throughout the generations it was open to popular misunderstanding and nationalistic distortion. The people were prone to believe that Yahweh was merely a national god, like Chemosh of Moab (Judg. 11:24; cf. II Kings 3:27 and the Moabite Stone), whose sovereignty was contingent upon the fortunes of Israel and who could be mobilized to serve national interests. Against this view the prophets raised a mighty protest. They insisted that Israel belonged to Yahweh, not vice versa. He had laid his personal claim upon them by his mighty and benevolent deeds, and had called them to fulfil their historical and social responsibility within his purpose. Far from being tied to his people, Yahweh could cast them off and, in so doing, could demonstrate his sovereignty. Why Yahweh chose to set his affection upon Israel is left unexplained. Certainly it is not accounted for in the OT by saying that Israel was religiously or culturally superior to other peoples (cf. Deut. 7:7-10). In Israel's deepest moments of faith, the consciousness of election was not the occasion for boasting, but for wonder, gratitude, and faith. Election, like revelation, stresses God's initiative in making himself known within the history of a particular people.

The meaning of Yahweh's choice of Israel is expressed by means of an analogy drawn from political experience, that of the covenant. It has been suggested that the covenant form was influenced by suzerainty treaties of the ancient Near East as known, e.g., among the Hittites. On the basis of his benevolent deeds, the suzerain establishes a covenant with his vassal, promising him protection and security. And the vassal, grateful for his sovereign's benevolence, promises obedience to the stipulations of the suzerainty treaty. Analogously, the covenant with Israel is a covenant of grace. The story of the covenant making (Exod. 19–24) is preceded by the story of what Yahweh had done for his people by delivering them from the pharaoh's yoke (Exod. 1–15). Even the concise summary of Israel's covenant responsibilities found in the Decalogue is preceded by a historical prologue which proclaims Yahweh's mighty act of deliverance (Exod. 20:2). Thus Israel's legal responsibility was motivated by gratitude for what Yahweh, their Lord, had done on their behalf (Exod. 19:3-6). Israel's ancient kerygma or proclamation of Yahweh's saving deeds, found in an old cultic credo now embedded in the book of Deuteronomy (26:5-10; cf. Josh. 24:1-13), became the theological nucleus around which the traditions of the Pentateuch were organized. *See* J.

The covenant, being a term of relationship, provides the basis for the knowledge of God to which the OT bears witness. Primarily this is not intellectual knowledge, for God is not an idea of the mind or an object in man's world. Rather, it is personal knowledge given within an I-and-Thou relation. Yahweh has "known" Israel, says Amos (3:2). Here the verb "know" (ידע) signifies Yahweh's redemptive choice of Israel as manifested in the Exodus and other events of Israel's history (cf. Amos 2:9-10). It expresses the meaning of the verb "choose" (בחר) or, in a more general sense, the meaning of the covenant relationship initiated by God. Israel, in turn, knows God by name. This knowledge of God, as Hosea emphasizes, involves trust, loyalty, and faithfulness—in other words, everything implied in Israel's covenant responsibility (Hos. 4:1, 6). The prophets deal with the problem of Israel's broken relationship with God, and they look beyond the present to the time when, in the relationship of a new covenant, men will "know" Yahweh in true faithfulness (Jer. 31:31-34; Hos. 2:14-23—H 2:16-25).

C. *THE PRESENCE OF YAHWEH WITH HIS PEOPLE.* Israel's history, as we have seen, is primarily covenant history—i.e., it is a history with Yahweh. To tell the story adequately, one would have to review the whole pilgrimage of Israel, beginning especially with the Exodus, and to study the various ways in which prophets, priests, and narrators interpreted the divine action in the unfolding sacred history.

Throughout the years, when the ancient tradition was being reinterpreted and supplemented with new insights into God's continuing activity, one conviction remained constant. It is summed up in the affirmation: "Yahweh is with us" (Isa. 7:14; Hos. 11:9; Amos 5:14; cf. Joel 2:27; Zech. 8:23). In manifold ways the OT bears witness to the belief in the real presence of Yahweh in the midst of his people. He "comes down" to rescue his people from Egyptian oppression and to summon Moses as a leader; he appears in a storm at the Battle of Megiddo to continue his "righteous acts" (RSV "triumphs") on behalf of his embattled people (Judg. 5:11; cf. Mic. 6:5); he promises Joshua that he will go with him during the invasion of Canaan (Josh. 1:9); he performs the SIGNS AND WONDERS which give assurance that he is immediately present. According to Israel, Yahweh is not removed from the historical world. He is here—not as a mystical presence, but as the Leader who goes before his people and teaches them the way wherein they should walk. "For what great nation is there that has a god so near to it as the LORD our God is to us, whenever we call upon him?" (Deut. 4:7.)

1. Theophanies. The sense of the immediate nearness of Yahweh finds expression in various theophanies (*see* THEOPHANY). Chief of these is the theophany associated with the giving of the law at Sinai (Exod. 19; 20:18-22). The traditional storm imagery (earthquake, wind, and fire; cf. I Kings 19:11-12) serves to emphasize the holiness and majesty of Yahweh's appearing, a theme which is recapitulated in the Deuteronomic address (Deut. 4:11-14). The nearness of God excites the greatest wonder and dread, for in the time of his visitation men realize that he is the holy God who comes from another sphere and whose presence poses a threat to man's ordinary world (*see* § D1 *below*). When he draws near, men realize that he is not just a God at hand, who can be localized and confined, but he is a God afar off (Jer. 23:23) whose judgments cannot be escaped by anyone (Ps. 139; Amos 9:1-4).

Thus Israel's faith expresses a religious polarity: on the one hand, Yahweh is above and beyond man's historical world of time and space; and on the other, he visits men and makes his personal presence known. Some circles, like the priestly school that produced Gen. 1, emphasize the transcendence and separation of God from his world, while others, like the Yahwist, stress—sometimes with naïve anthropomorphism—his immediate presence and direct appearance to individuals. In Israel's faith, however, these two emphases are not contradictory or mutually exclusive, but both are experiential elements in man's knowledge of God.

2. Concrete manifestations of God's presence. Yahweh's presence with his people during their historical pilgrimage was, so to speak, objectified or given concrete expression in various traditional ways.

a. Ark and tent of meeting. Early traditions gathered around the ARK OF THE COVENANT, a wooden chest which apparently was regarded as the throne on which Yahweh was seated invisibly "above the cherubim" (I Sam. 4:4; II Kings 19:15). As long as the ark was in Israel's camp, the people had an objective, visible sign of Yahweh's presence in their midst (cf. I Sam. 4:3-9). Enthroned upon the ark, he acted as their guide during the wilderness wandering (Num. 10:33), their protagonist in warfare (Num. 10:35-36), and their ever-present leader during the invasion of Canaan (Josh. 3–6). When the ark was captured during the Philistine wars, this was a dismal crisis, for it was believed that "the glory has departed from Israel" (I Sam. 4:21-22); and when it was brought by David to Jerusalem, the occasion was one of ecstatic rejoicing (I Sam. 6:13, 19; II Sam. 6; cf. I Sam. 6:13).

According to a different type of tradition, Yahweh

came down from heaven now and then in a cloud to the tent of meeting (*see* TABERNACLE) in order to meet Moses and to speak with him "face to face, as a man speaks to his friend" (Exod. 33:7-11; cf. Num. 11:16, 24-26; 12:4; Deut. 31:14-15). Thus the portable tent shrine was a place of rendezvous perhaps for tribal assembly but primarily for revelation to Moses. While the ark signified God's abiding presence, the tent symbolized his holy distance from his people (Exod. 33:7). Priestly tradition combines both views by saying that the ark was housed in the tabernacle.

b. The angel of Yahweh. The notion that Yahweh is surrounded by a council of heavenly beings who do his bidding (*see* HOSTS) is found throughout the OT. In the late OT period this view developed into an elaborate angelology (*see* ANGEL). In the early tradition, however, the expression מלאך (lit., "messenger") did not necessarily mean a heavenly intermediary between God and man, for Israel's faith found expression in the conviction that Yahweh himself was actively present in the world. Of particular interest are a number of passages which identify the messenger with Yahweh himself. The narrator speaks alternately of the angel and of Yahweh (Gen. 21:17; 22:11, 15-16; 31:11-13; Exod. 3:2-5; Judg. 6:11-24; etc.), and in one instance affirms that Yahweh's name or very self (*see* GOD, NAMES OF, § A) is in the guiding angel (Exod. 23:20-21). In these cases the angel is the form of Yahweh's appearance in a specific situation. He appears in human guise, but not in a genuine incarnation. In this way the tradition attempts to express both Yahweh's heavenly lordship and his personal presence in the world.

c. The face of Yahweh. The ultimate background of the conception of God's FACE is the practice of beholding the statue of a deity in the temple. Although Israelite religion strictly prohibited such images, the expression "to see the face of God" came to mean in a general sense appearing at the sanctuary or having communion with God (Exod. 23:15, 17; 34:20, 23-24; Pss. 24:6; 42:2—H 42:3; Isa. 1:12). In a further metaphorical refinement Yahweh's face signified his gracious help and presence (Pss. 11:7; 17:15). But in one interesting passage (Exod. 33:14-15), Moses is promised that Yahweh's face (RSV "presence") will accompany the people in their wilderness sojourn; this promise is perhaps to be associated with the ark (cf. Num. 10:33). Though Yahweh's heavenly lordship is maintained, his face or presence leads and saves his people (cf. Deut. 4:37; Isa. 63:9).

d. The glory of Yahweh. In priestly circles the GLORY of Yahweh is a characteristic theme. Yahweh's glory (כבוד) is not only his honor and majesty as disclosed particularly in his mighty deeds and kingly rule (Ps. 29:9; Isa. 6:3; 42:8; Ezek. 28:22); it is, especially in Ezekiel and P, a fiery envelope of light which shields him from sight when he appears in the world (Exod. 24:15-17; Ezek. 1; cf. Ps. 97). Yahweh's glory settles down over the tabernacle (Exod. 40:34-38) or fills the Jerusalem temple (I Kings 8:10-11; Ezek. 8:4; 9:3; 10:4, 18-19; 43:1-5), thus assuring Israel that God truly makes himself present to his people.

e. The name of Yahweh. In Deuteronomic circles the ancient notion of Yahweh's enthronement upon the ark was replaced by the theology of the name. Yahweh himself dwells in heaven, but he causes his name to dwell in his sanctuary (Deut. 12:5, 11, 21; 14:23-24; 26:2; I Kings 11:36; 14:21; etc.). Since, according to ancient psychology, the name was the bearer of a person's self, this was tantamount to saying that Yahweh himself, without being localized or limited to a particular space, was truly present with his people. *See* GOD, NAMES OF, § A.

3. Word, Spirit, Wisdom. The revelation of God in the world is expressed in other ways which came to have more decisive theological significance. Yahweh acts in the world through his WORD. In ancient psychology, the spoken word was not a mere disturbance of sound waves: it was an outgoing expression of the person of the speaker, a kind of extension of his self. Thus the "word of the Lord" came to the prophets with the authority and power of Yahweh himself. Yahweh's word is powerful in history, to destroy and to build (Jer. 1:9-10). When Yahweh speaks, his word does not return empty, but accomplishes the purpose for which he sent it forth (Isa. 55:10-11; cf. 45:23). His word stands forever (Isa. 40:8). Moreover, God's word is not only the expression of his personal presence in the world, bringing judgment and salvation to the people (Pss. 107:20; 130:5; Isa. 5:24), it is also the agency of his creation (as in the P creation story in Gen. 1; cf. Ps. 33:6; John 1:1-5), and of his continuing providential activity (Ps. 147:12-20).

The SPIRIT is not identical with God but is the agency of his historical activity in the world. The Hebrew word רוח also means "wind," and suggests the idea of power, movement, activity. The divine רוח empowers men to perform the tasks to which God calls them, whether the charismatic heroes of old (Judg. 6:34; 14:6, 19), the prophets (Num. 11:24-29; I Sam. 10:10; Mic. 3:8; cf. Joel 2:28—H 3:1), the messianic king (Isa. 11:2), or the Servant of the Lord (Isa. 42:1; cf. 61:1). Yahweh's holy Spirit has been the saving power within Israel's history from the first (Isa. 63:11), it is the sign of his presence from which no man can escape (Ps. 139:7; cf. 51:11—H 51:13), and it is the dynamic which moves history toward the goal of a new age and a new creation (Isa. 44:3; Ezek. 36:26-27; 37; Joel 2:28—H 3:1).

WISDOM has its major source in the ancient traditions of the East. By the time of Jeremiah, however, it was recognized that the sage, along with the prophet and the priest, was an agent of Yahweh (Jer. 18:18). Israel's sages came to emphasize the cosmic status of wisdom, and to personify it as the agent of God's creation and the providential ordering of the world (Job 28; Prov. 8:22-31). In the period of late Judaism, it was identified with the Torah (Ecclus. 24). Thus, by being related to the revealing word and action of Yahweh in Israel's history, it provided a preparation for the NT doctrine of the incarnate Logos (John 1).

In all these ways Israel's faith attempts to reckon with Yahweh's heavenly lordship and his active presence in the world. The OT stands opposed to any religious or philosophical view which excludes the involvement of deity in the change and contingency of earthly affairs. Since the earth is the Lord's (Ps. 24:1), it is the historical stage on which he visits men, acts to accomplish his purpose, and makes known his holy presence. Although the OT has no systematic formation in philosophical terms equivalent to transcendence and immanence, the central conviction of Israel's faith is that the eternal, supramundane God enters into and acts in the temporal sphere of human existence.

4. Anthropomorphism. As we have seen in the above discussion, Israel's faith in various ways sought to avoid the extremes of either removing God from the world into a heavenly sphere, or making him so much a part of the world that his deity is limited. The latter extreme provided a great temptation to Israel, for other religions, such as that of Egypt, boldly portrayed deities in human and animal form and advocated image-worship. Thus the gods were not only humanized, but animalized and materialized. Israel's faith, however, raised a strict prohibition against making any material, graven image of Yahweh or conceiving him in the likeness of anything in the realm of creation (Exod. 20:4). Deuteronomic tradition amplified the second commandment of the Decalogue by saying that at Sinai the people heard only Yahweh's voice, but saw no form (Deut. 4:12, 15-18), even though he spoke with them "face to face" (5:4). That Yahweh cannot be likened to anyone or anthing, but is incomparable in majesty, wisdom, and power, is the proclamation of Second Isaiah (Isa. 40:12-26; *see* § D6 *below*).

Despite these protests, the doctrine of the spirituality of God has no place in the OT. The one apparent exception is Isa. 31:3:

> The Egyptians are men, and not God;
> and their horses are flesh, and not spirit.

Even here, however, the issue is not the spirituality of God in opposition to anything material, but that of his vitality as opposed to the creaturely weakness upon which an alliance with Egypt rests (cf. vs. 1). Yahweh is not pure spirit, for his Spirit, like his Word, is the agency of his activity (*see* § C3 *above*). He is invisible and incomparable; he is exalted above all that is earthly; but Israel's theological thinking does not allow speaking of him in the abstract. With characteristic concreteness and historical interest, Israel speaks of Yahweh in highly personal terms, attributing to him human form (anthropomorphism) and human feelings (anthropopathism).

It is true that some parts of the OT are more naïvely anthropomorphic than others. The Yahwist, e.g., delights in bold anthropomorphisms: Yahweh walks in the garden of Eden, closes the door of the ark, smells the fragrance of Noah's sacrifice, comes down from heaven to see what men are doing at the tower of Babel, clogs the wheels of the Egyptian chariots, chases Moses in the wilderness, etc. Doubtless many of these features were inherited from the ancient popular tradition which the Yahwist received and incorporated into his over-all scheme of historical interpretation (*see* J). In any case, this picturesque language—e.g., in Gen. 2–3—is infused with a sense of divine sovereignty which far exceeds human limitations. The Elohist tends to avoid bold anthropomorphism by putting Yahweh (or Elohim) in touch with men through dreams and visions (Gen. 15:1; 20:3, 6; 28:12; Num. 12:6) or through angelic visitors (Gen. 21:17; 22:11, 15). This theological reserve undoubtedly is motivated in part by the attempt to place Moses in a special class; for "with him I speak mouth to mouth, clearly, and not in dark speech; and he beholds the form of Yahweh" (Num. 12:6-8; cf. Deut. 34:10). In priestly circles, out of which came the P material of the Pentateuch and the Chronicler's history, there is a more consistent and self-conscious effort to stress the unapproachable majesty and transcendence of God. In the P creation story, e.g. (Gen. 1), Creation is accomplished solely by the Word of the God who is absolutely holy and sovereign. But not even the priestly theologians could escape anthropomorphism, as indicated in the conception of God ruling as King over his heavenly council (Gen. 1:26; *see* HOSTS) and the notion of man's being made in God's image (5:1-3; *see* IMAGE OF GOD). Ezekiel, a priestly prophet, cautiously described the appearance of Yahweh—veiled within the blinding radiance of his glory—as a "likeness as it were of a human form" (Ezek. 1:26-28; cf. 8:2; Dan. 7:9-10).

To some degree or other, then, anthropomorphism appears in all circles and periods of OT tradition. Many anthropomorphisms undoubtedly have only a metaphorical meaning—e.g., the references to God's hands, ears, mouth, eyes, finger, feet, etc. But something more than metaphor is involved; for the OT, without engaging in metaphysical speculation, unhesitantly and consistently views Yahweh as a distinct person. (He is always spoken of as a man; but sexual characteristics are excluded, for he has no female counterpart.) Admittedly this concrete, human language is qualified, for

> God is not man, that he should lie,
> or a son of man, that he should repent
> (Num. 23:19; cf. I Sam. 15:29;
> Mal. 3:6)—

i.e., he is faithful to his word and brings it to pass. Since he is God and not man (Hos. 11:9), his thoughts and ways surpass human understanding (Isa. 55:8-9). Nevertheless, anthropomorphism is indigenous to a faith which views God in terms of historical actions and relationships rather than in terms of natural power or impersonal being. Indeed, Israel broke with the theriomorphism (representation of deity in animal form) of ancient religion and insisted that language drawn from personal relationships was most adequate for expressing faith in Yahweh. To him are ascribed the characteristics of personality: wisdom, will, purpose, love, anger, anguish, patience, hatred, jealousy, joy, etc. His covenant relationship with his people is described in images drawn from political life (king, judge, shepherd) or from family life (father, husband, kinsman; *see* GOD, NAMES OF, § D2). According to Second Isaiah, Yahweh is Israel's Redeemer; this term is derived from ancient family law, in which the kinsman had the obligation to vindicate the right of another member of the family (Isa. 41:14; 44:24; 47:4; cf. Job 19:25). *See* REDEEM.

In the OT anthropomorphism finds its finest expression in Hosea's description of Yahweh's heartbroken fatherly anguish over his prodigal son Israel

(Hos. 11) or in the portrayal of the compassionate longing of a husband to be reconciled with his fickle wife (chs. 1–3). And this is an anticipation of the supreme anthropomorphism of the Christian faith, which declares that God has revealed himself in the form of a person (John 1; Phil. 2:1-11). Any attempt to depersonalize God would be a violation of the biblical message, which, with various accents, affirms that he is the divine Thou who enters into fellowship with man and deals with him personally in the affairs of his history.

D. *THE TRAITS OF YAHWEH.* The OT does not purport to give information about what God is in himself, for the central concern is God's relation to man and man's relation to God—in a word, the covenant. A Jewish philosopher has observed that the Bible is not man's theology, but God's anthropology —i.e., instead of dealing with the nature of God (his attributes or being-in-himself), it enables man to know himself and what is required of him in the light of God's dealings. Nevertheless, just as the self, in its relation with other persons, discloses certain traits or characteristics, so God's relations with his people provide the basis for theological understanding of who God is and of his character as known within the covenant.

1. Holiness. The experience of the holy (*see* HOLINESS) was not peculiar to Israel's faith, but was deeply rooted in ancient religion. The holy is the numinous, the wholly other, not just in the sense of an overwhelming mystery that evokes awe but in the sense of divine power, impersonal and amoral in character, which threatens man's existence and excites dread. What is holy (persons, objects, places) must be carefully quarantined from the ordinary, profane sphere, lest its power break forth and destroy men (cf. Exod. 19:12, 21-23).

Ancient taboo conceptions clung to Sinai-Horeb, the ark (II Sam. 6:6-10), cultic vessels (Num. 16:36-40—H 17:1-5), the altar (Exod. 29:37), laws regarding what was clean or unclean, and mixture of seeds (Deut. 22:9). It was even supposed that holiness, like a contagion, could be transferred (Lev. 6:18, 27—H 6:11, 20; Ezek. 44:19; Hag. 2:12-13). Holiness, then, is fundamentally a mysterious energy which fills men with fear, rather than confidence, precisely because it is otherworldly—i.e., beyond anything known or conceivable in the ordinary world. The ancient cultus was based upon the necessity of separating the holy realm from the profane in order that, by the observance of the proper rites, man might be able to deal with and even control the holy.

In Israel's experience, however, the holy was identified with the dynamic will of Yahweh. He is preeminently the "holy God" (Josh. 24:19), whose sovereign will arouses fear and reverence, and at times he seems even to have a demonic aspect (Exod. 4:24-26). Ancient popular conception persisted, but no longer was holiness regarded as an impersonal force which could arbitrarily destroy or bless men. It is Yahweh, the divine Thou, who is holy (Isa. 8:12-13). Especially when contemplating his marvelous acts in history, men think of him as the God who is terrible (נורא; Deut. 7:21; 10:17; Ps. 76:12—H 76:13).

> Who is like thee, majestic in holiness,
> terrible in glorious deeds, doing wonders?
> (Exod. 15:11.)

See FEAR.

In priestly theology, holiness is the essential deity of God, which distinguishes him infinitely from creaturely and sinful man, making it necessary for cultic propriety, lest one offend the divine majesty (Lev. 10:1-3; Num. 1:48-53; 16). But it is also emphasized that God, through his act of revelation, has made Israel holy by separating her unto himself from the nations (cf. Exod. 19:6) and by establishing the cultus to sanctify the people. Israel's holiness, then, is based on her relation to the Holy God, rather than on any intrinsic qualities of her life. Not only does Yahweh claim a people for himself; he also claims objects, institutions, seasons, places, and special persons for himself, thus making them holy. Yahweh's sovereignty over Israel infuses things and relationships with holiness. Indeed, the meaning of Israel's cultus is expressed in the formula: "You shall be holy; for I Yahweh your God am holy" (Lev. 19:2).

The ethical dimension of holiness, to which the Holiness Code (Lev. 17–26) attests more than much priestly teaching, was given special prominence by the prophets, sometimes with such radical fervor that apparently the whole existing cultus stood under condemnation. Access to God is not on the basis of cultic performance, but on the basis of concern for the social responsibilities of the covenant community (Isa. 1:12-17; Jer. 7; Amos 5:21-24; Hos. 6:6). Both Isaiah and Second Isaiah call Yahweh the "Holy One of Israel" (Isa. 1:4; 5:19, 24; 10:17; 40:25; 41:14, 20; etc.). For Isaiah, holiness is not just the measure of the infinite gulf between the sublimity of God and the creatureliness of man; it is the awesome contrast between God's purity and man's sin (Isa. 6:1-5; cf. Pss. 15; 24:3-6; Hab. 1:12-13). For

> Yahweh of hosts is exalted in justice,
> and the Holy God shows himself holy in righteousness
> (Isa. 5:16).

Thus holiness is the divine power which breaks forth in wrath (*see* § D4 *below*) against Israel like a consuming fire (10:17), threatening the future of Israel. Yet the prophet knows, out of his own experience of the purging fire of forgiveness (6:6-7), that the divine purpose is to cleanse and refine in order that Israel may become a holy people (1:24-26).

Yahweh's activity in history is a manifestation of his holiness (Ezek. 20:41; 28:22, 25). The remembrance of Yahweh's mighty deed at the time of the Exodus prompts a poet to exclaim that he is "majestic in holiness" (Exod. 15:11). Confidence in his power to deliver leads Israel to say that "there is none holy like Yahweh" (I Sam. 2:2). In the last analysis, the holiness which distinguishes the divine from the human is manifest in God's power to deliver, a gracious power which surpasses all human strength and understanding. This is the thought that stirs Second Isaiah to poetic praise. Israel's God, incomparable in majesty and power (Isa. 40:25; 45:9-13), manifests his holiness in the redemption of Israel and the world (Isa. 41:14, 20; 43:3, 14-15; 47:4).

2. Jealousy. Yahweh's holiness and his JEALOUSY are so closely related that the latter is only the expression of the former (Josh. 24:19). Israel's God is known characteristically as the "jealous God" (Exod. 20:5; 34:14). The Hebrew word קנאה can be translated both by "jealousy" and by "zeal" (note the use of the word in Isa. 9:7—H 9:6). It is significant that the two words used in English translation are derived from the same Greek root. The term refers to the ardor with which Yahweh maintains his sovereignty and upholds the covenant welfare of his people.

Divine jealousy is frequently associated with the first commandment of the Decalogue. Yahweh wills to be Lord alone; the covenant requires that for Israel there shall be no other God. Any deviation from this central loyalty in order to serve "other gods" is a violation of Yahweh's holiness, in consequence of which his zeal breaks forth to punish the offenders (Exod. 34:12-16; Deut. 4:23-24; 6:14-15; Josh. 24:19-20). Thus jealousy or zeal overlaps in meaning with wrath, both being expressions of divine holiness (Deut. 32:16).

Like other traits of Yahweh to be considered below, "jealousy" is an analogical term based on human personality (*see* § C4 *above*). In the most intensively personal terms it expresses Yahweh's dealings with Israel. Israel did not have to reckon with an impersonal force or a vague numinous reality, but with the energetic, personal will of the God who had revealed himself in her history by benevolent deeds. He had set his affection upon Israel, and, in grateful response, Israel was under the obligation to serve him with heart, soul, and strength. His jealousy was the expression of his zealous will to be Lord and to uphold the covenant, lest Israel sink into the paganism of surrounding culture. In times of crisis, when the community was being weakened from within or without, men like Elijah rose up to display a corresponding zeal for Yahweh's covenant (I Kings 19:10; cf. II Kings 10:16).

It is erroneous to suppose that jealousy is a primitive idea which was gradually sloughed off in the refinement of Israel's faith. In a time when the easy-going tolerance of other religions threatened to corrode or absorb Israel's faith, prophets insisted upon unswerving fidelity to the God of the covenant. This passionate exclusivism, based upon Yahweh's claim to be the Lord alone, was the dynamic that led from a practical monotheism in the early period to a full-blown affirmation of Yahweh's sovereignty over all history and creation. *See* § D6 *below*.

3. Beneficence. Within the covenant community Yahweh was known as the God of חסד, a word which is often translated "lovingkindness" (KJV) or "steadfast love" (RSV; *see* LOVE). In an old liturgical passage, found in Exod. 34:6-7 and summarized in numerous other contexts (Num. 14:18; Neh. 9:17, 31; Pss. 86:15; 103:8; 145:8; Joel 2:13; Jonah 4:2), it is proclaimed that Yahweh's name or self (*see* GOD, NAMES OF, § A) is distinguished by this trait above all. Many voices in the OT affirm that Yahweh is worthy of the highest praise for his wonderful deeds of חסד (Pss. 17:7; 25:10; 103:17-18; 106:7, 45; 107:8, 15, 21, 31; 136; etc.).

When applied to Yahweh, חסד refers especially to his beneficent action on behalf of the weak and helpless. The God of Israel was known and worshiped as the gracious benefactor of his people. In their time of greatest distress, when they were slaves in Egypt, he intervened to deliver. The Sinai covenant, like the suzerainty treaties of the ancient world, was based on the sovereign's deeds of benevolence which evoked the people's gratitude and sense of obligation (Exod. 20:2; 24). The people pledged themselves to obedience in response to the gracious initiative and saving power of their deliverer. Because the covenant presupposes God's power on behalf of the powerless, it is understandable that in some passages of the OT חסד and "covenant" (ברית) are used in close association (Deut. 7:9, 12; I Kings 8:23; Ps. 89:28—H 89:29; Isa. 54:10).

Since Yahweh's חסד is a demonstration of marvelous beneficence, Israel confessed that only upon him could the people rely for strength and welfare. Again and again Israel, or individuals within the community, appealed to Yahweh to "show חסד" or to render assistance "according to thy חסד" (Gen. 24:12; II Sam. 2:6; I Kings 3:6-9; Ps. 51:1—H 51:3; etc.). The parallelism with such words as "faithfulness" or "truth" (Gen. 24:27; 32:10—H 32:11; Pss. 25:10; 40:10-11—H 40:11-12; 61:7—H 61:8; 85:10—H 85:11) testifies that Yahweh's power is not governed by caprice, but by a fundamental and never-failing constancy and trustworthiness. His is a love that is steadfast. Devotees of other ancient religions found it necessary to use magical, cultic means to propitiate the favor of the deity or to secure protection from an arbitrary exercise of divine power; but Yahweh's inner disposition, as manifest in his great historical deeds, was one of favor toward his people. His will, therefore, could be trusted, even when it was difficult to understand. Confident that man's times are in God's hand, the righteous man could live in dark days by faithfulness (Hab. 2:4). To be sure, Yahweh's חסד was not an indulgent affection, for his jealousy, as we have seen, demanded exclusive worship; and, though he was slow to anger, his wrath visited judgment upon the people's sins (Exod. 34:6-7). But his beneficent disposition toward his people was steady and consistent, instead of being subject to variableness or whim. Israel, therefore, could say thankfully that

> Yahweh is good;
> his חסד endures for ever
> (Pss. 100:5; 106:1;
> 107:1; Jer. 33:11).

In doing חסד, Yahweh is not bound by a legal responsibility (although the unconditional covenant with David seems to introduce this idea; II Sam. 7:15; 22:51; I Kings 3:6); rather, the inner incentive lies hidden within his holiness and freedom. From a strictly legal point of view, the sin of Israel should have been requited with total destruction; but Yahweh's actions disclose that he is long-suffering, patient, merciful, ready to forgive. Hosea's statement:

> I am God and not man,
> the Holy One in your midst
> (11:9),

is based on the conviction that Yahweh's חסד is greater and deeper than Israel's fickle infidelity. It is somewhat irrational, in that it exceeds what men have a right to expect or claim. Although Hosea's message is infused with a sense of Yahweh's holy love (*see below*), it is also based upon the ancient conception of חסד as a beneficent action, unilateral in character, which is directed toward one in need regardless of condition or merit. In the New Covenant, according to Hosea, Yahweh will betroth Israel to himself in חסד and mercy (Hos. 2:19-20—H 2:21-22; cf. Isa. 54:7-8; Jer. 16:5). חסד thus approaches the NT conception of χάρις or GRACE. By universalizing what was known through Israel's covenant history, psalmists affirmed that Yahweh's חסד fills the whole earth (Pss. 33:5; 36:5-6—H 36:6-7; 145:9) and that creation itself is the work of his חסד (Ps. 136:1-9).

4. Wrath and love. Just as anger and love are closely related psychologically, so theologically the two must be considered together (*see* WRATH OF GOD; LOVE IN THE OT). The pertinent Hebrew words refer to strong spontaneous feelings of a human personality and are used analogously to express the personal relation between Yahweh and his people. This anthropopathism must be understood within the I-and-thou relation of the covenant. *See* § C4 *above.*

The wrath of God is not a naïve way of saying that men bring inexorable disaster upon themselves when they break a system of laws or defy an impersonal fate. In the OT men are related personally to God himself, rather than to a structure of moral laws or principles. His wrath, therefore, is the energetic manifestation of his will toward his people. The human counterpart of God's wrath is the experience of guilt in consequence of a personal offense against the divine will (Ps. 51:3-4—H 51:5-6). Although this guilt may be brought to consciousness by the catastrophes of history, as prophetically interpreted, it may also be occasioned by a sense of the absence of God—i.e., the despairing realization that God is hiding his face (Deut. 31:17-18; *see* § B1 *above*) and, without intervention, is leaving men to suffer the consequences of their own folly.

Wrath is not the basic disposition of God toward his people. The tradition affirms that Yahweh is "slow to anger." With complete freedom, he can restrain his anger for the time being or can "repent" —i.e., alter his proposed action in the light of a changed human situation (Jer. 18:7-10; Amos 7:1-6). His anger is not a wild outbreak of rage, or a demonic impulse of his being; it is, rather, a temporary reaction evoked by specific violations of covenant responsibilities.

Furthermore, divine wrath, like jealousy-zeal (*see above*), with which it is often associated (Num. 25:11; Deut. 4:24; 6:15; Josh. 24:19-20), is directed toward upholding the welfare of the covenant community. It is, so to speak, embraced within and limited by the redemptive intention of God. The prophets believed that the contemporary sins of Israel were so grave that God in his wrath would bring upon them a terrible day of judgment; but they also perceived that this judgment had a positive meaning insofar as it was the prelude to the purification and renewal of the people. Thus Second Isaiah affirms that Yahweh's wrath was but for "a moment," while his compassion is based on "everlasting חסד" (Isa. 54:7-8). חסד is a constant, while wrath is a passing, characteristic of Yahweh's relation to his people.

Especially under the influence of Hosea, Israel came to realize that the deepest dimension of God's wrath is love. As the prophet reflects on these apparently paradoxical traits, fierce anger and ardent love seem to struggle within the mystery of the divine personality (Hos. 11). Yahweh's love is a holy love, surpassing all human understanding or analogy. Like a father's dealing with his wayward son, or like a husband's gracious dealings with his unfaithful wife, Yahweh's wrath is only the expression of a deep and holy love which ardently seeks to correct, discipline, and ultimately make possible a new relationship. Although the prophet seems unable to fathom the depth of the divine mystery in the present, he is confident that the power of Yahweh's love will triumph eschatologically. Thus the day of wrath, under whose dark shadow the prophets saw their contemporary situation, would be superseded by a time when God in love would make all things new—a vision which fires the poetic imagination of Second Isaiah (Isa. 40:2; 49:14-15).

5. Righteousness. To understand the righteousness (צדק, צדקה) of God (*see* RIGHTEOUSNESS IN THE OT), we must lay aside forensic notions of legal principles or ideal norms which have become associated with the English word which is used in translation. Righteousness is a characteristic of Yahweh's activity on behalf of his people, and therefore overlaps in meaning with other terms which describe his saving activity, especially חסד (Ps. 40:10—H 40:11; Hos. 2:19—H 2:21; 10:12).

In the book of Judges, the judge (שופט) is a man of action. His role is to obtain justice (משפט) for Israel in times of crisis and perhaps also, in some instances, to help individuals to receive justice in specific cases. Analogously, Yahweh is Israel's שופט, who by his power maintains the covenant community (*see* GOD, NAMES OF, § D3). The giving of the law at Sinai was the sign of his salvation—i.e., his upholding of the community's welfare by bringing all relationships and regulations under the governance of his personal will. Moreover, his acts in history are called his righteous (i.e., saving) deeds (Judg. 5:11; I Sam. 12:7; Ps. 103:6; Mic. 6:5).

The term "righteousness," then, has a dynamic, personal meaning within the covenant community. It is primarily a social or relational concept which presupposes, not relation to an absolute norm, but relation to another person or persons. Not all of life's relationships are the same, of course. The king stands in relation to his subject (and vice versa), a father to his son, and the sojourner in relation to native residents. If each party fulfils the requirements of a particular relationship, righteousness ensues; if not, the life of the community is impaired, it lacks welfare (שלום). Righteousness is the characteristic of one who re-establishes a man in his rightful place within the community, or vindicates and upholds the community when it is threatened by outside powers.

Israel turns to Yahweh for vindication, for righteousness belongs to him. As the prophets emphasized, Yahweh is the guardian of the social rights of the poor, the oppressed, and the legally helpless. He demands that righteousness characterize all the relationships of the community (Amos 5:24), and, when men fail, he intervenes to upset the oppressive order and set things right (cf. I Kings 21). In the Psalms we hear the voices of people who appeal to Yahweh's righteousness (Pss. 4:1—H 4:2; 143:1), confident that he can justify them—i.e., restore them to their proper place within the community (7; 10; 26; 35; 43). When the poor and the needy have no helper, they turn to him for deliverance (72:12), for he comes to judge the peoples (96:13; 98:9). And Israel relies upon Yahweh for help against her foes, for to Yahweh belongs "vengeance"—i.e., the power of vindication (Deut. 32:35-36; Isa. 34:8; 35:4). *See* VENGEANCE.

In a manner consistent with the meaning of the word from ancient times, Second Isaiah announces that Yahweh's righteousness is equivalent to his salvation or deliverance (Isa. 45:8, 13; 46:13; 51:5-6, 8). He is "a righteous God and a Savior" (45:21). He is the Redeemer (*see* REDEEM), whose task, as in family law, is to restore the justice of his people (43:1; 49:7, 26; cf. 60:16). Moreover, his saving activity, revealed in the Righteous One, the SERVANT, is not only on behalf of Israel but extends also to the nations (49:5-6). The issue of the Servant's suffering is that many are acquitted or accounted righteous. Through his life and witness the nations are restored to a new relationship to God (53:11; cf. vs. 5), and justice is established in the earth (42:4).

6. The only and unique Lord. Israel's ancient confession of faith was made in a polytheistic setting. Admittedly the religions of the Fertile Crescent, by the time of Moses, had moved far beyond primitive polydemonism toward an ordered, monarchic polytheism, and at times, as in the case of Akh-en-Aton's reform in Egypt (*ca.* 1370-1353 B.C.), seemed to tend toward explicit monotheism. Despite these developments, however, nature religion is basically polytheistic, for the powers of nature are manifold. Israel's faith, however, is based upon the worship of the one Lord, who is not a natural power, but whose sovereign will is revealed historically—pre-eminently in the one event, the Exodus. The question arises, then, as to whether Israel's faith unlike nature religions, was essentially monotheistic.

We have already seen that the jealousy of Yahweh, a unique doctrine in the tolerant atmosphere of polytheism, provided the dynamic which eventually embraced all of life, history, and the universe within the sovereignty of the God of Israel (*see* § D2 *above*). Since Yahweh had demonstrated his saving power by beneficently rescuing his people from Egyptian oppression, Israel was beholden to him alone. The first commandment of the Decalogue, which follows immediately upon the "good news" of Yahweh's saving deeds, is a stern reminder that Israel is to have "no other gods before me" (Exod. 20:3). This commandment, which is paralleled in other ancient legislation (Exod. 22:20—H 20:19; 23:13), clearly means that within the cultic community of Israel, Yahweh wills to be the only God. He will share Israel's worship with no other god, and no idols or images of him are to be made. Unlike the gods of other peoples, he has no female partner; this fact is underscored strikingly by the absence of a word for "goddess" in the Hebrew language.

It is highly doubtful, however, whether Israel's faith in the Mosaic period should be called monotheistic in the usual sense of the word. The question about the name of God (Exod. 3:13) presupposes a polytheistic context, although, as we have seen, the disclosure of the special name, Yahweh, has deeper religious implications (*see* GOD, NAMES OF). The Mosaic affirmation: "There is no other God besides Yahweh," was at first a confessional declaration made by the community in thanksgiving for Yahweh's mighty deed of deliverance in the Exodus. It represents the language of worship and should not be construed as a reflective judgment that there are no other gods at all. From the very first it was realized that Yahweh is unique, in the sense that his historical power is incomparable to any other god (see Exod. 15:11).

The power of "other gods" to seduce Israel from the covenant loyalty was demonstrated from the time of the entrance into Canaan. Indeed, much of the OT, explicitly or implicitly, bears witness to the violence of the struggle waged under the banner of the first commandment of the Decalogue. In the course of time, as Israel stepped upon a larger historical stage, the implications of Yahweh's jealous claim to be the Lord of the whole of life were seen in wider and deeper perspective. During the early monarchy, perhaps in the reign of Solomon, when Israel's political and cultural horizons had vastly enlarged, a prophetic writer (designated by scholars as the Yahwist; *see* PENTATEUCH) interpreted the whole of human history, beginning with the Creation, as being under the sovereign control and purpose of Yahweh, the God who had revealed himself in Israel's sacred history. In the ninth century, when expansion of Phoenician culture brought the accompanying temptation to worship the Phoenician Baal-Melkart, Elijah threw down the challenge in a manner reminiscent of Joshua's "Choose this day whom you will serve" (cf. Josh. 24:15). Elijah's question: Who is God—Baal or Yahweh? was not raised abstractly, but in terms of sovereignty, of power to act. Measured by this standard, the Baal was laughed into meaningless unreality (I Kings 18:17-46). In the eighth century Amos maintained an eloquent silence about other gods, while insisting strenuously that Yahweh's sovereignty controls the affairs of nations other than Israel (Amos 1:1–2:3; 9:7). A few years later, Isaiah scorned the gods (אלהים) of the nations as worthless idols (אלילים, "nothings") in comparison with the power and majesty of Yahweh (Isa. 2:8, 18; 10:10; 19:3). And a century later Jeremiah denounced the gods as "vapor" (Jer. 2:5; 10:8; 14:22) or "no gods" (2:11; 5:7).

Beginning with the time of Jeremiah, Israel's faith seems to have become more self-consciously monotheistic. The great confession of Judaism, the Shema ("Hear, O Israel"; Deut. 6:4-9), probably dates from about the time of Josiah's reform (621 B.C.), although it surely rests on a much older religious tradition. Unfortunately, the meaning of the Hebrew is uncertain. It is possible to translate: "Yahweh, our God, is one Yahweh"—in which case the Shema affirms that Yahweh cannot be divided into several Yahweh manifestations (poly-Yahwism), like the Baals of different sanctuaries. Or we may translate: "Yahweh is our God, Yahweh alone"—in which case the Shema affirms that Yahweh is the only and the unique God. The latter interpretation is supported by other Deuteronomic passages, which affirm, on the basis of the incomparable power and majesty of Yahweh's historical revelation, that "Yahweh is God; there is no other besides him" (Deut. 4:32-39; see especially vs. 35).

Israelite monotheism comes to its finest expression in the prophecy of Second Isaiah. The downfall of the Israelite nation, far from spelling the death of Israel's God, brought the opportunity for faith to perceive Yahweh's sovereignty in the widest possible dimensions. Yahweh is God alone, unique and incomparable in wisdom, majesty, and power, the Lord of all human history and the Creator of heaven and earth (Isa. 41:28-29; 42:17; 43:10-11; 44:7-8; 45:5-6, 14-17, 21-22; 46:1-2, 8-11; etc.). It is noteworthy, however, that this prophet does not reach this conclusion along a pathway of reflective monism, but by expounding a historical monotheism. He perceives that the divine will behind and within all history is precisely that of the God who chose to reveal himself historically to Israel. The God who called Abraham from the East, who delivered his people from Egypt, who was on the verge of accomplishing a new exodus from Babylonian exile, is the sovereign who alone controls the destinies of the nations. The prophet ridicules the gods of the nations as man-made constructs because they have no power to act. They are historically dumb, for they cannot announce in advance a historical purpose and bring it to fulfilment. They are as pitifully weak as man, for they too are at the mercy of the changes and fortunes of the passing years. But Israel's God is God alone, the "first and the last," for his eternal majesty spans history from beginning to end (*see* GOD, NAMES OF, § D4*b*). His inexhaustible power not only supports the whole creation but is mighty to deliver Israel from despair and guilt and to bring all mankind into the sphere of his redeeming work. Second Isaiah's theology of world history requires a historical monotheism.

Thus Israel, during the period between Moses and Second Isaiah, came to a clearer and deeper awareness of Yahweh's sovereignty. But the issue of monotheism should not be overemphasized. For, defined merely in terms of intellectual belief in one God, monotheism is not the heart of Israel's faith. Job's problem, e.g., was not that of belief in one God (on this matter he could readily have agreed with his friends), but was that of his relation to God and God's relation to him. His wild protests were not silenced until, in faith, he came to know that the Sovereign of the universe spoke to him with compassion and concern. The poem of Job is a forceful reminder that biblical faith is not equivalent to a rationally unified structure of thought, such as the word "monotheism" often suggests. In the modern period reconstructions of Israel's religious history have been based too much upon the notion of an ascending intellectual development from crude levels of Mosaic faith to the heights of monotheism in Second Isaiah.

There is a vast qualitative difference between the monotheism of, e.g., Akh-en-aton of Egypt and the "practical monotheism" of the Mosaic period. As we have seen, the axis of Israel's faith, from the time of Moses on, was the covenant assurance: "I am Yahweh, your God," and the covenant claim: "You are my people." The emphasis falls, not upon Yahweh's existence, but upon his action in Israel's history. Thus the typical argument against other "gods" was that they have no meaning within Israel's sacred history—they have not been "known" by the people or their fathers (Deut. 13:1, 6-11; 28:64; Jer. 16:13; 19:4). The only God Israel knows is the God who had "known" them by bringing them out of Egypt (Deut. 13:1-5; Amos 3:2). He wills to be absolutely sovereign over their lives, and through Israel to manifest his sovereignty over the whole of human history from beginning to end. The goal of history will be realized, according to a well-known prophecy, when the nations come to Jerusalem in order that they may know the God who has spoken through Israel's sacred history (Isa. 2:1-4; Mic. 4:1-4; *see* § B2 *above*).

E. *THE PURPOSE OF GOD.* Modern views of history (progressive, Marxist) are profoundly indebted to the biblical understanding of the dynamic and purposeful character of what we call the human drama. Against oriental religions or philosophies which affirm that existence is illusion (maya) or which assert that history turns in ever-repeating circles after the manner of the cycles of nature, Israel's faith affirms that man's historical life is a dramatic story which presses toward the fulfilment of purpose. This teleological emphasis, however, cannot be reduced to secular terms, as though the activity of God were not essential to the story. For the basic conviction of the biblical view is that God himself is present in the historical struggle, directing the course of human affairs toward his own end.

1. Incipient eschatology. The doctrine of the *eschata* or "last things" (*see* ESCHATOLOGY OF THE OT) was elaborated during the postexilic period into a vision of the final resolution of the historical conflict and the consummation of all things in the purpose of God. Although this doctrine, under the influence of Zoroastrian thought, found special expression in APOCALYPTICISM, its source lay far back at the very spring of Israel's faith. From the first, Israel knew Yahweh as the God who was actively leading his people into the future. Since his will was the determining factor in historical affairs, as in the contest with the pharaoh (Exod. 1–15), the conquest of Canaan (Joshua), or the battle with Canaanite forces at Megiddo (Judg. 5), history was the narration of his actions—the rehearsal of his "righteous deeds" (Judg. 5:11; RSV "triumphs"). Therefore events, as interpreted prophetically, had a holy character, for in them Yahweh disclosed his energetic zeal to be worshiped as Lord and to fulfil his purpose for Israel.

An early expression of the voluntaristic character of Yahweh's historical revelation was the theme of the divine PROMISE. This theme may have been inherited from the religion of "the fathers" in the pre-Mosaic period. In any case, it was one of the fundamental convictions which governed the exposition of the Mosaic faith in the early period of oral tradition, and eventually it came to be the leading theme of the historical epic of the Yahwist (*see* J). Thus in Gen. 12:1-3, Israel's sacred history opens with the call of Abraham (the ancestor and representative of the Israelite community) and Yahweh's threefold promise to him. The careers of the patriarchs, according to this view, were not an aimless seminomadic wandering, but a pilgrimage under the sign of the promise, Yahweh himself being the leader and guide. It may be that the Yahwist, writing in the dazzling light of the achievements of David and Solomon, thought that this promise was on the verge of being realized. But subsequent prophets affirmed that Yahweh intended something more for his people than the mere possession of Canaan or the prestige of being a great nation. The Day of Yahweh was not "light" (prosperity, national victory, prestige), but darkness (Amos 5:18-20); only by going through the shadowy valley of suffering and death could Yahweh's people inherit the promise which he held before them (Hos. 2:14-23—H 2:16-25).

2. God's will for Israel: community. In many ways the OT testifies that Yahweh's will is that Israel should be a "people"—not a people like the rest of the nations, but a special or peculiar people bound together by covenant loyalty to their God and to one another (Num. 23:9). "I will be their God and they will be my people"—this covenant declaration summarizes the divine intention which underlies the Israelite community and its history. For this purpose, according to the exodus tradition, he rescued them from Egyptian slavery and led them through the wilderness to the mount of the covenant (Exod. 19–24). For this purpose, he performed his "righteous acts" in the historical struggle when Israel's very existence was imperiled (Judg. 5). And for this purpose he raised up prophets to instruct them in the obligations involved in being Israel, the "people of God." The covenant implies that God wills to enter into relationship with his people and that he wills for his people to live in fellowship with him.

The prophets saw that the community was impaired by Israel's sins. Instead of remembering gratefully Yahweh's gracious deeds and living in a faithful relation to him and in a responsible relation to other members of the community (Mic. 6:1-8), the people preferred to go their own way, serving the attractive gods of the world and following the devices and desires of their hearts. Israel was not "whole" (תמים) with Yahweh (cf. Deut. 18:13); righteousness and justice were lacking (Isa. 5:1-7); and the "peace" (שלום) or welfare of the community was destroyed. Yahweh's zeal to uphold the covenant expressed itself in wrath (*see* § D4 *above*), as the pre-exilic prophets testified in the historical crises of their day. But his purpose for his people was SALVATION. He willed the restoration of the health, wholeness, and welfare of the community in order that "Not my people" might become "My people" in a new covenant relationship (Hos. 2:23—H 2:25). His saving purpose would be realized in the new covenant (Jer. 31:31-34; cf. the "covenant of peace" [Ezek. 34:25; 37:26; cf. Isa. 55:3; 61:8]) and in the new age which he would introduce (Isa. 40–55). The full implications of the doctrine of the new Israel were developed in the NT doctrine of the church. *See* CHURCH, IDEA OF.

The action of God, then, was directed toward RECONCILIATION. This motif was developed by priestly circles in terms of the meaning of SACRIFICE. In its deepest meaning, sacrifice was not a way to placate God and thereby change his disposition toward his people, but a means of expiation which God himself had provided in order that the health and holiness of the community might be preserved. The doctrine of sacrificial atonement reaches its high point in the OT in the portrait of the Suffering Servant, whose vicarious suffering, humiliation, and death are interpreted as God's means of reconciling his people to himself and thereby restoring them to welfare (שלום) and health (Isa. 53:5, 11).

3. The salvation of Israel and mankind. At the deepest levels of prophecy it was understood that Yahweh's saving purpose was not confined to Israel, but that it included all mankind. Indeed, God's will for man is community, for "it is not good that the man should be alone" (Gen. 2:18). Man, as God's creature, is a social being, whose selfhood is given to him in his relation to God and to his fellow man. One of the implications of the doctrine of CREATION is that God wills to enter into relationship with man, just as he wills that man should acknowledge his dependence upon his Creator. Although man in history (Gen. 4–11) attempts to live in such a way as to frustrate or deny God's intention, his restlessness and confusion testify to the truth that he cannot find true life outside community: fellowship with God and his fellow man in the bond of the covenant.

Thus the deepest insight into Israel's ELECTION or special calling is that God has chosen Israel to be the historical agent of world-wide blessing. The promise given to Abraham, according to the Yahwist (Gen. 12:1-3), includes the announcement that in Yahweh's purpose Abraham's people will be a blessing for all the families of the earth. This teaching about Israel's election is transposed into a richer key by Second Isaiah, who announces that God's redeeming activity is not confined to his people, even though it begins there, but his salvation reaches to the ends of the earth. The mysterious figure of the Servant of the Lord is the agent of God's purpose to bring light to the nations and to bring all men within the orbit of Yahweh's saving activity, which Israel had come to know through her sacred history (Isa. 42:6; 49:8; 53).

Admittedly, Israel did not always understand her calling in this universal perspective. In some eschatological literature, which is infused with nationalism, the nations are brought under such severe divine judgment that seemingly they have no place in God's purpose. But the more authentic strain of prophecy stresses that Yahweh is the saving Lord of the nations. In the last days the nations will learn peace by going to Jerusalem in order to acknowledge his sovereignty (Isa. 2:1-4). People of the nations will take hold of the robe of a Jew and ask to go with him, for "we have heard that God is with you" (Zech. 8:23; cf. 2:11—H 2:15; 14:16). The books of Ruth and Jonah were released as warnings against a narrow interpretation which limited the boundaries of the elect community. The proselytizing zeal of Judaism in the late OT period shows a recognition that Gentiles could be included within the covenant (Matt. 23:15).

Still, the OT was never able to remove completely the taint of nationalism. The messianic HOPE came to be colored with a passionate longing for the restoration of the national kingdom of David. The NT, however, draws heavily upon the message of Second Isaiah, identifying Jesus with the Suffering Servant, by whose sacrifice the doors of the kingdom have been thrown open to all men (Acts 8:26-35). The Christian faith rests upon the proclamation that God has brought Israel's sacred history to climax and fulfilment in Jesus Christ (Heb. 1:1-2), and the NT expounds the universal implications of the promise made to Abraham (Acts 3:25; Gal. 3:8).

Bibliography. G. Quell, in *TWNT,* vol. III (1938): "El und Elohim im AT," pp. 79-90; "Der alttestamentliche Gottesname," pp. 1056-80. W. Eichrodt, *Theologie des Alten Testaments,* vols. I–III (1933, 1935, 1939). P. Heinisch, *Theologie des Alten Testaments* (1940). M. Burrows, *An Outline of Biblical Theology* (1946), ch. 3. H. W. Robinson, *Inspiration and Revelation in the OT* (1946), pp. 1-159. O. J. Baab, *The Theology of the OT* (1949). M. Buber, *The Prophetic Faith* (1949). O. Procksch, *Theologie des Alten Testaments* (1950). H. H. Rowley, *The Biblical Doctrine of Election* (1950). G. E. Wright, *God Who Acts: Biblical Theology as Recital,* Studies in Biblical Theology, no. 8 (1952); "The Faith of Israel," *IB,* I (1952), 349-89. L. Köhler, *OT Theology* (1953). G. von Rad, *Theologie des Alten Testaments,* vol. I (1957). E. Jacob, *Theology of the OT* (1958). T. C. Vriezen, *An Outline of OT Theology* (1958). G. A. F. Knight, *A Christian Theology of the OT* (1959).

B. W. Anderson

GOD, NT. The NT, recognizing in the Incarnation the supreme revelation of God, concentrates on Jesus Christ, and therefore is less explicit than the OT about the great, basic characteristics of God himself. These are regarded as axiomatic and are assumed. This, however, is not for a moment to suggest that Christ is worshiped instead of God; rather, God is worshiped through Jesus Christ. Moreover, there can be culled from the NT a number of great affirmations about the unity and transcendence of God, his creatorhood, his supremacy over nature, and his revelation within it. But almost always, impersonal terms are avoided in favor of personal, and an active, dynamic conception of God pervades the NT. Most important of all, he is designated as Father. This conception, although not itself new, was evidently enormously deepened and enriched by the life and words of Jesus, and the idea of the fatherhood of God has ever since dominated Christian thinking. Not that this deepened intimacy reduces man's reverence and awe before God. On the contrary, it enhances them. The judgeship, the majesty, and the holiness of God are among the axioms of NT thought, though this, be it noted, does not alter the good news that the Judge is himself the one who takes the initiative in the work of reconciliation. The fatherhood of God, potentially universal, is an actuality in the lives of those who, in and through Christ, and by the power of the Holy Spirit, are able to cry, "Abba, Father."

The doctrine of the Trinity is not explicit in the NT, but its seeds are discernible. The fact of Christ and the experience of the Holy Spirit are already making it impossible to interpret the unity of God in terms of a "dead," undifferentiated monad. Particularly striking is the NT evidence for the conception of a God who achieves his limitless designs by a self-limitation: his omnipotence, omnipresence, omniscience, are all treated, not as abstract ideas but as expressed in terms of personality—i.e., in terms which, in that sense, are limiting. Most clearly of all, God is self-limited in the Incarnation—the "scandal of particularity"—the sharp focal point to which God, submitting himself to the Cross, contracts the beam of his light, so as ultimately to diffuse it without limit. In keeping with this conception of God as essentially not less than personal and as distinct from his creation, the NT conceives of man's contact with God, not in terms of deification (apotheosis), or of mystical identification or absorption, nor even (in this life) in terms of vision, but in terms rather of personal relationship, fellowship, communion. In a word, it is summed up in "Abba! Father!"

1. Terminology of God in the NT. (ὁ) θεός (which is the commonest LXX translation for אלהים or אל) almost always in the NT denotes the one God of monotheistic faith. Of the many gods of paganism, this title is used either in the reported words of pagans, or by Christians in order to be repudiated (Acts 12:22; 14:11; 17:23; 19:26-27 [θεά, "goddess"], 37; 28:6; I Cor. 8:5; Gal. 4:8; II Thess. 2:4). In II Cor. 4:4 ("the god of this world") it means, presumably, the devil, the spirit of "worldliness"; and in Phil. 3:19 ("their god is the belly") it is used in reference to sensuality taking the place of an object of worship.

The use or nonuse of the definite article is not necessarily an index of meaning; stylistic and syntactical considerations may often be in the main determinative. Cf., e.g., II Cor. 11:11 (ὁ θεὸς οἶδεν) with I Thess. 2:5 (θεὸς μάρτυς); Rom. 8:31 (εἰ ὁ θεὸς ὑπὲρ ἡμῶν) with Rom. 8:33 (ἐκλεκτῶν θεοῦ; θεὸς ὁ δικαιῶν).

For the application of (ὁ) θεός to Christ, *see* Christ; Divinity of Christ. Once, in John 10:34-35 (=Ps. 82:6), it is applied (at least in the NT context) to human beings.

There are several words compounded with θεός, which require here no detailed treatment: ἄθεος, "without God" (Eph. 2:12); θεοδίδακτος, "taught by God" (I Thess. 4:9); θεομαχεῖν, "fight against God" (Acts 23:9 KJV); θεομάχος, "opposing God" (Acts 5:39); θεόπνευστος, "inspired by God" (II Tim. 3:16 [*see* Inspiration and Revelation]); θεοσέβεια, "religion" (I Tim. 2:10); θεοσεβής, "a worshiper of God" (John 9:31); θεοστυγής, "hater of God" (Rom. 1:30 [*see* § 5*b below*]); φιλόθεος, "lover of God" (II Tim. 3:4).

For other designations of God ("Almighty," "Lord," etc.), *see especially* § 3 *below.*

2. God revealed in Jesus Christ.

How shall I sing that majesty
Which angels do admire?
Let dust in dust and silence lie;
Sing, sing, ye heavenly choir.

Yet, if a mortal must try to find words for an infinite

theme, the writer on the NT conception of God has at least this advantage: though "no one has ever seen God," yet "the only Son, who is in the bosom of the Father, he has made him known" (John 1:18). That is to say, the NT definition of God is to be found in Jesus Christ, who "is the image of the invisible God" (Col. 1:15; cf. II Cor. 4:4), who "reflects the glory of God and bears the very stamp of his nature" (Heb. 1:3), who is Emmanuel, God with us (Matt. 1:23). In fact, the NT makes little attempt to describe God except in terms of Christ: "He who has seen me has seen the Father" (John 14:9); and the word "Lord" (κύριος), which commonly stands in the LXX for the proper name of God, is in the NT more often applied to Jesus, except in OT quotations. (For good OT usage, outside direct quotations, however, see Luke 1:16; 2:9.)

It needs to be said at once that in no way does this emphasis on Christ as the supreme revelation of God involve the NT writers in worship of Christ instead of God; the regular formula is "God through Christ" or "in Christ" or even "and Christ" (cf. Rev. 22:13, "the Alpha and the Omega," of Christ, with 1:8, of God). Although the work of Christ is recognized as identical with the work of God himself, expressions of worship, adoration, and prayer are generally offered through him to God (Rom. 16:27; Jude 25; but contrast II Pet. 3:18); and divine blessings are usually spoken of as from God and from the Lord Jesus Christ (Rom. 1:7; II Cor. 13:14; etc.; though "the grace of the Lord Jesus Christ," without further addition, often appears in farewell formulas: I Cor. 16:23, etc.).

The vision in Rev. 4 (cf. 20:11; 21:5) represents the only attempt in the NT to portray God (*see* THEOPHANY); and even here it is by means of hint, allusion, and symbol (cf. Isa. 6; Ezek. 1). The richest "definition" of God is as the "Father of our Lord Jesus Christ" (Rom. 15:6; cf. II Cor. 11:31; Eph. 1:3, 17; Col. 1:3; I Pet. 1:3; *see* JESUS CHRIST). But since the NT assumes, while modifying and enriching, the OT conception of God, *see also* GOD, OT VIEW OF.

3. Unity and transcendence. That God is one is alluded to as an established assumption (Mark 12:29 ff; John 17:3; Rom. 3:30; 16:27; I Cor. 8:4-6; Gal. 3:20; Eph. 4:6; I Tim. 1:17; 2:5; Jas. 2:19; Jude 25). So are his unique goodness, truth, and wisdom (Mark 10:18; Rom. 3:4; 16:27), and his supremacy and ineluctable purpose. Heaven is his throne; he is eternally to be blessed; he controls all earthly powers (Matt. 5:34; 23:22; Rom. 9:5, 14 ff; 13:1; etc.). He is recognized as Creator, exercising vigilant care over all CREATION; he dresses the flowers and feeds the birds, and not a sparrow falls without his knowledge (Matt. 6:30; 10:29; 19:4; Mark 13:19; Luke 12:24; Acts 4:24; 17:24; Rom. 1:18 ff; Eph. 3:9; I Tim. 4:3; I Pet. 4:19; Rev. 4:11). As Creator, he is expressly distinguished from his creation (Rom. 1:25), although he is also immanent in all (Eph. 4:6), and (though this is less typical of the NT) all are in him (Acts 17:28). Everything has been created by him and through him and for him (Rom. 11:36; cf. I Cor. 8:6). Ultimately, according to I Cor. 15:28, he will be (revealed to be) himself "everything" (πάντα). But so "pantheistic" a phrase, if it is to be pressed at all (which is doubtful), is at any rate reserved for the final consummation. References to the revelation of God through "nature" occur in Acts 14:17; Rom. 1:20, but are notoriously rare, the whole weight being thrown on his revelation in his dealings with man, and, most of all, in the Incarnation.

The transcendence of God is explicitly alluded to. The term common to Jews and Gentiles, "Most High," is used; and there are famous phrases such as: "the King of ages, immortal, invisible, the only God" (I Tim. 1:17); "the blessed and only Sovereign, the King of kings and Lord of lords, who alone has immortality and dwells in unapproachable light, whom no man has ever seen or can see. To him be honor and eternal dominion. Amen" (I Tim. 6:15-16; cf. Rom. 1:20-23; 9:5; Rev. 4:8). The Jewish reverential periphrases for God are sometimes used (though among them is not "the Name," absolutely) —e.g.: "the Blessed," "Power" (Mark 14:61-62), "heaven" (Luke 15:18; cf. the frequent Matthean phrase "the kingdom of heaven"), "the Wisdom of God" (Luke 11:49), "the Majestic Glory" (II Pet. 1:17); and in a passive verb there may sometimes be detected the Jewish reverential avoidance of explicitly naming God as the subject of an active verb (e.g., Mark 4:11: "To you has been given" may be a circumlocution for "God has given you"). The "Almighty" (παντοκράτωρ; *see* LORD OF HOSTS) occurs not only in direct OT quotations but also, in Revelation, is adopted into the seer's own vocabulary, where also God is the "Alpha and the Omega, . . . who is and who was and who is to come" (Rev. 1:8, etc.; yet cf. 22:13, the "Alpha and the Omega" of Christ).

God is the one who wields absolute authority, as a potter does over his clay (Rom. 9:19 ff; cf. Matt. 10:28; Luke 12:5—or is this the devil? *see* AUTHORITY; PREDESTINATION); and the very conception of the KINGDOM OF GOD implies his supremacy and ultimate victory (cf. Rom. 14:11: "Every tongue shall give praise to God"). He is called Savior in Luke 1:47; I Tim. 1:1; 2:3; 4:10; Tit. 1:3; 2:10; 3:4; Jude 25; and is associated with salvation (Luke 1:69 ff; 3:6 [quotation from Isa. 40]; II Thess. 2:13; Rev. 7:10; 12:10; 19:1), and with the vindication of his people (Luke 1:68; 7:16; 18:7; Rom. 8:33; 11:26 [quotation from Isa. 59]). But "Savior" (like "Lord"; *see* § 2 *above*) is more often applied to Jesus. *See* SALVATION.

But these affirmations of the supremacy of God are not so made that the evil rampant in the world is minimized and ignored. On the contrary, it is described in very definite, personal, demonic terms. Nor is God represented as a dictator, riding to his goal roughshod over human will. "Despotic" terms are rarely used in the NT, and then sometimes merely in a conscious slave-master metaphor (Luke 2:29; Acts 4:24; II Tim. 2:21; Rev. 6:10—all δεσπότης, though variously rendered in the RSV; this term is applied also to Jesus in II Peter and Jude). In general, God is described in terms of personality: at the very least, he is not less than personal—and personality is the highest category known to men; and in keeping with this is the very frequent reference to his GRACE, a word describing his gracious personal relationship with us. Correspondingly, his archenemy is portrayed in terms of personal disobedience—i.e., of the rejection of his grace and of reaction against perfect personality (*see* DEMON; SATAN). The conquest of evil by God is assured: it is no evenly balanced conflict, as in dualism, between a god of good and a god of evil (Rom. 16:20); yet neither is it achieved by subpersonal means (see Matt. 4:8-10—the temptation to Christ to use methods other than God's). It is achieved by reconciliation (II Cor. 5:19; Col. 1: 20); and this means redemptive suffering. *See* ATONEMENT.

4. Impersonal terms avoided, in favor of personal. The NT, like the OT, tends to avoid metaphysical definitions and abstract terms. Only once is God called "the Deity" (τὸ θεῖον [Acts 17:29], in an address to a more or less philosophical audience; the term, used by Philo and Josephus, does not occur in the LXX). Only once each are abstract words for "deity" found (θειότης [Rom. 1:20]; θεότης [Col. 2: 9]). Twice God is equated with what seem, at first, to be great impersonal ideas: "God is light," "God is love" (I John 1:5; 4:8). But it soon becomes clear that the words "light" and "love" are used here, as in the Fourth Gospel, not impersonally, but to denote character and activity. "God is light" means that God, being the very source of light (cf. Jas. 1: 17), may be relied upon to act with absolute consistency and dazzling integrity, and that he cannot tolerate falsehood in any shape or form (I John *passim;* Rev. 22:15). "God is love" is expanded into: "In this the love of God was made manifest among us, that God sent his only Son into the world, so that we might live through him" (I John 4:9; cf. John 3: 16); and: "We love, because he first loved us" (I John 4:19). Even the love for God, which is man's proper function (Luke 10:27, etc.), is itself God's own gift to man. Thus "God is love" is an essentially active and dynamic statement—anything but abstract or static. "God is spirit" (John 4:24) seems to mean simply that God is not material, and therefore not localized in any one shrine or tied to externals. Similarly, the frequent phrase "the glory of God," except where it describes God's glorious plan for men, or an action done "to God's honor," mostly means (in keeping with its OT antecedents): "God manifesting himself among men" (e.g., John 11:40; Acts 7:2; Rom. 6:4; Eph. 3:16; Heb. 1:3; *see* GLORY, OT AND NT). Thus, these apparently abstract words, "light," "love," "spirit," "glory," are no real exception to the rule that the NT doctrine of God tends to avoid impersonal terms.

Indeed, if we compare with the language of the NT the great absolutes habitually applied by religion to God, the results are striking. Any theist would agree that God, by definition, must be almighty, omnipresent, omniscient. But (as is shown in § 7 *below*), the NT interprets all these in the light of God's self-limitation in the Incarnation. Moreover, if God is acknowledged as inscrutable (Rom. 11:33), yet the *via negativa*—namely, to define God by what he is *not*—is, in general, alien to the NT. Generally in the NT he is described anthropomorphically. He is the God whose character is revealed in human history (e.g., Revelation *passim*), and, most of all, in the Incarnation. The mighty deeds of Jesus are the "finger of God" at work (Luke 11:20). Just as, to the Hebrews, he was the God who brought them up out of Egypt and made a nation of them, so, to Christians, he is the God "who brought again from the dead our Lord Jesus" and made an eternal covenant with his people (Heb. 13:20; cf. Acts 3:25). God's "oath," his promise, is a recurrent theme (Acts 2:30; 7:17; 26:6; Rom. 11:29; II Cor. 1:20; Heb. 6:17). The irreversibility of God's promise, this "oath" by which scripture picturesquely describes him as binding himself, and which the Christian sees as taking shape in Christ (II Cor. 1:20—Christ the affirmation of all God's promises; *see* AMEN), is the basis of the Christian hope for final victory for the kingdom of God.

In keeping with this active conception of God in both Hebrew and Christian thought is the designation of him, in contrast to the dead, dumb idols, as the living God and the God who speaks—through creation, through history, and, most clearly, through Christ (Acts 14:15, 17; Rom. 1:20; I Cor. 12:2; I Thess. 1:9; I Tim. 6:17; Heb. 1:1-2). God, himself essentially alive, gives life to all (Mark 12:27; Acts 17:25; Rom. 4:17; 6:23; I Tim. 3:15). His aliveness judges whatever of death is in us: "It is a fearful thing to fall into the hands of the living God" (Heb. 10:31). Again, in contrast to the unreality of idols (I Cor. 8:4), he is the one who is "real" or true (I John 5:20—though this is possibly of Christ; cf. John 7:28), and his reality judges all pretense, lying, and hypocrisy (I John 5:21; Rev. 22:15; etc.).

5. God as Father. ***a. In the life and teaching of Jesus.*** Jesus himself, to judge by the reflection of his teaching and attitude in the NT, gave a new depth to the conception of God as Father (*see* TEACHING OF JESUS). Adumbrated in the OT and extended to early Judaism, the conception itself was nothing new. Indeed, outside Judaism also, the idea was common enough, whether in polytheistic mythology (Homer's "Father Zeus") or in philosophical thought (Plato's "Maker and Father of this universe" [*Timaeus* 28C]). For generations the Jews, at any rate, had declared, not, indeed, that they were in some sense physically descended from God (in the manner of pagan mythology), but that, spiritually and morally and by his choice of them to be his people, he had become their Father (so John 8:41, 54). But Jesus appears not only to have been sparing with the use of designations other than "Father," but also to have exhibited, through his life as well as through his words, a new attitude of sonship. It is true that other designations are found in his reported words: Simply "God," or (in OT quotation) "the Lord your God," is fairly frequent, but never in address to God (except in the cry from Ps. 22). "Lord" (κύριος) occurs at Mark 5:19 ("how much the Lord has done for you"); 13:20 ("if the Lord had not shortened the days"); and at Matt. 11.25; Luke 10:21 ("Lord of heaven and earth," but preceded by "Father"); but otherwise only in direct quotations from the OT. "The Most High" (ὕψιστος) occurs at Luke 6:35 (otherwise only on the lips of others, including an angel and a demoniac). "Power" (Mark 14:62) and "the power of God" (Luke 22:69), at the trial of Jesus, evidently represent an ordinary Jewish circumlocution. And there is the cry from Ps. 22: "My God, my God" (Matt. 27:46; Mark 15:34). Further, Jesus teaches constantly about the kingdom (or kingship) of God; but he who exercises this kingly sway is referred to, not as king (except, perhaps, in Matt. 5:35—Jerusalem is the "city of the great King"; cf. Gabriel's "stand in the presence of God," as in a king's court [Luke 1:19]), but as Father.

This being said, it must not be supposed, however, that the name "Father" as used by Jesus is attested by all the gospel traditions in such frequency as it appears in Matthew and John. These (together with the Johannine letters) are the writings which have familiarized the name to Christian readers. Nonetheless, the designation "Father" on the lips of Jesus is found in all the gospel traditions—Mark, the common ground of Matthew and Luke, and the peculiarly Lukan material, as well as that peculiar to Matthew and to John; and it is clearly implied by some of the parables or analogies (e.g., Luke 15:11-32). But, more than this, the baptism of Jesus marked him as Son of God in a special sense, his experience of God as Father is reflected in his way of life, and it appears that he used a form of the Aramaic word for "Father" which contemporary Jews seldom or never applied to God. ABBA in the gospels occurs only at Mark 14:36; but since the same Aramaic word is echoed by Rom. 8:15; Gal. 4:6, there is no need to doubt that it is a genuine word of Jesus; and, representing a form of address to human fathers, it reflects in Jesus an unprecedented simplicity and directness of approach to God.

b. In the life and words of Christians. But did Jesus teach his disciples to share precisely the same approach to God as his own? It is sometimes said that he deliberately distinguished between his own unique closeness to the Father and their secondary relationship. But, while it is true that the NT shows no shadow of doubt as to the uniqueness of Christ's status (*see* CHRIST)—he "called God his Father, making himself equal with God" (John 5:18; cf. 19:7)—yet it may be questioned whether he did teach his disciples to use a different mode of address to God from that which he himself adopted. It is true that he is sometimes represented, in all three Synoptists, as speaking to the disciples of "your (thy) Father," and that he is not recorded in any of them as using "our Father" in such a way as to include himself. (For the question whether the phrase "our Father" is original even in the Lord's Prayer, *see* LORD'S PRAYER.) Yet the only instance of a fully explicit contrast between Christ's use for himself and his intention as to his disciples' use, seems to emphasize the transmission to them of his own intimacy: John 20:17, "my Father and your Father, . . . my God and your God," may imply that, while there is indeed a distinction, yet the disciples are to receive from the unique Son a derived sonship ("my Father *who is also* your Father," as though the Greek were τὸν καὶ). In any case, Paul uses precisely the same "Abba" (Rom. 8:15; Gal. 4:6), and, incidentally, uses "my God" (Phil. 1:3; 4:19: this, not in the vocative as in Ps. 22, etc., but in reference to God, is paralleled only by John 20:17).

It is true, however, that only Jesus is represented in the NT as using the phrase "my Father" not only in vocative address but also in reference to God. This does not occur in Mark, but four times in Luke and many times in Matthew and John (cf. Rev. 2:27; 3:5, 21). Nevertheless, this does not alter the conclusion that the mission of Jesus seems to have been so to reveal and impart his sonship that—although in a most important sense unique—it might nevertheless be entered into and shared: Matt. 11:27; Luke 10:22 ("No one knows . . . who the Father is except the Son and any one to whom the Son chooses to reveal him"); Rom. 8:29 (he is the "first-born among many brethren"); Heb. 2:11 ("He is not ashamed to call them brethren"). Moreover, if the "SON OF MAN" is a collective, or even a representative, concept, then the relationship is intended to be shared by the "saints of the Most High" (Dan. 7:18, etc.). It is the spirit of sonship which links Jesus and his own in the common cry "Abba." In Rev. 21:7, the famous messianic phrase from II Sam. 7:14: "I will be his father, and he shall be my son" (cf. Ps. 89:26-27), becomes, in an adapted form, a promise for anyone who conquers: "I will be his God, and he shall be my son." It must be emphasized, however, that, whatever is implied by the new intimacy given by Christ to the name Father, it is an intimacy which deepens, rather than detracts from, the sense of God's majesty. The Lord's Prayer is a model of reverence coupled with simple trust. Whether or not the characteristically, though not exclusively, Matthean phrase "heavenly Father" (or "your Father who is in heaven") is original, it well represents this combination (cf. Heb. 12:9: "the Father of spirits," contrasted with "earthly fathers"). So do the phrases "Holy Father" and "O righteous Father" of John 17:11, 25.

The HOLINESS of God is not so frequently alluded to in the NT as in the OT (*see* GOD, OT), but the idea is assumed as axiomatic. See II Cor. 7:1; Heb. 12:10; I Pet. 1:15 ff ("As he who called you is holy, be holy yourselves in all your conduct; since it is written, 'You shall be holy, for I am holy' [Lev. 11:44, etc.]. And if you invoke as Father him who judges each one impartially according to his deeds, conduct yourselves with fear"); Rev. 6:10; and, more particularly, Rev. 4:8, where the great "thrice holy" of the SERAPHIM in Isa. 6:3 is repeated by the four living creatures in or around the throne of God. This "thrice holy" (*trishagion; ter sanctus*) came to be a constant element in the Eucharistic worship of the Christian church. Once again, it may be that Christ's acceptance of the role of the Son of man implied this sense of adoration combined with intimacy toward the Almighty (Dan. 7:9, etc.).

The cry "Abba," then, is first and foremost a profession of absolute obedience, a recognition of the absolute authority of God; and this new intimacy positively deepens the sense of awe (cf. I Pet. 1:17). This is further illustrated by the content of the temptation which followed Christ's designation as "Son"; for here Jesus is tempted to abuse his sonship, and his reply is: " 'You shall not tempt the Lord your God.'. . .

> 'You shall worship the Lord your God
> and him only shall you serve' "
> (Matt. 4:7, 10;

cf. Luke 4:8, 12; *see* TEMPT; TEMPTATION OF JESUS). In short, fatherhood, as applied to God, epitomizes his sovereignty as voluntarily acknowledged, and only adds to the awe of his judgments. For he is the Judge of all (Rom. 14:10-12; Heb. 12:23; *see* DAY OF JUDGMENT); and his wrath (*see* WRATH OF GOD; FEAR) is the more terrible because it is, not anger in the commonly accepted sense, but the fierce indignation against evil and the verdict upon it of one who, as Father, himself suffers in his own judgments. There is nothing "soft" about this fatherhood; there is an astringent quality in it (Rom. 11:22: "the kindness and the severity of God").

It is not despite, but because of, this severity that he is also the God of mercy, the God of hope, of peace, of comfort, of graciousness, the Father of mercies, able to forgive (Mark 2:7; Rom. 15:5, 13, 33; 16:20; II Cor. 1:3; 7:6; 13:11; Phil. 4:7, 9; I Thess. 5:23; Heb. 13:20; I Pet. 5:10; II John 3; etc.). He cannot be "bribed" or "propitiated" (*see* PROPITIATION; Luke 18:13; Acts 10:4, 31, can hardly be invoked as serious evidence to the contrary); but he voluntarily accepts, as Father, the cost of reconciliation. There are very few passages in the NT where it is not clear that the estrangement between man and God is on man's side, not God's. At most, it is possible to find two or three formal exceptions to this rule. The compound θεοστυγεῖς (Rom. 1:30), though translated "haters of God" in the RSV, might mean "hated by God"; and ἐχθροί (Rom. 11:28), translated "enemies of God" in the RSV, might imply enmity on the part of God. So, too, that Jesus offered himself as a sacrifice to God (Eph. 5:2; cf. Heb. 9:14) and intercedes with God for men (Rom. 8:34; Heb. 7:25) could be made to point in the same direction, were these passages to be read in isolation. But so constantly does the NT stress the initiative of God himself in reconciling (Rom. 5:8; II Cor. 5:19; etc.) that such an interpretation is excluded. And whatever is implied by the WRATH OF GOD it does not mean what is meant by "anger" in ordinary parlance. It is the white heat of a love which cares too much for the sinner to treat his sin as indifferent. It is a part, not a contradiction, of the love of God. We have yet to find a word which conveys, in our language, such a suffering-and-redemptive anger. This is not to ignore the problem of such apparently "vengeful" passages as Rom. 2:8-9; II Thess. 1:6-10; Revelation *passim*. It is only to say that they must be viewed in the light of the evidence just alluded to.

In Eph. 3:14-15 occurs the phrase "the Father, from whom every family in heaven and on earth is named." "Family" (πατριά) is not the same as "fatherhood" (πατριότης), and the ERV-ASV mg. "Gr. *fatherhood*" is not justified as a translation. But if the meaning is that, wherever a family (*patria*) is found, it derives its name from the supreme Father (*Pater*), the ultimate result is much the same: God is the origin of "paternity" and of family life everywhere. It may be that, in this particular passage, the meaning is even wider: that, just as Greek philosophy and Stoicism called God the Father of the universe, so here he is seen as the origin of all the "families" of beings, not only human but supra- or subhuman. But still the play on words, and the essential meaning, remain. Similarly Matt. 23:9: "Call no man your father on earth, for you have one Father, who is in heaven," points to God as the source of real fatherhood. In keeping with this, the NT sometimes uses "the Father," absolutely, in reference to God (as distinct from the vocative, in address to him), in the way which was to become familiar in the trinitarian formula. This use on the lips of Jesus himself is found in Mark 13:32 (=Matt. 24:36); otherwise only in Matt. 11:27 (=Luke 10:22); 28:19 (trinitarian formula); Luke 9:26; Acts 1:4, 7 (the risen Christ speaks); and frequently in John. Otherwise than on the lips of Jesus, it is found (with or without God) in John 1:14, 18; Acts 2:33; Rom. 6:4; I Cor. 8:6; 15:24; Gal. 1:1, 3; Eph. 2:18; 3:14; 5:20; 6:23; Phil. 2:11; Col. 1:12; 3:17; I Thess. 1:1; II Tim. 1:2; Tit. 1:4; Jas. 1:27; 3:9; I Pet. 1:2; II Pet. 1:17; I John 1:2-3; 2:1, 13, 15-16, 22-24; 3:1; 4:14; II John 3-4, 9; Jude 1.

c. Only potentially universal. But is God, then, the Father of all mankind indiscriminately? The NT answer seems to be: Potentially, yes; in actuality, not yet (*see* ADOPTION; CHILDREN OF GOD). Potentially, no doubt, all men are sons of God: "For we are indeed his offspring" (Acts 17:28; cf. Luke 3:38: "Adam, the son of God"—though neither passage is typical of the NT). But they are not such actually, until they become such by adoption (Rom. 8:15; Gal. 4:6). Just as, in the OT, God is universal Creator, but is a Father in a special sense to Israel (Exod. 4:22; Jer. 31:9; Hos. 11:1; cf. John 8:41-44, 54-55), so, in the NT, "children of God" is a term for Christians, not for all men as such: "No one comes to the Father, but by me" (John 14:6). Yet, precisely because the relationship is thus defined as moral and religious, not racial or national, it has the potentiality of becoming universal. If man's response to the fatherhood of God is limited, God's redemptive seeking after man knows no bounds. It is the same principle as comes most clearly into focus in the Incarnation itself—God's unique Son, born into a particular race and family at a given date in such a way as to be God's universal and all-time salvation (*see* § 7 *below*). And perhaps it is significant in the same sense, that redemption is, in the NT, closely associated with creation, suggesting the universal scope of the one as of the other: in Jas. 1:18 there is some doubt as to which creation is intended—whether the "first" creation (of the universe), or the "new" creation (of the redeemed humanity). For the association of the two, see II Cor. 5:17; Gal. 6:15; Col. 1:16-20.

d. Linguistic data. The combination of the words "God" and "Father" in the NT presents considerable variety, according to the use or omission of the definite article and of the copula: "God the Father of our Lord Jesus Christ," "the God and Father," etc.; and there is usually a good deal of textual variation at each occurrence. It is probably in a large measure a matter more of rhythm and of syntactical propriety than of essential meaning, although, no doubt, there is a discernible difference in force between "God who is also the Father of our Lord" and "he who is the God and Father of our Lord."

6. Trinity. In keeping with the conception of God as Father, and with the emphasis on his personality, is the discovery that his unity is not a simple, "dead," and undifferentiated unity. The love of God is the activity of Jesus (Rom. 5:8); the Son "is in the bosom of the Father" (John 1:18); Father and Son are reciprocal (Matt. 11:27; Luke 10:22; John 17:21; etc.). Moreover, after the life, death, and resurrection of Jesus, the HOLY SPIRIT becomes in a new way available and intelligible as the presence of God among his people through Jesus Christ and as the character of Jesus Christ within and among them (John 7:39; Acts 2:33; II Cor. 3:4-18; etc.). And thus, although a strictly trinitarian formula occurs in the NT only at Matt. 28:19 (at I John 5:7 it is notoriously an interpolation and only in a very late text), and although a doctrine of the Trinity is nowhere in the NT made explicit, the seeds of a trinitarian understanding of God are undoubtedly sown; and it is indicative of the direction in which the wind of NT thought is already blowing that there are several impressive instances of threefold (if not of technically trinitarian) expressions rising spontaneously to the lips of the Christian: I Cor. 12:4-6; II Cor. 13:14; Eph. 4:4-6;

II Thess. 2:13-14; I Pet. 1:1-2. The striking and unique statement (I Cor. 15:28) that ultimately the Son shall be subject to God, who will then be "everything" (πάντα), does not, in view of the whole trend of Pauline thought, permit of interpretation as the heresy of an "economic" Trinity in later times, so as to imply that God is manifest only successively as "Son" and "Father." *See* TRINITY.

7. Self-limitation. One of the most striking consequences arising from the conception of God thus far outlined is his voluntary self-limitation. This has already been alluded to in general terms above (§ 4). Pursuing it a little further, it is clear now that the key to its understanding is the fatherhood of God as interpreted by and in Jesus Christ. Thus, God's omnipotence is indeed asserted and assumed (Rom. 9; Rev. 1:8; Mark 10:27; Luke 1:37); but it is delimited by such phrases as "he remains faithful—for he cannot deny himself" (II Tim. 2:13—perhaps of Christ, but equally applicable to God; cf. Tit. 1:2). God is self-limited, that is to say, by his own consistency of character. The strongest human characters are those of whom we say: "He *could* not lie, he *could* not do a mean thing." So, the faithfulness of God implies his inability to be inconsistent or faithless. Similarly, his omnipresence, less explicit in the NT than, e.g., in Ps. 139, is known to the Christian chiefly in terms of God's Holy Spirit—his essentially personal presence (I Cor. 3:16 ff; II Cor. 3:17; 6:16; Eph. 2:22), from which only sin can exclude: "He is not far from each one of us" (Acts 17:27), though the rebellious "shall suffer the punishment of . . . exclusion from the presence of the Lord" (II Thess. 1:9; cf. John 9:31: "God does not listen to sinners"). Correspondingly, too, his omniscience is expressed mostly in terms of character, personality, and active dealing with persons. Undeniably, God is the God who knows the hearts of all men (Acts 1:24; 15:8; cf. I Sam. 16:7; Luke 16:15; Rom. 2:16; I Cor. 4:5); "your Father knows what you need before you ask him" (Matt. 6:8); he "sees in secret" (Matt. 6:4, etc.); "before him no creature is hidden, but all are open and laid bare to the eyes of him with whom we have to do" (Heb. 4:13); he has no favorites (Acts 10:34; Rom. 2:11; 14:12; Gal. 2:6; Col. 3:25). And yet, in another sense, his "knowledge" is specialized: he "foreknew" his own (Rom. 8:29; cf. Eph. 1:4; *see* FOREKNOWLEDGE), choosing them, in Christ, with a view to bringing the whole creation within the ambit of his purpose (cf. Luke 7:30; Acts 2:23; Rom. 9:11; Eph. 2:10; etc.). *See* ELECTION.

The NT, in other words, constantly represents God as content to achieve his purposes by self-limitation, by specialization, by selection, by contraction in order to expand. The idea of the chosen people, familiar in the OT and continued into the NT (God is the God of Abraham, Isaac, and Jacob [Acts 3:13; 7; etc.]), is among the most obvious examples. That God should thus select might seem to contradict his impartiality, were it not for the missionary purpose for which the selection is made (a Jonah for Nineveh, a Paul for the Gentiles). The very meaning of HOLINESS is affirmed in the NT as no segregating, but as an inclusive, redemptive quality. Thus in II Cor. 6:16 the OT promise to Israel:

> I will live in them and move among them,
> and I will be their God,

is applied to the Christian church as a whole—Jewish and Gentile alike. And the very climax of this purpose is the Incarnation itself—a colossal *reculer pour mieux sauter*. In one man, of a given race, at a certain time in history, at a particular spot on this planet, the eternal Word of God became flesh. No election or specialization could be more drastic: it is what has been called the "scandal of particularity." But it is in order to save the whole world that God thus limits himself: "I, when I am lifted up from the earth, will draw all men to myself" (John 12:32); "God was in Christ reconciling the world to himself" (II Cor. 5:19), and he "desires all men to be saved and to come to the knowledge of the truth" (I Tim. 2:4). God's almighty power and wisdom express themselves most characteristically in the acceptance of what the world calls weakness or foolishness (I Cor. 1:25 ff; 3:19; cf. II Cor. 13:4).

It is probable that in Acts 20:28 the correct reading is "the Lord" (i.e., Jesus; cf. Rev. 5:9), and that the verse is wrongly interpreted to mean that God obtained the church "with his own blood." The "blood of God," startling enough in Ignatius (Eph. 1.1), is hard to credit in the NT. But, even so, a God who himself enters into the sufferings caused by sin is certainly implied (whether or not deducible from this verse) by the close association of the Father with the Son throughout NT thought. A God "who justifies the ungodly" (Rom. 4:5) and yet remains "true though every man be false" (Rom. 3:4) can only be a God who himself enters into the cost of redemption (*see* JUSTIFICATION). "Patripassianism," as a heresy, is the failure to distinguish Father and Son, not the affirmation that the Father suffers in the Son. The Cross is God's own act (John 13:31-32; 17:1-5), and in it he himself enters into redemptive suffering. This all means that the classic idea of God's impassibility requires to be qualified in the light of the NT. Impassibility is, in fact, never there asserted of him. The nearest approach is: "God cannot be tempted with evil" (Jas. 1:13)—and it is perhaps significant that even this is a moral, rather than a metaphysical, matter. As for a Lucretian aloofness and freedom from suffering, this is precisely what the Incarnation denies. Thus, the great absolutes of philosophical thought about God run up, in the NT, into a picture of God as perfect personality, wielding in an absolute degree those qualities which we recognize as best in human character, and which are seen, perfectly exemplified on an individual scale, in Jesus; and the apparent limitations turn out to be, after all, precisely the universalizing of God's kingly rule. It is thus, and only thus, that God will ultimately be vindicated as himself the sum of things, absolutely all-embracing (I Cor. 15:28).

8. Man's contact with God. In keeping with the biblical distinction between the Creator and his creation, the NT never presents man's true end in terms of deification (apotheosis), but rather as perfect fellowship with God. The nearest approach to the apotheosis idea anywhere in the NT is the unique phrase: "that . . . you may . . . become partakers of the divine nature" (II Pet. 1:4); and even this, it is to be noted, is in terms, not of some magical change of substance, but of character: "that . . . you may escape from the corruption *that is in the world because* *of passion.*" In other words, as with Paul, so with this writer, eternal life is not an endowment independent of character, but is the realization of a true relationship with the good God. Moreover, this true relationship is so described as to safeguard the individuality of the believer. The NT offers no room for a mysticism of absorption or merging in God—loss of individuality in identification with him; it speaks rather of communion, participation, fellowship. The relationship is—to use a popular term—of the "I-thou" type, not a merging such as to lose the personality. This does not preclude terms of incorporation. Paul uses "in Christ" (ἐν χριστῷ), etc., and, though rarely, "in God" (ἐν θεῷ); and the Johannine writings freely use ἐν θεῷ (John 3:21; I John 4:16; etc.). The believer "dwells," "acts," or "is" in God. But that this is still a matter of a fully personal relationship is made clear by the fact that the condition for it is obedience: it is a conscious relationship of manhood responding to the divine love with willing obedience; and it is perfectly summed up in the sonship of Jesus. Exactly as his subordination to the Father (John 14:28; I Cor. 15:28) constitutes his unity with him (John 10:30; 14:9), so for man the right relationship is on the same pattern of filial obedience (Rom. 8:15-16). To see God is, in the OT, a terrifying, perhaps a fatal, experience (Judg. 13:22, etc.). In the NT: "No one has ever seen God; the only Son . . . has made him known" (John 1:18; cf. 14:9: "He who has seen me has seen the Father"). In any other sense, the vision of God is reserved for the future (Rev. 22:4; perhaps even Matt. 5:8). To "know" God means to respond to his "knowledge" of or approach to us (Gal. 4:8-9). The last word, as the first, is Christ himself. It is "in Christ," and by virtue of the same Spirit which dwelt in him, that the Christian is enabled, by adoption, to utter that same cry, "Abba! Father!" which epitomizes the relation on earth between the unique Son and his Father. *See also* ACCESS.

Bibliography. G. Dalman, *The Words of Jesus* (English trans., 1909); J. K. Mozley, *The Doctrine of God* (1928); W. R. Matthews, *God in Christian Thought and Experience* (1930), especially chs. 3–4; T. W. Manson, *The Teaching of Jesus* (1935); J. Burnaby, *The Belief of Christendom* (1959). See also works on the theology of the NT (e.g., F. C. Grant, R. Bultmann, E. Stauffer, P. Feine).

On "Abba," besides Kittel (*TWNT*) and Dalman, see: G. Kittel, *Lexicographia Sacra* (*Theol.* occasional papers; 1938), pp. 15-16; S. V. McCasland, *JBL*, LXXII (1953), 79 ff.

On the fatherhood of God more generally, see: F. J. Foakes-Jackson and K. Lake, eds., *The Beginnings of Christianity*, I (1920), 401-2; H. F. D. Sparks, "The Doctrine of the Divine Fatherhood in the Gospels," in D. E. Nineham, ed., *Studies in the Gospels* (1955); H. W. Montefiore, *JNTS*, vol. 3, no. 1 (Nov., 1956), pp. 31 ff.

C. F. D. MOULE

GOD, SON OF. *See* SON OF GOD.

GODLESS. The translation of several pejorative terms.

1. In the OT. Commonly the word so translated is חנף, chiefly in Job (8:13; 13:16; 15:34; 17:8; 20:5; 27:8; 34:30; 36:13), but also in Prov. 11:9; Isa. 9:17; 10:6; 33:14. Cognates occur in other Semitic languages, with the connotations of "ruthless," "perverse," and "deceitful." The expression חנפי לב of Job 36:13 has a parallel in Ugaritic *ḥnp lb*, applied to the ruthless goddess Anath. The KJV regularly translated this word as "hypocrite(s)," "hypocritical." Other words rendered "godless" in the OT are: זדים, "proud ones" (Pss. 119:51, 69, 78, 85, 122; KJV THE PROUD); בליעל, "worthlessness" (II Sam. 23:6; KJV SONS OF BELIAL; WORTHLESS [KJV UNGODLY] in Prov. 16:27; 19:28); אונים, "powerful ones" (Prov. 11:7; KJV UNJUST MEN); לא חסיד, UNGODLY (Ps. 43:1); עויל, UNGODLY (Job 16:11; 18:21; KJV WICKED in Job 18:21); KJV רשע, UNGODLY (II Chr. 19:2; Pss. 1:1, 4-6; 3:7; 73:12; RSV WICKED). חנף in Isa. 32:6 and חנפה in Jer. 23:15 are translated "ungodliness" (KJV HYPOCRISY; PROFANENESS). In II Sam. 22:5; Ps. 18:4 the KJV translates the phrase נחלי בליעל by "floods of ungodly men" (RSV "torrents of perdition").

2. In the NT. Βέβηλος (KJV PROFANE) is rendered "godless" by the RSV (I Tim. 4:7; 6:20; II Tim. 2:16) except in I Tim. 1:9, where it agrees with the KJV. Ἀσεβής (Rom. 4:5; 5:6; I Tim. 1:9; I Pet. 4:18 KJV [RSV IMPIOUS]; II Pet. 2:5; 3:7; Jude 4, 51) is rendered "ungodly" and ἀσέβεια (Rom. 1:18; 11:26; II Tim. 2:16) "ungodliness," except in Tit. 2:12 (IRRELIGION). The verb ἀσεβέω, "be irreverent, act irreverently" (II Pet. 2:6; Jude 15), is defined by "ungodly."

See also BELIAL; EVIL; FOLLY. M. H. POPE

GODLY. The translation of a number of terms in the Bible. The common OT term for "godly," "loyal," "pious," is חסיד (alternately SAINTS; FAITHFUL [ONES]; HOLY; GOOD MAN). Once (Mal. 2:15) אלהים (*'aelôhîm*), "God," used attributively, is translated "godly." Similarly, in the NT, τοῦ θεοῦ (II Cor. 1:12) and κατὰ θεόν (7:9-11) are rendered "godly." Other words rendered "godly" and "godliness" in the NT are the adjective εὐσεβής (II Pet. 2:9), the adverb εὐσεβῶς (II Tim. 3:12; Tit. 2:12), and the noun εὐσέβεια (I Tim. 2:2; 4:7-8; 6:3, 5-6, 11; Tit. 1:1; II Pet. 1:3, 6-7; 3:11). In II John 6, where the KJV translates ἀξίως τοῦ θεοῦ "after a godly sort," the RSV has "as befits God's service." In I Tim. 1:4 for the KJV "godly edifying" (οἰκονομίαν θεοῦ) the RSV has "divine training." For θεοσέβεια in I Tim. 2:10 the RSV has "religion" instead of the KJV "godliness."

See also FEAR; GODLESS; HASIDIM; SAINT; WORSHIP IN THE NT. M. H. POPE

GOEL gō ēl′. *See* REDEEMER.

GOG gŏg [גוג; Akkad. *gagu*, precious golden object] (I Chr. 5:4). Eponym of a Reubenite family.

Bibliography. M. Noth, *Die israelitischen Personennamen* (1928), p. 223.

GOG AND MAGOG gŏg, mā′gŏg [גוג, מגוג, king *and* his land; Γώγ, Μαγώγ]. Gog, chief prince of Meshech, came from the land of Magog; in Ezek. 38–39 he leads the evil forces which rise up to war against Yahweh in a climactic battle. In Rev. 20:8, however, Magog, by some strange process, is no longer a country but a fellow culprit with Gog in the Battle of Armageddon.

Ezek. 38–39 is developed as follows:

I. Prophecy that Gog will be destroyed, ch. 38
  A. Destruction foretold, vss. 1-6
  B. Attack on Israel predicted, vss. 7-13
  C. God will triumph, vss. 14-23
II. Overthrow of Gog, ch. 39
  A. Military defeat, vss. 1-6
  B. Weapons burned, vss. 7-10
  C. Burial of destroyed army, vss. 11-16
  D. Sacrifice of the mighty, vss. 16-20
  E. Glory of Yahweh, vss. 21-24
  F. Return from captivity, vss. 25-29

Many have attempted to identify Gog with some historical monarch or military figure, but no certainty on this point has been attained. Gyges, the king of Lydia who is the *Gûgû* in the records of Ashurbanipal, has been suggested, but with no more reason than phonetic resemblance between the two names. Some have sought the answer in mythology, where the person Gog might represent evil darkness set in array against the light of God.

Whatever the origins of the names, we may be sure that the picture portrays the "ends of the earth" as contemporaries understood them, rising against Yahweh. These included Persia, Cush, Put, Gomer, Togarmah, Sheba, Dedan, and Tarshish. They were the kingdoms of the world which would rise against the kingdom of God, as epitomized in restored Israel, but the attack was doomed to failure. One would expect such an attack to originate in the N, from which so many invasions had come in the past. This, then, was not meant to be understood as a reference to past or future literal history but involves rather the profound insight that ultimately the tension between good and evil must be resolved.

Much misunderstanding has clustered around the Gog-Magog cycle, especially among people who look always to the future for the meaning of religion and who seek exact fulfilment for every prophecy. The Hebrew word ראש, which is used in the adjectival sense meaning "chief" (Ezek. 39:1), has no relationship to Russia, nor does Meshech refer to Moscow, as has been alleged. C. G. Howie

GOIIM goi'ĭm [גוים]. **1.** A people (the word may be translated "nations" or "Gentiles") who, led by King Tidal, along with three Eastern kings, attacked the Cities of the Valley (Gen. 14:1, 9). They may have been non-Semitic tribes who lived to the N. They have been identified with the Hittites because of the resemblance of the name Tidal to the royal Hittite name Tudhaliash, and less reasonably to the Guti (in NE Mesopotamia).

2. A people mentioned in Josh. 12:23, where a king of Goiim in Galilee(?) was among those defeated by Joshua. Perhaps this was a migrating group, possibly related to the Philistines. "Galilee" (RSV) is with the LXX; the MT has "Gilgal"; but the reference may be to Gilgal (Jiljulich) N of Aphek, although it has also been identified with Harosheth-ha-goiim of Judg. 4:2.

Bibliography. W. F. Albright, *BASOR,* 11 (1923), 8. *Cambridge Ancient History,* II (1924), 375; cf. L. H. Grollenberg, *Atlas of the Bible* (1956), Index, p. 164. H. R. Hall, *The Ancient History of the Near East* (1935), pp. 194-95.
J. P. Harland

GOLAN gō'lən [גולן]. A city of Manasseh in Bashan, and a district of the same name. Golan was selected by Moses as one of the three cities of refuge E of the Jordan (Deut. 4:43; Josh. 20:8) and was one of the Levitical cities (Josh. 21:27; I Chr. 6:71—H 6:56). Josephus speaks of a division of the former Bashan called Gaulanitis, for the most part a flat and fertile tableland and in his time densely populated; it is apparently the same as the modern Jaulan, which is bounded by the Jordan on the W, the Yarmuk on the S, and Mount Hermon to the NE. Eusebius refers to Gaulan or Golan as a very large settlement in his time. It may be Sahem el-Jolan, which lies on the E bank of the River el-'Allan. S. Cohen

GOLD. Probably the first metal known to man, because it is found in nature in a pure state and thus does not require metallurgical processes except refining. Gold occurs in the Bible hundreds of times,

Courtesy of the Oriental Institute, the University of Chicago

34. Goldworking: weighing and recording, melting for casting (upper scenes); preparing the finished objects (lower scenes); from the tomb of Mereru-ka, Saqqarah, reign of Teti, Sixth Dynasty (2350-2200 B.C.)

and both in the OT and NT more frequently than any other metal. It is often mentioned together with silver, and it is noteworthy that in the majority of cases silver comes first, reflecting the memory of the oldest period, when gold was less valued than silver. Fig. GOL 34.

Besides the common זהב, there are several other words for "gold" in the OT—viz., בצר, חרוץ, כתם, סגור, פז. The different names must represent varieties depending on the degree of purity and color, but the exact meanings are unknown to us, and they are often rendered "pure gold," "fine gold," "choice gold," etc.

In the NT "gold" (χρυσιόν, χρυσός; cf. χρυσέος, "golden") was among the gifts offered by the Wise Men (Matt. 2:11). The Twelve sent out by Jesus were instructed to take no gold, silver, or copper (i.e., coins) in their belts (Matt. 10:9; cf. Acts 3:6; 20:33). For gold adornments, see I Tim. 2:9; I Pet. 3:3; Rev. 1:13; 18:16; etc. The city of the New Jerusalem was made of gold (Rev. 21:18, 21).

The traditional source of gold is the Land of Ophir (I Kings 9:28; 10:11; Job 22:24; etc.), although

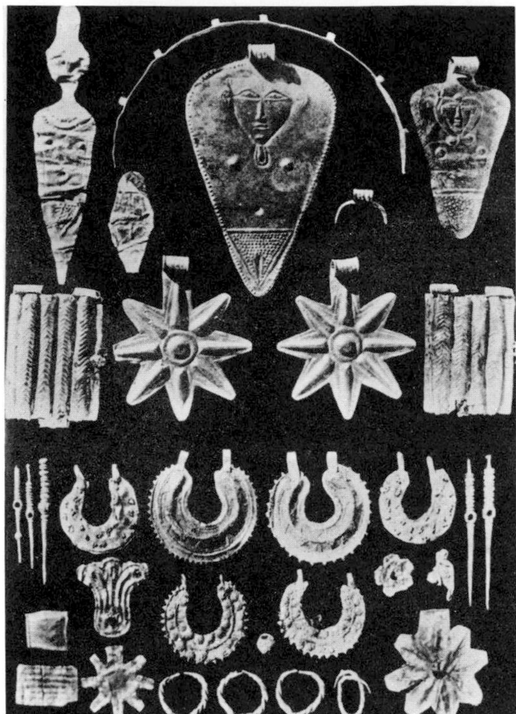

Courtesy of the Palestine Archaeological Museum, Jerusalem, Jordan

35. Gold work from Tell el-'Ajjul (*ca.* fourteenth-thirteenth centuries B.C.)

Havilah and Parvaim (Gen. 2:11-12; II Chr. 3:6) are mentioned too. That Ophir was actually a source of supply was recently confirmed by the find of a pottery fragment of the eighth century B.C. near Jaffa-Tel Aviv with an incised inscription in Hebrew: "Gold of Ophir to Beth Horon, 40 Sheqel" (Fig. OPH 11). A large quantity of gold must have come via Egypt from Nubia (modern Sudan), the name of which means "gold" in ancient Egyptian.

Although the Bible mentions a great variety of gold objects, sometimes large ones, they must have been molten down anciently for their value. In excavations, mainly small objects such as earrings, finger rings, beads, etc., are being found. From Beth-shan and Tell el-'Ajjul came several pendants with figures of female deities incised upon them.* A unique sample, of unknown provenance, is a golden signet ring with a seal inscribed with the Hebrew name Shaphat, still in the bezel. Fig. GOL 35.

See also METALLURGY.

Bibliography. W. M. F. Petrie, *Ancient Gaza* (1934), vol. IV, pl. XIII. B. Maisler, "Two Hebrew Ostraca from Tell Qasile," *JNES,* X (1951), 265-67, pl. XI B. See also various excavation reports. I. BEN-DOR

GOLDEN CALF. *See* CALF, GOLDEN.

GOLDEN RULE, THE. A modern designation for Jesus' command to do to others as you wish them to do to you (Matt. 7:12; Luke 6:31). The origin of this title is obscure. The rule is cited as early as 1674 as the "Golden Law." "Golden" signifies an inestimable value and utility. "Rule" refers not to a legal regulation but to an ideal moral principle.

In both Matthew and Luke the saying appears in a discourse by Jesus in a summarizing position, but in different contexts. Matthew climaxes some of Jesus' commands about prayer with the rule and adds: "This is the law and the prophets." Luke places the rule at the conclusion of Jesus' teachings about love of enemies and about gifts, but without reference to the law and the prophets.

Jesus' formulation of the Golden Rule is his own original wording of older Jewish precepts. He exalts the one who does rather than the one who receives. The greatness of this rule is matched only by its difficulty in practice. Its universal scope covers all dealings with others. Its simplicity pierces the dark complexities of human relationships with a clear guiding light. Its meaning for followers of Jesus must be correlated with the rest of his teaching and with his own example in conduct. It cannot properly be taken alone as an adequate guide for Christian living. Its truth, creatively and imaginatively applied in all human situations, moves men to a mutual good beyond all calculation.

Christians prefer the positive form and Jews the negative form of the rule. Arguments about which is superior are useless. Both religions give the Golden Rule in either form as God's will. In Jewish literature, prior to or near the time of Jesus, the negative form of the rule appears in various places: in Tob. 4:15: "What you hate, do not do to anyone"; in Aristeas 207, where it approaches an affirmative form; in Hillel's answer (Shab. 31*a*) to a heathen inquirer who wanted to be taught the whole law quickly (Hillel also declared the command to be the "whole law"); in the Palestinian Targum (Jerusalem I) at the end of Lev. 19:18 as an explanation of loving one's neighbor; in Philo (cited by Euseb. *Preparation* VIII.7.6). This love of neighbor and regard for his honor and property, "dear to thee as thine own" (Ab. 2.10, 12; cf. Ecclus. 31:15), indicate that positive aspects of the rule were also taught. In early Christian writings the negative form of the rule probably underlies Paul's statement that love does no wrong to a neighbor (Rom. 13:10); it is stated negatively in Did. 1:2, where it is part of the "Way of Life" which requires love of God and neighbor; it likewise appears in the Western text (Codex D) of Acts 15:20, 29. Numerous quotations of the positive form of the rule are quoted from the gospels by various church fathers.

Though Jesus gave his own wording to the Golden Rule, the thought in it is widespread in ethical and religious teachings of many peoples. Confucius taught the negative form. Ideals of conduct somewhat similar to the rule are known in the literature of the early Greeks and Romans and in the tenets of Hinduism, Buddhism, and Islam.

Bibliography. I. Abraham, *Studies in Pharisaism and the Gospel,* First Series (1917), pp. 18-29; G. B. King, "The 'Negative' Golden Rule," *JR,* VIII (1928), 268-79; L. J. Philippides, *Die "Goldene Regel," religionsgeschichtlich untersucht* (1929). D. M. BECK

GOLDSMITH [צורף, the refiner]. Goldsmiths are referred to frequently in the OT. They seem to have formed guilds (Neh. 3:8, 31-32). They made jewelry, idols, etc., either of solid gold or of beaten gold. For the goldsmith engaged in idol manufacture, see Isa. 40:19; 41:7; 46:6; Jer. 10:9, 14; 51:17.

The art of the goldsmith was very high during the Middle Bronze Age, when a special technique "granulation" was developed, consisting of tiny globules of gold arranged in patterns and soldered onto a gold surface.

Bibliography. C. R. Williams, *Gold and Silver Jewelry* (1924); W. M. F. Petrie, *Ancient Gaza* (1934), vol. IV, pls. XIII-XX.

I. BEN-DOR

GOLGOTHA gŏl′gə thə [Γολγοθά, skull; transliteration of Aram. גלגלתא, Heb. גלגלת; *also translated* κρανίον (cf. Luke 23:33; Judg. 9:53 LXX; II Kings 9:35); Lat. *calvaria* (Vulg.)]. The Jerusalem site of the crucifixion of Jesus of Nazareth and two others condemned under the Roman procurator Pontius Pilate.

The term appears twice in the OT, in the literal sense, referring to the skull of SISERA (Judg. 9:53) and the skull of JEZEBEL (II Kings 9:35). It appears in the NT only in the story of the Crucifixion (Matt. 27:33; Mark 15:22; John 19:17). In all these places the proper Greek equivalent is the single word κρανίον, which in Luke 23:33 is given as the name of the site without mention of the Semitic form "Golgotha." The proper Vulg. form everywhere is *calvaria,* which may be transliterated into the English term "Calvary," or translated as "skull." Hence, an English version may give the name of the site as Golgotha, Cranium, Calvary, or Skull.

It is not known why the place was so called. The simplest conjecture is that the skull symbolized death as meted out in this place of execution. Jerome (Commentary on Matt. 27:33) suggested that here skulls lay about unburied; and yet such was not the custom in Jerusalem. Again, there was an early Christian tradition that the skull of Adam was buried under the cross (Origen on Matt. 27:33), as is commonly pictured in medieval art; yet this is clearly a theological development from the name rather than an explanation of its origin. Still another suggestion was first made in the nineteenth century, that a certain hill in Jerusalem (from a particular angle) had the form of a skull; but this belated recognition of a profile demands imagination and an easy credulity.

Where was Golgotha? All that can be said with confidence is that the execution would have occurred outside the city wall; this is assumed also in John 19:20; Heb. 13:12. Some propose that it was on a hill, because it could be observed from a distance (Mark 15:40 and parallels). It is said to be near a road, because there were passers-by (Mark 15:29). Only John 19:41 states that the tomb was near, in a garden. Yet all these suggestions, even if they were considered to be cogent, do not inform us as to the site. Eusebius (Onom.) places Golgotha N of Mount Zion, a direction in accord with two sites now pointed out to travelers: "Calvary," now within the Church of the Holy Sepulcher, and "Gordon's Calvary."

Prior to the fourth century, Christians showed no interest in identifying the place of the Crucifixion. *Ca.* 325, Eusebius wrote that the Emperor Constantine directed Bishop Macarius to ascertain the sites of the Crucifixion and of the entombment and the Resurrection, which were presumed to lie together. A century later it was explained that the bishop was guided to the true sites through a vision of the Queen Mother Helena. After removing a Hadrianic temple of Aphrodite, Constantine erected there the two churches: Golgotha and Anastasis, where stands today the Church of the Holy Sepulcher, inside the present walls.

As one enters its door, one observes stairs on the right which mount to a balcony with altars. This rise of about fifteen feet is actually natural rock, and is the site which Constantine accepted as Golgotha and originally enclosed within an open court. A short distance to the W, beyond a hollow, he erected the Church of the Anastasis on the site identified as the tomb. Although the Holy Sepulcher complex has been destroyed and rebuilt many times, these two neighboring sites have remained fixed since the fourth century. The earliest reports of Constantine's two churches come to us from the Bordeaux Pilgrim (A.D. 333) and Eusebius (335), the latter of whom attended the dedication ceremony. To any other doubts of an authentic site must be added the further problem that archaeologists have not yet succeeded in establishing the course of the first-century Second North Wall, *outside* which Golgotha lay (cf. Jos. War V.iv.2).

In 1842 Otto Thenius of Dresden proposed that a rocky hill 250 yards NE of the Damascus Gate was Golgotha. He argued that it was the Jewish place of stoning, lay outside the city, and showed the form of a skull. In 1885, General Charles ("Chinese") Gordon also accepted this site, declaring that it formed the head of a long skeletal rock formation. Colonel Condor has also agreed to this identification, but the site is generally known as "Gordon's Calvary." Additional confirmation is claimed from the existence of the "garden tomb" nearby, involved in a joint claim of authenticity. This garden tomb lies in an area of Byzantine burial caves, and was discovered and exploited within the last century (*see* HOLY SEPULCHRE). No other proposed sites have been taken seriously.

Bibliography. G. Dalman, *Sacred Sites and Ways* (1935), pp. 346-81; J. W. Crowfoot, *Early Churches in Palestine* (1941), pp. 9-21; J. Finegan, *Light from the Ancient Past* (1946), pp. 433-38.

K. W. CLARK

GOLIATH gə lī′əth [גלית]. The Philistine champion who was slain in combat by David in the Valley of Elah* (I Sam. 17). Goliath is included among the descendants of the giants (רפאים), who, probably as foreign mercenaries serving with the Philistines, took up their residence in Gath (II Sam. 21:22; I Chr. 20: 8). His enormous stature and herculean armor struck terror into the army of Saul during the forty days he defiantly challenged it to provide a champion for a trial by combat, whose outcome would determine the fate of the war (cf. II Sam. 2:14 ff; *see bibliography*). Fig. ELA 21.

The youthful David arrived with provisions from home for his brothers at the theater of war in time to hear Goliath hurl his defiant challenge. However motivated, whether by the opportunity for an unknown youth to gain sudden fame—and a royal princess—or, more probably, by the deep religious resentment for the stinging reproaches of a foreigner, David offered himself as a combatant. After each disdained his opponent, David slung a stone that felled the giant, and quickly decapitated the champion of the Philistines, who now fled panic-stricken from the battle. Fig. SLI 68.

The armor of Goliath was dedicated by David to Yahweh (I Sam. 21:9; cf. I Sam. 17:54 [?]); Ahimelech the priest later returned the sword of Goliath to David in his flight from Saul. Although some sources credit David with the slaying of Goliath (I Sam. 17; 21:9; 22:10; cf. Ps. 151 LXX), this feat is elsewhere attributed to ELHANAN 1 (II Sam. 21:19; cf. I Chr. 20:5).

Bibliography. Livy *Historia* I. 24-25; S. N. Kramer, *Enmerkar and the Lord of Aratta* (1925), 11, 458-62, 476-78; J. B. Pritchard, ed., "The Tale of Si-nuhe," *ANET* (2nd ed., 1955), p. 20, ll. 109-45. E. R. DALGLISH

GOMER gō'mər [גמר]. **1.** Eldest son of Japheth (Gen. 10:2-3; I Chr. 1:5-6), and father of a people (Ezek. 38:6), whose name is to be equated with Assyrian *Gi-mir-ra-a,* Greek Κιμμέριοι. In the eighth century B.C. the Cimmerians, Indo-European nomads, invaded Asia Minor via the Caucasus under pressure of the SCYTHIANS (*see* ASHKENAZ). Greek, Assyrian, and archaeological sources are available for the reconstruction of their migrations and raids.

During the reign of Sargon (722-705) the Cimmerians attacked Urartu (*see* ARARAT) and also invaded Tabal (*see* TUBAL), where Sargon interfered. They were averted to the W of Asia Minor, where the Phrygian kingdom (*see* MESHECH) was destroyed by their raids. Its capital, Gordion, was burned and ransacked, and the Phrygian king Midas-Mita committed suicide (*ca.* 695 B.C.). Esarhaddon (681-669) again had to cope with the Cimmerians, whose king Teushpa he defeated. The Cimmerian threat was still serious during the reign of Ashurbanipal (669-626), when Assyrian support was sought by the peoples of Asia Minor (e.g., Tabal and LYDIA). One of the Cimmerian leaders, Tugdamme-Lygdamis, was defeated in Cilicia. The final expulsion of the Cimmerians was brought about by Alyattes of Lydia (*ca.* 605-560).

No settlements or fortresses have been identified as Cimmerian in character. Herodotus' characterization of their wars as raids has so far been borne out by archaeological evidence.

Bibliography. P. Naster, *L'Asie Mineure et l'Assyrie aux VIIIe et VIIe siècles avant Jésus-Christ* (1938), pp. 90-100; K. Bittel, *Kleinasiatische Studien* (1942), pp. 54-66. M. J. MELLINK

2. The wife of the prophet HOSEA; daughter of Diblaim (Hos. 1:3). Her unfaithfulness in marriage was used by the prophet as a dramatic parable of Israel's unfaithfulness to God.

GOMORRAH gə môr'ə —mŏr'— [עמרה]. One of the "cities of the Valley," which was destroyed by the Lord in his wrath over its wickedness (Gen. 13:10; 19:24-28; Deut. 29:23; Isa. 13:19; Jer. 49:18; 50:40; Amos 4:11). Gomorrah is first mentioned in defining the territory of the Canaanites (Gen. 10:19). Birsha king of Gomorrah, along with the kings of the other four cities, was attacked by, and later joined battle with, Chedorlaomer and his three Eastern allies in the Valley of Siddim (Gen. 14:2, 8). The depravity and consequent destruction of Gomorrah are held up as an example or warning (Deut. 29:23; 32:32; Isa. 1:9-10; 13:19; Jer. 23:14; 49:18; 50:40; Amos 4:11; Zeph. 2:9; Matt. 10:15; Rom. 9:29; II Pet. 2:6; Jude 7).

Usually Gomorrah is mentioned along with Sodom alone (seven times), but twice with all the cities of the Valley (Gen. 14:2, 8) and once with three, Zoar being omitted (Deut. 29:23). Gomorrah, though not mentioned, is included in the Pentapolis, or "Five Cities" (Wisd. Sol. 10:16), and in references to the destruction of the cities of the Valley (Gen. 19:25, 29).

Gomorrah is probably to be located under the waters of the S part of the Dead Sea, which area may once have been the fertile Valley of Siddim. Possibly Gomorrah may have been the northernmost of the five cities and situated by the stream Seil 'Esal.

See map and bibliography under SODOM.

J. P. HARLAND

GONG [χαλκός, copper] (I Cor. 13:1); KJV BRASS. A percussion instrument making a loud noise, probably used in the temple worship (*see* MUSIC § C). The reference may be to a form of cymbals. *See* MUSICAL INSTRUMENTS § B1*b*.

GOOD [טוב]. As shown already by the ancient translations, a word with a very wide extent of meanings. The LXX renders it mainly by ἀγαθός ("good"); e.g., Exod. 3:8: "a good and broad land"; II Sam. 18:27: "a good man, [bringing] good tidings") or by καλός ("beautiful"; e.g., Gen. 1:4: "The light was good"; Josh. 23:15: Yahweh's "good words"). In the same way (but not always in the same places) the Vulg. varies between *bonus* (e.g., Gen. 1:4; Exod. 3:8) and *pulcher* (e.g., Gen. 6:2: "The daughters of men were fair").

In Hebrew, טוב means that a person or a thing is in accordance with the acknowledged practical, moral or religious standards. Rebekah and the Persian queens are good-looking (Gen. 24:16; Esth. 1:11; 2:2). It is not good for a man to stay alone, but a good thing to find a wife, and even better is the love of a kissing friend (Gen. 2:8; Prov. 18:22; Song of S. 1:2). A good wine goes down smoothly, a good fig or a good honey is sweet, and it is good to eat honey but not good to eat too much of it (Song of S. 7:9; Judg. 9:11; Prov. 24:13; 25:16). A good age is a long life and a living dog better than a dead lion, but it is best not to be born at all (Judg. 8:32; Eccl. 9:4; 4:3; cf. 6:3). At least it is better to live in the corner of a housetop than to share the house with a contentious woman (Prov. 21:9; 25:24; cf. 21:19).

These standards are based on the joyful or hard happenings of daily life without moral or religious reflections, but these experiences themselves may include moral factors. To exhibit them is a main concern of the old oriental and Israelite WISDOM literature moralizing the good. The personified Wisdom gives good precepts, and it is better to get her than to get silver or gold, better to listen to the rebuke of a wise man than to the song of fools (Prov. 4:2; 3:14; cf. 8:19; 16:16; Eccl. 7:5). It is better to be slow to anger than to take a city (Prov. 16:32; cf. Eccl. 7:8;

9:16). It is not good to show partiality or to be without knowledge and to make haste (Prov. 19:2; 21:5). A crooked-minded man will not have the good time which he who keeps understanding will find (Prov. 19:8). For the Israelite wisdom, such knowledge and understanding includes the precepts of Yahweh delivered by Moses and the prophets (e.g., Neh. 9:13; Mic. 6:8; cf. Ps. 119:39; 1QS I.2-6). They have to be learned by every grown-up member of the Israelite nation able to discern good and evil (cf. Deut. 1:39; Isa. 7:15). Yahweh's precepts are good because he himself is good (e.g., Ps. 136:1)—indeed, the only one who is "good" (Matt. 19:17; Mark 10:18; Luke 18: 19). By revealing his commands he set before the people life and good, death and evil (Deut. 30:15), and it was the utmost earnest of his judgment when his people's sin obliged him to give them statutes that were not good, "by which they could not have life" (Ezek. 20:25). Yahweh has shown his goodness in Israel's history—e.g., in the sending of Ezra (Ezra 7:9)—and it is the duty of the Levites and of the congregation to confess that he is good (I Chr. 16:34; doxology). His goodness being mainly his grace and care for the humble-minded and the poor, to seek him and to seek good, to hate evil and to love good (Amos 5:6, 14-15), becomes synonymous with seeking justice, correcting oppression, defending the fatherless, and pleading for the widow (Isa. 1:12-17). As a reward for such an attitude God gives to his people the good land, victory, and other goods, to the single Israelite good health, richness, and long life. But the pious has the experience that all these goods are nothing in comparison with God himself, apart from whom he has no good and whose nearness is good for him even in the greatest needs and sorrows (Pss. 16:2; 73:28).

The same extension from a purely practical sense, via moralization, to a religious feeling may be shown for the opposite idea. There are bad things in the hereabouts—illness, poverty, and untimely death. There are foolish men who act against the counsels of Wisdom and so destroy their lives (e.g., Prov. 6: 32). But worst of all is the "wicked" man (רשע) who forgets God's ordinances, God's goodness, and God himself (e.g., Jer. 2:19). On account of the wide extent of both terms the totality of life may be described by the antithesis of "knowledge of good and evil" (e.g., Gen. 3:5), perhaps especially in the sexual field. It is man's tragedy that he learns what is good by contrast, by acting Evil—i.e., against God's commandment.

Bibliography. J. Hempel, *Das Ethos des Alten Testaments* (1938); W. Eichrodt, *Theologie des Alten Testaments,* III (1939), 44 ff; N. H. Snaith, *The Distinctive Ideas of the OT* (4th ed., 1950), pp. 51 ff; H. J. Stoebe, "Gut und Böse in der Jahwistischen Quelle des Pentateuch," *ZAW,* 65 (1953), 188-204; G. W. Buchanan, "The OT Meaning of the Knowledge of Good and Evil," *JBL,* 75 (1956), 114-20; H. H. Rowley, *The Faith of Israel* (1956), pp. 124 ff (the "good life"); P. van Imschoot, *Théologie de l'AT,* II (1956); R. Gordis, "The Knowledge of Good and Evil in the OT and the Qumran Scrolls," *JBL,* 76 (1957), 123-38; T. C. Vriezen, *Theologie des AT in Grundzügen* (1957), pp. 271 ff; N. Krieger, "Zu Gen 1 und Gen 2-3," *ZAW,* 70 (1958), 265-69. J. Hempel

GOODMAN. KJV archaism used to translate איש (Prov. 7:19; RSV HUSBAND) and οἰκοδεσπότης. *See* Householder.

GOPHER WOOD [עצי גפר, *'aṣê gōpher*]. The material from which Noah was instructed to make the ark (*see* Ark of Noah). The phrase appears only in Gen. 6:14 (P), and no cognates have been found. Some link עצי גפר with the last word in the verse, כפר (*kōpher*), "pitch," thus suggesting a resinous wood, like the conifers. Others have associated it with the Mesopotamian *kufa* boat, made of twigs and palm leaves sealed with bitumen (cf. Exod. 2:3: lit., "ark of reeds"). Regardless of the etymology of the word, it seems likely that the Priestly writer had in mind conifers (or perhaps more specifically cypresses—*Cupressus sempervirens* var. *horizontalis* Mill., Gord.) commonly used in shipbuilding. Every suggestion, however, appears to be gratuitous.

See also Flora § A8*b;* Cypress.

Bibliography. *Jewish Encyclopedia* (1904), VI, 45-46.

J. C. Trever

GORGIAS gôr′jəs [Γοργιάς]. One of the generals who, with Ptolemy and Nicanor, was a friend of the king, appointed by Lysias to lead the campaign against Judas Maccabeus. In I Macc. 4:1 ff, Gorgias was the actual commander, and in II Macc. 8:9 he is noted as a "general and a man of great experience in military service." Becoming governor of the district of Jamnia, he maintained mercenary troops and kept up a continuous warfare against the Jews at every opportunity. Judas was victorious over Nicanor and Gorgias in the Plains of Judea.

Gorgias marched with his army at night, expecting to smite Judas' army suddenly. But Judas heard of it and left camp to attack the Syrian army in Emmaus. Gorgias entered Judas' camp at night, and, finding it empty, surmised that the Jews were fleeing. At daybreak Gorgias realized that he had been trapped. Judas pursued his army, defeating it near Jamnia.

Two generals of the Hasmoneans, Joseph and Azariah, who disobeyed Judas' instructions, were defeated by Gorgias (I Macc. 5:61). They imagined that they could perform some heroic deed, but they were not of the Hasmonean family, through whom deliverance was given to Israel. S. B. Hoenig

GORTYNA gôr tī′nə [Γόρτυνα]. Alternately: GORTYN [Γορτύν]. A city located in a plain on the River Letheus in S central Crete. It was several miles from the sea; Metallum and Lebena were its ports. In classical times it was of Cretan cities second only to Cnossus in size and importance, and had temples to Apollo Pythius, Artemis, and Zeus. Though Cnossus and Gortyna joined in a league to control Crete, they spent much of their time in hostility to each other. Under the Romans, Gortyna became the metropolis of the island. In 1884, near Hagii Deka, the so-called Gortyna Law Code, a Greek inscription, was found on a wall twenty-seven feet long and five feet high. It dates *ca.* 450 B.C. and gives revisions and additions to earlier codes; it deals mainly with laws concerning family relations, family property, inheritance, and slaves. I Macc. 15:23 lists Gortyna alone of Cretan cities among the places to which the Romans *ca.* 139 B.C. sent letters on behalf of the Jews. This letter to Gortyna shows that there were Jews living there at that time.

Bibliography. I. Köhler and E. Ziebarth, *Das Stadtrecht von Gortyn und seine Beziehung zum gemeingriechischen Recht* (1912); E. Kirsten and W. Kraiker, *Griechenlandkunde* (1955), ch. 11, especially pp. 288-91.

F. V. Filson

GOSHEN gō'shən [גֹּשֶׁן; LXX Γεσεμ].

1. A place name in the phrase "land of Goshen," which appears in the general description of territory occupied by Joshua's forces (cf. Josh. 10:41; 11:16). It apparently refers to the hill-country region between Hebron and the Negeb, perhaps named after a city of the region.

2. A city of Judah located in the hill-country district of Debir (Josh. 15:51), and possibly once the chief city of a region bearing the same name (*cf.* 1 *above*). It is sometimes identified with modern Zahariyeh, *ca.* twelve miles SW of Hebron.

V. R. Gold

3. The area of Egypt, probably in the NE part of the Delta, occupied by the Israelites from the time of Joseph to the Exodus.

That Goshen designated a region in the E part of the Nile Delta is more or less certain from the notice given in Gen. 46:28 that Goshen was to be the intermediate meeting point for Joseph and his father, Israel, the former going up from his Egyptian residence, the latter coming down from Canaan. We are further informed by various references in the narrative of Gen. 46–47 that (*a*) Goshen was reckoned as a part of Egypt and not merely bordering on it, and (*b*) it was an area specifically for grazing. Twice (47:6, 11) Goshen is described as the "best of the land," and in the latter passage is equated with the "land of Rameses," which appears to be a definite geographical designation.

Little information further can be gleaned from the MT without entering upon the vexing question of the route of the Exodus (*see* Exodus, Route of). The first lap of that journey was from Rameses to Succoth; if we assume that Rameses refers to the Delta residence of the pharaoh and that Succoth is to be identified with Tell el-Maskhutah in the Wadi Tumeilat, we may then conclude that Goshen refers to the land around Rameses, in agreement with the association mentioned above. In such a case, precise localization of Goshen depends on the identification of Rameses, itself not a simple task, for Egyptologists are far from unanimous in their localization of the Delta residence of Rameses—if, indeed, this is what is meant by OT "Rameses." Great caution is necessary in making such an identification, since literally dozens of places in the Delta bore names containing the element "Rameses." The insistence, without further textual and topological evidence, that a particular one of these is the biblical city would elicit little scholarly support.

In two places (Gen. 45:10; 46:34) the MT "Goshen" is replaced in the LXX by the phrase Γεσεμ Αραβιας, the Arabian "Gesem." Until recently this has been interpreted as a reference to a Gesem in the Egyptian nome Arabia, whose capital, according to the classical geographer Ptolemeus, was Phacussa, modern Faqus. A prolonged effort to find mention of an Egyptian town or region named Gesem (or Goshen) in this general area has led to no positive results, since the supposed Egyptian forms *Gsm, Qsm,* so often quoted in this connection, rest on very questionable philological grounds. It may be taken as fairly certain that the name Goshen is not of Egyptian origin, but, like Succoth, Baal-zephon, Migdol, and Zilu (Sillo), is Semitic and attests, like them, to a long Semitic occupation of the E Delta before the New Kingdom; such a contention is supported by the existence of a town of the same name in Judah (e.g., Josh. 10:41). Quite recently a very interesting suggestion has been made concerning the Γεσεμ Αραβιας of the LXX: that such a change on the part of the LXX translators resulted from a remembrance of Gesem (Geshem; Neh. 2:19; 6:1-2, 6), the Arabian king, foe of Nehemiah, whose name has been found on silver bowls discovered in the vicinity of Tell el-Maskhutah. If his kingdom extended, as is suggested, from Judah in the N to Dedan (al-ʻUla) in the S and westward into the E Delta, it most probably included the area traditionally identified as Goshen. Because Goshen is not Gesem, however, one must assume that the LXX is an interpretation on the part of the translators, for whom the term "Goshen" was no longer current.

Bibliography. A. H. Gardiner, "The Supposed Egyptian Equivalent of the Name of Goshen," *JEA,* 5 (1918), 218-23; P. Mallon, "Les hebreux en Egypte," *Orientalia,* 3 (1921), 91-101; A. H. Gardiner, "The Geography of the Exodus: An Answer to Professor Naville and Others," *JEA,* 10 (1924), 94-95; E. Naville, "The Geography of the Exodus," *JEA,* 10 (1924), 18-39; W. F. Albright, "New Light on Early Recensions of the Hebrew Bible," *BASOR,* 140 (1955), 30-31.

T. O. Lambdin

GOSPEL (MESSAGE).

1. The term. *a. Etymology.* "Gospel" is the modern form of the Anglo-Saxon word "god-spell," a story from or about a god, and is a rendering of the Latin *evangelium.* The term was, however, understood popularly as meaning "good tidings" (e.g., Isa. 40:9; 52:7; Luke 2:10) or "glad tidings" (Rom. 10:15), where the RSV usually translates "good news," and has been used in this sense in the Protestant translations of the Bible since Tyndale. The Latin term goes back to the Greek word εὐαγγέλιον, which is found in the NT only. The LXX has only the verb εὐαγγελίζεσθαι, which in the older translations is rendered "to preach," "to tell," or "to publish," except for Isa. 40:9; 52:7; 61:1, where the KJV has "to bring [or to publish] good tidings." In Isa. 40:9 the RSV translates "herald of good tidings."

The Greek verb, in turn, is a rendition of the Hebrew בשׂר. As many Hebrew verbs, it has an ambivalent meaning, designating the public announcement of something wrought by God—e.g., a defeat (I Sam. 4:17) or a deliverance (Ps. 96:2)—that is of special importance to the group or collectivity which receives the news. It seems that particularly through Deutero-Isaiah the verb became a specific term of the theology of salvation. In his prophecies, the participle מבשׂר designates the messenger of God who announces the arrival of divine blessings. In intertestamental Judaism the verb regularly has a supernatural agent. Hence the Greek verb εὐαγγελίζειν or εὐαγγελίζεσθαι, meaning "to act as the bringer of good news," offered itself to the LXX for the rendering of בשׂר, particularly since the Greek verb also usually had a numinous connotation, referring to the operation of good luck (τύχη). The verb could, therefore, easily be adopted by the NT writers as a technical term. Luke (twenty-five times) and Paul (twenty-one times) make frequent use of it. Matthew has it only once, in a reference to Isaiah (Matt. 11:5); it is completely absent from Mark, James, and John, except for Revelation (two times).

b. Usage. It is obvious that the popularity of the verb in some NT writers is dependent upon their appreciation of the LXX, and especially of Isaiah. Different is the history of the noun εὐαγγέλιον, which is found eight times in Mark, four times in Matthew, sixty times in Paul's letters, including the Pastorals (four times), yet is absent not only from John, Hebrews, and James, but also from Luke. In the secular usage of classical and koine Greek, εὐαγγέλιον denotes the reward for good news, given either to the messenger or to the gods, who have wrought the felicitous event, while εὐαγγελία designates good news. Like μαρτύριον and μαρτυρία, the noun in -ιον designates the activity, and the noun *in-in-ía* the subject matter with which the action is concerned. The anomalous usage, by which εὐαγγέλιον was employed as designating "good news," hardly goes back to the Hebrew. For while בשׂרה may mean both good news and the reward of good news, it is, unlike the corresponding verb, never used in a religious sense. In the Greek inscriptions of Priene of 9 B.C., the birthday of Caesar Augustus is hailed as being "for the world the beginning of good news." A similar usage can be found in other Hellenistic documents. The Semitic idea that the king's ascension to the throne brings blessing to his people has obviously been coupled with the Hellenistic usage of εὐαγγέλιον as the public announcement of this event.

This origin of the religious use and new meaning of εὐαγγέλιον makes it appear improbable that Jesus himself should have used the noun or its Semitic equivalent. It is remarkable that neither Luke nor John uses the noun at all; that in the two instances in which, according to Mark (8:35; 10:29), Jesus speaks of losing one's life "for my sake and the gospel," the Synoptic parallels omit the reference to the gospel; and that the phrase "to preach the gospel" in Mark 13:10; 14:9 (and 16:15) presupposes the verb בשׂר rather than the noun.

c. Synonyms. Our surmise that Jesus did not use the noun is supported by the fact that in the NT a frequent synonym of εὐαγγέλιον is "word" (λόγος, ῥῆμα), and that all the verbs used in connection with "gospel" are also applied to "word" (e.g., "proclaim," "obey," "announce," "hear," "confirm," "speak," "have," "give," "come"). Certain of these verbs, when used absolutely, are obviously employed as synonyms of εὐαγγελίζεσθαι—e.g., κηρύσσειν, καταγγέλειν—and should be rendered accordingly. Similarly, when John's Gospel refers to Jesus' λαλεῖν, it means a qualified speaking—viz., the proclamation of the gospel. A full understanding of the nature and meaning of the gospel has, therefore, to include whatever is said in the Bible concerning the WORD of God and its proclamation.

"Word" (דבר) in the OT goes back to a root which means "back" or "background," and thus differs from the sensory perception of an object by the fact that it brings to light what "stands behind" it—i.e., what makes it to be what it is. With reference to a person, the word he speaks, or his speeches, express his purpose or intention. Furthermore, "word" in biblical parlance is always a communication from will to will; it is not merely descriptive of the essence of a thing. To the Greek mind, word and thinking go together, whereas for the Hebraic mind, the word is a mode of action. It is, therefore, primarily a spoken word, and even when written down, it still serves to express the speaker's intention. Accordingly, the gospel, too, is a divine word that manifests (φανερόω, ἀποκαλύπτω) God's ultimate purpose, and it is, therefore, a call to action or response.

The specific mode of communication implied in εὐαγγελίζεσθαι is best brought to light by the two synonyms κηρύσσειν and καταγγέλειν, and by the interchangeable use of κήρυγμα ("proclamation") and "gospel." The person who proclaims the good news does not act on his own authority. He is a herald (κῆρυξ) of the superior who sends him—i.e., of God, or his messenger—and announces what he has been commissioned to say. What he proclaims, however, is God's word, which in the Bible is not a manifestation of the "background" or the "secret" of things other than God, but invariably an expression of God's will or purpose. It is, therefore, addressed to the hearer's very self, not to his understanding or aspirations only, and thus concerns him in his personal totality of body and mind.

God's speaking is, therefore, the first act in the realization of a divine plan. Consequently, its truthfulness cannot be checked by the hearer by means of criteria which he has at his disposal, as is the case with scientific or philosophical notions and ideas. Rather, God's word authenticates itself by bringing about the things about whose realization it speaks (e.g., Isa. 55:10-13). This is not done by a miraculous power which the herald or the evangelizer possesses, nor by a kind of *mana* inherent in the words of a prophecy, but rather by the fact that, by speaking the word, God indicates that he is about to carry out the intention intimated in his word. Accordingly, the divine work promised can be considered as completed, once the revealing word has been spoken, though a wide temporal interval separates its inception from the ultimate goal.

d. Development. The historical development seems to have taken the following course: Jesus used the verb בשׂר or its Aramaic equivalent with reference to the saving message which he proclaimed, and which he called "the word" or "the word of God." The Greek-speaking church, guided by the verb εὐαγγελίζεσθαι, introduced the term εὐαγγέλιον, provided by the religious language of the age, into the vocabulary of nascent Christianity, endowing it with the characteristics of "the word." The term "gospel" was originally linked to the saving message of Jesus. Matthew, e.g., differentiates between Jesus' teaching and healing, on the one hand, and his proclaiming the gospel, on the other (Matt. 4:23; 9:35; cf. Luke 9:2; perhaps also Luke 20:21). The beginning of Mark's Gospel seems to indicate, however, that at the time of its writing, "gospel" was used in certain circles also as a designation of the whole public ministry of Jesus, not of the message brought by him only. One can easily see how, from Mark's usage, the term would develop in the second century into designating a book in which that gospel was described, though the church was anxious to insist on the oneness of the good news. The books were called "The Good News [singular] According to [κατά] Matthew," etc.

2. Formal characteristics. ***a. Proclamation of facts.*** The gospel is not the statement of a propositional truth that is being taught, but rather the proclamation of a fact that is announced by God (κηρύσσειν, ἀπαγγέλλειν). It is not to be identified with what C. H. Dodd (*The Apostolic Preaching*), on the basis of I Cor. 15:1-7 and similar passages, has termed the "kerygma"—viz., an enumeration of certain events in the life of Jesus. They are enumerated there as evidences of the truthfulness of the gospel. The gospel itself, as the NT writers understood it, is the divine proclamation of the realization of the final stage of God's plan of salvation, announced to the whole of mankind. What God himself had promised, and what people had hoped and waited for, is now becoming real. In the divinely wrought event, the scripture of the OT is fulfilled (cf., e.g., "in accordance with the scriptures" in I Cor. 15:3-4 and the many references to OT prophecies in the gospels and in Acts).

This redemptive activity is a novel event in the history of mankind, although it has long been foretold (e.g., Acts 8:35; 13:32-33; Rom. 1:2; 16:26; I Pet. 1:11-12; cf. I Cor. 10:4), and thus the gospel itself is something new. A new age has started (e.g., Rom. 3:21; II Cor. 5:17; Eph. 2:13; 3:10), and people are now living in eschatological time. Its good could not be attained at an earlier moment (e.g., I Pet. 1:11-12), yet it is equally true that with its proclamation people must not hope for another salvation (I Cor. 3:11-12). Its universal goal makes it necessary to announce it to all mankind (e.g., Matt. 24:14; 28:19; Mark 13:10; Rom. 1:16; 10:17; Col. 1:28), and hence Paul is so insistent on proclaiming it to the Gentiles also, and not to the Jews only (e.g., Acts 14:7; 15:21; 16:10; 17:18; Rom. 15:20; I Cor. 15:1-2; II Cor. 10:16; 11:7; Gal. 1:8, 11; 4:13; etc.).

Its newness does not exhaust itself in the fact that a hitherto unknown activity of God now comes to light. Rather, the gospel itself is part of a new activity of God, and thus confronts people with new possibilities and opportunities, as well as with new demands. While good things are announced to Israel in the OT (e.g., I Kings 1:42; Ps. 40:10; Isa. 52:7), we can speak only in an indirect way of the gospel in the OT (e.g., Rev. 10:7), for ontologically there is a world of difference between the promise of a reality and that reality itself. This explains the fact that when the gospel was announced to the Jews, they were perplexed and amazed (Mark 1:27=Luke 4:36; Matt. 22:22=Mark 12:17=Luke 20:26; Acts 2:7; 4:13; cf. also Matt. 8:27=Luke 8:25), and many of them remained outside that reality (Mark 4:11; I Cor. 5:12-13; Col. 4:5; I Thess. 4:12; Rev. 22:15).

b. Purpose. The purpose of the divine communication is not to enrich man's mind with new notions, but rather to announce to him salvation (σωτηρία; Acts 4:12; 13:26; Rom. 1:16; 13:11; II Cor. 6:2; Eph. 1:13; Phil. 2:12; II Thess. 2:13; etc.)—i.e., a condition by which his life will be made by God what it has not been previously, a true life. The gospel is always spoken of as a divine activity performed for the benefit of men. For this reason it is called εὐαγγέλιον, which signifies good or glad news, and "joy" is therefore a key word of the gospel (e.g., Luke 2:10; Acts 13:52; Rom. 14:17; I Thess. 1:6; Phil. 3:1; 4:4; etc.). The reason for this joy is the fact that the gospel is not a human discovery of what God is doing, but rather a fact which God brings to the knowledge of man. Man is not only able to know it, but also destined to be aware of it, and this is brought about in such a manner that the individual can realize that God is doing so for his benefit. The Lord makes it plain thereby that he has a people here on earth, for whose sake the final act of redemption is performed. Already in the provisional gospel of the OT, the prophet speaks of God's flock (Isa. 40:11) and reminds the cities of Judah that God is "your God" (Isa. 40:9). Bultmann is right, therefore, when he underlines the "existential" character of the gospel. He errs, however, by interpreting it in individualistic terms, and by substituting the timeless encounter with God for the experience of God's redemptive activity in eschatological time. The purpose of the gospel is to lead people away from the worthless things to the only true good (Acts 14:15). It is somewhat misleading, however, to emphasize the polemical element in the proclamation of the primitive church. While its message implies the rejection of both Judaism and paganism, it is nevertheless primarily positive—i.e., the assurance of God's final redemptive work. It is true, however, that the gospel is not always and by all received as good news. The goal toward which it points and the way to that goal are so contrary to man's expectations and wishes that it gives him offense (σκάνδαλον; e.g., I Cor. 1:23; cf. Rom. 1:16; II Tim. 1:8). Immediate acceptance is the exception rather than the rule (Matt. 11:5-6=Luke 7:22-23; Matt. 13:21=Mark 4:17; Matt. 13:57=Mark 6:3; Matt. 15:12; 24:10; 26:21=Mark 14:27; John 16:1; Rom. 9:33), and only by a radical fight against one's nature can one succeed in overcoming the offense (Matt. 5:29-30; 18:8-9).

In the NT the gospel is called the "word of God" (forty times), the "word of the Lord" (eight times), or simply the "word" (forty times), over against seventy-three occurrences of the term εὐαγγέλιον. The statistical evidence shows that for the primitive church's understanding of the gospel the emphasis fell upon the fact that it was a divine communication. It is not, however, for this reason, thought of as a verbal statement primarily, but rather as an event which manifests its divine purpose. John, therefore, will say that the "word of life" is something "which we have heard, which we have seen with our eyes, which we have looked upon and touched with our hands" (I John 1:1). The gospel is not a human theory concerning salvation, but rather a divine work. This fact, in turn, explains why the NT writers can say so confidently that the gospel is truthful or the word of truth (II Cor. 6:7; Eph. 1:13; Col. 1:5; Jas. 1:18) or that the word is reliable (I Tim. 1:15; 3:1; 4:9; II Tim. 2:11; Tit. 3:8). From the many words which God has spoken under the Old Covenant, the gospel differs by being his final and decisive word (Heb. 1:2). There are different ways of presenting it, but the basic facts proclaimed therein do not differ (e.g., Gal. 1:6-9; I Cor. 3:5-9). The starting point of its proclamation is not what people want to receive, but rather what goods God is offering to them.

But being the disclosure of the μυστήριον—i.e., the divine purpose of salvation—the gospel cannot be measured by the criteria of philosophy and science (I Cor. 1:17-31), because it speaks of the realization of a goal which not only has been completely unknown thus far (Rom. 16:25-26; Col. 1:26; 4:3; cf. Tit. 1:2-3; Rev. 10:7), but also utterly transcends the goods which can be realized by means of earthly factors (Rom. 11:33-36). The "messianic secret" is, therefore, an essential element of the gospel. Jesus was anxious to guard it lest his redemptive role should be mistaken as that of a miracle-worker.

c. Author. Though the gospel enters the human mind only through earthly media, it has, nevertheless, its origin in God himself (e.g., I Thess. 2:13). It is the "gospel of God" (Mark 1:14; Rom. 1:1; I Thess. 2:2, 9)—i.e., the good that God himself proclaims (e.g., Acts 10:36; 13:26; Rom. 1:1; Tit. 1:3; Rev. 10:7). Through it he calls people to himself (II Thess. 2:14). No man has, therefore, the right to fetter it (II Cor. 4:2)—i.e., to make it subservient to his cause or interests—or to use it as a source of income (II Cor. 2:17). The divine origin manifests itself in the fact that God himself chooses the people who are to proclaim it (e.g., Rom. 1:1; Gal. 2:8), and entrusts it to them (Gal. 2:7; I Thess. 2:4; cf. I Tim. 1:11; Tit. 1:3). They are thereby taken into the service of God, and are his servants (Luke 1:2; Acts 6:4; II Cor. 4:1) or slaves (Rom. 1:1; Gal. 1:10; Eph. 3:7; Col. 1:23; II Pet. 1:1; cf. Jer. 25:4; Dan. 9:10; Amos 3:7). These people are so filled with the sense of mission that they would feel miserable if they did not engage in their ministry or if they withheld part of the message (e.g., I Cor. 9:16; cf. Jer. 1:17).

In turn, nobody can make himself a messenger of the gospel. He has to be sent into his work. In the NT, the phrase "to be sent," absolutely used, means to be commissioned as a messenger of the gospel (e.g., Matt. 10:5; Mark 6:7, with reference to the Twelve; John 3:17, with reference to the Son). This also is signified by the title APOSTLE. This term, designating in Jewish Greek a person sent on an official errand on behalf of the chosen people, characterizes in NT parlance their office as that of proclaiming the gospel. Their "boldness" in proclaiming the good news is evidence of their vocation (I Thess. 1:5). Whether the term "evangelist," which is found only three times in the NT (Acts 21:8; Eph. 4:11; II Tim. 4:5), is to be identified with "apostle" is doubtful. The verb εὐαγγελίζεσθαι, "to proclaim good news," from which the noun "evangelist" is derived, is used in a broader sense in the NT than the activity implied in the term "apostle." The apostle is a person who, on account of his call, is enabled to bear witness to the divine origin of the gospel (e.g., Acts 8:25; I Thess. 2:4; cf. Luke 1:2; Acts 1:8), whereas others who are sent out by the apostles simply proclaim what they have heard from them. The "evangelists" who are mentioned in the NT are probably people who had special gifts of giving the gospel its literary form, first in the period of oral tradition and then in its written form.

In the proclamation of the gospel, Jesus occupies the central place. The gospel is εὐαγγέλιον Ἰησοῦ χριστοῦ (Mark 1:1) or simply τοῦ χριστοῦ (e.g., Rom. 15:19; I Cor. 9:12; II Cor. 2:12; 4:4; Gal. 1:7; Phil. 1:27)—i.e., the divine message that Jesus is the Christ. It is he to whom it was given first and in its entirety (Matt. 11:27). He is, according to Acts 10:36; Eph. 2:17, the messenger announced in Isa. 52:7. Matthew and Mark, therefore, characterize his whole ministry occasionally as one of proclaiming the good news (Matt. 4:17; Mark 1:14-15), and the Lukan story of Jesus in the synagogue of Nazareth (Luke 4:16-30) has probably the same programmatic function. But Jesus, too, knows himself as sent (e.g., Matt. 15:24; Mark 9:37; Luke 9:48; John 4:34), and therefore cannot but proclaim the Father's will and message (e.g., John 1:18; 8:28). In view of the intimate relationship in which he stands to the Father, he can emphasize that whatever aspect of the gospel he proclaims is the truth (cf. the phrase "Truly, I say to you"—e.g., Matt. 6:2, 5; 8:10; 13:17; Mark 3:28; 9:1; 11:23; Luke 4:24; 18:17; 21:32; and frequently in John). The proclamation with which he commissions the apostles consists, therefore, in all that he had authoritatively communicated to them (Matt. 28:20).

In view of this commission, it seems at first sight strange that Paul should speak in a number of instances of "my gospel" (Rom. 2:16; 16:25; II Tim. 2:8) or "our gospel" (II Cor. 4:3; I Thess. 1:5; II Thess. 2:14; cf. I Cor. 15:1; Gal. 1:11; 2:2; etc.). The expression cannot mean "my personal interpretation of the gospel," for Paul states clearly that he is bound by the gospel (e.g., Col. 4:4) and cannot take liberties with it. As his own view, it would lack the authority that he claims for himself as an apostle. Rather, the phrase indicates the firm band by which he is tied to the gospel. The gospel is one, and no special gospel has been revealed to him. But he, with his individuality, his special gifts, insights, and experiences, has been made a part of the gospel, so that he has a particular function in its proclamation. He has a special message for the Gentiles (Gal. 2:7).

But Jesus is more than the first recipient and the propagator of the good news. In his ministry, he is himself the good announced. He is God's power and wisdom (I Cor. 1:24); our peace (Eph. 2:14); the end of the law (Rom. 10:4); our righteousness, consecration, and redemption (I Cor. 1:30). The great "I am" statements in John (6:35; 8:12; 10:7, 11; 14:6; 15:1) have the same function. In his whole ministry, Jesus is himself the gospel.

d. Gospel as process. This fact leads to the realization that both the term "gospel" and the term "word of God" are not confined to designating a message. Rather, it is a process in which the messenger and his activity, as well as the result of his proclamation —viz., the faith of the believers—are integral parts. This fact is more obvious in the Greek texts. In the English versions the noun εὐαγγέλιον is several times rendered by the phrase "preaching" or "proclaiming the gospel" (e.g., II Cor. 2:12, where the Greek text has "I came for the sake of the gospel"). The word of God that runs and triumphs in this world (II Thess. 3:1) is identical with the missionary activity of the church (Mark 8:35; 10:29; Acts 14:3; 20:32; cf. Rom. 15:19; I Cor. 9:14, 18; I Thess. 1:5; 4:15). Whatever happens to the apostles happens to the gospel (Phil. 1; 2:22). Paul has been singled out "for the gospel"—i.e., for its propagation (Rom. 1:1)—and he is not ashamed of this activity (Rom. 1:16), because through it God is powerfully at work to save people (e.g., I Thess. 2:13; cf. I Cor. 4:15). Inasmuch as it is through Jesus that the gospel has been authoritatively announced, the missionary activity—i.e., the gospel—is the word of the risen Christ (e.g., Rom. 10:17; Col. 3:16), not the teaching of Jesus only, as has sometimes been surmised. Not by repeating the words of Jesus, but by proclaiming the gospel, do the apostles enable people to hear the Lord (Luke 10:16). This fact explains the relative freedom with which the early church handled the text of Jesus' sayings. The divine authorship is also the reason why, in Rev. 14:6, the gospel is called "everlasting" (not "eternal")—i.e., surviving the vicissitudes of history (Mark 13:31; I Pet. 1:25, quoting Isa. 40:8).

The missionary proclamation, however, does not automatically bring the assurance of divine salvation to people. While the gospel has a universal appeal, it is the word of God for those only who "listen" to it—i.e., take it seriously as a divine message (e.g., Mark 4:3, 9, 12, 15-16, 20, 23-24, and parallels)—and who "do the truth" (I John 1:6; cf. Jas. 1:22-23). People must walk worthy of it (I Thess. 2:12; Phil. 1:27; cf. Col. 1:10). The gospel demands acceptance (e.g., Acts 8:14; 11:1; 17:11; I Thess. 1:6; 2:13; Jas. 1:21), "obedience" (e.g., Rom. 6:17; 10:16; Phil. 2:12; II Thess. 1:8; 3:14; Heb. 5:9; I Pet. 2:8; 3:1), and appropriation; it has "to be eaten" (Jer. 15:16; Rev. 10:9-10; cf. John 6:51).

3. The message. ***a. General characteristics.*** What is it that the NT writers proclaim? It is the divinely wrought realization of a good which is of decisive significance for all men. Man is a slave of the cosmic forces. But the gospel announces that now through God's redemptive work he has been delivered from the bondage which made it impossible for him to lead a true life (e.g., Luke 21:28; John 8:32, 36; Rom. 3:24; 6:18, 22; 8:23; I Cor. 7:22; Gal. 5:1; Eph. 1:7; I Pet. 1:19). The Synoptists and the Apocalyptist call that goal "God's kingdom" (e.g., Matt. 3:2; 4:17; 13:11; Mark 1:15; 4:11; Luke 8:10; Rev. 1:6, 9; 5:10; 19:16); John speaks of regeneration and spiritual or everlasting life (e.g., John 3:3, 15; 20:31), and he is followed therein by I Peter (e.g., 1:3; 2:2). In Hebrews it is described as the establishment of the new people of God (e.g., 12:22; 13:20), whereas Paul most frequently characterizes it as the coming of "salvation," σωτηρία (e.g., Rom. 1:16; 10:10; 13:11; I Cor. 9:22; Eph. 1:13; Phil. 1:28; I Thess. 5:9; I Tim. 1:15; cf. Rom. 8:24; I Cor. 1:18; 9:22).

These differences of terminology reflect the diversity of the spiritual background of the writers or the groups to which they belonged. They all, however, have two features in common. First, the term "kingdom of God" makes clear that God is not in the first place concerned with man, but rather with the vindication of his glory (e.g., Matt. 19:28; 24:30; 25:31 and parallels; John 11:4; 17:5; Rom. 3:7; I Cor. 2:8; II Cor. 4:6; Eph. 1:12; I Thess. 2:12) in a world which is in rebellion against him (e.g., Rom. 1:23; 2:8; 10:21). That the process in which he establishes his kingly rule should bring salvation to mankind is, therefore, good news for mankind, because it is an evidence of God's grace (Acts 14:3; 20:32; I Pet. 1:13). Secondly, all of them proclaim in the name of God that this good will certainly be presented to the believers, because God has already taken the first step toward its realization. In other words, the gospel is not a doctrine of divine properties—e.g., his love, fatherhood, or grace—but rather the proclamation of a divine activity in history. For Mark, the saving process starts with the appearance of the Baptist; the other evangelists and Paul see it in the birth of Jesus (e.g., Matt. 1:21; Luke 2:10-11; John 1:14; Rom. 1:3; Gal. 4:4). They are unanimously agreed, however, that the process has reached its most important stage in the public ministry of Jesus. For in that fact the divine purpose has been publicly proclaimed (e.g., Rom. 16:25; Eph. 6:19; cf. Isa. 52:7; Luke 4:21).

The center of the gospel is not the idea of "ultimate reality" underlying all existence (Tillich), nor the myth of the descent of the heavenly Redeemer (Bultmann), but rather a historical fact which is essential for the working out of God's redemptive purpose. The significance which the life and ministry of Jesus have for the salvation of mankind is interpreted in various ways in the NT—e.g., as atoning sacrifice, ransom, service, vicarious suffering, representative penalty, or as the origin of new life. But there is agreement throughout the NT that the public ministry of Jesus is not by itself the goal of God's plan, but rather the indispensable means for its accomplishment. In the course of the second century, however, and as a result of increasing Hellenization, the gospel lost its eschatological character, and the Incarnation or the Cross was interpreted as completing, rather than starting, salvation.

b. Eschatological character. In the NT proclamation, the KINGDOM OF GOD approaches (Matt. 4:17; 10:7; Mark 1:15; Luke 10:9); i.e., the kingly rule of God is being established in this world, but this process will not be completed until the final victory of Christ (Rev. 11:15; cf. Acts 1:6). The Christians are not yet "saved"—i.e., brought to a full life in the strict sense of the word; they are σῳζόμενοι (I Cor. 1:18; cf. 15:2)—i.e., rendered ready for that condition. God has begun his good work in them but not yet completed it (e.g., Phil. 1:6; Col. 1:23). While God has sealed his gospel with the death of Christ and the gift of the Spirit (e.g., Rom. 8:23; II Cor. 1:22), the believers have not yet reached their destination, and they may slide back (e.g., Col. 1:22-23; Heb. 8:12; cf. II Cor. 11:2; Eph. 5:27). Hence, it is natural that the gospel should include warnings to be watchful (e.g., Matt. 24:42-43; 25:13; Mark 13:33, 35, 37; Luke 12:37-38; I Cor. 16:13; Eph. 6:18; I Thess. 5: 6; I Pet. 4:7; Rev. 3:3; cf. Matt. 22:11-13). The DAY OF THE LORD or of the SON OF MAN (e.g., Matt. 7: 22; 10:15; 11:22; 24:36, 42; Mark 13:32; Luke 17: 21), which is the clinching event in the work of redemption, still lies ahead (John 6:39-40, 44, 54; 12: 48; Rom. 2:16; I Cor. 1:8; 3:13; 5:5; Eph. 4:30; Phil. 1:6, 10; 2:16; I Thess. 5:2, 4; II Thess. 1:10), or, according to another terminology, not until the coming in glory of the Son of man (e.g., Matt. 24:30, 42; 26:64; Mark 13:26; 14:62; Luke 21:27; I Cor. 11:26; Eph. 5:6; Heb. 10:37; cf. Rev. 1:4, 8; 4:8; 22:17 [ὁ ἐρχόμενος]) or the PAROUSIA (e.g., Matt. 24:3, 27, 37, 39; I Cor. 15:23; 16:17; I Thess. 2:19; 3:13; 4:15; II Thess. 2:8; Jas. 5:7-8; II Pet. 1:16; 3:4, 12; I John 2:28) will the full restoration of the universe take place (Matt. 17:11; Mark 9:12; Acts 1:6; 3:21; cf. Rom. 8:19-20). All that God in his grace does for the believers is but a preliminary work "that in the coming ages he might show the immeasurable riches of his grace in kindness toward us in Christ Jesus" (Eph. 2:7). The glory of Jesus as God's chosen instrument of redemption has not yet been revealed (ἀποκαλύπτω; Luke 17:30; Rom. 8:18; I Cor. 1:7; II Thess. 1:7; I Pet. 1:5, 7, 13; 4:13; 5:1) or manifested (φανερόω; John 7:4; Col. 3:4; I John 2:28; 3:2).

That closing event will not be a blessing for all. For it is also a day of judgment (II Pet. 2:9; 3:7; I John 4:17) or of wrath (Rom. 2:5) and visitation (I Pet. 2:12), to which all men will be subjected (II Cor. 5:10; cf. Eph. 5:12-13). The coming of Christ offers an opportunity to escape condemnation (Rom. 8:1; cf. John 5:24), but only to those who keep his word. As in the OT, the judgment of doom is the inescapable alternative to salvation (Matt. 7:19; 24: 37-39; Luke 17:28 ff; 21:34-35; II Cor. 1:18 ff; I Pet. 4:17), and it is from this final judgment that the gospel offers escape (e.g., Matt. 3:7; Luke 3:7; John 3: 36; Rom. 1:18; 4:15; 5:9; Eph. 2:3; Col. 3:6; Rev. 6:16; 16:19). Moreover, the life everlasting is not a matter of experience yet for the believer. It is only by faith (Eph. 2:8) and hope (Rom. 8:24) that we anticipate our salvation.

c. The divine good. God's ultimate goal is described in the gospel both negatively and positively. It is a removal of all that renders human life worthless, such as poverty, lack of freedom, invalidity, oppression (Luke 4:18=Isa. 61:1), in a physical as well as a spiritual sense; furthermore, sorrow, want, persecution (Matt. 5:4, 6, 10), pain, anguish, and death (e.g., Rev. 21:4; cf. I Cor. 15:55-56), and above all sin (e.g., Matt. 26:28; Luke 24:47; Rom. 3:25; Heb. 9:26). Positively, God's goal is life everlasting (e.g., John 20:31)—i.e., righteousness, peace, and joy in the Holy Spirit (Rom. 14:17)—which results from Christ's victory over all the cosmic forces (e.g., Rom. 8:28, 35-39; I Cor. 15:24; Phil. 2:10). The Christian life is not described as a gradual approach or development toward this goal—though there are degrees of spiritual life (e.g., Matt. 25:14-30; Luke 19:11-27) —but rather as an existence in which, despite difficulties, dangers, and shortcomings, we can be sure of eventually obtaining the goods of salvation, because God has destined the believers for them. They are called a divine inheritance (e.g., Acts 20:32; 26:18; Rom. 8:17; Eph. 1:11, 14, 18; Col. 1:12; 3:24; Heb. 9:15; I Pet. 1:4), a safe heavenly deposit (e.g., Col. 1:5; cf. I Tim. 1:12; II Tim. 4:8), or a heavenly treasure (Mark 10:21; Luke 12:33; 18:22; cf. II Cor. 4:7). We can rightly consider them as belonging to us, but we will not be able to use and enjoy them fully until the DAY OF THE LORD.

The divine good offered in the gospel is realized in history but not by history. It consists of participation in the kingdom of heaven or of God, and the kingdom is the manifestation of a divine purpose in history. Its operation becomes visible, above all, in the life and ministry of Jesus Christ. He, however, is not a mere revelation of God's purpose, for that would mean that God operated in everything and everywhere in a saving manner, which manifestly he does not. Rather, Jesus is described as the actual realization of God's plan of redemption (οἰκονομία; Eph. 1: 10; 3:2, 9; Col. 1:25; or θέλημα; e.g., Matt. 6:10; 26: 42; Luke 22:42; John 4:34; 5:30; 6:38; Rom. 1:10; I Cor. 1:1; Gal. 1:4; Eph. 1:9; Heb. 10:7; I Pet. 2: 15; I John 5:14; cf. Acts 13:46). Over against God's redemptive work under the Old Covenant or the dispensation of the law, God's way of dealing with men through Jesus is an entirely new one. Jesus is, therefore, contrasted with the Law of Moses (e.g., John 1:17; 6:32; 7:19; Rom. 10:5; cf. Rom. 5:20; Gal. 3: 17) and the priestly system of the OT (e.g., Heb. 7: 23–10:18).

The primitive church expressed the fact that Jesus starts the actualization of God's redemptive plan by calling him, in conformity with OT prophecies, the Messiah or Christ—i.e., the Anointed One; and Jesus saw in the fact that Peter could confess him so an evidence of a divine revelation given to his disciples (Matt. 16:17; there is no ground for considering this passage spurious), and that his saving work was progressing. Jesus called himself the Son (Matt. 11: 27; 21:37-38; Luke 10:22; John 3:35; 5:19), meaning thereby Son of God (Matt. 26:64 and parallels; cf. Matt. 4:1-11; Luke 4:1-13), and expressed thereby the fact that what he did in his public ministry was effective because it was not an isolated historical event, but rather the supreme manifestation of the life-giving activity of God. The primitive church adopted the two titles and added that of Lord, indicating thereby that Jesus had successfully overcome the opposition of the powers of evil in this world. His resurrection was evidence of his lordship. The adoption of these OT titles shows that, notwithstanding the historical contrast between the work of Jesus and the Old Covenant, both are stages of redemptive history. The ministry of Jesus is the fulfilment of the OT predictions (e.g., Luke 24:27; Acts 3:22) and the antitype of the OT types (e.g., John 3:14; I Cor. 10: 2; Rev. 15:3; and the Transfiguration, Matt. 17:1-8 and parallels). *See* CHRIST.

Jesus' life makes manifest that the goal pursued by

God is the same intimate fellowship of children with their father (Matt. 5:9, 45; Luke 6:35; Rom. 8:16, 21; Gal. 3:26; Eph. 1:5; 5:1; I John 3:1, 10) that Jesus had with God (e.g., John 10:38; 14:11). This goal is reached through belief in Christ. In the believers, the Savior calls forth what had characterized him as the Son of God—viz., knowledge of God's redemptive plan (e.g., Matt. 11:27; John 10:15; 17: 25), willingness to do his will (e.g., Matt. 26:42; Luke 22:42; John 4:34; 5:30; cf. Matt. 5:18), and power to overcome the forces of evil in this world (e.g., Matt. 10:1; Mark 6:7; Luke 9:1). His strength is that of the messianic age (cf. Mark 1:7), and his miracles are, therefore, anticipations of the world to come, from which all antidivine powers will be excluded. But the secret of the messianic power consists in not opposing evil (Matt. 5:39; Rom. 12:21), and this will result in suffering. However, suffering which springs from a strictly positive and constructive life —i.e., from love—eventually triumphs over evil. Thereby the glory of the perfection of God's life is revealed (Matt. 5:48; II Cor. 4:4). Accordingly, the believers are not only healed, delivered from demoniac possession, comforted, and forgiven, but also born again—i.e., made capable of a life in harmony with God's saving plan (e.g., Matt. 18:3; John 3:3; 5:24; I Cor. 4:15; Eph. 2:1, 5; 6:15; II Tim. 2:10; Jas. 1:18; I Pet. 1:3, 23; I John 3:14)—and reconciled with God and the world (e.g., Rom. 5:10; II Cor. 5:18-20; cf. Rom. 5:1; Eph. 6:5). Their very conversion is the work of Christ (Rom. 1:16-17; Phil. 1:27). Their faith and their love result from the fact that he changes them into his likeness (Rom. 8:29; II Cor. 3:18; Phil. 3:21; I John 3:2; cf. Col. 1:4), and from faith and love results the comprehension (ἐπίγνωσις) of God's redemptive work (e.g., I Cor. 13:12; Eph. 1:17; 4:13; Col. 1:6, 9-10; 2:2; I Tim. 2:4; II Pet. 1:2-3). Thus the believers are established (e.g., Rom. 1:11; II Cor. 1:21; Eph. 6:13; I Thess. 3:2; II Pet. 1:12)—i.e., enabled to look steadfastly toward their goal in a world of flux, uncertainty, and confusion. Through the gospel (I Cor. 9:23)—i.e., through belief in Jesus—his followers not only receive all they need to be true men (e.g., Matt. 6:8; 7:7, 11; Luke 22:35; Phil. 4:11; Jas. 1:5; I John 2: 27), but are also enabled to do everything that is required of them (II Cor. 12:9-10; Eph. 6:10-11, 13; Phil. 2:18; 4:13; Col. 1:11; II Tim. 4:17). Though there will be sufferings and afflictions in their Christian life, these too result from the fact that the life of Christ is reproduced in them (Rom. 8:17; II Cor. 4: 10; Gal. 6:17; Eph. 3:13; Phil. 1:20, 29; 4:13; I Thess. 1:6; 2:14).

d. Holy history. Thus, not only the ministry of Jesus, but also the church, is proclaimed in the gospel. The story of the ministry of Jesus, taken by itself, would reveal the superiority and divinity of Jesus only, but would not cogently imply his saving significance. The way, however, in which the gospel is spread under the guidance of Christ, especially the discovery of a non-Jewish way of faith, but also the love which the Christians show for all people, reveals the universal goal of the gospel (e.g., Col. 1:5-6, 23, 28; I Thess. 1:7; II Thess. 3:1). Its power (Rom. 1: 16) is brought to light in the signs and miracles performed by those who proclaim it (e.g., Matt. 10:1; Mark 6:7; 16:17; Luke 9:1; Acts 14:3; I Cor. 2:4; I Thess. 1:5), in the numerical growth of the church (e.g., Acts 19:20; cf. I Cor. 1:18; II Cor. 6:7), in the fruits it bears, especially faith and love (e.g., Matt. 13:23 and parallels; John 15:1-16; Rom. 6:22; II Cor. 4:4; Eph. 5:9; Col. 1:4-6; I Thess. 2:8), for which reason it is also called a gospel of peace (Eph. 6:15). In turn, when their conduct is evil, it is not they but the word of God that is disparaged and scoffed at (Tit. 2:5). As the word of truth (e.g., II Cor. 6:7; Eph. 1:13; Col. 1:5; Jas. 1:18), the gospel authenticates itself in the congregation by so completely taking control of the lives of people (II Cor. 2:14) that in their being and actions they become its witnesses (Matt. 10:18; 24:14; Mark 13:9; Acts 1:8; 3:15; 13:31-32; 22:15; I Cor. 15:15; Gal. 5:3; Eph. 4:17; cf. I Pet. 2:12); i.e., they are ready to make a stand for it and to identify themselves with Christ's cause, no matter what the consequences will be (e.g., Rom. 16:25; I Cor. 15:1; Eph. 6:14; Phil. 1:12-14). The calm and steadfastness of believers in times of persecution and oppression brings out the truthfulness of the gospel (e.g., Phil. 1:7, 16). Finally, in the ongoing character of these manifestations, the NT recognizes the gospel as the "living and abiding word of God" (I Pet. 1:23). The first converts, e.g., are the first fruits presaging a rich crop (Rom. 16:5; I Cor. 16:15; Rev. 14:4) or mighty wells of living water (John 4:14) to quell the spiritual thirst of many.

Thus in the fact that their life is the realization of the gospel—i.e., the light (Eph. 5:13)—the believers experience it as the gospel of grace (I Pet. 1:13; cf. Acts 14:3; 20:32) and the love of Christ (Eph. 3:19), which comes to them and seeks them despite their sinfulness (Eph. 2:1-4). In their serving the gospel, it is the heavenly Christ or the grace of God in them who is active (I Cor. 15:10; II Cor. 6:7; Eph. 1:13; 3:17), and the life of the church is, therefore, the "gospel of the glory of Christ" (II Cor. 4:4, 10-11; cf. Phil. 1:20).

Bibliography. O. Cone, *The Gospel and Its Earliest Interpretations* (1893); W. P. DuBose, *The Gospel in the Gospels* (1906); M. Burrows, "The Origin of the Term 'Gospel,'" *JBL*, XLIV (1925), 21-33; O. A. Petty, *Did the Christian Use of the Term τὸ εὐαγγέλιον Originate with Paul?* (1925); G. A. Deissmann, *Light from the Ancient East* (1927), pp. 370-72; J. Schniewind, *Evangelion, Ursprung und erste Gestalt des Begriffs Evangelium* (1927); M. J. Lagrange, *L'Évangile de Jésus-Christ* (2nd ed., 1928); M. Dibelius, *The Message of Jesus* (English trans.; 1933); W. H. P. Hatch, "The Primitive Christian Message," *JBL*, LVIII (1934), 1-13; E. Molland, *Das paulinische Evangelium* (1934); C. H. Dodd, *The Apostolic Preaching and Its Development* (1936); R. Asting, *Die Verkündigung im Urchristentum* (1939); E. Percy, *Die Botschaft Jesu* (1953); B. Reicke, "A Synopsis of Early Christian Preaching," in A. J. Fridrichsen, ed., *The Root and the Vine* (1953); H. A. Blair, *A Creed Before the Creeds* (1955); L. Cerfaux, *La voix vivante de l'Évangile au début de l'Église* (1956).

O. A. PIPER

GOSPEL, APOCRYPHAL ə pŏk'rə fəl. A form of composition suggested by the canonical gospels. The apocryphal gospels fall into three classes: (*a*) early gospels, presumably superficially similar in outward form to the canonical gospels, and known to us solely from occasional references and quotations in the fathers; (*b*) infancy gospels; (*c*) passion gospels. For further description and a list of those to which separate articles are devoted herein, *see* APOCRYPHA, NT. M. S. ENSLIN

GOSPELS. The sole literary form that is peculiar to Christianity. The oldest exemplar of this form available to us is the writing which the church has long called the Gospel According to Mark (*see* MARK, GOSPEL OF). It probably is also the first ever written, in spite of the "many" predecessors mentioned in Luke 1:1 who had "undertaken to compile a *diegesis*" ("treatise, account," not "gospel"!) of related content. We cannot know with certainty just how rhetorical this "many" may be, but similar prologues from Hellenistic literature indicate that this word was conventional in such a passage (it may well be the most "literary" sentence in the whole NT) and suggest that it may mean only "more than one": Mark itself and perhaps the hypothetical Q, which, though not a "gospel," was an "account." *See* Q.

The anonymous compiler of Mark unwittingly invented a new genre of literature—unwittingly because he shows himself an unliterary man unacquainted with high literature, either Semitic or Greek, and ambitious for no literary glory but only to record the message of salvation. Unintentionally he also contributed the eventual name of this new form, which was derived from, but not identical with, the title he gave his book. The present title, "Gospel According to Mark," uniform with the titles of the other three gospels, is a by-product of the compiling of the NT into one collection. This title did not replace the original one; the latter remained, but now as the first sentence of the text itself: "The beginning of the gospel of Jesus Christ, the Son of God." "Gospel" here, however, is not this or any book, but the evangel, the Christian good news (*see* GOSPEL). Many commentators consider John the Baptist to be meant by the word "beginning"; if so, this title belongs only to the small section 1:2-11. But it is more likely that ἀρχή ("beginning") has here its not uncommon meaning "origin." In that case the original title named the whole book quite appropriately: Origin of the Jesus-Christ-Son-of-God Evangel. Just when this title was abbreviated to the single word "gospel" ("evangel") to denote any book of the same type as Mark, there is no way of knowing. The first sure testimony to such usage is the occurrence of the plural ("the memoirs . . . which are called *Gospels*") in Just. Apol. I.66, written probably A.D. 150-60 (cf. Diogn. 11.6).

To ask what a gospel is, is really to ask what Mark is. Mark is the folk book of the folk called Christian. As such, it is primarily a mirror of the life of this folk during the two generations until the book was written down. This mirror reflects the community's recent origin, but reflects only so much of its origin and of him who was its impetus and continuing guide as was relevant to the ongoing life of the community.

But this was a sacral community, the church. Therefore, one must speak more precisely of Mark—i.e., ecclesiologically: Mark, as the folk book of the church, is its cult legend. In it the church is assuring itself of its own existence, its possibility of existing, its reason for existing, and its ways of existing (proclamation, sacraments, prayer, exorcism, eschatological expectation, incipient polity), and particularly of its relation to deeds and words of Jesus of Nazareth, above all to his death and resurrection.

The writer, who never speaks in the first person or addresses his readers in the second person, is more editor-compiler than author. Having at his disposal, not by research but by participating in the life of the church, some ninety mostly unconnected anecdotes, he puts them together almost at random, sometimes grouping them by resemblance in content (it may be a single word), sometimes arbitrarily juxtaposing them with a meaningless "and then" or "in those days." (Only rarely is a geographical or chronological datum inherently anchored in the very substance of a tradition; then the preceding generalization does not hold.) Just as it makes no difference for preaching today *when* Jesus healed the blind man but only that he did so, neither did it matter to preaching before Mark—nor does it really matter in Mark; it only seems to do so, because a written document, unlike living memory, cannot contain all things at once but only seriatim.

Matthew (*see* MATTHEW, GOSPEL OF) has been aptly called an expanded edition of Mark. Luke (*see* LUKE, GOSPEL OF) shows some will toward a more literary and more historical product, but that will was largely frustrated by the very nature of the source materials inherited from Mark and Q; Luke undoubtedly has more polish than Mark, but its character is basically predetermined by Mark. Within the canon only John shows a decided development beyond the type established in Mark. Its author—the only really tangible author-personality among the evangelists—has well-nigh converted the unconscious folk art of Mark into a new art form of the high arts, something akin to drama: a personal confession of faith which deals in sovereign freedom with the traditional materials. If we possessed more than we do of the early Jewish apocryphal gospel(s) and the main body of the Gospel of Peter, we could better say to what extent they are rectilinear developments of the canonical gospels. The INFANCY GOSPELS have more in common with the Hellenistic novel than with the canonical gospels.

The gospels have no literary ancestors. They do have analogies. The best analogy would have to have three qualifications: (*a*) ultimate provenience in folk tradition; (*b*) a numinous character associated with continuing religious use; (*c*) a content of both words and deeds. In varying proportions these qualifications are filled by the *Apophthegmata Patrum* (a corpus of stories known in Greek, Latin, and Sahidic about the piety of the anchorites in the Sketic Desert —long read for the edification of monks), by the various folk anthologies concerning Francis of Assisi, and by the traditions concerning the Great Maggid (the successor and chief disciple of the eighteenth-century founder of Chassidism; both men were soon accorded great veneration). The first collection lacks any single, unifying, central figure; the other two had less official approval than the first. In any case, they are only analogies to the gospels.

Canonization inhibited the further development of the form, but some consider the lives of Jesus, which flourished in the eighteenth and nineteenth centuries, as a modern mutation of the gospel form. *See also* JESUS CHRIST; SYNOPTIC PROBLEM. K. GROBEL

GOSSIP. The conversation or light talk (tittle-tattle) of a newsmonger and a tattler (Ezek. 36:3; II Cor. 12:20); or an intentional slanderer (Jer. 9:4—H 9:3) and a hater of God (Rom. 1:29). Several terms are used to denote "gossip," "gossiping," or "one who gossips." In the OT, דבה (Ezek. 36:3) is translated "evil gossip" (KJV "an infamy"); רכיל is translated "he who goes about gossiping" in Prov. 20:19 (KJV "he that goeth about as a talebearer"), but elsewhere this term is variously rendered as "whisperer," "slanderer," "he who goes about as a talebearer." In the NT, ψιθυριστής (Rom. 1:29; KJV "whisperers") and φλύαρος (I Tim. 5:13; KJV "tattlers") are translated "gossips," and ψιθυρισμός (II Cor. 12:20) is translated "gossip" (KJV "whisperings").

According to Prov. 20:19, he who goes about gossiping unavoidably reveals secrets. Gossips are likely to be idlers, according to I Tim. 5:13—i.e., either lazy or careless in their use of time and energy. In his Second Letter to the Corinthians, Paul attempted to move them to repentance (12:19-21); as a part of this attempt he listed certain sins which he feared he would find, were he to visit them. In this list he ranked gossip with quarreling, jealousy, anger, selfishness, slander, conceit, and disorder. An even sharper condemnation of gossips is implicit in Rom. 1:29-30. H. F. BECK

GOTHIC VERSION. A translation made by Bishop Ulfilas *ca.* A.D. 365. This version is the oldest surviving literary remains of a Teutonic dialect. *See* VERSIONS, ANCIENT, § 6.

GOTHOLIAH gŏth'ə lī'ə [Γοθολίας]; KJV GOTHOLIAS —əs. Apoc. form of ATHALIAH 3.

GOTHONIEL gō thŏn'ĭ əl [Γοθονιήλ=עתניאל] (Jth. 6:15). The father of Chabris, one of the elders of Judith's city of Bethulia.

GOUGING EYES. The verb נקר, "bore, pick, dig, hollow out," is often used with "eye" as the accusative. In Judg. 16:21; I Sam. 11:2—H 11:3 this verb is translated "gouge" (cf. Num. 16:14; Job 30:17, where the accusative should be noted; Prov. 30:17; Isa. 51:1).

According to I Sam. 11:1-4, the men of Jabesh sued Nahash the Ammonite for peace after he had besieged their lands; the Ammonite king accepted their request on condition that the right eyes of all the men of Jabesh be gouged out. This attempt to make the men of Jabesh the laughingstock of the surrounding peoples was influential in arousing Saul to a position of military leadership in Israel. The Ammonite king probably intended no more than an insult, though some interpreters suggest that he meant to render the men of Jabesh unfit for war.

The custom of gouging out the eyes of captives was widespread. The Assyrians commonly blinded their captives with sharp instruments and are pictured doing so on their own monuments. The Philistines put out Samson's eyes before carrying him off to the prison at Gaza (Judg. 16:21). When the Babylonians captured Jerusalem in 586, they slew the sons of Zedekiah before his eyes, and then they put out his eyes and carried him into captivity (II Kings 25:7). H. F. BECK

GOURD. The KJV identification of the PLANT (קיקיון, *qîqāyôn*) in Jonah 4:6-7, 9-10 (cf. vs. 5!). The RSV avoids identifying this plant. The LXX uses κολοκύνθη, "gourd"; the Vulg. *hederam*, "ivy." The KJV and the ERV-ASV translate "gourd," with "Palma Christi" (also "palmcrist," the castor bean, *Ricinus communis* L.) in the margin. The *Cucurbita lagenaria* L., the "bottle-gourd" (also called *Lagenaria leucantha* [Duch.] Rusby), often used for booths and trellises in the Near East, fits the context and is claimed by some scholars to be the plant intended; thus the translation "gourd." The castor bean has been the usual identification. The Egyptian name, *kiki*, for the castor bean, and other linguistic arguments have led to this conclusion. The evidence is inconclusive.

See also FLORA § A16*a;* JONAH. For other references to gourds, *see* GOURDS, WILD.

Bibliography. I. Löw, *Die Flora der Juden*, I:2 (1928), 608-11; H. N. and A. L. Moldenke, *Plants of the Bible* (1952), pp. 203-4. J. C. TREVER

GOURDS, WILD [פקעת, *paqqū'ôth;* פקעים, *peqā'îm;* *root in cognate languages means* to crack, burst]. Wild vines with a poisonous fruit, probably *Citrullus colocynthis* (L.) Schrad.* *Paqqū'ôth* (feminine plural) appears only in II Kings 4:39 (LXX τολύπη,

36. Wild gourd (*Citrullus colocynthis*)

"gourd"), described as a wild vine (lit., "vine of the field"). One of the "sons of the prophets" at Gilgal, during a famine, gathered the fruit from these vines for food. The men were made ill, and they appealed to Elisha for help. "VINE OF SODOM" (Deut. 32:32) probably refers to the same plant. Fig. GOU 36.

Peqā'îm (masculine plural) is used to describe the shape of the carved decorations on the cedar paneling of the nave of Solomon's temple (I Kings 6:18; KJV "knops") and of the two rows of bronze decorations directly beneath the rim of the "molten sea" (I Kings 7:24). The exact significance of these decorations is not clear. Elsewhere they consist of "cherubim, palm trees, and open flowers" (I Kings 6:29, 32,

35). In II Chr. 4:3 the decorations under the rim of the "molten sea" are said to be "oxen" (KJV; Hebrew *beqārîm*), apparently an error (cf. "oxen" in the next verse, referring to the pedestals) for "gourds" (so RSV, following I Kings 7:24).

See also FLORA § A14*d;* SEA, MOLTEN.

Bibliography. H. N. and A. L. Moldenke, *Plants of the Bible* (1952), pp. 78-80. J. C. TREVER

GOVERNMENT. Biblical data on the various forms and procedures of Israelite-Jewish government and political administration are incidental to, yet integrally part of, the writers' and editors' presentation of the historical experience of their people, an experience extending over a period of some fifteen hundred years. Although we may distinguish between the biblical writers' and editors' interpretation of Israel's history and the empirical facts of that history, the latter no less than the former bear the stamp of a revolutionary conviction that harks back to the period of Israel's earliest consciousness of its peoplehood: the belief that man stands apart from nature in a special relationship with the sole creative source of all reality—namely, with God. Since this theory of the divine-human relationship marked Israel off from the other cultures and civilizations of the ancient Near East, constituted the ordering principle of their society, and is ultimately responsible for the existence of the Bible itself, it must be regarded as fundamental and formative for the Bible's account of Israelite-Jewish political norms and institutions (*see* COVENANT; ELECTION). The same master conviction defines the biblical counterparts of the psychological and sociological prepossessions which generally determine, or at least help to constitute, a people's choice and development of its political forms and institutions: conceptions of human personality, interpersonal relationships (particularly, in the present connection, the reciprocal relationship between leaders and followers), and modes of social structuring and stratification (*see* SOUL; TRIBE; FAMILY; etc.). While Israel inherited, shared, absorbed, or was influenced by the conceptions of these matters which appear elsewhere in the cultures and civilizations of the ancient Near East, they confront us in the Bible under the "sign of the covenant," hence transformed, transvalued, or otherwise modified.

A. *NOMADIC ISRAEL.* The Israelites' own traditions of their remotest origins and of their history before they established themselves in Canaan exhibit familiar acquaintance with the two main modes of life in the ancient Near East and the social, economic, and political institutions of each: that of the nomad or seminomad keeper of flocks and herds in the desert steppe (*see* NOMADISM), and that of the town-dwelling cultivator of crops in the sown land. While these traditions only later assumed the form in which they are now before us in the Pentateuch, they were already circulating when at least some of the Israelite tribes were nomads in the desert steppes. Brought into Canaan from the desert, they still occasionally reflect the early Israelite nomad's aversion to the urban life of the sown. This motif, e.g., appears in the tradition which makes of Cain, the first murderer, a "tiller of the ground" (Gen. 4:2) and the first builder of a city (Gen. 4:17); it can be glimpsed again in the narratives about Lot (Gen. 14; 19) and the misfortunes which beset him when he quit the nomadic life and took up settled residence in the city of Sodom. In pointed contrast with Lot (Gen. 13), the prospering eponymous ancestor of the Hebrews, Abram, is represented as having left the Mesopotamian cities of Ur and Haran, or their environs, to wander with flocks and herds in the Canaanite steppelands (Gen. 11:31; 12:5-6).

Such steppe-born criticism of life in the sown persisted beyond the conquest and settlement of Canaan to influence all later Israelite social and political thought and institutions. The attitudes reflected in and engendered by this criticism are those to which Samuel appealed in his famous excoriation of monarchy (I Sam. 8:11-18)—and which, parenthetically, make it unnecessary to assume that such a speech could not have been uttered in the premonarchic period. These same attitudes underlie, reinforce, even make possible, the prophets' denunciations of various manifestations of the syncretizing Canaanite-Israelite culture (e.g., Hosea). The nomad's abhorrence of urban life in the sown so far persisted in one postconquest Israelite group—the Rechabites—that they raised it to the level of a sacred, defining principle (Jer. 35:2-10). *See* RECHAB.

1. "Primitive democracy." Among both the town-dwelling peasants of ancient Mesopotamia, Syria, and Canaan and the pastoral nomads of the abutting steppelands, the earliest forms of political life were democratic. Autocratic institutions, including monarchical rule, were developed in the cities of the sown as responses to needs which an earlier "primitive democracy" could not successfully meet, while democratic forms persisted among the wandering tribes of the desert steppe. Ultimate sovereign power, in this "primitive democracy" or "primitive theocratic socialism," was vested in an assembly of all free men, though most public business was in the hands of a group of elders consisting of the heads of families and other leading personalities (*see* ELDER). Important decisions of legislative or judicial character were arrived at by consensus. Executive authority, normally left to the elders, was in time of war or other emergency delegated to the man or men deemed most capable of achieving a favorable outcome.

The changes whereby such a democracy gave way to a centralized monarchic system have been successfully traced in Sumerian and Old Assyrian records of the third pre-Christian millennium. The process was one in which the earlier democracy's provision for delegated, short-term executive authority in times of crisis was extended and permanently institutionalized, while the authority of the popular assembly and of the elders was completely subordinated to that of the executive.

Allowing for certain differences in the Syrian-Canaanite sector of the Fertile Crescent, such as rulership based on kinship and the lack of a genuinely indigenous civilization capable of imposing its norms on those entering it from without, the institutions of various nomad invaders, including those of Israel, passed through a parallel process. In the case of Israel, however, the covenant-consciousness of her people constituted a further decisive difference which prevented her monarchical institutions from functioning as they did in Mesopotamia or even among the kindred Syrian-Canaanite peoples; and it is the covenant-stamped "primitive democracy" of Israel which enabled her to survive the destruction of her monarchies.

2. Social and political affiliation. As with many other nomadic peoples, common descent, rather than common residence within a specific geographical area, naturally constituted the primary criterion of affiliation in preconquest Israel and the basis of her political organization. Even after the conquest of Canaan, this genealogical principle was never fully transcended, but, having been used to determine and to name the various tribal areas of settlement, later managed to survive the monarchy which it never ceased to plague (e.g., II Sam. 20:1; I Kings 12:16) and which sought to annul or to neutralize it (e.g., I Kings 4:7-19). The Israelite was born into a "household" (בית) or "father's house" (בית אב) which was part of a "clan" or "family" (אלף, משפחה) belonging to a "tribe" (שבט, מטה); all these together comprised the "people" (עם) of Israel (Num. 2:34; Josh. 7:14) or "sons of Israel" (בני ישראל). In early Israelite consciousness these terms were not nearly so mathematically graded as such passages as those just cited might seem to indicate. Dan, e.g., generally called a tribe, is sometimes referred to as a clan (Judg. 18:2); so, too, is Judah (Judg. 17:7). Similarly, the household or father's house is not always clearly differentiated from the family or clan; the paschal lamb, e.g., which the Israelites are told to "take . . . according to their fathers' houses, a lamb for a household" (Exod. 12:3), was to be slaughtered "according to your families" (vs. 21). If the terms overlap and merge into one another, this is because all basically refer to kinship circles radiating out from the "father" as a center, a "soul" which included everything that pertained to him and in which whatever larger whole of which he was a part was felt to be present. As biblical usage amply demonstrates, however, all these terms go beyond a mechanically applied notion of consanguinity; even the narrowest in point of kinship, the "house," could be used to designate the Rechabites, meaning all who chose to follow the nomadic ideal as promulgated by Jonadab son of Rechab (Jer. 35:18) and not merely the latter's own offspring. Thus the terms refer to collectivities or communities which are homogeneous in point of one or more characteristics shared by their members, characteristics which might be not only those of a shared germ plasm, but also religious, moral, social, economic, and political. Just as "son of a prophet" did not necessarily mean a person whose father was a prophet, so a "son of Israel" did not necessarily mean one whose father was literally a carrier of the genes of the patriarchs, but one who shared the characteristics—history, way of life, and destiny—that constituted the "people" of Israel.

3. Political authority and administration. Politically speaking, the most important of these focuses of affiliation were the tribe and the people as a whole. For Israel's nomadic period our sources exhibit the tribes as united through the Sinaitic covenant and under a charismatic leader; the political institutions described are therefore those of the people as a whole, but there can be little doubt that the same, or very similar, institutions prevailed in the individual tribe. As between the political functioning of a single tribe and of a group of tribes, the most important difference would seem to lie in the altered responsibilities of the tribal chief (cf. Num. 1:4, 16; 13:2), many of whose leadership functions would now pass to the charismatic leader of the whole people; while other duties, the necessity to discharge which would arise out of the linking of the tribes, would be assigned to him by the supreme leader (see, e.g., Num. 1:1-16; *see also below*).

The primary political institution of nomadic Israel was, as already indicated, the public ASSEMBLY, called the קהל and the עדה, generally translated as CONGREGATION. Both these terms, which are practically synonymous, mean all the adult males (Num. 26:2) of the people as convoked and gathered (=קהל), or as convened and assembled at stated times (=עדה), for public-welfare purposes; of the two, עדה is probably the more specifically technical in this sense. This assembly was the prime source of all authority over the people and the effective guarantor of all policy. Its most important members, achieving the dignity by seniority and experience, were the "elders" (זקנים); it was they, e.g., who accepted the leadership of Moses and of Aaron while Israel was yet in Egypt (Exod. 3:16; 4:29-31). They were neither a separate body, like a senate, nor, in any formal political sense, the official representatives of the assembly; rather, they were the assembly itself, in the ancient Hebrew manner of regarding a whole as completely present in its most characteristic parts. Whenever, therefore, the assembly was required for some action or decision, yet could not all be present, the elders would act as the entire body (see, e.g., Exod. 18:12; 24:1-2; Num. 11:16; Deut. 31:28, 30).

Besides the elders, mention is made of the "leaders of the congregation" (נשיאי העדה; Exod. 16:22; Num. 16:2; 32:2), the "summoned (ones) of the assembly" (קריאי העדה; Num. 1:16; 26:9), those "summoned to the assembly meeting" (קריאי מועד; Num. 16:2): the able and influential men whose presence was considered indispensable, but who might not, unless specially summoned, heed the trumpet call signaling the assembly's convocation (Num. 16:7).

The assembly functioned both deliberatively and judicially; an example of the former is the consideration of the report of the ten spies (Num. 13:26–14:4); of the latter, the hearing of the grievance of the daughters of Zelophehad (Num. 27:1-4); and, as in the case of the sabbath violator, its members might execute capital offenders (Num. 15:32-36). They naturally figured largely in the cult system (e.g., Lev. 4:13-21; 8:3; 9:5; Num. 8:9-10; 15:22-26), in war and the division of booty (Num. 22:3-4 [קהל= "horde"]; 31:26), and in the allocation of conquered territory (Num. 32:2-5; Josh. 18–19). They participated in the making of covenants, human (Josh. 9:15) and divine (Exod. 19:7-8; 24:1-4); were the immediate addressees of such far-reaching legislation as that declaring the equality of the alien and the native Israelite (Num. 15:15; הקהל should be translated "O assembly"); and were the natural audience of important compositions, like Moses' Song (Deut. 31:30–32:43).

The assembly's role in the initiation and execution of policies and laws was essentially passive, being consultative, corroboratory, and permissive, while the active role was in the hands of a supreme leader and those to whom he either delegated his powers or chose for the performance of specific functions. But the acceptance and confirmation of a leader, even if divinely commissioned, was, as mentioned above, the assembly's prerogative; and they had the power to depose him and to appoint another in his stead (Num. 14:1-4). This democratic motif was sufficiently strong to survive the transformation of Israel's political institutions in Canaan and to reassert itself at various junctures in her history under the monarchies (e.g., I Kings 12:3, 20; II Chr. 23:3). How strong it was in Israel's nomadic period, how well aware Israel was of the difference between a democratically sanctioned and limited leadership and monarchic despotism, is clearly seen in the taunt, hurled by Dathan and Abiram, that Moses was aspiring to royal authority (Num. 16:13). Regarded politically, indeed, each of the numerous "murmurings" of the people reported in the narratives of the Pentateuch (e.g., Exod. 14:10-12; 15:24-25; 16:2-3; 17:2-3; Num. 14:1-5; 16:1-11; etc.) was a threat to depose Moses from the leadership if the condition which caused the complaint were not abated. Although commissioned to the leadership by God—rather, precisely because he was believed to be so commissioned—he could be secure in it only so long as success and prosperity, the manifestations of the divine favor and sanction, attended his efforts and those of his appointees. Lack of prosperity, the losing of a battle (e.g., Josh. 7:2-9), or any kind of failure was attributable to a withdrawal of the divine power from the leader, and unless rectified or otherwise explained (e.g., Josh. 7:10-12), would have resulted in appointment of another leader. Failure of a succession of such leaders would inevitably have meant dissolution of the tribal confederacy, with its several components free to go their separate ways.

To aid him in the carrying out of his responsibilities, which, of course, were not merely political but extended over every aspect of the people's life, a supreme leader like Moses could and did delegate his authority to others. Such appointments might be for *ad hoc* purposes, such as for a census (Num. 1:1-16), for the construction of the tabernacle and the ark (Exod. 35:30 ff), or for a scouting mission (Num. 13); or they might be of a more permanent character, such as the institution of a judiciary (Exod. 18:13-26) or of a military organization (Num. 31:3-6, 14, 48-49, 52-54; Deut. 1:15). The tribal chiefs (נשיאי מטות אבותם [Num. 1:16; 7]; ראשי שבטיכם [Deut. 1:15]) were the most likely and politically tactful candidates for such offices, particularly that of JUDGE (שופט; see Num. 25:5) and of military commander (שר; קצין [Josh. 10:24]). Also at the leader's disposal were the people's own officers (שוטרים; Exod. 5:6-19 [RSV "foremen"]; Deut. 1:15; 20:5-9; Josh. 1:10; 3:2; 8:33, *see* OFFICER), at least some of whom were elders (Num. 11:16), men who saw to it that the people did what was expected of them. It was in his capacity as supreme leader that Moses installed Aaron and his sons in the priesthood (Exod. 28:1; Lev. 8; Num. 3:3-4) and assigned the Levites to specialized cult service (Num. 8:5-26). Perhaps not the least tribute to Moses' skill as the supreme political leader of nomadic Israel's turbulent and unstable tribal confederacy was the fact that he was able to ordain his own war adjutant, Joshua (Exod. 17:9), as his successor (Num. 27:15-23).

B. *ISRAEL AS A TRIBAL CONFEDERACY IN CANAAN.* Only as a covenanted tribal confederacy under skilful and experienced leadership could Israel have planned (e.g., Josh. 10) and carried out the military operations which, in the latter part of the thirteenth century B.C., weakened the Canaanite city-state feudalisms enough to permit a precarious grasp on portions of Transjordan and the central Palestinian hill country. During the next two centuries, a period of near-anarchy, the Israelite tribes had to fight to maintain these positions against the encroachments of other nomadic groups (e.g., the Midianites [Judg. 6]) and of neighboring peoples (e.g., the Moabite-Ammonite-Amalekite coalition [Judg. 3:12-30]; the recently arrived Philistines [Judg. 3:31; 13–16; I Sam. 4; etc.]), and to avoid extermination or reduction to slavery at the hands of the indigenous Canaanites (e.g., Judg. 4–5). In and from these positions they accomplished the transition to sedentary life in towns and villages, settling by clans and "fathers' houses" in territories allotted to and named after the tribes (Josh. 14–17; cf. Judg. 1); a tribe or clan which could not settle in, or lost, a territory originally allotted to it, "spied out" and took another as its "inheritance" (so Dan: Josh. 19:40-48; Judg. 1:34; 18). Such of the native population as the Israelite tribes were unable or found it inexpedient to drive out continued to "dwell among them," subjected to forced labor (Judg. 1:30) or peaceably sharing a town (vs. 29); in other cases, Israelite tribes "dwelt among the Canaanites" (vss. 31-33).

The passage to sedentary life in the sown, had it been at the outset a haphazard process of infiltration instead of the deliberately intended enterprise of a covenanted confederacy of tribes under strong charismatic leadership, would much sooner have shown a far greater degree of assimilation to Canaanite political institutions than both the biblical and the available extrabiblical evidence permit us to trace. In sharp contrast to the feudal city-kingdoms of Canaan; the centralized monarchies of Edom, Moab, and Ammon; and the warrior-caste "tyrannies" of the Philistines, Israel's political organization at this time continued to be that of a loosely articulated tribal confederation, whose main principle of cohesion was the "covenant" with their God into which they had entered under the guidance of Moses; this cohesion had palpable representation in the "ark of the covenant," enshrined first at Gilgal and later at Shiloh (Josh. 18:1). The terms of the covenant (cf. Josh. 24:25), marking as they did a revolutionary break with the mythopoeic thought and nature-centered cults of the surrounding cultures, provided a rationale of the Israelite tribes' steppe-derived and genealogy-based political institutions which enabled these, with some modifications, to withstand fundamental revisions until the time of David, nearly two hundred years thence.

Early Israelite thinking, however, could not create a democracy functioning on the national level; the settlement of the tribes in different parts of the land, and the failure to provide for a permanent supreme leadership of the sort for which a precedent was at hand in Joshua's succession to Moses (*see above*), meant rather a refocusing and scaling down of the characteristic older political forms for use on the local and regional levels. The covenant outlook was itself inevitably corroded by the tendencies to syncretism latent in the historical circumstances. When, therefore, necessity later compelled the Israelites again to unite their forces under a supreme political leadership, the form of the latter could only be influenced, not fundamentally determined, by their covenant-derived ideas. Kingship (*see* KING), when it came, was essentially foreign, naturalized in Israel but not native to her.

1. Political organization and action. As Israel settled down in the areas which bore the tribal names, the tribes themselves retained importance as territorially grouped aggregates of the towns and villages in which the clans and "houses" lived; but it was the urban communities which now constituted the basic political units. Our sources, to be sure, are replete with accounts of tribal, intertribal, and joint tribal actions of political and military character; until the eve of the monarchy, defense against foreign enemies was left to the several tribes rather than to the whole confederacy. Within these accounts, however, tribal terms are ambiguous, not merely in the sense of territorial versus human-group reference (e.g., Judg. 5:14, 17-18; cf. the Hebrew usage which permits a noun like "house" to signify the people of the house), but also as regards the political organization implied. When, e.g., we read (Judg. 11:8) that the "elders of Gilead" asked Jephtha to become "head over all the inhabitants of Gilead," we do not know whether these elders were acting as part of Gilead's public assembly, as a duly constituted body composed of one elder from each village and town of Gilead, or simply as a random group who felt sure enough of their prestige to be able to make such an offer (Judg. 10:17-18). Moreover, only one action making specific mention of the public assembly of all Israel is recorded before the time of Samuel, the king-maker: that in which the Benjaminites were requited for the "wanton crime" committed by the men of Benjaminite Gibeah whom their fellow tribesmen refused to hand over for justice (Judg. 20-21). This was a case which outraged Israel's covenant conscience and probed the essential principle upon which the confederacy rested.

Every Israelite now lived in an urban community and was at least theoretically a member of its public assembly, which met daily "at the gate" (e.g., Ruth 3:11 [Hebrew "all the gate of my people" = RSV "all my fellow townsmen"]; 4:1, 9-10). Here all the public business of the community was transacted, messages requiring publication were received (Judg. 6:34-35; 19:29-30), and political issues were debated and decided (Judg. 9:1-3). Actually, it was the elders, the heads of households and scions of important clans, who made the decisions; they were the mighty men of worth and valor (גבורי החיל; e.g., Judg. 6:12; of Boaz, in Ruth 2:1, RSV "man of wealth"), the nuclei of communal life and its authoritative upholders. One of these men might gain such prestige that the rest would generally defer to him. Such a man is depicted in Job 29:7-25, a classical description of an urban public assembly and the manner in which it carried on its business; the terms שרים ("princes"; vs. 9) and נגידים ("nobles"; vs. 10) of this passage, and others like נדיבים ("nobles"; Job 34:18) and נשיאים ("chiefs"; Josh. 22:14), are practically synonyms for these powerful elders, each emphasizing a particular nuance of the same basic conception (*see* PRINCE; NOBLES). In many cases the ruling elders all derived from a single, dominant family or clan; thus Ophrah, Gideon's city, belonged to the Abiezrites (Judg. 6:24), while the Gileadite villages "called Havvoth-jair" were in the hands of the thirty sons of Jair (Judg. 10:3); the Shechemites voluntarily accepted the dominance of Gaal son of Ebed and his clan, though they were but newcomers to the city, in order to rid themselves of Abimelech, whom they had previously accepted as their king, and of his deputy, Zebul (Judg. 9:26-41; Zebul is designated פקיד in vs. 28 and שר־העיר in vs. 30).

The elder-controlled city briefly outlined above remained the central core of Israelite political life to the exilic period; the law administered at the gates of such communities is still to be discerned in the book of Deuteronomy and in the Book of the Covenant. *See* COVENANT, BOOK OF THE.

Jealous of their independent sovereignty though they were, the communities of the several tribal territories and the tribes themselves recognized the need or desirability of concerted action for certain purposes and in certain circumstances. Of these, the most obvious was that of defense against foreign aggression; only less obvious was the need to protect the confederacy's own principle of cohesion, as demonstrated in the measures taken against the Benjaminites. On the positive side, if not quite so urgent, there was the common need to determine what ought and what ought not to be done in Israel (II Sam. 13:12), especially "every great matter" and "hard cases"

(Exod. 18:22, 26). Thus, there were joint undertakings and interests which the clans and tribes felt duty-bound to share; loss of honor and reproach were the usual penalties for failure to participate (e.g., Judg. 5:15-17), though harsher sanctions might be imposed (Judg. 21:8-12); conversely, an unsummoned tribe, aggrieved by the implied aspersion of their honor and fearing the insecurity of exclusion from Israel, might resent to the point of hostility an omitted invitation (Judg. 8:1-3; 12:1-3). A message circulated through the communities of each tribal territory called out the clans (Judg. 6:34-35; a trumpet call sufficed to summon the Abiezrites, Gideon's own kinsmen); as the decision to participate rested with the clans, the message itself had to be effectively persuasive, and extraordinary means were occasionally used to make it so (Judg. 19:29-30; I Sam. 11:7). The senders of these messages were usually acknowledged leaders (e.g., Barak [Judg. 4:10]) or elders (I Sam. 11:3), but they might also be individuals with a case of transcendent importance (e.g., the Levite of Judg. 19:29).

2. The judges. The conditioned anarchy (cf. Judg. 17:6; 21:25) of the Israelite tribal confederacy depicted above could neither brook nor produce a supreme leadership such as that earlier exemplified by Moses and Joshua. The unbroken series of successes which would have been demanded of this sort of leadership as the guaranty of its divine sanction was simply not possible in the historical circumstances. The Israelites' traditions and covenant-consciousness, however, could and did combine with the political necessities of their circumstances to produce a more limited type of leadership—limited temporally to the surmounting of crises, and limited functionally to the rendering of judicial decisions in the spirit of Israel's unique attitude to life.

Hence emerged the figures whom we, not quite correctly, call the judges (*see* JUDGE). All of them were regarded as endowed with a special God-given strength and favor—a "charism," to adapt a Greek term—which, joined with their own powers, enabled them to perform the tasks they undertook on Israel's behalf (Judg. 6:14). Their charism, while not that of a Moses, was thought of as differing from the latter's only in degree. The accession of this divine endowment is frequently, though variously, described in the scriptural accounts: through prophecy (Barak [Judg. 4:6-9]); mediated by an angel or directly bestowed (Gideon [Judg. 6:12-24]); through military victory (Jephthah [Judg. 11:9]); through birth-annunciation and Naziriteship (Samson [Judg. 13:2-5]); etc. In other cases—e.g., the so-called "minor judges" (Judg. 10:1-5; 12:8-15)—such details are not recounted; but since to the Hebrew mind any outstanding human achievement indicates an accretion of strength derived from God, these must also be regarded as charismatic leaders.

Depending, as we are told of such leaders, that they (*a*) "delivered," (*b*) "delivered and judged," or (*c*) simply "judged" Israel, we may distinguish their several main types. Examples of the "deliverer" are Ehud (Judg. 3:15), Shamgar (Judg. 3:31), and Gideon (Judg. 6:14, 36); of the "deliverer-judge," Othniel (Judg. 3:9-10), Tola (Judg. 10:1-2), Jephtha (Judg. 11:33; 12:7), and Samson (Judg. 13:5; 15:18, 20); and of the "judge" only, Jair (Judg. 10:3-5), Ibzan (Judg. 12:8-10), Elon (Judg. 12:11-12), and Abdon (Judg. 12:13-15). (Of this list, Samson should probably be reckoned a "deliverer" rather than a "deliverer-judge," but the evidence seems to oppose the like reclassification of Jephtha suggested by some scholars.) We are also told of the prophetess Deborah (Judg. 4:4-5) and of the prophet Samuel (I Sam. 7:15-17), as well as of the priest Eli (I Sam. 4:18; probably, however, a redactional addition), that they "judged Israel"—references whose contexts make it clear that the function of the premonarchical "judge" (שופט) was juridical rather than gubernatorial. The "deliverer" (מושיע), as the passages cited above show, was primarily a military leader; in Hebrew, the term means one who not merely liberates others from some threatened disaster, but who opens to them the possibility of continuous self-development to the utmost of their capacities (the root meaning of ישע is "to be wide, capacious"), the *sine qua non* of שלום ("peace, well-being"). It is the "deliverer" in this latter, positive sense who most readily appropriates the rulership function in premonarchical Israel. As such a deliverer Gideon was offered the rulership of Israel (Judg. 8:22; the Hebrew term used here is exact: משל־בנו, "rule over us," not, as at 9:14, מלך־עלינו, "be king over us"; rulership, not kingship, was offered to Gideon and his house, but only to the third generation; every king is, of course, a ruler, but not every ruler is a king). Jephtha's ability to "deliver," not his ability to "judge," caused the people of Gilead to make "him head and leader over them" (Judg. 11:8-11; the Hebrew word for "leader" here, קצין, probably means "military commander," though it is derived from a root which means "to decide" and is related to the Arabic *qâḍi*^{n}, "judge"); there was nothing, it should be added, to preclude a "deliverer," any more than a prophet or prophetess, from also functioning as a "judge."

3. The emergence of kingship. For some two hundred years the Israelite tribal confederacy sought, through temporary charismatic leaders, to meet the obvious need of a central political authority. It was only when experience had proved temporary devices to be completely inadequate, and when, in addition, Philistine victories (I Sam. 4:1-10) posed the threat of extinction to the confederacy and of enslavement to its population (cf. I Sam. 11), that Israel at long last instituted a monarchy (*ca.* 1020 B.C.). The delay has its ultimate explanation in the fundamental character of a society whose cohesion centered in a divine covenant and whose major units were jealous of their covenant-sanctioned autonomy. Strictly speaking, such a society could not adopt a monarchy on the Canaanite city-state pattern without fundamental subversion of the principle of its identity; the attempt of Abimelech to create a monarchy of this kind ended, as it was bound to do, in complete failure (Judg. 9).

A charismatic leadership that was temporary, on the other hand, was not inconsistent with Israel's basic constitution, but was not always available when needed and could not be depended upon to outlast the crisis which evoked it. The offer to make Gideon, his son, and his grandson (but not beyond) in turn "ruler" (Judg. 8:22) must be understood as an effort to solve the leadership problem on Israelite premises through an extension of the charism's temporal limits; Gideon's refusal of the offer (vs. 23) represents, in its insistence upon the theocratic principle, a conservative Israelite's denial that any change was necessary.

The attempt of SAMUEL to solve the problem through a continuing (possibly hereditary) judiciary, in addition to foundering on the moral unfitness of his own sons (I Sam. 8:1-5), failed to provide for the sustained military leadership and executive authority required to contain the Philistine threat. As Samuel's own effort shows, he was not opposed to introduction of a permanent centralization of political authority as such, but only to setting up the "deliverer," the military leader, rather than the "judge," as the supreme political officer in Israel. The disadvantages of a monarch who was primarily a military leader were graphically pointed out by Samuel (I Sam. 8: 11-18), but the people's insistence upon a king who could fight their battles (I Sam. 8:20) was not to be denied. Accordingly, SAUL son of Kish, having been designated by Samuel, the priest-prophet-judge who was the prime representative of Israel's sacred covenant tradition (I Sam. 10:1), having been accepted and acclaimed by all save "some worthless fellows" (vs. 27) at a public assembly held at Mizpah (vss. 17, 24), and having proved his charism by a victory over the Ammonites (I Sam. 11), was made Israel's first king by the people "before the LORD in Gilgal" (vs. 15).

Saul's kingship was still far more an Israelite charismatic leadership than a genuine monarchy. All that we are told of the leadership of a Gideon or a Jephthah is paralleled by what we are told of Saul's, only with some magnification of scope. Keeping his residence at Benjaminite Gibeah among his own kinsmen (I Sam. 15:34), he made no real effort to reign over Israel beyond constituting an entourage (14:47-52). Chief among the entourage were his near kinsman and army commander, Abner (vs. 50); his son Jonathan; his armor-bearer, David of Judean Bethlehem (16:21); and even a foreigner, Doeg the Edomite (21:7—H 21:8; 22:9, 18).

Nevertheless, Saul's leadership brought at least two new features into Israel's political life. First, he bore a title, "king" (מלך), which Israel had encountered among the Canaanites and other neighboring peoples but which she had never willingly conferred upon any native leader; the foreignness both of the concept and of the title is clearly stated in our sources (I Sam. 8:5, 19-20). Secondly, he was "anointed" king (10:1)—a ceremony hitherto reserved in Israel only for persons and objects functioning within the cultus (cf. Gen. 31:13; Exod. 40:9-15; Num. 3:3; etc.), but not used for the investment of a leader whose responsibility extended beyond the cultus (cf. Num. 27:15-23). That the anointment of a king was a Canaanite usage is attested by a letter found at Tell el-Amarna; as naturalized in Israel, it signified public recognition and acknowledgment that the anointed one was divinely designated and charismatically endowed (cf. II Kings 11:12); while a priest (I Kings 1:39) or a prophet (I Kings 19:16) might perform the act of anointing, this could be done by the people themselves without such mediation (e.g., II Sam. 2:4), and "to anoint" came to mean simply "to make king."

C. *THE ISRAELITE MONARCHIES.* Saul lacked the political skill necessary to mitigate, much less to resolve, the inherent contradiction between the monarchy and the covenant-centered institutions of the confederacy; this was the basic cause of his quarrel with Samuel, the kernel of fact in the narratives of the rupture (I Sam. 13:8-14; 15). The true founder of a united Israelite kingdom was DAVID of Judean Bethlehem, Saul's armor-bearer, a superb military leader and a consummate politician. It may be doubted that Samuel anointed David before the latter joined Saul's entourage (I Sam. 16:1-13; the account seems a secondary recasting of 9:15-17 combined with 10:20-21), but David's exploits, in addition to being a sufficient attestation of the charismatic character of his leadership, soon earned him Saul's jealous enmity as a contender for the kingship (I Sam. 18:5-16). Even as a fugitive from Saul's murderous wrath David astutely managed to add a dimension to the kingship which he felt would sooner or later be his: he proclaimed the inviolability of the anointed king's person as integral to Israel's sacred covenant tradition (I Sam. 24:6; 26:8-11); thus, at a stroke, he both gave increased stability to the throne and soothed the tradition-derived criticism of the monarchic institution. The same combination of military ability and political sagacity enabled David to create a Palestinian-Syrian empire, a tremendous personal achievement even when allowance is made for the contemporary weakness of the Egyptian and Mesopotamian powers. Before his career was over, he had become king over Judah (II Sam. 2:4), Israel and Benjamin (5:3), Jerusalem (5:6-10; cf. 24:18-20), and Ammon (12:30); ruled the Arameans of Damascus and the Edomites, in whose territories he installed garrisons (8:6, 14); reduced Moab to vassalage (8:2); and subdued the Philistines, the Amalekites, and the kingdom of Zobah (8:11-12).

This empire, however, was united only in David's own person; even its Judean-Israelite core was not an indivisible unity, but two kingdoms separated geographically by a third, David's personal city-kingdom of Jerusalem. As David had become king over Judah and over N Israel in virtue of two distinct political actions, the older confederacy could no longer develop into a genuinely amalgamated monarchic state. The opportunity presented by the successful repression of Absalom's rebellion to blur the division, if not to obliterate it, was lost in a quarrel between the Judeans and the Israelites over the king's restoration (II Sam. 19:41-43). The attendant rebellion led by the Benjaminite, Sheba son of Bichri (20:1-2), though it too was put down, contributed to the maintenance of a separateness which the administrative measures of SOLOMON, David's successor (I Kings 4:7-19), could not efface, and which at Solomon's death resulted in the establishment of N Israel as an independent kingdom (I Kings 12).

Thereafter the two kingdoms (Jerusalem having remained united with Judah) went their separate ways, now fighting each other (I Kings 14:30; 15:6), now acting in concert (I Kings 22:2-4; II Kings 9: 16), until each came to a sorry end—Israel, the N state, being destroyed by the Assyrians (722-721 B.C.; II Kings 17:6), and Judah by the Neo-Babylonian Chaldeans (587 B.C.; II Kings 25:1-7). Each conformed to the monarchic pattern created by David and developed administratively by Solomon.

The chief constitutional difference between the two kingdoms lay in their respective succession principles. In Judah, which had anointed the Judean tribesman David as their king (II Sam. 2:4), where David had bequeathed the monarchy to his son Solomon (I Kings 1:30, 35), and which, at the disruption, remained loyal to Solomon's son REHOBOAM (I Kings 12:21), the principle of hereditary succession became firmly entrenched. Even when, as not infrequently happened, assassination removed one Davidide from the Judean throne, none but another Davidide could succeed him (e.g., II Kings 12:19-21—H 12:20-22; 14:18-21).

In N Israel, on the other hand, hereditary succession had gained no real foothold in the brief and unhappy reign of ISHBAAL (Ish-bosheth), Saul's son, whose kingdom passed to David (II Sam. 2:8-10; 4:5–5:3); the ending of Saul's "dynasty" with the death of Ishbaal could thus be paralleled by the ending of David's upon the death of Solomon. At the disruption, a public assembly made JEROBOAM (1) son of Nebat "king over all Israel" (I Kings 12:20); the precedent followed in this act was that of Saul: just as the latter had been designated to the kingship by the prophet Samuel, so Jeroboam had been chosen by the prophet Ahijah the Shilonite (I Kings 11:29-31). The custom of prophetic designation continued until the time of Jehu; while attended by execution of the reigning king and his heirs (e.g., Baasha [I Kings 15:27-29; 16:2]; Jehu [II Kings 9]), it was at least preferable to the outright violence which was the sole succession principle during the last twenty years of the kingdom's existence (II Kings 15:10, 14, 25, 30). The importance of prophetic designation is illustrated by the case of Zimri (I Kings 16:8-20), who, having usurped power without such sanction, could rule only for seven days before being succeeded by Omri. The latter, whose kingship was legitimized by the Israelite militia and corroborated by victory over a similarly legitimized rival (I Kings 16:16, 21-22), was able to pass the throne on to three of his descendants over a period of some thirty years; but the prophetically designated Jehu was the founder of a dynasty that lasted for about a century. A prophetic divine word thus characterizes the bloody succession which followed the downfall of Jehu's dynasty:

> They made kings, but not through me.
> They set up princes, but without my knowledge
> (Hos. 8:4).

1. The king. In Judah and N Israel the king was neither himself a god, like the Egyptian Pharaoh, nor, as in Mesopotamia, a divinely chosen means of integrating human life with that of the gods. The Israelite and Judean kings were primarily human, secular figures whose cult functions differed from those of every other nonpriestly and non-Levitic Israelite merely in degree, but not in kind. Only secondarily, in virtue of the fact that they were heir to the priest-kingship of Jerusalem (Gen. 14:18; Ps. 110:4), could the Davidides be regarded as priests (II Sam. 8:18) or occasionally exercise priestly prerogatives (II Sam. 24:25; I Kings 3:3-4, 15). It was a typically astute political maneuver on David's part to take advantage of his Jerusalem priest-kingship in order to bring the ark of the covenant, the sacred symbol of the cohesion of the old Israelite tribal confederacy, up to Jerusalem (II Sam. 6); the inherited priest-kingship also permitted Solomon to build the temple and the royal palace (I Kings 6–7) in immediate proximity to each other (cf. II Kings 11:4-16). Royal sacerdotalism, however, had its critics (e.g., the reason alleged for the rejection of Saul [I Sam. 13:8-14]; cf. Uzziah [II Chr. 26:16-21; 27:2]), and in Ezekiel's ideal reconstruction of Jerusalem the contiguity of palace and temple was expressly proscribed (Ezek. 43:7-8). Despite the influence exerted by population fusion and cultural syncretism, despite the outright paganism of many N Israelite and Judean kings, the religious character of Israel's human kingship was basically and essentially that of the earlier charismatic leader; "divine-king" conceptions, insofar as they came into Israel's culture from without, never became fully integral to the human institution, but were ultimately absorbed into the Hebrew-Jewish conception of God.

The king's duties and responsibilities were those of the charismatic "deliverer-judge"; his powers and privileges were modeled upon those common to the royal absolutisms of the ancient Near East, but they were limited by vested local and regional interests and were conditioned by a criticism based on the values of the covenant tradition. Like the deliverer-judge, the king succored his people; even individuals might appeal to him for aid (II Sam. 14:4; II Kings 6:26), or come before him for justice (II Sam. 15:1-6; I Kings 3:16-28). What the monarch meant to his people is eloquently stated in a lament over the fall of Judah:

> The breath of our nostrils, the LORD's anointed,
> was taken in their pits,
> he of whom we said, "Under his shadow
> we shall live among the nations"
> (Lam. 4:20).

Unlike the older charismatic leader, however, who as *primus inter pares* was a rallying point and personalized center for the forces of the entire community, the king was elevated to a position above the people. Surrounded by an army of professional soldiers (e.g., II Sam. 8:18; 15:18-22; 20:7; I Kings 1:38; II Kings 11:4), his harem (II Sam. 3:2-5; 5:13-16; I Kings 11:1-3), his high officials (e.g., I Kings 4:2-6), and a host of other retainers (e.g., II Sam. 16:16; II Kings 25:19; Isa. 3:2-3), the king was supervened upon Israelite society and isolated from the people as a whole. His entire entourage was merely an extension of the king's own person; strictly speaking, the monarchy was not a state, but a man doing everything possible to enhance his personal greatness and glory.

There were limits, however, to a king's arbitrary self-glorification. David's purchase of Araunah's threshing floor at full price (II Sam. 24:24) shows his respect for the covenant tradition and for family-property law; limited by Israelite tradition, AHAB (2) did not himself dare to force expropriation of

Naboth's vineyard but allowed his Phoenician queen, who was significantly not thus inhibited, to obtain the property for him through having Naboth judicially murdered (I Kings 21:1-16). Arbitrary extensions of the royal prerogative evoked sharp criticism from prophetic upholders of the covenant tradition (e.g., Isa. 5:8; Hos. 5:10; Mic. 2:1-2), a criticism echoed in Ezekiel's ideal reconstruction which stresses the importance of restricting the extent of the king's domain (Ezek. 45:7-9). The Deuteronomic "law of the king" (Deut. 17:14-20), together with its insistence that the king identify himself completely with the covenant tradition, voices some typical grievances which historic experience with the monarchy produced among covenant-loyal Israelites. The reform of JOSIAH is a prime example, though by no means the only one, of the effect which such criticism might produce upon a king (II Kings 22:8–23:25). But within the bounds imposed by Israel's age-and-covenant-sanctioned custom (משפט) and idea of right (צדקה)—sometimes, indeed, outside these bounds—the king did as he thought best with and for a people whose destiny was scarcely distinguishable from his own either in their consciousness or in his.

2. The functioning of the kingship. The relationship between the king and the people was, on a larger scale, that which earlier obtained between a charismatic leader and those who recognized his chieftainship. The king's responsibility was great: for good and for ill, his actions were believed to involve not only himself and his house, but the entire people (e.g., II Sam. 24:17). This relationship, however, was personal and psychological, expressed in the covenant between king and people (e.g., II Sam. 3:21; 5:1-3; II Kings 23:3; Jer. 34:8-10); it was not a relationship that expressed itself in a stable series of impersonal political and administrative forms. King and people encountered and mutually affected each other, but the monarchy could never organize this encounter into an all-embracing and coherent administrative system. The king's administrative devices served only his own purposes; while they might help him fulfil the responsibilities undertaken by him on the people's behalf, they were instituted primarily as the instrumentalities of his demands upon the people rather than to promote the general welfare.

Local government under the monarchy, therefore, was not much different from what it had been under the tribal confederacy. As before, authority was in the hands of the public assembly with its elders and other leading men (e.g., I Kings 21:8; II Kings 10:1). Now, however, in some of the larger towns there was also a royal deputy, a שר, who acted on the king's behalf and protected his interests ("governor"; I Kings 22:26; II Kings 23:8); Ahab had deputies in the "districts" (מדינות; probably the older Solomonic tax districts, discussed below; *see* DISTRICT) of N Israel (I Kings 20:15), but whether these are to be distinguished from the town שרים is not clear. Relations between the deputy and the elders may not always have been smooth, as an instance during Abimelech's much earlier and abortive kingship of Shechem allows us to infer (Judg. 9). Still, so long as the king's requirements were fulfilled, there would be little occasion for interference by a deputy in a town's internal affairs. The king himself, on the other hand, might be guided by the counsel of the elders of a town or area in a matter which directly concerned its people (e.g., Ahab and the "elders of the land" [I Kings 20:7-9]). The most important effect of the monarchy upon the local communities was social rather than political. The king's service created a small army of officials who, while in many cases recruited from the old leading families, in effect constituted a new quasi-feudal aristocracy (cf. Samuel's warning [I Sam. 8:14-15]); a special and limited ruling class, in Judah and Jerusalem they were distinguished from "the people" as "princes" (Jer. 26:11-12; 34:10, 19).

a. Civil administration. The king "reigned . . . and . . . administered justice and equity to all his people" (II Sam. 8:15); these functions he either carried out directly himself or delegated to his "servants" (עבדים). The latter is the commonest generic designation (e.g., II Sam. 13:24) of men employed by a king in various official capacities (e.g., military [II Sam. 2:12-13]; diplomatic and intelligence [10:2-3]; member of royal investigating commission [II Kings 22:12-13]; merchant marine [I Kings 9:26-28]; etc.); the seals of several such officials are among archaeologically recovered artifacts of the period of the monarchies: "Shema, servant of Jeroboam" (probably Jeroboam II); "Obadiah, servant of the king" (probably later than the Obadiah of I Kings 18:1-3, "who was over the household" of Ahab); "Abijah, servant of Uzziah," and "Shebaniah, servant of Uzziah"; "Ushna, servant of Ahaz"; "Jaazaniah, servant of the king" (cf. II Kings 25:23; Jer. 40:8). From the reigns of David and Solomon, however, most departments of the king's business were staffed by officers whose functions are specifically or technically termed in our sources (see, e.g., the lists of David's high officials given at II Sam. 8:16-18 [repeated at I Chr. 18:15-17 with characteristic substitution of "chief officials" for "priests" in the allusion to David's sons]; II Sam. 20:23-26; and of Solomon's at I Kings 4:2-6). For internal affairs—civil and domestic administration—the most important officerships were the following:

a) The "one who is over the house" (אשר על־הבית; I Kings 4:6; 18:3, 6; II Kings 18:18, 37; 19:2; Isa. 22:15, 20-22): this office, apparently instituted by Solomon, subsequently became next in importance to that of the king himself; the person holding it was not merely a palace major-domo or STEWARD, but the king's vizier or prime minister. Isa. 22:20-22 is an admirable description of the importance and dignity of the position. The "Shebna" whom Isaiah threatened with deprivation of this authority (vss. 15-19) has been conjecturally restored as the (effaced) name in a recently deciphered tomb inscription, now in the British Museum, which specifically mentions the "one who is over the house." Similar epigraphic validation of the scriptural references to this high office is furnished by a clay seal impression of Jeremiah's day, found at Lachish, which reads: "Belonging-to-Gedaliah [w]ho is over the hou[se]." If, as is commonly accepted, the seal's owner was the Gedaliah son of Ahikam whom Nebuchadnezzar appointed as his commissioner in Judea (*see* § D1 *below*), it is probably merely fortuitous that no scriptural text records him to have been "over the house" in the last days of the Judean monarchy.

b) The Recorder (המזכיר; II Sam. 8:16 [I Chr. 18:15]; 20:24; I Kings 4:3; II Kings 18:18, 37; II Chr. 34:8): it has recently been suggested that this official was an Israelite analogue of the Egyptian royal herald. As such, his duties would include: the reporting of news to the king, announcement and interpretation to others of the sovereign's will, regulation of royal audiences and of court protocol, and supervision of the monarch's travel arrangements. Hezekiah's recorder was one of the three-man delegation sent to learn the Assyrian demands when Sennacherib invaded the country (II Kings 18:17-36); and Josiah's was a member of the commission sent by the king to arrange for the repair of the temple (II Chr. 34:8-14; cf. II Kings 22:3-7).

c) The secretary (סופר; II Sam. 8:17 [I Chr. 18:16]; 20:25; I Kings 4:3; II Kings 12:10; 22:3, 8-14; 25:19; Jer. 36:10, 12; 37:15, 20; etc.; *see* Scribes): wherever writing, recording, or tabulation of an official character had to be done, the task was entrusted to the trained professional known by this title. The royal or chief secretary doubtless had a corps of such "scribes" at his disposal; in Jeremiah's day, the "secretary's chamber" was apparently a hall large enough to hold a considerable number of people (Jer. 36:10, 12), while the former "house of Jonathan the secretary" was converted into a multi-celled prison (37:15-16). Solomon had two chief secretaries, sons of a father who held the same office under David; the name of the father appears variantly in the several lists, but seems to have been Egyptian, and he may have been imported by David to install a royal secretariat on Egyptian lines to serve the needs of the vastly expanded kingdom.

d) The "one in charge of forced labor" (אשר על־המס; II Sam. 20:24; I Kings 4:6; 5:14—H 5:28; 11:28; 12:18): the superintendent of the *corvée,* the man who raised and organized the compulsory labor gangs (consisting primarily of war captives and the remaining Canaanite population [I Kings 9:20-21] but also apparently of Israelites [I Kings 5:13—H 5:27]) employed on the king's heavy work projects. This official too must have had many subordinates; one such was Jeroboam, who later became king of N Israel (I Kings 11:28). Jeroboam's ability must have been extraordinary for his previous experience not to have barred him from the kingship. The "one in charge of forced labor" could hardly be a popular figure, and it is not surprising to read that Rehoboam's *corvée* superintendent was stoned to death (I Kings 12:18).

e) The "(one) over the district officers" (על־הנצבים; I Kings 4:5, 7, 27—H 5:7; cf. 22:47—H 22:48 ["deputy"]): this was the king's chief collector of internal revenue. Solomon divided N Israel into twelve administrative districts; in each there was an "officer," responsible to the chief collector, who was required to supply the king and his household with enough food for one month of the year, to administer the king's own properties, and to collect other imports and taxes (I Kings 4:7-28); David had presumably earlier inaugurated a similar system in Judah. With the king's deputies in the larger towns (*see above*), the district officials, and the chief revenue officer at court, the tax system was the best-organized administrative device of the monarchic period. The Samarian Ostraca of the early eighth century furnish archaeological documentation of continuation of the revenue system in the Northern Kingdom, while for Judah there is attestation to the same effect in the numerous jar handles stamped למלך—i.e., "belonging to the king." The productivity of his revenue system was a main factor in Solomon's extraordinarily successful foreign trade (I Kings 5:10-11—H 5:24-25), conducted through his overland "traders" (I Kings 10:28-29), and the "servants" of his merchant fleet (I Kings 9:26-28; cf. Jehoshaphat's unsuccessful venture in sea-borne commerce [I Kings 22:48-49—H 22:49-50]).

f) "Judges and officers" (שופטים ושוטרים; Deut. 16:18-20; 17:8-13; I Chr. 23:4; 26:29; II Chr. 19:5-8; etc.; *see* Judge; Officer): constituting an officially recognized judiciary, these appeared in the towns during the monarchic period and began to replace the earlier, rather freer methods of obtaining and dispensing justice. Exactly when and how the change was effected is uncertain, although for Judea tradition ascribes it to Jehoshaphat (874-849 B.C.; II Chr. 19:5-8); in the Northern Kingdom, as the Naboth case shows, the judicial process was still in the hands of the "elders and the nobles" during Ahab's reign (874-853 B.C.; I Kings 21:8-14). The town judge's function (Deut. 16:18-20), like that of the king himself in dispensing justice (e.g., II Sam. 14:4-11; 15:2-4; I Kings 3:16-28), grew out of the older Israelite custom whereby the weak sought the help of the strong in vindication of their covenant-sanctioned right and claims. The judicial "officer," as the term's usage in nonjudicial contexts implies (cf. Deut. 20:5, 8-9; Josh. 1:10-11; etc.; *see* § A3 *above*), marshaled and directed the people of the community whenever they had any role to play in a juridical matter—e.g., in the execution of a sentence. Since the Babylonian cognate (*šaṭâru*) of the term's Hebrew root means "to write," it is frequently asserted that the שוטר was a scribe or notary public, but this is dubious.

g) The Counselor (יועץ; II Sam. 15:12; 16:20-23; I Kings 12:6-10; I Chr. 27:32; II Chr. 22:3-4; 25:16; Prov. 24:6; Isa. 1:26; 3:3; etc.): this person may not always have had official status, but his function was filled during every reign. The king's greatest requirement, if he was successfully to carry out the responsibilities of ruling and of administering justice, was an "understanding mind to . . . discern between good and evil" (I Kings 3:9; cf. II Sam. 14:17). To achieve this, he availed himself of counsel, both superhuman—not only through prophet and priest, but through the "diviner . . . , the skilful magician and the expert in charms" (Isa. 3:3)—and human: the counselor. The royal counselor par excellence was David's, Ahithophel, whose "counsel . . . was as if one consulted the oracle of God" (II Sam. 16:23).

b. War and diplomacy. The king's army was at once his means of fulfilling his function as a "deliverer" (II Kings 13:5; 14:27) and the foundation of his power (e.g., II Kings 9:4-13). Despite full realization of the risks involved (II Sam. 18:3; 21:15-17), nearly every king participated in warfare, and some, like Ahab (I Kings 22:34-37) and Josiah (II Kings 23:29), died in battle. Identified with and dependent upon the army as he was, the king did his utmost to maintain it at maximum possible efficiency.

Thus David, while not disdaining the tribal militia (II Sam. 10:17; 24:1-9), professionalized the army (the "Mighty Men" [גבורים; II Sam. 10:7; 23:8-39]; "picked men of Israel" [בחורי ישראל, *Qere;* II Sam. 10:9]; "servants of David" [עבדי דוד; II Sam. 11:17]), and employed foreign mercenaries (the "Cherethites and Pelethites" [II Sam. 8:18]; the "Gittites" from the Philistine city of Gath [II Sam. 15:18]; cf. the "Carite" or Carian mercenaries of II Kings 11:4, 19). Though David seems to have cared little for chariots and horsemen (II Sam. 8:4), Solomon introduced them on a grand scale (I Kings 9:19; 10:26; cf. Deut. 17:16); the N Israelite kings made extensive use of them in their almost constant fighting against the Arameans ("Syrians"; e.g., I Kings 20:26; II Kings 13:7). These armed forces were staffed by officers, commonly designated "commanders" (שרים), of various degrees and kinds of authority. Under the king himself, the highest military post was that of "commander of the army": Abner held this office under Saul (I Sam. 14:50; 17:55; II Sam. 2:8); Joab under David (II Sam. 8:16; 20:23); Benaiah, David's commander of mercenaries (II Sam. 8:18; 20:23), under Solomon (I Kings 4:4); and Omri under Elah (I Kings 16:16). Mercenary troops were under the direct orders of their own commanders (II Sam. 15:18-22; II Kings 11:4), although these, as the example of Benaiah shows, might be responsible to an Israelite general. The chariotry constituted a separately organized and officered component of the army (I Kings 9:22; 16:8 [which indicates a bipartite subdivision of this force]). The infantry had the "commanders of thousands . . . hundreds . . . and fifties," if not also of "tens," given as the standard table of organization of the whole people at Exod. 18:21, 25; Deut. 1:15 (I Sam. 18:13; II Sam. 18:1; II Kings 1: 9-14; etc.). Among the infantry, there probably were separately commanded special contingents, such as the archers and חלוצי צבא ("men armed for war": light-armed troops? shock troops?) of II Chr. 17:18-19.

Diplomacy, always closely associated with war, was another chief preoccupation of the Israelite and Judean kings. It was employed by them in circumstances of belligerency for such purposes as the following: (*a*) to effect coalitions (e.g., II Kings 3: 6-8); (*b*) to avert or procure relief from attack (I Kings 15:18-19; II Kings 12:17-18; 16:7-9: 18:14); (*c*) to negotiate the terms of cessation of hostilities (I Kings 20:1-12, 31-35); (*d*) to provoke hostilities (II Kings 14:8-10); and (*e*) to establish covenants and peace (II Sam. 3:12-16; 10:19). Less bellicose uses and occasions of diplomacy were: (*a*) the arrangement of royal marriages (I Kings 3:1 [dowry, 9:16]; 11:1-3; 16:31); (*b*) the negotiation of trade-and-service agreements (II Sam. 5:11; I Kings 5:1-12—H 5:15-26; 9:27-28; 20:34); (*c*) to exchange felicitations and condolences (II Sam. 8:9-10; 10:1-2); (*d*) in the reception of visiting royalties or their envoys (I Kings 9:10-14; 10; II Kings 20:12-13); and (*e*) during royal visits abroad (II Kings 16:10). Such negotiations might be carried on at personal high-level meetings by the royal heads of state, who would address or refer to one another as "brother" (I Kings 9:12-13; 20:32-34). More often, however, they were handled by ambassadors (צירים; Ethiopian [Isa. 18:2]; "envoy" [Prov. 13:17]; "messenger" [25:13]; "servants" [e.g., II Sam. 10:2]; *see* AMBASSADOR), or specially designated delegations comprised of the king's highest officials (II Kings 18:18); but most frequently foreign affairs were negotiated through oral or written diplomatic correspondence conveyed by "messengers" (מלאכים; e.g., I Kings 20:2, 5, 9-12; II Kings 14:8-10).

D. *ISRAEL AND JUDAH UNDER ORIENTAL IMPERIALISM.* From the reign of the Assyrian king Tiglath-pileser III (745-727 B.C.) to the defeat inflicted by Alexander the Great upon Darius III Codomannus at the Battle of Issus (333 B.C.), the Near East was dominated in turn by the Assyrian (to 609), Neo-Babylonian (to 539), and Persian empires. The Assyrians extinguished the N Israelite state (721) and made vassals of the Judean kings. Judah, destroyed as a kingdom by the Babylonians (587), was permitted under Persian hegemony to become the seat of a province where, toward the end of the fifth century, semi-autonomous political authority passed into the hands of the high priests of the restored temple at Jerusalem.

1. Assyrian and Chaldean domination. The Assyrian policy of exchanging the ruling classes of territories incorporated into their empire resulted in the transfer of many N Israelites to Mesopotamia and Media (II Kings 15:29; 17:6; 18:11) and their replacement by a considerable body of foreigners, including Babylonians and Syrians (II Kings 17:24). The former Israelite kingdom, according to our rather scanty information, was reorganized into the four Assyrian provinces of Megiddo, Dor, Gilead, and Samaria ("Samerina"), each under an Assyrian governor (*bêl paḫâti*); the title of a subordinate official, "head of cities" (*rab alâni*), which occurs in a cuneiform document found at Samaria, suggests an Assyrian provincial counterpart of the Solomonic chief revenue officer (*see* § C2*a above*). Judea, on the other hand, was not incorporated into the Assyrian provincial organization but was ruled through such puppet kings as Manasseh (*ca.* 687-642 B.C.; II Kings 21). This policy, successful enough while Assyrian power was at full tide, could not be made to work once that tide had turned; Josiah (*ca.* 640-609; II Kings 22–23) asserted his independence of a weakened Assyrian control and could even dream of a reunited Israelite kingdom. But what was possible during Assyrian decline could not be achieved against the rising might of their Chaldean heirs, the masters of the Neo-Babylonian Empire; and the attempts of Jehoiakim (*ca.* 609-597; II Kings 24:1) and Zedekiah (597-587; II Kings 24:20) to follow Josiah's example only succeeded in convincing the Chaldeans that a vassal king in Judea was altogether too dangerous to tolerate. Accordingly, they broke down the walls of Jerusalem (II Kings 25:10), thus rendering it incapable of defense, and abolished the kingship and installed Gedaliah son of Ahikam (cf. II Kings 22:12, 14; Jer. 26:24) as their commissioner (פקיד; RSV "governor") at Mizpah (II Kings 25:22; Jer. 40:5). In this way Judea was added to the provincial organization which the Chaldeans had taken over from their Assyrian predecessors; administratively, it was probably merely a district attached to the province of Samaria, since the

Judean territory was now in Edomite hands while the W portions were absorbed in the Philistine province of Ashdod. Unlike the Assyrians, however, the Chaldeans did not replace the people whom they deported to Babylon with colonists from other parts of their empire, and it is possible that the commissionership was entrusted to other Judeans after the assassination of Gedaliah (II Kings 25:25).

2. Persian rule. With the conquest of Egypt by Cambyses in 525, the Persian imperial power became the greatest yet seen in the ancient world. Its rulers sought to preserve their empire by fostering the religious and cultural traditions of the subject peoples, even allowing them a measure of autonomy, while maintaining a firm grip on the real political and military power. For the Jews, both in Judea and in the Diaspora (*see* DISPERSION) of Egypt (cf. Jer. 42:15–43:7 and the Elephantine Papyri) and of Mesopotamia-Media, this policy had important consequences. Cyrus decreed (538) the rebuilding of the temple at Jerusalem (Ezra 6:3-5), entrusting the task to "one whose name was SHESH-BAZZAR" (Ezra 5: 14-16), who is frequently, though not certainly, identified with the Shenazzar listed among the sons of the Judean king Jehoiachin at I Chr. 3:18. But the disturbed condition of Judea, to which the prophet Haggai alludes in his rebuke that "you busy yourself each with his own house" (Hag. 1:9), allowed Shesh-bazzar scarcely to commence the laying of the temple's foundations before the work was halted. By the time it could be resumed, a Davidide, ZERUBBABEL, in whom both Haggai and Zechariah thought they saw the messianic inaugurator of the prophetically foretold, earthly kingdom of God (Hag. 2:20-23; Zech. 4:6-10; 6:9-14 [with restoration of "Zerubbabel" for "Joshua" in 6:11?]), was "governor of Judah" (פחת יהודה; Hag. 1:1, 14; 2:2, 21). Whether or not Zerubbabel lost his governorship (or deputy governorship) because of his participation in this episode of eschatological excitement is unknown. He is not expressly named as governor in the official correspondence about resumption of work on the sanctuary, which passed between the satrap of Beyond the River (פחת עבר־נהרא; the satrapy included most of Syria and Palestine), in association with his provincial governors (אפרסכיא), and Darius I (Ezra 5:6–6:12), in which Darius confirmed Cyrus' decree. Instead, both the satrap and the king mention the "elders of the Jews" (Ezra 5:9; 6:7) as those in charge at Jerusalem, with additional allusion in the king's letter to the "governor of the Jews" (פחת יהודיא; 6:7). At any rate, according to Ezra 6:14-18, it was the "elders of the Jews," rather than a governor, who presided over the completion and dedication of the "house of God" in the spring of 515 B.C., and thus gave a heart to their little satrapal province as well as a symbol of cohesion to the scattered Jewish communities of the world.

How and by whom Judean affairs were administered for the next fifty years is unknown. Shortly after the middle of the fifth century, however, NEHEMIAH the son of Hacaliah, a descendant of Babylonian exiles who had become cupbearer to the Persian king, was appointed GOVERNOR of the province of Judah (Neh. 5:14) and officially permitted to rebuild Jerusalem, including the renewal of its walls (Neh. 2:4-8; cf. Ezra 4:7-22). Judah thus became a province in its own right, apart from Samaria, if indeed it did not already have this status. Despite the opposition of his jealous fellow provincial governors, Sanballat of Samaria and Tobiah of Ammon, and of Geshem, the powerful and influential king of the Qedarite Arabs (as we now know from an Aramaic votive inscription on a silver vessel recently acquired by the Brooklyn Museum), Nehemiah succeeded in making Jerusalem the capital of a flourishing province. He had already found the province (מדינה; Neh. 1:3; 7:6) divided into districts (פלך; Neh. 3:9, 12, 14-18) or half-districts (חצי־פלך; 3:16-18), with a שר ("ruler") over each; he instituted a security system, to the command of which he appointed a "captain [RSV 'governor'] of the castle" (שר הבירה; Neh. 7:2-3), made provision for a genealogical registry (7:5), corrected various economic (5: 1-15) and religious abuses (7:61-65; 13:4-28), and recovenanted the people "to walk in God's law" (ch. 10).

In addition to the governor, who might himself be of Persian extraction—in 408 B.C., as we are informed by an Aramaic papyrus from Elephantine (Cowley, no. 30), one Bagoas (Bagohi) was "governor of Judea" (בגוה פחת יהוד)—and the Zadokite high priest of the temple, a third official achieved great importance under Persian imperial rule: the SCRIBE (הסופר; Aramaic ספרא). Since it was Persian policy to encourage subject peoples to live by their own religious traditions and laws, the need arose for trained experts who could interpret and transmit such materials. In Judea this function was discharged by scribes who were either themselves priests, like Ezra (the "priest, the scribe of the law of the God of heaven" [Ezra 7:21]), or Levites (cf. II Chr. 34: 13). The "scribe skilled in the Torah [law] of Moses which the LORD the God of Israel had given . . . set his heart to search [RSV 'study'] . . . and to do it, and to teach his statutes and ordinances in Israel" (Ezra 7:6, 10). Whether a Nehemiah or a Bagoas, it was the governor's duty to place this "law" into effect in the province of Judea, as it was the high priest's duty to preside over the temple cultus prescribed by that same law.

E. *JEWISH POLITICAL INSTITUTIONS IN HELLENISTIC AND ROMAN TIMES.* The basic structure of the religion-centered commonwealth which came into being on Judean soil under Persian rule persisted, though with marked modification of its characteristic features, to the destruction of the temple in A.D. 70. The high priesthood might be merged with the governorship (as under the Ptolemies and Seleucids) and even with an independent kingship (as with the Hasmoneans), or it might be altogether deprived of political authority (as in Herodian and Roman times), but the office endured so long as the temple was in existence. The scribe (Ecclus. 38: 24–39:11) retained his importance as adviser to foreign potentates and as the custodian, exegete, and teacher of the Torah-based Jewish tradition: out of his office evolved not only the "lawyer" and the "scribe" of NT times (e.g., Matt. 13:52; 22:35; 23: 1-3; Luke 11:45-46), but the "teacher" and "rabbi" (Matt. 23:8; Acts 5:34) as well. Local government by town assembly, "rulers," and "elders" went on much as before (e.g., Jth. 7:23), while the districts—extended, contracted, or revised according to shifting political circumstances—seem to have constituted the territorial units of the various taxation systems (e.g., I Macc. 11:28; Jos. Antiq. XII.iv.1) until the reorganizations of Pompey and Gabinius (Antiq. XIV.iv.4, v.4).

1. The independent Hasmonean commonwealth. The attempt, by ruling high priests, during the reign of the Seleucid king Antiochus IV (175-163 B.C.), to Hellenize Jewish religious and political institutions—including the transformation of Jerusalem into a Greek polis—met the fierce resistance of loyalist Jews and ended in failure. At a "great assembly [142 B.C.] of the priests and the people and the rulers of the nation and the elders of the country, . . . Simon the son of Mattathias, a priest of the sons of Joarib" was elected "leader and high priest for ever, until a trustworthy prophet should arise" (i.e., until the soon-expected eschatological consummation; I Macc. 14:28-29, 41). Within this recovenanted commonwealth (חבר; the term occurs both on the Maccabean coinage and in the "Damascus" Fragments) arose the later parties of the Sadducees, Pharisees, and Essenes, who differed among themselves on questions of religious law, doctrine, and national policy. To the scandal of the Pharisees and Essenes, the successors of Simon's son, John Hyrcanus (134-104 B.C.), added the title "king" to that of high priest. Backed by mercenary troops, the Hasmoneans' exercise of despotic authority was nevertheless inhibited by the Pharisees, who, in the reign of Alexander Janneus (103-76 B.C.), led the people in rebellion; and their tyranny was further tempered by the "senate," or body of elders and leading men, which had come down from earlier times (γερουσία; cf. I Macc. 12:6; Jos. Antiq. XIII.xvi.5).

2. Roman rule. The independent Hasmonean commonwealth was ended in 63 B.C. by the Romans, who thereafter ruled Judea through such client-kings as the Herodians or more directly through their own legates and procurators. The one significant, natively Jewish, political institution of this time was the Sanhedrin (συνέδριον=סנהדרין; Matt. 26:59; Acts 5:21; cf. the Mishna tractate of the same name), which, as a national council, represented the interests of the Jewish population before their Herodian or Roman rulers. Whether this Sanhedrin is identical with the institution described in Tannaitic sources, which was a supreme judicial tribunal (בית דין) and which claimed legislative and executive authority as well, is not clear. In any case, neither the Herodians nor the Sanhedrin had any more real authority during NT times than the Romans, for their own imperial purposes, might allow: the devices of effective government in Judea and Palestine were essentially the counterparts of those employed in provincial administration elsewhere in the Empire. *See* AGRIPPA; ETHNARCH; HEROD; HERODIANS; PILATE; PROCURATOR; ROMAN EMPIRE; SANHEDRIN; TETRARCH.

Bibliography. J. Pedersen, *Israel: Its Life and Culture,* I–II (1926), 12-60; III–IV (1940), 1-106 and *passim.* H. Frankfort, *Kingship and the Gods* (1948), *passim,* and especially pp. 337-44. R. Gordis, "Democratic Origins in Ancient Israel—the Biblical *'Ēdāh,*" *Alexander Marx Jubilee Volume* (1950), pp. 369-88. A. Alt, "Das Königtum in den Reichen Israel und Juda," *VT,* I (1951), 2-22. S. W. Baron, *A Social and Religious History of the Jews,* I (1952), 32-62, 212-49. M. Weber, *Ancient Judaism* (1952), 3-146, 267-335. A. G. Barrois, *Manuel d'archéologie biblique,* II (1953), 38-86. B. Mazar (Maisler), under ארץ ישראל ("דברי הימים"), אנציקלופדיה מקראית, I (1955), 679-741. S. Mowinckel, *He That Cometh* (1956), pp. 21-95. G. E. Wright, *Biblical Archaeology* (1957), pp. 69-97, 120-79, 199-210. M. Noth, "Gott, König, Volk im AT," *Gesammelte Studien zum AT* (1957), pp. 188-229; *The History of Israel* (1958), pp. 53-108 and *passim.* R. de Vaux, *Les institutions de l'AT,* vol. I: *Le nomadisme et ses survivances* (1958).

I. RABINOWITZ

GOVERNMENTS [κυβερνήσεις] (I Cor. 12:28). The KJV translation of a term used by Paul to denote one of God's *charismata,* or spiritual gifts given to the church (RSV "administrators"). It is not a synonym for a specific office or order of ministry. Its close association with HELPS has led some critics to see in these terms an allusion to the ministries performed by bishops, elders, and deacons, or the "leaders" (cf. Rom. 12:8; I Thess. 5:12). The metaphor contained in the Greek word recalls a "helmsman" of a ship. In the LXX the word occurs in Prov. 1:5; 11:14; 24:6, to describe the "counsels of the wise." M. H. SHEPHERD, JR.

GOVERNOR. The ruler set up by kings to be over a specific territory or province. He governs the area by authority of the supreme monarch, not in his own right. Joseph was a governor in Egypt under Pharaoh (שליט; cf. the Arabic title "sultan"; Gen. 42:6; cf. Eccl. 7:19; 10:5; cf. Gen. 45:26 with Acts 7:10). Gedaliah was appointed governor by the king of Babylon (Jer. 40:5). Daniel was governor of the wise men in Babylon (Dan. 2:48). Persian governors mentioned in the Bible include Tattenai, Shesh-bazzar, Zerubbabel, Nehemiah (Ezra 5:3, 14; Neh. 5:14; Hag. 1:1), who were over Judah. The Hebrew משל, used in Jer. 30:21, is for any ruler and could include an absolute ruler (Josh. 12:2; Ps. 105:20). The legates and procurators were governors under Rome (Luke 2:2; 3:1; Acts 23:24; 24:27). *See* PROCURATOR.

The "governor" (KJV) of the temple was the chief officer, who had authority over the temple environs (*see* OVERSEER). One such officer, Pashhur, put Jeremiah in stocks (Jer. 20:1). The RSV "officer" is a better translation of פקיד. The *Hiph'il* of this root is translated "made governor" in reference to the appointment of Gedaliah (Jer. 40:5; 41:2; cf. II Kings 25:22).

The "governor" (KJV) of the army was the "commander" (RSV) of a unit. However, חקק has in its root a concept of "decree," and so in the book of Judges includes the judges or the rulers themselves (Judg. 5:9, 14; cf. Gen. 49:10). So it is even used of God (Isa. 33:22).

In II Chr. 28:7, נגיד is "governor" of the palace, according to the KJV, but "commander" in the RSV (cf. II Chr. 32:21). This is the ruler or prince, even at times the king himself (II Sam. 5:2; I Chr. 29:22). The RSV uses "governor" in II Chr. 19:11. Similarly the נשיא is the chief prince in each tribe, or the "leader" in Solomon's kingdom (II Chr. 1:2). Perhaps this is comparable to the modern Bedouin sheik.

The leading prince (שר) of a city was sometimes called the "governor"—e.g., Amon (I Kings 22:26), Joshua (II Kings 23:8), and Ma-aseiah (II Chr. 34:

8). Occasionally this term is used as the governor of the temple (I Chr. 24:5 KJV). The prince of a district is called a governor in the RSV (I Kings 20:14). It is probable that שר is also used in the general sense of "ruler of the people" (II Chr. 23:20; Jer. 30:21). God is such a ruler (Ps. 22:28).

The most popular Hebrew term for "governor" is פחה. This is a loan word from the Akkadian *bêl paḫâti*, "lord of a district." It is sometimes translated "ruler" in the RSV. These officers are usually less than the king, as suggested in I Kings 20:24, but seem to have military power. They may have been captains in Assyria (II Kings 18:24). They were governors of Babylon (Jer. 51:23), of Medea (Jer. 51:28). The Persian governors in Palestine are so indicated (Neh. 2:7; cf. Hag. 1:1; Mal. 1:8). These were, of course, appointed by the king (Ezra 5:14). The Aramaic form occurs in Ezra 5:3, etc., for Tattenai, the SATRAP. The satrap in the story of Esther seems to be a civil governor or a deputy of the king (Esth. 3:12, etc.). The word is rarely used for the governors under Solomon (I Kings 10:15; II Chr. 9:14).

The governor of a captured city is sometimes called in Akkadian *šaknu*. In Hebrew and Aramaic, סגנים are rulers or "prefects." Only in Daniel does the translation "governor" occur (Dan. 2:48; 3:2; 6:7; etc.). *See* DEPUTY.

A title of honor became "governor" (KJV) in the Persian period. The RSV prefers "governor" for the Persian loan word תרשתא in Ezra 2:63; Neh. 7:65; 8:9; etc. The titles in Ezra 4:9 are confused, but APHARSACHITES seem to be a minor official and not a gentilic name.

In Zech. 9:7; 12:5-6, the KJV has "governor" for אלף (LXX χιλίαρχος). However, both the context and the poetic form favor the simple RSV translation, "clan." *See* CHIEF.

In the Apoc. "governor" is used to translate general terms for leadership, such as ἄρχων, δεσπότης, στρατηγός, etc.

In the NT the word ἡγεμών appears for the Roman legates and procurators and the proconsuls. These officials were administrators of a territory or province for the Roman emperor (I Pet. 2:14). Some had the Roman legion under them, while others were dependent on a general for army support. The system of appointment varied greatly. Tenure was generally one year, but many reappointments occurred. These governors administered the law and had power of life and death (Matt. 10:18; Mark 13:9; Luke 21:12). Quirinius was a proconsul (Luke 2:2) who may have had two terms of office under Tiberius. Pontius Pilate (Luke 3:1, etc.), Felix (Acts 23:24, etc.), and Festus (Acts 24:27, etc.) were procurators. The verb is used of Joseph, who was viceroy under Pharaoh (Acts 7:10). So the prophecy of Micah sees the Messiah as such a ruler under God (Matt. 2:6; cf. Mic. 5:1-2).

Similarly, one who is less than a king, but who serves as his deputy, is the ETHNARCH (ἐθνάρχης). Simon Maccabeus is called an ethnarch (I Macc. 14:47; Jos. Antiq. XIII.vi.6). In Damascus, Paul was apprehended by the governor ruling for King Aretas (II Cor. 11:32).

The ruler or governor of the feast (ἀρχιτρίκλινος) perhaps could be considered the deputy of the householder. He was the steward of the couch, the table master, or dining-room supervisor (John 2:8-9). He may also have served as master of the feast and regulated the drinking (Ecclus. 32:1).

The tutor or steward (οἰκονόμος) who acted as a "guardian" (RSV) to a child is called "governor" in the KJV (Gal. 4:2; cf. Luke 12:42; I Cor. 4:2). Likewise the "pilot" (RSV) of a ship is a "governor" (Jas. 3:4 KJV). *See* STEWARD.

C. U. WOLF

GOZAN gō′zăn [גוזן; Akkad. *Guzana*]. A city and district (on or near the Euphrates), through which the Habor River flowed. The place had been conquered by kings of Assyria prior to Sennacherib's invasion (701 B.C.) of Judah, according to II Kings 19:12=Isa. 37:12. In the ninth year of Hosea king of Israel, the Assyrian monarch Shalmaneser exiled some Israelites to Assyrian territory, including the region of the Habor, which is called the "River of Gozan" (II Kings 17:6; 18:11). In I Chr. 5:26, however, we find "Habor, Hara, and the river [of] Gozan"). Gozan is apparently the same as Gausanitis (Γαυζανῖτις), mentioned by Ptolemy (V.18).

C. H. GORDON

GRABA. KJV Apoc. form of HAGABAH.

GRACE. In the specifically Christian sense of the word, God's unmerited free, spontaneous love for sinful man, revealed and made effective in Jesus Christ. As such it lies at the very heart of the Christian gospel, and is one of its most distinctive features.

Some anticipations of this meaning of the word occur in the OT, but it is in the NT that its fullest significance is to be found. Nor is this found equally in all parts of the NT. In some books the use of the word hardly differs from that already familiar in secular Greek and in the Greek of the LXX. It is to Paul above all others that we owe the special significance the word has come to bear in the vocabulary of Christian faith. We do not know that it was he who first endowed it with this meaning, but it is certainly he more than any other who by his letters established it in the language of the church.

The Greek word which is normally translated in our English versions as "grace" is χάρις, and it is primarily the uses of this word which must here be examined. It must be borne in mind, however, that the truth conveyed by this word is very often present in the Bible in contexts where the word itself is not precisely used.

1. The meaning of χάρις
   a. In secular Greek
   b. In the LXX
2. "Grace" in the Pauline letters
   a. The grace of God
   b. The grace of our Lord Jesus Christ
   c. Grace in relation to human need
   d. The quality of grace
   e. With the meaning of "greeting" and "thanks"
3. Note on its use in the Pastoral letters
4. Grace in the non-Pauline writings of the NT
   a. The gospels
   b. Acts
   c. Hebrews

d. James
e. I Peter
f. II Peter
g. Jude
h. Revelation
5. The idea of grace apart from the use of the word "grace"
6. Conclusion
Bibliography

1. The meaning of χάρις. ***a. In secular Greek.*** One common meaning of the word is "pleasantness" or "attractiveness." An instance of this within the NT may be found in Luke 4:22, where it is used to describe the impression which the words of Jesus made on his hearers: "All . . . wondered at the words of grace" (ERV-ASV). Perhaps, too, this is the significance in Col. 4:6: "Let your speech be always with grace" (ERV-ASV).

The word may also mean a kindly attitude, and so approval or favor. This too finds its place in the NT. In Luke 1:30 Mary has "found favor with God," and in Luke 2:52 Jesus increased "in favor with God and man." It is similarly used in Acts 2:47; 7:10.

The word could also mean appreciation of a favor or a kindness, and so came to mean "thanks." In I Cor. 10:30, e.g., the Greek word χάριτι is rendered in the RSV as "with thankfulness." The common phrase χάριν ἔχω, which one would expect to mean "I receive a favor," is normally translated as "I am thankful" or "I thank" (as in Luke 17:9).

In the papyri and elsewhere the common phrase for "Thanks be to the gods" is χάρις τοῖς θεοῖς. In the NT it is modified for the use of Christians into χάρις τῷ θεῷ ("Thanks be to God"; Rom. 6:17; I Cor. 15:57; II Cor. 8:16).

b. In the LXX. Χάρις is the usual translation of the Hebrew word חן, which means "favor," as in the phrase "find favor in his eyes" (and so corresponds to the second meaning of χάρις, as noted above, in secular Greek). It can be used of men in their relationship to one another. A man, e.g., finds "favor" with one whom he regards as a superior, or from whom he seeks a concession (cf. Ruth 2:2). It is also used of man in his relationship to God. Usually it is the righteous man or one prepared to become righteous who thus "finds favor" with God. It is, however, always God who confers the favor on man. It would be quite inappropriate to speak of man's conferring favor on God.

The Hebrew word חן is therefore an equivalent of the Greek word χάρις only in this very limited sense. It falls far short of the fuller meaning which χάρις came to bear in the NT. Indeed, if this fuller meaning is to be represented at all by a Hebrew word, it is the word חסד (*ḥêsêd*) to which we should turn. This word is, however, usually translated in the LXX by the Greek word ἔλεος ("mercy"). For further discussion of the use of חסד in the OT, *see* § 5 *below.*

The word χάρις is used also in the Apoc., though not so frequently as to make it a characteristic word. It occurs seventy-five times in all, and of these occurrences twenty-nine are to be found in Ecclesiasticus.

2. "Grace" in the Pauline letters. The meanings attached to the word χάρις in the Greek version of the OT and in the Apoc. are not notably different from those already familiar in secular Greek, though, understandably enough, the word is used far more frequently in relation to God. These same usages of the word are found also in several parts of the NT. There is, however, a distinctive use of the word in the NT, and it is this which we usually have in mind when we speak of "grace" in its Christian significance. This sense of the word occurs predominantly in the Pauline writings, but not exclusively so. It is this distinctive NT meaning of the word which must now be examined.

It becomes clear merely from a count of the occurrences of χάρις in the different books of the NT how predominantly it is a Pauline word. It is not used at all in Matthew, Mark, I John, III John, and Jude. In II John it occurs once only, and in James, II Peter, and Revelation twice each; 3 times in the Fourth Gospel (all in the Prologue), 6 in Luke, 8 in Hebrews, 10 in I Peter, and 17 in Acts. In all these non-Pauline books the word appears only 51 times, and of these occurrences 27 are in Acts and I Peter, which on other grounds have been thought to have close links with Pauline teaching. In contrast with this, 101 instances of it occur in the Pauline corpus of letters, twice as many as in all the rest of the NT together, and in much smaller compass. The 101 instances in the Pauline writings occur in 156 pages, and the 51 instances in the rest of the NT in 512 pages.

The numbers alone prove that χάρις must be regarded as a characteristic word of Pauline writing. But over and above the significance of the numbers, the word comes to bear a special meaning in these letters. It is made the vehicle of a profoundly important element in Paul's understanding and proclamation of the gospel.

a. The grace of God. The Pauline phrase about grace which is most familiar to us is that which occurs in the commonly used benediction, derived from II Cor. 13:13: "the grace of the Lord Jesus Christ." It is misleading, however, to assume from this that in Paul's writings grace is associated with Christ rather than with God. In fact, the phrases "the grace of God" and "grace from God" occur even more frequently than "the grace of Christ." Almost every letter opens with the greeting: "Grace and peace from God," and grace is frequently spoken of as a gift bestowed by God, both upon Paul himself (I Cor. 15:10; Eph. 3:7) and upon others (II Cor. 6:1; 8:1; 9:14).

It is true that the means by which the grace of God is mediated to men is pre-eminently Jesus Christ —his incarnation, death, and resurrection. What God has done and still does for men in Jesus Christ, his Son, is God's outstanding act of grace. The grace of Jesus Christ, therefore, is not to be thought of as other than the grace of God, but rather as an expression of it. Indeed, Paul speaks in one continuous phrase of the "grace of our God and the Lord Jesus Christ" (II Thess. 1:12; cf. Rom. 5:15; I Cor. 1:3).

God is the source from which grace comes to man. Jesus Christ is the God-ordained means by which this grace most effectively reaches man in his need.

b. The grace of our Lord Jesus Christ. For the believer, therefore, the grace of God is actualized and made effective for human need in Jesus Christ. Paul speaks of the "grace of God and the free gift in the grace of . . . Jesus Christ" (Rom. 5:15).

The context where the "grace of Christ" most frequently occurs is the closing benediction of the letters, once in the familiar threefold benediction of II Cor. 13:13, but usually as a complete blessing in itself (Rom. 16:20; I Cor. 16:23; Gal. 6:18; Phil. 4:23; I Thess. 5:28; II Thess. 3:18).

The context, however, which gives the surest clue to its meaning for Paul is II Cor. 8:9, where it is used to interpret the significance of the incarnation: "You know the grace of our Lord Jesus Christ, that though he was rich, yet for your sake he became poor, so that by his poverty you might become rich." The grace of God is first and foremost evidenced in the incredibly generous and utterly unexpected action he took in coming in Christ to this world of sinful men. The grace of Christ is seen in his obedient fulfilment of his Father's gracious purpose, first by becoming man at all, by the humble courtesy of his lowly birth, by the compassion and dauntless courage of his life and ministry, by the steadfast faithfulness which led him to the Cross, and by the mighty power of his resurrection and ascension—and all accomplished "for our sake," though there was nothing in man that was even faintly worthy of it.

c. Grace in relation to human need. Grace is offered by God to man with the special purpose of accomplishing for man good things which he cannot achieve for himself. It is quite the reverse of a reward for good conduct; it is rather a means of rescuing him from his own deep failure and from his helplessness to overcome it.

In Paul's teaching it is particularly related to justification—i.e., God's acceptance of man as "righteous" and free from guilt. By the grace of God sinful man may be forgiven, and, in spite of his obvious and, indeed, acknowledged wrongdoing, treated by God as if he were innocent. *See* JUSTIFICATION.

In contemporary Judaism it was normally believed that a man gained acceptance with God (i.e., was justified) by sustained obedience to his commands. Paul, however, had proved the futility of this. Man could not by his own endeavors fulfil the whole, perfect will of God, especially when that will was applied to inward desire and motive as well as to outward act. Moreover, even if present obedience were possible, how could one atone for the sins of the past? For Paul the Jew, the guilt of past sin had become an unendurable, and yet an irremovable, burden. Part of the utter wonder of what Christ did for him was this, that when he yielded himself to Christ in trust and willingness to be commanded, this deep misery of guilt, this aching hopelessness of moral failure, was banished. Its removal was not due to anything that he or any other man had done or could do. It was all God's doing through Christ. Why had God so acted? Only because it must be his nature so to act. He was incredibly generous and compassionate, far beyond what man could have ever dreamed possible. This is what Paul tries to express when he speaks of the "grace of God in Christ." We are "justified by his [God's] grace as a gift, through the redemption which is in Christ Jesus" (Rom. 3:24).

All that God had done for man in Christ was, for Paul, brought to a sharp focus in Christ's death upon the cross. The grace of God is more than ever evident there. So Paul is able to speak of our being justified "by his blood" (Rom. 5:9), as well as by his grace.

In Ephesians the blessing which God confers on man through Christ is called "salvation," rather than justification (either by Paul himself, or by a disciple of his most skilfully expounding his master's message). But with even greater emphasis salvation is ascribed solely to the action of God's grace: "By grace you have been saved" (Eph. 2:5). And three verses later the same affirmation is repeated, this time in direct relation to faith: "By grace you have been saved through faith." Thus we have a comprehensive summary of the separate truths expressed in Rom. 3:24 ("justified by grace"); Rom. 5:1 ("justified by faith").

Election also is ascribed to the grace of God. In Rom. 11:5-6 God's choice of the people of Israel, and also of the faithful remnant among them, is the act of his grace, since it was based not at all on any merit in them.

Since man's acceptance with God is all God's doing (II Cor. 5:18)—i.e., it is all of grace—it is only to be expected that in Paul's letters "grace" is sharply contrasted with words which were commonly used to describe man's own endeavors to achieve status with God.

It is, e.g., the antithesis of law (Rom. 6:14-15), since a devout Jew was accustomed to assume that it was through obedience to the law that he could gain acceptance with God. To be "under the law" means to base one's life on this assumption. Paul, however, declares that it is the believer's privilege to be "under grace"—i.e., his acceptance with God is not something he must try to achieve by his own merits, but accept as a gracious, undeserved gift from God.

Successful obedience to the commands of the law came to be known as "works" (achievements), and these too are put in contrast to "grace" (Rom. 11:6).

What makes man unacceptable with God is his disobedience to God's will, his sin. Since grace makes a man acceptable to God in spite of his sin, and thereby brings him his one hope of conquering sin, through the strength and joy which comes from his restored relationship to God, grace and sin are also set in sharp contrast with each other (Rom. 6:1).

The grace of God in Christ not only brings salvation to sinful man, but also assigns to those who are saved special tasks in the service of God. It was by the grace of God that Paul was appointed an apostle, and commissioned to carry the gospel to the Gentiles. There was nothing in him, he knew, which made him suitable for it or deserving of it. It was a commission of which he felt utterly unworthy. But the spiritual and moral equipment which he needed for the fulfilment of the task was supplied to him as the gift of God's grace. God had chosen him, commanded and equipped him. "His grace was bestowed upon me," writes the apostle (I Cor. 15:9-10 ERV-ASV; cf. Rom. 1:5; I Cor. 3:10; Gal. 2:9; Eph. 3:7).

"My grace is sufficient for you," is the promise he received from the Lord (II Cor. 12:9).

It is not only the high rank of apostleship which is bestowed by the grace of God. All the various endowments which believers are enabled to bring to the corporate life of the church are called χαρίσματα ("gifts of grace"). They include prophecy, service, exhortation, teaching, etc. (Rom. 12:6-8), and also "miracles, healings, helps, governments, tongues" (I Cor. 12:28-31 ERV-ASV). The gifts "differ according to the grace given to us." And the greatest of all these χαρίσματα, far outstripping more spectacular gifts such as tongues, is "love."

In Rom. 5:2 Paul speaks of "this grace in which we stand" as though the whole status of a Christian, in his utter dependence on God in Christ, may be described as "grace" (cf. I Pet. 3:7; 5:12; Acts 13:43).

d. The quality of grace. Grace is, first, a free gift. It is never man's due, nor is it conferred as a reward (Rom. 4:4). In Eph. 2:8 it is called a "gift" (δῶρον), but more usually in this connection the stronger word δωρέα ("free gift") is used (Rom. 5:15; II Cor. 9:15; Eph. 3:7; 4:7). The phrase "the grace which was *given* to me" recurs constantly.

Grace is abundant. In connection with grace there often occur words which emphasize the unlimited extent of the gift. It "abounds" (περισσεύω; Rom. 5:15; II Cor. 4:15). It is multiplied (πλεονάζω; II Cor. 4:15). It exceeds expectation (Eph. 2:7). This overflowing abundance is suggested also in the phrase "the riches of his grace" (Eph. 1:7; 2:7).

It is through faith. Grace is frequently associated with faith, that response in man which accepts the offer of God's grace (Eph. 2:8). Theologians differ about the extent to which faith is a response of the will, for which the man concerned may be held responsible, and how far even faith itself is the gift of God's grace, as Phil. 1:29 suggests (cf. also Acts 18:27). Something of a paradox marks Christian experience at this point. The believer is utterly sure that "it is all God's doing," but he also knows that at some point he has had to say "yes" when he might have said "no."

Paul's writings confirm this paradox of belief. There is much in his letters to emphasize how from beginning to end the Christian life is the work of God's grace. There are, however, significant warnings, which make it clear that he knows that there is that in man which can accept and which can refuse and withstand God's proffered grace.

The former emphasis has led to the doctrines of "irresistible grace" and of predestination. These find support in the suggestion that God determines the destiny of individuals before their birth (Rom. 9, especially vss. 10-13), and in Rom. 10–11, with the special reference to grace in 11:5-6. Against this, however, must be set the words in which Paul explicitly acknowledges that grace may be resisted and thwarted by man. E.g., he writes in Gal. 2:21 of "making void" (ERV-ASV; RSV "nullify") the grace of God; and in Gal. 5:4 he chides his readers because they have "fallen away" from grace. He pleads too with the Corinthians that they do not "accept the grace of God in vain" (II Cor. 6:1).

Grace, therefore, does not override man's will and violate his responsibility; and that in man which enables grace to be effective in his life is what Paul calls "faith."

Finally, the grace of God is an active and effective power from God, bringing merciful aid to man. It is not a theoretical characteristic of the divine nature. It signifies rather the energetic initiative which God has taken and still takes in Christ to heal the breach between man and God, and repair the ruins in man's soul. Indeed, there are passages where grace is almost equated with power: "My grace is sufficient for you, for my power is made perfect in weakness" (II Cor. 12:9; cf. also I Cor. 15:10).

Indeed, it is probably an error to think of grace (or righteousness) as some separate entity, belonging to God and able to be dispensed by God. The "grace of God" means "God in his graciousness," and is a mode of speech, describing God himself, in his personal and gracious approach to man.

Grace is also a quality of Christian character. For Paul, "grace" usually means the grace of God as bestowed on man in Christ. More than this, however, it is one of those divine activities which can reproduce itself in the human lives of those who receive it. Certainly it is never used of man in his attitude to God, but it may be used of a Christian man in his relationship to his fellows. In this respect it is like love (ἀγάπη), which is fundamentally God's love for man, but the word can also be used of the Christian man's love for his fellow men. So too "grace" is primarily the characteristic of God's dealings with man, but can also be used of the relationship of man to man (as in Eph. 4:29; Col. 4:6).

In a further sense, derived from this, it is applied to the generous contribution which Christians make for the relief of their less fortunate fellows (I Cor. 16:3; cf. II Cor. 1:15; 8:4, 6, 19). In this last context Paul links together very closely the grace of God in Christ toward man (II Cor. 8:9) and the generosity toward his fellows which this should awaken in man (vss. 4, 6, 19).

e. "Greetings" and "thanks." In addition, Paul uses χάρις as the normal greeting with which he begins his letters ("grace and peace to you"), and "grace be with you" is his farewell greeting. Paul, indeed, may have been the originator of this use of χάρις as a Christian greeting. Certainly he used it regularly. In origin it was an adaptation for Christian purposes of the ordinary greeting of secular letters, familiar to us from the papyri: χαῖρε or χαίρετε ("rejoice"). The similarity of the verbal form χαίρω to the noun χάρις made the change easy and understandable. Superficially it is a slight change; in significance it is an enormous one.

Besides these rather particular uses of χάρις, Paul also avails himself occasionally of the current secular uses. The phrase χάρις τῷ θεῷ, e.g., occurs frequently in the ordinary sense of "thanks be to God" (as in II Cor. 8:16).

3. "Grace" in the Pastoral letters. Not many modern scholars regard these letters as coming direct from the apostle's hand, though it is probable that some portions of genuine letters have been included in them. It is appropriate, therefore, that a note on their use of "grace" should be added separately.

In these three letters "grace" occurs thirteen times. Six of these occurrences are found in the normal

Pauline greetings at the beginning and the end of the three letters. Two others appear in the common idiom χάριν ἔχω ("I thank"). The other five uses (I Tim. 1:14; II Tim. 1:9; 2:1; Tit. 2:11; 3:7) have a distinctively Pauline flavor about them. None of them occurs in a passage which is generally regarded as Pauline; yet they sound Pauline: grace abounds, and the writer speaks of being saved, justified, called, strengthened, by grace. But it may well be that the similarities to the Pauline phraseology come from a close imitation of his vocabulary.

4. Grace in the non-Pauline writings of the NT. ***a. The gospels.*** The word is not used at all in Matthew and Mark. In Luke there are six instances of it, but it is used in each case as in secular Greek, with the meaning of "pleasantness," "kindliness," "favor," or "thanks." There is no case of a recognizably Pauline usage, though it is possible that something of a deeper meaning may lie behind the characterization of the words of Jesus as "words of grace" (4:22 ERV-ASV).

In John the word occurs only four times, all four within the space of four verses in the Prologue (1:14-17). Here "grace" is combined with "truth," as if they are being presented as complementary to each other, together comprehending the totality of the gospel message (in a way somewhat similar to that in which Paul combines the "kindness and the severity" of God in Rom. 11:22). In the same context grace is contrasted with law, as with a lower level of religious life. It seems probable that something of the more developed meaning of the word, which we found in the Pauline writings, is to be recognized here.

b. Acts. Here the LXX (and secular) use of the word, meaning "favor," appears frequently, as in 2:47; 7:10, 46. In some other contexts, however, the word carries something of the Pauline emphasis. E.g., salvation is through grace (15:11), and so, indeed, even is "faith" (18:27). The grace of God is both the content of the gospel message (20:24, 32; 14:3) and the explanation of missionary success among the Gentiles (11:23). As in Rom. 5:2, it may be used to describe the status of the believer in his dependence on God (13:43); and in greetings of farewell, friends are committed to the grace of God or of Christ (14:26; 15:40).

c. Hebrews. The characteristic Pauline use of "grace" is not clearly present in this letter, though there are some contexts where the meaning clearly transcends its normal significance in the LXX.

The reading in 2:9 is uncertain, but the more commonly accepted one speaks of Christ's tasting death for everyone "by the grace of God." To associate grace with the self-giving of Christ on the cross "for everyone" is a Pauline emphasis.

In 13:25 we meet the benediction: "Grace be with all of you," which is familiar in the Pauline writings. In 12:28 (ERV-ASV) and perhaps 12:15, the grace of God is that which provides power for man to obey God, and in 13:9 it is that by which the "heart is strengthened." The "Spirit of grace" in 10:29 is the Holy Spirit, and the "throne of grace" is probably a periphrasis for God himself, from whom grace comes to our aid in times of need (4:16).

Here, therefore, grace is descriptive of God's loving concern and readiness to aid all who turn to him in need; but it is not specifically related to God's giving of himself to man in Christ and in the bestowal of salvation.

d. James. In this letter "grace" is used twice, and both times in connection with a quotation from the LXX (Prov. 3:34). We cannot be sure, therefore, that there is any distinctively Christian meaning in James's use of the word (4:6).

e. I Peter. In this letter "grace" is used more frequently, in proportion to its length, than in any other non-Pauline writing. In some respects it approaches Paul's usage. In the initial greeting, e.g., "grace" is combined with "peace." It is named the "grace of God," but it is related to God's action in Christ (1:10, 13; 5:10). It is also used to describe the privileged status of a believer in relation to God in 5:12; 3:7, where it is called the "grace of life" (cf. Acts 13:43; Rom. 5:2). In 2:19-20 it is applied to a gracious act or bearing which gains God's approval. In 4:10 grace is bestowed on believers in order to equip them with a "gracious gift" (χάρισμα) for the sake of others, and such gifts vary because grace itself is varied (ποικίλη). In 5:5 the word occurs in the same quotation from Prov. 3:34 as that found in James. *See* § 4*d above.*

Along with Acts, I Peter comes nearer in its use of "grace" to the distinctive Pauline meaning of the word than the other books of the NT.

f. II Peter. Apart from the initial greeting (1:2), which is like that in I Pet. 1:2, the only use of "grace" is at 3:18, where it occurs in the familiar phrase "grow in grace," which has been commonly interpreted to mean "grow in Christian character and goodness." It may be, however, that the phrase should be related closely to the name of Jesus, which follows: "grow in the grace and knowledge of our Lord and Savior Jesus Christ."

g. Jude. In vs. 4 certain men are condemned because they "pervert the grace of our God into licentiousness," presuming on God's forgiveness in order to persist in sin. It is the same abuse of grace which is denounced by Paul in Rom. 6:1.

h. Revelation. There is no use of "grace" in this book except in the opening and closing greetings, which correspond closely to those used by Paul.

5. The idea of grace apart from the use of the word "grace." So far we have confined ourselves largely to the use of the word "grace" in the NT and the Greek version of the OT. The truth about God, which the word "grace" is intended to represent, is, however, far more widespread in the Bible than the use of the word itself.

In the OT, e.g., we examined mainly the uses of חן, the Hebrew word translated in the LXX as χάρις. In many respects, however, the developed Christian meaning of grace is more akin to the Hebrew חסד, although this in the LXX is most commonly rendered by ἔλεος ("mercy"). חסד has, therefore, usually been translated into English as "mercy." The committee which translated the RSV found this single word inadequate, since חסד means a "loyal devotion grounded in love which goes beyond legal obligation and can be depended on to the utmost." This clearly has much in common with what Paul meant by "grace." The RSV translates it as "steadfast love." It is true that this "steadfast love" is normally directed toward God's chosen people, bound to him by the covenant and living in obedience to it ("such as keep his covenant"), but there are a few striking instances where חסד is shown by God to sinful and undeserving people. E.g., God promises to David that his חסד will not depart from his offspring, even if they "commit iniquity" (II Sam. 7:15); and in Isa. 54:8 God's חסד is offered to disobedient people (cf. also Ps. 103: 10-11). These are, however, only rare exceptions, but they do indicate a certain anticipation of NT teaching.

Apart, however, from the use of any particular word, we find sometimes in the OT a wondering awareness of God's willingness to forgive those who are utterly undeserving of it. It is present, e.g., in Pss. 32; 51; 130; 143. God's love for sinners also shines through the passages known as the "Servant Songs" in Isaiah. Ezekiel hears God proclaiming to his faithless people: "You shall be clean from all your uncleannesses, and from all your idols I will cleanse you" (36:25-29). In the book of Jonah, moreover, God is revealed as one who has mercy even upon the sinful heathen. Further, the fact that God chose Israel to be his own people must be attributed entirely to his "grace." It was not based on any merit in them. So too his deliverance of them out of Egypt was another act of grace, and not at all a reward for their good conduct.

In the gospels the word "grace" hardly appears at all in the full Pauline sense, but God's gracious dealings with his children are the theme of the gospels. It is human need, not merit, which brings Christ to this earth. The whole ministry of Jesus is an act of grace. His loving concern for the outcasts of society earns for him the scornful title "friend of sinners." He himself declares that he came not to call the righteous but sinners.

His teaching also expounds what his life illustrates. The father who welcomes home a worthless son with a generosity which bears no relation to the boy's merits is not unworthy to reflect a truth about God himself (Luke 15:11-24). The heartbroken tax collector, with nothing to plead before God but his own desperate need and penitence, is accepted ("justified") rather than the law-abiding Pharisee whose good conduct is made the ground of his self-assurance (Luke 18:14). In the parable of the workers in the vineyard (Matt. 20:1-15) the master's treatment of the workers far exceeds the requirements of justice. It is their need and his most unusual generosity which determine his action, not their achievements. Similarly God's dealings with men, says Jesus, are not based on a niggardly calculation of what each one deserves, but handed out in almost reckless extravagance, "good measure, pressed down, shaken together, running over" (Luke 6:38).

For Paul everything about Jesus speaks of the grace of God. His coming to earth at all is a supreme act of "grace" (II Cor. 8:9). Phil. 2:5-8 also proclaims this same act of grace, though the word is not applied to it; here, however, it is not only the Incarnation which is the proof of God's astonishing mercy, but also the death of Jesus. Rom. 5:6-11 presses home the same truth ("While we were yet helpless, . . . Christ died for the ungodly"). Nor is it only what Christ did for us, but what he still does through his risen presence and the gift of the Spirit, which proclaims his grace. It has been claimed, e.g., for Rom. 8 that the whole chapter is just an exposition of grace, though the word itself is not named. The same is true of Rom. 6:23; II Cor. 5:14-21; and many other passages.

6. Conclusion. The current uses of "grace" in secular Greek find their place within the NT, but the meaning of "favor" (an undeserved kindness) predominates. This meaning of the word readily lent itself to the deeper Christian significance which came to be attached to it. In Paul's letters it is applied particularly to God's uncovenanted, undeserved mercy toward man in Jesus, both in his incarnation and death and in his risen life. From this grace come to man the blessing of forgiveness, peace with God, salvation, strength for obedience to God, and gifts for service in his church.

Bibliography. G. P. Wetter, *Charis* (1913). J. Moffatt, *Grace in the NT* (1931). W. Manson, "Grace in the NT," in W. T. Whitley, ed., *The Doctrine of Grace* (1932), pp. 33-60. R. Bultmann, *The Theology of the NT* (1952), I, 288-92; II, 210-11. C. R. Smith, *The Bible Doctrine of Grace* (1956).

C. L. MITTON

GRACIOUS. *See* GRACE.

GRAFT; KJV GRAFF. The verb used in Rom. 11: 17-24 to translate ἐγκεντρίζω. A slip of a cultivated plant is inserted (grafted) into the stock of a common one. Paul used the figure to illustrate how Gentile believers had been grafted into the stock of faithless Israel, but he warned that the new branch could be cut away if it proved fruitless.

S. A. CARTLEDGE

GRAIN [בר, *bar;* דגן, *dāghān;* שבר, *šebher;* Ugar. *dgn;* κόκκος; σῖτος]. The edible seeds of certain cultivated grasses which provide a staple food for man, especially BARLEY; WHEAT. Many Hebrew and Greek words are associated with the above specific references to grain. The KJV usually uses the Old English "corn" to translate these words, but the almost exclusive use of "corn" for Indian maize in America has necessitated a change in the American versions.

Other words used for various kinds of grain are: גרש (*gereś*), "crushed grain" (Lev. 2:14, 16); כרמל (*karmel*), "fresh ears" (Lev. 2:14; 23:14; II Kings 4: 42); מלילה (*m^e^lîlâ*), "ear" (of grain; Deut. 23:25—H 23:26); ערמה (*'^a^rēmâ*), "heap of grain" (Ruth 3:7; Neh. 13:15; Jer. 50:26; cf. II Chr. 31:6-9; Song of S. 7:2—H 7:3); קלי (*qālî*), "parched grain" (Lev. 23:14; Ruth 2:14; I Sam. 17:17; 25:18; II Sam. 17:28); קמה (*qāmâ*), σπόριμα, "standing grain" (Exod. 22:6—H 22:5; Deut. 16:9; 23:25—H 23:26; Matt. 12:1; Mark 2:23; Luke 6:1); קמח (*qemaḥ*), "flour" or "meal" (Gen. 18:6; Num. 5:15; Judg. 6:19; Isa. 47:2; Hos. 8:7; etc.; *see* FLOUR); ריפות (*rîphôth*), "crushed grain" (II Sam. 17:19; Prov. 27:22); שבלת (*šibbōleth*), στάχυς, "ear" (of grain; Gen. 41:5-6; Ruth 2:2; Job 24:24; Isa. 17:5 [cf. Judg. 12:6]; Matt. 12:1; Mark 2:23; Luke 6:1).

The KJV uses "corn" occasionally for several other related Hebrew words: בליל (*bālîl;* Job 24:6; RSV FODDER; cf. Job 6:5; Isa. 30:24); בן (*ben;* Isa. 21:10; lit., "son of [a threshing floor]"); גדיש (*gādhîš;* Exod. 22:6—H 22:5; RSV STACKED GRAIN; cf.

Judg. 15:5); גרן (*gōren;* Deut. 16:13; RSV THRESHING FLOOR); and עבור (*'ābhûr;* Josh. 5:11-12; RSV PRODUCE).

The principal kinds of grain used for food in biblical times were: דחן (*dōḥan,* MILLET; Ezek. 4:9); חטה (*ḥiṭṭâ,* WHEAT; Gen. 30:14; *etc.*); כסמת (*kussemeth,* emmer [or SPELT?]; Exod. 9:32; etc.); שערה (*śe'ōrâ,* BARLEY; Exod. 9:31; etc.). The KJV mentions also RYE; FITCHES, but these were mistranslations for "spelt" (or "emmer"?).

The broad Plain of Esdraelon is the "breadbasket" of Israel today, much as it was in biblical times. Many of the broad valleys in Galilee provide fertile fields for grain. The ancient Philistine Plain along the S coast, much of the Plain of Sharon, and the valleys of Sorek and Elah in the Shephelah are still main grain-producing areas in Israel. Every available valley in the rough hill country of W Jordan is used for grain, even among the myriad olive trees. Many a rocky hillside or terrace produces its small plot of grain. The high W plateau of Transjordan has always been an important grain-producing area. For discussion of the implements used in biblical times, *see* AGRICULTURE § 4.

Grain-growing supplied frequent metaphors for prophet and apostle, as the above references show. Jesus' inimitable parables of the sower (Matt. 13:3-23; Mark 4:3-20), the weeds among the wheat (Matt. 13:24-30), the growth of the seed (Mark 4:26-29), the rich man and his barns (Luke 12:16-21), and other references to grain are still forceful vehicles of his message (see also I Cor. 15:35-38). *See* AGRICULTURE § 8.

The vital importance of grain crops to the people of the ancient Near East led to elaborate FERTILITY CULTS, worship designed to gain the favor of the goddess of fertility. Such goddesses are depicted on ancient cylinder seals, identified by stalks of grain projecting from their shoulders or garments. The adoption of these cults from the Canaanites by the Hebrew peasants brought forth the invective of the OT prophets, who viewed such practices as rebellion against Yahweh.

Several excavations of biblical cities have yielded remains of grain (mostly carbonized) and storage jars. The limestone plaque found in 1908 in the ruins of ancient Gezer is a late-tenth-century-B.C. agricultural calendar which mentions "grain-planting" and "barley harvest," and implies the wheat harvest (*see* INSCRIPTIONS). The Feast of Weeks (PENTECOST; Lev. 23:15-22; Deut. 16:9-12) was celebrated seven weeks (fifty days) after the beginning of the barley harvest, when the wheat harvest had been completed. *See* WEEKS, FEAST OF.

See also AGRICULTURE; CALENDAR; FLORA § A1; WINNOWING. J. C. TREVER

GRANARY. A storage place for winnowed grain, ranging from large jars to large pits.

Hebrew vocabulary abounds in terms for storage places, but not all clearly refer to granaries. מגורה occurs twice—Hag. 2:19 (RSV "barn"); Joel 1:17—in contexts which indicate granaries. אסם may refer to granaries in Deut. 28:8 (RSV "barn"; KJV "storehouse"); Prov. 3:10 ("barn"). In the RSV, מאבום is translated "granary" in Jer. 50:26.

Courtesy of the Oriental Institute, the University of Chicago

37. Large grain storage pit at Megiddo, with pair of winding stairs; Stratum III (*ca.* 780-650 B.C.)

In Matt. 3:12; Luke 3:17, ἀποθήκην is used for a place to store grain.

Excavations of Palestinian sites have revealed various methods of storing grain.* In 1953 at Tell es-Sultan (Jericho) a room was cleared containing twelve or more Middle Bronze storage jars, many with charred grain remaining in them. At Tell Jemmeh a large number of grain pits, some as large as twenty-five feet in diameter, were excavated. At Beisan was found a silo made of bricks, more than twelve feet in diameter and nearly as deep. In addition to these methods of storage, caves and dry cisterns may have been used. It was probably in the Late Bronze and Early Iron ages that large central granaries first became widespread in Palestine. *See also* STORE CITIES. Fig. GRA 37.

Bibliography. A. G. Barrois, *Manuel d'archéologie biblique,* I (1939), 315-17. H. N. RICHARDSON

GRAPE, GRAPES. *See* VINE, VINEYARD, §§ *3e, 5a.*

GRASS [דשא, חציר, ירק, עשב; χόρτος]. It is unlikely that the Hebrew distinguished carefully between the various grasses and grasslike herbs. The most general term in the OT for "grass" is עשב, which is used both of fodder for beasts (Deut. 11:15) and of food for men (Gen. 1:29; PLANT, as frequently elsewhere; KJV HERB). חציר is more strictly "grass." It is used of fodder, but not of human food (Ps. 104:14); of the growth on housetops (Ps. 129:6); etc. דשא (Aramaic דתא) refers to newly grown forage plants (II Sam. 23:4; Job 6:5). ירק (Num. 22:4) literally means "green," and is used by metonymy for "grass."

The short-lived character of grass is used to symbolize the temporary nature of man's life (Ps. 90:5); its profusion signifies fruitfulness and prosperity (Isa. 66:14). God's provision of grass for men and animals is one example of his providential care (Ps. 104:14), its failure in time of drought a sign of his displeasure (Jer. 14:5).

In the NT, "grass" (χόρτος) is likewise used to illustrate both God's providential care (Matt. 6:30) and man's transitoriness (Jas. 1:10-11).

R. W. Corney

GRASSHOPPER [ארבה (Nah. 3:15, 17; KJV *in* Judg. 6:5; 7:12; Job 39:20; Jer. 46:23), crowd, swarm, Akkad. *aribu,* Ugar. *irby,* Amharic *anbētā, usually* LOCUST; חגב, *cf.* Arab. *ḥajab,* hide, cover (*alternately* LOCUST); KJV גוב, גובי, swarm, multitude, *from* גבה, collect (RSV Locust)]. Even today "grasshopper" and "locust" are often used interchangeably, but "locust" is more correctly used to designate only the gregarious phase of certain short-horned grasshoppers (Acridiidae). The true grasshopper, then, is either a member of the long-horned family (Tettigoniidae), or is a solitary (non-migratory) phase of a short-horned species. Both families belong to the order Orthoptera. Actually, only a few species of Acridids produce swarms of the gregarious phase and can be called locusts. All the rest are grasshoppers. Figs. GRA 38; LOC 33-35.

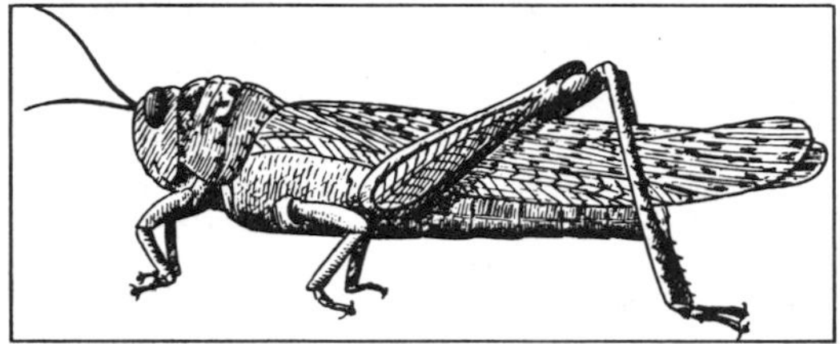

From Bodenheimer, *Animals of the Bible* (Tel Aviv: The Dvir Company Ltd.)

38. Short-horned grasshopper (*Anacridium aegyptium*)

In all stages of its life, the grasshopper destroys vegetation (Judg. 6:5; II Chr. 7:13; Eccl. 12:5[?]; Amos 7:1-2; Nah. 3:15). It is also used in various metaphors: The inhabitants of the earth are as insignificant as grasshoppers (Isa. 40:22), and so are Israel's spies (Num. 13:33). War horses on the offensive are like grasshoppers (Job 39:20). Israel's enemies, like grasshoppers, lay waste her land (Judg. 6:5; Jer. 46:23; Amos 7:1; Nah. 3:15). Nineveh's destroyers, like grasshoppers, left as suddenly as they came (Nah. 3:16-17). They, like the sand and the stars, are countless (Judg. 6:5; 7:12; Jer. 46:23; Nah. 3:15-17).

The חגב is one of four orthopterous insects listed as clean (Lev. 11:22; *see* Bald Locust). Only the thorax, either dried or broiled, minus head, viscera, wings, and legs, was thus eaten.

See also Fauna § F2.

Bibliography. S. H. Skaife, *African Insect Life* (1953); C. B. Williams, *Insect Migration* (1958). *See also* bibliography under Bald Locust.

W. W. Frerichs

GRATING [מכבר, lattice-work]; KJV GRATE. A bronze network or lattice (רשת) on the altar of burnt offering before the tabernacle (Exod. 27:4; 35:16; 38:4-5, 30; 39:39). The grating was to be placed under (תחת) a ledge of the altar, halfway down the side. The meaning is obscure, and the ledge is not otherwise described. The grating was to have rings at each of its four corners, through which carrying poles were inserted; this suggests that it might have formed a "collar" around the Altar, perhaps under a projection (the "ledge") like those on horned altars found at Megiddo and elsewhere.

E. M. Good

GRATITUDE. No motif more adequately reveals the nature of biblical faith than does gratitude or thanksgiving. With three unimportant exceptions (Luke 17:9; Acts 24:3; Rom. 16:4), thanks is always rendered unto God. It occurs only within the context of the covenant relationship. And it is always prompted by a concrete act of the covenant God within history.

In the OT, ידה is the verb "to give thanks," תודה the noun "thanksgiving." In the NT, εὐχαριστέω is most frequently employed verbally, while ἐξομολογέομαι (Matt. 11:25 = Luke 10:21) and ἀνθομολογέομαι (Luke 2:38) appear infrequently. Εὐχαριστία, "thankfulness," and χάρις, "thanks," are the nouns, εὐχάριστος the adjective "thankful."

1. In the OT. In the OT, thanksgiving forms the special note of the Psalter. Yet Israel's gratitude rings throughout her history. We are told that King David appointed certain Levites "to invoke, to thank, and to praise the Lord" (I Chr. 16:4; cf. vss. 7, 41; 23:30; 25:3; Neh. 12:46); this practice was continued by Solomon (II Chr. 5:13; 7:6), by Hezekiah (II Chr. 31:2), and by the returned exiles (Neh. 11:17; 12:24, 27, 31, 38, 40).

Thanksgiving played an integral part in Israel's cult. Festival processions on the way to Zion filled the air with "glad shouts and songs of thanksgiving" (Ps. 42:4). Entrance into the temple was with thanksgiving (Pss. 95:2; 100:4), and the service of worship contained melodies of gratitude (Ps. 147:7). Sacrifices, given as payment of a vow, were accompanied by thanks (Ps. 54:6; cf. Jonah 2:9), which sometimes took the place of the burnt offering (Ps. 69:30). "Judgments" before the altar of Yahweh were made with thanksgiving (Ps. 26:7). And all the tribes of Israel went up to Jerusalem to give thanks to the name of the Lord (Ps. 122:4).

Always Israel's gratitude was motivated by faith:

> O give thanks to the Lord, for he is good,
> for his steadfast love endures for ever!

(Pss. 106:1; 107:1; 118:1, 29; 136:1 [cf. vss. 3, 26]; I Chr. 16:4, 34, 41; cf. II Chr. 7:3; Ezra 3:11; Jer. 33:11).

Israel thanked Yahweh because he remained ever faithful to his covenant with her (Pss. 100:4; 107:8; 118:19; 138:2; 57:9). His faithfulness was manifested in many ways: in his protection of the nation and the individual from their enemies (Pss. 7:17; 28:7; 35:18; 44:8; 54:6; 79:13; 118:21; 138:1); in his deliverance of the needy from judgment (Ps. 109:30), from prison (Ps. 142:7), and from death (Pss. 30:12; 86:12; Isa. 38:18-19; cf. Ps. 138:2); in his righteous judgment, which put down the wicked and exalted the godly (Pss. 52:9; 75:1; 92:1; 140:13); in his forgiveness of his sinful people (Ps. 30:4; Isa. 12:1); in his wonderful provision for his chosen nation (Pss. 111:1; 145:10). These were Yahweh's mighty works of righteousness, of faithfulness to his covenant, and Israel's response was one of gratitude for his covenant love. Indeed, such gratitude was, on Israel's part, the condition for the proper fulfilment of her covenantal duties, for out of such gratitude was born the willingness to obey the laws of the covenant. Only in the power of the gospel could Israel truly come to fulfilment of the law.

2. In the NT. The NT differs little from the OT. Perhaps because Jesus often prayed alone (Mark 6:46), few of his thanksgivings are preserved in the tradition (Mark 8:6 = Matt. 15:36 = John 6:11, 23; Mark 14:23 = Matt. 26:27 = Luke 22:17; I Cor. 11:24; Matt. 11:25 = Luke 10:21; John 11:41). However, the angels' exclamation of Rev. 7:12 finds echo throughout the NT: "Blessing and glory and wisdom and thanksgiving and honor and power and might be to our God for ever and ever! Amen." Those who knew Jesus in the flesh thanked God for his work (Luke 17:16) and for his person (Luke 2:38). Those following after, and especially the apostle Paul, thanked God continually for that which was wrought by his power (Rom. 1:8; 7:25): for Jesus Christ (II Cor. 9:15), for a share in the coming kingdom (Col. 1:12; cf. II Thess. 2:13), for strength to proclaim the gospel (I Tim. 1:12), for special spiritual gifts (I Cor. 14:18; cf. Rom. 14:6), for physical sustenance (Acts 27:35; Rom. 14:6; I Cor. 10:30), for earthly joys (I Tim. 4:3), for the spread of the faith (II Cor. 2:14), for the love and the faith of the brethren (Rom. 6:17; I Cor. 1:4; II Cor. 8:16; Eph. 1:16; Phil. 1:3; Col. 1:3; I Thess. 1:2; 2:13; 3:9; II Thess. 1:3; Philem. 4), for the guidance of God (I Cor. 1:14). These were not just pious prayers set down by the writers. They were heartfelt thanksgivings poured out to God for that which God, through Christ and his Spirit, was accomplishing in the early church. The authors' gratitude was response to the concrete action of God within history.

Hence the NT writers urged their fellow Christians to be also thus grateful (Eph. 5:4; Col. 3:15). It would seem a strange exhortation, for gratitude cannot be commanded, but must spring spontaneously from the heart. As it stands in the NT, it forms simply another call to faith—a call to recognize that which God has done, to receive the benefits of his actions, to nurture such benefits in the soul, and to witness to them to the world. Only where gratitude was present was there true faith (cf. Rom. 1:21), for gratitude was the only faithful response possible to God's gift in Christ (cf. I Cor. 15:57). Indeed, the power to give thanks was itself given "in Christ," and thanksgivings were to be rendered through his power (Col. 3:17) and in his name (Eph. 5:20). The Christian was, then, to abound in thanksgiving (Col. 2:7), to pray with thanksgiving (Col. 4:2; Phil. 4:6; I Tim. 2:1), to witness to the gospel by being intelligibly thankful (I Cor. 14:16-17). This was the will of God for him (I Thess. 5:18). As he so responded, and as he served his faith rightly, the power of the gospel would spread to produce new thanksgivings (II Cor. 9:11-12; 1:11), all to the glory of God (II Cor. 4:15).

Gratitude lay at the heart of biblical faith because it formed the only proper response to that which had happened in history—namely, God's salvation of his people. E. R. ACHTEMEIER

GRAVE [קבורה ,קבר (*alternately* TOMB), שאול (*alternately* SHEOL); τάφος (Rom. 3:13; KJV SEPULCHRE); KJV בעי (Job 30:24; *cf.* RSV), שחת (Job 33:22; RSV PIT); KJV ᾅδης (RSV DEATH)]. An excavated place for the burial of the deceased. Context of biblical passages seldom makes clear whether the place was a trench in the soil or a cave cut in stone. The former may be intended in II Kings 13:21; Ps. 49:14; Tob. 8:9, 18. Artificial or natural caves shaped for the purpose were common (*see* TOMB). W. L. REED

GRAVEL [חצץ; KJV מעה, *see below*]. The word is used figuratively with reference to the consequences of deceitfulness (Prov. 20:17), and also in reference to the suffering which Zion receives at the hand of the Lord (Lam. 3:16; KJV GRAVEL STONES).

In Isa. 48:19 KJV, מעה is rendered "gravel"; the RSV "GRAINS [of sand]" supports the parallelism of the verse more adequately. H. F. BECK

GRAVEN IMAGE [פסילים ,פסל]. An image carved from stone, metal, or wood, mentioned in the OT (e.g., Deut. 27:15; Judg. 17:3-4; II Chr. 34:3; Nah. 1:14) with the molten image (מסכה) as an idol forbidden to the Hebrews. The graven image differed from the molten in that the latter was cast in a mold, whereas the former was sculptured.

Graven images were widely used in the ancient Near East for the purpose of representing the various deities. They are not mentioned in Genesis or in connection with the patriarchs and their travels in the land of Canaan; but according to Deut. 7:5; 12:3, they were used by the Canaanites. The making of the graven image was expressly forbidden to the Hebrews in the Decalogue (Exod. 20:4; Deut. 5:8), where it is implied that such images were made in the forms of animals, birds, and the human figure (cf. Deut. 4:16). They are also condemned elsewhere in the Pentateuch (Lev. 26:1; Deut. 4:23, 25; 27:15), and by certain prophets (e.g., Isa. 10:10; 21:9; 30:22; Jer. 8:19; 10:14; 51:47; Hos. 11:2; Mic. 1:7; 5:13; Nah. 1:14; Hab. 2:18). According to Judg. 17:1-4, a graven image of silver was made by a silversmith for the family of Micah, who lived in the hill country of Ephraim, and it was used in the worship of Yahweh. That they were also made of wood and could be burned, is implied in Deut. 7:5. Manasseh is condemned for having made graven images (II Chr. 33:19; cf. II Kings 21:7), and they were destroyed during the reformation of Josiah (II Chr. 34:4). W. L. REED

GRAVING TOOL [חרט]. A cutting implement with which the sculptor shaped his statue from the rough cast form. With this tool Aaron formed the golden calf (Exod. 32:4; *see* ART; CALF, GOLDEN). The same Hebrew word is used for a style of writing in Isa. 8:1. L. E. TOOMBS

GRAY. A translation of the Hebrew verb שיב and more frequently the noun שיבה, suggesting "old age" in terms of gray hairs or gray head (Gen. 42:38; 44:29, 31; Deut. 32:25; I Sam. 12:2; Job 15:10; Ps. 71:18; Prov. 20:29; Isa. 46:4; Hos. 7:9). The three Greek words γῆρας, πολιαί, and πρεσβύτης, all denoting "old age," are employed in the LXX.

See also COLORS. C. L. WICKWIRE

GREAT [μέγας, μεγάλη]. A title which, along with "Power" (Acts 8:9-10), should probably be interpreted against the background of the SIMON MAGUS legend, according to which he claimed the title as one who possessed divine power. He said "that he himself was somebody great." The people said of him: "This man is that power of God which is called Great." A century later, Justin (Apol. I.26) said that during the reign of Claudius, Simon Magus had gone to Rome, where he had been honored as a god; and that all the Samaritans, and some persons of other nations, regarded him as the first god (πρῶτον θεόν).

The nearest linguistic parallel to the title "Great" is the inscription of Saïttaï in Lydia: "One god in heaven, heavenly Moon, great power of the immortal God." Also he quotes from *Aelius Aristides* 37, 28 K: "Athena as the power of Zeus."

The NT is familiar with δύναμις, "power," as an angelic or demonic being (Rom. 8:38; I Cor. 15:24; Eph. 1:21; I Pet. 3:22). Ign. Eph. 13.1 has "the powers of Satan." *The Martyrdom of Polycarp* (14.1) has "God of angels and powers." Mark 14:62 uses "Power" as a metonym for God: "sitting at the right hand of Power." Not satisfied with the simple metonym, Luke expands it in 22:69 to "power of God."

There are thus at least four distinct ways of interpreting "Power" and "Great" with reference to Simon. He might consider himself like Athena as the power of God; like the moon as the great power of God; as an angel or demon; or as God himself. If we could rely on the legend of Justin's time, we would say that Simon claimed to be God. This is what his later followers asserted he was. But in view of the uncertain quality of the sources, one can safely venture no more than to point out the possibilities.

Bibliography. W. Bauer, *A Greek-English Lexicon of the NT and Other Early Christian Literature* (1957): μέγας, p. 499, and δύναμις, p. 207, where the literature is cited.

S. V. McCasland

39. The title page of the Great Bible (A.D. 1539)

GREAT BIBLE, THE. The first authorized version of the English Bible, edited by Miles Coverdale at Cromwell's request in 1539. Because of its size it was called the Great Bible. It was essentially Tyndale's translation without his marginal notes. It is sometimes called the Cranmer Bible because Archbishop Cranmer wrote a preface to the second edition.

Aided by competent scholars in Hebrew and Greek, Coverdale accomplished his task of preparing the text but had to go to Paris to secure a press capable of publishing the large Bible he had planned. The Inquisition authorities interfered, and the project was transferred to London, where the work was completed. *See* Versions, English, § 4.

Fig. GRE 39. J. R. Branton

GREAT LIZARD [צָב; *cf.* Syr. *'abhā,* lizard; Arab. *ḍabb,* lizard]; KJV TORTOISE. It is probable, from its context in Lev. 11:29 and in view of the cognates cited above, that צב (*ṣābh*) designates a kind of lizard, and this supposition is supported by the Targ., the Peshitta, and the LXX (which uses "land crocodile"; cf. Herodotus IV.192). Tristram follows Bochart in identifying the lizard in question with *Uromastix spinipes* (of the family *Agamidae*), which is *ca.* eighteen inches long and is called *ḍabb* by the Arabs.

See also Fauna § D; Lizard.

W. S. McCullough

GREAT OWL [ינשוף (*yanshûph in* Lev. 11:17; Deut. 14:16; *yanshôph in* Isa. 34:11), *possibly* blower, *from* נשף, to blow; *cf.* נשף, twilight; LXX-Vulg. ibis (Lev. 11:17; Isa. 34:11), swan (Deut. 14:16); Targ. (Onq.) קיפופא, owl]. Alternately: OWL (Isa. 34:11); IBIS (Lev. 11:17). The term often applied to the great horned or eagle owls, the largest and most powerful of all the owls, the species in Egypt being the *Bubo bubo ascalaphus* (of the subfamily Bubonidae).

Tristram noted the presence of the Great Owl in Palestine in the nineteenth century, but whether it can be identified with ינשוף is quite uncertain. G. R. Driver (*see bibliography*) favors the screech owl, *Tyto alba erlangeri.* The translation "ibis" (Lev. 11:17) is not correct, for according to Isa. 34:11, the ינשוף is found in Edomite ruins, which would not be the normal habitat of a wading bird.

Bibliography. G. R. Driver, *PEQ* (April, 1955), p. 15.

W. S. McCullough

GREAT SEA [הים הגדול]. The name by which the Mediterranean Sea was known by the peoples of the Near East. Its divisions included the Levant (Phoenician), the Aegean, the Adriatic, the Ionian, and the Tyrrhenian seas.

The Hebrews doubtless referred to the Mediterranean as the Great Sea (Num. 34:6; Josh. 1:4; Ezek. 47:10; etc.) because it was larger than the other seas (*see* Sea) with which they were acquainted. It was also referred to as the "western sea" (הים האחרון; Deut. 11:24; 34:2; Joel 2:20; Zech. 14:8). To the ancient Hebrews the great sea lay behind them when they faced E to determine the cardinal directions. The Mediterranean Sea is also intended by the term ים יפוא (Ezra 3:7; RSV "sea, to Joppa"; KJV "sea of Joppa"). In Exod. 23:31 it is referred to as the "sea of the Philistines." As can be judged by the context of the passages involved, the Mediterranean

John C. Trever

(*a*) *Cedars of Lebanon* near Tripoli

John C. Trever

(*c*) *The giant reed* (Arundo Donax), the *qaneh* of the OT, at En-gedi

John C. Trever

(*b*) *En-gedi,* showing reeds with the Dead Sea in the distance

PLATE IX

John C. Trever

(*a*) *Oleanders* in Wadi Nimrin on the way to Amman

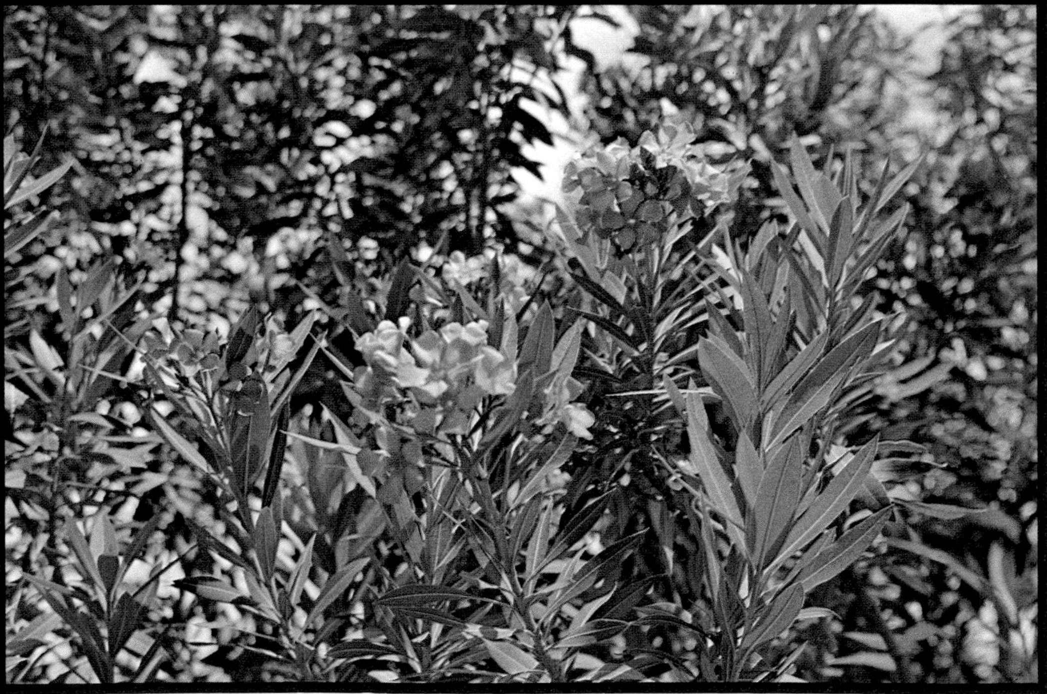

John C. Trever

(*b*) *Oleanders* along the Sea of Galilee

PLATE X

John C. Trever

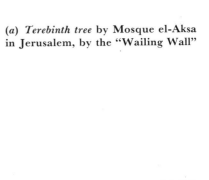

(*a*) *Terebinth tree* by Mosque el-Aksa in Jerusalem, by the "Wailing Wall"

John C. Trever

(*b*) *Two varieties of cistus* (rose?) in Jerusalem

John C. Trever

(*c*) *Pomegranate* in bloom, by the Sea of Galilee

Herbert G. May

(*d*) *Pomegranate tree* in August, near Gibeon

John C. Trever

(*e*) *Pomegranate fruit* in the Valley of Eshcol, near Hebron

PLATE XI

John C. Trever

(*a*) *Cluster of mustard, poppies, and wild barley* in the Valley of Elah

John C. Trever

(*b*) *Fig tree* with springtime figs, the *pagga* of the OT

John C. Trever

(*c*) *Cluster of anemones*

John C. Trever

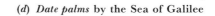

(*d*) *Date palms* by the Sea of Galilee

John C. Trever

(*e*) *Acacia hedge* in bloom

John C. Trever

(*f*) *Acacia tortillus,* the "shittim tree," near En-gedi

PLATE XII

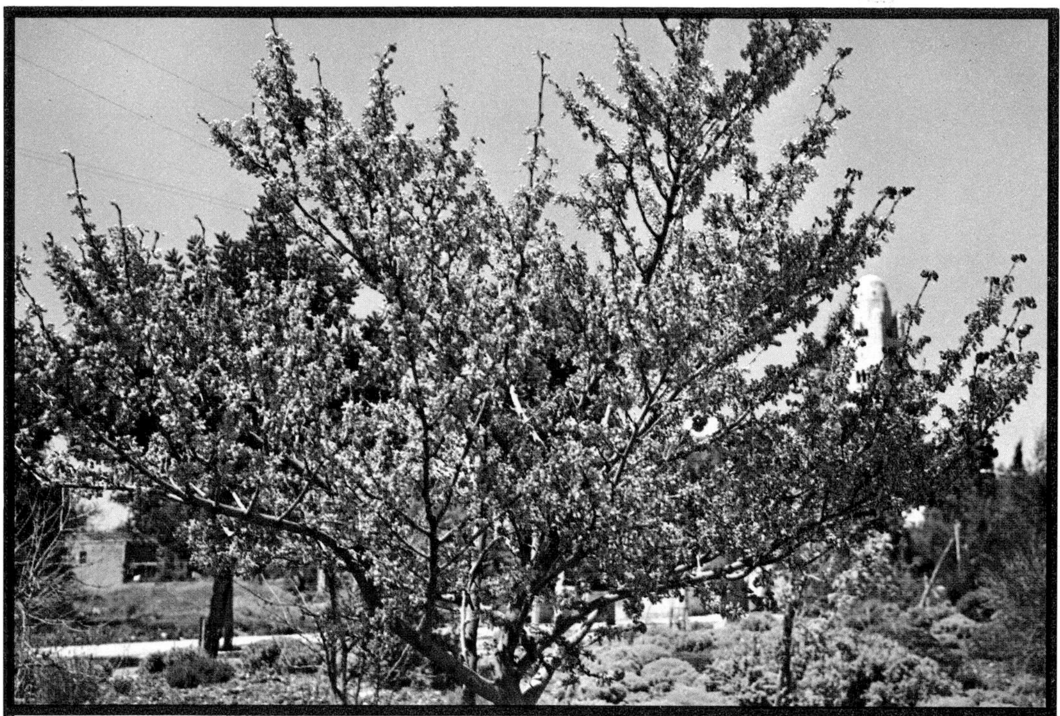

John C. Trever

(*a*) *Redbud tree* in Jerusalem

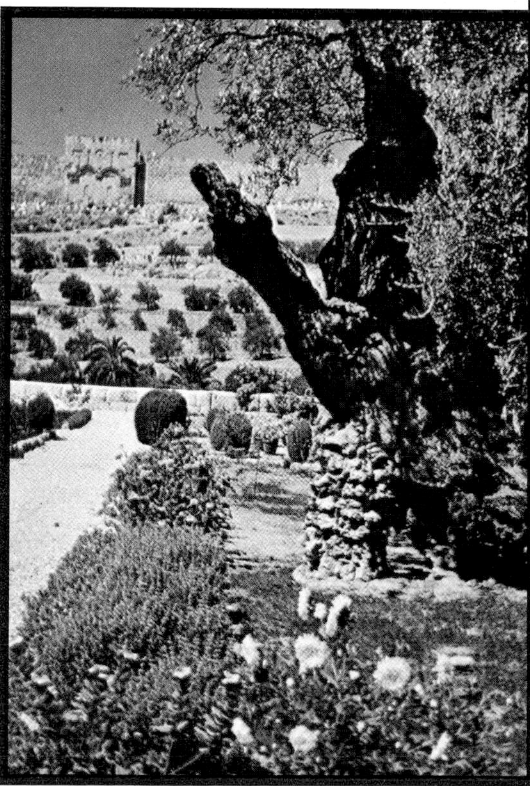

Herbert G. May

(*b*) *The Garden of Gethsemane,* ancient olive tree to the right, the "Golden Gate" of the city wall of Jerusalem in the background across the Kidron Valley

PLATE XIII

John C. Trever

(*a*) ***Thistles,*** **on the Plain of Sharon near Tel Aviv**

John C. Trever

(*b*) ***Thistles*** **("rolling thing" in Isa. 17:13 KJV) near Beer-sheba**

John C. Trever

(*c*) ***Thorn bush***

PLATE XIV

(*a*) *The River Nile* at crest, with date palms, S of Cairo, Egypt

Herbert G. May

Herbert G. May

(*b*) *Almond tree* in bloom in late February near Jerusalem. See Eccl. 12:5; Jer. 1:11.

PLATE XV

John C. Trever

(*a*) *Dill* in a wheat field at Beit Sahur, near Bethlehem in the vicinity of the "Shepherds' Field"

John C. Trever

(*b*) *Tamarisk tree* in bloom, by the Jordan River near Dagania

John C. Trever

(*c*) *Broom tree* in a wadi in the Negeb

John C. Trever

(*d*) *"Valley of the Maidens"* with fruit orchard, vineyard, and wheat field, by the village of Turmus 'Aiyah near ancient Shiloh

PLATE XVI

Sea is often designated in the OT simply as "the sea" (הים; Josh. 16:8; I Kings 5:9; 18:43; Jer. 46:18; Jonah 1:4), and similarly in the NT (θάλασσα, "seaside"; Acts 10:6, 32).

The Mediterranean is an inland ocean extending about 2,200 miles from Gibraltar to the Lebanon coast, and varying in width from *ca.* one hundred to six hundred miles. Geological studies have determined that the sea was formed during the Tertiary period from a larger ocean, called the Tethys. The movement of continental blocks between Europe and North Africa resulted in the formation of several basins of considerable variation in depth, and the mountains near the shores of the sea.

Unlike their neighbors the Phoenicians, who were famous for their fleets which sailed to many Mediterranean lands, the Hebrews were not a seafaring people. In the time of Solomon a fleet of ships was built on the Red Sea at EZION-GEBER and operated with the assistance of the Phoenicians (I Kings 9:26-27). Jehoshaphat was less successful, for his ships were wrecked in the same harbor (I Kings 22:47-49).

There is no record of similar ventures on the Mediterrean undertaken by the Hebrew people. This has been explained in part as being due to the desert origin of the people, which caused them to fear the sea. However, in view of the use of the Red Sea, which offered a reasonably good harbor at Ezion-geber, and the fact that the Phoenicians were successful sailors, although some of their ancestors were desert Semites, the Hebrew attitude toward the Mediterranean is probably to be explained by the absence of good harbors.

The Palestinian coast line of less than one hundred miles between Phoenicia and Philistia had no natural harbors from which fleets might operate. Ships could stop in fair weather at some of the Hebrew coastal towns (*see* DOR; JOPPA; ACCO); and some coastal shipping was possible, as in the time of Solomon, when timber from Lebanon was brought in rafts to Joppa (II Chr. 2:16). As an agricultural people, whose roads, rather than seas, were the important lanes of commerce, the Hebrews tended to look inland rather than to the sea in the development of their culture.

When the Hebrews described the territory of Canaan, they referred to the Great Sea as its W border (Num. 34:6; Josh. 9:1). According to Josh. 15:12, for the territory of Judah, "the west boundary was the Great Sea with its coast-line." In a similar way the records of the military exploits of such Assyrian and Babylonian kings as Ashurnasirpal II, Shalmaneser III, and Nebuchadnezzar refer to advances that were made to the Great Sea or the "upper sea" (Mediterranean).

Although the Hebrews often referred to Yahweh's power over the RED SEA, they do not mention or imply very frequently a similar power over the Mediterranean Sea. Yet from the instances where it is reported that Yahweh causes a storm on the sea (Jonah 1:4), rules the raging of the sea (Ps. 89:9), and extends his power over the sea (Isa. 23:11), it is evident that Yahweh was thought of as having jurisdiction over the seas.

The extensive use of the Mediterranean by the Phoenicians and the Greeks was continued by the Romans, who referred to it as "Our Sea." Following the conquest of Palestine by Pompey in 63 B.C., traffic on the Mediterranean increased as merchants, envoys, soldiers, and teachers made their way back and forth from Rome to the Near East. Ships from Alexandria, loaded with grain, sailed for Italy, and when their captains failed to take account of the dangers from the winter storms for which the sea is noted, shipwreck was the prospect (Acts 27:6, 11). The development of traffic on the Mediterranean during NT times helped to make possible the missionary activity of Paul, Silas, Barnabas, and others.

W. L. REED

GREAT SYNAGOGUE. *See* SYNAGOGUE.

GREAVES [מצחה]. A protective covering about the shank of the leg. The only occurrence of the word is at I Sam. 17:6, where the armor of Goliath is described as including מצחת נחשת, which almost certainly should be plural, as in the Versions, to read: מצחות נחשת, "greaves of bronze." J. W. WEVERS

GRECIANS. *See* HELLENISTS.

GREECE [Ἑλλάς]; GREEKS [Ἕλληνες].

1. Biblical usage
2. Settlement of the homeland
3. Era of colonization
4. Early culture and religion
5. Age of kings and nobles
6. Rise of democracy
7. Crisis of the fifth century
8. Climax of Greek culture
9. Age of Hellenism

Bibliography

1. Biblical usage. In the OT a number of obscure geographical and ethnographical references have been interpreted to mean Greece or the Greeks, especially Javan, the fourth son of Japheth (Gen. 10:2, 4; I Chr. 1:5, 7; Isa. 66:19; Ezek. 27:13), and perhaps also Dodanim; Gog and Magog (Lydia?); the Philistines (*see below*); the "isles" (Cyprus, Crete, the islands of the Aegean?); and the "kingdom of the North" (the Seleucid Empire). The name Greece occurs explicitly in Dan. 8:21; 10:20; 11:2; Zech. 9:13; and Greeks are mentioned in Joel 3:6. In the NT, the KJV "Grecians" is now usually interpreted as HELLENISTS in Acts 6:1; 9:29, and as Greeks in Acts 11:20; elsewhere the KJV "Greeks" is retained (e.g., John 12:20; Acts 14:1; 16:1, 3, and elsewhere in Acts; Rom. 1:14, 16; 10:12; I Cor. 1:22, 24; Gal. 2:3; 3:28). John 19:20; Acts 21:37; Rev. 9:11 refer to the Greek language, which is, indeed, the language of the NT itself; while Acts 17:12 refers to Greek women in Thessalonica. The usage in Mark 7:26 ("the woman was a Greek, a Syrophoenician by birth" [RSV 1952; "race" in RSV 1946]), is not unusual, since in the first century "Greek" was a cultural term, not ethnographic, and meant anyone who spoke the language, somewhat as in Lower Canada "English" simply means non-French.

The obscurity of the earlier OT references suggests the wide gulf which separated the two civilizations, Semitic and Indo-European, the one occupying the S "grassland," the other the N—a cleavage which continued throughout ancient history and reached all levels of culture, especially intellectual, artistic, and religious. It gave the point to Tertullian's "What has Jerusalem to do with Athens?"—i.e., the church with Greek culture (Presc. Her. 7). Yet in the end both contributed to the civilization which followed, and to the rise of the Christian religion. Many modern scholars believe that their contributions were of equal importance.

2. Settlement of the homeland. The ancient Greek homeland comprised the S end of the Balkan peninsula, between the thirty-sixth and fortieth parallels (Philadelphia, Pennsylvania, is also on the fortieth), and between twenty degrees and twenty-five degrees in E longitude. But in reality the ancient Greek world included three main areas: the S part of the Balkan Peninsula, W Asia Minor and the islands of the Aegean Sea, and South Italy and Sicily; even in the sixth century the Greek settlements in South Italy were called "Great Hellas" (*Magna Graecia*). As with most other ancient peoples about the Mediterranean, the settlement of the Greeks was the result of invasions which began in prehistoric times, and then later of expansion due to colonization. The original population of the Aegean basin was already settled there by 3000 B.C. These were the "Aegeans," for their civilization was an island culture; but they also occupied the mainland to the E and the W. Into this area came the Greeks, a branch of the Indo-Europeans. Their four main stocks, in their order of immigration, were: (*a*) the Achaeans, who came down overland from the N and the E *ca.* 2000–1900 B.C. and settled chiefly in the central Peloponnesus (Arcadia) and in Thessaly, Boeotia, and the NE Aegean (the Aeolians in Lesbos and on the mainland N of Smyrna); (*b*) the Dorians *ca.* 1500-1200 B.C., who settled the E Peloponnesus and the Isthmus (Argolis, Laconia), Crete, the islands of the S Aegean from Cythera to Rhodes, and the SW corner of Asia Minor; (*c*) the Ionians, who occupied Attica, Euboea, the islands of the middle Aegean, and the mainland of W Asia Minor from Phocaea to Miletus; and (*d*) the Aetolians, who occupied W central Greece, the N Peloponnese, Elis, Aetolia, and the islands offshore. The records of these migrations were the unwritten legends and traditions, some of them embedded in popular myth; and it is possible that in the confusion of the early period some stocks occupied areas from which they were later dislodged; the division of territory just outlined is that of the ultimate settlement, in historical times. It goes far to explain the political disunity and rivalry which characterized later Greek history and prevented the establishment of a Greek empire, like those of Egypt, Assyria, Persia, and Rome. It is not yet certain in which order the invaders came, though the one just given is most probable, in view of the ultimate location of the various groups.

Another as-yet-unsolved problem is the relation of the invading Greeks to the older inhabitants (traditionally called the "Pelasgians") and, especially, to the Minoans in Crete. The decipherment of the Minoan script now indicates that its latest form was Greek—the earlier form had close affinities with Akkadian. But the character of the people, their customs, standards of living, sports, and art reflect a stage of development far beyond that of the invaders from the N, and have ties—or at least afford parallels—not only with Egypt and the East but also with Anatolia. Further, the relation between the Minoans of Crete and the Mycenaeans on the mainland (in Argos, Tiryns, Mycenae, and even early Athens) is still uncertain. Were these originally Minoan settlements? Or did the proto-Greek mainlanders, who settled in Greece during some earlier invasion than the Achaean, cross over to Crete and there establish a powerful thalassocracy (the "sea kings" of Crete, *ca.* 2000 B.C.) and develop a luxurious civilization comparable only to that of the oriental empires? Life about the Mediterranean was hazardous in those days (see Thucydides, bk. I), and the invading hosts from the N were desperate, urged on by the dual pangs of hunger for food and for land. Like the swarming Celts of later centuries, or still later the barbarian Vandals and Goths who swept down from Central and Northern Europe in the third to fifth centuries of our era, these early Greeks destroyed, absorbed, salvaged, or transformed whatever stood in their way. What survived was in many cases only a name; in others, architectural ruins, primitive religious rites, a mingling of racial strains, or surviving political institutions—e.g., city kingship, or the helots in S Greece.

Ca. 1200-1100 B.C. a Greek expedition conquered and destroyed the prosperous city of Ilium, or Troy, near the entrance to the Dardanelles or Hellespont, on the NW coast of Asia Minor. Earlier still, *ca.* 1400 B.C., the Greek invaders had sacked and destroyed Cnossus in Crete, the center of the Minoan civilization; the survivors were scattered all over the E Mediterranean, some of them eventually, in the thirteenth century, settling on a strip of seacoast in S Palestine—the people known as the Philistines, who in time gave their name to that whole country. Still another wave of Indo-European invaders, *ca.* 1200 B.C., swept down the original route, then finding the Greek Peninsula already occupied, crossed over and destroyed the Hittite Empire in central and E Asia Minor. The story of this chaotic period is told in moving scenes depicted on the Egyptian monuments (see J. H. Breasted, *Ancient Times*, figs. 152, 153, 233), where the Egyptian troops, aided by mercenaries from Sardinia, drive back the northern invaders. It may be that it was during this period that the Etruscans were forced out of Lydia in SW Asia Minor and settled in Italy, N of the Tiber.

3. Era of colonization. Eventually the Greeks settled down, built cities, cultivated the land, absorbed the survivors of the earlier cultures on the mainland and in the islands, and made the Greek language, though still—and always—spoken in a variety of dialects, the common tongue of the entire Hellenic world. The earliest Greeks were not a maritime people, but it was not long before the necessities of their new situation—the two mainlands E and W, Ionia and Greece, being divided and yet at the same time united by the Aegean Sea, studded with islands like giant steppingstones—compelled them to become seafarers. In time they became the best sailors in the ancient world. Another factor which turned them to the sea was their own increasing population (which may, of course, have led to the original migrations) and the demand for a greater food supply; this supply was to be had from the sea—the Aegean abounded in fish. But even a greater amount of food could not wholly meet the requirements, and so by the eighth century a tide of colonization was in full course. The distant coasts of the Black Sea, all the shores of Sicily, S Italy (from the "heel" southward and westward around the "toe" and northward as far as Naples—i.e., Neapolis or "new city"), Corsica, S Gaul (chiefly Marseilles = Massilia), even E and S Spain, North Africa (Cyrene), and the delta of the Nile—all these far-flung locations and areas were settled during the two centuries between 750 and 550 B.C. In every case the dialect, religion, customs, and institutions of the founding city and its ancestral stock were maintained. No colony was permitted to infringe upon the political or economic rights of the mother city. This led in time to great friction, as in the pretexts with which the Peloponnesian Wars began (in 459-446 and 431-404 B.C.), and perpetuated the disunity which prevented the Greeks from making a common stand against Carthage (in Sicily) and Rome (in Magna Graecia), with the result that the vast enterprise of Greek colonization came eventually to nothing, politically. On the other hand, the social, religious, intellectual, and cultural consequences of this vast expansion were of untold benefit throughout all later European and Western history.

4. Early culture and religion. The earliest social structure was the nomadic tribe with its council of elders, but this gave place to the city king, like the Mycenaean (even in Homer), with its inevitable consequence, the "city-state," the most characteristic of Greek political institutions. This was an area of land with a group of towns dominated by one outstanding city which laid claim to them and administered the territory as a separate state. The age of the kings (*ca.* 1000-750 B.C.) was a period of slow development of the arts and of commerce. At first the Phoenicians dominated the maritime trade of the E Mediterranean, even of the Aegean, but the Greeks soon learned from them the building and navigation of ships, the manufacture of potteries and fabrics, and—most important of all—the alphabet, which was the foundation of a written language and eventually of a literature. The Greeks perfected the Semitic alphabet by adding vowels—a vast improvement. This early Phoenician trade probably accounts for the traces of "orientalism" in the earliest Greek art—e.g., the winged sphinx, the Assyrian tree of life, the palm, the lion motif. The same influence, with similar results, may be traced in ancient Etruscan art.

The "literature" of the age was—like that of its later parallel, the heroic age in Northern Europe—the oral tradition of ballads and popular epics of wars, battles, horsemanship, adventure at sea and in distant lands. These provided the subject matter of the *Iliad* and the *Odyssey,* which were given final form by Homer (*ca.* 800-700 B.C.), as the tale of the last days of the conquest of Troy and the story of Odysseus' oft-delayed and far-wandering journey homeward to Ithaca.

Woven into the texture of these epics, and of the Homeric hymns and "epic cycle" that followed them, are the still surviving ideas, religious and social, of the "age of chivalry" which now lay far back in the past. Homer's gods are personal beings, very human in character—far too human, the later Greek philosophers and the early Christian fathers agreed in saying—but certainly a long way removed from the fetishes, numina, or vague spirits of a "primitive" age of animism. Supreme among the gods, who now dwelt on Olympus, was Zeus, the "god of the bright blue sky," who was at the same time the thunderer, the rain-bringer, the avenging god whose lightning stroke could blast and destroy. The ancient earth-mother, *Gē,* or the Great Mother (*Magna Mater,* as the Latins called her—originally she was their *Terra Mater*) of the ancient Aegeans and Anatolians, was also retained; she was the one who made the crops grow and rendered the soil fertile, bringing forth food for men and beasts—the goddess Demeter (or *Gē Mētēr*) was the patroness of the earliest grain-growing in Attica; her cultus lay at the heart of the world-famous Eleusinian mysteries, which later gathered to themselves high and noble ideas and ideals of ethics and the hope of a blissful life to come. Apollo, already the sun-god, the deadly archer; his sister, Artemis, the huntress, the swift and painless slayer of women, and eventually the guardian of mothers giving birth to children; Athena, the patroness of the arts of peace, the inventress of the carding, spinning, and weaving of wool, of pottery-making, and of the cultivation of the olive; Dionysus, originally a tree god, now patron of the vine; Hermes, the messenger of the gods; Aphrodite, goddess of love; Ares, god of war; Poseidon, the "earth-shaker," ruler of the seas; Hera, the wife of Zeus; Hades, god of the underworld (also called Pluto, the "wealthy" one); and Hephaestus, the Vulcan of ancient Greece—these were the chief denizens of Olympus, some of them native pre-Greek deities, some of them purely Greek, and some of them imported from the area of Anatolia or Cyprus.

The influence of Homer, whose poems, along with those of Hesiod, became virtually the "Bible of the Greeks," was far-reaching and long-lasting. To the very end of classical antiquity and even to some extent afterward, the conception of these "shining ones" enshrined in Homer's verse remained the norm for the Greek idea of deity and for all thought about the gods. To this epical panorama of divinity Hesiod added (*ca.* 700) the standard genealogy of the gods, in his *Theogony*—i.e., his account of their origin, birth, and relations to one another. As Herodotus said (II.53), it was Homer and Hesiod who invented the "theology" of the Greeks. What they really did was only arrange and systematize a body of traditional religious lore.

5. Age of kings and nobles. Following the age of the kings came that of the nobles, who, like the Italian nobility of the Renaissance, were too full of energy to live quiet lives as landowners, magistrates, or priests. The land of Greece, like that of Scotland or Switzerland, was broken up geographically into many glens or cantons, which tended more and more to preserve and cultivate their own dialectic, economic, and religious peculiarities. The mountains of Greece, and also the Aegean Sea with its many islands and archipelagoes, prevented the establishment of any lasting political unity or even any complete and permanent cultural solidarity. The four main divisions, from early times, were Argos and Sparta in the Peloponnese, Athens and Thebes in the N. Nothing like the great empires of the East, or even the limited empire of the Hittites (also in a mountainous region), was ever achieved, except for the brief Athenian sea empire following the repulse of the Persians early in the fifth century.

This geographical handicap is the background of the rise of the nobles (i.e., the well-born) and their unhindered advance in power, taking the place of the earlier kings (cf. the social parallel in Rome, after the expulsion of the Etruscan kings *ca.* 500 B.C.). These noblemen enjoyed their wealth and luxury, their vast lands and overseas trade, their occasional ventures in piracy (like certain European noblemen in the seventeenth century)—all at the expense of the poverty and misery of the peasants. Hesiod's poems also echo the cry of the oppressed poor, and the demand (like an ancient *Piers Plowman*) for justice and equality of opportunity, if not of inheritance. This period, like the classical period of the OT history, set the background and norm for all later religion in the Greek world: hence its importance for any true appraisal of the place of Greek religious thought in the "preparation for the gospel."

By 650 B.C. kingship had become unknown; by 600 B.C. the nobles also were on the wane—their place was taken by local tyrants, "new" men, without birth or background (like those in Cicero's day or in nineteenth-century England or America), who by sheer force of arms, strategy, cleverness, or terrorism seized power in the cities and administered them for their own benefit. The vast overseas expansion of the Greek colonies and the great increase in Greek manufacture and commerce, the continuing overpopulation and resulting restlessness of city-dwellers and peasants alike, in the Greek homeland—these factors gave the tyrants their opportunity. They promised all good things to the landless and hungry, freedom to the oppressed, restoration to the exiled; but, once securely in power, they forgot all these earlier commitments. However, in spite of tyranny and oppression, trade continued to increase and wealth to accumulate. Metal coinage had been adopted in the early seventh century, and within a hundred years a capitalist class was in evidence—men whose wealth was in money, not merely lands and goods, slaves, factories, or mines, and who were in a position to lend their capital at a high rate of interest—eighteen per cent was usual! As the poet Alcaeus remarked: "Money [not manners, as in a later age!] maketh man" (Fragment 81 Edmonds).

6. Rise of democracy. It was against this background of commercial middle-class capitalism, of rural poverty, of irresponsible government by the local nobility, and especially, during the sixth century, the rule of the tyrants—who were ancient "dictators" or "leaders"—that the democratic movement got under way. Laws were passed to check the power of individuals, but often without success. Some of the tyrants, e.g., were ostracized and sent into exile, only to organize a following and return to seize their lost position of control. However, the irresistible drive and energy of the Hellene surmounted all obstacles, political and economic, and the advancement of Greek culture went steadily forward, hand in hand with the demand for democratic self-rule.

The great lyric poets set forth the varying moods and longings, beliefs and standards, of their age: Pindar, the popular celebrant of athletic prowess in the games; Sappho, whose haunting love poetry still moves us deeply; Tyrtaeus, the Spartan soldiers' poet who sang of arms and the battle for liberty. Architecture and sculpture were developing rapidly in new directions, away from the earthbound, flat-roofed Egyptian temple to the more ethereal Greek style, with fluted columns, sloping roof, and decorated frieze; the crude painted wooden statues of gods and men were supplanted by majestic, permanent works in marble, also painted. The rise of Greek law was paralleled by nobler religious conceptions, with purer and higher ethical ideas which were applied not only to human relations but also to the gods, and also by the notion of a righteous judgment to take place after death in the court of Minos and Rhadamanthus. Gods could no longer do evil and be excused for it—like the wayward and capricious nobles they imitated; even the gods must do justly, if they are to deserve to be called gods. This principle, strongly affirmed a century later by the dramatist Euripides, was anticipated even in the sixth century, with its cry for social justice and agrarian reform. There was also a marked development in physical science, philosophy, music, mathematics, and geography. All this took place in the age of the tyrants, which ended *ca.* 500 B.C., the date which, as we have seen, marked the expulsion of the kings from Rome and the establishment of the republic.

7. Crisis of the fifth century. Scarcely had democracy gained its first permanent foothold in Greece than it was called to face its most crucial trial. Ever since 549 B.C., when Cyrus became king of Media, the Persian Empire had been pressing steadily westward. By 546 Sardes, the capital of Lydia in W Asia Minor, had fallen, and Croesus, its famous king, had become a prisoner. All the Near East was soon in the hands of Cyrus, the "Great King" (the later title of the Persian emperors); in 525 his son Cambyses overran Egypt, so that the Persians now controlled all of Western Asia as far as the Aegean Sea and the Hellespont, and Northeast Africa as well. On the European mainland, Thrace, including the W shore of the Black Sea and the N coast of the Aegean, was soon added, as was also Cyrenaica, W of Egypt. This meant that they now held a third of the Greek world (Ionia, the W end of Asia Minor), and it looked as if the whole Balkan Peninsula, whose S part was the Greek homeland, would soon be overwhelmed. The countless armies of the Persians, supplemented by mercenary troops and levies from all the nations of "the West" (i.e., W of the Euphrates) seemed irresistible. In 490 B.C. a huge fleet under Darius I crossed the Aegean from Samos, sailed into the straits between Euboea and Attica, and landed at the Bay of Marathon. Their guide was the exiled tyrant Hippias, son of Peisistratus, who hoped thus to regain control of Athens. The landing of the Persians sent a shock of horror throughout Greece. The Athenians hastily sent messengers to ask Sparta for aid in the defense, and mustered their comparatively small citizen army under Callimachus

—approximately ten thousand Greeks to face twenty thousand to twenty-five thousand Persians. The Greek general Miltiades, who knew Persian strategy at first hand, counseled attack as the best defense (a strategy now identified with the French general Foch), and led the Greeks to bar the Persian advance upon Athens. A thousand Greeks arrived from Plataea to augment the force of the defenders, and when the Persians finally advanced, the Greeks fell upon their flank and by a tactic of "encirclement" crushed their two wings and made effective the close-drawn line of Greek spears, against which Persian arrows were useless. The Persian defeat was complete. The Greeks had lost two hundred men, the Persians six thousand.

But the Persian threat to Greek freedom was not removed, and the Greeks, now fully roused, decided to adopt a policy of preparedness. Themistocles advocated a strong navy, in order to fend off any further attack by sea. In fact, the next Persian ruler, Xerxes, was fully determined to do this very thing, by the use of Phoenician ships and seamen. He also induced the Carthaginians, it is thought, to attack Sicily. Thus the whole Semitic world was poising an avalanche which was to descend upon all that remained of the world of Greek civilization. By heroic measures of persistence and persuasion, Themistocles induced the Athenians to prepare a fleet. Although all of Greece was asked to combine for the defense, only Athens and Sparta made preparations. The blow fell in the summer of 480 B.C., ten years after the first attack, and the Persian forces advanced both overland across the Hellespont and then southward along the coast, and also by sea, likewise along the coast. Against the horde of Persian infantry, the Spartan king Leonidas with five thousand men undertook to check them at the Pass of Thermopylae near the Gulf of Malia, *ca.* ninety miles NW of Athens. His allies promptly dispersed, leaving only three hundred Spartans to hold the pass.

But the Persians were not to be checked at one point. Led by a Greek traitor, some of their troops crossed the mountains and attacked Leonidas from the rear, wiping out this valiant and immortal band, and also sending two hundred ships around Euboea to attack the Athenian fleet from their rear. But a storm destroyed this Persian task force, and the Greek fleet withdrew to the Bay of Salamis, just W of Athens. Meanwhile the Persian land forces moved southward and soon set fire to the city of Athens; the roads of Attica were dark with the multitudes of dusky warriors from the East, as the Greek refugees looked back and saw their homes and the homes of their gods devoured by the flames—a scene as horrible as the burning of Troy or of Sardes. Themistocles now sent out a false report that the Greek fleet was intending to slip away and flee; but the Persians were determined to hold the Greeks in the trap—their main fleet now controlled both exits of the bay—and so Xerxes seated himself on a high throne overlooking the scene, prepared to enjoy it. Penned in, and desperate, the Greeks once more followed the strategy of offensive defense and attacked. Their smaller numbers and their more maneuverable ships had a decided advantage, while the huge mass of the Persian fleet, crowded together in a confused huddle and almost unable to maneuver at all, was soon at a decided disadvantage. The battle lasted all day, and at the end the Persian fleet was a total wreck, and Greece was saved. Fearing now that the Greek fleet would cut off his return via the Hellespont, Xerxes retreated northward.

If only the strategy of Themistocles had prevailed, the Persians would never have escaped—and all later history would have been quite different! As it was, Xerxes recrossed the Hellespont and returned to Persia, leaving fifty thousand men in Thessaly under Mardonius, who attacked again the following spring. But his easy victory in Attica was turned to swift defeat when the Spartans under Pausanias crossed the Isthmus and threatened his rear. He withdrew to Plataea, where once more the Greek spear proved superior, at close quarters, to the Persian arrow, and only the Persian cavalry saved the army from extinction. Mardonius himself was slain. The feelings aroused in this great crisis are forever enshrined in Aeschylus' drama *The Persians*.

8. Climax of Greek culture. The tragic element in human history is nowhere more evident than in the history of Greece during the following decades. The heroic stand of Athens and Sparta against overwhelming odds, and the surprising victory—some said the gods and the ancient heroes, e.g., Agamemnon and Ajax, had joined the struggle—should have led to several centuries of peace and unity; alas, the Doric strain and the Ionic were too inharmonious. Athens loved freedom, Sparta order; Athens culture, Sparta discipline; Athens creative talent, Sparta concentrated political power. Which was the better choice should be obvious: Athens is still a great city; a plain covered with olive groves hides the spot where Sparta once stood.

In the years following the Persian invasions Athens determined to follow an independent policy, not bound to that of Sparta. In spite of Spartan objection, Themistocles rebuilt the walls of Athens and fortified its port, Piraeus. The Athenian fleet was soon dominant everywhere in the Aegean. A democratic "empire" arose, centered in the Delian League —its headquarters were the island of Delos, sacred to Apollo. The triumphant citizenry of Athens soon got out of hand; the old struggle of the people versus the nobles was revived; the ancient courts (e.g., the Areopagus) were restricted in range and authority; the highest offices of the state were opened to all classes; and the citizen jury, with six thousand members, undertook to try all cases. Chaos threatened; but again a leader came forward—the brilliant Pericles, under whom Athens soon regained her ancient glory, and even far surpassed it. The buildings on the Acropolis, especially the Parthenon, dedicated to Athena, the presiding and protecting goddess of the city, are the permanent record of the achievements of this era. But alas, the administration of Pericles saw the outbreak of war between Athens and Sparta—the long struggle, in two phases (459-446, 431-404 B.C.), which ended with both contestants crippled and exhausted, and no match for the fresh crises which arose in the following century.

But it was the glorious age of Athens' greatest splendor. Wealth and power, partly derived from contributions by the allies in the Delian League

—now in reality the Athenian Sea Empire—and an abundance of slaves, artisans, foreign traders and craftsmen, artists, poets, philosophers, teachers (including the sophists), actors, athletes, military and naval experts, scientists, physicians, historians, religious teachers—these characterized and filled the Athens of this period. It was now the heart, soul, and mind of all Greece, indeed of the whole Hellenic world. Even peoples outside—e.g., the Romans—undertook to learn from Greece, at first only by way of imitation and translation, in later centuries by wholesale adoption and importation.

The greatest writers of Greece belong to this period—i.e., the fifth century and the early decades of the fourth: the dramatists Aeschylus and Sophocles, with their profound interpretations of the traditional religion and history of Greece, the ancient myths and legends, their deep reading of the meaning of human life in the light of this interpreted tradition; Euripides, with his criticism of every strain of falsity and pretense, whether in religion or in the standards of society, in politics or in the everyday behavior of men; Aristophanes, with his uproarious critique of his contemporaries in the kaleidoscopic *comédie humaine;* Menander, with his penetrating, Shakespearian insight into the inmost recesses of the human heart and mind; Socrates, with his endless questioning, determined to force men, especially young men, to find some surer standing ground of conviction than the fluctuating mass of opinion handed down by their ancestors, or the views of the majority, or the prejudices of their class (the well-to-do, for the most part); Plato, with his profound reinterpretation of Socrates as the prophet of a world of eternal reality, expressed in the "ideas" of things rather than in their material embodiment—i.e., in mathematical relations and ratios, in musical harmony, and in all the truth, beauty, and goodness in the world; and Aristotle, the first "universal" mind, a scientist, a philosopher, a logician, a teacher, an encyclopedist who took all knowledge for his field of interest and research, and placed all posterity in his debt by his organized investigations and analyses.

A little later these were followed by Zeno, Cleanthes, and Chrysippus, the great leaders of the early STOICS, who taught men to live, free and brave, in a world which threatened to crush all independent thought and action; by Epicurus, who taught men to find happiness in spite of misery (he himself suffered from kidney stone all his life), and to live quietly amid the turmoil of political chaos (*see* EPICUREANS). Much earlier had come the historians—Herodotus, the "father of history," who for all his objective and fascinating journalism took a psychological, even a theological, view of events, and studied the conflict between East and West, from the Trojan War to the Persian, as the inevitable struggle between two opposing and utterly different types of mind; Thucydides, a participant in the great conflict between Athens and Sparta as an officer in the Athenian army, whose clear, cool portrayal and analysis of facts set the standard of first-rate historical writing for all time; Xenophon, whose historical works enable us to see how the world looked—especially the Eastern world (in his *Anabasis* and *Education of Cyrus*)—to a Greek farmer and soldier of the fourth century. All these men and many more—not even mentioning the orators—were creative minds of the highest order; they belonged to these two centuries, the fifth and the fourth, and they show how little the political and social conditions of an age determine the manifestations of genius. How little, and yet how much: for surely no other city-state—certainly not Sparta, certainly no non-Greek city in that age—produced anything like this galaxy of genius, whatever its outward conditions of prosperity or adversity, war or peace, luxury or hunger. But it was produced in spite of the handicaps of political disunity, confusion, and eventually chaos.

In the W the course of events ran parallel to those in the homeland. The Carthaginian attack on Sicily failed; it is said that the Greek victory at Himera took place on the same day as the battle of Salamis. But the exposed position of Sicily and South Italy imperiled the Greek foothold in the W, and even after the defeat of the Sicilian Expedition sent by Athens against Syracuse in 413, the peril continued. It was not many decades before the W Greeks were caught between the contending powers of Rome and Carthage, with the result that from 264 B.C. all of South Italy, and from 241 B.C. all of Sicily, became Roman territory. *See* GREEK RELIGION AND PHILOSOPHY; RHETORIC AND ORATORY.

9. Age of Hellenism. In the East, the weakened state of both N and S Greece, as a result of the long Peloponnesian War, led to continued efforts by outside powers to overwhelm the Greek homeland. The Persians, twice defeated, undertook no further invasion; but what they had failed to accomplish by force of arms, they still hoped to achieve by intrigue. In this they were likewise unsuccessful, especially after Philip of Macedon defeated the Greeks at Chaeronea in 338 B.C. and made himself the champion of Greek interests everywhere. In 334 his son Alexander, who had been educated by Aristotle and was fully conversant with Greek thought, political as well as philosophical, and also with Greek literature (his favorite author was Homer), undertook a war of revenge against Persia—revenge for the conquest of the Ionian cities on the E coast of the Aegean and also for the assassination of his father in 336. The story of Alexander's conquest of Asia Minor, the Syrian and Palestinian coast, Egypt, Mesopotamia, Babylon, Media, Parthia, Bactria—in brief, of the whole Near and Middle East as far as the territories lying immediately beyond the Indus River—is one of the chief epics in military history. Darius III was defeated at Issus in 333 B.C. and again at Arbela in 331, after which Alexander became his successor as "Great King" of the East. His further conquests carried the Greek language, Greek traditions, Greek art, and Greek ideas to the borders of India.

Although Alexander himself died soon after his return to Babylon (in 323 B.C.), his decade of conquest had opened the whole East to the infiltration of Western ideas; the next three hundred years are known as the Hellenistic—or even the Alexandrine—age. Thus, stricken and defeated Greece, after only a century and a half of democracy (in Athens from *ca.* 500 B.C. to 338), passed on the torch of Western civilization and culture to new hands, which carried it to the farthest reaches of the ancient world. Alexander was followed by his generals and their successors, and his new-won empire soon fell apart, chiefly into three main divisions: Egypt, ruled by the Ptolemies; Asia Minor, Syria, and the East, ruled by the Seleucids; Macedonia, ruled by the Antigonids. In the early third century (282 B.C.) the kingdom of Pergamum freed itself, and in the East the Parthians and Persians broke away. By 198 Macedonia had fallen before the advancing Roman power, and in 146 it became a Roman province. In the same year Corinth was captured and destroyed by Lucius Mummius, and Greece became the Roman province of Achaia. It is thus known in the NT (e.g., Acts 18:12).

But the story of ancient Greece, tragic as it is in its later stages and in its end—i.e., politically and socially—was far from finished as far as its real meaning for mankind was concerned, and especially for the history of the Christian religion. "Captive Greece captivated her conqueror" (Horace *Epistles* II.1.156), and Rome eagerly absorbed all it could from Greek culture. Greek art and literature, Greek sculpture and architecture, were not only imitated in Rome and elsewhere in the West but actually transported there. Such Roman generals as Sulla and Lucullus took with them shiploads of artistic treasures. Even whole temples were taken down and shipped to Italy. (One of Sulla's ships was driven by storm to the coast of North Africa and sank in shallow water, where the stones of a Greek temple have been discovered lying on the bottom.) The Greek language and literature, Greek philosophy, and Greek religious thought and terminology, permeated the whole East, especially Egypt, Syria, and Asia Minor. As a result, the world was prepared, as the Greek church fathers insisted, for the coming of Christ and the preaching of the gospel. In Alexandria (founded by and named for Alexander in 331 B.C.), where the whole NE central quarter of the city was occupied by Jews, the Hebrew Bible was translated into Greek, and schools were established for the cultivation of Greek learning by Jews. Even Greek tragedies, epics, and books of philosophy were written there by Greco-Jewish authors. Such a work as the Wisdom of Solomon, written *ca.* 50 B.C., is an example of this process of cultural and religious cross-fertilization. Out of it all arose a whole religious vocabulary, centered in the SEPTUAGINT (the Greek translation of the Hebrew Bible together with additional books used in Alexandria), which the early Christians took over and used. Not only is the NT a Greek book, but all Christian literature down to the early third century, even in Rome and the West, and to this day in the East, is in Greek. What our grandfathers, using Baron Bunsen's term, called "the hand of God in history," is obvious, not only from the history of the Hebrews and of Judaism but also from the history of Greek civilization and culture. Both stories were tragic; but both Hellenism and Hebraism "died to live" and to pass on to the future the best they had achieved in the moral, intellectual, and spiritual adventure of ancient man.

Bibliography. W. S. Ferguson, *Hellenistic Athens* (1911); *Greek Imperialism* (1913). G. Murray, *History of Ancient Greek Literature* (3rd ed., 1917). R. W. Livingstone, ed., *The Legacy of Greece* (1921); *The Pageant of Greece* (1923). G. W. Botsford and E. G. Sihler, *Hellenic Civilization* (1924); *The Cambridge Ancient History,* vols. II-VII (1924 ff). M. I. Rostovtzeff, *History of the Ancient World,* vol. I (1926). L. Whibley, ed., *Companion to Greek Studies* (1906; 4th ed., 1931). A. E. Zimmern, *The Greek Commonwealth* (1911; 5th ed., 1931). J. H. Breasted, *Ancient Times: A History of the Early World* (1916; new rev. ed., 1935). C. N. Cochrane, *Christianity and Classical Culture* (1940). M. I. Rostovtzeff, *Social and Economic History of the Hellenistic World* (3 vols.; 1941). H. Bengston, *Griechische Geschichte* (1950). W. W. Tarn, *Hellenistic Civilization* (1927; 5th ed., 1952). F. C. Grant, *Hellenistic Religions* (1953). F. C. GRANT

GREED [בצע, COVETOUSNESS; GAIN; DISHONEST GAIN; EVIL GAIN; UNJUST GAIN; *also used participially* (Ps. 10:3; Prov. 15:27; Jer. 6:13; 8:10; cf. אוה *and* חמד)]. Various other Hebrew words are rendered "greed," "greediness," and "greedily" (I Sam. 2:29; Job 20:20; Ps. 57:4; Prov. 28:25; Ezek. 16:27; Hos. 4:8; Hab. 2:5).

In the NT, πλεονεξία (alternately COVETING; COVETOUSNESS) may be translated "greed," "greediness," or "greedy" (Eph. 4:19; I Thess. 2:5; II Pet. 2:3, 14; cf. I Cor. 5:10-11; 6:10; II Cor. 9:5).

Greediness often signifies an excessive longing for food and drink or avidity in the consumption of them. Such craving, whether for wealth or for food and drink, goes beyond reason and is an evidence of a crass sort of selfishness. It is regarded as a serious sin in both the OT and the NT. Greed is intolerable in the Israelitic priesthood (I Sam. 2:29), and in a Christian bishop or churchman (I Cor. 5:11; 6:9-10; Tit. 1:7). Unbridled greed leads to apostasy (Ps. 10:3), and to strife (Prov. 28:25). Jeremiah regarded the greediness of his people as a principal cause of their decline and impending subjugation to Babylon (6:13; 8:10; 22:17). Jesus warned against the danger of greediness (Luke 12:15), and Paul recognized it as a major sin (Rom. 1:29; Eph. 5:3). According to II Pet. 2:3, 14, greediness is one of the identifying characteristics of those false teachers who would mislead the members of the Christian community. H. F. BECK

GREEK LANGUAGE, THE. The student of the Bible is, for reasons which will appear, primarily interested in the Greek of the Hellenistic times, and therefore this article will be concerned almost entirely with that period.

A. *LACK OF UNITY.* The Greek language is not one language but many. It has been a "living" language—i.e., a spoken language—for more than three thousand years. Like all other living languages, Greek has experienced constant change. Therefore, the multiplicity is partly temporal, and it is possible to classify the Greek language in terms of periods of time. A useful—though very general—classification on this basis is:

Classical Greek	Before 300 B.C.
Hellenistic Greek	300 B.C.-A.D. 550
Byzantine Greek	A.D. 550-A.D. 1453
Modern Greek (or New Greek)	After A.D. 1453

The Indo-European family of languages, which includes Greek, has the common characteristic of reducing the number of forms as the centuries pass. In the early period the Greeks said, "I have been called up for service throughout the war," in only three words. This was done by adding prefixes, suffixes, and infixes to the stem of the words. This formation of words by putting parts together is called synthesis. In later periods they said this sentence with a series of words—as in the example given, where subject and tense and voice and purpose and duration have been separated from the stem and are expressed by helping words. This form of expression is called analysis. The Greek language has moved, through the four periods listed above, from synthesis to analysis. We are familiar with this movement in the history of our own language, which has moved from the synthesis of Anglo-Saxon, where the pronoun "that" had twenty-three forms in the singular number, to the analysis of modern English, where it has but one form.

However, the student of Greek must be constantly on his guard against the assumption that this trend is everywhere present in the same degree at the same time or that the change takes place at a fixed rate of speed in all generations. Language does not exist apart from individual human beings who use it. Some welcome change; some resist it. Moreover, historical events of a nonlinguistic nature have advanced or retarded change. In periods of political tumult —long-continued war, conquest and occupation by a foreign power, revolution, etc.—linguistic change proceeds apace. In periods of peace and prosperity with continued dominance by the same class or dynasty, linguistic change occurs but slowly. Solidly established schools (or, at least, established teachers) slow up change in usage. Thus schoolteachers today retard—though they cannot prevent—the extension of the use of "It's me!"

This leads easily to the assertion that diversity in the Greek language springs from diversity in cultural levels. There is a Greek literary language and a popular Greek language. In some periods these are close together; in others, far apart. In the classical period, Attic prose was not far from the spoken language of the day; but poetry was quite a distance from the language of conversation. In modern Greek, poetry early identified itself with the popular language, while prose strained after a purified form of the language. This tension between bookish language and talk has been variously resolved at different times and in different places.

Still a third diversity existed in the Greek language—particularly in the classical period. The Greek people spoke and wrote a number of local dialects. The spoken dialects were not easily understood by Greeks to whom they were not native. Yet strong forces drove the Greeks toward a common dialect. These forces, in an ascending order of importance, were commerce, literature, and empire. An instance of the commercial influence is reported by Quintilian (A.D. 35-95), who says that a mixture of Attic, Ionic, Doric, and Aeolic was called Sardismos—probably from Sardis. The Ionic dialect was for a time a common language of literature, including scientific literature. But the political pre-eminence of Athens gradually made the Attic dialect the literary language of Greece.

B. *HELLENISTIC GREEK.* 1. Origins. Scholars have suggested various hypotheses as to the sources of the Hellenistic Greek language, but more and more agreement has been reached in favor of the Attic dialect as its major source. Some scholars posit the existence of a business Greek language in the fifth century B.C. which was based on the Attic dialect with many non-Attic elements in it. The fifth century B.C. in Greece saw two common languages—one, Ionic; the other, Attic. The Ionic was essentially a literary language, but it had no empire to sustain or advance it. Since Ionia was related to the Attic Empire and since the Attic dialect itself was influenced by earlier literature, the resultant mixture of these two into a common language characterizes what we call the Hellenistic Koine.

2. Characteristics of Hellenistic Greek. Hellenistic Greek itself was not a single language. It contains two major divisions: literary Greek, which tended to be artificial in the sense that it was separated from the spoken language; and what is usually called Koine, or common Greek, which was close to the spoken language.

a. Literary Greek. Hellenistic literary prose was an artificial language to a marked degree. Every author used "learned" materials, both in vocabulary and in grammar, although the amount of use varied widely from author to author. From the first century B.C. on, the imitation of the Greek of the classical period, the Golden Age, is a definite and recognizable movement in Greek literature. This movement is called Atticism, and it consists essentially of the use of archaisms and obsolete or obsolescent forms. Atticism is due to the impact of classical literature and of the rhetorician's emphasis on style. If all our contemporary authors regarded Elizabethan literature as the norm in vocabulary, grammar, and syntax, we would have something analogous to the role played by Atticism in the Greek of the Hellenistic period.

No one can succeed in complete imitation of the language of a previous age. Among authors in the Hellenistic period the range of achievement in the imitation of classical Greek usage is very wide. This variation in the amount of imitation can be seen on a reduced scale within the pages of the Greek NT. The NT has less of this literary character than any other piece of literature that comes to us out of the Hellenistic age. Yet in the NT, Luke ranks highest in approximation of Attic usage; Revelation ranks lowest. Even within the limited extent of the NT, it is not possible to speak of Atticism as if it were a single thing constant in degree.

The attempt of literary and educated people to keep a language close to the standards of a day that is gone is always hazardous, but it was especially so in the Hellenistic period. This period was ushered in with the collapse of Greek independence and the establishment of the empire of Alexander the Great. Alexander's conquests carried the Greek language rapidly over large areas of the Mediterranean world. Alexander's championship of Greek culture was itself a potent force toward linguistic change, and this championship was one thing that all his heirs agreed in carrying on. The result was that in the early part of the Hellenistic period enormous numbers of people learned the Greek language in adulthood as a second language. For most of these people a limited knowledge of the spoken language was the maximum achievement, with the inevitable result of the loss of dialectical peculiarities and literary refinements.

A further factor that contributed to the simplification of the language was the political turmoil that characterized the centuries preceding Augustus. In the wars of succession and conquest, a stable, dominant, cultured class devoted to carrying on a high literary tradition was an impossibility, and in this social confusion free from restraints and barriers imposed by schoolteachers, linguistic change went on at a very rapid pace indeed.

b. Nonliterary or Koine Greek. The nonliterary Hellenistic Greek is usually called the Koine. This Greek word is actually an adjective modifying the word "language" or "dialect," and means the "common language" in a double sense.

The Koine is a common language in the first place in that it is the language of the common people who are not schooled men or littérateurs, but it should be admitted at once that the degree of commonness in this sense varies widely from individual to individual. There was no standard Koine. There was nothing like Luther's Bible in its unifying influence on the new German language. There was no one document produced in this period which was used everywhere and exercised a dominant formative influence.

This makes it exceedingly difficult to define the Koine in the sense of popular functioning. It cannot mean that the most illiterate production is the best Koine. There are documents among the Greek papyri in which practically all rules of Greek grammar are violated. Are we to characterize the Koine on the basis of such documents as a popular language that puts the subject of the verb in the accusative case? This is a ridiculous extreme.

To avoid this extreme, we must recognize that a grammar is not possible for the Koine as it is possible for Attic Greek in the classical period. In the popular Koine each author's grammar must be written. The best that a Koine grammar can do is to indicate the direction in which development is moving and what forces are at work.

This assertion is based on a definition of the Koine as "that popular Greek language of the Hellenistic period which shows life and development in comparison with the usage of the past." This implies clearly that he who would know the Koine must know earlier Greek as well. Otherwise, he lacks the base line from which the definition of the Koine moves. For this reason, students of Koine Greek and of the Greek Bible need a knowledge of classical Greek if they are to carry their studies beyond the elementary level or into areas broader than a very specific problem may delimit.

There is another definition of the Koine that is somewhat, but not much, broader: that it is the sum total of the development of the Greek of common and commercial speech from the time of Alexander the Great to the close of ancient history. This definition is broad enough to include Koine Greek with some literary quality—such as the writings of Polybius, Josephus, and the Wisdom of Solomon in the Greek OT.

But Koine in its meaning of "common" also connotes "widespread," "not restricted in area of usage." The Koine Greek is the common language of the Mediterranean world in the sense that it is not a dialect, restricted to a geographical area. No one has yet succeeded in writing a dialectology of the Koine. Attempts have been made to establish regional usages, but these have not been widely accepted by scholarship. The Koine has remained a common language.

Yet the original, native non-Greek languages continued to be used throughout the Hellenistic period. The Koine Greek was the bridge between these alien islands of language. It was in no sense the "King's English"; it was not even the language of the capital of the empire. Thus, it rested upon its practical usefulness rather than upon the universally accepted tradition of great literature or the imperial power of its homeland. This meant that it was open to modification to a very unusual degree but that most of these modifications went in the direction of clarity and intelligibility and simplification and adaptation to the spoken speech.

This nonliterary Greek was vigorous, alive, and fresh with the tang of everyday living. (See the discussion of the Koine in Colwell and Mantey, *A Hellenistic Greek Reader* [1939], pp. 5-7, from which the following paragraphs have heavily drawn.) Radermacher coins a great phrase when he says: "The Hellenistic Period loved the living expressions." This is the common element of all vernaculars. In the Koine it meant the use of the historical present in narration, the use of the vivid present tense for the future, the use of the perfect in a present sense, a preference for superlatives over comparatives and for direct rather than indirect discourse. There is a constant overstriving for emphasis characteristic of any naïve, unschooled author. The college freshman underlines at least one word in a sentence for emphasis; his narratives fall inevitably into the historical present. False emphases like "the very same," "each and every," "very unique," "one of the most," garnish his compositions; and they had their counterparts in the nonliterary Koine of the NT period.

The vernacular strives as hard for clarity as it does for emphasis. This leads to that overfulness of expression characteristic of the modern newspaper as of the Greek Koine. Pronouns are used as subjects for verbs that do not need them; they are sprinkled lavishly through each clause. Parenthetical glosses distend the body of innumerable sentences. Prepositions and adverbs pile up before and after verbs; compound verbs are preferred to the simple forms; prepositional phrases replace the simple case, etc.

The heavy emphasis and redundancy of the Koine is offset by its simplicity. Insofar as it is a language of the people, it lacks or ignores those subtleties of expression which delighted the great minds of the Golden Age of Greek literature. The loss of the dual and the optative is due not only to the general "tendency" of the Greek language to abandon inflection but also to the limitations of low-brow thinking. The simplicity of much of the Koine is due to the lack of subtlety and sophistication in its authors. That glory of Attic prose, a wealth of connectives adequate to express the most minute differences in the relationship of clauses, is one of the last elements of the language to be mastered by the modern schoolboy. In the ancient world the use of all these conjunctions was beyond the powers of the Egyptian merchant and the Roman soldier—not only beyond his ability but also outside his needs. Therefore the Koine knows few conjunctions. Its favorite is "and," and the paratactic style of the six-year-old describing a visit to the zoo frequently occurs. Co-ordinate clauses far outnumber subordinate in this as in many other vernaculars. If the Koine resembles Hebrew in this area, it does so in the same way that it resembles Anglo-Saxon.

Uneducated people simplify their language by selecting one of the many linguistic formulas available to them for a particular purpose. Take, e.g., the expression of purpose itself. In classical Greek there were at least half a dozen ways of expressing purpose. Two of these were the use of the infinitive to express purpose and the use of a conjunction, ὅπως or ἵνα, with the subjunctive mood to express purpose. In the nonliterary Koine the people chose ἵνα with the subjunctive as their favorite method of expressing purpose.

Interestingly enough, the use of the infinitive in the Hellenistic period shows contrasting trends. The infinitive was an ambiguous element in syntax—partaking of the nature of the noun but also definitely sharing some of the functions of the verb. The users of the literary Greek language in the Hellenistic period increased its use of the infinitive as a noun and maintained, to some extent, the use of the infinitive to express purpose. But on the other hand, the nonliterary Koine rapidly substituted dependent clauses for the infinitive. In the popular language in the modern period, the infinitive has almost completely vanished.

One of the common processes for simplifying language is the creation of new forms by analogy with the old. Thus in Hellenistic Greek an unusual form like the accusative χαριν was regularized into χαριτα, and so with many other forms.

Another cause of simplification was changes in pronunciation. By the second century A.D. such changes from the classical period were extensive. At least five vowels shared the pronunciation of the long *iota: iota, omicron-iota, epsilon-iota, upsilon,* and *eta*. The *iota* adscript lost significance in pronunciation. *Alpha-iota* became confused with *epsilon*. *Omicron* and *omega* lost their distinction, and in general quantities of vowels were ignored. The accent had changed into a stressed accent.

One result of these changes in pronunciation was the confusion in pronunciation of forms spelled differently. This led in time to the adoption of one of these forms to the exclusion of the others.

But the language of the people is not all simple and bare. Where a more sophisticated writer (at least in the Golden Age) would avoid the poetic and learned word in writing simple prose, the Koine author often belongs to a class that welcomes the most garish style with the reverent sigh, "He talks just like a book!" There is often a bookish flavor in the Koine; poetic phrases, archaic words, learned tags, are used to give it color.

This ancient Greek vernacular is beyond description except in paradox. Its language was robust but limited, vulgar but exalted by simplicity, bare but colorful; it was so varied as to make all generalities inaccurate when applied to it.

C. *SOURCES FOR KOINE GREEK.* 1. The Greek Bible. Any list of sources for the study of the Greek of the Hellenistic period is determined by the purpose of a particular study. For the purposes of this article, the most influential literature produced in Greek in this period is the Greek Bible. Within this body of literature the NT has the greater value as

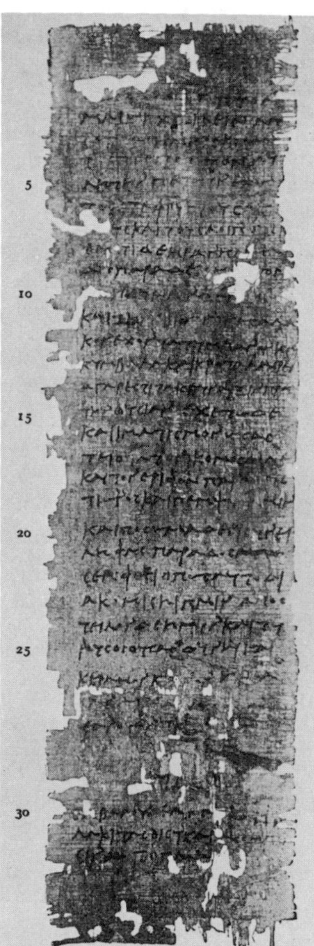

Courtesy of Hodder & Stoughton Ltd.

40. Letter from Demophon, a wealthy Egyptian, to Ptolemeus, a police official; a papyrus from Hibeh (*ca.* 245 B.C.)

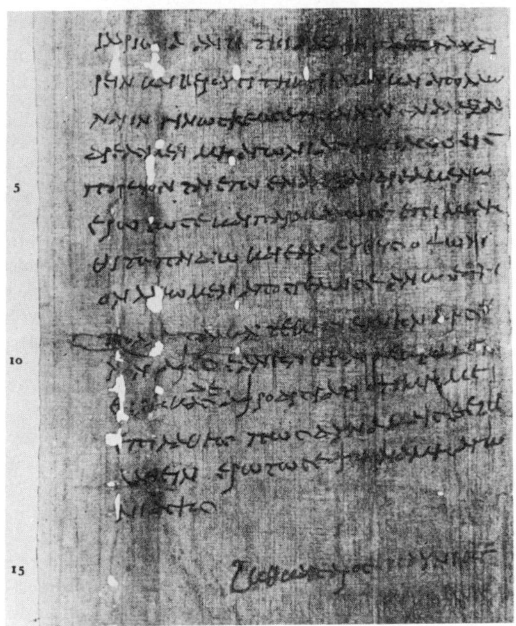

Courtesy of Hodder & Stoughton Ltd.

41. Letter from Hilarion, an Egyptian laborer, to Alis his wife; a papyrus written at Alexandria, June 17, 1 B.C.

being written originally in Greek, whereas the Greek OT is a translation. Since the Greek NT language is much closer to the nonliterary Koine than to the learned Greek of the period, this document itself becomes a primary source for the study of the language and, in turn, determines the selection of related documents from other writings of the period.

But before turning to the list of documents, a general word of caution against editors must be given. All the early printings of the documents from this period are suspect, for their editors were educated in the strictest grammar of classical Greek and in many instances changed the wordings of the MS sources to bring them into conformity with the Greek standards which they had been taught in the schoolroom. In the study of any of these documents, the student must look for a so-called "critical edition" produced in recent times with a frank report of linguistic peculiarities as they appear in the MS sources. In the case of the NT itself, this means the use of a text no earlier than Tischendorf or Westcott and Hort (*see* TEXT, NT), supplemented by the study of a critical apparatus that gives the variations in particular MSS. The first printings of the Greek NT are not dependable witnesses to spelling and syntax of the original Greek NT. In the church fathers the same thing is true. Migne's *Patrologia graeca* is untrustworthy, and critical editions of the church fathers—such as the series of the Berlin Academy, *Die Griechische Christliche Schriftsteller der ersten drei Jahrhunderten*—are to be employed. Similarly, in the early editions of the non-Christian writers, care must be taken not to be misled by the editor's "corrections" of the readings of his source.

2. Nonbiblical sources. Since the Greek Bible is of major importance in terms of current interest for the study of Koine Greek, a full discussion of the Greek Bible is postponed at this point. Here we turn to those nonbiblical sources which contribute to our understanding of the Greek of the Hellenistic period: Greek papyri, ostraca, and inscriptions. This is a grouping of documents according to the materials* upon which they are written. Papyri are documents written upon sheets of ancient paper, for the most part Egyptian. The ostraca are documents written on pieces of broken pottery, and the inscriptions are usually inscribed on stone. Figs. GRE 40-41.

There are, of course, literary documents written on ancient paper. The literature of the classical Greek period and the Greek Bible were at times written on papyrus, but we here eliminate all these literary papyri from consideration. Here our concern is with the so-called "nonliterary" papyri.

Among these documents we find, not only nonliterary material, but also almost illiterate material. Some of these documents are written by individuals who had little spelling and less grammar. These extremely "uneducated" documents must, of course, be used with the greatest care in generalizations about the Greek language in this period, but the number of documents is so great and the types of documents so numerous that these extreme cases can be ignored and still leave a tremendous body of material for study.

At least fifty thousand documents have been published in this field. There are personal documents, business documents, legal documents, official documents. There are family letters, love letters, orders to a tenant farmer, tax receipts, bills of sale, marriage contracts, divorce contracts, adoptions, wills, business contracts of all kinds—from a contract hiring an orchestra and dancers to a contract placing a boy as apprentice to a weaver; accounts from business of every type and from households, from temples, from government monopolies. There are records of lawsuits; there are court proceedings and judgments. In a word, these documents cover the range of documents in a complex society. For a list of publications that give an adequate sampling of these materials *see bibliography*.

Along with the variety in content goes the variety in cultural level. But generally speaking, these documents are closer to the spoken language of the people than they are to the Atticizing literary language of the period. One says this without denying that business documents are written with business formulas and that legal documents have their own legal formulas, and that in each you find the technical vocabulary appropriate to the content. Still the generalization remains: the nonliterary papyri are a valuable and extensive source for a knowledge of the nonliterary language and usage of the Hellenistic period.

In the case of the ostraca, the range of content is much narrower. These bits of pottery are the poor man's writing material, and they are used for accounts and tax receipts, particularly the latter, but not for very much else. Thus, while they have a contribution to make to the study of the Greek language, it is much more limited in scope than the contribution of the nonliterary papyri.

In the opposite direction, the same thing is true of the inscriptions. The inscriptions have a wider range than the ostraca and a much more limited range than the papyri. They are dominated by sepulchral and official inscriptions. They are usually formularized to a high degree. But there are exceptions to all these statements, and important linguistic material has been found in the inscriptions of this period.

Scholars have studied this material extensively for the light it may shed on our knowledge of the Greek language. There has been extensive grammatical study of the papyri written in the pre-Christian period. Grammars and lexicons have been developed with primary attention to the materials found here, but much still remains to be done in the writing of a grammar of the papyri in the Roman period.

3. The writings of Epictetus. Many students of Hellenistic Greek list Epictetus as the primary source for a knowledge of the nonliterary Koine. Epictetus was a Stoic philosopher born *ca.* A.D. 60, whose diatribes or sermons were recorded by his pupil Arrian. They are extensive in number, and they provide us with fine examples of the style of a popular lecturer at the turn of the first century A.D. There are striking parallels between Epictetus and some of Paul's writings, even in matters of style. Beyond this, in vocabulary, grammar, and syntax, these diatribes are a rich source of information for the nonliterary Koine.

4. Noncanonical Christian documents. The writings of some of the earliest Christian fathers have been formed by accident of publication into a collection called "THE APOSTOLIC FATHERS." These writings contain much of value for the student of the Greek of this period. They are available in a variety of editions.

The books that are often referred to as NT Apocrypha (*see* APOCRYPHA, NT) should be used in this study. The noncanonical gospels, acts, epistles, and apocalypses, particularly the acts that were produced in the late second and early third centuries, contain linguistic material of a high value. Much of this apocryphal literature comes out of popular Christianity, and it is closer to the language of everyday life than it is to the language of the schoolmen. The Acts of Paul, for example, contains much that is relevant.

It may be added that even the writings of the more sophisticated Greek fathers after the year 200 have something to contribute to our knowledge of the Koine.

5. Pagan authors. Beyond Epictetus, there are other writers of the period whose language, while not as colloquial as his, still contains many elements characteristic of the Koine.

Philo of Byzantium, from as early as the second century B.C., shows evidences of developing Koine in inflection and syntax and vocabulary. Radermacher, in his essay on the Koine, lists several dozen linguistic items of agreement with the nonliterary Koine. In some cases Philo changes from Attic usage to Koine usage; in some matters he stays with the Attic against the Koine.

Apollodorus the Mythographer is another writer of this period. Whether or not he is to be identified with the historian of the same name, his writings are to be dated not far from the beginning of the Christian era. He writes in the Koine—in inflection, in vocabulary, in spelling, and in syntax. In comparison with the language of Philo of Byzantium, the language of Apollodorus shows a decided descent to the vulgar speech.

The term "vulgar" applied to the Koine should not mislead us, for many writers of considerable culture and skill have "vulgar" linguistic elements. There are many writers whose works fall between the peaks of literary excellence and the valleys of vulgar speech. The writings of Artemidorus and the historian Diodorus are somewhat between Philo and Apollodorus on the one hand and Strabo the Geographer or Plutarch on the other. Nicolaus of Damascus, the historian, and Josephus should probably be ranked somewhere near Diodorus and Apollodorus.

It is clear that the available sources for an extensive knowledge of nonliterary Greek of this period are numerous, and that they range in value for this purpose along a continuum that reaches all the way to the writings of even such an Atticist as Dionysius of Halicarnassus.

D. *THE GREEK BIBLE.* The Greek Bible is today the most important book written in the Koine. Within that linguistic mélange, it is hard to locate it accurately. It is less common (in the vulgar sense) than the papyri; it is less literary than the writings of the Atticists. Generally speaking, Atticism has touched it but little, yet it has an "Atticism" of its own. Most of the OT is translation Greek, and for that large part the Semitic original was a sacred language to be changed as little as possible in translation. For the NT writers the Greek OT itself had a position of prestige analogous to that held by Attic in the esteem of cultured Greeks. Semitic elements entered through this detour, as well as through the primitive Aramaic elements in the authentic tradition of Jesus' teaching. Linguistically this volume, the Greek Bible, is a worthy representative of the variety of the Koine. Its individual books run the gamut from slavish translation to free composition, from the vulgar Greek of Revelation to the cultured Greek of the Wisdom of Solomon. In this as in many other aspects it gives a reliable picture of the contemporary Koine.

1. The Greek OT. The Greek OT is the most extensive work written in the Koine and the most varied in quality. There is more than one Greek OT. The best known is the translation known as the SEPTUAGINT—so called from the tradition that it was made by seventy (or seventy-two) translators. But there were several other translations with which the student should gain some acquaintance. The best known of these is Theodotion's translation (*see* THEODOTION), at the end of the second century A.D.—a revision of a Greek translation by the Hebrew text—which is well known because Theodotion's Daniel replaced the LXX Daniel in most MSS. Earlier than Theod., but more fragmentary, are two other Greek Old Testaments: the first, a slavishly literal version made about A.D. 130 by a Jewish proselyte named Aquila (*see* AQUILA'S VERSION); the second, which aimed at accuracy and at being good Greek, was made *ca.* A.D. 170 by SYMMACHUS, an Ebionite Christian.

Wurthwein unhesitatingly characterizes the language of the LXX as the "Koine, the common Greek language of the Hellenistic period." The number of Hebraisms and Aramaisms is relatively small. In general, the translation is not slavishly literal. Subordination frequently replaces the constant Hebrew co-ordination, either through the use of the Greek participle or through the use of subordinate clauses. As many as twelve different translations of a single Hebrew word can be found. Moreover, the translators occasionally Hellenized the concepts, and thus the language, of their Hebrew original. "The hand of Yahweh" became δύναμις τοῦ κυρίου (Josh. 4:24). Therefore, the student of the LXX cannot always find the clue to the understanding of the Greek in the Hebrew text—it may lie in Egyptian usages contemporary with the translators. But the closeness in translation varies from book to book and from section to section, as does the style and linguistic quality of the Greek. An objective and expert judgment of this diversity in style and idiom is the linguistic classification of H. St. John Thackeray in his *Grammar of the OT in Greek.* This is a rough classification into groups from the point of view of style. If the point of view were excellence as translation, the grouping would change considerably. A summary of this classification follows:

Translations

Good Koine Greek: the Pentateuch; Joshua (part); Isaiah; I Maccabees.

Indifferent Greek: Jer. 1–28; Ezekiel (except 36: 24–38); the minor prophets, I and II Chronicles (except the last few chapters of II Chronicles), I Kingdoms, II Kingdoms 1:1–11:1; III Kingdoms 2:1–21: 43; Psalms; Ecclesiasticus; Judith.

Literal or unintelligent versions (style akin to that of Theod. in many books): Jer. 29–51 with Bar. 1:1–3:8; Judges (in the text of Codex Vaticanus) with Ruth; II Kingdoms 11:2–III Kingdoms 2:11; III Kingdoms 22; IV Kingdoms; Song of Solomon; Lamentations; Daniel (in the version of Theod.); II Esdras (in the version of Aq.); Ecclesiastes (in the version of Aq.).

Paraphrases and Free Renderings

Literary: I Esdras with Daniel (in the LXX—in part); Esther; Job; Proverbs.

Free Greek—Works Composed in Greek

Literary and Atticistic: Wisdom of Solomon; Epistle of Jeremiah; Bar. 3:9 on; II, III, and IV Maccabees.

Vernacular: Tobit (in both forms of the text). Thackeray suggests that Tobit should perhaps be placed under paraphrases; he leaves open the question of whether or not Tobit had a Hebrew original.

The first part of the OT to be translated into Greek was the Pentateuch, the translation of which was begun about the middle of the third century B.C. The rest of the books of the Hebrew canon were translated from time to time, and it is probable that most, if not all, of them existed in Greek by the beginning of the Christian era. In the study of some of the Dead Sea Scrolls, F. M. Cross has found a Hebrew text of the LXX. This confirmation of the accuracy of our later copies of the LXX increases its importance for the study of the Koine, for it places it very early in the Hellenistic period, where the number of sources is not large.

2. The Greek NT. The Greek of the NT is the Koine of the first two centuries A.D. It is now generally agreed by NT scholars that the books as we have them were written in Greek. As was the case in the LXX, the quality of the language varies for two reasons: the strength of the Semitic element and the extent of the author's culture.

No one denies the presence of a Semitic element in the Greek NT. Its extent is vigorously debated. At the minimum, it must be admitted that all authentic sayings of Jesus in the Greek gospels are translations of an Aramaic original; that in the NT extensive quotations from the OT were usually made from the LXX; and also that the Semitic elements of the Greek OT were a Semitizing influence on the authors of the NT books. At the maximum this Semitic element has been claimed to include all four gospels and much of Acts, since a few extremists claim that these are translations of Semitic originals. Aramaisms or Semitisms can usually be paralleled in original Koine Greek, although a small number cannot. But frequency of usage of some of these surpasses their frequency in Koine usage. The general opinion as to the maximum extent of Semitic influence traces it back either to Semitic originals of a few sources or to the authors' habit of thinking in Aramaic while writing in Greek.

The variation in the cultural level of the various books is not as wide in the NT as in the Greek OT. No NT book is as Atticistic as the Wisdom of Solomon, although Revelation is as "common" in quality as anything in the OT. Revelation is certainly the least cultured of the NT books in language. Yet even it stands definitely above large numbers of the papyri. Matthew and Mark correspond roughly to what Thackeray calls the "indifferent" Greek of the OT. Linguistically John is not very far above the vernacular; but Luke, Acts, and Hebrews reveal a more advanced knowledge of the language. The identity of Paul's style with that of the contemporary Stoic preachers is now recognized, and James also has linguistic affinities with these popular preachers.

Radermacher's characterization of the Greek of the NT is illuminating. After emphasizing the uniformity of the Koine vis-à-vis geographical dialects, he claims that the lower degree of uniformity in the Greek NT is due to the strongly marked personalities of the authors. Yet their common theological interest was a unifying factor unknown to pagan writers in general. In declensions, verb inflection, and use of the article with names, the NT stands on comparatively high ground. But it is part of the nonliterary Koine in the extension in use of the infinitive with τοῦ, the extensive replacement of the infinitive by ἵνα (which does not occur in Hebrews, James, or the Petrine letters). In the use of prepositions the NT (especially John, Hebrews, I and II Peter, and Revelation) agrees with Epictetus.

The place of the Greek NT within the Koine is defined also by comparison with the Greek OT. This comparison is especially valuable if one's interest lies in the Semitic element in NT Greek. In general, the NT is living Greek to a much higher degree. The historical present is rare in the OT, but common in the gospels.

In the area of vocabulary, Radermacher claims that little is to be expected from comparing the NT and learned authors. But the establishment of the meaning of words in the NT must be sought in contemporary nonliterary Koine writings, in the papyri, and in the inscriptions. Older Greek sources can be used only with caution, since changes in meaning have now been established for many words. Later Greek usage in grammar and syntax often supports the NT. The wealth of comparable material is so great that a NT word's meaning is not to be accepted without some support in nonbiblical Greek.

In the discussion of the nonliterary Koine attention was called to some of the outstanding characteristics of the popular Greek language in the NT period. Practically every one of the characteristics listed there for the Koine is valid also as a characteristic of the Greek NT. In addition to these, attention may be called to the following usages in the NT: The comparative degree often serves for the superlative, and the superlative is frequently used in the sense of "very." The dual number is gone, and the optative mood is vanishing. Prepositions are more fluid in meaning and, as compared with the classical usage, are often confused in use. The future tense shrinks outside the indicative mood. Periphrastic verb forms have increased in frequency. Diminutive forms (always popular in vernaculars) are very common. The middle voice has lost ground to the passive and to the active plus pronoun. Rare inflectional forms tend to conform to the alternative dominant pattern. The accusative case has gained at the expense of the dative.

E. *THE DISCOVERY OF THE KOINE.* After the Christian movement had acquired educated leaders and entered the learned tradition of the Empire, it studied its Greek scriptures against the background of classical Greek literature and language. The constant and careful comparison of the Greek NT, for example, with these classical sources uncovered a long list of divergences in vocabulary, inflections, and syntax. In vocabulary, Thayer's revision and translation of Grimm's lexicon—*Greek-English Lexicon of the NT,* published in 1866—lists 450 words which occur only in the NT and have no parallel elsewhere. This list is a little longer than it should be, since Thayer's own lexicon includes parallels for a few of these words. These peculiarities were explained in one of two ways. In the first place, they were identified as "Hebraisms" due to the Semitic background of the Scriptures. In the second place, they were explained by the sacredness of its content. Thus, for example, in the matter of syntax a German scholar explained the peculiarities of NT usage as due to the influence of the Holy Spirit, so that NT Greek could be called the "language of the Holy Ghost." This scholar argued that the Holy Spirit changed the language of any people who received a divine revelation and that this adequately explained deviations in NT Greek from the usage of the classical period.

One man is to be given the credit for the discovery of the Koine—a German pastor named Adolf Deissmann. Even though one or two perceptive scholars had noted the true character of NT Greek as early as the middle of the nineteenth century, their statements made no impression on general opinion. Deissmann, on a visit to a friend in Marburg, found a volume of Greek papyri from Egypt, and leafing through this publication, he was struck by the similarity to the Greek of the NT. He followed up this observation with continued study, and his publications of his findings finally led to general acceptance of the position that the peculiarities of the Greek NT were, for the most part, to be explained by reference to the nonliterary Greek, the popular colloquial language of the period. He first published his results in two volumes of *Bible Studies* (1895, 1897) and later on in the justly popular *Light from the Ancient East* (1908).

His work influenced the brilliant British grammarian, James Hope Moulton, who championed the same position in his very influential writing and publishing, and also influenced grammarians in Germany, notably Radermacher and Debrunner. Many other scholars carried on the study of the Koine in the fields of grammar and lexicography. In NT lexicography Walter Bauer's work is still producing results. In his Introduction to his Fourth Edition (published in the Arndt-Gingrich Greek-English Lexicon) he lists twenty words which were not included in the Fourth Edition but which he has found in non-Christian Greek literature. He lists also twenty-seven items which appeared in the Fourth Edition as "Jewish peculiarities" but which have now been found in pagan sources. These most recent extensions of Deissmann's efforts are further tribute to his insight. Seldom in the history of scholarship has the work of one man been more influential in rewriting an entire chapter in the book of knowledge.

Bibliography. The OT text: A. E. Brooke and N. McLean, *The OT in Greek According to the Text of Codex Vaticanus* (1906—): this larger Cambridge edition repeats and improves in details the text made familiar to students for some years in the manual edition of H. B. Swete; in this larger work, the text is supplemented by the evidence of a valuable selected apparatus, which includes all the uncials, all early versions, much important patristic evidence, and a small group of minuscules. E. Wurthwein, *Der Text Des Alten Testaments* (1952), is a fine brief summary of current scholarly information on the study of the Greek OT.

The NT text and studies: C. Tischendorf, *Novum Testamentum Graece . . . editio critica octava maior* (1869-72)—a critical text with a good apparatus, now antiquated by subsequent discoveries; the text is, in general, similar to that of Westcott and Hort. B. F. Westcott and F. J. A. Hort, *The NT in the Original Greek* (vol. I: *The Text;* vol. II: *Introduction and Appendix;* 1882), has practically become the standard text of the Greek NT in England and, to a lesser degree, in America; the text itself has no critical apparatus, but the second volume gives a classic discussion of methods and principles of textual criticism; the lexicon by Hickie, which is often bound with the text, is not recommended. H. von Soden, *Die Schriften des Neuen Testaments in ihrer ältesten erreichbaren Textgestalt* (vol. I, 1902-10; vol. II, 1913): Von Soden's theory of the history of the text has been severely criticized and generally repudiated by scholarship; as a result, his text has not been accepted for scholarly study, but his work is an invaluable introduction to the study of the medieval MSS of the NT. A. Rahlfs, *Septuaginta* (1935), appears in a two-volume student edition and a one-volume de luxe edition; the text is based on the three older MSS as a primary source, but much additional evidence is given in the apparatus; the volumes of this work as they are published by the Göttingen LXX Society are the result of the most thorough study of the text of the LXX. E. Nestle, *Novum Testamentum Graece cum apparatu critico curavit* (22nd ed. by Erwin Nestle, 1956), is the best edition for classroom use. It gives variant readings in a critical apparatus which is periodically revised. It contains the evidence of the Beatty and other papyri and Codex Koridethi. Cross references are given in the margins, OT sources being identified. Verse divisions are plainly indicated. Most of the equipment of the medieval Greek MSS is reproduced. The text is derived from those of Weiss, Tischendorf, and Hort; it is quite close to that of Westcott and Hort. A. Debrunner, *Friedrich Blass' Grammatik des neutestamentlichen Griechisch* (7th ed., 1943), is the best of the formal grammars of the Greek NT; the same author's *Geschichte der Griechischen Sprache. II Grundfragen und Grundzüge des Nachklassischen Griechisch* (1954) is brief but valuable, and contains good bibliographies. L. Radermacher, *Koine* (1947); *Neutestamentliche Grammatik: Das Griechisch des Neuen Testaments im Zusammenhang mit der Volkssprache* (2nd ed., 1925)—the latter is not a formal grammar but a most interesting discussion in essay form, which integrates NT usage in the popular language of its period. J. H. Moulton, *A Grammar of NT Greek,* vol. I: *Prolegomena* (1908), is still the most valuable general discussion of NT Greek in English; his *Introduction to the Study of NT Greek* (5th ed., rev. H. G. Meecham, 1955), is the best of the Introductions; with this is bound "A First Reader in NT Greek." C. F. D. Moule, *An Idiom Book of NT Greek* (1953), is a worthy supplement to J. H. Moulton's work.

Good lexicons are: H. G. Liddell and R. Scott, *A Greek-English Lexicon* (ed. H. S. Jones and R. McKenzie; 1940), the standard lexicon for the study of Greek of the classical period. J. H. Moulton and G. Milligan, *The Vocabulary of the Greek Testament Illustrated from the Papyri and Other Non-Literary Sources* (1942), contains extensive quotation of parallels to NT usage. *A Greek-English Lexicon of the NT and Other Early Christian Literature,* trans. and ed. by W. F. Arndt and F. W. Gingrich from W. Bauer's *Griechisch-deutsches Wörterbuch zu den Schriften des Neuen Testaments und der übrigen Urchristlichen Literatur* (1957), the best lexicon for students of the Greek NT.

A brief general discussion of the language of the NT by B. M. Metzger appears in *IB,* VII (1951), 43-59.

E. C. COLWELL

GREEK RELIGION AND PHILOSOPHY. This article deals chiefly with the new forms of religious life and the new lines of philosophical speculation and ethical theory which developed in the Greek world following the conquests of Alexander the Great (died 323 B.C.), through the last three centuries before Christ and the first centuries of the Christian era.

1. Introduction
2. The old gods and the old cults
3. Personal religion: private associations
4. Oriental religions in the Greek world
   a. Egyptian cults
   b. Anatolian cults
   c. Syrian cults
   d. Persian cults
5. The mystery religions
6. Ruler-worship and deification
7. Fortune and Fate; astral religion and astrology; magic
8. The philosophical schools
   a. Decline of the older schools; Skepticism in the Academy
   b. The Cynics
   c. The Stoics
   d. The Epicureans
   e. Theosophy and Gnosis

Bibliography

1. Introduction. The rise of Macedon put an end to the independence of the Greek city-states; after the Battle of Chaeronea (338 B.C.), which left Philip of Macedon undisputed master of the whole Greek Peninsula, they were nothing more than municipalities within an empire governed by a military autocrat.

But the loss of political independence did not carry with it the extinction of Greek civilization. On the contrary, the Macedonians, victorious in the struggle for the mastery of Greece, made themselves the standard-bearers of the culture which the city-states, especially Athens, had brought to incomparable peaks of glory. Alexander the Great had his imagination fired by the exploits of the Homeric warriors, and thought of himself as a new Achilles, destined to lead the Greeks to victory over an infinitely greater Troy. The Greek philosopher Aristotle was Alexander's tutor. Every movement of his armies was preceded and followed by sacrifices to the Greek gods. In the realm of the spirit, Macedon was a province of conquered Greece. By the middle of the third century, the Macedonian dialect had given way to the Common Greek, now an international language, as completely as any of the regional dialects of the peninsula and the islands. New cities, largely peopled with Greeks and Macedonians, partly colonies of veterans, partly settlers from the homeland, were founded all over the East. Thousands upon thousands of Greeks proved ready to emigrate to the new foundations, to take advantage of the glowing opportunities offered to the tradesman, the artisan, the architect, the musician, the sculptor, and the administrator. Settlers of other nations also came, but were quickly assimilated to the Greeks, adopting the Greek language and giving their children a Greek education. Even the Jews, who could not be wholly assimilated, so far forgot their native language that translations of their scriptures had to be made into Greek for their benefit.

The effects of Hellenization made themselves felt as far E as Bactria and India, and extended ultimately to China and Japan; but it was in Western Asia and in Egypt that the process was carried on most intensively. In these regions, Macedonian rulers maintained their power for from two to three centuries. Alexandria in Egypt, the greatest of the new foundations, rose to the commercial and scientific leadership of the whole Greek world. New Greek cities in Asia Minor, Syria, and Mesopotamia—the Antiochs, the Seleucias, the Attaleias, the Stratoniceias, the Philadelphias—became flourishing centers of Greek cultural, as well as commercial, activity. The incorporation of these regions into the Roman Empire brought no break in the continuity of culture, for Greek continued to be the official language in Rome's eastern provinces, and the civil service was almost wholly manned by Greeks.

The movement of traffic did not flow always in the one direction. For nearly two centuries, indeed, the brilliant culture of Greece seemed to win an easy dominance, promoted as it was by the policy of the kings and supported by the technical superiority of the Greeks in almost every field that required skill and ingenuity. But the kingdoms of the Ptolemies and the Seleucids were the heirs of cultures more ancient than the Greek, and the latent resources of the Orient were not long in coming into play. By the middle of the second century B.C., the native forces of Syria, Babylonia, Persia, and Egypt were making themselves felt with ever-increasing force.

Even before the time of Alexander, oriental cults had begun to secure a following in the Greek homeland, and they now began both to revive in their own regions and to expand westward, not only into Greece but also to Rome and ultimately to Rome's western provinces as well.

The result was a wide and deep fusion of Greek and oriental elements to form a mixed culture, which we call "Hellenistic" or sometimes "Greco-Roman" —inaccurately, for it is really Greco-oriental—in which the oriental becomes more and more dominant, even though the language which carries it continues to be Greek. In religion, the great characteristic of the period is syncretism, the fusion of cults and the identification of the gods of one nation with those of another, with the corresponding growth of a tendency toward monotheism, often taking the form of a solar pantheism, and the doctrine that all the gods of the nations are variant manifestations of the one divine power that rules the universe. The astral religion of Babylonia wins a wide adherence, and in its wake comes astrology, with its dead weight of fatalism, inevitably promoting recourse to magic to break the chains of fate, or to mystery initiations to deliver from its power. In philosophy, the dominant school is Stoicism, first taught by the Phoenician Zeno, and always far more Semitic than Greek in spirit. All the schools are characterized by individualism and its complementary universalism; they are essentially philosophies of conduct, based on despair of the world as it is, concerned to teach man how to live as an individual in the cosmos, a citizen of a world-state which never existed and never could exist. And in the later stages, culminating in Neoplatonism, they tend more and more to detach man altogether from mundane things and to bid him seek his fulfilment in another world, the world of pure spirit, in ecstatic union with the divine.

2. The old gods and the old cults. The emergence of significant new forms of religious expression in the Greek world and the growth of personal religion must not blind us to the solid fact of the continued vitality and even resurgence of the traditional religion during the same period. The sense that all nature was instinct with divinity showed no signs of fading; the ancient tokens of reverence were still paid to the manifold spirits of wood and stream, fountain and cavern, sea and hill; the primeval rites of the family and of the farm—of birth, puberty, marriage, and death, of seedtime and harvest—were maintained unchanged. The civic religion was likewise observed in most of its forms. Though undermined by the criticisms of the philosophers and sophists, and shaken by the fall of the states which had looked to them for protection, the old gods continued to receive on a grand scale the public worship of the Greek communities.

Every effort to restore the fabric of the city-states was accompanied by at least as much care for the renewal of the public religion as for the restoration of the finances and the limited rebuilding of the armed forces that was permitted. Every city continued to provide for the regular sacrifices to its tutelary deities and for the priesthoods which offered them. Zeus Polieus and Athena Polias, warders of the city, are not abandoned by their worshipers simply because they have failed to protect them from their enemies; or at least, the loss of faith is not reflected in any diminution of the public cult. In the old cities, indeed, little energy is shown in the building of new temples; the temple of Zeus Olympius at Athens, begun *ca.* 300 B.C., was not completed until the Emperor Hadrian took it in hand more than four hundred years later. But Greek architects and masons were busy with the construction of new temples to the Greek gods in all the new foundations of Alexander and of the Macedonian dynasts who followed him. The immense altar of Zeus at Pergamum (the "Satan's throne" of Rev. 2:13), built by Attalus I to commemorate his victories over the Gauls, exceeded in magnificence any Greek altar of earlier times. In Syria, the Seleucid kings adored Apollo as the patron of the dynasty and honored him with statues, temples, and groves. In Egypt, it was Dionysus who received special honors from the ruling dynasty, and one of them (Ptolemy IV Philopator) was prepared to resort to persecution to advance his policy of identifying Dionysus with the high gods of his subjects, including the God of Israel. The Greeks who settled abroad were ready enough to worship the local divinities, but they did not for that abandon their own ancestral gods.

Zeus especially attained a matchless renown. In philosophy, his name became the symbol for the very idea of divinity; and in cult he was identified with the high god of every nation—with Sabazios in Phrygia, with Hadad in Syria (Zeus-Adados), with Amon-Re in Egypt, with the Hittite deity Teshub at Doliche in Commagene (Zeus Dolichenos), and with a host of lesser divinities. It was the attempt to establish him in the temple of Jerusalem as Zeus Ouranios (Baal-Shamem), by identification with the God of Israel, which precipitated the revolt of the Maccabees.

In all parts of the Greek world, festivals flourished. Athens continued to observe the Panathenaea and the Greater and Lesser Dionysia, and revived in greater splendor the quadrennial Delia. Toward 200 B.C., Magnesia on the Meander consecrated its territories to its gods, restored its main temples, and established new annual and quadrennial festivals, with games and sacrifices, to which all the Greek cities were invited to send participants. The same kind of thing was happening everywhere; a list of the new festivals would fill a column.

The old Greek religion had suffered severe blows, but it was far from ready to die. If other proof of its vitality were needed, it would be seen in the fact that after displacing the ancient Phoenician religion at Carthage in the fourth century, it transformed the whole structure of Roman religion from the middle of the third century onward. Jupiter is recast in the image of Zeus;* Minerva becomes a Roman Pallas; the unimportant Roman water numen Neptune takes on the stature of the mighty Poseidon; and so through the whole pantheon. Images of the Roman gods are created on the Greek models, and Greek rites previously unknown to the staid practices of ancient Rome are introduced on a grand scale. In the first Christian century, Paul traveled through cities filled with images and altars; and a hundred years after him, Pausanias describes a Greek world which in the outward aspects of religion, at least, showed no sign of decay of its old cults. Fig. ZEU 2.

3. Personal religion: private associations. There is evidence, nonetheless, that the religious needs of the time could no longer be wholly satisfied within the compass of the old cults of city, phratry, and tribe. Before the time of Alexander, it had been a risky business for a citizen to profess a private religion; the authorities looked upon such a thing as outright sedition. In the Hellenistic period, on the other hand, we observe a remarkable growth of private religious associations which stand apart from the organized structure of the civic religion. These cult groups (θίασοι, ἔρανοι) were of various kinds. Some of them were almost of the nature of guilds—of merchants, of artists, of musicians, of old schoolfellows; and in these the religious interest was generally subordinate to the social, though each group had its temple and altar and paid its devotions to the god of its choice. There were many, however, which were formed for no other purpose than to worship the particular god to whom they were consecrated. Sometimes they would choose one of the old Greek gods as the object of their devotion—Athena, Apollo, Hermes, Poseidon; more frequently Aphrodite; and most frequently of all, Dionysus, whose cult offered an ecstatic escape from the ugliness and despair of the times in the abandonment of the mystic. But even more significant is the number of associations that were formed for the worship of an alien god. A thiasos of the Egyptian Ammon is found at the Piraeus early in the third century; fifty years later, we hear of an association of worshipers of Serapis; within the next generation Serapis is joined by Isis and Anubis, and in the following century by Harpocrates (Horus the Child). The Phoenician Adonis and the Great Mother from Phrygia have each a thiasos which worships them under their native rites. The islands of Delos and Rhodes were as hospitable as Athens. The Egyptian gods were worshiped there by their thiasoi in the third century; and the Syrian goddess Atargatis, identified by the Greeks with Aphrodite, probably was introduced into Delos long before the building of the temple which was dedicated to her in 128 B.C. Serapis and Isis had their groups of devotees in almost all the islands of the Aegean; and the deities of Syria and of Asia Minor were scarcely less popular.

Some of the cities, notably Athens, passed legislation from time to time to regulate the activities of these cult associations, but it was seldom that they were taken under the control of the community and made part of the official religion. Membership in them was always voluntary, and consequently involved a more personal relationship to the god and a more active participation in the rites of worship than could be found in the state cults. They afforded an avenue of religious expression and a measure of satisfaction of religious aspirations and needs which the established cults could not provide. In some cases they overcame the barriers of tribe and family, of race and social status. Thracians and Libyans, Phrygians and Syrians, could be members of thiasoi which were largely made up of Greeks; and some associations admitted slaves. The common worship of the patron divinity created a new tie of brotherhood and a sense of fellowship which was no longer felt in attachment to the city or the tribe, and which was open to men who had abandoned these attachments by migrating abroad. In many of them, the bond was sealed and maintained by sacramental rites. In the long perspective of history, their chief significance lies in the fact that they were the channels by which the oriental religions found entrance into the Greek homeland and so began their momentous penetration of the Western world.

4. Oriental religions in the Greek world. The victorious expansion of the oriental religions is one of the most conspicuous features of the age. The first place among them belongs to the cult of Serapis, with whom is associated the ancient Egyptian goddess Isis, who gathers to herself the cults of numerous mother goddesses of Greece and Asia and becomes the prototype of the Christian Madonna. Next come the Syrian and Babylonian religions, manifold in form and character, which carry the worship of the sun and the heavenly bodies and the deadly superstitions of astrology over the whole Mediterranean world. A number of Anatolian cults—of Sabazios, of Men-Tyrannos, of the Great Mother, of the Ephesian Artemis—also win devotees abroad. Iranian elements are contributed to the vast amalgam from an early period, but the great advances of Mithraism belong to a later time.

a. Egyptian cults. The god Serapis is from the beginning a compound deity, partly Egyptian and partly Greek. His cult was introduced in Egypt by the first Ptolemy in the later years of the fourth century. According to legend, Ptolemy was commanded in a dream to fetch the god—that is, his image—from Sinope in Pontus, where he was worshiped as a god of the underworld by all the coastal peoples of the Euxine. At Memphis he was identified with Osiris, the Egyptian lord of the realm of the departed, and associated with the cult of the Apis-bull; his name, which is found early at Memphis in the form "Oserapis," is clearly a Greek transliteration of the Egyptian Oser-Hapi (Osiris-Apis). A magnificent cult statue was designed for him by the Greek sculptor Bryaxis, who drew upon the classical types of Zeus, Hades (Pluto), and Asclepius, and set on his head as a crown the modius, a round corn measure. He is thus from the beginning conceived as a universal god, lord of the underworld as of the heavens, healer of diseases and giver of corn and wine, and able to offer his worshipers a blessed life beyond the grave. Later we find him identified with the sun-god, and bearing such compound titles as Zeus Helios Great Serapis. In the ordering of his cult, the Eumolpid Timotheus, one of the hereditary guardians of the Eleusinian mysteries of Demeter, was brought from Eleusis to be associated with the Egyptian priest Manetho; this would suggest that elements of the Eleusinian ritual were incorporated into the liturgy, which in the main appears to have been translated from the Egyptian formulas of the Osiris cult. The great Serapeum constructed at Alexandria by Ptolemy was built on the Egyptian pattern, and the priesthood was at first purely Egyptian, of sacerdotal race; but the devotees were nearly all Greeks, Macedonians, and other foreigners. Among them, the new cult had immediate and enduring success. The first hymns to Serapis are said to have been composed by the scholar-statesman Demetrius of Phalerum, who had been cured of blindness by the god. The court poets joined in his praises, and a vast literature quickly grew up, telling of his "philanthropia."

The cult of Serapis was carried into the Greek homeland in the first instance by Greeks returning from Egypt. In the islands of the Aegean and in Asia Minor, it may have been promoted by the Ptolemies in support of their imperial aims; but most of the early sanctuaries are surprisingly modest constructions, and it is more than likely that the cult owed its rapid spread mainly to the zeal of its followers, organized in the private associations mentioned above. In the course of the third century B.C., Serapis has his worshipers in nearly all the Greek coastal cities and in Boeotia, in many parts of Asia Minor and on the shores of the Euxine. In the second century, he makes his way eastward into Babylonia and even to India, and westward to S Italy and so to Rome. In the face of prolonged and determined opposition from the Roman authorities, the cult continued to win adherents in the capital and in all Italy, until at last the Flavian emperors and after them the Antonines and the Severi were glad to lend it the countenance of the court and even to walk in its processions.

Once established in Greek and Roman territories, Serapis opened the way for the goddess Isis, who proved to have a far greater popular appeal. In the old Egyptian religion she was the sister and wife of Osiris, faithful and true, who sought and gathered together the fragments of his corpse, dismembered by his enemy Set (Typho), and by her magic powers restored it to life; and by him she conceived and bore Horus, who overcame Set and avenged his father. Among the Greeks, she became the great goddess of the sea, the kindly and powerful protector of sailors; and she somehow gathered to herself all the female deities of the eastern Mediterranean. In the aretalogies she is identified with Artemis, Aphrodite, Demeter, Hecate, Hera, Hestia, Astarte, Nanai, the Great Mother, and many lesser divinities. She is hailed as the mistress of every land, the queen of heaven, the star of the sea, the diadem of life, and by many other epithets; she is Health, Fortune, Righteousness; she is "Isis of ten thousand names" (μυριώνυμος). It is she who has established among men all the arts and crafts, all the institutions of social life, the rites of religion, and the principles of morality; she is the perpetual helper of the human race; and she has power over Destiny (Heimarmenê)—her worshiper is set free from the bondage of fate, and she can even prolong his life beyond the appointed limits.

The Isis cult offered gaudy public ceremonies to attract devotees and impressive secret rites to bind them to the service of the goddess. The two great festivals of the year were the Heuresis (εὕρεσις; Latin *inventio*), the Finding of Osiris, in the autumn; and the Launching of the Ship (πλοιαφέσια; Latin *navigium Isidis*) in the spring, at the opening of navigation. At the Heuresis, the worshipers witnessed and participated in the dramatic re-enactment of the death of Osiris at the hands of Set, the sorrowful search of Isis for the members of her husband, and her joy in finding him and restoring him to life. The action ends with the proclamation of the priest: "Be of good cheer, O Mystae! now that the god has been saved; for there shall be salvation for you out of your distresses" (Firmicus Maternus *De Errore Profanarum Religionum* 22). At the Launching, a carnival-like procession with flowers, lamps and torches, flute players and choirs of singers, devotees clad in linen and carrying sistra, priests bearing the insignia of the goddess, with images and sacred animals, made its way through the streets to the harbor and committed the sacred bark of Isis to the sea. It then returned to the temple, where the scribe read prayers for ships and seafarers, for the state and its rulers. After that, all kissed the feet of the goddess and so went home. Throughout the year, sacrifices were offered to the goddess daily, and private offerings could be presented at any time. Her temples were open for prayer and meditation, and—unique in the ancient world—benches were arranged before the images for the use of her adorers.

The public cult was supplemented by private disciplines resembling a penitential cure of souls. The Roman satirist Juvenal, bitterly hostile to all oriental influences in Italy, speaks with scorn of proud Roman ladies who would drag themselves on their knees over the frozen ground of the Campus Martius at the behest of the priest of Isis. The candidate for initiation must submit to long fasts and vigils in the temple, and must surrender much of his wealth, as well as his person, to the goddess. She rewards him with the affection of a mother and with her divine protection against all the baleful influences of the world.

b. Anatolian cults. Of the Anatolian cults, the oldest and most widespread was that of the Great Mother, called Ma or Cybele or Agdistis (under the latter name, a bisexual deity) and several other names. By the Greeks she was identified with Rhea, the mother of the Olympian gods; with Demeter (Δημήτηρ, "Mother Earth"); and with ARTEMIS. In most forms of her cult, her son and consort, Attis, is associated with her. Her temples were organized as powerful landholding corporations, owning thousands of slaves and served by multitudes of eunuchs and sacred prostitutes, ministers of the fertility cult. These temples were states within the state, and their powers were only partially curbed by the Hellenistic rulers. The cult had received accretions from many sources over the centuries—Phrygian and Hittite, Syrian and Persian—so that in Hellenistic times it presents a complex and confusing picture. In some centers, the male god has acquired the major role and is identified with Zeus; elsewhere the Mother has taken on the traits of the Persian Anahita (Anaitis) and adopted the Persian fire worship into her cult. Her temple-state at Ephesus had long maintained close relations with the Greek city, which revered her as the Artemis of the Ephesians and marked its coinage with her symbol, the bee, until the end of the fourth century B.C., when Lysimachus brought the temple under civil control. Elsewhere in Asia Minor, the Mother had many Greek worshipers; she and Attis are mentioned in Asian inscriptions of the Hellenistic period more frequently than all the Greek gods together. Private associations which worshiped her under the name of Meter

(Μήτηρ, "Mother") are found in Athens from the fourth century on, and occasionally in other parts of the Greek world; and there were some few groups of worshipers of Attis. The great foreign conquests of the goddess were not in the Greek world, which probably found her cult too unrestrainedly orgiastic; it is in Rome and the Latin West that she makes her deepest impress, at a later period.

The moon-god Men also held vast temple-states in all the regions of Asia Minor, ruled by his priests and owning thousands of slaves. Under the cult name of Men-Tyrannos he is worshiped by an association of slaves at Cape Sunium in Attica; he and the sun-god Helios share a sanctuary at Delos; and in the first century B.C., his name is linked with Pan and the Nymphs at Athens in supplications for rain. Rites of purification and expiation are prescribed for all who approach him. He seems to have gathered to himself all the sparse remnants of moon cults which survived in ancient Greece; but he never became a major deity outside Anatolia. In his homeland, he continued high in honor among natives and Greek settlers alike. He is the guardian of the graves, and his image commonly appears on gravestones. One of his altars bears the inscription "One God in the heavens, Men Tyrannos, Great Power of the Immortal God."

Of much greater importance is the Phrygian deity Sabazios, identified by the Greeks now with Zeus, now with Dionysus; the mystic formula "Bull begets Snake and Snake begets Bull" recalls crude myths of the birth of Persephone from Demeter and of Dionysus-Zagreus from Persephone, both begotten by Zeus, first as Bull, then as Snake. The peculiar identification with the God of Israel may have been suggested by the similarity of the name to Sabaoth (Lord "of hosts"), or to the cult title Sabbatistes ("Sabbath-God"); and by the epithet Hypsistos ("Most High"), often given to Sabazios and widely used by the Jews in Greek synagogue inscriptions and other references to their own deity. The most striking feature of the initiation ritual of this cult was the drawing of a snake through the bosom of the candidate, who thus drew into himself the powers of the god and was brought into mystical union with him. Rites of purification have an important place in the preparation for admission to the mysteries; they hold before men the hope of vindication in a judgment after death, and of a joyous immortality. The mysteries of Sabazios were celebrated at Athens before the end of the fifth century, apparently without the secrecy which was required by other such cults; the wider extension to the limits of the Roman Empire awaits the second century of our era and appears to accompany the cult of the Great Mother. The insignia of the god are numerous and varied—bull, ram, snake, toad, lizard, pine cone and palm tree, barley ears, agricultural tools, often a goblet; on the later monuments, solar and astral symbols abound, as Sabazios is identified with Helios. A distinctive cult object is the bronze hand, used as a votive offering or an amulet. It is always found in the form of the "Latin benediction"—the thumb and the first two fingers stretched out, the third and fourth fingers closed against the palm, the whole surmounted front and back with a profusion of the god's insignia and often with tiny heads, male and female. The name of the god is probably derived from *sabaia* (σάβαια, "beer"), and it may well be that in his cult beer took the place of the wine in the cult of Dionysus in promoting ecstasy by intoxication; but this feature is overlaid with a fantastic abundance of elements from the most diverse sources. The syncretism of the period here receives its most ample expression.

c. Syrian cults. The success of the Syrian gods in winning devotees abroad is relatively limited. The great sky-god Hadad is identified with Zeus and receives a cult at Delos and elsewhere under the name of Zeus-Adados. His consort ATARGATIS, or Derceto, is more widely worshiped. To the Greeks, and also to the Romans, she is pre-eminently the "Syrian goddess," and is regarded as a form of Aphrodite (Venus). Like the Artemis of the Ephesians, she is a form of the Great Mother of Anatolia. A number of local bels were identified with Zeus, and the cults of some few of them grew to a more than local significance; for instance, the bel of Mount Kasios, enshrined in the form of a conical stone, is worshiped by the Greeks of the nearby Seleucia in Pieria under the cult title of Zeus Kasios, and his cult is carried into Egypt and to Delos, to Epidaurus, and to Corcyra. And the black stone of Emesa became still more famous in later times (A.D. 218), when it was carried to Rome by an emperor who himself took its name, Elagabalus, and made it the principal symbol of Sol Invictus, the "Unconquered Sun." Under Aurelian (A.D. 272) it was the bel of Palmyra who was accorded the same honor. The hammer-wielding god of Dolichê in neighboring Commagene, originally a Hittite deity dear to the wandering tribe of iron-workers called the Chalybes, became first Zeus Dolichenos and then under the Romans received the resounding titles of Jupiter Optimus Maximus Dolichenus Sol Invictus and was borne to all parts of the Empire, even as far as Hadrian's Wall, in the camps of the legions. The dominant sun worship of the later Empire owed much to the sun cults of Syria.

But Syria plays its greatest role in the history of Hellenistic religion as the intermediary by which the astral religion of Babylonia passed into the Western world and entered into its long association with Greek science and philosophy in the formation of the imposing structure of astrology, which took shape in Egypt in the second century B.C. and exercised an extraordinary dominance over the minds of men until modern times. *See* § 7 *below*.

d. Persian cults. The influence of Mazdaism, the pure and lofty religion taught by Zoroaster, was inestimably great in the realm of religious thought. To the later Judaism it contributed cardinal elements of its eschatological doctrine, of resurrection and judgment to come, of angels and demons, of a prince of demonic powers almost rivaling the supreme god —no inconsiderable part of the general framework of thought which was inherited by early Christianity. In the Greek world there is no evidence of such significant acceptance of Zoroastrian ideas, except insofar as they contribute to the radical dualism of the Gnostic schools. The Persian cults that win adherents in the Hellenistic kingdoms belong rather to the older strata of pre-Zoroastrian Persia. Ahura Mazda, the "Wise Lord" exalted by Zoroaster as the One God, is hardly ever encountered; in the kingdom of Commagene, whose kings boasted of a mingled Greek and Persian ancestry, he is identified with Zeus and is represented in the vast monument of Nimrud Dagh by a colossal statue bearing the compounded name of Zeus Oromasdes. The Persian sun-god Mithras is represented in the same monument under the composite title Apollo Mithras Helios Hermes; in the kingdom of Pontus he is the patron deity of the royal house, and kings are called Mithradates in his honor; he is worshiped also by the pirates of the Cilician coast, the most deadly sea rovers of antiquity. In and after the second century A.D. he becomes the favorite god of the Roman legionaries, who make grottoes and erect altars for him in their garrison posts all over the Empire; with the growth of solar religion in the later Empire, he is identified with Sol Invictus. The goddess Anahita sometimes appears as his consort. More frequently she has her own temples and worshipers, in company with or in identification with the Great Mother, sometimes with the Artemis of the Ephesians; the fire cult is practiced on her altars and from them is adopted into other cults of Anatolia. In Pontus and in Armenia she was long the principal female deity. None of the Persian cults has left any important traces in the Greek peninsula itself or in the Aegean islands.

5. The mysteries. In earlier times, two main types of mystery cult were practiced in the Greek world: the mysteries of Demeter at Eleusis in Attica, and the mysteries of Dionysus in many different places, wherever groups of Bacchants were formed to celebrate them. In Hellenistic times, the thiasoi of Dionysus multiplied in the Greek world, especially in the Hellenized regions of the East; new mysteries of the Eleusinian type were founded in other cities, and Eleusinian priests were called to aid in the institution or in the reorganization of cults in Asia and in Egypt. At the same time, most of the oriental religions which were invading the Greek world came in the form of mystery cults with initiations and sacraments, with the promise of immortality and the ecstasy of participation in the life of the divinity.

The Eleusinian mysteries were celebrated under the direction of their hereditary custodians, the family of Eumolpides—one of the few professional priesthoods known to Greek religion. Admission was obtained individually through ceremonies of initiation, which were open to all of Hellenic race, including women and even, on occasion, slaves; yet they were administered by the Athenian state as part of the official religion, and the whole population of Attica participated in the rites. In its origins, undoubtedly pre-Hellenic, the worship of Eleusis was an agrarian fertility cult, meant to ensure that Earth would bring forth her increase. Two pairs of divinities are involved: Demeter (Mother Earth) and her Daughter (Kore—the Maiden), and Pluto (Wealth) with his consort, Persephone. But Kore has long since become identified with Persephone, and Pluto with Hades the lord of the underworld; so that the Maiden is at once the daughter of Earth and the queen of the world of the dead. The myth in the earliest form in which it has come down to us (the Homeric Hymn to Demeter—seventh century B.C.) is already composite. The rape of Persephone by Hades-Pluto, the barren fields, the quest of Demeter for her lost daughter, the return of the Maiden from the underworld, and the restoration of verdure—this in itself is a clear enough representation of the seasonal crop cycle, and lends itself readily to the promise of a new life for man beyond the grave. With this is combined a story of Demeter's care for the royal child of Eleusis, on whom she would have bestowed immortality by a bath of fire, had she not been interrupted by the ill-timed intrusion of the terrified parents. The goddess herself establishes the rites by which she is to be worshiped and appoints her own priesthood. To those who are initiated, she promises a blessed immortality and a participation in the divine nature. "Happy is that man who has seen these things," the Hymn proclaims, "but he who has had no part in the rites shall never have an equal lot in the dark realms of death." The atmosphere of this cult was not frenzied or ecstatic, but quietly joyful; and it appears to have made in the main for the elevation of the religious spirit in Greece.

The mysteries of Dionysus are of an entirely different character, though they lead to the same goal of participation in the divine nature and the consequent immortality. They are marked in their beginnings by a wildness and frenzy amounting to madness, which they never wholly lose, though they are greatly tamed and disciplined in the mature culture of the Greek cities. Dionysus himself is not a native deity of the Greeks or of the land before them; he is of Thracian origin, and when he first invades the Greek world, he provokes a mingling of attraction and repulsion and wins his way against bitter opposition. His devotees are mastered by a religious intoxication, by a sacred madness. They wear the hides or horns of animals, and course wildly over the mountain trails and pastures by night to the sound of flutes and the shouts of "Evoe." Springs of water and of wine break out beside them, and honey drops from the woven myrtle wands (*thyrsoi*) which they bear. Demeter is the goddess of the grain, and of nature in its cultivated aspects; Dionysus is the god of the vine, and of nature in her wildness, her untamed savagery. His "Maenads" (mad women) come upon a flock of sheep or goats, slay them, tear them to pieces with their hands, and devour them raw; sometimes it is an unhappy man, spying on their revels in a spirit hostile to the god and to the Bacchic rites, who is thus encountered and slain and devoured. In all this savagery, it is the spirit of the god himself that possesses the devotees; and it is he himself, incarnate in the beast or the man who is devoured, on whom the worshipers feed and whom they take into themselves.

The night revels on the mountains, the devouring of raw flesh, the savage frenzies of which the older stories tell, had ceased to be practiced by the Greeks long before the Alexandrian age. The mysteries are celebrated by private brotherhoods which are often companies of artists, musicians, or craftsmen, and sometimes, especially in Pythagorean circles in Western Hellas (Sicily and S Italy), schools of philosophers and statesmen. It is held among them that the rites and doctrines have been laid down in ancient times by Orpheus. Of most significance is the "Orphic" doctrine of the soul as the divine element in man, buried in the body as in a tomb and attaining its full freedom and purity only when it is delivered from the sepulchre of the body. The crude and savage myth of Dionysus-Zagreus is related both to the wild frenzies of the early cult and to the developed doctrine of the soul. Dionysus, child of Zeus by Semele, is torn to pieces and devoured by the Titans; the Titans are blasted by the lightning of Zeus, and out of their ashes is created man, who thus possesses a dual nature—part divine and part titanic, mutually hostile. The soul, the divine part that derives from Dionysus, can be set free from its unnatural union with the titanic nature only as it is liberated from the body; but it can be progressively purified of its defilements by ascetic disciplines, especially by abstinence from flesh, by ritual purifications, and by sacramental rites, often of a magical character. It can pass through a cycle of existences and experience reincarnation in various forms; there is a Purgatory in which the last defilements can be removed; and the soul can finally proclaim that it has escaped from the "sorrowful weary wheel," that it is of the "blessed race" of the gods, and that it has entered into immortality. This doctrine appealed to some of the noblest of the Greeks. Pythagoras was its greatest convert, and his disciples were organized as Orphic thiasoi. It profoundly influenced Pindar, in whose poetry it has found moving expression; and it underlies the doctrine of the soul which is set forth by Plato in the Phaedo and the Phaedrus. Indirectly also it has played a great part in the historical development of Christian ideas of the soul.

6. Ruler cults and deification. The practice of according divine honors to sovereigns is one of the most conspicuous features of public religion in the period. In part this was a device of statecraft, a political scheme for giving the support of religious sanctions to a naked military dictatorship; and in part it was facilitated by oriental ideas of the divinity of kings, especially the Egyptian recognition of the Pharaoh as the "living Horus," the son of Osiris, a veritable incarnation of the divine powers. But these were secondary and subsidiary factors. From the earliest times the Greeks themselves had accorded divine honors to men who had distinguished themselves by outstanding services to their fellows or by exceptional exploits in war. Such honors were not, indeed, rendered to their rulers; but it was a general custom for the founders of cities or of colonies to be honored with a public cult after death. These, as a rule, remained local observances, but as manifestations of religion they are not essentially different from the cult accorded to mythical or semimythical "heroes" such as Theseus at Athens or Bellerophon at Corinth; and closely related to these are cults of wide appeal such as those of Herakles and of Asclepius, the deified physician. In all of them is reflected the feeling that the nature of man is akin to the nature of the gods, that a kind of concentration of divine virtue is manifested in the exceptional man; and the not ignoble thought that the nature of the divine is most truly revealed in the nature of man at its highest and best. Something of this feeling appears again in the legend that Plato was conceived in the womb of his mother through a visitation of Apollo, in the veneration of his image by his disciples of the first generation, and in the dedication of an altar to him by Aristotle. Moreover, the political theories of both Plato and Aristotle had envisaged the ideal ruler as a man whose gifts lifted him above the common human stature, above the restraints of the law which applied to others, a man who walked among mortals as a god.

These hero cults were not rendered in the Greek world to living men, but to the mighty dead who were held to have attained immortality. Lysander alone, victor in the decisive battle of Aegospotami (406 B.C.), which ended the maritime supremacy of Athens, was accorded honors akin to those of the heroes. The Spartans set up his statue among a group of gods at Delphi, in the memorial which they dedicated after the victory; several cities erected altars to him; games and festivals were instituted in his honor. In 336, Philip of Macedon had his own statue carried in procession with those of the twelve gods of Olympus. It remained for Alexander to claim in full measure for himself the status of a god among men. He traced his descent from Zeus through Herakles and Achilles; at the Oasis of Ammon in the Western Desert, he had himself formally recognized as son of the supreme Egyptian deity, whom the Greeks identified with Zeus; at Susa, he received from his Persian subjects the reverence (προσκύνησις) which they were accustomed to offer to their own sovereigns, but sought in vain to extort the same servile homage from Macedonians and Greeks. Nonetheless, a certain recognition of his divinity was made by the Greek cities when they gave the title of *theoroi* to the envoys whom they sent to his court, for this was reserved for officials charged with religious functions such as inquiries of the Delphic oracle. After his death his corpse was carried to Memphis by Ptolemy, then satrap of Egypt; and he was given a cult and a priesthood, which were in the next reign transferred to Alexandria.

The earliest Ptolemies do not seem to have received divine honors in their lifetime, but were honored after death as the "Savior Gods, Brother Gods, Manifest Gods." By the fifth generation they have come to terms with the Egyptian priesthoods and have been admitted to the traditional place of the Pharaohs in the state religion. The first Seleucids were likewise deified after death—Seleucus I as Zeus the Victor (Nicator) and Antiochus I as Apollo the Savior. But Antiochus II styles himself Theos (God), and Antiochus IV (Epiphanes) regards himself and receives worship as the manifest form of a deity (Apollo or Zeus). Most remarkable of all, perhaps, violet-crowned Athens herself votes divine honors to Demetrius Poliorcetes ("the Besieger"), the greatest sea captain of the age, in gratitude and admiration for his prowess in freeing the city from the rule of Demetrius of Phalerum and the Macedonian pretender Cassander (307 B.C.). By a decree of the Athenian assembly, Demetrius and his father Antigonus are hailed as "savior gods"; their arrival is likened to the coming of Demeter and Dionysus; an altar to Demetrius *Kataibates* ("the Alighter") is erected on the spot where he descended from his chariot; pictures of him and his father are woven into the Peplos, the great Robe of Athena, among the likenesses of the gods. In a hymn composed for him in 290, he is lauded as the only god, the son of Poseidon and Aphrodite; while the other gods are far away or have no ears to hear or take no thought for Athens, Demetrius is beheld in his living presence, not in wood or stone; and to him they pray: "Give us peace, Beloved."

When Rome began to extend her conquests into the kingdoms of the Eastern Mediterranean, she was still a republic without any permanent head. Altars and temples were now dedicated by the Hellenistic cities to Rome, the city-goddess, the personification of the Roman state or people. And even in republican times governors were given priesthoods, and cultic observances were ordained in their honor. The ruler cult was transferred to the great proconsuls. The successive war lords of the first century B.C.—Sulla, Pompey, Julius Caesar, Antony—were flattered in the same ways. Caesar is addressed by the cities of Asia as the "God Manifest, sprung from Ares and Aphrodite, the common Savior of the life of men." It was a matter of course that, once the civil wars were ended, the victor should be accorded no lesser honors. Cities were eager for the privilege of building temples to Augustus; and he is given the highest titles of divinity—God and Savior, Zeus Eleutherios, Apollo Eleutherios, the Lord. Games were instituted in his honor, and sacrifices offered on his altars.

7. Fortune and Fate; astral religion and astrology; magic. The ruler cult was the religion of success, the deification of power and will in the men who shaped events and determined the course of history. Such titles as "Savior" and "Benefactor" (Soter, Euergetes) were given partly in flattery, partly in hope; though in part, especially in the case of Augustus, they expressed the gratitude of war-weary peoples to the man who had brought at long last an era of peace. But to many men of those disordered times, it seemed as if success and failure were apportioned by impersonal cosmic forces, mightier far than the war lords, and making sport of the farsighted schemes of statesmen. To some it appeared that chance ruled the world; the supreme deity was Tyche (Τύχη, "Fortune"). The cities of Greece had begun to institute cults of Tyche early in the fourth century, and in Hellenistic times she becomes the city-goddess almost everywhere, in place of the older patron deities such as Athena Polias. She is represented in sculpture under a form created by Eutychides for the Tyche of Antioch *ca.* 300 B.C. Fortune was a capricious goddess, lifting a man to the heights today and dashing his pride tomorrow. There was no security for the wise in his wisdom, for the rich in his wealth, for the righteous man in his integrity, or for the mighty in his strength; all alike were at the mercy of Fortune. On the other side, the defeated could hope that the turn of her wheel might bring him victory, the destitute that he would lay hands on a windfall, and the man of low degree that he might be lifted to eminence. "Speak no more of Mind," writes Menander (*ca.* 300 B.C.), "for the human mind is nothing, while that of Tyche—whether this be a divine breath [πνεῦμα] or a mind—this it is that directs the course of all things and causes every turn and saves all things; but mortal forethought is vapor and vanity" (Fragment 482).

To others the ruling power was Fate (Ἀνάγκη, "Necessity"; or Εἱμαρμένη, "Destiny"), governing all things with the iron rod of determinism. Fate might be conceived as an all-wise Providence, or even personified as the will of Zeus; but man was still left with the sense of helplessness and frustration, subject to the decrees of a power that no supplication could move and no wisdom circumvent.

This conviction of the all-embracing rule of Fate received strong support from the star worship which was introduced into the Greek world in the fourth century; and still more from the concomitant progress of astrology, which made significant advances over the Greek world in the third century, and by 150 B.C. had become one of the chief preoccupations of scientists and philosophers. The notion that the heavenly bodies are divine is by no means unknown to the Greeks of earlier times; it was reckoned to Anaxagoras for gross impiety that he held the sun and the moon to be mere stone and earth; but this belief did not find expression in cultic observances, apart from some rites of the sun and the moon (Helios and Selene) of minor importance. Plato (or one of his immediate disciples) in the *Epinomis* recognizes that the knowledge of the astral deities has been borrowed by the Greeks from non-Greeks, but is confident that "the Greeks will learn to worship them in a truly nobler and more righteous fashion," and holds that they "must be named first as the visible gods, and the greatest, most worshipful, and clear-sighted of them all" (secs. 988A, 984D). The home of the astral religion was Babylonia, where the worship of the "host of heaven" had been practiced from a remote antiquity. From Babylonia, star worship spread into Syria and Egypt, and so over the whole of the Greek and Roman world. Chaldean astrologers, often charlatans playing on the credulity of the masses, but sometimes prophets of the astral religion, won followers in all lands; and astrology took captive the highest thought of mankind.

The Greek mind had been prepared for the invasion of astralism by the speculations of the Pythagoreans, of Plato in his later years, and of Aristotle. In the unchanging regularity of the courses of the heavenly bodies they perceived evidences of true divinity. In the fourth century, the astronomer Eudoxus of Cnidus and the botanist Theophrastus speak with skeptical wonder of the Chaldean horoscopes, by which they profess to foretell not only the weather but also the future of individuals and of nations. *Ca.* 280, the Babylonian Berossus opened a school of astrology on the island of Cos, and published a treatise on its doctrines. In the second century, astrology became one of the main preoccupations of Greek philosophy and science. Carneades the Skeptic exposed its weaknesses, and Panaetius, the greatest Stoic teacher of the time, rejected it; but Stoicism generally treated it as an integral part of its doctrine of Providence. Hipparchus of Nicaea, the unrivaled master of mathematics and astronomy, gave it his unqualified support, and indeed assured its future triumph by refuting the heliocentric theory of Aristarchus of Samos, which would have cut away its roots. The basic textbooks of the system were brought out in Egypt around the middle of the second century under the names of Nechepso-Petosiris and of Hermes Trismegistus, the name given by the Greeks to the Egyptian deity Thoth, the scribe of the gods and the revealer of the sciences and arts and of all occult wisdom. Posidonius of Apamea, disciple and successor of Panaetius and teacher of Cicero, the guiding and representative genius of the first century B.C., incorporated astrology into his system of Platonized Stoicism and made it the queen of the sciences. The dominion thus secured was to endure for centuries.

Astrology combined the appeal of science with that of religion. The casting of horoscopes was an exacting scientific task, requiring an advanced proficiency in astronomy and mathematics; the professional practitioners were not unjustifiably known as "mathematicians." Once their presuppositions were granted, their methods were rigorously scientific; and the utmost confidence was placed in their predictions. If they were falsified by the event, the mistake could always be attributed to the dishonesty of the astrologer, to an error in computation, or to a failure to take into account all the complex factors; the validity of the method was not called in question, any more than the science of medicine is discredited today by errors in diagnosis. The exact science which could predict with infallible accuracy the eclipses of the sun and the moon lent its authority to the prediction of events in human life.

In its Hellenized form, astrology was based upon the doctrine of universal "sympathy" (συμπάθεια τῶν ὅλων). The heavens and the earth are so bound together in a unity of all life that whatever comes to pass in the higher world is exactly reproduced in the lower. But as the heavenly bodies are divinities, it is their movements that determine the events of earth. Influences emanating from the stars flow continually upon men, shaping the character and destiny of every individual and the fate of every nation. The horoscope that shows the configuration of the heavens at the moment of a man's birth can be interpreted to reveal the exact number of days that he is destined to live, and the fortunes that will attend him. Thus astrology carries with it an absolute fatalism, inflexible as the courses of the stars.

Within this system, the planets are the governing powers. Among them are reckoned the sun and the moon, as well as the five true planets known to ancient astronomy—Ares, Hermes, Zeus, Aphrodite, and Cronos (or, to give them their more familiar Latin names—Mars, Mercury, Jupiter, Venus, and Saturn). Each planet is so identified with the god whose name it bears as to share his mythological personality and impart it to the individual born while it is in the ascendant. Thus Ares-Mars imparts martial qualities; Zeus-Jupiter (Jove) makes a man jovial; the irresistible influences of Venus provide an excuse for amorous adventures; the moon makes for lunacy; and so forth. The seven-day planetary week was established in this age; each planet had its day in turn, to which it gave its name—the names which we still employ in their Teutonic equivalents. Time itself becomes a god (Aeon), and all its subdivisions are deified—the Months and the Seasons, the Hours and the Days. More and more the Sun came to be regarded as the leader of the heavenly host, the supreme and dominant Intelligence of the cosmos. In its highest form, this doctrine teaches that the Sun is the visible symbol of the supreme Mind, the glorious image of the invisible fiery essence that is the spirit of the universe. The syncretistic and monotheistic tendencies in ancient religion lead under the direction of astrology toward a solar pantheism.

The astral religion had profound effects in the whole domain of religious thought. It changed the very conception of deity, and it promoted a new conception of the origin and destiny of the human soul. The divine stars might be given the names of the traditional gods, but they were not burdened with the traditional anthropomorphism and the immorality of the myths. The unceasing regularity of their movements was a token of the perfect order, harmony, and intelligence which reigned among them. And they were eternal. The traditional gods were indeed immortal (ἀθάνατοι, "deathless"), but they had their beginnings and were the descendants of an older race which had held the supremacy before them. The stars were the same yesterday and today and forever, eternal and unchanging. And the human soul was a fragment of the same fiery essence. Driven by some compulsion, it had descended from its ethereal home to be entombed for a time in an earthly body and to contract the defilements of earth. Its high destiny was to return to its starry abode, purging itself of its defilements by stages as it passed through the seven spheres ruled by the seven planets, till it attained the unmingled light of the heaven of heavens. The life to come is no longer conceived as that of strengthless shades in a gloomy underworld, but as that of pure spirits liberated from every burden to enjoy the bliss of an astral paradise. And for many, the contemplation of the stars seemed to give foretastes of this eternal joy. A mystic ecstasy possessed them as they felt themselves rapt in a sublime communion with the divinities in the heavens, and knew that in their inmost selves they were akin to the gods.

Despite these brighter aspects, astrology was, broadly speaking, a burden to the mind of man, by reason of its overpowering fatalism. The Stoic might hold it the part of a wise man to see in the decrees of Fate the wisdom of an all-ruling Providence, and to learn submission, even to find joy and freedom in submission, to make his will one with the universal will which could in no case be deflected. But mankind generally sought escape from the iron clasp of Destiny. Some hoped to win release through the mysteries, by dedication to some god who was mightier even than Fate. And far more had recourse to magic. Amulets and incantations, rites and spells, invocations of gods of outlandish names—these could always be provided by the practitioners of the magic arts to ward off a baneful influence of one's evil star, or even to prolong one's days beyond the appointed term. The great numbers of magical papyri that have been found and published, and the countless amulets and charms, show clearly enough the prevalence of the resort to magic by all classes of the population, and prepare us for the statement of the first Christian historian that when the practitioners of Ephesus brought their books of magic to burn them publicly at the preaching of Paul, the value of them was calculated at fifty thousand pieces of silver (Acts 19:19).

8. The philosophical schools. The primary feature of the post-Aristotelian philosophy is that it is no longer concerned with the city-state and with the life of man within the community of his city, but with man as an individual in the mighty cosmos, the one eternal city common to gods and men, of which any earthly state could be only a shadow. The city-state was in decline even when Plato and Aristotle were elaborating political systems which viewed the life of man wholly in terms of his place in the corporate life of the city. With the clearest realization of the faults, weaknesses, and limitations of every city known to them (and Aristotle is said to have studied the constitutions of over one hundred), they still thought of man as a ζῷον πολιτικόν (Aristotle's phrase)—a "living being formed for the life of the city"; and they inquired into the ends of his life in relation to the manifold scope for every kind of activity afforded by the city, and sought in their political theory to frame the constitution of a city in which man might live life to the full. The events of the fourth century shattered the ancient pattern of the autonomous city beyond repair, and at the same time brought men into an incomparably vaster political structure, which in the time of Alexander included all the cities of Greece and the sprawling empires of Western and Central Asia, stretching from the Adriatic Sea to the frontiers of India and seeming to embrace the whole of mankind. Neither this undigested and unstable empire of Alexander nor the vast imperial states which succeeded it could in any sense replace the city as the focus of man's loyalties and the theater of his moral and spiritual life. The philosophers of Hellenistic times could make nothing of limited loyalties of nation or of class, nor could they profitably point man toward the fulfilment of life in relation to a corporate system within which he had no longer any real significance. These military autocracies administered by permanent officials could not be envisaged as the locus of man's highest life. The task now was to establish the significance of the individual in himself, apart from any social nexus, and to point out a way of attaining the good life without the supports and opportunities of a social order. The main concern of thought is the theory and practice of ethics, and that, the ethics of the autonomous individual.

a. Decline of the older schools; Skepticism in the Academy. As in religion the old cults survived, so in philosophy the great schools which Plato and Aristotle had founded, the Academy and the Lyceum respectively, continued their activity, but with diminishing vitality and with slight influence upon the general mind. The Peripatetics, as the members of the Lyceum were called, devoted themselves mainly to descriptive work in the natural sciences, to the accumulation and study of flora and fauna from the conquered regions of the East, to the making of libraries, and to encyclopedic work of various kinds. Theophrastus, the greatest botanist of antiquity, and Demetrius of Phalerum, who founded the great library of Alexandria for Ptolemy Philadelphus, were both Peripatetics. The Academy devoted its energies chiefly to dialectic, and became little more than a parasite on other schools, content to expose the logical fallacies and absurdities of Epicurean and Stoic doctrine and to profess an ultimate skepticism about the very possibility of knowledge. Their criticisms were acute and penetrating, especially those of Carneades, the great master of the Middle Academy (*ca.* 150 B.C.); but as they had nothing constructive to offer, they went largely unheeded, except insofar as they forced some modifications in Stoic theory. The influence of Plato, always very great, was not exercised through his successors in the Academy, but through his own writings, which continued to be widely read.

b. The Cynics. The Cynic philosophers never formed an organized school like the Academy or the Lyceum, but were rather a succession of solitary prophets, preaching the pursuit of individual freedom by the disregard of everything but wisdom and virtue, challenging all the conventions of society and all the superstitions of religion, and calling upon men to follow no law but that of nature. Antisthenes, the first of the line, a disciple of Socrates and a contemporary of Plato, struck out the lines of conduct and the ruling theories that were to characterize the Cynic teachers. An ascetic frugality satisfied with the barest necessities of existence; a complete disregard for pain; scorn of every kind of luxury and ostentation; and mordant criticism of human follies, weaknesses, and vanities marked his daily life. All the conventions of society, even its graces and manners, came under his lash. He held that wisdom and virtue were the only things to be desired, and thought of himself as a Herakles, wrestling incessantly and enduring endless labors in the pursuit of virtue. He felt that he had a mission, under a divine compulsion, to tear away the shams of life and to expose every kind of hypocrisy and humbug. His searing rebukes he compared to the bitter remedies which a physician prescribes for the healing of his patients; and he anticipates an element of the gospel story in his reply to those who criticized him for keeping company with evil men. "Physicians too are with the sick," he said, "but they do not catch the fever."

But the name of Antisthenes has been almost forgotten in the greater fame of his disciple Diogenes, who, with his home in a tub, his lantern, his staff and his beggar's wallet, and his biting retorts to great and small, became a legend in his own lifetime. The name Cynic (κυνικός, from κύων, "dog") was applied first to him in revulsion against his practice of performing his natural functions in public, like a dog, wherever he happened to be. This and other grotesque and offensive behavior was to him the consistent application of the maxim that virtue consists in living according to nature; such actions did not keep the Athenians from esteeming him highly, or detract from his power of winning men by his discourse. His challenging way of life seemed to offer a kind of armor against Fortune; caring nothing for the gifts that Fortune could bring, he cared nothing for the reverses that she might have in store. The name of "dog" he would not reject; when Alexander introduced himself as "Alexander the great King," Diogenes replied: "And I am Diogenes the Dog." But he thought of himself as the hound of Zeus, commissioned to rebuke the faults of mankind and to turn men's hearts to virtue—the true virtue which wisdom teaches, not the sham virtue of current convention.

The Cynics, like Socrates, would not leave men alone. Theirs was no cloistered philosophy, but an aggressive missionary appeal which preached in the market place and the crossroads, using every means to compel men to listen. In the long run, their influence on the world was mediated chiefly through Stoicism, a philosophy at once more comprehensive and more humane, equally insistent on virtue as the only good, but less stringent in its demands on human nature. And for their street preaching, they developed the form known as the diatribe, which was inherited by the early Christian preachers of the gospel, especially for moral exhortation.

c. The Stoics. The Stoic philosophy derives its name from the Painted Stoa ("porch," or more properly "colonnade") in the agora of Athens, where the founder of the school, the Cypriot Zeno, lectured to his disciples from *ca.* 304 B.C. to his death in 263. Under a succession of able exponents, continuing over a period of five hundred years, it became far and away the most influential of all philosophies of the time, and for the majority of cultivated men it virtually occupied the whole sphere of religion.

Zeno began his philosophical work as a disciple of the Cynic Crates, but in his developed system he found a means of relating the unbridled individualism of the Cynic to universal principles. He continued to build on the principle that virtue is the highest—indeed, the only—good; and that virtuous living consists in living in conformity with nature; but he combined with this the doctrine that the essential nature of the individual is one with the essential nature of the universe. The individual who would live in accordance with his own nature must therefore live in accordance with that right reason (Logos) which is the governing principle of all things, and may be called Zeus, or Providence, or Destiny. Zeno is as radical as any Cynic in his criticism of conventional morality, of social sham, and of standards of conduct that are accepted merely because they are traditional. All things must be brought to the test of Reason, but Reason is a universal principle, at once the soul of the world and the soul of man, a general law to which all things are subject. Freedom for man is not, therefore, the arbitrary rejection of every restraint, but the voluntary acceptance of the universal will which must be obeyed by all whether they will it or not. So we have a famous prayer of Cleanthes, the disciple and successor of Zeno: "Lead me, O Zeus, and thou, O Destiny, whithersoever I am appointed by you to go; for I will follow you without delay. And though I be unwilling to go, because I have fallen into wrongdoing—I will follow, nonetheless." To this the Roman Seneca added the line which became a proverb: "The Fates lead him who is willing; they constrain him who is unwilling."

Accepting Destiny as the rule of a wise and beneficent Providence, the Stoic has no concern for changes in his outward circumstances. Reverses of fortune are matters of indifference to him, for they are determined by the creative reason which rules all things and is one with the reason enthroned in his own heart; and they do not impair the integrity of his inward self. By a rigorous self-discipline, he has cultivated an apathy (ἀπάθεια) which renders him insensitive to pain and pleasure, success and misfortune. He has learned, in whatsoever state he is, to be self-sufficient (αὐτάρκης).

The Stoic could speak of man, in Aristotle's phrase, as a ζῶον πολιτικόν—a "living being formed for the life of the city"; but the true city of his habitation was nothing less than the universe itself, the "City of God" (of Zeus), the "home common to gods and men, of which both are citizens." Zeno may himself have been directly influenced by Alexander the Great's noble vision of Concord (ὁμόνοια), of a union of hearts which should transcend the ancient prejudices of race. More probably, king and philosopher alike grasped something which was in the very air of the times, which corresponded to the realities of the age. At all events, the Stoic conception of Reason as the determining principle in man abstracted from the individual everything that belonged to race or social status (and, indeed, everything that characterized him as an individual), to fix wholly upon that which he shared in some measure with every other man and with the universe itself. The one distinction that matters is the distinction of wisdom and folly—of virtuous living in keeping with the right reason (ὀρθὸς λόγος) which governs all things, and of senseless rebellion which issues in wickedness. It is a Stoic inspiration that prompts the words of Menander: "No man is an alien to me, if he be a good man; Nature is one in all men, and it is character that establishes kinship" (Fragment 602). Such a philosophy, it may be remarked, was admirably suited—was, indeed, imperatively demanded—to meet the needs of vast empires, which could not found a lasting system of government upon the superiority of one race. Stoic philosophers became the confidants and advisers of kings and emperors; and in the second century A.D. a Stoic philosopher, Marcus Aurelius Antoninus, himself ascended the imperial throne.

The Stoic conception of deity owed nothing to the popular religion of Greece. The divine is a material substance which permeates the whole of things. It may be described as spirit (πνεῦμα), but in this terminology spirit is itself a material substance—air or breath—moving through all things and holding them in unity by a certain power of tension (τονικὴ δύναμις). It is the germinative reason (σπερματικὸς λόγος), the general law, the providence (πρόνοια) or destiny (εἱμαρμένη) which governs all things with wisdom and goodness. The Stoic deity is essentially pantheistic and impersonal, even though the language (especially in Cleanthes and Epictetus) is often charged with the fervor of deep personal devotion. The name of Zeus may be used as a symbol, and the gods of the nations may be regarded as symbols of different aspects or activities of the one universal Power; and the myths may be interpreted as allegories of the divine nature; Stoicism thus accommodates itself to the popular religion rather than attacking it. Still more readily it accommodates itself to astrology, for it finds its own doctrine of Destiny or Providence confirmed by the unvarying regularity of the stars in their courses. If all things are predetermined, it is no long step to hold that they can be predicted, and the way is open for divination of every kind. But there is no thought of a personal deity who can aid man or comfort him. There is nothing greater than the spark of divinity within himself, a fragment of the fiery substance which is the soul of the world. "You are primary; you are a particle [ἀπόσπασμα] of God; you have within you something which is a part of him" (Epictetus *Discourses* II.8.10). *See also* STOICS.

d. The Epicureans. Epicurus, the founder of this school, settled in Athens in 306 B.C. after a few years of teaching philosophy in other cities, and there he remained for the rest of his life (died 270), in the company of the friends who gathered around him in his famous Garden. His school is often called the Garden, as that of Zeno is called the Porch (Stoa). For him, the one end of human life was happiness, or sweetness (ἡδονή), and he taught that this was to be found through knowledge of the true nature of things, which would deliver men from fear (fear of the gods and fear of death), the destroyer of all happiness; through withdrawal from public activity of every kind into a life of quiet obscurity (λάθε βίωσας, "live unnoticed"); through the cultivation of an inward calm that nothing can shake (ἀταραξία, "tranquillity," or better, "imperturbability"); and through friendship (φιλία).

The interests and aims of Epicurus were wholly practical, not in the least speculative. Holding that "pleasure is the beginning and the end of living the blessed life" (*Epicurus to Menoeceus* 128), he framed all his doctrines with a view to teaching men how to live pleasurably. Virtue is not itself the end, for even virtue is not pursued for its own sake, but for the sake of happiness, as medicines are taken not for their own sake but to promote health. At times, this line of thought leads him to view justice as nothing more than expediency, and even to hold that "injustice is not evil in itself, but only in the fear that it arouses out of the notion that it will be discovered by the avengers appointed to deal with such matters" (*Kyriai Doxai* 34). Yet he also teaches that the only happy life is the life of virtue. "Prudence teaches that it is not possible to live pleasurably without living prudently, nobly, and justly; nor to live prudently, nobly, and justly without living pleasurably; for the virtues are organically united with the life of pleasure, and the life of pleasure is inseparable from them" (*Epicurus to Menoeceus* 132; cf. *Kyriai Doxai* 5).

The pleasure he sets as the end of life is not ignobly conceived. It is not to be found in endless revelry, love-making, feasting on the best foods, or other self-indulgence, but in "sober reasoning, searching out the causes of every choice and every rejection, and banishing the notions through which the greatest tumult possesses the souls of men" (*Epicurus to Menoeceus* 132). He and his circle lived frugally and despised luxury and extravagance.

Among the notions that must be banished as the cause of tumults in the soul, the first place belongs to the common beliefs about the gods. Epicurus would make no terms with the popular religion. Gods indeed there are, but they are not such as the multitudes believe. They dwell far off in the spaces between the worlds and take no thought for mankind; they live the life of undisturbed tranquillity, which is the perfection of happiness and the goal of the wise man's aspiration. Such beings, blessed and incorruptible, have no troubles in themselves and bring no troubles on others. They are not to be dreaded, as if they were maleficent, nor is there any need to placate them with sacrifices and offerings; the worship of the wise man will be wholly adoration. The astral deities have no more to be said for them than the gods of the popular religion; the stars are not divine beings, but masses of fire. The Stoic conception of Destiny as the supreme divinity is absurd; the wise man "laughs to scorn the Destiny which is introduced by some as the mistress of all things." No conscious wisdom moves and directs the world; everything is sufficiently explained through mechanical causation.

The physical theories of Epicurus, largely based upon the atomism of Democritus, are elaborated for the sole purpose of showing that no divine intervention need be postulated to account for the world or the heavens or for anything that takes place within them. He is not interested in natural science for its own sake; he affirms that if men had never been affected with fear at such things as storms, eclipses, falling stars, etc., there would never have been any need to study natural science. He offers a variety of physical explanations of natural phenomena, but one contents him as much as another. He wants only to dispel the notion that these things take place at the command or by the design and will of any divinity. The movement of the atoms accounts for everything, even for the invariable recurrences of the courses of the stars.

The fear of death is removed by the doctrine that death is extinction. The soul, like the body, is composed of atoms; and with the death of the body, the soul disintegrates into the atoms of which it is composed. Death is the end of sentient existence; the terrors of the afterlife vanish as unreal. And with the fear of death, most of the fears that haunt men in life are banished also. "There is nothing to be dreaded in life by him who has truly grasped that there is nothing to be dreaded in ceasing to live" (*Epicurus to Menoeceus* 125). The hope of immortality is gladly abandoned for the sake of abolishing all dread of what may follow death; and it is even suggested that the sweetness of life is prized all the more highly, when "men seek the fruits not of the longest but of the sweetest time" (*ibid.* 126). *See also* EPICUREANS.

e. Theosophy and Gnosis. From about the beginning of the first century B.C., rationalism enters upon a long decline in the Greek world. There is evidence of a spreading disillusionment with philosophy as an avenue to apprehension of the truth, combined with a growing demand for authority, for a revelation. Along with this comes a new concern for the soul, and the truth that is sought is the truth that will enable the soul to attain its high destiny. Since the time of Plato and even earlier, many Greeks had come to think of the soul as something distinct from the body, belonging to a higher order of existence, endowed with powers of reason and insight which are impaired and held in check by the association with the body. In the later Hellenistic times, there is a growing conviction that the soul is a divine essence which has somehow fallen into an evil condition; as this belief becomes widely dominant, it has profound effects on philosophy and religion, determining the objectives of both. The interest in ethics, which had been the chief concern of Zeno and Epicurus and indeed of all the schools, is subordinated to the quest for the salvation of the soul, and this salvation is conceived in terms of the freeing of the soul from the bondage of the body and its ascent to the realm of pure divine being, its true home.

The dialogues of Plato contributed in no small measure to this development. In the *Phaedo* (64B-67D), philosophy is described as a "practice of dying" (μελέτη θανάτου), on the ground that it seeks the release, or loosing, or separation, of the soul from the body (ἀπαλλαγή, λῦσις, χωρισμὸς ψυχῆς ἀπὸ σώματος); and again in the *Theaetetus,* in a digression on the contemplative life (172C-176C), the aim of the philosopher is seen as a "flight" (φυγή) from mortality and an assimilation to God insofar as this is possible (ὁμοίωσις τῷ θεῷ κατὰ τὸ δυνατόν). In this later period, the Academy shakes itself loose from its long alliance with Skepticism, and turning to the mystical element in Plato, sets out on the long road to Plotinus and the Neoplatonic mysticism which was to make inestimable contributions to the mystical theology of the church through the following centuries. In this school, Reason never wholly lost her rightful throne, though after Plotinus she is forced into an uneasy coupling with mediumistic divination and the strangely enticing techniques of theurgy, which is nothing else than the direction of magical practices toward religious ends.

Neo-Pythagoreanism has a widening vogue. Less a philosophical school than an association of religious communities, it presents Pythagoras as a divinely inspired sage, even as a divinity—Apollo himself. His wisdom is transmitted orally as an esoteric doctrine, guarded in the circles of his disciples; every discussion is ended with his *ipse dixit* (αὐτὸς ἔφα). Even Plato, it is alleged, was a disciple of Pythagoras, and his philosophical doctrines rest, not upon the cogency of his dialectic, but upon the authority of the prophetic word of Pythagoras. This school makes much of a mysticism of numbers, imposes a strict vegetarianism, teaches a doctrine of transmigration, and holds that in this life the body is the prison house in which the soul is confined to do penance for faults committed in a former existence.

But in the general estimation the sages of Greece were held to be far inferior to the wise men of the Orient; it was widely supposed that Egypt, Chaldea, Persia, India, were depositories of an ancient wisdom and that the wisest of the Greeks were mere children beside the priests of Re, the Magi, the "Gymnosophists" of India; for some, Judea too was a home of wisdom. Pythagoras, Democritus, Plato—all the teachers of Greece were now imagined to have sat at the feet of Eastern teachers. Babylonian and Persian sages—Ostanes and Zoroaster—were now given as the authors of theosophical treaties. Hermes Trismegistus (the Egyptian deity Thoth in his Greek dress), already the source of astrological lore, is now presented as the revealer of saving truth in a theosophical literature which ranges from the loftiest and purest mystical philosophy to alchemy and magic. The sacred book, venerated and accorded authority in proportion to its antiquity, is the vehicle of all these Eastern revelations. In such an atmosphere, Jewish and Christian apologists make much of the supposed antiquity of the OT scriptures. Moses was centuries older than Plato, hence far more authoritative; indeed, Plato learned from his writings, and the Platonic philosophy is already to be found in the book of Genesis. A Neo-Pythagorean of the second century A.D. (Numenius) is willing to admit that Plato is nothing else than an "Atticizing Moses."

All the theosophies of these manifold schools may be called "gnostic" in the sense that they teach that knowledge (gnosis)—i.e., knowledge of the revealed doctrine of God, World, and Soul—is itself salvation. The materials employed in the construction are drawn from many quarters; they exhibit again the syncretism which characterizes all the religious thought and activity of the period. Oriental elements from various sources—Iranian, Egyptian, Syrian, Babylonian—are inextricably mingled with the Greek substratum of religious thought, which is itself compounded of Platonic idealism, shamanistic notions of the soul, and some tenets of the Stoic philosophy. Astrology usually enters largely into the mixture. The redemption of the soul is pictured in terms of an ascent through the spheres, guarded as they are by the mighty divinities enthroned in—rather, embodied in—the planets. In a number of the systems—most of them hardly deserve such a name—the planet-divinities are hostile powers who seek to resist the ascent of the soul; the true deity is high above them all, wholly transcendental, invisible, unknowable except insofar as he chooses to make himself known. It is sometimes taught that the soul cannot escape from this material world except through the intervention of a redeemer who descends through the spheres and returns victorious over the planets who control them—"the world Rulers of this present darkness" (Eph. 6:12).

The Gnostic systems which constituted a great danger to Christianity throughout the second century belong within this general climate of religious thought; in another sense, the same might be said of Catholic Christianity as well, though the differences are radical. The Christian (heretical) Gnostics turned Christ into a mythological figure, making him one of the emanations which they conceived as mediators between the supreme God, essentially incapable of contact with the material universe, and the human soul, essentially one with the divine, but imprisoned in a material body as the consequence of some accident within the divine pleroma. Paul is evidently dealing with some incipient form of such Gnosticism when he affirms that Christ is the "image of the invisible God," and that "in him all the fulness [pleroma] of God was pleased to dwell" (Col. 1:15, 19). And the church never failed to hold to the essential unity of the spiritual and the material—things visible and things invisible are alike the creation of the one God, the Father Almighty; and all his creation is good.

Bibliography. Sources: The sources include practically all the extant literature of the period, together with many thousands of inscriptions and papyri and masses of archaeological material from the excavations of sacred sites all over the Near East. Pausanias' *Description of Greece* (trans. with extensive annotations by J. G. Frazer; 6 vols.; 1890) is a mine of information about the religious antiquities of the second century A.D.; Strabo's *Geography* adds much local detail from a century earlier. Excellent selections of epigraphic material are found in W. Dittenberger, *Orientis Graecae Inscriptiones Selectae* (2 vols.; 1903-5); *Sylloge Inscriptionum Graecarum* (4 vols.; 3rd ed., 1915-24); and in C. Michel, *Recueil d'Inscriptions Grecques* (1900; *Suppléments,* 1912, 1927). A representative selection of papyri with English translations is available in A. S. Hunt and C. C. Edgar, eds., *Select Papyri* (2 vols.; 1932-34). For a wider range of documents in English translation, see E. Bevan, *Later Greek Religion* (1927); F. C. Grant, *Hellenistic Religions* (1953); E. Barker, *From Alexander to Constantine* (1956). For illustration, see J. Leipoldt, *Die Religionen in der Umwelt des Urchristentums* (1926), in H. Haas, ed., *Bilderatlas zur Religionsgeschichte*.

General works: L. Gernet and A. Boulanger, *Le Genie Grec dans la Religion* (1932), pt. III. M. Nilsson, *Geschichte der Griechischen Religion,* vol. II: "Die hellenistische und römische Zeit" (1950), is incomparable in scope and quality. On the general history and culture, see: P. Wendland, *Die hellenistisch-römische Kultur in ihren Beziehungen zu Judentum und Christentum* (2nd and 3rd eds., 1912); J. Kaerst, *Geschichte des Hellenismus,* vol. II (1926); P. Jouguet, *Macedonian Imperialism and the Hellenization of the Orient* (trans. M. R. Dobie; 1928); M. W. Rostovtzeff, *Social and Economic History of the Hellenistic World* (3 vols.; 1941); W. W. Tarn, *Hellenistic Civilization* (3rd ed., rev. G. T. Griffith, 1952).

On the old gods and the old cults (§ 2 *above*): L. R. Farnell, *Cults of the Greek States* (5 vols.; 1896-1909); W. K. C. Guthrie, *The Greeks and Their Gods* (1937); A. B. Cook, *Zeus* (3 vols.; 1914-40).

On personal religion and on oriental religions in the Greek world (§§ 3-4 *above*): Apuleius *The Golden Ass,* especially bk. 11; Plutarch *Concerning Isis and Osiris;* Sallustius *Concerning the Gods and the Universe;* R. Reitzenstein, *Die hellenistische Mysterienreligionen* (3rd ed., 1926); F. Cumont, *Les Religions Orientales dans le Paganisme Romain* (4th ed., 1929; English trans. of 2nd ed., 1911); A. D. Nock, *Conversion* (1933); K. Prümm, "Mystèries," in L. Pirot, A. Robert, and H. Cazelle, eds., *Supplément au Dictionnaire de la Bible,* vol. VI, fasc. XXX (1957), cols. 1-225.

On the mystery religions (§ 5 *above*): *See bibliography* for §§ 3-4 *above;* also Euripides *The Bacchae;* the Homeric *Hymn to Demeter;* N. Turchi, *Fontes historiae mysteriorum aevi hellenistici* (1930).

On ruler-worship and deification (§ 6 *above*): L. R. Farnell, *Greek Hero Cults and Ideas of Immortality* (1921); M. Nilsson, *Geschichte der Griechischen Religion* (1950), pp. 125-275; E. Barker, *From Alexander to Constantine* (1956), Index under "Deification."

On Fortune and Fate, astral religion and astrology, and magic (§ 7 *above*): F. Cumont, *Astrology and Religion Among the Greeks and Romans* (1912); F. Boll, *Sternglaube und Sterndeutung* (4th ed., rev. W. Gundel, 1931); O. Neugebauer, "The History of Ancient Astronomy: Problems and Methods," *JNES,* IV (1945), 1 ff. Current bibliography in *Isis.*

On the philosophical schools (§ 8 *above*): E. Zeller, *The Stoics, Epicureans and Sceptics* (trans. O. J. Reichel; 1880); E. Caird, *The Evolution of Theology in the Greek Philosophers,* vol. II (1904); J. Geffcken, *Der Ausgang des griechisch-römischen Heidentums* (1920); A. M. J. Festugière, *La Révélation d'Hermès Trismégiste* (4 vols.; 1944-49); E. R. Dodds, *The Greeks and the Irrational* (1951); G. Quispel, *Gnosis als Weltreligion* (1951); H. Leisegang, *Die Gnosis* (3rd ed., 1955); R. M. Grant, *Gnosticism and Early Christianity* (1959). *See also* the bibliographies under EPICUREANS; STOICS.

On the relation of Greek cults and philosophies to Judaism and Christianity: T. R. Glover, *The Conflict of Religions in the Early Roman Empire* (1909); P. Wendland, *Die hellenistisch-römische Kultur in ihren Beziehungen zu Judentum und Christentum* (2nd and 3rd eds., 1912); A. Deissmann, *Licht vom Osten* (4th ed. rev., 1923); W. R. Halliday, *The Pagan Background of Early Christianity* (1925); S. Angus, *The Religious Quests of the Graeco-Roman World* (1929); R. Bultmann, *Primitive Christianity in Its Contemporary Setting* (trans. R. H. Fuller; 1956); and nearly all the articles in the *Reallexikon für Antike und Christentum.*

F. W. BEARE

GREEK VERSIONS. The most important ancient version of the OT is the SEPTUAGINT, which, according to tradition, was made in the third century B.C. by seventy translators at the request of Ptolemy Philadelphus (*see* VERSIONS, ANCIENT, § 2*a*). Modern Greek translations of both OT and NT (*see* VERSIONS, MEDIEVAL AND MODERN, § 4) began to appear in the eleventh century. B. M. METZGER

GREEN. The translation of several words, most frequently of ירק. This word generally refers to vegetation (Gen. 1:30; 9:3; Exod. 10:15; Job 39:8; Ps. 37:2). Its derivative ירקרק identifies the yellow-green of gold (Ps. 68:13) or plague spots (Lev. 13:49; 14:37).

The adjective רענן (from the verb רען), which appears occasionally in allusions to places of idolatrous practices (cf. Deut. 12:2; I Kings 14:23; etc.) and is rendered "green," refers primarily to the luxuriance of trees. Elsewhere in the OT, רענן, translated as "green," denotes that which is luxuriant or flourishing and healthy.

Although the terms חי, דשא, לח, אב, and רטב are sometimes construed as "green," their basic reference is to that which is living, growing, fresh, and new, rather than to color.

In the NT, χλωρός is employed to designate the green of vegetation (cf. Mark 6:39; Rev. 8:7; etc.).

See also COLORS. C. L. WICKWIRE

GREETING. *See* SALUTATION.

GREYHOUND. KJV translation of זרזיר מתנים (Prov. 30:31; RSV STRUTTING COCK). *See* COCK; FAUNA § B6*c*.

GRIDDLE [מחבת] (Lev. 2:5). A thick pottery plate with small depressions like a waffle iron. After David's day, when iron became common, this metal was also used for griddles (cf. Ezek. 4:3).

GRIEF. *See* SUFFERING.

GRINDING. The process by which grain was made into flour by being rubbed between two rough stones, sometimes especially prepared for the purpose, and operated by hand or turned by an animal. *See* MILL.

GRISLED. KJV archaism used to translate the plural adjective ברדים. *See* DAPPLED; COLORS.

GROVE. KJV translation of אשרה (RSV ASHERAH) and אשל (Gen. 21:33; RSV TAMARISK).

GUARD [טבח, משמעת, משמר, רץ; κουστωδία (KJV WATCH), σπεκουλάτωρ (Mark 6:27; KJV EXECUTIONER), σωματοφύλαξ; KJV στρατοπεδάρχης (Acts 28:16; *cf.* RSV)]. A man or body of troops assigned to protect a person or thing.

The word טבח, "guard" (Gen. 37:36; 39:1; 40:3 ff; II Kings 25:8 ff; Jer. 39:9 ff), is derived from the root טבח, "to slaughter," and designates the special troops of an Egyptian or Babylonian king; the connection of meaning is uncertain, though it has been plausibly conjectured that the royal guard originally also prepared the sacrificial food for the king. The Israelite royal guard was called רצים (lit., "runners"—i.e., the outrunners or royal escort). They kept watch at the palace doors, had charge over the guardroom in which the king's treasures were kept (cf. I Kings 14:27-28), and accompanied the royal chariot (I Kings

1:5). The משמעת (from שמע, "to hear, obey"; hence, those who obeyed the personal orders of the king) was the bodyguard; David is mentioned as the captain of Saul's bodyguard (I Sam. 22:14); and Benaiah, of David's (II Sam. 23:23; I Chr. 11:25). The word משמר denotes chiefly the place of confinement and only later came to mean "those who keep watch" (Neh. 4:22-23; Ezek. 38:7).

The Greek word σωματοφύλαξ is a word which literally means "bodyguard." Darius had three young men in his personal bodyguard (I Esd. 3:4); a bodyguard is also attested for Holofernes (Jth. 12:7) and for Ptolemy IV Philopator (III Macc. 2:23).

The word "guard" is seldom found in the NT. The Greek κουστωδία is a Latin borrowing (*custodia*) used of the Roman guard set over Jesus' grave (Matt. 27:65-66; 28:11), whereas σπεκουλάτωρ, also of Latin origin (*speculator*), occurs but once (Mark 6:27). In Imperial Rome the *speculatores* were the bodyguard attached to the emperor's person. In the Mark passage the meaning is extended to members of Herod Antipas' guard (not "executioner" as in the KJV).

See also FOOTMAN; PRAETORIAN GUARD.

Bibliography. J. Kromayer and G. Veith, *Heerwesen und Kriegführung der Griechen und Römer* (*Handbuch des Altertumswissenschaft* IV, 3.2; 1928), pp. 392, 489-90.

J. W. WEVERS

GUARD, COURT OF THE [חצר המטרה] (Jer. 32:8, 12; 33:1; 37:21; 38:6, 13, 28; 39:14-15); KJV COURT OF THE PRISON. Apparently an open court in the palace complex which was reserved for detention of prisoners, at least during the time of the siege of Jerusalem. Here Jeremiah was confined, but he could continue his prophesying and even carry on necessary business transactions with the aid of his secretary. H. G. MAY

GUARD, GATE OF THE [שער המטרה] (Neh. 12:39); KJV PRISON GATE. Possibly a gate of the palace compound in Jerusalem, although the context would favor its identification with the city gate HAMMIPHKAD, or MUSTER GATE; *see* map under NEHEMIAH. *See also* JERUSALEM § 7*b*. G. A. BARROIS

GUARDIAN [ἐπίτροπος]; KJV PROTECTOR (II Macc. 11:1; etc.); TUTOR (Gal. 4:2). The adult legally responsible for the person and property of a minor. In a general sense the Greek word means "manager" ("steward" in Matt. 20:8; Luke 8:3) or "governor" (a verbal form is used of Pilate in Luke 3:1 in some MSS); but in specific legal usage it is the regular term for the guardian of a minor, and in this sense it is found in rabbinic literature as a loan word. In the Apoc., Lysias is called the guardian of the young Syrian king Antiochus Eupator (II Macc. 11:1; 13:2; 14:2; cf. I Macc. 3:32-33; 6:15-17). The sole NT occurrence of the word in this sense is in Gal. 4:2, where Paul is presenting his argument that the Jewish law was an instrument of temporary validity until the appearance of Christ.

The RSV uses the English word in II Kings 10:1, 5: "guardians of the sons of Ahab." The Hebrew here (אמן) has the general sense of "support," "nourish," "confirm," etc.

See also CUSTODIAN.

Bibliography. S. Eger, "Rechtswörter und Rechtsbilder in den Paulinischen Briefen," *ZNW*, 18 (1918), 105-8, gives references to papyri; E. D. Burton, *Galatians*, ICC (1920), pp. 211-15; S. Belkin, "The Problem of Paul's Background," *JBL*, LIV (1935), 52-55, gives references to Philo and rabbinic literature.

A. WIKGREN

GUDGODAH. *See* HOR-HAGGIDGAD.

GUEST [קראים, *lit.* called; ἀνακείμενος, *lit.* reclining; καταλύω, *lit.* relax; ξενίζω, receive as a guest, entertain]. One invited to a feast or the like (I Kings 1:41, 49; Prov. 9:18; Zeph. 1:7; Matt. 22:10-11), or provided with lodging (Luke 19:7). The "guest room" of Mark 14:14; Luke 22:11 and the "inn" of Luke 2:7 represent the same Greek word (κατάλυμα). *See* HOSPITALITY; MEALS.

S. A. CARTLEDGE

GUEST ROOM [κατάλυμα]; KJV GUEST CHAMBER. The room in which Jesus and the disciples celebrated the Last Supper (Mark 14:14; Luke 22:11). The word occurs as "inn" in Luke 2:7.

The guest room would be a single room where travelers could sleep. As used here, it is the room, borrowed or rented specifically for the eating of the Passover meal, by pilgrims to the Passover. It is therefore a temporary lodging place. E. M. GOOD

GUIDEPOSTS [תמרורים; *cf.* תמר, post (RSV scarecrows; Jer. 10:5); תימרה, column (Joel 2:30—H 3:3; Song of S. 3:6); Arab. *'amār*, sign; *'amar*, heap of stones]; KJV HIGH HEAPS. A word which occurs only in Jer. 31:21, where it appears to be a synonym for WAYMARK. W. S. McCULLOUGH

GUILE [מרמה (Gen. 27:35; DECEIT *in* Ps. 34:13—H 34:14; FRAUD *in* Ps. 55:11); שקר (Ps. 119:78; *more commonly* FALSE); משאון (Prov. 26:26); δόλος]. Crafty or deceitful cunning; treachery; duplicity; deceit. To beguile someone is to deceive him. Suitable antonyms of "guile" are "honesty" and "sincerity." The use of "guile" with reference to a stratagem or a trick or wile is now obsolete but nonetheless suggestive. In Rom. 16:19 Paul urges the Roman Christians to be "wise as to what is good and guileless (ἀκέραιος) as to what is evil." Presumably his hope was that sincere and honest Christians should learn to distinguish between right and wrong and thus maintain their moral integrity. According to John 1:47, Jesus commended Nathanael because there was no guile in him. Jesus is commended to the readers of I Peter (2:22) as one who committed no sin and whose lips were free of guile. According to the same letter (3:10):

> He that would love life
> and see good days,
> let him keep his tongue from evil
> and his lips from speaking guile.

According to Gen. 27:35, Isaac readily admitted to Esau that Jacob had come with guile in order to steal his brother's birthright (cf. Ps. 119:78; Prov. 26:26).

H. F. BECK

GUILT. *See* SIN.

GUILT OFFERING. *See* SACRIFICE AND OFFERINGS § A4*b*.

GULF. *See* CHASM.

GULL. *See* SEA GULL.

GUM [נכאת, *n^e^khôth;* Arab. *naka'at;* LXX θυμίαμα, incense]. A product of trade gathered from the resin of an herb or shrub, possibly the *Astragalus gummifer* Lab. or *Astragalus tragacantha* L. It was carried down to Egypt by Ishmaelites from Gilead, along with balm and myrrh (Gen. 37:25; KJV SPICERY); and it was sent by Jacob to Joseph in Egypt as one of the "choice fruits of the land," along with balm, honey, myrrh, pistachio nuts, and almonds (Gen. 43:11; KJV SPICES). Many plants in the Near East exude resins which became important items of ancient trade.

See also BALM; FLORA §§ A7*b, i-j, l;* MASTIC; MYRRH; SPICES; STACTE.

Bibliography. I. Löw, *Die Flora der Juden,* II (1924), 419-24; G. E. Post, *Flora of Syria, Palestine and Sinai,* I (1932), 373-408. J. C. TREVER

GUNI gū'nī [גוני, *cf.* Arab. *ğūnun*]; GUNITES —nīts. **1.** The second son of Naphtali (Gen. 46:24; Num. 26:48; I Chr. 7:13); ancestral head of the Gunites (Num. 26:48).

2. A Gadite (I Chr. 5:15).

See also LXX variants in II Sam. 23:32; I Chr. 11:34.

GUR gûr [גור] (II Kings 9:27). An ascent near Ibleam where Jehu's men wounded Ahaziah king of Judah.

GURBAAL gûr'bāl [גור בעל] (II Chr. 26:7). A city occupied by Arabs, possibly in the neighborhood of Edom. Uzziah numbered it among his conquests, and perhaps changed its name to the more pleasing one of JAGUR. The LXX translation, "rock of Baal," points to a reading that was either *ṣûr-ba'al* (Hebrew) or *ṭûr-ba'al* (Aramaic). On the other hand, Egyptian lists mention a town called *Kr-b'r,* which may be Gurbaal. S. COHEN

GUTTER. KJV translation of רהטים (RSV RUNNEL) in Gen. 30:38, 41, and of צנור (RSV WATER SHAFT) in II Sam. 5:8. *See* WATER WORKS; JERUSALEM § 5*a.*

GYMNASIUM [γυμνάσιον]. A place of physical exercise for Greek youths; a school of training, sometimes used in a wider sense—e.g., of a philosophical school. Great resentment was felt by many of the Jews at the attempt of Antiochus Epiphanes to introduce the Greek way of life among them (*see* ANTIOCHUS § 4). He established a gymnasium in Jerusalem (I Macc. 1:14; II Macc. 4:12). For the Greek the gymnasium, no less than the assembly and the theater, was an essential part of life; it trained the body in harmony and beauty and provided a social club for the youth who banded themselves into guilds of *epheboi* which had their headquarters at the gymnasium.

Paul and the Christians in general do not appear to have felt such keen resentment against the activities of the gymnasium, and the apostle goes so far as to use them as metaphors illustrating the Christian life (I Cor. 9:24-27; Gal. 2:2; 5:7; Phil. 1:30; 2:16). Γυμνασία (exercise in the gymnasium) is mentioned in I Tim. 4:8 in order to point out, after the manner of Paul, that bodily exercises have a legitimate, though limited, place in life, and in order to compare the spiritual training of the Christian.

But two centuries before this, it was the gymnasium and the practices associated with it that angered the pious Jews, the HASIDIM, and that were the cause of the Maccabean Revolt (*see* MACCABEES). One cause of offense was that on stripping naked for the exercises the young Jew made his circumcision obvious to all, and therefore became reluctant to have his own baby boys circumcised. Moreover, the cult of the body seemed almost like idolatry to the more conservative-minded Jews; certainly it was closely associated with a nation of idolaters. In addition to this, those who met in the gymnasium attended in Greek clothes, and part of the dress of the *ephebos* was the broad-brimmed felt hat called the *petasus,* which was objectionable because it was associated with the god Hermes. *See* DISCUS. N. TURNER

H. The abbreviation for "Holiness Code," which designates a legal section of P material consisting of Lev. 17-26. Its compilation is usually assigned to the seventh-sixth century B.C. Close affinities with Ezekiel are apparent, but priority is disputed. *See* PENTATEUCH. D. N. FREEDMAN

HAAHASHTARI hā'ə hăsh'tə rī [האחשתרי, the Ahashtarites] (I Chr. 4:6). A family of the tribe of Judah.

Bibliography. M. Noth, *Die israelitischen Personennamen* (1928), p. 236.

HABAIAH hə bā'yə [חביה, Yahu has hidden (*i.e.*, protected)]; KJV OBDIA ŏb dī'ə [Codex A 'Οβδιά] in I Esd. 5:38. Alternately: HOBAIAH hō bā'yə (Neh. 7:63). Eponym of one of the families of returned exiles claiming priestly descent, but unable to document their claim, and therefore denied the rights of the priesthood, at least temporarily (Ezra 2:61; cf. vss. 62-63; Neh. 7:63; I Esd. 5:38).

B. T. DAHLBERG

HABACUC hăb'ə kək. Douay Version form of HABAKKUK.

HABAKKUK hə băk'ək [חבקוק; LXX 'Αμβακούμ; Vulg. *Habacuc*]. A cultic prophet of Judah who lived during the last days of Josiah (640-609 B.C.) and under the reign of Jehoiakim (609-598 B.C.). The book which bears his name is eighth among the minor prophets in the OT canon. *See* map "Palestine: Micah, Nahum, Habakkuk, Zephaniah," under ZEPHANIAH, BOOK OF.

1. Name
2. Nature of the book
3. The lamentation and prayer liturgy
   a. Title and opening lament
   b. The oracle of Yahweh
   c. The prophet's protest
   d. The watchtower
   e. The five woes
4. The Dead Sea Scroll commentary
5. The psalm
6. Religious teachings

Bibliography

1. Name. The origin of the name Habakkuk is uncertain. Nöldeke derives it from the Arabic *hibhkatun,* "dwarf." Noth derives it from an Akkadian plant name, *ḫambaḳûḳu,* which is more probable. Mowinckel calls attention to the legend in the LXX of Bel and the Dragon, in the title of which the prophet is called "Habakkuk, son of Jesus of the tribe of Levi" (vs. 1). If that tradition is correct, Habakkuk was linked definitely to the priesthood.

2. Nature of the book. Many scholars consider the book to constitute a unity, possibly a liturgy for a day of penitence. The Dead Sea Scroll of Habakkuk, however, does not include ch. 3—a theophanic hymn—and this omission suggests to some critics that only chs. 1-2 are authentic.

Direct divine utterance, spoken through the mouth of an official and authorized mediator or cultic prophet, had its place within the liturgy of any particular day in the cultus of ancient Israel. Many psalms show that such a liturgy had poetic and musical form. From the beginning the word of divine revelation in Israel was clothed in poetic, rhythmical, metrical form. The same must have been the case as regards the words of revelation in the liturgy of the temple. The psalms are not always the expression of one mood or one voice. In many of them are expressed various moods and motifs, and in the actual rendering they are compositions of a cultic-liturgical nature.

It fell to the temple prophets in the cultus of Judah to attend to the position of the temple singers. Songs sung in the name of the congregation were undoubtedly sung by such singers. One would not be in error to assume that the cultic songs of the individual which were sung in connection with such rites of purification as are associated with the rituals of lamentation, while sung in the name of the congregation, would actually be rendered by professionals, the temple singers.

As Mowinckel has shown, not many of the common people were at home in the appropriate ritual details which were particularly fitting for the psalm's rendition. The songs were not sung with music books before them, but from memory. It is likely that most of the songs came from the hearts and minds of the men who belonged to the profession of temple singers.

If the prophet Habakkuk was such a prophet, he was very familiar with cultic compositions. The first two chapters of his book are in the form of a lamentation and prayer liturgy.

3. The lamentation and prayer liturgy (chs. 1-2). ***a. Title and opening lament (1:1-4).*** Following the title (1:1), which introduces the book as the "oracle of God," comes the prophetic lament. The date is approximately 598 B.C. The first destructive blow of the Babylonians' (Chaldeans') might has fallen upon Judah. That which the prophet Jeremiah had clearly foreseen as certain has happened. Here is a note frequently to be sounded in Judah, and it is destined to continue for some time—the note of national lamentation: "O LORD, how long?" It is a cry for help, but God does not seem to hear. Habakkuk sees, taking place before his very eyes, and seemingly ignored by God, destruction and violence on a vast scale. Law has surrendered to force, so that righteousness has no opportunity. The wicked are strong enough to throttle the power of justice. According to some scholars, he who utters these words is confronted by the Chaldeans, a "bitter and hasty nation" (vs. 6), whose standard of justice has in it no social concern for the rights of other nations, and whose plans of ruthless conquest embrace the then-known inhabited world. Other critics, however, maintain that the lament reflects the domestic situation in Judah before the Battle of Carchemish (605 B.C.).

b. The oracle of Yahweh (1:5-11). What is taking place in history has meaning. The prophet discerns that it is the mighty God who, at this very moment, is using the powerful Chaldean nation set on world conquest. The emergence of this ruthless and cruel world power in the Near East began in 612 B.C., when Nabopolassar came into power, and Nineveh—famed capital of Assyria, and for centuries the terror of small powers such as Judah—fell before his superior might. No unillumined eye could see anything good for Judah or for the entire Near East in what was being done by the Chaldeans, that ruthless nation which knew no right but might (1:11).

c. The prophet's protest (1:12-17). One is not surprised at Habakkuk's protest to God, whom he addresses as "from everlasting," "my Holy One," the sole deity of his own worship. He is convinced that God's purpose in contemporary history is that the Chaldeans express upon Judah the Lord's judgment and his chastisement (vs. 12). But how can this be? How can the pure eyes of God endure to look on with equanimity while he sees a pitiless nation like the Chaldeans swallowing up a people more righteous than itself (vs. 13)? How can he let the Judeans be taken on the Chaldean hook, and dragged out with the Chaldean seine? How can he permit the Chaldeans to sap Judah's strength, then make it possible for them to deal just as mercilessly with peoples other than Judah and just as helpless as Judah is over against such pagan power (vss. 14-17)?

d. The watchtower (2:1-5). It was one of the great and insistent questions which have never been adequately answered. Habakkuk evidently had a high retreat to which he was accustomed to go, where he might brood over his problems and await, in receptivity, God's message in such an hour when he desperately needed light. He designated his retreat as "the tower"; it was his "watch," his "lookout," to which he went to await in eager spiritual receptivity Yahweh's word. His purpose was to "look forth to see what he [Yahweh] will say to me," in answer to the question he had posed in 1:17. Is the Chaldean nation to be permitted by God to keep on mastering nation after nation, "to bring all of them up with a hook," to "drag them out with his net," to pull them along with his seine, and thus dominate and absorb people after people with impunity?

There came to him that day a vision experience in which the holy God mediated to him on behalf of his nation one of the greatest messages of OT religion. The message was of such importance that he felt a divine impulse to write it succinctly and plainly upon tablets such as were used for the writing down of prophetic messages. The message was to be written in large characters so that even a runner could see it and read it without stopping (2:2). The content of it was to be an abiding truth which one must wait for in spiritual sensitivity and with hushed eagerness of expectation (vs. 3). The truth may seem to be slow in coming, but the prophet is patiently to "wait for it." Then comes the reply.

To this simple but profound revelation which the prophet is about to receive, there are two parts. "He whose soul is not upright in him shall fail" (vs. 4*a*). I.e., the nation or person that proceeds upon a policy that is not erect, upright, honest, just, or morally straight, shall fail. Despotism, ruthless domination on the part of nation or man, is bound to fail. The present Chaldean policy of cruel dealing with peoples such as it can and does overpower will not triumph. Its pitiless power is but seeming power.

The second part of the revelation (vs. 4*b*) is the positive putting of the great truth: "The righteous [be it nation or person] shall live by his faith." The Hebrew word for "FAITH" is אמונה, from the verbal root אמן, meaning "confirm, support" (*cf.* AMEN).

In 2:5 the Dead Sea Scroll of Habakkuk reads, instead of "Wine is treacherous," "Wealth is treacherous," which in the context most likely gives a more correct reading.

e. The five woes (2:6-19). Habakkuk lifted up against the figure of the arrogant, wealthy oppressor (the Chaldeans) a taunt song, in a series of five woes. While the meaning was perforce veiled, every loyal Judean saw clearly what he meant, and found utterance for his own passionate and bottled-up indignation against the Chaldean nation.

a) The first woe (vss. 6*b*-8) deals with Nebuchadrezzar's lust for tribute from the nations he conquered. The prophet viewed him as a merciless creditor, exacting from his conquered peoples heavy impost.

b) The second woe (vs. 9) lifts into the open the purpose of the Chaldean pillage and plunder—to make the empire so strong materially that no nation would dare challenge it.

c) The third woe (vss. 12-13) focuses upon the cruelty of the Chaldean oppressor, for Nebuchadrezzar used the naked human strength of his captives to erect the cities which he built or rebuilt, so that no national power could challenge his dominance. Vs. 14 is an almost word-for-word quotation from Isa. 11:9*b*, and the thought of it is appropriate in the present context.

d) The fourth woe (vss. 15-16*c*) solemnly teaches that the Chaldean dealings toward his neighbors in merciless power will rebound upon the Chaldean nation itself. The primeval dragons of Chaos and Disorder—the "beasts" of vs. 17, Leviathan and Behemoth—in the hour of judgment will bring upon the proud Chaldeans shattering destruction.

e) The fifth and last woe (vs. 19) is a rebuke to the Chaldean worship of their gods, Bel, Shamash, and Marduk, whose cult was performed at the Babylonian temples with elegance, pomp, and brilliancy. The concluding verse (20) brings a vivid contrast between the man-made idols, brilliantly overlaid with gold and silver yet utterly lifeless (vs. 19), and the invisible but potently present Lord in his holy temple, before whose majestic face the entire earth is summoned to awed silence.

4. The Dead Sea Scroll commentary. Scholars have discovered in the Dead Sea Scroll on Hab. 1-2 about fifty readings which vary from the received MT of the OT, a few of which seem reasonably conclusive. The oft-debated reading "Chaldeans" in 1:6 is confirmed. For Hab. 1:11 Elliger rightly accepts the scroll's rendering: "And he makes his might his God." The Habakkuk Commentary on 1:17 omits the interrogative particle so as to read: "Therefore he bares his sword continually slaying nations and has no pity," thus suggesting merciless slaughter.

5. The psalm (ch. 3). The fact that the Dead Sea Scroll of the Habakkuk Commentary neither contains nor refers to the book of Habakkuk supports the long-held view of many scholars that ch. 3 was not part of the original Habakkuk. G. B. Gray views it as having been derived from some psalm collection. S. R. Driver calls attention to the nature of its content, viewing it as a lyric ode, sublime in poetic conception and splendid in diction, and he ranks it along with the finest Hebrew poetry in the OT. In the form of a vision experience, the poet describes Yahweh's decisive struggle with his enemies, issuing in their ultimate and final defeat. Not unlike an ancient "dithyrambic" Greek hymn, it has a wild and frantic nature for it is written in an ardent vein.

After an opening title (vs. 1), in which a final editor designates ch. 3 as a "prayer of Habakkuk the prophet," comes a majestic poem on Yahweh's advent (vss. 2-15). There are echoes in it of the earlier theophanies of Deut. 33; Judg. 5 (cf. also Ps. 77).

The poet remembers Yahweh's work (vs. 2), and he pictures the holy God coming from Teman in Edom, marching across Paran, which lies between Sinai and Kadesh-Barnea (vss. 3-4). God's destructive power is pictured in mythological terms (vss. 5-7). Yahweh has battled with the powerful forces of primeval chaos (vss. 8-11). Now it is with the destructive Chaldeans that the mighty God is angry, as he goes forth to save his people (vss. 12-15).

The poet is greatly stirred by his vision and is left trembling, almost consumed, with deep feeling (vs. 16 *ab*). But now he turns from fearful awe to calm trust in Yahweh's ultimate intervention, in judgment upon the Chaldean (vs. 16*c*).

The prophetic liturgy and the psalm now conclude in triumph (vss. 17-19). It is a heartfelt cry of trust in God, a magnificent expression of the victory of faith over all misfortune and loss.

6. Religious teachings. The little book of Habakkuk is filled with truths which stand at the core of Hebrew religion: History has meaning if one takes the long view and judges events from the perspective of faith. Uprightness in the soul is necessary for individuals and nations alike. The righteous shall live by his faith. Wealth is treacherous as a basis of human dependence for security. Ruthless dealings rebound upon the doer. God can overrule an evil nation for his righteous purpose. Evil is bound to fail in the end, even though it may seem victorious. There is no might but right. Trust in God is the only sure basis of strength, regardless of external situations. The ultimate of faith is joy in communion with God.

Bibliography. S. R. Driver, ed., *The Minor Prophets,* New Century Bible, vol. II (1906). O. Procksch, *Die kleinen prophetischen Schriften vor dem Exil* (1910). J. M. P. Smith *et al., A Critical and Exegetical Commentary on Micah, Zephaniah, Nahum, Habakkuk, Obadiah, and Joel,* ICC (1911). A. B. Davidson, *The Books of Nahum, Habakkuk and Zephaniah,* Cambridge Bible (1920). G. A. Smith, *The Book of the Twelve Prophets* (1929). G. W. Wade and G. G. Stonehouse, *The Books of the Prophets Zephaniah, Nahum and Habakkuk,* WC (1929). E. Sellin, *Das Zwölfprophetenbuch* (1930). J. Lachmann, *Das Buch Habakuk* (1932). H. Junker, *Die zwölf kleinen Propheten* (1938). W. Lüthi, *Habakuk rechtet mit Gott* (1946). M. Wittenburg, *Habakuk* (1949). J. Coppens, *Les douze Petits Prophètes: Bréviaire du prophétisme* (1950). K. Elliger, *Das Buch der zwölf kleinen Propheten,* vol. II (1950). M. Schumpp, *Das Buch der zwölf Propheten* (1950). F. Horst, *Die zwölf kleinen Propheten* (1954). P. Trinquet, *Joel, Abdias, Habacuc* (1954). C. L. Taylor, Jr., Introduction and Exegesis of Habakkuk, *IB,* VI (1956), 973-1003. W. Vischer, *Der Prophet Habakuk* (1958).

Special studies: A. F. Kirkpatrick, *The Doctrine of the Prophets* (1932). W. Staerk, "Zu Hab. 1:5-11; Geschichte oder Mythos?" *ZAW,* LI (1933), 1-28. G. R. Driver, "Linguistic and Textual Problems: Minor Prophets III, Habakkuk," *JTS,* XXXIX (1938), 394-98. E. A. Leslie, *The Prophets Tell Their Own Story* (1939). P. Humbert, *Problèmes du livre d'Habacuc* (1944). A. T. Pearson, *The Problem of Unity and Date in Habakkuk* (1948). H. Schmidt, "Ein Psalm im Buche Habakkuk," *ZAW,* LXII (1949), 52-63 (on Hab. 1:2-4, 12-13; 3:18-19). M. Stenzel, "Hab. 2:1-4, 5*a*," *Bibl.,* XXXIII (1952), 506-10. D. M. Lloyd-Jones, *From Fear to Faith; Studies in the Book of Habakkuk* (1953). E. Osswald, "Zur Hermeneutik des Habakuk-Kommentars," *ZAW,* 68 (1956), 243-56.

Studies on Hab. 3: F. C. Burkitt, "The Psalm of Habakkuk," *JTS* (1915), pp. 62-85. F. J. Stephens, "The Babylonian Dragon Myth in Hab. 3," *JBL,* XLIII (1924), 290-93. H. Bévenot, "Le Cantique Habacuc," *RB,* XLII (1933), 499-525. T. H. Gaster, "The Battle of the Rain and the Sea," *Iraq,* IV (1937), 21-32. W. A. Irwin, "The Mythological Background of Hab. 3," *Journal of Near Eastern Studies,* I (1942), 10-40. W. F. Albright, "The Interpretation of Hab. 3:4," in H. H. Rowley, ed., *Studies in OT Prophecy* (1950), pp. 1-18. M. Delcor, "La geste de Yahvé au temps de l'Exode et l'espérance du psalmiste en Hab. iii," *Miscellanea biblica B. Ubach* (1953), pp. 287-302. S. Mowinckel, "Zum Psalm des Habakuk," *Theologische Zeitschrift,* IX (1953), 1-22. P. Béguerie, "Le psaume d'Habacuc," *Études sur les Prophètes d'Israël* (1954), pp. 53-84. "Psalm Criticism Between 1900 and 1935," *Vetus Testamentum,* 5 (1955), 13-33.

Studies on the Qumran Commentary on Hab. 1–2: W. H. Brownlee, "The Jerusalem Habakkuk Scroll," *BASOR,* CXII (1948), 8-18; "Further Light on Habakkuk," *BASOR,* CXIV (1949), 9-10. M. Delcor, *Les manuscrits de la Mer Morte; essai sur le Midrasch d'Habacuc* (1951). H. E. Del Medico, *Deux manuscrits hébreux de la Mer Morte* (1951). W. H. Brownlee, "The Historical Allusions of the DS Habakkuk Midrash," *BASOR,* CXXVI (1952), 10-20. M. Delcor, "Où en est le problème du Midrash d'Habacuc?" *RHR,* CXLII (1952), 129-46. H. H. Rowley, *The Zadokite Fragments and the Dead Sea Scrolls* (1952). K. Elliger, *Studien zum Habakuk-Kommentar vom Toten Meer* (1953). C. Detaye, *Le cadre historique du Midrash d'Habacuc* (1954). F. F. Bruce, *The Teacher of Righteousness in the Qumran Texts* (1956). H. H. Rowley, "The Teacher of Righteousness and the Dead Sea Scrolls," *Bulletin of the John Rylands Library,* vol. L (1957).

E. A. Leslie

HABAZZINIAH hăb'ə zĭ nī'ə [חבצניה] (Jer. 35:3); KJV HABAZINIAH. Grandfather of the Rechabites who were tested by Jeremiah.

HABBACUC. KJV Apoc. form of Habakkuk.

HABERGEON hăb'ər jən. KJV translation of שריון (II Chr. 26:14; Neh. 4:16—H 4:10; RSV Coat of Mail); שריה (Job 41:26—H 41:18; RSV Javelin); תחרא (Exod. 28:32; 39:23; RSV Garment). A habergeon is a defensive armor, originally for the neck and shoulders but later reaching the thighs and even below the knees. *See* WEAPONS AND IMPLEMENTS OF WAR. W. S. McCULLOUGH

HABIRU, HAPIRU hä'bĭ ro͞o, —pĭ— [Akkad. *ḫabiru, ḫapiru;* Ugar. *'prm;* Egyp. *'apir*]. The name of a group of people. Whether *ḫabiru* or *ḫapiru* should be considered the correct reading cannot be decided with certainty; both readings seem to be possible. As to this question, it should perhaps be kept in mind that *b* and *p* are interchangeable in some cases. Thus, e.g., a *b* in Hebrew may sometimes correspond to a *p* in Ugaritic. In Akkadian signs exist which may be read with a *b* or a *p*. Accordingly, the two forms *ḫabiru* and *ḫapiru* may be local varieties. This may be so in Akkadian, and, provided that Ugaritic, *'prm* and Hebrew *'brm* are etymologically related, we have the same interchange there. *Ḫabiru* is most likely of West Semitic origin, which is apparent from the first consonant, ', in Hebrew, Ugaritic, and Egyptian. The word seems originally to have been, not an ethnic term, but rather the denotation of a social class, though this is very uncertain. The problem of the Habiru was exhaustingly discussed at the fourth international Conference of Assyriologists. The volume published by J. Bottéro containing the material (*see bibliography*) shows how completely scholarly opinion diverges on practically every point, also on the question of etymology. Nor can the Sumerian ideogram *SA.GAZ* (with several variants—e.g., *SAG.GAZ*) be explained. One Akkadian word or another may be adduced for comparison; but since the word, as has been mentioned, is undoubtedly of West Semitic origin, an Akkadian correspondent does not necessarily occur in the material known.

The earliest occurrence of the Habiru is found in texts dating from the Third Dynasty of Ur (roughly *ca.* 2050 B.C.). From that time on, they are mentioned in texts from all important archives in the Near East and thus appear in the second millennium spread over a wide area. They occur, e.g., in Mesopotamia in the reigns of Warad-Sin and Rim-Sin of Larsa and in the reign of Hammurabi of Babylon. They are mentioned in texts from Mari in the reigns of Yasmaḫ-Addu and Zimri-Lim, who were contemporaries of Hammurabi; in texts from Alalaḫ, Nuzi, Boghazköy; and, finally, in the Amarna Letters. In texts from Ras Shamra we find the corresponding word *'prm.*

As to their social position, the Habiru often appear in the service of one king or another, and more particularly, in many cases as soldiers. As to their names, some Habiru people have West Semitic names, but there are also Habiru who have Akkadian and even non-Semitic names. The same is true of the *'prm* of the Ras Shamra Texts, who seem to be of a heterogeneous ethnic character having only their social position in common. Such facts have led scholars to believe that Habiru is not an ethnic term but rather denotes some kind of social group. This is particularly clear in lists from Boghazköy (KUB IX, 34; IX, 4; HT, 6; KUB VII, 42). There Habiru are mentioned in lists of social classes. It is important to note that they are mentioned in the second part of the list, the lower classes. They seem to occupy a position between the free citizens and the slaves and may accordingly be some kind of clients. In some texts the gods of the Habiru are mentioned; this indicates that they were a real class of the society.

On the other hand, there are texts where "Habiru" seems to be more of a gentilic term. This is so, e.g., in texts from Mari, where Habiru operate in bands as seminomads in the region from the Ḫabur to the Baliḫ and the Euphrates. Also in texts from Alalaḫ, Habiru seems to be an ethnic group: King Idrimi dwelt for seven years among the Habiru soldiers. They lived in groups together and seem to have been a special class of the population, though the term may also have had the special denotation of "soldier" or "officer." In the Amarna Letters the Habiru people appear as a separate ethnic group having West Semitic names.

From these few examples it is evident that the Habiru sometimes seem to be a social class, while in other cases they are most likely an ethnic group. The word may originally have been an appellative which developed into an ethnic term. In that case we may compare "Habiru" with "Canaanite," which also originally may have denoted a social class (merchant; *see* CANAAN), and "Amorite," for in Mesopotamia the Amorites were also apparently a social group. In Gen. 14, where (*ca.* 1700 B.C.) Abraham is called העברי, "the Hebrew," there is no indication of the meaning of the word "Hebrew." It may denote an ethnic group, but also a social class. But generally the term "Hebrew" in the OT is an ethnic term. It seems probable that Habiru is an Akkadian form related to Hebrew העברי, and, in all probability, the Hebrews were a branch of the Habiru.

Bibliography. J. Bottéro, *Le problème des Habiru à la 4e rencontre assyriologique internationale,* Cahiers de la Société asiatique, vol. XII (1954); M. Greenberg, *The Ḫab/piru* (1955). These two volumes contain all the material and many valuable comments on the relevant texts and problems.

A. HALDAR

HABOR hā'bôr [חבור]. A tributary of the Euphrates, flowing into the latter from the NE. The Habor (Assyrian "Khabur") watered a heavily settled valley

From *Atlas of the Bible* (Thomas Nelson & Sons Limited)

1. The Habor River, a tributary of the Euphrates

in antiquity, as the many mounds of buried cities attest. Some of the Israelites were exiled to the banks of the Habor by Shalmaneser in King Hosea's ninth year (II Kings 17:6; 18:11; I Chr. 5:26).

Fig. HAB 1. C. H. GORDON

HACALIAH hăk'ə lī'ə [חכליה] (Neh. 1:1; 10:1); KJV HACHALIAH. The father of Nehemiah. The frequently proposed interpretation of the name as "Wait for Yahu" is unlikely, since such a verb form in a name is unprecedented in the OT.

HACHILAH hə kī'lə, hăk'ĭ lə [חכילה]. A hill in the neighborhood of Ziph where David took refuge when pursued by Saul (I Sam. 23:19; 26:1). It is described as being near the wilderness of Jeshimon, which would place it in the neighborhood of Hebron, but the site has not been identified. S. COHEN

HACHMONI hăk'mō nī [חכמוני, *from a place name*(?)]; HACHMONITE —nīt. **1.** The family of Jashobeam, one of David's Mighty Men (I Chr. 11:11). Jashobeam is called a Tachemonite in II Sam. 23:8, probably because of a textual error.

2. The family of Jehiel, a servant of David (I Chr. 27:32, where the word should be rendered "Hachmonite" as in 11:11, since both are the same in Hebrew).

Bibliography. M. Noth, *Die israelitischen Personennamen* (1928), p. 232. H. H. GUTHRIE, JR.

HADAD hā'dăd [הדד, אדד, thunderer(?); Akkad. *Adad, Addu, Haddu;* Ugar. *Hd*]; KJV HADAR —där in Gen. 25:15. Alternately: HADAR [הדר] (Gen. 36:39). **1.** The eighth son of Ishmael (Gen. 25:15; I Chr. 1:30).

2. A king of Edom (Gen. 36:35-36; I Chr. 1:46-47).

3. Another king of Edom (Gen. 36:36; I Chr. 1:50-51). Gen. 36:39 should, with some forty Hebrew MSS, as well as with other witnesses to the text, be read "Hadad" instead of "Hadar."

4. A member of the royal house of EDOM who escaped to Egypt when David conquered Edom, and then later return to his homeland to revolt against Solomon (I Kings 11:14, 17, 19, 21, 25). The Hebrew actually reads "Adad" for the first "Hadad" in I Kings 11:17, and it has been conjectured that I Kings 11:14 ff combines two accounts, one of Hadad the Edomite and the other of Adad the Midianite. Convincing reasons have been given (*see bibliography*) for identifying this Hadad with 3 *above*.

Bibliography. A. M. Honeyman, "The Evidence for Regnal Names Among the Hebrews," *JBL*, LXVII (1948), pp. 13-25; W. F. Albright, *Archaeology and the Religion of Israel* (3rd ed., 1953), pp. 73 ff.

Courtesy of the Pierpont Morgan Library

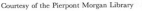

2. Offering being made to the storm-god Hadad, with one foot on the mountain and holding a saw in his hand; from the First Babylonian Dynasty

5. The ancient Semitic storm-god who as the great Baal of the Ugaritic pantheon figured in the struggle of the religion of Israel against Canaanite religion. *See* BAAL (DEITY); UGARIT.

Fig. HAD 2. H. H. GUTHRIE, JR.

HADADEZER hăd'ə dē'zər [הדדעזר; Akkad. *Adad-idri,* Hadad is help]; KJV HADAREZER hā'dər ē'zər [הדרעזר] in II Sam. 10:16, 19; I Chr. 18:3, 5, 7-10; 19:16, 19. A king of Zobah, defeated by David. The most powerful Aramean ruler of his day, Hadadezer extended his control as far as the Upper Euphrates, seizing territory formerly held by Assyria. The weak Ashurrabi II (1012-972 B.C.) was unable to check him. The conflict between Zobah and Israel had begun in the reign of Saul.

The OT preserves three accounts of campaigns by David which involved Hadadezer: (*a*) II Sam. 10:6-14, where a coalition of Aramean rulers who had come to the relief of the besieged city of Rabbah of the Ammonites were defeated by Joab (*see* HANUN 1); (*b*) 10:15-18, which describes a battle at HELAM between David and a new army of Hadadezer under his commander Shobach. Again the Arameans were defeated, and "all the kings who were servants of Hadadezer . . . made peace with Israel"; and (*c*) 8:3-8, which tells of a defeat inflicted on Hadadezer "as he went to restore his power at the river Euphrates." A second battle defeated the troops of Damascus who were coming to Hadadezer's aid. Some critics maintain that each account describes a different campaign; others feel that (*b*) and (*c*) deal with the same series of events.

The final result of the Aramean wars was that David garrisoned Damascus and exacted a tribute from Hadadezer. This gave him virtual control of the Transjordan trade as well as the rich copper deposits of the *biqa'*.

Bibliography. T. H. Robinson, *A History of Israel*, I (1951), 201, 237-38; G. E. Wright, *Biblical Archaeology* (1957), p. 124; M. Noth, *The History of Israel* (1958), pp. 194-96. Contrast E. G. H. Kraeling, *Aram and Israel* (1918), pp. 42-44; M. F. Unger, *Israel and the Arameans of Damascus* (1957), pp. 42-48.
R. W. CORNEY

HADADRIMMON hā'dăd rĭm'ən [הדדרמון, *from* Hadad (*probably* thunder; *cf.* Arab. *hadda,* thunder) *plus* Rimmon (*probably* RIMMON 3)]. A deity for whom public mourning was made in the great central plain of Palestine by Megiddo (Zech. 12:11).

Hadad is known from the Ras Shamra Texts as the proper name of BAAL, the Amorite storm-god, also identified with the vegetation he stimulated. The mourning mentioned in Zech. 12:11 was probably a rite which had its mythical counterpart in the mourning for the dead Baal by his sister, the goddess Anat.

Bibliography. M. Jastrow, *The Religion of Babylonia and Assyria* (1898), pp. 156-61. For further bibliography, *see* BAAL (DEITY). J. GRAY

HADAR hā'där. **1.** KJV form of HADAD, SON OF ISHMAEL (Gen. 25:15).

2. Variant of HADAD 3 (Gen. 36:39).

HADAREZER. KJV alternate form of HADADEZER.

HADASHAH hə dăsh'ə [חדשה, new] (Josh. 15:37). A village of Judah in the Shephelah district of Lachish. It was located in the vicinity of MORESHETH-GATH, but precise identification remains uncertain.

HADASSAH hə dăs'ə [Aram. הדסה=הדס, myrtle; *or* Akkad. *ḫadaššatu,* bride] (Esth. 2:7). Either the original Hebrew name of ESTHER or a title given to her. If the latter, Hadassah would be the Akkadian "bride," a title used for Ishtar.

HADATTAH. *See* HAZOR-HADATTAH.

HADES hā'dēz. *See* DEAD, ABODE OF THE; GEHENNA.

HADID hā'dĭd [חדיד, sharp; Αδιδα]. A town of Benjamin overlooking the coastal plain at the NW extremity of the Shephelah. It was one of a cluster of towns situated near the mouth of the Valley of Aijalon, and with Lod (Lydda) and Ono it constituted the ancestral homeland of more than 720 exiles who returned from the Babylonian exile (Ezra 2:33; Neh. 7:37; 11:34).

All OT references to the site are postexilic; but, in addition to the implication of the OT references, its early date is indicated by its inclusion on the Karnak list of Thut-mose III and its description in the Mishna as a walled city since the days of Joshua ('Arak. 9.6).

It is probably to be identified with modern el-Haditheh, between three and four miles NE of Lydda, and with Adida (I Macc. 12:38; 13:13; Josephus). The site was fortified by Simon Maccabeus before he met Trypho (Jos. Antiq. XIII.vi.5; I Macc. 12:38), and by Vespasian before he went against Jerusalem (Jos. War IV.ix.1). It was near this site, also, that the Nabatean Aretas III defeated Alexander Janneus (Jos. Antiq. XIII.xv.2).

W. H. MORTON

HADLAI hăd'lī [חדלי; Arab. *ḥadlun,* fat] (II Chr. 28:12). An Ephraimite person or family.

Bibliography. M. Noth, *Die israelitischen Personennamen* (1928), p. 226.

HADORAM hə dôr'əm [הדורם, Haddu (Hadad) is exalted]. **1.** An Arabian tribe, called the first-born of Joktan (Gen. 10:27; I Chr. 1:21) and possibly located in Yemen. *See also* UZAL.

2. Son of Tou the king of Hamath (I Chr. 18:10). The parallel passage in II Sam. 8:10 reads "Joram," which should probably be emended to "Hadoram."

3. An official of Rehoboam who was in charge of the forced labor (II Chr. 10:18); the same as Adoram (I Kings 12:18) and Adoniram (4:6). S. COHEN

HADRACH hăd'răk [חדרך, Aram. חזרך, *the inscription of king Zkr;* Akkad. *Ḫatarikka*]. A town in the NW part of Lebanon.

HA-ELEPH hā ē'lĭf [האלף] (Josh. 18:28); KJV ELEPH ē'lĕf. A city in Benjamin. The name is probably to be read with the preceding word, "Zela," as "Zela-ha-eleph," and is perhaps modern Salah, between Jerusalem and Gibeon. *See* ZELAH.

HAG, NIGHT. *See* NIGHT HAG.

HAGAB hā'găb [חגב, grasshopper, locust]; KJV Apoc. AGABA ăg'ə bə. Head of a family of NETHINIM among the returned exiles (Ezra 2:46; I Esd. 5:30). The name is lacking in the parallel Neh. 7:48.

HAGABAH hăg'ə bə [חגבה, grasshopper, locust] (Ezra 2:45); KJV Apoc. GRABA grä'bə [Codex A, Γαβά]. Alternately: HAGABA [חגבא] (Neh. 7:48). Head of a family of NETHINIM among the returned exiles; evidently to be distinguished from HAGAB (Ezra 2:46; but note the absence of Hagab in Neh. 7:48).

HAGAR hā'gär [הגר; Ἅγαρ (KJV AGAR)]. The handmaid of Sarah whom she gave as a concubine to Abraham and who became the mother of Ishmael.

The Hagar stories have been preserved primarily by J (Gen. 16:1*b*-2, 4-14) and E (21:8-21), with a few verses from P (16:1*a*, 3, 15-16). Most scholars think that the J and E traditions were originally parallel, both depicting the expulsion of Hagar and Ishmael from the family of Abraham. The insertion of vs. 9 in ch. 16 provided the connecting link between the two.

In the first story (16:1-16) Hagar is identified as the Egyptian handmaid of the barren Sarai. Since Yahweh's promise to Abram (12:1 ff) was endangered by her barrenness, Sarai gave Hagar to him for children—a custom paralleled elsewhere in Genesis (Rachel and Leah in 30:3, 9), as well as in the NUZI texts. When Hagar became pregnant, she assumed an arrogant attitude that infuriated her mistress. With Abram's permission, Sarai treated Hagar so harshly that she fled defiantly into the Wilderness of Shur, an area between Beer-sheba and Egypt. At a spring the angel of Yahweh appeared to announce that she was to bear a son from whom would come a multitude of descendants and whose name was to be Ishmael ("God has heard"), because "God had heard" her in her affliction. Ishmael would be a real Bedouin, a "wild ass of a man," fierce and warlike. Because of this theophany, she named the well BEER-LAHAI-ROI, the "well of one who sees and lives."

The second story (21:8-21) presumably occurred several years after the birth of Ishmael. At a feast Sarah saw Ishmael playing with her recently weaned child, Isaac, and was seized by the fear that Hagar's boy might become an heir alongside her own. She demanded of a reluctant Abraham the expulsion of Hagar and Ishmael. Weak and pathetic, Hagar fled to the dry Wilderness of Beer-sheba, where death for her child seemed certain until the angel of God showed her a well. He assured her that "God had heard" the voice of the crying Ishmael, who would not die but would become a great nation. And Ishmael grew up to live in the Wilderness of Paran, to become an expert with the bow, and to marry an Egyptian woman.

The Hagar traditions reflect the belief of the Hebrews that they were related to the wild, warlike Bedouin peoples to the S of Palestine, whose eponymous ancestor was ISHMAEL. Like the Hebrews, they too had Abraham as their father, but their ancestral mother, of course, was the inferior concubine Hagar. Whether there is a relation between the Hagrites (*see* HAGRITE) of I Chr. 5:10, 19-20; Ps. 83:6—H 83:7 and Hagar is not certain, but it is likely, since two of the sons of Ishmael (Gen. 25:15) are Hagrites (I Chr. 5:19).

In the NT, Paul makes allegorical use of the Hagar story (Gal. 4:21-31). Hagar and her son stand for the slavery of the old covenant, in contrast to the freedom of the new covenant typified by Isaac, the son of the free woman. M. NEWMAN

HAGARENE. KJV alternate form of HAGRITE.

HAGGADAH hə gä′də [הַגָּדָה, narration]. All scriptural interpretation which is nonlegal or narrative in character, and which aims at the development of inner piety and religious devotion. As such, Haggadah supplements HALACHAH as a source of Jewish teaching, the latter telling the son of Israel what duty is, the former stirring in him the will to an eager performance of this duty. The Haggadic method of instruction is by means of story, saga, legend, parable, homily, maxim, proverbs, and wise sayings. The same method and often also the same material are employed by the NT in imparting its teachings; nevertheless, insofar as the NT is not a work of scriptural interpretation and is not associated with the Halachah, it cannot be said to contain any Haggadah in the strictly technical sense of the term.

Bibliography. R. T. Herford, *Talmud and Apocrypha* (1933); I. Epstein, *Judaism* (rev. ed., 1945). I. EPSTEIN

HAGGAI hăg′ī, —ī [חַגַּי; LXX ʼΑγγαῖος]. The tenth in the series of twelve short prophetic books which forms the concluding section of the OT. *See* map "Palestine: Haggai, Zechariah, Malachi," under ZECHARIAH, BOOK OF.

A. *THE PROPHET.* The name Haggai is derived from the word for "a festival," which would suggest that the prophet was born on some feast day. Little or nothing is known of his background. He is referred to simply as "the prophet" (1:1, etc.; Ezra 5:1; 6:14), and no ancestry is given. He would appear, however, from this description, to have been a conspicuous figure, and Jewish tradition has it that he was known as a prophet in Babylon during the Exile.

On the evidence of 1:1 he was active in Jerusalem in 520 B.C.; this may suggest that he had made his way there sometime before this date. He does not appear to have been of the priestly caste, since he asks the priests' guidance on a matter of Levitical practice (2:11-13). If 2:3 implies that he had seen the temple before its destruction in 586, he was a very old man when he became one of the prime movers for its restoration in 520. In association with ZECHARIAH (Ezra 4:24–5:1; 6:14; Zech. 1:16) he rouses the people of Jerusalem and their leaders ZERUBBABEL and JOSHUA (3) to undertake this task; and it would appear to be largely because of his energy and enthusiasm, as indicated in his oracles, that the work of restoration was begun almost immediately after his first appeal, and completed within four years (Ezra 6:15).

In later Talmudic tradition Haggai was associated with Zechariah and Malachi as joint founder of the "Great Synagogue," and it was considered that with the death of these, the last of the prophets, the Holy Spirit departed from Israel. A number of psalms are attributed to Haggai and Zechariah in the LXX, Vulg., and Peshitta (e.g., Pss. 138; 146–149); this may account for the Christian, as opposed to the Jewish, tradition that the prophet was of priestly descent.

B. *THE BOOK.* Haggai is the first of the collection of prophecies dating from the postexilic period; the others are Zechariah and Malachi. Haggai is the shortest of the three, comprising merely two chapters totaling thirty-eight verses. These are made up of four utterances delivered within the space of four months in the second year of the reign of Darius I Hystaspis, king of Persia (522-486)—i.e., in 520. The form of the book would suggest that these oracles were collected by someone other than the prophet himself. Haggai is referred to throughout in the third person and is described impersonally as "the prophet." Moreover, the book serves as a record of the effect of the prophet's words, as well as a collection of his utterances. It is, of course, possible that Haggai himself compiled the book and chose to refer to himself in the third person, but the general view is that the compilation was done by some unknown disciple not long after the time at which the oracles were first delivered.

1. Historical background. Despite the Chronicler's impressive account of the return of the Jews to Jerusalem from exile as being the main result of the conquest of Babylon by CYRUS in 539 and, indeed, as being the chief motive behind Cyrus' campaigns, both the return and its sequel appear to have been much more prosaic than the narrative of Ezra 1–3 would suggest. According to the text of the Cylinder of Cyrus, when the victorious Persian king had taken possession of the territories of Babylon, he gave general permission to racial minorities exiled there to return to their own countries if they wished to do so.

Contrary to the Chronicler's rosy picture of a mass return of the exiled Jews to Palestine and the immediate undertaking of the rebuilding of the temple, it seems more probable that only some of the Jews availed themselves of this opportunity, and that their first task was to eke out some kind of existence in a land that had suffered much ever since its capital city had been destroyed fifty years earlier.

Under the leadership of Shesh-bazzar, who is described as the "prince of Judah" (Ezra 1:8) and "governor" (5:14), which presumably means that he was the first ruler of what was now the Persian province of Judah, it is possible that in 537 (i.e., the second year after the return; cf. Ezra 3:8-13) the repatriated exiles laid the foundations of a new temple amid the ruins of Jerusalem, as indicated in Ezra 5:16. If they did so, there is no indication in the books of Haggai and Zechariah that they had proceeded any further with its building.

It is more probable that the Chronicler, writing his narrative over two centuries later, has given an idealized account of what actually happened. In his desire to credit the returning exiles with a religious zeal to fulfil the hopes of Second Isaiah and Ezekiel, he has invested the early days of the return with a fervor to which the more sober contemporary evidence of Haggai and Zechariah lends no support. The impression conveyed by both these writings would tend to confirm the view that it was not until the emergence of Haggai as an inspired leader that any serious steps were taken to restore the dilapidated temple at all, and that the rebuilding did not, in fact, start until 520 (i.e., the second year of Darius I), under the governorship of Zerubbabel (ch. 1).

Many Jews had preferred to remain in Babylon (Jos. Antiq. XI.iii), including those who had established themselves most successfully. Those who returned not only were presumably not possessed of abundant means, but also whatever zeal they had for the restoration of the house of the Lord was tempered by finding themselves among people who had become reconciled to the sight of the ruined sanctuary.

The destruction of the temple in 586 by the army of Nebuchadnezzar (II Kings 25:9) would mean the breaching of the walls and the disappearance of the shrine and adjacent buildings, but the whole area with its courts would still be available as a sacred place for those who were minded to worship. An altar for burnt offerings was no difficult matter to erect, if, indeed, the old one had been destroyed, and there is evidence that this was in use (Jer. 41:5; cf. Hag. 2:14) and that priests were in attendance (Lam. 1:4). There are more somber indications in both Jeremiah and Ezekiel (e.g., Jer. 7:17-19; Ezek. 8:9-18) that pagan cults, including the worship of Ishtar, Tammuz, and the sun, had established themselves side by side with the worship of Yahweh. Even if these were conditions which obtained before the fall of Jerusalem, it would be more than likely that they persisted after the visible reminders of the superiority of Yahweh-worship had vanished.

Economic conditions, too, must further have lowered the morale of those who were left among the fragments of the Jewish state. The devastation of the Babylonian conquest was heightened both by harrying tactics on the part of the petty kingdoms which surrounded Judah, and later by the marauding Persian army under Cambyses on its way to invade Egypt in 525. When in addition to this we remember the gloomy picture drawn by the book of Haggai of a people crippled by a succession of bad harvests, with subsequent poverty, it is difficult to think that the period between the return and the emergence of Haggai as a leader can have been anything other than a dispiriting struggle for existence, far less one of religious enthusiasm. Concern for the rebuilding of the temple must have been the least of the anxieties of the sorely tried people of Jerusalem.

But outside Palestine big events were afoot. When Darius I succeeded Cambyses as ruler of the Persian Empire in 522, revolts broke out throughout the subject provinces. The supremacy of the Gentile masters of the world was threatened. To a prophetic mind such as that of Haggai, accustomed to look for the leading of Yahweh in the signs of the times, this must have suggested the prelude to the end event of history, the final destruction of the power of the Gentiles and the establishment of the messianic kingdom. With Zerubbabel, a scion of the house of David (I Chr. 3:17-19), installed as governor of Judah, and assuming in the prophet's mind messianic status, the time appeared to be ripe for the rehabilitation of the house of the Lord, so that Yahweh might return to his people, as Ezekiel and Second Isaiah had foretold, to establish his throne in Zion (Isa. 52:7-10; Ezek. 43:4-5). It was in such a situation that Haggai uttered the oracles which are contained in this book.

2. The four prophecies. ***a. Ch. 1.*** In August-September, 520, Haggai appeals to Zerubbabel and Joshua, the high priest, to rally the people to the rebuilding of the shattered temple. He accuses the people of Jerusalem who were in a position to help of being more concerned about their own comforts than that the house of the Lord should be restored. The disasters of drought and bad harvests from which they have suffered are nothing but God's punishment for their impious neglect. The prophet's words have an immediate effect, and, within three weeks, work on the temple commences.

b. 2:1-9. A month later Haggai has to appeal again. Apparently the builders had lost heart. They felt that the new temple could never compare with the glories of its predecessor. Haggai encourages them with the promise of the speedy advent of the messianic kingdom and the downfall of the Gentiles. Their treasures will flow to Jerusalem to enrich the new house of the Lord (cf. Zech. 2:8-9).

c. 2:10-19. The meaning of the third oracle, delivered two months later still (i.e., November-December, 520), is rather obscure. Some commentators prefer to rearrange the order. But, taken as it stands, it suggests that the prophet secures a decision from the priests to the effect that ritual uncleanness is more contagious than ritual holiness, and applies this to the rebuilding of the temple. He may mean that the previous unwillingness of the people to rebuild the temple had tainted their service of Yahweh, with consequent disaster to themselves; but that now that the work had started, their prosperity was assured. On the other hand, "this people" (vs. 14) may refer to the Samaritans (cf. Ezra 4:1-5), in which case Haggai is recommending that their offer of help should be rejected on the grounds that they are undesirable associates—presumably, at this pre-Nehemiah-Ezra stage, on political rather than religious grounds.

d. 2:20-23. In the last oracle, uttered on the same day as the preceding one, Haggai proclaims the impending end of Gentile domination in the Day of the Lord, and declares Zerubbabel to be the messianic king.

C. *THE SIGNIFICANCE OF HAGGAI.* The value of the book is historical rather than religious. The prophecies may originally have been connected with the cultic rites of the New Year Festival, but they represent a sad decline from the ethical vigor and conviction of those of the pre-exilic prophets. Haggai's chief concern is the re-establishment of the cultus, the shell rather than the kernel. While it may be true that without the shell the kernel withers, there are lacking here the profound insights into the nature of worship which we find in Amos or Jeremiah. Haggai takes the superficial view that material prosperity is assured provided the mechanics of worship are guaranteed.

Yet on a long-term view it must be said that, without the temple and the Judaism which centered on it, the legacy of the great prophets would have been quickly dissipated, and Christianity would have had no foundations on which to build. Haggai deserves to be remembered for his contribution to this. Zerubbabel was not the Messiah, as Haggai imagined, and the messianic age when it came did not bring about the downfall of the Gentiles and the enrichment of the temple, as the prophet expected; but the hope and encouragement which Haggai's message brought to the dejected community of Judah at that time was, in the providence of God, a significant milestone in the *Praeparatio Evangelica.*

From a historical point of view the value of the book is, of course, that together with the book of Zechariah it forms a corrective to the inaccuracies of the Chronicler and sheds welcome light on the obscure period between the fall of Jerusalem and the achievements of Nehemiah. *See* TEMPLE, JERUSALEM.

Bibliography. Commentaries: S. R. Driver, Century Bible (1906); H. G. Mitchell, ICC (1912); W. E. Barnes, Cambridge Bible (1917); G. A. Smith, EB (1928); E. Sellin, KAT (1929); F. Horst, HAT (1954); D. Winton Thomas, *IB*, vol. VI (1956). See also Introductions to the literature of the OT by Driver, Pfeiffer, Bentzen, etc.

For background see L. E. Browne, *Early Judaism* (1920).

Special study: P. F. Bloomhardt, "The Poems of Haggai," *HUCA*, V (1928) 153-95. W. NEIL

HAGGEDOLIM hăg'ə dō'lĭm [הגדולים, the great ones, *or* the high priests] (Neh. 11:14); KJV ONE OF THE GREAT MEN. The father of Zabdiel, a priest. Either the KJV is correct in translating the word (cf. LXX), or the text is corrupt.

HAGGERI. KJV form of HAGRI.

HAGGI hăg'ī [חגי, born on a feast day; *cf. personal names* חגי (HAGGAI), חגית, חגיה]; HAGGITES hăg'ītes. The second son of Gad; ancestral head of the "family of the Haggites" (Gen. 46:16; Num. 26:15).

HAGGIAH hă gī'ə [חגיה, festal (*i.e.*, born on a festival day]. A Levite; descendant of Merari (I Chr. 6:30—H 6:15). The last element of this name is not theophorous but hypocoristic.

Bibliography. M. Noth, *Die israelitischen Personennamen* (1928), p. 222. B. T. DAHLBERG

HAGGITES. *See* HAGGI.

HAGGITH hăg'ĭth [חגית, born on the feast day; *cf. personal names* Haggai, Haggi]. A wife of David; mother of Adonijah, who later claimed the throne (II Sam. 3:4; I Kings 1:5, 11; 2:13; I Chr. 3:2).

HAGIA. KJV Apoc. form of HATTIL.

HAGIOGRAPHA hăg'ĭ ŏg'rə fə, hā'jĭ— [כתובים, writings; ἁγιογραφα, holy writings]. The term (transliterated from Greek) used for the third division of the Hebrew Bible, the Writings. In contrast to the other two (the Law and the Prophets), it is a miscellaneous collection of eleven (in Hebrew) varied books which achieved canonization separately (*see* CANON OF THE OT). Printed Hebrew texts, following German and French MSS, place these books in the following order: (*a*) three large poetical books (Psalms, Proverbs, Job); (*b*) the five scrolls (Megilloth) which came to be read in the synagogues at five great feasts (Song of Solomon, Ruth, Lamentations, Ecclesiastes, Esther); (*c*) a book of late prophecy (Daniel); and (*d*) two books of postexilic history (Ezra-Nehemiah, Chronicles). English Bibles follow the Greek and consequently arrange these books in a different order. F. T. SCHUMACHER

HAGRI hăg'rī [הגרי] (I Chr. 11:38); KJV HAGGERI hăg'ə rī. Father of Mibhar, one of the Mighty Men in David's army. Instead of "Mibhar the son of Hagri" the parallel passage in II Sam. 23:36 has "Bani the Gadite," and this is preferred by commentators. R. F. SCHNELL

HAGRITE hăg'rīt [הגרי, descendant of Hagar(?)] (I Chr. 27:30—H 27:31); KJV HAGERITE hăg'ərīt. HAGRITES [הגריאים, הגראים, הגרים] (I Chr. 5:10, 19-20: Ps. 83:6—H 83:7); KJV HAGARITES [הגריאים, הגראים] in I Chr. 5:10, 19-20; KJV HAGARENES hăg'ə rēnz [הגרים] in Ps. 83:6—H 83:7. A pastoral Bedouin tribe living in the region E of Gilead. They are named with Moab, Edom, Ishmaelites, and other enemies of Israel who dwelt in the Transjordan (Ps. 83:6—H 83:7). They are likely the same people as the 'Αγρᾶιοι referred to by the Greek geographers Strabo, Ptolemy, and Pliny.

In the time of Saul the tribe of Reuben, perhaps with the assistance of the other Transjordan tribes, extended its territory to the edge of the desert by conquering the Hagrites (I Chr. 5:10, 19-22). When David organized his kingdom, Jaziz the Hagrite was given oversight of the flocks (I Chr. 27:30). The ethnological relationship of the Hagrites with Hagar the mother of Ishmael (Gen. 16) is uncertain.

"Sons of Hagar" (οἱ υἱοί 'Αγαρ; KJV "Agarenes") are mentioned in connection with Teman in Bar. 3:23. Their identification here is not significant. The passage is reminiscent of the tradition of the wisdom of the East, mentioned also in I Kings 4:30—H 5:10; Jer. 49:7; Obad. 8.

Bibliography. E. Meyer, *Die Israeliten und ihre Nachbarstämme* (1906), p. 328. R. F. SCHNELL

HAHIROTH. *See* PI-HAHIROTH.

HAI. KJV alternate form of AI.

HAIL, HAILSTONES [ברד, אלגביש; χάλαζα]. Hail occurs only as the result of violent turbulence in fully developed cumulo-nimbus clouds, and frequently accompanies severe thunderstorms. Raindrops within the cloud are carried to great heights where the temperature is below 0° F; the ice pellets grow in size as they are carried up and down. When they eventually fall to earth, they may be hailstones ½-1 inch in diameter, capable of damaging field crops and even of injuring men and animals. In exceptional conditions they may be even larger; hailstones weighing 10 ounces have been recorded in England and some weighing 24 ounces in Nebraska. In October, 1937, in the coastal plain near Tel Aviv, roof tiles were broken by hailstones.

Hailstorms are recorded in the Bible as ruining crops (Exod. 9:18-34; Hag. 2:17) and striking down men and animals in the open (Exod. 9:25; Josh. 10:11), and as accompanied by lightning (Exod. 9:23; Ps. 18:12-13—H 18:13-14; Rev. 11:19), storm winds (Ezek. 13:11), driving rain (Isa. 28:17), and snow (Job 38:22). The hailstones which killed the Amorites at Gibeon must have come from an exceptionally heavy cumulo-nimbus behind which "the sun stood still [remained] . . . until the nation took vengeance on their enemies" (Josh. 10:11-13). *See* PALESTINE, CLIMATE OF.

Bibliography. D. Ashbel, *Introduction to Meteorology* (1940), pp. 246-47 (in Hebrew); G. Kimble and R. Bush, *The Weather* (1946), pp. 112-14.

R. B. Y. SCOTT

HAIR [שֵׂעָר, שַׂעֲרָה; θρίξ, κόμη]. The hair's capacity for constant growth has always made it seem an important seat of life and, therefore, religiously significant. The most notable example of this in the Bible is in the case of the NAZIRITE vow (Num. 6:1-21; Judg. 13:5; 16:17; I Sam. 1:11), one aspect of which was to allow the hair to grow long so that it might be presented to God as an offering (Num. 6:18; Acts 18:18; 21:23-24). Samson's hair, in the final form of the story (Judg. 13:5), appears to have been left long in fulfilment of such a vow, although originally it had a more primitive significance as the repository of his strength (Judg. 16:19, 22). The shaving of the head in mourning (Job 1:20; Isa. 15:2; Jer. 41:5; 47:5; 48:37; Ezek. 7:18) and the offering of the hair to the dead were part of ancient religious practice, but forbidden to the Hebrews (Deut. 14:1). Indeed, the complete shaving of the head was forbidden to them for any purpose (Lev. 19:27; cf. Jer. 9:26; Ezek. 44:20).

In the OT, long hair on men was greatly admired (II Sam. 14:25-26; cf. Song of S. 5:2, 11), but in the NT it is frowned upon as contrary to nature (I Cor. 11:14). Although women wore their hair long (I Cor. 11:15), the biblical writers deplore the excessive ornamentation of it (Isa. 3:24; I Pet. 3:3).

The hair is a symbol of the fine (Judg. 20:16), the small (Luke 21:18), and the numerous (Matt. 10:30).

Fig. COS 49.

R. C. DENTAN

HAIRCLOTH [בַּעַל שֵׂעָר]. A term used in II Kings 1:8 ("He wore a garment of haircloth"), where the KJV translates: "He was a hairy man." The versions support the KJV meaning, but the RSV translation is obviously right in view of the phraseology in Matt. 3:4; Mark 1:6.

See also HAIR; DRESS AND ORNAMENTS.

J. M. MYERS

HAKKATAN hăk'ə tăn [הַקָּטָן, the small one; Apoc. 'Ακαταν]; KJV Apoc. ACATAN ăk'—. A member of the family of Azgad; the father of a certain Johanan, who returned to Jerusalem from the Babylonian exile with Ezra (Ezra 8:12; I Esd. 8:38).

HAKKOZ hăk'ŏz [הַקּוֹץ, the thorn; Apoc. 'Ακκώς]; KJV KOZ kŏz in Ezra 2:61; Neh. 3:4, 21; 7:63; KJV ACCOZ ăk'ŏz in I Esd. 5:38. Alternately: ACCOS ăk'ŏs (I Macc. 8:17).

The eponym of a family of priests in David's time (I Chr. 24:10). Members of this family were among those unable to document their claim to priestly rank after the Exile and so were suspended from sacerdotal office (Ezra 2:61; cf. Neh. 7:63; I Esd. 5:38). It is perhaps this family that is represented by the Uriah who helped repair the wall of Jerusalem (Neh. 3:4, 21). Presumably the Eupolemus sent by Judas Maccabeus as member of an embassy to Rome was a scion of this house (I Macc. 8:17).

See also KOZ.

B. T. DAHLBERG

HAKUPHA hə kū'fə [חֲקוּפָא, crooked; Apoc. 'Ακουφά, 'Ακειφά, 'Αχειφά]; KJV Apoc. ACIPHA ə sī'fə. Head of a family of postexilic temple servants of lower rank (Ezra 2:51; Neh. 7:53). *See* NETHINIM.

HALACHAH hä'lä kä' [הֲלָכָה, *from root* to walk, *with reference to* Exod. 18:20]. The authoritative Jewish way of life as expressed in moral law and ritual precept. It embraces the whole body of Jewish teaching, legislation, and practices which have proceeded from the interpretation and reinterpretation of the laws of the Bible through an unbroken succession of generations of Jewish teachers from Ezra onward; it also includes adaptations or modifications from time to time made applicable to changed conditions of life—economic, domestic, political, social—by spiritual leaders. Although legalistic in content, the Halachah is designed to bring all human occupations into relation with the service of God and to establish the supremacy of the divine will as the measure of all directions and strivings of human life.

See also TALMUD.

I. EPSTEIN

HALAH hā'lə [חֲלַח]. A city or district in the Assyrian Empire, to which Shalmaneser exiled some of the Israelites in the ninth year of King Hosea (II Kings 17:6; 18:11; see I Chr. 5:26 for Pul or Tiglath-pileser's exiling of Israelites to Halah). The RSV makes a common conjectural emendation in Obad. 20, reading "the exiles in Halah" for "the exile of this host" (cf. KJV).

C. H. GORDON

HALAK, MOUNT hā'lăk [הָהָר הֶחָלָק, bald mountain]. A mountain mentioned as the S limit of the conquest of Joshua (Josh. 11:17; 12:7). It is described as being "on the way leading up to Seir" (cf. RSV "that rises toward Seir"), the wooded slopes E of the Arabah. The name and site are preserved in the Jebel Halaq on the NW side of the Wadi Marra, N of 'Abdeh.

S. COHEN

HALAKAH. A variant spelling of HALACHAH.

HALF-SHEKEL TAX [δίδραχμον]. The temple tax (see Matt. 17:24) required annually of every Jew. A half-shekel was worth approximately two Attic drachmas, or about thirty-six cents. *See* TAXES.

HALF-TRIBE [חצי שבט]. A term used chiefly in Joshua and I Chronicles (elsewhere only in Numbers and Deuteronomy), always with reference to MANASSEH. After Moses and his troops had defeated Sihon of Heshbon and Og of Bashan, half the tribe of Manasseh, like Reuben and Gad, requested permission to settle E of the Jordan River. Permission was granted on condition that they lead the military invasion of Canaan and help in the establishment of settlements W of the Jordan (Num. 32, especially vss. 33-42; Deut. 3:12-13; 29:8; Josh. 12:4-6; 18:7). When these conditions had been met, the half-tribe of Manasseh returned with Reuben and Gad to the E of the Jordan (Josh. 1:12-18; 4:12). The half-tribe of Manasseh which settled E of the Jordan was given a part of the territory of Gilead and all of Bashan (Deut. 3:13-15; Josh. 13:29-33); the other half-tribe settled in central Palestine, in a region bounded by Ephraim on the S, Issachar on the NE, and Asher on the NW (Josh. 17:5-10); however, boundary lines among these tribes do not seem to have been clearly established (see Josh. 16:9; 17:11).

See also TRIBE. H. F. BECK

HALHUL hăl'hŭl [חלחול] (Josh. 15:58). A city of Judah in the hill-country district of Beth-zur; identified with Halhul, four miles N of Hebron. In NT times Alulos (Halhul) was near the S border of the territory of Aelia Capitolina (Jerusalem).

V. R. GOLD

HALI hā'lī [חלי] (Josh. 19:25). A border town in the territory of Asher. According to the context, it must be near Helkath, but its exact location is unknown.

HALICARNASSUS hăl'ə kär năs'əs [Ἁλικαρνασσός]. A Greek city founded as a Dorian colony in Caria of Asia Minor. It was located on the NW shore of the Ceramic Gulf and had an excellent harbor. Heights at the site permitted unusually strong fortifications. Before Alexander the Great destroyed the city in reprisal for its support of the Persians, it was the largest and strongest city in CARIA. After this destruction in 334 B.C. it never regained its former greatness, but it continued to be important in commerce and cultural life. It was noted as the location of the tomb of King Mausolus (377-353 B.C.). Erected by his sister and wife, Artemisia, this monument was included among the seven wonders of the ancient world, and the noun "mausoleum" derives from it. Among the noted writers of Halicarnassus were the historians Herodotus and Dionysius. A modern village, Bodrum, occupies a portion of the ancient city site.

Halicarnassus was Greek in its life and culture. Because of its wide commercial and cultural ties, however, its population was of mixed origin. There is clear evidence from the last two centuries B.C. that numbers of Jews lived there. I Macc. 15:23 states that *ca.* 139 B.C. the Romans sent letters to the city to urge that the Jews there be protected in their life and worship. Josephus (Antiq. XIV.x.23) quotes a decree which the people of the city passed, probably in the middle of the first century B.C., stating "that those Jewish men and women who so wish may observe their Sabbaths and perform their sacred rites in accordance with the Jewish laws, and may build places of prayer near the sea, in accordance with their native custom."

Bibliography. Strabo *Geography* XIV.2.16-17; C. T. Newton, *Travels and Discoveries in the Levant,* II (1865), 58-146; D. Magie, *Roman Rule in Asia Minor* (1950), especially pp. 86-87, 909-11. F. V. FILSON

HALL. 1. A hall or room (לשכה; KJV "parlor") connected with the sanctuary, in which the sacrificial meal was eaten, and to which Saul and his servant were invited by Samuel (I Sam. 9:22). Some scholars emend the present corrupt Hebrew text of I Sam. 1:9 to read "in the hall" instead of "in Shiloh," because of its reference to eating the sacrificial meal. The same word apparently underlies the LXX translation of I Sam. 1:18: "Then the woman went her way and entered the hall and ate and drank with her husband." לשכה is also used of the chambers of various officials in the temple at Jerusalem (II Kings 23:11; Jer. 35:2, 4; 36:10; Ezek. 40:17, 38) and of a scribe's room in the palace (Jer. 36:12, 20-21).

2. The Hall of Pillars (אולם העמודים; KJV "porch of pillars"; I Kings 7:6), part of King Solomon's PALACE buildings. Some scholars take this hall to be a pillared porch at the entrance of the House of the Forest of Lebanon, with the Hall of Judgment (*see* 3 *below*) at the other end. Others see it as a separate building, possibly an entrance hall to the whole palace complex. Such a pillared entrance hall has been

Courtesy of the Oriental Institute, the University of Chicago

3. Excavation which shows the three drum bases on the porch of a palace at Tell Tainat, built in the eighth century B.C.

found in the palace and temple complex at Tell Tainat in Syria, dating from the eighth century B.C. Figs. HAL 3; TEM 20.

3. The Hall of the Throne (אולם הכסא; KJV "porch for the throne"), or Hall of Judgment (אלם המשפט; KJV "porch of judgment"; I Kings 7:7), another of Solomon's buildings.* In it was the royal throne, and here the kings gave their legal judgments. The dimensions of this hall are not given, but its splendor is suggested by the cedar paneling from floor to rafters. Its position in relation to the other buildings must be conjectured. Some have made it a chamber at one end of the House of the Forest of Lebanon, with that building and its pillared porch providing an impressive entranceway to it. Others have made it an audience chamber at the entrance to the royal residence itself. The latter seems to have been the relation of judgment hall to palace in the royal buildings of Darius at Persepolis four hundred years later. Figs. HOU 32-33; PER 33.

4. The king's hall (בית המלך; KJV "king's house"), the audience chamber of the Persian king Ahasuerus (Xerxes) at Susa (Esth. 5:1). That this passage refers to a specific hall within the palace, rather than to the palace as a whole (as in Esth. 2:8-9, 13; 4:13), seems evident from the wording of 5:1. The ruins of the royal audience chamber of Darius and Xerxes at Susa (called "Apadana," lit. "hall of pillars") have been excavated. It was a great room 193 feet square with six rows of pillars, six pillars in each row, supporting the roof. The pillars were 7 feet around and 65 feet high, with capitals formed of the forequarters of two bulls facing outward. On three sides of the hall were porches, each with two rows of these same fine columns. In this room was the throne of King Xerxes, where he sat in audience and in judgment. *See* PALACE § 1.

5. The banqueting hall (Aramaic בית משתיא; KJV "banquet house") of King Belshazzar, the scene of the feast and the handwriting on the wall (Dan. 5: 10). The corresponding Hebrew words (בית משתה) are used in Esth. 7:8; Eccl. 7:2; Jer. 16:8, to describe rooms of a more private nature. In this case, however, it is a great audience chamber. The throne room of the kings of Babylon has been excavated. It was a rectangular room *ca.* 50 feet by 160 feet and probably had a great vaulted roof. The floors were paved with brick, and the plastered walls were decorated with colorful scenes in tile. A doubly recessed niche in the S wall faced the main entrance, and, from his throne in this niche, the king commanded the attention of all those in the hall and could be seen also by people in the paved court outside. This hall was very likely the scene of Belshazzar's feast.

6. The KJV translation of αὐλή in Luke 22:55 (RSV "courtyard"; cf. Matt. 26:58, 69; Mark 14:54, 66; John 18:15; in all of which the KJV has "palace" and the RSV "court" or "courtyard"). It usually means an enclosed but unroofed space. In the LXX of Exod. 27:9 and in Rev. 11:2 it designates the courtyard of the tabernacle or temple.

7. The KJV translation of αὐλή and πραιτώριον, in reference to the official residence of the governor. In Jerusalem this was Pilate's quarters in the fortress of Antonia (Mark 15:16; KJV "the hall [αὐλή], called Praetorium"; RSV "the palace [that is, the praetorium]"). In Caesarea it was Herod's headquarters (Acts 23:35). Here, and in Matt. 27:27; John 18:28, 33; 19:9, the KJV has "judgment hall" but the RSV, more literally, "praetorium."

Bibliography. R. Koldewey, *Excavations at Babylon* (1914), pp. 103 ff; A. T. Olmstead, *History of the Persian Empire* (1948), pp. 280 ff; J. A. Montgomery and H. S. Gehman, *Critical and Exegetical Commentary on the Books of Kings*, ICC (1951), pp. 164-65; A. Parrot, *Temple of Jerusalem* (1957), pp. 19-21.

S. V. FAWCETT

HALLEL hăl'əl, Heb. hə lāl' [הלל, praise thou (the Lord); *cf.* HALLELUJAH)]. A song of praise to the Lord. To praise the Lord was one of the duties of the Levites (II Chr. 7:6; Ezra 3:11) and of the daily morning prayer (Pss. 145-50).

The "Egyptian" Hallel (Pss. 113-18; cf. 114:1), according to a tradition of the first century A.D., was composed by Moses. It was recited in the homes at the Passover meal (Matt. 26:30), in the temple and in the synagogues at the great annual festivals and at the day of the New Moon. It celebrates God's great deeds from the Exodus till the messianic time.

The "Great" Hallel (Pss. 120-36, or 135-36, or even 136 only) praises God for having given rain (135:1) and food to all flesh (136:25).

Bibliography. H. L. Strack and P. Billerbeck, *Kommentar zum NT aus Talmud und Midrasch,* I (1922), 845 ff; I. Elbogen, *Der jüdische Gottesdienst* (2nd ed., 1924), pp. 494 ff.

J. HEMPEL

HALLELUJAH hăl'ə lo͞o'yə [הללו־יה, הללויה, praise (ye) the Lord]. The form of doxology used in the fifth book of Psalms and in the work of the Chronicler.

1. Philological questions
2. Cultic use
    a. In the Psalms
    b. Outside the Jerusalem cult
    c. In the Christian churches

Bibliography

1. Philological questions. The intensive stem of the root הלל (*pi'el:* "to praise"; *pu'al:* "to be praised"; *hithpa'el:* "to praise oneself") is used in both a secular and a religious sense. The servants of Pharaoh praise Sarah for her beauty (Gen. 12:15; cf. II Sam. 14:25 [Absalom]; contrast Ecclus. 11:2). The virgins are praised on their wedding day (Ps. 78:63), or Tyre for the power of the town (Ezek. 26: 17). The king may praise himself for his weapons (I Kings 20:11; cf. Prov. 27:2; Jer. 9:22-23) as the people praise their king (II Chr. 23:12). In the same way the Philistines praise their god Dagon (Judg. 16:24) and the Israelites Yahweh (e.g., I Chr. 23:5; Jer. 20:13), his word (Ps. 56:4—H 56:5), or his name (e.g., Ps. 113:1; Isa. 62:9 in 1QIs[a]). He is praised by them (e.g., I Chr. 16:25) as by the fathers in the Jerusalem temple before the Exile (Isa. 64:10). The heathen praise themselves by their idols (Ps. 97:7), as the Israelites do by Yahweh (e.g., I Chr. 16:10; Isa. 44:6; 45:25).

This use is the reason for the Jewish interpretation of the cultic exclamation "Hallelujah" as an imperative: "Praise!" with "Yah" (abbreviation of "Yahweh," as, e.g., in Pss. 68:18—H 68:19; 77:11—H 77: 12) as its object. According to this understanding it may be followed by הללו את־יהוה ("Praise Yahweh") and הללוהו ("Praise him"; Ps. 148:1) or by הללו אל ("Praise God"; Ps. 150:3). But there is a Jewish tradition that this interpretation is secondary and "Hallelujah" a very ancient enthusiastic cultic shout not containing the divine name. It is indeed astonishing that there is no clear example of the use of the verb הלל with "Yahweh" as its object before Deutero-Isaiah and that "Hallelujah" is to be found only even later. Side by side with AMEN it closes the fourth book of Psalms (Ps. 106:48). It appears in the MT at the opening (Pss. 106:1; 111:1; 112:1) or at the end of some psalms (104:35; 105:45; 115-117; *see* HALLEL), or in both places (113; 135; 146-150). It may be that the verb הלל had before the Exile a profane and "heathenish" sense, making it not worthy to be used for the God of Israel. In any case, there is no reason to see in "Hallelujah" the root of the Israelite hymns. The custom of starting songs of praise with an imperative is older than the Israelite literature or the "Hallelujah" in the Psalms.

The LXX, followed by the Vulg. and most of the modern translations, does not translate "Hallelujah." The η of their ἀλληλουια is still unexplained. Theod. uses αἰνεῖτε τὸν ὄν ("Praise the One").

2. Cultic use. ***a. In the Psalms.*** The psalms containing "Hallelujah" praise the Lord for his power and his wisdom in the creation of the world (Ps. 104) or in the history of Israel, especially in the liberation from Egypt (105; 106; 135). His mighty blessings are far stronger than those of the idols (115), so that the heathen too shall sing it (117). In the life of the single pious man God's life-giving strength is no less visible and adorable (116). The group of the so-called "Hallelujah psalms" (146-150) combines all these motives in a general praise of all that God did, does, and will do. The work of the Chronicler shows the manner of its use, especially in the Jerusalem cult. "Hallelujah" is sung as an antiphony by the different choirs (Ps. 135:19 ff; cf. I Chr. 16:25) or by the congregation (I Chr. 16:36; 29:8 ff); this singing is the main duty of the Levites according to the rule believed to be instituted by David (e.g., I Chr. 23:5; Neh. 12:24). During a certain period "Hallelujah" was repeated after every verse of the Hallel.

b. Outside the Jerusalem cult. "Hallelujah" appears in III Macc. 7:13; the Egyptian Jews, saved from the king's elephants, sang it going home in Alexandria. In the Last Days the streets of the redeemed Jerusalem will sing it (Tob. 13:18), and Rev. 19:1 ff waits for the great choir of the angels, the twenty-four elders, and the four living creatures, who will celebrate by this acclamation the salvation and glory and power of God and the marriage of the Lamb. The Christian-Gnostic Odes of Solomon have "Hallelujah" at the end of each poem.

c. In the Christian churches. The use of "Hallelujah" in the Christian churches varies. In the Eastern churches it has a long and living tradition with a great musical richness. In Bethlehem, Jerome found it sung by the congregation after the lessons, and he persuaded Pope Damasus to introduce it in Rome into the service at Easter. This custom extended more and more, until Gregory I introduced it into all services. To avoid some abuses arising with the custom of singing the final syllable, "jah," at great length with many tones, he connected it with a short verse (e.g., Pss. 5:2; 7:12; 85:8; 95:1; 98:1; 147:12). During the Middle Ages the custom arose of combining the melody of this final syllable with some words in Latin or the vernacular languages. These so-called "sequences" are perhaps the most important root for the religious popular songs and canticles from the thirteenth to the sixteenth century and of the Protestant chorals. Luther accepted (1523) the "Hallelujah" after the lessons as "eternal voice of the church, no less eternal than the memory of his passion and his victory," but banished it (without remaining success) in 1526. The Missale Romanum and the Protestant liturgies retaining its general outlines have a double "Hallelujah" between Easter and Pentecost, but do not sing it during the fasting times.

Bibliography. M. Jastrow, Jr., "The Origin of the Form יה for the Divine Name," *ZAW*, 16 (1896), 1-16; P. Wagner and F. Cabrol in *Dictionnaire d'archéologie chrétienne et de liturgie*, I (1907), 1226-46; T. J. O'Mahony in *Catholic Encyclopedia*, I (1907), 319-20; L. Petit in *Dictionnaire de théologie catholique*, I (1909), 836-39; T. Nöldeke, "Halleluja," *BZAW*, 33 (1918), 376-80; I. Elbogen, *Der jüdische Gottesdienst in seiner geschichtlichen Entwicklung* (2nd ed., 1924); J. Beckmann in *Leiturgia*, II (1955), 71-75; M. Reisel, *The Mysterious Name of Y.H.W.H.* (1957); E. Lohse, *RGG*, III (1959), 38.

J. Hempel

HALLOHESH hă lō'hĕsh [הלוחש, the whisperer—*evidently the professional title of a charmer*]. The father of Shallum, who, with his daughters, helped repair the walls of Jerusalem under Nehemiah (Neh. 3:12). The name also appears among those who sealed Ezra's covenant (Neh. 10:24—H 10:25).

M. Newman

HALLOW. *See* Holiness.

HALT. KJV alternate translation of χωλός. *See* Lame.

HAM hăm [חם, *perhaps hypocoristicon with* West Semitic *Ḫammu; cf. personal name* חמואל; Χαμ; Vulg. *Cham; identifications with* Egyp. *km and* Coptic *kême are no longer favored*]. **1.** The second of Noah's three sons (Gen. 5:32; 6:10; I Chr. 1:4). With his wife, Ham joined his married brothers and his father in the ark. After the Flood he shared in the divine blessing and covenant (Gen. 9:1-17). *See* Noah § 1.

However, the early J story tells that when Noah awoke from his drunken sleep and "knew what his youngest son had done to him," he cursed Canaan—not Ham—and condemned him to the service of Shem and Japheth, his brothers (Gen. 9:20-27). It seems best, form-critically, to separate this story from the flood tradition and to infer that the original order of Noah's sons was: Shem, Japheth, Canaan. To harmonize the two accounts, an editor identified Ham as the father of Canaan in vss. 18, 22. *See* Shem § 2; Canaan 1.

The sons of Ham are listed in Gen. 10:6; I Chr. 1:8 as Cush, Egypt, Put, and Canaan. For "Hamites," *see* Man, Ethnic Divisions of. L. Hicks

2. The name used in Pss. 78:51; 105:23, 27; 106:22 as a poetical synonym of *Miṣráyim* (Egypt), since he is the eponymous father of the Hamites, of whom Egypt is a member nation (Gen. 10).

HAM (CITY) [הם]. A city of the Zuzim in the region E of the Jordan, which was smitten by Chedorlaomer and his allies in the time of Abraham (Gen. 14:5). The city is mentioned again as Huma, no. 118 in the list of Thut-mose III. The name is preserved in the modern village of Ham on the Wadi er-Rejeileh (also called Wadi Ham), *ca.* four miles S of Irbid. The tell (Tell Ham) nearby, which marks the site of the ancient city, shows evidence of a settlement in the Bronze and Iron ages and the remains of a triple wall built of very large stones.

Bibliography. N. Glueck, *AASOR*, XXV-XXVIII (1951), 165-66.

S. Cohen

HAMAN hā'mən [המן]. The prime minister of the Persian king Ahasuerus and an enemy of the Jews in the book of Esther.

The son of Hammedatha (Esth. 3:1, etc.), Haman

is also called an Agagite in 3:1, 10; 8:3, 5; 9:24. This designation is probably intended to relate him to Agag, the Amalekite enemy of Saul of Kish in I Sam. 15.

Because Mordecai, a Jew of the line of Kish and the uncle of Esther, refused to bow before him, Haman contrived a plot to destroy all the Jews in the dominion of Ahasuerus. He specially prepared a gallows on which to hang Mordecai. But through the intervention of Esther, who was also the wife of Ahasuerus, Haman's plot was revealed, and he met the fate he had planned for Mordecai. In the subsequent purge by the Jews of their enemies, Haman's ten sons were killed too (9:6-10).

Some scholars view the story of Esther as reflecting a mythological struggle between the gods of Babylon and Elam, with Haman identified as the Elamite god Humman. Others regard it as romantic fiction created in connection with the Feast of Purim. Still others believe it records a genuine event of the fifth century B.C. in which the Jews in Persia survived a threatened persecution. In this case, Haman was probably a historical figure. M. NEWMAN

HAMATH hā'măth [חמת, חמת רבה; Akkad. *Amātu(m);* Aram. חמת; Egypt. *Ḥmtu;* Ημαθι; Arab. *Ḥamāt*]; KJV HEMATH hē'— in I Chr. 2:55; 13:5; Amos 6:14; KJV Apoc. AMATHIS; HAMATHITE hā'mə thīt. **1.** An important town situated on the Orontes in Syria; modern Nahr el-'Asi. It is in the valley on both sides of the river at the railway between Aleppo and Damascus, a little S of 35° latitude. At this spot the valley is on a level of 1,015 feet above the sea. Hamath was during long periods the center of an independent kingdom, the S frontier of which was the N frontier of the Israelite kingdom (cf. Num. 13:21; Josh. 13:5; Judg. 3:3). This was probably also the case during the reign of King David (cf. II Sam. 8; 10; 12:26-31).

The history of Hamath is fairly well known, thanks to a Danish excavation conducted by H. Ingholt (*see bibliography*). The earliest period of settlement known goes back to Neolithic times, and the excavator was able to uncover twelve layers. Level H seems to correspond to the Old Babylonian period. From the Hyksos period there are no findings, a fact which may indicate military devastation. In the Amarna age the town was the center of an Amorite kingdom (*see* AMORITES), but it seems to have been conquered by the famous Abdi-Ashirta, who played a political role and subdued a large territory in Syria, trying to be on friendly terms both with Egyptians and with Hittites.

Hamath is one of the important centers of the findings of Hittite hieroglyphic inscriptions. In the time of David, Hamath was the capital of an important kingdom, with which David collaborated. The latter conquered King Hadadezer of Zobah and perhaps this was possible through the help of Toi king of Hamath, whereas the king of Zobah was allied with Damascus (cf. II Sam. 8:3-12). Jeroboam II seems to have re-established the frontiers of the Israelite kingdom, so that the S frontier of Hamath again became the N frontier of the Israelite kingdom (cf. II Kings 14:25 ff; however, a textual error is not excluded). This would mean that Jeroboam recaptured

From *Atlas of the Bible* (Thomas Nelson & Sons Limited)

4. Hamath on the Orontes River

the regions which had previously been taken by Damascus and Hamath. The power of the kingdom of Hamath is recognizable in Assyrian royal inscriptions. The inscription of Zakir king of Hamath and L'sh, is also an important testimony. The latter inscription is furthermore of essential import for our knowledge of the language of that time. Shalmaneser II says he conquered several towns in Syria, among others Hamath and Damascus. Still more decisive was the victory of Sargon II. At that time an Assyrian type of cult was practiced at Hamath. *See bibliography.*

In the Hellenistic age Hamath was still of importance. In the reign of Antiochus IV its name was changed into Epiphania (Ἐπιφάνεια). During the Maccabean War, Hamath became the theater of war, when, according to I Macc. 12:24-25, the centurions of Demetrius stationed their armies in its territory.

In the Islamic age Hamath preserved its importance as a center of Christians. The Arab historian Dimashqi tells us about the Christian Easter (cf. Dimashqi, translated by Mehren, p. 408).

Today Hamath offers picturesque views to the tourist—e.g., its famous water wheels. But it is also an important commercial and industrial town (textiles in the first place).

Fig. HAM 4.

Bibliography. R. Dussaud, *Topographie historique de la Syrie antique et médiévale* (1927); H. Ingholt, *Rapport préliminaire sur sept campagnes de fouilles à Hama en Syrie, 1932-38* (1940); P. Hitti, *History of Syria* (1951); J. Læssøe, "A Prayer to Ea, Shamash, and Marduk, from Hama," *Iraq,* vol. XVIII, no. 1 (1956).

2. A town which was also called Hamath-Zobah (II Chr. 8:3), or ZOBAH, situated S of 1 *above* (cf. II Sam. 8:9; II Chr. 8:3-4). This town is perhaps also mentioned in Ezek. 47:17, and it is probably the same town as Zobah. A. HALDAR

HAMATH, ENTRANCE OF [לבא חמת, *lᵉbhô ḥᵃmāth*]. The N border of the ideal limits of the Promised Land (Num. 34:8), and of the possession of the tribes of Israel in the New Age (Ezek. 47:15; 48:1). Solomon's kingdom extended from the Brook of Egypt (Wadi el-'Arish) to the entrance of Hamath (I Kings 8:65), and the kingdom of Israel at the time of Jeroboam reached northward to the entrance of Hamath (II Kings 14:25; see also Amos 6:14).

It was somewhere in the Valley of On (el-Biqa') between the Lebanon and Anti-lebanon Mountains. Some would place it in the lower part of this valley, between Mount Hermon and Mount Lebanon; in

Num. 13:21 it is mentioned with Rehob (Beth-rehob) near Dan. However, the association with Zedad (modern Sadad) and Hazar-enan (modern Qaryatein?), SE of Kadesh on the Orontes, suggests it should be placed in the territory of Riblah. It would have marked the S border of the territory controlled by Hamath.

It is not improbable, as some have suggested, that "entrance to Hamath" is to be rendered rather "Labo-hamath," the name of a town, to be identified with modern Lebweh on the Orontes below Riblah, commanding the watershed between the Orontes and the Leontes rivers. H. G. MAY

HAMATH-ZOBAH hā'măth zō'bə [חמת צובה]. A designation of the town of ZOBAH in II Chr. 8:3.

HAMITES. *See* MAN, ETHNIC DIVISIONS OF.

HAMMATH hăm'ăth [חמת, hot spring]; KJV HEMATH hĕm'əth in I Chr. 2:55. **1.** The "father" of Rechab (I Chr. 2:55), or the home of the Kenites of the family of Rechab. Considered as a place, this was probably in Judah, the Negeb, or farther S.

2. A fortified town in Naphtali (Josh. 19:35). It is located at Hammam Tabariyeh, a hot springs just S of Tiberias on the W shore of the Sea of Galilee. Hammath is almost certainly the same as the Levitical town known as Hammon in I Chr. 6:76—H 6:61 and Hammoth-dor in Josh. 21:32.

Bibliography. L. H. Vincent, "Les Fouilles Juives in d'el-Ḥamman, a Tibériade," *RB,* 31 (1922), 115-22.
G. W. VAN BEEK

HAMMEDATHA hăm'ə dā'thə [המדתא, *perhaps from* Pers. *mah-data,* given by the moon]; KJV AMADATHA ăm'—. The father of Haman, archenemy of the Jews in the book of Esther (3:1, 10; 8:5; 9:10, 24).

HAMMELECH hăm'ə lĕk. KJV translation of המלך ("the king") in Jer. 36:26; 38:6. Instead of "the son of Hammelech," the RSV translates "the king's son." This phrase may refer to any member of the royal household.

HAMMER. The hammer stone, a smooth or shaped stone held in the hand, was employed from earliest times down through the biblical period. Beginning in the Bronze Age, the stone was sometimes perforated for better grip or to receive a handle. Mallets of bone or wood were used in all periods but are rarely preserved for the excavator. The hafted hammer with a metal head is rare in Palestine, perhaps because of the paucity of metal and the fact that stone was a satisfactory substitute, whereas tools and weapons with a cutting edge required metal.

The term מקבה, "hammer," is used of the tool of the stonemason (I Kings 6:7) and of the smith (Isa. 44:12), and of the mallet for driving pegs (Judg. 4:21; cf. 5:26, where the RSV "MALLET" is more accurate than the KJV "hammer" for הלמות). What distinction there is, if any, between this tool and the פטיש (hammer of the smith; Isa. 41:7; cf. Jer. 50:23) is not known. The פטיש of Jer. 23:29 is a stonemason's tool. The Greek equivalent of this word is σφῦρα, which means any type of hammer or mallet and is connected with forging in Ecclus. 38:28. כילפות, "hammers" (a loan word from Akkadian *kalapati;* Ps. 74:6), has also been thought to refer to axes or hatchets or to iron-tipped beams; the context refers to weapons of destruction used on wood. In Jer. 51:20 "hammer" (KJV BATTLE AX) translates מפץ (from נפץ, "to shatter"); this context and Ezek. 9:2, where the same root appears, favor the translation "battle ax" or "war club."

See also WEAPONS AND IMPLEMENTS OF WAR.

Bibliography. R. A. S. Macalister, *Gezer II* (1912), p. 245; W. M. F. Petrie, *Tools and Weapons* (1917), pp. 40-41, plates XLV-XLVI, LXXVIII; G. Loud, *Megiddo II* (1948), vol. II, plate 289:1; C. Singer *et al.,* eds., *A History of Technology* (1954), pp. 129-32, 608-9. R. W. FUNK

HAMMOLECHETH hă mŏl'ə kĕth [המלכת, she who reigns] (I Chr. 7:18); KJV HAMMOLEKETH. An eponym; probably originally a divine title; sister of Gilead and ancestor of several tribal families of Manasseh.

Bibliography. G. B. Gray, *Hebrew Proper Names* (1896), pp. 115-16; E. L. Curtis, *Chronicles,* ICC (1910), p. 152.
B. T. DAHLBERG

HAMMON hăm'ən [חמון, hot spring(?)]. **1.** A border town in Asher (Josh. 19:28). It is perhaps to be identified with Umm el-'Awamid, a site located near the coast approximately five miles NE of Ras en-Naqurah.

2. A Levitical town in Naphtali (I Chr. 6:76—H 6:61). *See* HAMMATH 2. G. W. VAN BEEK

HAMMOTH-DOR hăm'əth dôr' [חמת דאר] (Josh. 21:32). A Levitical town in Naphtali. *See* HAMMATH 2.

HAMMUEL hăm'yōō əl [חמואל; *cf.* Arab. *al-ḥumam*]; KJV HAMUEL. A family or clan of the tribe of Simeon (I Chr. 4:26).

Bibliography. M. Noth, *Die israelitischen Personennamen* (1928), p. 79; G. Ryckmans, *Les noms propres sud-sémitiques* (1934-35), II, 60. H. H. GUTHRIE, JR.

HAMMURABI hăm'ə rä'bĭ. The sixth king of the First Dynasty of Babylon (1792-1750 B.C.); son of Sin-muballit, and father of Samsu-iluna.

The history of the reign of King Hammurabi is known only in its outlines, although we have more and better evidence for his reign than for that of any other king of his dynasty. Apart from royal inscriptions (stelae, foundation tablets, bricks, and a clay cone), there are a large number of political and administrative letters and—more important still—the official names given to the forty-two years during which Hammurabi ruled over Babylon. These names refer to all kinds of royal activities, such as the building of city walls, the dedication of votive offerings, the erecting of statues in temples, other pious works, and, of course, wars. It is the nature of this evidence that it offers only a small selection of "historical facts," which often have to be interpreted in order to be usable. The historical section of the preamble to the Code of Hammurabi* presents more evidence as to the maximum extent of his kingdom than any

Courtesy of the Oriental Institute, the University of Chicago

5. Stele containing the Code of Hammurabi; at the top the sun-god Shamash extends the ring and rod to Hammurabi, who stands as a worshiper before him; from Susa (eighteenth century B.C.)

other inscription, though its tenor is clearly hymnic and not historical and factual. It mentions all the major cities ruled by Hammurabi, at the same time extolling the pious deeds and social acts performed in these places by him. There exist two more stone inscriptions referring to Hammurabi; but they are, curiously enough, of poetic content, which is extremely rare for texts on this type of writing material. The first is on a very broken basalt stela found in Ur. Here Hammurabi himself speaks in a bilingual (Sumerian and Akkadian) inscription of his achievements. He mentions his conquest of the distant mountain regions of Gutium, Subartu, and Tukrish, "whose language is confused." The second is an inscription on a broken statue, which addresses the king in Sumerian and Akkadian, in hymnic terms. The building inscriptions refer to the repairing of temples, among them those of Babylon, Borsippa, Larsa, and Zabalam, and to the construction of city walls, especially that of Sippar. Some are written in Sumerian and some in Akkadian. The correspondence of Hammurabi consists mainly of letters he sent to various high administrative officials touching mostly on legal and administrative matters. They amount to *ca.* 140 letters, and their style bespeaks a well-established bureaucratic tradition. Hammurabi's political letters come from the archive in Mari; there are three letters addressed by him to court officials and one directly to Zimri-Lim, king of Mari. In the same archive has been found the copy of a letter sent by Zimri-Lim to Hammurabi and fifteen more letters, containing references to Hammurabi, written by political emissaries of Mari stationed at the court of Hammurabi in Babylon. Figs. HAM 5; LAW 18.

In the history of Mesopotamia, Hammurabi and his period represent a crucial phase in the development of Babylonian civilization as well as in the history of the city of Babylon. Under the five kings who sat on the throne of Babylon in the hundred years before him, the city had led an inconspicuous existence. These rulers repeatedly conquered and lost the neighboring city of Kish, and made some ineffective campaigns along and beyond the Tigris. We shall never know to what extent Babylon was politically independent during that period, since we cannot expect its kings to have reported such matters, but it can safely be assumed that the political status of Babylon repeatedly shifted from independence to more or less effective control by Isin or Larsa. Since in the date formulas of Sin-muballit, the father of Hammurabi, more cities are mentioned than in those of any of his predecessors, it seems that Babylon's rise to power started at that time. Still, Sin-muballit had to confine his warlike acts to the S (a victory over Ur, a conquest of Isin), because Shamshi-Adad I of Assyria was then an important power in the N. When Hammurabi "entered the house of his father"—this peculiar expression is used only with respect to Hammurabi and his two predecessors—this danger had passed and Hammurabi took the opportunity to embark on what seems to have been a policy of military expansion. From his seventh to his eleventh year he conquered Uruk and—in an alliance with Rim-Sin of Larsa—Isin; he destroyed Malgûm, crossed the Tigris into Emutbal, and went upstream along the Euphrates as far as Rāpiqu. The following years up to the twenty-ninth have names that do not refer to war, and this seems to indicate a period of consolidation and organization of the realm. Therefore it is somewhat astonishing to find Hammurabi from his thirtieth year to the end of his reign engaged in nearly uninterrupted warfare. The very first of these year names strikes what seems an ominous note: "(year in which) the leader, beloved of Marduk, after having defeated the army which Elam—(coming) from the frontier of Marhashi, together with Subartu, Gutium, Eshnunna and Malgi—had raised in masses, organized through the power of the great gods (the empire of) Sumer and Akkad." Most of the names of the war years refer to such coalitions, such as the year 32 (to Eshnunna, Subartu, and Gutium), the year 37 (Sutium, Turukku, Kakmu, and Subartu), and the year 39 (Subartu); while the year 31 mentions the victory over Rim-Sin, the year 35 the dismantling of Mari and Malgium, and the year 38 a defeat inflicted on Eshnunna. It seems that these continual "victories" mostly against the peoples to the N and the NW present at best an offensive defensive of Hammurabi against the pressure of invading mountaineers or peoples set in motion by such events. The second period of wars seems to have reduced rather than extended his realm, to which he now likes to refer as "Sumer and Akkad," as none of his predecessors in Babylon could do. In fact, the last years of Hammurabi are named after clearly defensive measures to which he resorted in the N of the country: walls along the Tigris and the Euphrates (year 42) and the fortification of Sippar by means of a wall of piled-up earth (year 43). This was either an emergency measure or a technique made necessary by special circumstances. We do not know anything about the military situation at the time of the death of Hammurabi, but a letter exists which sheds an interesting light on the circumstances accompanying the accession to the throne of his son Samsu-iluna. The letter is badly damaged. In it the new king writes to a high official of the realm: "The king, my father, is s[ick] and I sat myself on the throne in order to [. . .] the country." In the balance of the tablet, Samsu-iluna announces his first act as king, which concerns the remission of the debts of certain social classes, an act to which the Old Babylonian kings had to resort periodically to remedy the economic pressure upon the lower classes of the population. Even if Samsu-iluna succeeded in stabilizing the political and military situation, it remains uncertain how much of Babylonia, apart from the capital, was held by the five kings of the dynasty who followed Hammurabi and ruled for 150 years more, each ascending the throne of his father. One thing, however, remains as the enduring success of the rule of Hammurabi: all later kings of Babylonia resided in Babylon, the other cities becoming provincial from then on; and this new situation was recognized throughout the entire country, with the exception of the region around the mouths of the two rivers, where inaccessible marshes and poor communications created a refuge for separatist and unorthodox groups for many millenniums. The "Sea Country," which rose with the decline of power of Babylon, is only the first of the political organizations which grew up in that region. *See* CHALDEA.

During the peaceful period between the twelfth and the thirtieth year, Babylonia seems to have become not only prosperous and politically important but also a center of learning. Hammurabi was the first king of his dynasty to leave us royal inscriptions correctly styled in Sumerian. It is possible that the fall of Larsa led to the migration of scribes to the new capital, but nothing of the Old Babylonian text material possibly kept in the Babylon of the First Babylonian Dynasty is accessible, since the water table of the region has risen and excavation cannot touch these levels. The centuries which followed the reign of Hammurabi became something like the golden age to which the numerous Old Babylonian literary texts bear eloquent witness. This was even realized a millennium later in Assyria. We have a letter found in Nineveh (Harper, *Assyrian and Babylonian Letters,* no. 255), in which a Neo-Assyrian scholar writes to his king, most likely Ashurbanipal, that he has brought from Babylon some originals from the time of "Ammurapi the king." Intimately connected with the name of Hammurabi is, of course, the law code which bears his name, a copy of which was found in the library of Ashurbanipal. Other copies are extant.

The name Hammurabi belongs to those Semitic but not Akkadian personal names which begin to appear in cuneiform texts quite early (end of the third millennium and Akkad period) and can be found during the reign of the Dynasty of Hammurabi all over Mesopotamia and as far W as the coast of the Mediterranean. The language of the people who bear these names—as far as it can be reconstructed from these names, which are mostly theophoric—is referred to in the scholarly literature as "Eastern Canaanite," "West Semitic," or "Amorite," but the provenience of this people and their role in Mesopotamian history are still subjects of discussion. Apart from some rulers of Larsa (ruling at the time of the first kings of the Hammurabi Dynasty), Hammurabi is the first king to have such a name, and it should be pointed out that Hammurabi's father and two more kings before him had truly Akkadian personal names. The name Hammurabi itself appears in the texts of Mari as a royal name, twice in a dynasty ruling in Aleppo and once as the name of the king of a country called Kurda (reading and location uncertain). This tellingly illustrates the role and political importance of the ethnic and social group which bore such names. According to the spelling of the name Hammurabi in the cuneiform alphabetic system of writing of Ugarit, it should be transcribed *Hammu-rapi* (note the variants with *Ammu-* and *-rapi'*). The meaning of the name is still a moot question: the first element is doubtless theophoric, and the second refers to healing, but a reliable translation cannot be given. It should be mentioned that the biblical king name Amraphel (Gen. 14:1, 9) has been connected with Hammurabi ever since the early days of Assyriology.

Bibliography. F. M. T. Boehl, *Hammurabi, King of Babylon, in the Setting of His Time* (1946). A. L. OPPENHEIM

HAMONAH hə mō′nə [המונה, multitude] (Ezek. 39:16). A city where Gog hordes are to be destroyed after the unsuccessful attack on Israel by this force of evil, according to the prophecy of Ezekiel.

HAMON-GOG hā′mən gŏg′ [המון גוג, multitude of Gog] (Ezek. 39:11, 15). A valley in Transjordan where the multitude of dead from the armies of Gog are to be buried, according to the prophecy of Ezekiel.

HAMOR hā′mōr [חמור, he-ass; Εμμωρ]. The father of Shechem, killed with him in revenge by Simeon and Levi (Gen. 34; cf. Judg. 9:28; *see* SHECHEM 1). From the sons of Hamor, Jacob purchased land upon which he erected an altar (Gen. 33:19) and wherein Joseph was later buried (Josh. 24:32). However, Stephen confused Shechem with Mach-pelah (Acts 7:16; KJV EMMOR; cf. Gen. 23; 48:22; 50:13, 25). *See also* SHECHEM 4. L. HICKS

HAMRAN hăm′răn [חמרן] (I Chr. 1:41); KJV AMRAM ăm′răm. The first son of clan chief Dishon. The name used in Gen. 36:26 is Hemdan.

HAMSTRING [עקר]. A verb meaning "to cut the muscle tendon of the thigh." In the Bible the reference is to oxen (Gen. 49:6) and horses (Josh. 11:6, 9; II Sam. 8:4; I Chr. 18:4), hence to the great tendon at the back of the hock of the hind leg. To hamstring an animal completely disables or lames it.

J. A. SANDERS

HAMUEL. KJV form of HAMMUEL.

HAMUL hā′məl [חמול, spared; Samar. חמואל; LXX Ἰεμουήλ, Ἰαμουήλ]; HAMULITES —mə līts. Grandson of Judah, and younger son of Perez (Gen. 46:12; Num. 26:21 [LXX B 'Ιαμούν]; I Chr. 2:5); ancestral head of the Hamulites (Num. 26:21).

HAMUTAL hə mū'təl [*Qere* חמוטל, *Kethibh* חמיטל, חם *plus* טל, *probably* father-in-law is protection; *cf. bibliography*]. Wife of Josiah; mother of Jehoahaz and Zedekiah (II Kings 23:31; 24:18; cf. Jer. 52:1).

Bibliography. H. Bauer, *ZAW*, XLVIII (1930), 80. D. Harvey

HANAMEL hăn'ə mēl [חנמאל, *possibly from* חנן אל, God is gracious]; KJV HANAMEEL —mēl. Son of Shallum, Jeremiah's uncle (Jer. 32:7-9), from whom the prophet purchased a field at Anathoth during the siege of Jerusalem.

HANAN hā'nən [חנן, *evidently a shortened form of* חנניה *or* אלחנן, Yahu has been gracious]. **1.** A descendant of Benjamin (I Chr. 8:23).

2. A Benjaminite who was an ancestor of Saul (I Chr. 8:38; 9:44).

3. One of David's Mighty Men (I Chr. 11:43).

4. The head of a prophetic guild that occupied a chamber in the temple (Jer. 35:4).

5. The head of a family of Nethinim (temple servants) that returned to Palestine after the Exile (Ezra 2:46; Neh. 7:49; cf. I Esd. 5:30).

6. An assistant to the temple treasurers appointed by Nehemiah (Neh. 13:13).

7. A Levite who helped to interpret the law at the assembly of Ezra (Neh. 8:7) and also sealed the covenant (Neh. 10:10—H 10:11).

8. Another man who sealed Ezra's covenant (Neh. 10:22—H 10:23).

9. Yet another who sealed the covenant (Neh. 10: 26—H 10:27). M. Newman

HANANEL, TOWER OF hăn'ə nĕl [מגדל חננאל] (Neh. 3:1; 12:39; Jer. 31:38; Zech. 14:10); KJV HANANEEL —nēl. A tower of the N rampart of Jerusalem. The person for whom it was named is not known. Covering the approach to the temple, it was replaced by the βᾶρις mentioned by Josephus (Antiq. XV.xi.2), and by the Antonia Tower (*see* Antonia, Tower of). *See* map under Nehemiah. *See also* Jerusalem §§ *6e, 7b*. G. A. Barrois

HANANI hə nā'nī [חנני, *short form of* Hananiah; 'Ανανίας]; KJV Apoc. ANANIAS ăn'ə nī'əs. **1.** The father of the prophet Jehu (I Kings 16:1, 7; II Chr. 19:2; 20:34). In a story invented by the Chronicler, "Hanani the seer" is probably meant to be the same person (II Chr. 16:7).

2. A postexilic family of Levitical singers of the Heman group (I Chr. 25:4, 25). *See* Heman 3; Music.

3. A priest who divorced his foreign wife in the time of Ezra (Ezra 10:20; I Esd. 9:21).

4. A brother or kinsman of Nehemiah whose tidings of conditions in Judah prompted Nehemiah's work and who later was one of those put in charge of Jerusalem (Neh. 1:2; 7:2). *See* Hananiah 8.

5. A musician at the dedication of the walls of Jerusalem (Neh. 12:36); he may be connected with 3 *above.*

Bibliography. M. Noth, *Die israelitischen Personennamen* (1928), p. 187. H. H. Guthrie, Jr.

HANANIAH hăn'ə nī'ə [חנניהו, חנניה, Yahu has been gracious; 'Ανανίας]; KJV Apoc. ANANIAS ăn'ə nī'əs. **1.** An officer in the army of Uzziah (II Chr. 26:11).

2. The father of a "prince" (administrative official) in the time of Jeremiah (Jer. 36:12).

3. A prophet who, in opposition to Jeremiah, predicted the early fall of Nebuchadnezzar and the early return of those exiled from Judah in 597 (Jer. 28:1, 5, 10-17). The account in Jer. 28 is interesting as an example of the problem of false prophets and of the role of symbolic actions in prophetism. *See* Prophet.

4. Grandfather or family of a sentry who arrested Jeremiah on the charge of deserting to the Babylonians (Jer. 37:13).

5. A postexilic descendant of David; son of Zerubbabel (I Chr. 3:19, 21).

6. A postexilic person or family of the tribe of Benjamin (I Chr. 8:24).

7. A postexilic family of singers of the Heman group (I Chr. 25:4, 23). *See* Heman 3; Music.

8. One of those who divorced their foreign wives in the time of Ezra (Ezra 10:28; I Esd. 9:29). *See* 10 *below.*

9. A "perfumer," or ointment maker, who helped restore the walls of Jerusalem under Nehemiah (Neh. 3:8). *See* 10 *below.*

10. A repairer of the walls of Jerusalem under Nehemiah (Neh. 3:30); he may be the same as 9 *above,* though the confusion of the lists makes it difficult to tell. Actually 8, 9, and 12 could all refer to the same person.

11. The "governor of the castle"; one of those whom Nehemiah put in charge of Jerusalem (Neh. 7:2). The Hebrew of the verse could mean "my brother Hanani—that is, Hananiah the governor of the castle." "Hanani," in Hebrew, is a shortened form of "Hananiah." *See* Hanani 4.

12. A "chief of the people" who signed the pledge of reform in postexilic times (Neh. 10:23). *See* 10 *above.*

13. A priest in the time of Nehemiah; listed as one of the trumpeters at the dedication of the wall of Jerusalem (Neh. 12:12, 41).

14. One of the three youths who figure in the stories in the book of Daniel and its apocryphal additions (Dan. 1:6-7, 11, 19). *See* Shadrach; Song of the Three Young Men.

Bibliography. M. Noth, *Die israelitischen Personennamen* (1928), p. 187; D. Diringer, *Le Iscrizione Antico-Ebraiche Palestinesi* (1934), p. 351. H. H. Guthrie, Jr.

HAND [יד; χείρ]. Besides the numerous passages in which the Bible uses "hand" simply to designate a part of the body, there are many others in which the word has a metaphorical sense. Most numerous are those in which it occurs as a picturesque symbol of "power" (Ps. 78:42 KJV; Heb. 10:31); the phrase "(to deliver) into, or out of, the hand" is a very common example (Exod. 3:8; Judg. 4:2). In many passages of the original Hebrew the word יד appears in this sense where the English translations make use of a different word: e.g., Exod. 14:31 ("work"); Lev. 5:7 ("afford"; lit., "if his hand does not reach"); Josh. 8:20 ("power"). Sometimes the idea of "power" is weakened to "possession" (Gen. 35:4 KJV).

The word can also be used, like the words for many other parts of the human body, by metonymy, for "person" or in place of a personal pronoun (Isa. 35:3). Note the phrases "at your hand" (Isa. 1:12 KJV), meaning merely "from you"; and "by the hand of" (Lev. 8:36 KJV), meaning merely "by" (cf. RSV).

There are many references to the "hand" (i.e., the "power") of God (Isa. 41:20; Luke 1:66). Notable are such phrases as "outstretched hand" (Jer. 21:5); "strong hand" (Exod. 6:1); "strength of hand" (Exod. 13:3); and the expression "The hand of the LORD was upon him," meaning "He was seized by the prophetic ecstasy" (Ezek. 1:3).

In Hebrew the word "hand" can sometimes mean "side" (II Sam. 15:2 MT), as in the English phrase "right, or left, hand." Peculiar to Hebrew is the use of יד in the sense of "monument" (II Sam. 18:18)—perhaps recalling a type of Phoenician monument on which a hand was engraved—and also, possibly, "phallus" (Isa. 57:8; RSV "nakedness").

R. C. DENTAN

HANDBAG. *See* BAG § 1.

HANDBREADTH [טפח]. A measure based on the width of the hand at the base of the fingers; *ca.* three inches. Six handbreadths were equal to the common cubit, and Ezekiel's cubit (Ezek. 40:5) had an extra handbreadth. This unit was a standard measure in Egypt. *See* WEIGHTS AND MEASURES §§ D1, 4*c*.

O. R. SELLERS

HANDKERCHIEF. The word used in Acts 19:12 to translate σουδάριον, which is really a Latin word from the root meaning "sweat." It may refer to a piece of cloth like our handkerchiefs, used to wipe away sweat, or to a towel-like head dressing, such as the kaffiyeh still used by the Arabs. The same Greek word is used in Luke 19:20; John 11:44; 20:7, where the KJV translates "napkin" and the RSV either "napkin" or "cloth." In Acts the "handkerchief" was used to bring power from Paul for the healing of the sick. The same term designates in Luke 19:20 the wrapping for the pound to be buried in the earth, and in John the cloth with which the face of the dead was covered.

S. A. CARTLEDGE

HANDMAID. *See* MAID.

HANDPIKE [מקל יד, a staff (or rod) of the hand] (Ezek. 39:9); KJV HANDSTAVE. A long wooden staff with a pointed metal head; used as a weapon by foot soldiers.

It is clear from Ezek. 39:9-10 that the "staff of the hand" is a weapon and that at least part of it is of wood, but nothing else is certain. It may have been a quarterstaff, a thrusting spear or pike, a javelin, or a battle-ax.

See WEAPONS AND IMPLEMENTS OF WAR.

Bibliography. For photographs of Egyptian battle axes, see W. C. Hayes, *The Scepter of Egypt* (1953), p. 282.

W. S. MCCULLOUGH

HANDS, LAYING ON OF. A ceremony occurring in both the OT and the NT in various contexts and meanings:

a) In the burnt offerings and sin offerings of the OT sacrificial cultus, the offerers were directed to lay their hands on the victims before they were slain (Exod. 29:10; Lev. 1:4; 4:4, 24, 29, 33; 8:14; Num. 8:10, 12; II Chr. 29:23). It has sometimes been held that this act signified a transference of guilt from the offerer to the victim. But the OT speaks of such a transference of guilt only in the case of the laying on of hands upon the scapegoat (Lev. 16:21). In the case of the sin offerings, the ceremony may have meant nothing more than a setting apart of the victim in consecration to its sacred purpose. This is suggested by the ceremony described in Lev. 24:14, where a blasphemer has hands laid upon him by all who heard his cursing, before he is taken out to be stoned. Certainly there was no transference of guilt in this case, though it might involve a transfer of ritual defilement. Philo (*On the Special Laws* I.203-4) understood the laying on of hands upon the victim as a sign of the offerer's pure intention and blameless life.

b) Laying on of hands was also used to impart a blessing. So Jacob blessed the children of Joseph (Gen. 48:14), and Jesus blessed the little children (Matt. 19:15; Mark 10:13, 16). Related to this was the "lifting up" of outstretched hands to invoke a blessing upon a group, such as the priestly benediction (Lev. 9:22), or Jesus' parting blessing to his disciples at his ascension (Luke 24:50). Possibly in the same range of ideas was Jesus' use at times of laying on of hands in healing the sick (Mark 5:23; 6:5; 16:18; Luke 4:40; 13:13). Here the underlying idea seems to be a transference of spiritual wholeness and physical vitality. Likewise, Ananias laid hands on Paul that Paul might regain his sight (Acts 9:12, 17); and Paul so healed the father of Publius in Malta (Acts 28:8). Cf. also Acts 5:12, where the hands of the apostles work signs and wonders, chiefly in acts of healing.

Another type of blessing was the conveyance of the Holy Spirit by the laying on of hands, in such passages as Acts 8:18-19; 19:6—often taken, with the reference in Heb. 6:2, as the basis of the church's rite of confirmation following upon baptism. But in Acts this gift of the Spirit is more particularly linked with outward, visible manifestations of the Spirit's activity, as in "speaking with tongues."

c) A special type of blessing through laying on of hands occurs in rites of ordination. So Moses ordained Joshua as his successor (Num. 27:18, 23; Deut. 34:9)—a ceremony adopted in later times for ordination to the rabbinate, which may well have been the source of Christian rites of ordination. It should be noted, however, that Moses conveyed to Joshua a commission; he did not convey thereby the "spirit of wisdom," for Joshua already possessed this. The ordination was an outward sign of recognition of Joshua's spiritual qualifications, and gave him authority to exercise an office of leadership in the congregation of God's people.

In the NT ordination has the same sense. The SEVEN, selected on the basis of their spiritual gifts already evident, were ordained by the TWELVE by prayer and the laying on of hands (Acts 6:6); and

Paul and Barnabas were likewise commissioned and dismissed for their missionary journey by the prophets and teachers at Antioch (Acts 13:3). In the Pastorals, however, the laying on of hands in ordination is associated with the imparting of a spiritual gift (I Tim. 4:14; II Tim. 1:6). But in I Tim. 5:22, the ceremony probably refers, not to ordination, but to the reconciliation of penitents. Thus in later church usage, one finds a variety of associations of the ceremony: confirmation, ordination, healing, reconciling penitents, and the imparting of blessings upon both persons and objects.

Bibliography. J. Behm, *Die Handauflegung im Urchristentum* (1911). H. P. Smith, "The Laying on of Hands," *AJT,* XVII (1913), 47-62. B. S. Easton, "Jewish and Early Christian Ordination," *ATR,* V (1922-23), 308-19; VI (1923-24), 285-95; abridged in *Early Christianity. The Purpose of Acts and Other Papers* (1955), pp. 135-43. J. Coppens, *L'imposition des mains et les rites connexes dans le NT et dans l'Eglise ancienne* (1925). S. New, "The Name, Baptism, and the Laying on of Hands," in F. J. Foakes-Jackson and K. Lake, *The Beginnings of Christianity,* V (1933), 121-40. J. Newman, *Semikhah* (1950). N. Adler, *Taufe und Handauflegung* (1951). A. Ehrhardt, "Jewish and Christian Ordination," *Journal of Ecclesiastical History,* V (1954), 125-38. M. H. SHEPHERD, JR.

HANDSTAVE. KJV form of HANDPIKE.

HANES hā'nīz [חנס] (Isa. 30:4). The late name of the capital of the twentieth Upper Egyptian nome. The Greeks, identifying the local deity Herishef with Hercules, renamed the city Heracleopolis, the epithet Magna being added to distinguish it from the similarly named city of Lower Egypt. The native Egyptian name reflected in the Hebrew was *Ḥwt-nn-nsw,* "the house of the royal child"; a Late Assyrian transcription *Ḫininši* is also attested.

T. O. LAMBDIN

HANGING [תלה; LXX κρεμάννυμι]. After having been put to death, public enemies and criminals might be hanged as a further degradation or a public warning (Gen. 40:19; Josh. 8:29; 10:26; II Sam. 4:12). Biblical law does not recognize hanging as a form of execution, but permits it afterward on condition that the corpse be taken down and buried the selfsame day (Deut. 21:22-23). A hanged man is considered polluting and an "insult to God" (קללת אלהים; LXX κεκατηραμένος ὑπὸ Θεοῦ, "accursed of God" [cf. Gal. 3:13]; for the NT application of the Deuteronomy passage to crucified persons [Acts 5:30; 10:39; Gal. 3:13] cf. 4Qp Nah. 7–8; but Tosef. Sanh. 9.6 understands "insult to God" in the sense that man is God's image). Josh. 8:29; 10:27 record that the corpses of the Canaanite kings were taken down and buried at sundown on the day they were hanged; contrast the prolonged exposure by the Egyptians (Gen. 40:19), the Philistines (I Sam. 31: 10), and David (II Sam. 21:10-14).

According to Jos. Antiq. IV.viii.24, all executed criminals were afterward hanged. The Mishna (Sanh. 6.4) prescribes hanging only for those put to death by stoning—according to one opinion, only for blasphemers and idolaters.

The gallows (עץ; LXX ξύλον) is described in the Mishna as a gibbet; the dead man's hands were tied together and slung over the arm. Since impaling was practiced in Persia (Herodotus III.125, 159), this may be meant by תלה in Esth. 2:23; 5:14; 7:9 (LXX σταυρόω, "impale"), 10; 9:13-14.

Hanging oneself (ἀπάγχω, "strangle," LXX for חנק) is referred to twice (II Sam. 17:23; Matt. 27:5).

The meaning of הוקיע, "hang" (Num. 25:4; II Sam. 21:6, 9, 13), is obscure. It may be gathered only that some religious significance (cf. "for/before YHWH") is involved. In II Sam. 21 the bodies of the victims are subjected to a prolonged exposure before burial.

Bibliography. For the 4Qp Nahum passage, see *JBL,* LXXV (1956), 91. On הוקיע, see S. R. Driver, *Notes on the Hebrew Text of the Book of Samuel* (2nd ed., 1913), p. 351.

M. GREENBERG

HANGINGS [קלעים; תכלת, blue material (Esth. 1:6); בתים, *probably* woven garments, *from* Arab. *batt;* KJV מסך (RSV SCREEN)]. Drapes. The hangings which surrounded the court of the tabernacle (Exod. 27:9-18; 35:17; 38:9-18; 39:40) were made of fine twined linen and were hung from pillars 5 cubits (*ca.* 7.5 feet) high (Exod. 27:18). On the N and S sides of the tabernacle court, the hangings extended for 100 cubits (*ca.* 150 feet) and on the E and W sides of the court for 50 cubits (*ca.* 75 feet). There were also hangings on each side of the gate to the court, 15 cubits (*ca.* 22.5 feet) in length. The hangings were to be carried, according to the priestly writers, by the Levitical family of Gershon (Num. 3:26; 4:26). *See* TABERNACLE.

Before the gate of the tabernacle court were hangings (KJV; RSV SCREEN) of richly colored material and fine twined linen (Exod. 27:16), on which was embroidery. This screen hung from four pillars and measured 20 by 5 cubits (*ca.* 7.5 feet; Exod. 38:18). A similarly constructed screen, 25 cubits in length, hung at the door of the tent of meeting (Exod. 26:36-37). Both these screens or sets of hangings were carried by the family of Gershon (Num. 3:25-26).

The hangings mentioned in Esth. 1:6 were of blue material, and nothing more can be known of them. The hangings the women wove for the ASHERAH (II Kings 23:7) were probably cultic garments (cf. etymology above). E. M. GOOD

HANIEL. KJV form of HANNIEL in I Chr. 7:39.

HANNAH hăn'ə [חנה, *from* חן, grace]. **1.** Wife of Elkanah the Ephraimite; mother of Samuel (I Sam. 1:2-20). For many years she was barren. Finally, during the family's annual visit to the sanctuary at Shiloh, she made a vow that if granted a son, she would dedicate the child to God (1:11). After this the child Samuel was born. As soon as possible, Hannah dedicated him to the service of God in the sanctuary of Shiloh, saying that "as long as he lives, he is lent to the LORD" (vs. 28). Hannah subsequently had other sons and daughters (2:21). The psalm attributed to her (2:1-10) seems to have been introduced from some other context.

2. KJV Apoc. form of ANNA 2. D. HARVEY

HANNATHON hăn'ə thŏn [חנתן] (Josh. 19:14). A border town in Zebulun. It is mentioned twice in the Amarna Tablets (EA, nos. 8, 245, where it is spelled *Ḫinnatuni* and *Ḫinatuna* respectively) of the fourteenth century B.C., and once in the annals of Tiglath-pileser III.

Hannathon is perhaps located at Tell el-Bedeiwiyeh, a site occupied in the Middle Bronze, Late Bronze, Iron I (i.e., *ca.* 2000-900), and Islamic periods, approximately six miles N of Nazareth; strong arguments have also been advanced for identifying it with el-Harbaj at the S end of the Plain of Acco.

Bibliography. W. F. Albright, "Some Archaeological and Topographical Results of a Trip Through Palestine," *BASOR*, 11 (1923), 11; "Contributions to the Historical Geography of Palestine," *AASOR*, 2-3 (1923), 23-24. G. W. Van Beek

HANNIEL hăn'ĭ əl [חַנִּיאֵל, God has been gracious]; KJV HANIEL in I Chr. 7:39. **1.** A Manassite leader, son of Ephod (Num. 34:23). He was one of those appointed, under the oversight of Eleazar and Joshua, to superintend the distribution of the W Jordanian territory among the ten tribes to be settled in that area of Canaan. The meaning of the name Hanniel and of other names in this account underscores Israel's dependence upon God for the new life in Canaan.

2. A leader or warrior of Asher; a son of Ulla (I Chr. 7:39).

Bibliography. M. Noth, *Die israelitischen Personennamen* (1928), pp. 35, 92, 187. R. F. Johnson

HANOCH hā'nŏk [חֲנוֹךְ, חֲנֹךְ, wise(?), *or* follower(?)]; KJV HENOCH hē'nŏk in I Chr. 1:33; HANOCHITES —īts. **1.** Eponym of a Midianite clan whose ancestry is traced to Abraham through Keturah (Gen. 25:4; I Chr. 1:33).

2. Eponym of a Reubenite clan (Gen. 46:9; Exod. 6:14; Num. 26:5; I Chr. 5:3).

Bibliography. M. Noth, *Die israelitischen Personennamen* (1928), p. 228; W. F. Albright, "The Babylonian Material in the Predeuteronomic Primeval History," *JBL*, LVIII (1939), 96. H. H. Guthrie, Jr.

HANUKKAH hä'nə kə [חֲנֻכָּה, consecration, dedication]. The Feast of Rededication. After Judas Maccabeus had cleansed the temple from the pollution of pagan worship (165 B.C.), the twenty-fifth of Chislev (December) was kept annually in memory of this.

See also Dedication, Feast of. N. Turner

HANUN hā'nən [חָנוּן, gracious, *an abbreviation of* Hananiah(?) *or* Hananiel(?), Yahu (*or* El) has been gracious]. **1.** King of the Ammonites. His insult to the ambassadors of David caused Israel to besiege Rabbah. Hanun called on Hadadezer for aid, and the siege was apparently postponed until the end of the Aramean wars (II Sam. 10:1-14). Then, despite stiff resistance by Hanun, the city was captured and the inhabitants reduced to slavery (11:1; 12:26-31). David appointed Hanun's brother Shobi in his place (17:27).

2. An inhabitant of Zanoah who helped repair two sections of the Jerusalem wall under Nehemiah (Neh. 3:13, 30). In the latter passage he is called the "sixth son of Zalaph," a phrase without parallel in the genealogical lists. Perhaps it is a corruption of "inhabitants of Zanoah." R. W. Corney

HAPHARAIM hăf'ə rā'əm [חֲפָרַיִם] (Josh. 19:19); KJV HAPHRAIM hăf rā'əm. A town in Issachar. Hapharaim (spelled *ḥprm*, no. 18) also appears in the Shishak list of conquered Palestinian towns (*ca.* 918 B.C.). It is probably located at et-Taiyibeh, approximately nine miles NW of Beth-shan.

Bibliography. W. F. Albright, "The Jordan Valley in the Bronze Age," *AASOR*, VI (1926), 35; "The Topography of the Tribe of Issachar," *ZAW* (1926), 227-28. G. W. Van Beek

HAPPINESS. Usually the human condition of well-being which comes with God's blessing or as divine reward for righteousness. Happiness is expressed in Hebrew idiomatically by אַשְׁרֵי, "Happy is . . . ," and in the LXX and the NT by μακάριος. The English versions appear to render the Hebrew term indiscriminately with "happy" or "blessed," and the preferred translation in the NT is "blessed."

The word "blessed" is appropriate, since man's happiness is recognized either as the fruit of God's freely given blessing or as a divinely granted reward for human merit. Both testaments contain examples of happiness as a gift: "Blessed is he whom thou dost choose and bring near" (Ps. 65:4—H 65:5); "Blessed are those who are invited to the marriage supper" (Rev. 19:9); and both contain examples of happiness as the reward for merit: "Blessed is he who considers the poor!" (Ps. 41:1—H 41:2); "Happy is he who is kind to the poor" (Prov. 14:21); "When you give a feast, invite the poor, the maimed, the lame, the blind, and you will be blessed, because they cannot repay you. You will be repaid at the resurrection of the just" (Luke 14:13-14).

The end of this last passage, in Luke, suggests an area, however, in which the NT adds a feature absent in the OT. It concerns the nature of this happiness. In the NT as well as the OT happiness is health and success, life and offspring, security and plenty (Deut. 33:29; Pss. 1:1-3; 41:2—H 41:3; 128:2; Prov. 8:34-36; 16:20; Isa. 32:20, but also Matt. 24:46-47; Luke 1:42; Jas. 1:12; Ps. 127:5, which is tragically reversed in Luke 23:29). The new note, particularly evident in the beatitudes, is the prospective nature of happiness there: "Your reward is great in heaven" (Luke 6:23; cf. Matt. 5:3-12; Rev. 14:13). *See also* Joy. S. H. Blank

HAPPIZZEZ hăp'ə zĕz [הַפִּצֵּץ, *tribal name* (*cf.* Beth-pazzez)] (I Chr. 24:15); KJV APHSES ăf'sēs. A descendant of Aaron (cf. I Chr. 24:1-6, 19); the eponym of one of the courses of temple priests under King David.

HARA hâr'ə [הָרָא, the mountain *or* the highland; LXX L Αρραν; *omitted in* LXX AB *and* Syr.]. The place to which the king of Assyria exiled the Hebrew tribes Reuben, Gad, and half of Manasseh, according to I Chr. 5:26. Since it is listed with places in N Mesopotamia, in the vicinity of Gozan (Ptolemy's Gausanitis, modern Tell Halaf), some have regarded Hara as the local designation of the mountainous region N of Gozan-Guzana (the classical Mons Masius and modern Karja Baghlar).

Because I Chr. 5:26 appears to be a faulty rendition of II Kings 17:6; 18:11, where instead of "Hara" the Hebrew text has "the cities of Media" and the

LXX has "the mountains of Media," some have regarded Hara as a corruption of the latter. It would then designate the mountainous district E of the Tigris River Valley. The Arabs subsequently called those highlands El Gebal ("the Mountain"). Less likely is the suggestion that "Hara" is a corruption of the name Harhar (חרחר), a Median city conquered by King Sargon of Assyria and colonized by him with captives from other countries. Tobit, an exile to Assyria, communicated with fellow Jews who had been transported to Media (Tob. 1:14-15).

R. A. Bowman

HARADAH hə rā'də [חרדה] (Num. 33:24-25). A stopping place in the journey of the Israelites from Sinai. The location is unknown.

HARAN hâr'ən [הרן, *earlier* mountaineer, *but perhaps* sanctuary; חרן (*in* 2 *below*)]. **1.** Son of Terah; brother of Abram (Abraham) and Nahor; father of Lot, Milcah, and Iscah. Haran died in Ur while his father was still alive (Gen. 11:26-31).

2. A Judahite; son of Caleb and his concubine Ephah (I Chr. 2:46).

3. A Levite; son of Gershonite Shimei (I Chr. 23:9).

L. Hicks

HARAN (PLACE) [חרן; Akkad. *Ḫarrânu;* Χαρράν]; KJV NT CHARRAN kâr'ən. A city of N Mesopotamia (now Turkey) where Abraham lived (Gen. 11:31; see also Acts 7:2, 4); where his father, Terah, died (Gen. 11:32); and whence Abraham migrated to Canaan (12:4-5). The kinsmen of the patriarchs continued to dwell as Arameans in Haran; Rebekah, daughter of Bethuel, was brought from there by Eliezer as bride for Isaac (Gen. 24); and later Jacob fled there (27:43; 28:10; 29:4) to dwell with Laban. Jacob married Laban's daughters, Leah and Rachel, in Haran, and all his children (the eponymous ancestors of the tribes) except Benjamin were born there, according to the OT tradition (Gen. 29:32–30:24).

The devotion of Haran to the moon cult of Babylonia indicates that the city was founded by the Third Dynasty of Ur, perhaps *ca.* 2000 B.C. That the Haran neighborhood was the scene of commercial colonies from the S is clear from recently discovered

From *Atlas of the Bible* (Thomas Nelson & Sons Limited)

6. Modern Harran, the biblical Haran, the chief tell to the left, with characteristic small houses of N Syria in the foreground

cuneiform tablets. Ezek. 27:23 lists Haran among the famous commercial cities. II Kings 19:12 (=Isa. 37:12) states that the ancestors of Sennacherib had devastated Haran along with other cities.

Current excavations in Haran (Harran) have revealed a long and continuous history from Assyro-Babylonian through Islamic times. Deep into the Christian period, Haran remained a stronghold of lunar paganism.

Fig. HAR 6.

C. H. Gordon

HARARITE hâr'ə rīt [(ה)הררי, הררי, (ה)ארדי]. A gentilic adjective of an unidentified tribe, predicated of the fathers of three members of the Mighty Men of David known as the "Thirty": Agee (II Sam. 23:11), father of Shammah; Shammah (II Sam. 23:33; Shagee in I Chr. 11:34), father of Jonathan; and Sharar (II Sam. 23:33; Sachar in I Chr. 11:35), father of Ahiam.

E. R. Dalglish

HARBONA här bō'nə [חרבונא, חרבונה, *perhaps from* Pers. *kherban,* donkey-driver]. One of the seven eunuchs who served as chamberlains for Ahasuerus (Esth. 1:10). He suggested that Haman be hanged upon the gallows he had prepared for Mordecai (7:9).

M. Newman

HARBOR [λιμήν] (Acts 27:12); KJV HAVEN. The word is used in the account of Paul's voyage to Rome with reference to Fair Havens near Lasea in Crete, and Phoenix, a port of Crete.

HARDEN THE HEART. A phrase, used to translate various verbs, expressing a firm set of mind, stubbornness, indifference, callousness, insensibility, inability to understand (cf. חזק, "make strong, unyielding" [Exod. 4:21; 14:4, 17; Josh. 11:20]; קשה, "make sharp, hard" [Exod. 7:3; Ps. 95:8]; קשה, "make firm, stubborn" [Isa. 63:17]; אמץ, "be bold, make obstinate" [Deut. 15:7]; כבד, "be heavy, insensible" [Exod. 8:15, 32; 9:7, 34; I Sam. 6:6]; φωρόω, "be callous" [Mark 6:52; cf. 8:17; John 12:40]; σκληρύνω, "be dry, hard" [Heb. 3:8, 15; 4:7]). In describing events from the standpoint of the divine purpose and redemptive activity, the biblical writers speak of God's hardening men's hearts (Exod. 4:21; 7:3; 14:4, 17; Deut. 2:30; Josh. 11:20; Isa. 63:17). At the same time they avow men harden their own hearts (Exod. 8:32; 9:34-35; Deut. 15:7; I Sam. 6:6; II Chr. 36:13). They found no apparent inconsistency in ascribing this activity both to God and to men. For men, by acting in accordance with their own self-will, were carrying out the divine purpose. This mind-set was characterized as Israel's sin, manifesting a lack of faith and a rebellious spirit (cf. Ps. 95:8; John 12:40; Heb. 3:8, 15; 4:7). The NT writers give it as the reason the disciples did not understand Jesus' actions (Mark 6:52; cf. 8:17).

Bibliography. J. Skinner, *Isaiah,* I, Century Bible (1915), 50; S. R. Driver, *Exodus,* CB (1918), pp. 53-54.

V. H. Kooy

HARE [ארנבת; *cf.* Ugar. *anhb;* Akkad. *annabu;* Arab. *'arnab;* Syr. *'arnbâ*]. Any of several herbivorous rodents of the family Leporidae. Bodenheimer speaks of the common hare of Palestine as *Lepus europaeus judaeus,* which is somewhat smaller than the average hare, whereas Tristram mentions the *Lepus syriacus* as the common hare of the N regions, this being the size and color of the English hare. Other species are occasionally encountered. The hare's close relative, the rabbit (*Lepus cuniculus*), has never existed in the lands of the Bible.

The OT (Lev. 11:6; Deut. 14:7) refers to the hare only to indicate that it is an unclean animal, but its assertion that the hare is a ruminant is contrary to fact. Probably, as in the case of the hyrax (*see* ROCK BADGER), some movements of the mouth and jaws have been erroneously interpreted as cud-chewing.

W. S. MCCULLOUGH

HAREL. *See* Ariel.

HAREPH hâr'ĕf [חרף, autumn, *or* sharp] (I Chr. 2:51). The founder of Beth-Gader.

Bibliography. M. Noth, *Die israelitischen Personennamen* (1928), p. 228; D. Diringer, *Le Inscrizioni Antico-Ebraiche Palestinesi* (1934), p. 196. H. H. GUTHRIE, JR.

HARETH. KJV form of HERETH.

HARHAIAH här hā'yə [חרהיה, *or* חרחיה] (Neh. 3:8). The father of Uzziel, who helped repair the walls of Jerusalem under Nehemiah—i.e., unless the passage is to be emended עזיאל בן־חבר הצורפים "Uzziel a member of the guild of goldsmiths." M. NEWMAN

HARHAS här'hăs [חרחס] (II Kings 22:14). Alternately: hăz'rə [חסרה] (II Chr. 34:22). Grandfather of Shallum, husband of Huldah, the prophetess consulted about Josiah's book of the law.

HAR-HERES här hĭr'ĭz [הר חרס, mountain of the sun] (Judg. 1:35); KJV MOUNT HERES. A mountain near Aijalon; probably identical with the border fortress of BETH-SHEMESH (Josh. 15:10; 21:16) and IR-SHEMESH (Josh. 19:41). Har, no. 77 of the list of Thut-mose III (*ca.* 1490-1436), is perhaps Har-heres.

V. R. GOLD

HARHUR här'hûr [חרחור, *possibly* raven]. Eponym of a family of temple servants listed among the returned exiles (Ezra 2:51; Neh. 7:53). The name is replaced by two others in I Esd. 5:31.

Bibliography. M. Noth, *Die israelitischen Personennamen* (1928), p. 230. B. T. DAHLBERG

HARIM hâr'ĭm [חרם, dedicated (to God); Χαρμή]; KJV Apoc. CARME kär'mĭ (I Esd. 5:25). **1.** A descendant of Aaron; eponym of a priestly house in the reign of King David (I Chr. 24:8); mentioned also among the exiles returned from Babylon (Ezra 2:39; Neh. 7:42; I Esd. 5:25; cf. Neh. 12:15; *see also* REHUM).

2. Eponym of a nonpriestly family among the returned exiles (Ezra 2:32; Neh. 7:35; lacking in I Esd. 5:22), some of whom also had to divorce their foreign wives later under Ezra (Ezra 10:31). The name is lacking in I Esd. 9:32.

3. A priest who signed Ezra's covenant (Neh. 10:5).

4. One of the chiefs of the people, signatory to Ezra's covenant (Neh. 10:27).

Bibliography. M. Noth, *Die israelitischen Personennamen* (1928), pp. 136-37, 216. B. T. DAHLBERG

HARIPH hâr'ĭf [חריף, *either* sharp *or* autumn]. Head of a family that resided in Jerusalem after the Exile (Neh. 7:24; cf. I Esd. 5:16), and also one of those who sealed Ezra's covenant (Neh. 10:19—H 10:20). In Ezra 2:18 the corresponding name is Jorah (יורה, "autumn rain"), which is perhaps the equivalent of Hariph. M. NEWMAN

HARLOT. *See* PROSTITUTION.

HARMON här'mən [ההרמונה] (Amos 4:3); KJV THE PALACE. The text where this hapax legomenon occurs is unfortunately corrupt. The name Harmon appears nowhere else in the Bible, and no place by this name is known. Many of the older versions have presupposed, not a proper noun, but a common noun (ארמון), meaning "palace" (see KJV), though there is by no means any consistency among the ancient versions or commentaries. The Targ. to Amos 4:3 interprets the expression as "beyond the mountains of Armenia." The LXX reads "the mountain of Romman." Ibn Ezra understands the meaning as "behind the wall of Samaria."

On the basis of the LXX the reference might be to a hill E of Bethel called Rimmon (רמון; Judg. 20: 45, 47; cf. Josh. 15:32; 19:13).

Scholars have made many suggestions, among which are the readings "naked" (ערמות), "devoted to destruction" (ההרמתנה), and "Harmon."

J. A. SANDERS

HARMONY OF THE GOSPELS. The gospels arranged in parallel columns for careful comparison. The name "harmony" was borrowed from music by A. Osiander (1537) in allusion to the pleasant accord of a four-tone chord. From Osiander to Griesbach (1774), harmonies characteristically included all four gospels; Griesbach initiated the special type of harmony (named by him "synopsis") which includes only the first three gospels. Today most scholars agree that a four-gospel harmony does justice neither to the Gospel of John nor to the Synoptics, but that a three-gospel harmony (or synopsis) is indispensable. The order of Mark now prevails.

Forerunners of the (post-Reformation) harmony were: (*a*) the second-century Diatessaron of Tatian (a composite gospel woven together from strands of all four, and perhaps a fifth), which is lost but is mainly recoverable from medieval adaptations of it; (*b*) the third-century Diatessaron of Ammonius of Alexandria, completely lost, which used Matthew as backbone; (*c*) the ten Canons of Eusebius, ingenious tables of parallel references, easily accessible today in the inner margin of Nestle's *Novum Testamentum Graece*.

Bibliography. The most useful current harmonies are: Huck-Lietzmann, *Synopse der drei ersten Evangelien* (Greek); *Gospel Parallels* (Huck's arrangement, using RSV text; English).

K. GROBEL

HARNEPHER här'nə fər [חרנפר; Egyp. *ḥr-nfr*, Horus is merciful]. A place or family in Asher (I Chr. 7:36).

Bibliography. M. Noth, *Die israelitischen Personennamen* (1928), pp. 63-64.

HARNESS. KJV form of BREASTPLATE in I Kings 22:34; II Chr. 18:33 and of MYRRH in II Chr. 9:24.

HAROD hâr'ŏd [חרד, trembling(?)]; HARODITE —īt; HARORITE hā'rôr īt. **1.** A spring, the site of Gideon's encampment while preparing for battle with the Midianites (Judg. 7:1), and possibly the unnamed fountain where Saul made camp against the Philistines (I Sam. 29:1). It is generally identified with 'Ain Jalud, a spring located on a NW spur of Mount Gilboa. G. W. VAN BEEK

2. The home of two of David's men, Shammah and Elika. The KJV translates חררי, חרורי, "Harodite" in II Sam. 23:25; "Harorite" in I Chr. 11:27. Similarity between Hebrew "r" and "d" probably accounts for the confusion in spelling, and "Harod" is doubtless correct in both places. O. R. SELLERS

HAROEH hə rō'ə [הראה, the seer] (I Chr. 2:52). Son of Shobal; probably the same as Reaiah in I Chr. 4:2.

HARORITE. *See* HAROD 2.

HAROSHETH-HAGOIIM hə rō'shĕth hə goi'īm [חרשת הגוים] (Judg. 4:2, 13, 16); KJV HAROSHETH OF THE GENTILES. A Canaanite town; the home of Sisera, who was defeated by Israel under Barak and Deborah. Its location remains unknown, although attempts have been made to identify it with Tell 'Amr or Tell el-Harbaj. Archaeological soundings conducted at Tell 'Amr have shown that it was probably not occupied before the tenth century B.C., more than a century after the historic battle with Sisera was fought. Tell el-Harbaj, on the other hand, is perhaps better suited to the topographical requirements of Helkath. It is possible that Harosheth-hagoiim is the *Muḫrashti* of the Amarna Letters (EA no. 335:17); if this is the case, it should probably be sought in the Plain of Sharon. G. W. VAN BEEK

HARP [κιθάρα] (I Macc. 4:54); KJV CITHERN sĭth'ərn. A Greek stringed instrument listed with lutes and cymbals as used in the celebration at the time of the rededication of the temple on the twenty-fifth of Chislev, 165 B.C. (cf. I Macc. 13:51, and the Aramaic transliteration in Dan. 3:5, 7); it was pictured on Jewish coins of the Rebellion. Perhaps of Semitic origin (Hebrew כנור), the cithara or cithern was an elaborate lyre with eleven or twelve strings of equal length strung over a wooden sound box and fastened to tuning pegs on a crossbar, plucked with either the left or the right hand. It was used independently or with other instruments and also to accompany voices in singing.

The KJV uses "harp" to translate κινύρα (RSV LUTE) in I Macc. 4:54. *See* MUSICAL INSTRUMENTS § B1*d*.

For "harp" in the OT, *see* MUSICAL INSTRUMENTS § B4*c*.

Bibliography. C. Sachs, *The History of Musical Instruments* (1940); O. R. Sellers, "Musical Instruments of Israel," *BA*, IV (1941), 36-38. E. W. SAUNDERS

HARPOON [שכה, *cf.* Akkad. *šakāku,* be pointed, *šikkatu,* nail, point] (Job 41:7—H 40:31); KJV BARBED IRON. Mentioned in parallelism with fishing spears (צלצל דגים), as an inadequate weapon for catching the sea monster Leviathan. *See* FISHER.

HARROW [שדד]. The harrow as a special tool is not known in ancient Egypt and probably did not exist in ancient Palestine. However, Job 39:10; Isa. 28:24; Hos. 10:11 clearly refer to some process other than plowing. The meaning of the verb שדד in these passages is not clear, and authorities differ on the sense of it, taking it to mean either cross plowing (doubtful), making of border furrows, or the dragging of branches to smooth the soil over the seed (probable). H. N. RICHARDSON

HARSHA här'shə [חרשא, mute, *or* taciturn]. Alternately: CHAREA [Χαρεά] (I Esd. 5:32). Eponym of family of temple servants listed among the returning exiles (Ezra 2:52; Neh. 7:54).

Bibliography. M. Noth, *Die israelitischen Personennamen* (1928), p. 228. B. T. DAHLBERG

HART [איל; *cf.* Ugar. *'yl,* deer, buck; Arab. *'ayyil,* hart, mountain goat; Akkad. *ajalu,* hart]. Alternately: STAG. The adult male of the Red Deer (*Cervus elaphus*). The Red Deer is one of the most typical members of the DEER family, as well as one of the most widely distributed. The general color of the pelage varies slightly with the season, but it tends toward a reddish brown. The height of a mature specimen is *ca.* four feet at the shoulder.

Various OT references (Deut. 12:15, 22; 14:5; 15:22; I Kings 4:23—H 5:3) indicate that the איל was an available, as well as an edible, game animal, that it was a ruminant, and probably that it was a deer. It can only be described as a reasonable hypothesis that the deer thus designated was the Red Deer. Other biblical references allude to the hart's leaping (Isa. 35:6), and to its need for water and food (Ps. 42:1—H 42:2; Lam. 1:6). In Song of S. 2:9, 17; 8:14 the hart's strength and agility, doubtless often observed, account for the simile applied to the beloved. W. S. MCCULLOUGH

HARUM hâr'əm [הרום] (I Chr. 4:8). Eponym of a family of the tribe of Judah.

HARUMAPH hə rōō'măf [חרומף, *probably* mutilated nose, *from* חרם *plus* אף; *cf.* Lev. 21:18] (Neh. 3:10). The father of Jedaiah, who helped repair the walls of Jerusalem in the time of Nehemiah.

HARUPHITE hə rōō'fīt [*Kethibh* חריפי, *Qere* חרופי, *from* חרף, sharp *or* autumn(?)] (I Chr. 12:5—H 12:6). The gentilic designation of Shephatiah, one of the Benjaminite warriors who joined David at Ziklag. It is possible that there is some relation between this designation and the Calebite Hareph (חרף) of I Chr. 2:51 or the Hariph (חריף) family of Neh. 7:24; 10:19—H 10:20, but the context suggests an unknown place name, Hareph or Hariph. M. NEWMAN

HARUZ hâr'ŭz [חרוץ, gold(?), *or* eager(?)] (II Kings 21:19). Maternal grandfather of Amon. His name is probably Arabic, and his place of origin Jotbah.

HARVEST. The gathering of the crops. The Gezer Calendar provides a clue to the harvest seasons in ancient Israel. Olives were harvested at the beginning of the year—i.e., the middle of September to the middle of November (*see* CALENDAR), by beating the trees with long sticks (Deut. 24:20; Isa. 17:6). In March-April flax was harvested by cutting it off

Courtesy of Staatliche Museen, Berlin

7. Scene of the harvesting of flax, from a bas relief of a tomb of Pa-heri at el-Kab; Eighteenth Dynasty (1550-1350 B.C.)

near the ground, then laying the stalks out to dry (Josh. 2:6).* The harvesting of barley (*see* BARLEY HARVEST) took place in April or early May, while the wheat harvest occurred in May-June (*see* REAPING). During August-September the summer fruits—figs, grapes, and pomegranates—were harvested. Fig. HAR 7.

Bibliography. G. H. Dalman, *Arbeit und Sitte,* V (1937), 23 ff; W. F. Albright, *BASOR,* 92 (1943), 16 ff; G. E. Wright, *Biblical Archaeology* (1957), pp. 180 ff.

H. N. RICHARDSON

HASADIAH hăs′ə dī′ə [חסדיה, Yahu has been faithful; 'Ασαδαίος; Vulg. *Sedei*]; KJV Apoc. ASADIAS ăs′ə dī′əs. **1.** One of Zerubbabel's sons (I Chr. 3:20).

2. Son of Hilkiah, and ancestor of Baruch (Bar. 1:1).

HASENUAH. KJV form of HASSENUAH in I Chr. 9:7.

HASHABIAH hăsh′ə bī′ə [חשביה, חשביהו, Yahu has taken account (*i.e., of childlessness and has given a child*); Apoc. Σαβίας (I Esd. 1:9)]; KJV MALCHIJAH măl kī′jə in Ezra 10:25; KJV Apoc. ASSABIAS ăs′ə bī′əs. Alternately: ASIBIAS ['Ασιβίας] (I Esd. 9:26). **1.** A Levite listed as ancestor of a musician of the sanctuary (I Chr. 6:45—H 6:30).

2. A Levite, ancestor of Shemaiah, a returned exile (I Chr. 9:14; Neh. 11:15).

3. A Levite, son of Jeduthun; listed among the musicians set apart by David to prophesy with music in the sanctuary (I Chr. 25:3, 19).

4. A Hebronite, mentioned as a royal deputy under King David for the area W of the Jordan River (I Chr. 26:30).

5. A chief officer of the Levites under King David (I Chr. 27:17).

6. A chief of the Levites under King Josiah (II Chr. 35:9; I Esd. 1:9).

7. A Merarite Levite among those who joined Ezra's company at the River Ahava and who were entrusted with the temple treasures being brought to Jerusalem (Ezra 8:19, 24); perhaps to be identified with the Levite of the same name among those signing Ezra's covenant (Neh. 10:11), perhaps also with the temple musician mentioned in Neh. 12:24.

8. One of the laymen among those persuaded by Ezra to divorce their foreign wives (Ezra 10:25, where read with RSV "Hashabiah" instead of MT-KJV "Malchijah" [MT and KJV]; *cf.* ASIBIAS in I Esd. 9:26 ['Ασιβίας=חשביה]).

9. A builder of Nehemiah's wall (Neh. 3:17).

10. A Levite, descendant of Asaph (Neh. 11:22).

11. A priest of the house of Hilkiah in the time of Joiakim the high priest (Neh. 12:21).

Bibliography. M. Noth, *Die israelitischen Personennamen* (1928), pp. 21, 189.

B. T. DAHLBERG

HASHABNAH hə shăb′nə [חשבנה, *perhaps a corruption of* חשביה, Yahu has considered, *but more probably a shortened form of* חשבניה, Yahu has considered me] (Neh. 10:25—H 10:26). One of those who sealed Ezra's covenant.

HASHABNEIAH hăsh′əb nē′yə [חשבניה, *perhaps a corruption of* חשביה, Yahu has considered, *but more probably a shortened form of* חשבניה, Yahu has considered me]. **1.** The father of Hattush, who helped repair the walls of Jerusalem in the time of Nehemiah (Neh. 3:10).

2. A Levite who participated in a liturgical blessing of Yahweh in the time of Ezra (Neh. 9:5). The Syr. reading, חשביה, suggests that he might be identical with the Levite Hashabiah of Ezra 8:19, 24; Neh. 10:11—H 10:12; 11:22; 12:24.

M. NEWMAN

HASHBADDANAH hăsh băd′ə nə [חשבדנה, *possibly a corruption of* חשביה, Yahu has considered, *as the* Syr. *suggests, or of* חשבניה, Yahu has considered me]. One of the men, possibly a Levite (*see* HASHABNEIAH 2), who stood on Ezra's left hand when the Law was read at the great assembly (Neh. 8:4).

M. NEWMAN

HASHEM hā′shĕm [חשם]. A Gizonite who was a member of the Mighty Men of David known as the "Thirty" (I Chr. 11:34). *See* JASHEN.

HASHMONAH hăsh mō′nə [חשמנה] (Num. 33:29-30). A stopping place along the route of Israel's journey from Sinai.

HASHUB. KJV alternate form of HASSHUB.

HASHUBAH hə shōō′bə [חשבה, *perhaps* consideration; *since a feminine passive participle is not appropriate for a male, it possibly should be vocalized either ḥašābhâ* *as a shortened form of ḥ^a^shabhyâ,* Yahu has considered, *with the hypocoristic ending, or simply as ḥ^a^shubh,* considered (of Yahu)] (I Chr. 3:20). A son of Zerubbabel.

M. NEWMAN

HASHUM hā'shəm [חשם; Arab. *ḫatimun,* broad-nosed; Ασομ]; KJV Apoc. ASOM ā'səm. Eponym or head of one of the families that returned from exile (Ezra 2:19; 10:33; Neh. 7:22; 8:4; 10:18; I Esd. 9:33). I Esd. 9:44, which parallels Neh. 8:4, has the name Lothasubus in place of Hashum.

Bibliography. M. Noth, *Die israelitischen Personennamen* (1928), p. 227.

H. H. GUTHRIE, JR.

HASHUPHA. KJV form of HASUPHA.

HASIDEANS hăs'ə dē'ənz [Ἀσιδαίοι = חסידים, *ḥ^a^sîdhîm*]. A militant religious community which participated in the Maccabean Revolt. They were zealous for the law, but their origins, organization, and ultimate purposes are unknown. *See* MACCABEES.

1. OT background. *Ḥ^a^sîdhîm* (generally translated "saints") are mentioned in several psalms as faithful Israelites who fear, trust, and depend upon the Lord. Ps. 149 is particularly important:

> Sing to the LORD a new song,
> his praise in the assembly of the *ḥ^a^sîdhîm!*
> . . . .
> Let the high praises of God be in their throats
> and two-eged swords in their hands,
> to wreak vengeance on the nations
> and chastisement on the peoples,
> . . . .
> to execute on them the judgment written!
> This is glory for all his *ḥ^a^sîdhîm.*

2. In the Maccabean period. The Hasideans are referred to in I Macc. 2:42; 7:13; II Macc. 14:6. They are not mentioned as a newly formed party, and it is probable that they existed in the pre-Maccabean period. Soon after the Maccabees revolted, "there united with them a company of Hasideans, mighty warriors of Israel, every one who offered himself willingly for the law" (I Macc. 2:42).

There is no sound basis for the widely held notion that the Hasideans were interested only in religious reform and not in national independence. There was an occasion in the early years of the war when certain scribes of the Hasideans sued for peace. During the parley their negotiators were perfidiously seized and killed (I Macc. 7:12-16). The folly of trusting the enemy was thus made clear, and the main body of Hasideans presumably continued to support Judas (cf. II Macc. 14:6).

After the war, during the struggle for power in the newly established revolutionary state, party conflict seems to have developed between the Hasideans and the Maccabeans over the question of the legitimacy of the Maccabean claims to the high priesthood. This conflict can be dated as early as the composition of I Maccabees; for its author, a court historian of the later Maccabees, disparages the legal interpretations of the Hasidean scribes of his time by drawing attention to the rueful mistake of those Hasidean scribes who during the revolution had misplaced their trust in a priestly family which, though legitimate from their point of view, had turned out to be neither trustworthy nor just (7:12-18).

The later PHARISEES and ESSENES probably developed out of rival wings of this postrevolutionary Hasidean party.

Bibliography. V. Aptowitzer, *Parteipolitik der Hasmonäerzeit im rabbinischen und pseude-epigraphischen Schrifttum* (1927); J. C. Dancy, *A Commentary on I Maccabees* (1954).

W. R. FARMER

HASIDIM hăs'ə dĭm [חסידים, *ḥ^a^sîdhîm*], *masculine plural of* HASID hä'sĭd [חסיד, *ḥāsîdh*]. The term *hasid* applies to one who practices *hesed* (חסד, *ḥésedh*). These cognate words have been the subject of much study and discussion in recent decades. The word *hesed* is frequently associated with "covenant" (ברית, *b^e^rîth*), and the two terms comprehend to a large extent the same obligations, as indicated by the expression "to keep covenant and *hesed*" (Deut. 7:9). The covenant is established by rites, but *hesed* is the quality which results from the maintenance and implementation of the covenant. In the broadest sense, *hesed* denotes the joint liability, the mutual obligation, of persons who are involved in social, economic, or political relationships, or who belong together in any way. It has been succinctly defined as the "virtue that knits together society." The term is applied to the angels' rescue of Lot (Gen. 19:19); the loyalty of wife to husband, son to father, daughter-in-law to mother-in-law (Gen. 20:13; 47:29; Ruth 1:8); the rewarding of a spy (Judg. 1:24); the friendship between David and Jonathan (I Sam. 20:8; II Sam. 9:1); the loyalty of a subject to the king (II Sam. 3:8; II Chr. 24:22); leniency of victor to vanquished (I Kings 20:31); the ideals which the good wife and mother seeks to inculcate in the members of her household (Prov. 31:26). Translators have found the word difficult to render adequately. The LXX and the Vulg. generally rendered ἔλεος and *misericordia,* and the older English versions have for the most part "mercy," but sometimes "kindness" or "loving kindness." The basic meaning of the word, however, appears to be "loyalty," and so the RSV renders it in some instances where the reference is to human relations (I Sam. 20:15; II Sam. 2:5; 3:8; 16:17; I Kings 2:7; Ps. 101:1; Prov. 3:3; 14:22; 16:6; 19:22; 20:6, 8; Jonah 2:8), or "loyally" in the idiom "to do *hesed* with (someone)" (עשה חסד עם; Gen. 21:23; 24:49; 47:29; II Sam. 10:2; I Kings 2:7; I Chr. 19:2); but in other instances the word is rendered "kindness" or "kindly." The plural of the word (*ḥ^a^sādhîm*), as applied to the proofs of loyalty shown in the good life, is translated "good deeds" (II Chr. 32:32; 35:26; Neh. 13:14). However, where *hesed* applies to God's dealings with man, the RSV chooses "steadfast love" as the regular rendering of the word. Once the expression "the *hesed* of the Lord," in reference to the covenant of friendship between David and Jonathan (I Sam. 20:14), is rendered "the loyal love of the LORD." In Job 37:13 the word is translated "love," without qualification.

A *hasid* is a person characterized by *hesed,* a man of *hesed* (איש חסד, *'îš ḥesedh;* Prov. 11:17; Isa. 57:1). The form *hasid* applies almost exclusively to man; apart from Ps. 145:17; Jer. 3:12, it is never used of God in the OT, the Talmud, or later Jewish literature. As applied to man, it denotes man's ideal loyalty to God within the community of the faithful. Accordingly, the English versions generally render *hasidim* as "saints," and the RSV retains this rendering in thirteen cases (Pss. 16:3; 30:4; 31:23; 37:28; 79:2; 85:8; 97:10; 116:15; 132:9, 16; 145:10; 148:14; Prov. 2:8). In a few passages the RSV has changed the KJV "saints" to "faithful (ones)" (I Sam. 2:9; Pss. 50:5; 89:19; 149:1, 5, 9), and the KJV "holy" to "godly" (Deut. 33:8; Pss. 16:10; 86:2), "good man" to "godly man" (Mic. 7:2); "godly" is retained in Pss. 4:3; 12:1; 32:6. In Ps. 18:26 (=II Sam. 22:26) the RSV has substituted "loyal" for KJV "merciful."

In the passages noted above in which the RSV has retained the rendering "saints," the word has in each case a possessive suffix referring to the Lord; thus the term is used as a collective designation of Israel as a religious community, "the saints of the Lord" (note especially Pss. 85:8; 148:14; 149:1). There was, doubtless, a stage in which the mere fact of belonging to the chosen people was title to the designation *hasid,* but with the development of ethical monotheism the term came to have moral and spiritual implications. This is especially clear in Pss. 37:28-29; 97:10-11, where the word stands in synonymous parallelism with "the righteous" (צדיקים, *ṣaddîqîm*), as contrasted with "the wicked." The versions attempted to convey the ethical and spiritual connotations of the term. Aq. and Symm. translate ὅσιος "saintly." The LXX and Origen render εὐσεβής or εὐλαβής, "reverent." The Targ. mostly retains the Hebrew word, but in a few places substitutes "righteous" (צדיק, *ṣaddîq*) or "pure" (זכא, *zākhâ*). Syr. generally renders "righteous" (זדיקא, *zaddîqâ*), but also "holy" (חסיא, *ḥāsᵉyâ*), "pure" (גבא, *gābhâ*).

Bibliography. N. Glueck, *Das Wort ḥesed im alttestamentlichen Sprachgebrauch,* BZAW, vol. 47 (1927); W. F. Lofthouse, "Chen and Chesed in the OT," *ZAW,* 20 (1933), 29-35; N. H. Snaith, *The Distinctive Ideas of the OT* (1944); H. J. Stoebe, "Die Bedeutung des Wortes häsäd im AT," *Vetus Testamentum,* 2 (1952), 244-54; R. Sorg, *Hesed and Hasid in the Psalms* (1953); W. L. Reed, "Some Implications of *ḥēn* for OT Religion," *JBL,* 73 (1954), 36-41; A. R. Johnson, "Hesed and Hasid," *Interpretationes ad Vetus Testamentum Pertinentes Sigmundo Mowinckel Septuagenario Missae* (1955), pp. 100-112.

M. H. Pope

HASMONEANS hăz′mə nē′ənz [חשמונאי; ʼΑσαμωναῖος]. The family name of the dynasty of Jewish high priests and kings who ruled from 142 to 63 B.C. The early members form the theme of I Maccabees, the book which seeks to portray them as the family divinely ordained to save Israel (see especially 5:62). The very earliest members are sometimes known as the MACCABEES. This, however, is a name which strictly should only be applied to one of their number, Judas Maccabeus, a son of Mattathias (*see* MATTATHIAS 1), and the founder of this illustrious family (*see* JUDAS 10). The ascendancy of this family procured for the Jewish people a sixty-five-year period of peace and freedom, between periods of Greek and Roman supremacy.

1. Hasmoneus
2. The rise of the family
3. The rule of the Hasmoneans (142-63 B.C.)
   a. Simon
   b. John Hyrcanus
   c. Judas Aristobulus I
   d. Alexander Janneus
   e. Alexandra
   f. Aristobulus II
4. The end of the Hasmoneans (63-7 B.C.)
5. Achievement of the Hasmoneans

Bibliography

1. Hasmoneus. The family derives its name from ʼΑσαμωναῖος, the great-grandfather of Mattathias, according to Josephus (Antiq. XVI.vii.1). We know almost nothing of this person. It may even have been a name borne by Mattathias himself. In any case, the name itself probably ultimately derives from a place name—HESHMON or HASHMONAH—though it has been variously interpreted as meaning "fruitfulness," "temperer of steel," and "wealthy."

2. The rise of the family. The name Hasmonean does not occur in the books of Maccabees, but is drawn from Josephus (Antiq. XX.viii.11; xx.10), who refers to the "sons of Asmoneus," to the "Asmoneans," and to the "Asmonean family." Moreover, we have one instance in the Mishna (*see* TALMUD) where Judas Maccabeus and his brother are called "Hasmoneans" (*Middōth* 1.6), and one or two similar references in later Jewish literature. The family first steps into the pages of history in 167 B.C., when the brave priest at MODIN resists the Seleucid king's demand for sacrifice to the heathen gods and slays the king's officer and a Jew who was complying. This entailed for Mattathias a flight to the mountains, whence he and his five sons and many loyal Jews who followed him descended from time to time to pull down altars, forcibly circumcise children, and put apostates to death. When, after a short time, the old man died, his son Judas Maccabeus assumed the leadership of the rebellion. Living up to his reputation of a "lion in his deeds, like a lion's cub roaring for prey" (I Macc. 3:4), Judas excelled in guerrilla warfare, and after defeating at Emmaus the three Syrian generals who were sent against him, Judas had to meet the Syrian regent himself, Lysias (*see* LYSIAS [SYRIAN]). As a result, peace was made, which gave the Jews complete freedom of worship, and Judas completely cleared the temple of idolatry and instituted the Rededication Feast in 165 (*see* DEDICATION, FEAST OF).

But the Maccabees did not rest; they found that minorities of Jews were maltreated in some places, and they did not like the fortified citadel which Lysias had built in Jerusalem and which housed Syrian troops (*see* JERUSALEM § 9); and, besides, Judea was not free. Judas therefore continued the fight until his valiant death at Elasa in 161 (I Macc. 9:1-22). His brother Jonathan (*see* MACCABEES) then became military leader of the Maccabees and continued the struggle with spasmodic attacks upon the Syrian army, and resisted the spread of Hellenization. As time went on, the Seleucid dynasty in Antioch was weakening, was often glad of Jonathan's help, and could not afford to support Hellenizing high priests in Jerusalem against popular disapproval. This increased the prestige of the Hasmonean house and their adherents. The Hasmonean dynasty can be said to have had its beginnings when Jonathan, ten years before the Jews gained complete independence, prudently allowed himself to be appointed high priest by the upstart Syrian king or pretender, Alexander Balas (*see* ALEXANDER 2), in whose negligent reign the Jews were left to their own devices.

As Balas was too preoccupied with his personal struggles, the Hasmoneans thrived unmolested, and in the next reign the Seleucid power conceded to Jonathan a good deal of territory in Samaria and almost complete freedom from taxation. Jonathan now became a powerful influence in the struggles for the throne by various Seleucid claimants. His army was capable of waging successful battles on behalf of any claimant, but he was tricked into being captured in 143, and then killed by a Syrian pretender. He was succeeded by his brother SIMON MACCABEUS as captain and as high priest, with the nation behind him. Simon continued with the fortifications which Jonathan had commenced in Jerusalem, and was granted one concession after another from Antioch. His final victory was to overcome the Syrian citadel in Jerusalem, the Acra, and to demand of Demetrius II that at last the Jewish people might be free of their overlords and the yoke of the heathen removed (I Macc. 13:33-52). The last of Mattathias' sons had demonstrated that the blood of the Maccabees had not been shed in vain.

3. The rule of the Hasmoneans (142-63 B.C.)

a. Simon (141-135). In 141, by his own people, Simon was given the title of ethnarch or governor, and the right of hereditary succession was granted to his heirs (I Macc. 14:41-49). All this was inscribed on a tablet which was placed in the temple. A new age was seen to have dawned, and documents were dated from it. Coins were struck. An independent treaty was concluded with Rome and Sparta. A period of peace did much to strengthen the prosperity of Judea and to prove the administrative gifts, priestly integrity, and meticulous justice of Simon. He was perhaps the best ruler the Jews ever had in the postexilic period, though he was not their king. He promoted literature and the arts, trade and farming. Unfortunately, tragedy marred the end of his rule, and in his old age Judea was treacherously invaded by the king of Syria, Antiochus VII (*see* ANTIOCHUS 7). The two sons, Judas and John, to whom Simon entrusted the campaign, inflicted a decisive defeat on the Syrian general near Modin. All went peacefully and prosperously for two more years, until in 135 Simon and two of his sons perished at DOK at the hand of his son-in-law and chief rival for power, Ptolemy son of Abub. One son escaped and assumed his father's offices of governor and high priest before his rival could reach Jerusalem. He was John, commonly known as Hyrcanus, who had been in charge of the fortress Gazara.

b. John Hyrcanus (135-105). His long regime began somewhat unfortunately, because he agreed to the demand of the Seleucid king Antiochus VII Sidetes, after Jerusalem had been besieged for a whole year and the wall broken down, to disarm his troops and to pay a heavy indemnity. However, there was soon a turn in the tide of fortune, and John Hyrcanus quickly ended his temporary humiliation. He seized the opportunity afforded by the death of Antiochus in 128 and the disputes about the succession which followed, to cease paying the indemnity and to extend the borders of Jewish territory: E of the Jordan, and northward to include Shechem and the Samaritans, whose rival temple on Mount Gerizim he destroyed (*see* GERIZIM, MOUNT) *ca.* 109, and southward to include IDUMEA (the old Edom). He compelled the Idumeans to become Jews and observe the whole law. In spite of this, however, the Jews themselves for the future never regarded the Idumeans as anything but Edomites and semiheathen. The savage revenge which Hyrcanus took upon the Samaritans must, in part at least, have been dictated by the irritating aloofness of the SAMARITANS during the Maccabean struggles; they had always been bitterly hostile to the Judeans and had resisted both Maccabean influence on the one hand and Hellenization on the other. John Hyrcanus had then a double reason for paying off old scores.

He considerably strengthened the defenses of his country by building fortresses and concluding a useful treaty with Rome. His prestige increased: men looked upon him as a prophet as well as a high-priestly prince; his name began to appear inscribed on the Judean coinage; he hired foreign mercenaries to help fight his campaigns.

One very important development took place during the high priesthood of John Hyrcanus—the transfer of his sympathies from the popular Pharisaic to the noble Sadducean party. The Pharisees openly resented the hint that Hyrcanus, who had hitherto been much under their influence, might venture to assume royal status; they looked upon the house of David alone as the true royal family. The earlier Hasmoneans had been predominantly pious and zealous for the law after the fashion of the later Pharisees. Both parties were by now becoming powerful, religiously and politically, and more and more mutually antagonistic, but it is not certain beyond all doubt that they were known as yet by the names of Pharisee and Sadducee. Josephus reports that Hyrcanus was overtly condemned as a usurper by a member of the popular party and challenged to surrender the high priesthood because he had no claim to it (Jos. Antiq. XIII.x.5-6). The story is repeated in the Talmud, but it looks like a Pharisaic invention with the motive of ascribing opposition to the Hasmonean claims as early as possible.

Hyrcanus' move toward the more politically minded and aristocratic party had the greater significance and importance in that it set the direction for future development in the Hasmonean dynasty. John Hyrcanus undoubtedly set the precedent by developing Hellenistic sympathies, and departing from the simpler ideals of the earlier members of his family. The names of his three young sons were changed from Judas, Mattathias, and Jonathan (glorious names!) to Aristobulus, Antigonus, and Alexander Janneus.

Politically it was a very successful period for the Jews, great strides being made toward the full restoration of the royal Davidic throne of Judah and the complete safety and independence of the state. We know too little about his latter years, but Aristobulus and Antigonus proved themselves valiant soldiers when their father left them in charge of the siege of the city of Samaria. This Greek colony appealed to Syria, to Antiochus Cyzicenus (*see* ANTI-

OCHUS 9), who came only to be ignominiously defeated by the two brothers. Samaria eventually fell, and was utterly destroyed. News of these victories delighted the heart of the old priest in Jerusalem, Hyrcanus. But they also saddened the hearts of many of the more pious Pharisees, who thought that the high priesthood was in danger of being profaned by worldly ambition.

Coins from this regime have been found in the ruins of the Qumran community (*see* DEAD SEA SCROLLS), and the sect which resided there may well have originated at this period, perhaps as a protest against the prevailing Hasmonean worldliness. Messianic psalms were written at this time, with John Hyrcanus as the probable hero, and it was largely because of the greatness and glory of his period of priesthood and governorship that second-century conceptions of the Messiah often centered round the hope of a priestly ruler, descended from Levi like the Hasmoneans.

It has been held, but not by most investigators, that Hyrcanus was the first of the Hasmonean rulers to take the title of king; it is more likely that this was true of his eldest son, Judas Aristobulus I (*see* § 3*c below*). With John Hyrcanus the Hasmonean rulers passed forever their highest peak of nobility and religious devotion. The rest of them aimed at being little more than secular monarchs, and few achieved anything better than the average in moral character. The difference between the second- and first-century Hasmoneans is in this way particularly marked. In consequence, the messianic hopes of the best minds in the nation tended to turn away from the Priest idea to that of the SON OF MAN—a supernatural figure far removed from this world, and not in the slightest modeled on the Hasmonean priest-kings!

c. Judas Aristobulus I (104). Before he died, Hyrcanus had decided that his widow should retain the civil power at his death, while his eldest son, Aristobulus, should assume the high priesthood. But Aristobulus was anything but pious; all his ambitions were political, and after ruthlessly imprisoning (according to Josephus) all the family except his brother Antigonus, and allowing his mother to die of hunger in prison, he not only seized the civil power, but also proclaimed himself as Aristobulus, King of the Jews. He was, however, careful that foreign nations should be more aware of this than the Jews themselves. On his coins he appears only as Judas, his Jewish name, and merely as high priest, not king.

He continued his father's work of strengthening the nation. He extended its boundaries northward, beyond Samaria and Scythopolis, by conquering those Itureans who inhabited "Galilee of the Gentiles," as it came to be called, in a very short reign of only one year. The Galilee in which Jesus was brought up was really the creation of Aristobulus, who forcibly proselytized a race which was essentially or largely Gentile, making them accept circumcision and all the beliefs and customs of the Jews. The family of which Mary came belonged, of course, to Judea, but it is likely that some of the apostles of Jesus, chosen by the Sea of Galilee and near to Capernaum, were of mixed Syrian and Greek descent, whose forebears were forced into Judaism by the sword of the Hasmonean kings.

Aristobulus moved much further than his father away from the ideals of the Maccabees. Whether or not he called himself *Philhellene* ("friend of the Greek"), he behaved accordingly. It is the more remarkable, therefore, that in common with other Hasmoneans he should have displayed so conspicuously the proselytizing spirit.

Out of jealousy and suspicion, and urged on by his queen, Salome Alexandra (*see* ALEXANDRA; *see also* § 3*e below*), he had unwittingly caused Antigonus, for whom he had some affection, to be murdered by his bodyguard. It is said to the credit of Aristobulus that his painful death was hastened by his remorse for the crime against his brother.

d. Alexander Janneus (104-78). Aristobulus was succeeded by a brother whom he had imprisoned and who was now released by his sister-in-law. His name, Jonathan, or Jannai, was Hellenized into Janneus, and in addition he took the Greek name Alexander. This does not mean that he favored Greek culture in any way, as Aristobulus had done. Like his brother, however, he was ambitious to complete his father's work of conquering and Judaizing all Coele-Syria (N Palestine), and he did finally succeed in Gaza in the S (*ca.* 96 B.C.) and all the towns except Ascalon on the W coast S of Mount Carmel, and in extending the kingdom to Gadara and other cities E of Jordan.

In him the Hasmonean dynasty really reached its height territorially. But the subjugation of so many cultured Greek cities had a demoralizing effect on the civilization of Coele-Syria: prosperity declined in field and city, and everywhere the scars from the wars from which his reign was scarcely ever free were visible. In the words of Ps. 2, which may have been composed in this reign, it was his warlike aim to receive the heathen for his inheritance, the utmost parts of earth for his possession, and to bruise them with an iron rod, breaking them in pieces like a potter's vessel. It was seldom indeed that any foe, even Egypt or Syria, was able to thwart his designs for very long.

Unfortunately for him, he was considerably hindered by troubles nearer home, and these very largely centered around the enmity of the Pharisees, to whom he appeared thoroughly disreputable. Their opposition might have remained harmless enough, but in overcoming it Alexander Janneus stooped to every kind of savagery. The Pharisees probably owed their origin to the HASIDIM, the "pious ones," in the reign of Antiochus Epiphanes. Sometimes they had assisted the Maccabees in the struggle for independence, but at other times they had remained aloof, especially after Judas Maccabeus had begun to display merely political ambitions. All their zeal had been for the law and in support of characteristically Jewish institutions against Hellenistic ones, and they did not desire war and glory for their own sake. They became less and less sympathetic toward the Hasmonean house and increasingly critical of the legality of its claims to the high priesthood and royal status. The Hasmonean house, in its turn, though it had risen to power in the first place through the pious zeal of the Hasidim and their successors, was now finding itself more in line with the other powerful and rich families of Judea. And these were Sadducees. Sympathies and antipathies reached a critically acute stage in the days of Alexander Janneus. Of course, although Josephus himself is not prejudiced against the Sadducean king, we can never be sure how far the report which the Jewish historian gives of the king's atrocities has been previously colored by Pharisaic bitterness against him. This record of Janneus in his home affairs is one of the most disgraceful in the annals of dictatorship. Briefly it is as follows:

During a celebration of the Feast of Tabernacles, he was officiating in the temple as high priest when disapproval of an immoral, drunken, bloodthirsty scoundrel in such a place impelled the people to hurl at him, not only insulting words, but also the citron fruit which they carried at the feast. Another important detail is gleaned from the Talmud tractate Sukkah: instead of pouring the water libation on the altar, as he should have done according to Pharisaic opinion, he had poured it over his own feet. It may well be that Janneus was in this way declaring himself publicly on the side of the Sadducees, sharing their contempt for this Pharisaic ritual of pouring water, the origin of which is said to have been the need for rain at that time of year to fill the cisterns in Jerusalem. The Sadducees were mainly the country aristocracy, not concerned with the filling of cisterns in the city, whereas the Pharisees were largely city dwellers without easy access to the countryman's wells and streams. The Sadducees regarded the libation as a layman's invention, unnecessary and rather slighting to the priesthood, as it came but five days after the impressive prayers of the Day of Atonement. Alexander Janneus would then be risking his life, and certainly his popularity, thus to mock the people's prayer for rain at the end of the festival; and he was at least declaring his sincere adherence to Sadducean beliefs and the dignity of the priesthood.

Whether this was a dangerous rising or not, Janneus did not prevent his wild Asian mercenaries from falling upon the outraged crowds with some savagery, and killing six thousand, if Josephus is right. Jerusalem was nearly always in a ferment after this, and when Janneus returned ignominiously from an engagement with the Nabatean king beyond the Jordan, and entered Jerusalem with practically no army, it was the signal for a determined revolt sponsored by the Pharisees in 94 B.C. After six years of civil war (*ca.* 88 B.C.), they and the people called to their aid a Seleucid king Demetrius III Eucerus (*see* DEMETRIUS 4)—ironically enough, a descendant of the Antiochus Epiphanes against whom their ancestors had risen under the brave leadership of Janneus' forebears!

Janneus and his mercenaries were decisively crushed at Shechem, and then an acute problem arose. Were the Jews to return to Seleucid domination? According to a commentary on Nahum, discovered at Qumran, it looks as if Demetrius was expecting to march into Jerusalem. Many were horrified at the idea and, as the lesser of the evils, returned to support the Hasmonean, who had fled to the mountains. It was a tragic step, because according to this grim account Janneus soon captured the remaining leaders of the revolt. He then lay drinking among his concubines (so Josephus tells us), looking down upon a ghastly scene: eight hundred crosses with men upon them, and by many a cross the dying man's wife and children, cut to death before his eyes.

The spirit of the Pharisees was at a low ebb after this. There was no more thought of active resistance, and thousands fled from the wicked man's dominion. The Pharisees had hope of a life to come, where God rewards and requites, but they left Jerusalem with much bitterness in their hearts, despising the rich and influential Sadducees more than before. Their cry must have been something like this: "Woe to you mighty, who oppress the righteous. The day of your destruction will come!" (I Enoch 96:8 orig. tr.). The noble families had done nothing to restrain the tyrant from his lawless deeds.

It has been pointed out that disposal of political enemies by crucifixion is attributed to a figure called the Lion of Wrath in one of the biblical commentaries (on Nahum) which were discovered at Qumran near the Dead Sea (*see* DEAD SEA SCROLLS). It is therefore suggested that the Lion is no other than Alexander Janneus, and that the Qumran community in whose library the scrolls were found consisted of a group of pious Judeans and their priests who escaped from Janneus and settled in the desert with a rival high priest. The community had its own leader, as we gather from the Commentary on Habakkuk, one of the Qumran scrolls, who was named the Teacher of Righteousness. He was persecuted by another figure called the Wicked Priest. The latter may be identical with the Lion of Wrath (in the Nahum Commentary). It cannot be proved that the Teacher was actually crucified, but this has been surmised in view of the reputation of Alexander Janneus as gleaned from Josephus. But there is as yet no evidence for the existence of any rival high priest, much less that the Teacher was such. There is a great deal to be said for the view that the Wicked Priest and the Lion of Wrath are intended to be Alexander Janneus, and that the Qumran community began with the persecuted Pharisees and others who fled from Jerusalem during his reign. Coins of the reigns of Hyrcanus and his sons were found in the ruins of the first building at Qumran, proving that the community did already exist at this time. The prominent Pharisee, Simon ben Shetach, may even be the Teacher of Righteousness and leader of this community; at least he sought to hide himself from his brother-in-law, as we gather from rabbinical stories. Moreover, Janneus was reputed to be the son of a captive slave girl, and one of the Dead Sea Scrolls does, indeed, breathe a pious sigh for the time when bastards and sons of strangers will be debarred from the restored temple. On the other hand, this same calumny was hurled by the Pharisees, according to some evidence (*see* § 3*b above*), at Janneus' father. Again, little can be made of the fact that both the Lion and Alexander Janneus may have been fond of crucifying opponents.

A warrior all his life, Janneus waged several more campaigns against Syria, Arabia, and other neighbors, and died while fighting on the other side of Jordan in 78 B.C.

He bequeathed his throne to Alexandra, the widow of his brother and apparently his own wife too, and the high priesthood to his son. Whether or not he himself urged Alexandra to make peace with the Pharisees, as Josephus describes, this is certainly what she did. It is not impossible that the aged and tired villain, wracked by the pains which were the penalty of an impure life, had already read the vengeance written upon the faces of those men of the people whom he had savagely oppressed.

e. Alexandra (78-69). Salome—to give her her Hebrew name—ruled wisely and piously during nine years of unwonted peace, allowing the Pharisees a wide measure of control over internal affairs but retaining foreign policy in her own control. There were two sons: Hyrcanus the high priest, who was of little moment, and his younger brother, Aristobulus, who was a man of much greater competence and initiative, and in consequence was not allowed any say in affairs of state. Aristobulus had never sympathized with his father's enemies, nor with the apparent desire of his mother to placate them. He saw that the Pharisees were recalling the banished, releasing prisoners, and planning a revenge against those who had counseled his father to execute the eight hundred rebels. Several of them in their turn suffered crucifixion. Not unnaturally, the noble Sadducean houses, despising Alexandra for the change of front for which she was responsible, looked to the younger son for leadership and helped him to stir up trouble against his mother. This they were able to do, because they were of the military class and had the fortresses under their control. His mother was bound to relent and do her best to curb the excesses of the Pharisees. However, when the aged lady became ill and was desirous of leaving her throne to the eldest son, the meek Hyrcanus, Aristobulus was determined to obtain it for himself, and to this end he gained control of some of the strongest fortresses in the country. He raised an army of his own; and because the Queen had given orders that he must be resisted, he was preparing to attack Jerusalem when his mother died.

f. Aristobulus II (69-63). At Alexandra's death, against her own wishes Hyrcanus had to make way for his younger brother, after a battle at Jericho, and he retired into private life. He was an indolent and peace-loving man. If an unscrupulous intriguer had not worked upon the elder brother's unmanly fears, no danger would have appeared from that quarter. An Idumean named Antipater, whose son was to become Herod the Great, persuaded Hyrcanus that he needed protection against his ruthless brother and induced him to seek this protection in Petra at the hands of the Nabatean Aretas III, king of Arabia. *See* NABATEANS.

Antipater, whose father had been governor of Idumea, and who himself was now an influential person in Jerusalem, was seeking only his own advantage by standing behind the effeminate Hyrcanus. He had against him both the determined Aristobulus and most of the old aristocratic families, but he played his hand well.

Aretas promised to support Hyrcanus and to help him to regain the throne of Judea and the high priesthood from Aristobulus, but in return he demanded Hyrcanus' promise to restore the twelve cities which their father had captured from the Arabians. The plan was put into execution and worked well. The younger brother had to flee when he was defeated and his troops had deserted him. The Pharisees were not sympathetic toward him, for he had shown during his mother's reign that he hated them, and they willingly helped the Arabians lay siege to him and the priests on the temple mount in Jerusalem in 65 B.C. A period of bitter civil strife then began. During the siege, according to Josephus, a man named Onias, whose prayers for rain in drought had previously been wondrously answered, was brought forward by the followers of Hyrcanus, who required him to curse Aristobulus. But instead of this, Onias impressively asked God to listen to the prayers of neither side; and for this he was stoned to death. It has been suggested that he was the Teacher of Righteousness who was persecuted by the Wicked Priest, according to the Habakkuk Commentary among the DEAD SEA SCROLLS, and it is suggested that the Wicked Priest is either Aristobulus II or Hyrcanus or both; although there are some points which seem to favor the identification, most of the detailed evidence is hardly impressive enough to bear this conclusion to the exclusion of other possibilities.

All might have gone well for the fortunes of Hyrcanus, had not both the Hasmonean princes separately appealed to Rome to assist them, for Rome had now taken over the collapsed Syrian power and under Pompey was extending her sway to the Euphrates. Marcus Scaurus, Pompey's legate in Syria, had already departed for Jerusalem to make capital out of the quarrel. He gave his verdict in favor of Aristobulus, having been promised large sums of money from both brothers, and ordered the king of Arabia to withdraw on pain of being declared an enemy of Rome. The Idumean Antipater and other supporters of Hyrcanus had no intention of abandoning the struggle for power, and they sent an embassage personally to the Roman commander-in-chief, Pompey, at Damascus in 63. Aristobulus himself did the same thing! Moreover, there was a third and popular deputation received by Pompey, probably from the Pharisees, to which the great man was far more likely to listen, which advocated that Rome should favor neither prince but rather that he should assume the political government himself, abolishing the monarchy altogether and allowing only the theocratic rule of the priests.

While Pompey was slowly making up his mind, Aristobulus became discontented and occupied the fortress of Alexandrium. Pompey received this as a threat and marched against him. Surrendering the stronghold, Aristobulus retired into Jerusalem and awaited attack. Even then, when Pompey advanced, Aristobulus went to him and sought peace, offering to open the gates and pay a price, but his followers in Jerusalem kept the gates shut when Gabinius was sent for the money. Pompey imprisoned Aristobulus for this and succeeded in entering the city, because the party of Hyrcanus and Antipater, now swollen in numbers by many who were alarmed by the proximity of Roman troops, opened the gates. But Aristobulus' party, though bereft of their king, retreated to the fortified temple mount, which had a precipice almost all round it, and defended themselves. There was a siege of three months. The walls of the mount were finally breached by Pompey's battering rams, the temple was entered, the priests were cut down as they ministered at the altar, and twelve thousand Jews were slaughtered by Pompey's men (63 B.C.). The Roman commander now proceeded to profane the temple still more by entering the Holy of holies, to see what riches were there, but he took nothing away and afterward ordered that the place should be rehallowed and the worship continue as usual. He took away much of the territory of Judea and did not depart from Jerusalem without leaving there a Roman garrison. The horrors of these dreadful months live again for us in the pious songs of the period: the PSALMS OF SOLOMON.

This was the end of the reign of Aristobulus II. He and his family were carried off by Pompey, and in 61 he was led captive through the streets of Rome, fortunate not to have been executed as so many of his supporters were. Hyrcanus, the elder brother, was allowed to function as high priest and ethnarch, without the title of king, although he is generally known as Hyrcanus II. It was therefore the end of the Hasmonean dynasty in any real sense of the word. Tribute must now be paid to Rome, and Judea was to come under the supervision of the Roman proconsul of Syria. The downfall largely came about through the stupid folly, to which this house was prone, of so eagerly calling for the assistance of foreign powers in internal strife. At the same time, it has to be granted that it is doubtful whether even in the most fortunate circumstances the wisest of Jewish rulers could have maintained the independence of his people once the Romans had entered upon the ruins of the Syrian Empire.

4. The end of the Hasmoneans (63-7 B.C.). But we must follow the life of Aristobulus II a little further to its sad end. The Idumean Antipater had prudently shown himself well disposed toward the Romans, and he wielded considerable power for the moment. He might have been overthrown by the repeated attempts of Aristobulus' branch of the Hasmonean family to regain power and unite Coele-Syria, which was divided by Gabinius into five administrative districts; but the Romans invariably came to the Idumean's help. In 57, Alexander, the son of Aristobulus II, who had escaped before reaching Rome, rose against Antipater but was defeated and captured; the next year it was Aristobulus himself and his other son, Antigonus, who had escaped captivity; the next year again, it was Alexander who led the rebellion. Gabinius crushed each of these risings. In 53 there seemed to be an opportunity for the Jews when Gabinius' successor, Crassus, had been defeated by the Parthians at Carrhae, but the Jewish rebellion under Pitholaus was crushed by the next proconsul, Cassius (51), who sold many thousands of Jews as slaves. However, Aristobulus was released by Julius Caesar after he had seized the power in Rome in 49, and the intention was to send him with an army against Antipater and the party of Pompey in Syria, but before setting out, Aristobulus was poisoned by the supporters of Pompey. In the same year, 49, his son Alexander was beheaded by order of Pompey himself in Antioch.

At the ascendancy of Julius Caesar, after Pompey's assassination in 48, Antipater artfully placed himself on the winning side once more. He became Caesar's devoted friend and gave him considerable assistance during his Egyptian campaign. In return, the five divisions made by Gabinius were happily abolished and Judea was united under the high priest Hyrcanus, who once again enjoyed the hereditary political functions which Gabinius and Pompey had taken away; and Hyrcanus was called "ethnarch," while Antipater served Rome as procurator (47 B.C.). No taxation need now be paid to Rome, and the laws and customs of the Jews were thoroughly respected. They were exempt from military service with the Roman legions, which were now withdrawn from Judea. Territories which had been seized were restored, including the valuable seaport of Joppa. Julius Caesar proved himself kindly disposed toward the Jews, both in Judea and in Alexandria. Caesar was murdered in 44; but although Antipater was quick enough to transfer his allegiance to the new power of Cassius, his brilliant career was suddenly cut short by the poisoning hand of a Jewish rival for power in 43. Because he was an Idumean, he was never popular with the Jewish people. Antipater had, however, procured for his eldest son, Phasael, appointment as governor of Jerusalem: and for his second son, Herod (*see* HEROD [FAMILY]), appointment as governor of Galilee. The Idumean brothers, after Caesar's assassination and the victory of Antony and Octavian over Brutus and Cassius in 42, were able to gain the ear of Mark Antony and to silence all the accusations of the Sadducean nobility against them. Once again Hyrcanus was reduced to being no more than high priest, while Herod and his brother were granted powers of government with the title of "tetrarch."

But at this point Antigonus (whose Hebrew name, Mattathias, appears on his coins), the surviving son of Aristobulus II, who had already pleaded his cause unsuccessfully before Julius Caesar, made one last determined attempt to regain his father's kingdom in 40 B.C. Herod defeated him in battle, but the Hasmonean won the support of the fierce invading Parthians who had temporarily broken the Roman power in Syria and who proclaimed him king. It was the last brief glory of the Hasmonean house. Both Phasael and Hyrcanus were captured by the Parthians, and Phasael committed suicide. His young brother Herod fled to his friends at Rome. The high priest Hyrcanus was carried off and barbarously treated. The Roman senate then declared that Herod was king of Judea, and the next year (39) he landed at Ptolemaïs and declared war on Antigonus, Mark Antony's soldiers having dealt with the Parthian menace. Although this war lasted for more than two difficult years, Herod was finally successful. He took Jerusalem at last, with the assistance of Antony's legate Sosius and of the Roman legions, and he slaughtered all his opponents among the Sadducean aristocracy. King Antigonus II was captured, and was beheaded in Antioch—the first king to suffer thus at the hands of Rome. With him the Hasmonean story really closes, for Herod was now firmly on the throne of Judea (37 B.C.).

And yet this noble house and lineage does not quite pass into oblivion, for Herod had already married Mariamne, the Hasmonean princess. She was granddaughter of Aristobulus II through her father, Alexander, and also granddaughter of Hyrcanus II, through her mother, Alexandra. In her person, therefore, were united those two branches of the Hasmonean house which were so bitterly at feud. Her brother Aristobulus, hardly more than a boy, was high priest. During the first few years of the reign of Mariamne's husband, that extraordinary king in fits of jealous suspicion murdered in turn the young high priest Aristobulus III in 35, the aged grandfather Hyrcanus II in 30, Mariamne herself in 29, and her mother, Alexandra, in 28.

After these ruthless crimes there remained but two males who might be termed Hasmoneans: Herod's own children by the Hasmonean Mariamne. They were Alexander and Aristobulus. Their father ordered these two strangled to death in 7 B.C., at the very place where he had married their mother, and so he freed himself at last from any possible fear of Hasmonean rivalry or any sentimental attachment, on the part of his people, to a noble house.

5. Achievement of the Hasmoneans. The achievement of the Hasmoneans, during the century of their ascendancy, was distinguished and permanent. They were the means by which Judaism and the Jewish state became a force to be reckoned with, even by the Romans, marked out conspicuously from neighboring religions and cultures, the object as well as the subject of many bitter feelings—particularly on the part of its nearest neighbors, the Samaritans. They had brought some other nations too under their rule and, not content with simple conquest, had impressed them beneath a religious yoke. This outthrust of empire was all lost under the Herodians, who failed to see as clearly as the Hasmoneans that the first essential was to preserve the Jewish state in the face of hostile heathen neighbors, however bloodthirsty the tactics by which this end was achieved. Only so, it seemed to the Hasmoneans, could the worship of God and the wholesome teaching of the Law and the Prophets be preserved forevermore. In any case, the Herodians did not feel that such a destiny was worth so great a sacrifice.

Within the state, alongside the continuance of the temple and its sacrifices, the increased study and reading of the Law, which had been fostered under Hasmonean rule, resulted in a great impetus being given to scribal activity in the way of copying, studying, and teaching the Bible (*see* SCRIBE). It was the most permanent legacy of their rule, even more than the growth of the great parties, Pharisaic and Sadducean, and the bitter antipathy between them, which was so obvious a feature of the period. *See* PHARISEES; SADDUCEES.

Together with reverence for the Scriptures went the belief in doctrines which owed their origin to the experiences of Hasmonean days: RESURRECTION of the dead and the hope of a future life after death.

In conclusion, it would not be wide of the mark to suggest that all the foundation stones of modern Jewry were well and truly laid during the period of Hasmonean rule.

Bibliography. Jos. Antiq. XII.v ff; War I.ii ff. F. W. Madden, *Coins of the Jews* (1881). E. Schürer, *A History of the Jewish People* (English trans., 1891), I, 212-399. E. Bevan, *Jerusalem Under the High Priests* (1904). J. Juster, *Les Juifs dans l'empire romain* (1914). V. Aptowitzer, *Parteipolitik der Hasmonäerzeit* . . . (1927). *Cambridge Ancient History,* vol. IX (1932); vol. X (1934). W. O. E. Oesterley, *The Jews and Judaism During the Greek Period* (1941). R. Marcus, *Proceedings of the American Academy for Jewish Research,* 16 (1946-47), 97-181; "Selected Bibliography (1920-45) of the Jews in the Hellenistic-Roman Period." F.-M. Abel, *Les Livres des Maccabées* (1949), especially pp. 3-4 and bibliography on pp. lx ff. W. R. Farmer, *Maccabees, Zealots and Josephus* (1956).

On Alexander Janneus, see: H. Loewe in *Judaism and Christianity* (1937), I, 123-30. J. M. Allegro, *The Dead Sea Scrolls* (1956), pp. 94-100.

N. TURNER

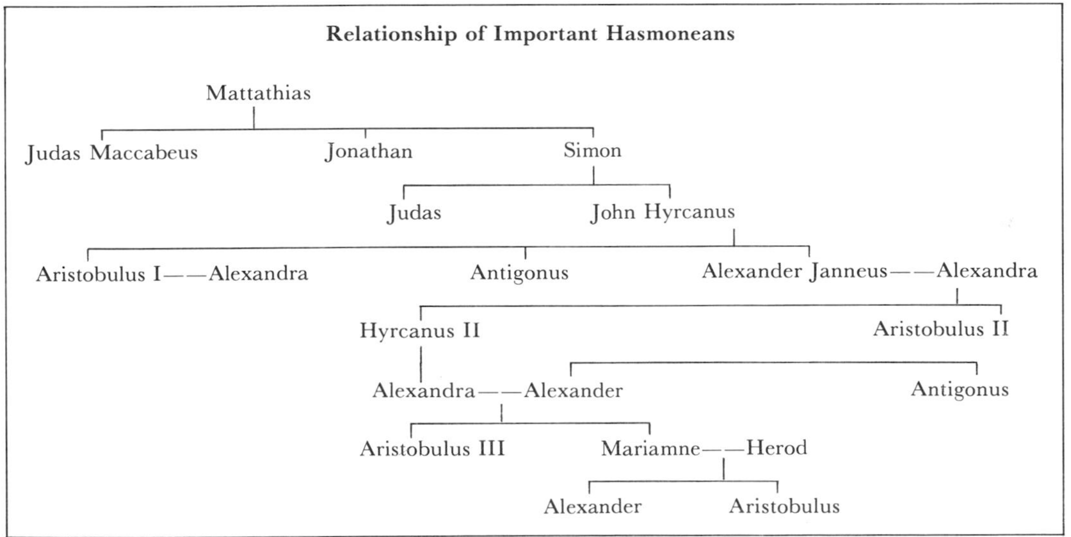

HASRAH hăz'rə [חַסְרָה]; KJV Apoc. AZARA ăz'ə rə. **1.** Chronicles form of HARHAS.

2. Head of a family of temple servants who returned with Zerubbabel (I Esd. 5:31). The name is omitted in the parallels Ezra 2:49; Neh. 7:51. *See* NETHINIM.

HASSENAAH. Alternate form of SENAAH.

HASSENUAH hăs'ə no͞o'ə [הסנאה, הסנואה, the hated women]; KJV HASENUAH in I Chr. 9:7; KJV SENUAH sə no͞o'ə in Neh. 11:9. A postexilic Benjaminite family name (I Chr. 9:7; Neh. 11:9). "Hodaviah" in I Chr. 9:7 could be a corruption of

"Judah," in which case both references would be to the same person. "SENAAH" is probably a variant of "Hassenuah." H. H. GUTHRIE, JR.

HASSHUB hăsh'əb [חַשּׁוּב, *possibly* considerate, *but more probably a shortened form of* חֲשַׁבְיָה, Yahu has considered]; KJV usually HASHUB hā'shŭb. **1.** A member of the Merari clan of the tribe of Levi, and the father of a certain Shemaiah who settled in Jerusalem after the Exile (I Chr. 9:14; Neh. 11:15).

2. Either one man who had two assignments in rebuilding the walls of Jerusalem in the time of Nehemiah, or two builders with the same name (Neh. 3:11, 23).

3. One of those who sealed the covenant in the time of Ezra (Neh. 10:23—H 10:24).

M. NEWMAN

HASSOPHERETH. *See* SOPHERETH.

HASUPHA hə sōō'fə [חֲשׂוּפָא (Ezra 2:43), חֲשֻׂפָא (Neh. 7:46), swift; *cf.* Arab. *ḫašūfun;* Apoc. Ἀσιφά]; KJV HASHUPHA hə shōō'fə in Neh. 7:46; KJV ASIPHA ə sĭf'ə in I Esd. 5:29. Eponym of a family of temple servants among the returned exiles (Ezra 2:43; Neh. 7:46; I Esd. 5:29).

Bibliography. M. Noth, *Die israelitischen Personennamen* (1928), p. 226. B. T. DAHLBERG

HAT [Aram. כַּרְבְּלָה; *cf.* Akkad. *karballatu,* helmet, cap]. One of the articles of clothing with which the three Hebrews were cast into the furnace (Dan. 3:21).

HATACH. KJV form of HATHACH.

HATCHET [כַּשִּׁיל] (Ps. 74:6); KJV AX. One of the instruments used in breaking down the carved wood of the sanctuary; perhaps the axe of a woodcutter.

HATE, HATRED [שׂנא; μισεῖν]. Dislike, antipathy, aversion, between persons, in a variety of human relationships (cf. Gen. 26:27; 29:31,33; Judg. 11:7; 14:16; II Sam. 13:15).

1. In the OT. In the OT the concept derives its peculiar religious meaning from the notion that God hates. The troublesome passage: "Yet I have loved Jacob but I have hated Esau" (Mal. 1:2-3) provides a clue to understanding. God's hatred is the counterpart of his ELECTION love. Jacob he loves in his election; ESAU he hates in his rejection. And so God's enemies are Israel's enemies and vice versa; they are those who hate God (Num. 10:35; Deut. 7:15; 33:11). God hates evil, and so Israel must hate evil (Exod. 18:21; Ps. 97:10; Amos 5:15). In the Psalms the enemies of God and Israel are frequently portrayed (Pss. 34:21; 35:19; 38:19; 83:1-8), and God is petitioned for help against the enemies who hate him and his people (Pss. 68:1-2; 83; 139:19-22). God hates idolatry and false worship (Deut. 12:31; 16:22; Jer. 44:4 ff). Israel's worship can become the object of God's hatred when there is lack of obedience to his commandments (Hos. 9:15; Amos 5:21; Mal. 2:13-16).

It is important to recognize that while in the concrete historical situations the term "hate" could have had an emotional connotation, as a concept it is based essentially upon the religious commitment to reject and turn away from those who deny God and his laws. There is no sharp distinction between the power of evil and the actor; nor is there, in general, any explicit emphasis on overcoming hate with love. In the OT the one clear prohibition of hatred is in the case of the brother (Lev. 19:17; Deut. 19:11). In the eschatological dualism of the Qumran writings there is a new emphasis on God's hatred of the spirit of darkness, which holds dominion over the wicked (1QS 3.26–4.1). But, as in the canonical Psalms, the Qumran sectarians are called to separate themselves from the wicked and hate them, though they are under rigorous obligation to love their fellow sectarians.

2. In the NT. In the teachings of Jesus there is no holy hate against men. Rather, he admonishes his disciples to love all men, even their enemies (Luke 6:27). Nevertheless, the disciples are not removed from the hatred of the world (Matt. 10:37; Luke 14:26), and increasing hatred is one of the signs of the approaching consummation of the kingdom (Matt. 10:22; 24:9; Mark 13:13; Luke 21:17). The difficult passage enjoining hatred of family and self (Luke 14:26; cf. Matt. 10:37), one of Jesus' most paradoxical utterances, is intended to stress the unconditional character of discipleship. All that the disciple should love most, including himself (*see* LOVE IN THE NT), must not stand between him and his Master. "Hatred" is used here almost synonymously with "denying the self" (Mark 8:34: ἀπαρνησάσθω ἑαυτόν; cf. Luke 9:23). Discipleship may involve leaving home and family—even death.

The NT in general reflects the principles in Jesus' teaching (Luke 6:27). While life in the old age was characterized by hate (Tit. 3:3), life in the new age is characterized by love (Rom. 13:8 ff; I John 2:9, 11; 3:14; 4:20), which overcomes evil and hatred. Evil deeds are hated, but not persons (Jude 23; Rev. 2:6). Renunciation or hatred of wickedness is motivated by God's love for sinners, revealed in Jesus Christ (Rom. 5:8), and it moves the disciple toward love for man held captive by wickedness.

Especially in the Gospel and Letters of John the sharp antithesis between the life of love and of hate is drawn. Hatred, though intensely personal, assumes almost cosmic dimensions in its demonic opposition to God's love. It is the basis of unbelief, evil deeds (John 3:20), and murder (I John 3:15). Only through the infinite love of God actively revealed in Jesus Christ is such hatred overcome (John 3:16-17). The mission of the church is to reveal this love to the world, which continues in hate (John 17:14, 20-26).

F. W. YOUNG

HATHACH hā'thăk [הֲתָךְ, *perhaps from* Pers. *hataka,* good] (Esth. 4:5-6, 9-10); KJV HATACH hăt'ək. A eunuch of Ahasuerus appointed to attend Queen Esther. It was through him that she learned from Mordecai about Haman's plot against the Jews.

M. NEWMAN

HATHATH hā'thăth [חֲתַת, weakness(?)]. A Calebite family (I Chr. 4:13).

Bibliography. M. Noth, *Die israelitischen Personennamen* (1928), p. 227.

HATIPHA hə tī′fə [חֲטִיפָא, seized (*e.g., as a captive in childhood*) Ἀτιφά] KJV Apoc. ATIPHA ə—. Eponym of a family of temple servants among the returned exiles (Ezra 2:54; Neh. 7:56; cf. I Esd. 5:32).

Bibliography. M. Noth, *Die israelitischen Personennamen* (1928), p. 232. B. T. DAHLBERG

HATITA hə tī′tə [חֲטִיטָא; Apoc. Ατητα]; KJV Apoc. TETA tē′tə. A family of gatekeepers (Ezra 2:42; Neh. 7:45; I Esd. 5:28).

HATTIL hăt′əl [חַטִּיל; Arab. *ḫaṭila,* talkative; Apoc. Αγια]; KJV Apoc. HAGIA hā′gĭ ə. A family of SOLOMON'S SERVANTS (Ezra 2:57; Neh. 7:59; I Esd. 5:34).

Bibliography. M. Noth, *Die israelitischen Personennamen* (1928), p. 229. H. H. GUTHRIE, JR.

HATTUSH hăt′ŭsh [חַטּוּשׁ; Ἁττους]; KJV Apoc. LETTUS lĕt′əs. **1.** A postexilic descendant of David who returned to Judah with Ezra (I Chr. 3:22; Ezra 8:2; I Esd. 8:29); called the grandson of Shecaniah in I Chronicles, but his son in Ezra.

2. A repairer of the wall of Jerusalem under Nehemiah (Neh. 3:10); some identify him with 1 *above.*

3. A postexilic priest who signed the pledge of reform (Neh. 10:4; 12:2). The name is probably missing from Neh. 12:14 through an error in transmission. H. H. GUTHRIE, JR.

HAUGHTINESS. *See* PRIDE.

HAURAN hôr′ən [חַוְרָן]. A district E of the Jordan and the Sea of Galilee, and N of the Yarmuk River. The name appears only in Ezek. 47:16, 18, where it marks the NE limit of Ezekiel's ideal land of Israel. The name, however, is old, for it is mentioned in Egyptian texts of the Nineteenth Dynasty as *Huruna.* It was occupied apparently by the kings of Damascus after the division of the Israelite kingdom and is mentioned as *Ḫaurânu* in the inscriptions of Shalmaneser III of Assyria, who devastated it in 842 B.C. Tiglath-pileser III overran it in 732 and founded two districts there with centers at Metuna and Karnaim; Ashurbanipal crushed a revolt there. Despite these destructive wars the district flourished because of the fertility of its lava soil, and during the Greco-Roman period, when it was known as Auranities, it served as the granary of Palestine.

Both Jews and Greeks were settled there in large numbers in the fourth century B.C. and after, and the region was coveted by the Nabateans and so changed hands frequently. It was conquered by the Maccabeans in the second century, but came under Nabatean control in 90 B.C., when the Nabateans won a victory over Alexander Janneus. Pompey in turn annexed it to the DECAPOLIS, but Augustus returned it to Herod the Great, who settled numerous Jews from Babylonia there. After the death of Herod, this territory fell to his son Herod Philip (cf. Luke 3:1); in A.D. 37 Caligula bestowed it, with the rest of the tetrarchy of Philip, upon his favorite Herod Agrippa I, and it was ruled by the latter's son, Agrippa II, until the great war against Rome (66-73). Hauran was again under Nabatean control from 85 to 106, when Trajan finally added it to the Roman province of Syria. The region still bears the name of el-Hauran. S. COHEN

HAVEN [חוֹף (*twice in* Gen. 49:13; *once* SHORE); מָבוֹא (KJV ENTERING IN), coming in, entrance; KJV λιμήν (RSV HARBOR)]; THEIR DESIRED HAVEN [מְחוֹז חֶפְצָם (Ps. 107:30), *lit.,* the city (Akkad. *maḫāzu*) of their desire]. Used primarily in the nautical sense, as a place which offers safe anchorage and station for ships. *See* HARBOR. H. F. BECK

HAVILAH hăv′ə lə [חֲוִילָה, *perhaps a diminutive of* חוֹל, sand, *and so* a stretch of sand]. A land mentioned in the story of the Garden of Eden as producing excellent gold, bdellium gum, and the *shoham* ("onyx") stone, and as being surrounded by the River Pishon (Gen. 2:11-12). The name occurs also in the genealogies, first as a son of Cush (Gen. 10:7; I Chr. 1:9), and next as a son of Joktan (Gen. 10:29; I Chr. 1:23). The Ishmaelites are also said to have lived in the territory from Havilah to Shur (Gen. 25:18). However, the passage (I Sam. 15:7) which states that Saul pursued the Amalekites from Havilah to Shur cannot be correct, since the first locality is obviously in the S of Judah; hence it is probably to be emended to Hachilah, a hill mentioned elsewhere (I Sam. 23:19; 26:1, 3).

Opinions as to the location of Havilah have differed widely. Most of them considered the Havilah of Arabia and that of the Garden of Eden story as two different localities. The former is sometimes placed on the Persian Gulf, but the most widely accepted location is on the W coast of Arabia, N of Yemen, where a region named Haulan is known from a Sabean inscription. The latter is placed variously in India, under the assumption that the Pishon is the Indus or the Ganges, or in Somaliland, where there was a town called Avalis (modern Zeila). Glaser, on the other hand, argues that all the passages refer to the same country and that it is to be located in the Yemama, in the region around Riyadh; the Pishon is identified by him with the Wadi el-Dawasir. The products of Havilah reported in Gen. 2 give the impression of a real Arabian country, as gold and fragrant gums were found in many parts of Arabia, and the *shoham* stone, the *sâmtu* of the Assyrians, was probably malachite.

Bibliography. E. Glaser, *Skizze der Geschichte und Geographie Arabiens,* II (1890), 319-26; J. A. Montgomery, *Arabia and the Bible* (1934), pp. 38-40. S. COHEN

HAVVOTH-JAIR hăv′ŏth jā′ər [חַוֺּת יָאִיר, villages of Jair]; KJV usually HAVOTH-JAIR hā′—; KJV BASHAN-HAVOTH-JAIR bā′shən— in Deut. 3:14. A group of villages located in Bashan in Gilead, sixty according to Deut. 3:4, but only thirty according to Judg. 10:4. There are no fewer than three accounts in the Scriptures of how these villages received their name. According to Num. 32:41; Deut. 3:14, these cities were in Bashan and were taken by "Jair the son of Manasseh"—i.e., the Jair clan of the Manasseh group. In the latter passage the KJV gives the name as Bashan-havoth-jair; but the words *'eth habbāshān* make no sense in the context and are probably a marginal gloss to the word "Argob" above, which is given as the exact site of the villages. In I Chr. 2:21-24 there is mention of a connection between the clans of Manasseh and those of Judah: Hezron, the grandson of Judah, was married to the daughter of Machir of Gilead and had a son named Segub. Segub's son Jair is said to have made extensive conquests, including Geshur and Aram, which in other passages are regarded as independent; Kenath, which is elsewhere said to have been taken by Nobah (Num. 32:42); and these villages, which are given his name. Finally, in Judg. 10:3-4, there is mention of a judge, Jair the Gileadite, who had thirty sons who ruled over thirty cities which were named after their father.

These three explanations of the name Havvoth-jair represent various traditions that arose to explain the name. The account in Chronicles is obviously a Judean attempt to claim a relationship with Manasseh and assert a claim to rule over the territory of Gilead. The account of Jair the judge is suspicious; his entire story looks like a late endeavor to bring the number of judges up to twelve (*see* JUDGES, BOOK OF). The first account, assuming that the conquest was made by a clan rather than an individual, appears most likely to be historical. S. COHEN

HAWK [נץ; קאת (Isa. 34:11; *alternately* PELICAN; VULTURE)]. Any of several small to medium-sized diurnal birds of prey of the suborder Falcones, of which the sparrow hawks, goshawks, and harriers comprise the subfamily Accipitrinae. There are over twenty species of sparrow hawk alone, the commonest being *Accipter nisus*. This latter bird, as well as the marsh harrier (*Circus aeruginosus*) and the hen harrier (*Circus cyaneus*), was fairly common in Palestine in Tristram's time. It is a reasonable assumption that נץ (*nēṣ*) designates this group of birds (cf. "according to its kind" in Lev. 11:16), which are declared to be unclean. The reference in Job 39:26 may be to the migratory habits of some members of the hawk family.

See also FAUNA § B1. W. S. MCCULLOUGH

HAY [χόρτος (I Cor. 3:12); KJV חציר (RSV GRASS)]. Hay is not usually used in the Near East. *See* GRASS.

HAZAEL hā′zĭ əl [חזהאל, חזאל; Akkad. *Ḫaza'ilu*, God sees]. King of Damascus *ca.* 841–*ca.* 798 B.C.

A usurper, whom the Assyrians called a "son of a nobody," a person without royal antecedents, Hazael was a servant of Ben-Hadad I of Damascus. When informed by the prophet Elisha that he was to be king of Damascus, and anointed by him (I Kings 19:15-16), Hazael murdered his master (II Kings 8:13-15) and seized the throne of Damascus (*ca.* 841 B.C.)

At once Hazael attacked Ramoth-gilead, which Joram of Israel had recaptured, and he seriously wounded King Joram in the battle (II Kings 8:28-29). In 841 B.C. only Hazael resisted the Assyrian Shalmaneser III in Syria. Damascus was besieged, and its environs were destroyed, but Hazael was not taken. After another unsuccessful assault on Damascus in 837 B.C., Shalmaneser III left Hazael to his own devices in the W.

Hazael menaced the kingdoms of both Israel and Judah (II Kings 13:22) throughout the reigns of Jehu (841-813) and Jehoahaz (813-798). From Jehu he took all Israelite lands E of the Jordan River (II Kings 10:32-33; Amos 1:3); and through constant attack and oppression during the reign of Jehoahaz, Hazael humbled Israel and seriously reduced its military force (II Kings 13:1-3, 7, 22). He conquered all Philistia S of Aphek (LXX L of II Kings 13:22) and captured the city of Gath (12:17), thereby dominating the Arabian caravan routes which reached the Mediterranean Sea in Philistia. When Hazael threatened to approach Jerusalem, King Joash of Judah bribed him with rich treasure stripped from his palace and temple at Jerusalem to stay away from Jerusalem (II Kings 12:17-18; cf. II Chr. 24:23-24).

When the Assyrian Adad-nirari III came to Syria (*ca.* 804 B.C.), he received submission and rich tribute from a king of Damascus whom he called *ma-ri'* (Aramaic "lord"). De Vaux perhaps rightly identifies Hazael with *mari'*, although some are inclined to consider Hazael's successor, his less successful son, Ben-hadad II, as that king of Damascus. A label found with the remains of an "ivory couch" at modern Arslan Tash, the ancient Assyrian provincial capital, *Ḫadâtu*, marks the bed as "belonging to our lord Hazael." It may well have been part of the booty taken by Adad-nirari III from *Mari'*.

A mighty warrior and perhaps the greatest king of Damascus, Hazael was also a builder who adorned his capital. As late as the time of Josephus (A.D. 37-100), Hazael and Ben-hadad were worshiped at Damascus because of their benefactions to the city (Jos. Antiq. IX.iv.6). At some time toward the end of the reign of Jehoahaz of Israel (died 798 B.C.) or at the beginning of the reign of Jehoash (798-782), Hazael died and was succeeded by his son Ben-hadad II, as both the Bible (II Kings 13:24) and the Aramaic Zakir Inscription (lines 4-5) inform us.

Bibliography. E. Kraeling, *Aram and Israel* (1918); R. de Vaux, "La chronologie de Hazael et de Benhadad III, Rois de Damas," *RB*, XLIII (1934), 512-18; F. Rosenthal, "Zakir Inscription," in J. B. Pritchard, ed., *ANET* (2nd ed., 1955), pp. 501-2; M. F. Unger, *Israel and the Aramaeans of Damascus* (1957), pp. 75-82, 160-63. R. A. BOWMAN

HAZAIAH hə zā′yə [חזיה, Yahu has seen] (Neh. 11:5). An ancestor of a certain Maaseiah, who was a Jewish lay leader living in postexilic Jerusalem.

HAZAR-ADDAR hā′zər ăd′ər [חצר אדר] (Num. 34:4). *See* HEZRON 2; ADDAR.

HAZAR-ENAN hā′zər ē′nən [חצר עינון, חצר עינן; LXX Ασεζναειμ, Ασερναιν, *etc.*]. Alternately: HAZAR-ENON (Ezek. 47:17-18; 48:1). According to Num. 34:7-10, a city on the frontier between Palestine and Hammath (cf. Ezek. 47:16-17). It is identified with modern Hadr at the foot of Mount Hermon.

HAZAR-GADDAH hā′zər găd′ə [חצר גדה] (Josh. 15:27). A city in the S part of Judah, mentioned between Moladah and Heshmon. The element "Gaddah" in the name suggests that it may have been a shrine of Gad, the god of fortune. The site is unknown.

HAZAR-HATTICON. KJV form of HAZER-HATTICON.

HAZARMAVETH hā'zər mā'vĭth [חצרמות]. A Semitic people descended from Shem through Joktan (Gen. 10:26; I Chr. 1:20), who settled in the Wadi Hadhramaut in S Arabia. This valley, which parallels the coast for *ca.* two hundred miles, became the center of a flourishing state with its capital at Shabwa. The economy of Hadhramaut was based on its control of the frankincense groves of Dhofar in certain periods; of the caravan route westward to Qataban, Saba, and Ma'in; and of Cana, the major frankincense port in Arabia.

The history of this state is little known. It appears to have enjoyed two periods of great power, in the fifth century B.C. and again in the first and second centuries A.D. There have been two archaeological excavations in this area—one at Hureidha, which brought to light a small temple belonging to the fifth-second centuries B.C.; and a sounding at Shabwa, which revealed a mausoleum of *ca.* the first century A.D. or slightly later.

Bibliography. R. A. B. Hamilton, "Six Weeks in Shabwa," *Geographical Journal*, 100 (1942), 107-23; G. Caton Thompson, *The Tombs and Moon Temple of Hureidha* (*Hadhramaut;* 1944); H. von Wissmann and M. Höfner, *Beiträge zur historischen Geographie des vorislamischen Südarabien* (1952), *passim;* W. F. Albright, "The Chronology of the Minaean Kings of Arabia," *BASOR,* 129 (1953), 22; W. L. Brown and A. F. L. Beeston, "Sculptures and Inscriptions from Shabwa," *JRAS* (1954), pp. 43-62.

G. W. VAN BEEK

HAZAR-SHUAL hā'zər shōō'əl [חצר שועל, jackal court]. A town of Simeon in the extreme S of Judah, always mentioned in close relationship with Beer-sheba (Josh. 15:28; 19:3; I Chr. 4:28). It was occupied by the Jews after the Exile (Neh. 11:27). The name suggests that it was originally occupied by a Canaanite clan with a jackal as its totem.

S. COHEN

HAZAR-SUSAH hā'zər sōō'sə [חצר סוסה, horse court] (Josh. 19:5); **HAZAR-SUSIM** —sōō'sĭm [חצר סוסים] (I Chr. 4:31). A city of Simeon in the SW part of Judah. As the name indicates, it was a sort of stables where Solomon kept the horses he imported from Egypt and sold to the Hittites and Syrians (I Kings 4:26; 9:19; 10:29; cf. also the mention of cities of horsemen in II Chr. 8:6). Its site is probably Sbalat Abu Susein in the plain E of the Wadi Far'ah.

See also SOLOMON § 5. S. COHEN

HAZAZON-TAMAR hăz'ə zŏn tā'mər [חצצן תמר] (Gen. 14:7; II Chr. 20:2); KJV HAZEZON-TAMAR in Gen. 14:7. A city of the Amorites which was conquered by Chedorlaomer and his allies (Gen. 14:7). It was apparently not far from Sodom and the other cities of the plain; in II Chr. 20:2 it is identified with EN-GEDI on the W side of the Dead Sea. It may be the same as the TAMAR fortified by Solomon (I Kings 9:18) and located by Ezekiel in the SE corner of the land of Israel (Ezek. 47:19; 48:28). The name is preserved in the Wadi Hasasa NW of 'Ain-jidi.

See also ZIZ, ASCENT OF. S. COHEN

HAZEL. KJV translation of לוז (RSV correctly ALMOND) in Gen. 30:37.

HAZELELPONI. KJV form of HAZZELELPONI.

HAZER-HATTICON hā'zər hăt'ə kŏn [חצר התיכון, middle court] (Ezek. 47:16); KJV HAZAR-HATTICON. A place mentioned by Ezekiel as the NE corner of his ideal boundary of Israel. The form is peculiar and is probably a scribal error for "Hazar-enon."

HAZERIM hə zĭr'ĭm. KJV transliteration of חצרים ("unwalled permanent settlements") in Deut. 2:23. The RSV translates "villages," as in Gen. 25:16; Josh. 13:23; etc., rather than interpreting as a place name.

HAZEROTH hə zĭr'ŏth [חצרות, enclosure, settlement]. A camping place of the Israelites after Kibroth-hattaavah (Num. 33:17-18; 11:35; 12:16; Deut. 1:1). Here Miriam and Aaron disputed with Moses over his marriage with a Cushite woman, and over his unique position as the sole mediator between God and his people (cf. Num. 12:2). Perhaps the place is to be identified with 'Ain Khadra, NE of the traditional Mount Sinai, on the way to 'Aqabah.

Bibliography. W. M. F. Petrie, *Researches in Sinai* (1906), p. 262; F.-M. Abel, *Géographie de la Palestine*, II (1938), 214, 344.

J. L. MIHELIC

HAZEZON-TAMAR. KJV form of HAZAZON-TAMAR in Gen. 14:7.

HAZIEL hā'zĭ əl [חזיאל, vision of God] (I Chr. 23:9). A Gershonite Levite.

Bibliography. M. Noth, *Die israelitischen Personennamen* (1928), p. 198.

HAZO hā'zō [חזו] (Gen. 22:22). The fifth son of Nahor and Milcah; probably to be identified with the mountainous, uninviting region of Hazu in N Arabia, which is mentioned in Esarhaddon's Arabian campaign. *See* BUZ.

HAZOR hā'zôr [חצור, an enclosure]. **1.** Tell el-Qedah* on the Wadi Waqqas, five miles SW of Lake Huleh, ten miles N of the Sea of Galilee. The huge tell dominates the Plain of Huleh and the ancient Via Maris, a trade route from Egypt to the N and the E. Figs. HAZ 8-9.

Hazor is named in the nineteenth-century Execration Texts from Egypt, the Mari Letters (eighteenth century), lists of conquered Palestinian cities (Thutmose III, Amen-hotep II, Sethos I), and in the Amarna Letters, as well as in the Bible.

Hazor was a Canaanite royal city whose king, Jabin, headed the N Canaanite coalition against Joshua. The alliance was defeated, and Hazor was sacked (Josh. 11:1-15; 12:19). *Ca.* a century later, Deborah and Barak led a revolt against another Jabin (a dynastic name?), who ruled N Israel. The

Courtesy of the Magnes Press, the Hebrew University, Jerusalem, Israel

8. Tell el-Qedah (Hazor), air view looking N. The "Lower City" lay on the larger rectangular plateau to the N of the tell proper.

Courtesy of the Magnes Press, the Hebrew University, Jerusalem, Israel

9. Air view of Tell el-Qedah (Hazor), looking SE

issue was decided in Israel's favor at the Battle of Taanach (*ca.* 1125), when Jabin's forces under Sisera were routed (Judg. 4–5). To protect the Plain of Huleh, Solomon rebuilt and fortified Hazor. Some two hundred years later, in 732, Tiglath-pileser III captured Hazor (II Kings 15:29). Jonathan successfully fought the forces of the Seleucid king Demetrius II, in the Plain of Hazor in 147 (I Macc. 11:67; Jos. Antiq. XIII.v.7).

John Garstang made a trial dig in 1928, but systematic excavation of Hazor began with Yigael Yadin's work in 1955-56.* Within the huge rectangular enclosure, protected by a typical Hyksos *terre pisée* wall, were discovered cities from the Hyksos, Amarna, and post-Amarna periods, the last one possibly destroyed by Joshua. This part of Hazor, the "Lower City," was not rebuilt after the destruction of the second Late Bronze Age city. A discovery of great interest in this area was a series of four superimposed Canaanite temples, the latest of which had a plan which broadly resembled that of Solomon's temple. *See* TEMPLES § 2*a*. Figs. HAZ 10; TEM 44; ALT 21.

On the tell itself, twenty-one strata have been excavated, the last stratum dating back to 2750-2500 B.C. Hazor's most flourishing period was during the period when the "Lower City" was built (*see above*). After Joshua's conquest in the late thirteenth century B.C., two cities, presumably Israelite and much poorer than the last Canaanite city, preceded Solomon's extensive rebuilding of Hazor as a garrison

Courtesy of the American Schools of Oriental Research

10. Aerial view of the excavations at Hazor

city (cf. I Kings 9:15). Stratum X has provided a well-constructed casemate wall, typical for the period, and another Solomonic city gate like those found at Megiddo and Gezer. The following city suffered perhaps from the depredations of Ben-hadad of Damascus (cf. II Chr. 16:4) early in the ninth century.

Over this city, Ahab (*ca.* 869-850) rebuilt the city, erecting a large public building (a storehouse?) which was reused by his successors (Stratum IV) and a heavily fortified citadel on the W tip of the mound. In the buildings of the next city, belonging to wealthy merchants of the time of Jeroboam II (786-746), were found the first Hebrew inscriptions in Galilee from the period of the monarchy. Above this were the ruins of the city which Tiglath-pileser III destroyed in 732. The three-foot layer of ashes in the citadel testifies to the violence of the destruction. The city was rebuilt but abandoned in the early seventh century. The Persians used the citadel in the fifth and fourth centuries. The final stage of the citadel was Hellenistic.

2. A city of Judah in the Negeb (Josh. 15:23). It should probably be read with "Ithnan"—"Hazor-ithnan" (cf. "Hazor-hadattah"; LXX B Ασοσιωναιν); it may be identified with el-Jebariyeh, on the Wadi Umm Ethnan, near Bir Hafir, *ca.* 8¾ miles SE of el-ʿAuja.

3. A city of Judah in the Negeb (KJV). It should be read with the following word as HAZOR-HADATTAH (so RSV).

4. Same as KERIOTH-HEZRON (Josh. 15:25).

5. A city N of Jerusalem reoccupied by Benjaminites after the Exile (Neh. 11:33). The name is preserved in Khirbet Hazzur, W of Beit Hanina; the ancient site is probably nearby el-Burj.

6. A still unknown place in the Arabian Desert E of Palestine which Nebuchadrezzar despoiled in 598 B.C., providing the theme of one of Jeremiah's oracles (Jer. 49:28-33). Whether it refers to a single place or to a group of tribes remains unclear. Berossus (*ca.* 330-250), quoted by Josephus (Apion I.xix), mentions the capture of Arabia by Nebuchadrezzar.

Bibliography. Y. Yadin *et al.*, *Hazor I. An Account of the First Season of Excavations* (1958). Y. Yadin, *Archaeology*, 10 (1957), 83-92; *IEJ*, 6 (1956), 120-27; 7 (1957), 118-23; 8 (1958), 1-14; 9 (1959), 75-88; *BA*, 19 (1956), 2-11; 20 (1957), 34-47; 21 (1958), 30-47; 22 (1959), 2-20. V. R. GOLD

HAZOR-HADATTAH hā'zôr hə dăt'ə [חצר חדתה, new Hazor, *if the second word is* Aram.; *cf.* Euseb. Onom. Ασως τὴν καίνην] (Josh. 15:25); KJV HAZOR, HADATTAH. A village of Judah in the Negeb district of Beer-sheba. It is possibly to be located at el-Hudeira, a region SW of Tuwani toward the Dead Sea. V. R. GOLD

HAZZELELPONI hăz'ə lĕl pō'nī [הצללפוני; *text corrupt*]; KJV HAZELELPONI hă'—. A sister of certain descendants of Judah mentioned in I Chr. 4:3.

HE hā [ה, *h* (*Hê*)]. The fifth letter of the Hebrew ALPHABET as placed in the KJV at the head of the fifth section of the acrostic psalm, Ps. 119, where each verse of this section of the psalm begins with this letter.

HEAD [ראש; κεφαλή]. A term used both literally and metaphorically in the Bible. The basic meaning of "head" is the uppermost part of the body, either of men (Gen. 48:14) or of animals (Exod. 12:9). In an extended sense it is an appropriate name for the topmost part of anything—i.e., a tower (Gen. 11:4), a lampstand (Zech. 4:2), mountains (Isa. 2:2), or trees (II Sam. 5:24); in all these instances the English versions translate by some such word as "top." It may also be used in the sense of "point of beginning"—e.g., of rivers (Gen. 2:10 KJV), streets (Ezek. 16:25), or periods of time (Exod. 12:2; Judg. 7:19; Ezek. 40:1; the English versions translate "beginning"). In some passages it is the equivalent of the English word "sum" (as in Num. 1:2 KJV; ראש). The phrase "head stone of the corner" in Ps. 118:22 KJV and in the passages in the NT in which it is quoted (e.g., Matt. 21:42) has the meaning of "cornerstone."

The word "head" in the Bible is never connected with the intelligence. The ancient Hebrews were unaware of the function of the brain and, indeed, had no name for it; the intellectual powers were believed to be situated in the HEART.

A characteristic biblical usage, apparently unknown to secular Greek, is that of the term "head" for the leading member of a family (Exod. 6:14) or community (Deut. 33:5). Consequently it can be used to mean simply "source of authority," as in depicting the superiority of man to woman in marriage (Eph. 5:23).

The most distinctive theological use of the word "head" occurs in Ephesians and Colossians, where it describes the relationship of Christ to the church (Eph. 4:15; 5:23; Col. 1:18; 2:19) and the created universe (Eph. 1:22; Col. 2:10). While the starting point of this image may well be the OT use of the word "head" for the leading person of a community, it is developed and elaborated to an extent which has no biblical precedent and is perhaps influenced to some extent by Gnostic or quasi-Gnostic conceptions. R. C. DENTAN

HEADBAND. 1. שבים (Isa. 3:18); KJV CAUL. Probably a head ornament of gold or silver.

2. KJV translation of קשרים in Isa. 3:20. *See* SASH.

HEADDRESS [פאר, *from* Egyp. *pyr*] (Isa. 3:20); KJV BONNET. A head-covering for women, ornamental in character. It was wound about the head (cf. Ezek. 24:17) without any under cover. The Hebrew word is also used of the GARLAND of the bridegroom (Isa. 61:10; cf. vs. 3); the TURBAN worn by men (Ezek. 24:17, 23); and the priest's linen CAP (Ezek. 44:18). J. M. MYERS

HEALING, HEALTH. Healing may be described in terms of the curing or restoring to health of a sick person, whether by promoting the closure of wounds, repairing the results of accidents or surgical disease, or administering effective treatment for specific pathological conditions of the body or mind. Health is frequently given the minimum definition of the absence of disease, but a state of clinical health involves definite positive considerations also. A person may be described as healthy when he exhibits that state of body and mind in which all the functions are being discharged harmoniously. It is not necessary for all parts of the body to be absolutely free from disease for a person to be in a state of clinical health, since the normal degeneration of aging tissues may render the harmony of body and mind in a minor key. The Hebrew *shālēm* ("healthy, whole") is a cognate of *shālôm* ("peace").

1. Health and longevity in the Bible
2. Health and environment
3. Prophylactic nature of the Mosaic code
   a. The sabbath
   b. Laws regarding edible foods
   c. Circumcision
   d. Sexual relationships
   e. Sexual hygiene
   f. Cleanliness
   g. Sanitation
4. Health and healing in the OT
5. The approach of Jesus to health and healing
6. Health and healing in the NT
7. Materia medica of the Bible

Bibliography

1. Health and longevity in the Bible. In antiquity, as in all ages, health was a highly prized possession among the Near Eastern peoples. The Hebrews tended to think of health primarily in terms of physical strength and well-being. Mental or emotional disturbances were generally related to some specific organ of the body (*see* DISEASE). The pastoral and agricultural pursuits of the Hebrews made a robust physique desirable, and even when urban centers developed during the monarchy, their inhabitants continued to cherish the ideal of bodily vigor and health. The weakling and the invalid constituted an object of contempt among the ancient Hebrews, and despite the legislation which was designed to protect such categories as the maimed, halt, and blind, the structure of society contrived to make life very difficult indeed for anyone who was not in full possession of his faculties. A brief summary of the qualities the ideally healthy Hebrew enshrined in his person are found in reference to David, who was "skilful in playing, a man of valor, a man of war, prudent in speech, and a man of good presence; and the LORD is with him" (I Sam. 16:18). In Ecclus. 30:14, health was regarded as the greatest of all earthly benedictions.

Whenever blessings were invoked, length of days was invariably one of the benefits most frequently enjoined. However, if the life of the individual was prolonged beyond the ideal of threescore and ten years (Ps. 90:10), hardship and sorrow were only to be expected as the logical outcome. In actual fact, the general life expectancy was nearer sixty than seventy years, and it was only the exceptional individual who attained to the traditional age of Moses (cf. Gen. 6:3). In ancient Egypt it was customary to recognize a long and prosperous life by saying that a man lived to be a hundred and ten years old, and this age was ascribed to Joseph (Gen. 50:26). The advanced years of the antediluvians are modestly estimated when compared with those of analogous personages in early Babylonian mythology. There are many problems attached to the numerology of the Semitic writings generally, and it is probable that the advanced ages ascribed to Seth, Enoch, and others are symbolical or eponymous, and not primarily literal. Eccl. 12:1-8 furnishes in allegorical language a gloomy description of advanced old age.

2. Health and environment. The land of Palestine does not appear to have been the seat of endemic infection in antiquity, as were Mesopotamia and Egypt. The river valleys and wadis did not normally afford a breeding ground for mosquitoes, while the incidence of imported diseases was probably considerably less than in countries with flourishing trade connections. The open-air life of the patriarchal nomads and the agricultural pursuits of the sedentary farmers of the monarchy contributed to the health and well-being of the populace. Even with the rise of an urban proletariat in the eighth century B.C., the over-all situation was not appreciably affected, and it was only at a comparatively late period of OT history that the cities became overcrowded.

It is very difficult to say whether the ancient Hebrews enjoyed better health than their modern counterparts. Considerations of living conditions then and now make a comparison odious in a great many respects. Again, some diseases which were scourges in the ancient world have now largely disappeared, while others which were unknown in antiquity have become very common. Furthermore, it is only within recent years that many of the diseases which have been prevalent for countless centuries of human existence have been described at all carefully. However, it is possible to speak with certainty upon one point. There can be no question that infant mortality was extremely heavy in antiquity. One estimate has claimed that in Egypt only three out of every ten children born into a family could expect to survive to adulthood. A comparable state of affairs doubtless existed in ancient Canaan, and was produced in part by lack of hygiene, environmental considerations, and neglect of elementary precautions for safeguarding public health.

In earlier phases of Hebrew thought, disease was regarded as a divine visitation consequent upon disobedience or sin, and this penal theory persisted in the popular mind throughout the entire biblical period. But other etiological factors were also envisaged, including the work of the adversary (Job 2:7) under divine permission, spirits of deafness or dumbness (Mark 9:17), and parental sin (John 9:2). There appears to have been comparatively little awareness of the fact that the principle of cause and effect enshrined in the dictum about a person's reaping what he sowed might also apply to disease on the natural level (cf. Ecclus. 37:30-31). Because of the consistent spiritualizing of pathological phenomena, the general biblical view of the incidence of disease related it more or less directly to divine interposition. Since God was the physician of his people, it followed that healing constituted a manifest token of his forgiveness. Health itself could be maintained by a punctilious observance of the divine commands throughout life, and if this discipline of the spirit was undertaken consistently, the blessing of material prosperity would be added to physical and mental health (cf. Exod. 15:26). *See* DISEASE.

3. Prophylactic nature of the Mosaic code. An important legislative step to counteract the effects of ignorance in matters of personal and communal hygiene was taken in the enactment of the sanitary sections of the Mosaic code. These portions of the Law are obviously of great antiquity, and represent a considerable advance upon the medical concepts of other ancient Near Eastern peoples. They legislated for the time when the Hebrews would be a sedentary people occupying their promised land, and they furnished the basis for all subsequent formulation of public-health enactments. The Mosaic law was notable for its complete repudiation of the authority and use of magic. Whereas contemporary civilizations uniformly regarded the incidence of disease as the result of demonic activity, the ancient Hebrews held that everything, good and evil alike, ultimately proceeded from the omnipotent Lord of the universe. By establishing Yahweh's moral supremacy they obviated the need for magical mediation, and placed the entire disease situation on a spiritual footing whereby the personal relationship which existed between the individual and his God was the determinative factor.

This did not exempt the righteous from sickness any more than it condemned the wicked to lifelong affliction. What it did, however, was to make clear that disease was conditioned largely by factors of a moral and spiritual, rather than a primarily physical, nature.

In view of the commonly accepted theory regarding the incidence of disease in antiquity, the moral concepts of holiness contained in the law indicated a new approach to the problem of sickness. The emphasis was now laid on the prevention of disease rather than its cure. If a man pursued a life of spiritual fellowship with God, he was entertaining the most valuable safeguard possible against sickness. But if, when disease arose, he attempted to cure it, he was trespassing upon the prerogatives of the Great Physician and interfering with functions which lay solely within the operation of divine discretion. Thus the primary emphasis of the law in this respect was prophylaxis, and because of this unique therapeutic emphasis Moses may well be spoken of as the father of preventive medicine. In the medical enactments of the Pentateuch, social hygiene was elevated to the level of a science, and the precepts of the Mosaic era survive to the present as a model of sanitary and hygienic insight.

The medical code received its most comprehensive expression in Leviticus. This is, in effect, a priestly handbook. Such a procedure accords fully with the practice, consistently found in antiquity, which committed to the priesthood the responsibility of instructing the people in all branches of knowledge. The medical clauses of Leviticus are thus seen to be extremely old compilations, and probably antedate other source material for the book. Upon examination it will be seen that the Mosaic prophylactic sanitary code comprises seven basic principles, as follows:

a. The sabbath. The custom of observing certain days during each month on which normal business or professional activity was suspended had its roots in the religion of the Old Akkadian period (*ca.* 2360-2180 B.C.) of Mesopotamian history—if, indeed, it did not originate at a still earlier period (*see* SABBATH). The earliest Mesopotamian calendars were based on lunar phases, and when the ancient Babylonians incorporated Sumerian calendars into their own culture, they interpreted the lunar phases in the light of the activities of superhuman beings as they might be related to human society. Each day of the month was dedicated to one or more deities of the Babylonian pantheon, and a type of horoscope was drawn up which stated whether or not the particular day was propitious, and what kind of activity might be pursued without fear of divine reprisal.

In the older Babylonian calendars there were nine principal days upon which virtually all activity ceased, while lesser restrictions were imposed upon other days of the month. A revision of this procedure was adopted during the reign of Ashurbanipal, in which the phases of the moon were represented by the seventh, fourteenth, twenty-first, and twenty-eighth days respectively. Thus the month was divided into four periods of seven days each, and the first week of each month commenced with the new moon. The day which followed the fourteenth of each month was known as *shapattu* or *shabattu,* which in the business life of Sumeria and Babylonia indicated the middle of the month, when work was interrupted for a short time. Ashurbanipal's calendar forbade work on days which fell in the series of seven mentioned above. On these days of restricted activity the people were counseled to refrain from work, and to propitiate the deities. It is important to notice, however, that the days themselves were not called by the name *shapattu,* this term being reserved for the day of the full moon.

While the Hebrew sabbath was perhaps associated with the new moon at an earlier period, it was essentially an expression of cultic life from the Mosaic period onward. The legislation in Exod. 31:13-17 specifically mentions physical rest as an important element of sabbath observance in conjunction with the worship of the Deity. Even domesticated animals were furnished with the opportunity for physical rest under the provisions of sabbath law (Exod. 23:12). The aim of the enactments concerning the sabbath may thus be said to be twofold: (*a*) The religious aspect of the observance was intended to furnish men with an opportunity for mental and spiritual re-creation. (*b*) The relaxation of physical effort at properly regulated intervals appears to have been enjoined for the purpose of maintaining physical vigor at a consistent level of functional efficiency.

For reasons which are difficult to determine, the principle of one rest day in seven is most adequately suited to the normal operating capacity of the human body. Different ratios such as one in six or one in eight have been tried, but have failed to achieve the success encountered with the ratio of one in seven. The sensitive nature of physical mechanisms is such that the body requires regular periods of rest and cessation from normal occupational activities; otherwise a breakdown will occur. Just as the degree of physical and mental restoration obtained from sleep determines to a considerable extent the subsequent performance of the body, so the re-creation of physical and mental states by the proper observance of a sabbath will govern the degree of well-being which the individual can normally expect. The idea of the sabbath thus emerges as a prophylactic and therapeutic principle of fundamental significance for the physical and spiritual health of the individual and the community alike.

The Mosaic law extended the concept of the sabbath to the land itself, as a safeguard against the depletion of its mineral reserves. Every seventh year after the harvest had been gathered in, the law (Lev. 25:2-7) stipulated that the land should be left fallow for a year, to ensure the continued fertility of the ground.

b. Laws regarding edible foods. If the prophylactic concepts enshrined in sabbath observance were intended to promote individual and social well-being, the legislation concerning the varieties of food which could be eaten beneficially was evidently enacted to serve as a guide for maintaining health and vigor. The dietary rules of the Pentateuch are by far the most scientific of their kind to be found in the ancient Near East, for, in the main, other nations adjusted their diets to the dictates of tradition, without respect to specific formulations of law. Accordingly, potential foodstuffs were regarded as either "clean" or "unclean," although careful delineation of these two categories appears to have been avoided except for Hebrew religious practice. While the rationale of this principle is unknown, its antiquity cannot be questioned, for it was recognized as a long-established procedure at the time of the Flood (Gen. 7:2).

Some scholars have suggested that this classification took its rise in the system of primitive taboos, or that it was connected with totemism in early times. While some of the forbidden animals and birds did, in fact, constitute nome-emblems in ancient Egypt and were associated with the fetishistic worship of that land, it is impossible to argue toward such origins as far as Mesopotamian religion is concerned, since it did not pass through a totemistic stage. In ancient Egypt, those animals and birds which were considered sacred through their being associated with particular deities were forbidden for food. While the Hebrew enactments concerning clean and unclean categories may have been in part a reaction against the cult worship of Egypt or a protest against fetishism, it would appear that principles of a vastly different order from the magical were in view when the food laws were promulgated.

These enactments may be summarized by saying that vegetarianism was not restricted in any way except that the fruit of newly planted trees was forbidden for food. An elementary rule was provided so as to leave no doubt as to the limits of clean and unclean categories of animals. Only those which chewed the cud and parted the hoof were suitable for food, since they were exclusively vegetarian (Lev. 11:3-8; Deut. 14:4-8). All blood was to be drained from the tissues before the flesh was regarded as suitable for cooking and eating. Under no circumstances was the flesh of an animal which had died from natural causes to be eaten (Deut. 14:21). The fat which surrounded the kidneys and abdominal viscera was also excluded by law from the Hebrew diet. Of the aquatic creatures, those which had fins and scales were considered clean, while the unclean fowls included the rapacious, aquatic, and predatory species (Lev. 11:13-19). All insects were prohibited for food except locusts.

That these rules were designed specifically to protect the individual and communal health of the Hebrews is evident from the following considerations. There is far less probability of contracting food poisoning from the flesh of vegetarian animals under subtropical climatic conditions than would be the case if the Carnivora were eaten. The flesh of the pig is particularly dangerous in this respect, being the intermediate host for several parasitic organisms of differing degrees of severity. The organism *Trichinella spirilis* occurs in partially or improperly cooked pork, and if ingested, its larvae mature in the intestine. The parasitic worm thus produced propagates great numbers of larvae, which migrate to the muscles, where they become encapsuled. Symptoms of this disease (*trichiniasis* or trichinosis) include malaise, fever, edema of the face and legs. One of the diagnostic features is an increase in the quantity of eosinophiles (normally three per cent) in the blood.

Tapeworm infestation as a result of eating pork is considerably more common than trichinosis. The pig is the intermediate host for a parasitic worm known as *Taenia solium,* which in a developed form is often as much as ten feet in length. In man, the definitive host, the worm develops from the *Cysticercus cellulosae* parasite present in measly, raw, or improperly cooked pork. Occasionally this infestation leads to the formation of nodules in the brain or the skeletal muscles (*somatic taeniasis*), with resultant epileptiform symptoms.

Along with some other animals, the pig is also the intermediate host for the parasitic *Echinococcus granulosus* (a species of small tapeworm), which in its larval stage in man is the cause of hydatid (cystic) tumors in the liver, lungs, and other parts of the body. A further disease, conveyed in particular by pigs and rodents, is toxoplasmosis. Animals can derive the disease through eating the flesh of other animals which have become infected, while in man, those who already have trichinosis generally exhibit a proportionally greater susceptibility to toxoplasmosis than those who are uninfected with the *Trichinella* organism. The protozoan *Toxoplasma* is found in the form of a cyst, known as the pseudocyst, and this structure enables the parasite to resist the action of gastric juices or the uneven heat resulting from inadequate cooking of the meat.

While the flesh of the pig has always been one of the chief sources of tapeworm infestation, it must be remembered that the ruminants proper are not themselves wholly free from parasitic organisms. Bovine flesh is occasionally the intermediate host for the beef tapeworm *Taenia saginata,* and man, the definitive host, acquires the parasite through ingesting the organism *Cysticercus bovis* in the improperly cooked flesh of an infected animal. The developed intestinal worm is almost twice the size of the *Taenia solium* parasite mentioned above.

It is quite probable that the strictures against eating the flesh of all animals, birds, and rodents without discrimination was also intended to safeguard the Hebrews against the incidence of tularemia. This disease is normally transmitted to man through the bite of a fly known as *Chrysops discalis,* as well as through other insects. It can also be acquired by the casual handling of an animal carcass which has previously been infected in this way, or as the result of a bite by an infected animal. The symptoms resemble those of undulant fever and bubonic plague, and have a general debilitating effect upon the victim.

The Hebrews shared the traditions of the ancient Near East generally in restricting their dietary attention to those aquatic creatures which had fins and scales. The exclusion of all edible Crustacea from the diet of the Hebrews removed one possible source of epidemic disease. Many of these organisms live on sewage and putrefying substances, and are not infrequently the cause of typhoid and the paratyphoid fevers. However, even certain varieties of clean fish can convey tularemia, while fish may also be the intermediate host for the huge parasitic worm *Diphyllobothrium latum,* which often grows to about thirty feet in length.

The risk of infection by the parasitic organisms dealt with above is by no means as far removed from modern occidental society as some writers are inclined to think, despite the stringent nature of most contemporary food laws. If this is the case, similar threats to individual and communal health among the ancient Hebrews were infinitely greater. The preservation of animal flesh for any length of time under subtropical climatic conditions is virtually impossible without proper refrigeration. Even if meat was comparatively fresh when it was consumed by the ancient Hebrews, their methods of cooking would seldom ensure that any parasitic organisms which might be lurking in the tissues would be consistently destroyed. Under such conditions the prophylactic approach is the best method of ensuring comparative freedom from infestation by parasitic worms, or from poisoning through contact with contaminated foodstuffs.

This concern for public health also expressed itself in the emphasis placed on the protection of food and water from pollution by unclean objects (Lev. 11:31-38). Prophylactic considerations were basic to this legislation, which when followed would go far toward preventing the incidence of food-borne polioencephalitis, the enteric fevers, food poisoning, and the parasitic worms. Insistence on the safeguarding of a clean supply of water was the most effective means of forestalling the rise and dissemination of diseases such as amoebiasis, the fevers of the enteric group, cholera, bilharziasis, and spirochetal jaundice. These prophylactic measures, which constitute a fundamental part of any system of public health, were of particular importance for the welfare of a nation living under primitive conditions in a subtropical region of the earth.

c. Circumcision. In the ancient world, CIRCUMCISION was not only a quasi-religious rite, but also the mark of initiation into a tribe or the sign of acquired manhood. The Egyptians regarded it as the hallmark of a cultured people, and also associated hygienic considerations with it. Among the Jews, however, it claimed an overriding religious significance through its association with the Covenant. It was the only form of physical mutilation which the law sanctioned, all the others being regarded as heathen in nature and origin. In antiquity the practice of circumcision was thought to have certain positive hygienic values, and was widely believed to prevent venereal disease and carbuncles. Fecundity was also thought to result from resection of the prepuce, although on what grounds it is difficult to determine. Modern medicine recommends circumcision as a means of preventing cancer of the penis. As a purely hygienic procedure there is much to be said for circumcision in instances where a constricted opening of the prepuce (phimosis) causes irritation of the glans penis by confining an accumulation of smegma proximate to the *corona glandis*. If the prepuce is particularly small in circumference, it may interfere to some extent with micturition.

d. Sexual relationships. The laws governing sexual union were based on the concept of the family as a social unit, and precluded intermarriage, polygamy, polyandry, and marriage of the matriarchal variety (the latter was extremely common in ancient Egypt). Even the union between a man and his paternal half sister, a not infrequent occurrence in the patriarchal period (cf. Gen. 20:12), was forbidden by Levitical law. Endogamy was prescribed for the Hebrew people, partly as a safeguard against contact with neighboring heathen races. But because of the dangers implicit in endogamy, the Mosaic law (Lev. 18:6-18) made it clear that marriage was forbidden within certain prescribed degrees of blood relationship, and thereby branded as incestuous many of the unions which were common in nations other than Israel. Into the category of prohibited degrees came uterine sisters and half sisters, stepdaughters, daughters of a stepson or a stepdaughter, and the sister of a living wife. If a man entered into marital union with any of the foregoing, he had transgressed the limits established by the law.

The purpose of this legislation, the most elaborate of its kind in antiquity, may be understood from religious, sociological, and biological standpoints. The moral nature of the Covenant demanded morality in the "chosen people," and thus precluded abhorrent sexual practices such as incest. In view of the widespread sexual deviations associated with religion in the ancient Near East, the regulating of sexual function for the Hebrews was a matter of paramount importance if they were to witness creditably to the morality of their Deity.

Sociologically, a lack of restraint in marriage with close relatives would have the effect of subordinating the rights and privileges of society as a whole to the dictates of a few dominant families. If the latter centralized and monopolized land and wealth through intermarriage, the welfare of the nation would be in jeopardy, while the families themselves would inevitably be plagued with jealousy and intrigue.

Biologically, the alleged detriments resulting from union within the prohibited degrees of consanguinity and affinity are held to include diminution in fecundity and deterioration of physical and mental vigor. In actual fact, there is no adequate physiological reason for regarding consanguineous unions as particularly dangerous for the body and mind.

e. Sexual hygiene. The provisions for individual sexual hygiene form an important part of the Levitical prophylactic approach to health. The act of coition was associated with concepts of uncleanness, as is the case among certain primitive peoples, and after sexual congress the participants were required to wash in water (Lev. 15:16-18). It is probable that the feelings of uncleanness which the law attached to coition were intended to serve as a form of control over sexual activity, and as a safeguard against the promiscuity of the Canaanites or other contemporary nations. The religious sanctions which the law thus imposed would invest the entire matter of sexual relations with a specifically moral character consonant with the covenant relationship.

The presence of blood, forbidden in all forms to the Hebrews, meant that menstruation was a particularly defiling occurrence, involving seven days of uncleanness (Lev. 15:19-24). The diffusive nature of the ceremonial defilement was such that any object of contact with a woman during the period of the menses was considered unclean. Levitical law took cognizance of the possibility of intercourse during menstruation, a practice which apparently was not uncommon in contemporary society, and legislated against it vigorously. In Lev. 15:24 any man who came into physical contact with the menstrual discharge was considered ceremonially unclean for seven days, but in Lev. 20:18 the deliberate practice of coition during the catamenia was forbidden. It would appear from this legislation that sexual activity was specifically designated as the means of procreation and not as an end in itself. *Coitus interruptus* was held to be an improper use of natural instinct and function (cf. Gen. 38:9). On purely medical grounds, abstinence from sexual intercourse during menstruation is held to prevent the incidence of nonspecific urethritis, which may arise through such a practice.

In instances of *menostaxis* (unduly prolonged menstruation) or *menorrhagia* (profuse menstruation), the woman was regarded as unclean throughout the period of discharge and for seven further days, after which appropriate ceremonies were prescribed for cleansing (Lev. 15:25-30). The fact that bleeding occurred during parturition meant that childbirth was surrounded with certain degrees of defilement, although the baby itself was always considered to be ceremonially clean. The defiling influence of the lochia subsequent to the birth of a female child was regarded as more diffusive than that for male offspring, and the period of uncleanness was extended accordingly (Lev. 12:2-5). Under normal circumstances the parents did not cohabit again after parturition until the baby had been weaned, a period which was not infrequently as long as two years.

Defilement also occurred from seminal emissions, and could be removed by washing when a prescribed period of time had elapsed. Deviations of sexual practice such as homosexuality (Lev. 18:22) and bestiality (Lev. 18:23) were rigidly condemned in the Mosaic code.

These laws employed religious sanctions to enforce specific restrictions upon human sexual behavior, and at the same time they laid considerable stress on the importance of personal hygiene during a stage in the development of the Hebrew nation when such matters were wont to be regarded with varying degrees of indifference. The prescribing of a period of isolation prior to the renewal of ceremonial cleanliness was an important aspect of the prophylactic approach implicit in this legislation.

f. Cleanliness. Among the Hebrews great emphasis was placed upon the washing of the body, despite the frequent shortages of water which occurred at different times each year. Under normal circumstances, ceremonial defilement could be removed by washing, after an appropriate period of isolation. When lepers were declared ceremonially clean, the washing of the clothes and the body constituted an important part of the purification ritual (Lev. 14:2-32). Ablutions were also prominent in the exercise of the priestly office (Exod. 30:18-21), and in a general religious sense were symbolic of the removal of sin or moral defilement.

From the standpoint of prophylaxis and general hygiene, the stress laid on the cleansing of anything which might be suspected of defilement was of fundamental importance. By this means the risk of communicating disease through contagion or fomites would be reduced appreciably, while the isolation of potential carriers of disease for a specified period of time would also help to control the incidence of disease. *See* DISEASE; LEPROSY.

g. Sanitation. The nomadic tribes of antiquity paid scant attention to sanitary practices, and this indifference was doubtless one of the major reasons for the rise and spread of epidemic disease. Mosaic legislation laid down carefully regulated sanitary procedures for the Israelites. Armies in the field were required to dispose of all excreta by burial (Deut. 23:12-13), a practice which provided for effective control of feces, urine, and fly-infestation. In general, sanitary rules were strictly enjoined for military forces, and the description of the precautions adopted after a battle with the Midianites (Num. 31:7-24) shows that isolation of victor and vanquished was required, prior to ceremonial ablutions.

The significance of the sanitary regulations is out of all proportion to the amount of space which they occupied in the Mosaic prophylactic legislation as a whole. A measure of control over air-borne and fly-borne plagues was afforded; this was of immeasurable importance for individual and communal health in preventing the outbreak of devastating epidemics. Thus an advanced degree of protection from infectious disease was afforded if the prescribed rules for sanitation, isolation, and hygiene were followed. The prophylactic approach was the special contribution of the Hebrews to medical theory, and the principles enshrined in the Pentateuch are in harmony with the basic precepts of contemporary preventive medicine.

4. Health and healing in the OT. In the light of earlier observations (*see* § 3 *above*) it will appear that health was a divine gift, and along with material prosperity was confidently expected by the faithful in Israel. When disease occurred, however, the sufferer could only look to God, the Physician of his people, for healing and recovery. To postexilic Judaism, recourse to human aid was precluded on the ground that such a procedure would usurp divine prerogatives in this respect; only the exceptional individual such as Asa (II Chr. 16:12) consulted physicians. The prophets occasionally gave advice concerning treatment to those who were sick, and also furnished prognoses from time to time (*see* MEDICINE). But because sickness was a spiritual matter, in the last analysis, healing could only properly be expected to follow a revival or revitalizing of the relationship between the individual and God. Thus, apart from a few folk remedies, there is no outline of medical treatment for disease as such in the OT, because such systematized therapeutics simply did not exist among the ancient Hebrews.

5. The approach of Jesus to health and healing. While Jesus Christ did not attempt to explain disease, his attitude toward its presence in the lives of individuals marked a considerable advance in thought on the consensus of OT opinion regarding sickness and disease. Instead of manifesting an attitude of contempt toward the weak and the sick, Jesus showed in his first recorded sermon that his earthly ministry was closely bound up with the frail and feeble of body and soul.

In the first instance, Jesus was firmly convinced of his Father's purpose for human wholeness and salvation (John 3:16; 10:10), and never once supported the OT concept of disease as a punishment sent by God. Instead, he frequently envisaged the incidence of disease as the result of evil producing an imbalance within the personality. Jesus viewed the individual as an essential unity of body and mind. This holistic emphasis was as far removed from the Greek concept of the body as a prison house for the soul as it was from the outlook of Descartes in a later period. Cartesian philosophy divided the personality into physical (*substantia extensa*) and mental (*substantia cogitans*) categories, considering the latter alone to be the proper sphere of operation of the church.

Because the view which Jesus took contemplated the individual as an integer, he was able to envisage more clearly than his predecessors the influence of body and mind upon each other. While he was always concerned to heal the sick in body, he invariably paid close attention to the mind and spirit of the sufferer. Insofar as they are recorded in any detail, his interviews with sick people seem to have had as one of their aims the uncovering of evidence pointing to a deficient relationship between the sufferer and his environment. His encounter with the Samaritan woman (John 4) transformed what might have been a casual conversation into a powerful therapeutic analysis which penetrated her outward poise, revealed the chaos and conflict in her emotional life, and confronted her with the person of the living Christ as the answer to her deepest needs. This interview is a superb example of nondirective counseling, and could serve as a model for psychotherapists.

Any knowledge of Jesus' approach to healing must rest largely upon inference, since his curative acts were a spontaneous expression of his sympathy and a sign of the kingdom of God, and did not constitute clinical demonstrations of therapeutic techniques. Nevertheless, certain principles appear consistently in the approach he adopted toward disease and healing. He disavowed entirely the idea that sickness was sent by God as a punitive measure, nor did he encourage the belief that the sufferer ought to remain ill in order to acquire courage or learn patience. On the one occasion where the sufferer raised the possibility that it might not, after all, be the will of Christ for healing to take place (Matt. 8:2-3; Mark 1:40; Luke 5:12-13), Jesus was at pains to banish the implied suggestion immediately, and proceeded to heal the leper forthwith.

Fundamental to all his healing activity was his conviction that disease was not an established part of the divine order of things. In some instances he actually attributed the incidence of illness to the operation of evil in human life (cf. Luke 13:16). Since his avowed mission was to destroy the works of the Devil, it followed that he would make every effort to heal the sick and diseased. Consequently, he responded to the disease situation by healing the sufferer whenever he was confronted with sickness. The circumstances of the case largely determined the mechanisms or techniques he employed, but these were generally secondary to his persistent desire to grapple with the sin which so frequently lay behind the specific ailment.

His ministry, therefore, was as much to the mind as to the body. His precepts in the Sermon on the Mount and elsewhere dealing with human motives and the deep workings of the mind show by implication that he was acutely aware of the place emotional conflict, resentment, fear, anxiety, hatred, and the like had in the genesis of disease. So much is this the case that it has been said in recent years that the most assured findings of modern psychiatry constitute but one small part of the distilled wisdom contained in the Sermon on the Mount.

Jesus was cognizant of the fact that the presence of a bias toward evil in the human personality provided ample opportunity for the functioning of sin in the individual life. Consequently, his analysis of specific situations was directed at resolving the state of spiritual turmoil and conflict, thereby severing the roots of psychogenic disease. Modern psychiatric investigation has shown that this conflict takes place in the unconscious mind, a largely uncharted area of the human personality in which such dynamics as faith, hope, the will to live, fear, and other emotional states are held to be rooted. It was to this realm, where so many of the disorders which afflict mind and body have their beginning, that the healing influence and spiritual authority of Christ penetrated. Such anticipation of certain contemporary psychotherapeutic techniques occurs in the gospel record of some miracles of healing in which suggestion and other psychological mechanisms were employed. It is interesting to note that the techniques were modified for differing individuals, indicating that Jesus had diagnosed the patient's ailment accurately and was aware of the factors which had contributed to its incidence.

There are good reasons for believing that in his healing activity Jesus was endeavoring to raise the sufferers whom he encountered to a more advanced degree of spirituality. It was his desire that men should be won for the divine kingdom, and share in the powers and energies which were manifested in the relationship existing between him and his Father, for this ultimately constituted his mission to humanity (cf. Luke 7:21-22). Entrance to this realm of the spirit presupposed the operation of divine love on the one hand, and on the other a degree of faith manifested either by the sick person or by someone connected with him. This faith was to be distinguished from credulity, suggestibility, and the like, for the dynamic nature of the emotional response involved a measure of conscious intelligent commitment of the person to the will of God in Christ. Though the degree of participation in faith varied with different individuals, the gospel narratives make it clear that some measure of faith was normally evoked by Jesus as a condition of healing (cf. Matt. 9:29; Luke 17:19; 18:42). Certain healings took place without specific mention of faith being present (cf. Matt. 9:1-8; 12:9-13), but it is obviously implicit in the sufferer's response to the words of Jesus. In other healings there is no mention of the attitude of the sick person in this respect (cf. Luke 13:11-13; 14:4; 22:51), which may in part be because the miracles of healing were incidental to other considerations.

In any assessment of such an approach to health and healing it must always be remembered that the therapeutic activity of Jesus included significant spiritual, as well as psychological, considerations, directed at the restoration of the entire personality. These healings cannot be explained satisfactorily on the simple assumption that he was a shrewd psychologist who dismissed a wide variety of psychoneurotic conditions by means of adroit techniques which were in advance of contemporary practice. While psychological theories can throw much light on the healing work of Jesus, they cannot of themselves explain it fully.

Matthew (8:17) envisaged Christ's healing ministry as a fulfilment of the statement in Isa. 53:4 concerning the work of the divinely appointed Servant. In this respect the evangelist interpreted the prophetic oracle more accurately than many modern English versions, which speak of the Servant's bearing "griefs" and "sorrows." The Hebrew text of this verse employs the simple words for "diseases" and "pains" (so RSV mg.), which relates the healing of sickness directly to the work of the servant. If the Christian church is correct in its traditional interpretation of the Isaiah Servant passages in terms of the atonement on Calvary, it would appear that the incarnate Lord dealt also with disease and sickness on the cross as well as with human sin—i.e., his atonement avails for the whole personality, body as well as soul. On this basis, therefore, it is theoretically justifiable to appeal to the finished work of Jesus for physical healing as well as for spiritual restoration.

6. Healing and health in the NT. The restoration of the sick formed part of subsequent apostolic practice, in conformity with the expressed will of Christ. In the days immediately after Pentecost many healings took place at the hands of the apostles (Acts 2:

43; 5:12; 8:7), and the pathology dealt with was as varied as that which had confronted Jesus. In the main, however, the healings were achieved by a powerful degree of suggestion linked to the faith of the sufferer, and do not appear to reflect consistently that variety of approach or that depth of spiritual perception which Jesus had manifested in his miracles. As time passed, the treatment of disease became more uniform, employing the formula of the name or the power of Christ in response to the expectant trust of the sufferer. It would also appear that particular techniques such as anointing and prayer (Jas. 5:14-15) were employed by the senior Christians in the community as a means of healing disease. From the experience of Paul with Trophimus at Miletus (II Tim. 4:20) it may be concluded that the healing power given to the apostles diminished with the passing of time. Whatever the explanation of the illness of Trophimus, it is clear that he would not have remained sick had Jesus been present. For discussion of the general pathology of the NT, *see* DISEASE.

7. Materia medica of the Bible. There is little mention of galenicals and empirical materia medica in biblical literature, despite the abundance of herbs and other therapeutic substances in Palestine. Consequently, there are no pharmacopoeias or formularies extant such as have survived from Mesopotamian and Egyptian cultures.* However, certain substances were used in a general therapeutic sense, and can be classified in terms of their use as fumigants, culinary herbs, or specifically curative substances. Fig. HEA 11.

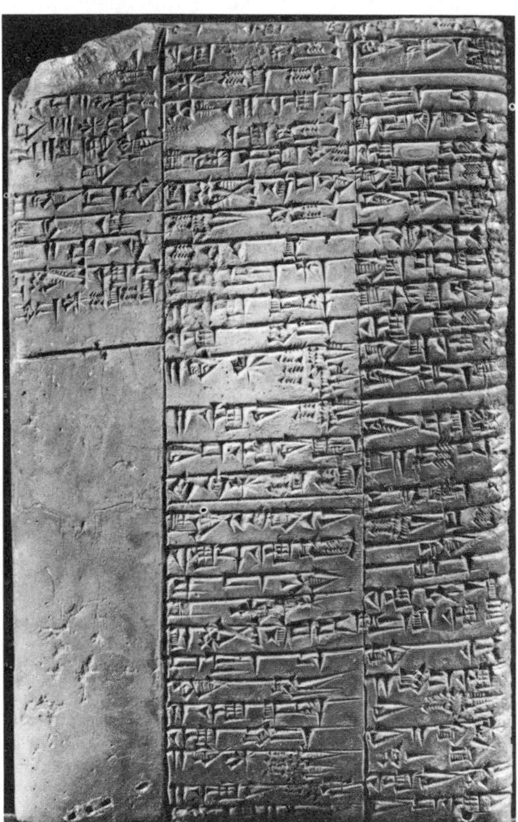

Courtesy of the University Museum of the University of Pennsylvania

11. A Sumerian "medical" tablet from Nippur (late third millennium B.C.)

INCENSE was the most important member of the first class, and consisted of a mixture of aromatic substances (Exod. 30:34-36). While its primary function was to honor God in the worship of the sanctuary, it probably served as a fumigant and deodorant also. The use of aromatic oils and perfumes for personal hygiene was dictated by climatic and other considerations. Myrtle, saffron, aloes, cassia, myrrh, spikenard, and cinnamon also came within this category. The symbolic anointing of a host or guest was an indication of respect (Ruth 3:3; II Sam. 12:20), while discontinuance of anointing indicated personal grief (Deut. 28:40).

Therapeutic substances in use among the Hebrews included the renowned balm of Gilead (*see* GILEAD, BALM OF) as an unguent preparation. A number of herbs were employed as gastric stimulants, tonics, rubefacients, and carminatives. Of these the more commonly found were fennel, dill, spelt, cumin, anise, and the caper berry. Carbonate of soda was often boiled with olive oil to make soap, or alternatively certain plants of the saltwort and glasswort families were used as an alkali instead of the carbonate of soda (natron). Olive oil was frequently administered internally and externally, sometimes being mixed with wine to furnish astringent and antiseptic qualities.

Herbs of a culinary nature played a prominent part in Hebrew diet. In addition to dill, fennel, cumin, anise, and spelt, the labiate herbs such as marjoram, thyme, mint, and sage were widely used. Anise seeds were popular as a condiment in cookery, as was cinnamon. The "bitter herbs" (Exod. 12:8) probably consisted of lettuce, endive, chicory, and water cress. Although there were many poisonous plants in Palestine, they do not appear to have been employed for criminal purposes.

Bibliography. H. P. Newsholme, *Health, Disease and Integration* (1929); C. R. Smith, *A Physician Examines the Bible* (1950); H. W. Frost, *Miraculous Healing* (1951); R. K. Harrison, "Medicine of the Bible," *Canadian Association of Medical Students and Internes Journal*, vol. X, no. 1 (1951), pp. 17-20; H. N. and A. L. Moldenke, *Plants of the Bible* (1952); A. R. Short, *The Bible and Modern Medicine* (1953), pp. 27-46.

R. K. HARRISON

HEALING, GIFTS OF. Primitive Christianity possessed miraculous powers, including the power to heal (Acts 2:22; 3:16; 4:30). Paul mentions gifts of healing in his list of spiritual gifts (I Cor. 12:10, 28).

1. The healing ministry of Jesus. From the beginning of his ministry Jesus performed healing miracles (Mark 1:29-32, 40-45). "The power of the Lord," says Luke, "was with him to heal" (5:17). His enemies attributed this power to Satan (Mark 3:22); Jesus said it was of God (Matt. 12:28; Luke 11:20). In the power of the Spirit he began his ministry (Mark 1:10; Luke 4:18-19), proclaiming the kingdom (Mark 1:14-15), and affirming that healing was a sign, among others, that the rule of God, the "acceptable year of the Lord," had been inaugurated (Matt. 11:5; Luke 4:19; 7:22), the predicted character of the new age realized (Isa. 35:5-6; 61:1-2). He sent forth his disciples with authority "to heal every disease and every infirmity" (Matt. 10:1). Mark reports their success (6:13), and Luke sees this success as evidence of the kingdom's nearness (10:9).

2. The healing ministry of the church. The healing activity of Jesus and his disciples explains the place of healing in the primitive church. The gift is conferred by the Spirit (I Cor. 12:10, 28); the Spirit is given by the exalted Christ (Acts 2:33); the mighty works, including healing, are signs of the messianic age (Acts 2:16-21; Joel 2:28-31); believers have been "transferred" into the "kingdom of [God's] beloved Son" (Col. 1:13); the "powers of the age to come" have entered the present (Heb. 6:5), and Christ's power has been delegated to all who believe on him. People are astonished at the healing work of Peter and Paul and Philip (Acts 3:11; 5:15; 8:9-13; 14:8-10). Faith "in the name [person] of Jesus" (Acts 3:6, 16; cf. Matt. 9:27-31; Mark 5:34; 9:14-27), prayer and anointing with oil (Jas. 5:14-15; cf. Mark 6:13), and the "laying on of hands" (Acts 9:12, 17; 28:8; cf. Matt. 9:18; Mark 5:23), all belong to the healing process. Healing and the forgiveness of sins also go together (Jas. 5:16; cf. Mark 2:3-12; Ps. 103:3).

The NT gifts of healing are an integral part of the mission and message of Jesus, and of the early church's consciousness of their fulfilment, and must not be confused with psychiatry, or faith healing, however impressive the parallels, or however significant the light modern therapeutic practices may throw upon them.

Bibliography. A. Richardson, *The Miracle-Stories of the Gospels* (1941); S. V. McCasland, *By the Finger of God* (1951); L. D. Weatherhead, *Psychology, Religion and Healing* (rev. ed., 1954).

E. ANDREWS

HEAP OF STONES [גל אבנים]; HEAP [גל]. A symbol used in several different ways. A heap of stones raised over a slain person served as a reminder of his shameful conduct and, probably, as a warning that the place was tainted (*see* STONING). A heap of stones was raised over the body of Achan after he and his family had been stoned and burned (Josh. 7:26). A similar heap was raised over the body of the king of Ai after he had been hanged by Joshua (8:29). A heap was also raised over the pit where Joab and his men threw the body of Absalom (II Sam. 18:17).

A heap of stones was made as a witness to the compact which was drawn up between Jacob and Laban (Gen. 31:46-52; *see* GALEED).

Such phrases as "HEAP OF RUINS" and "STONE HEAP" occur as variant translations of the Hebrew phrase and often bear a distinct connotation: A place which has become a heap of ruins (i.e., the stones of the destroyed buildings) is a reminder of the fate which God has in store for the sinful (Isa. 25:2). To warn that a city or house or an altar will become a stone heap is to announce impending destruction (Job 15:28; Isa. 37:26; Jer. 9:11—H 9:10; 51:37; Hos. 12:11—H 12:12). The ancient Israelite, as the modern Arab peasant, thought that such heaps of stones were inhabited by evil or dangerous spirits (see Isa. 13:21; 34:14; cf. Job 8:17).

H. F. BECK

HEART. In biblical psychology, the central and unifying organ of personal life. Like all primitive peoples, the ancient Hebrews did not make a sharp distinction between physical and psychic powers and tended to attribute psychological functions to certain organs of the body. Of all such organs the heart was the chief; it was the innermost spring of individual life, the ultimate source of all its physical, intellectual, emotional, and volitional energies, and consequently the part of man through which he normally achieved contact with the divine. In the recesses of the heart dwelt the thoughts, plans, attitudes, fears, and hopes which determined the character of an individual; here also God (and, in the NT, the power of evil) could work in secret to transform that character by implanting new thoughts and feelings.

There are three Hebrew words for "heart": לב, לבב, and לבה (the latter used only eight times), but there is no distinction in meaning. All are normally translated in the LXX by καρδία (occasionally νοῦς or διάνοια), which is also the word used in the NT. The conception of heart in the NT is identical with that in the OT.

1. A part of the physical body. The word "heart" is only rarely used in a purely physical sense, as in I Sam. 25:37; II Kings 9:24.

That the Hebrews thought of the heart as the center of physical vitality is shown by occasional references to strengthening it by food (Judg. 19:5) and making it glad with wine (Ps. 104:15), although it is obvious that in this usage the word carries psychological overtones also.

A rare idiom uses the word "heart" to designate the inner part of the sea (Exod. 15:8) or of the earth (Matt. 12:40).

2. The seat of psychic life. Ordinarily the term "heart" means only incidentally the physical organ and denotes primarily the psyche at its deepest level. In this sense it is sometimes equivalent to רוח (SPIRIT; Pss. 51:10; 143:4) or קרב (RSV "inward mind"; Ps. 64:6).

a. The seat of the emotions. All the emotions of which a person is capable may be attributed to the heart. The heart can be glad (Prov. 27:11; Acts 14:17), sad (Neh. 2:2), troubled (II Kings 6:11 KJV), courageous (II Sam. 17:10), discouraged (Num. 32:7), fearful (Isa. 35:4), envious (Prov. 23:17), trustful (Prov. 31:11), generous (II Chr. 29:31), moved by hatred (Lev. 19:17) or love (Deut. 13:3). The emotions of the heart are sometimes pictured vividly and concretely: it is said to fail (Gen. 42:28), to faint (Gen. 45:26), to melt (Ps. 22:14), to tremble (I Sam. 28:5), to throb (Ps. 38:10), to flutter (Isa. 21:4 ASV), to grow hot (Deut. 19:6 KJV; Luke 24:32), to be sick (Prov. 13:12), to be broken (Ps. 69:20). The heart is also the seat of the appetites and desires (Ps. 37:4), both bad (Rom. 1:24) and good (Rom. 10:1).

b. The seat of the intellect. More distinctively Hebrew than the thought of the heart as the seat of the emotions is the conception that it is the center of intellectual life. The process of cogitation takes place in the heart (Judg. 5:16; Mark 2:6); thoughts belong there (I Chr. 29:18); and there one meditates on the deep things of life (Ps. 4:4; Luke 2:19). Because of its concrete character, the Hebrew language can hardly express the idea "to think" except by the phrase "to say in the heart" (Gen. 27:41 KJV; Ps. 10:6 KJV). With the heart man makes his plans (Prov. 16:9 KJV) and seeks knowledge and understanding (Eccl. 8:16 KJV). The heart is the storehouse of memory (Prov. 3:3; Luke 1:66). So intimate is the connection of heart and thought that the English versions (especially the RSV) sometimes render לב or לבב by "UNDERSTANDING" (Job 12:3) or "MIND" (Jer. 7:31). "To steal the heart" means "to deceive the mind" (II Sam. 15:6). WISDOM, in the sense of "skill," is a quality of the heart (Exod. 31:6 KJV), as is wisdom in the wider sense (I Kings 10:24 KJV).

c. The seat of the volition and the moral life. From the idea that the heart is the center of the intellectual life it is a natural step to the thought that it is the center of the will and hence of the moral life. The heart can plan wicked deeds (Prov. 6:18) and may become basically perverted (Prov. 11:20 KJV; Heb. 3:12); as such it can be a spring pouring forth wickedness (Matt. 15:19). It may be lifted up with pride (Deut. 8:14); it may become hardened (Zech. 7:12; Matt. 19:8: σκληροκαρδία), fat (Ps. 119:70), stubborn (Jer. 3:17), godless (Job 36:13), or turned away from God (I Kings 11:2). The hard or stubborn heart is sometimes described as "uncircumcised" (Jer. 9:26; Acts 7:51). One may depend too much on his own heart (Num. 15:39) or have a deceived heart (Isa. 44:20 KJV) or a hypocritical, "double" heart (Ps. 12:2). What is to be desired in man is that he have a "tender," not a hardened, heart (II Kings 22:19 KJV: רך). The good heart is one that is perfect (I Kings 8:61 KJV: שלם) or blameless (Ps. 119: 80: תמים), clean (Ps. 51:10: טהור), upright (Ps. 32:11: ישר), honest and good (Luke 8:15), pure (Matt. 5:8), single (Eph. 6:5), circumcised (Jer. 4:4; Rom. 2:29), or broken (Ps. 34:18). The idea of "perfection" or "wholeness," the most comprehensive of the terms, is also conveyed by the phrase "with all the heart" (Deut. 6:5; בכל לבב). Man can, if he will, cleanse (Ps. 73:13) or renew (Ezek. 18:31 KJV) his heart. The heart is capable of education; one can set his heart to seek God (II Chr. 12:14) or the law (Ezra 7:10), apply it to the search for understanding (Prov. 2:2), or guide it in the right way (Prov. 23:19 KJV). But the human heart in general is corrupt (Jer. 17:9), undependable (Prov. 28:26 KJV), and full of evil (Gen. 8:21; Eccl. 9:3).

3. The point of contact with God. The heart, as the innermost spring of the human personality, is directly open to God and subject to his influence. The heart speaks to God (Ps. 27:8) and trusts him (Ps. 28:7); the word of God dwells in it (Deut. 30: 14), and there faith takes its rise (Rom. 10:10). God looks upon the heart (I Sam. 16:7), knows its secrets (Ps. 44:21; Acts 1:24: καρδιογνώστης), and can test its moral quality (Ps. 17:3). For his mysterious purposes he can harden it (Exod. 4:21), but can also turn it to good (Ezra 6:22). He can put his fear into it (Jer. 32:40) or inspire it with new purposes (Neh. 2:12; Rev. 17:17). In the NT the devil has a similar power (John 13:2; Acts 5:3). God can give man an understanding heart (I Kings 3:9 KJV) or take all understanding (לב) away (Job 12:24). Even the hearts of kings are subject to God's control (Prov. 21:1); he fashions the hearts of all (Ps. 33:15).

Since the heart naturally inclines to evil, hope for its betterment must lie rather in God's transforming grace than in any educational activity on the part of man. Sometime in the future, it was believed, God would write his law in men's hearts (Jer. 31:33). The same God who could change the heart of a man into the heart of an animal (Dan. 4:16 KJV) was able to create for man a new heart (Ps. 51:10); one day he would take away the old, hardened heart of Israel and put a new, receptive heart in its place (Ezek. 36:26). In the NT, God is said to have shone (II Cor. 4:6), to have given the down payment of the Spirit (II Cor. 1:22), and to have poured forth his love in men's hearts (Rom. 5:5); there Christ could dwell (Eph. 3:17), and the peace of Christ might reign (Col. 3:15).

4. The equivalent of the personality. Since the term "heart" can mean the totality of the feelings, thoughts, and desires of a man, traced back to their deepest source in his inner life, it sometimes has almost the value of the modern psychological term "personality."

Occasionally it is connected with the reins (KIDNEYS) as an almost equivalent term (Jer. 11:20 KJV: כליות ולב). This usage shows how dangerous it would be to attribute to Hebrew psychology too precise an allocation of psychic functions to particular physical organs. For the Hebrews the personality was diffused through the whole of the body, and the assignment of special functions to particular organs was loose and often inconsistent.

In many cases the word "heart" is used in a weakened, nonspecific sense in which it may quite properly be replaced by a word simply designating the person; e.g., "My heart shall not fear" (Ps. 27:3) means little more than "*I* shall not fear." Often the word "self" can be used as a precise synonym for it; e.g., "Abraham . . . said in his heart" (Gen. 17:17) means only ". . . said to himself" (cf. KJV and RSV).

Bibliography. E. Hatch, *Essays in Biblical Greek* (1889), pp. 94 ff; C. A. Briggs, "A Study of the Use of לב and לבב in the OT," *Semitic Studies in Memory of A. Kohut* (1897); P. Joüon, "Locutions hébraïques avec la préposition על devant לב, לבב," *Bibl.*, 5 (1924), 49-53; A. R. Johnson, *The Vitality of the Individual in the Thought of Ancient Israel* (1949); F. H. von Meyenfeldt, *Het Hart (Leb, Lebab) in Het Oude Testament* (with English summary; 1950); R. Bultmann, *Theology of the NT* (trans. K. Grobel; 1954), I, 220-27.

R. C. DENTAN

HEARTH [יקוד, מוקדה (KJV BURNING); KJV אח (RSV BRAZIER), כיור (RSV BLAZING POT; *see* POT), מוקד (RSV FURNACE), הראל *and* אריאל (*see below*)]. In biblical times the hearth was a depression in the floor for the cooking of food.

In Ezek. 43, הראל, *har'ēl* (vs. 15), and אריאל, *'arî'ēl* (vs. 16), are translated "altar hearth" (KJV "altar"). This was the uppermost stage or ledge of the altar of burnt offering, upon which the sacrifice was laid. Cf. Lev. 6:9.

See also ARCHITECTURE; HOUSE; ARIEL; ALTAR.

O. R. SELLERS

HEAT AND COLD. Extremes of atmospheric temperature, annual and daily (Gen. 8:22). General terms for "heat" are חם (Gen. 18:1; Job 24:19; Jer. 17:8) and καῦμα (Rev. 7:16; 16:9); for "cold," קרה (Job 24:7; 37:9; Ps. 147:17; Prov. 25:20), קר (Gen. 8:22), and ψῦχος (John 18:18; Acts 28:2; II Cor. 11:27). As causing extreme discomfort, the preferred terms are חרב (lit., "dessicating heat"; Gen. 31:40; Isa. 25:4; etc.); חרבון, "heat" (Ps. 32:4); καύσων, "scorching heat" (Matt. 20:12; Luke 12:55; cf. Jas. 1:11); קרח, "cold" (Gen. 31:40) or "frost" (Jer. 36:30); and קרה, "cold" (Prov. 25:20). The direct heat of the sun is חמה (Ps. 19:6—H 19:7), or καύσων (Jas. 1:11). In the LXX, καύσων sometimes translates קדים (e.g., Hos. 12:1—H 12:2), the hot, dry EAST WIND; and this may be intended in Luke 12:55. The emotional heat of anger is חמה (cf. Gen. 27:44; II Kings 22:13; Isa. 42:25; etc.) or חרון (cf. Deut. 13:18; Josh. 7:26; Nah. 1:6; etc.).

See also PALESTINE, CLIMATE OF; SUMMER AND WINTER. R. B. Y. SCOTT

HEATH. KJV translation of ערער, *'ar'ār*, in Jer. 17:6 (RSV SHRUB); 48:6 (RSV WILD ASS). The true heath, *Erica vagans* L. (and other species), rarely is found in Bible lands and does not fit the geographical associations of the passages. The most widely accepted identification is the JUNIPER.

See also FLORA § A9*g*. J. C. TREVER

HEATHEN [גוים; ἔθνη]. *See* NATIONS.

HEAVE OFFERING. KJV translation of תרומה (RSV HOLY THINGS), the portions of sacrifices and offerings which were set apart, removed, or taken up ("heaved") for Yahweh and the priests. *See* SACRIFICE AND OFFERINGS § C3-4.

HEAVEN [שמים; οὐρανός]. The word "heaven" is used in the Bible in two senses: (*a*) In the larger sense, it denotes the upper part of the cosmic ocean, which envelops the earth. It is therefore conceived as made of water; indeed, in Akkadian and Arabic the cognate words are used by metonymy to mean "rain." (*b*) In the narrower sense—with which we are here primarily concerned—"heaven" denotes the immediate ceiling or canopy of the earth—i.e., the sky, pictured as a septum stretched across the cosmic ocean to prevent its water from overflowing. This septum is variously portrayed.

1. Heaven as a metal strip
2. Heaven as a curtain
3. Heaven as a garment
4. The windows of heaven
5. The bottles of heaven
6. The promptuaries of heaven
7. The stages of heaven
8. The pillars of heaven

Bibliography

1. Heaven as a metal strip. The standard Hebrew term for the celestial septum is רקיע (Gen. 1:6-8; Pss. 19:1; 150:1; Dan. 12:3). This is usually rendered "firmament," after LXX στερέωμα and Vulg. *firmamentum.* But the word denotes properly a strip of hammered metal; and this picture is, in fact, elaborated in Job 26:13, where God is said to polish it by breathing upon it with his wind, even as a man might breathe on a mirror for the same purpose (cf. 37:18). The conception finds a perfect parallel in the "brazen heaven" of Homer (*Iliad* V.425, 504; *Odyssey* III.2) and Pindar (*Pyth.*, X.22; *Nem.*, VI.13); while, somewhat similarly, heaven is described both in ancient Egyptian sources and occasionally by Homer as made of iron. In the same vein, too, the pavement of heaven—i.e., the firmament—is described in Exod. 24:10 as, literally, "of the appearance of lapis lazuli [ספיר; LXX σαπφειρος]"—a concept which recurs in Mesopotamian sources and which is repeated in the apocalyptic visions of Enoch (14:9-10; 71:5) and in later rabbinic literature (e.g., Genesis Rabbah 4.12). *See bibliography* § 1.

2. Heaven as a curtain. Alternatively, the expanse is portrayed as a strip of gauze or muslin (דק) stretched like a tent (Isa. 40:22) or spread like a curtain (Ps. 104:2). This, too, has interesting parallels. In the Rig Veda (VIII.6.5), heaven is said to be stretched out like a hide. In the Egyptian Book of the Dead (ch. 85), it is described as a "skin" (*šet*); and in the Finnish Kalevala as an embroidered cloth; and the same imagery is frequent in German popular riddles. *See bibliography* § 2.

3. Heaven as a garment. Lastly, heaven is regarded as a garment. This concept, however, develops in two ways. On the one hand, the garment is pictured as an outspread blanket, even as an Arab spreads his cloak to sleep on it. On the other hand, it is portrayed as a mantle or wrap in which God enfolds himself. This latter idea is especially well attested in other cultures. Thus—to cite but a few examples—in the Iranian Zend Avesta (Yasht 13.3; Yasna 30.5), the supreme god, Mazda, is said to wear the heavens as an embroidered robe; while in Teutonic mythology Odin wears an azure mantle, representing the sky; and among the Ewe-speaking Negroes of Africa, the azure sky is the veil with which Morwa, the supreme god, covers his face. It is especially the star-spangled night sky that lends itself to this imagery. The Mesopotamians often describe it as a "variegated garment" (*burummu;* cf. ברומים in Ezek. 27:24), and the moon in particular is said to be attired in the "robe of heaven" (*nalbaš šamê*). *See bibliography* § 3.

The picture of heaven as a garment is arrestingly developed in the LXX version of Job 14:12:

> So man lies down and rises not again;
> till the heavens are no more he will not awake,

where, by different vocalization of the consonantal text (viz., *BᵉLôTH*, "wear out," for MT *BiLTî*, "are no more"), the ultimate dissolution of the heavens is portrayed as "becoming unstitched" (οὐ μὴ συρραφῇ).

4. The windows of heaven. The firmament, or celestial dam, was believed to be punctuated at intervals by grilles or sluices (ארבות [Gen. 7:11; 8:2; II Kings 7:2, 19; Isa. 24:18; Mal. 3:10], "windows of heaven"; but cf. LXX καταρράκται [Isa. 24:18 θυρίδες]; Vulg. *cataractae*), through which the rain was released in due measure. In the Ras Shamra Texts these are termed more neutrally "cracks" or "fissures" (*bdqt;* בדק in II Chr. 34:10; Ecclus. 50:1), and this has inspired the attractive suggestion that the same word should be recognized also (for MT very similar ברקים) in Ps. 135:7; Jer. 10:13; 51:16, thus yielding the sense: "He maketh fissures [instead of 'lightnings'] for the rain." These sluices have their counterparts in the "springs" or "fountains" (מעינות תהום; Gen. 7:11; cf. Prov. 8:24, 28) through which the waters of the nether ocean were made to issue.

5. The bottles of heaven. The celestial waters were also conceived as being stored in skins or bottles (i.e., clouds), which were tilted and emptied by God at his good pleasure (Job 38:37). This concept, too, is not unparalleled elsewhere. A common Turkish expression for "It rains" is, "The bottles are emptied," while in the Rig Veda (V.83.7-8), the rain-god Parjanya is invoked to "draw downward thine opened water-skin." In the same way, too, the Peruvians believed in a rain-goddess who sat in the clouds emptying a pitcher; and similar ideas are entertained in Teutonic mythology. Moreover, in the Ugaritic Poem of Baal (I*AB, vi, 7), that god of rainfall is instructed to take "thy clouds, thy buckets [*mdlk*], thy rains." *See bibliography* § 4.

6. The promptuaries of heaven. In the heavens were located the storehouses or promptuaries (אוצרות) of the winds (Ps. 135:7; Jer. 10:13; 51:16; Enoch 18:1; II Esd. 4:5), the hail (Job 38:22), and darkness (Isa. 45:3)—a notion developed in considerable and fantastic detail in the visions of Enoch (17:3; 18:1; 41:4; 60:12-24; 69:23; 71:4, 9).

7. The stages of heaven. The concept of successive stages or strata of heaven is nowhere explicitly articulated in the OT, for the expression "heaven of heavens" (Deut. 10:14; cf. I Kings 8:27; Ps. 48:4) is probably no more than an ordinary Hebrew superlative. In the Pseudep., however (e.g., Test. Levi 3; Slavonic Enoch), we do indeed encounter that notion of the seven heavens which was later to become a commonplace of Jewish and Arabic folklore (cf. Talmud, Ḥag. 12*a;* Koran, Sura 22.4), and which likewise obtains in many other cultures—e.g., Hindu, Siberian, Turkish, Sumatran. In the NT, on the other hand, only three strata appear to be recognized (II Cor. 12:2). This alternative likewise appears in rabbinic sources, while in the ancient Mesopotamian myth of Etana there are similarly only three stages, in the uppermost of which dwells the supreme god, Anu.

8. The pillars of heaven. Heaven was thought to rest upon pillars (Job 26:11; cf. Milton, *Paradise Regained,* book IV, line 455: "the pillar's frame of heaven"; *Comus,* line 597: "the pillar'd firmament"). This conception, too, is common to many other peoples, and was entertained in antiquity by the Egyptians, the Iranians, and the Greeks. The number of the pillars is not stated in the OT, but the common view in other cultures was that there were four of them, situated at each of the cardinal points. *See bibliography* § 5.

For theological aspects of heaven, *see* KINGDOM OF GOD, OF HEAVEN; ANGELS.

Bibliography. 1. On heaven made of iron, Egyptian: Devirea, *Mélanges d'archéologie égyptienne et assyrienne,* I (1873), 9. Greek: *Odyssey* XV.329; XVIII.565. On heaven of lapis lazuli: B. Meissner, *Babylonien und Assyrien,* II (1920), 108.

2. On heaven as a curtain: H. Güntert, *Von der Sprache der Götter und Geister* (1921), p. 142. For the notion in German popular riddles: L. Strackerjan, *Sagen aus dem Herzogtum Oldenburg* (2nd ed., 1909), II, 108.

3. On heaven as a garment: R. Eisler, *Weltenmantel und Himmelszelt* (1910). T. H. Gaster, *Thespis* (1950), p. 186. On Akkadian *nalbaš šamê:* S. Langdon, *JRAS* (1925), pp. 717-18. E. Weidner, *Archiv für Orientforschung,* VII (1931), 115-16. On *burummu:* P. Jensen, *Kosmologie der Babylonier* (1890), pp. 6-7.

4. On the bottles of heaven: G. de la Vega, *Commentarios reales* (trans. C. R. Markham; 1867-71), II, 27. J. Grimm, *Teutonic Mythology* (trans. F. Stalybrass; 1880), p. 593. G. Jacob, *Altarabische Parallelen sum AT* (1897), p. 20.

5. On the pillars of heaven, Egyptian: G. Maspero, *Revue archéologique,* N.S. XXIV (1877), 322. Iranian: I. Scheftelowitz, *Die altpersische Religion und das Judenthum* (1920), p. 106. Greek: O. Gruppe, *Griechische Mythologie* (1906), p. 382.

T. H. GASTER

HEAVEN, HOST OF. *See* HOSTS, HOST OF HEAVEN.

HEBER hē'bər [חבר, comrade]; HEBERITES —be rīts. **1.** Eponym of an important clan of the tribe of Asher (Gen. 46:17; Num. 26:45; I Chr. 7:31-32); sometimes connected with the HABIRU.

2. A Kenite; the husband of Jael, the woman who killed Sisera (Judg. 4:11, 17, 21; 5:24). Considerations of meter make it probable that "the wife of Heber the Kenite" was inserted into Judg. 5:24 under the influence of Judg. 4.

3. A man or family of the tribe of Judah, founder of Soco (I Chr. 4:18).

4. A family of the tribe of Benjamin (I Chr. 8:17); probably to be identified with Eber in I Chr. 8:12.

Bibliography. M. Noth, *Die israelitischen Personennamen* (1928), p. 222.

H. H. GUTHRIE, JR.

HEBREW hē'broo͞ [עברי; LXX *generally* Ἑβραῖος, ὁ περάτης *in* Gen. 14:13]. The name of the ancestor Eber is probably a construction from the name of the people. A definitive etymology cannot be given. עברי is a term denoting the Israelites and is often used by foreigners (Gen. 39:14; Exod. 1:16; etc.). The word is also used by the Hebrews as a name for themselves (Exod. 1:19, etc.). In such a case "Hebrew" and "Israelite" would be interchangeable. According to other passages, the Hebrews are a separate ethnic group in Canaan, though closely related to the Israelites (*see* ISRAEL, NAMES AND ASSOCIATIONS OF). In Num. 24:23 ff the Hebrews appear as an important nation comparable to Assur. On the possible connection between עברי and *Ḫabiru, see* HABIRU.

According to the genealogical table (Gen. 10:21 ff), the ancestor of the Hebrews is called Eber, son of Shem, and several people are included in his descendants. Of these Abraham, Nahor, and Lot deserve particular mention. According to the OT, Abraham is the ancestor of the Hebrews, Nahor the ancestor of the Arameans, and Lot the ancestor of the Moabites and the Ammonites. In order to illustrate the character of such genealogies, it may be remarked that in Mari texts Nahor occurs as a name of a town. The genealogies are accordingly constructions, and individuals appearing in them may reflect ancient ethnic groups, towns, or countries. In Gen. 14, Abraham is the Hebrew, and he is said to be an ally of the AMORITES having their center at Hebron. According to the traditions of Genesis, Abraham migrated from Ur in Mesopotamia, and these traditions undoubtedly reflect an early migration. Later invasions into Canaan are reflected in the traditions about the exodus from Egypt and the entrance into Canaan under Joshua. Perhaps this invasion from the S may be connected with various groups entering Canaan after the expulsion of the Hyksos from Egypt in the early sixteenth century. On this account several migrations probably took place during more than a century.

The Hebrew language is a branch of Canaanite and Amorite, or rather Canaanite and Amorite are ancestral dialects through the merging of which the growth of biblical Hebrew may be explained. Undoubtedly, non-Semitic languages also influenced the development of Hebrew (cf. the Amarna Letters). Some OT texts, moreover, are written in a language of a more ancient structure than others. Foremost among such texts are the poetic texts of the Psalms and parts of the prophetical books. The poetic structure is much the same as that of Ugaritic. Biblical Hebrew, the closest relative of which is Moabite (Mesha Inscription), is the result of the linguistic development which took place since the time when Ugaritic texts were written. Through the discovery of the MSS in the cave in Qumran NW of the Dead Sea, texts are now known which make it evident that the Hebrew of that time (*ca.* A.D. 100) showed a number of differences from the Hebrew of the MT.

Of linguistic differences between Hebrew and Ugaritic some examples may be mentioned. The following sounds have merged into each other: *ḥ* and *ḫ*, ʾ and *ġ;* furthermore, the sibilants show a number of differences. In Hebrew a definite article is used, though less consistently in poetical texts, which is an archaic feature. The case endings, still occurring in Ugaritic, have been dropped. The verbal system of Hebrew also shows a number of differences, and the use of the tense is a problem which cannot be said to be definitely settled. The fact that the problem of the tenses of Ugaritic has not yet been completely solved makes a brief survey rather unprofitable.

A. HALDAR

HEBREW LANGUAGE. With the exception of the small sections Ezra 4:8–6:18; 7:12-26; Jer. 10:11; Dan. 2:4*b*–7:28, which are in the ARAMAIC LANGUAGE, and a number of odd words and names in a variety of languages, the canonical books of the OT are in the Hebrew language. Since the language of the Arameans is called Aramaic (ארמית), one might have expected the language of the Hebrews to be called Hebrew (עברית), but, instead, it is called the "language [lip] of Canaan" (Isa. 19:18), and Judean (יהודית) the "language of Judah" (Neh. 13:24; Isa. 36:11). In the NT, "in Hebrew" (Ἑβραϊστί, derived from the Aramaic *ʿibhray;* John 5:2; 19:13) and "in the Hebrew dialect" (τῇ Ἑβραΐδι διαλέκτῳ; Acts 21:40) are used to designate both Hebrew and the locally spoken Aramaic, as is Josephus' "language of the Hebrews" (γλῶσσα τῶν Ἑβραίων). "Hebrew" (עברית) is used only in the later rabbinic literature, which even then often prefers to use the phrase "sacred tongue" to distinguish it from the "vulgar tongue." From Ἑβραῖος came the Latin *Hebraeus,* the source of our English word "Hebrew."

1. Hebrew among the Semitic languages. Hebrew is one of the Semitic languages (*see* SEMITES) and shares the general characteristics of that language group in its preference for triliteral roots, the consonantal dominance in its stems, hesitancy to form compound words, and simplicity of sentence structure. More specifically it belongs to the Canaanitish branch of the NW Semitic group, so that its closest connections are with the other members of that branch—viz., Ugaritic, Phoenician, Moabitish, and Edomitish. These Canaanitish languages are doubtless that "tongue of the West land" mentioned in Assyrian inscriptions, and of which we have evidence from names and words in Egyptian inscriptions as early as the nineteenth century B.C., in cuneiform inscriptions from the fifteenth century, and in actual texts from the people themselves in Byblian inscriptions dating perhaps from the eighteenth century B.C., the Ugaritic texts from Ras Shamra of the fourteenth century, and a number of fragmentary inscriptions as yet only partially understood, dating from between the eighteenth and twelfth centuries B.C. The indications are that this Canaanitish was not a homogeneous language, even in those early times, but that as there was an E Canaanitish, of which we have evidence from names in Akkadian, so in Canaan itself there was some difference between the dialects of N Canaanitish and what we may call S Canaanitish. Both the Byblian inscriptions and those of Serabit el-Khadem reveal the fact that Semitic-speaking people in this area were laboring to adapt Egyptian hieroglyphic signs to form a Semitic alphabet, and the Ugaritic texts use an alphabet based on cuneiform signs, so it is certain that Canaanitish was being written long before the Hebrews entered the land.

There have been advocates of a fantastic theory that Hebrew was the autochthonous language of Canaan, but the number of non-Semitic place names, along with the presence of non-Semitic words in the Canaanitish languages, words which would seem to have been adopted from the tongues of the pre-Semitic inhabitants, are sufficient evidence that no Semitic-speaking group was autochthonous there. The biblical tradition is that the ancestors of the Hebrews were associated with the incoming Arameans, whose language belongs to the other branch of the NW Semitic group (*see* ARAMAIC LANGUAGE). These early Hebrews entered the S area of Palestine, settled at first in the hilly districts, and only gradually expanded to the plains. As they settled, they adopted the local dialect of S Canaanitish, modifying it somewhat by their earlier Aramaic speech habits, and the resultant language developed into the Hebrew of historic times.

2. The early monuments of the language. The earliest monumental evidence of it is the Gezer Calendar of perhaps the tenth century B.C., but there are Samarian ostraca of the ninth (or maybe eighth) century, the Siloam Inscription of the eighth century, graffiti and seal and jar-handle inscriptions from the ninth to the sixth centuries, and the Lachish Letters from the sixth century. Some of the early songs and other passages embedded in the OT may have been composed as early as the tenth century B.C., though we have them only in the form in which they were transmitted by much later scribes. In view of the plentiful evidence for early use of writing in Palestine, there is no need to doubt that the Hebrews themselves could have been writing their language as early as the tenth century B.C. It is clear that in the early period there was no homogeneous language, for the Gezer Calendar shows a S dialect which differs somewhat from the N dialect in the ostraca from Samaria, while the story in Judg. 12:4-6 enshrines a memory that northerners could be recognized by details of their pronunciation. It was the Jerusalem dialect, as the dialect of the chief city, which gradually imposed itself as the standard literary dialect.

3. The script. The Byblian inscriptions use over a hundred characters for writing their language, but this is apparently because there are multiple forms for the same sign to indicate differences in pronunciation, just as in Ugaritic there are three signs for the א to indicate its pronunciation with "a" or "i" or "u." Ugaritic also, however, has variant forms for certain signs where no difference of pronunciation is to be assumed, and among its thirty-one signs are three which seem to represent foreign sounds in non-Semitic words. S Arabian uses twenty-nine signs and Arabic twenty-eight, though in Arabic several signs are distinguished from one another only by diacritical points. The earliest Hebrew writing so far known uses a form of the old Canaanitish alphabet of twenty-two characters, such as is used in the Phoenician and Zinjirli inscriptions. That the language had a wider range of sounds than these signs could express is clear from transcriptions in Egyptian, Greek, and Latin, where at times a distinction is kept between *ḥ* and *ẖ*, ʿ and *ġ*, *ś* and *š*, just as in Arabic script, though in the Hebrew script ח has to serve for both *ḥ* and *ẖ*, ע for both ʿ and *ġ*, and ש for both *ś* and *š*. Later the Masoretes used a dot to distinguish *sl* from *s* in the "square script," derived from an Aramaic development of the early Canaanitish script. Another group of consonants—viz., בגדכפת—had a double pronunciation, later indicated by the presence or absence of a dot, distinguishing *b* from *bh*, *g* from *gh*, *d* from *dh*, *k* from *kh*, *p* from *ph*, and *t* from *th*, some of which have separate signs in other Semitic scripts. Reduplicated consonants are not normally reduplicated in the writing. Some of the earlier fragmentary Palestinian inscriptions read downward in Chinese fashion. The Ugaritic inscriptions normally read from left to right, like Akkadian, though odd inscriptions in this script found in Palestine read from right to left. Some of the S Arabian inscriptions, like early Greek inscriptions, read boustrophedon (alternately right to left, left to right), but Hebrew, like the majority of Semitic languages, is written from right to left.

4. Phonetics of Hebrew. The four peculiar features of the consonantal system are: (*a*) the gutturals א, ʾ (for the glottal stop); ה, *h;* ח, for both *ḥ* and *ẖ;* ע, for both ʿ and *ġ;* (*b*) the emphatics, ט, *ṭ*, beside ת, *t;* ק, *q*, beside כ, *k;* צ, *ṣ*, beside ס, *s;* (*c*) the fact that בגדכפת have a double pronunciation according to whether they are or are not preceded by a vowel sound; (*d*) the profusion of sibilants: ס, *s;* ז, *z;* שׁ, *š;* שׂ, *ś;* and צ, *ṣ*. The consonantal system for the written language is shown in Table 1.

Table 1

	Bilabials	Labiodentals	Interdentals	Coronal-Alveolars	Emphatics	Palato-Alveolars	Palatals	Velars	Uvulars	Pharyngals	Glottals
Plosives	p פּ; b בּ			t תּ; d דּ	ṭ ט			k כּ; g גּ	q ק	h ה	ʾ א
Fricatives	w ו	ph פ; bh ב	th ת; dh ד				y י	kh כ; gh ג	ẖ ח; ġ ע	ḥ ח; ʿ ע	
Sibilants				s ס; z ז	ṣ צ	š שׁ	ś שׂ				
Liquids				l ל; r ר							
Nasals	m מ			n נ							

In the ancient form of writing, consonants alone were written, and there was no indication of the vocalization. A first step toward vocalization was the use of ו, י, and ה, and to a lesser extent א, to represent, at first finally and later medially also, the lengthened vowels. This appears at a relatively early date in the inscriptions, apparently as a borrowing from Aramaic, but its use was somewhat haphazard. The Old Greek translation of the OT (LXX) shows that they were not used consistently in the Hebrew text from which that was translated, or at least not distributed in the same way as they are in our printed text. Their use in the Dead Sea Scrolls, and indeed the variants in their use even in relatively late Hebrew MSS, indicate that they were always regarded as a secondary element in the text. Vocalization beyond this was not absolutely necessary when the language was a living language, and so books and newspapers in modern Hebrew, as in Arabic, are printed without vocalization. As Hebrew came to be less and less the language of common intercourse, however, it was needful to have some way of indicating more fully the vocalization, and this was done by the so-called "pointing"—i.e., providing the consonants with small signs, written above, within, or below them, to indicate the vowels with which they are to be pronounced. Three such systems of vocalization are known. The system ordinarily used in printed texts of the OT is the Tiberian system worked out by the Masoretes of the School of Tiberias. It is a predominantly infralinear system, with signs for *a* and *ā*, *e* and *ē*, *i* and *ī*, *o* and *ō*, *u* and *ū*, a sign to mark the vowelless consonant, signs for the helping vowel *Šᵉwâ*, and dots to distinguish *š* from *ś*, the "hard" as against the "soft" pronunciation of *b, g, d, k, p, t*, and reduplication. Two older systems, both supralinear, are the Babylonian and the Palestinian, which appear in certain groups of MSS, and demonstrate that these systems were introduced only gradually, for at first only ambiguous words were pointed—i.e., these helps to the pronunciation were inserted only where they were felt necessary.

All three systems are the work of the schools, and would seem to have appeared first in Mesopotamia, being based on the system of notation worked out there in the fifth century to mark the pronunciation of the Syr. Bible. Thus at best they represent only late tradition as to the pronunciation; the system of Tiberias reached its final form perhaps not much earlier than A.D. 800. Jerome in the fourth century complained of this lack of vocalization in the texts and tried to represent in Latin transcription the way he heard words pronounced by his Jewish teachers. From these transcriptions of Jerome, along with the even earlier transcriptions in the LXX and in the works of Origen, it is possible to work back to some understanding of an earlier pronunciation which proves to be nearer that of classical Arabic. The Tiberian system of signs is given in Table 2.

There was no punctuation in the early writing and often not even word division. In some inscriptions words are separated by a dot or a stroke, but the evidence of the LXX shows that its translators used Hebrew MSS where the writing, if not *scriptio continua*, was at least defective in word division. One

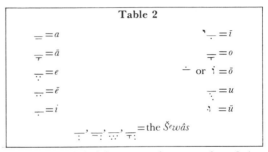

Table 2

◌ַ = *a*	◌ִי = *ī*
◌ָ = *ā*	◌ָ = *o*
◌ֶ = *e*	◌ֹ or וֹ = *ō*
◌ֵ = *ē*	◌ֻ = *u*
◌ִ = *i*	וּ = *ū*

◌ְ, ◌ֲ, ◌ֱ, ◌ֳ = the *Šᵉwâs*

attempt at minimizing some elements of confusion arising from this defective writing was the reserving of a special form of ךםןףץ as final letters, but this came into use only gradually. The Masoretes who worked out the signs for vocalization also worked out another set of signs to serve as marks of punctuation, and yet further signs to guide readers to the proper cantillation of the text. These signs are of late date and are of two kinds, one for the poetical books of the OT and a somewhat different system for the prose books.

5. Grammar. ***a. Historical.*** The early writers of Hebrew would have been as little conscious of grammar as were the pre-Islamic Arab poets. The various attempts at etymologizing in the OT writings are merely folk etymologies and are no evidence of linguistic interest. As any language, however, comes more and more into use as a literary medium, it tends to become "fixed." This is a gradual process, and in the case of Hebrew may be considered to have gained impetus when the Jerusalem dialect, perhaps as early as the United Kingdom under David and Solomon, came to be regarded as the standard form of the language. The body of inscriptional material in Hebrew is so small and fragmentary that any study of the grammatical forms must of necessity be based on the text of the OT. That text, however, has suffered so much at the hands of copyists, as we see not only from the deuterographs in the OT, but from the forms in the Dead Sea Isaiah Scroll (IQ Isa[a]), as well as at the hands of those devoted laborers on the text, the Masoretes, that it is doubtful if we can ever obtain any clear picture of this process of "fixing," since we are never sure which forms were written by the author and which are due to later hands. The great number of variants for certain grammatical forms recorded in our Hebrew grammars suggests there was a period of considerable uncertainty before a standard form imposed itself. It has been pointed out that in Ezek. 13:20-22 there are three different ways of forming the suffix for the second person plural, and in Isa. 32:9-11 there are different ways of forming the feminine plural of the imperative. It is possible that some of the anomalous grammatical forms, and some elements of vocabulary—e.g., the use of שפחה beside אמה for "handmaid," of צעיר beside קטן for "small," of מורה beside תער for "razor," etc.—may be dialectal, but this is not necessarily so, and no attempt has yet succeeded in distinguishing in detail dialectic strata in the text of the OT.

Historical development in the language is discernible. The language of the poetical books, e.g., is often more archaic, preserving older forms and constructions as well as older elements of vocabulary in

Hebrew as it has in other languages. The fact that this poetical archaism may be affected does not detract from its value as evidence for historically older forms. Similarly the language of such books as Ezra-Nehemiah, Chronicles, the Song of Songs, Ecclesiastes, and Esther reveals a later form of Hebrew, showing a development of certain grammatical forms, a use of particles foreign to the older language, an increase of Aramaisms, and a characteristic adoption of elements of vocabulary from surrounding cultures. The literature produced in the period after the close of the canon uses a language which shows even further development—so great, indeed, as to warrant distinguishing Mishnaic Hebrew from biblical Hebrew. Still further development in the post-Mishnaic period and the Middle Ages marks rabbinic Hebrew, while the revival of the language in the nineteenth and twentieth centuries has produced modern Hebrew.

There has been continuous cultivation of Hebrew as a literary language from the tenth century B.C. to modern times, but whether there was continuity as a spoken language is debatable. The incident in II Kings 18:26-36 is clear evidence that it was the spoken language in Jerusalem when Sennacherib was before the city in *ca.* 701 B.C., yet when Ezra after the "return" read the Law to the people, they needed interpreters to make the meaning plain (Neh. 8:2-8). That Hebrew continued to be written in the intertestamental period is evident both from the inscriptional material and from such works as Ecclesiasticus and the nonbiblical material from Qumran, but this gives the impression of being composition in a learned language, not in a vernacular. The language of the Mishna has been cited as evidence that Hebrew was still a spoken language, but even the fact that it uses good Hebrew words not to be found in the OT does not necessarily mean that they were drawn from living speech, for many words from the older language could have been preserved in literary sources, though they do not happen to occur in what has survived to us as the OT. It is not impossible that Hebrew may have continued to be spoken in limited circles of pious Jews on through the Middle Ages, but this would seem to have been in the way in which Latin continued to be spoken as an ecclesiastical language, rather than as a vernacular.

b. Descriptive. The grammatical characteristics of biblical Hebrew may be briefly summarized. All grammatical categories are, of course, merely abstractions invented for the purpose of describing the structure of any language, and the commonly used Latin terminology is unfortunately not very well adapted for the description of Semitic languages. In general Hebrew follows the common Semitic grammatical pattern. Words, which are combined in meaningful arrangements to form sentences, belong to three categories: nouns, which are names of realities, concrete or abstract; verbs, which indicate activities; and particles, which indicate varying types of relationship among nouns and verbs. Particles may suffer modification but not inflection. Nouns and verbs may be inflected by internal modification, or by the affixing of preformatives or afformatives or both. The triradical stem is the essential element for both form and meaning. Thus from the stem *KTB,* concerned with writing, Arabic, e.g., uses *KaTaBa* ("he wrote"), *KaTaBtum* ("ye wrote"), *yaKTuBu* ("he writes"), *naKTuBu* ("we write"), *litaKTuBa* ("that she may write"), *'uKTuBū* ("write ye"), *KaTiB* ("a writer"), *KiTāB* ("a book"), *KuTuB* ("books"), *maKTaB* ("an office"—i.e., a place where writing is done), *maKTaBah* ("a library"), *KuTTāB* ("an elementary school"—where writing is taught), *taKāTaBa* ("he was in correspondence with"), *KuTiBa* ("it was written"), *KuTuBī* ("bookseller"), *iKtiTāB* ("to inscribe one's name in a register"), *KiTāBah* ("a deed or record"), etc., etc. Hebrew follows this general pattern. Two genders are recognized, masculine and feminine; three persons, the speaker, the one addressed, and the one absent; two numbers, singular and plural, though there are still some fragments of the dual remaining.

The noun includes pronouns, adjectives, and the numerals. There is a definite article הַ, derived, apparently, from an old demonstrative. It is prefixed with reduplication, actual or virtual, of the following consonant—e.g., *sûs* = "a horse," but *hassûs* = "the horse"; *'îr* = "a city," but *hā'îr* (for *ha''îr*) = "the city." Personal pronouns have two forms, an independent form and an affixed form which may be used with nouns, verbs, and particles. E.g., *'anî* is the independent pronoun for the first person singular in *'anî hammélekh* ("I am the king"), but it is the suffix *-nî* in *himlakhtánî* ("thou hast made me king"), the suffix *-î* in *malkî* ("my king") or *mālakh 'alāy* ("he ruled over me"), and the prefix *-'e* in *'emlōkh* ("I shall reign"). The interrogative and relative pronouns are particles. The personal pronouns of the third person serve also as demonstratives, but the other demonstratives are particles, though as demonstratives they may take the article. The indefinite pronouns are expressed by common nouns specialized in meaning for this pronominal service.

Nouns were probably at one time inflected for three cases, with the endings *-u, -a, -i,* in the singular, as in Ugaritic and Arabic, but these were early lost, though traces of them are probably to be seen in such words as *Methûšā'ēl* (cf. Akkadian *mutu šā ili*), *layelâ* ("by night"), *ṣāphônâ* ("northward"), and *Penî'ēl* beside *Penû'ēl.* The possessive is indicated mostly by the construct state—i.e., a shortened form of the noun, where shortening is possible—before the pronominal suffixes or before the associated word; e.g., *haddābhār* = "the word," but *debhārô* = "his word" —the word of him—and *debhār hammélekh* = "the king's word." Feminines may be formed from masculines by the suffix *-â*, representing an older *-ath* which appears in the construct state—e.g., *sûs* ("horse"), *sûsâ* ("mare"), *sûsath hazzāqēn* ("the old man's mare"). Some feminines retain the *-th* ending —e.g., *šelîšîth* ("a third"), *'Ammônîth* ("an Ammonitess"). A plural is formed for the masculine by the suffix *-îm,* which is shortened to *-ê* in the construct, and by changing *-ath* to *-ôth* for the feminine—e.g., *sûsîm* ("horses"), *sûsê hazzāqēn* ("the old man's horses"), *sûsôth* ("mares"). The dual ending *-áyim* (construct *-ê*) is for the most part limited to things which go in pairs, and may be added to either a masculine or a feminine form—e.g., *qéren* ("a horn"), *qarnáyim* ("two horns"), *šāphâ* ("a lip"), *šephātháyim* ("two lips"), *śiphthê hazzāqēn* ("the two lips of the old man"). The object may be expressed by the pronominal suffix attached to the verb—e.g., *yišmorkā* ("he will keep thee"); or by the noun as object standing after the verb—e.g., *tišmōr hammiṣwâ* ("thou wilt keep the commandment"); or by the noun as object preceded by the particle *ēth*—e.g., *nišmōr ēth hassḗther* ("we shall keep the secret").

Adjectives behave as do the nouns. Thus *ṭôbh* ("good") forms a feminine singular *ṭôbhâ,* a masculine plural *ṭōbhîm,* and a feminine plural *ṭôbhôth.* Adjectives may be either predicative or attributive—e.g., *ṭôbh hammélekh* ("the king is good"), or *hammélekh haṭṭôbh* ("the good king")—agreeing with their nouns in number and gender. There are no comparative or superlative forms. The comparative is expressed by using *min* ("from") in the sense of "than"—e.g., *ṭôbh min zāhābh* ("better than gold"); and the superlative is expressed by the article—e.g., *sûsô haṭṭôbh* ("his best horse"), *bittî haqqᵉṭannâ* ("my youngest daughter").

There are cardinal, ordinal, and multiplicative numerals. Of the cardinals, "one" is an adjective which follows its noun—e.g., *pār 'eḥādh* ("one ox"), *pārâ 'eḥath* ("one cow"). "Two" is a noun in the dual, masculine *šᵉnáyim,* feminine *šᵉtháyim,* and agrees in gender with the noun to which it stands in construct state—e.g., *šᵉnê pārîm* ("two oxen"), *šᵉthê pārôth* ("two cows"). "Three" to "ten" are nouns which disagree in gender with the nouns to which they stand in construct state—e.g., *šēšeth pārîm*="six oxen," but *šēš pārôth*="six cows." The tens are the plurals of the units—e.g., *šiššîm* ("sixty")—except "twenty," which is the plural of "ten." They are the same for both masculine and feminine. There are special words for "hundred," "thousand," and "ten thousand." There are ordinals form "first" to "tenth" which are adjectives, but beyond "tenth" the cardinal numbers are used for the ordinals also. The multiplicatives are the feminine dual of each numeral—e.g., *šibh'āthâyim* ("sevenfold").

Nouns may be either original or derivative. זאב ("a wolf"), חול ("sand"), שמש ("sun"), are original nouns; but *yābhāl* ("a stream"), *yabbéleth* ("flowing"), *yōbhēl* ("a protracted sound"), *yūbhāl* ("a river"), *yᵉbhûl* and *bûl* ("produce of the field"), *mabbûl* ("inundation"), are all derivatives from a stem *YBL* ("to flow forth"). Thus the participles, infinitives, and gerundives of the verb are properly derived nouns.

The verb is inflected for number, person, and gender. Thus *yikhtōbh* ("he will write"), *tikhtōbh* ("she will write"), *nikhtōbh* ("we shall write"), *tikhtᵉbhū* ("ye [masculine] will write"), *tikhtóbhnā* ("ye [feminine] will write"). There are no true tenses, but there are three states—viz., perfect, imperfect, and imperative. *Kāthábhtî* means "I wrote," "I have written," "I did write"—i.e., the action is complete, finished, perfect. *'Ekhtōbh* means "I write," "I am writing," "I shall write," "I may, might, or ought to write"—i.e., the action is unfinished, incomplete, imperfect. *Kᵉthōbh* means "write," the command to do the action. A distinction is marked between transitives and two types of intransitives (called statives), the one originally indicating a transient and the other a permanent state. There are certain modifications of the imperfect, a somewhat shortened form of the second and third persons (which, however, now for the most part coincides with the ordinary imperfect), for the jussive ("let him write," "may he write," "do not write"), a somewhat lengthened form for the first person for the cohortative ("O let me write"), and an emphatic or energetic form with a suffixed *-n.* This energetic form occurs also in the imperative, which has in addition a somewhat lengthened form for the emphatic imperative.

The characteristic feature of the verb, however, is its system of derived stems to represent aspects of the verbal action. Classical Arabic knows fifteen of these, of which ten are in common use, though neither in Arabic nor in Hebrew are all of them necessarily in use for every verb. Hebrew normally uses seven, all of them fully inflected for number, gender, and person, and forming infinitives and participles. The simple form is the *Qal*—e.g., כתב ("he wrote"). A prefixed *n-* makes the *Niph'al* נכתב, which is properly a reflexive of the *Qal*—e.g., טמא ("he was unclean"), נטמא ("he defiled himself")—though sometimes it denotes reciprocal action—e.g., נלחמו ("they fought one another"); but most commonly it is used as a passive—e.g., נשגב ("he has been exalted"). A reduplicated middle radical gives the *Pi'ēl,* whose general sense is intensive of the *Qal*—e.g., שבר="he broke," but שבר (*shibbēr*)="he broke in pieces"; though it sometimes has a causative sense—e.g., למד ("he learned"), למד (*limmēdh,* "he taught"; i.e., he caused to learn). The *Pu'al* is properly the passive of the *Pi'ēl*—e.g., רום ("he rose"), in the *Pi'ēl* "he raised" and the *Pu'al* "he was raised." The prefix *hith-* makes the *Hithpa'ēl,* whose proper meaning is the reflexive of the *Pi'ēl*—e.g., התרומם ("he exalted himself"). At times, however, it signifies reciprocal action (e.g., ראה="he saw," but תתראו="ye look on one another"); or to make a show of being (e.g., נביא ="a "prophet," and התנבא="he pretended to be a prophet"); or to indicate the action of the verb on oneself (e.g., לקח="he took," but התלקח="he took hold on himself"). A prefixed *hi-* with internal *-i-* makes the *Hiph'īl* whose meaning is causative of the *Qal* (e.g., מלך="he reigned"—i.e., he was king—but המליך="he made someone king"), though sometimes it is declaratory (e.g., צדק="he was righteous," but הצדיק="he justified"—i.e., he declared righteous). Prefixed *ho-* makes the *Hoph'al* which is the passive of the *Hiph'īl*—e.g., המלך ("he was made king"). There are also several rarer derived stems such as *Po'ēl, Po'al, Hithpo'ēl, Pa'lēl, Pe'al'al, Pilpēl, Hithpalpēl,* and some quadriliteral verbs.

Particles are of various kinds. There is an interrogative particle ה to introduce questions, also אי ("where?"), which may be compounded—e.g., איה ("where?"), איך ("how?"), מאין ("whence?"), אנה ("whither?"). The interrogative pronouns are מי ("who?") and מה ("what?"). Some particles are merely connective. The commonest of these is ו ("and"), but there are או ("or"), גם ("also"), אולם ("but"), כי ("because"), כן ("thus, so"), פן ("lest"). The negative particle is לא, and the prohibitive particle אל. The conditional particles are אם, לו, and לולי ("if"). Other particles are prepositional, some of them inseparable from their words—e.g., ל ("to, for"), ב ("in, at, by, with"), כ ("like"); whereas others are independent—e.g., מן ("from"—which, however, may be prefixed), על ("upon"), אל ("unto"), את ("with"),

עַד ("unto"). Another את is used before nouns as the sign of the definite object. Other particles are ejaculatory—e.g., אֲהָהּ ("ah!"), אָח ("alas!"), אוי ("woe!"), הוי ("alas!"), הַס ("hist!"), אֲלוֹ ("behold!"), הֵן ("lo!"). There are no real adverbs in Hebrew. Many nouns in special constructions serve to express what we would express by an adverb, and some of the particles have an adverbial sense—e.g., אָז ("then"), טֶרֶם ("not yet"), and the negative בַּל.

c. Syntax. With this limited grammatical apparatus, it cannot be expected that biblical Hebrew should have the flexibility and adaptability that classical Greek has as an instrument for the expression of thought. It is remarkable, however, with what skill the biblical writers have used the resources of the language. The syntax is comparatively simple, like that of all the older Semitic languages. Sentences are of two kinds, nominal and verbal. In such a sentence as אתם המעט מכל העמים ("Ye are the least of all peoples"), the verb "to be" is understood between the subject and the predicate. Where the verb is expressed, it commonly precedes its subject—e.g., ותוצא הארץ דשא ("And the earth brought forth herbage"); though this is but following the general tendency to give precedence to the predicate—e.g., צדיק יהוה ("Righteous is Yahweh")—except when the subject is to receive the emphasis—e.g., את העם העביר אתו ("The people, them did he make pass over"). Prepositional phrases commonly precede the verb—e.g., "In the beginning God created the heavens." Negative, interrogative, and other particles also commonly precede the verb, but the sentence order normally is predicate, subject, object, words denoting closer specification. The adjective when attributive generally follows its noun and agrees with it in number, gender, and in definiteness or indefiniteness.

There is no verb "to have"; the possessive particles serve instead—e.g., "I shall have peace" is "It will be peaceful for me"; and "They had bitumen for mortar" is "And bitumen was to them for mortar." Hebrew also lacks that useful preposition "of," so common in Aramaic. Instead it sometimes uses the adjective—e.g., "the altar of bronze" is "the bronze altar"; sometimes the preposition מן ("from")—e.g., וגם משרי ישראל ("and also some of the princes of Israel"). Most commonly, however, it is expressed by putting the two nouns in construct—e.g., סוסי המלך ("the-horses-of the king"). There may be several such nouns following one another in construct—e.g., "the-rest-of the-number-of the-bows-of the-warriors-of the-children-of Qedar"—but no attribute can break in between two nouns in construct, nor is it usual for more than one noun to be in construct to the same word. Thus "a great heap of stones" is "heap of stones a great one," and "to the prayer and supplication of thy servant" is "to the prayer of thy servant and to the supplication of him," though exceptionally there occurs "the knowledge and fear of Yahweh" (דעת ויראת יהוה). The great defect of this construction is that it is not possible by it to express the indefiniteness of one member and the definiteness of the other at the same time. מזמור דויד is "the psalm of David," but "a psalm of David" has to be מזמור לדויד (a psalm belonging to David). On the other hand, this construct state permits such expressions as "hill of my holiness" for "my holy hill," "man of the land" for "husbandman," etc., which add much to the variety and elegance of diction.

Sentence formation in early Hebrew was almost exclusively paratactic, whole strings of sentences being connected merely by "and," with very little use of subordinate sentences. The monotony, however, is relieved by skilful use of the possibilities inherent in the telic and atelic sense of the perfect and imperfect, and the variations of meaning suggestible by variations in the use of derived stems. Since the perfect is telic, it can be used for things conceptually finished and complete as well as for those actually so. Thus God says to Abraham: "To thy seed do I give this land," but as God's giving is something already fulfilled, it is: "To thy seed I have given this land." Similarly an abiding state of affairs may be considered as something already complete, so the psalmist says: "I have hated [i.e., I hate] those who seek after vanities." For this reason "I know" is commonly "I have known." Conditional sentences may be regarded as conceptually complete, and so they use the perfect—e.g., אם־לא הביאתיו ("if I do not bring him back"). There is also a characteristic use of the imperative to replace a conditional sentence, as when Joseph says: "This do and live," for "If you do this, you will live." Similarly the imperfect, since it is atelic, may be used for things which have not yet happened—e.g., for "and no herb of the field had as yet sprung up" the writer uses יצמח ("is springing up"); or for things which are conceptually incomplete, though they have happened—e.g., ואד יעלה מן הארץ ("and a mist came up from the earth"). Likewise it may be used for the frequentative—e.g., "and his mother makes [i.e., used to make] for him a little jacket"; and where we would use "ought"—e.g., מעשים אשר לא יעשו ("deeds that ought not to be done").

The most characteristic construction made possible by this telic and atelic sense, however, is that known as the *waw*-conversive construction, which is found also in other Canaanitish languages. In this, since the verb has properly nothing to do with time, but with completeness or incompleteness, it is customary, when a narrative passage begins with an imperfect, to have all the succeeding verbs in the perfect introduced by *waw,* or if it begins with a perfect, to have all the succeeding verbs in the imperfect introduced by *waw.* Thus Gen. 3:22 reads literally: "lest he put forth his hand and has taken also of the tree of life and has eaten and has lived for ever." I.e., the imperfect here denotes the emergent action, and all the other actions are regarded as conceptually complete as results of it. Further variety and ease of diction are given by idiomatic use of infinitives and participles—e.g., וכי ימות מת ("and should anyone die"), or ויצא יצוא ושוב ("and it went to and fro"), or המלך תמלך עלינו ("perhaps thou wouldst reign over us").

6. Poetic forms. Hebrew poetry, like the poetry of other languages, preserved many archaic forms and constructions, along with a definite poetic style and vocabulary. There is no regular rhyming, but there is a rhythmic structure dependent on the accent, and a characteristic feature of parallelism, such as seems to have been used in earlier Canaanitish literature. There is occasional strophic arrangement in poetry, and even some poetical pieces arranged in stanzas with a refrain, but all attempts to find generally applicable strophic schemes in biblical Hebrew have failed. For further details of poetic structure, *see* POETRY.

7. Loan words in Hebrew. There is a not inconsiderable body of borrowed vocabulary in biblical Hebrew—i.e., words which are not originally Hebrew but were borrowed from surrounding peoples, adopted into Hebrew, and used with as little sense of their foreign origin as there is when speakers of English use such words as "piano" or "solo," which were borrowed from Italian. Some of these borrowed words, such as תנור ("oven"), זית ("olive"), רמון ("pomegranate"), בדלח ("bdellium"), ארגון־ארגמן ("purple"), כנור ("harp"), for which no satisfactory etymology has yet been suggested, may be words which came from the pre-Semitic inhabitants of the land, or words borrowed from one or another of the non-Semitic peoples with whom the Hebrews were in contact but of whose languages we have no adequate record. Such words as סוס ("horse"), ברזל ("iron"), פלגש ("concubine"), may belong to this latter class, for it seems probable that שריון ("coat of mail") and ישפה ("jasper") may be of Hurrian origin, and כובע ("helmet") a word taken from Hittite. Other groups of words may be traced with some confidence to the sources from which they came. One group is from Akkadian, in some cases ultimately from Sumerian through Akkadian. Several Hebrew names of months are Akkadian. Words connected with governmental administration, such as מדה and אשכר ("tribute"); סגן and פחה as names for civil officials; רב־מג, תרתן, and רב־שקה for military officers; בלו and מכס ("tax"); שטר and טפסר ("scribe"); הלך ("feudal service"); גרה ("legal currency"); אגרת ("edict"); and the names of such social classes as מסכן ("poor man"), אמן ("artisan"), אכר ("farmer"), נקד ("sheep farmer"), מלח ("seafaring man"), פחר ("potter"), are further examples. Another group is of Egyptian origin. Such luxury articles as שש ("fine linen"), אבנט ("a scarf"), הבנים ("ebony"), טבעת ("a seal"), קסת ("a writer's palette"), כתם ("fine gold"), אח ("a brazier"), משי ("silken material"), צי ("a ship"), אחלמה ("amethyst"), לשם ("opal"), פח ("a metal plate"), are examples. One interesting word is שנהבים ("ivory"), where the שן is the ordinary Hebrew word for "tooth," but הבים represents the Egyptian word for "elephant." Words for other luxury articles seem to have come with the articles from India. Such words are פטדה ("topaz"), כרכם ("saffron"), תכי ("peacock"), אהלות ("aloes"), כרפס ("cotton fabric"), ספיר ("sapphire"). In writings from the Persian period we find words of Iranian origin, such as דת ("law"), פתגם ("edict"), גנזך ("treasury"), גזבר ("treasurer"), אחשדרפן ("satrap"), אדרכון ("a daric"), פרדס ("park, garden"), אחשתרן ("royal courtier"), פרתמים ("nobles"), פתבג ("food ration"), and many others. סרן ("city ruler") seems to be a Philistine word.

8. Later Hebrew. Already in the later books of the OT and in the Hebrew of Ecclesiasticus there is evidence that Hebrew is being written as a learned language (לשון החכמים) rather than as a living vernacular. In part this was because of the increasing spread of Aramaic as the language of common intercourse, but partly it was because the Hebrew which was still in use, and which Rabbi Meir pleads may be preserved as the speech of the pious, had itself undergone great changes. This later form of the language became Mishnaic Hebrew, technically the language of the Mishna which was codified *ca.* A.D. 200, but used for the language in the form it had from *ca.* 200 B.C. to *ca.* A.D. 500, and known mainly from the works of the Tannaim and the early Amoraim. It differs considerably from biblical Hebrew in vocabulary, grammar, style of diction, and even in pronunciation, for the constantly occurring confusion among the consonants—נתאלמלה beside נתארמלה, כאור beside כעור, אזהרה beside הזהרה, טעה beside תעה, קרסם beside כרסם, הפקר beside הבקר, etc. —can only mean that these sounds were no longer as carefully distinguished in pronunciation as they had been in the older language.

There are changes in the pronouns. אנו appears as the plural of אני. אתם is used for both masculine and feminine, while אתן, which nowhere occurs for the second feminine plural, is used at times for the second masculine plural, as הן is for the third masculine plural, while in the suffixed pronouns *-n* commonly occurs instead of *-m* for the third masculine plural. The relative אשר is replaced by the form ש, which occurs sporadically in biblical Hebrew, and this added to the particle ל is used as a new possessive pronoun which can even take pronominal suffixes—e.g., שלי ("mine"—that which is to me). As a demonstrative זו replaces זאת, and by prefixing אי a new interrogative איזה, איזו ("which?") is formed.

In the verb, not only are there many new verbs which are not found in biblical Hebrew, and new meanings given to others which are there, but there is considerable change in the use of the aspects in the derived stems, some verbs not occurring in stems in which they are used in biblical Hebrew, and others in stems in which they are not used there, while some of the stems, particularly the *Pi'ēl*, are greatly extended in range. Most important, however, is the development of new aspects in derived forms. The old *Pu'al* survives for the most part only in the participle, whereas the *Hoph'al* becomes extremely common, and new formations such as the *Shaph'ēl*, *Pil'ēl*, *Pir'ēl*, *Pilpēl*, *Nithpa'ēl*, hardly, if at all, represented in biblical Hebrew, are in frequent use. There is also a significant development of quadriliterals, and even quinqueliterals appear. Variations in the verbal inflections are but few, the most important being the dropping of any distinction between masculine and feminine plural in the endings of the imperfect and imperative. The *waw*-consecutive construction almost completely disappears, but, on the other hand, there is a great extension of the use of the verb "to be" (היה) with participles, and the use of participles with the infinitive, or the participle with attached pronouns, to express varieties of verbal action.

In the nouns there is considerable expansion in the matter of derived forms and in the use of diminutives. The *-th* feminine ending and the *-īn* plural ending, which occur occasionally in biblical Hebrew, are much more commonly used, and there is a somewhat fuller use of the dual. In particles, again, there is much extension of use, especially in combinations used to take the place of adverbs. Such common particles as כי, פן, גם, almost pass out of use, but new particles such as שמא, אלא, and an extended use of

שׁ are noticeable. The את, which in biblical Hebrew indicated the definite object, has become a demonstrative and can take the suffixed pronouns.

The vocabulary was greatly enriched in this period by borrowings from Aramaic and from Greek and Latin, as well as by new formations from old roots. In part this was needed because of the very different nature of the documents that had to be written in Mishnaic Hebrew. To a large extent these were concerned with matters of everyday life in an environment culturally different from that of the biblical writers, and there were no biblical words for many of these matters. To some extent writers might draw on old Hebrew vocabulary not represented in our remains of biblical Hebrew, and at times they could use biblical words in new meanings, but often they were driven to form new words, or to borrow them from the surrounding cultures.

This Hebrew developed even further in the succeeding period to become rabbinical Hebrew, which, for the most part, was a literary medium among people who spoke many different vernaculars. In this period the language was greatly influenced by Arabic, under which influence its poetry even developed quantitative meters and used rhyme.

Bibliography. General: L. Metmann, *Der hebräische Sprache; ihre Geschichte und lexikalische Entwicklung seit Abschluss des Kanons* (1904). H. Torczyner, "Hebräische Sprache," *Encyclopaedia Judaica,* vol. VII (1931), cols. 1,031-66. E. A. Speiser, "The Pronunciation of Hebrew Based Chiefly on Transliterations in the Hexapla," *JQR,* XVI (1926), 343-82; XXIII (1933), 233-65; XXIV (1933), 9-46. D. Diringer, *Le iscrizioni antico-ebraiche palestinesi* (1934). A. Sperber, "Hebrew Based upon Greek and Latin Transliterations," *HUCA,* XII-XIII (1937/38), 103-274. H. Torczyner, *The Lachish Letters* (1938). A. Goetze, *Accent and Vocalism in Hebrew* (1939). Z. S. Harris, *Development of the Canaanite Dialects* (1939). H. Torczyner, *Te'udhoth Lakish* (1940). A. Sperber, "Hebrew Based upon Biblical Passages in Parallel Transmission," *HUCA,* XIV (1939), 153-249; "Hebrew Phonology," *HUCA,* XVI (1941), 415-82. S. Moscati, *L'Epigrafia ebraica antica* (1951); *Stato e problemi dell'epigrafia ebraica antica* (1952). F. M. Cross and D. N. Freedman, *Early Hebrew Orthography* (1952).

Poetry: G. B. Gray, *The Forms of Hebrew Poetry* (1915). A. Brung, *Die Rhythmus der alttestamentlichen Dichtung* (1930). T. H. Robinson, "Some Principles of Hebrew Metrics," *ZAW,* XIII (1936), 28-43.

Grammars: F. E. König, *Historischkritisches Lehrgebäude der hebräischen Sprache* (3 vols.; 1881-97). W. Gesenius, *Hebräische Grammatik* (1909; English trans. A. E. Cowley, 1910). Bauer and Leander, *Historische Grammatik der hebräischen Sprache des Alten Testaments* (1918-22). P. Joüon, *Grammaire de l'hébreu biblique* (1923). G. Bergsträsser, *Hebräische Grammatik,* I (1918); II (1929). A. Sperber, "Hebrew Grammar: A New Approach," *JBL* (1943), pp. 137-262. M. Lambert, *Traité de grammaire hébraïque* (1946). O. Grether, *Hebräische Grammatik* (2 vols.; 1951).

Grammatical problems: G. R. Driver, *Problems of the Hebrew Verbal System* (1936). M. Sekine, "Das Wesen des althebräischen Verbalausdrucks," *ZAW,* LVIII (1940/41), 133-41. E. Brønno, *Studien über hebräische Morphologie* (1943). F. R. Blake, *A Resurvey of Hebrew Tenses* (1951). V. Christian, *Untersuchungen zur Laut- und Formenlehre des Hebräischen* (1953).

Syntax: S. R. Driver, *A Treatise on the Use of the Tenses in Hebrew* (1881). A. Müller, *Outlines of Hebrew Syntax* (1882). C. Brockelmann, *Hebräische Syntax* (1956).

Lexicons: F. Brown, S. R. Driver, and C. A. Briggs, *A Hebrew and English Lexicon of the OT* (1906). G. Dalman, *Aramäisch-neuhebräisches Handwörterbuch zu Targum, Talmud und Midrasch* (1938). F. Buhl, *Wilhelm Gesenius' hebräisches und aramäisches Handwörterbuch über das Alte Testament* (1949). E. Ben Yehuda, *Thesaurus totius Hebraitatis et veteris et recentioris* (15 vols.; 1908-53). Koehler and Baumgartner, *Lexicon in Veteris Testamenti Libros* (1953).

Concordances: G. Lisowsky, *Concordantiae Veteris Testamenti* (1955). S. Mandelkern, *Biblorum sacrorum Concordantiae* (1955).

Script: S. Yeivin, *Tôldhôth hakkthābh ha'ibhrî* (1938). G. R. Driver, *Semitic Writing, from Pictograph to Alphabet* (1954).

Mishnaic Hebrew: A. Geiger, *Lehr-und Lesebuch zur Sprache der Mischnah* (1845). J. H. Weiss, *Mishpat lshôn hammishnâ* (1867). M. H. Segal, *A Grammar of Mishnaic Hebrew* (1927; Hebrew ed., 1936).

Modern Hebrew: E. M. Lipschutz, *Vom lebendigen Hebräisch* (1920). S. Spiegel, *Hebrew Reborn* (1930). Yardeni and Rabinowitz, *The Grammar of Our Language* (1943). Z. Har Zahav, *Diqdûq hallāshôn ha'ibrîth* (3 vols.; 1951—). A. Jeffery

HEBREW RELIGION, HISTORY OF. The religion of Israel was a phenomenon unique in the ancient world. First appearing coincident with the emergence of the Israelite people in the thirteenth century B.C., it had a history of approximately a thousand years before issuing in the Judaism of the immediate pre-Christian centuries. Though this history brought a great development of ideas, and involved many changes, it did not constitute an evolution from lower forms of religion to higher, as it was once the custom to describe it. Israel's faith retained throughout the essential and distinctive character with which it began. For fuller discussion and other opinions, *see bibliography; see also* ISRAEL, HISTORY OF.

- A. The religion of the patriarchs
- B. The formative period
  - 1. Sources of knowledge
  - 2. The covenant society
    - *a.* The Exodus and the covenant at Sinai
    - *b.* The covenant form
    - *c.* The obligations of covenant
    - *d.* Covenant and promise
  - 3. The God of early Israel
    - *a.* Yahweh the God of Israel
    - *b.* Yahweh alone is God
    - *c.* The nature of Israel's God
  - 4. The institutions of early Israel
    - *a.* The tribal league
    - *b.* The central shrine and its clergy
    - *c.* The cult
    - *d.* Covenant law and its development
- C. From the judges to the eighth century
  - 1. The rise of the monarchy and its significance
    - *a.* Organization of life under the crown
    - *b.* Cultural adaptation
    - *c.* Social and economic changes
    - *d.* The new religious center in Jerusalem
  - 2. Religion in the Divided Monarchy
    - *a.* Religion and the state in Judah
    - *b.* Religion and the state in Israel
    - *c.* Paganizing tendencies in Israel
    - *d.* Social disintegration
- D. From the eighth century to the fall of Jerusalem
  - 1. The first of the classical prophets
    - *a.* The earlier prophets
    - *b.* Prophets of the eighth century in Israel
    - *c.* Prophets of the eighth century in Judah
  - 2. The reform movement in Judah
    - *a.* The reform of Hezekiah
    - *b.* The reform of Josiah

A. *THE RELIGION OF THE PATRIARCHS.* Though Israel's distinctive religion began with Moses, it was prepared for by that of the PATRIARCHS. These were part of a seminomadic migration which brought new population to Palestine in the first half of the second millennium B.C. Their religion, as seen from evidence in Genesis and from extrabiblical texts both contemporary and later, was of a distinctive sort quite different from the official paganisms of the surrounding lands. Their God was the God of the clan, the personal God of the clan chief. This may be seen from certain archaic names for the Deity in Genesis —e.g., "the God [perhaps 'Shield,' as in 15:1] of Abraham" (e.g., 31:53); "the Fear [properly 'Kinsman'] of Isaac" (31:42); "the Mighty One [Champion] of Jacob" (49:24). It is also illustrated in early personal names such as Abiram, Ahiram, Abiezer, Ahiezer, Abimelech, Ahimelech, and the like, in which the God is spoken of as the "(divine) father/brother" of the worshiper. The patriarchal God was the unseen head of the clan, whom the clan father had undertaken to serve and to trust, and whose promises of the blessings of land and seed (e.g., Gen. 15) he had received. To this God, whose cult was simple and presided over by the clan father himself, the clan gave supreme, if not exclusive, devotion.

As the patriarchs entered Palestine, their cults were carried on at local shrines, and their gods no doubt identified with the gods worshiped there. The patriarchs worshiped God under the name El, which is the name of a Canaanite god but also a general word for "the god." Such names as El-Shaddai (Gen. 17:1; Exod. 6:3; etc.), El-Elyon (Gen. 14:18), El-Olam (Gen. 21:33), El-Ro'i (Gen. 16:13), are instanced (*see* GOD, NAMES OF). While these gods were worshiped locally, the patriarchal deity was no local numen but the patron deity of the clan over whose fortunes he watched. As the patriarchal stock passed into Israel, whether via Egypt or through later absorption, their gods were identified with Yahweh (cf. Exod. 6:3) and their traditions (*see* TRADITION, ORAL) normalized as those of all Israel. Their religion, especially with its sense of an intimate bond between God and people supported by covenant and promise, profoundly influenced the faith of Israel. The pattern of the patriarchal covenant, different from that of Sinai and no mere back-projection of it, also lived on. It is probable that much of Israel's legal tradition (*see* § B4*d below*), strikingly akin to that of Mesopotamia, came to her through her own patriarchal ancestors rather than through Canaanite mediation.

B. *THE FORMATIVE PERIOD.* Israel's religion began, as Israel did, in the events of the Exodus and Sinai. Its founder was MOSES. Though it adapted practices of pre-Mosaic origin, and borrowed others, its distinctive character is evident from the beginning.

1. Sources of knowledge. Since the Pentateuchal documents are all of later date (*see* BIBLICAL CRITICISM 1; PENTATEUCH), it is necessary to guard against anachronism in describing the religion of earliest Israel. Studies in shorter units of tradition have, however, revealed a considerable body of material apparently stemming from Israel's formative period (tenth century and before). This includes a number of cultic confessions (Deut. 6:20-25; 26:5-10*a;* Josh. 24:1-13) and poems (e.g., Gen. 49; Exod. 15:1-18; the poetry of Num. 23–24; Deut. 33; Judg. 5; Pss. 29; 68; etc.). Moreover, both the Decalogue (*see* TEN COMMANDMENTS) in its original form and the Book of the Covenant (Exod. 21–23; 34) go back to the early period, as does the basis of the laws of D and, in part, of H; and the parent of J and E, containing the major themes of both, was also in existence in the period of the Judges. (*See* PENTATEUCH.) From material of this sort a fair picture of Israel's religion in the formative period may be drawn. While one cannot always separate pre- from post-Conquest features, there is little reason to assume that Israel's faith fundamentally altered its character with that event.

2. The covenant society. Israel's religion did not center in an idea of God, but in the memory of a historical event as interpreted by faith, and in response to that event in covenant. This event was the exodus from Egypt.

a. The Exodus and the covenant at Sinai. Whatever the events in detail, there can be little doubt that a group of Hebrews, who had been held as state slaves in Egypt, were led thence by Moses at the behest of a "new" God, Yahweh, to the accompaniment of happenings so marvelous that they were never forgotten. This rescue was interpreted as an act of Yahweh's unmerited favor calling a people from bondage to himself. There is also no reason to doubt—again, whatever the details—that these Hebrews then moved to Sinai, where, in solemn ceremony, they made covenant with Yahweh to be his people. A new society was thus formed where none had been before, in which the basis of obligation was that covenant response to the favor of Yahweh already experienced. Israel's religion was founded upon belief in her ELECTION by Yahweh and her COVENANT with him. Though both notions were refined in course of time, both were basic from the beginning.

b. The covenant form. The covenant form, best seen in the Decalogue, is an ancient one which has its closest parallel in certain Hittite suzerainty treaties of a day slightly before that of Moses. In these the Great King addresses his vassals and, reminding them of his benevolent acts which obligate them to gratitude (cf. the preamble of the Decalogue), lays down the stipulations which he imposes and which they are to accept (cf. the body of the Decalogue). These typically include the prohibition of foreign relations save through the Great King, and of enmity with others of his vassals. Response to the call to arms is required (Judg. 5:13-18, 23; 21:8-12); and unlimited trust is to be reposed in the Great King.

Vassals are to appear before him annually with tribute (Deut. 26:5-10*a;* I Sam. 1:21) and are to submit all controversies with other vassals to him (Deut. 17:8-13[?]). A copy of the treaty is to be placed in the shrine and periodically read publicly (Deut. 10:5; 31:9-13). Sanctions are supplied by a series of BLESSINGS AND CURSINGS invoking the gods (Deut. 28). Such features as these illustrate both the antiquity of the covenant form and something of its meaning: Israel began as a federation of clans, bound to live in sacred truce with one another under the suzerainty of Yahweh.

c. The obligations of covenant. The covenant was no bargain between equals, but a vassal's acceptance of the overlord's terms. Early Israel was a primitive theocracy in which Yahweh was king. The symbols of her cult—e.g., the ARK OF THE COVENANT, which was Yahweh's throne (Num. 10:35-36); Moses' rod; the URIM AND THUMMIN—were the symbols of his rule. The notion of the kingship of Yahweh is thus, in its roots, quite old (e.g., Exod. 15:18; Num. 23:21; Judg. 8:22-23; Ps. 68:24). Israel had come into being through her covenant acceptance of Yahweh's favor and rule; covenant could, therefore, be maintained only so long as the Overlord's stipulations were met. The heart of these was (cf. the two parts of the Decalogue) that Israel honor Yahweh and have nothing to do with any other god, and that she strictly obey his law in all dealings with the covenant brother. These stipulations explain the direction of the later prophetic attack on the national sin, and also the importance of law in Israel at all periods of her history.

d. Covenant and promise. A note of HOPE and PROMISE is also primitive. This had been an original element in the religion of the patriarchs, from which background the nucleus of Israel had come. And Yahweh's call to Israel in Egypt had come precisely as one to a new future and to hope. Moreover, the covenant form itself, though laden with obligation, carried the implicit assurance that, obligation met, the Overlord's favor would be continued. The earliest poems (*see* § B1 *above*) reveal a robust confidence that Israel will be assured her land, given all material blessings, made a great people victorious over all her foes: who blesses her will be blessed, who curses her will be cursed (Num. 24:9; cf. Gen. 12:3). This is in no sense an eschatology (*see* ESCHATOLOGY OF THE OT); but the seeds of it lie here.

3. The God of early Israel. Though Israel's religion did not center in a doctrine, her notion of God was nevertheless unique from the beginning (*see* GOD, OT).

a. Yahweh the God of Israel. The God of Israel was called Yahweh. Though there is no agreement as to the meaning of this name, it is probably best taken as a causative of the verb "to be," and part of a formula (cf. Exod. 3:14): "He Causes to Be What Comes into Existence," which has parallels in Egyptian texts. In the course of time the original meaning was lost, and Yahweh became merely a proper name; but the name shows that Israel's God was from the beginning no local nature deity, but a high God of cosmic domain. Whether or not a God called Yahweh was worshiped before Moses—say in Jethro's clan—is unknown. This is not impossible, but the evidence is indecisive; the name Yahweh is nowhere attested before Moses. But even if such a cult existed, a new character was imparted to it by Moses which made it a new thing. The religion of Yahweh, as we know it, began with him.

b. Yahweh alone is God. From the beginning Israel was forbidden to worship any god but Yahweh (e.g., Exod. 20:3; 22:20). Though she repeatedly did so, this was never excused or condoned: Yahweh is a jealous God who brooks no rival (Exod. 20:5). And, so marvelous were his acts, Israel did not conceive of him as having any rival. He created the universe quite alone (Gen. 2:4*b*-25); he has no pantheon, no consort (the Hebrew lacks a word for "goddess"), and no progeny. For this reason, Israel created no myth (*see* MYTH, MYTHOLOGY [OT]), nor borrowed any except to devitalize it. Her earliest poems (e.g., Exod. 15:1-18) show that she was emancipated from mythopoeic thought from the beginning. Yahweh was, of course, at all periods thought of as surrounded by his heavenly host (*see* HOST OF HEAVEN), his "holy ones" (e.g., Deut. 33:2; Ps. 29:1); and at times there was the temptation to accord these beings worship. But this was always censured. In Israel's faith there was place for but one God; even the gods of the patriarchs survived only in identification with Yahweh, not as subordinate deities.

To ask if this was monotheism is to pose a question foreign to the thought of ancient man. Early Israel did not explicitly deny that other gods existed; indeed, there are passages where their existence is naïvely assumed (e.g., Exod. 18:11; Judg. 11:24; I Sam. 26:19)—though this occurs in late passages as well (e.g., II Chr. 2:5) and may be in part an accommodation of language. Yet Israel's faith was not a mere monolatry or a henotheism, for, if the existence of other gods was not denied, neither was their status as gods tolerantly granted. To Israel only one God was *God;* the other gods, deprived of part in creation, function in the cosmos, power over events, and cult, were robbed of all that made them gods—in short, were rendered nonentities, were "undeified." Though the full implications of it were not drawn until much later, in this practical sense Israel's faith was monotheistic from the beginning.

c. The nature of Israel's God. Yahweh differed from the pagan gods of the ancient world in his essential nature. Though conceived of anthropomorphically, no image of him (*see* IDOL) could be made (Exod. 20:4). Nor was he identified with any heavenly body, or natural force or function. Though manifesting his power through nature (cf. the poems under § B1 *above*), no one aspect of nature was more characteristic of him than another. And, though he conferred the blessings of fertility (e.g., Gen. 49:25-26; Deut. 33:13-16), he was in no sense a fertility god. In Israel's faith nature, though not lifeless, was robbed of personality. It was not, in fact, primarily in the repeatable events of nature, but in unrepeatable historical events, that Yahweh manifested himself; and in these events, unlike the pagan gods, he acted purposively. These purposive acts of Yahweh were the basis of Israel's obligation to him. Israel's religion, therefore, offered no ritual technique for manipulating the unseen powers of nature for selfish ends. Her God was no pagan maintainer of *status quo* to be appeased by ritual, but one who had called her from bondage to a new future as his people, and who demanded of her obedience. Sacrifice, important as it was, could thus never properly be regarded as a mere technique. And, though it was popularly practiced, Israel had no place for magic (e.g., Exod. 20:7; 22:18; I Sam. 28:9; *see* DIVINATION; MAGIC).

4. The institutions of early Israel. Israel's faith expressed itself in certain tangible institutions. Chief among these was her tribal league, with its central shrine, its cult and sacred occasions, and, above all, its law.

a. The tribal league. Israel began her history as a league of twelve tribes (*see* TRIBE). It was an organization not unlike the amphictyony of a somewhat later period in Greece and Italy, or the league of Arab clans formed by Mohammed. Though reaching definitive form after the Conquest as new elements—some Canaanite, some of the stock of Israel's own ancestors—were absorbed (cf. Josh. 24), it was an expression of the covenant pattern of Sinai. Israel was a sacral league of clans united in covenant with Yahweh. There was no machinery of statehood whatever. The clans enjoyed complete independence, being obligated only to assist in the care of the central shrine and to respond to the call to arms. In times of danger there would arise a man endowed with the divine Spirit (e.g., Judg. 3:10; 11:29), a charismatic leader called a JUDGE, who would rally the clans against the foe. But the authority of the judge was not permanent, and in no case hereditary. He was in no sense a king. To early Israel the institution of kingship was foreign and repugnant (cf. Judg. 8:22-23; 9:7-15). The tribal league persisted for some two hundred years, and in it Israel's distinctive institutions gained normative form.

b. The central shrine and its clergy. The focal point of the league was the tent shrine (*see* TABERNACLE) housing the ark of the covenant. A heritage of the wilderness days, it came finally to rest in SHILOH, where it remained as long as the tribal league endured. There the clans would gather on feast days to seek the presence of Yahweh and renew their allegiance to him. Other shrines, many of ancient origin, existed and were tolerated; but Shiloh was the heart of the covenant league. Though a permanent structure may have been built there (I Sam. 1:9; 3:3), the tent tradition persisted (II Sam. 6:17; 7:6-7). This shrine had a clergy (*see* PRIESTS AND LEVITES) claiming Levitic lineage, which was apparently hereditary (I Sam. 1-3). Though the later theory that all cultic personnel must be of the clan Levi did not then obtain, Levites enjoyed a great prestige, no doubt because Moses himself was of that clan (cf. Judg. 17:7-13; 18:30). But since "Levite" could also refer to a class (i.e., one pledged by vow), men of various clans who were of this class came gradually to be reckoned to Levi (e.g., SAMUEL 1; cf. I Sam. 1:1; I Chr. 6:28).

c. The cult. As was true of all ancient religions, Israel's cult involved various kinds of sacrifice (*see* SACRIFICE AND OFFERINGS). Since our major source (Lev. 1-7) applied to the later temple, a precise description of early sacrificial ritual is impossible. In the wilderness it was certainly simple, and scarcely central, though it cannot be argued (e.g., from Jer. 7:21-23; Amos 5:21-27) that there was none. Since, as archaeology has shown, Hebrew sacrifice had many parallels with Canaanite practice, we may assume that as Israel entered Palestine and absorbed elements sedentary there, together with their shrines and cultic traditions, her worship was enriched by borrowing. Though this brought the danger that pagan rites, and a pagan theory of sacrifice, would creep in, borrowing was not indiscriminate (e.g., human sacrifice, fertility rites, the notion of sacrifice as food for the god or a thing *opus operatum,* were foreign to official Israelite theory), and what was borrowed was given the rationale of Yahwistic faith.

But at the heart of Israelite cultus was not sacrifice, but certain great annual feasts (Exod. 23:14-17; 34:18-24): PASSOVER; WEEKS; Ingathering (*see* BOOTHS, FEAST OF; *see also* FEASTS AND FASTS). All these were older than Israel and, except for Passover, of agricultural origin. But Israel gave them a new interpretation, making them no longer nature festivals but celebrations of Yahweh's historic acts in the Exodus. Though these feasts were probably celebrated locally as well as at Shiloh, there is evidence for a great annual feast at the central shrine at the New Year (Judg. 21:19; I Sam. 1:3, 21), when the tribesmen would bring their tribute to Yahweh. Probably in connection with this, perhaps every seven years (Deut. 31:9-13), there would be a ceremony of covenant renewal when Yahweh's acts were recited and his law read, and allegiance to him renewed. Israel's cult was thus no "history-less" maintainer of material well-being, but precisely a reminder of history. In connection with it, her sacred traditions (*see* TRADITION, ORAL) were repeated and given normative form.

d. Covenant law and its development. Since Israel's existence was based on her covenant with Yahweh, covenant law was a central factor in her life from the beginning (*see* LAW IN THE OT). Her legal tradition began with Moses and reached normative form in the earliest period; the Book of the Covenant (Exod. 21-23; 34) represents the legal practice of the tribal league.

Laws fall into two general categories as regards form: casuistic ("if a man—," etc.) and apodictic ("thou shalt [not]"). The former have numerous parallels in the Mesopotamian law codes, while the latter—best seen in the Decalogue—are Israel's distinctive contribution and state the basic stipulations of covenant.

We may assume that as need arose to apply these stipulations to tangible situations, Israel drew upon the legal tradition of her environment. Most of this borrowing was done soon after the Conquest, and probably from elements of the same stock as her ancestors who had been absorbed by her, rather than from her Canaanite neighbors. But such borrowing was not indiscriminate; and the whole was made an expression of Israel's covenant faith.

Law was normally administered by the village elders in accordance with tradition. The priest had the duty of deciding hard cases (cf. Deut. 17:8-13), whether by oracle or by ordeal (Num. 5:11-31), or from superior knowledge of the law; he had also the duty of giving instruction on the basis of the law. The "minor judges" (Judg. 10:1-5; 12:8-15) may have been men chosen by the representatives of the clans to interpret the law as it concerned all Israel, and to adjudicate disputes between clans (*see* JUDGE).

C. *FROM THE JUDGES TO THE EIGHTH CENTURY.* This was a period of adjustment to new situations, of the disintegration of old patterns and the intrusion of new ones. Israel's religion was involved and, to some degree, its essential character threatened. Of the various forces in play, none was more significant than the supersession of the tribal league by the monarchy.

1. The rise of the monarchy and its significance. Israel was driven to set up a monarchy when the tribal league was destroyed by the Philistines late in the eleventh century (I Sam. 4). The change brought her material glory, but also an inner transformation of her society which affected her religion profoundly.

a. Organization of life under the crown. The monarchy brought the end of the old order. The first king, SAUL, a leader of the old type who was made king by popular acclamation (I Sam. 11), effected no essential change in Israel's structure. Because of his own instability, and his inability to overcome tribal independence and tensions between the old order and the new, he failed. But DAVID succeeded. First becoming king over Judah with Philistine consent and popular acclaim (II Sam. 2:1-4), he was later acclaimed king by the N tribes as well in solemn covenant (II Sam. 5:1-3); all Israel was thus united in the king's person. Seizing JERUSALEM, a city thitherto Canaanite, as his capital (II Sam. 5:6-10), he also conquered the other Canaanite cities of Palestine and incorporated them in the state, and subsequently won a sizable foreign empire. Since the state was created by David and centered in his person, it was necessary that a son succeed him—which SOLOMON did. The principle of charismatic leadership thus gave way to dynastic succession. As the state was progressively organized under the crown, the tribal system became of less practical importance, till finally (I Kings 4:7-19) it was replaced by twelve administrative districts. Though the tribal league lived on as a sacral tradition, the basis of social obligation was no longer Yahweh's covenant, but the state. A certain weakening of the covenant idea was inevitable.

b. Cultural adaptation. Adaptation had been going on since the Conquest first brought Israel into contact with the superior material culture of CANAAN. As she adopted the agrarian life, she was tempted to take up the practice of the fertility cult (*see* FERTILITY CULTS; BAAL [DEITY]), or to regard Yahweh as a god of fertility. This was especially so since she had absorbed into her structure peoples sedentary in the land, both Canaanites and others who were partly Canaanite in culture. Though these became worshipers of Yahweh, their local cults continued. There was thus always the danger that Israel's faith would assimilate beliefs and practices incompatible with it.

The monarchy speeded up the process. Jerusalem had been a Canaanite city with an ancient cultic tradition. Moreover, David and Solomon incorporated thousands of Canaanites into the state, most of whom became no more than nominal Yahwists, if that. As Solomon made treaties with surrounding lands, sealing them by marriage, the cults of his foreign wives were fostered in Jerusalem (I Kings 11:1-8). Most profitable of these treaties was that with TYRE, center of Canaanite culture. Solomon's TEMPLE, built by Canaanite architects (I Kings 7:13-14) on a Canaanite pattern, introduced in its symbolism many features thitherto foreign to Israel. Further, since Israel had no tradition of monarchy, she was forced to model the institutions of state in part on forms borrowed from outside, possibly via Canaanite mediation (*see* KING). Though these features were harmonized with the national religion, rites and concepts theretofore unknown were introduced. Withal, a reduction of stress on the events of the Exodus and Sinai as the foundations of faith and society was inevitable.

c. Social and economic changes. These were both sudden and drastic. Early Israel had been a nation of small farmers with little commerce and less industry. A clan society with none of the feudalism of the Canaanite states, she had no ruling class, no social distinctions or extremes of wealth and poverty. This was all changed. Solomon's commercial and industrial ventures, though state monopolies, raised the living standard of the nation and allowed some, especially by contrast, to grow rich. The court grew very rich. As royal projects drew people to the cities, urban population grew apace, with an attendant weakening of tribal ties and traditions. Moreover, the demands of state required a burden of taxation which bore heavily. Plagued by a chronic fiscal dilemma, Solomon ultimately drafted his subjects into forced labor for the state (I Kings 5:13-18)—a wholly "un-Israelite" measure. As life was regulated under the crown, and as Canaanites with a feudal background and no conception of the covenant order were absorbed, notions of aristocracy and class distinction began to intrude (I Kings 12:1-15). The solidarity of Israelite society was weakened.

d. The new religious center in Jerusalem. However great the break, David sought to link his state with the old order. By installing the ark (*see* ARK OF THE COVENANT) in Jerusalem (II Sam. 6), and by appointing ABIATHAR of the house of ELI as one of its two chief priests (II Sam. 20:25; cf. I Sam. 14:3; 22:20), he was able to advertise the state as the patron and protector of the national religious heritage. Solomon's temple added to its prestige. Although some (II Sam. 7:5-7) thought the temple a dangerous innovation, and although other shrines were freely tolerated, the link that was to bind the future of Israel's faith to Jerusalem had been forged. The temple was both the national shrine of the Israelite people and a royal installation, the dynastic shrine of the house of David. It was supported and controlled by the state (I Kings 2:26-27). While kingship in Israel did not follow patterns observable elsewhere in the ancient world, the KING played a central role in the cult (e.g., I Kings 8). An official state cult had begun. The dogma was developed that Yahweh had chosen Zion as his seat and promised to David an eternal dynasty (e.g., II Sam. 7:8-17; 23:1-7; I Kings 11:13, 32). This provided the monarchy with a sacral basis and harmonized it with Israel's ancestral faith.

The temple cult was early enriched as regards its SACRIFICES and FEASTS, and as regards MUSIC and psalmody (*see* POETRY [HEBREW]; PSALMS, BOOK OF; WORSHIP IN THE OT). Literary activity flourished as the traditions of the past were collected and written down. Works such as that of the Yahwist (*see* J) and the "Court History of David" (II Sam. 9–20: I Kings 1–2) were composed approximately in the reign of Solomon, while other tales of the heroic past were also given written form (*see* JUDGES, BOOK OF; SAMUEL, BOOKS OF).

2. Religion in the Divided Monarchy. Because of economic and sectional grievances, and because of tension between the old order and the new, the N tribes rebelled when Solomon died, and thereafter went their own way. Religious developments in the two states in some respects ran parallel, in others followed entirely different patterns.

a. Religion and the state in Judah. Throughout her history Judah remained loyal to the house of David. David, who had brought the nation to its Golden Age, in which the promise inherent in the national religion seemed all but fulfilled, made an unforgettable impression. Later generations idealized him and desired no future save in terms of a restoration of the glories of his rule.

The theological basis of the state was Yahweh's choice of Zion and David. Reaffirmed in the cult (e.g., Pss. 2; 72; 89; 110; 132), this became the national dogma. Each new KING was hailed at his accession as Yahweh's "son" (Ps. 2:7) whom Yahweh would defend. Though he was required to do justice (Ps. 72:1-4, 12-14) on pain of chastisement, the dynasty was eternal (Ps. 89:1-4, 19-37; II Sam. 7:12-16) and would triumph over all its foes (Pss. 2:10-11; 72:8-11; 110:5-6).

This dogma, plus the prestige of the temple with its Levitical tradition, gave to Judah a remarkable stability and helped to guard her from extremes of apostasy. Yet it meant a further shift from the ancient notion of covenant. The Davidic covenant was of a different type from that of Sinai, and in tension with it. In it—somewhat as in the patriarchal covenant—the relationship of God and nation was unconditional and based on promise. To suggest that the nation could fall was to suggest that Yahweh could break covenant. An obscuring of the reciprocal obligations of covenant was inevitable; stress shifted from obedience to covenant law to meticulous celebration of the ritual. As religion tended to become the maintainer of the national well-being, a subtle paganizing of Israel's faith entered in.

Yet it was in this official cult that hope and promise were given definitive form. The royal ideal, though cruelly frustrated by circumstance, was not surrendered but intensified. The hope persisted that a future king, perhaps the next one, would make the promises actual. As the element of promise indigenous to Israel's faith was shaped by the dynastic ideal, there were sown the seeds of the hope of the MESSIAH (*see also* ESCHATOLOGY OF THE OT).

b. Religion and the state in Israel. The N state began without dynastic tradition or official cult. Nor was it ever permanently successful in establishing a dynasty; the notion of hereditary rule was in tension with the older tradition of the tribal league. Selection of kings by prophetic designation and popular acclamation (e.g., I Kings 11:26-40; 12:20), though increasingly a fiction, continued in principle at least till the days of Jehu (II Kings 9:1-13). The result of this was an extreme political instability. An official cult, however, was established. Both to counteract the prestige of Jerusalem and to provide his state with religious sanctions, JEROBOAM I designated (I Kings 12:26-33) BETHEL and DAN, both ancient cult places claiming a Levitical tradition, as official shrines. The former, at least, retained this status as long as Israel existed (Amos 7:10-13). At both, the invisible Yahweh was conceived as standing or enthroned on a bull (*see* CALF, GOLDEN). The bull, though conceptually a parallel of the cherubim (*see* CHERUB) of the Jerusalem temple (I Kings 8:6-7), had associations with the fertility cult and was thus an entering wedge for syncretistic tendencies. At Bethel, Jeroboam instituted an annual autumn festival to counteract the similar one held in Jerusalem. In all this Jeroboam probably built on ancient tradition and was able to pose as a reformer.

c. Paganizing tendencies in Israel. To these the N state was peculiarly liable. The greater part of the Canaanites absorbed by Israel was within her borders. And since the official shrines lacked the prestige of Jerusalem, other shrines, many with cults of pre-Mosaic origin, were equally popular. It was easy for pagan practices and notions to infiltrate the national religion. In many minds Yahweh and Baal differed but little. In the ninth century Israel was threatened with the official introduction of a foreign paganism when JEZEBEL, wife of AHAB 2, sought to make the cult of the Tyrian Baal the religion of the court. Many Israelites became overtly pagan, and those who resisted (*see* ELIJAH THE PROPHET; ELISHA) were persecuted. Though this threat was ended (II Kings 9–10) by the purge of JEHU 1, native varieties of paganism flourished unmolested. By the eighth century Israel, even her official cult, was shot through with pagan practices (cf. Hosea, *passim*). The notion of covenant had been so completely prostituted that the prophets could not appeal to it. Obligation was discharged by sacrifice and ritual (e.g., Amos 4:4-5; 5:21-24), and the promises—perhaps a survival of the patriarchal pattern of covenant—were regarded as unconditional. Israel hoped for the Day of Yahweh (*see* DAY OF THE LORD), when all the promises would be made actual (Amos 5:18-20); it was not believed that Yahweh could or would judge his people (Hos. 6:1-3).

d. Social disintegration. Society meanwhile progressively disintegrated. The trends begun with Solomon, though checked at times, were never reversed. As the tribal system became only a memory, as Canaanites of feudal background with no notion of covenant were absorbed, as the national religion was progressively paganized and its obligation satisfied by ritual, covenant law inevitably ceased to have meaning, and abuses ran wild. Though both Israel and Judah knew political and economic vicissitudes, in the mid-eighth century they were as well off as they had been since Solomon. But in Israel, at least, society was torn asunder (cf. Amos, *passim*). Wealthy landholders amassed property and dispossessed and enslaved the poor. The courts, disregarding covenant law, were instruments of injustice. Venality, dishonesty, personal immorality, and debauchery were the rule. Israel's society, uprooted from the pattern which had given it birth, was without moral standard. And though in Judah, where society was more homogeneous and less open to foreign influence, the schism was less severe, the same tendencies operated there also (cf. Isaiah and Micah, *passim*).

D. *FROM THE EIGHTH CENTURY TO THE FALL OF JERUSALEM.* Protest against these social trends was not slow in coming. About the middle of the eighth century there began the flowering of the prophetic movement in classical form. After the destruction of Israel and until the fall of Jerusalem in 587, this flowering continued, and there were several significant efforts at reform.

1. The first of the classical prophets. The prophets, though a new and creative phenomenon in the history of Israel's religion, are not to be described, as they so often have been, as the great spiritual pioneers who discovered ethical monotheism. On the contrary, they were heirs of a tradition centuries old who attacked abuses and pronounced judgment upon them in the light of the covenant faith of Israel's past (*see* PROPHET, PROPHETISM).

a. The earlier prophets. Prophets had been active in Israel since the days of Saul, when bands of them in ecstatic frenzy (I Sam. 10:5-6, 10-13) roused their fellows to fight the holy wars of Yahweh against the Philistine masters. Later we find them, at times on good terms with the state yet reserving the right to criticize it (e.g., II Sam. 7:1-17; 12:1-15; 24) in the light of a more ancient tradition (*see* NATHAN 2; GAD 1), at times taking direct action against it (e.g., I Kings 11:26-40). After the schism, they were active in both states, but especially in Israel, where the clan-league tradition was stronger. They knew a burst of activity during the Aramean wars of Ahab, when they both encouraged the king (I Kings 20:13-14, 28) and rebuked him (I Kings 20:35-42) in the light of the ancient tradition of the holy war. Jezebel's policy (*see* § C2*c above*) faced them with a crisis. As stout nationalists, they opposed it and met a persecution (I Kings 18:4) in the face of which some gave in. A schism thus arose in their ranks, with certain of them (*see* MICAIAH 3) obliged to oppose both the state and their fellow prophets as well (e.g., I Kings 22:1-28). Jehu's purge, which they backed (II Kings 9:1-10), probably satisfied most of them; making peace with the state, they placed their patriotic fervor at its disposal. As professional functionaries of court and shrine, many of them became venal, prostituting their office for reward (e.g., Mic. 3:5, 11). Though standing in the same ancient tradition, the classical prophets held these professionals in contempt, and broke with them (e.g., Amos 7:14-15; Mic. 3:5-8).

b. Prophets of the eighth century in Israel. The first two prophets, AMOS and HOSEA, addressed the N state in the generation before its fall. They attacked the national sin, Amos principally social injustice, Hosea principally syncretism and apostasy. They viewed this sin against the background of Yahweh's past gracious acts toward Israel (e.g., Amos 2:9-12; 3:1-2; Hos. 11:1-4; 13:4-6) and the obligations of covenant, the major stipulations of which idolatry and injustice had violated. Hosea classically described the covenant as Yahweh's marriage of Israel (e.g., 2:2-13), and her idolatry as unforgivable adultery. Rejecting the empty, paganized cult, and the notion that Yahweh's promises were unconditional (e.g., Amos 5:18-24), both preached a message of judgment. Though they called for penitence, they were sure that the nation was doomed. Yet, unlike their predecessors, neither they nor the prophets who followed them sought to overthrow the state by revolution: Yahweh, the divine Overlord, will execute sentence through foreign foes who are the agents of his judgment.

Yet, for all this, the note of promise was not given up. Though barely implicit in Amos, it is quite strong in Hosea, who told how Israel the faithless wife, disciplined in catastrophe, would again be betrothed to Yahweh (e.g., 2:14-23). Hope thus rested beyond calamity in a new gracious act of Yahweh like that of the Exodus.

c. Prophets of the eighth century in Judah. As Israel collapsed, the prophetic movement was carried forward in Judah by ISAIAH and MICAH. Their attack followed the pattern of Amos and Hosea, and likewise moved from an understanding of the reciprocal nature of Yahweh's covenant: all injustice, idolatrous practice, and rebellion against Yahweh was viewed as breaches of the covenant stipulations. Isaiah and Micah also attacked the external cult by which the nation hoped to satisfy God's demands (e.g., Isa. 1: 10-20), and its corrupt clergy (e.g., Mic. 3:5-12). They preached a message of judgment, in the case of Micah (3:12)—and the young Isaiah, too (e.g., 5:1-7; 6:11-12)—as total as that of Amos.

But Isaiah, in particular, was influenced by the official theology of the Davidic covenant. His message was, in fact, a powerful reaffirmation of that theology, and a summons to the nation to trust in its promises. This explains his seemingly contradictory political advice: in 735/734 he begged AHAZ not to fear the coalition that sought to dethrone him, but to trust in his official theology and send no tribute to Assyria (7:1-9, 10-17; *see* IMMANUEL); in 714-711 he warned HEZEKIAH (1) not to rebel against Assyria, but to trust in Yahweh (e.g., 14:32; 18:1-6; 20); and, when rebellion was subsequently made (705-701), denounced it and the alliance with Egypt which supported it as rebellion against Yahweh (e.g., 28: 14-22; 29:15; 30:1-17); and yet, when the Assyrians laid siege to Jerusalem, it was Isaiah who urged Hezekiah to hold out in reliance upon the promises to David (e.g., 37:21-29, 33-35). To Isaiah the sole hope of Judah was to trust in Yahweh (e.g., 30:15). And to this hope he gave a classical form. As in the Davidic covenant, sinful Judah will be disciplined, but not cast off utterly (e.g., 10:24-27, 28-34). The discipline will serve to purge her dross away, leaving a chastened and purified remnant (1:24-26; 10:20-21) —if no more than that (10:22-23). Isaiah's hope was positively expressed in terms of the dynastic ideal (9:2-7; 11:1-9), the promise of a just and victorious king of David's line who would establish Yahweh's eternal rule of peace. Here the hope of the Messiah, normative in later Judaism, took shape.

2. The reform movement in Judah. Judah had always oscillated between periods of religious laxity and efforts at reform. In the late eighth century, for a variety of reasons, the reform movement gained momentum.

a. The reform of Hezekiah. In submitting to Assyria, AHAZ had been forced to give official recognition to Assyria's gods (II Kings 16:5-20). Other pagan cults were also fostered (II Kings 16:2-4), and a time of religious laxity ensued. As the Assyrian cults were offensive not only to loyal Yahwists but to all patriotic citizens as well, Hezekiah's struggle for independence naturally led to their removal, and also awakened a nationalistic reaction against all religious features considered foreign. Prophetic threats of a fate for Jerusalem similar to that of Samaria (Mic. 3:12; cf. Jer. 26:16-19) also played a part. Pagan cults of all kinds were abolished (II Kings 18:1-7), and even (vs. 4) objects of ancient origin thitherto thought unobjectionable (*see* NEHUSHTAN). Effort was also made (cf. vss. 4, 22) to close outlying shrines of Yahweh where pagan practices had flourished. Further, moved by the dream of an Israel once more united under the throne of David, Hezekiah made an attempt—with indifferent success—to induce the N tribes to participate (II Chr. 30:1, 10-12). The Assyrian's reconstitution of the shrine of Bethel (II Kings 17:25-28) was quite likely a countermeasure to this. *See* HEZEKIAH 1.

Hezekiah's reform did not endure; the people were not ready for it. When MANASSEH (2) resumed loyalty to Assyria, the Assyrian cults were reinstated, and a period of general apostasy ensued (II Kings 21:1-16). All sorts of pagan rites, including those of the fertility cult, DIVINATION, MAGIC, and even human sacrifice (vs. 6), were fostered. The heavenly bodies (vs. 5) were apparently regarded as members of the pantheon and accorded worship (*see* HOST OF HEAVEN). Israel's religion was in danger of becoming a polytheism. Those who protested were apparently (vs. 16) repressed, and the reform movement driven underground.

b. The reform of Josiah. The collapse of Assyria during the reign of JOSIAH left Judah free, and this was the signal for the most sweeping reform of her history. Josiah's reform, like Hezekiah's, was in part a facet of resurgent nationalism aimed at purging the nation of everything foreign. It also had the support of such prophets as ZEPHANIAH (1) and JEREMIAH, both of whom pronounced judgment on the nation for its idolatry. It fed, too, on the uneasiness which world events had awakened, and which evoked in Judah as elsewhere a search for security in the surer things of the past. The reform had been in progress for some years (II Chr. 34:3, 8) when (in 622) it was given new impetus and direction by the discovery, in the course of the purification of the temple, of a "book of the law" (II Kings 22:3–23:3). This was almost certainly some form of the book of DEUTERONOMY, whose laws reach back ultimately to the legal tradition of the tribal league and which, apparently handed down in N Israel, had presumably been brought to Jerusalem after the fall of Samaria and re-edited there in the reign of Hezekiah or Manasseh. Reflecting faithfully the reciprocal nature of the Mosaic covenant, Deuteronomy declares that the national hope lies in keeping covenant, while idolatry and disobedience lead inevitably to ruin.

The reform was thus a rediscovery of the Mosaic covenant and an attempt to put it into practice. It issued (II Kings 23:4-14, 21-25) in a ruthless purge of all pagan cults and practices, both native and foreign. It also abolished shrines of Yahweh throughout Judah and centralized all worship in Jerusalem (vs. 8). As Josiah annexed the territory of the erstwhile N state, the reform was extended there also (II Kings 23:15-20; II Chr. 34:6-7). The ideal of a purified Israel united under the throne of David seemed in fair way to be realized. The reform had the good effect of ridding the land, if only temporarily, of pagan practices. And, since the demands of the law were moral, and since Josiah was himself a just man (Jer. 22:15-16), the worst social abuses were certainly checked. Centralization was, however, resisted and never accepted by many (II Kings 23:9), while in Jerusalem, whose clergy had gained an unhealthy monopoly, the reform tended to issue in purely cultic activity (e.g., Jer. 6:16-21; 7:21-23). The written law was elevated at the expense of the prophetic word (Jer. 8:8-9); and the confidence grew that, the demands of covenant law having been met by cultic reform and ritual, the national safety had been secured (Jer. 6:14; 8:11).

3. The last days of Judah. With Josiah's death in 609 (II Kings 23:29-30) Judah's independence ended. Subject first to Egypt, then to Babylon, she was destroyed by the latter in 587 after a prior deportation in 597. These events put Israel's faith to its severest test.

a. The spiritual crisis of Judah. Josiah's violent death and the end of independence seemed to many a contradiction of the Deuteronomic theology. Under JEHOIAKIM the reform, already wearing thin, was abandoned, and pagan cults returned in force. Yet clergy and people alike clung to the official dogma that the national safety was assured by the presence of Yahweh's temple (Jer. 7:4) and by his promises to David. To deny this was to accuse him of breaking covenant (Jer. 26:8-11). Down to the end a miraculous intervention was expected (Jer. 21:2) as in the days of Hezekiah (Isa. 37:36-37). The fall of the nation threw the truth of the national religion, as popularly understood, into question. Why has Yahweh not been faithful to his promises? Has he been defeated by mightier gods? Or is it that he is not just (Jer. 31:29; Lam. 5:7; Ezek. 18:2, 25, 29)? If the tragedy could not be interpreted in terms of Yahweh's power and justice, Israel's faith would perish.

b. Prophets of the last days of Judah. Israel's faith was saved in good part by prophets who addressed the nation in its darkest hour. In all of them (*see* JEREMIAH; EZEKIEL; HABAKKUK; LAMENTATIONS, BOOK OF) the problem of the divine justice is to the fore. All, though in different ways, explained the calamity as Yahweh's righteous judgment on the national sin. This is almost the whole burden of Jeremiah, who, declaring that covenant had been broken, rejected the popular trust in the permanence of temple (7:1-15) and dynasty (21:12–22:30) utterly. He saw the Babylonians as the instruments of divine judgment (e.g., 4:5-8, 11-18; 5:10-17), and called Judah to accept their yoke (chs. 27–28); since she would not do this, he pronounced her doom. Ezekiel, too, declared (chs. 8–11) that Yahweh had quitted his temple and doomed the nation for its sins; the calamity was not only his doing, but positively his vindication of himself as righteous and sovereign Lord (14:21-23; 20:33-38). Explained thus, tragedy could not destroy Israel's faith.

The prophets prepared for the survival of faith in other ways. Jeremiah's rejection of the official cult and his insistence on a repentant heart (e.g., 4:4, 14; cf. Ezek. 18:31, etc.), prepared for the time when faith must go on without cult—a thing to the ancient mind impossible. Ezekiel's individualizing of the problem of the divine justice (ch. 18), mechanical though it seems, served to release men from a fatalistic burden of inherited guilt and from the despair into which they had fallen (33:10; 37:11). The summons of both to individual decision laid the foundation for a new community of faith, the old national-cultic community having been destroyed. And both assured their people that God had not forsaken them even in the land of their exile (e.g., Jer. 29:10-14; Ezek. 11:16). Both regarded the Exile as an interim, a purification, out of which Yahweh would call his people as once from Egypt (e.g., Jer. 24; Ezek. 20:33-38). Hope to both of them thus lay in a new act of divine grace, creating a new and purified people: to Jeremiah (31:31-34) the making of a new covenant, to Ezekiel (e.g., ch. 37) the resurrection of the dead nation by Yahweh's spirit and the establishment with it of an eternal COVENANT of peace. Exiled Israel was thus not left hopeless, but could look forward to the promise of a new future.

E. *THE EXILE AND BEYOND.* The EXILE was a watershed in the history of Israel's religion. While the postexilic community in no sense broke with the faith of old Israel, it nevertheless gave that faith a new form. In the Exile and beyond it, Judaism was born.

1. Israel in exile. In 587 Jewish life in Palestine was totally disrupted. Though Jews continued to live around about Jerusalem, they were few and poor. It was with the exiles in Babylon, though themselves not very numerous, that the future of faith rested.

a. The Exile and Israel's faith. Grievous emergency though the Exile was, Israel's faith persisted through it with an amazing tenacity. The legal, cultic, and historical traditions of the past were jealously guarded, handed down, and, in some cases, edited (e.g., the historical corpus, Deuteronomy through Kings) during the Exile. The sayings of the prophets were likewise preserved and their collection carried forward, for in these the exiles found both explanation of their plight, and hope. Yet, for all that, the danger to faith remained grave. Many still viewed the national disaster as proof of Yahweh's powerlessness, and these were acutely tempted to turn to the worship of the presumably mightier gods of Babylon (cf. Ezek. 20:32; Isa. 40–48, *passim*). Moreover, the Exile had uprooted Israel and opened before her vast new horizons. Her faith could no longer continue as a national cult with limited national perspective; it had to adapt itself, to understand its position with relation to the great nations and their gods as never before, if it was to survive.

b. Reinterpretation of Israel's faith: Second Isaiah. As Babylon was about to fall to Cyrus (539), the so-called Second Isaiah (*see* ISAIAH) supplied both the needed adaptation and the profoundest interpretation of the national suffering that had yet been given. With the comforting assurance that the penalty for sin had now been paid, he declared that the Exile was soon to end (e.g., 40:1-11). There had been no "divorce" between Yahweh and Israel (50:1; ch. 54); Yahweh would now for the sake of his honor and purpose forgive her and come to her rescue (42:18–43:7; 43:8–44:5; ch. 48). There would be a great new exodus (e.g., 43:14-21; 48:20-21), with Yahweh leading his flock in triumphal procession through the desert back to Zion, there to establish his kingly rule of peace (e.g., 52:1-12). Hebrew monotheism is here given clearest expression. The gods of the nations are not gods at all; none is God but Yahweh, who is creator, who alone has prepared a purpose in history and can bring it to fruition (chs. 40–48). Even Cyrus is the unknowing instrument of that purpose (44:24–45:8). Israel is Yahweh's chosen witness before the world that he is God (e.g., 43:8-13); it is his intention that all people will see his mighty acts and recognize him as such (e.g., 45:9-25). Yet Israel's role is not to be a passive one; she is to be Yahweh's servant to bring the light of his rule to the nations (e.g., 42:1-9; 49:1-6). The notes of promise and of obligation inherent in Israel's faith, as well as her exclusive recognition of Yahweh as God, were thus placed in world-wide perspective.

In the figure of the SERVANT OF THE LORD the prophet gave the national suffering and the national hope profound reinterpretation (especially 42:1-4; 49:1-6; 50:4-9; 52:13–53:12). Yahweh's purpose is to triumph through his Servant, who, persecuted and rejected, brings the light of his truth to the world, and who, having made himself a sin offering (53:10), is vindicated and victorious. Israel's hope was thus given an entirely novel pattern quite different from the popular one, and one richly played upon in the NT. While the Servant is more than a picture of suffering Israel, the calling of the Servant is nevertheless hers (e.g., 50:10); as she obeys this calling, her sufferings vicariously serve God's redemptive purpose.

2. The rise of Judaism. Having conquered Babylon, Cyrus allowed the Jews to re-establish their life in Palestine, and a number of them returned thither. After many difficulties the TEMPLE was rebuilt (520-516) and its cult resumed. But it was not until the coming of EZRA (3), approximately a century later, that the community was organized in stable form. In that community the beliefs and practices of Judaism developed.

a. The holy people: particularism vs. universalism. The postexilic community was a church rather than a nation. It understood itself as the remnant of Israel, called by God's grace out of bondage in the new exodus and summoned to live as his people under his law. This obligation it formally assumed in solemn covenant with Ezra as its representative (Neh. 8–10). It saw as its destiny, therefore, to realize in itself the covenant ideal of a "kingdom of priests and a holy nation" (Exod. 19:6). It was not a national unit or, strictly speaking, an ethnic one—there were foreigners and proselytes (e.g., Isa. 56:1-8) in its midst—but a community bounded by covenant and law. Since the Jews were surrounded by pagans on all sides, the danger of assimilation had to be combatted vigorously (Ezra 9–10; Neh. 13:15-31) lest they be swallowed up altogether. This led to a growing particularism and a tension with the universalism implicit in monotheistic faith. Jews tended to draw apart from GENTILES, from SAMARITANS, and even from those of their own number who did not keep the law. Proselytes (*see* PROSELYTE) were welcomed (e.g., Isa. 56:6-8; 66:18-21; Zech. 8:20-23) and accorded equality before the law (cf. Lev. 19:34; 24:22); and before NT times vast numbers of them had been made. Yet Judaism did not become an actively missionary religion; the tendency was to look down on the Gentiles and to wish as few dealings with them as possible—a tendency rebuked in the book of JONAH. This tension was one which continued unresolved in Judaism, and which carried over into the infant church.

b. The idea of God. In Judaism monotheism triumphed completely. While there were always Jews who readily yielded to foreign customs, the hard core of Judaism turned from paganism and idolatry resolutely. The tendency was to exalt GOD yet more and more. Although ANTHROPOMORPHISM in describing him could not be dispensed with, later OT literature shows a noticeable trend away from it. The divine name, Yahweh, came to be considered ineffable; various substitutes for it, and devices to guard one from pronouncing it, were developed. There was much reflection on God's acts of creation and providence, as seen, e.g., in the later PSALMS and WISDOM literature. There was a profound devotional piety, again illustrated in the later psalms, and an equally profound concern for the conduct of the good life, seen especially in the later wisdom literature. A tendency to find an almost mechanical relationship between one's deeds—specifically one's observance of the law—and one's fortunes, whether good or ill, evoked an early protest in the book of JOB, and later in a much more skeptical vein in ECCLESIASTES. Yet in all this Judaism had no doubt that her God alone was God, sovereign in all things and just in all his ways. *See* WORSHIP IN THE OT.

As God was exalted above his creation, great play was allowed for the role of angelic beings (Yahweh had always had his heavenly host) in carrying out his will (*see* ANGEL; HOST OF HEAVEN); at least by the Maccabean period (cf. Dan. 12:1) these had become distinct personalities. Partly from reflection on the problem of theodicy, partly owing to outside influence, the figure of SATAN, originally a member of Yahweh's court whose function it was to accuse evildoers (e.g., Job 1-2; Zech. 3:1-2), emerged as the great adversary of God who tempts men to evil (cf. II Sam. 24:1; I Chr. 21:1). By the immediate pre-Christian centuries (*see* APOCALYPTICISM; DEAD SEA SCROLLS; ESSENES) a dualistic tendency which viewed the world as a battleground of good and evil, light and darkness, had established itself. Yet no proper dualism emerged, for even here God remained the sovereign Lord in whose providence all things occur.

c. The future hope of Judaism. Hope for the future, always present in Israel's faith, continued; expressing itself partly in inherited forms, partly in new ones, it issued in a complex eschatology (*see* ESCHATOLOGY OF THE OT; ESCHATOLOGY OF THE APOCRYPHA AND PSEUDEPIGRAPHA). The old national hope of the messianic king early attached itself (Hag. 2:20-23; Zech. 6:9-14) to ZERUBBABEL, only to be bitterly disappointed. It seems thereafter to have been pushed somewhat into the background. Although it continued strong till NT times and after, it was divorced from the existing order and attached to the new order which God would establish at the end of history (on the notion of a messiah of Levi, or of Joseph, *see* MESSIAH; on the notion of new covenant as taken up by Jewish sects, *see* ESSENES; DEAD SEA SCROLLS). Later Hebrew prophecy turned almost entirely from present history to the last events of Yahweh's judgment and the establishment of his triumphant rule (e.g., Isa. 24-27; Ezek. 38-39; Joel [*see* JOEL, BOOK OF]; Zech. 9-14 [*see* ZECHARIAH, BOOK OF]). As prophecy died out, and as hope was shaped by concepts borrowed from outside, there issued the phenomenon of APOCALYPTICISM, a literature which is concerned to describe in cryptic language, usually under the device of pseudonymity, the final cosmic struggle between God and evil. First instanced in the second century B.C. (*see* DANIEL), it flourished through the first century A.D. (*see* PSEUDEPIGRAPHA; REVELATION, BOOK OF). In this literature there appears the figure of the SON OF MAN, originally a corporate representation of the true Israel (Dan. 7:13-14), but later (*see* ENOCH, BOOK OF) a pre-existent heavenly deliverer who would come in glory at the end of days.

Probably in good part from reflection on the problem of justice, Judaism began to develop a belief in the RESURRECTION, a thing unknown in old Israel. The concept itself was a borrowed one, but it was adapted to the faith of Judaism. First appearing (Isa. 26:19) as a resurrection of the faithful, the notion of a resurrection both to eternal life and to eternal shame was developed (Dan. 12:2) and became popular in Judaism. But this was not yet unanimously accepted in NT times (e.g., Mark 12:18-27; Acts 23:6-10).

d. The place of the law in Judaism. The most characteristic feature of Judaism was its stress on keeping the law (*see* LAW [IN THE OT; IN FIRST-CENTURY JUDAISM]). In fact, to be a Jew was to keep the law. The obligations of covenant law had been a primitive feature in Israel's religion; in Judaism this received a logical but one-sided development. The prophets had explained the Exile as a result of breach of covenant law; and this naturally led men to take law more seriously, especially since, cult and nation having been destroyed, the law alone remained as the mark of a Jew. And the postexilic community had been constituted (Neh. 8-10) precisely in a covenant committing it to the observance of the (now written) law. As hope of the reconstitution of the old order was given up, and hope pushed to the end of history, the law was accorded absolute validity for regulating conduct in the present age. Not only was covenant obligation to be fulfilled and God's favor gained by the keeping of it; it became virtually the whole content of obligation. Though the temple cult was carried on—the law specified it!—it became of somewhat vestigial importance; the old Levitical function of teaching was far more central. Every village had its SYNAGOGUE, where the law was read and expounded. The law superseded both priestly lot and technical oracle, and prophetic word, as the giver of the divine will; prophecy ceased in Israel.

Judaism gradually developed a fixed, if unofficial,

canon of scripture (*see* CANON OF THE OT). The PENTATEUCH had authoritative status from the time of Ezra or soon after; and to this were subsequently added the books of the prophets. By the second century B.C. most of the books of the OT as we know it were regarded as holy scripture. But the Pentateuch, as law par excellence, retained the pre-eminent position. Judaism became a religion of the Book, committed to the observance of written law; the highest virtue was the study and keeping of it (cf. Pss. 1; 19:7-14; 119; etc.). As effort was made to apply the law to tangible situations, there gradually arose a body of oral law aimed at further defining its meaning. There was also the desire to build a "fence" around the law lest it be broken inadvertently. As law grew more massive, there arose a class of scribes (*see* SCRIBE; RABBI)—in NT times mostly PHARISEES—who devoted themselves wholly to studying it and teaching it. Although the oral law grew apart from the priestly class (*see* SADDUCEES) in general, it became the hallmark of Judaism and was ultimately crystallized in the TALMUD. The law expressed the Jewish ideal of a people holy to God; it enabled Judaism to survive when its temple and cult were finally destroyed (A.D. 70). The NT, however, affirms that this whole history of faith found its conclusion in Christ, who is the fulfilment of its law and its hope, and who gave to his church, the Israel according to the Spirit, the awaited new covenant. *See* CHRIST, CHRISTOLOGY; CHURCH, IDEA OF.

Bibliography. J. Pedersen, *Israel, Its Life and Culture,* I–II (1926); III–IV (1940). M. Noth, *Das System der zwölf Stämme Israels* (1930); *Die Gesetze im Pentateuch* (1940; reprinted, *Gesammelte Studien zum AT* [1957], pp. 9-141). A. Alt, *Der Gott der Väter* (1921; reprinted, *Kleine Schriften,* I [1953], 1-78): fundamental for religion of the patriarchs; *Die Ursprünge des israelitischen Rechts* (1934; reprinted, *Kleine Schriften,* I [1953], 278-332). H. W. Robinson, *Inspiration and Revelation in the OT* (1946). G. E. Wright, *The OT Against Its Environment* (1950); "The Faith of Israel," *IB,* I (1952), 349-89. J. Muilenburg, "The History of the Religion of Israel," *IB,* I (1952), 292-348: a convenient treatment with further bibliography including older works. H. J. Kraus, *Gottesdienst in Israel* (1954). G. E. Mendenhall, *Law and Covenant in Israel and the Ancient Near East* (1955): important for the covenant form and its history. S. Mowinckel, *He That Cometh* (English trans.; 1956). H. H. Rowley, *The Faith of Israel* (1956). W. F. Albright, *Archaeology and the Religion of Israel* (3rd ed., 1953); *From the Stone Age to Christianity* (3rd ed., 1957): both of fundamental importance. B. W. Anderson, *Understanding the OT* (1957): an excellent popular treatment. W. Eichrodt, "Religionsgeschichte Israels," *Historia Mundi,* II (n.d.), 377-448; *Theologie des ATs,* I (5th ed., 1957); II–III (2nd ed., 1948). J. BRIGHT

HEBREWS, GOSPEL ACCORDING TO THE. A lost Greek gospel current in the Decapolis and Egypt in the second century, probably to be identified with the Gospel of the Ebionites (*see* EBIONITES, GOSPEL OF), and quite distinct from the Aramaic targum of the Greek Matthew known as the Gospel of the Nazarenes. *See* NAZARENES, GOSPEL OF.

Eusebius refers to this writing several times. Among the books which some Christians reject was counted the "Gospel according to the Hebrews in which those of the Hebrews who have accepted Christ take special pleasure" (Hist. III.25.5). The Ebionites who "wholly rejected Paul and called him an apostate from the law . . . used only the gospel called According to the Hebrews and made little account of the rest" (Hist. III.27.4). That this writing was current in the second century is evidenced by the fact that Hegesippus made extracts from it (Euseb. Hist. IV.22.8). That it was known in Egypt is evidenced from citations from it by both Clement and Origen.

Owing in no small part to Jerome's mistaken claim to have "translated into Greek and Latin speech" the Gospel According to the Hebrews "which Origen often uses" (*On Illustrious Men* 2), and to the medley of citations which he appropriates, in part from those which Origen had made of this gospel, in part from those apparently made by Apollinaris from the totally distinct Gospel of the Nazarenes, the widest confusion as to the nature and content of the Gospel According to the Hebrews has prevailed. This confusion is heightened by Jerome's word: "In the gospel which the Nazarenes and Ebionites use, which I have lately translated into Greek from the Hebrew, and which is called by most people the original of Matthew" (*On Matt.* 12:13). Many have regarded it as parallel to, if not actually anterior to, our canonical gospels and a source of at least equal historical value. Few would so regard it today. That it, like the other apocryphal gospels, is subsequent to and heavily dependent upon the canonical four may be safely hazarded. The results of certain researches would seem to warrant extreme caution in any attempt to reconstruct its content from the citations by Jerome. Most of the latter may safely be ascribed to the Gospel of the Nazarenes; Jerome has taken these quotations from Apollinaris' commentaries.

Apparently this Greek Gospel According to the Hebrews, while heavily dependent upon Matthew, was a totally different book. According to the Stichometry of Nicephorus, it was approximately three hundred *stichoi* shorter than our Matthew. Dependence upon Luke-Acts is as marked as upon Matthew. Quotations from Hegesippus, Origen, and Eusebius indicate that the writing was the product of Jewish-Christian thought of the sort properly styled Ebionite. James was the central figure, presented in sharp and even hostile contrast to Paul, and clearly outranked Peter. It was to James, not to Peter, that Jesus made his first postresurrection appearance. Apparently Peter was not regarded as the chief of the Twelve. In the list of the Twelve, John's name is first, Simon's third.

While many of the citations from Jerome, which have commonly been regarded as from this gospel and which have tended to suggest its marked similarity to our Matthew, must be left aside when attempting to discover its content and nature, the quotations from soberer and more reliable writers are revealing. According to Eusebius (*Theophany* 4.2), it contained a variant tradition of the parable of the entrusted funds ("talents," "pounds"). Clearly dependent upon both the Matthean and Lukan forms of this parable, it shows the evidence of later reflection. Three servants are distinguished: one multiplied his money by trading; one hid it and returned it intact but without increase; one squandered it on harlots and flute girls. The second received a rebuke; it was to the third that the severer penalty was given. Eusebius also records (Hist. III.37.17) that this gospel contained the story of the woman taken in adultery, originally a part of none of our canonical gospels, but now standing in many MSS in John, in some in Luke. That the story was not unlike one told by Papias is remarked by Eusebius, but the conclusion reached by many scholars that Papias had drawn it from the Gospel According to the Hebrews is utterly unwarranted and highly improbable.

Origen twice cites from this gospel a word of Jesus: "Even now did my mother the Holy Spirit take me by one of my hairs and carried me away unto the great mountain Tabor . . ." (*On John* 2:12; *On Jeremiah,* homily 15.4). That this is but a bit of haggadic amplification of the story of the Temptation, suggested by the famed experiences of Ezekiel (Ezek. 8:3) and Habakkuk (Bel 33-39), would seem obvious. The saying, twice quoted by Clement but in slightly variant forms, is of interest, if not revelatory of the essential nature of this gospel: "He that wondereth shall reign, and he that reigneth shall rest" (Misc. I.9.45), and: "He shall not cease from seeking until he find, and having found he will be amazed, and having been amazed he will reign, and having reigned he will rest" (Misc. V.14.96). This saying is identical with one of the OXYRHYNCHUS SAYINGS OF JESUS and has suggested to many scholars the possibility that the latter sayings are essentially excerpts from this lost gospel.

The suggestion that the title "Gospel According to the Hebrews" was the one given it by its author, and the alternative proposal that it was an indication of its original language, are both equally unlikely. Rather, the title would seem to reflect the disparaging recognition on the part of those who knew and rejected this gospel, that it was the gospel belonging to the Jewish Christians and employed by them. Origen's cautious preface to quotations from it: "And if any accept the Gospel according to the Hebrews," or: "If any accept that saying," may well reflect his own awareness that while this writing was not heretical in the sense that many of the apocrypha were, it was yet far from akin to those commonly accepted by the orthodox. If the tone was as anti-Pauline as has been suggested, his caution is not surprising.

Bibliography. For a somewhat different appraisal, see M. R. James, *The Apocryphal NT* (1924), pp. 1-9 (which collects all the traditional quotations). Other rewarding studies are to be found in E. Hennecke, *Handbuch zu den neutestamentlichen Apokryphen* (1904); A. Schmidtke, *Judenchristliche Evangelien* (1911); B. W. Bacon, *Studies in Matthew* (1930), especially pp. 478-95; J. Schoeps, *Theologie und Geschichte des Judenchristentums* (1950).

M. S. ENSLIN

HEBREWS, HISTORY OF. *See* ISRAEL, HISTORY OF.

HEBREWS, LETTER TO THE [πρὸς Ἑβραίους]. In most editions the nineteenth book of the NT canon, being placed between the thirteen letters of Paul and the Catholic letters. So it is located in the Latin MSS, but most of the Greek MSS have it between II Thessalonians and I Timothy. Although we call Hebrews a "letter," it has no author's name and no addressee, nor can we recognize any specific occasion or purpose. There is no prescript and the letter commences immediately with a theological treatise; but it ends with greetings. It was not written by Paul; style, form, and Christology speak against such authorship, and nothing speaks for it (*see* § 3 *below*).

The Western part of the early church refused until the end of the fourth century to acknowledge the canonicity of Hebrews because it was not written by Paul. Later the Western church accepted the Eastern theory of its Pauline origin. It was not before Augustine accepted the canon, which Athanasius had laid down in his Thirty-ninth Easter Letter (367), and Pope Innocent I (405) agreed upon all twenty-seven books, that Hebrews became a fully acknowledged part of the NT canon in East and West.

1. Composition and contents
2. Form and purpose
3. Authorship, destination, and date
4. Theological significance
   a. Eschatology
   b. Christology
   c. The admonitions
5. Historical setting

Bibliography

1. Composition and contents. It has been said that our letter presents in many respects the "riddle of the NT," that it is solitary among early Christian writings, "without father, without mother, and without genealogy."

At first sight we have an uncomplicated composition:

I. The superiority of the Son over angels and Moses, 1:1-4:13
II. Jesus the true High Priest, 4:14-6:20
III. Jesus and his sacrifice, 7:1-10:18
IV. Exhortations for steadfastness in faith, 10:19-12:29
V. Different exhortations and final salutation, ch. 13

Some scholars prefer another outline and try to find the rhetorical pattern of later Greek admonitory speeches: the "Prooimion" (chs. 1-4); the "Diegesis" (chs. 5-6); the "Parenesis" (chs. 7-10); the "Epilogos" (chs. 11-13). Yet there are only a few phrases in Hebrews which justify the rhetorical scheme as underlying the letter.

Though christological parts are regularly followed by parenetical (or hortatory) ones, the author does not fail to include admonitions even inside the dogmatical sections (2:1 ff; 3:7 ff; 5:11 ff). Indeed, it seems as if Christology is used as a means for the support of the exhortations. There is a constant rhythm between theology and moral appeal, which reminds one somewhat of passages in IV Maccabees and Philo. The whole thus can be called a "word of exhortation" (13:22), although the theological and christological parts are of special significance. An older tradition of confessional formulas is taken up and organically included (e.g., 1:3; 4:12-13; 7:3, 26; 13:14).

The integrity of the letter is not questionable, except the final verses (13:22-25), which have a noticeable Pauline touch not to be found anywhere else in the book. Yet this could be by chance, and the phrase "those who come from Italy" says nothing for or against the authenticity (for reasons against, *see* § 2 *below*).

2. Form and purpose. It is significant that neither the word "letter" (ἐπιστολή) nor the term "to write" (γράφειν) occurs. Instead, we find the terms "word," "speech," "proclamation" (λόγος). No specific references to the concrete situation of the original readers are present. The general remarks about the neglect of their meetings (10:25) and the enduring of persecutions (10:32-34) could probably be made about many of the larger congregations of the postapostolic age. The admonition about the singleness of penitence, beginning with 5:11, referring to the dullness of the hearers—"You need milk, not solid food" (vs. 12)—seems to have no concrete addressee, since in 6:9 the author asserts: "Yet in your case, beloved, we feel sure of better things that belong to salvation." Thus it may be said that Hebrews is a unique book in the NT canon, especially as regards its literary character. To use the categories of A. Deissmann, one is obliged to say it is not a real "letter," but an "epistle"—i.e., a literary piece of art meant for general reading (cf. CLEMENT, EPISTLE OF). The final salutation (13:22-25), alone speaking against such a literary evaluation, could be explained as the attempt to transform the "epistle" into a "letter." *See* LETTER.

The epistolary character does not exclude the possibility, and even probability, that a sermon or lecture has been used. The exceptionally good style and the acquaintance with the rhetorical forms of Hellenism, features which Hebrews has in common with Philo or the Wisdom of Solomon, suggest the teacher or preacher. The many changes from the "we" to the "you" and to the individual "I" point in the same direction. The assumption then would be that we have before us a written sermon, which in its form and style is akin to the Jewish-Hellenistic homily of the synagogue. This does not require that Hebrews was originally composed as one sermon—namely, on Pss. 94–110—to which the phrase (2:1) "to what we have heard" could refer. On the contrary, it is more probable that we have in this epistle several sermons combined and collected by the author himself.

The form is further characterized by an extensive use of the OT in the LXX, although the author does not stay with the verbal text (1:8 may have a corrupted text; passages from Deuteronomy in 1:6; 10:30; 12:15; 13:5 are not quoted according to the LXX). Out of thirty-two quotations ten are taken from Psalms. In addition there are many allusions. The method is primarily marked by a christological interpretation (see, e.g., 1:5 ff; 2:6 ff, 12 ff; 10:5 ff) which uses different exegetical approaches: the allegorical exegesis, following Philo, is often used (e.g., 7:2-3; 13:10-14; see also 3:6; 10:20; 12:22), but the typological exegesis is predominant. When Moses and Jesus are discussed together in 3:1-6, it is more a case of simple comparison; but the whole passage 7:1–10:18 is a typological section. In 8:6-13 the Old Covenant is the type for the New Covenant as antitype. And the motif of I Cor. 10:1-10 is repeated in Heb. 3:7–4:13—the Israel of the wilderness being presented as the typological figure of the Christian church. All this is not only a matter of form, but of theological significance, insofar as the author regards Christianity in the historical continuity with Israel and Judaism, despite his constant stress upon its superiority.

3. Authorship, destination, and date. There is common agreement today that Paul is not the author of Hebrews. A long history of assertions and hypotheses has led to this point. It is possible that Clement of Rome (although similarities between Clement and Hebrews can be explained by the use by both of traditional liturgical formulas), and the "Shepherd of Hermas" knew Hebrews; but Marcion, the Roman presbyter Gaius (Euseb. Hist. VI.20.3), and the Muratorian Fragment do not mention the epistle. The earliest witness is Clement of Alexandria (Euseb. Hist. VI.14.4), who mentions the title πρὸς Ἑβραίους and tells that Paul wrote the letter in the Hebrew language, while Luke translated it into Greek. He further tries to explain why Paul did not mention his own name at the beginning, by asserting that in writing to Hebrews the apostle wished to avoid arousing in them a possible antagonism, especially since he was known as the Apostle to the Gentiles. Origen follows the same tradition, but obviously has his doubts. He differentiates: the ideas are Pauline; the expression and style come from somebody else. He concludes: "Who really wrote the letter is known to God alone" (Euseb. Hist. VI.25). Tertullian (*De Pudicitia* 20) brings up the name of Barnabas as the author of the Letter to the Hebrews —a theory which has had its advocates even up to present times. Luther suggested Apollos; Calvin either Clement of Rome or Luke. W. Manson has suggested that our letter could be rooted in a circle like the one reflected in the speech of Stephen in Acts.

Hebrews was taken as Pauline until the Reformation, when Erasmus vigorously fought for a change in this opinion. The Tridentinian Council (April 8, 1546) decided for the Pauline authorship; the Pontifical Bible Commission of Rome (June 24, 1914) added, however, that one is not obliged to assume that Paul gave to the letter its final form. Who then is the author? We do not have the sources any longer to make a clear decision, except that it is not Paul. All other theories are no more than possibilities. The question then arises, whether we can approximately determine the spiritual atmosphere out of which the author wrote (*see* § 4 *below*).

On the basis of the title "To the Hebrews" the first readers were understood to be Jewish Christians. Yet nothing can be derived from the title as such, which originally was outside the rolled papyrus letter and probably was never copied. It seems as if the present title is a mere hypothesis derived from the content of the letter. Special Jewish Christian features are missing. No references are made to circumcision or worship of the temple or ritual law in general. The general acquaintance with the OT was the same with Gentile Christians.

As places to which the epistle was sent, Alexandria, Rome, Palestine, and, more specifically, Jerusalem, have been mentioned. The considerations which speak against Jewish Christians speak also against Jerusalem. A Hellenistic milieu is more probable. For Alexandria no weighty arguments can be given, except perhaps that atmosphere and terminology point to a kinship with Philo's writing. But this would say nothing as to the original readers, although it might give a hint as to the spiritual home of the author.

For Rome as destination, more can be said. Not only has I Clement the earliest allusion to Hebrews, but it is also noteworthy that Rome always preserved a tradition that Paul was not the author. The salutation by "those who come from Italy" (13:24) goes better with the assumption that these were living outside Italy and sending their greetings homeward. (For the opposite thesis, see Codex A in its subscription: "written from Rome.") Some of the exhortations —they have endured and must still endure persecution (10:32 ff; 12:4); they stood in specific need of steadfastness; they must be loyal to the confessions, having patience in view of the nearness of the end— such admonitions, though reflecting the general situation of Christianity at the end of the first century, would support the Rome hypothesis. On the other hand, nothing is said explicitly about the Neronian persecution, nothing about Peter's and Paul's martyrdom (13:7 should not be used as a reference!). Although nothing can be said conclusively, Rome as the place of destination has the highest probability.

What can be said about the date? Some scholars have argued from silence that Peter and Paul were still alive, since Nero's persecution is not mentioned, and one should—Rome as destination being presupposed—go back to the time *ca.* A.D. 60. Other scholars have assumed that the Jewish cult was still going on and the temple not yet destroyed, since Hebrews refers to these in the present tense. But today it is agreed that the present tense was always demanded for the interpretation of the Jewish law, as can be seen with Josephus, Mishna, and Talmud. Further, it is apparent that the author has no personal knowledge of the cult in the temple.

The close relation of Hebrews to writings like I Clement and even the Revelation of John, and to ideas to be found in Luke, speak for the time at the end of the first century—i.e., the time of Domitian (81-96). The problems of the postapostolic era are the concern of the Letter to the Hebrews.

4. Theological significance. The constant discussion of the Jewish cult and the use throughout of the OT serve the purpose of proving the absolute superiority of God's revelation in Christ for a Hellenistic world. The theology of Hebrews is that of a Hellenistic Christianity of the postapostolic age. These points explain why two themes are very much in the center of our epistle—namely:

a. Eschatology. Hebrews stresses the coming of the end, assuming that the Christian church is endangered by its neglect of this truth (12:1 ff). In the opening verses of ch. 1 the present time is called "these last days"; 2:5 speaks of the "world to come." The forces of the coming aeon are already breaking in (6:5). The eschatology is not used for speculations—as with II Peter (*see* PETER, SECOND LETTER OF) or REVELATION—and is not the reaction to a general postponement idea, but is emphasized for a practical purpose —namely, to overcome the weariness and weakening of faith. A twofold aspect of eschatology can be seen —pointing on the one hand to a future action of God, to the coming of Christ Jesus, and pointing on the other to the present as the time of definite transition from an old to a new aeon. "Therefore do not throw away your confidence, which has a great reward. For you have need of endurance, so that you may do the will of God and receive what is promised.

> " 'For yet a little while,
> and the coming one shall come and shall not tarry' "
> (10:35-37).

When he comes, the Christians can expect an epoch of salvation, a period of "rest," an everlasting "sabbath." We are waiting for the "city which is to come" (13:14). Yet just because there is this certainty of a near-fulfilment of God's "promises," Christians should disassociate themselves from the world and live as strangers upon the earth (11:13). The accent of eschatological hope is laid upon the future, but in spite of its nearness it is not conceived as imminent in the way it is with Paul (*see* ESCHATOLOGY OF THE NT). One cannot say that this eschatology is the typical apocalyptic one, although it contains some features of it. But while the anticipation of a future event is stressed, Christ is regarded as having "appeared once for all at the end of the age" (9:26). This affirmation of an eschatological present is rather Gnostic than Jewish.

Connected with the eschatology is the motif of pilgrimage (see especially 3:7–4:13). Thus Israel as the people wandering through the wilderness can be recognized as the prototype of Christianity. We have our gospel not as a possession, but as promise (εὐαγγέλιον as ἐπαγγελία), and therefore the danger of APOSTASY is at hand. Yet in this pilgrimage of God's people—meaning Christianity (4:9; 11:25; 13: 12)—we have Christ as leader (2:10; see further 12:2). This motif is carried through the epistle (notice the verbs προσέρχεσθαι [10:22; 11:6; 12:18, 22]; ἐξέρχεσθαι [13:13]; ἀναστρέφεσθαι [10:33; 13:7]; or in 12:1: "Let us run . . . the race that is set before us"). Of course, this means practically that the present is a militant pilgrimage in which Christ is the forerunner and Christians are to follow in his steps, by suffering. It is the way to the heavenly Jerusalem, the "new and living way" (10:20).

This motif can be found also in Philo, where it is called the "kingly way" (cf. *De Opif. Mundi* 69; *De Mutat. Nom.* 179 ff, etc.). But since there is no direct dependence of Hebrews on Philo, one has to assume a common source. Ernst Käsemann discovered it in pre-Christian Gnostic writings—namely, Mandean literature, Hermetica, the Acts of Thomas, the Odes of Solomon. The Gnostic idea and mythology have been used, but the application of them to Christianity, and the necessary transformation involved, is the work of the author of Hebrews.

b. Christology. The Christology of Hebrews is immediately developed in the opening chapter (vss. 1-4). God "has spoken to us by a Son, whom he appointed the heir of all things, through whom also he created the world." After the redemption "he sat down at the right hand of the Majesty on high" and "obtained the name" of "Son." In the following quotations from the OT, Christ is even "God" (1:8-9) and "Lord" (1:10), later on "Son of God" (4:14). In the very center Christ is described as the "high priest" (7:1 ff). There is no possibility of differentiating between the sonship and the high priesthood of Christ; they are identified (cf. 5:5-6). When in 1:2; 5:7 Jesus in his earthly days seems to possess the sonship, we must recognize that it is used here proleptically, in anticipation. In fact, he was enthroned as Son after his ascension (the passages 1:5 ff give the enthronement; the term "first born" [πρωτότοκος] refers to the universal rulership). Yet he was preexistent and participated in God's creation (1:2). This means Jesus as Son during his historical lifetime was a *Christus absconditus,* a "hidden Christ." There is obviously a common line in Hebrews and Phil. 2:5-11 (*see* PHILIPPIANS, LETTER TO THE; KENOSIS). They both use an earlier pattern, probably the Gnostic "Anthropos" myth. The gift of "the name" (ὄνομα) is the final glorification after suffering and crucifixion; in Hebrews it is the name "Son"; in Phil. 2:9 ff it is "Lord." Christ Jesus is seen as the decisive revelation of God. He is God's representative in the midst of this world and is our representative in heaven before God. In other words, he is the mediator (ὁ μεσίτης; Heb. 8:6; 9:15; 12:24—in all three cases connected with διαθήκη). Although he is seen in the succession of preceding words of God, he is now the final one and has a cosmic power superior to angels, Moses, Aaron, Melchizedec, and this-worldly priests. Yet the ultimate victory will come when after the Parousia all angels and men will kneel before him and the rulership of his kingdom will be perfect.

There is no explicit mentioning of Christ's resurrection—an allusion may appear in 13:20—but it is presupposed whenever exaltation and enthronement in heaven are spoken of. The accent is upon his being in heaven. In the same way, the crucifixion is not explicitly referred to, but is everywhere presupposed. It is interpreted in two ways: as the purification of our sins (cf. 1:3) and as the victory over death. In winning the latter he had to be real man "of the same nature" (2:14) as we are. He had to suffer and to undergo temptations. Especially the point of being tempted is stressed (2:18: "Because he himself has suffered and been tempted, he is able to help those who are tempted"; cf. 4:15; see also 5:8), not so much in order to enrich the Christology, but to emphasize the soteriological aspect. In this connection Christ's being without sin (χωρὶς ἁμαρτίας; 4:15 [cf. 9:28]) is asserted. Thus he revealed himself as the very Messiah, the perfect one forever (5:9; 7:28). His death is seen as the consequence of his incarnation and as resulting primarily in the destruction of the power of death (2:14) for all who follow him in faith.

The concept of Christ as the high priest (ἀρχιερεύς) runs through the letter as a whole, just as that of his being the Son. In both instances Christ is the eschatological representation. The idea does not occur anywhere else in the NT canon (but cf. I Clem. 36: 1; 61:3; 64:1; Ign. Phila. 9:1; each time in liturgical context). The work of the high priest comprises earth and heaven. By his death he unlocks the door to the eternal sanctuary in heaven. He receives the initiation for the heavenly cult and enables all believers to follow him as the forerunner (6:20). His work means atonement for the sins of men. The soteriological aspect is explained in 7:1–10:18, yet has been assumed since 2:14. In 2:17 the title of high priest is used as if known to the readers. It may be that it was known from liturgical usage in the congregation. It is known that the "historical" high priest had to be a descendant of Aaron. In the DEAD SEA SCROLLS the one of the two mentioned messiahs—namely, the priestly one—is named as Messiah of Aaron. He is just the same as the high priest of Hebrews, who is identified with Jesus of Nazareth. With Philo the LOGOS is also the high priest. Hellenistic and Jewish traditions come together in this title and figure, which seems to be a well-known messianic metaphor, again going back to pre-Christian Gnostic conceptions that are connected with the terms of an ἀρχηγός and πρόδρομος.

In Heb. 5:1-4 it is said about the high priest: (*a*) that he is called by God, just as Aaron was (5:4); (*b*) that he is chosen from among men (5:1); (*c*) that he acts on behalf of men—i.e., he is priest (5:1); (*d*) that he can deal gently with men (5:2)—i.e., he has "compassion"; (*e*) that he himself is beset with weakness (5:2); (*f*) that he is bound to offer sacrifice for himself (5:3); (*g*) that he is bound to offer sacrifice for the sins of the people (5:3). These characteristics and functions of the high priest explain the work of Christ Jesus. Yet, the functions do not really correspond to the historical Christ Jesus. Therefore, we find the emphasis in 5:5-6 that he "did not exalt himself to be made a high priest, but was appointed" by God and called "Son" and nominated a "priest for ever, after the order of Melchizedek."

The unique Melchizedek passages of Hebrews (cf. Philo *On Abraham* 235; yet Melchizedek is never called *high* priest with Philo, Josephus, or the LXX) go back to Ps. 110:4 and perhaps again to earliest liturgical traditions (see Heb. 3:1; 4:14; 10:23; see also above to 2:16). This tradition was taken up already in 5:10; 6:20; yet is unfolded in 7:1 ff. Who is Melchizedek? According to etymology "Ṣedeḳ is King" (מלכי־צדק; Gen. 14:18) or later with Heb. 7: 2: "by translation of his name, king of righteousness." Probably he is meant as the primeval man who returns as Messiah, like such figures as Moses, Elijah, or Metatron, Sem or Michael. He is held here in higher respect than in the OT. Since we have, with Philo, Melchizedek as "priest of God" and as Logos, one must assume a common tradition, which is Gnostic in its origin. For the christological theme the correspondence of type and antitype is significant, having in common the eternal priesthood: "Resembling the Son of God he continues a priest for ever" (7:3). The repetition of Melchizedek in Christ refers to his eschatological and concluding role as Messiah. The typological picture demonstrates how Jesus is interpreted in a cultic direction, according to Ps. 110, and yet without losing the identity of his historicity and exaltation.

The Christology of Hebrews is strictly connected with soteriology. The theme "Son" is connected with that of "the sons"—i.e., the believers (2:5–3:6). The point of departure was the citation of Ps. 8 and its reference to "man" and "the son of man." The interrelation is historical and sacramental as well as symbolic. The specific terms "faith" (πίστις) and "confession" (ὁμολογία) point to this. We have in 11:1 the famous verse: "Now faith is the assurance of things hoped for, the conviction of things not seen." Is this to be taken as a Christian definition? As it stands, it is more a phenomenological description than a theological definition. Yet other sayings of Hebrews can supplement 11:1. Remarkable is the strict connection of faith and hope (ἐλπίς or ὑπόστασις: cf. 6:11; 10:22). Hope, as well as faith, has as subject the promises of God (ἐπαγγελία). In other words, they are conditioned by the future. On the other hand, faith is (as with Paul) obedience toward the Word of God (3:7 ff)—to that word which God has finally spoken in Christ Jesus—and demands steadfastness (6:12) and patience (10:36; 12:1). This Word of God means God himself and his revelation in Christ Jesus. More than in other books of the NT canon, this "faith" becomes "faithfulness." And here enters the often used term "confession" (ὁμολογία; see 3:1; 4:14; 10:23), which seems to refer to a liturgical action and to the actualization of faith in the life of following Christ's example. The confession is man's response to God's action in Christ.

c. The admonitions. The theological-christological intention of Hebrews leads to the primary point of the ethical admonitions. As in PAUL, who connects always the indicative of being with the imperative of becoming (cf. Rom. 6), we find in our epistle a consistent connection of Christology-soteriology and following parenesis, or exhortation (*see* § 2 *above*). Whenever Hebrews speaks of "Son and sons," of the first-born in the singular (1:6) and the plural (12:23), of the forerunner, of the Christian "pilgrimage," an ethical implication is given. Yet we do not find, as with Paul, concrete ethical demands. The admonitions are primarily concerned with the danger of APOSTASY or weariness and lack of hope. In order to strengthen their steadfastness, the author calls the repetition of repentance "impossible" (6:4-6). All this is also reflected when faith is perceived as faithfulness and sin more as the weakening of faithfulness than as disobedience or actual deed.

5. Historical setting. The previous section referred several times to Gnostic sources used by the author for his Christology and eschatology, especially for his motif of the Christian pilgrimage. This historical perspective seems to be more justified than that in which Hebrews is seen in the exclusive context of rabbinism. Even the general nearness to Philo is better explained by acknowledging a Jewish Gnosis. Yet our author makes use of this Gnostic material in his own independent way and does it throughout, consistently taking his Christology for the primary point of admonition. Future research has to elaborate further the historical setting of Hebrews.

Bibliography. Commentaries by J. Moffatt (1924); T. H. Robinson (1933); O. Michel (8th ed., 1949); G. Spicq (1952-53). E. F. Scott, *The Epistle to the Hebrews* (1922); W. Manson, *The Epistle to the Hebrews* (1951); E. Käsemann, *Das wandernde Gottesvolk* (2nd ed., 1957).

E. DINKLER

HEBRON hē'brən [חברון, association, league]; HEBRONITES —īts. **1.** A Levite, third son of Kohath; named in P (Exod. 6:18; Num. 3:19) and Chronicles (I Chr. 6:2, 18; 23:12). From him were reckoned the Hebronites and "the sons of Hebron" (15:9; 23:19; 24:23).

2. Son of Mareshah in a Calebite genealogy; father of Korah, Tappuah, Rekem, and Shema. Possibly the reference is to the city of this name (I Chr. 2:42-43).

Bibliography. M. Noth, *Die israelitischen Personennamen* (1928), p. 222.

T. M. MAUCH

HEBRON (CITY). 1. A city nineteen miles S of Jerusalem, 13½ miles S-SW of Bethlehem.* It lies on the E side of a valley and has an unusually abundant water supply (wells and springs). From its

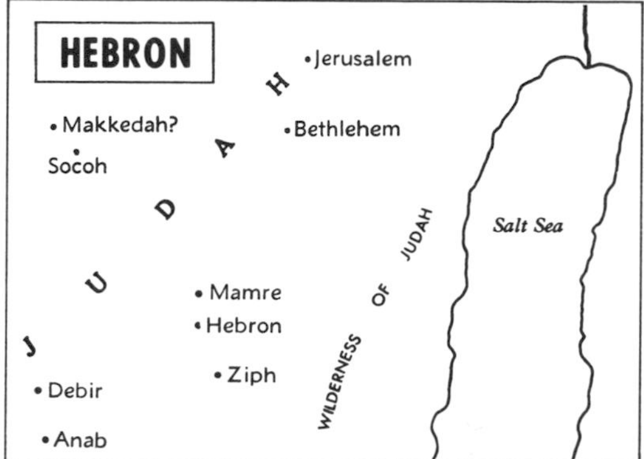

founding to the time of the Crusades, Hebron was built on the hill er-Rumeideh, just W of the modern city. On it are examples of pottery from the end of the Bronze Age on, and on its summit are remains of an ancient wall and other ruins (called Deir el-Arba'in). The modern city is built around the tombs of the patriarchs. Fig. HEB 12.

The present name of the city, el-Khalil (er-Rahman), "the friend [of the merciful one—i.e., God]" is reminiscent of an appellation for Abraham found, e.g., in II Chr. 20:7; Isa. 41:8; Jub. 19:9; Philo (in *On Sobriety:* ὁ θεοφιλής); Jas. 2:23. The mosque over the cave is called the Haram el-Khalil, the "sacred precinct of the friend [of the merciful one]." Fig. HEB 13.

Hebron was a Canaanite royal city in the hill country of Judah, founded seven years before the

From *Atlas of the Bible* (Thomas Nelson & Sons Limited)

12. Aerial view of the setting for the ancient city of Hebron

From *Atlas of the Bible* (Thomas Nelson & Sons Limited)
13. The town of Hebron

(re)building of Zoan (Tanis, earlier Avaris) in Egypt (Num. 13:22) or *ca.* the middle of the fourteenth century B.C. This tradition is supported by the patriarchal narrative in which the references are to Mamre, just N of Hebron, with the latter serving chiefly as a location point for the hearers (and readers) of a later date (cf. Gen. 13:18; 23:19; 35: 27; 37:14). In Abraham's day, a time of considerable unrest in the region, there was at least one Hittite clan in the vicinity, as well as Amorites, for Abraham had to purchase the cave for a family sepulchre from a Hittite chieftain named Ephron (Gen. 23:8; cf. 14: 13; *see* MACHPELAH).

At the time of its founding, it was called Kiriath-arba (Tetrapolis, or "fourfold" city) and later came to be called Hebron (Gen. 23:2; 35:27; Josh. 15:54; 20:7; 21:11; Neh. 11:25). The historical relationship between the two names is unclear. The biblical tradition relates the earlier name to one Arba, the great hero of the Anakim, "the giants," a people mentioned in the conquest narrative (Num. 13:22; Josh. 14:15; 15:13), and possibly in the twentieth-century Egyptian execration texts. The biblical tradition is probably etiological but may conceal within it a reference to a historical event which escapes us at present.

In the fourteenth century the Hebron region was ruled for a time by a local prince, Shuwardata, who appears in several of the Amarna Letters. In the first unsuccessful attempt at conquest, by approaching Canaan from the S, Moses' spies reconnoitered around Hebron and elsewhere to determine the strength of their prospective adversaries. Three clans of the Anakim (Sheshai, Ahiman, and Talmai) lived at Hebron at this time, early in the thirteenth century (Num. 13:22). After about a generation the successful attack against Canaan was launched from the E.

This time Hoham, king of Hebron, died at the hand of Joshua and his forces in the latter's victory over the S Canaanite coalition led by Adonizedek of Jerusalem in the Battle of Makkedah (Josh. 10:1-27). Hebron itself was destroyed and its population devoted to the sword along with Debir, Anab, and other hill-country cities (Josh. 10:36-37; 11:21-22). Archaeological evidence indicates immediate Israelite occupation of Debir (cf., however, Judg. 1:11-12), but Hebron seems to have been reoccupied by the three clans of the Anakim and was not effectively controlled by the Israelites until its recapture by Caleb's forces after Joshua's death (Josh. 14:13 ff; 15:13-14; Judg. 1:10, 19-20; cf. Josh. 10:36-39; 11: 21-22). The biblical account is not entirely clear on this matter, however. The account of Caleb's capture of Hebron could simply be one phase of the campaign of occupation under Joshua's general leadership—or a continuation of it after Joshua's death. Hebron was designated a Levitical city and a city of refuge (Josh. 20:7; 21:10-13; I Chr. 6:57). In the royal administrative reorganization, it became a district capital (Josh. 15:54).

Hebron is prominent in the story of David's early career. It was one of the cities to receive a gift from David for services rendered him and his men; the gift was taken from the booty captured from the Amalekites after David's successful pursuit of them, in reprisal for their sack of Ziklag (I Sam. 30:31). He was anointed "king of Judah," and for the first 7½ years of his reign it was capital of the S kingdom; while Ishbosheth (Ishbaal), Saul's son, ruled the N from Mahanaim. Several of David's sons, including Absalom, were born at Hebron. As a result of a personal affront, Ishbosheth's general, Abner, defected and was in the process of bringing the N into David's camp when he was treacherously killed by Joab and his brother for Abner's slaying of their brother in the course of an engagement which had begun at the Pool of Gibeon. Abner was buried in Hebron. After Abner's death, two of Ishbosheth's captains assassinated him, decapitated him, and took his head to David at Hebron, hoping for a bounty. Instead, David had them killed for their treachery, and had Ishbosheth's head buried in Abner's grave. After Ishbosheth's death, the N was united with the S, and the capital moved to the newly captured Jerusalem, from which David ruled the remaining 33 years of his reign (II Sam. 2:1-5:5; I Kings 2:11; I Chr. 3: 1-4; 29:27).

Hebron became the headquarters for Absalom's abortive revolt against his father, David (II Sam. 15: 7-10). Rehoboam (*ca.* 922-915) had the fortifications of Hebron strengthened (II Chr. 11:5, 10). The tentative reading "field of Abram" in the list of Palestinian places captured by Shishak in *ca.* 918 B.C. may refer to Hebron, in which case it is the first extra-biblical association of Abraham and the region of Hebron. Hebron was probably occupied by Sennacherib in 701 and destroyed by Nebuchadrezzar in 587, though there is no specific biblical reference to either so far as Hebron is concerned. From the eighth-century jar handles found at various sites, on which the legend "belonging to the king: Hebron" (or Ziph or Soco or Memshath) appears, it seems that Hebron may have been a royal pottery during this period.

During the Exile the region of Hebron was occupied by the Idumeans (Edomites), in whose hands it remained until 164, when Judas Maccabeus captured and burned it, destroying the walls and towers which protected it (I Macc. 5:65; cf. Jos. Antiq. XII. viii.6). Except for its fortifications, apparently, it was rebuilt, and during the reign of Herod the Great pretentious buildings were erected over the site of the Cave of Machpelah and on the site of MAMRE; part of the former remains in the mosque now standing on the site. In A.D. 68, Simon, one of the Jewish revolutionaries, raided Hebron for supplies (Jos. War

IV.ix.7); later that year, Cerealius, one of Vespasian's officers, captured and burned the city (Jos. War IV. ix.9). It is not mentioned in the NT, and references to it during the Byzantine period are concerned only with the tomb of the patriarchs there; it belonged to the Diocese of Eleutheropolis. During the Crusades the Praesidium Sancti Abrahae was erected nearby. In 1168 it became the seat of a bishopric, but it was returned to Muslim rule in 1187.

Bibliography. F.-M. Abel, *Géographie de la Palestine,* vol. II (1938); H. H. Rowley, *From Joseph to Joshua* (1950); R. de Vaux, "Macpélah," *Dictionnaire de la Bible, Supplément,* vol. V (1953), cols. 620-21; G. E. Wright, *Biblical Archaeology* (1957).

2. KJV translation in Josh. 19:28. The Hebrew is better rendered עברן, EBRON, in the RSV. However, it should be read עבדון, ABDON, with some Hebrew MSS; Josh. 21:30; I Chr. 6:74—H 6:59.

V. R. GOLD

HEDGE. Properly, the translation of the noun משוכה (alternately מסוכה), the verb שוך (alternately שכך), referring to a thorn hedge (*see* THISTLES), and the noun φραγμός, a fence of any kind. Occasionally, however, "hedge" has been used to render גדר (alternately גדרה), a stone WALL or FENCE. Hedges were constructed to protect vineyards (*see* VINE) from predators (Ps. 80:12-13—H 80:13-14; Isa. 5:5; Matt. 21:33; Mark 12:1). Indeed, the whole countryside could be regarded as consisting of either highways or hedges (Luke 14:23). Figuratively the verb "hedge (in or about)" is used to express both God's protection (Job 1:10) and his constraint (Job 3:23; Lam. 3:7; Hos. 2:6—H 2:8) of a person. Micah complains that even "the most upright is sharper than a thorn hedge" (7:4 KJV).

J. F. ROSS

HEDGEHOG [קפוד, קפד, *probably from* קפד (*Pi'el*), to roll up; *cf.* Arab. *qunfudh,* hedgehog; Syr. *qûfdâ,* hedgehog, porcupine]; KJV BITTERN. Alternately: PORCUPINE (Isa. 34:11); KJV BITTERN (Isa. 14:23; Zeph. 2:14). Any of the genus Erinaceus, small insect-eating mammals, *ca.* ten to twelve inches long, covered with a coat of short spines and having the power to roll themselves up in self-protection into a ball-like form. Three species of hedgehog are reported by Bodenheimer as found in modern Palestine.

The three OT passages in which קפוד (*qippôd*) occurs describe inhabited areas which are to become desolate and the home of various wild creatures. The word probably means "hedgehog," but in Zeph. 2:14 this can be so only if it is assumed that the columns and capitals of Nineveh's buildings have fallen to the ground.

The "porcupine" of Isa. 34:11 is a rodent of the family Hystricidae, and although exclusively vegetable-eating and more than twice the size of a hedgehog it bears a superficial resemblance to the latter in having the protection of quills or spines. Porcupines are found in modern Palestine, where, Tristram records, they are "commonly believed by the natives to be a larger species of hedgehog."

See also FAUNA § A2*b*. W. S. MCCULLOUGH

HEEL, LIFTED. The phrase הגדיל עלי עקב (lit., "made great the heel[?] against me") is translated "has lifted his heel against me" in Ps. 41:9 (cf. John 13:18). The expression refers to the cruel treachery of friends, who, in line with Semitic custom, have interpreted the sick man's distress as divine punishment, and have made him an object of social rejection. It may have no reference whatever to raising the heel to kick one, as a means of attack (cf. Hos. 12:3: עקב, "to attack at the heel," treated as the root of "Jacob" in Gen. 25:26; 27:36), or to the cunning of a wrestler (as πτέρναν would suggest in John 13: 18), and may simply mean "has turned his back on me," or "has turned his heel on me."

It is possible that the word עקב, translated "heel" (but also meaning "reward," or as an adverb "because"), is misplaced from the end of vs. 11, or is an early gloss. הגדיל is never used in the OT in the sense of "lift up" or "raise," but always "to act proudly," "to magnify oneself." The phrase הגדיל עלי occurs elsewhere (e.g., Job. 19:15; Pss. 35:26; 55:12). Moreover, the context of Ps. 41:9 suggests words rather than deeds (as "lifted his heel" would indicate). The LXX, however, had the full phrase (reading "has magnified his supplanting of me"). The NT (John 13:18) follows neither the MT nor the LXX but reads: "has lifted his heel against me." Jesus applies the words to the treachery of Judas, who, by turning on Jesus, brought fresh significance to these words. The NT phrase means "acted treacherously," and applies to deeds. But the emphasis would seem to be that one, with whom one was bound by a covenant of peace, who partook of one's bread, had violated the laws of hospitality, and had turned on his host.

Bibliography. G. H. A. Ewald, *Commentary on the Psalms* (trans. E. Johnson; 1880), I, 191-95; T. K. Cheyne, *The Book of Psalms,* I (1904), 183; R. Kittel, *Die Psalmen* (1922), p. 147.

V. H. KOOY

HEGAI hĕg'ī [הגי, הגא (Esth. 2:3), *probably from* Pers.; *cf.* 'Ηγίας, an officer of Xerxes (Herodotus 9.33; Ctesias *Persians* 24] (Esth. 2:3, 8, 15); KJV HEGE hĕg'ī in Esth. 2:3. A eunuch of Ahasuerus, in charge of the women.

HEGEMONIDES hĕj'ə mō'nə dēz ['Ηγεμονίδης = ἡγεμών, guide(?)] (II Macc. 13:24); KJV PRINCIPAL. Syrian officer appointed by Antiochus as "governor from Ptolemais to Gerar" at the time Antiochus was compelled to withdraw to Antioch to deal with the revolt under Philip.

J. C. SWAIM

HEGLAM hĕg'ləm [הגלם, he carried them into exile] (I Chr. 8:7). Son of Ehud, and the father of Uzza and Ahihud; Heglam is given as an alternative for the hypocoristic name Gera.

The descent of Ehud is not specified in this section of the genealogical table. According to Judg. 3: 15, a Benjaminite by the name of Gera was the father of Ehud. Presumably the Gera of I Chr. 8:7 was a descendant of Benjamin, through Bela, though the relationship in this case is more remote than with the Gera of vs. 3, who was clearly identified as the son of Bela and the grandson of Benjamin. It is possible that this grandson of Benjamin is to be identified as the father of both Ehud and the Shimei who cursed David (II Sam. 16:5; 19:16-17, 19; I Kings 2:8), and therefore as the founder of the Benjaminite family or clan which bore the same name (Gen. 46:21; contrast Num. 26:38-40). H. F. BECK

HEIFER [עגלה; עגלת בקר (*correctly* YOUNG COW *in* Isa. 7:21); פרה, *see* COW; δάμαλις]. The heifer was used on the threshing floor (Hos. 10:11; cf. Deut. 25:4) and presumably for other agricultural work. A three-year-old heifer was used in the Lord's covenant with Abraham (Gen. 15:9). Samuel sacrificed a heifer (I Sam. 16:2). The neck of a heifer was broken in expiating murder by an unknown assailant (Deut. 21:1-9; cf. M. Soṭ. 9.1-9; Ker. 6.2; Par. 1.1).

The term "heifer" is applied figuratively to his Philistine wife by Samson (Judg. 14:18), to Egypt (Jer. 46:20), to Babylon (Jer. 50:11), to Israel in her stubbornness (Hos. 4:16, where, however, the word is פרה, "cow"), and to a docile Ephraim (Hos. 10:11). The heifer at grass is a symbol of wantonness in Jer. 50:11.

The KJV "heifer of three years old" (Isa. 15:5; Jer. 48:34) is taken by most commentators to be a place name, Eglath-shelishiyah (so RSV).

For the red heifer of Num. 19:1-10 (the word is פרה and should be translated "cow"; cf. δάμαλις in Heb. 9:13), *see* RED HEIFER.

The "heifers" (עגלות) of Beth-aven (Bethel) in Hos. 10:5 should be read "calf" (עגל; cf. LXX, Syr.; so RSV). *See* CALF, GOLDEN. W. S. MCCULLOUGH

HEIR [יורש, one who inherits; κληρονόμος]. The son of an owner of property. The heir, while still a child, was no better than a slave. Although the potential owner of the entire estate, he was under guardians and trustees until the date set by the father (Gal. 4:1-2).

Through Christ men cease to be slaves and become sons and heirs (Gal. 4:4-7). The Son has been appointed heir of all things, so that he reflects the glory of God (Heb. 1:2-3). Noah became an heir of the righteousness that faith produces (11:7), and Isaac and Jacob are also heirs of the promise that God made to Abraham (vs. 9). The poor, and men and women alike, are all "heirs of the grace of life" (I Pet. 3:7).

See also INHERITANCE. O. J. BAAB

HELAH hē'lə [חלאה, necklace] (I Chr. 4:5, 7). One of the two wives of Ashhur, descendant of Judah and ancestor of Tekoa.

HELAM hē'ləm [חילם, חלאם]. A city near the N boundary of Gilead, where David defeated the Syrians (II Sam. 10:16-17). It was also read by the LXX in Ezek. 47:16 and located between Hamath and Damascus. It is the same as the *Ḥl'm* of the Egyptian Execration Texts (1850-1825 B.C.) and the ALEMA of I Macc. 5:26. S. COHEN

HELBAH hĕl'bə [חלבה] (Judg. 1:31). A town in Asher, from which the Israelites could not expel the Canaanite population. Helbah is generally considered to be the same as AHLAB, because of the similarity of their consonants; both are corrupt variants of MAHALAB. G. W. VAN BEEK

HELBON hĕl'bŏn [חלבון; Akkad. *Ḫilbūnu;* Arab. *Ḥelbūn*] (Ezek. 27:18). A town mentioned in the lamentation for Tyre; particularly famous for its wine. It is identified with modern Helbun, NW of Damascus in a region of Anti-lebanon where also today the cultivation of the vine is important. A. HALDAR

HELCHIAH. KJV Apoc. form of HILKIAH 6 in I Esd. 8:1.

HELDAI hĕl'dī [חלדי, mole (animal); חלם (Zech. 6:14)]. Alternately: HELED hē'lĕd [חלד, mole] (I Chr. 11:30); HELEB hē'lĕb [חלב] (II Sam. 23:29); KJV HELEM hē'lĕm in Zech. 6:14. **1.** One of David's MIGHTY MEN; a Netophathite (II Sam. 23:29; I Chr. 11:30; 27:15). The name should be read either "Heldai" (I Chr. 27:15) or "Heled" (I Chr. 11:30), both of which are from the same root. "Heleb" (II Sam. 23:29) must be an error.

2. One of those who brought gold and silver with which the prophet Zechariah was to make a crown for Joshua the high priest (Zech. 6:10, 14). "Helem" in 6:14 (Hebrew and KJV) must be an error.

Bibliography. M. Noth, *Die israelitischen Personennamen* (1928), p. 230. H. H. GUTHRIE, JR.

HELECH hē'lĕk [חילך] (Ezek. 27:11); KJV THINE ARMY. Possibly the name of the country of Cilicia, in SE Asia Minor.

Assyrian records refer to part of the region of CILICIA under the name of Hilakku. The earliest mention appears under Shalmaneser III (858-824 B.C.). Hilakku was presumably conquered by Sargon *ca.* 720 B.C. and given to a vassal prince. The country revolted against Sennacherib in 696 and again under Esarhaddon (680-669). It sent tribute to Ashurbanipal *ca.* 668/7, perhaps in fear of the Cimmerian invasions. *See* GOMER.

The reading of "Helech" among the mercenaries of Tyre is consistent with the warlike character of the Cilicians with their Phoenician contacts attested for the seventh century B.C. and later. It seems preferable to the KJV "thine army."

Bibliography. For Hilakku, see P. Naster, *L'Asie Mineure et l'Assyrie aux VIIIe et VIIe siècles avant Jésus-Christ* (1938). M. J. MELLINK

HELED. An alternate form of HELDAI.

HELEK hē'lĕk [חלק, portion, lot]; HELEKITES —lə kīts. A member of the tribe of Manasseh, of the family of the Helekites (Num. 26:30). He is listed as one of the male descendants of Manasseh the son of Joseph (Josh. 17:2; cf. vs. 1; also Num. 27:29, where Helek's lineage is traced back to Joseph through Gilead, Machir, and Manasseh). W. L. REED

HELEM. KJV form of HELDAI 2; HELER.

HELEPH hē'lĕf [חלף] (Josh. 19:33). A border town in Naphtali. Khirbet 'Arbathah, located a short distance to the NE of Mount Tabor, has been suggested as a possible identification, but this is uncertain.

Bibliography. A. Saarisalo, *The Boundary Between Issachar and Naphtali* (1927), pp. 27-28, 122-24. G. W. VAN BEEK

HELER hē'lər [הלם] (I Chr. 7:35; RSV in error); KJV HELEM hē'lĕm. A family of the tribe of Asher.

This name should probably be HOTHAM (cf. I Chr. 7:32).

HELEZ hē'lĕz [חלץ, he has saved (*shortened form*); *cf.* Phoen. חלצבעל, Baal has saved]. **1.** One of David's MIGHTY MEN (II Sam. 23:26; I Chr. 11:27; 27:10). II Samuel calls him "the PALTITE"; I Chronicles "the PELONITE." Since LXX A reads "the Peolonite" in II Samuel and since I Chr. 27:10 says Helez is an Ephraimite, "the Pelonite" is probably correct.

2. A family of the tribe of Judah (I Chr. 2:39).

Bibliography. M. Noth, *Die israelitischen Personennamen* (1928), p. 180. H. H. GUTHRIE, JR.

HELI hē'lī ['Ηλί=עלי, Eli]. **1.** The father (according to some, the grandfather) of Joseph in the genealogy of Jesus (Luke 3:23).

2. Douay Version form of ELI; also KJV form in II Esd. 1:2. F. W. GINGRICH

HELIAS. KJV Apoc. form of ELIJAH.

HELIODORUS hē'lĭ ə dôr'əs ['Ηλιόδωρος]. A high official in the court of the Seleucid king Seleucus IV Philopator, who was sent to confiscate temple moneys at Jerusalem for the royal treasury; he became the object of divine vengeance, according to a story told in II Macc. 3 and repeated with some differences in IV Macc. 3:19–4:14. A temple official named Simon falsely represented the situation with reference to deposits in the temple treasury to Apollonius, the governor of Coele Syria and Phoenicia; Apollonius then reported it to the king. When Heliodorus attempted to enter the treasury, he was attacked and dreadfully beaten by a horseman in golden armor and two youths who appeared miraculously. At the intervention of the high priest Onias III, the stricken man was saved and lived to tell how the power of God defended his dwelling place.

According to Appian (*Syrian Wars* 45), Heliodorus was a dear friend of Seleucus IV; an inscription found in the temple of Apollo at Delos suggests that Heliodorus was a prominent officer in the court. In 175 B.C. he attempted to usurp the throne by assassinating the king, only to be driven out by Eumenes and Attalus, who put Seleucus' brother Antiochus on the throne.

Bibliography. W. Otto in Pauly-Wissowa, *Realencyklopädie*, VIII (1913), 12-15; A. Bouché-Leclercq, *Histoire des Séleucides* (1913-14), pp. 239 ff; E. R. Bevan, *Cambridge Ancient History*, VIII (1930), 490 ff. E. W. SAUNDERS

HELIOPOLIS hē'lĭ ŏp'ə lĭs [בית שמש, house of the sun; LXX ἡλίου πόλεως] (Jer. 43:13); KJV BETH-SHEMESH bĕth shē'mĕsh. The capital of the Thirteenth Lower Egyptian nome, situated at the S vertex of the Nile Delta.

1. Name and references
2. Heliopolitan theology
3. A cult center
4. Archaeological finds

Bibliography

1. Name and references. Heliopolis, one of the most important cities of ancient Egypt, was situated near the site occupied today by the village of Matariyah, by Tell Hisn, just NE of modern Cairo. The Egyptian called the city *iwnw* (or *inw*), which is borrowed in Hebrew as *'Ôn* (also Aven) and is found in cuneiform inscriptions as *Anu* (Middle Babylonian) and *Unu* (Late Assyrian). On is mentioned in Gen. 41:45, 50; 46:20, where Potiphera is referred to as the priest of On. Elsewhere, other than in Jer. 43:13, Heliopolis is mentioned only obliquely, as in Isa. 19:18, where we should possibly read עיר החרס (*'îr haḥeres*), "City of the Sun." The latter passage has a textual problem in the relevant phrase: the MT has *haheres,* not *haḥeres.* The reading *haḥeres,* which is probably a reference to Heliopolis in view of the Egyptian context of the verse, is supported by several MSS, as well as by Symm. and the Vulg. It is noteworthy that outside the Genesis narrative none of the references to Heliopolis (if, indeed, this is the correct understanding of them) is direct—Aven, Beth-shemesh, and Ir-haheres.

2. Heliopolitan theology. Heliopolis is perhaps best known as the home of the Heliopolitan theology, which had assumed its basic form as early as the Third Dynasty. According to this system the chief deity was Atum, syncretized with Re into Atum-Re, the sun-god, who dominated the Great Ennead, consisting of Shu (atmosphere); Tefnut (moisture); Geb (earth); Nut (sky); ISIS; OSIRIS; Seth; and Nephthys. This ennead was adopted also by the Memphite theologians, who altered it by making Ptah the central figure, and, indeed, the emanation and manifestation of the ennead itself.

3. A cult center. Although Heliopolis played no important political role in Egyptian history, it remained one of its most outstanding cult centers until Saïte times. Among the numerous objects of veneration to be found in Heliopolis were (*a*) the steer-god Mnevis, (*b*) the stone fetish known as the *benben* (prototype of the OBELISK), (*c*) the phoenix, a symbol of the birth of Atum, and (*d*) the *iwn* pillar, presumably the fetish from which the city took its name. Note that Jer. 43:13 mentions Heliopolis specifically with reference to its function as a cult city and the site most commonly associated with the obelisk.

4. Archaeological finds. The present site is relatively poor in archaeological remains and, according to Petrie, shows no evidence of ancient occupation after the Saïte period (Twenty-sixth Dynasty). This would support the statement of Strabo (XVII.805-6) that the city was laid waste by Cambyses. Among the items of unusual archaeological interest is a curious enclosure surrounded by a ringwall with rounded corners. Though it was identified by Petrie as a Hyksos fort, further investigation by Ricke suggests that the "fort bank" was actually the retaining wall of a primitive mound of sand upon which stood the *benben.* This would symbolize, then, the primordial hillock on which Atum stood when he first emerged from the waters of Nun (chaos). Further noteworthy remains are the large temple area of Atum-Re-Harakhte and the still standing obelisk of Sesostris I (Twelfth Dynasty).

Bibliography. W. M. F. Petrie, *Heliopolis, Kafr Ammar, and Shurafa* (1915), pp. 1-7; H. Ricke, "Eine Inventartafel aus Heliopolis im Turiner Museum," *ZA*, 71 (1935), 111-33;

A. H. Gardiner, *Ancient Egyptian Onomastica* (Text), II (1947), 144-46; H. Bonnet, *Reallexikon der ägyptischen Religionsgeschichte* (1952), pp. 543-45. T. O. LAMBDIN

HELKAI hĕl'kī [חלקי, *perhaps contracted from* חלקיהו, my portion is Yahu] (Neh. 12:15). A priest, head of the house of Meraioth in the days of Joiakim the high priest.

Bibliography. M. Noth, *Die israelitischen Personennamen* (1928), pp. 38, 163-64. B. T. DAHLBERG

HELKATH hĕl'kăth [חלקת] (Josh. 19:25; 21:31). Alternately: HUKOK hŏŏ'kŏk [חוקק] (I Chr. 6:75—H 6:60). A Levitical border town in Asher. The first historical mention of Helkath is in the Thut-mose III list of towns (Egyptian *Ḫrgt*).

Perhaps the town is to be identified with Tell el-Harbaj, a low mound of *ca.* six acres, located at the S end of the Plain of Acco and occupied in the Early Bronze (*ca.* 3000-2100), Late Bronze (*ca.* 1550-1200), and Iron I (*ca.* 1200-900) periods.

Bibliography. British School of Archaeology Jerusalem Bulletin 2 (1922), pp. 10-17; 4 (1924), 45-46. A. Alt, "Die Reise," *PJ*, 25 (1929), 38-39. G. W. VAN BEEK

HELKATH-HAZZURIM hĕl'kăth hăzh'ŏŏ rĭm [חלקת הצרים, field of sharp rocks (flints) *or* swords(?), field of adversaries(?)] (II Sam. 2:16). An area, presumably near the Pool of Gibeon, so called as the scene of the "tournament of champions" in which twelve of Joab's men of war dueled with twelve from the ranks of Abner, each thrusting his sword into his opponent's side. Some scholars emend to חלקת הצדים "field of the sides" (see RSV mg.). W. H. MORTON

HELKIAS. KJV Apoc. form of HILKIAH.

HELL. *See* DEAD, ABODE OF THE; GEHENNA.

HELLENISM hĕl'ə nĭz əm. The Greek spirit, character, or civilization, especially the higher culture or humanism of the ancient Hellenes; in modern writers, an enthusiasm for or devotion to this culture. But among historians the term now means the civilization which spread over the Mediterranean world, including the Near East, as a result of Alexander's conquests in the decade 334-325 B.C.

Unfortunately, the aggressive actions of the philhellene party in Jerusalem, early in the second century B.C., led to a crisis under Antiochus IV (*see* MACCABEES, BOOKS OF) and the consequent long Maccabean war of independence. It also created internal tensions within Judaism, resulting in attitudes of exclusiveness and superiority which continued for centuries, and were overcome only in early Christianity (see Acts 15; Galatians). F. C. GRANT

HELLENISTS hĕl'ə nĭsts; KJV GRECIANS grē'shən**z**. Greek-speaking Jews referred to in Acts 6:1; 9:29, and as a variant reading in 11:20. They are contrasted with the "Hebrews"—i.e., Jews who spoke Hebrew (or Aramaic). The tension between the two groups is reflected in Acts 6-7 and elsewhere, and doubtless intensified the problem of the admission of Gentiles to the church, reflected in Acts 15; Gal. 1-2. According to Acts 2:5-6, the foreign-born Jews living in Jerusalem spoke various languages. It may be assumed that in the first century they also spoke Greek, for it was commonly spoken throughout the lands of the Near and Middle East, of which the nations mentioned in Acts 2:9 ff are examples. It was probably these "foreigners" who were designated by the term "Hellenists," rather than Gentiles.

The theory that the term means "Greeks"—i.e., non-Jews—is improbable on several grounds: (*a*) The story itself and the material in Acts 1-5 presuppose the spread of the church among Jews, in Jerusalem; (*b*) the problem of the daily "distribution" implies a much larger group of complainants than a mere infiltration of "Greeks"; (*c*) Philo distinguished between the "Hebrews" and "us"—i.e., the Greek-speaking Jews (*Confusion of Tongues* 26); (*d*) Chrysostom, whose native tongue was Koine Greek, stated explicitly that "Hellenists" meant "Greek-speaking" (*Homily* XIV, on Acts 6:1); (*e*) the account of the conversion of Gentiles (Acts 10:45; 15:3) relates something *new;* (*f*) the whole later conflict over the admission of Gentiles—i.e., without circumcision and observance of the Jewish law—would have been impossible had Gentiles been present in the church from the beginning.

That the variant reading (perhaps an attempted "correction") in Acts 11:20 is erroneous (cf. the reverse variation in 9:29, Codex A) is obvious from the context: "To the Greeks *also*" marks a new stage in the spread of the gospel.

Bibliography. Among the commentaries, see especially E. Haenchen in the Meyer series (1956). H. J. Cadbury in *Beginnings of Christianity* (1920 ff), IV, 64; V, 59-74. E. Lohmeyer, "Das Abendmahl in der Urgemeinde," *JBL*, 56 (1937), 217-52. See further references in W. F. Arndt and F. W. Gingrich, *A Greek-English Lexicon of the NT* (1957). F. C. GRANT

HELMET [כובע, קובע; περικεφαλαία]. A defensive headgear worn in battle, ordinarily probably made of leather for soldiers (II Chr. 26:14; Jer. 46:4; Ezek. 23:24; 27:10; 38:5) but of bronze for royalty and heroes (I Sam. 17:5, 38). It probably consisted of a cap with a long flap to cover the cheek and ears—hence the correct rendering by the LXX as περικεφαλαία (cf. also Eph. 6:17; I Thess. 5:8). In contrast to the Syrian-Hittite helmet, that of the Assyrians and Babylonians was pointed.

In symbolic usage, the Lord is pictured wearing a helmet of salvation (Isa. 59:17). The "armor" of the Christian includes the helmet of salvation (Eph. 6:17), and his helmet is the hope of salvation (I Thess. 5:8). In Pss. 60:7—H 60:9; 108:8—H 108:9 God describes Ephraim as מעוז ראשי (KJV "the strength of mine head"), interpreted in the RSV as "my helmet." J. W. WEVERS

HELON hē'lŏn [חלן, חלון; *if from* חיל *plus diminutive -ōn,* strength, power; LXX Χαιλον] (Num. 1:9; 2:7; 7:24, 29; 10:16). A Zebulunite; the father of Eliab.

HELPERS [ἀντιλήμψεις]; KJV HELPS. One of the charismata, or "gifts of the Spirit," named by Paul in I Cor. 12:28, among the several functions exercised by members of the church for the benefit of one another (cf. Rom. 12:7). It is not the title of an office or ministerial order, though it has often been identified with the ministry of deacons (*see* DEACON). In classical Greek and in the LXX, the word is common in the sense of "lend a hand" to help one in some work. The verb form occurs in Luke 10:40 as a synonym of Martha's household service. In the Pauline context, the word is suggestively placed between the gifts of healing and of administration.

M. H. SHEPHERD, JR.

HEM. 1. A KJV alternate translation of שׁוּל. *See* SKIRT 2.

2. KJV translation of κράσπεδον in Matt. 9:20; 14:36. *See* FRINGE.

HEMAM hē'măm. KJV-MT translation of הימם in Gen. 36:22. The word, probably related to הימן (I Kings 5:11) as אונם (Gen. 36:23) is to אונן (Gen. 38:4), is incorrectly translated HEMAN by the RSV (LXX Αιμαν). Hemam was the second son of the clan chief Lotan, and an ancestor of a Horite subclan in Edom. The name is given in I Chr. 1:39 as HOMAM.

L. HICKS

HEMAN hē'mən [הימן, faithful; הימם, *see* HEMAM]. **1.** A Horite (Gen. 36:22; MT-KJV HEMAM). *See* HOMAM.

2. A "wise man" of the "sons of Mahol" (guild of dancers in the days of Solomon; I Kings 4:31—H 5:11). In I Chr. 2:6 he is called a son of Zerah, a name which the Chronicler may have derived from "Ezrahite" (Ps. 88—H 88:1; *see* ETHAN). Both an Edomite and a Canaanite ancestry have been adduced for Heman. He is probably the same as 3 *below*.

3. A Kohathite, son of Joel; one of the leaders of the temple musicians under David and Solomon (I Chr. 6:33-47—H 6:18-32; 15:17, 19; 16:41; II Chr. 5:12; *see* ASAPH; ETHAN; JEDUTHUN). He is called a seer (I Chr. 25:5) and "prophesied" to musical instruments (vs. 1). Perhaps the guild of Heman was originally a guild of cultic prophets (cf. Jer. 35:4) which was later transformed into a musical guild.

Bibliography. J. A. Montgomery, *Arabia and the Bible* (1934), pp. 169-74; contrast W. F. Albright, *Archaeology and the Religion of Israel* (1956), pp. 126-27. See also: S. Mowinckel, *Psalmenstudien,* III (1923), 17-18. A. R. Johnson, "The Prophet in Israelite Worship," *ET,* XLVII (1935-36), 312-19. R. H. Pfeiffer, *Introduction to the OT* (1948), pp. 621-22, 639.

R. W. CORNEY

HEMATH. KJV alternate form of HAMATH 1.

HEMDAN hĕm'dăn [חמדן, *from* חמד, desire, take pleasure in (?); *cf.* Old South Arab. *proper names* חמד *and* חמדן] (Gen. 36:26). The first son of clan chief Dishon; ancestor of a native Horite subclan in Edom. The name occurs in I Chr. 1:41 as חמרן, HAMRAN.

L. HICKS

HEMLOCK. KJV translation of לענה (RSV WORMWOOD) in Amos 6:12 and of ראשׁ (RSV POISONOUS WEEDS) in Hos. 10:4. *See* FLORA § A14*a;* GALL; POISON; WORMWOOD.

HEMORRHAGE [ῥύσις]. Any bleeding or flow of blood, whether visible or concealed, profuse or sporadic. In the OT hemorrhage brought with it ceremonial defilement, thus imposing serious restrictions upon the individual's religious and social life. Blood was deemed sacred, and all contact with it was strictly prohibited.

The woman with hemorrhage (Matt. 9:20-22; Mark 5:25-34; Luke 8:43-48) probably had a *uterine fibromyoma* (fibroid). The "bloody flux" (Acts 28:8 KJV) was evidently the intestinal bleeding of dysentery (so RSV).

R. K. HARRISON

HEN (PERSON). KJV translation of חן ("favor") in Zech. 6:14. It is probable, however, that the original reading was "Josiah," as in the Syr. and vs. 10. *See* JOSIAH 2.

HEN [ὄρνις, bird, cock, hen] (Matt. 23:37; Luke 13:34). The female of the domestic fowl and of various other birds. Ὄρνις can mean the female of any bird. For figures involving birds to describe God's relation to Israel, cf. Deut. 32:11; Pss. 17:8; 36:7—H 36:8; 91:4; Isa. 31:5; etc. The words of the Lord to Israel in II Esd. 1:30: "I gathered you as a hen gathers her brood under her wings," are thought to be part of a second-century Christian interpolation in this apocalypse.

See also COCK.

W. S. MCCULLOUGH

HENA hĕn'ə [הנע; LXX Ανα, Αναγ, *etc.*]. A town mentioned in II Kings 18:34; 19:13; Isa. 37:13. Its location is not known. In II Kings 18:13-36 it is related that the Assyrian king Sennacherib, who then was out on an expedition against Jerusalem, sent his envoys from his headquarters at Lachish to persuade Hezekiah to give up his anti-Assyrian policy. The Assyrian envoys stated that Hezekiah would have no success. Other kings had tried the same but without result. To illustrate this statement, the fate of other cities, including Hena, was referred to.

A. HALDAR

HENADAD hĕn'ə dăd [חנדד, *perhaps* favor of Hadad (weather deity)]. The eponym for a Levitical house of priests mentioned in connection with the building of the temple under Zerubbabel (Ezra 3:9), the repair of the Jerusalem wall in the time of Nehemiah (Neh. 3:18, 24), and the signing of Ezra's covenant (Neh. 10:9).

B. T. DAHLBERG

HENNA [כפר, *kōpher;* κύπρος]; KJV CAMPHIRE. A fragrant flowering shrub or tree, *Lawsonia inermis* L., which is common in the Middle East.

In Song of S. 1:14 the lover is likened to the fragrant cluster of the henna blossoms "in [from?] the vineyards of Engedi," where the tree has been found. In 4:13-14 the tree is listed with NARD; SAFFRON; CALAMUS; CINNAMON; and FRANKINCENSE in a metaphor in praise of the bride.

Kᵉphārîm in Song of S. 7:11—H 7:12, usually translated "villages," may also refer to "henna flowers" (cf. Amer. Trans.).

See also COSMETICS; FLORA § A7*d*.

Fig. HEN 14.

Bibliography. H. N. and A. L. Moldenke, *Plants of the Bible* (1952), pp. 124-25.

J. C. TREVER

14. Henna

HENOCH hē′nək. Douay Version form of ENOCH; KJV form of ENOCH 1 in I Chr. 1:3; KJV form of HANOCH in I Chr. 1:33.

HEPHER hē′fər [חפר, help(?)]; HEPHERITES —fə rīts. **1.** Eponym of a clan of the tribe of Manasseh or of Gilead (Num. 26:32-33; 27:1; Josh. 17:2-3). *See* EPHER 3.

2. A man or family of the tribe of Judah (I Chr. 4:6).

3. One of David's MIGHTY MEN (I Chr. 11:36); the text differs from that in II Sam. 23:34, and both may be corrupt.

Bibliography. M. Noth, *Die israelitischen Personennamen* (1928), p. 155. H. H. GUTHRIE, JR.

4. A Canaanite city whose king was defeated by Joshua (Josh. 12:17) and which later figures in the listing of Solomon's administrative districts. "All the land of Hepher" was under the jurisdiction of Ben-hesed, one of Solomon's officials; and, with ARUBBOTH and SOCO, it composed the third administrative district (I Kings 4:10). Hepher is listed, together with Arubboth, on an early-eighth-century ostracon; and both have been identified with the places mentioned above.

The exact location of Hepher is unknown; Hafireh, *ca.* two miles E of Arubboth, and Tell Ibshar have been suggested.

Bibliography. W. F. Albright, "The Administrative Divisions of Israel and Judah," *JPOS*, V (1925), 28-31.

W. L. REED

HEPHZIBAH hĕf′zĭ bə [חפצי־בה; חפץ *plus* ב, my delight is in her]. **1.** The wife of King Hezekiah, and the mother of Manasseh (II Kings 21:1).

2. Symbolic name for the restored Jerusalem, when God's "delight" will again be in her (Isa. 62:4 KJV). The RSV translates: "My delight is in her."

D. HARVEY

HERALD. An officer making state or royal proclamations public, or bearing ceremonial messages between princes and powers. There is no evidence that he carried challenges (*see* AMBASSADOR; INTERPRETER). The word כרוזא in Dan. 3:4 translates a Greek loan word, κῆρυξ, which is also used in the NT for "one who proclaims" (I Tim. 2:7; II Tim. 1:11; II Pet. 2:5). In Daniel it has its original meaning. In the NT it is used metaphorically for the "preacher," and is so translated in Timothy. Peter applies the word to the warning of Noah. The term "herald" is used also in the phrase "herald of good tidings" to translate the participial phrase מבשרת (Isa. 40:9; 41:27; KJV "that bringest good tidings"). In this phrase is the OT gospel. The metaphor suggests the preacher is a herald in that he bears a message or proclamation given him by the heavenly King.

C. U. WOLF

HERB. The translation of:

a) ארה (II Kings 4:39). In Ugaritic *'ar* is found parallel to *šblt* (שבלת, EAR OF GRAIN), indicating that a cereal or grain is meant here, rather than an herb. *See* SHIBBOLETH.

b) Λάχανον (Luke 11:42; KJV also in Matt. 13:32 and parallels; Rom. 14:2), a cultivated, as opposed to a wild, plant.

See also GRASS.

Bibliography. A. E. Rüthy, *Die Pflanze und ihre Teile* (1942), pp. 38-39. R. W. CORNEY

HERCULES hûr′kyə lēz [Ἡρακλῆς] (II Macc. 4:19). Hercules, god of the Olympic games held in Tyre every five years, was substituted as king of the city for the old Phoenician god, Melkart, and honors were paid to Hercules in Tyre (cf. Strabo *Geography* 16.2.23). Jason sent ambassadors from Jerusalem to convey three thousand silver drachmas for the sacrifice to the god. But the escort thought it inappropriate that the money should be used for such pagan sacrifice. It was used instead for fitting out some ships. S. B. HOENIG

HERD. *See* SHEEP; CATTLE.

HERDSMAN [רעה ,נוקד]; KJV HERDMAN. The KEEPER of domestic animals that go in flocks or herds (Gen. 13:7-8; 26:20; I Sam. 21:7). Joseph's brethren, Saul, and others kept cattle. Herdsmen were important in all ages of Israel's history (II Chr. 26:10; 32:28-29; etc.).

The word נוקד is used only twice in the OT: once of AMOS in his description of his OCCUPATION before the call to preach (7:14), and once to describe MESHA king of Moab (II Kings 3:4; SHEEP BREEDER). This is usually interpreted as referring to the lay origin of Amos and the wealth of Mesha. Recent study on the basis of Ugaritic by the Scandinavian school cast doubt on this conclusion. Perhaps נוקד is used of Amos and Mesha as an official priestly title. *See* DRESSER OF SYCAMORE TREES.

Bibliography. A. Haldar, *Vetus Testamentum*, 1 (Oct., 1951), 293 ff. C. U. WOLF

HERES, ASCENT OF hĭr′ĭz [מעלה החרס, ascent of the sun]. A place where Gideon turned back from pursuing the Midianites (Judg. 8:13). The reading is doubtful; the KJV translates the words "before the sun was up" and Aq. and Symm. both read מלמעלה ההרים, "from up in the mountains." S. COHEN

HERES, CITY OF. *See* SUN, CITY OF THE.

HERES, MOUNT. KJV form of HAR-HERES. *See also* HERES, ASCENT OF.

HERESH hĭr′ĕsh [חרש, mute, *or* taciturn] (I Chr. 9:15). A Levite listed among the returned exiles. The name is lacking in the parallel Neh. 11:15-16.

HERESY [ἡ αἵρησις]. Originally, a school, sect, faction; later, the opposite of orthodoxy.

In Hellenistic Greece the term "heresy" meant a philosophical school with its special doctrine. The usage was similar in Judaism—e.g., the school or party of the PHARISEES; the SADDUCEES; the ESSENES; etc. The Hebraic-rabbinic equivalent of the word is גדבה or מין, the latter of which refers usually to inner-Jewish factions.

The NT language is influenced by Hellenistic and Jewish terminology—e.g., Acts 24:5, where Paul's opponents call him a "ringleader of the sect of the Nazarenes," thus designating Christianity as a sect (*see* NAZARENE) and using language similar to Josephus and the rabbinic sources (cf. Acts 5:17; 15:5; 26:5).

The new Christian usage of the term, with reference to inner-Christian factions, began as soon as a Christian church was established. Church and heresy became excluding entities—i.e., the Greek term was used in a bad sense (I Cor. 11:18-19; Gal. 5:20), yet without the technical meaning of "schism" (τὸ σχίσμα, "separation," "division"), which seems to refer to a dogmatic and organizational break. An exegetical difficulty exists with regard to I Cor. 11:18-19, where αἵρησις and σχίσμα appear side by side. The passage indicates that with "schism" the parties of I Cor. 1:10 ff are meant, while heretic factions seem to be understood as possible or even necessary before the end time. II Pet. 2:1 speaks of "false prophets" who "secretly bring in destructive heresies." The exegetical and theological question arises whether the church is able to tolerate "heresies," at the same time being forced to reject the possibility of "schisms." E. DINKLER

HERETH hĭr′ĕth [חרת] (I Sam. 22:5); KJV HARETH hâr′—. A forest between Adullam and Giloh in which David hid after his sojourn in Moab; possibly to be located around Kharas, a hamlet near Khirbet Qila (*see* KEILAH), *ca.* 6½ miles E of Beit Jibrin (Eleutheropolis). V. R. GOLD

HERITAGE. There is no clear distinction in the Hebrew Bible between the terms "INHERITANCE" and "heritage." The KJV generally uses "heritage" to designate those things, both spiritual and material, which come from God (Job 20:29). The RSV uses "inheritance" in material matters (Num. 27:7) and "heritage" in spiritual (Pss. 94:14; 136:22).

Land and territory were believed to come into possession of Hebrew families by heritage. They were theirs by divine gift, not by conquest (Num. 26:53). They then passed from generation to generation by inheritance (Num. 36:7). Spiritual qualities, relationships with God, even assured material prosperity, were accepted as part of the heritage (Ps. 16:5-6). W. G. WILLIAMS

HERMAS, SHEPHERD OF hûr′məs. An apocalyptic work by a Roman prophet Hermas, whom ecclesiastical tradition since Origen uncritically identified with the personage named in Rom. 16:14. The Muratorian Canon of the Roman church (*ca.* A.D. 200) states that the work was written when Hermas' brother, Pius, was bishop of Rome—i.e., *ca.* 140. This date may well mark the completion and publication of the Shepherd; but internal evidence, supported by the MS tradition, suggests that the first four Visions, at least, may be as early as the beginning of the second century. In Vision II.4.3, reference is made to Clement as one entrusted to send the book to other communities. It is possible that this Clement is the reputed third bishop of Rome and author of a letter of the Roman church to the Corinthians. *See* CLEMENT, EPISTLE OF.

The Shepherd has three principal divisions: five Visions, twelve Mandates or Commandments, and ten Similitudes or Parables (though these last are more allegorical in character than parabolic). Vision V serves as an introduction to the Mandates; and Mandate XII leads into the first Similitude. There are, however, Mandates scattered among the Visions and Similitudes; and Visions also occur in the Similitudes. Similitude IX, the lengthiest of its group, takes up and develops Vision III, and actually appears to be the beginning of a fourth major division, since Hermas introduces it by the statement: "After I had written the commandments and parables of the Shepherd."

In the first four Visions, the revealer is a woman named Rhoda, identified by Hermas as his onetime mistress when he was a slave. She is actually a Sibylline figure, who in successive transformations from an elderly lady to a young and beautiful woman is a symbolic representation of the church. With Vision V, a figure garbed as a shepherd and named the Angel of Penitence takes over the role of revealer; and from this personage the work derives its title.

The principal theme of Hermas' apocalypse is the revelation of a "second chance" of repentance to baptized Christians, in view of an impending persecution and the second coming of the Lord. This penitence will avail to save even those who have committed the most grievous sins, including apostasy. Hence Hermas' teaching has been understood as a significant modification of a rigoristic tradition in the church that refused reconciliation to Christians excommunicated for serious offenses committed after baptism (cf. Heb. 6:4-8; 10:26-29; 12:16-17). There is, however, no notion of a penitential system in Hermas, such as developed a generation later in the Catholic Church. The offer of respite is extraordinary, and linked to an imminent crisis. It is not possible to identify precisely the occasion of this crisis, although some critics have connected it with the tradition of a "new remission of sins preached in the third year of Trajan" (A.D. 100), mentioned in a book by a Jewish Christian heretic Elkesai (cf. Hippolytus *Against Heresies* IX.8).

The Shepherd is replete with moralistic instructions. In Vision III.8.3-8, a series of personified Christian virtues supports a "tower" that is symbolic of the church. The chief one is faith, defined as "that by which the elect of the Lord are saved." The other virtues (each one successively portrayed as a daughter of the preceding virtue) are: self-control, simplicity, knowledge, innocence, reverence, and love. "Whoever serves them and has strength to persevere in their works will have his dwelling in the tower with the saints of God." Salvation requires right doing no less than right believing; and remission of sins is made contingent upon keeping the commandments. Hermas is the first Christian moralist to promote the idea of works of supererogation over and beyond the commandments, for which the reward is a "more surpassing glory and esteem from God"—specific examples of which are the refraining of a widowed person from remarriage (Mandate IV.4), and the performing of a fast in order to provide food for the poor and needy (Similitude V.3).

The root of sin, in Hermas' view, is "double-mindedness" (cf. Jas. 1:8; 4:8). From it issue blasphemy, hypocrisy, jealousy, dishonesty, pride, lust, and contentiousness. He is vehement in denunciation of the rich, nor does he spare to reprimand the church's hierarchy for its factiousness (Vision III.9.7-9) and avarice (Similitude IX.26.2-3). No respecter of persons, Hermas remarks upon his own sins as a father and a man of business, and upon those of his shrewish wife and unruly, faithless children. His portrayal of ordinary Christian living in his time belies the idealistic notion that many have of the church in that age. It should be said, however, that many critics consider the autobiographical details in the Shepherd to be fictitious. Altogether Hermas pictures the church as a very mixed society on this earth, comparable to the conception in the Matthean parable of the wheat and the weeds.

Fundamentally, the source of Hermas' ethical principles is to be found in Hellenistic Jewish moral teaching, but slightly recast with Christian perspectives. In this respect his outlook is very similar to the ethical teaching of the Testament of the Twelve Patriarchs, the Two Ways material in the DIDACHE, and the Letter of James. Of special interest is his theory of two kinds of "spirits" or "angels" in man, both good and evil respectively, which has an interesting parallel in the instruction on the "two spirits" in the Essene Manual of Discipline (1QS III.13–IV.26). This theory is particularly developed in Mandates V-VIII.

Apart from his ecclesiology, there is little in Hermas to interest the student of doctrine. He believed that the apostles and teachers, after their death, preached to and baptized those who had died before them (Similitude IX.16.5)—an interesting extension of the doctrine of the descent into Hades. His Christology exhibits adoptionist tendencies as regards the Lord's manhood (Similitude V.6.1); and he distinctly identifies the Son of God with the Holy Spirit (Similitude IX.1.1), and, in another passage, with Michael, the chief of the angels (Similitude VIII.3.2-3).

Hermas' culture was very limited. His style is of mediocre quality, and betrays numerous Semitisms and Latinisms. He can be very confused in working out details of his allegories. Some of the scenario of his visions and similitudes shows striking resemblances to the *Tabula* of Pseudo-Cebes, and several critics have sought parallels to his themes and images in pagan erotic novels and in the Hermetic writings. He occasionally cites the OT, and he knows several apocrypha. The closest parallels to his apocalyptic are to be found in II Esdras. In one place (Vision II.3.4) he refers a citation to a Jewish book (otherwise unknown) of Eldad and Modat (for the names, cf. Num. 11:26).

To students of the history of the NT canon, Hermas is disappointing. He appears to have known Matthew and Mark, less probably Luke and John. He reflects some of Paul's letters, Hebrews, I Peter, and Revelation. The close parallels of outlook and vocabulary between Hermas and the Letter of James are insufficient to prove direct literary dependence one way or the other.

The Shepherd was highly esteemed by the ante-Nicene fathers, who considered it inspired. It was widely used for the moral instruction of catechumens. In Egypt, it enjoyed a quasi-canonical authority; and, with the pseudo-Epistle of Barnabas, it was included, after the books of the NT, in the Codex Sinaiticus (fourth century). No complete text of the original Greek is extant, for both Codex Sinaiticus and a fifteenth-century Codex Athensis are defective. Of the numerous fragments among Greek papyri, the most important by reason of age (second half of the third century) are the sixty-two leaves in the possession of the University of Michigan (edited by C. Bonner in 1934). Two Latin versions are extant—one of them almost contemporaneous with Hermas—and these are essential for reconstructing the text. There are also important Coptic fragments, a single fragment in Middle Persian, and a defective version in Ethiopic. Strangely, no relics of a Syriac version have come to light.

See also APOSTOLIC FATHERS.

Bibliography. Best critical texts: M. Whittaker, *Die apostolischen Väter,* I: *Der Hirt des Hermas* (1956; in the Corpus of the Berlin Academy). R. Joly, *Hermas, Le Pasteur* (Sources Chrétiennes, no. 53; 1958), with French translation, Introduction, and Notes.

The standard commentary is that of M. Dibelius in H. Lietzmann, *Handbuch zum NT,* Ergänzungsband (1923).

For extensive bibliography, see Joly's edition and J. Quasten, *Patrology,* I (1950), 97-105.

Special studies: K. Lake, "The Shepherd of Hermas and Christian Life in Rome in the Second Century," *HTR,* IV (1911), 25-46. O. D. Watkin, *A History of Penance* (1920), I, 47-72. W. J. Wilson, "The Career of the Prophet Hermas," *HTR,* XX (1927), 21-62. D. W. Riddle, "The Messages of the Shepherd of Hermas: A Study in Social Control," *JR,* VII (1927), 561-77. O. J. F. Seitz, "Relationship of the Shepherd of Hermas to the Epistle of James," *JBL,* LXIII (1944), 131-40. J. P. Audet, "Affinités littéraires et doctrinales du Manuel de Discipline," *RB,* LX (1953), 41-82. R. Joly, "La doctrine pénitentielle du Pasteur d'Hermas et l'exégèse récente," *RHR,* CXLVII (1955), 32-49. K. Rahner, "Die Busslehre im Hirten des Hermas," *Zeitschrift für katholische Theologie,* LXXVII (1955), 385-431. P. Carrington, *The Early Christian Church* (1957), I, 391-409; II, 91-94. H. Chadwick, "The New Edition of Hermas," *JTS,* N.S. VIII (1957), 274-80.

M. H. SHEPHERD, JR.

HERMES hûr′mēz [Ἑρμῆς, *perhaps from* ἕρμα, prop, rock, cairn, *etc., but possibly non-Greek in origin*]. **1.** A Greek deity, son of Zeus and half brother of Apollo, whom he resembles without attaining his moral significance. He is the master thief and trickster, the god who brings good luck, honestly or dishonestly, hence the patron alike of thieves and of traders; he is the herald of the gods, and therefore carries the herald's staff, which often becomes a magic wand in his hands; and he is the god of eloquence. He seldom receives a public cult, but is widely worshiped in the religion of the family as a fertility-god. This is probably his primary and most primitive aspect, and is reflected in the pillar with phallus, surmounted with bust, which represented him at the house door. Under another serious aspect, he is Psychopompos, the Marshaler of souls, who guides the dead along the road to the realm of Hades. In the astral religion he is identified with the planet Mercury; and in the syncretism of Hellenistic times, he is identified with the Egyptian god Thoth and given the epithet Trismegistus, "thrice-great," and becomes the great revealer of the way to the attainment of immortality.

At Lystra the superstitious people took the apostles for gods in the likeness of men: "Barnabas they called Zeus, and Paul, because he was the chief speaker, they called Hermes" (Acts 14:12). It was Hermes in his character as god of eloquence and divine herald that they had in mind.

2. An individual greeted by Paul in Rom. 16:14, about whom nothing further is known.

F. W. BEARE

HERMOGENES hər mŏj'ə nēz [Ἑρμογένης, born of Hermes] (II Tim. 1:15). Someone mentioned with PHYGELUS and "all who are in Asia" as having deserted Paul—for theological reasons, and/or for fear of sharing Paul's fate in Rome. In the Acts of Paul (2:1, 4, 11-14) Hermogenes is described as a coppersmith and, with Demas, as "full of hypocrisy" (cf. also Jos. Apion I.xxiii; Suetonius *Domitian* 10).

B. H. THROCKMORTON, JR.

HERMON, MOUNT hûr'mən [חרמון, *from* חרם, *in the Hiph'il* consecrate—*i.e.*, a consecrated place, a sanctuary; LXX Αερμων]; HERMONITES —mə nīts. The mountain which forms the S spur of the Anti-lebanon Range. According to Deut. 3:9, its name varied in the various dialects of Syria and Palestine, its Amorite name being שניר, its Sidonian שריון (for this name cf. now also the Ras Shamra Texts). In Deut. 4:48 we find the name שיאן. In I Chr. 5:23 differentiation is made between Senīr, Hermon, and Baal-hermon, and in the Song of Songs between Shenir and Hermon. Perhaps SENIR was the name of a N part of Anti-lebanon.

Mount Hermon reaches a height of *ca.* 9,100 feet above the sea and offers a majestic view from far distances. Its crown is to be seen from many places in Palestine. Because it is covered with snow during a great part of the year, the Arabs call it Jebel el-Sheikh, the "gray-haired mountain," or Jebel el-Thalj, the "mountain of the snow." From Mount Hermon the water comes which flows in the rivers of N Hauran; and furthermore, the sources of the Jordan are to be found on its slopes. Fig. JOR 26.

The impressive view of Mount Hermon has always fascinated the human mind, and since times immemorial it has been a sacred mountain. Its Hebrew name may perhaps be taken as an allusion to

15. Mount Hermon from the E

this fact. In Judg. 3:3 the name is Mount Baal-hermon, which indicates that a local Baal was worshiped there, as was the case in many other places (cf. I Chr. 5:23). In Ps. 133:3, Mount Hermon is associated with the dew, a well-known symbol of the vegetation-deities. In a treaty between the Hittites and the Amorites from *ca.* 1350 B.C., Mount Hermon is alluded to as a sacred mountain; this text may be the oldest known mentioning of that fact. Mount Hermon was used as a cult place also in later periods, as is shown by the fact that a Greek inscription has been found describing the local god of the mountain. It is also mentioned in I Enoch and by Eusebius. Jerome describes the cult place on the S peak called Qasr 'Antar.

Fig. HER 15.

A. HALDAR

HEROD (FAMILY) hĕr'əd [הורדוס; Ἡρῴδης]. The dynasty which under Rome ruled Jewish Palestine 37 B.C.–A.D. 70.

A. Family origins
B. Herod the Great
   1. Youth
   2. Governor of Galilee
   3. King
      a. Consolidation (37-25 B.C.)
      b. Prosperity (25-13 B.C.)
      c. Domestic troubles (13-4 B.C.)
   4. Assessment
C. Archelaus
D. Herod Philip
E. Herod Antipas
F. Agrippa I
G. Agrippa II
H. In the NT
   1. Agrippa I
   2. Agrippa II
   3. Herod Antipas
   4. Archelaus
   5. Aristobulus
   6. Drusilla
   7. Bernice
   8. Felix
   9. Herod the Great
   10. Herod Philip
   11. Herodians
   12. Herodias
   13. Philip
   14. Salome
   15. Summary
Bibliography

A. *FAMILY ORIGINS.* The family of Herod rose to significance in the reign of the Hasmonean queen Salome Alexandra.

She and Alexander Janneus (*see* JANNEUS, ALEXANDER) had two sons, the elder HYRCANUS II, the younger ARISTOBULUS. When Janneus died in 78 B.C., Salome retained the throne, but the high priesthood, for which only males were eligible (*see* PRIESTS AND LEVITES), went to Hyrcanus II, who was in line for the throne also. The younger Aristobulus attempted to seize the throne; Salome Alexandra's sudden death (69) saved her from being deposed by her own son.

Hyrcanus was crowned king; but Aristobulus, aided by mercenaries and Sadducees, arose in direct rebellion and defeated Hyrcanus. To Aristobulus went the crown and the high priesthood. The brothers made a public show of reconciliation in the temple at Jerusalem, so that an income from revenues of the high priesthood was assigned to Hyrcanus. That the reconciliation did not endure is ascribed by Josephus to Antipater, the father of Herod.

The grandfather of Herod had also borne the name ANTIPATER; Herod's father was known also by the shorter name Antipas. The first Antipater had been designated by Janneus and Alexandra as "general" (στρατηγός) of Idumea, of which land Antipater was a native. It seems clear from Josephus that the grandfather was already dead at the time of the controversy between Hyrcanus II and Aristobulus.

Josephus calls the second Antipater an "old and bitterly hated foe" of Aristobulus, but abstains from justifying the epithet. He pauses in his *Jewish War* merely to mention Antipater's Idumean background, and in Antiq. XIV.i.3 briefly to discuss it. He cites NICOLAS of Damascus, a Gentile historian, to the effect that Antipater was of a principal Jewish family of Babylonia which had come to Judea, but he charges Nicolas with the wish to flatter and incur favor with the family of Herod. The Idumean origin is referred to very often in Josephus and is alluded to in rabbinic literature (Sot. 7.8).

A later legend (in Just. Dial. 52; and Julius Africanus, cited in Euseb. Hist. I.7.11) makes Antipater the son of a temple slave of Apollo at Ashkelon in Philistia. Writers on Herod and his family, even in modern times, treat the dynasty more as novelists than as students of history. The frequent view depicts Antipater as a crafty self-seeker, devoid of worthy attributes. Josephus, though scarcely an admirer of Antipater, does allude (Antiq. XIV.vi.2-3; viii.1) to affirmative qualities possessed by Herod's father.

Antipater regarded himself as a Jew and was so regarded by his contemporaries. The portrait of Antipater in Josephus is itself not a consistent one; some (e.g., Schuerer) explain the inconsistencies as due to the different sources, favorable and unfavorable, which Josephus utilized without editing, while others (e.g., Laqueur) contend that Josephus grew in anti-Herodian feeling between the time of his first account of the dynasty in *The Jewish War* and the later occasion when he composed a parallel account in *Antiquities*. Any summary of Antipater is the more reliable as it adheres closely to what he did (as far as we can know it).

In the issue between Hyrcanus II and Aristobulus, Hyrcanus was content to accept the subordinate position accorded to him after the reconciliation. Hyrcanus' passive nature is stressed by Josephus (Antiq. XIII.xvi.1; XIV.i.3; War I.x.4; Laqueur doubts the authenticity of Josephus' report). The initiative to change matters, however, was supplied by Antipater, whose position, official or unofficial, remains unspecified.

Ultimately Antipater's pressure had an effect; Hyrcanus determined to flee to Aretas III, king of the neighboring Nabateans, for safety and help. Prior to the flight, Antipater had visited Aretas and received the latter's assurances of help.

Aretas defeated Aristobulus, who fled from the battle to Jerusalem; on Passover, troops of Aretas and Jews who had joined Hyrcanus besieged the temple.

At this juncture (65 B.C.), the Roman general Scaurus, who had been sent to Syria by Pompey, arrived in Judea. In 64, Hyrcanus and Aristobulus appeared before Pompey at Damascus to press their rival claims; so, too, did some Jews who asked that the brothers be rejected and that theocracy be restored. Josephus relates that Hyrcanus' statement of his case "was supported by more than a thousand of the most reputable Jews, whom Antipater had provided for that purpose" (Antiq. XIV.iii.2).

Pompey deferred his decision. When certain promises were broken by Aristobulus, Pompey moved against the Holy City, which, torn by internal strife, fell to the Romans (63). When Josephus summarizes the event as a calamity, he omits mention of Antipater, blaming rather Hyrcanus II and Aristobulus (Antiq. XIV.iv.5). Hyrcanus, "because in various ways he had been useful to" Pompey, was restored as high priest; Jerusalem was made tributary to the Romans and placed administratively under the legate of the province of Syria.

The Roman conquest began to extend southward beyond Palestine; Antipater was assigned by Hyrcanus and by Scaurus to tasks which he did well.

Aristobulus and his two sons, Alexander and Antigonus, separately tried unsuccessful revolts (Alexander in 57; Aristobulus the same year; Antigonus in 56; Alexander in 55). Josephus next states (War I.viii.7) that "Gabinius [the Roman governor] then proceeded to Jerusalem, where he reorganized the government in accordance with Antipater's wishes." Gabinius "sent Antipater, who was a man of good sense, to the unruly elements, to see whether he could put a stop to their unruly behavior . . . but he could not restrain Alexander" (Antiq. XIV.vi.3).

Josephus relates the activities of C. Cassius Longinus (of Shakespeare's *Julius Caesar*) in 53-51, the chief incident of which was the slaying at Antipater's request of Peitholaus, a Jewish general who was carrying on the unextinguished revolt initiated by Aristobulus. At this point, Josephus (War I.viii.9; Antiq. XIV.vii.3) pauses to relate that Antipater had married a woman named Cypros, of an illustrious "Arabian" (probably Nabatean) family; and he lists their children as four sons, Phasael, Herod, Joseph, Pheroras, and a daughter, Salome.

After Julius Caesar became master of Rome (49), he released Aristobulus from a prison in Rome, and

A Partial Genealogy of the Family of Herod

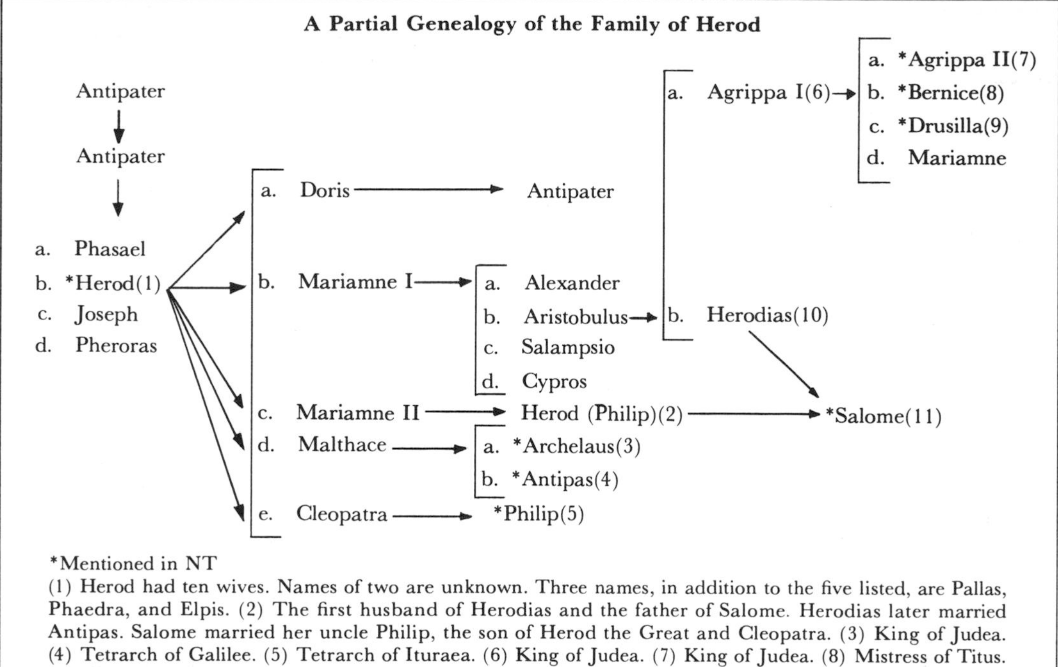

*Mentioned in NT
(1) Herod had ten wives. Names of two are unknown. Three names, in addition to the five listed, are Pallas, Phaedra, and Elpis. (2) The first husband of Herodias and the father of Salome. Herodias later married Antipas. Salome married her uncle Philip, the son of Herod the Great and Cleopatra. (3) King of Judea. (4) Tetrarch of Galilee. (5) Tetrarch of Ituraea. (6) King of Judea. (7) King of Judea. (8) Mistress of Titus. (9) Wife of Festus. (10) First the wife of (2), then of (4); the mother of (11)

sent him to Syria to fight the Pompeyites; but Aristobulus was poisoned by friends of Pompey. Caesar, fighting in Egypt in 48-47, received help from Antipater, who received several wounds in combat. To please Antipater, Caesar made him a Roman citizen and confirmed Hyrcanus as high priest.

Caesar disregarded some charges brought by Antigonus, and upheld Antipater, now procurator (ἐπίτροπος) of Judea, and permitted Hyrcanus to rebuild Jerusalem and to be known as "ethnarch" as well as high priest (Antiq. XIV.viii.5; War I.x.2-3).

Antipater appealed to the restless Judean populace to be loyal to Hyrcanus; Josephus comments (War I.x.3; Antiq. XIV.ix.1) that "while he spoke in this strain, he took the country into his own hands, finding Hyrcanus indolent and without the energy necessary to a king." Antipater appointed his son Phasael governor of Jerusalem and his son Herod governor of Galilee.

Antipater "was courted by the nation as if he were king. . . . Notwithstanding this, his affection for Hyrcanus and loyalty to him underwent no change" (War I.x.5).

After the death of Caesar (44), Cassius took control of Syria and levied tribute on the Jews. Antipater arranged for his sons and others to help collect the money. Among these was one Malichus, whose life Antipater had previously saved. After Cassius departed from Syria, Malichus bribed a butler to poison Antipater (43); Herod killed Malichus by stabbing him (War I.xi.4; Antiq. XIV.xi.4); the former passage eulogizes Antipater as a "man of great energy in the conduct of affairs, whose crowning merit was that he recovered and preserved the kingdom for Hyrcanus"; the latter, "a man distinguished for piety, justice, and devotion to his country."

B. *HEROD THE GREAT*. 1. Youth. Herod was the second of Antipater's five children. On the premise that Herod was seventy at the time of his death (see War I.xxxiii.1; Antiq. XVII.viii.1), his birth may be set in 73 B.C. Josephus (Antiq. XIV.ix.2) incorrectly designates him as only fifteen in 47. In War I.xxi.13, Josephus speaks of his great physical constitution and precision in the use of the javelin and the bow. A passage (War I.x.7) speaks of Hyrcanus' love for him. The father's position undoubtedly was the lever that moved Herod into the governorship of Galilee.

2. Governor of Galilee. The title Herod bore was στρατηγός; its precise connotation is unknown. He quickly (47) aroused admiration among Galilean Jews and Roman officials in Syria at his promptness in capturing and executing a "brigand" Ezekias and some followers. In Hyrcanus' court, however, malicious people charged that Herod (and Phasael) were acting dictatorially; Herod was charged with having violated Jewish law in the execution of Ezekias and others. Hyrcanus ordered Herod to trial. The account in Antiq. XIV is more bitter toward Herod than that in War I.

The accounts of Herod's trial in *The Jewish War* and *Antiquities* contain glaring contradictions. They agree on little more than the fear of Hyrcanus and most of the Sanhedrin of condemning Herod, and of Hyrcanus' directing an acquittal. Herod emerged from the farce stronger than before. He even contemplated deposing Hyrcanus.

The Roman governor of Syria, Sextus Caesar, appointed Herod a Roman official as governor of Coele-Syria (and possibly Samaria). Now (46) Herod's career became intertwined in the affairs of Rome in Syria.

Sextus Caesar, a relative of Julius Caesar, was murdered by Bassus, a partisan of Julius' foe Pompey; Antipater, a friend of Julius, sent troops under his two sons against Bassus. This minor war dragged on indecisively for almost three years. After the murder of Caesar in 44, Cassius came to Syria; Herod, Phasael, and Malichus were among those designated to raise certain required taxes.

As the alignment of Octavius Caesar and Antony against Brutus and Cassius became crystallized, Cassius reappointed Herod as governor, or possibly "procurator"—the accounts diverge—of all Syria, promising to appoint him king of Judea when the war was concluded (War I.xi.3; Antiq. XIV.xi.2).

Herod quieted turbulent Samaria and then marched toward Jerusalem (43). Antigonus, son of Aristobulus, again raised troops to invade Judea. Herod defeated these (42) and was acclaimed in Jerusalem, where previously he had been regarded with hostility. By this time Herod had a wife, Doris, and, by her, a son, Antipater. Doris is described by Josephus as a native of Jerusalem (Thackeray errs in rendering "native" by "Jewess"; cf. Marcus; Otto asserts, beyond the evidence, that she was an Idumean). Herod became betrothed to Mariamne, the granddaughter of Hyrcanus II. However fraught it was to be with ultimate personal disaster, the latter betrothal won him an acceptance in Judean circles.

Jewish leaders came to Antony, who had taken up residence in Syria, to lay accusations against Herod and Phasael. The outcome was that Antony appointed Herod and Phasael "tetrarchs."

Two years later a Parthian prince, Pacorus, joined with Antigonus in the effort to place the latter on the throne held by Hyrcanus. Thereby began a complicated series of incidents, the end result of which was to bring the career of Herod to its first climax. The invaders besieged Jerusalem and were partly successful. Opposed to them were the forces of Phasael and Herod (War I.xiii.2 says, undoubtedly mistakenly, Phasael and Hyrcanus; Antiq. XIV.xiii.3, Phasael and Herod). It is evident that nothing less than civil war was under way. Daily skirmishes between the opposing forces took place.

But when Pentecost brought hosts of pilgrims to Jerusalem, a Parthian general, named like the prince Pacorus, proposed to Phasael that he negotiate a cessation of the war with the Parthian king Barzaphranes. Though Herod was suspicious of the good faith of the proposal, Phasael decided to go and to take Hyrcanus with him. They met the Parthian king in Galilee. After negotiations, Hyrcanus and Phasael were treacherously put in chains; simultaneously a Parthian detachment, left behind in Jerusalem, tried to induce Herod to accompany them outside the walls of Jerusalem. Learning about Phasael, Herod set off for Masada with his troops and close relatives. After some vicissitudes, Herod moved on to Petra (Sela), the capital of the Nabatean kingdom.

Back in Jerusalem, the Parthians began a pillage, which they extended into other parts of Judea. Antigonus was made king. To guard against the possible restoration of Hyrcanus, Antigonus mutilated him, permanently disqualifying Hyrcanus from the high priesthood (Lev. 21:17 ff). Phasael died, either through suicide or poisoning or in battle.

Instead of help from the Nabatean king, Herod found orders to leave Nabatea promptly. He went to Egypt and then to Rome, where he was received graciously by Antony and Octavius Caesar (probably in December, 40). The Romans had good reason to despise Antigonus for having joined up with their foes, the Parthians; accordingly, Antony and Octavius, with Senate confirmation, named Herod the king of Judea (confirmed outside Josephus by Strabo XVI. 765; Appian *Civil Wars* V.75; Tac. Hist. V.9). We now encounter Herod, no longer as a governor or tetrarch, but as a king, and in the ensuing contentions against Antigonus, the stake is no longer that of indirect control of Judea, but that of kingship itself.

In late 39, Herod sailed from Italy. He marched through Galilee, paused to capture Joppa, and then moved on to Masada, where his relatives were under attack. Next, supported by Roman forces, he encamped on the W side of Jerusalem. Instead of attacking immediately, he had a proclamation made of his willingness to forget the offenses committed against him by his enemies. To this propaganda campaign Antigonus replied (Antiq. XIV.xv.2; *The Jewish War* is silent) that Herod was a "commoner and an Idumean, that is, a half-Jew." (When Antiq. XIV.viii.1 and XX.viii.7 are joined to the passage quoted, and are regarded in light of the forced conversions of the Idumeans by John Hyrcanus [Antiq. XIII.ix.1], they refute adequately the tendency of some interpreters to regard Herod, not alone as a usurper—this he was—but also as a Gentile. This judgment is not affected by the statement in Antiq. XIX.vii.3 that Herod was more akin to the Greeks than to the Jews, for the issue here is his cultural interests, not his formal affiliations.)

Idumea, Samaria, and Galilee had come over to Herod, though garrisons of Antigonus remained to be reduced and rebellion in Galilee to be put down. Herod moved on to Jerusalem to resume the interrupted siege. Meanwhile he married his betrothed Mariamne. A long and bitter siege resulted in victory. Antigonus fell captive to Sossius, who departed to join Antony, taking Antigonus with him.

According to Antiq. XV.i.2, Herod gave Antony a large bribe to persuade the Romans to put Antigonus out of the way; War I.xviii.3 tells simply that Antigonus fell beneath the ax.

With the death of Antigonus and the end of the Hasmonean dynasty, Herod ceased to be the nominee for king; he became the king in reality (37).

3. King. Though some scholars divide Herod's reign slightly differently, it is convenient to divide his reign, 37-4 B.C., into three parts: consolidation (37-25); prosperity (25-13); domestic trouble (13-4). *Antiquities* gives much more detail of Herod's reign than does *The Jewish War*. Contradictions and inconsistencies exist between the two accounts; moreover, there are contradictions even within *Antiquities*, which is the basis for the ensuing paraphrase.

a. Consolidation (37-25 B.C.). Internal problems were an immediately pressing concern, such as the need (War I.xviii.2) to stop the foreign allies from profaning the temple and pillaging Jerusalem; Herod accomplished this by distributing rewards (i.e., bribes) to the Romans for their services.

As to the Jews, Herod conferred high honors on

those closely allied to him, and exterminated the loyal followers of Antigonus. For those who were partisans of neither, Herod had to find a suitable solution. Two Pharisees, Sameas and Pollio, members of the Sanhedrin, Herod treated with deference, because Pollio had recommended that the gates of Jerusalem be opened to Herod at the time of his attack in 37. On other members of the Sanhedrin he took bitter vengeance. It is likely that Herod deprived the Sanhedrin of its civil powers, limiting it to religious affairs.

Historians have often wished to equate protagonists and opponents in these struggles with Sadducees and Pharisees, or with patriots and "assimilationists." The debated question of the emergence of the RABBI in this time has increased speculation. Rabbinic literature (e.g., *Pirqe Aboth* I) speaks of successions of *Zugoth* ("pairs") of luminaries, but is devoid of any firm chronology. It is difficult to weave this rabbinic material in with that provided by Josephus; Christian scholars have been guilty of ignoring it almost entirely, and some Jewish scholars of seeing more than is visible.

Two active Hasmoneans, Hyrcanus II and Aristobulus, were threats to Herod. Hyrcanus II, no longer eligible to the high priesthood, had gone to Babylon, there to be received with a warm welcome. Herod invited him to return to Judea, promising to share the throne with him. Initially he treated him with honor, calling him "father." But subsequently his treatment changed. Aristobulus was Herod's wife's brother. It might have been reasonable to designate Aristobulus the high priest, but Herod ignored Aristobulus and called Ananelus to the position.

The action incensed his mother-in-law, Alexandra. She wrote to Cleopatra to intercede with Antony, to appoint Aristobulus the high priest. (It will be recalled that Antony had supplanted Caesar in the affection of this queen of Egypt, and had thereby become virtually a slave to her.) Aristobulus was then only sixteen. Herod avoided the issue by unseating Ananelus and appointing Aristobulus high priest.

When Aristobulus officiated at the temple on Pentecost, the great public acclaim for the young Hasmonean sealed his fate. A little later, Herod, sojourning at Jericho, invited Aristobulus to visit him. The day was hot, and a bathing party took place. Herod playfully ducked Aristobulus under the water, till the young man drowned.

Alexandra believed the death was murder. She sent a report to Cleopatra, who persuaded Antony to summon Herod for an accounting; Herod was under obligation to go. But now more involved family affairs intrude. Herod's mother, Cypros, and his sister, Salome, commoners by birth and Idumeans by extraction, were treated to humiliations by Mariamne and Alexandra; Herod resented the slights. When he departed to see Antony, he put Mariamne and Alexandra under the surveillance of his uncle Joseph, who was also Salome's husband. Herod was aware that Antony could, and might, sentence him to death; he enjoined Joseph in strict secrecy that in that event Joseph should kill Mariamne, whose beauty was known to the lascivious Antony. Indeed, Cypros and Salome had told Herod that Mariamne had often committed adultery and that she had sent Antony a picture of herself, as though to exhibit that which might attract Antony's well-known lust.

Herod's eloquence, and his bribery, won over Antony. But on his return to Jerusalem, Herod heard from Salome an accusation that Mariamne and Joseph had committed adultery. Herod questioned Mariamne and was satisfied with her denial. However, she demanded to know why he had secretly instructed Joseph to kill her if he, Herod, were slain by Antony. Herod, suspicious, concluded that her knowledge of the secret could have come only if she and Joseph had really committed adultery. He had Joseph put to death; and he was torn, now as later, between love and murderous hatred of Mariamne (35 or 34).

Civil war broke out (32) between Antony and Octavius. Herod was assigned by Antony, at Cleopatra's instigation, to make war on the Nabateans, for Cleopatra hoped that when the two kingdoms had weakened each other, she could absorb both. Initially Herod was victorious over the Nabateans, but the tide of war was turned by troops of Cleopatra, who treacherously attacked Herod and defeated him. When a destructive earthquake added to Herod's predicament, he sent to Nabatea envoys to sue for peace, but the Nabateans slew them. Mustering his troops, Herod routed the foe and returned home.

Some few months later, Antony was defeated by Octavius at Actium (September, 31). Herod thought it necessary that Octavius (now Augustus) should regard him as the only possible ruler of Judea. This he accomplished by charging Hyrcanus II with plotting with the king of the Nabateans (Antiq. XV.vi.2), and thereupon having Hyrcanus killed. Other accounts do not bear out either indiscretion or treachery on Hyrcanus' part (Antiq. XV.vi.3-4).

On setting out to see Augustus, Herod considered it prudent to prevent Alexandra from stirring up revolt. He sent her and Mariamne to Alexandrium under two reliable custodians, Joseph and Soemus, with instructions that in the case of Herod's death they should kill the two women. (The similarity of circumstances between Herod's visit to Antony and this visit to Augustus raises questions debated by scholars. To discuss the problems here is impossible; note only that in *The Jewish War*, Herod is reported to have slain Mariamne and Joseph on returning from Antony in 35 or 34; in *Antiquities* he slew Mariamne and Soemus on returning from Augustus in 29). Herod won over Augustus and received confirmation of his royal rank.

Herod was never able to accept sanely the reality that Mariamne was dead. Alexandra, Mariamne's mother, was killed a year later. Three years later, Herod slew his brother-in-law Castobar, the man whom Salome had married after Herod had slain her first husband.

***b. Prosperity** (25-13 B.C.).* Josephus begins the second period by specifying how Herod ruptured Jewish law. His violations include the introduction of quinquennial games in honor of Caesar and the building of a theater in Jerusalem and an amphitheater nearby. In 24 he erected a royal palace; he built or rebuilt a good many fortresses and Gentile temples; on the seacoast he built a harbor, a city which he named Caesarea, and many other buildings. *See bibliography*. Figs. CAE 1; PAL 3.

Such a period of prosperity rested on the confidence and good will reposed in Herod by Augustus. Antiq. XVII.ix.6 states that Herod was called "friend and confederate"—apparently a title conferrable upon a local king by the Romans. Considerable scholarly debate exists on this title; at stake is the question of the measure of autonomy Herod possessed. Herod, however obsequious he was to Rome, was no petty or insignificant ruler; he was an important king. Thus, his two sons by Mariamne he sent to Rome "to enjoy the company of Caesar." Augustus, visiting Syria in 20, received him graciously (Antiq. XV.x.3).

His infidelity to Judaism was not inconsistent with his rebuilding the temple in Jerusalem (*ca.* 20). Josephus (Antiq. XV.xi.1) calls it the most glorious of his actions; rabbinic literature (B.B. 4*a*) states that "one who has not seen Herod's temple has never seen a beautiful building." The rabbis suggest also that the edifice was his "atonement for having slain so many sages of Israel" (*Numbers Rabba* IV.14).

Herod married again another Mariamne, alluded to as Mariamne II. His wives totaled ten (Josephus is incorrect in War I.xxviii.4). We know of at least fifteen children, of whom ten were sons. A striving for power, for succession to the throne, or even usurpation of it, was inevitable. This struggle focuses initially on Antipater III, a son by Herod's first wife Doris. When Herod had married Mariamne I, he had pushed Doris and Antipater aside. Having slain Mariamne, he restored Doris to favor, centering his affection on Antipater. But he had two sons (three, but one died in infancy) by Mariamne I: Alexander and Aristobulus; these he sent to Rome to be educated.

Antipater III, Doris' son, regarded succession as his. But to Alexander and Aristobulus the real succession required Hasmonean blood, which they, through their mother, possessed, while Antipater did not. We need not make our way through the maze of machinations, plots, lies, and treacheries and artificial reconciliations used by the sons to discredit one another. Herod came to lack the ability to separate truth from lies. The very prosperity of the period, releasing him from obligations to external affairs, made him in these internal ones all the more involved and wavering. Not alone by his children, but also by the marital tribulations and excursions of his sister Salome and his brother Pheroras, was he unsettled.

c. Domestic troubles (13-4 B.C.). The rivalries between Antipater III and the sons of Mariamne I came into the open after 13. In 8, Herod took both Alexander and Aristobulus into custody on a charge of treason. At Caesar's instruction his sons were tried at Berytus (Beirut) by a court of Romans and of Herod's relatives. Both were condemned to death and executed in 7 or 6.

The family feuds were not over. Alexander had left two sons, and these Antipater regarded as a continuing threat. In 5, Antipater was brought to trial for instigating the poisoning of Pheroras and for plotting ventures against Herod.

In the midst of the trial proceedings a rebellion arose, directed largely at removing from the temple a golden eagle which Herod had had put over the main gate, in contravention of Jewish law. Herod's guard arrested those guilty of sedition. Fatally sick, Herod mustered strength to attend their trial and to denounce them.

Herod's physical strength was rapidly failing. He ordered the immediate execution of Antipater. Five days later Herod died.

4. Assessment. The murders, the violence, and the usurpation of the throne by Herod are acts not capable of being condoned. Historians frequently infer that Herod was completely a villain and his foes, so it would seem, heroes. A more just judgment would view him in his own context, where pretension to royalty, or its possession, carried with it the supposed obligation to the most ignoble conduct. The internecine struggles in Judea paralleled those in Rome itself, and duplicated those in the Roman provinces.

What can be said in greatest condemnation of Herod was not that he was worse than or different from other provincial kings, but that he was fully as bad as they were. Of adherence to Jewish ethics or fidelity to Jewish law or standards there is not one trace in Josephus' account; on the contrary, there are a number of passages which reflect his indifference and unconcern.

Herod was a Jew only by birth, the offspring of converts to Judaism. In his actions he was no more Jewish than were the petty Gentile monarchs with whom his offspring or relatives intermarried. He was the king of Judea, but never in any sense a Jewish king.

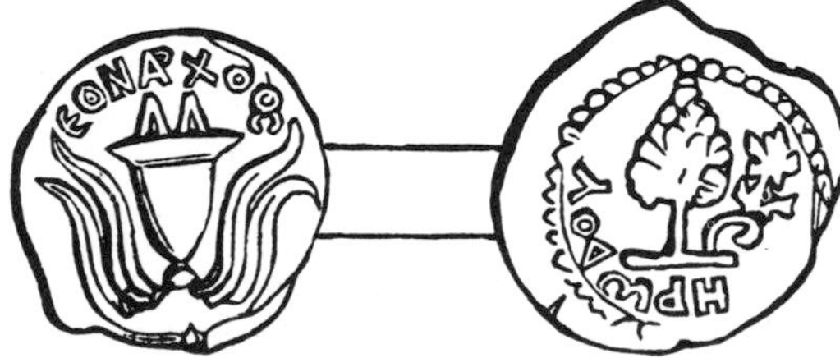

16. Copper coin of Herod the Great

Certainly his unadmirable career discloses qualities which, if addressed to worthy purposes, would have appeared admirable. His rise to power took place at a time of civil war and of internal upheavals. His skill in his maneuvers with Roman officials was matched by his military prowess. He carved a respected, relatively tranquil kingdom out of an important segment of the Roman Empire, and within that kingdom he bought, at a high price, a relatively high degree of order and peace.

Fig. HER 16.

C. *ARCHELAUS.* Archelaus (Ἀρχέλαυς), son of Herod and Malthace, was named in his father's codicil as the principal successor—i.e., as king—while two brothers (*see* §§ D-E *below*) were named tetrarchs of limited territories.

Archelaus was aware of the broad hostility of the Jews to his family. He sought to avert difficulties by the double step of placating his own countrymen through kindliness and forbearance (thereby acting in sharp contrast to his father) and by the gesture of deferring his ascension to the throne until the kingship willed to him by his father could be confirmed by Rome.

His intent in the first case was frustrated by a revolt in 4 B.C. In the second case, he journeyed to Rome, accompanied by many members of his family; ostensibly they were to support him in his petition to receive Roman recognition. Herod had left a will (War I.xxxii.7), which named Antipas king, and the codicil (War I.xxxiii.7), which made Antipas only a tetrarch, and Archelaus king. Antipas also journeyed to Rome, to contest with his brother for the kingship. There ensued typical machinations.

Before a decision could be rendered, a third Jewish deputation was in Rome, to plead for autonomy and to bring charges against both the deceased Herod and Archelaus. By now, Philip, a third son of Herod, was also in Rome.

Augustus' decision divided the kingdom into halves. Over one half he named Archelaus as ethnarch, but deferred the title of king until Archelaus might show that he merited it. The other half Augustus split into two parts; Antipas became the tetrarch of Galilee and Perea, and Philip the tetrarch of Batanea, Trachonitis, Auranitis, and other small places. Archelaus became ethnarch of Judea, Idumea, and Samaria (War II.vi.3).

The brutal treatment by Archelaus of Jews and Samaritans led to the arrival in Rome of deputations from both to denounce him to Augustus. After a trial, Archelaus was banished to France, in A.D. 6. His territory was reduced to a province, under a PROCURATOR, Coponius (6-9). Archelaus died sometime after 18 (Strabo XVI.765).

D. *HEROD PHILIP.* The tetrarchy of Herod Philip, son of Herod and Cleopatra, included Batanea, Trachonitis, and nearby districts. Josephus tells us virtually nothing of his reign, though he mentions the founding of CAESAREA PHILIPPI (War II.ix.1), modern Banias. It is likely that Philip did not found the city, but rather renamed it on rebuilding and enlarging it. From the absence of details about Philip's reign, it is a frequent practice to summarize it, as does Josephus, as one of tranquillity and prosperity.

Confusion in Josephus is reflected in scholarly literature about Philip's marital life. A son of Herod, known in Josephus also as Herod, was married to HERODIAS (*see* § H12 *below*), granddaughter of Herod the Great and Mariamne I and daughter of Aristobulus and Bernice. Thereafter, Herodias married Herod Antipas (*see* § E *below*). It was this Herodias, when she was Antipas' wife, who was instrumental in the death of John the Baptist. But was her first husband Herod II, or was he the tetrarch Philip? The NT alludes to the first husband as Philip. Josephus records only one marriage of the tetrarch Philip, that to Salome, the daughter of Herodias. The solution is likely to be that Mark 6:17 errs in speaking of Herodias as the wife of Philip; the corrected reading would be Herod II. Philip's wife, then, was not Herodias, but rather her daughter, Salome, who had danced before Antipas.

When Philip died without issue in 34, his tetrarchy was for three years attached to Syria (Antiq. XVIII. iv.6), but in 37 it was assigned to Agrippa I (*see* § F *below*).

E. *HEROD ANTIPAS.* Herod Antipas (date of birth unknown) was a younger brother of Archelaus, and like him the son of Herod and Malthace. His contest for the kingship in 4 B.C. (*see* § C *above*) ended unsuccessfully. However, he was named tetrarch of Galilee and Perea. A builder like his father, he founded a city, Tiberias, named for the Roman emperor Tiberius. He chose for the site an ancient burial ground, with the result that Jews shunned the place as ritually unclean (cf. Num. 19:14); so Antipas had to import Gentiles in order to have a population.

His half brother, the tetrarch Philip (*see* § D *above*), was married to Salome, daughter of Herodias. (Herodias was the daughter of Aristobulus and granddaughter of Herod the Great.) Herodias, in turn, was married to another half brother, Herod II. Antipas met Herodias and became enamored of her. As he already had a wife, the daughter of the Nabatean king Aretas (her name is not given), Antipas divorced her, and she returned to her father. Then Antipas married Herodias.

John the Baptist was put to death by Antipas. Josephus gives as the reason Antipas' fear of rebellion; the gospels (Matt. 14:1-12; Mark 6:17-18; Luke 3: 19-20) give as the reason John's denunciation of Antipas' marital irregularity (the tetrarch is uniformly called Herod, not Antipas, in the NT).

War broke out in 36 between Antipas and Aretas, and Antipas' army was destroyed. Tiberius died, and Caligula became emperor; to Agrippa, the brother of Herodias, was given the territory previously held by the tetrarch Philip (who had died in 34), but Agrippa received the title of king (37). After Agrippa had come to Palestine (38-39), Herodias persuaded Antipas that they should go to Rome so that Antipas might also gain a more royal title. Agrippa, however, had in readiness some damning charges against Antipas, with the result that Antipas was banished to Lyons in France (39). Herodias accompanied him there. Antipas' tetrarchy was given to Agrippa. (The accounts in Antiq. XVIII.vii and War II are often in minor contradiction.)

F. *AGRIPPA I.* After the banishment of Archelaus in A.D. 6, his territory (primarily Judea) was administered by a Roman PROCURATOR.

Agrippa, son of Herod the Great's son Aristobulus, had been taken to Rome (4 B.C.) by his mother when he was six years old. In A.D. 23 or 29 (the date is uncertain), financial need brought him to Palestine. Moody, he contemplated suicide. An appeal to his sister Herodias brought Agrippa an appointment from his brother-in-law, the tetrarch Herod Antipas, as the overseer of markets in Tiberias. But a quarrel with Antipas soon ended this employment. For a short while, Agrippa was with the Roman governor Flaccus, but his acceptance of bribes made him move on. He succeeded in borrowing money in Alexandria to move on to Rome (36). There he succeeded in becoming a protégé of the heir apparent, Caligula. When indiscreetly he expressed openly the wish that Caligula would soon succeed Tiberius, the latter cast Agrippa into jail.

Some six months later (37), Caligula acceded to the throne, granting to Agrippa the tetrarchy of Philip (*see* § D *above*) with the title of king, and also the tetrarchy in Syria of LYSANIUS.

A year later (38) Agrippa set out for Judea. His vessel stopped at Alexandria, and thereupon a bitter persecution of Alexandrian Jews broke out.

On arriving in Palestine, Agrippa incurred the jealousy of Herod Antipas (*see* § E *above*); thereafter Antipas lost his tetrarchy, which came to be added (40) to Agrippa's possession.

A year later, chancing to be in Rome when Caligula was murdered, Agrippa was helpful in the ascent of Claudius to the Roman throne; as a result Judea and Samaria, which had been under procurators, were added to his territories, so that Agrippa ruled over virtually the same land that his grandfather Herod had ruled over.

Agrippa reigned as king A.D. 41-44. He died at the age of fifty-four, survived by three daughters (Bernice, Mariamne, and Drusilla) and by a seventeen-year-old son (Antiq. XIX.ix.1) also named Agrippa. Because the younger Agrippa was still a minor, the kingdom was temporarily reduced to a province.

G. *AGRIPPA II.* Apparently Agrippa II was in Rome when his father died (44). Being a minor, hence unable to come to his father's throne, he used his influence on behalf of the Jews who were undergoing tribulations in Judea, especially under the procurators Ventidius Cumanus (48-52) and Felix (52-60).

At the age of twenty-three (probably in 56), Agrippa II succeeded an uncle and brother-in-law, Herod, to the throne of Chalcis in modern Lebanon (Antiq. XX.v.2; War II.xii.1). In 53, Agrippa II relinquished the throne of Chalcis and received instead a larger territory formerly within the tetrarchy of Philip (*see* § D *above*). A little later, possibly in 61, Nero, the Roman emperor, added to his territory portions of Galilee and Perea; thereby Agrippa was king over part of Judea. Agrippa had, and exercised, the right to appoint or remove the high priest.

Little is related about Agrippa II in subsequent times, and this little is most unfavorable. With his sister Bernice (the widow of his uncle Herod of Chalcis) he appears to have been involved in incest, both before and after she married one Polemon of Cilicia (Antiq. XX.vii.3; cf. Juvenal *Satires* VI.156-60).

When the rebellion against Rome broke out in 66, Agrippa's troops participated in the assault on Jerusalem by Cestius Gallus (War II.xvii.9). It is a fair summary to say that Agrippa was undeviatingly on the side of the Romans. He entertained the general Vespasian in 67; he went with Vespasian and Titus to Rome in 68 for the purpose of calling on the new emperor, Galba, who was murdered before Agrippa reached Rome (War IV.ix.2). Vespasian was now elected emperor; Agrippa returned to Palestine to take the oath to the new emperor. At the end of the war, in 70, Agrippa had additional territories added to his possessions (War VII.ii.1; v.1). Apparently he and Bernice moved to Rome *ca.* 75. There Bernice was the mistress of Titus, as she had been previously in Palestine (Tac. Hist. II.2). After 75 we know only this about Agrippa—that he corresponded with Josephus about the latter's book *The Jewish War* (see Jos. *Life* LXV; Apion I.9). Agrippa died apparently *ca.* 100. Josephus mentions neither wife nor children; it is often inferred from a passage in Suk. 27*a* that he had two wives. With the death of Agrippa II the Herodian dynasty came to an end.

17. Copper coin with profile of Herod Agrippa II

Fig. HER 17.

H. *IN THE NT.* Virtually all that is told in the NT about members of the family of Herod is lacking in Josephus; and where it is not lacking, it is usually at variance.

But, to anticipate what will emerge in detail *below*, the Herodian family was scarcely approached via archives or historical research by NT writers. Conservative Christians have expended considerable effort to justify what the NT tells about Herod and/or his family. Radical Christian scholars or secular historians have discounted the NT materials as both legendary and tendentious. *See bibliography.*

1. Agrippa I. Acts 12:1-23 relates that Agrippa (called only Herod in the text) persecuted the church, slaying James the son of Zebedee and arresting Peter. Peter was released from prison by an angel. Agrippa had the sentries put to death. Thereafter, angry with the people of Tyre and Sidon, he responded to their appeal with a speech. The people, obsequiously, "shouted, 'The voice of a god, and not of man.' Immediately an angel of the Lord smote him, because he did not give God the glory; and he was eaten by worms and died" (Acts 12:22-23).

In Jos. Antiq. XIX.viii.2, a lugubrious account of Agrippa's death relates that Agrippa at Caesarea, on seeing an owl (a bird of ill omen to him) sitting on the awning of the theater, was seized with abdominal pains, taken to his palace, and died there five days later. The contents of Acts 12:1-23 is totally absent from Josephus.

2. Agrippa II. After Paul has appealed to Caesar in the presence of Festus (Acts 25:1-12), it is related that when Agrippa (II) and (his sister) Bernice arrived at Caesarea, Festus laid Paul's case before the king. The next day Paul appeared before them in the audience hall (25:13-27). Agrippa gave Paul permission to speak, after which Paul asked (26:27-28): "'King Agrippa, do you believe the prophets? I know that you believe.' And Agrippa said to Paul, 'In a short time you think to make me a Christian!'" Agrippa and Festus agreed that Paul had done nothing to deserve death or imprisonment. "Agrippa said to Festus, 'This man could have been set free if he had not appealed to Caesar'" (26:32). Though G. H. C. Macgregor will "admit perhaps the apologetic coloring in the narrative, without however questioning the substantial accuracy of the main facts," he states that "many critics have found the narrative . . . frankly incredible" (*IB*, IX, 318-19). Not one word of the narrative is found in Josephus.

3. Herod Antipas. The passage in Mark 6:14-29, with its rather full parallel in Matt. 14:1-12 and oblique parallels in Luke 3:19-20; 9:7-9, relates the circumstances of the death of John the Baptist. Mark 6:14 surprisingly calls Antipas "king"; Luke 3:1 properly designates him "tetrarch." "Antipas" does not appear as part of his name in the NT.

The account in Josephus of the death of John is bare; that in the gospels is embroidered by the well-known story of the dance of Salome (unnamed in the gospels), whose mother, Herodias, was Antipas' second wife. Antipas had divorced his first wife (a Nabatean princess whose name is unknown) and then taken Herodias away from his half brother Herod. Mark 6:17 names the brother as Philip, as do some, though not all, of the texts of Matt. 14:3. A half brother Philip is known to have married this Salome.

The NT knows nothing of the "seven veils" in which developing legend dressed Salome. Indeed, it is the view of most commentators that the passage, beyond verifying the statement of Josephus that Antipas put John to death, is merely legendary embellishment.

Antipas figures in a brief passage, Luke 13:31-33. It relates that Pharisees told Jesus that Herod wanted to kill him. Jesus replied: "Go and tell that fox, 'Behold, I cast out demons.' " (The fox represents destructiveness, rather than merely craftiness.) The context of the passage is strange, for J. M. Creed writes: "It appears out of place; Jesus is depicted as already on the way to Jerusalem. . . . It has been plausibly suggested that . . . some hostile activity on Herod's part . . . has disappeared from the present Gospel."

In a third passage, found only in Luke 23:6-12, Pilate, learning that Jesus was a Galilean, brought him to Antipas, who chanced to be in Jerusalem then. Jesus answered none of Antipas' questions. Herod and his soldiers "treated him with contempt and mocked him; then, arraying him in gorgeous apparel, he sent him back to Pilate. And Herod and Pilate became friends with each other that very day." The absence of a comparable passage in Mark, Matthew, and John suggests strongly that this passage is legendary. The passage is hearkened back to in Acts 4:25-26. The purpose of it may have been to transfer the mockery of Jesus from the Roman soldiers (Mark 15:16-17) to Antipas. Creed says: "Luke was perhaps glad to transfer the outrage from the soldiery of Rome to the soldiery of the local tetrarch. In the apocryphal Gospel of Peter, the responsibility of Antipas, rather than of Pilate, for the condemnation of Jesus, is magnified."

4. Archelaus. *See* § C *above.* Only Matthew mentions him (2:22), relating that when Joseph "heard that Archelaus reigned over Judea in place of his father Herod, he was afraid to go there."

5. Aristobulus. Paul in Rom. 16:10 sends greetings to the "family of Aristobulus." His identity is unknown. The conjecture that this Aristobulus was, indeed, the grandson of Herod the Great (Jos. War II.ii.6; Antiq. XX.i.2) is farfetched.

6. Drusilla. The third and youngest daughter of Agrippa I. She was married briefly at the age of fourteen to Azizus, King of Emessa, probably in 52. In 53 or 54 she married the Roman (and Gentile) procurator of Palestine, Felix (*see* § H8 *below* for the passing mention of her in Acts 24:24).

7. Bernice. The sister of Agrippa II. *See* §§ G, H2, *above.*

8. Felix. Not properly a Herodian himself, he can be listed here because one of his three wives, Drusilla, was a Herodian. Felix was procurator of Judea 52-60 (Acts 23:24–24:27).

9. Herod the Great. Luke 1:5 states laconically that the events described in the gospel began "in the days of Herod, king of Judea"; no other mention of Herod is made in Luke.

Matt. 2:1 relates that "Jesus was born in Bethlehem of Judea in the days of Herod the King." There follows the narrative of the wise men from the East, who have seen the star; of Herod's summoning and questioning the three; of their journey to Bethlehem and departure without fulfilling Herod's mandate to report to him about the Christ child; of the flight of Joseph to Egypt to save Jesus from the "slaughter of the innocents"; of Herod's death (2:1-19). The material is absent from Josephus.

Those who have assessed this material have expressed a range of judgment from full confidence in reliability through full skepticism. This latter judgment is to be preferred, though it falls short, in the case of Matthew, of indicating the extent to which the childhood of Moses seems repeated in the childhood of Jesus—namely, the narrow escape, while a baby, from death at the hands of a wicked king, and the call out of Egypt, this as part of a deliberate design in Matthew to depict Jesus as a new Moses.

Another difficulty rests in the datum supplied by Luke 2:2 of the census in the time of Quirinius (*see* Chronology of the NT § A1*b*). The price of skepticism as to the reliability of ascribing the birth of Jesus to the last year of the reign of Herod the Great is that the precise year of his birth becomes quite unknown. It is, however, the price which strict historical study demands.

The problem involved is in the character of NT data. The question is whether it is history or legend.

10. Herod Philip. The first husband of Herodias (she later married Herod Antipas); given in Mark 6:17 as Philip. *See* § H3 *above.*

11. Herodians. *See* Herodians.

12. Herodias. Mentioned in Mark 6:17-29 and its parallel, Matt. 14:3-12, and in an oblique parallel, Luke 3:19-20, she was the second wife of Herod Antipas, and he was her second husband. Her first husband was Antipas' half brother Herod. *See* § H3 *above.*

Herodias' father was Aristobulus, son of Herod the Great. Her mother was a niece of Herod the Great (Bernice, daughter of Herod's sister, Salome). Herodias had by her first husband a daughter named Salome.

13. Philip. Mentioned in Luke 3:1, he was a son of Herod the Great and of Cleopatra of Jerusalem (Antiq. XVII.i.3). His tetrarchy was E and NE of the Sea of Galilee. For these regions Luke gives the name of Ituraea and Trachonitis; Josephus differs on this (Antiq. XVII.viii.1; xi.4; War II.vi.3).

Philip plays no role in the gospel. The mention of him is in Luke's fixing of the chronology of the activities of John the Baptist. The city of Caesarea Philippi (Mark 8:27) was founded by him. Beth-saida

(Luke 9:10) was also in his territory. Philip married Salome (*see* § H14 *below*), the daughter of Herodias (*see* § H12 *above*).

14. Salome. The daughter of Herodias (*see* § H12 *above*), Salome is known by name from Josephus; the daughter unnamed in the gospels (Matt. 14:3-12; Mark 6:17-29; Luke 3:19-20) is unquestionably this Salome.

Salome danced before her stepfather, Herod Antipas, on his birthday. In gratitude he offered her whatever she wished; and she wished, and received on a platter, the head of JOHN THE BAPTIST. *See* § H3 *above*.

Josephus is silent on the incident. The student is often surprised at how relatively bare the NT account is. The weight of liberal scholarship regards it as legendary.

On the assumption of a historically reliable account, the problem of the age of Salome at the time of the incident is frequently raised. On the one hand, she appears as yet unbetrothed to Philip (*see* § H13 *above*); on the other hand, she had been born to Herodias when the latter was still married to Salome's father, Herod (*see* § H10 *above*). Philip, her husband, would appear to have been fifty at the time of the incident; it is argued by some that Salome could scarcely have been the young maiden at this time that Mark implies she was, if she married a man of fifty. Accordingly, some have supposed that if Salome danced at all, she must have been forty-five or fifty.

After the death of Salome's husband Philip in 34, she married a relative named Aristobulus, the prince of Chalcis, and bore him three children (Antiq. XVIII.v.4).

15. Summary. The judgment that the gospels are religious tracts rather than exercises in historical research is borne out by the examination of the passages which mention the members of the Herod family. The contents of these passages not only fail of mention in Josephus, but even are out of accord in significant details; they include materials inevitably to be classified as legendary; their total import is small, being only extensive enough to afford the evangelists sporadic opportunity for weaving into the accounts in the gospels or Acts materials which seek to relate Christianity to its Jewish background. Indeed, when Luke-Acts is separated from Mark and Matthew, the increased sparsity of the mention of the family of Herod becomes underlined. The old theory of Krenkel (*Josephus and Lukas* [1894]) that Luke utilized Josephus as a source, though carelessly, is not supported by the material on the family of Herod. This theory can be held only by attributing to Luke something more than mere carelessness—namely, tendentiousness and unrestrained imagination; for if what Luke-Acts tells us about the family of Herod is legendary, then Josephus is definitely not the source for the particular legends.

The NT material on Herod's family adds virtually nothing to knowledge of them. It increases the perplexities rather than illuminating dark places.

Bibliography. E. Schürer, *A History of the Jewish People in the Time of Jesus Christ* (English trans., 1872, from the 2nd German ed.), is antiquated in some of its bibliography but remains a standard work of reference. Schürer's detailed study of the problems of the NT references to the Herodian family should be consulted. The best study of Herod, marred by occasional excess of speculation, is W. Otto, *Herodes* (1913), published as an offprint from Pauly-Wissowa, *Realencyklopädie der klassischen Altertumswissenschaften;* for the same Encyclopedia, Otto also wrote articles on the Herodians, Herodias, and Herod Agrippa, incomparably superior to any other writings on these persons. Josephus is the basic source of information, and hence the student might be alert to the Loeb Classical Library translations, especially the volumes of *Antiquities* prepared by R. Marcus, whose explanatory notes are virtually a commentary; H. St. J. Thackeray is quite good on *The Jewish War*. Ch. 5 of R. Laqueur, *Der jüdische Historiker Flavius Josephus: Ein biographischer Versuch auf neuer quellenkritischer Grundlage,* merits both attention and ultimate rejection. F.-M. Abel, *Histoire de la Palestine* (1952), vol. I, pt. 2, pp. 287-503, is an admirable work. On Herod's violations of Jewish law, see J. Juster, *Les Juifs dans l'empire romain* (1914), II, 128-29; L. Finkelstein, *The Pharisees* (2nd ed., 1940), II, 684-85. More recent works are admirably listed in R. Marcus, "A Selected Bibliography (1920-1945) of the Jews in the Hellenistic-Roman Period," *Proceedings of the American Academy for Jewish Research,* XVI (1947), 98-181.

S. SANDMEL

HERODIANS hĭ rō'dĭ ənz [ʽΗρῳδιανοί]. Literally, adherent of Herod, or of his dynasty. *See* HEROD (FAMILY).

In three unquestioned passages (Mark 3:6; 12:13= Matt. 22:16), the Herodians are mentioned as opponents of Jesus, along with the Pharisees. The term is never found in Luke or John. Matt. 12:14 (=Mark 3:6) omits Mark's mention of the Herodians, as does the parallel in Luke 6:11. Matt. 22:16 (=Mark 12: 13) carries over the mention of them in Mark, but Luke 20:20 does not. Another passage, Mark 8:15, varies in the MSS, for a few (e.g., Chester Beatty Papyrus 45, W, and Θ) read "leaven of the Herodians" rather than the usually accepted reading "leaven of Herod." The parallel to this passage, Matt. 16:6, does not read "Herod" or "Herodians," but rather "SADDUCEES," while Luke 12:1 warns only against the "leaven of the Pharisees, which is hypocrisy."

The problem, or series of problems, involved, includes: (*a*) an identification of "the Herodians" in a manner more specific than simply as adherents either of a Herod or of the Herodian dynasty; (*b*) an answer to the problem of Luke's apparent full avoidance of the term "Herodians" and Matthew's partial avoidance of it; (*c*) the identification, found among commentators, of the Herodians with Sadducees, this through bringing together Mark 8:15; Matt. 16:6.

Older literature states that the Herodians were the "adherents of the dynasty of Herod, who made common cause with the Pharisees against Jesus." Gould (1896) identifies them as "those among the Jews who, in more or less veiled opposition to the Roman procuratorship, desired the restoration of the national kingdom under one or other of the sons of Herod."

Modern scholarship, for the most part, lacks the sense of certainty found in these earlier interpreters. Thus Branscomb (*see bibliography*) states that "who these Herodians were is uncertain." Guignebert (*see bibliography*) says: "What the Gospels tell us of the evil intentions of the 'Herodians' . . . is very vague, and cannot be analyzed into facts." While Wilfred L. Knox (*see bibliography*) terms the Herodians a "body of Jewish opinion which seriously regarded the rule of the Herodian dynasty as the best solution of the Jewish problem," he declares that "it may indeed be doubted whether Mark really knew who they were."

Two explanations are cited, and rejected, by Jerome (in his commentary on Matt. 22:15), one from Origen and one from Pseudo-Tertullian. The first of these supposed that those willing to pay tribute to Caesar were called Herodians by their opponents; the second, that the Herodians were those who believed Herod to be the Christ. Again, Epiphanius (*Panarion* XX.1) mentions the Herodians as the twentieth in his list of heresies. E. Bickerman (*see bibliography*), after summarizing and dismissing various such theories, declares himself in favor of regarding the Herodians as followers of Herod Antipas (*see* HEROD [FAMILY] § E). If some specific identification of the Herodians must be made, Bickerman's is as convincing as any.

However, reverting to the problems listed above, several suggestions may be made: (*a*) Mark and Matthew can lay no claim to historical precision; and even if they could, the three allusions to the Herodians are so vague that the Herodians cannot truly be identified. (*b*) The avoidance of the term, in Matthew partially and in Luke completely, is probably the result of a deliberate correction of Mark, possibly out of a desire to reject improbable explanations of the type cited above from Origen and Epiphanius. (*c*) There is nothing in Matthew which actually identifies the Herodians with the Sadducees, for Matt. 16:6 merely substitutes the Sadducees for Mark's Herodians; while Luke 20:20, parallel to Mark 12:13 and to Matt. 22:16, omits the Herodians entirely, abstains from a specific substitution, and relates instead that the questioners of Jesus were "suborned spies" (Creed [*see bibliography*]). There is, then, no direct statement in the gospels which equates Herodians and Sadducees.

Bibliography. W. Otto, "Herodians," in Pauly-Wissowa, *Realencyklopädie der klassischen Altertumswissenschaften*, Supplement II, p. 200—a superior article. B. W. Bacon, "Pharisees and Herodians in Mark," *JBL,* XXXIX (1920), 102-12; "The Leaven of the Pharisees," *Studies in Matthew* (1930), pp. 511-17. J. M. Creed, *The Gospel According to St. Luke* (1930), p. 247. C. A. H. Guignebert, *Jesus* (English trans., S. H. Hooke, 1935), p. 188. B. H. Branscomb, *The Gospel of Mark* (1937), p. 61. E. Bickerman, *RB,* XLVII (1938), 184-97. H. H. Rowley, "The Herodians in the Gospels," *JTS,* XLI (1940), 14-27. W. L. Knox, "Church and State in the NT," *Journal of Roman Studies,* XXXIX (1949), 23 ff; *The Sources of the Synoptic Gospels,* I: *St. Mark* (1953), 10.

S. SANDMEL

HERODIAS hĭ rō'dĭ əs ['Ηρῳδιάς]. A wife of Herod Antipas, and the daughter of Aristobulus and Bernice. Aristobulus was the son of Herod the Great; Bernice was Herod's niece, the daughter of his sister Salome (*see* HEROD [FAMILY] § H7). Herodias' exact dates are unknown beyond her belonging in the first half of the first century A.D.

Herodias was married initially to the half brother of her father. She bore this husband a daughter named Salome. The husband-uncle is known in Mark 6:17 as Philip, and so too in some of the texts of Matt. 14:3. It is more likely, however, that his true name was Herod, and not Philip, for there was still another brother who carried the name Philip.

Herod Antipas was a half brother of the first husband of Herodias. Antipas had divorced his first wife, a Nabatean princess, to make room for Herodias, and wooed her away from his half brother. An account in the gospels (Mark 6:17-29; Matt. 14:3-12; cf. Luke 3:19-20), lacking in Josephus, relates that JOHN THE BAPTIST had denounced this marital irregularity; the daughter, Salome, after a dance, in vengeance demanded and received John's head on a platter.

Josephus relates that when Agrippa I (*see* HEROD [FAMILY] § H1), her brother, came to the throne of Judea in A.D. 41, Herodias prevailed upon the reluctant Antipas to go to Rome to petition the Emperor Caligula to supplant Agrippa and to name Antipas the king (*see* CALIGULA). Instead, however, the emperor banished Antipas to Lyons, in Gaul, and Herodias accompanied him there.

Bibliography. Jos. Antiq. XVIII.v.1-2; vii.1-2; War I.xxix.1; II.ix.6. *See also* the bibliography under HEROD [FAMILY].

S. SANDMEL

HERODION hĭ rō'dĭ ən ['Ηρῳδίων]. A Christian man greeted in Rom. 16:11 by Paul, who called him a kinsman—i.e., fellow countryman (Jew; cf. Rom. 9:3).

F. W. GINGRICH

HERODIUM hĭ rō'dĭ əm ['Ηρώδειον]. A fortress-palace and tomb monument some four miles SE of Bethlehem. It was built and named by Herod the Great for himself. The conical-shaped, artificially heightened hill, on top of which the ruins of the Herodian citadel are still visible, gives a striking appearance from many points in S Judea. It is known in modern times as Jebel el-Fureidis ("hill of paradise") or Frank Mountain. Fig. TEK 7.

Herodium was both a desert retreat and part of a chain of fortresses Herod erected or rebuilt in the wilderness to protect his kingdom; among the latter were Alexandrium; Hyrcania; MASADA; and MACHAERUS. At the time Herod fled S before the Parthians in 40 B.C., he was attacked by hostile Jews; near the site where he was later to build Herodium, he inflicted on them a severe defeat, and so was able to make his way to Rome and claim his kingdom (Jos. War I.viii.8); Antiq. XIV.xiii.9). He subsequently erected a fortress called Herodium on the Idumean frontier, the location of which is unknown, and the luxurious palace by the same name near Bethlehem (Jos. War I.xxi.10). The latter, at his express request, was also to be his tomb; when he died at Jericho (4 B.C.), a grand funeral procession proceeded by way of Jerusalem to Herodium, where he was interred (Jos. War I.xxiii.9).

Under Roman administration Herodium was the capital of one of eleven toparchies (Jos. War III.iii.5). During the events of A.D. 68-69, Simon, a leader of a rebel band, sent Eleazar to request the capitulation of Herodium, but the move was unsuccessful (Jos. War IV.ix.5). As one of the three last strongholds of Jewish resistance (the other two being Machaerus and Masada), Herodium was reduced by Lucilius Bassus in A.D. 72 (Jos. War IV.ix.10). Thus ended its brief but illustrious existence.

The brief description given by Josephus (War

I.xxi.10), together with recent observations of the ruins, provides the essential details of the structure. Herod had artificially raised and crowned the hill with a ring of three concentric walls with round towers standing at the four cardinal directions. At the foot of the mountain he erected other palaces, buildings, pools, and terraces appropriate to a palatial retreat. A grand stairway of two hundred white marble steps mounted to the citadel. An aqueduct to bring in an abundant water supply was constructed at great expense.

Bibliography. E. Robinson, *Biblical Researches in Palestine,* I (1874), 478-81; C. Schick, *ZDPV,* 3 (1880), 88-99 (with plan); E. Schürer, *A History of the Jewish People* (English trans.; 1891), division I, vol. I, pp. 435-36, 467; F.-M. Abel, *Géographie,* II (1938), 348. R. W. FUNK

HERODOTUS hĭ rŏd′ə təs. A Greek historian of the fifth century B.C. He was called by Cicero the "father of history" (Laws I.1).

1. Life. We know little of his life other than what we learn indirectly from his *History*. Suidas gives his parents' names as Lyxis and Dryo (or Rhoio). He was born in Halicarnassus, probably *ca.* 484 B.C., where the prevailing dialect was Ionic. Later, sometime after 454, he lived in Athens, where he was probably acquainted with Pericles and Sophocles. In 445 or shortly thereafter, he went to Thurii, where he took part in the founding of the new colony initiated by Pericles. Suidas tells us that Herodotus was buried in the market place of Thurii; but there was another tradition that he died in Pella. We do not know where or when he died, but his death must have occurred *ca.* 424. In *ca.* 440 he may have returned to Athens from Thurii, where he lived until the outbreak of the Peloponnesian War in 431; but this is disputed. Some scholars believe he never left Thurii permanently. It was probably during this later period of his life that he did his more extensive traveling in Asia and Egypt and wrote his famous *History*.

2. Travels. Herodotus' *History* is based largely on the data he collected during his travels. The chronology of his journeys is a subject of dispute. Suffice it to say that he traveled widely and visited such places as the coasts of the Euxine, Babylonia, Phoenicia, Egypt, and probably Cyrene.

3. Herodotus' *History*. The main subject of the *History* is the relation between the Greeks and the oriental powers from the accession of Croesus to the end of the Persian Wars and the capture of Sestus in 479/78 B.C. His work is divided into nine books: the first three deal with the reigns of Cyrus and Cambyses and the accession of Darius, and with the rise of Persian power. The second three deal with the reign of Darius, Persian failure in Scythia and at Marathon, and Greek failure in Ionia. The third triad describes the reign of Xerxes and the defeat of Persia by Greece.

Writing when the policy of Athens was being severely criticized, at the beginning of her conflict with Sparta, Herodotus emphasizes the contributions which Athens made to Greece.

Cicero, as mentioned above, called Herodotus the "father of history"; but the Israelites, not to mention others, produced earlier histories. Herodotus' history has an epic flavor; it is a Homeric account of the Persian Wars. It seeks to discover causes of great events, but the author's perspective in this regard is seriously limited.

4. Sources. Herodotus' sources include: (*a*) the testimony of eyewitnesses, on which he relies heavily and which is valuable for his recent history; (*b*) traditions: he is skeptical of marvels except ancient ones; (*c*) archaeological material; (*d*) written sources, which seem to lie behind his list of satrapies (III.89-97), his description of the Royal Road (V.52-53), and his list of the Persian army (VII.61-99).

B. H. THROCKMORTON, JR.

HERON [אנפה (Lev. 11:19; Deut. 14:18), *cf.* אנף, to be angry; Akkad. *anpatu, an unidentified bird;* Targ. (Onq.) אבו, vulture, kite; LXX χαραδριός, *possibly* a plover, *see below;* Vulg. *charadrius*]. Any of a family (Ardeidae) of wading birds with a long, thin neck and long legs, whose haunt is water of every kind and whose food is fish and other water animals. Tristram testifies that at least seven varieties of heron were common in the lake regions of Palestine in his day. We might therefore expect the heron to be mentioned in a list of OT birds.

The two biblical references to אנפה indicate an unclean bird, while the phrase "according to its kind" (Lev. 11:19) suggests a bird of which several species were known. Otherwise it cannot be identified. The LXX word, χαραδριός, is used by Aristotle to indicate a bird found at the seaside with gulls and nesting in cliffs (*History of Animals* 593*b*, 15; 615*a*, 1); and by Aristophanes for a river bird (*Birds* 1141).

If we suppose that water or wading birds are near the end of the two biblical lists, אנפה may be a species of heron (so Bodenheimer; *see* FAUNA § B5; cf. LXX above); G. R. Driver (*see bibliography*), however, favors the cormorant.

Bibliography. G. R. Driver, *PEQ* (1955), pp. 17-18.

W. S. MCCULLOUGH

HESED hē′sĕd. KJV form. *See* BEN-HESED.

HESHBON hĕsh′bŏn [חשבון; Ἑσεβῶν]; KJV Apoc. ESEBON ĕs′ĭ bŏn. An important city in the N part of Greater Moab; it is the modern Hesban, located just S of the Wadi Hesban, *ca.* fifty miles due E of Jerusalem. It is frequently called the city of Sihon, king of the Amorites, who wrested the whole territory from the Moabites as far as the River Arnon (Wadi Mojib); he made it his capital, and the appellation may indicate that the city was built by him. After Sihon was defeated by the Israelites, Heshbon was rebuilt and populated by the tribe of Reuben and later by the Gadites (Num. 21; 32; Josh. 13:17, 26; 21:39; I Chr. 6:81). The region about it was bitterly contested between Moab and Israel; it was probably conquered by the former under Eglon (Judg. 3:12 ff) and won back by the latter through the efforts of the judges (I Sam. 12:9, 11). The territory then remained permanently Israelite until after the death of Ahab (853 B.C.), when MESHA of Moab reconquered it in his great campaign. From that time on, it remained in Moabite hands and is mentioned more than once in the oracles directed against Moab (Isa. 15:4; 16:8-9; Jer. 48:2, 33-34). *Ca.* 600, Heshbon seems to have fallen into the hands of the Ammonites (Jer. 49:3), who had made some claims to the territory (Judg. 11:26). In the Hellenistic period it was part of the Nabatean kingdom; it was reconquered by Alexander Janneus (103-76), but was allowed full autonomy, including the right of striking its own coins (Jos. Antiq. XIII.xv.4). After the fall of the Jewish state, Heshbon was annexed to the Roman province of Syria.

Bibliography. A. Musil, *Arabia Petraea I Moab* (1907), pp. 383-88; N. Glueck, *AASOR,* XVIII-XIX (1939), 242-51.

S. Cohen

HESHMON hĕsh'mŏn [חשמון] (Josh. 15:27). A town in the SW part of Judah, near Beth-pelet. It may be the source of the adjective "Hasmonean," the Talmudic designation for the Maccabees.

HETH hĕth [חת]. The eponym of the Hittites in the Table of Nations (Gen. 10:15; I Chr. 1:13); the Hittites (KJV "sons of Heth") appear in the story of the acquisition of the cave of Machpelah by Abraham (Gen. 23; 25:10; 49:32); the marrying of the "Hittite women" (KJV "daughters of Heth"), or "Canaanite women" (KJV "daughters of Canaan"), by Jacob was discouraged by Rebekah and Isaac (cf. Gen. 27: 46; 28:1, 8). I. J. Gelb

HETHLON hĕth'lŏn [חתלן]. A place on the hypothetical N border of Israel, according to Ezekiel (47: 15; 48:1). Possibly it is identical with Heitela, E of Tripolis in Lebanon.

HEWERS OF WOOD [חטבי עצים]. One of the lowest classes of Servant. The Gibeonites preferred such Slavery to death (Josh. 9:21, 23, 27). These workers are to be distinguished from those who felled trees for building purposes (II Chr. 2:9-10; Jer. 46: 22) to be used by the Carpenter or craftsmen (*see* Crafts). These are really the gatherers of firewood —an endless, dull task. The lowliness is clearly indicated in Deut. 29:11, where these hewers of wood are among the last in the listing of covenanting people (vs. 10).

See also Drawers of Water. C. U. Wolf

HEXATEUCH hĕx'ə to͝ok, —tūk. The modern scholarly designation of the first six books of the Bible (i.e., the Pentateuch plus Joshua). The identification of the Hexateuch as the basic literary unit in the larger history of Israel (Genesis–II Kings) was regarded as a major contribution of critical scholarship, and as the indispensable corollary of source analysis. It had been apparent to scholars for a long time that the Pentateuch, traditionally understood to be the work of Moses, was not only a composite of different strands, but the truncated section of a more extensive composition. It must have included the book of Joshua, at least, if there was to be a suitable conclusion to the story of Israel's beginnings. The theme of the Promised Land is paramount in the Pentateuch; it is firmly established in the book of Genesis, and reinforced in the narrative of the deliverance from Egypt and wanderings in the wilderness; it demands the fulfilment related in the story of the conquest and settlement found in Joshua. It is unthinkable that the narrative should have ended before relating these decisive events. Just as the recognition of the total literary pattern pointed to the inclusion of Joshua, source analysis located the familiar Pentateuchal sources in that book. The composite narrative was assigned to JE, while the boundary lists and other technical data were apparently the work of P. The whole book bore the unmistakable stamp of Deuteronomic redaction.

The relationship of Joshua to the following books, especially Judges, was also considered. It was thought by some that J, and possibly E, carried the narrative of Israel's settlement down through the period of the judges into the time of David (or Solomon), when the promise of the land was finally and totally achieved. J and E have been identified in Judges, and in the "two sources" of Samuel, but the evidence is by no means decisive. It was recognized that the books of Judges, Samuel, and Kings had undergone the same sort of Deuteronomic editing as Joshua, but it was thought that this activity was undertaken by different members of a so-called Deuteronomic school, and did not necessarily signify an organic interrelationship. The clinching argument for the Hexateuch as an independent literary work rested upon the evidence for P. It was generally agreed that P was present in Joshua but did not extend beyond it. Since P provided the framework for the Pentateuch, this meant that the redactor (R_{JEDP}) must also have included Joshua in his compilation. That the structure of Joshua is essentially Deuteronomic rather than Priestly was a source of concern, but not sufficient to undermine the "Hexateuchal" solution. There the matter rested.

In recent scholarship the Hexateuchal reconstruction has come under suspicion, and the Hexateuch itself has disintegrated. It is by no means certain that the sources in Joshua are the same as those in the Pentateuch. Prominent scholars have argued that J and E are not to be found in Joshua, but end substantially in the book of Numbers; that the lists in Joshua may be P-type material but not necessarily P; and finally that Joshua in its present form is part of the great Deuteronomic history extending from Deuteronomy through II Kings, and does not therefore belong to a Pentateuchal complex. It is clear that the Hexateuch and the Deuteronomic history represent overlapping and conflicting reconstructions of the major units in the basic biblical narrative (Genesis–II Kings). In this larger work, Joshua is a middle term, with strong connections in both directions (i.e., as a suitable conclusion to the story of the occupation of the land, and as an indispensable link in the whole story of Israel from entry to exit). It would, nevertheless, appear that the principal division in the Genesis–Kings narrative comes between Numbers and Deuteronomy, which not only stands apart from the preceding books, but quite clearly constitutes a beginning, the introduction to the history (Joshua–Kings) which follows. The claims made for the essential integrity of the Deuteronomic history have more evidence to commend them than those of the Hexateuch. The main difficulty with this approach is that it leaves the so-called Tetrateuch (the first four books) as a mere torso. The original arguments about the truncation of the story at the end of the Pentateuch apply even more strongly to the Tetrateuch. It is difficult, if not impossible, to escape the conclusion that JE included an account of the conquest and settlement in the land. It is altogether possible that fragments of this narrative are embedded in the book of Joshua (and even Judges), although the evidence is scanty, since the book has been extensively revised and is now an integral part of the Deuteronomic history.

It may be best to postulate the existence of two major and slightly overlapping works covering the books from Genesis through Kings: (*a*) the JEP history, incorporating the JE narrative along with archival data of the Tetrateuch plus an account of the conquest and settlement in the Promised Land (parallel to and possibly including some materials in the book of Joshua); (*b*) the Deuteronomic history, beginning with Moses' farewell speeches (including a summary of preceding events) and coming down to the fall of Judah and the Exile. These two works were amalgamated by an editor who inserted the Deuteronomic history at the appropriate place in the JEP narrative (i.e., at the end of the wanderings). He either removed the last part of the JEP account or blended it into the present book of Joshua. Still later the present division at the end of the book of Deuteronomy into the Pentateuch and the Former Prophets was made, but on the basis of religious and not literary considerations. The term "Hexateuch" has proved useful in the history of criticism, and reflects an important era in biblical scholarship. But it is doubtful whether the literary composition it designated ever existed as an independent entity.

Bibliography. The classic presentation in English of the Hexateuchal analysis and its defense is J. E. Carpenter and G. Harford-Battersby, eds., *The Hexateuch* (2 vols.; 1900). See also the Introductions by S. R. Driver, *Introduction to the Literature of the OT* (9th ed., 1913); A. Bentzen, *Introduction to the OT* (2 vols.; 1948); R. H. Pfeiffer, *Introduction to the OT* (2nd ed., 1949). The discussion in *The OT and Modern Study* (1951), chs. 3-4, is helpful. A later word is to be found in O. Eissfeldt, *Einleitung in das AT* (2nd ed., 1956). See also G. W. Anderson, *A Critical Introduction to the OT* (1959); Y. Kaufmann, *The Religion of Israel* (1960).

D. N. FREEDMAN

HEZEKI. KJV form of HIZKI.

HEZEKIAH hĕz'ə kī'ə [(ו)חזקיה, Yahu (is) my strength; 'Εζεκίας]; KJV alternately HIZKIAH hĭz kī'ə (Zeph. 1:1), HIZKIJAH —jə (Neh. 10:17), EZEKIAS ĕz'ə kī'əs (Matt. 1:9-10). **1.** King of Judah *ca.* 715-687 B.C.; son and successor of Ahaz.

The full form of the name appears in the MT and has been found on a contemporary ostracon from Jerusalem. In Assyrian inscriptions the name is "vocalized" as *Ha-za-qi-(i)a-ú.*

Hezekiah came to the throne at the age of twenty-five and reigned twenty-nine years (II Kings 18:2; II Chr. 29:1). His mother was Abi the daughter of Zechariah (ABIJAH in II Chr. 29:1; Abi is a caritative of Abijah). The date of his accession seems to be fixed by Sennacherib's campaign in 701, which took place in the fourteenth year of King Hezekiah (II Kings 18:13). The terminal date of his reign must be after the accession of Tirhakah (Taharqo), mentioned in II Kings 19:9. Egyptian sources indicate that Tirhakah became king *ca.* 689.

Hezekiah was remembered by later generations as an able and vigorous ruler and a pious king (II Kings 18:5; cf. 23:25). Another aspect of the reign is indicated by the reference, perhaps authentic, to the "proverbs of Solomon which the men of Hezekiah king of Judah copied" (Prov. 25–29). Hezekiah came to the throne at a critical time in the history of Judah. Aram had fallen to Tiglath-pileser in 732, and had been made into four Assyrian provinces. A similar fate overtook Israel in 722-721 at the hands of Sargon II. Judah had been seriously weakened by the Syro-Ephraimitic War and by attacks on her territory by Edomites and Philistines during the reign of Ahaz. The annual payment of tribute to Assyria was an intolerable burden upon her resources. Further, religious conditions under Ahaz had become chaotic. The urgent demand of the time was for political and religious reform. The alternative was the fate of the surrounding nations—servitude to Assyria. Isaiah had pleaded with Ahaz to have faith in Yahweh, but to no avail. Now men were beginning to see that only the power of Yahweh could save them from the might of Assyria.

That a religious reform took place is unquestionable. Even during the reign of Ahaz a reform party was probably in existence in Judah. The prophetic words spoken by Amos and Hosea had come to terrible fulfilment in the destruction of the N kingdom. Was a like fate to befall Judah? The N disaster was powerfully used by the contemporary prophets Isaiah and Micah to point the moral of a return to the worship of Yahweh. It may be contended that Hezekiah's interests were largely political, and that he was influenced by political motives, but the line of distinction between religious enthusiasm and patriotism was not always sharply drawn in ancient Israel. In this regard the position and the influence of Isaiah are especially to be noted. Hezekiah removed the high places, broke down the pillars, and cut down the Asherah (II Kings 18:4). He even destroyed the brass serpent which had been preserved in the temple and was said to have been made by Moses. Such measures would not have the support of the whole people, and the inevitable reaction came during the reign of Hezekiah's son Manasseh.

The Chronicler has a long account of the religious reformation in II Chr. 29–31. The cleansing and sanctifying of the temple and the restoration of the temple cult (ch. 29) were followed by a great celebration of the Passover, in which certain people of the former N kingdom participated (ch. 30). Then the whole land, including Ephraim and Manasseh, was cleansed of idolatry (31:1). The rest of ch. 31 describes further reformation measures carried out by Hezekiah. To this religious reformation Kings has only one corresponding verse (II Kings 18:4). To what extent, then, can the information found in the Chronicles be regarded as historical? So much of it seems to reflect the Chronicler's own special viewpoint and interest.

The tendency has been to disregard in large measure the account of the Chronicler. Such a judgment, however, is unwarranted. The Chronicler has preserved material based on reliable traditions. It is true that Isaiah makes no specific reference to such a reformation. This is very surprising unless the prophet saw that the real motive was not a religious one at all. At the same time it must be noted that to the Assyrian Rabshakeh is attributed the reference to high places and altars removed by Hezekiah (II Kings 18:22). A religious reformation occurred which was only in part successful. This reform movement extended also to the former N kingdom. There is no reason to doubt the statement that Hezekiah's messengers met with little success in Ephraim and Manasseh, but won a limited response in Asher and Zebulun farther to the N (II Chr. 30:10-11). A reason for this may be suggested: Under the Assyrians, Bethel again became important as a cult center (II Kings 17:27-28). The Assyrians probably saw the importance of a rival place of worship to Jerusalem and so permitted the worship of Yahweh at Bethel. That the sending of messengers to the N by Hezekiah had political implications is certain.

Hezekiah's other concern was to strengthen Judah politically. He does not appear to have committed any act of open rebellion against Assyria for some years. During this period, however, it is probable that, with an eye to the future, he began to strengthen the defenses of Jerusalem. In particular, he cut through the solid rock in order to bring the water of the Gihon Spring into the city (II Kings 20:20; II Chr. 32:30).* This remarkable feat is recorded in the contemporary Siloam Inscription. In his inscriptions for his eleventh year—i.e., 711—Sargon records a victorious campaign against Aziru king of Ashdod, which he made into an Assyrian province. He also claims that Ashdod sought help from Judah and Egypt. Apparently Hezekiah did not join in this rebellion. But with Sargon's death in 705 and the accession of Sennacherib an entirely new situation developed, and there is evidence of widespread intrigue. To this time is to be attributed the embassy sent by Merodach-baladan king of Babylon to Hezekiah (II Kings 20:12-15; Isa. 39:1-4). He had established himself in S Mesopotamia and offered stubborn resistance to Assyrian attempts to overthrow him. To the same period belongs the re-emergence of Egypt on the world scene under a strong ruler, the Ethiopian Shabako (the Tirhakah of II Kings 19:9). The time seemed opportune for rebellion, and in all probability Hezekiah intrigued openly both with Babylon and with Egypt against Assyria. "He rebelled against the king of Assyria, and would not serve him"—i.e., he withheld tribute from him (II Kings 18:7*b*). "He [also] smote the Philistines as far as Gaza and its territory, from watchtower to fortified city" (vs. 8). This is probably to be interpreted as a purely local matter. During the reign of Ahaz the Philistines had raided the Shephelah and the Negeb, and seized some of the cities of Judah (II Chr. 28:18; cf. Isa. 14:28 ff). In the unsettled situation that prevailed at Sargon's death Hezekiah saw his opportunity to retaliate. It is possible, however, that he had a wider object in mind—to foment rebellion against Assyria. The prophet Isaiah seems to have opposed the rebellion. Fig. HEZ 18.

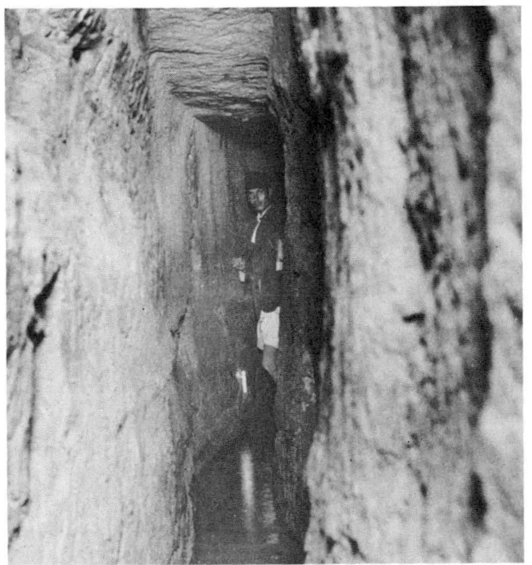

18. The Siloam tunnel, erected in Jerusalem by Hezekiah king of Judah (715-687 B.C.)

After settling affairs, at least temporarily, in the E in two campaigns, Sennacherib turned to the W. This third campaign is very well documented in Assyrian sources* and can be supplemented by the biblical record (II Kings 18:13–19:37; II Chr. 32:1-22; Isa. 36–37). In 701 Sennacherib invaded Palestine and in an extensive campaign put down the rebellion. A large Egyptian and Ethiopian army had marched N to relieve Ekron, to which Sennacherib had laid siege, but it was defeated. Ekron was captured, and Padi its king, who had remained loyal to Assyria and as a result had been handed over to Hezekiah as a prisoner, was again set on the throne. Then Sennacherib turned against the fortified cities of Judah and seized them (II Kings 18:13). He claims to have conquered forty-six of them, together with the small villages around about. Among them were the exceedingly strong fortress city of Lachish (vs. 14) and Debir. Sennacherib's famous reliefs depict the siege of Lachish and the captives passing before the king. The exact sequence of events is not clear. While the siege of Lachish was still in progress, Hezekiah sent a message to Sennacherib, offering to surrender and promising to pay whatever tribute was imposed upon him (vs. 14*a*). Presumably most of the fortified cities of Judah had already fallen, and Hezekiah saw that further resistance was useless. He may also have wished to save the capital city from the same fate which had overtaken the others. The Assyrian king demanded an enormous tribute of three hundred talents of silver and thirty of gold (vs. 14*b*). The Assyrian records contain an even larger figure—eight hundred talents of silver. To obtain this sum, Hezekiah took all the silver from the temple and the royal treasuries. He also "stripped the gold from the doors of the temple of the LORD, and from the doorposts which Hezekiah king of Judah had overlaid and gave it to the king of Assyria" (vs. 16). This datum is of considerable interest, and indicates that the king had restored and adorned the temple. Not only this, but the Assyrian inscriptions give a picture of considerable wealth and luxury in Judah at this time (cf. II Chr. 32:27-29). They also reveal how thorough were the preparations which Hezekiah had made for rebellion, and advance a reason for his capitulation—the desertion of his mercenaries. Fig. INS 12.

II Kings 18:17–19:37 raises many difficult problems. Hezekiah had already submitted, but these verses tell of still further demands made by Sennacherib, calling for complete surrender. Further, they seem to consist of parallel accounts—18:17–19:7; 19:8-37. Their historicity is open to question. It is possible that during the siege of Lachish, which Sennacherib had difficulty in capturing, he sent part of his army under the Rabshakeh to Jerusalem in order to pin down Hezekiah's forces. The city was besieged but was not captured. After some time the Rabshakeh returned from Jerusalem—no reason is given for his return—and joined the king of Assyria, who was then fighting against Libnah (II Kings 19:8). Apparently Lachish had fallen by this time. The siege of Libnah was interrupted by the news of the approach of an Egyptian army under Tirhakah king of Ethiopia (vs. 9). But Tirhakah only became king of Egypt *ca.* 689. Sennacherib's Annals in regard to this campaign break off abruptly with the statement that he "laid waste the large district of Judah and made the overbearing and proud Hezekiah, its king, bow in submission." The probable explanation is that events at home demanded his return, and he withdrew (II Kings 19:7).

From the evidence available to us it is not possible to reconstruct the history of subsequent events. Kings records an Assyrian invasion which was remembered because of a plague which decimated the Assyrian army (II Kings 19:35). If this had any connection with Tirhakah, it presumably occurred after his accession *ca.* 689, unless it is assumed that he had not yet become king. As against the hypothesis of one campaign carried out by Sennacherib against Hezekiah, it seems preferable to adopt the hypothesis of two campaigns and to assume a second Assyrian invasion of Palestine between 689 and 686, the year of Hezekiah's death. The circumstances were again propitious. In 691 the Assyrians sustained a defeat at the hands of the Babylonians and the Elamites at Khalulê. Hezekiah revolted again, with the backing of Tirhakah. It would appear that considerable confusion arose regarding Sennacherib's activities in Palestine, and the accounts of two originally separate campaigns were telescoped into one.

Bibliography. R. P. Dougherty, "Sennacherib and the Walled Cities of Palestine," *JBL,* XLIX (1930), 160-71. E. G. Kraeling, "The Death of Sennacherib," *JAOS,* 53 (1933), 335 ff. W. O. E. Oesterley and T. H. Robinson, *A History of Israel,* I (2nd ed., 1934), 385 ff. H. H. Rowley, "Zadok and Nehushtan," *JBL,* LVIII (1939), 113 ff. J. A. Montgomery, *The Books of Kings,* ICC (1951), pp. 480-518. J. Simons, *Jerusalem in the OT* (1952), pp. 207, 222 ff, 292 ff, 327 ff. A. Alt, *Kleine Schriften zur Geschichte des Volkes Israel,* II (1953), 242-49. J. B. Pritchard, ed., *ANET* (2nd ed., 1955), pp. 287-88, 321. W. Rudolph, *Chronikbücher* (1955), pp. 293-315. W. F. Albright, "New Light from Egypt on the Chronology and History of Israel and Judah," *BASOR,* 130 (1953), 4-11 (especially 8-11); "Further Light on Synchronisms Between Egypt and Asia in the Period 935-685 B.C.," *BASOR,* 141 (1956), 23-27 (especially 23-26). M. Noth, *Geschichte Israels* (3rd ed., 1956), pp. 239 ff. G. E. Wright, *Biblical Archaeology* (1957), pp. 164-72.

2. One of the ancestors of the prophet Zephaniah (Zeph. 1:1).

3. Son of Neariah, descendant of the royal family of Judah (I Chr. 3:23).

4. Head of a family whose descendants returned with Nehemiah from the Babylonian exile (Ezra 2:16; Neh. 7:21). The Babylonian name was Ater. Both names occur in Neh. 10:17 among the number of those who set their seal to the covenant.

H. B. MacLean

HEZION hē'zĭ ən [חזיון, *from* Arab. *hadwa'*, one with pendulous ears] (I Kings 15:18). Grandfather of Ben-hadad I of Syria.

HEZIR hē'zər [חזיר, swine, boar]. **1.** A descendant of Aaron; eponym of a priestly house in the reign of King David (I Chr. 24:15).

2. One of the chiefs of the people signatory to the covenant of Ezra (Neh. 10:20).

HEZRO hĕz'rō [חצרו] (II Sam. 23:35 *Kethibh;* I Chr. 11:37); KJV HEZRAI —rī [חצרי] in II Sam. 23:35 (*Qere;* LXX). A Carmelite who is numbered among the Mighty Men of David known as the "Thirty."

HEZRON hĕz'rən [חצרון, חצרן, *from place name*(?); 'Εσρωμ]; KJV NT ESROM ĕs'rŏm; HEZRONITES —rə nīts. **1.** Eponym of a clan of the tribe of Reuben (Gen. 46:9; Exod. 6:14; Num. 26:6; I Chr. 5:3).

2. Eponym of a clan of the tribe of Judah (Gen. 46:12; Num. 26:21; Ruth 4:18-19; I Chr. 2:5, 9, 18, 21, 24-25; 4:1; Matt. 1:3; Luke 3:33).

H. H. Guthrie, Jr.

3. A city on the S border of Canaan, between Kadesh-barnea and Addar (Josh. 15:3). In the parallel passage in Num. 34:4 it is combined with the latter as Hazar-addar. It is not the same as Kerioth-hezron, another city in the S of Judah. *See* Kerioth.

S. Cohen

HIDDAI hĭd'ī [הדי] (II Sam. 23:30). One of the Mighty Men of David known as the "Thirty." He came from the brooks of Gaash in the hill country of Ephraim. In I Chr. 11:32 he is called Hurai (חורי).

HIDDEKEL hĭd'ə kĕl [חדקל, *from* Assyro-Babylonian *Idiglat/Idignat, from* Sumer. *Idigna*] (Gen. 2:14; Dan. 10:4 KJV; RSV TIGRIS). The Hebrew name of the River Tigris. *See* Tigris.

HIDE, HIDDEN. *See* Revelation.

HIEL hī'əl [חיאל, God lives]. A Bethelite who rebuilt the city of Jericho in the days of Ahab, and the loss of whose sons is interpreted to be the fulfilment of an ancient curse uttered by Joshua. It is recorded that when Joshua destroyed the city of Jericho, he pronounced a grievous curse upon whoever should rebuild it and stipulated that

> At the cost of his first-born shall he lay its foundation,
> And at the cost of his youngest son shall he set up its gates (Josh. 6:26).

Centuries later, in the days of Ahab, Hiel undertook the hazardous task of rebuilding Jericho and thereby violated the curse. During the reconstruction Hiel suffered the loss of his eldest son, Abiram, and his youngest son, Segub. These deaths may have occurred through natural causes or by immolation as foundation sacrifices. The historian, however, attributes them to the nemesis of the curse of Joshua (Josh. 6:26 LXX; I Kings 16:34).

E. R. Dalglish

HIERAPOLIS hī'ə răp'ə lĭs ['Ιεράπολις, 'Ιερὰ Πόλις, the holy city]. A town in the SW of Asia Minor.

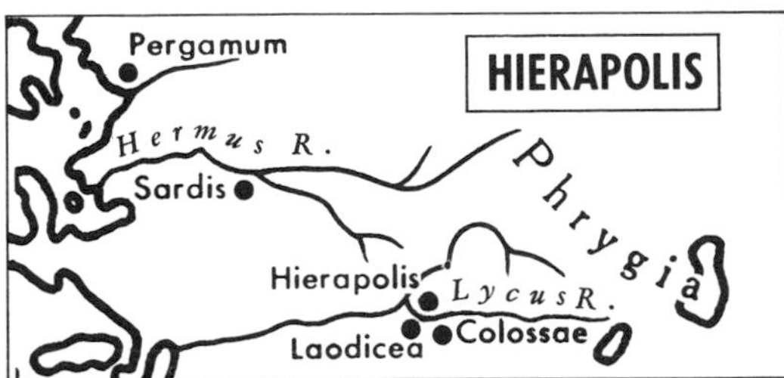

Hierapolis is one of the important Hellenistic and Roman cities in the Lycus Valley in the extreme SW of Phrygia. It is situated on a terrace overlooking the N bank of this river, some six miles N of Laodicea and ten miles W of Colossae. The terrace of Hierapolis, nicknamed Pamukkale ("cotton castle") in modern times, is famous for its continuing geological transformation. Hot mineral springs issue from the rock in the city, and the waters streaming down the cliffs have deposited limestone in large formations, the surface of which is made of gleaming white "frozen cascades."

These hot springs were originally associated with another miraculous phenomenon—a cave filled with lethal vapors. Only eunuch priests were able to escape alive from this Plutonium or Charoneion, considered an entrance to the underworld (Strabo XII. 629). The cave was no longer there in the fourth century A.D., but in ancient times a local Phrygian cult seems to have been attached to the spot. This early sanctuary could have given the city its name of Hieropolis, "city of the *hieron* (sanctuary)," a form which preceded the later official name of Hierapolis, the "holy city."

The foundation of Hierapolis as a city seems to be due to Eumenes II of Pergamum (197-160 B.C.). From a cult center it became an active commercial competitor of its neighbors in the Lycus Valley. Here too the textile industries were particularly celebrated. The organization of the craftsmen into guilds is attested for such specialists as wool workers, carpet weavers, and purple dyers. The position of the city was strategic (its plateau rising some three hundred feet above the river valley), and of commercial advantage, as it lay on a branch road leading from the main E-W highway to the Hermus Valley and Sardis. Moreover, Hierapolis had its hot medicinal springs as an added attraction for visitors.

The city continued its prosperous existence under the Romans as part of the province of Asia. It suffered from the earthquakes which also affected Laodicea (Tacitus XIV.27), but apparently it was rebuilt on an extensive scale. The most interesting aspect of the religious history of Hierapolis is the transformation of the old and primitive cult site, with its cave and worship of the Great Goddess (who appears on local coins), into the center of Christianity (attested by Col. 4:13). Justinian made the city a metropolis, and its bishops often appear in Byzantine lists.

The ruins of Hierapolis have been explored but not excavated. The city plan follows the grid system. A colonnaded main street runs NW to SE, other streets cross it at right angles, and the public buildings follow the same orientation. Most noticeable are the ruins of Roman baths combined with a gymnasium,* in which some vaults are still standing. These baths must have been the center of residence for visitors who came to seek the cure of hot baths at Hierapolis. A large apsidal building stands E of the baths next to the main street, and another, similar one to the N of the N gate. Although there are several crosses cut into the arches, these two Roman buildings do not seem to have been designed as churches, although the S one may have been converted. A church of the fourth or fifth century A.D. has been recognized in a smaller building near the N gate. Fig. HIE 19.

Courtesy of Ahmet Dönmez

19. Ruins of baths at Hierapolis

The theater and the city wall are the only irregular elements in the city plan. The preservation of the theater is good and its location spectacular, overlooking the city and the Lycus Valley.

Much information regarding the inhabitants of Hierapolis was gathered from its cemeteries to the N and the E. Some 1,200 sarcophagi were counted, most of them of simple shape, but some prominent mausoleums serving as family graves.

Bibliography. W. M. Ramsay, *The Cities and Bishoprics of Phrygia*, I (1895), 84-121; C. Humann *et al.*, *Altertümer von Hierapolis* (Jahrbuch des deutschen archäologischen Instituts, Ergänzungsheft IV; 1898); D. Magie, *Roman Rule in Asia Minor* (1950), pp. 127-28.

M. J. Mellink

HIEREEL. KJV Apoc. form of Jehiel.

HIEREMOTH. KJV Apoc. form of Jeremoth.

HIERIELUS. KJV Apoc. form of Jehiel.

HIERMAS. KJV Apoc. form of Ramiah.

HIEROGLYPHS hī'rə glĭfs [ἱερός, sacred; γλυφή, carving]. The pictographic symbols used in the ancient Egyptian system of writing. Normally in use on stone inscriptions, hieroglyphs were occasionally written with a pen on papyrus. An abbreviated, cur-

Courtesy of the University Museum of the University of Pennsylvania

20. Hieroglyphs on a limestone fragment from a tomb wall, Twenty-sixth Dynasty in Egypt (663-525 B.C.)

From *Atlas of the Bible* (Thomas Nelson & Sons Limited)

21. Hieroglyphs from the temple of Sesostris, built *ca.* 1950 B.C., and destroyed by Amenophis III in the fifteenth century and replaced by the hall of columns of Karnak

sive form of this script was very early developed, known as hieratic, which was further simplified in the Persian period to become demotic. A different system of hieroglyphic script was developed by the Hittites to write one of their languages.

See also WRITING AND WRITING MATERIALS. Figs. HIE 20-21.

R. J. WILLIAMS

HIERONYMUS hī'ə rŏn'ə məs ['Ιερώνυμος]. One of the district governors (στρατηγοί) in Palestine under Antiochus V. He and his fellow governors, Timotheus, Apollonius, and Demophon, "would not let [the citizens] live quietly and in peace" (II Macc. 12:2).

J. C. SWAIM

HIGGAYON hĭ gā'yŏn. *See* MUSIC.

HIGH PLACE, SANCTUARY. The religious place of sacrifice, worship, and festival. So largely does the place of worship figure in the Bible that about twenty terms or expressions are employed. "High place" is the rendering of "BAMAH"; "sanctuary" translates three Hebrew words: קדש, "holiness"; מקדש, "place of holiness"; and דביר, "oracle, inner sanctuary, the holy of holies" (containing ark, cherubim, and mercy seat). In the NT "sanctuary" appears but nine times to render ναός (Matt. 23:35), οἶκος (Luke 11:51), σκηνή (Heb. 8:2, 5; 9:1, 8), and ἅγια (Heb. 9:24; 10: 19; 13:11) in descriptions of both Herod's temple and the heavenly sanctuary.

High places were essentially Canaanite—apparently from as early as the second half of the third millennium—and then Israelite sanctuaries, situated on high hills and associated with green trees and leafy oaks. They could be open-air or roofed sanctuaries and were also frequently equipped with houses and halls or buildings of various kinds (I Kings 12:31; 13:32; II Kings 17:32; 23:9), including raised platforms as at Beth-shan and other places.* Equipped with altars of sacrifice, incense, stone pillars, trees and/or poles, and water, they were the objects of Yahweh's wrath (Lev. 26:30; Ps. 78:58). Israel was bidden to destroy them on entering Canaan (Num. 33:52; Deut. 33:29). They were partially removed by Asa (II Chr. 14:3, 5; but cf. 17:6), and destroyed by Hezekiah (II Kings 18:4) and Josiah (II Kings 23: 8, etc.). Many were built by Solomon (I Kings 11:7), Rehoboam (I Kings 14:23; II Chr. 21:11), and many kings of N Israel (II Kings 17:9). They are said not to have been removed by no fewer than six kings: Asa (I Kings 15:14), Jehoshaphat (I Kings 22:43), Jehoash (II Kings 12:3), Amaziah (II Kings 14:4), Azariah (II Kings 15:4), and Jotham (II Kings 15: 35); and to have been restored by Manasseh (II Kings 21:3; II Chr. 33:3; etc.). Figs. HIG 22-23.

The editors of Kings displayed a certain whitewashing tendency when they associated Solomon with the high place at Gibeon (I Kings 3:4), as did the Chronicler in mentioning in connection with the same shrine the tabernacle (I Chr. 16:39; 21:29) and the tent of meeting (II Chr. 1:3, 13). Yahweh was worshiped at high places (II Chr. 33:11, 17). On them sacrifices and incense were offered (I Sam. 9:12; I Kings 3:3; etc.) in Moab (Jer. 48:35) as in Israel (II Kings 16:4; II Chr. 28:4; Ezek. 6:3, 6; etc.). Worshipers ate (I Sam. 9:13), wept (Isa. 15:2), and prayed (Isa. 16:2; 56:7) at high places; prophets (I Sam. 10:5-13) and priests (II Kings 23:5, 9, 20, etc.) frequented them and resided at them. I-II Kings especially show that they were centers of very great activity for private devotion, official ceremonies, and annual festivals.

"Sanctuary," on the other hand, represents places of mainly Israelite and Yahwistic worship, and the

Courtesy of the University Museum of the University of Pennsylvania

22. Great stepped altar in the Mekal temple of Thutmose III, fourteenth(?) century B.C.; from Beth-shan

Courtesy of Denis Baly

23. The high place at Petra

word should be studied in connection with named sanctuaries like Gilgal near Jericho, Bethel, Shechem, Beer-sheba, Gibeon, and especially the amphictyonic shrine at Shiloh, and the temple at Jerusalem. The first word, קדש, is used frequently of the tabernacle in the desert and its component parts (Exodus; Leviticus; Numbers), of Solomon's temple (I Kings; Psalms), of Judah figuratively (Ps. 114:2), and of the New Jerusalem (Isa. 62:9), and some twenty-five times in the phrase "Shekel of the sanctuary" (Exodus; Leviticus; Numbers). The second word is מקדש, which has the same root as the first—viz., "holiness, separation"—but is distinguished by having "m" for its first letter, thereby indicating, as so often in Hebrew, "the place of," or where the holiness is to be found. This second word describes the TABERNACLE of the Exodus (Exodus; Leviticus; Numbers); the TEMPLE at Jerusalem (Exod. 15:17; I-II Chronicles; Neh. 10:39—H 10:40; Mal. 2:11; etc.); the New Jerusalem (Isa. 60:13; Ezek. 37:26, 28); and also sanctuaries at Shechem (Josh. 24:26), Bethel (Amos 7:13), and Moab (Isa. 16:12).

The sanctuary or temple is the constant and central feature of most of the OT and is implied in most parts of the NT. They often originate by divine designation through dream or theophanic visitation, as the stories of Abraham (Gen. 12:7), Jacob (Gen. 28:10-17), Moses (Exod. 3:12), Gideon (Judg. 6), or David (II Sam. 24) show. Otherwise they are founded by the patriarchs or heroes of Israel. It is a natural corollary of this that the pattern of the sanctuary is also revealed (Exod. 25:9, 40; Num. 8:4; I Chr. 28:19; Acts 7:44; Heb. 8:5), so that there is a presumption that the earthly sanctuary is a copy of the heavenly sanctuary (Isa. 14:13; Heb. 8:5; 9:23-24). This theory of the cosmic significance of the sanctuary—e.g., Solomon's temple—must be understood in the light of the Egyptian and Syrian structures which are partly the prototypes of Solomon's temple, and anticipate its symbolism; and also in the light of Sinai-Horeb, which is the prototype sanctuary of the Israelites, and which thus conveys a historical dimension to the purposes of the sanctuary and cult in Israel.

The narrative and prophetic works of the OT, not to mention the Psalms, show the importance of the sanctuary, but there is also the evidence of the laws. Thus the first positive law following the Decalogue is a law of the altar, and "altar" means a sanctuary, however rudimentary. The block of P law in Exod. 25-31 begins with the offering for the building of the sanctuary (cf. chs. 35-40). The Code of Holiness (Lev. 17-26) begins with a law, the aim of which is to establish the necessity and uniqueness of the one sanctuary, and the laws of Deuteronomy begin in ch. 12 with exactly the same aim. Likewise Ezekiel's law begins in ch. 40 with the sanctuary (cf. Zech. 1:16). The laws clearly show the priority of the sanctuary for Israel, and Hag. 1 points to the same theme. Small harvests and an inflationary economy (Hag. 1:6) occur because the people attend to their own homes and are not concerned to rebuild the temple (vs. 9). Sanctuaries mean prosperity because they are the centers of blessing. Though Solomon built his sanctuary as a royal chapel, as had many kings and emperors in the Fertile Crescent, yet it is intended as a medium for the blessing of Israel. At Ras Shamra the gods themselves help to erect Baal's temple and so create and maintain well-being (cf. Isa. 2:2=Mic. 4:1; Isa. 60:13; Ezek. 37:26, 28; 47:1-12).

There is a very close connection between the Israelite sanctuary and the divine name. Where Yahweh records his name, there he visits and from there he blesses (Exod. 20:24; cf. I Chr. 22:19; II Chr. 20:8; Ps. 74:7). Note, too, the close connection in such passages as "defiling my sanctuary and profaning my holy name" (Lev. 20:3).

Sanctuaries were places of pilgrimage (Exod. 5:1, etc.; I Sam. 1:3; I Kings 12:26-27; Hos. 4:15; Amos 5:5), and as such meeting places for people (Ps. 29:2). The larger and more important shrines—e.g., the amphictyonic shrine of Judges and I Samuel—or the great high place at Gibeon would attract greater crowds. There thus inheres in the very idea of the sanctuary an aspect of centrality and unity. At these sanctuaries there were sights to be seen (Pss. 27:4; 63:2—63:3; 68:24; 84:7; etc.); oracles of advice, help, and answered prayer to be procured (I Sam. 1:17; Pss. 27:4; 85:8; etc.); sacrifices to be offered, incense to be burned, and all the manifold activities appropriate to ancient worship, instruction, and atonement for sin. Festival and fast alike belong to the sanctuary, as do light and truth and life.

It is inevitable that in Canaan, so prone to syncretism, the sanctuaries—Solomon's not excluded—should show signs of foreign features. Thus the ancient conceptions of the temple as, among other things, the bond or center of the land or lands is implied in several OT passages. The tabernacle of the desert is in the center of the camp (Exod. 25:8; Lev. 15:31; Num. 2:2). There are likewise a number of references to the midst of the earth (Ps. 74:12; Isa.

19:24), which, like Isa. 2; Mic. 4, imply the presence of the sanctuary. The same is true of the sanctuary planned by Ezekiel (Ezek. 37:28; 43:8-10, 15; 48:21; cf. Zech. 2:10-11; 8:3, 8). Some (sacred) places in the vicinity of Shechem (Judg. 9:37) and Jerusalem (Ezek. 38:12) are described by the word "navel"—center of land and earth respectively. Yet this geographical centrality of the sacred place is overshadowed in the Bible by that personal centrality which belongs to the great figures of the Bible, such as Abraham (Gen. 12:3); the Davidic king (Pss. 2; 89; etc.); the Suffering Servant of Isa. 53; Jesus on the cross (John 12:32). Yet this geographical and personal centrality become one in the figure of God himself as the sanctuary or asylum of Israel (cf. Exod. 21:14; I Kings 1:50; Ezek. 11:16; but not Isa. 8:14, where the text is unsound). Thus Jesus' word to the woman of Samaria that sanctuary worship will pass away anticipates the words: "I saw no temple in the city, for its temple is the Lord God the Almighty and the Lamb" (Rev. 21:22; cf. vs. 24; 22:2). Sanctuaries of all kinds are thus temporary, in themselves plots of ground with buildings witnessing to the divine claim that the earth is the Lord's, and pointing to the day when earth like heaven will acknowledge the divine sovereignty. In that day sanctuaries will be no more, for all space, like time, property, and life, will be God's.

Bibliography. A. von Gall, *Altisraelitische Kultstatten* (1898); G. Westphal, *Jahwes Wohnstätten* (1908); P. Volz, *Biblische Altertümer* (1914), pp. 14-23; R. Storr, *Die Frömmigkeit im Alten Israel* (1928), pp. 192-93; T. Oestreicher, "Reichstempel und Ortsheiligtümer in Israel," *Beiträge zur Förderung christlicher Theologie*, vol. XXXIII, no. 3 (1930); E. König, "Zentralkultstätte und Kultuszentralisierung im alten Israel," *Beiträge zur Förderung christlicher Theologie*, vol. XXXIV, no. 3 (1931); F. Jeremias, "Das orientalische Heiligtum," ΑΓΓΕΛΟΣ *Archiv für neutestamentliche Zeitgeschichte und Kulturkunde*, IV (1932), 56-69; W. F. Albright, *Archaeology and the Religion of Israel* (1942), pp. 103-7; G. E. Wright, "The Significance of the Temple in the Ancient Near East; Part III: The Temple in Palestine-Syria," *BA*, vol. VII, no. 4 (1944), pp. 65-77; R. Brinker, *The Influence of Sanctuaries in Early Israel* (1946)—very good; C. C. McCown, "Hebrew High Places and Cult Remains," *JBL*, LXIX (1950), 205-19; A. Schwarzenbach, *Die geographische Terminologie im Hebräischen des ATs* (1954), pp. 12-16; W. F. Albright, "The High Place in Ancient Palestine," *Volume du Congrès, Strasbourg* (Supplement to *VT*, IV; 1957), pp. 242-58; S. Iwry, *"Maṣṣēbāh* and *Bāmāh* in IQ Isaiah[A] 6 13," *JBL*, LXXVI (1957), 225-32.

G. Henton Davies

HIGH PRIEST. *See* Chief Priest; Priests and Levites.

HIGHER GATE. *See* Upper Gate.

HIGHEST HEAVEN(S) [שמי השמים, heaven of heavens] (I Kings 8:27; II Chr. 2:6; 6:18); KJV HEAVEN OF HEAVENS. Since the word "heaven" (שמים) was also used by the Hebrews in the narrower sense of "firmament," or "ceiling of the earth," the "highest heaven" denoted the canopy believed to be in turn suspended over that expanse. In Mesopotamian and later Jewish folklore, the sky was conceived as consisting of several superimposed layers. The "highest heaven" might therefore also designate the uppermost of these. Called in Akkadian the "heaven of Anu" (*šamê ša* [d]*Anim*), it was there that the supreme god had his supernal dwelling. *See* Heaven; Sky.

In Deut. 10:14; Neh. 9:6, the RSV inconsistently retains the older rendering, "heaven of heavens."

T. H. Gaster

HIGHWAY [מסלה, a built-up road, *from* סלל, to cast up *or* build up (a highway), *from* Akkad. *sulû*, highway; מסלול, Akkad. *mušlalu;* דרך, way, road (KJV *alternately* WAY); KJV ארחה (RSV CARAVAN), חוץ (RSV STREET); KJV διεξόδους τῶν ὁδῶν (RSV THOROUGHFARE), ὁδός (RSV STREET; ROADSIDE)]. In addition to its literal usage, the term "highway" is occasionally used figuratively (Prov. 15:19; 16:17; Jer. 18:15; 31:21). In Isa. 11:16; 35:8; 40:3 (cf. 62:10), it designates the road of the returning exiles (see also Isa. 19:23).

See also King's Highway; Road; Travel and Communication.

H. F. Beck

HILEN hī'lən [חילן]. A village in the hill country of Judah, assigned to the Levitical family of Kohath (I Chr. 6:58—H 6:43). *Cf.* Holon 1.

HILKIAH hĭl kī'ə [חלקיה, חלקיהו, my portion is Yahu]; Χελκίας]; KJV Apoc. once **HELKIAS** hĕl kī'əs (I Esd. 1:8); once **HELCHIAH** hĕl kī'ə (I Esd. 8:1); also **CHELCIAS** kĕl'shĭ əs (Bar. 1:1, 7; Sus. 2, 29, 63). **1.** A Merarite Levite antedating King David (I Chr. 6:45—H 6:30).

2. Another Merarite Levite, contemporary of David (I Chr. 26:11).

3. The father of Eliakim, an officer over King Hezekiah's household (II Kings 18:18, 26; Isa. 22:20; 36:3).

4. The father of Jeremiah the prophet (Jer. 1:1).

5. The father of Gemariah, an ambassador of King Zedekiah to Nebuchadnezzar (Jer. 29:3).

6. A high priest in the reign of King Josiah, who aided the latter's religious reforms and who found the Book of the Law in the temple (II Kings 22:4-14; I Chr. 6:13—H 5:39; II Chr. 34:9-22; 35:8; cf. I Esd. 1:8; *see* Deuteronomy; Josiah); an ancestor of Ezra, according to Ezra 7:1 (cf. I Esd. 8:1).

7. A chief of the priests among the returned exiles (Neh. 12:7); also a priestly house mentioned from the postexilic period (vs. 21), perhaps represented as well by earlier priests of this name (*cf.* 1, 2, 6, *above*).

8. One of those who stood beside Ezra at the public reading of the law; probably a layman (Neh. 8:4). I Esd. 9:43 reads "Hezekiah."

9. According to Bar. 1:1, 7, an ancestor of Baruch, Jeremiah's servant.

10. The father of Susanna (Sus. 2, 29, 63 [with Theod.]; also vs. 7 LXX).

Bibliography. M. Noth, *Die israelitischen Personennamen* (1928), pp. 18, 163-64.

B. T. Dahlberg

HILL, HILL COUNTRY. A land elevation such as those in the central ridge of Palestine (*see* Palestine, Geography of); usually, but not always, distinguished from a mountain in being lower or less distinct as a peak. *See* Mount.

The common Hebrew word for "hill" is גבעה; it is used in referring to elevated terrain in a general way (Gen. 49:26), to a specific elevation (Exod. 17: 9), and to natural elevations such as those on which the pagan rites of the Canaanites were conducted and adopted by some of the Israelites (Deut. 12:2; I Kings 14:23). Although the Hebrew word הר is often translated "mountain" (Gen. 31:54; Exod. 3:1; etc.), it is also rendered "hill" (Judg. 16:3; Pss. 2:6; 121:1; etc.). The term עפל is translated "hill" in II Kings 5:24 (KJV TOWER); Isa. 32:14 (KJV FORT); Mic. 4: 8 (KJV STRONGHOLD). Although the meaning of עפל is uncertain (*see* OPHEL), it probably designated a natural hill rather than an artificial tower. In the NT βουνός is rendered "hill" (Luke 3:5; 23:30), as is also ὄρος (Matt. 5:14; Luke 4:29; KJV "hill" in Luke 9:37 [RSV MOUNTAIN]).

In many passages where the KJV renders הר as "mountain" or "mount," most modern English translations, including the RSV, use "hill country" (Gen. 31:23; Num. 13:17; Deut. 1:7; Josh. 9:1; etc.). Because there is not a sharp distinction among "mountain," "hill," and "hill country," the choice of the proper English word is difficult and requires a knowledge of the geography of Palestine. In view of the fact that the elevations in the Palestine and E Jordan areas seldom rise above three thousand feet, it is preferable to refer to them as "hills" or "hill country" (cf. "hill country of Seir" in Gen. 36:8; "hill country of Gilead" in Deut. 3:12; "hill country of Judah and Israel" in Josh. 11:21; "hill country of Naphtali" in 20:7), especially when an area, rather than an isolated peak, is intended. W. L. REED

HILLEL (THE ELDER) hĭl'əl. A Talmudic sage and a leading scholar in the development of the oral law (*ca.* 60 B.C.–A.D. 20).

Although the Talmudic sources preserve a number of anecdotes about Hillel, and sayings, parables, and (two) enactments by him, the data for a full-length sketch are much too meager. Hillel was a native of Babylonia who came to Palestine in order to continue his studies in the advanced Palestinian academies, principally those of the great "expositors," Shemaiah and Abtalyon. The story about his diligence, despite poverty, later became a popular tale. His eminent abilities were recognized when he established his view on an important legal problem to the satisfaction of the halachic authorities of his time, the Bene Batyra: that the obligation to bring the paschal offering overrides sabbath prohibitions. As these halachic authorities may have been a special commission for temple ritual, Hillel's erudition and skill in the give-and-take with them would therefore be no small matter. The sources state that he was thereupon appointed Nasi, which has been said to mean head of that temple commission. Hillel's championing of the use of sophisticated hermeneutic principles was of special significance for the development of Talmudic method and study, and for both the expansion and the deepening of the concept of the oral Torah. The seven rules, whose application he urged in the interpretation of scripture, were later the basis and model of still additional principles of exegesis—e.g., the thirteen rules of Rabbi Ishmael.

In contrast to his colleague Shammai and Shammai's school, Hillel and the school over which he presided, Bet Hillel, were inclined most often to a liberal rather than conservative interpretation of the demands of the law; so, too, it was the Hillelite view that the opportunities for study ought to be made more liberal than the Shammaites were prepared to make them.

The sources delight in repeating a number of anecdotes, all of them contrasting the proverbial patience of Hillel with the impatience and irascibility of Shammai, the most famous anecdote being the one of the proselyte who wanted to learn the whole Torah while standing on one foot. After Shammai had rebuffed him, the proselyte came to Hillel. "What is hateful to thee do not do to thy fellowman," Hillel told him; "this is the whole Torah; all else is commentary. Now go learn that!"

Pirke Aboth quotes more sayings by Hillel than by any other single sage. Among the better known of these are: "Be of the disciples of Aaron, loving peace and pursuing peace, loving mankind and drawing them to the Torah." "If not I for myself, who then? And being for myself, what am I? And if not now, when?" Several maxims by Hillel occur also in other Talmudic sources.

Hillel was responsible for two major enactments which constitute far-reaching adaptations of biblical law: one (the *prozbul*) in regard to the cancellation of debts in the sabbatical year (Deut. 15:2), and one in connection with the sale of houses in fortified cities (Lev. 25:29-30). Descendants of Hillel inherited his position of Nasi, and one of these was Rabbi Judah the Prince (*ca.* A.D. 220), the redactor of the Mishna. In effect, the Hillelite emphasis proved to be dominant in Pharisaic and Talmudic Judaism, thus determining actually the direction taken by classical Judaism ever since.

Bibliography. A. Kaminka, "Hillel's Life and Work," *JQR*, XXX (1939-40), 107-22; J. Goldin, "Hillel the Elder," *JR*, XXVI (1946), 263-77; L. Finkelstein, *Ha-Perushim ve-Anshe Keneset Ha-Gedolah* (1950), pp. 1-16; N. N. Glatzer, *Hillel the Elder: The Emergence of Classical Judaism* (1956).

J. GOLDIN

HIN hĭn [הין]. A liquid measure of *ca.* an American gallon; one sixth of a bath. *See* WEIGHTS AND MEASURES § C4*g*.

HIND [אילה, *feminine of* איל, *see* HART; *cf.* Ugar. *aylt*, doe, hind]. The adult female of the Red Deer, especially after the third year. For the uncertainty about the precise meaning of the word translated "hind," *see* HART.

The OT references to the hind allude to her calving (Job 39:1; Jer. 14:5; possibly Gen. 49:21; Ps. 29:9), and to her surefootedness (II Sam. 22:34; Ps. 18:33—H 18:34; Hab. 3:19), though it should be noted that deer, generally speaking, live in wooded or grass country, not in rocky surroundings. The hind's grace and seeming gentleness explain the metaphor for one's wife in Prov. 5:19; the significance of the reference to Naphtali as a hind in Gen. 49:21 is obscured by the uncertain text. In the title of Ps. 22—H 22:1 the phrase "The Hind of the Dawn" is presumably a musical notation, referring possibly to a well-known melody. For the use of "hind" in the oath in Song of S. 2:7; 3:5, *see* GAZELLE.

W. S. McCULLOUGH

HIND OF THE DAWN. *See* MUSIC.

HINGE [ציר; Akkad. *ṣirru*]. Probably a metal hinge pole piece or pivot attached to a door and fitted into a socket (Prov. 26:14); a sluggard turning on his bed is compared to a door turning on its pivot. פתות (I Kings 7:50) is translated "hinges" in the KJV, but the RSV uses "sockets." The meaning is uncertain.

See also DOOR; SOCKET. O. R. SELLERS

HINNOM, VALLEY OF THE SON OF hĭn'əm [גיא, גי בן הנם] (Josh. 15:8; 18:16; II Chr. 28:3; 33:6; Jer. 7:31-32; 19:2, 6; 32:35) [RSV VALLEY OF BEN-HINNOM]. *Alternately:* VALLEY OF THE SONS (KJV CHILDREN) OF HINNOM [גי בני הנם] (II Kings 23:10); VALLEY OF HINNOM [גיא הנם] (Neh. 11:30; KJV also Josh. 15:8; 18:16). A deep valley S of Jerusalem, which marked the limit between the tribes of Benjamin and Judah (Josh. 15:8; 18:16). According to Jeremiah 19:2, the Gate Harsith, or POTSHERD GATE, led from the city into this valley. It is commonly identified with the Wadi er-Rababi, which at first runs N-S beneath the W walls of the Old City, and then turns sharply to the E in the direction of the Kidron (*see* KIDRON, BROOK). There is little textual support for a hypothesis according to which the name of Hinnom applied originally to the ravine of the Tyropoeon E of the city of David, and that it would have been transferred to the Wadi er-Rababi in the time of the monarchy.

The books of Kings, Chronicles, and Jeremiah mention repeatedly the cults rendered to foreign gods and the sacrifices of children cremated in honor of Baal and Molech, toward the junction of the valley with the Kidron, at the place called TOPHETH (II Kings 23:10; II Chr. 28:3; 33:6; Jer. 32:35). Thus the Valley of Hinnom became so notorious that Jeremiah could dispense with pronouncing the name when he condemned the cults of "the valley" (Jer. 2:23), which would be called "Valley of Slaughter" in the Day of Vengeance (Jer. 7:31-32; 19:5-6). The memory of the rituals of cremation gave birth to the notion of the hell of fire, γέεννα τοῦ πυρός (Matt. 5:22), a transcription of the Hebrew גיא הנם (*see* GEHENNA). The Valley of Hinnom is given as the N limit of postexilic settlements scattered throughout the old territory of Judah and Simeon, as far S as Beer-sheba (Neh. 11:30).

24. The Valley of Hinnom

Jewish and early Christian tombs, ranging from the Roman to the Byzantine periods, are still visible on the steep cliffs on the S side of the valley, where a well-founded tradition places the Potter's Field, bought for the burial of paupers with Judas' silver. *See* AKELDAMA; JERUSALEM § 12. *See* map under JERUSALEM.

Fig. HIN 24.

Bibliography. G. A. Smith, *Jerusalem*, I (1907), 170-80; H. Vincent, *Jérusalem Antique* (1912), pp. 124-34; G. Dalman, *Jerusalem und sein Gelände* (1930), pp. 199-207; F.-M. Abel, *Géographie de la Palestine*, I (1933), 401-2; J. Simons, *Jerusalem in the OT* (1952), pp. 10-12, 52, note 2. G. A. BARROIS

HIPPOPOTAMUS [בהמות, *plural of* בהמה, beast, CATTLE] (Job 40:15 RSV mg.; KJV-RSV BEHEMOTH). A large, thick-skinned amphibious ungulate mammal of the family *Hippopotamidae,* with an enormous head, a bulky, hairless body, and short legs; now found only in the rivers of Africa.

The animal described in Job 40:15-24 has been variously identified, but the view that it is a hippopotamus (which Bodenheimer dismisses too lightly; *see* FAUNA § A2*e*ii), is less open to objection than any alternative. The plural of בהמה, *b^e^hēmâ,* to designate the hippopotamus is doubtless used with intensive force (a plural of "majesty"): this was probably the largest animal, with the possible exception of the elephant, known to the author. How well he was acquainted with the hippopotamus we do not know. Even though he may have seen the animal, in his poem he treats it freely, and he may even echo some popular beliefs (e.g., vs. 19*a*). His only serious zoological error is his reference to the tail; the short tail (*ca.* nine inches) of this animal hardly justifies what is said in vs. 17*a*.

Apart from any knowledge the author had of the Egyptian hippopotamus (cf. Herodotus II.71), he may have been familiar with a Palestinian species. There is now evidence from Tell Qasileh, near Tel Aviv, of hippopotamus remains on the coastal plain of Palestine dating from the twelfth to the fourth centuries B.C. Swamps in N Galilee and in the Jordan Valley may also have harbored the hippopotamus during the same period.

Bibliography. G. Haas, *BASOR,* 132 (Dec., 1953), 30-34.
W. S. MCCULLOUGH

HIRAH hī'rə [חירה; LXX Ιρας]. Judah's Adullamite associate (Gen. 38:1, 12, 20-23). In vs. 12 (cf. also vs. 20) the LXX and the Vulg. read "his shepherd" (*rō'ēhû*) for "his friend" (*rē'ēhû*).

HIRAM hī'rəm [חירם, חירום; *an abbreviation of* אחירם (Ahiram), the brother (God) is exalted, *or* brother of the exalted one]. Alternately: HURAM [חורם] (Chronicles). **1.** King of TYRE (986-935 B.C.); a contemporary of David and Solomon. In the tenth century B.C. there seems to have been a tremendous expansion of the Phoenician commercial empire, and by the middle of Hiram's reign the colonies of Gades and Tartessus (Tarshish) in Spain had been founded.

The historian Menander attributes to Hiram I an extensive building program, the institution of a new feast for the Tyrian deity Melcart, and the suppression of a revolt by the inhabitants of Utica or Citium (Jos. Antiq. VIII.v.3; cf. Herodotus II.44). Hiram's friendship with David and Solomon was probably based on a mutual need. Israel lacked the technical skills necessary for the advancement of her material culture; Phoenicia was deficient in agricultural production.

The OT implies that Hiram's first contact with Israel—the supplying of workmen and raw material for the palace of David (II Sam. 5:11)—took place shortly after the capture of Jerusalem, which happened before Hiram became king. Either the OT has mistakenly named Hiram instead of his father Abibaal (Jos. Antiq. VIII.v.3), or, as seems more likely, the OT has placed the contact with Hiram too early. Recognition from a ruler as well established as Hiram would be more likely to follow David's defeat of the Philistines, an event which doubtless called the attention of the surrounding nations to this new monarch.

Hiram likewise made a treaty with Solomon (I Kings 5:12—H 5:26), who seems to have married a Sidonian princess (I Kings 11:1; cf. Ps. 45:12—H 45:13[?]). Again Hiram supplied the Israelites with cedar and skilled labor for their building program, in return for wheat and olive oil (I Kings 5:1-11—H 5:15-25; II Chr. 2:1-16—H 1:18–2:15; cf. Jos. Antiq. VIII.ii.6-8, who assures his readers that the correspondence could still be found in the Tyrian archives). Official buildings dating from this period show many signs of Phoenician influence in design and execution. *See* MEGIDDO § 3*d*.

Hiram also aided Solomon in his commercial enterprises by supplying ships and seamen for the merchant fleet which operated out of the port of EZION-GEBER (I Kings 9:26-28; 10:11, 22; II Chr. 8:17-18; 9:10, 21). No doubt, Hiram received a share of the profits; perhaps he was given the right to base a fleet of his own in Solomon's port. The Chronicler's statement that Solomon traded with the Phoenician colony of Tarshish (II Chr. 9:21) is the result of his misunderstanding the term "ships of Tarshish" (I Kings 10:22). "Tarshish" refers to the class of the ships, not their destination. *See* SHIPS AND SAILING.

When Solomon's ambitious building program proved too great a strain on his treasury, he was forced to sell to Hiram twenty cities, apparently located on the coastal plain between Carmel and the Phoenician territory (*see* CABUL). Perhaps the ceded district included the port of ACCO, which is missing from the province list of Solomon (I Kings 4:8-19), though it lay within the boundaries of David's kingdom (II Sam. 24:5-7).

2. Same as HURAM 3.

Bibliography. W. F. Albright, "The Role of the Canaanites in the History of Civilization," *Studies in the History of Culture* (1942), pp. 37-46; M. Noth, *The History of Israel* (1958), pp. 210, 212.

R. W. CORNEY

HIRCANUS. KJV form of HYRCANUS.

HIRELING. A servant or other worker paid WAGES.

HISS [שׁרק]. A sound made by forcing the breath between the tongue and the teeth; used to express astonishment (I Kings 9:8; Jer. 18:16; 19:8; 49:17; 50:13) or derision (Lam. 2:15-16; Ezek. 27:36). It is often accompanied by wagging the head (Lam. 2:15), clapping the hands (Lam. 2:15), gnashing the teeth (Lam. 2:16), shaking the fist (Zeph. 2:15). One suspects at times it was used when passing ruins, as a protection from the demons of destruction (cf. II Chr. 29:8; Jer. 19:8; 25:9, 18; 29:18; 51:37; Mic. 6:16).

V. H. KOOY

HISTORY. A theological approach to history seeks to outline the biblical interpretation of history, conceived as a movement purposed and controlled by God, who is Lord of history, and further to ask whether this conception of history as a series of happenings "according to the definite plan and foreknowledge of God" (Acts 2:23) is one to which Christians today can subscribe with undivided conscience. History is one thing; a theological interpretation of history may be quite another. The distinction may be expressed as that between history (*Geschichte*) and "sacred" or "salvation" history (*Heilsgeschichte*). The problems to be discussed are the relation of *Heilsgeschichte* to *Geschichte,* and whether the foundations of the *Geschichte* are sufficient to bear the superstructure of *Heilsgeschichte* which faith has built upon them.

A. *"EVENT" AND "FACT."* The word "fact" is from Latin *factum,* "thing done," and a fact is generally taken to mean something that has really happened, as distinct from any conclusions that may be drawn from it. Yet it is now almost a commonplace to say that "there are no bare facts for the historian." This is because any two observers of even a single contemporary event can nearly always be relied upon to report it in ways that not only differ but may, in part at least, appear to contradict one another.

NT historical writing is, as historical writings go, near to, though not contemporary with, the events it records. In the accounts of the Resurrection, the First Gospel has it that "an angel of the Lord descended from heaven" (Matt. 28:2), the Second that "they saw a young man sitting" (Mark 16:5), the Third that "two men stood by them" (Luke 24:4), and the Fourth that Mary "saw two angels in white, sitting" (John 20:12). But whether or not we believe that the Resurrection took place, it would be unwarranted skepticism to base denial of it upon the "discrepancies" in the gospels. On the contrary, the unself-conscious independence of the narratives is some testimony to the essential veracity of the story.

OT history is of events often long past. And when the record is of a series of happenings over a long period of time—much more, the history of an entire people—it is often difficult to determine how much is fact and how much interpretation. If there are no longer any "bare facts" for the historian, it is convenient to define a fact of history as an event together with the (inevitable) interpretation that enters into the recollecting and recording of it. (German can make the distinction between *Geschehen,* "happening," and *Historie.*) Such a new "fact" can be a powerful motive force in the life of a people. Indeed, a nation's life and character can be even more powerfully influenced by what it believes to have been its history than it is by events long past, which anyhow are now only "remembered" as they are embodied in the national tradition. (This is not to say that the tradition is pure fabrication or to degrade belief into credulity.) E.g., the Hebrews escaped from Egypt and crossed the Red Sea. So much was event that can be reduced to physical terms. The Egyptians may have seen, and a modern reader may see, no more in it than that. But the Hebrews believed that they owed their "deliverance"—this was to introduce *Heilsgeschichte* as distinct from *Geschehen* or even *Geschichte,* "escape"—to Yahweh—*Heilsgeschichte* again. This faith was continually deepened with the passage of the years and the assurance that Yahweh was still with them, and it is not too much to say that the whole edifice of Jewish religion and morality rests upon it.

It is pertinent at this stage to say something about the issue that arises between those who hold strongly conservative views about Bible history and the so-called "critics." The former believe, often passionately, that every Bible narrative or statement is "fact" in the sense that things happened exactly as described. They make no distinction between event and fact as they have been defined here. *Geschichte* is *Heilsgeschichte,* and *Heilsgeschichte, Geschichte.* This means that duplicate stories which appear to contradict each other—e.g., the sister-wife stories in Gen. 12:10-20; 20; 26:1-11—must be made to agree by what is often forced and labored exegesis. The "critic" is not in this predicament. He finds many indications that history in OT times was not, and cannot be expected to have been, written in the manner of modern histories. It was not academic-scientific. Critics may, and do, differ among themselves about just how much OT historical writing may be labeled *Geschichte.* But so long as they are reasonably conservative in their treatment of the *Geschichte*—and most critics nowadays are—and so long as they share the Christian faith in the *Heilsgeschichte*—as almost all of them do—the differences between fundamentalist and critic may be less acute than they often are believed to be.

B. *METHODS OF HISTORICAL WRITING.* Historiography, which deals with methods of historical writing, has nothing directly to do with the interpretation of history, though a historian's method of dealing with his materials often gives the clue to his interpretation of history. There are three types of historical literature: (*a*) narrative or descriptive; (*b*) didactic or pragmatic; (*c*) scientific or genetic.

1. Narrative. The simplest form of narrative history consists of annals; but even annals, by what they record and by what they leave unrecorded, afford some key to the outlook of the annalist. It is probable that the "Book of the Chronicles [Hebrew "acts of the days"] of the kings of Israel [and Judah]," to which the books of Kings refer (I Kings 14:19, etc.), was mainly annals. Such unconnected statements in the account of Solomon's reign as that "then Solomon built a high place" (I Kings 11:7) may also have been excerpted from annals of the reign. But the finest piece of descriptive historical writing in the OT—or, indeed, anywhere before Herodotus—is the "court history" of David (II Sam. 9-I Kings 2). This reads as if it was written by at least a near contemporary. It is objective, it never moralizes, and yet it leaves the impression that the writer was fully aware that David's trouble with his sons was due to his own lack of self-discipline, though this is never said.

2. Didactic. Most OT historical writing is didactic, "history with a purpose." This applies particularly to the historical retrospects in Deuteronomy and to the books of Judges and Kings. Many scholars believe that the whole of Deuteronomy–II Kings was originally one work—the "Deuteronomic history"—which was later subdivided. Samuel is less moralizing than Kings, mainly because in three quarters of it the hero is David, who was, by Deuteronomic standards, the ideal king, and moralizing historians let themselves go more readily when there are evils to be denounced than when there is good to be commended. "Ahab the son of Omri did evil in the sight of Yahweh more than all that were before him" (I Kings 16:30). This, with minor variations, is typical; only two kings, Hezekiah (II Kings 18:4-5) and Josiah (II Kings 22:2; 23:25), both of them kings of Judah, receive unqualified praise. The Deuteronomic historians were more concerned to point the moral for their contemporaries than to give an unbiased account of the past.

3. Scientific. A modern academic historian must write as well as he can, but he is more concerned to show how events are related to the economic-social and spiritual movements from which they derive, than to be entertaining or instructive. The last thing he will do is moralize, though he may, if his work is on a big canvas, attempt a "philosophy of history." Of this "genetic" type of history there is nothing in the OT, if only because the documentary sources to which a "scholar," had there been any such in OT times, could have access and from which he could develop a technique of research and writing, were meager in the extreme compared with the wealth of materials at the disposal of the historian today. OT prophets and historical writers were not concerned with pure history. And yet, paradoxically enough, they did attempt something which, if it cannot be called a philosophy of history, was nevertheless an interpretation of history viewed, as it were, *sub specie aeternitatis.* This interpretation of history is to be found, not so much in the Deuteronomic writings, which were largely moralizings on comparatively recent happenings viewed from the standpoint of the law of the one legitimate sanctuary, but in the sagas of the Pentateuch and in the prophetical writings.

C. *THE OT INTERPRETATION OF HISTORY.* **1. The primeval history.** The first eleven chapters of Genesis are not quite like anything else in the OT. They describe the creation of the world and the beginnings of civilization down to approximately the time when writing began to be employed in Babylonia and something like historical records could be kept. Some of the stories, of the Creation and the Flood, have points of similarity to, and were almost certainly ultimately derived from, Babylonian mythology. (The word "mythology" is used in a variety of meanings. Mention of it here prompts the remark that *Heilsgeschichte* is not mythology in the sense the word generally bears in the current "demythologizing" controversy. To "demythologize" is to restate *theological* concepts in terms which are not at variance with scientific cosmology. The relation between *Heilsgeschichte* and *Geschichte* is not quite the same as that between prescientific mythological, and "demythologized" theological, concepts.)

The materials in the primeval history—again those relating to the Creation and the Flood—are in duplicate, of which some parts are commonly assigned to the P and other parts to the J strata of the PENTATEUCH. There are differences of presentation as between P and J, but in this short summary the differences may be neglected (as may also such sigla as J^1, J^2, L, and S), and Gen. 1–11 may be treated as a unit.

Briefly, the world had its origin in the creative will of God. Man's place in it is that of a creature, a creature superior, indeed, to all other creatures, in that he is created "in the image and likeness of God," but nevertheless a creature. His position in relation to God, who created him, on the one hand, and to the world in which he finds himself, on the other, differs from that of all other creatures. He is to have universal dominion, but he must not attempt to usurp the authority of the Creator. His disobedience to the divine injunction had disastrous consequences, culminating in the Flood, from which only Noah and his family were preserved. Immediately after the Flood, God is said to have established a covenant with Noah and his descendants and all living creatures, to the effect that never again should there be a flood to destroy the earth (Gen. 9:9-11). The story continues with the dispersal of Noah's descendants over the earth. The Japhethites are (roughly) the European peoples, the Hamites the African, and the descendants of Shem the Semites. Europe and Africa lay more or less beyond the geographical horizons of the genealogists of Gen. 10–11. The center of their world was occupied by the Semites, of whom Eber (עבר; Gen. 10:21; 11:14), the ancestor of the Hebrews (עברים), receives particular mention. Five generations after Eber comes Terah, the father of Abram, Nahor, and Haran (Gen. 11:16-27), and the stage is set for the call of Abram/Abraham.

2. The sagas. The sagas are those stories in Genesis–Numbers, and Joshua–Judges, which are generally assigned to the JE tradition. There is now less confidence than there was in labeling paragraphs, still less verses and parts of verses, as from the documents J and E; and sigla like J^1, J^2, E^1, E^2, are best treated as tentative. Nevertheless, the differences between JE and P are clearly recognizable and are admitted even by the "traditio-historical" school. For the present purpose it matters little whether stories come from J or from E. We may even give them no labels at all and still discern in them a definite interpretation of history. They bear the impress of a master mind, and they received very nearly their present shape (whether orally or in writing is little matter) fairly early in the period of the monarchy, probably between 1000 and 850 B.C. Later amplifications of the Deuteronomists (D) and the Priestly school (P) keep to the essential pattern of this archetypal interpretation.

The story begins with Yahweh's summons to Abram/Abraham to leave Ur of the Chaldeans and go "to the land that I will show you" (Gen. 12:1), a land which is to be given to his descendants (vs. 7). But already, together with concern for Abraham and his descendants, there is a note of universalism: "By you all the families of the earth will bless themselves" (vs. 3). The central arch of the whole edifice is the complex of stories in Exodus about the institution of the Passover, the Exodus itself, and the covenant ceremonies and giving of the law on Mount Sinai. The story reaches its conclusion in the triumphant conquest of the Promised Land.

This conclusion is reached only after a long series of contretemps. First, Abraham has no son. Sarah is taken for a time into the harem of Pharaoh (Gen. 12:10-20). As she continues to be barren, Abraham anticipates that one of his slaves must be his heir (15:3). When at length Ishmael is born, his mother is the Egyptian slave Hagar (Gen. 16). At long last Sarah bears Isaac, and Ishmael and the Arabs disappear from the story (25:1-18). When Isaac grows up, there is difficulty in finding a suitable wife for him (Gen. 24). For a time Rebekah also is barren, and of the twin boys she later bears, it is Jacob, the younger, who secures the birthright, by stratagems of dubious morality. Jacob in his turn must seek a wife among his Aramean kinsfolk and at the same time keep out of the way of the irate Esau, whose descendants also in due course disappear from the main thread of the story (Gen. 36). In his old age Jacob migrates to Egypt to escape famine in Canaan. There he and his family are provided for by Joseph, who, after being sold by his own brothers, had been given up as dead. After the death of Joseph the Israelites are slaves for a long time in Egypt. And so on.

Even after the Exodus, the Israelites for their persistent grumblings are condemned to wander for a generation in the wilderness before they may enter the Promised Land. The whole story is instinct with the faith that the purpose of God must finally be realized, despite all obstinacies of nature and of men. This faith may be summed up in the words of Joseph to his brothers: "So it was not you who sent me here, but God. . . . You meant evil against me; but God meant it for good" (Gen. 45:8; 50:20).

3. The prophets. ***a. The past.*** The pre-exilic prophets have surprisingly little to say about the patriarchal tradition. Abraham is not mentioned except in Mic. 7:20, probably a late passage. Hosea refers to Jacob (12:3-4—H 12:4-5), and there is an echo of this in Jer. 9:4—H 9:3: "Every brother will altogether overreach" (עקוב יעקב, "do the Jacob"). In Amos the names Isaac, Jacob, and Joseph are only appellations of the nation Israel. It is not until the Prophet of the Exile that the patriarchal tradition becomes prominent, with particular reference to Abraham (Isa. 41:8-9; 51:2; 63:16; cf. Ezek. 33:24).

The Exodus and the wilderness wanderings, on the other hand, are prominent in Amos (Amos 2:9-11; 3:1-2), and Hosea seems to say that Yahweh's first meeting with Israel dates from the Egyptian oppression and deliverance (Hos. 11:1; 12:9—H 12:10; 13:4; cf. Ezek. 20:5-6; Amos 3:1-2). Hosea (2:2-23—H 2:4-25; 9:10) and Jeremiah (2:2-3) picture the wilderness wanderings as a kind of honeymoon time in which Israel was married to Yahweh and entirely happy in him. If this seems at variance with the incident of the golden calf and the ungrateful complainings which are such a feature of the stories in Exodus and Numbers, it may be that the idealization of the wilderness period was intended to throw into greater relief the later apostasy of Israel, which is depicted in the darkest colors (Jer. 2:5-28; cf. Hos. 2; Amos 2:10-12). Ezekiel (20:5-8) even carries back the apostasy of Israel to the time of the Egyptian bondage. Apostasy is the theme, too, in the Deuteronomic framework of the stories in Judges.

Prominent in Deutero-Isaiah is the conception of the divine choice or "election" of Israel (Isa. 41:8-9; 44:1-2). It is a feature also of Deuteronomy (Deut. 4:37; 7:6-7), and although the verb "choose" is not used, the conception of election is implicit in the Genesis saga of Abraham.

b. The present. The prophets were not cloudy idealists, now rhapsodizing, now lamenting, over Israel's past. They were uncompromising realists. Yahweh was Lord of history, now as well as in the past. He was not concerned only with the domestic fortunes and morals of Israel. His judgments were universal in their reach. Amos asserted that Yahweh would call Moab to account for a cruelty perpetrated upon Edom (Amos 2:1-3). Isaiah has Yahweh apostrophize the Assyrians as the "rod of my anger," with which he will chastise his own people, Israel (Isa. 10:5-11). But if the Assyrians take matters into their own hands and with overweening pride exceed the bounds of their commission, Yahweh will not spare them either (Isa. 10:12-15). In Jeremiah, Yahweh speaks of "Nebuchadrezzar the king of Babylon, my servant" (Jer. 25:9). Nebuchadrezzar and his Babylonians are Yahweh's agents and as such are invincible until the divine purpose through them is accomplished (Jer. 27:8; 37:9-10). The political extinction of the Hebrew kingdoms and the deportations of their peoples were not, as the prophets saw it, the work of ruthless military powers free to treat small nations exactly as they pleased. They were judgments of the "Holy One of Israel." Toward the end of the Exile, Deutero-Isaiah hailed the rise of another non-Israelite agent of Yahweh—this time a deliverer, not a destroyer. He was Cyrus, who is dignified by Yahweh with the titles "my shepherd" (Isa. 44:28) and "anointed" (Hebrew *messiah;* Isa. 45:1).

c. The future. History, for the prophets, was not a meaningless succession of recurring cycles of events. It began with Creation (as distinct from emanation), it had all along been under the control of Yahweh, and it was moving toward a purposed end. In other words, the prophets were eschatological in their thinking. There are those who hesitate to use the word "eschatology" for any view of the future which is not conceived in terms of the dualistic conception of two worlds, one "on this side" and the other "on that side" of the time series. Such a contrast has no place in the minds of the prophets. The end is within the time series, and, speaking generally, is brought about on the plane of this world. (The general sense of the Hebrew word "eternity," עולם, is "long duration.") But it is convenient to use the word "eschatology" for OT visions of the future, so long as we are clear about the restricted sense in which we are using it.

Prophetic conceptions of the future may, in general, be summed up in the expression "the kingdom (or kingly rule) of God," although the expression does not always occur in any given "forward-looking" passage. In Isa. 40–55 there is expectation of the near-approaching advent of Yahweh, who is coming *in propria persona* and whose "glory" will be revealed for "all flesh" to see (Isa. 40:3-5). The details of this "new Exodus" are largely conceived in terms of the Exodus and wilderness wanderings of long ago (e.g., 41:17-20; 43:16-21). In Joel (2:28-29—H 3:1-2) there is promise of the "pouring out" of Yahweh's spirit "on all flesh." In Isa. 65:17-25 the ideal future is pictured in terms of a return to paradisal peace, the feeding together of Herbivora and Carnivora (cf. Isa. 11:6-9), and longevity and material abundance for mankind (cf. Isa. 25:6-8). Only in Isa. 26:19 and the apocalyptic Dan. 12:2-3 does the expectation of a blessed future life find unambiguous expression, and even then the expectation is of a resurrection to life upon this earth. In some descriptions of the kingdom of God, though not in all, there appears the figure of the messianic king, of the lineage of David (Isa. 11:1-9; Mic. 5:2-3—H 5:1-2; Zech. 9:9). In Isa. 52:13–53:12 and some related passages we read of the atoning death of a suffering SERVANT OF THE LORD. The religious insight and depth of these passages is so profound that their real significance was not perceived until Jesus interpreted them as referring to himself.

All in all, the OT makes upon us the impression of its incompleteness. It seems to look forward to a consummation that lies beyond itself. This is the more striking because there is no rigidity about its expectations of the future. It is as if it labors to express what so far was inexpressible.

D. THE NT INTERPRETATION OF THE OT. The OT ends, somewhat hesitantly, on a note of expectation. The NT begins, without any hesitancy at all, on the note of fulfilment. This NT fulfilment is everywhere related to the OT expectation. The two Testaments are a unity; neither is self-explanatory nor can be properly understood without the other. It is as if all the loose ends of the OT promises are gathered together, to find their culmination, and explanation, in a unique event of history, the coming of Christ, and all that followed upon that coming. The key fitted the lock perfectly, or so at least the writers of the NT believed. This is the testimony of Jesus himself (Luke 4:16-21; 24:25-27, 44-47), of the Synoptic gospels (Mark 1:1-8 and parallels), of the Prologue to the Fourth Gospel (John 1:1-17), of the speeches of Peter and Stephen in Acts (2:14-36;

7), of Paul (Rom. 9–11; Gal. 4:1-5), of I Peter (1:1-12), and of the Letter to the Hebrews (1:1 *et passim*). It is needless to multiply references; if we could succeed in unraveling this thread that runs through the NT, what would be left would be almost as colorless as the gospels would be without the miracles of Jesus.

E. *VALIDITY OF THE BIBLICAL INTERPRETATION.* It might be considered sufficient simply to outline, as objectively as possible, the biblical interpretation of history, and then leave the result to the dispassionate judgment of the reader. But this would seem lacking in courage, not to say wanting in candor. We are asked to believe that an assortment of writers, all of them (with the exception of Luke) Jews, none of them (not even Luke; see Luke 1:1-4) a scientific historian, on the basis of a series of happenings of minor political importance that took place almost before history, as we understand it, had got well under way, had already discerned the meaning and purpose of history. What they affirm can be summed up in the opening words of the Letter to the Hebrews: "In many and various ways God spoke of old to our fathers by the prophets; but in these last days he has spoken to us by a Son, whom he appointed the heir of all things" (1:1-2). Even if "in these last days" (ἐπ' ἐσχάτου τῶν ἡμερῶν τουτῶν) should mean no more than "recently," it is clear from I Cor. 10:11 (τὰ τέλη τῶν αἰώνων) and I Pet. 1:20 (ἐπ' ἐσχάτου τῶν χρόνων), and from much else in the NT, that the first Christians believed that the coming of Christ was the culmination of history. Obviously they were mistaken if they supposed they were living at the end of time. But they were not thinking in terms of time as measured by a celestial timepiece. The end, the τέλος, lay in the quality of finality of the revelation in Christ. Christ was for them the full, and final, revelation of God to man. And there seems no reason why the "final" revelation should not have been given to man as early in history as he was able to grasp something of its import. How otherwise should he have any light by which to steer his perilous course? This is not to say that there was no "revelation" of God to Athens and to Rome. It is only to say that for the knowledge of God, the Bible is normative for as long as time shall last. *Heilsgeschichte* is the standard by which *Geschichte* will be forever judged.

Another problem must be faced. For the pre-exilic prophets, as we have seen, Yahweh's relations with Israel appear to have begun with the Exodus, though they were presumably familiar with the patriarchal tradition, which was current at least a century earlier. This does not mean that the name Yahweh was unknown before the time of Moses. There is every reason to believe it was known. There is good reason to believe it was known to the Midianite-Kenites (*see* KENITES; MIDIAN; HEBREW RELIGION), but Exod. 6:2-3 says distinctly that it was not previously known to the Israelites. It is probable that the Genesis saga was prefixed, so to speak, to an Israelite *Heilsgeschichte* whose primary impulse was the Exodus, and that some of it was originally of Canaanite provenance. The testimony of archaeology is that the milieu of the patriarchal stories is that of the second millennium B.C., in which they are located, not that of the first millennium, in which the older critics supposed they were "written." Yet it is difficult to determine in any detail just what, or how much, *Geschichte* lies behind the *Heilsgeschichte* of Genesis. He would be a rash historian who denied the historicity of Abraham. It is probable, on the other hand, that Jacob and Joseph were originally gods (cf. the *Y'qb-'r* and *Yshp-'r* of the Karnak pylons of Thut-mose III), although Jacob, as he is portrayed in Genesis, is a character psychologically convincing, a typical Israelite. Noah is the Utnapishtim of Babylonian mythology. Some of the figures in Genesis may be types, rather than individuals we may expect to meet in the afterlife. The sagaman whom we call "J" was in some sort like a biographer who researches into the antecedents of his hero. The modern biographer will set down nothing he cannot document accurately. J, on the other hand, when he would relate the antecedents of Israel, had to make do with folk traditions, part Israelite, part Canaanite, which he adapted with consummate skill to the Israelite *Heilsgeschichte*. It is little matter: the arch of the biblical interpretation of history is set firmly upon the two pillars of the Egyptian oppression and the Exodus in the OT, and the Cross and the Resurrection in the NT.

It remains to be asked whether the biblical interpretation of history is one to which an intelligent man can subscribe with an undivided conscience. Of course, if we start from the conclusion that we "should recognize in the development of human destinies [only] the play of the contingent and the unforeseen" (H. A. L. Fisher, Preface to *A History of Europe*), there is nothing further to be said. (The biblical interpretation of history by no means excludes the play of the contingent and the unforeseen.) But if we approach the question from the standpoint of Christian faith—and this is not to forfeit intellectual honesty and respectability—our conclusion may be that the biblical interpretation of history is, at least in broad outline, right.

We are to take the *Geschichte* as it is outlined in ISRAEL, HISTORY OF, and such articles on NT history as are relevant, and ask whether the interpretation we ourselves put upon it accords with the biblical *Heilsgeschichte*. This may seem a delicate tightrope exercise, the more so because *Heilsgeschichte* has a way of becoming an integral factor in history—the last words of Mattathias (I Macc. 2:49-68) illustrate this very clearly—and because it is probably as impossible completely to empty biblical history of *Heilsgeschichte* as it is completely to demythologize theology.

The Jews are an extraordinary people. Some part of their distinction in modern times may be due to their reactions to the harsh treatment meted out to them in the Middle Ages, but it is equally a heritage from OT times and from the OT *Heilsgeschichte*. They always were a gifted and "peculiar" people. Moses is their counterpart to Pericles; the Yahwist can vie with Homer, the prophets with the Greek tragedians. There was not the variety of genius in Israel that there was in Greece, but the testimony of Israel is the more striking and significant because it was so dominated by intense awareness of God. The NT is the record of events without parallel in history, and nothing since has been the same as it would have been if Christ had never come. The promise to Abraham, "by you all the families of the earth will bless themselves," may seem inadequately fulfilled if we judge it by the halfhearted attempts of the Jews in postexilic times to evangelize the Gentiles. But Christ was a Jew, and no exclusiveness of the Jews could hinder the fulfilment of their mission in him. The *Geschichte* which produced the Bible is, take it by and large, only explicable in terms of the biblical *Heilsgeschichte*. In short, biblical history *is* salvation history.

Bibliography. J. Skinner, *I and II Kings* (Century Bible), pp. 3-18, describes OT and modern methods of historical writing. *The Kingdom of God and History*, the Church, Community, and State Series, III (1938), contains essays on the meaning of history against the background preceding World War II, by H. G. Wood, C. H. Dodd, E. R. Bevan, C. Dawson, E. W. Lyman, P. J. Tillich, H. D. Wendland, and O. Piper; the essay by Dodd is especially relevant. C. H. Dodd, *The Authority of the Bible* (2nd ed., 1938). H. W. Robinson, *Redemption and Revelation* (1942), especially Introduction, pt. I, and pt. II, chs. 9-10; *Inspiration and Revelation in the OT* (1946), especially pt. III. E. Jacob, *La tradition historique en Israël* (1946). C. R. North, *The OT Interpretation of History* (1946). S. H. Hooke, *In the Beginning*, Clarendon Bible, OT, vol. VI (1947)—for the primeval history and sagas. M. Noth, *Überlieferungsgeschichte des Pentateuch* (1948), is valuable for the early history but inclined to be "nihilistic." H. H. Rowley, *The Biblical Doctrine of Election* (1950). C. R. North, "Pentateuchal Criticism," in H. H. Rowley, ed., *The OT and Modern Study* (1951). G. E. Wright, *God Who Acts: Biblical Theology* (1952).

C. R. NORTH

HISTORY OF ABDIAS, APOSTOLIC. *See* ABDIAS, APOSTOLIC HISTORY OF.

HISTORY OF JOSEPH THE CARPENTER. *See* JOSEPH THE CARPENTER, HISTORY OF.

HITTITES hĭt′īts [*singular* חתי, חתית, *plural* חתים, חתית, *from the form Hatti, attested in cuneiform sources*]. A people of the ancient Near East. Parallel with this gentilic formation, the form "Heth" (the eponym of the Hittites), as well as forms standing for "sons of Heth" and "daughters of Heth," occur in the OT.

1. History of the Hittites
2. Hittite languages
3. Use of the term "Hittite"
4. Hittites in the OT

Bibliography

1. History of the Hittites. The original Hittites were a people who lived in central Anatolia and spoke a non-Indo-European language called Hattic or Proto-Hittite. This language is known to us only from scattered personal and geographical names in the Old Assyrian inscriptions from Cappadocia (*ca.* 2000 B.C.) and from a small number of inscriptions a few centuries later. With the invasion of Indo-European elements at the beginning of the second millennium B.C., the original Hittite state expanded into an empire covering vast territories in Anatolia and Syria. The farthest S expansion is marked by the ephemeral conquest of Babylon by the Hittite king Mursilis (*ca.* 1600 B.C.) on the one side, and by the mention of Hittites in the OT on the other. *Ca.* 1200 B.C., the Hittite Empire fell apart under the impact of the invasions of various peoples from across the Aegean, among whom the Phrygians, close relatives of the Balkan Thracians, must have played the lead-

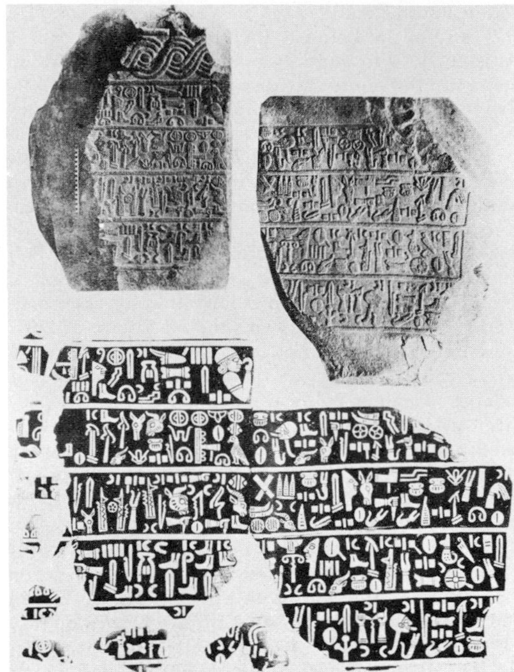

Courtesy of the Oriental Institute, the University of Chicago

25. Several inscriptions, found at Carchemish, in Hittite hieroglyphs

ing role. For a few centuries the history of Anatolia is covered by an almost total darkness. Out of it no great state emerged comparable in size and power with the Hittite Empire. The whole area once occupied by the Hittites was thereupon divided into small kingdoms and principalities with the main centers around Kayseri, Tyana, and Malatya in Anatolia, and Carchemish, Aleppo, and Hamath in N Syria. These states soon came in contact with the Assyrians, whose conquering drive westward was continually threatening their very existence. One by one they fell prey to the expanding power of Assyria. The year 717 B.C., in which Carchemish was conquered by the Assyrian king Sargon II, marks the end of the independence of the last of the small Hittite states. Fig. HIT 25.

2. Hittite languages. One of the chief languages of the Hittite Empire was cuneiform Hittite, the decipherment of which, initiated in 1915 by the Czech scholar B. Hrozný, has progressed so far in the following years through the concerted efforts of E. Forrer, J. Friedrich, A. Goetze, F. Sommer, and E. H. Sturtevant—to name only the chief scholars—that the language is now considered fully deciphered. Cuneiform Hittite is an Indo-European language of the centum group, as best exemplified by the preservation of the velar in such words as *kartis* ("heart") or *luk* ("to kindle"), and of the labiovelar in such words as *kwis* ("who") or *kwen* ("to strike"). Although restricted in its spoken use to the area around Ḫattusas (modern Boghazköy),* the capital of the empire, cuneiform Hittite was the official language of the empire, as can be gathered from the fact that in this language were written the historical annals, proclamations, laws, and treaties with foreign states. The language

Courtesy of the Oriental Institute, the University of Chicago

26. Ḫattusas (modern Boghazköy), capital of the ancient Hittite Kingdom

is attested from *ca.* 1600-1200 B.C. The second most important language of the Hittite Empire was hieroglyphic Hittite, the decipherment of which was achieved during the last twenty years through the effective collaboration of five scholars of such diverse national origin as H. T. Bossert, E. Forrer, I. J. Gelb, B. Hrozný, and P. Meriggi.* Hieroglyphic Hittite is doubtless an Indo-European language and was spoken throughout the Hittite Empire from *ca.* 1600 to 700 B.C. Much less well known are Luwian and Palaic, two still different Indo-European languages. Figs. HIT 26; CAR 10; CAL 3.

3. Use of the term "Hittite." In common usage the term "Hittite" has at least three different meanings, as it can stand for: (*a*) the native non-Indo-European Hittites, called "Hattians," who lived in central Anatolia; (*b*) the so-called "cuneiform Hittites," or Nesians—i.e., the people who originally lived around the capital Ḫattusas and used an Indo-European language preserved in a cuneiform writing borrowed from Mesopotamia; and (*c*) the so-called "hieroglyphic Hittites," who were originally at home in the S parts of the empire and used another Indo-European language preserved in a hieroglyphic form of writing of local origin. To the Assyrians and Hebrews, the term "Hittites" covered all the inhabitants of the original Hittite Empire plus its dependencies, irrespective of their linguistic or ethnic affiliation.

4. Hittites in the OT. In the consideration of Hittite history two main periods can be distinguished: the period before 1200 B.C. and the period after this date. In the first period the Hittite Empire, centered in inner Anatolia, extended southward toward the N reaches of Syria, but never as far S as Palestine. In the second period, small Hittite kingdoms and principalities covered vast areas in Anatolia and Syria, none of them extending S of the Lebanon and Anti-Lebanon. The appearance of Hittites in Palestine according to the OT is a historical enigma, for which only tentative interpretations can be offered.

Several names of individuals with a Hittite background are known from the OT. Ephron the Hittite sells a burial ground, Machpelah, situated before Mamre, near Hebron, to Abraham (Gen. 23:10; 25:9; 49:29-30; 50:13). Abraham calls himself a foreigner and a settler, while the Hittites are called native to the area. Judith, the daughter of Beeri the Hittite, and Basemath, the daughter of Elon the Hittite, are married to Esau, while he is staying in the area of Beer-sheba (Gen. 26:34; a different tradition, naming Adah, the daughter of Elon the Hittite, is found in Gen. 36:2). The custom of taking Hittite women as wives, discouraged by Rebekah and Isaac in the case of Jacob (cf. Gen. 27:46; 28:1), was followed in later times by Solomon (I Kings 11:1). Ahimelech the Hittite was a contemporary of David (I Sam. 26:6), as was also Uriah the Hittite, whose wife, Bathsheba the daughter of Eliam, was taken by David (II Sam. 11; 12:9-10; 23:39; I Kings 15:5; I Chr. 11:41). All the names of the Hittites listed above are Semitic, with the exception of the name of Uriah, for which a possible Hurrian etymology has been suggested. Thus it is clear that the Hittites living in Palestine, no matter what the memory or tradition of their ethnic background might have been, represented a group of people fully assimilated to the surrounding Semitic population.

The only exact indications concerning the geographical location of the Hittites in Palestine come from the stories dated to the time of Abraham and Esau, which place the Hittites in the area of Hebron and Beer-sheba in Judah. The reminder of Ezekiel to the city of Jerusalem that her father was an Amorite and her mother a Hittite (Ezek. 16:3, 45) again places the Hittites in the same general area. Not so clear are the implications of the story about an unnamed native of Luz (later renamed Bethel), who, after his life was spared when the Israelites took that city, went into the land of the Hittites and built another city Luz there (Judg. 1:26). The conclusion that a man settling in the land of the Hittites would likely be a Hittite himself, though plausible enough, cannot be proved at the present. If this is correct, then the story confirms the localization of the Hittites in S Palestine. Finally, we should recall the reference to the Hittites living in the hill country (Num. 13:29), apparently that of Judah and of some neighboring areas.

Nothing constructive on the localization of Hittites in Palestine can be obtained from the twenty-two references to Hittites listed among the people who were believed to represent the original inhabitants of Palestine before the coming of the Israelites. The lists are quite irregular in their structure; some list only two peoples and some as many as seven. Disregarding the lists of peoples mentioned in Gen. 15:19-21; Ezra 9:1 (where Kenites, Kenizzites, etc., are mentioned), the names of the seven peoples are: Canaanites, Hittites, Amorites, Perizzites, Hivites, Jebusites, and Girgashites. Indicative of the importance attached to the Hittites in these schematic lists is the fact that Hittites are mentioned six times in the first place and nine times in the second, overshadowed only by the Canaanites in the order of listing.

The table of nations lists Heth, along with Sidon, the Jebusites, the Amorites, the Girgashites, the Hivites, the Arkites, the Sinites, the Arvadites, the Zemarites, and the Hamathites, as the sons of Canaan the son of Ham (Gen. 10:15-18; I Chr. 1:13-16). Hittites are here listed as Canaanites, together with the Phoenicians and the pre-Hebrew peoples of Palestine; the Indo-European background of the Hittites had long been forgotten by the author(s) of the table of nations.

The remaining five references to Hittites in the

OT all pertain to areas outside Palestine proper. One reference, in the story of the unnamed man who founded the city Luz in the land of the Hittites (Judg. 1:26), has been discussed above. The promise given by Yahweh to the children of Israel: "From the wilderness and this Lebanon as far as the great river, the river Euphrates, all the land of the Hittites to the Great Sea toward the going down of the sun shall be your territory" (Josh. 1:4), is difficult to evaluate, since it covers not only Palestine but also vast territories beyond, up to the banks of the Euphrates. The area between the Mediterranean and the Euphrates was under some form of political control by the Hittites, but only in very ancient patriarchal times could it be imagined that some nomadic ancestors of the Hebrews lived or roamed in that faraway area N of Palestine. In its northernmost extension, David's empire reached Kadesh on the Orontes, if we can rely on the reconstruction of a damaged passage in II Sam. 24:6, which, in accordance with a LXX version, reads: "to the land of the Hittites, towards Kadesh."

Besides these three mentions of the land of the Hittites, the OT has two references to the kings of the Hittites, neither of which can be placed within an exact geographical frame. One passage refers to Solomon's buying chariots and horses and reselling them to the kings of the Hittites and the kings of the Arameans (I Kings 10:29 and similarly in II Chr. 1:17); and the other names the kings of the Hittites and the kings of the Egyptians as allies of Joram king of Israel against the Arameans (II Kings 7:6).

In résumé of the foregoing discussion, it can be said that the OT sources mentioning the Hittites can be divided into two classes: those referring to the non-Palestinian Hittites and those referring to the Hittites living in Palestine.

The OT sources in which the non-Palestinian Hittites are mentioned are very few in number—five at the most—and they all refer to the land of the Hittites and Hittite kings, to be located somewhere N of Palestine. The plural form of "kings" agrees well with the political situation of Greater Syria after 1200 B.C., during which time this whole vast area was subdivided into a large number of small kingdoms and principalities, all called "Hittite" in the Assyrian sources, irrespective of their ethnic background, whether Hittite, Hurrian, Aramaic, or Phoenician. The term "Hittite," used for the various Syrian states, goes back to a period before 1200 B.C., during which the Anatolian Hittites exercised full political control over large parts of Syria, especially those situated close to the Assyrian Empire.

All other OT sources mention Hittites as living peacefully in Palestine in the midst of the native populations, be they Hebrew or not. Although quantitatively they are much more numerous than the sources referring to the non-Palestinian Hittites, they are not explicit enough to allow general conclusions. As far as the sources show, the Hittites seem to be living in the hill country of Judah, they bear Semitic names corresponding to those of their neighbors, and, otherwise, they seem to be fully assimilated to the surrounding population.

Courtesy of Staatliche Museen, Berlin

27. Bas relief of seven Hittite prisoners, possibly from scene depicting the Battle of Kadesh; probably from time of Ramses II (1301-1234 B.C.)

Courtesy of Staatliche Museen, Berlin

28. Hittite prisoners, on faïence tile, probably from the time of Ramses III (*ca.* 1195-1164 B.C.)

The presence of Hittites in Palestine is a historical problem, for which several interpretations can be offered, none of them conclusive. According to one interpretation, the Hittites of Palestine are leftovers from a period in which the Hittites, originally Anatolian, controlled politically the whole of Greater Syria, including Palestine. This interpretation is not in accordance with the Assyrian sources, which generally locate the states called "Hittite" in an area situated N of Palestine. However, there is one exception to this, found in the Annals of Sargon II of Assyria and repeated in his "Display Inscription," wherein the population of the Palestinian Ashdod is called "Hittite." Some new evidence possibly bearing on the presence of Hittites in Palestine was discovered by Forrer (*see biblography*) on a cuneiform Hittite tablet from the archives of Boghazköy. The interpretation of the tablet has its difficulties, but there is no doubt that it contains a reference to Hittites of the Anatolian city Kurustamma living in the "land of Miṣri" at the time of the Hittite king Mursilis II (*ca.* 1330 B.C.). The "land of Miṣri" may indicate generally the territories under Egyptian control, including Palestine. No constructive suggestions can be offered as to the reasons why these particular Hittites emigrated to Egyptian-occupied territories. An entirely different interpretation of the presence of Palestinian Hittites in the OT might be suggested if we replaced with "Horites" the name "Hittites" in many, if not most, of the OT passages. This would involve a change of only one consonant, namely ת to ר, in the Hebrew consonantal text, and this would be paleographically admissible. It has always appeared strange that the HORITES, or Hurrians, who played such an important role in the history of Syria and Palestine in the second millennium B.C., have received very scant mention in the OT, far out of proportion to their real importance. By replacing "Hittites," when the term designates people living in Palestine, with "Hurrians," we may obtain a picture which is fully compatible with our knowledge of Hurrian history.

Figs. HIT 27-28.

Bibliography. J. Garstang, *The Hittite Empire* (1930). E. O. Forrer, "The Hittites in Palestine," *PEQ*, LXVIII (1936), 190-209; LXIX (1937), 100-115. F. F. Bruce, *The Hittites and the OT* (1948)—a popular account. O. R. Gurney, *The Hittites* (1952), especially pp. 59-62. A. Goetze, *Kleinasien* (2nd ed., 1958). I. J. GELB

HIVITE hĭv'īt, hī'vīt [חִוִּי, *always with the article, and usually used collectively*]. The Hivites were one of the nations prominent in Canaan before the Israelite settlement.

The term appears usually in the stereotyped list of nations expelled by the Israelites (Exod. 3:8, 17; 13:5; 23:23, 28; 33:2; 34:11; Deut. 7:1; 20:17; Josh. 3:10; 9:1; 11:3; 12:8; 24:11; Judg. 3:5; I Kings 9:20= II Chr. 8:7). But such instances tell us little about the people, and the same is true of the genealogical entry in Gen. 10:17 (=I Chr. 1:15).

The remaining notices of the Hivites, though few in number, supply better data. Gen. 34:2 applies the term to Hamor, father of Shechem. The inhabitants of Gibeon, to the N of Jerusalem, are identified as Hivites (Josh. 9:7; 11:19). Hivite cities are encountered on the way between Sidon and Beer-sheba (II Sam. 24:7), and Hivite settlements are placed in Mount Lebanon (Judg. 3:3) and even at the foot of Hermon (Josh. 11:3). Lastly, according to the LXX reading of a mutilated MT passage, the Israelite conquest left in its wake "deserted places of the Hivites and the Amorites" (Isa. 17:9). All this would seem to argue for the Hivites an original role of outstanding significance. Yet there is not a trace of such a people in any extrabiblical source.

Internal evidence may help to clear up this apparent mystery. In the consonantal writing of Hebrew the names for the Hivites (חוי), the HORITES (חרי), and the HITTITES (חתי) differ from one another by their respective middle letters alone. This was bound to lead to some textual confusion. Thus the MT itself speaks of "Zibeon the Hivite" in Gen. 36:2, but lists the same person as a Horite in vs. 20. Moreover, the LXX has "Horites" for the MT "Hivites" in Gen. 34:2; Josh. 9:7; and conversely, the "Hivites" of the LXX text at Isa. 17:9 reflects Hebrew *ḥry*, corrupted in the MT to *ḥrš*. Finally, the LXX speaks of Hittites in Josh. 11:3, whereas the MT refers to Horites.

The Horites in particular (*see* HURRIANS) would readily account for the prominence and the location that the MT assigns to the Hivites. Hurrian personal names are attested from Central Palestine, including Shechem (cf. Gen. 34:2), not to mention Lebanon and inland Syria. Furthermore, it is worth noting that in the stereotyped lists of nations the Hivites are mentioned usually before the Jebusites (*see* JEBUS), whose Hurrian affiliations are now well known; here, too, therefore, Hivites might well stand for "Horites." Why, then, were these names interchanged?

The assumption of a purely graphic confusion could account for some of the instances, but hardly for all of them. A plausible explanation must be sought elsewhere. We know that tradition identified the Horites with the pre-Edomite population of Seir, a region with which the Hurrians had apparently little, if anything, in common. On the other hand, the Hivites are located in Palestine precisely where the Hurrians were established. Since the name "Horites" came to be pre-empted for another group—perhaps because of etymological interference ("cave-dwellers"; *see* HORITES)—the designation "Hivites," which was probably secondary and limited at the start, came to be applied eventually to the Hurrians proper. The LXX, however, as well as some internal evidence in the MT (Gen. 34:2; Isa. 17:9), would still seem to point to actual conditions at an earlier time.

Bibliography. E. Meyer, *Die Israeliten und deren Nachbarstämme* (1906), pp. 328-45; E. A. Speiser, *AASOR*, XIII (1933), 26-31. E. A. SPEISER

HIZKI hĭz'kī [חִזְקִי, O my strength (*invocation to deity*)] (I Chr. 8:17); KJV HEZEKI həz'ə kī. A descendant of Benjamin.

Bibliography. M. Noth, *Die israelitischen Personennamen* (1928), pp. 38, 160.

HIZKIAH. Alternate form of HEZEKIAH.

HIZKIJAH. KJV alternate form of HEZEKIAH.

HOBAB hō'băb [חֹבָב]. Father-in-law of Moses (Num. 10:29; Judg. 4:11). Conflicting traditions as to the name of Moses' father-in-law are preserved. In addition to Hobab, JETHRO priest of Midian (Exod. 3:1; 18:1) and Reuel (Exod. 2:18) are so named. There is also uncertainty in the identification of Hobab, since he is described as a Midianite in Num. 10:29, a Kenite in Judg. 4:11. "Hobab" may possibly once have stood in Exod. 2:18, "Reuel" then being a clan designation in that verse. Some LXX MS evidence indicates that Judg. 1:16 once read "Hobab the Kenite."

Moses urged Hobab to accompany the Israelites as guide through the wilderness; and although the account in Num. 10:29-31 leaves his decision in doubt, Judg. 1:16 would suggest that he did guide them. R. F. JOHNSON

HOBAH hō'bə [חוֹבָה; Akkad. *Abu(m)*; Amarna *Ube, Abi*]. A country the capital of which was Damascus.

According to Gen. 14:15, Hobah was situated "on the left hand of Damascus"—i.e., "north of Damascus" (so RSV). Various attempts have been made at the identification of Hobah; e.g., Qabun or Hobah, NW of Damascus. According to the letters from Tell el-Amarna, however, Ube seems to have been a territory, the capital of which was Damascus. Before the sixteenth century the name of Damascus is unknown, and probably another town was the center of the settlement of the Damascene. The mound Tell el-Salihiye, situated *ca.* ten miles E of Damascus, is the largest mound to be found in the region, which may favor the view that the capital was situated there in the early periods. Accordingly Hobah was probably the name of this place, which later lost its importance when Damascus became the capital of the territory. The mound of Tell el-Salihiye shows that there was a place of settlement since prehistoric times, and in the Old Babylonian period there was an important town which was fortified and may have been a defense against enemies coming from the E.

A. HALDAR

HOBAIAH. Alternate form of HABAIAH.

HOD hŏd [הוד, majesty (*probably a shortened form*)] (I Chr. 7:37). Eponym of a family in the tribe of Asher.

Bibliography. M. Noth, *Die israelitischen Personennamen* (1928), p. 146.

HODAVIAH hŏd'ə vī'ə [הודויה, הודויהו (*in* I Chr. 3:24 *Kethibh* הודיוהו), give thanks to Yahu]; KJV HODAIAH hō dā'yə in I Chr. 3:24. Alternately: HODEVAH hō dē'və [הודוה, *although Qere* הודיה] (Neh. 7:43). **1.** A descendant of King David (I Chr. 3:24).

2. One of the heads of the half-tribe of Manasseh (I Chr. 5:24).

3. A Benjaminite (I Chr. 9:7).

4. Ancestor of a family of Levites among the returned exiles (Ezra 2:40; Neh. 7:43; lacking in I Esd. 5:26; cf. Ezra 3:9, where apparently this name is replaced by Judah, possibly in error).

Bibliography. M. Noth, *Die israelitischen Personennamen* (1928), pp. 32, 194-95, 219. B. T. DAHLBERG

HODESH hō'dĕsh [חדש, new moon]. Wife of Shaharaim, a Benjaminite (I Chr. 8:9; but the text here is corrupt).

Bibliography. E. L. Curtis, *Chronicles,* ICC (1910), pp. 159-60.

HODEVAH. Alternate form of HODAVIAH 4.

HODIAH hō dī'ə [הודיה, Yahu is splendor; Apoc. Αὐταίας]; KJV HODIJAH hō dī'jə in Nehemiah; KJV Apoc. AUTEAS ô tē'əs. **1.** Husband of a woman of Judah (I Chr. 4:19; KJV here renders the text incorrectly).

2. One of the Levites who interpreted the law to the people when Ezra read it publicly (Neh. 8:7; cf. I Esd. 9:48) and who helped lead the worship on the day of penitence (Neh. 9:5). Doubtless he was one of the two Levites signatory to the covenant of Ezra (Neh. 10:10 or 13).

3. Another Levite, signatory to Ezra's covenant (Neh. 10:10 or 10:13).

4. A chief of the people, signatory to Ezra's covenant (Neh. 10:18). B. T. DAHLBERG

HOE [מעדר, *from* עדר, to hoe] (Isa. 7:25 [KJV MATTOCK]; verbal form in Isa. 5:6; 7:25 [KJV DIG]). The hoe was used for loosening the soil and cutting out weeds around trees, bushes, and vines. *See* MATTOCK.

HOGLAH hŏg'lə [חגלה, partridge]. One of the five daughters of Zelophehad of Manasseh (Num. 26:33; 27:1; 36:11; Josh. 17:3 [all P]). It is probable that the names of the five daughters were originally the names of Canaanite towns (*see* BETH-HOGLAH). The name Hoglah appears in the eighth-century Samaria Ostraca.

M. NEWMAN

HOHAM hō'hăm [הוהם] (Josh. 10:3). King of Hebron. He was one of five confederate kings in the Amorite coalition which attempted to halt Joshua's invasion of the territory SW of Jerusalem.

HOLIDAY [יום טוב, a good day]. A happy or festal day. The biblical reference is to the feast of PURIM celebrating deliverance from Israel's enemies (Esth. 8:17; 9:22; cf. I Sam. 25:8). It was a time of feasting and drinking (excess being permitted), giving of dainties to one another, and showing charity to the poor. This was the only secular holiday in the Jewish calendar for the expression of the lighter side of life. It was celebrated with feasting, games, merriment, playing of mummers, masquerading, noisemaking, etc.

In the postbiblical period the phrase "good day" refers to any holy day or festival day.

V. H. KOOY

HOLINESS. The "given" undergirding and pervading all religion; the distinctive mark and signature of the divine. More than any other term, "holiness" gives expression to the essential nature of the "sacred." It is therefore to be understood, not as one attribute among other attributes, but as the innermost reality to which all others are related. Even the sum of all the attributes and activities of "the holy" is insufficient to exhaust its meaning, for to the one who has experienced its presence there is always a plus, a "something more," which resists formulation or definition. Its connotations are as diverse as the cultures which seek to describe its mysterious nature, but common to all is an awareness of an undefined and uncanny energy, a sense of the numinous (cf. Latin *numen*), of the imponderable and incomprehensible, an inarticulate feeling of an inviolable potency outside and beyond, removed and distant, yet at the same time near and "fascinating," invading the everyday world of normal experience—what Rudolf Otto has described as the *mysterium tremendum.* Primitive societies seek to do justice to the maleficent and beneficent powers of "the holy" in such words as "mana" and "taboo," but these positive and negative forces are present wherever "the holy" is present. Holiness thus extends into every area of existence.

In the Bible "holiness" is related, e.g., to the world of nature and of history, to the realm of human experience and conduct, to the election-covenant life of Israel, to the psychophysical life of the individual, and even to the destiny of nations. There it is the revelation of the holy presence which gives rise to the impulse to worship; where the Holy One manifests himself in the *hieros logos* as in the theophanies, altars and sanctuaries are erected to bring the event and word to holy immediacy and realization. Wherever God's presence is felt, there men encounter the wonder and mystery of holiness. It is, therefore, the religious word κατ' ἐξοχήν. While it often denotes a state or condition, it is for ancient Israel primarily an activity and a speaking which eventuate in relationship.

A. *IN THE OT.* 1. Etymology and usage. The root *qdš* is found in several Semitic languages. It is present, e.g., in the Phoenician inscriptions, notably those of the twelfth-century Yehimilk and the later Eshmunazar sarcophagus, and also in the Ugaritic texts (*qdš*, "sanctuary" [Aqhat I.27, 45; II.16]; *bn qdš*, "sons of holiness" [137.21, 38]). Its provenance is probably Canaanite. But these passages cast no clear light on the etymology of the word. While many theories have been advanced as to its origin, only two need be considered here:

The first associates the root קדש with a hypothetical primitive root קד, whence קדקד, "crown of head," "hairy crown" (cf. Ugaritic *qdqd*), inferentially "cutting." According to this view, the root קדש is related to חדש, "to be new" ("cut off"; cf. קצב and חצב, קצף and חצף, קצר and חצר). In all these cases the meaning of "separation" is paramount. While the linguistic argument cannot be said by any means to be coercive, it must be admitted that the meaning suits the major associations of the word both in the history of religions (cf. τέμνειν and τέμενος; Latin *sancire* and *sanctus;* Polynesian *tapu* and *tabu*) and in the OT and NT.

The second theory connects the root with the Akkadian *qadašu,* "to be bright" or "to shine," synonymous with *ellu*[m], "clear," "bright." Semantically this satisfies a number of biblical contexts—above all, the not infrequent associations of קדש with FIRE and GLORY (כבוד).

Nevertheless, the more elemental meaning seems to lie with "separation." This is also confirmed by an examination of the more striking antonyms of קדש. Of these the most important is חל, "profane" or "common" (Lev. 10:10 P; I Sam. 21:5-6; Ezek. 22:26; 44:23). The verbal root חלל ("to profane," "to pollute," etc.) expresses the antithesis even more forcefully than the noun חל. The prophet Ezekiel, with his profound sense of the divine holiness and of the sanctity of the temple and its cult, employs the word frequently in notable contexts (7:24; 20:9, 14, 22; 22:8; etc.) as does the writer of the Holiness Code (Lev. 21:9, 12; 22:2, 32). Where holiness is treated as though it belonged to the sphere of the secular or common, without fear and awe, there it is profaned. Another term relating to the same vocabulary is חרם, *ḥérem* (lit., "devoted" [to Yahweh], hence "set apart": "Every devoted thing is most holy to Yahweh": כל חרם קדש קדשים הוא ליהוה [Lev. 27:28 P]). Especially in the holy war the *ḥérem* plays an important role, for all the spoil is Yahweh's; it must therefore be "devoted" to him by being destroyed. When Achan violates the *ḥérem,* he and his blood relatives are exterminated, and the Israelites must sanctify themselves (התקדשו) before they may again engage in holy encounter. Yahweh claims what belongs to him (Josh. 6:17-18; 7:1, 10-13).

Allied to the foregoing terms is the root נזר, "to dedicate," "to consecrate," "to separate" (Lev. 15:31; 22:2; Ezek. 14:7; Hos. 9:10; Zech. 7:3). The Nazirite is one who is dedicated to God: "All the days of his separation [נזרו] he is holy to Yahweh" (קדש הוא ליהוה; Num. 6:8; cf. Judg. 13:5, 7).

In the LXX, קדש and its derived forms are almost invariably rendered by ἅγιος and its congeners, ἁγιότης, ἁγιωσύνη, ἁγιαζειν, ἁγιασμός, etc. While ἅγιος occurs in classical Greek as early as Herodotus, it appears more frequently in the Hellenistic period, probably because of oriental influence. Be that as it may, the linguistic usage of the NT seems to have been profoundly influenced by the LXX. The adjective קדוש is rendered by ἅγιος and καθαρος (only Num. 5:17); the verb variously by καθαρὸν εἶναι (Isa. 65:5), δοξάζειν (Isa. 5:16), καθαρίζειν (Job. 1:5), etc.

2. Associations of holiness. A scrutiny of the terminology most frequently associated with "holiness" reveals not only its vast range and diversity of usage, but also the richness of its connotation and its peculiar imagery.

a. Holiness and fire. Most striking is the frequent association of holiness and fire. It is in fire that Yahweh manifests himself most characteristically, especially in the great theophanies from the time of Moses on (Exod. 3:2-3; 19:18; 24:17; Deut. 4:12, 24; 5:22-27; 9:3; Ps. 18:8-14 = II Sam. 22:9-15; Ezek. 1:4-28; Hab. 3:3-4); these and many other passages are often directly related to holiness. The divine manifestation in judgment, too, is characteristically in fire, especially on the Day of the Lord (Isa. 34: 8-10; Zeph. 1:18; cf. Isa. 9:18-19; Amos 1:3–2:16). Again, the practices of the cult are intimately and specifically connected with fire, and the emphasis upon holiness in all these contexts is noteworthy (Lev. 2:3, 9-10; 6:16-18; 7:3-5; 10:1-3: "unholy fire"; 16:27; 21:6-10; etc.). The substantives of fire imagery are frequent throughout the OT, often in passages where holiness is directly mentioned: "light," "heat," "smoke," "flame," "coals," "furnace," "caldron," "ashes," "brimstone." Similarly the verbs reflect this same symbolism: "scorch," "blaze," "consume," "burn," "kindle," "glow," "warm," "quench," etc. It is the seraphim, "the fiery ones" (cf. שרף, "to burn"), who sing, "Holy, holy, holy," before the throne of Yahweh, and one of them takes the glowing coal from the altar (cf. the cherubim in Ezek. 10:6-8). It will be observed that a number of the terms *below* which belong to the terminology of holiness reflect the same imagery of fire.

The NT perpetuates the same usage, especially, of course, in the language of judgment (Luke 12:49; Heb. 12:26-29: "Our God is a consuming fire"), in reference to the Holy Spirit (Matt. 3:11; Acts 2:1-4), and in allusions to the Mosaic or Sinaitic theophany (Acts 7:30), the visions of Isaiah and Ezekiel (Rev. 4:4-11), and the Day of the Lord (I Cor. 3:12-15).

*b. **Holiness and jealousy.*** Yahweh is a jealous God (אל קנא; *see* JEALOUSY). It belongs to his nature to maintain the uniqueness and integrity of his deity. The *mysterium tremendum* is revealed in the passionate zeal and drive of his holy being. "God is a devouring fire, a jealous God" (Deut. 4:24). Such a holy God demands exclusive worship (Josh. 24:19; Exod. 20: 3, 5: אל קנא כי אנכי יהוה אלהיך). The dynamistic and daemonic force of his holy jealousy is great, so much so that it seems at times almost identical with holiness itself. His very name is Jealous (Exod. 34:14 J; cf. Deut. 4:24; 6:15; Ezek. 39:25; also Exod. 4:24-26 J). His unpredictable "passionateness," the drive of the divine pathos, is intimately involved with his jealousy, and expresses the vitality and intense urgency of his holy activity. It is in this context that we must read passages which refer to Yahweh's "hate" (Ps. 11:5; Isa. 1:14; Hos. 9:15; Amos 5:21; Mal. 1:3); he cannot tolerate worship, the human response to his manifested holiness, that is in defiance of his essential and innermost nature. This is equally true of references to his vengeance or vindication (cf. Isa. 63:2-3; Ezekiel *passim*). It is important that verses like these always be understood in their contextual relations, where sometimes we read of Yahweh's "repenting" or relenting (Jer. 18:8; 26:3, 13, 19), which belongs to the same dynamic terminology as jealousy, vengeance, and wrath.

*c. **Holiness and wrath.*** Closely connected with the foregoing is Yahweh's manifestation of holy wrath (*see* WRATH OF GOD). Here again the association with heat and fire is prominent. Anthropomorphisms and anthropopathisms are especially frequent in the descriptions of the divine punishment. When Nadab and Abihu offer "unholy fire," fire comes forth from Yahweh to consume them, for "I will show myself holy among those who are near me" (Lev. 10:1-3). Considering the major role that divine judgment plays in the Bible, it is not surprising that the terminology should be rich (חרון אף חמה קצף עבור זעם) and that the NT is quite as emphatic as the OT upon the ὀργὴ θεοῦ. The Day of Yahweh is a day of wrath (Ezek. 7:5-13; Zeph. 1:14-18). It is clear that in all the passages where Yahweh's wrath is mentioned we have to do with a holy manifestation, even when the word "holy" is not mentioned. Elsewhere the symbolic patterns are clear, as in Ezekiel's prophecy against Gog (chs. 38–39), particularly in 38:18-23, where the imagery of wrath and holiness is portrayed in almost unexampled concentration and vividness.

*d. **Holiness and fear.*** The biblical understanding of holiness includes the large and diversified sphere of dread, terror, awe, reverence, and FEAR. This elemental response to the holy is compounded of numerous and varied feelings. The terminology is therefore correspondingly rich and diverse. When Jacob awakens from his sleep, he is afraid and says: "How awesome [נורא] is this place! This is none other than the house of God." The motif of the "terrible" persists throughout the OT. Yahweh is "holy and terrible" (Pss. 89:7; 99:3; 111:9); holy in his terrible works (Exod. 15:11; II Sam. 7:23; Pss. 66:3, 5; 145:6; Isa. 64:3); holy above all in the Exodus (Exod. 15: 11, 15; Deut. 26:8; Ps. 106:22), the events of the covenant (Exod. 19 J and E; cf. 34:12), and the Conquest (Exod. 23:27; Josh. 5:1–11:9). For a proper grasp of this aspect of the divine holiness, it is essential to observe the contexts. The word "terrible" is characteristically associated with "great." Yahweh is a great and terrible God (Deut. 7:21); a great and terrible God who keeps covenant (Neh. 1:5); Israel praises his great and terrible name (Ps. 99:3); Yahweh is great and terrible above all that are around him (Ps. 89:7—H 89:8). Again, Yahweh is terrible in his sanctuary, but the words which follow give the word substance:

> The God of Israel,
> he gives power and strength to his people
> (Ps. 68:35—H 68:36).

It is clear that one moves in a spacious area of holiness here. The nuances of the word are with majesty, sublimity, awe, augustness, and reverence. God's terrible judgment is an assertion of his sovereignty, as often in Ezekiel: "that they may know that I am Yahweh." Before his coming the heavens and earth quake (Exod. 19; Ps. 68:7-8—H 68:8-9).

*e. **Holiness and "remoteness."*** The consciousness of the radical cleavage between the human and the divine is rooted in *taboo,* and is illustrated in the law of the *ḥērem* (חרם), in which man is forbidden to appropriate what belongs to God, and in the frequent prohibitions against profanation. The holy is unapproachable; man must not "come near" (קרב) to it. Thus Moses must not come near, for the place on which he stands is קדש (Exod. 3:5 J; cf. Josh. 5:15). When Yahweh is about to descend on Sinai, the whole mountain is placed out of bounds; whoever touches it will die (Exod. 19:12-13, 20-24 J). Whoever touches holy things will experience the same fate (Num. 18:3). No man may see God and live (Exod. 33:20 J); whoever gazes at Sinai when Yahweh comes down will perish (Exod. 19:21; cf. Judg. 13:

22). When the men of Bethshemesh violate the sanctity of the ark by looking into it, a great slaughter ensues, and in terror they cry out: "Who is able to stand before Yahweh, this holy God?" (I Sam. 6:20). When the ark falls into the hands of the Philistines, the consequences are appalling (II Sam. 6–7). As Hempel has shown, the piety of Israel is pervaded throughout by this sense of distance from the holy (*Abstandsgefühl*). God is God and man man (Pss. 8: 5; 9:20; Isa. 31:3; Hos. 11:9*b*).

f. Holiness and cleanness. The contrast between "holy" (קדש) and "profane" (חל) is sometimes paralleled by the contrast between "clean" (טהור) and "unclean" (טמא; Lev. 10:10; Ezek. 22:26; 44:23; *see* CLEAN AND UNCLEAN). The relation between the two contrasts is so intimate as often to suggest identity of meaning. So reference is made to the cleansing and hallowing (or consecrating) of the altar (Lev. 16:19; Ezek. 43:26) or of the temple (II Chr. 29: 15-16) or of the walls of Jerusalem (Neh. 12:30). Nevertheless, the two are not synonymous; purity or cleanness is an aspect of holiness, though a major aspect, as is seen in the numerous cultic and ceremonial references, especially in the book of Leviticus (11:32; 13:6, 34, 58; 15:13, 28; cf. Ezek. 24:13; 36: 25). To be sure, there are notable passages in which the words move in the moral or ethical sphere, as in Job. 17:9; Hab. 1:13; in the striking description of the words of Yahweh in Ps. 12:6—H 12:7; and in the fervent petitions of Ps. 51:10—H 51:12: "Create [ברא] in me a clean heart [לב טהור], O God" (cf. I Sam. 20:26).

g. Holiness and majesty. Another complex of terms is related to the quality and character of holiness: "majesty," "splendor," "honor," "beauty," "glory," "spaciousness," etc. While each of these may be represented by a distinctive term in Hebrew, they tend to coalesce in their connotations, as is made clear by an examination of their renderings in the RSV. Yahweh is "majestic in holiness" (Exod. 15:11; בקדש נאדר). As Israel's holy King he is clothed in majesty—*rex majestatis* (Ps. 93:1; גאות)—in honor and majesty (Ps. 104:1; הוד והדר), with terrible majesty (Job 37:22; נורא הוד). Honor and majesty go before him (I Chr. 16:27; Pss. 96:6; 111:3); therefore Israel's holy choirs exult and hymn his praises (Pss. 104:31-35; 145:5; 148:13), and properly so, for in the sanctuary they contemplate the "beauty of Yahweh" (Ps. 27:4; נעם יהוה). His name is majestic (אדיר) in all the earth (Ps. 8:1); the glory of the Holy One (הודו) is above the heavens and earth (Ps. 148:13; Hab. 3:3). There are overtones of the aesthetic in these ascriptions; their nuances include "graciousness," "goodness," "pleasantness," but also "awe," "reverence," "power," and "honor." Majesty has other dimensions also, as we see in the ominous refrains of Isaiah's poem on the Day of Yahweh, where awfulness, terror, sublimity, and the *tremendum* are present (Ps. 114; Isa. 2:2, 10, 19, 21 [מהדר גאונו]; cf. Job 37:22).

h. Holiness as unsearchable, incomprehensible, and incomparable. Each of these terms has its own particular linguistic and literary associations, but they are grouped here for the sake of brevity. The deep things of God no man can fathom; the limits and mysteries of his ways are beyond all human wit and ken (Job 11:3-12). His knowledge is too wonderful for the psalmist; it is so high that none can reach up or out to it (Ps. 139:6). God's understanding is unsearchable, for no man can penetrate it with his designs and thoughts (Isa. 40:13-14; I Cor. 2:11). He is incomparable in his holiness. From the beginning Yahweh was Israel's invisible Lord, invisible yet sovereign; his holiness cannot be fashioned or bodied forth in anything man can see. There is none among the gods like him in his holiness (Exod. 15:11; I Sam. 2:2; Ps. 77:13—H 77:14; Isa. 40:18-20, 25-26). Yahweh's uniqueness is the uniqueness of his holiness. Therefore, all comparisons are futile, for to find an adequate image or figure would be somehow to dispose over him. God is in heaven and man on earth (Eccl. 5:2).

i. The holy as "wonderful." The ways of God are not man's ways (Isa. 55:8-9); they are beyond his calculation, grasp, or control, for they are holy (Ps. 77:13; *see* MIRACLE; SIGNS AND WONDERS). He appears when men least expect him; the element of "surprise" and amazement is therefore a concomitant of the theophanies (Gen. 28:17; Judg. 6:22-23; cf. Ezek. 1:28*b*). Nor must man inquire after his name, because it is "Wonderful" (Judg. 13:18; פלאי). The unconsumed burning bush is an extraordinary sight (Exod. 3:2). Before Yahweh performs wonders in Israel, the people must sanctify themselves to him (Josh. 3:5). Man may search out the "hidden things" of God (Job 13:24; Isa. 45:15; 48:6; Jer. 33:3), but he cannot find them out, for they are "too wonderful" (Job 42:3). Yet Israel never ceases to proclaim his wonderful deeds (Exod. 15:11; Deut. 26:8; Pss. 9:1; 105:2; 106:7; 107:8, 15, 21, 31); she rests upon his promise that he will yet perform marvelous acts, wonderful and marvelous (הפלא ופלא להפליא), and praises "him who alone does great wonders" (Ps. 136:4).

j. The holy as "great" (גדול). The adjective has connotations of extraordinary power; they suggest spaciousness, magnitude, and vastness, as in Ps. 104: 1: "O Yahweh my God, thou art very great!" or Ps. 95:3: "For Yahweh is a great God." The force of such passages is seen in the way they are related to the other key words we have been examining, as in the frequent association of "great" and "terrible" (*see* § A2*d above*). When the psalmist contemplates the holiness of Yahweh, he exclaims: "What god is great like our God?" (Ps. 77:13). In an awesome passage tense with deep feeling and striking imagery, Ezekiel reports the divine oracle: "So I will show my greatness and my holiness [התגדלתי והתקדשתי] and make myself known [ונודעתי] in the eyes of many nations" (38:23). This motif of Yahweh's "greatness" is further illustrated by the large number of passages where the adjective "great" precedes the acts of God or the things that belong to him. Thus the Day of Yahweh is a great day (Zeph. 1:14).

k. The holy as exalted. The Holy One of Israel is "high and lifted up" (רם ונשא; Isa. 6:1); he is "exalted" (נשגב), for he dwells "on high" (מרום; Isa. 33:5). He is called *Elyon* (עליון), "Most High." Although this becomes a title for God (Pss. 7:17; 9:2; 50:14; 57:2—H 57:3; etc.), the original connotations of "exaltation," "supremacy," and "loftiness" are seldom lost (Pss. 47:4; 91:9; Dan. 4:2, 17, 25, 32;

5:18). He is exalted in strength and power (Job 36: 22*a;* Ps. 21:13—H 21:14), among the nations and in the whole earth (Ps. 57:5, 11). On the Day of Yahweh he is against all the proud pretensions of civilization and culture, all those things that are proud and haughty and lifted up (Isa. 2:12-15): "Yahweh alone will be exalted in that day" (vss. 11, 17*c*). The *locus classicus* for the Holy One as exalted is Isa. 57:15:

> Thus says the high and lofty One
> who inhabits eternity, whose name is Holy:
> "I dwell in the high and holy place,
> and also with him who is of a contrite and humble spirit."

Again, it is to be observed that many of these contexts appear in the liturgies and celebrations of the cult, in the outbursts of adoration.

l. The holiness of the living God. The "life" of Yahweh and his holiness are closely joined. The divine oath: "As I live," and the human counterpart: "As Yahweh lives" (I Kings 17:12), belong to the same language as does holiness. The living God is a holy God; his "life" is holy life (Deut. 32:40; Josh. 3:10; Pss. 42:2; 84:2-4; Jer. 10:10). This is superbly illustrated in Deut. 5:23-26, where the holiness terminology and symbolism are extraordinarily rich. Here the major theme throughout is life and death. To "hear" the words of God and to "see" him should mean certain death, and yet—here is the wonder of Yahweh's holiness—man still lives, lives by his grace. This is the meaning too of the "Fear not" of the theophanies after the divine self-disclosure. A NT writer summarizes the OT awesomeness before the holy: "It is a fearful thing to fall into the hands of the living God" (Heb. 10:31). Holiness means judgment and death, yet the Holy One consecrates men to his service, equips them with holy powers, in wrath remembers mercy, and calls men to life in his presence. See Deut. 30:15-20; Pss. 36:9; 99; 136; Jer. 1:5; 2:13; 10:6-10; 17:12-13.

m. Summary. The following observations emerge from the foregoing discussion:

a) Holiness cannot be simply equated with perfection or righteousness; this would be to defy the meaning of many passages. The connotations of the word are broader; moreover, some contexts, such as those concerning the ark, have little moral content.

b) The various ascriptions associated with holiness must be read in their total context. Again and again they coalesce, and it is only by discerning their full range that the meaning of holiness can be grasped.

c) Almost throughout, the symbolism of fire is employed, both in the contexts of fire imagery where holiness is not mentioned and in holiness contexts where fire is not mentioned, as well as where they are expressly associated.

d) The foregoing discussion of terminology is by no means exhaustive; other relationships are present also, as, e.g., with "power" and "might." The force of holiness is felt in every sphere of existence. It has been called the source of all other kinds of energy. It is this connection which explains holiness as an agency of judgment, redemption, and grace.

e) There is considerable theological diversity in the biblical understanding of holiness. We have to do with both old and new. The old sometimes belongs to the ideology of holiness among other peoples, as, e.g., in the localization of the holy at particular spots, or in the purificatory practices, or in the presence of sacred harlots in the sanctuaries, קדשות and קדשים; the new belongs to all that is distinctive of Yahweh as he reveals himself in the election-covenant events of the Mosaic age.

3. Holiness historically revealed. Definitions and descriptions are in themselves inadequate ways of portraying the reality of the divine holiness in the OT and the NT. It is rather as holiness is revealed in holy words and holy events that we encounter its power, the effects it produces upon those who experience its presence, and its concrete and diverse manifestations. It is the purpose of the following discussion, therefore, to call attention to the historical revelation of the holy God of Israel in several of the major periods of Israel's faith.

a. In the Yahwist and Elohist sources in Genesis. These do not contain the word "holy," but there are several contexts where its reality is felt, as in Abram's intercession in behalf of Sodom and Gomorrah: "Behold, I have taken upon myself to speak to the Lord, I who am but dust and ashes" (Gen. 18:27 J). Here the patriarch is overcome with a sense of creatureliness before the awesome mystery of Yahweh. Similarly in the vision at Bethel, Jacob feels the dread and darkness of holiness when he awakens. The best example, however, is Yahweh's covenant with Abram in ch. 15. Dread and great darkness fall upon the patriarch after the strange preparation for the sacrifice; "when the sun had gone down and it was dark, behold, a smoking fire pot and a flaming torch passed between these pieces." It is significant that the passage is sometimes thought to be proleptic of Sinai.

b. In J and E. In the early accounts of the revelation to Moses (J and E) holiness assumes a place of central importance. Here we have a personal holy encounter between Moses and Yahweh. Moses may not approach the bush because the land about it is קדש, but the voice which speaks from the bush is Yahweh's. It is a concrete historical experience with a personal holy God. Similarly in the revelation to Israel at the Mount the holy God speaks to the people out of the midst of the fire, engaging them in a particular relationship and calling them to decision. The Decalogue (Exod. 20:1-17) and the later Torah belong to the same context of holiness. The whole of Exod. 19 is a living narrative in which everything is holy, and Yahweh's promise that Israel will be a holy nation (גוי קדוש; vs. 6) is thus given its appropriate setting as are the extensive תורות which follow (20:1–23:33; cf. Exod. 24, another holy engagement also followed by תורות). Exod. 15 is later than the Mosaic age, but it preserves an authentic memory in its remarkable stress upon holiness and its major relationships and activities (vss. 11, 13, 16).

Yahweh's entrance into a holy compact with a people at Sinai is the *fons et origo* of the life of the holy people (עם קדוש) and the beginning of that movement which continued, albeit in often confused and broken ways, through the holy wars of the Conquest and the proclamation of the prophets, into the NT, where it was remembered, deepened, and granted fresh perspectives. Israel could confess:

"Yahweh our God is holy!" (Ps. 99:9) because Yahweh had made himself known as a holy God, spoken his holy name, required holy statutes, ordained holy times and seasons, and appointed to his service holy men whose mission it was to perform his holy will, fulfil his holy purpose, and live in holy obedience.

c. In the book of Joshua. Joshua repeats many Mosaic motifs, including the episode of the holy ground (5:13-15). In the account of the violation of the *ḥērem* (Josh. 7), the people must be "sanctified," and in the covenant at Shechem (Josh. 24) significantly the emphasis upon Yahweh as a holy and jealous God is preserved. While the book of Judges contains the root קדש but once (17:3) and that in a special source, we have vivid accounts of charismatic endowment in connection with the holy war. The Spirit of Yahweh (רוח יהוה) rushes upon or clothes the leaders and fills them with extraordinary powers. Yahweh as the איש מלחמה is in the midst of the camp and wreaks terrible havoc and confusion on the foe. War is a holy undertaking, and the participants are therefore holy. The stories of the ark (I Sam. 3:1–7:2) illustrate the supernatural powers of the sacred palladium and the deadly effects upon those who violate its sanctity. But whatever primitive aspects these stories possess—and they are many—it is well to be reminded that the ark was the throne on which Yahweh was seated invisibly as Israel's king. The tragic vicissitudes in the Philistine cities and Uzzah's fatal misadventure (II Sam. 6:6-9) reveal the terrible and impersonal force of the taboo; there is little here to suggest the influence of Mosaic and covenantal faith. Yet the account must also be read in its larger framework.

d. In the Prophets. The prophets of Israel were heirs of a holy tradition reaching back to the time of Moses, in which Yahweh's holy will and purpose were determinative for the existence and destiny of the holy people. The cultic songs and liturgies praised and exalted his holy activity (e.g., Exod. 15), and the cultic laws were Israel's response to the demands of the covenant relation (Exod. 19:5-6; 20:23–23:33). Both exercised a strong influence upon the prophets, upon their theology as well as upon the literary forms in which it found expression. The affirmation "Yahweh our God is holy" now becomes articulate in the identification of the nature of Yahweh with the holy. That Yahweh swears by his holiness (קדשו; Amos 4:2) is tantamount to his swearing by himself (נפשו; Amos 6:8).

Hosea accentuates the ancient motif of the holy presence "in your midst" (11:9; cf. Exod. 34:9; Num. 5:3; 14:14; Josh. 24:5) and gives to it a depth of meaning transcending the legal-institutional interpretations of the covenant bond. The personal inwardness of the holy relation, as well as the defiance of conventional structures, give him a place in Israel's holiness theology surpassed by no other. While full justice is given to the destructive and punitive activities of holiness, it now finds deeper expression in the conquering holy love rooted in the covenantal bond of grace:

> I am God and not man,
> the Holy One in your midst,
> and I will not come to destroy.

With Isaiah of Jerusalem the absoluteness of the divine holiness is carried to unprecedented heights: Yahweh is the "Holy One of Israel" (1:4; 5:19, 24; 10:20; 12:6; 17:7; 29:19, 23; 30:11-12, 15). He is King absolutely and Holy One absolutely, but holiness is primary. He is the sovereign Holy One. But what gives substance to Isaiah's theology of holiness is the way in which the traditional motifs associated with holiness (*see* § A2 *above*) receive fresh and powerful reformulation (cf., e.g., the fire symbolism in 10:16-17; 30:27-28; 31:9). It is clear that the cult has exercised a profound influence upon the prophet, just as he, in turn, was destined to influence both his prophetic successors, Habakkuk (1:12-13; 3:3—H 3:2), Ezekiel (5:11; 28:22, 25; 36:22-23), and Second Isaiah, and the priestly teachers and legislators (the Holiness Code and the P legislation).

Second Isaiah was just as radical in his reformulation of the contexts and dynamic qualities of the holy as was Isaiah. For here Yahweh is not only the Holy One absolutely (Isa. 40:25; 41:14-16; 43:3; 45:11; 47:4; 48:17; 49:7; 55:5), but more especially the Holy One in relation to his redemptive activity (41:14; 43:3, 14; 47:4; 48:17; 49:7; 54:5). Yet the Prophet of the Exile is not projecting anything new, for the holiness of Yahweh's redemption from slavery belonged to the traditions which he above all others appropriated, albeit in eschatological dimensions.

It is clear from the foregoing discussion that the prophets of Israel have oriented holiness to the major stream of biblical faith, which had its beginnings in the religion of Moses. Yet holiness has also been deepened and transformed by a more exclusive emphasis upon the personal: the holiness of God is personal holiness and is active in the whole realm of history as well as in the lives of his servants the prophets. It is against this background that we are to understand the "ethical" character of holiness. To understand Isaiah's conception of Yahweh's holiness, it is not sufficient to cite references; we must view them in their historical contexts. When in his vision the prophet hears the trisagion of the seraphim, he sees himself as he is before Yahweh's majestic and penetrating holiness. He is stricken (אוי לי "woe is me"), utterly undone or "destroyed" (נדמיתי), a man of unclean lips (כי איש טמא שפתים אנכי), dwelling among a people that is unclean. Only the atonement through holy fire from the altar can avail him. He has seen the King:

> Yahweh of hosts is exalted in justice
> [ויגבה במשפט],
> and the Holy God shows himself holy in righteousness
> [האל הקדוש נקדש בצדקה] (Isa. 5:16).

The distance between the holy and the profane appears in the contrast between man's sin and God's utter perfection. Yet holiness is not simply identified with moral categories; the transcendence, "otherness," and exalted majesty of Yahweh still remain after the moral categories are exhausted (cf. Isa. 31:1).

Again, the holiness of God is now understood more clearly as active, less as a condition or state of being or even supernatural energy and more as an expression of his will and purpose. It manifests itself in judgment and destruction, notably in Isaiah (1:4-9;

5:13-16; 30:8-14), especially on the Day of Yahweh (2:6-22), and in Ezekiel (28:22; 36:20-32; 38:17-23), but in the other prophets too (Amos 4:2-3; 6:8; cf. chs. 1-2; Mic. 1:2-4; cf., however, Hos. 11:9). It is active in mercy and grace, in redemption and salvation (Isa. 10:20-23; 12:6; 17:7-9; 29:19-21; see also Second Isaiah *above*).

Notable, too, is the divine self-manifestation. This is expressed in a variety of syntactical forms (e.g., *pi'el, hithpa'el,* but especially the *niph'al*) and the theologoumena of revelation: "glory" (כבוד), "honor" (הוד), "majesty" (הדר), and "name" (שם)—all, of course, in the immediate contexts of "holiness" (קדש). In the sight of all the nations God manifests his holiness (Ezek. 20:31; 28:25; 36:23; 38:23), for his holy name must not be profaned among them; therefore he acts for his name's sake only (למען שמי; Ezek. 20: 44; 36:22-23; 39:25) that it may be vindicated (36: 23: וקדשתי את שמי הגדולה) and no longer profaned. Ezekiel's awareness of the divine holiness is more awesome, more sublime and majestic, more cosmic and "tremendous," than that of his prophetic predecessors, precisely because he, more than any other, knows the horror of profanation. For him sin is, above all, a profaning of what is holy and of him who is holy. God shows his holiness, too, in his act of calling the prophets to his service, as we recognize particularly in Jeremiah (1:5; 23:9), the most subjective of the prophets, who therefore suffered most from the compulsions and restraints of his holy calling. From all this it can be seen that holiness is not confined solely to the sphere of the cult, but extends itself to the peoples of the world and to world history.

Holiness and GLORY (כבוד) are closely related. The latter is employed for the external manifestation of Yahweh. It is probable that both have their original phenomenological associations with fire, holiness stressing its heat and power and danger, and glory its light, radiance, glow, etc. Naturally they tend to coalesce at times, but together they form a vast and impressive, indeed central, theology of revelation.

e. The priestly development. In considering the place of holiness in priestly life and practice, it is essential to recognize that the relatively late sources, the Holiness and Priestly codes, often reflect attitudes and activities which are not only very early but also contemporary with the preaching ministries of the prophets. Again, it is important to keep in mind that a substantial portion of the OT belongs to the priestly stratum of Israel's faith. The modern tendency to exalt prophetic religion has often had the effect of obscuring a major and important part of Israel's religious life and actual religious practice. Thus the faith of Israel is viewed in a distorted perspective. Finally, it is precarious to draw a sharp line between prophet and priest. The two had much more in common than we are accustomed to think. Not only were they mutually indebted to each other, but both belonged to the same cult and both were therefore dedicated to the common life and work of holiness. Nevertheless, within this common world of faith there are movements and directions of which we must take account, more particularly in the exilic and postexilic period (after 587 B.C.).

a) The true Israelite must know what is holy and what is not, in order that he may worship his God properly and that he may protect himself from harm and defilement (Lev. 10; 16; 22:17-33). As the emphasis upon the cult grew, the distinctions between the holy and the profane, the clean and the unclean, were not only more sharply drawn than heretofore, but were subjected to elaborate casuistic development. Moreover, the conceptions of the holy tended to be increasingly limited to the realm of the cult and its objects: holy garments (Exod. 28:2, 4; 29:21; 31: 10), holy offerings (Exod. 28:36; Lev. 19:8), holy priestly crown (Exod. 29:6; 39:30), holy flesh (Exod. 29:37), anointing oil (Exod. 30:31-37; Num. 35:25; Ps. 89:20); the tabernacle and its furnishings (Exod. 40:9), holy fruit (Lev. 19:24) and food (Lev. 22:14; Ezra 2:63). Laws of purification to ensure cultic purity became increasingly important (Lev. 21; Mal. 1:10-14). Holy times were also rigorously observed, holy days and holy seasons—the sabbath above all, for it was viewed as the very purpose of God's creation of the heavens and earth. The Priestly historian brings his account of creation to a culmination in its sanctification: "God blessed the seventh day and hallowed it [ויקדש]." Thus creation is drawn into the sphere of holiness, and the name of God is hallowed in the creation of men. The true order then becomes sanctification, creation, worship; thus God's holy purpose is realized.

b) Yet all this must not be construed to imply the exclusion of the ethical stress of the prophets. On the contrary, as we have seen, men like Isaiah and Ezekiel left their impress upon the theology and rituals of the cult. This is illustrated both in the songs, hymns, and prayers of the temple worship and in the legal formulations of the Holiness and Priestly codes. Such "Torah liturgies" as Pss. 15; 24:3-5; Isa. 33:14*b*-16; 56:1-8 describe the kind of Israelite who may enter into Yahweh's presence. Only he who is of pure heart (בר לבב) and real integrity (תמים) may "look on Yahweh's face." Lev. 19 is a superb example of the meaning of holiness in the life of the faithful son of the covenant. Here, as elsewhere in the Holiness Code, the solemn words "I am Yahweh your God" are repeated again and again, but it is the topic sentence which gives point and substance to this mighty self-asseveration: "You shall be holy; for I am holy, Yahweh your God" (vs. 2). These words are now applied to every facet of Israel's existence, but wherever men are involved with each other holiness means love—love to neighbor, to the resident alien, the blind, the deaf, and the slave. Significantly, the chapter comes to its climax by pointing out that this God to whom Israel owes its devotion is the one who revealed himself in the great act of redemption from slavery. *See* WORSHIP IN THE OT.

c) Holiness as the personal nature of Yahweh finds living expression in the worship and theology of the Name (השם). Where Yahweh causes his name to be remembered (יזכיר), there worship takes place, for it is there that the sanctuary arises, the name is spoken, addressed, and called upon. Not a spatial image but a spoken word is central. This emphasis is particularly strong in Deuteronomy, but Ezekiel makes much of it in Yahweh's sanctification of his name and his acting "for his name's sake." Similarly, the Holiness and Priestly codes employ the term frequently, and it appears also in the hymnic literature (I Chr. 16:10, 35; Pss. 33:21; 103:1), always as an expression of intensely personal relation to the personal Holy One.

B. *IN THE NT*. 1. Etymology and usage. Of the various terms employed by the ancient Greeks to express the idea of holiness—ἵερος, ὅσιος, σέμνος, ἅγιος, ἅγνος—the word ἅγιος is least frequent. On the other hand, in biblical usage it is precisely ἅγιος which receives the pre-eminence over all others. The other terms are also present, to be sure: e.g., ἵερος (II Tim. 3:15); ὅσιος (Acts 2:27; 13:34, quoted from Isa. 55:3; Heb. 7:26); σέμνος (I Tim. 3:8; Tit. 2:2); ἅγνος (II Cor. 6:6; 7:11; I Tim. 5:22); but it is ἅγιος and its derivatives which occur most frequently and in a great variety of syntactical and semantic associations. The reason is not far to seek. The Septuagintal translators sought to do justice to the OT usage of קדש and its cognates, to the historico-ethical meanings which were attached to it, and to the personal nature of the holy as was expressed, e.g., in its connection with compassion, love, and mercy. They employed the word ἅγιος, but gave to it a latitude and depth for which the Greeks possessed nothing remotely similar. For our understanding of the word, then, we are indebted to its Semitic background as it is found in the canonical writings of the Old Covenant.

In the Hellenistic period ἅγιος is employed as an epithet for the gods, especially the Egyptian and Syrian, like Isis, Serapis, and Baal; thence it is applied to the Greek divinities, above all in the mystery religions. Oriental influence is perceptible in this later usage, so that ἅγιος is close to the Hebrew קדש. In the apocryphal literature the canonical usage is perpetuated. Allusion is made to the holiness of Jerusalem (Tob. 13:9; I Macc. 2:7), of the temple (I Esd. 1:53; II Macc. 5:15), of the altar (Ecclus. 45:10), of the sabbath (Tob. 2:1; II Macc. 5:25), of the covenant (I Macc. 1:15, 63), also of the heavens (Wisd. Sol. 9:10), of the angels (Tob. 11:14; 12:15), of the Spirit (Wisd. Sol. 1:5; Ecclus. 48:12) and particularly of God (Tob. 12:12, 15; Ecclus. 23:9; II Macc. 14:36). The authors or translators of these works render קדש in essentially the same manner. In rabbinical literature too the linguistic practice is by and large that of the OT. Among the most frequent appellations for the Deity is "the Holy One" (הקדוש). Since the holy name was too sacred to be pronounced, such titles became more and more common and impressive; indeed, "the Name" (השם) itself becomes a surrogate for "Yahweh." Allusions are made to the Holy Spirit also (רוח הקדש) in the texts of the third century. The Scriptures are regarded as holy, the Torah above all, and those who obey it are sometimes called holy.

2. The NT understanding of holiness. The OT, then, forms the firm basis upon which the NT understanding of holiness is built. There is variety, of course, as within the OT, and this is of two kinds: (*a*) difference in nuance according to the nature of the particular context and (*b*) a radical reorientation because of the faith that the Messiah had come in Jesus and that through him God had brought into existence a new age and a new creation. We encounter many of the same associations of ἅγιος with other terms, as in the OT: e.g., "fire" (Luke 3:16; Acts 2:3; I Cor. 3:13; Heb. 12:29; Rev. 4:5-6), "wrath" (Rom. 1:18; 2:5-10; 5:9; I Thess. 1:10; Heb. 4:3), "cleanness" and "purity" (Luke 11:37-41; Acts 21:28; II Cor. 7:1; Eph. 5:26; Heb. 9:13-14), "majesty" (Heb. 8:1-2; II Pet. 1:16-18), "exaltation" (Phil. 2:9; Heb. 7:26). The author of the Letter to the Hebrews, in describing Christ as the heavenly high priest, brings some of these ascriptions together (7:26): "holy" (ὅσιος), "blameless" (ἄκακος), "unstained" (ἀμίαντας), "separated from sinners" (κεχωρισμένος ἀπὸ τῶν ἁμαρτωλῶν), "exalted above the heavens" (ὑψηλότερος τῶν οὐρανῶν; cf. Col. 3:12-13). The prevailingly cultic usage of the terminology of holiness in the OT is found in the NT too, often in places where we do not suspect its presence. But what distinguishes the NT preoccupation with holiness from the OT more than aught else is its predication of holiness to the Spirit of God (*see* HOLY SPIRIT). The OT employs the expression "holy Spirit" only three times (Ps. 51:11—H 51:13; Isa. 63:10-11), whereas the NT has it more often than all other occurrences of the word "holy," about ninety times. Sanctification plays a correspondingly great role.

a. The holiness of God. The NT reaffirms the OT confession: "The Lord our God is holy," but it is surprising that it does so relatively seldom. It is obviously one of those major expressions of faith which were assumed. In the LORD'S PRAYER the first petition, "Hallowed be thy name" (Ἁγιασθήτω τὸ ὄνομά σου; Matt. 6:9; Luke 11:2), corresponds to contemporary Jewish usage, not only in its phraseology but also in its association with prayer for the coming of the kingdom. The subject here is God, not man. His name is his person, as in the OT (*see* § A3*d above;* also Ezek. 20:41; 38:16). The petition, like the whole prayer, is eschatologically oriented. What is more, the hallowing of the Name, with its opposite, the profanation of the Name, was "the most characteristic feature of Jewish ethics both as principle and as motive" (G. F. Moore [*see bibliography*]), yet the roots of this understanding lie deeply embedded in the OT. The apocalyptic seer places the trisagion of Isa. 6:3 in a sublime setting by combining it with Ezekiel's vision (Rev. 4:6*b*-10); the four living creatures round the throne sing ceaselessly:

> Holy, holy, holy, is the Lord God Almighty
> [ὁ παντοκράτωρ],
> who was and is and is to come!

and they "give glory [δόξα] and honor [τιμὴ] and thanks [εὐχαριστία] to him who is seated on the throne." Again, in another canticle of praise, the "song of Moses, the servant of God, and the song of the Lamb," a whole series of awesome ascriptions belonging to holiness terminology ("great," "wonderful," "almighty," "just," "true," "King of the ages," "fear," etc.) culminates: "For thou only art holy" (cf. Ps. 99 and especially Rev. 16:4-7). It is notable that in both the OT and the NT the theme of holiness is expressed in the ultimate lyricism of adoration. In I Peter, too, the holiness of God is affirmed, now in the impressive setting of the vocation of the people of God: "As he who called you is holy, be holy yourselves in all your conduct" (1:15; cf. Exod. 19:3*b*-8), and the admonition is enforced by the central words of the Holiness Code, Israel's election to holiness: "You shall be holy, for I am holy" (I Pet. 1:16). Significantly, the following verse speaks of God as Father and of his redemptive work through the precious blood of Christ. Finally, in the high-priestly prayer of John 17, in words of great intensity and solemnity, Jesus addresses God as Holy Father (πατὲρ ἅγιε). Here the tensions between the divine distance and nearness are resolved (cf. Isa. 57:15) and are reminiscent of the Lord's Prayer: "Father, may thy name be sanctified." It is in praise, holy calling, and prayer, then, that the holiness of God is celebrated by the early Christians as it was also in the exultation, vocation, and worship of the children of the old covenant.

b. The holiness of Jesus Christ. The ascription of holiness to Jesus appears only infrequently in the NT (Mark 1:24; Luke 1:35; 4:34; John 6:69; Acts 3:14; 4:27, 30; I John 2:20; Rev. 3:7). One reason for this may be the large place assumed by the activity of the Holy Spirit in the thought and worship of the early Christians; perhaps, too, other titles and appellations drawn from traditional messianic phraseology were felt to be more immediately apposite. At the same time, when Jesus is called "the Holy One" (cf. הקדוש), it is generally a messianic ascription. Thus he who came at the end of the age to destroy the world of demons is confessed by the demons to be "the Holy One of God" (ὁ ἅγιος τοῦ Θεοῦ; Mark 1:24; Luke 4:34).

In Luke the holiness of Jesus is already related to his birth in words filled with awe and wonder. The angel addresses Mary:

> The Holy Spirit will come upon you,
> and the power of the Most High will overshadow you;
> therefore the child to be born will be called holy,
> the Son of God (1:35; cf. Matt. 1:20).

In the Benedictus (Luke 1:68-79) and elsewhere the echoes of the holy-war terminology, now applied to Christ's mighty works of deliverance, are plainly heard.

The Fourth Gospel transforms the Petrine confession into a solemn declaration of faith: "We have believed [πεπιστεύκαμεν], and have come to know [ἐγνώκαμεν], that you are the Holy One of God [ὁ ἅγιος τοῦ Θεοῦ]" (6:69).

In I John the reference is probably to Christ when the writer addresses his followers: "You have been anointed by the Holy One" (2:20).

Again in the high-priestly prayer we encounter the motif which is present *mutatis mutandis* in the OT, notably in Ezekiel in the divine self-sanctifying: "For their sake I consecrate myself [ἁγιάζω ἐμαυτόν], that they also may be consecrated [ἡγιασμένοι] in truth" (John 17:19).

The introduction to the letter to the church of Philadelphia (Rev. 3:7), as so often in Revelation, adds fresh nuances to the title: "The words of the holy one, the true one, who has the key of David."

The book of Acts follows its own course by identifying the Holy One with the Servant of the Lord of Second Isaiah. Thus Jesus is called God's servant (τὸν παῖδα αὐτοῦ), the Holy and Righteous One (ἅγιον καὶ δίκαιον) whom he has glorified (3:14; see Isa. 44:23; 49:3; 53:11; 55:5). Peter and John and their friends rejoice in the signs and wonders performed "through the name of thy holy servant Jesus" (τοῦ ἁγίου παιδός σου Ἰησοῦ; Acts 4:30). Whatever the original identification of the Servant may have been, here there is no question that it is understood messianically, that it is the Messiah who is holy, and that Jesus has fulfilled the "messianic" expectations.

The writer of the Letter to the Hebrews, while not ascribing the title of the Holy One to Christ, nevertheless has much to say of his sanctifying office (*see* SANCTIFICATION). Both as high priest (cf. Ps. 106:16: קדוש יהוה) and as sacrificial offering, Christ is the mediator of a new covenant, purifies the conscience from dead works (Heb. 9:13-15), abolishes the old sacrifices, so that "we have been sanctified through the offering of the body of Jesus Christ once for all" (Heb. 10:1, 10, 14; 13:12-13). It is clear that the mind of the writer has been thoroughly imbued with OT covenantal, sacerdotal, and sacrificial thought and that it serves him well for the elaboration of his theology of the mediatorial work of Christ (cf. Exod. 19:6; Leviticus; Jer. 31:31-34).

c. The holiness of the church. The NT church is successor to the worshiping community of the old covenant and sees its beginnings in its memories and expectations (*see* CHURCH, IDEA OF; CHURCH, LIFE AND ORGANIZATION OF; CHURCH, WORSHIP OF). In its appropriation of the sacred writings of Israel with their anticipation of the new age, the new covenant, the new creation, the new birth in water and in Spirit, the new heart, it possessed the categories and symbols out of which the new age was to be interpreted. The ancient accounts of the establishment of sanctuaries through the holy presence and the *hieros logos;* the remembering, celebrating, teaching, sacrificing, and confessing activities of the ongoing life of the cult; the sacred objects like the ark or the altar or the temple furnishings; the temple itself, with its elaborate paraphernalia and imagery; the cultic personnel; the life and worship of the synagogue; the liturgical development in hymns and prayers—to all these the church was heir. Where it did not appropriate the old forms and images, it was destined to enter into dialogue and encounter with the categories in the light of the emergence of the decisively new in the revelation and redemption of Jesus the Christ. Thus the idea of the holy people (עם קדוש) perpetuated itself in the early Christian worshiping community (Exod. 19:6; Heb. 9:15-22; 12:18-24; I Pet. 1:14-16; 2:9-10; see also Rom. 11:13-16; Eph. 2:12). Once the Gentiles were "separated" from the commonwealth of Israel (τῆς πολιτείας τοῦ Ἰσραήλ), strangers to the covenants of promise, "without God in the world," but now they are "brought near" in the blood of Christ, who has reconciled them to God in one body through the Cross, so that they are no longer strangers but members of the household of God, built upon the foundation of the apostles and prophets, Christ Jesus being the chief cornerstone in whom the whole structure is joined together; and they have become a "holy temple in the Lord" (Eph. 2:11-22). They are called to a new life, called to be saints (κλητοῖς ἁγίοις; Rom. 1:7; I Cor. 1:2), yet they are Abraham's children if they "do what is right"

(I Pet. 3:15; *see* SAINT). The distinctively moral connotations of ἅγιος are by no means clear in Paul; the moral transformation wrought in the life of the Christian on which he lays great stress is not called holiness. But the writer of Ephesians is at great pains to describe the life of the ἅγιοι (5:2-20), as is the writer of Colossians (3:5-17), who, in addressing "God's chosen ones, holy and beloved," describes the nature of the new life in Christ and brings his admonitions to a great finale: "Whatever you do, in word or deed, do everything in the name of the Lord Jesus, giving thanks to God the Father through him." If the vocabulary of holiness is not attributed to God and Christ as often as we should expect, it nevertheless permeates the whole NT as it does the OT, by the activity of the Holy Spirit, by the life and conduct of "the saints," by its intimate association with other central words like "elect," "beloved," "faithful," and by the allusions to "holy prophets" (Acts 3:21), "holy apostles" (Eph. 3:5), "holy calling" (II Tim. 1:9), "holy scriptures" (Rom. 1:2), "holy covenant" (Luke 1:72), "holy law" (Rom. 7:12; II Pet. 2:21), and by its constant dependence upon the OT scriptures.

Bibliography. W. W. Graf von Baudissin, *Studien zur semitischen Religionsgeschichte,* vol. II (1878); H. Cremer and J. Kögel, *Biblisch-theologisch Wörterbuch* (11 Auflage, 1923), pp. 34-62. G. F. Moore, *Judaism* (2 vols.; 1927), II, 100-111. J. Begrich, "Heilig," *Religion in Geschichte und Gegenwart* (Zweite Auflage, 1928), cols. 1714-21. R. Asting, *Die Heiligkeit im Urchristentum* (1930). J. Hänel, *Die Religion der Heiligkeit* (1931). J. Hempel, *Gott und Mensch im AT* (1936). R. Otto, *The Idea of the Holy* (trans. J. W. Harvey; 10th ed., 1946). J. Pedersen, *Israel: Its Life and Culture* (2 vols.; 1926, 1947). O. Procksch, *Theologie des alten Testaments* (1950). W. Eichrodt, *Theologie des alten Testaments,* Teil I: "Gott und Volk" (5. neubearbeitete Auflage, 1957), pp. 176-85 and *passim.*

J. MUILENBURG

HOLINESS CODE. *See* PENTATEUCH.

HOLM TREE [תרזה, *tirzâ*(?); πρῖνον] (Isa. 44:14; KJV CYPRESS). A tree used both for firewood and for idol manufacture. Some botanists identify *tirzâ* with the holm oak, *Quercus ilex* L., a small, holly-like evergreen oak. Sus. 58 is a clear reference to this oak, where it is a tree in the garden of Joakim in Babylon.

The translation "holm tree" in Isa. 44:14 is confusing, since the true holm is a holly, *Ilex aquifolium.* The holm oak hardly suits the context. The root רזה, meaning "to be lean," might support the identification with the slender cypress, *Cupressus sempervirens* var. *pyramidalis,* so common in Bible lands. The context implies either a conifer or an oak.

See also CYPRESS; FIR; PLANE TREE.

J. C. TREVER

HOLOFERNES hŏl'ə fûr'nēz ['Ολοφέρνης; *cf.* 'ολοφρονέω, be crafty, deceitful]. The Assyrian general, commissioned by King Nebuchadnezzar to subdue the "whole west country" (Jth. 2:6), who met ultimate defeat at the hands of a woman.

Leading a well-equipped army of 120,000 foot soldiers and 12,000 cavalry, Holofernes established a reign of terror in Mediterranean lands, seeking everywhere to destroy all worship except that of Nebuchadnezzar. Threatening to invade Judea, he was warned by Achior the Ammonite that the people who dwelt there were under the protection of a god who was invincible. The swash-buckling General Holofernes brushed aside the advice of Achior and laid siege to Judea. In desperation, the Hebrews urged their leaders to surrender. The widowed Judith, obtaining permission to pass through the lines, beguiled the mighty warrior with her charms. When he was drunk, she cut off his head and won deliverance for her people.

He who had been second only in power to Nebuchadnezzar was disarmed by a woman's beauty. This has been a favorite theme of artists (using him as an example of defeated pride, Dante [*Purgatorio* XII.59] places him in the Circle of the Proud).

Under Artaxerxes III a general named Holofernes invaded Asia Minor (Diodorus Siculus *History* 31.19. 2-3).

J. C. SWAIM

HOLON hō'lŏn [חלן, חלון, sandy(?)]. **1.** A village of Judah in the hill-country district of Debir (Josh. 15:51); designated a Kohathite Levitical city (Josh. 21:15; cf. I Chr. 6:58; HILEN). The usual identification with Khirbet 'Alin, near Jala, NW of Hebron, would place it more properly in the province of Beth-zur (Josh. 15:58-59) rather than that of Debir.

V. R. GOLD

2. A town in the tableland of Moab, mentioned with Jahzah, Mephaath, and others (Jer. 48:21). Its site is unknown.

HOLY ARRAY. *See* ARRAY, HOLY.

HOLY GHOST. *See* HOLY SPIRIT.

HOLY OF HOLIES ["Αγια 'Αγίων] (Heb. 9:3); KJV HOLIEST OF ALL. The inmost sanctuary of the temple. *See* MOST HOLY PLACE; TABERNACLE; TEMPLE, JERUSALEM.

HOLY ONE, THE [קדוש; ὁ ἅγιος]; THE HOLY ONE OF ISRAEL [קדוש ישראל]. In the OT, the title of Yahweh, Israel's God, especially in the prophecy of Isaiah (1:4; 5:19, 24; 10:17, 20) and of Second Isaiah (40:25; 41:14, 16, 20; 43:3, 14-15). In the NT the title is applied to the Messiah (Mark 1:24; Acts 3:14; cf. I John 2:20).

See GOD, OT VIEW OF, § 4*a*.

B. W. ANDERSON

HOLY PLACE [קדש, מקום קדש]. The TABERNACLE or tent of meeting; the courts, inner room, and outer room of the tabernacle; the TEMPLE and its precincts (cf. Exod. 26:33; 28:29; 29:31; 38:24; 40:9; Lev. 6:9, 19-20; 10:4, 17-18; etc.).

HOLY SEPULCHRE [קבר; τάφος *or* μνῆμα *or* μνημεῖον; Vulg. *sepulcrum*]. The Jerusalem cave where Jesus of Nazareth was entombed.

In the OT and NT there are numerous references to TOMBS, and in the NT there are three different Greek words for this term. The "holy sepulchre" refers to all those instances in the NT where the reference is to the tomb of Jesus, although it is nowhere described as "holy." Mark and Luke imply, and Matt. 27:60 specifies, that the tomb belonged to Joseph of Arimathea, and they state he had hewn it out himself. They say nothing about its location.

Mark does not state—though the three other gospels add it—that no burial had previously been made in this tomb. The account of John is quite different from the others, as it casually notes that there was a garden there with a new tomb in it, and because the Preparation Day was about to begin, they laid Jesus therein (implying that this was a tentative measure).

There is no record from the first three Christian centuries that any place had been marked as the holy sepulchre. Eusebius recounts that the Emperor Constantine directed Bishop Macarius to ascertain this site, and that divine guidance led him to locate the tomb despite the fact that it was buried and needed to be excavated. Constantine then erected over this tomb the Church of the Anastasis, a circular domed structure which replaced Hadrian's Temple of Aphrodite, which was at the same time demolished. This new church stood at the W end of a large court, within which also he built the Church of Golgotha. Constantine's development of these holy sites was first attested by the Bordeaux Pilgrim and Eusebius, who were his contemporaries. The site thus chosen for the holy sepulchre is the one now marked by the Aedicule within the domed rotunda of the later and larger Church of the Holy Sepulchre, inside the present walls. Figs. HOL 29-30.

Courtesy of the Philosophical Library

29. Bell tower and dome of the Church of the Holy Sepulchre

Courtesy of the Philosophical Library

30. Court and façade of the Church of the Holy Sepulchre

There is one other site which has been accepted by many as the holy sepulchre, generally known as the "garden tomb." It is a short distance N of the Damascus Gate, on the W side of "Gordon's Calvary" (*see* GOLGOTHA). It came to attention *ca.* 1867 and more recently has been cultivated into an attractive and quiet spot. Actually, this rock-cut tomb is one of many in the area, so that even the argument of the proximity to Golgotha lends no support for validity. The "garden tomb" and "Gordon's Calvary" may stand or fall together as authentic sites.

Bibliography. G. Dalman, *Sacred Sites and Ways* (1935), pp. 346-81; C. W. Crowfoot, *Early Churches in Palestine* (1941), pp. 9-21; C. C. McCown, *The Ladder of Progress in Palestine* (1943), pp. 244-53; L. Farmer, *We Saw the Holy City* (rev. ed., 1953), pp. 146-63. K. W. CLARK

HOLY SPIRIT [רוח קדש; πνεῦμα ἅγιον]. The mysterious power of God, conceived in the first place as the mode of God's activity, manifested especially in supernatural revelation to selected individuals and in their being possessed by a force which gave them marvelous strength, courage, wisdom, and the knowledge of God's will and his dealings with men; later identified with the personal presence of God, and regarded as the distinctive endowment of his people; and in the NT understood as the mode of God's operation in the church, made possible through the work of Christ and mediating the glorified Christ to his people and the church to its exalted Head.

1. OT conceptions of the Spirit. ***a. As possessing Israel's heroes.*** The Spirit of the Lord is regarded as the source of the endowment of Israel's heroes with extraordinary physical strength (Judg. 14:6, 19; 15:14). It is a supernatural and unpredictable power, which takes possession of a man, and controls his actions like a tremendous inner force. In such contexts "spirit" retains something of its original meaning of "wind." As the wind seizes upon the dust of the ground and animates it, blowing it where it will, like a live object, so the divine Spirit animates the human personality. Occasionally the Spirit, conceived in this fashion as a quasi-physical force, lays hold of a man physically, so as to raise him up and set him on his feet (Ezek. 2:2; 3:12, 24) and even, apparently, to transport him from one place to another (11:24; cf. the action of the "angel of the Lord" in Bel 36). The action of the Spirit in taking possession of a person can be dramatically described as "clothing itself" with the human being, putting him on like an outward garment, so completely does the Spirit become the dynamic inner power which energizes the possessed person (Judg. 6:34; cf. ERV mg.).

b. As inspiring rulers. The Spirit, however, is principally thought of as the source of mental and spiritual perception and abilities, for it is the divine activity which inspires certain specially favored individuals and so heightens their natural powers by its supernatural energy as to bestow upon them all those qualities which they need in order to fulfil their calling successfully. It is by the action of the Spirit that kings and rulers receive the gifts necessary for leadership. The judges, in particular, are represented as Spirit-possessed men, gifted with qualities that enable them to govern Israel and save her from her oppressors; thus it is said of Othniel that "the Spirit of the LORD came upon him, and he judged Israel," and it was under the influence of the Spirit of the Lord that Gideon roused the tribes to repel the hostile Midianites and Jephthah advanced against the Ammonitish invaders (Judg. 3:10; 6:34; 11:29). Saul was similarly empowered to lead Israel to the relief of Jabesh-gilead (I Sam. 11:6). Of more significance in the history of the OT belief in the working of the Spirit is the Spirit-possession of David after Saul had anointed him (I Sam. 16:13). As the divinely chosen king of Israel, David was a Spirit-filled ruler, and it is significant that it was after his choice and anointing that the Spirit of the Lord is said to have departed from Saul.

Hence the expectations associated with the house of David point to the hope of a ruler pre-eminently endowed with the Spirit of God. The ideal figure of an inspired king, as it is portrayed by Isaiah (11:2), has the distinctive characteristic of Spirit-possession, through which he receives the sevenfold abundance of those gifts that are the special qualities of a wise and just ruler. This inward unction with the Spirit is evidently thought of as having an outward counterpart in the external rite of anointing (cf. Ps. 89:20-21). This link between the ideas of anointing and of Spirit-possession reappears in connection with the SERVANT OF THE LORD (Isa. 42:1) and the divinely sent prophet of Isa. 61:1, and in this respect associates these figures with that of the Israelite monarch. The primitive church's conception of the messiahship of Jesus owes much to the two last-named passages, no doubt because he had himself interpreted his mission in terms of the Servant and the prophet of Isa. 61 (if these can properly be separated).

In the OT, however, the conception of a messianic bearer of the Spirit plays little part. It appears more explicitly in the postcanonical literature, as, e.g., in an echo of Isaiah's prophecy: "The Lord of Spirits seated him on the throne of his glory, and the Spirit of righteousness was poured out upon him" (Enoch 62:2; cf. 49:3). The idea that the future Messiah (*see* MESSIAH [JEWISH]) would be the bearer of the Spirit became fused with the expectation of a universal outpouring of the Spirit at the end of the present age. The general blessings of the future are associated particularly with the resting of the Spirit upon the Messiah (Pss. Sol. 17:42), and the Testament of Levi, if it is to be reckoned as a pre-Christian document, affords evidence for the hope that as a consequence of the saving activity of the "high priest" the Spirit of the Lord will come upon his people (18).

The NT sees the fulfilment of the hope of a Spirit-possessed Messiah in the coming of the Spirit upon Jesus at his baptism (Matt. 3:16; Mark 1:10; Luke 3:21; John 1:33), when "God anointed Jesus of Nazareth with the Holy Spirit and with power" (Acts 10:38). *See* CHRIST.

c. As transferred from ruler to ruler. The Spirit, as the proper endowment of the ruler of God's people, is sometimes thought of as being transferred from one Spirit-possessed individual to another when the latter is commissioned as his predecessor's representative or alter ego. Thus "Joshua the son of Nun was full of the spirit of wisdom, for Moses had laid his hands upon him; so the people of Israel obeyed him" (Deut. 34:9; but cf. Num. 27:18-23, where Joshua is described as being already "a man in whom is the spirit" before his commissioning).

d. As inspiring the prophets. The primary manifestation of the activity of the Spirit in the OT is prophecy (*see* PROPHET). The dreams of Joseph were recognized by Pharaoh as inspired divination: Joseph was a man "in whom is the Spirit of God" (Gen. 41:38). Through David, as one who delivers inspired oracles, "the Spirit of the LORD speaks" (II Sam. 23:2); the false prophet Zedekiah the son of Chenaanah claims that the Spirit of the Lord is within him, so that if his adversary Micaiah is really a prophet, this must imply that the Spirit has left him and gone to Micaiah (I Kings 22:24). The true prophet may declare boldly:

> I am filled with power,
> with the Spirit of the LORD,
> and with justice and might,
> to declare to Jacob his transgression
> and to Israel his sin (Mic. 3:8).

The parallel between Spirit and power is to be noted. In the "Second Isaiah" (*see* ISAIAH) the prophet's inspiration is said to come from "the Lord GOD . . . and his Spirit" (Isa. 48:16); in this passage the Spirit is conceived more personally, as virtually synonymous with the presence of God himself. The mission of the prophet of Isa. 61:1 is carried out under the inspiration and authentication of the Spirit with which he has been anointed by the Lord; and when the Spirit of the Lord "falls upon" Ezekiel, he is enabled to hear the message of doom which he is commissioned to declare to Israel (Ezek. 11:5). By his Spirit the Lord sent "the law and the words" through the prophets (Zech. 7:12), and it was by the

Spirit that God sent his warnings to Israel through the prophets (Neh. 9:30). It is particularly as the Spirit of prophecy that Joel pictures the expected future outpouring of the Spirit on all flesh, so that prophesying, dreams, and visions will no longer be restricted to a few specially chosen individuals (Joel 2:28-29). Thus the prayer attributed to Moses (Num. 11:29) would be fulfilled, and all the Lord's people would become prophets through the action of the Lord in putting his Spirit upon them.

The outward manifestation of the spirit of prophecy is primarily to be seen in ecstatic phenomena. When the Lord takes of the Spirit which was upon Moses and distributes it to the seventy elders of Israel who are to become assistants to Moses in the government of the people, they prophesy for so long as the inspiration of the Spirit comes upon them. The fact that they are Spirit-possessed is immediately obvious, as it is in the case of Eldad and Medad, who "prophesied in the camp" (Num. 11:25-26). They are evidently recognizable by the entire community as ecstatics. Similarly, when Saul encounters the band of prophets descending from a high place with their music, he is immediately infected by their ecstatic enthusiasm; the Spirit of the Lord comes "mightily" upon him, he prophesies with them, and is "turned into another man" (I Sam. 10: 6, 10), so that "when all who knew him before saw how he prophesied with the prophets, the people said to one another, 'What has come over the son of Kish? Is Saul also among the prophets?' " The infection of prophetic ecstasy is even stronger in the case of messengers of Saul, and finally of the king himself, when they see the company of prophets prophesying and Samuel standing as head over them (I Sam. 19: 20-24); the Spirit passes over, as it were, to them against their will, so that the purpose of their mission is frustrated. On this occasion, we are given some indication of the more bizarre manifestations of the prophetic spirit; Saul "stripped off his clothes, and he too prophesied before Samuel, and lay naked all that day and all that night."

The Spirit-possessed prophet may move unexpectedly and mysteriously from place to place under the compelling power of the divine energy (I Kings 18:12), and where the Spirit may have caught up a prophet and "cast him upon some mountain or into some valley," it may well be useless to seek him (II Kings 2:16). It is the Spirit which seizes the prophet and enables him, in a trance and in visions, to see what is taking place at a great distance from where he stands. Ezekiel, closely identifying the "hand" and the "spirit" of the Lord, declares that "he put forth the form of a hand, and took me by a lock of my head; and the Spirit lifted me up between earth and heaven, and brought me in visions of God to Jerusalem" (Ezek. 8:3). Later, "the Spirit lifted me up and brought me in the vision by the Spirit of God into Chaldea" (11:24), and under the influence of the Spirit he is brought into the temple to receive the vision of its renewed glory (43:5). The ecstatic prophet is pre-eminently the "man of the spirit" (Hos. 9:7).

In the case of the Hebrew prophets, however, the inspiration of the Spirit, with its accompanying outward manifestations, is a temporary and passing phenomenon. Only in respect of the greatest figures of the OT can it be said that the Spirit comes to possess a man permanently, so that his life is altogether controlled by its influence. This is indicated in the case of Moses, who was so completely a man of the Spirit that the Spirit which rested upon him could be extended by the divine action to embrace the elders, who thus became a kind of extension of his own Spirit-possessed personality (Num. 11:17, 25). It is also implied in the story of Elijah, a double portion of whose divine spirit is transferred to Elisha, so that the disciple is able to perform the same wonders as those of his master (II Kings 2:9, 15; cf. vss. 8, 14). The latter narrative is interesting in that the endowment of Elisha with the spirit of Elijah is consequent upon the ascension of Elijah into heaven, and is conditional upon the disciple's being enabled to witness his master's glorification. When these events have happened, Elisha becomes the Spirit-possessed successor, or rather alter ego, of the great prophet. It is obvious from the narrative of Acts 1–2 that the typology of the passage has profoundly influenced the Lukan account of the reception by his disciples of the Spirit which rested upon Jesus, as a consequence of his glorification, which they themselves were privileged to witness.

e. As effecting sanctification and judgment. The phenomena of ecstasy are not, however, the most important effects of Spirit-possession, nor are they a necessary proof of it. The Spirit is the source of all intellectual and spiritual gifts, whether they be the artistry of Bezalel (Exod. 31:2) or the understanding and wisdom with which Daniel interpreted dreams (Dan. 5:14 RSV mg.). It is the inspiration of the men of wisdom (Ecclus. 39:6) and so can be identified with the WISDOM of God (Wisd. Sol. 9:17). The effects of the operation of the Spirit are seen by the great prophets, not merely in the ecstatic ravings of the enthusiast, but in the permanent establishment of justice and righteousness among the people of God. This transformation of the world into a place of righteousness is expected in the days when "the Spirit is poured upon us from on high" (Isa. 32:15). It is the guarantee and sign of the covenant promises of God (Hag. 2:5), and of their fulfilment in the acts of God toward the restored community (Zech. 4:6). Above all, the Spirit is the activity of God in sanctification, both of the covenant people (Isa. 59:21), who will be enabled by their possession of the Spirit within them to observe the commandments of God (Ezek. 36:27; cf. 39:29), and of the individual, who may pray:

> Create in me a clean heart, O God,
> and put a new and right spirit within me.
> Cast me not away from thy presence,
> and take not thy holy Spirit from me
> (Ps. 51:10-11).

f. As the presence of God with Israel. The divine Spirit is the mode of God's judgment on his people, and is thus associated by Isaiah with the cleansing of Jerusalem in the day of deliverance for the faithful remnant of the covenant people "by a spirit of judgment and by a spirit of burning" (Isa. 4:4). This prophecy has influenced the NT account of John the Baptist's expectation of the future baptism "with the

Holy Spirit" (Matt. 3:11; Luke 3:16). Through the Spirit's action God's justice and righteousness are to be established in Israel in the age of fulfilment (Isa. 32:15-17). For Israel, as for the individual, the Spirit is the medium by which God teaches man to do his will, and leads him onward in the right way of life (Ps. 143:10). Its activity is associated especially with the establishment of God's covenant with Israel, and the deliverance of the Exodus. God "put in the midst of them his holy Spirit" and "caused his glorious arm to go at the right hand of Moses" (Isa. 63:11-12). Here the Spirit is equated with the "arm" of the Lord, and represents the active presence of God among his people, saving them from their enemies and constituting them the people of the covenant. The Spirit is "holy," as being the active mode of the operation on earth of the transcendent God, and is virtually identified with the being of God himself. The Spirit is personally conceived—no mere power or influence, but the object of a possible personal relationship. Israel's disloyalty to God is a rebellion against his Spirit:

> But they rebelled
> and grieved his holy Spirit;
> therefore he turned to be their enemy,
> and himself fought against them
> (Isa. 63:10);

and the action of God in leading Israel in the exodus wanderings is equated with the personal activity of God himself: "The Spirit of the LORD gave them rest" (vs. 14).

As the personal power of God, effective in the moral and spiritual transformation of his people, the Spirit will be the inner principle of the life of the restored community. The bestowal by God of his Spirit will bring about a renewal of the covenant relationship between God and Israel, enabling the people to observe his laws and truly to belong to him (Ezek. 11:19-20). To receive the Spirit will be the decisive turning point in Israel's repentance (Ezek. 18:31, where the new human spirit of the restored community is the effect of the operation of the Spirit of God, as 36:26-27 makes clear). Through the divine Spirit there will be a transformation of the human character, so that a "heart of flesh" replaces the "heart of stone" of the days of Israel's transgression.

g. In eschatological expectation. As we have already seen, the prophetic hope of the coming of God's Spirit, conceived in this ethical fashion, upon the people of the covenant is part of, or rather one aspect of, the blessedness of the age of fulfilment. In the OT this possession of the Spirit by the whole people of God belongs to the sphere of eschatological expectation. As an object of hope, the Spirit-possession of Israel is associated with divine judgment (Isa. 4:4), the ideal ruler (Isa. 11:2), and, above all, with the renewal of Israel as the people of the covenant (Isa. 32:15; Ezek. 11:19; 36:26; Joel 3:1), and with their repentance in the last days (Zech. 12:10) and restoration. The Second Isaiah links this renewal through the Spirit with the role of Israel as the servant of God, and dramatically compares the working of the Spirit in the re-creation of the nation with the transformation of the desert by streams of water (Isa. 44:3). This metaphor of the new life brought about by the creative Spirit was to exert a powerful influence on the development of Christian imagery.

h. In creation. The Spirit, as the mode of God's re-creation of his chosen people, is re-enacting a part already assigned to it in the creation of all things. The "breath," "wind," or "Spirit" of God is the creative power which brings life to the formless chaos in the beginning of all things (Gen. 1:2), and, as equated with the "word" of God, is the agent by whom God made the heavens (Ps. 33:6). The "breath" or "Spirit" of God gives life to the animal creation, and when it is taken from them, they revert to dust (Ps. 104:29-30; cf. Gen. 2:7). In these last instances the thought is primarily of the "inbreathing" by God of the life principle or "soul" of living creatures, but although this life principle is not to be identified with the actual Spirit of God, it is represented by the Hebrew writers as an effect of its operation. A new creation of life through the Spirit's agency is described in Ezekiel's vision of the dry bones (Ezek. 37:9-14). A human person is therefore one whom God, by the action of his Spirit and "breath," has formed from the clay:

> The spirit of God has made me,
> and the breath of the Almighty gives me life
> (Job 33:4; cf. 34:14-15).

In the postcanonical literature the Spirit and the Word of God are still spoken of as the means whereby God has brought all things into being (Jth. 16:14), and in the Wisdom of Solomon (1:7) the divine Spirit is described, possibly under the influence of Stoic conceptions of the all-pervading pneuma, as "filling" the universe and holding all things together as a rational bond of cohesion.

i. In relation to the being of God. The thought of the OT is interested in the activity of God rather than in the metaphysical problem of his being; and it follows that little is said by Hebrew writers about the inner relationship of the Spirit to God. God's Spirit is apprehended in its operation, and this operation is recognized as the working of God himself. Nevertheless, it is occasionally implied that the Spirit of God is identical either with the being of God, so that what God is the Spirit is also, or with his personality. Thus Isaiah contrasts "flesh," in the sense of what is material and belonging solely to the order of the world, with what is "spirit"—i.e., partaking of the transcendent divine nature:

> The Egyptians are men, and not God;
> and their horses are flesh, and not spirit
> (Isa. 31:3).

He also sets in parallel the "mouth" and the "Spirit" of the Lord: the Spirit, like the "mouth" by which God utters his commands, is here the person of God in his relation to men (Isa. 34:16). God's Spirit is identified by the Second Isaiah with the personality, or mind, of the Lord (Isa. 40:13), and, as has been noted above, the Spirit is recognized in one passage as the personal presence of the Lord, whom his people grieve by their unfaithfulness (Isa. 63:10-14), being here equated with the "angel" of God (vs. 9), who is the Lord himself as present among the covenant people. *See* GOD, OT VIEW OF.

2. Intertestamental developments. There are few developments in the intertestamental period which radically affect the NT conception of the nature and work of the Holy Spirit. In the main, the Spirit continues to be thought of as being, pre-eminently, the Spirit of prophecy, manifested in the distant past in such great figures as Elijah (Ecclus. 48:12) or Isaiah (vs. 24), but which was now no longer present in Israel. Contemporary prophecy had fallen into discredit (cf. Zech. 13:2-6), and for the present the Spirit of prophecy was believed to lie dormant, as it were, even though special inspiration might be granted to an individual, such as Ezra, who prayed for the sending of the Holy Spirit to enable him to rewrite the books of the Law which had perished (II Esd. 14:22). In this instance, however, no fresh revelation was granted. Ezra's inspiration is that of the scribe, recording and expounding the written Word, rather than the prophetic spirit; and it was generally acknowledged that prophecy was not to be looked for in the present age (I Macc. 9:27). A "faithful prophet"—i.e., one truly inspired—remained a distant hope (I Macc. 4:46; 14:41). The eschatological expectation persisted of a future outpouring of the Spirit on Israel, associated at times with a coming deliverer of God's people (Pss. Sol. 17:37; 18:7; Test. Levi 18:7; Test. Judah 24:2).

3. NT teachings. ***a. The Spirit and John's mission.*** The long-awaited fulfilment of the hope of a general renewal of the prophetic Spirit was seen by JOHN THE BAPTIST to be approaching. Luke, indeed, seeks to show that the events which immediately preceded the work of Jesus and were, in a sense, themselves a part of the gospel were already taking place in the setting of a new upsurge of the long dormant Spirit of prophecy, prophecy being the inspired announcement of the coming fulfilment, of which the child John is to be the forerunner. Elizabeth and Zechariah are "filled with the Holy Spirit." Simeon is likewise inspired to recognize the Christ in Jesus and to proclaim his mission to bring light to the Gentiles (the role of the Servant) and glory to Israel (Luke 2:25-32). This emphasis on a renewal of the Spirit of prophecy as the prelude to the gospel is peculiar to Luke; but the synoptic tradition agrees in seeing John himself as a Spirit-possessed prophet (cf. Matt. 11:9; Mark 11:32), endowed with the Spirit from before his birth (Luke 1:15). His mission was to prepare a faithful remnant of Israel, by repentance associated with the outward sign of cleansing by baptism in the Jordan, to face the coming judgment; it was also a preparation for a future baptism with the Holy Spirit (Matt. 3:11; Mark 1:8; Luke 3:16), and at least in one aspect the symbolism of his baptism, recalling the metaphorical language in which the OT prophets had likened the action of the Spirit to that of water in the desert, fits this preparation.

John's baptism, however, was not in itself an effective sign of the fulfilment of the ancient hope of a general outpouring of the Spirit. This hope still lay in the future, though John himself believed it to be imminent. The last days had not yet dawned, and his mission was no more than a preparation for the fulfilment. The promised outpouring of the Spirit waited, according to the common testimony of the NT writers, until the saving work of the Messiah should have been completed. These events were, however, nearer at hand than John himself at first realized. The baptism with the Holy Spirit of which he had spoken actually took place, so far as one of his followers was concerned, when Jesus came to be baptized by him. From that decisive moment the age of hope already began to give place to the age of fulfilment. Hence when John had received from his messengers the news that the messianic signs were being visibly enacted, he receded from the scene, as the evangelists understood it, his work of preparation being done and the age of the new covenant having been ushered in by his prophetic call to Israel (Matt. 11:2-15; Luke 7:18-30; 16:16). In the light of the age of fulfilment, however, John's mission itself took on something of the character of the gospel, by anticipation (Mark 1:1; Luke 3:18).

b. In Christ's baptism. The great turning point in the biblical history is the BAPTISM of Jesus, when the Spirit descended upon him, anointing him (Acts 10:38) as the messianic Son of God, followed, after the completion of his saving work in death, resurrection, and ascension, by the general bestowal of the Spirit which had rested upon him to all his disciples at Pentecost. The baptism is therefore the first of the gospel events, after the prelude formed by the mission of John. It is the "anointing" of the Christ with the Spirit, and is accordingly given an important place in the summary of the apostolic preaching which Luke puts into the mouth of Peter (Acts 10:38). Implicit allusions to it occur elsewhere in Acts (4:27; 13:24-25). Whereas the people as a whole had been baptized by John as a remnant elected to await the dawning of the age of fulfilment, Jesus received in his own person the promised outpouring of the Spirit. With this was associated the proclamation from heaven of his divine sonship (Matt. 3:17; Mark 1:11; Luke 3:22). Sonship and Spirit-possession are, in fact, identical. The evangelists distinguish the "descent" or "remaining" (John 1:33) of the Spirit upon Jesus from the temporary and partial Spirit-possession of a prophetic enthusiast. It is not a mere possession by an impersonal force, but rather a state of personal union with God the Father, a continuous and enduring endowment with the authority and power (cf. Matt. 7:29; Mark 1:22; Luke 4:32, 36) which characterized his ministry and resulted from that union. This distinction is expressed in the imagery of the descent of the dove (Matt. 3:16; Mark 1:10; Luke 3:22; John 1:32). The Spirit is not a mere prophetic inspiration; it descends "in bodily form," as Luke pictures it (3:22), resting upon the Messiah with the fullest endowment of divine power. This does not imply that the permanent unction with the Spirit has not certain moments of particularly high exaltation (cf. Luke 10:21), but it asserts the completeness of this Spirit-possession which is identical with sonship. The actual symbolism of the dove is obscure. It may be that it is intended to recall Noah's dove, the harbinger of the first covenant between God and man; the Spirit comes upon Jesus as the Christ, and opens the way toward the new covenant in which all Israel will know the Lord through the indwelling of his Spirit.

c. In Mark and Matthew. The Synoptic gospels contain few references to the Holy Spirit, although it is to be noted that Luke, writing from a different standpoint from that of Mark, and with a larger perspective in view, embracing the gospel events from the birth of John to the proclamation of Christ in Rome, adds an emphasis of his own to the relatively meager sayings about the Spirit which he found in Mark and Q. This comparative lack of allusions to the Spirit is entirely natural, and is in accordance with the general theology of the NT as a whole; for the dispensation of the Spirit belongs to the age of the church, the time following the death, resurrection, and ascension of the Lord, on which the coming of the Spirit upon God's people depended.

Mark, after telling his readers about the baptismal descent of the Spirit upon Jesus and the proclamation of his divine sonship by the heavenly voice, explains that it was under the compulsion of the Spirit that Jesus immediately retreated to the desert to grapple with the temptation by the devil (Mark 1:12). Mark does not tell us explicitly that the Spirit was the divine principle and energy of the ministry of Jesus and the proclamation of the kingdom of God; but the fact that this was so, as Luke explains less ambiguously, is implicit in the Markan saying about the blasphemy against the Holy Spirit (Mark 3:29). The direct and total opposition to Jesus' mission, which ascribed the signs of the kingdom (the casting out of demons) to the power of evil, is blasphemy against the Holy Spirit itself. Hence this is the ultimate sin, the final rejection of God as manifested in his active presence in the mighty works of Jesus. " 'Truly, I say to you, all sins will be forgiven the sons of men, and whatever blasphemies they utter; but whoever blasphemes against the Holy Spirit never has forgiveness, but is guilty of an eternal sin'—for they had said, 'He has an unclean spirit' " (Mark 3:28-30).

A version of this saying which occurs in Luke 12:10, and is found alongside the Markan form in Matt. 12:31-32, contrasts the blasphemy against the Holy Spirit, not with all other sin, but specifically with "speaking a word against the Son of man." Here the emphasis lies on the distinction between Jesus as he presented himself to the public view in his earthly ministry, disclosing his true character only to the eye of faith and only in signs and parables, with the Spirit itself as the inner motive and principle of his great works. The opposition of the scribes was deliberate and conscious, an ultimate rejection of the saving activity of God in the person of Jesus. Luke gives his own interpretation to this blasphemy, bringing the saying into direct relation with another Markan passage (Mark 13:11) in which the immediate inspiration of the Spirit is promised to those who confess Christ under stress of persecution.

Mark's allusion to the Spirit in this context represents an exception to his general rule of not alluding to the Spirit, the principle of the postresurrection life of Christians, in his account of the preresurrection ministry of Jesus except insofar as it was necessary for him to indicate the Spirit-possession of Jesus himself. In the so-called Little Apocalypse, Mark is describing Christ's prophecy of the postresurrection age when his followers would be subject to persecution. Hence he can properly lay emphasis on the inspiration of the Spirit which would be experienced by faithful confessors in that missionary and martyr situation. The Christian disciple is told not to be anxious how he is to make his defense of the faith when he is put on trial: "But say whatever is given you in that hour, for it is not you who speak, but the Holy Spirit." Luke reproduces this promise, in a different context (Luke 12:12), but immediately precedes it with a warning against apostasy: "He who denies me before men will be denied before the angels of God. And every one who speaks a word against the Son of man will be forgiven; but he who blasphemes against the Holy Spirit will not be forgiven" (Luke 12:9-10). The blasphemy against the Spirit has thus been transferred in thought from the context of Christ's ministry to that of the situation of the missionary church. It has come to be identified with apostasy, the unforgivable sin, which stands over against the steadfast confession of the martyr, testifying to Christ under the direct inspiration of the Holy Spirit (cf. Acts 7:55; Heb. 6:4-6; I John 5:16).

Matthew has reproduced the Markan statement that Jesus went into the wilderness under the compulsion of the Spirit, though both he and Luke speak of the Spirit as "leading" rather than "driving" Jesus (Matt. 4:1; cf. Mark 1:12; Luke 4:1). He has included the saying about the blasphemy against the Spirit (Matt. 12:31-32) both in the Markan form and in that which appears in Luke and may be considered to be the Q version. He also includes a saying (Matt. 12:28) which occurs in a slightly different form in Luke (11:20). This saying makes explicit the fact implied in Mark that it is by the operation of the Spirit in his ministry that Jesus performs the mighty works which are the sign of the approach of the KINGDOM OF GOD in his own person. The kingdom is already present by anticipation in the works which are done through the agency of the Spirit, and the chief sign of this is the defeat and destruction of the demonic powers of evil: "If it is by the Spirit of God that I cast out demons, then the kingdom of God has come upon you." Luke has the same saying (11:20) with the difference that "finger" replaces "Spirit." This is probably to be accounted for by a desire on the part of Luke to introduce a reminiscence of Exod. 8:19; in any case, the concept of the "finger," "hand," or "arm" of the Lord, as a symbol of the active presence of God, is very close in OT thought to that of the "Spirit" of the Lord. The works of Jesus betoken the present operation of the Spirit, bringing about an anticipation in the ministry of Jesus of the promised times of the end, the age of fulfilment for Israel. This saying is directly related to the blasphemy against the Spirit by which the opponents of Jesus attribute his works to the devil.

Matthew's explicit assertion that the Spirit is the energizing principle of the mighty works of Jesus is reinforced by his use of the Second Isaiah's description of the "Servant of the Lord" in order to present his readers with a picture of the Galilean ministry:

> Behold, my servant whom I have chosen,
> my beloved with whom my soul is well pleased.
> I will put my Spirit upon him,
> and he shall proclaim justice to the Gentiles
> (Matt. 12:18, citing Isa. 42:1-2).

Jesus is the Servant, possessed of the Spirit of God for the execution of his saving mission.

Looking forward from the ministry of Jesus to the mission of the postresurrection church, Matthew reproduces the Markan promise of a direct inspiration of the Spirit for the confessor in times of persecution (Matt. 10:20), placing it in the setting of the instructions delivered by the Lord to the Twelve at the outset of their mission. In this gospel, too, there occurs the command of the risen Lord to his disciples to "make disciples of all nations, baptizing them in the name of the Father and of the Son and of the Holy Spirit" (Matt. 28:19). This is a passage which was to prove of immense significance in the later development of the doctrine of the Trinity and of the personality and divinity of the Holy Spirit. Indeed, in its liturgical use in connection with baptism, it may be regarded as a primary source of the theologically formulated doctrine of later centuries. There is no evidence to show that this text is not an authentic part of the Gospel of Matthew; and although the baptismal practice of the apostolic church, so far as we can infer it from the NT, does not appear to have included the use of the threefold name, it may well be that in certain quarters it was already so employed by the last decade or two of the first century. The association of the Holy Spirit in a personal manner with "God" and "the Lord Jesus Christ" is already attested for a considerably earlier date by Paul's concluding prayer in II Cor. 13:14, and the Matthean liturgical formula represents only a somewhat more consciously theological expression of the same belief. It is good evidence that the Spirit was being recognized as fully divine, and by implication as fully personal, in other circles besides the Johannine, at a relatively early date.

d. In the Third Gospel. In the Lukan writings there is considerably more emphasis on the operation of the Spirit than in the other Synoptics. Luke sees the Spirit as active in a great renewal of prophecy before the birth of John, and in John's own mission; the Spirit rests on Jesus, and in its power he carries out his mighty works; after the death, resurrection, and ascension of Jesus, the same Spirit which rested upon him is bestowed upon the community of his followers, so that the work of the Spirit links together, and binds into a single operation of God, the whole series of events which began in the Jerusalem temple at the annunciation to Zechariah and reached a climax in the free proclamation of the kingdom of God in the capital city of the Gentile world by the leading apostle.

In the setting of renewed inspiration and prophecy, the birth of Jesus is announced to Mary. Just as the Spirit was the creative agency of God in the formation of the world, so the Spirit will come upon Mary and enable her to become miraculously the mother of the promised Messiah (Luke 1:35). Matthew, too, explains that Mary "was found to be with child of the Holy Spirit," and narrates the appearance of the angel to Joseph, telling him in a dream not to fear to take "Mary your wife, for that which is conceived in her is of the Holy Spirit" (Matt. 1:18, 20). In this Matthean account the birth of Jesus fulfils the prophecy of Isa. 7:14 (as the LXX version suggested its meaning to be) by being brought about through the supernatural action of the divine power of the Spirit, working the miracle of his virgin birth; but no more is told to the reader than the bare fact. In Luke, on the other hand, the nature of the Spirit's activity is more explicitly described: the Spirit is equated with the "power of the Most High," and it is said to "come upon" Mary and "overshadow" her. This recalls the operation of the Spirit in creation, and Luke's choice of the word "overshadow" is evidently also intended to point to the association of this action of the Spirit with the "overshadowing" of the cloud of the divine presence at the announcement of the sonship of Jesus to the disciples at the Transfiguration (Luke 9:35). The evangelist may possibly also wish his readers to see a parallel between the promise of the coming of the Spirit upon Mary and the promise of the coming of the Spirit upon the apostles after the Resurrection (cf. Luke 24:49; Acts 1:4, 8).

The opening of the ministry of Jesus is, in Luke's account, characterized by the working of the Spirit in him, after its descent at the Jordan. Luke adds to the Markan narrative of the compulsion of the Spirit, which took Jesus into the wilderness, the statement that it was like a prophet of old, "full of the Holy Spirit" (cf. Mic. 3:8), that Jesus returned from the Jordan, when he was "led by the Spirit for forty days in the wilderness" (Luke 4:1-2). After the temptations, Jesus "returned in the power of the Spirit into Galilee" to begin his teaching in the synagogues (Luke 4:14). This added emphasis on the Spirit's role in the earthly ministry of Jesus is characteristic of Luke's editorial insertions and additional notes, and of the various slight but subtle alterations which he makes in his material, both Markan and non-Markan so far as the critic can judge of the latter.

One of the most important passages which exemplify such additions and alterations is the dramatic episode of the proclamation by Jesus of the purpose of his mission in the synagogue at Nazareth, a passage which is probably basically Markan and has been greatly enlarged and placed in a new context by Luke in order to serve as an introduction to the central theme of both the Third Gospel and Acts (Luke 4:16-30). Here Jesus declares himself to be the prophet announced in Isa. 61:1-2, a figure who would probably be identified both by himself and by his audience with the Servant of the Lord. He is the ideally Spirit-possessed prophet, sent out with the unction of the Spirit to proclaim good news (Luke 4:18). This is the key to the Lukan picture of Jesus, and of the church which was to carry on the same mission after his death and resurrection had made it possible for the Spirit with which he was anointed to be bestowed on his people in their turn.

It is possible that the reader is intended to be reminded occasionally at other points in Luke's narrative that Jesus was the great prophet of Isa. 61, identified with the "prophet like Moses" of Deut. 18:15 (cf. Acts 3:22; 7:37; and the implied parallel between Jesus and Moses in Luke 24:19; Acts 7:22). Thus Jesus is greeted as a "great prophet" after the raising of the widow's son (Luke 7:16), and Simon the Pharisee is already to consider the question whether or not Jesus is a prophet, or, according to a variant reading, "the prophet"—i.e., the prophet like Moses (Luke 7:39). Jesus may again be implicitly identified with the prophet of Isa. 61 at Acts 4:27. It is more important to notice that, according to

Luke, the profound and exultant expression of complete personal union between Jesus and the Father, recorded on the occasion when the mission of the Seventy had demonstrated the power of the kingdom of God and the destruction of Satan, was a moment of rejoicing "in the Holy Spirit" (Luke 10:21). The inspiration of the Spirit mediates this most intimate personal bond. It is a relationship to God in which the disciples of Jesus will be enabled in some measure to share. Hence, for Luke the supreme object of Christian prayer is the gift of the Holy Spirit: "If you then, who are evil, know how to give good gifts to your children, how much more will the heavenly Father give the Holy Spirit to those who ask him?" (Luke 11:13). The Matthean version of this saying (Matt. 7:11) contains no reference to the Spirit, and it is probable that Luke has altered the form of the saying as he found it in Q. Along with this saying the variant reading in Luke 11:2 must be considered. This gives the petition: "May the Holy Spirit come upon us and cleanse us," in place of: "Thy kingdom come." Its MS attestation is very slight, but, besides being known to Gregory of Nyssa and Maximus the Confessor, it was also read by Marcion and stood, apparently, in his text of Luke instead of "Hallowed be thy name." It is at least possible that this reading is not due to Marcion himself but is original in Luke. It would certainly be in harmony with Luke's conception of the Spirit as the primary object of prayer.

The Lukan use of the sayings about the inspiration of the confessor and the blasphemy against the Spirit have already been discussed. This gospel ends with the announcement by the risen Lord that the divine promise is about to be fulfilled, when the disciples will be "clothed with power from on high" (Luke 24:49). The second volume of Luke's work describes how this came about, and presents a ministry of the church in the power of the Spirit, parallel with that of Jesus.

e. In Acts. This fulfilment waits upon the glorification of Jesus, completed in his ascension. Thereafter the Lord himself is in heaven, until the final consummation (Acts 3:21). He is no longer with his disciples (Luke 24:44); but the Spirit is the link between the ascended Lord and those to whom he has covenanted to administer it, like the servants in the parable of the pounds (Luke 19:11-27; cf. Luke 22:29-30; Acts 1:6-8). The Spirit is the same as that which rested upon Jesus, and it can even be called the "Spirit of Jesus" (Acts 16:7). Thus, although the risen Christ appears in Luke to be far removed from his people on earth, the Spirit supplies the personal link which makes it possible for the works of Jesus to be continued in his name by his followers.

The coming of the Spirit, as the result of the completion of the mission of Jesus, is the fulfilment of John's prophecy of a coming "baptism" with the Holy Spirit (Acts 1:5). That this is a participation in the same Spirit which operated in Jesus is emphasized in Luke's assertion that it was "through the Holy Spirit" that the risen Lord gave his final commandment to his apostles (vs. 2). This is the fulfilment of the promise of a general outpouring of the Spirit; the followers of Christ will participate in his own baptism with the Spirit. It is conceived by Luke in terms of the Spirit of prophecy, which is now the power and motive principle of the church's missionary witness to Christ throughout the world. The coming of the Spirit enables the apostles to receive power, and so to become witnesses to the end of the earth (vs. 8). Luke reminds us, in the speech ascribed to Peter (vs. 16), that the same Spirit had been the inspiration of the OT prophecies, so that there is a direct continuity between the activities of the prophet and those of the apostle. He then describes the coming of the Spirit on the day of Pentecost, interpreting this as the fulfilment of Joel's prophecy of a universal outpouring of the Spirit of prophecy (Acts 2:16-21).

Since the Spirit is, in Luke's view, pre-eminently the inspiration and dynamic principle of the missionary enterprise, it is appropriate that he should depict the Pentecostal event as an onrush of divine power, like the wind or the *ruach* of the OT in its more concrete and physical manifestations, and that its coming should be symbolized in terms of tongues "as of fire," distributed and resting upon the apostles. The purpose of the Spirit's onrush is to bestow upon them the gifts most needed for the mission to the whole world, represented by the crowd drawn together in Jerusalem "from every nation under heaven" (Acts 2:2-5). This fulfilment of the words of Joel has been made possible by the resurrection and glorification of Jesus: "Being therefore exalted at the right hand of God, and having received from the Father the promise of the Holy Spirit, he has poured out this which you see and hear" (Acts 2:33).

The gift is not something confined to the original witnesses who were supernaturally empowered on the day of Pentecost. "The promise," said Peter in his speech to the Pentecost crowd, "is to you and to your children and to all that are far off" (Acts 2:39). It is to be received by those who, like the followers of John, repent and are baptized for the forgiveness of sins (Acts 2:38). The vitally important difference between John's baptism and the Christian baptism, which is an effective sign of the bestowal of the Spirit, is that the latter is "in the name of Jesus Messiah." It is as the people of the Christ, the renewed Israel, that those who repent now receive the fulfilment of what in John's preaching could only be a promise for the future. The quality of life evinced by this Spirit-possessed community is summed up by Luke in Acts 2:42-47, where the frequent association of the Spirit with joy and gladness is strikingly emphasized. Spirit-possession is also the mark of the apostolic witness who confesses Christ in times of danger. Peter is acting under the inspiration of the Spirit when he testifies to the assembled rulers of Israel (Acts 4:8), and the "boldness" of Peter and John (vs. 13) is a typical manifestation of this inspiration. Once again, this inspiration of the Christian missionaries is associated with a reminder that the work of the Spirit in testifying to the gospel is continuous with the inspiration of the OT prophets (vss. 25-26). The prayer of the assembled church (vss. 24-30) asks that God will grant them "to speak . . . with all boldness," and the prayer is answered by a renewed assurance that the Spirit is the power and inspiration of their mission; Pentecost is, as it were, confirmed in this new situation of danger and persecution: "The place in which they were gathered together was shaken; and they were all filled with the Holy Spirit and spoke the word of God with boldness" (vs. 31). Thus the Spirit, indwelling the community of Christian believers and inspiring their mission, can be adduced as the chief testimony to the truth of the apostolic preaching: "We are witnesses to these things, and so is the Holy Spirit whom God has given to those who obey him" (5:32).

Certain outstanding leaders of the mission are described as being pre-eminently possessed by the Holy Spirit. Stephen, in particular, fulfils the Lord's promise that the confessor of the faith under persecution would be directly inspired. In his disputations with the members of the Hellenist synagogues in Jerusalem, Stephen's inspiration made him invincible: "They could not withstand the wisdom and the Spirit with which he spoke" (6:10); and it is especially in his witness as a martyr that his inspiration through the Spirit reaches its highest point. "Full of the Holy Spirit" (7:55), he is enabled to see the heavens opened and to receive a vision of the Son of man in glory. Paul is similarly "filled with the Holy Spirit" when he withstands the efforts of Bar-Jesus to oppose the proclamation of the gospel (13:9).

Other leaders are also specially marked out as being Spirit-possessed. This is true of the Seven (6:3, 5), of Barnabas (11:24), and of Paul after his conversion, when the touch of Ananias brings him healing for his blindness and participation in the Pentecostal gift which had been received by the earliest believers (9:17). There is no necessary contradiction between this special endowment and the general impression given by the early chapters of Acts that the whole church was the Spirit-possessed community of the new covenant. Luke's chief interest is in the work of the Spirit in the furtherance of the church's world-wide mission. He therefore concentrates his attention upon the specifically missionary gifts of the Spirit (*see* SPIRITUAL GIFTS). There are some who are endowed with peculiar powers of eloquence or the doing of mighty works, and are leaders of the mission in a special sense; there are also those who have special gifts of prophecy. In such cases the operation of the Spirit is manifested in "tongues" (*see* TONGUES, GIFT OF), prophesying, and other unusual phenomena. Thus the narrative of Acts includes the episodes of the Christian prophet Agabus, whose inspiration closely resembles that of the prophets of the OT, including the exercise of prophetic symbolism (11:28; 21:11); other prophets at Antioch (13:1); and the prophesying and speaking with tongues of the twelve disciples whom Paul met at Ephesus (19:6). On the other hand, the Spirit is also the life principle of the community as a whole, where its manifestations are to be seen rather in the common life, brotherhood, and joy. Its presence is expressed in the institution of common property, so that an offense against the unity of the whole body, motivated by dishonest self-interest, is a sin against the Holy Spirit (4:32-37; 5:3, 9). When the church in a particular area is at peace and is being consolidated, its way of life can be described as "walking in the fear of the Lord and in the comfort of the Holy Spirit" (9:31). This life in the Spirit is especially characterized by joy (13:52).

Above all, in Luke's picture of the life of the primitive church, the Spirit is the guiding and controlling power of the world-wide mission. Through the inspiration of the Spirit, Philip is instructed to join the Ethiopian eunuch (8:29), and when his task is accomplished, Philip is removed to other spheres of activity by the agency of the Spirit (vs. 39). It is through the direct guidance of the Spirit that Peter is induced to meet the envoys of Cornelius and go with them to Caesarea (10:19; 11:12). The Spirit directs the church at Antioch to send out Barnabas and Saul as their missionaries to the Gentile countries of Asia Minor (13:2), and it is in the consciousness of the Spirit's guidance that they set out on their journey (13:4). The COUNCIL OF JERUSALEM sends its instructions to the Gentile brethren in Antioch, Syria, and Cilicia in the confidence that its decision has been due to the direct guidance of the Spirit: "It has seemed good to the Holy Spirit and to us" (15:28). On the second missionary journey the Spirit dictates to Paul and Silas how the strategy of the mission is to be pursued. On this journey the province of Asia is not to be evangelized, nor are the apostle and his companion allowed to go into Bithynia; the Spirit's guidance brings them perforce to Troas, where the call will come to take the gospel overseas to Macedonia (16:6-7). Luke does not tell us how this guidance was mediated; but we should probably infer that it was received through prophetic insight, in the manner in which the Hebrew prophets had discerned the divine command to go to particular places and carry out particular tasks. We have already noticed that it is in connection with this guidance of the missionary preachers that the Spirit is specifically described as the "Spirit of Jesus." Paul's decision on his third journey to leave Asia and revisit Greece is similarly made under the compulsion of the Spirit: "Paul resolved in the Spirit to pass through Macedonia." The decision is his own rational resolve; but it is arrived at in the consciousness of the leading of the purposive divine power which is the driving force of the entire missionary enterprise (19:21).

As another instance of the Spirit's direction of the church's mission we may reckon the appointment of the ministry. The elders of the Ephesian congregation were made "guardians" or "overseers" in the church by the action of the Spirit (20:28). The allusion here is probably to the selection of these men by some person or persons gifted with prophetic insight, perhaps Paul himself, acting, as he believed, under inspiration.

In the course of Paul's last journey to Jerusalem, the prophetic Spirit is also active in warning him of the dangers and difficulties which await him (20:22-23). The narrative of his visit to Tyre and to Caesarea suggests that these warnings were conveyed through revelations to prophets, as well, perhaps, as to Paul himself directly.

The question how Luke conceives the Spirit to have been received by the ordinary members of the Christian society is notoriously difficult to answer. It is a central theme of Lukan theology that the age of fulfilment has dawned and that its characteristic mark is the outpouring of the Spirit in accordance with the ancient prophetic hope. The Spirit, therefore, with which Luke so constantly associates the idea of divine power (cf. Luke 1:17; 4:14; 5:17; 6:19; Acts 1:5, 8; 10:38), is now the possession of the community as a whole. Pentecost, with the descent of the Spirit upon the nucleus of the church, corresponds to the "anointing" of Jesus himself with the same Spirit (cf. Luke 4:16-30). It inaugurates the age of the church and its world-wide mission, and is represented as being an antitype of the proclamation of the Law at Sinai (cf. Jub. 6:17, 19; Philo *On the Special Laws* 2.189; *On the Decalogue* 33.35), and perhaps also of the episode of Babel (cf. Gen. 11:1-9). The promise is made by Peter in his speech to the Pentecost crowd that the gift of the Spirit will now be available to all who repent and are baptized in the name of Jesus Christ (Acts 2:38), and it is clear from the rest of the narrative that this promise was fulfilled and that the church is a Spirit-possessed body. Here it would appear that the rite of baptism has become, for the Christian, the effective sign of the reception of the Spirit, being the outward means by which he enters upon every aspect of his calling. This would be in line with the explicit teaching of Paul and the general implications of the NT as a whole.

On the other hand, in the case of Cornelius and his household, the Spirit "fell on" the converts as they were listening to Peter's preaching, as an immediate gift bestowed by God without human agency. Their baptism followed, and was a consequence of, their Spirit-possession, not the means by which they received it (10:44-48). This episode, however, is obviously exceptional. It is a turning point in the church's mission, at which the will of God that Gentiles should be received into the community and baptized is miraculously demonstrated in a way which overcomes and sets at rest all doubts and scruples. It is a Gentile Pentecost (cf. 11:15-17; 15:8-9), a fact to which attention is repeatedly drawn in the course of the controversy about the admission of Gentiles. Spirit-possession, too, means in this case participation in the prophetic gifts (speaking with tongues) which were given at Pentecost to the original leaders of the Christian mission. Though the relationship between the entire community's experience of the Spirit and special prophetic endowments is never unambiguously expressed in Luke's writings, it is clear that he implies a distinction between them.

The same ambiguity probably accounts for the apparent contradiction between Acts 2:38 and the narrative of the Samaritan converts who were baptized by Philip but whose reception of the Spirit was delayed until Peter and John had come from Jerusalem and laid their hands upon the new believers (8:12-17). Here, again, we find a major turning point in the missionary enterprise, the admission to the community of non-Jews, members of the odious Samaritan schismatic sect. Once again, Spirit-possession is being thought of in terms of prophetic inspiration. It appears from the narrative that it might have been expected that the Samaritan converts would have shown some manifestation of the Spirit, which must presumably have taken the form of ecstatic phenomena. This did not occur, and it took place only when the two chief leaders of the original Jerusalem church had come to Samaria and given converts a sign of their full acceptance into the hitherto Jewish society of the church. When Peter and John give them a token of "solidarity"—almost, indeed, of personal identification—they begin to manifest their possession by the Spirit in so obvious a manner that Simon the magician seeks to purchase the power of conferring so marvelous a gift (8:19). Two things make this incident highly exceptional: the great step forward is being taken of bringing the gospel to non-Jews and incorporating them into the church in fellowship with the Jews of Jerusalem, and the new nucleus of the mission in Samaria is granted exceptional and visibly manifest signs of the extension to it of the prophetic gifts of Pentecost. It is extremely unlikely that Luke intends the story of the preaching at Samaria to be regarded as typical of the church's normal missionary work, or that it would be right to infer from this story that a "Spirit baptism" was regularly conferred upon converts by the imposition of hands, baptism in water being only a preliminary rite in preparation for this.

In the case of Paul (9:17-18) it is not clear whether reception of the Spirit was mediated in his baptism or whether it preceded it, being associated with the act of Ananias in laying his hands on Paul for the restoration of his sight. The probability is that the imposition of hands was here a sign and means of healing, and that the promised gift of the Spirit came when he "rose and was baptized." If Luke's story is accurate, this interpretation of it would seem to be borne out by Paul's own teaching on baptism.

At Ephesus (19:2-6) Paul met disciples who had been baptized, not with the Christian baptism "in the name of the Lord Jesus," but only with "John's baptism" of preparation for the coming of Jesus. They had accordingly not received the Holy Spirit when they were converted (19:2), nor even heard that the Holy Spirit "is" (i.e., that the age of the Spirit has come and that the Spirit is available to all believers). The status of these men is obscure. They may have been followers of John, but their designation as "disciples" and the reference to their "believing," which means "conversion," suggests rather that they were converts made by Apollos whose original belief was apparently some form of acceptance of Jesus, which nevertheless stopped short of an understanding of the postresurrection, postascension, and postpentecostal situation (18:24-26). They were baptized by Paul "in the name of the Lord Jesus," and "when Paul had laid his hands upon them, the Holy Spirit came on them; and they spoke with tongues and prophesied" (19:6). These disciples form the nucleus of the church at Ephesus, the main center of Gentile Christianity in Paul's lifetime. The Pentecostal endowment of special gifts of the Spirit, in the form of "tongues" and prophesying, is extended to these particularly important disciples at the time of another notable moment in the progress of the universal mission. It is mediated by the sign of self-identification given to them by the chief apostle of the Gentile communities, himself pre-eminently possessed of the Spirit.

In harmony with the Spirit-guided and -empowered mission of the Christian preachers, the inspired prophets of the Old Covenant continue to give their witness. The resistance of the old Israel to the gospel, described as resistance to the Holy Spirit (7:51), was thus foreshadowed by the prophecy of Isaiah through which the Spirit gave warning of the opposition the mission would meet from the Jews (28:25).

The Lukan conception of the Spirit, though it can

scarcely be said to include that of full personality, is nevertheless rich and varied. Attempts have been made to distinguish different shades of meaning corresponding to the instances of the use of "the Holy Spirit" (with the definite article) and "Holy Spirit" (without the article). The former occurs twenty times in Luke-Acts, the latter eighteen times. But no rigid distinction can be made here. It remains true that Luke shares the general NT theology of the Spirit as manifested in the baptism of Jesus and becoming the possession of the Christian community as a consequence of his saving work, but that he superimposes, as it were, on this common belief his own peculiar insistence on the Spirit as the guide and dynamic power of the world-wide mission, manifested in prophetic *charismata* ("gifts of the Spirit"), first in Jerusalem and then especially in the new churches of the Samaritan and Gentile worlds.

One peculiar passage remains to be mentioned. Apollos is described as "being fervent in spirit" (Acts 18:25), and as speaking and teaching the things concerning Jesus, speaking boldly in the synagogue. At that time he "knew only the baptism of John," and Acts 19:2-3 shows that this indicates a rudimentary stage of discipleship which did not include an understanding of the postpentecostal situation. In view of the general teaching of Luke-Acts it is hard to see how such a person could be a sharer in the Spirit, the inspiration of the church of the baptized, for which John's baptism had been merely a preparation; he could hardly be said to have entered with the more fully instructed Christians into the age of fulfilment. A possible explanation is that "spirit" here means his own spirit, and not the Spirit of God (so RSV). Yet the boldness of speech which is ascribed to him is usually a mark of the Spirit's activity. Perhaps, therefore, he is to be reckoned as a sharer, in an unusual manner, of the Spirit which possessed the missionary church, and, if this is so, his case warns us not to try to use the Lukan writings as a basis for working out any overrigid formulations concerning the work of the Spirit in the church. As in the episode of Cornelius, the operation of the Spirit is free and uncontrolled.

f. In Pauline theology. Paul says little about the relation of the Spirit to Jesus during his earthly life. According to Paul's "gospel," which no doubt reflects the primitive tradition which he had himself received, Jesus was "descended from David according to the flesh and designated the Son of God in power according to the Spirit of holiness by his resurrection from the dead" (Rom. 1:3-4). Here, in this virtual anticipation of a "two-natures" Christology, the "Spirit of holiness" or Holy Spirit is almost equivalent to the divine principle in Jesus. The operation of the power of God in him denotes his divine sonship, as his human descent marks him out as the Davidic Messiah; and this sonship is proved by the fact of the Resurrection (*see* RESURRECTION IN THE NT). More important, in the thought of Paul, is his conception of the Spirit as the mode of Christ's presence in and among his people. The Spirit, in the Lukan writings, is the link between the ascended Christ in heaven and his people on earth. In Paul the link is more intimate: Christ dwells in the believer and in the community; the believer is "in Christ," and the community is the "body of Christ." The mode by which this mutual indwelling takes place, and by which Christ is made the life principle of the church and the church is united to its head, is the Spirit, which is the Spirit of Christ himself.

The new life in which Christians share through grace, responded to by faith—i.e., the life of the resurrection anticipated in the present time—is a state of being "in the Spirit" (Rom. 8:9). This does not denote a condition of prophetic ecstasy. It includes the whole content of the Christian life, the deep personal union with Christ made possible by grace. It is a state in which the Spirit of God dwells in the believers. The "Spirit of God" is now recognized as the "Spirit of Christ" (8:9): "Any one who does not have the Spirit of Christ does not belong to him." To "have the Spirit of Christ" is the same as experiencing Christ himself: "If Christ is in you, . . . your spirits are alive" (vs. 10). This again is equated with the indwelling of the "Spirit of him who raised Jesus from the dead" (vs. 11). The Spirit is not substantially identical with Christ; but the Spirit mediates Christ to the church and the church to Christ. The Spirit makes the risen and glorified Christ present to the individual Christian and to the church collectively; it is in the Spirit that the believer and the church are united to the Lord. Hence the Spirit and Christ may be spoken of interchangeably as the principle of the new life and the sphere of man's access by grace and faith to God the Father. The Spirit is the "Spirit of Jesus Christ" (Phil. 1:19). It is thus the decisive test of the authenticity of supposed prophetic inspiration to determine the relation of its content to the basic Christian faith in Christ as Lord. There can be no revelation of the Spirit which contradicts this; and, on the other hand, the confession of Christ as Lord is a sure indication of the working of the true Spirit of God. "No one speaking by the Spirit of God ever says 'Jesus be cursed!' and no one can say 'Jesus is Lord' except by the Holy Spirit" (I Cor. 12:3).

Since the Spirit is the mode of the Christian's apprehension of the risen Christ, it is possible for Paul to set together in his thought, in parallel as it were, "the Lord Jesus Christ," "God," and "the Holy Spirit" (II Cor. 13:14), and the necessary implication of this is that the Spirit has come to be understood as personal. Yet Paul's identification of the Spirit of God with the operation of the risen Christ in and among his people does not lead him to make a substantial identification of the Spirit as a divine "person" with Christ as a divine "person." His statement: "Now the Lord is the Spirit" (II Cor. 3:17) is not to be read in this sense. It is not an ontological statement about the Godhead. In its context Paul has been contrasting the dispensation of the Spirit with that of the law. Speaking of the glory of the former as compared with the lesser glory of the latter, he uses the passage in which the glory reflected in the face of Moses was described in Exodus (34:29-35). This leads him to consider the blindness of the Jews, who cannot discern the true meaning of the OT; they do not see that it leads to the new covenant of the Spirit, replacing the old dispensation of the law; their eyes are blindfolded. Yet, just as Moses laid aside the veil that covered his face, when he went in to commune with God (Exod. 34:34), so when the Jews similarly turn to the Lord, the veil will be removed from their minds and they will understand. In their case, the phrase "the Lord" means "the Spirit," the principle of the new life in Christ.

As the motive and principle of the new life "in Christ," the Spirit stands in sharp contrast to the Law (*see* LAW IN THE NT), the principle of man's relationship to God under the old dispensation. To return to the bondage of the law would mean separation from Christ and abandonment of the Christian hope, guaranteed by the indwelling of the Spirit (Gal. 5:5). The new covenant, brought into effect by Christ, is a relationship to God consisting in and depending upon the indwelling of God's Spirit, and not a legal relationship embodied in a written code. The latter cannot give life: "The written code kills, but the Spirit gives life" (II Cor. 3:6). The Spirit ("the LORD" of Exod. 34:34) effects a transformation into the likeness of Christ, "from one degree of glory to another" (II Cor. 3:18).

Release from the law and its condemnation means a discharge from servitude and an entry into the new life in which the Spirit is both the motive and principle of life in Christ and also the sphere in which that life is lived: "We serve not under the old written code but in the new life of the Spirit" (Rom. 7:6). This new principle may itself be termed a new law, the "law of the Spirit of life in Christ Jesus"; but it is of a totally different kind from the old law, which is the "law of sin and death" (Rom. 8:2). It is a principle of life which could never be attained through the performance of supposedly meritorious legal works; it is given only through "hearing" the gospel "with faith" (Gal. 3:2). It is significant that the Christian experience of life in the Spirit is so real and vivid that Paul can use it as a convincing argument to the Galatians who are being led back to legalism by false teachers: "Did you receive the Spirit by works of the law, or by hearing with faith?"

To abandon the gospel of grace and revert to legalism would be to exchange life in the Spirit for life "in the flesh" (cf. Gal. 3:3). The flesh (*see* FLESH [NT]) is man's human nature in its unredeemed state, as alienated from God. It is in itself incapable of responding to the Spirit, and it represents a principle which is wholly at enmity with the Spirit and is to be done to death or "crucified" by those who are united with Christ in his death and in his resurrection to the new life which is Spirit-controlled and Spirit-motivated. Those who are walking by the Spirit must contend against the hostile principle of the flesh, and Paul reminds his hearers of the contrast between the works of the flesh and the "fruit of the Spirit," which is seen in the qualities of the Christian life, beginning with love, joy, and peace (Gal. 5:16-25). Life in the flesh results in corruption; life in the Spirit is eternal life (Gal. 6:8). Christians are those who "walk not according to the flesh but according to the Spirit . . . set their minds on the things of the Spirit. To set the mind on the flesh is death, but to set the mind on the Spirit is life and peace" (Rom. 8:4-6). Those in whom the Spirit of God dwells are not in the flesh but in the Spirit (vs. 9), and by the Spirit they put to death the deeds of the body—i.e., in this case, the flesh (vs. 13). The promise of the Spirit was thus reserved for those who could receive it through faith, not for those who sought salvation in legal works; the covenant of the Spirit is therefore intended for the Gentiles (Gal. 3:14).

The Spirit is Christ's Spirit, the Spirit of the Son of God, and the Christian, indwelt by the Spirit, enters into a new relationship to God, that of a son to his Father. Through the Spirit, Christians are enabled to address God as Father, and the proof that they are sons of God is the indwelling Spirit, which cries out in them "Abba! Father!" (Gal. 4:6). The Spirit testifies to our spirit that we are sons of God, and fellow heirs with Christ (Rom. 8:14-17).

Through the Spirit, with its assurance of sonship toward God, the Christian has access to the Father and communion with him. Through Christ both Jew and Gentile "have access in one Spirit to the Father" (Eph. 2:18). In the Spirit man can speak to God, for the Spirit prays within him, interceding "for the saints according to the will of God." Although man cannot pray as he ought, the Spirit "intercedes for us with sighs too deep for words" (Rom. 8:26-27). Hence Paul exhorts his readers to "pray at all times in the Spirit, with all prayer and supplication" (Eph. 6:18). The indwelling of the Spirit gives man his peculiar rights and dignity (I Thess. 4:8). It is this indwelling which is the distinctive mark of the Christian life (Rom. 8:9). It is the mode of Christ's own indwelling (Eph. 3:16-17). "Participation in the Spirit" is the common experience of all Christians (Phil. 2:1), producing the fellowship of the Spirit which Paul mentions in II Cor. 13:14 (unless this should be rendered "participation in the Spirit" with the RSV mg.). The individual who is united to Christ enters into a union with him in one Spirit; he "becomes one spirit with him" (I Cor. 6:17). His physical body is therefore sacred, as a temple of the Spirit (I Cor. 6:19). Similarly, the community as a whole is a temple in which God's Spirit dwells. Strife and factions destroy the holy temple of the corporate body (I Cor. 3:16-17); and the church collectively is a structure into which its various members are built together as a "dwelling place of God in the Spirit" (Eph. 2:22).

The one Spirit is thus the ground of the church's unity as the one body of Christ in which all worldly or fleshly divisions are transcended (I Cor. 12:13; Eph. 2:18; 4:3-4). *See* CHURCH, IDEA OF.

Present possession of the Spirit is a guarantee and first installment of the total redemption which is to be entered into hereafter. It is the ground of Christian hope. It is the first fruits, the anticipation in part of the harvest which awaits Christians at the end (Rom. 8:23), the guarantee of the total redemption which will include the transformation of the body into a spiritual body (II Cor. 5:5). By his possession of the Spirit the believer is marked out as God's property, bearing his distinguishing mark or ownership, his "seal" by which the Christian is assured of final redemption (II Cor. 1:22; Eph. 1:13; 4:30).

The supreme manifestation of the working of the Spirit is love (*see* LOVE IN THE NT). Through the gift of the Spirit, God's love is outpoured in the hearts of Christians (Rom. 5:5); and it is the source of the love which binds the Christian body together (Rom.

15:30; Col. 1:8). The panegyric on love in I Cor. 13 is intended to show that, of all the manifestations of the Spirit, love is the climax. Joy is also associated with the presence of the Spirit, even in defiance of earthly tribulations (I Thess. 1:6), and this is a mark or characteristic of the kingdom of God (Rom. 14: 17). It springs from the power of the Spirit to inspire and maintain Christian hope (Rom. 15:13); for the Spirit reveals the true nature and meaning of the divine purpose (Eph. 3:5).

All Christians are thus partakers of the Spirit, who should "be filled with the Spirit" (Eph. 5:18) and "aglow with the Spirit" (Rom. 12:11). All have entered upon this state of life in the Spirit through acceptance of the gospel and baptism (cf. the baptismal context of Paul's teaching on the Spirit in Rom. 6–8, the baptismal allusion in I Cor. 6:11, and the explicit statement in I Cor. 12:13).

At the same time, the Spirit is manifested in certain special endowments for particular purposes. As in Luke's writings, the Spirit is the dynamic force and the guide inspiring the apostolic mission, attesting the gospel and commending it with power (Rom. 15:19; I Cor. 2:4; I Thess. 1:5), inspiring Paul himself (I Cor. 2:10) and enabling him to convey the gospel to those whom the same Spirit disposes to receive it (I Cor. 2:13-14). The Spirit characterizes his labors (II Cor. 6:6) and enables him to present his ministry to the Gentiles as a priestly offering to God (Rom. 15:16), for his converts are consecrated by the Spirit (II Thess. 2:13). It is in the consciousness of his inspiration, too, that Paul wrestles with the problem of Israel's rejection of his gospel (Rom. 9:1). The Spirit remains the Spirit of prophecy, manifested in prophesying, tongues, and ecstatic utterances (I Thess. 5:19; cf. Eph. 5:18-19). At Corinth these gifts were being cultivated in the community to excess, and in ways which led to pride and the self-righteousness of an elite of spiritually gifted persons. Hence, while Paul allows the value of prophetic and ecstatic gifts, he insists that not only these, but all forms of service in the church are equally the work of the Spirit, and that the greatest gift is love (I Cor. 12:4-31; 13). He also prefers prophecy, with its intelligible and rationally communicated utterance, to "tongues" which need a special gift of interpretation. In any case, church order is not to be disturbed by the exercise of ecstatic speech in the congregation (I Cor. 14:1-35, a passage which indicates that liturgical utterances [vss. 15-16] might be directly inspired).

g. In the Pastoral letters, Hebrews, I and II Peter, and Jude. The Pastoral letters add little to the teaching of the acknowledged Pauline letters. At I Tim. 3:16, a liturgical fragment, Christ's vindication "in the Spirit"—i.e., in respect of the operation in him of the Spirit of God—is contrasted with his manifestation in the flesh—i.e., in the conditions of his human life and death. By the Spirit prophetic guidance is available to the church (I Tim. 4:1), and the indwelling Spirit enables the truth of Christianity to be preserved inviolate (II Tim. 1:14). Regeneration and renewal in the Holy Spirit—that is to say, the new life in the Spirit—is effected for all Christians through the baptismal washing (Tit. 3:5).

The Letter to the Hebrews contains little on this subject. The Spirit speaks through the Scriptures (Heb. 3:7; 10:15), sometimes through typological interpretation of the OT (Heb. 9:8). It was through the Spirit that Christ carried out his self-offering to God (9:14); Christians become partakers of the Spirit through their baptism (6:4); apostasy is an outrage against the Spirit of grace (10:29); and the special gifts of the Spirit authenticate the church's preaching (2:4).

I Peter mentions the inspiration of the prophets to speak of Christ; they were possessed by the Spirit of Christ even under the old covenant (I Pet. 1:11). It also speaks of the sanctification of Christians by the Spirit to be the people of God (1:2). II Peter contributes a very definite affirmation of the inspiration of the OT prophecies by the Spirit: "Men moved by the Holy Spirit spoke from God" (II Pet. 1:21). Jude contrasts the worldly schismatics, who are devoid of the Spirit, with those who continue to pray in the Spirit (Jude 19-20).

h. In Johannine theology. The Johannine literature is far richer in its doctrine of the Spirit. Christ is uniquely possessed of the Spirit (John 1:32-33) as the Son and the envoy of God (cf. John 3:34). The Christian is one who experiences a new birth of the Spirit —i.e., a birth to a new life in the Spirit, contrasted with ordinary fleshly birth (3:5-8; cf. 1:13). It is a birth of water and the Spirit (3:5)—this phrase echoes the ancient imagery in which the prophets likened the action of the divine Spirit to life-giving water and which would be intended by the evangelist to indicate to his readers Christian baptism; and it denotes being born "anew," or possibly "from above" (3:3, 7), or perhaps both.

The new birth in the Spirit is not available until Christ's work is accomplished and he is glorified. The Fourth Gospel makes explicit the implication of the Synoptic narratives that "the Spirit had not been given" [lit., 'was not yet'], because Jesus was not yet glorified" (7:39). Before Christ's glorification in death and resurrection, his disciples are instructed about the coming of the Spirit, who is now spoken of in fully personal terms as the "Counselor" or "Paraclete" who is to dwell with and in them, as the Spirit of truth (14:17), mediating to them a full understanding of the meaning of Christ's person and work (14:26), and bearing witness to Christ in and through the witness of those who are Christ's followers, being sent by the glorified Christ from the Father (15:26-27). His coming, which waits upon the physical departure of Jesus, will effect judgment through declaring the vindication of Jesus, the defeat of the devil, and the exposure of those who have rejected Jesus (16:7-11). The Spirit is to be the guide into all the truth, for he will mediate Christ to believers (16: 13-15). *See* PARACLETE.

When the Resurrection has taken place, the gift of the Spirit is bestowed on Christ's followers by his creative inbreathing (20:22), empowering them for their mission of forgiveness and judgment.

All Christians are anointed, as the people of the Spirit-possessed Messiah, with the unction of the Spirit (cf. I John 2:20). The Spirit is the assurance of Christ's indwelling presence (I John 3:24). The Spirit witnesses to the reality of Christ's incarnation, with the water and the blood of his death and of the

Christian sacraments (I John 5:7-8); and the acknowledgment that "Jesus Christ has come in the flesh" is the criterion of the Spirit's inspiration in the church (I John 4:2). For further discussion of the Spirit in the Fourth Gospel, *see* JOHN, GOSPEL OF, § 4.

In Revelation the Spirit is once again the inspiration of the prophet, declaring a message through the prophet's utterances (Rev. 1:10; 2:7, etc.; 4:2; 14:13; 21:10), the prophetic Spirit being identified with the "testimony of Jesus" (19:10); and in the expectant cry of the church to its Lord, "Come," the Spirit itself is speaking (22:17).

Bibliography. H. B. Swete, *The Holy Spirit in the NT* (1910); H. Leisegang, *Pneuma Hagion* (1922); E. F. Scott, *The Spirit in the NT* (1923); F. Buchsel, *Der Geist Gottes im NT* (1926); H. W. Robinson, *The Christian Experience of the Holy Spirit* (1928); F. C. Synge, "The Spirit in the Pauline Epistles," *Church Quarterly Review*, vol. 119, no. 237 (1934); N. H. Snaith, *The Doctrine of the Holy Spirit* (1937); C. Williams, *The Descent of the Dove* (1939); C. K. Barrett, *The Holy Spirit and the Gospel Tradition* (1947); G. W. H. Lampe, *The Seal of the Spirit* (1951); J. G. Davies, *The Spirit, the Church and the Sacraments* (1954).

G. W. H. LAMPE

HOMAM hō'măm [הומם; LXX Αιμαν] (I Chr. 1:39). A Horite in Edom. *See* HEMAM.

HOMER hō'mər [חמר]. A dry measure equal to ten ephahs (Ezek. 45:11), related to the Akkadian *imeru*, which means "ass" and is presumably the load that an ass should carry. Various estimates put its volume between 3.8 and 6.6 bushels. An equal measure was the cor.

See also WEIGHTS AND MEASURES § C4*a*.

O. R. SELLERS

HOMICIDE. *See* CRIMES AND PUNISHMENTS § 3*b*.

HOMOSEXUALITY. Homosexual relations are forbidden as an abomination worthy of death (Lev. 18:22; 20:13). The wages of homosexuality may not be used in God's house for the payment of any vow (Deut. 23:18; cf. Judg. 19:22). The Hebrew reads literally: "wages of a dog," a word that possibly designates a sacred male prostitute. *See* PROSTITUTION.

Homosexuals (μαλακός; KJV "effeminate") are among those condemned by the apostle Paul (I Cor. 6:9; cf. Rom. 1:27). The law is laid down for the ungodly and sinners, including the sodomites (I Tim. 1:10). Jude 7 recalls that Sodom and Gomorrah indulged in "unnatural lust" and were punished by eternal fire. "Sex perversion, disorder in marriage, adultery," are some of the idolatrous evils denounced in another document (Wisd. Sol. 14:26).

Sacred homosexual prostitution in connection with foreign cults may have been one factor in the strong biblical repudiation of homosexuality. The houses of male prostitutes were destroyed by King Josiah (II Kings 23:7; cf. I Kings 14:24; 15:12; 22:46). *See* SODOMITE.

Bibliography. D. S. Bailey, *Homosexuality and the Western Tradition* (1955); W. G. Cole, *Sex and Love in the Bible* (1959).

O. J. BAAB

HONEY [דבש, נפת; μέλι]. The honey of the Bible was of three kinds: (*a*) a thick grape syrup (Arabic *dibs*); (*b*) wild honey ("honey from [RSV 'out of'] the rock" [Deut. 32:13; Ps. 81:16—H 81:17]; cf. the honey found in a lion's carcass [Judg. 14:8], or in a forest [I Sam. 14:25]; cf. also the honey eaten by John the Baptist [Matt. 3:4; Mark 1:6]); and (*c*) honey from domesticated bees (cited as a "produce of the field" in II Chr. 31:5).

Honey is called one of the necessities of life (Ecclus. 39:26) and is often mentioned in lists of foodstuffs or good things of the land (Gen. 43:11; Deut. 8:8; II Sam. 17:29; I Kings 14:3; cf. Ezek. 16:13, etc.; on the phrase "a land flowing with milk and honey," *see* MILK). Because honey fermented easily, it was prohibited in burnt offerings, along with leaven (Lev. 2:11); honey was widely used in sacrifices elsewhere in the ancient Near East, however.

The sweetness of honey is often used in metaphorical expressions (Judg. 14:18; Pss. 19:10—H 19:11; 119:103; Prov. 5:3; 16:24; Ezek. 3:3; Rev. 10:9-10). For the "curds and honey" eaten by the child Immanuel (Isa. 7:15), *see* CURDS. *See also* BEE.

Bibliography. H. M. Ransome, *The Sacred Bee* (1937).

J. F. ROSS

HONOR [*usually* כבוד (*more often* GLORY), *from* כבד; *also* גדולה, greatness, dignity; הדר *and its derivatives*, to prefer, to give the place of preference; הוד, weight, splendor, majesty; יקר, value; תפארת, beauty, glory; LXX δόξα; NT *usually* τιμάω *and its derivatives; also* δόξα (*more often* GLORY)]; PLACE OF HONOR [πρωτοκλισία]; WORTHY OF HONOR [σεμνός]; HONORABLE [καλός]. High respect, esteem, or reverence shown to, received from, or felt in regard to another person. Particularly in the OT, however, the term refers to a possession of a person, closely connected with his position in the community. The possession of valor, property, wealth, wisdom, or high position is an indication of a man's honor (Gen. 45:13; SPLENDOR).

Honor and GLORY are closely connected in the Bible, both terminologically and theologically. Also, in the RSV a number of instances may be noted in which "MAJESTY," "SPLENDOR," and similar terms are used rather than "honor." Conversely, the RSV occasionally has "honor" where the KJV and other versions use other words (Gen. 30:20; I Sam. 2:8; etc.).

By far the majority of occurrences of the term "honor" in the OT refer to the honor of man. This is true largely because, as indicated above, the same words may be rendered "glory," "splendor," "majesty," etc. These latter terms have generally been selected by the translators when the reference is to God's glory or honor. Man's honor is clearly understood to be a gift of God (Pss. 8:5—H 8:6; 62:7—H 62:8; 71:21). It consists in all those gifts or blessings which extend and enhance the personality (i.e., the SOUL, נפש) of man: wealth, property, wisdom, valor. Man displays his honor through his readiness to give, to share honor with his fellows. His honor may be lost through misfortune or through disobedience to God. Those who build up honor for themselves are roundly denounced by the prophets (Isa. 1:23; Amos 5:11-12; 8:4-5; etc.). A man's honor must be employed in the maintenance of wholeness (שלום) within the life of the community. Thus honor is closely connected with justice, righteousness, and peace—key terms in the covenant vocabulary of the OT. Dishonor, accordingly, is equally closely connected with sin. Of particular importance in the OT is the honor due to father and mother (Exod. 20:12; Deut. 5:16); this commandment also occurs six times in the NT.

The NT also uses the term "honor" primarily in reference to man. It contains numerous admonitions, however, against a person's seeking honor for himself: the place of honor at feasts (Luke 14:7-8; 20:46) or the honor one has in virtue of his office (Heb. 5:4). The Christian is urged to bestow honor freely and gladly upon those to whom honor is due (Rom. 12:10; Phil. 2:29; I Tim. 5:3; 6:1; etc.). Should he be required to suffer dishonor, this need not indicate either his faithlessness to his calling as a man or his infidelity to God. On the contrary, it may be a mark of his discipleship (II Cor. 6:8).

All glory and honor and dominion are to be conferred upon God, both because he is worthy of honor as God (I Tim. 1:17; 6:16; Rev. 4:9; 7:12) and because he is the source of all honor (II Pet. 1:17; Rev. 4:11). Jesus also has been "crowned with glory and honor because of the suffering of death" (Heb. 2:9); the Lamb who was slain is worthy "to receive power and wealth and wisdom and might and honor and glory and blessing" (Rev. 5:12-13). It is incumbent upon the Christian to "honor Christ in the body" (Phil. 1:20), to "give God the glory" (or "honor"; Acts 12:23), which apparently means to acknowledge the sovereignty and honor of the Deity (cf. Josh. 7:19). To withhold the honor due to God or to his Son is sin.

See also BLESSING; SHAME.

Bibliography. W. Caspari, *Die Bedeutungen der Wortsippe* כבד *im Hebräischen* (1908); J. Pedersen, *Israel, Its Life and Culture*, I-II (1926), 213-44. W. HARRELSON

HOOK. The translation of several words:

a) וו; a gold (Exod. 26:32) or silver (27:10) hook attached to the pillars of the tabernacle. The various hangings of the tabernacle were suspended from these hooks.

b) חח, inserted in the nose (II Kings 19:28) or jaw (Ezek. 29:4) of animals (19:4-9) or captives (II Chr. 33:11). To it would be attached a rope by which the captor could lead his prisoner. In Exod. 35:22 the word refers to a type of jewelry, possibly a brooch.

c) חכה (Isa. 19:8; Hab. 1:15); צנה or צנ (Job 40:24; Amos 4:2); סיר דוגה (Amos 4:2): all fish hooks (*see* FISHING). In Job 40:24 the MT is בעיניו, "with his eyes" (so KJV). The RSV reads בצנים, "with hooks."

d) שפתים (Ezek. 40:43), a word of doubtful meaning. The LXX reads "edges."

e) Ἄγκιστρον (Matt. 17:27), a fish hook. It is a general term for "hook" in classical Greek.

See also PRUNING HOOK.

Bibliography. J. B. Pritchard, ed., *ANEP* (1954), figs. 447, 524. R. W. CORNEY

HOOPOE hōō'pōō [דוכיפת, *dûkhîphath, possibly onomatopoeic; cf.* דוך, to pound, beat, *and cf. the hoopoe's habit of striking the ground with its beak; cf.* Demotic *qqpt*, hoopoe; Syr. *qaqûphâ,* hoopoe; Vulg. *upupa*, hoopoe; LXX ἔποψ, hoopoe (Lev. 11:19); πορφυρίων, water hen (Deut. 14:18); Targ. (Onq.) woodcock]; KJV LAPWING. Any of a family (Upupidae) of Old World nonpasserine birds (Genus Upapa), having a head crest of erectile plumes and a long, slender, curved bill. In Tristram's time it was a summer visitor to Palestine and "tolerably common in all parts of the country." That דוכיפת designates this bird is reasonably certain. The hoopoe's search for grubs and small insects in such repulsive places as dunghills may account for its being classed among Israel's unclean birds. W. S. MCCULLOUGH

HOPE. In English usage the word "hope" covers a wide range of meanings, and nowhere is this more apparent than in the Bible. In the OT "hope" is the translation of many Hebrew words, each with its own diverse associations. And in the English NT, although there are fewer Greek antecedents, these antecedents often convey an unsuspected wealth of meaning. In both OT and NT, therefore, the word "hope," whether as noun or as verb, points to ranges of experience and truth which are often missed in casual reading. To be sure, in both the OT and the NT the concept occurs in ordinary speech without significant overtones. But the predominant usage falls in theological contexts which give to the word many complex implications. In these contexts there is a high degree of continuity between the OT and the NT. The existence of hope springs from the covenants made by God with his people. Hope links together the two parties of the covenant: God is man's hope; therefore, man hopes in God. Hope is intricately involved in the total pattern of divine action and human response.

A. *HOPE IN THE OT.* The words more frequently used to connote "hope" are בטח, חסה, יחל, קוה, and שבר. In the LXX these and some ten other Hebrew constructions are on occasion rendered by the Greek noun ἐλπίς and the verb ἐλπίζειν; but none of the Hebrew terms is translated exclusively thus. Other Greek renderings are πεποίθεναι ("to trust"), ὑπομένειν ("to endure"), and προσδοκᾶν ("to expect" and "to await"). In both Hebrew and Greek, the noun often accents the ground or the object of expectation, while the verb more often accents the human attitude of hoping.

1. In common speech. בטח in its various forms often bespeaks a present condition of security and prosperity, which produces a feeling of complacency and self-sufficiency. A man is at ease, fearing no threats and confident that the future will sustain his security (Judg. 18:7, 9-10, 27; Isa. 32:9-10; 47:10; Zeph. 2:15). קוה gives a stronger sense that man's fate is wholly dependent upon future contingency.

Even though a tree is cut down, it will sprout again; therefore, there is hope for it. But there is no hope for a man who dies (Job 14:7). When God cuts off a man, leaving him Sheol as his only home, man's hope is gone, because he has no future (Job 17:15; 19:10; 27:8). Conversely, so long as man has a future, he has hope (Prov. 23:18; 24:14). Very often hope indicates the confidence which one man vests in another (Judg. 9:26; Mic. 7:5), but there are men who have no hope and in whom it would be folly to trust (Prov. 26:12; 29:20). When man's confidence rests on ephemeral resources, his hopes are doomed to futility. This is true when he relies on armies and fortresses (Isa. 31:1-3; 36:4-9; Hos. 10:13), on riches (Job 31:24; Pss. 49:6-12; 52:7; Prov. 11:28), on houses (Job 18:14; Isa. 32:9-14), or on sorcery and idols (Ps. 115:4-8; Isa. 44:9-20; 47:9-15). The basic question is not whether hopes are good or bad, but whether they are futile or valid. A hope that is not firmly grounded ensures disappointment, shame, and disaster (Pss. 25:2, 20; 31:1; 71:1; Prov. 10:28; Isa. 32:9-14; Ezek. 37:11).

2. In theological contexts. The basis of ultimate confidence is therefore the chief issue facing man. Throughout the OT, God is recognized as the "hope of Israel" (Jer. 14:8). He alone makes men dwell in safety. He alone offers promises for the future which can be relied on, for his faithful and steadfast love guarantees the fulfilment of his word. By dread deeds he delivers all who take refuge in him, and thus becomes the hope (חסה) of all the ends of the earth (Pss. 65:5; 71:4-5). Many are the images which articulate this conviction that God alone provides at once the source and the object of man's trust. He is a rock which cannot be moved (Deut. 32:4, 15, 18; Pss. 18:2, 31, 46; 62:2, 6-7; Isa. 26:4; 30:29). He is a refuge and fortress which offer ultimate security for the poor and the righteous in the midst of their affliction (Pss. 14:6; 61:3; 73:28; 91:9; 94:22; Prov. 14:26; Ezek. 34:27-28). Hope is defined, not so much by the distinct shape of specific desires and expectations, as by the fact that it springs from God's creative and sustaining power and that it moves toward a good which is congruent with that power.

With what attitudes do men respond to this God who is in himself their hope? These attitudes in their multiplicity and interdependence constitute hope as response. We may distinguish four attitudes: (*a*) a trust in God, through which one commits his cause to the Lord, holds fast to him, and lives in serenity and peace under his present protection (here בטח is the key word; cf. Job 11:18; Pss. 9:10; 22:8-9; 40:4; Prov. 22:19; Isa. 26:3; Jer. 17:7); (*b*) a ready eagerness to take refuge in him from one's foes, and to rely on him for speedy deliverance (here חסה is the key word; cf. Pss. 5:11; 7:1; 16:1; 17:7; 18:2, 30; 25:20; 36:7; 37:40); (*c*) the confident expectation of good, of future gladness which becomes the occasion for present rejoicing (Ps. 13:5; Prov. 10:28; 11:23); (*d*) a waiting in patience and courage for the Lord to bring his salvation. The recognition of delay in the promised help prompts endurance in the midst of present adversity (here יחל is the key word; cf. Pss. 31:24; 33:18-22; 38:15; 42:5, 11; 69:3; 71:12-14; 119:114-16; 130:6-8; Isa. 51:5).

Hope as a living, present bond between the God of hope and the hoping Israel thus becomes a major definition of the life of the righteous community. Because this hope cannot be reduced to specific objects of future desiring, it is not immediately destroyed by unexpected shifts in human fortunes. It frees men from anxiety, but not from the necessity for patient endurance. It is quite incompatible with the fear of human enemies, but entirely compatible with the fear of God, for this fear, too, is an expression of confidence in God as the only source of ultimate security. It gives to man's existence a future-orientation, without investing all reliance on a specific historical goal and without diminishing the source of confidence in God's mighty work in the past and the present.

B. *HOPE IN THE NT.* "Hope" (ἐλπίς, ἐλπίζειν) is a primary term in the NT vocabulary, appearing in all the major books, although rarely in the gospels and not at all in Revelation. (Absence of the word by no means indicates the absence of the reality.) The word appears only as a noun or verb, and never in adjectival or adverbial form, probably because the accent does not fall on subjective feelings (e.g., "hopeful," "hopefully") but on the objective alignment of forces determining the human situation. For the same reason, the noun does not invite adjectival modifiers—e.g., good or bad hopes.

1. In common speech. In fewer than one fourth of its occurrences in the NT, "hope" describes a human situation quite apart from any religious content. Here it denotes an expectation concerning the future which accords (usually) with a person's desire and serves as a basis for speech or action. In planting seed, the farmer desires and expects a harvest (I Cor. 9:10). In lending his money, the lender desires and expects a return (Luke 6:35). Paul wants and plans to send Timothy to Philippi (Phil. 2:19, 23), or he expects to visit a church soon (Rom. 15:24; cf. I Tim. 3:14; II John 12; III John 14). So strongly, however, does the accent fall on expectation rather than desire, that one can lose hope even when his desire remains (Acts 16:19; 27:20). Hope then stands or falls with the dependability of the expectation. The basis of expectation thus becomes the decisive constituent of hope. It is with this basis that the theological use of the word primarily deals.

2. In theological contexts. Here "hope" involves all facets of the manifold relationships of God and his people. God is the author and source of hope, its sustaining power, and its unseen yet certain object. Each of these relations is subject to multiple and varied articulation. But common to all is the conviction that because hope is God-grounded, God-sustained, and God-directed, hope is a reality within which men may dwell. Hope is simultaneously the response among his people to his activity among them. As a description of this response, hope is expectation expressed in faith, confidence, patience, endurance, and eagerness. Different writers stress different features of this complex but living structure.

***a.* Paul.** To Paul, God is the source and ground of hope, the "God of hope" (Rom. 15:13). One may correctly infer from the remarkable statement in Rom. 8:20 that it is God who in hope subjects creation to futility. Hope rests upon God's calling and upon his PROMISE (Rom. 4:17-21). This explains why there can be but one hope (Eph. 4:4). The gospel, which proclaims one promise and one calling, mediates hope (Col. 1:23). The hope which constitutes the ground of faith's expectancy is so objectively certain that it is virtually synonymous with the destiny promised by God, the inheritance to which God's people are called (Rom. 5:2; 12:12; Eph. 1:18; Col. 1:23; I Thess. 5:8).

The power to hope is conveyed from God to men through the Holy Spirit, which dwells in their hearts (Rom. 5:5; 15:13; Gal. 5:5). It is synonymous with the living, indwelling Christ, who is "in you, the hope of glory" (Col. 1:27). Just as the new life of believers is constituted simultaneously by their living in Christ and by Christ's living in them, so too their hope is in Christ, and their hope is Christ active in them. As the "first fruits" of the Spirit, hope is the assurance of the full harvest (Rom. 8:23-30; Eph. 1:13).

The object hoped for in Paul's thought is everywhere the continuation and completion of this work of Father, Son, and Spirit. This completion, although a single end, is capable of flexible description: "sharing the glory of God" (Rom. 5:2); the "glorious liberty of the children of God" (Rom. 8:21); the "redemption of our bodies" (Rom. 8:23); "righteousness" (Gal. 5:5); "being changed into his likeness" (II Cor. 3:12-18); acquiring possession of the inheritance (Eph. 1:14).

As a human response to God's activity, hope is for Paul closely associated with unshakable confidence (Rom. 4:18; 5:5), with rejoicing (Rom. 5:2; 12:12), with steadfast endurance (Rom. 5:4; 8:25; 12:12; I Thess. 1:3), with boldness (II Cor. 3:12; Phil. 1:20), with freedom (Rom. 8:21; Gal. 5:5), with peace (Rom. 5:1; 12:13; Eph. 2:13 ff), and with love (I Cor. 13:7). Noteworthy is the frequent appearance of the famous triad: faith, hope, love (Rom. 5:1-5; I Cor. 13; Eph. 4:1-6; I Thess. 1:3; 5:8), not as separate virtues, but as mutual, interacting gifts of the Spirit. Also noteworthy is the recognition of the mysterious, paradoxical, and "offensive" character of hope in Christ. Faith exhibits a confidence which is strengthened, not weakened, by the apparent impossibility of the promise (Rom. 4:16-25). Hope is conveyed only by the Spirit and deals with "what no eye has seen" (I Cor. 2:9-16). It thrives on trials, and on the experience of sufferings (Rom. 5:1-5; 8:17; 12:12; II Cor. 1:3-7). In hope, the church participates in the futility and bondage of the whole creation, where the sons of God are conspicuous by their weakness as well as by their patience (Rom. 8:18-27). Hope derives its inner structure from the victory over death wrought in the death-resurrection of Jesus Christ (I Cor. 15; I Thess. 4). Finally, it should be noted that hope is at once corporate and personal, both in its source in God and in its manifestation in men. It is coextensive with the covenant, the promise, the calling, by which the existence of God's people is sustained. The hope of Abraham has archetypal validity for all Abraham's true descendants. Gentiles who through Christ are united to the commonwealth of Israel receive the hope which is embodied in the "covenants of promise" (Eph. 2:12). In Christ as the new Adam, the "one man," God offers "acquittal and life" to all men and thus includes all creation within the scope of redemption (Rom. 5–8; I Cor. 15). Those who share the life of this new Man are bound together into one hope.

b. Luke-Acts. Luke uses "hope" in its theological context less frequently, and with a less complex and subtle cluster of associations. Hope is quite simply the desire and expectation of a Messiah who will redeem Israel (Luke 24:21). This expectation, so prominent in Israel, was the reason for the disciples' loyalty to Jesus, and consequently the reason for their despair at his death. Although the Cross seemed to demonstrate the frustration of this hope, visitation from the risen Lord brought the certainty of its fulfilment.

This fulfilment was not, however, realized apart from the work of the risen Lord in "opening the Scriptures" and in opening the disciples' eyes (Luke 24:31-32). For Luke, the ultimate ground of hope is God (Acts 24:15), whose promise to the fathers is fulfilled in the resurrection of Jesus Christ (Acts 26: 6-7). Faith in this resurrection had given David assurance of a destiny which enabled him to "dwell in hope" (Acts 2:26). The apostle Paul was attacked by Jews and placed on trial before the Romans because of his confident proclamation that God's fulfilment of his promise in the resurrection of the dead is nothing less than the vindication of Israel's hope (Acts 24:15; 26:6-7). Paul's defense of this hope stands or falls with the credibility of God's exaltation of Jesus from the dead (Acts 26:8).

It is through the Resurrection and the Ascension that the promised Holy Spirit is given, and this Spirit enables men to see what prophets and kings had long hoped to see—the overcoming of death by life (Acts 2:16-36) through the coming of the Messiah. In Acts the link between the OT and the new era is constituted by the one promise and the one hope. The opposition between the apostles and the Jews (not Israel) developed over the resurrection of Jesus, which in fulfilment of the promise constitutes the "hope of Israel" (Acts 28:20).

c. Hebrews. It is characteristic of Hebrews to use an article with ἐλπίς, "*the* hope," and thus to stress, not the subjective manifestation, but the objective ground and goal. Here, as throughout the Bible, the hope is grounded firmly on the covenant promise and oath of God: "He who promised is faithful" (10:23; cf. 6:16-18; 7:20-21).

Also stressed is the conviction that because Jesus is its surety, this is a better promise and a better covenant. The covenant is now supported by the "power of an indestructible life," and hence the corresponding hope is a better one (7:16-19). The superiority is seen in the twin facts (*a*) that the Day is now drawing near (10:25) and (*b*) that today we can draw near to God. Those who now share the wilderness wandering can also enter today the promised rest (4:1-3). Those who now constitute the temple, and the house of God, now have access through the veil into the Holy of holies (6:19-20). The process of entering, however, is a continuous one—of moving toward the End as the pilgrim or the runner (11:1–12:3). "Things hoped for" are there now behind the veil to be manifested in the coming Day. They are unseen but nonetheless real. The substance of things hoped for is witnessed to by such faith as that of Abel, Enoch, Noah, and Abraham.

This faith (the subjective appropriation of the objective hope) is variously described and fully illustrated: the confident and obedient heart, the opposite of the hard hearts which induced the Israelites to reject Moses in the wilderness (3:6-19); the courageous and patient endurance, far removed from apathy and sluggishness, by which Abraham obtained the promise (6:11-18); the unwavering and untiring confession, supported by love and good works, which all pilgrims of faith have demonstrated (10:23–12:3). The hope which is set before men produces and vindicates the faith by which they seize it.

It is because Jesus is the surety of the promise that he is also pioneer and perfecter of faith (12:2). His faithful obedience unto death thus becomes the mediator of the new covenant and the supreme example of how to lay hold of the better hope. Because of his entrance as priest into the Holy of holies, our hope is located where he is. Being there, it serves as a perfect anchor of the soul (6:19). Men cannot see the anchor, but by faith they grasp it (11:1).

d. I Peter. "Hope" is a salient word in I Peter, which has rightly been called the letter of hope. The central motifs of NT thought here receive succinct and lucid explication. Hope is a mark of rebirth through God's mercy (1:3). The new life is participation in the resurrection of Jesus Christ; therefore, hope is the power of this life. Birth into hope is birth into an inheritance which comprises both the coming salvation and the present status as heirs. Hope is both present and future in the same sense that the revelation of God's glory is present and future (1:13, 21). It is the eschatological gift which now enables men to depend wholly on the coming glory (1:13, 20). The source and sustainer of this confident and patient expectancy is God (1:21). Hope is man's way of reverencing Christ as Lord (3:15). The Christian's hope not only marks the boundary between his former and his new life; it also marks the boundary with the world. Hope, in fact, is the issue at stake in persecution (cf. Acts; Hebrews). It is something to be confessed, defended, explained on the witness stand. The defense which best conforms to the hope employs gentleness, courage, forgiveness, and reverence (3:10-16). As in Paul, the prime corollaries of hope are faith, joy, and love (1:3-9). Hope is that expectation of the coming grace which is manifested by sober obedience and holiness.

e. Conclusion. As in the OT, so in the NT, no single word is sufficient for expressing the reality of hope. E.g., the word ἐλπίς rarely occurs in the Synoptic gospels, yet there is no diminution of hope. Here God's promise and gift of his kingdom is assumed to be the ground and object of man's expectation. The message and work of Jesus are described as the answer to man's longing for redemption (among the key words are προσδοκᾶν and προσδέχεσθαι; Matt. 11:3; Mark 15:43; Luke 2:25, 38; 3:15; 7:19-20; 12:36, 46; 23:51). Everywhere Jesus commands his disciples to seek first God's kingdom, surrendering all other desires and claims. He requires of them constant alertness (γρηγορεῖν; Mark 13:34-35; 14:34-38; Luke 12:37) and patient endurance (ὑπομένειν; Matt. 10:22; Luke 8:15; 21:19).

So, too, in the book of Revelation, the relationship of the Messiah to his people is full of hope, even though the word is absent. He is the ALPHA AND OMEGA, the victorious King, who promises to those who conquer full participation in his sovereignty. This promise elicits a loyalty which takes the form of keen expectancy, of continual wakefulness (Rev. 3:2-3; 16:15), and of unwearying patience (2:2, 19; 3:10). To share in Jesus and his kingdom is inseparable from accepting his affliction and endurance (1:9). Such endurance is an essential component of faith (13:10; 14:12). Thus throughout the Bible, the thought of hope fuses together the reality of God as the source and goal of expectation and the totality of faith's response: trust, eagerness, patient endurance, and joyful assurance.

Bibliography. A. Pott, *Das Hoffen im NT* (1915); M. A. C. Warren, *Truth of Vision* (1948); J. Daniélou, *Advent* (1950); J. A. T. Robinson, *In the End, God* (1950); J. Marsh, *Fullness of Time* (1952); C. F. D. Moule, *Meaning of Hope* (1953); Advisory Commission, World Council of Churches, *Christ, Hope of the World* (1954); E. Brunner, *Eternal Hope* (1954); J. E. Fison, *Christian Hope* (1954); P. S. Minear, *Christian Hope and the Second Coming* (1954); J. A. T. Robinson, *Jesus and His Coming* (1957).

P. S. MINEAR

HOPHNI AND PHINEHAS hŏf'nī, fĭn'ĭ əs [חפני, tadpole, *from* Egyp. *ḥfn(r);* פנחס, פינחס, the Negro, *from* Egyp. *pə nḥśj*]. The two sons of Eli who with him were priests of Yahweh at Shiloh (I Sam. 1:3). The narrative calls them "sons of Belial" (i.e., worthless, utterly depraved; *see* BELIAL) and tells how they "had no regard for the LORD" (2:12): they "treated the offering of the LORD with contempt" (vs. 17). They took meat as they liked for themselves before the sacrifice was offered to God; and whenever a man who was sacrificing protested, they threatened to carry through their wishes by force if necessary (vss. 13-16). A later hand accentuated their abuse of the priestly office by saying that they lay with women who served at the sanctuary (vs. 22*b*). They ignored Eli's rebuke, and Eli did not reform them (vss. 22-25; 3:13). Because of their unchecked sin the doom of the house of Eli was declared by an unidentified man of God (2:27-36, probably a late insertion to give divine sanction to the Zadokites as the only legitimate priests; *see* PRIESTS AND LEVITES) and by Samuel (3:11-18). Hophni and Phinehas accompanied the ARK OF THE COVENANT to the battlefield at Aphek (4:4) and were slain in the disastrous battle with the Philistines (vss. 11, 17). When the news came to Shiloh, Eli died (vs. 18), and the wife of Phinehas gave birth prematurely to Ichabod (vss. 19-22). The genealogy in 14:3 (which makes Phinehas the grandfather of the Ahijah who accompanied the ark in the reign of Saul) is intrusive, and connection by means of a brother is unusual in a genealogy. Like 2:27-36 and perhaps from the same hand, 14:3*a* probably is an interpolation designed to place all the priests of this period under the rejection of the house of Eli in favor of the Zadokites.

Bibliography. M. Noth, *Die israelitischen Personennamen* (1928), p. 63; G. Caird, Exegesis of I Samuel, *IB*, II (1953), 887, 950; L. Koehler and W. Baumgartner, eds., *Lexicon in Veteris Testamenti Libros* (1953), pp. 321, 759.

T. M. MAUCH

HOPHRA hŏf'rə [חפרע, *from* Egyp. *w'ḥ-ib-r'*, the heart of (the sun-god) Ra endures; LXX Οὐαφρῆ;

Herodotus ʼΑπρίης]. A pharaoh (588-569 B.C.) of the Twenty-sixth Dynasty. Jeremiah (44:30) prophesied that he was to suffer the same fate at the hands of his enemies as Zedekiah had suffered at the hands of Nebuchadrezzar.

Hophra succeeded his father, Psammetichus, and ruled at Saïs in the Delta. Early in his reign he invaded Palestine and Phoenicia, and he incited Zedekiah to revolt against Babylon (Jer. 37:5). After this revolt failed and Nebuchadrezzar took Jerusalem, Hophra received a few Jewish refugees, including Jeremiah, into the Delta town of Tahpanhes, probably Daphnae (43:7). Hophra's rule was marked by the use of Greek mercenaries in unwise military expeditions. Finally a young relative, Amasis, was proclaimed king in opposition to Hophra in 569 B.C. Hophra tried to defeat Amasis in a campaign in 566, but was killed, in conformance with Jeremiah's prophecy.

Bibliography. *Cambridge Ancient History*, II (1925), 213-15, 301-3; 399-401; P. G. Elgood, *The Later Dynasties of Egypt* (1951), pp. 95-102. J. A. WILSON

HOPPING LOCUST; KJV CANKERWORM. *See* LOCUST § 1*d*.

HOR hôr [הר, *hōr*, mountain(?); *always* הר ההר, *hōr hā-hār*, Mount Hor—*lit.*, Hor, the mountain]. **1.** A mountain on the border of Edom where, according to one tradition, Aaron died and was buried (Num. 20:22; 21:4; 33:37; Deut. 32:50). On the other hand, Deut. 10:6, following another tradition, states that he died and was buried at Moserah.

Josephus identifies Mount Hor with one of the mountains in the vicinity of Petra (Antiq. IV.iv.7). Tradition has localized it on Jebel Harun, the mountain of Aaron, which is a 4,800-foot twin-topped sandstone mountain, the highest and the most rugged in Edom's mountain range.* On the summit of Jebel Harun is a tomb allegedly belonging to Aaron, the upper part of which is a Mohammedan mosque. The tomb, however, is probably a rebuilt Christian church from the period of Emperor Justinian (527-65). Fig. HOR 31.

31. Traditional site of Mount Hor, Jebel Harun, the highest peak in Edom

This tradition, which places Hor in the midst of Edomite territory, and not on its border (Num. 20:22), is open to serious doubts. Since Edom denied Israel's request for permission to pass through its territory, and implemented this denial with a strong military border force (Num. 20:17-21; Deut. 2:8), Israel could not have reached Jebel Harun without crossing Edom. Jebel Madurah, a place *ca.* fifteen miles from Kadesh, has been suggested as the most likely site for Hor. Its topography is also such that the impressive ceremony of transferring the high-priestly office from father to son (Num. 20:22-29) could be performed "in the sight of all the congregation," while Jebel Harun is both too high and too inaccessible for people to witness what happened on its top. However, the data are insufficient to make the identification of Hor certain.

2. Another mountain peak called by the same name (Num. 34:7-8). It was to mark the N limit of Israel's inheritance. It was probably some prominent peak in the Lebanon Mountain Range. Both Mount Hermon and Jebel Akkar, a NE spur of Lebanon, have been suggested as the possible location for this second Mount Hor.

Bibliography. E. Robinson, *Researches in Palestine* (1841), II, 651-53; E. H. Palmer, *The Desert of the Exodus* (1872), pp. 364-65; C. Trumbull, *Kadesh-barnea* (1884), pp. 127-39; H. Bauer, "Die hebräischen Eigennamen als sprachliche Erkenntnisquelle," *ZAW*, 48 (1930), 74; E. G. Kraeling, *Bible Atlas* (1956), pp. 118-19. J. L. MIHELIC

HORAM hôr'ăm [הרם] (Josh. 10:33). A king of Gezer, defeated and slain when he tried to relieve the victorious siege of Lachish by Joshua.

HOREB, MOUNT. *See* SINAI, MOUNT.

HOREM hôr'ĕm [חרם, sacred] (Josh. 19:38). A fortified town in the territory of Naphtali. The context indicates that it was in the hill country of N Galilee, but the exact site is unknown.

HORESH hôr'ĕsh [חרש, forest] (I Sam. 23:15-19); KJV A (THE) WOOD. A place in the Wilderness of Ziph at which David hid from Saul for a time, and the scene of a compact between David and Jonathan; usually identified with Khirbet Khoreisa, *ca.* 1⅔ miles from Tell Ziph and *ca.* 6 miles S of Hebron.

V. R. GOLD

HOR-HAGGIDGAD hôr'hə gĭd'găd [חר הגדגד, hole *or* cavern of Gidgad]; KJV HOR-HAGIDGAD. Alternately: GUDGODAH gŭd gō'də [גדגדה] (Deut. 10:7). A stopping place of the Israelites in the wilderness. In Num. 33:31-33 the order of travel is Moseroth, Bene-jaakan, Hor-haggidgad, Jotbathah; whereas in Deut. 10:6-7 it is Beeroth Bene-jaakan, Moserah, Gudgodah, Jotbathah.

It has been proposed, but is phonetically not probable, that the site might be identified with Wadi Ghadaghed, a stream which flows into Wadi Jerafeh, which in turn empties itself into Wadi el-Jeib in the region of Arabah. J. L. MIHELIC

HORI hôr'ī [חרי, LXX Χορρι (1 *below*); חורי, LXX Σουρι (2 *below*); *see* HORITES]. **1.** The first son of Lotan; ancestor of a Horite subclan in Edom (Gen. 36:22; I Chr. 1:39).

2. The father of Shaphat, a Simeonite (Num. 13:5). L. HICKS

HORITE hôr'īt [חרי, *plural* חרים, *with the article*]. **1.** In the MT, a name specialized for the early population of Seir, the country later occupied by the Edomites (Gen. 14:6; Deut. 2:12, 22). In one passage, moreover (Gen. 36:2), the MT reading "Hivite" is plainly a textual error for "Horite" (cf. vs. 20).

2. The LXX reads "Horites" for "HIVITES" in Gen. 34:2; Josh. 9:7; both these passages deal with inhabitants of Central Palestine, as distinct from the MT "Horites." Conversely, the LXX reads Ευαῖοι, "Hivites," in Isa. 17:9, where the MT has החרש, evidently a corruption of החרי, "the Horites." The land involved here is Palestine proper. It follows that these Horites-Hivites are not to be confused with the pre-Edomite Horites—a fact still apparent to the LXX, and not unknown to earlier Hebrew tradition. Such W Horites have to be connected with the extra-biblical HURRIANS. In local usage they were more commonly designated as Hivites.

There are two valid reasons for separating Horites 1 *above* from Hurrians: (*a*) Their personal names (Gen. 36:20-30) do not conform to Hurrian patterns, but are instead Semitic; (*b*) there is no archaeological evidence whatever for Hurrian settlements in Edom, or in Transjordan in general. Consequently, the dual use of the term "Horite" must be ascribed (just as in the case of Cush) to accidental similarity in sound. When referring to the Horites of the MT, the Hebrew term is Semitic in origin, probably "cave-dweller," as tradition has explained it all along. In its other use, the word goes back to Hurrian (stem *ḫuru* or *ḫurw*). The need for maintaining a distinction between the two usages led to gradual disuse of "Horite" in the sense of "Hurrian" and the eventual replacement of that doublet by "Hivite."

Bibliography. E. Meyer, *Die Israeliten und deren Nachbarstämme* (1906); E. A. Speiser, *AASOR* (1933), pp. 26-31.

E. A. SPEISER

HORMAH hôr'mə [חרמה, devotion]. A city of Simeon in the S of Judah in the neighborhood of Ziklag (Josh. 15:30; 19:4; I Chr. 4:30). The meaning of the name is ambiguous, as it may mean "the greatest sanctity" or "complete destruction" as a burnt offering to a deity. According to one story the Israelites, after the return of the spies and the doom pronounced on their generation, made a desperate and futile attempt to invade the hill country and were beaten back as far as Hormah (Num. 14:45; Deut. 1:44). In these passages Hormah may be used anachronistically to indicate the exact place, or a Canaanite city of that name may have been in existence at the time. Another account, however, derives the name of the place from the fact that the Israelites, annoyed by the attacks of the king of Arad, turned and devastated the region and called it Hormah (Num. 21:3). Finally, there is a statement that the tribes of Judah and Simeon joined to destroy the city of ZEPHAT, which they renamed Hormah (Judg. 1:17). The city is also included in the list of kings conquered by Joshua (Josh. 12:14), but this list is a summation of all the Israelite conquests in W Canaan. It was one of the cities to which David sent some of the spoil from the defeat of the Amalekites, apparently because of hospitality to him while he was an outcast (I Sam. 30:30).

Opinions as to the probable location of Hormah vary according to the possible direction of the Israelite attack as related in Num. 21. If it came from the S, the most likely site would be Tell el-Milh, *ca.* seven miles E of Beer-sheba. If it came from the SW, the logical place would be Tell esh-Sheri'ah, *ca.* twelve miles NW of that city. S. COHEN

HORN. *See* MUSICAL INSTRUMENTS.

HORNET [צרעה, depression, discouragement; Arab. *ḍar'a,* be abased]. An insect of the order Hymenoptera; actually a WASP, but larger and more dangerous. The species most common in Palestine is the large, yellow, red-brown *Vespa orientalis*. Like the ant and the bee, the hornet is a social insect with specialized phases (male drones, queen, workers). The *Vespa orientalis* is the most important enemy of the honeybee, for whose workers it lies in ambush near the hives, and whose hives, if unprotected, it invades and destroys. Hornets of the tropical species are easily aroused and sting anyone disturbing them. A colony lives in a many-celled nest, usually suspended from a branch, and made of a kind of paper manufactured from bits of wood rasped off by the workers. By the end of the season as many as ten thousand hornets may inhabit such a nest.

The biblical passages which contain צרעה (Exod. 23:28; Deut. 7:20; Josh. 24:12) all refer to a divine intervention on Israel's behalf in driving out the inhabitants of Canaan. Koehler (Koehler-Baumgartner, *Lexicon*) does not recognize "hornet" as being a possible translation, accepting rather "depression" or "discouragement," from צרע, "be abased" (*contrast* FAUNA § F4*b*); but the fierce nature of this insect, as well as its habit of paralyzing its prey before sucking out its vital fluids, is well suited to the context. Interpreted as a metaphor, Yahweh's preparatory onslaught would so numb the Canaanites that they would be unable to defend themselves against the Hebrew tribes. It indicates that Yahweh played as much the decisive role in the conquest of Canaan as he had in the exodus from Egypt. W. W. FRERICHS

HORONAIM hôr'ə nā'əm [חרנים, חרונים, *probably* two caves, holes]. A town of Moab, mentioned with other Moabite cities in the oracles against Moab (Isa. 15:5; Jer. 48:3, 34). It was apparently at the foot of a descent (Jer. 48:5), but its exact location is uncertain. Mesha fought against Hauronen (חורנן; *see* MOABITE STONE) and took it. Alexander Janneus (103-76) took Oronain ('Ωρωναίν) with other cities from the Arabs, but Hyrcanus restored them to Aretas (Jos. Antiq. XIII.xv.4; XIV.i.4).

In II Sam. 13:34 the RSV translates "from the Horonaim road" for the Hebrew "from the road behind him." The reference is probably to Upper and

Lower BETH-HORON, "Horonaim" being understood as a dual form of Horon. E. D. GROHMAN

HORONITE hôr′ə nīt [חרני, citizen of Horonaim, *or more probably* of Beth-horon]. An epithet used with the name of Sanballat, who opposed Nehemiah in the restoration of Jerusalem (Neh. 2:10, 19; 13:28).

HORSE. The horse played an increasing part in war, travel, and hunting in the Near East from the middle of the second millennium B.C. and in Israel from the time of Solomon.

1. Words for "horse"
2. Introduction in the Near East
3. Uses
   a. In war
   b. In transportation
   c. In hunting
   d. As food
   e. In threshing
   f. In the cult
4. Trade in horses
5. Care and equipment
6. Characteristics and actions
7. Comparisons and figurative references
8. Supernatural horses
   a. In the OT
   b. In the Apoc.
   c. In the NT

Bibliography

1. Words for "horse." Hebrew words meaning "horse" are:

a) סוס (138 times; e.g., Gen. 47:17); the feminine, סוסה, occurs in Song of S. 1:9 (RSV "mare"; KJV "horses").

b) פרש (Isa. 28:28 [text doubtful]; Joel 2:4 [RSV "horses"]; Ezek. 27:14 [RSV "war horses"]). In these cases the KJV translates HORSEMEN, the more common meaning. In II Sam. 1:6, בעלי הפרשים (lit. "possessors of horses") is translated "horsemen."

c) אביר (Judg. 5:22 [RSV "steeds"; KJV MIGHTY ONES, the root meaning]; Jer. 8:16 [RSV "stallions"; KJV STRONG ONES]; Jer. 47:3 [RSV "stallions"; KJV BULLS]).

d) רכש (I Kings 4:28—H 5:8 [RSV "swift steeds"; KJV DROMEDARIES]; Esth. 8:10, 14 [RSV "swift horses"; KJV MULES]; Mic. 1:13 [RSV "steeds"; KJV SWIFT BEAST]).

e) בני הרמכים (Esth. 8:10 [RSV "bred from the royal stud"; KJV YOUNG DROMEDARIES]; lit. "the offspring of the swift mares").

The Greek word ἵππος, "horse," appears in Jas. 3:3 and 14 times in Revelation (e.g., 6:2).

2. Introduction in the Near East. The horse was probably first domesticated in the steppes of S Russia and Central Asia. The commonest Hebrew word for "horse," סוס, *sûs,* and its Akkadian and Egyptian cognates (*sīsû* and *ssm.t, śśm.t*) seem to be of Aryan origin. Horses are not included among the animals of the Hebrew patriarchs in the early second millennium B.C. Horses are mentioned in the Cappadocian Tablets (nineteenth century B.C.), but not so frequently as asses. The Aryan Mitanni introduced the two-wheeled battle chariot with war horses into N Mesopotamia in the eighteenth century B.C. About the same time the Kassites, using horses and chariots, gained control of Babylonia. During the Hyksos period (eighteenth-sixteenth centuries B.C.) the horse and the chariot came into Egypt. Amarna letters of the fourteenth century B.C. indicate that horses were then used in Palestine. Cavalry, introduced by the Medes and Cimmerians, was employed in Mesopotamia from the twelfth century B.C. onward. Fig. CAM 6.

3. Uses. In the ancient Near East the horse was used for war, for transportation and hunting by the wealthy, but not for agriculture and very little for bearing or pulling burdens.

a. In war. The majority of the biblical references to the horse are connected with war.

The Bible refers to the war horses with chariots of the Egyptians (Exod. 14:9), the Canaanites (Judg. 5:22), the Syrians (I Kings 20:1), the Assyrians (Isa. 5:28), the Chaldeans (Jer. 4:13), and the Medes and Chaldeans (Nah. 3:2). War horses were ridden by the Philistines (II Sam. 1:6), the Syrians (I Kings 20:20), the Medes and Persians (Jer. 50:42), the soldiers of Magog (Ezek. 38:4), and the Romans (Acts 23:23, 32). The enemies of God in the last times will use horses (Zech. 14:15; Rev. 19:18). The Egyptians and Assyrians have left many reliefs of their war horses and chariots. Figs. CAM 6; CHA 24-25; GAZ 12.

There was considerable opposition to the horse in Israel as a symbol of pagan luxury and dependence on physical power for defense. Moses (Deut. 17:16) and Samuel (I Sam. 8:11) warned Israel that a king might multiply horses for pleasure and for war like the pagans. Psalmists (Pss. 20:7—H 20:8; 33:17) and prophets (Isa. 31:1; Ezek. 17:15) condemned trusting in horses rather than in the Lord for victory. As a sign of the peacefulness of the messianic kingdom, the king comes riding on an ass, not a horse, and chariots and war horses are to be abolished (Zech. 9:9-10).

In the face of this opposition, it is not surprising that the introduction of the war horse in Israel was gradual. Following divine instructions, Joshua hamstrung the horses of the Canaanites (Josh. 11:6, 9). David hamstrung most of the horses captured from Zobah, but kept enough for a hundred chariots (II Sam. 8:4). Solomon is reported to have had variously forty thousand and four thousand stalls for his horses (I Kings 4:26; II Chr. 9:25; *see* STALLS). King Ahab's horses are mentioned in I Kings 18:5, and records of Shalmaneser III state that Ahab furnished two thousand chariots in the coalition against Assyria. Jehoshaphat of Judah also had war horses, presumably with chariots (I Kings 22:4; II Kings 3:7). With irony Rabshakeh, the Assyrian general, offered Hezekiah two thousand horses, if the latter could furnish riders, knowing that Judah did not have so many horsemen (II Kings 18:23). Sennacherib's annals list many horses among the booty taken from the cities of Judah, and this is illustrated by a relief, originally in Nineveh, showing a chariot and horses from Lachish.

b. In transportation. The horse furnished transportation for royalty, nobility, and the wealthy in the ancient Near East. As a sign of honor, Joseph rode in Pharaoh's second horse-drawn chariot (Gen. 41:43). Absalom made a display by riding in a horse-drawn chariot (II Sam. 15:1). Naaman traveled from Syria with horses and chariots to visit Elisha in Israel (II Kings 5:9). Horses were used to transport the body of Amaziah to Jerusalem (II Kings 14:20). Horses became so common in Jerusalem that the royal palace had a special horse gate (II Chr. 23:15), and a gate of the city was called the Horse Gate (Neh. 3:28; Jer. 31:40). Jer. 17:25; 22:4 promise that Davidic kings would continue riding in chariots and princes on horses, on condition of national obedience. Isa. 66:20 predicts that the exiles would return on horses, and the Jews returning under Zerubbabel had 736 horses (Ezra 2:66). A postexilic prophet sees even the horses of the messianic kingdom as holy to the Lord (Zech. 14:20). The important place of the horse in Persian society is illustrated by Mordecai's honor of riding the royal horse (Esth. 6:8-11).* Egyptian, Assyrian, and Persian reliefs show the king riding in a horse-drawn chariot on state occasions. Fig. OX 18.

c. In hunting. The only biblical mention of hunting by horse is Job 39:18, with reference to the ostrich. Hunting by kings in chariots (Egypt, Assyria) or on horseback (Assyria) was depicted in reliefs (Assyria) and paintings (Egypt).

d. As food. The eating of horse meat was forbidden by the principle of the Mosaic law in Lev. 11:4. II Kings 7:13 may imply that horses were eaten in Samaria during a siege.

e. In threshing. As it stands, Isa. 28:28 refers to the use of horses in threshing grain, but the text and interpretation of the verse are uncertain.

f. In the cult. Among the reforms of Josiah was the removal of the horses and chariots which his idolatrous predecessors had dedicated to the sun (II Kings 23:11). These may have been used in religious processions. With the Babylonian sun-god, Shamash, were associated a charioteer and presumably a chariot and horses. Helios, the Greek sun-god, was also represented in poem (Homeric Hymns III.69) and in sculpture (E pediment of the Parthenon) as riding in a chariot with horses.

4. Trade in horses. According to Gen. 47:17, Joseph gave the people of Egypt grain in exchange for their horses. One of Solomon's commercial ventures was the selling of horses from Egypt and from Kue—i.e., Cilicia (not KJV "linen yarn"), at the rate of 150 shekels of silver (I Kings 10:28). The Tyrians secured horses and war horses for trade from Beth-togarmah (Ezek. 27:14), in Armenia, also a source of horses for Mesopotamia.

5. Care and equipment. The words translated "bred from the royal stud" (Esth. 8:10) mean literally "offspring of swift mares" and may indicate breeding for speed. Solomon kept horses in stalls and fed them barley and straw (I Kings 4:26, 28—H 5:6, 8), the food of modern Arab horses. In MEGIDDO there have been found stalls and feeding troughs from Solomon's time sufficient for about 450 horses. A horse's harness (Jer. 46:4) might consist of a bridle (Ps. 32:9) and a bit (Jas. 3:3), and sometimes a saddlecloth was used (Ezek. 27:20). Bells were attached to the harness as decoration (Zech. 14:20). A whip was used to urge on a horse (Prov. 26:3).

6. Characteristics and actions. Some of the characteristics of the horse noted in the Bible are: swiftness (Jer. 4:13; Hab. 1:8); strength (Job 39:19; Ps. 147:10); neighing when excited by sexual urge (Jer. 5:8) or by battle (Jer. 8:16); stamping (Jer. 47:3); leaping (Job 39:20); sure-footedness (Isa. 63:13); hardness of hoof (Isa. 5:28); inability to run on rocks (Amos 6:12); need of a bridle for restraint (Ps. 32:9); and stubbornness when unbroken (Ecclus. 30:8). The Bible's most detailed and animated description of the horse is in Job 39:19-25.

7. Comparisons and figurative references. The characteristics of the horse are the basis for comparisons and figurative references to it in the poetical and prophetic books of the Bible. Men should not be like horses in need of the restraint of a bridle (Ps. 32:9). A damsel is compared in beauty to a mare of Pharaoh (Song of S. 1:9). The Israelites in the desert were like horses in not stumbling (Isa. 63:13). Evil men of Jerusalem lust for their neighbors' wives like neighing stallions (Jer. 5:8). The wicked go their way like a horse plunging into battle (Jer. 12:5). The rejoicing of the Chaldeans over plunder is like the neighing of stallions (Jer. 50:11; the number of references to the horse in Jeremiah is noteworthy). The sexuality of stallions is a picture of the evils of Egyptian idoltary (Ezek. 23:20). Locusts are compared to horses in appearance and in running (Joel 2:4). As it is unnatural for horses to run on rocks, so the people have perverted justice into poison (Amos 6:12). The Lord rides a chariot with horses, figures of power and majesty (Hab. 3:8, 15). God will make Judah like a triumphant war horse (Zech. 10:3). The supernatural locusts of judgment are compared to horses in appearance and to chariots with horses in sound (Rev. 9:7, 9).

8. Supernatural horses. ***a. In the OT.*** Elijah is taken up to heaven by a chariot and horses of fire (II Kings 2:11). The eyes of Elisha's servant are opened to see chariots and horses of fire around them (II Kings 6:17). In a vision Zechariah sees angelic horsemen on horses of different colors (red, sorrel, and white) who patrol the earth (Zech. 1:8). In Zech. 6:2-3, 6, the prophet sees four chariots with red, black, white, and dappled horses respectively. Here the colors of the horses seem to be associated with the four directions.

b. In the Apoc. According to II Macc. 3:25, the Seleucid chancellor Heliodorus, when about to rob the temple in Jerusalem, was attacked by a supernatural horseman. When Antiochus made his second attack on Egypt, heavenly horsemen are said to have been observed in the sky over Jerusalem (II Macc. 5:2-3). Five heavenly horsemen are said to have aided Judas in fighting against the Seleucids (II Macc. 10:29).

c. In the NT. In Rev. 6:2, 4-5, 8, the colors of the four horses are symbolic of the judgments inflicted on the earth by their riders: white=conquest, red=slaughter, black=famine, pale=death. Judgment is also executed by cavalry with supernatural horses with teeth like lions and serpentlike tails (Rev. 9:17, 19). Christ and his hosts ride to victory on white horses (Rev. 19:11, 14, 19, 21). *See* FAUNA § A1*a*.

Bibliography. B. Meissner, *Babylonien und Assyrien,* I (1920), 61, 87, 92-93, 218, 259, 295, 333. A. Erman and H. Ranke, *Aegypten und aegyptisches Leben im Altertum* (1923), pp. 583-86, 615. B. Meissner, *Babylonien und Assyrien,* II (1925), 318, 412,

427. S. Bodenheimer, *Animal Life in Palestine* (1935), pp. 126-28. M. Hilzheimer, "The Evolution of the Domestic Horse," *Antiquity*, IX (1935), 133-39. H. G. May, "Some Aspects of Solar Worship at Jerusalem," *ZAW*, XIV (1937), 269-81. A.-G. Barrois, *Manuel d'archéologie biblique*, I (1939), 284-85, 337-38. E. D. Van Beuren, *The Fauna of Ancient Mesopotamia as Represented in Art, Analecta Orientalia*, XVIII (1939), 28-34. J. Wiesner, *Fahren und Reiten in Alteuropa und im Alten Orient, Der Alte Orient*, Band XXXVIII, Heft 2-4 (1939). W. F. Albright, *Archaeology and the Religion of Israel* (1942), pp. 139, 213. A.-G. Barrois, *Manuel d'archéologie biblique*, II (1953), 89-91, 216, 229, 233, 290-91. K. Galling, "Der Ehrenname Elisas und die Entrückung Elias," *ZThK*, LIII (1956), 129-48 (wishes to increase the places where פרשים is translated "horses"). F. Hančar, *Das Pferd in prähistorischer Zeit* (1956).

J. A. THOMPSON

HORSE GATE [שער הסוסים]. A gate of Jerusalem, leading to the Kidron (*see* KIDRON, BROOK), toward the SE angle of the temple area, in the vicinity of the palace (Jer. 31:40). This gate was restored by Nehemiah (Neh. 3:28). *See* map under NEHEMIAH. *See also* JERUSALEM. G. A. BARROIS

HORSELEACH. KJV form of LEECH.

HORSEMAN [פרש; רכב; רכב סוס, rider on a horse; ἱππεύς]; HORSEMEN [ἱππικόν; Rev. 9:16; RSV CAVALRY]. One who rides a horse, usually in battle. *See* CHARIOT; HORSE; WAR, METHODS OF.

HOSAH hō'zə [חסה, refuge]. **1.** A Levite of the family of Merari; one of the gatekeepers of the tent David pitched for the ark when he brought it into Jerusalem (I Chr. 16:38). He and his thirteen sons and brethren were subsequently included in the expanded organization of the gatekeepers and were responsible for the posting of six guards for the W gate of Shallecheth (I Chr. 26:10-19; *see* JERUSALEM).

E. R. DALGLISH

2. A border town in the territory allotted to Asher (Josh. 19:29). According to the context, it was in the vicinity of Tyre, but no certain identification has been made.

HOSANNA. The Vulg. transliteration of הושיעה־נא, "Save us, we beseech thee" (Ps. 118:25; cf. II Sam. 14:4; Ps. 20:9—H 20:10), in Matt. 21:9; Mark 11:9; John 12:13.

In Ps. 118, which forms a part of the HALLEL, a pilgrim who was rejected like a worthless stone is now recognized to be a righteous man. He enters the temple to thank Yahweh for his goodness, and he is greeted by the priests as coming in the name of Yahweh. In vs. 25 he asks God for more help and greater success. This verse was sung in the liturgy of the Feast of Tabernacles (*see* BOOTHS, FEAST OF) once a day and seven times on the seventh day by the priests during their circuit(s) around the altar. When they did so, the congregation waved their lulab, consisting of branches of myrtle, willow, and a palm leaf (Jos. Antiq. III.x.4; cf. III Macc. 10:6-7). These branches themselves were sometimes called "Hosanna."

In Jewish postbiblical texts "Hosanna" is connected with messianic hopes; the man coming in the name of Yahweh is understood as the Messiah. But this interpretation seems to be much older. Together with the combination of the lulab and the "Hosanna," it would best explain the situation at Jesus' entry into Jerusalem. The people, wearing palm leaves, greet him as the Son of David, for whose coming they have asked God in the highest (as for the advent of the king in Ps. 20:9—H 20:10). Through him the kingdom of "our father David" is coming (only Mark); he is the king of Israel (only John).

In the Christian churches Matt. 21:9 got its place in connection with the threefold "Holy" preceding the consecration of the elements in the Holy Communion, seldom after the Eucharistic meal (cf. Did. 10:6): "The grace may come, this world may perish, Hosanna to the God of David"; Apostolic Constitutions 8:13).

Bibliography. F. C. Burkitt, *JTS*, 17 (1916), 139-49; I. Elbogen, *Der jüdische Gottesdienst in seiner geschichtlichen Entwicklung* (2nd ed., 1924); J. Brinktrine, *Römische Quartalschrift für Altertumskunde*, 35 (1927), 303 ff; E. Werner, " 'Hosanna' in the Gospels," *JBL*, 65 (1946), 97-122; J. S. Kennard, Jr., " 'Hosanna' and the Purpose of Jesus," *JBL*, 67 (1948), 171-76; G. Rietschel, *Lehrbuch der Liturgik*, I (2nd ed., ed. P. Graff; 1951), 236 ff; W. Reindell, *Leiturgia*, II (1955), 454 ff; J. J. Petuchowski, *"Hoshi'a na* in Psalm CXVIII, 25—a prayer for rain," *Vetus Testamentum*, 5 (1955), 266-71.

J. HEMPEL

HOSEA (MAN AND BOOK) hō zā'ə [הושע]. The name of the first book of the twelve prophets in the OT canon—second, however, to Amos chronologically. The name is the same in Hebrew as that of the last king of Israel, Hoshea (II Kings 17:1) and the original name of Joshua (Num. 13:16; Deut. 32:44).

1. The prophet
2. Variant interpretations
3. Date and composition
4. Text and style
5. The theology of Hosea

Bibliography

1. The prophet. Hosea occupies a unique place among the prophets of the OT as the only one of the writing prophets who had his home in Israel. Men such as Elijah and Micaiah a century earlier had left behind them a great prophetic tradition in the Northern Kingdom, but by the middle of the eighth century B.C. it was largely forgotten. There were still prophets in the land, but they were of such a degenerate type that Amos, when he went N to deliver his oracles at Bethel, scorned to be counted one of them (Amos 7:14). Hosea was to accuse prophets and priests alike of complete irresponsibility in their office, and, in their ignorance of the true nature of God, of guiding the people into pagan practices rather than into a pure faith (4:4-6).

So different is Hosea from Amos in character, outlook, and style that it is difficult to find any sure trace of Amos' influence in his writings; yet it remains likely that there is a relation between Amos' brief but powerful ministry in the N and Hosea's appearance not more than a few years later as the one genuine prophetic voice that the eighth century was to produce in Israel. The followers of Amos were the first to preserve the oracles of a prophet. The followers of Hosea, in gathering together both his oracles and certain biographical matter concerning him, were thus continuing a recently established

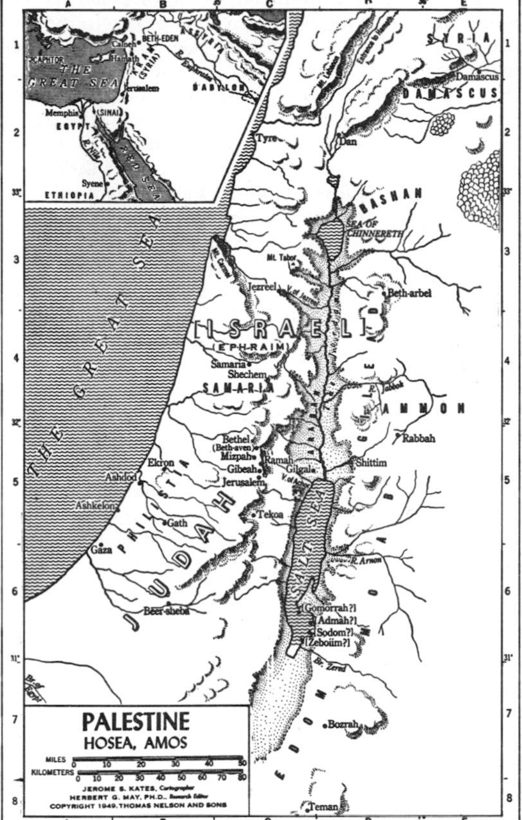

tradition, and we may assume a community of interest between the followers of the two prophets. Both books received editing in Judah. The fact that both prophets found themselves in bitter and irreconcilable conflict with the official priests and prophets adds to the likelihood that those who were spiritually awakened by them would make common cause.

The interpretation of the book of Hosea has been made extremely difficult by uncertainty about the meaning of certain references to the prophet's family life in chs. 1; 3. As sometimes happens in such instances, the basic uncertainty has led to wide variations of interpretation at this one point, and widely different conceptions of the prophet. Therefore, the collection of oracles in chs. 4–13, which are remarkably consistent in their character, should be taken as a basis for the understanding of Hosea and his ministry.

The book falls naturally into three divisions. Chs. 1–3 are distinguished by their references to Hosea's personal experience in marriage, his relation with his wife being interpreted as a parable of Yahweh's relation with Israel. All three of these chapters as they stand proclaim judgment but end on a hopeful note, envisaging a day of restoration for Israel beyond the inescapable day of judgment. Chs. 4–13 consist of brief oracles which expose the corruption of the nation, the irresponsibility of priests and prophets, the unfitness of kings and princes to rule, the spiritual degeneracy of the population, conditions which make it impossible for Israel to continue much longer as a nation. Such inner weaknesses invite destruction at the hands of an invader. Doom is certain, and in these chapters no word is spoken which points beyond the doom. Then in ch. 14 the darkness lifts and again the note of hope is sounded. One of the basic questions to which an answer must be found is whether the passages expressing hope for the more distant future are original to Hosea or have been added, as in some other prophetic books, by a later editor who knew that judgment was not God's final word to Israel.

The acceptance of chs. 4–13 as basic in understanding Hosea makes impossible the kind of erratic judgments concerning him which have been only too common, which build him up as the prophet of God's tender love in sharp contrast to Amos as the prophet of God's unquenchable wrath. For Hosea as for Amos, the wages of sin is death. His proclamations of God's judgment upon the sins of Israel are as severe as any to be found in the book of Amos. At no point in the entire book is there any suggestion that Israel can escape the coming disaster. Where hope is expressed in chs. 1–3; 14, it is not hope that the judgment may not come, but hope for a new beginning beyond the judgment.

2. Variant interpretations. Chs. 1–3 constitute a single unit, containing biographical and autobiographical material in chs. 1; 3 and a sermon to Israel in ch. 2, but bound together by the fact that all three use the marriage relationship as a likeness of God's relation to Israel and the disruption of the marriage relation by the adultery of the wife as a likeness of Israel's response to God. For centuries these chapters have furnished interpreters with major difficulties. It has seemed to dishonor God and to impeach his holiness to take literally the statement of 1:2 that God commanded Hosea to marry a harlot or the statement of 3:1 that God commanded him to reunite himself with the same harlot after she had disgraced his home.

Jewish interpreters in medieval times, such as Maimonides, Aben Ezra, and Kimchi, insisted that no such marriage ever actually took place. The whole transaction—command of God, marriage, birth of children, disruption of marriage, and later restoration—was the substance of a prophetic dream or vision, as when Ezekiel in a vision reported himself seized by the hair and transported to Jerusalem (Ezek. 8:3). Others understand Hosea's marriage as a prophetic allegory, from which they say we should no more deduce the character of the actual marriage than we should deduce the character of his (or Isaiah's) children from the names that are given them as signs to the nation. A variation of this is the view of Luther and Osiander that Gomer and her children were merely called adulterous for parabolic purposes but were actually not so. Thus chs. 1; 3 would be read allegorically in the same fashion as ch. 2. But this seems to overlook emphatic differences between ch. 2 and chs. 1; 3. The impression of biographical and autobiographical content is too strong to be completely suppressed.

At the opposite extreme is what may be termed the realistic interpretation, which insists that the biographical details of chs. 1; 3 are to be taken literally. Thus Gomer must be understood as already an acknowledged harlot at the time God commanded Hosea to marry her. Each step in Hosea's marriage relation was taken, not on any impulse of his own, but at the command of God. In short, his marriage, the birth of his children, the disruption of his home, and the restoration of Gomer to the home were acts performed in obedience to God in order to make his marriage the medium by which God might speak to Israel. The difficulty of this theory is twofold: it is grotesque to imagine a prophet's deliberately establishing a marriage with a harlot in order to act out a parable of God's relation with Israel, and Hosea pictures the marriage relation of God and Israel as having been true and idyllic in its earliest stage (2:15; 11:1).

Perhaps the most popular interpretation in recent years has been the romantic one which applies a considerable measure of imagination to the biographical material in chs. 1; 3, reconstructs the marriage experience of the prophet and finds in it the key to the prophet's message, his discovery of a redemptive love in his own relation with his wife becoming for him the revelation of God's redemptive love for Israel. Behind this theory lies the assumption that before the time of Hosea no one in Israel had had any comprehension of covenant love between God and Israel, that Israel's earlier religion was semipagan, with fear as its predominant characteristic. Thus Amos was seen as the discoverer of ethical monotheism and Hosea as the discoverer of the divine love. More recent scholarship has revised the picture of Israelite religion in the period from Moses to Amos and Hosea, validating a prophetic tradition in which the covenant relation between God and Israel was central and there was an understanding of God that prepared the way for Amos and Hosea, so that they can no longer be represented as such startling innovators. Nevertheless, the romantic theory persists in varying forms.

This interpretation is found as early as 1737, when Gebhard suggested that Gomer's disposition to harlotry was not manifest until sometime after the marriage. Some evidence of this was seen in the fact that in 1:2 she is called, not a harlot, but a woman "of harlotry." The theory was taken up and developed by an impressive array of major scholars. The marriage experience of Hosea was reconstructed somewhat as follows: Hosea entered upon marriage with Gomer with no suspicion of trouble and with the expectation of years of happiness before him. He named his first child Jezreel as a warning to the royal house that soon God's judgment must fall upon it for the butchery of Jezreel. Thus far there was no indication of trouble in the home. But upon the birth of a second child, a girl, Hosea realized that his wife had been unfaithful to him; so he named the child "Not pitied." A third child he disowned entirely, naming him "Not my people." So ends the biographical element in ch. 1. When ch. 3 opens, the wife is being offered for sale in a slave market. The intervening time, therefore, has to be bridged by assuming that Gomer, after the birth of her third child, left the home and became a common harlot, that misfortune eventually overtook her, and that she was on the point of being sold as a slave when Hosea sought her out once more. At God's command he bought her back but did not immediately restore her to the home, rather fixing for her a time of discipline and preparation that the marriage relation might be renewed on a new basis. Then, in contemplation of all that had happened, or perhaps at some point in the midst of the experience, Hosea recognized the parallel between his own marriage and that of God with Israel and leaped to the conclusion that there was in God's heart a love for Israel like his own passionate and persistent love for Gomer. Some carried this theory to great lengths. One scholar asserts that not only did Hosea's marriage experience give his life its decisive direction, but the passion of his nature which made him persist in his love for Gomer was later sublimated into a love for his children (11:1-3) and an inner sympathy even with animals (vss. 4-7).

This theory is subject to serious criticisms. Mention has already been made of the long tradition of God's covenant love for Israel. The severity of God's judgment in an Amos had behind it the intensity of God's love that would not let his people go without a struggle. Far from discovering God's love for Israel through his marriage experience, Hosea declared God's love to have been evident from the very beginning of the nation's life (11:1) and his own conduct in marriage to be a human reproduction and representation of the divine reality. A second difficulty is that in the text of chs. 1; 3 each act of Hosea is the prophetic act of a prophet with the purpose of conveying a specific message to the nation. It is very difficult to go behind these parabolic acts and reconstruct a personal history. The names of Hosea's children dare not be taken as indications of Gomer's conduct any more than deductions would be made concerning Isaiah's family life from the strange names he gave his children, "The spoil speeds, the prey hastes," and "A remnant shall return." Also it is plain that Hosea had long been a prophet, long enough for the birth of three children (most likely *ca.* six years in the East), before the events of ch. 3, and that the present record of the experiences would be written still later, so that chs. 1; 3 dare not be interpreted as describing the experiences that made him a prophet. The most that can be said is that Hosea seems to have been tragically unfortunate in his marriage, to have seen in it a human parable of God's relation with Israel, and to have acted out in relation to his wife a parable of God's redemptive love for Israel.

There are yet other theories of interpretation. Thomas Aquinas, followed by Sebastian Schmidt (1687), tried to avoid the offensiveness of the account by supposing that Hosea took Gomer, not as his wife, but as a concubine. It is hard to see that this is less offensive. A more widely held view was that the harlotry of Gomer, as of Israel, was meant to be understood, not as physical, but as spiritual harlotry. One scholar denies that the woman in ch. 3 is Gomer. The two chapters, he says, do not present a continuous story. Ch. 1 narrates Hosea's marriage to a woman who shares the religious apostasy of the nation and the naming of his children in such a way as to declare to the nation its approaching doom. Ch. 3 describes a purely symbolic act of the prophet which has nothing to do with his marriage: he buys a harlot in the market place in order to declare parabolically God's readiness to purchase a sinful nation out of its slavery. This theory is based almost entirely upon the supposition that Hosea would never have described his own wife merely as "a woman" (3:1). Others read ch. 3 as Hosea's own account of the same marriage that is described in ch. 1, although 3:1 speaks, not of "marrying," but of "loving." The total effect of the multiplicity of theories should be to make us exercise great restraint in imaginative reconstructions and careful to base our interpretation of the prophet, not on tentative hypotheses, but rather upon solid evidence of his mind.

3. Date and composition. The period of Hosea's ministry is described in 1:1 in somewhat puzzling terms. The hand of a Judean editor can be recognized in the naming first of four Judean kings, then of only one Israelite king, Jeroboam, in spite of the fact that Hosea's entire ministry was in Israel. For Hosea to have been active until the time of the fourth Judean king, Hezekiah (725-697), would have required an extremely long ministry, while the completion of his ministry during the reign of Jeroboam II (787-747) would have made it extremely short. The prophecy of the fall of the house of Jehu (1:4), which occurred with the death of Jeroboam's son, Zechariah, in 746, makes it likely that Hosea began his ministry in 747 shortly before Jeroboam's death. This is supported by the absence of references to any era of prosperity such as we find in Amos' oracles, delivered in the immediately preceding period. Rather, Hosea's words mirror a state of confusion and anarchy such as became characteristic of Israel after 746, when one king followed the other in quick succession and the land was full of violence (5:1; 7:3-7; 9:15; 13:10-11). The length of Hosea's ministry is uncertain. Absence of any reference to the Syro-Ephraimitish war of 734 makes it likely that it terminated before this date.

The development of Hosea's ministry and the process by which his book came into its present form are closely related problems. It is significant that the names given to the prophet's three children over a period of at least six years strike the same note of inescapable doom that is conveyed by the oracles in chs. 4–13, and also in 2:2-13. This suggests that in the first stage of Hosea's ministry he dinned into the ears of his people the certainty of judgment. But always in the background, ready to break through, was another, seemingly contradictory note, the plaintive note of God's heartbrokenness at the sin and ruin of his people. But even this injured love of God could not relieve the darkness of judgment.

Some scholars believe that only these oracles of doom are original to Hosea, and that, where hope breaks in, it is the product of a later editor (1:10-11; 2:14-23;14). But they must reckon with ch. 3, which comes from the hand of Hosea himself. Plainly there came a point in Hosea's ministry when he could no longer believe that judgment was God's last word. Beyond the judgment day he saw a new beginning for Israel with God and proclaimed it to the nation by his own redemption of his wayward Gomer. It was therefore Hosea himself who added vss. 1, 14-23, to the oracle of doom 2:2-13, transforming it into an oracle of redemption, and who wrote ch. 14 as a new conclusion to his collection of oracles to proclaim the possibility of redemption and restoration for a repentant people once they have been cleansed and humbled by the judgment. It would be at this same time that he set down his autobiographical note which is preserved in ch. 3.

The first sign of a hand other than Hosea's at work upon the book is in ch. 1, where the writer speaks of Hosea in the third person. Fortunately this editor identifies himself rather plainly. His Judean nationality is evident, not only in the superscription, in which Judean kings precede the king of Israel, but also in vs. 7, which refers to the deliverance of Judah from disaster, most likely that of 722, though it may have been that of 701. This writer, in telling of Hosea's marriage and the naming of his children, had before him chs. 2–3, and, following their lead, described Gomer as a woman of "harlotry." Also, under the influence of chs. 2–3 he added vss. 10-11 in ch. 1 in order to relieve the gloom of vss. 2-9, showing his identity again, however, in his concern that Judah should be united with Israel in the future day of redemption.

There are frequent references to Judah throughout the book, and these have sometimes been thought to be entirely later additions (e.g., K. Marti believed that Hosea never once spoke of Judah). No good reason, however, can be found for questioning the authenticity of many of them (e.g., 5:10, 12-14; 6:4; 8:14). To the prophets the two kingdoms constituted one people of God, and it was as natural for Hosea to include Judah in his oracles of judgment as it was for Amos to choose Bethel as the scene of his ministry. But when words of warning are addressed to Judah (e.g., 4:15; 6:11) or words of praise (e.g., 11:12) or words of hope for a united Davidic kingdom (e.g., 3:5), it is clearly the hand of a later Judean editor at work; how much later we cannot say. The final verse of ch. 14 is sharply distinguished from all that precedes, having the character of proverbial wisdom rather than that of a prophetic oracle. Its date is most likely very late.

Some scholars (*see bibliography*) assume that only those parts of Hosea are genuine that proclaim doom, and that all suggestions of hope are from the hands of later editors. As an antidote to sentimentalism, which has concealed the character of Hosea as a prophet of inescapable doom, these writings have value, but they are forced to do violence to the text in order to make it fit the theory. Batten (*see bibliography*) denies ch. 3 to Hosea, eliminates all reference to Gomer's character from ch. 1, and then announces triumphantly that Gomer has been cruelly slandered. Hosea's character as a prophet of doom may be maintained without resorting to such measures and while recognizing the essential integrity of the present text of the book.

4. Text and style. The text of Hosea confronts the interpreter with great and often insuperable obstacles because of its frequently confused and corrupt state. There may be wide differences in translation, as different interpreters make varying reconstructions of the text. The LXX is often of great help in recovering the original, not only of individual words, but even of whole sentences.

In style Hosea differs greatly from Amos. His oracles are brief and pointed and employ none of the devices for cumulative effect which make some of Amos' sermons so powerful. The sensitive, passionate nature of Hosea shows plainly in his ways of speech. Where Amos thunders, Hosea pleads. Where Amos gives the impression of iron strength and of a judgment that moves relentlessly down upon the nation, Hosea sounds like a man who is torn and bleeding within himself because of the harsh words of judgment which it is his duty to proclaim. In this he is similar to Jeremiah. His oracles are the brief outcries of a tortured soul, carrying passion in every word, too passionate for their form to show any careful calculation for effect. They are like staccato blows at the heart of the nation, with an evangelical passion that at times comes close to that of Second Isaiah.

5. The theology of Hosea. The entire book of Hosea has its focus in the relation of God to Israel. In this Hosea is distinguished from Amos, for whom the universal sovereignty of God forms the background of all his thinking. Hosea sets little emphasis upon God's sovereignty, and he has nothing to say about his care or concern for other nations. What God is to Israel and what Israel is to God engages his whole attention. Also within Israel, his approach to the sins of the nation is different from that of Amos. Amos' passionate concern is that the ordinary citizen in Israel is being trampled upon, cheated, and debased. It is the absence of common justice that shocks him. Hosea sees the same evils, the irresponsibility of the rulers, the corruption of priests and prophets, the degeneracy of the cult, but for him these are all merely signs of a deeper evil, the repudiation by Israel of its covenant relation with God. He does not exempt the people from responsibility but includes them with princes and priests in a common guilt. The nation has forsaken its husband, Yahweh, and has played the harlot by setting its trust upon the Baals, upon its own military forces and upon foreign alliances. Sin is not defined in any legalistic way by Hosea; for him the essence of sin for Israel is to rely upon anyone or anything other than God for the guidance and sustaining of its life. For this reason idolatry of any kind receives severe censure from Hosea.

Two key words in Hosea's theology are חסד, which may be translated "faithful love," and דעת אלהים, "knowledge of God." חסד denotes the loyalty and devotion that may be expected in a relationship of love, and therefore is used of God's attitude toward Israel, as well as of the response for which he hopes from Israel. It has a third dimension when it describes the attitude toward one another of Israelites who are bound together within the covenant. The same חסד which has determined God's dealings with them as a nation is meant to determine their dealings with one another. Here Hosea roots his ethics firmly in his theology. The conduct of Israelites is to be a reflection of the nature of God. At one point (6:6) Hosea seems almost to equate חסד with knowledge of God. They are two ways of describing the essence of the covenant relation. By knowledge of God he very clearly has in mind something far beyond intellectual apprehension. It is a knowledge which is possible only in a personal relation in which the entire existence of the knower is involved. To know God is to respond to him in faithful love and to have the whole of life determined by the understanding of oneself and one's fellow men that becomes possible in this relation. *See* LOVE IN THE OT.

Hosea sees the election of Israel in historical perspective. Israel's special relation with Yahweh did not begin yesterday but has compassed its entire history as a nation. He looks back to the days of the Exodus as the idyllic honeymoon in the marriage of Yahweh with Israel (2:15; 11:1). At that time the leadership in the life of Israel was in the hands of a prophet and not in the hands of a king (12:13). God was Israel's king and husband and father. But from the earliest days of settlement in Palestine the covenant was broken. The worship of the people became corrupted into Baal-worship, and the trust of the people became fixed upon kings and armies and foreign alliances rather than upon God. That which alone has given Israel a purpose in its life has been the uniqueness of its relation with God, and with the destruction of this relation the very basis of its continued existence among the nations has been taken away (8:8). It is clear that, for Hosea, the covenant, while it binds Israel to God, does not bind God to Israel in such a way as to encourage any false confidence or self-righteousness. God's covenant love for Israel is such that in spite of the nation's sin, he cannot lightly give them up (11:8). It breaks his heart to have his covenant partner turn from him. But the relation is a personal one, which can be maintained only when there is faithfulness in both partners.

Hosea interprets God's judgment upon sin and unfaithfulness, not as arbitrary acts, but as consequences which issue from the nature of sin itself. The disruption of the covenant relation results in a vanishing from the life of the nation of all knowledge of God and all faithful love. The priests, whose task it is to teach the nation to know God, are themselves without the knowledge which they are to communicate (4:4-6). This blindness and ignorance and incapacity for faithful love plunge the whole of society into disorder. Without knowledge of God, men are without the kind of understanding which makes possible healthful relations with one another, and all the institutions of society are corrupted (4:4). Hosea used the likeness of sowing and reaping to represent the causal relationship between human conduct and national consequences. They who sow the wind must reap the whirlwind (8:7; cf. 10:13). The incurring of guilt brings death (13:1). But he knows that it is equally true that the sowing of righteousness will bring a harvest of salvation (10:12).

Perhaps it was in his own marriage situation that Hosea came to see most clearly the fearful dilemma of man's evil. Sin, by its disruption of the personal relation on which life depends, brings blindness, callousness, and despair, which lead to yet more violent sin. The human being, once started on this disastrous downhill course, is helpless to stop the tragic cumulative process. There must be an intervention from beyond. Someone, with love for the sinner in spite of the sin, must break in upon the deadly process and by sheer grace create for the prisoner of sin and death the possibility of a new beginning. This was Hosea's final word concerning God. Israel by her sin might bring herself to the very verge of slavery and self-destruction, but God would not give her up. When she had tasted the bitterness of judgment, he would intervene and open the way for restoration of the covenant and a new future.

Bibliography. Commentaries: A. Wünsche, *Der Prophet Hosea übersetzt und erklärt, mit Benutzung der Targumim der jüdischen Ausleger Raschi, Aben Ezra und David Kimchi* (1868). C. F. Keil, *Commentary on the Twelve Minor Prophets* (German, 1866; English trans., 1880). W. Nowack, *Der Prophet Hosea erklärt* (1880). F. Hitzig, *Die zwölf kleinen Propheten* (4th ed. by H. Steiner; 1881). T. K. Cheyne, *Hosea with Notes and Introduction*, Cambridge Bible (1884). C. von Orelli, *The Twelve Minor Prophets* (German, 1888; trans. J. S. Banks, 1893). J. J. P. Valeton, Jr., *Amos en Hosea* (1894; German ed., 1898). J. Wellhausen, *Die kleinen Propheten, übersetzt und erklärt* (3rd ed., 1898). K. Marti, *Dodekpropheton,* KHC (1903). R. F. Horton, *The Minor Prophets, Hosea-Micah,* New Century Bible (1904). B. Duhm, *Die zwölf Propheten* (1910). W. R. Harper, *Amos and Hosea,* ICC (1910). J. M. P. Smith, *Amos, Hosea and Micah* (1914). W. Nowack, *Die kleinen Propheten übersetzt und erklärt* (later ed., 1922). H. Gressmann, *Die Schriften des AT,* pt. II (2nd ed., 1931). E. Sellin, *Die kleinen Propheten,* KAT (1932). G. A. Smith, *The Book of the Twelve Prophets,* vol. I (rev. ed., 1940). G. Brillet, *Amos et Hosée* (1946). A. Weiser, "Die kleinen Propheten," *AT Deutsch* (1949). T. H. Robinson and F. Horst, "Die zwölf kleinen Propheten," *HAT* (1954). N. H. Snaith, *Amos, Hosea and Micah* (1956).

Special studies: A. B. Davidson, "The Prophet Hosea," *Exp.,* IX (1879), 241-64. J. Bewer, "The Story of Hosea's Marriage," *AJSL,* 22 (1906), 120-30. K. Budde, *Der Schluss des Buches Hosea, Toy Festschrift* (1912), pp. 205-11. W. Baumgartner, *Kennen Amos und Hosea eine Heils-Eschatalogie?* (1913). A. Heerman, "Ehe und Kinder des Propheten Hosea," *ZAW,* 40 (1922), 287-312. K. Budde, "Der Abschnitt Hosea 1-3," *TSK,* 96/97 (1925), 1-89; "Zu Text und Auslegung des Buches Hosea," *JBL,* 45 (1926), 280-97. F. Prätorius, *Die Gedichte des Hosea* (1926). K. Budde, *JBL,* 53 (1934), 118-33; "Hosea 1 and 3," *Theologische Blätter,* 13 (1934), 337-43. H. S. Nyberg, *Studien zum Hoseabuch* (1935). T. H. Robinson, "Die Ehe des Hosea," *TSK,* 106 (1935), 301-13. H. G. May, "An Interpretation of the Names of Hosea's Children," *JBL,* 55 (1936), 285-91. T. C. Vriezen, *Hosea: Profeet en Cultuur* (1941). H. W. Robinson, *The Hebrew Prophets* (1948). A. D. Tushingham, "A Reconsideration of Hosea 1-3," *JNES,* 12 (1953), 150-59. F. Buck, *Die Liebe Gottes beim Propheten Osee* (1953). H. H. Rowley, "The Marriage of Hosea," *Bulletin of the John Rylands Library,* XXXIX (1956), 200-233. G. Östborn, *Yahweh and Baal: Studies in the Book of Hosea* (1956). F. S. North, "Solution of Hosea's Marital Problems by Critical Analysis," *JNES,* 16 (1957), 128—. H. H. Wolff, *Dodekapropheten* (1957—). G. Farr, "The Concept of Grace in the Book of Hosea," *ZAW,* 29 (1958), 98-106.

On the assumption that only those portions of Hosea are genuine that proclaim doom, see L. W. Batten, "Hosea's Message and Marriage," *JBL,* 48 (1929), 257-73. R. E. Wolfe, *Meet Amos and Hosea* (1945), follows Batten's lead. Essentially the same viewpoint is supported by W. F. Stinespring, "Hosea, Prophet of Doom," *Crozer Quarterly,* 27 (1950), 200-207.

J. D. Smart

HOSEN. KJV for Aramaic פטיש (RSV Tunic) in Dan. 3:21. "Hosen" is an archaic term for "hose," "leggings."

HOSHAIAH hō shā'yə [הושעיה, Yahu has saved]. **1.** One of the princes of Judah who participated in the processional at the time of the dedication of the rebuilt walls of Jerusalem (Neh. 12:32).

2. The father of Azariah (Jer. 42:1—G 49:1; 43:2) or Jezaniah (42:1 MT), who was a leader among the Jews after the fall of Jerusalem. He seems to have been a Maacathite (40:8).

M. Newman

HOSHAMA hŏsh'ə mə [הושמע, *contracted from* יהושמע, Yahu has heard] (I Chr. 3:18). One of the seven sons of Jehoiachin.

Bibliography. M. Noth, *Die israelitischen Personennamen* (1928), pp. 107n, 185.

HOSHEA hō shē'ə [הושע, may Yahu save]; KJV OSHEA ō— in Num. 13:8, 16.

1. The original name of Joshua the son of Nun, an Ephraimite (Num. 13:8). The name was changed by Moses (vs. 16).

2. One of David's officers set over the Ephraimites; son of Azaziah (I Chr. 27:20).

3. The prophet whose Hebrew name has been commonly Anglicized as Hosea.

4. The last king of Israel (*ca.* 732-724 B.C.); son of Elah. Murderer and successor of Pekah, Hoshea was taken captive by Shalmaneser V.

The name is probably a shortened form of (*a*) יושיע and יהו, "Let Yahu save"; or (*b*) הושעיהו, "Yahu saves." The latter has been found in the Lachish Letters. The name appears as *A-ú-si-'* in Assyrian inscriptions.

Hoshea became king as the result of a conspiracy, in which he murdered Pekah. Tiglath-pileser claims that he placed Hoshea on the throne. In a sense both statements are correct, for Hoshea could not have become king without the approval of Assyria. He reigned for nine years (II Kings 17:1).

The usual moral judgment is passed on him by the Deuteronomic writer: "He did what was evil in the sight of the Lord." In Hoshea's case, however, the judgment is not absolute, for these words are added: "yet not as the kings of Israel who were before him" (II Kings 17:2). This may very well be a historical reminiscence based on a trustworthy tradition.

Assyria still dominated the scene. Tiglath-pileser III died in 727 and was succeeded by his son Shalmaneser V. Until that year Hoshea continued to pay tribute to Tiglath-pileser. The burden, however, finally became intolerable, and he revolted, probably at Tiglath-pileser's death, before his successor was able to establish himself. The revolt seems to have been widespread and had the promised support of Egypt. The name of the Egyptian king is given as סוא (So; II Kings 17:4). This should probably be vocalized differently and read as "Sewe" (cf. Assyrian *Sibe*). In the Annals of Sargon for his second year the name appears with the title *turtanuu* (cf. the *tartan* of Isa. 20:1)—i.e., "commander-in-chief." It is possible that at this time he was the commander-in-chief and only later became king. Egyptian influence may have been felt in Samaria even prior to this time (cf. Hos. 7:8, 11, 16; 11:5). In 724, Shalmaneser marched against Hoshea, who capitulated and again paid tribute (II Kings 17:3). But Shalmaneser "found treachery" in him, so he took him prisoner and besieged Samaria (vss. 4-5). The siege lasted three years—a fact which indicates something of the strength of its defenses. In the meantime Shalmaneser died and was succeeded by Sargon II (722-721). The latter finally subdued the city, as he claims in the annals for his first year—i.e., 722-721—and frequently elsewhere.

There is confusion in the biblical record in regard

to the name of the Assyrian king. II Kings 17:6 says simply: "In the ninth year of Hoshea the king of Assyria captured Samaria." The parallel account in 18:9-10 states that "Shalmaneser king of Assyria came up against Samaria and besieged it and at the end of three years he [MT 'they'] took it." It continues with the indefinite phrase: "Samaria was taken."

The precise figure given by Sargon of 27,290 prisoners carried off contrasts sharply with II Kings 17:18: "[The Lord] removed them [i.e., Israel] out of his sight; none was left but the tribe of Judah only"—a statement which can be true only in a general sense. As a result of Sargon's deportation of the leading citizens, calculated at about one twentieth of the total population of the land, Israel as a kingdom ceased to exist. The captive Israelites were carried off to Assyria and were resettled in "Halah, and on the Habor, the river of Gozan, and in the cities of the Medes" (vs. 6). To take their place, Sargon imported colonists "from Babylon, Cuthah, Avva, Hamath, and Sepharvaim and placed them in the cities of Samaria" (vs. 24). These new colonists brought with them their own cults.

Bibliography. H. G. May, "The Deportation of Israel" and "The Israelites in Exile," *BA*, VI (1943), 57-60. A. Alt, *Kleine Schriften zur Geschichte des Volkes Israel,* II (1953), 188-205, 226-34. J. B. Pritchard, ed., *ANET* (2nd ed., 1955), pp. 284-85. W. F. Albright, "New Light from Egypt on the Chronology and History of Israel and Judah," *BASOR,* no. 130 (1953), pp. 4-11, especially pp. 8-11; "Further Light on Synchronisms Between Egypt and Asia in the Period 935-685 B.C.," *BASOR,* no. 141 (1956), pp. 23-27, especially pp. 23-26. M. Noth, *Geschichte Israels* (3rd ed., 1956), pp. 236 ff. G. E. Wright, *Biblical Archaeology* (1957), pp. 160-63.

5. One of those who set their seal to the covenant in the time of Nehemiah-Ezra (Neh. 10:23—H 10:24).

H. B. MacLean

HOSPITALITY [φιλοξενία] (Rom. 12:13; Heb. 13:2; I Clem. 1:2; 10:7; 11:1; 12:1; Herm. Mand. 8:10; cf. I Tim. 3:2; Tit. 1:8; I Pet. 4:9). Entertainment of a stranger (sojourner) as a guest; recognized as a sacred duty throughout the Mediterranean world, and more heartily and stringently kept than many a written law. While the word does not appear in the OT, the custom is evidenced, particularly in the patriarchal stories (Gen. 18:1-8; 19:1-11; 24:14-61; cf. Judg. 19:10-25). In the NT the practice provides the background for many of the details in the life of Jesus and the early Christian community. *See also* GUEST; SOJOURNER.

1. Among the Hebrews. The main practices stem from nomadic life, when public inns were a rarity and every stranger a potential enemy. Hospitality was discharged more from fear and for protection than from generosity. One might even entertain the deity or his messengers (cf. Gen. 18:1-8; 19:1, 3; Heb. 13:2). Moreover, the host never knew when he himself would be dependent on others. The guest was treated with respect and honor and was provided with provender for his animals, water for his feet, rest, and a sumptuous feast. He enjoyed protection, even if he were an enemy, for three days and thirty-six hours after eating with the host (the time sustained by his food). Hospitality was to the Bedouin what almsgiving was to the later Jews—an expression of righteousness. A traveler entering a city would come to the open place, and there, unless a breach of etiquette occurred, someone would invite him to his home and grant him the customary graces (Gen. 19:1-3; Judg. 19:15-21).

2. Among the Christians. The NT describes Jesus as dependent on hospitality for his daily care and lodging (Matt. 8:20; 9:10; Mark 7:24; 14:3; Luke 7:36; 8:3; 9:52; 10:38; 14:1; 19:5; John 12:2). It is assumed in the sending forth of the apostles (Matt. 10:5-15; Mark 6:7-11; Luke 9:2-5; 10:4-11). And it accounts to a considerable degree for the extensive journeys of the early Christian missionaries (cf. Acts 16:15; 18:27; III John 5-6), and the retention of the "living voice" of the gospel. Christians, in their travels, would seek out Christian brethren, partly for protection but mainly to share fellowship and worship. Churches shared their gospel tradition, the collection (possibly in the form of eucharistic elements; cf. Just. Apol. 1.67), their homes (Acts 16:15; 18:27; Herm. Sim. 8:10; Arist. Apol. 15:7), and provided labor for those desiring to settle in their midst (Did. 12). On hearing of poverty, they contributed to the necessity of the saints (Rom. 15:26-27; II Cor. 9:1-2; cf. Phil. 4:10, 14-18). Hospitality was the chief bond which brought the churches a sense of unity. The Roman church, as the church of the imperial capital, came to supremacy partly through its constant concern for Christians everywhere.

Certainly such a practice was bound to be abused by idlers and pretenders. Precautions early were taken to test the genuineness of a Christian traveler and to forestall his becoming a burden to the Christian community (cf. I John 4:1; II John 7-11; Did. 11-12).

Bibliography. J. L. Burkhardt, *Notes on the Bedouins and Wahabys,* I (1831), 338-50; C. M. Doughty, *Arabia Deserta,* I (1888), 228; A. von Harnack, *The Expansion of Christianity in the First Three Centuries,* I (trans. and ed. J. Moffatt; 1904), 181-249; J. Pedersen, *Israel,* I-II (1926), 356-58; W. R. Smith, *Religion of the Semites* (3rd ed., 1927), pp. 75-78; D. W. Riddle, "Early Christian Hospitality," *JBL,* 57 (1938), 141-54.

V. H. Kooy

HOSTAGES [בני תערובות, sons of pledging]. Persons held as security against revolt or aggression.

The Hebrew word תערובות is an abstract plural substantive from ערב, "to take or give a pledge"; hence the phrase בני תערובות literally means "sons of pledging." The LXX misunderstood the word as deriving from ערב, "to mix"; hence the odd misrendering "sons of commingling."

The word "hostages" occurs only in II Kings 14:14=II Chr. 25:24 in the account of Jehoash' victory over Amaziah of Judah. Amaziah was captured, part of Jerusalem's walls were broken down, much booty was removed to Samaria, and hostages were taken to ensure the future good behavior of the Judean king.

See also SURETY.

J. W. Wevers

HOSTS, HOST OF HEAVEN. In the OT the God of Israel is frequently called "Yahweh [God] of hosts" (יהוה [אלהי] צבאות), for that is his "name" (Isa. 47:4; 51:15; Jer. 10:16; 31:35; Amos 5:27)—i.e., his personal nature (*see* GOD, NAMES OF, § 1). The epithet expresses Yahweh's sovereign might and majesty in history, but the precise meaning of the "hosts" which stand at his command is uncertain. The ambiguity of the epithet is inherent in the words "host," "hosts" (צבא, צבאות), whose range of meaning extends from earth to heaven.

Basically, צבא is a military term. It is used most frequently to indicate a body of men organized for war—i.e., an army (Gen. 21:22, 32, E; 26:26 J; Judg. 4:2, 7; 9:29; I Sam. 12:9; II Sam. 3:23; Isa. 34:2; Jer. 51:3; etc.). Also it may mean the act of war, or warfare (Num. 1:3, 20 P; Deut. 24:5; Josh. 22:12, 33; I Sam. 28:1; etc.), or, by an extension of meaning, may designate a term of hard service (Job 7:1; Isa. 40:2; Dan. 10:1). In late priestly literature it is sometimes used of the service of the Levites in the sanctuary (Num. 4:3, 23, 30, 35, 39, 43; 8:24-25).

Since the realms of earth and heaven were closely related in ancient thought, it was believed that the same kind of organized military array was found in the heavenly sphere. Thus the celestial bodies—the sun, moon, and stars—were regarded as an army, the "heavenly host" (צבא השמים). In the astrological cults of antiquity it was believed that the celestial bodies were animated by divine spirits and thus constituted a living army which controlled human destiny. The temptation for Israel to worship them proved to be irresistible, especially in the time when Assyrian and Babylonian cultural influence was strong (Deut. 4:19; 17:3; II Kings 17:16; 21:3, 5 [=II Chr. 33:3, 5]; 23:4-5; Jer. 8:2; 19:13; Zeph. 1:5). This paganism was effectively answered by Israel's doctrine of creation, which affirmed that the heavenly host were God's creatures, ordained to perform a special function and marshaled at his command (Gen. 1:14-19; 2:1; Neh. 9:6; Pss. 33:6; 103:21; 148:2; Isa. 40:26; 45:12). *See* CREATION § 2.

Moreover, included in the conception of the heavenly host is the idea of the angels (better, "messengers"; *see* ANGEL) who are associated with Yahweh in his rule. On the analogy of divine assemblies known in Canaan and Babylonia, Israel conceived of Yahweh as a king who presides over his heavenly council, composed of angelic servants or "sons of God" (*see below*). Micaiah's vision is expressed in these words: "I saw Yahweh sitting on his throne, and all the host of heaven standing beside him on his right hand and on his left" (I Kings 22:19; cf. Gen. 1:26; Job 1–2; Ps. 82; Isa. 6). From time to time, divine messengers were sent forth from the council to accomplish Yahweh's purpose, as we learn from the Prologue to the book of Job. Tradition relates that Joshua, just before leading his army to attack Jericho, was met by one of these angels, who introduced himself as the "commander of the host [צבא] of Yahweh" (Josh. 5:14). The angelic host (cf. Luke 2:13) was conceived of as a mighty army, in the service of Yahweh. Thus when Jacob was met by a band of angels, according to Gen. 32:1-2—H 32:2-3, he exclaimed: "This is God's army!" (מחנה אלהים).

At various times and in various circles of Israelite tradition all these ideas were associated with the epithet "Yahweh of hosts." Here we are dealing with an old cultic name whose original meaning was given within the context of holy war (*see* WAR, IDEAS OF). Interestingly, the epithet does not occur at all in the Pentateuch or Joshua and Judges, but first appears in Israelite tradition in connection with the amphictyonic sanctuary of Shiloh, where an annual sacrifice to Yahweh of hosts was held (I Sam. 1:3, 11). At Shiloh was stationed the "ark of the covenant of Yahweh of hosts, who is enthroned on the cherubim" (I Sam. 4:4)—a war palladium whose presence in Israel's camp gave assurance that Yahweh himself was conducting Israel's battles (Num. 10:35-36; I Sam. 4:1–7:2; cf. II Sam. 11:11; 15:24-26). David inherited the conception of holy war that was inherent in the epithet "Yahweh of hosts" (note Saul's exercise of the ban upon Amalek in the name of Yahweh of hosts [I Sam. 15:2-3]), and transferred the central sanctuary from the then defunct Shiloh to his capital city of Jerusalem, which he appropriately consecrated by bringing into it the ark of Yahweh of hosts (II Sam. 6:2-19; note especially vss. 2, 18). Although the conception of holy war was soon superseded by a new, nationalistic ideology, the cultic epithet was thereafter associated in a special sense with Jerusalem, where the ark rested within the temple (II Sam. 7:8, 26; Ps. 46:4-7—H 46:5-8; Isa. 6:3; 37:16, 32=II Kings 19:16, 31). The military meaning of "hosts" is clearly set forth in I Sam. 17:45, where David is represented as saying that he fights in the name of Yahweh of hosts, who is the "God of the armies [מערכות] of Israel." Elsewhere Israel's troops are designated as צבאות whom Yahweh leads to victory (Exod. 6:26; 7:4; 12:17, 41, 51), and this is often implied when the epithet is used (I Sam. 15:2; II Sam. 5:10; 6:18). According to Ps. 24:7-10, the King of glory is Yahweh of hosts: "Yahweh strong and mighty, Yahweh mighty in battle"; and the lifting of the gates may presuppose a ceremony of bringing the ark into the temple. Another psalmist laments Yahweh's apparent rejection of his people by saying: "Thou dost not go forth, O God, with our armies" (צבאותינו; Ps. 60:10—H 60:12=108:11—H 108:12; cf. 44:9—H 44:10).

Believing that the powers of heaven and earth are under Yahweh's lordship, the author of the Song of Deborah sensed no contradiction between Yahweh's summons of Israel to holy war through a charismatic leader and the idea that the heavenly host—the stars in their courses—were marshaled to fight for Israel (Judg. 5:20). But the meaning of the old cultic epithet "Yahweh of hosts" inevitably shifted when, in the time of David, the tribal confederacy began to vanish and Israel's religious traditions were reoriented in terms of the new nationalism. Under the new circumstances holy war, as practiced formerly when the ark was carried into battle, became obsolete. Moreover, the surviving belief that Yahweh was on Israel's side in war was repudiated by a line of prophets, beginning with Amos, who insisted that the Day of Yahweh would be a day of darkness and defeat for Israel (Amos 5:18-20).

The name "Yahweh of hosts" occurs predominantly in the literature of the prophets (247 out of some 285 times), which is a clear indication that in their vocabulary "hosts" was not synonymous with Israel's armies. To be sure, the prophets did not surrender the ancient idea of Yahweh's action in the military sphere but rather inverted it, as it were, by insisting that Yahweh was turning military forces against his people in order to judge them for their sins. Whenever the epithet "Yahweh of hosts" is used by pre-exilic prophets, invariably it has the dynamic meaning it formerly had in the days of the amphictyony: Yahweh of hosts acts in the historical arena to accomplish his sovereign purpose (Isa. 1:9, 24; 2:12; 3:15; 5:9, 16, 24; 21:10; Jer. 5:14; 6:6, 9; 8:3; 35:17; 38:17; Amos 5:14-17, 27; 6:8; Nah. 2:13—H 2:14; Hab. 2:13; etc.). Moreover, at the deepest level of prophetic insight it was perceived that Yahweh of hosts brings a redemption which surpasses and transcends all nationalistic hopes (Isa. 44:6; 45:13; 47:4; 48:2; 51:15; 54:5; Mic. 4:4), and, indeed, a psalmist affirmed that the God of Israel "makes wars cease to the end of the earth" (Ps. 46:8-11).

In reinterpreting Yahweh's power, expressed in the traditional cultic epithet, the prophets had at their disposal the conception of the heavenly council, referred to above. Micaiah's vision of Yahweh enthroned in majesty and surrounded by the host of heaven is echoed in the account of Isaiah's inaugural vision (Isa. 6), and this in turn is echoed in Isa. 40:1-11. Indeed, Yahweh's prophets insisted that they spoke with an authoritative "Thus saith the LORD" because they had been drawn into Yahweh's council, while the false prophets had not (Jer. 23:18, 22; cf. Isa. 6:8; 40:6; Amos 3:7). During the prophetic period, the idea of the heavenly council posed both a danger and an opportunity for Israel's faith. The danger lay in the fact that, owing to the undefined constituency of the council, pagan deities could be admitted and, in popular syncretistic faith, could be venerated along with Yahweh. The seriousness of this threat can be seen from the action of Manasseh, who constructed altars to the "host of heaven" in the Jerusalem temple, where Yahweh demanded the exclusive worship of his people (II Kings 21:3-5; cf. 23:4-5; Deut. 4:19; Jer. 8:2; 19:13). On the other hand, the threat also provided the opportunity to understand Yahweh's power and majesty in concrete and vivid terms. Pagan deities were absorbed into the heavenly council and were given the subordinate status of messengers or servants of Yahweh of hosts (Exod. 15:11; Pss. 29; 89:5-8—H 89:6-9). The members in good standing are those divine beings who hearken to their sovereign's will (Pss. 103:21; 148:1-6). According to Ps. 82, those "sons of God" who fail to perform their appointed function are banished and sentenced to die like men. In an apocalyptic passage it is stated that in the end time

> Yahweh will punish
> the host of heaven, in heaven,
> and the kings of the earth, on the earth
> (Isa. 24:21).

Thus the epithet "Yahweh of hosts" sums up the Israelite faith that Yahweh alone is Lord in heaven and on earth. The One whom the heavenly host praise is also exalted in the earth and, above the tumult of history, commands: "Be still, and know that I am God" (Ps. 46:10).

The above discussion has been based on the assumption that it is proper to translate "Yahweh *of* hosts," thus indicating a genitive relationship, which is clearly the case in the expanded form "Yahweh, God of hosts" (*see* LORD OF HOSTS). Along different lines, however, the view has been advanced that both terms of the epithet are independent grammatically and thus stand in apposition, on the analogy of "Yahweh El Elyon" or "Yahweh El Olam" (*see* GOD, NAMES OF, §§ C2*b-c*). According to this hypothesis, צבאות is an intensive abstract plural (cf. "Elohim") which means "Sabaothic Power"—i.e., "mightiness" or "the mighty one." The juxtaposition of the two divine names, one derived from Israel's Mosaic tradition and the other perhaps from Canaanite circles, first occurred in the ancient central sanctuary of Shiloh, where Israelite faith was influenced by Canaanite motifs. Thus Yahweh was identified with Sabaoth, enthroned upon the cherubim (in the fashion of other throne scenes represented in Canaanite art), and extolled as the God who is elevated above all powers. Although this view (*Jahwe, der Zebaothhafte*) is grammatically possible, it advocates an abstraction of thought which is not characteristic of the Hebrew mind. Therefore, the concrete meaning of "Yahweh of hosts," which expresses either the historical dynamism of holy war or the sovereign decree issued with the heavenly council, is preferable. Admittedly, in the course of time צבאות lost its specific meaning and became more abstract. This is evident in the LXX, where the translators sometimes treat Σαβαώθ as a divine proper name (cf. Rom. 9:29; Jas. 5:4), sometimes suggest that Kyrios includes all powers in himself (κύριος τῶν δυνήμεων), and most frequently construe the Hebrew to mean "the Lord Omnipotent" (κύριος παντοκράτωρ).

Bibliography. S. R. Driver, "Lord of Hosts," *HDB,* III (1900), 137-38. E. Kautzsch, "Zebaoth," *Realenzyklopädie für protest. Theologie und Kirche* (3 Aufl., 1908), XXI, 620-27. W. F. Arnold, *The Ephod and the Ark* (1917), pp. 142-48. B. N. Wambacq, *L'épithète divine Jahvé Sᵉbaôt* (1947); see the review by W. F. Albright, *JBL,* 67 (1948), 377-81. W. Eichrodt, *Theologie des ATs,* I (1948), 89-90. J. Obermann, "The Divine Name YHWH in the Light of Recent Discoveries," *JBL,* LXVIII (1949), especially 309-14. O. Eissfeldt, "Jahwe Zebaoth," *Miscellanea academica Berolinensia,* vol. II, no. 2 (1950), pp. 128-50. V. Maag, "Jahwes Heerscharen," *Festschrift L. Köhler* (1950), pp. 27 ff. L. Köhler, *OT Theology* (1958).

B. W. ANDERSON

HOSTS, LORD OF. *See* LORD OF HOSTS.

HOTHAM hō'thəm [חותם, seal, signet ring]; KJV HOTHAN hō'thən in I Chr. 11:44. **1.** A member of the tribe of Asher (I Chr. 7:32). In vs. 35, הלם, Helem (RSV "Heler"), is apparently the same person.

2. An Aroerite (*see* AROER), father of two of David's Mighty Men (I Chr. 11:44).

B. T. DAHLBERG

HOTHIR hō'thər [הותיר]. One of the sons of Heman who assisted in the instrumental music in the worship in the house of Yahweh (I Chr. 25:4). He obtained for his allotted time of service the twenty-first lot of the twenty-four divisions (vs. 28). Some scholars, however, believe that I Chr. 25:4, from the name Hananiah to the end of the verse, is a misplaced, fragmentary psalm of lamentation.

Bibliography. W. Rudolph, *Chronikbücher,* HAT (1955), includes relevant bibliography.

E. R. DALGLISH

HOUR [Aram. שׁעה, glance, twinkling; ὥρα, hour]. **1.** KJV translation in the phrase "the same hour" in Dan. 3:6, 15; 4:33; 5:5. The RSV translates "immediately," as the Aramaic indicates, not a period of time, but a point in time (cf. Dan. 4:19). The OT knows no system of equal hours for dividing the day. *See* DAY; NIGHT; TIME; WATCH.

2. The NT designation of a definite period (e.g., Matt. 20:1-12; Mark 15:25); also used loosely (e.g., Matt. 8:13 KJV) or metaphorically (e.g., Matt. 26:45). By NT times the Jews were counting twelve hours each in the day and in the night (cf. John 11:9). Sundials and water clocks were in use for marking the hours. *See* DIAL AND SUNDIAL. S. J. DE VRIES

HOUSE [בית; *so* Aram; Akkad. *bitu;* Ugar. *bt;* Arab. *bayt;* οἰκία, οἶκος]. A word used some two thousand times throughout the Bible referring to an abode, varying from the simplest home of a peasant to the palace (house of the king) and the temple (house of God). In Egypt, Mesopotamia, and the lowlands of Syria and Palestine, builders of houses used mud or sun-dried brick, while in the hills of Palestine they used mostly stone, which was abundant. Wood was used for roofing and for some superstructure. As civilization developed in Egypt, stone was quarried from the cliffs and used in some of the better houses. In Palestine the earliest known houses are the mud houses in Jericho. *See* JERICHO § 2.

Etymology of בית is uncertain; some consider it derived from a root meaning "go in," "spend the night," with the implication that the house was principally a refuge from nocturnal dangers and bad weather. From earliest historical times, however, there were throughout the Near East houses designed for comfortable living. Excavations at AI disclosed impressive houses with thick walls from the Early Bronze Age (*ca.* 3000-2100). At Tell Beit Mirsim (DEBIR) foundations of the Middle Bronze Age (*ca.* 2100-1550) show thick, well-constructed walls. The house of Lot at Sodom (Gen. 19:1-11), presumably of the Middle Bronze Age, reputedly was strong enough to hold off a mob temporarily.

In biblical times most houses were in cities, towns, or villages. The agricultural population had houses in settlements from which members went out to cultivate their fields or tend their flocks. There are few instances of separate military posts or community houses, like the one at Qumran, away from towns. From excavations it appears that during the time of Israel and Judah cities became more congested, with the result that houses were smaller, walls thinner, and planning less careful. There were exceptions, as in official houses in MEGIDDO.

At every period covered in the Bible there was a variety of dwelling. The house of a free man or an official would face a street and adjoin other houses. It might be part of the city wall with a window opening to the outside (Josh. 2:15-21; II Cor. 11:33). Probably it would be rectangular with an open court in front. The door would be of wood with a wooden beam as the lintel and two upright posts as jambs. There would be a room for domestic animals, sleeping quarters, and a central room with a hearth for cooking and braziers for heating. Smoke would go out through open windows, which could be closed by latticework. The ceiling would be of wooden beams plastered over with clay. Some of the flooring would be of plaster or stone. Steps would lead to the roof, where there would be a guest room (II Kings 4:10). The surface of the roof would be of clay, which regularly had to be replenished and rolled, as in many houses today. In the spring grass might grow briefly on the housetop (Ps. 129:6; Isa. 37:27).

The term בית has a variety of meanings, as "inside" (Gen. 6:14); a receptacle for a corpse, called "eternal home" (Eccl. 12:5); any dwelling, as a spider's web (Job 8:14).

Both Hebrew and Greek words for "house," as in English, many times refer to the family. To build a house, then, may mean to produce a family (Exod. 1:21; Ruth 4:11; Matt. 12:25; John 4:53). *See* ARCHITECTURE. O. R. SELLERS

HOUSE OF THE FOREST OF LEBANON lĕb'ə nən [בית יער הלבנון]; *in short* HOUSE OF THE FOREST (Isa. 22:8). A part of Solomon's palace in Jerusalem, named for its cedar pillars and wallboards imported from Mount Lebanon. It is described as a rectangular building divided by three (Hebrew four) rows of pillars, with an upper story of chambers distributed in (three) rows of fifteen each (I Kings 7:2-5). It was organically connected with the other public rooms of the palace, namely the Hall of Pillars, perhaps to be amended into "Waiting Hall" (העומדים instead of העמודים), and the Hall of the Throne, as

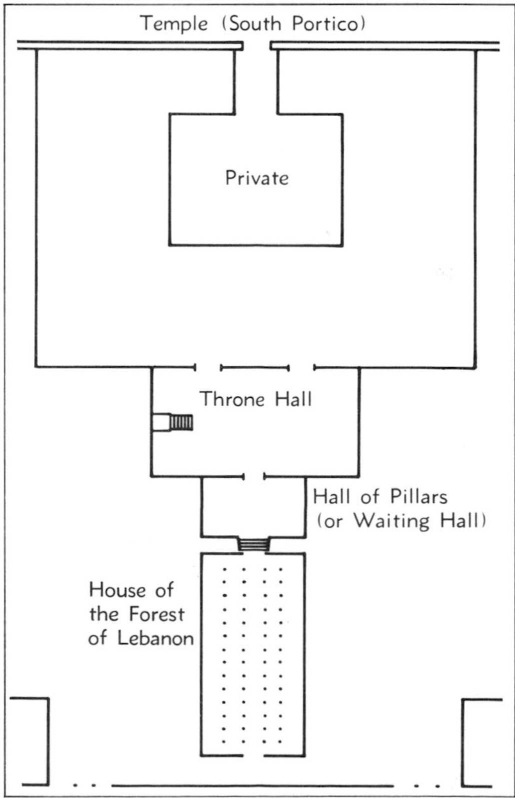

Courtesy of J. Gabalda & Cie., Paris

32. Suggested arrangement of the buildings of Solomon's palace at Jerusalem, according to L.-H. Vincent (*Jerusalem de l'AT*, vol. II, fig. 134, p. 428, by L.-H. Vincent and A.-M. Steve)

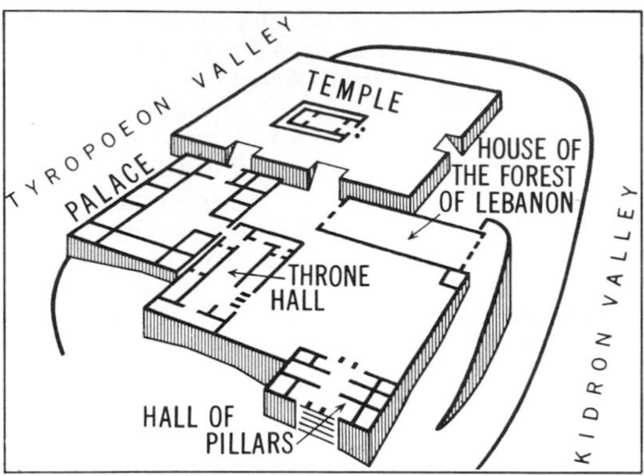

From Kurt Galling, *Biblisches Reallexikon* (Tübingen: J. C. B. Mohr)

33. Suggested arrangements of the Solomonic temple and palace complex

well as with the private apartments of the king (palace) and of the daughter of Pharaoh (I Kings 7: 6-8). Various references are made to the golden shields (of the guard), the ivory throne, and the precious vessels that were kept in the House of the Forest (I Kings 10:17, 21; II Chr. 9:16, 20; Isa. 22: 8). The palace compound was located to the S of the courtyard of Solomon's temple and belonged to the same architectural ensemble, combining God's house and the house of the king, his representative on earth. The exact location and layout of the palace remain highly hypothetical, in the absence of definite archaeological information. *See* PALACE; TEMPLE (JERUSALEM); HALL.

Figs. HOU 32-33.

Bibliography. K. Galling, *Biblisches Reallexikon* (1937), p. 411; J. Simons, *Jerusalem in the OT* (1952), pp. 130, 436; H. Vincent, *Jérusalem de l'Ancien Testament,* II (1956), 423-31.

G. A. BARROIS

HOUSEHOLD DUTIES, LIST OF. *See* LISTS, ETHICAL.

HOUSEHOLD OF GOD [οἶκος θεοῦ (I Tim. 3:15); ὁίκος τοῦ θεοῦ (I Pet. 4:17); οἰκεῖοι τοῦ θεοῦ (Eph. 2: 19)]. The community of believers, the members of the household which constitutes the church. *See* CHURCH, IDEA OF.

HOUSEHOLDER [οἰκοδεσπότης] (Matt. 20:1). A house steward or master of the house. The Greek word occurs twelve times in the Synoptic gospels, and nowhere else in the NT. In the parable of Matt. 20:1 ff, Jesus makes the point that God deals with men as the householder deals with his laborers.

B. H. THROCKMORTON, JR.

HOWLING CREATURES [אחים, *cf.* Arab. *'aḫḫa,* to cough, *or aḫū,* strange, foreign] (Isa. 13:21); KJV DOLEFUL CREATURES. The context suggests some wild creatures not normally to be found in houses (cf. LXX ἦχος, "sound, noise"). Koehler (*Lexicon,* p. 26) favors "eagle-owls," and G. R. Driver (*PEQ* [May-Oct., 1955], p. 134) "hyaenas."

W. S. MCCULLOUGH

HOZAI hō'zī [חוזי]. Author of some "sayings" in which the record of Manasseh's life was preserved, according to the Hebrew text of II Chr. 33:19. One Hebrew MS and the LXX (τῶν ὁρώντων) read "of the seers" (חוזים; so RSV), and this is generally preferred. Some commentators, however, take the MT as a reference to an otherwise unknown prophet. A third alternative is to rearrange the consonants of the Hebrew text to read חזיו, "his [i.e., Manasseh's] seers."

J. M. WARD

HUKKOK hŭk'ŏk [חוקק]. A border town in the territory of Naphtali (Josh. 19:34). It is generally identified with Yaquq, approximately three miles W of CHINNEROTH, overlooking the plain.

HUKOK. Alternate form of HELKATH.

HUL hŭl [חול]. The second son of Aram, and a grandson of Shem, according to Gen. 10:23; in I Chr. 1:17, the seventh son of Shem (but see LXX A).

HULDAH hŭl'də [חלדה, *possibly from* חלד, weasel]. A prophetess; wife of Shallum, "keeper of the wardrobe" (II Kings 22:14). She was the one consulted when King Josiah sent to "inquire of the LORD" after finding the Book of the Law in the temple. She prophesied God's judgment upon the nation, but peace for Josiah because of his repentance (vss. 16-20). It was after this consultation that Josiah carried out his religious reform (23:1-25). Huldah's prophecy is of interest in connection with the question of fulfilment of prophecy (Josiah was later killed), and also for the unusual example of a woman's acting in this capacity (cf. Deborah in Judg. 4:4; Anna in Luke 2:36).

D. HARVEY

HUMANITY OF CHRIST. The idea found in the NT that Jesus Christ was truly human in every respect, despite the emphasis on his divinity (*see* DIVINITY OF CHRIST).

The earliest gospel, Mark, appears to teach that Jesus' knowledge was limited (13:32), and quotes Jesus as disclaiming to be good in the absolute sense (10:18: "Why do you call me good? No one is good but God alone"). The cry from the cross: "My God, my God, why hast thou forsaken me?" (15:34), can be understood as an expression of true humanity.

The Gospel of Luke affirms that Jesus grew "in wisdom and in stature, and in favor with God and man" (2:52). The gospels throughout reflect a life of human activity, and Jesus was regarded by most of his contemporaries as a teacher and prophet.

The Gospel of John, which has the most developed Christology of any NT book, pictures Jesus as fatigued and thirsting (4:6-7; 19:28) and includes the story that when his side was pierced, blood and water came out (19:34), perhaps in order to guard against the idea that his sufferings were illusory.

The Pauline letters emphasize Jesus' origin from a Jewish family and the human limitations under which he lived (Rom. 9:5; II Cor. 13:4; Gal. 4:4; Phil. 2:7-8).

The Letter to the Hebrews teaches that Christ is a high priest who can have compassion for human weakness, since he was tempted in every way, yet without sin (4:14; cf. Matt. 4:1-11 = Luke 4:1-13); also that Christ was perfected through his sufferings (Heb. 2:10), shared human flesh and blood (2:14), and cried out to God and learned obedience through what he suffered (5:7-8).

The Pastoral letters refer to him as the "man Christ Jesus" (I Tim. 2:5). *See also* CHRIST §§ 5, 9; KENOSIS.

S. E. JOHNSON

HUMILITY [צנע, ענוה, עני; ταπεινός, πραΰς, *and related words*]. A situation of lowliness or affliction, and a characteristic way of acting toward God and man; opposite to pride, arrogance, and violence. There is not a clear distinction between humility and MEEKNESS or PATIENCE. At first the humble are the poor or afflicted, but later humility is separated from socio-economic connotations to refer to subjective traits of character; the words translated by this English word have relatively little to do with one's self-valuation apart from ways of acting toward others.

1. In the OT. The great emphasis upon humility in both Judaism and Christianity must be traced back to its roots in the beginnings of Israel. The pre-Mosaic ancient world was, like the later Greco-Roman world, very sensitive to social status, so much so that the overturning of the normal social distinctions was calamity and chaos. The beginnings of Israel were tied up with rejection of such aristocratic stratification of society. Acutely aware of their lowly origins as state slaves in Egypt (Exod. 1:11; Deut. 26:6), and of the goodness of Yahweh, who delivered them from an intolerable affliction, they could never regard Yahweh as the upholder of a social system built on pride and wealth. On the contrary, it is Yahweh who delivers the humble, but brings down the haughty (cf. I Sam. 2:7; II Sam. 22:28). The concept of humility is thus in the OT almost exclusively tied up with human beings who are in affliction, poverty, and suffering; only rarely does ענוה occur as an abstraction (and in relatively late passages), designating a purely subjective trait of character. Humility is the state of the POOR and afflicted (עני and אביון), whose situation is one in which they must acknowledge their own helplessness and utter dependence upon God. Yahweh himself humbles man, whether it be Pharaoh (Exod. 10:3) or Israel in the wilderness (Deut. 8:2, 16), in order that man may know that he does not live by bread alone, and that it is by Yahweh's power that he obtains wealth. The Deuteronomists warn against pride in power on the ground that Yahweh's choice of Israel was based, not on human strength and achievements, but on divine love and promise to the fathers (Deut. 7:7-8). By attributing to Yahweh the source of all wealth and power, these two major sources of human pride and arrogance were brought under control (cf. Jer. 9:23-24). On the other hand, the humble poor are the constant concern of Yahweh, from the oldest law codes (Exod. 23:6, 11; cf. Deut. 15:4, 7, 11; 24:14) throughout the prophets. Utterly dependent, they were evidently increasingly preyed upon by the wealthy and powerful, who acted with violence and arrogance and are thus equated with the enemies of Yahweh in all the pre-exilic prophets (Isa. 3:14-15; Jer. 2:34, *et passim;* Amos 2:6-7; 4:1). It is most likely that this horror of violent actions against the helpless was constant from the time of Moses on. On the other hand, the humility of the poor became the symbol of the righteous God-fearer from Moses (Num. 12:3), and especially after the destruction of Jerusalem. Zephaniah had already nearly equated righteousness and humility (2:3; 3:12-13) and Micah (6:8) had identified humility as the requirement of God, but in the Psalms particularly the afflicted is almost a technical term for the God-fearing pious (Pss. 22:26; 25:9; 147:6; *et passim*). It is probable that there is a direct connection between these uses and the HASIDIM of the Maccabean period, since a direct connection is seen between suffering and the maintenance of religious integrity.

2. In the NT. Only rarely does humility in the NT have the objective aspect of poverty, affliction, or low social status so characteristic of OT uses. Matt. 5:5 may have such underlying connotations, but is obviously a reminiscence of Ps. 37:11, as Luke 1:52 takes up I Sam. 2:7. In Acts 20:19, Paul mentions humility together with tears and trials; this suggests the old connection. However, it is in connection with Jesus himself as Messiah that the motif of humility and also of affliction occurs most frequently. Matt. 21:4-5 applies to him the prophecy of Zech. 9:9, in which the religious ideal of humility has already been attributed to the king. The same is true in Matt. 11:29, where there is the same emphasis upon peace and nonviolence. It is possible that the OT narratives of Saul (I Sam. 10:21-23) and David (16:11-12) are also deliberate attributions of humility to the earliest kings. This humility of the sovereign is, at any rate, not a new motif in the NT, connected as it is with the OT, where it reflects theological concepts of sovereignty which contrast most sharply with ancient paganism, even though the ritual humiliation of the king does play a part in the Babylonian Akitu Festival. *See* ASSYRIA AND BABYLONIA.

The vast majority of references to humility in the NT refer to subjective traits of character not tied up with an objective situation of affliction or poverty. Humility appears in many catalogues of Christian virtues in the letters, sometimes connected with the example of Jesus (I Cor. 4:21; II Cor. 10:1; Phil. 2:8) and sometimes connected with OT passages which emphasized God's concern for and protection of the poor and resistance to the proud (II Cor. 7:6; Jas. 4:6). Humility is sometimes contrasted deliberately with violence (I Cor. 4:21; Gal. 6:1; II Tim. 2:25). Christian humility means a lack of concern for one's own prestige (Rom. 12:16; cf. Matt. 18:4; 23:12; Luke 14:11; II Cor. 11:7), and consequently valuation of others above self (Phil. 2:3). In Jas. 1:10 the old expectation of the exaltation of the poor and humbling of the rich is to be realized in the Christian community, but the economic difference is now irrelevant.

From the frequency of references in the NT, one may conclude that humility is regarded as a most important trait of early Christian life. Since it is primarily an attitude and mode of acting in regard to one's fellow men, it does away with selfish pride, arrogance, and especially violence, and furnishes the possibility of peace and harmony within the community. It also, however, withdrew the normal foundations of authority in human society, which are usually to be found in prestige and power. This conflict between humility and prestige appears throughout the OT, and perhaps is to be found in the temptation narratives, but certainly is dealt with by Paul in Phil. 2:5-13. The resolution of the religious necessity of humility and at the same time of authority is to be found in the Cross—and the Resurrection. Nothing could more forcefully indicate that for early Christians, the two are to be harmonized only in the act of God, not in exempting religious authorities from humility, nor in reducing humility to ritual acts or a false self-denigration.

Bibliography. A. Rahlfs, עני *und* ענו *in den Psalmen* (1892); A. Causse, *Les 'Pauvres' d'Israël* (1922); R. Storr, *Die Frömmigkeit im AT* (1928), pp. 159-60; H. Birkeland, *'āni und 'ānāw in den Psalmen* (1933); A. Gelin, *Les pauvres de Yahvé* (1954); T. C. Vriezen, *An Outline of OT Theology* (1958), p. 313.

G. E. MENDENHALL

HUMOR. Subject indexes in library catalogues often use the caption "Wit and Humor" rather than "Humor" alone. This usage is appropriate to an investigation of humor in the Bible. Religion is serious, and the Bible is basically a serious book. However, the Bible, like any other great literature, has its lighter moments, especially its quick perception of the incongruous, which is the essence of wit. Another aspect of wit is the ability to make a neat turn of speech; it is obvious to all that the Bible abounds in this sort of thing. We should also keep in mind Whipple's classic descriptions: "Wit is abrupt, darting, scornful, and tosses its analogies in your face; humor is slow and shy, insinuating its fun into your heart."

Not only is the Bible a serious book; it is also an ancient and mostly oriental book, originally written in languages little known to ordinary Occidentals today, and evincing only a few instances of contact with the European or Western world. Because of the verbal and intellectual subtlety of humor, it is the literary quality most easily lost in translation. "In other words," says Leacock, "translation of humor from one language to another, from one age to another, from one thought to another, is almost impossible." Almost, it might be added, but not altogether impossible. Some of the Bible's humor is already fairly well recognized, and more of it can be pointed out or explained. Modern translations often provide help by adding an explanation in brackets or in a footnote.

IRONY AND SATIRE are special forms of humor, usually with a didactic or moralistic purpose.

One of the most common kinds of humor (or rather, wit) in the Bible (and perhaps everywhere) is the pun, a form of wordplay or paronomasia. Paronomasia, or wordplay in general, goes far beyond mere humor in the Bible, because of the oriental fondness for this sort of thing. Learned dissertations have been written on the subject (*see bibliography*), attesting its prime importance. Casanowicz lists some five hundred wordplays from the OT, and Russell adds at least two hundred from the NT. Obviously, only a few of the more striking examples can be mentioned or discussed here. Not all of these could be called humorous in the modern sense, but certainly they are all witty, and were so intended by the original speakers and writers. It has been said that the pun is the lowest form of humor; the people of Bible times would not have agreed; to them words were more serious and significant than to us.

Genesis provides some of the best plays on words, especially in connection with proper names. The Garden of Eden story, in spite of serious implications such as the introduction of sin into the world, has a lightness of touch that has long been recognized. Who has not smiled at the indecent haste with which the guilty pair clothe themselves and try to hide among the trees? And how sadly yet ludicrously human it is when the man blames the woman and she in turn blames the serpent! The whole atmosphere contrasts sharply with the austere account of Creation that precedes (1:1–2:4*a; see* DOCUMENTS). In this atmosphere the pun is at home; we are prepared to understand the earthy nature of mankind by an untranslatable pun at the beginning of the story (2:7): "Then the LORD God formed man [*ādhām*] of dust from the ground [*adhāmâ*]." Likewise, in the passage on the formation of the woman from a rib of the man (which has given rise to no end of humorous remarks), the close relationship between man and woman is asserted, and then clinched by a telling pun, which is not altogether lost in English (2:23):

> This at last is bone of my bones
> and flesh of my flesh;
> she shall be called Wo*man* [*ishshâ*],
> because she was taken out of *Man* [*îsh*].

Near the end of the story the woman, destined to become the mother of the race, receives an appropriate personal name; and again the occasion calls for a pun (3:20): "The man called his wife's name Eve [*ḥawwâ*], because she was the mother of all living [*ḥay*]."

The famous story of the Tower of Babel, or Babylon, as we now call it, is in similar vein. The language barrier is a tragic problem among men, as the biblical writer senses when he makes it the result of man's sinful pride and ambition; but it also has its comic aspects—the other person's language often sounds ludicrous, as though it were mere babbling. Thus arises the opportunity for the pun on the name of the tower (11:9). By using the form "Babylon," Moffatt makes the pun very close in English, thus: "Hence it was called Babylon [*bābhel*], because it was there that the Eternal made a babble [*bālal*] of the language of the whole earth."

The names of the PATRIARCHS give fruitful occasion for punning. Abram and Abraham suggest "father" (*ābh*) plus another word (17:5). Isaac (*yiṣḥaq*) suggests the verb "to laugh" or "to enjoy oneself" (17:17, 19; 21:6; 26:8). Ishmael sounds like the verb "to hear" or "give heed" (16:11; 17:20). Esau suggests "hairy" (25:25). Edom is very similar to the word for "red" (25:30). Jacob suggests both "heel-holder" and "supplanter" (25:26; 27:36; Hos. 12:2-3). Joseph may be compared with the verbs "take away" (*'āsaph;* Gen. 30:23) or "add" (*yāsaph;* 30:24). Manasseh suggests "forgetfulness" (41:51), and Ephraim can be connected with a verb meaning "to be fruitful" (41:52; Hos. 9:16; 14:8).

The prophets also use puns, often with ironical, sarcastic, or satirical force, to make their monitory message more vivid (*see* IRONY AND SATIRE). Thus their humor is of a somewhat grimmer sort than that found in Genesis. Only a few selected examples can be given: "*Gilgal* shall go into *galling* exile [*gālâ*]" (Amos 5:5; cf. Amer. Trans. and Moffatt). The most famous and the grimmest pun in the Prophets occurs in Amos 8:1-2: "Thus the Lord GOD showed me . . . a basket of summer fruit [*qayiṣ*]. . . . Then the LORD said to me, 'The end [*qēṣ*] has come upon my people Israel.' " This figure is very vivid, for not only does the word for "summer fruit" sound like the word for "end," but obviously the fruit is conceived of as being overripe to add to the effect of doom (see Moffatt).

The splendid paronomasia in Hos. 8:7 is usually lost in English:

> The standing grain [*qāmāh*] has no heads [*ṣemaḥ*],
> it shall yield no meal [*qemaḥ*]

(note the rhyming free translation of Moffatt). Hos. 12:11—H 12:12 has another pun on Gilgal:

> If in *Gilgal* they sacrifice bulls,
> their altars also shall be like stone heaps [*gallîm*].

Because of its strong feeling and high literary style throughout, wordplays are found in all parts of the book of Isaiah. A few examples must suffice: "Ah [*hôi*], sinful nation [*gôi*]" (1:4); "*eat* the good" or "be *eaten* by the sword" (1:19-20); "to terrify ['*a*rōṣ] the earth ['*āreṣ*]" (2:19);

> He looked for justice [*mishpāṭ*],
> but behold, bloodshed [*miśpāḥ*];
> for righteousness [*ṣ*e*dāqâ*],
> but behold, a cry [*ṣ*e'*āqâ*]!
> (5:7);

note 17:12; 21:2 in any translation, though none does justice to the original; "There shall be moaning [*ta'*a*niyyâ*] and groaning [*wa'*a*niyyâ*]" (29:2); "a sacrifice [*zebhaḥ*] in Bozrah, a great slaughter [*ṭebhaḥ*] in the land of Edom" (34:6); "Wild beasts [*ṣiyyîm*] shall meet with hyenas ['*iyyîm*]" (34:14); "He makes them . . . like driven stubble [*qash*] with his bow [*qashtô*]" (41:2); "like a wife forsaken ['*a*zubhâ] and grieved ['*a*ṣûbhath] in spirit" (54:6); "a rush [*sheṣeph*] of wrath [*qeṣeph*]" (54:8 Moffatt).

Mic. 1:10-14 contains a series of wordplays of this type. Unfortunately the text is not in good order, and most translations give no hint of the original flavor. *The Interpreter's Bible* and the translations of Knox and Moffatt (especially the latter) do give some help.

The most telling pun in Jeremiah, comparable to that in Amos 8:2 and setting the theological tone for the entire book, is that in 1:11-12: "I [Jeremiah] said, 'I see a rod of almond [*shāqēdh;* Moffatt 'wake-tree'].' Then the LORD said to me, 'You have seen well, for I am watching [*shōqēdh;* Moffatt 'wakeful'] over my word to perform it.' " Horror, a very grim form of humor, is well expressed in 2:12: "Be appalled [*shōmmû*], O heavens [*shāmayim*], at this"; note in the following verse the contrasting figures, "living waters" and "broken cisterns." The call to repentance in ch. 3 plays upon two meanings of the verb *shûbhâ*, "to turn," "return," "turn away": "Return [*shûbhâ*], faithless [*m*e*shûbhâ;* Moffatt 'turncoat'] Israel" (vs. 12); "Return [*shûbhû*], O faithless [*shôbhābhîm*] children" (vs. 14);

> Return [*shûbhû*], O faithless [*shôbhābhîm*] sons,
> I will heal your faithlessness [*m*e*shûbhōth*]
> (vs. 22).

The feeling in this last verse is no longer satirical humor, but deep pathos; this shows the range of moods which the pun could express.

Our final prophetic example, typical of a group, is from Zech. 9:5: "Ashkelon shall see [*tērê*] it, and be afraid [*têrâ*]." A number of the forms of the Hebrew verbs meaning "to see" and "to fear" are similar, with the result of about fifteen plays on these two words in the OT.

The WISDOM literature naturally makes use of wordplays and other forms of wit. Examples are:

> A stupid [*nābhûbh*] man will get understanding [*yillābhēbh*],
> when a wild ass's colt is born a man (Job 11:12);

"The companion [*rō'ê*] of fools will suffer harm [*yērôa'*]" (Prov. 13:20); "There are friends [*rē'îm*] who *pretend to be friends* [*hitrô'ēa'*, similar to a word meaning "be harmful"; *double-entendre*]" (Prov. 18:24); "Who has woe ['*ôy*]? Who has sorrow ['*a*bhôy]?" (Prov. 23:29)—a part of the satire on the drunkard.

The APOCRYPHA are, for the most part, translated works; therefore many of their wordplays are lost. However, Susanna contains two clever and bitter puns in the Greek (both LXX and Theod.), which are worthy of mention here: " 'Under which tree did you see them meet?' He answered, 'Under a mastic tree [*schînon*].' And Daniel said, 'You have told a fine lie against your own life, for already the angel of God has received the sentence from God, and he will cut [*schisei*, 'split'] you in two' " (vss. 54-55 Goodspeed); " 'Under which tree did you catch them embracing each other?' . . . 'Under a liveoak tree [*prînon*].' And Daniel said to him, '. . . the angel of God is waiting with his sword to saw [*prisai*] you in two' " (vss. 58-59 Goodspeed). Note, in addition to the wordplays, that the names of the trees rhyme—they are both lies!

The translation problem also affects, to some extent, the presentation of wordplays from the Greek NT (*see* ARAMAIC). Yet much of the Greek NT is not translation; in some cases the wordplays are preserved, and in other cases the Greek itself gives occasion for new wordplays (as was probably the case also in the passage from Susanna presented above). Hence it is not difficult to collect examples from the NT. Most of them are witty, rather than humorous; some are very serious.

Underlying Matt. 1:21 is a pun on a proper name, similar to those presented from Genesis. The idea presented is basic to NT thought—namely, that Jesus is savior; but the pun is not even preserved in Greek, to say nothing of English. Yet the original import of the verse cannot be understood without reference to it: "She will bear a son, and you shall call his name Jesus [original form *yēshû'*a], for he will save [*yāsha'*] his people from their sins." A good humorous, satirical pun occurs in Matt. 6:16: "They disfigure [*aphanizousin*] their faces that they may figure [*phanôsin*] in public as fasting" (Russell). Probably the most famous wordplay in the NT is that in Matt. 16:18, fairly well preserved in Greek, but lost in English: "You are Peter [Greek *petros;* Aramaic *kēphâ*], and on this rock [Greek *petra;* Aramaic *kēphâ*] I will build my church." Note John 3:8, where the same word (*pneuma*) means both "wind" and "Spirit." In II Cor. 1:21 occurs a significant wordplay on the root meaning of the word "Christ": "It is God who establishes us with you in Christ [the 'Anointed' One], and has commissioned [*chrisas*, 'anointed' (Goodspeed) or 'christened'] us." In I John 2:19 the same

Greek phrase (*ex hēmôn*) is repeated with an opposite meaning: "They went out *from us,* but they were not *of us.*"

In conclusion, reference may be made to a few more general or extended passages of humorous import.

Outstanding is the story of Samson (Judg. 13–16). Pfeiffer's characterization is most apt: "The hero lacks the refinement of a Joseph or an Achilles, but possesses traits dear to simple and healthy rural folk. Always brawling and excelling all rivals in muscular strength, this uncouth fellow is no match for feminine wiles. But under the rough exterior there is a witty if untutored mind, quick at repartee, an instinctive devotion to his own people, and a dogged determination in avenging wrongs, which culminates in a self-inflicted heroic death. Samson is a sort of irresponsible and uncontrollable Till Eulenspiegel or Peer Gynt."

By combining two translations (Moffatt and RSV) of Samson's exulting cry after the jawbone incident (15:16), we can sense something of the flavor of the more humorous parts of the entire narrative:

With the jawbone of an ass,
  I have piled them in a mass!
With the jawbone of an ass,
  I have slain a thousand men!

Other OT passages to be noted are: Lamech's boast (Gen. 4:23-24); Noah's drunkenness (Gen. 9: 18-27); Abraham's bargaining with the Lord (Gen. 18:22-33); the various instances of Jacob's clever trickery (Gen. 25:21–32:1); the story of the attempts of the angel to impede the progress of Balaam and his ass (Num. 22:21-35); Ehud's stabbing of the obese Eglon (Judg. 3:15-27); the rout of the Midianites (Judg. 7:19-22); Jotham's fable or parable (Judg. 9:7-20); Abimelech's death at the hands of a woman (Judg. 9:50-54); the ruse by which the Benjaminites obtained wives (Judg. 21:15-24); the slaying of Goliath (I Sam. 17); David's frustration of Nabal (I Sam. 25), whose name means "fool" (vs. 25); Elijah's ridiculing the prophets of Baal on Mount Carmel (I Kings 18:26-29; sarcastic and satirical); Micaiah's irony (I Kings 22:15); the extravagant actions of Ezra and Nehemiah (Ezra 9:3; Neh. 13:25; unintentionally humorous); Haman's unwittingly being the cause of honoring his enemy Mordecai (Esth. 6:1-11); Haman's hanging on his own gallows (Esth. 5: 14–7:10); Job's bitter irony (Job 12:2); the sluggard (Prov. 6:6-11; 24:30-34; 26:13-16); the scolding wife (Prov. 21:9, 19; 25:24); the drunkard (Prov. 23:29-35); the fool (Prov. 26:1-12; 27:22); "A living dog is better than a dead lion" (Eccl. 9:4); the satirical ridicule of IDOLATRY (cf. Elijah; Pss. 115:2-8; 135:15-18; Isa. 2:8, 18-21; 40:19-20; 44:9-20; 45:16; 46:1; Jer. 10:1-10; Hos. 4:17; 8:4-6; 13:1-2); Nebuchadnezzar's madness ("made to eat grass like an ox" [Dan. 4]); Jonah's absurd sulking (Jonah 4:1-9); Micah's mockery (Mic. 2:6-7, 11); Nahum's gleeful taunts over Nineveh (Nah. 3).

In the Apoc.: Holofernes' being overcome by the wiles of a woman (Jth. 12–13); Daniel's trapping the guilty old men (Sus. 51-59); the detection of the fraud of the priests of Bel (Bel 19-22); the bursting of the great dragon or serpent (Bel 23-28).

In the NT: the mote (RSV "speck") and the beam (RSV "log"; Matt. 7:3-5; Luke 6:41-42); the outwitting of the Pharisees (Matt. 22:15-22; Mark 12:13-17) and the Sadducees (Matt. 22:23-33; Mark 12:18-27); "straining out a gnat and swallowing a camel" (Matt. 23:24); "whitewashed tombs" (Matt. 23:27; cf. Acts 23:3); Peter's impetuous overconfidence (Matt. 26:33-35; Mark 14:29-31; Luke 22:33-34); "better to marry than to burn" (I Cor. 7:9 KJV); Paul's ridicule of misconduct in worship (I Cor. 11: 22).

Bibliography. E. P. Whipple, *Literature and Life* (1871), p. 91; I. M. Casanowicz, *Paronomasia in the OT* (1894)—a Johns Hopkins dissertation, and a very valuable study; E. Russell, *Paronomasia and Kindred Phenomena in the NT* (1920)—a University of Chicago dissertation, and a useful supplement to Casanowicz; D. Zuver, *Salvation by Laughter* (1933); S. Leacock, *Humor: Its Theory and Technique* (1935), p. 226; F. Rosenthal, *Humor in Early Islam* (1956).

W. F. STINESPRING

HUMTAH hŭm'tə [חמטה, place of lizards(?)] (Josh. 15:54). A village of Judah in the hill-country district of Hebron. The present location is unknown.

HUNCHBACK [גבן, curved, crook-backed]. A type of person cited in the Holiness Code (Lev. 21:20) as unfit for priestly service, although he was permitted to partake of holy food (the priest's portion). The priest was a sacred person, consecrated to Yahweh, and thus was to have no blemish, spiritual or physical.

V. H. KOOY

HUNDRED, TOWER OF THE [מגדל המאה, *migdal hammē'â*]; KJV TOWER OF MEAH mē'ə. A tower of the N rampart of Jerusalem restored by Nehemiah (Neh. 3:1; 12:39). It is listed immediately before the Tower of Hananel (*see* JERUSALEM § 7*b*). It is very possible that the mention of the Tower of the Hundred may result from an artificial insertion into the text of Neh. 3:1. G. A. BARROIS

HUNDREDWEIGHT. The measure used in the translation of ὡς ταλαντιαία, "heavy as a hundredweight" (Rev. 16:21). The KJV translates "about the weight of a talent," and the RSV interprets the talent as *ca.* a hundred pounds. *See* WEIGHTS AND MEASURES § B4*k*. O. R. SELLERS

HUNTING [ציד, *ṣayyādh,* hunter (Jer. 16:16; *emended* Prov. 6:5); ציד, *ṣayidh,* hunter (Gen. 10:9; 25:27; *Qerê* Gen. 27:3; *also* RSV GAME, KJV VENISON); צוד, to hunt; למצודה (KJV to be hunted, RSV for prey; lit., for hunting; Ezek. 13:21; *elsewhere used of the hunting* SNARE: Ezek. 12:13; 17:20; etc.); מדח, hunted (*participle;* Isa. 13:14)]. The pursuit of wild animals for food, protection, or pleasure.

Although the purely hunting phase of human culture was long past before the biblical period began, the hunt must still have provided an important supplementary source of food, especially in the semi-nomadic stage. Hunting with dogs is attested for the immediately pre-Israelite period in Palestine by the Egyptian story *The Tale of Si-nuhe.* Two hunters from the early time are mentioned by name in the OT: Nimrod (Gen. 10:9) and Esau (Gen. 25:27).

With the coming of city life and the development of trade, the economic importance of hunting declined further, but it remained significant enough to be the subject of a law in Lev. 17:13 and of one of

Courtesy of the Trustees of the British Museum

34. Assyrian hunters using bow and arrow to shoot birds and other game; from a bas relief on the palace of Sargon II (721-705 B.C.) at Khorsabad

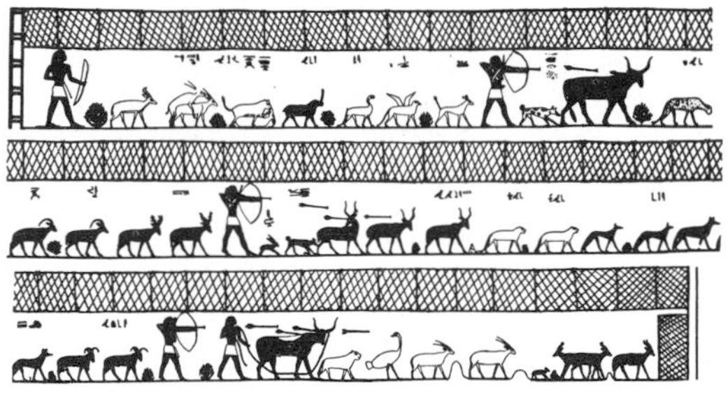

35. Hunting in the desert, showing the use of bow and arrows and netting; from tomb of Amen-em-hep at Beni-hasan, Twelfth Dynasty (1971-1928 B.C.)

the proverbs (12:27; cf. Ecclus. 36:19). Deut. 14:5 includes wild game among the animals permitted as food (e.g., the hart, gazelle, roebuck, wild goat, ibex, antelope, and mountain-sheep; *see* FAUNA), and these must have been obtained by hunting. Many common game animals, such as the hare and wild pig,* were, however, prohibited by the dietary laws (Lev. 11:6). The OT has few references to the hunting of four-footed beasts, but the fowler with his nets and snares* is a common figure; understandably so, since Palestine lies on the main flight routes of the migratory birds. Nevertheless, a rather low opinion of hunting as a profession seems to have prevailed in Israel, for Esau, who lived by the hunt, is regarded as uncivilized by contrast with Jacob the herdsman (Gen. 25:27). Figs. HUN 34-35; TRA 76.

The hunting weapons specifically mentioned in the OT are the bow and arrow (Gen. 27:3) and, by implication, the sling (I Sam. 17:40). Ancient Near Eastern art shows the lasso and spear in use for hunting, and traps, nets, and deadfalls are described in the OT. In hunting wild animals for protection or to rid the community of a dangerous beast or pest, the more military weapons—spear, sword, and club—were used (I Sam. 17:40; Ps. 23:4). The OT records several incidents of killing animals in self-protection (Judg. 14:6; I Sam. 17:34-37; II Sam. 23:20), and describes the shepherd as equipped with club and sling for the defense of his flocks. *See* WEAPONS; TRAPS.

In communities where the chase is a substantial source of food, the battue method of hunting was employed from antiquity, and is still in use. The villagers form a cordon, and beat forward over the ground, with loud shouts and the pounding of drums or sticks, driving the frightened game before them into a blind canyon, a corral of nets, or a prepared pit, where it is easily killed. Allusions to this type of hunting may be present in OT references to the fear inspired by confined spaces (Job 18:11; Ps. 18:5), and especially the prophetic linking of "terror" and "the pit" (Isa. 24:17-18; Jer. 48:43-44). Fig. HUN 36.

Hunting for pleasure was the privilege of kings and nobles. Phoenician, Assyrian,* and Egyptian art shows royal personages hunting from the chariot while hunting dogs join in the chase (*ANEP* 183-84, 190). Such royal sport is not referred to in the OT, either because the mountainous terrain of Palestine made it impossible or because the OT writers had too little interest in such matters to record them. Josephus, however, states that Herod enjoyed hunting on horseback, a practice introduced by the Persians (War I.xxi.13). Fig. ASS 102.

Courtesy of the Trustees of the British Museum

36. An Assyrian bas relief showing two footmen with shields and daggers assisting Ashurnasirpal (883-859 B.C.) in a lion hunt; from Nimrud

The patience required of the hunter and the deadly intent of the hunt provided a suitable metaphor, often used in both the OT and the NT, for persistent and inexorable pursuit with intent to destroy (cf. I Sam. 24:11; Job 10:16; Jer. 16:16; Mic. 7:2; Mark 12:13; Luke 11:54; I Tim. 3:7; II Tim. 2:26). The strangest use of the hunting metaphor is Ezek. 13:18, 21, where sorceresses who attempt to destroy life by their magic are said to be hunting souls.

Bibliography. F. von Oppenheim, *Der Tell Halaf* (1931), pp. 133-38; K. Galling, *Biblisches Reallexikon* (1937), pp. 286-90; G. Gerleman, *Contributions to the OT Terminology of the Chase* (1946); J. B. Pritchard, *ANEP* (1954), pp. 56-60.

L. E. TOOMBS

HUPHAM hū'fəm [חופם, *a tribal name*]; HUPHAMITES —fə mīts. Alternately: HUPPIM hŭp'ĭm [חפים (Gen. 46:21); חפם (I Chr. 7:12)]; probably HURAM hū'rəm [חורם] (I Chr. 8:5). An eponym; listed as a son of Benjamin (Gen. 46:21 [cf. Jub. 44:25]; Num. 26:39; I Chr. 7:12); inserted erroneously in I Chr. 7:15. The context of "Huram" in I Chr. 8:5 suggests that "Hupham" be read here.

Bibliography. E. L. Curtis, *Chronicles*, ICC (1910), pp. 150, 152-53, 158.

B. T. DAHLBERG

HUPPAH hŭp'ə [חפה, canopy (*perhaps referring to divine protection*)] (I Chr. 24:13). A priest contemporaneous with King David.

HUPPIM. Alternate form of HUPHAM.

HUR hûr [חוּר, *perhaps* child (*originally a pet name; cf.* Akkad. *ḫūru*), *or perhaps shortened from* אשחור, ASHHUR, *or perhaps related to gentilic* חרי, HORITES]. **1.** An eponym; listed as a descendant of Judah; son of Caleb and Ephrath, and an ancestor of Bezalel the craftsman (I Chr. 2:19-20; cf. Exod. 31:2); but listed also as a son of Judah (I Chr. 4:1); again, listed as the "first-born of Ephrathah the father of Bethlehem" (I Chr. 4:4; cf. 2:50). Possibly he is to be identified with the Ashhur who was the son of Caleb and Ephrathah (I Chr. 2:24, as the RSV emends; cf. vs. 19; 4:4-5). Possibly this lineage is represented in 2, 4, and 5 *below*. But it is worth while to note that this name comes into association with the gentilic חרי, "Horite" (i.e., "Hurrian"; e.g., Gen. 36:20; *see* HORITES), since both "Seir the Horite" and Hur are listed as having among their descendants Shobal (Gen. 36:20; I Chr. 2:50; cf. I Chr. 4:1, where he is the brother of Hur) and Manahath or the Manahathites (Gen. 36:23; I Chr. 2:54; cf. also Ezer [אצר] in Gen. 36:21; Ezer [עזר] in I Chr. 4:4).

2. Moses' assistant, who with Aaron supported Moses' upraised hands during the battle with Amalek (Exod. 17:10-12) and who, with Aaron, presided over the government of the people during Moses' absence (24:14). The Jewish historian Josephus (*ca.* A.D. 100) thought he was the husband of Moses' sister Miriam (Antiq. III.ii.4).

3. One of the five kings of Midian slain by the Israelites under Moses (Num. 31:8; Josh. 13:21).

4. Father or family name of Solomon's purveyor in the hill country of Ephraim (I Kings 4:8; *see* 1 *above;* also BEN-HUR).

5. Father or family name of a certain Rephaiah, who helped repair the wall of Jerusalem in the time of Nehemiah (Neh. 3:9).

Bibliography. E. L. Curtis, *Chronicles,* ICC (1910), pp. 89-90; M. Noth, *Die israelitischen Personennamen* (1928), p. 221.

B. T. DAHLBERG

HURAI. Alternate form of HUDDAI.

HURAM hyo͝or'əm [חוּרָם]. Alternately: HURAM-ABI ho͞o'rəm ä'bī [חורם אבי, חורם אביו, Huram is my father] (II Chr. 2:13—H 2:12; 4:16); HIRAM hī'rəm [חירם, brother of the exalted one] (Samuel, Kings). **1.** A Benjaminite (I Chr. 8:5). Probably his name should be read "Hupham" (cf. Num. 26:39).

2. Same as HIRAM 1.

3. Chief architect of Solomon's temple. In I Kings 7:14 he is said to be the son of a man of Tyre and a woman of Naphtali; II Chr. 2:14—H 2:13 makes his mother a Danite. The Chronicler calls him Huram-abi—a name which he may have created by combining "Hiram" (I Kings 7:13) with "ab" from the second element of "Oholiab," the name of a Danite who helped build the tabernacle (Exod. 31:6). The list of Huram's talents (II Chr. 2:7, 14—H 2:6, 13; cf. I Kings 7:14) is taken from Exod. 31:1-6; 35:35.

Bibliography. M. Noth, *Die israelitischen Personennamen* (1928), p. 242; A. Brunet, "Le Chroniste et ses sources," *RB,* LXI (1954), 358-59.

R. W. CORNEY

HURI hyo͝or'ī [חוּרִי, *perhaps* child (*originally a pet name; cf.* Akkad. *ḫūru*)] (I Chr. 5:14). A Gadite.

Bibliography. M. Noth, *Die israelitischen Personennamen* (1928), pp. 38, 221.

B. T. DAHLBERG

HURRIANS ho͝or'ī ənz. The name of a people widely diffused throughout most of the ancient Near East; referred to in the Bible as HORITES; HIVITES; and Jebusites (*see* JEBUS). Various social customs of the patriarchal age can be traced back to the Hurrians (*see* NUZI), whose language, moreover, left its mark on Hebrew and Northwest Semitic phonology.

1. In extrabiblical sources. The Hurrians were spread more widely in the ancient Near East than any other people before the Arameans. Although their original home has to be sought in the general region of Armenia, the Hurrians were settled in historical times not only in adjacent areas of Anatolia and Syria but also as far E as the district of Arrapkha (modern Kirkuk), which included Nuzi, and as far S as Central Palestine. It is this exceptional expansion that long kept scholars from recognizing diverse units of the far-flung Hurrians as branches of the same people. The ties between biblical Horites, the dominant ethnic element of the kingdom of Mitanni, and the bearers of certain unusual personal names from Mesopotamia were by no means apparent at first glance.

The necessary key was provided by the Hittite archives from Boghazköy. Included among these were texts and passages in a language expressly labeled as *ḫurli-li,* "Hurlian," which could then be linked up with lands and people elsewhere designated as *Ḫurri.* This language, in turn, proved to be the same as the speech of Mitanni—previously discovered at AMARNA—in which the pertinent gentilic form appeared as *ḫurw-oḫe* and *ḫurr-oḫe.* The basic stem, then, had to be *ḫuru-* or *ḫurw-,* which became *ḫurli-* in Hittite and *ḫurri* elsewhere; it was manifestly a native term. The corresponding gentilic in Ugaritic proved to be *ḫry.* Inevitably, the biblical חרי, "Horite," as applied to an ethnic group attested in Central Palestine, fell into line, inasmuch as Hurrian personal names had been discovered in that same area. And the reason for the Egyptian designation of Palestine as *Ḫr* (=*Ḫuru*), which was introduced in the New Kingdom, likewise ceased to be a puzzle. Thus in the space of a few years Hurrians had been certified by name all the way from Anatolia to Egypt.

Before long it became possible to recognize Hurrian elements even without the benefit of the appropriate ethnic or linguistic label. This result was brought about by steady progress in the recovery of the Hurrian language. Unrelated to any of the linguistic stocks previously established for that region—such as Semitic, Sumerian, and Indo-European—Hurrian has generic affinities only with Urartian (the language of ancient Armenia); its only likely modern relatives would have to be sought among the Caucasic family, with which Hurrian shares certain structural features.

The Hurrians flourished from the middle of the third to the end of the second millennium B.C. Their greatest political accomplishment was the Mitanni Empire, with its center in the Middle Euphrates Valley, in the vicinity of Harran (biblical Haran). At its height, *ca.* the middle of the second millennium,

Mitanni dominated Assyria, apart from extending to Arrapkha and Nuzi in the E and Alalakh in the W. But the cultural role of the Hurrians outstripped by far their political authority, both in time and in space. They were sufficiently important at Mari, in the Hammurabi period, to have religious compositions in their own language included in the local archives. Hurrian texts of a few centuries later have been found at Boghazköy, as has already been indicated, and also in UGARIT, where the material comprises not only unilingual compositions but also a short Sumero-Hurrian vocabulary and a brief Akkado-Hurrian bilingual. The Amarna Letters, furthermore, contain numerous Hurrian technical terms and glosses, aside from the long Mitanni letter of Tushratta, which was composed in classical Hurrian.

Having borrowed extensively from Mesopotamian culture, back in the third millennium, the Hurrians were that much better equipped to serve as teachers to their Hittite neighbors in regard to writing, literature, law, religion, and art; small wonder that the Hittite vocabulary teems with Hurrian loan words. Although deeply indebted to Mesopotamia, the Hurrians have left ample evidence of their independent cultural achievements, notably in the fields of art, literature, and social practices.

2. In the Bible. Because of greater distance from their main centers, the Hurrians were much less influential in Palestine than in Syria and Anatolia. Nevertheless, their impact on the Israelites was far from negligible. This can be traced to two separate points of contact. One was in Central Mesopotamia: since the home of the patriarchs was in thc Haran region, which was also the center of Hurrian authority, the Hebrew forefathers were exposed there directly to Hurrian influence (*see* NUZI). The other was in Canaan: as an important component of the pre-Israelite population, the Hurrians were bound to leave some mark on the Israelite settlers.

One unexpected trace of the presence of Hurrians in Canaan is linguistic. In common with Phoenician and Aramaic, Hebrew changes its stops *b g d k p t,* when they are undoubled and postvocalic, to corresponding spirants (transliterated as *bh gh dh kh ph th* herein). Such a pattern is foreign to Semitic, but indigenous to Hurrian. Since spirantization occurs precisely where Semitic and Hurrian were in intimate contact, but is absent elsewhere, and since the process can now be synchronized with the period of maximum Hurrian expansion, it is apparent that the practice was copied by West Semitic from Hurrian.

The presence of Hurrians in Palestine proper is witnessed independently by cuneiform sources. In the Amarna Letters (fourteenth century B.C.) the ruler of Jerusalem, which was then a Jebusite center, bears a name meaning "Servant of Ḫepa." The first word is represented by a logogram (originally a picture sign), so that its actual form is still uncertain. The rest, however, stands for the Hurrian mother-goddess, thus testifying to the Hurrian background of the Jebusites. This conclusion is supported by the Jebusite name in II Sam. 24:16, where the consonantal text gives *'wrnh* (traditionally Araunah), which can now be explained as a form of Hurrian *ewri,* "lord." There is, further, the evidence of the cuneiform tablets from Tell Ta'annek (biblical Taanach), dating from the middle of the second millennium B.C., which contain a large proportion of Hurrian personal names. Moreover, a contemporary tablet from Shechem also lists names that may well be Hurrian. It is thus clear that in the patriarchal age Hurrians were settled in Central Palestine in considerable numbers.

The Bible does not fail to reflect these conditions. The pertinent references, however, are to be found under other ethnic headings. One such term, as has just been indicated, is "Jebusite." Another, more widely used, one is "Hivite." Gen. 34:2 connects Hamor the Hivite directly with Shechem. Gibeon, which was situated a short distance to the N of Jerusalem, was a Hivite center (Josh. 9:7; 11:19). And Hivite settlements are recorded for Mount Lebanon (Judg. 3:3) and Hermon (Josh. 11:3), districts otherwise known for their Hurrian connections. It follows, therefore, that the term "Hivites" somehow came to refer to Hurrians. This equation is confirmed by indirect textual evidence. In one instance the MT interchanges "Hivites" (Gen. 36:2) with "Horites" or "Hurrians" (36:20). The LXX substitutes χορραῖοι for the MT חוי in Gen. 36:2; Josh. 9:7, the Greek form still retaining the double "r" sound of *Ḫurri;* and conversely, the LXX Ευαῖοι at Isa. 17:9 points to an original MT חרי, "Horite," for the present חרש (see RSV text and mg.; *see* HORITES § 2). The term "Hivites," then, was apparently a local name for Hurrians—another such being "Jebusites"—which gradually replaced "Horites," perhaps in order to avoid confusion with the unrelated namesakes in Seir.

In the light of the foregoing evidence, we are now in a much better position to appreciate the Shechemite agitation against Abimelech, of which a vivid account is given in Judg. 9. Abimelech had usurped the throne at Shechem by first trading on his blood ties with the Shechemites through his mother's line. It was a dangerous argument, for eventually his opponents turned it against him by reminding the citizenry that their ruler was the son of the Israelite Jerubbaal; and in so doing, they harped on the fact that true Shechemites were descendants of Hamor (vs. 28). Now Hamor is identified in Gen. 36:2 as a "Hivite" (MT), which the LXX equates with "Horite." What is more, the main point of that chapter is that the Hamorites were uncircumcised, which in Canaan would be tantamount to non-Semitic. The bitterness of the war against Abimelech can scarcely be ascribed to political or clannish differences alone. The whole issue, however, gains immeasurably in sharpness and importance when it is viewed as a symptom of the deeper cleavage between the heterogeneous societies of Hurrians and Israelites. Thus the course of cultural co-operation between the two communities was not uniformly smooth or constructive.

In summary, there is more Hurrian matter in the Bible than is generally realized. Further research is bound to add to what is already known on the subject.

Bibliography. On the people and their culture: E. A. Speiser, "Ethnic Movements in the Near East in the Second Millennium B.C.," *AASOR,* XIII (1933), 13-54; A. Götze, *Hethiter, Churriter und Assyrer* (1936); I. J. Gelb, *Hurrians and Subarians*

(1944); E. A. Speiser, "Hurrians and Subarians," *JAOS,* LXVIII (1948), 1-13.

On the language: E. A. Speiser, "Introduction to Hurrian," *AASOR,* vol. XX (1941).

On Hurrians (Horites) in Palestine: E. Meyer, *Die Israeliten und deren Nachbarstämme* (1906), pp. 328-44; W. F. Albright, "A Teacher to a Man of Shechem About 1400 B.C.," *BASOR,* LXXXVI (1942), 28-31; "A Prince of Taanach in the Fifteenth Century B.C.," *BASOR,* XCIV (1944), 12-27; B. Landsberger, *Journal of Cuneiform Studies,* LVIII (1954), 59.

E. A. SPEISER

HURRICANE. The translation of סופה in Ps. 83:15—H 83:16 (elsewhere STORM; WHIRLWIND).

HUS hŭs. Douay Version form of Uz.

HUSBAND AND WIFE. *See* FAMILY; MARRIAGE.

HUSBANDRY. The tilling of the soil. This term, along with "husbandman," is used in the KJV but is not employed in the recent translations. אכר is translated in the RSV by such words as "plowman" (Isa. 61:5), "farmer" (II Chr. 26:10; Jer. 14:4; 31:24; 51:23; Amos 5:16), and "tiller of the soil" (Joel 1:11). Such phrases as איש האדמה (Gen. 9:20) and איש־עבד אדמה are now translated "tiller of the soil." In I Cor. 3:9, γεώργιον has become "field." In other NT passages the KJV "husbandman" has become "householder," since originally "husbandman" meant "master of the house." *See* AGRICULTURE.

H. N. RICHARDSON

HUSHAH hōōsh'ə [חושה, haste(?)]; HUSHATHITE —thīt. A village in Judah's hill country (I Chr. 4:4); the home of one of David's Mighty Men (II Sam. 23:27; cf. II Sam. 21:18; I Chr. 27:11). It is identified with Husan, SW of Bethlehem.

HUSHAI hōōsh'ī [חושי]. An Archite who served the exiled David as a spy in Jerusalem during the rebellion of Absalom. Deeply aggrieved, with coat rent and earth upon his head, Hushai would have joined the company of David at the Mount of Olives, whither they had fled from Jerusalem when its capitulation to Absalom appeared imminent (II Sam. 15:32). At the instance of the king, however, he returned to the capital and was received as a royal adviser by the unsuspecting Absalom (16:15-19). The plan of AHITHOPHEL to attack the forces of David without delay was successfully opposed by Hushai, who thus gave David time to escape beyond the Jordan (17:5 ff). The espionage of Hushai at the court of Absalom was supported by the priests Abiathar and Zadok, each of whose sons acted as couriers to David (vss. 15 ff). Absalom's discovery of this treasonable activity and the subsequent silence of the narrative concerning Hushai suggest an ominous end of the "friend of David." This title appears to be equivalent to the office of the "king's friend" (I Chr. 27:33; cf. II Sam. 15:32 LXX; 15:37; 16:16; I Kings 4:5), which Hushai held under David.

He is probably to be identified with the father of BAANA (2), one of the prefects of Solomon (I Kings 4:16).

E. R. DALGLISH

HUSHAM hōōsh'əm [חשם, חושם; LXX Ἀσόμ] (Gen. 36:34-35; I Chr. 1:45-46). A Temanite, third king in Edom "before any king reigned over the Israelites."

HUSHATHITE. *See* HUSHAH.

HUSHIM hōōsh'ĭm [חשים, חושים, חשם]. **1.** Son of Dan (Gen. 46:23). The name occurs in Num. 26:42 as Shuham, by an interchange of consonants.

2. Son of Aher, a Benjaminite (I Chr. 7:12; text uncertain).

3. A wife of Shaharaim, a Benjaminite, and the mother of Abitub and Elpaal (I Chr. 8:8, 11; text uncertain).

L. HICKS

HUSK. KJV translation of זג (Num. 6:4; RSV SKINS; צקלן (II Kings 4:42; RSV SACK); κεράτιον (Luke 15:16; RSV POD).

HUT. The translation of מלונה (from לין, לון, "to lodge, pass the night") in Isa. 24:20 (KJV COTTAGE). In the catastrophic outburst of terror which the author envisions, the earth itself "sways like a hut." The same Hebrew noun occurs elsewhere only in Isa. 1:8 (LODGE).

E. M. GOOD

HUZ. KJV form of Uz.

HUZZAB hŭz'əb. KJV translation of הצב (Nah. 2:7), an obscure word translated "its mistress" (i.e., the palace') by the RSV. Alternative suggestions include: (*a*) Nineveh, the Assyrian queen (thus Targ.), or a goddess (these take the word as a noun with cryptic denotation); (*b*) if it is a verb, a passive form of נצב, "be established" or possibly "be decreed" (the LXX apparently presupposes this root and translates "the foundation"; but this could hardly be the subject of the following verbs in vs. 7), or a passive of יצא, "be brought forth." All nouns proposed are guesses, while any verb would leave the sentence without a proper subject ("palace" in vs. 6 is masculine and so does not fit the feminine verbs in vs. 7).

J. M. WARD

HYDASPES hī dăs'pēz [Ὑδάσπης] (Jth. 1:6). A river in the Elymais. The Vulg. reads *Jadason,* the Syr. *Ulay* (cf. Dan. 8:2). This river cannot be identical with the Hydaspes (=Vitasta) in the Punjab. The Greek might be corrupt for the Χοάσπις, now the Kerhah, which flows into the delta at the mouth of the Euphrates and Tigris.

P. WINTER

HYENA [אי (KJV WILD BEAST OF THE ISLAND[S]), *cf.* Arab. *'ibn āwī,* jackal, fox; צבעים, *proper name* ZEBOIM, *lit.* hyenas (*singular* צבוע *or* צבע); *cf.* Arab. *ḍabu'*; Syr. *'aph'ā*]. Any of certain stockily built carnivorous mammals of the genus Hyaena, placed zoologically between the cats (Felidae) and the dogs (Canidae). Usually feeding on carrion, the hyena is regarded as cowardly and cruel. Its cry is a disagreeable, unearthly sound. Tristram described the striped hyena (*Hyaena striata*) as being, in the nineteenth century, the commonest of the beasts of prey in Palestine, next to the jackal (*NHB* 107-9). If this situation obtained in the biblical period, it is strange that the Bible does not contain more allusions to this animal. As matters stand, hyenas have furnished the place name Zeboim (cf. the proper name Zibeon in Gen. 36:2, etc.). Whether אִי, cited above, means "hyena" is uncertain; it is at least an animal occupying deserted human habitations.

W. S. McCullough

HYKSOS hĭk'sōs. A term applied originally by the priest-historian Manetho (*ca.* 280 B.C.) to the rulers of Egypt assigned to the Fifteenth and Sixteenth Dynasties, but extended by modern scholars to designate the ethnically composite group which dominated Egypt and most of the Syro-Palestinian area during MB II (*ca.* 1800-1550 B.C.).

It is generally agreed that Manetho's translation of the word "Hyksos" as "shepherd kings" is only partially correct, and that the word is simply a rendering of Egyptian *ḥqꜣw ḫꜣswt*, "rulers of foreign countries." The beginnings of Hyksos control in Egypt are obscure, owing to the paucity of written sources from the period, but it appears that their invasion of the Nile Valley from the NE took place during the period of anarchy and political dissolution which followed the powerful Twelfth Dynasty (*ca.* 1991-1792 B.C.), and that the first Hyksos dynasty—the Fifteenth, according to traditional Egyptian accounts—was established in the Delta with its capital at Avaris *ca.* 1730 B.C. It apparently supplanted the Fourteenth Dynasty, then centered at Khois in the Delta, and was concurrent with the latter half of the Thirteenth Dynasty at Thebes in Upper Egypt. It is probable that the ruling powers at Thebes were vassals to the Hyksos domination during the Fifteenth and Sixteenth Dynasties in the N, but there is no clear evidence that the Hyksos actually controlled the territory of Thebes and the country to the S.

Growing dissatisfaction with the foreign domination of the N led to positive action on the part of Kamose, the last Egyptian ruler of the Seventeenth Dynasty at Thebes. While details of his campaign against the Hyksos are lacking, one may assume that he succeeded in driving them from Middle Egypt and confined them to the Delta region. The expulsion of the Hyksos from Egypt was accomplished by Ahmose (*ca.* 1570-1545 B.C.), the first ruler of the Eighteenth Dynasty. His campaigns against the Hyksos resulted finally in the destruction of their capital at Avaris, after which the king pursued them to S Palestine and besieged them at Sharuhen (Tell el-Far'ah) for three years.

It is certain from both archaeological and philological evidence that the Hyksos were not an ethnic unity. Because the Hyksos in Egypt adopted the language of that country, the linguistic evidence for affiliations with other ethnic groups consists primarily of personal names. Among these, only Semitic has been identified with certainty, but other considerations make it more than probable that both Hurrian and Indo-European elements were also present. These conclusions appear all the more certain when the Hyksos migration is viewed in the light of the general ethnic movements during the first half of the second millennium B.C. in which Hurrian and Indo-European peoples gained domination over much of the Near East.

The archaeological remains of Hyksos sites in Palestine are characterized by large fortifications of beaten earth with a sloping revetment and a surrounding moat; examples occur at Tell Beit Mirsim, OT Jericho, and Hazor. Also associated with the invasion of the Hyksos are the use of horse-and-chariot in warfare, which the Egyptians were quick to adopt, a more common use of bronze and the concomitant superiority in weapons, and special skills in numerous crafts such as metallurgy and jewelry.

Bibliography. R. M. Engberg, *The Hyksos Reconsidered* (1939); A. Alt, *Die Herkunft der Hyksos in neuer Sicht* (*Berichte über die Verhandlungen der sächsischen Akademie der Wissenschaften zu Leipzig;* 1954).

T. O. Lambdin

HYMENAEUS hī'mə nē'əs [Ὑμέναιος, hymeneal, *or* pertaining to marriage]. Mentioned with Alexander in I Tim. 1:20 and with Philetus in II Tim. 2: 17 as a Christian (of Ephesus[?]; cf. I Tim. 1:3) who taught false doctrine.

In I Tim. 1:19, Hymenaeus is said to have rejected his conscience—probably in rejecting right beliefs—and to have "made shipwreck of [his] faith." "Paul" had therefore delivered him and Alexander to Satan (cf. I Cor. 5:5)—i.e., he had put them out of the church, making them *ipso facto* subject to the powers of evil. The hope was that as a result of excommunication Hymenaeus and Alexander would "learn not to blaspheme" (I Tim. 1:20) and not to misrepresent the truth. Here, as in the Corinthians passage, deliverance to Satan was intended to be ultimately beneficial.

In II Tim. 2:16, Timothy is told to avoid the (Gnostic?) "profane jargon" (Moffatt) used by men like Hymenaeus and Philetus, which was undermining the faith of some believers. Hymenaeus denied the resurrection of the body by affirming that "the resurrection [was] past already" (vs. 18). Just when and in what way Hymenaeus believed the resurrection had already happened in the lives of believers is not said; but the probability is that he taught that the resurrection took place at baptism. His view may have stemmed from a misunderstanding of Rom. 6:1-11; Col. 3:1 (cf. John 17:3) and was probably related to a similar notion referred to in the Church Fathers. E.g., Irenaeus tells of Menander, who taught that his disciples "obtain the resurrection by being baptized into him, and are no more able to die, but remain youthful and immortal" (Iren. Her. I.23.5; cf. also Tert. *On the Soul* 50; Just. Apol. I.26). Closely related is the view that the resurrection takes place when one becomes acquainted with the truth, the truth often believed to be communicated at baptism. E.g., Simon and Carpocrates denied the possibility of the resurrection of the body but held that the resurrection from the dead was simply an acquaintance with the truth which they taught (Iren. Her. II.31.2; cf. Tert. *On the Resurrection of the Flesh* XIX). A less likely possibility is that Hymenaeus taught that the resurrection takes place in one's children (cf. Acts of Paul 2:14; Ecclus. 30:4).

B. H. Throckmorton, Jr.

HYMNS. The earliest Christians received from Judaism the use of psalms and religious songs both in public, liturgical cult and in private, informal devotions. The production of psalms among the Jews did not abate with the editorial completion of the canonical Psalter, but continued uninterrupted. One may note the psalms contained in the Apoc., notably the SONG OF THE THREE YOUNG MEN and Prayer of Manasseh (*see* MANASSEH, PRAYER OF), the Pharisaic collection of eighteen PSALMS OF SOLOMON from the middle of the first century B.C., and the "Psalms of Thanksgiving" found in the MSS of the Qumran sect of Essenes (*see* DEAD SEA SCROLLS). In this same tradition of psalmody, inspired by the religious poetry of the OT, must be placed the cento of Rom. 3:13-18, the hymn of Rev. 15:3-4, and the messianic psalms of Palestinian Jewish Christianity preserved in the narratives of Luke 1–2: the Gloria in Excelsis; MAGNIFICAT; BENEDICTUS; and NUNC DIMITTIS.

The "hymn" sung by Jesus with the Twelve at the conclusion of the Last Supper (Mark 14:26; Matt. 26:30) was probably the Hallel, or Pss. 113–18, particularly associated with the celebration of the chief Jewish festivals. The church's adoption of the OT psalms in its own worship was inevitable, if only for the reason that Jesus used them, as did all devout Jews, in his own devotions, and that he viewed them as a prophecy of himself (cf. especially Mark 12:10-11, 35-37, and parallels; Luke 24:44). Indeed, there is greater evidence for the use of the Psalter by the church in the first two centuries as a prophetic book than as a liturgical hymnal. Of an estimated 287 quotations of the OT contained in the NT writings, 116 are from the Psalter.

References to song in the church's worship of NT times are abundant (Acts 2:47; I Cor. 14:15, 26; Eph. 5:19; Col. 3:16; Jas. 5:13), but they are so general in character that one cannot say that it was drawn exclusively from the canonical Psalter. The same is true of the hymns sung as personal devotions by Paul and Silas in the jail at Philippi (Acts 16:25). The evidence of Col. 3:16 (parallel in Eph. 5:19) suggests a variety of types of religious songs. Attempts of commentators to distinguish "psalms, hymns, and spiritual songs" as referring to OT psalms and Christian compositions of both a formal and a spontaneous nature are suggestive; but the classification cannot be rigidly applied. The NT does contain, however, a few fragments of early Christian hymnody, in addition to the psalms of Luke 1–2; and these give us some idea of its richness and variety. A baptismal hymn is probably cited in Eph. 5:14, a creedal or confessional type in I Tim. 3:16. Hymns of a doxology character are to be found in I Tim. 6:15-16, and notably in Rev. 4:8, 11; 5:9, 12-13; 7:10, 12; 11:15; 19:1-2, 6-8. The inspiration of these doxologies was most likely the similar acclamations of praise in use in the Greek-speaking synagogues of the Jewish Dispersion. Several other NT passages have been held by some critics to be based on hymns: the Prologue of John's Gospel; the Pauline christological summaries in Phil. 2:6-11; Col. 1:15-20, and the cento of OT texts in Rom. 9:33; I Pet. 2:6-7. Hymnal forms, such as these, were valuable for evangelistic and didactic purposes no less than for worship.

The production of Christian hymns accumulated during the second century, although only one collection has come down to us—the forty-two baptismal hymns of the Syrian church known as the Odes of Solomon, in the parallel verse form of the canonical Psalter. Especially favored were hymns in honor of Christ, in the style of the Greek metrical ode, such as the hymn "Bridle of Untamed Colts," appended to Clement of Alexandria's *Instructor*—a hymn still used in modern church hymnals (*see also* Euseb. Hist. V.28.4). The "hymn [*carmen*] to Christ as to a god," referred to by Pliny the Younger (*Letters* X.97), has been variously interpreted: as a hymn, antiphonal psalmody, litany, or ritual formula such as the baptismal promises and creed. The Gnostics and other heretical groups made much use of metrical hymns, finding them, no doubt, an effective medium for the propaganda of their peculiar theological views. Their success may be measured by the reaction in orthodox circles, about the turn of the third century, against the use in the liturgy of all nonbiblical psalms and hymns. It was not until the middle of the fourth century that Christian hymnody once more blossomed in the church's worship. However, in private devotion and informal gatherings, such as the AGAPE, Christians continued to find an outlet for singing "new songs."

Bibliography. J. B. Lightfoot, *St. Paul's Epistles to the Colossians and Philemon* (rev. ed., 1892), pp. 222-23. J. Kroll, *Die christliche Hymnodik bis zu Clemens von Alexandreia* (1921); "Die Hymnendichtung des frühen Christentums," *Die Antike*, II (1926), 258-81. E. G. Selwyn, *The First Epistle of St. Peter* (1949), pp. 273-77. J. Quasten, "Carmen," *Reallexikon für Antike und Christentum,* II (1954), 905-8.

M. H. SHEPHERD, JR.

HYPOCRISY, HYPOCRITE [ὑπόκρισις, ὑποκριτής]. Originally, in the context of Greek drama, the act of playing a part and the one who plays a part. The terms were also used metaphorically to signify the action of feigning to be what one is not. In English only the metaphorical meaning remained, with the prevailing signification of the simulation of goodness. This context of meaning which originated from the Greek drama has no place in OT thought and hence no comparable Hebrew terms. The RSV reflects this fact by eliminating the words "hypocrisy" and "hypocrite" from their translations of the OT, whereas the KJV used them.

1. OT meaning. The Hebrew root frequently translated "hyprocrisy" or "hypocrite" in earlier versions is חנף. The RSV regularly translates the Hebrew by the English "godless" (Job 8:13; 15:34; Isa. 33:14; etc.) where the KJV has "hypocrite." We can gain an understanding of the meaning of the Hebrew root חנף from those passages where a synonym is conjoined in familiar parallelism. Most common synonyms are מרע, "evildoer" (Isa. 9:17); חטאים, "sinners" (Isa. 33:14); רשעים, "wicked" (Job 20:5). In some passages light is shed on the meaning by the use of an antithetical Hebrew word placed in parallelism, such as צדיקים, "righteous," in Prov. 11:9.

The terms most frequently used by the LXX to translate the root חנף are ἄνομος and πονηρός (Isa. 9:17; "godless," "wicked"); ἀσεβής (Isa. 33:14; "godless," "impious"). The verb form of the Hebrew occurs numerous times meaning "pollute" or "corrupt" (Num. 35:33; Ps. 106:38; Isa. 24:5; Jer. 3:1). From this it can be seen that the Hebrew root חנף means radical opposition to God and the wickedness of the one so opposed. This stands in sharp contrast with

English "hypocrisy," meaning basically "pretense" and "simulation of goodness." In two passages of Theod.'s translation of Job (34:30; 36:13), later incorporated into the LXX, the Hebrew חנף is translated by Greek ὑποκριτής. This, in addition to similar occurrences in Aq. and Symm., seems to imply that Greek-speaking Jews had come to understand ὑπόκρισις in other than its normal Greek metaphorical meaning of "pretending to be what one is not."

2. In the NT. This background in the OT and Hebrew is very significant for interpreting the words ὑπόκρισις and ὑποκριτής in the NT, especially in the words of Jesus. The Greek meaning was as alien to Aramaic as to Hebrew. It is unlikely that Jesus in the many passages where he is reported to have attacked the Pharisees as "hypocrites" was attacking them for simulating goodness. This is substantiated by the several instances in the Synoptic gospels where in the same saying we have alternate readings. E.g., the reading "their hypocrisy" in Mark 12:15 becomes "their malice" (πονηρίαν) in Matt. 22:18 and "their craftiness" (πανουργίαν) in Luke 20:23. The words "the hypocrites" in Matt. 24:51 alternate with "the unfaithful" (ἀπίστων) in Luke 12:46. Jesus does not attack the Pharisees for insincerity in feigning goodness, though they knew they were evil. On the contrary, it is because they are so self-righteously convinced of their goodness that he castigates them. Their blindness sets them in opposition to God. They not only lock men out of the kingdom of God (Matt. 23:13) but also make them children of Gehenna (vs. 15). They are compared to unmarked graves, which by their uncleanness contaminate those who walk upon them (Luke 11:44). This is consistently the field of meaning in the many sayings where Jesus uses the terms "hypocrisy" and "hypocrite" according to the Greek NT.

In the few instances of the terms elsewhere in the NT we find the same meaning. It is the term used by Paul to describe the actions of the Christian Jews, including Peter and Barnabas, at Antioch (Gal. 2:14). The term "insincerely" does not do full justice to the phrase ἐν ὑποκρίσει. Paul is condemning their irresponsible breach of good faith in renouncing an original agreement, not their pretense (see also I Tim. 4:2; I Pet. 2:1). The only passage in the NT which clearly retains the original Greek meaning is the verb form used in Luke 20:20, where the scribes and high priests send spies who "pretended to be sincere" (ὑποκρινομένους). In view of the Gentile background of the author of Luke, this is not surprising. With this one exception the occurrences of "hypocrisy" and "hypocrite" in the NT must be understood against the background of the peculiar development of meaning in Jewish thought and the OT.

Bibliography. E. Hatch, *Essays in Biblical Greek* (1889), pp. 91-93. D. Matheson, " 'Actors' Christ's Word of Scorn," *ET*, XLI (April, 1930), 333-34. L. H. Marshall, *The Challenge of NT Ethics* (1947), pp. 60-62. F. W. Young

HYRCANUS hûr kā'nəs [Ὑρκανός, *perhaps from* Hyrcania, *to which many Jews had been transported*] (II Macc. 3:11); KJV HIRCANUS. A man who, for some reason or other, had a great deal of money deposited in the temple about the time of the visit of

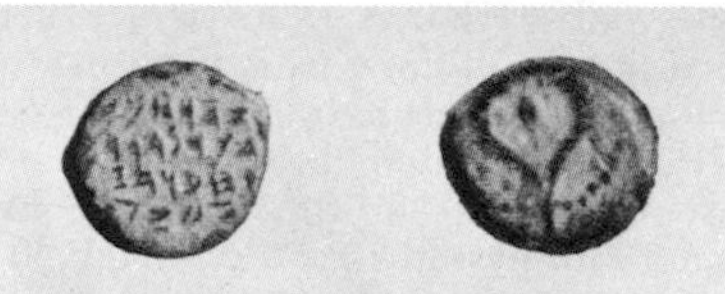

Courtesy of the Trustees of the British Museum

37. Coin of John Hyrcanus (135-104 B.C.)

the notorious Heliodorus. He was of high rank, and the son of Tobias (1). Fig. HYR 37.

For the more important John Hyrcanus and Hyrcanus II, *see* Hasmoneans §§ 3*b,f*, 4.

N. Turner

HYSSOP hĭs'əp [אזוב, *'ēzôbh;* ὕσσωπος]. A small, bushy plant, probably the *Origanum maru* L., the Syrian marjoram (called in Arabic *ṣa'tar*). For centuries arguments have raged over the identification of אזוב, largely because of the occurrence of ὕσσωπος in John 19:29. The eleven other occurrences of "hyssop" offer little difficulty of identification, though the meaning of the Greek is not fully established. It was clearly not the Southern European hyssop, *Hyssopus officinalis* L., characterized by its blue flowers, which is not native to the Holy Land.

The use of a "bunch of hyssop" as a brush for daubing the lintels of the Hebrew homes with blood from the sacrificed lamb at the first Passover (Exod. 12:22) seems to have established the tradition for most of the other references. The Levitical laws for the cleansing of Leprosy (Lev. 14:4, 6, 49, 51-52) and the rite of the Red Heifer (Num. 19:6, 18) involved the use of אזוב (no reference to a "bunch,"

38. Hyssop

however) along with "Cedar wood" and "Scarlet stuff." In the former laws the hyssop, together with the cedar wood and the scarlet stuff, is dipped in the blood of a sacrificed bird and sprinkled seven times on the person or the house to be cleansed of leprosy. In the latter law the cedar wood, the scarlet stuff, and the hyssop are burned with the sacrificial red heifer.

The writer of Kings says of Solomon: "He spoke of trees, from the cedar . . . to the hyssop that grows out of the wall" (I Kings 4:33—H 5:13). Here the expression means all flora, from the greatest of trees to the most humble shrub. In the familiar penitential psalm attributed to David, the king refers to the symbolic use of hyssop in the cleansing ceremony ("Purge me with hyssop"; Ps. 51:7—H 51:9).

Heb. 9:19 refers to Moses' reading of the Old Covenant at Sinai (Exod. 24:6-8) and sealing it by sprinkling blood and water over the book and the people with "scarlet wool and hyssop." The OT passage, however, makes no reference to hyssop in this case.

Hyssop was used to administer vinegar to Jesus on the cross, according to John 19:29, while Matt. 27:48; Mark 15:36 mention a REED. Since hyssop seems inconsistent with this scene, some scholars consider ὕσσωπος here to refer to the *Sorghum vulgare* L. as the "reed" used. Others emend ὑσσώπῳ περιθέντες to ὑσσῷ προπεριθέντες, reading: "They put . . . on a pike" (Amer. Trans.). Could it be that the variation from the Synoptics was intentional, and that John used ὕσσωπος with a symbolic meaning? Hyssop formed an integral part of OT redemptive theology. Another suggestion is that hyssop *and* the sponge were put on a reed (not mentioned), thus adding the cooling effect of the hyssop leaves, for which they are noted.

See also CLEAN; CRUCIFIXION; FLORA § A9*j*.

Fig. HYS 38.

Bibliography. I. Löw, *Die Flora der Juden*, II (1924), 72-73, 84-101; L. Baldensperger and G. M. Crowfoot, "Hyssop," *PEQ*, 63 (1931), 89-98; E. J. Goodspeed, *Problems of NT Translation* (1945), pp. 115-16; H. N. and A. L. Moldenke, *Plants of the Bible* (1952), pp. 160-62.

J. C. TREVER

I AM [אהיה] (Exod. 3:14). The formula which gives an opaque explanation of the meaning of the sacred name Yahweh (יהוה). In its full form, "I am that [or what] I am" or perhaps "I cause to be what is," it represents a wordplay on the root of the word "Yahweh," "to be, to come to pass." It has been suggested that the "I am" sayings of the Fourth Gospel (John 6:35; 14:6; etc.) echo the Exodus passage. *See* GOD, NAMES OF, § B3. B. W. ANDERSON

IBEX [דישון, *cf.* דוש, to tread; Akkad. *daššu,* buck of gazelle] (Deut. 14:5); KJV PYGARG. A species of WILD GOAT. The wild goat of the OT is generally thought to be the ibex, but the meaning of דישון is not known, although the antelope has been suggested. *See also* FAUNA § A2*f*iii. W. S. MCCULLOUGH

IBHAR ĭb'här [יבחר, he (El *or* Yahweh) chooses]. One of the sons of David who were born at Jerusalem. His mother is given the status of a wife, and not a concubine (II Sam. 5:15; I Chr. 3:6; 14:5).

IBIS ī'bĭs [ינשוף] (Lev. 11:17); KJV GREAT OWL. A wading bird (of the family Threskiornithidae) found on the margins of rivers and lakes. It was not in Palestine in the nineteenth century, although it may have been there in the biblical period. It is doubtful if ינשוף means "ibis"; the RSV follows the LXX and the Vulg. in this translation in Lev. 11:17 but uses "GREAT OWL" in Deut. 14:16.

The ibis was a well-known bird in ancient Egypt (*Threskiornis aethiopica aethiopica*), where it was sacred to the god Thot(h). Its association with Egyptian religion, and its consumption of mollusks, crustaceans, etc., would undoubtedly have made it unacceptable as food to the Hebrews. W. S. MCCULLOUGH

IBLEAM ĭb'lĭ əm [יבלעם]. A city in the territory of Issachar listed among the cities in Issachar and Asher which were given to Manasseh, and from which the Manassites were not able to drive out the Canaanites (Josh. 17:11-12; Judg. 1:27). Ibleam is mentioned in a list of cities conquered by Thut-mose III, who claims to have brought it, with many other Palestinian cities, under his control (during the fifteenth century B.C.). Ibleam probably was not conquered by the Israelites until the time of David.

It is reasonably certain that Ibleam was one of the LEVITICAL CITIES and that it is identical with BILEAM (I Chr. 6:70—H 6:55; some MSS of the LXX read "Ibleam" [Ιεβλααμ]). The LXX of Josh. 21:25 also lists Ibleam as one of the cities allotted to the Levites. Probably the Hebrew text of this verse does not mention Ibleam, because "Gath-rimmon," which is in Dan, not in Manasseh, was copied by mistake from the preceding verse.

Ahaziah king of Judah was wounded by Jehu's soldiers at Ibleam near the ascent of GUR (II Kings 9:27). Most modern English translations of II Kings 15:10 read "Ibleam" on the basis of one Greek MS which has Ιεβλααμ where the Hebrew reads "before the people" (קבל עם). If this is correct, Zechariah king of Israel was assassinated at Ibleam by Shallum.

Ibleam has been identified with modern Bel'ameh near Jenin. W. L. REED

IBNEIAH ĭb nē'yə [יבניה, Yahu builds up] (I Chr. 9:8). A Benjaminite who returned from exile in Babylon.

IBNIJAH ĭb nī'jə [יבניה, may Yahu build up (*i.e.,* grant posterity)]. A Benjaminite (I Chr. 9:8*b*); possibly the same as Ibneiah (9:8*a*).

Bibliography. M. Noth, *Die israelitischen Personennamen* (1928), p. 212; F. S. Brown, S. R. Driver, and C. A. Briggs, eds., *Hebrew-English Lexicon of the OT* (1955), p. 125.
B. T. DAHLBERG

IBRI ĭb'rī [עברי, a Hebrew, *but perhaps corrupted from* עבדי, servant] (I Chr. 24:27). A Merarite Levite, contemporary of David.

Bibliography. M. Noth, *Die israelitischen Personennamen* (1928), p. 252; cf. pp. 38, 137.

IBSAM ĭb'săm [יבשם, fragrance of balsam] (I Chr. 7:2); KJV JIBSAM jĭb'—. A man of the tribe of Issachar.

IBZAN ĭb'zăn [אבצן, swift; Arab. *'abūṣun,* swift (horse)] (Judg. 12:8-10). A so-called minor judge whose thirty sons and thirty daughters were married to persons outside his clan.

In the stories of the judges Ibzan appears next after Jephthah. The site of his seven-year career, and presumably the location of his tomb, is given simply as Bethlehem. Early commentators beginning with Josephus assumed this to be the famous Bethlehem of Judah. Therefore Ibzan was traditionally understood to be Boaz, husband of Ruth and ancestor of David. More likely the city was the site of modern Bet Laḥm, on the border of Zebulun and Asher, *ca.* ten miles N of Megiddo and seven miles W-NW of Nazareth. If, as seems likely, the various judges were understood as representing their respective tribes, since the next-mentioned judge, Elon, was a Zebulunite, Ibzan was probably regarded as the judge representing the tribe of Asher.

The mention of his large family, whose numbers are exceeded only by Gideon and Abdon, indicates his wealth. The reference to his children's extra-clan marriages indicates his wide influence and high esteem outside his own immediate circle.

The name Ibzan is mentioned nowhere else and

does not seem to be related to the place name Ebez (Josh. 19:20). As so few details of his career are given, some commentators consider Ibzan to be a late editor's unhistorical invention to fill chronological space between Jephthah and Samson (so also Elon and Abdon). Others consider that on these minor judges—including, before Jephthah, Tola and Jair—what is given is authentic information, based on official records, about persons who occupied the central office in Israelite society before the rise of the monarchy.

See also JUDGE; JUDGES, BOOK OF, § E1.

Bibliography. G. F. Moore, *Judges,* ICC (1895), pp. 310, 312; C. F. Burney, *Judges* (1930), pp. 289-90, 334; M. Noth, *Die israelitischen Personennamen* (1928), p. 226; *History of Israel* (1958), pp. 99-102. C. F. KRAFT

ICE. *See* SNOW; PALESTINE, CLIMATE OF.

ICHABOD ĭk'ə bŏd [אי־כבוד, where is the glory? *or* inglorious (ἀδοξία; Jos. Antiq. V.xi.4) *or* alas the glory (LXX Οὐαὶ Βαρχαβωδ)]. Son of Phinehas. He received his name from the great catastrophe which befell Israel at the time of his birth—the capture by the Philistines of the ark, which was Israel's "glory," the source of her worth and greatness. Stunned by news of this disaster and by the death of both her husband and her father-in-law (Eli), Ichabod's mother died after giving him birth (I Sam. 4:19-21).

For the relationship of Ichabod to Ahijah (I Sam. 14:3), *see* ELI. R. W. CORNEY

ICONIUM ī kō'nĭ əm ['Ικονιόν, 'Εικονιόν] (Acts 13–16; II Tim. 3:11). A city in S central Asia Minor visited by Paul and Barnabas on their first recorded missionary journey; now the Turkish provincial capital Konya.

It was considered the capital of Lycaonia during the Greek and Roman empires. Highways from Syria to Ephesus and Rome went through Iconium, and this made it a place of vast trade. With its beautiful plains, made productive by the streams from the Pisidian Mountains, it was a center of grain and fruits, known especially for its plum and apricot orchards and its fields of wheat and flax. An old proverb said, "See all the world; but see Konia [Iconium]," for it was considered one of the most beautiful and fertile sites in the world. Iconium became a large and wealthy city in later Roman and Byzantine times, a metropolis with its seat for the archbishop.

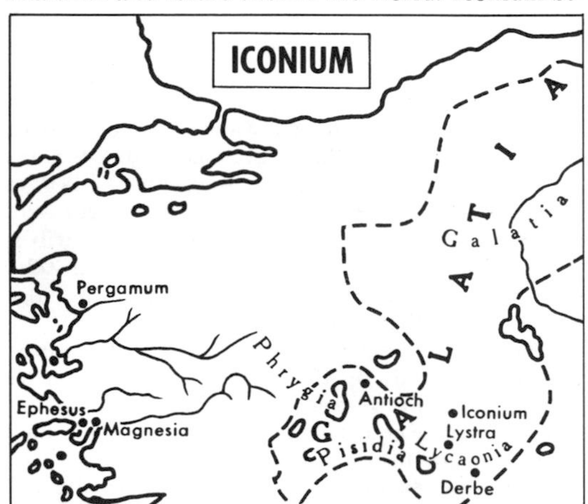

Xenophon in the fourth century B.C. (*Anabasis* I.2.19) is the first historian to mention Iconium, when he tells of Cyrus' travels to the E and his coming to "Iconium, the last city of Phrygia; thence he pursued his route through Lycaonia." Cicero (*ad Familiares* XV.55.2), Strabo (*Geography* XII.6.1), and Pliny (N.H. V.25) speak in their writings of Iconium as a city of Lycaonia. The inhabitants of Iconium regarded themselves as of Phrygian, rather than Lycaonian, extraction, since they used the Phrygian language. In A.D. 163 one at the trial of Justin Martyr referred to himself as a slave from Iconium in Phrygia; and Bishop Firmilian at the Council of Iconium (235) spoke of Iconium as in Phrygia. A legend is related to Stephanus regarding King Annakos of Iconium, after whose death the Deluge destroyed the entire population, who were called Phrygians.

In the third century B.C., Iconium was ruled and largely Hellenized by the Seleucid kings of Syria; but after the Battle of Magnesia in 187 B.C. it was placed under the rule of the king of Pergamum, though he never took possession of it; and by 165 B.C. it was governed by the Galatae. In 129 B.C., Iconium with Galatia came under the government of the Pontic kings. Mark Antony in 39 B.C. gave it to Polamon, but in 36 B.C. he placed it under Antymas, who at that time became king of Galatia. In 25 B.C., at the death of Antymas, Iconium became a part of the province Galatia, and was thus incorporated into the Roman Empire.

In NT times Iconium was considered, along with Antioch (Pisidia), Lystra, and Derbe, as belonging to the Roman province of Galatia. Paul and Barnabas on their first recorded missionary journey proceeded to Iconium after their first visit to Antioch in Pisidia, where they made many Gentile converts; at Iconium they preached to Jews and Gentiles in the synagogue, but left for Lystra and Derbe when both Gentiles and Jews threatened to stone them; the Jews from Iconium and Antioch pursued Paul to Lystra, where they stoned him and dragged him out of the city; in Iconium, as in other cities on his first recorded journey, Paul left elders in the church. Timothy was well spoken of in Iconium; a later reference is made to Paul's persecutions and sufferings at Iconium; the city was the principal setting for the Acts of Paul and Thecla. By the beginning of the Christian era Iconium was completely Hellenized. If the S Galatian theory is correct, then Paul's Letter to the Galatians would have been directed to Iconium, Lystra, Derbe, and Antioch (Pisidia); and I Peter would have been sent to these churches (I Pet. 1:2).

Claudius (41-54) gave Iconium the name Claudiconium, which showed its strong Roman sympathies; and under Hadrian (117-38) it was made a Roman colony. In 235 one of the early church councils was held there. In 295, Diocletian created the province Pisidia, with Iconium as one of its principal cities, Antioch being the capital; but in 372, Iconium became the principal city and capital of the new province Lycaonia. After 660 and the coming of Islam,

Iconium was victimized for three centuries by Arab raids, and it fell into the hands of the Arabs in 708, but was never taken by the caliphs. It was included in the Byzantine Empire until the eleventh century, with its prosperity culminating in 1097, when it was made the capital of the Seljuk Empire. After Frederick I (Frederick Barbarossa) captured Iconium in 1190, it remained permanently a Turkish city, with the Christians dwelling six miles to the N in Tsille. Today it is called Konya (also Konia, Koniah), and is the capital of the province Konya in S central Turkey.

See also GALATIA; GALATIANS, LETTER TO THE; PAUL AND THECLA, ACTS OF; PHRYGIA; LYCAONIA.

Bibliography. W. M. Ramsay, *The Cities of St. Paul* (1908), pp. 317-82; W. M. Calder and J. Keil, eds., *Anatolian Studies* (1939), pp. xxiv, xxviii-xxix, xxxiii, 60, 67, 69, 103, 225, 234, 238, 395; J. Finegan, *Light from the Ancient Past* (1946), pp. 260-64. T. S. KEPLER

IDALAH ĭd'ə lə [ידאלה] (Josh. 19:15). A town in Zebulun. It is generally identified with Khirbet el-Hawarah, a site just S of BETHLEHEM 2.

IDBASH ĭd'băsh [ידבש, honey-sweet] (I Chr. 4:3). A man of Judah; son of Etam.

IDDO ĭd'ō [אדו (6 *below*), *perhaps an abbreviated form of* אדון, LORD; ידו (2, 8 *below*), *possibly an abbreviated form of* ידעיה, Yahu has known; עדא (3 *below*), עדו (1, 4-5, *below*), עדוא (7 *below*), *probably abbreviated forms of* עדיה, Yahu has adorned]; KJV Apoc. ADDO ăd'ō (I Esd. 6:1); SADDEUS săd'ĭ əs (I Esd. 8:45); DADDEUS dăd'— (I Esd. 8:46); EDES ē'dēz (I Esd. 9:35). **1.** A Levite of the clan of Gershom (I Chr. 6:21—H 6:6), who evidently is called Adaiah (עדיה) in vs. 41—H vs. 16.

2. The son of a certain Zechariah, and the man appointed by David as chief over the Manassites in Gilead (I Chr. 27:21).

3. The father of Abinadab, an administrative officer of Solomon in Mahanaim (I Kings 4:14).

4. A seer and prophet cited as an authority for the reigns of Solomon (II Chr. 9:29), Rehoboam (12:15), and Abijah (13:22). In 9:29, *Kethibh* is יעדי, and *Qere* is יעדו.

5. The grandfather of the prophet Zechariah (Zech. 1:1, 7). In vs. 7, as well as in Ezra 5:1; 6:14 (cf. I Esd. 6:1), his name is spelled עדוא. He is possibly the same as 7 *below*.

6. The head of a group of temple servants from Casiphia who provided cultic servants to accompany Ezra in his return to Jerusalem (Ezra 8:17; I Esd. 8:45-46).

7. The head of a family of priests that returned to Jerusalem after the Exile (Neh. 12:4, 16). He is possibly the same as 5 *above*.

8. One of those compelled by Ezra to give up their foreign wives (I Esd. 9:35). He is called Jaddai in Ezra 10:43. M. NEWMAN

IDLENESS [עצלות, *from* העצל, be slow, sluggish; ἀτάκτως]. The neglect of proper duties; depending upon the generosity and toil of others. A theme of Hebrew wisdom was that indolence led to poverty and want (Prov. 19:15; Eccl. 10:18; Tob. 4:13). A good wife (Prov. 31:27) "does not eat the bread of idleness"; she will not sit down inactive, eating the bread of those who work. She is always well occupied, supervising all that goes on in her household. She earns her bread (Prov. 31:27; cf. II Thess. 3:8, 10).

Paul reproved the idlers at Thessalonica for walking disorderly (ἀτάκτως, "out of ranks") and not in accordance with the tradition handed down by him (II Thess. 3:6, 8). They were truant from responsibilities, busybodies, meddling in the affairs of the brotherhood, and throwing the burden of their maintenance on hard-working and charitable brethren. Such were no longer to be sustained by the community (vs. 10).

In the Papyri ἀτάκτως means "to play truant from work"—i.e., "absenteeism" (P. Oxy. 275, 725). Among the Thessalonians this condition appears to have been something of long standing and not due simply to the expected Parousia.

Bibliography. J. E. Frame, *Thessalonians,* ICC (1912), pp. 297-310; W. Neil, *The Epistle of Paul to the Thessalonians* (1950), p. 124. V. H. KOOY

IDOL. A transliteration of the Greek εἴδωλον, "image."

Specifically the term denotes the image of a god when such is the object of worship, but any material symbol of the supernatural which is the object of worship may be so termed. The latter usage, like the application of the term "idol" to the unworthy object, concrete or abstract, of obsession, is secondary from a linguistic point of view.

In the English version of the OT "idol" is the general translation for a variety of words. Some of these—e.g., סמל (II Chr. 33:7, 15); ציר (Isa. 48:5); גלול (Lev. 26:30; Deut. 29:17; I Kings 15:12; 21:26; II Kings 17:12; 21:11, 21; 23:24; Ezek. 6:4-6, 9; 8:10; 14:3-7; 16:36; 18:6, 12, etc.); פסל (Exod. 20:4; Deut. 4:16, 23, 25; 5:8; II Kings 21:7; Isa. 40:19-20; 42:17; 44:9; 48:5; Nah. 1:14; Hab. 2:18); צלם (Num. 33:52; II Kings 11:18; II Chr. 23:17; Ezek. 7:20; 16:17); and עצבים (I Sam. 31:9; II Sam. 5:21; Pss. 106:36, 38; 115:4; Isa. 10:11; Hos. 4:17; 8:6; Zech. 13:2)—actually mean graven images. Other images, probably anthropomorphic, with which the Hebrews were familiar were תרפים.

These words apparently designated images of household gods in the patriarchal period (Gen. 31:19, 34-35). Unlike the other words cited, this word does not by its etymology, which is uncertain, suggest idols or graven images; and teraphim were not, like these words, images of alien deities. An etymological connection with Assyrian *tarpu,* "specter," is possible, in which case teraphim may signify images of dead ancestors or ancient kin-gods; this explanation would be in accord with the store which Laban set on his teraphim which were stolen by Rachel (Gen. 31:19 ff). There is, however, no evidence of the actual worship of these, and in historical times in Israel they were used in divination (Ezek. 21:26; Zech. 10:2). Nevertheless, they are associated with graven or molten images (Judg. 18:14, 17) and with images in the round (II Kings 23:24).

In addition to words signifying actual images sculptured or cast in the round, there are a number of circumlocutions which express Hebrew abomination or contempt for alien gods, and may or may not refer to plastic images of these. Such words are אימה, "an object of terror" (Jer. 50:38); מפלצת, "a cause of trembling" (I Kings 15:13; II Chr. 15:16); שקוץ, "abomination" (II Chr. 15:8); און, "vanity" (Isa. 66: 3); and אליל, *ælîl,* "a nonentity" (Lev. 19:4; 26:1; I Chr. 16:26; Pss. 96:5; 97:7; Isa. 2:8, 18, 20; 10:10-11; 19:13; 31:7; Hab. 2:18; Zech. 11:17). The last word, cognate with an Arabic root meaning "to annihilate," is very commonly used in the OT and is a wordplay on אל, *'ēl,* or אלהים, the generic name for "god." There is a similar wordplay between עצב, "shape," and עצב, "grief," in Isa. 48:5. In certain cases these circumlocutions denote alien gods, which were represented by images; in other cases—e.g., Lev. 19:4; 26:1; I Kings 15:13; II Chr. 15:16; Isa. 2:20; 31:7; 48:5; Jer. 50:38—the context indicates that actual images are denoted.

Aside from the bulls which were a conspicuous feature of the cult sponsored by Jeroboam I at Bethel and Dan (*see* IDOLATRY), the Israelites would seem to have been familiar with idols of the Canaanite deities Baal, Ashera, and Astarte at least from the time of Solomon, whose liberal proclivities permitted the worship of gods of neighboring peoples by his foreign harem in Jerusalem. The Baal temple built by Ahab at Samaria (I Kings 16:32) doubtless contained an image of the god either sculptured in the round or in relief like the god Resheph and the goddesses Anat and Astarte from the Late Bronze Age sanctuaries at Beth-shan, but this is a matter of conjecture. The nature of the "horrible thing," or "object of trembling," set up to the mother-goddess Ashera by Maacah, the mother of Asa, in Jerusalem (I Kings 15:13) is likewise uncertain, and may or may not have been an anthropomorphic image or, as has been suggested, a phallic emblem. From the account of the reformation of Josiah (II Kings 23) it is apparent that many symbols of Canaanite worship and other pagan cults, like sun worship, had been in use in Jerusalem, and that even in the exilic period the miserable remnants of the Jerusalem community could resort to the use at least of drawings or reliefs of gods and cult animals, if not to actual idols in the ruins of the temple (Ezek. 8:10).

This familiarity on the part of the Hebrews with material representations of local deities is the more intelligible when we consider the limited area of the settled land in Palestine occupied by the Hebrews in OT times and the proximity of Phoenicians, Syrians, and Philistines, to say nothing of the local Canaanites, who did not scruple to use idols. Baal, or Hadad,* the Canaanite god of winter storms and rain, is known from sculpture from Ras Shamra* and from statuettes from the same site and from Megiddo and Lachish in Palestine in the Late Bronze Age as a warrior-god striding forth in a short kilt and brandishing a mace and a thunderbolt as a spear.* His helmet is adorned with the horns of his cult animal, the bull. The Canaanite goddess Anat, the sister of Baal, is known as a warrior-goddess from a Ras Shamra relief, and Astarte is represented regularly in Egyptian reliefs from the Late Bronze Age as a naked female, usually standing upon a lion. From various Palestinian sites of the Late Bronze Age and

Courtesy of James B. Pritchard

1. Storm-god, perhaps Adad, on the back of a bull; from Arslan Tash

Early Iron Age come clay-molded figurines of a naked female with pudenda and breasts emphasized. The coiffure of certain of these suggests that of the Egyptian cow-goddess Hathor, with whom Astarte was often identified, but it is doubtful if these "Astarte plaques," as they are called, were properly objects of worship. Though derived from representations of this fertility-goddess, they may simply have served as amulets to prompt on the principle of imitative magic fertility in communities where progeny was almost an obsession. These figurines have a long history throughout the Near East from the Neolithic period, where highly stylized forms of the female figure appear. Figs. HAD 2; IDO 1; UGA 7, 10-11; UGA 6.

In Palestine and even from Ras Shamra no life-sized idol survives, though the story of the mishap of Dagon at Ashdod (I Sam. 5:1-4) indicates that such anthropomorphic images, either life-sized or colossal, must have been known.

In the period of the Hebrew settlement the story of Micah in the Danite migration (Judg. 17–18) indicates that graven and molten images and other concrete objects such as the ephod were used, presumably in the cult of Yahweh (*see* IDOLATRY § 3). After the seventh century, however, the worship of Yahweh was divested of all suggestion of images. Thereafter, any use of idols in Israel was introduced *ab extra,* as in the struggling Jerusalem community in the exilic period (Ezek. 8) and notably in the Seleucid period, when the pagan nature cults were revived in the provinces, and Hellenistic cults, such as that of

Olympian Zeus, complete with anthropomorphic image, were set up in the temple in Jerusalem (Dan. 11:31). Such attempts, however, in the interests of political and cultural uniformity, were resolutely opposed by the hard core of Judaism.

In the early Christian community practices connected with idols again became a problem, though in the NT the references to idols (e.g., Acts 7:41; 15:20, 29; 21:25; Rom. 2:22; I Cor. 8:1, 7, 10; 10:28; II Cor. 6:16; I Thess. 1:9; I John 5:21; Rev. 2:14, 20; 9:20) are generally not specifically to images but to the worship of alien gods in which the idol in the Greco-Roman age might signify much or little (*see* IDOLATRY § 4). In Christian as in Hebrew writings, "idol" or "mere image" is a convenient form of abuse for pagan worship. In I Cor. 8:4; 10:19; 12:2, however, Paul seems to refer to the actual image as having no more than its material significance.

In Rom. 2:22, referring to the Jew's abhorrence of "idols" in the context of the Decalogue, and in the famous definition of the duties of Gentile converts in the eyes of the primitive Hebrew Christian community in Acts 15:20, the term "idols" probably signifies the worship of actual images, though in the last passage (Acts 15:29), in view of the reference to communion feasts in the temples of pagan gods (cf. I Cor. 8:1 ff; Rev. 2:14, 20; *see* IDOLATRY), it is not clear that "pollutions of idols" means the use of images rather than communion feasts, ritual prostitution—ostensibly as a rite of imitative magic—and other practices associated with the worship of alien gods.

Bibliography. R. Dussaud, *Les découvertes de Ras Shamra (Ugarit) et l'AT* (1941); J. B. Pritchard, *Palestinian Figurines in Relation to Certain Goddesses Known Through Literature* (1944); A. G. Barrois, *Manuel d'archéologie biblique* (1953), pp. 389-98.

J. GRAY

IDOLATRY [εἰδωλολατρία]. Idol-worship; worship of images. Taken literally in the OT, idolatry may signify the worship of alien gods, generally represented by concrete images or idols (*see* IDOL), or the use of such symbols in the worship of Yahweh. In the NT, where the worship of alien gods is not denoted, the term is used figuratively of undue obsession with any object less than God.

1. Idolatry in alien cults
2. Relation of Israel to alien cults
3. Concrete symbols in Yahwism
4. Idolatry in the NT

Bibliography

1. Idolatry in alien cults. The various gods of Mesopotamia, Canaan, and Egypt were represented in sculpture in the round or in relief as anthropomorphic figures. In Egypt, however, though the chief gods were depicted in human form, most of the numerous deities were depicted also with the chief physical characteristics of animals—e.g., Horus with the head of a falcon,* Anubis with the head of a jackal,* Hathor with the horns of a cow. This theriomorphism is probably the survival of a primitive local totemism, such as is regularly found in primitive societies of Central Africa, with which ancient Egyptian culture had certain fundamental affinities. In Syria and Palestine also documents and sculpture from the latter part of the second millennium and from the first millennium B.C. indicate the association of certain deities with certain animals. Thus in the Ras Shamra Texts the senior god El is termed "the bull" and is represented probably on the sculpture of an unnamed deity with bull's horns. Baal is also depicted as an active warrior in a helmet garnished with the bull's horns. The bull features in the case of El and Baal probably symbolize their procreative powers. Resheph, the god of plague and mass destruction, is represented in Egyptian sculpture from the fourteenth and thirteenth centuries with a helmet and gazelle horns, suggesting probably the desert as the source of untoward influences, such as sirocco winds, locusts, and possibly marauding nomads. The Canaanite fertility-goddess Astarte (biblical ASHTAROTH)* was associated with the lion and in a late Egyptian sculpture from the Ptolemaic period bears the head of a lion. These, however, may be simply cases of the use of images as concrete imagery, a grosser case of the anthropomorphic and vivid figurative language in which even the Hebrews found it necessary to speak of Yahweh. No doubt, such concrete symbols of the gods tended in popular thought to supplant the attributes they symbolized, and it was certainly no part of Hebrew or Christian polemic against such cults to represent them otherwise than in their abuse. Nevertheless, the Canaanite texts from Ras Shamra show evidences, though slight, of a more enlightened theology, and the animals in question, as Jeroboam's bulls at Bethel and Dan, and as similar animals in N Syria and Anatolia, may have been, not images of the Canaanite deities, but rather pedestals or symbols of their presence, as the ark was the symbol of the presence of Yahweh (Num. 10:35-36). Well known as an object of Canaanite worship is Asherah, now known explicitly from the Ras Shamra Texts as the mother-goddess and con-

In the Brooklyn Museum Collection

2. A hawk, wearing a crown, represents the god Horus.

sort of El. Often Asherah appears to be misunderstood in the versions of the OT—e.g., II Kings 23:4, 6 (LXX τῷ ἄλσει, "to the grove"; cf. ERV "to the Asherah"). The narrative of Gideon's destruction of the fertility shrine of Ophrah (Judg. 6:25 ff) indicates that the Asherah was by the altar of Baal, and the fact that Gideon burnt his offering to Yahweh with the Asherah which he had cut down indicates that it was of wood. The Hebrew text mentions literally עצי האשרה, "the trees of the Asherah," and this is probably the source of the belief that the Asherah was a grove. We are not bound, however, to render the Hebrew word עצי so literally, and it may signify simply "wood." A single object seems to be denoted—either a natural tree or a wooden pole as a stylized tree—the term "Asherah" either signifying its "erect" position or being the name of the Canaanite mother-goddess whom it symbolized as the repository of fruitfulness. The association of the mother-goddess with a tree, moreover, may have been suggested by primitive Semitic animism, where, as among Arab peasants to the present day, certain, mostly conspicuous, trees, thickets, wells, and rocks are thought to be the abode of *welis* (*genii loci*), many of whom may be the survivors of ancient Baalim (*see* BAAL). Figs. IDO 2; JAC 5; ASH 91.

2. Relation of Israel to alien cults. At various crises in the history of Israel there was a tendency to adopt the local Canaanite cults either in principle or in detail. This tendency is condemned generally by the protagonists of Israelite monotheism as "idolatry" or rather "idols," a term which visualizes either actual images or the forces acknowledged and worshiped—whether with or without images is not always certain (*see* IDOL). In considering the condemnation of idolatry in Israel we must bear in mind the varying degrees to which Israel assimilated the culture of Canaan.

In settling to the new life of the agriculturist in Palestine, the Hebrew nomads naturally adopted various rites, particularly associated with imitative magic, appropriate to seasons of transition, such as the beginning and end of harvest, and the New Year festival. The last, which was associated with the Feast of Tabernacles, was the chief seasonal festival in the peasant's year, and from Zech. 14:16 it is apparent that the kingship of God was a prominent theme of that festival. Psalms and passages in the Prophets on this theme reveal a striking affinity in imagery and subject matter with the Ras Shamra myth of the kingship of BAAL. Here the Hebrews seized upon the Canaanite expression of faith in Providence in nature and adapted it to their own peculiar ethos as the expression of their faith in Providence in history and the moral order. The popular tendency, however, was to remain satisfied, as the Canaanites had been, with the rites designed to secure the material benefits of nature, and this is the substance of Hosea's censure of his contemporaries. This preoccupation with the material fruits of creation rather than with the nature and will of the Creator himself is idolatry in the general sense (cf. Rom. 1:25).

Apart from this Canaanite fertility cult thinly disguised under the name of Yahweh, there were periodic efforts of a more deliberate nature to establish it in more detail. The Deuteronomic version of the Hebrew settlement in Judges regards the progress and recession of the settlement as related to fidelity to the ancestral faith and their apostasy to the cult of Canaanite Baal and Ashtaroth. The degree of accuracy in this sweeping condemnation is impossible to determine, and it may amount to no more than the adoption of seasonal rituals without undue emphasis on the characters of the Canaanite gods. In the cults of Dan and Bethel sponsored by Jeroboam I the bull symbols indicate Baal, the celebration of whose kingship was—to judge from the Ras Shamra Texts—the high light of the nature cult of Canaan. Here Jeroboam seems simply to have adapted the cult of Baal to that of Yahweh in the New Year festival, in which the stability of God's order and that of his community were affirmed in the celebration of God as King (I Kings 12:32). Under Ahab, however, the king's affiance with the Phoenician princess Jezebel stimulated a more deliberate reaction to the Canaanite fertility cult. Ahab established the cult of Baal of Sidon at Samaria (I Kings 16:32) in a temple, which was the scene of Jehu's bloody extermination of the house of Omri (II Kings 10). In Judah the liberal policy of Solomon had encouraged the cults of his foreign wives, and in the reign of his grandson Asa we read of an "abominable image" (מפלצת) having been set up by the queen mother, Maacah, to Asherah (I Kings 15:13). From the accounts of the reforms of Hezekiah (II Kings 18:4) and Josiah (II Kings 23) it is apparent that Canaanite idolatry in its crude form, as well as the cult of Chemosh—"Milcom"—from beyond Jordan, astral worship, and the worship of the sun with the horse as its cult animal, had pervaded Jerusalem and the temple itself. These reforms, of course, had also the purpose of a political demonstration, prompted by the signs of the decay of Assyria, which had so long dominated Palestine. With the death of Josiah and the relapse of Judah into political insignificance in face of the rising power of Babylon, there was a recrudescence of the grosser forms of idolatry in the temple itself, including theriomorphic images or figures drawn in the temple (Ezek. 8:10), the worship of the vegetation-god Tammuz (Ezek. 8:14) and of the sun (Ezek. 8:16). In the disillusionment of postexilic times Isa. 65:2-7 indicates the tendency to resort to heathenish practices and even obscene rites, where the flesh of unclean animals like swine (Isa. 65:4) and mice (Isa. 66:17) was eaten and dogs were sacrificed (Isa. 66:3). This, however, was in the poor Jewish community of Palestine; in the Jewish communities in Mesopotamia, which were the real representatives of the traditions of the race, the imposing cults of Babylonia were regarded with supreme contempt, and local idolatry was reduced to absurdity (Isa. 40:18-26; 44:9-20; 46:1-2). The Seleucid suzerains of Palestine in the second century B.C. revived the worship of local fertility-gods in the provinces, in the Hauran, Transjordan, and the Philistine coast, and endeavored to establish the worship of Hellenistic deities in Judah and in the temple itself with "the abomination that makes desolate" (Dan. 11:31), the statue of Olympian Zeus. Such cults, however, like the cult of Augustus established by Herod the Great at Samaria, were imposed *ab extra* and resolutely resisted by the Jews.

The extent to which the Hebrews in the pre-Mosaic period may have shared in the grosser forms of religion current in the Near East is a matter of conjecture. The practice of totemism among the ancestors of the Hebrews must remain an interesting hypothesis suggested by the designation of certain tribes, families, and individuals, and distinction which the historical Hebrews drew between clean and unclean animals, and the taboo on the flesh of certain animals. The crude animal cult to which Ezekiel alludes (8:10), though possibly a survival of primitive totemism, far from being a revival of native Hebrew totemism after almost a millennium, is more likely to have been an alien importation like the cults of Tammuz and the sun mentioned in the same context. The various places hallowed in patriarchal tradition by theophanies, such as the terebinths of Mamre and Shechem,* the wells of Beer-sheba and Beer-lahai-roi, and the stone of Bethel, suggest that primitive animism was an element in the faith of the early Hebrews, though to classify this as idolatry depends on the worshiper's conception of the power present at such places. On the evidence of theophoric names of Amorite contemporaries of the earlier patriarchs living in similar conditions, we have little doubt that the Pentateuch, in spite of a tendency to theological anachronism, in presenting the relation between God and the patriarchs as a social one is fundamentally true to fact. Fig. TER 51.

3. Concrete symbols in Yahwism. In the patriarchal tradition, in spite of its idyllic cast, there is a certain amount of evidence of unorthodox liberality in religion. Josh. 24:2 alludes to the worship of other gods than Yahweh in Mesopotamia in patriarchal times, though Gen. 12:1 ff in the account of the migration from Mesopotamia makes no mention of alien worship, and it may well be that Josh. 24:2 is visualizing the worship by various Hebrew septs of several kin-gods to whom they stood in a social relationship.

The worship of any other god than Yahweh and the use of any image in his worship are forbidden in the Decalogue (Exod. 20:3-4); and in the apodictic laws, which Alt regards as the oldest specifically Israelite elements in the Book of the Covenant (Exod. 20:22–23:33), images of gold and silver are expressly forbidden (Exod. 20:23). In this latter enactment, which according to Alt would antedate the Decalogue by some three or four centuries, it is to be noted that the Hebrew text does not forbid the representation of Yahweh, but only the use of images of other gods besides him. Thus it is possible that some concrete representation of Yahweh, or at least a symbol of his presence, was used until the time of the formulation of the Decalogue in the E body of Pentateuchal tradition, which is generally dated in the eighth century B.C. An argument for this view is that the idiom "to placate God" means literally "to sweeten the face of God," and in certain passages the MT which is rendered "to appear before God" is an obvious modification of an original phrase meaning "to see the face of God" (e.g., Exod. 23:15; 34:23; Deut. 16:16; I Sam. 1:22; Ps. 42:3). The former expression may refer to the anointing of some concrete object, such as the standing stone which Jacob anointed at Bethel (Gen. 28:18-19). The representation of a god by a rough stone block was known in the case of the local Nabatean god Dusares, and the term "the Rock" applied to Yahweh may refer to such a concrete representation. A concrete object of worship was visualized in Judg. 8:24 ff, which describes how Gideon used the gold ornaments from the spoils of the Midianites to make an "ephod" which he set up as a cult object in his native Ophrah. The actual nature of the ephod in early Israel is not certain, but it was apparently a garment (I Sam. 2:18; II Sam. 6:14) either worn or carried by a priest (I Sam. 14:3) and used in divination (I Sam. 23:6 ff; 30:7 ff). In the time of Saul the ephod had its place in the sanctuary of Nob, and behind it was kept Goliath's sword, a trophy of the wars of Yahweh (I Sam. 21:9). This passage and the narrative of Gideon suggest a free-standing object, but neither excludes the possibility that the ephod might be of cloth or sheet metal, worn by the priest or hung over some symbol of the presence of Yahweh and so, through the sacred lots, the medium of the revelation of his will (cf. Exod. 28:6 ff). In Hos. 3:4 the ephod is visualized as a vital element in the cult of Yahweh. Here its association with a pillar or standing stone may indicate that the latter represented Yahweh, or at least marked the place where he was to be found, and the ephod may have been draped over it. In the story of Micah in the Danite migration an ephod is associated with a graven and molten image (Judg. 17:4-5; 18:14), though there is no suggestion that the object of worship was other than Yahweh. It is noteworthy that Hosea mentions ephod, teraphim, and standing stone without condemnation as necessary cult objects in the cult of Yahweh.

The last two passages do nothing to clarify the nature of teraphim, though from Ezek. 21:21; Zech. 10:2 it is apparent that they were used in divination. Their use is condemned in I Sam. 15:23. There teraphim might be taken as parallel to "divination" (קסם) in the preceding colon, but it might also be taken in apposition to "vanity" (און), the preceding word. Since this term generally signifies idols or idolatry, teraphim might also have this significance here. The same difficulty applies to the mention of teraphim in the account of Josiah's reformation in II Kings 23:24, where the term is associated with various illegitimate means of divination in what precedes, but with images in the round with what follows. In I Sam. 19:13, 16, where teraphim (RSV "image") were used to counterfeit David in bed, it is generally held that an anthropomorphic image, a household god, was denoted, but Albright seems nearer the truth in regarding teraphim here as a bundle of rags, in support of which view a root *trp*, "to wear out, languish," may now be cited from the Ras Shamra Texts. From Gen. 31:19 ff, however, we see that teraphim were portable images, and are actually called the "gods" of Laban (Gen. 31:30). No doubt these were the familiar domestic deities represented by clay figurines often found in boxes beneath the corner of the floor of ancient Mesopotamian dwelling houses. Whatever their actual nature and significance in early Israel, they were apparently considered quite legitimate in certain quarters until the time of Hosea, though the passage in I Sam. 15:23 indicates that at an earlier time the use of teraphim was not above suspicion. By the time of Josiah the teraphim were definitely abused and as such uncompromisingly condemned.

A theriomorphic cult object, the precise nature of which and its actual use in the cult of Yahweh are very obscure, was the brazen serpent, Nehushtan. The serpent is associated in sculpture from Egypt and Canaan in the Late Bronze Age (1600-1200 B.C.) with the goddess Astarte, and serpents in clay and metals were found in the excavation of Gezer. The serpent, renewing its skin every year, was the fitting symbol of the goddess of fertility, but it is unlikely that Nehushtan had such significance in Jerusalem. Hebrew tradition in Num. 21:8-9; II Kings 18:4 regards it as a prophylactic amulet associated with Moses in the desert period. The fact that it seems to have been used in the Wadi Arabah in the vicinity of the ancient copper mines suggests that it was some symbol in the worship of the native smiths, or Kenites, who were allies of the Hebrews and also worshipers of Yahweh. However this may be, the brazen serpent at Jerusalem had outlived its practical purpose and so was abolished by Hezekiah.

4. Idolatry in the NT. In the NT, idolatry, meaning the worship of gods other than the one living and true God, and the use of images, is characteristic of the life of the heathen. The difficulties of the early Christian communities in a pagan world are particularized in the practical problem of Christians' eating meat which had been part of an animal sacrificed to a heathen god or "idol" (I Cor. 8; 10:14 ff; Rev. 2:14, 20). This seems to refer to the eating of such meat in a communal meal in fellowship with heathen rather than to the buying of meat for private consumption in the open market. For the more sophisticated among the heathen in the Greco-Roman world this communion meal, primarily a means of reintegrating the community and its god, had a merely social significance, and certain enlightened Christians felt themselves free to partake of such meals without prejudice. In the mind of certain less enlightened Christians, however, the religious association of such meals prevailed, and for their sakes the practice was condemned by Paul, who nevertheless implies that the fact that the idols or gods of the heathen have no real existence means that the meat of their sacrifices is not really harmful.

Higher thought in the Greco-Roman world had really outgrown idolatry and the old cults of Greece and Rome. This attitude is symbolized for Paul by the altar at Athens "to an unknown god" (Acts 17:23). Mystery religions, however, where the individual or community sought to appropriate the experiences of dying and rising nature deities such as Osiris or Triptolemus, were very popular, and the emperor cult was already by the time of Paul accepted, at least in the Eastern Mediterranean. Indeed, Herod the Great had already established the cult of Augustus at Samaria, and Caligula proposed to set up the cult with his image in the temple at Jerusalem—an episode to which Mark 13:14, citing Dan. 11:31, may refer.

In general "idolatry" is used figuratively in the NT, especially in the Pauline letters, and signifies obsession with created things instead of devotion to the Creator (e.g., Eph. 5:5; Phil. 3:19, where gluttony and covetousness are said to be "idolatry").

Bibliography. W. R. Smith, *The OT in the Jewish Church* (1892), pp. 165-213, 221-28, 240-44; S. I. Curtiss, *Primitive Semitic Religion Today* (1902); W. R. Smith, *The Religion of the Semites* (1927); S. A. Cook, *The Religion of Ancient Palestine in the Light of Archaeology* (1930); W. Schmidt, *The Origin and Growth of Religion* (English Trans. H. J. Rose; 1931), pp. 62, 72, 75, 267; W. C. Graham and H. G. May, *Culture and Conscience* (1936); H. Frankfort, *Kingship and the Gods* (1948); S. Mowinckel, *Han som Kommer* (1951), pp. 24-43; A. G. Barrois, *Manuel d'archéologie biblique*, II (1953), 82, 324-459; M. Noth, *Die Welt des AT* (1957), pp. 221-36. J. GRAY

IDUEL. Alternate name of ARIEL.

IDUMEA ĭd'yo͞o mē'ə [Ἰδουμαία, Ἰδουμέα, (land) of the Edomites]. A term used in the LXX and Josephus for Edom, the region SE of the Dead Sea. After the Exile, it refers to the region S of Judea occupied by Edomite refugees from the growing pressure of the Nabateans, an Arab tribe which took over the ancient Edomite homeland.

Idumean authority eventually extended as far N as Beth-zur, fifteen miles S of Jerusalem. In the Herodian dynasty, the Idumeans provided the native ruling house in Palestine for nearly a century and a half. Throughout the Seleucid, Hasmonean, and Herodian periods, Idumea changed hands frequently. In 164 B.C., Judas Maccabeus fortified Beth-zur against an independent Idumea (I Macc. 4:61) and ravaged its territory (5:3, 65). In 125, John Hyrcanus annexed it to the Hasmonean state. In 63 Pompey detached it from Judea, but in 37 Herod the Great, an Idumean, reannexed it to Judea. During the next century this exchange continued until it finally became a permanent part of the province of Syria under the rule of the procurator of Judea after the First Revolt.

See also EDOM; SEIR.

Bibliography. A. Robert, "Idumée," *Dictionnaire de la Bible, Supplément*, vol. 4, cols. 195-99. V. R. GOLD

IEZER ī ē'zər; IEZERITES —zə rīts. Contraction of ABIEZER.

IGAL ī'găl [יִגְאָל, may (God) redeem; KJV IGEAL ī'gĭ əl in I Chr. 3:22. **1.** The spy from Issachar among the twelve spies sent out by Moses to search out Canaan (Num. 13:7).

2. One of David's Mighty Men (II Sam. 23:36). Cf. I Chr. 11:38, where apparently this name is replaced by Joel (יואל).

3. A descendant of King David through King Jehoiachin (I Chr. 3:22).

Bibliography. M. Noth, *Die israelitischen Personennamen* (1928), pp. 28, 200. B. T. DAHLBERG

IGDALIAH ĭg'də lī'ə [יגדליהו, Yahu is great] (Jer. 35:4). An obscure Judean prophet whose grandsons had a chamber in the temple under Josiah.

IGEAL. KJV alternate form of IGAL.

IGNATIUS, EPISTLES OF ĭg nā'shəs. Seven letters by a bishop (reputedly the second) of Antioch in Syria, written in two successive stages of a journey through Asia Minor while he was being conducted to Rome as a prisoner condemned to fight and die in the wild-beast shows. From Smyrna were sent the letters to the churches of Ephesus, Magnesia, Tralles, and Rome; from Troas, the ones to the churches of Philadelphia and Smyrna, and a personal letter to Polycarp, bishop of Smyrna. The original collection and preservation of these letters was due to the initiative of Polycarp. *See* POLYCARP, EPISTLE OF.

In the fourth century these letters were expanded by an Arian interpolator, and later ages witnessed further expansion of the corpus by the addition of a number of spurious letters. There also exists in Syriac an abridged recension of three of the letters. Legendary Acts of Ignatius' martyrdom, composed in the fifth and sixth centuries, are historically worthless, but important witnesses for the text of the letter to the Roman church. The researches of Theodor Zahn (1873) and J. B. Lightfoot (1885) in sifting the genuine from the spurious in the textual tradition of Ignatius have won universal acceptance; and students should beware of using texts or translations of Ignatius published prior to the work of these two scholars.

We know nothing certain about Ignatius except what is revealed in these letters. His name is a Latin form which has suggested to some a servile origin. We do not know how or when he became a Christian or a bishop. He apparently left the church in Syria in turmoil; but whether this was cause or effect of his arrest, we cannot tell. To Eusebius alone (Hist. III.36) we are indebted for the information that he suffered under Trajan (A.D. 98-117). Internal criticism of the letters tends to confirm this dating, particularly in view of Ignatius' knowledge and use of NT writings. A few critics argue for a later date. Unfortunately, the date of Polycarp's letter, our earliest witness to Ignatius, depends upon the date of Ignatius' martyrdom itself. Irenaeus (V.28.4) quotes Rom. 4:1 as by "a certain one of us," which suggests that Ignatius was long dead. Origen (*Homily VI on Luke*) cites Ign. Eph. 19:1 and describes Ignatius as "second bishop of Antioch after Peter."

The immediate appeal of Ignatius' letters is their revelation of a sensitive, intense mystic, both proud of and humbled by his sufferings for Christ's sake. He communicates vividly the physical horror and the spiritual exaltation of his martyrdom. His letter to the Romans is an urgent plea that they do nothing to hinder his becoming an "imitator of the suffering of my God." He earnestly longs to "reach the presence of God," by being "ground by the teeth of the wild beasts, so that I may be found pure bread of Christ." Ignatius claimed the gifts of prophetic utterance (Ign. Phila. 7:1) and visions of heavenly things (Ign. Trall. 5). But it is an exaggeration of certain modern critics when they describe him as a man of abnormal psychology and neurotic temper.

In all his letters to the Asian churches Ignatius was a strenuous advocate of the authority of the hierarchy of bishops, presbyters, and deacons, and of the need for unity in the churches under these ministers. His writings are the earliest unmistakable witness to the governance of the churches by these threefold orders of ministry, and in particular by the monarchical episcopate (*see* MINISTRY, CHRISTIAN). He would allow no meetings of any kind in the churches without the knowledge and authorization of the bishop. Yet he shows no hint of any doctrine of apostolic succession in the ministry. His advocacy of episcopal rights stemmed apparently from practical, rather than theoretical, considerations. By reason of his liturgical and pastoral oversight the bishop was responsible for preserving his flock from the dangers then threatening the integrity of the apostolic faith and teaching.

This theological crisis had two roots. On the one hand, the Asian churches were being subjected to powerful Judaizing tendencies, both speculative and cultic (Ign. Magn. 8-10; Ign. Phila. 6-9; cf. similar warnings in Rev. 2:9; 3:9). On the other hand, these churches were infiltrated with teachers of the Docetic heresy that denied the historic reality of the Lord's birth, life, death, and resurrection in the flesh, and affirmed that his human nature was only a semblance (Ign. Eph. 7-9; Ign. Magn. 11; Ign. Trall. 9-11; Ign. Smyr. 1-7; Ign. Polyc. 3). The teaching was the same as that condemned in I John 4:2-3. Against this denial of the "flesh and blood" of Christ, whether in Incarnation or in sacrament, Ignatius was passionately aroused to express his dread, anger, and contempt. He took the outrage of Docetic heresy personally—to say that Christ's sufferings were only a semblance was equivalent to affirming that his own martyrdom for Christ in the body of flesh was unreal (Ign. Trall. 10; Ign. Smyr. 4).

Ignatius is the first Christian writer to use the term "Catholic Church" (Ign. Smyr. 8:2); and he takes "catholic" to mean "orthodox." His doctrine of the Godhead and of the person of Christ is remarkably agreeable to the dogmatic definitions of later times. His ringing assertions of the reality of the Incarnation are frequently phrased in ways that suggest dependence upon creedal formulas. He affirms the Davidic descent of Jesus, his virgin birth, his baptism by John, his crucifixion under Pilate and Herod, and his bodily resurrection. He is familiar with a theological speculation concerning the star that appeared at Jesus' birth (more developed than what is suggested by Matt. 2:2; cf. Ign. Eph. 19). He accepts the doctrine of the descent into Hades, to raise the prophets of old from the dead (Ign. Magn. 9:2). He shows little interest in the Second Coming.

The OT is not often reflected in Ignatius' letters. He seems to have preferred the authority of a living tradition of faith to subtle exegesis of texts (see the much-discussed passage about the "archives" and the "gospel" in Ign. Phila. 8:2). His gospel traditions are closest to Matthew, and he probably cites Matt. 3:15 textually in Ign. Smyr. 1:1. Critics differ respecting his knowledge of John. There are strong affinities of thought and outlook between Ignatius and the Fourth Evangelist, and some striking parallels of phrase—Christ as the "door" (Ign. Phila. 9:1), "living water" and "bread of God" (Ign. Rom. 7:2-3), and the Spirit who "knows whence he comes and whither he goes" (Ign. Phila. 7:1). In Ign. Smyr. 3:2, Ignatius cites an apocryphon of the risen Lord, which Origen knew in the Preaching of Peter, Jerome in the Gospel According to the Hebrews. Ignatius was well acquainted with the letters of Paul, especially Ephesians; and he recalls associations of Paul with the church in Ephesus (Ign. Eph. 12:2), and of Peter and Paul with the church in Rome (Ign. Rom. 4:3). Dependence of Ignatius upon other

NT writings cannot be demonstrated, though there are occasional verbal parallels with Acts and Hebrews.

Ignatius' style is popular, replete with vivid metaphor and quotable maxims, generally lucid, and free of all bombast. It is not cultivated, but there are traces of Hellenistic vocabulary and rhetoric. It is intensely personal, and Ignatius has the gift of communicating in words the passion with which he held his convictions.

Bibliography. The fundamental work is J. B. Lightfoot, *The Apostolic Fathers,* pt. II: *S. Ignatius, S. Polycarp* (3 vols.; 2nd ed., 1889). See also the texts, translations, and commentaries listed in the bibliography under APOSTOLIC FATHERS, to which should be added: J. H. Srawley, *The Epistles of St. Ignatius* (1935); T. Camelot, *Ignace d'Antioche, Lettres* (Sources Chrétiennes, 10; 1951).

Important monographs: H. Schlier, *Religionsgeschichtliche Untersuchungen zu den Ignatiusbriefen* (1929); J. Moffatt, "Ignatius of Antioch—A Study in Personal Religion," *JR,* X (1930), 169-86; F. A. Schilling, *The Mysticism of Ignatius of Antioch* (1932); C. C. Richardson, *The Christianity of Ignatius of Antioch* (1935); J. Moffatt, "An Approach to Ignatius," *HTR,* XXIX (1936), 1-38; C. Maurer, *Ignatius von Antiochien und das Johannesevangelium* (1949); R. Bultmann, "Ignatius und Paulus," in J. N. Sevenster and W. C. van Unnik, eds., *Studia Paulina* (1953), pp. 37-51; E. Molland, "The Heretics Combatted by Ignatius of Antioch," *The Journal of Ecclesiastical History,* V (1954), 1-6.

See also bibliographies under BISHOP; MINISTRY, CHRISTIAN.

M. H. SHEPHERD, JR.

IGNORANCE [שגגה, שגיאה (RSV *generally* ERROR; SIN), unwitting sin; ἄγνοια, ἀγνωσία, ἀγνόημα]; IGNORANT [ἀγνοέω, uninformed; ἰδιῶται, uneducated]. In the OT, unwitting or inadvertent sin, which, although less serious than conscious transgression, involves guilt and requires atonement.

שגגה is a somewhat technical name for this kind of sin, and is found, outside Eccl. 5:6—H 5:5; 10:5, only in legislative passages (Lev. 4:2, 22, 27; 5:5-18; 22:14; Num. 15:24-29; 35:11, 15; Josh. 20:3, 9). This sin is plainly contrasted with deliberate and flagrant offenses, those committed "with a high hand" (Num. 15:30; cf. Ps. 19:13—H 19:14), for which there is no cultic atonement. Similar words are משוגה (Job 19:4) and משגה (Gen. 43:12), meaning "error."

The Hebrew roots שגג and שגה convey the basic idea of "erring" or "going astray," often with the expressed or implied causation of ignorance. This may be a physical straying (Deut. 27:18; Ezek. 34:6), drunken staggering (Isa. 28:7), emotional infatuation (Prov. 5:19-20), or intellectual and moral error (Gen. 43:12; Job 12:16; Prov. 19:27). In the priestly legislation and in Ezek. 45:20 it is brought into a ritual context where it is dealt with as a sin before God.

It is apparent that for the Hebrew even a sin of ignorance was taken seriously as incurring guilt, not only upon the sinner himself, but often upon the whole community. The fact that he was not aware of his wrongdoing (the element of ignorance is clearly stated in Lev. 4:13-14, 22-23, 27-28; 5:2-4; 22:14; Num. 15:24) does not excuse him. Guilt automatically attaches itself to the deed. That this conception is a remnant from an earlier, dynamistic mentality seems likely in cases where the unwitting sin violates ritual or taboo (e.g., Lev. 4:3; 5:14-16; 22:14; cf. I Sam. 14:24 LXX). However, this sin could occur "in any of the things which the LORD has commanded not to be done" (Lev. 4:2, etc.), so that the consciousness of guilt attaching to it ought to be viewed, at least in its later expressions, as arising from a deep and truly spiritual insight into the pervasiveness of sin. When a sin of inadvertence came to light, restitution was required (Lev. 22:14), and prescribed sacrifices were carried out in order that it might be forgiven (cf. Num. 15:22-29, elaborated in Lev. 4; 5:14-16). *See* SACRIFICE AND OFFERINGS.

That a sin committed in ignorance was considered less serious than a deliberate sin, despite its culpability, appears very clearly in the provision of cities of refuge for those guilty of manslaughter (Deut. 19: 4-10; Josh. 20:2-6, 9). The fact that a death had been caused without deliberate intent removed it from liability to blood-vengeance. *See* CITY OF REFUGE.

Other passages where these words indicate sins of ignorance are Job 6:24; 19:4; Ps. 19:12—H 19:13; Eccl. 5:6—H 5:5. Otherwise the Bible furnishes many instances of unknowing sins (e.g., Gen. 20:9; Num. 22:34; Deut. 22:8). The Greek ἀγνοέω, ἄγνοια, occasionally employed in the LXX to translate forms of these roots, appear in this meaning in II Macc. 11: 31; Heb. 5:2. It is, of course, considered a serious transgression to lead others into these sins (Prov. 28:10; Isa. 28:7).

By extension of meaning these words come simply to stand for all sin viewed as culpable error, with or without the element of inadvertency. OT passages with this meaning are I Sam. 26:21; Ps. 119:10, 21, 67, 118; Prov. 5:23; 20:1; Eccl. 10:5. The same usage appears in Tob. 3:3; Jth. 5:20; Ecclus. 23:2-3; I Macc. 13:39; Heb. 9:7 (cf. also Ecclus. 51:19). *See* SIN; FOLLY; WISDOM.

More Hellenistically, the NT generally speaks of ignorance as the want of KNOWLEDGE. As such it may be exclusively an intellectual matter, or it may incline to the OT notion of culpable ignorance in a religious sense.

In the purely intellectual sense, the concept of "ignorance" appears in various shades of meaning. It indicates lack of personal acquaintance (II Cor. 6:9; Gal. 1:22; cf. Wisd. Sol. 19:14), the absence of awareness or orientation (Acts 17:23; Rom. 2:4; II Cor. 2:11; cf. Wisd. Sol. 7:12; III Macc. 5:27), the lack of comprehension (Mark 9:32; Luke 9:45; Rom. 6:3; 7:1; I Pet. 2:15; II Pet. 2:12), or a refusal to acknowledge (I Cor. 14:38; cf. vs. 37). A common Pauline formula is: "I would not have you ignorant" (KJV)—i.e., "Be aware, comprehend" (Rom. 1:13; 11:25; I Cor. 10:1; 12:1; II Cor. 1:8; I Thess. 4:13).

Intellectual ignorance can, however, lead to sin; in fact, ignorance of God and of the gospel is identical with spiritual estrangement and apostasy. Thus the Jews' ignorance in crucifying Jesus (Acts 3:17) and Paul's ignorance in persecuting the Christians (I Tim. 1:13) approach both in culpability and in forgivability the OT sin of שגגה. Equally serious is the failure of the Jews to acknowledge Christ (Acts 13:27) and to understand the true "righteousness" of God (Rom. 10:3), and the failure of the Gentiles to know the true God (Acts 17:30; I Cor. 15:34; Eph.

4:18; I Pet. 1:14; cf. Wisd. Sol. 13:1; 14:18, 22; 15:11; II Macc. 4:40), particularly when they ignore the light of natural knowledge (cf. Rom. 1:21; II Pet. 3:5).

S. J. DE VRIES

IIM ī'ĭm [עיים, heaps, ruins]. **1.** One (Josh. 15:29) of a list of cities "in the extreme South," which were allotted to the tribe of Judah.

Bibliography. F. M. Cross, Jr., and G. E. Wright, "The Boundary and Province Lists of the Kingdom of Judah," *JBL,* LXXV (1956), 202-26.

2. KJV form of IYIM (Num. 33:45). *See* IYE-ABARIM.

E. D. GROHMAN

IJE-ABARIM. KJV form of IYE-ABARIM.

IJON ī'jŏn [עיון]. An important Israelite town in the extreme N of Palestine. It is probably located in Merj 'Ayyun, between the watershed of the Litani River and Mount Hermon, but the exact site is unknown. The generally proposed identification of Ijon with Tell ed-Dibbin is doubtful, because surface explorations have failed to yield evidence of occupation in Iron II (*ca.* 900-600), required by the biblical narrative.

Ijon was among the Israelite towns captured by Ben-hadad of Damascus during the reign of Baasha (I Kings 15:20; II Chr. 16:4). Tiglath-pileser III of Assyria also took the town and deported its inhabitants in the time of Pekah (*ca.* 733 B.C.).

Bibliography. A. Jirku, "Neue Forschungen in Syrien und Palästina," *ZDMG,* N.F. 11 (1933), 188.

G. W. VAN BEEK

IKHNATON. *See* AKH-EN-ATON.

IKKESH ĭk'ĭsh [עקש]. A Tekoite whose son Ira was a member of the company of David's heroes known as the "Thirty" (II Sam. 23:26; I Chr. 11:28) and the officer in charge of the Davidic militia for the sixth month (I Chr. 27:9).

ILAI ī'lī [עילי] (I Chr. 11:29). An Ahohite who was a member of the Mighty Men of David known as the "Thirty." In II Sam. 23:28 he is called ZALMON.

ILIADUN ĭ lī'ə dən ['Ειλιαδούν (B), Ιλιαδουν (A), Ελιαδουν (Luc.)] (I Esd. 5:58); KJV ELIADUN. Ancestor of some of the Levites who rebuilt the temple. The name is omitted in the parallel Ezra 3:9, unless it is to be identified with Henadad.

C. T. FRITSCH

ILLEGITIMATE CHILD [νόθος]. *See* BASTARD.

ILLYRICUM ĭ lĭr'ə kəm [τὸ 'Ιλλυρικόν] (Rom. 15:19). A Roman province on the E coast of the Adriatic Sea.

The limits of this area were variable (Suetonius *Tiberius* 16; Appian *Illyrian Wars* 1) and often indeterminate, but in general it may be said to have been bounded by Pannonia on the N, Moesia on the E, Epirus on the S, and the Adriatic on the W. The inhabitants were the Illyrians (οἱ 'Ιλλυριοί), and the land was often called Illyris (ἡ 'Ιλλυρίς) or Illyria (ἡ 'Ιλλυρία). Strabo (VII.317) describes the Illyrian seaboard as very well supplied with harbors both on the coast and on the neighboring islands, and says that the coastal lands were sunny and fertile but the inland regions mountainous and cold. He also speaks of the wildness and the piratical habits of the people.

The Greeks came in contact with the Illyrians when Chersikrates of Corinth settled on the island of Corcyra and expelled the Liburnians, members of an Illyrian tribe (Strabo VII.315), this being narrated by Strabo (VI.269) in connection with the founding of SYRACUSE by Archias in the eighth century B.C. In succeeding centuries Greek colonies were established in Illyria, notably at Salona near Spalato. The kings of MACEDONIA warred repeatedly against the Illyrians, and in 359/358 B.C., Philip II defeated their king Bardylis in a severely contested battle (Diodorus XVI.4). When the Gauls invaded Greece (279 B.C.), they sent one of their armies against the Illyrians and the Macedonians (Pausanias X.19.7). Illyrian acts of aggression against the Greek colonies and of piracy against both Greek and Roman shipping reached a climax under Queen Teuta and led to war with Rome in 229 B.C. As he narrates these events, Polybius (II.12) remarks that "the Illyrians were then not the enemies of this people or that, but the common enemies of all." Although Teuta surrendered large parts of Illyria to the Romans, the conflict with Rome continued intermittently for a long time. In 168 B.C. a Roman army under the praetor L. Anicius overcame the Illyrian people, and in the settlement of the following year Illyricum was divided into three parts (Livy XLV.26.15; 43.4). Regular Roman government was still not established in the region, but in 59 B.C., Caesar was granted the governorship of Illyricum for a period of five years (Dio XXXVIII.8.5). In 35-33 B.C., Octavian campaigned in Illyria and, as Appian (*Illyrian Wars* 28) narrates, subdued the whole country, not only parts which had revolted from the Romans but also parts which had never been under their rule before. *Ca.* 11 B.C., after Tiberius had put down a rebellion of the Dalmatians (*see* DALMATIA), the region was placed under Augustus as an imperial province (Dio LIV.34.4). Yet again in A.D. 6 there was a great revolt of the Dalmatians as well as the Pannonians, but this too was suppressed by Tiberius after three years of fighting (Dio LV.29-34). Only then could it be said that Illyricum was fully integrated as a province in the Roman Empire.

It is uncertain whether Paul means in Rom. 15:19 that he had actually preached in Illyricum, or simply names this province as marking the W limit of the Eastern world, in the strategic centers of which he had planted the gospel (*see bibliography*). Christianity is known in Illyricum from the third century, Salona being an important center.

Bibliography. Vulić, "Illyricum," *Pauly-Wissowa,* IX, i (1914), cols. 1085-88; Fluss, "Illyrioi," *Pauly-Wissowa,* Suplement V (1931), cols. 311-45; H. Lietzmann, *Handbuch zum NT* 8, *An die Römer* (4th ed., 1933), p. 121; J. Knox, Exegesis of Romans, *IB,* IX (1954), 645-46.

J. FINEGAN

IMAGE. *See* GRAVEN IMAGE; MOLTEN IMAGE; IDOL.

IMAGE, IMAGERY. A graphic description, or pictorial representation of reality and truth, as opposed to abstract thought. The Oriental had a love for the concrete and the practical. He expressed his ideas pictorially, and he had a special gift for story and the ability to make his figures come alive with a few, well-chosen phrases. Contemplation was in terms of life situation. There was no metaphysical search for absolute goodness, beauty, truth. The Hebrew was too practical for that. There was search for truth in the present experience, for the good under existing circumstances. Greed was portrayed by a picture of a greedy man; love, by an example of loving; fear, by an experience of terror. Here the distinction between the historical and the imaginative, between fact and figure, is not clear-cut. This makes the problem of ascertaining the actual historical facts of the Bible extremely difficult. It also accounts for the incessant use of proverb, story, and parable in teaching.

For the ancient Hebrew, the secular and the sacred were one. He was dominated by the idea of God, and accepted the world as an expression of the divine personality. God was ever near at hand. The phenomena of nature, the movements of men and of nations, the fortunes and woes of life, were related to his direct action and control (cf. Isa. 45:5-7; Amos 3:6*b*). Hence the abundance of anthropomorphisms. When the Israelite expressed his faith, it was in terms of experience; when he spoke of God, it was in terms of his mighty acts.

The imagery of the Bible is expressive of the life of the Hebrews, who lived between the desert and the sea, dependent upon the land for existence, threatened by politically ambitious neighbors to the N and to the S. The hopes and fears of the people, together with the waverings of faith and apostasy, in all periods of their history—nomadic, agricultural, dynastic, exilic, colonial—are expressed in the imagery of the day.

The imagery of the OT is rich and expressive in its variety, and taken from the most common and elemental experiences of life—e.g., speaking and hearing, walking, birth, marriage, adultery, judging, are given deep religious and ethical import. God is described as father (Isa. 1:2; 50:1), husband (Jer. 2:2; Hos. 2:16), teacher (Isa. 28:26), healer (Jer. 30:17), shepherd (Ps. 23:1; Jer. 31:10), judge (Isa. 2:4), king (Isa. 33:22), warrior (Jer. 20:11), winnower (Jer. 15:7), husbandman (Isa. 5:2-7), smelter (Isa. 1:25), builder (Jer. 31:4), harvester (Jer. 8:13), giver of rain (Jer. 5:24), leader of the blind (Isa. 42:16), stranger and wayfarer (Jer. 14:8), etc. Israel is depicted as one diseased (Isa. 1:5-6), a faithless wife (Jer. 3:20), a wild vine (Jer. 2:21), a wild ass (Jer. 2:24), well-fed stallions (Jer. 5:8), cows of Bashan (Amos 4:1), as well as God's servant (Jer. 30:10), his beloved (Jer. 11:15), bride (Jer. 2:2), vineyard (Isa. 5:1-7), heritage (Jer. 12:7-9).

The NT is equally rich in imagery. Jesus speaks of the kingdom of God in terms of a man sowing seed (Matt. 13:24-30), treasure hid in a field (vs. 44), a net cast into the sea (vss. 47-50). He finds religious truth in a shepherd's seeking a lost sheep (Luke 15:4-7), children at play (7:31-35), men at prayer (18:9-14), a woman preparing dough (Matt. 13:33). Light, water, wind, bread, wine, salt, a lamp, a vine, a road, all became expressive of religious truth.

Again, salvation is portrayed in figures drawn from the law court, the slave market, the market place, the mystery cults, the temple service, and the family sphere. Again, this is to say nothing of the elaborate and rich imagery depicted in the cosmology and eschatology of the Bible.

What the biblical writer accomplished by imagery was to relate faith to the life situation and experience of man. To the modern interpreter this peculiarity presents the problem of distance and antiquity. He lives in a new day, with a new culture and new thought-forms. The problem of interpretation and reinterpretation, the presenting of the gospel in terms of contemporary imagery, is the ever-current need. This is one of the most important tasks of the biblical scholar if he is to help make the faith relevant for his day. *See* ANTHROPOMORPHISM; SYMBOL.

Bibliography. D. B. Macdonald, *The Hebrew Literary Genius* (1933); J. Muilenburg, "The Ethics of the Prophet," *Moral Principles of Action* (ed. R. N. Anshen; 1952), pp. 527-42; S. Terrien, "The Anthropology of God," *Union Seminary Quarterly Review*, vol. XIII, no. 1 (1957), pp. 13-17.

V. H. KOOY

IMAGE OF GOD. In elucidating the meaning of "image of God" in the OT, it is necessary to discount the theological speculation of which it has been the subject throughout the Christian centuries. We must also look at the expression in isolation from the "sea change" which it underwent when it was taken up into NT thought. Only in this way can we do justice to both the OT and the NT conception.

The P narrative in Genesis tells that man was made in the image of God. The primary reference is to concrete resemblance, but we must credit the writer with some intention to convey an abstract idea —viz., that of human personality in its relation to God. The OT never suggests that the image of God was lost by the Fall.

In the NT the image of God is something which (in all but two cases) does not belong to man. It is identified with Christ, image now being the perfect reflection of the prototype. Through his relation to Christ the believer is transformed into the same image. This is both an eschatological hope and (in some measure) a present reality.

1. In the OT. ***a. The evidence.*** The primary OT evidence is limited in scope. The passages to be considered are: Gen. 1:26-27; 5:1-3; 9:1-7 (all in the P source and clearly written with reference to one another), to which must be added the poetical treatment of the theme, Ps. 8, even though the expression "image of God" does not actually occur in it. Though not strictly relevant, two references in the Apoc. should perhaps be mentioned: Ecclus. 17:3; Wisd. Sol. 2:23-24; to which may be added Wisd. Sol. 7:25.

b. Linguistic considerations. A few preliminary observations on the linguistic problem may be helpful. In Gen. 1:26 two words are used, צלם ("image") and

דמות ("likeness"). When we are told in Gen. 1:27 that the proposal made in 1:26 was carried into effect, only the former of these words is used. Gen. 5:1 uses the second word only (sometimes regarded as a redactional gloss), and 9:6 the first. In 5:3, where we find the expression used of the resemblance between Adam and his son Seth, both words occur, but in reverse order. To complicate interpretation, the use of the particles which go with the nouns is not consistent. In 5:1, דמות has the particle which goes with צלם in 1:26-27, whereas in 5:3 the particles are interchanged, though in some forty-five MSS the reading has been harmonized with 1:26.

In 1:26 the particle with צלם may be regarded as a *beth essentiae*—i.e., as signifying identity. Though the point is debatable, the particle with דמות, which normally signifies "resemblance," may occasionally be used to express identity. This would give us virtually "as the image and likeness." On the other hand, we may translate "in [or after] the image" and "after the likeness" (cf. RSV). The choice is difficult and seems to depend on the way in which the terms צלם and דמות are understood.

The word צלם occurs seventeen times in the OT. Five of the occurrences are in the passages under consideration. In ten of the other cases the meaning is plainly concrete ("statue," "model," "picture"). In the remaining two (Pss. 39:6—H 39:7; 73:20) the translations "shadow," "dream," seem appropriate. It is a matter of debate whether or not צלם in these two cases should be regarded as actually a different word coming from a distinct Arabic root, the word in the other ten cases coming from an Arabic root meaning "cut." If we accept the view that there are two separate roots, it becomes more difficult not to take the five occurrences in Genesis in a strictly concrete sense. If we vote for a single root only, we may say that, on the polarity principle, the word צלם may be concrete at one end of the scale and abstract at the other, regarding the occurrences in Genesis as perhaps somewhere in the middle. One interesting suggestion is that צלם in the context might be derived from the second Arabic root and explained as "shadow picture." The most prevalent opinion today is that צלם should be given a concrete meaning in the first instance, but that a certain flexibility of meaning should be allowed for.

The second term in Gen. 1:26, דמות, has more the appearance of being abstract in meaning, and it actually is so used in certain instances of its occurrence. It may also, however, be used concretely as meaning a "plan."

That in 1:26 two words are used may imply that the author was struggling to express a difficult idea or wished to obviate the danger of צלם being taken in too concrete a sense. The linguistic evidence which has been thus summarily reviewed would suggest that there is not much difference in meaning between the two nouns or, indeed, as used here, between the two particles.

*c. **Interpretation.*** The attempt must now be made to determine the meaning of the statements of the priestly writer. For evidence of the variety of scholarly opinions, *see bibliography*.

At the one extreme are those who take the words צלם and דמות in the most strictly concrete sense and declare the meaning to be, either that man is a concrete image of God in respect of literal physical resemblance, or that he is made after an actual concrete model or image of God. One translation of a disputed passage in the Gilgamesh Epic (*Altorientalische Texte zum AT* I 80 ff or *ANET* 73-99) might seem to support this second suggestion. The word *zikru,* however, probably does not mean "model" but rather "mental image." A mythological reference to the making of men in the image of a god in a Babylonian or Sumerian epic (there are various examples which could be cited) is conceivable, but the fact that the priestly writer is at pains elsewhere in Gen. 1 to exclude mythology would suggest that here too he may be deliberately rejecting mythology. Certainly there is no trace here of the Babylonian belief that man had in his veins the blood of a god. It is possible that the clear separation in Gen. 1:27 of the statement about the distinction between man and woman from that about man's being made in the image of God may imply a rejection of the view found in a Sumerian liturgy that men and women were made after the image of a god and a goddess respectively.

At the other extreme are the interpretations which depart entirely from the concrete meaning of צלם and offer a purely spiritual interpretation, using words like "personality," "self-consciousness," "self-determination," "immortality" (cf. Wisd. Sol. 2:23-24), "reason," "ability to pass judgment," "freedom of the will," "moral capacity."

The image of God is something which the priestly writer believes to be characteristic of all men (not specially of the king, as in Egypt). He makes no reference to the narrative of the Fall, and he gives as the reason for the command not to commit murder, given after the Flood, that man was made, and therefore presumably still is, in the image of God. This disposes of the dogmatic interpretation which goes back to Justin and Irenaeus that the צלם is reason, which man retained after the Fall, whereas the דמות is *justitia originalis,* which he lost.

Man's resemblance to God is analogous to Seth's resemblance to his father, Adam. This makes it certain that physical resemblance must not be excluded. We still talk of a boy's being the living image of his father.

The manner in which the creation of man is introduced in 1:26 and the fact that the passage 9:1-7 implies that human life has a greater sanctity than animal life and that this difference is linked with the image of God imply that the writer intends by the phrase "image of God" to express in some way man's peculiar dignity. That there is any intention on the part of the writer of 1:26-27 to imply that, as the woman is the "thou" of the man, so man is the "thou" of God, is more doubtful, though perhaps not impossible. The idea that there is any reference to the relationships within the Godhead must be rejected.

If we start with the possibility that the writer is thinking of man as the image of God in the sense in which a statue can represent the absent ruler (cf. Dan. 3), it will be seen that immediately man acquires dignity and authority as God's representative. It is possible that there is some implied reference to man's erect posture as compared with the animals.

Man and the animals are distinct, and the distinction must not be obscured (Lev. 20:15-16). The possibility that a physical resemblance between God and man is intended should not be excluded on the ground of Deut. 4:15-24. Though no תמונה ("form") was seen at Horeb, it is not denied that God has form, and that he has is clearly the implication of certain theophanies described in the OT (e.g., Isa. 6; Ezek. 1). In the OT there is a curious oscillation between the belief that God cannot be seen and that he can be seen. What the writer in Genesis says is, not that man may make an image of God—this he would have strenuously denied—but that God has made man an image of himself. By stating likeness, he also implies distance. It should also be recognized that to assert external resemblance does not exclude spiritual resemblance. The OT does not treat man as a duality of soul and body. Moreover, anthropomorphisms are used in speaking of God and are not a sign of primitive thought. On the other hand, it is true that P avoids anthropomorphic language as much as possible, and this creates a probability that, when P uses the concrete term צלם, he may well be seeking to convey an abstract idea.

Perhaps we may conclude that, while much of the thought that there is an external resemblance between God and man may be present—Ezekiel, who was a priest, has it, however cautiously he states it—P seems to have reached a measure of abstraction. We may not go far wrong if we say that for him the image of God means personality, provided we remember this must not be understood in the sense of the autonomous, self-legislating self of the philosophers. Man is determined by God as his Creator. By "image of God" may be meant what gives authority, and that God has made him to exercise such may imply responsibility.

Though the image of God must not be defined in terms of the task of ruling over the lower creation, or of ability to do so (cf. Ecclus. 17:3), the two are closely connected. This appears also in Ps. 8, which speaks of God's condescension to, and care of, man and his granting him a status little less than divine and royal honors that he may exercise his rule. The glory and honor with which man is crowned suggest both external beauty and inward dignity. The mythological account of the king of Tyre in Eden (Ezek. 28:12, 17) implies an endowment of beauty and also of wisdom. We may say that Ps. 8 implies dignity and authority and nobility of appearance as God's gift to man to fit him for his cultural task (cf. Gen. 1:26, 28).

2. In the NT. ***a. Traces of the OT view in the NT.*** The OT view of the image of God appears without alteration in two passages of the NT—viz., I Cor. 11:7; Jas. 3:9. It is important to notice that in the former passage, εἰκών (the LXX translation of צלם) is coupled with δόξα (cf. Ps. 8), whereas James uses ὁμοίωσις (the LXX translation of דמות). In the same way in Rom. 1:23, ὁμοίωμα is used of "likeness" (דמות), whereas εἰκών seems to mean something more than "image" in the sense of "likeness"—in fact, to signify what completely corresponds to the "prototype," that of which the εἰκών is the "likeness." This change of meaning of εἰκών is also shown in Heb. 10:1, where it is contrasted with σκιά.

b. The NT transformation of the idea. It is this change of meaning of the term εἰκών (the LXX equivalent of צלם) from "likeness" to "perfect reflection of the prototype" which is determinative for the NT. Nothing could make clearer the tremendous impact of the revelation of God in Christ than the fact that it has almost completely obliterated the thought of man as being in the image of God and replaced it with the thought of Christ as being the image of God, that being understood in the sense of perfect correspondence to the divine prototype. In Wisd. Sol. 7: 25-26, Wisdom had been described as a "pure emanation of the glory of the Almighty," a "reflection of eternal light," a "spotless mirror of the working of God," the "image of his goodness." This description is applied to Christ as the Son in Heb. 1:3: "He reflects the glory of God and bears the very stamp of his nature," and this opening assertion of the writer governs his conviction throughout his letter that in Christ reality had come to take the place of shadow.

It is a central theme of the Johannine writings (though the expression "image of God" is not used) that in Christ, who became flesh, a "glory as of the only Son from the Father" became visible (John 1: 14), and that to see Christ was to see the Father (John 12:45; 14:9). I John 3:2 is occupied with the thought that, while men are God's children already, an even more glorious destiny is in store—viz., a likeness to God or, it may be, to Christ, in whom God is visible. It is in Paul's thought that the change of view is most fully worked out.

c. The Pauline view. It is in the Pauline writings that the new thought of Christ as the image of God is most fully worked out and brought into relation with the question of man's destiny. In Col. 1:15 it is stated that Christ, the "beloved Son" (vs. 13), "is the image of the invisible God," while in II Cor. 4:4 we read of "Christ, who is the likeness of God." In both cases the word used is εἰκών. Paul is concerned above all, however, with the practical consequences of this. What interests him is not a philosophy but his gospel. What seems to have happened is that Paul, accepting an exegesis of Gen. 1–2 such as we find in Philo in the distinction he draws between the heavenly man (Gen. 1:26) and the earthly man (Gen. 2:7), identifies man as the image of God (Gen. 1:26) with Christ, as Philo identified him with the Logos. This is worked out in detail in I Cor. 15:45-46 in the contrast between ὁ πρῶτος ἄνθρωπος 'Αδάμ, the first Adam who became at his creation a living soul (נפש חיה) made of the dust and therefore χοϊκός, and ὁ ἔσχατος (δεύτερος) ἄνθρωπος, the last or second Adam, who was a life-giving spirit (cf. II Cor. 3:18: "the Lord who is the Spirit"). If there is any connection here with the Iranian Anthropos myth, it is noticeable that Paul says nothing of the pre-existence of Christ as man—indeed, seems deliberately, by the terminology he uses, to avoid doing so—though elsewhere he speaks of Christ's pre-existence freely (see Col. 1:15: "the first-born of all creation"; Phil. 2:6: "though he was in the form of God"). The man from heaven (I Cor. 15:47) is not pre-existent man. This means that Paul's identification of Christ with the man in the image of God of Gen. 1:26 springs, not from a cosmological, but from a soteriological, concern.

Paul's mind is filled with the thought that it is only in relation with Christ that man can attain the likeness to God which at the first (Gen. 1:26) was only man's in promise. In Phil. 2:6-8 he speaks of Christ's exchanging the form (μορφή) of God, which was his by right, to assume the form of a servant and the likeness of men, μορφή—in both cases, meaning "mode of existence."

As Christians are in this Christ, the relationship will work itself out in the relationships existing in the Christian community. In Col. 3:15 the exchanging of the old man (nature) for the new, "which is being renewed in knowledge after the image of its creator," will bring about a community in which racial, religious, and social distinctions will no longer have any meaning, "but Christ is all, and in all" (cf. Eph. 4:22-24).

Above all, Christians must "put on love, which binds everything together in perfect harmony" (Col. 3:14). It is in God's plan for men that they should "be conformed [συμμόρφους] to the image of his Son" (Rom. 8:29) and therefore, since there is no distinction, to the image of God. This is an eschatological hope, but it is also in some real measure a present reality, for "we all, with unveiled face, beholding the glory of the Lord, are being changed into his likeness from one degree of glory to another; for this comes from the Lord who is the Spirit" (II Cor. 3:18; cf. Phil. 3:20-21).

Bibliography. W. Eichrodt, *Theologie des AT* (2nd rev. ed., 1935), II, 60-65; G. Kittel, "Der übertragene Gebrauch von 'Bild' in NT," *BWANT,* II (1935), 393-96; G. von Rad, "Die Gottesebenbildlichkeit im AT," *BWANT,* II (1935), 387-90; P. Humbert, " 'L'Imago Dei' dans l'AT," *Études sur le récit du paradis et de la chute dans la Genèse* (1940), ch. 5, pp. 153-75; T. C. Vriezen, "La Création de l'homme d'après l'image de Dieu," *OTS,* II (1943), 87-105; W. Zimmerli, *I Mose I-II Die Urgeschichte,* I (1943), 75-100; L. Köhler, "Die Grundstelle der Imago-Dei Lehre, Gen. 1:26," *Theologische Zeitschrift* 4, Jg. 1 (1948), pp. 16-22; H. Schrade, *Der Verborgene Gott* (1949), p. 316; F. Horst, "Face to Face: The Biblical Doctrine of the Image of God," *Interpretation,* vol. IV, no. 3 (1950), pp. 259-70; L. Köhler, *Theologie des AT* (3rd ed., 1953), pp. 134-35; E. Jacob, *Théologie de l'AT* (1955), pp. 135-40; G. von Rad, *Das Erste Buch Mose: Genesis* (4th ed., 1956), pp. 44-47.

N. W. PORTEOUS

IMAGINATION. This noun in the older English versions (together with its cognate verb) is a source of misconception to the modern reader, since it ordinarily has the obsolete sense of "plotting or devising evil" rather than the current sense of "the power of freely forming mental images," a concept entirely unfamiliar to the ancient Hebrews, who were not given to fantasy and who conceived of mental activity primarily in terms of preparation for action (*see* MIND). In Prov. 6:18; Lam. 3:60-61, where the word "imaginations" is found in the KJV, the underlying Hebrew word is מחשבות, which means literally "thoughts," but is more accurately translated by the RSV as "plans" and "devices." The Hebrew word יצר, for which the RSV retains the translation "imagination" in two places (Gen. 6:5; 8:21), does indeed seem to mean the power of forming mental images, but presumably also as a prelude to action, and in three of the five instances in the KJV obviously a bad action. In only two late passages (I Chr. 28:9; 29:18) does the English word have a good, or at least a neutral, sense. Here, as in Deut. 31:21, the RSV translates "purposes" or "plans." In the later rabbinic view the word יצר was taken to mean "impulse," and the conception arose that the יצר הטוב ("the good impulse") and the יצר הרע ("the bad impulse") were elements in the human personality.

The general confusion created by the use of the word "imagination" in the KJV is even worse confounded by its being used in a series of passages (e.g., Deut. 29:19; Jer. 3:17) to translate the Hebrew שרירות, which properly means "stubbornness" and is so translated in the RSV (though usually by means of an adverb rather than the noun).

The situation with respect to the use of the word in the NT is essentially the same as that in the OT. The words διαλογισμοῖς and λογισμοὺς in Rom. 1:21; II Cor. 10:5, which the KJV, taking account of the bad sense implied by the contexts, translates "imaginations," would be more accurately rendered "reasonings" (cf. RSV). The RSV has retained "imagination" only in Luke 1:51 (for διάνοια, "thought"), presumably because of its liturgical familiarity, and added it in Acts 17:29 to translate ἐνθύμησις (KJV "device"). R. C. DENTAN

IMALKUE ĭ măl'kyo͞o ĭ ['Ιμαλκουέ=ימלכו; Vulg. *Emalchuel*] (I Macc. 11:39); KJV SIMALCUE sī'məl kū'ī. Someone described as "the Arab, who was bringing up Antiochus, the young son of Alexander." It is clear from Greek and Roman writers, as well as from the scriptures (II Sam. 4:4; II Kings 10:2; 11:2), that the companion of a young prince in the ancient world occupied a position of honor and importance. Josephus (Antiq. XIII.v.1) describes Imalkue as "an Arabian prince who had charge of the young Antiochus." At a time when "the troops were murmuring against Demetrius," Trypho, formerly "one of Alexander's supporters," saw an opportunity to set up a rival to Demetrius and sought the aid of Imalkue in a plot to proclaim Alexander's son as King Antiochus VI (I Macc. 11:38-40). The plot was successful, and when Antiochus "began to reign and put on the crown," "all the troops that Demetrius had cast off gathered around him, and they fought against Demetrius, and he fled and was routed" (vss. 54-55). J. C. SWAIM

IMLAH ĭm'lə [ימלה (Kings), ימלא (Chronicles), he is full(?); *a name known in Palmyrene*]. The father of the prophet Micaiah (I Kings 22:8-9; II Chr. 18:7-8).

IMMANENCE. A philosophical term often used to express the biblical view that while God is elevated in majesty (transcendent), he is also actively present in human affairs. *See* GOD, OT VIEW OF, § C; INCARNATION.

IMMANUEL ĭ măn'yo͞o əl [עמנו אל, God is with us; 1QIs[a] עמנואל; LXX 'Εμμανουήλ]; KJV EMMANUEL in Matt. 1:23. A symbolic name to be given to the child whose birth was foretold by Isaiah as the sign to Ahaz and his court that God would deliver them from their enemies (Isa. 7:14; 8:8). In the NT this name is applied similarly to Jesus.

1. Historical circumstances
2. Lexical problems

3. Exegetical problems
4. History of interpretation
   a. An OT parallel
   b. Early Christian
   c. Jewish
   d. Critical
5. Suggested solution
Bibliography

1. Historical circumstances. In 734 B.C., Judah was threatened by kings REZIN of Syria (Aram) and PEKAH of Israel (Isa. 7:1-2). Their purpose was to compel AHAZ to join a coalition against TIGLATH-PILESER of Assyria. If he refused to comply, they intended to depose the Davidic dynasty and set up in its place "the son of Tabeel" (*see* TABEEL 1), probably an Aramean. Ahaz was inclined to appeal for help to Tiglath-pileser, and he subsequently took this course (II Kings 16:7 ff). Isaiah was instructed by God to meet Ahaz at a place outside Jerusalem as he was inspecting the defenses of the city. He was to take with him his son SHEAR-JASHUB and assure the king that if he had faith in God, he had nothing to fear from Rezin and Pekah, who were only "two smoldering stumps of fire-brands" on the point of being extinguished. Ahaz was unconvinced.

At some time later Isaiah confronted Ahaz in the presence of the court (Isa. 7:10-13) and offered him a "sign" from Yahweh. The sign might be anything he asked, either from the underworld ("Sheol") or from heaven. Ahaz declined to ask, saying that it was not for him to put God to the test (cf. Deut. 6:16). Whether this was pious timidity on his part, or whether he was masking hypocrisy under a show of piety, is not certain, but Isaiah's forthright indignation points to the latter. He seems to say that Ahaz has renounced his allegiance to Yahweh ("your God" in vs. 11 has become "my God" in vs. 13). Then he goes on: "Therefore the Lord himself will give you [plural] a sign: See, the young woman is [or perhaps will be] pregnant and will give birth to a son, and will give him the name Immanuel." Then follow particulars of the fortunes of the infant Immanuel and what appears to be an assurance that within a comparatively short time the danger to Judah will have passed.

2. Lexical problems. The word translated "young woman" is עלמה. "Virgin" (RSV mg.; KJV) is based on the LXX and Matt. 1:23 (παρθένος). The Hebrew for "virgin" is בתולה, which could be further defined to avoid ambiguity (Gen. 24:16). The word עלמה properly denotes a young woman of marriageable age. Although it must have been a common enough word, it is comparatively little used (Gen. 24:43; Exod. 2:8; Ps. 68:25—H 68:26; Prov. 30:19; Song of S. 1:3; 6:8; Isa. 7:14; and, doubtfully, in one or two psalm titles); the corresponding masculine form, עלם, is used in I Sam. 17:56; 20:22. None of the examples (not even Prov. 30:19) is inconsistent with virginity, unless Isa. 7:14 should be translated: "The young woman is [already] pregnant" (on which *see below*). The word may have denoted a woman until the birth of her first child, though there is no proof of this. On the other hand, in Ugaritic the corresponding words *ġlmt* and *btlt* are both used of the goddess Anat, who was not *virgo intacta,* and in Palmyrene the plural is used of harlots.

Another problem is the force of the article in "the young woman." The article is sometimes used in describing a situation vivid to the imagination, as in II Sam. 17:17 (cf. G-K § 126q, r); so "a young woman" (RSV). Or it could be used "generically" (G-K § 126m); hence "*any* young woman," or even "young women." As between the present "is pregnant" and the future "shall be pregnant," the Hebrew can mean either, but the close similarity to Gen. 16:11 is in favor of the first alternative.

The word "sign" (אות) can be used of either natural (Gen. 1:14; 9:12; 17:11; Exod. 3:12; I Sam. 10:7, 9) or supernatural (Exod. 4:8-9; Isa. 38:7, 22) phenomena. When it denotes the latter it is sometimes conjoined with מופת ("portent" or "wonder"), as in Exod. 7:3; Deut. 4:34. In Isa. 7:11 the proffered sign was, to judge from the context, to be supernatural; in vs. 14 it could be natural, the closest parallel being Exod. 3:12, where the meaning is: "This shall be the evidence or proof that it is I who have sent you: when you have done what I tell you, you and the people you have delivered shall worship me here." In other words, the sign is verified as subsequent events happen according to prediction.

3. Exegetical problems. Opinion has been sharply divided on whether the "sign" is a promise or a threat. In vs. 11 it is clearly a promise. But since Ahaz is obdurate (vs. 12), the promise, many suppose, is turned to a threat in vss. 14-17. The arguments for this are: (*a*) The wider context, vss. 18-25, gives a picture of general desolation; (*b*) the word "therefore" (vs. 14) introduces a threat in 1:24; 5:13, 24; (*c*) the name Immanuel could mean "God be with us" in the sense "God help us!" (*d*) "butter and honey" indicate privation.

The contrary arguments are: (*a*) The desolation in vss. 18-20, 23-25, may well be that of the dominions of Pekah and Rezin, as in 8:1-4. Vss. 21-22, which picture depopulation and return to a pastoral economy, may apply to Judah, and the situation is consistent with Isaiah's doctrine of the remnant. Isaiah nowhere promises that Judah will be unscathed. In vs. 17 the prosaic "the king of Assyria" is widely regarded as a marginal gloss, and the meaning would then be that Judah will enjoy prosperity such as it had not known since the disruption of Solomon's kingdom, the inference being that the sundered kingdoms will be reunited.

b) "Therefore" can introduce a promise (cf. Jer. 16:14-15), and the meaning would then be: "In the circumstances, since you will not ask for a sign, though Yahweh has offered it, he will have to give it you himself."

c) In all similar annunciation passages (Gen. 16:11; 17:19; Judg. 13:3, 5; Matt. 1:21; Luke 1:13 ff, 31 ff) the birth of the child bodes good. This is equally true of the extrabiblical parallels (*see* § 5 *below*). Also the refrain: "Yahweh of hosts is with us" (Ps. 46:7, 11—H 46:8, 12; cf. I Kings 8:57) is always on a note of confidence.

d) For the Hebrews the Promised Land was a "land flowing with milk and honey." "Butter" (חמאה) was made with aromatic herbs from the richest part of the milk (Prov. 30:33), and butter, milk, and honey were luxury foods (Gen. 18:8; Deut. 32:14; Judg. 5:25; II Sam. 17:29; Job 20:17; 29:6). In

Babylonia they were ingredients in cultic ceremonies, and in Ugaritic texts fruitfulness is accompanied by abundance of butter (*ḥm't*=חמאת) and milk (*ḥlb*=חלב). In late Jewish texts (Sibylline Oracles V.282; II Enoch 8.5-6) the righteous are to eat milk and honey in paradise. The association of "butter and honey" with privation may, however, be true insofar as they were given to those who had recently been in privation (cf. Judg. 5:25; II Sam. 17:29), or the inference may be that the crops have been devastated.

4. History of interpretation. ***a. An OT parallel.*** A passage similar to Isa. 7:14 is Mic. 5:3—H 5:2:

> Therefore he shall give them up until the time
> when she who is in travail has brought forth.

If this is from Isaiah's contemporary Micah, it may be an independent prophecy. Many think it is later than Micah himself, in which case it may be an interpretation of Isaiah. It is in vaguer terms than Isa. 7:14, but it is to be noted that in both passages the birth of the child is to be followed by what appears to be the reunion of Israel and Judah (Isa. 7:17; Mic. 5:3*b*).

b. Early Christian. The earliest clear interpretation is Matt. 1:22-23, in which the Immanuel oracle is taken as a prophecy of the virgin birth of Christ. This interpretation lay ready to hand in the LXX rendering ἡ παρθένος. It was almost unchallenged in Christendom until the end of the eighteenth century, notwithstanding that in the Isaiah context the sign must have been something relevant to the situation in which Ahaz found himself. Indeed, it is clearly indicated that by the time the child is able to discriminate between foods he likes and foods he does not like (for this interpretation of "to refuse the evil and choose the good," see II Sam. 19:35)—i.e., by the time he is weaned—Syria and Ephraim will be devastated. Damascus was destroyed in 733-732 B.C.

c. Jewish. The Jews reacted strongly against the Christian interpretation, and in the Greek translations of Aq., Symm., and Theod. they substituted νεᾶνις for παρθένος. They maintained that Immanuel was Hezekiah, the first-born son of Ahaz. The Christian reply to this was that if Ahaz reigned sixteen years (II Kings 16:2) and Hezekiah was twenty-five years old when he came to the throne (II Kings 18:2), Hezekiah must already have been nine years old when the Immanuel prophecy was uttered. Accordingly, medieval Jewish scholars came to identify the עלמה with either the wife of Isaiah or another wife of Ahaz. The objections to the wife of Isaiah are that elsewhere the prophet refers to her as "the prophetess" (8:3) and that since she had already borne one child, Shear-jashub, she could hardly be called עלמה.

d. Critical. From the end of the eighteenth century the traditional Christian interpretation was being increasingly abandoned. By the turn of the twentieth century it was common for critical scholars to take the article in הָעַלְמָה generically and to make the sign mean little more than an assurance that within a year the situation would have changed so much for the better that women bearing male children would be calling their boys Immanuel. This implied that the Immanuel sign was no longer to be taken as having any messianic significance, such as might still be assumed for Isa. 9:1-7; 11:1-9. And it must be conceded that the NT is not regulative for the interpretation of the OT; e.g., Matt. 2:15 cannot make the original meaning of Hos. 11:1 anything other than that God delivered Israel from Egypt at the Exodus.

5. Suggested solution. The view summarized in § 4 *above* has never gone unchallenged. Isolated scholars, not fundamentalists, have maintained something like the traditional interpretation, this in view of the many ancient myths which tell of the virgin birth of a wonder child. There must, it is postulated from Isa. 7:14; Mic. 5:3, have been a similar popular expectation in Israel.

This postulate has been strengthened by a passage in a Ras Shamra text: *hl ġlmt tld b*(*n*), "See! the *ġlmt* shall give birth to a son" (Nikkal and the Kathirat, line 7), which, with the omission of a single word, is the same as in Isa. 7:14. In another text (II Aqhat II.1 ff), Danel cries: *k yld bn ly,* "for a son is born to me" (cf. Isa. 9:6). This makes it difficult to disassociate the Immanuel sign from the messianic passages in Isa. 9; 11. In the Ras Shamra Texts the children are the offspring of divine, or at least royal, marriages. It is therefore probable that the Immanuel sign is to be interpreted in the context of a widespread divine-royal annunciation formula, in which the words *btlt* and *ġlmt* ("virgin" and "young woman"), which are frequently used together, had a cultic, rather than a biological, signification. (This is without prejudice to the historicity of the nativity story in Matt. 1, where ἡ παρθένος certainly means *virgo intacta* and the story is one the historicity of which must be decided on its merits.) The likelihood is that the "young woman" of Isa. 7:14 was the wife of Ahaz and that she was thought to share something of the sacral character of the king her husband (*see* KING § 4). In this case the original Immanuel may have been Hezekiah. The objection that Hezekiah was already born when the Immanuel sign was given (*see* § 4*c above*) is not fatal: II Kings 16:2; 18:2, if taken exactly as they stand, seem to be in need of some correction, since they would make Ahaz only eleven years older than his son Hezekiah.

There is no indication that Hezekiah or any contemporary of Isaiah was actually named Immanuel. For that matter, the names in Isa. 9:6—H 9:5 are honorific rather than personal. Nor, on the traditional interpretation, was Jesus called Immanuel, except subsequently, and occasionally, in the language of devotion. It is true that Isaiah apostrophizes Immanuel in 8:8: "Its outspread wings will fill the breadth of your land, O Immanu-el." The attempt has sometimes been made to read this as ". . . the breadth of the land, for God is with us" (as in vs. 10—this without change of the Hebrew consonants). But such a reading makes nonsense in the context, and in the Qumran scroll of Isaiah the letter *kaph* is clearly a pronominal suffix in the expression "your land." That Isaiah should address Immanuel in a single lyrical passage is not proof that an actual Immanuel was at that time on the throne of Judah. The only names similar to Immanuel are, so far as is known, Immadiyahu, "Yah(u) is with me," on an early Hebrew seal, and Immanuiah, "Yah(weh) is with us," in a papyrus from Elephantine (fifth century B.C.).

It is obvious that the problems presented by Isa. 7:14 ff are complicated and that in the present state of our knowledge no final answer to them can be given. There have been Protestant scholars, not fundamentalists, who have favored the traditional interpretation that the sign is a direct prediction of Christ; also, Catholic scholars who have only accepted the traditional interpretation with reservations. The difficulty is to see how a long range prediction could have any intelligible meaning for Ahaz, the more so since Isa. 7:14 ff appears to say that the child, whether or not he is already conceived, will be born within a comparatively short time.

The possibility must be considered that a prophecy may have a proximate fulfilment which nevertheless does not exhaust its meaning. If we say that the original Immanuel was Hezekiah, we are not saying that the further application of the sign to Jesus in the NT was unwarranted fantasy. The widespread ancient myth of the dying and rising god bears a certain superficial resemblance to the NT account of the death and resurrection of Christ. This does not mean that the death and resurrection of Christ are mythical. It means that the Christian gospel is the historicization of ideas and longings which, for all their crudity, are, and were intended by God to be, a *praeparatio evangelica*. Or, it is generally agreed today that the kings in Pss. 2; 45; 110 were actual reigning kings of Israel or Judah; the author of the Letter to the Hebrews, not inappropriately, gives to the Psalms a messianic-christological interpretation. It is a far cry from early expectations of a wonder child to the Incarnation of God in Christ. The complex of messianic oracles in Isa. 7; 9; 11 is the middle term between them.

Bibliography. In addition to the Commentaries on Isa. 1-39 listed under ISAIAH, see: F. Giesebrecht, "Die Emmanuelweissagung," *TSK,* LXI (1888), 217-46; K. Fullerton, "Immanuel," *AJSL,* XXXIV (1918), 256-83; E. Norden, *Die Geburt des Kindes* (1924); R. Kittel, *Die hellenistische Mysterienreligion und das AT* (1924); H. Gressmann, *Der Messias* (1929), pp. 235-42; E. G. Kraeling, "The Immanuel Prophecy," *JBL,* L (1931), 277-97; W. C. Graham, "Isaiah's Part in the Syro-Ephraimitic Crisis," *AJSL,* L (1934), 201-16; C. B. Hansen, "Immanuel," *Dansk teologisk tidsskrift,* III (1940), 31-47; J. J. Stamm, "La prophétie d'Emmanuel," *Revue de Théologie et de Philosophie,* N.S. XXXII (1944), 97-123; G. Widengren, "Hieros gamos och underjordvistelse," *Religion och Bibel,* VII (1948), 17-46; E. Hammershaimb, "The Immanuel Sign," *Studia Theologica,* III (1949), 124-42; J. Coppens, "La prophétie de la 'almah," *Ephemerides Theologicae Lovanienses,* XXVIII (1952), 648-78; S. Mowinckel, *He That Cometh* (trans. G. W. Anderson; 1956), pp. 110-19; N. Gottwald, "Immanuel as the Prophet's Son," *Vetus Testamentum,* 8 (1958), 36-47; J. Lindblom, *A Study of the Immanuel Section in Isaiah, Isa. vii.1-ix.6* (1958). C. R. NORTH

IMMER ĭm'ər [Aram. אמר, lamb (-village); Apoc. (A) 'Εμμηρούθ (I Esd. 5:24), 'Εμμήρ (I Esd. 9:21); Apoc. (B) 'Αλλάρ (I Esd. 5:36)]; KJV Apoc. MERUTH mē'rəth (I Esd. 5:24), EMMER ĕm'ər (I Esd. 9:21), AALAR ā'ə lər (I Esd. 5:36). **1.** A priest or priestly house first listed as a contemporary of David in I Chr. 24:14. Pashhur, Jeremiah's priestly opponent, is identified with this family (Jer. 20:1), and other members are prominently mentioned from the postexilic period. The line is represented among the priests returned from Babylon (I Chr. 9:12; Ezra 2:37; cf. Neh. 7:40; I Esd. 5:24). Two of them were among those persuaded by Ezra to divorce their foreign wives (Ezra 10:20; I Esd. 9:21). One Zadok of this house helped repair the wall of Jerusalem under Nehemiah (Neh. 3:29), and they are included in the list of priests resident in Jerusalem after the Exile (Neh. 11:13). B. T. DAHLBERG

2. A Babylonian place, unidentified, from which Jewish exiles, who could not prove their ancestry with genealogical records, returned to Palestine (Ezra 2:59; Neh. 7:61; I Esd. 5:36). Later Jewish records mention a Kefar Imra ("lamb-village") in the Jerusalem Talmud (Ta'an. IV.69*a;* cf. Lamentations Rabbah on II.2: נמרא). R. A. BOWMAN

IMMORALITY [πορνεία]. Some kind of unlawful sexual intercourse. The RSV sometimes translates "fornication" (the usual KJV translation), "unchastity," and in two cases "impurity" in the phrase "impure passion" (τοῦ θυμοῦ τῆς πορνείας; Rev. 14:8; 18:3). Paul speaks of a case of immorality involving a man's living with his father's wife (I Cor. 5:1); he fears he will find many cases of (sexual) immorality in Corinth (II Cor. 12:21). He lists immorality as one of the works of the flesh (Gal. 5:19); he says that the man who engages in immorality sins against his own body (I Cor. 6:18) and will not inherit the kingdom of God (I Cor. 6:9-10; Gal. 5:19-21; cf. Eph. 5:3, 5). Because of the temptation of immorality, it is better for each person to marry (I Cor. 7:2). Christians are not to associate with "immoral" Christians (I Cor. 5:11).

In Revelation "immorality" is often used figuratively in the sense of apostasy from God, or idolatry, as in the OT (cf. II Kings 9:22; Jer. 3:2, 9; Hos. 6:10; Rev. 2:21; 9:21). B. H. THROCKMORTON, JR.

IMMORTALITY [ἀθανασία (I Cor. 15:53); ἀφθαρσία (Rom. 2:7), *lit.,* incorruptibility]. Once a relationship between Yahweh and DEATH had been affirmed, there could be hope of a victory over death; for where Yahweh reigns, life must dominate. If Yahweh can cure persons dying of illness, he can also make manifest his power over death, once death's work is finished. The assertion that Yahweh is a living god is a central theme of the OT (Pss. 18:46—H 18:47; 42:2—H 42:3; 84:2—H 84:3; etc.; Jer. 23:36; Hos. 1:10—H 2:1). The affirmation of his eternity is only the consequence of his existence. The living God stands in contrast both to the pagan deities, who are only dead idols (II Kings 19:4, 16; Ps. 106:28; Jer. 10:11), and to men, who are mortal.

The life that Yahweh possesses is, moreover, a source of life that he puts at the service of his faithfulness to men and his covenant with them. Thus Yahweh can restore a life weakened by illness and sin—an action presented as a revivification, expressed with the help of the root חיה (Job 33:19-26; Pss. 30:2-3—H 30:3-4; 56:13—H 56:14; 71:20; 143:11). Nothing prevents Yahweh from exercising this regenerating power, once death has completed its work. The OT mentions several cases of persons' being restored to life by Elijah and Elisha—the son of the widow of Zarephath (I Kings 17:17-21), the son of the Shunammite (II Kings 4:18-37), and the body of an anonymous individual reanimated by contact with the bones of Elisha (II Kings 13:20-21). In these instances the resurrections are more akin to the cure of the very ill than to the final resurrection. They occur shortly after death, when the body has not yet been reduced to dust, and they only prolong life. A more definitive victory over death occurs in the taking up to God of certain privileged individuals. Thus Enoch (Gen. 5:24) and Elijah (II Kings 2:10-11) were taken by God (לקח) without dying. Pseudepigraphic tradition ascribes a similar fate to Moses by interpreting Deut. 34:5 in the sense of a taking away (cf. Asmp. Moses 11:9 ff). These examples have been considered to be premonitory signs of a more general reality.

Faith in immortality was oriented in two main directions:

a) The idea of a possible return to life gained wider and wider acceptance. The Israelites could not remain unaffected by the Canaanite belief in the death and resurrection of a divinity who symbolized the life of nature. The faithful linked themselves with the idea of death and resurrection within the cult. Certain expressions employed by the Israelites in their own religion may be adapted from the faith of the Canaanites. Thus Hos. 6:1 ff perhaps imitates a liturgical theme of a cult celebrating the death and resurrection of the god. The lament for King Jehoiakim might likewise be borrowed from Canaanite ritual (Jer. 22:18). It is not impossible that Israel may have shared with its neighbors a belief in the immortality of the king (cf. Ezek. 34:24; 37:24), although this idea should be explored only with extreme caution. It should be emphasized, on the other hand, that this mystical attitude toward nature, which is the essence of Canaanite religion, served to render the Israelites very cautious in speculating about eternity.

Probably the idea of the resurrection of the dead underlies certain images in which the future of the Israelitic people is presented as a resurrection. In addition to the text of Hosea already cited, the vision of the prophet Ezekiel (ch. 37) may be mentioned. The precision with which this text describes the reanimation of the bones of the dead and the coming out from the tombs seems to suggest that certain precise ideas relative to death underlie these images. In the fourth song of the Servant of Yahweh, a long, probably immortal, life is mentioned. This life is granted him as a compensation for his sufferings and death, which are accepted as an expiation for the sins of others (Isa. 53:8, 10). In Dan. 12:2 resurrection is extended to a greater number (רבים). It is not yet a question of the resurrection of all, but of many, and this resurrection will be twofold in nature, being followed by the recompensing of some and the punishment of others. The resurrection is born from the Maccabean wars and from the problem presented to faith by the martyrdom of so many just people, who should normally have been rewarded with the blessings of this life. It is definitively conceived as a form of retribution. Isa. 26:19 in speaking of "thy dead" probably also refers to the martyrs.

As well as being an expression of retribution, the resurrection appears as the logical and necessary consequence of the extension of Yahweh's reign over the whole earth. When Yahweh becomes king, death will be destroyed forever (Isa. 25:8), and the host on high will be punished, together with Leviathan and the other powers who keep the dead captive in Sheol (24:21; 27:1 ff). At the same time Yahweh will spread over the earth a "dew of light" (26:19—H 29:19), the resurrection being thus identified with a new creation more perfect than the first. For the author of Ps. 22, the resurrection likewise forms part of the triumph of the reign of Yahweh (vss. 29-30). Israelitic faith was perhaps influenced by the Iranian religion in certain aspects of the idea of resurrection—e.g., in the association of the resurrection with retribution and with the messianic hope. On the other hand, hope of an eternal life based on the immortality of the soul is entirely foreign to the OT, and the cosmic myth of the destruction and renewal of the world, which was basic in Iran, was far less important in Israel than was faith in the power and justice of Yahweh.

b) The second current of thought is not characterized by a consideration of the possibilities and modes of resurrection. It is a matter of faith which, trusting to God for the choice of a solution, asks no other certitude than communion with him. This attitude, which may be termed mystic, occurs in several psalms. The author of Ps. 16 is not concerned with what will happen after death, but for him communion with Yahweh is so strong a reality that it could not be destroyed by death. Since Yahweh is the living god, this communion likewise means to the psalmist a life after death. A similar hope is perhaps expressed in Ps. 17:15, even though the allusion to resurrection is not obvious there. In Pss. 49; 73 the psalmists seem to find a possible solution to the problem of death in the taking up to God of certain privileged beings (cf. the use of the verb לקח, "take," in Pss. 49:15—H 49:16; 73:24). The author of Ps. 49 is certain that since he has been just and faithful, death will not be for him the inexorably destructive force that it will be for the ungodly. The author of Ps. 73, threatened with a premature and unjust death, knows that even if death takes place, it cannot end his communion with God, which no power can destroy. This is already the triumphal faith expressed by the apostle Paul at the end of Rom. 8, that nothing can separate from God's love a man who knows he has been chosen by God. The same attitude appears in Job 19:26, where primary emphasis is put neither on retribution on earth nor on the resurrection, but on the certainty of "seeing" God, a term which always means communion with God, generally through the cult. Job's faith is in knowing that his communion with God will exist, whatever happens, and this precisely at a time when sight and reasoning seem to prove the contrary.

It is this profoundly religious current which contributed the most strongly to transforming the idea of the resurrection into a living faith. With the triumph of a clearly individualistic doctrine of retribution, the ideas of immortality and resurrection came to occupy an increasingly important place in Judaism. These ideas, however, were far from receiving unanimous acceptance. They are clearly rejected by Ecclesiasticus, Judith, Tobit, Baruch, and I Maccabees (cf. I Macc. 2:49, 70), and the Sadducean party remains faithful to this position. An affirmative attitude is expressed in II Macc. 7:9 ff, in the parables of Enoch, in the book of Baruch, and in the Testaments of the Twelve Patriarchs (particularly that of Judah). The terms of Isa. 26:19; Dan. 12:2 are re-employed and made explicit, although numerous variations occur in these writings as to the mode and place of resurrection and as to the nature of the resuscitated bodies.

The texts of Qumran speak now of a resurrection of the just (1QH XI.12), now of an "eternal joy in a life without end" in the shining world of God and the angels (1QS IV.7-8). In the writings of Alexandrine Judaism the idea of a resurrection is replaced by that of the immortality of souls near God (Wisd. Sol. 3:1 ff; 9:15; IV Maccabees). Popular Judaism compromised between the beliefs inherited from the OT and the Greek or Greco-Iranian ideas. In Enoch 22 the "spirits of the souls of the dead" are distributed in Sheol among four compartments—which is already a form of judgment—and have an independent existence while waiting to resume a bodily form on the day of resurrection. The same combination of the doctrine of the immortality of the soul with that of the resurrection (which sometimes leads to original points of view), reappears in II Esdras (IV Ezra), particularly in ch. 7. An analogous attitude may be found in the NT, where, besides the clear assertion of corporal resurrection, is found a belief in immortality and in a life near God immediately following death (cf. Luke 16:24). Jesus, however, by insisting on the reality and omnipotence of the living God in speaking of life after death, rejoins the fundamental assertions of the OT, passing over contemporaneous Judaic belief (Matt. 22:23; Mark 12:26).

Bibliography. J. Touzard, "Le développement de la doctrine de l'immortalité dans l'AT," *RB* (1898), pp. 207 ff. L. F. Burney, *Israel's Hope of Immortality* (1909). W. V. Baudissin, *Adonis und Eshmun* (1911); "Alttestamentliches 'ḥajjim' Leben in der Bedeutung von Glück," *Festschrift* (ed. Sachau; 1913), pp. 143-61; J. Lindblom, *Das ewige Leben* (1914). A. Bertholet, "The Pre-Christian Belief in the Resurrection of the Body," *AJT* (1916), pp. 1 ff. E. Sellin, "Die alttestamentliche Hoffnung auf Auferstehung und ewiges Leben," *NKZ* (1919), pp. 232 ff. F. Noetscher, *Altorientalischer und alttestamentlicher Auferstehungsglauben* (1926). W. Baumgartner, "Der Auferstehungsglauben im Alten Orient," *Zeitschrift für Missionskunde und Religionswissenschaft* (1933), pp. 193-214. J. Schmid, "Der Ewigkeitsbegriff im AT," *AA* (1940). A. T. Nikolainen, "Der Auferstehungsglaube in der Bibel und ihrer Umwelt," *Annales Acad. Scient. fennicae* (1944). W. Bieder, "Auferstehung des Fleisches oder des Leibes?" *Theologische Zeitschrift* (1945), pp. 105 ff. H. Birkeland, "The Belief of the Resurrection of the Dead in the OT," *Studia Theologica* (Lund, 1950), pp. 60-78. L. Rost, "Alttestamentliche Wurzeln der ersten Auferstehung," *In Memoriam E. Lohmeyer* (1951), pp. 67 ff. J. Guillet, "Les sources scriptuaires de la foi en la résurrection de la chair," *Bible et Vie chrétienne* (1953), p. 40. G. Molin, "Entwicklung und Motive der Auferstehung vom AT bis zur rabbinischen Zeit," *Judaica* (1953), pp. 225 ff. H. J. Franken, *The Mystical Communion with YHWH in the Book of Psalms* (1954).

See also bibliography under DEATH.

E. JACOB

IMNA ĭm'nə [יִמְנָע, may he (God) preserve] (I Chr. 7:35). A descendant of Asher.

Bibliography. M. Noth, *Die israelitischen Personennamen* (1928), pp. 28, 197.

IMNAH ĭm'nə [יִמְנָה, luck, good fortune]; KJV JIMNA jĭm'— in Num. 26:44; KJV JIMNAH in Gen. 46:17. **1.** An eponym; listed as a son of Asher (Gen. 46:17 [cf. Jub. 44:21]; Num. 26:44; I Chr. 7:30).

2. A Levite; the father of Kore, a contemporary of King Hezekiah (II Chr. 31:14).

Bibliography. M. Noth, *Die israelitischen Personennamen* (1928), p. 224.

B. T. DAHLBERG

IMPALEMENT. An ancient Near Eastern method of execution, whereby a spiked stake was set in the ground (or wall) and a living body thrust upon it (usually between the legs). In Ezra 6:11 (וּזְקִיף יִתְמְחֵא; lit., "and being raised up, let him be stuck on it") this is set as the penalty for altering the edict of Darius relative to rebuilding the temple; a timber of the offender's house is used. Impalement was practiced by the Assyrians for prisoners of war, deserters,

3. Victims impaled by the Assyrians on the hill; from an Assyrian relief

and malefactors guilty of the more horrible crimes or unnatural vice.* Darius is said to have impaled three thousand when he took the city of Babylon (Herodotus Hist. 3.159). Fig. IMP 3.

Some scholars feel the biblical references Num. 25:4; Deut. 21:22-23; Josh. 8:29; II Sam. 21:6, 9; Esth. 9:14 refer to impalement. *See* HANGING.

Bibliography. A. H. Layard, *Babylon and Nineveh* (1853), p. 335n; W. D. Birch and T. G. Pinches, *The Bronze Ornaments of the Palace Gates of Balawat* (1902), pp. 2*b*, 4*b*, 10*a*; A. T. Olmstead, *History of Assyria* (1923), pp. 87, 112, 114, 144, 177, 308, 551.

V. H. KOOY

IMPEDIMENT IN SPEECH [μογιλάλος]. Labored speech; a disturbance of the organ of speech causing one to speak with difficulty—i.e., to make no intelligible sounds (Mark 7:32). The ancient versions understood the term here to mean "mute, dumb."

While Mark 7:37 (ἀλάλους, "speechless") suggests "mute" or "dumb," vs. 35 (ἐλάλει ὀρθῶς, "He spoke plainly") and the alternative reading of a number of MSS in vs. 32 (μογγιλάλον, "hoarse of speech") would indicate that the man with an impediment in his speech was unintelligible in his speaking, rather than without the faculty of speech.

The phraseology was undoubtedly meant by the author to recall the messianic passage Isa. 35:5-6 (where μογιλάλος is used in the LXX to translate אִלֵּם, "dumb"), as indicated by the concluding comment of the people: "He has done all things well; he even makes the deaf hear and the dumb speak" (vs. 37).

The word occurs also in Exod. 4:11 Aq., Symm., and Theod. (LXX δυσκωφος, "injured in one of the senses," "deaf," "mute"), and in Isa. 56:10 Aq. (LXX ἐνεόι, "silent from terror or amazement").

Bibliography. H. B. Swete, *The Gospel According to St. Mark* (1898), p. 151; J. M. Lagrange, *Evangile selon Saint Marc* (1920), p. 187; V. Taylor, *The Gospel According to Saint Mark* (1952), pp. 353-54. V. H. KOOY

IMPRISONMENT. *See* CRIMES AND PUNISHMENTS.

IMPURITY. *See* CLEAN AND UNCLEAN.

IMRAH ĭm′rə [ימרה, may he rebel(?); *or read* ימנע, Imna(?); *see bibliography*] (I Chr. 7:36). A descendant of Asher.

Bibliography. M. Noth, *Die israelitischen Personennamen* (1928), p. 246.

IMRI ĭm′rī [אמרי, *contraction of* אמריהו, Yahu has uttered, *or* Yahu has promised]. **1.** Ancestor of one of the returned exiles (I Chr. 9:4); possibly to be identified with the AMARIAH of the parallel Neh. 11:4.

2. The father of the Zaccur who helped repair the wall of Jerusalem in the time of Nehemiah (Neh. 3:2).

Bibliography. M. Noth, *Die israelitischen Personennamen* (1928), pp. 38, 173. B. T. DAHLBERG

INCANTATIONS. Ceremonial chants used by magicians to exorcise malevolent spirits and to heal the sick. The technique of the magicians engaged in this work consisted of two distinct parts: (*a*) the chanting of these incantations—i.e., the pronouncement of "words of power"; and (*b*) the performance of prescribed acts—i.e., the use of certain substances charged with supernatural potency.

The quality of the ingredients employed by the "physicians" varied in accordance with the nature of the sickness, but the spells, which constituted the most important element of the whole procedure, remained, to a degree, stereotyped in form. These were collected and classified by the conjuration priests into special "incantation series" for the ready use of the practitioners. The Babylonian incantation commonly consisted of three parts: (*a*) the invocation of the names of the great gods by the magician in whose behalf he acted; (*b*) the identification of the spirit (or sorcerer) which caused the sickness; and (*c*) the call on the demon to leave the body of the sufferer, which often ended with the words: "By heaven be ye exorcised! By earth be ye exorcised!"

We have no extant text of a Palestinian incantation from the biblical period. The OT terms חובר חברים (lit., "one who mutters sounds") and מלחש (lit., "one who whispers"; Ps. 58:5—H 58:6) probably refer to the art of chanting incantations (*see* ENCHANTER). Acts 19:13 reports that "itinerant Jewish exorcists [in Ephesus] undertook to pronounce the name of the Lord Jesus over those who had evil spirits." The invocation of the name of Jesus was part of an incantation formula used by these exorcists. That incantation manuals, similar to those in use in Egypt and Babylonia, were in circulation in Ephesus and could be obtained at a price seems to be clear from vs. 19, in which we are informed that "a number of those who practiced magic arts brought their books together and burned them in the sight of all; and they counted the value of them and found it came to fifty thousand pieces of silver." *See* EXORCISM. I. MENDELSOHN

INCARNATION ĭn′kär nā′shən [Lat. *incarnatio*, being or taking flesh]. God's becoming man; more particularly, in Christian usage, the revelation of God in the human life of Jesus of Nazareth. The Christian use of the term was derived from the Latin version of John 1:14, and is frequent in Latin Christian authors from the fourth century onward.

1. Fundamental significance. ***a. Generally.*** Incarnation signifies the assumption by a divine being of human or animal form. More is meant than simply divine influence, however continuous, as, e.g., in the case of the prophets of Israel or the imams (divinely appointed leaders) of Mohammedanism. The elevation of a human being to divine honors—properly speaking, apotheosis—is also to be distinguished from incarnation. The idea of incarnation is found in various religions, but its most serious expression is its use in Christian theology with reference to Christ.

In Hinduism, Rama, the hero of the epic *Ramayana*, was regarded as divine, and, probably later, as an incarnation of the god Vishnu. Buddhism can think of the Buddha as an incarnation of Vishnu. In ancient Egyptian religion the deities could be thought of as incarnate in men or animals; and dead men could become incarnate again (this borders on the belief in metempsychosis or the transmigration of souls). More particularly, the king in Egypt was an incarnation of one of the gods. The theory was that his father in the act of begetting was really the god Ra, who had assumed the father's body. One sect of Muslims, the Shiites, believe that Allah became incarnate in the Prophet's son-in-law Ali.

The incarnations of subordinate deities are not very significant, nor are repeated incarnations of the same deity. More noteworthy is the conception of an incarnation of the one God, as in Hinduism. Distinctive of Christianity is the note of finality in the thought of Christ's incarnation. Incarnation cannot mean so much in Hinduism as in Christianity, because of the pantheistic presuppositions of Hinduism—viz., that the divine (Brahma) is not transcendent but all-pervasive; moreover, Hinduism attaches no significance to personality and individuality.

b. Christian. John 1:14 is the fundamental affirmation of Christianity. The fullest revelation of God was personal, in a particular life. For Jesus ben Joseph, carpenter of Nazareth, 6 B.C.-A.D. 30, was no mere Galilean, or Jew, a man of the first century A.D. He was the incarnation of God. In his actual, Jewish life the life and power of God were in action (John 10:30; 14:10). He was the revelation not only of human potentialities as carpenter, teacher, and prophet, but also of divine truth and power. Henceforward God was to be addressed, in the circle of his adherents, as the "Father of our Lord Jesus Christ." And this means much more than that Christ was an avatar, or temporary manifestation of deity—a conception congenial to other faiths. Nor was the theory known as adoptionism acceptable. According to this theory Jesus was adopted, or promoted, to divine status at a certain point in his earthly career, because of his resistance to temptation, his moral achievement, etc. Although some features of the most primitive preaching of the church lend plausibility to this theory, it was early defined as heresy—i.e., as not adequate to the true stature of Christ. He was divine throughout the whole period of his humanity. From the very beginning of his earthly existence he was God incarnate, although, by an ineluctable paradox in the Christian affirmation, his humanity was fully real.

In his flesh the Logos—i.e., mind—of God was expressed. He not merely conveys or mediates that mind, like the Hebrew prophets, but, so John assures us, he is to be identified with it, and his human life made God's mind personally present and real before men in an unprecedented manner. The opening verses of the Letter to the Hebrews make the same assertion.

The coming of Christ is explicable in terms of the Logos conception—i.e., roughly speaking, in terms of the best human thinking up to that date about God and his self-communication to the world. All that men had truly discerned about God is illuminated, and brought to a focus, in Christ. The eternal, cosmic, mediating principle between God and the world is no longer a philosophic term, but a human life. In the life of Jesus, as the Christian tradition bears witness to it, can be discerned the mode of operation of the universe. The meaning of the universe and the nature of God are related to the nature of Christ. For he is the Logos, the eternal Son of God, on whom the universe depends. *See* CHRIST.

The question may be raised, How much more is implied by incarnation than by REVELATION? Roughly speaking, the Logos doctrine explains revelation adequately enough. The Logos stands for God as revealed—i.e., not for his transcendent being or inner nature, but for that of God which can be projected into the world and become immanent. In the OT and Hellenistic Judaism this was expressed in terms of WISDOM. John goes further when he declares that the Logos became immanent in a human life. This is more than speaking of revelation at a point in history, or of a climax of revelation. Incarnation is the final form of revelation. The revelation vouchsafed in Christ so much surpasses other revelation as to make John assert that other revelations do not count (1:18; 10:8; 14:6). And in the earlier gospel tradition one finds Jesus saying that the mutual knowledge of Father and Son is now available to those "to whom the Son chooses to reveal him" (Matt. 11:27). The ultimate goal of knowing and being known by God (cf. I Cor. 13:12; Gal. 4:9; Col. 1:9-10) is brought within reach through Christ's ministry among men.

A doctrine of the Incarnation must take some account of the ATONEMENT, because the revelation Christ brought was not complete until his passion and resurrection. It is not only Christ's birth as a man, but also his whole life and achievement which give him supreme significance both as revealer of the divine concern for man and as solver of the human problem. He came into the world to deal with sin (Rom. 8:3), to make goodness possible, to bring men into a harmonious relationship with their Creator (Rom. 5–8), to impart that knowledge of God without which man cannot truly live (John 10:10; 20:31).

His achievement was not simply his, qua man; for God was operating in and through him. This is clear in the witness of the NT, and it is this twofold aspect of his person which the later doctrine of the two natures, the divine and the human, was formulated to conserve. The paradox of God incarnate, of Christ as God-Man, is typical of the whole operation of God as our redeemer. And it may be argued that apart from belief in the Incarnation we cannot ultimately believe in Christ as redeemer.

2. In the gospels. ***a. Mark.*** Mark's Gospel has no birth narrative or genealogy, but it gives prominence to Jesus' divine sonship. Jesus is acclaimed "my beloved Son" by a heavenly voice at his baptism and transfiguration (1:11; 9:7). The question whether these were private experiences of Jesus, or whether they represent a wider awareness of his function at that time, cannot be taken up here. The Baptism and the Transfiguration are cardinal moments in Jesus' ministry, however they are to be interpreted in detail. Of lesser importance, though noteworthy in Mark's narrative, is the recognition of Jesus' divine nature by demons (3:11; 5:7; etc.) and by the centurion at the Cross (15:39).

The christological parable generally referred to as that of the laborers in the vineyard (12:1-11) is primarily intended to illustrate, not Israel's recalcitrance, but the martyrdom of God's final messenger to them, who is no less than his Son. Two new points are made about Jesus' sonship: It is distinguished from the relationship of other servants of God to him—i.e., it is a unique relationship—and it is destined to lead to self-sacrifice in death. The parable is told, as it were, under the shadow of the cross, and in this we can be sure that we have Jesus' own conception of his destiny. For the uniqueness of his relationship to the Father we refer also to 13:32, and to the account of the agony in Gethsemane, where the retention of the Aramaic *Abba* (14:36)—an actual memory of Jesus at prayer, as overheard both at Gethsemane and elsewhere—expresses the relationship more intimately. This is accentuated by Matthew, who reiterates "My Father" (Matt. 26:39-44). This *Abba* is more significant than the *Abinu* (Our Father) of the Jewish Prayer Book, and also than the "Our Father" of the Lord's Prayer.

The historical accuracy of the accounts of Jesus' trial is more doubtful. In Mark 14:61-62 Jesus accepts the high priest's charge that he claimed to be the "Son of the Blessed" (i.e., God). This is intended as a synonym for "Messiah." In the Lukan account we note that the claim to messiahship and the claim to sonship are differentiated (Luke 22:67-70).

b. Matthew and Luke. Mark's statement of the basic Christology is taken up into the developed Christologies of Matthew and Luke. The distinctively Matthean and Lukan features, such as their stress on Jesus' kingship (Matthew) or on his humanity (Luke), are not so relevant to his incarnation and sonship. The theme of Jesus as the one who establishes the kingdom of God is also more emphasized in Matthew and Luke than in Mark. The KINGDOM OF GOD means the divine, redemptive activity in which Jesus was the central actor. But Jesus' relationship with God is not precisely defined in passages about the kingdom. As inaugurator of the kingdom he is differentiated from all other men, even from those who could justifiably be called heralds of the kingdom—e.g., the prophets of Israel, culminating in John the Baptist. As Messiah, Jesus himself is King of Israel, and this receives some prominence, especially in Matt. 2:1-11 (cf. Mark 15:1-32; John 18:33–19:22).

For our purpose the most significant additional materials furnished by Matthew and Luke are their accounts of the birth of Jesus and the notable Logion which they derive from the primitive sayings source Q (Matt. 11:25-27; Luke 10:21-22).

The birth narratives of Matthew's and Luke's gospels testify that, though the birth of Christ (and his consequent humanity) was real, his paternity was divine rather than human. In the intention of both evangelists, it is not so much the virginity of Mary as the activity of the Holy Spirit which is emphasized.

According to Luke (1:26-38), Mary's child was conceived without human sexual relationship, but through the activity of the divine grace (χάρις; vs. 30), spirit, and power (πνεῦμα and δύναμις; vs. 35). He was Son of God in a unique sense, and Messiah (1:32-33; 2:11). The Magnificat (Luke 1:46-55) interprets this as one of the saving acts of God for Israel; similarly the Benedictus (Luke 1:68-79; cf. 2:25-32, 38). Mary has the unique honor of being the instrument of this divine action, but no special glorification of her as the virgin mother is intended in the Lukan record (cf. 11:27-28).

Matthew, like Luke, connects the birth of Jesus with the action of the Holy Spirit (Matt. 1:20), and with messiahship (2:1-6). He mentions also the significance of the name Jesus (1:21; cf. Luke 1:31). Peculiar to Matthew is the reference to Isa. 7:14 (1:23), where the Hebrew does not imply virginity in the strict sense, and the main emphasis is on the birth of a child who shall bring the presence of God near to men. Matthew makes more than Luke does of the significance of the birth of Jesus for the Gentile world (cf. Matt. 2:1-11 with Luke 2:32*a*).

The absence of human paternity is just as much emphasized by Matthew (1:18-20) as by Luke. The fact of incarnation and this particular manner of its achievement appear to be inseparable in these two accounts. Modern criticism of the gospels is inclined to label them legendary, and to pronounce the virgin birth unhistorical and, in view of the silence of the other NT sources about it, not essential to Christian faith. It may be held, however, that acceptance of the fact of an unprecedented divine incursion into human conditions of life presupposes willingness to admit unprecedented circumstances in the *manner* of its inauguration. Moreover, two features in these accounts of the birth, in addition to the physical miracle, should be remembered: The Isaiah quotation in Matthew indicates that the birth of Christ, whether normal or miraculous as a biological event, was part of the eternal purpose of God. Secondly, both writers have something to say about the spiritual preparation of the parents (Matt. 1:20-21; Luke 1:26-38), without whose sensitiveness to divine action the physical event could not have happened in their home.

Certainly the reality of Christ's birth is affirmed in these birth narratives. He was truly born, and his body was not a mere semblance, as the heresy known as DOCETISM supposed (Col. 2:8-9; I John 4:1-3). This type of spiritualizing, which cannot take seriously the idea of incarnation, has its parallel in some forms of Buddhist thought which conceived of Buddha as having a purely spiritual body, and as having been born in a special manner, unsoiled by the impurities of conception, etc. *See also* VIRGIN BIRTH.

Matt. 11:25-27 (=Luke 10:21-22)—there can be no doubt about the genuineness of this saying—mirrors Jesus' own consciousness of dependence on God and of mission to make him known to men. The relationship of Father and Son is one of mutual intimacy and recognition. The Father is of such a character as to grant the revelation of himself to the humble upon earth, and of this revelation the Son is the sole mediator. His earthly existence is the outcome of that divine purpose (note the Johannine parallel, to be examined below, John 1:14, 18). The verb form "have been delivered" must signify the heavenly or pretemporal equipment of Jesus—i.e., the preparation for incarnation—rather than incarnation itself. On this divine authority, which Jesus possesses and which he can transmit to his own representatives when his earthly mission is terminated, we may compare Matt. 28:18. For the thought of his actual mission to the world, which is not explicitly referred to in Matt. 11:27, we may note Luke 4:43, where the words "I was sent for this purpose" —viz., to preach the good news of God's kingdom—are made to refer to his incarnation—a subtle alteration of Mark 1:38*c*.

Matt. 11:25-27 undoubtedly portrays Jesus' self-consciousness. It is perverse to make this saying refer to a sonship Jesus shares with all who have knowledge of God. In this passage, as in Mark 12:1-11, Jesus' own conviction and insight are preserved. Similarly, on the peculiar intimacy with which Jesus felt himself to be in relation to God, we may rely on Matt. 10:32-33; 15:13; 16:17; 18:10-14, 35 (mostly peculiar to Matthew), and four passages peculiar to Luke: 22:29; 23:34, 46; 24:49.

The unique sonship of Jesus stands out in contrast with a general sonship which is predicated of all who believe in God and accept him as Father—e.g., Luke 6:35-36 (cf. Matt. 5:48); 12:30-32; 15:11-32; 16:24; Matt. 5:9, 16; 6:9; 21:28-31; 23:9; 25:34. From Luke 8:19-21 (=Mark 3:31-35); 11:27-28, we may infer that Jesus dissuaded people from special veneration for himself or his mother. For him the question of personal dignity or birth is never so important as doing the will of God. What matters above all is the relation with God created by obedience. Even incarnation is not an honor for which he is willing to be congratulated.

c. John. In John's Gospel the Incarnation has special prominence. Whereas in the Synoptics Jesus' divine sonship, though its uniqueness is affirmed, is synonymous with messiahship, in the Fourth Gospel its eternal aspect is much more emphasized, and the sonship and messiahship of Jesus are considered, not simply in terms of his ministry in Palestine at a particular period of time (though the reality of Jesus' human life, and the whole setting in history, are definitely presupposed by John), but in their relationship to the eternal being of God, ontologically rather than historically.

This is most evident in the opening section of the gospel (1:1-18). John does not commence, as Mark does, with the baptism of Jesus; nor even, as do Matthew and Luke, with his birth and its immediate antecedents. John opens his gospel concerning Jesus of Nazareth with a reference to creation, and before creation to the timeless existence of God: the very opening words, "In the beginning," are identical with the opening words of the OT and were intended to recall the creation narrative of Gen. 1 and the creative Word upon which everything depends. The ministry of Jesus, according to John, is part of the self-communication of God to man, and is grounded in the mystery of the nature of the eternal God. For what was manifested in the activity of Jesus was nothing less than the Word—i.e., that in God which mediates between God and the world. The term "Word" had enjoyed considerable currency in religion and philosophy before John wrote his gospel. In Greek (Logos, λόγος) it signifies both reason and spoken word—i.e., inner thought and outward expression. (*See* WORD; MEDIATION § C8*b*.) John chose the term and applied it to Jesus because his earthly life and ministry were actually the revealing of the divine purpose to men, and needed to be understood, not as mere historical event, but as carrying that divine significance. In and through him God was imparting himself. His words were "spirit and life" (6:63; cf. 4:24, "God is spirit"). His acts were "signs" —i.e., of the presence and power of God (2:11, etc.).

In conceiving that the work of Jesus could be described as the operation of the Logos, John has to state emphatically—here going beyond all previous teachers, whether Jewish or non-Jewish—that the Logos actually entered the human sphere in the sense of *becoming* a human being: the Word became flesh (1:14). The choice of the word "flesh" rather than simply "man" is deliberate; it signifies humanity in its physical aspect, where its affinity with animals and its differentiation from God is most patent. The precise meaning of the verb "became" is difficult to determine, and perhaps it is unwise to attempt to define it too precisely. After all, it is a statement of the central paradox of the Christian faith. As distinguished from the verb "to be," which is used in vs. 1, it signifies coming into existence, as in vs. 3 ("were made") and vs. 10 ("was made") and vs. 17 ("came"). Thus the fleshly existence of the Word began with the human life of Jesus of Nazareth. On the other hand, something less than the full identification of the eternal Word with flesh is intended; for the Word is still the subject, imparting through the "flesh" grace and truth and glory; moreover, at this point it passes over into the term "Son," whose continued existence "in the Father" as well as in the earthly life of Jesus is maintained throughout the gospel. The more specific word for generation, which is used in vs. 13, is avoided in vs. 14. But it cannot be expected that a single verb should fix finally the sense in which the divine was really present among men in a human body. The divine Logos entered, not merely the mind, but the body (flesh) of a particular man.

The eternal thus entering history, and being, as it were, concentrated in a single human life, poses an insuperable philosophical problem, admittedly. This aspect of the Incarnation has been called, in G. Kittel's memorable phrase, the "scandal of particularity." But John felt that nothing short of this must be affirmed if the significance of the historic life of Jesus, as Christian experience had come to evaluate it, was to be brought out as a manifestation of ultimate reality. Having pondered this and having decided to express this in terms of the Logos, John felt that he must break the bounds of the Logos doctrine as previously understood and develop his argument to the culminating assertion that the Logos became flesh.

We note that in this gospel this "becoming" is the focal point, as it were, the decisive event for human salvation; this, rather than the successive experiences and achievements of the earthly ministry of Jesus, culminating in the Cross and the Resurrection. In other words, the Fourth Gospel is the fountainhead of the type of Christian theology which is called incarnational.

This difference of emphasis, as compared with other NT writings, must not be treated as an outright contrast. The necessity of Christ's passion, and his significance as the Lamb of God who takes away the world's sin (1:29; I John 3:5; 4:10) are also emphasized in this gospel. Moreover, the effect of the Incarnation is declared to be enlightenment (1:5, 9); regeneration (1:12-13); true, eternal life (3:15-17; 5:26; 17:2-3; 20:31; I John 4:9).

Nevertheless, this focusing on revelation rather than on atonement, and on the divine initiative in entering upon the human stage rather than on Christ's dealing with the human problem, by his teaching, healing, sacrificial death, etc., is new and significant. There is a notable, small group of passages in which Christ is described as the Son of man, who came down from heaven (3:13-15; 6:33-39, 62; 8:14*b;* 12:32-34; 13:3). Probably the Gnostic myth of the Redeemer who descends from the heavenly to the terrestrial sphere, and whose ascent again makes possible liberation for men, has exerted some influence on John in these passages; the significant difference, however, is that for Jesus the ascent was possible only after his meeting the opposition of men and the power of darkness, and after a lifting up on the cross (12:32, and the whole context vss. 31-39); exaltation in glory had to be preceded by exaltation in suffering and death. The descent of Christ for this earthly ministry is never called his taking flesh, as in 1:14. But it makes the entry into the earthly sphere the decisive factor for human salvation, and tends to place the emphasis on the commencement of the Redeemer's career rather than on its culmination in sacrificial suffering. In the Johannine conception incarnation involves atonement, not atonement, incarnation.

In 1:14 the Incarnation means revelation of the divine glory and dwelling (lit., "tabernacling") among men. The implied reference to Exod. 29:42-43; 33:7-9, suggests that the coming of Jesus is God's presence upon earth. No tabernacle is now necessary, no Jerusalem temple either (4:21-24); God can be known and worshiped in and through Christ. *See also* GLORY; TABERNACLE.

The opposition of human society to him who came as the revelation of God is frankly recorded in this gospel, often in terms of the antithesis of light and darkness (1:4-5, 9-11; 3:19-21; 6:60-71; 8:37-59; 12:37-43; 15:18-23; 17:14). The presence of the Revealer forces men into the valley of decision, and they must either respond with faith or remain in darkness.

After the announcement of the Incarnation at 1:14 the term "Logos" is laid aside, and throughout the rest of the gospel Christ is referred to, and refers to himself, mainly as the Son of God. ("Son of man" also is a frequent title, but it does not predominate.) For the full understanding of what incarnation means, therefore, the implications of divine sonship must be drawn out. 3:16-18 grounds the mission of the Son in the divine love for the world. This is a change from the more metaphysical vocabulary of Logos and revelation to the ethical term which John shares with other NT writers, and which is a characteristic Christian term deriving from the Master himself. It is here used for the motive of divine self-revelation and incarnation, and thus we learn that the significance of love in human relationships is to be seen in the self-giving of God himself. The divine self-giving which prompted the incarnation, and was complemented by Christ's self-sacrifice, is the heart of the gospel and the sole hope of man. We hear elsewhere in John's Gospel of the Father's love for the Son (3:35; 10:17; 15:9-10; 17:23-26) and of the Son's love for the Father (14:31; 15:10), as well as of the Son's love for his own (13:1, 34; 14:21; 15:9-13). John has, in fact, used the idea of love to interpret the nature of God, the process of revelation and redemption, and moral relationships within the redeemed community, the church. For this we may refer to the First Letter (I John 3:11-24; 4:7–5:5).

On the equality of the Son with the Father see 5:18-23; 10:29-30, 37-38; 14:8-11. His pre-existence is of course implied (cf. 5:17; 8:57-58). On the mission of the Son see 4:34; 5:37; 6:38-39; 9:33; 12:44-46. The incarnate Christ is represented as saying: "I am in the Father and the Father in me" (14:10; cf. I John 2:23). This is his sole claim to authority in the church or to significance for humanity, and the doctrine of the Incarnation safeguards this. It is difficult to reconcile this with doctrines of his self-emptying (Kenosis) derived from Phil. 2:6-8. *See also* SON OF GOD.

3. In Acts and the letters. ***a. Acts.*** The Christology of Acts might be described as adoptionist rather than incarnational. Christ appears as a "man attested to you . . . with mighty works" (2:22); as God's servant, the "Holy and Righteous One" (3:13-14; also 4:27; cf. 8:32-34); as the prophet whom God had promised to raise up (3:22); as one "anointed . . . with the Holy Spirit and with power" (10:38). All this adds up to Messiah (9:22; 17:3; 18:5, 28) and final judge of mankind (10:42; 17:31). As Messiah he can also be called Son of God (9:20), but this seems to contain no suggestion about his divine origin.

> Thou art my Son,
> today I have begotten thee,

taken from Ps. 2:7, is applied to him in one passage (13:33), but the thought is not of his birth but of his resurrection, and of the fulfilment of God's purpose through him, a greater boon even than the Mosaic law (vs. 39).

Christ's lordship is asserted (2:36), especially in the Pauline speeches (16:31; 20:24, 35; 22:8-10; 23:11; 26:15).

b. I-II Peter. I Peter is more concerned with the passion of Christ and his coming again (his apocalypse, 1:13; or manifestation, 5:4) than with his first coming. But in 1:20 that first coming is referred to as a realization in time of a divine decision before the beginning of time (cf. II Tim. 1:9-10). This realization in time is the prelude to the end of time—a conviction shared by most of the early Christians and rooted in the primitive proclamation (Acts 2:16-17; Heb. 1:1-2). The imminence of the end makes the second manifesting of Christ more prominent in the thought of I Peter than the first (the same verb, φανερόω, is used in both 1:20 and 5:4. Similarly in the Johannine writings it means both Incarnation [I John 1:2; 3:5, 8] and Second Coming [I John 2:28; 3:2]).

II Peter asserts the reality or historicity of Christ's earthly career; it was no myth (1:16). The same noun is used here for Christ's first coming as is used in 3:4 for his final coming (παρουσία, a parallel to the double sense of "manifest" in I Peter).

c. Paul. For Paul's understanding of the Incarnation, as in the case of other authors, all statements about Christ's divine sonship are in a general way relevant. But three passages stand out as of major relevance:

a) Gal. 4:4-5: In the divine control of history, which is the background of the argument of chs. 3–4 in this letter, the period before Christ was, for the Jews in particular, and by implication for mankind generally, "under the law"—i.e., a period when men were subject to the guidance of the Mosaic law or other moral codes. This, as Paul sees it, was a kind of slavery, from which men needed to be liberated. True righteousness of life was not attainable under these conditions (3:11, 21*b*). But this was in the divine plan merely a preparatory dispensation (3:24: "The law was our custodian until Christ came"). God's intention was that goodness should be achieved (3:24*b:* "that we might be justified by faith") and the ideal society realized (3:26-29); and the coming of Christ was the means of this achievement. That is the point of "when the time had fully come" (4:4). The object was the desired liberation (4:5; 5:1), by which the former slaves became freemen, in fact attained the status of divine sonship, the highest expectation of old Israel, and a sharing in the privileged status of Christ himself (4:5-7; 3:26). Christ came as the emissary from the Creator, in fact his Son, and as a power superior to all authorities which tyrannized over mankind (cf. 4:8-9).

In conferring freedom he had to submit to human conditions both of heredity, "born of woman," and of social and physical environment, "born under the law" (4:4*b*). The implication of "born of woman" is the reality of his human birth; it was not an appearance only, nor a legend. Nothing is implied here about the virginity of his mother. The miracle resides, not in the physical conditions, but in the divine overruling and purpose suggested by "when the time had fully come, God sent forth his Son." Paul's other two references to Christ's birth simply record that he was by physical descent a Jew (Rom. 1:3; 9:5). Galatians is not more explicit as to how Christ's coming secured these benefits, but we may refer to Rom. 8:3-4, where the purpose of the Incarnation is given as "for sin"—i.e., to deal with the problem created by man's sin. Man, left to his own resources ("the flesh"), even with the guidance of a moral code (the law), could not achieve the good life (fulfil the "just requirement of the law"). This need has been met by Christ's coming into human life ("in the likeness of sinful flesh"). Somehow—again no full explication is offered—he has removed the limiting factor ("condemned sin") and liberated mankind (vs. 2) and provided new moral resources (the Spirit; vss. 2, 5-11).

Christ so confronts men with the righteousness of God that it becomes available for them, and the human problem is transformed (I Cor. 1:24, 30; II Cor. 5:21; Phil. 3:9). There is no specific reference to incarnation in these passages. We may speak of a divine indwelling in Christ (II Cor. 5:19). Whatever metaphor may be used for the mode of God's control of Christ, it is definite that he is God's representative, through whom the divine plan for human redemption is made operative.

b) Phil. 2:6-8: The second main passage refers to the birth and death of Christ, the beginning and end of his earthly life, as his humiliation and self-emptying. His pre-existence is assumed, and is somewhat loosely described as existence "in the form of God." Equality with God was his by right, not a status to be laboriously acquired. Becoming a man meant renouncing that heavenly status, and by comparison humanity was utter slavery (7*b*). But he was prepared for this sacrifice and extended it to the point of dying a slave's death (8*b*). Paul makes no use of the idea of sonship here. Incarnation meant a temporary laying aside of divinity, and its outcome was the attainment of lordship (9-11); inescapably involved in it was "death on a cross." Neither here nor in Rom. 8:3 does "likeness" (7*b*) imply any lack of the full reality of manhood. Paul cannot be charged with Docetism, the view that Christ's body was not real (referred to in I John 4:2; II John 7). The metaphor of emptying which is used here has a good parallel in II Cor. 8:9, where Christ's earthly ministry is thought of as voluntary self-impoverishment. In both passages the paradox of the Incarnation is stressed. It was alien to Jewish messianic expectations. Some scholars admit Hellenistic influence here —e.g., the idea of a Redeemer who comes down from heaven, makes contact with human beings imprisoned on earth, awakes their latent divinity, and liberates them to return with him to the heavenly sphere. We have already noted the possible influence of this conception on the Johannine Son of man. The theory of some that Phil. 2:5-11 is a pre-Pauline hymn does not affect our interpretation. (Similar views are held by some about Col. 1:15-20.) There is certainly a poetic or liturgical quality in the language, which should warn us against imposing a too-precise theological meaning on such words as "form," "emptied."

Paul would agree that in assuming human nature Christ did not assume liability to sin (cf. II Cor. 5:21). In the language of later theology, Christ took upon him perfect, not fallen, manhood. For definite assertion of his sinlessness cf. Heb. 4:15.

In two important passages (Rom. 5:12-21; I Cor. 15:45-47) Christ is spoken of as second Adam, as realizing the ideal which the first Adam—i.e., mankind as a whole—failed to attain. This means that Christ opened a new possibility for human life. His own achievement is made available to those who attach themselves to him, by faith, in the church. To quote the language of later theologians again, "He became what we are that we might become what he is."

c) Col. 1:15-20: This passage does not explicitly mention the coming of Christ, but gives us Paul's maturest thought about his pre-existence and divine status. Jewish conceptions of WISDOM undoubtedly contributed to Paul's Christology here.

Christ is God's likeness or image (vs. 15, also II Cor. 4:4). The term was used of the Logos (in Philo) and Wisdom (Wisd. Sol. 7:26), as well as of man in the creation narrative (Gen. 1:26). This divine intention, which actual man never realized, is realized in Christ, who does show forth the invisible God to the world of men. There must be reference in this to Christ's earthly life, although the passage continues with reference to his pre-existence before creation and his activity as agent of creation (vss. 15*b*-16). The universe was created by his agency—here the thought is precisely that of the conception of wisdom in Prov. 8; Wisd. Sol. 7—and to serve his ends ("through him and for him")—that is an extra touch of Paul's: Christ is the Lord who will also preside over a final consummation (cf. Eph. 1:10; 4:13-15). Christ is the principle of cohesion or stability in the universe (vs. 17). His headship in the universe and of mankind generally is paralleled by his headship in the redeemed society, the church, though this was established by his resurrection—viz., at the conclusion of his ministry as a man (vs. 18).

His work can be described as reconciliation in the whole universe (vs. 20)—i.e., the removal of hindrances and the production of harmony, not among men only but also among heavenly beings. For this Christ has unlimited divine support and accreditation: "In him all the fulness of God was pleased to dwell" (vs. 19). Is this a reference to the Incarnation, or to Christ's pre-incarnation status? Probably the former, since vs. 20 definitely means his ministry on earth, including his passion (cf. "bodily," 2:9; *see* PLEROMA).

Christ's presence in the world and in the church is the divulging of the "mystery" of God's purpose which had previously been hidden (Col. 1:26-27; 2:2-3; I Cor. 2:7).

d. The Pastoral letters. The Pastorals offer isolated references to Christ's incarnation. The writer has greater aptitude for an impressive phrase than for sustained theological argument. "Christ Jesus came into the world to save sinners" (I Tim. 1:15); the thought moves quickly from incarnation to atonement, which was its main purpose, as in Tit. 2:11; 3:4-5. He was "manifested in the flesh" (I Tim. 3:16). This reads like a quotation from a rudimentary creed. We have the verb "manifest" again in II Tim. 1:10, together with a cognate noun for the Incarnation, whereas the cognate noun signifies the final coming in I Tim. 6:14; II Tim. 4:1, 8; Tit. 2:13.

In II Tim. 1:10 again incarnation is the prelude to Christ's work of abolishing death and conferring the new light of true life and immortality.

In two memorable phrases (Tit. 2:11; 3:4) the "appearing" of Christ is due to the grace or goodness or loving kindness of God which has in view the salvation of all mankind.

e. Hebrews. In this letter the Incarnation is not stressed in and for itself, but as the prelude to Christ's dealing with sin, the basis of mankind's greatest need. This required the blood of self-sacrifice (9:22), and so, the author might argue, the sacrificial death which Christ actually offered presupposed his human birth.

In contrast with the prophets who brought earlier revelation, Christ is God's son (1:2), his first-born (1:6; cf. Col. 1:15-18). All the dignity and intimate relationship to God which this implies is emphatically, though very succinctly, stated in 1:2-4. Adequate exposition is impossible here. The language is influenced by descriptions of Wisdom, and there are parallels in John 1:1-5; II Cor. 4:4; Col. 1:15. Christ is pre-existent, the agent of creation and maintenance of the world, and of the redemption of man ("purification for sins," 1:3*b*, as also 5:9: "source of eternal salvation"; cf. 9:12).

His actual birth is not mentioned, either in the manner of Matt. 1–2; Luke 1–2; or in that of John 1:14. But his superiority, not of degree but of nature, not only to prophets but also to angels, is brought out (1:5–2:8), and to Moses (3:1-6), Joshua (4:1-8), and the Jewish high priest (5–10). His life on earth meant identification with mankind (2:9-18). Christ "partook of the same nature" (vs. 14) as the "descendants of Abraham"—i.e., he was born a Jew. This self-subjection involved death and the conquest of the devil (vs. 14*b*), a hard discipline (5:8) accepted in response to God's call (5:4-5; 10:5-9). The reality of his temptation is stressed (2:18; 4:15), but also his sinlessness (4:15; 7:26; cf. 2:10; 5:9). His sinlessness is generally implied rather than asserted in the NT, but cf. John 7:18; 8:46; II Cor. 5:21; I Pet. 2:22.

Though Hebrews is explicit on Christ's personal perfection, it is mainly concerned with the efficacy of his ministry: this also was perfect (argued in somewhat Platonic terms, 8:1-7) in relation to past, present, and future (8:13; 7:25; 13:8). According to this line of thought the Incarnation was simply the commencement of this fully efficacious ministry by which sin and death, and the Devil who was held to cause them, were overcome. The once-for-all-ness of this achievement is underlined (7:28; 9:26). It was final and unrepeatable. Christ's life was eternal in quality, in that Johannine sense which includes moral perfection and divinity as well as timelessness (7:15-28). The purpose of his incarnation was not simply to live, or teach, or leave an example; but to effect atonement—i.e., to liberate man from all that prevents his obeying the will of God.

4. In the OT. The transcendence and holiness of God is axiomatic in the thought of the OT, and therefore incarnation cannot so easily be accommodated as it would be in a more immanental conception. Nevertheless, as partial anticipations of the NT doctrine the following points should be noted:

a) God is close to men, controlling human action (e.g., Gen. 41:32).

b) Man has a certain affinity with God (Gen. 1:26).

c) God bestows his spirit upon those who have special tasks to perform, ministering to his purpose (*see* SPIRIT). Most significant here are prophets, high priest, and Messiah; also the king, whose precise relationship to God is the subject of current debate. *See* MEDIATION § C6; SERVANT OF LORD.

d) Isa. 7:14 is not a reference to incarnation in the NT sense; but it does imply that in some human lives God's presence is particularly known. The idea of a mother's being "pregnant by no mortal" (as Philo says of Moses' wife Zipporah) is later.

e) There is important teaching about divine self-manifestation—e.g., by angel, word, wisdom. *See* MEDIATION § C8*a*.

f) Pre-existence implies, to the Hebrew mind, nothing ontological about the being in question, but simply that his function is according to the purpose of God. It was held by some rabbis that not only Messiah, but also the Law and the temple were created before the world. This is not pre-existence in the metaphysical or Platonic sense, nor as implied in John 1; Col. 1. Neither OT nor later Judaism seems to hold that the Messiah really existed before his actual appearance; all passages that can be appealed to as evidence of such a belief (Ps. 72:5; 110:3; I Enoch 48:3, 6; Asmp. Moses 1:14) are to be understood otherwise.

To accept the Johannine identification of the Messiah, insofar as represented in Jesus, with the Logos, and the affirmation of the incarnation of the Logos, is to break the bounds both of pre-existence and of messiahship as previously understood. The Incarnation had no real precedent. The impact of Christ was like new wine potent to burst old bottles. On this whole subject, *see also* CHRIST.

Bibliography. Biblical material: A. E. J. Rawlinson, *The NT Doctrine of the Christ* (1926); Strack-Billerbeck, *Kommentar zum NT*, II (1928), 333-52; W. D. Davies, *Paul and Rabbinic Judaism* (1948); C. H. Dodd, *The Interpretation of the Fourth Gospel* (1953); G. V. Jones, *Christology and Myth in the NT* (1956).

On Christology in general: L. S. Thornton, *The Incarnate Lord* (1928); K. Barth, *Dogmatik*, I.2 (1938), 134-221; J. M. Creed, *The Divinity of Jesus Christ* (1938); D. M. Baillie, *God Was in Christ* (1948); A. R. Vine, *An Approach to Christology* (1948).

E. C. BLACKMAN

INCENSE [קטרת, smoke, odor of (burning) sacrifice; θυμίαμα (KJV *alternately* ODORS); KJV לבונה (RSV *usually* FRANKINCENSE; *alternately* INCENSE (I Chr. 9:29; Jer. 41:5); SMOKE (Ps. 66:15), *see below*]. A compound of gums and spices intended to be burned; the perfume arising from these substances when burned.

"Incense" is the KJV translation of two Hebrew words, קטרת and לבונה (Isa. 43:23; 60:6; 66:3; Jer. 6:20; 17:26; 41:5), which were at an early time quite distinct in meaning in Israel. Later the second word (lit., "frankincense") came to be practically synonymous with the first. The distinction between these two words is usually maintained in the RSV.

The term קטרת was first used with reference to the smoke of the sacrificial victims (Deut. 33:10; Ps. 66: 15; Isa. 1:13), and the *Pi'el* form of the verb means "cause to smoke" upon the altar (I Sam. 2:15-16; Jer. 19:13; 44:21, 23; Hos. 4:13; 11:2; Hab. 1:16). Subsequently the term was used with reference to the smoke of frankincense and other aromatics, of the incense offering (Exod. 30:8), and of the material burned in the offering (Lev. 10:1; Ezek. 8:11). The meaning "incense" probably belongs clearly to the term for the first time in Ezek. 8:11; 16:18; 23:41. This connotation, which refers specifically to the material burned in the offering, is used frequently in P.

Incense compounded according to a specified formula (Exod. 30:34-38) was used extensively in the ritual of the temple (Exod. 25:6; 35:8, 28; 37:29; etc.). This pure incense was compounded of equal parts of stacte, onycha, galbanum, and frankincense, plus a seasoning of salt. In Herodian times, according to Josephus, there were thirteen ingredients in the pure incense (War V.v.5). Pure incense, which could not be made or used for secular purposes (Exod. 30: 37-38; Lev. 10:1-11), was burned on the altar of incense (Exod. 30:1 ff; 40:5; Lev. 4:7; I Chr. 28:18), which was in the temple just before the veil of the holy of holies. This altar was a replica in miniature of the altar of burnt offering (Exod. 30:1-10); it was flanked on the S by the seven-branched lampstand and on the N by the table of the bread of the Presence. Incense was burned on this altar by the high priest each morning and evening (Exod. 30:1 ff; cf. Luke 1:8-11). Once a year, on the DAY OF ATONEMENT, the high priest was directed to carry a censer of burning incense when he entered the holy of holies and approached the mercy seat (Lev. 16:12-13).

Virtually all Pentateuchal references to the offering of incense occur in the Priestly Code; this fact led Wellhausen and Kuenen to the conclusion that the offering of incense was a late refinement of the cultus and perhaps a result of the influence of heathen religious rites (II Chr. 34:25; Jer. 11:12-17; 48:35). It is, of course, noteworthy that the eighth-century prophets made no allusion to such a feature in the cultus. Nevertheless, there is no conclusive proof that the offering of incense was unknown in Israel before the seventh century. Israelitic religious tradition regarded the offering as an ancient one and as a local parallel to a practice which was widely known among the worshipers of false divinities (II Chr. 34:25; Jer. 48:35; cf. Lev. 26:30; II Chr. 14:5; 34:4, 7; Isa. 17: 8; 27:9; Ezek. 6:4, 6).

The offering of incense came to bear several significations in the Israelitic tradition. Purificatory powers were attributed to the burning of incense in time of plague (Numbers), and probably the burning of incense was thought to have a sanitary influence in places of slaughter and sacrifice. Incense was regarded as a costly offering (Song of S. 3:6; 4:6, 14; cf. Isa. 60:6; Matt. 2:11; Rev. 18:13), and therefore a suitable one for princes and leaders (Num. 7:14, 20; incense may also have been of some peculiar significance in the rites of consecration). The Israelite, like many another ancient, assumed that the deity, like his people, would enjoy the fragrance of burning incense; he therefore offered it to the deity whom he wished to honor, as also to heads of state and honored guests (I Kings 11:8; II Kings 22:17; 23:5; Jer. 1:16; 7:9; 11:13; 19:13; 32:29; 44:17 ff; Ezek. 6:13; 23:41; Dan. 2:46). According to Deut. 33:10, these offerings of incense were well received by the God of Israel; it was therefore assumed that they were effective in making atonement before him (Lev. 16, especially vss. 12-13; Num. 16:46-48). It is perhaps in light of this belief that in both the OT and the NT an interesting parallel relationship between the offering of incense and of prayer is suggested (Ps. 141:2; Rev. 5:8; 8:3-4; cf. Luke 1:10). The fragrance of the incense was symbolic of the prayers of the faithful.

The offering of incense is treated as a very sacred rite wherever mentioned in the OT. Technically the prerogative of making the offering belonged to the high priest, and unqualified persons who presumed to make it were sometimes struck dead (Num. 16; cf. the Chronicler's account of Uzziah's leprosy in II Chr. 26:16-21). Aaron's sons were smitten because they offered the incense improperly (Lev. 10:1-2). Both John Hyrcanus (Jos. Antiq. XIII.x.3), and Zechariah (Luke 1:8-23) received divine revelations while offering incense. This last passage indicates that the offering of incense was no longer the prerogative of the high priest in Herodian times.

See also INCENSE, ALTAR OF; SACRIFICE AND OFFERINGS; WORSHIP IN THE OT. H. F. BECK

INCENSE, DISH FOR [כף, palm of the hand]; KJV SPOON. A type of shallow golden bowl used as a CENSER.

Lists of the furnishings of both the TABERNACLE (Num. 7:14, 20; etc.) and the TEMPLE (I Kings 7:50) include a number of these incense vessels, made of pure gold. In the tabernacle they are associated with the table for the BREAD OF THE PRESENCE. There were twelve such vessels, each weighing ten shekels of gold by the temple standard (Num. 7:84-86). They are mentioned again in the account of the building of Solomon's temple (I Kings 7:50=II Chr. 4:22), and of its repair under Joash (II Chr. 24:14), and they were among the plunder taken by the Babylonians in 586 B.C. (II Kings 25:14=Jer. 52:18-19).

The function of these vessels indicates that they were shallow bowls, and the Babylonian cognate of their Hebrew name has this sense, but the literal meaning of the Hebrew "palm of the hand," suggests that they may be related to a class of shallow stone bowls found at several sites in Palestine and Syria, including Tell Beit Mirsim and Megiddo. These have hollow handles into which a wooden pipe was probably attached so that the incense in the bowl could be kept burning by blowing through it. They are often carved with lions' heads and other cultic symbols, and a number of them have a hand carved in relief on the bottom, so that the interior of the bowl was almost literally the palm of the hand.

Bibliography. W. F. Albright, "The Fourth Joint Campaign of Excavation at Tell Beit Mirsim," *BASOR,* 47 (1932), 15; G. E. Wright, "Solomon's Temple Reconstructed," *BA,* vol. IV (1941).

L. E. Toombs

INCENSE ALTAR [מזבח קטרת]. This term, which refers (Exod. 30:27) to the altar of incense of the wilderness sanctuary, may also be applied to the "golden altar" of the temple of Solomon (I Kings 7:48; missing in 6:20), as Isa. 6:6 suggests. That the offering of incense was not introduced in Israel until the sixth century B.C. is surely not correct, even if it did not find more general usage, particularly in "family worship," until more recent times (cf. I Sam. 2:28; Isa. 43:23; Jer. 6:20). According to Exod. 30:1 ff, the incense altar, which was intended to be portable, consisted of a gold-overlaid table with horns, measuring one cubit by one cubit by two cubits. In the equipment of the interior of the new temple in Ezek. 41:1 ff the incense altar is missing; but this description, from a secondary source, is fragmentary. Perhaps the incense altar was considered pagan by the author (see Ezek. 8:11). I Macc. 1:21; 4:49 give an account of an incense altar in legitimate worship, whereas Josephus does not—which is probably accidental. Offerings of incense were also presented in the Jewish colony at Elephantine (cf. *ANET* 492).

The term חמן (*ḥammân*), attested among the Nabateans and the Palmyreans, designates a (small) incense altar, just as in the OT; it is not, as has been suggested, "sun statues" or, with the KJV, "images," which are meant by the plural of the term in the OT

Courtesy of the Oriental Institute, the University of Chicago

4. Pottery incense stand, from Megiddo, Stratum VI (*ca.* 1150-1100 B.C.)

Courtesy of the Oriental Institute, the University of Chicago

5. Limestone horned incense altar from Megiddo (*ca.* tenth century B.C.)

(חמנים; Lev. 26:30; II Chr. 14:5; 34:7; Isa. 17:8; Ezek. 6:4, 6), but rather with the RSV, "(incense) altars." They are regarded as pagan and are condemned.

If we disregard the clay incense holders which can be traced in Palestine up until the end of the second century (Figs. INC 4; LIL 29; ART 66), we can identify two types for the period between the tenth and the fifth century. One is a rectangular hewn block of stone—often provided with a decorative border—with a depression in the upper surface and (in most cases) horns on four corners; the smallest specimen is from the eleventh to the tenth century, from Tell Beit Mirsim; other examples are known from Megiddo (Figs. INC 5; MEG 32), Shechem (E. Sellin, "Die Ausgrabung von Sichem," *ZDPV,* 49 [1926], 232-33), and Gezer (*AOB* 444). As the exceptionally high—0.90 meter—altar of Shechem demonstrates (cf. *BRL* 19), there were incense altars with attached base or podium, and the smaller models were probably also placed on the large altars of burnt offerings or table altars (*Depositaltäre*) at times (cf. II Chr. 34:4). Fig. INC 6.

A second, more recent type, the חמנים, which probably comes from Arabia, is the cuboid incense altar, usually with four low feet. These have come to light in Gezer, Tell Jemmeh, Cyprus (cf. K. Galling, "Archäologischer Jahresbericht," *ZDPV,* 52 [1929], 247-48), S Arabia (Fig. INC 7), and also in Uruk, Babylon, and Asshur (L. Ziegler). These little limestone incense altars (sixth to fifth century) are especially numerous in Lachish (O. Tufnell *et al., Lachish III* [1953], plates 68-70); one of them has an Aramaic inscription beginning with the word "incense offering."

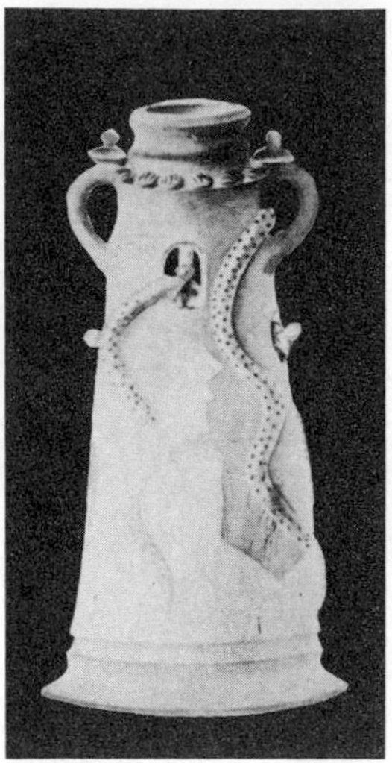

Courtesy of the University Museum of the University of Pennsylvania

6. Cylindrical incense stand from Beth-shan (*ca.* eleventh century B.C.)

Courtesy of the University Museum of the University of Pennsylvania

7. Limestone incense altar with S Arabic inscriptions on the sides (third to first century B.C.)

Bibliography. M. Löhr, *Das Räucheropfer im AT* (1927). H. G. May, *Material Remains of the Megiddo Cult* (1935). K. Elliger, "Chammanim-Masseben?" *ZAW,* 57 (1939), 236-65; "Der Sinn des Wortes chamman," *ZDPV,* 66 (1943), 129-39. H. Ingholt, "Le sens du mot Ḥamman," *Melanges syriens offerts à M. R. Dussaud,* II (1939/40), 795-802. L. Ziegler, "Tonkästen aus Uruk, Babylon und Assur," *ZA,* 13 (1948), 224-40. R. De Langhe, "L'autel d'or," *Anal. Bibl.,* X (1959), 342-60. M. Haran, "The Use of Incense," *VT,* X (1960), 113-29. K. GALLING

INCEST. The translation of תבל (KJV CONFUSION) in Lev. 20:12 (PERVERSION in Lev. 18:23; KJV CONFUSION). A number of examples of incest, or sexual intercourse between persons too closely related for normal marriage, may be observed in the Bible (Gen. 19:31-35; 20:2, 12; 35:22; 49:4; II Sam. 13:14; Ezek. 22:10-11; I Cor. 5:1). The writer of the book of Jubilees states that the sons of Adam married their sisters (Jub. 4). This allusion and the one concerning Lot and his daughters (Gen. 19:31-35) show that one alleged reason for incest was to populate the earth. Some of the illustrations exhibit the influence of sexual passion, whereas others were doubtless affected by the existence of subfamilies, children with the same mother, who were not intimately related to one another (e.g., Lev. 18:9: a daughter "born at home or born abroad"). Further, in a polygamous society a son, when he inherited his father's estate, may have inherited also his father's wives, except, of course, his own mother (II Sam. 3:6-11).

Sexual intercourse with the following classes of women was prohibited: "any one near of kin," the mother, any other wife of one's father, a sister, the daughter of a son or daughter, a father's wife's daughter, a father's sister, a mother's sister, an aunt, a daughter-in-law, a sister-in-law (Lev. 18:6-16), or one's mother-in-law (Deut. 27:23). The penalty for incest was childlessness (Lev. 20:21) or death (vss. 11-13)—by fire if a man took a wife and her mother also. Whoever committed various "abominations," including incest, was to be cut off from his people (18:29). With respect to the case of incest in the Corinthian church, Paul says: "Let him who has done this be removed from among you. . . . You are to deliver this man to Satan for the destruction of the flesh" (I Cor. 5:2, 5). The emphasis upon exogamous marriage, as well as opposition to incestuous practices by the idolatrous Canaanites (Lev. 20:23), serves to explain the biblical attitude on this matter. *See* MARRIAGE.

Bibliography. For the text of law codes on incest, see J. B. Pritchard, ed., *ANET* (2nd ed., 1955). O. J. BAAB

INDIA [הדו (Esth. 1:1; 8:9), *probably from* Old Pers. *hi*ⁿ*duš, from* Sanskrit *síndhu,* stream—*i.e.,* the Indus River]. A country in Asia S of the Himalaya Mountains, referred to twice in Esther as marking the E limits of Ahasuerus' (Xerxes') kingdom.

Persian inscriptions make it clear that India was a province of the Achaemenid Empire (559-330 B.C.), but they say nothing about its extent. In view of the limited data on India which Herodotus of the fifth century B.C. was able to glean (III.94-106; IV.40, 44), it is not surprising that the OT writers, living in their rather circumscribed world, should have known nothing about such a distant land. Some hearsay about it may have drifted into Palestine when the latter was part of Achaemenid Persia, but it was not until after the time of Alexander the Great (died 323 B.C.) that the Mediterranean world was properly informed about the Indus Valley and its peoples. This is the age to which Esther belongs, as does I Maccabees. The latter suggests that in the second century B.C. the Seleucids still used war elephants (possibly Indian) and Indian mahouts (I Macc. 6:37), though the statement in I Macc. 8:8 that Antiochus III (223-187 B.C.) had control of any part of India, if the text is sound, is incorrect.

Despite the growth of geographical knowledge in the Hellenistic and early Roman periods, and the considerable Roman trade with India, via Egypt and the Red Sea, the NT is just as ignorant of, or indifferent to, India as is the OT. W. S. MCCULLOUGH

INDIAN DRIVER [ὁ Ἰνδὸς αὐτοῦ] (I Macc. 6:37); KJV INDIAN. An elephant driver. Each war elephant of Antiochus V is said to have had its Indian driver. N. TURNER

INDICTMENT [ריב]. A formal charge or complaint in a court of justice. ריב is a technical legal term for "a case at law," "to conduct a legal suit," "to lay a case before one" (Job 31:35; Jer. 25:31; Hos. 12:2; cf. Isa. 3:13-15; Jer. 2:9; Hos. 4:1; Mic. 6:2). This term, in the sense of "indictment," is used exclusively of God, who brings a case against the wicked (the elders of Israel in Isa. 3:13-14; the nation in Jer. 2:9 [cf. Mic. 6:2]; the inhabitants of Israel in Hos. 4:1; Judah[?] and Jacob in Hos. 12:2; the nations in Jer. 25:31) for their moral and spiritual condition. Job, in maintaining his innocence, cries out for the indictment written by his adversary (Job 31:35). In Mic. 6:2 we have a picture of such a cosmically constituted court. The hills, mountains, and foundations of the earth are the jury; God is the prosecutor; and Israel is in the witness box. V. H. Kooy

INDIVIDUAL, INDIVIDUALISM. *See* MAN, NATURE OF.

INFANCY GOSPELS. Narratives purporting to tell of the birth of the Virgin and of the birth and childhood of Jesus. For further treatment and a list of those to which articles are devoted herein, *see* APOCRYPHA, NT.

INGATHERING, FEAST OF. *See* BOOTHS, FEAST OF.

INHERITANCE. One Hebrew term commonly translated "inheritance" has related meanings as well. The RSV sometimes uses the word "HERITAGE," especially when a spiritual sense is intended (*see below*). It parallels rather closely a Greek term in the NT, where it is adapted to a Christian frame of reference. Israel herself is called the inheritance of Yahweh, even as the "people," Mount Zion, and the temple are so designated. A special application of the term "inheritance" is made by the NT writers.

1. Relevant terms and concepts
2. Inheritance of a father's possessions
3. Legislation on inheritance
   a. Son of a slave girl
   b. Right of the first-born
   c. Rights of daughters
   d. The status of the widow
   e. Other categories
4. Canaan as Israel's inheritance
5. Israel as the inheritance of Yahweh
6. Inheritance in the NT

Bibliography

1. Relevant terms and concepts. Based on נחל, "give," "bestow," the idea of "inheritance" is indicated usually by נחלה. The related meanings "property," "possession," should also be noted. Associated with the word, especially in connection with the distribution of the land of Canaan to the various tribes, is the meaning of "portion (tract, territory)." The Greek has κληρονομία, a noun from a verb which means "to inherit." In the strict legal sense, both biblical words relate to the process of receiving possessions by descent or to that which is so received, as against that which is received—devised—by means of a will. A more general meaning is "to possess as having been handed down from the past," or, in the context of the Bible, as either having been handed down from the father or fathers or given by God. In many instances of biblical usage, the theological meaning of the word goes beyond the legalistic. Apart from any legal process, it may characterize the bestowal of a gift or possession upon his people by a merciful God, in fulfilment of a promise or as a reward for obedience. A Greek word, cognate to the one named above, κλῆρος signifies what is assigned by lot, or portion. The first meaning connotes the process of casting lots, but this meaning is lost, and a theological one takes its place. *See* §§ 4-5 *below*.

2. Inheritance of a father's possessions. Scattered indications of inheritance customs and practices are insufficient to provide a complete understanding of this subject, but they do furnish useful clues. The right of inheritance was vigorously defended by the prophet Elijah. Ahab had tried by legal means to acquire Naboth's vineyard, but Naboth had refused, saying: "The LORD forbid that I should give you the inheritance of my fathers" (I Kings 21:3). Naboth's right to preserve and transmit his inheritance from his fathers to his sons was circumvented by false charges of crimes calling for the death penalty.

Rachel and Leah, wives of Jacob, protested to the God of Bethel that their father had denied them their property rights (Gen. 31:14, 16). This episode in Genesis reveals only the desire of Jacob's wives to inherit from their father and gives no clear account of any particular custom.

A man's inheritance is so much a part of his life that it is spoken of as his house:

> They [the wicked] oppress a man and his house,
> a man and his inheritance (Mic. 2:2).

Righteousness enables a father to leave an inheritance to his children and to their children as well, while the sinner can leave nothing (Prov. 13:22).

The request that Jesus direct a man's brother to divide his inheritance with him may reflect the concern of a brother who is not the first-born (Luke 12:13).

3. Legislation governing inheritance. Laws aimed at the control of inheritance are few in the Bible. For reasons that are not entirely clear, certain classes of persons in the community are singled out for special attention with respect to inheritance. These include the son of a slave girl or concubine, the first-born son, daughters, and the widow.

a. The son of a slave girl. The right to inherit was evidently not materially affected by the status of the mother. Sarah needed to take special action in order to prevent the son of the slave girl Hagar from inheriting along with Sarah's son, Isaac, and from inheriting as the first-born, at that (Gen. 21:10). The Babylonian Code (CH) provides that if a slave girl bears children and their father accepts them as his children, they are to share equally with the children of the wife in their father's estate as his heirs (section 170). But if the father fails to acknowledge them, they have no claim on his estate. However, in this event they shall be set free (section 171). It is noteworthy that Abimelech the son of a concubine asserted his claim to inherit against the claims of the sons of his father's wives (Judg. 8:30-31). A slave who acts wisely will have pre-eminence over a son who behaves shamefully, and he will "share the inheritance as one of the brothers" (Prov. 17:2). An interesting variant is the law enabling the prince of the Jewish theocratic state to give an inheritance to a slave (Ezek. 46:16-17), who, however, must return it if he is liberated.

b. Right of the first-born. The first-born is to receive double the portion of his father's possessions given to other sons (Deut. 21:15-17). Reuben was the first-born of Israel; "but because he polluted his father's couch [see Gen. 49:4], his birthright was given to the sons of Joseph" (I Chr. 5:1). I.e., Reuben's violation of the law against incest denied him the benefit of the law governing the rights of the first-born son. The story of Isaac's blessing to Jacob before he died suggests that the right of the first-born may have been formally conferred by a verbal blessing from the aged father (Gen. 27:4) in connection with a ceremonial meal. Once the words of the blessing had been pronounced, their effect was irrevocable (vs. 37). Custom, however, was doubtless sufficient to ensure that the inheritance was distributed in accordance with this right, whether or not a formal ceremony took place.

c. Rights of daughters. In view of the patriarchal form of the Hebrew family, the rights of sons were pre-eminent. These rights determined the succession to the father's name and possessions. But what happened in the event there were daughters but no sons? This problem is handled in considerable detail in Num. 27:1-11. A man had five daughters and no sons. Moses gave the decision that in such cases the father's inheritance should go to the daughter(s). If he had no daughters, his possessions should go to his brother. If he had no brother, then they should go to his father's brothers. If there were none, the property should go to the next of kin. This procedure was to become a statute for the entire nation, Moses decreed. To prevent the inheritance from going to another tribe, a ruling prohibited daughters from marrying outside the tribe of their father (Num. 36:6). Whether because of changes brought about by the Exile and subsequent events or because of the effect of this law, the book of Job records that Job's three daughters received an inheritance along with their brothers (42:15).

d. Status of the widow. No provision is made for the security of the widow through a provision that she inherit a portion of her late husband's property. Reasons for this singular omission have been advanced, such as the view that death before old age is a calamity, a punishment for sin, the effects of which extended to the wife who was left behind (*see* WIDOW). But the widow was not entirely unprotected by law and custom. The requirement of the levirate marriage (*see* MARRIAGE § 1*g*) may have provided for the inheritance of property. To preserve both the name and the inheritance of the family, the remarriage of the widow was required. The remarriage of the widow to each of six brothers under the operation of the levirate law (Matt. 22:24-26) thus continuously provided for her, apparently until her death, because she had no children by any of her husbands. Here and in the LXX the term "son," which appears in the Deuteronomic statement of the levirate law, becomes "children," possibly under the influence of the law permitting the inheritance of daughters in Num. 27.

e. Other categories. Inheritance of a king's possessions and royal office was not automatic in Israel, although the right of the FIRST-BORN was evidently operative as a rule. Succession to the throne might be decided by the help of a king's harem and his counselors (I Kings 1:27-28). The resident alien was allotted land in the restored community as an inheritance (Ezek. 47:20), provided he had children. His inheritance—i.e., assignment of land—would be decided by the identity of the tribe with which he lived. Priests were to have no inheritance (44:28). The fate of a rebellious son is drastic in Deut. 21:18-21: there is no question of cutting him off as an heir; he must be destroyed.

4. Canaan as Israel's inheritance. Canaan was the land that God had promised and delivered to his people (Deut. 4:21; 19:14). The basis of this belief is succinctly stated in the Lord's words to Joshua: "You shall cause this people to inherit the land which I swore to their fathers to give them" (Josh. 1: 6; cf. 13:6-7, etc.; 23:4-5). Jeremiah refers to this land as that which was given to the fathers of Israel and Judah "for a heritage . . . , a heritage most beauteous of all nations" (3:18-19; cf. 12:14). This land was distributed among the various tribes of Israel, divided according to the size of each tribe (Num. 26:52-62; 33:54). Precise areas of land were specified for the tribes, each portion being located in relation to the one adjoining (Ezek. 48:1-7). Although the priests had no inheritance of land, because God is their inheritance, they shall share the offerings of grain and meat that are brought by the people (44:28-30).

5. Israel as the inheritance of Yahweh. Central to Israel's life are the holy temple and the land around it. These too are God's inheritance (Ps. 79:1). Israel is the tribe of the Lord's inheritance (Jer. 10: 16). A similar use of the term appears in some passages (Deut. 9:26, 29; Ps. 28:9; etc.) where God's people are called his heritage. Because of Israel's treachery, God has forsaken his house, abandoned his heritage (Jer. 12:7); rejected by him, she has become like an enraged lion (vs. 8). Even though she is the Lord's inheritance, Israel has polluted the land with her "detestable idols" and has "filled [his] inheritance with their abominations" (16:18). Babylon is the plunderer of God's heritage—i.e., Israel (Jer. 50:11; cf. 51:19).

As a consequence of her nature as the inheritance or heritage of her God, Israel—or members of the Israelite community—undergoes certain types of experience which are also described as a heritage from the Lord. Destruction is the "heritage which oppressors receive from the Almighty" (Job 27:13). God will make the nations the heritage of his anointed one, the king on Zion, his holy hill (Ps. 2:6-8). The heritage of the blameless and upright ones "will abide for ever," for they are the true people of God (37:18). God has given his people, who are his true inheritance, the "heritage of the nations"—i.e., control over them as a possession (111:6). The Servant of the Lord receives divine protection as a heritage (Isa. 54:17); and those who honor the sabbath shall receive the heritage of Jacob their father—namely, divine approval (58:14). The tribes of Jacob are to be gathered in one place where they will receive their inheritance as it was of old—namely, Jerusalem and the greatness which this city once symbolized (Ecclus. 36:11). And the honorable man transmits to his descendants a good inheritance of uprightness (41:10-11). The priesthood is the "heritage" of the Levites (Josh. 18:7), and the Lord's testimonies are the "heritage" of the psalmist forever (Ps. 119:111).

6. Inheritance in the NT. Apart from the use of "inheritance" as the transmission of property from a father to his son in some of the parables of Jesus (Matt. 21:38; Mark 12:1-8; Luke 15:11-12), the NT employs this concept largely in a spiritual and theological sense. Thus eternal life is a benefit that can be inherited (Luke 18:18). The inheritance of God will be given to the elders of Ephesus in terms of the "word of his grace" (Acts 20:32). Abraham and his descendants did not receive the promise that they would inherit the world through the law, but through the "righteousness of faith" (Rom. 4:13). God's kingdom cannot be inherited by men who are immoral (I Cor. 6:9-10); the Holy Spirit is a guarantee of "his glorious inheritance in the saints" (Eph. 1:18). To share in the inheritance of the saints, men must be delivered from the dominion of darkness and transferred to the kingdom of his beloved son (Col. 1:12-13). This inheritance is a reward for obedience by the faithful (3:24). The promises of the gospel are inherited through patience and faith (Heb. 6:12); and "those who are called may receive the promised eternal inheritance" (9:15; cf. Heb. 11:8; I Pet. 1:4, 18). In the Dead Sea Scrolls appears a similar figure. God's chosen ones will obtain from him an inheritance of righteousness, strength, and glory (1QM XI.7-8).

Bibliography. A. Deimel, *Codex Hammurabi* (1930); M. Noth, *Die Gesetze im Pentateuch* (1940); E. Neufeld, *Ancient Hebrew Marriage Laws* (1944); T. J. Meek, *Hebrew Origins* (rev. ed., 1950), pp. 77-78; J. B. Pritchard, ed., *ANET* (2nd ed., 1955).

O. J. Baab

INIQUITY. *See* Sin.

INK [דיו; μέλαν] (Jer. 36:18; II Cor. 3:3; II John 12; III John 13). Writing fluid made from soot or lampblack mixed with gum arabic. Red ink was also made by substituting red iron oxide for the carbon. *See* Writing and Writing Materials.

INKHORN, WRITER'S. KJV translation of קסת הספר (RSV Writing Case).

INLAY. A piece of material fitted or molded into a recess in the surface of another body. In Ezekiel's lament over Tyre, which is likened to a ship (27:1-9), vs. 6*b* is somewhat obscure, although the first three (Hebrew) words, translated: "They made your deck (or boards) of ivory," are textually sound. As it is incredible, particularly in an otherwise plausible description, that the deck of any ship should be made of ivory, the RSV has tried to reduce the difficulty of this verse by the rendition: "They made your deck . . . inlaid with ivory."

It is probable that various objects, described elsewhere in the OT as being "of ivory," were in fact inlaid with ivory. Solomon's throne (I Kings 10:18) was likely of wood, with extensive ivory and gold inlay. Similarly we may interpret the "beds of ivory" in Amos 6:4. This inlaid furniture was sufficiently prized to be part of Hezekiah's tribute to Sennacherib in 701 B.C., for we learn that the latter received, among other things, "couches (inlaid) with ivory, *nîmedu*-chairs (inlaid) with ivory" (*ANET* 288). The ivory buildings mentioned in I Kings 22:39; Ps. 45:8—H 45:9; Amos 3:15, were doubtless structures characterized by the generous use of ivory inlay on doors and paneling (*see bibliography*). Figs. INL 8; IVO 18.

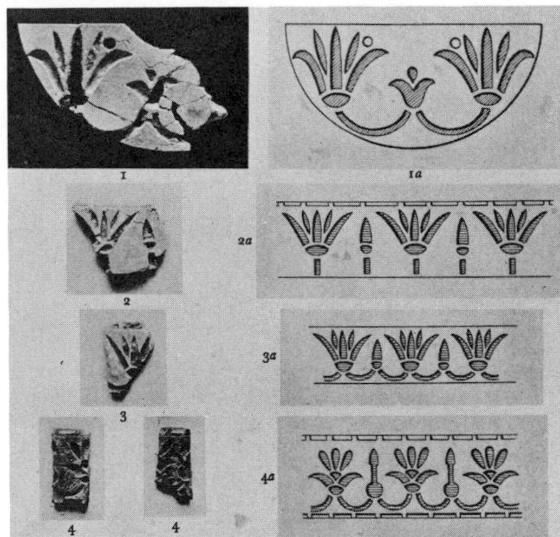

By permission of the Palestine Exploration Fund

8. Ivory inlays from Samaria (first half of ninth century): (1, 1*a*) lotus flowers and a lily; (2, 2*a*) lotus flowers and buds; (3, 3*a*) chain of lotus and buds; (4, 4*a*) chain of palmettes and buds

In Esth. 1:6 the description of the floor of the banqueting court is probably to be taken (with RSV) as a "mosaic pavement."

Inlay has played a continuous part in the decorative art of the Near East from Sumerian to modern times, the earliest inlays being made from bone, mother-of-pearl, and shell. *See* Ivory.

Bibliography. For a survey of inlays, enamels, and fine ivory work, to *ca.* 500 B.C., see C. Singer, E. J. Holmyard, and A. R. Hall, eds., *A History of Technology*, I (1954), 659-83. For an account of ivories from inlays in doors and paneling, unearthed at Samaria and believed to have come from the ninth century B.C., see J. W. Crowfoot, *Early Ivories from Samaria* (1938).

W. S. McCullough

INN [מלון (RSV LODGING PLACE; Gen. 42:27; 43:21; Exod. 4:24); κατάλυμα (Luke 2:7), πανδοχεῖον (Luke 10:35)]. A word used for several different kinds of shelter or dwelling.

1. In the OT. The Hebrew word by etymology is a "place to spend the night" (see Josh. 4:3), and it is used of the camping place of an individual (Jer. 9:2—H 9:1), a family (Exod. 4:24), a caravan (Gen. 42:27; 43:21), an army (II Kings 19:23 [RSV "retreat"]; Isa. 10:29), or even a nation (Josh. 4:3, 8). Perhaps a simple shelter for desert travelers is meant in Jer. 9:2—H 9:1, but in none of the other references is any structure demanded by the context. So the KJV "inn" for the references in Genesis and Exodus is misleading. When travelers did not find lodging in private houses, they often camped in the open (Gen. 19:2; 28:11; Judg. 19:15).

"Geruth Chimham" (Jer. 41:17) could be translated "habitation of Chimham" (KJV) or "Chimham's Inn" (Amer. Trans.), but the text and meaning are uncertain. This place was near, not in, Bethlehem, and the gap in time makes the identification with the "inn" of Luke 2:7 unlikely.

The Targ. of Josh. 2:1 calls Rahab פונדקיתא, "innkeeper," and Josephus (Antiq. V.i.2) so describes her also. It is possible that Rahab combined the professions of harlot and innkeeper, as was sometimes done in Roman times also. It is noteworthy that this Aramaic word for "innkeeper" and the words in rabbinic sources for "inn" (פונדק, from Greek πανδοχεῖον; and אושפיזא, from Latin *hospitium*) are of foreign origin, perhaps indicating that the organized hostel was an importation into the Near East.

2. In the NT. In Bethlehem, Joseph and Mary could find no room in the "inn" (Luke 2:7). The root meaning of the Greek word καταλύμα is a "place to loose one's burden." Here the word does not mean a hotel, but perhaps the village guest house, like the modern Arabic *maḍâfah*. The same word is used of the "guest room" where Jesus and the disciples ate their last supper together (Mark 14:14; Luke 22:11). According to a Greek inscription of the first century A.D., a man named Theodotus provided a hospice (καταλύμα) with rooms and a water supply for Jewish pilgrims in Jerusalem. Fig. SYN 94. *See also* JERUSALEM § 12.

The Good Samaritan took the wounded traveler to an "inn" (πανδοχεῖον; Luke 10:34). Since this hostel had an "innkeeper" (πανδοχεύς; vs. 35), who could supply food and care to the wounded man, it was more like an inn in the modern sense than that of Luke 2:7. By coincidence, the Mishna (Yeb. XVI.7) relates that some Levites going along the same road from Jerusalem eastward left a sick companion at an inn (פונדוק) in charge of the woman innkeeper (פונדקית). This may have been the same inn as that of Luke 10:34.

The inn of the Good Samaritan has been traditionally identified with Khan el-Ahmar, or more commonly with Khan Hathrur (or Hatrur), midway on the road between Jerusalem and Jericho. This khan, or caravansary, consists of a building with arched door, and a large court, in the center of which is a well. The inn of Jesus' day may have had a similar plan.

In Fragments of an Unknown Gospel a leper says to Jesus that he contracted the disease by eating with lepers in an "inn" (πανδοχεῖον).

Bibliography. A. Bertholet, *Die Stellung der Israeliten und der Juden zu den Fremden* (1896), p. 24; G. Dalman, *Sacred Sites and Ways* (trans. P. L. Levertoff; 1935), pp. 41-43, 244-45; E. F. F. Bishop, *Jesus of Palestine* (1955), pp. 41-45.

J. A. THOMPSON

INNER, INWARD MAN [ὁ ἔσω ἄνθρωπος]. The meaning of this phrase in Paul's theology may be found in his view of personality (see Rom. 7:22-23), in which he sees the self as comprised of three elements: (*a*) the "inmost self," in which the law of God dwells and which in Rom. 7:23 he equates with reason (νοῦς); (*b*) "my members" (τοῖς μέλεσίν μου), which in Rom. 7:18 he calls "my flesh" (τῇ σαρκί μου) and which in this sense means the innate desires that in their natural state accept no law standing in the way of their satisfaction; and (*c*) the conscious "I" (ἐγώ), which is aware of both reason and desire. Every "person" includes these three "selves," each of which in its role speaks as "I." Man's predicament is that the inner self of reason is in conflict with the self of desire, which by its nature recognizes no law.

Elsewhere (II Cor. 3:17-18; Eph. 3:16) Paul indicates that the Lord, or Spirit, dwells in the Christian's inner self, providing grace necessary to bring the flesh under discipline.

A reflection of Paul's understanding of the self occurs in Freud's analysis of personality into superego, id, and ego.

Bibliography. S. V. McCasland, *By the Finger of God* (1951), pp. 21-30; J. Knox, *IB*, IX (1954), 498-505.

S. V. MCCASLAND

INNOCENCE; KJV INNOCENCY. The condition of one who has not offended God; freedom from sin and guilt.

1. In the OT. In the RSV of the OT this noun occurs only three times (Gen. 20:5; Pss. 26:6; 73:13), though the adjective is found frequently. The Hebrew root נקה (adjective נקי), which it regularly translates, has the primary meaning of "clean" or "free from"—thus, "free from guilt, innocent" (e.g., Exod. 23:7; II Kings 24:4). The person so described has refrained from transgression of God's will or commandment in his relations both to God and to man. The RSV frequently translates the same Hebrew root by "guiltless" (e.g., Exod. 20:7; Deut. 5:11; Jer. 2:34). Closely allied in meaning is the Hebrew root תם, which the RSV translates "righteous" or "blameless" when moving in this sphere of thought, denoting more positively the status of completeness or integrity (Gen. 7:1; Job 1:1; Ps. 18:23). This positive emphasis is further reflected in other passages, where תם is translated "perfect" (e.g., Lev. 22:21; Job 36:4; Ps. 18:30). The Hebrew צדיק (*see* RIGHTEOUSNESS), with the same positive nuance, is eight times translated "innocent" by the RSV (e.g., Gen. 20:4; Deut. 25:1; Job 9:15). The LXX usually translates δίκαιος ("right, just, righteous"). All three roots move in the same sphere of meaning.

Innocence throughout the OT is conceived basically in moral terms. That this innocence is relative is necessitated by the OT view of human sinfulness (*see* SIN). Nevertheless, with the growing tendency to equate God's will with the Torah, there was a corollary tendency to define innocence in terms of keeping the Torah. The OT never departs from the conviction that only God can create a right heart and remove sin. But the growing tendency toward emphasis on Torah as the objective criterion for judging innocence was accompanied by an absolutizing and moralizing of the concept of innocence.

2. In the NT. In the RSV of the NT the adjective "innocent" is found eight times, translating four different Greek terms: ἀκέραιος ("unmixed, pure"; Matt. 10:16; Phil. 2:15), ἀθῷος ("free from"; Matt.

27:4, 24), δίκαιος ("upright, just, righteous"; Matt. 23:35; Luke 23:47), κάθαρος ("clean, pure"; Acts 18:6; 20:26). The first two Greek terms convey the negative and the last two the more positive meaning. Several other Greek words (ἄμωμος, ἀνέγκλητος, ἄμεμπτος, ἄκακος) translated "blameless" by the RSV are closely associated in meaning to these four. The disciples are to be "innocent as doves" (Matt. 27:24); Paul is innocent of the fate of those who will not hear the gospel which he has responsibly preached (Acts 18:6).

In the NT it is primarily in relation to God's will revealed through Jesus Christ that innocence is judged. However, innocence in the NT must ultimately be understood, not merely in moral, but in eschatological terms. The Christian is only relatively innocent in the moral sense, since only Jesus Christ was truly innocent—really free from sin and guilt (Luke 23:47; cf. I Pet. 1:19). With Adam the Christian is a creature whose sense of guilt reveals that his innocence is lost. But in the Second Adam, Jesus Christ, he is confronted with the possibility of restoration in the innocence of God's only faithful Man. Insofar as the Christian can be called innocent, it is as he is forgiven and becomes a new creature through Christ. To be innocent in this ultimate sense involves the full consummation of the new age already inaugurated by Christ. It is only Christ who can present him "holy and blameless" (Col. 1:22; cf. Eph. 5:27) and "guiltless in the day of our Lord Jesus" (I Cor. 1:8; cf. I Thess. 5:23). Innocence in any ultimate sense for the Christian is not something he attains, claims, or possesses on his own. It is a gift of God revealed and given through faith in Jesus Christ (Eph. 1:4); its full meaning and consequences await the final disclosure in the Day of the Lord.

F. W. Young

INNOCENTS, SLAUGHTER OF THE. An incident recorded in Matt. 2:16-18, where it is part of the narrative of 2:1-18. A messianic prediction by Magi or astrologers that a child should be born in Bethlehem who would be "king of the Jews" is understood by Herod the Great as referring to a royal claimant. When the Magi flee to avoid questioning, Herod in a rage orders the death of all male children in Bethlehem two years of age or less (perhaps twenty to thirty in number). The evangelist finds in this a fulfilment of Jer. 31:15—G 38:15; but the connection of this verse with Bethlehem is not clear, as Ramah, traditional burial place of Rachel, is *ca.* ten miles N of Jerusalem (cf. Gen. 35:17; 48:7). *See* Ephrathah 2.

The motif of the story is familiar, and recalls the account of Pharaoh and Moses in Exod. 1-2. However, the character and deeds of Herod, especially in his last years, would make such an act quite plausible, although no other evidence for it exists. Josephus' silence may be part of his general suppression of messianic data. He recounts similar and worse atrocities—e.g., Herod's order to mark his own death by the slaying of one member of each family (Antiq. XVII.vi.5-6).

See also Jesus Christ; Ramah 3.

Bibliography. A. H. McNeille, *The Gospel According to St. Matthew* (1915), pp. 19-20; P. Saintyves, "Le massacre des Innocents ou la persécution de l'Enfant Prédestiné," *Congrès d'histoire du Christianisme*, I (1928), 229-72.

A. Wikgren

INQUIRE OF GOD [שׁאל, to ask, consult; דרשׁ, to seek, resort to; בקר, to inquire]. To seek divine guidance through the consultation of oracle, priest, prophet, or God himself. In the early period of Israel's history the Deity was consulted through the priest (Judg. 18:14, 17; I Sam. 22:10), or through the seer, the precursor of the prophet (I Sam. 9:9). Priest and prophet were both connected with the sanctuary, and both were diviners. The priest divined by sacred lot, Urim and Thummim (cf. Num. 27:21; I Sam. 14:36-42); ephod (I Sam. 23:9-13; 30:8); and perhaps also by teraphim, sacred images (Judg. 18:14), and sacrifice (Hos. 3:4). How the prophet divined is not known. Seeing and hearing were his specialty. He used ecstatic vision, and at times music was employed (cf. I Sam. 10:5; II Kings 3:15).

The Deity was consulted on numerous matters of personal and public welfare (cf. I Sam. 9:9). More particularly, the king would inquire of the Deity, before going to battle, to create victory in his soul and assure himself of victory (I Sam. 23:2, 4; II Sam. 5:19, 23; II Kings 3:11; II Chr. 18:4, 6-7; cf. Judg. 1:1; 20:23).

While dreams, Urim, and prophet were the recognized means to ascertain the divine will (I Sam. 28:6), many others existed—e.g., mediums and wizards (I Sam. 28:3; Isa. 8:19; cf. Deut. 18:10-11), necromancers (I Sam. 28:8; Isa. 8:19; cf. Deut. 18:11), teraphim (Judg. 17:5; 18:13-14, 17-18, 20; Hos. 3:4; Zech. 10:2), pillar (Hos. 3:4), ark (Judg. 20:27), altar (II Kings 16:15)—to say nothing of the consultation of foreign deities such as Baal-zebub (II Kings 1:2-3, 16) and Milcom (Zeph. 1:5).

With the rise of prophetic schools, consultation of the Deity was predominantly through the prophet. The earlier prophets used stimulated ecstasy to ascertain the divine will; the later prophets relied more on inspiration and prophetic insight. The fall of the nation brought prophecy into disrepute (because of the false prophets), and the priest in postexilic Judaism rose to the foreground. However, since the time of Solomon, the wise man (or sage) was frequently consulted as to the divine will in matters of daily life (cf. Jer. 18:18). With the rise of the synagogue, direct consultation of the Deity through prayer came more and more in vogue, until in NT times we have prayer as the chief means to inquire of God. Christians were taught to pray in the name of the Lord Jesus (John 14:13-14; 15:16; 16:23, 26; cf. Acts 2:21; Rom. 10:13).

See also Ark; Divination; Ephod; Priests and Levites; Prophet; Seer.

Bibliography. W. R. Arnold, *Ephod and Ark* (1917); J. Pedersen, *Israel*, I-II (1926), 141-44; A. Guillaume, *Prophecy and Divination* (1938).

V. H. Kooy

INSCRIPTION ON THE CROSS [ἐπιγραφή]. KJV alternately: SUPERSCRIPTION (Mark 15:26; Luke 23:38). The sign attached to Jesus' cross to indicate the crime alleged against him, the crime for which he was condemned. *See also* Cross; Trial of Jesus.

The word αἰτία (RSV "charge"; KJV "accusation") is used in reference to the inscription in Matt. 27:37; Mark 15:26. John 19:19-20 uses the word τίτλον, "title." The basic meaning of αἰτία is the cause or reason for an action. This use appears often in the LXX and contemporary Greek literature, as well as in the NT (e.g., Luke 8:47; Acts 10:21; 22: 24; II Tim. 1:12; Tit. 1:13). From these it takes on the legal meanings of "accusation" (Acts 25:18), "charge or ground for complaint" (Matt. 19:3; John 18:38; 19:4, 6; Acts 23:28; 25:27), and "ground for capital punishment" (αἰτια θανάτου; Acts 13:28; 28:18). The last two are involved at Matt. 27:37; Mark 15:26. The authors of Luke and John may have recoiled at applying so opprobrious a term in Jesus' case, and so changed it.

The wording of the inscription varies in the four gospels, but all contain the definitive phrase "the King of the Jews." This shows, on the one hand, that Jesus was convicted of insurrection, his personal claims being interpreted as opposed to the authority of Rome (*see* TRIAL OF JESUS). On the other hand, the phrase exhibits the contempt in which the Jews were held by their Roman masters. The cross stood close to a main road out of Jerusalem, where Jewish passers-by must see the inscription and sense the derision. The Fourth Gospel strongly underscores this (John 19:20-32). The words, it says, were in Hebrew, Latin, and Greek; hence none who saw it could fail to understand. The Jewish authorities complained to Pilate, asking that the inscription be changed to: "This man said, I am King of the Jews." Pilate, however, refused to alter it. PIERSON PARKER

INSCRIPTIONS. During the past century or so, the understanding of the Bible has been revolutionized by the mass of written documents recovered from the ancient Near East. The story of the decipherment of the scripts in which they were written and the recovery of the many languages employed has all the elements of suspense and romance.

In this article the term "inscriptions" is understood to mean any written documents, whether on stone, clay, papyrus, or any other material (*see* WRITING AND WRITING MATERIALS). The exigencies of space preclude any exhaustive listing of texts or full discussion of their significance. Brief references to documents of greatest interest to students of the Bible must suffice. It will be convenient to divide these texts into five groups according to the languages in which they are written.

1. Egyptian
2. Sumerian and Akkadian
3. Canaanite
4. Aramaic
5. Greek

Bibliography

1. Egyptian. With the successful decipherment of the ROSETTA STONE* by Champollion in 1822, it became possible for scholars to read the hitherto enigmatic hieroglyphs inscribed on Egyptian temples, tombs, stelae, obelisks, etc., as well as the even more extensive materials written in hieratic and demotic script on leather, papyrus, etc., thus rendering this great body of material available to scholars. Fig. ROS 19.

One of the classics of Egyptian literature, preserved on many papyri and ostraca, is the Story of Si-nuhe. It narrates the adventures of a self-exiled official of the early Twelfth Dynasty who took refuge in Syria on the assassination of King Amen-em-het I, *ca.* 1962 B.C. The vivid picture it affords of seminomadic life is a valuable contemporary illustration of the background against which the patriarchal narratives in the book of Genesis are set.

From the end of the Twelfth or beginning of the Thirteenth Dynasty, during the nineteenth and eighteenth centuries B.C., a number of pottery bowls and figurines have come to light. On these were inscribed a series of curses directed against real or potential enemies of the state. The bowls were then ritually smashed to accomplish the magical destruction of these foes. Among the names of persons and places recorded in these Execration Texts are many Asiatic ones (e.g., Ashkelon, Jerusalem, Achshaph, Shechem), from which may be deduced the political conditions

Courtesy of the University Museum of the University of Pennsylvania

9. A stele of Seti I, giving an account of the King's victory over a coalition of Asiatic princes; found at Beth-shan

in Syria-Palestine during this period. They show a patriarchal organization, e.g., rather than that of the later city-states. From the same time (*ca.* 1740) comes a papyrus which contains a list of ninety-five slaves, many of them Semites.

Much important information may be derived from the topographical lists, cataloguing the conquests of Thut-mose III (*ca.* 1490-1436) of the Eighteenth Dynasty, inscribed in the temple of Amon at Karnak. Together with his "annals," recorded on the same building, these lists serve to document the history of the Palestinian city-states such as Megiddo, Gezer, Taanach, Aijalon, etc., during the expansion of the Egyptian Empire. The names of places in Palestine contained in the later lists of Ramses II (*ca.* 1290-1223) on the Ramesseum at Thebes and of Ramses III (*ca.* 1179-1147) at Medinet Habu are mere copies of the earlier list of Thut-mose. The much later Karnak list of Sheshonk I (*ca.* 940-919), whom the OT calls SHISHAK, records 156 cities of Syria-Palestine which he claims to have captured; this is not a mere copy, but contains many names not to be found in the earlier lists. This invasion of Palestine in the fifth year of Rehoboam is referred to in the OT (I Kings 14:25-26; somewhat expanded in II Chr. 12:2-9).

A papyrus of *ca.* 1300 relates an episode, legendary in character, concerning a general of Thut-mose III who was responsible for the capture of the town of Joppa. In it we find the prototype of the story of "Ali Baba and the Forty Thieves."

A number of Egyptian inscriptions have turned up at various sites in Palestine. Three stelae, one of Ramses II and two of his predecessor Seti I (*ca.* 1303-1290), come from BETH-SHAN, which was occupied by an Egyptian garrison. The larger stela of Seti tells of the capture of Beth-shan by the ruler of Hamath and its relief by Seti. The smaller one mentions "the *'apiru* [*see* HABIRU] of Mount Yarumtu," and is evidence of a later invasion by Seti. Fig. INS 9.

An outstanding literary work of the reign of AKH-EN-ATON (*ca.* 1360-1353) is his great hymn to the god Aton, carved in hieroglyphs on a tomb at Tell el-Amarna. Rightly regarded as a major document of the Atonist "heresy," this work draws upon elements from the earlier Hymn to Amon, speaking of the sun-god's benefactions and lauding him as creator and sustainer of the universe. The supposed monotheistic tendencies in the hymn are mere literary clichés which are to be found already in the polytheistic Hymn to Amon, and are part of the universalism in religion which was characteristic of the Empire. Reference has frequently been made to the striking similarity of this hymn to Ps. 104, but direct literary dependence is most unlikely. It is probable, however, that the Hebrew writer drew upon Egyptian sources for these ideas which pervaded later Egyptian religious works.

During the Nineteenth Dynasty, in the third year of MER-NE-PTAH (*ca.* 1223-1211), revolts seem to have occasioned a punitive expedition into Syria-Palestine. Although no such campaign is recorded in the OT, there is some evidence to suggest that it did take place. Two years later, Mer-ne-ptah faced a far more serious threat to Egyptian security when the Libyans, supported by the Sea Peoples, attempted to invade his borders. To commemorate his achievements on both these occasions, Mer-ne-ptah inscribed a series of hymns of victory on a stela which he set up in his mortuary temple at Thebes, meanwhile carving a duplicate on the temple of Amon at Karnak. In the final strophe the pharaoh makes the sole reference to Israel to be found in any Egyptian text:

> Canaan is plundered with every evil;
> Ashkelon is taken; Gezer is captured;
> Yanoam is made non-existent;
> Israel lies desolate; its seed is no more.[1]

The name Israel is written in such a way as to suggest that the people was an important one, although not yet permanently established.

The short story was first developed as a literary genre in Egypt, from whence the art was passed to the Hebrews. A fine example of the Egyptian genius for storytelling is the Tale of the Two Brothers, preserved in a MS of *ca.* 1225. Of particular interest is the close resemblance which the first part of the story bears to the account of Joseph and Potiphar's wife (Gen. 39).

The Sea Peoples, who had been repulsed by Mer-ne-ptah, made a full-scale assault on Egypt by land and sea during the reign of Ramses III (*ca.* 1179-1147) of the Twentieth Dynasty. These Indo-European folk, who had established themselves in the E Mediterranean, included such groups as the Achaeans, Tyrsenians, Lycians, Teucrians, and others who later gave their names to Sardinia and Sicily. Among them were also the PHILISTINES, who settled on the Palestinian coastal plain after they were driven back by Ramses. The records of these naval and land battles were inscribed on Ramses' mortuary temple at Medinet Habu.

A tale of the Twenty-first Dynasty, *ca.* 1100, relates the experiences of an Egyptian temple official by the name of Wen-Amon who was dispatched to purchase timber in Byblos for the bark of the god Amon. The story, with wry humor, makes clear the depths to which Egyptian prestige had sunk by this time. In the course of the tale mention is made of an episode in which "the god seized" a priest and "made him possessed." This instance of prophetic frenzy in Syria is of great interest in view of the OT accounts of ecstatic prophecy in Israel. *See* ECSTASY.

Egypt, famed for her wise men, produced many didactic treatises written for the instruction of officials' sons, such as the Old Kingdom writings of Ptah-hotep. In her declining years this tradition was maintained and at some period, probably during the eleventh century, the Wisdom of Amenemope made its appearance. Exhibiting a high ethical tone and an emphasis on personal piety characteristic of the times in which it was written, the work has special significance for biblical studies. The very close parallelism between parts of this document and Prov. 22:17–23:14 is such as to suggest literary dependence of the latter on the Egyptian work.

At the end of the fourth century B.C. the tomb of an Egyptian official by the name of Petosiris was adorned with a series of hieroglyphic texts. Among

[1] From D. W. Thomas, ed., *Documents from OT Times,* published by Thomas Nelson & Sons.

Courtesy of George C. Cameron, American Schools of Oriental Research and the University of Michigan

10. The cliff at Behistun, with Darius I relief and inscription in three languages: Old Persian, Elamite, and Akkadian

these were some of a didactic nature which seem to have been influenced by OT literature, notably Ps. 128.

Finally, in a demotic MS of the first century A.D. there occurs a tale which, despite its late date, is purely Egyptian in character. This is the story of a man whose son, possessed of magical powers, led him through the halls of the underworld. In it can be found the prototype of the parable of the rich man and Lazarus (Luke 1:19-31).

2. Sumerian and Akkadian. The key to the decipherment of the CUNEIFORM scripts was the great rock inscription of Darius I at Behistun.* Unlike the Rosetta Stone, which provided a Greek version of the Egyptian texts, Darius' record of his suppression of the revolts which followed his accession was inscribed in three unknown languages: Old Persian, Elamite, and Akkadian. Rawlinson, who first copied the text in 1837, succeeded in deciphering the Old Persian version in 1846, and the Akkadian version shortly afterward. As a result of this achievement, the riches of the Sumerian and Akkadian literatures, written in the same script, were at last revealed.

Some texts are written on stone, but the vast majority are on clay tablets. The amazing extent of these treasures first become apparent with the discovery in 1853 of the royal library of Ashurbanipal (668-633) at Nineveh. Although this was the largest, similar libraries have been found going back as early as Sargon II (721-705). Figs. INS 10; PER 38-39.

The Sumerian King List, compiled *ca.* 2065, records the reigns of the earliest rulers in Mesopotamia and indicates that the line was interrupted by a memorable flood. The eight antediluvian kings are given reigns totaling 241,200 years (the last ruling 18,600)! A late form of the list preserved by Berossus (281-261) enumerates ten such kings, with a total of 432,000 years. Such astronomical figures recall the OT record of the longevity of the ten patriarchs from Adam to Noah (Gen. 5).

The early Sumerian supremacy was interrupted by the Semitic Old Akkadian Dynasty founded by Sargon I (*ca.* 2360). A legendary account of his birth has been preserved in which he is said to have been placed in a basket of rushes and set afloat in the river, to be rescued by an irrigation official. The similarity of this story to that of Moses (Exod. 2:1-10) is obvious.

It was in Mesopotamia that the first legal "codes" were produced. Most famous of all is that of HAMMURABI (*ca.* 1728-1686),* inscribed on a magnificent stela, with copies on clay tablets. This great work was a compilation of laws already in existence, many of them translated from Sumerian, and was intended as a supplement and amendment to the common law of his day. Recent discoveries have revealed that, far from being the earliest such "code," this was one of a series. Similar collections of laws are known from the reigns of Ur-Nammu (*ca.* 2060) of Ur, Bilalama (*ca.* 1930) of Eshnunna, and Lipit-Ishtar (*ca.* 1865) of Isin. The Middle Assyrian laws, probably of the fifteenth century, are similar in content and refer to levirate marriage (cf. Deut. 25:5-10). This development of a legal tradition was transmitted to the West, giving rise to the Hittite "code." Not only do such collections illuminate the Mosaic legislation in the OT (*see* LAW IN THE OT), but they also suggest how the tradition and form (though not necessarily the content) of the latter had their origin. Fig. HAM 5.

Two sites have unexpectedly yielded great numbers of texts which have shed much welcome light on the early narratives in Genesis. The first is MARI on the middle Euphrates, where over twenty thousand tablets from the nineteenth and eighteenth centuries have been recovered from the archives of the palace. Among the letters is preserved some correspondence with Hammurabi himself. Since the region was predominantly Amorite in population (*see* AMORITES), these texts supply much information for the background of the Hebrew patriarchal period.

The second group of texts, numbering many thousands of tablets from the fifteenth and fourteenth centuries, comes from the site of ancient NUZI in NE Mesopotamia. This was an area inhabited largely by Hurrians, in the OT called HORITES, although the language used in the texts is Akkadian. These business and legal documents have provided a clue to the understanding of many of the legal practices preserved in the patriarchal narratives of the OT, such as the selling of the birthright, and the fact that the possession of the household gods (*see* TERAPHIM) virtually gave title to an estate.

At the site of ancient Alalakh in the Turkish Hatay, the statue of King Idrimi (*ca.* 1450), accompanied by a long biographical inscription, has recently been recovered. The account which it contains of a man, estranged by jealousy from his elder brothers but later, after having become king, reconciled to them, may be reflected in the OT story of Joseph.

The reigns of Amen-hotep III (*ca.* 1397-1360) and his son Akh-en-Aton (*ca.* 1360-1353) witnessed the breakup of Egypt's Asiatic possessions. The stirring events of these days are graphically portrayed in the state archives of Akh-en-Aton unearthed at TELL EL-AMARNA in Middle Egypt. These consist of nearly four hundred clay tablets written in Akkadian, which was at this time the language of international diplomacy. The documents include letters to and from the petty rulers of the city-states in Syria-Palestine which were under Egyptian suzerainty, such as Byblos, Tyre, Megiddo, Jerusalem, etc. The HABIRU figure prominently in these letters as a people whose invasions led to the collapse of Egyptian domination. Of great importance also is the language of these texts, for not only do they betray Canaanite grammatical and lexical features, but they also contain a large number of Canaanite glosses which are invaluable for a knowledge of the Canaanite (Hebrew) language of the period.

The epic had its rise in Mesopotamia. To honor the Babylonian god Marduk, a great poem of seven tablets was composed in which earlier Sumerian ideas of COSMOGONY were incorporated. This Creation Epic was recited annually as a part of the New Year's festival to celebrate the triumph of the hero Marduk over the forces of chaos, represented by the goddess Tiamat. This victory, achieved by his weapons the storm winds, reflects the annual conflict in nature between the floods and the winds in springtime, just as the description of creation in the epic is a portrayal of the continuous formation of alluvial Mesopotamia through the deposit of silt. The motif of the fight between Marduk and Tiamat was later transmitted to Canaanite and Hebrew literature (*see* LEVIATHAN); indeed, the name Tiamat is etymologically akin to the Hebrew *tᵉhōm* (Gen. 1:2; *see* ABYSS). The epic tells how, in order to relieve the gods of menial tasks, man was created from the blood of one of the gods. In other Sumerian and Akkadian myths the substance used is clay mingled with divine blood.

The Epic of Gilgamesh, which goes back to Old Babylonian times and utilizes earlier Sumerian sources, achieved even greater popularity, as the versions in Hittite and Hurrian testify. It relates, in the course of twelve tablets, the adventures of Gilgamesh and his boon companion Enkidu.* When the latter dies, Gilgamesh embarks on a search for immortality, which leads him to the abode of Utnapishtim, the hero of the flood. In the eleventh tablet Utnapishtim recounts the flood story in a form remarkably similar to that in Gen. 6–8 (*see* FLOOD [GENESIS]). This account, based on the Sumerian story of Ziusudra, is similar to others in Akkadian texts, such as the Atrahasis Epic. Fig. FLO 18.

Mesopotamian wisdom literature, unlike that of Egypt, is characterized by extensive collections of proverbs, both in Sumerian and in Akkadian, a custom which the Hebrews adopted in the book of Proverbs. The discussion of theodicy likewise has no counterpart in Egypt, but is represented by four works, one Sumerian, the others Akkadian: a Sumerian poem, perhaps as early as 2000; a poem from the reign of Ammiditana (*ca.* 1619-1583); the Acrostic Dialogue or Babylonian Theodicy, from the Kassite period; the slightly later Poem of the Righteous Sufferer. These all pave the way for the later Hebrew discussions of the same problem (Job; Pss. 37; 49; 73).

A common literary genre in Mesopotamian religious literature is the penitential psalm. Its influence on Hebrew psalmody is seen in such examples as Ps. 51.

The royal annals of the Assyrian kings afford a valuable supplement to the historical books of the

Courtesy of the Trustees of the British Museum

11. Scenes from the "Black Obelisk" of Shalmaneser III (858-824 B.C.), from Nimrud, showing tributes being brought to Shalmaneser III by Sua the Gilzanite (left) and Jehu "son of Omri" (right)

Bible, and Mesopotamian methods of recording events may well have served as models for Hebrew historiography. Those of most direct interest for the OT begin with Shalmaneser III (858-824), whose "monolith inscription" tells of his battle at Qarqar on the Orontes River in 854 against a coalition of twelve kings, including Ahab of Israel, who supplied the largest contingent. On his "black obelisk"* he describes (and illustrates with a relief) the submission of Jehu of Israel. Neither of these facts is mentioned in the OT. Tiglath-pileser III (744-727) records how Menahem of Israel paid tribute (cf. II Kings 15:19-20) and mentions the Syro-Ephraimite War, which involved Ahaz of Judah (cf. II Kings 16:5-18). The destruction of Samaria and the deportation of the Israelite population (cf. II Kings 18:9-12) are recounted by Sargon II (721-705). The description of the siege of Jerusalem in the reign of Hezekiah by Sennacherib (704-681)* supplements the OT account (II Kings 18–19=Isa. 36–37). The annals of Esarhaddon (680-669) mention Manasseh as a vassal, and those of Ashurbanipal (668-633) describe his invasion of Syria-Palestine and Egypt. Figs. INS 11-12.

Four Babylonian chronicles give a graphic account of the fall of Nineveh and fix the date as 612. The description of the collapse of the Assyrian Empire makes the death of Josiah at the hands of Pharaoh Neco (II Kings 23:29) intelligible. The chronicles also fix the date of the capture and destruction of Jerusalem. Most remarkable of all is a group of three hundred tablets from Babylon, dated between 595 and 570, during the reign of Nebuchadnezzar II (605-562). These list the rations of oil and barley for persons maintained by the royal commis-

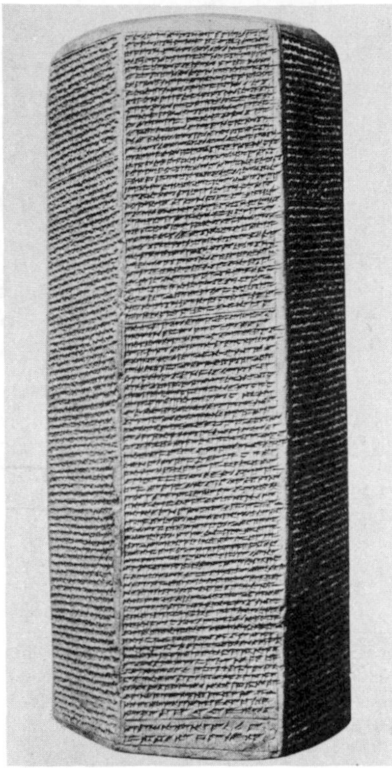

Courtesy of the Oriental Institute, the University of Chicago

12. Clay prism containing the annals of Sennacherib (704-681 B.C.)

sariat, among whom appear none other than Jehoiachin, the exiled king of Judah, and his five sons (cf. II Kings 25:27-30).

A poem by a Babylonian priest denounces the reign of Nabonidus (555-539) and recognizes Cyrus II (557-529) as the heaven-sent world ruler in terms reminiscent of the sentiments expressed by the prophet in Isa. 40–55. Cyrus himself has left a cylinder relating the fall of Babylon and indicating that he allowed various exiled peoples in his new domains to return to their own lands.

3. Canaanite. The discovery at Ras Shamra, ancient UGARIT on the N Syrian coast, of an archive of hundreds of clay tablets inscribed in an alphabetic cuneiform script and in a language which proved to be an early form of Canaanite was destined to have far-reaching effects on OT studies.* These mythological poems of the fifteenth and fourteenth centuries are of great linguistic importance and have contributed not a little to the understanding of Hebrew vocabulary in the OT. But even more significant is the fact that OT poetic literature is permeated by literary reminiscences of these epics. Moreover, they richly illustrate the religious beliefs and practices denounced by such prophets as Hosea. Figs. UGA 2; WRI 28.

A number of inscriptions discovered at the Egyptian turquoise mines in the Sinai Peninsula have provided the evidence for the origin of the alphabetic scripts which produced the Hebrew alphabet and ultimately our own (*see* ALPHABET).* These proto-Sinaitic inscriptions, to be dated *ca.* 1500, were written with

From *Zeitschrift des Deutschen Palästina-Vereins;* by permission of Otto Harrassowitz, Wiesbaden, Germany

13. Inscribed plaque from Shechem in alphabetic script (*ca.* 1650 B.C.)

signs derived from Egyptian hieroglyphs on the acrophonic principle. Three short inscriptions in the same script have turned up at Gezer, Lachish, and Shechem. Figs. WRI 29; INS 13.

From the thirteenth and twelfth centuries comes a series of alphabetic inscriptions from such sites as Beth-shemesh, Byblos, and Lachish,* as well as inscribed arrowheads. These are of great importance in illustrating the development of the script from the proto-Sinaitic texts to the Phoenician inscriptions of the tenth century at Byblos (*see* EPIGRAPHY).* The latter, six in number, together with the later Phoenician inscriptions, such as that of Kilamuwa from Zenjirli, contribute valuable data for the history of PHOENICIA. They also provide evidence for the orthography of the Hebrew in the earliest portions of the OT. Figs. LAC 4; GEB 15.

The longest Phoenician inscription to date was recently discovered at Karatepe in E Cilicia. From it may be obtained much information about the kingdom of the Danunians (one of the Sea Peoples) in the latter part of the eighth century. This great inscription, which actually contains three versions of the text in Phoenician, is also bilingual, for the same text, with minor differences, appears in two versions written in hieroglyphic Hittite. The text affords a brilliant confirmation of the successful attempts of scholars to decipher this new language and script (*see* HITTITES). Its greatest contribution in this connection will be the new lexical information it provides.

The MOABITE STONE, a monument erected *ca.* 840 by Mesha, king of Moab, is the only important inscription in the Moabite dialect.* It tells how the Israelite ruler Omri conquered N Moab and further recounts a victory over Israel not mentioned in the OT. Fig. MOA 66.

The earliest Hebrew inscription is a limestone plaque from GEZER, to be dated *ca.* 925. This interesting text is an agricultural calendar, probably a schoolboy's exercise. Fig. CAL 2.

Of great interest is the group of about seventy Hebrew ostraca from SAMARIA (town), consisting of invoices for the deliveries of oil and wine to the royal treasury between *ca.* 778 and 770. These texts, contemporary with Jeroboam II of Israel and the

Copyright: The Matson Photo Service

14. The Siloam Inscription, in Hebrew, found at the end of Hezekiah's tunnel, tells of the workmen's boring the tunnel from opposite ends and finally meeting.

prophets Amos and Hosea, are of extreme value for Hebrew paleography, showing as they do the development of the cursive hand, as well as for the language, being written in the N Israelite dialect, like the Gezer Calendar.

In 1880 a lad accidentally discovered a Hebrew inscription in the ancient tunnel leading from the Gihon spring to the Pool of SILOAM at Jerusalem. It proved to contain a description of the engineering feat by which the tunnel was excavated during the reign of Hezekiah to withstand the siege of Sennacherib *ca.* 701 (II Kings 20:20; cf. II Chr. 32:2-4, 30). Fig. INS 14.

Twenty-one ostraca were recovered from the excavations during 1935-38 at LACHISH, to be dated *ca.* 589, just before the capture of the town by Nebuchadnezzar in the time of Jeremiah and Zedekiah. In addition to business documents and lists of names, there are several letters addressed to Yaosh, the military governor of Lachish.* The importance of these inscribed potsherds for a knowledge of the Hebrew of the time of Jeremiah is enormous. As in the case of the Siloam Inscription, they are composed in the S dialect of Judah. Fig. INS 15.

Copyright: By permission of the Trustees of the late Sir Henry S. Wellcome

15. Lachish Letter No. 4, written with pen and ink on pottery, is a letter from a field officer to his commanding officer; written in the late summer of 589 B.C.

Some hundreds of Hebrew inscriptions are to be found on miscellaneous objects, such as seals, weights, jar-handle stamps, ossuaries, coins, etc. Often these are of particular interest, like the recently excavated jar handle stamped with the name of Gibeon,* which confirms the tentative identification of the site. One seal bears the legend "Shema, liegeman of Jeroboam" (II), another has "Ushna, liegeman of Ahaz," and two others, bearing the names of Gedaliah and Jaazaniah, were found at Lachish among remains of the period just before the Exile. Four weights, inscribed with the word פים, have clarified the meaning of this enigmatic expression in I Sam. 13:21. OSSUARIES yield a rich store of Jewish names. Fig. GIB 30.

From the Phoenician colony of Carthage come two Punic inscriptions of the fourth century B.C. These are sacrificial tariffs, listing sacrifices with the payments due the priests and the apportionment of the sacrificial victims. They display a marked resemblance to the ritual and practice of the sacrificial system outlined in the Priestly Code. *See* SACRIFICE AND OFFERINGS.

Until recently the earliest Hebrew MSS of the OT were of the ninth century A.D. The one possible exception was the NASH PAPYRUS from Egypt, which contains the Decalogue and Shema. This fragment, perhaps to be dated late in the second century B.C., is of importance both paleographically and as evidence that Hebrew could still be read by Jews in Egypt. The sensational discoveries of the DEAD SEA SCROLLS from 1947 on, however, have yielded MSS earlier by a millennium (*see* TEXT, OT).* The wealth of information they furnish with regard to the literature and beliefs of the sectarian community which produced them can scarcely be overestimated. Figs. DEA 20-21.

4. Aramaic. A stela, found near Aleppo, was erected *ca.* 860 to Melcarth, the god of Tyre, by

"Ben-hadad [I], the son of Tabrimmon, the son of Hezion, king of Syria," thus confirming the succession as given in I Kings 15:18.* This ruler, who aided Asa, king of Judah, against Baasha of Israel, is thus shown on epigraphic grounds to be a contemporary of Elijah and Elisha (cf. II Kings 8:7-15; this Ben-hadad is usually considered to be the second king of this name). Fig. BEN 28.

According to II Kings 8:15, Hazael usurped the throne of Ben-hadad I, as Assyrian inscriptions also affirm. A brief Aramaic inscription on one of the ivories from Arslan Tash in N Syria gives the name of Hazael. An Assyrian inventory list records these ivories as part of the booty captured from Syria by Shalmaneser III. Hazael's son and successor was Ben-hadad II (usually regarded as III; cf. II Kings 13:24); this fact was confirmed by the stela of Zakir, king of Hamath and Lu'ash, erected *ca.* 775. Zakir relates how he defeated a coalition of kings led by Ben-hadad.

The longest Old Aramaic text yet found, to be dated *ca.* 750, comes from Sujin. This, together with three other eighth-century inscriptions from Zenjirli, provides contemporary material for the history of the Aramaic kingdoms. Two grave inscriptions from Nerab and an ostracon containing a letter found at Ashur, all of the seventh century, complete the corpus of Old Aramaic inscriptions.

Many documents coming from the sites of Jewish military colonies have been found in Egypt. These letters and business and legal documents are written in Imperial Aramaic, the lingua franca of the Persian Empire. They include 110 papyri from Saqqarah, Edfu, Hermopolis Magna, and especially Elephantine (*see* Elephantine Papyri),* in addition to some 350 ostraca from Elephantine and at least thirteen letters to administrative officials written on leather. Although a few are dated in the sixth and third centuries B.C., the bulk of the texts comes from the fifth century. They are important for a knowledge of the Aramaic of the period, which is somewhat earlier than that of the Aramaic sections of the OT. The light they shed on the religious practices of Jewish colonists in Egypt is also considerable, indicating as they do the existence of a temple at Elephantine subsequent to the Deuteronomic legislation in favor of a single sanctuary at Jerusalem. Recently a still earlier papyrus was found at Saqqarah, to be dated *ca.* 603. Written by a ruler of a Palestinian town (Ashkelon?) to Pharaoh (probably Neco II), it refers to Nebuchadnezzar's invasion. Fig. ELE 25.

Three silver vessels now in the Brooklyn Museum bear Aramaic inscriptions referring to Gashmu, king of Kedar. If these are to be connected with a Lihyanite inscription associating a man of the same name with the Persian governor of Dedan, it may well be that we are dealing with the very Gashmu or Geshem of Neh. 2:19; 6:1, 6.

Among minor inscriptions of a later period may be mentioned an ossuary of the first century A.D. with the legend: "Here were brought the bones of Uzziah, king of Judah. Do not open!"* Apart from its historical interest, the text is important as an example of the Aramaic of Jesus' time. An altar from Palmyra, bearing the word חמן, has proved that the object so designated in the OT is not a "sun image" as in the KJV, but an Incense Altar. Fig. UZZ 19.

5. Greek. The "Balustrade" Inscription, which survives in two Greek copies from Herod's temple in Jerusalem, reads: "No foreigner is to enter within the balustrade and enclosure around the temple. Whoever is caught will render himself liable to the consequent penalty of death" (cf. Acts 21:28-29).

Another inscription from Jerusalem provides the oldest evidence of a synagogue in Palestine. It commemorates the construction of a synagogue by Theodotus, a "ruler of the synagogue."* Since the description of this Theodotus suggests that he was a freedman, perhaps this was the "synagogue of the Freedmen" mentioned in Acts 6:9. Fig. SYN 94.

An inscription from Delphi proves that Gallio was proconsul of Achaia in A.D. 52. This fact is of importance for the chronology of Paul (cf. Acts 18:12).

The sands of Egypt have yielded up masses of Greek papyri. Two letters, of the year 259 B.C., come from Tubias—i.e., Tobiah—who held the same position under Ptolemy II that his ancestor the Ammonite Tobiah (2) held under Artaxerxes I (Neh. 2:10). Most of these papyri come from the Faiyum, from such sites as Arsinoë, Tebtunis, Gurob, and especially Oxyrhynchus. They are letters; business and legal documents; literary works, including the famous Oxyrhynchus Sayings of Jesus;* etc.; and they shed a flood of light on the daily life of the early centuries A.D. Of great significance also is the evidence they afford for the Koine, or nonliterary Greek of the day, which is the form of Greek used by the NT writers. Fig. OXY 19.

Bibliography. Translations of many of the inscriptions discussed herein, together with bibliographies, are contained in J. B. Pritchard, ed., *ANET* (2nd ed., 1955); D. W. Thomas, ed., *Documents from OT Times* (1958).

The following are supplementary: F. L. Griffith, *Stories of the High Priests of Memphis* (1900), pp. 142-207; cf. H. Gressmann, "Vom reichen Mann und armen Lazarus," *Abhandlungen der preussischen Akademie der Wissenschaften zu Berlin, Philosophisch-historische Klasse* (1918). G. A. Cooke, *Text-Book of North-Semitic Inscriptions* (1903); cf. W. F. Albright, "Phoenician Inscriptions of the Tenth Century B.C. from Byblus," *JAOS,* LXVII (1947), 153-60; D. Diringer, *Le iscrizioni antico-ebraiche palestinesi* (1934). C. C. Edgar, "Selected Papyri from the Archives of Zenon," *Annales du Service des Antiquités,* XVIII (1918), 164-66, 231-32. "A Greek Synagogue Inscription from Jerusalem," *BASOR,* IV (1921), 13-14. L. H. Vincent, "Découverte de la 'Synagogue des affranchis' à Jérusalem," *RB,* XXX (1921), 247-77. G. Lefebvre, *Le tombeau de Petosiris* (1923-24). W. F. Albright, "The Discovery of an Aramaic Inscription Relating to King Uzziah," *BASOR,* XLIV (1931), 8-10. "The Proconsulship of Gallio," in F. J. Foakes-Jackson and K. Lake, *The Beginnings of Christianity,* V (1933), 460-64. J. Simons, *Handbook for the Study of Egyptian Topographical Lists* (1937). W. F. Albright, "The Early Alphabetic Inscriptions from Sinai," *BASOR,* CX (1948), 6-22. H. L. Ginsberg, "An Aramaic Contemporary of the Lachish Letters," *BASOR,* CXI (1948), 24-27. S. Smith, *The Statue of Idrimi* (1949); cf. W. F. Albright, *BASOR,* CXVIII (1950), 14-20. W. F. Albright, "The Smaller Beth-shan Stele of Sethos I," *BASOR,* CXXV (1952), 24-32. W. C. Hayes, *A Papyrus of the Late Middle Kingdom* (1955), pp. 87-89; cf. W. F. Albright, *JAOS,* LXXIV (1954), 222-33. I. Rabinowitz, "Aramaic Inscriptions of the Fifth Century B.C.E.," *JNES,* XV (1956), 1-9; cf. F. M. Cross, Jr., *BA,* XVIII (1955), 46-47. R. J. Williams, "Theodicy in the Ancient Near East," *Canadian Journal of Theology,* II (1956), 14-26. D. J. Wiseman, *Chronicles of Chaldaean Kings* (1956); cf. D. N. Freedman, *BA,* XIX (1956), 50-60.

R. J. Williams

INSECTS. The phrase שרץ העוף (Lev. 11:20-21, 23; Deut. 14:19) is translated "winged insects" (KJV FOWLS THAT CREEP; FLYING CREEPING THING[S]; CREEPING THING THAT FLIETH; *see* CREEPING THINGS). On insects as a class, *see* FAUNA § F.

The "winged insects" of Lev. 11:20-23 include the LOCUST. It illustrates the prescientific character of the biblical age that any of these insects should be referred to as having four feet, though the edible ones are said to have leaping legs in addition to their four feet (cf. M. Hullin 3.7; Talmud Hullin 65*a*-66*a*).

W. S. MCCULLOUGH

INSIGHT [בים, בינה, תבונה]. The intellectual and spiritual capacity to discern the nature of things; the power of discernment and discrimination (Ezra 8:16; Prov. 1:2; 2:3; 3:5; 4:1, 5, 7; 7:4; 8:14; 9:6, 10; Eph. 1:9; 3:4; cf. II Sam. 14:17, 20; Wisd. Sol. 7:7, 17-21). In biblical thought insight, like wisdom, is a gift from God (Eccl. 2:26; Wisd. Sol. 7:27; cf. 7:7; I Cor. 2:2-16; Jas. 1:5-8), and is a somewhat permanent mental and spiritual endowment. The desire for it is preponderantly pragmatic; it is essential for the guidance of life. Man's intellect, apart from God, will not lead him aright (Prov. 3:5).

Insight is coupled with wisdom (Prov. 1:2; 4:5, 7; 7:4; 8:14; 9:10; Eph. 1:9), understanding (Prov. 2:3), and counsel (Prov. 8:14), to all of which it is intimately related. It brings to man intellectual perception (Prov. 2:3); knowledge of the deep things of God (Job 11:7; 28; Jer. 9:23-24; Wisd. Sol. 9:13-18; I Cor. 2:10-11), of the counsel of God (Wisd. Sol. 9:13, 17), of good and evil (II Sam. 14:17; I Kings 3:9), of all things on earth (II Sam. 14:20), of things pleasing to God (Eccl. 2:26; Wisd. Sol. 9:18); and skill in arranging things so as to lead to a desired end (Prov. 8:14). Such knowledge is regarded as revelation. In Ezra 8:16, the term "men of insight" refers to intelligent leaders—i.e., teachers.

By this gift man is able to perceive the spiritual in the material, to see in human history the divine activity, in Jesus of Nazareth the Christ of God. *See also* WISDOM; UNDERSTANDING.

Bibliography. M. Burrows, *An Outline of Biblical Theology* (1946), pp. 31-33; W. Eichrodt, *Theologie des Alten Testaments*, II (Dritte Auflage; 1950), 38; O. Procksch, *Theologie des Alten Testaments* (1950), pp. 476-80; L. Koehler, *OT Theology* (trans. A. S. Todd; 1957), p. 146.

V. H. KOOY

INSPIRATION AND REVELATION. The verb "to inspire" is found in a number of passages in the RSV, where it does not translate any single word in Hebrew or Greek but has been supplied in order to clarify the sense of the original. In such instances it denotes the action of God in bestowing wisdom or skill on a particular individual, or the operation of the HOLY SPIRIT in guiding the minds of prophets or stimulating the members of the Christian community either to spiritual joy or to the performance of the various functions and offices by which the fellowship of the whole body is maintained and strengthened.

God may thus "put it into the heart of" (RSV "inspire") the skilful artist Bezalel to teach his craft (Exod. 35:34). The wise king, as a servant of God, whose mind is directed by the Lord, utters "inspired decisions"—i.e., oracles or wise decrees (Prov. 16:10; קסם; LXX μαντεῖον). The word "inspire" is used by the RSV in order to bring out the meaning of such passages as Matt. 22:43; Mark 12:36, where David, as a prophet, is quoted as having spoken of Christ "in the Spirit"—i.e., under the guidance of the Spirit of God; Luke 2:27, where Simeon, as a Spirit-possessed prophet, comes into the temple under impulse of the Spirit to greet the Christ; I Tim. 1:18, which speaks of the stimulus provided for Timothy's Christian career by the prophecies which marked him out for selection as a leader in the church. In I Cor. 12:11 we are told that the Spirit "operates" (ἐνεργεῖ; RSV "apportions") the various gifts needed by the members of the community for their different kinds of service; here the RSV explains that these are the result of the Spirit's inspiration. Similarly, the "joy of the Holy Spirit" which fills the Christians of Thessalonica in their reception of the gospel, despite the persecution and affliction with which its coming had been associated, is rightly described by the RSV as "inspired by the Holy Spirit" (I Thess. 1:6).

1. Inspiration and scripture. ***a. General view of the OT as inspired.*** The Greek term for "inspired" (θεόπνευστος, "God-breathed") occurs only once in the Bible (II Tim. 3:16) and then with reference to the OT scriptures: "All scripture is inspired by God and profitable for teaching, for reproof, for correction, and for training in righteousness," or, as the passage should perhaps be rendered: "Every scripture inspired by God is also profitable . . ." (RSV mg.). The word indicates that God has in some manner breathed into these writings his own creative Spirit, just as he breathed life into man when he formed him out of the dust of the ground (Gen. 2:7). The Scriptures have been in some way infused with the life-giving power of the Spirit of God.

So much is clear from the use of this term. It is, however, not easy to determine in what sense the writer of this letter thought of the Scriptures as being inspired. "Inspiration" is a quality of persons rather than of writings as such, and there can be little doubt that what is meant is that the scriptures of the OT are the product of men who were specially inspired and empowered by the divine Spirit. The concept was a familiar one in the Greek world. Oracles, e.g., were regarded as inspired because they were delivered by persons who were supernaturally possessed by a divine power and spoke under the compulsion of a mysterious afflatus which controlled, and in a measure superseded, the exercise of their natural faculties. The writer of II Timothy is certainly thinking of the Scriptures as the writings of men who wrote under the guidance and in the power of the divine Spirit. The Scriptures—i.e., the Law, the Prophets, and such other writings as the Psalms—were written by men who were given peculiar insight into the ways and purposes of God, so that their message was to be regarded as essentially God's word to his people.

b. Christian interpretation of the OT. The setting of the Law and the Prophets as sacred books in Judaism, followed by the gradual definition of the rest of the CANON of the OT scriptures, already rested upon the belief that God had uniquely revealed himself to certain minds which he had empowered to receive his self-disclosure. The Christian church looked at the Scriptures from a different standpoint. At a very early date, it carried through a most remarkable revolution in the understanding of the OT. This is reflected in the account Luke gives of the journey to Emmaus, when the risen Lord expounded to his disciples "in all the scriptures the things concerning himself," "beginning with Moses and all the prophets" (Luke 24:27). The Bible was now read as a Christian book. It was a collection of writings whose focus and central point was Christ. The Scriptures, in fact, were a book about Christ. The Law, properly understood, pointed forward to him and spoke of him in types and figures, as the writer to the Hebrews pointed out at length; the prophets foretold Christ in fuller detail and with greater clarity; and for the purpose of this exegesis David, the ancestor of Christ according to the flesh, was himself one of the prophets, an inspired seer who spoke plainly about Christ in the Psalms. This reinterpretation of the Scriptures is known to us chiefly through the way in which the authors of the NT use the Greek Bible; but the process must date back to a time before the establishment of the Hellenist churches. The justification of the Christian gospel from the pages of the Scriptures must have been an essential task of the missionary preacher who sought to commend his message to Jews; and without a scriptural armory no apologetic addressed to Jewish audiences would have been possible. The peculiar collection of proof texts used by Matthew may indicate an early stage in the process of assembling evidence to prove that, properly understood, the Scriptures spoke of Christ. Indeed, it is likely that the reinterpretation was begun by Jesus himself, as he used passages of Deuteronomy to define his mission against misconceptions of it suggested to him by the devil (Matt. 4:1-10; Luke 4:1-12), and worked out his vocation in terms of the Son of man and the Servant of the Lord.

c. Inspiration of the prophets. This drastic change in the understanding of the OT led to a new conception of the inspiration of the ancient writers. They had been accepted as men who had been endowed with a singular understanding of the ways of God, and hence as men who spoke the word of God to his people. Now it was seen that "in many and various ways God spoke of old to our fathers by the prophets; but in these last days he has spoken to us by a Son" (Heb. 1:1-2). In Christ there was to be discerned God's final and complete word to man. This word was not discontinuous with what God had declared in former times through the mouth of the prophets and such inspired writers as David in the Psalms. On the contrary, the prophets of Israel were now seen as men who were moved by the Spirit of God to witness to Christ and his coming before the event took place. Their inspiration was now thought of as a special gift which enabled them, not simply to discern the significance of God's acts in history as a whole, but rather to foresee and proclaim the dispensation of the Incarnation. This view of the function of the OT teachers is well summed up in the opening discourse in I Peter: "The prophets who prophesied of the grace that was to be yours searched and inquired about this salvation; they inquired what person or time was indicated by the Spirit of Christ within them when predicting the sufferings of Christ and the subsequent glory. It was revealed to them that they were serving not themselves but you, in the things which have now been announced to you by those who preached the good news to you through the Holy Spirit sent from heaven, things into which angels long to look" (I Pet. 1:10-12).

The prophets of the Old Covenant are thus regarded as men who were divinely empowered to predict the sufferings of Christ and the subsequent glory. This reflects the use that was actually made of their writings by the primitive church's missionaries and teachers. Their value lay in the fact that in them the Spirit had borne witness to Christ. As the Fourth Gospel represents Jesus as saying to the Jews: "You search the scriptures, because you think that in them you have eternal life; and it is they that bear witness to me" (John 5:39), and: "If you believed Moses, you would believe me, for he wrote of me. But if you do not believe his writings, how will you believe my words?" (vss. 46-47). Moses wrote about Christ; the Scriptures bear witness to him. The Spirit instructed the prophets about the fulfilment of God's purposes in Christ. *See* PROPHET.

d. Inspiration proved by the Holy Spirit in the church. The Scriptures can be understood, however, in the sense which their inspired authors intended, only if the reader possesses the key to their interpretation. Without this, the reader would be in the same position as the Ethiopian who, on reading the Servant poems, could only ask whether the prophet was speaking of himself or of some other man, and needed to be enlightened by the Christian evangelist before he could discern that the prophet was foretelling Jesus (Acts 8:34-35). The key was supplied by the apostles and the other missionaries who bore testimony to Christ under the guidance and in the power of the same Spirit who had inspired the prophets to bear witness beforehand. The ministry of the prophets and of the apostles is continuous; in essentials it is the same ministry, for the same Spirit speaks in both and their testimony is the same. Its expression is different, for the former spoke before the event, indicating it in mysterious images and types, whereas the latter were sent to point to the fulfilment, and to declare the gospel openly. Looking back to the prophetic writings in the light of the witness of the apostolic church, one could see that "no prophecy of scripture is a matter of one's own interpretation, because no prophecy ever came by the impulse of man, but men moved by the Holy Spirit spoke from God" (II Pet. 1:20-21, a variant reading being: ". . . moved by the Holy Spirit holy men of God spoke" [RSV mg.]). The prophecies are to be interpreted by an objective standard; they are not capriciously given oracles, each related to particular individual circumstances, but are divinely revealed words whose meaning is declared in Christ. The Holy Spirit, who is now active in the church's proclamation of the gospel, moved the saints of old to speak as they did.

There is thus a double movement of thought, as it were, in the primitive church's understanding of the inspiration of the prophetic writers: (*a*) It accepts their works as a body of sacred scriptures, uniquely authoritative as embodying the word of God to his people. It has taken them over from Judaism with this value already set upon them. It therefore looks to them for evidences for the gospel, and seeks to prove the truth of the Christian understanding of the life, death, and resurrection of Jesus on the basis of OT texts. An essential part of the earliest Christian preaching is that "Christ died for our sins in accordance with the scriptures, that he was buried, that he was raised on the third day in accordance with the scriptures" (I Cor. 15:3-4). The evidence of the inspired prophets, enshrined in the written Bible, is an actual part of the gospel as Paul had received it and as he handed it on in turn to his own converts. The missionary speeches of the apostles, so far as we may judge from the narrative of Acts, when they were not directed to purely Gentile audiences, like the speeches of Paul at Lystra and Athens, were mainly concerned to show the necessary connection and harmony between the Christian message and the prophecies of the OT, the latter embracing, not only the prophetical books in the narrower sense, but also all those parts of the scripture which could be understood in a new sense as alluding in some way to Christ or to the situation of Christ's church. The inspiration of the ancient prophets, a matter on which both the missionaries and their hearers were fully agreed, could be appealed to as a guarantee of the truth of the gospel. (*b*) At the same time, the movement of thought runs in the other direction. The inspiration of the prophets is attested in a new way, by reason of the fact that their utterances have found a fulfilment in the events of the gospel and the age of the church.

That the Scriptures have so been fulfilled can be shown by the apostles on the basis of their personal testimony. Their witness is guaranteed by the authority of the inspired prophets and is in itself a new attestation of the fact that the Spirit of God moved those prophets so that their writings are supremely authoritative for the Christian. Hence the early Christian writers ascribe to the prophetic scriptures the value of the words of God himself. According to Mark, Jesus asserted the divine inspiration of David in the messianic Ps. 110. The citation of the first verse of this psalm is introduced with the words: "David himself, in the Holy Spirit, declared" (Mark 12:36). The RSV gives the right sense of this verse when it translates: "David himself, inspired by the Holy Spirit, declared." David was speaking as an inspired prophet possessed by the Spirit and enabled by the Spirit to declare the truth about God's purposes. It is God himself who spoke through the prophets. As Zechariah said in his hymn of praise:

> [God] has raised up a horn of salvation for us
> in the house of his servant David,
> as he spoke by the mouth of his holy prophets from of old
> (Luke 1:69-70).

The gospel of Christ was "promised beforehand" by God "through his prophets in the holy scriptures" (Rom. 1:2). A psalm prophetical of the condition of the church can therefore be ascribed directly to the Holy Spirit: "Therefore, as the Holy Spirit says,

> 'Today, when you hear his voice,
> do not harden your hearts' "
> (Heb. 3:7).

It may be that the phrase rendered by the RSV "it is said," introducing a quotation of Ps. 68, should rather be translated "he says," indicating that God himself speaks in the psalm (Eph. 4:8), but this is uncertain. God, at any rate, speaks in the Scriptures, in harmony with, and subordinately to, the final utterance of his word in Christ.

2. Inspiration of apostolic preaching. The apostles and the other Christian missionaries witness to the events the prophets foresaw. Hence the foundation of the church is "the apostles and prophets" (Eph. 2:20). The prophets are conjoined with the apostles because through them both the same Spirit testifies to Christ. Both are inspired. The apostles, as the representatives and envoys of Christ, are inspired by the Spirit to testify to him. They are to be received as Christ himself, for they bear Christ to their hearers (cf. Matt. 10:40). Their witness is the witness of the Spirit himself: "When the Counselor comes, whom I shall send to you from the Father, even the Spirit of truth, who proceeds from the Father, he will bear witness to me; and you also are witnesses, because you have been with me from the beginning" (John 15:26). The Spirit attests the gospel and commends it to those who listen to the apostolic preaching. At Thessalonica, Paul presented the gospel "in power and in the Holy Spirit" (I Thess. 1:5)—a phrase which probably indicates both the inspiration of the preacher and the witness of the Spirit in the hearts of his audience. So, too, Paul declares: "Christ has wrought through me to win obedience from the Gentiles, by word and deed, by the power of signs and wonders, by the power of the Holy Spirit" (Rom. 15:18-19). His message did not rest upon any wisdom or persuasive eloquence of his own, but it was presented "in demonstration of the Spirit and power" (I Cor. 2:4). The apostle was inspired by the Spirit to proclaim the gospel in word and deed. He was inspired by the Spirit to grasp the meaning of God's promises (I Cor. 2:10). It is as one inspired by the Spirit that Paul approaches and grapples with the problem of Israel's disobedience (Rom. 9:1). The Pauline letters bear out in detail what is said in the gospels and Acts concerning the inspiration of the apostolic missionaries (*see* HOLY SPIRIT), and their inspiration is continuous with that of the inspired writers of the Scriptures. Whether or not Paul conceived himself in his letters to be writing "Scriptures," he certainly believed that the inspiration which enabled him to grasp and to proclaim the Christian gospel was the operation of the same Spirit who had spoken in the prophets of the OT. *See* PREACHING; APOSTLE; MINISTRY.

3. Inspiration of Christians. ***a. Martyrs and other confessors.*** The Spirit that inspired the prophets to foretell the coming of Christ and to proclaim the gospel in advance, often in words which inevitably remained obscure until their fulfilment, testified to Christ in a special way in the mouth of his disciples when they publicly acknowledged him. A definite promise that those who confessed Christ under the stress of persecution would receive an immediate inspiration of the Spirit was contained in the gospels, and was the NT basis of the later belief that the martyr or the confessor was pre-eminently a "spiritual" man, one possessed by the Spirit in a unique degree, whose words were therefore such as to carry supreme authority. The warning given by Jesus to his disciples that they must expect to suffer persecution is followed by the promise: "When they bring you to trial and deliver you up, do not be anxious beforehand what you are to say; but say whatever is given you in that hour, for it is not you who speak, but the Holy Spirit" (Mark 13:11). Matthew, rewriting this section of Mark, puts this promise into the context of the instructions given by Jesus to the Twelve and makes the nature of the promised inspiration clearer: "It is not you who speak, but the Spirit of your Father speaking through you" (Matt. 10:20). Luke sets in contrast with the confessor's possession of this special inspiration of the Spirit the unforgivable blasphemy against the Spirit committed by the person who rejects the divine assistance, refuses the Spirit's inspiration, and apostatizes, denying Christ (Luke 12:8-12). The promise of the PARACLETE, related by the Fourth Evangelist, also places the witness which the Spirit will bear to Christ, along with, and througn, his disciples, in the context of a warning that the disciples of Jesus will be hated and persecuted as he himself was (John 15:18-27). Running through the entire gospel tradition, therefore, there is the thought that the highest degree of inspiration is given to the Christian who confesses Christ when he is on trial for his faith. Inspiration is in itself the witness of the Spirit of God to Christ; and the Spirit is most truly and perfectly active in the testimony of the martyr.

The great example of the fulfilment of this promise of inspiration is to be seen in the story of STEPHEN. It is in the Spirit that he contends against the enemies of Christ (Acts 6:10). When he is arrested, on charges which are essentially those upon which Jesus himself had been condemned in the high priest's court (vss. 11-13), he is transfigured in countenance as he prepares to make his defense. His speech is not a defense in the proper sense; he does not defend himself against the charges which have been preferred against him. It is, rather, a proclamation of the gospel in terms of scriptural fulfilment. For the Christian confessor a trial was the great opportunity for the preaching of the gospel; and in Luke's picture of Stephen's apologia we see the inspired Christian confessor bearing witness to Christ and using for this purpose the inspired utterances of the ancient scriptures and the understanding which the inspired prophets had of the long story of God's dealings with his covenant people. When his hearers break in on his speech and are about to kill him, he is filled with the Holy Spirit (7:55), and enabled in an ecstasy to "see the heavens opened and the Son of man standing at the right hand of God" (vs. 56). The manner of his death, as Luke records it, is strongly reminiscent of the death of Jesus. The martyr is one who shares in a supreme sense in the death of Jesus, being indwelt by the same Spirit which belonged to Jesus.

The confessor who suffers for his faith is thus a uniquely inspired man. It is this conviction which underlies the early origin of the Christian belief in the special sanctity of the martyrs and prompted the development of a cult of the saints. Nevertheless, it is not only confession of Christ under persecution which is the work of the Spirit. All acknowledgment of the lordship of Christ is his work, and it is because of the inspiration of the Spirit that any man can make his profession of faith. "I want you to understand," says Paul to the Corinthians, "that no one speaking by the Spirit of God ever says 'Jesus be cursed!' and no one can say 'Jesus is Lord' except by the Holy Spirit" (I Cor. 12:3). This passage raises difficulties of interpretation, but it is likely that Paul is referring to a profession of faith in Christ made by the new convert at his baptism. We may compare: "If you confess with your lips that Jesus is Lord and believe in your heart that God raised him from the dead, you will be saved" (Rom. 10:9). No one, then, can make his initial confession of faith in Christ as Lord (cf. the early form of baptismal creed in the "Western" text of Acts 8:37, RSV mg.), without the inspiration of the Spirit. We may say that all inspiration of the Spirit, according to the NT, is related to the testimony of men to Christ: to the testimony of the martyr, to that of the apostolic missionary, and to that of every believer as he comes to conversion. The fact that the Spirit inspires the convert to profess his creed of belief in Christ when he comes to his baptism, and yet that the bestowal on him of the living presence of the Spirit is something which the evidence of the NT makes us assign to the convert's baptismal and postbaptismal experience, is paradoxical. Christians are those who have received the Spirit as a result of their conversion; the Spirit's coming to them is a result and consequence of their baptism and its profession of faith; yet it is because of the inspiration of the Spirit, as a prevenient act, that the Christian is enabled to confess Christ in the first place. Here is an aspect of the constant paradox of grace.

b. In the corporate life of the church. Since the Spirit's inspiration is experienced by all who acknowledge Christ, the whole community of the church can be said to be inspired. They are a people who are "taught of God." The Christians at Thessalonica "have been taught by God"—i.e., through the inspiration of the Spirit—"to love one another" (I Thess. 4:9). Speaking of the Christian's possession of the Spirit, the "anointing" by which they are truly the people of the Messiah, John says: "The anointing which you received from him abides in you, and you have no need that any one should teach you; as his anointing teaches you about everything, and is true, and is no lie, just as it has taught you, abide in him" (I John 2:27). The Christian community is a body of those who are inspired by the Spirit. Such inspiration is no longer the privilege of a few individual prophets, selected to receive a special revelation of the purposes of God; it is granted to the whole society insofar as it is possessed by the Spirit, who mediates to it the presence of the glorified Christ. They are "taught by God," in the sense that the Spirit is given to them to bring the words of Jesus to their remembrance, to illuminate their meaning, and so to guide them into all the truth (cf. John 14:26; 16:12-14). In this inspired community the prophecy is fulfilled: "And they shall all be taught by God" (Isa. 54:13, cited at John 6:45). *See* CHURCH, IDEA OF.

There is thus a continuous operation of the Spirit in the prophets and other inspired individuals in the Old Covenant, and hence in their words as written down and set apart as "scripture," in the testimony to Christ of the apostles, the confessors, and the ordinary Christian believers, and in the church collectively.

c. As related to ecstatic speech. It remains true that the NT speaks of certain classes of persons who are endowed with a peculiar degree of inspiration, or rather, who experience the operation of the Spirit in a remarkable and unusual mode. The most important of these are the ecstatics, endowed with the gift of tongues (*see* TONGUES, GIFT OF), and the prophets within the Christian church (*see* PROPHET IN THE NT). Paul is concerned (I Cor. 12–14) to insist that the obvious and spectacular inspiration which enables some to speak with tongues and others to interpret what has thus been said in a state of ecstatic possession is only one among the many manifestations of the activity of the Spirit within the Spirit-possessed community of the church. Speaking with tongues is listed by Paul relatively low in his enumeration of the operations of the Spirit among the members of the Christian society (I Cor. 12:10, 28-29), and he is evidently anxious to dispel the idea, so prevalent in the congregation at Corinth, that a person who has been inspired to "speak in a tongue" has received a special divine favor which marks him out as a more advanced and "spiritual" Christian than his fellows. He is also insistent that the gift of prophecy ought to be more highly valued than that of tongues. The latter is a peculiarly individual gift, useless for the edification of the congregation as a whole: "For one who speaks in a tongue speaks not to men but to God; for no one understands him, but he utters mysteries in the Spirit" (I Cor. 14:2). Prophecy, however, is intelligible. It conduces to the instruction and edification of the whole body. Even an unbeliever or outsider, should he enter the congregation when all are prophesying, will be impressed with the sense that God is present in the assembly; whereas if they were speaking with tongues, such an intruder could only conclude that he had come into a crowd of madmen (I Cor. 14:23-25).

Prophecy is to be preferred because the prophet can be understood by his hearers without the need for an interpreter with a peculiar inspiration of the Spirit to enable him to grasp the meaning of what has been said: "He who prophesies is greater than he who speaks in tongues, unless some one interprets, so that the church may be edified" (I Cor. 14:5). Paul will not allow that speaking with tongues is beneficial to the community, unless the ecstatic utterances can be translated into intelligible speech, or unless the inspired person can somehow preserve at the same time his normal exercise of his own reason. This is especially true in the case of liturgical prayer and praise in the congregation. "I will pray with the Spirit [RSV 'spirit'] and I will pray with the mind also; I will sing with the Spirit [RSV 'spirit'] and I will sing with the mind also. Otherwise, if you bless with the Spirit [RSV 'spirit'], how can any one in the position of an outsider say the 'Amen' to your thanksgiving when he does not know what you are saying? For you may give thanks well enough, but the other man is not edified" (I Cor. 14:15-17). The reference here is probably to the Eucharistic liturgy. The celebrant might make his prayer "in the Spirit," in a state of ecstatic possession; but his unintelligible utterances will not benefit the congregation. The prophet, on the other hand, is rational. He is inspired; he speaks in the Spirit; but his inspiration does not suspend his ordinary rational faculties. "The spirits of prophets are subject to prophets"; the speaker does not lose control of himself (I Cor. 14:32).

In the controversy with the Montanists, orthodox apologists were accustomed to maintain that genuine prophecy did not involve the suspension of the prophet's rational consciousness. Irrational inspiration was a mark of the false prophet. We know too little of the nature of the prophetic gift in the primitive church to be able to test this claim, apart from the words of Paul quoted above. Such men as Agabus behave in the manner of the prophets of the OT, declaring the will of God in a particular situation. It seems probable, however, that the chief task of the Christian prophet was to unlock the meaning of the Scriptures in the light of the inspiration of the Spirit of Christ. Prophets are associated with teachers by Paul (I Cor. 12:28), as well as with apostles and evangelists (cf. Eph. 4:11). On the whole it seems improbable that their inspiration took the form of speaking in ecstatic trances; they are, rather, missionary preachers.

The OT prophet was essentially a man inspired to interpret God's dealings with man. He was conscious of being entrusted with a word of God, so that his speech could be prefaced with "Thus saith the Lord"; but to what extent the great "canonical" prophets, as well as the members of prophetic guilds at an earlier stage, were ecstatics is hard to determine (*see* PROPHET). Certainly, the outward signs of Spirit-possession were no sure guarantee that the prophet was genuinely speaking under the compulsion of the Spirit of God (cf. Deut. 13:1-5; I Kings 22:19-28; Jer. 20:7-18). Whether the prophet was really inspired to receive and declare the meaning of God's acts in history (cf. Jer. 7:25; 25:4; Hos. 6:5; Amos 3:7) could be determined only by the content of his message and not by external phenomena. So far as the OT is concerned, the test of prophetic inspiration lay in the effects and results of the prophet's message; from the standpoint of the NT writers it lay primarily in the relation of his message to Christ. *See* SPIRITUAL GIFTS.

Bibliography. W. Sanday, *Inspiration* (1893); H. W. Robinson, *Inspiration and Revelation in the OT* (1944); F. W. Camfield, *Revelation and the Holy Spirit* (1945); E. Brunner, *Revelation and Reason* (1946); A. Farrer, *The Glass of Vision* (1948); J. K. S. Reid, *The Authority of Scripture* (1957).

G. W. H. LAMPE

INSTINCT. A word which occurs in the phrases "creatures of instinct" (II Pet. 2:12) and "by instinct" (Jude 10). The Greek, ἄλογος, means simply "without reason." The same word is found in Acts 25:27 with the sense of "contrary to reason" (RSV "unreasonable").

Jude speaks of blasphemers who know "by instinct," or "by nature." II Peter speaks of false prophets who are merely "creatures of instinct." Perhaps this means that they are "creatures of nature"—i.e., with no intellectual or spiritual life.

B. H. THROCKMORTON, JR.

INSTRUCTION. *See* TEACHING.

INSTRUMENTS. *See* ALTAR; MUSICAL INSTRUMENTS; THRESHING; WEAPONS AND IMPLEMENTS OF WAR.

INTEGRITY [תם, תמה, תמים]. The state or quality of being complete, well adjusted. The term is extracted from practical evaluation, not legal phraseology. It implies sincerity of heart and motive, singleness of purpose, genuineness, truthfulness, uprightness (cf. Gen. 20:5-6; I Kings 9:4; Pss. 7:8; 25:21; 26:1, 11; 41:12; 101:2; Prov. 2:7; 10:9; 19:1; 20:7; 28:6). In biblical thought moral character is not judged by any absolute or ideal (as in Greek philosophy), but by relationship to God. God sets the standard by which man is judged. That man alone is perfect who is so in the judgment of God. Integrity thus marks the man who walks with singlehearted devotion to God and honorable behavior to men (Prov. 25:21). Noah (Gen. 6:9), Abraham (Gen. 17:1), Jacob (Gen. 25:27), David (I Kings 9:4), and Job (Job 1:1, 8; 2:3) are described as possessing this quality.

Integrity brings its own reward: preservation from enemies (Pss. 25:21; 41:12), redemption from destruction (26:11; 41:12), guidance for living (Prov. 11:3). He who has it has the Lord as his shield (2:7), walks securely (10:9), remains in the land (2:21). Blessed are his sons (20:7).

Assertions of integrity and innocence do not indicate a spirit of self-righteousness and self-satisfaction (as in Luke 18:11-12). The great religious souls who profess integrity—David, Job, the psalmist, Paul—are also most keenly aware of personal sin (II Sam. 12:13; 24:17; Job 13:26; 14:16-17; Pss. 51:5; 69:5; I Cor. 15:9; I Tim. 1:15). The whole drama of redemption is centered on the possibility of the sinner walking in uprightness before God.

While the term "integrity" scarcely occurs in the NT (only Tit. 2:7), the concept is current enough. The Baptist demands integrity in daily life from the penitents (Luke 3:8-14); Jesus enjoins purity of heart (Matt. 5:8), singleness of eye (Matt. 6:22; cf. Luke 11:34-36), purity of motive (Matt. 6:1-6, 16-18); and there are numerous injunctions to truthfulness, sincerity, and genuineness as fundamental to Christian character and conduct.

See also RIGHTEOUSNESS.

Bibliography. A. F. Kirkpatrick, *The Book of Psalms*, I Cambridge Bible (1914), pp. lxxxvii, lxxxviii; J. Pedersen, *Israel,* I-II (1926), 363-76; L. Koehler, *OT Theology* (trans. A. S. Todd; 1957), pp. 166-68.

V. H. KOOY

INTERCESSION. *See* PRAYER; MEDIATOR.

INTERDICT [אסר, אסרא]. A legal term signifying a prohibitory decree, a prohibition (Dan. 6:7-9, 12-13, 15). The biblical references are to a written decree of Darius banning a petition (prayer) to any god, or man, for thirty days, except the king. The presupposition is that the king alone is to be treated as god, or the only authentic representative of the deity. The prohibition was to be binding on all subjects, and irrevocable according to the laws of the Medes and the Persians (Dan. 6:8, 12; cf. Esth. 1:19; 8:8). Such an ordinance, while not impossible, is utterly out of keeping with what we know of the religious policy of Persian kings, but may well reflect the religious situation of the Hellenistic era.

V. H. KOOY

INTEREST [נשך; τόκος]; KJV USURY. The sum paid by a borrower for the use of the borrowed capital.

Other Hebrew words for "interest" are תרבית and מרבית, rendered in the RSV by "increase." Instead of "interest" and "increase," the KJV has invariably "usury," which in the mind of the translators of the time had not the derogative connotation it has taken in our days. They were perfectly aware, however, of the prohibitions and restrictions expressed in the Law, of the excessive rates charged by unscrupulous lenders at all times, and of the fact that some medieval theologians had condemned the practice of lending money for interest.

For a detailed discussion of the various types of interest mentioned in the Bible, *see* DEBT.

G. A. BARROIS

INTERMEDIARY [μεσίτης] (Gal. 3:19-20); KJV MEDIATOR. *See* MEDIATOR.

INTERPRETATION, HISTORY AND PRINCIPLES OF. Interpretation represents either of two technical words, "exegesis" or "hermeneutics," which were originally synonyms but now are arbitrarily distinguished: exegesis, the detailed specific explication of a text; hermeneutics, the theory underlying such explication. Interpretation will here be treated primarily in the sense of hermeneutics.

1. The necessity of interpretation. Any not simply naïve product of the human mind, even if contemporary and in one's own idiom, invites, perhaps demands, interpretation; the invitation turns the more insistently into demand the farther the product may be from one's own time or idiom, or both. Such a product may be a painting or sculpture, a symphony or drama, a law code or a document of religion. The Bible contains thoughts now between two and three millenniums old, formulated within an environment alien to our own, and written in two Semitic languages (Hebrew and Aramaic) and an Indo-European language (Hellenistic Greek) remote from our own—three clamorous demands for interpretation. But it is a fourth fact about the Bible which, for the Christian, makes interpretation of it the most poignant demand for interpretation in our entire culture: its claim to authority, a claim rather modestly made within the Bible, but categorically made for it by the group (the church) within which it has its life.

There is, of course, already interpretation within the Bible, not merely of dreams (Gen. 40; Daniel; cf. Acts 10–11) or riddles (Judg. 14; Dan. 5) or figurative speech (John 2:21; 21:19; and often) which may occur in the text, nor merely of the OT within the NT (Matthew; Hebrews; *et passim*), but also of older OT passages in younger ones (Jer. 31:29-30 in Ezek. 18; the books of Samuel and Kings in the books of Chronicles) and of the older NT in its youngest portions (Matt. 10:10 in I Tim. 5:18). Furthermore, there is a subtle web of interpretation lying between the two testaments: the fact that the NT writers always quote the OT, not in Hebrew, but in Greek. But every translation is inevitably to some degree (and often to a high degree) an interpretation—in fact, one of the common meanings of *interpretatio*, since Cicero's time at the latest, is "translation." For every translator "carries over" into the new language only what he understands the original language to be saying; in other words, between the translator's reading of the original and his transmutation of it there lies a fundamental act of interpretation: it is only what he *thinks* the original means that he *can* translate.

Two basic questions have agitated the history of biblical interpretation: (*a*) How many meanings may a given passage have? and (*b*) To what extent must or may interpretation be governed by a tradition of interpretation recognized as authoritative?

2. How many meanings? The now obvious answer that a passage of scripture, as of any other literature, has just one meaning unless there is exceptional indication of double meaning, far from being obvious, had to be won through the travail of many centuries. The underlying cause of this struggle was a misunderstanding of the divine authority of the Bible, complicated by various theories of verbal inspiration. With only occasional exceptions, until the Reformation the church and its scholars took for granted multiple meaning in scripture.

a. The Alexandrian answer. It was fateful for a thousand years of interpretation that the first great Christian exegete, Origen (*ca.* 185-254), lived and worked in the city of the learned Jewish interpreter Philo of Alexandria (*ca.* 25 B.C.–A.D. 40). Though two centuries and a new religion separated Origen the Christian from Philo the Jew, Origen worked in a literary milieu deeply conditioned by the chameleonlike art of allegory, which had arisen in Greek rationalistic interpretation of mythology and had been cultivated by Hellenistic Jewish forerunners of Philo (Letter of Aristeas; Aristobulus) but found its great virtuoso in that philosopher himself. Like Philo, Origen was not systematically interested in finding a true plurality (three or more) of meanings in a given passage, but only in finding the "deeper meaning," which he was more than willing to find everywhere, even when he accepted and valued the literal meaning, but in which he was particularly interested when he found the obvious sense untrue, unworthy, or impossible. Writers on Origen often leave the impression that he regularly set forth three meanings of a passage: its "flesh," its "soul," and its "spirit," in accordance with *On First Principles* IV.1, where such interpretation is recommended in order that three kinds of men may be edified: the simple man by the "flesh" of a text (the obvious sense), he who has ascended a certain way by its "soul," and the perfect man (I Cor. 2:6-7 is cited in full) by the "spiritual law which 'has but a shadow of the good things to come' " (Heb. 10:1). (Note that this definition of the "spirit" of a passage fully equates it with the later patristic *anagoge*.) But this is theory, not practice. So is Homily V.1 on Leviticus, where the same scheme is mentioned but only the sense called "anima," which one "takes by surprise" within the literal text, is pursued. (Here there is also the interesting statement that God made the corpus for those who were before us, the anima for us, and the spiritus for future believers.) In his exegetical works he only rarely pursues a third meaning, and where he does (e.g., Homily II.6 on Genesis), the third meaning is likely to be moral (i.e., tropological) rather than anagogic. Nevertheless, both his formulated theory and his practice were fertilely influential after him, in spite of the church's official anathema upon him three centuries after his death.

What the church condemned was his theological results, not the exegetical method by which he had reached them. The church had too well learned from him to use his own method for it to be able to condemn Origen the exegete along with Origen the theologian.

Origen's hermeneutic legacy was (*a*) the unrestricted assumption of at least a second meaning lying universally beneath the letter and to be found by allegory; (*b*) a great fund of clever allegory to countless texts of both testaments; (*c*) a theory of the threefold meaning of scripture.

b. The Antiochene protest. Within the ancient church there arose only one noteworthy protest against allegorical exegesis—that of the School of Antioch. Its great names were: Diodorus of Tarsus (died 394), Theodore of Mopsuestia (died 428), and Theodoret of Cyrrhus (died 460), plus their great popularizer, Chrysostom the homilist (*ca.* 347-407). The School of Antioch was not without later influence in Asia Minor and the West (*see below*), but its main stream "went underground" from the Greek-speaking world eastward into the Syriac-speaking interior of Syria, first 150 miles to Edessa, then another 150 miles to Nisibis, and remained effective for centuries in the Nestorian church, whose founder (Nestorius; died *ca.* 451) had been probably a personal and certainly a loyal pupil of Theodore himself. Unfortunately the writings of the real founder of the school (Diodorus) exist only in vestiges, barely enough to suggest the powerful impetus he gave to his great pupil Theodore, who is the only one of this school who is reasonably tangible to us, because more of his work is preserved. His hermeneutically most suggestive work—five books *Adversus Allegoricos*—has perished, either by neglect or, more likely, by the official censorship of the allegorizing majority. It doubtless contained sharp words like his remark on Zech. 1:9-10: "It is full of utter inanity [ἀνοίας], or, to come nearer the truth, of insanity [φρενοβλαβείας], to assert that whenever there is mention of both an 'angel' and 'the Lord' the OT is thereby [i.e., with 'angel'] speaking of the Son of God." Theodore himself bears out in the prefaces to his commentaries on the minor prophets what Photius long after says of his exegesis: "He did his utmost to avoid allegories; he made his interpretation according to the *historia* [i.e., according to the literal account]."

Theodore insists that "the narratives of events of olden time are not fictitious" (Preface to Joel) but were written down "for the great advantage of those then living" (Preface to Jonah); and in his reaction against the allegorists he is often amazingly reluctant to find direct predictions of Christ, doubtless because they had found reference to Jesus and Christian institutions in almost every line of the OT. He declares the following to be nonmessianic: Hos. 11:1; Mic. 4:1-3; 5:1-2; Hag. 2:10; Zech. 11:12-15; 12:10; Mal. 1:11; 4:5-6. For introducing the sole occurrence in the NT of any form of the Greek root on which the word "allegory" is formed, Theodore criticizes Paul (on Gal. 4:24): "He [Paul] calls comparison of events [accomplished] by juxtaposing past and present events—'allegory.' " But this is not allegory in Theodore's sense. Paul was speaking inexactly, nontechnically, and the allegorists, he says, abuse Paul's inexact use of the word when they take it technically as authority for resolving scripture into a series of allegories.

A modern exegete almost feels that he hears a colleague speaking when he finds such insights in Theodore. Protestant writers often wax lyric and hyperbolic when they speculate on "what might have been" if Theodore's hermeneutics had not sunk with the anathema on Nestorius, even hinting that Reformation exegesis might have emerged a thousand years earlier than it did. Certainly the course of exegesis would have been incomparably more sober and would have been spared many a blind alley, but these enthusiasts fail to see that the double meaning which Theodore so valiantly excluded with one hand, as allegory, he and the whole School of Antioch admitted with the other hand—as typology. Admittedly there is a difference in degree, but the underlying assumption of dual (if not plural) meaning is the same. Thus, in his typological sense, Theodore finds the following passages indirectly messianic (i.e., alluding to Jesus of Nazareth): Pss. 15—H 16; 54—H 55; 88—H 89; Joel 2:28-29; Amos 9:11; Zech. 9:9; Mal. 3:1. Even the justly famous School of Antioch leaves us with two meanings of scripture, the *historia* and the *typus*.

Two weak bridges bring some slight influence of Antiochene hermeneutics into the West: Jerome and Junilius Africanus. In the 370's Jerome had studied at Antioch, hearing among others Apollinaris of Laodicea (Jerome's Letter 84 to Pemmachius, § 4), a contemporary of Diodorus (who, himself, had probably already left Antioch for Tarsus). Judging from the fragments of his work preserved in the catenae, Apollinaris' exegesis shared the Antiochene characteristics of sobriety, insight, and avoidance of allegory. Where the many-sided and often self-contradictory Jerome sets himself to unfold the literal or historical sense, as he does countless times, it is not unreasonably assumed that the seed of his Antiochene teacher is bearing fruit; but this is only one facet of Jerome.

The other bridge, much later, was Junilius, a high palace official of African origin, at Constantinople *ca.* 550. He wrote in his native Latin *Instituta regularia divinae legis,* owing its content, he confesses (dedicatory letter), to Paulus Persa (probably Paul of Basra), who was intimately connected with the Nestorian academy at Nisibis, where the methods and insights of Theodore of Mopsuestia were still thriving.

c. The triumph of allegory. By and large the exegesis of the great church, both Latin and Greek, flowed on as if the School of Antioch had never been. Origen had established the method which triumphed. As we have seen, Origen had called the three meanings of scripture its body, its soul, and its spirit. But his terminology was still in flux: for the derived meaning(s) he also used the learned terms "anagoge," "allegory," and "tropology," but for him the first two were synonyms and the third differs very little. He also used *theoria* in the sense of "allegory." (The Antiochenes used *theoria* as the antithesis to "allegory," and the equivalent of their own "typology"—but one may say that "typology" was only their special brand of "allegory" in the widest sense of the latter word.) Pupils of Origen distinguished between allegory and anagoge: they are one in origin but separate in teleology. The goal of allegory is Christology and ecclesiology; that of anagoge, the eschatology of the individual. Tropology is also allegorical in character, allegory applied to ethical living (τρόπος means both "figure of speech" and "moral character").

Within two hundred years of Origen's death John Cassianus formulated for his monks in Marseilles (*ca.* 425) a fourfold theory of hermeneutics which uses exactly the terminology that crops out again and again through the next thousand years. The two basic kinds of interpretation are: (*a*) historical and (*b*) spiritual; but the latter has three subspecies: (*a*) tropology, (*b*) allegory, and (*c*) anagoge. (Cassian's great contemporary and theological opponent, Augustine, has his own hermeneutic tetrad: history, aetiology, analogy, and allegory, of which the middle two are of non-Origenic provenance.) What Origen himself might have indicated as either of two synonymous series of three—history, allegory, tropology, or: history, anagoge, tropology (the two respective middle terms being interchangeable)—has here been conflated into a single series of four members by simple addition.

Jerome, just before Cassianus, seems never to have brought into one sentence a formal fourfold theory of hermeneutics; like many another exegete after him, he professes to follow a threefold scheme: by combining two of Origen's key passages, I Thess. 5:23 and Prov. 22:20 (which he rendered *Ecce, descripsi tibi eam tripliciter*), he concludes: "The description in our hearts is threefold; so is the rule [for the interpretation] of the Scriptures," and says that we must understand them according to "history," "tropology," and *intelligentia spiritualis* (Epistle to *Hedibiam* CXX. 12). The third term is vague but probably equals allegory. The missing term is "anagoge." But Jerome is quite familiar with it—e.g., in his Isaiah Commentary: in the Preface to book V he says that the next book will be "tropological" in method, but in the Preface to book VI he says that both books VI and VII will deal with "anagoge." For him, as for Origen, the words are virtually synonymous. Many times in the body of the Isaiah Commentary he uses the word "anagoge" (cf. also *Epistle* CXX.8) so that centuries of exegetes whom his great prestige drew into his following could, not unreasonably, believe they were following him in a fourfold method because he had himself tacitly added one to his theoretical three.

So for a thousand years the exegete could choose either a twofold sense (the literal or historical and the mystical or spiritual sense) or a threefold (several different groups of terms) or a fourfold—and still remain within the hermeneutic tradition of Alexandria. Sometime in the scholastic period a mnemonic couplet was devised which became very popular:

> *Littera gesta docet, quid credas allegoria,*
> *moralis quid agas, quo tendas anagogia.*

"The letter teaches the events, allegory what you are to believe, the moral sense what you are to do, anagoge whither you are to strive."

It is a curious fact that medieval Jewish exegesis also knew and used a fourfold theory of interpretation. It also had its mnemonic device, the single word "PaRaDiSe," whose four Hebrew consonants yielded the initials of four key words: *peshat* ("spread out," the obvious literal meaning), *remez* ("hint," typological or allegorical meaning), *derash* ("search," a meaning derived by research according to the *middoth* [rules]), and *sod* ("secret," mystical meaning). If the fourth term can be understood as at least including the secrets of life hereafter (i.e., anagoge), then three of the rabbinic terms are equatable with three of the patristic four, and only the equation "tropology = *derash*" remains doubtful. (Since tropology always refers to conduct, one would expect "halachah" as its equivalent; can *derash* here mean "halachah" arrived at by midrashic methods? Surely the Beth ham-midrash was a place primarily for the study of halachah, not of haggadah, and many of the early midrashim were halachic.) But even a 75-per-cent correlation requires some explanation. Do the two quadriform series resemble each other by chance or by dependence, and if the latter, in which direction?

Since the church has been so often and so deeply indebted to the synagogue, it might be so here, too. But the only really old evidence for this scheme must be sought in the Mishnaic story (Chagiga 14*b*) of the four scholars who got into "paradise" and all came to grief except Rabbi Akiba, and can be found there only by allegorizing the story itself: PRDS the fourfold scheme of interpretation, each of the scholars representing one kind! But the story really means by "paradise" the enticing garden of speculation on the two theosophic subjects—the "works of creation" (Gen. 1) and the "works of the chariot" (Ezek. 1) mentioned in the story—a paradise to avoid if one is not Akiba. The actual mnemonic word "paradise," with its specific four pendants, seems first to occur in the Zohar (thirteenth century; Spain). The twelfth century seems to have been a time of relatively peaceful discussion between learned Jews and Christians, particularly in France; then, if not before, the Christian schematization appears to have brought about the similar system in certain Jewish circles—viz., the cabalists and their public. Not that the rabbis needed to learn anything from the outside about any one of these four methods of interpretation! They had long used all of them, and many more, for finding remotely derived "meanings."

d. Jewish influences. But the direction of dependence was certainly the reverse in a much more important matter: Jewish scholars brought the church the first dawning since the School of Antioch of central, though not sole, interest in the literal meaning of scripture. Through the latter half of the eleventh century there taught and wrote at Troyes in Champagne the great reformer of Jewish exegesis of the Bible (and the Talmud): Rabbi Solomon ben Isaac, better known by his acrostic nickname, Rashi. Though some of his pupils carried through the master's ideas more radically and consistently than he had, Rashi nevertheless gave the real impetus. In regard to choice between the literal sense and the midrashic nonliteral meaning(s), his commentary on the Pentateuch is not so much a clear break with the past as it is a strong shift in emphasis: his intention is to find the literal meaning. He is too loyal a traditionalist to ignore the welter of inventive exegeses of the past, but he also sifts them, passing on only those which seem to him somewhat compatible with the literal meaning. Thus on Gen. 3:8 he says: "There are many haggadic midrashim on this passage . . . but I have no intention other than to indicate the simple sense of the Bible, and, besides that, to incorporate such statements of the haggadah as expound the words of the Bible appropriately." Or on Gen. 49:22: "There are still many more haggadic midrashim on this, but this is the one which best expounds the actual wording of the text." So he comes to the conclusion: "Therefore I say let Scripture be expounded according to its simple meaning, each word in its proper context—and let the midrash-interpretation be only a hint" (on Exod. 6:2-9).

Among Rashi's distinguished pupils were Joseph Kara, Rashi's own two grandsons Samuel ben Meir (Rashbam) and Jacob Tam, and a pupil of the latter, Joseph Bekhor Shor. For us the most important is Rashbam, whose commentary on the Pentateuch has been called the "most illustrious product" of the school of Rashi. In it at Gen. 37:2 he says: "But our teacher Solomon, my mother's father, . . . already set his mind to explaining the simple meaning of Scripture. I myself . . . argued with and before him and he admitted to me that if he had time he would feel himself obliged to compose new commentaries according to the literal explanations which are turning up every day anew." This the grandson was more or less doing for him in writing the commentary where these words stand.

How did knowledge of the Rashi school of commentaries, written in Hebrew, cross the barrier of language and religion into Christian scholarship? Until recently it has been conventional to assert that Nicholas of Lyra was the mediator; undoubtedly he was one factor, but there was another very important, earlier one: the school of St. Victor in the persons of three teachers, Hugh, Richard, and Andrew, all called "of St. Victor." St. Victor was a chapter of canons regular (not monks) of the rule of St. Augustine founded at Paris in 1110 (the decade in which Rashi had died at Troyes, *ca.* eighty miles away). Its canons conducted a theological school, of which Hugh was an early master. His interest in the present connection is twofold: while he was far from abandoning mystical meanings he had a clear grasp and insistence upon the literal meaning as basic; and his *Notulae* on the Octateuch (*MPL,* CLXXV, 29-114) frequently offer exegetic insights of "Hebrews" or of "a Hebrew" which are not to be found in his revered Jerome, but which are found either in the works of Rashi or in those of Hugh's contemporaries Joseph Kara and Rashbam. Hugh never gives the names of his Jewish authorities; but since it was a convention of the time not to name one's contemporary Christian authorities, Hugh had all the more reason to suppress the names of his contemporary "infidel" authorities.

Hugh's ideas and methods lived on in two pupils who succeeded him, Richard (a Scot) and Andrew (probably an Englishman). Richard, best known for inheriting his master's mysticism, is noteworthy here only for his own statement (*De Concordia Temporum; MPL,* CLXXV) that he had consulted "writings of the Jews" (not scripture: *scripta,* not *scriptura*) *per Judaeos*—"with the help of Jews" (apparently an admission that he could not read medieval Hebrew but sought personal help from those who could).

Andrew of St. Victor is the heir and perfecter of the hermeneutics of their master Hugh, going so far in devotion to the literal meaning that he interpreted Isa. 7:14 literally (and Jewishly, as he admits), thereby evoking a shocked refutation by Richard in two books *De Emanuele.* Andrew's method is to give first the (traditional) Christian explanation, then the Jewish. But since he assumes the first to be more or less known, the latter unknown, he often gives more space to the Jewish view, which he may refute or leave unanswered, or frankly adopt. Like his teacher Hugh, he leaves his Jewish informants unnamed; they are *Hebraei* or a *Hebraeus.* Frequently what they report coincides with recorded interpretations of Rashi. But Andrew also knows some interpretations of his own contemporary, the very sober Rabbi Joseph Bekhor Shor. Andrew in the latter half of the twelfth century, though remaining a Christian, had become a disciple of Rashi's literal method as developed by his pupils. Andrew's work was not quite forgotten in the succeeding centuries. His interpretations, though without his name, are frequently cited in the *Historia Scholastica* of Peter the Eater (Comestor). In the next generation Stephen Langton often cites him by name. In the fourteenth century Nicholas of Lyra cites both Master Andrew and his Jewish originals. But the canons of St. Victor had not succeeded in persuading the church to concentrate upon the literal sense of scripture.

e. Nicholas of Lyra. A Franciscan professor at the University of Paris, Nicholas (died *ca.* 1349) from Lyra in Normandy, has the distinction of being the author of the first Bible commentary ever printed (*Postillae Perpetuae* [Rome, 1471-72]). Its eighty-five books were usually divided into five huge folio tomes, but, with accumulated annotations by others, later editions grew to six and seven folios. (Pope could think of nothing more hugely forbidding to symbolize a dull library: "De Lyra here a dreadful front extends" [*Dunciad,* bk. 1, l. 153]). All through the first two centuries of printing it was reprinted in many countries, editions, and forms. A decade before Luther's emergence a Strasbourg writer reports a proverb: "*Nisi Lira lirasset, nemo doctorum in Bibliam saltesset*" ("Had Lyra not played his lyre, none of the learned would have danced into the Bible"). Another (later?) form of the proverb may be a Protestant rejoinder to this implied belittling of direct Bible study: "*Si Lyra non lyrasset totus mundus delirasset*" (". . . all the world would have gone mad")—with a second pun on *de Lyra!* But the classical form of the jingle is an anti-Lutheran innuendo that Luther owed all his biblical learning to Nicholas: "*Si Lyra non lyrasset Lutherus non saltasset*" (". . . Luther would not have danced").

Actually this giant work is two commentaries: the first fifty books go through the whole of scripture, giving a professedly literal interpretation. The other thirty-five books, called *Moralitates* (in the incunabula, *Moralia*), cover the same ground with a mystical commentary. The second Prologue ("Concerning the author's intention and method of procedure") to the first fifty books is significant. He no more than Rashi rejects the nonliteral senses, but he considers the literal sense basic: "All [senses] presuppose the literal as a foundation . . . : thus a mystical exposition at variance with the literal sense is to be regarded as improper and tactless, or, other things being equal, as at the least not very decent or tactful." Only the literal sense, not the mystical, can furnish an argument for proving or clearing up any doubt. Besides, the literal sense has suffered at the hands of interpreters who usually were little interested in it and smothered it under their countless mystical interpretations. "I intend to insist upon the literal sense and sometimes to insert very few and brief mystical expositions, albeit rarely." He will use not only the catholic doctors but also "what the Hebrews have said, particularly Rabbi Solomon [Rashi] who has done more than the rest to clear up the literal sense." But the purpose of these fifty books of labor was only to furnish a firm support for the thirty-five books of the mystical commentary, which find abundant room for all three of the traditional mystical meanings. Nicholas is still solidly within the patristic-scholastic tradition, but the fact that he treats the literal and the mystic senses separately and does so in the ratio 50/35 is the portent of a more radical possibility in the future.

f. Martin Luther. Luther began in the old hermeneutic tradition. "When I was a monk, I was an expert in allegories. I allegorized everything" (*Table Talk* I.136; his earliest lectures on Psalms [1513-16; *WA* 3, 4] abundantly document this statement). "So I hated Lyra beyond all interpreters because he so diligently pursued the literal meaning. But now for this very recommendation I place him ahead of almost all interpreters of Scripture" (*WA* 42[377]). "Since that time when I began to embrace the historical meaning I have always abhorred allegories and have not used them unless either the text itself exhibited them or [allegorical] interpretations could be cited from the New Testament" (*WA* 42[173]).

Particularly in his lectures on Genesis (*WA* 42) Luther constantly cites Lyra. On 2:9 (*WA* 42[71]) he says: "All these things are literal [*historica*] as I strongly warn you, lest the unwary reader be tripped up by the Fathers who forsake the *historia* and hunt allegories. The reason I love Lyra and place him among the best is that he everywhere retains and pursues *historia,* although he lets himself be overcome by the authority of the Fathers, and sometimes it deflects him by their example from the right meaning to tactless allegories." The thing to seek is faith in the Pauline sense. "So it is not to be wondered at that those who do not seek this [faith] in *historiis* seek the shades of allegory as pleasant paths to go strolling in" (*WA* 42:377). Again mentioning Lyra, he refers to the "well-known rule" in theological schools "that Scripture is to be understood in a fourfold sense," which he describes and then rejects with the ironic remark: "For all of me, let each one of them overflow with its meaning! But our effort will be placed above all in this: to arrive at one simple, germane, and sure literal sense—if we are to treat sacred things aright. For I consider the ascription of several senses to Scripture to be not merely dangerous and useless for teaching but even to cancel the authority of Scripture whose meaning ought to be always one and the same. . . . Lyra thinks that the studies of students are aided by this rule so that they may get themselves out of the more obscure places. But I judge otherwise and decide that it is neither safe nor useful to follow this rule in the Church" (*WA* 42:567-67).

In a certain sense Luther was willing to tolerate "allegory." "I hold simple literal meanings to be of the highest importance; I do not particularly approve of allegories. For allegories ought to be employed as if they were ornaments and amplifications. For clearly they are to teaching as color is to building; color neither constructs nor supports the house but only decorates it." He proceeds to "decorate" with two little allegories and then goes on: "If one wants to play with allegories, he will do it very comfortably if he refers this [Isa. 13] to the Law and the Gospel. Let Cyrus be the Law and that power of Babylon be directed against the haughty consciousness of the self-righteous." But he is lecturing to students: is this not a parody on the game of allegory? He finishes seriously: "Had not this business with the Pope kept me in the simple text of the Bible, I would have become an idle trifler with allegories like St. Jerome and Origen. . . . You, therefore, learn by my example and beware—and pursue everywhere simple stories [literal meanings] and the naked text. Afterwards it may be that you can treat allegories without peril, as we see that Paul also brought up an allegory by way of ornament" (*WA* 25:142). In his own practice Luther seems to have excepted from his category of allegory references that he considered christological, excepted them because to him they only doubled what the NT told him directly (literally); at any rate, he was much inclined to find, not merely messianic allusions, but explicit references to Jesus Christ in OT passages where modern exegetes find only the former or neither.

Although Luther's principle of the simple literal meaning of scripture only slowly gained recognition, it never has been lacking in any generation of the Protestant church, even when other interests have eclipsed it. For the further thread of the history of interpretation, *see* BIBLICAL CRITICISM.

3. The authority of tradition. The other main factor in the history of interpretation owes its importance largely to the uncertainties of Alexandrine hermeneutics: if scripture or a particular scripture has no certain, dependable meaning, some other authority beside it or above it is necessary to guide faith and conduct. Such an authority was ready at hand in the concept "tradition." By it the second century had meant the sum total of that which had been passed on by the apostles, written or unwritten, but the third and fourth centuries understood tradition to be distinct from scripture: tradition is the unwritten ongoing life of the church handed down in unbroken succession from the apostles—indeed, tradition *is* the church. Augustine himself, with his high estimate of scripture, once says: "I would not believe the gospel if the authority of the catholic Church did not impel me to do so" (*Against the Epistle of Manichaeus Called Fundamental* I.5; *MPL,* XLII, 176). From the context it is clear that he means: the Christian accepts the canon of scripture only on the endorsement of the church—it was the church which established and maintains the canon.

But it was a young contemporary and theological opponent of Augustine, Vincent, a monk at Lerinum, who coined the formulation of the tradition principle that became classic: "Care is to be taken that we hold that which has been believed everywhere, always, by everybody" (*Commonitorium* II, *MPL,* L, 640). This is his circumlocution for the tradition which is the church's norm even over the understanding of scripture: "It is necessary . . . that the line of prophetic and apostolic interpretation be guided by the norm of the ecclesiastical and catholic sense." Throughout the Middle Ages this assumption of an authoritative tradition governing interpretation tended either to insulate the church's scholars from interpreting the Bible itself or to distort every attempt to do so. Abelard dared to show that what "everybody" had "always" believed "everywhere" was exceedingly problematic, because one father's "Yes" stood against another's "No" in countless cases (*Sic et Non;* twelfth century), and incurred for his daring the condemnation of the church. Perhaps aware that his literal interpretations were a departure from the multiple-meaning tradition, and hence possibly suspect, Nicholas of Lyra wrote (Preface 2 to the *Postillae*): "I protest that I do not intend to assert or determine anything that has not been manifestly determined by Sacred Scripture *or by the authority of the Church*. . . . Wherefore I submit all I have said or shall say to the correction of Holy Mother Church and of all learned men."

Before Luther, Wyclif was in this respect already thoroughly Protestant: "Though there were a hundred popes and every monk were made a cardinal, their opinion in matters of faith is to be valued only insofar as it is founded upon Scripture" (Trialogion IV c. 7). Luther himself came only gradually to the position of declaring the sole authority of scripture —but it was his discovery of Rom. 1:17 within scripture which led him to this position. In matters of faith ecclesiastical tradition had to submit to the highest authority: scripture. (In matters of ritual and liturgy Luther conceded tradition more, sometimes determinative, authority side by side with scripture.) The Council of Trent felt obliged to define its stand on scripture and tradition: "The Council accepts all the books of the Old and New Testament [enumerated] and also the traditions pertaining either to faith or morals . . . with the *same respectful affection and reverence*." Actually, since "tradition" at any given moment is the mind of the church, a slightly later decision of the same council placed tradition above scripture: "It is for Mother Church to judge of the true sense and interpretation of the holy Scriptures." Tradition and the mind of the church have become one. But just where is the mind of the church to be found? Roman Catholics received the answer from the Vatican Council (1869): in the Pope; since then it is he who, as the embodiment of Catholic tradition, decides what scripture means.

But for Protestant interpretation the conditions necessary for critical understanding were present when it had been accepted that scripture has one simple meaning and that it neither has nor can tolerate human authority. *See* BIBLICAL CRITICISM.

Bibliography. L. Diestel, *Geschichte des Alten Testamentes in der christlichen Kirche* (1869); F. W. Farrar, *History of Interpretation* (1886); W. Bacher, *Die jüdische Bibelexegese vom Anfange des zehnten bis zum Ende des fünfzehnten Jahrhunderts* (1892); G. H. Gilbert, *Interpretation of the Bible, A Short History* (1908); E. von Dobschütz, "Vom vierfachen Schriftsinn," *Harnack-Ehrung* (1921), pp. 1-13; B. Smalley, *The Study of the Bible in the Middle Ages* (1941); R. M. Grant, *The Bible in the Church* (1948).

K. GROBEL

INTERPRETER [מליץ]. One who translates languages; one who makes known the will of another, such as an AMBASSADOR; one who unfolds the meaning of what is said, seen, or dreamed by another. Joseph uses an interpreter when his brothers are still to be confused and tested (Gen. 42:23). On the other hand, he solves the riddle or interprets the dreams of others (40:22; 41:13). In Job 33:23; Isa. 43:27 the interpreter is an intermediary between God and man, a spokesman or ambassador for God (*see* MEDIATOR). In the NT the verb "interpret" is used in reference to explaining the speech of those with the gift of tongues (I Cor. 14:28), expounding scriptures (Luke 24:27), or translating foreign languages (Acts 9:36).

C. U. WOLF

IOB yōb [יוב; Samar.-LXX Ἰασούβ] (Gen. 46:13); KJV JOB jōb. Third son of Issachar. The parallel lists in Num. 26:24; I Chr. 7:1 (especially the *Qere*) indicate that "Jashub" was the original reading.

IOTA ī ō'tə [ἰῶτα]. The smallest letter of the Greek alphabet. It also has generally been regarded in Matt. 5:18 as representing the Hebrew *yodh* as the smallest of the Hebrew alphabet. While some doubts have been expressed about distinguishing the *yodh* and *waw* in regard to size in certain periods and scripts, it is probably safe to say that in the "square" script of the first century A.D. such a distinction was possible and is reflected in Matthew. The RSV here simply transliterates the Greek word: "Not an iota, not a dot, will pass from the law." The KJV rendering, "JOT," goes back to Tyndale's "one iott," probably itself influenced by the Vulg. *iota unam*. *See also* DOT.

A. WIKGREN

IPHDEIAH ĭf dē'yə [יפדיה, may Yahu ransom] (I Chr. 8:25); KJV IPHEDEIAH ĭf'ə dē'yə. A Benjaminite.

Bibliography. M. Noth, *Die israelitischen Personennamen* (1928), pp. 28, 200.

IPHTAH ĭf'tə [יפתח, he (God) opens] (Josh. 15:43); KJV JIPTAH jĭp'tə. A village of Judah in the Shephelah district of Libnah-Mareshah; possibly modern Tarqumiya, E of Lachish.

IPHTAH-EL ĭf'tə ĕl' [יפתח־אל, let El open, *or* El opens] (Josh. 19:14, 27); KJV JIPHTHAH-EL jĭf'thä ĕl'. A valley on the border between Zebulun and Asher. It is probably to be identified with Wadi el-Melek, NW of Nazareth.

IR ĭr [עיר, *perhaps* ass's colt] (I Chr. 7:12). Apparently a Benjaminite; perhaps to be identified with IRI (I Chr. 7:7).

Bibliography. M. Noth, *Die israelitischen Personennamen* (1928), p. 230.

IRA ī'rə [עירא]. **1.** A Jairite who was included among the officers of David as his priest—an office not necessarily sacerdotal in character (II Sam. 20:26). In the similar catalogues of Davidic officials the office of priest (II Sam. 8:18) is interpreted to mean "chief official in the service of the king" (I Chr. 18:17).

2. An Ithrite who belonged to the company of the Mighty Men of David known as the "Thirty" (II Sam. 23:38; I Chr. 11:40).

3. Son of Ikkesh, and one of the Mighty Men of David (II Sam. 23:26; I Chr. 11:28) who also served as captain in charge of the Davidic militia for the sixth month (I Chr. 27:9).

E. R. DALGLISH

IRAD ī'răd [עירד] (Gen. 4:18). In the Yahwistic tradition, an antediluvian patriarch of the line of Cain, and father of Mehujael. The parallel member in the Priestly Sethite list is Jared.

IRAM ī'răm [עירם]. An Edomite clan chief (Gen. 36:43 [LXX Ζαφωιμ, Ζαφωει]; I Chr. 1:54 [LXX Ηραμ, Ζαφωειν]).

IRI ī'rī [עירי, *perhaps same as* עיר, Ir] (I Chr. 7:7). A Benjaminite.

IRIJAH ī rī'jə [יראייה, Yahu sees] (Jer. 37:13-14). A Benjaminite sentry, presumably at Anathoth, who arrested Jeremiah as a deserter to the Chaldeans when he went to claim his inheritance.

IRNAHASH ĭr nā'hăsh [עיר נחש, city of a serpent; *perhaps originally* city of copper—Copperopolis] (I Chr. 4:12). A city of Judah whose location is unknown. The reference to "Valley of Craftsmen" (גיא חרשים; vs. 14) may indicate the time of composition of this section (cf. Neh. 11:35). If the reference in Nehemiah could be validly compared, Irnahash should be sought N of Jerusalem, in the territory of Benjamin.

The suggestion of Deir Nahhas, near Beit Jibrin, should not be ignored, however. Reference to Khirbet en-Nahas, near the N end of the Arabah, is tempting but improbable. V. R. Gold

IRON (CITY). KJV form of Yiron.

IRON [ברזל, Akkad. *parzillu,* Ugar. *bršl, all apparently derived from* Hitt. *barzillu; biblical* Aram. פרזל; σίδηρος, *adjective* σιδηροῦς].

1. Origin of ironworking
2. Tubal-cain
3. Iron in Palestine
4. Literary metaphors derived from iron

Bibliography

1. Origin of ironworking. Beads made of meteoric iron were used in Egypt as far back as predynastic times. Apart from these, only five iron objects have been found before the end of the Eighteenth Dynasty. Four of these are probably more recent than the date their finders gave them. The fifth, now only an iron mass but once probably an iron object, adhering to Sixth-Dynasty-type copper adzes, has been tested and shown to be of nonmeteoric origin, although it could be merely a lump of iron smelted accidentally and found to be useless since the method of working iron red hot was not then known (so Lucas). It is practically certain that the art of smelting and working iron was discovered by the Hittites of Asia Minor *ca.* the middle of the second millennium B.C. The fact that the word for "iron" in Akkadian, Hebrew, Ugaritic, and Aramaic seems to be a loan word from Hittite supports this view. It is true that very few iron objects dating from the Hittite period have been found in Anatolia, but this is doubtless to be accounted for by the tendency of iron to rust away quickly. A letter of the Hittite king Hattusilis III (1275-1250 B.C.) to one of his contemporaries, probably the king of Assyria, implies that in the thirteenth century B.C. the Hittite area was recognized to be the source of iron: "'As for the good iron which you wrote about to me, good iron is not available in my sealhouse in Kizzuwatna [a district in south-east Asia Minor]. That it is a bad time for producing iron I have written. They will produce good iron, but as yet they will not have finished. When they have finished I shall send it to you. To-day now I am dispatching an iron daggerblade to you." (O. R. Gurney, *The Hittites* [2nd ed., 1954], p. 83).

2. Tubal-cain. Hebrew tradition associates the beginnings of ironworking with a figure called Tubal-cain (Gen. 4:22). This figure is undoubtedly composite and represents a merger of two different traditions concerning the origin of metalworking (*see* Metallurgy). It is usually maintained that the form Tubal is due merely to the desire of the author to achieve an assonance with the preceding Jubal and that it can have no possible connection with the Tubal of Northeastern Asia Minor, who are associated in tradition with metalworking (cf. Ezek. 27:13; Herodotus 3.94). But this contention is dominated by the idea that the J source, to which Gen. 4 belongs, is of ninth-century-B.C. date, at which time the Hebrews seem to have known nothing of the Tubal. Tubal and the associated Meshech first appear in Hebrew literature in the book of Ezekiel (sixth century B.C.) and in Gen. 10:2. But the date of the J source is open to question; it may well come from the hand of the pre-P author of the book of Genesis, who may be dated in the early postexilic period. This was a time when the geographical horizons of the Hebrews were considerably enlarged by the incorporation of Asia Minor, as well as of Palestine, in the Persian Empire.

Tubal and Meshech seem to have moved into Asia Minor *ca.* 1200 B.C. and to have inherited the Hittite skill in the mining and smelting of iron. Since they were the leading craftsmen in iron at the time when the Hebrew tradition took shape, the origin of the art was attributed to them rather than to their Hittite predecessors and teachers. The tradition is valid to the extent that it points to the N as the region from which iron reached Palestine; cf. Jeremiah's "iron from the north" (15:12).

3. Iron in Palestine. The use of iron seems to have spread very slowly, because it was difficult to produce and because the first iron smelted was doubtless not much harder than hammered copper or bronze. Furthermore, it required heating before being worked, and this necessitated a great expenditure of fuel, whereas copper and bronze could be worked cold.

It is generally believed that iron was introduced into Palestine by the Philistines, but if the latter came from Crete rather than from Anatolia, this is unlikely. According to Hebrew tradition, the Canaanites possessed iron at the time of Joshua's invasion and thus before the arrival of the Philistines *ca.* 1190 B.C. Thus Josh. 6:24 states that iron objects were found in the house of Rahab the harlot; 22:8 lists iron among the spoil taken from the Canaanites; and Num. 31:22 lists it among the booty taken from the Midianites. Furthermore, Moses is said to have forbidden the Israelites to employ any iron tool when they built an altar on Mount Ebal (read "Gerizim" in Deut. 27:4). The historical value of references to iron in late sources may be questioned, but there seems no reason for questioning the statements in Josh. 17:16; Judg. 1:19 that the Canaanites of Beth-shean, the Valley of Jezreel, and the Coastal Plain possessed iron chariots at the time of Joshua.

Although the Philistines may not have introduced iron to Palestine, they soon gained access to a considerable supply for themselves, as the story of Goliath implies (I Sam. 17). The iron tip of the giant's spear is said to have weighed six hundred shekels (over sixteen pounds; vs. 7). When the Philistines conquered the Hebrews, they did not permit them to have smiths of their own, and so prevented them from equipping themselves with up-to-date weapons. This made it necessary for the Hebrews, whenever their implements and tools needed sharpening or repairing, to resort to the Philistine smiths, who charged them exorbitant prices (I Sam. 13:19-22). These tools were doubtless of copper or bronze, not of iron. The only iron object from this period found in Hebrew territory is a plowpoint from Gibeah, Saul's capital.

For a long time the Hebrews continued to be handicapped in the struggles with their neighbors by their lack of metal, whereas at least one of their foes, Jabin king of Hazor, is said to have possessed nine hundred iron chariots (Judg. 4:3). The situation changed with the establishment of a Hebrew monarchy. David followed the example of other kings in making metal one of the main prizes of war (II Sam. 8:8). This may have been the way he obtained the "great stores of iron" (I Chr. 22:3) which were later used for making nails for the gates of the temple, although I Chr. 29:7 claims that the iron (100,000 talents of it, equivalent to over 7,500,000 pounds!) was donated by the people. Iron tools were in use in Transjordan in David's time, for after conquering the Ammonites he is said to have "set them to labor with saws and iron picks and iron axes" (II Sam. 12:31=I Chr. 20:3). (For iron mines in Hebrew territory, *see* MINING.) In the sixth century B.C., Tyre was importing iron, but the corrupt condition of the text of Ezek. 27:19 makes it impossible to tell whence she obtained it. In the stories of Elijah and Elisha there are two references to iron: in one we read of a prophet named Zedekiah making a set of iron horns for himself and prancing around in front of kings Ahab and Jehoshaphat at Samaria (I Kings 22:11); in the other story we hear of a prophet chopping down trees along the Jordan with an iron axe (II Kings 6:5).

4. Literary metaphors derived from iron. The literary metaphors derived from iron all seem to be of relatively late date, as is to be expected. Thus iron is used as a symbol of hardness and strength or of harshness in Deut. 28:48 (a "yoke of iron"), in Isa. 48:4 (an "iron sinew"), in Job 19:24; Jer. 17:1 (a "pen of iron"), in Ps. 2:9; Rev. 2:27; 12:5; 19:15 (a "rod of iron"), and in Ps. 105:18 (a "collar of iron"). In Dan. 7:7 the crushing might of the fourth beast is symbolized by its having "great iron teeth," with which it devoured and broke in pieces. Most striking of all is the simile in Prov. 27:17:

> Iron sharpens iron,
> and one man sharpens another.

Bibliography. A. Lucas, *Ancient Egyptian Materials and Industries* (2nd ed., 1934), pp. 193-200, 405-7; G. A. Wainwright, "The Coming of Iron," *Antiquity,* X (1936), 5-24; R. J. Forbes, "The Coming of Iron," *Ex Oriente Lux,* IX (1944), 6-14; W. F. Albright, "Cilicia and Babylonia under the Chaldaean Kings," *BASOR,* 120 (1950), 22-25.

F. V. WINNETT

IRONS [ברזל] (Ps. 107:10). A reference either to fetters or to chains (cf. Pss. 105:18; 149:8; III Macc. 3:25; IV Macc. 11:10), suggesting the custom of binding prisoners shut up in a dungeon with chains (cf. Job 36:8; Acts 12:6; 16:26), or to the iron bars which strengthen the prison gates (cf. Ps. 107:10, 16; Isa. 45:2). The term is used figuratively for the condition of those who reject the commandments of God.

V. H. KOOY

IRONSMITH [חרש ברזל] (Isa. 44:12); KJV SMITH. One who works with IRON, both smelting the ore and casting the finished pieces. The Hittites and the Philistines had a monopoly of such craftsmen until the time of David (Judg. 1:19; I Sam. 13:19-21). The iron swords (I Sam. 17:7) and chariots (Josh. 17:16) gave the Israelites an inferior position. Smiths also made axe heads (Deut. 19:5), chains (Pss. 105:18; 107:10; etc.), chisels (Job 19:24), idols (Dan. 5:4), prison bars (Acts 12:10), etc.

See also METALLURGY; CRAFTS. C. U. WOLF

IRONY AND SATIRE. Irony is defined by *Webster's New International Dictionary* as a "sort of humor, ridicule, or light sarcasm, which adopts a mode of speech the intended implication of which is the opposite of the literal sense of the words." Satire is defined by the same authority as a "literary composition holding up human or individual vices or folly, or abuses or shortcomings of any kind, to reprobation by means of ridicule, derision, burlesque, or other method of intensifying incongruities, usually with an intent to provoke amendment." Dudley Zuver says: "In general, satire and irony can be distinguished from humor in being more moralistic and disciplinary in intent." Ronald Knox makes this distinction: "Irony is content to describe men exactly as they are, to accept them professedly, at their own valuation, and then to laugh up its sleeve. . . . Satire . . . is born to scourge the persistent and ever-recurrent follies of the human creature as such." *See also* HUMOR.

1. Irony. There are numerous examples of irony in the Bible. From the OT, these may be noted: the mockery of supposing that man can be equal to God (Gen. 3:5, 22; 11:6); false reasons for the failure of Sisera to return (Judg. 5:28-30); "You only hate me" (Judg. 14:16); Samson's straight-faced lies to Delilah (Judg. 16:7, 11, 13); Solomon's command: "Cut the living child in two" (I Kings 3:25 Amer. Trans.); Elijah's sarcastic taunting of the prophets of Baal (I Kings 18:27; *see* § 2 *below*); Micaiah's mocking answer to Ahab (I Kings 22:15); Job's bitter answer to his friends (Job 12:2); God's challenge to Job (Job 40:10-14; cf. Gen. 3:5); the mistaken notions of God's enemies (Pss. 2:3-4; 83:3-4); the downfall of the great (Isa. 14:9-17; 23:4, 16; Ezek. 28:2); the deluded Ephraimites (Hos. 6:1-3); "offspring of Canaan and not of Judah" (Sus. 56).

In the NT: "I do not know you" (Matt. 25:12; cf. 7:23; Luke 13:25-27); "I reap where I have not sowed" (Matt. 25:26); Jesus' answer to Judas ("Friend"!) and the crowd (Matt. 26:50, 55, the latter more like sarcasm); the mockery of the crowd (Matt. 26:68; 27:40-43, 49; John 19:3); "Can anything good come out of Nazareth?" (John 1:46); "him who is without sin among you" (John 8:7); "Do you too want to become his disciples?" (John 9:27); Jesus' answer to Peter (John 13:38); the contemptuous epithet of "King" spoken by Pilate (John 19:14-15, 19); "Shall I commend you [for gluttony and drunkenness]?" (I Cor. 11:22); "Go in peace, be warmed and filled" (Jas. 2:16).

2. Satire. This is a more extended form of expression than irony; in fact, it may use irony, sarcasm, invective, burlesque, ridicule, and all similar devices. One should remember, however, that invective alone is not satire. Satire must manifest the lightness of wit and humor, yet have a serious purpose to reform some widespread evil or folly. The outstanding example in the Bible is the prophets' bitter criticism of the corrupt society in which they lived. The terrific impact of this satire is often avoided or evaded by readers or exegetes who wish to see the Bible as a book entirely of sweetness and light (e.g., the many absurdly sentimental interpretations of the life and theology of Hosea). In general, the extent of satire in the Bible is probably unknown to many. Some of the outstanding examples may be mentioned here:

The satire on the reign of Solomon in particular and the monarchy in general (Deut. 17:14-20; I Sam. 8:10-18; cf. I Kings 9:15-11:40) seems clear. Jotham's fable or parable against the evil deeds of Abimelech (Judg. 9:4-20; this passage is also antimonarchical in tendency) is notable for its literary form and style.

The book of Job (*see* JOB, BOOK OF) is a masterpiece from many points of view, including that of satire. The whole effort of Job in the debate (nine speeches) constitutes, not only a personal defense, but a satire on the conventional religious ideas of the day, especially the dogma of perfect and exact retribution, or justness of reward, for the deeds of men on this earth. Even the so-called "friends" add to this effect by the very stuffiness and conventionality of their attack. We have here also the quality of dramatic irony, since the reader knows from the Prologue that Job really is innocent. On the other hand, the praise of Wisdom (ch. 28) and the speeches of the Lord (chs. 38-41) constitute a sort of countersatire on the obviously earthbound and personally conditioned views of Job and those who would agree with him. In spite of the decision rendered in the Epilogue, it would seem from one point of view in the book that both sides in the debate stood in need of correction such as might be stimulated by satire.

Another wisdom book with satirical content is Ecclesiastes. As in Job, there is sharp reaction against the orthodox thought of the author's day, especially the idea of just deserts for all in the best of all possible worlds. There are flashes of sardonic wit, such as: "Vanity of vanities! All is vanity" (1:2; 12:8), and: "A living dog is better than a dead lion" (9:4); yet the author never criticizes God as does Job, and he may have been contending for a better conception of God and a more wholesome view of life.

The book of Proverbs, by its very nature of offering comments on morals and manners, contains a certain amount of satire. Some of its more vividly satirical passages are: on the victim of an evil (KJV "strange") woman (5:1-20; 6:23-33; 7:4-27 [note vss. 7, 22-23]; 9:13-18 [the woman here personifies all folly]; 22:14; 30:20; cf. Ecclus. 9:2-9); on the sluggard or lazy man (6:6-11; 13:4; 18:9; 21:25; 22:13; 26:13-16; cf. Ecclus. 22:1-2); on the drunkard (20:1; 21:17; 23:19-21, 29-35 [note delirium tremens in vs. 33]; cf. Ecclus. 31:25-30); on gluttony (23:1-3; cf. Ecclus. 31:12-24); on the fool (10:8, 14, 23; 14:7, 24; 15:5, 7, 14, 21; 16:22; 17:7, 10, 12, 16, 21, 24-25, 28; 18:2, 6-7; 21:20; 22:3, 15; 26:3-12; 27:22; 29:9, 11, 20). It should be noted that all this is prefaced by praise of wisdom (1:20-2:22), personified as a chaste and beautiful woman—an effort by one of the later writers of the book to present the cure for the satirized follies.

As noted above, the most significant strain of satire in the OT is that in the books of the prophets (*see* PROPHET). It should be remembered that this satire is directed against the prophets' own people and culture. It is easy to criticize foreigners; it is less easy and requires far more courage to attack the evils in one's own society.

This satire may be said to emerge in the story of ELIJAH THE PROPHET and the prophets of Baal on Mount Carmel (I Kings 18:16-46). It is clear that a large part of Israel has gone over to the worship of Baal, and the tendency of this story is to show how ridiculous are Baalism and those who follow it. Another satire, this time directed against the sycophantic professional prophets of Yahweh, who say only what the king wants to hear, is seen in the story of Micaiah (*see* MICAIAH 3) from the same period (I Kings 22:5-38).

A century later the literary prophets began to satirize conditions in the Hebrew states. Amos and Hosea spoke directly to the N kingdom of Israel, trying to avert its downfall. Practically the whole book of Amos should be read in this connection (2:6-9:8*b;* 9:8*c*-15 were probably added later). Note particularly 4:1-5, beginning with "cows of Bashan" (overfat women); also the climactic pun in 8:2 (*see* HUMOR for explanation). The message of Hosea is similar, but even more bitter (2:2-13 [note vs. 7—H 9]; 4-10 [note 4:16; 6:4; 8:6; 10:11]; 11:12-13:16—H 12:1-14:1 [note 13:2, 16—H 14:1]).

Isaiah and Micah also satirized Israel from their vantage point in Judah (Isa. 28:1-4; Mic. 1:6-8), and then, especially after the fall of Israel, turned their barbs even more trenchantly upon their own nation and its self-righteousness (Isa. 1:2-23; 3:13-26; 5:1-7, 22-24; 28:7-22; 29:1-4; 30:8-17; 31:1-3; 32:9-14; Mic. 2:1-11; 3; cf. Zeph. 1:2-13).

Jeremiah and Ezekiel spoke in similar vein to Judah just before its downfall (Jer. 1:4-23:29, omitting 3:14-18; 10:1-16, 23-25; 12:14-17; 16:14-15, 19-20; 17:19-27; 23:1-8 [note 2:23-28]; Ezek. 4-9; 11:1-12; 12-16 [note the especially bitter satire in ch. 16]; 20:45-24:14 [note ch. 23]).

Each of these prophets criticized the ruling monarch of his day; hence the antimonarchical satire pointed out above may have had its origin in the preaching of the prophets.

The prophets criticized, ridiculed, and satirized the idolatry and corruption of their own kings, cities, and people. Amos included some neighboring nations in his sweep before castigating Israel most of all (1:3-2:16). Isaiah probably uttered oracles against Assyria, Philistia, Damascus, and Egypt (10:12-15; 14:28-32; 17:1-3; 20). Jeremiah prophesied against Egypt (44:30; 46:3-12). Other, more chauvinistic writers hurled even more fiery verbal darts at foreign nations, so that we have a whole library of "antiforeign oracles," some added to the books of the earlier prophets, some standing alone or added to later prophets (Isa. 13:2-22; 14:3-21 [very satirical]; 15:1–16:11; 9:1-15; 23:1-16; 37:22-29; Jer. 46:13–51:58; Lam. 4:21-22; Ezek. 25–32; 35:1–36:15; Joel 3:19-21—H 4:19-21; Obadiah; Nah. 2–3; Zeph. 2; Zech. 9:1-7; 14:12-19; cf. Ps. 137:7-9).

Closely related is the ridicule of foreign idolatry, in contrast to condemnation of idolatry practiced by Hebrews (I Sam. 5:1-7 [cf. I Kings 12:28-30]; Pss. 115:4-8; 135:15-18; Isa. 44:9-20; 45:16; 46:1 [cf. 57:3-13]; Jer. 10:1-16).

Much of the book of Daniel has a similar satirical cast. Ch. 1 satirizes foreign "wisdom" and eating habits. In ch. 2, the helpless ignorance of the Chaldeans is the first target; then the collapse of the great image with feet of clay is a double satire against foreign nations and idols—the image representing both. Again, in ch. 3, the three Jews make a great image and a great king look ridiculous. In ch. 4, a great foreign potentate goes ridiculously mad; some regard this as a satire on Antiochus Epiphanes. Ch. 5 satirizes licentiousness, idolatry, and the ignorance of foreign magicians. Again, in ch. 6, a mighty foreign king is brought down to humility. In the rest of the book the mightiest foreign kingdoms are shown under the guise of strange beasts as transitory and of little significance compared with the immortal kingdom of the saints.

The book of Jonah presents a satire of a very different type, more like that of the earlier prophets. A broad-minded Jew ridicules his own people, represented by the rebellious prophet, Jonah, for their lack of missionary zeal, their prejudice against foreigners, and their failure to understand a God of love.

In the Apoc., the book of Judith again satirizes the impotence of foreign potentates. Wisdom of Solomon contains another satire against idolatry (13:10–14:31; 15:7–16:1). The Epistle of Jeremiah (Bar. 6) has a similar theme. The same is true of Bel and the Dragon.

In the NT, the principal satire is that in the gospels against the scribes and the Pharisees for their hypocrisy. The bulk of the material is in Matt. 23; Luke 11:39-54, with other scattered references such as Mark 2:16-17; Luke 5:30-35; 6:7-11; 15:1-10. Note also Paul's attack on the Judaizers (Phil. 3:2, 19) and the castigation of the rich in Jas. 5:1-6 (cf. Mark 10:25). Finally, of course, comes the well-known satire on Rome in Revelation. The wicked city and its empire are first represented under the guise of strange beasts, as are the foreign kingdoms in the book of Daniel (Rev. 13; *see above*); then Rome is disguised for further vituperation as the great harlot-city of Babylon, a favorite target of the antiforeign satirists of the OT (14:8; 16:18–19:3). The city and all its allied potentates in the end go down to perdition as the apocalyptic author vents his bitterest mockery and sarcasm upon them (19:17-21).

Bibliography. H. Lesêtre, "Ironie," *VDB,* III (1903), 924-25; R. A. Knox, *Essays in Satire* (1928), p. 23; D. Zuver, *Salvation by Laughter* (1933), p. 17; D. Worcester, *The Art of Satire* (1940). W. F. Stinespring

IRPEEL ĭr'pĭ əl [ירפאל, God heals] (Josh. 18:27). A town allotted to the tribe of Benjamin. The associated towns suggest a site in the hill country NW of Jerusalem. The most likely is Rafat, N of Gibeon and 6½ miles NW of Jerusalem. W. H. Morton

IRRIGATION. Artificial means of watering crops; used throughout Bible times in the form of aqueducts, cisterns, dams, canals, etc. *See* Agriculture.

IR-SHEMESH ĭr shĕm'ĭsh [עיר שמש, city of the sun] (Josh. 19:41). A city of Dan; probably identical with Beth-shemesh.

IRU ī'ro͞o [עירו] (I Chr. 4:15). A son of Caleb; listed in the genealogy of the tribe of Judah.

ISAAC ī'zĭk [יצחק, ישחק, *see* § 1 *below;* Ἰσαάκ]. The son of Abraham's "old age." Isaac was born in his father's hundredth year (Gen. 21:5, 7). He married Rebekah when he was 40 years old (24:64; 25:20) and became the father of Esau and Jacob at age 60 (Gen. 25:26*b;* I Chr. 1:34). Isaac died at Hebron when he was 180 years old (Gen. 35:27-29) and was buried with his wife in the cave at Mach-pelah (49:31).

1. Etymology
2. Isaac in the OT
   a. Birth of Isaac
   b. Isaac and Ishmael
   c. Sacrifice of Isaac
   d. Isaac and Rebekah
   e. Birth of Esau and Jacob
   f. Isaac and Abimelech
   g. Isaac's blessing
   h. Death of Isaac
3. Isaac in the NT

Bibliography

1. Etymology. The name Isaac, from the verb צחק, means "he laughs" (or "he will laugh"), as does the variant from שחק at Ps. 105:9; Jer. 33:26; Amos 7:9, 16. The several OT etymologies play on this meaning. In the J narrative Sarah laughs in derision at Yahweh's promise of a son, because she is old (Gen. 18:12-15). In E she sees herself as the object of laughter (21:6), or, possibly, as laughing for joy at Isaac's birth (KJV). But E alludes to another explanation also in vs. 9 when Ishmael is pictured as "sporting" with Isaac. מצחק may mean "laughing at" in the sense of "mocking" (so ASV; also Gen. 17:17; 18:12-15; Judg. 16:25; Ps. 2:4) or "laughing with" in the sense of (sexual) play (Gen. 26:8 [RSV "fondling"]; Exod. 32:6). In P it is Abraham who laughs at the divine promise (Gen. 17:17-19).

But these are popular (*Volksetymologien*), not accurate, etymologies. יצחק, an imperfect-tense formation like יעקוב (Jacob § A), is best regarded as a shortened form of an original theophorous name. A divine element—most probably אל (cf. ישמעאל; *see* Ishmael 1)—should be supplied, and the full form translated: "Let (may) God laugh"—i.e., look with kind affection toward the bearer. (In the Canaanite religious texts from Ugarit [§ 4], *'El* frequently laughs [*ẓḥq/ṣḥq*]).

2. Isaac in the OT. In comparison with the towering Abraham, the complex Jacob, and the noble Joseph, the Isaac of the OT story is weak both in character and in portrayal. In both these respects it is true that "an Abraham is apt to be followed by an Isaac." Of the biblical patriarchs, strictly defined (*see* Patriarchs § 2), he is patently the least significant.

The Isaac cycle of stories was probably formed and preserved in the cultic centers at Beer-sheba and Beer-lahai-roi, where he was esteemed as the regional hero and patron. His life revolves chiefly around these centers (Gen. 21; 22:19; 26:23, 33; 28:10 [Beer-sheba]; and 24:62; 25:11 [Beer-lahai-roi]). Further, whatever its original place in Israel's traditions, the Isaac story creates the initial impression of serving primarily as a link between the major narratives about Abraham and Jacob. E.g., with the possible exception of the sections showing Isaac's relations with Abimelech (*see* § 2*f below*), in no unit of the present story does Isaac emerge as the leading figure for whose purpose alone the events are recounted.

Nevertheless, in Genesis as now constructed, it not only serves quite successfully as the genealogical link between the Abraham and Jacob cycles but also makes its own distinctive contribution to the theological themes in the patriarchal history. For, first of all, Isaac is the child of promise, a living sign of God's faithful and gracious dealing with Israel (*see* § 2*a below*). The God who promised has also fulfilled. He is dependable, and Israel can trust in him. But more, he is faithful even when Israel is weak and vacillating. Vague and insignificant though Isaac appears, he remains nevertheless a major channel through whom God works salvation for Israel and mediates his grace to future generations. Standing in this position, Isaac is seen, therefore, also as the man of blessing. *See* § 2*f below*.

***a. Birth of Isaac* (*Gen. 21:1-7*).** The first word spoken about Isaac's birth declares him to be the child of divine promise. Although Abraham is old and his barren wife, Sarah, is past the normal expectation of childbearing, God has promised them a son of their own (15:4; 17:15-19 [P]; 18:9-15 [J]; cf. 15:5 [E]; *see* Abraham §§ C1*g, j*). Now, after Abraham has reached the age of a hundred years, God makes good his word. Sarah conceives and bears a son, whom she calls Isaac, saying: "God has made laughter for me; every one who hears will laugh over me" (21:6; but cf. KJV; *see* § 1 *above*). With his name Isaac, the child stands as an inescapable sign of God's faithfulness in the face of Sarah's incredulity.

But the parents are grateful; and, as a proper son of the covenant, Isaac is circumcised on the eighth day (vs. 4; cf. Luke 1:59; 2:21; Acts 7:8; Phil. 3:5).

***b. Isaac and Ishmael* (*Gen. 21:8-14; 25:9-11*).** Sarah's lack of faith in God's ability to perform his promise that Isaac will inherit the divine blessing leads to the expulsion of Ishmael. On the day of the festal celebration of Isaac's weaning, Sarah is greatly disturbed to see Ishmael sporting "with her son Isaac" (not in the MT; supplied from the LXX). The exact nature of the "offense" is not clear (*see* § 1 *above*). But however the relationship is expressed, Ishmael's intimacy with Isaac leads Sarah to question whether the son of the handmaid may share in, or even usurp, the inheritance of her own son. She compels Abraham to drive out Ishmael and his mother.

Abraham is distressed. But God suffers him to comply with Sarah's desperate action, assuring him of Isaac's unassailable position: "Through Isaac shall your descendants be named" (vs. 12*b;* cf. Rom. 9:7; Heb. 11:18). Not through Ishmael, the child of human impatience and unfaith (*see* Abraham §§ C1*i*, 2*c;* Ishmael 1), nor any collateral line, however worthy, but through Isaac, the child granted by God's grace, the divine promises will be transmitted to Israel (cf. Gal. 4:21-31). Therefore, Abraham may assist in Hagar's dismissal, knowing that her son, though he continues a neighbor, will not threaten Isaac's future (Gen. 21:14).

The tradition here accounts for the historic situation that the Israelites and Ishmaelites represent collateral lines of descent from Abraham and live as neighbors, the latter occupying the territory lying principally to the E (cf. ארץ קדם in 25:6; ארץ בני קדם in 29:1) of Palestine. *See* Palestine, Geography of; Arabians § 2.

The biblical narrative brings Isaac and Ishmael together again only upon the occasion of Abraham's death (25:9-11*a*).

***c. The sacrifice of Isaac* (*22:1-19*).** As is the case with Jesus in the gospels (Luke 2:41-51), only one episode is known about the childhood of Isaac. Since Isaac knows what a sacrifice entails and is old enough to carry a load of wood (vs. 6), he is portrayed, not as a small child, but as at least a lad. The story of the "sacrifice" of Isaac (called by later Jews the "binding of Isaac," עקדת יצחק) is a superb example of the Elohist's narrative art. The issue of faith and obedience dominates the whole story. It pictures father and son, in journeying to the land of Moriah, intimately sharing the pathos of the hour. As they walk together (vss. 6*b*, 8*b*), each bearing the materials by which the father expects to offer up the life of his only beloved son—Ishmael having been sent away previously (*see* § 2*b above*)—they share also a deep faith. Abraham trusts that God knows what he has asked and that Isaac will respond in obedience; Isaac relies upon the wisdom and love of his father and, perhaps by his example, also upon God's providence (vss. 6-8; cf. Wisd. Sol. 10:5; Heb. 11:17-19). Isaac's question: "Where is the lamb for a burnt offering?" (vs. 7*b*), seems to go beyond innocent curiosity and betrays an intuition that this is no common journey on which his father leads him. Accordingly, the picture of Isaac sensing the solemnity of the occasion and yet walking in perfect obedience, while carrying the wood upon which he is to be sacrificed, ranks among the most christological portraits found in the OT.

For his part Abraham, for his faithfulness, receives his son, as it were, a second time (cf. Gen. 21:1-3). The "gift" of Isaac is especially significant here, in view of Abraham's earlier gross lack of faith in fathering a son by Hagar (*see* Abraham §§ C1*i*, 2*c*), for it demonstrates God's unshakable fidelity to his promise.

***d. Isaac and Rebekah* (*24:62-67*).** When Abraham is old, he sends his trusted servant back to the region of Haran (*see* Aram-naharaim) to obtain from his own kindred a wife for Isaac (24:1-61; *see* Abraham § C1*m*). By this he wishes to maintain, principally at least, purity of religion, not of race; for the religion of Nahor's family is of the same basic type as Abraham's (*see* Patriarchs § 5; Nahor 2). But he is very insistent that Isaac not be taken there, even if it be the only means of his obtaining a wife. For Abraham is the possessor of "this land" (vs. 7), and Isaac must inherit the promise. To leave Canaan would be a signal act of infidelity. The faithful servant is entrusted with the double responsibility of preventing Isaac from marrying a native Canaanitess and yet from leaving the Promised Land. With this commission the servant goes and finds Rebekah. Rebekah, the sister of LABAN, sharing something of the steward's own sense of destiny, agrees to accompany him back to Palestine and marry Isaac, whom she has never seen. In this compelling scene, which introduces her to the reader, Rebekah displays something of the resolution of will and independence of action which characterize her later in the Isaac story.

The scene depicting the first meeting of the future couple, though brief, is colorful and winsome (vss. 62-67). Isaac has just come up to the region of Hebron, Abraham's residence according to J (13:18; 18:1 [=Mamre]), from Beer-lahai-roi, which is located farther in the Negeb (24:62*b*, or "the wilderness of Beer-lahai-roi"; see Commentaries). Presumably he has been told of his father's intent and has come to Hebron to await the servant's return, because he goes out into the field in the evening "to meditate" (the precise meaning of the verb שוח is uncertain), sees the caravan approaching, and walks out to meet it. His curiosity is matched by Rebekah's, for when she sees her groom-to-be, she "falls off" the camel, and she veils her face. The lasting impression of the narrative is that the pair enjoy love at first sight. He marries her and is "comforted after his mother's death" (but the text is not in order; probably notice of Abraham's death originally stood here, or in the preceding verses).

***e. Birth of Esau and Jacob* (*25:19-28*).** Like Sarah, who was to be a "mother of nations" (17:16*b; see* SARAH), Rebekah is barren. In the over-all context of the promise of continuing descendants in the house of Abraham (12:7; 13:16 [J]; 15:5 [E]; 17:2-3 [P]; cf. 24:60 [J]), Rebekah's barrenness creates a major test of faith in Yahweh. Instead of resorting to despair or self-willed action (*see* ABRAHAM §§ C1*i*, C2*c*), Isaac meets the temptation with prayer (25:21*a*). Isaac's patient faith is set in a high light by the Priestly chronology, for according to it Rebekah remained childless for twenty years (cf. vss. 20*a*, 26*b*). Yahweh was gracious to Isaac: he "granted his prayer [lit., 'allowed himself to be entreated by him,' ויעתר לו], and Rebekah his wife conceived" (vs. 21).

With the birth of the twins Esau and Jacob, Yahweh's promise concerning Isaac is fulfilled and the patriarch's faith and prayer exonerated. And in the oracle characterizing the future of these two (vs. 23), this promise is renewed implicitly by the words "nations" and "peoples," as it is explicitly at 26:3-5 (*see* § 2*f below*). But also, with the birth of twins who are in conflict with each other (vss. 22*a*, 23*b*, 26*a*, 29-34; cf. 27:41-45), the promise is again threatened. Further, the conflict between the sons is reflected in, and the threat deepened by, the divided loyalty of their parents; for Isaac loved the roving hunter, ESAU, but Rebekah loved the "quiet" Jacob (25:28; *see* JACOB § C1).

***f. Isaac and Abimelech* (*ch. 26*).** Only in his dealings with ABIMELECH does Isaac stand out as a person in his own right. Previous episodes have seen him subordinated to his father or his wife, and the remaining sections weave his story into the narrative of his sons. Perhaps here, then, Israel's distinctive picture of Isaac may be sought. The portrait of Isaac which dominates all his dealings in this chapter is that of the man of blessing.

Yahweh's initial theophany to Isaac, when he had taken refuge in GERAR from the famine, sounds this note clearly: "Sojourn in this land, and I will be with you, and will bless you" (vs. 3*a*). The obstacle created by the famine to the working out of the patriarchal promise of land and seed (12:7; 13:15) is overcome by divine protection, as is also the threat posed by Rebekah's beauty (vss. 6-11). Isaac sowed in that land "and reaped in the same year a hundredfold," because "Yahweh blessed him, and the man became rich, and gained more and more until he became very wealthy" (vss. 12-13). His prodigious success is the natural and inevitable effect of the divine blessing which he bore. In the borderland between the natives and the Israelites (the "valley of Gerar"), Isaac was also successful in obtaining plentiful sources of water, so vital for life in Palestine. Since Yahweh prospered his efforts, he would surely become "fruitful in the land" (vss. 17-22).

When Isaac returned to Beer-sheba, Yahweh again appeared to him, identifying himself as the "God of Abraham your father" and repeating the promise of blessing. By erecting an altar there, Isaac bound his family to the same God worshiped by his father (vss. 23-25; cf. 21:25-33). *See* PATRIARCHS § 5.

The final episode emphasizes further the theme of blessing. Abimelech and two high officials (*see* PHICOL) come to Isaac in the patriarch's own land and request a covenant with him because, they acknowledge, "you are now the blessed of Yahweh" (ברוך יהוה; vs. 29).

***g. Isaac's blessing* (*ch. 27*).** The theme of blessing dominates also the final, most poignant scene in Isaac's life. Not knowing the day of his death, the man of blessing wishes to communicate this blessing to his older son. However, through crass deceit, initiated by the mother herself, the younger son, who has previously gained the family birthright (*see* JACOB § C1*b*), now steals the patriarchal benediction. The pathetic and shocking story is masterfully told by the Yahwist. The aged, blind father, uncertain of his son yet wishing to believe in him, finally satisfies himself by the kiss, and gives to his undeserving son his deathbed blessing (vss. 1-30).

With Esau's anguished cry ("Bless me, even me also, O my father!" vs. 34), which severs the father's vain hold on the hope that he has nevertheless been right, the scene reaches its dramatic height. Isaac knows that the blessing he has solemnly communicated to Jacob can be neither recalled nor annulled, for it comes from God (*see* JACOB § C1*c*). The brokenhearted father can only take some of the words of the blessing and pronounce them over Esau as a mitigated curse (vss. 39-40; cf. vs. 28). The results of the affair seem tragic: Isaac dies, knowing he has given his blessing to a lying, deceitful son; Esau hates his brother and seeks occasion to kill him; and Jacob flees from the land promised to him, never to see his mother again (vss. 41-45 [J]; but see P's explanation, 27:46–28:9). Yet in the skein of tragedy God has been at work; and Jacob's blasphemous assertion (27:20) is, in the ultimate issue, true (cf. Heb. 11:20).

h. The death of Isaac **(*Gen. 35:27-29*).** When he was 180 years old, Isaac died at Hebron, and was buried by his sons Esau and Jacob in the cave of MACH-PELAH, where Abraham and Sarah lay and where he had buried Rebekah (35:27-29; 49:32). The phrase "old and full of days" (35:29) is seen as evidence of the blessing manifesting itself in his life. *See* BLESSEDNESS.

3. Isaac in the NT. The most important aspect of the Genesis story dealt with in the NT is, obviously, the sacrifice of Isaac (*see* § 2*c above*). Although Paul did not develop the relation between the sacrifice of Abraham's only beloved son and that of Christ, his reminder that "we, brethren, like Isaac, are children of promise" (Gal. 4:28; cf. Rom. 9:6-13) points suggestively in that direction. As Isaac was obedient unto the point of death, so Christ offered himself in perfect obedience to the Father's will; and it is in the same sacrificial self-giving that the Christian is called to share. Isaac's sacrifice would serve as a "type" (τύπος), first for Christ, who fulfilled it perfectly, then also for Christians, who are Abraham's seed after the Spirit (*see* ABRAHAM § E). The early Christian church developed this latent concept quite fully (Barn. 7:3; Clement of Alexandria *Paedagogica* I.5.1; Strom. 2.5; Iren. Her. 4.4; and especially Origen), and it had a parallel development in post-biblical Judaism. *See* the Isaac theme in the article by Schoeps in the *bibliography*.

Bibliography. J. Pedersen, *Israel,* I-II (1926), 190-212; M. Noth, *Die israelitischen Personennamen* (1928), pp. 210, 218; H. J. Schoeps, "The Sacrifice of Isaac in Paul's Theology," *JBL,* LXV (1946), 385-92; D. Lerch, *Isaak's Opferung christlich gedeutet* (1950); J. J. Stamm, "Der Name Isaak," *Festschrift für Albert Schaedelin* (1950), pp. 33 ff; E. A. Speiser, "I know not the Day of my Death," *JBL,* LXXIV (1955), 252-56.

For historical background and religion of the patriarchal period, *see* bibliography under PATRIARCHS. For description of some Genesis commentaries, *see* bibliography under ABRAHAM.

L. HICKS

ISAI ī'zī. Douay Version form of JESSE.

ISAIAH ī zā'ə [ישעיהו, ישעיה, Yah(weh) is salvation]. KJV alternately: ESAIAS ĭ zā'əs [*twenty-one times in the* NT, *from* LXX 'Ησαίας]. The name of the first of the "major" prophets (always ישעיהו) and of the book (ישעיה) in which his prophecies have been preserved.

The spelling current in the eighth century B.C. was ישעיהו. The shorter ישעיה was later and is found in the Elephantine Papyri (Cowley 5.16; 8.33; 9.21). The name is similar in meaning to Joshua (יהושע) or Jesus (ישוע), and Hosea (הושע), also to Elisha (אלישע, "God is salvation"). Other individuals are named ישעיהו and ישעיה in the OT, but for these the RSV has kept the KJV spelling JESHAIAH.

- A. The prophet
  - 1. His life
    - *a.* Early ministry
    - *b.* Withdrawal from public life
    - *c.* Middle years
    - *d.* Later ministry
  - 2. His personality
  - 3. His theology
    - *a.* Yahweh's sovereignty
    - *b.* Yahweh's holiness
    - *c.* Human sin
    - *d.* Faith in Yahweh
    - *e.* The remnant
    - *f.* The Messiah
- B. The book
  - 1. Chs. 1–39
    - *a.* Composition
    - *b.* Contents
  - 2. Chs. 40–55
    - *a.* Historical background
    - *b.* Authorship
    - *c.* The author
    - *d.* Structure
    - *e.* Contents
    - *f.* Interpretation
    - *g.* Theology
  - 3. Chs. 56–66
    - *a.* Authorship and date
    - *b.* Contents
  - 4. Text
- Bibliography

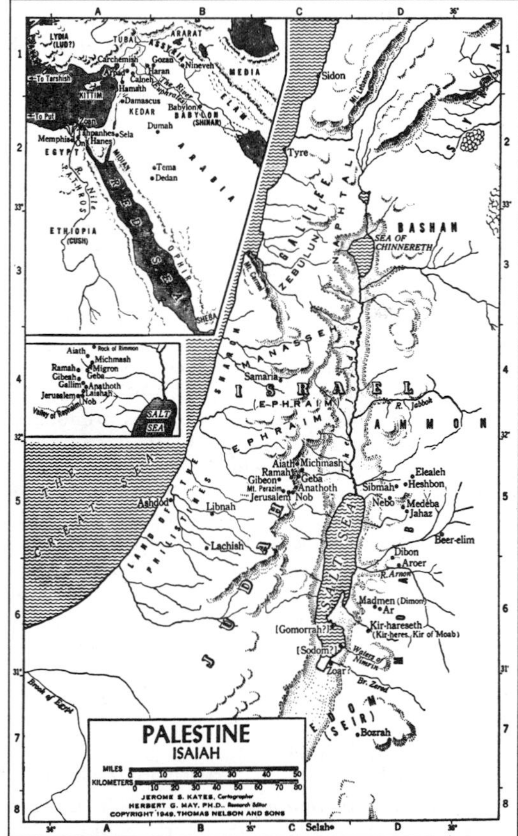

A. *THE PROPHET.* Isaiah's life and ministry must be seen against the historical background of his time. *See* ISRAEL, HISTORY OF, § 9; ASSYRIA AND BABYLONIA § C.

1. His life. What is related of Isaiah's life in the book of Isaiah is supplemented in part by II Kings, especially 18:13-20:21, which is parallel, with some variations, to Isa. 36-39. He was the son of a certain Amoz (אמוץ), who is not to be confused with the prophet Amos (עמוס). It may be assumed that he was born in Jerusalem, about, or shortly before, 760. His call came to him "in the year that King Uzziah died" (6:1), *ca.* 742.* He was married and refers to his wife as "the prophetess" (8:3). He had sons to whom he gave the symbolical names SHEAR-JASHUB and MAHER-SHALAL-HASH-BAZ. His ministry extended over more than forty years, during the reigns of four kings of Judah—Uzziah, Jotham, Ahaz, and Hezekiah (1:1). The last we hear of him is on the occasion of Sennacherib's threat to Jerusalem (701), when he was appealed to by Hezekiah and his court. Tradition has it that Isaiah was sawn asunder in the reign of Manasseh (*see* ISAIAH, ASCENSION OF). This legend may be older than the Letter to the Hebrews (cf. Heb. 11:37) and is perhaps based upon II Kings 21:16. It is impossible to determine whether or not it contains an element of truth. Fig. UZZ 19.

a. Early ministry (742-734). Isaiah's call came to him in the temple. Assuming, as we must, that his account of it is of something he actually experienced, and not so much imaginative description, he must have stood in or very near the sanctuary, and it is not fanciful to suppose that he was, like Jeremiah and Ezekiel, a priest, or perhaps a prophet attached to the temple. It may be taken as certain that he began at once to prophesy and that his message was one of condemnation of the religious and social-economic evils of his time (6:9-10). Most of the contents of chs. 1-5 accord well with this. It is clear that Isaiah had no illusions about the obduracy of his people. He came into public prominence at the time of the Syro-Ephraimitic invasion of Judah in 734 B.C. He always appears to have had easier access to the king and the court than we can suppose was possible for the ordinary citizen; the assumption that he belonged to the aristocracy is confirmed by all that we read of him, as well as by his literary style. It was now that Isaiah made his pronouncement of the birth of IMMANUEL. He was uncompromisingly opposed to Ahaz' plan to cast himself on the protection of Assyria, and he maintained his stand against alliances with foreign powers throughout his ministry. He saw clearly that such alliances would compromise the religious as well as the political freedom of his country (cf. II Kings 16:10-18). Accordingly, the motive underlying his counsel was more religious than political: the prophet believed that faith in Yahweh was a sufficient guarantee of divine protection. Not to have faith was to court disaster:

> If you will not believe,
> surely you shall not be established (7:9).

b. Withdrawal from public life (734-715). Isaiah was no conspirator against the state; and after Ahaz concluded the Assyrian alliance, Isaiah announced his intention to keep silence and to wait for Yahweh (8:16-18). The present Hebrew text speaks of his "disciples." Although there is some doubt about the originality of this reading, there is every reason to believe that the prophets did gather disciples and that it was to such like-minded spirits that we owe the preservation of much of their teaching. At the least, Isaiah's attitude was that his own name and the names of his children would continue to witness as "signs and portents" from Yahweh. But we cannot point with certainty to any public utterances of his between 734 and the death of Ahaz in 715.

c. Middle years (715-705). When Ahaz was succeeded by Hezekiah, Isaiah was once more able to speak freely. An utterance on Philistia is dated "in the year that King Ahaz died" (14:28-32). Hezekiah only waited for an opportunity to break with the foreign policy of his father. The messianic passages 9:2-7—H 9:1-6; 11:1-9 cannot be dated with any certainty. Their optimism is not decisive evidence against their composition in Ahaz' reign, but it is more likely that they come from a time when the outlook was brighter. In 711, the year that the Assyrian TARTAN captured the Philistine stronghold of Ashdod, Isaiah was bidden to go naked and barefoot as a sign and portent (cf. 8:18) of the fate that awaited Egypt and Ethiopia (ch. 20; cf. ch. 18; 19: 1-15). This he did for three years. The motive was doubtless to dissuade Hezekiah from becoming involved in Egyptian intrigues against Assyria. At the same time Isaiah could hardly be blind to the increasing ruthlessness of Assyria. He was from the beginning convinced that Yahweh's chastisement was coming to Judah. It was also clear to him that Assyria was the instrument of this chastisement (10: 5-10). But he was equally convinced that it was not in the divine purpose that Zion, the earthly habitation of Yahweh, should be given over to the Assyrians to be spoiled and plundered. This may be the reason why invective against Jerusalem and its inhabitants is not so prominent in the middle years as it had been earlier.

d. Later ministry (705-701). The death of Sargon II (*see* SARGON 2) in 705 was the signal for a general revolt against Assyria. The embassy of MERODACH-BALADAN of Babylon (ch. 39), although its setting in the book of Isaiah is later than the time of Hezekiah's illness (ch. 38), which itself was subsequent to the invasion of Sennacherib in 701 (chs. 36-37), must have been *ca.* 703. It is clear from the story that Hezekiah was being drawn into a coalition against Assyria. Isaiah's policy of nonparticipation was the same as it had always been. He stigmatized the alliance as a "covenant with death and Sheol" (28:15). Egypt as an ally was wholly undependable (30:1-5; 31). SENNACHERIB, having crushed Merodach-baladan, moved swiftly against the Philistine cities, with whom (and probably with Egypt) Hezekiah had now compromised himself. The biblical account of the campaign in II Kings 18:13-37; Isa. 36 is supplemented by the Cylinder of Sennacherib, which tells how the citizens of Ekron delivered their king Padi to Hezekiah. An Assyrian detachment was sent to invest Jerusalem, and Sennacherib describes how he shut up Hezekiah "like a caged bird in Jerusalem his royal city." In this crisis Hezekiah sent to Isaiah the entreaty: "Lift up your prayer for the remnant that is left" (II Kings 19:4; Isa. 37:4). Isaiah interpreted the insolence of Sennacherib's envoys as mockery and reviling of the "Holy One of Israel."

His answer was unhesitating: he declared in Yahweh's name that Sennacherib should go back by the way he had come, "for I will defend this city to save it, for my own sake and for the sake of my servant David" (II Kings 19:34; Isa. 37:35). At the same time Isaiah saw no excuse for levity on the part of the populace; 22:1-4 may come from a time earlier than Sennacherib's invasion, but it would be no less relevant in 701 than it had always been.

2. His personality. So long as it was believed that the entire book of Isaiah was written by the prophet himself, Isaiah was assumed to be the greatest, as he was the first in time, of the major prophets. Today not even the whole of chs. 1–39 is thought to come from him. Accordingly, his stature may seem less than it was, and there are those who reckon Jeremiah and/or Deutero-Isaiah as at least his equals. To discuss which was the greatest of the prophets is futile. Amos, Hosea, Isaiah, Jeremiah, Ezekiel, and Deutero-Isaiah, to name those who may be considered "major" in the nonliterary sense, have common characteristics and qualities. The differences between them are largely those dictated by the circumstances of their times. Notwithstanding that the word "genius" is nowadays loosely and all too frequently used, it is the only word that does justice to Isaiah. His literary output is still considerable, and his ministry lasted for more than a generation. He was a poet-seer and at the same time a man of action, a statesman unerring in judgment. As a young man he was mature in both, and as a man in his sixties he had lost nothing of his mastery in either. Ezekiel could be bizarre; Isaiah was sanity itself. Jeremiah was sometimes unsure of himself, even unsure of Yahweh. Isaiah never was; there is no evidence that he ever had to wait for Yahweh's instruction in an emergency (contrast Jer. 28:11-14; 42:1-7).

Isaiah never felt under unwilling compulsion, notwithstanding that after his call he could speak of Yahweh's "strong hand" being "upon" him (8:11). His answer to Yahweh's call for a volunteer was the free-will offering of himself: "I heard the voice of the Lord saying, 'Whom shall I send, and who will go for us?' Then I said, 'Here I am! Send me' " (6:8). His gifts of mind and imagination; his social position as, it may be assumed, a member of the aristocracy; his private and family life—all were dedicated to a service he never regretted and from which he never looked back. He was fearless and frank in the presence of majesty; he could pour withering scorn on the pretensions of a state official (22:15-25); he was scathing in his denunciations of gluttony, land greed, and social injustice (5:8-23); he told the society beauties of his time exactly what Yahweh thought of them, without any mincing of words (3:16-26); and his compassion for the unprivileged never made him pander to the mob (22:1-3). He must have been far and away the greatest man of his time.

Isaiah's consistency was not the consistency of a "little mind." His policy of nonalliance was the right one for his time, though we are not at liberty to argue from it that alliances between nations are always and everywhere immoral. His doctrine of the inviolability of Zion was justified, and if its signal vindication and his own immense prestige converted it into a dogma whch a century later had baneful consequences (cf. Jer. 7:1-15), this was no fault of his.

Isaiah, like all great poets, must have been born a poet. But his experience at his call gave an incandescent quality to his genius. His style is simple and direct, without the elaboration of the later Second Isaiah (this is no depreciation of Second Isaiah). That he knew how a vineyard was prepared (5:1-2), or what a derelict hut in a garden looked like (1:8), or was familiar with the bovine patience of domestic animals (1:3), is not remarkable. There were no mammoth cities in his day. But the majesty of his description of Yahweh's coming in judgment is superb (2:10-21). The skill with which he begins the love song of "my beloved" about his vineyard, until as he proceeds it is "my beloved" (Yahweh) himself who is singing, is perfect. Like other poet-prophets (Jer. 1:11-12; Amos 8:1-2), he is not ashamed of a pun; but it is an apt pun, even when it is intentionally harsh: "He expected justice [*mishpāṭ*], but instead, bloodshed [*miśpāḥ*]; righteousness [*ṣ^edhāqâ*], but instead, a cry [*ṣ^e'āqâ*]" (5:7 [orig. tr.]). If, to be a genius of the first rank, a man must be at once a creative artist and a man of affairs, Isaiah must be accorded his place among the select few. And his was genius heightened by utter consecration to the service of God.

3. His theology. The outstanding emphases in Isaiah's theology are already explicit or implicit in the account of his call (ch. 6).

a. Yahweh's sovereignty. "Monotheism" is an abstract noun, and the eighteenth century Deists were monotheists. Isaiah did not say, as the Prophet of the Exile did (Isa. 45:6, 22-23), that there is no God but Yahweh. But from what he does say, it is inconceivable that he thought of any other "god" as having real existence: "The whole earth is full of his [Yahweh's] glory" (6:3). Idols are אלילים, "worthless things," "nonentities" (2:8, 18, 20-21), the "work of men's hands" (37:19; cf. 2:8; Ps. 115:4). It is Yahweh who determines the course of history. The Assyrians appear invincible, but they are only a rod in Yahweh's hand, and if they overstep the bounds of their commission, Yahweh will not spare them (10:5-19).

b. Yahweh's holiness. "Holiness" is another abstract noun, and it is probable, though not certain, that the original idea underlying the root קדש was that of (physical) separation (*see* HOLINESS). All Semitic "gods" were "holy," but the word had no ethical connotation. The temple prostitutes of Akkadian and Canaanite religion were "holy women." Isaiah saw Yahweh in majestic exaltation. The attendant seraphim shielded themselves from the dazzling radiance as they cried: "Holy, holy, holy is Yahweh of hosts" (6:3). The threefold "Holy" (Trisagion) was the Hebrew way of expressing the superlative, "most holy." Holiness in such a context is not a negative absence of moral impurity; it is not positive moral perfection, that and no more. It has still the "numinous" quality which had always attached to it. Yahweh's holiness is his perfect moral purity combined with his transcendent exaltation. That holiness has a moral content had been anticipated by Amos (Amos 4:2), who voiced Yahweh's demand for justice and righteousness (5:24). But it was Isaiah who laid the main emphasis upon Yahweh's holiness, who first, and often (twelve times), called Yahweh the "Holy One of Israel," and forever sealed the bond between holiness and righteousness.

c. Human sin. That Yahweh's holiness must express itself in judgment upon human sin is evident from the immediate impact it made upon Isaiah: "I said: 'Woe is me! For I am lost; for I am a man of unclean lips, and I dwell in the midst of a people of unclean lips; for my eyes have seen the King, Yahweh of hosts.'" Sin is uncleanness; it is also rebellion against Yahweh (1:2). The whole body of society is tainted with it (1:4-6). Sacrifices are no remedy for it (1:11-15) but only make matters worse. The inevitable consequence of man's sensuality, self-sufficiency, pride, and injustice was a fearful expectation of judgment. Amos had already announced such a judgment, the "day of Yahweh" upon Israel (Amos 5:18-20). In Isaiah the day of Yahweh is to be universal in its scope (2:6-22).

d. Faith in Yahweh. There is only one remedy for man's self-reliance and resort to his own expedients, and this is faith in Yahweh. This strikes a new note in prophecy and finds expression in two passages which sum up Isaiah's positive testimony. In 7:9: "If you will not believe [*ta'aminû;* Hiph'il], you shall not be established [*tē'āmēnû;* Niph'al]," the play on words can be conveyed by some such rendering as: "If you will not be sure, you cannot be secure," or by making the contrast between "faith" and the now obsolete colloquial "staith." The other passage is 28:16: "He who believes will not be in haste," meaning that he will not get panicky. Closely related in thought is 30:15:

> In returning and rest you shall be saved;
> in quietness and in trust shall be your strength,

this attitude being contrasted (vs. 16) with feverish reliance upon horses, which will only suffice for ignominious flight.

e. The remnant. Amos (5:15) had spoken of the "remnant of Joseph" (N Israel), which should survive catastrophe, as of something to which Yahweh might be "gracious." It is probable that the last clause in Isa. 6:13: "The holy seed is its stump," is a gloss—it is not in the LXX. Nevertheless, the doctrine of the remnant must early have taken shape in Isaiah's mind. His little son SHEAR-JASHUB, "A remnant will return," was old enough to accompany his father on foot to the encounter with Ahaz in 734 B.C. (*see* IMMANUEL § 1). At first the name was a "sign and portent" of sinister import (8:18). Even if 10:20-23; 11:11, 16, should not be from Isaiah, it is certain that Isaiah looked for something more than a bare survival of Judah. Yahweh was

> laying in Zion for a foundation
> a stone, a tested stone,
> a precious cornerstone, of a sure foundation
> (28:16).

"My disciples" (8:16) may be suspect (*see* § A1*b above*), but the very book of Isaiah, not to speak of the postexilic Jewish community, is evidence that a purified remnant did survive. The doctrine of the remnant has been of immense significance in the subsequent history both of Judaism and of Christianity.

f. The Messiah. Isaiah's messianic teaching is not free from perplexity. This may be because it was more incidental than central to his teaching. The prophet was in declared opposition to the policy of Ahaz. He was not uncritical of Hezekiah (ch. 39), but his conviction of the inviolability of Zion was for him a higher compulsion than denunciation of what might be interpreted as the pro-Egyptian leanings of the king, and in the crisis of 701 he stood firmly by Hezekiah. Expectation of a future messiah was largely born of dissatisfaction with the reigning kings, and it is not antecedently improbable that Isaiah should have made messianic pronouncements. The "Immanuel" prophecy, no matter how it should be interpreted (*see* IMMANUEL), was such a pronouncement. With it 9:2-7—H 9:1-6; 11:1-9 make up a trilogy. But it is difficult to determine whether the "perfect" tenses of 9:2-7 are "prophetic perfects" referring to the future, or whether the passage celebrated the birth, or perhaps the enthronement, of a contemporary prince. 11:1-9 has often been denied to Isaiah, on the ground that it is written from the standpoint of the Exile—the "stump of Jesse" has already been cut down (vs. 1); but the present trend of opinion is to regard the passage as Isaianic. Even so it may refer to a contemporary king (Hezekiah?) of whom great things were expected, rather than in the first instance to a future messiah. What is said of the "Messiah" in both 9:2-7; 11:1-9 is in terms of then current kingship ideology (*see* KING § 7). The king was a sacred, and, in some sort, semidivine person. But for all his endowment, it is clear that he is only a vicegerent, entirely subordinate to Yahweh: "The zeal of Yahweh of hosts will do this" (9:7). 32:1-8 is in general terms, and the parallelism of "king" and "princes" in vs. 1 shows that it is a description of society in conditions where kings "reign in righteousness" and princes "rule in justice."

B. *THE BOOK.* In all printed Hebrew Bibles "Isaiah" is the first of the "Latter Prophets" (Isaiah, Jeremiah, Ezekiel, and "the Twelve"). It is so also in the oldest Hebrew MS codices (tenth and eleventh centuries A.D.). The Qumran scrolls give no indication of where their copyists would have placed Isaiah in the order of prophets. Some later MSS place Isaiah after Ezekiel, and a passage in the Talmud (B.B. 14*b*) has it that this is the correct order and that Isaiah was composed by the "men of Hezekiah." This recalls Prov. 25:1 and may indicate that Jewish scholars were not satisfied that the entire book was from the pen of Isaiah. Such, indeed, is the general view today. But that the book as we know it went by the name of Isaiah by *ca.* 180 B.C., is clear from Ecclus. 48:17-25, which refers to the historical section (Isa. 36–39) and then goes on to say of Isaiah:

> By the spirit of might he saw the last things,
> and comforted those who mourned in Zion

(cf. Isa. 40:1). This is confirmed by the somewhat later Qumran scrolls.

There is an obvious break in the subject matter of the book at the end of ch. 39, and another almost equally obvious at the end of 55. Even if chs. 40–66 are predictive prophecy from the pen of Isaiah, it is convenient to deal with the sixty-six chapters under separate headings (1–39; 40–55; 56–66), without, at the outset, pronouncing on the authorship of chs. 40–66.

1. Chs. 1-39. ***a. Composition.*** The occurrence of subsidiary titles (1:1; 2:1; 13:1; etc.) suggests that the book was in part compiled from smaller units and collections. The following main divisions are fairly clear: (*a*) ch. 1, a collection of prophetic pronouncements; (*b*) chs. 2–12, mainly concerned with "Judah and Jerusalem," ascribed in a title (2:1) to Isaiah; (*c*) chs. 13–23, pronouncements mainly concerned with foreign nations; (*d*) chs. 24–27, an eschatological prophecy or prophecies; (*e*) chs. 28–33, a collection of "woes" dealing with the relationship of Judah to Assyria; (*f*) chs. 34–35, two eschatological prophecies; (*g*) chs. 36–39, historical narratives.

But it is an oversimplification of the problem to suppose that Isa. 1–39 was formed by the addition of some seven originally independent booklets. A feature of the prophetical books is that they consist of three types of materials generally denoted by (*a*) utterances of the prophets, for the most part short, and usually in verse; (*b*) stories about the prophets, in prose and in the third person; (*c*) passages of autobiography, mainly prose but sometimes with verse intermingled (cf. Isa. 6). Now if 2:1 was intended as the superscription to chs. 2–12, it is clear that the section contains *a, b,* and *c* materials: chs. 2–5 are prophecies; chs. 6; 8 are autobiographical; ch. 7 is biographical; and chs. 9–12 are again prophecies. The processes by which even chs. 1–39, without the addition of chs. 40–55; 56–66, assumed their present form, are complicated and obscure. It is likely enough that chs. 13–23; 24–27; and, with modifications, 36–39 were complete and separate entities before they were incorporated in the book as we have it today, but how the materials in the other main sections were assembled in their present order we can sometimes only conjecture. One main principle of association would seem to have been "catchwords." E.g., 1:10-17 is clearly distinct from 1:2-9, but the one begins, as the other ends, with the mention of Sodom and Gomorrah. A similar catchword is the "woe" (six times) of ch. 5 (cf. 28:1; 29:1 [in Hebrew], 15; 30:1; 31:1; 33:1). Two other sets of consecutive passages begin: "In that day" (7:18, 20, 21, 23; 19:16, 18, 19, 23, 24). Chs. 13–23 consist of what must originally have been separate pieces; the majority of them now have in common an introductory: "The oracle concerning," which stands outside the poem proper. The Hebrew is משא (from a root "to lift up"—i.e., the voice) in the construct state. "Pronouncement on" perhaps better conveys the meaning to the modern reader, though some of these passages are oracular enough in the usual sense of the word.

b. Contents. The contents of chs. 1–39 may be grouped and summarized as follows:

Ch. 1: This contains some five (ERV) or more short poems, mostly denunciations but with some promises. The title (vs. 1), with its enumeration of "kings of Judah," must be postexilic. While most of the sections are presumably early, the description in vss. 7-9 best suits the conditions during Sennacherib's invasion. Unlike most prophetic oracles, vss. 2-9 are put in the mouth of the prophet, not Yahweh. Heaven and earth are called to hear Yahweh's verdict on his people's ingratitude. The description of the diseased body politic well illustrates the concept of corporate personality. Vss. 10-17 are related to the preceding by the figure of Sodom and Gomorrah, here examples of wickedness, there of destruction. Their theme is the futility of sacrifices (cf. Jer. 7:22-23; Hos. 6:6; 8:11-14; Amos 5:21-24; Mic. 6:6-8). The alternative to repentance is destruction (vss. 18-20). Vss. 27-31 are generally thought to be a later consolation, offsetting the preceding denunciations; this may well be, but we can no longer assume it. It is an oversimplification to suppose that the preexilic prophets were concerned only with judgment.

Chs. 2–12: The superscription 2:1 may refer to chs. 2–12, since the next heading is at 13:1, or it may refer only to 2:2-4. These verses are found with minor variations, and the addition of another verse, in Mic. 4:1-4. They may well have been anonymous, and the conception of Zion as a center of pilgrimage for all "nations" (Micah "peoples") is not otherwise attested until the Exile (*see* §§ B2*e*, 3*b*, *below*). The theme of 2:5-22 is the coming "day of Yahweh," which will spell doom for idolatry and human pride.

3:1-15 pronounces the doom of rapacious rulers. This is followed (3:16–4:1; cf. Amos 4:1-3) by denunciation of frivolous women whose love of luxury can only be satisfied as their consorts "grind the face of the poor." (The inventory of luxuries in vss. 18-23 is prose, probably later amplification.) 4:2-6 is descriptive of Zion, which has been purified by judgment. It is as near prose as a prophetic utterance can be. In thought and expression it reads as if it is later than Isaiah, but it is a fine example of the way the spirit of Isaiah continued to influence later generations.

The vineyard song, 5:1-7, viewed only as a poem, is a work of consummate art. It is evidently based on popular vintage songs (cf. 56:12) and begins with a quick movement (meter 3:2 and 2:2), which appropriately passes at vs. 4 into longer and heavier rhythm (3:3 and 2:2:2; *see* POETRY [HEBREW]). 5:8-24 contains a series of "woes" ("Shame . . . !") on the privileged classes, landowners who evict small farmers, drunkards, skeptics no longer capable of making moral distinctions, and venal judges. Their enormities will have inevitable consequences—"Therefore . . ." (vss. 13-24)—and the tragedy is that the crimes of those who are privileged must drag down all society in a common ruin. The concluding verses of ch. 5 (25-30) relate to the downfall of N Israel at the hands of Assyria and are best read as the conclusion of 9:8-21 (note the refrain at the end of vs. 25 and cf. 9:12, 17, 21).

The account of Isaiah's call (ch. 6) is autobiographical and is too well known to need description (*see* §§ A3*a-c above*). It is likely that vss. 9-13 are proleptic, colored by the prophet's experience of the obstinacy of his people.

Chs. 7–8 relate to the Syro-Ephraimitic invasion of 734 (*see* IMMANUEL; SHEAR-JASHUB; MAHER-SHALAL-HASH-BAZ). Ch. 7 is biographical, ch. 8 autobiographical.

9:1—H 8:23 is prose, a connecting link between

the preceding pronouncement of doom and the messianic passage following (9:2-7—H 9:1-6, for which *see* § A3*f above*). 9:8-21—H 9:7-20, of which 5:25-30 (*see above*) is the conclusion, relates to the coming downfall of N Israel. It is presumably earlier than the fall of Samaria and may picture the dynastic struggles which preceded the final catastrophe. 10:1-4, notwithstanding that it concludes with the refrain:

> For all this his anger is not turned away
> and his hand is stretched out still,

has more in common with the "woes" of 5:8-23. It is directed against "those who decree iniquitous decrees . . . and rob the poor of my [Yahweh's] people" —i.e., Judah.

10:5-19 illustrates, as well as any passage in the OT, the Hebrew conviction that Yahweh is Lord of history. Its relevance for the present century is obvious. The Assyrians were an utterly ruthless military power. They are the unconscious instrument of Yahweh, a rod in his hand to chastise his own people. There is no criticism of them in chs. 7–8, but here their arrogance cries aloud for retribution. They have exceeded the bounds of their commission, but they are powerless to exceed the bounds of Yahweh's purpose. Vs. 12: "When the Lord has finished all his work on Mount Zion and on Jerusalem he will punish the arrogant boasting of the king of Assyria and his haughty pride," is probably secondary, but it sums up the situation as well as anything could. In 10:20-23 the conception of the remnant (*see* § A3*e above; see also* SHEAR-JASHUB; REMNANT SHALL RETURN) finds expression in both its aspects, of doom and of promise. The promise of deliverance from Assyria is closely related to vss. 5-19 and to the subsequent assurance to Hezekiah (37:6-7). The chapter concludes with a vivid description of an army (Assyrian[?] or Syro-Ephraimite; cf. 7:1-2) marching from N to S against Jerusalem.

Ch. 11 is a picture of the messianic age. For vss. 1-9 *see* § A3*f above*. They are more eschatological in tone than 9:2-7 and are remarkable for the conception of the sevenfold (cf. Rev. 1:4) spirit of Yahweh, which shall "rest" on the king as his permanent endowment, not "rush" upon him as in the earlier accounts of the "judges" (Judg. 14:6; I Sam. 10:6). The passage has contributed to later apocalyptic imagery (cf. vs. 4*b* with Rev. 1:16). The picture of the messianic age is continued in 11:10-16, which is almost certainly postexilic, and closes with two short hymns of thanksgiving (12:1-2, 3-6).

Chs. 13–23: These chapters are mainly concerned with foreign peoples and are similar to collections in Jer. 46–51; Ezek. 25–32. The heading משא ("Oracle" or "Pronouncement") occurs ten times in the section.

Although the "oracle concerning Babylon" (ch. 13) is said to be that "which Isaiah the son of Amoz saw" (vs. 1), it is almost certainly from a later time. The coming destruction is "near" (vs. 6), and the reference to the Medes (vs. 17) points to a date *ca.* 540. The taunt song against "Babylon" (14:4-21), which may here be a symbolic name, is a separate poem and is joined to the preceding by verses (14:1-3) which presuppose the Exile. The passages on the overthrow of Assyria (14:24-27) and the premature rejoicing of Philistia (14:28-32) are Isaianic.

The "oracle concerning Moab" (chs. 15–16) is full of obscurities, and parts of it (15:2-7; 16:6-11) are found also in Jer. 48:29-38. If the editorial note 16:13-14 is right, it may be that Isaiah made use of an earlier poem.

The "oracle concerning Damascus" (17:1-6) pronounces doom on both Syria and Ephraim. It is Isaianic, *ca.* 734, and should be read against the background of 7:1–8:4. 17:9-11 is directed against the widespread cult of ADONIS (TAMMUZ): "pleasant plants" (vs. 10) is better rendered "gardens for Adonis" (cf. ERV mg.); at least, this is what it means. The concluding verses of the chapter (12-14) sound like Isaiah but cannot be exactly dated.

Chs. 18–19 are "concerning Egypt" (19:1). The poetical sections (18:1–19:15) confirm the mean opinion Isaiah had of reliance upon Egypt (cf. 30:1-7; 31:1-3). The occasion may have been the establishment of the twenty-fifth (Ethiopian) dynasty (cf. 18:1), which attempted to revive the ancient glory of the country. 19:16-25 contains five prose passages beginning: "In that day." They are not from Isaiah, but they are unique in that they envisage a time when Egypt and Assyria, who had so long and so often been Israel's and each other's foes, will worship Yahweh together with Israel (vss. 23-25).

Ch. 20 is biographical and unlike anything else in chs. 13–23. Its place here is, no doubt, due to its community of subject with chs. 18–19.

Ch. 21 contains three pronouncements, on the "wilderness of the sea" (vss. 1-10), "Dumah" (vss. 11-12), and Arabia (vss. 13-16). The enigmatical "wilderness of the sea" (מדבר ים) can hardly be right. The LXX reads "wilderness" simply, and the first Qumran scroll has "words" (דברים). The original was perhaps "pronouncement on the wilderness." The passage, with its references to Elam and Media (vs. 2) and the fall of Babylon (vs. 9), recalls chs. 13–14 and dates from about the same time. For "Dumah" (vs. 11) the LXX reads "Edom," interpreting rightly, as the following "Seir" shows. "What of the night?" means either: "How much longer will the night last?" or perhaps: "What will follow the night?"

22:1-14 is a pronouncement on the "valley of vision." It obviously relates to Jerusalem, and the "valley" must have been somewhere in its vicinity, perhaps the Valley of Hinnom (cf. Jer. 7:31-34). The passage is in two parts (vss. 1-8*a*, 12-14), with connective verses (8*b*-11) in prose. Isaiah protests against the premature and reckless levity of the inhabitants of Jerusalem: they rely on their own resources without regard to Yahweh. The date that comes readiest to mind is 701 B.C., but another possibility is 711, when Sargon took Ashdod (cf. 20:1) and might have been expected to follow this with an attack on Jerusalem. 22:15-25 is an invective against Shebna, the major-domo of the palace, and an announcement that he will be replaced by Eliakim. The date must be prior to 701, since by then (cf. 36:3; 37:2) Eliakim was major-domo and Shebna subordinate to him.

The pronouncement on Tyre (ch. 23) foretells the doom of the seaports of Phoenicia. There were so many unsuccessful sieges of Tyre between the eighth century and its capture by Alexander the Great, that it is impossible to determine which of them Isa. 23

describes, or, it may be, anticipates. Tyre was, at the most, on the periphery of Isaiah's interest. The passage should be read in conjunction with the more elaborate Ezek. 26–28.

Chs. 24–27: These chapters have often been described as an "apocalypse," and they are more like apocalypse than anything else in the OT, with the exception of Dan. 7–12. But while they are certainly eschatological, they lack the differentiae of apocalypse proper—pseudonymity, symbolism, and the like (*see* APOCALYPTICISM § 2). Similar materials are found at the ends of other prophetical books (e.g., Isa. 63–66; Joel 3:9-21—H 4:9-21; Zech. 12–14). It is not obvious that the chapters are a unity: the eschatological passages are interspersed with some lovely lyrical passages (25:1-5, 9; 26:1-6), and it may be that the arrangement of the several pieces is on the principle of alternating woe and weal. Specially noteworthy is 25:7, which promises that Yahweh "will destroy" (lit., "swallow up") the "veil that is spread over all nations," this being followed (vs. 8) with words which have been taken up in part into Paul's "Death is swallowed up in victory" (I Cor. 15:54), and in part into the NT Apocalypse (Rev. 7:17). Note also 26:19, one of only two passages in the OT—the other is Dan. 12:2—in which the doctrine of the resurrection of the dead finds expression. No clear historical background is discernible for Isa. 24–27, and the general opinion is that the chapters are some of the latest in the OT.

Chs. 28–33: These are mainly Isaianic. They open with a "woe" against the "drunkards of Ephraim," which must be earlier than the fall of Samaria. But for the most part the contents are from the later period of Isaiah's ministry, when Judah was dallying with the Egyptian alliance (cf. 30:1-7; 31:1-3). Isaiah is scathing in his denunciation of the blindness and incompetence of the rulers of Jerusalem (28:14-15; 29:13-16), but he never wavers in his conviction that Yahweh's purpose for Zion was something which no folly of man could gainsay (28:16; 30:15), even though destruction should overwhelm all else (28:22). The concluding chapter (33) in this section reads like a prophetic liturgy, and it is probably from a time much later than Isaiah's.

Chs. 34–35: These contain two eschatological poems. The first (ch. 34) describes Yahweh's judgment "against all the nations" (vs. 2), with particular reference to "Edom" (vss. 5-6). The feud between Israel and Edom (Jacob and Esau) was of long standing and reached its height when the Edomites took advantage of their "brothers" in the catastrophe of 586 B.C. (cf. Ps. 137:7; Ezek. 35; Obad. 10-12). But it is likely that in the present context "Edom" is "typical" of those who are enemies of the Jews and thereby become the enemies of God. The well-known ch. 35 is in complete contrast to the preceding, and, in its descriptions of the desert become oasis and the highway back to Zion, has affinities to chs. 40–55.

Chs. 36–39: These historical narratives are parallel to II Kings 18:13–20:19, but omit II Kings 18:14-16 and insert the psalm of Hezekiah (Isa. 38:9-20). The section looks like an appendix similar to that which closes the book of Jeremiah (Jer. 52 is parallel to II Kings 24:18–25:30) and suggests that the book of Isaiah once closed with ch. 39.

2. Chs. 40–55. It is almost unanimously agreed that the historical background of at least chs. 40–48 is the Babylonian exile (sixth century B.C.). In chs. 56–66 the background appears to be Palestinian, though it reads more like Palestine after than before the Exile. Hardly anyone today denies that chs. 49–55 are from the author of chs. 40–48, notwithstanding that chs. 49–55 contain no references to Babylon. It is convenient to distinguish between chs. 40–55 and chs. 56–66, even if (as some hold) both sections are from the same author. The question is whether chs. 40–55(66) are "long-range" prophecy from the pen of the eighth-century Isaiah, or whether they come from an author or authors living during (40–55) and after (56–66) the Exile. A very few scholars believe that chs. 40–66, together, perhaps, with chs. 34–35, are a unity from *ca.* 400 B.C. This involves either deleting "Cyrus" in 44:28; 45:1, or regarding him as a "type."

a. Historical background. If the text of 44:28; 45:1 is sound and Cyrus is the historical CYRUS, king of Persia, it is clear that we must interpret chs. 40–48(55) against the background of the Exile, even if Isaiah of Jerusalem was their author. In 39:5-8 Isaiah is said to have predicted the Exile. In chs. 40–48 this has come about: the Jews have been despoiled (42:24-25) by the Babylonian-Chaldeans (47:6) in whose land they now are (48:20). Assyria, the world power in Isaiah's day, is not mentioned except as an oppressor in the undefined past (52:4). The Exile is represented as accomplished fact. Jerusalem and the temple appear to be in ruins but are to be built through the agency of Cyrus (44:26-28; cf. 45:13). Babylon is to be humiliated (43:14; 46–47). Release is coming to the Jews (40:1-11), and the overwhelming impression we receive is that it is coming soon (46:13; 51:5, 14).

b. Authorship. If chs. 40–55 had not been preserved as part of the "book of the prophet Isaiah," and we were left to determine from internal evidence when the (in that case) anonymous author lived and wrote, it is safe to assume that the answer would be that he wrote sometime between the rise of Cyrus and the fall of Babylon. This, indeed, is the normal "critical" opinion today. But to say so is, as some devoutly believe, to deny the inerrancy of the Bible, since in the NT Isa. 40:3 is cited as from "Isaiah the prophet" (Mark 1:2-3; though vs. 2*b* is actually from Mal. 3:1!). The belief that Isaiah was the author of the entire book that bears his name was current by the early part of the second century B.C., and was taken for granted in the NT (Matt. 12:17; Acts 8:30) and probably by Jesus himself. The question is whether there is reason to suppose that Jesus would, on a question of this kind, have voiced any other view than that which was current in his time, even if he had known there was a "Second Isaiah." He had something other to do than to instruct his generation in matters which had no relevance for them, however much they may exercise our minds today.

That prophecy, and, in particular, Isa. 40–55, contains a large element of prediction, is not in doubt. Nor are there wanting passages which predict the distant future (e.g., Isa. 2:2-4). But such passages are mostly brief and in general terms. A prophecy of sixteen consecutive chapters, giving a detailed account of what was to happen two centuries after it was written, would be unique in the prophetical writings, and it is difficult to see what purpose it could serve for Isaiah's contemporaries. Scholars who conclude that it dates from the sixth century B.C. are as devout and conscientious as those who believe it was written in the eighth, and they are equally persuaded that it is the "word of God." Their case rests finally upon 48:6-7:

From this time forth I make you hear new things,
hidden things which you have not known.
They are created now, not long ago;
before today you have never heard of them.

If the passage was written by the eighth-century Isaiah, and if the "new things" relate to the time of Cyrus, it could not be said: "You have never heard of them," unless, of course, chs. 40–55 were "hidden" in the sense that they were not put into circulation but went "underground" for nearly two centuries, to be brought to light during the Exile. But the conception of "hidden things" as "sealed apocrypha" (cf. Dan. 8:26; 12:4, 9; Rev. 10:4; 22:10) is, so far as we have any evidence, considerably later than the time of the pre-exilic Isaiah (Isa. 8:16 does not refer to a sealed "book" but to oral "teaching").

c. The author. Nothing is known of the author, who is generally referred to as Second Isaiah, or Deutero-Isaiah, occasionally the "Babylonian Isaiah." It is probable that he lived in Babylonia, though Palestine, and even the Lebanon or Egypt, have been suggested. His only reference to himself is in the LXX, Vulg., and first Qumran scroll reading of 40:6: "And I said" (cf. ERV mg.), but it is by no means certain that this was the original reading. It is likely enough that in the earlier part of his ministry the prophet was precluded from speaking in public; otherwise he might well have been silenced by the Babylonian authorities. But 55:1-5 reads like public proclamation, and it is easy to imagine that as Babylon fell, he was free to come into the open. He had no illusions about the "blindness" of his fellow exiles (cf. 42:18-25; 48:1-11), and it may well be that he encountered opposition from them (see on 45:9-13). It is not improbable that there is an autobiographical element in 50:4-9, and some have maintained that he was himself the Suffering Servant (in which case 49:1-6 will be autobiographical). This is improbable; but whoever the SERVANT OF THE LORD was, it would be surprising if something of the prophet's own experience had not contributed to the portrait of him.

d. Structure. So long as chs. 40–55 were thought to come from the eighth-century Isaiah, it was assumed that they were part of a "written book," as, indeed, were all the prophetical writings. Not until the second decade of the present century did those even who assigned them to Second Isaiah begin seriously to think otherwise. There had been a growing recognition that the prophets were primarily "speakers" rather than writers and that the prophetical books as we have them are precipitates from the originally "spoken word." It was recognized that Second Isaiah bears more of the marks of a written composition than do, e.g., the utterances of Amos. But Second Isaiah's work is repetitive, and there is in it much overlapping. If he was a prophet, he must, it was urged, like his predecessors, have been himself a speaker. Accordingly, for a number of years, the dominant view has been that Deutero-Isaiah consists of some fifty originally independent pieces or poems delivered orally. How these pieces came to be related to one another in the order in which we have them, has been the subject of much discussion. One theory is that they were juxtaposed on the "catchword" or domino principle (*see* § B1*a above*): thus a passage beginning "Fear not" (feminine; 41:14) is placed after another ending "Fear not" (masculine; 41:13). Similarly, passages beginning "Hearken to me" (51:1, 7) and "Listen to me" (51:4), or "Awake, awake" (51:9; 52:1), and "Rouse yourself" (51:17), are found in near contexts. This principle of arrangement could be the prophet's own, but an arrangement so mechanical, if the suggestion is right, is more likely to be that of his disciples than of the master himself.

A closer inspection reveals that Isa. 40–55 is a shapely and orderly document, in which the several pieces are preserved in relatively logical and even chronological order. Thus, in chs. 40–48 the address is generally to Jacob-Israel, in chs. 49–55 to Zion-Jerusalem. Cyrus and Babylon are named in chs. 40–48, never in chs. 49–55. In chs. 40–48, but never in chs. 49–55, there are polemics against the idol-gods, summonses to assize-inquests, and appeals to the fulfilment of former prophecies. Of the references, implicit (first in 41:2, 25) and explicit (44:28; 45:1), to Cyrus, it is significant that Cyrus is not named until he is directly addressed, as if by that time there was no further need for anonymity and veiled allusions. All this points to the chapters' being in approximately chronological order.

There is reason to think that some of the short passages which have been supposed to be independent units, are really parts of longer poems. E.g., the four short pieces 40:1-2, 3-5, 6-8, 9-11, may have been composed separately, but together they were intended as a programmatic prelude to the whole work. Similarly, 41:1-16 is a unit (*see* § B2*e below;* the paragraph divisions in the RSV sometimes mark "strophes," as well as separate poems). A comparison of 42:10-17 with Pss. 96; 98; 149 makes it probable that the Isaiah passage is a unit, since no one proposes to divide the psalms into separate compositions.

At the other extreme from the "small-units" theory, it is thought by some that Isa. 40–55 is a poem, or series of poems, carefully arranged by Deutero-Isaiah himself. The difficulty of this theory is that no two scholars agree, or are ever likely to agree, on where the larger units begin and end. The truth probably lies somewhere between the two extremes. But the whole is sufficiently well arranged for us to say with some confidence that it bears the stamp of Deutero-Isaiah's own personality, and in it we can discern his theological conceptions in some logical sequence.

e. Contents. The contents of chs. 40–55 may be grouped and summarized as follows:

Chs. 40–48: The prophecy opens (40:1-11) with a series of proclamations announcing Jerusalem's approaching deliverance from her "warfare" (RSV mg. "time of service"; cf. Job 7:1: "hard service").

Her guilt is pardoned, and it is as if she had served a double sentence. We are probably to understand that the prophet overhears announcements made in the divine assembly (cf. I Kings 22:19-22; Isa. 6). A herald gives orders for a processional highway to be prepared across the desert between Babylonia (presumably) and Jerusalem. Yahweh is coming in person, and all mankind is to witness his "glory." Then follows a passage in which all human "steadfastness" (RSV "beauty") is said to be as evanescent as the flower of the field, in contrast with the "word of our God," which "will stand for ever." Finally, Jerusalem is to announce to her daughter cities of Judah the imminent approach of Yahweh. He is bringing with him the exiles he has delivered, tending his flock with an arm both strong and tender.

The prelude over, the main themes are taken up. 40:12-31 describes Yahweh in a series of questions, some of them certainly, all of them probably, by Yahweh himself, as the Incomparable. He created the world without instruction or agency, either of man or of gods which are only fashioned by men. He is Lord of the nations and leader into battle of the starry hosts of heaven. From where he sits enthroned upon the overarching vault of the earth, the inhabitants of the world look as numerous, and as small, as grasshoppers. Yet no assurance of the creative might of God can bring relief to souls in anguish, and after all the weary years of exile Jacob-Israel feels that his "way" is hid from, and his "just right" disregarded by, God. He should know that the Creator, who faints not nor is weary, gives power to the faint and strength to those who, unlike himself (vs. 26), have none. Those who wait expectantly for Yahweh acquire fresh strength, strength that sustains them not only in heroic ventures that demand soaring flight or swift running, but also in the drudging walk of life: "They shall walk and not faint."

In 41:1-7 the nations are summoned to an assize-inquest to inquire who it is that has "stirred up one from the east whom victory meets at every step." The answer is that it is Yahweh, who controls history, "calling the generations [of mankind] from the beginning." The monotheistic formula: "I am He [than whom there is none other]" recurs several times in subsequent chapters. The victor from the E is, by general consent, Cyrus. Vss. 8-10 (note the adversative "but") are a continuation of what precedes. The coastlands "are afraid" (vs. 5), but Israel is not to fear (vs. 10; the verbs are the same in the Hebrew). Israel is called by Yahweh "my servant." Vss. 11-16 are a further continuation of the same theme, notwithstanding that in vss. 11-13 there is a change of meter (3:2 instead of 3:3), and in vss. 14-16 Jacob-Israel is addressed in the feminine (this is due to the word "worm," which is feminine; in vss. 15-16 the gender reverts to the masculine). The more violent Israel's enemies become, the less is their power to harm (vss. 11-13). Indeed, the despised and puny "worm" shall become a giant threshing sledge, capable of pulverizing mountains (vss. 14-16).

In 41:17-20 the theme of the processional highway (40:3-4) is amplified. The inhospitable desert will be abundantly supplied with water and adorned with forest trees. These, apparently, are not saplings, which are to be "planted" and must slowly grow to maturity; they are to be "placed" and will presumably be mature trees. The return from Babylon is to be a second and more wonderful exodus. Deutero-Isaiah has frequent allusions to the exodus from Egypt, and his thought is steeped in the hallowed traditions of his people.

41:21-29 is another unity. The nations have already been summoned to the bar of judgment (vs. 1). Now it is the turn of their gods. Can they foretell the future, or do they understand the significance of the "former things"? Let them do anything, either good or ill, and show at least some sign of life and animation! Yahweh declares that they are nothing at all. Herodotus relates that when Croesus of Lydia was forced to encounter Cyrus, he sent gifts to all the oracles of Greece that he might know the outcome of the campaign. He was told that he would destroy a great empire, but the oracles were careful not to say that it would be his own. In vss. 25-29 Yahweh asserts, as an example of his ability to determine the course of events, that it is he who has stirred up the conqueror from the NE. But when he looks for a like ability elsewhere, neither the heathen nor "these" (their gods) have anything to say.

For 42:1-4, *see* SERVANT OF THE LORD. 42:5-9 is thought by some to be either a separate Servant Song or a continuation of the preceding. As it stands, the "you" of vs. 6 is best understood as referring to the Servant (so RSV; cf. "a covenant to the people"). It is possible that the verses were originally addressed to Israel, that the subject of the infinitives in vs. 7 was Yahweh, and that the passage has been adapted as a follow-up to the song (the words "a light to the nations" [vs. 6] are not in the LXX or in the closely related Hebrew of 49:8; they may have been filled in from 49:6). The problem is a difficult one, and reference should be made to the commentaries. A striking feature of the passage is the "hymnic" introduction (vs. 5), in which the attributes of Yahweh are extolled in a series of participial relative clauses. This is characteristic of Deutero-Isaiah (cf. 43:1; 45:18; etc.).

Reference to Pss. 96; 98 indicates that 42:10-17 is a unity. The psalms begin with the summons to "sing to Yahweh a new song" and end with the announcement of his coming to judge the world. The Isaiah passage follows a similar pattern. The anthropomorphic figures of Yahweh as a berserk warrior (vs. 13) and a woman in travail (vs. 14) may strike the modern reader as bizarre, if not repellent. But in the context of the Exile they are not inappropriate. It is Yahweh's zeal for the helpless enslaved that moves him to speak so (cf. 59:15-18; 63:1-6). In the sequel, when Christ came, it was not to slay but to be crucified.

The last verses of ch. 42 (18-25) are uncompromisingly frank about the "blindness" of Yahweh's servant Israel. The prophet makes it clear that the disaster which had overtaken his people was due to their sins, not the inevitable fate of a small people in the path of a ruthless empire. 43:1-7, with its initial "But now," is a continuation of the preceding paragraph, and pictures the reversal of Israel's fortunes. Yahweh has "redeemed" (*see* REDEEM) Israel (the general sense of "redeemer" in Deutero-Isaiah is "protector"). Neither water nor fire can harm her, since God will be with her. He will gather his children ("my sons . . . and my daughters") from the four points of the compass, to which they have been driven. He alone is God (43:8-13), and the Israelites, notwithstanding that they are blind and deaf, are his witnesses to the nations, who are once more pictured as assembled in a world-wide court.

A comparison of the RSV rendering of 43:14 with the KJV and the ERV indicates that the meaning of the text is uncertain, but it is clear that disaster is to overtake Babylon. This is followed (43:15-21) by a reference to the disaster which overtook Egypt at the Red Sea. (The verb forms in vss. 16-17, most of them participles, should be translated by past tenses: "made," "brought forth," "lay down."). The wonders of the second exodus will even surpass those of the first, and the theme of "rivers in the desert" (cf. 41:18) is amplified by saying that even the wild creatures of the waste will join in honoring Yahweh.

The meaning of 43:22-24 is not that Israel had not offered sacrifices during the Exile—how could she?—but that the sacrifices she offered in the days of her independence were prompted by self-indulgence and did not honor Yahweh at all. Translate: "It was not upon me that you called . . . to the point of becoming weary of me." The references to "sheep" (KJV-ERV "small cattle") and "sweet cane" (cf. Jer. 6:20) seem derogatory. But Yahweh had not "burdened" (lit., "put to slave labor"; cf. Exod. 1:13) his people with offerings; on the contrary, they had burdened him with their sins. Nevertheless, it was his nature to "blot out" their rebellions, though they had first to endure heavy chastisement.

In 44:1-8 the reference to "water on the thirsty land" (vs. 3) does not refer to the watered desert of 41:18; 43:20, but to the outpouring of Yahweh's spirit for the increase of Israel's population, which may have become inadequate to ensure maintenance of the prosperity of the homeland. Vs. 5 seems to anticipate that Gentile proselytes will join themselves to Israel. 44:6-8 refers to what are now the familiar themes of Yahweh's sole deity and his ability to predict the future: the RSV rendering of vs. 7 is based upon a slight but widely accepted conjectural emendation.

The satire on the making of idols (44:9-20) is more elaborate than anything else of the kind in the prophecy. It is printed in the RSV as prose, but there are many traces of parallelism in it. It has often been thought to be a late insertion. This cannot be affirmed with confidence. Whoever the author may have been, the passage is based on accurate observation. "One log for fuel and deity"; it is ludicrous. Worse, it is stupid (vs. 19), a pathetic delusion (vs. 20).

44:21-23 is perhaps the original continuation of vs. 8; otherwise the reference to "these things" is obscure. These verses lead up to a further declaration (vss. 24-28) that Yahweh is the sole Creator and that Cyrus, now actually named, is the appointed agent to fulfil Yahweh's "purpose" to rebuild Jerusalem and the temple.

Ch. 45 is mainly concerned with Cyrus. Yahweh has already called him "my shepherd"—in the OT the word "shepherd," when used metaphorically, always refers to a ruler. Now he is addressed as his "anointed" (משיח, "messiah"), a word nowhere else used of a foreigner, who does not "know" Yahweh (vs. 4) and so is his unconscious instrument. Vss. 9-13 are probably addressed to Jews who might be scandalized that Yahweh should be said to employ a non-Israelite to carry out his purposes. It is possible that Cyrus is addressed in vs. 14—the pronoun suffixes for "you" can be read as masculine, without changing the consonantal text—but this cannot be regarded as certain. The chapter rises to a magnificent climax. God's creation is orderly (vs. 18), and his word is clear (vs. 19). All the ends of the earth are bidden to turn to him and be saved; such is the declared and unalterable purpose of him who is at once "a righteous God and a Savior."

Bel (Marduk) and Nebo (Nabu) in ch. 46 were the gods of Babylon and Borsippa respectively and were related in the Babylonian pantheon as father and son. They are contrasted, as gods which have to be carried on the backs of pack animals in a vain attempt to deposit them in safety, with Yahweh, who carries his people from birth to old age. They are incapable of self-movement, nor can they save their anguished devotees. Again the chapter closes with the assertion of Yahweh's sole deity and the accomplishment of his purpose through Cyrus, a "bird of prey from the east."

Ch. 47 is a "taunt song" (cf. 13:1–14:23) addressed to Babylon. She who had been the mistress of kingdoms will be degraded to a menial drudge. She has exceeded her commission by maltreating Yahweh's people. None of her enchanters or astrologers will be able to stave off her ruin.

Ch. 48 asserts that Yahweh long ago announced the disaster that would overtake Israel. This was in order that, when it came, Israel might have no occasion for attributing it to anything else but her own obstinacy. The passage is harsher in tone than anything else in the "prophet of consolation," and it has sometimes been thought that the original words of consolation have been expanded by an interlinear commentary of condemnation (vss. 1*b*, 2, 4, 5*b*, 7*b*, 8*b*-10). This view is not so common as it once was. Vss. 17-19 portray something almost like divine anguish in the face of Israel's obstinacy (cf. Luke 13:34). The chapter closes with a summons to leave Babylon (vss. 20-21), and the references to the first exodus are intended to inspire confidence in the equal safety of the second.

Chs. 49–55: Nearly all the leading ideas of Deutero-Isaiah find expression in the first half of his prophecy. What we find in chs. 49–55 is mostly amplification of them, with particular reference to Yahweh's purpose to rehabilitate Jerusalem.

49:1-6 is the second of the so-called Servant Songs (*see* SERVANT OF THE LORD). It is followed by verses which have much the same relation to it as 42:5-9 has to 42:1-4, but in this case the passage has even more clearly the marks of a declaration of the release and safe conduct of the returning exiles. Yahweh can less readily forget Zion than a mother can forget the child she has borne (vss. 14-16). The rebuilt city will be too small for its inhabitants (vss. 17-21). At Yahweh's signal the nations, led by kings and their consorts, will conduct Zion's children home with deference and even homage (vss. 22-23), and those who had tyrannized over them will in their panic consume one another in internecine war.

Chs. 50–54 contain two songs of the Servant of the Lord: 50:4-9(11); 52:13–53:12. For the rest the chapters are mainly concerned with the rehabilitation of Zion-Jerusalem. In 50:1-3; 52:1-2; 54 the city is pictured as the "wife" of Yahweh. This figure is not uncommon in the OT (cf. Jer. 2:2; Ezek. 16; Hos. 2) and is continued in the NT in the conception of the church (Eph. 5:25-27) or the new Jerusalem (Rev. 21:2, 9) as the bride of Christ. After all they had endured of separation from their homeland, Yahweh's people might conclude that he had formally divorced their mother (cf. Deut. 24:1) or sold them (her children) to some creditor (cf. Exod. 21:7; II Kings 4:1; Neh. 5:5, 8; Matt. 18:25). The meaning of 50:1, which is correctly translated in the RSV (contrast KJV), is that Yahweh has not given Zion any bill of divorce, and to think of him as having any creditors is preposterous. On the contrary, the Exile was consequent to his people's sins (vs. 2).

In the well-known final chapter (55) the gifts of God are as *ex gratia* and as universal as anywhere in the Bible. Vss. 3-4 are sometimes interpreted as an assurance that the Davidic monarchy will be restored. Another and more probable interpretation is that the covenant with David will now be remade with the people as a whole (the pronouns "you" and "your" in vs. 3 are plural in the Hebrew). At the same time it is urged that delay in accepting the proffered grace may be fatal (vss. 6-7). Yahweh's "thoughts" and "ways" are not as the thoughts and ways of men (vss. 8-9). His "word" and purpose will as assuredly be fulfilled as that rain and snow fructify the earth (vss. 10-11). The prophecy concludes on the same note as that with which it began. We should judge that the liberation edict of Cyrus (cf. Ezra 1:1-4) had not yet been published. The closing sentence may be rendered: "It shall be to Yahweh for a memorial, an everlasting inscription which shall never be effaced," as though the way back through the desert is to be kept in perpetuity as a commemorative park.

f. Interpretation. The conclusion of the preceding paragraph raises the question whether the exuberant language of the prophet is to be taken literally, or whether it is only so much poetic hyperbole. Did he expect the journey back to Palestine to be effected in the wonderful way he describes? And, if he did, must we set him down as a deluded enthusiast? Was he, in fact, a poet-prophet of the sixth century? Or was he a poet of *ca.* 400 whose imagery need not be taken literally? If he was the former, it may be argued that if events did not happen as he expected, his "theology" has no firm foundation.

It is hardly necessary to say that there was no "return" from exile on the scale and in the miraculous way Deutero-Isaiah expected. Indeed, there does not appear to have been any considerable return until the time of Ezra (*ca.* 400 B.C.). The evidence of Haggai and Isa. 56–66 is that conditions in Jerusalem were depressing until Nehemiah rebuilt the walls (444 B.C.). The "glory of the LORD" was not revealed with the immediacy and fulness the prophet seems to have expected.

This, however, is not to discredit Deutero-Isaiah. The matter may be expressed in this way: Deutero-Isaiah is the last of the great prophets, and in his message we see the culmination of revelation which may be said to have begun through Moses and was intensified in the prophets, particularly Isaiah, of the eighth century. It is as if the Prophet of the Exile reached the crest of a range looking out over a wide prospect to the coming of Christ (*see* SERVANT OF THE LORD). The NT gospels take their cue from the "evangelist of the OT" (Mark 1:1-3 and parallels), and Christ, as it has been said, "served himself heir" to the mission of the Servant. But the vision of any great prophet is "foreshortened." He sees the distant as near and depicts it in outlines of amazing clarity. And a prophet, like any artist, must depict what he sees in a medium (in this case poetry) suitable to his theme and in the idiom of his time. Deutero-Isaiah was steeped in the traditions of his people, and his descriptions of salvation were inspired by the epic of the Exodus, which in the course of the centuries had come to have all the radiance of "salvation history." Had there been no NT sequel, we might have had to say that the prophet's theology had little foundation to sustain it. As it is, in the context of Scripture as a whole, it is right to say that his message has been "transfigured" and that its basic conceptions are authenticated.

g. Theology. It is permissible to speak of the "theology" of Deutero-Isaiah, notwithstanding that it is not systematically formulated. All his thinking is determined by his conception of Yahweh as the sole Creator of the universe, Lord of history, Savior of Israel his chosen people and, indeed, of all mankind. His whole outlook is theocentric. Yet there is no trace in it of pantheistic monism. Yahweh is represented as saying: "I am He [than whom there is none other]." This is in marked contrast with the Vedantic philosophy, which says to man: "That art thou [than which there is nought else]." Yet Yahweh's care and concern for the world did not cease when he had created it. There is, of course, no hint of the modern concept of "continuous creation," but Yahweh is said to have "created" Israel (43:1, 7, 15), and the word is used even of contemporary happenings (41:20). This is as far removed from a stark or abstract theism as it is from pantheism: in the "berserker rage" passage (42:13-14) something like anguish is attributed to Yahweh. Whoever the perfect Servant of the Lord may have been, suffering is the means by which he fulfils his mission. The range of verbs and nouns which the prophet uses to describe Yahweh's relation to the Israel he "loves" (43:4) is very wide: he is Savior, Redeemer, King, Shepherd; he calls, chooses, strengthens, and takes by the hand. The most obvious link with proto-Isaiah is the conception of Yahweh as the "Holy One of Israel" (thirteen times in Proto-, eleven in Deutero-Isaiah). The expression is infrequent outside the book of Isaiah, and Isaiah was the first to use it. But there is a difference in emphasis between the two prophets: in Proto-Isaiah the major emphasis is upon Yahweh as judge (1:4; 5:19, 24; etc.); in Deutero-Isaiah it is always upon his saving power and protection.

3. Chs. 56–66. This section of Isaiah presents problems of which there is so far no agreed solution.

The divergencies of view may be briefly indicated. A small minority of scholars believe that chs. 40–66, together with, perhaps, chs. 34–35, are from one author. Others think that chs. 56–66 are not from Deutero-Isaiah. Of them, some think they are a unity, by a disciple of Deutero-Isaiah; others, the majority, that they are from several authors, most of whom were disciples of Deutero-Isaiah. In either case, "Trito-Isaiah" is a convenient designation.

a. Authorship and date. The general background is Palestinian, and it is arguable that some parts at least could be pre-exilic (e.g., 57:1-13 is very much in the vein of Ezek. 16; 23). On the other hand, passages like chs. 60–62 are so like Deutero-Isaiah that if they had been included in chs. 40–55, there would be little disposition to doubt that they are his. It has often been argued that the references to the temple (56:5, 7; 60:7) and the walls of Jerusalem (60:10) are proof that the temple had been rebuilt but that the walls had not. This would indicate a date between 516 and 444. But what is said about the temple may be in expectation of the future rather than description of the present, very much as 62:6 must be anticipation of the rebuilding of the walls, if the chapters are a unity and the walls had not yet been built. In 63:7–64:11 the temple is in ruins, from which we must suppose that the passage dates from shortly after 586, unless—which is questionable—disaster had befallen the 516 temple.

On the whole, chs. 56–66 are not so clearly a unity as are chs. 40–55. Even in chs. 60–62, which are so like Deutero-Isaiah, there are significant differences of emphasis: e.g., in 62:11 there is obvious literary affinity to 40:10, but instead of "Behold, the Lord Yahweh comes," we have: "Behold, your salvation comes," as if studiously to avoid the idea, so prominent in chs. 40–55, of Yahweh's triumphal march in person; similarly, "Prepare the way of Yahweh" (40:3) becomes: "Prepare the way for the people" (62:10).

The broad difference of emphasis between chs. 56–66 and chs. 40–55 is this: in chs. 40–55 Yahweh is coming to the immediate help of his people, and it is they who need to be roused from their hopelessness and despondency; in chs. 56–66 it is Yahweh who seems reluctant, while the people clamor for his coming; passages like

> O that thou wouldst rend the heavens and come down
> (64:1);
>
> We look for justice, but there is none,
> for salvation, but it is far from us
> (59:11);
>
> Give him no rest
> until he establishes Jerusalem
> (62:7)

would sound out of place in chs. 40–55.

The probable solution of the problem of chs. 56–66 is that which is most widely favored—namely, that "Trito-Isaiah" is from a number of authors who were in the tradition of Deutero-Isaiah. In that case the several pieces may date from various times between 538 and 444 or even later. 63:7–64:12 is similar in tone to Lamentations and may date from early in the Exile. For the rest, it is difficult to assert with confidence dates before or after the period 520 (Haggai-Zechariah) to 516 (dedication of the second temple). Earlier "Trito-Isaiah" critics were inclined to a date not long before Nehemiah (444) and interpreted passages like 65:1-7; 66:1-4 as polemic against the Samaritans; but little is known in detail about the Samaritan Schism. More recently the tendency has been to favor dates *ca.* 516. This would account better for the close similarities between Trito- and Deutero-Isaiah. It must be admitted that the history of the Jewish community in the first half of the fifth century is very obscure.

Trito-Isaiah shares with Deutero- and Proto-Isaiah the emphasis upon Yahweh as the "Holy One of Israel" (60:9, 14; cf. 57:15). We are to think of the eighth-century Isaiah as having created a tradition which continued to be a living and potent force for some three centuries.

b. Contents. The emphasis upon the ordinances of religion in 56:1-8 is almost wholly foreign to the chapters preceding. There is no mention of the sabbath in Deutero-Isaiah. Here, to keep the sabbath and to refrain from doing evil are in parallel clauses. Justice (משפט) and righteousness (צדקה) have many nuances in Deutero-Isaiah; in this context they have a cultic-legal flavor. The passage is an assurance to foreign proselytes and (Jewish) eunuchs that if they hold fast by Yahweh's covenant, they shall have equal access to Yahweh in his temple with born and unmutilated Jews. In this there is something of the catholicity of Deutero-Isaiah, and the verses appear to be a protest against an exclusiveness which became all too common in postexilic times.

56:9–57:13 is a scathing invective against corrupt religious leaders (56:9–57:2) and licentious nature-worship (57:3-13). It could well be pre-exilic, but there is insufficient reason to suppose that the practices condemned did not persist after the Exile. The remaining verses of ch. 57 are entirely in the spirit of Deutero-Isaiah. The transcendent God dwells with the man "who is of a contrite and humble spirit." This paradox is expressed with a simplicity that makes it sound entirely natural. It is not said that God *in spite of* his holiness dwells with the lowly and meek, but that he "dwells" (so the Hebrew) in eternity *and* with the lowly and meek.

There is evidence that during the Exile regular fasts were observed (Zech. 7:1-7; 8:18-19). There is always danger that statutory religious observances can come to lack sincerity. From Isa. 58:1-12 it appears that fasting made people quarrelsome and that on fast days they engaged in business (vs. 3 RSV mg.) and bullied their workers. The prophet is bidden to ask them whether they can properly call this fasting. This denunciation of social unrighteousness is entirely in the spirit of the pre-exilic prophets. In 58:13-14 the sabbath is to be treated as holy ground, a day when business is to be put aside (vs. 13 RSV mg.). The passage is brief but has the same moral fervor as the preceding.

The theme of ch. 59 is that Yahweh's delay in coming to the help of his people is not due to inability on his part but to their sins. A vivid description of these is followed by a community lament and confession. Finally, Yahweh himself takes the initiative and intervenes, coming in judgment like a pent-up stream (vs. 19 ERV mg.). He will come as Redeemer (so RSV rightly, as against KJV). There is no thought of incarnation, but in the light of the NT sequel the interpretation of the KJV has a certain justification and even inevitability.

The general similarity of chs. 60–62 to Deutero-Isaiah has already been noted. The section can be divided into three parts according to the present chapter divisions. Ch. 60 opens with a magnificent description of the sunrise glory of Yahweh upon Jerusalem while the rest of the world still lies in darkness. The nations are attracted to the brightness and themselves bring back the exiles. The Holy City shall be mistress of the nations; foreigners will rebuild her walls, and their kings be her servants. The material and moral prosperity of Zion will be without precedent. There will be no more need of sun and moon, because Yahweh will be her everlasting light (cf. Rev. 21:23).

The opening verses of ch. 61 were read by Jesus in the synagogue at Nazareth at the beginning of his ministry (Luke 4:16-20), with the significant omission of the words "and the day of vengeance of our God." They have sometimes been taken as a Servant Song, but it is more probable that the speaker is the prophet. The rest of the chapter is very similar to the chapter preceding. A glorious future awaits the Jews, who are collectively to exercise the same priestly functions in the world-wide community of the people of God as the priests exercise toward lay Israelites.

62:1-5 reverts to the theme of Zion as the bride of Yahweh (cf. 50:1-2; 54; *see* BEULAH). For the meaningless "your sons" (vs. 5) read, with only a vowel change, "your builder"—i.e., Yahweh. Yahweh will station watchmen on the walls of Jerusalem to remind him continually of his promise to make the city a "praise in the earth" (vs. 7).

The dramatic poem 63:1-6 has literary affinities with 59:15-20; 61:2, and recalls the figure of the berserk warrior of 42:13. Antiphonal voices are heard. The first must be that of the prophet; the second is the voice of Yahweh, solitary, and mighty in power and salvation. The words: "I have trodden the wine press alone" (vs. 3) have sometimes in the language of devotion been interpreted of Christ's agony on the Cross. This was not the intention of the writer. Nevertheless, in the light of the sequel, it has a measure of justification (see on 42:13).

63:7–64:12 is one of the most moving passages in the OT. It is a community lament, in which appeal is made to Yahweh's steadfast love manifested in the past history of his people. The words "in all their affliction" should be joined to the end of 63:8, and vs. 9 should be translated: "It was neither envoy nor messenger, but his own presence [lit., 'face'] that saved them" (cf. Exod. 33:14). This is supported by the parallelism and by the LXX, and is even closer to the MT. "In all their affliction he was afflicted" is hardly normal OT doctrine, though there are approximations to it in passages like Isa. 42:13-14. The whole is an impassioned appeal to Yahweh to come to the deliverance of his people. The passage is significant in that twice in it the spirit of Yahweh is called "his holy Spirit" (elsewhere in the OT only Ps. 51:11—H 51:13), and it is often noted that there is a measure of hypostatization in the conception of the Spirit (cf. "They . . . grieved his holy Spirit"; one cannot "grieve" an abstract quality).

The difference between the RSV and KJV translations of 65:1 should be noted. The former is correct: "I was ready to be found by those who did not seek me." God is ready to be found, but he is not found by those who will not trouble to seek him. This is appropriately followed by a denunciation of ghoulish worship. Yet God will not destroy the whole people (vss. 8-10), though destruction awaits those who deliver themselves over to gods like Gad ("luck") and Meni ("fate"; vss. 11-12). The chapter concludes with descriptions of a new creation and the long life of those who shall live in the redeemed community.

The concluding chapter (66) moves between the two poles of judgment and salvation. The most natural interpretation of the first paragraph is that it dates from *ca.* 520 and is a protest against temple and sacrifice as such. However this may be, the verses are the clearest foreshadowing in the OT of the dominical word: "God is spirit, and those who worship him must worship in spirit and truth" (John 4:24).

In conclusion, although on a first reading chs. 56–66 seem uneven in quality and hardly on the same level of inspiration as Deutero-Isaiah, the oftener they are read the more are they seen to contain some of the unforgettable passages in the OT.

4. Text. The text of Isaiah has, on the whole, been well preserved; indeed, a glance at the footnotes to Kittel's *Biblica Hebraica* is sufficient to indicate that it presents fewer problems than do the majority of the other prophetical writings. Even before the discovery of the DEAD SEA SCROLLS, the attitude of scholars toward the text was already becoming markedly more conservative than it had been at the beginning of the present century (*see* TEXT, OT). If a passage appears to be seriously corrupt and the versions provide no solution, it is now widely agreed that purely conjectural emendation is of little value. There is always the possibility that a passage which has defied interpretation may become clear as knowledge of the languages cognate with Hebrew increases (e.g., the word עשיר, "rich," in 53:9 has long been a puzzle, and it has been usual to emend it to עשי רע, "evil doers"; but it now appears that it is cognate with Arabic *ġuthr*[un], "rabble" or "dregs" [of humanity], of which it is a sound philological equivalent). There are two Dead Sea Scrolls of Isaiah. One (1QIs[a]) is complete, and the other (1QIs[b]) fragmentary. MS *b* is almost word for word the same as the MT. MS *a* has many readings different from those of the MT, and although some few of them may be superior, the majority are only differences of orthography. The two Dead Sea MSS go to show that the MT was substantially fixed by the beginning of the Christian era—a conclusion which few would have dared assert with confidence before the discovery of the scrolls.

Bibliography. Commentaries on the whole book: B. Duhm, *Das Buch Jesaia übersetzt und erklärt* (4th ed., 1922), first separated the Servant Songs and assigned chs. 56–66 to Trito-Isaiah; free with the text but still valuable. J. Skinner, *The Cambridge Bible* (2 vols.; rev. ed., 1925). F. Feldmann, *Das*

Buch Isaias übersetzt und erklärt, Exegetisches Handbuch zum AT, 14 Bd. (2 vols.; 1925-26). G. A. Smith, *The Book of Isaiah* (2 vols.; 2nd ed., 1927). J. Fischer, *Das Buch Isaias übersetzt und erklärt,* Die Heilige Schrift des ATs, VII Bd. (2 vols.; 1939). E. J. Kissane, *The Book of Isaiah* (2 vols.; 1941-43).

Commentaries on chs. 1-39: G. B. Gray, ICC (1912), for chs. 1-27 only. O. Procksch, *Jesaia I übersetzt und erklärt,* KAT, Bd. IX.1 (1930). R. B. Y. Scott, Introduction and Exegesis of Isa. 1-39, *IB,* V (1956), 151-381.

Commentaries on chs. 40-55(66): R. Levy, Deutero-Isaiah (1925). C. C. Torrey, *The Second Isaiah: A New Interpretation* (1928), takes chs. 34-35; 40-66 as a unity dating *ca.* 400. P. Volz, *Jesaia II übersetzt und erklärt,* KAT, Bd. IX.2 (1932). J. Muilenburg, Introduction and Exegesis of Isa. 40-66, *IB,* V (1956), 381-773.

Special studies: H. Gressmann, "Die literarische Analyse Deuterojesajas," *ZAW,* XXXIV (1914), 254-97. L. Köhler, *Deuterojesaja (Jesaja 40-55) stilkritisch untersucht,* BZAW, vol. XXXVII (1923). K. Elliger, *Deuterojesaja in seinem Verhältnis zu Deuterojesaja,* BWANT, 4 Folge, Heft 11 (1933). L. Glahn and L. Köhler, *Der Prophet der Heimkehr* (1934). J. Begrich, *Studien zu Deuterojesaja,* BWANT, 4 Folge, Heft 25 (1938). J. Lindblom, *Die Jesaja Apocalypse Jes. 24-27* (1938). S. Smith, *Isaiah Chapters XL-LV: Literary Criticism and History* (1944). M. Burrows, ed., *The Dead Sea Scrolls of St. Mark's Monastery,* vol. I (1950).

The standard Introductions to the OT may also be consulted, especially those of S. R. Driver, Bentzen, Eissfeldt (2nd ed., 1956), Oesterley and T. H. Robinson, Pfeiffer, Sellin (8th ed., ed. L. Rost; 1950), and Weiser (2nd ed., 1949).

See also bibliographies under IMMANUEL; SERVANT OF THE LORD.

C. R. NORTH

ISAIAH, ASCENSION OF. A pseudepigraph, a combination of three earlier sources: the Martyrdom of Isaiah (Jewish) and the Testament of Hezekiah and the Vision of Isaiah (both Christian). Origen (third century) and IV Baruch (second or third century) both refer to the death of Isaiah by being sawed in two, in a manner to indicate acquaintance with the Martyrdom. Justin Martyr, Tertullian, and the Talmud (see also Heb. 11:37) testify to the early currency of the legend, if not of the book itself. External testimony to the existence of the Testament as a separate work is given by Cedrenus (beginning of the twelfth century), who cites 4.12 as being from the Testament of Hezekiah. Still earlier, a fifth- or sixth-century Greek Amherst papyrus contains 2.4–4.4, comprising parts of both the Martyrdom and the Testament.

A Vision of Isaiah is included in the Montfaucon list of apocryphal books based on MSS from the tenth century and later. A Latin text, printed in 1522 from a MS now lost, and reprinted by Gieseler in 1832, contains the Vision alone, as does the Slavonic version, which gives the title, the Vision of Isaiah. Latin fragments from the fifth or sixth century contain part of the Martyrdom (2.4-13) and of the Vision (7.1-19). The Vercelli Acts of Peter 24 (*ca.* A.D. 200) quotes a prophecy concerning the birth of Jesus which may be from 11.14 of the Vision. Jerome cites 11.34 from an Ascension of Isaiah, and Epiphanius quotes two different passages from the same work, saying that it was used by the Hieracites and by the Archontics, two early-fourth-century heresies. The complete text of the Ascension, so-named, is in the Ethiopic version, first published by Laurence in 1819, and later, in 1877, by Dillmann. A twelfth-century Greek MS (published by Gebhardt in 1878) contains the entire work, but in an abbreviated and rearranged form. Referred to as the Greek Legend, it seems to reflect the tripartite origin of the Ascension, since it describes the work as the prophecy, apocalypse, and martyrdom of Isaiah.

The Martyrdom was probably written in Hebrew or Aramaic, then translated into Greek. The rest was originally in Greek. The Ethiopic, Latin, and Slavonic go back to Greek texts. The latter two do not have 11.2-22, a somewhat Docetic account of Jesus' birth, but this may be an omission for doctrinal reasons. The text throughout is corrupt, but for the most part the corruptions are of a minor character.

The patristic and textual data, as well as internal evidence, seem to support the identification by Charles of the several sources, with some editorial redactions: the Martyrdom of Isaiah in 1.1-2*b*, 6*b*-13*a*; 2.1–3.12 (save for the mention of the ascension of Jesus in 2.9); and in 5.2-14; the Testament of Hezekiah in 3.13*b*–4.18; and the Vision of Isaiah in 6.1–11.40. The redactions are 1.2*b*-6*a* (an introduction to the whole work); 1.13*a*; a phrase in 2.9; 3.13*a*; 4.19–5.1*a*, 15-16; 11.41-43 (a conclusion).

1. The Martyrdom of Isaiah. This is a Jewish midrash of II Kings 21:16, which summarizes Manasseh's evil deeds. Accordingly, Isaiah makes certain dire predictions concerning Manasseh, the servant of Beliar-Sammael, who will climax his evil deeds by having Isaiah sawed in two. Belchira, a false prophet, speaking for Beliar-Sammael, tempted Isaiah by offering him freedom and the reverence of Manasseh, the princes, and the people if he would say that his prophecies were lies. Isaiah resisted this temptation, and, upheld by the Holy Spirit, died bravely.

As previously noted, the manner of Isaiah's death became a part of both Jewish and Christian tradition. Isaiah's temptation shows some similarities—but this is all—to that of Jesus. The work may be pre-Christian, but more probably belongs to the first century A.D.; it is certainly no later than the early second century.

2. The Testament of Hezekiah. Here (3.13*b*–4.18) is a Christian apocalypse purporting to be a vision of Isaiah's which he related to Hezekiah. Isaiah briefly predicts the descent of the Beloved (Christ) from the seventh heaven, his incarnation, the Twelve, the fact that he taught, his tortures by the Jews and his crucifixion, the Twelve being offended by him, the watch at the tomb, the Resurrection, his commission to the Twelve to teach all nations about the Crucifixion and the Resurrection, and his ascension to the seventh heaven.

Next, and still briefly, Isaiah prophesies about the early church (the "plant") and the working of the Holy Spirit. However, with the approach of the Second Advent there will be much falling away; the leaders, elders, and shepherds will be lawless and contentious, as will be many believers. There will be a decrease of true prophets, and the prophets of the OT will be ignored.

Then Beliar, the Satanic ruler of this world, will descend from his place in the firmament, assuming the form of the lawless royal matricide (i.e., Nero). He will persecute the church and will put one of the Twelve (Peter?) to death. Acting and speaking like the Beloved, he will perform miracles. Calling himself God, he will place his image in the cities so that people can worship and sacrifice to him. Many Christians will follow him; those who are faithful (including some who knew Jesus personally) will go to the desert to await the Beloved's return. Beliar-Nero (both an ANTICHRIST and a pseudo Christ) will hold sway three years, seven months, and twenty-seven days (the 1,335 days of Dan. 12:12).

The Lord will then return with his army of angels and holy ones; he will defeat Beliar and his hosts, dragging them into Gehenna. A messianic reign of unstated duration will follow; it will be shared by the godly who are still alive and by the saints who have gone to the seventh heaven (a first resurrection). After this messianic period the righteous will ascend to the seventh heaven, clothed in spiritual bodies ("garments") in place of their earthly bodies. A rebuke of the visible world ruled over by Beliar will precede a second resurrection and judgment of the godless, whom the Beloved will annihilate by fire. Presumably, though this is not stated, he then will return to the seventh heaven.

This little apocalypse has a Neronic Antichrist passage resembling that in Rev. 13 (see also Mark 13; II Thess. 2:1-12). The eschatological pattern is also remarkably similar: the destruction by Christ of the Antichrist and his armies, the first resurrection of the righteous only who share in a messianic interim, a second resurrection and judgment, and the destruction of the wicked by fire. The differences, it would seem, preclude the dependence of one upon the other; they both reflect the same Christian tradition. Unlike Revelation, the Testament has the final dwelling of the righteous in the seventh heaven; also, the resurrected (as in Paul and II Enoch) have spiritual, not physical, bodies.

There are also some striking similarities to the Matthean account of the Crucifixion and the Resurrection, with the offense of the Twelve, the guard at the tomb, and the postresurrection commission to the disciples. However, in the light of marked differences from the canonical gospels, it is possible that here again there is a common dependence upon Christian traditions.

The Testament has been dated as early as A.D. 68. This may well be too early. However, the statement that there would be some who knew Jesus living at the time of his second advent, together with the resemblances to Revelation, might indicate a late-first-century or early-second-century date. The simple church organization, with elders, shepherds, and a diminishing number of prophets, indicates a similar period, as does the blame placed upon the Jews alone for the crucifixion of Jesus. The complete silence concerning Paul (even though Peter's martyrdom is mentioned) may indicate a time prior to the publication of Acts and of Paul's letters, or to an early-second-century period when Paul was in eclipse.

3. The Vision of Isaiah. The Vision (6.1–11.40) is the longest source. It shows similarities in language to the Testament, but is more Gnostic than apocalyptic, with the Beloved a kind of Gnostic redeemer rather than an apocalyptic messiah.

Isaiah had a vision in which he left his earthly body and was taken up into the seventh heaven by an angelic guide. The seventh heaven was the abode of God, the Beloved, and the Holy Spirit, as well as the righteous dead from the time of Adam (however, other righteous dead are in Sheol), clothed in their spiritual bodies. He was shown the garments (spiritual bodies), crowns, and thrones that were reserved for the believers when they reached the seventh heaven. Sammael (also called the Adversary) dwelt in the firmament and controlled the earth, which, like physical bodies, seemingly is evil.

Isaiah heard God bidding the Lord Christ to descend to the earth, and also to the lower regions. In his descent he assumed the form of the angels of each heaven, and of the firmament and air as well, thereby disguising himself.

A birth narrative, somewhat Docetic in nature, is then presented. The Virgin Mary is with child, but, because of a visit by the angel of the Spirit (the Holy Spirit), Joseph does not put her away. Two months after her marvelous conception Mary looked and saw a babe and was astonished, for she had no pain, nor were there any visible signs of a birth. She reared the child without revealing who he was. When he was grown, he performed signs and miracles (nothing is said about his teaching). The Adversary caused the Jews to deliver him to the king to be crucified. The Beloved then descended to Sheol; next, after the third day he arose, remained on earth for a time (in 9.16 for 545 days), and commissioned the Twelve. He then ascended to the seventh heaven, and seated himself at the right hand of the Great Glory, with the Holy Spirit at God's left. Isaiah is assured that in the last days he (and presumably others of the righteous) will go to the seventh heaven to receive their heavenly garments.

A Gnostic movement (possibly Ophite) described by Irenaeus in his *Against Heresies* I.30 provides the best parallel for the Vision. Following an account of an elaborate Gnostic myth, it is stated that the pre-existent Christ descended from the seventh heaven to earth, disguising himself in the form of the residents of each heaven on entering it. In the meantime a certain Jesus, born of a Virgin, was prepared to be the pure receptacle for the descended Christ. Christ, then, united with Jesus, possibly at the time of baptism, thus forming Jesus Christ. Many of the disciples were unaware of his true identity. He began to work miracles, to heal, and to announce the unknown "Father." When the "powers" decided to destroy him, Christ departed from Jesus, who then was crucified. However, Christ assisted Jesus in rising from the dead; this was a spiritual, not a physical, resurrection, so that his disciples at first did not recognize him. He remained on earth eighteen months (cf. the 545 days in Vision 9.16), he received knowledge, and he taught some of his disciples the great mysteries. He was then received into heaven, where he sat down at the right hand of Ialdabaoth. Here he would receive those who had known Jesus Christ, after they had put off their earthly bodies of flesh.

The Vision seems to be a modification of this Gnostic scheme—lacking, of course, its fantastic mythology and its extreme Gnosticism. If so, this would tend to place the Vision in the latter part of the second century. There are some similarities between the birth story of the Vision and that in Ign. Eph. 19 (first part of first century), and of the Infancy Gospel of James 19 (late second century). The possible citation of the Vision in the Vercelli Acts of Peter 24 (*ca.* 200) fits in with the other data.

It is quite evident that the Ascension as a whole was in circulation by the beginning of the fourth century; it may well have been compiled earlier, but where or by whom is unknown. The suggestion that Hieracas, a heretic in Egypt at the beginning of the fourth century, was the redactor is plausible, but is without any proof. If the component sources are as early as is generally supposed, then the work deserves more attention than it has usually received.

Bibliography. G. Beer, "Das Martyrium Jesajae," in Kautzsch, *Die Apokryphen und Pseudepigraphen des Alten Testaments* (1900), II, 119-27. R. H. Charles, *The Ascension of Isaiah* (trans. from the Ethiopic Version, which, together with the New Greek Fragment, the Latin Versions, and the Latin Translation of the Slavonic Version, is here published in full; 1900). J. Fleming, "Himmelfahrt des Jesaja," in Hennecke, *Handbuch zu den Neutestamentlichen Apokryphen* (1904), pp. 323-31 (Introduction and critical notes). R. H. Charles, "The Martyrdom of Isaiah," *The Apoc. and Pseudep. of the OT* (1913), II, 155-62. R. H. Charles and G. H. Box, *The Ascension of Isaiah* (1919; trans. by Charles, Introduction by Box). V. Burch, "The Literary Unity of the Ascensio Isaiae," *JTS,* XX (1919), 17-23; "Material for the Interpretation of the Ascensio Isaiae," *JTS,* XXI (1920), 249-65. J. Flemming and H. Duensing, "Die Himmelfahrt des Jesaja," in Hennecke, *Neutestamentlichen Apokryphen* (2nd ed., 1924), pp. 303-14 (German translation). A. L. Davies, "Ascension of Isaiah," in Hastings, *Dictionary of the Apostolic Church,* I (1915-18), 99-102.

M. Rist

ISAIAS ī zā'əs. Douay Version form of Isaiah.

ISCAH ĭz'kə [יסכה] (Gen. 11:29). A daughter of Haran, and the sister of Milcah.

ISDAEL. KJV Apoc. form of Giddel.

ISHBAAL ĭsh'bāl [איש־בעל, man of Baal]. Alternately: ESHBAAL ĕsh'— [אשבעל, man of Baal, *or* Baal exists] (I Chr. 8:33; 9:39). The name Ishbaal is not found in the Bible. Because of the hesitancy to pronounce the name "Baal," Ishbosheth was substituted.

Ishbaal-Ishbosheth was ruler of the N tribes of Israel after the death of Saul. He struggled unsuccessfully with David for the leadership of all the tribes. The Chronicler, anxious to avoid anything which would cast doubt on the legitimacy of David's reign, makes no mention of this chapter in Israel's history.

After the defeat of Israel by the Philistines at Mount Gilboa, and the death of Saul and his older sons (I Sam. 31), the ambitious Abner took Ishbaal, one of the surviving sons of Saul, and proclaimed him king. The crowning took place at Mahanaim in Transjordan (II Sam. 2:8), no doubt because the territory W of the Jordan was under Philistine control (I Sam. 31:7). In II Sam. 2:9 it is claimed that Ishbaal ruled over Gilead, Asher (reading "Asherites" for "Ashurites"), Jezreel, Ephraim, Benjamin, and all Israel. That "all Israel" did not follow Ishbaal is clear from the following verse, where it is stated that the house of Judah followed David. The boundary between the areas controlled by David and Ishbaal seems to have been the Aijalon Valley (vss. 12-13). Whatever control Ishbaal exercised over the territory W of the Jordan was probably due to his submitting himself to Philistine overlordship. Indeed, both David and Ishbaal may well have started their careers as Philistine vassals (*see* Achish). Perhaps the Philistines hoped that conflict between the two contenders for rule in Israel would provide a check to the development of any single strong power in Palestine.

A long civil war soon broke out between the two parties (II Sam. 2:12-17; the precise nature of the "play"—*Pi'el* of שחק, "to laugh"—of the young men which caused the outbreak of hostilities is not clear; the context indicates some sort of tournament). The tide of war ran steadily in David's favor (3:1).

The N tribes were handicapped by lack of strong leadership. The real power was Abner, whom the weak Ishbaal seemed unable to check (II Sam. 3:6). When Abner appropriated for himself one of Saul's concubines—an act which may well have indicated that Abner had designs on the throne (cf. II Sam. 16:22; I Kings 2:22)—Ishbaal for once objected. Abner asserted his loyalty and immediately began plotting to transfer the allegiance of the N tribes to David (II Sam. 3:7-19).

Joab's murder of Abner frustrated this attempt (II Sam. 3:26-27). But without Abner the cause of the N tribes was in dire straits. Once his commander was gone, Ishbaal seems to have given up all hope of holding his crown, and Israel found itself practically without leadership (4:1). Ishbaal was soon murdered in his sleep by two of his captains, and the last block to David's complete control was removed (4:5-12; cf. the account of the murder of the Egyptian Amen-em-het).

In II Sam. 2:10 it is stated that Ishbaal was forty years old when he began to rule, and that his reign lasted two years. Both these figures have been questioned. Abner's treatment of Ishbaal is more understandable if the king was still a minor when crowned; his youth would also explain why he apparently was not present at the Battle of Mount Gilboa. At any rate, forty years is much too old, for this would make Ishbaal *ca.* twenty-eight years old when his father was anointed, an event which took place when Saul was a "young man" (I Sam. 9:2).

It is likewise argued that the length of his reign must have been roughly the same as the rule of David at Hebron, since the capture of Jerusalem and the transfer of the capital appears to have followed closely upon the acknowledgment of David as king of all Israel (II Sam. 5:1-9). David's reign at Hebron is given as 7½ years (2:11; 5:5).

Bibliography. J. B. Pritchard, ed., *ANET* (2nd ed., 1955), p. 418; E. Voegelin, *Israel and Revelation* (1956), pp. 254-55; M. Noth, *The History of Israel* (1958), pp. 183-86.

R. W. Corney

ISHBAH ĭsh'bə [ישבח, *perhaps* may (God's wrath) be allayed] (I Chr. 4:17). A descendant of Judah; son of Mered and Bithiah the daughter of Pharaoh. The KJV follows a corrupt text.

Bibliography. M. Noth, *Die israelitischen Personennamen,* pp. 28, 211.

ISHBAK ĭsh'băk [ישבק; *cf. personal name* שובק (Neh. 10:25)]. Fifth son of Abraham and Keturah (Gen. 25:2 [LXX Ιεσβοκ]; I Chr. 1:32 [LXX A Ιεσβοκ; LXX B Σοβακ]).

ISHBI-BENOB ĭsh'bī bē'nōb [ישבו בנב (*Kethibh*), ישבי בנב (*Qere*)] (II Sam. 21:16). A Philistine giant who was slain by Abishai when he threatened the life of David. However, the verse presents serious difficulties principally because "Ishbi-benob" is clearly translatable as "they abode in Nob" (better, "Gob"—cf. vss. 18-19). With the dissolution of the name of the giant, one of the simplest of the various resultant reconstructions of vss. 15-16 posits that some such words as "Now there was a warrior" be placed after the words "and they abode at Gob."

Bibliography. A. Schulz, "Die Bücher Samuel," *EH* (1920).
E. R. Dalglish

ISHBOSHETH ĭsh bō'shĭth [איש־בשת, man of shame]. Alternately: ESHBAAL ĕsh'bāl [אשבעל, man of Baal, *or* Baal exists] (I Chr. 8:33; 9:39). King of Israel after the death of Saul. The name was originally Ishbaal. During the period of the judges and the early monarchy many Hebrew names were compounded with "Baal," a word which can mean "master" or "possessor," and which may have been applied to Yahweh without any thought of connecting him with the Canaanite fertility gods. By the time of David such formations had all but ceased. The violence of the prophetic attack on Baal-worship (cf. Hos. 2:16—H 2:18) made later generations hesitant about pronouncing the name "Baal," and "bosheth" ("shame") was substituted.

Bibliography. G. B. Gray, *Studies in Hebrew Personal Names* (1896), pp. 120-36; W. F. Albright, *Archaeology and the Religion of Israel* (1956), p. 207.
R. W. Corney

ISH-HAI ĭsh'hī [אישחי (*Kethibh*), אישחה (*Qere*)]. The name used in the title "the son of Ish-hai," used of Benaiah in II Sam. 23:20 RSV mg. The *Qere* reading, "valiant man" (so RSV text), which is probably to be preferred, is found also in I Chr. 11:22.
C. T. Fritsch

ISHHOD ĭsh'hŏd [אישהוד, man of vigor] (I Chr. 7:18); KJV ISHOD ĭsh'ŏd. A Manassite, son of Hammolecheth the sister of Gilead. The names are eponymous.

Bibliography. M. Noth, *Die israelitischen Personennamen* (1928), p. 225.

ISHI ĭsh'ī [ישעי, (God) has saved]. **1.** A Jerahmeelite (I Chr. 2:31).

2. A man of Judah (I Chr. 4:20).

3. A Simeonite (I Chr. 4:42).

4. A chief of the half-tribe of Manasseh (I Chr. 5:24).

Bibliography. M. Noth, *Die israelitischen Personennamen* (1928), pp. 38, 176.

ISHI (NAME OF GOD). KJV translation of אישי (RSV MY HUSBAND) in Hos. 2:16. This is the name to be used by Israel in addressing God in the day of redemption, instead of the pagan Baali, in which Israel's God was confused with the Canaanite Baal.
J. D. Smart

ISHIAH. KJV form of Isshiah.

ISHIJAH. KJV form of Isshijah.

ISHMA ĭsh'mə [ישמא, *hypocoristic for* ישמע, may (God) hear] (I Chr. 4:3). A descendant of Judah.

Bibliography. M. Noth, *Die israelitischen Personennamen* (1928), pp. 28, 39, 198.

ISHMAEL ĭsh'mĭ əl [ישמעאל, *see below;* LXX Ἰσμαηλ]; KJV Apoc. ISMAEL ĭs'mĭ əl. The first and oldest etymological reference to "Ishmael" is also the most explicit: the child is to be named Ishmael (ישמעאל) because the Lord "has given heed" (שמע) to the mother's affliction (Gen. 16:11). Since this is from the J Source, "Yahweh" occurs as the divine name; but it must originally have been "Elohim" or better "El," as the name itself and the prevalence of the "El religion" in Genesis would indicate (*see* God, Names of, §§ C1-2). Two other passages allude to the meaning of the name: one from the Elohist (21:17*b*); one from the Priestly writer (17:20*a*). Although both employ the verb שמע, "to hear," in the perfect tense (however, cf. 21:17*aα*), "Ishmael" reflects a formation with the imperfect (probably originally *yishma*ʻ*'ēl,* like the Hebrew personal name *yishmaʻyāh(û);* cf. Elephantine יהוישמע). It is best translated as a jussive, "May God hear," though "God hears" and "God shall hear" are permissible. Significantly, the analogous form to this OT name now appears in the Mari Texts as *Ya-áš-ma-aḫ-AN* (VI.22.16). *See* Mari; Patriarchs § 3*a*.

1. Son of Abraham by Hagar; older half brother of Isaac (Gen. 25:12; I Chr. 1:28).

Despite the fact that the traditions about Ishmael are carried by all three sources comprising Genesis (ch. 16; 17:18-27; 21:8-21), little is said about the person himself.

The Yahwist, other than furnishing the clearest etymology (*see above*), tells that Ishmael "shall be a wild ass of a man, his hand against every man and every man's hand against him; and he shall dwell over against all his kinsmen" (16:12). But this is more in the nature of an ethnic etiology, referring to the Ishmaelites, than a biographical contribution.

The Elohist adds that Sarah (technically, Sarai; *see* Sarah) saw Ishmael "playing [מצחק] with her son Isaac" (lacking in the MT; supplied from the LXX and the Vulg.) on the day when the latter was weaned and, through jealousy for Isaac if not also for herself, forced Abram (*see* Abraham §§ A1-2) to cast out Hagar and Ishmael into the wilderness. "God heard" the voice of the lad, however, and saved them by providing a well of water at Beer-sheba. Under the protection of God, Ishmael grew up in the wilderness of Paran. Hagar procured for him a wife from her own country, Egypt (21:8-21). E's note that Ishmael "became an expert with the bow" (vs. 20*b*) points beyond the man to the people. His accounting for the separation of Ishmael from Isaac, similar to J's statement at 16:12*b,* is also more ethnic than personal.

From the Priestly writer come a few personal data, but these are brief. Ishmael was born when Abraham was 86 years old, and was named by his father (16:15-16); he was circumcised at the age of 13 (17:

22-27); when Abraham died, Ishmael joined Isaac in the burial (25:9); and Ishmael lived 137 years (vs. 17). Moreover, P furnishes statistics on Ishmael's descendants: his twelve sons (25:12-16; given also at I Chr. 1:29-31), who dwelt from Havilah to Shur (Gen. 25:18); and a daughter Mahalath, Nebaioth's sister (28:9; identified as Basemath at 36:3 [P]; cf. 36:10, 13, 17). But again, these lists are more pertinent for the Ishmaelites than for Ishmael.

But if these few verses tell little about Ishmael the man, they say a great deal about Ishmael the child as a witness to man's despair and God's goodness.

God had promised Abraham and Sarah a son (15:4; 17:16, 19, 21; 18:10, 14). Yet they doubted that he could fulfil his promise (17:17; 18:12-15; cf. 15:2-3) and, despairing, forced the issue by using Hagar as a substitute (16:1-6). Then, even after God had made good his promise through the birth of Isaac himself, Sarah, with Abraham consenting, drove Hagar and Ishmael into the wilderness, because she still feared that God might renege in the future and allow the "son of this slave woman" to become a joint heir with her son, Isaac (21:8-10; see Paul's famous use of this incident in Gal. 4:21-31). Ch. 21 is not, therefore, just a N version of ch. 16 but shows a progression of man's doubt. Ishmael, the very child of Sarah's despair (ch. 16), instead of serving as a confirmation of God's goodness, becomes for Sarah and Abraham a living threat to the promise. Regardless of ameliorating circumstances such as the ten years' wait (16:3), the slave's contempt (vs. 4), and the mistress' hurt (vs. 5), or personal concern such as Abraham's care for mother and child (21:11, 14; but cf. 16:6), the Ishmael story in its present construction portrays the tension between faith and doubt. So viewed, it condemns Abraham, Sarah, and Hagar alike as guilty of lack of faith.

Conversely, through Ishmael, God proves himself dependable and gracious. He is "faithful" in performing his promises to each person. Not only does he give Isaac to Abraham and Sarah as their own child, but he hears Hagar and saves Ishmael also, making him—for Abraham's sake (21:13)—into a great nation, headed by his sons as "twelve princes" (16:10; 17:20; 21:13, 18; 25:16).

Bibliography. S. R. Driver, *The Book of Genesis,* WC (1926), pp. 180-84, 209-13, 241-44; M. Noth, *Die israelitischen Personennamen* (1928), p. 198; G. von Rad, *Das erste Buch Mose,* ATD 3 (1952), pp. 160-72, 196-201; M. Noth, "Remarks on the Sixth Volume of Mari Texts," *Journal of Semitic Studies,* I (1956), 325.

2. The third son of the Benjaminite Azel, a descendant of Saul (I Chr. 8:38; 9:44).

3. The father of Zebadiah, who was "governor [הנגיד] of the house of Judah" during the reign of Jehoshaphat (II Chr. 19:11).

4. Son of Jehohanan. One of the "commanders of hundreds" who helped bring the royal child Joash to the throne (II Chr. 23:1).

5. Son of Nethaniah. As a member "of the royal family" (מזרע המלוכה) of Judah (II Kings 25:25), Ishmael acted as leader of the "captains of the forces" (שרי החילים) who overthrew the Judean puppet government established by Nebuchadnezzar in 586 B.C. With the assistance of ten of his cohorts, and apparently at the instigation of the Ammonite king (Jer. 40:14*a;* cf. 41:10*b,* 15), Ishmael went into Mizpah and killed Gedaliah, along with his fellow Jews and the Chaldean (Babylonian) soldiers "who happened to be there" (40:7-10, 13-16; 41:1-3). Later by treachery he slew also seventy Israelites who had come to Mizpah to worship (41:4-9). The rest of the citizens of Mizpah he took captive, intending to carry them over to the Ammonites. These were rescued by Johanan (*see* JOHANAN 6), though Ishmael and eight comrades completed their flight successfully (vss. 10-15; omitted in the summary account in II Kings 25:23-25). *See* GEDALIAH 4; NEBUCHADREZZAR.

6. Pashhurite who put away his foreign wife during Ezra's reforms (Ezra 10:22). L. HICKS

ISHMAELITES ĭsh'mĭ ə līts [ישמעאלי, ישמעלי, ישמעאלים, *for etymology, see* ISHMAEL] (Gen. 37:25, 27-28; 39:1; Judg. 8:24; I Chr. 2:17; 27:30; Ps. 83:6—H 83:7); KJV often ISHMEELITES. A gentilic term applied without specific geographical or racial reference (just as *k*ᵉ*na'anî,* "merchant," was applied to the Canaanites) to wandering caravan traders, tent-dwellers, and camel-herders who dwelt in settlements or nomadic camps in the desert regions of North Arabia between HAVILAH, Egypt, and the Euphrates (Gen. 25:18) from the early second millennium until at least the eighth-seventh century B.C.

1. Origin. The Ishmaelites traced their descent from their eponymous ancestor Ishmael, the son of Abraham by his handmaid Hagar (Gen. 25:18-19). Since Ishmael's mother was an Egyptian (Gen. 16:1), it is implied that the Ishmaelites had some Egyptian blood in their veins, and a late tradition holds that Ishmael's wife, who is nowhere mentioned in the OT, was also an Egyptian (cf. Jos. Antiq. I.xii.2).

2. The Ishmaelites and Joseph. The Ishmaelites as such are mentioned only a few times. The earliest instance is in the story of Joseph, who was sold by his brothers to an incense-bearing caravan of Ishmaelites coming from Gilead (Gen. 37:25, 27-28; 39:1). Two strands of tradition appear to be interwoven in this story (*see* MIDIANITES). Many scholars consider the use of the term "Ishmaelites" here, like the mention of camels (*see* CAMEL), to be anachronistic, since, according to the patriarchal genealogies, Ishmael himself would appear to have been a fairly close contemporary of Joseph. However, as pointed out above, the Ishmaelites were primarily nomadic caravan traders without specific geographical or racial reference, so that rigid chronological relationships need not be implied.

3. Ishmaelites and Midianites. In the period of the judges we find the Ishmaelites in close connection with Midianites. When Gideon had defeated the latter, he requested the men of Israel to give him the earrings they had taken as spoil from the Midianites: "For they had golden earrings, because they [i.e., the Midianites] were Ishmaelites" (Judg. 8:24). The designation "Ishmaelites" here is presumably synonymous with "nomadic traders," as both the Midianites and the Ishmaelites belonged to nomadic groups, although each reckoned their origin from a slightly different source.

4. Other references to Ishmaelites. In the last OT occurrence of the Ishmaelites as an ethnic group (Ps. 83:6—H 83:7), they are mentioned with the Edomites in a list of conspirators against Israel. The majority of scholars have held that Ps. 83 is very late; some even date it to the era of the Maccabees. There is nothing, in either the style or the content of the psalm, that warrants such a late date. A careful study of the historical period in which the peoples flourished who are named in the psalm (vss. 6-8—H 7-9), shows that the historical context which may have evoked the writing need not be any later than the eighth century.

Two individual Ishmaelites are named by the Chronicler: Abigail, David's sister, married "Jether the Ishmaelite" (I Chr. 2:17), and the official in charge of the camels in David's administrative organization is named "Obil the Ishmaelite" (27:30).

5. Descendants of the Ishmaelites. Twelve princes (eponyms of tribes or districts) are said to have sprung from Ishmael (Gen. 17:20; 25:12-16), causing the Hebrews to acknowledge that the descendants of Ishmael had become a "great nation" (Gen. 21:18). A number of the names of these descendants appear in historical records outside the biblical narrative, and such Ishmaelite congeners as Nebaioth, Kedar, Adbeel, Dumah, Massa, and Tema are mentioned in Assyrian texts dating from the eighth-seventh century B.C. Mibsam, Mishma, and Hadad have so far not been identified in any extra-biblical sources. The first two appear again in I Chr. 4:24-25 as Simeonite clans, probably affiliated with Arab clans in S Judah. Jetur, Naphish, and Kedemah form another homogeneous group; Jetur is associated with the powerful tribe of the Hagarenes (*see* HAGRITES), frequently cited in the Assyrian records, and Kedemah designates descendants of the *Bᵉnē Qedem* (*see* EAST, PEOPLE OF THE), more or less mixed with Qedar. All these Ishmaelite stocks are represented as quartered, in general, to the E of Palestine in the Syrian Desert, and flourishing primarily in the first centuries of the first millennium B.C. In the first century A.D., Josephus (Antiq. I.xii.2) connected the Ishmaelites with Arabia in general, but throughout the OT they are clearly distinguished from the descendants of Joktan, who peopled the Arabian Peninsula.

Bibliography. E. Meyer, *Die Israeliten und ihre Nachbarstämme* (1906), pp. 261, 322-28, 390; F.-M. Abel, *Géographie de la Palestine* (1933), I, 294-97; W. F. Albright, "The Biblical Tribe of Massa' and Some Congeners," *Studi orientalistici in onore di G. Levi della Vida* (1956), pp. 1-14.

G. M. LANDES

ISHMAIAH ĭsh mā'yə [ישמעיהו, Yahu hears]; KJV ISMAIAH ĭs mā'yə in I Chr. 12:4. **1.** One of the disaffected Benjaminite warriors who joined the proscribed band of David at Ziklag (I Chr. 12:4). He is represented as a leader of the "Thirty," a legion of military merit, presumably composed of Benjaminite worthies in this early stage of David's career, and different from the later Davidic "Thirty."

2. An officer and a leader of the tribe of Zebulun in the Davidic era (I Chr. 27:19). E. R. DALGLISH

ISHMEELITES. KJV alternate form of ISHMAELITES.

ISHMERAI ĭsh'mə rī [ישמרי, may (God) preserve] (I Chr. 8:18). A Benjaminite.

Bibliography. M. Noth, *Die israelitischen Personennamen* (1928), pp. 28, 38, 196.

ISHOD. KJV form of ISHHOD.

ISHPAH ĭsh'pə [ישפה, *possibly from* ישפט, may (God) judge] (I Chr. 8:16); KJV ISPA ĭs'pə. A Benjaminite.

Bibliography. M. Noth, *Die israelitischen Personennamen* (1928), p. 248, no. 773.

ISHPAN ĭsh'păn [ישפן, *possibly from* ישפט, may (God) judge] (I Chr. 8:22). A Benjaminite.

Bibliography. M. Noth, *Die israelitischen Personennamen* (1928), p. 248, no. 774.

ISHTAR ĭsh'tär. The Babylonian fertility-goddess —originally masculine—Athtar, the Venus Star (*see* LUCIFER; SHAHAR; SHALEM 2). Ishtar was the most potent goddess in Mesopotamian religion, playing the same role in the fertility cult as Anat at Ras Shamra and ASHTORETH in Palestine. Like the former goddess and Isis in Egypt and Demeter in Greece, Ishtar is associated with the dying vegetation-deity, in this case TAMMUZ. From early in the second millennium her warlike character was recognized, and in the Assyrian period she was revered beside the national god Assur as a goddess of war, and in fact was termed Belit, the mistress par excellence.

On the possibility of her cult among the Hebrews at the end of the Monarchy, *see* QUEEN OF HEAVEN.

See also ASSYRIA AND BABYLONIA.

Bibliography. M. Jastrow, *The Religion of Babylonia and Assyria* (1898), pp. 202-6; J. Bottéro, *La religion babylonienne* (1952), pp. 37-38; J. B. Pritchard, ed., *ANET* (2nd ed., 1955), pp. 83-85, 106-9; *Larousse Encyclopedia of Mythology* (1959), pp. 57-58; E. O. James, *The Ancient Gods* (1960), pp. 78-80.

J. GRAY

ISH-TOB ĭsh'tŏb. KJV reading for "men of TOB."

ISHUAH. *See* ISHVAH.

ISHUAI, ISHUI. KJV forms of ISHVI.

ISHVAH ĭsh'və [ישוה, *perhaps from* שוה, to be like, resemble; LXX Ιεσουα, Ιεσσαι, Ισουα]; KJV ISHUAH ĭsh'o͞o ə in Gen. 46:17; ISUAH ĭs'o͞o ə in I Chr. 7:30. Second son of Asher; descended from Jacob and Zilpah (Gen. 46:17; I Chr. 7:30). Since the name is lacking in the parallel list in Num. 26:44, it may be a variant form of ISHVI.

ISHVI ĭsh'vī [ישוי, *possibly* crippled in the hand]; ISHVITES —vīts; KJV ISHUAI ĭsh'o͞o ə in I Chr. 7:30; ISHUI in I Sam. 14:49; ISUI ĭs'o͞o ī in Gen. 46:17; JESUI jĕs'o͞o ī in Num. 26:44. **1.** An eponym; listed as a son of Asher (Gen. 46:17 [cf. Jub. 44:21]; Num. 26:44; I Chr. 7:30).

2. A son of King Saul (I Sam. 14:49).

Bibliography. M. Noth, *Die israelitischen Personennamen* (1928), p. 227. B. T. DAHLBERG

ISIS ī'sĭs. An Egyptian goddess; the wife of Osiris and the mother of Horus.

Isis was worshiped in ancient Egypt from the earliest historical period as the supreme mother-goddess and as a personification of the creative power of the soil. Although she may have been originally a local predynastic deity of the Lower Egyptian nome of Sebennytus, her principle attributes were well defined by the time of the Pyramid Texts, and evidence points to her having attained her universal character at a very early date. By a constant syncretic process

16. Isis, seated on her throne, holds King Seti I (1318-1301 B.C.) on her lap; from Abydos

whereby she was identified with numerous Semitic, Greek, and Roman deities, her cult eventually spread over nearly all the ancient world. Her cults survived in the Roman world until the sixth century A.D.

Figs. ISI 16; EGY 18.

Bibliography. S. A. B. Mercer, *The Religion of Ancient Egypt* (1949), pp. 198-202; J. Černý, *Ancient Egyptian Religion* (1952), *passim.* T. O. LAMBDIN

ISLAND, ISLE [אִי אִיִּים; νῆσος, νησίον]. The islands of the Mediterranean are referred to in the biblical references in which these words are found.

The hope is expressed in Ps. 72:10 that the kings of the isles will render tribute to the Hebrew king. According to Isa. 40:15, the Lord's power extends over islands. The same idea may be implied in Ezek. 26:18, although it is possible that אִין, אִיִּים, may refer to the Phoenician coastland (cf. vs. 15) rather than to the islands of the Mediterranean Sea. The eschatological imagery of Isa. 42:15 in the phrase: "I will turn the rivers into islands," is a unique use of אִיִּים (some scholars have suggested that the text should be emended to read צִיִּים, "dry land").

In the NT, specific islands of the Mediterranean Sea are referred to by name. Among them are the islands of CYPRUS (Acts 13:4, 6); CAUDA (27:16); MALTA (28:1). Although they are not designated as islands, the islands of CRETE; RHODES; and COS are also mentioned in connection with the travels of Paul.

The Hebrew אִיִּים, as can be judged by the context of the passages where it occurs, frequently does not mean "island" but "coast" or "coastland" (*see* COAST). It is so rendered correctly by the RSV in certain passages where the KJV has "island" or "isle" (Gen. 10:5; Esth. 10:1; Ps. 97:1; Isa. 11:11; Jer. 2:10; etc.). The same word in Isa. 13:22; 34:14; Jer. 50:39 is rendered "island" by the KJV (RSV correctly HYENA; JACKAL). W. L. REED

ISMACHIAH ĭz'mə kī'ə [יִסְמַכְיָהוּ, Yahu sustains] (II Chr. 31:13). A temple officer of third rank.

ISMAEL ĭs'mĭ əl. Douay Version and KJV Apoc. form of ISHMAEL.

ISMAIAH. KJV form of ISHMAIAH 1.

ISPAH. KJV form of ISHPAH.

ISRAEL, HISTORY OF (ISRAELITES). The history of Israel can scarcely begin before the time of Jacob, who is represented in the Bible as the ancestor of the twelve tribes. The Bible opens, however, with cosmogonic traditions, and bridges the gap between Creation and the patriarchs by a series of genealogies, into which ancient stories have been woven. While some of these stories embody profound spiritual teaching and are of high value for the study of biblical thought, they cannot be treated by the historian as materials for any scientific account of the course of events. Their similarity to Babylonian traditions has long been recognized, even though the vast difference in spirit and in religious outlook between the Babylonian and the biblical stories demands equal recognition (*see* GENESIS; CREATION; FLOOD). Our knowledge of Canaanite mythology has now been greatly increased, chiefly through the discovery of the Ras Shamra Texts (*see* UGARIT). Nothing comparable with the biblical stories is known from Canaanite sources, and we may have reasonable confidence that there is historical substance in the biblical tradition that Israel's ancestors derived from Babylonia. Abram, the grandfather of Jacob, or Israel, is said to have left Ur and migrated with his family to Haran, and thence to have gone to Palestine. Since Ur was the principal seat of the worship of Sin, and the same god was the chief deity of Haran, some ancient connection between these cities is probable, and migration from the one to the other is not unlikely. Nevertheless, Israel's links with N Mesopotamia seem to have been closer than with Babylonia, and in Deut. 26:5 Jacob is represented as a "wandering Aramean."

1. The patriarchal age. Some scholars have found no historical value in the traditions about the patriarchs, who were formerly thought to be mere personifications of tribes—though this view was always questioned by some scholars. In Gen. 10 we find many tribal names treated as the names of individuals and fitted into a genealogy, and it is characteristic of Hebrew thinking to personify a group, and to speak of Amalek or Moab with a singular verb when a whole people is meant. There is nothing antecedently impossible, therefore, in the supposition that in the patriarchal traditions group experiences were represented as those of individuals. In Gen. 34, indeed, the cities of Hamor and Shechem are represented as father and son. It is impossible to carry such a theory through all the patriarchal traditions, however, and especially so in the case of Abraham, whose singularly exalted character bears the stamp of individuality. Even if these stories were originally told about tribes, they might still have some historical substance, and they could not be lightly dismissed as without value for the historian.

It is true that of none of these stories do we have independent confirmation from other ancient or contemporary sources. Nevertheless, our recent knowledge of the ancient Near East from archaeological discoveries has made it clear that contemporary customs of the period in which the patriarchs are located are accurately reflected in the biblical stories. Wellhausen affirmed that "we attain to no historical knowledge of the patriarchs, but only of the times when the stories about them arose in the Israelite people; this later age is here unconsciously projected, in its inner and outer features, into hoar antiquity, and is reflected there like a glorified mirage" (*Prolegomena to the History of Israel*). But this is precisely what we do not find. Customs which are not attested for the period to which the creation of the stories is attributed are reflected in these traditions. Yet texts which have been found at NUZI and MARI show that similar customs prevailed in Mesopotamia in the first half of the second millennium B.C. (*see bibliography*). A modern writer, using all the resources of great libraries, may write a historical novel that accurately reflects the conditions of the age in which he sets his story. But the biblical narratives cannot be supposed to have had such an origin, and when we find here striking examples of the true reflection of ancient customs, we can only conclude that they have been handed down in tradition. There is thus some reason to believe that the stories in which they are embodied were also handed down, and that the substance of the stories was faithfully transmitted. Hence there is a much greater disposition today to allow that there is some reliable historical substance in the stories.

We must, however, beware of going to the other extreme, and treating all these stories uncritically as scientific history. They are sagas, rather than history, and the recovery of history from them can only be in broad and general terms, and is only to be achieved with patience and by the careful study of the stories themselves and of known contemporary history. That Israel's ancestors came from Babylonia to N Mesopotamia and thence into Palestine, and that later some of them went into Egypt and subsequently were reduced to taskwork and then brought out of Egypt, there seems no reason to doubt—the more so as no obvious motive for the creation of such stories, if they were not true, lies to hand. Many of the individual stories preserve reliable traditions, though in evaluating these traditions one finds it impossible to consider the patriarchal age without relation to the Mosaic age.

The chronological problems attaching to this period are complex in the extreme, and it may be said at once that there is no general agreement about them. The biblical statements contained in Gen. 12:4; 21:5; 25:26; 47:9; Exod. 12:40; I Kings 6:1 would bring the migration of Abram from Ur into the twenty-first century B.C., and the Exodus into the middle of the fifteenth century. There is only one passage which sets Abram in relation to world history, and this is Gen. 14, a passage which has by many been held to be very late, but which many today believe to be quite ancient. Its use for historical purposes, however, is beset with difficulties. It makes Abram the contemporary of AMRAPHEL, king of Shinar. This king is often held to be HAMMURABI of Babylon, though the equation of the names is far from sure and has long been challenged. Hammurabi was formerly believed to belong to the twenty-first century B.C., and this perhaps contributed to the acceptance of the equation. But in the light of recent knowledge, and especially that gained from texts recovered from Mari, it is now certain that Hammurabi belonged to a much later period, and he is today placed either wholly within the eighteenth century or in the eighteenth and seventeenth centuries. If the equation of Amraphel with Hammurabi is retained, therefore, there are serious difficulties about the biblical chronology, while if it is abandoned, we have no passage which sets Abram in the framework of known history. For any reconstruction we must therefore start from the Exodus.

2. Moses and the Exodus. At the beginning of the century the Exodus was dated by most scholars of all schools, including the most conservative, in the thirteenth century B.C. More recently many scholars have moved back to the fifteenth century, and when

Garstang dated the fall of Jericho, on the basis of his excavations there, at the end of that century, this date became widely adopted. There were, however, many difficulties. For the biblical traditions represent the Israelites as engaged on taskwork in cities of the Nile Delta region for a Pharaoh who had his court in the neighborhood. Our knowledge of Egyptian history of the fifteenth century B.C. provides no suitable background for these traditions. Moreover, Exod. 1:11 gives the names of the cities on which the Israelites were set to work as Pithom and Raamses (*see* RAMESES [CITY]). These names have to be rejected as a later addition if the fifteenth-century date is retained. Furthermore, Palestinian archaeology has established that the main wave of destruction of Canaanite cities fell toward the end of the thirteenth century, and all probability would suggest that this destruction was at the hands of the Israelites. In favor of the fifteenth-century date for the Exodus, it is argued that the Amarna Letters (*see* TELL EL-AMARNA), written by Palestinian princes to the Egyptian court in the first half of the fourteenth century and appealing for help against enemies who are called by the ideogram SA-GAZ or by the name HABIRU, reflect from the Canaanite side the incursion of the Israelites who had come from Egypt. Since these letters ask for small reinforcements of fifty, or in one case as few as ten, soldiers, it is hard to reconcile them with the biblical tradition.

The recent excavations at JERICHO have brought Garstang's conclusions into question, and it is increasingly recognized that we have here a special problem and that the date of the fall of this city cannot be made the sole determining factor in considering the date of the Exodus.

On the other hand, any simple acceptance of the thirteenth-century date involves us in other difficulties. The shortening of the period of the judges is got over by the view that the judges were local heroes, rather than a succession of national leaders. The "Israel stele" of MER-NE-PTAH brings us incontestable evidence of the presence of Israel in Palestine when they would be barely out of Egypt on this late-date view. This difficulty is countered by the observation that Israel does not appear to be a settled people, like the others mentioned in the stele. More difficult to explain is the fact that the wave of destruction of S Palestinian cities, such as LACHISH, fell almost immediately after the Israelites would have left Egypt on this view, whereas the biblical tradition is of an initial, unsuccessful attempt on the S. Here scholars have fallen back on the view that not all the tribes went into Egypt, and that some were in Palestine while the others were in Egypt. This view is supported by the fact that there is some evidence from contemporary sources that some of the tribes were in Palestine at a time when on any view the Israelites are represented as being in Egypt. The crucial difficulty here concerns the tribe of Levi. For there is much evidence in the OT that links the tribe of Levi with the S and with Judah, whereas Moses is represented as a Levite and as the bringer out of Egypt of the tribes which were there. Some have argued that the word "Levi" simply means "priest," but against this we have the evidence of Gen. 34; 49:5-7, which associates Levi with Simeon, and predicts a common fate for both. That they did not share a common fate is certain, and it is therefore probable that Gen. 49:5-7 is an ancient oracle, coming from a time when it seemed likely that they would share a common fate, and when, therefore, Levi was a secular tribe.

Combining as much biblical evidence as possible with the extrabiblical evidence, one may put forward the view that the migration of Jacob and his sons from Mesopotamia fell early in the Amarna age, at the beginning of the fifteenth century B.C., and that this group formed part of the Habiru tribes, which were, however, far more widespread in the ancient Near East, and are not to be simply equated with the children of Israel. For detailed treatment of this view, *see bibliography*.

In that age there seem to have been two main attacks, one from the N and the other from the S. The treachery of Simeon and Levi at Shechem would fall in this age, and would perhaps indicate a group that advanced into the center of the country, but failed to maintain itself. The other associated groups moved much more slowly northward, and the archaeological evidence that points to destruction of S cities more than a century later is to be connected with their exploits. The story of Joseph's being taken into Egypt is placed shortly after the Shechem incident in the Bible, and if this is to be relied on, we should still be in the Amarna age for Joseph's rise to power. In that period the heretic Pharaoh AKH-EN-ATON broke with the Theban priesthood of Amen, that had hitherto provided the chief ministers of state, and proscribed the worship of Amen, making the worship of the sun-god, whose symbol was the sun-disk Aton, the sole permitted worship. Such a Pharaoh would have to look round for talent elsewhere for the service of the state, and this period would offer a suitable background for the story of Joseph. Moreover, we are told that Joseph was given as wife the daughter of the priest of On (Gen. 41:50). In no age would it have been a greater honor to be given the daughter of the priest of the sun-god as wife. The descent of a small group of Joseph's kindred into Egypt after his being taken there could rest on a subsequent migration, perhaps especially of some of the Levites and Simeonites who had failed to establish themselves in Shechem, while others of these tribes may have fallen back on Judah—the Simeonites to achieve some territorial settlement in the S for a time, prior to their early disappearance from history, while Levi gradually took on a functional character and became priests.

The period between the death of Joseph and the rise of the oppressing Pharaoh is passed over in a single verse in the Bible, and was probably quite short. The time of the sojourn in Egypt is given as 430 years in Exod. 12:40 (though this is halved in the LXX), but the biblical genealogies are uniformly inconsistent with this. The period is commonly put at four generations, with a maximum of seven in the case of Zelophehad's daughters and a minimum of three in the case of Moses. It would therefore seem likely that the sojourn in Egypt lasted about 130 years. The Pharaoh of the Oppression would then be Ramses II (*see* RAMSES 2), who is known to have undertaken building operations in the Nile Delta region in the reign of his father, Seti I, and to have continued them in his own reign. This fact would provide an appropriate setting for the taskwork of the Israelites and for the Moses story, as well as for the names of the store cities preserved in the Bible. The Israelites who were led out by Moses would be mainly the Joseph tribes, but with Levite elements, to which Moses certainly belonged, and Levites would be connected both with the groups which had not gone into Egypt and with those which had. The tribes led out of Egypt would not, on this view, have spent a long period in the wilderness before attacking the center of Palestine across the Jordan under Joshua. It has to be remembered that in the biblical account thirty-eight of the forty years between the Exodus and the Conquest are said to have been spent at Kadesh, and the wandering proper was limited to two years. It may be that the long sojourn at Kadesh preceded the earlier entry in the time of Jacob, and it is the combining of the two movements into a single story which has resulted in the linking of the long sojourn at Kadesh and the short period of later wandering into a single period of forty years.

This view finds substantial historicity in the traditions of the Bible, though it disentangles them into two separate strands. It should be noted that no view accepts all the statements of the Bible as they stand, but that every view either openly or silently dismisses what it cannot use. The view indicated here represents a greater integration of biblical and extrabiblical evidence than can be found in any other, and while it cannot be presented as in any sense certain, it offers a reasonable working hypothesis. The only major pieces of archaeological evidence which provide difficulties are provided by Jericho and AI, the latter of which seems to have been destroyed long before the time of Joshua, on any possible view of the Exodus. Both these difficulties lie, not alone against the present view, but against every other. Apart from these all the evidence of archaeology falls into place.

It will be seen that substantial historicity is here allowed to the Joseph story. It is also allowed to the story of Moses. Neither of these stories can be regarded as strict history in all its details, and certainly the numbers of those led out by Moses must have been greatly multiplied. But this does not mean that there is no core of reliably ascertainable fact. Some writers have dismissed the whole story of Moses as worthless from a historical point of view and as created by faith. This does not seem likely. Granted that none of the actual events of the Exodus can be shown to be referred to in contemporary nonbiblical records, it has yet to be remembered that the known history of the fourteenth and thirteenth centuries provides a background which suits the biblical stories. Moreover, it is antecedently unlikely that any people would invent the story that it had been reduced to taskwork in a foreign country, if there were no substance in the story. It is similarly unlikely that any people would have invented the story that in its deliverance it took no active part itself, if it had fought its way out. Nor would any people have invented the story that it had been delivered by a God it had not hitherto acknowledged as its own God, if it had not substantial reasons for believing it.

The religious significance of the work of Moses is not in question here. Politically he was the creator of the nation, or at least of those elements which he led. From an oppression which lasted down to *ca.* the middle of the thirteenth century, he led these tribes into the desert and filled them with a national consciousness, as well as with the sense that they had been chosen by the Yahweh in whose name he had led them out, to whom they had committed themselves by the Covenant, and with the confidence that this God would give them a settled home in Canaan.

3. Joshua and the judges. Joshua is represented as the leader of the united tribes of Israel, and as achieving the conquest and division of the entire land. At the same time, in Judg. 1 the conquest is attributed to separate tribes, or small groups of tribes. This is probably the more accurate account. To Joshua, the Ephraimite, the leader of the Joseph tribes and their associates who had come from Egypt, should be attributed the securing for Israel of a foothold in the central part of the country. That he won a great victory at Aijalon is not to be doubted, since an ancient poem, which commemorated this victory, links it with his memory (Josh. 10:12-13). This poem may well be contemporary with the events of which it sings. In the S the kindred tribes who had not gone into Egypt were in the same age extending their influence and pressing steadily northward, and it may well be that Joshua in some way gave them support. It is improbable, however, that he succeeded in linking up with Judah, since we find that in a later age a Canaanite belt still separated Judah from the N tribes. The feeling that all the Israelite tribes were of a common stock, even though their settlement came in different waves, would seem to be well grounded in fact. The sense of kinship among the tribes and also the tensions that existed among them are alike to be understood, if we recognize a common origin, but a long period of separate history before they came together for a short time in the United Monarchy.

On the view presented above, it is not necessary to shorten the period of the judges to *ca.* a century and a half between Joshua and the rise of Saul. The judges were tribal heroes, rather than national heroes, and the chronological framework in which they are set in the book of Judges comes from the Deuteronomic school of a later age, and is to be differentiated from the content of the traditions themselves. If some of the tribes had been continuously in the land from the time of Jacob, some of the stories may well come from the period before the time of Moses and Joshua. The earliest of the major judges, of whom alone we have traditions preserved, was OTHNIEL, who belonged to the S group, and whose exploits were probably stated to be against the neighboring Edomites in the earliest form of the tradition. The confusion of Edom and Aram is a common one in the Bible, and the expansion of Aram to Aramnaharaim, or Mesopotamia (Judg. 3:8), may postdate the confusion here.

It has been suggested that the Israelite tribes formed an amphictyony, pledged by a religious oath to help one another, with an amphictyonic shrine as the center of their confederation. One may doubt whether there was any twelve-tribe amphictyony at this date, for one finds little evidence of it in the period of the judges. At the same time, the prominence of shrines in the narrative must be recognized, and it seems more likely that at various times there were alliances of groups of tribes, these alliances being sealed at sanctuaries. The variety of shrines mentioned seems to tell against an amphictyony of all the tribes with a central amphictyonic shrine.

The exploit of Ehud was against the Moabites, who were extending their power W of the Jordan; that of Gideon was against the Midianites, who were similarly extending their power; that of Jephthah was against the Ammonites on the E of Jordan; those of Samson against the Philistines. It will be observed that all of these were non-Canaanite foes, and the Israelite leaders were fighting the battles of the Canaanites, no less than their own. It is not surprising, therefore, that while in times of crisis the Israelites were conscious of their racial and religious distinction from the Canaanites, there was not a little fusion and intermarriage during this postsettlement period. That the fusion brought a measure of religious syncretism, involving the worship of Israelites at Canaanite shrines and the following of Canaanite religious customs, is clearly recognized in the Bible, and is understandable.

In the case of only one of the judges was the enemy Canaanite. This is in many ways the most important of the stories of the judges. Sisera of Harosheth was extending his power from the Vale of Esdraelon over the Israelite tribes N and S of the vale, until Deborah, a prophetess, urged Barak to summon the tribes on both sides to combine against the foe. The subsequent victory, in which the Israelites routed the far better equipped enemy, was due in no small part to a storm which immobilized the chariots of Sisera, and in which the Israelites found the hand of their God. The victory was celebrated in a magnificent poem (Judg. 5), which is doubtless contemporary, and which is therefore a historical document of the utmost importance (*see* DEBORAH 1). In the prose account, which precedes the poem, the victory over Sisera has been combined with the account of a victory over Jabin of Hazor, won by two N tribes, originally quite separate from it. In the book of Joshua the victory over Jabin and the destruction of his city is attributed to Joshua (Josh. 11). Sisera was defeated by a larger combination of Israelite tribes than had hitherto come together in any single operation. Various tribes are praised or blamed in the poem for giving or withholding aid, but the measure of the blame varies, and this does not suggest that all the tribes were under a common amphictyonic oath to give aid. Judah is not mentioned for praise or blame, and this is probably because Judah was still separated from the N tribes by a Canaanite belt, and it would have been unrealistic to expect any help from that quarter.

Samson, the last of the major judges, performed feats of personal heroism against the PHILISTINES, who here come prominently before us for the first time. The Philistines were a people who effected a foothold on the Mediterranean coast early in the twelfth century B.C., probably as a part of the movement of peoples and wide disturbances in the E Mediterranean following the fall of the Minoan Empire, though there is no evidence that the Philistines had come from Crete itself. Gradually they extended their sway up the coast and into the hinterland, until they became the most dangerous menace to both Israelites and Canaanites. The migration of the tribe of Dan to its N home, recorded in the appendix to the book of Judges, was doubtless due directly or indirectly to the pressure of the Philistines.

The book of Judges is of the utmost importance for the study of the social and political conditions in the postsettlement period, as well as for the study of the religious conditions. There was little lasting cohesion among the Israelite tribes, and more than once intertribal jealousies led to internal war among the tribes. At one time the son of Gideon by a Canaanite wife attempted to establish a monarchy (*see* ABIMELECH), with an authority based on force instead of the moral authority of a leadership based on charismatic gifts freely recognized by the tribes; but this attempt came to a speedy end.

The most serious internal strife among the Hebrew tribes is recorded in the appendix to the book of Judges, when other tribes combined against Benjamin after the incident concerning the Levite's concubine (Judg. 19–21). The story itself is full of interest for the light it sheds on the times, but also because it prepares the way for things that follow.

4. The rise of the monarchy. The rise of Saul and the establishment of the monarchy was mainly due to the extension of Philistine power to the heart of the land. In the time of Eli, who was the priest of SHILOH, where the ancient symbol of the ark, which had come down from the time of Moses, was kept, the Philistine pressure was strong, and a battle was fought at Aphek. Here the ark was carried onto the battlefield as the guarantee of the presence of the national God, Yahweh. Instead of the hoped-for succor, however, disaster ensued. The ark itself was captured and taken as a trophy, and Shiloh was destroyed. Eli collapsed and died on hearing the news of the defeat, and the whole of the central highlands came into the power of the enemy. Israel lay defenseless and leaderless. The Philistines soon returned the ark, but its sanctuary had been destroyed, and it lay neglected in Kiriath-jearim for many years, while Philistine influence continued dominant.

The rise of the monarchy to meet this situation was due to prophetic inspiration. Prophecy is a phenomenon by no means limited to Israel, and it is now known that it was found in Mesopotamia as well as in Syria quite anciently (*see* PROPHET). The rising against Sisera had been due to the activity of a prophetess, and from now on, we find frequent evidences of the political as well as religious activities of the prophets of Israel. The man who had most to do with the establishment of the monarchy was Samuel, though it is clear that there were prophetic bands who fostered patriotic and religious feelings. Samuel is depicted as a judge, though he does not fit into the pattern of the judges of the book of Judges, and in one story is represented as a man of local fame before the emergence of SAUL.

That two accounts of the rise of the monarchy are combined in the Bible is well known. The earlier represents Saul as first privately anointed by the prophet Samuel (*see* SAMUEL 1) in the name of Yahweh, with the commission to deliver the Israelites from Philistine power. At the same time the Jephthah story and the story of the war with Benjamin also seem to lead up to the same climax. Saul's first exploit was against the Ammonites, who were renewing the pressure on the E of Jordan from which Jephthah had given relief. After the war with the Benjaminites, the people of Jabesh-gilead had intermarried with the Benjaminites, as they had stood aside from the war. Hence, when they were now pressed by the Ammonites, they appealed to the tribe of Benjamin for help, and Saul took the lead against the enemy with conspicuous success. The Philistines would be unconcerned with this incident, which seemed likely only to weaken the Israelites and not to menace themselves. But Saul turned against the Philistines the strength and popular support he had gained by this exploit, and the Philistines were driven out of the center of the land and Saul was acclaimed as king. The Philistines still controlled the coastal region and the vale of Esdraelon, and in the subsequent encounters with Saul they tried first to force their way inland, and then later to attack from the N. As the result of the latter thrust Saul was killed on the fatal field of Gilboa, and Philistine power was re-established W of the Jordan.

Some idea of the real achievement of Saul may be gained by noting the scenes of his battles with the Philistines. At the beginning of his reign they were in the heart of the country, until the victory at Michmash drove them out. Later, they sought to go up the defiles that led directly from their own chief cities into the hill country, but the battle of Ephes-dammim, with which the story of David's victory over Goliath is associated, checked their attempt. At the end of Saul's reign it was by the wide detour and approach from the N that they were able to re-enter. The moodiness of Saul, which is given prominence in the Bible, should not lessen the historian's recognition of the service he rendered his people during the years he led them.

5. The reign of David. Already, before the death of Saul, the attention of the reader of the Bible is directed to David, of whose life we are given a more detailed account than we have of any other OT character (*see* DAVID). At first he was a supporter of Saul, until the king's jealousy of his popularity turned him into an outlaw, who fled for refuge to the Philistines and then became the dependent of one of the Philistine leaders. On the death of Saul, Ish-bosheth succeeded his father as king, but had his headquarters E of the Jordan. He can have had little real authority W of the Jordan, where Philistine influence was again paramount, and even E of the Jordan he counted for but little, all real power being in the hands of his general, Abner. Meanwhile, David extended his influence in Judah, where he was recognized as king. At once war ensued between him and Ish-bosheth. This war the Philistines were content to watch unmoved. At first there would be a certain benevolent neutrality toward David, since he owed some allegiance to the king of Gath, but they would welcome the struggle with Ish-bosheth as calculated to weaken both groups of Israelites, and to prevent David from becoming too powerful. Again they miscalculated, as they had done at the time of Saul's rise. Ish-bosheth's cause languished, and when Abner made overtures to David, he was killed by David's general, Joab, as the result of a blood feud which the war had created. Ish-bosheth was thereafter murdered, and David was recognized as the king of all Israel. This brought Judah into a closer union with the N tribes than had hitherto been known.

David quickly turned his arms against Jerusalem, which till now had remained a Jebusite town. It is probable that in the war with the Philistines, Jerusalem had recognized that her interests and those of the Israelite tribes were common, and no embarrassment had been caused to Saul while he was defending the land against them. But in the encounter between David and Ish-bosheth the situation was different. David's relations with the Philistines would not commend him to the Jebusites, and this stronghold in his path must have hampered him in dealing with Saul's son. Hence, no sooner was David acclaimed as king of all Israel than he turned to attack Jerusalem. The natural strength of the city gave its people a sense of security against such means of attack as were available to David. By a bold and skilful ruse, however, the city was entered and captured, though David was too wise to treat its people harshly, or to destroy its defenses.

It was at once clear to the Philistines that David was no longer a dependent, but a menace to their power, and they quickly tried to suppress him. It was now too late, however. Just as Saul had turned against them the strength he had developed in the encounter with the Ammonites, so David faced them with a strength they had watched him acquire. Instead of yielding to their attack, therefore, David turned the tables on them, and was able to reduce them to dependence on him. His position was now much stronger than Saul's had ever been, and he was not long in exploiting the situation and reducing the surrounding states one by one to a similar recognition of his overlordship. In consequence he soon established himself as the head of a kingdom greater than that ruled by any other Israelite king during all the history of the people. That this was in part due to his own and Joab's military gifts is beyond question. But it should be remembered that it was also in part due to the international situation of his time. In an earlier age Egyptian power had been dominant in the whole region, just as in later ages Assyrian, Babylonian, and Persian power was dominant. During the brief period of the United Monarchy none of the greater neighboring powers was in a position to interfere in Palestine, and the union of the Israelite tribes under skilful leadership made them the strongest unit within that little world, and gave to David an opportunity that did not recur.

This is not to attribute the success of David simply to good fortune. The situation offered the opportunity, but David's skill enabled him to seize it. His genius is seen in his transfer of his capital to Jerusalem after its capture. This would seem to have alienated some Israelite sentiment, but David was anxious to enlist the natural strength of the city, and the prestige it had long enjoyed, on his own side. The wisdom of his choice was matched by the measures he took to attach Israelite sentiment to the city. He brought the long-neglected ark into the city. As a sacred object linked with the name of Moses, it made Jerusalem an Israelite center no less than a Jebusite; and since the ark was no longer kept in a famous shrine, no sentiment could be offended by its elevation to prominence again. Hitherto the ark had been associated with the N tribe of Ephraim, while David's personal links with the tribe of Judah ensured its support at this stage. More important was the clear declaration implicit in this act that the national religion lay at the base of David's kingdom, and that the worship of Yahweh was to be its unifying force. For despite the tribal independence and often separate history, all the Israelite tribes had come to recognize Yahweh as their God, by whatever diverse ways they had come to this recognition.

David's rule did not continue to be popular among all his subjects, however. The disappearance of the menace of foreign foes removed one of the major unifying forces, and the newly found unity of the Israelite tribes began to disintegrate. Even David's own tribe of Judah became disaffected, as is clear from the fact that when Absalom raised the standard of revolt, he did so in Hebron. At this time David was able to find refuge E of the Jordan, in the place where Ish-bosheth had maintained himself after the death of Saul. The hostility of Saul's own tribe of Benjamin is to be understood, and is clear from the fact that at the time of the king's flight before Absalom, Shimei could openly curse him with impunity. Later Sheba, from the same tribe, led a revolt against David, which seemed at first likely to be dangerous, until the seasoned and ruthless Joab took charge of the campaign. It must be remembered, also, that despite the glory of David's reign, to which later generations looked back with some wistfulness, his subjects in his own day were conscious of the burdens of war, arising, not alone from the hazards of battle which they were compelled to face, but also from the frequent neglect of their own occupations. For David imposed forced labor on his subjects, and established the system which aroused deep resentment in the time of Solomon.

6. The reign of Solomon. When David's end seemed near, his eldest surviving son, Adonijah, assumed that the succession would be his, and made his plans to meet the expected situation. He was foiled by the prophet Nathan and the queen Bathsheba. When David had committed adultery with Bathsheba and had had her husband, Uriah the Hittite, virtually murdered, Nathan had rebuked the king in the name of Yahweh (II Sam. 12). Afterward, however, Nathan was on the side of Bathsheba, and it was because of his resource that her son secured the throne. Various rivalries played their part in the situation. During the time of his outlawry in the reign of Saul, David had been accompanied by Abiathar, the sole survivor of the family of Eli who had escaped the massacre which Saul had ordered. In Jerusalem, however, we find Abiathar beside Zadok, who was perhaps the Jebusite priest in the city before David captured it. That there was rivalry between them is certain, and we find Abiathar supporting Adonijah and Zadok supporting Solomon. Similarly we find David's field commander, Joab, on the side of Adonijah, but Benaiah, the captain of the king's bodyguard, on the side of Solomon. By a swift stroke, planned by Nathan, Solomon was proclaimed king on David's orders, before the death of his father, and the succession thereby secured.

Later generations accorded Solomon a reputation for wisdom which his subjects might have disputed, and we find the works known as the wisdom literature freely ascribed to him. That there was a certain splendor about his reign may be recognized, but it was largely a hollow splendor. Solomon's reign was predominantly one of peace, in contrast to the constant wars whereby David had established and maintained his kingdom. It might therefore have been expected that the country would enjoy prosperity, in which people and king would share. Instead, the people faced ever harder conditions, while the court grew in size and splendor.

The sources of Solomon's wealth were many. He levied heavy taxes on his own people, requiring both goods and services from them. His country was divided into twelve districts, charged with the maintenance of the court for a month in turn, and since approximately equal districts would be needed, the tribal divisions were ignored. This would inevitably add to the dissatisfaction the levies must in any case have aroused. Moreover, Judah seems to have been given a privileged position, and so the feeling was increased. For the king's many building enterprises forced labor was used, doubtless in a far more burdensome form than the reign of David had seen. The subject peoples were also forced to contribute, probably under harsher conditions than the Israelites. Again, the tolls that were levied on the transit trade that passed through the land went to swell the king's exchequer. During many of the periods of peace the land knew, such tolls went to the exchequer of some foreign sovereign, in Egypt or Assyria or Babylonia. During other periods several of the small states must have levied their toll on the trade that passed from Asia Minor and Mesopotamia to Egypt. The reign of Solomon was the one period of peace when the Israelite king controlled this area, and drew the profit from this trade. Again, Solomon engaged in state trading enterprises. He fitted out a fleet of ships which sailed down the Red Sea and as far as India, engaging in commerce which brought various exotic products into the land and no small profit to the coffers of the king. In the neighborhood of the port of EZION-GEBER, from which his ships sailed, he had copper mines, which are unmentioned in the Bible, but which archaeology has uncovered. These were doubtless worked by slave labor. From all these sources, it is not surprising that the king acquired a wealth which seemed to his contemporaries to be vast, perhaps the more so since his subjects were given so little opportunity to share it.

Great building enterprises were undertaken. The most famous building was the temple, which Solomon built to house the ark, and which later became the sole sanctuary where sacrifice to Yahweh was recognized as legitimate by the Jews. It was not built by the king to be the sole sanctuary, however, and there is ample evidence that he visited other shrines. The temple was intended to be the royal shrine, and it was attached to the king's palace, which exceeded it in size, and probably in splendor. In various parts of the land the king established depots, of which some were to provide for the large number of chariots which he maintained. At MEGIDDO stables have been discovered by archaeologists, and there can be little doubt that these were built for Solomon. So costly was his court and so many his enterprises, that despite his wealth he was not able to meet all his obligations, and he was forced to cede some cities to the king of Tyre in payment for the services of the skilled craftsmen placed at his disposal and materials imported from abroad.

Solomon entered into numerous foreign alliances, including one with the Pharaoh of Egypt, as well as his alliance with the great maritime power of Tyre. These alliances were sealed by marriages with foreign princesses, which brought religious and cultural influences into the land which were unwelcome to the devotees of the national religion of Israel. For now, as so frequently, religion became the focus for all the discontent with which the land seethed, and when the time was ripe, it was the prophets who directed the discontent.

7. The Divided Kingdom. Already, during the reign of Solomon, the discontent was smoldering, and the prophet Ahijah encouraged Jeroboam, who was one of the king's officers in charge of the *corvée,* to lead a revolt. News reached Solomon, however, and he took swift action against Jeroboam, who escaped to Egypt and remained there until the king's death, placing himself under the protection of the reigning Pharaoh—who was not, needless to say, the Pharaoh with whom Solomon had allied himself by marriage, but of another dynasty, which had by now gained control of the country. Throughout his reign Solomon does not seem to have had to face any outbreak of rebellion within the country, as David had done, and may not have realized the strength of feeling his oppressive reign had aroused. Before the end of his life, however, he had seen clear signs that the little empire he had inherited was cracking. Some of the neighboring states had broken away and secured their independence, and the revolt of Damascus brought into being a kingdom which was later to become a serious threat to Israel.

On the death of Solomon, Jeroboam returned from Egypt, and soon became the leader of the dissident elements in the N. The tribes gathered at Shechem to demand reform before they pledged their loyalty to Rehoboam, the son of Solomon. The story of Rehoboam's disdainful answer is familiar. It showed that he and some of the court circle were still quite unaware of the state of feeling in the land, and Rehoboam was completely unprepared for the open revolt which at once broke out, under the leadership of Jeroboam.

It would be unfair to attribute the rebellion solely to the foolish answer the new king had given. A more adroit handling of the situation might have surmounted the peril, but the real causes were deep-seated, and it may well be that the Disruption would have come in any case. It has been said above that under Solomon, Judah seems to have enjoyed a favored position; and jealousy of this position played its part in the situation. In the period of the judges intertribal jealousy among the tribes of the N had more than once led to friction, and it is not surprising that there was feeling against the privileged position of Judah, which had so recently come into the stream of Israelite life. On the view presented above, Judah had entered the land quite separately from the Joseph tribes, and in a different age, and though they recognized a common origin and shared a common religion, they had for long had a separate history, because of the Canaanite belt across the land. To conciliate this feeling would have meant that Rehoboam would forfeit the support of his own tribe, and he could have little certainty that the dissidents would at once rally to his side. To respect the tribal divisions would have meant an immediate reorganization of the land, and to lighten taxation and abandon the *corvée* would have struck at once at the life of the swollen and luxurious court Rehoboam had inherited, and would have turned its members into enemies. To cut expenditure when circumstances compelled was one thing; to do so in response to a demand whose seriousness neither the king nor the court could recognize would have been another, and would have been interpreted by friend and foe as weakness. While recognizing the folly of the answer that touched off the rebellion, it is fair to recognize that the new king was in a real difficulty, which was not of his making.

Still more important, we should not forget the part the prophets played at this time. AHIJAH, a N prophet, had instigated the rebellion; and after it had broken out, a S prophet, Shemaiah, paralyzed Rehoboam's arm when he planned to suppress the rebellion. Prophets of N and S therefore favored the Disruption. That they were moved in part by the sufferings of the people is doubtless true, and we should not suppose that the prophets of the eighth century were the first to feel indignation at social injustice and oppression. On the other hand, we should not forget that Ahijah and his fellow prophets were also interested in the national religion and were concerned to fight all that imperiled it. At the time of the establishment of the monarchy, the prophets realized that the Philistine domination was a menace to the religion of Yahwism, since a God who was powerless to defend his people, as Yahweh had seemed in the battle of Aphek, would be likely to lose their confidence. Now, however, the menace was more insidious. The foreign alliances of Solomon had brought Israel into the stream of international life in a way she had not hitherto known in her history; and this in turn brought religious and cultural influences into the land that the prophets could not but view with alarm. The Disruption was the final blow at the little empire which David had established, to which later generations looked back with wistfulness. But the prophets preferred religious purity to political power.

The relatively brief period during which all the Israelite tribes had been united in a single kingdom had left a permanent deposit of the greatest importance. For during this period the traditions of N and S had been brought together and amalgamated into a single corpus. It is generally believed that among the sources of the Pentateuch there are two early documents, one coming from the N and the other from the S, and these probably took their separate shape after the Disruption. Both, however, were collections of traditions of N and S, and the United Monarchy had left an enduring mark on these traditions, which in part determined the form in which they have come down to us.

When Jeroboam led the N tribes in revolt, the S tribe of Judah continued to be loyal to Rehoboam. From now on until the destruction of Samaria the two kingdoms continued to be separate, sometimes warring with each other, the smaller kingdom sometimes accepting a position of dependence on the other. The S kingdom remained true to the dynasty of David, save that for a few years Athaliah ruled the land. The N kingdom had frequent changes of dynasty, however, and throughout its checkered history had less stability than the S. Not infrequently these changes of dynasty were due to prophetic incitement, and we sometimes find that the prophet who had instigated an insurrection quickly turned against the man of his choice, just as Samuel had turned against Saul. Jeroboam himself did not long retain prophetic support. In the books of Kings he is constantly condemned from the Deuteronomic standpoint of the compiler because he elevated the sanctuaries of Bethel and Dan into national shrines. The priesthood of Dan claimed descent from Moses, while Bethel is associated in the traditions with the patriarchs. Neither shrine was first created by Jeroboam, and both had continued through the period of the United Monarchy to function as shrines, just as other sanctuaries in the land had. Solomon's temple later became the only sanctuary to be recognized as legitimate, but, as has been observed above, it was not built to be the sole sanctuary, but to be the royal shrine. It was therefore natural that Jeroboam should desire a royal shrine, though in actual fact he had two. Both were recognized as Yahweh shrines, and it is probable that the bull images which stood in them were not thought of as images of Yahweh, but as the pedestals of an imageless God. Their condemnation by the Deuteronomist is to be understood. We should not suppose, however, that the N was religiously inferior to the S. For long the religious leaders belonged to the N. Elijah and Elisha were both N prophets, and in the eighth century Amos, though a southerner, prophesied in the N, and Hosea was a northerner.

Not long after the Disruption the Pharaoh of Egypt, SHISHAK, led an expedition against the land. His own inscription shows that this was not to support Jeroboam against Rehoboam's attempts to reduce the revolted tribes to obedience, as the reader of the biblical account might suppose, but was against both the little kingdoms. One of the first effects of the Disruption, therefore, was to expose both kingdoms anew to perils from without. In the subsequent times of friction between the two states, the S kingdom, with a shortsightedness it was often to show, appealed on occasion to the kingdom of Damascus to come to its aid by an attack from the N. Gradually the Arameans of Damascus increased their power, until they became a serious menace to the Israelites.

Early in the ninth century the N Israelite kingdom went through a period of revolution when there were three aspirants to the throne. One was quickly eliminated, but for a time the other two continued their rivalry, until Omri emerged as the sole king (*see* OMRI, KING). He was an abler leader than the few verses devoted to him in the Bible would suggest. To him was due the choice of Samaria for the capital. Hitherto the N capital had been moved about, but for some time had been at TIRZAH. The choice of Samaria showed something of the strategic insight David had shown in moving to Jerusalem, though Samaria was not already a famous city, but had to be created by Omri. In order to strengthen himself against Damascus, Omri made an alliance with the maritime power of Tyre, and his son Ahab married a Tyrian princess. Under Omri's leadership the N kingdom showed a new strength, and he was able to reconquer Moab, as we learn from the MOABITE STONE. This monument was prepared for Mesha, the king of Moab of whom we read in II Kings 3, and it tells us that for forty years the Moabites had been subject to Israel.

In the reign of Omri's son Ahab, the evil effects of the Tyrian alliance became apparent. For the queen, JEZEBEL, was a forceful personality, whose ideas of the position of a king were other than those of the Israelites, as the story of Naboth's vineyard eloquently testifies. Tyrian cultural and religious influence was widely felt in the land, and it inevitably roused prophetic opposition. Such opposition the queen would not brook, and the sanctity of the person of the prophets was not recognized.

The S kingdom was at this time friendly to the N, and both flourished. The S king, Jehoshaphat, was able to re-establish control over the S route to Ezion-geber, and even attempted to renew the maritime trade that Solomon had maintained. An alliance between the two kingdoms was sealed by the marriage of Ahab and Jezebel's daughter Athaliah to the son of Jehoshaphat. Subsequent events showed that the S kingdom was not regarded as an equal partner in the alliance.

It is of interest to note that though the prophet Elijah (*see* ELIJAH THE PROPHET) was bitterly opposed to Jezebel and all the Tyrian influence, and though in this reign his great conflict with the prophets of the Tyrian god took place on Mount Carmel, whenever it came to a conflict with Damascus, the prophet was on the side of his people. Later we find the same thing with ELISHA. Though he was opposed to the court, and ultimately instigated the revolution which brought Jehu to the throne, he was regarded by the Arameans as their most powerful enemy, because of the support he always gave to the Israelite king. In Ahab's reign Damascus made a determined attempt to conquer Israel. This ended in a defeat which brought the king of Damascus into the hands of Ahab as a prisoner. To the consternation of the prophets, Ahab treated his prisoner with generosity and made a treaty with him. Our external sources show that this was less quixotic than might appear. At this time Assyrian power was waxing, and her influence and arms were already known in the W. In 853 B.C., which must have fallen shortly after Ahab's treaty with Ben-hadad, Assyria was met by a confederation of W states at the battle of Qarqar. Here a large Israelite contingent was found, including a considerable force of chariots, which probably consisted of those ceded to Ahab by Ben-hadad. The Assyrians claimed the victory, but at least their advance was halted, and they do not boast of any large fruits of the victory. In effect, therefore, this concerted action was a triumph for the W states.

Statesmanship did not long outlive the triumph, however. Ahab called on Ben-hadad to implement the provisions of the treaty he had made and restore Israelite districts E of the Jordan which had earlier been annexed; and when Ben-hadad refused, war broke out anew between Israel and Damascus. Here it is to be noted that one prophet opposed Ahab's adventure, though all the other prophets—prophets of Yahweh and not of Baal—supported him, just as Elijah and Elisha consistently supported their country against foreign foes. Only the prophet Micaiah (*see* MICAIAH 3) proved to be a true prophet, and in the battle which ensued Ahab met his end, despite the fact that Jehoshaphat had reluctantly been drawn into the adventure and had been compelled to wear the royal robes.

Within a few years the prophets judged that the time was ripe for another revolution in the N. This time they sought to promote revolution in the Damascus kingdom as well as in Israel, doubtless to prevent Aramean exploitation of the situation in Israel. In fact, the Damascus revolution took place first, and advantage was taken of Israel's weakness. This time Jehu was the chosen vessel of the prophets for the revolution against the dynasty of Omri, and the revolution swept away the kings of both Israel and Judah; the queen mother, Jezebel; and large numbers of the royal house. Despite the zeal for Yahwism which Jehu showed, the prophets were not long in turning against his house, though before it came to an end, it attained a splendor the N kingdom had not hitherto known.

Jehu sought to make up for his weakness against Damascus, now that the alliance with Tyre was completely broken, by sending tribute to the Assyrian king. This shortsighted policy of buying security against a nearer menace by welcoming a farther one, we find repeatedly in both kingdoms; and it is a tragic fact that the nearest approach to statesmanship, shown by Omri and Ahab, was ruined by the baneful influence of Jezebel and the religious opposition she aroused. Jehu found temporary relief against Damascus, but soon Assyria was occupied with her own troubles, and for some years Israel had to face continual pressure from Damascus with little relief through Assyrian activity in the W. It was not until toward the end of the ninth century that the Aramean pressure was relaxed.

In the meantime Jehu's revolution had affected the S kingdom as well as the N. The king of Judah had been among his victims, and Athaliah, the queen mother and daughter of Ahab, at once seized the power and put to death all the surviving members of the royal house, with the exception of the boy Joash, whose life was preserved by the high priest, Jehoiada. After six years he was presented in the temple by Jehoiada and acclaimed king, while Athaliah was swept away. For a time the kingdom was administered by the high priest, but later, when the king assumed the power, there was friction between Joash and his former guardian. This took the form of a dispute as to whether the maintenance of the temple fabric should be a charge on the king's revenues or on those of the priests. In the end a compromise was reached, and a system which continued to the days of Josiah, two centuries later, was established.

With the advent of the eighth century there was an improvement in the fortunes of both kingdoms. Renewed Assyrian activity in the W had weakened the Aramean kingdom, but had then given place to further Assyrian inactivity in this area, and as there was now peace between Israel and Judah, each kingdom had been able to protect itself, and even to expand its power against its neighbors. In the N kingdom the long reign of Jeroboam II saw a revival which brought a greater measure of prosperity than had been seen since the Disruption. Unhappily the prosperity was not shared by all classes, and it but served to breed social evils which proved a menace to the stability of the state. Wealth was concentrated in the hands of a small class, and many of the small peasant farmers found themselves dispossessed of their lands and reduced to the position of serfs. The courts were venial, and the poor were denied the protection of the law. In such a situation the prophets championed the rights of the oppressed, as their predecessors had done, and championed them in the name of religion and not merely in the name of humanity. Amos and Hosea belonged to the time of Jeroboam and the period immediately following, and their prophecies give a vivid insight into the social ills of the time. They show that the forms of religion were still maintained—indeed, splendidly maintained. Nevertheless, in the prophetic view Israel's religion consisted, not simply in the observance of ritual, but in the maintenance of a covenant which bound the people to God and to one another. "You shall love the Lord your God . . . , and your neighbor as yourself," is a fitting summary of the prophetic demand no less than of Christ's.

In the S kingdom Uzziah's long reign fell largely at the same time as Jeroboam's in the N, and it saw a similar prosperity and some expansion against Judah's neighbors in the S. That it brought similar ills in its train is clear from the prophecies of Isaiah and Micah, though the work of both prophets fell somewhat later.

8. The fall of Samaria. To the prophet the collapse of the N kingdom was due to its weakness and disloyalty; to the historian it was due to the irresistible power of a revived Assyria. The prophet was aware of this power, and regarded it as the divine means of disciplining Israel; the historian is aware of the part the seething discontent within the land and the bitter divisions among the little W states played in exposing them to the new peril. In 745 B.C., Tiglath-pileser seized the Assyrian throne, and soon showed himself a vigorous and ruthless ruler. The system of deportation of conquered peoples which he began was continued by his successors, and this inevitably checked the recovery of the states once reduced to dependence. Before Assyrian arms brought menace to Israel, however, the inner weakness of the state was manifest. For after the death of Jeroboam II there were frequent revolutions, and no king continued long on the throne. One party pinned its faith to Egypt and another favored submission to Assyria, with a resulting inner strife that ensured that no policy should be successful. In 734 B.C. there was an attempt to revive an anti-Assyrian alliance in the W, and Israel joined with Damascus to bring pressure on Judah to join it. Instead of joining the alliance, Ahaz, the king of Judah, appealed to Assyria for help, in continuance of the already noted policy of embracing a more distant menace to avoid a nearer. The prophet Isaiah had only contempt for the W allies, though he did not favor the appeal for Assyrian aid. This aid brought relief; it also brought the end of the Damascus kingdom, and so brought the dreaded foe to the borders of Israel. Within a few years the Assyrians were on Israelite soil, and after a stubborn resistance Samaria was captured, many of its citizens deported, and the N kingdom had come to an end.

9. The kingdom of Judah. One of the most vexed questions of OT chronology concerns the date of Hezekiah's accession to the throne, since the biblical data do not seem to be self-consistent (*see* CHRONOLOGY OF THE OT). There is therefore disagreement among scholars as to whether he was already on the throne at the time of the fall of Samaria. In any case, Judah was not involved in the disaster of her neighbor, and this little kingdom survived for a further century and a half. She was now the buffer state between Assyria and Egypt, and therefore the scene of constant intrigue. It was not only Egypt that intrigued here. Babylon was restless under Assyrian rule, and Merodach-baladan, a Chaldean, twice sought to head a revolt in the E and to free Babylon from Assyria under his own rule. His embassy to Hezekiah (II Kings 20) was concerned with more than the king's health, and was doubtless directed toward the fomentation of rebellion in the W to synchronize with the rebellion in the E. Both of Merodach-baladan's bids for power in Babylon were crushed, the second by Sennacherib before the W plans were ripe.

In 711 B.C., Hezekiah seems to have maintained the policy of submission to Assyria which he had inherited from Ahaz, at a time when Assyrian arms were moving toward Egypt along the coast road through Philistia. A few years later, however, he was drawn into the alliance in which doubtless Merodach-baladan's envoys had been interested. Revolt in the W, with Egyptian backing, was planned, and in preparation for it Hezekiah sought to bring the same pressure on his Philistine neighbors as Samaria and Damascus had sought to bring on Ahaz. Padi, the king of Ekron, was carried to Jerusalem, and the city was brought into the alliance. Hezekiah strengthened the defenses of Jerusalem, and constructed the SILOAM tunnel to ensure the water supply of the city. He also carried through a religious reform, which was doubtless closely linked with the revolt. For Assyria imposed the worship of her gods on conquered peoples, and the altar which Ahaz had built in Jerusalem following his submission to Assyria (II Kings 16:10 ff) was an expression of the recognition of Assyrian gods. Any revolt against Assyria would therefore involve the repudiation of her gods, and the revival of the national religion. In this revival Hezekiah incorporated reform, and the most significant feature of this reform, abortive though it proved, was the centralization of Judah's religion in Jerusalem.

The prophet Isaiah did not favor the rebellion, and perceived that it could not succeed, though he consistently promised that Jerusalem itself should be spared. When Sennacherib moved against the W, the whole of Judah, with the exception of Jerusalem, was soon overrun. Hezekiah yielded without a struggle, and handed over Padi to be restored to his throne, and paid a heavy fine. Thereafter we read of the investment of Jerusalem by Assyrian troops, the closing of the gates with the support of Isaiah, and the deliverance of the city through a plague which broke out in the Assyrian camp, compelling the withdrawal of the enemy, who had moved to meet an advancing Egyptian army. While in the Bible this reads as the account of a single campaign, many scholars believe that two separate campaigns of Sennacherib are here telescoped.

In any case the reform of Hezekiah seems to have collapsed with the revolt associated with it. His successor, Manasseh, pursued the policy of submission to Assyria, and when Assyrian arms were carried into Egypt, which was conquered for a short time, Manasseh loyally supplied contingents. Manasseh's reign saw the greatest expansion of Assyrian power; before its end, however, that power was already crumbling. New foes were now appearing from the Caucasus, invading the Assyrian dominions from the N, and though for a time they were successfully met and diverted, the menace remained. Yet when Assyria fell, it fell from inner weakness as much as from external pressure. After the long reign of Ashurbanipal, the Assyrian throne knew little stability, and revolt was soon widespread. In Babylon, Nabopolassar appeared, to renew—this time successfully—the attempt of Merodach-baladan to establish a Chaldean dynasty there. In the W, Josiah revolted in alliance with other little states, which dreamed anew of freedom. That Josiah carried through a religious reform is in no way surprising, and that he should seek to give leadership to Israel as well as to Judah is not surprising. For Israel had no surviving royal house, and Israel's interest in liberation was the same as Judah's. The reform again centralized religion in Jerusalem, but this time on the basis of a book which was discovered in the temple, and which is identified by almost all scholars with the book of Deuteronomy, or at least with its core. Babylon secured her independence, and in alliance with the Medes she overthrew Assyria. In 612 B.C., Nineveh was destroyed, and though the capital was transferred to Harran, that also fell two years later.

Meanwhile Egypt, traditionally the foe of Assyria, had come to the help of the tottering empire. This may have been in part because she feared the upstart powers attacking Assyria, and in part in order that she might extend her own powers W of the Euphrates. Certainly when Assyria fell, she sought to occupy that W area, and whatever measure of freedom Josiah might have enjoyed now came to an end. The Pharaoh at once sought to consolidate his own power in the W in readiness for the inevitable struggle with Babylon, and Judah was quickly reduced to obedience, while Josiah perished for his resistance. In 605 B.C. the battle of Carchemish settled the fate of the W states. Here Nebuchadrezzar, the son of Nabopolassar, conquered Neco, who hastily withdrew to Egypt, and Egypt itself was spared invasion only through the death of Nabopolassar, which compelled Nebuchadrezzar to return to Babylon without delay to secure the kingdom for himself. It is now known that the battle of Carchemish did not finally decide the issue. A few years later Babylon was forced to meet another threat from Egypt, and another battle was fought in the S.

10. The fall of Jerusalem. Not even yet could the W believe that the new power would endure. On the death of Josiah, his younger son had been placed on the throne, but he was quickly removed by Neco in favor of Jehoiakim, who promised obedience. This obedience was in turn pledged to Babylon after the battle of Carchemish, but Jehoiakim looked for the opportunity to revolt, and later did so. Josiah's reform had collapsed with his revolt, and the suppressed shrines were soon functioning once more. Jehoiakim's revolt was short-lived when Nebuchadrezzar moved against him and his allies. Before the Chaldean armies appeared at the gates of Jerusalem, the king had died and his son Jehoiachin had succeeded him. The city surrendered, and Jehoiachin was carried off to Babylon to face a long captivity. We now know from surviving tablets that children were born to him there, and we have particulars of the allowances of food made to the king and his family (cf. E. F. Weidner [*see bibliography*]). Meanwhile his uncle, Zedekiah, had been placed on the throne in Jerusalem. Many of the leading people of the city had been carried away with Jehoiachin, and the weak Zedekiah, with no wise counselors to guide him, save the prophet Jeremiah, whose advice he had not the strength to take, became drawn into fresh Egyptian plots and rebelled against Babylon once more, bringing down on himself and his people the horrors of the long siege of Jerusalem, and ultimately the destruction of the city and the temple, and the end of the kingdom of David. In the surviving Lachish Letters we have contemporary records from a time shortly before the fall of Jerusalem, and while they add little to our knowledge of events, they reveal the tension and recrimination that marked the closing stages of the resistance to Nebuchadrezzar. *See* LACHISH.

11. The Exile and restoration. Large numbers of the people were carried away to Babylon when Jerusalem fell. Soon fresh troubles came upon the unhappy people left behind, for Gedaliah, who had been made governor by the conqueror, was murdered, and his companions fled to take refuge in Egypt, taking Jeremiah the prophet with them. In the years that followed, the Edomites pressed in on the people of Judah who survived, leaving bitter memories that long persisted; but otherwise we have little knowledge of the state of the land. The exiles seem to have cherished in an alien land the faith they had been frequently reproved by prophets for forsaking, and while there were doubtless some who were absorbed into the community among which they lived, there were others who maintained their separateness and cherished the hope of restoration to their land. In this they were helped by the prophet Ezekiel, whose despair for Jerusalem before its fall was matched by his hope of a new temple and a reorganized cultus. Many of the exiles gradually settled down in Babylonia, and a century later we find a successful firm of Jewish bankers there.

Nebuchadrezzar was not only a great warrior, but also a wise and enlightened ruler, whose inscriptions tell of his works of peace more than of his victories (*see* NEBUCHADREZZAR). No comparable ruler of this line followed him. After his death there were a few years of disorder, during which three rulers followed him, and then NABONIDUS seized the throne. For most of his reign he lived in Tema, leaving the administration of the state in the hands of his son Belshazzar. From a surviving lampoon in verse we know of the contempt in which Nabonidus was held, and a fragment from Qumran describes him as mad. The land was seething with discontent, and was in no state to meet a new peril which had arisen. CYRUS, king of Anshan, had become king of Persia, and then revolted against his overlord, the Median king, and within a few years had conquered Croesus, king of Lydia. Here was a clear menace to the Babylonian kingdom, and before long the arms of Cyrus were directed against it.

Among the Jewish exiles was the prophet whom we call Deutero-Isaiah, who quickly perceived the significance of the new star on the horizon, and heartened his people with the promise of deliverance. Cyrus won a victory at Opis, and shortly afterward Babylon fell without a blow, and the Babylonian Empire was annexed to the Persian. Cyrus soon gave the Jews permission to return to their land and to rebuild their temple. A few seem to have returned, but the rebuilding of the temple was delayed. The enthusiasm of hopes was exchanged for the hard realities of rebuilding their homes and their life among the dispirited people they found in Judea.

12. The Persian period. Of the history of the Jews in the Persian period relatively little is known. On the death of Cyrus, Cambyses became king, and during his reign Egypt was added to the Persian Empire. We learn from the ELEPHANTINE PAPYRI, which were found in Egypt *ca.* the beginning of the twentieth century, that there was already a Jewish colony in the island of Elephantine, opposite Assuan, when Cambyses invaded Egypt, and that the Jews had a temple of their own God there, which Cambyses left undisturbed. How far back this colony went can only be conjectured. It continued to exist for more than a century after the Persian invasion, and it became a Persian military outpost.

Cambyses did not return from his Egyptian campaign. One Gaumata laid claim to the throne, giving himself out to be Smerdis, brother of Cambyses, who had been put to death by the king before setting out for Egypt. For a time it looked as though the Persian Empire would fall to pieces, the various provinces each taking advantage of the situation to resume their independence. At this time ZERUBBABEL, who was of the house of David, was the governor of Jerusalem. It is not surprising, therefore, that the Jews should have dreamed of the restoration of the kingdom of David, and before long we find the prophets Haggai and Zechariah calling for the rebuilding of the temple, and seeking to revive the national life on the basis of the national religion.

Meanwhile Darius Hystaspis, who was a kinsman of Cyrus, though not in the direct line of succession, assumed the leadership, and quickly eliminated Gaumata, and then set to work to reduce the provinces one by one to obedience. In this he was completely successful, and before long the Persian Empire was restored, and then given a more solid organization than it had yet had. Before the Jews were reduced, the rebuilding of the temple had been begun, and Zechariah had visions of Zerubbabel and the high priest standing side by side as the crowned heads of the restored Jewish state. Suddenly Zerubbabel disappears from the picture, and we can only suppose that in some unrecorded way Judea came again under the Persian sway and Zerubbabel was eliminated for his rebellion. Nevertheless, the building of the temple continued. The Samaritan community appealed to the king to stop this, but the people of Jerusalem were able to produce the authority to rebuild the temple granted by Cyrus, and they were allowed to continue the work, and in 516 B.C. it was completed. From the beginning the Persian religious policy toward subject peoples was more enlightened than the Assyrian policy had been, and it was under the Persian rule that Judaism was established.

For the next half century we have no secure knowledge of Jewish history. We read of an abortive attempt to rebuild the walls of the city in the reign of Artaxerxes (Ezra 4:7-24), and this was almost certainly Artaxerxes I. Again, there was an appeal to the court against this rebuilding from Samaria, this time successful, and the king ordered the forcible interference with the work, pending his further pleasure. It is probably this blow to the Jerusalem community which lies behind the grief of Nehemiah on his receiving news from the city (Neh. 1:4), and it would explain his nervousness in asking the king for permission to renew the rebuilding.

That the mission of Nehemiah fell in the twentieth year of Artaxerxes I admits now of little question. His adversary was SANBALLAT, who is known from the Elephantine Papyri to have been the governor of Samaria, and at the end of the fifth century Sanballat was still governor, though the actual administration was then in the hands of his sons. The extreme caution of Nehemiah in laying his plans and the extreme speed with which he carried through the work of rebuilding the walls would alike be explained by the recent abortive attempt. Nehemiah was anxious to complete the work before there could be any renewed appeal to the court.

The mission of Ezra is less easy to place. We are told that he was sent to Jerusalem in the seventh year of Artaxerxes, and if this was also Artaxerxes I, it fell before Nehemiah's mission. The Chronicler clearly believed that Ezra was sent to put into effect the "law of the Lord" before Nehemiah came to restore the walls, but that Ezra delayed to carry out his mission for thirteen years and first read the law after Nehemiah had arrived. The abortive attempt to rebuild the walls would then appear to have fallen after Ezra's arrival, though it is nowhere associated with his name. Many scholars believe, however, that the work of Ezra lay in the reign of Artaxerxes II, and this greatly eases the difficulties. Both men are represented as having exercised independent civil and religious authority, and if both were in the city together, this is hard to understand. Both dealt with the question of mixed marriages. When Nehemiah returned to Jerusalem after reporting to the court, he found that there had been intermarriage between the family of Sanballat and that of the Jerusalem high priest, and also another enemy, Tobiah the Ammonite, was installed in a room in the temple. It was therefore political conditions that angered him, and led him to attack mixed marriages. Ezra's action was religiously inspired, and was directed against the threat that such marriages brought to the religious purity of the Jews. While the chronological problems attaching to the work of these two men cannot be settled with certainty, it seems likely that the work of Ezra should be placed later than that of Nehemiah. Some scholars would place Ezra in the reign of Artaxerxes I, but shortly after the second visit of Nehemiah. This would hardly allow time for the evil of mixed marriages to have become serious once more after Nehemiah had forcibly dissolved such marriages. To place Ezra's mission in the seventh year of Artaxerxes II would allow an adequate period for this. *See bibliography.*

The work of Ezra was the enforcement of a religious law which he brought from Babylon. It is not necessary to suppose that this was a new and unheard-of law. It may well have been heard of in Palestine as well as in Babylonia, and the fact that it was accepted as the law of Moses would suggest that this was so. Whether it was the completed Pentateuch or the Priestly Code is not agreed, but in either case it became accepted by the Samaritans no less than by the Jews, and its origin was therefore clearly not attributed to Ezra. By putting this law into force Ezra gave to Judaism the character it continued to have down to NT times.

One of the vexed questions of Jewish history is that of the Samaritan Schism. Throughout the postexilic period there were recurrent crises between the Jews and Samaria, though these seem to have been political rather than religious. Since the Samaritans accepted the Pentateuch, which must have included the law book of Ezra, the final breach cannot have taken place until after the mission of Ezra, but it appears to have been final before the work of the Chronicler, who left the N kingdom entirely out of his history so far as this could be done, and who seems to have regarded the N community as no true part of Israel. *See bibliography.*

13. The Greek period. For the remainder of the Persian period we have little secure knowledge of Jewish history. With the rise of Alexander the Jews soon passed into his power, and from extrabiblical sources we learn that when the conqueror passed through Palestine, he was received by the high priest. Alexander advanced into Egypt and there founded Alexandria, which seems from the start to have contained a Jewish colony. This colony inevitably soon became Greek-speaking, and it was for them that the Bible was translated into Greek. The translation of the Pentateuch is ascribed by tradition to the middle of the following century, and this is probably reliable. It must be remembered, however, that there was a considerable Jewish Diaspora in other lands, and with the spread of Greek power the Greek language became widely current, so that for other Jewish communities Greek renderings would be valuable. How far the Alexandrian rendering spread elsewhere, or how far there were other local renderings which ultimately influenced what came to be known as the LXX, cannot be known with certainty.

When Alexander came to his early end, his generals fell to quarreling, and for some years the history of the period became rather like a kaleidoscope. Gradually there emerged three principal divisions, of which two concerned the Jews. These were the Ptolemaic kingdom of Egypt and the Seleucid kingdom, which included Asia Minor, Syria, Babylonia, and a rather nebulous claim to the more E conquests of Alexander, somewhat fitfully renewed from time to time. These two kingdoms are referred to in the book of Daniel as those of the S and the N respectively. Palestine soon fell within the sphere of the Ptolemies, and for more than a century continued to owe them allegiance. Nevertheless, the Seleucids claimed that it belonged to them of right. Seleucus I, who established the Seleucid kingdom, had once been a fugitive at the court of Ptolemy I, with whose help he set out to secure for himself the largest slice of the empire of Alexander. Before the battle of Ipsus it had been agreed among the victorious allies that in the event of victory Palestine should fall to Ptolemy, but the contingents of Ptolemy arrived too late to take part in the battle, and Seleucus held that the agreement was void. Since Ptolemy's troops had occupied Palestine, and since Seleucus was too conscious of his debt to Ptolemy to use force against him, he contented himself with a protest. The result was that Palestine was a bone of contention between the two houses for a century. Of the conflicts and alliances between the Seleucids and the Ptolemies, briefly summarized in Dan. 11, it is unnecessary here to treat. It must suffice to say that following the battle of Paneion, in 198 B.C., Palestine passed to the rule of the Seleucids. Antiochus III had sought twenty years earlier to wrest this region from the Ptolemies, but had failed. When he now succeeded, there were Jews who welcomed the change. It was not long, however, before they took a different view.

At this time there were inner dissensions among the Jews. The Greek kingdoms, while separately governed, claimed to be parts of the undivided empire of Alexander, and both continued Alexander's policy of spreading Greek culture and marrying it to the culture of the E. There were Jews who favored the spread of Greek culture and welcomed its influence, while there were others who clung to the separatism which Ezra had stamped deeply upon Judaism, and held aloof from it. Political and religious considerations were soon woven together. The high-priestly house of Onias stood over against the house of the Tobiads, who, before the change-over to the Seleucid rule, had secured from the Ptolemies the tax-farming rights which had formerly belonged to the high priest. Hence the Oniads favored the change to Seleucid rule. They soon found that they had secured no advantage from the change, however. The Tobiads secured their position with their new masters, and neither religiously nor politically had the Oniads strengthened theirs. It is only in the light of these internal and external factors that the conflict of the Maccabean age can be understood.

14. The Maccabean age. Antiochus III became involved in war with Rome a few years after his annexation of Palestine, and at the battle of Magnesia in 190 B.C. he was defeated and compelled to forfeit his control of Asia Minor and to pay a large indemnity. His successor, Seleucus IV, inherited an exchequer depleted by wars, and a reduced kingdom to provide the indemnity. The high taxation this involved contributed to the unpopularity of Seleucid rule. When Seleucus turned to robbing temples to supply his needs, and sent his representative to rob the Jerusalem temple, this unpopularity among the Jews was increased, even though the attempt to rob the temple was foiled. Religious loyalty, nationalism, and resentment at oppressive taxation united one section of the people, while the pro-Seleucid elements reacted more strongly in favor of Greek culture.

When Seleucus was murdered by Heliodorus, who proclaimed the infant son of Seleucus as king, with the real power in his own hands, Antiochus, brother of Seleucus, soon landed in Syria to eliminate Heliodorus and to take his nephew under his own protection, and then to eliminate him and leave himself on the throne (*see* ANTIOCHUS 4). Antiochus had been a hostage in Rome, but had been replaced by Demetrius, the son and rightful successor of Seleucus. Antiochus was not, therefore, the heir to the throne, and it is not surprising that the elements in Palestine who were disaffected toward the Seleucids disputed his title to rule them. Antiochus, who became known as Antiochus Epiphanes, was not long in seeking to exploit dynastic troubles in Egypt in order to get possession of the Ptolemaic kingdom. His nephews, the two disputing Ptolemies, hastened to make up their quarrels, perhaps moved by the fate of the son of Seleucus. Before long, Antiochus made an open move against Egypt, but this time was foiled by the ambassador of Rome, to whose Senate Egypt had appealed for help.

Humiliated and angry, Antiochus fell back on Jerusalem. Here he found a complex situation. Already before this, Onias had been removed from office through inner Jewish intrigues, and the high priesthood had been bartered to the highest bidder. Deep personal feelings had been aroused, and all the religiously loyal had been driven to the side of Onias. This high priest had been himself put to death before the time we have now reached, but the bitter divisions continued. Now Antiochus determined to destroy the religion of Judaism, since he judged that though religious and political considerations were woven together in the opposition to himself, this opposition would collapse if its religious root were extirpated. It has been said that it was the policy of the Greek rulers to foster Greek culture. Antiochus therefore now pursued this policy in Palestine with greater vigor and violence than any of his predecessors. All the practices of the Jewish faith were forbidden, the temple was desecrated and turned into a shrine of Zeus, and the Jews were ordered to eat unclean foods and to sacrifice to idols.

It was this situation which brought about the

Jewish revolt under the Maccabees. Led at first by Judas Maccabeus, the rebels scored initial successes against the forces sent by Antiochus, until the temple was recovered, cleansed, and rededicated, though a Seleucid garrison continued to occupy the citadel in Jerusalem. The death of Antiochus in the E led to a period of confusion in the Seleucid kingdom, with upstarts and pretenders taking part in the internal wars that followed. Judas Maccabeus was himself killed in 161 B.C., but he was followed by his brothers Jonathan and Simon in turn, and these took advantage of the troubles in Syria to barter their support now to one and now to another, so as to secure their own position and to gain Jewish independence. The result was the Hasmonean rule, which continued down to the Roman annexation of Palestine. The Maccabean family was a priestly house, though not in the high-priestly line. The successors of Judas nevertheless assumed the high priesthood, and later took the title of king, thus combining in a single person these two offices, save for a period when the civil office was held by a woman.

It was this period which saw the rise of the Jewish parties known as Pharisees and Sadducees. Other Jewish sects seem also to have been born in the second century B.C. According to Josephus the Essenes already existed in the middle of that century. By many writers the sect of the DEAD SEA SCROLLS is identified with the Essenes. Whether or not this identification is allowed, it is commonly believed that the sect of the Scrolls took its origin in some way from the troubles of the Maccabean age, though there is less agreement as to when the Teacher of Righteousness of that sect lived.

15. The Roman period. At the end of the second century there was much tension between the Pharisees and the Sadducees, and this continued into the first century, when, under Alexander Janneus, the Pharisees were ranged in opposition to the king, whose enemies at one point invoked the aid of Demetrius III against him. Arising from this, a large number of the Pharisees were crucified by Janneus. In the middle of the first century, however, Palestine became involved in the Roman civil wars, and the army of Pompey came to Jerusalem and brought the Jews under Roman control. Soon Herod, an Idumean, skilfully exploited the dissensions in the Hasmonean family, and secured from Rome the title of king, though he had yet to win his kingdom, which was, of course, still subject to Rome. He succeeded in winning his kingdom, and by his adroitness in dealing with the ever-changing situation arising from the civil wars among the Romans, he continued to hold the kingdom until his death in 4 B.C. In some ways he served the Jews well, though he was never loved by them and was always regarded as an alien. His ruthless cruelty was experienced by members of his own family, as well as by large numbers of his subjects, and despite the outer splendor of his reign and the building achievements which he could claim, including the undertaking of the rebuilding of the temple, he won no gratitude. *See* HEROD [FAMILY].

After his death his kingdom was divided among members of his family; Archelaus secured the rule of Judea for a few years, until he was displaced and Judea was brought under direct Roman rule. The other parts of Herod's kingdom continued to be ruled by members of the Herodian house, though still with responsibility to Rome. Again deep divisions developed among the Jews. Some cherished bitter hostility to the Romans and to all who supported them, while others sought by co-operation with Rome to further Jewish interests—and their own at the same time. The Roman rulers rarely understood the Jewish character, and were themselves of varying ability and worth. The situation therefore went from bad to worse, until in A.D. 66 the Jewish Revolt broke out. The course of the war is recounted by Josephus in *The Jewish War*. It was marked by fanaticism and bitter excesses even among those who fought the Romans, and despite the heroism of the rebels and the religious loyalty that made them observe the sabbath and maintain the sacrifices of the temple even when in the direst straits, the issue was the destruction of Jerusalem and the temple in A.D. 70. For a time the Roman armies were commanded by Vespasian, until he was called to wear the purple. The final capture of Jerusalem was made by his son Titus (*see* TITUS, EMPEROR). Among the treasures carried away by Titus, and displayed at his triumph, were the table of shewbread from the temple, the golden candlestick, and a roll of the Law. The temple itself was destroyed completely, and has never been rebuilt. It was not destroyed, however, until its work was complete. It symbolized the religion of Israel, with its high achievement, its pure monotheism, its noble prophetic teaching, and its deep personal piety. Its sacrifices might pass, as the author of the Letter to the Hebrews says, for they had been superseded by the sacrifice of enduring efficacy at Calvary. But the table, the candlestick, and the Law were fittingly carried to Rome, to symbolize the dissemination in the wider world of the faith that had sprung from Judaism—the faith whose supreme sacrament centers in a table, whose Lord is the light of the world, and whose roots are so firmly embedded in Israel's history that without the Old Covenant it cannot be fully understood.

Bibliography. J. W. Rothstein, *Juden und Samaritaner*, BWAT, vol. 3 (1908). E. Schürer, *Geschichte des jüdischen Volkes im Zeitalter Jesu Christi* (3 vols.; 4th ed., 1901-9). R. Kittel, *Geschichte des Volkes Israel,* I (6th ed., 1923); II (6th ed., 1925); III (1927-29). A. Schlatter, *Geschichte Israels von Alexander dem Grossen bis Hadrian* (3rd ed., 1925). W. Kolbe, *Beiträge zur syrischen und jüdischen Geschichte,* BWANT, N.F. 10 (1926). H. H. Schaeder, *Esra der Schreiber* (1930). A. Jirku, *Geschichte des Volkes Israel* (1931). E. Meyer, *Geschichte des Altertums,* II (2 vols.; 2nd ed., 1928-31). A. T. Olmstead, *History of Palestine and Syria to the Macedonian Conquest* (1931). W. F. Albright, *The Archaeology of Palestine and the Bible* (1932). A. Lods, *Israel from Its Beginnings to the Middle of the Eighth Century* (English trans. S. H. Hooke; 1932). W. O. E. Oesterley and T. H. Robinson, *A History of Israel* (2 vols.; 1932). E. Bickermann, *Der Gott der Makkabäer. Untersuchungen über Sinn und Ursprung der makkabäischen Erhebung* (1937). A. Lods, *The Prophets and the Rise of Judaism* (English trans. S. H. Hooke; 1937). A. H. M. Jones, *The Herods of Judea* (1938). E. F. Weidner, "Jojachin, König von Juda, in babylonischen Keilschrifttexten," *Mélanges syriens,* II (1939), 923 ff. W. F. Albright, *The Archaeology of Palestine* (1949). T. J. Meek, *Hebrew Origins* (2nd ed., 1950). H. H. Rowley, *From Joseph to Joshua* (1950); "Recent Discovery and the Patriarchal Age," *The Servant of the Lord* (1952), pp. 217 ff; also "The Chronological Order of Ezra and Nehemiah," pp. 131 ff. F.-M. Abel, *Histoire de la Palestine depuis la conquête d'Alexandre jusqu'à* *l'invasion arabe* (2 vols.; 1952). W. F. Albright, *The Biblical Period* (1952). A. Alt, *Kleine Schriften zur Geschichte des Volkes Israel* (2 vols.; 1953). J. B. Pritchard, ed., *ANET* (2nd ed., 1955). G. Ricciotti, *The History of Israel* (trans. C. della Penta and R. T. A. Murphy; 2 vols.; 1955). H. H. Rowley, "Sanballat and the Samaritan Temple," *Bulletin of the John Rylands Library*, XXXVIII (1955-56), 166 ff. D. J. Wiseman, *Chronicles of Chaldaean Kings* (1956). M. F. Unger, *Israel and the Aramaeans of Damascus* (1957). G. E. Wright, *Biblical Archaeology* (1957). M. Noth, *Gesammelte Studien zum AT* (1957); *Die Welt des ATs* (3rd ed., 1957); *History of Israel* (1958). J. Bright, *History of Israel* (1959).

Bible atlases: P. Lemaire and D. Baldi, *Atlante Storico della Bibbia* (1955). L. H. Grollenberg, *Atlas of the Bible* (trans. and ed. J. M. H. Reid and H. H. Rowley; 1956). E. G. Kraeling, *Rand McNally Bible Atlas* (1956). G. E. Wright and F. V. Filson, *The Westminster Historical Atlas to the Bible* (2nd ed., 1956).

H. H. Rowley

ISRAEL, KINGDOM OF.

See Israel, History of, §§ 7-8.

ISRAEL, NAMES AND ASSOCIATIONS OF.

1. The name of Jacob the patriarch. In Gen. 32:22 ff we are told about Elohim's wrestling with Jacob, and that because of this the latter's name was changed and he should be called Israel. This story contains an etymology of the name, what we may call a popular etymology, according to which the meaning of the name would be "El wrestles." It is commonly admitted that this interpretation cannot be said to give the real meaning of the name, and, of course, it is impossible to present decisive arguments for any etymology of a name like Israel. However, the most probable interpretation is that which connects the name Israel with the root *išr/'šr*, "reliable," "successful," "happy." It may be mentioned that in cuneiform texts there are names almost identical: *Išrē-il, Ašri-ilišu.* It seems hard to assume that such names should be explained in another way than Israel. If Israel is etymologically connected with Ašer, we are faced with the possibility that Israel is originally connected with the ancient Canaanite gods of fertility, Ašer being the male counterpart of Ašera, which is one name of the Canaanite goddess of fertility. In that case, the name Israel refers to the Canaanite substratum of OT religion, and Jacob's change of name may then refer to a merging of the tribes entering from the E with a Canaanite religious community. The "Rock of Israel" (Gen. 49:24) has been referred to in this connection as being an allusion to the cult stone (massebah) and parallel to the "Mighty One of Jacob," the latter expression referring to the bull as the symbol of the god of fertility.

2. A designation of the people of Israel as a whole. According to the OT traditions of the growth of the Israelite nation, the patriarchs were the earliest ancestors of the people. In the scholarly discussion of these figures several theories have been advocated. According to one theory, they were real historical persons; according to another they are to be regarded as cult heroes. Since the traditions of the patriarchs were created much later than the time they reflect, they have received many features from later periods, and they can by no means be considered real historical sources. In all probability they reflect early migrations of various ethnic groups, a number of which later merged with one another. As a matter of fact, they have been associated with cult centers, Abraham with Hebron, Isaac with Beer-sheba, and Jacob with Bethel.

In the traditions about the sojourn in Egypt and the Exodus from there, the wandering through the desert and entering into Canaan under Joshua, the name of "Israel," or more commonly the "children of Israel," is used about the Israelite people as a whole, and accordingly the twelve tribes of Israel all appear in these traditions. It is true, in several passages the term "Hebrews" is used. In the sections of the OT dealing with the people after the invasion of Canaan, "Israel" is used as a designation of the people as a whole (Deuteronomy–Samuel), consisting of twelve tribes. If we compare various lists of the twelve tribes, a few variations are found. In Gen. 49 we encounter the twelve sons of Jacob, whereas in Deut. 33 the tribe of Simeon is omitted and the tribe of Joseph is divided into two tribes, Ephraim and Manasseh. The system of the twelve tribes is now admitted to have originated in Palestine, and accordingly, this system as applied to earlier periods is not historical. The traditions about the early periods may be said to be a schematic outline of historical events during many centuries.

3. A designation of the inhabitants of the N kingdom. In passages like II Sam. 2:9, 17; 3:10; 19:41; 20:1; I Kings 12:16, the name Israel is used about the N tribes, whose center is Ephraim. The mountain of Israel is found in Josh. 11:16, 21. After the division of the United Kingdom into two, Israel is the name of the N kingdom (I Kings 14:19, etc.) Other expressions are, e.g., the "house of Israel" (I Kings 12:21; Hos. 5;1; Amos 5:1; Mic. 1:5; etc.).

4. A designation of the inhabitants of the S kingdom. In some passages Israel is used about the S kingdom (e.g., Isa. 5:7; Mic. 3:1). This is particularly the case after the fall of the N kingdom.

5. A designation of a cult community. The name Israel has come into use as a designation of the Israelite people, and from an early time particularly of the N tribes, in Canaan. In this development Canaanite elements played an important role, several of the Israelite tribes being Canaanite or other ethnic groups. But when the Israelite nation became conscious of its national characteristics, it was the belief in the national god Yahweh that was the basis of the Israelite nation. Because of this belief not only was the name Israel used as a designation of the cult unity bound up with the worship of Yahweh, but also the figure of Israel became a religious ideal (see, e.g., Isa. 1:3; 4:2; 49:3). This religious basis of the national consciousness is particularly to be observed in the idea of the people of Israel as the people chosen by Yahweh, and in the idea of the covenant. These ideas are the chief recurrent theme in the whole OT conception of the history of the Israelite people. Since the idea of the Israelite people as Yahweh's chosen people was especially connected with the temple of Jerusalem onward from the period when that temple became the only legitimate cult place, these religious ideas have remained the basis of the national consciousness of the Jews through the ages. As an example it may be mentioned that the name Israel was used by the Maccabeans to designate the kingdom of the Jews, and this is the case with the Jewish kingdom in Palestine of the present day.

Bibliography. G. A. Danell, *Studies in the Name of Israel in the OT* (1946), with further references; I. Engnell, review of Danell's book in *Symbolae Biblicae Upsalienses,* no. 7 (1946).

A. HALDAR

ISRAEL, RELIGION OF. *See* HEBREW RELIGION.

ISRAEL, SOCIAL AND ECONOMIC DEVELOPMENT OF. The people of Israel, dwelling in Palestine, experienced a long and complex social and economic development, extending through several stages of cultural evolution.

1. The nomadic stage. Israel, like the other Semitic peoples of antiquity, had its origins in the Arabian Desert, particularly in its N stretches. Contrary to the nationalized, biblical tradition, Israel emerged from the desert and established itself in Palestine, not as a single, united people, but rather as separate, independent, or, at the most, loosely federated clans or tribes. During this pre-Palestine, desert period the Israelites lived as nomads, the only way of life which the desert permits. Their wealth consisted primarily of sheep and goats. The problem of food supply for themselves and their animals confronted them constantly. *See* NOMADISM.

Their religious belief and practice were correspondingly primitive. Their gods they conceived of as supernatural powers responsible for their existence, both as individuals and as clan or tribal groups, and whose immediate, divine task was therefore to provide for their physical needs, to make both their women and their animals fertile, to guarantee their safety during their desert wanderings, and to give them victory over all enemies. Each clan or tribe, a complete social unit unto itself in every respect, had its own particular deity, a god of distinctly local character, thought to dwell in some one, single spot—a mountain perhaps, or a life-giving spring of water. *See* HEBREW RELIGION.

These ancient Semitic, desert clans, for the most part at least, practiced beena MARRIAGE, and accordingly traced kinship through the mothers alone. Endogamy was strictly prohibited. The women of a clan received visits, either momentary or prolonged, from men of other clans. The offspring of such matings belonged to the clan of the mother. Fatherhood, frequently—perhaps usually—unknown, was inconsequential. Many scholars maintain that the more primitive Semitic society was patriarchal, or that it also had fratriarchal and matriarchal elements, being primarily patriarchal.

Within the clan absolute social equality and democracy prevailed. Everyone was equal in every respect. Clan action was initiated only upon the decision of its male members, or at least of the oldest, most experienced, and presumably therefore wisest, among them—in other words, the elders. Right and wrong were determined primarily by custom and tradition. Those male members recognized as the most authoritative custodians of time-honored customs and traditions functioned as judges. Conformity to ancient custom and tradition was the norm in rendering judgment. But the principle of absolute democracy withheld from these so-called judges, or even from the clan itself, authority to enforce their judgments. Public opinion within the clan alone exercised this power. Any member of the clan might, if he chose, disregard the decision of the judges. But in such case public opinion might expel him from the clan, deprive him of all privileges of membership therein, including protection by both clan deity and kinsmen, and force him out into solitary and exceedingly precarious desert existence (cf. Gen. 4: 14).

2. The agricultural stage. The country of Palestine divides naturally into two distinct sections. An imaginary, E-W line just N of Jerusalem would effectively mark this division. N of this line the country is, as a whole, fertile and well watered. Accordingly agriculture has always been the basic occupation of its population. S of this line the country is, in the main, poorly watered, sterile, and in places even barren. Therefore, its dominant occupation in biblical times was sheep-raising.

This S section was conquered and settled by the clans of Judah *ca.* the middle of the thirteenth century B.C. They entered from the S, led by the Levite Moses. Firmly established in this southernmost section of Palestine, their way of life changed but little from what it had been of old. David it was who finally welded these clans into the single tribe of Judah, and this tribe, in turn, through integration with other seminomadic clans and tribes in the far S, into the kingdom of Judah in its initial stage, with himself functioning as king.

N of this imaginary line conditions differed radically, both because of the relative fertility of this section and its consequent ability to support a larger and more densely settled population and because of earlier entrance of Israelites into it. Here Israelites first established themselves permanently in the district N of the Valley of Jezreel *ca.* 1400. The occupation of the entire N section was completed by other nomadic or seminomadic Israelites certainly not later than 1300. Not impossibly with some of these the transition from clan to tribal organization may have begun prior to entrance into the land. On the other hand, the tribe of Manasseh certainly evolved within Palestine through the fusion, following the protracted and devastating forays of marauding Midianite nomads and their ultimate conquest by Gideon, of the decimated clans of Machir, Jair, and Abiezer, and quite probably of remnants of other neighboring clans as well. Moreover, that the nomadic spirit of democracy still persisted in the thought and culture of these clans is evidenced by Gideon's absolute refusal to accept the proffered kingship (Judg. 8:22-23). Obviously the very concept of royalty, with its absolute authority, particularly over kinsmen, was abhorrent to him.

This second group of invading Israelite clans and tribes seem to have established themselves at first in the more mountainous section of Central Palestine, bordering the Jordan Valley. Confrontation by a common enemy, the native Canaanites, and also the consciousness of a common, desert background, culture, and religion, tended to draw these N Israelite clans and tribes together upon occasion into loose, intertribal federation. Such was the case at the decisive Battle of Taanach (Judg. 4–5). However, even in this battle only those tribes immediately contiguous to the Valley of Jezreel, and therefore directly endangered by the federation against them of Canaanite city-states within the Valley, participated. This victory established definitive Israelite domination of this entire N section of the country.

Now firmly settled in the land, these N Israelite clans and tribes quickly absorbed much of the Canaanite way of life, its agricultural techniques and institutions, its language, and its religion. Eventually, however, with the progressive integration of the surviving Canaanite population with their Israelite conquerors, and with this the termination of the earlier, common, Canaanite danger, the impulse to intertribal federation gradually weakened. The tribes N of the Valley of Jezreel and likewise, to some extent at least, those E of the Jordan, and also the tribe of Dan to the SW, along the seacoast, relaxed in considerable measure their sense of intertribal obligation and tended to go each its own way. In consequence the tribes of Central Palestine, Ephraim, Manasseh, and Benjamin, came to constitute a sort of tribal federation, still rather loose, but decidedly more closely integrated than anything previously existent among the N Israelites. In the main, especially for these tribes of Central Palestine, this was a period of steadily expanding life and culture, growing prosperity, sense of security, and belonging to the land.

However, the advent of the PHILISTINES, early in the twelfth century, changed all this. Migrating from Crete, they eventually established themselves along the S Palestinian coastland. They contributed to West Asiatic culture knowledge of the production of iron and the fabrication of iron weapons and tools. Eventually they undertook to expand their territory. Early in the twelfth century the whole of Central Palestine, from the N border of Benjamin to the N edge of the Valley of Jezreel, had come under repressive Philistine domination.

However, a half century or so later the prophet Samuel, realizing that a leader and deliverer would hardly arise either from Ephraim, his own tribe, or from equally crushed and dispirited Manasseh, turned his gaze farther afield, to the kindred and still unconquered tribe of Benjamin. He understood that to achieve this goal a much closer and more effective and stable organization than the former, loose, intertribal federation was imperative. Accordingly, when chance brought to him the Benjaminite Saul, and this too at a most auspicious moment, the New Year's Day, Samuel, convinced that Yahweh had chosen this man and sent him to him for a purpose, anointed Saul as king (I Sam. 9:1–10:1)—king over a united Israel, but a united Israel which, for the moment, consisted, and that merely in theory and hope, of only Benjamin and the remnant of conquered Ephraim and Manasseh. Thus Israel became a monarchy.

Saul's entire reign was devoted to unremitting but fruitless warfare against the Philistines. The failure of the Ephraimites and Manassites to rally to him compelled him to operate almost entirely on the defensive. Small wonder that he failed completely in the task Samuel had laid upon him. With his death Benjamin too came completely under Philistine domination.

David, Saul's successor, was a man of extraordinary ability. Operating primarily from his assured position as king of Judah and only secondarily from that of being Saul's son-in-law—and therefore, in conformity with one rule of succession to the kingship current among Western Semites in that relatively early day, also king of Benjamin and the N tribes—David captured the hitherto impregnable Canaanite city-state, Jerusalem. Through Jerusalem passed the all-important trade route leading upward from South Arabia, through Ezion-geber, at the N tip of the Gulf of Aqabah, then through the lower Arabah, Judah, Israel, and onward to Tyre. Now in complete control of this one, indispensable avenue of communication between N and S, David joined the two kingdoms of Judah and Israel into the so-called United Kingdom, and strengthened this union by enforcing his claim to Michal, Saul's daughter, as his wife, and thereby his right of succession to Saul as king of Israel (II Sam. 3:12-16). The Philistines were reduced to vassalage. And, taking advantage of the contemporary low ebb of power of the surrounding nations, Egypt, the Hittites, Assyria, and Babylonia, David established an Israelite empire, which extended from Ezion-geber northward to Kadesh on the Orontes, and from the Mediterranean coast as far N as Mount Carmel and thence from the Lebanon Mountains eastward to the Great Desert. Naturally within this United Kingdom of Israel, under David's able and aggressive leadership, his own tribe, Judah, was dominant.

3. The international-commercial stage. Shortly before this time, the final decade of the eleventh century, Tyre had become the commercial metropolis of the world. The new united Israel was Tyre's immediate neighbor, linked to it directly by the trade route from Ezion-geber through Jerusalem. Relations of friendship and alliance were quickly established. Tyrian merchants began to frequent Israel, bartering the commodities of foreign lands for Israel's products. The establishment of the Davidic empire inaugurated a period of relative peace for all Western Asia, which endured for well over a half century. The people of Palestine could now, as never before, undisturbedly carry on their normal occupations. Now the Israelite farmers of the N began to raise crops far in excess of local needs. This surplus they could dispose of to these Phoenician merchants. Steadily this process expanded. Foreign commodities became increasingly plenteous, and with this slowly but surely the standard of living rose. In due time a merchant class evolved. Their activities expanded steadily, and their wealth and influence increased correspondingly. More and more they centered their transactions, and with this their residence, in the cities, where they could operate upon an ever widening and more remunerative scale. They built luxurious homes and acquired servants and slaves. They traveled about in horse-drawn chariots, carrying on their manifold enterprises. Their women and children were garbed in foreign textures, and foreign commodities to an ever-increasing extent satisfied their daily needs. The cities grew in size, wealth, and economic power, and among them especially Jerusalem, the capital. Class distinctions gradually evolved, and a city-dwelling aristocracy, consisting in the main of court personnel, military dignitaries, government officials, and wealthy merchants, soon asserted itself, which contrasted strikingly with the mass of the people, the peasants of the N and the shepherds and small farmers of the S. As might be expected, the agricultural N, having far more to barter, advanced further and more rapidly in this economic and attendant cultural evolution than did the pastoral S.

This program, inaugurated by David, was greatly expanded by his very able son and successor, Solomon. Relations with Tyre were drawn closer, while at the same time Israel inaugurated direct commercial contacts with neighboring nations. Traffic in horses and chariots was cultivated particularly (I Kings 10:14-29). The mineral resources of the country, and especially the copper mines in the Arabah, were exploited extensively, in the main by slave labor. And Solomon even developed Ezion-geber as a seaport and from there with his own fleet began to exploit the potentially rich commerce of the Red Sea and the Indian Ocean (I Kings 9:26-28). Steadily the wealth of the nation grew; its international role expanded; and its way of life, its social organization, and its culture were transformed, particularly for its urban population. Likewise during this period, largely in response to the demands of empire administration and the promotion of international commerce, scribal activity increased, and Hebrew literature had its beginnings.

Quite naturally the stronghold of this new, evolving Israelite culture was Jerusalem, the capital. Other cities, particularly in the agricultural N, throve and underwent corresponding social and cultural transformation, but in far less degree than Jerusalem. And equally naturally, a decided division and more or less latent antagonism in cultural and religious outlook and practice sprang up between the progressive and class-conscious city-dwellers, particularly those of Jerusalem, and the rural population, the conservative-minded farmers of the N and the decidedly reactionary shepherds of the S.

With the death of Solomon the Israelite empire dissolved, and also the United Kingdom resolved itself into its two component parts, the agricultural N and the predominantly pastoral S, organized thenceforth as two distinct kingdoms, Israel and Judah. At times a state of hostility—of varying intensity, however—kept the two nations apart. But, in the main, the more or less conscious realization of joint dependence upon a common source of self-sufficiency—viz., undisturbed control of the trade route from Ezion-geber to Tyre—tended to maintain peaceful, and occasionally even co-operative, relations between them, to link both of them together to Tyre, and likewise to bring both into natural competition with and active hostility to Aram.

Immediately following the division of the kingdom and the resultant termination of international contacts, Israel, the Northern Kingdom, reverted to its earlier agricultural economy. Under Ahab, however, and again apparently under Jeroboam II, mediated by renewed, close, co-operative relations with both Judah and Tyre, international commerce flourished anew, and urban life, with its attendant social class distinctions, expanded greatly, especially in the thriving N. It was in large measure these circumstances, and particularly those of social and economic character, such as the steady increase in wealth and power of the rich, their luxurious, self-indulgent living, their dishonest business practices and the attendant, steadily expanding oppression and enslavement of the poor, which seemed to contravene in every way the democratic manner of life instituted by Yahweh for his people and accepted by them as a basic condition of their covenant relationship with him, which summoned to action the two shepherd-prophets, Elijah in the reign of Ahab, and Amos in the reign of Jeroboam II.

In Judah conditions remained much as they had been. If anything, the contrast between Jerusalem, with its distinctly urban cultural and social stratification, and Judah proper, with its rural, predominantly pastoral population—the so-called *'am ha'areṣ*, "people of the land" (cf. II Kings 11:14, 18-20)—became even more clearly defined. After this general pattern economic, social, and cultural conditions persisted, in Israel until its final overthrow by the Assyrians in 721, and likewise in Judah until its conquest by the Babylonians in 586.

4. The postexilic period. The Babylonian conqueror, Nebuchadnezzar, captured, laid in ruins, and carried off to exile in distant Babylonia large sections of the population, not only of Jerusalem (II Kings 24:11-16; 25:22), but also of all the other fortified cities of Judah. With this, urban life and its attendant economic and social circumstances and activities came to a sudden and complete end. Only the lower social strata, in large measure the rural population, remained resident in the land. Farming and grazing became again the dominant occupations, and the general culture of the Judean community reverted very largely to the agricultural level, with the attendant revival of the long-outgrown agricultural way of life and many of its distinctive institutions. During the early portion of this exilic period life for these Judean farmers in their native land seems to have been difficult indeed. Gradually, however, despite occasional poor crops, the economy of the people seems to have become satisfactorily stabilized, and some, and perhaps even many, to have prospered sufficiently for them to dwell in ceiled houses and even to seem economically capable of rebuilding the temple (Hag. 1:2-11). During this seventy-year period, throughout which the temple lay in ruins (586-516), these Judean farmers seem to have, quite naturally, expanded the role of the SYNAGOGUE as the center of local religious observance, and in such measure that it apparently satisfied all their needs of worship, with the result that their initial response to Haggai's plea that they rebuild the temple was apparently one of indifference at the very least.

The message of that exalted prophet Deutero-Isaiah (*see* ISAIAH) plainly influenced the thought and program of this Judean community far more than it did those of the Babylonian Jewish exiles, to whom it was primarily directed. It proclaimed the absolute unity and universal character and authority of Yahweh, Israel's native deity, as the one, sole God of the world, the unity of the world itself and of mankind therein in conformity with the divine plan, the impending realization of this world unity through the establishment of a world empire by Cyrus the Persian, chosen for this service by Yahweh and destined by him to be the world king, his messiah (Isa. 45:1). It proclaimed further that Israel was no longer a political entity, a nation, but was rather a people, Yahweh's people, chosen by him to be his servant, the agent of his purposed salvation for all mankind, and for the discharge of this service destined to be restored by Cyrus from exile in Babylonia to the cherished homeland.

The closing years of the Babylonian exile found the Jewish community of Palestine divided into two distinct parties, which may aptly be termed the nationalists and the universalists. Both parties, responding in this one respect to Deutero-Isaiah's message, were definitely universalistic in principle and program. The nationalists cherished the eager hope for regained Jewish political independence and the reestablishment of the ancient Judean kingdom under a line of kings of the divinely chosen, ever-enduring Davidic dynasty. The suicide of Cambyses in 522 B.C., and with this the sudden collapse of the short-lived dynasty of Cyrus, coupled with the attendant chaos and the seemingly impending collapse of the Persian Empire, encouraged these nationalists in their hopes and plans. They readily accepted Deutero-Isaiah's thought of a divinely purposed world empire, but, rejecting a portion of the prophet's full message, held that Yahweh, truly the one, universal God, but nevertheless Israel's own god primarily, could never have intended that any people other than Israel should permanently administer this world empire, nor any dynasty other than that of David rule over it eternally. Moreover, the time was ripe, so they believed, for the achievement of their program. The result was the altogether futile rebellion of Zerubbabel in 520-519 (Hag. 2:20-23; Zech. 4:6-7*a*).

With the collapse of the Zerubbabel rebellion the universalists came to the fore. This party apparently accepted the Deutero-Isaianic message and program practically *in toto*. With the aid of the Persian government the second temple was erected and was formally dedicated upon the New Year's Day of 516. This was a significant moment indeed. Conforming to the basic theme of Deutero-Isaiah's message, that Yahweh had chosen Israel, not at all to be a nation, ruled by a king of the Davidic line, but rather to be his people, his servant, the agent of his salvation of all mankind, these universalists now transformed the former Jewish nation into a people, a religious people, a theocracy, under the meaningful name *q^ehal Yahweh*, the "community of Yahweh," a community whose true and sole king was Yahweh himself, and whose natural, earthly representative and spokesman was the chief priest of the new temple. Furthermore, accepting, apparently unconditionally, the role of Israel as Yahweh's servant, the agent of his purposed world salvation, these universalists inaugurated an active program of proselytism, which apparently won many converts to Judaism and admission into the "community of Yahweh." This program continued in effect so long as this second temple stood and the universalist party remained dominant. This was, however, only thirty years.

It came to a sudden and catastrophic end through a second attempt at rebellion from Persia by the nationalists at the death of Darius I late in 486. This rebellion was crushed by Xerxes, Darius I's successor, quickly and ruthlessly by permitting and encouraging Judah's immediate and bitterly hostile neighbors, Edom, Moab, Ammon, and the Philistines, to invade the country. They encountered practically no resistance from the nationalists, who relied entirely upon Yahweh's presumptive promise to himself subdue all nations beneath them (Deut. 20:10-20) and thus establish the destined Jewish world empire. The country was ravaged, Jerusalem was taken, and its walls and gates were destroyed. The second temple was burned to the ground. Many of the people were massacred pitilessly, while others, taken captive, were sold, in the slave markets of Tyre and Gaza, unto the farthest corners of the then known world (Joel 3:1-8—H 4:1-8). The Jewish community of Judea was left but a tiny, pitiful remnant of its former self (Neh. 1:2-3).

With the return, in 458, from Babylonian exile of Ezra and his band and the erection by him of the third temple, with Persian authorization and support, conditions within the Jewish community of Palestine became slowly but steadily stable once again. Urban life began to revive in Jerusalem. The rebuilding of the city walls by Nehemiah in 444 stimulated this trend greatly. That portion of the Jewish community in Babylonia of which Ezra and his followers were representative had faced a constant challenge. Accepting Jeremiah's message, especially as reinterpreted by their fellow Zadokite, Ezekiel, of Yahweh's purpose eventually to restore exiled Israel to its native land, take it again as his people, give it a new heart, purged of all impulse to sin (Ezek. 36:16-36), and enter into a new, and now an eternal, covenant with it (Jer. 24:4-7; 31:30-33), this community was faced with a perplexing problem, how to resist assimilation and preserve its Jewish identity in a foreign land, amid a strange people, and under the compulsions of a variant and, in many respects, superior culture, so that they might be ready for the day of fulfilment of Yahweh's announced purpose with them. The solution of this problem was a program of strict Jewish separatism and particularism, the complete antithesis of the program of the universalist party of the Jewish community of Palestine, and likewise in considerable measure of that of the nationalists.

This Babylonian program of Jewish particularism and separatism Ezra sought quite naturally to impose upon the Jewish community of Palestine. Proselytism to Judaism was halted completely, and intermarriage with foreigners was prohibited. To the former universalist doctrine of the religious peoplehood of Israel, as opposed to political nationhood, Ezra and his followers subscribed fully. But for them this was an exclusive, not an inclusive, Jewish peoplehood. Israel was a people apart from all the other peoples of the world, Yahweh's people and his alone. Both Ezra and Nehemiah still designated the Jewish people by the now traditional name *qᵉhal Yahweh,* the "community of Yahweh" (Ezra 10:12, 14; Neh. 7:66; 8:17). However, by the close of the fifth century a new term, *'ᵃdat Yisra'el,* the "congregation of Israel," had supplanted the older term (cf. Exod. 12:3, 6, 47; II Chr. 5:6). The particularistic, almost racial implications of this term, especially when contrasted with its antecedent term, *qᵉhal Yahweh,* are unmistakable. As a further manifestation of the extreme particularism of the Ezranic movement and of the institutions it fostered, the penalty of excommunication, of "cutting off," of expulsion from the "congregation of Israel" for the transgression of those principles which safeguarded the Jewish integrity of this "congregation" and linked it in proper relationship with Yahweh, was instituted already in Ezra's day. And as a still further manifestation of the now dominant spirit of extreme particularism, the SAMARITANS and likewise the contemporary Jewish community of Egypt, both regarded as sprung from marriage with non-Jews, were regarded as not true Jews, and so were excluded from the "congregation of Israel."

With the erection of the third temple by Ezra, the entrenchment therein, after a prolonged struggle with the Levitical priests of the second temple, of the Zadokite or Aaronide priests as the dominant priestly functionaries (Ezek. 44:10-16), with their compilation, during the final quarter of the fifth century B.C., of the major stratum of the Priestly Code (*see* LAW [IN THE OT]), and with the adoption of a new, luni-solar calendar and the regulation of the festivals and other ritual occasions thereby, the character of official Judaism and the way of life of the Jewish people for the ensuing five centuries became fixed.

The Hasmonean kingdom came into being as the result of the desperate reaction of the Jewish people to the drastic transformation of their religion which Antiochus IV of Syria sought to impose upon them. The HASMONEANS were not of the Davidic line. Theirs was not at all the restored Judean kingdom, as this had been envisaged of old and of which memories still lingered in certain circles. The first Hasmonean rulers administered the kingdom in responsible and traditionally democratic manner. The later Hasmonean kings became more autocratic. Under them a court party and a resultant aristocracy, with attendant social class distinctions, tended to evolve once again. In no small measure the struggle between the two parties, the Sadducees and the Pharisees, reflected the resultant situation. Under Herod and his successors (*see* HEROD [FAMILY]) this process expanded notably. But this aristocracy represented always something foreign to the true, democratic spirit of the Jewish people, superimposed upon and more or less consciously resented by them. Throughout the Herodian era, until the destruction of the temple by the Romans in A.D. 70 and the end of the Jewish state, the lines of demarcation between this aristocracy and the people at large were clearly defined, with a resultant strengthening of the traditional spirit of democracy within the Jewish people.

Bibliography. W. R. Smith, *Kinship and Marriage in Early Arabia* (1885); J. Benzinger, *Hebräische Archäologie* (1894); W. R. Smith, *The Religion of the Semites* (3rd ed., 1927); A. Lods, *Israel* (1932); M. Burrows, *The Basis of Israelite Marriage* (1938); D. Jacobson, *The Social Background of the OT* (1942); E. Neufeld, *Ancient Hebrew Marriage Laws* (1944); J. Morgenstern, various studies in the Calendars of Ancient Israel in *HUCA,* I (1924), 13-78; III (1926), 77-107; X (1935), 1-148; XXI (1948), 365-496; *Vetus Testamentum,* V (1955), 34-76; "Beena Marriage (Matriarchate) in Ancient Israel," *ZAW,* N.F., VI (1929), 91-110; VIII (1931), 46-58; "Amos Studies, III," *HUCA,* XV (1940), 59-304 (also in book form, 1941); "Jerusalem—485 B.C., I," *HUCA,* XXVII (1956), 101-79; XXVIII (1958), 15-47.

J. MORGENSTERN

ISSACHAR ĭs'ə kər [יִשָּׂשכָר, *probably a verbal form: Yašaśkir,* May (God) show mercy; NT Ἰσαχάρ]. **1.** The ninth son of Jacob, and the eponymous ancestor of one of the twelve tribes. He was the first of those sons born later to Leah (Gen. 30:18, giving the folk etymology of the name, "man of reward"); for this reason in the enumerations of the descendants of Jacob he is always mentioned together with Zebulun and directly after the older full brothers (Gen. 35:23; 46:13; Exod. 1:3; cf. I Chr. 3:1).

The tribe of Issachar belongs with the tribe of Zebulun as Manasseh does with Ephraim. They are full-blooded members of the Leah group, but within it they are taken together as a unit. Their territories border each other, and on the border they have a common sanctuary on Mount Tabor. For this reason, too, a common saying is devoted to them in the Blessing of Moses (Deut. 33:18-19):

> Rejoice, Zebulun, in your going out;
> and Issachar, in your tents.
> They shall call peoples to their mountain;
> there they offer right sacrifices.

Obviously Tabor is meant, and the "peoples" are the related tribes. The most important thing is that they are named together at the beginning of the saying, and, indeed, in contrast to Gen. 30:18, etc., Zebulun before Issachar, exactly the same as with the two Joseph tribes at the close of the preceding Joseph saying, and, likewise, the younger before the older. The conclusion might be that, like Manasseh and Ephraim, Issachar and Zebulun developed separately only under the influence of their geographical setting, and that they were very much more closely associated in the first period of their occupation of the land.

Later each of them had its own destiny. And perhaps it can also be inferred from the arrangement of the names in the Blessing of Moses that Issachar, like Manasseh, once lost the priority. The Issachar statement of the Blessing of Jacob (Gen. 49:14-15), which is again preceded by the Zebulun statement, indicates this from quite a different point of view. There the tribe is compared to a strong ass which can no longer rise between its loaded saddle baskets (השפתים,

RSV "sheepfolds"). It is reproved for having become a serf in this pleasant land. This can only mean that in the territory described in Josh. 19:17-23 between Tabor and the S end of the Lake of Chinnereth in the N and the valley of the River Jalud in the S, where a series of Canaanite cities lay, the tribe sought and found contact with them, and this was condemned by the remaining tribes. Light may perhaps be thrown on Issachar's fate by one of the Amarna Letters which was newly published by Thureau-Dangin in 1922, in which the prince of Megiddo complains that management of the lands of the devastated city of Shunem (Solem) falls on him alone; he must bring in people from far away for the purpose. From this, Alt concluded that in the long run help could be procured and Pharaoh would reap his harvest only if Shunem were newly settled. Shunem lay in what was later Issacharite territory. Alt asked the not-unjustified question as to whether it were not possible that in just such a circumstance Issachar—or at least parts of the tribe—might have been taken into service by a ruler. In this way the biting scorn concerning the "slave at forced labor" (serf) who "bowed his shoulder to bear" (Gen. 49:15) finds, undoubtedly, a suitable explanation. In any case, Issachar at one time went through a crisis. Nevertheless, the tribe maintained itself as an equal in the twelve-tribe scheme.

Obviously Issachar was able to rehabilitate itself in the period before the kings. Perhaps this happened as a result of its brave action in the Battle of Deborah. Issachar is mentioned with praise in the Song of Deborah (Judg. 5:15, after Zebulun), while the parallel prose account does not speak of the tribe at all, although it refers to Zebulun and Naphtali. The tribe even furnished once the "proclaimer of the law" of the amphictyony in the person of the "minor judge" Tola (Judg. 10:1). In Solomon's arrangement of administrative districts Issachar's territory formed an independent province (I Kings 4:17). In Baasha the tribe furnished a king for the N kingdom (15:27). From then on, an Israelite royal residence, Jezreel, was situated in the territory of Issachar, probably because the property of the discredited royal family of Baasha had been confiscated as royal domain. Issachar was assigned and also filled the important role of bridge between the N and the S as long as the Plain of Jezreel was in Canaanite hands. It was, indeed, the only Israelite tribe to settle from the beginning in the territory which was long occupied by old Canaanite city-states. For this it paid at times with its independence, but it withstood the test.

In the later literature Issachar appears primarily in statistical contexts. In the lists of the Priestly Code it regularly has its place before Zebulun, always along with the Leah tribes (Num. 1:8, 28-29; 13:7; 26:23-25), sometimes immediately after Judah as the first (Num. 2:5; 7:18; 10:15); Num. 34:26 constitutes the only exception, insofar as Zebulun ranks ahead of Issachar and the list of the land-allotment commission is arranged geographically to some extent. In Deut. 27:12, Issachar stands with the tribes who bless. In Josh. 19, Issachar's lot is given after that of Zebulun. In the list of the Levite cities Issachar leads the third group, in one instance (Josh. 21:6 = I Chr. 6:62—H 6:47); and in the other instance, the E half-tribe of Manasseh is still put ahead of it (Josh. 21:28 = I Chr. 6:72—H 6:57), while Zebulun is shoved into the fourth group. In Ezek. 48:25 the tribe receives the third strip of land in the S—before Zebulun; and in vs. 33, the middle S gate—before Zebulun. In the lists of Chronicles, too, Issachar has priority (I Chr. 12:32—H 12:33, where Issachar even gets special praise; 27:18), as well as in the narrative portions (I Chr. 12:40—H 12:41; II Chr. 30:18). In the arrangement of I Chr. 4-7 the extended genealogy of Issachar may be found in 7:1-5, while that of Zebulun is missing. The NT does not deviate from the rule, in that it puts Issachar ahead of Zebulun in the list of the sealed (Rev. 7:7).

For the territory of Issachar, *see* TRIBES, TERRITORIES OF, § 4.

See also the bibliography under ASHER.

Bibliography. A. Alt, "Neues über Palästina aus dem Archiv Amenophis IV," *PJB,* XXV (1924), 22-44 = *Kleine Schriften,* III (1959), 158 ff.

2. Son of Obed-edom; a Levite gatekeeper at the time of David (I Chr. 26:5). K. ELLIGER

ISSHIAH ĭ shī'ə [ישיה, ישיהו, *perhaps* may Yahu forget (one's sin), *or* Yahu has caused (one) to forget (bereavement)]; KJV ISHIAH in I Chr. 7:3; JESIAH jĕ sī'ə in I Chr. 12:6; 23:20. **1.** A man of the tribe of Issachar (I Chr. 7:3).

2. One of David's Mighty Men (I Chr. 12:6).

3. A Levite, son of Uzziel (I Chr. 23:20; 24:25).

4. A Levite, chief of the family of Rehabiah (I Chr. 24:21), and accordingly descended from Moses (cf. 23:14-17).

Bibliography. M. Noth, *Die israelitischen Personennamen* (1928), pp. 28, 211. B. T. DAHLBERG

ISSHIJAH ĭ shī'jə [ישיה, may Yahu forget] (Ezra 10:31); KJV ISHIJAH. One of those forced by Ezra to give up their foreign wives. The name perhaps appears as Ἀσσιας in the parallel I Esd. 9:32.

ISSUE. KJV translation of זוב, מקור, αἱμοῤῥέω, and ῥύσις, all referring to a DISCHARGE as from a suppurating sore or wound; a bodily secretion, whether venereal or not.

ISSUE OF BLOOD. KJV translation of αἱμορροοῦσα (RSV HEMORRHAGE) in Matt. 9:20.

ISTALCURUS ĭs'təl kyŏŏr'əs [Ἰστάλκουρος]. According to I Esd. 8:40, the father of Uthai, one of the "sons of Bigvai" who returned from the Exile with Ezra "in the reign of Artaxerxes." But apparently "Uthai the son of Istalcurus" is a corruption of "Uthai and Zaccur" in the parallel Ezra 8:14. *See* ZACCUR 5. J. C. SWAIM

ISUAH. KJV alternate form of ISHVAH.

ISUI. KJV alternate form of ISHVI 1.

ITALIAN COHORT ĭ tăl'yən kō'hôrt [σπεῖρα Ἰταλική] (Acts 10:1). A unit of the Roman army. Inscriptions attest the presence of *Cohors II Italica* (*civium Romanorum voluntariorum*) at Caesarea in A.D. 69-157. Although there is no clear evidence to show that *Cohors II* or any other Italian cohort was present in Caesarea before 69, Luke probably had this cohort in mind. He would have understood that it was made up, for the most part, of troops mustered in Italy and possessing Roman citizenship, whether free-born or freedmen.

See also COHORT; AUGUSTAN COHORT; CORNELIUS.

Bibliography. T. R. S. Broughton, "The Roman Army," in F. J. Foakes-Jackson and K. Lake, eds., *The Beginnings of Christianity,* pt. I, vol. V (1933), pp. 427-45, note xxxiii. See especially pp. 441-43. F. D. GEALY

ITALY ĭt'ə lĭ [ἡ 'Ιταλία]. A long peninsula between the Tyrrhenian and Adriatic seas.

From the Alps in the N to the sea in the S, Italy has a length of some 700 miles, and its breadth is from 100 to 150 miles. The mountain chain of the Apennines forms the backbone of the peninsula. Fertile plains and valleys are to be found particularly on the W side. The largest river is the Tiber, which flows between Etruria and Latium. S of this is the extremely fertile Campania. The best harbors are at Naples and Genoa on the W, and at Brindisi, ancient Brundisium, on the E.

According to Antiochus of Syracuse, a historian of the fifth century B.C. quoted by Dionysius of Halicarnassus (I.12.35), Italy derived its name from a King Italos ('Ιταλός) who ruled in the thirteenth century B.C. in the extreme SW part or "toe" of the Italian boot. The name thus applied originally only to this region. It was gradually extended in its application northward until the Rubicon River, which flowed into the Adriatic N of Ariminum, was the N boundary between Roman Italy and Cisalpine Gaul (Appian *Civil Wars* II.35). In popular usage, indeed, Italy meant the entire land as far as the foot of the Alps (Polybius V.29).

Italy is mentioned in the NT in Acts 18:2; 27:1, 6; Heb. 13:24; while Acts 10:1 refers to the ITALIAN COHORT. Places in Italy which are mentioned in the NT include: FORUM OF APPIUS; PUTEOLI; RHEGIUM; ROME; THREE TAVERNS. *See also* ROMAN EMPIRE.

Bibliography. Philipp, Lackeit, and Scherling, "Italia," *Pauly-Wissowa,* Supplement III (1918), cols. 1246-1302. J. FINEGAN

ITCH [נתק] (Lev. 13:30; 14:54); KJV SCALL. One possibility of differential diagnosis where LEPROSY was suspected. A fourteen-day quarantine period sufficed to establish its identity. It may have been *alopecia areata,* which produces restricted patches of baldness; *tinea tonsurans* or *tinea sycosis* (varieties of ringworm). R. K. HARRISON

ITHAI ĭth'ī [אתי] (I Chr. 11:31). Son of Ribai of Gibeah of the Benjaminites; numbered among the Mighty Men of David known as the "Thirty." In the parallel catalogue he is called Ittai (*see* ITTAI 2; II Sam. 23:29).

ITHAMAR ĭth'ə mär [איתמר, *perhaps* island of palms]. A figure known only in P, Chronicles, and Ezra; the fourth of the sons of Aaron: Nadab, Abihu, Eleazar, Ithamar (Exod. 6:23; Num. 26:60; I Chr. 6:3; 24:1). These names interconnect various traditions concerning the priesthood (*see* PRIESTS AND LEVITES). After the Return, the problem of the constitution of the priesthood was resolved by ascribing to David the following arrangement: sixteen courses of priests of the descendants of Eleazar (Zadok reckoned as the son of Eleazar), eight courses of priests of the descendants of Ithamar (non-Zadokite priests; I Chr. 24:1-19). Postexilic tradition stated that four sons of Aaron were consecrated to the priestly office (Exod. 28:1; Num. 3:2-3; cf. Num. 20: 25-28). The rejection of Nadab and Abihu left Eleazar and Ithamar pre-eminent (Lev. 10; Num. 3:4; I Chr. 24:2). Eleazar became the chief figure through whom priestly descent was traced to Aaron. However, tradition concerning Ithamar asserted that in the wilderness he was the leader over all the Levites (Exod. 38:21), over the Gershonites (Num. 4:28), over the Merarites (vs. 33; 7:8). The house of Eli was descended from Ithamar, according to comparison of I Sam. 14:3; 22:9; I Chr. 24:3. A family of Ithamarite priests (who had become prominent in Babylonia) returned with Ezra (Ezra 8:2; I Esd. 8:29).

Bibliography. Westphal, "Aaron und die Aaroniden," *ZAW,* XXVI (1906), 222-25; T. Meek, "Aaronites and Zadokites," *AJSL,* XLV (1929), 158-60, 165; K. Möhlenbrink, "Die levitischen Überlieferungen des ATs," *ZAW,* LII (1934), 214-15, 217-19, 225; W. Rudolph, *Ezra und Nehemiah,* HAT (1949), pp. 79-81; R. Bowman, Exegesis of Ezra, *IB,* III (1954), 632. T. M. MAUCH

ITHIEL ĭth'ĭ əl [איתיאל, *probably* God is with me; *cf.* עמנואל]. **1.** An ancestor of the Benjaminite Sallu, who resided in Jerusalem after the Exile (Neh. 11:7).

2. One of two people in Prov. 30:1 to whom Agur addressed his words, the other being UCAL. M. NEWMAN

ITHLAH ĭth'lə [יתלה, a hanging (*or* lofty) place] (Josh. 19:42); KJV JETHLAH jĕth'lə. A village of the tribe of Dan. The site is unknown.

ITHMAH ĭth'mə [יתמה] (I Chr. 11:46). A Moabite whose name is included in the sixteen names added by the Chronicler to the catalogue of the Davidic Mighty Men known as the "Thirty."

ITHNAN ĭth'năn [יתנן] (Josh. 15:23). A city in the S of Judah, near Ziph. The name may be connected with ETHNAN, a descendant of Judah (I Chr. 4:7). Its site is unknown.

ITHRA ĭth'rə [יתרא]. The father of Amasa. He was married to David's sister Abigail (Abigal in II Sam. 17:25). According to II Sam. 17:25 he is called Ithra the Israelite; but a better reading is provided in I Chr. 2:17, where his name is given as Jether the Ishmaelite (cf. II Sam. 17:25 LXX^{A}; I Kings 2:5, 32). E. R. DALGLISH

ITHRAN ĭth'răn [יתרן; *cf. personal names* יתרא, יתר, אביתר, יתרו]. **1.** Son of clan chief Dishon; ancestor of a native Horite subclan in Edom (Gen. 36:26; I Chr. 1:41).

2. Son of Zophah, an Asherite (I Chr. 7:37).

ITHREAM ĭth'rĭ əm [יתרעם] (II Sam. 3:5; I Chr. 3:3). The sixth son of David; born of David's wife Eglah in Hebron.

ITHRITES ĭth'rīts [יִתְרִי, *perhaps* abundant *or* preeminent)]. A tribe or clan associated with KIRIATH-JEARIM (I Chr. 2:53). Two of David's Mighty Men were Ithrites (II Sam. 23:38; I Chr. 11:40).

ITTAH-KAZIN. KJV form of ETH-KAZIN.

ITTAI ĭt'ī [אִתַּי]. **1.** A devoted Philistine soldier, exiled from his native city of Gath, who with six hundred of his followers and their families accompanied David, despite the latter's magnanimous dissuasion, when the king fled from Jerusalem at the outbreak of Absalom's rebellion (II Sam. 15:19-22). Ittai shared the command of the forces of David with Joab and Abishai in the battle of the forest of Ephraim, when the rebellion of Absalom was effectively crushed (II Sam. 18:2 ff).

2. Son of Ribai of Gibeah of the Benjaminites; numbered among the Mighty Men of David known as the "Thirty" (II Sam. 23:29). In I Chr. 11:31 he is called Ithai.

E. R. DALGLISH

ITURAEA ĭt'yŏŏr ē'ə, —ŏŏr— ['Ιτουραῖοι *or* 'Ιτουραία(χώρα); *related to* יְטוּר; LXX Ιετουρ, Ιεττουρ]. A region NE of Galilee in the Anti-lebanon country settled by Arab people of Ishmaelite stock; included in the tetrarchy of Philip in Luke 3:1. The people known from the second century B.C. on as 'Ιτουραῖοι are undoubtedly the same tribe as the descendants of Ishmael's son Jetur (Gen. 25:15), referred to in I Chr. 5:19 as enemies of the tribes of Reuben, Gad, and Manasseh.

1. Location. Historical geographers have found it difficult to define the boundaries of Ituraea, since the references in ancient literature are often confusing and ambiguous. The Ituraeans of N Palestine are frequently mentioned by Greek and Roman writers, but it is not certain whether Ituraea and TRACHONITIS were wholly distinct districts or overlapped or were identical. Strabo (*Geography* XVI.2.16, 18) appears to locate the kingdom of the Ituraeans in Anti-lebanon in the Beqa' Valley, with its capital at Chalcis, carefully distinguishing it from the territory of the Trachons. Josephus certainly understands the Ituraeans to live N of Galilee, for he describes a campaign against them by Aristobulus I (105-104 B.C.), who annexed part of their land to Judea and forcibly circumcised their people (Antiq. XIII.xi.3). Originally the Ituraeans were a hill-country people living on the W slope of Anti-lebanon, perhaps in the larger Lebanon region toward Phoenicia. In the first century B.C. under the rulers Ptolemy and Lysanius the kingdom encompassed its largest area, extending westward to the sea, eastward to Damascus, and including the lands of Panias and Ulatha in the S down to and perhaps including the N borders of Galilee. After the death of Lysanius in 36 B.C., the kingdom may have been divided into several smaller districts (*see* § 2 *below*) of which one small tetrarchy was inherited by Herod Philip in 4 B.C. (Jos. Antiq. XVII.xi.4; Luke 3:1); some scholars, however, have believed that in NT times Ituraea and Trachonitis referred to the same territory.

2. History. To the Greeks and the Romans the Ituraeans were known as an uncivilized bandit people, designated both as Syrians and as Arabians, and renowned for their skill as bowmen, as references in Vergil, Lucan, Cicero, and Strabo attest. Their name as a people appears first in the second century B.C. Shortly before the beginning of Roman rule in Palestine, they formed a strong confederacy scattered through the entire Lebanon region, ruled by a certain Ptolemy, the son of Mennaeus (*ca.* 85-40 B.C.), "who possessed Massyas and the mountainous country of the Ituraeans" (Strabo *Geography* XVI.ii.10) and probably the surrounding territory. Pompey destroyed many of his fortified places in the Lebanon and probably reduced somewhat the extent of the empire. The tribal principality was inherited by his son Lysanius I, who is called "king of the Ituraeans" by Dio Cassius (XLIX.32). At his death in 36 B.C. at the instigation of Antony, large portions of the principality were given to Cleopatra (Plutarch *Antony* 36; cf. Jos. Antiq. XV.iv.1-2). Our knowledge of the subsequent history is confused by incomplete sources, but the former empire probably suffered division into at least four parts whose individual histories can be partially traced. In 20 B.C., Herod the Great received from Augustus the tetrarchy of Zenodorus, successor to Lysanius and vassal of Cleopatra. Part of this tetrarchy was inherited in 4 B.C. by Herod's son Philip (Luke 3:1) and ruled still later by the Agrippas after Philip's death in A.D. 34.

Another section of the principality which centered in the city of Abila, the "tetrarchy of Lysanius," was bestowed upon Herod Agrippa I in A.D. 41 by Claudius (cf. Jos. Antiq. XIX.v.1; XX.vii.1). This Lysanius has often been identified with the earlier ruler of the Ituraean kingdom (cf. Luke 3:1). However, an Abilene inscription (*Corpus Inscriptorium Graecarum* 4521) and an inscription at Heliopolis (4523) lead to the conclusion that Josephus is referring to a younger tetrarch of the same name who governed Abila before A.D. 37, thus supporting the chronological note of Luke.

In 38 the kingdom of a certain Soemus of the Ituraeans was seized by Caligula and later incorporated into the province of Syria. It probably consisted of the N territory below Heliopolis (Baalbek) to Laodicea (Dio Cassius LIX.12; Tac. Ann. XII.23), the tetrarchy of Arca.

A final section known as the kingdom of Chalcis, the center of the earlier principality, was given to a grandson of Herod the Great known as Herod of Chalcis, by Claudius in 41; it subsequently passed in 50 to Herod Agrippa II when it was enlarged to include all of Philip's tetrarchy, Abilene, and Arca, and incorporated at Agrippa's death *ca.* 93 into the province of Syria.

Bibliography. E. Schürer, *History of the Jewish People in the Time of Jesus Christ,* div. 1, vol. II (1900), 325-44 (with extensive bibliography); G. A. Smith, *Historical Geography of the Holy Land* (9th ed., 1902), pp. 544-47; Pauly-Wissowa, *Real-Encyklopädie,* vol. IX (1916), cols. 2377-80.

E. W. SAUNDERS

IVAH. KJV form of IVVAH.

IVORY [שֵׁן, tooth; ἐλεφάντινος]. Ivory was carved for inlaid decoration (*see* INLAY) on thrones (I Kings 10:18; II Chr. 9:17), beds (Amos 6:4), houses (I Kings 22:39; Ps. 45:8; Amos 3:15), and possibly on

Copyright: By permission of the Trustees of the late Sir Henry S. Wellcome

17. Ivory flasks, from Lachish

decks of ships (Ezek. 27:6 RSV). To the uses to which ivory was put, as attested by the biblical references, are now to be added others discovered in archaeological excavations in Palestine and the ancient Near East: boxes, gaming boards, cosmetic spoons and jars, figurines, amulets, and combs. Fig. ART 67.

One source for ivory used in carving is suggested by I Kings 10:22, where Solomon is said to have had a "fleet of ships of TARSHISH," which once every three years used to bring gold, silver, ivory, etc. In Ezek. 27:15, Rhodes (Hebrew Dedan) is mentioned in connection with "ivory tusks" (lit., "horns of ivory "). From sources outside the Bible it is known that large herds of elephants roamed N Syria in the second millennium B.C. In the fifteenth century B.C., Amen-em-heb, a soldier of Thut-mose III, tells of an elephant hunt in Ni on which 120 elephants were captured (*ANET* 241). Tiglath-pileser I, Assyrian king of the eleventh century, captured and slew elephants in the country of Harran (*ARAB* I, 247). In the ninth century, Ashurbanipal II reported the slaying of thirty elephants and collecting live specimens for a zoo (*ARAB* I, 519-20). Up until the middle of the ninth century, when the elephant may have become extinct there, tusks from elephants were available from N Syria. Pictorial representation of an elephant appears on the Black Obelisk of Shalmaneser III, where the tribute from Musri is represented. Fig. ELE 24.

In Amos 3:15; 6:4 ivory is mentioned as a token of wealth and luxury. This association of ivory with luxury items is confirmed by lists of booty taken from Palestine by Egyptian and Assyrian conquerors. Among the objects taken from Megiddo by Thutmose III in 1468 B.C. were: "6 carrying-chairs of that enemy, of ivory, ebony, and *carob*-wood, worked with

Courtesy of the Oriental Institute, the University of Chicago

18. A reconstruction drawing of an ivory inlay with a plant ornament; from Megiddo (1350-1150 B.C.)

Courtesy of the Oriental Institute, the University of Chicago

19. A single ivory comb with an ibex and a dog in relief; from Megiddo (1350-1150 B.C.)

gold" (*ANET* 237). Adad-nirari (810-783 B.C.) listed as tribute from Damascus, "a bed (inlaid) with ivory, a *nimattu*-couch mounted and inlaid with ivory" (*ANET* 282). Sennacherib's account of tribute paid him in 701 B.C. by Hezekiah listed: "couches (inlaid) with ivory, *nîmedu*-chairs (inlaid) with ivory" (*ANET* 288).

A great wealth of "Phoenician" ivory has come from excavations in Palestine and Syria, and specimens of carved work have been found scattered from Cyprus to Ur in Lower Mesopotamia. An inventory of these carved ivories (*see bibliography*) lists 1,271 separate objects. While ivory has been found at Tell

Courtesy of the Oriental Institute, the University of Chicago

20. A double ivory comb with lion and trees in relief; from the treasury in the palace of the princes at Megiddo (1350-1150 B.C.)

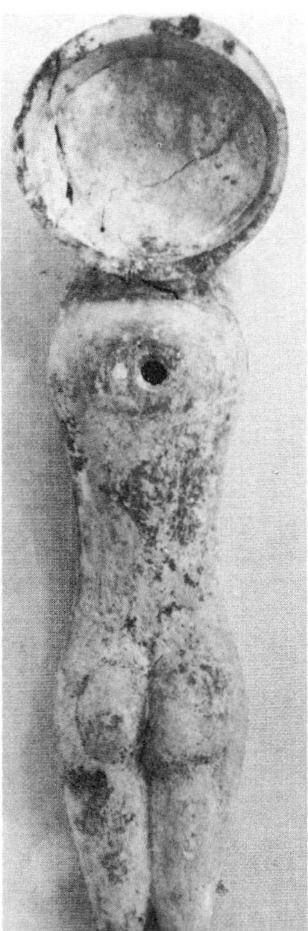

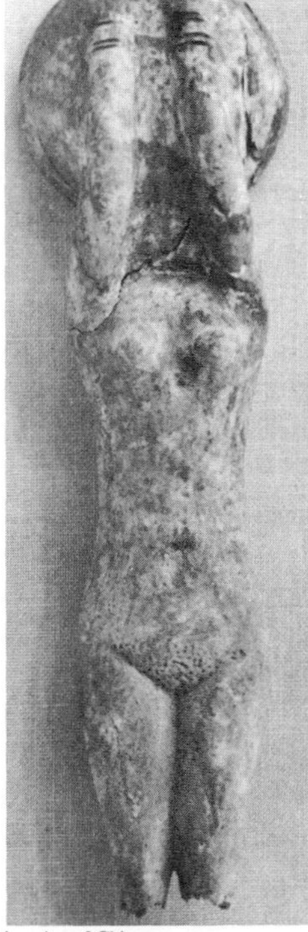

Courtesy of the Oriental Institute, the University of Chicago

21. Opposite sides of an ivory spoon with female figurine handles, from Megiddo (1350-1150 B.C.)

Courtesy of the Palestine Archaeological Museum, Jerusalem, Jordan

22. Ivory found at Samaria, showing lion grappling with bull; from Ahab's palace (ninth century B.C.)

el-Far'ah (in the S; Figs. ART 68-69), Tell ed-Duweir (Fig. IVO 17), el-Jish, and Beisan, the most important collections of Palestinian ivories have come from Megiddo and from Samaria (Figs. ART 70; LIO 32). In 1932 a hoard of 383 pieces of carved work was discovered at Megiddo and attributed by the excavator to the period of 1350-1150 B.C. (Figs. BAN 18-19; IVO 18-20). On one piece (Fig. ART 70), probably an inlay for furniture, was depicted a prince of Megiddo seated on a sphinx throne and celebrating a military victory. Gaming boards, cosmetic spoons, boxes, and a rich variety of other objects constituted this hoard of ivory, which may well have represented the treasure of an "ivory-collector" (Fig. IVO 21). The ivories found at Samaria, thought to belong to the ninth century, contain decorated panels with frame and tendon on the side for attaching to furniture or woodwork (Figs. INL 8; IVO 22). These pieces, to judge from a partly worked carving, were probably carved at Samaria and belong to the period of Ahab (Fig. ART 71).

Pl. XXIV.

Bibliography. J. W. and G. M. Crowfoot, *Early Ivories from Samaria* (1938); G. Loud, *The Megiddo Ivories* (1939); C. Decamps de Mertzenfeld, *Inventaire commenté des ivoires phéniciens et apparentés découverts dans le proche-orient* (1954); J. B. Pritchard, *ANEP* (1954), figs. 125-32; R. D. Barnett, *A Catalogue of Nimrud Ivories and Other Examples of Ancient Near Eastern Ivories* (1957).

J. B. PRITCHARD

IVVAH ĭv'ə [עִוָּה] (II Kings 18:34; 19:13; Isa. 37:13); KJV IVAH ī'və. A town; the site is unknown. In II Kings 18:13-36 the envoys of the Assyrian king Sennacherib, trying to persuade the Judean king Hezekiah to give up his policy against Assyria, referred to the fate of other towns: Hamath, Arpad, Sepharvaim, Hena, and Ivvah (cf. II Kings 19:13; Isa. 37:13).

A. HALDAR

IVY [κισσός]. According to II Macc. 6:7, when the Dionysiac festival took place, Antiochus compelled Jews to march in the procession for DIONYSUS wearing ivy wreaths. Dionysus, or Bacchus, was the pagan god of the vine and its produce, and ivy was sacred to him. Cf. III Macc. 2:29, a reference to Jews' being branded with an ivy leaf.

B. H. THROCKMORTON, JR.

IYE-ABARIM ī'yə ăb'ə rĭm [עיי העברים, heaps of the regions beyond, *or perhaps* heaps of the passes]; KJV IJE-ABARIM ī'jə—. A stopping place of the Israelites, following Oboth, and preceding the "Valley of Zered" (Num. 21:11-12; *see* ZERED, BROOK) or Dibon-gad (33:44-45). Iye-abarim was in the wilderness on the SE border of Moab. It is tentatively located by some in the region of Mahaiy, a strong Moabite fortress dominating the ascent from the Brook Zered. E. D. GROHMAN

IYIM ī'yĭm [עיים] (Num. 33:45); KJV IIM. A shortened form of IYE-ABARIM.

IYYAR ē'yär [איר]. The second month of the Hebrew CALENDAR; earlier known as Ziv.

IZHAR ĭz'här [יצהר, *perhaps* may (the deity) shine forth, *or* may (the deity) show himself exalted]; KJV IZEHAR ĭz'ə här in Num. 3:19; JEZOAR jə zō'ər in I Chr. 4:7 (but cf. 2 *below*); IZHARITES —hə-rīts. **1.** A Levite, son of Kohath; eponym of a tribal family (Exod. 6:18, 21; Num. 3:19, 27; 16:1; I Chr. 6:2, 18, 38: 23:12, 18).

2. In I Chr. 4:7 a variant of ZOHAR (*Kethibh* יצחר; *Qere* וצחר, "and Zohar").

Bibliography. M. Noth, *Die israelitischen Personennamen* (1928), pp. 205, 225, 255. B. T. DAHLBERG

IZLIAH ĭz lī'ə [יזליאה; *cf.* Arab. *jazalījun*, eternal= long-living(?)] (I Chr. 8:18); KJV JEZLIAH jĕz—. A Benjaminite.

Bibliography. M. Noth, *Die israelitischen Personennamen* (1928), p. 246.

IZRAHIAH ĭz'rə hī'ə [יזרחיה, may Yahu arise, shine forth (*i.e.,* as a star)] (I Chr. 7:3). A descendant of Issachar.

Bibliography. M. Noth, *Die israelitischen Personennamen* (1928), pp. 28, 205, 216.

IZRAHITE ĭz'rə hīt [יזרח, may (the deity) shine forth] (I Chr. 27:8). A man of a family or town called Izrah. The name occurs only once and with the definite article. Perhaps it is to be identified with ZERAHITE (I Chr. 27:11).

Bibliography. M. Noth, *Die israelitischen Personennamen* (1928), p. 205. B. T. DAHLBERG

IZRI ĭz'rī [יצרי, *perhaps contraction for* Yahu has fashioned, *or perhaps for* צרי (Zeri), mastic balsam] (I Chr. 25:11). A temple musician; and if identified with ZERI (I Chr. 25:3), a descendant of Jeduthun.

Bibliography. M. Noth, *Die israelitischen Personennamen* (1928), p. 247; cf. p. 223. B. T. DAHLBERG

IZZIAH ĭ zī'ə [יזיה, may Yahu sprinkle, purify] (Ezra 10:25; I Esd. 9:26); KJV Apoc. EDDIAS ĕ dī'əs. One of those compelled by Ezra to put away their foreign wives.

J. One of the principal narrative sources or strata of the PENTATEUCH. The symbol is derived from the personal name of God, Jehovah (or more accurately Yahweh, from יהוה), the use of which is characteristic of this source. It is commonly regarded as Judahite in origin, and somewhat earlier than E (tenth-ninth centuries B.C.). D. N. FREEDMAN

JAAKAN jā'ə kăn [יעקן; LXX Ιωκαν] (I Chr. 1:42); KJV JAKAN jā'kən. Third son of clan chief Ezer; ancestor of a native Horite subclan in Edom. He is probably to be associated with Bene-jaakan in Num. 33:31-32, and with Beeroth Bene-jaakan in Deut. 10:6.

The original form of the name is not clear. Cf. ועקן (LXX καὶ Ιωυκαμ καὶ Ουκαν), translated "and Akan," in Gen. 36:27. L. HICKS

JAAKOBAH jā'ə kō'bə [יעקבה, may (the deity) protect] (I Chr. 4:36). A prince of the tribe of Simeon.

Bibliography. M. Noth, *Die israelitischen Personennamen* (1928), pp. 28, 38, 46, 197.

JAALA jā'ə lə [יעלא, ibex] (Neh. 7:58). Alternately: JAALAH [יעלה; 'Ιεηλί] (Ezra 2:56; I Esd. 5:33); KJV Apoc. JEELI jē'lī. Eponym of a family of "Solomon's servants" listed among the returned exiles.

JAALAM. KJV form of JALAM.

JAANAI. KJV form of JANAI.

JAAR jā'ər [יער, forest] (Ps. 132:6); KJV THE WOOD. A place appearing in parallel with Ephrathah; usually thought to be the same as KIRIATH-JEARIM.

JAARE-OREGIM jā'ə rĭ ôr'ə jĭm [יערי ארגים]. An obvious textual corruption of "Jair" and a transcriptional error that imported "oregim" ("weavers") from the following line (II Sam. 21:19; cf. I Chr. 20:5; *see* ELHANAN 1; JAIR 4).

JAARESHIAH jâr'ə shī'ə [יערשיה, may Yahu plant; *cf.* Akkad. *erêsu,* plant] (I Chr. 8:27); KJV JARESHIAH. A Benjaminite.

Bibliography. M. Noth, *Die israelitischen Personennamen* (1928), pp. 28, 203.

JAASAU, JAASAI. KJV and ERV mg. forms of JAASU.

JAASIEL jā ā'zĭ əl [יעשיאל, God does]; KJV JASIEL jā'— in I Chr. 11:47. **1.** Son of Abner; an officer and leader of the tribe of Benjamin during the reign of David (I Chr. 27:21).

2. A Mezobaite whose name appears among the sixteen names added by the Chronicler to the catalogue of the Davidic Mighty Men known as the "Thirty" (I Chr. 11:47). The difficulty involved in the gentilic name has been resolved by some interpreters as equivalent to "from Zobah." E. R. DALGLISH

JAASU jā'ə sōō [יעשי (*Kethibh*), יעשו (*Qere*), *probably a shortened form of* יעשיאל *or* יעשיה(ו), may God (or Yahu) make] (Ezra 10:37); KJV JAASAU —sô. One of those compelled by Ezra to give up their foreign wives.

JAAZANIAH jā ăz'ə nī'ə [יאזניהו, Yahu hears]. Alternately: JEZANIAH jĕz — (Jer. 40:8; cf. 42:1). "Jaazaniah son of Tob-shillem" is mentioned in Lachish Ostracon I (*see* LACHISH) from the early sixth century B.C. It was apparently a common name at that time.

Courtesy of the American Schools of Oriental Research

1. Impression of the seal of Jaazaniah, from Tell en-Nasbeh

1. A Judean, son of Maacathi, or the Maacathite, (II Kings 25:23; Jer. 40:8), who remained under Gedaliah after the Exile. If Hoshaiah (Jer. 42:1) was a Maacathite, his son was the same Jezaniah mentioned in Jer. 40:8; although the latter may refer to Azariah son of Hoshaiah (cf. 43:2), as the LXX shows (see RSV).

Fig. JAA 1.

2. A Rechabite, son of Jeremiah (not the prophet), tested by the prophet Jeremiah in Jehoiakim's reign (Jer. 35:3).

3. Son of Shaphan, appearing, in a vision of Ezekiel, among the idolatrous elders of Israel (Ezek. 8:11).

4. Son of Azzur, one of the twenty-five Judean elders in one of Ezekiel's visions (Ezek. 11:1). J. M. WARD

JAAZER. KJV alternate form of JAZER.

JAAZIAH jā'ə zī'ə [יעזיהו, may Yahu nourish; *cf.* Arab. *rad̲ā*)] (I Chr. 24:26-27). A Levite, son of Merari.

Bibliography. On the problem of identification of this name, see E. L. Curtis, *Chronicles*, ICC (1910), p. 274; J. D. Davis, *The Westminster Dictionary of the Bible* (rev. H. S. Gehman; 1944), p. 276. On etymology, see M. Noth, *Die israelitischen Personennamen* (1928), pp. 28, 203. B. T. DAHLBERG

JAAZIEL jā ā'zī əl [יעזיאל, may God nourish; *cf.* Arab. *rad̲ā*] (I Chr. 15:18). Alternately: AZIEL ā'— [עזיאל, *originally same form as above*] (I Chr. 15: 20). One of the musicians accompanying the ark on its removal from the house of Obed-edom. This name is probably also to be read in I Chr. 16:5 for "Jeiel" (*see* JEHIEL 1), which is doubtless a copyist's error.

Bibliography. M. Noth, *Die israelitischen Personennamen* (1928), pp. 27-28, 203. B. T. DAHLBERG

JABAL jā'bəl [יבל; LXX Ἰωβέλ] (Gen. 4:20). The first son of Lamech and Adah; progenitor of nomadic shepherds.

JABBOK jăb'ək [יבק]. One of the principal E tributaries of the Jordan; the modern Nahr ez-Zerqa, so called from its blue waters. It rises in a spring near 'Amman (the biblical Rabbah of the Ammonites), flows N for some miles, then turns and flows westward through an ever-deepening canyon, ending in a fertile delta and emptying into the Jordan *ca.* fifteen miles N of the Dead Sea. Its total length is *ca.* fifty miles, and its average rate of descent is *ca.* eighty feet to a mile, so that its current is strong and steady. The name Jabbok may be derived from the sound of the gurgling of its waters. It was when Jacob crossed the Jabbok that he had his nocturnal encounter with a spirit that wrestled with him all night and gave him a new name, Israel, at dawn (Gen. 32:22-29); the word used for "he wrestled" (*yē'âbhēq*) may be a pun on the name Jabbok.

With its steep banks, the river was a natural boundary; the early S-N stretch formed the W boundary of Ammon, regarded as very strong (Num. 21:24), and the lower courses formed the boundary between the kingdoms of Sihon and Og (Judg. 11: 22). The lower courses also divided Gilead into two parts (Deut. 3:12, 16; Josh. 12:2-6), S Gilead being called here "the half of Gilead" and N Gilead "the rest of Gilead." The cities that lay on or near its course included Gerasa, Mahanaim, Penuel, Succoth, and Adam, while numerous tells, of whose identity the Bible gives no indication, point to the density of the population in ancient times in the Jabbok Valley.

Fig. JAB 2. S. COHEN

Courtesy of Herbert G. May

2. Valley of the Jabbok River

JABESH jā'bĭsh [יבש, יביש, dry]. **1.** Same as JABESH-GILEAD.

2. The father of King Shallum of Israel (II Kings 15:10, 13-14). Jabesh here may be a geographical rather than a personal name, for "Shallum the son of Jabesh" may mean that Shallum was a native of the town of Jabesh. Cf. "the son of Tabeel" (Isa. 7: 6), which refers to a person whose home was in the land of Tabeel in NW Palestine or SW Syria, a place known to us in an Assyrian inscription from Calah. So also "Jehu the son of Omri" in the Assyrian records means "Jehu of Beth-omri," the official name of Samaria; and "Shamgar the son of Anath" in Judg. 3:31 means "Shamgar of Beth-anath," a town in the Galilee area.

Bibliography. M. Noth, *Die israelitischen Personennamen* (1928), p. 244; W. F. Albright, "The Son of Tabeel (Isaiah 7:6)," *BASOR*, CXL (1955), 34-35. H. G. MAY

JABESH-GILEAD jā'bĭsh gĭl'ĭ əd [יבש גלעד, יביש גלעד, Jabesh of GILEAD]; also JABESH [יבש, יביש] (I Sam. 11:1, 3, 5, 9, 10; 31:12, 13; I Chr. 10:2). A city E of the Jordan with significant associations with the career of Saul.

1. Location. The name of Wadi el-Yabis (River Jabesh), which flows into the Jordan from the E some twenty air miles S of the Sea of Galilee, points to the general area in which the site must be located. It was placed by Eusebius six miles from Pella on the road to Gerasa, which would support its location at Tell el-Maqlub, overlooking the N side of the wadi in the broken hill country of N Gilead. But the biblical accounts of overnight communications with Bezek and Beth-shan (*see* § 2 *below*) favor identifica-

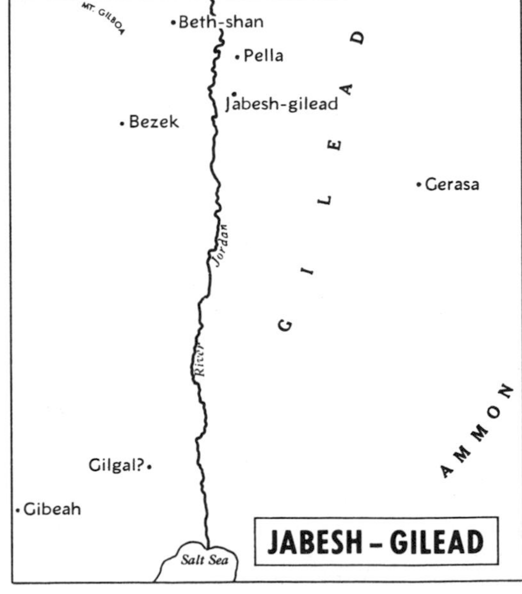

tion with the joint site of Tell el-Meqbereh–Tell Abu Kharaz farther W, overlooking from the N the broadening out and merging of the wadi with the Jordan Valley. From Tell Abu Kharaz one can see to the NW Tell el-Husn, the site of the city of Beth-shan. This is one of the richest sections of the fertile N half of the E side of the Jordan Valley.

Tell Abu Kharaz was a great fortress towering over Tell el-Meqbereh, which was probably the residential section of the city. Examination of potsherds on the surface of the site has disclosed that it was occupied in the Early Bronze, Middle Bronze, and Iron Age (EB I-II, EB IV–MB I, MB II, Iron I-II), and to the Roman and Byzantine periods. The place was first occupied *ca.* 3200 B.C. Potsherds from the thirteenth to the sixth centuries B.C., from Israelite times, predominated.

2. History. The biblical history of Jabesh-gilead is closely connected with that of Gibeah of Benjamin. Early ties between the two areas may be reflected in the account of marital relations of Machir (i.e., Gilead) and Benjamin in I Chr. 7:15 (cf. vs. 12).

Jabesh-gilead first appears in Judg. 21. As punishment for not participating in the war against Gibeah and the Benjaminites, Israel put it to the sword, saving only four hundred virgins. These were given as wives to four hundred of the six hundred warriors who were the only Benjaminites to escape in the destruction of their tribe. Although this story has folkloric embellishments and is variously interpreted by scholars, its essential historicity is supported by the total biblical picture of intertribal conflicts, in particular those between the West Jordan and the Transjordan tribes. The story also helps explain subsequent relations between Jabesh-gilead and Gibeah. The site was apparently reoccupied soon after this incident, presumably by neighboring Gileadites.

The bonds between their descendants and the Benjaminites were strengthened when Saul rescued Jabesh-gilead from Nahash the Ammonite, who had laid siege to it and demanded as a condition for capitulation that he might gouge out the right eyes of the men of the city. Its elders sent messengers through Israel for help. Saul and the people of Gibeah responded, and Saul mustered an army at Bezek (Khirbet Ibziq?) at the edge of the hills overlooking the Jordan Valley from the W. Saul and his men made a forced march at night into the valley and across the Jordan to arrive at Jabesh-gilead at dawn; it was a distance of only about ten miles as the bird flies, but for Saul's army hardly an easy trip over such terrain. He attacked the Ammonites from the morning watch to the heat of the day, defeating and scattering them. This incident marked the effective beginning of the monarchy, and Saul was made king at the Gilgal sanctuary (I Sam. 11).

When Saul and his sons had been slain on Mount Gilboa and their bodies hung on the wall of Beth-shan by the Philistines, all the valiant men of Jabesh-gilead crossed the Jordan and rescued the corpses. The approximately nineteen-mile trip to Beth-shan and back was made during the night. They burned the bodies and buried the bones in honor under the tamarisk tree at Jabesh, holding a seven-day mourning fast (I Sam. 31:8-13; I Chr. 10:8-12). David commended the Jabeshites for their act (II Sam. 2:4*b*-7), seeking in vain that they recognize his kingship. After he had later established his rule over both Judah and Israel, David brought from Jabesh-gilead the bones of Saul and Jonathan and buried them in the family tomb at Zela in Benjamin (II Sam. 21:12-14).

Bibliography. N. Glueck, *The River Jordan* (1946); "Explorations in Eastern Palestine, IV," *AASOR*, XXV-XXVIII (1951), Pt. I, 268-75. Contrast M. Noth, "Jabes-Gilead: Ein Beitrag zur Methode AT Topographie," *ZDPV*, LXIX (1953), 28-41.

H. G. MAY

JABEZ jā'bĭz [יַעְבֵּץ, *see* 1 *below*]. **1.** A name introduced abruptly into a list of descendants of Judah (I Chr. 4: 9-10); possibly the ZOBEBAH of vs. 8 is corrupted from this name. The folk etymology in this passage derives יַעְבֵּץ from עצב—i.e., "he gives pain (or sorrow)." He is perhaps the eponym of the community of this name.

Bibliography. E. L. Curtis, *Chronicles*, ICC (1910), p. 107.

B. T. DAHLBERG

2. A place in Judah, perhaps near Bethlehem, where several families of scribes lived (I Chr. 2:55).

JABIN jā'bĭn [יָבִין, one who perceives(?)]. **1.** King of Hazor, defeated and executed by Joshua (Josh. 11:1). A confederacy of Canaanite kings, promoted by Jabin, was organized in the area W and N of the Sea of Galilee upon receipt of news of Joshua's victories elsewhere in Canaan. Although equipped with horses and chariots, the Canaanite forces were defeated at the Waters of Merom; and Jabin's city, Hazor, SW of Lake Huleh, was burned. Other cities in the region were not razed but were occupied by the Israelites. With the exception of some oversimplifications, Josh. 11 appears a reliable account of the Israelite campaign in N Canaan.

2. King of Canaan, reigning in Hazor, whose forces under the command of Sisera were defeated by Deborah and Barak in battle at the River Kishon (Judg. 4:2, 7, 17, 23-24; Ps. 83:9—H 83:10). Jabin was hardly king of Canaan, but rather a Canaanite king of Hazor, whose career has now been confused with that of SISERA. Sisera, "who dwelt in Harosheth-ha-goiim," was most likely king of that settlement and spearhead of a Canaanite coalition to resist Israelite encroachment upon the Plain of Esdraelon. Whether Jabin has been introduced secondarily from Josh. 11 into the account of Sisera's defeat is uncertain.

R. F. JOHNSON

JABNEEL jăb'nĭ əl [יַבְנְאֵל, God causes to be built]. Alternately: JABNEH jăb'nə [יַבְנֵה] (II Chr. 26:6); Apoc. JAMNIA jăm'nĭ ə [Ἰάμνεια]. **1.** The westernmost location point on the N border of Judah (Josh. 15:11); modern Yebna, four miles inland from the Mediterranean Sea and nine miles N-NE of Ashdod.

In the course of his reign, Uzziah (*ca.* 783-742 B.C.) recaptured Jabneh from the Philistines by breaching its wall (II Chr. 26:6 ff).

Jamnia is mentioned with other cities along the Syro-Palestinian coast as being alarmed at the approach of Holofernes (Jth. 2:28). Because of its easily defended position, Jamnia served as a base of operations for the Seleucid generals, Georgias (I Macc. 4:15; 5:58), Apollonius (10:69), and Cendebeus (15:40). According to II Macc. 12:8, Judas Maccabeus captured and burned Jamnia in 164 B.C. to prevent a rumored atrocity against his countrymen. Josephus, however, attributes the capture and sack of Jamnia to Simon in 142 (Antiq. XIII.vi.7). In 80, it appears in the list of cities under the control of Alexander Janneus (Jos. Antiq. XIII.xv.4).

In 63 B.C., Pompey occupied Jamnia (Jos. War I.vii.7; cf. Antiq. XIV.iv.4), and a few years later Gabinius ordered it rebuilt (War I.viii.4; cf. Antiq. XIV.v.3). After the death of Cleopatra, Herod added it to his domain (cf. War I.xx.3; Antiq. XV.vii.3). Herod first presented it to his sister Salome and later to the Empress Livia. Under Tiberius (A.D. 14-37) it was administered by an imperial official.

Jamnia appears in the events leading up to the First Revolt (cf. Jos. War II.xvi.1-2), and after the revolt it became the "center-in-exile" of the Sanhedrin, the Beth-Din, which continued to meet in Jamnia until the beginning of the Second Revolt in 132. It is probably best known for the meeting of the Synod of Jamnia, *ca.* 100, in which the collection of Jewish sacred writings was reviewed and conclusions were reached which have had great significance for both Jew and Christian in matters pertaining to the canon of the OT.

2. A village in S Naphthali (Josh. 19:33); possibly to be identified with Khirbet Yamma, W-SW of the Sea of Galilee.

V. R. GOLD

JABNEH. Alternate form of JABNEEL.

JACAN jā'kən [יעכן] (I Chr. 5:13); KJV JACHAN. A Gadite.

JACHIN jā'kən [יכין, he (*i.e.*, the deity) establishes, *or* he will establish; *shortened form of* יהויכין (יויכין); *cf. also* Phoen. *ykn'l;* Akkad. *Jakini; see* JACHIN AND BOAZ; JEHOIACHIN]; JACHINITES —kə nīts. **1.** The fourth of six sons of Simeon in Gen. 46:10; Exod. 6:15, but the third of five (Ohad being omitted) in Num. 26:12. He is probably identical with Jarib, who occurs in the parallel list of Simeon's sons in I Chr. 4:24. Also, he is the ancestral head of the "family of the Jachinites" (Num. 26:12).

2. The priest to whom the twenty-first lot fell when David divided the officials for temple service (I Chr. 24:17); eponymous head of a priestly house living in Jerusalem (I Chr. 9:10; Neh. 11:10).

L. HICKS

JACHIN AND BOAZ jā'kən, bō'ăz [יכין, he will establish; בעז, *be'ōz,* in strength of]. Twin pillars of cast bronze erected on each side of the entrance to Solomon's temple (I Kings 7:15-22, 41-42; II Kings 25:16-17; II Chr. 3:13, 15-17; Jer. 52:17, 20-23). The descriptions of the pillars are not clear, and the sources differ as to their dimensions—height, 18 cubits in Kings and Jeremiah MT, 35 cubits in Chronicles and Jeremiah LXX; circumference, 12 cubits in Kings MT and Jeremiah, but 14 cubits in I Kings 7:15 LXX; height of capitals, 5 cubits, except 3 cubits in II Kings 25:17. The function and symbolism of the pillars and the meaning of their names have given rise to many hypotheses.

The pillars are said to have been hollow (Jer. 52:21), with a thickness of four fingers, or 1/6 cubit (1 cubit = 17.7 inches). On top of each pillar was a bowl-shaped capital 5 cubits in height, decorated with a checkered design, lily leaves, or petals to a height of 4 cubits, and wreathed with strings of pomegranates. Although the primary source (I Kings 7:19, 21, MT) is vague as to the relation of the pillars to the vestibule of the temple, and the dubious LXX addition to 7:22 suggests that they carried the architrave, it is almost certain that Jachin and Boaz were free-standing columns "in front of the temple" (II Chr. 3:17). Their function was decorative, symbolic, and cultic, like the other bronze furnishings of the temple with which they are listed. The proportions of diameter to height are not those of structural pillars; this may explain the doubling of the height in later tradition. Most important is the analogy of such free-standing columns in front of temples at

Courtesy of the Oriental Institute, the University of Chicago

3. Restoration of the façade of the inner temple of Nabu at Khorsabad, showing two pillars before the temple

Courtesy of the Oriental Institute, the University of Chicago

4. Column base of temple at Tell Tainat (*ca.* eighth century B.C.)

Khorsabad, Tyre, Paphos, and elsewhere. Particularly striking is the finding in front of the temple of Sin at Khorsabad of a cylindrical bronze casing 29½ feet in length, comparable to the height of the Jachin and Boaz pillars. Fig. JAC 3.

In a Canaanite temple excavated at HAZOR two

round basalt pillar bases were found in the porch on each side of the entrance. Cf. the two-pillar bases of the Tell Tainat temple (*see* TEMPLES).* These were not free-standing pillars. Fig. JAC 4.

The proportions and form of the pillars, surmounted by their bowl capitals (cf. Zech. 4:3), accord with Albright's view that they served as giant incense stands, or as cressets, on the analogy of the cressets pictured in a third-century-B.C. tomb at Marisa and those in front of a temple at Paphos shown on Roman coins. There is no biblical reference to their cultic use (with the possible exception of Isa. 4:5), and it is possible that their function was symbolic only. They have been interpreted as stylized forms of the standing stones and sacred poles of Canaanite shrines (Gen. 28:18; Deut. 12:3), of the "pillars of heaven" (Job 26:11), and as the mountains between which the sun was believed to rise. Doubtless the symbolism was multiple and developed in the course of time. Architecturally they are descended from the standing stones and detached pillars of Canaanite and Assyrian temples, but their meaning in Solomon's temple must be related to their distinctive names. The twin pillars at Gadeira mentioned by Posidonius bore inscriptions. One such at Lagash erected by Gudea was called: "Ellil, king of the stormy whirlwind . . . has chosen Gudea."

It seems probable that the names of the pillars in Solomon's royal temple (cf. Amos 7:13), where he officiated as principal priest (I Kings 7:14, 22; 8:64), were derived from the initial words of dynastic inscriptions like that of Gudea. In Gen. 31:45, 49, a named pillar serves as a perpetual witness to a solemn covenant. In II Kings 11:14; 23:3 it is specially noted that the king "stood by the pillar," suggesting its special significance for the king. The verb הכין, "establish," is prominent in OT dynastic oracles (cf. II Sam. 7:12-13, 16; I Kings 2:24; Ps. 89:3-4—H 89:4-5; Isa. 9:6; etc.), and the first pillar may have borne an inscription like: "He will establish [*yākîn*] the throne of David forever." The second inscription may also have had dynastic significance—e.g., "In the strength of [*beʿōz*] of Yahweh shall the king rejoice" (cf. Ps. 21:1—H 21:2)—or it may have had a mythological or cultic reference (cf. Pss. 74:13; 96:6).

Bibliography. K. Möhlenbrink, *Der Tempel Salomos* (1932), pp. 110-15. R. B. Y. Scott, "The Pillars Jachin and Boaz," *JBL*, LVIII (1939), 143-39. W. F. Albright, *Archaeology and the Religion of Israel* (1942), pp. 138-48; "Two Cressets from Marisa and the Pillars of Jachin and Boaz," *BASOR*, 85 (1942), 18-27. H. G. May, "The Two Pillars Before the Temple of Solomon," *BASOR*, 88 (1942), 19-27. P. L. Garber, "Reconstructing Solomon's Temple," *BA*, XIV (1951), 8-10. A. Parrot, *Le Temple de Jérusalem* (1954), pp. 14-20.

R. B. Y. SCOTT

JACINTH jā'sĭnth [לשם, *lešem* (KJV LIGURE, *from* LXX λιγύριον, Vulg. *ligurius*); NT ὑάκινθος]. A reddish-orange stone, a variety of zircon. An adjectival form of the NT word (ὑακίνθινος) is used in Rev. 9:17 ("sapphire"; RSV mg. "hyacinth"). It is a stone in the breastpiece of judgment (Exod. 28:19; 39:12). It is the eleventh jewel in the foundation of the wall of the New Jerusalem (Rev. 21:20), and an adjectival form of the Greek word (ὑακίνθινος) describes the breastplates of the riders in the vision in Rev. 9:17 (RSV SAPPHIRE; RSV mg. HYACINTH). *See also* JEWELS AND PRECIOUS STONES § 2.

W. E. STAPLES

JACKAL [שועל, *see* FOX; תן (*plural* תנים *in* Isa. 13:22, *etc.;* תנין *in* Neh. 2:13; Lam. 4:3; תנות *in* Mal. 1:3; KJV DRAGON, SEA MONSTER]. Any of certain carnivorous mammals of the genus Canis Aureus, of the family Canidae, smaller than the true wolf, with a shorter tail than the latter. The jackal moves about mostly in packs and usually at night. Its food is small mammals, poultry, fruit, vegetables, etc., and, unlike the fox, it will eat carrion and other refuse. In India it is said to suffer much in extremely hot weather, and in biblical Palestine it may have been very sensitive to unusual drought and heat (cf. Jer. 14:6).

Courtesy of the Cairo Museum; photo courtesy of the Metropolitan Museum of Art

5. The god Anubis as a jackal, lying on a funerary chest; from the tomb of Tut-ankh-Amon at Thebes

Although its cry is a distinctive wailing howl, which must have been familiar to most Hebrew villagers, there is only a single allusion to this sound (Mic. 1:8). Apart from one reference to the suckling of its young (Lam. 4:3), and another to a "Jackal's Well" outside Jerusalem (Neh. 2:13), most of the other OT passages relate to jackals' prowling around ruins and desertlike areas. Babylon (Isa. 13:22; Jer. 50:39; 51:37), Edom (Isa. 34:13), Hazor (Jer. 49:33), the cities of Judah (Jer. 10:22), Jerusalem (Jer. 9:11—H 9:10), Mount Zion (Lam. 5:18), Esau (Mal. 1:3), are specifically mentioned as being, or as destined to be, the resorts of jackals. In Ps. 63:10—H 63:11 the psalmist's enemies are to be prey for jackals, whereas in 44:19—H 44:20 the psalmist's lament is that this is the sad lot of Israel (cf. Job's complaint in Job 30:29). In the messianic age the desolate haunts of jackals will bring forth vegetation (Isa. 35:7), and the jackals and other wild animals will rejoice in the Lord's gift of plenteous water in the wilderness (Isa. 43:20).

Fig. JAC 5. W. S. MCCULLOUGH

JACKAL'S WELL [עין התנין, fountain of the *tannîn* (*a mythological monster*)] (Neh. 2:13); KJV DRAGON

WELL. A well or fountain accessible from the VALLEY GATE outside Jerusalem. It has been identified by some with EN-ROGEL. A location in the upper tract of the Valley of Hinnom (*see* HINNOM, VALLEY OF) suits the context better.

See also JERUSALEM §§ 2, 7*b*. G. A. BARROIS

JACOB jā'kəb [יעקב, יעקוב, *see* JACOB (ISRAEL) § 1; LXX *and* NT 'Ιακώβ; Vulg. *Jacob*]. **1.** *See* JACOB (ISRAEL).

2. Son of Matthan and father of Mary's husband, Joseph (Matt. 1:15-16). *See* GENEALOGY OF CHRIST.

JACOB (ISRAEL). Son of Isaac and Rebekah; younger twin brother of Esau; and husband of Leah and Rachel (Gen. 25:21-26; 29:21-30). Because Jacob is also called Israel (32:28; 49:2), his twelve sons are the "sons of Israel" (Exod. 1:1; I Chr. 2:1).

A. *ETYMOLOGY.* Genesis gives two etymologies of the name Jacob. The primary reference occurs, as is usual, in the birth narrative: the younger twin is called *Ya'aqōbh* because at birth he was holding his brother's heel (*'āqēbh;* 25:26 J). In the second passage, when the younger steals the older brother's blessing, Esau affirms that Jacob is rightly named, "for he has supplanted me [*wayya'qᵉbhēnî*] these two

times" (27:36). Here the verb *'āqabh,* really a denominative from *'āqēbh* and so "to seize by the heel," carries by extension the meaning "to overreach" (cf. Ps. 49:5—H 49:6).

Further, two passages outside Genesis clearly play upon the name Jacob. Jer. 9:4*b*—H 9:3*b* makes a twofold allusion to the traditional etymology: "For every brother is a supplanter [*'āqôbh ya'qōbh*]." Hos. 12:3*a*—H 12:4*a* brings to mind both the strict and extended meanings of the verb *'āqabh* in saying of Jacob: "In the womb he took his brother by the heel."

Accordingly, the biblical form *Ya'aqōbh* should mean "He overreaches" or "He will overreach." Cf. also the OT proper names יעקבה and עקוב.

Nevertheless, these traditional explanations have the appearance of popular etymologies (*Volksetymologien*), with which Genesis abounds (e.g., Cain, Seth, Abraham, Reuben). Quite likely the original name was different in form and meaning.

In all probability the name Jacob was originally theophorous, the divine element of which—commonly *'ēl*—is now missing (like Isaac, Joseph, Jephthah; *see* ISHMAEL 1). The restored form would then be *Ya'aqōbh-'ēl* or, as a jussive, *Ya'aqubh-'ēl.* This is parallel in form with the Palestinian place name *Yaqob-el,* appearing in the lists of the Pharaoh Thutmose III (1490-1436 B.C.); with *Ya'qub-Har,* the name of a Semitic chieftain of the early Hyksos period; and with the personal name *Ya-a' (AḪ)-qu-ub-ilu,* attested at Chagar Bazar (*ca.* 1725 B.C.).

The root עקב is general Semitic and occurs in the Arabic personal names *'Aqba'* and *'Aqabtu/'Aqbatu,* in Akkadian *Aqbi-il* and *(Ḫ)aqba-aḫum* at Mari, in the Aramaic inscriptions at Hatra, and perhaps in Syriac עקבאלהא and Palmyrene בלעקב. As a noun meaning "heel" it occurs in Hebrew, Aramaic, Syriac, Arabic, Ugaritic, and Akkadian. However, the meanings of the verb are not clear, and the biblical etymologies may even represent a deliberate obscuring of an earlier meaning. "To guard, watch, or protect" has been suggested (cf. South Arabic and Ethiopic *'aqaba* and North Arabic *mi'qab*[un]). Accordingly, "Jacob" could mean "May God protect!"; but this is uncertain.

In conclusion, Jacob was not uniquely a biblical name but an ancient member of the Near Eastern onomastica.

B. *SOURCES OF THE JACOB TRADITION.* **1. The written sources.** The written sources from which the present biblical narrative was constructed are the documents identified by Pentateuchal criticism as J, E, and P (*see* PENTATEUCH §§ A3, 5). The following is, mainly, the analysis made by Martin Noth: From the Yahwist come 25:21-26*a,* 27-34; 27:1-45; 28:10, 11*a*α, 13-16, 19; 29:1-35; 30:1*a*α, 3*b*β, 4, 5, 7-16, 20*a*β*b,* 21, 24-43; 31:1, 3, 17, 18*a*α, 19*a,* 20, 21*a*α*b,* 22, 23, 25*b,* 26*a*α, 27, 30*a,* 31, 36*a,* 38-40, 46-49, 51-53*a;* 32:4-14*a,* 23-33; 33:1-3, 6, 7, 12-17, 18*b;* 34:1-31; 35:21, 22*a;* 37:3*a,* 4, 5*a,* 6-21, 25-27, 28*a*β*b;* 38:1-30; 42:1*b,* 4, 5, 38; 43:1-13, 14*a*α*b;* 45:25-28; 46:1*a*α, 5*b,* 28-34; 47:29-31; [49:2-28]; 50:1-10*a,* 14. From the Elohist come 28:11*a*β*b,* 12, 17, 18, 20-22; 30:1*a*β*b,* 2, 3*ab*α, 6, 17, 18-20*a*α, 22, 23; 31:2, 4-16, 19*b,* 21*a*β, 24, 25*a,* 26*a*β*b,* 28, 29, 30*b,* 32-35, 36*b,* 37, 41-45, 50, 53*b,* 54; 32:1-3, 14*b*-22; 33:4, 5, 8-11, 19, 20; 35:1-5, 7, 8, 14, 16-20; 37:3*b,* 31-35; 42:1*a,* 2, 3, 29-37; 46:1*a*β*b*-5*a;* 47:7-12; 48:1, 2, 7-22; 50:10*b,* 11. From the Priestly writer come 25:26*b;* 27:46–28:9; 31:18*a*β*b;* 33:18*a;* 35:6, 9-13*a,* 15, 22*b*-29; 31:1, 2*a*α*b;* 46:6-27; 47:27*b,* 28; 49:1*a,* 29-33; 50:12, 13.

But these documents were not the earliest sources. At the beginning Jacob stories were popular in the S, in Transjordan, and even in Haran, as well as at Bethel and Shechem. From these areas they found their way into larger cycles of legend, on which the principal written documents later drew.

2. The earlier cycles. It would seem desirable, therefore, to get behind these written documents to the earlier strata of Jacob legends which, though part may have been in written form, were originally oral traditions. By critical analysis Hermann Gunkel delineated four strata of Jacob stories, now stacked on top of one another like layers of soil. By removing each layer in reverse chronological order—i.e., the uppermost, and thus latest, stratum first—he felt that he reached down to the core of the Jacob tradition.

First and oldest of the strata are the narratives about Jacob and Esau. These, contained in Gen. 25:21-27:45; 32:4-33:17, are the "real kernel of the Jacob tradition." The Jacob of this stage is the shepherd who bests the hunter. His name is simply a common proper name, not infrequent in Palestine or Mesopotamia. *See* § A *above.*

Next oldest are the narratives about Jacob and Laban (29:15-32:1). In these the clever young shepherd outwits the older, more experienced shepherd, who attempts to take advantage of him.

Originally these stories circulated as independent traditions about the several principals; for this, according to Gunkel, is the basic feature of oral tradition, that "each story existed by itself as a separate entity." However, Jacob was basically the same type of figure in both cycles, and later they were combined, the Jacob-Laban tales being set in the midst of the older, Jacob-Esau group. The union was effected by having Jacob flee from Esau in Palestine to Laban in Mesopotamia. Then, after having despoiled Laban, Jacob returns to Palestine, where Esau awaits him.

Superimposed on this combined narrative is a third layer of stories about theophanies and holy places. Having earlier been honored independently in the particular localities where they were at home, they were incorporated into the composite story at the various points where Jacob was brought into contact with the sites they concern. These pericopes served also to effect the transition from one cycle to another. So, e.g., the Bethel story (28:11-22) becomes a link between the first part of the Jacob-Esau cycle and the Laban narrative, and the Mahanaim (32:1-2—H 32:2-3) and Peniel (vss. 22-32—H 22-33) units mark the return to the Esau cycle. At this point in the tradition, Jacob was raised to the status of national ancestor; Esau became associated with Edom, and Laban with Aram (Syria). The Shechem notice (33:18-20) both concludes the Esau cycle and introduces the Dinah legend (ch. 34).

Finally, stories about Jacob's children, their birth and destiny, form the top, and latest, layer. Since Jacob-Israel was held to be the ancestor of the nation, his sons were ranked as the heads of the twelve tribes of Israel. At this final stage Jacob is no longer the "skilled shepherd" of the Esau and Laban narratives nor the "fearless foeman" of the Peniel scene; he appears, rather, as the aged father who is reunited in Egypt with his favorite son, Joseph, and as the honorable patriarch who blesses the people that will bear his name.

3. The unified story. Gunkel's investigation attempted to get behind the composite narrative by isolating the smallest units in Israel's earliest traditions. In dealing with the forms and cycles of ancient saga, oral as well as written, it made a historic advance over the purely literary documentary analysis of Wellhausen. It does not, however, represent the final approach to the Genesis narratives. After analysis must come synthesis. Ultimately the stories must be put together again and, with understanding increased, read in their present setting as organic, carefully considered portions of a unified epic. The resulting story is Israel's faithful assertion that the God who made all the peoples on earth has been at work in her own history in a special way, calling the patriarchs to a destiny he is able to fulfil even when they least deserve it.

The Jacob story, then, must finally be read as a whole, and as an integral part of a canon which is Holy Scripture.

C. *JACOB IN GENESIS*. In its broadest reaches the Jacob story comprises half the book of Genesis. The account of his birth comes in ch. 25 and his burial in ch. 50.

1. Jacob and Esau. ***a. The birth of Jacob and Esau (Gen. 25:21-28).*** The first word about Jacob is that he was given in answer to prayer. Rebekah, like Sarah (11:30; 16:1-2), was barren. When Isaac prayed for his wife, "Yahweh allowed himself to be entreated by him" (*see* ISAAC § 2*e*), and Rebekah gave birth to twin boys. The first was named Esau because he was hairy (*see* ESAU § 1). The second was named Jacob because he came forth holding his brother's heel (*see* § 1 *above*). Esau became skilled at hunting, and a man of the field, whom Isaac loved "because he ate of his game." Jacob, in contrast, was "a quiet man [איש תם, 'a settled, orderly, and well-integrated man'], dwelling in tents"; and Rebekah loved him.

The birth ensured Isaac that the promise of the land of Canaan and of numerous descendants, which God made to Abraham and repeated to him, would be fulfilled. He had sons from whom "nations" would come (25:23).

Yet this promise was immediately placed in jeopardy. For at the very beginning a note of conflict between the two sons was sounded, and it was echoed in the partiality of the parents. Family hostility gravely threatened the patriarchal promise of land and seed. Under this tension Jacob must live.

Yet the initial scene of the Jacob story foreshadowed also the resolution of the tension and guaranteed the fulfilment of the promise. Jacob, by divine oracle, would triumph (vs. 23). The end is obvious to the reader, regardless of the problems to be met.

b. Jacob obtains Esau's birthright (25:29-34). The paradox in Jacob's life is immediately illustrated in the first specific story told about him. When Esau, the carefree hunter, came in from a fruitless chase, and learned that the careful shepherd had prepared food, he bargained away his birthright (בכרה; *see* FIRST-BORN) for a batch of stuff, the name of which he did not even know (lit., "this red, this red stuff"; vs. 30*a*).

An element of fraud, not now sufficiently clear, may have been involved in the transaction. E.g., Jacob may have deliberately disguised the nature of his brew. His insistence on the irretractable oath (vs. 33; cf. Josh. 9:19) seems to be a protection against the discovery of deception. Also, deliberate deceit here would clarify Esau's later accusation (Gen. 27:36: "these two times"). At any rate, by patience and foresight, Jacob gained the right of precedence which by birth was not his. God's oracle (25:23) was working itself out. Yet with good fortune came also the hostility which would later imperil his life (27:41).

c. Jacob steals Esau's blessing (ch. 27). Being old and fearing that he might die suddenly, Isaac charged Esau to prepare for him savory food, that he might pass on to his first-born son the patriarchal blessing his soul carried (cf. vs. 4*b*). But while Esau was out innocently hunting, Jacob hearkened to his mother's stratagem and, after cautiously satisfying himself on the risk, carried off the deceit with boldness. And to his crass lies (vss. 19, 24) he added shocking blasphemy ("Because Yahweh your God granted me success"; 27:20; cf. 24:12). The pathos of the occasion is deepened by the aged father's blindness. Torn by suspicion and doubt ("The voice is Jacob's voice, but the hands are the hands of Esau"; vs. 22), the blind father finally pronounced upon Jacob the deathbed benediction (vss. 27*b*-29; cf. 24:1-9; ch. 49).

Here the blessing is not directly from God. The word itself is active, Isaac communicates it, and even Jacob helps fashion the conditions under which it is given. So with Esau's curse. The blessing can be neither recalled nor shared (vss. 37-38). Only an ill fortune remains for Esau (vss. 39-40).

2. Jacob in Haran. ***a. The vision at Bethel (28:10-22).*** En route to Haran from Beer-sheba, Jacob lodged at the ancient Canaanite sanctuary-city Bethel (*see* BETHEL [SANCTUARY]). There, in a nocturnal vision, Yahweh appeared to him, identified himself as the God of his fathers (cf. 12:7; 13:14-17; 26:3-5; *see* PATRIARCHS § 5), repeated to him the promise of the land and seed, set him to a universal mission (*see* ABRAHAM § A4), and assured him of a divinely guided prosperity. Jacob acknowledged the awesomeness of that place where he had met God, by solemnly naming it Bethel and binding himself to the patriarchal God by personal oath.

Theologically the importance of this scene may first have been to legitimize Yahweh-worship at this pre-Israelite cultic center. But as one of the principal passages in which God deals with Jacob directly and declares his personal direction of the patriarch's destiny, it serves now as a manifest guide to the interpretation of the Jacob story as a whole. *See* § E *below*.

b. Jacob and Laban (chs. 29-31). This ancient cycle, laid in Aram-naharaim and featuring the family of LABAN, now interrupts the Palestinian-oriented Jacob-Esau story. The union of the two narratives links the Hebrew patriarchs with their Aramean kinsmen.

In the first of these narratives (29:1-30) Jacob marries Leah and Rachel. Having come to the region of Haran, Jacob met Laban's beautiful daughter RACHEL, whom he loved at first sight (vss. 10-11, 18, 20). Laban took his nephew home and agreed to give him Rachel in exchange for seven years' service with his flocks. Jacob not only fulfilled the bargain honorably but also, because of his blessing, brought to his uncle great prosperity (cf. 30:27-30). Laban, however, deceived Jacob, making him take the elder and less attractive sister, LEAH. Once more Jacob agreed to serve seven years for his favorite, Rachel, and was faithful to his word.

The second narrative (29:31–30:24) tells of Jacob's children. Twelve children were born to Jacob during his long service in Mesopotamia. From the disdained Leah came Reuben, Simeon, Levi, Judah, Issachar, Zebulun, and Dinah; and from her maid ZILPAH came Gad and Asher. The beloved Rachel, being barren (29:31; 30:1-2; cf. 11:30; 25:21), gave her maid BILHAH to Jacob, in order to obtain children by her (30:3-8; *see* ABRAHAM § C1*i*). Bilhah bore Dan and Naphtali. Finally, Rachel herself bore Joseph, an answer to her prayer (vss. 22-24).

The names of the children are, most likely, shortened forms of originally theophorous names whose earlier meaning is hidden by the popular etymologies given here (*see* § A *above; see also* NAME § C2). Regardless of the historical difficulties involved, the picture of Israel as a unit of twelve members, articulated into smaller groups and yet sharing common parentage and common allegiance, must rest on a valid tradition; and its basis may be sought here. *See* TRIBE.

The present story of Jacob's return to Palestine, involving the reasons for this major decision (31:1-2, 3, 13); the question of Laban's bargain for an equitable distribution of their common gain (30:25-43); and the ethical issues involved in Jacob's departure, Rachel's theft of her father's household gods (31:19; *see* TERAPHIM), Laban's accusation against his son-in-law (vss. 25-35), and Jacob's angry oath of clearance (vss. 36-42), has woven together conflicting traditions and makes a simple picture difficult to gain.

Nevertheless, from this presentation of the several episodes, the conclusion is clear that in the midst of the all-too-human quarrels over family and fortune God is at work, protecting and prospering his blessed (31:38-42), as even Laban (30:27) and his daughters (31:16; cf. vss. 5-13) acknowledged. And in their final scene, when the two parted at Mizpah, Laban, by requesting Jacob to cut a covenant of peace with him, admitted Jacob's favored position as the carrier of divine blessing. *See* LABAN § 3.

3. The return of Jacob. ***a. Mahanaim and Peniel (ch. 32).*** As Jacob approached the land of which by divine promise he was heir, a band of angels met him (vss. 1-2—H 2-3), perhaps symbolizing for him once again God's protection. *See* MAHANAIM.

But at the JABBOK he was met by "a man" (איש) who wrestled with him until daybreak. In a show of magnificent courage Jacob prevailed and won from the antagonist a blessing which entailed the change of Jacob's name to ISRAEL. Fig. JAC 6.

Courtesy of Herbert G. May

6. Bridge across the Jabbok River at the point of the ancient ford (see Gen. 32, Jacob's wrestling with the angel)

In this story, which combines the etymologies of Israel and PENIEL and an ancient cultic etiology (vs. 32), a major key for the interpretation of Jacob's life is given. For Jacob did not wrestle with a river demon or the devil or Esau or even his own alter ego, but with One who was able to bless him and change his name, and this is God himself (as P states clearly in 35:9-15; cf. Gen. 17:5, 15; Isa. 62:4; Hos. 2:23; 12:3-4—H 12:4-5; Matt. 16:17-18). The persistent struggle with God which issues in a divine blessing must be seen as characteristic, not only of Jacob the man, but also of Israel the nation.

b. Reconciliation with Esau (ch. 33). Fearful that his brother's hostility had not subsided during the years, Jacob approached the dreaded meeting with his usual careful cleverness, seeking both to pacify his wronged twin and to protect himself and his family from attack (32:3-9, 13-21; 33:1-3). To his stratagems, however, he added prayer (32:9-12). In this prayer to his father's God, which brings together the divine action in the past (vs. 9*b*), the need of the present (vs. 11), and the promise for the future (vs. 12), a pattern of Jacob's whole life may be seen. Amid all the tragic tangles in his human relations, Jacob realized that ultimately it was God with whom he dealt.

In an appealing scene of great tenderness Jacob met Esau and was received back with magnanimity and affection.

4. Jacob the patriarch (chs. 34–50). The twins separated, to meet again only at their father's death (35:27-29). Esau went to Seir and there became the ancestor of a nation, thus fulfilling the divine promise (25:23; cf. 27:39-40; 33:16; ch. 36; *see* ESAU; EDOM). Jacob remained in Palestine to assume his inheritance.

The rest of the Jacob narrative focuses not so much on the patriarch himself as upon the places and people associated with him.

Leaving Esau, Jacob journeyed to SUCCOTH; then to Shechem, where he bought ground and built an altar (33:17-20). From there he went, by divine command, to Bethel (*see* BETHEL [SANCTUARY]) and received a theophany which repeated the patriarchal promises. Once again he responded with worship (35:1-15). Jacob and his family continued southward (cf. 12:9). During this journey Rachel died in childbirth and was buried on the way to Ephrath (Bethlehem; 35:16-20). Jacob joined Isaac at Mamre (Hebron) and there buried his father in the family sepulchre (35:27-29; cf. 49:31). Finally, when severe famine gripped Canaan, Jacob and his sons set out for Egypt. At Beer-sheba he received further assurance of God's favor (46:1-4). In Egypt he dwelt "in the land of Goshen" until his death.

This part of the story of Jacob is told principally in terms not only of places but also of persons. It is, in fact, primarily a family history. Jacob's return to Canaan brought his family immediately into conflict with the sons of Hamor (ch. 34). Rachel's death was the occasion of Benjamin's birth, an event marking a certain climax in the narration, for it is followed by a short list of Jacob's twelve sons (35:22*b*-26) and a lengthy genealogy of the descendants of Esau (ch. 36).

Moreover, the final chapter in Jacob's life, that intertwined with the Joseph story (chs. 37; 39–50; *see* JOSEPH SON OF JACOB), is an intimate family portrait. Regardless of a cosmopolitan context, it contrasts the internal conflicts of jealousy and hate with the ennobling power of love and forgiveness. At the story's end Jacob bestows a patriarchal blessing upon Ephraim and Manasseh (48:8-20) and then upon his own sons (ch. 49; *see* BLESSINGS AND CURSINGS). God's promise to Jacob was fulfilled; at his death the Egyptians paid him great homage, and his sons buried him at Machpelah with Abraham and Isaac (49:29–50:14; cf. 27:28-29; 46:3-4).

Although this story is a moving "family history," it is not thereby a secular narration but the disclosure of God at work through people and places. *See* § E *below.*

D. *JACOB IN THE REST OF THE BIBLE.* As an individual Jacob is not frequently mentioned. He is remembered as a child of favor (Mal. 1:2; Rom. 9: 10-13), an heir of the divine promise (Heb. 11:9), and a man of blessing (Heb. 11:20-21).

As Israel's third great patriarch (*see* PATRIARCHS § 2) Jacob is often linked with ABRAHAM (*see* §§ D-E) and Isaac. So the God of Abraham, Isaac, and Jacob, who is the same as El Shaddai (Exod. 6:3) and Yahweh (3:6, 15; *see* GOD, NAMES OF, § B2) remembered his covenant (2:24; 32:13; Deut. 29:12), had compassion on Israel (II Kings 13:23), and glorified his servant Jesus (Acts 3:13). The patriarchs are alive with him (Mark 12:26-27) and sit at his table in the kingdom of heaven (Matt. 8:11).

However, as the representative of the nation whose name he bears, Jacob appears quite frequently. Israel is the "house of Jacob" (Luke 1:33); its God is the "King of Jacob" (Isa. 41:21); and his temple is a "habitation for the God of Jacob" (Acts 7:46). This figure of Jacob (Israel) reaches its height when applied to the Servant of the Lord (Isa. 41:8; 44:1-2, 21; 48:20; cf. 49:3), of whom Jesus is the perfect example (Matt. 8:17; 12:15-21; Mark 1:11; 9:2-8; 10:45; Luke 2:30-32; John 1:19-23; Acts 8:26-39; Heb. 9:28; I Pet. 2:22-25).

E. *THEOLOGICAL SIGNIFICANCE.* Jacob's story is a story of conflict. The note of conflict which is heard even before his birth (Gen. 25:22-23) reverberates throughout the entire narrative. Having twice supplanted Esau, Jacob flees to Haran. But with Laban, Jacob must engage in a protracted struggle, resolved only after he has left for Palestine. The mood of the scene in which Jacob returns to Esau is pregnant with the threat of hostility and fear. Even in the "Joseph section" most of the scenes depicting Jacob's relations with his sons are fraught with concern. In short, Jacob is beset with dangers from every area—the natural (famine), the human (Esau and Laban), and the divine (the "man" at the Jabbok). Upon each occasion his inheritance of the blessing is threatened.

Moreover, this situation is made more complex by the sharp edge of Jacob's personality. The character of Jacob the clever, mendacious supplanter projects so prominently from the narrative that it is difficult to bring the story into proper focus. The reader frequently feels that the deceitful Jacob deserves to be forsaken, left to face alone the full force of his dangers. No other patriarchal narrative is so inescapably dominated by the character of the man himself; and this tends to distort the evaluation of every incident.

Yet the paradox of the Jacob story is that its very domination by personal, secular concerns, which tend to alienate the reader and obscure his judgment, provides also a key to its underlying theology. With the other patriarchs God acts directly. In the story of Jacob, however, he seems mostly to have withdrawn from the active scene. But God is no less at work here, ordering the course of history for his purposes, as the Bethel and Peniel theophanies demonstrate. He works, however, through unworthy persons and unsavory situations. It is Israel's belief that in the tangled web of conflict and tragedy which Jacob weaves and then falls into himself, God's guiding hand, though half-hidden, is nonetheless present. Thus, when Jacob rises to a height of blasphemy unprecedented in the patriarchal history and declares to his blind father that he has found game so quickly "because the LORD your God granted me success" (27:20), he utters also the most profoundly true explanation of his career.

In many spots Jacob's story is distasteful, in others delightful. But whatever the original purpose of its separated parts, the present narrative was written to instruct, not to amuse, its readers. To see its proper role in the great theological epic of the patriarchs, the reader has to recapitulate Jacob's own discovery that "surely the LORD is in this place; and I did not know it" (28:16).

Bibliography. Among the many good Commentaries on Genesis, H. Gunkel, *HKAT* (4th ed., 1917), is distinguished by richness of detail and form-critical analysis; and G. von Rad, *ATD,* vol. 4 (1953), by its theological perception. For fuller reference, *see* the bibliographies under GENESIS; PATRIARCHS.

Special studies: H. Gunkel, *What Remains of the OT* (1928), pp. 151-86; M. Noth, *Die israelitischen Personennamen* (1928), pp. 177-78, 207-9; C. H. Gordon, "The Story of Jacob and Laban in the Light of the Nuzi Tablets," *BASOR,* LXVI (1937), 25-27; W. F. Albright, "A Third Revision of the Early Chronology of Western Asia," *BASOR,* LXXXVIII (1942), 36; M. Noth, *Überlieferungsgeschichte des Pentateuch* (1948), pp. 58-62, 95-111, 160-71; A. Alt, "Die Wallfahrt von Sichem nach Bethel," *Kleine Schriften zur Geschichte des Volkes Israels* (1953), I, 79-88; M. Noth, "Mari und Israel," *Geschichte und Altes Testament* (Alt Festschrift; 1953), pp. 142-52; B. D.

Napier, *From Faith to Faith* (1955), pp. 70-80, 80-97; J. Muilenburg, "The Birth of Benjamin," *JBL*, LXXV (1956), 194-201; V. Maag, "Jakob-Esau-Edom," *Theologische Zeitschrift*, 6 (1957), 418-29; G. von Rad, *Theologie des ATs* (1957), I, 135-40, 169-77; S. Mowinckel, "'Rahelstämme' und Leastämme,'" *Von Ugarit nach Qumran* (Eissfeldt Festschrift; 1958), pp. 129-50; M. Noth, *The History of Israel* (1958), pp. 1-7, 53-84, 120-26. L. Hicks

JACOB'S WELL [πηγὴ τοῦ Ἰακώβ] (John 4:3-12). The well where Jesus met the Samaritan woman.

The earliest reference to Jacob's Well is the gospel account, for the OT mentions no such well. The narrative implies a well-established tradition that "Jacob's well was there." It was along the road at or near a city of Samaria called Sychar, which is probably identified with Shechem (Tell Balâṭah). The identification of Jacob's Well as *Bîr Ya'qûb* is supported unanimously by Jewish, Samaritan, Christian, and Muslim tradition. This tradition is as early as the Bordeaux Pilgrim (*ca.* A.D. 333). The well is certainly ancient and is generally accepted as the one referred to in the Gospel of John. However, there is no evidence aside from tradition that it was dug by or dates from the time of Jacob, "who gave us the well" (John 4:12).

Bîr Ya'kûb, at the foot of Mount Gerizim, is 1½ miles SE of Nablus. It is at a road junction, just N of the place where the roads from Jerusalem and the Jordan Valley join. At the well the road divides again, one fork going to Nablus and the other to roads leading N and E to Jenin and the Jordan Valley.

The well, at present seventy-five feet deep, is partly filled with debris. The water never rises near the top; as the woman said: "The well is deep" (John 4:11). It is *ca.* eight feet in diameter, but it narrows toward the top, which is covered with a large stone with a hole in it. The upper portion of the well is lined with masonry, but the lower portion is cut in the soft limestone. The water is cool and refreshing. It is both a cistern (φρέαρ) and a spring (πηγή), for it appears to be fed by surface water as well as by underground sources (cf. John 4:6, 11).

Courtesy of Harriet-Louise H. Patterson

7. Site of Jacob's Well, within the unroofed church right of center; Mount Ebal in the background

In the fourth century A.D. a cruciform church was built on the site with the well at the crossing. There are also remains here of a Crusader church which was destroyed in the twelfth century. It is now the property of the Greek Orthodox Chuch, which has a walled enclosure and an unfinished church at the site. Today one goes down a stairway below ground into the remains of a crypt of the Crusader church to reach the top of the well.

Fig. JAC 7; Pl. XXXI*a*.

Bibliography. W. Sanday, *Sacred Sites of the Gospels* (1903), pp. 31-33; G. Dalman, *Orte und Wege Jesu* (1919), pp. 207-11. D. C. Pellett

JACUBUS. KJV Apoc. form of Akkub 4.

JADA jā'də [ידע, (God) has cared] (I Chr. 2:28, 32). A Jerahmeelite, son of Onam.

Bibliography. M. Noth, *Die israelitischen Personennamen* (1928), p. 181.

JADDAI jăd'ī [ידו (*Kethibh*), ידי (*Qere*)] (Ezra 10:43); KJV JADAU jā'dô. Same as Iddo 3.

JADDUA jăj'o͞o ə [ידוע]. **1.** A chief of the people and signatory to the covenant (Neh. 10:21—H 10:22.)

2. Son of Jonathan (though this may be an error for "Johanan"), and high priest three generations after Eliashib (Neh. 12:11, 22; "Jaddua" may be a late addition in vs. 22). He was the last high priest named in the OT, holding office probably in the time of Alexander the Great, with whom he was linked by Josephus (Antiq. XI.viii.2). *See* Priests and Levites. J. M. Ward

JADDUS jăd'əs [Ἰαδδούς (B), Ιοδδους (A), Ακκους (Luc.)] (I Esd. 5:38); KJV ADDUS ăd'əs. A man who married Agia, one of the daughters of Barzillai, and took the name of his father-in-law. In the parallels Ezra 2:61; Neh. 7:63, he is called simply by his adopted name. After the return under Zerubbabel his descendants were excluded from serving as priests, since their genealogy was not found in the priestly register. C. T. Fritsch

JADON jā'dŏn [ידון, frail one, *from* Arab. *wdn*(?), *or possibly a shortened form of the name* ידניה, Yahu rules (*found in the* Elephantine Papyri] (Neh. 3:7). A Meronothite who worked with Melatiah the Gibeonite and the men of Gibeon and of Mizpah in repairing the walls of Jerusalem during the time of Nehemiah. Meronoth (cf. I Chr. 27:30) is probably to be identified with modern Beit Unia, three miles NW of Gibeon. If the KJV of Neh. 3:7*b* is correct, perhaps the work of these men extended to the place where the Persian governor had his seat in Jerusalem. M. Newman

JAEL jā'əl [יעל, mountain goat]. The Bedouin woman who killed the Canaanite leader Sisera after his defeat by the Israelites. According to the Song of Deborah (Judg. 5:2-31), she used true nomadic guile, bringing out milk—a sign of hospitality—to the fugitive Sisera when he sought refuge at her tent. Sisera, accepting the bait, took the "lordly bowl" in his hands, and was probably struck down by Jael just as he bent his head to the dish (vss. 24-27). The later prose account turns the exploit into treachery, having Sisera killed after he had eaten, and misunderstanding the original weapon of the poem (4:17-22).

The description of Jael as the "wife of Heber the Kenite" (5:24) may have been introduced into the poem from 4:17, where it belongs. It is possible that some exploit of the wife of Heber has been combined with that of Jael. It is also entirely possible that Jael was a Kenite woman, for the Kenites were ancient allies of Judah (see 1:16). A northern origin for Jael might be more probable, however, considering the location of the battle and the fact that Judah is not listed as one of the warring tribes.

The reference to Jael in 5:6 has been questioned on the basis of both the history and the meter of the poem.

See also DEBORAH 2. D. HARVEY

JAGUR jā'gər [יגור] (Josh. 15:21). A city in the SE part of Judah, near the border of Edom. It may be the same as GUR-BAAL. A possible site is Tell Ghurr, ten miles E of Beer-sheba.

JAH, YAH jä, yä [יה]. An abbreviated form of the sacred name Yahweh, as in the Hebrew text of Exod. 15:2 or in the liturgical expression "Hallelujah" ("praise Yah[weh]"). *See* GOD, NAMES OF, § B.

JAHATH jā'hăth [יחת, *perhaps* (God) will snatch up]. **1.** A descendant of Judah (I Chr. 4:2).

2. An eponym; a Gershonite Levite (I Chr. 6:20, 43; 23:10-11).

3. An Izharite Levite (I Chr. 24:22).

4. A Merarite Levite; an overseer of the workmen repairing the temple in the reign of King Josiah (II Chr. 34:12).

Bibliography. F. S. Brown, S. R. Driver, and C. A. Briggs, eds., *Hebrew-English Lexicon of the OT* (1955), p. 367.
B. T. DAHLBERG

JAHAZ jā'hăz [יהץ, יהצה, *perhaps* a trodden *or* open place]. Alternately: JAHZAH jä'zə; KJV JAHAZA jə hā'zə; JAHAZAH. A city in Transjordan, where the Israelites defeated the Amorite king Sihon, when he refused permission to pass through his territory (Num. 21:23; Deut. 2:32; Judg. 11:20). Jahaz was assigned by Moses to the tribe of Reuben (Josh. 13: 18). The city with its pasture lands was given to the Merarite Levites (Josh. 21:36; I Chr. 6:78—H 6:63). Later it was taken by Moab (Isa. 15:4; Jer. 48:21, 34), to whom it had probably originally belonged before Sihon's conquest. Mesha (*see* MOABITE STONE) said that the king of Israel had built Jahaz and dwelt there while fighting Moab. However, Chemosh drove out the king of Israel, and Mesha took Jahaz in order to attach it to the district of Dibon.

Jahaz would seem to be N of the Arnon, not far from Dibon, but its site has not been identified. One suggested identification is Jalul, 3½ miles E of Medeba. Another is Khirbet et-Teim, a mile SW of Medeba. A third is Umm el-Walid, 7½ miles SE of Medeba, but the remains there do not seem to antedate the Nabatean period. E. D. GROHMAN

JAHAZIAH. KJV form of JAHZEIAH.

JAHAZIEL jə hā'zĭ əl [יחזיאל, may God see; Apoc. Ἰεζηλος]; KJV Apoc. JEZELUS jə zē'ləs. **1.** One of the Mighty Men who came to David at Ziklag (I Chr. 12:4—H 12:5).

2. One of the priests appointed by David to blow trumpets before the ark of the covenant (I Chr. 16:6).

3. A Korahite Levite listed as contemporaneous with David (I Chr. 23:19; 24:23).

4. A Levite of the sons of Asaph who prophesied before King Jehoshaphat concerning battle with Ammon and Moab (II Chr. 20:14).

5. The father of one Shecaniah among the exiles who returned from Babylon (Ezra 8:5; cf. I Esd. 8:32).

Bibliography. M. Noth, *Die israelitischen Personennamen* (1928), pp. 27-28, 198. B. T. DAHLBERG

JAHDAI jä'dī [יהדי, may (God) lead; *cf.* Syr. *and* Arab. root *h-d-j*] (I Chr. 2:47). A descendant of Judah.

Bibliography. M. Noth, *Die israelitischen Personennamen* (1928), p. 196.

JAHDIEL jä'dĭ əl [יחדיאל, may God rejoice (in his works)] (I Chr. 5:24). A chief in the half-tribe of Manasseh.

Bibliography. M. Noth, *Die israelitischen Personennamen* (1928), p. 210.

JAHDO jä'dō [יחדו, may (God) rejoice (in his works), *from* חדה] (I Chr. 5:14). A Gadite.

Bibliography. M. Noth, *Die israelitischen Personennamen* (1928), pp. 28, 210.

JAHEL jā'əl. Douay Version form of JAEL.

JAHLEEL jä'lĭ əl [יחלאל, may God show himself friendly(?)]; JAHLEELITES —ə līts. Third son of Zebulun, and ancestor of the Jahleelites (Gen. 46:14; Num. 26:26).

Bibliography. M. Noth, *Die israelitischen Personennamen* (1928), p. 204.

JAHMAI jä'mī [יחמי, may (God) protect] (I Chr. 7:2). A descendant of Issachar; son of Tola.

Bibliography. M. Noth, *Die israelitischen Personennamen* (1928), pp. 28, 196, 216.

JAHVEH jä'və [יהוה]. A vocalized form of the four consonants of the Israelite sacred name for God; more properly, YAHWEH. *See* GOD, NAMES OF § B.

JAHZAH. Alternate form of JAHAZ.

JAHZEEL jä'zĭ əl [יחצאל, may God distribute, *or* may God grant good fortune]; JAHZEELITES —ə līts. Alternately: JAHZIEL [יחציאל] (I Chr. 7: 13). An eponym; descendant of Naphtali (Gen. 46: 24 [cf. Jub. 44:30]; Num. 26:48; I Chr. 7:13), and founder of a tribal family (Num. 26:48).

Bibliography. M. Noth, *Die israelitischen Personennamen* (1928), pp. 27-28, 204. B. T. DAHLBERG

JAHZEIAH jä zē'ə [יחזיה, may Yahu see] (Ezra 10: 15); KJV JAHAZIAH jä hə—. One of the four men who opposed Ezra's action in regard to foreign wives.

JAHZERAH jä'zə rə [יחזרה, *possibly,* prudent; *cf.* Arab. *ḥadhira*] (I Chr. 9:12). Ancestor of a priest among the returned exiles. The name parallels Ahzai in Neh. 11:13.

Bibliography. R. A. Bowman, Exegesis of Nehemiah, *IB,* III (1954), 775-76; M. Noth, *Die israelitischen Personennamen* (1928), p. 228. B. T. DAHLBERG

JAHZIEL. Alternate form of JAHZEEL.

JAIR jā'ər [יאיר, may (the deity) shine forth; *in* I Chr. 20:5, *Kethibh* יעור, *Qere* יעיר, may (God) arouse (*see* 4 *below*)].

1. An eponym (cf. II Sam. 20:26); a son of Manasseh. He occupied a number of villages in Gilead in the region of Argob (Num. 32:41; Deut. 3:14; Josh. 13:30; I Kings 4:13; cf. I Chr. 2:22, where his father is Segub of Judah, and his mother a daughter of Machir of Manasseh). *See* HAVVOTH-JAIR; JAIRITE.

2. A Gileadite who judged Israel twenty-two years (Judg. 10:3, 5); he and his sons had thirty cities. The name is doubtless related to 1 *above. See* HAVVOTH-JAIR.

3. A Benjaminite, possibly related to 1 *above;* ancestor of Esther's guardian, Mordecai (Esth. 2:5).

4. Father of the Elhanan who killed the brother of Goliath, according to I Chr. 20:5; or who, according to II Sam. 21:19, killed Goliath himself (where read "Jair" [יעיר] for "Jaareoregim"; the latter spelling is a copyist's error due to homoeoteleuton; cf. MT).

Bibliography. M. Noth, *Die israelitischen Personennamen* (1928), pp. 7, 28, 204, 216. B. T. DAHLBERG

JAIRITE, THE jā'ə rīt [היארי] (II Sam. 20:26). A patronymic used only to describe Ira the priest of David, and indicative of descent from JAIR (1) the son of Manasseh, whose descendants resided in Gilead (Num. 32:41; Deut. 3:14; etc.).

JAIRUS jā ī'rəs ['Ιάϊρος, W-H Ιάειρος; KJV Apoc. יאיר, *see* 2 *below*]. **1.** A synagogue official ("ruler") whose dead daughter, aged twelve, was raised by Jesus (Mark 5:21-24, 35-43; Luke 8:40-42, 49-56; Matt. 9:18-19, 23-26, though Matthew abstains from mentioning Jairus by name).

In all three accounts the narrative is interrupted by an account of a woman who had had a flow of blood for twelve years. Scholars have puzzled that the one narrative encases the other, for they have in common little more than the commending of faith and the number twelve.

The name could well have been repeated in Mark 5:35-36, 38, 40, but is not; two good ancient MSS (D and *it*) omit "Jairus by name" from Mark 5:22; some scholars suggest that only Luke's text carried the name, and that the presence of this name in his text is a product of a tendency in late times to supply names which were unknown in the more primitive tradition.

Matthew's version of the story is much condensed; it is one in a succession of ten miracle narratives. Luke's account has some details quite different from those of Mark. Mark 5:41 portrays Jesus as saying in Aramaic: " 'Talitha cumi'; which means, 'Little girl, I say to you, arise.' " Luke and Matthew omit this Aramaic, Luke portraying Jesus as saying: " 'Child, arise,' " while Matthew relates Jesus "took her by the hand, and the girl arose." In Acts 9:36-43 a Dorcas died; her name means "gazelle," which in Aramaic, according to vs. 36, is *Tabitha:* "Peter . . . knelt down and prayed; then turning to the body he said, 'Tabitha, rise.' " Commentators have noticed the similarities in the Tabitha account and that of Jairus' daughter, and some have thought the one to be a doublet of the other.

The Hebrew of Jairus might well be יעיר ("he will awaken") rather than יאיר ("he will enlighten"); this is cited by those who regard the narrative as a legendary resurrection.

Other commentators suppose that possibly the girl was not dead, but only in a trance. Branscomb comments in opposition that the evangelist did not take literally the words, "The child is not dead but asleep"; if he had done so, "there would have been no miracle to relate." It is reasonable to conclude that all three evangelists intended the narrative to be a bit of wonder-working by Jesus, not a mere error by the parents.

Bibliography. E. Plummer, *St. Luke,* ICC (1901), p. 237; E. Klostermann, *Das Markusevangelium* (4th ed., 1950); W. E. Bundy, *Jesus and the First Three Gospels* (1955).

2. KJV translation of יאיר (RSV JAIR 3) in Add. Esth. 11:2 ('Ιάειρου B ℵ L, ἰάτρου A).

S. SANDMEL

JAKAN. KJV alternate form of JAAKAN.

JAKEH jā'kə [יקה, prudent, *from* Arab. *wāqin; participle active* I *of w-q-j*=be wary] (Prov. 30:1). Apparently the father or ancestor of Agur, a wisdom sage. The verse forms a title to the passage following it and has been variously interpreted.

Bibliography. C. H. Toy, *Proverbs,* ICC (1916), pp. 518-19; M. Noth, *Die israelitischen Personennamen* (1928), p. 228; C. T. Fritsch, Exegesis of Proverbs, *IB,* IV (1955), 947.

B. T. DAHLBERG

JAKIM jā'kĭm [יקים, may (the deity) establish]. **1.** A Benjaminite (I Chr. 8:19).

2. A priest, descendant of Aaron (I Chr. 24:12).

Bibliography. M. Noth, *Die israelitischen Personennamen* (1928), pp. 28, 200.

JALAM jā'ləm [יעלם, young man]; KJV JAALAM jā'ə ləm. An Edomite clan chief; second son of Esau and Oholibamah (Gen. 36:5, 14, 18; I Chr. 1:35).

JALON jā'lŏn [ילון] (I Chr. 4:17). A descendant of Judah.

JAMB [איל] (Ezek. 40:9–41:3); KJV POST. In Ezekiel's vision the jambs were decorative, and not merely structural, parts of a gate. *See* ARCHITECTURE; TEMPLE, JERUSALEM.

JAMBRES. *See* JANNES AND JAMBRES.

JAMBRI jăm'brī ['Ιαμβρί] (I Macc. 9:36). A tribe, presumably the Amorites (cf. the reading in Jos. Antiq. XIII.xi: "the sons of Amaraios"). When Jonathan became leader and left the command of the irregular troops to John, the sons of Jambri from

Medeba (which is noted in Num. 21:31 as a city of the Amorites) made John captive and took everything that he had. Jonathan and Simon took revenge by ambushing a wedding party of the sons of Jambri, killing many, and taking their spoils.

Bibliography. S. Tedesche and S. Zeitlin, *I Maccabees* (1950).

S. B. HOENIG

JAMES jāmz ['Ιάκωβος, *Hellenized form of* 'Ιακώβ (*see* JACOB); Lat. Jacobus, Jacomus]. A variant form of the name Jacob. The extent of identity among the various persons named James in the NT is much discussed. Some or all of those listed under 2-5 *below* are considered by many to be the same person.

1. One of the sons of Zebedee; one of the twelve disciples of Jesus (Matt. 4:21; 10:2; 17:1; Mark 1:19, 29; 3:17; 5:37; 9:2; 10:35, 41; 13:3; 14:33; Luke 5:10; 6:14; 8:51; 9:28, 54; Acts 1:13; 12:2). Jesus' call of James and his brother John (*see* JOHN THE APOSTLE), the sons of Zebedee, who were fishermen in the Sea of Galilee, is related in connection with the call of two other brothers, Peter and Andrew (Matt. 4:18-22; Mark 1:16-20). The call of these four disciples was the first event after the beginning of the ministry, according to Mark and Matthew. Luke, who places the story later, tells it differently, mentioning only Peter, James, and John (Luke 5:1-11). That James and John left their father with the hired servants (Mark 1:20) indicates that they were working in a family business, though Mark mentions the point to stress their obedience. Luke adds that James and John were partners of Peter (Luke 5:10).

In the lists of the Twelve, James and John always form a group of four with Peter and Andrew. Sometimes the sons of Zebedee are named after Peter and Andrew (Matt. 10:2; Luke 6:14); sometimes they come between them (Mark 3:16-18; Acts 1:13). The latter order reflects the priority of the new relationship to Jesus over the human relationship of Peter and Andrew.

James was probably the older brother, since he is usually mentioned first, and John is sometimes identified as the "brother of James" (Mark 3:17; 5:37; *cf.* Matt. 10:2; 17:1). However, Luke and Acts sometimes name John first or call James the brother of John (Luke 8:51; 9:28; Acts 1:13; 12:2), probably because John was a well-known "pillar" of the church after James's death (Gal. 2:9).

Mark alone records that Jesus gave James and John the special name BOANERGES, or "sons of thunder" (Mark 3:17).

Peter and James and John form a special group of disciples on three occasions recorded in the gospels, in addition to the occasion of their call as described by Luke. At the home of Jairus, Jesus permitted only these three from the circle of disciples to go with him to the child (Mark 5:37; Luke 8:51; Matthew omits this detail). Again, at the Transfiguration, Jesus chose these three to ascend the mountain with him (Matt. 17:1; Mark 9:2; Luke 9:28). Finally, in Gethsemane they were again chosen to accompany Jesus (Matt. 26:37; Mark 14:33; Luke omits this detail). Similarly, according to Mark, James and John went with Jesus to the home of Peter and Andrew (Mark 1:29); and it was Peter, James, John, and Andrew who asked about the signs of the coming Judgment (Mark 13:3).

James and John appear together in two other places. In Luke 9:51-56 they ask Jesus whether he wants them to call down fire from heaven on the Samaritan village that would not receive Jesus and his disciples. In this story James and John, with their allusion to Elijah (II Kings 1:10-12), represent the old way in contrast to the way of Jesus. Later copyists have expanded the text to explain the conclusion. "He . . . rebuked them" (Luke 9:55) is interpreted in some MSS by the addition of: "You do not know what manner of spirit you are of"; many others also add the saying: "For the son of man came not to destroy men's lives but to save them" (cf. Luke 19:10).

The other episode in which the two brothers appear together is when they requested places at Jesus' right and left hand in his coming glory (Matt. 20:20-28; Mark 10:35-45). In Matthew it is their mother who makes the ambitious request, though Jesus replies directly to James and John; in Mark the two brothers speak for themselves. The answer of Jesus is a double one: to the brothers, a prediction that they will drink the cup that he drinks, and to the rest of the Twelve, in response to their grumbling at James and John, words on true greatness—to be great means to be slave or servant of all. The section on greatness (Matt. 20:24-28; Mark 10:41-45) is used in a different setting in Luke 22:24-27, and may not be originally part of the story of James and John. Both in this story and in the story of the Samaritan village, the focus falls on Jesus rather than on James and John, except as their human desires, perhaps emphasized by their human relationship to each other, make their words a foil for the words and purpose of Jesus.

With the rest of the Eleven, James was a witness of the Resurrection. But the narratives of the Resurrection do not make any special mention of him, except that the sons of Zebedee are listed as present on the shore of the Sea of Galilee when Jesus appeared to the disciples there (John 21:1-8)—this story shows striking parallels to the original call of Peter, James, and John, as told in Luke 5:1-11.

James is the only one of the Twelve whose martyrdom is related in the NT, and probably he was the first of them to be put to death. According to Acts, Herod Agrippa I, king of Palestine A.D. 42-44, executed James as part of a wider move of persecution which included the arrest of Peter (Acts 12:1-3). That James was prominent enough to be singled out for execution may indicate that Peter, James, and John formed a special group among the leaders of the church in Jerusalem, as they had among the followers of Jesus. However, though Peter and John are mentioned together in Acts (3:1, etc.), the martyrdom is the only episode related of James.

Later, legendary stories expand the narrative of Acts. Clement of Alexandria (*ca.* 200) writes that James forgave his accuser (quoted by Euseb. Hist. II.9.2-3). The apocryphal Apostolic History of Abdias (*see* ABDIAS, APOSTOLIC HISTORY OF) describes James's miracles and controversies, which culminate in his execution by Herod. But his known early death led to James's receiving little attention in the growth of legendary stories about the apostles. A later legend (sixth or seventh century) told that he preached in Spain, and it was also believed that he was buried there. In Christian tradition James the son of Zebedee is known as James the Great, in contrast to James the son of Alphaeus, who is known as James the Less.

Some interpreters think that James was a cousin of Jesus, on the basis of a comparison of the lists of women present at the Crucifixion. In Matt. 27:56 the mother of the sons of Zebedee is one of these; she is often identified with the Salome listed in Mark 15:40 (*see* SALOME 2). If a further identification can be made, of the mother of the sons of Zebedee (Matt. 27:56) with "[Jesus'] mother's sister" (John 19:25), then James's mother was the sister of Mary the mother of Jesus. This theory assumes, probably rightly, that in John 19:25 "his mother's sister" is a different person from "Mary the wife of Clopas" (*see* 5 *below*). But it is very improbable that James was a cousin of Jesus. In view of the interest of the early church in relatives of Jesus, it is very likely that if he had been, this fact would have been prominent in early tradition, but it is not. Furthermore, it is doubtful that the various lists of women present at the Crucifixion can be harmonized, since they represent various traditions. Matthew and Mark state that they name only a few women of many, and it is not necessarily the case that the individuals mentioned in the various gospels are the same persons.

2. The son of Alphaeus; one of the twelve disciples of Jesus (Matt. 10:3; Mark 3:18; Luke 6:15; Acts 1:13). He heads the third group of four disciples in each list of the Twelve, but is not mentioned by name in any episode recorded in the gospels or Acts.

Since the disciple Levi is also called a son of Alphaeus (Mark 2:14), it has been suggested that James and Levi were brothers. But this is not likely, since they are not associated in any way in the gospels. Even on the assumption that Levi is an alternative name for Matthew (who is never called a son of Alphaeus), Matthew is never paired with James the son of Alphaeus in the lists of the Twelve, though Peter and Andrew, and James and John, are paired as brothers (*see* ALPHAEUS; LEVI 4; MATTHEW, APOSTLE). It is quite possible that James the son of Alphaeus is the same person as James the son of Mary. *See* 3 *below.*

A number of early forms of the text substitute the name "James the son of Alphaeus" for "Levi the son of Alphaeus" in Mark's story of the call of the tax collector. This alteration is not found in Luke's narrative of the call of Levi (Luke 5:27), while Matthew reads the name "Matthew" in the parallel (Matt. 9:9). Though the sources offering the reading "James" in Mark 2:14 represent a variety of early traditions, this variant reading is not original and does not give the clue to another James, nor to information that James the son of Alphaeus was a tax collector; but rather it represents an attempt, different from the tradition of Matthew, to identify Levi as one of the Twelve.

3. One of the sons of Mary (*see* MARY 4). The mother is mentioned as present at the Crucifixion (Matt. 27:56; Mark 15:40), and at the discovery of the empty tomb (Mark 16:1; Luke 24:10). This James had a brother Joses (*see* JOSES 1) or Joseph, and was known as James the "less" (Mark 15:40 KJV) or "younger" (RSV), perhaps because of his small stature. It is often thought that James the son of Mary was a cousin of Jesus, but this theory is extremely improbable (*see* 5 *below*). It is possible that James the son of Mary is to be identified with the son of Alphaeus. *See* 2 *above.*

4. The father of Judas (Luke 6:16; Acts 1:13). In the lists of Luke and Acts, Judas the son of James is one of the Twelve. The Greek reads "Judas of James." The KJV translates "Judas the brother of James"; and on the assumption that these two were brothers, this James has often been identified with James the brother of Jesus, who had a brother named Judas (Matt. 13:55; Mark 6:3; *cf.* JUDE 1), and often as well with James the son of Alphaeus and James the son of Mary. It is exceedingly unlikely that these persons are all the same (*see* 5 *below*). In any case, it is probable that this James was the father, not the brother, of the disciple Judas, and as such it is doubtful that he is otherwise known in the NT. *See* JUDAS 8.

5. A brother of the Lord. He is listed first among the brothers of Jesus, presumably as the oldest of them (Matt. 13:55; Mark 6:3). Paul met James the Lord's brother in Jerusalem on his first visit, three years after his conversion (Gal. 1:19). There can be little doubt that the same person is referred to simply as James in Acts 12:17; 15:13; 21:18; I Cor. 15:7; Gal. 2:9, 12; and is probably intended in Jas. 1:1; Jude 1.

The relationship between James and Jesus has been much discussed (*see* BROTHERS OF THE LORD). NT and early Christian writers refer to James as a "brother" of Jesus, and the natural interpretation of the language of that period is the literal one, that James was a son of Joseph and Mary, younger than Jesus. Though this view was rejected by most of the ancient church, it is probably correct.

Belief in the perpetual virginity of Mary led to the development of the view that Jesus and James were foster brothers. The legend of Mary's betrothal to Joseph, an elderly widower with children, developed early. It may be read in the Protevangelium of James (*see* JAMES, PROTEVANGELIUM OF). Thus, it was believed, Joseph's sons were known as the brothers of the Lord. This theory was widely accepted during the early centuries of Christian history, and is still the prevailing view of the Eastern churches. The principal difficulty with it is that it is based on accounts of the lives of Joseph and Mary which are essentially legendary and nonhistorical.

Another, later view is that James and Jesus were cousins. By identifying James with James the son of Alphaeus (*see* 2 *above*), it was believed that he was one of the Twelve. By identifying him also with James the son of Mary (*see* 3 *above*), it was held that he was a cousin of Jesus. As in the theory that James the son of Zebedee was a cousin of Jesus, this conclusion was reached through a study of the lists of women present at the Crucifixion. By comparing Matt. 27:56 with John 19:25, and punctuating the latter verse to read: "his mother, and his mother's sister Mary the wife of Clopas, and Mary Magdalene," students have concluded that Mary the mother of James was Mary of Clopas, and that she, rather than the wife of Zebedee, was the sister of Jesus' mother. If James the brother of the Lord is James the son of Mary, and if the identification of the Mary of Matthew and the Mary of John is correct, then James was a cousin, not a brother, of Jesus. Another theory established the relationship through a tradition that CLOPAS, identified with Alphaeus, was a brother of Joseph. Either of these chains of identification is very improbable. Nonetheless, the view that James and Jesus were cousins became current in the Western church and is current in the Roman Catholic Church. By his identification with James the son of Alphaeus, James is known in Christian tradition as "James the Less" (from Mark 15:40 KJV), in contrast to James the Great, the son of Zebedee.

James apparently was not a disciple during the ministry of Jesus (Matt. 12:46-50; Mark 3:31-35; Luke 8:19-21; John 7:5). Yet he was a witness of the Resurrection (I Cor. 15:7), and he appeared very early as an important leader in Jerusalem. Though he was not one of the Twelve, James was apparently regarded as an apostle. This is the most natural meaning of Gal. 1:19: "I saw none of the other apostles except James the Lord's brother." It has been suggested that James became an apostle as a replacement for James the son of Zebedee, since Acts first mentions him after the death of the latter. It is more probable, however, that in the early church there were more than twelve apostles from the beginning, since I Cor. 15:5-7 mentions the Twelve separately from "all the apostles." James, like the Eleven and Paul, became an apostle by the appearance of the risen Christ to him, commissioning him to be a specially authorized witness to the Resurrection. Though he apparently stayed in Jerusalem, in contrast to other apostles and other brothers of the Lord who traveled (I Cor. 9:5), his vocation is apparent when Paul refers to the agreement that James, Peter, and John should go to the Jews, while Paul should go to the Gentiles (Gal. 2:9). Thus the beginning and basis of James's position in the church was not his human relationship to Jesus, but his special relationship by faith to the risen Christ. *See* APOSTLE.

From James's presence in Paul's list of those to whom the risen Christ had appeared, it is clear that James shared the eschatological faith of the first Christians, that God would establish a new age through Christ. James was at one with Paul in believing that the new faith in Christ was for Gentiles as well as for Jews, and they agreed as well that Gentiles did not have to follow the Jewish law (Gal. 2:6-10; cf. Acts 15:12-21). James's own special vocation, however, was to the Jews (Gal. 2:9). Perhaps James and many other Jewish Christians believed that the mission to the Jews would pave the way for the salvation of the Gentiles, as is suggested by Acts 15:16-18, quoting Amos 9:11-12 (LXX). Paul, on the other hand, believed that the salvation of the Gentiles would unexpectedly precede the conversion of the Jews (Rom. 10-11). It is difficult, however, to know James's thought in detail, especially since the speeches in Acts are not literal records of the words of the speakers.

Ancient tradition presents James as combining the new faith in the Resurrection with a strong loyalty to the Jewish law. Most scholars find that this tradition reflects his real sympathy with the law, though the later traditions greatly exaggerate his legalism. In Galatians and Acts, James is not presented as a rigid follower of the law. Probably James the brother of the Lord is the James of the Letter of James (Jas. 1:1; cf. Jude 1). Whether the letter was written by him, or whether, as is more likely, it is a collection of Christian teaching presented in his name at a later time, its emphasis on common-sense morality rather than legalism shows that James was not remembered as a strict follower of the Mosaic law. *See* JAMES, LETTER OF.

In Gal. 2:1-10, Paul says that in a private conference at Jerusalem the "pillars," James, Peter, and John, accepted him without qualification, except that he should remember the "poor" (perhaps the saints of Jerusalem). The context shows that the discussion centered on circumcision, and that Paul was not required to ask circumcision of his Gentile converts, since they did not have to follow the law.

Acts 15:1-29 presents an account of a public conference about Paul's work, which cannot be completely harmonized with Galatians, though most scholars think that Acts and Galatians are reporting the same conference. In Acts the issue of circumcision drops into the background, and James proposes certain minimum requirements to be followed by non-Jewish believers; these proposals are then adopted as the so-called "apostolic decree." In the usual text Gentiles are required to "abstain from the pollution of idols and from unchastity and from what is strangled and from blood" (Acts 15:20). This is a series of predominantly ceremonial requirements apparently designed to make easier the table fellowship within the church, between Jews and those who did not follow Jewish dietary practices. Some "Western" forms of the text omit "what is strangled"; their shorter list, which some scholars consider the original form, can be seen as involving primarily moral rather than ceremonial requirements, though either list can be interpreted with either emphasis. In either case, Acts shows James playing a mediating position between a group of Jewish Christians who wished all believers to follow the law, and Gentile Christians on whom the obligation of the law as such was not laid. Whether the details of the decree can be attributed to James is a difficult question, since Paul says nothing about it in Galatians. If the decree was adopted before Paul wrote Galatians, he may have ignored it because he thought that it was temporary or local. But many scholars think that the differences between Acts and Galatians are most easily resolved by supposing that the decree comes from a somewhat later period, and has been inserted at this point by the author of Acts because it deals with the relations between Jewish and Gentile Christians. If this theory is correct, then it is problematical to what extent the rules of the decree present the point of view of James. In any case these rules attributed to James did not become regular requirements laid on Gentile Christians. *See* COUNCIL OF JERUSALEM.

When Paul resisted Peter's refusal to eat with Gentile Christians at Antioch, apparently after his conference with the leaders at Jerusalem, the turning point in Peter's refusal was the coming of "certain men . . . from James" (Gal. 2:12). They claimed James's support for requiring the full observance of Jewish dietary laws among Jewish Christians, but it is not possible to be sure that they represented him accurately in the matter of Jewish and Gentile Christians' eating together, or even that he was as anxious to follow the old traditions as they asserted. Similarly James is shown in Acts as joining with the elders of the church in Jerusalem in advising Paul to share in a temple ceremony (Acts 21:17-26). Here again, the story indicates James's reverence for the old pattern of piety, but does not clearly show how he related it to his new faith. Perhaps James represented a group of Christians who continued to celebrate the temple worship, while Stephen (Acts 7) represented a group which rejected the temple.

Thus the NT references to James show that he was devoted to the old Jewish tradition, yet willing to modify it in the light of the newness of God's action in Christ. A background for this combination of concern for both law and eschatology is found in some Jewish apocalyptic writings (*see* APOCALYPTICISM) and in the DEAD SEA SCROLLS. Later tradition among Jewish Christians remembered and exaggerated James's devotion to the law, almost to the neglect of his faith in the new action of God in Christ. According to Hegesippus, writing *ca.* 180 (quoted by Euseb. Hist. II.23.4-18), James was a NAZIRITE and spent so much time on his knees in intercession for the people that his knees grew horny like a camel's. He was thought to have been so pious that he was revered by all as "the Just" (a title perhaps transferred from Christ; cf. Acts 3:14; 7:52; 22: 14). This picture of devotion to the law is full of legendary traits; in it James almost becomes himself a mediator between God and man. E.g., Hegesippus portrays James as a priest in his intercession for the people, though he could not have belonged to the priestly group, and he makes his faith in Christ so secret that the "Jews and scribes and Pharisees" ask him to restrain the people from believing in Christ. Though James was not so offensive to the Jewish leaders as was Paul, it is very improbable that he was honored by them for his piety; eventually they put him to death (*see below*). The exaggerated picture of James's Jewish piety reflects a later period, when Jewish and Gentile Christians had separated. It does not represent the conditions of the first Christian generation, though some scholars have wrongly used this picture of James to reconstruct an early Christianity which fell apart almost from the beginning in a conflict over the law.

By tradition James was the first "bishop" of Jerusalem (Clement of Alexandria, quoted by Euseb. Hist. II.1.3). Jewish Christianity exalted James to a position above Peter and Paul. The Gospel According to the Hebrews (*see* HEBREWS, GOSPEL ACCORDING TO THE) presents the resurrected Christ as appearing first to James, and apparently presupposes that James, unlike the others, never doubted the Resurrection. The *Clementine Homilies* and *Clementine Recognitions*, which are romances about the life of CLEMENT dating from the fourth century but partly based on Jewish Christian sources of an earlier time, call James "bishop of bishops." In these writings Peter and the other apostles are accredited by James (*Clementine Recognitions* IV.35). James is presented as sending out the apostles in the Coptic Gnostic "Letter of James" of the Jung Codex. As in Hegesippus' tradition about his piety, this honoring of James is a Jewish Christian attempt to exalt the one remembered as their leader to the position of true guide of the first Christians. James was not a "bishop" in the later sense of the term. But both Galatians and Acts confirm the conclusion, exaggerated in these later writings, that James was the most respected and authoritative leader in Jerusalem for most of the first Christian generation. Though Paul's independence of Jerusalem was acknowledged (Gal. 2:6-10), the fact that his position had to be discussed with James and the other "pillars" shows that authority in Jerusalem also meant, in the first generation, recognition in other churches.

The basis of James's position in the church was his relation to the Risen Christ, but the fact that he was of the family of Jesus no doubt strengthened his authority. Jesus himself repudiated the ties of family as a basis for importance among his followers (Matt. 12:48-50; Mark 3:33-35; Luke 8:21). Nonetheless, the role of the family in leadership in the ancient Near East makes it probable that many Christians honored James as a brother of Jesus, especially since they were keenly aware that Jesus and his brothers were of the family of David, the promised messianic line. That there was some recognition of James's human relationship to Jesus is made more probable by the fact that after the death of James and the destruction of Jerusalem, another relative of Jesus, named Simeon, came into a position of leadership (Hegesippus, in Euseb. Hist. IV.22.4; cf. III.11-12). The succession Jesus-James-Simeon has led some students to find in early Jewish Christianity an approach to a dynastic pattern of leadership, a Christian "caliphate." It is probable that this way of ensuring continuity in the church did commend itself to some Christians, but it proved to be only a temporary experiment.

Two separate traditions tell that James was put to death shortly before the destruction of Jerusalem in 70. According to the Jewish historian Josephus, writing *ca.* 94, James with "certain others" was stoned in 62 at the instigation of the Sadducee high priest Ananus, as one of his first acts as high priest. Ananus was able to carry out the execution because the newly appointed Roman procurator, Albinus, had not yet arrived in Palestine (Jos. Antiq. XX.ix. 197-203). It is possible that the others who were put to death were also Christians, but this is not stated. This passage has been suspected of being a Christian interpolation in the text of Josephus, but it shows no obvious Christian bias and fits Josephus' usual interpretation of the Sadducee party. Thus there is little doubt that James was put to death by the priestly authorities in the early sixties, perhaps as part of a wider move of opposition to Christianity.

Another account of the death of James comes from Hegesippus, in the passage cited above to describe his piety. According to Hegesippus, James met his death after being presented to the people at Passover to give his impartial judgment about Jesus. When he proclaimed Jesus as the Son of man, seated at

God's right hand, he was cast down from the temple, stoned, and clubbed to death. Hegesippus agrees with Josephus that James was put to death by priestly authorities in the sixties, though he puts the episode shortly before the siege of 66. But the details of his story are legendary.

Bibliography. T. Zahn, "Brüder und Vettern Jesu," *Forschungen zur Geschichte des neutestamentlichen Kanons und der altchristlichen Literatur,* vol. VI, pt. II (1900), pp. 225-364; J. B. Mayor, *The Epistle of St. James* (3rd ed., 1913), pp. i-lxv; H. J. Schoeps, *Theologie und Geschichte des Judenchristentums* (1949), pp. 122-26, 256-70; H. von Campenhausen, "Die Nachfolge des Jakobus," *Zeitschrift für Kirchengeschichte,* LXIII (1950-51), 133-44; E. Stauffer, "Zum Kalifat des Jakobus," *Zeitschrift für Religions- und Geistesgeschichte,* IV (1952), 193-214; J. Munck, *Paulus und die Heilsgeschichte* (1954), pp. 103-11, 233-37; G. Quispel, Neue Funde zur valentinianischen Gnosis," *Zeitschrift für Religions- und Geistesgeschichte,* VI (1954), 291-92; L. E. Elliott-Binns, *Galilean Christianity* (1956); E. J. Goodspeed, *The Twelve* (1957); S. E. Johnson, "The Dead Sea Manual of Discipline and the Jerusalem Church of Acts," in K. Stendahl, ed., *The Scrolls and the NT* (1957), pp. 129-42.

W. A. BEARDSLEE

JAMES, APOCALYPSE OF [יַעֲקֹב; Ἰάκωβος]. A Gnostic writing found at Chenoboskion in Egypt in 1946 in no fewer than three editions, two in one codex, the third in another codex and in a hitherto unknown Coptic dialect. This writing is apparently totally distinct from the apocryphon quoted in an encomium on John the Baptist (*see bibliography*), and may conceivably be related to the "discourses" which Hippolytus (*Heresies* V.2) reports the Naasenes claimed had been handed down to Mariamne by James the brother of the Lord, concerning primordial man and the triple principle of the universe.

For further discussion of Gnostic apocrypha, *see* APOCRYPHA, NT.

Bibliography. E. A. W. Budge, *Coptic Apocrypha* (1913), p. 348.

M. S. ENSLIN

JAMES, ASCENTS OF [Ἀναβαθμοὶ Ἰακώβου]. A writing mentioned only by Epiphanius (*Heresies* XXX.16). According to him it was a book used by the Ebionites; it represented James the brother of the Lord as speaking against the temple and sacrifices, and was bitterly anti-Pauline. Paul was a Greek; desiring to wed the daughter of the high priest, he got himself circumcised and became a proselyte; but, failing to win his bride, he became enraged and wrote tirades against the law and circumcision. *See* APOCRYPHA, NT.

It has been plausibly conjectured that the book described the ascents of James up the temple steps, whence he addressed the multitude. Reflections of the writing have been seen in the Clementine *Recognitions* (I.66-71), where James is represented ascending the steps on seven consecutive days, only at last to be flung down and left for dead by "the enemy" (Saul of Tarsus). It has been suggested that the familiar story of James's martyrdom, quoted by Eusebius (Hist. II.3-18) from Hegesippus (*ca.* A.D. 175), may well have been the grand finale of these ascents, recounting, as it does, James's address from the pinnacle of the temple, his being hurled from this lofty height, his stoning, and his subsequent death by a laundryman's club.

Bibliography. For an account of conjectures about the writing and the possibility of its connection with an otherwise unknown Jewish-Christian Acts of the Apostles, see H. J. Schoeps, *Theologie und Geschichte des Judenchristentums* (1949), pp. 381-456.

M. S. ENSLIN

JAMES, LETTER OF. The twentieth book in the NT and the first of the so-called CATHOLIC LETTERS.

1. History
   a. Authorship
   b. Reading public
   c. Date
   d. Place of composition
   e. Purpose
2. Message
   a. Genuineness versus pretense
   b. Credentials of leaders
   c. Christian godliness
3. Text

Bibliography

1. History. ***a. Authorship.*** The author identifies himself simply as "James, a servant of God and of the Lord Jesus Christ" (1:1). More specifically, he says he is a teacher (3:1). His excellent Greek style, varied vocabulary, use of the diatribe form, suggest a Greek background. He thought and taught in Koine Greek. His public was as clearly Greek.

The issues with which James of Jerusalem was concerned do not appear in this letter. Author and audience knew Paul through his published letters only. The problems treated by James had grown out of a misuse of such Pauline emphases as love and faith to justify moral inertia and acts of partiality. The soundness of Paul's positions is assumed by James. The sort of antagonism toward Paul manifested by many Jewish Christians nowhere appears in James (cf. Rom. 2:17–4:25; Gal. 1–3).

Eusebius says that in the *Hypotyposes,* Clement of Alexandria gave concise explanations of "all of the Canonical Scriptures, not passing over even the disputed writings." He explains that by the latter he means "the Epistle of Jude and the remaining Catholic Epistles, and the Epistle of Barnabas, and the Apocalypse known as Peter's" (Hist. VI.14.1). No extant statement by Clement substantiates Eusebius' representation. Eusebius himself regarded James, the Lord's brother, whom he calls an apostle, as the author, but he clearly knew the status of the letter was debatable because of uncertainty regarding its authorship. *See* CANON, NT.

Origen is the earliest of the fathers to refer explicitly to James (Commentary on John XIX.23). He seems to have popularized the letter in Alexandria, and under Alexandrian influence its acceptance spread throughout the church. In the East, from the time of Origen, James was generally treated as having been written by the Lord's brother. Eusebius' references to its doubtful status (Hist. II.23.24-25; III.35.3) probably described his knowledge of contrary opinions in Syria and the West.

In Syrian centers like Antioch and Edessa, James was recognized by the fifth century. I John, I Peter, and James were the three Catholics included in the PESHITTA, and James may have been translated for inclusion in that version. In Syrian centers remote from Greek influences, James remained doubtful.

The church in the West came to know James through leaders who had traveled in the East. Hilary of Poitiers (A.D. 356-58) was the first Westerner to refer to the letter as by "the apostle James" (*On the Trinity* IV.8). Jerome included James in the Vulg. version and quoted it in his writings. Augustine's canon was identical with Jerome's, and his espousal of the letter was reflected in its adoption as canonical at the councils of Hippo in 393 and Carthage in 397 and 419. Augustine was the first African father to use James.

Authorship of James by the Lord's brother is rendered unlikely by the fact that prior to Origen it was unknown outside the locality of its origin and was thereafter accepted hesitantly in Syria and the West. Apostolicity early became a credential for canonicity, and skepticism about its authorship accounts for the slowness with which James won its way. Jerome, who was largely responsible for the acceptance of James in the West, thought the Lord's brother wrote it, but he knew the tradition of its pseudonymity and reported that it was thought "by some to have been published by someone else" in James's name, and gradually "as time went on . . . gained authority" (*On Illustrious Men* II).

The tradition of authenticity thus hinges on the judgment of Origen. He may have known an earlier tradition to this effect. Just as possibly, his opinion may have been based on inferences from allusions to James in Acts and in Paul's letters.

Whatever the origin of the tradition, it represented the impression the author of the letter himself probably intended to create. His description of himself (1:1) suggests that he wrote in the name of James of Jerusalem, now a revered figure of a relatively remote past, in whose spirit he intended to speak. The names of Paul, Peter, and John were already associated with influential letters. The name of James, popularized in Acts and Galatians, was, however, available, and could be effectively used in accordance with current literary practice.

b. Reading public. The letter describes its reading public as the "twelve tribes in the dispersion" (1:1). Jewish tribal divisions disappeared centuries before the Christian era, so that it is needlessly literalistic to interpret this address to mean Jews or Jewish Christians. Nothing in the letter suggests the Jewish origin of the readers. The sins condemned are human, not Jewish. The "perfect law, the law of liberty" (1:25), refers, not to the Mosaic system, but to the Christian law of love (cf. Barn. 2.1, 6; Just. Dial. 12.3). James shows no awareness of the antagonistic groups of Paul's time (cf. Acts 15; Gal. 2–3). The address is clearly a designation of Christendom as the spiritual Israel (cf. Matt. 3:9; 12:46-50; Acts 10:34-37; Rom. 4:16; 9:6-8; Gal. 3:7-9; 6:16; Eph. 1:1; I Pet. 1:1; Rev. 7:4-17; 21:10-15).

c. Date. The literary connections of James are the principal basis for an approximate date. The letter does not quote earlier Christian writings. Rather clearly, however, its author knew Romans, I Corinthians, Galatians, and Ephesians, which means that he knew them as members of a published collection. The concern of James and II Peter with the misuse of Paul by heretics strongly suggests A.D. 125-50.

Though in all cases indecisive and requiring detailed discussion, parallels both verbal and ideological suggest James's knowledge of Matthew, Luke, Hebrews, I Peter, Hermas, and I Clement, in addition to Paul's published letters. Paul's letters were published *ca.* A.D. 95. Between 95 and the date of Origen's use of James, the most significant datum is the concern of James and II Peter with the misuse of Paul's teaching. Paul's letters enjoyed a tremendous vogue for the quarter of a century following their publication. Because of the espousal of Paul by heretics during the second quarter of the second century, however, Paul's letters waned in popularity. James apparently originated in this period of waning popularity—i.e., A.D. 125-50.

d. Place of composition. The author's basic interest is the "good life" (3:13). Obedience to the "perfect law" is the foundation of the "good life" (1:25). These emphases so closely resemble those of Matthew and the Didache as to suggest Syrian Antioch as the common place of origin. The hesitancy with which James was accepted in the Syrian canon, however, makes this view less plausible.

More probably, Origen found the letter at Caesarea and brought it with him to Alexandria. Until then it had apparently enjoyed a purely local circulation. Origen's appreciation of it gained an extension of its appeal. A Caesarean origin would explain affinities of the letter with Jesus' teaching as preserved in non-Markan written sources used by Matthew and Luke. The location also fits the comparatively early acceptance of James in the Greek church in the East.

e. Purpose. Faced with serious misuse of Paul's teaching on love and faith, a Greek Christian teacher of the first quarter of the second century wrote a letter in the name of James, whose authority Paul had recognized and with whose approval he had done his missionary work (Acts 15:12-41; Gal. 1:19). He was moved to write because "foolish fellows" (2:20), like the "ignorant and unstable" of II Pet. 3:16, had distorted Paul's emphases "to their own destruction" and the confusion of the church. James condemns an understanding of love that condones "partiality" (2:1-13), and that justifies inertia by equating faith with orthodoxy (2:14-26). Love and faith require commitment to the "perfect law, the law of liberty." The result of such commitment is perseverance in obeying that law. James intended to exalt genuineness and condemn sham. He wrote to insist that religiousness be morally energetic and socially redemptive. He proposed to arouse the conscience of the church on issues confused in the preaching of incompetent and heretical leaders.

2. Message. The theme of James is the "righteousness of God" (1:20), meaning the righteousness God approves. The letter is an exposition of this theme under three broad headings:

I. Genuineness versus pretense, 1:2–2:26
II. Credentials of leaders, 3:1-18
III. Christian godliness, 4–5

Somewhat more specifically, James insists that righteousness involves performance, not merely perception of truth. A piety that is exclusively devotional or intellectual is counterfeit. Effective piety is a synthesis of endurance (1:2-18), obedience (1:19-27), impartiality (2:1-13), integrity (2:14-26), discipline

(3:1–4:10), humility (4:11–5:6), patience (5:7-11), prayerfulness (5:12-18), and love (5:19-20).

The superscription (1:1) sets the tone of the message. Its point of view is more definitely theological than moralistic. The author describes himself as a "servant [δοῦλος] of God and of the Lord Jesus Christ." This is the equivalent of saying that God has no competitors for his devotion. He utterly belongs to God and desires to be used in bringing God's will to pass. His acknowledgment of Jesus Christ as Lord gives his service to God its most fruitful norm (cf. Rom. 10:9-13). The author is, in other words, a Christian, distinguished from other Christians only in having assumed the role of a teacher (3:1).

Under the analogy of the "twelve tribes in the dispersion," James addresses the church in its wholeness as the spiritual Israel. "The dispersion" (ἡ διασπορά) described the Jews as separated from their homeland and scattered among alien nations (cf. Jer. 15:4-7; Dan. 9:7; John 7:35; I Pet. 1:1). In the first century, three fourths of all Jews in the Roman world were so scattered. They found it advantageous to live outside Palestine, and most of them had emigrated for this reason. Sentimentally, however, the dispersion was regarded as lamentable, and it was felt that God's providence would be fulfilled by reunion in their homeland (cf. Isa. 40:1-5; 43:5-19; 49:22-25; 66:20-23). Applied to the church, "the dispersion" described Christians as temporarily residing in a hostile world, and as looking toward the bliss of a heavenly homeland. Christians, wherever located, were united by the hope of being together eternally (John 14:1-3; 17:10-20; Gal. 4:26; Phil. 3:20-21; Heb. 12:22-29; 13:14; I Pet. 1:1; Rev. 21–22).

a. Genuineness versus pretense. The emphasis on genuineness is positively stated in 1:2-18. Exposure of pretense in 1:19–2:26 complements the analysis of genuineness and clarifies its meaning. Constituent elements in true religion are unwavering constancy, maturity of character, expectant prayerfulness, heavenly wisdom, joy based on preference for true values, confident hope, objectivity in self-judgment.

The trials (πειρασμοί) James discusses are related to πειρατής, from which the English word "pirate" comes. A pirate attacks with a view to taking valuables from their owner. Satan is called ὁ πειράζων (Matt. 4:3; cf. I Cor. 7:5; 10:13; I Thess. 3:5). By analogy, "trials" assault men of faith and tend to create skepticism of God's providence. Instead of jeopardizing faith, however, trials should enhance it by enriching its elements. Christians should be glad to have their faith subjected to critical appraisal. Accordingly, they are to count it unmixed joy (πᾶσαν χαράν) when variegated trials (ποικίλοις πειρασμοῖς) come. Trials make the elements of true faith stand out in bold relief.

Constancy (ὑπομονή) is the inner principle of faith. It is staying power. Adversity brings out this aspect of faith and develops it (cf. Rom. 5:3-5). Constancy is prerequisite to perfection (τελείωσις; cf. Heb. 12:2, τελειωτής τῆς πίστεως, where Christ is described as raising faith to its ultimate expression). James urges a mature, as against a partially developed, faith (1:4: ἔργον τέλειον ἐχέτω; cf. 2:22). This is comparable to Paul's idea of faith working itself out in love (Rom. 6; Gal. 5:6; cf. John 17:4). Maturity of character is the goal of faith, and James thinks trials foster maturity (1:2-4).

This perfection is nurtured by prayer that is undoubting (μηδὲν διακρινόμενος)—i.e., faith whose inner principle is the constancy developed in trial (1:5-8). The wind-tossed sea and the irresolution of a double-minded man (ἀνὴρ δίψυχος) are analogies for ineffective faith. When a man prays, he must face one way—toward God—and ignore all else. The object of such prayer is wisdom, a religious equivalent of the worldly man's capacity for achieving success based on discernment and determination. God bestows such wisdom impartially and generously in answer to undoubting faith. God matches prayer of this quality with generosity: he "gives to all men generously." His impartial generosity in bestowing wisdom is man's warrant for praying.

Poverty and wealth illustrate the trials James discusses (1:9-12). Both the gaining of wealth and its loss typify the circumstances of Christians. Joy in the midst of adversity discloses the wisdom God gives. The ephemeral character of riches, discerned by wisdom, is illustrated by flowers that "fade and die." Moral growth in adversity is, by contrast, heavenly wealth (cf. I Cor. 7:17-24). The reward of steadfastness and perfection is the "crown of life which God has promised to those who love him" (1:12). Genuine faith enables men to face the future unafraid. God's reward is eternal, not ephemeral. God's victor's wreath is a "crown of life"—i.e., eternal life (cf. John 3:15; 10:10; Rom. 2:7; I Cor. 9:25; Rev. 2:7-10).

James next examines the origin of trials, which are more easily occasions for temptation than for joy (1:13-18). If God is regarded as sending trials, Christians will tend to yield and sin. So James insists that though trials may be so met as to please God, their origin cannot be attributed to God. Like Paul (cf. I Cor. 10:9-13), James destroys the self-excusing sinner's chief defense. God as God is untemptable (ἀπείραστος) and does not violate his character by tempting men. Nor is Satan responsible (cf. Enoch 69:4-15). Temptation is from within; man's inner life is the source. By their own desires (ὑπὸ τῆς ἰδίας ἐπιθυμίας) men are enticed. As the author pursues these figures of hunting, desire becomes temptation's bait, and the lured man finds death, not a "crown of life" (cf. Rom. 6:15-23; 8:5-30). Invariably, from God come "every good endowment and every perfect gift." God is undeviating, and in him "there is no variation or shadow due to change" (1:17). Truth, as revelation in its totality, supplies men with a guide for achieving the crown of life (1:18).

In 1:19–2:26, James complements his exposition of genuineness by exposing pretense to view. Right response to instruction is the keynote in 1:19-27. Moral consistency as the foundation of worship is the theme in ch. 2.

Appropriate performance is made the test of good listening (1:19-27). Attentiveness is important, but as the condition of discovery of duty. Execution of duty is the listener's primary concern. The teacher's words are lures to action. One who divorces hearing from doing is like "a man who observes his natural face in a mirror . . . and goes away and at once forgets what he was like" (1:23-24).

Scriptural revelation and inner conviction support James's contention (cf. Rom. 5:1-11). Truth inwrought in man's heart (ἔμφυτος λόγος) and revealed in the Scriptures forms the substance of Christian teaching. Interpretation of man to himself and exposition of historical revelation are the teacher's twofold task. For the Christian, truth is always imperative, never merely descriptive.

The Greek word θρησκεία, translated "religion" (1:27), describes religion in terms of observances and rites, both external. James contends that actual sanctity takes precedence over rites. To control the tongue and manifest sympathy with "orphans and widows" is to "keep oneself unstained from the world." Deeds that express love, not rites, constitute genuine purity.

Partiality (προσωποληψία), based on outer circumstances, betrays religion (2:1-7). Two excuses for so perverting Christianity are refuted in 2:8-12, 14-26. In 2:1-7, James contends that faith alone makes men Christian. Religion is debased when churchmen classify men by worldly norms. Non-Christian outsiders have, presumably, visited church services. Fawning before them is an effort to win them to membership. Granting success, such members would be Christian in appearance only. James insists that rich visitors be so treated as to show them that true wealth belongs to the realm of faith. The criteria of the kingdom, not the world, control God's judgment and should dictate the attitudes of churchmen.

The "royal law" (2:8) is clearly the Christian law of love. Partiality has been excused as an observance of this law. Deference to rich visitors has masqueraded as redemptive love. James brands such pretense as a caricature of evangelism (2:8-13). Evangelism is futile, he contends, if it leaves men ignorant of moral values implicit in the gospel. They will be unmercifully judged who cater to the rich, because they are unfair in leaving the rich uninstructed regarding true wealth.

Faith has also been caricatured as a substitute for living by Christian standards (2:14-26). This is a second instance of sham. Christians are πιστοί, but faith as commitment is energetic, not apathetic (cf. Gal. 5:6, 13-26; 6:2-4; I Thess. 1:3). Demons, Abraham, Rahab, are three analogies for the energetic quality of saving faith. James's contrast is between two grades of faith, or between nominal and actual Christians. Faith and the behavior it implies are halves of an indivisible whole. Instead of discussing faith and works on a Pauline precedent, James deals with faith conceived to be either living or dead. The one effectively saves; the other is useless—i.e., dead (νεκρός)—in that it accomplishes nothing.

b. Credentials of leaders. In 3:1-12, the church leader is called teacher, and in 3:13-18, wise man. The discussion throughout reflects the atmosphere of the second century and tends to locate James in the context of the Didache and the Pastoral letters. James makes it clear that personal qualities, not status, are important. In view of temptations teachers face, James urges that few nominate themselves for the role. Being a teacher, he knows the severity with which God will judge teachers (ἐιδοτες ὅτι μείζον κρίμα λημψόμεθα; 3:1).

Wisdom implies a reasoned view of life. Whether earthly or heavenly, it proposes conduct designed to win success. Criteria belong to the realm in which success is sought. In 5:19-20, James describes as truth the body of revelation that guides men in godliness. The wise man is expected to exemplify and urge this truth as the basis for success—i.e., salvation. Irresponsibility in speech has been reprimanded already (cf. 1:19, 26; 2:12). Such irresponsibility in a teacher implicates the church. It is singled out, now, as the most prevalent of the "many mistakes" Christians make. Control of the tongue thus typifies the thoroughly disciplined life. It is the mark of maturity (τέλειος ἀνήρ). Because few Christians are so disciplined, the number of aspirants for teaching should be kept to the minimum (3:1-12).

A too passionate zeal for one's own views is apt to be the undoing of the wise man (3:13-18). Controversialism is, therefore, a less desirable evidence of wisdom than meekness, purity, peaceableness, gentleness, reasonableness, mercy—the elements that compose the wisdom that "comes from above." By contrast, earthly wisdom involves "jealousy and selfish ambition . . . , disorder and every vile practice," precisely because it is "unspiritual" and "devilish." Heavenly wisdom is the leader's best credential, and with it he must be endowed "from above."

c. Christian godliness. Worldiness and godliness, briefly contrasted in 3:13-18, are now elaborately analyzed. In 4:1–5:6 worldliness is portrayed and censured, and in 5:7-20 the Christian virtues are urged on the basis of the nearness of the "coming of the Lord" and the inspiring examples of Job and Elijah as representative prophets. Worldliness is examined under three manifestations: double-mindedness, or "friendship with the world" (4:1-12); presumptuousness, illustrated by traders who plan with no thought of God (4:13-17); and devotion to pleasure (5:1-6).

Worldly wisdom has been described as "earthly, unspiritual, devilish," and as finding fruition in "jealousy and selfish ambition . . . , disorder and every vile practice" (3:14-16). Prevalence of this wisdom constitutes "friendship with the world" (4:1-12). It explains the generally lost condition of the world. The church has not remedied this state of affairs because, instead of employing the wisdom that "comes down from above," it has accepted the worldliness which breeds "wars" and "fightings."

This "friendship with the world" makes desire (ἐπιθυμία) the norm of behavior (4:2). It may take many forms: pleasure-madness, acquisitiveness, double-mindedness, pride (cf. Luke 12:16-21). Inner tensions and social confusion are its results. The mark of godliness, by contrast, is humility; and to the humble, God "gives more grace" (4:7). Spiritual values alone satisfy man's spirit, because God himself bestows that spirit.

Desire to possess correlates the thought of 4:1-12 with that of 4:13-17. The traders whose one thought is to "get gain" are, presumably, nominal Christians. They know "what is right" but fail to do it (4:17). Their self-confidence causes them to omit God from their plans. They never say, "If the Lord wills" (4: 13-16).

That there were rich Christians is implied in 1:9-10. Wealth, like desire, is now condemned as a false and frustrating goal (5:1-6). The rich, whether

Christians or not, exhibit the folly of making wealth life's goal. James pleads that Christians make the Lord their "portion." As with the rich man in Luke 16:19-31, the prospect for the rich is the judgment of the Lord of hosts. When the "miseries" of that judgment befall them, they will "weep and howl." The inhumanities of their money-madness make them objects of God's wrath. The transitoriness of riches (5:1-3), inhumanities involved in acquiring them (5:4, 6), the sensuality they engender (5:5), combine to require God's condemnation.

In 5:7-20, James turns to the positive commendation of qualities that mark men as friends of God. These qualities are patience (μακροθυμία; 5:7-10), steadfastness (ὑπομονή; 5:11), truthfulness (ἤτω δὲ ὑμῶν τὸ ναὶ ναί καὶ τὸ οὒ οὔ; 5:12), confident prayerfulness (5:13-18), readiness to confess one's sins (5:15-16), and active concern for the salvation of sinners (5:19-20).

Instead of bitter retaliation against those who by "fraud" have kept back the wages of the laborers, and who have "lived on the earth in luxury," and who have "killed the righteous man," Christians are urged to be patient (μακροθυμήσατε). This patience is closely related to expectancy ("The Judge is standing at the doors," as in II Thess. 2:5). It is in view of the "coming of the Lord" that patience is obligatory. The farmer and the prophets illustrate this expectant calmness (5:7-10).

Steadfastness (ὑπομονή) is akin to patience, but specifically describes the man whom no suffering can frighten (5:11). It is patience manifested in unwavering constancy (cf. 1:2-4). Job is the great exemplar of this virtue, and its justification is found in the compassion of the Lord. The injunction against swearing (5:12) is conceivably a condemnation of malediction in contrast with patience. More probably, it has the meaning of Matt. 5:34-37, where the oath guarantees truth. James, like Jesus, pleads for a rigorous integrity that obviates the need for swearing. The "fraud" used in holding back the "wages of the laborers" typifies the evil system that necessitates oaths.

Prayer taps divine sources of strength (5:13-18). Whatever the problem (suffering, sickness, sin, frustration), the "prayer of faith" (cf. 1:6) puts the Christian in touch with ultimate sources of help. It is the Christian's principal reliance in life's vicissitudes. Confession of sins (5:15-16; cf. Rom. 14:11) is primarily Godward and is thus an aspect of prayer. It is manward also, and so looks toward prayer for "one another" by Christians.

Finally, Christians who bring a wandering brother back to the truth will save the sinner's soul "from death and will cover a multitude of sins" (5:19-20). "The truth" is the body of revealed norms, religious and moral, recognized by the church for guidance in godliness. They who "wander from the truth" have in some way violated this revelation. Such "wandering" is serious and conceivably threatens death. It is not, however, irremediable (cf. Heb. 6:4-8; Herm. Vis. II.2.4-8). Not only so, but he who "brings back a sinner" will "cover" his own sins, even though they be "a multitude" (cf. Prov. 10:12; I Pet. 4:8; I Clem. 49:5).

3. Text. The history of James in the third and fourth centuries does not coincide with that of the other CATHOLIC LETTERS. The study of its text is for this reason unencumbered by problems that attend the remainder of the group. The first version of James does not antedate the fourth century. Materials of primary importance for the study of the text are the Greek uncial and minuscule MSS and the various versions of the Greek text. References to James in the writings of early church fathers are extremely limited in number.

Codex Vaticanus of the early uncials best preserves the text. There the text of James is comparatively free of emendations. Vaticanus is probably the oldest extant Greek MS of the letter.

The correction of texts was widespread at a very early date, and most of the significant variants in the text of James were extant by the fourth century. A comparison of the collations of uncial MSS shows few instances of significant variants in which Vaticanus stands alone. Its readings show less evidence of emendation than the solitary witness of uncials ℵ, A, and C. In combination with Sinaiticus or Alexandrinus, there is no instance of emendation, whereas uncial combinations excluding Vaticanus are relatively numerous. The preference in Vaticanus for shorter readings distinguishes it from Sinaiticus. The readings of Codex Ephraem do not differ appreciably from Alexandrinus.

The text of James in Codex Alexandrinus is more closely related to the cursive Codex 33 than to any of the uncials. In fifteen readings, A and 33 stand together without corroboration of other uncials. Most of these, however, represent deliberate correction. Deviations from the witness of earlier uncials in such ninth-century uncials as K, L, and P yield few readings free from suspicion. Emendation in the interest of improvement of style and the explanation of the text characterizes these ninth-century uncials. They represent the Antiochian text and are of first importance as the textual basis of later MSS that underlie the texts of Erasmus and the Complutensian Polyglot.

Until the middle of the third century, Greek was the official language of the church in the West. Under Pope Callistus, Latin supplanted Greek, and a translation of the Greek text became necessary. The Old Latin version was the result. Individual MSS of this version show pronounced textual variation. The exact origin of this version is not known, but it enjoyed wide circulation in North Africa. The best extant witnesses to the Old Latin for James are the ninth-century Codex Corbeiensis and Speculum Pseudo-Augustini. They both testify to a common Greek text of which, apparently, a single translation was made. Of older Greek uncials, their closest affinities are with Vaticanus, which means that they represent a Neutral type of text. Both, however, have undergone a greater degree of emendation than Vaticanus. In the Armenian Version, the text of the Catholic epistles corresponds most closely to the text of Vaticanus. *See* TEXT, NT.

Bibliography. J. B. Mayor, *The Epistle of James* (1892); J. H. Ropes, *The Epistle of James,* ICC (1916); R. J. Knowling, *The Epistle of James,* Westminster Series (1922); F. Hauck, "Der Brief des Jakobus," *Kommentar zum NT* (1926); J. Moffatt, *The General Epistles,* Moffatt NT Commentary (1928); A. Meyer, *Das Raetsel des Jakobusbriefes* (1930); H. Windisch, "Die katholischen Briefe," 3rd ed., reworked by H. Preisker, in *Handbuch zum NT* (1951); F. Hauck, *Die Kirchenbriefe* (7th ed., 1954); M. Dibelius, *Der Brief des Jakobus* (8th ed., prepared by H. Greeven; Meyer Series; 1956); B. S. Easton, Introduction and Exegesis of James, *IB*, XII (1957), 3-74.

A. E. BARNETT

JAMES, PROTEVANGELIUM OF prō'tĭ văn jĕl'ĭ əm. The earliest of the infancy gospels, recounting the birth, childhood, adolescence, token marriage, supernatural pregnancy, and delivery of Mary. Together with the Gospel of Thomas (*see* THOMAS, GOSPEL OF), it was the chief source of several other infancy gospels. Its original title appears to have been History of James Concerning the Birth of Mary; Origen refers to it as the Book of James. The title Gospel of James the Less, under which it was condemned in the Gelasian Decree, is not earlier than the fourth century. It was first styled Protevangelium (i.e., Protogospel) of James by its sixteenth-century discoverer, Guillaume Postel.

The earliest certain reference to this writing is by Origen, who cites it as the source of the tradition that Jesus' brothers were "sons of Joseph by a former wife whom he had married before Mary." His added comment: "Now these who say so wish to preserve the honor of Mary in virginity to the end" (*On Matthew* 10.17), accurately describes the apparent purpose of the author, who claimed in the concluding section to be James, head of the Jerusalem church: "Now I, James, who wrote this history in Jerusalem, when there arose a tumult when Herod died, withdrew myself into the wilderness until the tumult ceased in Jerusalem. Glorifying the Lord God who gave me the gift and wisdom to write this history."

The writing tells the story of the birth and early years of Mary. Like Samuel—the story clearly reflects the OT narrative—she is born to Anna and Joachim in answer to the bitter prayers of the long-barren woman and her husband, after an angelic visitation to each separately (cf. the same note in the story of the birth of Samson). At the age of three, in accord with the earlier vow of the mother, Mary is brought to the temple and seated by the priest upon the third step of the altar. She is brought up in the temple as a sort of Jewish vestal virgin, "as a dove that is nurtured" and fed solicitously by angels, until, reaching the age of twelve, she becomes a problem.

In answer to the advice of his fellow priests the high priest Zacharias enters the holy of holies, prays, and receives divine direction for her betrothal to that one of the widowers of the people who shall be designated by a divine portent. Her betrothal to Joseph follows, for from his rod a dove flies out and lights upon his head. Joseph's unwillingness to be made a "laughingstock to the children of Israel" is silenced by a warning reference to the fates of Dathan, Abiram, and Korah, and he takes her to his house, while he himself goes "to build his buildings."

Then follows, as a sort of interlude, the story of her selection by the priests, as one of the pure virgins of the tribe of David, to weave the "true purple and scarlet" portion of the veil of the temple. "At that season Zacharias became dumb and Samuel was in his stead until the time when Zacharias again spake." Mary, while filling her pitcher with water, hears the word: "Hail, thou art highly favored—blessed art thou among women." As she is spinning the thread for the temple veil, an angel appears and announces the birth of a son, whom she shall name Jesus. When the spinning is completed, Mary visits Elizabeth. "Now she was sixteen years old when these mysteries came to pass."

Joseph, now returning from his building and finding her six-months pregnant, reproaches her, but is admonished in a dream. Later he is accused by Annas the scribe; but when he and Mary drink the waters of conviction with no ill effect, the high priest is convinced of their innocence.

Then follows the decree of Augustus, the trip to Bethlehem (apparently from Jerusalem), where Mary is left in a cave while Joseph seeks a midwife. At this point the narrative changes without warning to the first person, with Joseph the speaker, describing first the sudden and complete cessation of all action in nature and mankind, and then his conversation with a midwife.

The narrative changes back to the third person, with the birth of the baby in the cave, the testimony of the midwife and Salome that even after the birth Mary is a virgin, and the restoration, by contact with the infant Jesus, of Salome's hand, which has "fallen away from her in fire" because of her unbelief in Mary's virginity.

Then follows the story of the Wise Men and the star (which stands over the head of the cave). In fear of Herod's decree, Mary wraps the young child and hides him in an ox manger.

Then follows the story of the miraculous escape of John the Baptist, for whom, his mother hears, Herod is searching. She flees to the hill country, and finding no place of escape, groans aloud: "O mountain of God, receive thou a mother with her child. And immediately the mountain clave asunder and took her in."

Then follows the death of Zacharias, who is arrested and slain by the officers of the enraged Herod. The priests enter the temple, find blood congealed by the altar, and are informed by an angelic voice of the murder of Zacharias. Symeon is elected by lot to take his place and is promised that he shall not see death until he shall see the Christ in the flesh. With the claim to authority (quoted above) and a brief benediction the document ends.

This résumé of contents reveals that the birth stories in Matthew and Luke are the principal sources. In a manner similar to that in which the other type of infancy gospels—namely, the Gospel of Thomas and its imitators—sought to fill in the "hidden years" of Jesus' boyhood, this nameless author has "filled in" for Mary. Considerable ingenuity is displayed in braiding into the purely imaginative story many biblical touches, with a total disregard of their original setting. There seems no slightest trace of what might be properly styled independent tradition, while attempts to see this account as the earlier source of the stories in Matthew and Luke are manifestly absurd.

That the story as we now have it is all the product of one author is most unlikely. The sudden introduction of Joseph as the narrator of one section; the story of the choice of Mary to be one of the makers of the veil of the temple; the unexplained lapse of four years, during which Joseph is seemingly absent from home "building his buildings"—Mary was twelve at the time of her marriage, sixteen when found to be pregnant; the long section at the end having to do with Zacharias and his death, have suggested to several investigators that at least two narratives have been woven together, and hypotheses of an Apocryphon of Joseph and also one of Zacharias have been offered.

Touches from folklore are clearly to be seen, as in the reference to the cave as the site of the divine birth—a common motif far earlier than the Christian legend—and the supernatural and portentous hush that held all nature speechless. These suggest a familiarity on the part of the teller or tellers of this tale with popular legend and tradition, but to what extent they and the other variations evidence the formal use of other written sources is at best uncertain. That the author knew stories of Isis and of the vestal virgins is entirely likely; his reference to the years Mary spent in the temple is nevertheless adequately explained on the basis of the story of the boy Samuel, while the statement that the aged prophetess Anna—no less a female—"did not depart from the temple" (Luke 2:37) is not to be overlooked.

That the story was composed in Greek in the second century, very probably in Egypt, and had acquired its present form prior to Epiphanius, is widely recognized. Many MSS containing the text in whole or in part are extant. Most of them are not earlier than the tenth century, although one may be dated in the ninth, and occasional fragments still earlier. Versions from the Greek are extant in Syriac, Armenian, and Coptic. Whether a Latin version was ever made is uncertain. At any rate, none is known.

Although early pronounced heretical, the Protevangelium of James has had a very wide influence. The source, as already stated, for many other apocryphal writings, notably the Gospel of Pseudo-Matthew (*see* PSEUDO-MATTHEW, GOSPEL OF) and those dependent upon this, it is summarized in the *Golden Legend,* compiled by Jacobus de Voragine in the thirteenth century. It was the principal, if indirect, source of the cult of Saint Anne and the Feast of the Presentation of the Virgin in the Temple, and the inspiration of many of the masterpieces of such Italian painters as Giotto, Raphael, and Titian.

See also APROCRYPHA, NT.

Bibliography. An English translation is given by M. R. James, *The Apocryphal NT* (1924), pp. 38-49. Brief descriptions with convenient bibliographies of editions and studies are to be found in B. Altaner, *Patrologie* (2nd ed., 1950), pp. 50-51; J. Quasten, *Patrology* (1950), I, 118-22. M. S. ENSLIN

JAMES THE GREAT, ACTS OF. One of the many romances styled apocryphal Acts (*see* ACTS, APOCRYPHAL; APOCRYPHA, NT), purporting to set forth the adventures and martyrdom of James the son of Zebedee, in amplification of the bare notice in the canonical Acts. It is extant only in Latin, as bk. IV of the Apostolic History of Abdias (*see* ABDIAS, APOSTOLIC HISTORY OF), although it is possible that there was an earlier Greek original, of which no trace has come down save an apparent quotation by Clement of Alexandria in his lost *Hypotyposes,* in which James forgives his accuser while en route to martyrdom (Euseb. Hist. II.9.1-3).

James is represented as being in constant conflict with the magician Hermogenes and his disciple Philetus (cf. II Tim. 1:15; 2:17), the latter of whom he finally converts and empowers to perform miracles. The bare mention in the canonical Acts of James's martyrdom is, of course, amplified. After a dispute with the Jews, in which James quotes many pat prophetic passages from the OT, he is beheaded, together with a scribe named Josias, whom James converts and pardons.

The book is a commonplace tale of magical wonders, influenced by the earlier legend of Peter in constant conflict with his archopponent, Simon Magus.

Bibliography. A brief résumé of the contents of the book is found in M. R. James, *The Apocryphal NT* (1924), pp. 463-64.
M. S. ENSLIN

JAMIN jā'mĭn [ימין, good fortune; Apoc. 'Ιάδινος]; JAMINITES —mĭ nīts; KJV Apoc. ADINUS ə dī'nəs. **1.** An eponym; son of Simeon (Gen. 46:10 [cf. Jub. 44:13]; Exod. 6:15; Num. 26:12; I Chr. 4:24).

2. A Jerahmeelite (I Chr. 2:27).

3. One of the Levites who helped interpret the law to the people at the public reading by Ezra (Neh. 8:7; I Esd. 9:48). B. T. DAHLBERG

JAMLECH jăm'lĕk [ימלך, may (the deity) give dominion] (I Chr. 4:34; cf. vs. 38). A Simeonite and family prince.

JAMNIA. *See* JABNEEL.

JANAI jā'nī [יעני, may (the deity) answer] (I Chr. 5:12); KJV JAANAI jā'ə nī. A Gadite.

Bibliography. M. Noth, *Die israelitischen Personennamen* (1928), pp. 27-28, 198.

JANIM jăn'ĭm [ינים] (Josh. 15:53); KJV JANUM jā'nəm [*Qere* ינחם]. A village of Judah in the hill-country district of Hebron; possibly to be identified with Beni Na'im, E of Hebron.

JANNAI jăn'ī ['Ιανναί] (Luke 3:24); KJV JANNA jăn'ə. An ancestor of Jesus.

JANNES AND JAMBRES jăn'ĭz, jăm'brĭz ['Ιαννῆς καὶ 'Ιαμβρῆς (Μαμβρῆς)=יוחני וממרא; Aram. (Targ.) ינים וימברים (*cf.* Gr.)]. The legendary Egyptian magicians who opposed Moses and Aaron and duplicated their miracles to discredit them (Exod. 7:11-12, 22), and who came to typify heretical opponents to truth in Jewish and Christian circles (cf. II Tim. 3:8). In Exodus they are anonymous, and the names do not occur in the OT, Philo, or Josephus. But they are common in late Jewish and in Christian sources, and are partly attested in pagan writers. The names may be Grecized Aramaic, and may all derive from forms of "John." Certain references in Origen and the Decree of Gelasius (*see below*) attest the existence of an apocryphon, perhaps in the first century A.D., describing and condemning their activities.

The non-Jewish sources are brief, simply identifying them as outstanding magicians living after Zoroaster, one (Numenius) associating them with the Exodus episode. Two of the three pagan references name only Jannes (Pliny Nat. Hist. XXX.2.11; Lucius Apuleius *Apology* II.90). These are from the first and second centuries respectively. The Neoplatonic Numenius (second century), as cited by Origen (*Against Celsus* IV.51) and Eusebius (*Preparation for the Gospel* IX.8), mention both. The two are also named in various Christian sources, the earliest, besides II Timothy, being Origen (*On Matt.* 23:37; 27:9), Cyprian (*On the Unity of the Church* 16), Acts of Pilate 5; Apostolic Constitutions VIII.1, and the so-called Decree of Gelasius (sixth century).

In the late Jewish and Samaritan sources an extensive legendary tradition developed about them in connection with the Exodus account, and they were also associated with the eschatological conflict between good and evil as false prophets and antagonists of God and Israel. They were connected with the figure of Bileam (Balaam) and with Beliar (Belial). The earliest written tradition which mentions them (Damascus Document 7.18-19; *ca.* 100 B.C.) speaks of Belial as "setting up" or "rearing up" Jannes and his brother in opposition to Moses and Aaron, and the Jerusalem Targ. to Exodus (22:22) makes them the wizard sons of Balaam, as do various rabbinic sources (*see bibliography*). In this tradition they escape with Balaam to Ethiopia and usurp the throne of the king, Kikanos. But they are routed through the intervention of Moses and flee to Egypt, where they become Pharaoh's head magicians. According to another legend, they become proselytes to Judaism and join in the Exodus. Cf. the title of the book referred to in the Decree of Gelasius: *Poenitentia Jannis et Mamre*. The names BALAAM (Bileam) and BELIAL apparently were confused in the various legends.

Bibliography. E. Schürer, *Geschichte des jüdischen Volkes* (3rd ed., 1909), III, 402-5, gives the text of the pagan and Christian sources and references to the Jewish accounts; H. L. Strack and P. Billerbeck, *Kommentar zum NT aus Talmud und Midrasch*, III (1926), 661 ff; M. Gaster, *The Asatir* (1927), pp. 80-99, etc. (on the Samaritan documents and beliefs); J. Bidez and F. Cumont, *Les Mages hellénisés* (1938), pp. 11-14 (for the pagan references); H. Odeberg and A. Oepke in R. Kittel, *TWNT*, III (1938), 192-93, 990-91, give data on the origin, spelling, etc., of the names; L. Ginzberg, *The Legends of the Jews* (7 vols.; 1910-39), contains the legendary materials and references to the rabbinic sources; M. Dibelius, *Die Pastoralbriefe* (1955), pp. 87-88.

A. WIKGREN

JANNEUS jă nē'əs [ינאי, *from* יונתן, Jonathan; Ἰανναῖος]. King of Judea *ca.* 103-76 B.C.; also called Alexander (Ἀλέξανδρος); son of John Hyrcanus. His half brother Aristobulus I, on becoming king, imprisoned Alexander. But when Aristobulus died, after a year's reign, Alexander succeeded him and also married the childless widow. He then became high priest and thus did not violate the law of levirate marriage, which prevents a high priest from marrying a widow. Perhaps the notion that a high priest is not permitted to marry in a levirate manner was a later measure.

Alexander Janneus was concerned with imperialism. He besieged Ptolemaïs (Acre) but was repulsed by Ptolemy Lathyrus and suffered great losses. He was saved only when Cleopatra sent two Jewish generals to help Alexander against her banished son,

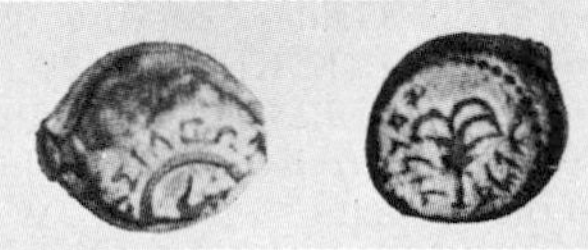

Courtesy of the Trustees of the British Museum

8. Coin of Alexander Janneus

Ptolemy Lathyrus. She was dissuaded from annexing Judea only by these generals. In new campaigns Alexander Janneus suffered losses also in NE Palestine. He was most successful in his expedition against Philistia and Gaza. The rift between the Pharisees and the Sadducees is set by the Talmud as occurring in his day (Ḳid. 66*b*).

Friction developed between Janneus and the Pharisees, who disliked his warlike tactics but sought only religious observances. They also resented his assumption of the title "king." Alexander sided with the Sadducees, and in a ceremony on the Feast of Booths the people pelted him with their citrons. He allowed the mercenaries free run, and they killed six thousand Pharisees.

Janneus was unsuccessful against the Arabs and returned to find the Pharisees opposed to him, seeking his death as a condition for lasting peace. They negotiated with Demetrius III to fight against their own king. However, in time they repented of their act and left the Syrians, to turn toward Alexander. Alexander treated them cruelly, executing eight hundred Pharisees before the eyes of their wives and children, while he feasted with his courtesans. Many Pharisees then emigrated to Syria or Egypt.

Alexander continucd his warlike campaigns, battling against the Arab king Aretas, but was shamefully defeated by him. Even though he was afflicted with disease, he continued his warlike activities, suffering much the last three years of his life. His wife, Salome, was entrusted with the civil government. On his deathbed, he counseled her to be friendly with the Pharisees but only to fear the hypocrites therein (Soṭ. 22*b*). Despite his cruelty the Pharisees gave him last honors.

Alexander's main purpose was to increase the boundaries of Judea. Hence he came into conflict with the Pharisees on political matters. All his gains were temporary, for his reign brought about excessive hardships later to his people.

The Talmud narrates many incidents of his association with his brother-in-law Simon ben Shetah, one of the leaders of the Great Sanhedrin. Alexander's wife, Salome Alexandra, succeeded him as ruler, introducing a favorable Pharisaic rule.

Fig. JAN 8.

Bibliography. For the original narrative in Josephus, see Antiq. XIII.xiii; War I.iv. See also: J. Derenbourg, *Essai sur l'histoire de la Palestine* (1867), pp. 86, 99 ff; E. Schürer, *The History of the Jewish People in the Time of Jesus Christ* (1891), div. 1, vol. I, pp. 295 ff; L. Ginzberg, "Alexander Jannaeus," *Jewish Encyclopedia*, I (1902), 353; R. H. Pfeiffer, *History of NT Times* (1949), pp. 21 ff, 190.

S. B. HOENIG

JANOAH jə nō'ə [ינוח]; KJV JANOHAH —hə in Josh. 16:6-7. **1.** A border town in Ephraim (Josh. 16:6-7). It is identified with Khirbet Yanun, *ca.* seven miles SE of Shechem.

2. A town in N Galilee, captured by Tiglath-pileser III of Assyria (II Kings 15:29). The site is uncertain, but it must have been located between Abel-beth-maacah and Kedesh (cf. Josh. 19:37), according to the context. G. W. VAN BEEK

JANUM. KJV form of JANIM.

JAPHETH jā'fĭth [יפת, *see* § 1 *below;* Ιαφεθ]. The second son of Noah.

1. Etymology. OT tradition connects *yâpheth* (pausal form of *yépheth*) with the Hebrew verb פתה: "God enlarge [יפת] Japheth" (so RSV), or "May God make Japheth spacious" (Gen. 9:27 [J]). This folk etymology may have carried theological as well as geographical connotations.

No positive connection has been established with *Kafti,* the Egyptian designation of the (Eteo-)Cretans, or with the Greek Titan Japetos (Ιαπετος), the father of Atlas and Prometheus.

2. The blessing of Japheth. When Noah became drunk from the wine of his vineyard and lay uncovered in his tent, "his youngest son" breeched the laws of Hebrew modesty—though apparently without premeditation—by seeing the nakedness of his father. The two older brothers, walking backward, covered Noah (Gen. 9:20-23). Upon awaking, Noah cursed Canaan, making him the lowest of slaves to his brothers (*see* CANAANITES § 1). Then, after blessing SHEM (§ 2), he said:

> God [אלהים] enlarge Japheth,
> and let him dwell in the tents of Shem;
> and let Canaan be his slave (vs. 27).

This story presents such a different view of Noah's life and family from that given in the flood account that they are best considered separate traditions. There are strong indications that this J tradition of Noah the vinegrower knew that patriarch's three sons as Shem, Japheth, and Canaan. To harmonize this version with the Priestly list, an editor would then have added Ham as Canaan's father in vss. 18, 22.

The people who are to dwell with the Hebrews in Canaan are, most probably, the PHILISTINES. Although the Hittites have also been proposed, 10:18 links them with the descendants of Ham.

Accordingly, Von Rad postulates, the Yahwist picked up this ancient piece and placed it here to show why the Israelites (Shem) do not have sole possession of the land promised to their fathers. It had been God's will from the beginning, as Noah himself prophesied, that the Philistines (Japheth) would also have a share in Canaan.

3. The table of nations. In the Priestly genealogy Japheth is the youngest of Noah's three sons and the father of Gomer, Magog, Madai, Javan, Tubal, Meshech, and Tiras (Gen. 10:1-2; cf. I Chr. 1:4-5). Since this table is really a "map in literary form," it presents Japheth as the ancestor of those ancient peoples who lived to the W and the N of the Hebrews—principally those dwelling in the regions adjacent to the Aegean, Black, and Caspian seas (*see* MAN, ETHNIC DIVISIONS OF). These are mainly the components of the Indo-European family of nations whose area stretched from the S coasts of Europe to Persia.

Bibliography. F. M. T. Böhl, *Kanaanäer und Hebräer* (1911), pp. 19, 68-69; G. von Rad, *Das erste Buch Mose,* ATD, 2 (1949), pp. 111-22; W. Brandenstein, "Bemerkungen zur Völkertafel in der Genesis," *Festschrift Albert Debrunner* (1954), pp. 63-83. L. HICKS

JAPHIA jə fī'ə [יפיע, may (the deity) shine(?)]. **1.** King of Lachish, SW of Jerusalem (Josh. 10:3). He was one of five confederate kings in the Amorite coalition that attempted to halt Joshua's invasion.

2. A son of David, born after David had become king in Jerusalem (II Sam. 5:15; I Chr. 3:7; 14:6).

Bibliography. M. Noth, *Die israelitischen Personennamen* (1928), pp. 204-5. R. F. JOHNSON

3. A border town in Zebulun (Josh. 19:13). It is identified with Yafa, a site less than two miles SW of Nazareth. The remains of an early synagogue have been found there.

JAPHLET jăf'lĭt [יפלט, may (the deity) deliver] (I Chr. 7:32-33). An Asherite, son of Heber.

JAPHLETITES jăf'lə tīts [יפלטי] (Josh. 16:3); KJV JAPHLETI —tī. A clan whose location helps to mark the S boundary of Ephraim in an area E of Gezer.

JAPHO. KJV form of JOPPA in Josh. 19:46.

JAR. *See* POTTERY; VESSELS.

JARAH jâr'ə [יערה, honeycomb, *but perhaps read* יעדה (B, A, Ιαδά)] (I Chr. 9:42). A descendant of King Saul. Instead of this name I Chr. 8:36 has Jehoaddah (יהועדה).

Bibliography. M. Noth, *Die israelitischen Personennamen* (1928), p. 246; cf. p. 245. B. T. DAHLBERG

JAREB jâr'ĭb. KJV translation of ירב, as the name of a king, in Hos. 5:13; 10:6. More likely מלכי רב, "great king" (so RSV), should be read, as apposition or title of the Assyrian king mentioned there.

JARED jâr'ĭd [ירד; 'Ιάρεδ]. An antediluvian patriarch of the line of Seth; father of Enoch (Gen. 5:15-20; I Chr. 1:2; Luke 3:37). *See also* JERED; IRAD.

JARESIAH. KJV form of JAARESHIAH.

JARHA jär'hə [ירחע] (I Chr. 2:34-35). Egyptian servant of Sheshan, a Jerahmeelite, who gave his daughter as wife to the former.

JARIB jâr'ĭb [יריב, *a shortened form of* יויריב, may Yahu contend]; KJV Apoc. JORIBAS jə rī'bəs (I Esd. 8:44); JORIBUS (I Esd. 9:19). **1.** A son of Simeon, according to I Chr. 4:24, but not mentioned in Gen. 46:10; Exod. 6:15; Num. 26:12.

2. One of the leading men who assisted Ezra in securing temple servants before the return to Palestine (Ezra 8:16; I Esd. 8:44).

3. One of the priests compelled by Ezra to give up their foreign wives (Ezra 10:18; I Esd. 9:19).

M. NEWMAN

JARIMOTH. KJV Apoc. alternate form of JEREMOTH.

JARMUTH jär′mŭth [ירמות, a height]. **1.** A city of Judah situated on an easily defended hill, Khirbet Yarmuk, eight miles N-NE of Eleutheropolis (Beit Jibrin).

It was one of five Canaanite royal cities which attempted to halt Joshua's invasion, but the coalition was defeated and the kings executed at Makkedah (Josh. 10:3, 5, 22 ff; 12:11). It became a part of the Shephelah province of Zorah-Azekah (15:35), and after the Exile it was reoccupied by Jewish returnees (Neh. 11:29).

In a cuneiform letter from *ca.* 1365, found at Tell el-Hesi (Eglon), Yaramu (Jarmuth) is a town ruled by a robber chief who is answerable only to the Egyptian officials.

2. A Levitical town in Issachar (Josh. 21:29). This should perhaps be read Remath (with LXX B), the initial *yodh* being a scribal reminiscence of the famous town in Judah. It would then be the RAMOTH of I Chr. 6:73—H 6:58 and Remeth of Josh. 19:21.

Bibliography. W. F. Albright, "A Case of Lese-Majeste in Pre-Israelite Lachish," *BASOR,* no. 87 (1942), p. 36, note 30; Albright, "The List of Levitic Cities," *Louis Ginzberg Jubilee Volume* (English section; 1945). V. R. GOLD

JAROAH jə rō′ə [ירוח, soft, delicate; *cf.* Arab. *wariḫa*] (I Chr. 5:14). A Gadite.

Bibliography. M. Noth, *Die israelitischen Personennamen* (1928), p. 226.

JASAEL. KJV Apoc. form of SHEAL.

JASHAR, BOOK OF jā′shər [ספר הישר, book of the upright one(?), *see below*]; KJV JASHER. A written document mentioned as though well known and containing Joshua's poetic address to the sun and the moon (Josh. 10:12-13), David's lament over Saul and Jonathan (II Sam. 1:17-27), and probably (*see below*) Solomon's original words of dedication of the temple (I Kings 8:12-13).

Reference is made to the above-mentioned poetic quotations of Joshua and David as having been "written in the Book of Jashar" (Josh. 10:13; II Sam. 1:18). Using exactly the language of Josh. 10:13, the writer in the LXX rhetorically asks whether Solomon's quotation was not written in the Book of "Song." On the assumption that this statement accidentally dropped out of the MT (the entire quotation appears in the LXX after Solomon's long prayer of I Kings 8:14-53) and that by accidental transposition of two Hebrew letters the LXX read "Song" (שיר) instead of "Jashar" (ישר), most scholars consider I Kings 8:12-13 to be a third quotation from the lost Book of Jashar.

The term "Jashar" is a fairly common Hebrew word meaning "one who [or that which] is straight, honest, just, righteous, upright." Therefore it is assumed that the title "Book of the Upright [One]" refers either to the historical heroic individuals who are the subjects of its contents or to all Israel as the upright people. If the latter, the title may be related to JESHURUN.

The three quotations from the Book of Jashar are all poetry. Because of this fact, and because the term "Jashar" in the title has never been satisfactorily explained and yet has obvious similarity to various verb forms of the root שיר, "to sing," a few scholars hold that the LXX rendering "Book of Song," rather than "Book of the Upright [One]," is the correct original title.

The nature of this book must be inferred from its three quotations, for there is no other evidence. It seems to have been an ancient national song book, the antiquity of which is suggested in part by the relatively poor state of preservation of the Hebrew text of each poem.

The book must have contained a variety of songs, for each of the extant ones is very different from the others. The first is apparently a very old incantation to Yahweh's heavenly bodies to prolong daylight—or perhaps to lengthen predawn darkness—until Israel has time enough to complete victory over its Amorite enemies. The second, an authentic literary monument to David's poetic skill, is a remarkable appreciation of both the national significance and the personal friendship of the tragic heroes involved. The third, reminiscent of Ugaritic parallels but probably an authentic utterance of Solomon on the occasion, is an ancient song establishing God's supremacy over nature and ritual.

The origin of the Book of Jashar is uncertain. Some think it was a written collection begun in premonarchic Israel and expanded from time to time. Others regard it as the compilation of oral tradition not earlier than the days of Solomon and perhaps much later. Probably it was the beginning of sacred literary archives established at the height of the monarchy in order to preserve some of the most notable traditions of Israel. Its nearest parallel was apparently the Book of the Wars of the Lord (Num. 21:14). In fact, some scholars would identify these two books as one (*see further* WARS OF THE LORD, BOOK OF). There has been speculation as to whether the Song of Deborah (Judg. 5), the Song of Miriam (Exod. 15:21), and the like may not have been included in these extraordinarily important ancient anthologies of Israel's heroic past. But there is no record of such.

The intriguing and mysterious nature of the Book of Jashar has given rise through the centuries to both false identifications and imitations of the book. Certain ancient Jewish commentators considered the title a reference to the Torah. A medieval Book of Jashar paralleled a portion of the pseudepigraphic Testament of Judah. Other medieval rabbinical works have received the same title. Worthless modern forgeries claiming to be discoveries of this long-lost book have occasionally appeared, the most recent of which was in a fifth edition in 1953.

Bibliography. H. St. J. Thackeray, "New Light on the Book of Jashar," *JTS,* XI (1909-10), 518-32; S. Mowinckel, "Hat es ein israelitisches Nationalepos gegeben?" *ZAW,* N.F. XII (1935), 130-52; J. A. Montgomery, *Kings* ICC (1951), pp. 189-92; E. Nielsen, *Oral Tradition* (1954), ch. 3.

C. F. KRAFT

JASHEN jā′shən [ישן] (II Sam. 23:32). A member of the Mighty Men of David known as the "Thirty." The MT of II Sam. 23:32 reads "the sons of Jashen," while the parallel passage in I Chr. 11:34 has "the sons of Hashem the Gizonite." It is manifest that in both instances the words "the sons of" (בני) are dittographic and repeat the ending of the name Shaalbonite (שעלבני). The gentilic name of Jashen has dropped out of the text of II Sam. 23:32 but is given as "the Gizonite" in I Chr. 11:34. The name of the hero in the original catalogue would then seem to have been "Jashen/Hashem the GIZONITE."

E. R. DALGLISH

JASHER. KJV form of JASHAR. *See* JASHAR, BOOK OF.

JASHOBEAM jə shō'bĭ əm [ישבעם]. **1.** A Hachmonite who is described as the son of Zabdiel and a descendant of Perez; the chief of the "Three," the highest command among the Mighty Men of David. He was personally credited with 300 enemy casualties in one encounter (I Chr. 11:11). He was also in command of the 24,000 men of the Davidic militia that served for the first month of the year (I Chr. 27:2-3).

The text of II Sam. 23:8 differs considerably from that of I Chr. 11:11 and may be reconstructed in the following manner: The reading "Josheb-basshebeth," which the KJV renders "that sat in the seat," is probably a corruption of the name Ishbaal (LXX 'Ιεβοσθε—i.e., איש־בשת; Lucian 'Ιεσβααλ—i.e., אישבעל; the original name אשבעל was apparently changed to אשבשת, then corrupted to ישב בשבת). The gentilic "Tachmonite" (KJV) or "Tahchemonite" (RSV) should no doubt be read "Hachmonite" in accordance with I Chr. 11:11. The reading of שלשה for שלשי (שלושים—I Chr. 11:11) and the RSV rendering of "Three" rather than the KJV "captains" appear justified in view of II Sam. 23:9, 13, 18-19, 22-23; I Chr. 11:12, 18, 21, 25; and are supported by the LXX of II Sam. 23:8 and the reading of Lucian there and in I Chr. 11:11. The words "Adino the Eznite" are a KJV transliteration of an unintelligible phrase which interprets the expression as a personal name of the "Tachmonite." However, it seems best to adopt the reading of I Chr. 11:11 and to translate "he wielded his spear" (RSV). The Chronicler's reading of "three hundred" seems preferable to the text of II Sam. 23:8, where "eight hundred" is found.

In summary, the reconstructed text of II Sam. 23:8 may be rendered: "Ishbaal, a Hachmonite; he was chief of the three; he wielded his spear against three hundred whom he slew at one time."

2. One of the disaffected Benjaminite warriors who joined the proscribed band of David at Ziklag (I Chr. 12:6). It seems best to interpret his description as a Korahite as having reference to the place of his origin.

E. R. DALGLISH

JASHUB jā'shəb [ישוב, may (the deity) return; 'Ιάσουβος]; JASHUBITES —shə bīts; KJV Apoc. JASUBUS jə sōō'bəs. **1.** An eponym; descendant of Asher (Num. 26:24; I Chr. 7:1). He is called Iob (KJV Job) in Gen. 46:13, but this is a copyist's error (cf. Jub. 44:17).

2. One of the men persuaded by Ezra to divorce their foreign wives (Ezra 10:29; I Esd. 9:30).

Bibliography. M. Noth, *Die israelitischen Personennamen* (1928), pp. 28, 199.

B. T. DAHLBERG

JASHUBI-LEHEM jə shōō'bī lē'hĕm. KJV translation of ישבי לחם, as the name of a man of Judah, in I Chr. 4:22. The RSV reads: ישבו לחם, "They returned to Lehem"; the reading should probably be: [ו]ישבו להם, "but they returned." *See* LEHEM.

JASIEL. KJV form of JAASIEL 2.

JASON jā'sən ['Ιάσων, Greek *substitute for* Joshua]. **1.** Jason I, high priest in 174-171 B.C.

He was the brother of Onias III, whom he supplanted as high priest. (Some scholars believe he was a son of Joseph ben Tobias and his brothers were Simon, Onias-Menelaus, Lysimachus, and Alcimus-Eliakim.) When Onias III fled to Egypt, Joshua-Jason maneuvered to obtain the priesthood. The office of high priest should have gone to Onias IV, son of Onias III, by inheritance, but Jason brought about a deviation which ultimately led to the decline of the priesthood, and it was dominated by the sons of Joseph. Jason promised to build gymnasiums in Jerusalem and to give a great sum of money to King Antiochus for confirmation of the office. He influenced changes for Hellenism and made Jerusalemites "citizens of Antioch" (II Macc. 4:8 ff). He also sent representatives to the Olympic games at Tyre, to give three thousand silver drachmas for sacrifice to Hercules. Even the escort thought this wrong, and through the intervention of these escorts the money intended for pagan sacrifice by Jason was converted into fitting out ships (vss. 18-20).

The sons of Joseph, however, found Jason to be too conservative in his notion of Hellenization, and he was deposed by his cousin Onias (called Menelaus), brother of Simon the Captain, of the family of Tobias, when the latter conveyed a sum of money to Antiochus. A false rumor had spread that Antiochus had died, and Jason then attacked Jerusalem, killing his own countrymen unmercifully. Jason fought against Onias-Menelaus, driving the latter out of Jerusalem; but Antiochus, who had to abandon his attack on Egypt because of Roman intervention, attacked Jerusalem and aided Onias-Menelaus. Jason was forced to flee to the Ammonites, to Transjordan, and remain there.

Accused before Aretas, ruler of the Arabs, he had to flee from city to city, despised as a tormentor of his fatherland. He could not find asylum in Egypt because Onias, his predecessor, was there and because it was known that Jason had been pro-Seleucid though he had fought Antiochus. He died as an exile among the Lacedaemonians and had no one to mourn him. He was accursed because he was not buried in the sepulchre of his fathers (II Macc. 5:10).

Bibliography. S. Tedesche and S. Zeitlin, *The Second Book of the Maccabees* (1954), pp. 7 (note 11), 13.

2. Jason II, son of ELEAZAR (10); one of the delegation sent to Rome by Judas Maccabeus to establish a treaty of friendship and alliance (I Macc. 8:17).

3. Jason of Cyrene. He was recognized as the author of II Maccabees, a history of Judas Maccabeus and his brothers, written in five books. The Epitomist, an Antiochean Jew, condensed it. Jason may have supplied the basic facts, but many chapters seem to be the adornment and rhetoric of Epitomist.

The abridgment shows remnants of beautiful style of Judeo-Hellenistic literature. Some scholars think that the Hebrew *Jossipon* may have traces of Jason's original work.

We do not know when he lived. Jason's work is the only authentic document of the civil war among Jews in the period before the Hasmoneans (II Macc. 2:23 ff).

Bibliography. C. C. Torrey, *The Apocryphal Literature* (1945), pp. 78 ff; R. H. Pfeiffer, *History of NT Times* (1949), pp. 506 ff, 514; S. Tedesche and S. Zeitlin, *The Second Book of Maccabees* (1954), pp. 20 ff; A. Tcherikover and A. Fuks, *Corpus Papyrorum Judaicarum,* I (1957), 47. S. B. HOENIG

4. Paul's host at Thessalonica (Acts 17:5-7, 9), who was haled before the politarchs when the mob could not find Paul. He was freed upon giving security to keep the peace. The Jason mentioned as sending a greeting in Rom. 16:21 was in Corinth when this letter was written, but it is possible that he was the same as the one in Acts; if so, he was a Jew ("kinsman" = "fellow countryman").

F. W. GINGRICH

JASPER. A green chalcedony. The word is used to translate:

a) יהלם, *yah^a^lôm* (KJV and elsewhere RSV DIAMOND), a stone in the covering of the king of Tyre (Ezek. 28:13).

b) ישפה, *yāš^e^phê* (cf. Persian *yashm;* Arabic *yashb* or *yaṣb;* Akkadian *ašpu;* LXX ονύχιον; Vulg. *beryllus*), a stone in the breastpiece of judgment (Exod. 28:20; 39:13). In Ezek. 28:13 this word is translated "ONYX" (cf. LXX), while יהלם, elsewhere "diamond," is "jasper."

c) Ἴασπις, used with carnelian in the description of the one on the throne (Rev. 4:3), the radiance of the glory of God (21:11), the walls of the city (21:18). It was the first jewel in the foundation of the wall of the New Jerusalem (21:19).

W. E. STAPLES

JASUBUS. KJV Apoc. form of JASHUB.

JATAL. KJV Apoc. alternate form of ATER.

JATHAN jā'thən [Ἰαθάν (BA), Ναθαν(א)] (Tob. 5:13); KJV **JONATHAS** jŏn'ə thəs. Son of Shemaiah, and brother of Ananias. They were kinsmen of Tobit, who fondly recalls his accompanying Ananias and Jathan to Jerusalem for worship. J. C. SWAIM

JATHNIEL jăth'nĭ əl [יתניאל] (I Chr. 26:2). A Korahite gatekeeper of the sanctuary.

Bibliography. On the etymological obscurity, see M. Noth, *Die israelitischen Personennamen* (1928), p. 248, no. 782.

JATTIR jăt'ər [יתיר, pre-eminence(?)]. A Levitical city of Judah in the hill-country district of Debir (Josh. 15:48; 21:14; I Chr. 6:57—H 6:42). Jattir shared in David's booty from the Amalekites (I Sam. 30:27). The site is modern Khirbet 'Attir, *ca.* thirteen miles S-SW of Hebron. V. R. GOLD

JAVAN jā'vən [יון; Arab. *Yûbān*] (Gen. 10:2, 4; I Chr. 1:5, 7; see also Isa. 66:19; Ezek. 27:13; Dan. 8:21; 10:20; 11:2; Joel 3:6—H 4:6; Zech. 9:13, which are references to the descendants of Javan and their lands; also the somewhat obscure reference in the Hebrew text of Ezek. 27:19). The fourth son of JAPHETH son of Noah (Gen. 10:1-2); and the father of Elishah, Tarshish, Kittim, and Dodanim (or Rodanim; Gen. 10:4; cf. I Chr. 1:5, 7). The name is generally understood to refer to the descendants of Japheth through Javan, and to their W lands (Gen. 10:5)—Ionia (which corresponds etymologically with the name of Javan and which denotes GREECE, including Asia Minor and Macedonia); CYPRUS; RHODES; and at least a part of Syria.

Javan is mentioned in Isa. 66:19 as one of the distant nations which will witness the future manifestation of God's glory. The sons of the Javanites (the Greeks) are referred to in Joel 3:6—H 4:6 as slave traders who purchased Jewish captives from the Phoenicians and the Philistines. Javan is also mentioned in the oracle against Tyre in the book of Ezekiel (27:13), again with reference to their involvement in the slave traffic and other commercial activities. According to Zech. 9:13, Judah and Ephraim, the sons of Zion, will serve as God's warriors in wreaking vengeance upon the sons of Javan (Greece). The references in Daniel to the king (8:21), the prince (10:20), and the kingdom of Javan (11:2), allude to the Greco-Macedonian Empire, and reflect an extension of the original identification of Javan with the Ionian colonies in Asia Minor.

Javan is mentioned in the Hebrew text of Ezek. 27:19 as a place or people with whom Tyre carried on commercial relations. The verse presents textual difficulties (the Hebrew text was read by the LXX as ויין, "and wine"; cf. the RSV including the mg.). Those who retain the Hebrew text identify Javan with a Greek colony or an Arab tribe in Arabia.

The Ionians are referred to in Assyrian records, in the cuneiform inscriptions of Darius and in Egyptian records from the times of Ramses II.

Bibliography. B. Stade, *Das Volk Javan* (1880); M. Lidzbarski, *Handbuch der nordsemitischen Epigraphik* (1898), p. 287*a;* J. Skinner, ICC (1910), pp. 196-200; D. D. Luckenbill, "Jadanan and Javan," *Zeitschrift für Assyriologie,* 28 (1913), 92-99; C. F. Lehmann-Haupt, "Zur Erwähnung der Ionier in altorientalischen Quellen," *Klio,* 27 (N.F. 10; 1934), 74-83, 286-94; E. Herzfeld, *Altpersische Inschriften* (1938), no. 14, pp. 27 ff. H. F. BECK

JAVELIN. *See* WEAPONS AND IMPLEMENTS OF WAR § 3*c*.

JAZER jā'zər [יעזר, יעזיר]; KJV **JAAZER** jā ā'zər in Num. 21:32; 32:35. A fortified Amorite city in Gilead, in a district that was disputed by the Israelites, Moabites, and Ammonites.

1. History. After the defeat of Sihon, king of the Amorites, Moses sent spies out to Jazer and subsequently occupied the town (Num. 21:32), which was later fortified by the Gadites to whom it was assigned (Num. 32:1, 34-35). Later it became a Levitical city (Josh. 21:39). The region was noted for its pasture lands and for its fruits and vines (Isa. 16:8-9; Jer. 48:32). Jazer was important as a border post against an attack from Ammon, and during the reign of David the city was garrisoned by Judahites from

Hebron (I Chr. 26:31). After the death of Ahab (853 B.C.), the entire region was conquered by Mesha of Moab; and from that time on, the city is mentioned as an important city of Moab, in the books of Isaiah and Jeremiah. In Hellenistic times the city was under the rule of the Ammonites, from whom it was retaken by Judas Maccabeus (I Macc. 5:8).

2. Location. Jazer was situated not far from the border of Ammon, in this case the river Jabbok as it flows N from Amman (Rabboth-ammon). The LXX, which RSV follows, reads: "Jazer was the boundary of the Ammonites," instead of: "The boundary of the Ammonites was strong (עז)" (Num. 21:24). Eusebius and Jerome speak of a place named Azer or Iazer, about ten Roman miles W of Rabbah of the Ammonites. The site that best suits this location is the ruin called Kom Yajuz, which occupies a splendid defensive location between the Wadi Kom and the Wadi Yajuz.

Bibliography. I. Press, *Entziklopedia Eretz Yisrael*, IV (1955), 399-400; N. Glueck, "Explorations in Eastern Palestine, III," *AASOR*, XVIII-XIX (1939), 178-81. Contrast G. M. Landes, "The Fountain at Jazer," *BASOR*, 144 (1956), 30-37.

S. COHEN

JAZIZ jā'zĭz [יזיז] (I Chr. 27:30—H 27:31). A Hagrite who was one of the royal stewards of David in charge of the flocks.

JEALOUSY. The biblical idea of jealousy includes the range of attitudes from the intense hatred of man for man in envy to the positive emotion of single-minded zeal. The English words "zeal" and "jealousy" are both derived from Greek ζηλόω, "to be jealous," which is itself derived from ζέω, "to boil." The term "jealousy" is used for both man and God, both as "jealousy of" something and as "jealousy for" something. The line between the two meanings is very thin, and context alone determines which is applicable.

1. Terminology
   a. In Hebrew
   b. In LXX Greek
   c. In NT Greek
2. In the OT
   a. Human jealousy
   b. Man's jealousy for God
   c. The jealousy of God
3. In postbiblical Judaism
4. In the NT
   a. Envy
   b. Zeal

Bibliography

1. Terminology. The word "jealousy" and its allied terms ("envy," "zeal," "passion," "fury") occur a number of times in the Bible, to translate several Hebrew and Greek terms.

a. In Hebrew. The root usually translated "to be jealous" is קנא, the root meaning of which is perhaps "to become red in the face." The verb (perhaps denominative, always in *pi'el* and *hiph'il*) and the noun קנאה are the normal terms for all kinds of jealousy (cf. Gen. 37:11; II Sam. 21:2; Zech. 1:14). Two intensive nominal forms, *qannā'* and *qannô'*, are used only of God (Exod. 20:5; Deut. 5:9; Josh. 24:19; Nah. 1:2). In I Sam. 2:32 the RSV, probably correcting מעון to עין, "eye," translates "envious eye," supplying "envious" from the context. In Ps. 68:16—H 68:17 "envy" renders רצד, a *hapax legomenon* connoting stealthy and hostile watching (cf. Arabic *raṣada*, "to lie in wait with hostile intent").

b. In LXX Greek. The usual LXX translation of קנא and its cognates is ζηλόω (Isa. 11:13) and the nouns ζῆλος (Num. 25:11), ζήλωσις (Num. 5:14, 30), ζηλωτός (Exod. 20:5), and ζηλοτυπία (Num. 5:15). The cognate παραζηλόω occurs in Deut. 32:21; I Kings 14:22; Ecclus. 30:3; παροργίζω, "to provoke to anger," is found in Ps. 105:16—H 106:16; and παροξύνω, "to infuriate," in Deut. 32:16. In Ezek. 36:5 קנאה is rendered by θυμός, "wrath" (RSV "hot jealousy"); and in Prov. 14:30 καρδία αἰσθητική, "a perceptive heart" (RSV "passion"), perhaps mistranslates קנאה.

c. In NT Greek. The NT derived its terminology from the LXX, though not all terms of the LXX are used. ζηλόω and its cognates ζηλεύω (only Rev. 3:19), ζῆλος (Acts 5:17), ζηλωτής (I Cor. 14:12; *see* ZEALOT), and παραζηλόω (Rom. 11:11) are used for the whole range of meanings. Φθονέω (only Gal. 5:26) and the noun φθόνος (Matt. 27:18) denote human envy, though φθόνος is used in Jas. 4:5 for divine jealousy.

2. In the OT. For the OT jealousy is the emotion of single-minded devotion, which when turned upon the self, produces hatred or envy of others; or when turned beyond the self, produces overpowering zeal leading to total selflessness.

a. Human jealousy. Human jealousy may be either envy of or zeal for another. The Philistines envy Isaac his great possessions (Gen. 26:14), and Rachel is jealous of Leah's ability to bear children (Gen. 30:1). Ps. 106:16 describes the opposition to Moses by Dathan and Abiram (Num. 16) as jealousy. The pious are not to be jealous of evildoers (Ps. 37:1; Prov. 24:1, 19) or of the fortunes of the wicked (Ps. 73:3; Prov. 3:31; 23:17). Jealousy causes vengeful fury (Prov. 6:34) and produces a kind of spiritual death (Job 5:2; Prov. 14:30; Song of S. 8:6). But jealousy is also suspicion, as in the prescriptions of an offering and trial by ordeal for a wife suspected of infidelity (Num. 5:14-30). *See* BITTER.

The jealousy which produces positive devotion to others is exemplified by Joshua's desire to forbid Eldad and Medad from prophesying, which Moses rebukes, wishing that the whole nation would prophesy (Num. 11:26-29). David makes restitution to the Gibeonites for Saul's misdirected jealousy for Israel and Judah in seeking to slaughter them (II Sam. 21:2).

b. Man's jealousy for God. Phinehas' murder of an Israelite and his Midianite bride is commended by Yahweh as being "jealous with my jealousy" (Num. 25:11-13, a favorite example of zeal in later Judaism; cf. Ecclus. 45:23; I Macc. 2:26; IV Macc. 18:12; Sanh. 81*b;* Numbers Rabbah 20.25). Jehu's jealousy for Yahweh is likewise expressed by the slaughter of Ahab's family (II Kings 10:16). Elijah pleads that he has been "very jealous for Yahweh" (I Kings 19:10, 14). A less destructive devotion is expressed in Pss. 69:9—H 69:10 (jealousy for the temple); 119:139 (a jealousy in response to neglect of Yahweh's words).

c. The jealousy of God. The divine jealousy is also expressed in two directions. It is, on the one hand, provoked by idolatry, which is usurpation of the divine prerogatives (Deut. 32:16, 21; Ps. 78:58; Ezek. 8:3, 5), or by disobedience, implying a heedlessness of commitment (Deut. 4:24; I Kings 14:22; Isa. 59:17 ["fury"]). Wilful departure from the covenant causes the jealousy of God to break forth in destructive judgment (Deut. 29:20—H 29:19; Ps. 79:5; Ezek. 5:13; 16:38, 42; 23:25; Nah. 1:2; Zeph. 1:18; 3:8; *see* FIRE; DAY OF THE LORD). But Yahweh is also jealous because of his holiness (Josh. 24:19; Ezek. 39:25; *see* HOLINESS). Covenantal jealousy demands totality of obedience (Exod. 20:5; Deut. 5:9; 6:15), for in Yahweh's covenantal activity, "his name is Jealous" (Exod. 34:14). *See* COVENANT.

The divine jealousy, however, is the principle of God's protection of his people. It is his zeal which will provide the remnant of Israel with its life (II Kings 19:31; Isa. 37:32), which will maintain the messianic kingdom forever (Isa. 9:7—H 9:6). His jealousy blazes against the foes of his exiled people (Isa. 42:13; Ezek. 36:5-6; 38:19) and shames their adversaries (Isa. 26:11). His jealousy for Judah is both wrath against her adversaries and compassion for Jerusalem (Zech. 1:14-16; 8:2). The cry of the faithful in the straits of a locust plague arouses Yahweh's jealousy and his pity (Joel 2:18).

3. In postbiblical Judaism. The jealousy of God tends to fall into the background in both the Apoc. and the Pseudep. and in the rabbinic literature. The omniscience of God is a "jealous ear [which] hears all things" (Wisd. Sol. 1:10), and his jealousy is his "whole armor" (Wisd. Sol. 5:17). But Rabbi Jonathan interpreted Nah. 1:2 as meaning that God overcomes his own jealousy (Genesis Rabbah 49.8).

Human jealousy in its two characteristic directions appears in this literature. "Jealousy and anger shorten life" (Ecclus. 30:24), but righteous jealousy for the law is commended (I Macc. 2:27, 50; II Macc. 4:2). Envy is the opposite of love (Test. Gad 7:7; Test. Simeon 4:7) and is cast out by the fear of God (Test. Simeon 3:4-6; *see* FEAR) and by humility (Test. Gad 5:3). Pious zeal, however, is praised, for "the zealous come early for the performance of religious duties" (R.H. 32*b;* cf. Pes. 4*a*).

4. In the NT. As in the intertestamental literature, the jealousy of God takes the background in the NT. The author of Hebrews foresees judgment as a "fury of fire" (πύρος ζῆλος) against God's adversaries (10:27). Paul fears that the Corinthians' idol-worship will "provoke the Lord to jealousy" (παραζηλόω; I Cor. 10:22), though he feels for them a "divine jealousy" (ζηλῶ γὰρ ὑμᾶς θεοῦ ζῆλῳ; II Cor. 11:2), a covenantal jealousy put in terms of betrothal (*see* LOVE [NT]). The author of James quotes an unknown source, perhaps a paraphrase of Exod. 20:5: "He yearns jealously [πρὸς φθόνον ἐπιποθεῖ] over the spirit which he has made to dwell in us" (Jas. 4:5).

a. Envy. Jealousy of others for the NT is the antithesis of love (I Cor. 13:4; II Cor. 12:20; Jas. 3:14, 16; 4:2). It is listed by Paul among the "works of the flesh" (Gal. 5:20 [ζῆλος], 21 [φθόνος]). All the uses of φθόνος and φθονέω, save that of Jas. 4:5, fall into this negative category (Matt. 27:18; Mark 15:10; Rom. 1:29; Gal. 5:26; Phil. 1:15; I Tim. 6:4; Tit. 3:3; I Pet. 2:1). The author of Acts ascribes jealousy to the Jews' treatment of the early church (Acts 5:17; 13:45; 17:5).

b. Zeal. The positive pole of jealousy is found in the NT, particularly in Paul, who feels that the "godly grief" engendered by the Corinthians' repentance produced zeal (II Cor. 7:11) of a kind which inspires the other churches (II Cor. 9:2). Paul finds this pious jealousy admirable in the Jews (Rom. 10:2; cf. Acts 21:20; 22:3), and he feels that it characterized his own life before his conversion (Gal. 1:14; Phil. 3:6). But Paul hopes that his ministry will provoke the Jews to yet more jealousy for God's truth, which may bring them salvation (Rom. 11:11, 14). The church must have zeal for the Spirit and its manifestations (I Cor. 12:31; 14:1, 12, 39). But zeal must be focused on the proper end. Those who corrupt the Galatians do so out of false zeal, so that their zeal may be reciprocated (Gal. 4:17-18).

Other writers commend zeal for "good deeds" (Tit. 2:14) and for "what is right" (I Pet. 3:13). It is the exclusive devotion which produces repentance in the face of chastening persecution (Rev. 3:19).

Bibliography. F. Küchler, "Der Gedanke des Eifers Jahwehs im AT," *ZAW*, 28 (1908), 42-52. B. Reicke, *Diakonie, Festfreude und Zelos in Verbindung mit der altchristlichen Agapenfeier* (1951). E. M. GOOD

JEALOUSY, ORDEAL OF [מנחת קנאת, cereal offering of jealousy]. A test which was devised to determine if a woman suspected of adultery was guilty or not. She had to drink holy water mixed with dust after she had taken a solemn oath, the "oath of the curse," while holding the "cereal offering of jealousy." If she was guilty, her body would swell and her thigh fall away; if innocent, she should be free to conceive children (Num. 5:12-28; cf. Code of Hammurabi, section 132).

See also JEALOUSY. O. J. BAAB

JEARIM, MOUNT jē'ə rĭm [הר יערים, mountain of forests] (Josh. 15:10). A mountain on the N border of Judah; probably identical with Mount Seir (*see* SEIR 2), on which is located the modern village of Saris, *ca.* nine miles N of Jerusalem. V. R. GOLD

JEATHERAI jē ăth'ə rī [יאתרי] (I Chr. 6:21); KJV JEATERAI —ăt—. Probably a scribal error for ETHNI.

JEBERECHIAH jĭ bĕr'ə kī'ə [יברכיה, Yahu blesses] (Isa. 8:2). The father of Zechariah.

JEBUS jē'bəs [יבוס]; JEBUSITE jĕb'yə sīt [יבסי, יבוסי]; KJV JEBUSI jĕb'yə sī [יבוסי] in Josh. 18:16, 28. Originally the name of a clan, the Jebusites, in control of Jerusalem before the conquest of the city by David. The Hebrew word יבוסי (*yᵉbhûsî*), with the ending *î* characteristic of the names of clans and nations, was reproduced by the KJV in Josh. 18:16, 28, instead of the more usual form, "Jebusite." The name Jebus occurs in Judg. 19:10-11 with the explanation "that is, Jerusalem," and in I Chr. 11:4-5, where Jerusalem is glossed "that is Jebus, where the Jebusites were." One may conclude from these passages, not that Jebus was the primitive name of Jerusalem, but rather that Jebus was derived from the name of the clan which occupied the site, as, e.g., Paris (in Latin

Lutetia Parisiorum) was named for the tribe of the *Parisii*. The toponym Jebus may well have been forged by late biblical writers unaware of the fact that the name Jerusalem, which they regarded as sacred, actually did antedate the first appearance of the Hebrews in Palestine, and was of pagan origin (*see* JERUSALEM § 1). The list of the principal cities of the tribe of Benjamin (Josh. 18:28 MT) mentions "the Jebusi, which is in Jerusalem," probably to be interpreted "the city of the Jebusi . . . ," rather than "Jebus (that is, Jerusalem)," as in the RSV. The etymology of the name of the clan is unknown.

The clan of the Jebusi or the Jebusites (generally in the singular in Hebrew with a collective sense), is mentioned in Gen. 10:16, together with other clans allegedly issued from Canaan (*see* CANAANITES), on the same line as the AMORITES. Accordingly, Josephus classifies the Jebusites among the Canaanites (Antiq. VII.iii.1). The Jebusites are listed on a par with the Amorites, the Canaanites, and the Girgashites in Gen. 15:21. However, the (Jebusite) king of Jerusalem, Adonizedek, is counted as one of the five confederate Amorite kings who opposed Joshua (Josh. 10:5). Onomatology confirms to some extent the Amorite background of the Jebusites, whose listing among the people of Canaan probably results from geographical, rather than ethnological, considerations, inasmuch as the Amorites and their kindred are mentioned as inhabiting the highlands of Palestine, thus being surrounded by, or living in the midst of, the Canaanite populations of the lowlands, which occupied the Mediterranean seaboard and the valley of the Jordan (Num. 13:29).

Jerusalem, the city of the Jebusites, was claimed in theory by the tribe of Benjamin in the division of the soil of Canaan (Josh. 18:28). As a matter of fact, the boundary between Judah and Benjamin ran along the Valley of Hinnom (*see* HINNOM, VALLEY OF THE SON OF), to the S of the "shoulder of the Jebusite" (Josh. 15:8; 18:16). The imprecision of the biblical text makes it inadvisable to speculate too heavily concerning its bearing on the topography of primitive Jerusalem. The location and the general layout of the city, however, have been ascertained by archaeology (*see* DAVID, CITY OF; ZION). Jerusalem was not occupied by the Israelites as they overran the land of Canaan under Joshua, and the town and its suburbs remained as a foreign enclave (Josh. 15: 63). In this passage, Jerusalem is mentioned in connection with Judah, probably by implicit reference to the later status of the city as the capital of the S kingdom. The independence of Jerusalem from Hebrew rule in the time of the judges is further evidenced by the story of the Levite of Mount Ephraim who, journeying from Bethlehem northward, passes in view of the presumably hostile city of the Jebusites (Judg. 19:10-12).

The capture of the stronghold of Zion by David put an end to the domination of the Jebusites (II Sam. 5:6-7; I Chr. 11:4-6). The survivors submitted to the Israelites, and David, after he had made the city his capital, purchased from a Jebusite, ARAUNAH, or Ornan, the rocky hilltop used as a threshing floor to the N of the city of David, with a view to building a permanent structure for housing the ark of the covenant (II Sam. 24:18-25; I Chr. 21:15, 18-28).

Bibliography. G. A. Smith, *Jerusalem,* I (1907), 266-67; G. Dalman, *Jerusalem und sein Gelände* (1930), pp. 82-83; F.-M. Abel, *Géographie de la Palestine,* I (1933), 320-21; J. Simons, *Jerusalem in the OT* (1952), pp. 60-61, 246-47.

G. A. BARROIS

JECAMIAH. KJV form of JEKAMIAH.

JECHOLIAH. KJV alternate form of JECOLIAH.

JECHONIAH; KJV JECHONIAS. Apoc. and NT forms of JECONIAH 1.

JECOLIAH jĕk'ə lī'ə [יכליהו, יכליה (II Chr. 26:3 *Qere*), יכיליה (II Chr. 26:3 *Kethibh*), Yahu is able] (II Kings 15:2; II Chr. 26:3); KJV JECHOLIAH in II Kings 15:2. The mother of King Azariah (Uzziah).

JECONIAH jĕk'ə nī'ə [יכניה; Ιεχονιας]; Apoc. and NT JECHONIAH; KJV Apoc. JECONIAS —əs; KJV NT JECHONIAS. **1.** Alternate name of JEHOIACHIN, king of Judah.

2. A Levite of the reign of Josiah (I Esd. 1:9); same as Conaniah in II Chr. 35:9.

JEDAIAH jĭ dā'yə [ידיה (1-2 *below*), Yahu has favored; ידעיה (3-7 *below*), Yahu knows]; KJV Apoc. JEDDU jĕd'ōō. **1.** A Simeonite (I Chr. 4:37).

2. One of those who helped to repair the wall of Jerusalem (Neh. 3:10).

Bibliography. M. Noth, *Die israelitischen Personennamen* (1928), p. 182.

3. A descendant of Aaron; eponym of a priestly house mentioned from the time of David (I Chr. 24: 7) and listed among the returned exiles (I Chr. 9: 10; Ezra 2:36; cf. Neh. 7:39; I Esd. 5:24). The individuals and families listed below are doubtless a part of this priestly line, but the exact relationships cannot be determined; and the distinctions, if any, among the various subjects referred to by this name cannot be clearly drawn.

4. One of the priests among those resident in postexilic Jerusalem (Neh. 11:10).

5. A priest among the returned exiles, related to a priestly house of this name (Neh. 12:6, 19).

6. Evidently another priest related to another priestly house of this name (Neh. 12:7, 21).

7. One of the returned exiles who brought contributions from Babylon for the Jerusalem community (Zech. 6:10, 14).

Bibliography. On the occurrence of this name in Neh. 12, see R. A. Bowman, Exegesis of Nehemiah, *IB,* III (1954), 785.

B. T. DAHLBERG

JEDEUS. KJV Apoc. form of ADAIAH.

JEDIAEL jĭ dī'əl [ידיעאל, known of God]. **1.** An eponym; a Benjaminite, according to I Chr. 7:6, 10-11; but the genealogy may originally have been that of Zebulun.

2. One of David's Mighty Men (I Chr. 11:45).

3. One of the Manassites who deserted to David while the latter served with the Philistines (I Chr. 12:20).

4. A Korahite gatekeeper in the reign of David (I Chr. 26:2).

Bibliography. On this name in I Chr. 7, see E. L. Curtis and A. A. Madsen, *Chronicles,* ICC (1910), pp. 145-49. On etymology, see M. Noth, *Die israelitischen Personennamen* (1928), pp. 13, 35, 90, 181. B. T. DAHLBERG

JEDIDAH jĭ dī′də [ידידה, beloved, lovely] (II Kings 22:1). The mother of King Josiah.

JEDIDIAH jĕd′ə dī′ə [ידידיה, beloved of Yah(weh)] (II Sam. 12:25). A name given to Solomon by Nathan at the instance of Yahweh and indicative of Yahweh's love for Solomon and of the gracious restoration of the erring David.

JEDUTHUN jĭ do͞o′thən [ידותון, ידתון, ידיתון (*properly* Jedithun)]. **1.** A Levitical singer of the time of David. He is associated with Asaph and Heman (I Chr. 25:1; II Chr. 5:12). Elsewhere the third associate of Asaph and Heman is Ethan (I Chr. 15:17), suggesting that the names Ethan and Jeduthun refer to the same person. If so, Jeduthun (whose ancestry is nowhere given by the Chronicler) would become a member of the Levitical family of Merari (I Chr. 6:44—H 6:29). Perhaps the name Jeduthun is derived from the psalm tone (*see* 2 *below*), which originally may have read "upon the hands of Ethan" (לידי איתן).

Jeduthun is said to "prophesy" (I Chr. 25:1, 3) and is called the "king's seer" (II Chr. 35:15; cf. I Esd. 1:15; *see* EDDINUS). Possibly the guild which traced its origin to Jeduthun was originally a prophetic guild, which by the time of the second temple had become a guild of singers. *See* HEMAN.

In I Chr. 16:38, 42, Jeduthun is mistakenly made the father of the gatekeepers. The first of these verses may be a gloss by one who found Obed-edom mentioned as a singer in I Chr. 15:21. Perhaps some words have fallen out of the text between "the sons of Jeduthun" and "were appointed to the gate" in vs. 42. *See* PSALMS, BOOK OF.

2. A psalm tone ("according to Jeduthun"; titles of Pss. 39, reading על ידותון for לידותון; 62; 77).

Bibliography. P. de Lagarde, *Übersicht über die im aramäischen, arabischen und hebräischen übliche Bildung der Nomina* (1889), p. 121; S. Mowinckel, *Psalmenstudien,* III (1923), 17-18; A. R. Johnson, "The Prophet in Israelite Worship," *ET,* XLVII (1935-36), 312-19. R. W. CORNEY

JEELI. KJV Apoc. form of JAALAH.

JEELUS. KJV Apoc. alternate form of JEHIEL.

JEEZER; JEEZERITES. KJV alternate form of ABIEZER.

JEGAR-SAHADUTHA jē′gər sā′ə do͞o′thə [יגר שהדותא, witness heap] (Gen. 31:47). The Aramaic name given by Laban to the heap of stones set up by him and Jacob. There is no indication that this became the basis of a place name, as was the case with the corresponding Hebrew term GALEED.

S. COHEN

JEHALLELEL jĭ hăl′ə ləl [יהללאל, may God shine forth]; KJV JEHALELEEL jē′hə lē′lĭ əl in I Chr. 4:16; JEHALELEL jĭ hăl′ə ləl in II Chr. 29:12. **1.** An eponym; a descendant of Judah (I Chr. 4:16).

2. A Merarite Levite (II Chr. 29:12).

Bibliography. M. Noth, *Die israelitischen Personennamen* (1928), pp. 28, 205, 208, 216. B. T. DAHLBERG

JEHDEIAH jĕ dē′yə [יחדיהו, may Yahu rejoice (*i.e.,* in his works)]. **1.** A Levite identified in I Chr. 24:20 with the reign of King David.

2. A Meronothite; official in charge of David's she-asses (I Chr. 27:30).

Bibliography. M. Noth, *Die israelitischen Personennamen* (1928), pp. 28, 210. B. T. DAHLBERG

JEHEZKEL jĭ hĕz′kĕl [יחזקאל, may God strengthen] (I Chr. 24:16); KJV JEHEZEKEL —ə kĕl. An eponym; a priest descended from Aaron.

Bibliography. M. Noth, *Die israelitischen Personennamen* (1928), pp. 28, 202.

JEHIAH jĭ hī′ə [יחיה, Yah(weh) lives] (I Chr. 15:24). A Levite who was appointed as a gatekeeper for the ark when it was brought to Jerusalem by David.

JEHIEL jĭ hī′əl [יחיאל, may God enliven; KJV יעואל *in* I Chr. 9:35; 11:44 (RSV JEIEL 2-3)]; KJV Apoc. HIEREEL hī ĕr′ĭ əl ['Ιερεήλ (B, A)] (I Esd. 9:21); HIERIELUS hī ĕr′ĭ ē′ləs ['Ιεζρίηλος (A)] (I Esd. 9:27); JEELUS jĭ ē′ləs ['Ιεήλ (A)] (I Esd. 8:92—G 8:89); JEZELUS jə zē′ləs ['Ιεζήλου] (I Esd. 8:35); SYELUS sĭ ē′ləs ['Ησύηλος] (I Esd. 1:8). Alternately: JEHUEL jĭ ho͞o′əl [*Kethibh* יחואל, *Qere* יחיאל] (II Chr. 29:14). **1.** A Levite musician among those ministering before the ark in Jerusalem (I Chr. 15:18, 20; 16:5).

2. A Gershonite Levite; chief of the house of Laadan (I Chr. 23:8). He was in charge of the temple treasury in David's reign (29:8), and he was founder of a priestly family called Jehieli (I Chr. 26:21-22).

3. An instructor or adviser to David's sons (I Chr. 27:32).

4. A son of King Jehoshaphat of Judah (II Chr. 21:2).

5. One of the Levites assisting the reforms of King Hezekiah (II Chr. 29:14), and later a temple overseer in his reign (31:13).

6. A ruler of the temple during the reforms of King Josiah (II Chr. 35:8).

7. The father of one of the exiles returning with Ezra from Babylon (Ezra 8:9; cf. I Esd. 8:35).

8. The father of the Shecaniah associated with Ezra's marriage reforms (Ezra 10:2; cf. I Esd. 8:92), and perhaps the same Jehiel who was among those induced to divorce their foreign wives (Ezra 10:26; cf. I Esd. 9:27).

9. A priest among those persuaded by Ezra to divorce their foreign wives (Ezra 10:21; cf. I Esd. 9:21).

Bibliography. M. Noth, *Die israelitischen Personennamen* (1928), pp. 28, 90, 206. B. T. DAHLBERG

JEHIELI jĭ hī′ə lī [יחילי] (I Chr. 26:21-22). Gentilic of JEHIEL 2.

JEHIZKIAH jē′hĭz kī′ə [יחזקיה, יחזקיהו] (II Chr. 28:12). Son of Shallum; a chief of Ephraim.

JEHOADDAH jĭ hō′ə də [יהועדה, *perhaps a corruption of* יערה, Jarah (I Chr. 9:42), *or* יהוידה, Jehoiada] (I Chr. 8:36). An obscure Benjaminite.

JEHOADDAN jĭ hō′ə dən [יהועדן, *probably* Yahu is delight] (II Chr. 25:1); JEHOADDIN —dĭn [יהועדין (*Kethibh*)] (II Kings 14:2). The mother of King Amaziah.

JEHOAHAZ jĭ hō′ə hăz [יהואחז, Yahu has grasped *or* taken hold of]. Alternately: JOAHAZ jō′ə hăz [יואחז, *a contraction of* יהואחז] (II Chr. 34:8). **1.** King of Judah *ca.* 842 B.C.; youngest son and successor of Joram.

"Jehoahaz" is a variant of "Ahaziah" (cf. II Chr. 21:17; 22:1). In the former case the divine name appears as a prefix, in the latter as a suffix. *See* AHAZIAH 2.

2. King of Israel *ca.* 815-801 B.C.; son and successor of Jehu.

Jehoahaz is said to have reigned for seventeen years (II Kings 13:1). But the synchronisms of 13:1, 10, require a correction to fifteen.

The text of II Kings 13:1-9, which describes his reign, is confused. It is clear, however, that Israel was overrun by the Syrians under Hazael and his son Ben-hadad (vs. 3; cf. vs. 22; for the situation in Judah, cf. 12:17-18). The survival of the Asherah in Samaria was the ostensible reason for Israel's overthrow (13:6). The N kingdom was reduced to the status of a subject nation. This is borne out by the description of the military forces left to Jehoahaz. They consisted of only "fifty horsemen and ten chariots and ten thousand footmen" (vs. 7). Contrast the forces ascribed to King Ahab in Assyrian sources at the Battle of Qarqar, "two thousand chariots and ten thousand footmen." The number of ten thousand footmen (vs. 7*a*) is open to serious question in view of the statement that "the king of Syria had destroyed them [i.e., Israel's military forces] and made them like the dust at threshing" (vs. 7*b*). The clear implication is that Israel's armed might was almost totally destroyed. In the light of this situation the reference to the "might" of Jehoahaz in the summary of his reign (vs. 8) is clearly a mere formula.

Vss. 4-6 give the impression of being an intrusion in the present text. The attempted identifications of the "savior" (vs. 5) have proved improbable.

The archaeological evidence bears out this description. Megiddo seems to have been destroyed at this time and was not rebuilt until a later period.

Bibliography. J. B. Bury *et al.*, eds., *Cambridge Ancient History*, III (1925), 375-76.

3. King of Judah 609-608 B.C.; son and successor of Josiah, carried into captivity to Egypt by Pharaoh Neco.

In our sources this king is called by two names—Jehoahaz and Shallum (I Chr. 3:15; Jer. 22:10 ff). The probable explanation is that Shallum was his personal name. He assumed a throne name—Jehoahaz—when he became king. Cf. a similar change of name in the cases of Eliakim/Jehoiakim (II Kings 23:34), Jeconiah (Coniah)/Jehoiachin (Joiachin; II Kings 24:6; Jer. 22:24; 24:1; Ezek. 1:2), Mattaniah/Zedekiah (II Kings 24:17). Names compounded with "Yahu" were common.

Jehoahaz came to the throne at the age of twenty-three and reigned three months in Jerusalem (II Kings 23:31; II Chr. 36:2). His mother's name was Hamutal (or Hamital). She was the daughter of Jeremiah of Libnah (probably by a diplomatic marriage; cf. II Kings 19:8).

According to the family tree in I Chr. 3:15, Shallum was the youngest of Josiah's four sons. There must, therefore, have been some special reason why he was made king by the "people of the land" instead of his elder brother. It may be that Eliakim/Jehoiakim had already shown pro-Egyptian tendencies. This would be especially resented in view of the circumstances of the death of the popular Josiah. It is possible that he was Josiah's "brother," but in the light of the evidence such a conclusion is not convincing.

Jehoahaz succeeded to the throne in tragic circumstances. With Josiah's death at Megiddo (609) Judah's dream of independence and a revival of the old Davidic empire was rudely shattered. She had escaped from Assyrian domination only to become a province of Egypt. After a brief reign of three months Jehoahaz was summoned by Pharaoh Neco to Riblah on the Orontes. This was the capital of Coele-Syria at the time, and here Neco had set up his headquarters. Jehoahaz was made a prisoner and tribute was imposed on Judah to the extent of a hundred talents of silver and ten(?) talents of gold. Neco made Eliakim king and changed his name to Jehoiakim. Jehoahaz was taken to Egypt, where he died.

The exile of Jehoahaz to Egypt was the occasion of Jeremiah's dirge (22:10-12), where he called on the people to lament for Jehoahaz, who was about to go away, never again to see his native land. Cf. also the reference to Jehoahaz in Ezek. 19:3, with its description of him as a "young lion."

Bibliography. W. F. Albright, "The Seal of Eliakim and the Latest Pre-exilic History," *JBL,* LI (1932), 77-106; F.-M. Abel, *Géographie de la Palestine,* II (1938), 436-37; A. M. Honeyman, "The Evidence for Regnal Names Among the Hebrews," *JBL,* LXVII (1948), 13-25; D. J. Wiseman, *Chronicles of Chaldean Kings* (1956), pp. 18 ff.

H. B. MACLEAN

JEHOASH. Alternate form of JOASH.

JEHOHANAN jē′hō hā′nən [יהוחנן, Yahu has been gracious; *cf.* JOHANAN; Apoc. 'Ιωανάν (A, I Esd. 9:1), 'Ιωάννης (I Esd. 9:29)]; KJV alternately JOHANAN jō hā′nən (Ezra 10:6; Neh. 6:18); JOANAN jō ā′nən (I Esd. 9:1); JOHANNES jō hăn′ĭz (I Esd. 9:29). **1.** A Korahite Levite; gatekeeper of the sanctuary (I Chr. 26:3).

2. One of King Jehoshaphat's captains (II Chr. 17:15).

3. The father of Ishmael, a commander who supported Jehoiada's revolt against Athaliah (II Chr. 23:1).

4. The owner of the chamber to which Ezra withdrew for fasting (Ezra 10:6; I Esd. 9:1); called the "son of Eliashib." If, as seems probable, he can be identified with the Johanan of Neh. 12:22, who is evidently a grandson of Eliashib, the high priest of Nehemiah's time (3:1), his connection with Ezra offers an important clue to the chronology of Ezra-Nehemiah. *See* JOHANAN 9.

5. One of the Israelites, contemporaries of Ezra, who had married foreign wives (Ezra 10:28; I Esd. 9:29).

6. A son of Tobiah the Ammonite; contemporary of Nehemiah. His Jewish wife was a daughter of Meshullam, who helped repair the wall of Jerusalem (Neh. 6:18; cf. 3:4, 30).

7. A priest in the time of the high priest Joiakim (Neh. 12:13).

8. One of the priests officiating at the dedication of the Jerusalem wall during Nehemiah's term as governor (Neh. 12:42).

Bibliography. M. Noth, *Die israelitischen Personennamen* (1928), pp. 21, 62, 187.

B. T. DAHLBERG

JEHOIACHIN jĭ hoi'ə kĭn [יהויכין, *in* Ezek. 1:2 יויכין (*properly* Joiachin), Y establishes]. Alternately: JECONIAH jĕk'ə nī'ə [יכניה, יכוניה, יכניהו, Y exists (?) *or* Y protects (?) *or* let Y establish (?)] (I Chr. 3:16-17; Esth. 2:6; Jer. 24:1; 27:20; 28:4; 29:2); CONIAH kō nī'ə [כניהו, *a contraction of the preceding*] (Jer. 22:24, 28; 37:1); JECHONIAH, KJV JECHONIAS ['Ιεχονίας] (Matt. 1:11-12). King of Judah 598-597, son and successor of Jehoiakim, carried into exile by Nebuchadrezzar.

In contemporary inscriptions the name appears as *Yaukîn*, which might be anglicized "Jauchin." This and the related forms Jehoiachin and Joiachin probably represent his throne name, given to him when he became king, while Jeconiah (Coniah) was his personal or private name. Compare how his father Eliakim became Jehoiakim (II Kings 23:34) and his uncle Shallum was also called Jehoahaz (II Kings 23:30; I Chr. 3:15; Jer. 22:11).

Jehoiachin became king in December of 598 at the age of eighteen and reigned for three months (II Kings 24:8). According to II Chr. 36:9 he was eight years old and reigned for three months and ten days, but the Babylonian tablets mentioned below and the mention of his wives in II Kings 24:15 make it clear he was eighteen years old. His mother was Nehushta, the daughter of Elnathan of Jerusalem, possibly the same Elnathan mentioned in Jer. 26:22; 36:12, 25; see also the contemporary Elnathan in an inscription from Lachish (Lachish Letter No. 3, line 15). The prominence given her suggests her great influence in the briefly reported events.

Jehoiachin inherited a disintegrating kingdom, with Judah in rebellion against Nebuchadrezzar's overlordship (*see* ISRAEL, HISTORY OF). His father Jehoiakim may have been assassinated in a palace revolt by elements unsympathetic with his policies, and this may help explain Jehoiachin's apparently quick capitulation. The Babylonian Chronicle, based on the official annals of the Babylonian kings, supplements the biblical narratives and establishes the chronology for the end of Jehoiachin's reign.* It informs us that in the seventh year of Nebuchadrezzar's reign, in the month Chislev (December, 598), Nebuchadrezzar mustered his troops and marched to the Hatti-land (Syria-Palestine). He encamped against the "city of Judah" (Jerusalem), and on the second day of the month Adar (March 16, 597, or more exactly March 15/16, since the Babylonians reckoned the day from sunset to sunset) he seized the city and captured the king. He appointed there a king of his own choice, and took heavy tribute, which he sent to Babylon. The captured king was, of course, Jehoiachin, and the king of his own choice was Jehoiachin's uncle (II Chr. 36:10 has "brother"), Mattaniah, now named Zedekiah. The biblical accounts relate that Jehoiachin submitted and, along with his mother, his wives, his officials, and others, was carried into exile. Jer. 52:28 numbers the exiles at this time as 3,023, but II Kings 24:14 reports 10,000. Fig. JEH 9.

The exile of Jehoiachin was the occasion for oracles of Jeremiah (13:18-19; 22:24-30; cf. 24:1-10), which mention also Jehoiachin's mother. Jeremiah believed Jehoiachin would not return from exile, and that his offspring would not rule again in Judah. The prophet Hananiah, by contrast, predicted the return of Jehoiachin within two years (Jer. 28:3-4, 11). Others doubtless had similar hopes and still reckoned Jehoiachin as the legitimate king. Jehoiachin's own hopes for return and restoration are reflected in Jeremiah's oracle (22:24-30). Ezekiel dated his oracles, not according to the reign of Zedekiah, but by the exile of King Jehoiachin (1:2; 8:1; etc.), perhaps reflecting the exile's view of Jehoiachin's continuing royal status.

Zedekiah may have been regarded by many as only a provisional ruler, in anticipation of Jehoiachin's return. Two stamped jar handles from the excavations of Tell Beit Mirsim (Kiriath-sepher) and one from Beth-shemesh, belonging to the time of Zedekiah, bore the inscription לאליקם נער יוכן, "Belonging to Eliakim, steward of *Yaukîn*."* Eliakim was steward of the crown property, which was thus kept intact and protected while Jehoiachin was in exile, that it might be his when he returned. It is possible that Gedaliah, who was governor of Judah after Zedekiah was deposed, may also have been regarded as a provisional ruler. Fig. JEH 10.

The Babylonians themselves may have intended the eventual restoration of Jehoiachin, if circumstances would make it advisable. We may compare Manasseh's exile and return (II Chr. 33:11-13). Jehoiachin continued to bear the title of king of Judah in Babylon. On tablets found in Babylon listing deliveries of rations in oil, barley, etc., to captives and skilled workmen, *Yaukîn* king of Judah and his five sons are mentioned. The tablets also contain references to other Judeans, to inhabitants of Ashkelon, Tyre, Byblos, and Arvad, and to Egyptians, Elamites, Lydians, and others. They are dated from the tenth to the thirty-fifth year of Nebuchadrezzar (595-570 B.C.). One of the tablets mentioning Jehoiachin is dated 592. The reference to distribution of rations to him and the mention of his five sons suggest that he was not in prison but was living a fairly normal life in Babylonia. Perhaps an attempted escape later resulted in his imprisonment. In II Kings 25:27-30; Jer. 52:31-34 we are informed of his release from prison by Evil-merodach (Amel-Marduk) on a date which, according to one possible reckoning, represents March 20 or 22, 560 (561). Jehoiachin's seat was set above that of other kings with him in Babylon, and he dined at the table of Evil-merodach, who gave him a regular daily allow-

9. Babylonian chronicle, recording the Battle of Carchemish (605 B.C.) and the capture of Jerusalem (597 B.C.)

ance of food as long as he lived. His elevation at this time may have engendered great hopes among the exiles, perhaps even bordering on messianic expectations.

Jehoiachin altogether had seven sons, whose names are listed in I Chr. 3:17. It has been suggested that the name of one of them, Shenazzar, perhaps to be read Sin-ab-usur, may be corrupted to Sheshbazzar in Ezra 1:8, etc.; and so he may have been the first leader or governor of Judah after the return. He was succeeded by a grandson of Jehoiachin, Zerubbabel, who became the center of an unsuccessful attempt to restore the throne.

In the genealogy in Matt. 1:11-12 Jechoniah (Jehoiachin) is given as the son of Josiah, the name of Jehoiakim being absent from the list. In the Apoc., Baruch reads his book in the hearing of Jeconiah and other exiles in Babylon (Bar. 1:3), and in I Esd. 1:43 Joakim (Jehoiakim) appears as an error for Jehoiachin.

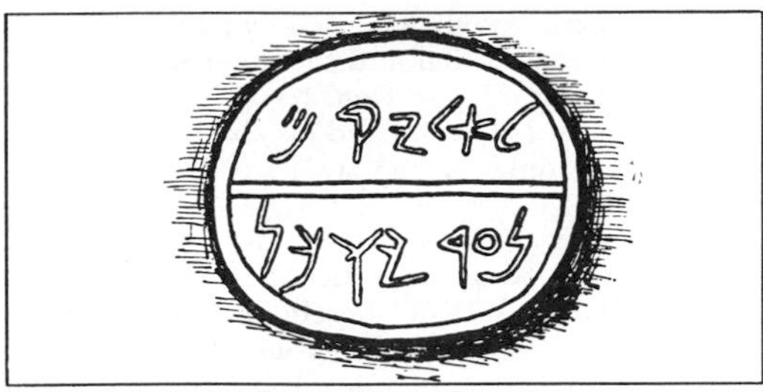

Courtesy of the American Schools of Oriental Research

10. Seal of Eliakim, steward of Jehoiachin; unearthed at Beth-shemesh

Bibliography. W. F. Albright, "The Seal of Eliakim," *JBL,* LI (1932), 77-106; "King Jehoiachin in Exile," *BA,* V (1942), 49-55. H. G. May, "Three Hebrew Seals and the Status of Exiled Jehoiachin," *AJSL,* LVI (1939), 146-48. E. F. Weidner, "Jojachin, König von Juda, in babylonischen Keilscrifttexten," *Mélanges Syriens,* II (1939), 923-35. J. B. Pritchard, ed., *ANET* (2nd ed., 1955), p. 308. D. J. Wiseman, *Chronicles of the Chaldean Kings* (1956), pp. 32-35, 72-73.

H. G. MAY

JEHOIADA jĭ hoi′ə də [יהוידע, Yahu knows *or* has regarded; *same as* יוידע, Joiada]. **1.** The father of the Benaiah who commanded King David's mercenaries (II Sam. 8:18; 20:23; 23:20, 22; I Kings 1:8–2:46) and who served under Solomon also (I Kings 4:4; cf. I Chr. 11:22, 24; 18:17; 27:5; in the last passage he is called "the priest"). It is doubtless this same Jehoiada who, according to the Chronicler, joined forces with David at Hebron and is called a "prince" (נגיד) and identified with the house of Aaron (I Chr. 12:27). *See* BENAIAH; DAVID.

2. According to I Chr. 27:34, the successor to Ahithophel as King David's counselor; the son of Benaiah, and presumably the grandson of 1 *above.* But it is possible that the genealogical order has been inverted here through a scribal error and that this individual is identical with 1 *above.*

3. The high priest in Jerusalem who organized and led the coup that overthrew Queen Athaliah of Judah (*ca.* 842-837 B.C.), together with the Baal cult that she supported, and established the boy king Joash (Jehoash) on the throne (II Kings 11:4-21; cf. vss. 1-3). Jehoiada apparently acted as regent for the new king during the latter's minority, and later inspired Joash' rehabilitation of the temple of the Lord (12:1-6). In the parallel account in II Chr. 22:10–24:27, Jehosheba (Jehoshabeath), the royal aunt of Joash who saved and hid the infant prince when Athaliah killed the other male heirs to the throne, is represented as the wife of Jehoiada, thus making him the new king's uncle (22:10-12). In the latter account it is related further that after Jehoiada's death his son, Zechariah, was executed by King Joash for having criticized conditions in Judah, for which death in turn Joash suffered divine punishment through military defeat and assassination (24:17-27). *See also* ATHALIAH; JEHOSHEBA; JOASH.

Bibliography. W. O. E. Oesterley and T. H. Robinson, *A History of Israel,* I (1932), 350-53.

4. A priest in the time of Jeremiah the prophet (Jer. 29:26).

5. Alternate form of JOIADA 2; KJV form of JOIADA 1.

B. T. DAHLBERG

JEHOIAKIM jĭ hoi′ə kĭm [יהויקים, יויקים (Neh. 12:10-12, 26; *properly* JOIAKIM), Y raises up]. King of Judah *ca.* 609-598 B.C.; son of Josiah, and brother of Jehoahaz.

In contemporary documents the name appears as Yaukîm. This is an abbreviation of Joiakim (or Jehoiakim). These related forms in all probability represent his throne name. His given name was Eliakim (II Kings 23:34; II Chr. 36:4), but Pharaoh Neco changed his name to Jehoiakim (*see* JEHOIACHIN). The change of name may very well have been deliberate on the part of the pharaoh, to appeal to Israel's national pride.

On the evidence of I Chr. 3:15, Jehoiakim was the second son of Josiah. He succeeded to the throne when his younger brother Jehoahaz was deposed by Pharaoh Neco after a reign of only three months.

Jehoiakim became king at the age of twenty-five and reigned eleven years in Jerusalem (II Kings 23:36; II Chr. 36:5). His mother was Zebidah, daughter of Pedaiah of Rumah (II Kings 23:36) in Galilee. He may have been passed over as his father's immediate successor because of his pro-Egyptian leanings. That he had some influence with Egypt is clear from the story of the flight and death of the prophet Uriah (Jer. 26:20 ff). This would also account for Neco's choice of him. Neco further laid the land of Judah under heavy tribute—a hundred shekels of silver and ten(?) talents of gold (II Kings 23:33; II Chr. 36:3). This sum Jehoiakim obtained by levying a tax upon the whole land (II Kings 23:35). That the king put some of the money thus obtained to his own personal use seems clear from Jeremiah's oracle of woe against him (Jer. 22:13 ff).

Our knowledge of events following the death of King Josiah at Megiddo (609) has been increased considerably by the appearance of four hitherto unpublished texts of the Babylonian Chronicle. Previously our main source of information for this period was the extract from Berossus, contained in Jos. Antiq. X.xi.1. Exact details are still lacking, but after the Battle of Megiddo (609) Assyria as an empire does not again appear in the picture. The world powers are Egypt and the Medo-Babylonian Empire. From 609 to 605 Nabopolassar of Babylon and his son Nebuchadrezzar were engaged in a number of campaigns against the hill folk on the S Urartian border. At the same time the Egyptians held a strong position at Carchemish on the Euphrates, from which the Babylonians were apparently unable to dislodge them, despite repeated attempts to do so. The general picture is that Egypt managed to retain the initiative. Nabopolassar himself returned to Babylon, where he died in August, 605.

Meantime, probably in May-June, 605, Nebuchadrezzar, now in sole command of the Babylonian army, attacked the Egyptians at Carchemish. He claims to have routed them completely in the decisive battle that followed. The Babylonian Chronicle records that even those who escaped were overtaken in the district of Hamath, and "not a single man escaped to his own country." Nebuchadrezzar pursued his attack to the W and "conquered the whole area of the Hatti-country" (i.e., Syria-Palestine). The biblical record confirms this account. "The king of Egypt did not come again out of his land, for the king of Babylon had taken all that belonged to the king of Egypt from the Brook of Egypt to the river Euphrates" (II Kings 24:7). These events must have occurred before August, 605, when Nebuchadrezzar was recalled to Babylon by the news of his father's death.

The date is important also from the point of view of chronology. Jeremiah (46:2) assigns the Battle of Carchemish to the fourth year of Jehoiakim. This enables us to date both the Battle of Megiddo and the death of Josiah. It also fixes the date of the reign of Jehoahaz and the accession of Jehoiakim.

As a result of Nebuchadrezzar's victory over Egypt, Jehoiakim transferred his allegiance to him, but his actual submission (II Kings 24:1*a*) probably took place in the first year of Nebuchadrezzar's reign —i.e., 604-603, when he marched with his army through the Hatti territory and received heavy tribute from all its kings.

For three years Jehoiakim acknowledged Babylonian suzerainty. Then he rebelled (II Kings 24:1*b*). The occasion appears to have been an indecisive battle of great ferocity fought near the Egyptian border between the Babylonians and the Egyptians in 601-600. The Babylonian Chronicle does not mention either the date or the place of this battle, nor is any reference made to it in our present Egyptian sources. Casualties were very heavy on both sides, and the clear implication is that Nebuchadrezzar was compelled to break off the campaign. After the battle he withdrew to Babylonia, where he remained for almost two years. This interval he spent in reequipping his military forces, especially his chariotry. Egypt was apparently in no position to move toward the conquest of Syria-Palestine. It is clear, however, that she continued her policy of intrigue, and apparently she was sufficiently strong to make an attack to the N and capture Gaza (Jer. 47:1). Jehoiakim's revolt against Nebuchadrezzar, against the advice of Jeremiah (cf. Jer. 27:9-11), was probably due to Egyptian influence at his court. In the circumstances Nebuchadrezzar dispatched bands of Chaldeans and enlisted the aid of the Syrians, the Moabites, and the Ammonites in an attempt to put down the rebellion (II Kings 24:2). Apparently these efforts were unsuccessful, and in 598 Nebuchadrezzar himself was again in Judah at the head of his armies and laid siege to Jerusalem. The Babylonian Chronicle enables us to date the succession of events. In the seventh year of the reign of Nebuchadrezzar, in the month of Chislev (i.e., December, 598), he mustered his troops, marched to Hatti land, and besieged the "city of Judah" (i.e., Jerusalem). The city was captured on the second day of the month Adar (i.e., March 15/16, 597), and the king taken prisoner. The captured king was Jehoiachin, who reigned for three months. Thus December, 598, marks not only his accession but also the death of Jehoiakim.

The probable explanation of the Chronicler's statement: "Against him came up Nebuchadrezzar king of Babylon, and bound him in fetters to take him to Babylon. Nebuchadrezzar also carried part of the vessels of the house of the LORD to Babylon and put them in his palace" (II Chr. 36:6-7), is that this is a conclusion which the Chronicler drew from the report of Berossus that among the captives captured by Nebuchadrezzar in 605 were Jews, and that he decorated the temple of Bel and the other temples with the spoils of war (cf. also Dan. 1:1-2).

The reign of Jehoiakim and his character form the subject of a number of the oracles of JEREMIAH (cf., e.g., Jer. 36).

The manner of the king's death is problematical. The writer of Kings says that he "slept with his fathers" (II Kings 24:6), thereby indicating that he died a peaceful death. The Chronicler, on the other hand, makes no mention of his death. In this connection Jeremiah's two oracles relating to Jehoiakim's death must be considered. No lament would be made for him. He would be buried with the "burial of an ass," "dragged and cast forth beyond the gates of Jerusalem" (Jer. 22:18-19). "His dead body shall be cast out to the heat by day and the frost by night" (36:30). The Chronicler's omission of any notice of his death is understandable if II Chr. 36:6 means that Jehoiakim was carried off in fetters to Babylon, where he died. Such an interpretation of the verse, however, does not seem probable. It declares that Jehoiakim was bound in fetters with the intention of taking him to Babylon. But the plan was apparently given up, for some reason which is not recorded. The most likely explanation for the ignorance of the sources regarding his death would seem to be that he was murdered by supporters of the pro-Babylonian party. The king's pro-Egyptian policy had brought the armies of Nebuchadrezzar to the gates of Jerusalem. He paid the penalty for this policy with his life. If this surmise is correct, it would explain, at least in part, why Jehoiachin, the son and successor of Jehoiakim, surrendered so quickly to the Babylonians. In these circumstances Jeremiah's prophecies may very well have been fulfilled and the king's body left unburied. It is an interesting suggestion that the phrase הנמצא עליו (II Chr. 36:8) means "that happened to him because of these things" (RSV "which he did") and is an actual reference to Jeremiah's prophecies.

In the genealogical list in Matt. 1, Jehoiakim's name is missing; only Jechoniah (Jehoiachin) is mentioned by name as the son of Josiah. The name Joakim (Jehoiakim) in I Esd. 1:43 should be read as Jehoiachin (so RSV).

Bibliography. F.-M. Abel, *Géographie de la Palestine,* II (1938), 438; A. M. Honeyman, "The Evidence for Regnal Names Among the Hebrews," *JBL,* LXVII (1948), 13-25; J. Bright, "A New Letter in Aramaic, Written to a Pharaoh of Egypt," *BA,* XII (1949), 46-52; H. L. Ginsberg, *Alexander Marx Jubilee Volume* (1950), pp. 439 ff; W. F. Albright, Review of a Critical and Exegetical Commentary on the Books of Kings, *JBL,* LXXI (1952), 253; J. P. Hyatt, "New Light on Nebuchadrezzar and Judean History," *JBL,* LXXV (1956), 277-84; D. J. Wiseman, *Chronicles of Chaldean Kings* (1956), pp. 20-32, 65-75; G. E. Wright, *Biblical Archeology* (1957), pp. 175 ff.

H. B. MACLEAN

JEHOIARIB jĭ hoi′ə rĭb [יהויריב, may Yahu contend (*i.e.,* in behalf of one)]. Descendant of Aaron; eponym of a priestly house identified in I Chr. 24:7 with the reign of King David and represented among those who returned from the Babylonian exile (I Chr. 9:10; the same as JOIARIB in Neh. 11:10).

Bibliography. M. Noth, *Die israelitischen Personennamen* (1928), pp. 28, 201.

B. T. DAHLBERG

JEHONADAB. Alternate form of JONADAB.

JEHONATHAN jĭ hŏn'ə thən [יְהוֹנָתָן, Yahu has given]. **1.** One of the Levites who, in company with the princes of Judah and some priests, instructed the people in the law during an itinerant teaching mission in the cities of Judah in the third year of Jehoshaphat (II Chr. 17:8).

2. The head of the postexilic priestly family of Shemaiah (Neh. 10:8; 12:6) in the days of the high priesthood of Joiakim the son of Jeshua (12:18; cf. vss. 10, 12, 26).

3. KJV form of JONATHAN in I Chr. 27:25.

E. R. DALGLISH

JEHORAM. Alternate form of JORAM.

JEHOSHABEATH. Alternate form of JEHOSHEBA.

JEHOSHAPHAT jĭ hŏsh'ə fət, —hō'shə— [יְהוֹשָׁפָט, Yahu judges *or* has judged; Ἰωσαφάτ]; KJV JOSAPHAT jŏs'ə făt (Matt. 1:8). Alternately: JOSHAPHAT jŏsh'ə făt [יוֹשָׁפָט, *a contraction of* יְהוֹשָׁפָט] (I Chr. 11:43; 15:24). **1.** One of the priests who took part in the procession when the ark of God was brought from the house of Obed-edom the Gittite to the city of David. His task was to blow a trumpet before the ark (I Chr. 15:24).

2. Recorder ("[the king's] 'remembrancer' " is a better translation of the Hebrew title מַזְכִּיר) in the administrations of David and Solomon; son of Ahilud (II Sam. 8:16; 20:24; I Kings 4:3; I Chr. 18:15). He is always listed as one of the chief officials of the kingdom.

3. One of Solomon's twelve administrative officers, with responsibility for the district of Issachar; son of Paruah (I Kings 4:17). The task of each of the officers was to provide food for the king and his household for one month each year (vs. 7).

4. King of Judah *ca.* 837-849 B.C.; son and successor of Asa.

Jehoshaphat became king at the age of thirty-five and reigned for twenty-five years. His mother was Azubah daughter of Shilhi (I Kings 22:42; II Chr. 20:31).

The reign of Jehoshaphat was marked by the end of the warfare which had gone on continuously between Israel and Judah since the death of Solomon (I Kings 22:44). The kings of the two countries entered into an alliance which was later confirmed by the marriage of Ahab's daughter Athaliah to Jehoram, son and heir of Jehoshaphat (II Kings 8:18, 27; cf. II Chr. 18:1)—an alliance which in the end was to prove disastrous. The immediate result, however, was a revival of strength in both kingdoms, though Judah clearly occupied a subordinate position. This is evidenced in the account of the Israelite attack on Ramoth-gilead (I Kings 22:1 ff), which comes from a prophetic source. Jehoshaphat was on a state visit to Ahab when he was persuaded to join in an attempt to recover Ramoth-gilead for Israel. But he was unwilling to set out without divine approval. With one accord Ahab's prophets, four hundred in number, announced the success of the contemplated expedition. Jehoshaphat, however, was not satisfied, and grudgingly Ahab sent for Micaiah son of Imlah. Micaiah first agreed with the other prophets, but later declared the vision he had seen. Israel would be "scattered upon the mountains, as sheep that have no shepherd." Despite this prophetic word the planned attack on Ramoth-gilead was carried through, and in the ensuing battle Ahab was mortally wounded. The news of his death was followed by the rout of the allied armies. The writer of Kings makes no mention of Jehoshaphat's further part in the action. Presumably he withdrew to Jerusalem. The Chronicler, however, records a word of censure uttered against him by Jehu the son of Hanani the seer (II Chr. 19:1-3). Judah's position at this time is further corroborated by the story of the attack on Moab (II Kings 3:4 ff). Historically, this alliance was probably the result of a double pressure from Assyria and Aram.

Jehoshaphat proved to be an able ruler and succeeded in bringing Edom under his control. The importance of this success lay in the fact that it gave Judah command of most of the caravan routes from Arabia and brought increased wealth to the S kingdom (II Chr. 17:5; 18:1).

The incident recorded in I Kings 22:47-49 (cf. II Chr. 20:35-37) must have occurred toward the end of Jehoshaphat's reign, as Ahaziah son of Ahab was then king of Israel. The text of I Kings 22:47-48 is corrupt and requires correction. It seems probable that Jehoshaphat had appointed a deputy over Edom, and that an attempt was made to revive maritime trade with Arabia. The first ship to be built was wrecked at Ezion-geber. Thereupon Ahaziah of Israel offered help to man a fleet, but Jehoshaphat would not agree to his proposal. It is clear that his refusal was based on the fear of N encroachment upon his territory. The matter of the control of the trade routes was also doubtless involved.

There is no reason to doubt the essential historicity of the incident recorded in II Kings 3:4 ff, where the kings of Israel, Judah, and Edom undertook a war against Moab, which had revolted from Israel. It is questionable, however, if Edom had a king at this time (cf. I Kings 22:47; II Kings 8:20).

The Chronicler gives a long and detailed account of Jehoshaphat's achievements (II Chr. 17–20). He fortified cities in Judah and placed garrison troops also in the cities of Ephraim which Asa his father had taken (17:1-2). He was feared and held in the highest regard by all the surrounding peoples. Philistines and Arabs alike brought him tribute and gifts (vss. 10-13). He had a mighty army (vss. 14-19). The figures are not reliable, but the passage probably gives a historical picture of the organization of the army. II Chr. 20:1-30 records a great victory over a combined force of Moabites, Ammonites, and Meunites at En-gedi. The story appears to be based upon a reliable tradition, which has been extensively worked over by the Chronicler. It is not a parallel to II Kings 3:4-27. Noteworthy in this connection is the account of a great penitential assembly gathered together "to seek help from the LORD" in a time of crisis. In the midst of the waiting people "the Spirit of the LORD came upon Jahaziel the son of Zechariah, . . . a Levite of the sons of Asaph," and he proclaimed the word of Yahweh. In all probability this reflects a common Israelite religious practice.

In addition, Jehoshaphat carried out a systematic teaching program among the people of Judah. Certain of the princes, Levites, and priests were sent throughout the land to instruct the people in the "book of the law of the LORD" (II Chr. 17:7-9). Vs. 8, with its emphasis on the prominent position occupied by the Levites, is demonstrably a reading back into the time of Jehoshaphat of conditions which prevailed in the Chronicler's own day. Vss. 7, 9, may rest on an old tradition. The scope of the "book of the law of the LORD" is unknown. By his own example Jehoshaphat openly encouraged the worship of Yahweh in the land. He also introduced a very important administrative change (19:5-11). Prior to his time justice had been administered by the local elders in the various communities. Jehoshaphat appointed judges in all the fortified cities of Judah. He also established a court of final appeal in Jerusalem, made up of Levites, priests, and heads of families, with the chief priest and the governor of the house of Judah in charge. The similarities between II Chr. 19:5-11 and Deut. 16:18-20; 17:8-13 are obvious. The divergences are probably to be explained by the situation existing in the time of the Chronicler. That his source told of such a judicial reform initiated by Jehoshaphat seems certain. The suggestion that II Chr. 17:7-9 is perhaps a doubtlet of 19:4-11 is an interesting one and may be correct.

In the Chronicler's account of the wars of Jehoshaphat the numbers are quite unreliable. In like manner his picture of the reforms carried out by the king bears upon it the stamp of the postexilic period. But that reforms took place is beyond question.

It seems probable that the fortresses and store cities which Jehoshaphat built in Judah (II Chr. 17:12-13) are to be understood in the light of a province system existing in Judah—a fact to which Rehoboam's comparable list (11:5-12) also points. Like Rehoboam, Jehoshaphat appointed his sons over some of these fortified cities (21:2-3). If Josh. 15:20-62 is the province list of Judah and dates from the reign of Jehoshaphat, as has been suggested, we have at hand a picture of the extent of the kingdom of Judah at this time.

Jehoshaphat may have acted as regent for his father, Asa, after the king was incapacitated in his thirty-ninth year.

Bibliography. N. Glueck, "The Third Season of Excavation at Tell el-Kheleifeh," *BASOR,* no. 79 (1940), pp. 2-18, especially p. 8; W. F. Albright, "The Judicial Reform of Jehoshaphat," *Alexander Marx Jubilee Volume* (1950), pp. 61-82; A. Alt, *Kleine Schriften zur Geschichte des Volkes Israel,* II (1953), 276-88; M. Noth, *Das Buch Josua* (2nd ed., 1953), pp. 73-123; W. Rudolph, *Chronikbücher* (1955), pp. 249-65; F. M. Cross and G. E. Wright, "The Boundary and Province Lists of the Kingdom of Judah," *JBL,* LXXV (1956), 202-26.

5. The father of Jehu, who exterminated the dynasty of Omri; and son of Nimshi (II Kings 9:2, 14). In I Kings 19:16; II Kings 9:20; II Chr. 22:7, Jehu is called the "son of Nimshi," but this is his grandfather's name. H. B. MACLEAN

JEHOSHAPHAT, VALLEY OF [עמק יהושפט]. A valley in which God shall summon the nations to be judged in the days of the messianic restoration of Judah and Jerusalem, according to Joel 3:2, 12. The intent of this text is symbolical rather than geographical, as may be inferred from the etymology of the name, "Yahweh shall judge," or from Joel 3:14, where the same valley is called "valley of decision" (עמק החרוץ), in the sense of a judicial decision or a verdict.

A few Jewish commentators, followed by the majority of early and medieval Christian exegetes, however, interpreted the toponym realistically. Kimchi supposes that a valley near Jerusalem would have been named for a monument built by King Jehoshaphat (*see* JEHOSHAPHAT 4). The Valley of Jehoshaphat has been identified at times with the Valley of Hinnom (*see* HINNOM, VALLEY OF THE SON OF), and, ever since the fourth century A.D., with the Valley of the Kidron (*see* KIDRON, BROOK), on the basis of speculations concerning God's vengeance in the day of judgment, of which the destruction of idols burnt in the Kidron by reformer kings was regarded as a type. This artificial exegesis has left traces in the Vulg.'s rendering of Jerusalem's MUSTER GATE as *Porta Judicialis,* "Gate of Judgment," in Neh. 3:31, according to a current meaning of the root *pqd* ("to visit," "to punish"). The associations of the Kidron Valley with the theme of Judgment survive in various Moslem legends concerning the so-called Golden Gate, on the E front of the Ḥaram esh-Sherīf or temple area. The upper tract of the Kidron Valley opposite the Golden Gate is referred to as the Djahannum (Gehenna), and the two doors of the gate, which shall be closed to unbelievers and all evil men, are known as the door of mercy and the door of contrition. The groups of Christian hermits and nuns who were seeking shelter from the wrath to come, and who repaired to miscellaneous caves and desecrated rock-cut tombs on either bank of the Kidron, were incorporated in the Laura, or monastic foundation, of the "Valley of Jehoshaphat," as early as the sixth century. A later monastery, built in the twelfth century near the church of the Tomb of Mary, bore the title of Saint Mary of Josaphat, and the city gate leading to the bridge of the Kidron, called today Bāb Sitti Mariam, Gate of Saint Mary, and also (erroneously) Saint Stephen's Gate, was known until the fourteenth century as Gate of the Valley of Josaphat.

The fanciful identification of the Valley of Jehoshaphat with the Kidron remains extremely popular among tourists and pilgrims, no doubt because of the countless tombstones and monuments of the Jewish cemeteries, which call to mind the day when the dead shall rise from their graves to face the sovereign Judge.

Bibliography. H. Vincent and F.-M. Abel, *Jérusalem Nouvelle,* IV (1926), 813-16, 849-52; J. Simons, *Jerusalem in the OT* (1952), pp. 10, 372. G. A. BARROIS

JEHOSHEBA jĭ hŏsh′ə bə [יהושבע, Yahu is abundance, wholeness; *cf.* Bathsheba, Elisheba]. Alternately: JEHOSHABEATH jē′hō shăb′ĭ əth [יהושבעת] (II Chr. 22:11). The daughter of King Jehoram of Judah (II Kings 11:2). When Ahaziah was killed in Jehu's revolt, the queen mother, Athaliah, destroyed the rest of the royal family and reigned herself. Jehosheba saved Joash from this destruction, hiding him for six years, until Jehoiada could make him king. According to Chronicles, she was the wife of Jehoiada. D. HARVEY

JEHOSHUA; JEHOSHUAH. KJV alternate forms of JOSHUA.

JEHOVAH jĭ hō'və. An artificial form, often attributed to Petrus Galatinus in *ca.* A.D. 1520, which results from the combination of the consonants of the Tetragrammaton (*see* YAHWEH) with the substitute vowel reading which was introduced when the MT was fixed during the sixth-seventh centuries A.D. The pre-Masoretic text was consonantal, vowels being supplied by the reader from a knowledge of the language. In the postexilic period (after 538 B.C.), however, the sacred name was withdrawn from popular usage for fear that it would be profaned. Of the various substitutes that were employed, the chief was "Adonai" ("Lord"), the vowels of which the Masoretes as a rule added to the consonants "YHWH" to indicate that "Adonai" should be read. The combination of the two—the Tetragrammaton and the vowels of "Adonai"—yields the artificial name which appeared in early editions of the KJV. The RSV, following ancient synagogue practice, renders "the LORD."

See also GOD, NAMES OF, § B.

B. W. ANDERSON

JEHOVAH-JIREH jĭ hō'və jī'rə. KJV translation of יהוה יראה (RSV lit., THE LORD WILL PROVIDE) in Gen. 22:14. This is the designation Abraham gave to the location where God provided a ram to be sacrificed in Isaac's stead. The equally possible reading "Yahweh will see" is less likely in the context, where divine providence is apparently the theme (vss. 8, 12).

The location of the site is unknown. Tradition, with Rashi, Ibn Ezra, etc., has always associated the story with the location of the Solomonic temple. Scholarship has offered the alternative suggestion that the sanctuary of the oak of Moreh at Shechem was originally intended. J. A. SANDERS

JEHOVAH-NISSI jĭ hō'və nĭs'ī. KJV translation of יהוה נסי (RSV lit., THE LORD IS MY BANNER) in Exod. 17:15. This was Moses' designation of the altar which he had erected as a memorial after the victory over the Amalekites. God was regarded as the rallying point for the Israelite army, and the name יהוה was their battle cry (cf. Judg. 7:20; Ps. 20:7). J. L. MIHELIC

JEHOVAH-SHALOM jĭ hō'və shā'ləm. KJV translation of יהוה שלום (RSV lit., THE LORD IS PEACE), the name of the altar erected by Gideon at Ophrah (Judg. 6:24).

JEHOZABAD jĭ hō'zə băd [יהוזבד, Yahu gives; *cf.* JOZABAD]. **1.** Son of Shomer; one of the servants of Joash who murdered the king at Millo (II Kings 12:21—H 12:22). In the parallel version (II Chr. 24:26) he is called the son of Shimrith the Moabitess.

2. A temple gatekeeper, son of Obed-edom (I Chr. 26:4).

3. A Benjaminite commander under Jehoshaphat (II Chr. 17:18). J. M. WARD

JEHOZADAK. Alternate form of JOZADAK.

JEHU jē'hū [יהוא, he is Yahu]. **1.** King of Israel *ca.* 842-815 B.C. He succeeded to the throne after the murder of Joram, last of the Omride dynasty.

The original vocalization was probably יוהוא (*Yōhu*) or יהוא (*Yāhu*). In cuneiform texts the name is found as *Ja-u-a.*

Jehu was the son of Jehoshaphat, son of Nimshi (II Kings 9:2). It is clear that in the phrase "son of Nimshi" (vs. 20) "son" is used in the general sense of "descendant." Actually he was the grandson of Nimshi. He reigned in Samaria for twenty-eight years (10:36).

II Kings 9:1–10:28 gives a detailed account of Jehu's rebellion against the house of Omri. It comes from a prophetic source, roughly contemporary with the events it describes. The movement had full prophetic backing. The note of censure, which appears in II Kings 10:29 ff; Hos. 1:4, is the result of later reflection. Certain features of this bloody revolution are noteworthy:

a) It was prophet-inspired. Whether Elijah had anything to do with it or not (I Kings 19:15-18), the motive was a religious one. Elijah's very name, "Yahweh is God," indicates his attitude toward the worship of any other god in Israel, and the episode on Mount Carmel (18:17 ff) his blazing passion for Yahweh alone. It is clear that the worship of the Tyrian Baal-Melcarth and Astarte, imported into Israel by the Tyrian Jezebel, was regarded by the prophets as an insult to Yahweh the God of Israel, and must therefore be completely destroyed. The opportune moment arrived in the time of Elisha. The Israelite army was on guard at Ramoth-gilead against Hazael, king of Syria (II Kings 9:14*b*-15*a*). King Joram had been wounded in the campaign there, and had returned to Jezreel to recuperate. Elisha summoned one of the sons of the prophets and bade him go to Ramoth-gilead, seek out Jehu, one of the army commanders, and privately anoint him king over Israel in the name of Yahweh. Then he was to make his escape as quickly as possible (9:1-3). The elements of speed and secrecy are stressed in Elisha's orders (vs. 3).

The young man executed his commission. It is probable that the command to exterminate the house of Ahab (vss. 7-10*a*) did not belong in the original statement. The hesitancy of Jehu in announcing to his fellow commanders the purpose of the prophet's visit gives every appearance of an actual event. On their insistence, however, he told them what had happened. They immediately proclaimed him king, and Jehu made preparations to drive to Jezreel, after taking precautions that news of the events at Ramoth-gilead should not reach that city. Then he set out with a company of chariots. As they drew near to Jezreel, the watchman on duty reported to King Joram that a company was approaching. Joram ordered messengers on horseback to be sent out to meet them, but they did not come back. Suspicious of what this meant, Joram ordered his royal chariot to be made ready; and he and Ahaziah king of Judah, who was paying him a visit, drove, each in his own chariot, to meet Jehu. They met him at the plot of ground which had belonged to Naboth the Jezreelite. Queen Jezebel had been responsible for the murder of Naboth, and his property had then come into the possession of King Ahab (I Kings 21: 17 ff). In ruthless manner Joram was slain by Jehu and his body tossed on the plot that had formerly belonged to Naboth. Thus Elijah's prophecy was fulfilled (I Kings 21:17 ff). Ahaziah king of Judah tried to escape, but was pursued, overtaken, and seriously wounded at Ibleam. He died at Megiddo. Then Jehu came to Jezreel, where Jezebel awaited him in state. On his orders she was thrown into the street from an upper window, trampled on by the horses, and eaten by dogs (II Kings 9:30-37). Perhaps the character of Jehu is to be seen in the words: "He went in and ate and drank" (vs. 34), just as if nothing unusual had happened.

The murder of the kings of Israel and Judah, together with the queen mother, was followed by the slaughter of Ahab's whole family in Samaria, some seventy persons in all (II Kings 10:1). By a clever ruse Jehu challenged the loyalty of the city's leaders. He invited them to choose the best and fittest of the king's sons and set him on his father's throne and fight for him and his father's house. When they protested their loyalty to him, Jehu ordered the heads of all the members of Ahab's family to be sent to him at Jezreel, where he exhibited them at the city gate. Then he slew all who were left of Ahab's family in Jezreel, together with all who had held high official positions (II Kings 10:1-11). Thereafter he went to Samaria.

On his way there he met the royal party from Judah coming to visit the royal family in Samaria. The place of meeting was at Beth-eked of the Shepherds (II Kings 10:12)—i.e., the "shearing house of the shepherds." This place has not certainly been identified. Jehu gave orders that the whole party should be taken alive and slaughtered. In this blood bath forty-two persons perished (vs. 14). The figure may be a round number, but if so, one would expect forty instead.

The religious element in the revolt was again demonstrated by the fact that Jehonadab, son of Rechab, is pictured as giving his wholehearted support to Jehu (II Kings 10:15-16). The Rechabites were fanatical in their devotion to Yahweh. They had neither gardens nor vineyards. They refused to drink wine. They lived in tents and would not build houses. The ideal they had was the simple life of the desert (Jer. 35). The association of the Rechabite leader with Jehu is indicative of the spirit of discontent that prevailed in Israel at this time. Jehonadab was remembered as taking part with Jehu in the blood purge that followed.

Arrived in Samaria, Jehu completed the destruction of the house of Ahab (II Kings 10:17). He then proceeded to the wholesale extermination of both the cult and the worshipers of Baal. That this incident is historical is not to be doubted, but that it involved all the worshipers of Baal "throughout all Israel" (vs. 21) is open to question. Under the pretense of offering a great sacrifice to Baal, Jehu summoned all the Baal-worshipers to the house of Baal which Ahab had built in Samaria (I Kings 16:32). Jehonadab son of Rechab had part with him in the events that followed. Orders were issued that every single person present was to be slain. These orders were carried out. Then the house of Baal itself was demolished and the pillar of Baal broken in pieces. The site became a latrine, and its evil reputation was remembered even in the writer's own day.

One may question Jehu's real religious zeal for Yahweh in all these events, but that a religious motive was present is unquestionable. The cult of Baal-Melcarth had been exterminated from Israel, or at least it had been drastically curtailed. It is to be remembered, however, that a similar thing had happened before (I Kings 18), but Baal-worship had survived. And the same thing occurred again.

b) An economic factor was also involved. The Omride rulers had brought about a considerable change in the fortunes of Israel. Prior to this time Israel's economic prosperity had depended upon the small peasant farmer. He owned his own plot of land by inalienable right and expected to hand it down to his descendants. There were larger farms, but these were the exception rather than the rule. Omri's choice of Samaria as his new capital city, and particularly his alliance with Phoenicia, affected the whole destiny of Israel. Wealth began to appear in Israel as the result of increased trade, and a new merchant class arose. The contrast between rich and poor became sharper as the years passed, and this contrast was heightened as a result of periods of drought. Men long remembered the great drought which occurred in Ahab's reign, with its accompanying famine in the land (I Kings 17). The result was that the wealthy merchants loaned money at extortionate rates to the peasants, and when they were unable to pay, confiscated their land and enslaved their families. There is no question that the incident of Naboth's vineyard (I Kings 21) aroused popular discontent and fed the flames of revolt. Presumably other similar travesties of justice had occurred.

c) It is equally clear that there was dissatisfaction in the army. Plans for revolution had already been made. These only awaited a suitable opportunity to put them into effect. This opportunity came with the absence of Joram when the army was defending Ramoth-gilead. Thus the stage was set for Jehu's purge of the land.

But it went too far. From the religious point of view it accomplished its purpose: There was no longer any chance of successfully establishing a rival worship to that of Yahweh in Israel. From the political point of view, however, it was a major disaster. Israel's former allies, Phoenicia and Judah, had been permanently antagonized. The prophetic hatred of Jezebel's Tyrian deities may account for Jehu's savage revenge on Jezebel and all her followers, but it is difficult to find any real justification for the murder of the royal family of Judah. Israel now stood alone, and she paid the penalty. Hazael king of Aram seems to have completely overrun Transjordan at this time and annexed it (II Kings 10:32-33; cf. Amos 1:3). Clearly Jehu was not in a position to challenge him, despite the reference to "all his might" in the summary of his reign (II Kings 10:34). The Assyrian inscriptions furnish further details of the situation. In 842 Shalmaneser III marched against Aram. He claims to have inflicted a defeat on Hazael of Damascus, and besieged him in Damascus, but did not succeed in capturing the city. He then proceeded to Phoenicia, where he placed a stele with his image as king on the cliff of Ba'li-ra'si. On the cliff at the mouth of the Dog River in Lebanon an image is pointed out which may be the one erected by Shalmaneser III. In the course of this campaign Shalmaneser received tribute from the inhabitants of Tyre and Sidon and from Jehu, son of Omri (*Ia-ú-a mār Ḫu-um-ri-i*). The tribute consisted of gold, silver, vessels made of these metals, and wooden objects, the exact nature of which is unknown. Shalmaneser's famous Black Obelisk shows Jehu actually presenting these tokens of his submission. It is also of interest as portraying Israelites for the first time, as far as we know. *Ca.* 837 the Assyrians again raided Syrian territory, but thereafter were taken up with their own affairs till 805. The general picture during this period is one of constant aggression by Aram against both Israel and Judah. It is probable that at this time Megiddo was destroyed by Hazael.

It is to be noted that the Chronicler gives only a very brief summary of the events recorded in II Kings 9:1-10:28 (II Chr. 22:8-9). The reason is clear: He was not interested in Jehu. He was interested only in the fate of Ahaziah.

Bibliography. E. G. Kraeling, *Aram and Israel* (1918), pp. 73-84; M. Noth, *Die israelitischen Personennamen* (1928), p. 143; J. A. Montgomery, "Ascetic Strains in Early Judaism," *JBL*, LI (1932), 183 ff; F.-M. Abel, *Géographie de la Palestine*, II (1938), 271; R. S. Lamon and G. M. Shipton, *Megiddo I*, XLII (1939), 8 ff; J. B. Pritchard, ed., *ANET* (2nd ed., 1955), p. 281; G. E. Wright, *Biblical Archaeology* (1957), pp. 156 ff.

2. A prophet, son of Hanani, who foretold the destruction of Baasha's house (I Kings 16:1, 7, 12). The same name is given to the prophet who censured Jehoshaphat king of Judah for joining with Ahab king of Israel in the attack on Ramoth-gilead (II Chr. 19:2). In II Chr. 20:34 are mentioned the "chronicles of Jehu the son of Hanani, which are recorded in the Book of the Kings of Israel."

3. A Benjaminite from Anathoth; one of David's Mighty Men who came to him at Ziklag (I Chr. 12:3).

4. A Judahite, of the family of Jerahmeel; son of Obed (I Chr. 2:38).

5. A Simeonite; son of Joshibiah, head of a father's house (I Chr. 4:35). H. B. MACLEAN

JEHUBBAH jĭ hŭb'ə [יחבה; *Qere:* חבה, *perhaps contracted from* חביה, (God) has hidden (someone from danger)] (I Chr. 7:34). A descendant of Asher.

Bibliography. M. Noth, *Die israelitischen Personennamen* (1928), p. 242; cf. p. 178 n. B. T. DAHLBERG

JEHUCAL jĭ hū'kəl [יהוכל, Yahu is mighty] (Jer. 37:3); JUCAL jōō'kəl [יוכל] (Jer. 38:1). Son of Shelemiah; a courtier of Zedekiah.

JEHUD jē'hŭd [יהד, praise] (Josh. 19:45). A Danite village; identified with modern el-Yahudiyeh, eight miles SE of Jaffa. The LXX reads "Jazur" (modern Yazur) here—probably a variant reading, not a scribal error.

JEHUDI jĭ hū'dī [יהודי, Jew, Judean]. The prince, son of Nethaniah, who brought Jeremiah's scribe Baruch to the court and read his scroll to Jehoiakim (Jer. 36:14, 21, 23). His name (lit., "the Judahite") may be due to the fact that he was a naturalized Judean, since his great-grandfather was named Cushi (lit., "the Cushite"). J. M. WARD

JEHUDIJAH jē'hə dī'jə. KJV translation of יהדיה (RSV JEWISH) in I Chr. 4:18. The word is not a proper name; it appears with the definite article and means "woman of Judah," to distinguish this one of Mered's wives from another, who was Egyptian.

JEHUEL. Alternate form of JEHIEL.

JEHUSH. KJV alternate form of JEUSH.

JEIEL jĭ ī'əl [יעיאל, God has healed *or* preserved (*cf.* Arab. *w'j*); *Kethibh* יעואל (I Chr. 9:35; 11:44; II Chr. 26:11)]; KJV JEHIEL jĭ hī'əl in I Chr. 9:35; 11:44. Alternately: OCHIEL ō kī'əl ['Οχίηλος] (I Esd. 1:9). **1.** A chief of the tribe of Reuben (I Chr. 5:7).

2. Ancestor of the inhabitants of Gibeon and of King Saul (I Chr. 9:35; cf. 8:29, as emended in the RSV).

3. One of David's Mighty Men (I Chr. 11:44); possibly identical with 1 *above*.

4. A Levite represented both as gatekeeper and as musician (I Chr. 15:18, 21; 16:5*b*). Jehiah apparently stands for this name in I Chr. 15:24.

5. In I Chr. 16:5*a*, probably a copyist's error for JAAZIEL.

6. A Levite of the sons of Asaph (II Chr. 20:14).

7. King Uzziah's secretary who prepared the military lists mentioned in II Chr. 26:11.

8. A chief of the Levites in the time of Josiah (II Chr. 35:9). Ochiel appears in the parallel I Esd. 1:9.

9. One of the Jews who put away their foreign wives in obedience to Ezra's decree (Ezra 10:43). The name is absent from the parallel I Esd. 9:35.

10. KJV form (correctly) of JEUEL 2-3.

Bibliography. W. Rudolph, *Esra und Nehemia* (1949), p. 78.
B. T. DAHLBERG

JEKABZEEL. Alternate form of KABZEEL.

JEKAMEAM jĕk'ə mē'əm [יקמעם, may *'am* (divine kinsman) raise up] (I Chr. 23:19; 24:23). A Levite, son of Hebron.

Bibliography. M. Noth, *Die israelitischen Personennamen* (1928), pp. 76-79, 200.

JEKAMIAH jĕk'ə mī'ə [יקמיה, may Yahu establish]; KJV JECAMIAH in I Chr. 3:18. **1.** A Jerahmeelite (I Chr. 2:41).

2. One of the sons of King Jehoiachin (I Chr. 3:18).

JEKUTHIEL jĭ kū'thĭ əl [יקותיאל, may God nourish; *cf.* Arab. *qāta*] (I Chr. 4:18). An eponym; descendant of Judah through Mered.

Bibliography. M. Noth, *Die israelitischen Personennamen* (1928), pp. 36, 203.

JEMIMAH jĭ mī'mə [ימימה, *perhaps* dove] (Job 42:14); KJV JEMIMA. The first of Job's three daughters born to him when his fortunes were restored.

JEMNAAN. KJV Apoc. form of JABNEEL; JAMNIA.

JEMUEL jĕm'yōō əl [ימואל] (Gen. 46:10; Exod. 6: 15). The first son of Simeon; same as NEMUEL.

JEPHTE jĕf'tĭ. Douay Version form of JEPHTHAH.

JEPHTHAH jĕf'thə [יפתח, he opens, *see below;* Ἰεφθάε (Heb. 11:32; KJV JEPHTHAE)]. Gileadite warrior who, as "ruler" or "judge," delivered Israel from the Ammonites, sacrificed his daughter in fulfilment of a vow, and defeated the Ephraimites (Judg. 11:1–12:7).

1. The name
2. Critical problems
3. Jephthah and the Ammonites
4. Jephthah and his daughter
5. Jephthah and the Ephraimites
6. Jephthah's significance

Bibliography

1. The name. The Hebrew name Jephthah appears also as a place name, IPHTAH (Josh. 15:43). It is a shortened form of IPHTAHEL, a place name meaning "El (God) opens (the womb)" or "El (God) frees (the captive)" (Josh. 19:14, 27); the same name also appears in Old South Arabic. Related are the Hebrew personal name PETHAHIAH, meaning "Yahweh has opened" (I Chr. 24:16; Ezra 10:23; Neh. 9:5; 11:24), and the name Japtih-Adda in the Tell El-Amarna Tablets.

2. Critical problems. The biblical story of Jephthah contains a number of puzzling literary and historical problems. It is preceded by a long introduction (Judg. 10:6-16) and includes what has been called a "great interpolation" (11:12-28). The introduction summarizes the period of the judges thus far in language and theology similar to that of the introduction to all the stories of the judges (2:6–3:6). It is probably by the same Deuteronomic editor. The faithless Israelites have fallen successively into the worship of seven foreign gods; hence angry Yahweh has sold them into the hands of seven foreign nations, until they have cried for deliverance. This introduction gives special attention to oppression by the Philistines and the Ammonites (11:7-9) and hence was evidently intended to introduce the subsequent stories of both Samson and Jephthah. *See* JUDGES, BOOK OF, § C2*i*.

The long interpolation, Jephthah's diplomatic negotiations with the enemy, mentions the Ammonites only in the introduction (11:12-15) and the conclusion (vss. 27-28). The body of the argument concerns the Moabites and is based upon the accounts in Num. 20–22, despite the fact that it was EHUD who had encountered the Moabites, and Jephthah's calling was to deliver Israel from the eighteen-year menace of the Ammonites (10:8, 17-18). Historical precedents cited are the Israelite forefathers' having by-passed Moab on their journey from Egypt to the Promised Land, having won the now-disputed territory N of Moab between the rivers Arnon and Jabbok from Amorite—not Moabite or Ammonite—King Sihon and held it for the intervening three hundred years (*see* JUDGES, BOOK OF, § E, on the chronology), and not having been challenged by war with Moabite King Balak at the time. The religious view taken is that, since the Israelite God, Yahweh, had long ago given them their territory, the invaders should confine themselves to the territory their own god had won for them. The god mentioned is CHEMOSH, national deity of the Moabites, not the Ammonites, and he is evidently respected by the writer as having power as the enemy's national deity.

Some interpreters explain this confusion between Moabite and Ammonite history as due to the fact that this interpolation was written perhaps in the seventh century B.C., when distinctions even between national deities were blurred because the Ammonites were taking over declining Moab's territory. *See further* AMMON; MOAB.

Because of the problems above indicated and other internal inconsistencies in the Jephthah story, some scholars have concluded that there were originally two very different narratives of Jephthah. In the earlier one, a continuation of the old J narrative of the Hexateuch, Jephthah was a Gileadite driven from home because of his illegitimate parentage, and he was the leader of a bandit gang. Recalled by the promise of rulership, he saved his people from the Ammonites, and subsequently massacred escaping Ephraimites at the fords of the Jordan. In the later narrative, a continuation of E, Jephthah, who was a respectable householder living in Mizpah, saved his people from the Moabites and sacrificed his daughter in fulfilment of a vow. With some differences in detail, some interpreters have seen the latter only as Jephthah's true story, the former as the otherwise lost story of another Gileadite, JAIR.

It is possible, however, with the exception of the interpolation in 11:12-28, to interpret the story of Jephthah as a fairly consistent early account of the first real defense of Transjordan territory and of the career of a historical Jephthah, centering in his charismatic leadership in defeating the Ammonites, his vow and its fulfilment, and his intertribal struggle with jealous Ephraimites.

3. Jephthah and the Ammonites. The Ammonites' territory was on the border of the Arabian Desert E of both Gilead and Moab, their capital Rabbath-ammon (modern Amman). Jephthah's call was in response to their pushing W in perhaps the early eleventh century B.C.

The selection of Jephthah is the story of crisis-motivated popular demand that an obviously God-empowered leader become practical dictator, despite his low family background (Judg. 10:17–11:11). Because Jephthah's mother was a harlot, whose son therefore could not share in any family inheritance, Jephthah had been banished from home, probably with clan approval (11:1, 7). His father may have been unknown (the language of 11:1*b*-3*a* and the concept of the territory Gilead as a personal name are probably from a late editor). As leader of an outlaw band Jephthah conducted successful raiding parties from his center at TOB, perhaps some fifteen miles E of Ramoth-gilead, the location later of Syrian allies of the enemy Ammonites (cf. Jephthah's outlaw activities, including a possible league with allies of Ammon, with those of David and his league with enemy Philistines: I Sam. 21:10–22:2; 28:1-2; 29; II Sam. 10:6-8).

In the crisis Jephthah was offered the position of "chief" or "ruler" (קצין, RSV "leader"; Judg. 11:6,

11; Arabic "one who decides judicially"; used only here in Judges, but elsewhere in Josh. 10:24; Prov. 6:7; 25:15; Isa. 1:10; 3:6-7; 22:3; Dan. 11:18; Mic. 3:1, 9). When his mission was successfully accomplished, his position was to be permanent, but he is later recorded as having been judge only six years before his death and burial in his Gileadite city (Judg. 12:7).

At a sacred place, Mizpah in Gilead (site unknown), Jephthah was consecrated in a solemn ceremony of holy words: "The Lord was witness" (lit., "hearer"); all the words were spoken "before the LORD" (11:10-11). Immediately thereafter (if, as seems likely, vs. 29 is the sequel of vs. 11), Jephthah's charismatic leadership became clear, for "the spirit of the LORD came upon Jephthah" (vs. 29; exactly the language used of Othniel in 3:10; cf. Ehud and Gideon).

The named sites of the routes of Jephthah's collection of troops from Gilead and E Jordan Manasseh (vs. 29) and of his battles, probably to the E, are unknown. But because of his decisive victory over the Ammonites, they caused no more trouble until the days of Saul (I Sam. 11).

4. Jephthah and his daughter. The central concern in the story of Jephthah is his vow and its fulfilment, as the explanation of an old Israelite annual four-day feast of lamentation (Judg. 11:30-31, 34-40). Jephthah's vow, made perhaps at his consecration, was not rash, but deliberate. Expecting great things of Yahweh, he promised his best in return, human sacrifice. Such sacrifice was not infrequent in Israel; it was usually made as a desperate, last-resort measure of securing divine favor (cf. II Kings 16:3; 17:17; 21:6; Jer. 7:31; Mic. 6:7; *see* SACRIFICE AND OFFERINGS § B4). Jephthah's bitter sorrow lay in the fact that God did not intervene (as with Abraham in Gen. 22), perhaps by letting only a slave be the first to come forth from his house. This Jephthah must have hoped, for the sacrifice had been postponed until after victory; it was not the prelude to battle. Instead of a slave, God took his "absolutely only child" (as vs. 34 emphasizes) when she welcomed her father, as would be expected, by the custom begun by Miriam at the Exodus from Egypt (Exod. 15:20-21; cf. I Sam. 18:6-7). Unlike the gory details of Aeschylus' portrayal of the sacrifice of Agamemnon's daughter Iphigenia, the Hebrew storyteller with fine sensitivity shows Jephthah's bitter grief and his daughter's courageous self-denial, born of respect for her father's faith, and then leaves the outcome to the reader's imagination.

On the plane of social custom the emphasis upon Jephthah's daughter's virginity points up the fact that she had neither husband nor father of her child to rescue her from her father's vow. That she was not sacrificed but became founder of an order of perpetual virgins is a medieval idea. On the plane of folk tale or cult legend the story and its resultant custom were related to the prevalent Near Eastern fertility cults. In one form of the cult there were "women weeping for Tammuz" (Ezek. 8:14), dead Babylonian god of vegetation who had been killed at the onset of the dry season by his enemies and was then sought in the underworld by his wife, Ishtar (*see* TAMMUZ; cf. Egyptian Osiris and Isis, Canaanite Baal or Adonis and Ashtarte). Such women weepers were the "companions" (Judg. 11:37-38; cf. "my love" in Song of S. 1:9) who accompanied Jephthah's daughter on her two-month mountain vigil. Possibly in this form of the nature-worship the weeping was over the feared perpetual virginity of Ishtar or Ashtarte, Mother Earth—hence no agricultural crops in the foreseeable future.

5. Jephthah and the Ephraimites. Jephthah's conflict with the Ephraimites could have been a private feud between a few individuals, which in the subsequent telling was blown up to become a tribal affair (Judg. 12:1-6). Perhaps a few "fugitives of Ephraim" (vs. 4), onetime W Jordan Ephraimites now living as colonists in Gilead, incensed because they did not feel included, contrary to his intent, in Jephthah's call to battle, made trouble. GIDEON had dealt with a similar situation by persuasion and flattery (Judg. 8:1-3). Not so Jephthah. In the subsequent struggle, according to the exaggerated figures, 42,000 Ephraimites trying to return to their W Jordan homeland were massacred when detected, because of their inability to pronounce SHIBBOLETH.

6. Jephthah's significance. Jephthah's victories stopped Ammonite invasions until the days of Saul, some decades later. His massacre of Ephraimites, only an incident in the intertribal conflict with that haughty people (*see* EPHRAIM 1), gives the Hebrew student evidence of early dialect differences among the Israelites. Religiously Jephthah's career was distinguished by his charismatic adventuring and success as evidence of divine favor; and his indomitable will, revealed in his overcoming personal grief and sacrificing his daughter, was memorable in establishing an Israelite custom. As one of the chief "judges" he was remembered as one of Yahweh's chief deliverers of his people (I Sam. 12:11) and celebrated by the author of the NT Letter to the Hebrews as one of the heroes of faith (Heb. 11:32).

Bibliography. G. F. Moore, *Judges,* ICC (1895), pp. 275-310. K. Tallqvist, *Assyrian Personal Names* (1914), p. 92. M. Noth, *Die israelitischen Personennamen* (1928), pp. 28-29, 179, 200. C. F. Burney, *Judges* (1930), pp. 293-334. G. Ryckmans, *Les noms propres sud-sémitiques,* I-III (1934-35), 74. J. Pedersen, *Israel: Its Life and Culture,* I-II (1926), 44-45, 216, 218-19, 224, 317; III-IV (1940), 34, 37-38, 325-27, 381, 450, 703. H. M. Orlinsky, "Critical Notes on Gen. 39:14, 17; Judg. 11:37," *JBL,* LXI (1942), 92-97. C. A. Simpson, *Composition of the Book of Judges* (1957), pp. 45-53, 99-100, 112-13, 128-29, 142-45. M. Noth, *History of Israel* (1958), pp. 61, 157-59.

C. F. KRAFT

JEPHUNNEH jĭ fŭn'ə [יְפֻנֶּה, may he (God) turn(?) *or* turned(?)]. **1.** The father of Caleb (Num. 13:6; 14:6, 30, 38; 26:65; 32:12; 34:19; Deut. 1:36; Josh. 14:6, 13-14; 15:13; 21:12; I Chr. 4:15; 6:56). Jephunneh is identified as a member of the tribe of Judah and, on occasion, as a Kenizzite (e.g., Num. 32:12).

2. Son of Jether; included in the genealogy of the tribe of Asher (I Chr. 7:38).

Bibliography. M. Noth, *Die israelitischen Personennamen* (1928), pp. 28, 199. R. F. JOHNSON

JERAH jĭr ə [יֶרַח, moon] (Gen. 10:26; I Chr. 1:20). A son of Joktan, and hence probably the name of an Arabian locality. Since it is mentioned next to Hazarmaweth (Hadramaut), it was probably located on the Mahra coast, where a city called Jerakon Kome is mentioned by Ptolemy. S. COHEN

JERAHMEEL jĭ rä′mĭ əl [ירחמאל, may *El* (the deity) have compassion]; JERAHMEELITES —ə līts. Alternately: JEREMIEL jə rĕm′ĭ əl [Ἰερεμιήλ] (II Esd. 4:36); KJV URIEL yo͞o′rĭ əl. **1.** A Semitic tribe first mentioned as living in S Judah, where David came into contact with them during his forays out of Ziklag, while he was a fugitive from Saul (I Sam. 27:10; 30:29). Only in the postexilic period is Jerahmeel listed as a Hebrew clan, of the tribe of Judah (I Chr. 2:9, 25-27, 33, 42; cf. vss. 3-5). It is believed that this clan, along with others such as the Calebites (cf. 2:9, 18; Chelubai=Caleb), was gradually forced northward after 586 B.C. by Edomite incursions from the S and the E, until it attached itself to the Jewish communities around Jerusalem. *See bibliography.*

2. A Levite; son of a certain Kish (not Saul's father; I Chr. 24:29).

3. An officer under King Jehoiakim (*ca.* 609-598 B.C.) and contemporary with the prophet Jeremiah (Jer. 36:26). Although a "son of the king" (not KJV "Hammelech," which only transliterates the Hebrew phrase, "the king"), he can scarcely be a son of Jehoiakim if the latter was only thirty years old at the time (cf. II Kings 23:36; Jer. 36:9). He was perhaps the king's brother or had some other relation to royalty.

4. The archangel Jeremiel (also Ramiel or Remiel), appointed over the resurrection (I Enoch 20:8; cf. II Esd. 4:36; II Bar. 55:3). *See bibliography.*

Bibliography. On the Jerahmeelite clan, see: W. O. E. Oesterley and T. H. Robinson, *A History of Israel* (1932), I, 101, 135; II, 55. W. A. L. Elmslie, Exegesis of I Chronicles, *IB*, III (1954), 353. For a radical theory in this connection that has become a curiosity in the history of biblical criticism, see T. K. Cheyne, "Jerahmeel," section 4, *Encyclopaedia Biblica* (1901), vol. II, cols. 2365-66.

On Jeremiel, see R. H. Charles, "Enoch," and G. H. Box, "IV Esdras," in R. H. Charles, ed., *The Apoc. and Pseudep. of the OT* (1913), II, 512, 567 (note 36).

See also K. Kohler, "Angelology," *The Jewish Encyclopedia*, I (1901), 590. B. T. DAHLBERG

JERASH jĕr′ăsh. Modern Arabic name of GERASA.

JERECHUS. KJV Apoc. form of JERICHO.

JERED jĭr′ĕd [ירד, rose]. **1.** An eponym; a descendant of Judah through Mered (I Chr. 4:18).

Bibliography. M. Noth, *Die israelitischen Personennamen* (1928), p. 231.

2. KJV form of JARED.

JEREMAI jĕr′ə mī [ירמי, *perhaps* fat one, *from* Arab. *warima;* Apoc. Ἰερεμιας] (Ezra 10:33; I Esd. 9:34); KJV Apoc. JEREMIAS jĕr′ə mī′əs. One of those compelled by Ezra to give up their foreign wives.

JEREMIAH jĕr′ə mī′ə [ירמיה, ירמיהו, *perhaps* may Yahu loosen (the womb), *or* may Yahu lift up; Ἰερεμίας]; KJV JEREMIAS —əs in Ecclus. 49:6; Matt. 16:14; JEREMY —mĭ in I Esdras; Matt. 2:17; 27:9. **1.** One of the "Mighty Men" who joined David at Ziklag (I Chr. 12:4—H 12:5).

2. Another warrior, a Gadite, who joined David at Ziklag (I Chr. 12:10).

3. A third warrior, also a Gadite, who joined David at Ziklag (I Chr. 12:13).

4. A Manassite, head of a father's house (I Chr. 5:24).

5. The father of Hamutal, wife of King Josiah and mother of King Jehoahaz (II Kings 23:31) and King Zedekiah (24:18).

6. *See* JEREMIAH THE PROPHET.

7. The father of Jaazaniah, a Rechabite contemporaneous with Jeremiah the prophet (Jer. 35:3).

8. A priest who returned from Babylon with Zerubbabel (Neh. 12:1); a priestly house is also represented by this name (vs. 12).

9. One of the priests signatory to the covenant of Ezra (Neh. 10:2).

10. One of the princes of Judah among those officiating at the dedication of the Jerusalem wall under Nehemiah (Neh. 12:34).

Bibliography. M. Noth, *Die israelitischen Personennamen* (1928), pp. 36, 201. B. T. DAHLBERG

JEREMIAH, LAMENTATIONS OF. *See* LAMENTATIONS, BOOK OF.

JEREMIAH, LETTER OF. A letter purporting to be written by Jeremiah to the exiles of Judea at the time of their deportation to Babylon by Nebuchadrezzar and warning them of the length of their captivity and of the danger of apostasy. It is rambling and fragmentary and difficult to analyze because of its illogical and repetitious structure. In some Greek MSS and in the KJV it follows Baruch, without a break, as though it were the sixth chapter of Baruch.

The Letter of Jeremiah, or Jeremy, as it is sometimes called, is not a letter, nor was it written by Jeremiah. The unknown author, who lived much later than the prophet, was influenced by Jeremiah's letter to the exiles of 597 (Jer. 29:1-23) to write this so-called letter. However, where Jeremiah had exhorted the exiles to mistrust the false prophets in their midst, the so-called Jeremiah went further and warned the exiles to beware lest they be attracted by the Babylonian gods, because these idols had no power or life.

Jeremiah addresses his letter "to those who were to be led captive to Babylon by the king of the Babylonians, to make known unto them in accordance with what had been commanded to him by God" (vs. 1). The people are not yet in exile, and the name of Jeremiah does not even occur in the letter itself. This work is more of a sermon than a letter. After an Introduction (vss. 1-7), the rest of the sermon of seventy-three verses is divided into ten parts, each of which reiterates the lifelessness of wooden and metal images and their uselessness as objects of worship. There is no logic or order in the whole work, and it is tiresomely repetitious, but the homily is broken up into portions by a refrain repeated eleven times, emphasizing his exhortation: "Thereby they are known not to be gods; therefore, fear them not" (vss. 16, 23, 29, 30, 40, 44, 49, 52, 54, 56, 69).

The author mentions only two religious practices characteristic of Babylonia, the mourning for dying gods, like Tammuz in vss. 31-32—G 30-31, and the maiden's sacrifice (vs. 43). The letter was almost certainly inspired by Isa. 44:9-20; Jer. 10:1-16. These prophets were denouncing Gentile idolaters, but they also intended to show their own people the vileness of idolatrous practice and to warn them against it. This was the sole purpose of this anonymous writer.

The exact date is difficult to determine. Backsliding from faith was a frequent fact in Israel during times of peace. It is well known that many Jews were attracted to alien cults throughout the Greek period, 300 B.C. onward, so that the warning in the letter might have been uttered any time during this period. It might have been written in the time of John Hyrcanus or a hundred years later. The reference in vs. 3: "So when ye come into Babylon ye shall remain for . . . seven generations," indicates, according to one scholar, a date *ca.* 306 B.C. or some thirty years after the arrival of Alexander in Babylon. Another scholar places the date near the end of the second century B.C.

Many scholars are of the opinion that the letter was originally written in Greek, but this is improbable if the date at the end of the fourth century is accepted. Others are of the opinion that Hebrew is the original language, finding throughout peculiarities which suggest translation from a Hebrew original; and still others hold to the theory of an Aramaic original. C. C. Torrey (*see bibliography*) defends this view. He believes that in II Macc. 2:1-2 the reference to instruction given by the prophet Jeremiah to "those who were being deported" and the exhortation not "to be led astray in their thoughts upon seeing the gold and silver statues and their adornment," are undoubtedly references to this letter. The passage in II Maccabees is in an Aramaic letter sent by the authorities in Jerusalem to the Jews in the year 124 B.C.; and this, Torrey believes, shows that the letter, in its original Aramaic form, was held in high esteem.

Bibliography. O. F. Fritzsche, *Handbuch zu der Apocrypha* (1851), p. 206; R. H. Charles, *Apoc. and Pseudep.* (1913); W. O. E. Oesterley, *Books of the Apoc.* (1914); H. St. J. Thackeray, *Some Aspects of the Greek OT* (1927); C. C. Torrey, *The Apocryphal Literature* (1945); R. H. Pfeiffer, *History of NT Times with Introduction to the Apoc.* (1949); S. Tedesche and S. Zeitlin, *I and II Maccabees* (1950). S. TEDESCHE

JEREMIAH THE PROPHET. One of the major prophets, whose activity spans the period 626–*ca.* 580 B.C. and whose book is second in the canonical order of the Prophets.

- A. The man and his times
  - 1. The age of Jeremiah
    - *a.* The Near East
    - *b.* Judah
  - 2. Personality of the prophet
- B. Life and ministry
  - 1. 626-621
  - 2. From the reformation of 621 to the death of Josiah
  - 3. From 609 to the Battle of Carchemish
  - 4. From Carchemish to the first deportation in 598
  - 5. From 598 to the fall of Jerusalem in 587
- C. Theology
  - 1. The word of God
  - 2. Knowledge of God
  - 3. Yahweh's activity
    - *a.* In the life of the prophet
    - *b.* In the life of the people
    - *c.* In the history of nations
    - *d.* In the universe
  - 4. Sin and judgment; repentance and forgiveness
  - 5. Eschatology
- D. The book
  - 1. General character
  - 2. Major divisions of the book
  - 3. Composition
  - 4. The Baruch Scroll
  - 5. Prophecies against Judah and Jerusalem
  - 6. The biographical narratives
  - 7. The Deuteronomic additions
  - 8. The Little Book of Comfort
  - 9. The oracles against the nations
  - 10. Historical appendix
  - 11. Text
- Bibliography

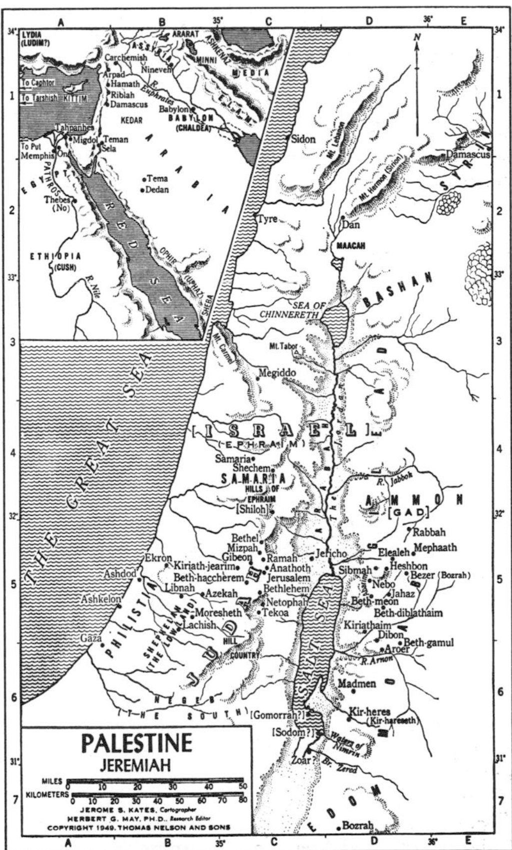

A. *THE MAN AND HIS TIMES.* 1. The age of Jeremiah. *a. The Near East.* The death of ASHURBANIPAL in *ca.* 631 signaled revolt within the Assyrian Empire. In 626, Chaldea under NABOPOLASSAR declared its independence. A period of conflict followed. The Babylonian Chronicle admirably supplements the OT record for the years 626-623, 616-594 B.C. (*see bibliography*). By 616, Nabopolassar had pressed his campaign into Assyria. Shortly afterward the Medes under Cyaxares intervened. In 614 they captured Asshur. The Chaldeans, arriving too late to aid in the attack, forged an alliance with them, and the allies, joined by the Umman-manda, besieged Nineveh. The city fell in 612. Meanwhile Egypt, under Psammetichus (663-609), came to the support of the Assyrian army at Harran, but the city was taken in 610. The next year NECO (609-593), successor to Psammetichus, went to relieve the hard-pressed Assyrians. At Megiddo he met Josiah, king of Judah, whom he put to death. He arrived too late to be of help to his Assyrian ally, however, for the Chaldeans were already in command. The issue between Chaldea and Egypt was settled in 605 in the important Battle of Carchemish, where NEBUCHADREZZAR, son of Nabopolassar, won a decisive victory. "At that time," the Chronicle reports, "Nebuchadrezzar conquered the whole of Hatti." The future of the Near East lay with Chaldea until the rise of Cyrus a half century later.

b. Judah. Manasseh's long reign of fifty-five years (687-642; *see* MANASSEH) was one of almost complete subservience to Assyria. His son Amon (*see* AMON 1), after a reign of two years (642-640), was assassinated in an anti-Assyrian coup. He was in turn succeeded by JOSIAH, a child of eight years (640-609). According to the Chronicler (II Chr. 34:3), while still a youth "he began to seek the God of David his father; and in the twelfth year began to purge Judah and Jerusalem" of the syncretistic cults. This may preserve an authentic reminiscence, for it is difficult to believe that the reformation was suddenly initiated in 621 as the consequence of the discovery of the Book of the Law. Moreover, it seems likely that it was the result of the labors of the anti-Assyrian party long active underground during Manasseh's reign. It is singular that the Chronicler's date for the beginning of the reforms coincides with the year of the Chaldean revolt. Josiah's reformation gave notice that Judah's vassalage was at an end. His designs were national and political as well as religious. In keeping with contemporary aspirations, he sought to reestablish the kingdom of David. It is probable, as Alt (*see bibliography*) and Noth (*see bibliography*) have shown, that Josh. 15:21-62; 18:21-28 reflect the boundaries of the new United Kingdom. But the reformation described in II Kings 23:1-25, probably an extract from the royal annals, also sought to return Israel to her ancient heritage in the old Shechemite amphictyony. The Covenant Book, contained within the book of Deuteronomy, rested on the foundations of Mosaic religion, but it was a greatly expanded version of that faith, expressed in the categories, language, and literary style of the seventh century B.C.

In 609, Neco went to the aid of the dying Assyria. Josiah met him at Megiddo, according to the Chronicler with a military force (II Chr. 35:20-24); if so, his designs may have been to impede the Egyptian advance and thus to render support to Chaldea. But the venture ended disastrously, for Josiah was slain. Meanwhile Jehoahaz, Josiah's second son, was anointed king of Judah. Neco forthwith summoned him to Riblah and made his elder brother king, assigning him the regnal name of JEHOIAKIM (609-598). Three years after the fall of Carchemish in 605, the Judean king withheld tribute, and bands of marauding Chaldeans, Syrians, Moabites, and Ammonites invaded the land (II Kings 24:2). Again in 598, Jehoiakim refused tribute; this time Jerusalem was subjected to terrible siege. Many of its foremost citizens and skilled artisans were carried into exile. JEHOIACHIN, who had meanwhile ascended the throne, was carried to Babylon, where he received the preferential treatment of a captive monarch. The following years were hectic and confused. Judah was split between pro-Chaldean and pro-Egyptian factions. The book of Jeremiah presents a vivid picture of this period. The prophet was the victim of the nationalistic hysteria of those who favored revolt. In 588 the Chaldean army laid siege to Jerusalem, and on the ninth of Ab, a year and a half later, entered the city. The temple was destroyed, and the kingdom of Judah came to a disastrous end. Zedekiah (598-587; *see* ZEDEKIAH, KING OF JUDAH) was blinded and sent to Babylon as a captive of war. In contrast to the relatively merciful treatment accorded her in 597, Judah was now made a Babylonian province with Gedaliah of the family of Shaphan as its governor.

See also ASSYRIA AND BABYLONIA; ISRAEL, HISTORY OF.

2. Personality of the prophet. Not only is the age of Jeremiah extraordinarily well documented with a great diversity of literary materials, but the life of the man, who, more than any other, was called to speak to that age, is richer in the variety of its literary witnesses than that of any other of the prophets of ancient Israel; indeed, the sources for his biography and prophetic career are not only more extensive in their range but also more revealing and searching in their portrait of the man. Already in his call we can discern the beginning of those tensions which were to disturb him throughout his life. His poetry, of which we have a substantial deposit, possesses a lyrical quality, an afflatus and emotional power, a wealth of imagery, a sensuousness and passionateness, a revelation of changing moods and tempers, unrivaled in the records of Semitic antiquity. His self-disclosures in the so-called "confessions" are the most intimate and unglossed, the most inward and authentic, of any that have been preserved to us from ancient times; in this respect Jeremiah comes closer to Paul, Augustine, and Luther than any other of the OT prophets. So much a part of him is this preoccupation with the interior life that personal ejaculations and outcries intrude upon his prophecies, especially in the war poems (4:10, 19-21, 23-26), but also elsewhere (16:19-20; cf. 8:18–9:2—H 8:18–9:1). But alongside the prophet's own poetic effusions lie long prose narratives, straightforward and unembellished, perhaps by his amanuensis Baruch, which constitute a second major source for our knowledge of the man. Finally, there is a substantial number of passages bearing a strong Deuteronomic stamp, which supplement what Jeremiah has to tell us about himself. *See* § D *below*.

The portrait which emerges from an examination of these literary records is one of a very sensitive man, quickly responsive to the vicissitudes of life about him, with a capacity to set down in words all that he observed and felt and suffered, all that had come to him from Yahweh, however much they might offend his tendencies toward self-centeredness and pride. To the world of nature, in all its varied manifestations, he was sensitive and percipient: the blossoming of the almond in early spring (1:11-12); the hot air of the sirocco (4:11); the migratory impulse of the stork and the times of the turtledove, swallow, and crane (8:7); the fierce, inchoate drive of the young camel and the sexual lust of the wild ass (2:23-24); and even the pathos of the heavens and the earth (2:12; 4:23-26, 28). Throughout his life he suffered the torment of being set apart from others: from his fellow countrymen; from the various classes of priests, prophets, and statesmen; from the members of his own family (12:6); and from all who participated in the everyday pleasures of life. He was denied the comfort and joy of wife and family (16:1-2). Yet he was sustained by an awareness of God's presence with him, inconstant and fleeting though it sometimes was (1:8, 19; 14:8-9; 15:20), of Yahweh's contending in his behalf like a dread warrior (20:11), of the power of the divine word (1:9; 15:16, 19; 20:8-9; 23:29); and by memories of Israel's election-covenant past (2:2*b*-3). Like Moses he was called to be God's mouth (15:19). Yet he was sore afflicted by a sense of alienation from God (14:8-9; 15:18; 17:17; 20:7). It was this sensitive and passionate man who was called to be a prophet to the nations (1:5); an intercessor for the people, yet denied this role when he most desired it (11:14; 14:11-12); a gleaner in the vineyard (6:9); a refiner and tester (6:27-30); an Israelite Cassandra discredited in an age of peril; a speaker of parables and himself a parable (13:1-11; 18:1-3; 19:1-2, 10-11); a "fortified city, an iron pillar, and bronze walls, against the whole land" (1:18; 15:20). Jeremiah addresses his own people during the four decades before the Chaldean conquest of 587 B.C. with a directness and power unmatched by any of his contemporaries; yet it was he more than any other who gave expression to a piety, faith, and hope, and indeed a theology, which made it possible for Judah to survive the disasters of the nation's fall, the destruction of the temple, and the end of the Davidic dynasty.

B. *LIFE AND MINISTRY.* Jeremiah was born in the village of Anathoth, modern Ras el-Kharubbeh, *ca.* two miles NE of Jerusalem, the son of Hilkiah, a priest, possibly a descendant of Abiathar, whom Solomon expelled to Anathoth shortly after his accession to the throne (I Kings 2:26). The town belonged to the tribe of Benjamin, for which Jeremiah seems to have had special concern and affection (Jer. 6:1; 11:18-23; 31:15). While we are not informed concerning his early years, it is apparent that he was reared in the traditions of his fathers. Even in his earliest poems he reveals a firm grasp of the election-covenant faith of the Mosaic age, akin to Hosea's understanding of it and particularly as it was to be revealed in the Deuteronomic Book of the Covenant a few years later. His prophetic predecessors left a deep impression upon him, above all Hosea, who prophesied in the turbulent closing years of the N kingdom. He had experienced the apostasies of Manasseh's reign, and his revulsion to its syncretistic practices is reflected in his earliest oracles.

The prophet's call came in the year 626 B.C. How old he was at the time we do not know, but he was probably only a youth (1:6). The report of the call may well come from a later period in his life; like Isaiah's vision, it reflects, not only a profound awareness of the significance of his mission, but also a realization that he is called to prophesy to the nations. Like Moses, he shrinks from the burden that is laid on his shoulders, but the power of the divine word overcomes him (1:9). His divine commission is

> over nations and over kingdoms,
> to pluck up and to break down,
> to destroy and to overthrow,
> to build and to plant.

Two visions follow the narrative of the call. The first is of an almond rod (שקד), which through paronomasia signifies God's watching (שקד) over his word to bring it to fruition (1:11-12). In the second (1:13-19) Jeremiah sees a boiling caldron "facing away from the north." This is symbolic of the imminent coming of the foe from the N. The terrible invasion is God's judgment against Judah for her apostasy to other gods.

The prophetic ministry of Jeremiah falls into the following periods:

a) From his call to the reformation of 621
b) From the reformation to the death of Josiah (609)
c) From 609 to the Battle of Carchemish (605)
d) From Carchemish to the first deportation (598)
e) From 598 to the destruction of Jerusalem (587)

1. 626-621. Jeremiah's prophetic activity during this period is directed to two major concerns: (*a*) the prevailing religious corruption of the time, the seductive lure of the nature cults, and Judah's spiritual insensateness; and (*b*) the imminent invasion of the foe from the N. Yahweh remembers Israel's early devotion (חסד), her love (אהבה) as a bride, the years of wandering in the wilderness when she covenanted with him to be his people (2:2-3). But now an appalling thing has happened: Israel has exchanged her God for other gods. The fathers, priests, rulers, and prophets have all forsaken Yahweh. The people engage in the licentious rites of the fertility cults (2:20, 27; 3:2-3); some are attracted by Egypt, others by Assyria (2:18).

> Where are your gods
> that you made for yourself?

Jeremiah exclaims (2:28). So he issues an urgent plea for Judah to turn from her gross infidelity and to return to Yahweh (3:1, 12, 14, 20, 22; 4:1). The influence of Hosea upon the young prophet is apparent in these oracles. The central theme of harlotry is the same in both, as is the emphasis upon the father-son relation, the bridal days in the wilderness, the lure of Egypt and Assyria, but more especially Yahweh's covenant with his people, the bond sealed in steadfast or covenantal love (חסד).

In the poems on the foe from the N, Jeremiah achieves the loftiest height of lyrical expression. Much controversy has raged over the identity of this foe. Formerly, on the basis of the account in Herodotus (I.103-5), it was identified with the SCYTHIANS from the region beyond the Caucasus, perhaps the Umman-manda of the cuneiform inscriptions. But this view has been subjected to trenchant attack by

F. Wilke (*see bibliography*) and has been rejected by many modern scholars. Others have thought of the Chaldeans and Medes who destroyed Nineveh in 612; still others of the Chaldeans (i.e., Neo-Babylonians) alone. But the latter view demands altering the text of 1:2 (cf. 25:3; 36:2) from the "thirteenth year" to the "twenty-third year." It is perhaps better to hold that the reference was originally to the Scythians, but that it was altered by Jeremiah himself in the light of later events, when the invasion came from the Babylonians. In these poems we see Jeremiah torn and at times even convulsed by Yahweh's revelation to him that the imminent war is his judgment upon Judah, on the one hand, and by his passionate concern for his own people, on the other (4:19-20). But what is more, the mind of the prophet has become a field of battle, where disaster follows hard upon disaster; his own writhing is the interior psychological counterpart of the awful events which are impending. For him they are already happening.

2. From the reformation of 621 to the death of Josiah. There was much in the reformation of JOSIAH (*see* § A1*b above*) of which the prophet might approve: the return to the election-covenant faith of the Mosaic age and the Shechemite amphictyony, the stress upon the holy people and their unique relation to Yahweh, the divine love for Israel and the moving appeal for a responding love on the part of Israel, the extirpation of all Canaanite and Assyrian worship, the call to responsibility, and the humanitarian requirements. But unfortunately it is uncertain whether we have any record at all of Jeremiah's activity during the years following the reformation. It may be, however, that ch. 11 gives an authentic account of Jeremiah's early support of the movement. That the language contains much Deuteronomic phraseology is unquestionable, but this need not militate against its historicity. We may well believe, not merely that Jeremiah gave his approval to the great reforming movement, but that at the command of Yahweh he proclaimed its words in Jerusalem, urging the people to obey them. More than this we do not know; the period, so far as our record goes, seems to be one of complete silence. It may well have been a time of relative peace for Judah despite the fateful struggle going on in Mesopotamia, a period in which the king and his supporters were able to implement their national goals and to resuscitate the ebbing covenantal faith of Sinai and Shechem. If so, it was to receive a terrible reversal in the tragic death of the king at Megiddo (609). When Jehoahaz was taken to Riblah some three months later, Jeremiah indited a lament:

> Weep not for him who is dead,
> nor bemoan him;
> but weep bitterly for him who goes away,
> for he shall return no more
> to see his native land.

3. From 609 to the Battle of Carchemish. It was a dark hour for Judah, but Jehoiakim was not the man to meet it. At the beginning of his reign, possibly on the occasion of his coronation (26:1), Jeremiah went to the temple at the command of Yahweh to deliver a sermon against the excessive trust in the temple as a source of deliverance in this time of crisis. The reformation had sought to centralize worship there and had bred a superstitious trust in its efficacy. But the place in and of itself was no harbor of refuge; Yahweh is present to those whose lives are in conformity with his will and purpose: "Amend your ways and your doings, and I will let you dwell in this place" (7:3). When those who come to worship in the temple violate all the requirements of the covenant, making it a veritable den of robbers, it will suffer the fate of Shiloh in the time of Eli and Samuel (7:1-15).

The address caused consternation among the temple priests and prophets, and they pronounced their verdict upon the prophet: "You shall die." The princes came to the New Gate of the temple, and there Jeremiah was tried. He defended himself by saying that he had spoken at the behest of God, then repeated the substance of his address and warned them of the evil consequences upon themselves if he was put to death. The princes and the people rose to the prophet's defense, accepting his word that he had spoken in the name of Yahweh and invoking the instance of the prophet Micah in the eighth century, who had prophesied in very similar terms (Mic. 3:12). The verdict is not given, but Ahikam the son of Shaphan took Jeremiah under his protection (ch. 26). Uriah, another prophet, who had prophesied in words like Jeremiah's, fled to Egypt, but was returned to Jerusalem, where he was put to death by Jehoiakim (vss. 20-23).

Jehoiakim proved to be an unscrupulous and oppressive monarch, self-seeking and luxury-loving. The reforming movement suffered a serious reversal during his reign (7:17-19, 30-31; 11:9-13). Jeremiah's proclamations in its support were deeply resented, especially by his townsmen at Anathoth, who sought to dispose of him (11:18-23). His temple address shows very clearly, however, that he had begun by this time to have serious reservations concerning popular attitudes toward the reformation, for the people were exaggerating the value of purely cultic acts to the exclusion of the ethical imperatives which the Book of the Covenant had so strongly emphasized. If Jeremiah opposed the excessive trust in the temple as merely a spatial refuge, he was equally outspoken concerning the efficacy of sacrificial offerings solely as cultic acts (6:20; 7:21-24; 11:15-16; 17:1).

Again and again he exhorted his countrymen to obedience (7:23-29; 22:1-5), and persisted in his call to repentance and change of heart (8:4-7; 9:5), although he came to feel that their moral sense had become so atrophied that repentance was impossible (8:4-7). "They do not know me," is the judgment that sounds again and again. Jeremiah sought to intercede for his people, but so grievous was their insensateness that Yahweh forbade him (7:16; 11:14; 14:11-12; cf. 15:1). Against Jehoiakim he launched a bitter invective, detailing his enormities and contrasting them with the exemplary conduct of Josiah, his father (22:13-17), and followed it with a sinister lament: "With the burial of an ass he shall be buried" (vss. 18*b*-19).

The fall of Carchemish to Nebuchadrezzar in 605 seems to have registered a profound effect upon the prophet. It was in that year that he was commanded by Yahweh to transcribe all his prophecies from the beginning of his prophetic ministry in 626. He himself was debarred from the temple precincts, doubtless because of such episodes as the temple discourse, and Baruch was ordered to read the scroll on a great national day of fasting before all the people. So serious was the indictment that it was called to the king's attention. The princes saw to it that Baruch and Jeremiah went into hiding, but Jehudi was commanded to read the scroll to the king in the winter house where fire was burning in the brazier. As he completed three or four columns, the king would cut them from the scroll with a penknife and cast them into the blaze. Jeremiah was commanded to dictate his prophecies once more. He did so, but added to them "many similar words," including a denunciation of Jehoiakim's act of sacrilege and a pronouncement of dire punishment (ch. 36). A vivid poem celebrating the overthrow of Egypt at Carchemish, reminiscent of the war poetry of 4:5–6:30, is given in Jer. 46:3-12. It may well be Jeremiah's own composition.

It was probably about this time that the prophet suffered another humiliation. Returning from Tophet, where he had been prophesying, he stood in the court of the temple and proclaimed an oracle of imminent doom upon Jerusalem. When Pashhur the priest heard it, he beat the prophet, put him in stocks in the upper Benjamin Gate of the temple, and left him there for the night. Jeremiah was prepared: he delivered an even more terrible indictment of Pashhur and accompanied it with his original invective (19:14–20:6). Such experiences as these did not leave Jeremiah unscathed; he was deeply wounded by them, and the interior self-disclosures which are interspersed in his book follow naturally upon this period of rejection and contumely.

4. From Carchemish to the first deportation in 598. As the fateful year of 626 had marked the beginning of Jeremiah's prophetic career, the year of the fall of Carchemish (605) seems to have marked the beginning of a new period of his activity. It is likely that it is to this time that we are to assign his interior dialogical encounters with Yahweh, the so-called "confessions," although they may well be earlier. To this time too we may assign the symbolic prophecies, in which Yahweh's word was acted out in dramatic form. In the confessional laments Jeremiah reveals his innermost thoughts and feelings. He grieves that he was born a man of strife and contention (15:10), of hostility and indignation (15:17). He recalls hours when God's words were the delight of his heart (15:16), but when at the same time he suffered the anguish of isolation and alienation: "I sat alone, because thy hand was upon me" (15:17). He was separated from everyone, but the depths of his despair came in his sense of God's absence. Yahweh had become to him an unreliable wadi whose waters fail (15:18). He even accuses God of deceiving him (20:7; cf. 14:8). In utter desperation he cries out:

> Why is my pain unceasing,
> my wound incurable?
> (15:18).

These laments of the prophet are remarkable for their fluctuation of feeling and mood, the constant ebb and flow from faith to doubt, from courage to despair, from compassion to hostility (11:18-21; 20:11-12). There is egocentricity in these outcries, but what is most remarkable is that they are usually overcome by God's word (12:5-6; 15:19-21). Jeremiah hears Yahweh canceling his claims, ignoring his complaints, admonishing him to return—to utter what is precious and to cast out what is worthless, so that he may be Yahweh's mouth (15:19). Again, in many contexts Jeremiah's declarations about himself are transformed by the divine first-person causative: his knowing is God's causing him to know (11:18); his returning is God's causing him to return (15:19). At times he approaches blasphemy (20:7), but he does not hesitate to expose his thoughts. In the symbolic prophecies he plays the role of Yahweh himself, as in the acted parable of the linen waistcloth (13:1-11) or the potter's earthen flask (19:1-2, 10).

It was in this period also that Jeremiah brought the Rechabites, who refused to drink wine, to the temple as an example of obedience to the disobedient men of Judah (ch. 35). When in 598 Jehoiakim refused tribute to Babylonia and the city was subjected to siege, Jeremiah uttered a vehement oracle of doom against its inhabitants (10:17-18), but when the city was taken, he identified himself with its fate in a poignant and beautiful lament (13:15-17). Yet the tragedy only confirmed his conviction that Judah's sufferings were the result of its defection from Yahweh (15:5-9). When Jehoiachin was taken to Babylon as a captive, Jeremiah refused to offer any hope for his return or for the resumption of the Davidic dynasty (22:24-30).

5. From 598 to the fall of Jerusalem in 587. Zedekiah, another son of Josiah and full brother of the lamented Jehoahaz, came to the throne at the age of twenty-one. He was neither tyrannical nor prodigal like Jehoiakim, but was incapable of coping with the forces arrayed against him. He lacked force and stability of character. That he came to the throne at the command of Nebuchadrezzar made him suspect to the nationalists in Judah. He was friendly to Jeremiah and often called on him for counsel. But there were many popular prophets who predicted an imminent return to the exiles, the restoration of the temple treasures, and divine judgment upon Nebuchadrezzar. These Jeremiah strenuously opposed. He lamented the ungodliness of priest and prophet (23:9-12) and urged the people not to listen to the optimistic predictions of the prophets (vss. 16-17), declaring that they were dreamers of dreams, deceivers intent on making the people forget the prophetic Word, thieves of authentic divine oracles, crying: "Thus says Yahweh," when they had not listened to him (vss. 23-32).

The issue came to a dramatic head in 594 on the occasion of a gathering in Jerusalem of representatives of the smaller powers, who had doubtless come to plan concerted action against Babylonia. Jeremiah, at the command of Yahweh, placed thongs and yoke bars on his neck and addressed them with an oracle. The sovereignty of nations is in the power of the Creator of the earth, and it is for him to dispose of nations as he will. Nebuchadrezzar is his servant, and to him has been given all the lands;

therefore, they must subject themselves to his rule (27:1-11).

Later in the year he was confronted by the prophet Hananiah in the presence of a crowd of priests, prophets, and people gathered in the temple. Hananiah proclaimed the imminent defeat of Babylon, the return of the exiles, and the restoration of the temple treasures. This was Jeremiah's wish too, but he reminded Hananiah that the former prophets gave no such pleasant assurances and that the prophet who proclaims peace will be justified only by the event. Hananiah then took the yoke bars from Jeremiah's neck and broke them, saying this was a symbol of the rupture of Chaldean power. Jeremiah left, but sometime later returned with bars of iron and reminded Hananiah that he had not been sent by Yahweh (ch. 28).

Perhaps it was at this time that Jeremiah wrote a letter to the exiles urging them not to be deceived by the dreams of the diviners and prophets, because the exile would be long. They must therefore seek the welfare of the land of their captivity, "for in its welfare you will find your welfare" (29:1-14).

Zedekiah was unable to hold out against the demand for resistance, and Jeremiah's support of his policy gave him no strength. Nebuchadrezzar and his army descended upon Judah and Jerusalem. The city was surrounded and the towns of Judah systematically destroyed. In the Lachish Ostraca we have contemporary documents from this period which show many interesting affinities with the book of Jeremiah (*ANET* 321-22). Jeremiah went to Zedekiah to warn him that the city would be burned but that he would die in peace (34:1-6). During the siege Zedekiah made a covenant with the people to liberate all the slaves, but in a short time they were taken back by their masters. Jeremiah reproached them severely and told them that they would suffer grievously for this breach of good faith (34:8-22). When the siege was lifted at the approach of the Egyptian army *ca*. 588, Zedekiah sent a deputation to Jeremiah asking him to pray for the city, but the prophet replied that the relief was only temporary and that the city would certainly be destroyed (37:1-10). He sought, however, to take advantage of the respite and set out to go to the land of Benjamin, presumably to Anathoth, but was arrested by a sentry at the Benjamin Gate and accused of desertion, which he denied. He was forthwith beaten by the princes and placed in custody (37:11-15).

Jeremiah languished there for some time, until Zedekiah sent for him secretly and asked him if there was any word from Yahweh. Jeremiah replied: "There is . . . You shall be delivered into the hand of the king of Babylon" (37:17). He then besought the king not to return him to the prison; his request was granted, but he was placed in the court of the guard (37:16-21). While there, but after the siege was resumed, Jeremiah purchased a field from his cousin Hanamel, since the right of redemption belonged to him. This act he interpreted as a sign that normal commercial actions such as these would again take place (32:1-15). Jeremiah persisted in counseling capitulation, even by individual citizens; it was a choice of life or death. The princes demanded his life, and Zedekiah was unable to defend him. He was cast into a cistern of the court of the guard, but was later rescued by Ebed-melech (38:1-13). A poignant interview with the king followed shortly after. Jeremiah feared for his life, and the king was in the depths of despair. But the prophet again counseled surrender. The king feared revenge by the Jewish deserters, however. Jeremiah agreed to the king's request that he make no reference to the real substance of the interview to the princes (vss. 14-28).

The Babylonians captured Jerusalem on the ninth of Ab, 587 (Jer. 39:1-2; II Kings 25:8-21). Nebuchadrezzar had given orders to Nebuzaradan, the captain of the guard, to show Jeremiah special consideration. He was released from confinement, and elected to go to Mizpah to join Gedaliah, the grandson of Shaphan, who had been appointed governor of the newly created Chaldean province. After the disastrous events in which Gedaliah and many of the Jews were slain, the new leaders turned to Jeremiah to request that he pray to Yahweh for counsel; Jeremiah acceded to their request, and after ten days the word of Yahweh came to him. It was Yahweh's will that they remain in the land, trust themselves to the mercy of the Chaldeans, and give up all plans of going to Egypt. The leaders were enraged, accused Baruch of instigating him against them, and set out for Egypt, taking Jeremiah and Baruch with them. Of the prophet's life in Egypt we know little. An account is preserved of a symbolic action, which was designed to show that Nebuchadrezzar would devastate Egypt. It may have been in Egypt that Baruch compiled his master's prophecies and added to them his own memoirs of the fateful years during which he served him as amanuensis. Included was a special collection, known as the "little book of comfort" (chs. 30–31), parts of which remind one of the style of his early years, but others suggest the hope of restoration. Most significant is the prophecy of the new covenant (31:31-34), in which Judah would receive a new Torah inscribed on the heart and all would know Yahweh in a new relation because their sins and iniquities would be forgiven.

C. *THEOLOGY*. The thought and faith of Jeremiah are so intimately interwoven that it is impossible to isolate one from the other. Whether we can speak of his theology in any strict construction of the term may be questioned, for nowhere does he endeavor to delineate his thought into a nicely articulated system. Here we are concerned rather with a poetic mind given to rich and variegated imagery; with a living, moving, historical relationship between God and man; with autobiographical transcripts of interior experience and biographical accounts with abundant circumstantial detail. From the beginning to the end of his life it is with Yahweh that the prophet has to do, not with a transcendent Being separated from human life and history but with One who is transcendent, to be sure, but also a personal Lord active in the concrete intimacies of life, in the life and history of the chosen people, in the affairs of the nations, and in the universe of creation. Behind all these lie the traditions of the election-covenant faith; a story of perpetual vicissitudes; a cultic life of venerable institutions, celebrations, and rituals; and a constant emergence of new situations in which the revelation becomes concrete, unique, and alive, yet related to revelatory events and words of the past and oriented to the future in foreboding and hope. Again, the language and literary modes are such as to resist intellectual formulations, which it is likely the prophet would not have understood or would have deemed inadequate to his meaning. So abundant and striking are his imagery and symbolism that a general or abstract terminology deprives his thought of what is often most alive and most significant.

1. The word of God. In Jeremiah the theology of the Word reaches its culmination. Throughout his life he is aware that it is his destiny to proclaim Yahweh's דבר. The hour of his call is the arrival of God's word to him. The divine words are placed in his mouth, words which are to extend to nations and kingdoms with overwhelming consequences. The דבר has Yahweh's intention and will in it, and it is alive with the divine energy and sovereignty. In his conflicts with the popular prophets of his day, he is compelled to discern the nature of God's revelation to him. They too speak in the name of Yahweh, but Jeremiah denies that they have been sent (23:21), that they have stood in the divine council (23:18, 22), that they have been addressed (23:21). They dream dreams, but these dreams are their own (23:25-28); they have no knowledge (14:18); they are propagators of lies (5:31; 14:14; 23:26-27, 32); above all, they deceive the people by their optimism, rehearsing the old text of the holy-war ecstatics: "Go up and prosper," the unreflected שלום of their wishes. To these facile preachers Jeremiah has no easy reply, for the Word is for him something with which he has himself to contend. But he knows it is nothing over which man has disposal (23:18); it cannot be induced at will. It is given, even against one's own wishes (28:6-7). To it the true prophet must subject himself in obedience, listening, waiting. For Jeremiah it formed the line of battle where he waged his terrible conflicts. To him Yahweh's word was like blazing fire, a hammer crushing the rocks in pieces, a reproach and derision (20:7-9; 23:29). Its source was not to be discovered in the exigencies of contemporary politics nor in the charismatic seizures of the ecstatics but in the purpose and activity of God (29:26). In the travail of prayer Jeremiah waited for the Word, and at times he waited long (15:10-21; 42:1-7). He knew what it was to tremble and stagger like a drunken man because of the impact of Yahweh's holy words (23:9).

2. Knowledge of God. The acute problem which the word of God could pose for Jeremiah is reflected in his meditation upon the knowledge of God, upon the relationship between God's knowing and his own knowing, and upon the mystery of his own self-consciousness and his profound awareness of being apprehended and grasped. Jeremiah reports a momentous divine self-asseveration: "I am the Knowing One" (29:23; cf. RSV: "I am the one who knows"). The life of faith is being known of God. So Jeremiah is aware of Yahweh's foreknowledge of him (1:5), and more than once he appeals to God's knowing of him in earnest cries (12:3; cf. 11:18; 15:15; 17:16). He finds it necessary again and again to translate his simple declaratives in the *qal* stem into the divine causatives in the *hiph'il.* Yahweh knows the plans and devices of men (18:23; 29:11). It is obvious that Yahweh's knowing of Jeremiah is more than cognitive; it is rather an activity of relationship, an interior and prior being—apprehended. But man has a "knowledge" of God too, although the prophet is never bold enough to say that he possesses it. Yet he chides the priests because they have no knowledge of God (2:8), the poor because "they do not know the way of Yahweh" (5:4), the foolish people who do not know him (4:22). They turn to other gods whom they do not know (7:9). Even the stork in the heavens knows her times, but Israel does not know Yahweh's משפט (8:7). Yet in the time of the new covenant, Israel will no longer be admonished: "Know Yahweh," for they shall know him, both small and great, through Yahweh's forgiveness of their sins.

3. Yahweh's activity. ***a. In the life of the prophet.*** Yahweh's activity in Jeremiah's life is best understood by an examination of the many verbs in which he is addressed, more particularly in the call and confessional laments. Here we have Jeremiah's most inward "theology" *in nuce.* We confine ourselves to the divine first-person verbs: "I knew you," "I consecrated you" (הקדשתיך), "I appointed you," "I send you," "I command you," "I am with you," "I have put my words in your mouth," "I have set you over nations," etc. (1:5-10). It is in lines such as these that we come to grasp what Yahweh's presence meant to Jeremiah.

b. In the life of the people. Underlying all that Jeremiah has to say concerning Israel, whether in judgment, exhortation, or promise, is the memory of its election to be the people of Yahweh. This is at once the source of its uniqueness, the meaning of its existence, and the expression of the divine purpose within its life. Israel is separated to Yahweh as holy (קדוש), the first fruits of his harvest (2:3), a choice vine of pure seed (2:21), his beloved (11:15; 12:7), his heritage (12:7-9), his vineyard (12:10), his flock (13:17), his first-born (31:9). In the first of his recorded oracles Jeremiah tells of Yahweh's participating in Israel's time by his remembering the devotion (חסד) of her youth, her love (אהבה) as a bride, following him (לכת אחרי) in the wilderness (2:2).

Only seldom do we encounter a specific reference to the covenant (14:21; 31:32), but the terminology associated with it is certainly present (7:23; 11:3-8; 24:7); the requirements and laws to which appeal is made have their source in the covenant, as does the grace which exceeds all of Israel's performance. Permeating all the prophet's thought is the realization that Israel belongs to Yahweh and that her existence stands upon the foundation of an ultimate demand of obedience and service and with it the joyous expression of thanksgiving. This relationship is described in terms of the two most intimate bonds in the family life of the Orient; of the father to his son and the bride to her husband. It is clear that Jeremiah is heavily indebted to Hosea here, but he makes the imagery his own (2:2; 3:4, 19, 22; 31:9, 18-20). Elsewhere (18:1-11) Yahweh is portrayed as the Potter and Israel the clay in his hands. He is sovereign over her life: "He reworked it into another vessel, as it seemed good to the potter to do." Yet, paradoxically, she is accountable to him, and his action is determined by her conduct.

c. In the history of nations. The nations, too, are under Yahweh's gracious sovereignty. Nebuchadrezzar is his servant (27:6), the instrument of his purpose (vss. 6-9). The appeal in this context to Yahweh's creation of the earth (vs. 5) is merely prelude to the assertion of his sovereignty over the nations. Similarly, the foe from the N is the divine judgment against Israel. In the dark days after the downfall of Judah, Yahweh assures the remnant at Mizpah that they need not fear Babylon, because he is able to deliver and save them (42:11-12).

d. In the universe. Yahweh created the earth and all the living creatures which inhabit it (27:5). It is therefore his to govern as he will (27:4-11; cf. 18:1-11). The whole created universe, with its fixed order and purpose, is assurance of his lordship over history (31:35-37). He gives the rain in its appointed season (5:24; 14:22); he determines the times of the stork, turtledove, swallow, and crane (8:7), as of men, even though they may defy the givenness of their times. Thus he is Lord of "times" and of space and demonstrates his sovereignty over all, not only in the affairs of nations (ch. 27) but also in the lives of men, as Jeremiah can witness from his own experience.

4. Sin and judgment; repentance and forgiveness. Yahweh has revealed his holy will through his Torah and in the ministry of priests and prophets. What is required of Israel is the kind of activity and conduct which characterize his rule over the earth: steadfast love, justice, and righteousness (9:23-24). These are not understood as ethical norms or ideals but as ways of divine action; nor are they understood solely as grounded in creation, although this is not excluded, but through revelation in call, consecration, election, and covenant. It is these latter events which determine the true nature of the people. Therefore, sin is viewed as unnatural, a violation of all that which Israel was destined to be through her commitment to Yahweh's proffered relationship (2:11, 21), a perversion of her true self. It is the stubborn refusal to know God (*see* § C2 *above*). It is a going away from him (2:5), a going after הבל, "worthlessness"; a refusal to inquire into the revelatory events of the *Heilsgeschichte* (2:6-8); a rejection of their "glory" and apostasy to other gods (2:11-12), forsaking Yahweh, the fountain of living waters, for "no gods" (vs. 11); a capitulation of the life lived in holy memory; a gross forgetting (שכח 2:32; 3:21); a perverting of their ways (3:21); the faithlessness of wayward sons (3:22); the forsaking and abandoning (עזב) of God (2:17, 19); the breaking of the bond between servant and master (2:20); harlotry (2:20, 25; 3:1); incorrigibility (2:30, 35); profligacy (2:36); disobedience (3:13); rebellion (2:29); marital infidelity (3:20); sickness (3:22); want of a sense of shame (3:3); and degenerateness (2:21). The stain of guilt is so deep it cannot be cleansed with lye (2:22); its drive is as compelling as that of the restive young camel and the lust of the wild ass (2:24), as ineradicable as the Ethiopian's skin or the leopard's spots (13:23). The consequence of sin is judgment. This belongs to Yahweh's righteous ordering of history. The misfortunes that befall a people are from God, and they are called forth by its guilt and disobedience and refusal to serve. The foe from the N is an instrument of punishment and discipline. Yet Yahweh's desire is always that his people turn from their past ways and return to him. Jeremiah echoes again and again the old prophetic cry: "Repent!" (3:1–4:4). If his people repent and swear:

> "As Yahweh lives,"
> in truth, in justice, and in uprightness,
> then nations shall bless themselves in him
> (cf. Gen. 12:1-3).

God calls his wayward sons back to him, and is eager to forgive (3:12*b*-14, 19-22*b*). The underlying basis of all that is said about the new covenant—indeed, the transforming event which brings it into existence—is Yahweh's forgiveness and his determination not to remember any more the iniquities of his people (31:31-34; cf. 2:2).

In this connection we may turn to the cult and its practices as means of reconciliation and deliverance. It is probable that Jeremiah himself was connected with the temple and its ministry (cf. chs. 7; 26). But the temple has no efficacy in and of itself and will be destroyed because its worshipers violate the spirit and attitude which true worship requires: repentance, contrition, and a changed life. Neither are sacrifices sufficient of themselves to ward off the imminent threat of national destruction. The true circumcision is circumcision of the mind and heart (4:4). Even the Torah may become a snare and a delusion through the false pen of the scribes (8:8). It is not probable that Jeremiah opposed any of these institutions as such; he saw them, however, as possible instruments of corruption and induration. The popular prophets could appeal legitimately to the assurance of Yahweh's presence with Israel, but they distorted and perverted it by failure to grasp the contingency which lay at the heart of the original covenantal bond (Exod. 19:5).

5. Eschatology. Jeremiah's expectations for the future are obscured by the presence of much material which does not belong to him. The book contains a number of passages which look forward to a complete restoration in the manner of Ezekiel and Second Isaiah (Jer. 23:1-8; 30:10-11, 18-22; 31:10-14, 23-25): the gathering of the remnant from the nations (23:3-4; 30:10-11; 31:10-14); the raising up of David, a righteous Branch (23:5-6); and the new exodus (23:7-8).

But there are other passages which have some claim to authenticity where the restoration motif is present. In the parable of the two baskets of figs (ch. 24) Yahweh through his grace regards as good those who have suffered the harshness of exile and promises them a new heart that they may become his people once more (24:4-7). In the letter to the exiles (29:4-14) all hopes of a speedy return are rejected; indeed, the prophet urges them to seek the welfare of their captors and to pray on their behalf. Yet he has a plan for them, a plan for welfare to give them a future to which they may look forward (29:11-12). We are on even surer ground in the account of Jeremiah's purchase of the field at Anathoth. Here too there is considerable expansion of the text, but the prophet's words to Baruch have every mark of genuineness. The latter is commanded to place the two deeds in an earthenware vessel "that they may last for a long time. For thus says the Yahweh of hosts, the God of Israel: Houses and fields and vineyards shall again be bought in this land" (32:9-15). In this chapter we hear again of the promise of one heart and one way, "for their own good and the good of their children after them" (vs. 39).

Finally, in the great oracle of the coming age, the prophecy of a new covenant, we have words which, while not from Jeremiah, are consistent, not only with the foregoing passages, but also with the tenor of much of his earlier utterances. The new covenant is not like the old; it will be engraved on the hearts of the men of Israel and Judah, and "they shall all know me" (*see* § C2 *above*), for Yahweh will forgive their iniquities, and his remembering of them (cf. 2:2) will not include their transgressions (31:31-34).

D. *THE BOOK.* Jeremiah is the second of the books of the major prophets in our present canon, but in an earlier period the first, following the books of Kings, which were also attributed to him (B.B. 14*b*-15*a*). More than any other book of the Bible it reveals the prophet's personal experiences and sufferings, as well as his own intimate self-disclosures. It is in this area that his influence upon subsequent writers and later piety has been most profound, notably the poems of the Psalter, the portraits of the Servant of the Lord in Second Isaiah, and the records of travail during the Maccabean age. The prophecy of the new covenant (31:31-34) influenced the writers of the NT (II Cor. 3:2-18; Heb. 8:6-11; cf. Matt. 26:28; Mark 14:24). While he was by no means the first in Israel to emphasize individualism, the example of his life and the poignancy of his laments and "confessions" left a deep impression upon his successors. It was hc, more than any other, who made it possible for Israel to meet the tragedy of the nation's downfall and the destruction of the temple in 587.

1. General character. Like the other great prophetic collections—Isaiah, Ezekiel, and the Book of the Twelve—the book of Jeremiah is a compilation—indeed, a compilation of compilations. It contains a great variety of literary types and forms. The two major types characteristic of the OT as a whole are abundantly represented and in a particularly striking fashion. The poetry assumes many guises: the ecstatic lyricism of the war songs (4:5*b*-8, 13-16, 19-22), the cosmic brooding of the imminent "end" (4:23-26), the intense subjectivity of the confessional laments (15:10-11, 15-20; 20:7-18), the unsparing and withering denunciation of the invectives with their accompanying threats (22:13-19), the pathetic effusion of intimate grief (13:15-17), the rhetorical and stylistic diversity of the poems against the foreign nations (46:3-12; 50:35-38; 51:1-58).

Similarly, the prose of the book has many forms: acted parables (13:1-11; 18:1-6; 19:1-2, 11-12), protracted sermonic discourse (7:1-15; 34:12-22), biographical narrative (chs. 26; 27–28; 36), letter (29:4-23, 25-28), vision (1:11-12, 13-14; ch. 24).

The literary units vary greatly in length, in both the poetry and the prose. Moreover, it is easy to recognize various literary strata by relative consistency of style in different parts of the book.

The variety in literary form and style calls attention to what is perhaps the most singular feature of the book's composition: the anomaly of numerous indications of systematic order and plan, on the one hand, and apparent confusion and disarray, on the other. It is clear as one reads through the whole book that it has gone through a long and complicated process. It is not the work of a single mind or the craft of a single writer. The history of its composition and growth is not to be explained, however, on a purely literary basis. It is probable that many of the poems and oracles circulated in the oral tradition before they were transcribed, and even in the course of oral transmission they underwent alteration and expansion. This, to be sure, is also true of the literary history of the book, in respect both of its individual literary units and its more extensive literary complexes. Intrusive material has disturbed the sequence and structure of the separate compositions as well as the manner in which they are arranged, of the *ipsissima verba* of the prophet Jeremiah as well as of the contributions of other writers. The impression of an involved literary history in which different compilers were active—sometimes, it would seem, in almost cavalier independence of one another—is confirmed by two further phenomena: (*a*) the substantial number of repetitions or literary duplications and (*b*) the divergences of the Greek text from the MT. Of the repetitions and duplications the following are illustrative:

6:12-15 and 8:10-12
10:12-16 and 51:15-19
16:14-15 and 23:7-8
23:5-6 and 33:15-16
23:19-20 and 30:23-24
30:10-11 and 46:27-28

Duplicates more or less similar to these appear in other books of the OT also—in Ezekiel, Second Isaiah, Joel, Obadiah, and others; the authenticity of each case must be examined by itself. In the Greek text of Jeremiah the oracles against the foreign nations (chs. 46–51) appear after 25:13 of our Hebrew and English texts (46:1–51:64 MT=25:15–45:5 LXX), and in a radically different order. Moreover, the LXX omits portions of the Hebrew text (27:20-22; 33:14-26; 39:3-14; 48:45-47). The presence of the foreign oracles in the second major section of the book conforms to the arrangement of such oracles in Isaiah (chs. 13–23) and Ezekiel (chs. 25–32).

Despite the foregoing demonstration of disarrangement of material, evidences are not wanting of systematic ordering and plan in the literary history of the book. There are, e.g., a number of collections which possess a certain homogeneity, some of them with appropriate headings or introductions, as in the oracles against the kings of Judah in 21:11–23:8, or against the prophets in 23:9-40, or the introduction to the "little book of comfort" (chs. 30–31; see 30:4), or the opening verse of the oracles against the nations (46:1; the closing phrase, "against all the nations," of 25:13*c* belongs here). Despite interruptions here and there, 4:5–6:30, with its vivid strophes on the foe from the N, forms a fairly unified literary whole, as does 2:2–4:4 on Israel's infidelity and apostasy and Yahweh's call to repentance. Moreover, the scroll which Jeremiah dictated to Baruch ben Neriah in 605 (see ch. 36) was certainly controlled by a dominant theme (vss. 2, 29). Signs of chronological arrangement are also present. The account of the prophet's call in ch. 1 is followed by a sequence of poems which are held by the majority of scholars to come from his earliest period. Chs. 37–44 are in excellent chronological order; elsewhere too the sequence of materials, while now disrupted, shows signs of an original chronological ordering (cf. chs. 26 ff).

The critical task is thus clear: to explain the extraordinary situation in the history of the book's composition, of order and plan on the one hand and of disorder and confusion on the other.

2. Major divisions of the book. The book may be outlined as follows:

I. Prophecies against Jerusalem and Judah, chs. 1–25
II. Biographical narratives about Jeremiah, chs. 26–45
III. Prophecies against the foreign nations, chs. 46–51
IV. Historical appendix, ch. 52

It is within the first major division of the book that we find the greatest amount of material stemming from Jeremiah. Among the passages which may be assigned to him with some confidence are the following: the call (1:4-19), invectives and calls to repentance (2:2–4:4), poems on the foe from the N (4:5–6:30; 8:14-17), confessional laments (11:18–12:6; 15:10-21; 17:12-18; 18:18-23; 20:7-18; cf. 8:18–9:3—H 8:18–9:2), laments for Judah and Jerusalem (9:4-11—H 9:3-10; 9:17-22—H 9:18-23), liturgy of drought (14:1–15:3), symbol of celibacy (16:1-13), oracles against the kings of Judah (21:11–23:8), oracles against the prophets (23:9-40), and the vision of the baskets of figs (ch. 24). There are other passages also which preserve authentic reminiscences of the prophet's activity and words like his temple discourse repeated in a condensed form but expanded with narrative detail in ch. 26 (7:1-15) and the prophet's support of the Deuteronomic reformation (11:1-17).

The second division (chs. 26–45) is almost exclusively prose and is in all probability the composition of Baruch (see 32:11-16; ch. 36; 43:1-7; ch. 45). The Little Book of Comfort (chs. 30–31) is an intrusion and contains both authentic Jeremianic material and additions from a later time.

The prophecies against the foreign nations (chs. 46–51) seem to have had a different literary history from the rest of the work. How much of this section, if any, comes from the prophet, it is difficult to say.

The final section is derived from II Kings 24:18–25:21, 27-39, but fortunately adds the important and reliable record of the numbers carried into captivity.

3. Composition. The modern phase of the critical study of the book of Jeremiah was inaugurated by the publication of the commentary by Bernhard Duhm in 1901 (*Das Buch Jeremia* in *KHC*). It is the merit of this work that it shows remarkable appreciation of the prophet's poetic style, but more especially that it recognizes for the first time the major literary strata of the book. Its defect is its too rigid limitation of the authentic materials to poems in a single meter (3′2′).

Sigmund Mowinckel advanced the study of the book in his monograph *Zur Komposition des Buches Jeremia* (1914). Here the literary strata were more clearly identified and explicated. Mowinckel recognized three major collections of material:

a) A compilation of authentic Jeremianic oracles, but without any introductory or concluding formulas: 1:4-10, 11-12, 13-16; 2:2*b*-9; 2:10-13; 2:14-28*a;* 2:29-37; 3:1-5, 19-20; 3:21–4:4; 4:5-10; 4:11*a*β-18; 4:19-22; 4:23-28; 4:29-31; 5:1-9; 5:10-14; 5:15-17; 5:20-31; 6:1-6*a;* 6:6*b*-8; 6:9-15; 6:16-19; 6:20-21; 6:22-26; 6:27-30; 8:4*a*β-12; 8:13; 8:14-17; 8:18-23; 9:1-8; 9:9-11; 9:16-21; 9:22-23; 9:24-25; 10:17-22; 11:15-16; 11:18-20, 22-23; 12:1-6; 12:7-12; 13:12-14; 13:15-27; 14:2-10; 14:11-16; 14:17*a*β–15:2; 15:5-9; 15:10-21; 16:1-13; 16:16-18, 21; 17:1-4; 17:9-10; 17:12, 14-18; 18:13-17; 18:18-23; 20:7-13; 20:14-18; 21:11*b*-12; 21:13-14; 22:6*a*β-9; 22:10-12; 22:13-19; 22:20-23; 22:24-30; 23:5-6; 23:9-15; 23:16-20; 23:21-24, 29; 24:1-10(?); 25:15-16, 27-38.

b) The work of the author of the book as a whole, a personal-historical composition:

1. 19:1-2, 10, 11*a,* 14–20:6
2. Ch. 26
3. Ch. 28
4. 29:24-32
5. Ch. 36
6. 37:1-10
7. 37:11-16
8. 37:17-21
9. 38:1-13
10. 38:14-28*a*
11. 38:28*b;* 39:3, 14; 40:2-12
12. 40:13–43:7
13. 43:8-13; 44:15-19, 24-30

Mowinckel denied Baruch's authorship of this work and assigned it to a date after Jeremiah's death, 580-480 B.C. According to him it was composed in Egypt.

c) A special source of pronounced Deuteronomic style with the characteristic formula of introduction: "The word which came to Jeremiah from Yahweh": 7:1–8:3; 11:1-5, 9-14; 18:1-12; 21:1-10; 25:1-11*a;* 32:1-2, 6-16, 24-44; 34:1-7; 34:8-22; 35:1-19; 44:1-14. The authenticity of all these utterances is rejected.

Mowinckel's work has had a profound influence on subsquent discussion. With significant reservations, especially with regard to dates and authenticity, it is accepted by Rudolph (*Jeremia,* in *HAT* [1947]) and substantially by H. G. May (*see bibliography*). The attack against his position has concentrated on his view of the date and authorship of *b* but more especially on his somewhat radical estimate of the *c* material. But his brilliant analysis succeeds in calling attention to the stylistic and ideological diversities within the book.

Another and perhaps more common approach to the composition of the book has been the attempt to reconstruct the scroll dictated to Baruch in 605.

4. The Baruch Scroll. In the fourth year of Jehoiakim, Jeremiah was commanded to dictate to Baruch all the "words" which he had spoken against Israel, Judah, and all the nations from the days of Josiah to the present. The scroll was read in the temple on a day of fasting, and the event was reported to the king, who commanded it to be read in his hearing. As he listened to it, he cast it several columns at a time into the fire of the brazier. Jeremiah was then ordered to dictate the scroll again, and to it he added "many similar words."

Is it possible to reconstruct this work? Many have thought so, but the results have not served to inspire much confidence. Yet certain criteria are present which should provide some clue: (*a*) the date, 626-605 B.C.; (*b*) the character of the oracles, certainly judgment and threat (36:3, 29); (*c*) the length (it was read three times in the course of a single day). If the substance of the scroll is present in our book, then it is likely that it is to be found in the first major division (chs. 1-25). Now 25:1-13 forms an admirable conclusion, and although it has doubtless received expansion, gives us certain data of some interest: the temporal limits are the same, as in ch. 36; the character of the prophecy is the same; and, above all, the final words refer to "everything written in this book" (25:13). It is obvious, however, that this cannot mean that Baruch's scroll was coextensive with these chapters; much would need to be excluded to conform to its length and character. J. P. Hyatt (*IB*, V, 787) suggests the following passages as belonging to the original document: 1:4-14, 17; 2:1-37; 3:1-5, 19-25; 4:1-8, 11-22, 27-31; 5:1-17, 20-31; 6:1-30; possibly 8:4-9:1. This is probably a minimum. Eissfeldt (*Einleitung in das Alte Testament,* p. 425) gives quite a different set of passages, including the great temple speech (7:1-8:3), the threat against Jerusalem (11:6-14) and Israel and Judah (13:1-14), and the denunciation of sabbath violation (17:19-27). Certainty on the matter is excluded, and this applies a fortiori to the expanded scroll, but it would seem likely that the original writing is contained within the compass of 1:4-25:13.

5. Prophecies against Judah and Jerusalem. A somewhat closer inspection of chs. 1-25 in historico-critical perspective will supplement our observations concerning its contents and the possibility of the presence of Baruch's scroll within its compass. The superscription (1:1-3) may be the work of Baruch or of the final editor or of both (vss. 1-2, 3). The present literary construction suggests the work of two hands by its twofold temporal setting. The rest of the chapter is devoted to the call (1:4-10, 11-12, 13-19). It is likely that none of it was reduced to writing until long after the event. Each pericope opens in the same fashion: "The word of Yahweh came to me, saying." It is possible that vss. 4-10 and 13-19 are parallel accounts of the call, the first representing substantially the report of Jeremiah himself, the second that of Baruch, though based upon Jeremiah's own account.

In ch. 3, vss. 6-12*a* and 15-18 are surely intrusive. They do not belong here. It is less certain that vss. 24-25 (rendered as prose in the RSV) are spurious; stylistic and structural features favor their originality.

In ch. 4, vss. 9-10 are certainly Jeremiah's, as are 11-12; they are literary fragments which were inserted here, the first because it represents the prophet's actual commentary, the second because it was related to the major theme of the foe. While vss. 23-27 seem difficult to credit to the prophet because of their "apocalyptic coloring," it is not safe to reject them on this account. In general, 4:5-6:30, like 2:2-4:4, represent fairly homogeneous sections.

The long prose section 7:1-8:3 is of quite a different style; the Deuteronomic cadence and terminology do not argue against essential authenticity, however. This is true also of the not dissimilar section in 11:1-12:6. That there are intrusions here is likely, but its general tenor is Jeremianic. The confessional laments are certainly genuine (11:18-12:6; 15:10-21; 17:12-18; 18:18-23; 20:7-18; cf. 8:18-9:3—H 8:18-9:2), as are the denunciations of the kings (21:11-23:8) and the popular prophets (23:9-40). In its present form ch. 24 is not Jeremiah's composition, but it is most probably based upon his report. The concluding section (25:1-13) is laden with Deuteronomic terminology, but it correctly witnesses to a crucial point in his prophetic ministry (cf. vs. 13 with chs. 36; 45).

6. The biographical narratives. This section includes 19:1-20:6; chs. 26-29; 32:1-45:5, with the deletion of minor passages such as 33:14-26. It covers the period from *ca.* 608 to Jeremiah's last days. The whole comprises a *Leidensgeschichte,* a memoir of the prophet's trials and sufferings.

The style of these narratives contrasts sharply with that of Jeremiah in his early period. It is straightforward, clear, and detailed. There is no reason to doubt the essential historical accuracy of this section. To be sure, Baruch reproduces the prophet's words in his own language, as Thucydides did the funeral oration of Pericles or the author of the book of Acts the speeches of Paul; yet it is precarious to make too much of this, for it is doubtful whether the prophet always indulged in the poetic flights of his early years. Moreover, there is not a little in these discourses which preserves the kind of personal detail and intimate reflections characteristic of the "confessions" in the first division of the book, as well as the vigorous forthrightness of the invectives and threats. It is apparent that an original order has been altered, as is seen, e.g., by the dating of ch. 26 at the beginning of Jehoiakim's reign and ch. 45 during his fourth year, while the intervening narratives (also disordered) fall partly in the reign of Zedekiah.

H. G. May has subjected this division of the book to a thoroughgoing critical analysis and reaches the conclusion that it cannot come from a contemporary of Jeremiah but must be dated, at the earliest, in the first half of the fifth century (*see bibliography*). John Bright (*see bibliography*) has assayed the same task with equal vigor and thoroughness and reaches radically different results. While his view of the precise nature of the compilatory character of the book is open to question, his defense of the narratives as trustworthy and the work of a contemporary is entirely successful.

Here we have Baruch's somewhat circumstantial and detailed yet, partly for this very reason, deeply moving account of the suffering and persecutions of his master. Some have supposed that it is he who is responsible for the book in substantially its present form; others see him as the compiler of Jeremiah's *ipsissima verba* with his own prose "passion story." The latter may indeed be the case; if so, we may well understand how his own language occasionally interrupts the prophet's own. It is also probable that we have duplicate accounts from Jeremiah and Baruch, comparable to 7:1-15 and ch. 26, as in 1:4-10, 13-19.

7. The Deuteronomic work. As we have seen, it was Duhm who first called attention to the distinctiveness of this "source," and he was seconded in his views by Mowinckel, who assigned it to Source *c*. There is no question that this material bears the stamp of Deuteronomic composition and style; the problem is whether it is in any sense Jeremiah's and whether it is historical. The problem is a complicated one, for not infrequently Baruch employs the same style and language. It is now increasingly recognized, however, that the practice of excision of so-called Deuteronomic language will not meet the situation. For it is very probable that this kind of speech was contemporary with the prophet, and it is not inconceivable that he may himself have employed it upon occasion, above all within the precincts of the temple or in his relationships to the cult. Yet it need not be contended that all the passages included within Mowinckel's *"c"* are Jeremiah's *ipsissima verba;* what is probable, however, is that they are in general dependent upon authentic historical information derived from the prophet himself. An excellent example is the account of the potter and the clay (18:1-12); that the nucleus is Jeremiah's can scarcely be questioned, even though it is certainly elaborated Deuteronomically. In a different way the same is true of chs. 32; 34–35.

8. The Little Book of Comfort. It is generally recognized that chs. 30–31, called the "Little Book of Comfort," represent an independent compilation, although some scholars have suggested that the work extended through ch. 33 (e.g., R. H. Pfeiffer [*see bibliography*]). While there is widespread disagreement concerning originality, date, and provenance, the following conclusions seem probable: (*a*) the little book is highly composite, representing very early oracles together with substantial additions from a much later period than Jeremiah's; (*b*) the dominating interest is with the N, and the original poems may well have had their provenance there; (*c*) the poetry which has the strongest claim for originality possesses the same vigor, imagery, and ecstatic quality of his earliest work and is therefore to be assigned to that period, conceivably during the period of silence from 621 to 609. The following passages probably come from this time: 30:5-7, 12-17, 23-24; 31:2-6, 7-9, 15-22. Other original material may have been reworked, but most of the rest is late. The important passage on the new covenant (31:31-34) "gives the substance of Jeremiah's thought, but not in his words" (Hyatt).

9. The oracles against the foreign nations. This, too, originally comprised a separate compilation and is comparable to similar collections in Isaiah (chs. 13–23), Ezekiel (chs. 25–32), and the Twelve (Amos 1:1–2:4). That its literary history is somewhat involved is suggested by the order of the poems in the LXX and by omissions in the latter. Hans Bardtke (*see bibliography*) has argued for the authenticity of most of these poems to the nations. There is much that is attractive in this view. Jeremiah was called to be a prophet to the nations, and it must be admitted that if the authenticity of oracles such as these could be demonstrated, the phrase would gain in propriety and cogency. The argument of style (cf. Pfeiffer's characterization, pp. 506-10) is not necessarily decisive against their genuineness, for it is certain that Jeremiah did not retain his fervor and imaginative genius and éclat throughout his life. The long period of suffering exacted a heavy toll. It is possible too that he may have prophesied in Egypt. The fact that the collection is independent may only mean that it was added later after the completion of the earlier compilation. The poem against Egypt (46:3-12) is probably genuine, and portions of other poems may go back to him. Bardtke's own reconstruction, however, is open to grave objections.

10. Historical appendix. The concluding chapter of the book, as we have seen, has been taken from II Kings 24:18–25:21, in the same manner as Isa. 36–39 was drawn from the same book. Notable is the extremely valuable report, probably drawn from an official record, preserved in Jer. 52:28-30. There is every reason to credit its reliability, and it is a great support for assessing the extent of the captivity.

11. Text. The Greek translation deviates from the text transmitted by the Masoretic scholars. Most notable is the location of the oracles against the nations; in the LXX they appear after 25:13 of our present text. What is more, they are ordered differently:

MT: Egypt (46), Philistines (47), Moab (48), Ammonites (49:1-6), Edom (49:7-22), Damascus (49:23-27), Kedar and Hazor (49:28-33), Elam (49:34-39), Babylon (50:1–51:58).

LXX: Elam, Egypt, Babylon, Philistines, Edom, Ammonites, Kedar, Damascus, Moab.

About one eighth of the Hebrew text is absent in the LXX. Most of these omissions are minor, representing individual verses or parts of verses; others are due to error, such as the homoeoteleuton of 39:4-13 and 51:44*b*-49*a;* still others are intentional—e.g., the omission of doublets in the Hebrew text (8:10-12; 30:10-11; 48:10-11). But some are to be explained only by their absence in the Hebrew *Vorlage* employed by the translators, as in 33:14-26. Stylistic and cultic interests may also have played a role. In assessing the relative superiority of one text over another, each case must be considered independently.

Bibliography. The relevant sections of the following critical introductions are recommended: Driver, Steuernagel, Eissfeldt, Pfeiffer, and Bentzen.

Commentaries: B. Duhm, *KHC,* vol. XI (1901). C. H. Cornill (1905). F. Giesebrecht in Nowack, *HKAT* (2nd ed., 1907). P. Volz, *KAT,* X (1922; 2nd ed., 1928). F. Noetscher in *Feldmann-Herkenne, Die Heilige Schrift des ATs,* VII, 2 (1934). W. Rudolph, *HAT,* vol. 12 (1947). A. Weiser, *ATD* (Jer. 1:1–25:13 [1952]; 25:14–52:34 [1955]). J. P. Hyatt, *IB,* V (1956), 777-1142.

Critical discussions of composition and related problems: F. Wilke, "Das Skythenproblem in Jeremiabuch," *BWAT,* 13 (1913), 222-54. S. Mowinckel, *Zur Komposition des Buches Jeremia* (1914). F. Horst, "Die Anfaenge des Propheten Jeremia," *ZAW,* 41 (1923), 94-153. T. H. Robinson, "Baruch's Roll," *ZAW,* 42 (1924). 209-21. A. Alt, *PJ,* XXI (1925), 100 ff. H. G. May, "The Chronology of Jeremiah's Oracles," *JNES,* 4 (1935), 217-27. H. Bardtke, "Jeremia, der Fremdvoelkerprophet," *ZAW,* 53 (1935), 209-39; 54 (1936), 240-62. G. von Rad, "Die Konfessionen Jeremias," *Evangelische Theologie* (1936), pp. 265-76. G. R. Driver, "Linguistic and Textual Problems: Jeremiah," *JQR,* 28 (1937/38), 97-129. H. Birkeland, *Zum hebraeischen Traditionswesen* (1938). For the theory that the Little Book of Comfort extends through ch. 33, see R. H. Pfeiffer, *Introduction to the OT* (1941), p. 501. H. G.

May, "Towards an Objective Approach to the Book of Jeremiah: the Biographer," *JBL*, 61 (1942), 139-55, shows the influence of Mowinckel; on the biographical narratives, see especially p. 152. S. Mowinckel, *Prophecy and Tradition* (1946). H. H. Rowley, "The Prophet Jeremiah and the Book of Deuteronomy," *Studies in OT Prophecy* (1950), pp. 157-74. J. P. Hyatt, "The Deuteronomic Edition of Jeremiah," *Vanderbilt Studies in the Humanities* (1951), pp. 71-95. J. Bright, "The Date of the Prose Sermons of Jeremiah," *JBL*, 70 (1951), 15-29. H. Kremers, "Leidensgemeinschaft mit Gott im AT," *Evangelische Theologie*, 13 (1953), 122-40. On the Babylonian Chronicle, see D. J. Wiseman, *Chronicles of Chaldean Kings* (1956). M. Noth, *History of Israel* (1958), pp. 271-74.

J. Muilenburg

JEREMIAS jĕr′ə mī′əs. Douay Version form of Jeremiah.

JEREMIEL. Alternate form of Jerahmeel 4 in II Esd. 4:36.

JEREMOTH jĕr′ə mŏth [ירמות, *yerēmôth*, swollen *or* obese (*with -ôth here hypocoristic*); Apoc. Ἱερεμώθ, Ἰαριμώθ; *see also* Jerimoth]; KJV twice JERIMOTH —ĭ mŏth (I Chr. 7:8; 27:19—but in the latter passage correctly, with the MT ירימות, a variant of the foregoing); KJV once RAMOTH rā′mŏth [*Kethibh* ירמות, *yerāmôth; Qere* רמות, *rāmôth*] (Ezra 10:29); KJV Apoc. HIEREMOTH hī ĕr′ə mŏth in I Esd. 9:27, 30; JARIMOTH jăr′ə mŏth in I Esd. 9:28. **1.** According to I Chr. 7:8 (cf. vs. 6), a Benjaminite; but the genealogy is probably Zebulunite.

Bibliography. E. L. Curtis and A. A. Madsen, *Chronicles*, ICC (1910), pp. 145-49.

2. A Benjaminite (I Chr. 8:14). "Jeroham" perhaps stands for this name in vs. 27.

3. A Merarite Levite (I Chr. 23:23; same as "Jerimoth" in 24:30).

4. A Levite of the "sons of Heman" (I Chr. 25:22; same as "Jerimoth" in vs. 4).

5. A chief of the tribe of Naphtali (I Chr. 27:19, where the KJV "Jerimoth" is proper).

6. One of the Jews who were listed as having foreign wives in the time of Ezra (Ezra 10:26; I Esd. 9:27).

7. Another Jew listed as having a foreign wife in the time of Ezra (Ezra 10:27; I Esd. 9:28).

8. A third Jew listed as having a foreign wife in the time of Ezra (Ezra 10:29; I Esd. 9:30).

Bibliography. M. Noth, *Die israelitischen Personennamen* (1928), pp. 39, 226.

B. T. Dahlberg

JEREMY. KJV Apoc. and NT alternate form of Jeremiah.

JEREMY, EPISTLE OF. *See* Jeremiah, Letter of.

JERIAH jĭ rī′ə [יריהו, may Yahu see (one's need)]. Alternately: JERIJAH —jə (I Chr. 26:31). A Kohathite Levite, son of Hebron (I Chr. 23:19; 24:23); listed as chief of the Hebronites in the time of King David (26:31).

Bibliography. M. Noth, *Die israelitischen Personennamen* (1928), p. 198.

B. T. Dahlberg

JERIBAI jĕr′ə bī [יריבי] (I Chr. 11:46). One of the sons of Elnaam whose names appear among the sixteen additional names that the Chronicler added to the catalogue (II Sam. 23) of the Mighty Men of David known as the "Thirty."

JERICHO jĕr′ə kō [יריחו, ירחו, יריחה]. The major city at the S end of the Jordan Valley; the key defense position for the W section of the wide plain. The OT city was located at Tell es-Sultan, the NT city at Tulul Abu el-ʿAlayiq. The former was built above one of the largest springs in all of Palestine, and this spring is still watering the extensive gardens of modern Jericho a mile or so downstream. The NT city was a mile S of the OT Jericho. It was located on both banks of the Wadi Qelt, where that magnificent canyon opens out into the great, broad plain of the Jordan.

1. OT Jericho
2. Neolithic Jericho
3. Intertestamental and NT Jericho
4. Roman and Byzantine Jericho

Bibliography

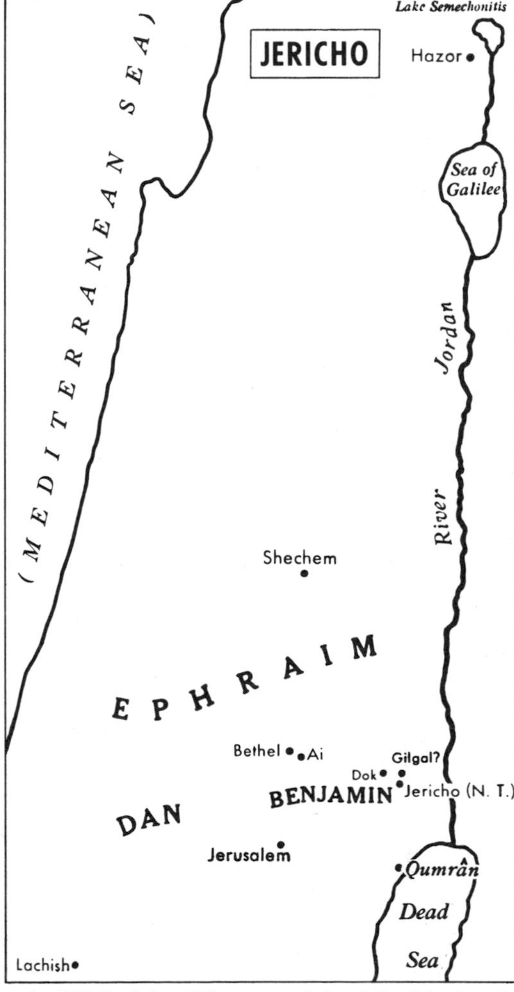

1. OT Jericho. The story of the fall of Jericho is very difficult of interpretation. Before the days of archaeological research the commentators could let their imagination have free rein, and this gave a mul-

Copyright: The Matson Photo Service

11. Air view of OT Jericho, showing the mound of Jericho in the foreground; in the distance are the Dead Sea and the mountains of Moab.

tiplicity of interpretations. Unfortunately the Jericho of Joshua's day still presents a highly technical problem even for the archaeologist, as only a small portion of that city survived to the present century. Today there is nothing left for the archaeologist to dig and thus double check the work of his predecessors. When, however, the fall of Jericho is studied in the light of the military campaigns which preceded it and followed it, the archaeologist can, at least in part, reconstruct the Jericho picture; and today archaeology is fast approaching a solution of the problem. Some space, however, must be devoted to the history of archaeological work at Jericho and the other key cities of Joshua's campaigns before and after Jericho.

Since the fall of Jericho is one of the most fascinating stories in all of scripture, it is not surprising to find that Jericho was one of the first cities in Palestine to be excavated. This work was done by Ernst Sellin and Carl Watzinger in 1907-11. Unfortunately this work was carried on before any accurate pottery calendar (*see* ARCHAEOLOGY § C3*a;* POTTERY § 2) had been worked out for Palestine. Indeed, the excavators gave only a minimum attention to pottery, specializing on striking forms rather than on an overall portrayal of the pottery. The city which Sellin identified as Israelite was actually centuries earlier —i.e., in the latter part of the Middle Bronze Age (seventeenth-sixteenth centuries).* Père Hugo Vincent, however, who later became known as the best pottery expert in Palestine, was an unofficial observer at the excavations, and he insisted that there was pottery of the final phase of Late Bronze Age—i.e., the thirteenth century—on the site. Figs. ALA 12; JER 11.

From 1929 to 1936 John Garstang worked on the mound. His major discovery was that the site was occupied in the Neolithic period, even before the invention of pottery. When he came to that part of the mound dealing with Bible times, however, Garstang found the site difficult to excavate and more difficult to interpret. Although he shifted his dating of various walls and levels several times, the general public knows his work best through a single study, *The Story of Jericho,* in which he dated Joshua's conquest at 1400-1388 B.C. He described Jericho as a four- or five-acre city surrounded by a double wall. The city was destroyed in a great conflagration apparently assisted by an earthquake. His description of the city seems to many readers to fit well into the Joshua story, and it is quoted or used in modified versions. But whatever date is now given by scholars to this particular destruction emphasized by Garstang, all agree that his date is more than a century earlier than the conquest of the cities described in the immediately following campaign, which began at Ai and ended at Hazor. Fig. JER 12.

Courtesy of Herbert G. May

12. Excavations of ancient Jericho

Garstang's work gave emphasis to the views of several scholars that the Israelites left Egypt at various times rather than in a single mass exodus under Moses. These scholars differed among themselves, but in general they separated Moses and Joshua by a strong time lag—some giving priority in time to one leader and some to the other. *See* JOSHUA, BOOK OF, § D1.

In 1952, Kathleen M. Kenyon began work on the mound. After five years of her work the archaeological picture is clearer, and the following conclusions now seem valid: Most of the mound is sixteenth century B.C. or earlier; indeed, the major depth of the mound is actually Neolithic.* In other words, most of the mound belongs to prehistoric times, and the last *big* city was something like three hundred years earlier than Moses. Unfortunately she has found that the small amount of the upper levels which had escaped destruction by wind and rain were those areas al-

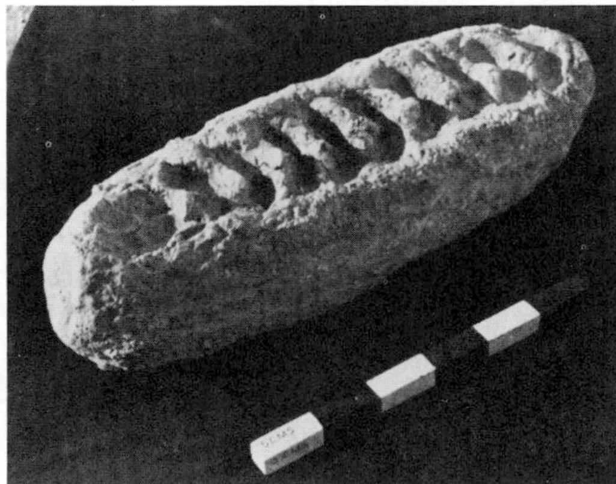

From Kathleen Kenyon, *Digging Up Jericho* (London: Ernest Benn Ltd.)

13. A thumb-impressed Neolithic brick, from Jericho

ready worked by the Germans and Garstang. Jericho was built of mud brick, and this is quickly disintegrated by both wind and rain. The same winds which furnished the forced draft for Solomon's smelters at EZION-GEBER (§ 2) had already been blasting away at the mud bricks of Jericho. One year the English excavations here were flooded by heavy rains. Even in the Neolithic area, Miss Kenyon found, stream channels had cut into parts of the mound. It therefore seems unlikely that anything new can be learned of thirteenth-century Jericho from the mound itself, although nearby tombs may prove very helpful in the future. One of the major tragedies of Palestinian archaeology is that the Germans excavated Jericho when archaeology was still an infant science. Figs. JER 13-15.

Since the archaeological evidence at Jericho is small, it is wise to move on to the remainder of Joshua's campaign to see what new light it may throw on the Jericho story. The capture of Bethel-Ai (*see* BETHEL [SANCTUARY] § 2) is shown by a terrific conflagration followed by a complete cultural change and deterioration in the city which replaced it. This pattern was repeated in the excavations of Lachish and Kiriath-sepher. Furthermore, the fall of LACHISH (§ 2) was dated by inscriptional material to *ca.* 1200 B.C. Tell el-Hesi, which is probably Eglon, was also destroyed *ca.* 1200 B.C. The importance of this S campaign is demonstrated in the Mer-ne-ptah inscription of the same general date (*see* INSCRIPTIONS § 1). This is the first mention of Israel in any inscription, and here the Egyptian king refers to Israel as a nation but as yet without specific boundaries. Even Joshua's northern campaign, which seems so

From *Syria* (1935); courtesy of the Librairie Orientaliste Paul Geuthner, Paris

14. Mask from Neolithic Jericho

From Kathleen Kenyon, *Digging Up Jericho* (London: Ernest Benn Ltd.)

15. Neolithic plastered skull, from Jericho

totally unrelated to the southern one, has now been confirmed by Israeli excavations at HAZOR, where the city was found to be very much larger and stronger than expected and where there is a wealth of pottery data belonging to the same period.

The success of such an extensive military campaign as these archaeological excavations have demonstrated and which included cities as far distant and as unrelated as Lachish and Hazor could hardly have been started in a local feud between the Bethel-Ai Canaanites and some Israelite clan. The preceding Transjordan campaign, however, had been an excellent preparatory action over equally long distances; and Glueck's researches in Transjordan show that the thirteenth century was the only possible date for that campaign. Jericho was the junction point of these two campaigns. It was the first city across the Jordan and the bridgehead in Cis-Jordan.

Turning now to the interpretation of this archaeological evidence of the two campaigns and of that found at Jericho itself, it looks as if Jericho was only a small city in Joshua's time. It probably used a section of the old brick walls of an earlier city for its defenses. That such brick walls do actually disappear rather easily can be seen at Kiriath-sepher (*see* DEBIR [Josh. 1:11-15]) in the Late Bronze Age, where the city wall is missing but where a street, concentric with that wall, still remains with the house foundations adjacent. That there was some occupation at Jericho in the thirteenth century is proved by some local imitations of Mycenean ware that have been found on the mound and in tombs. This is what Père Vincent maintained as far back as the German excavations.

Furthermore, not only is the city which Joshua conquered largely missing, but the next two cities that succeeded it, according to scripture, do not appear anywhere on the mound! The city of palm trees which Eglon captured and where he received tribute from Israel (Judg. 3:13) must have been Jericho, but no signs of this city have yet been found in the excavations. David's ambassadors, who had been insulted by the king of the Ammonites, stopped at Jericho until their beards were grown (II Sam. 10:5); but again the mound furnishes no remains of this town. Equally instructive is the fact that only a portion of the little city or "block house," which was a century earlier than Joshua's conquest, was preserved.

At the present time the interpretations of the Israelite conquest fit into two general categories, although each view has several modifying features. (*a*) Jericho was a small city captured in the same military campaign which saw Israel conquer Transjordan and then move successfully against some, but not all, of the major cities of W Palestine, going even as far N as the great fortress of Hazor. (*b*) The Israelite conquest extended over a considerable length of time and occurred in two or more waves. Those which took place earlier than the thirteenth century would be represented by three factors: (*i*) the fall of one of the older and stronger Jericho fortresses—i.e., those dug by Garstang; (*ii*) an earlier military conquest of central Palestine which made it possible for Joshua to reinstitute the law at Shechem without any prior military action; and (*iii*) other data referred to in the genealogical material of I Chronicles.

Although Joshua laid a heavy curse upon Jericho (Josh. 6:26), nevertheless when the conquered land was distributed, Jericho was credited to the tribe of Benjamin (Josh. 18:21), and the boundary between Benjamin and Ephraim was the road from Jericho to Bethel. The above curse is apparently referred to in the founding of Jericho by Hiel, the Bethelite (I Kings 16:34). The loss of his sons may well refer to a foundation sacrifice after the Canaanite pattern. Actually, however, archaeologists do not find too many such foundation sacrifices.

At one point on the mound the Germans found a heavy building with long rooms. They interpreted it as a reflection of Syrian architectural influence. Archaeologists now recognize this type of structure as an Israelite granary characteristic of the tenth and ninth centuries B.C. Since there were two cities on the site after Joshua's conquest, the founding of this city by Hiel may well refer to its elevation as a military depot as represented by the granary. Such a reserve depot was good military strategy at this time, as the wheat basket of Transjordan was a constant battleground between Israel and Syria.

There was a school of the prophets in Jericho at the time of Elijah's translation (II Kings 2:4-18). Elisha's first act after he took up Elijah's mantle was to purify the spring at Jericho (II Kings 2:19-22). Both Ezra and Nehemiah speak of a postexilic Jericho, listing the population of this Jericho as 345 (Ezra 2:34; Neh. 7:36), and Nehemiah also notes that the men of Jericho helped rebuild the walls of Jerusalem (Neh. 3:2). This Jericho was apparently like the Jericho of the days of the judges and David. These are the last OT references to the Jericho that was located at Tell es-Sultan—i.e., beside the great spring. The Jericho that we know from the intertestamental and NT periods was located along the Wadi Qelt a mile or so to the S.

2. Neolithic Jericho. But there is another phase of excavations at Tell es-Sultan that deserves notice—namely, the Neolithic period. This was discovered by Garstang, and he continued to dig down to a prepottery period (before 5000 B.C.); but it was Miss Kenyon who revealed the phenomenal nature of this Neolithic period. This phase of Jericho's history throws new light on the pre-Abrahamic chapters of Genesis. Miss Kenyon has demonstrated that civilization actually existed here several thousand years earlier than anyone had even dreamed of. Carbon 14 dating has confirmed this.

These Neolithic cities occupy forty-five feet of debris representing about twenty successive house levels! Equally significant is the size of these cities, for they were approximately eight acres in area—the same as many an OT city. Their houses had well-designed rooms characterized by the use of burnished plaster on both floors and walls. The flattened cigar-shaped bricks were thumbmarked for easier bonding.* The population used fine limestone dishes and a new type of quern; their flints were Tahunian (*see* PREHISTORY § 1). Fertility-cult objects common to later times were here also. There was a new religious factor, however, in the use of skulls, some of which had the features reproduced in plaster. They are true individualistic pieces of art in portrait sculpturing. Figs. JER 13; 15.

Among the earlier Neolithic phases was a military defense consisting of a solid stone tower thirty feet through, and for additional defense there was a twenty-seven-foot ditch cut out of solid rock. Still earlier there was a better tower with an interior stairway, where twenty steps are still intact, and each step is a three-foot dressed stone. The roof used even larger stones. These lowest levels represent a different culture, for the brick used was flat on the bottom but the tops were hog-backed. The houses were round and the walls battered. The objects found in the dwellings were also different from the later levels. Thus Jericho continues to add to its honor as the world's oldest city, and we must now date civilization several thousand years earlier.

3. Intertestamental and NT Jericho. Herod the Great founded NT Jericho, which is today represented by ruins called Tulul Abu el-ʻAlayiq. Jericho served as his winter capital, and its balmy winter climate was in striking contrast to the bone-chilling damp winter of Jerusalem. The city was located on the W edge of the Jordan plain where the Wadi Qelt opens out onto this plain. J. B. Pritchard reports a Chalcolithic and Early Bronze settlement here. Charles Warren and Ernst Sellin had both trenched this tell, but they reported little in the way of findings. J. L. Kelso excavated it for the American School of Oriental Research in 1950, and the following year J. B. Pritchard worked here.

A small Hellenistic fortress was erected here to guard the road from the Jordan Valley to Jerusalem. Bacchides is credited with fortifying Jericho (I Macc. 9:50); this was either his work or that of his opponents the Maccabees. Simon, one of the Maccabees, was treacherously killed at Jericho by his son-in-law Ptolemy (I Macc. 16:14-16). A second small tell across the wadi was probably originally built at the same time. Pompey captured two forts called Threx and Taurus at Jericho in 63 B.C.; and they are probably the same forts as those of the Maccabean period. A mountaintop on either bank of the Qelt was also a citadel of defense, especially Kypros on the S, which Herod the Great gave to his mother.

Herod's work on the site seems to fall into two phases, an early cut-stone period, where the masonry is similar to that used in other cities, and a later *opus reticulatum* phase. This latter reflects one of Herod's trips to Rome, for here on the Wadi Qelt are con-

Courtesy of James B. Pritchard

16. Excavated remains of Herodian gymnasium or palaestra(?) at NT Jericho, W of the tell

structions similar to those which Augustus was building on the Tiber. Anyone who has seen Pompeii has seen the same building phase that appears at Jericho. Although the buildings of the two cities are similar, Jericho was a much more expansive site with plenty of room for pools, parks, and villas, as well as the normal civic buildings of a Greco-Roman metropolis.* The Qelt ran through the city, and some of its major buildings were oriented to that stream. One of them was about two city blocks in length. Another had a grand stairway 150 feet long. There was a sunken garden with fifty statuary niches and a semicircular terraced garden in the center. At either end of this sunken garden were buildings, some walls of which were forty-one inches thick. Josephus reports that at the death of Herod the Great his palace and some of the other buildings of Jericho were burned, but his son Archelaus quickly restored the city. Fig. JER 16.

Zacchaeus, the most famous of all tax collectors, held an office which was highly remunerative, not only because of the fabulously rich balsam groves nearby, but also because Jericho was the winter capital of the kingdom. When Christ was entertained by Zacchaeus (Luke 19:1-10), it would be in one of the finest houses of the city, and it would compare with the best of Pompeii. The presence of sycamore trees in Jericho in connection with this story is testified to by the use of this timber in one of the earlier Hellenistic forts. Beggars were also found in these rich cities, for almsgiving was highly meritorious. Matthew, Mark, and Luke all tell of Christ's ministry to such beggars here at Jericho (Matt. 20:29-34; Mark 10:46-52; Luke 18:35-43). As Christ left the city, he entered at once into the great canyon of the Wadi Qelt, which carried the main road to Jerusalem. These same mountains had witnessed the scene of his temptations immediately after the baptism, and Jericho may well have summarized all the cities of this world in that temptation. Now at the close of his ministry Christ passed through the same mountain setting en route to Calvary, that final testing. This concludes the story of NT Jericho, but the city lived on for some time yet.

4. Roman and Byzantine Jericho. Archaeologists have not yet found any evidence of Jericho's destruction by Vespasian's army. Instead, he spared the city and stationed large garrisons here preparatory to the attack on Jerusalem. His troops, however, did destroy Khirbet Qumran (*see* DEAD SEA SCROLLS § 3), about seven miles to the S, at this time. The relationship of this Essene community to Jericho is still puzzling, for that puritanical group did not live at Qumran in the days when the profligate Herod had his winter capital there. Whether or not Herod the Great ordered them out, we do not know. Upon his death, however, they did return to their old center.

After Jerusalem was destroyed in A.D. 70, Jericho declined swiftly, and by the turn of the century the old capital had shrunk to a small garrison town. At the time of Bar Cocheba's Rebellion (A.D. 132-35), however, the city flared up briefly, for either the Romans or the Jews rebuilt one of the early forts. Roman Jericho was still located on this site when the Bordeaux Pilgrim passed through here in A.D. 333, but shortly thereafter the site was abandoned and Roman Jericho was replaced by a new Byzantine Jericho (Erikha) a mile or so to the E. Modern Jericho is built over this Byzantine site. When the Germans excavated OT Jericho, they found a little Byzantine occupation on that mound also.

Bibliography. E. Sellin and C. Watzinger, *Jericho, Die Ergebnisse der Ausgrabungen* (1913); J. and J. B. E. Garstang, *The Story of Jericho* (1948); J. L. Kelso and D. C. Baramki, *Excavations at NT Jericho and Khirbet en-Nitla* (1955); K. M. Kenyon, "Jericho, Its Setting in Near Eastern History," *Antiquity* (Dec., 1956), pp. 184-95; J. B. Pritchard, *The Excavations at Herodian Jericho, 1951* (1958). J. L. KELSO

JERIEL jĭr'ĭ əl [יריאל, may God see] (I Chr. 7:2). A descendant of Issachar.

JERIJAH. Alternate form of JERIAH.

JERIMOTH jĕr'ĭ mŏth [ירימות, *yerîmôth*, swollen *or* obese (*with -ôth here hypocoristic*); *see also* JEREMOTH]. **1.** According to I Chr. 7:7, a Benjaminite; but this genealogy is thought to be rather that of Zebulun.

Bibliography. E. L. Curtis and A. A. Madsen, *Chronicles*, ICC (1910), pp. 145-49.

2. A Benjaminite among those who joined forces with David at Ziklag (I Chr. 12:5—H 12:6).

3. A Merarite Levite (I Chr. 24:30; same as "Jeremoth" [*yerēmôth*] in 23:23).

4. A Levite of the "sons of Heman" (I Chr. 25:4; same as "Jeremoth" [*yerēmôth*] in 25:22).

5. A son of King David, and the father of Mahalath, a wife (and cousin) of King Rehoboam (II Chr. 11:18).

6. A Levite; one of those who helped supervise the temple treasuries in the reign of King Hezekiah (*ca.* 715-687 B.C.; II Chr. 31:13).

7. KJV form of JEREMOTH 1; 5 (correctly of the latter).

Bibliography. M. Noth, *Die israelitischen Personennamen* (1928), pp. 39, 226. B. T. DAHLBERG

JERIOTH jĕr'ĭ ŏth [יריעות, tents] (I Chr. 2:18). One of the wives of Caleb. The MT is obviously in disorder; either Jerioth is another name for Azubah, or Azubah was formerly the wife of another man called Jerioth.

Bibliography. G. Richter, "Untersuchungen zu den Geschlechtsregistern der Chronik I," *ZAW,* XXXIV (1914), 109-10. J. F. Ross

JEROBOAM jĕr'ə bō'əm [ירבעם, may the people grow numerous]. **1.** The first king of Israel (*ca.* 922-901 B.C.); son of Nebat. Jeroboam was chosen as king of the ten N tribes at the disruption of the kingdom following the death of Solomon.

The parallelism between the names of the two rivals Jeroboam and Rehoboam may very well be deliberate, and both may be throne names. In both cases the power of the people (עם) is stressed as against the power of the king. There may be a connection with the Babylonian "Hammurabi." *See* REHOBOAM.

Jeroboam reigned for twenty-two years (I Kings 14:20).

There are two accounts of Jeroboam, prior to his becoming king. These are contained in I Kings 11:26-40 and in the Greek supplement to I Kings 12:24 ff; 14:18 ff. According to the former, he was an Ephraimite from the village of Zeredah (the modern Deir Ghassaneh), SW of Shechem. His father was Nebat, and his mother Zeruah (i.e., "leprous"). She was a widow (I Kings 11:26). When next we hear of Jeroboam, he was a young man employed in fortification work which Solomon had ordered to be done in Jerusalem. His marked ability and industry brought him to the attention of the king, who appointed him overseer of the *corvée* of the house of Joseph (vss. 27-28; cf. 5:13 ff). As such, Jeroboam must have become aware of the deep resentment this system evoked among the people. This awareness may have caused him to rebel against the king and to side with the people. No open act of rebellion, however, is mentioned. Where such would be expected in the narrative, there appears the story of the prophet AHIJAH the Shilonite, who met Jeroboam one day as he was leaving Jerusalem. Ahijah symbolically tore his new robe into twelve pieces, gave ten of them to Jeroboam, and announced in the name of the Lord, the God of Israel, that on Solomon's death he would give ten tribes to Jeroboam, while one tribe would be left to Solomon's son, for the sake of David. The prophecy ended with the promise that if Jeroboam continued loyal and true to the Lord, his kingdom would endure (I Kings 11:29-39). "Solomon sought therefore to kill Jeroboam," but he fled to Egypt to the protection of Shishak king of Egypt, and there he remained until Solomon's death. It is clear that the connection between vs. 39 and vs. 40, if any, is a very loose one, inasmuch as the narrative records that "the two of them were alone in the open country" when Ahijah's prophecy was made. The same thing is true of the connection between vs. 28 and vs. 29.

Two points in particular in this story call for comment. Is this episode of Ahijah, which makes him the chief instigator of the revolt, historically trustworthy? That it may have a basis in fact is to be granted, but it does not belong in its present position. In this story of Jeroboam material taken from two different sources has been combined by the Deuteronomic editor of Kings. It does not account for Solomon's hostility and Jeroboam's consequent flight to Egypt, nor does it adequately explain the choice of Jeroboam as king on his return.

The probable explanation of the reference to ten tribes and one tribe in vss. 31-32, and again in vss. 35-36, is that it was customary in later times to speak of the ten tribes of the N, and of the S kingdom of Judah. At this time Benjamin may have been considered as part of Judah. It may not have recovered from the massacre of the people recorded in Judg. 19–21.

According to the latter account Jeroboam was an Ephraimite. His mother's name was Sarira, and she was a harlot. Consequently, no mention is made of his father's name. Solomon had made him overseer of the *corvée* of the house of Joseph. He built a city called Sarira on Mount Ephraim. He had three hundred chariots. Using the levies of Ephraim, he built the Akra and enclosed the city of David. Then he rebelled against Solomon, wishing to become king himself. Solomon therefore attempted to kill him, but he fled to Egypt to the protection of Sousakim (Shishak). There he remained until the death of Solomon. When word reached him that Solomon was dead, he wanted to return home, but Sousakim was unwilling to let him go. Parenthetically we learn that Jeroboam had married the Pharaoh's sister-in-law, who had borne him a son, Abia. Sousakim finally gave him permission to return. He came back to Sarira, where the tribes of Ephraim gathered to him, and there he built a fortress. Then follow the story of the sickness of his son, the prophecy of Ahijah, and the death of the child (cf. I Kings 14:1-18). After this Jeroboam came to Shechem, where he gathered the tribes together. This is followed by the prophecy of Samaias the Elamite (cf. I Kings 11:29 ff). The rest of the Greek supplement corresponds to the Hebrew text of I Kings 12:1-24.

Of the two accounts the Hebrew is to be preferred. It is more objective and impartial. The Greek account is clearly biased against Jeroboam. He had prophetic backing at first, even though it was later withdrawn. This may be the reason for the insertion of Ahijah's prophecy in I Kings 11:29-39.

When he heard of the death of Solomon, Jeroboam returned from Egypt. The present text of both Kings and Chronicles indicates that on his return he was summoned by the assembly of the N tribes to Shechem (I Kings 12:2-3; II Chr. 10:2-3), and that he took part in the complaint made to King Rehoboam to redress the grievances of the people. It is clear, however, from I Kings 12:20 that Jeroboam was not present at the discussions with the king, Only after Rehoboam had given his answer and the standard of revolt had been raised by the N, was Jeroboam called to the assembly and made king of the ten tribes. He had already demonstrated his ability. As an overseer he was familiar with the dissatisfaction of the people, and he had apparently sided with them against Solomon, who tried to kill him. This man was the people's choice.

A major task faced Jeroboam at the very outset. It was essential to consolidate the kingdom and to counteract the well-established position in which Jerusalem stood both politically and religiously, but actual details of the reign are absent. This may be due to two factors: (*a*) The violence of Shishak's invasion which occurred in the fifth year of King Rehoboam (*ca.* 918). It is now known from archaeological evidence that in this invasion Israel, as well as Judah, was laid waste, although the biblical record speaks only of the invasion of Judah. The young N kingdom, which had not had time to establish itself, fared worse than the S kingdom. Hence actual historical data of the period are missing. (*b*) Despite the evidence of I Kings 12:21-24; II Chr. 11:1-4, the historicity of which is questionable, it is extremely probable that Jeroboam was engaged in border warfare with Judah throughout his reign (I Kings 15:6; II Chr. 12:15*b;* cf. also I Kings 13:3-20). This may have engaged much of his attention.

Jeroboam fortified ("built") Shechem (I Kings 12: 25)—this has been confirmed by archaeology—and made it his capital. The cryptic statement that follows: "He went out from there and built Penuel," may indicate that he established a new capital there. This, however, appears unlikely. It is more probable that he established a strong point on the other side of the Jordan at Penuel on the Jabbok River, so as to be able to command the trade routes over the Jordan. He later moved to a new capital, Tirzah (14: 17), the modern Tell el-Far'ah, although this is not stated directly. Nor is any reason given for the change. From the military point of view, however, Shechem could have been defended only with difficulty.

Later Judean prejudice has colored the account of Jeroboam's so-called religious innovations to such an extent that it is difficult to assess their true value. Cf. the formula used by the Deuteronomist in passing judgment on most of the kings of the N kingdom: "He walked in the way of Jeroboam the son of Nebat, who made Israel to sin." Our sources consist of a late tradition (I Kings 12:26-31), and two stories which come from a prophetic source (I Kings 12:32–13:32; 14:1-18). Jeroboam would not have dared to substitute the worship of any other God in place of Yahweh with any hope of success. He therefore proceeded to reorganize the Yahweh cult on the basis of old traditions which were characteristic of the N tribes. For this purpose he chose two sites—Dan, in the far N, and Bethel. Bethel had been the scene of a theophany to Jacob (Gen. 28:10 ff), and Dan claimed connection with the family of Moses (Judg. 18:30). Further, tradition affirmed that the golden bull calf had been introduced into the Israelite cult by Aaron while Moses was still alive (Exod. 32). What Jeroboam did was to alter, not the worship of Yahweh, but the symbolism of the cult. For the cherubim of the S, which bore the invisible presence of Yahweh, Jeroboam substituted the bull. The change, as was almost inevitable, led to syncretistic worship, and it is questionable that Jeroboam was motivated by a real religious concern. Rather, political expediency dominated his action.

It is further stated that he made houses on high places (I Kings 12:31), but it is to be noted that removal of these is not attributed either to David or to Solomon. From the point of view of the temple priesthood in Jerusalem, he was guilty of an unpardonable crime in appointing non-Levitical priests to have charge of the cult (II Chr. 11:13-15; 13:9). Not only this, but he dared to burn incense himself—this was the prerogative of the priests—and he appointed a feast in the eighth month, similar to the feast held in Judah in the seventh month. It is probable that Jeroboam is here in line with the old Israelite practice, and that originally the feast was celebrated in the eighth month. Only later, with the change of calendar, did it come to fall in the seventh month.

The story of the nameless man of God (I Kings 13:1 ff) who came from Judah and appeared suddenly at Bethel while Jeroboam was burning incense at the altar, is of doubtful historical value. On the contrary, 14:1-18, which tells of the sickness of Jeroboam's son Abijah, of the visit of his mother in disguise to the prophet Ahijah, of his prediction of Abijah's death on her return home, and of the doom of Jeroboam's house, probably contains factual data. The parallel in the Greek in 12:24 g-n is to be noted, but the present Hebrew version is to be accepted. It gives a consistent picture. The movement which began under prophetic auspices and with prophetic backing ended in failure. Jeroboam proved unequal to the situation.

I Kings 14:19 refers to the "Book of the Chronicles of the kings of Israel" for the record of the wars of Jeroboam; but apart from the general statement (I Kings 14:30) that there was continual war between Rehoboam and Jeroboam, no details of specific battles are given. That the statement gives a true picture of existing conditions is, however, not to be doubted. II Chr. 13:3-19 purports to give details of one such battle between Abijah, Rehoboam's son, and Jeroboam which resulted in a great victory for the S kingdom. There is no reason to question the historicity of the battle which took place near Mount Zemaraim, in the neighborhood of Bethel in the hill country of Ephraim (II Chr. 13:4). The result was noteworthy. The Israelites fled before the men of Judah, and Abijah's forces took Bethel, Jeshanah, and Ephron, each with its villages (vs. 19). Jeshanah and Ephron both lay NE of Bethel. This warfare involved the border territory for the most part, as was only to be expected. That this territory frequently changed hands is evident from the story in I Kings 15:16. The details of the battle of Mount Zemaraim given by the Chronicler are historically unreliable. His account is colored by his theological viewpoint. The probability is that Abijah had made a covenant with the king of Syria, as is actually stated in I Kings 15:19; II Chr. 16:3. The Chronicler hints at an unusual kind of death for Jeroboam (II Chr. 13:20), but it is more likely that he died peacefully (I Kings 14: 20).

It is difficult to define precisely the line of demarcation which separated the two kingdoms. It appears probable that the territory of Benjamin was joined to Judah, although the N kingdom did not give up its claim to this territory without a struggle. The border seems to have passed through the territory formerly occupied by the Danites (cf. the mention of Zorah and Aijalon in the list of cities fortified by Rehoboam; II Chr. 11:10).

Bibliography. J. Skinner, *Kings,* Century Bible (*ca.* 1893), pp. 443 ff. J. Morgenstern, "Three Calendars of Ancient Israel," *HUCA,* I (1924), 67 ff. W. F. Albright, "Archaeological and Topographical Explorations in Palestine and Syria," *BASOR,* 49 (1933), 26 ff; *From the Stone Age to Christianity*

(1940), pp. 228 ff; "The Chronology of the Divided Monarchy," *BASOR,* 100 (1945), 16-22. T. J. Meek, *Hebrew Origins* (1950), pp. 160 ff. J. A. Montgomery, *The Book of Kings,* ICC (1951), pp. 242-67. E. R. Thiele, *The Mysterious Numbers of the Hebrew Kings* (1951), pp. 55 ff. W. F. Albright, "New Light from Egypt on the Chronology and History of Israel and Judah," *BASOR,* 130 (1953), 4-8. W. Harrelson, B. W. Anderson, and G. E. Wright, "Shechem, the 'Navel of the Land,'" *BA,* XX (1957), 2-32.

2. King of Israel *ca.* 786-746 B.C.; son and successor of Joash.

Jeroboam reigned for forty-one years (II Kings 14:23). The book of Kings furnishes but scant information about his achievements, but it is clear that under him the N kingdom attained a prosperity such as it had not known before. *See* AMOS; HOSEA.

The summary of the reign in II Kings 14:28 tells of all that Jeroboam did, "and his might, how he fought, and how he recovered for Israel Damascus and Hamath, which had belonged to Judah." The MT reads: "and how he recovered Damascus and Hamath for Judah in Israel." Perhaps two items have been telescoped here. The only word of the second that has survived is ליהודה ("to Judah"), which has been misplaced in the present text. The verse records an Israelite expansion to the N, involving Damascus and Hamath, and a further expansion to the S, involving Judah. This would seem to be borne out by the general statement that "he restored the border of Israel from the entrance of Hamath as far as the Sea of the Arabah" (vs. 25). These two terms expressed the N and S boundaries of Israel ideally (cf. Amos 6:14). An oracle to this effect had been given by the prophet Jonah the son of Amittai, who belonged to Gath-hepher (II Kings 14:25). To this prophet was assigned the later prophetic book which bears his name. He was clearly an intense nationalist, and as such stands over against his contemporaries Amos and Hosea (cf. Amos 6:13-14).

Details of Jeroboam's campaigns are almost entirely lacking. Amos has a reference to the conquest of Lo-debar and Karnaim (6:13) in Gilead.

The international situation was particularly favorable to Israel. Assyria was weak and managed to retain only a measure of control in the W by a series of campaigns against Damascus and Hamath. The Eponym Canon lists five such campaigns. In addition Damascus and Hamath vied bitterly with each other for mastery in Syria. Against this background Jeroboam's successes against both Hamath and Damascus are to be understood.

While the cult of Yahweh flourished as never before, Baalism still prevailed among a large number of the people. The Samaria Ostraca (*ca.* 778-770) indicate a large number of personal names formed with "Baal." According to Amos, everything in the land was crooked (8:7-9). A great gulf separated the rich and the poor. Trade was good; architecture and the arts flourished; but fundamentally the revival was unsound and could not last.

Bibliography. A Alt, Die syrische Staatenwelt vor dem Einbruch der Assyrer, *ZDMG,* 88 (1934), 233-58; F.-M. Abel, *Géographie de la Palestine,* II (1938), 341-42; E. R. Thiele, *The Mysterious Numbers of the Hebrew Kings* (1951), pp. 288 ff; J. B. Pritchard, ed., *ANET* (2nd ed., 1955), p. 321; M. Noth, *Geschichte Israels* (3rd ed., 1956), pp. 227-28; G. E. Wright, *Biblical Archaeology* (1957), pp. 157-60. H. B. MACLEAN

JEROHAM jĭ rō'hăm [ירחם, *perhaps* soft *or* delicate; *see bibliography*]. **1.** An Ephraimite, and the father or ancestor of Elkanah the father of Samuel (I Sam. 1:1). The Chronicler represents him as a Levite (I Chr. 6:27, 34).

2. A Benjaminite of Gedor (locality uncertain); father or ancestor of two of the men who joined David's forces at Ziklag (I Chr. 12:7); possibly related to 6 *below.*

3. Father or ancestor of one Azarel who was a chief officer over the tribe of Dan during the reign of King David (I Chr. 27:22).

4. Father or ancestor of a certain Azariah, one of the military officers involved in the uprising against Queen Athaliah which resulted in her execution (II Chr. 23:1).

5. A Benjaminite (I Chr. 8:27); perhaps the same as "Jeremoth" in 8:14, and perhaps identical with 6 *below.*

6. Father or ancestor of a Benjaminite among the residents of postexilic Jerusalem (I Chr. 9:8; absent in the parallel Neh. 11:7).

7. A priest resident in postexilic Jerusalem (I Chr. 9:12; Neh. 11:12).

Bibliography. M. Noth, *Die israelitischen Personennamen* (1928), p. 226. B. T. DAHLBERG

JERUBBAAL jĕr'ə bāl [ירבעל, Baal contends (*if the root of the verb is* ריב); Baal multiplies (*if the root is* רבב)]. The name given to Gideon when he broke down his father's Baal altar (Judg. 6:32), and thereafter stated to be Gideon's other name (7:1; 8:35) or used in place of "Gideon" (8:29; 9:1-2, 5, 16, 19, 24, 28, 57; I Sam. 12:11). The root meaning of the name expresses the power of Baal either to fight for himself or to make fruitful (*see above;* it is probably not "Baal teaches" or "founds," from the root ירה). As such it could originally have referred to Yahweh as the "Baal" or "lord" who has these qualities. Thus, as some interpret, it could have been Gideon's original name, or, according to others, the name of a person other than Gideon. In the context of Judg. 6:32, however, it seems clearly to be understood as ironically urging the impotent god Baal's defiance of Yahweh's hero. Thus under the anti-Baalism preaching of the prophets the name later was corrupted to Jerubbesheth in order to poke shame upon all Baal-worship and obliterate the Baal element in the word (cf. Ishbosheth for Ishbaal, and Mephibosheth for Meribaal).

Bibliography. J. Pedersen, *Israel: Its Life and Culture,* III-IV (1940), 205; M. Noth, *Die israelitischen Personennamen* (1928), pp. 77, 119-22, 206-7; W. F. Albright, *Archaeology and the Religion of Israel* (1946), p. 112; M. Noth, *History of Israel* (1958), pp. 152-53. C. F. KRAFT

JERUBBESHETH jĭ rŭb'ə shĕth [ירבשת, shame contends, *or* shame multiplies(?)] (II Sam. 11:21). The deformation of the name JERUBBAAL by substituting the word "shame" for the god name "Baal" in order to obliterate the Baal element in the original name (cf. Ishbosheth for Ishbaal, and Mephibosheth for Meribaal). C. F. KRAFT

JERUEL jĭ ro͞o'əl [ירואל, founded by God(?)] (II Chr. 20:16). A wilderness area between Tekoa and

En-gedi; scene of Jehoshaphat's defeat of the Ammonite-Moabite-Meunite coalition. For the name, cf. ירואל, Jeriel and Penuel-Peniel.

JERUSALEM jĭ rōō′sə ləm [ירושלם, foundation of Shalem; Ἱερουσαλήμ, Ἱεροσόλυμα]. The chief city of Palestine. Sacred to Jews and Christians to this day as the "city of the great King," and to Muslims as the third most holy city of Islam, Jerusalem outranks all other cities of the Bible in prominence and wealth of sacred associations. Under one name or another it appears in about two thirds of the books of the OT and about half of the books of the NT. Figs. JER 17-18; Pl. XXIX.

1. Names
2. Situation and general topography
3. Early history
   a. Prehistoric times
   b. The Early and Middle Bronze Ages
   c. Abraham at Jerusalem
   d. The Late Bronze Age
4. The period of conquest and settlement
   a. The conquest and division of the land
   b. The time of the judges
5. The early monarchy
   a. The reign of David
   b. The reign of Solomon
6. The kingdom of Judah
   a. Rehoboam, Asa, and Joash
   b. Amaziah, Uzziah, and Jotham
   c. Ahaz and Hezekiah; Isaiah and Micah
   d. Manasseh and Josiah; Zephaniah
   e. Jehoahaz, Jehoiakim, Jehoiachin, and Zedekiah; Jeremiah
7. The Exile and the Persian period
   a. Sheshbazzar and Zerubbabel
   b. Ezra and Nehemiah
   c. Visions of the future
8. The Greek period
9. The Hasmonean period
10. The early Roman period and the reign of Herod
11. The lifetime of Jesus
12. The apostolic period to the death of Agrippa I
13. From the death of Agrippa I to the fall of Jerusalem

Bibliography

1. Names. The name Jerusalem appears first in Egyptian "Execration Texts" of the nineteenth and eighteenth centuries B.C., in a form equivalent to *Urushalim.* In the Amarna Letters of the fourteenth century (*see* TELL EL-AMARNA) it is written *Urusalim.* Later Assyrian texts have the form *Urusilimmu.* In the Hebrew OT the Masoretic vowel points (*see* MASORA) indicate the pronunciation *yerûšālayim;* in the Aramaic parts of the OT, however, the pronunciation indicated is *yerûšālēm.* The Greek transliteration Ἱερουσαλήμ, used regularly in the LXX and often in the NT, follows the Aramaic pronunciation.

The meaning of the name is undoubtedly "foundation of Shalem." The traditional interpretation, "city of peace," is as inaccurate etymologically as it is inappropriate historically. The root *yrh* is used in Job 38:6 in the sense of "laying" a cornerstone; it appears also in other names (*see* JERUEL; JERIEL; JERIAH).

17. Jerusalem as seen from the Mount of Olives

Courtesy of the Arab Information Center, New York

18. Air view of Jerusalem, showing the Dome of the Rock Mosque to the right in the rectangular square, and the Kidron Valley in the right foreground

Jerusalem was evidently in early times a center of the worship of Shulmanu or SHALEM. In the Amarna Letters the city is apparently called Beth-shalem, the name Jerusalem being applied to the territory of which it is the capital.

The first name under which the city appears in the Bible is Salem, or more exactly Shalem, שלם (*see* § 3*c below*). This is clearly a shortened form, using only the name of the god and omitting the noun *Yeru* ("foundation of") or *Beth* ("house of"). The Egyptian texts mentioned above show that the longer name was older than the time of Abraham. In Ps. 76:2, Salem is used as a poetic name for Jerusalem.

Other names applied to the Holy City will be discussed in connection with the passages where they first appear. They include Moriah (*see* MORIAH 2; *cf.* § 3*c below*); JEBUS (*cf.* § 4*b below*); ZION (*cf.* § 5*a below*); City of David (*see* DAVID, CITY OF; *cf.* § 5*a below*); and Ariel (*see* ARIEL 2).

2. Situation and general topography. Jerusalem is located at approximately 31 degrees N latitude and 35 degrees E longitude. It lies on the central plateau at an altitude of *ca.* 2,500 feet above sea level. Its location makes it a natural center of the country, both commercially and politically. The main route between Shechem on the N and Hebron on the S meets here the road from Jericho and the Jordan Valley on the E and several converging routes from the Mediterranean on the W.

This is not the highest point in the country or even in the immediate vicinity. A traveler from any direction cannot see the city until he has crossed the hills "round about Jerusalem" (Ps. 125:2). This is especially true of the site of the earliest city, which was on the lowest of the hills occupied by Jerusalem in later centuries. Now outside the city altogether, this

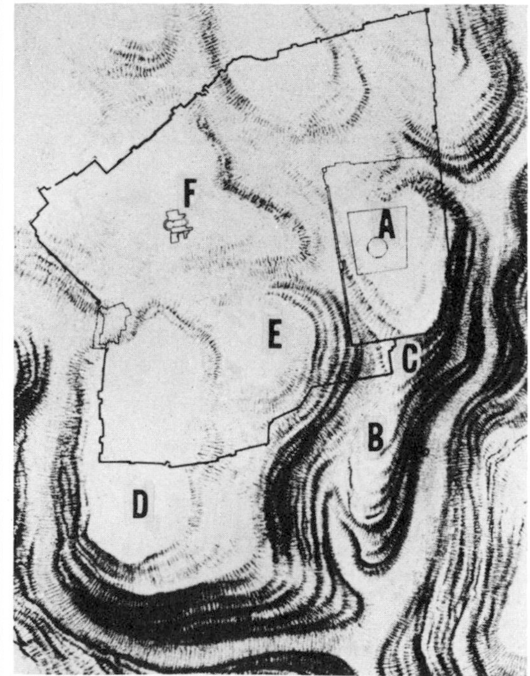

Millar Burrows

MAP I. Relief map of Jerusalem

hill is at the SE corner of the group of hills. All the subsequent expansion has been to the N and the W.

The principal features of the site can still be discerned, though at many points they have been greatly altered by natural erosion and even more by the hand of man, cutting and filling in, destroying and

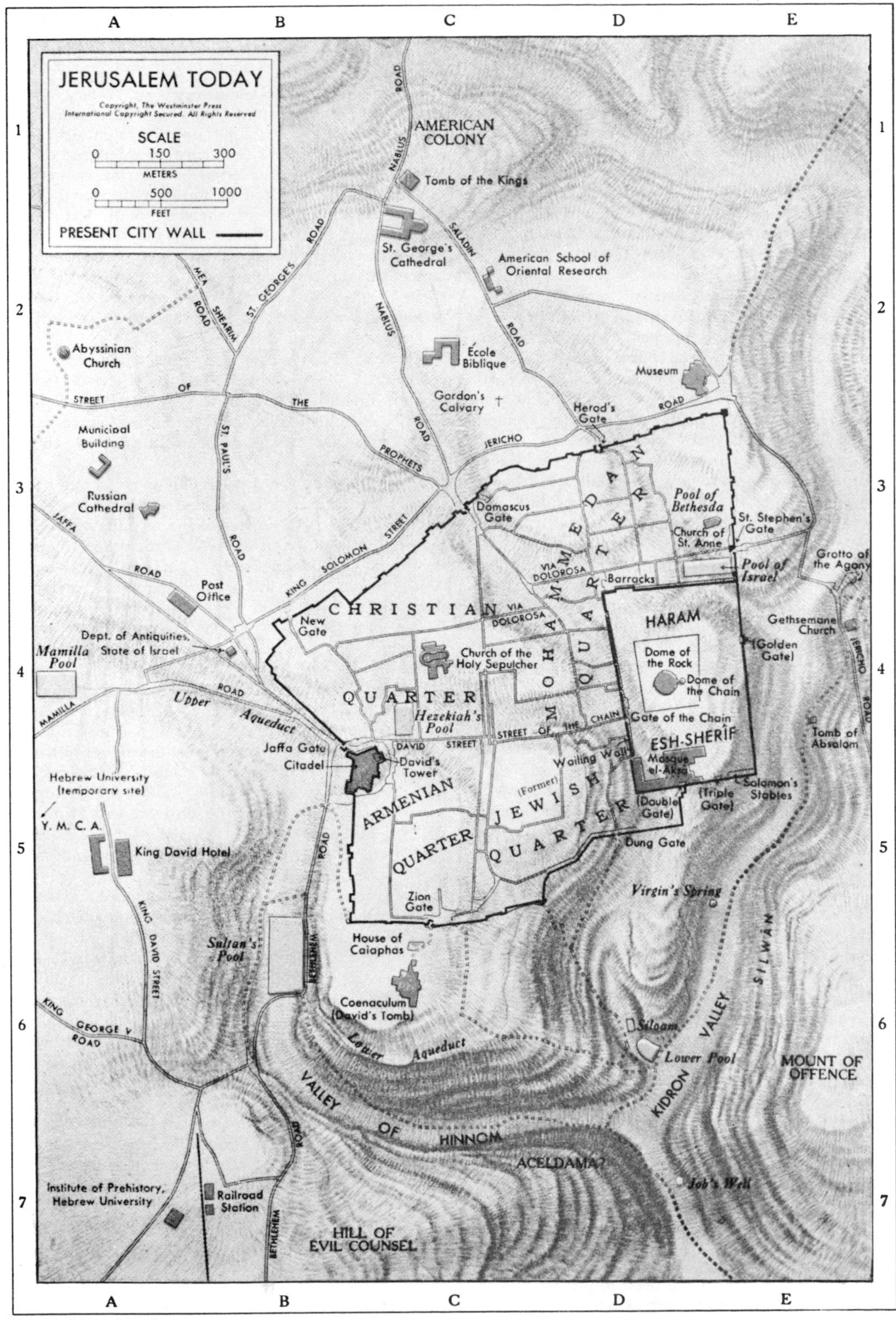

Courtesy of Westminster Press

19. Plan of Jerusalem today

rebuilding. The valleys, which were once deep ravines, have so filled with sediment and debris that in some places, especially where they pass through the city, they are now only slight depressions. Fig. JER 19.

A glance at Map I will give a better idea of the site than any description. The black lines mark the course of the sixteenth-century Turkish walls, enclosing what is now called the Old City. It will be seen that except on the N the city is surrounded by valleys. On the W and the S is the Valley of Hinnom or of the son of Hinnom (*see* HINNOM, VALLEY OF). On the E is the Kidron Valley (*see* KIDRON, BROOK).* Running through the city from N to S and dividing it into two very unequal parts is a central valley not named in the Bible but known in Roman times as the Tyropoeon, or Cheesemakers', Valley. Pl. XXV*a*.

There are three different Hebrew words for VALLEY. The Kidron is always designated as a *naḥal,* translated "brook," "torrent," or "ravine." The general word for "valley," *gē'*, is applied to the Hinnom Valley. The third word, *'ēmeq,* is used for such a relatively broad, level valley or plain as the Valley of Rephaim (*see* § 3*a below*), the Valley of Shaveh (*see* § 3*c below*), or the King's Valley (*see* § 5*a below*); in Jer. 31:40—H 31:39 it is used for the "valley of the dead bodies and the ashes" (*see* § 6*e below*).

The hill to the E of the central valley is highest and broadest at its N end (A), which is the Temple Mount (*see* TEMPLE). The long, narrow, relatively low S end of the E hill (B) is the site of the ancient City of David (*see* § 5*a below*). Between these two, above the narrowest part of the hill, is the part (C) called OPHEL.

The higher and much larger hill (D) on the W side of the central valley is cut off on the N by a smaller valley, which runs from W to E into the central valley, just below the site of the temple. Its course is followed by what modern visitors know as David Street. At the NE corner of this hill a knob or promontory (E) projects into the central valley. To the N and W of the two valleys is the hill on which stands the Church of the Holy Sepulchre (F; *see* § 11 *below*). To the NW and beyond the present walls the ground continues to rise to the modern Russian Compound.

The first settlement was located on the low, narrow SE hill because only there was a convenient supply of water available. At the bottom of the hill on the W edge of the Kidron Valley is an intermittent spring now called Umm ed-Daraj ("Mother of Steps"), 'Ain Sitti Miryam (the "Spring of My Lady Mary"), or the Virgin's Spring. In the Bible its name is GIHON. Another spring, EN-ROGEL,* is the present-day "Job's Well." It is *ca.* 250 yards to the S of the southernmost tip of the hill. The location of the JACKAL'S WELL, mentioned by Nehemiah, is uncertain (*see* § 7*b below*). It is clear in any case that the ancient city depended upon Gihon for water. *See* §§ 3*d,* 6*c below.* Fig. ENR 29.

3. Early history. ***a. Prehistoric times.*** In the Valley of Rephaim (*see* REPHAIM, VALLEY OF), to the W and SW of Jerusalem, have been found Paleolithic and Mesolithic flints like those associated elsewhere with the *Paleoanthropus Palestinensis* (*see* PREHISTORY). At Jerusalem itself pottery from the fourth millennium B.C. has been excavated. Apparently during the last part of that millennium the SE hill (B) was occupied by a people, probably Semites, who used pottery and metal.

b. The Early and Middle Bronze Ages. Pottery of the Early and Middle Bronze Ages (*see* ARCHAEOLOGY; POTTERY; *also* Fig. POT 63, nos. 3-4) demonstrates the occupation of the site during the third and early second millenniums, preceding and during the period of the HYKSOS. Judged by modern standards, the walled city of this period was very small, occupying only between eight and nine acres, but Jericho at that time was even smaller, and Shechem was not much larger. At the upper end, a little to the N of the spring, there was a sanctuary; the royal palace and cemetery lay below this, and the rest of the hill to its S tip was occupied by the city.

Remains of Early Bronze Age walls have been discovered on this part of the hill. By the end of that period, indeed, or early in the Middle Bronze Age, the city evidently expanded to the N, for traces of walls from that time have been found along the E side of Ophel (C).

The W wall of the pre-Israelite city has not been traced, but a large gate uncovered near what must have been the NW corner of the city may indicate the original position of the wall at this point, though the actual remains probably come from a later time. At the S end of the hill a stone stairway cut out of the rock has been excavated. There are indications that it may go back to the earliest period of settlement, possibly before any wall and gate were built here.

c. Abraham at Jerusalem. The incidents related in Gen. 14 took place during the Middle Bronze Age. The city here called SALEM was undoubtedly Jerusalem (*see* § 1 *above*). The Valley of Shaveh, identified for ancient readers as the King's Valley (vs. 17; *see* SHAVEH, VALLEY OF), may have been the open space at the juncture of the Kidron and Hinnom valleys; but the fact that it was the king of Sodom who met Abram there suggests that this place was down in the Jordan Valley.

The second time that Abraham came, or may have come, to Jerusalem was the occasion of the offering of Isaac (Gen. 22:1-19). The place is indicated only as "one of the mountains" in the "land of MORIAH," but in II Chr. 3:1 the place where Solomon built the temple is called Mount Moriah. Coming up from Beer-sheba, Abraham might well reach Jerusalem on the third day; he would not be able to see it from a great distance, but the phrase "afar off" need not imply this (vs. 4). The name Moriah is itself subject to some suspicion. The LXX reads "the high land"; the Syr. reads "the Amorite land," which may be correct. By the time II Chr. 3:1 was written, however, it was believed that the temple hill was the place where Isaac had almost been sacrificed.

After the marvelous deliverance of his son, Abraham named the place "The LORD will provide" (*see* JEHOVAH-JIREH). As the marginal notes of the RSV indicate, neither the name nor its context is at all clear. Apparently this name was never in common use for Jerusalem.

d. The Late Bronze Age. In the fifteenth century B.C. or thereabouts the Hurrians or HORITES came

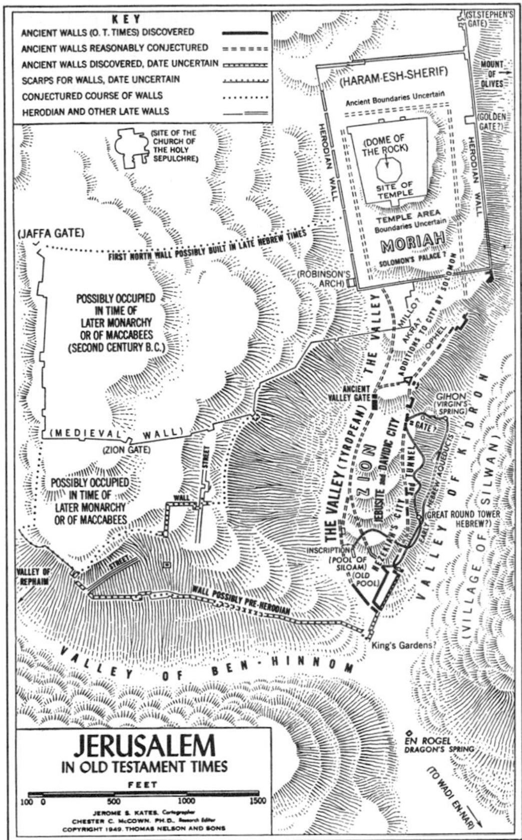

into Palestine. One of the writers of the Amarna Letters (*see* TELL EL-AMARNA) was *'Abd-Ḫiba* or *Arti-Ḫepa*, probably a Hurrian, who reigned at Jerusalem in the fourteenth century as a vassal of Egypt. The Hurrians introduced at Jerusalem, as elsewhere, improved methods of fortification. A strong masonry rampart which has been excavated on the E slope of Ophel (C) comes from this period. A later tower inserted in the rampart obscures its original form, but there are two curving sections, between which there was probably a gate. Farther S, at the end of the hill, have been found several lines of wall, one above another, which probably supported the successive stages of a similar rampart. The rulers of the city undertook also to ensure their water supply. At about the beginning of the Late Bronze Age several shafts and tunnels were cut in the solid rock above Gihon, affording access to the spring from inside the city.

4. The period of conquest and settlement. ***a. The conquest and division of the land.*** The capture of Ai and the submission of Gibeon so alarmed the king of Jerusalem, ADONI-ZEDEK, that he formed a coalition with four other kings and attacked Gibeon (Josh. 10:1-5). Joshua promptly and decisively crushed the coalition, and Adoni-zedek perished with his allies, but Jerusalem was not taken (vss. 6-43).

The city appears again in the description of the boundaries of Judah and Benjamin (Josh. 15:7-8; 18:16; *see* TRIBES, TERRITORIES OF). The points named in the boundary of Judah appear in the opposite order in the boundary of Benjamin. Coming up from the Jordan Valley, the line reaches En-rogel; thence it "goes up by the valley of the son of Hinnom at the southern shoulder of the Jebusite" (or more literally "to the shoulder of the Jebusite on the south") and on "up to the top of the mountain that lies over against the valley of Hinnom, on the west, at the northern end of the valley of Rephaim." All these points we have met before (*see* § 2 *above*), except the "shoulder of the Jebusite," of which 15:8 adds: "that is, Jerusalem."

That the Jebusites were the pre-Israelite inhabitants of Jerusalem is evident from many references (*see* JEBUS). The identification of the "shoulder of the Jebusite" with Jerusalem, however, raises questions, because proceeding from En-rogel, one turns W into the Valley of Hinnom before reaching the SE hill (B), which was the Jerusalem of Joshua's time. The "shoulder" must be the SW hill (D). It was doubtless held by the Jebusites and therefore may have been known by this name, even though it was outside the walled city. Later, when the explanation "that is, Jerusalem," was written, the city had spread over to the W hill. An alternative explanation is that the name Valley of Hinnom meant originally the central valley, the Tyropoeon (*see* § 2 *above*); but while this disposes of some difficulties, it raises others which make it unacceptable.

Judg. 1:1-8 reports that Judah and Simeon defeated and cruelly mutilated Adoni-bezek (*see above*), and that Judah captured Jerusalem, slaughtered the inhabitants, and burned the city. Apparently, however, the Jebusites soon reoccupied and rebuilt it. According to Josh. 15:63, "the Jebusites dwell with the people of Judah at Jerusalem to this day." Judg. 1:21 makes the same statement concerning the tribe of Benjamin.

b. The time of the judges. In Judg. 19:10-12 it is said that on the way back from Bethlehem the Levite and his concubine arrived at nightfall "opposite Jebus (that is, Jerusalem)." The Levite's servant proposed that they "turn aside to this city of the Jebusites," but the Levite refused to "turn aside into the city of foreigners." Just where the road was that brought the travelers "opposite" or "near" the city, yet would have required them to "turn aside" to enter it, we cannot tell. Possibly it was on the W side of the W hill.

The name Jebus occurs elsewhere only in I Chr. 11:4, which says that David and his followers "went to Jerusalem, that is Jebus, where the Jebusites were." The parallel in II Sam. 5:6 (*see* § 5*a below*) does not use this name. It is clearly not an older name than Jerusalem (*see* § 1 *above*). Perhaps it was used by the Hebrews to designate the city of the Jebusites.

5. The early monarchy. ***a. The reign of David.*** The account of the capture of Jerusalem by David in II Sam. 5:6-9 is obscure, and the text is undoubtedly corrupt. The parallel in I Chr. 11:4-8 does not resolve the difficulties. Without attempting to explain the references to the blind and the lame, which the Chronicler omits, we note first that "David took the stronghold of Zion, that is, the city of David." Here we first encounter the name ZION.

Was the "stronghold of Zion" the same as Jerusalem? The word "stronghold" would suggest a fortress or a fortified part of the city, but this would hardly be called the "city of David." Possibly "Jerusalem" had then a somewhat wider connotation than "Zion," but this is uncertain. The name Zion was applied in later times to the temple hill; still later tradition transferred it to the SW hill.

David's statement: "Whoever would smite the Jebusites, let him get up the water shaft" (II Sam. 5: 8), becomes in I Chr. 11:6: "Whoever shall smite the Jebusites first shall be chief and commander." The KJV borrows the last clause from I Chronicles to complete the sentence in II Samuel. The original text probably read something like this: "Whoever reaches the water shaft first and smites the Jebusites and the lame and blind, who are hated by David's soul, shall be chief and commander." The word translated "water shaft" appears elsewhere only in Ps. 42:7, where it means "cataracts" (KJV "waterspouts"). In II Sam. 5:8 it may mean the rock-cut shaft already mentioned (*see* § 3*d above*), by which access was afforded to the spring from within the city. Many, therefore, suppose that Joab climbed up this shaft and took the Jebusites by surprise. The verb here used, however, does not mean "get up" (RSV) but "touch" or "reach" (KJV "get up to"). What David challenged his men to accomplish was to fight their way up to the opening of the shaft and so cut off the Jebusites from their water supply.

Courtesy of Herbert G. May

20. Walls excavated on the SE hill of Jerusalem, part of which has been ascribed by some archaeologists as built in the time of David

David now made the stronghold his own dwelling place and "built the city round about from the Millo inward" (vs. 9). The term MILLO occurs again later (*see* §§ 5*b*, 6*a*, *c below*). Literally it means "filling," and it probably designates a place where a depression, a ditch, or a breach in the wall was filled in, but what or where this was we can only guess. On the W side of the E hill just to the S of the temple area, where the hill was originally very narrow, an accumulation of debris has filled in the curve of the valley and widened the hill. If this was the Millo, II Sam. 5:9 means that David's building extended to the S from this area. Portions of walls excavated on the SE hill have been attributed by archaeologists to David, but none can be dated with certainty in his time. Fig. JER 20.

The selection of Jerusalem as the royal capital was a step of great historic importance. Belonging to neither the N nor the S tribes, it facilitated the unification of the kingdom. It constituted also a personal domain for David and his descendants and so promoted the establishment of a long-lasting hereditary dynasty. David also made Jerusalem the religious capital of the nation by bringing the sacred ark to the city and setting up a tent for it, presumably near the palace (II Sam. 6). After building his own palace, David aspired to build a house for God too, but was not allowed to do so (II Sam. 7).

Where David's house was built (II Sam. 5:11) we cannot tell. A reference to it in Neh. 12:37 (*see* § 7*b below*) suggests that it was near the S end of the hill and on the E side. It was, no doubt, from a window of this house that Michal looked with disgust at her husband's undignified behavior when the ark was brought into the city (II Sam. 6:16, 20-23). From the roof of this house David saw Bathsheba bathing (11: 1-5). Here Uriah was brought before the king, and here he "slept at the door of the king's house" (vss. 6-13). Here David made Bathsheba his wife after having Uriah killed (vss. 14-27), and no doubt it was here that Nathan denounced his sin and brought him to repentance (ch. 12). In this house Absalom for a while supplanted his father (15:16, 35), until David was brought back after Absalom's death (19:11; 20:3).

Absalom's own house is mentioned (II Sam. 14:24, 31). We read also that he set up a monument for himself in the King's Valley (18:18). This may be the place mentioned in Gen. 14:17 (*see* § 3*c above*), but neither reference gives any clue to its location. It may have been in the space at the confluence of the Kidron, the Tyropoeon, and the Hinnom valleys. The word rendered "valley" in this case, however, suggests an even broader area. *See* VALLEY; *see also* § 2 *above*.

Fleeing from Jerusalem at the time of Absalom's revolt, David crossed the brook Kidron (*see* § 2 *above*) and "went up the ascent of the Mount of Olives" (15: 23, 30; *see* OLIVES, MOUNT OF), passing the "summit, where God was worshiped" (15:32; 16:1), and so going down to the Jordan Valley. During his absence he was informed of Absalom's doings by his spies, to whom a maidservant brought word while they hid at En-rogel (*see* § 2 *above*), until "a lad saw them, and told Absalom" (17:17-18).

The pathetic closing scenes of David's life (I Kings 1 ff) took place, no doubt, in the palace that Hiram's men had built for him (*see above*). When he died, he "was buried in the city of David" (2:10). Neh. 3:16 (*see* § 7*b below*) indicates that the "sepulchres of David" were near the S end of the SE hill on its E side. Remains of ancient tombs excavated in this area may indicate the place. The traditional site on the SW hill has no claim to authenticity; in David's time that hill was not "in the city of David." *See* TOMBS OF THE KINGS.

b. The reign of Solomon. When Adonijah attempted to seize the throne, he offered sacrifices "by the SERPENT'S STONE, which is beside En-rogel"* (I Kings 1:9). Aside from its being "beside En-rogel" (*see* §§ 2, 4*a*, 5*a above*), its location is unknown. Prompt action by Nathan led to the anointing of Solomon at Gihon (1:38-40; *see* § 2 *above*). Adonijah sought sanctuary at the altar (vs. 50). This was in the tent David had set up for the ark (*see* § 5*a above*), as is stated in connection with Joab's vain attempt to escape Solomon's wrath (2:28-34). Fig. ENR 29.

Solomon's most important act was undoubtedly

the building of the TEMPLE; it was only one, however, of his many building enterprises. In addition to the "house of the LORD" and "his own house," he built the "wall around Jerusalem" (I Kings 3:1; 9:15), not to mention many buildings at other places. The building of the temple required an extension of the city's walls to enclose and protect the holy precincts. From the NE corner of David's city the wall was carried to the N above the Kidron Valley. Its foundation was set in the rock nearly a hundred feet below the level of the ground at the bottom of the modern wall. About where the Golden Gate now stands, the wall turned and followed to the NW the S edge of a small valley now covered by the N part of the sacred area. After crossing the crest of the hill, it turned again to the left and proceeded southward, perhaps a little to the E of the present wall.

The SW corner of the present *ḥaram* or sacred enclosure juts out into the Tyropoeon Valley, which originally curved to the E near the position of the "Wailing Wall." Solomon's wall may have followed the valley to the SE until it reached the NW corner of the City of David; from this point it could follow the old wall of the SE hill. Whether it did so cannot be determined without our knowing whether Solomon enclosed the SW hill. This question cannot be answered at present.

Involved with it is the identification of "the Millo" which Solomon built (I Kings 9:15, 24; 11:27). The previous mention of the Millo in the story of David (*see* § 5*a above*) implies only that the place referred to was known by that name in the writer's time. The statements in I Kings 9; 11 may mean that Solomon merely rebuilt something which already existed, but they suggest that it was a new structure. In 11:27 it is connected with closing the "breach of the city of David." We do not know where or what this breach was. The word translated "breach" must mean here, as elsewhere (e.g., Neh. 6:1), a break in the city's fortifications, but what was built to fill this breach must have been something rather imposing to be included in the lists of Solomon's major achievements and to bear a special name for centuries. *See* §§ 6*a-c below*.

In Eccl. 2:6 the "Preacher, the son of David, king in Jerusalem," says that he made pools for irrigating his trees. This no doubt reflects a tradition that Solomon made some provision for Jerusalem's water supply. One of a series of ancient rock-cut channels, which led the overflow from Gihon to the lower end of the SE hill and the valleys below it, is plausibly attributed by archaeologists to Solomon. Just above the strong ancient wall across the mouth of the Tyropoeon Valley there is an older and lighter wall which seems to have been built to form a pool for the water from this channel; it may have been the work of Solomon (*see* SILOAM; *also* Fig. SIL 60). Both walls, however, may be later (*see* § 6 *below*). A similar channel, made to bring water to Jerusalem from what are traditionally known as Solomon's Pools, near Bethlehem, may go back in its earliest form to Solomon. *See* POOL.

Within the city there were other works of the royal builder. Along with the temple and the city wall "his own house" is mentioned (I Kings 3:1; 7:1, 8; 9:1, 15; *see* PALACE). With this are named also the HOUSE OF THE FOREST OF LEBANON, the Hall of Pillars, and the Hall of the Throne or Hall of Judgment, with incidental mention of the "great court" and the "other court back of the hall" (7:2-12; *see* HALL 2). There are references also to a house built by Solomon for his Egyptian wife (I Kings 7:8; 9:24). This great complex of buildings evidently lay in the area between the City of David and the temple. Figs. JER 17; HOU 32-33.

Less to his credit are the pagan altars which Solomon built for his foreign wives. Where these were located we are not told, except that the high place for Chemosh and Moab was "on the mountain east of Jerusalem," which was no doubt the southernmost summit of the Mount of Olives, now known as the Mount of Offense (I Kings 11:7-8). In spite of this apostasy, Solomon was buried in the City of David when he died (11:43).

6. The kingdom of Judah. Too many events at Jerusalem are recorded to be noted here. From here on, only events especially affecting the city itself and references to particular buildings or parts of the city will be considered.

a. Rehoboam, Asa, and Joash. In the reign of Rehoboam, the Egyptian king Shishak attacked Jerusalem and plundered both the temple and the palace (I Kings 14:25-26). Rehoboam and most of his successors continued to be buried in the City of David (14:31; 15:8; etc.). Asa, the third after Solomon, deposed his mother, who "had an abominable image made for Asherah," from the rank of queen mother, and the image was burned in the Kidron Valley (I Kings 15:13).

The next event involving topographical details at Jerusalem is the accession of Joash (II Kings 11). The young prince was crowned in the temple, after guards had been posted at the palace, at the "gate Sur" (*see* GATE; SUR), and at the "gate behind the guards" (vss. 5-6). Neither of these gates can be located. Presumably the "gate behind the guards" was the same as the "gate of the guards" (vs. 19), through which the new king was taken to his palace; it was therefore between the temple and the palace. In II Chr. 23:20 it is called the "upper gate" (*see* § 6*b below*). The gate Sur is called in II Chr. 23:5 the "Gate of the Foundation"; either name could be derived by a scribal error from the other.

When Athaliah came on the scene, she was seized by the guards and taken "through the horses' entrance to the king's house" (II Kings 11:16; cf. II Chr. 23:15: "into the entrance of the horse gate of the king's house"), where she was killed. The HORSE GATE appears again in Neh. 3:28; Jer. 31:40, both of which indicate a position on the E side of the hill, near the Kidron Valley. Since it obviously led from the temple to the palace, it must have been near the SE corner of the temple enclosure, not far from the city wall but probably not a part of it (*see* §§ 6*e*, 7*a-b below*).

Following the coronation of Joash, the temple of Baal was destroyed. Where this was is not indicated. Joash also repaired the temple. *See* TEMPLE, JERUSALEM, § A1*d*.

At about this time Jerusalem was threatened by Hazael, king of Syria. Joash bought security at the cost of all the treasures of the temple and the palace

(II Kings 12:17-18). According to the Chronicler, Jerusalem was attacked by the Syrians, and Joash was wounded (II Chr. 24:17-24). II Kings 12:20; II Chr. 24:25 agree that the servants of Joash conspired against him and killed him; the Chronicler, however, says that he was killed in his bed, while the account in Kings says that he was killed "in the house of Millo, on the way that goes down to Silla." Where Silla was is unknown; the "house of Millo" may or may not be the same Millo that was built by Solomon (*see* § 5*b above*). Like his predecessor, Joash was buried in the City of David (II Kings 12:21); the Chronicler adds, however, "but they did not bury him in the tombs of the kings" (II Chr. 24:25).

b. Amaziah, Uzziah, and Jotham. Amaziah, the successor of Joash, was defeated by Jehoash of Israel and taken captive at Beth-shemesh. Jehoash thereupon "came to Jerusalem, and broke down the wall of Jerusalem for four hundred cubits, from the Ephraim Gate to the Corner Gate" (II Kings 14:8-13). Other references to these two gates indicate their general position. *See* §§ 6*e*, 7*b below.*

The name of the Ephraim Gate suggests that a road to the N passed through it. When only the SE hill was occupied, a gate opening on the central valley would fulfil this purpose; by the time of Amaziah, however, the city wall almost certainly enclosed the SW hill also. Vestiges of an ancient wall, perhaps as old as the ninth century B.C., have been discovered, running E and W, a little to the S of the present David Street. At about the intersection of this line and the first street leading N to the Damascus Gate,* the top of a large Roman arch is now visible above ground. The Ephraim Gate of Amaziah's time probably stood at about this place. Fig. GAT 11.

The Corner Gate was then four hundred cubits (two hundred yards) away, probably at the W end of the wall just mentioned. This would put it at about the corner of the square in front of the present Citadel, where David Street begins its descent into the central valley. Because of the higher ground to the N and the W, this stretch of wall would be the most vulnerable in the city's defenses; and while Jehoash, coming from Beth-shemesh, would approach the city from the SW, he might well select this W portion of the N wall for destruction.

Important measures for the fortification of Jerusalem and other places are attributed to Amaziah's son Azariah, called also Uzziah. He "built towers in Jerusalem at the Corner Gate and at the Valley Gate and at the Angle, and fortified them" (II Chr. 26:9). The tower at the Corner Gate would strengthen the wall at a point where it had already been found to need special protection. The Valley Gate is mentioned here for the first time. It was in either the W or the S wall of the city. The SW corner, above the turn of the Valley of Hinnom, seems as likely a place as any. Where the ANGLE was is unknown. The Hebrew word may mean a recessed or inner angle, as distinguished from a projecting corner, but this is not certain. Other passages apply it to points in the city wall (*see* § 7*b below*); whether they refer to the same point mentioned here is not clear.

The only act with which Jotham is credited in II Kings is the building of the "upper gate of the house of the LORD" (15:35; *see* TEMPLE, JERUSALEM, § A1*d*). The Chronicler adds that Jotham "did much building on the wall of Ophel" (II Chr. 27:3).

c. Ahaz and Hezekiah; Isaiah and Micah. The momentous meeting of Ahaz with the prophet Isaiah recorded in Isa. 7 took place "at the end of the conduit of the upper pool on the highway to the FULLER'S FIELD." None of the topographical items here mentioned can be identified now. The "upper pool" has been located by different scholars on the N, E, S, and W sides of the city and even in the central valley. The other points are moved about accordingly. Almost exactly the same description of the place is given later in connection with another incident. *See below.*

The next chapter of Isaiah refers to the "waters of Shiloah that flow gently" (8:6). In the LXX this name takes the form SILOAM, as in the works of Josephus and in the gospels (*see* § 11 *below*). The Hebrew word means something like "conveyer." It would be an appropriate designation for one of the rock-cut channels which brought water from Gihon to and around the S end of the SE hill. Later this name was applied to Hezekiah's tunnel through the hill and the pool into which it emptied (*see below*), but these did not yet exist in the reign of Ahaz. The prophecy in Isa. 8:5-8 seems to reflect the situation after Ahaz had disregarded the warning of ch. 7 and had called Tiglath-pileser to his aid (II Kings 16:7).

In Hezekiah's reign Sennacherib "came up against all the fortified cities of Judah and took them" (II Kings 18:13). Hezekiah paid heavy tribute, despoiling both temple and palace (vss. 14-16), but Jerusalem was still threatened. Now occurred the incident referred to above: emissaries from Sennacherib came to Jerusalem to demand complete submission. "When they arrived, they came and stood by the conduit of the upper pool, which is on the highway to the Fuller's Field" (vs. 17). The conversation which ensued was heard by the people assembled on the wall (vs. 26). Apparently Hezekiah's officials were on the wall, while the Assyrian envoys stood below. Putting together the incidents of II Kings 18; Isa. 7, we learn only that the place described was outside the city wall but near it, on a highway, and beside a conduit which brought water to or from a pool. Fig. HEZ 18.

The term "upper pool" implies the existence of a "lower pool," and this name actually appears in Isa. 22:8-11. Here a king, probably Hezekiah, is said to have "looked to the weapons of the house of the forest" (presumably Solomon's House of the Forest of Lebanon; *see* § 5*b above*), and to have broken down houses "to fortify the wall" of Jerusalem. He is said also to have "collected the waters of the lower pool" and to have "made a reservoir between the walls for the water of the old pool." The old pool seems to be distinguished from the lower pool, although some commentators take vss. 9, 11, as referring to the same enterprise. The reservoir for the water of the old pool was evidently a new receptacle to receive water from that pool; collecting the waters of the lower pool, however, may mean either providing a receptacle for water from the pool or bringing the water together to fill it. The phrase "between the two walls" is intriguing, especially in view of the fact that a "gate between the two walls" near the "king's garden" is mentioned later (*see* § 6*e below*). If the same two walls are meant, a location near the mouth of the central valley is indicated for the reservoir of Isa. 22:11.

Further accounts of Hezekiah's defensive measures help to clarify the picture. II Kings 20:20 says that he "made the pool and the conduit and brought water into the city." II Chr. 32 gives a fuller account. Expecting an attack by Sennacherib, Hezekiah undertook "to stop the water of the springs that were outside the city" (vs. 3). This must mean Gihon in the Kidron Valley, the openings in the irrigation channels leading from it to the lower end of the hill, and En-rogel. The king and his men also "stopped all the springs and the brook that flowed through the land." The "brook" (*naḥal*) is probably the Kidron itself, which is regularly designated by this word. *See* § 2 *above*.

The same chapter says also: "This same Hezekiah closed the upper outlet of the waters of Gihon and directed them down to the west side of the city of David" (II Chr. 32:30). This refers undoubtedly to the "conduit" mentioned in II Kings 20:20, which still exists. It is a tunnel cut through the solid rock, twisting and turning for nearly six hundred yards from the spring to an opening in the central valley near its mouth. Just inside the opening was found in 1880 an inscription, in the alphabet of Hezekiah's time, recording the cutting of the tunnel by two teams who began at the ends and met in the middle. The proud memory of this achievement found expression centuries later in Ecclus. 48:17. *See* SILOAM.

All these facts, taken together, suggest a possible identification of the various pools and the reservoir that have been mentioned. The "reservoir between the two walls for the water of the old pool" was perhaps the pool into which Hezekiah's tunnel emptied, where the Pool of Siloam is now. The "two walls" between which it was made may have been those on both sides of the central valley, one being the ancient wall of the SE hill and the other a later one on the other side of the valley. The new reservoir received the water formerly stored in a pool near the spring in the Kidron Valley, called the "old pool" in Isa. 22:11 and the "upper pool" in II Kings 18:17; Isa. 7:3. The stopping of the "upper outlet of the waters of Gihon" (II Chr. 32:30) made this old upper pool useless. The spot where Isaiah met Ahaz and the Assyrian envoys later threatened Hezekiah was not beside this upper pool in the Kidron Valley, far below the city wall, but at the low S end of the hill, beside the conduit which, before the tunnel was made, brought water to irrigate the gardens in the valley. *See* § 5*b above*.

The lower pool, whose waters Hezekiah collected, was probably in the mouth of the central valley, just above the strong double wall which here crosses the valley and just below the spot where the new reservoir was made somewhat later. At this point there is still an old pool, now filled with earth, called *birkeṭ el-ḥamra*. At some time previous to the cutting of the Siloam tunnel, the conduit mentioned above was diverted and carried around the S end of the hill by a short tunnel, so that the water flowed into the pool in the central valley. Possibly Ahaz was having this done when Isaiah met him, but it is equally possible that Hezekiah had it done early in his reign, before the Assyrian threat had become formidable. Directing the conduit to this pool would then be what is meant by collecting the waters of the lower pool.

One thing seems clear: the central valley was by this time inside the city, and therefore at least some part of the SW hill was now within the walls. II Chr. 32:30 says that Hezekiah directed the waters of Gihon "down to the west side of the city of David"; II Kings 20:20 says that he "brought water into the city." There would have been no point in the elaborate enterprise of the tunnel and the pool if they had only conveyed the water to a place still open to a besieging army; nor would a wall merely enclosing the pool and the outlet of the tunnel have met the demands of the situation.

II Chr. 32:5 goes on to say that Hezekiah "built up all the wall that was broken down, and raised towers upon it, and outside it he built another wall; and he strengthened the Millo in the city of David." What the Millo was we still do not know (*see* § 5*b above*). The word translated "broken down" recalls the action of Jehoash of Israel in II Kings 14:13 (*see* § 6*b above*), but the reference here is probably not to that incident. Hezekiah "saw that the breaches of the city of David were many" and "broke down the houses to fortify the wall" (Isa. 22:9-10).

But what was the other wall which Hezekiah built? Conceivably it was merely one built outside the existing wall to reinforce it; more probably it enclosed a new portion of the expanded city. Not much later we hear of the "SECOND QUARTER" or Mishneh (*see* § 6*d below*). It is commonly supposed that this was an extension of the city to the N, beyond the old N wall. If so, it may also have been the area enclosed by Hezekiah's "other wall."

All Hezekiah's precautions would hardly have availed against a determined Assyrian attack, but at the moment of supreme peril Jerusalem was marvelously delivered (II Kings 19:20-37). Her doom, however, was only postponed. Isaiah's contemporary, Micah, denounced the corruption and oppression practiced by those who would "build Zion with blood and Jerusalem with wrong," and declared that because of them Zion would be "plowed as a field," Jerusalem would "become a heap of ruins," and the "mountain of the house" would become a "wooded height" (Mic. 3:10, 12). Isaiah himself promised Hezekiah only a respite during his own lifetime (II Kings 20:6, 16-19; Isa. 38:5-6; 39:5-8).

According to II Chr. 32:33, Hezekiah was buried "in the ascent of the tombs of the sons of David." One is reminded of the "stairs that go down from the City of David," mentioned in Neh. 3:15 near the "sepulchres of David." *See* § 7*b below*.

d. Manasseh and Josiah; Zephaniah. Very different from Hezekiah was Manasseh. All he is said in II Kings to have built is a succession of pagan places and objects of worship (21:3-5, 7). In addition to his idolatry he "shed very much innocent blood, till he had filled Jerusalem from one end to another" (vs. 16). His wickedness evoked the vivid prophecy that God would "wipe Jerusalem as one wipes a dish, wiping it and turning it upside down" (vs. 13). When Manasseh died, he "was buried in the garden of his house, in the garden of Uzza" (21:18; II Chr. 33:20 says simply "in his house").

The Chronicler adds the story of Manasseh's captivity and repentance, after which he removed all the pagan altars and idols he had set up and "restored the altar of the LORD" (II Chr. 33:15-16). He also "built an outer wall to the city of David west of Gihon, in the valley, to the entrance by the Fish Gate, and carried it round Ophel, and raised it to a very great height" (33:14). Being "west of Gihon, in the valley" (*naḥal*—i.e., the Kidron Valley), Manasseh's outer wall must have been on the E slope of the SE hill, below the older wall of the City of David and above the spring. To the N, Manasseh "carried it round Ophel." If his wall reached "to the entrance by the Fish Gate," it must have continued around the temple area on the E and the N. Obviously the points here mentioned are not given in the order of their location; the reference to Ophel is brought in, so to speak, as an afterthought.

The Fish Gate is here mentioned for the first time. From Neh. 3:3 it is clear that this was a gate in the N wall, about where it crossed the central valley (*see* § 7*b below*). In Zeph. 1:10 the Fish Gate is named along with the Second Quarter (*see below*). It is unlikely that for this whole distance Manasseh's wall ran outside the older wall and parallel to it. II Chr. 33:14 may be translated: "He built an outer wall for the city of David . . . and for the entrance into the Fish Gate; he also carried it around Ophel." If this interpretation is correct, it was only at the points mentioned that the wall was doubled.

Of the brief reign of Amon, who followed Manasseh's bad example, nothing of note for the history of Jerusalem is recorded. He was killed "in his house" and buried "in his tomb in the garden of Uzza" (II Kings 21:23, 26). His son Josiah returned to better ways and destroyed the pagan sanctuaries and idols of his predecessors (II Chr. 34:2 ff). The temple was repaired, and the finding of the Book of the Law led to a drastic reformation (II Kings 22:3-20; 23:1-25; *see* TEMPLE, JERUSALEM, § A1*d*). On hearing the book read, Josiah sent the high priest and his associates to consult the prophetess HULDAH, who "dwelt in Jerusalem in the Second Quarter" (22:14). The SECOND QUARTER, or Mishneh, is mentioned also by Zephaniah, who prophesied during the reign of Josiah (Zeph. 1:1). On the Day of the Lord, he says:

> A cry will be heard from the Fish Gate,
> a wail from the Second Quarter,
> a loud crash from the hills (1:10).

The fact that the Fish Gate and the Second Quarter appear together does not imply that they were in the same part of the city, but it is probable on other grounds that this gate was in the wall which enclosed the Second Quarter, N of the old city wall (*see* § 7*b below*). The wall enclosing the Second Quarter may have been, as we have seen, the "other wall" built by Hezekiah. *See* § 6*c above*.

Zephaniah continues (vs. 11):

> Wail, O inhabitants of the Mortar!
> For all the traders are no more;
> all who weigh out silver are cut off.

The Mortar is not mentioned elsewhere, and nothing can be inferred from this passage except that it was a commercial quarter of the city. The Targ. identifies Zephaniah's Mortar with the Kidron Valley, but modern scholars take it to be the depression between the E and W hills where the central valley is joined by the valley descending from the W. *See* § 2 *above*.

Several places in Jerusalem and its vicinity are named in the account of Josiah's reformation, but most of them cannot now be identified. For the writer's contemporaries the "high places of the gates that were at the entrance of the gate of Joshua the governor of the city, which were on one's left at the gate of the city" (II Kings 23:8), would be quite explicit, but we do not know any of the points mentioned. Equally unknown are the "chamber of Nathan-melech the chamberlain" (vs. 11) and the "upper chamber of Ahaz" (vs. 12). What is meant by the word in vs. 11 translated "precincts" by the RSV (KJV "suburbs") is obscure. The pillar by which the king stood (23:3) was, no doubt, the one mentioned in 11:14. *See* § 6*a above*.

Many of the idolatrous objects removed from the temple and the city were burned and pulverized in the "brook Kidron"—i.e., the Kidron Valley, conveniently near the temple and the palace (*see* § 2 *above*). S of the city, "in the valley of the sons of Hinnom," was TOPHETH, where child-sacrifices by fire were offered (vs. 10). Josiah "defiled" this and also Solomon's "high places that were east of Jerusalem, to the south of the mount of corruption" (vs. 13). The "mount of corruption" is identified by the Targum with the Mount of Olives, and this must be correct, because the Mount of Offense (*see* § 5*d above*) is just to the S of the Mount of Olives. *See* CORRUPTION, MOUNT OF.

e. Jehoahaz, Jehoiakim, Jehoiachin, and Zedekiah; Jeremiah. The death of Josiah was closely connected with the rise of the Neo-Babylonian Empire. After the brief reign of Jehoahaz, Jehoiakim came to the throne as a tool of Egypt; compelled to submit to the Babylonians, he soon rebelled but did not live to see the consequent investment and surrender of Jerusalem. His son Jehoiachin, after reigning only three months, was taken captive to Babylon with "all Jerusalem," leaving only the "poorest people of the land" (II Kings 23:36–24:16). Zedekiah held the throne for ten years, but then rebelled and brought upon his capital and kingdom the disaster of 587 (24:17-20).

During these tragic years, beginning back in the reign of Josiah, Jeremiah prophesied, and there is much about Jerusalem in his words. The sacrifice of children by fire at Topheth (*see* § 6*d above*) was repeatedly denounced by Jeremiah: in the days to come, he said, the place would be filled with the bodies of the people of Judah and would be called the "valley of Slaughter" (Jer. 7:32; 19:6). He pronounced this doom in the "Valley of Ben-hinnom at the entry of the Potsherd Gate" (19:2). The Valley of Ben-hinnom is, of course, the same as the Valley of Hinnom (*see* § 2 *above*). The Potsherd Gate is not mentioned elsewhere, but it obviously opened on this valley near Topheth. It may have been the same gate elsewhere called the Dung Gate. *See* § 7*b below*.

Several points in Jerusalem and its surroundings are named in Jer. 31:38-40. This is not a description of the city's growth in the days to come; its point is that not only the temple area, but the whole city and even the polluted valley S of it, "shall be sacred to the LORD." Other references to some of the places mentioned show that the prophet assumed the extent of the city as it was in his own day.

The tower of Hananel was at the NW corner of the temple enclosure (*see* § 7*b below*). The Corner Gate was at the W end of the N wall of the city (*see* § 6*b above*). These two points therefore mark the NE and NW limits of the city outside the temple area. As vs. 39 reads in the RSV, it suggests that the N limit will continue to the W "farther, straight to the hill Gareb." The Hebrew, however, says "upon the hill Gareb" (cf. KJV). The expression translated "straight" in the RSV (lit., "opposite it"; cf. KJV "over against it") does not imply that the line continues without a change of direction; a turn to the S at the Corner Gate is probably taken for granted, and the meaning is that from this point the line will continue straight ahead to the S along the edge of the W hill to its SW corner, where it will turn eastward toward Goah.

Neither Gareb nor Goah is mentioned elsewhere. Gareb is apparently the SW hill of Jerusalem; Goah must be something in or near the Valley of Hinnom. The word used for the "valley of the dead bodies and the ashes" indicates a broad, level surface (*'ēmeq; see* § 2 *above*); it is therefore undoubtedly the open E end of the Hinnom Valley, where Topheth was, and the bodies and ashes are those of the sacrifices by fire at that place (*see above* and § 6*d*). The "fields as far as the brook Kidron" must be in the area where the three valleys come together. It was in the "fields of the Kidron" that Josiah burned the pagan objects taken out of the temple. *See* § 6*d above.*

From this point the line turns N, following the E wall of the City of David to Ophel and the temple area. It ends at the "Horse Gate toward the east," probably the gate where Athaliah was killed (*see* § 6*a above*). Thus the boundary sketched by Jeremiah, beginning at the NW corner of the temple enclosure, ends at the SE corner of the palace area, S of the temple, and so encloses the whole city.

Most of the other topographical data in the book of Jeremiah are associated with the Temple. In 17:19 Jeremiah is told to "stand in the Benjamin Gate, by which the kings of Judah enter and by which they go out, and in all the gates of Jerusalem," and to denounce working and burden-bearing on the sabbath. Since the territory of Benjamin lay to the N and NE of Jerusalem, the entering and going out mentioned must mean coming from and going to the N or the NE. In 20:2 Jeremiah is confined "in the stocks that were in the upper Benjamin Gate of the house of the LORD." The implied lower gate of Benjamin may have been the one called simply the Benjamin Gate in 17:19 and elsewhere. It was probably a city gate, whereas the upper Benjamin Gate was a temple gate.

Jeremiah was on the way to the land of Benjamin when he was arrested and accused of deserting to the Chaldeans (37:12-13). The Chaldean army which had been besieging Jerusalem had just withdrawn (vss. 5, 11). This incident too suggests that the Benjamin Gate was near the NE corner of the city, in either the N or the E wall. The king was "sitting in the Benjamin Gate" when Ebed-melech came to intercede for Jeremiah (38:7); conceivably he was enjoying the sight of the area from which the besiegers had departed.

In Zech. 14:10 (*see* § 7*c below*) the Benjamin Gate marks the opposite extreme from the Corner Gate (*see above* and § 6*d*). Since other points in the same verse indicate the N and S limits of the city, these two gates evidently indicate the E and W limits. The Benjamin Gate was therefore probably in the E wall rather than the N wall. It may have been a gate designated elsewhere by another name, possibly the Muster Gate of Neh. 3:31. *See* § 7*b below.*

The dramatic scene of the reading and burning of Jeremiah's scroll took place in the king's "winter house" (36:22). We cannot identify this or the other places mentioned in the story of Jeremiah's imprisonments. Twice he was confined in the "court of the guard which was in the palace of the king of Judah" (32:2; 33:1; 37:21); he was even kept for a while in a cistern in this court (38:6-13). Meanwhile he had been imprisoned in the "house of Jonathan the secretary," which "had been made a prison" (37:15-20). After his release from the cistern, he "remained in the court of the guard until the day that Jerusalem was taken" (38:13, 28).

The account of the fall of Jerusalem in Jer. 39 says that the Babylonian princes and officers "came and sat in the middle gate" (vs. 3). Presumably this was in the N wall, perhaps the gate elsewhere called the Fish Gate (*see* § 7*b below*). Zedekiah fled in the opposite direction, "going out of the city at night by way of the king's garden through the gate between the two walls" (vs. 4; II Kings 25:4). In Neh. 3:15 (*see* § 7*b below*) the "king's garden" is placed near the S end of the City of David, apparently at the juncture of the three valleys. The "two walls" may have been the same as those between which Hezekiah had made a reservoir (*see* § 6*c above*). Possibly the gate here mentioned was Nehemiah's Dung Gate. *See* § 7*b below.*

7. The Exile and the Persian period. ***a. Sheshbazzar and Zerubbabel.*** Although the city had been left in ruins by the Chaldeans, returning refugees probably made some effort to worship, at least by prayer and lamentation, on the site of the temple. There is no authentic record of this, however. The first indication we have of any attempt at restoration is the statement of II Chr. 36:22-23; Ezra 1:1-4 that Cyrus issued a proclamation charging the Jewish exiles to go to Jerusalem and rebuild the temple. A group thereupon returned, taking with them the temple vessels, which Cyrus had entrusted to their leader, Sheshbazzar (1:8). Other groups evidently followed them at intervals. The rebuilding of the temple, undertaken by Zerubbabel and Jeshua, was stopped by their adversaries in the surrounding territory until the second year of Darius, 520 B.C. (Ezra 4:1-5, 24). Then, at the urging of Haggai and Zechariah, it was resumed and completed (Ezra 5–6; Hag. 1–2; Zech. 1–8).

So far we hear nothing of rebuilding the city itself. Zechariah receives assurance that the Lord will comfort Zion (1:17). Walls will not be needed (2:4-5). A charge that the Jews were rebuilding the city, however, was made in the reign of Xerxes and renewed in the reign of Artaxerxes I, who ordered the cessation of the enterprise (Ezra 4:6-23).

b. Ezra and Nehemiah. Ezra came to Jerusalem in the seventh year of ARTAXERXES (Ezra 7:1-10). One

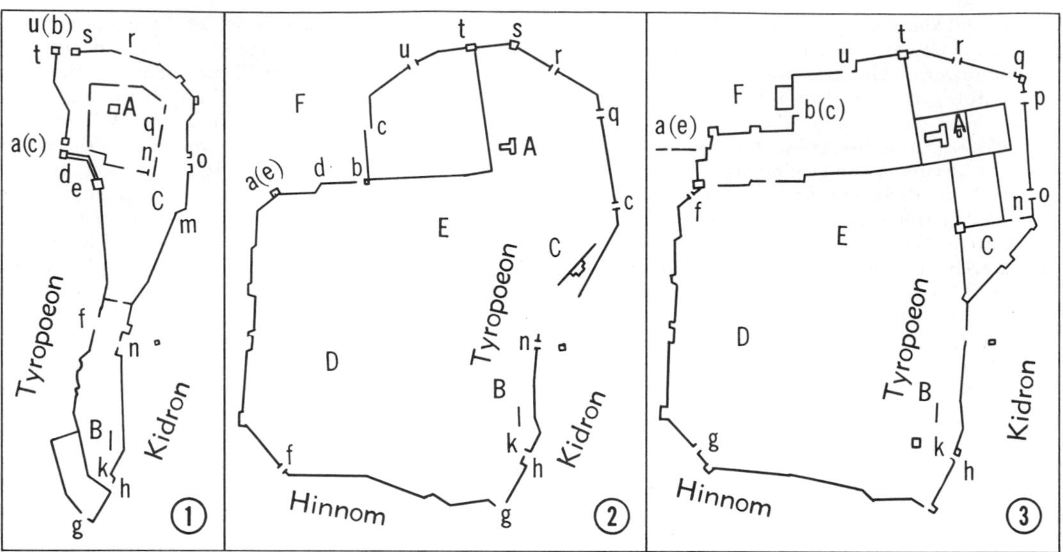

Millar Burrows

MAP II. Different conceptions of the plan of Nehemiah's Jerusalem: (1) Avi-Yonah; (2) Simons; (3) Vincent

may question which of the emperors who bore this name is meant; we shall assume that the reference is to Artaxerxes II (405-358 B.C.). In any case, it was in the twentieth year of Artaxerxes I (444 B.C.) that Nehemiah was authorized to go to Jerusalem and rebuild the walls (Neh. 2:1-8). The forcible interruption of the previous attempt to rebuild the wall in the reign of Artaxerxes (*see* § 7*a above*) probably caused the condition reported to Nehemiah (Neh. 1:3). His success in securing the emperor's approval was all the more remarkable.

Gates and other points in the wall are named in three passages concerning the work of Nehemiah: the account of his preliminary inspection by night (2:12-15), the account of the rebuilding of the wall (ch. 3), and the account of its dedication (12:31-43). Some of the same points and a few others are named in connection with the work of Ezra (Ezra 9; 10:1-7; Neh. 8; 9:1-4; 10:28-39; 13:1-3). For our present purpose all these may be considered together. For the sequence of events, *see* EZRA AND NEHEMIAH, BOOKS OF.

Several of the points specified have been encountered already; others, though not necessarily all, had existed before the exile. Possible locations of the points named in these passages are shown in Fig. NEH 13; three other views of outstanding scholars are given here in Map II, where the small letters indicate respectively the following points:

a. Corner Gate (*see* §§ 6*b*, *e*, 7*c*)
b. Gate of Ephraim (Neh. 8:16; 12:39; *see* § 6*b*)
c. Old Gate (Neh. 3:6; 12:39)
d. Broad Wall (Neh. 3:8; 12:38)
e. Tower of the Ovens, or Furnaces (Neh. 3:11; 12:38)
f. Valley Gate (Neh. 2:13; 3:13; *see* § 6*b*)
g. Dung Gate (Neh. 2:13; 3:13-14; 12:31)
h. Fountain Gate (Neh. 2:14; 3:15; 12:37)
i. King's Pool (Neh. 2:14)
j. Wall of the Pool of Shelah of the King's Garden (Neh. 3:15)
k. Stairs of the City of David (Neh. 3:15; 12:37)
l. Sepulchres of David (Neh. 3:16; *see* § 5*b*)
m. Angle (Neh. 3:19-20, 24-25)
n. Water Gate on the E (Neh. 3:26; 12:37)
o. Horse Gate (Neh. 3:28; *see* § 6*a*)
p. E Gate (Neh. 3:29)
q. Muster Gate (Neh. 3:31)
r. Sheep Gate (Neh. 3:1, 32; 12:39)
s. Tower of the Hundred (Neh. 3:1; 12:39)
t. Tower of Hananel (Neh. 3:1; 12:39; *see* § 6*e*)
u. Fish Gate (Neh. 3:3; 12:39; *see* § 6*d*)

The Corner Gate (a) is not mentioned in Ezra or Nehemiah; if it belonged at all to the wall repaired by Nehemiah, it must have been known by some other name in his time. Why the Gate of Ephraim (b), named in the account of the dedication of the wall, does not appear in the account of the rebuilding, can only be guessed. It is mentioned between the Old Gate (c) and the Broad Wall (d), but there seems to be no place for it there, and the other may not be strictly consecutive. Some scholars identify the Old Gate with the Ephraim Gate on the assumption that in Neh. 12:39 the two names are merely alternative designations of the same gate. The name "Old Gate" (more exactly "Gate of the Yeshanah") is probably a corruption of "Gate of the Mishneh" (*see* § 6*d above*). The name "Broad Wall" should perhaps be emended to "Wall of the Square" (cf. 8:16: the "square at the Water Gate" and the "square at the Gate of Ephraim"). The Tower of the Ovens (e) may have been the tower built by Uzziah at the Corner Gate (*see* § 6*b above*), but in this case the Corner Gate cannot be identified with any of those named in Nehemiah.

The Valley Gate (f) is not named in connection with the dedication of the wall, but it was clearly the point from which the two processions set out, proceeding in opposite directions and meeting at the temple (Neh. 12:31, 38, 40). It had been the point from which Nehemiah set out and to which he returned in his preliminary inspection of the wall (2:

13, 15), and we have encountered it before (*see* § 6*b above*). Its choice as the starting point of the two processions suggests that it was at the opposite corner of the city from the temple—i.e., the SW corner.

Between the Valley Gate and the Dung Gate (g) the JACKAL'S WELL is named in Neh. 2:13. Its location is uncertain; the hypothesis which identifies it with En-rogel (*see* § 2 *above*) is as likely as any. Possibly it was what Jeremiah called the Potsherd Gate (*see* § 6*e above*). If the Valley Gate was at the SW corner of the city, the Dung Gate was not far from the juncture of the Hinnom and Tyropoeon valleys. It may well have been at the S end of the ancient wall which crossed the mouth of the Tyropoeon Valley, where remains of an ancient gate have been found.

The Fountain Gate (h) was undoubtedly at the N end of the wall just mentioned, at the S tip of the E hill. In 2:14 it is followed by the "King's Pool" (i), and in 3:15 by the "wall of the Pool of Shelah of the king's garden" (j). The name of the Pool of Shelah recalls the Shiloah of Isa. 8:6 (*see* § 6*c above*), and the two names are probably only variant forms of the same word; in fact, some MSS read "Shiloah" in Neh. 3:15. It does not follow, of course, that the same canal or conduit is referred to in Neh. 3:15; Isa. 8:6.

The King's Pool and the Pool of Shelah may have been the same pool. Perhaps it lay at the end of the Tyropoeon Valley, where the *birket al-ḥamra* is now, just above the wall which crossed the mouth of the valley. The Lower Pool into which Hezekiah's tunnel emptied (*see* § 6*c above*), the King's Pool, and the Pool of Shelah would then all be one and the same, except for such changes as followed the cutting of the tunnel; and the word "Shelah" would refer here to the tunnel.

In that case it is strange that the Fountain Gate is named before the King's Pool in Neh. 2:14 and before the wall of the Pool of Shelah in 3:15. The gate may have been mentioned first in 3:15 as a more formidable item than the wall in the program of repairs, or it may have been repaired before the wall; but 2:14 is not so easily explained. Perhaps, therefore, the King's Pool lay outside the wall in the lower Kidron Valley. The Pool of Shelah, however, cannot be located there unless the text is in disorder, because the wall of this pool was built "as far as the stairs that go down from the City of David." These were at the S end of the SE hill, just where we are compelled to place the Fountain Gate. In 12:37 also the Fountain Gate is followed immediately by the "stairs of the city of David." Here we seem to strike solid rock, both literally and figuratively. The remains of a staircase cut in the rock at this point have been excavated, and there is no reason to doubt that they are the stairs in question.

Neh. 12:37 mentions next the "ascent of the wall," which suggests that here the wall itself ascended the slope to reach the top of the hill on the E side. This seems to be confirmed by steplike cuts in the rock, apparently for the foundation of successive sections of the wall.

From here on, we proceed northward along the E side of the hill. From the King's Pool, Nehemiah on his tour of inspection found no place for his beast to pass; he therefore "went up by the valley" (*naḥal*—i.e., the Kidron; *see* § 2 *above*), inspected the wall either by looking up from the bottom of the valley or by climbing the steep slope on foot, and then returned to the Valley Gate (2:14-15). The builders and the dedicatory procession moved along the top of the slope.

The next team of workers (3:16) "repaired to a point opposite the sepulchres of David, to the artificial pool, and to the house of the mighty men." David's tomb (l) was in the S part of the SE hill (*see* § 5*b above*). The artificial pool (lit., "made pool") must have been somewhere in the Kidron Valley, doubtless below Gihon and only a little farther N than the sepulchres of David. No more can be said of the house of the mighty men. The house of David mentioned in 12:37 was presumably the palace built by David on the SE hill (*see* § 5*a above*). Remains of a wall which may be the one repaired by Nehemiah have been uncovered along the E edge of the hill in this region, but their identity and date are not certain.

The next portion of wall designated is a "section opposite the ascent to the armory at the Angle" (3:19). The Angle (m) is mentioned also in vs. 20, and the same word appears again in vss. 24-25 (*see below*). Its exact meaning is uncertain. In II Chr. 26:9 it designates an unidentified place where Uzziah built a tower (*see* § 6*b above*). That we are now not far from the temple area is suggested by the next point named, the "house of Eliashib the high priest" (3:20).

A few more sections bring us "to the Angle and to the corner," and another group's assignment is "opposite the Angle and the tower projecting from the upper house of the king at the court of the guard." Here we are plainly in the vicinity of Solomon's palace, called the "upper house of the king," as distinguished from David's palace farther to the S. The court of the guard recalls Jeremiah's imprisonment (*see* § 6*e above*). Where the tower projecting from the palace was, we cannot tell.

The workers on the next section of the wall included "temple servants living on Ophel"; their portion extended "to a point opposite the Water Gate on the east and the projecting tower" (3:26). The following section was "opposite the great projecting tower as far as the wall of Ophel" (vs. 27). The wall of Ophel recalls Manasseh's wall around Ophel (*see* § 6*d above*). The "Water Gate on the east" (n) appears in Neh. 12:37 as the terminus of the first procession. Since the two companies came together at the temple (12:40), a position very close to the temple is indicated. This gate therefore cannot have been directly above Gihon, as its name suggests. The vicinity of the temple is indicated also by the fact that Ezra assembled the people to hear the law in the "square before the Water Gate" (Neh. 8:1, 3); this was also one of the places where booths were made for the ensuing festival (8:16).

The repeated references to projecting towers and the reappearance of the Angle after several sections of wall, not to mention the corner (3:25), are confusing. Possibly from the neighborhood of the house of Eliashib there were two walls under repair, some of the teams working on the W wall of Ophel and the S wall of the palace and temple area, while others carried the repair of the E wall up to the SE corner of that area. This would not, however, answer all the questions raised by the text, which has undoubtedly suffered from the mistakes of copyists who understood it no better than we do.

Some of the difficulty arises from the fact that the prepositions used do not always make clear whether what is named was a part of the wall itself or something inside or outside the city, mentioned merely as a point of reference. The Horse Gate (o), which comes next in Neh. 3:28, seems to be an entrance to the palace in II Kings 11:16; II Chr. 23:15 (*see* § 6*b above*). In Jer. 31:40 the "corner of the Horse Gate" marks the farthest extension of the city to the E (*see* § 6*c above*). Probably, therefore, the Horse Gate was a gate in the city wall, not far N of the corner where it became also the E wall of the temple enclosure.

The East Gate of Neh. 3:29 (p) is a temple gate, probably a gate of the inner court. The fact that the "upper chamber of the corner" comes between the Muster Gate and the Sheep Gate (3:31-32) favors the location of the Muster Gate (q) in the E wall near its N end. As noted *above* (§ 6*e*), Nehemiah's Muster Gate may have been the Benjamin Gate of Jeremiah and Zechariah.

At this time the N wall still followed the S slope of the valley which descended from the NW into the Kidron Valley, under the NE corner of the present sacred area. In this wall was the Sheep Gate (r), the starting point and end of the account of rebuilding (Neh. 3:1, 32) and the last point but one in the route of the second dedicatory procession (12:39). From the Sheep Gate the second company in the dedicatory procession, coming from the W, went on and "came to a halt at the Gate of the Guard" (Neh. 12:39). Unless this is to be identified with the Muster Gate, which seems unlikely, it must have been a gate of the inner temple court. It cannot be connected with the court of the guard of 3:25, for that was attached to the palace, S of the temple. *See* § 6*e above*.

To the W of the Sheep Gate in the N wall were two towers, the Tower of the Hundred (s) and the Tower of Hananel (t). They were evidently not far apart, at the northernmost point of the city wall, just before it turned slightly to the left and crossed the Tyropoeon Valley. The Tower of Hananel is named also in Jer. 31:38 (*see* § 6*e above*) and Zech. 14:10 (*see* § 7*c above*) to mark the N extent of the city.

The Fish Gate (u), mentioned only in Neh. 3:3; 12:39, was the N gate of the Mishneh (*see* § 6*d above*) in the Tyropoeon Valley, where the road from the N entered the city. Nehemiah speaks later of men from Tyre who lived in Jerusalem and sold fish even on the sabbath (13:16). From their market and perhaps their dwellings in the same quarter, this gate probably got its name.

c. Visions of the future. For the remainder of the Persian period we have little information concerning Jerusalem, but the writers of the time had much to say concerning the city's future glory. To list here the references to Jerusalem and Zion in the Psalms, the wisdom literature, and the late portions of the prophetic books would serve no purpose. In two prophetic passages, however, there are references which call for comment. Either or both may have come from the Greek instead of the Persian period, but in view of the uncertainty on this point it is convenient to discuss them here. The first is the prophecy of judgment in the Valley of Jehoshaphat in Joel 3:11-21 (*see* JEHOSHAPHAT, VALLEY OF). Tradition locates this in the upper Kidron Valley, but the prophet probably had no particular valley in mind. The Hebrew word used here (*'ēmeq*) does not, in fact, indicate such a steep, narrow valley as that of the Kidron (*see* § 2 *above*). The name, which means "Yahweh has judged," was probably meant to be understood symbolically, like the "valley of decision" in vs. 14. *See* DECISION, VALLEY OF.

The other passage is the vision of the judgment on the Mount of Olives and the future growth of Jerusalem in Zech. 14. The location of the Mount of Olives is familiar (*see* §§ 5*a-b*, 6*d above*, 11 *below*). The description of Jerusalem mentions as points in its periphery the Gate of Benjamin, the "place of the former gate," the Corner Gate, the Tower of Hananel, and the "king's wine presses." The Gate of Benjamin (*see* §§ 6*e*, 7*b above*) clearly marks the E extent of the city, as the Corner Gate (*see* §§ 6*b-c*, 7*b above*) marks its W limit. What the "former gate" was is unknown. It was probably a gate in the old N wall, perhaps the Ephraim Gate (*see* § 6*b above*), which had lost its previous importance after the enclosure of the Mishneh. *See* § 6*d above*.

The Tower of Hananel (*see* §§ 6*e*, 7*b above*) and the "king's wine presses" obviously designate respectively the N and S extent of the city. This indicates that the king's wine presses were in or near the Hinnom Valley, in the general region where the King's Pool and the King's Garden have been placed. *See* § 7*b above*. Fig. JER 18.

8. The Greek period. For more than a century after the conquests and death of Alexander the Great, Palestine was involved in the struggle between the Ptolemies of Egypt and the Seleucids of Syria. In 320 B.C., Ptolemy I captured Jerusalem. During most of the third century, while Palestine was under Egyptian rule, Jerusalem was secure and prosperous. A description of the city in the Letter of Aristeas, from about this time, notes especially the hilly nature of the site, with walls and streets going up and down across hills and valleys.

Our sources for this period are scanty, and there is little to report concerning Jerusalem. Excavations on both the E and the W hills have found remains of buildings and walls which can be attributed either to the Greek or to the Hasmonean period (*see* § 9 *below*), but they cannot be connected with anything recorded in the literature of the time. Buildings for athletic contests and dramatic presentations were apparently built in the Tyropoeon Valley, between the temple and the W hill. This area has never been thoroughly excavated. The tombs in the Kidron Valley traditionally called the tombs of Absalom, Jehoshaphat, James, and Zechariah, though commonly assigned to the time of Herod, are probably the result of a process of construction and reconstruction which began as far back as the third century B.C.

The fighting between Egypt and Syria caused much damage at Jerusalem, both directly and indirectly. When Palestine became a part of the Seleucid dominions (198 B.C.), special privileges and exemptions were granted to the Jews to repair the damage suffered by the city and the temple. This favorable treatment, however, soon gave way to more oppressive measures, including even an attempt to plunder the temple treasure (II Macc. 3).

Meanwhile the growing influence of Hellenistic culture had produced a division among the Jews themselves. This was intensified by the worldliness and venality of contenders for the high priesthood, who made this sacred office a matter of royal favor, purchased by bribes and political subservience. In the reign of Antiochus IV Epiphanes a violent conflict between two such rivals gave the king an occasion to desecrate and plunder the temple and massacre many of the people of Jerusalem. Later Antiochus sent a "chief collector of tribute, and he came to Jerusalem with a large force" (I Macc. 1:29). The city was plundered and burned, its houses and walls torn down, and many of its people killed or taken captive (vss. 30-32). "Then they fortified the city of David with a great strong wall and strong towers, and it became their citadel" (vs. 33). For years to come, this citadel (for the location *see* § 9 *below*) was to be a "great snare" and an "ambush against the sanctuary" (I Macc. 1:35-36; 3:45). The ensuing persecution provoked the Maccabean Revolt.

9. The Hasmonean period. In the tangled history of the MACCABEES and the HASMONEANS, Jerusalem was deeply involved. Devastated and in ruins, its population decimated, the city was controlled by the garrison in the Syrian citadel. Judas Maccabeus was able to purify and rededicate the temple (*see* TEMPLE, JERUSALEM, § B2) in 164 B.C., and even to fortify the sacred enclosure, while a part of his troops kept the Syrian garrison occupied (I Macc. 4:41, 60). Two years later, in the reign of Antiochus V Eupator, Judas besieged the citadel, but the king came to the relief of the garrison. Inducing the Jews by an offer of peace to admit him to the temple, he broke his oath and had the protecting wall destroyed (6:18-62).

Demetrius I made Alcimus high priest and sent Bacchides with him to Jerusalem to overthrow Judas. A group of Hasidim sought to make peace with these two and were promised safety, but sixty of them were treacherously seized and killed. Nicanor, who was sent later with an army, was defeated by Judas, and his soldiers "fled into the city of David" (7:32). Coming to Mount Zion, Nicanor mocked and threatened the priests, but not long thereafter he lost his life in the decisive battle of Adasa, and his head and right hand were exhibited by the triumphant rebels "just outside of Jerusalem" (vs. 47).

Bacchides and Alcimus were not sent again. After the death of Judas in the battle of Elasa, Jonathan fought against Bacchides, who now fortified many cities in Judea. "And he took the sons of the leading men of the land as hostages and put them under guard in the citadel at Jerusalem" (9:53). Alcimus ordered the wall of the inner temple court torn down, but died before the work was completed (vss. 54 ff). A few years later, when the throne of Demetrius was threatened by Alexander Epiphanes, both contestants tried to win the adherence of Jonathan, whose power had become formidable. Demetrius authorized him to recruit and equip troops and made the garrison in the citadel give up to him their hostages. Jonathan now undertook to restore the dismantled walls of Jerusalem "and encircle Mount Zion with squared stones" (10:11).

Not to be outdone, Alexander conferred the high priesthood upon Jonathan. Demetrius countered by offering extraordinary exemptions, declaring Jerusalem to be tax-free, undertaking to yield the citadel to Jonathan, and granting release to debtors who took refuge in the temple. The promise to give up the citadel, however, was not kept. After the accession of Demetrius II, Jonathan besieged the citadel. He obtained also from Demetrius the confirmation of his high priesthood and another promise to remove the Syrian garrison from the citadel, but this promise, like others before it, was broken.

Jonathan now transferred his allegiance to the rival king Antiochus VI and undertook "to build the walls of Jerusalem still higher, and to erect a high barrier between the citadel and the city to separate it from the city, in order to isolate it so that its garrison could neither buy nor sell" (I Macc. 12:36). A part of the E wall of the city above the Kidron Valley "had fallen, and he repaired the section called Chaphenatha" (vs. 37). The building of the barrier and the repairing of Chaphenatha were probably not connected but distinct items in the comprehensive effort to build up the city.

At the height of his success, Jonathan was deceived and imprisoned by Trypho, who was seeking to become king. Simon, last of the Maccabean brothers, now "hastened to complete the walls of Jerusalem, and he fortified it on every side" (13:10). Responding to appeals from the garrison of the citadel, Trypho attempted to come to their relief but was frustrated by a heavy snowfall. Simon now made peace with Demetrius, but continued to enforce an effective blockade of the citadel until the garrison was compelled to sue for peace. They were put out, the citadel was cleansed, and the Jews took possession in 141 B.C. (13:49-51; 14:36).

Jews were now settled in the citadel, and Simon "fortified it for the safety of the country and of the city, and built the walls of Jerusalem higher" (14:37). He also "strengthened the fortifications of the temple hill alongside the citadel, and he and his men dwelt there" (13:52). Presumably this means that they established themselves in the fortress at the NW corner of the sacred area, where the Tower of Hananel had formerly stood. *See* §§ 6*c*, 7*b above.*

The historian Josephus inserts at this point a tale which has seriously embarrassed scholars. To prevent any future control of the temple and the city from this point of vantage, he says, Simon demolished the citadel and had the whole "mountain" on which it stood cut down to a lower level than the temple. To accomplish this, says Josephus, the people worked day and night for three years (Antiq. XII.vi.7). What makes the whole episode incredible is that there is no area near the temple which is now lower but can be believed to have been higher at any time without the assumption of what has been called a geological monstrosity. The story also contradicts the statement of I Macc. 14:37 that Simon settled Jews in the citadel and fortified it.

Where then was this citadel (Greek ἄκρα)? I Macc. 1:33 identifies it with the fortified City of David. In 14:36 it appears as a fortress in the City of David. Josephus puts it in the "lower city," by which he clearly means the SE hill, where the ancient city of David lay (*see* §§ 1, 2, 5*a-b*, 6*a above*). A garrison in this position, however, could not have dominated the temple. Josephus evidently assumed that it was here, and this assumption may account for his idea that the SE hill had originally been higher than the temple hill.

To find a more convincing location for the citadel, one must assume that the designation "city of David" does not mean in I Maccabees what it means in the OT. Its application must have shifted from one place to another. This is by no means impossible or without parallel, though Josephus still knew that David's city was on the SE hill. Certainly the relations between the citadel and the temple and the great difficulty the Jews had in capturing the citadel are much clearer and more consistent on the supposition that the citadel was on the NE spur of the SW hill (Map I,E), across the valley from the temple. From this point one can still overlook the sacred area. Here the palace of the Hasmonean rulers stood later (*see below*). Some cutting in the rock when this palace was built, or perhaps even when Simon himself refortified the citadel, may have afforded the factual basis for a tradition which grew and was transformed into Josephus' tale of the leveling of the SE hill.

For several years after the capture of the citadel Jerusalem enjoyed peace. When Antiochus VII demanded that the citadel be turned over to him, with Joppa and Gazara, Simon bluntly refused (I Macc. 15:28-36). Shortly thereafter Cendebeus, the king's general, built up Kedron, fortified its gates, and stationed troops there to raid the highways of Judea (I Macc. 15:38-41; cf. 16:9). This cannot mean the Kidron Valley at Jerusalem, which had no gates and would be a poor place for such a purpose. No town named Kedron is known, but Gederoth in the coastal plain (Josh. 15:41; II Chr. 28:18) is undoubtedly meant.

After the assassination of Simon and the accession of his son John Hyrcanus, Antiochus VII invaded Judea and besieged Jerusalem, attacking it from the N, where the ground was as high outside as inside the walls. A shortage of water in the city was relieved by a heavy rain, but to forestall the danger of famine Hyrcanus put out of the city all the people except the fighting men. The poor wretches, not being allowed to pass through the king's lines, suffered horribly, and many died. The survivors were finally readmitted in the autumn at the time of the Feast of Tabernacles.

At the request of Hyrcanus, Antiochus now granted a week's truce and even sent a liberal offering for the festival. Encouraged by this generosity, Hyrcanus sued for peace. The king's demand that a Syrian garrison be established in the city was rejected, but his other terms were met, tribute and hostages were given, and after demolishing the city's fortifications he raised the siege.

A period of prosperity and conquest followed. To support his many military ventures, in which he used foreign mercenary troops, Hyrcanus plundered the tomb of David (*see* §§ 5*b*, 6*c*, 7*b above*). I Maccabees mentions as a major achievement of John Hyrcanus the "building of the walls which he built" (16:23). This probably means the rebuilding of the walls dismantled by Antiochus.

According to Josephus (Antiq. XVIII.iv.3), Hyrcanus also built a tower or fortress on the site later occupied by the fortress Antonia (*see* § 10 *below*), and "usually lived there." This was at the NW corner of the temple enclosure. Simon, as we have seen, had taken up residence in the temple precincts, probably at this same place. Aristobulus I, son and successor of John Hyrcanus, continued to live in the tower his father had built. He was lying sick there when his brother Antigonus, coming to visit him, was killed, because of a tragic misunderstanding, in a dark underground passage between the tower and the temple.

The reign of Alexander Janneus was decidedly eventful, but most of what occurred at Jerusalem was connected with the temple rather than the city. His notorious crucifixion of eight hundred captured rebels and slaughter of their wives and children, while he callously feasted with his concubines before the eyes of the horrified citizens, may have taken place at the palace, but there is nothing to prove this. The first definite reference to the palace occurs in the reign of his widow and successor, Alexandra. A delegation including her younger son Aristobulus appeared here before the queen and besought her to restrain the excesses of the Pharisees.

Later Aristobulus attempted to wrest the kingdom from his mother, whereupon she seized his wife and children as hostages and imprisoned them in the fortress N of the temple. Upon the death of the queen not long thereafter, her elder son Hyrcanus II, whom she had made high priest, was defeated in battle by Aristobulus and took refuge in the fortress where the wife and children of Aristobulus were imprisoned. The two brothers now met in the temple and made a solemn agreement, by which Aristobulus became king and occupied the palace, while Hyrcanus retired to the former dwelling of Aristobulus. Where this was is not indicated; the palace was, no doubt, the one opposite the temple on the E spur of the W hill (E).

Beguiled by the wily Idumean Antipater, Hyrcanus fled to Petra and took refuge with the Nabatean king Aretas, who attacked Aristobulus, defeated him, and besieged him in the temple at Jerusalem. Aristobulus, however, won the support of the Roman official whom Pompey had placed in charge of Syria. He promptly compelled Aretas to give up the siege. Aristobulus now took the offensive and decisively defeated Aretas and Hyrcanus.

All this, however, was the beginning of the end for the Hasmonean kingdom. When Pompey, returning from Armenia, heard the pleas of Aristobulus, Hyrcanus, and the Jews who wanted neither of them, he found Aristobulus so intransigent that he imprisoned him and besieged Jerusalem. The adherents of Hyrcanus admitted the Romans to the upper city on the W hill, enabling them to invest the temple on that side. There was at this time a bridge across the Tyropoeon Valley, but it was cut by the followers of Aristobulus. On the N the temple hill was protected by a strong wall above a little ravine and by a ditch connecting this ravine with the Tyropoeon Valley. Pompey filled the ravine and ditch and made a great ramp for his siege engines. After a siege of three months, the wall was breached, and a frightful mas-

Courtesy of Denis Baly

21. Remnant of E span of a bridge over Tyropoeon Valley; discovered in 1838 by Edward Robinson

sacre followed in the sacred area. Pompey destroyed the city walls but ordered that the temple be cleansed and the sacrifices renewed. Many of the people were carried off as slaves.

During the Hasmonean period the city had undergone considerable modification. The fortress built by John Hyrcanus N of the temple, the Hasmonean palace above the Tyropoeon Valley, and the bridge across the valley have been mentioned. The temple area was extended at its SW corner by partly filling in the Tyropoeon Valley, which curved to the E at this point. Remains of two phases of Hasmonean fortifications, both possibly from the time of John Hyrcanus, have been found at the NW corner of the city, in the present citadel. Other remains of walls at various points may have come from this time. *Cf.* Fig. JER 21.

10. The early Roman period and the reign of Herod. After the fall of Jerusalem in 63 B.C., Hyrcanus was left in charge as high priest and ethnarch. Attempting to rebuild the walls, he was restrained by the Romans. Twice in the next decade a son of Aristobulus named Alexander attempted to gain control; once Aristobulus himself with another son, Antigonus, made a similar effort. In spite of Pompey's consideration for the temple, its treasure was robbed by his lieutenant Crassus.

After the death of Pompey, Hyrcanus and Antipater allied themselves with Julius Caesar. Hyrcanus was confirmed as high priest and ethnarch, Antipater was made governor of Judea, and they were allowed to restore Jerusalem's walls. When Antigonus tried again to invade Palestine, he was defeated by Antipater's son Herod, then governor of Galilee. Later, when summoned before the Sanhedrin at Jerusalem for putting a bandit chief to death, Herod confounded that body by his bold demeanor but withdrew without resorting to violence.

After the assassination of Julius Caesar and the defeat of Brutus and Cassius, Mark Antony made Antipater's sons Phasael and Herod tetrarchs of Judea; but Antigonus, aided by the Parthians, attacked Jerusalem, made his way into the city, and besieged Phasael and Herod in the Hasmonean palace. Driven back, Antigonus was compelled to take refuge in the temple enclosure; but the people and the pilgrims who had come for the feast of Pentecost took his part, and Phasael and Herod were shut up again in the palace. Making a bold sally into what Josephus calls the suburb, the Mishneh of the OT (*see* §§ 6*a*, 7*b above*), Herod drove the people to the upper city on the W and the temple area on the E.

Phasael and Hyrcanus now tried to negotiate with the Parthian general, but he made them prisoners. Phasael committed suicide, and Hyrcanus was carried off to Babylonia. Herod slipped out of Jerusalem by night, took his family to Masada, and went to Rome, where the Senate appointed him king of the Jews. Meanwhile, however, the Parthians plundered Jerusalem, and for three years Antigonus ruled as king and high priest. In 37 B.C., Herod besieged the city, with the help of Roman troops. Again siege engines were set up before the N walls. The suburb was captured and then the temple, and once more there was frightful carnage in the sacred courts and the city, but Herod prevented his foreign soldiers from entering the temple or pillaging the city.

So began a long reign rivaling that of Solomon in the magnificence of its building enterprises at Jerusalem and elsewhere, though marked also by cruelty and tragedy. One of Herod's first undertakings was the rebuilding of the fortress at the NW corner of the temple area, which he named Antonia in honor of his patron Mark Antony (*see* ANTONIA, TOWER OF). He moved it a little to the N, on the ridge between the Tyropoeon Valley and the ravine which descended toward the SE. Protecting ditches and a large reservoir were cut in the solid rock. Excavations have disclosed the impressive form and extent of the new fortress, which Herod now used for several years as his own palace. It was connected with the temple enclosure both by stairways and by underground passages.

After the death of Herod's favorite wife, Mariamne, her mother tried to suborn the commanders of Antonia and the Hasmonean palace. The plot was foiled, but Herod's rule now became more despotic. Much of his building was done in this part of his reign. A theater and an amphitheater were built, as well as a xystus or place for athletic games, all apparently in the Tyropoeon Valley. These expressed Herod's interest in Hellenistic culture but alienated the Jewish religious leaders.

Herod built also a new palace at or near the site of the ancient Corner Gate (*see* §§ 6*b*, *e*, 7*a*, *c above*). It was strongly fortified and protected by three great towers, named Hippicus, Phasael, and Mariamne. The massive foundations of the present "Tower of David" belonged to one of these towers, either Phasael or Hippicus. The palace was abundantly supplied with water by an aqueduct or canal from a source perhaps as far away as the "Pools of Solomon" S of Bethlehem. Fig. WAT 6.

Herod's most famous building project was, of course, the reconstruction of the temple (*see* TEMPLE, JERUSALEM, § C). His extension of the sacred enclosure affected the topography of the city as a whole. Some enlargement had already been made at the SW corner, as we have seen (*see* § 9 *above*). Herod now extended the area both to the S and to the N, filling in not only the Tyropoeon Valley on the SW but also the ravine on the NE and the ditch across the ridge between the ravine and the Tyropoe-

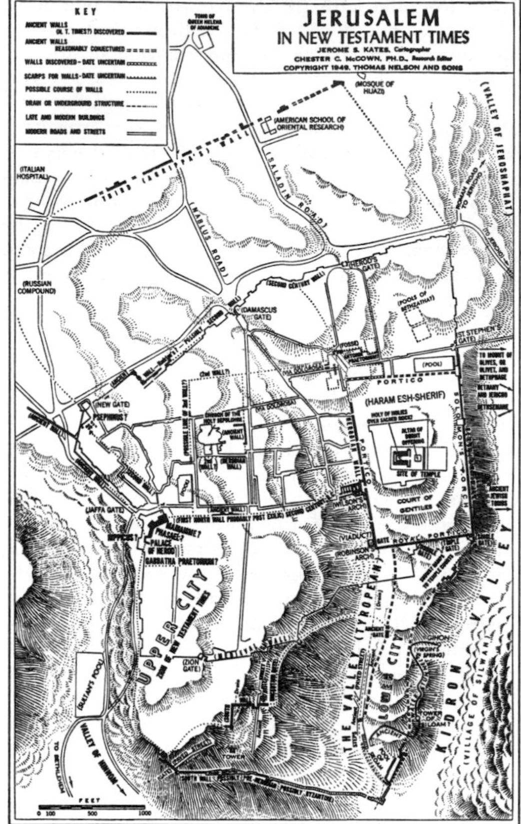

on Valley. The city wall also was pushed further to the N. The area on the S which had been occupied by the pre-exilic royal palace was now included in the temple enclosure.

Extension to the E and the W was prevented by the valleys, but there was considerable reconstruction of the walls. The famous "Wailing Wall" on the W side of the area, traditionally ascribed to Solomon, is a part of Herod's wall; other portions are to be seen on the S and E sides. Of the temple itself not a stone remains, but the sacred area remains to this day substantially as Herod left it, approximately twice as large as it had been before his time. From the main gate on the W side of the temple area, where a bridge had formerly crossed the Tyropoeon Valley (*see* § 9 *above*), Herod built a new viaduct following the line of the ancient N wall, now marked by the Street of the Chain.

To secure funds for his extravagant projects, according to Josephus, Herod broke into the tomb of David, as John Hyrcanus had done before him (*see* § 9 *above*); but when two of his guards were killed by a supernatural flame that burst out upon them, the frightened king withdrew and built a monument of white stone at the mouth of the tomb.

From the reign of Herod or near it come some of the ornamental tombs in the vicinity of Jerusalem. They contribute nothing to our purpose beyond the fact that they exhibit a rather clumsy attempt to copy Greco-Roman art.

11. The lifetime of Jesus. The opening events of the gospel story occurred during the last troubled years of Herod's reign. Only the vision of Zechariah in the temple (Luke 1:5-23), the appearance of the Wise Men before Herod (Matt. 2:1-12), and the presentation of the infant Jesus (Luke 2:22-38) are connected with Jerusalem. When Joseph learned that Herod was dead and his son Archelaus was reigning in his place, he avoided Judea and withdrew to Galilee (Matt. 2:19-22).

Archelaus had to put down rioting in the temple before he could even sail for Rome to secure the emperor's confirmation of his authority. During his absence the Roman official in charge at Jerusalem so enraged the people by his efforts to obtain the royal treasure that they rose against him at the Feast of Pentecost. Three bands attacked his forces, one to the N of the temple, another at the hippodrome in the Tyropoeon Valley, and the third at Herod's new palace. In a violent struggle on the W side of the temple area, the Romans burned the porticoes, penetrated the sacred area, and seized some of the temple; but the people's attack on the palace continued until the governor of Syria came and put down the insurrection.

Augustus appointed Archelaus ethnarch of Judea, Samaria, and Idumea. Within ten years, however, Archelaus' subjects appealed to the Emperor to remove him. In A.D. 6 he was banished to Gaul, and Judea came under the direct government of a Roman procurator. It must have been at about this time that Jesus came to Jerusalem with his parents for the Passover (Luke 2:41-51). In A.D. 6 he would have been about twelve years old. His awareness of the events of the time may be reflected by the reference in Luke 19:12-14 to a nobleman who "went into a far country to receive kingly power," but whose subjects sent an embassy to say that they did not want him as their king.

The procurators, not finding life at Jerusalem to their liking, made Caesarea their principal place of residence. An officer was left in charge at Jerusalem, with troops stationed at the Herodian palace and at Antonia. On their periodic visits to Jerusalem the procurators lived at the palace. Under the first four procurators nothing of great importance occurred at Jerusalem, but in A.D. 26 Pontius Pilate became procurator, and trouble arose at once. The first time he came to Jerusalem, he brought into the city by night troops carrying ensigns bearing the emperor's image. The previous procurators, out of deference to the religious scruples of the Jews, had refrained from introducing such images into the holy city. In the morning a delegation of the indignant citizens went to Pilate, who at once withdrew to Caesarea and a few days later had the ensigns removed.

Pilate undertook one notable project for Jerusalem—an aqueduct to bring a more adequate supply of water from the vicinity of Bethlehem. Herod, if not Solomon, had made a beginning in this direction by creating the lower of two aqueducts which can still be partially traced; the upper aqueduct was the work of Pilate. To pay for it he undertook to draw on the temple treasury, but the citizens angrily protested. Pilate had soldiers circulate in diguise among the people, killing or wounding many of them, and proceeded with the enterprise.

The Synoptic gospels say nothing of any visit to

Jerusalem by Jesus between the age of twelve and the last days of his life. The Gospel of John reports several incidents there during this interval. The cleansing of the temple and the conversation with Nicodemus take place at the Passover season shortly after the "first sign" at Cana (John 2:13–3:21). The healing of the lame man and the ensuing controversy are connected with another feast, not specified, at Jerusalem (ch. 5).

The place of this miracle is a pool called Bethesda, Bethsaida, or BETHZATHA. Josephus calls the quarter N of the temple Bezetha, and the two names were probably the same originally. The pool is said also to have been "by the sheep gate" (KJV "sheep market")—the Greek has only an adjective, but it is the same one used in the LXX for the Sheep Gate (*see* § *7b above*). The region N of the temple area seems therefore to be indicated. An old reservoir under a little church in the property of the White Fathers is commonly believed to be the pool of Bethzatha. This identification is as probable as any that has been suggested.

In John 7–8 a visit to Jerusalem at the Feast of Tabernacles is reported. After this, in ch. 9, comes the healing of the blind man who receives his sight after washing in the pool of Siloam. That this was identical with the present pool of Siloam, at the outlet of Hezekiah's tunnel (*see* §§ *6c, 7b above*), cannot be assumed, but it was undoubtedly in that vicinity. A tower in Siloam which fell and killed eighteen people is mentioned in Luke 13:4.

When Jesus saw his end approaching, he "set his face to go to Jerusalem" (Luke 9:51). It could not be, he said, "that a prophet should perish away from Jerusalem" (13:33); and he cried out in sorrow and compassion at the city which rejected his loving solicitude (vss. 34-35). At the end of the tragic journey, surrounded by people who spread garments and branches before him, he came to Jerusalem; but "when he drew near and saw the city," Luke tells us, "he wept over it" and foretold its destruction (19:41-44). About halfway down the W side of the Mount of Olives there is a chapel called *Dominus Flevit,* which is believed to mark the place where Jesus wept over Jerusalem. A more probable place is the point where one comes over the top of the hill and gets the first breath-taking view of the city.

Crossing the Kidron Valley, Jesus "entered Jerusalem, and went into the temple" (Mark 11:11). The cleansing of the temple and the teaching in its courts lie outside the scope of this article, but the disciples' amazement at the "wonderful stones" of the temple (Mark 13:1) recalls the remains of Herodian masonry still to be seen in the foundations of the sacred enclosure. *See* § 10 *above.*

For the "holy places" connected with the last week of Jesus' life on earth, we are dependent upon church traditions of uncertain age and value, in no case definitely attested earlier than the fourth century. It is disappointing not to be sure of the authenticity of these sites, yet perhaps it is better so. Veneration of sacred places may easily pass into idolatry. At all of them we can at least reverently recall the events associated with them by tradition, and respect the fervent faith of pilgrims who through the centuries have found here comfort and inspiration.

The place where the Last Supper of Jesus with his disciples was eaten is defined in the gospels only as a large upper room in a private house (Matt. 26:18; Mark 14:13-15; Luke 22:10-12). The traditional site of the upper room, called the Cenaculum, is on the SW hill outside the present walls. The slight claim of this tradition to authenticity is not enhanced by the fact that the tomb of David is alleged to have been at the same place.

Concerning the sites of other events we are no better informed. On the SW hill, just outside the Zion Gate, is the burying ground of the Armenian patriarchs. The adjoining buildings are believed to cover the site of the high priest's palace, where Jesus was arraigned before Caiaphas (Matt. 26:57; Mark 14:53; Luke 22:54). A chapel called the Prison of Christ indicates the place where Jesus is supposed to have been detained. Some think, however, that the high priest's palace was in what is now the garden of the Assumptionist fathers, a little farther to the E. According to John 18:13, Jesus was taken first to Annas, the father-in-law of Caiaphas, and only then to Caiaphas (vs. 24). The traditional site of the house of Annas is the Armenian Convent of the Olives near the Church of St. James, in the SW part of the Old City.

Tradition has long regarded a cave on the W side of the Tyropoeon Valley as the place where Peter wept after denying his Master (Matt. 26:75; Mark 14:72; Luke 22:62). Here once stood a church referred to by many pilgrims in the Middle Ages. Another grotto, farther to the S and W in the garden of the Assumptionist fathers, is thought by some to be the site of this church and of Peter's remorse. The whole series of events may have occurred in an entirely different part of the city.

In the morning Jesus was taken to Pilate. Matthew inserts here (27:3-10) the story of the death of Judas, which Luke relates in Acts 1:18-19. In both accounts, which are otherwise quite different, reference is made to a field called the Field of Blood or AKELDAMA, traditionally located on the hill directly S of the Valley of Hinnom. One tradition has it that Caiaphas had a country home on this hill, and the trial of Jesus before him was held there.

According to John 18:28 (cf. vs. 33 and 19:9), Jesus was taken to the PRAETORIUM to appear before Pilate. The Synoptic gospels do not name the place until later, when the soldiers are said to have taken Jesus into the praetorium (Matt. 27:27; Mark 15:16). It has been argued that Pilate's praetorium was at Herod's palace; most authorities, however, accept the tradition which identifies it with the fortress Antonia (*see* § 10 *above*). Ordinarily the procurator lived and held court at the palace, but at such a time as the Passover, when Jerusalem was crowded with pilgrims, he may well have made his headquarters at the fortress overlooking the temple. There is now a Muslim school on the rock above the NW corner of the sacred area, where once stood one of the towers of Antonia. In the courtyard of this school is the First Station of the Cross, marking the beginning of the Via Dolorosa. The trial of Jesus before Pilate probably occurred near this spot (Matt. 27:1-14; Mark 15:1-5; Luke 23:1-5; John 18:33-38; 19:8-11).

Luke alone records (23:5-11) an interruption of the

hearing before Pilate. Learning that Jesus was a Galilean, the Procurator tried to evade the problem before him by sending Jesus to Herod Antipas, a son of Herod the Great, who had been tetrarch of Galilee and Perea since his father's death. He had come to Jerusalem for the Passover. The supposed site of his house is marked by the little Greek chapel of Nicodemus in the NE part of the present Old City, not far from the site of Antonia. Other sites also have been suggested. The Old Hasmonean palace overlooking the Tyropoeon Valley (*see* § 9 *above*) may have been used by the royal visitor. In any case, Jesus, after refusing to answer Herod's question, was mocked and sent back to Pilate.

The crowd which clamored for Jesus' death and refused to accept Barabbas in his place (Matt. 27:15-26 and parallels) "did not enter the praetorium" (John 18:28). Pilate repeatedly went out to speak to the crowd and back into the praetorium to question Jesus further (John 18:29, 33, 38; 19:4, 9). Once he brought Jesus out and showed him to the crowd, saying: "Here is the man!" (19:5). Near the first station of the cross, where this is thought to have occurred, the street is spanned by a Roman arch traditionally known as the *Ecce Homo* arch. It is part of a triumphal arch of the time of Hadrian, a century later than the crucifixion of Jesus. Pl. XXVII*b*.

John 19:13 says that when Pilate found he could not satisfy the mob except by condemning Jesus to death, "he brought Jesus out and sat down on the judgment seat at a place called The Pavement, and in Hebrew, Gabbatha." The strongest evidence for the location of the praetorium at Antonia—and it is very impressive indeed—is a great stone pavement, more than 150 feet square, under the convent of Notre Dame de Sion across the street from the first station of the cross and a little to the W. The second-century arch just mentioned rests on it and is obviously later. Scratched in the pavement are the complicated diagrams of a Roman game. This was undoubtedly the courtyard of Antonia, and it is probably the very pavement on which Pilate's judgment seat was placed when he pronounced the sentence of death on Jesus. Here, too, in all probability, were posted some of the soldiers who took Jesus into the praetorium and cruelly mocked him (Matt. 27:27-31 = Mark 15:16-20; John 19:1-3).

According to John 19:17, Jesus "went out, bearing his own cross." The second station of the cross is at the foot of the ramp leading down to the street from the Muslim school; here the imposition of the cross is commemorated by pilgrims who follow the Via Dolorosa. The way now follows the street to the W. The incidents marked by the third and fourth stations of the cross are not recorded in the gospels. A broken column at the corner of the street which comes down from the Damascus Gate marks the third station, where Jesus is thought to have fallen under the weight of the cross. At the fourth station, where the Via Dolorosa turns the corner to the S, tradition says that Jesus met his mother. At the first corner to the right the way turns westward again. Here a little shrine with an inscription over the door marks the fifth station, where, it is supposed, Simon of Cyrene was compelled to carry the cross, though the Synoptic gospels imply that this was done at the beginning (Matt. 27:32; Mark 15:21; Luke 23:26).

The street now climbs the W side of the Tyropoeon Valley. About midway up the hill a piece of an old column in the wall of a building indicates the sixth station, where according to tradition Veronica wiped the Master's face. Where the ascending street meets another running straight S from the Damascus Gate, tradition says that there was a city gate in the first century called the Gate of Judgment because a notice of the sentence passed on Jesus was posted on it. A chapel at this corner marks the seventh station of the cross, where Jesus is thought to have fallen again in passing through the gate. There is nothing of this in the gospels, and it is unlikely that there was a city gate at exactly this spot, though there probably was one a little farther to the S. The question depends on the course of the city wall at the time of Jesus, which we shall have to consider presently.

Crossing the street and continuing up the hill to the W, one comes to the eighth station, marked by a cross carved in the wall of a Greek monastery. This is believed to be the place where Jesus spoke to the women of Jerusalem (Luke 23:27-31). From here on, the way is barred by the Greek monastery, and it is necessary to return to the corner, turn to the right, and proceed S to a flight of steps, from the top of which an alley leads to the door of a Coptic monastery. The ninth station, where Jesus is thought to have fallen a third time, is marked here by a column.

The last five of the fourteen stations of the cross are inside the vast Church of the Holy Sepulchre, four of them at the traditional site of Calvary and the last at the tomb itself (*see* SEPULCHRE, CHURCH OF THE HOLY). To reach the church from the ninth station, one must return to the steps and continue down the street to the S, turning to the right around the corner of a Russian convent and following the street toward the W to the court in front of the church.

Just inside the door of the church on the right is the elevated rock which tradition regards as GOLGOTHA or Calvary (Matt. 27:33; Mark 15:22; Luke 23:33; John 19:17). The question of its authenticity has been a subject of distressingly heated controversy. Western visitors are alienated by the childish legends told to pilgrims and tourists and the barbarous fashion in which the place is adorned. What is called Gordon's Calvary, N of the Old City, with its Garden Tomb, preserves an atmosphere more suited to devotion than the ancient Church of the Holy Sepulchre, but the arguments advanced for its authenticity have no historical value. The evidence for the traditional site itself is by no means conclusive; the arguments against it, however, are not cogent, and it remains more probable than any other site that has been suggested. The place where Jesus was crucified was certainly outside the city of that time. John 19:20 says that it was "near the city"; Heb. 13:12 preserves the memory that it was "outside the gate." We cannot trace the tradition of the site farther back than the fourth century A.D., when Constantine built his church there; but unless there had been such a tradition, he would hardly have selected a place which in his time was inside the city. The question therefore depends largely on the location of the city wall in the first century.

What is at issue is the "second wall," as Josephus calls it. The older wall lay farther to the S. Unfortunately Josephus does not describe the course of the second wall precisely. He says only that it began at a gate of the first wall called Gannath (i.e., the Garden Gate), that it enclosed the N quarter of the city, and that it ended at the fortress Antonia (War V.iv.2). On the location of the Gennath Gate authorities differ. If it was near the middle of the old wall, not far from the Tyropoeon Valley, the second wall ran northward well to the E of the hill occupied by the Church of the Holy Sepulchre. If, as seems more likely, the starting point was nearer the W end of the old wall, the second wall may have turned to the E either N or S of the traditional Calvary.

Archaeological evidence has been offered for both hypotheses. That advanced for the more northerly line, enclosing the traditional site, has been shown to be irrelevant. That advanced for the line farther S is more impressive but still not entirely conclusive; it consists of bits of ancient masonry and rock-cuttings which may or may not represent an ancient wall and moat. The existence of other Jewish tombs near the Holy Sepulchre supports the view that this area was outside the wall in the first century. Of course, even if it be granted that the city wall in the time of Jesus lay to the S and E of this place, it does not necessarily follow that the sacred events took place at exactly these particular spots. It is not too much to say, however, that the evidence, as far as it goes, favors this general vicinity.

Since neither the location of the praetorium nor the authenticity of the traditional Calvary can be definitely established, the route between them is of course still less certain, quite apart from the fact that the streets in the time of Jesus lay at many points far below the present level of the ground. The reports of pilgrims through the centuries, moreover, show that the stations of the cross have been variously located at different times and by different groups. The honest and enlightened pilgrim of today finds all this very disappointing. With a little exercise of historical imagination, however, he can still be deeply moved by the fact that somewhere on these very hills his Lord was condemned and crucified.

The eleventh and twelfth stations of the cross, on Calvary itself, commemorate the crucifixion and death of Jesus. The thirteenth station marks a traditional incident, the delivery of Jesus' body to his mother. The fourteenth station is at the Holy Sepulchre. The authenticity of this tomb, in the center of the great rotunda of the ancient church, stands or falls with the authenticity of Calvary. Around both of them the rock has been cut away to produce a level floor, so that they now stand up above the surrounding surface. If this is indeed the tomb of Joseph of Arimathea, in which he reverently laid the body of Jesus (Matt. 27:57-61; Mark 15:42-47; Luke 23:50-56; John 19:38-42), the level of the ground was then much more uneven and somewhat higher than it is now. According to John 19:41 (cf. 20:15), it was in a garden.

A detail in the record of the burial of Jesus is illustrated by a number of Jewish tombs of the period. Joseph, we read, "rolled a great stone to the door of the tomb" (Matt. 27:60), or, as Mark says, "against the door of the tomb" (15:46). In the tombs just mentioned, a circular slab resembling a millstone rolls in a groove so that it covers the opening but can be rolled back to gain access to the tomb. This explains the sealing of the tomb related in Matt. 27:62-66. One of the best examples, belonging unquestionably to the first century, is in the tomb of Helen of Adiabene, of which more will be said later. *See* § 12 *below*.

The Holy Sepulchre is the traditional site, of course, not only of the burial of Jesus but also of his resurrection. Here, it is believed, the women came to anoint the body and found the tomb open and empty (Matt. 28:1-10), and here the risen Lord appeared to Mary Magdalene (John 20:11-18).

A postresurrection appearance to the disciples at Jerusalem is related in Luke 24:33-49; in John 20:19-29 there are two such appearances, eight days apart. The place is not specified; tradition supposes that the disciples were gathered in the same upper room where the Last Supper had been eaten, but there is nothing to indicate this in the text. Acts 1:13 speaks of the "upper room, where they were staying," to which they returned after the Ascension. According to Acts 1:3-5, Jesus appeared repeatedly to the disciples "during forty days" and "charged them not to depart from Jerusalem" until they received the baptism of the Holy Spirit (cf. Luke 24:49).

In Acts 1:12 the Ascension is located on the "mount called Olivet"—i.e., the "Mount of Olives" (*see* §§ *5a-b, 6d, 7c above*); Luke 24:50 places it "as far as Bethany," on the E side of the Mount of Olives, but both the text and the meaning of the phrase rendered "as far as" are uncertain. Tradition points to a place on the summit of the mount, marked by an old chapel now converted into a mosque.

12. The apostolic period to the death of Agrippa I. The first recorded incident in the history of the apostolic church is the selection of Matthias to take the place of Judas among the twelve apostles (Acts 1:15-26). Where this took place is not stated. The eleven disciples had been devoting themselves to prayer "together with the women and Mary the mother of Jesus, and with his brothers" (vss. 12-14); vs. 15, however, speaks of a company of about a hundred and twenty, who could hardly have assembled in the upper room where the eleven were staying (vs. 13).

The fulfilment of the promise of the Holy Spirit at the Feast of Pentecost occurred when "they were all together in one place," not otherwise specified (Acts 2:1). At the sound of the speaking in tongues the multitude of pilgrims "from every nation under heaven" flocked together (vss. 5-6), and Peter addressed them (vss. 14 ff). This implies sufficient space for a considerable assembly, but there is nothing to indicate where it was.

Several incidents related in the early chapters of Acts may be passed over here, because they occurred at the temple (*see* TEMPLE, JERUSALEM, § C1). Even the "common prison" mentioned in 5:18 may have been connected with the sacred area. Where the disciples were gathered when they prayed for boldness to speak the word, and the place was shaken by the power that came to them (4:23-31), where they administered their common affairs (4:32–5:11), and where they ordained seven men to supervise the daily distribution (6:1-6), we have no means of telling. We do not know even in what quarter of the city all these things took place.

Among those who disputed with Stephen and instigated his arrest (6:9 ff) were "some of those who belonged to the synagogue of the Freedmen (as it was called)." A possible reference to this synagogue has been found in a Greek inscription discovered in a cistern on the SE hill of Jerusalem. It says that a synagogue, a guesthouse for strangers, and a bathing establishment were built by a man named Theodotus, son of Vettemus. From the fact that the father's name is Latin it has been inferred that he may have been an emancipated Jewish slave. The script of the inscription favors a date in the first century.

The place where Stephen was stoned to death is designated only as outside the city (Acts 7:58). There are two traditions concerning the site of this first Christian martyrdom. The Dominican Church of St. Stephen, on the Nablus Road N of the Damascus Gate, is built on the foundations of a fifth-century basilica, erected by the Empress Eudoxia to house the relics of the saint and to be her own mausoleum. Whether this was believed at that time to be the place where Stephen died is not clear, but the Crusaders who camped there later so regarded it. The rival site, marked by the Greek Chapel of St. Stephen, is beside the Jericho Road near the bottom of the Kidron Valley, below St. Stephen's Gate. It is attested at a slightly earlier date than the other.

The next incident located at Jerusalem is the criticism of Peter by the "circumcision party" after the conversion of Cornelius (Acts 11:1-8). Meanwhile much else had been happening at Jerusalem. Philo reports an incident which sounds like a variant version of Josephus' story of the ensigns (*see* § 11 *above*). Pilate, says Philo, had the name of the Emperor Tiberius inscribed on shields which were hung on the walls of the palace. The Jewish leaders, unable to induce Pilate to remove them, appealed to the emperor, who ordered the shields removed.

In A.D. 36 Pilate was deposed because of a cruel massacre of Samaritans. The Roman legate in Syria, Vitellius, appointed another procurator and came to Jerusalem himself at the Passover season. His liberal attitude greatly pleased the Jews. The priestly vestments for the festivals, which had been kept in the fortress Antonia since the days of the Hasmonean priest-kings, were now turned over to the priests to be kept in the temple. Before Vitellius left Jerusalem, word came that Tiberius had died and Caligula had become emperor (A.D. 37).

Vitellius and his successor, Petronius, dealt wisely with the Jews, but all chance of tranquillity at Jerusalem was lost when Caligula ordered his own image set up in the temple. Disaster was averted by the prudent procrastination of Petronius and the intercession of Agrippa, a grandson of Herod the Great whom Caligula had made king over the former territories of Philip and Antipas. The death of Caligula further allayed the excitement. The threatened desecration of the temple may well be what is meant by the "desolating sacrilege" in Matt. 24:15; Mark 13:14.

Caligula's successor, Claudius (A.D. 41-54), added Samaria and Judea to the domain of Agrippa, who now reigned as Agrippa I over the whole kingdom of Herod. A famine "in the days of Claudius," which necessitated sending relief from other places to the Jerusalem church, is recorded in Acts 11:27-30. On the whole, however, the reign of Agrippa seems to have been a time of prosperity. A generous patron of the temple and a strict observer of the law, at least while he was in Palestine, the king was idolized by the Jews.

His popularity was probably enhanced by his harsh treatment of the disciples at Jerusalem: he is the "Herod the king" who "laid violent hands upon some who belonged to the church," had James the brother of John put to death, and imprisoned Peter (Acts 12:1-5). Marvelously delivered from prison, Peter went to the house of Mark's mother, but the disciples gathered there could not believe it was really he (vss. 6-19). Where this house was we do not know. There is a tradition which places it where the Syrian Orthodox Monastery of St. Mark now stands in the Old City, not far S of David Street.

One enterprise of Agrippa I has occasioned much debate. The city had now spread beyond the wall to the N, occupying the "fourth hill," Bezetha (*see* § 11 *above*). To protect this new quarter Agrippa began to build what Josephus calls the third wall; but, fearing the emperor's displeasure, he abandoned the project when only the foundations had been laid. The course of the third wall is defined in some detail by Josephus, but the points of reference he names cannot all be identified.

Foundations of an ancient wall which have been uncovered some distance to the N of the city are believed by some archaeologists to be the remains of Agrippa's wall; others find good reason to reject this identification. The foundations are earlier than the Byzantine period, but their construction does not correspond to the description of Josephus. Their course also is not that of Agrippa's wall. It began at Hippicus, one of the towers of Herod's palace (*see* § 10 *above*), and extended northward to a great tower named Psephinus. Part of the foundations of this tower still survive at the base of the "Tower of Goliath" in the NW corner of the Old City.

At this point the wall turned to the E and passed opposite the site of the somewhat later tomb of Helen of Adiabene, the traditional "Tombs of the Kings" (*see* § 13 *below*). Josephus says that this tomb was *ca.* three stadia from the city—i.e., *ca.* five hundred yards, which is approximately the distance between it and the present N wall. The foundations in question are much nearer to Helen's tomb. Agrippa's wall, Josephus continues, passed through the royal caverns, meaning undoubtedly the so-called Quarries of Solomon, which run under the present N wall. At an unidentified tower called the "Fuller's Monument" the wall turned S above the Kidron Valley and rejoined the earlier wall.

What Josephus tells us about the third wall thus corresponds fairly closely with the present N wall of the Old City. Archaeological soundings have shown that Agrippa's wall did not follow exactly the line of the present wall, but probably ran a few feet to the N of it. When the wall considerably farther N was built is an unsolved problem, but it was apparently after the close of the NT period, probably in the second or third century.

13. From the death of Agrippa I to the First Revolt. Soon after Agrippa's death (A.D. 44) Queen Helen of Adiabene, a convert to Judaism, came to Jerusalem. Her palace on the SE hill is mentioned by Josephus in his account of the siege of A.D. 70 (*see* § 14 *below*). In the region N of the temple and outside Agrippa's unfinished wall she had a magnificent tomb made for herself and her family. Under the traditional name of the "Tombs of the Kings" it is still one of the most impressive sights of Jerusalem, a striking example of the mixed style of art which prevailed at that time in the Near East.

Most of the procurators sent by Rome after the death of Agrippa were corrupt and indifferent to Jewish traditions and aspirations. Disorder and messianic uprisings became more and more the order of the day, and contending factions arose among the Jews themselves. The temple was often desecrated by fighting and killing, as one high priest succeeded another. In A.D. 49-50 the Emperor Claudius gave the supervision of the temple and the right to appoint the high priests to Agrippa II, a son of Agrippa I, making him also king of a little kingdom in Syria. As his residence when in Jerusalem, he was given the old Hasmonean palace. *See* § 9 *above*.

Ca. a year later Felix became procurator. Although he married Agrippa's sister, his dealings with the Jews were far from sympathetic. The revolutionary party of the Zealots received especially harsh treatment. It was during this time that the apostle Paul came to Jerusalem and was attacked by a mob for allegedly bringing Greeks into the temple (Acts 21: 27-30). His life was saved by the intervention of the Roman tribune, who took him into the barracks for safety after allowing him to address the crowd from the steps (21:31–23:29). Presumably these barracks were in the fortress Antonia.

The conversation between Paul and the tribune includes a reference to the ASSASSINS and to an Egyptian who led some of them into the desert (21:38). This Egyptian was a Jew from Egypt who promised his followers that from the Mount of Olives they would see the walls of Jerusalem collapse at his command, and could then follow him into the city. Felix attacked them, killed over a hundred of them, and captured two hundred, but their leader escaped. Meanwhile disorders in Jerusalem and throughout the country increased. Felix put to death many brigands and agitators; but, being annoyed by the high priest, Jonathan, he allowed some of the brigands to enter the city, mingle with the worshipers at the temple, and kill Jonathan with the daggers they had concealed in their robes.

In A.D. 60 Felix was removed from office. His successor, Porcius Festus, won the approval of the less extreme elements of the population. Strife arose, however, between the aristocrats of Jerusalem and Agrippa II when the latter built a large dining hall at the top of the old Hasmonean palace, where he could observe what was going on in the temple enclosure as he took his meals. The Jewish leaders thereupon erected a high wall at the W edge of the inner court, cutting off the king's view. Festus ordered them to demolish the wall but let them appeal to the Emperor Nero, who allowed them to leave it standing.

Albinus, who followed Festus, was one of the worst of the procurators. At this time serious unemployment was created at Jerusalem by the completion of construction in the temple courts. A project to relieve the situation by reconstructing one of the temple gates was vetoed by Agrippa II, but he sanctioned an alternative project to pave the city with white stone. A little later Albinus, hearing that he was about to be displaced, tried to please the Jews by executing all the worst criminals in the prisons and releasing the rest.

Gessius Florus, the last procurator, was even worse than Albinus. As though bent on provoking rebellion, he allowed disorder to go unchecked, imprisoned Jews who protested, and misappropriated the funds of the temple. Troops were sent against a crowd at the temple who had demanded that the emperor intervene. Taking up his residence at the palace (presumably that of Herod the Great; *see* § 10 *above*), the procurator now set up his tribunal beside it and heard the supplications of the city's leading men, but then rejected their petitions and turned his troops loose against the people in the market place and streets of the upper city. Many leading Jews of Roman citizenship and rank were scourged and crucified before the procurator's tribunal. Josephus says that *ca.* 3,600 men, women, and children were killed that day. Horrified at the slaughter, Agrippa's sister Berenice (*see* HEROD [FAMILY] § H 7) tried repeatedly to induce Florus to have mercy, but in vain.

Some of the Jewish leaders and priests persuaded the multitude to desist from public lamentation, but Florus apparently did not want peace. Troops brought up from Caesarea fell upon a delegation which met them before the city gates, then pushed through the N quarter Bezetha (*see* § 10 *above*) in the hope of occupying the fortress Antonia and the temple area. Florus himself and his soldiers set out from the palace but were unable to reach Antonia, because the people stopped their passage through the narrow streets and threw darts at them from the housetops. The Jewish insurgents also destroyed the N cloisters of the temple, cutting off access from Antonia.

Florus now withdrew to Caesarea and reported to the legate of Syria that the Jews were in revolt against Rome. Charges against Florus himself were sent also by the Jewish leaders and Berenice. A tribune was sent to Jerusalem to investigate. Persuaded by Agrippa to walk around the city as far as Siloam accompanied only by one servant, the tribune was convinced that the population was peaceably disposed. When he was gone, however, the people, fearing that Nero would hold them responsible for the disorders, decided to send a delegation to Rome to complain against Florus. Agrippa considered this very unwise. Putting Berenice where she could be seen at the Hasmonean palace, he assembled the people at the xystus, a smooth area for athletic contests in the Tyropoeon Valley below the palace. His eloquence persuaded the people to abandon the project of complaining to Nero. When he urged submission to Florus, however, he was so violently opposed that he withdrew to his own kingdom.

The beginning of the war with Rome, in the opinion of Josephus, was the decision of the priests to receive no offering in the temple from any foreigner. This meant the rejection of the emperor's offerings. At the same time the customary sacrifices for rulers were stopped. The leading men of the city, unable to control the rebellion, now appealed to Florus and Agrippa for military assistance. Agrippa sent three thousand horsemen, by whose help the party opposing the revolt occupied the upper city of the W hill, while the insurgents controlled the temple area, the SE hill, and the Tyropoeon Valley. The fortress Antonia was still held by Roman troops.

In the ensuing struggle the party of moderation was soon driven from the upper city and shut up in the Herodian palace. The Hasmonean palace and the high priest's house were burned. The fortress Antonia also fell to the rebels, who burned it and slaughtered its garrison. When the Jews besieged in Herod's palace surrendered, the Romans took refuge in the towers of Hippicus, Phasael, and Mariamne. Eventually they too surrendered and were treacherously massacred.

All this was accomplished in spite of bitter factional struggles among the insurgents themselves. The rebels were now masters of the whole city. In the autumn of 66 the legate of Syria, Cestius Gallus, brought an army against them. The N quarter, Bezetha, was burned, but when his soldiers had reached the temple wall and undermined it, Cestius inexplicably recalled them and withdrew from the city.

All efforts among the Jews to avoid war were now abandoned, and the leaders at Jerusalem attempted to form a military organization. Nero sent his ablest general, Vespasian, to put down the revolt. Arriving in Palestine early in the year 67, Vespasian undertook to get control of the rest of the country before attacking Jerusalem. Time was thus given the rebels to make preparations, including the completion of the N wall which Agrippa I had begun (*see* § 12 *above*); but factional strife in the city, resulting even in frightful slaughter of Jews by Jews or by Idumeans brought in by one group to attack another, prevented effective action.

After a rapid succession of three emperors in one year following the death of Nero, Vespasian became emperor in 69 and went to Rome, leaving his son Titus to carry out the attack on Jerusalem. The story of the siege of 70 cannot be repeated here; its details are of no significance for the understanding of the Bible. The stratagems of the besieged sometimes imperiled the Roman soldiers and even Titus himself, but the end would have been certain even if the Jews had been united among themselves. The bloody strife within the walls between the factions which struggled for possession of different quarters of the city was more horrible than the siege itself.

Titus attacked the city from the NW and took one wall after another. To take the oldest and innermost wall, he set up great mounds or ramps of earth, one of them being near the pool Amygdalon, now known as the Patriarch's Bath or the Pool of Hezekiah. The fortress Antonia and the wall N of the temple were invested in like manner. The whole city was surrounded also by a wall more than five miles long.

Famine was soon added to the horrors of the siege, but the factions in the city continued their insensate fighting and killing. The N wall was finally breached by the battering rams of the Romans; the fortress Antonia was captured and dismantled, the sacred enclosure became a scene of frightful carnage, and the lower city was plundered and burned all the way down to the pool of Siloam. The upper city, too, was laid waste. Of Herod's palace only the three great towers remained standing to mark the site.

For both Judaism and Christianity the fall of Jerusalem and the destruction of the temple marked a turning point. The Christian community had escaped to Pella across the Jordan before the siege. No more incidents of biblical history are located at Jerusalem. Jesus had foretold the time when the city would be surrounded by armies, and her enemies would cast up a bank about her (Luke 19:43; 21:20); he had foreseen the ruin of the temple, leaving not one stone on another (Mark 13:2).

Since then the Holy City has gone through innumerable vicissitudes, rarely knowing peace for any length of time. Christians may well pray for the peace of Jerusalem (Ps. 122:6), remembering always at the same time that the true worship of God can never again be localized either there or at any other place on earth (John 4:21). The new Jerusalem of Rev. 21 is no earthly city, but one that will come down "out of heaven from God" (vs. 2).

Bibliography. J. Jeremias, *Jerusalem zur Zeit Jesu* (1923—); G. Dalman, *Jerusalem und sein Gelände* (1930); D. Baldi, *Enchiridion Locorum Sanctorum* (1935); J. Simons, *Jerusalem in the OT* (1952); L. H. Vincent, *Jérusalem de l'AT* (1954); M. Avi-Yonah, ed., *Sepher Yerushalayim* (*The Book of Jerusalem;* 1956).

M. Burrows

JERUSHA jĭ ro͞o'shə [ירושא, *from* ירש, possession] (II Kings 15:33); JERUSHAH [ירושה] (II Chr. 27:1). The mother of Jotham king of Judah.

JESHAIAH jĭ shā'yə [ישעיה, ישעיהו, Yahu has saved (*same spelling as for* Isaiah); Apoc. (A) Ἰεσσίας, Ὠσαίας; Apoc. (B) Ἐσιας *in* I Esd. 8:33]; KJV twice JESAIAH jə sā'yə (I Chr. 3:21; Neh. 11:7); KJV Apoc. JOSIAS jō sī'əs in I Esd. 8:33; OSAIAS ō sā'yəs in I Esd. 8:48. **1.** A descendant of King David in the postexilic period (I Chr. 3:21).

2. A Levite musician, one of the "sons of Jeduthun" (I Chr. 25:3, 15).

3. One of the Levites sharing supervision of the temple treasuries (I Chr. 26:25).

4. An Elamite among the Babylonian exiles who returned to Jerusalem with Ezra (Ezra 8:7; I Esd. 8:33).

5. A Merarite Levite in the same company (Ezra 8:19; I Esd. 8:48).

6. A Benjaminite ancestor of one of the residents of postexilic Jerusalem (Neh. 11:7). The name is not given in the parallel I Chr. 9:7-8.

B. T. Dahlberg

JESHANAH jĕsh'ə nə [ישנה (II Chr. 13:19), שן (I Sam. 7:12)]; KJV SHEN shĕn in I Sam. 7:12. One of the cities taken, with its villages, by Abijah in a war with Jeroboam I (II Chr. 13:19), suggesting a location on the border of Judah and Israel. "Jeshanah" is probably to be read for "Shen" in I Sam. 7:12, in view of the similarity of the names and the region involved.

Apparently the same place, called Isanas, was the headquarters of Pappus, general of Antigonus, where the forces of Herod the Great were victorious (Jos. Antiq. XIV.xv.12).

The most probable of several proposed locations is Burj el-Isaneh, *ca.* three miles N of Jifneh.

Bibliography. W. F. Albright, "Ophrah and Ephraim," *AASOR,* IV (1922-23), 125-26. W. L. Reed

JESHARELAH jĕsh'ə rē'lə [ישראלה] (I Chr. 25:14). A musician among the sons of Asaph during the time of David. The name is probably a corrupt form of Asharelah (vs. 2).

JESHEBEAB jĭ shĕb'ĭ ăb [ישבאב, *perhaps* may the father (*here secular*) endure (*i.e.,* enjoy prolonged life)] (I Chr. 24:13). A priest or priestly house, descended from Aaron.

Bibliography. M. Noth, *Die israelitischen Personennamen* (1928), p. 247; cf. p. 67n. B. T. Dahlberg

JESHER jē'shər [ישר, (the deity) shows himself just(?)] (I Chr. 2:18). A son of Caleb, listed in the genealogy of Judah.

Bibliography. M. Noth, *Die israelitischen Personennamen* (1928), p. 189.

JESHIMON jĭ shī'mən [הישימון, הישמן, a waste, a desert]. Alternately: DESERT; DESERT WASTES; WILDERNESS. **1.** A waste area in the neighborhood of Ziph (I Sam. 23:19, 24; 26:1, 3), N of the hill of Hachilah, and of Maon. The location seems to be a few miles S of Hebron.

2. KJV translation in Num. 21:20; 23:28 (RSV DESERT). It is a waste, overlooked from the top of Peor and from the top of Pisgah. The location would seem to be near the NE end of the Dead Sea, perhaps including the site of Beth-jeshimoth.

See also Desert; Wilderness. E. D. Grohman

JESHISHAI jĭ shĭsh'ī [ישישי, venerable(?)] (I Chr. 5:14). A Gadite.

JESHOHAIAH jĕsh'ə hā'yə [ישוחיה, *possibly* Yahu humbles] (I Chr. 4:36). A prince of the tribe of Simeon.

JESHUA jĕsh'ŏŏ ə [ישוע, Yahu is salvation]; KJV once JESHUAH (I Chr. 24:11); KJV Apoc. JESUS jē'zəs ['Ιησοῦς] (I Esd. 5:8, 24; 9:19, 48; Ecclus. 49:12); JESSUE jĕsh'ŏŏ ĭ ['Ιησουέ (A)] (I Esd. 5:26); JESU jē'zōō, jē'sōō ['Ιησοῦς] (I Esd. 8:63). Alternately: JOSHUA jŏsh'ŏŏ ə [יהושע, *variant of* ישוע (*in* Haggai *and* Zechariah)]. **1.** The form of JOSHUA used in Neh. 8:17. *See* Joshua Son of Nun.

2. A division of Aaronite priests identified by the Chronicler first with the time of David (I Chr. 24:11), and perhaps the same priestly house as is listed among the returning exiles in Ezra 2:36 (cf. Neh. 7:39; I Esd. 5:24); possibly represented also in 5 *below.*

3. A Levite who assisted in the distribution of the priests' allowances during the reign of Hezekiah (*ca.* 715-687 b.c.; II Chr. 31:15).

4. A subdivision of the (nonpriestly) clan of Pahath-Moab listed among the exiles returning from Babylon (Ezra 2:6; cf. Neh. 7:11; I Esd. 5:11 [RSV only]).

5. A high priest (in Haggai and Zechariah called Joshua); *ca.* 560-490 b.c.; son of Jozadak (Jehozadak), who was among the Jews taken into Babylonian captivity in 586 b.c. (I Chr. 6:15—H 5:41). Jeshua the high priest was contemporary with Zerubbabel the governor and the prophets Haggai and Zechariah in postexilic Jerusalem under the Persian king Darius Hystaspis (522-486).

The books of Haggai and Ezra generally mention his name and Zerubbabel's together as a pair, indicating respectively their ecclesiastical and civil leadership of the Jerusalem community, and one of the visions of Zechariah epitomizes this relationship as "the two anointed who stand by the Lord of the whole earth" (cf. Zech. 4:11-14).

Following Zerubbabel, who is first, Jeshua's name heads the Chronicler's lists of returned exiles (Ezra 2:2; Neh. 7:7; 12:1, 10, 26; cf. I Esd. 5:8). He shares with Zerubbabel the responsibility for building the Jerusalem temple, aroused and spurred on by the preaching of the prophets Haggai and Zechariah (Hag. 1:1, 12, 14; 2:2, 4; cf. Ezra 5:2; Ecclus. 49:11-12). Although the Chronicler projects the beginning of their reconstruction of the temple and its cult back into the time of the Persian king Cyrus—i.e., to the years immediately following the termination of the Exile in 538 b.c. (Ezra 3:2, 8; 4:3; cf. 1:1-2)—the work described in this connection is generally presumed to belong in the reign of Darius (*see* Ezra and Nehemiah, Books of; Haggai; Zerubbabel). Apparently Jeshua is one of those signified in Enoch 89:72—the others being Zerubbabel and either Ezra or Nehemiah—where are mentioned "three of those sheep" who "turned back and came and entered and began to build up all that had fallen down of that house." *See bibliography.*

Jeshua (or Joshua) is the subject of several of the prophet Zechariah's apocalyptic visions. In one the high priest appears before a heavenly court in which he is absolved of iniquity and his "filthy garments" are exchanged for clean apparel, and he as high priest is given jurisdiction over the temple (Zech. 3). The vision would appear to attempt an expression of divine sanction for the high priest's ecclesiastical authority in the face of doubts concerning the qualifications of a returned exile for the office. Zech. 6:9-14 (cf. 4:14) suggests, on the other hand, that the high priest is to have a supportive role vis-à-vis the royal throne as represented in the governor Zerubbabel, a ruler in the Davidic line. The phrasing of 6:12-13 anticipates that "the Branch"—i.e., Zerubbabel, not Joshua (as now in vs. 11)—was to receive the crown of David. However, the passage was emended later to read "Joshua" by a redactor who knew, after the event, that both civil and religious authority in Judah devolved finally upon the high priest after Persia withdrew all political power from the house of David. *See* Haggai; Priests and Levites; Zechariah; Zerubbabel.

Some of Joshua's family are listed among those contemporaries of Ezra who married foreign wives (Ezra 10:18; cf. I Esd. 9:19).

Bibliography. C. C. Torrey, *Ezra Studies* (1910), p. 319; L. W. Batten, *Ezra and Nehemiah,* ICC (1913), p. 107; R. H. Charles, "Book of Enoch," *Apoc. and Pseudep. of the OT* (1913), II 256; W. F. Albright, "Date and Personality of the Chronicler," *JBL,* XL (1921), 122; R. H. Pfeiffer, *Introduction to the OT* (1948), p. 605; D. W. Thomas, Exegesis of Zech. 1–8, *IB,* VI (1956), 1067-71, 1080.

6. A Levitical house or clan, perhaps descended from 3 *above,* among the exiles returning to Jerusalem from Babylon (Ezra 2:40; 8:33; cf. Neh. 7:43; 12:8, 24; I Esd. 5:26; 8:63). This is doubtless the family from whom is descended the Ezer son of Jeshua who worked on Nehemiah's wall (Neh. 3:19), and a representative of this house was among those who signed the "covenant of Ezra" (Neh. 10:9—H 10:10). The individuals following below are doubtless members of this family.

7. A Levite chief who helped supervise the work of rebuilding the temple in the days of Zerubbabel the governor and Jeshua the high priest (Ezra 3:9).

8. One of the Levites who interpreted the law as Ezra read from it before the people (Neh. 8:7; cf. I Esd. 9:48; but *see bibliography*). In Neh. 9:4-5 he and his colleagues direct the public service of worship.

Bibliography. R. A. Bowman, Exegesis of Nehemiah, *IB,* III (1954), 736-37.

B. T. Dahlberg

9. A town occupied by Jewish returnees from the Exile (Neh. 11:26); modern Tell es-Sa'wi, NE of Beer-sheba. *See also* Sheba 3.

JESHURUN jĕsh'ə rən [ישרון, *probably from* ישר, upright] (Deut. 32:15; 33:5, 26; Isa. 44:2); KJV JESURUN jĕs'ə rən. A variant form of the name Israel. It was usually regarded by scholars as a late and artificial construction after the analogy of the name Zebulun (*cf.* Jeduthun), but the two poems of Deut. 32–33 cannot now be regarded as late. It is perhaps best taken to be a hypocoristicon from the name Israel, occurring only in poetry, and conceivably intended to emphasize the root meaning, "upright." The LXX does not treat this as a proper name, but instead translates it very curiously with ἠγαπημένος, "beloved" (ἠγαπημένος 'Ισραὴλ in Isa. 44:2). The same Greek word occurs repeatedly as an appellative of Egyptian kings during the Greek period. Since the passage in Deutero-Isaiah connects the term with the Servant who is chosen, the corresponding Greek word occurs repeatedly as an adjective characterizing both Jesus (Eph. 1:6) and the NT church (Col. 3:12; I Thess. 1:4; II Thess. 2:13; Jude 1). In almost every passage the concept of Election is closely connected.

G. E. Mendenhall

JESIAH. KJV alternate form of Isshiah.

JESIMIEL jĭ sĭm'ĭ əl [ישימאל, may God establish] (I Chr. 4:36). A prince of the tribe of Simeon.

Bibliography. M. Noth, *Die israelitischen Personennamen* (1928), pp. 28, 36, 202.

JESSE jĕs'ĭ [ישי; אישי; 'Ιεσσαί]. The father of King David. He was of the tribe of Judah and resided in Jerusalem. Jesse is first introduced in the narrative which describes the visit of the prophet Samuel to Bethlehem to anoint, in the place of Saul, one of the sons of Jesse. When the prophet had called the guests to the sacrificial meal, he had pass in review before him all the sons of Jesse except David, but none was chosen. When David, the youngest son of Jesse, was finally summoned from tending the sheep, Samuel anointed him as the future king of Israel (I Sam. 16:1-13).

Somewhat later Jesse received messengers from King Saul, petitioning that David be sent to the court to alleviate the periodic mental depression of the monarch. Jesse not only acceded to this request but also sent along with his son a present of foodstuffs for the king. When a second request was made by Saul, that David be permitted to reside at the court, Jesse likewise granted it (I Sam. 16:14-23).

From another source in the book of Samuel it is recounted that on the occasion when Jesse sent David with provisions for his three eldest sons, who were serving in the army of Saul in the campaign against the Philistines in the valley of Elah, the famous encounter of David with the Philistine giant took place (I Sam. 17:12 ff).

Although Jesse is described as well advanced in years when David was but a lad (I Sam. 17:12), he appears to have survived a sojourn in the land of Moab, where David took his parents during the time of his proscription by Saul (22:3-4).

Jesse was the son of Obed and the grandson of the opulent Boaz, the hero of the story of Ruth (Ruth 4:17, 22; I Chr. 2:12; Matt. 1:5-6; Luke 3:32). He was the father of eight sons: Eliab, Abinadab, Shimea or Shammah, Nethanel, Raddai, Ozem, Elihu (I Chr. 27:18; *see bibliography*), and David; and two daughters: Zeruiah and Abigail (I Chr. 2:13-16). A discrepancy appears, however, when Abigail (called Abigal) is described as the daughter of Nahash (II Sam. 17:25). It has been proposed that in this verse the name Nahash is a textual importation from the following verse; or that Nahash is the wife of Jesse; or that Jesse may have contracted with the family of Nahash, king of Ammon, a beena marriage, in which the children would bear the maternal family name.

The designation of David as the "son of Jesse" was an opprobrious epithet used by those who were inimically disposed toward him, as Saul (I Sam. 20:27, 30-31; 22:7-8), Doeg (22:9), Nabal (25:10), and the ten tribes (I Kings 12:16). However, the designation subsequently achieved a continuing venerability (I Chr. 10:14; 29:26; Acts 13:22), while the similar expressions "shoot from the stump of Jesse" and "the root of Jesse" (Isa. 11:1, 10 = Rom. 15:12) became symbols in messianic prophecy.

Bibliography. W. Rudolph, *Chronikbücher* (1956), p. 180.

E. R. Dalglish

JESSUE. KJV Apoc. alternate form of Jeshua.

JESU. KJV Apoc. alternate form of Jeshua.

JESUI. KJV alternate form of Ishvi.

JESURUN. KJV alternate form of Jeshurun.

JESUS jē' zəs ['Ιησοῦς = יהושע, Joshua]. **1.** Grandfather of Jesus son of Sirach (Prologue to Ecclesiasticus).

2. Son of Sirach; author of ECCLESIASTICUS. *See* SIRACH, SON OF.

3. *See* JESUS CHRIST.

4. Jesus Barabbas. *See* BARABBAS.

5. Jesus Justus. *See* JUSTUS 3.

6. KJV Apoc. alternate form of JESHUA.

7. KJV translation in Acts 7:45; Heb. 4:8. *See* JOSHUA SON OF NUN. F. W. GINGRICH

JESUS, WISDOM OF. A Gnostic writing discovered at Chenoboskion in 1946 (*see* APOCRYPHA, NT), based on the Letter of Eugnostos (*see* EUGNOSTOS, LETTER OF), and in the form of a dialogue between the resurrected Jesus and twelve disciples and seven holy women. In an appendix Mary Magdalene (who played an important role in Gnostic literature) inquires regarding the origin and function of the disciples.

The precise relation of this document with the one bearing the same title in the famous Berlin MSS is still uncertain. M. S. ENSLIN

JESUS CHRIST. The personal name of the one whose title, "Christ" (or "the Christ"), gave its name to the Christian religion (Acts 11:26). The English form of the word goes back to the Latin (*Iesus*), which transliterates the Greek; but the original Hebrew form was *Joshua,* or more fully *Yehoshuah* ("Yahweh is salvation," or ". . . saves," or ". . . will save"), which Matthew (1:21) found especially significant, "for he [i.e., either Jesus or God] will save his people from their sins." This was an early Jewish Christian reflection on the meaning of Jesus' name; it would not have occurred to anyone but a believer. The name was fairly common in the first century; Josephus mentions nineteen persons called Jesus. The popularity may reflect the rising tide of nationalism which accompanied and followed the Maccabean War, and only increased under the Roman domination; for the first to bear the name was Joshua the son of Nun (Josh. 1:1), who led the Israelites in the conquest of Canaan. (Cf. Heb. 4:8, where the KJV reads "Jesus"—i.e., Joshua; the names were identical both in the NT and in the LXX. In Matt. 27:16-17 the MSS 1 etc. sy^{s} sy^{pal} and Origen read "Jesus Barabbas" to distinguish him from Jesus of Nazareth.)

In order to distinguish their Master from others of the name, the disciples used various phrases, such as "Jesus of Nazareth" (Luke 24:19), "Jesus, Son of David" (a messianic title; Mark 10:47), "the Galilean" (Mark 14:70), "the Nazarene" (Mark 14:67; cf. Matt. 26:71), "the prophet" (Matt. 21:11; Luke 7:39; 24:19). Perhaps significantly, the usual appellation "son of so-and-so" (naming his father) is not used: Jesus is described as "son of Joseph" only in Luke 4:22; John 1:45; 6:42 (contrast Mark 6:3: "the son of Mary," and Matt. 13:55: "the carpenter's son," though many scholars suspect that the text has been altered at this point, at least in Mark). None of these appellatives survived for very long in Greek-speaking Gentile Christianity (though "son of Mary" was revived in medieval devotion); the Gentile church preferred titles with a theological connotation. Even before the period of Paul's missionary activity—i.e., probably from the very beginning of Gentile Christianity—the title "Christ" (*Christos* = "anointed" = Messiah) had tended to become a proper name, either in the usual form, "Jesus Christ," or (less commonly) "Christ Jesus"—the latter order retained more of the original significance, "the Messiah Jesus." Throughout the later Christian church, in all its branches, "Jesus Christ" has been used as the proper name of Jesus.

The history of this title and its transformation into a proper noun reflects the earliest development of Christology, which began with a Jewish messianic concept and ended with the metaphysical idea of divine incarnation. It also reflects the spread of Christianity in the Greco-Roman world, where Greek and Latin proper nouns usually included two words, a personal name with an appellative, like Julius Caesar, Titius Justus, Diodorus Siculus, or Marcus Aurelius.

A. *SOURCES.* 1. Paul. The earliest literary reference to the birth of Jesus is in Paul's letter to the churches in Galatia (Gal. 4:4-5): "When the time had fully come, God sent forth his Son, born of a woman, born under the law, to redeem those who were under the law, so that we might receive adoption as sons." The statement is entirely theological and characteristically Pauline. The "fulness of time" probably means "at the end of the ages" (cf. Dan. 11:35; Tob. 14:5; Syr. Bar. 40:3; II Esd. 9:5; 11:44), rather than at the end of a particular sequence of historical events, preparatory to Christ's coming, or as a result of some special development of religious ideas or even of revelation (a view which is partly patristic, partly modern). "Born of a woman" is scarcely a reference to the Virgin Birth (though some read it: "born of *the* woman"); instead, like all anti-Gnostic, anti-Docetic language, including that of the Apostles' Creed, it meant: "He was truly born, of flesh and blood, not a phantom [i.e., a purely 'spiritual'] redeemer who appeared only to disappear and leave behind him a collection of esoteric doctrines" (cf. Job 14:1; 15:14; Heb. 2:14). "Born under the law" affirms that he was a Jew, a member of the sacred covenant with Israel, a fact attested by the whole NT and questioned only in the interest of bizarre modern "Aryan" or anti-Semitic theories.

Paul's statement is an example and illustration of his usual way of referring to the historical life of Jesus (cf. Rom. 1:3-4; II Cor. 5:16). The facts of Jesus' earthly life are presupposed, but not stated; Paul builds upon them, interprets or reinterprets them, but does not describe them. He presupposes that the story of Jesus is already familiar to his readers (as he does again in Gal. 3:1). The narratives of Jesus' life, teaching, ministry, death, and exaltation were undoubtedly a part both of the earliest Christian PREACHING (or kerygma) of the gospel, the new message of salvation, and also of the detailed teaching (didache; *see* CHURCH, LIFE AND ORGANIZATION OF) based upon the written OT as well as upon the church's oral tradition (cf. Luke 1:1-4). Hence the assumption that Paul's references to Jesus provide support for the "Christ myth" theory—popular *ca.* 1910, and occasionally revived—rests upon a strange and unrealistic view of Paul himself—i.e., his mind, his writings, and his public teaching. In particular, it rests upon a mistranslation of II Cor. 5:16: "From now on, . . . we regard no one from a human point of view; even though we once regarded Christ from a human point of view, we regard him thus no longer." This is no repudiation or minimizing of knowledge about the "earthly" Jesus, let alone an attempt to explain or qualify Paul's disregard for the facts of Jesus' life; instead, it shows Paul's insistence upon the supernatural, divine, and therefore absolute significance of Jesus' life, death, and resurrection (see vss. 17-19). Yet even this theological statement (like the one in Gal. 4:4) presupposes the historical facts which are at the basis of the discussion. So also do many other references in the Pauline letters. Occasionally, as in I Cor. 11:23-25 (the Last Supper); 15:3-8 (the resurrection appearances), Paul cites specific events. At other times one must read between the lines for references to the life of Jesus, as in Rom. 15:8; I Cor. 13; Gal. 3:1; Phil. 2:5-11. It is inconceivable that these are references to some "mythical" or purely legendary or otherwise unhistorical figure.

A similar situation is reflected elsewhere in the NT, outside the gospels, as in Heb. 13:12 (Jesus was crucified outside Jerusalem); II Pet. 1:17-18 (the Transfiguration). The events are presupposed, are referred to as already familiar to the readers, and are either cited as evidence or given a further interpretation.

2. The gospels. A consideration of the earliest references to Jesus, found not only in the letters of Paul but also in other early Christian writings outside the gospels (e.g., the apostolic fathers and the apologists), will prepare the modern reader to approach the main sources—the four gospels. These also are "theological" writings, whose purpose is either to convince their contemporaries that Jesus is divine and so to win them for eternal life (John 20:30-31), or to set forth a more satisfactory interpretation of the meaning of his life than the one proposed by Jewish or pagan opponents or by Docetic Gnostics (*see* GNOSTICISM). The inference is sometimes drawn that such theological or apologetic—not to say polemical—writings do not furnish adequate data for reconstructing the biography of Jesus or even for drawing a clear and consistent picture of his character, mission, and teaching. But it may be said in reply that it is precisely the variety found in the gospels and in their underlying traditions—a variety which survived and was really not greatly affected by the unifying theological interpretation—which provides us with the range and variety in testimony which are needful in interpreting the life of Jesus. But the gospels are not biographies of Jesus. Instead, they are the writing-down of the traditions of his earthly life, his teaching, death, and resurrection, as a part—the historical part—of the early Christian kerygma, the proclamation of the message of salvation in and through him, his work (in the past), and his coming PAROUSIA.

As a matter of fact, very few detailed biographies have come down to us from the ancient world: Cicero's (based on his letters), Alexander's (based on the memoirs of his generals), Caesar's (based on his "commentaries")—these are the chief examples. Such collections as Plutarch's *Parallel Lives of Famous Greeks and Romans,* or Suetonius' *Lives of the Twelve Caesars,* Eunapius' *Lives of the Sophists,* Diogenes Laertes' *Lives of the Philosophers,* are usually based on tradition, occasionally supplemented by documents. Tacitus' *Life of Agricola,* Josephus' *Autobiography* (= Antiq. XXI, in the second edition), are based on personal recollections. The oft-cited *Life of Apollonius of Tyana* by Philostratus (*ca.* A.D. 210) is not really a biography at all but a *Tendenzschrift,* possibly in imitation of the gospels, written "in praise of Apollonius" and for the purpose of supporting the revived pagan religion in the court of the Severi, especially at the request of the Empress Julia Domna. Xenophon's *Memorabilia of Socrates* was only an anecdotal memoir, designed to add further luster to the fame of this philosopher, who had left no writings to posterity. Hence it cannot be assumed that the church fell in with a custom already well established in providing itself with written records of the life of Jesus; instead, as the historians of ancient literature now recognize, the church created this type of literature to serve its own purposes. The material thus used was the oral tradition which had circulated in the church itself, from the beginning. The gospels were, therefore, not literary works, written for publication and wide dissemination in the Greek-speaking world of the first and second centuries, but represent the compilation and editing of the traditions as handed down within the church itself.

The reasons for writing were obvious: the age of the earlier "eyewitnesses and ministers of the word" (Luke 1:1-4) was drawing to a close; the stories from Jesus' life and his reported sayings, parables, controversies, and expositions of scripture—which the Christians used in their services of worship, as supplementing the readings from the OT—must be written down if they were to be preserved for continued use. The appeal to such Christian writings as were already in existence (e.g., Paul's letters) could conceivably—without the supplementing oral traditions of Jesus' life—be misinterpreted, e.g., in a Gnostic or other partisan direction; hence, for these and still other reasons, the necessity of writing down the tradition was strongly felt, and led to the composition of the four gospels—and of others—in the period following *ca.* A.D. 65. *See bibliography.*

a. The nature of the gospels. The nature of the gospels needs to be borne constantly in mind; for, although it is widely recognized that their purpose and character are "theological," the bearing of this upon their historical interpretation and use in writing the life of Jesus is often overlooked. As already in the pre-Pauline and Pauline tradition, the earthly life of Jesus is dominated by the figure of the risen and exalted Christ; it is the heavenly Lord, whose words and deeds during the period preceding his resurrection and exaltation are related here. The significance of "all that Jesus began to do and teach" (Acts 1:1) is found, not in the ongoing sequences of historical continuity, his personal influence, the growth of his fellowship, the results of his "founding" of a new religion—things a biography would record and emphasize—but in its relevance to the coming event of his resurrection, glorification, and final parousia. His life is interpreted as the climax of OT prophecy and preparation; his own words are given a deeper relevance to the future—i.e., the period in which the church was now living and witnessing to him; thus the whole tradition forms the main subject and substance of the early Christian propaganda, *the* GOSPEL or "good news" of salvation in and through the Lord Jesus Christ.

By the same process, words of early Christian prophets (as well as those of the OT) are occasionally added to the tradition, since they have been spoken "in his name," and are as authentic "words of the Lord" as were those of Jesus himself as he walked on earth (e.g., Rev. 1-3). The reconstruction of the life of Jesus and the recovery of his teaching in its earliest form—i.e., as delivered by Jesus himself—therefore involves a careful literary and historical examination of the gospels; for the original stratum of tradition must be distinguished from later levels, and then at the end it must be recognized that this earliest stratum is itself "theological"—i.e., interpreted or set forth in terms of a definite set of presuppositions regarding God's purposes and activities in this present age, preparatory to his fuller self-revelation in his acts in the age to come. There is no "bare" history, or "mere" or "pure" history; all history is interpreted history.

History has meaning, and so is remembered, only because it has been interpreted in one or another particular way. Nowhere is this principle more obvious than in the gospels.

The word "gospel" is from Old English *godspel,* "good spell"—i.e., "good news." (The association with God and substitution of "God" for "good" came later.) The English term thus meant, originally, what εὐαγγέλιον meant in NT Greek: the "good news" of salvation in the age to come. In this sense, the word was used chiefly by Paul (e.g., Gal. 1:6-9). The use of the term as referring to a book (i.e., the one containing this message of "good news") came only in the second century, as in Just. Apol. 1.66; Dial. 8.2; 11.3; 15.3; II Clem. 8.5; Ign. Phila. 8.2; Smyr. 7.2; Diognetus 11.6. Even so, the earliest usage still referred to the contents of the book—i.e., the subject of the fourfold gospel canon which was collected *ca.* A.D. 150. To this day, the titles of the books by the four evangelists are simply "[The Gospel] According to Matthew," "According to Mark," etc. The popular usage in the present day, "The Gospel of Matthew," "The Gospel of Mark," etc., with its question-begging assumption of authorship, was wholly unknown in the earliest period of the church history.

b. The Gospel of Mark. The earliest of the four was MARK, written probably late in the sixties, just before the fall of Jerusalem in A.D. 70. It contained the gospel—i.e., the tradition of Jesus' life and teaching, forming part of the Christian kerygma—as it circulated in and was cherished by the Christian community in Rome, where recently both Peter and Paul had died as martyrs, along with many others; the story, without names, is told by Tacitus in his *Annals* XV.44, where the massacre of the Christians is attributed to the Emperor Nero. Whether or not the author or editor—i.e., compiler—of this gospel was the Mark referred to in Acts 12:25; 13:13; 15:37-40; or in I Pet. 5:13, is uncertain. Marcus was a very common Roman name, in the first and second centuries, but Papias of Hierapolis (*ca.* 130) evidently assumed that all the NT passages just cited refer to Mark the evangelist (see Euseb. Hist. III.39.15).

The traditions preserved in Mark are arranged in a clearly recognizable order, which some scholars even believe to have been that of the early Jewish Christian ecclesiastical or liturgical year, from the Christian observance of Rosh Hashanah to Passover (=Easter), with additional lections for Passover week (or Holy Week) relating the last days of Jesus in Jerusalem, his death and burial. (*See bibliography.*) The story begins with the prophetic ministry and message of John the Baptist, Jesus' baptism and temptation, and his own ministry in Galilee after John was imprisoned; this ministry falls into two main parts, in Galilee and in Jerusalem. Even within these two divisions there are various sequences and collections of material which must go back to the oral tradition as it first began to be gathered about various subjects and grouped accordingly, either orally or (here and there) in writing. Thus the ministry in Galilee (1:14–10:52) consists of two parts:

a) Jesus' work in the towns about the Sea of Galilee (1:14–5:43), includes the events of a day in Capernaum, told with vivid detail (1:16-38), a series of controversies with the scribes (2:1–3:6; 3:22-30), a group of parables (4:1-34), and a collection of great miracle stories (4:35–5:43). It is impossible to assume that these groups represent any but the most general chronological scheme—Papias said that Mark wrote "by no means in order"!—or that they give us more than sample incidents and teachings from Jesus' ministry in his homeland, Galilee.

b) Chs. 6–10 of Mark recount a series of more distant journeys—i.e., outside Galilee (e.g., to the N, where two more or less parallel accounts are given of what may have been the same journey, in 6:30–7:37; 8:1-26), three more controversies (7:1-23; 8:11-12; 10:1-12), and the great central section of Mark on the "way of the cross" (8:27–10:45), which is clearly addressed to a martyr church, and culminates in the sublime saying recorded in 10:45; it includes a whole sequence of "discipleship" sayings (8:34-38; 9:33-50; 10:13-31, 35-45).

By ch. 10, Jesus is already on his way to Jerusalem, where his ministry is to culminate in his death (foreseen in 8:31; 9:31; 10:32 ff). Here is included another series of controversies (11:27–12:34, supplemented by vss. 35-40), the great apocalyptic discourse in ch. 13 (with material from the so-called "Little Apocalypse" in vss. 6-8, 14-20, 24-27), for which obviously there was no other, certainly no more appropriate, place than right where it is, at the conclusion of the Jerusalem ministry, and just preceding the passion narrative.

The narrative in chs. 14–15 is probably Mark's revision of the older Roman form of the passion narrative, which was known to all the Christian churches (cf. Gal. 3:1), but which took somewhat different form as it was studied, revised, and amplified in various places—or by various evangelists. The general course of events is the same in all the gospels; but the details vary greatly, for all the gospels come from a period before rigid canonization and the stereotyping of form and content precluded any further elaboration or revision of the story. Mark's passion narrative probably reached its climax in the testimony of the Roman centurion (15:39), to which was appended, naturally, the account of Jesus' burial. Finally, the account of the finding of the empty tomb (16:1-8) is Mark's closest approximation to the story of the Resurrection, which he entirely presupposed (as did every early Christian), and undoubtedly accepted in the sense in which it had long before been recounted and interpreted by Paul (cf. I Cor. 15:3-8), though his story also clearly implies the physical reality of the event.

It is now thought that the "blocks" of material found in Mark represent old pre-Markan sources—i.e., collections of gospel tradition. In addition, there are traces of early "sequences," in which the material probably had already been arranged for didactic use (e.g., the "discourse" on the washing of hands—i.e., ceremonial cleansing—as contained in Mark 7, or the discipleship theme which lies just under the surface and juts out repeatedly in 8:27–10:45). There is little question that the arrangement of the tradition had begun before Mark wrote. There were "sources of sources," even before the earliest gospel was written.

The importance of Mark's arrangement of the traditional material cannot be exaggerated. In spite of the rearrangements, omissions, and additions made by Luke and Matthew (*see* SYNOPTIC PROBLEM), Mark's order continued to dominate the presentation of the life of Jesus. It has been argued that it tallies with the order found in the speeches of Peter in the first half of Acts, and therefore must reflect the original, authentic sequence of events. But the theory that the speeches in Acts are derived from early sources is very questionable; and, by hypothesis, Luke had followed Mark in preparing the gospel which bears his name, and naturally did the same in writing its sequel, the book of Acts. There is a strong probability that Mark follows a trustworthy general sequence: John the Baptist, Jesus in Galilee, more distant journeys, the journey to Judea, his visit to Jerusalem, arrest, trial, death, resurrection. But this is no guarantee of details, and the late-nineteenth-century "Markan hypothesis," which assumed that the primitive "Petrine" Gospel of Mark retained the authentic recollections of an eyewitness, in the exact order of events, is now generally abandoned. Papias says, among other things, that Mark was not himself an eyewitness (contrary to modern theories which identify him with the young man in the garden in Mark 14:51-52), and also that—as mentioned above—he did not write "in order" (τάξει)—i.e., in correct sequence (contrast Luke 1:3—καθεξῆς). It is obvious that Mark's order is chronological only in its widest, most general outline; it is, in fact, far more topical than chronological. Mark's purpose was not that of a historian or biographer, but of a compiler of traditions—the traditions of the Roman church, now threatened with persecution and perhaps suppression. He wrote to encourage this martyr church, his fellow Christians, to stand fast and remain loyal to Christ in spite of outrage, torture, even death. *See* MARK, GOSPEL OF.

c. Luke and Matthew. The order of the other gospels is in general that of Mark, but each has its own plan and purpose. Luke-Acts, of which the gospel formed Part I, is an apologetic writing, designed to show that Christianity was not a subversive movement, and that neither Jesus nor Paul, nor the other apostles, nor the rank and file of Christians from the beginning of the Christian movement, had ever threatened public law and order or encouraged revolution against Rome. In fact, the Christians were entitled to the same rights and privileges at law which were accorded the Jews—i.e., the right to be let alone, and to worship freely, in accord with their ancient ways, the God of their fathers; for Christianity itself was a "way" within Judaism, on a par with that of the Pharisees, with whom they shared several of their main beliefs. In the gospel, Luke revises Mark, omitting two long sections, and inserting material from the "Sayings Source" ("Q"), chiefly in his long central section (9:51–18:14), which expands the material associated with the journey to Jerusalem (Mark 10:1) into a series of didactic sayings, parables, and incidents. The device is purely literary: Jesus leaves Galilee a second time (13:33), and yet at the end of the section he is no nearer Jerusalem than when he began (cf. 18:31). The bearing of this phenomenon of Lukan order, like that of Mark, upon the writing of the life of Jesus, will be made clear in what follows. It is obvious that the order is not chronological. *See* LUKE, GOSPEL OF.

The order of Matthew is the result of combining a series of subject sequences, where five great sections of narrative, in which Mark is followed closely, are each followed by a discourse summing up Jesus' teaching on a related topic. These topics are: (*a*) discipleship (narrative, 3–4:22; discourse, 4:23–7:27); (*b*) apostleship (narrative, 7:28–9:34; discourse, 9:35–10:42); (*c*) the hidden revelation (narrative, 11–12; discourse, 13:1-52); (*d*) church administration (narrative, 13:53–17:27; discourse, ch. 18; (*e*) the Last Judgment (narrative, chs. 19–22; discourse—a double discourse, one public, the other private—chs. 23–25). To this very formal didactic arrangement of the life and teachings of Jesus has been prefaced the nativity narrative in chs. 1–2, and following it the passion narrative (26–27) and the resurrection narrative (28), in all of which Matthew sets forth entirely independent tradition, revising Mark's passion and resurrection narratives to insert this special tradition. Clearly Matthew's topical and didactic order does not supply us with a chronology of the life of Jesus.

The material common to Luke and Matthew, outside that which they derive from Mark, is thought to represent still another source, now usually designated as "Q" (=*Quelle,* German for "source"). This seems to have been (like Mark's sources) an orderly arrangement of the tradition, in this case the sayings of Jesus together with various cognate material, and can be reconstructed with fair certainty. It is impossible to say, however, whether it was in written or stereotyped oral form—in the ancient Orient this was a distinction without a difference, as the latter form was as fixed as the former. In addition to Mark and Q, it is now held by most scholars that Matthew had special material of his own (M) and that so also had Luke (L), each a fairly homogeneous body of tradition with a distinct and characteristic vocabulary and set of presuppositions, theological and other. *See* MATTHEW, GOSPEL OF.

d. John. The order of John is even more formal and didactic. After the great hymn about the Logos in 1:1-18, into which the author has inserted references to John the Baptist, and the account of John the Baptist, his message, and his disciples (1:19-51)—several of whom leave him to follow Jesus—the book is divided into two main parts: (*a*) the manifestation of the incarnate Logos on earth, in chs. 2–12, including the seven great "signs" or proofs of Jesus' divine nature and power (2:1-11; 4:46-54; 5:2-9; 6:1-14; 6:16-21; 9:1-7; 11:1-44—not one of these is an exorcism, like those in the Synoptics, as if the foul demons dared not enter the presence of the incarnate Son of God); and (*b*) the story of Jesus' return to the Father (13:1–20:31; ch. 21 is an appendix), including the deeply moving supper discourses (chs. 14; 15–16) and the sublime high-priestly prayer (ch. 17). Although it was once thought that John presupposed the other gospels, which he undertook to supplement, correct, or perhaps even supplant, it is now generally held that both his material and his point of view are unique and cannot be explained by correlation or comparison with the Synoptics. In John it is the cosmic Christ of the Christian faith and worship at the end of the first century—or even early in the second—who speaks to his disciples, to the later church, to the world, and to the assailants and antagonists of the church. The process of selection and reinterpretation which began even before the gospels were written, and which made the living, present Christ, the church's Lord, the real subject—not a mere figure from the past, the historical Jesus of Nazareth, who died under Pontius Pilate *ca.* A.D. 29 or 30—has now reached its culmination.

This cosmic Christ is the head of his church, the Savior of the world, the one by whom men are to live forever (ch. 6), the Judge of all mankind who nevertheless judges no man (8:15; 12:47), since men judge themselves by their response or reaction to him—this purely theological interpretation of the gospel tradition has all but eclipsed the historical; and yet there are surviving historical traits in John which supplement the Synoptic accounts at important points. The long-recognized contrast between John and the Synoptics is certainly obvious, but it may easily be exaggerated: the Synoptics are also "theological," though to a lesser degree; John is also historical—i.e., contains historical tradition—though to a lesser degree. But it is not John's purpose to write either history or biography, but to prove that Christ, the incarnate Logos, was truly human, and not a phantom, as the Docetic Gnostics held, a divine being who appeared in human form but was incapable of suffering or dying. Hence we cannot take John's outline for a chronological one. *See* JOHN, GOSPEL OF.

e. No "harmony" of the gospels. Modern gospel research has abandoned the hopeless attempt to weave together the four gospels into one consecutive narrative, or even to arrange a "harmony" of the four separate narratives. Their divergent purposes and arrangement make this impossible. Instead, what is known as FORM CRITICISM, or better, form history (*Formgeschichte*), has taught us to recognize that in its original "form" the gospel tradition existed in separate pericopes (or roughly "paragraphs"), each a unit complete in itself and each reflecting the whole of Jesus' thought, attitude, purpose, and career—as a dewdrop reflects the whole sky, including the heavenly bodies. No single pericope presupposes any other—except in the passion narrative, which was the earliest consecutive arrangement of separate pericopes into a historical narrative—and none requires any other for its explanation. The same is true of Jesus' sayings: each is an independent unit, a shimmering jewel, rounded and complete in itself. The discourses in the gospels have been composed by gathering together and arranging these sayings in more or less homogeneous groups, as in the Sermon on the Mount (Matt. 5–7) or the earlier Q collection reflected in Luke 6:20-49, or the great discourses in John 14–16, where the structure is that of a catena (or "chain") of sayings on a common subject.

The marvelous fact is that, despite the divergent purposes of the evangelists, and the differing frames or classifications in which the sayings of Jesus have been collected—and probably were so collected before the evangelists wrote—the unique and distinctive character of Jesus stands out clearly and unmistakably, far more so than any other figure in the past whose life was recorded only in tradition (e.g., Moses or Pythagoras, Ezra, Hillel, or Akiba). The character and personality of Hippocrates cannot be recovered from the Hippocratic writings, or those of Homer, Herodotus, or Vergil from their so-called "lives." (The early lives of Francis of Assisi are different; they are Christian—i.e., post-Christian.) If we inquire what a community is likely to produce (by "projection" of the influence of its leader), an example may be found in the Hermetic writings, with their monotonous, uniform, impersonal didactic style and purely speculative or metaphysical type of spirituality. But the gospels have the freshness and vividness, as well as the variety, of all human life, and bear the stamp of their own self-evident authenticity. The later sayings—e.g., postresurrection or community sayings—reflect the mind and spirit of Christ and are as a rule entirely "in character." This is true even of many of the legendary accretions to the gospel story. A parallel may be seen in the discrepant lives of Alexander the Great, all the way from the legendary work of Pseudo-Callisthenes to the memoirs of his generals, reported by Arrian; the result is a composite, fairly homogeneous picture of their subject (see Arrian's *Anabasis of Alexander*).

f. Varieties in tradition. The gospel tradition embraces a variety of narrative forms: brief anecdotes from the life of Jesus, told in the simplest and most direct language (e.g., Mark 1:29-31); longer, more circumstantial, more elaborate narratives (e.g., Mark 6:30-44), especially the great miracle stories (e.g., Mark 5:1-20); purely legendary material (e.g., Mark 6:17-29); midrash, like the pious fiction of the rabbinical teachers or the medieval guides in the art of meditation who elaborated and impressed the teaching of a text by free use of the imagination (e.g., Matt. 2:1-12, 13-23; 27:3-10). It also includes a variety of didactic forms, some new, some old and familiar: the gnomic saying (e.g., Mark 4:9; 8:35; 9:40; 10:15; Luke 14:11); the prophetic utterance (Mark 1:15; 9:1); the scribal disputation or controversy (Mark 7:6-13; 12:35-37), usually concerned with the interpretation of scripture; the parable (Mark 4:3-8); the macarism or pronouncement of happiness: "Blessed are those who . . ." (e.g., Matt. 5:3-12; Luke 6:20-23; 10:23-24); worthy examples (Luke 10:29-37); the exposition of the OT, especially the Law (e.g., the series in Matt. 5:17-48); the commission of the disciples and predictions of their coming experiences (Matt. 9:35–11:1); apocalyptic forecasts (Matt. 23:37-39; Luke 19:39-44; 21:20-24); and the castigation of Jesus' enemies, chiefly the scribes and Pharisees (e.g., Matt. 23:1-36; Luke 16: 14-15).

The narratives, like the sayings and parables, were originally distinct, and were not at first parts of a continuous account of the life or ministry of Jesus. In fact, the few links which we find are wholly editorial. In the gospels, as in all traditional literature, sections which are retrospective and designed to bind the narrative together into a continuous story are always editorial (cf. Mark 8:16-21; Luke 22:35-38; 24:6-11; John 12:37-43). So also are the passages which look forward (e.g., Mark 8:31; 9:31; 10:32-34; 9:12*b;* Luke 2:34-35; 4:13; 9:31; 13:32-33, 35; 19:43). It is Luke who had done most, among the evangelists, to link the story of Jesus into one consecutive narrative. And yet, even in Luke these are only initial attempts to weave together the gospel story as a whole and give it literary unity—i.e., that unity which we expect in a work of history or biography. (As stated above, the earliest narrative to take continuous form was the basic passion narrative underlying Mark 14–15.)

g. Different types of tradition. The preservation of these divergent types of tradition was due entirely to their use in the early church, especially in preaching, in teaching, and in worship. The "place in life" (*Sitz im Leben*) of the parables and the miracle stories was probably the instruction of converts and of the faithful; that of the controversies with the scribes and Pharisees was the still-continuing contest of the church with its opponents, and especially the disagreements in the interpretation of scripture—e.g., the demands of the law and also the messianic prophecies; that of the prophetic and apocalyptic material was the apocalyptic interests of the church, which rose to great heights in times of crisis (e.g., under Gaius [A.D. 40], again under Nero just before the fall of Jerusalem [A.D. 69-70], or under Domitian, when Revelation was written, or later under Hadrian, when the second Jewish war against Rome broke out [A.D. 132]).

In its original form the gospel tradition—certainly its oldest portions—circulated in Aramaic, the language of Palestine in the first century. But it was not long before this was translated into the ordinary, everyday (koine) Greek of the Greco-Roman world outside. In fact, the Greek translation of the oldest pericopes had continued in use for a long time before they were collected into the gospels or even into the gospel sources. Many of the earliest Christians were bilingual (e.g., at Antioch), and the process of translation was probably sporadic, individual, and a little at a time—like the later Old Latin translation of the gospels themselves in North Africa and elsewhere. Thus some of Jesus' sayings have been transmitted in two or more different forms (they may, indeed, have circulated in more than one form in Aramaic, before the process of translation began). But in almost every case the essential content is the same, though the language differs (cf. the Beatitudes in Matt. 5:3-12 and in Luke 6:20-23, and the Woes in Luke 6:24-26).

The sayings and parables of Jesus reflect a world of thought quite different from that of the Pauline letters, and bear no trace whatsoever of the philosophical examination or discussion of religious problems: Jesus is the prophet (Matt. 21:11; Luke 24:19), who spoke simply, with inspired directness, the message from God to his contemporaries. If a few sayings of a similar character have crept into the tradition, either from the parallel tradition of Jewish wisdom teaching or from the utterances of early Christian prophets, they also are found to be "in character" and belong by right of identical spiritual insight with those of Jesus. So are the sayings which Jesus may have quoted from the OT and other religious writings: he quoted them only because they were relevant, and expressed his own point of view and convictions. A similar problem was faced, in the ancient world, by all schools or religious groups whose teaching was traditional—i.e., oral rather than written. The Muslim rule is noteworthy (the early Muslim teachers faced a similar problem); the Prophet said: "If the tradition is worthy of me, it can be accepted." There is no other rule, in cases where doubtful sayings are to be considered—e.g., those with secondary textual support (such as Luke 9:55; 23:34); or the so-called AGRAPHA, or unwritten sayings (those found outside the gospels—e.g., Acts 20:35); or the oracular utterances of apocalyptists speaking in the name of the risen Lord (e.g., Rev. 22:16).

h. The question of authenticity. The source and authenticity and the later elaboration of sayings which have to do with Jesus' own destined place in the kingdom of God (e.g., Mark 14:62) or his coming death and resurrection (8:31) must be considered in connection with Jesus' own self-consciousness and sense of mission, so far as these are reflected in the gospels (*see* § E *below*). The early church had no questions on this point. God's will was clear from scripture, once the key had been provided by Jesus' actual career, death, and resurrection; and if the OT contained the secret "hidden for ages and generations but now made manifest to his saints," must it not have been clear to Jesus himself? This is the presupposition of such passages as the confession of Peter, especially in its Matthean form (16:17 ff), and the whole of Jesus' life and teaching as set forth in John. Since the gospels were not biographies, nor records of the gradual disclosure of Christian truth to the believing church, after the Resurrection, the whole content of this new faith had to be moved back into the earthly life of Jesus. What was for him only an apprehension, a presentiment, a growing awareness, became for the church a positive conviction, an openly avowed certainty. How else could it be? If Jesus truly was now the glorified Messiah, awaiting in heaven, at God's right hand, the swiftly approaching hour when he should return on the clouds to conduct the Last Judgment, then must he not have been already the Messiah while he walked on earth? And must he not have been fully aware of all that awaited him, at the end of his earthly life and also afterward? A Messiah who did not know himself to be the Messiah was preposterous! A Messiah who was to turn the ancient messianic category upside down, and who was to suffer and die before beginning his reign in glory, but who knew nothing about the divine plan which led to this totally new role and its sovereign strategy, was equally inconceivable! Hence the motive which led to the reinterpretation and reformulation of some of Jesus' sayings, in the interest of making clear his own awareness of the supreme role which he was to play in the purposes of God, was a perfectly natural, indeed an inevitable, one. *See* CHRIST.

The question to be investigated is the extent to which the church has reinterpreted or re-emphasized Jesus' words, making him responsible (as in John) for the proclamation, during his own lifetime, of his own character, nature, and destiny. We have already seen that the gospel tradition, like all historical tradition everywhere, is interpreted tradition; uninterpreted history is meaningless. Nevertheless, we cannot escape the duty of drawing a line, if possible, at the point where interpretation passes over into reinterpretation, and where later convictions are read into the simpler early sayings and narratives. It is the same problem with which we are faced in the study of all ancient history, in the OT, in classical literature, and even in modern history and contemporary reporting. There are no infallible records anywhere; in the nature of the case, there cannot be, for we ourselves are far from infallible in understanding the records before us, and so were those who first composed them, compiled them, and transmitted them to posterity. It is asking too much—in fact, it is asking the impossible—to demand a clear, plain statement of "just what happened," or of "just what was said," without innuendo, overtone, allusion, or implicit reference of any kind. Only angels, not men, could ever grasp and understand such a record. We have this treasure "in earthen vessels" (II Cor. 4:7) —i.e., conditioned by all the limitations of human language, human understanding, the meaning of words, and especially the limits set to the unveiling of one person's inner consciousness to another. There are many questions we would like to ask, which can never be answered (cf. Acts 1:6 ff). History, all history, is based on probabilities.

3. The non-Christian sources. The non-Christian sources are few and slight. Tacitus, writing *ca.* 110, described (Ann. XV.44) the horrible tortures meted out by Nero to the Christians in Rome. He ostensibly punished them as the incendiaries who had fired the city in July, 64. One term used of them was probably "Chrestians," due to a popular misunderstanding found elsewhere in ancient literature (e.g., Suetonius *Life of Claudius* 25.4; see also Tert. Apol. 3). *Chrestus* meant "kind," while *christos* (in Greek and Latin) meant "anointed," or "smeared," and had no meaning either as a title or as a proper name. Josephus (writing *ca.* 90) mentions (Antiq. XX.ix.1) the stoning of James, "the brother of Jesus, the so-called Christ." (The longer passage in XVIII.iii.3 is now recognized to be an interpolation, for it begins: "This man was the Messiah." If Josephus had written this sentence, he would have been a Christian!) The old Slavonic version of Josephus' *War* mentions Jesus in several places, and even describes his personal appearance; but the hand of the interpolator is clearly evident. In the Babylonian Talmud (Sanh. 43*a*) is a reference to "Jeshu ha-Notsri," who "did signs and wonders and led Israel astray," whom "they hanged on the eve of Passover." But this is at best only a vague and distorted echo of the gospels, and contains no independent historical information. Even more fruitless is the identification of Jesus with the "Teacher of Righteousness" referred to in the Dead Sea Scrolls. There is no evidence to support this hypothesis.

As for later Christian writings, there are scattered sayings attributed to Jesus, such as the so-called Sayings of Jesus found at OXYRHYNCHUS; but they are chiefly Gnostic compositions, and one or two of them are thoroughly pantheistic. The same is true of those found at Nag Hammadi in 1945. The data contained in the apocryphal gospels (dated after 150) are mainly unreliable; their only authentic traces are derived from the canonical gospels. This is especially noteworthy in the "Fragments of an Unknown Gospel," published in 1935. *See* APOCRYPHA, NT.

4. Is a life of Jesus possible? The question is often asked, whether it is possible, on the basis of the tradition contained in the gospels, to write a life of Jesus. The diversity—in fact, the total disagreement—of the lives of Jesus produced during the past two centuries does not encourage optimism. The chronology of Jesus' ministry has been variously estimated, all the way from a few months—a year or less—to four years, or seven, or even twelve. In some lives the forced inclusion of John, with its totally different point of view (instead of Mark's theory of the "messianic secret," shared more or less by Luke and Matthew, John represents Jesus as announcing his divine nature from the outset), and even the substitution of John's three Passovers for the one in Mark, completely distorted what remained of the Markan order. The differences in the interpretation of Jesus' teaching, all the way from a social-ethical system of morals to the pure otherworldliness of "thoroughgoing" eschatology or the ultratheological view which in effect forces Jesus' teaching into agreement with Paul's (especially in Rom. 7), have resulted in totally divergent reconstructions of Jesus' life and ministry. Above all, the question of the so-called "messianic consciousness" of Jesus—i.e., his own view of his vocation, mission, career, and quasi-divine nature, as prophet, Messiah, or Son of man—and the question of the sense in which he used the term "Son of man," either with the connotations of divine exaltation and power (as in Daniel and I Enoch) or with those of lowly humanness (as in Ezekiel)—this twofold question has divided scholars, especially since 1900, into two or more irreconcilable camps. The result has been an impasse for scholars, and despair for laymen. Many of the theories advanced in recent times have been ephemeral, and are now of interest only to students of the history of research, comparable to the contemporaneous and now antiquated theories in physics and biology. Unfortunately, some of them are revived from time to time by ingenious writers—this could not happen in the field of natural science.

Nevertheless, the progress of modern research in this area is undeniable. For one thing, it is now more clearly recognized than ever before that the student needs a fuller equipment of knowledge than has sometimes been the case, and cannot trust to his own private and personal impressions derived from the careful reading of the English Bible. He needs ancient languages, and also should be familiar with ancient literature and history, not only classical but also Semitic, for the gospels contain originally Semitic (i.e., Aramaic) traditions in Greek translation; he should also be familiar with ancient historiography, and realize that there are questions which it is useless to ask. (E.g., it is a real question whether or not the ancient world—except for two or three exceptional Greek and Latin historians—had any conception of history comparable to the modern conception. Certainly our modern types of history and biography did not exist in the ancient world.) He must also realize that the criteria of the validity or authenticity of tradition were not at all what we demand—for the simple reason that the purpose of tradition, especially of religious tradition, was something entirely different from the annalistic recording of past events or incidents, speeches or sayings. The fortuitous accretion of cognate traditions, such as the Cynic teaching found in Matthew (e.g., 6:34*b*) and the Didache, or the added apocalyptic material from the Little Apocalypse in Mark 13 (e.g., vss. 24-27), or the ascetic sayings (e.g., Matt. 19:10-12), must be recognized, but must not lead to skepticism regarding the basic traditions, which remain unaffected. The influence of the OT, which was positive and factual and not merely formal (see Matt. 27:6-10 or John 19:23-24), must also be recognized—also without detracting from the substantial veracity of the basic tradition.

Finally, the student must realize that the ancient world had no interest in what we call "personality," the unique combination of physical and mental, emotional and spiritual characteristics which distinguishes the individual from all other men, and rouses the reader's curiosity to find out, if possible, the "secret" of his growth and development—why, or how, he turned out to be the "person" he was. No trace of this interest is to be found in the Bible, or in other ancient Semitic literature, and almost none in classical literature, until a very late period. It is significant that neither the Greeks nor the Romans had a word for this concept of "personality." Thus it will have to be recognized that we shall probably never get back to a fully detailed, photographically authentic account of Jesus' life and character, and to tape-recorded accuracy in the reproduction of his sayings. But this, it must be borne in mind, is what we must expect in the biography of any figure in the ancient world; we have no right to demand more, for it could never have been provided, under the circumstances and conditions of the early church.

The situation is similar to that of the NT text: we cannot hope to recover the autographs, and the best that modern textual scholarship can possibly achieve is an approximation to the readings of the majority of the MSS which were in circulation during the second century. Yet we will not despair! The probability is that the text, for all the thousands of variations in MSS, patristic quotations, and ancient versions, is correct to within one or two per cent. And in the case of the gospels, and their interpretation, and the resulting life of Jesus, the probability is that modern historical research is approaching a reliable consensus. It is like the restoration of an old master—e.g., Rembrandt's "Christ in the Garden," which turned out, when later incrustations and additions had been removed, to be a very different scene, "The Changing of the Guard"—but now has all the freshness and power of the original masterpiece. As we work back through the gospels and their underlying sources to the still earlier and really basic traditions, we are confronted, as never before, by a consistent and homogeneous figure whose voice rings across the centuries and still penetrates our inmost hearts. And we hear this voice all the clearer for the removal of secondary and really obstructing sounds, whether they be the voices of devout and consecrated disciples proclaiming their Lord, or the echoes of later theological discussion and debate. We are not, in fact, in any worse straits than the church has been since the end of the first century. What we have, in the end, is the separate pericopes, just as they are still read, and for many centuries have been read, in the church's liturgy.

The late-nineteenth- and early-twentieth-century dream of recovering the biography of Jesus on the basis of the gospels viewed as the "earliest sources for the life of Jesus," or of reconstructing in detail the history of the apostolic age on the basis of its "historical records and documents," was too ambitious, too modern, and really impossible. It was a mistake to describe the gospels, or the rest of the NT, in such terms. One might as well describe the works of Plato as the "earliest documents for the life of Socrates"—Plato was simply not trying to write the life of his master, but to carry on, apply, and elaborate certain fundamental principles which were apparently implicit in the older man's unwritten teaching. What we have, in lieu of a life of Jesus, is the fourfold gospel in the NT, to be studied with patience, discrimination, and the courageous use of our critical faculties—never forgetting that criticism (κρίσις—i.e., "judgment") is a positive tool, enabling us to distinguish between arguments, to weigh evidence, and to decide which is the more probable view or reading. There is no short cut to the achievement of the modern dream of a "purely historical life of Jesus." We are still where the church has always been, confronted with the four gospels and with the rest of the NT, which we are bidden to "search and examine" and apply, first of all, in our own lives. The task is essentially religious, not secular.

For several centuries it was held that the OT (i.e., prophecy and typology) was an authentic "source" for the life of Jesus. With the prevailing view of the inspiration of scripture, this was natural and inevitable. For several centuries the interpretation of the gospels, and of the Bible generally, from the point of view of systematic or dogmatic theology was unquestioned (Is not all divine truth one?), with the result that the gospels were forced to yield data which could readily be fitted into whatever dogmatic system was held by the commentator or exegete. Only with the rise of the modern historical-critical view of the Bible has the procedure been reversed, and the data of the gospels established first, and without regard to the requirements or presuppositions of systematic theology. The result thus far has been the liberation of exegesis and literary-historical criticism from the shackles of dogmatic theology, though the process is not yet complete; and the consequences, for theology generally, have also been advantageous, for it has been compelled to find its data in the immediate deliverances of religious faith, in general religious experience, and to rest its foundations upon a purely spiritual, self-consistent, self-authenticating view of religion—as may be seen in such modern theological systems as those of Paul Tillich and William Temple.

B. *BACKGROUND.* 1. Jesus the Galilean. Jesus was a GALILEAN (Mark 1:9, 14; 6:6). This fact was of far-reaching significance for his whole career. For Galilee was the "Circle of the Gentiles," *galil ha-goyim* (Matt. 4:15; Isa. 9:1), either because it was surrounded by foreign nations or because (in later times) the Jews there were surrounded by foreigners. This region, lying between Samaria in central Palestine and the mountains of Lebanon on the N border, and between the Mediterranean Sea on the W and the Jordan on the E, was fertile and populous in the first century. But it had not always been Jewish territory. In the days of Jesus there were many non-Jews, especially Syrians, Phoenicians, Arameans, Greeks, and Romans, living here. Some of these were descended from the peoples who had settled in Palestine during the Exile—i.e., the century or more following 597 B.C.—or earlier still, after the destruction of Samaria, then capital of the Northern Kingdom, in 722 B.C. Many had, no doubt, crowded into the land during the terrible days of the Maccabean War, which began in 168 B.C., when the MACCABEES had evacuated the whole Jewish population to Judea for safety. Later (104 B.C.) these foreigners were forced to accept Judaism. But Jesus' ancestors were purely Jewish, and traced their descent from King David.

In the Ten Towns (or DECAPOLIS) lived descendants of Alexander's veterans and other Greeks, together with the veterans of later campaigns, such as those of Pompey. The outlook of a Jewish boy growing to manhood in this region, surrounded by Gentiles, and in contact with foreigners from all parts of the world, was necessarily different from that of a citizen of Jerusalem or of any town in Judea. Across the broad, fertile Plain of Esdraelon lying S of Nazareth came the ancient caravan road from Egypt; it had followed the coast to the range of Mount Carmel, then crossed over the pass at Megiddo. Moving on to the N and E, it went up and over and down the hills of E Galilee, rounded the Lake of Galilee at Capernaum, and moved on into the distant NE, toward Damascus, Palmyra, Babylon, India, China! How could a boy fail to be impressed with the vastness of the world, with the improbability of God's exclusive concern for one people only, when daily before his eyes came "many from east and west" (Matt. 8:11), Gentiles who might be seeking not only the riches of this world but also the kingdom of God! Off to the W, he could catch a view of the broad sea, with its dark ships and their white sails, as the traders of the Western world and the troops of the Romans followed their coastal routes from land to land. Moreover, Galilee was an agricultural region, with widely diversified occupations: its small hillside fields produced grain (chiefly barley); its lake abounded with fish; its orchards grew figs, olives, and apples, with melons and cucumbers on the ground between the trees; its vineyards produced the rich grapes and tart wine preferred by the peasantry. By ancient standards, especially in the East, Galilee was very prosperous, and the description of conditions drawn by modern Marxists is refuted by the researches of historians and archaeologists. On the other hand, Ernest Renan's description of the happy Galilean fishermen, singing as they drew in their full nets, is too romantic—fishermen rarely sing as they work, and there were cares and burdens enough for all in those days.

It is impossible even to approximate the figures for the population of first-century Galilee. One scholar estimates a total of 5,000,000 to 6,000,000 for all Syria in the first century; for Galilee, *ca.* A.D. 68, about 400,000; for Jerusalem 100,000; for the (western) Diaspora as a whole, about 6,000,000. For Palestine as a whole, a figure of 800,000 to 1,000,000 has been proposed. But these are only guesses, though based on considerations which are used elsewhere in estimating ancient populations. There is no use in comparing figures for the present day, as Palestine is in a process of transition, and no one can predict its eventual population when stabilization is finally achieved.

2. Economic and political conditions. The economic and political situation was serious. For a hundred years Palestine had been free, though the Maccabean War, which had lasted twenty-five years (168-143 B.C.), was won only by a heroic expenditure of life and treasure; then in 63 B.C. came Pompey the Great, invited to come down from Antioch and settle the quarrel over the right of succession between the last two Maccabean brothers, Hyrcanus and Aristobulus II. Following this act of armed intervention, the Romans never withdrew. Herod the Great (40-4 B.C.) was an "allied king" (*rex socius*) of the Romans; his sons were permitted to succeed him only by Roman consent: ARCHELAUS (4 B.C.–A.D. 6) as ethnarch of Judea and Samaria, with the promise of kingship if he did well (he did not, and was removed in 10 years, and Roman procurators were appointed instead); Antipas as tetrarch of Galilee and Peraea (4 B.C.–A.D. 29); Philip as tetrarch in NE Palestine (4 B.C.–A.D. 26; cf. Luke 3:1-2). But the government of the Herods (*see* HEROD) was only a stopgap. Roman policy was consistent and continuous: the whole exposed E frontier, from the Black Sea to the Red, required the establishment of a continuous line of defense, since there was no natural frontier of mountains, rivers, or lakes. Two armies of swift-riding Parthians had invaded Palestine in 40 B.C., sacked several towns, and murdered their inhabitants; this must be prevented. The rich caravans which moved northward toward the upper Euphrates must be protected—the Romans even tried, later on, to control that river (e.g., at Dura-Europos) and made a temporarily successful attempt to include Armenia in their E frontier; but this was later abandoned by Hadrian.

The meaning of all this for Palestine, including little Galilee, was obvious. Like Belgium, like Alsace, like Poland, like every buffer state in all history, the land of the Jews was forcibly annexed, overrun, conquered, and reconquered again and again. The dreams of the founders of the Second Commonwealth —complete isolation from the surrounding nations, with freedom to worship God in his designated way in his own land—was impossible of realization. The Maccabean War had been won not only by the heroism and sacrifices of the Maccabees, but in consequence of the declining strength of the Seleucid Empire, itself caught between the advancing power of Rome (especially after the Battle of Magnesia in 189 B.C.) and its crumbling E and S support, and enfeebled by internal strife and disloyalty, especially dynastic. The insurgents in Jesus' days, the Zealots (*see* ZEALOT), were also devoted to the ancient ideal of a priestly theocracy, free from all foreign control; their battle cry was: "No King but God," as Josephus repeatedly informs us. But they were destined to fail —the old Maccabean dream was impossible of realization; the new Roman Empire of the first century A.D. was a wholly different force in world affairs than the tottering Seleucid Empire had been in the later second century B.C. The only contribution of the nationalists was negative: unrest, violence, internal tension and disorder, ending finally in open revolt, the emergence of the "cutthroats" (*sicarii*), and the reign of terror that preceded the fall of Jerusalem in A.D. 70.

This political situation also affected the economic conditions of the time. On the whole, the East was better off than the West, in the first century. Asia Minor and Syria contained many thriving centers of industry; Egypt was still the more or less unexploited treasure house of the ancient world, where the accumulated wealth of the Pharaohs had been ably conserved and enhanced during three centuries by the Ptolemies, and where a docile peasantry worked hard and long to produce and increase the resources of their masters. Under Rome, Egypt was looted. In the West, especially in Italy, two centuries of warfare had all but exhausted the agricultural population, the mainstay of a settled and prosperous economy. Greece had been overrun, ravaged, sacked, and largely depopulated; even in Cicero's time its decline was evident to all observers. The seizure and conveyance of the treasures of Greek art to Rome and the neighboring Italian villas; the influx into Italy of tens of thousands of slaves; their harsh and inhuman treatment by their masters, the *nouveaux riches* of the new empire—all these factors were to affect the early church in its westward advance. But in the East, conditions were still more or less patriarchal, and far less disturbed, except in Palestine. In Palestine the intransigent refusal of the Jews to accommodate themselves to the "wicked kingdom" (Rome), to accept the principle of taxation by a foreign power and occupation by a foreign army, even a token force, made it impossible for Palestine to share in the rising prosperity of the first and early second centuries. Added to this factor was the steady influx of Jews from abroad, who came here in order to pass their remaining years in the sacred land, and as near as possible to the sacred city on Mount Zion—a factor which complicated the already difficult problem of the food supply, in a country whose productivity was already in decline. (The ancient forests were gone, and the land was already becoming arid, as it has remained for centuries under Arab, Frank, and Turkish rule.)

Finally, the Roman tribute, designed to meet the

costs of occupation and defense, was imposed without regard to the sacred taxes, tithes, and other offerings which were set up as the only system of taxation—i.e., that of the priestly theocracy envisaged in the Pentateuch (*see* TAXES). It has been estimated that the total taxation, Roman and priestly, amounted to about 35-40 per cent of the total income of the nation. For an ancient people living under patriarchal conditions, with almost no margin between production and consumption, and threatened with famine every few years (twice in Herod's reign), this was an impossible economic burden, with no conceivable solution such as improved agriculture, industrial development, manufacture, or increased commerce. The combination of political friction and oppression (as it was viewed by most Jews) with a hopeless economic situation formed the background not only of the political history of Palestine in the first century, but also of the life and ministry of John the Baptist and of Jesus and the early Christian apostles.

3. The revival of messianism. For one thing, the rise and nationwide spread, not only of a revived and fanatically jingoist messianism, but also of a more esoteric apocalyptic eschatology, were both conditioned by this unhappy situation. If Jesus and John both firmly rejected the resort to violence, each in his own way, it was their answer to a widespread appeal which was steadily winning the masses and leading on to the catastrophe of the late sixties, the meaningless and futile tragedy of the war with Rome. But there were other leaders who did not hesitate to approve the movement and to make the most of it for personal ends; the years from the death of Herod to the outbreak of the war with Rome were filled with movements headed by fanatical adventurers, false prophets, even false messiahs whose deluded followers were led out to perish in the wilderness or to be cut down by the Roman cavalry (see Mark 13:5-6; Acts 5:36-37). If, here and there, scattered groups gathered to pray for the "redemption" of Israel (Luke 2:25; 24:21), it was because things had gone so far that no solution could be thought of short of direct divine intervention. If pious PHARISEES redoubled their vigils and prayers (Luke 18:12), and their scrupulous observance of all the detailed minutiae of the scribal interpretation of the law, it was in view of the growing crisis. Only the complacent "quisling" SADDUCEES washed their hands of the whole movement (John 11:48 ff), preferring to make the most of both worlds—their priestly patrimonies in the country and the omnipotent world power represented by their Roman friends and associates.

Off in the wilderness N of the Dead Sea, the ESSENES observed their special rites, chiefly baptismal, and studied their esoteric books. What Josephus tells us of them, and what Philo says about the Therapeutae in Egypt, is now elucidated in some measure by the DEAD SEA SCROLLS, though our information is still mainly derived from Josephus. But the Essenes also, like the apocalyptists, like many of the Pharisees, and like many of the early Christians, were pietists, quietists—i.e., escapists. The theory that the Essenes, or the Qumran community whose library contained the Dead Sea Scrolls, influenced John, or Jesus, or the early Christians, or the NT, is not convincing. Repeatedly, during the past decades, various scholars have tried to show that Jesus was an Essene, but the view is no more probable now than when it was first advanced. The "contacts" between the Dead Sea Scrolls and the Gospel of John, e.g., are not nearly so striking as those between the Gospel of John and other ancient writings, Greek, Hellenistic, or rabbinic. Hellenistic Judaism included a far greater variety of religious thought and speculation than is realized by those who have not studied its literature.

C. *JESUS' BIRTH.* **1. The two infancy narratives.** It is now widely recognized that the accounts of Jesus' birth in Matt. 1–2; Luke 1–2 were entirely independent in origin, and represent two different attempts by the later Synoptists to provide the account of Jesus' life with a proper beginning. The two genealogies (*see* GENEALOGY) well illustrate this independence; the view that one is the genealogy of Joseph, the other of Mary, is a perversion of the plain meaning of holy scripture. Matthew (1:1-17) traces Jesus' descent through the royal line from King David, and, earlier still, from Abraham—Jesus was a true Jew. Much of the material is taken directly from the OT (Ruth 4:18-22; I Chr. 2:1-15; 3:10-19). The list ends with: "Joseph the husband of Mary, of whom Jesus was born, who is called Christ," though some MSS, notably the Sinaitic Syr., read: "Joseph, to whom was betrothed the virgin Mary, was the father of Jesus who is called Christ." This latter is an impossible reading, in view of what follows in vss. 18-25, but may (as many now hold) contain the original conclusion of the genealogy: "Joseph was the father of Jesus who is called Christ"—the only possible conclusion, if the genealogy was to have any meaning. (Some take it to mean legal father, but this is an evasive and artificial explanation.) Luke's genealogy (3:23-38) reverses the order, and traces Jesus' ancestry, as the son ("as was supposed") of Joseph, through another line back to King David and Abraham (also using the material from I Chronicles and Ruth), but continuing back to "Adam, the son of God," as if descent from Abraham were not so important as from Adam, and the universal human nature which this involved. (So the rabbis often interpreted the descent of all mankind from Adam.)

2. Luke's narrative. The story of the annunciation, birth, and childhood of both Jesus and John, as told in Luke 1–2, is a weaving together of two infancy narratives, whose component parts can still be distinguished; and within the story of Jesus' birth and infancy, three strands are clearly marked: the story of the divine announcement (1:26-38); the birth of Jesus and the divine proclamation to the shepherds (2:1-20); the visit to the temple and the revelation to Simeon (2:21-40). The story of the visit to Elizabeth (1:39-56) is designed to tie together the two strands (the Johannine and the Nazarene), and may originally, as certain MS readings in vs. 46 suggest (by attributing the *Magnificat* to Elizabeth), have been Johannine material. The finished story is often described as the Lukan "idyll," and recalls the OT story of the birth and infancy of Samuel, which it frequently echoes (I Sam. 1–3). It is partly traditional, no doubt, but the telling is the work of an extraordinary literary artist. In it Luke has re-created (imaginatively) the long-vanished figures of the family of Jesus and of John, the atmosphere of simple but noble Jewish piety which dominated Jesus' home in Nazareth and influenced his whole development. The deep religious feeling which still throbs in the Lukan canticles (1:14-17, 32-33, 35, 46-55, 68-79; 2:14, 29-32, 34-35), the glowing hope of the coming national liberation and the restoration of the ancient Davidic kingdom, the profound motives of humility and loyalty and obedience to the divine will—all this is indispensable for understanding Jesus, his life and times, his teaching, and his personal character. The language and the thought are alike derived from the OT, especially the Psalms and the Prophets, and are continuous therewith (like the Psalms of Solomon, written *ca.* 50 B.C.). If Jesus' boyhood home had an influence upon the shaping of his mind, as it must have had; if the religious character and devotion of his parents had any influence upon him; if the atmosphere which surrounded his childhood conditioned in any way his later development (and how else could he have grown, if the Incarnation was real?), then we must suppose that the picture Luke draws in his first two chapters is true and realistic. In other words, the early surroundings of the One whom God "chose" and "sent" to his people and to all mankind must have been those of this humble, beautiful, consecrated Jewish home.

The central story in Luke's infancy narrative is the annunciation to Mary, the betrothed of Joseph, that she is to bear a son who

> will be great, and will be called the Son of the
> Most High;
> and the Lord God will give to him the throne of his
> father David,
> and he will reign over the house of Jacob for ever;
> and of his kingdom there will be no end (1:31-33).

This prophecy is, of course, in the language of the ancient hope of the Messiah, the glorious supernatural king who was to sit on David's throne, free the nation, and establish a purely religious and absolutely just theocratic utopia which would endure forever (see Ps. 72, for an OT example). The fact that Jesus never mounted an earthly throne, or desired to do so, only increases our debt to Luke for preserving this ancient conception and emphasis, deeply embedded in the old Palestinian tradition.

3. Matthew's narrative. By contrast, the story in Matthew (1–2) is far less inspiring; it resembles the fanciful but pedantic tales in the later Jewish midrash, which as a rule started with a text, or texts, and then "re-created the scene" by a free flight of fancy, often fabricating historical events to meet the needs of the exegete or preacher—much as modern writers often do in producing "religious" novels of the life of Moses, the Maccabees, or Christ. E.g., the verse in Isa. 7:14 which reads in the LXX (it is not the reading of the original Hebrew—i.e., of the canonical text of the Bible): "Behold, a [or the] virgin shall conceive and bear a son" (Matt. 1:23), is now interpreted as a prediction of Jesus' birth, although no suggestion of the idea (the Virgin Birth) is found anywhere else in the NT. (The phrase in Luke 1:34: "Since I know not a man," and the one in Luke 3:23: "as was supposed," are often viewed either as editorial additions or as later glosses added to the text of Luke under the influence of Matt. 1:18-25.) From an ancient Jewish point of view (see, e.g., Philo's accounts of the births of the patriarchs), a virginal conception would add nothing to the assurance of Jesus' future greatness; the idea is purely Hellenistic. Moreover, the question in Luke 1:34: "How shall this be?" (the RSV "How *can* this be?" is not supported by the Greek) refers not to the birth of a son, for Mary is about to be married, but to the glorious destiny of her son, described in vss. 32-33; and the angel's reply (in vs. 35), explaining how it is to be—through the "overshadowing" of the "Holy Spirit"—explains Jesus' character and destiny (as "holy," and "the Son of God"), not his birth. The question is a leading one—its sole purpose is to introduce the answer which follows. Luke has several of these "leading questions"—they are characteristic of his style (see 12:41; 13:23; Acts 1:6). Later Christian doctrine laid great emphasis upon the VIRGIN BIRTH; but for the gospels, and the NT writings generally, and their writers, it had little significance, and was probably unknown. (Even in the earliest form of the Apostles' Creed, in the second century, the emphasis is on "born," not on "virgin"—one purpose of the Creed was to rule out Docetic Gnosticism, with its phantom deity.) If, as moderns, we try to picture the scene, the old Italian painters Leonardo da Vinci and Antonello da Messina will help us: Mary is kneeling in prayer and meditation, with the Bible open before her, when the angel appears and addresses her. One wonders what passage she could have been reading. There is only one answer: the great messianic prediction in the book of the prophet Isaiah.

The concluding sections of Luke's infancy narrative (2:21-52) likewise stress the deep piety of Jesus' family, and his own response. They also suggest that the glorious future anticipated in the OT, and summarized in the angel's words to Mary, may not be readily or easily fulfilled (vss. 34-35), and that Jesus himself had to rise above family loyalty in his life of utter obedience to God (vs. 49)—the very demand he was later to make of his disciples (Luke 14:26). At the same time the universal extension of his gospel is foretold both by the angels (vs. 14), in language which must have reminded Theophilus of the imperial inscriptions in honor of Augustus, and by Simeon (vss. 29-32) in language which echoes the OT (cf. Isa. 42:6; 46:13; 49:6).

D. *JOHN THE BAPTIZER*. 1. His call to repentance. The earliest form of "gospel," still preserved in Mark and John and also reflected in Acts 10:36 ff, begins, not with the birth of Jesus, but with the coming of JOHN THE BAPTIST. The conclusion of John's work marked the "beginning of the gospel" (Mark 1:1, 14-15; Luke 16:16; Acts 1:22; 10:37; 13:25). Although there is some evidence of later rivalry between the followers of Jesus and those of John (e.g., Mark 2:18; Luke 5:33; 11:1; John 1:6-51; 3:22-30; 10:41; Acts 18:24–19:7), the view which eventually prevailed is that John was the "forerunner" or herald, whose chief function was to announce the coming of the Messiah (=Jesus) and to prepare the way for him by calling the nation to repentance (Mark 1:2-8; 9:11-13). For this reason Luke gives the multiple dating in 3:1-3. It is his only way of dating the beginning of Jesus' ministry, which he assumed, apparently, was a year in length (at least so Irenaeus interpreted Luke 4:19). The year referred to must have been A.D. 27 or 28 for the beginning of John's ministry, with the presumption that Jesus' ministry began in 28 or 29. At least this is as close an approximation as can be made; and for ancient chronology of either private or popular events, not public or official, this is very close. *See* CHRONOLOGY OF THE NT.

John's message was a call to repentance in preparation for the coming Judgment. Not only his garb but also his manner and his message suggested Elijah the Tishbite (Matt. 11:14; Luke 1:15-17; contrast John 1:21), who was expected to return at the end of the age (Mark 9:11 ff; Mal. 4:5-6). In fact, John took up where Malachi left off, and renewed the ancient prophet's denunciation of sin and wickedness, including the sin of adultery and the cruel "putting away" (divorce) of wives (Mal. 3:5; 2:13-16). John denounced Herod Antipas for his highhanded taking of his brother Philip's wife (Mark 6:17-18), which also involved (according to Josephus) the disgrace and abandonment of his first wife, a Nabatean princess, the daughter of King Aretas. Josephus says that Antipas put John in prison out of fear of his growing popularity, lest he should start an insurrection. The two explanations, by Mark and Josephus, are not incompatible; both stories are traditional.

By "repentance" John meant the biblical *teshubah,* "turning about"—i.e., the actual abandonment of sin, facing away from it, and "turning" to the Lord; and the seal of this thorough repentance was baptism, which was a self-administered rite of cleansing. It was like the baptism of proselytes, for whom it meant the washing away of all defilements contracted through contact with idolatry; in this case, the extraordinary feature was that it was required of born Jews. It was to be followed by the practice of a new and better righteousness, in obedience to the will of God (Luke 3:7-14). The literary analysis of Mark 1:8 and parallels suggests that the original form of John's saying (in Q) read: "I baptize you with water; he [the Coming Judge—i.e., either God himself or the Messenger of the Covenant] will baptize you with *fire."* Mark revised this to fit the current Christian situation, and read: "I have baptized you with water; but he will baptize you with the Holy Spirit." In editing Mark, Luke and Matthew conflated the two versions and read: "with the Holy Spirit and with fire," and then continued with the rest of the saying, which Mark had omitted: "His winnowing fork is in his hand. . . . The chaff he will burn with unquenchable fire." It has been thought that the Baptist here referred to the universal conflagration at the end of the age, an expectation found in Persian religious thought and also in Stoic teaching; but the reference to Malachi seems more probable (Mal. 3:2-3; 4:1-3), as more fully in harmony with Jewish eschatological expectations.

2. Relations between John and Jesus. The character of John is in sharp contrast with that of Jesus, throughout the gospel narratives which bring them together. John was an ascetic who renounced the world and its good things, lived in the desert, and preached a stern message of repentance based on the threat of judgment to come. Jesus, on the other hand, was the prophet of the kingdom of God, who was himself able to communicate to others, in word and deed, the mighty powers of the coming kingdom. This marked contrast between Jesus and John makes improbable the modern theory (based on John 1) that the two were closely associated for a time, but finally disagreed and separated, each going his own independent way as prophet and teacher. *See also* § E2 *below.*

3. Jesus' baptism and temptation. The specific point at which John's office as herald and forerunner was connected with Jesus' mission was the baptism of Jesus at the direction of John (Mark 1:9-11 and parallels; only Matthew [3:14-15] reflects the later difficulty of representing the sinless Jesus as accepting John's baptism, and he solves it by making Jesus the example of perfect obedience). At this moment, according to the Synoptics, Jesus becomes aware of his life's mission: the heavens open, the Holy Spirit descends upon him, and the voice of God declares: "Thou art my beloved Son; with thee I am well pleased." (The words "well pleased" mean that he is the one whom God has specially chosen for some divine mission.) The "Western" (*see* TEXT, NT) reading in Luke 3:22: "Today I have begotten thee" (cf. Ps. 2:7), is improbable after Luke's infancy narrative. It was this endowment with the Spirit which not only, according to Luke, led Jesus into the wilderness (4:1-2), where he was put to the test by Satan, but also equipped him for his public ministry in Galilee (4:14-15, 18; 5:17).

The story of the Temptation, briefly recounted by Mark (1:12-13) and more fully by Matthew (4:1-11) and Luke (4:1-13), is best understood as an account of the ordeal of the Messiah, in which he was put to the test in ways comparable to those of the people of Israel in the wilderness after the Exodus. The solution of the problem in each trial is a verse from the story of the Exodus (Deut. 8:3*b;* 6:16, 13). The fuller version, in Matthew and Luke, is probably from Q; Mark's is only a brief reference. In form, it is perhaps a meditation on the Deuteronomic story of the nation —somewhat as Luke's central section (9:51–18:14) clearly parallels Deuteronomy in many places—rather than an autobiographical narrative from Jesus' own lips. Once more it is clear that the sources of the gospels included the OT, which was viewed as of equal authenticity and authority for the life of Jesus with the church's own traditions.

Crossing this motif of the ordeal is another: the devil's attempt to ascertain Jesus' true nature, whether he is really the "Son of God" or not. This feature anticipates the later attempt of the demoniacs (or, in the ancient view, of the demons) in the gospel story, where they concluded that he was the Messiah and Son of God (Mark 1:34; Luke 4:34, 41). Jesus' victory over the tempter was decisive, but not permanent: the devil departed "until an opportune time," according to Luke (4:13), which probably meant until the Passion (22:46, 53*b*). The temptation narrative gives us an insight into a widespread early Christian view of Jesus, his nature, mission, and achievement, according to which his whole career was one of conflict with the powers of darkness, and reached its climax at the Cross, where defeat was turned into victory through the Resurrection. The view is also reflected in Paul (cf. Col. 2:15) and in Origen and other, later Christian writers, for whom Jesus' conflict with the powers of evil, ending in his victory over sin, Satan, and death, is the key to his whole career—and to the theology of the Incarnation and the Atonement. *See also* § F4 *below*.

E. *JESUS' MISSION AND MESSAGE.* 1. The beginning of the mission. Although the Gospel of John represents Jesus as a member of the Baptist's entourage, possibly even a follower and associate (as some scholars hold) who took away—with the prophet's full consent—some of John's own disciples when he returned to Galilee, the earlier gospels state only that Jesus' public ministry began after John had been imprisoned by Herod Antipas (Matt. 4:12; Mark 1:14; Luke 3:19-20; 4:14). His mission was primarily that of a prophet (Mark 1:15), teacher (Luke 4:15), and healer (Luke 4:40; 13:32) or exorcist (Luke 4:41; 6:17-19); his message was the announcement of the impending arrival of the reign (or kingdom) of God (Luke 4:43), and the requirements which were to be met before admission into this kingdom (Luke 6:20-23).

2. Jesus the prophet. Although the apparel and food of John the Baptist are described in the gospels (Mark 1:6), nothing is said of Jesus' personal appearance or habits—for the reason that there was nothing unusual about them (Matt. 11:18-19). The earliest representations of him in Christian art are only types, like the stern, majestic, sublime face that looks down from the ceiling of the sanctuary in Byzantine churches of the East, and in the West from Cefalù and Monreale to Ravenna and Aquileia; or, in modern art, like the well-known head of Christ by Heinrich Hofmann. His intrepid courage is clear from every page of the gospels (e.g., Luke 4:28-30; 13:31-33); at the same time his gentleness is evident from the attraction which he had for children (Mark 10:13-16)—something unusual in an ancient religious teacher, Jewish or other.

The popular estimate of him as a prophet is reflected in Luke 7:39, where Simon the Pharisee questions it. His own words presuppose it, more than once (e.g., Luke 4:24; 13:33). So does the beginning of the gospel story: Jesus is endowed with the Holy Spirit for the mission he is to carry out (Luke 3:22; 4:17-21). If this involved messiahship as well, that was an additional office. The gift of the Spirit constituted men *prophets* (I Sam. 10:10; Isa. 61:1-4; Mic. 3:8; Luke 1:15, 67; 4:18-19; I Pet. 1:10); it did not constitute them messiahs. Yet if John the Baptist was "more than a prophet" (Matt. 11:9), Jesus himself was undoubtedly also more (cf. Matt. 12:6). The discussion in John 7:40-42 over *the* prophet also implies that Jesus was popularly known as a prophet: "the prophet from Galilee." It was also the view reflected at the end of the gospel (Matt. 21:11; Luke 24:19) and in the early Palestinian church (Acts 2:22); though it was this prophet who became, by his resurrection, "both Lord and Christ" (Acts 2:36). This was the attitude of the "common people," the "great throng" who heard him gladly (Mark 12:37*b*) and hung on his words, not only in Galilee but also in Judea and Jerusalem—in fact, wherever he went; for the gospels make it clear that even when he withdrew into the wilderness (i.e., the uninhabited, open country), the crowds followed him, and whenever he arrived in a village, the people immediately gathered about him. As he spoke as an inspired prophet, his words were infallible (Mark 13:31) and must be accepted and obeyed. The ancient conception of prophet was as far from that of "lowly humanness" as it was from that of the religious or theological expert: in a monotheistic religion like Judaism, or as later in Islam, but also in the polytheistic religions of antiquity, a prophet was the direct mouthpiece of God. It was the highest possible conception, next to deity itself—which, in the Semitic religions, was impossible, since they ruled out all concepts of Incarnation.

Since John the Baptist was thought of as a prophet (Mark 11:32; this was also Jesus' view of him—Matt. 11:9-11; Mark 9:13), the question at once arose as to the relationship between the two. Not only Herod Antipas (Mark 6:14-16) but also the people (Mark 8:28) assumed that Jesus was John risen from the dead—these passages obviously belong later than Herod's murder of John. This was one view. Another, also reflected by Jesus himself, made John the expected *Elias redivivus* (Mal. 4:5; Mark 9:12-13; contrast John 1:21), so that Jesus and John could scarcely be identified. (The order of verses in Mark 9:9-13 is probably to be altered to agree with that in Matt. 17:9-13.) Their authority, as Jesus implied, was identical—from "heaven" (i.e., from God; Mark 11:27-33); both were inspired prophets, and both were rejected (Matt. 21:28-32). Yet John's preaching did not go beyond the coming Judgment (Luke 16:16), and never embraced the kingdom, which was Jesus' main subject of discourse. Not only in character, appearance, and message were they different, but also, and especially, in their mission. John was the forerunner, Jesus the fulfiller; this was the simple, pristine theology of the Palestinian church reflected in our earliest gospel sources.

3. The message of the kingdom of God. Jesus' conception of the KINGDOM OF GOD is not set forth systematically or dogmatically anywhere in the gospels. Instead, as elsewhere in the NT, it is assumed that the reader will understand what is meant. But the very terms used imply that it is eschatological: the reign of God is "at hand" (i.e., it has already drawn near (ἤγγικεν [Mark 1:15]; the verb ἐγγίζω is one of the new verbs [Aristotle and later; LXX] formed from an adverb—here ἐγγύς, which means "close by"; cf. Syriac Apocalypse of Baruch 85), and is still on its way; it "has come upon" (Luke 11:20) Jesus' contemporaries, though its full and final realization is still in the future (Luke 19:11); the time for its coming has been "fulfilled"—i.e., completed (Mark 1:15; for the term see Acts 2:1), and there will be no further delay; men must therefore repent, believe the good news, and prepare for the kingdom's arrival. What has become of John's prediction of the coming Judgment is not clear; apparently Jesus takes it for granted (cf. Luke 11:29-32, 50-51; 12:35–13:9; 13:25-30), though it is variously interpreted in the gospels; Luke seems to identify it with the fall of Jerusalem (13:34-35; 21:20-24); at least the fall of Jerusalem is a part of the drama of the final Judgment. The kingdom is to be the outward and visible manifestation of God's rule over the universe.

a. The meaning of "kingdom of God." Such a statement as that in Luke 17:21: "The kingdom of God is in the midst of you," is not to be taken otherwise.

Although frequently cited as an example of Jesus' "mysticism" or "inwardness," this interpretation rests chiefly upon the old translation, "within you," understood in the unfortunate modern sense of "you" as singular; the "you" (ὑμῶν) is plural (Jesus is addressing the Pharisees—vs. 20), and the contrast is not between an inward realization and an outward manifestation of the kingdom, but between a present realization (or perhaps a sudden coming) and a series of observable external "signs," events which could be taken as evidence of its gradual approach and would thus permit one to calculate the time which remained before its arrival—the favorite occupation of apocalyptists in all ages. The "signs" are already present in the "signs of the times"; and chiefly, it is Jesus himself, his teaching, his disciples, his followers, and the "mighty works" which God is doing through him (Luke 11:20, 29). Therefore the kingdom of God is already present, "in your midst," and there is no need to look for "signs and portents" in the skies or elsewhere in the natural order (cf. Mark 13:4). The theory that the kingdom of God is an inner state of mind, or of personal salvation, runs counter to the context of this verse, and also to the whole NT presentation of the idea.

It is strange, in view of the fact that Jesus clearly takes for granted his hearers' understanding of the term, that the phrase "kingdom of God" is not found in the OT or in later Jewish literature prior to or contemporary with Jesus' generation. Such expressions as "his [God's] kingdom," or "the kingdom of the Most High" are found in the OT (see Pss. 29:10; 47:7; 139:9; 145:11-13; Dan. 2:44; 4:3; Zech. 14:9); but here the meaning is God's universal sovereignty over nature and history. It is not something that "comes" only at the end of the age. It is eternal, and existed before the Creation; and yet it must "come" here in this world where human and demonic sin has led to a revolt against the divine rule. Even the apocalyptic literature makes no use of the term. And yet Jesus assumes that his ordinary hearers among the Galilean 'AM HA'AREZ will understand it! The most probable explanation seems to be that the term was not really a theological one at all, but popular, and was perhaps taken over from the Zealots, who "rejected the kingly and all other forms of government" (i.e., Greek or democratic; or Roman—i.e., senatorial or imperial—together with the procurators, and also the local Idumean dynasty of the Herods as allies of Rome), and insisted upon the sole sovereignty of God, who had chosen Israel for his own people. The great slogan of the Zealots, "No king but God," had been perverted and degraded by these fanatical freebooters, revolutionists, and murderers masking as religious and political liberators. But the term was perfectly appropriate on the lips of one whose purpose was entirely religious, and who looked forward to the establishment of God's reign, not by the violence of the sword (Matt. 26:52*b*) nor by the gathering of an army (John 6:15), but by the act of God himself, when he should "take his great power and reign" (cf. Rev. 11:17). The Zealot principle, and all other activistic principles, had been rejected by Jesus from the outset, according to the clear implications of the temptation narrative. His mission was to wait, prepare, convert; to heal the sick, exorcise demons, convert the sinful, and thus gather a consecrated people who would make ready for the full and final coming of God's reign. The "revolution" which would bring in the reign of God was entirely in God's hands.

b. The teaching of the parables. Many of Jesus' parables (*see* PARABLE) deal with the coming of the kingdom, though the precise meaning is not conveyed by such language as "the kingdom of God is like . . ." (e.g., Mark 4:26, 30-31; Luke 13:18, 20). A similar formula was used by the Jewish rabbis, and by the ancient wisdom teachers: "To what is the thing like, and with what shall we compare it?" I.e., the point of comparison with the kingdom of God is indicated in only a general way—the *subject* is the kingdom of God—and its precise teaching must be sought for by the hearer. Other parables (e.g., Luke 18:1-8, 9-14) have no such introduction, and some are not comparisons at all, but illustrative examples (e.g., Luke 14:7-32; 16:1-9, 19-31). The theory in Mark 4:11-12, that the parables were meant to conceal Jesus' teaching rather than to make it clear, is peculiar to Mark and Luke; Matt. 13:13 changes Mark's ἵνα to ὅτι, "because," and thus avoids the paradox; John has no parables, only allegories. Mark's theory, which is consonant with his theory of the "messianic secret" (i.e., Jesus' secret messiahship), may have seemed probable in a milieu of esoteric religious teachings—i.e., Rome in the sixties—but was surely out of place in Galilee in the twenties, especially in the circle of Jesus and his simple followers; and it is contradicted by the tradition contained later on in the same chapter (Mark 4:21-25, 33, 34*a*).

In spite of Mark's adverb, "of itself," in 4:28—the parable is omitted by Luke and Matthew—there is no suggestion of a mechanical "advance" or "spread" of the kingdom of God, as the result of human effort to "found" or "build" it; the whole point is that the kingdom, like the harvest, comes secretly, and the word αὐτομάτη ("of itself") emphasizes only the fact that one cannot watch it (cf. Luke 17:20, as above). Matthew's substituted parable of the weeds (Matt. 13:24-30, 36-43) has an entirely different point; here it is the presence of wickedness or the absence of devotion in the later church (cf. 24:12). The point in such a parable as that of the sower (Mark 4:3-8) is not the nature of the kingdom, but the response to the message of its coming and the call to repentance, as even Mark's pedestrian interpretation in 4:13-20 makes clear; nor does it imply that only a fourth of the hearers respond—a farmer whose seed was three-quarters wasted or lost would soon give up! The picture is really one of success—the size of the harvest (vs. 8). The same theme appears in the parables of the mustard seed and the leaven (Matt. 13:33; Mark 4:31-32): the results (the final response) are out of all proportion to the tiny beginnings! So also in the parable of the leaven (Matt. 13:33; Luke 13:21), where the eventual success of the process is assumed. The parables of hidden treasure, the pearl, and the net (Matt. 13:44-50), and of the trained scribe (51-52), found only in Matthew, are not descriptive of the kingdom, but of its joyful discovery, its priceless value, its universal range of appeal, its challenge and judgment of the unworthy, its deeper meanings as discovered (in scripture) by the trained scribe—i.e., the Christian teacher.

c. The "coming" of the kingdom. Jesus assumes that the kingdom is coming at once, in "this generation" (Mark 9:1; 13:30). Although "no sign shall be given" (Mark 8:12), the "signs of the time" are clear for all to see (Luke 11:16; 12:54 ff). The steadily growing unrest of the people, the tyranny of the foreign occupying power, the injustice of the rulers (seen in the death of John the Baptist), the impotence and inability of the religious authorities to deal with the situation—all these tensions and frustrations indicated that a crisis was impending. It was as clear to John and Jesus, and also to some others, no doubt, as the similar situation in centuries gone by had been to Amos, Jeremiah, and other prophets.

This "prophetic" interpretation of contemporary history is not to be confused with the "apocalyptic" (*see* APOCALYPTICISM), which is found in such works as Daniel, Enoch, IV Ezra, and in the Little Apocalypse underlying Mark 13 (vss. 3-4, 6-8, 14-20, 24-27; see especially vss. 4, 29); other apocalyptic features are the appearance of false messiahs and false prophets, as in vss. 6, 21 ff, of which the first century had many examples (cf. Matt. 7:21-23; Luke 6:46; 13:26-27). The "signs" described in Mark 13 contradict the principle: "No sign shall be given" (Mark 8:11-13, modified in Matt. 12:38-42; Luke 11:29-32; there are three stages in the development of the saying in the tradition). But the presuppositions of Mark 13 are derived not from Jesus' teaching, but from the Jewish-Christian Little Apocalypse. The details in Matt. 24:40; Luke 17:34-35 are derived from the Little Apocalypse via Mark 13:14-20. As in the OT crises, especially the fall of Jerusalem in 597-586, God's patience has been exhausted by this generation (Matt. 23:35-36; Luke 13:6-9).

The passage announcing the threat of doom is credited by Luke (11:49-50) to the "Wisdom of God," which may have been some apocryphal or apocalyptic work then in circulation; its fulfilment, as Luke clearly recognized, took place, not in an ending of the world or of its present order, but in the fall of Jerusalem in A.D. 70 (Luke 19:41-44; 21:20-24; he sees the whole eschatological gospel of Jesus through the lurid haze of this great catastrophe). The temple is to be destroyed (Mark 13:1-4), as well as the city. Not one stone will be left upon another in the beautiful new structure begun by Herod the Great and still far from completion in Jesus' day. Jesus weeps over the city (Luke 13:34-35)—the editorial addition in vs. 35*b*, which was found even in Q, must not mislead the interpreter; it no doubt refers to Jesus' triumphal entry on Palm Sunday (19:38). Similarly, Jesus warns the women of Jerusalem not to weep for him, but for themselves (Luke 23:28-31); some scholars think that all these Lukan passages concerning the fall of Jerusalem are related, perhaps derived from a common source. The tension of the times is clearly reflected likewise in Luke 12:49-50, where the "fire" and "water" of John's baptismal preaching are applied by Jesus to himself (cf. Mark 10:38). So also Luke 13:1-9 is no abstract discussion of theodicy, but a warning of the coming destruction of Jerusalem, whose terrors and dangers can be escaped only by repentance. Repeatedly Jesus warns that the coming of the Judgment, or the PAROUSIA of the Son of man, will be sudden, instantaneous, inescapable, and "without observation" other than the "signs of the times" (Matt. 24:26-27; Luke 17:20-37). As we have seen, the proper translation of Luke 17:21 is "in the midst of you"; the proper exegesis is suggested by vss. 23-24, where part of the saying is repeated. The kingdom is already here, in essence; its full manifestation in external reality will be instantaneous (cf. Mark 13:26). The Gnostic interpretation, "Whoever knows himself will find it," quoted in Huck's *Synopsis* and in *Gospel Parallels,* section 183, from *Oxyrhynchus Papyri,* 654 (2), is to be rejected, along with the ancient translation, *in animis vestris.* Further emphasis upon this suddenness of the final end is seen in the reference to the Flood and the burning of Sodom and Gomorrah (vss. 26-30), and other warnings, some of which are only conventional apocalyptic, but others are fresh and original (e.g., vs. 33, from Mark 8:35; and vss. 34-35, from Q). The saying about the vultures and the corpse (37*b*) points once more toward the contemporary scene: wherever there is evil, the Judgment will strike. The vultures remind us of the Erinyes in Greek religious thought.

d. The coming Parousia and Judgment. As later on in Paul's teaching ("the Day will disclose it"—I Cor. 3:13), so in that of Jesus, everything will be clear at the coming Judgment (Matt. 10:26-33; Luke 12:2-12). Again, this is eschatological teaching, not Gnostic (as in the saying quoted in Huck and in *Gospel Parallels* on § 155, from *Oxyrhynchus Papyri,* 654 [4]: "What is hid from you will be revealed to you.") Also as in current apocalyptic thought, only a few will be saved (Luke 13:22-24)—i.e., the "elect" (cf. Mark 13:22), or the "righteous" (Matt. 25:34), for whom the kingdom has been "prepared from the foundation of the world." Jesus does not say that these are identical with his followers, though it is assumed that his own disciples, who have renounced all to follow him, will receive the kingdom as a gift (Luke 12:32-33), and surely those who "hear the word of God and keep it" (viz., Jesus' true family; Mark 3:31-35; Luke 11:27-28) will be included. Such a saying as that about the apostles' twelve thrones (Matt. 19:28; Luke 22:28), though by definition belonging to Q, seems to have a wholly different background from the other kingdom sayings; it is ruled out by the pericope in Mark 10:35-45, where Jesus denies that he has authority to assign places of honor in the kingdom (though here also there are difficulties —the disciples' request would have been impossible after vss. 33-34, and vss. 38-40 are clearly a *vaticinium ex eventu;* the *Gospel of the Naassenes,* quoted in Huck and in *Gospel Parallels,* on § 192, undertook to get around the difficulty by reading: "Even if you drink . . .").

The real answer to the request and the continuation of the narrative is in vss. 41-44. The Son-of-man saying in vs. 45 is perhaps a reformulation of a saying of Jesus, made in the early church; cf. Luke's form of it in 22:27. The sublime account of the Last Judgment in Matt. 25:31-46 is not a "parable" but an illustrative story, and so is the one in Luke 16:19-31 (the rich man and Lazarus), which was based, apparently, on an old Egyptian tale of the judgment of souls after death. In view of the sudden coming of the kingdom, at the Parousia, Jesus' message is to *watch!* (Mark 13:37), with loins girded and lamps aflame (Luke 12:35-36; the parable of the watchful maidens, Matt. 25:1-13, elaborates this teaching); every Jew would recognize an added reference to the Passover celebration with its eschatological connotations (Exod. 12:11; cf. Mark 14:38; Luke 22:40; 21:34 ff, concluding the apocalyptic discourse, is an editorial cento based on Mark). Nevertheless, Jesus himself does not know the day or the hour of the impending Parousia of the Son of man or of the Judgment, which presumably is to follow (see Mark 13:32; cf. Acts 1:7). The text of Matt. 24:36 has probably been altered by the insertion of "nor the Son"; the addition is probably an inference from Matt. 25:13 (cf. 24:44; Luke 12:40, from Q), and the statement is strong enough without it. If Irenaeus and Origen had omitted the phrase, we should assume that it represented a theological interest; but when Eastern MSS omit it, this can scarcely be because of a theological presupposition. And if the words were not found in the original text of Matthew, the next inference is that they were likewise absent from Mark. The use of "the Son," absolutely, is not found elsewhere in Mark; it is found in Matthew (11:27), where, however, the Son's knowledge seems to rule out such a statement as the present one. The view that the gospel must first be preached to all nations (Mark 13:10; 14:9), and then will come the end (Matt. 24:14), is surely a later one. Contrast the idea set forth in I Cor. 15:24, which does not emphasize preaching. Finally, such a passage as Matt. 16: 17-19, the blessing of Peter and his promised preeminence in the church—if this is the true interpretation—is likewise a later addition to the gospel tradition. No such conception is found anywhere else in the NT, nor is it congruous with the course of early Christian history, so far as we know it.

e. Was the kingdom identical with the church? There are passages in which the kingdom is referred to as Christ's or the Son of man's (Matt. 13:41, where the kingdom is identified with the church; *see* CHURCH, IDEA OF); but these are late editorial revisions (especially in Matthew) which reflect the early Christian point of view (cf. John 18:36). So also are the passages which apparently identify the kingdom with the Jewish people or the Jewish church-state or the ancient covenant (e.g., Matt. 21:43). A striking saying about the new era which began after John's imprisonment (or death) appears in two different forms: "From the days of John the Baptist until now the kingdom of heaven has suffered violence [or has been coming violently], and men of violence take it by force" (Matt. 11:12); "The law and the prophets were until John; since then the good news of the kingdom of God is preached, and every one enters it violently" (Luke 16:16). "Kingdom of God" and "kingdom of heaven" are identical in meaning; the latter is only the reverent Jewish circumlocution to avoid using the word "God." Matthew's form of the saying looks back upon a period of violence which began with the Baptist's martyr death; here the kingdom is apparently the Jewish people, or the holy covenant, which has been ravaged and violated by "men of violence," including Herod, the Zealots, the Romans, and all who have had their will with the helpless nation: the very form of the saying is its interpretation. On the other hand, Luke's form pictures the beginning of the gospel (as also in Acts 10:37 ff), its public proclamation, and the ensuing popular response. This also is an interpretation. As both forms are interpretations, it is difficult to find a common element which can be described as the original saying of Jesus. This is also true of many other "detached" sayings preserved in the gospels, where no editorial interpretation or setting gives us a clue to the original meaning.

4. Jesus' ministry to the outcast. Jesus' ministry, as we have seen, was devoted to the "lost sheep of the house of Israel" (Matt. 10:6; Mark 2:14-17; cf. Ps. 147:2-3; Ezek. 34:6)—i.e., the Galilean 'AM HA'AREZ who were scorned by the religious leaders, the scribes, and by the model pietists, the PHARISEES, since they neglected the observance of the religious rules of strict Judaism such as those concerning the sabbath, tithes, the food laws, and avoidance of contacts with idolatry (i.e., with Gentiles). Their very occupations required them to disregard some of the rigid theoretical rules of the scribes—and even of the Torah. E.g., the cattle required watering and feeding, the cows and goats milking (Luke 13:15), even on the sabbath. Accidents and injuries required attention, even on the holy day (Luke 14:5). The later rabbis admitted the point that works of necessity and of mercy abrogate the letter of the law, but in the first century the rigorists seem to have prevailed. Such rules as that of CORBAN (Mark 7:10-11)—viz., the insistence that there could be no dispensation from vows dedicating property or income to God, even in cases of momentary anger or resentment (they were binding even when it meant neglect of one's parents, whose support the law required)—such abstract, theoretical, and inhuman interpretations of the law were egregious examples of uncontrolled legal professionalism. They help to account for the neglect of the law by many of the laity, and also explain the rift between them and their leaders ("This crowd, who do not know the law, are accursed!"—John 7:49).

It was to the neglected common people, who "heard him gladly," that Jesus devoted himself. His saying: "I was sent only to the lost sheep of the house of Israel," receives a curious emphasis and interpretation from its setting in Matt. 15:24, where it is assumed (as in 10:5, 23*b*) that it rules out any consideration of the needs of Gentiles; but the emphatic words are "lost sheep," not "Israel," and the verses in ch. 10 are now generally thought to reflect the views of the ultra-right-wing Jewish Christians in Jerusalem ("those about James") in the forties or fifties, rather than Jesus' own principles. But as a matter of fact, Jesus never began a ministry among the Gentiles, in spite of the suggestion in John 7:35. The charge against Jesus: "He eats with tax collectors and sinners" (Mark 2:13-17), was reiterated throughout his ministry (e.g., Luke 15:1). The strict Pharisee, who avoided contaminating contact with idolatry and with those who were careless of their own contacts with it, could not understand him (Luke 7:39). Jesus viewed his mission as "to call sinners" (Mark 2:17), rather than the "righteous"—i.e., the religious-minded and devout observers of Judaism.

In other words, the gospel was, from the outset, a gospel of redemption. The trilogy of parables in Luke

15 (the lost sheep, the lost coin, and the lost son) makes this clear: "There will be more joy in heaven [i.e., in the presence of God] over one sinner who repents" than over many of the "righteous" who "need no repentance," while God's welcome to the penitent is like that of a father receiving back again a beloved son who has become "lost." The parable of the marriage feast (Luke 14:16-24) pictures God's invitation as extended to the *'Am Ha'arez,* after the professionally pious have rejected it—the later interpretation of it as a reference to the Gentile mission is a sound application of the principle, but not a sound exegesis of the original meaning. E.g., the conversion of Zacchaeus (Luke 19:1-10) is an example of a recovery of the "lost" (cf. 3:13; the penitent is welcomed back as a true "son of Abraham" [3:8]). Blind Bartimaeus and others were saved by faith; Zacchaeus was saved by repentance. Keeping the commandments could lead to salvation (cf. Mark 10:19); but Zacchaeus was a sinner (Luke 19:7; this is not an insertion into the story but the necessary setting for vs. 9). The woman with the ointment in Simon's house (Luke 7:36-47) is a glowing picture of gratitude to Jesus for all he was doing for the poor and outcast, and for all that he meant to them. The final verses (48-50) are a typical Lukan "tag" which, as often, only confuses the story. The fact that the woman's sins are already forgiven is evident from her deep love and gratitude. The parallels in Matt. 26:6-13; Mark 14:3-9; John 12:3-8 move in another direction, and are interpreted as referring to Jesus' impending death. Did Jesus intend (at least eventually) a mission to Gentiles? Luke 4:25-27 may be understood to point that way, and also 13:29; but the evidence as a whole is against the theory. This was one charge his enemies did not bring against him—they might have done so had there been sufficient grounds for it (cf. John 7:35).

5. Jesus' teaching and Judaism. Jesus' teaching embraced, apparently, most of the basic beliefs and practices of religion as set forth in contemporary Judaism (though the gospels are not exhaustive). Centered in his proclamation of the coming kingdom (Luke 4:43), his preaching dealt with a whole series of correlated subjects. The fundamental revelation of God in the OT, and his character and purposes as therein revealed, are everywhere taken for granted. E.g., the parable of the workers in the vineyard (Matt. 20:1-16) is no illustration of a new economic theory, but a story to illustrate the overwhelming grace and goodness of God, which cannot be measured by human deserving. The goodness of the Creator is apparent even in nature; he sends his sun and his rain "on the evil and on the good" (Matt. 5:45), and cares for the birds of the air and the flowers of the field (Luke 12:22-31; cf. Ps. 147:8-9). Hence God is to be trusted for our daily needs (Mark 8:16-21); we must not yield to anxiety (Matt. 6:33). In fact, God always answers prayer, though not always as we wish (Matt. 7:7-11); hence the power of faith is unlimited (Luke 17:5-6): "With God all things are possible" (Matt. 19:26). It is only a step from this conviction to that of the unlimited power of prayer, and in Mark and Matthew of cursing (Matt. 17:20; 21:21-22; Mark 11:23-24; Luke 17:6; John 14:13-14; 16:23). The story of the importunate friend (Luke 11:5-8) illustrates this principle, as does also the parable of the unjust judge (Luke 18:1-8); constancy in prayer will achieve results, as it did in this case—if it succeeds with a wicked human judge, how much more with the Father in heaven! (Vs. 8*b* is another Lukan "tag," suggesting that the Christians—i.e., *the* faith, which is the Christian—may be exterminated before the Parousia, a possibility which must have seemed real in the days of Nero or Domitian, if not earlier.)

a. Absolute sincerity. In the practice of religion, absolute sincerity and singleness of purpose are required (Luke 11:34-35; 14:34-35; the parables of light, the lamp, the eye, and even salt are interpreted in this sense). There is no use in trying to escape this principle; to do so is only to deceive oneself: "Where your treasure is, there will your heart be also" (Luke 12:33-34). It is impossible to serve two masters (Matt. 6:24), and even in serving one master it is not possible to win merit: "When you have done all that is commanded you, say, 'We are mere undeserving slaves [not "unworthy," as in RSV, nor "worthless," but as slaves "non-remunerated"; cf. Antigonos of Socho in Pirke Aboth 1:3]; we have only done our duty' " (Luke 17:10). The actual practice of religion is what matters, not ardent professions of zeal or devotion (Matt. 7:21-27), and the outward act discloses the inner motive and disposition (Matt. 7:15-20; 12:33-35; 21:28-32). Even everyday prudence is invoked to support the appeal to repentance (Luke 12:57; 14:34-35; 16:1-13, the parable of the clever steward, followed by a series of admonitions or homiletical tags in verses 8*b*-13). The parable in 12:57-59 even urges reconciliation with God as a matter of common prudence. The parable of the talents (Matt. 25:14-30; Luke 19:11-27) likewise emphasizes the necessity of "putting religion in practice," though Luke's parallel is confused by conflation with another story—or parable—of a king seeking investiture, and in both (therefore in Q) the insertion of a verse from Mark 4:25 has obscured the meaning: the verse from Mark refers to learning, not to economic conditions. (The verses in Luke 12:47-48 about responsibility for service are only two tags attached to the preceding section, vss. 42-46; one is in vss. 47-48*a;* the other, in 48*b*, forms a simple quatrain.)

b. Love for one's neighbor. High among the duties of religion, as taught in Judaism and also by Jesus, is LOVE for one's neighbor, and even one's enemy (Luke 6:27-28, 32-36). This is not limited to fellow Jews. The finest example is in the illustrative story (not a "parable") of the good Samaritan (Luke 10:29-37), which explains what loving another "as thyself" means: it was at considerable risk, as well as expense, that the Samaritan rescued the wounded traveler, for he cared for him as he would for his own life. (Cf. Jesus' own attitude toward the Samaritan village [Luke 9:51-56], and the account in John 4:1-42.) Such sayings as those about reconciliation and forgiveness of enemies (Luke 17:4) or even about reproving an offender (Matt. 18:15-17) make the principle still clearer, in the undramatic situations of everyday life—though Matthew as usual is moving in the direction of canon law, and follows the sayings with the awesome parable of the unmerciful steward (18:23-35). Above all things, the sin of leading others into sin must be avoided (Mark 9:42-48).

c. Humility. The teaching on humility is very prominent, not only in the Beatitudes (Matt. 5:3-12; Luke 6:20-23), which describe the character pleasing to God and therefore requisite in those who are to enter his kingdom, but also repeatedly in the gospels: e.g., Matt. 18:4; 23:12; Mark 9:33-37; 10:15, 43-44; Luke 9:48; 14:7-11 (where it is combined with charity, vss. 12-14, introducing the parable of the great supper, vss. 15-24); 18:14, 17. The Beatitude, "Blessed are the poor *in spirit*," means "in their own estimation, aware of their own shortcomings and insufficiency"—the opposite of self-confidence in the approach to God. Jesus' whole concept of the kingdom of God rules out pride of place (Mark 10:35-45). God prefers the humble to the arrogant (Luke 18:9-14). He is greatest who serves (Mark 10:42-44). It is this demand of a lowly estimate of oneself which leads to the prohibition of censoriousness (Matt. 7:1-5).

d. The permanence of the law. Although the gospels are not in entire agreement (*see* § A4 *above*), Matthew at least insists that Jesus held the Jewish law to be permanently binding (Matt. 5:17-20; the saying in Luke 16:17 does not fit the context and may be a gloss—at best it is one of a group of supplementary sayings for which Luke had not found a suitable context in his narrative). In the Christian interpretation, the law is even harder to keep than in the scribal! The rest of Matt. 5 shows that mechanical piety will not do—nothing less than the imitation of the perfect love, compassion, mercy, and justice of God. The two great commandments in the law make for eternal life (Mark 12:28-31), as the friendly scribe recognized (vss. 32-34). The Torah really sets a very high goal for human effort, and cannot be easily observed, or observed 101 per cent, so as to achieve merit through either complete observance or "works of supererogation." Thus the Torah itself, in spite of the concession in Deut. 24:1-4, really requires monogamy and forbids divorce and remarriage (Mark 10:1-12). Such practices of religion as the three considered in Matt. 6:1-18 (almsgiving, prayer, and fasting) were not strictly rules governing all Jews at the time, though the first two were universally commended, and the third was increasingly in practice, especially among the Pharisees. (Jesus and his disciples did not fast—Mark 2:18-22—but the early Christians did.)

e. The Lord's Prayer. In its phraseology the LORD'S PRAYER (Matt. 6:9-13) closely resembles both the ancient form of Kaddish and some of the petitions in the earliest recensions of the Shemoneh Esreh or Eighteen Benedictions. The Lord's Prayer begins, as all Jewish prayers begin, with the praise of God, and is centered in the coming of his kingdom. "Hallowed be thy name" means, May God be recognized and worshiped everywhere. "Thy kingdom come," or "Thy reign begin," includes:

> Thy will be done,
> On earth as it is in heaven.

"Daily bread" means enough for daily needs. "Forgive us our debts" includes our failure to do good as well as our actual commission of wrong. "As we have forgiven" does not set a standard which God must meet, but means only that we have met the absolutely essential precondition to being heard by him (vss. 14-15). "Lead us not into temptation" means, as in other Jewish prayers, "Do not subject us to testing, do not compel us to face trials" (of the kind which often destroy men's faith in God; cf. Ecclus. 2:1-18); or possibly the final, eschatological tribulation, as in Albert Schweitzer's interpretation. "Deliver us from evil" means from the evils of life (as also in other Jewish prayers), not from wickedness. The ascription at the end, "For thine is the kingdom and the power and the glory, for ever," is a very early liturgical addition (cf. Did. 8.2; 10.5) based on I Chr. 29: 11-13.

The saying about the temple tax (Matt. 17:24-27) may be apocryphal—at least the story of the shekel in the fish's mouth must be a legend—but the saying in Mark 11:17: "My house shall be called a house of prayer for all nations," quoting Isa. 56:7, is certainly authentic. Moreover, Jesus' teaching shares many principles also found in Pharisaism—e.g., the doctrine of the resurrection (Mark 12:18-27, which may have been originally a "school debate," like the one on the grounds for divorce); but in Jesus' teaching all material concepts of the resurrection body were certainly ruled out.

f. His criticism of scribal teaching. On the other hand, Jesus' criticism of the scribal interpretation of the law, and also of the personal character of the religious leaders of his time, is clear in all the gospel sources. Mark 7:1-13 criticizes the mistaken tradition of the scribes, while vss. 14-23 state the real causes of defilement, which the scribes apparently overlook; Mark 8:15 criticizes the leaven of the Pharisees, and Luke 12:1 interprets this as the leaven of "hypocrisy"; the stern invectives in Matt. 23; Mark 12:37*b*-40; Luke 11:37–12:1 also charge them with greed as well as hypocrisy, with ostentation, the love of adulation, a merely external righteousness (or practice of religion)—e.g., the exact specification of tithes and the neglect of mercy and love, the increase of the burden of ceremonial rules upon the people, and the actual hindrance of those who would enter the kingdom of God. Luke 16:14-15 includes avarice as a Pharisaic vice; but this is scarcely reflected in their tradition—it was far more true of the affluent, worldly Sadducees. Moreover, the criticism of the leaders also included the people—"Like people, like priest" (Hos. 4:9). The parable of the wicked vineyard tenants (Mark 12:1-12) is a criticism, not of the leaders only, but of the nation; Luke 7:31-35 criticizes Jesus' contemporaries as a whole, in view of their failure to respond to either John's preaching or his own. (The woes on the Galilean towns, Luke 10:13 ff, may reflect a later view.)

g. Jesus' teaching on wealth. Jesus' teaching on wealth was probably more of a concern to the rich, landowning Sadducean high-priestly aristocracy than to either the scribes or Pharisees or the average "poor priest" living on his little patrimony somewhere in Judea or Galilee and performing his temple duty only two weeks in the year—like the prebends at Wells Cathedral in the Middle Ages. The praise of the widow offering her two "mites" (Mark 12:41-44) is caustic enough: "She has given more than all the others"; but the positive statement that riches are a hindrance to one's entering the kingdom of God (Mark 10:23-27), the story of the rich man and the beggar Lazarus (Luke 16:19-31), the demand of renunciation of property (Mark 10:17-31), and the total, sweeping principle of Luke 14:33: "Whoever of you does not renounce all that he has cannot be my disciple" (this emphasis is peculiar to Luke), and above all the parable of the rich fool (Luke 12:13-21) —these sayings must have seemed to many contemporaries to mark a total divergence, not only from the Jewish leaders and people and the practice of both, but from all traditional religion. It is noteworthy that this motive is not based on asceticism, or even on eschatology (the "interim ethics" to hold good until the kingdom comes), but upon the love, mercy, and goodness of God—and the love of neighbor that forms the heart of this religious ethic.

Jesus' ethic as a whole is neither scientific nor philosophical, in either the modern or the ancient sense. It cannot be lifted off its true base in the revealed religion of the OT, and set upon some other (Marxist, or Utilitarian, Aristotelian, or the "success" ethics of modern commercialism). The citation of the "Golden Rule" (Matt. 7:12; Luke 6:31; hence in Q) is only an added admonition, as it appears in the Sermon on the Mount, not an ethical principle of fundamental importance. It was a world-old adage, and circulated in its negative form in the Judaism of Hillel and of Jesus: "Do *not* do to others what you would *not* have them do to you." The strange and obscure gnomic saying found in Matt. 7:6, a chiastic quatrain: "Do not give dogs what is holy . . . ," is probably the conclusion of the sequence on the practice of piety: 6:1, 2-4, 5-8, 16-18. It is a quaint, even quasi-cynical, conclusion like 6:34 and the tags in the Didache, and means much the same as 10:13*b*-14 —i.e., do not waste your efforts on the unconvertible, who only oppose and revile you.

h. The scribes' reply. In their reply, the criticisms of Jesus by the scribes and Pharisees included his association with "sinners"—not necessarily wicked men, but lax, nonobservant Jews, who were despised by the official interpreters of the law and their lay followers, the Pharisaic "separatists." In Luke 7:39 the suspicion that Jesus cannot be a prophet, since he does not avoid contact with a "sinner," is openly voiced by Simon the Pharisee.

The charge brought by the scribes who came down from Jerusalem (Mark 3:22), more serious than the criticisms of the local scribes, maintained that Jesus was "possessed by Beelzebul, . . . the prince of demons," and thus exercised the undenied power of driving out other demons. Jesus' refutation of the charge is masterly: (*a*) a kingdom divided—as they thus represent Satan's to be—is on the way to ruin; (*b*) the fact that Jesus exorcises demons (which they cannot deny) shows that the "strong man" is already bound—the robber-baron is in chains, if the prisoners in his dungeons are being released; (*c*) if Jesus' exorcisms are effected by the authority and power of Beelzebul, by what power do the "sons" (disciples) of the scribes exorcise demons?—the libel must also apply to them; (*d*) but if, on the contrary, Jesus' exorcisms are done by the authority and power of God—i.e., his Holy Spirit—then the inference must follow that God's kingdom is close at hand, and has, in fact, "come upon you" (Matt. 12:25-29; Mark 3:23-30; Luke 11:17-22; Mark for some reason has omitted the crucial Q verse, the climax of the argument).

The criticism that Jesus undertook to forgive sins appears in Mark 2:5-7; Luke 7:49; but the middle part of the pericope (vss. 5*b*-10) is thought by many to be an insertion from another source, while Luke 7:49 belongs to the Lukan "tag"—the story is complete with vs. 47, where Jesus infers from the woman's gratitude that she is already forgiven. At least, the charge against Jesus is not repeated in the tradition, as it would have been had it been often made.

The criticism that he disregarded the sabbath was most serious, for it meant a breach, not of scribal tradition but of the law itself (Mark 2:23-28; 3:4; Luke 13:15-16; 14:3). Again, Jesus' refutation was not a denial of the fact, but its justification: works of mercy were at least on a par with works of necessity, if not a priority, and grave human need abrogates the requirement of the sabbath "rest"—which itself had been ordained for the benefit and welfare of men, not as an end in itself (Matt. 12:5; Mark 2:27; 3:1-6). The interpretation of "Son of man" in Mark 2:28 and parallels cannot be either "man" or Jesus himself; either interpretation would be contrary to his thought. It must be an inference drawn in the early church, in the course of the transmission of the tradition. The textual evidence in vss. 27-28 is complicated, and requires careful analysis; the pericope properly ends with vs. 27.

i. Jesus' criticism of the law. Thus Jesus' criticism of the scribal interpretation of the law, which the Pharisaic pietists adopted as their rule of life, went farther and included some parts of the law itself. E.g., the Torah permitted divorce under certain conditions, but hedged it about with provisions which would make for justice and equity (Deut. 24:1-4; *see* MARRIAGE). The scribal authorities, Hillel and Shammai and their followers, debated the meaning of the grounds to be alleged—viz., "some indecency" (in the wife)—some authorities arguing that it meant premarital sexual indulgence, others open adultery or fornication, still others incompetent housekeeping ("if she burns his bread"). Most of the interpretations were impossible, since they were covered by other regulations in the Torah; but Jesus swept them all aside (Mark 10:1-9). "From the beginning" God intended husbands and wives to be "joined together" in lifelong mutual fidelity. The Deuteronomic (=Mosaic) legislation was only a later concession to the hardness of human hearts, and could not possibly abrogate the fundamental principle laid down by the Creator (Gen. 2:24): "What therefore God has joined together [i.e., the principle of monogamic marriage], let not man put asunder." The added statement "in the house" (vs. 10, a regular Markan device for introducing additional material, especially from Q) is a categorical formulation of the principle, on the way to its incorporation in the church's canon law (see also Matt. 5:31-32; 19:9; Luke 16:18; I Cor. 7:10-16 shows that the apostle Paul found it necessary to allow a modification of the rule). The added verse, Mark 10:12, is a corollary which makes the rule applicable to both partners, since under Roman law a woman could divorce her husband; under Jewish law only the husband could divorce. This is an example of the way in which Jesus, a nonrabbinic, nonscribal lay teacher of religion, expounded the OT, and dealt with one of the problems which vexed the schools (Matt. 19:3).

In dealing with this and other religious and moral questions, Jesus appealed to the highest principles, the love, mercy, and justice of God, and took his stand upon a direct, intuitive understanding of God's will and requirements, not upon the scribal tradition of authoritative interpretations in the past (see Matt. 5:17-48; Mark 7:5-13). It was his freedom from scribal tradition, and his unhesitating rejection of scribal authority, culminating in his free and independent attitude toward the Scripture itself, which roused the antagonism of the religious authorities and resulted in his death. His teaching was a threat to their influence over the people, and to their whole system of religious interpretation and regulation. It was as a "heretic" who criticized and interfered with the national cultus that he was delivered to the Romans, on a trumped-up charge, and executed by them as a revolutionist.

j. Jesus' teaching of his disciples. Much of Jesus' teaching was addressed to his own disciples and to the larger group of followers who gathered about him wherever he went. The "Twelve" are listed four times in the NT (Matt. 10:2-4; Mark 3:14-19; Luke 6:13-16; Acts 1:13), though the lists do not entirely agree. This is not surprising in view of the fact that the names had been handed down by oral tradition (the great second-century rabbi and patriot Akiba had twelve disciples), but the total comes to fourteen in the various lists. The main purposes of Jesus' selection of disciples is stated in Mark 3:14-15: "to be with him, and to be sent out to preach [i.e., proclaim the gospel of the kingdom] and have authority [or power] to cast out demons"; i.e., they were to share, and to carry further, the mission and ministry of Jesus himself (cf. Mark 1:17, 39). The mission of the disciples (described in Matt. 9:35–10:16; Mark 6:6-13; Luke 9:1-5; 10:1-12, 16) illustrates this—though some of the details refer to the later, postresurrection mission of the early church in Palestine; they have been read back into the lifetime of Jesus. Although Luke assumes (12:33; 14:33) that every follower of Jesus was required to renounce all his possessions, this seems not actually to have been the case. In any event, the possibility of return to their usual occupations was still open (John 21:3), and the renunciation, for most of them, did not involve giving up great wealth (Mark 10:17-22 is exceptional).

k. Discipleship. Discipleship is a great privilege (Matt. 13:16-17), and therefore any sacrifice it requires must be met cheerfully and unhesitatingly. The way is narrow that leads to life (Matt. 7:13-14), and prudence must be exercised in choosing to follow Jesus (Luke 14:25-35)—the statements are largely negative; note the threefold "he *cannot* be my disciple." The saying about eunuchs in Matt. 19:10-12 is perhaps an Encratite addition to the gospel tradition; it really requires celibacy, which is impossible without the help of divine grace, as in Mark 10:27*b*. Yet the disciples are to be like their Master (Matt. 10:24-25) if they are to share his life; and he was unmarried. Nothing less than total renunciation is required (Mark 8:34-38; Luke adds "daily"), including the renunciation of family life—hyperbolically described as "hating" their next of kin, since the spread of the gospel produced intense frictions within families (Mark 10:28-31; Luke 9:57-62; 12:51-53; 14:26-27; domestic divisions were a feature in the anticipated conditions of the "latter days," according to the eschatological interpretation of Mic. 7:6, overlooking Mal. 4:6). For one thing, Jesus' disciples included women (Luke 8:1-3; cf. Acts 1:14), and in an ancient oriental household this might easily lead to disunity and separation, as it often did in the early centuries of the church's history, especially during the persecutions. The beautiful story of Mary and Martha (Luke 10:38-42) illustrates the requirement of singlehearted devotion. We should probably omit vs. 42*a*, which is unessential and complicates the story (as the gloss in Mark 8:14*b* did!), and which in view of the textual variants probably originated in a well-meaning gloss, followed by later attempts either to remedy or to improve it.

Persecution is foreseen as the lot of the disciples (Matt. 10:17-25; Mark 13:9-13; cf. John 15:21; 16:2), though some of the details probably reflect the conditions of tension and opposition in Palestine during the decades which led up to the final breach between the church and the synagogue. Yet the disciples are not to be anxious (Matt. 10:19-20; Luke 12:11-12); the Spirit will teach them what to say, when they are brought to trial (Luke) or will inspire their words and speak through them (Matthew). What is required is fearless confession of their discipleship (Matt. 10:26-33; Luke 12:2-12), since on the Day of Judgment the Son of man will surely deny the faithless and apostate (Mark 8:38; Luke 9:26; Matt. 10:33 has "I will deny," an example of the frequent interchange of "Son of man" and the first person singular of the verb in the "Son of man" sayings; Luke 12:9 has "he will be denied"). And yet the blessed promise is clear: "Those who receive you, receive me," and the cup of cold water given the persecuted or the imprisoned will not be forgotten (Matt. 10:40 ff).

For further details on Jesus' teaching, *see* SERMON ON THE MOUNT; TEACHING OF JESUS.

F. *THE MIGHTY WORKS.* 1. Healings and exorcisms. From the outset, Jesus' proclamation of the kingdom of God was accompanied by supernatural manifestations, chiefly exorcism and the healing of the sick. This was in marked contrast to the Baptist ("John did no miracle"—i.e., "sign"—John 10:41). Attempts have been made to analyze the descriptions of the various ailments treated, and the methods used by Jesus; but the diagnosis was only popular and traditional, not scientific, and the methods were chiefly prayer, the eliciting of faith on the part of the sick, and the firm, authoritative word of command by the healer.

Such ailments as possession by a "demon" (Mark 1:21-28, 32), fever (1:29-31), leprosy (1:40-45; cf. Luke 17:11-19), paralysis (Mark 2:1-12), a "withered" hand (3:1-6), chronic hemorrhage (5:25-34), deafness and muteness (7:31-37), blindness (8:22-26; 10:46-52), epilepsy (9:14-29), dropsy (Luke 14:1-6)—these are the ailments that commonly afflicted mankind in the ancient world, as the Greek medical writers and the great *Natural History* of the elder Pliny show. The continuous emphasis on healing in Mark justifies the description of this work as the "gospel of the mighty works of Jesus." And yet the emphasis is not altogether on his pre-eminence as a healer, and it is recognized that at Nazareth he failed (Mark 6:5-6; the exception clause sounds unreal after "not a single [οὐδεμίαν] mighty work," and must be a gloss); the explanation is the Nazarenes' lack of faith. Other "mighty works" included the restoration of the centurion's slave (Matt. 8:5-13; Luke 7:1-10; cf. John 4:46-53), Jairus' daughter (Mark 5:22-24, 35-43), the widow's son at Nain (Luke 7:11-17), the Syrophoenician's daughter (Mark 7:24-30), the woman with a "spirit of infirmity" (Luke 13:10-17). In none of these is the precise ailment suggested, though the last-named intimates that the weakness was due to an evil spirit. Even the "miraculous" catch of fish in Luke 5:1-11 may be accounted a "mighty work," or the stilling of the storm (Mark 4:35-41, which some view as an exorcism of the spirit of the storm), and certainly the exorcism of the "legion" which possessed the Gerasene demoniac (Mark 5:1-20), whose condition is vividly described—an ancient "terror of the glen." Perhaps the cursing of the fig tree (Mark 11:12-14, 20-26) should be included; according to Mark it was the only miracle performed in or near Jerusalem (excluding Jericho, which was several miles E of the city). Matthew tells the story in the true vein of miracle lore: the tree withers instantly (Matt. 21:19), and the story becomes a lesson in successful cursing (vss. 20-21)! But Mark's catena of sayings at the end is surely inappropriate here. Vss. 25-26 are probably both interpolated; both are based on Matt. 6:14-15, and neither of them is in Markan language or style. It scarcely needs to be said that this picture of a disappointed, resentful, and vindictive prophet or holy man is not worthy of Jesus, and conflicts with the usual representation of him in the gospels. It sounds more like Elijah, Elisha, or Mohammed. *See* MIRACLE.

2. Other miracles. Although healings and exorcisms provide the majority of the miracle stories in the Synoptics (cf. Luke 13:31-32), there are a few others which can scarcely be included in this category. One is the walking on the water (Mark 6:45-52), which has a parallel in the life of Buddha; the story as told in Matthew (14:22-33) is almost a parable of Peter's wavering faith (vss. 28-31), as seen in his "denials" of Jesus during the "trial" by the Sanhedrin (26:69-75). Luke omits both this miracle and the cursing of the fig tree.

The feeding of the multitude is told in two forms (the five thousand: Matt. 14:13-21; Mark 6:30-44; Luke 9:10-17; John 6:1-13; the four thousand: Matt. 15:32-39; Mark 8:1-10; Luke and John omit). The stories are two variant accounts of the same event, presumably; for when the problem of feeding the four thousand arises, the disciples make no reference to any earlier solution. The reference to both feedings, in Mark 8:16-21, is an editorial device to furnish a setting for the repeated saying (7:18; 8:17*c,* 18, 21). The whole outlook of the passage, and of the narratives of the feeding to which it refers, is diametrically opposed to the temptation narrative, where Jesus flatly refuses to satisfy hunger by performing a miracle (Matt. 4:3-4; Luke 4:3-4). (Does this explain Mark's omission of the fuller Q account of the Temptation—viz., because he held a different interpretation of the meaning of the feeding than that which the old tradition had set forth?) Many scholars now believe that the feeding was a kind of "eschatological sacrament," binding Jesus' followers to him and to one another in view of the approaching crisis.

Thus the miracle stories in the Synoptic gospels are mainly of one class, healing and exorcism. Those in John are in a different category, as "signs" of divine power, or even "epiphanies" of a divine being (John 2:11). That exorcisms and cures could be performed by others than Jesus is clear from his commission of the disciples to do both (Matt. 9:8; Luke 9:1-2; 10:9), from his reference to the "sons" of the scribes who practiced exorcism (Luke 11:19), from his refusal to interfere with the work of the stranger who was using his name (Mark 9:38-41), from the expectation that false prophets and messiahs would be able to do signs and wonders (Matt. 24:11, 24), and from the fact that his practice of exorcism and healing was not denied or included among the charges brought against him by his enemies. Even the occasional failure of exorcism is recognized (Luke 11:24-26).

Yet even during his ministry of extraordinarily successful healing and exorcism, Jesus could say: "No sign shall be given!" (Mark 8:12), and in the Fourth Gospel the failure of the "signs" to convince his adversaries is noted (John 12:37). All this is evidence of the slightness of the emphasis placed on the exercise of supernatural—or supernormal—powers in the early church. Paul, e.g., lays no emphasis on Jesus' "miracles"; he never, in fact, mentions them, though he does refer to his own "signs of an apostle" (Rom. 15:19; II Cor. 12:12). Even Jesus' resurrection is not, for Paul, either a "sign" or a "mighty work," but the supremely natural consequence of the victorious life and death of the Son of God.

3. The meaning of the "mighty works" for Jesus himself. In fact, the whole modern concept of "miracle," as a stupendous, inexplicable event which conflicts with or contradicts the "laws of nature," is useless when we try to explain the "mighty works" of Jesus. They were not indications of superior skill or even of a privately possessed supernatural power; instead, as in the OT, they were the "mighty works" of God, not man, though done *through* a prophet or other chosen person. The ministry of Jesus included healings and exorcisms in addition to teaching and proclaiming the message of the arriving kingdom; and these "mighty works" were evidence, not of the truth of his message, or of his own personal power or divine nature, but of the fact that the kingdom of God was really at hand. The powers of darkness were actually being rolled back, the "powers of the age to come" (Heb. 6:5) were already being manifested, now at the end of this present age. In a word, the whole concept, in the Synoptics, is eschatological; and if one inquires what the "mighty works" meant to Jesus himself, the answer is clear and unmistakable: "If it is by the Spirit of God [Luke reads "finger of God," which is an OT phrase meaning the same thing] that I cast out demons, then the kingdom of God has come upon you" (Matt. 12:28; Luke 11:20). The miracle stories in the Fourth Gospel belong in a different category, although three of them are also found in the Synoptics. They are basically "signs" of the divine person who performed them and of his heavenly "glory," which he had laid aside temporarily but incompletely on becoming man.

4. Significance of the Baptism and the Temptation. We are now in a position to look back and recognize the significance of the baptism and temptation narratives, located at the beginning of the story by Mark (the other Synoptists follow his order). The Baptism (Mark 1:9-11) was not, as some scholars have held, the "awakening of Jesus' messianic consciousness," or his "inauguration" as Son of God—a view reflected in the Western reading of Luke 3:22, but refuted by Paul's statement in Rom. 1:4, which is consonant with most of the NT; instead, the Baptism was Jesus' endowment with the Holy Spirit for his office and ministry as a prophet. Like all the prophets of the OT, like every prophet, even in the NT, there had to be a "call" and a "commission," and the outpouring of the Spirit upon him. But unlike the prophets of old, Jesus' endowment was permanent and was given, as the Fourth Gospel says, "without measure" (John 3:34). Unlike the earlier prophets, he neither committed a sin nor spoke a sinful word after his endowment with the Spirit (cf. John 8:46; II Cor. 5:21; I Pet. 2:22; see the Gospel According to the Hebrews, quoted by Jerome *Against the Pelagians* III.2, cited in Huck's *Synopsis* and in *Gospel Parallels,* on § 135).

The ordeal, through which he at once passed, was the test of his vocation, and proved him superior to the various diabolical proposals—short cuts devised to bring in God's kingdom, popular demagoguery, "signs and wonders," spectacular self-exploitation, the direct action of the Zealots and of other revolutionists. All these were the ways of Satan, not of God (cf. Mark 8:33). Instead, he must follow the way of simple obedience to the Spirit's guidance (Luke 4:1, 14, 18; 5:17; 6:19), one step at a time, without any "program" or "campaign" of action. *See also* §§ D3, E2, *above.*

So true is the temptation narrative to the whole character of Jesus as portrayed in the gospels that it provides the key to the beginning of his ministry, where the Synoptists have placed it (though they might well have considered such a location as Mark 8:27-29 or 31-38; or 14:32-42; or Luke 12:49-50; 13: 31; or 17:22-30). The fall of Satan (Luke 10:17-20) presumably belongs in the period of the mission of the disciples (i.e., the Twelve, who were sent out to exorcize; not the Seventy of Luke 10:1-12), but the binding of the strong man (Mark 3:27) must have been earlier (cf. John 12:31). The testing of Jesus in the wilderness takes forty days, as the testing of Israel in the wilderness (Deut. 2:7) took forty years. When it is over, the devil leaves him "until a more convenient opportunity" (ἄχρι καιρόυ—Luke 4:13; but see Acts 13:11—the phrase was common and untechnical).

The words spoken by the heavenly voice at the Baptism and those at the Transfiguration (Mark 9:7) are related, and the implications of the second, "Listen to him," may well have been implicit in the first. The scene is prophetic, as the association with Moses and Elijah suggests, though Luke has introduced a wholly new idea in 9:31-32: their conversation concerned Jesus' "exodus" from this life, to "enter into his glory" permanently (Luke 24:26). The Markan narrative may be composite; 9:5-6 (or even 4-6) may be secondary. Peter's words were admittedly irrelevant (vs. 6), and their purpose is apparently to emphasize the terror occasioned by the supernatural phenomenon. Some scholars interpret the incident as a postresurrection appearance of Jesus predated to the Galilean ministry; but whatever its origin, in the tradition, the story as now presented is an anticipation of the "glory that shall be" when Jesus has risen from the dead. Luke, of course, edits the passage with his central section in mind (cf. 9:51).

5. The question of messiahship. ***a. The journey to Caesarea Philippi.*** It is significant that according to the Synoptics (unlike the Fourth Gospel), Jesus did no "mighty works" of healing or exorcism outside Galilee, except for the healing of the Syrophoenician girl (Mark 7:24-30)—none in Judea except Bartimaeus at Jericho, where Mark represents him as teaching (10:1; 11:18; 12:1, 38). The journeys to the region of Tyre and Sidon (Mark 7:24) and Caesarea Philippi (8:27) were clearly not for the purpose of evangelizing the Gentiles, since Jesus preferred not to be recognized. Some writers have held that Jesus fled from Herod Antipas, thus acknowledging that his Galilean ministry had failed; others that he went away for a rest (as in Mark 6:31). The simple fact is, we do not know why he went away. It has been suspected that the journey to Tyre and Sidon was described in order to justify the reference in Luke 10: 13-14; but the latter is from Q, and the logic of the connection is hard to see. The Phoenician cities did not, as a matter of fact, repent, any more than ancient Nineveh at Jonah's preaching. The journey to Caesarea Philippi, like Jesus' withdrawal beyond the Jordan in John 10:40, may have been a "retreat"; but the evidence is lacking. Jesus' question, addressed to the disciples: "Who do men say that I am?" (Mark 8:27), and especially the answers: "John the Baptist," or "Elijah," or "one of the prophets," remind us of Herod's quandary (6:14-16). In the eyes of his contemporaries, even of his disciples, Jesus was a prophet, which meant an authorized and authoritative representative of God. If he was something even more, as some suspected—i.e., the Messiah—it is clear from the Synoptics that Jesus made no public claim to either the title or the office.

All the more singular then is the passage relating Peter's confession of faith (Mark 8:27-33), with Jesus' apparent acceptance of the description (which Matthew elaborates in 16:17-19) followed by the stern charge that they were to say nothing about it. This may, of course, be due to the theory of the "messianic secret" which Mark held (cf. 3:12; 9:9; etc.), but it is equally probable that Jesus had no intention of fulfilling the ancient hope of a great king who should arise, free the nation, destroy their enemies, restore its old boundaries, mount the throne of David, and thenceforth reign in bliss for many years—or forever—over a happy people. The "messianic hope" was too earth-bound, too this-worldly, too materialistic, even jingoistic, to match Jesus' concept of the kingdom of God. The modern insistence upon the historical reality of Jesus' "messianic consciousness" overlooks this fact, and also the fact that there is no direct line between Jesus' "messiahship" and the "divinity" of Christ. A great many impostors, both ancient and modern, have had a "messianic" consciousness. Jesus was something different, and far profounder, in his meaning for the world and for man's salvation. When Jesus rebuked Peter for protesting against his approaching rejection and death (Mark 8:32-33), it became clear that what Peter—and others—meant by messiahship was not at all Jesus' concept of his mission. It is in this light that the question in Mark 12:35-37*a:* "How can the Messiah be the Son of David?" is to be understood. Although the popular acclamation identified him with this coming nationalistic deliverer (cf. Mark 10:47-48; 11:9-10; for the interpretation, see Matt. 21:9, 15; Luke 19:38), and although the conviction of Jesus' descent from David was deeply embedded in Christian tradition, as Rom. 1:3 and the genealogies in Luke and Matthew show, it is clear that Jesus himself laid no emphasis upon it. Too many would-be deliverers claimed royal descent, and proved by their actions how remote were their aims from the true purposes of God. Jesus' aim was certainly nonpolitical (see the passage about tribute to Caesar: Mark 12:13-17).

b. Jesus did not proclaim his messiahship. Unlike some other religious leaders of the time, and unlike the portrayal in John, Jesus (according to the Synoptics) does not make himself the center of his teaching or demand submission or loyalty to himself as a condition of acceptance or admission to the kingdom of God. (The sayings that deal with loyalty in persecution even to the point of death obviously reflect the conditions of the early church, faced with opposition and the threat of extermination by either the Jewish synagogue or the Roman state or by both.) His whole concern was with the kingdom of God and its coming. The passion predictions (Mark 8:31; 9:31; 10:32-34 and parallels) are totally ignored in the narrative that follows, especially the passion narrative; they are not only based on the passion narrative itself, as brief summaries of the leading facts, but are projected backward into the Galilean ministry by Mark, presumably in order to show that Jesus was not taken unawares in Jerusalem and that he knew in advance what he was doing. But such incidental statements as those in Matt. 28:17; Mark 14:29, 31, 32-42, 47; 16:1, 3, 8; Luke 24:11, 21, are impossible on the assumption that the disciples had ever heard the three passion announcements.

Nor is the messianic claim the real ground of Jesus' condemnation, either by the Jewish authorities in Mark 14:53-65 or before the Roman governor in 15:1-5; in both cases the charge is trumped up and garbled, to make out Jesus a revolutionist or insurrectionist, as Luke 23:1-25 and even the passion narrative in John make clear. Moreover, the Synoptic accounts of Jesus' teaching contain no emphasis on his messiahship (as in John), but only the narratives of his life.

The reason for this distinction is probably Mark's interest in showing that Jesus was already Messiah during his earthly life, and that he acted accordingly; Mark was not interested in Jesus' teaching. When the later Synoptists revise and supplement Mark with material on Jesus' teaching, they do not edit it in the messianic direction. For the fundamental conviction of the earliest church was that Jesus became Messiah at his resurrection from the dead (Acts 2:36; Rom. 1:4), and Mark's theory of the secret messiahship during his preceding lifetime cannot really alter this principle.

c. The "Great Thanksgiving." Such a "christological" section, perhaps hymn, as the Great Thanksgiving (Matt. 11:25-27; Luke 10:21-22) is unique in the Synoptics, and sounds more like the discourses in John (cf. John 10:15). The "babes" are those of I Cor. 1:18–3:2, and of the central discipleship sequence in Mark (e.g., 9:42; see also Matt. 18:1-5, 6, 10, 14). The hymn is not Gnostic, though Luke reads almost as if it were: "No one knows who the Son *is*" (Marcion's variant, "No one *knew,*" is Gnostic). For the phrase "to know God" is perfectly biblical (cf. Isa. 11:9; Jer. 22:16; 31:34; Hos. 6:6; John 17:3), whereas "to know who [he] is" imports a speculative, metaphysical, nonbiblical, Gnostic turn of thought into the expression. The continuation of the hymn in a third stanza (Matt. 11:28-30) based on Ecclesiasticus 24:19-22; 51:23-24 (cf. Pss. Sol. 7:9) perhaps indicates the origin of the passage in early Christian devotion and meditation, like much of the material (also poetic) in the discourses of the Fourth Gospel. Finally, the blessing of Peter in Matt. 16:17-19, which implies a fully "messianic" consciousness and purpose on Jesus' part, is now widely recognized to be a bit of pious theorizing or fancy, in the interest of the supreme authority of Peter as the Christian interpreter of the law and the expounder of Christian duty, who possessed the right "to bind and to loose"—in the early Palestinian or Antiochene church, where Peter might have become the first pope, had Rome not claimed him. Cognate material on Peter is also found in Matthew, and even in Mark. But (*see* § E3*d above*) the total neglect or ignoring of this passage in the other gospels, and also especially in Acts and the Pauline letters, is sufficient proof of its apocryphal character.

As Origen observed long ago (*Against Celsus* I.48): "The whole life of Jesus proves that he avoided speaking of himself. . . . He preferred to make himself known as Messiah more by his works than by his words." His purpose was purely religious, and his submission to the will of God was complete. It is "out of character" when Jesus is represented as demanding submission to his own messianic authority, or even as claiming to be the Messiah. What was to be his own position in the coming kingdom he left entirely in the hands of God. It was the kingdom, not his own position in it, which was his sole and exclusive concern.

d. Jesus' authority as a teacher. Much has been made of the solemn tone of Jesus' reiterated pronouncements in the Sermon on the Mount: "You have heard that it was said. . . . But I say to you . . ." (Matt. 5:22, 28, 32, 34, 39, 44—from M), as if Jesus were asserting his own personal authority, superior to that of Moses. Perhaps this was the view of the author or compiler of Matthew, who viewed Jesus as the "second Moses" or "greater than Moses"; but in English translation it is largely the effect of the archaic King James Version, and was no doubt intentional, as the seventeenth-century translators shared the view. But in the tradition behind Matthew there was no emphasis on the speaker's own authority as contrasted with some other—as may be seen elsewhere in the gospels: e.g., Luke 10:24; 11:51; 12:4-5,

8, 22, 27, 37, 44, 59; 13:3, 5; 18:14; etc. Even in Matt. 5, and elsewhere in the Sermon on the Mount, the same manner of speech (i.e., with no contrasting emphasis) is found: e.g., 5:18, 20, 26; 6:2, 5, 16, 25, 29, etc. Even in the Fourth Gospel the striking "Truly, truly, I tell you" may be a final echo of this characteristic manner of speaking—too heavily stylized in the archaic translation: "Verily, verily, I say unto you." In such a turn of expression the human Jesus still stands before us, with *his* emphasis, which is not on personal authority but on the truth of what he is saying: "But, I *tell* you. . . ." In fact, this characteristic human tone carries far more weight than the formal "*I* say" or "It is *I* who say." It is a mistake to look for support of a theological doctrine (the divinity of Christ) in an archaic example of overtranslation. One does not do the same in interpreting Paul and other ancient writers (see I Cor. 7:29; 15:50; etc.).

There is no question that Jesus viewed himself and was viewed by others as a prophet; even incidental notes in both the discourses and the narratives of the gospels reflect this fact. But it is a question whether or not he also thought of himself as the Messiah—this would not be an alternative to the prophetic call, but an addition to it—for the texts which suggest it are open to question, and several of them are undoubtedly secondary and editorial. Further, the passages which represent Jesus as a prophet are clear and consistent, whereas those which represent him as claiming messiahship are not. The conception of messiahship ranges all the way from the nationalistic "son of David" type to the exalted "Son of man" conception found in Daniel and Enoch—it is a question if this latter conception should be called "messianic." If a choice must be made, it is probable that the first of these goes back to Jesus himself, while the second is due to the attribution to him of the exalted office of Judge at the Last Judgment, by others, especially in the early Palestinian church, perhaps even in Galilee.

Although the title "rabbi" is given to Jesus in the gospels, it is not probable that the title was in common use before the reorganization of the Jewish schools after the fall of Jerusalem in A.D. 70. Mark uses it in 9:5; 10:51; 11:21; 14:45; but the usage was rare, and the RSV correctly translates it "Master." It was essentially an academic term, "my teacher"; and although Jesus was a teacher, with disciples who accompanied him, and expounded the scripture, and debated with the scribes, it is much more probable that he was viewed, in his own lifetime, as a "wisdom" teacher—i.e., a lay teacher of religion, not a professional rabbi. The same is true of Paul, who deserves the title even less; he had no students or disciples, and no tradition (in the usual sense), and, like Jesus, his attitude toward the Law can never have been the characteristic rabbinic or scholastic attitude.

G. *THE DEATH OF JESUS.* 1. The forces against him. Although the Gospel of John represents Jesus as actively engaged in teaching and "performing signs," and debating with the Jewish authorities in Jerusalem, chiefly in the temple, the Synoptics describe him as centering his ministry in Galilee, and going to Jerusalem only for the final Passover. Even Mark pictures him as going up to the city as if walking in a dream (Mark 10:32), "as one whom a dream hath possessed," bent on laying down his life there as the "ransom for many." But it is doubtful if this can be harmonized with the actual events described in the passion narrative. Instead, Jesus is aware of the dangers confronting him, but does not flinch; he has faced opposition, even royal opposition, before (Luke 13:31). Like the men chosen for a raid behind enemy lines, or those in a flying squadron sent on a forlorn mission, he knows that the prospects are against his return to Galilee. But that he actually courted death, or went up to Jerusalem knowing that he was to die, seems suicidal and—as a part of the gospel story—unreal.

The forces arrayed against him were powerful: the scribes, jealous of his influence with the people and resentful of his independent exposition of the Scriptures, and of his criticism of their methods and their traditions; the Pharisees, stung by his riddling exposure of their weaknesses and failures; Herod Antipas, suspicious of Jesus' possible connection with the Zealots or with John the Baptist; the Sadducees, equally suspicious, and roused to fury by his interference with the routine of the temple worship; the Romans, concerned only with peace and security; and Pilate, concerned chiefly over his own waning popularity with the Jews—he had twice already driven them to riot, once over the introduction of the idolatrous legionary standards into Jerusalem, and once when he laid hands on the sacred treasure in the temple in order to build an aqueduct. Hence it was not surprising that Jesus faced the possibility, even the probability, of death at their hands.

2. Jesus in Jerusalem. According to Luke and Matthew (not Mark), the TRIUMPHAL ENTRY into Jerualem was followed at once by the "cleansing" of the temple, when Jesus drove the tradesmen and their wares out of the sacred enclosure, and refused to permit anyone to carry a vessel through the outer court—a casual profanation of the shrine by making it a short cut (Matt. 21:10-17; Mark 11:11, 15-19; Luke 19:45-48). This was an act which any OT prophet might have undertaken, though the early Christians no doubt viewed it as messianic (cf. Mal. 3:1*b*). Immediately, the temple authorities interrogated him, and he characteristically answered them with a question: By what authority did John [the Baptist] act? (Mark 11:27-33). It was a question they found inconvenient to answer. His teaching in the temple, according to Mark, was chiefly controversial, beginning with the parable of the wicked tenants (12:1-12), which was obviously aimed at the religious authorities. In its present form, it has been considerably edited, in an allegorical direction, not only by Luke and Matthew but even by Mark. The question over tribute to Caesar (Mark 12:13-17) was clearly designed to answer his dilemma over authority (11:28-30) by an even more serious one, since it required an answer which would either end his popularity or throw him into the hands of the Romans. But Jesus replied that both Caesar's demands and God's are to be met—Caesar's, which are not many (a few denarii), and God's, which are the whole of life.

The question regarding the RESURRECTION is also located here by Mark (12:18-27) and the other Synoptists. In his answer Jesus proves by their own methods of exegesis that the Torah itself teaches the survival of the departed, and therefore their resurrection, but not in a mundane or material sense as a mere restoration to earthly conditions or relations. The question of the Great Commandment which follows (Mark 12:28-34) ends the series of controversies and questions, in Mark, and shows the agreement of at least one scribe with Jesus' teaching, and his recognition that the love of God and of one's neighbor "is much more than all whole burnt offerings and sacrifices"—a remarkable admission in the very presence of Israel's sacrificial system. Jesus' commendation: "You are not far from the kingdom of God," is a pacific close to the incident, but the mood lasts only momentarily. The question of Jesus: "How can the scribes say that the Christ [the Messiah] is the son of David?" (Mark 12:35-37*a*), followed by the discourse against the scribes (37*b*-40, greatly enlarged in Matt. 23:1-36), the remark about the widow's offering of two "mites" (the smallest copper coins), and the prediction of the coming destruction of the temple (Mark 12:41–13:4), completes the setting for the passion narrative. It is painted in the darkest colors of which the evangelists are capable. (The Synoptic Apocalypse, Mark 13 and parallels, is an interlude; this was the only possible place for the material, in Mark's arrangement of the tradition.)

3. The Last Supper. The passion narrative proper opens with the plot of the Jewish authorities (Mark 14:1-2) to get rid of Jesus before the Passover, and Judas' agreement (vss. 10-11) to hand over Jesus to them secretly. Mark's basic narrative, derived, no doubt, from the old Roman passion narrative, is amplified by a series of insertions, such as the anointing in Bethany (vss. 3-9), and the preparation for the Passover (vss. 12-16, closely resembling the preparation for the Triumphal Entry in 11:1-7); but it must have contained the account of the LAST SUPPER (14:17-25), which was probably known to all Gentile Christians from the beginning (cf. I Cor. 11:23-26). Despite Mark's editorial treatment (vss. 12-16), this was probably not a Passover meal, but simply Jesus' last meal with his disciples—there is no mention of lamb or unleavened bread, and other features in the Passover meal are missing. The tone of vs. 25 is thoroughly eschatological, far more so than the similar note in the Passover Seder. Jesus' whole ministry of teaching, healing, preaching, and preparation for the kingdom of God had now reached a climax and crisis: if he was to die, it was not because his mission had been a failure, but only because the purposes of God led another way than the one he had anticipated. If the world—or the present order—was to end with his death (a note found in a late-first-century apocalypse, IV Ezra [=II Esdras] 7:29 ff: "My son the Messiah shall die, and all who draw human breath. . . . And after seven days the world, which is not yet awake, shall be roused"), God's purpose of redemption nevertheless still held good, and he would "drink the fruit of the vine" with the disciples once more "in the kingdom of God."

The whole purpose of the sacramental "institution" is clear from these words: Jesus is binding his disciples to himself, and himself to them, with bonds which even death cannot break or weaken. If he is to die, so are they. If the end of the age has finally arrived, they must together face the great transition. If the prospect of death now faces them, so also does the promise of resurrection. Apparent defeat is really the beginning of triumph—death is in fact only the mode, God's method, of bringing about the victory. Such invincible faith is the spirit, not only of the supper, but of the whole gospel of Jesus, and of the beginning of the Christian religion. The tense atmosphere of the hour, electric with powerful eschatological expectancy and surrounded by the dark night of earthly and demonic hostility (cf. John 13:30), still breathes in the passage about the two swords (Luke 22:35-38). Jesus speaks ironically: danger is abroad, you must go armed; now not only make for yourselves "purses that wax not old" (Luke 12:33) but a sword as well—the sword of the Spirit, as a later apostle said, and the breastplate of faith; for their battle is not with flesh and blood but with the principalities and the powers, the rulers of darkness who are closing in on them. But still they do not understand (Mark 8:21). "Here are two swords," they tell him, and he replies: "It is enough." As Chrysostom explained, this laconic reply only meant, "What an utterly insignificant arsenal!"

4. The arrest and Jewish "trial." After the supper the band withdrew to the Garden of Gethsemane, across the Kidron Valley on the E side of Jerusalem, where Jesus was wont to spend the night (John 18:1-2). It lay on the W slope of the Mount of Olives (Mark 14:26). Here Judas followed them with his rabble of slaves and temple police from the high priest's household, seized Jesus, and led him to the house of Annas, the old high priest, where the junto of high priests and members of the Sanhedrin was gathered. Although Mark represents the scene as a session of the SANHEDRIN, proceeding by orderly steps to a legal trial (14:53-65), a representation which Matthew and Luke follow, it is probable that the account in the Fourth Gospel is to be preferred (John 18:12-24). The so-called "Jewish trial," described in the Synoptics, contravenes Jewish legal procedure (as set forth in the Mishna, tractate Sanhedrin) at several important points, and implies that the Sanhedrin still possessed the right to try capital cases—which the rabbinic tradition denies for approximately this period ("forty years before the fall of Jerusalem"). But in John, the "trial" is only a private examination by the high priest, in which Jesus is asked about "his disciples and his teaching," whereupon Jesus replies that he has done nothing in secret, and that his teaching is well known (vss. 19-21). It is not strange that the early Christian tradition was ill informed on the subject. The hints contained in the Gospel of John as to the sources of its information (John 18:15-16, 26) are impressive, as is the whole story in John, including the chronology.

5. The Roman trial and the Crucifixion. But with the Roman trial the situation is different: in spite of editorial revisions, especially by Luke and John, the basic story is the same in John and the Synoptics. Pilate is informed that Jesus is an agitator and insurrectionist claiming to be "King of the Jews," and therefore a dangerous plotter against the Roman military regime in Palestine. Luke also states that they charged him with interfering in the collection of tribute (Luke 23:2; κωλύων means more than "forbidding"). But Pilate is not impressed. When he asks

Jesus if he is "the king of the Jews," Jesus replies: "You have said so"—which may mean either "Would you say so?" or "That is what you say," as well as "Yes, I am." (Cf. Luke 22:70 and Mark 14:62 in some MSS: "You say that I am"—which Luke certainly understands as an affirmation; but here, in all three Synoptics, the reply seems inconclusive, and Pilate ignores it.) Since Jesus made no further answer (Mark 15:5), Pilate informed the Jewish leaders that he found Jesus guiltless of the charges. But after three unsuccessful attempts to free his prisoner (the maneuver of sending him to Antipas is found only in Luke [23:6-16]), Pilate yields to the insistence of the high priests and elders, supported now by an excited mob, and orders Jesus scourged and crucified.

This was a most horrible, agonizing death, usually taking several days, during which the dehydrated body of the victim, exposed to sun and air, gradually shriveled. Only the most vicious criminals, traitors, brigands, and public enemies were condemned to this mode of execution. Sometimes their bodies were nailed, usually only tied, to low crosses, barely off the ground; and a guard was set to watch them and see that they did not escape or were not rescued by friends and accomplices. Along with Jesus were executed two "robbers" (Mark 15:27), really insurrectionists, as Josephus uses the term (cf. vs. 7).

The location of the scene was just outside one of the N gates of Jerusalem, on a hill called Golgotha ("Place of a Skull"). Mark gives the time, 9 A.M., and adds that from 12 to 3 there was darkness over the whole land (vss. 25, 33). Some of Mark's details, and more of Matthew's, Luke's, and John's, are derived from the OT, which to the early Christians was exactly as reliable and authentic a source as their own local tradition or the earliest written accounts of the Passion. One such detail may be the "cry of dereliction" (Mark 15:34), which is quoted from Ps. 22:1, but which some scholars take to be the proof that Jesus was reciting the Psalms as he hung on the cross, as Columban recited the Psalter standing waist deep in the cold river. But even so, it was not Jesus' last word. Mark says that he died with a mighty shout—of victory (vs. 37). Luke (23:46) keeps the victorious cry, but adds the words: "Father, into thy hands I commit my spirit!"—another verse from the Psalms (Ps. 31:5), and one which is surely by far the most appropriate, as it continues: "Thou hast redeemed me, O LORD, faithful God."

6. The Resurrection. The burial of Jesus was in a nearby garden, in a new grave or sepulchre belonging to a secret disciple, JOSEPH OF ARIMATHEA (Mark 15:42-47; John 19:38-42). The burial was only temporary, as the sabbath was now drawing near. When the sabbath was over, Jesus' women disciples would come and bury him permanently, with spices and ointments (Mark 15:47; 16:1). But when they arrived, as the story is told in the Synoptics, they found the tomb empty and were told by angels (Matthew: "an angel"; Mark: "a young man"; Luke: "two men"; John omits) that Jesus was risen. In Mark and Matthew, the women are bidden to go and tell the disciples that Jesus is preceding them on the way to Galilee. Luke alters this to read: "Remember what he told you, *while he was still in Galilee*"—viz., that he must die and rise again. In John there is no angel, and Jesus makes himself known, not to the disciples, but to Mary Magdalene—in one of the most beautiful and touching stories in all religious literature (John 20:1-18).

It is clear that several strands of tradition have been woven together in the Easter story. Luke's revision is motivated by his conviction (see Acts 1:4, 12, 14) that the disciples actually remained in Jerusalem, and did not return to Galilee. Matthew tries to fill out what seems missing in Mark's brief account (breaking off at 16:8, where the women, in spite of vs. 7, "said nothing to anyone"), and recounts an appearance of Jesus in Galilee (Matt. 28:16-20). Luke amplifies with the sublime story of the walk to Emmaus (24:13-35), followed by the appearance of Christ in Jerusalem (vss. 36-49), and the Ascension (vss. 50-53). Someone in the second century completed Mark's brief narrative of the open tomb with material (the longer ending in 16:9-20) taken from the other three canonical gospels, and even from Acts; while still another—or others—added the shorter ending (see RSV): "But they reported briefly to Peter and those with him all that they had been told. And after this, Jesus himself sent out by means of them, from east to west, the sacred and imperishable proclamation of eternal salvation." In addition to all this, the Washington MS, supported by certain Greek MSS referred to by Jerome in his *Against the Pelagians* II.15, has a long interpolation between vss. 14 and 15. *See* MARK, GOSPEL OF.

7. Theories of the Resurrection. It is not strange, accordingly, that various theories of the Resurrection have been propounded. In the age of rationalism, one popular theory explained Jesus' revival or resurrection as the effect of a night of rest in a cool rock tomb, which promptly restored the energies of a vigorous young man—a carpenter!—who had been on the cross for only six hours at most.

Early in the era of modern "psychological" interpretation, it was explained that a hysterical young woman, Mary of Magdala, who was in love with Jesus, came to the garden in the misty April morning, looking for his tomb, and finding one that happened to be open, immediately fell under the hallucination that the gardener (also astir at an early hour) was her lost Lord and Master.

Still other theories have been advanced, none of them very convincing, for they all assume a wholly corporeal idea of the risen body of Christ, quite contrary to the NT concept. The true starting point, for the earliest account of the Resurrection and the earliest conception of it, is I Cor. 15:3-8, where Paul lists in a series the appearances of the risen Lord to his disciples, and includes the manifestation to himself as the last in the series. This appearance of the risen Christ is described by Luke in Acts 9:3-7, but is only briefly hinted at by Paul in Gal. 1:11-17, where it is clearly a "revelation" (vs. 12: ἀποκάλυψις). In I Cor. 15:3-8, Paul uses the term which in the Greek OT (Paul's Bible) is repeatedly used for divine self-manifestations or theophanies, and which, when God or some supernatural being, such as an angel, is involved, never means "was seen by" but "made himself seen by"—i.e., "appeared to" (ὤφθη, a technical term in the "Jewish Greek" which the early church took over and made its own).

It is, therefore, a great mistake in interpretation to ignore the out-and-out supernatural character of the Resurrection, and try to explain it in some naturalistic way; it is equally a mistake to reduce the Resurrection to a mere revival or resuscitation of the body of Jesus, as "resurrected from the grave," reanimated, and merely transfigured or equipped with supernatural faculties or powers. Paul sounds the right note when he insists that "Christ being raised from the dead will never die again; death no longer has dominion over him" (Rom. 6:9). Hence "if any one is in Christ, he is a new creature," or, "there is the new creation"—i.e., the "new" creation, which is to take the place of the old, has already begun (II Cor. 5:17). The fulfilment of the gospel, with its eschatological hope, takes place in the "new being," the new existence which comes to pass "in Christ," and which was inaugurated by the event which we still call, inadequately, his "resurrection from the dead." *See* RESURRECTION OF CHRIST.

Bibliography. On the composition of the four gospels, see F. C. Grant, *The Gospels, Their Origin and Their Growth* (1957), especially chs. 1-3.

On the relation of Mark's traditions to the early Jewish Christian liturgical year, see P. Carrington, *The Primitive Christian Calendar* (1952).

On Jesus' ability to communicate to others the powers of the kingdom, see M. Dibelius, *Jesus* (1949), p. 58.

For the Washington MS interpolation between vss. 14-15 of Mark 16, see A. Huck, *Synopsis of the First Three Gospels* (1936), p. 213; B. H. Throckmorton, *Gospel Parallels* (2nd ed., 1957), p. 191.

Other works: E. Renan, *Life of Jesus* (1863). J. R. Seeley, *Ecce Homo* (1866). G. Dalman, *The Words of Jesus* (1902). O. Holtzmann, *The Life of Jesus* (1904). W. Sanday, *The Life of Christ in Recent Research* (1907); *Outlines of the Life of Christ* (rev. ed., 1908). A. Schweitzer, *The Quest of the Historical Jesus* (1910). T. R. Glover, *The Jesus of History* (1917). V. Taylor, *The Historical Evidence for the Virgin Birth* (1920). E. F. Scott, *The Ethical Teaching of Jesus* (1924). J. Klausner, *Jesus of Nazareth* (1925). F. C. Grant, *The Economic Background of the Gospels* (1926). W. Bauer, "Jesus der Galiläer," *Festgabe für Adolf Jülicher* (1927). S. J. Case, *Jesus, a New Biography* (1927). M. Goguel, *Au seuil de l'évangile: Jean Baptiste* (1928). B. S. Easton, *Christ in the Gospels* (1930). B. H. Branscomb, *Jesus and the Law of Moses* (1930); *The Teachings of Jesus* (1931). T. W. Manson, *The Teaching of Jesus* (1931). R. Bultmann, *Jesus and the Word* (1934). M. Dibelius, *From Tradition to Gospel* (1934); *Gospel Criticism and Christology* (1935). C. H. Dodd, *The Parables of the Kingdom* (1935). C. A. H. Guignebert, *Jesus* (1935). H. J. Cadbury, *The Peril of Modernizing Jesus* (1937). J. Héring, *Le royaume de Dieu et sa venue* (1937). J. Weiss, *The History of Primitive Christianity*, bk. I (2 vols.; 1937). B. S. Easton, *What Jesus Taught* (1938). L. Finkelstein, *The Pharisees* (2 vols.; 1938). P. Gardner-Smith, *The Christ of the Gospels* (1938). M.-J. Lagrange, *The Gospel of Jesus Christ* (2 vols.; 1938). M. Dibelius, *The Message of Jesus Christ* (1939). F. C. Grant, *The Gospel of the Kingdom* (1940). C. C. McCown, *The Search for the Real Jesus* (1940). D. E. Adams, *Man of God* (1941). J. Knox, *The Man Christ Jesus* (1941). A. Richardson, *The Miracle Stories in the Gospels* (1941). A. T. Olmstead, *Jesus in the Light of History* (1942). F. C. Grant, *The Earliest Gospel* (1943); *An Introduction to NT Thought* (1943). H. B. Sharman, *Son of Man and Kingdom of God* (1943). J. Knox, *Christ the Lord* (1945); *On the Meaning of Christ* (1947). M. Dibelius, *Jesus* (1949). T. W. Manson, *The Sayings of Jesus* (1949). R. H. Pfeiffer, *History of NT Times* (1949). M. Goguel, *The Life of Jesus* (1950). E. J. Goodspeed, *A Life of Jesus* (1950). A. N. Wilder, *Eschatology and Ethics in the Teaching of Jesus* (new ed., 1950). H. Windisch, *The Meaning of the Sermon on the Mount* (1951). J. Jeremias, *The Parables of Jesus* (1955). G. Bornkamm, *Jesus von Nazareth* (1956). O. Cullmann, *The State in the NT* (1956). W. R. Farmer, *Maccabees, Zealots, and Josephus* (1956). S. M. Gilmour, *The Gospel Jesus Preached* (1957). S. E. Johnson, *Jesus in His Homeland* (1957). J. Knox, *The Death of Christ* (1958). F. C. Grant, *Ancient Judaism and the NT* (1959), pt. III.

F. C. GRANT

JETHER jē'thər [יתר, abundance; *this form appears once* (Exod. 4:18) *for* יתרו (JETHRO)]. **1.** The oldest son of Gideon, one of the "judges" during Israel's period of settlement in Canaan. Jether was commanded by his father to slay the prisoners Zebah and Zalmunna, the "kings of Midian." He was afraid, however, and Gideon performed the act himself; the prisoners were spared the humiliation of execution by a boy (Judg. 8:20-21).

2. An Ishmaelite; father or ancestor of Amasa, whom Absalom, David's son, made commander of the army when Absalom rebelled against David (I Kings 2:5, 32; I Chr. 2:17). In II Sam. 17:25 he is called Ithra (יתרא).

3. A descendant of the tribe of Jerahmeel (I Chr. 2:32).

4. Son of a certain Ezrah mentioned in a list of descendants of Judah (I Chr. 4:17).

5. A descendant of the tribe of Asher (I Chr. 7:38); probably the same as Ithran (יתרן) in vs. 37.

B. T. DAHLBERG

JETHETH jē'thĕth [יתת; LXX A Ιεβερ, LXX B *and* Luc. Ιεθερ, *in* Gen. 36:40; LXX A Ιεθεθ, LXX B Ιεθετ, Luc. Ιεθερ, *in* I Chr. 1:51]. An Edomite clan chief; or perhaps "chief *of* Jepheth."

JETHLAH. KJV form of ITHLAH.

JETHRO jĕth'rō [יתרו, יתר]. Priest of Midian; the father-in-law of Moses (Exod. 3:1; 4:18; 18:1-2, 5-6, 12).

Moses' initial flight from Egypt led him to the land of Midian, where his protection of seven shepherdesses at a well subsequently brought him the hospitality of their father, Jethro, the priest of MIDIAN. Here Moses found not only refuge but also a bride, Zipporah, one of the seven daughters, and employment as shepherd for his father-in-law. The name of the deity Jethro served as priest is not explicitly disclosed, but when Jethro later met Moses and the Israelites after their exodus from Egypt, he affirmed that "Yahweh is greater than all gods" (Exod. 18:11). It is the combination of these roles of priest and father-in-law that makes Jethro of such moment in the story of Moses.

Tradition preserves two names, Hobab and Jethro, for the father-in-law of Moses. HOBAB evidently belongs to the J source and Jethro to the E. The name REUEL, which appears in the story of Moses' protection of the seven shepherdesses (Exod. 2:18), is apparently a misreading of the reference in Num. 10:29 to "Hobab the son of Reuel the Midianite, Moses' father-in-law." The J tradition records Moses' attempts to persuade his father-in-law to accompany the Israelites as guide through the wilderness to the Promised Land (Num. 10:29-32), but E reports only that Jethro "went his way to his own country" (Exod. 18:27). The early attachment of KENITES to Israel (Judg. 1:16; 4:11) is connected with their descent from Hobab, Moses' Kenite father-in-law

(J). Such information suggests that the father-in-law belonged to a Kenite ("smith") clan of Midianites and that he migrated with the Israelites to the Promised Land.

The figure of Jethro has attracted most attention, however, because of attempts to identify his priesthood as exercised in a pre-Mosiac Yahweh cult. According to this hypothesis, Yahweh was the tribal god of the Midianites or Kenites, and it was through his priest Jethro that Moses and the Israelites were introduced to the knowledge and service of Yahweh. Exod. 18 is interpreted as the initiation of Aaron and the elders of Israel into the cult of Yahweh at a sacrifice "offered" by Jethro (vs. 18; cf. RSV). In this view Israel derives not only cultic ceremony but also legal institutions from the Midianites. Jethro's proposal that Moses lighten his judicial burden by hearing only those cases in which he would "represent the people before God, and bring their cases to God" (vs. 19), is said to involve the introduction of the sacred lot (*see* LOTS) into Israel. Later Israelite piety, however, attempted to reduce the evidence of Israel's indebtedness to Midian and transformed Jethro in Exod. 18 from missionizing priest to visiting father-in-law escorting his daughter and her two sons to a reunion with Moses (vs. 5).

Undoubtedly, Israel derived cultic and cultural forms from its neighbors, although what the forms meant remained by no means necessarily the same. It is also unlikely that a later age would have invented Moses' intimate connection with Jethro and Midian, in view of the later hostility between Midianites and Israelites (cf. Judg. 6:2; Isa. 9:4—H 9:3). Yet these considerations cannot of themselves establish the validity of the hypothesis that Jethro transmitted Yahwism to Israel. It is significant that Moses did not mention to Jethro the disclosure of Yahweh's name and will after the theophany at the burning bush (Exod. 4:18), and when Jethro met Moses and the Israelites escaped from Egypt, he is repeatedly characterized as father-in-law but only once as priest (Exod. 18). His sacerdotal and hence evangelistic capacity appears distinctly minimized. Yet it remains a startling reminder of the comprehensiveness of OT religion that the initial and perhaps foremost proponent of Yahweh, "whose name is Jealous" (34:14), should have been sheltered, married, employed, and counseled within the precincts of a priest of Midian.

Bibliography. H. Gressmann, "Jethros Besuch bei Mose," *Mose und seine Zeit* (1913), pp. 161-80; M. Buber, "Jethro," *Moses* (1946), pp. 94-100.

R. F. JOHNSON

JETUR jē'tər [יטור]. A tribe descended from Ishmael (Gen. 25:15; I Chr. 1:31), which was at war with the Israelites of Transjordan (I Chr. 5:19). For its history, *see* ITURAEA.

JEUEL jōō'əl [יעואל]; KJV correctly JEIEL jĭ ī'əl [MT יעיאל, God has healed *or* preserved; *cf.* Arab. *w'j*] in II Chr. 29:13; Ezra 8:13. **1.** Chief of a father's house; listed among the returned exiles (I Chr. 9:6).

2. One of the Levites who took part in the reforms of King Hezekiah (II Chr. 29:13).

3. One of those who returned with Ezra from Babylon (Ezra 8:13; I Esd. 8:39).

Bibliography. W. Rudolph, *Esra und Nehemiah* (1949), p. 78.

B. T. DAHLBERG

JEUSH jē'ŭsh [יעוש, *perhaps* may (God) aid; *Kethibh* יעיש, *Qere* יעוש, *in* Gen. 36:5, 14; I Chr. 7:10]; KJV JEHUSH jē'hŭsh in I Chr. 8:39. **1.** An eponym; one of the sons of Esau born to him by Oholibamah (Gen. 36:5, 14). He and his brothers became Edomite chiefs (vs. 18; cf. I Chr. 1:35).

2. A Benjaminite, son of Bilhan (I Chr. 7:10).

3. A Benjaminite, son of Eshek, and apparently a descendant of King Saul (I Chr. 8:39).

4. A Gershonite Levite, and the house descended from him (I Chr. 23:10-11).

5. A son of King Rehoboam (II Chr. 11:19).

Bibliography. M. Noth, *Die israelitischen Personennamen* (1928), p. 196.

B. T. DAHLBERG

JEUZ jē'ŭz [יעוץ, *possibly* encouraged] (I Chr. 8:10). A Benjaminite.

JEW, JEWS, JEWESS jōō, jōōz, jōō'ĭs. In biblical terms, the members of the S state of Judah (Neh. 1: 2; Jer. 32:12; 40:11) or the postexilic people of Israel in contrast to Gentiles (Esth. 9:15-19; Dan. 3:8; Zech. 8:23; John 4:9; Acts 14:1) or the adherents of worship of Yahweh as done at Jerusalem after the Exile (*see* JUDAISM; Esth. 3:4-6; Dan. 3:8).

1. Etymology
2. OT usage
3. NT usage
4. "Jewess"
5. The Jews

Bibliography

1. Etymology. The English word "Jew," as well as the French *juif,* comes from Old French *giu.* This undoubtedly derives from the Latin *judaeus,* which is based on the Greek 'Ιουδαίος, an approximate transliteration of the Aramaic יהודאי and Hebrew יהודי.

2. OT usage. In the OT, יהודי ("Jew") is not used for members of the old tribe of Judah or even to distinguish persons of the Southern Kingdom from those of the Northern Kingdom (cf. איש יהודה in I Sam. 11:8; II Sam. 2:4; cf. II Kings 16:6). It is scarcely used until the kingdom of Judah had survived N Israel (II Kings 25:25; Jer. 38:19; 52:28-30). In postexilic times "Jew" refers to a subject of the Babylonian or Persian province of Judah or of the Maccabean state (Esth. 9:15-19; Neh. 4:1—H 3:33; Zech. 8:23; I Macc. 8:20; Jos. Antiq. XI.v.7) in contrast to Gentiles. The term is used to mean a member of the Jewish people or religion (Ezra 4:12; 5:5; Esth. 2:5; cf. especially Esth. 8:17: proselytes).

3. NT usage. In the NT, 'Ιουδαίος ("Jew") is used in contrast to "Gentiles" (John 2:6; Acts 14:1), to "Samaritans" (John 4:9), and to "proselytes" (Acts 2:10; cf. John 4:22). This would indicate that "Jew" in the NT is applied to one who is Jewish by both nationality and religion. It would appear that the factor of nationality was the stronger, for Jewish Christians are called Jews (Acts 21:39; Gal. 2:13; cf. John 8:31). On the other hand, one may be called a Jew, not by race or nationality, but because of his faith: "He is a Jew who is one inwardly" (Rom. 2: 28-29; cf. Rev. 2:9; 3:9). The NT at times rather indiscriminately speaks of Jews as antagonists to

Jesus, his ministry, the gospel, and his followers (Matt. 28:15; John 3:25; 5:10; 6:41, 52; 7:13; 8:48-57; 9:18, 22; 10:19, 31; 11:37; 12:10, 37; II Cor. 11:24; I Thess. 2:14-16; etc.). While this is particularly true in the Gospel of John, even here an attitude favorable to Jesus is evidenced among the Jews (11:33-36; 12:9-11; cf. 3:1) in contrast to their leaders (8:13, 16; 12:10, 19; 18:3, 12, 14).

4. "Jewess." This word occurs only once in the Bible (Ἰουδαία; Acts 24:24), for Drusilla, the wife of Felix. Timothy's mother is called a "Jewish woman who was a believer" (Acts 16:1). Mered's "other wife" is referred to as "his Jewish wife" in contrast to Bithiah, the daughter of Pharaoh (I Chr. 4:18). "Judith" (יהודית) is the name of Esau's wife, the daughter of Beeri the Hittite, as well as of the heroine of the apocryphal work Judith.

5. The Jews. As shown above, the usage of the term "Jew" was very fluid even in biblical times. It does not refer exclusively to members of the tribe of Judah. While it is freely used to indicate national origin, this usage begins only after the southern kingdom of Judah had survived the northern kingdom of Israel in the seventh century B.C. Soon, however, one was called a Jew, regardless of nationality, if he adhered to Judaism. Nonetheless, religion did not become the sole criterion by which to call oneself a Jew, as noted in the OT and NT passages (§§ 2-3 *above*), for proselytes were often distinguished as such, while those of racial or national origin were distinguished as Jews.

Today the term is even more fluid. There are Jews both by religion and by birth, by religion but not by birth, and by birth but not by religion. Race, nationality, physical type, language, culture, belief—none of these nor any combination of these will distinguish or identify the Jew. While it is without question that the Jews represent a clearly traceable continuum in the history of mankind, there is no least common denominator for the some twelve million people today who call themselves Jews. Indeed, perhaps the best that can be said is that he is a Jew who says he is.

Bibliography. J. Jacobs, "Jew (the Word)," *Jewish Encyclopedia*, VII (1904), 174-75; R. B. Gittelsohn, "What Is a Jew?" *Modern Jewish Problems* (1943), pp. 8-29; M. J. Herskovits, "Who Are the Jews?" in L. Finkelstein, ed., *The Jews*, II (1949), 1151-71; J. R. Marcus, *Early American Jewry*, vol. I (1951), p. viii.

J. A. SANDERS

JEWELER [חרש אבן, artificer of stone] (Exod. 28:11); KJV ENGRAVER. An artificer who cut inscriptions on precious stones. *See* ART; ENGRAVING; JEWELS AND PRECIOUS STONES.

JEWELS AND PRECIOUS STONES. Stones valued for rarity, beauty, or association, especially stones polished, cut, or engraved for use as ornaments; gems. The word כלי (lit., "thing," "anything made") is used specifically for "jewel" or "jewelry." אבנים יקרות, "precious or costly stones," refers to costly building stones and other objects, as well as jewels.

Pl. XVII.

1. General observations concerning jewels in the Bible
   a. Early reasons for regarding stones as precious
   b. Archaeological evidence for the quantity and sources of jewels and for the extent and processes of their manufacture
   c. Difficulties in making specific and accurate identification of jewels
2. Jewels named in the Bible and relevant archaeologically known materials
3. Noteworthy jewel passages
   a. Exod. 28:17-21; 39:10-14
   b. Job 28:12-19
   c. Ezek. 28:12-19
   d. Isa. 54:12
   e. Lists of precious stones
4. Rev. 21:19-20 and the symbolism of precious stones
   a. Precious stones and theophany
   b. Interpretation of the twelve stones in Philo and Josephus
   c. The heavenly city, New Jerusalem, and paradise

Bibliography

1. General observations concerning jewels in the Bible. ***a. Early reasons for regarding stones as precious.*** Gems, according to Pliny (died A.D. 79), are the concentrated beauty of the world. Aesthetic appreciation was probably not the earliest motivation for acquiring, preparing, and wearing stones. The desire for personal adornment (*see* DRESS AND ORNAMENTS) may have come first. Some think the early use of jewels was intended to secure for the wearer magical benefits associated with the stones (*see* AMULETS). The Egyptian Book of the Dead (*ca.* 1500 B.C.) refers to amulets in heart shapes made of lapis lazuli, green feldspar, carnelian, and serpentine. The *Lithica* poem of Orpheus (second century B.C.) tells of the magical properties of gems. The "magic stone" (אבן חן) which causes everything to prosper (Prov. 17:8) is suggestive of the amuletic power of jewels, but this idea is rarely found in biblical texts. With the beginnings of personal property and business, social, and political relations, the need on the part of unlettered folk to identify personal possessions, agreements, and communications caused stones to be prized as materials for SEALS AND SCARABS. One of the safest and soundest ways the ancients had to conserve great wealth was investment in jewels. They fluctuated little in value, could be readily sold if need be; they were light and small in size and could be readily carried or hidden away. Regard for jewels is likely to have been prompted in antiquity, as it has been at other times, for a variety of reasons.

b. Archaeological evidence for the quantity and sources of jewels and for the extent and processes of their manufacture. The Hebrew language does not have one specific word for "jewel"; it is only by context that the word usually translated "jewel," כלי, meaning "made or manufactured thing," has that significance; in Prov. 25:12; Song of S. 7:1—H 7:2 another word (חלי; plural חלאים) is used which means rather generally "ornament," as translated in the former passage. "Precious stones" is an original Hebrew expression which has come into the English language by Bible translations. The phrase itself appears fourteen times in the RSV, and there are other synonymous expressions such as "stones of remembrance," "costly stones," "stones for setting," "stones of fire," "precious jewel," "most rare jewel," "fair jewels," and "fine jewels." Job 28:10 is understood by some to affirm that God's "eye" has seen "every precious thing" (יקר)—i.e., every jewel. If one considers further the numerous references to separately named jewels, the part played by gem stones in OT literature appears to be as remarkable and significant as jewels themselves seem to have been to Bible peoples. Jewels were used for personal adornment (Exod. 11:2; Isa. 3:20; 61:10); for gifts and tokens of friendship (Gen. 41:42 [*see* SIGNET]; I Kings 10:2, 10; II Chr. 9:1, 9; Ezek. 16:11, 39; 23:26); for royal crowns (II Sam. 12:30; I Chr. 20:2; cf. Zech. 9:16); for royal garments (Ezek. 28:13); for the royal treasury (I Kings 10:11; I Chr. 29:2; II Chr. 9:10; 32:27); for the royal sanctuary (II Chr. 3:6; cf. Esth. 1:6; Dan. 11:38); and for the high priest's insignia (Exod. 28:15-21; 39:8-14; cf. Ecclus. 50:9). OT "jewelry," a closely related term, certainly included objects set with gems—e.g., the signet (Gen. 38:18), anklets, armlets, bracelets, crescents, earrings, and nose rings (*see* ANKLET; ARMLET; CRESCENT; EARRING). For the incorporation of jewels in an article to be worn, cf. the golden tomb mask of Tut-ankh-Amon (died 1349 B.C.), inlaid with lapis lazuli, calcite, obsidian, quartz, carnelian, and bits of colored glass.

It would appear that in contrast to the many kinds of jewels that were known, the early Israelites actually must have possessed small quantities of jewels, precious stones, or decorative minerals. In Palestinian excavations generally (cf. the exceptional fifteenth-fourteenth-century-B.C. collection found at Megiddo, the finds at Gezer, and the Ezion-geber necklace of carnelian, agate, alabaster, and glass beads), comparatively slight evidence for precious stones has been found. By contrast, engraved gems, along with elaborately tooled vessels of gold and silver, are among the common surviving Phoenician products (e.g., the rich finds at UGARIT and the contents of the royal tombs of Byblos, OT GEBAL, now in the National Museum, Beirut). Engraved jewels from the excavations in Greece are so numerous that by examples taken from them it is possible to trace the whole historical panorama of Greek art styles. The richness of Egyptian tomb collections in this regard is familiar knowledge.

Geological surveys indicate that in Palestine-Syria there are no gem deposits. In Egypt fifteen kinds of precious stones are to be found, six of them in more than one site, and in N Mesopotamia there are native deposits of four of the gem stones the ancients counted as precious. Such facts explain the reports that the Israelites received their precious stones from other lands and other peoples. Apart from an early quantity from Egypt in the form of manufactured jewelry (Exod. 3:22; 11:2; 12:35-36; 35:22) and other booty (e.g., Num. 31:50; Judg. 8:26), jewels came into Palestine through regional distributors, especially the traders of Phoenicia (Ezek. 28:13). The stones are said to have originated in OPHIR and in other parts of Arabia (I Kings 10:2; Ezek. 27:22), but the Arabians must have been mainly traders, too, as many of the most valued stones came from still more remote places—Asia and India have been suggested.

I Kings 20:34 indicates that foreign merchants had factories in the Samaria of Omri's time; the art of cutting and polishing stones probably became in time a local craft, the uncut stones, by necessity imported, remaining rare and quite expensive. In the Exodus period, however, as Egypt already possessed a fully developed gem-engraving industry in the Eighteenth Dynasty (1580-1350 B.C.), such Israelite workmen as OHOLIAB (Exod. 38:23), working with more abundant raw material, could have learned the art there. *See* ENGRAVING.

Cutting stones in facets to intensify brilliance by multiplying internal light reflection and refraction is a modern technique developed in Europe. The ancient method of stone dressing was that today called *en cabochon*—i.e., in rounded, convex forms with smooth or polished sides. The effect of natural colors was often further heightened through engraving. In stones of multilayered structure two or more colors might appear in the engraved designs. In this art the ancients excelled; the quality of their workmanship is rarely equaled by modern craftsmen equipped with mechanical tools and powerful magnifying instruments. The finest of the gem cutters' art (see a description, Ecclus. 38:27) is assumed in Exod. 28:9-11; 39:6, where instructions are given for the engraving of two multicolored, horizontally stratified stones (in Exodus, onyx—i.e., black and white; cf. Josephus: sardonyx—i.e., red and white), each with six tribe names, not in reverse as on a seal, but so as to be readable by the observer (the Lord; Exod. 28:12); i.e., white letters were cut into a red or black polished face, or the same technique was applied with a reversal of the colors.

c. Difficulties in making specific and accurate identification of jewels. The jewels named in the OT appear accidentally and in connection with the writers' primary interests. No catalogue appears or would be expected. Even with such a listing, the difficulties of positive identification of ancient jewels by modern terminology and classification would remain. The translating of terms was already complicated in biblical times. It is evident that the LXX translators in the third century B.C. had no more exact understanding of the Hebrew jewel names than had Jerome (*ca.* A.D. 400) of Hebrew or Greek terms when he translated the Latin Bible. English versions offer little more help; they tell us of the kinds of stones that were considered precious by the translators, rather than what the Bible means.

The broader consideration of jewels in the ancient world to which the subject of jewels in the Bible belongs is as yet indefinitely described. Only a fractional part of the ancient world is known archaeologically. The ancient writers shared the scientific limitations of their time; lacking modern methods of investigation such as chemical analysis and precision instruments of measurement and discrimination, they relied on examination and classification by color, weight, consistency, hardness, transparency, conductivity, friction, taste, and smell. From the large number of writers quoted by Pliny who made studies of stones between the time of Theophrastus (third century B.C.) and his own (first century A.D.), it is clear that there were some in the ancient world who, with all their superstitious beliefs, made remarkably close observations. Even so, exact identification is often impossible—e.g., in the same category defined by physical characteristics, especially color, an identical name is given to stones which modern analysis shows to be of quite different natures. The general accounts by modern writers of gems in antiquity vary because of the limited evidence upon which deductions are based or inability to use available modern techniques of identification. In the present state of our general knowledge, the most that can be offered is an alphabetical listing of jewels as named in the current English translations of the Bible, with references to special articles in this work, including in the list gem stones known archaeologically to have been available and used as jewels in the Bible lands and times.

2. Jewels named in the Bible and relevant archaeologically known materials. "Adamant" represented the hardest substance known, called *adamas,* "invincible." It translates *šāmîr,* probably "corundum," in Ezek. 3:9; Zech. 7:12. Diamonds became useful precious stones only with the fifteenth-century-A.D. discovery of how to cut them. The word *šamir* in Jer. 17:1 ("diamond") should be understood possibly to refer to a point of exceptionally hardened iron or a splinter of natural crystal (as corundum or rock crystal). The word *yahalōm* in Exod. 28:18; 39:11 ("diamond") refers to some very hard stone—perhaps, as the Ezekiel rendering suggests, jasper, a stone widely used in Egypt for engraving. *See also* ADAMANT; DIAMOND.

"Agate" translates *kadhkōdh* in Isa. 54:12; Ezek. 27:16, *šebhô* in Exod. 28:19; 39:12, and χαλκηδών in Rev. 21:19. Theophrastus states that in his day these quartz stones, with their banded structure adapted for engraving, were sold at great price; by Pliny's time agate had ceased to be a precious stone. It is well represented in Palestinian bead finds and in Egyptian beads. *See also* AGATE.

On "alabaster," *see* "calcite" *below. See also* ALABASTER.

Amber, though not a stone but fossilized resin, is known archaeologically to have been used especially with yellow gold by the ancients for personal jewelry; it was credited with medicinal qualities. *Ḥašmal* (Ezek. 1:4, 27; 8:2; "gleaming bronze") is a word of great uncertainty, possibly with primary emphasis on shining qualities, whether in bronze, AMBER, or electrum (cf. LXX ἤλεκτρον).

Amethyst, a purple quartz, is widely represented in the excavations in Palestine and Egypt and in many sorts, most of them variations of violet or wine color. Pliny brands as false an assertion of the magi that this stone was an effective preventive against intoxication. The Hebrew name *'aḥlāmâ* links the stone with dreams or dreaming (*ḥālām,* "to dream"; Exod. 28:19; 39:12). The NT name is 'Αμεθύστος (Rev. 21:20). Amethyst is frequent as beads in Palestinian excavations, and in Egyptian amulets, beads for necklaces, and bracelets and scarabs. It was rarely used by the Greeks. *See also* AMETHYST.

Basalt, a black volcanic rock available in Palestine as elsewhere in the Near East, was used in Egypt for scarabs and in Assyria for cylinder seals.

"Bdellium" (*bedhōlaḥ*) is of quite uncertain identification but indicates some type of precious material (Gen. 2:12; Num. 11:7, where the LXX understands bdellium as rock crystal). *See also* BDELLIUM.

"Beryl" (*taršîš* in Exod. 28:20; 39:13; Dan. 10:6; *šōham* in Ezek. 28:13; βήρυλλος in Rev. 21:20) is a stone usually of sea-green color, though it is known in other colors. The emerald is a superior variety of beryl. Beryl is not often represented in Palestinian finds. The numerous early Egyptian amulets once called beryl are proved, on further examination, to be green feldspar. *See also* BERYL.

Calcite is one of the commonest of minerals; alabaster, marble, and onyx are among its varieties. Alabaster was used in Egypt in thin plates for inlaid jewelry and furniture.

"Carbuncle" means currently a bright, deep red stone like a garnet cut *en cabochon* with smooth rounded sides. In the OT *bāreqeth* (Exod. 28:17; 39:10) is a glittering stone (*bārāq,* "lightning"); the LXX translation of *bāreqeth* suggests our emerald—i.e., gem-quality green beryl. *See also* CARBUNCLE.

"Carnelian" translates *'ōdhem* (Ezek. 28:13), σάρδιον (Rev. 21:20). Red stones, especially chalcedony, are among the most frequently excavated jewels in Palestine, where it is the favorite material for Hebrew seals, as well as in Egypt for scarabs and in Mesopotamia for engraved objects (it is mentioned three times in the Gilgamesh Epic) and in Greek and Roman engraved gems. *See also* CARNELIAN.

"Chalcedony" (KJV translation of χαλκηδών in Rev. 21:19), is the name of a class of quartz stones including carnelian, sardius, chrysoprase, agate, and onyx. These are frequent in Palestine excavations as beads and seals, occasionally in Egyptian beads and scarabs. Chalcedony ranked high with Greek gum cutters in the fifth and fourth centuries B.C. *See* CHALCEDONY.

"Chrysolite" (*taršîš* in Ezek. 1:16; 10:9; 28:13; χρυσόλιθος in Rev. 21:20), modern magnesium iron silicate (related to olivine and peridot), was Pliny's term for the present-day golden-yellow topaz. *See also* CHRYSOLITE.

"Chrysoprase" (χρυσόπρασος; Rev. 21:20) is somewhat uncertain. If it was the same as that known today, it was an apple-green, fine-grained variety of quartz. Some ancient Egyptian jewelry of this material has been identified. *See also* CHRYSOPRASE.

"Coral" (*râmôth* in Job 28:18; *penînîm* in Lam. 4:7) in the red variety, for which there is a similar Arabic word meaning "branches," was available from the Mediterranean Sea. A type of coral from the Red Sea was used for beads in Egypt. *See also* CORAL.

"Crystal" (*gābhîsh* in Job 28:18; *qeraḥ* in Ezek. 1:22; κρύσταλλος in Rev. 22:1) covers all transparent, almost colorless materials such as glass, "Iceland spar," rock crystal, etc. Crystal beads are found in OT Palestine. *See also* CRYSTAL.

On "diamond," *see* "adamant" *above. See also* DIAMOND.

"Emerald" now means a rich green beryl. Such stones are rare in excavations. Green feldspar and turquoise, with the same general color tones, frequently appear and may be what is meant by *nōphekh* (Exod. 28:18; 39:11; Ezek. 27:16; 28:13; in Ezek. 28:

13 "carbuncle)." *Bāreqeth* (Ezek. 28:13) is thought to be more likely our emerald. Both terms could have meant simply green precious stones. The NT terms are σμαράγδινος, σμάραγδος (Rev. 4:3; 21:19). *See also* EMERALD.

Emery and corundum dust were used as polishing and drilling abrasives.

Feldspar in many types, all aluminum silicates, is of frequent occurrence in excavations. Green feldspar, which is commonly confused with other green stones, appears to have been popular in Egypt as material for amulets and beads.

Flint, important in early antiquity for ornaments and tools, may have continued as a valued stone, at least among the less wealthy folk. In Job 28:9 it is referred to as a treasure of the earth. *See also* FLINT.

Garnet, as employed by Egypt, was a native dark red or reddish brown, translucent stone used for beads. The flame-colored garnet was largely used for Greek, Etruscan, and Roman engraved gems.

Glass in various colors is found in Egyptian excavations at least from the third millennium B.C. It is opaque and is used as a substitute for precious stones, especially in inlaying of ornaments and utensils. Note the glass beads found at Solomonic Ezion-geber.

Hematite as used in Egypt was black, opaque, and with a metallic luster, and it appears in beads, amulets, kohl sticks, scarabs, and small objects. In the red variety (sometimes called bloodstone) Mesopotamian seals and Hittite gems are found, as well as beads of the same material, throughout the ancient Near East. In Palestine hematite Hebrew seals and beads are known.

"Hyacinth" is a term taken from the Greek ὑάκινθος ("sapphire" in Rev. 9:17; 21:20), a blue precious stone (possibly including our modern sapphire) which in a yellow variety Pliny states was often made into gems by the ancients. *See* "jacinth" *below.*

"Jacinth" (*lešem;* Exod. 28:19; 39:12) refers to an orange-colored zircon. In Rev. 21:20 the Greek means "sapphire," "dusky red." *See also* JACINTH.

"Jasper" (*yāsh*[e]*phê* in Exod. 28:20; 39:13; *yah*[a]*lōm* in Ezek. 28:13; ἴασπις in Rev. 4:3; 21:11, 18-19) is a present-day opaque type of quartz usually red, brown, or yellow. Pliny describes ἴασπις as green and often transparent—i.e., apparently our translucent green chalcedony or plasma. It is uncertain whether the LXX equivalent constitutes a sure identification. This stone is frequent in Palestinian tombs and excavations and in Egyptian amulets, beads (usually red), and inlays. Green jasper was common for Greek gems. *See also* JASPER.

Lapis lazuli, a rich azure blue with "fool's gold" spangles, is abundantly represented: in the Mesopotamian literature (mentioned six times in the Gilgamesh Epic) and excavations; in Egypt, where it was an imported material from Western Asia for small jewelry and objects; in Palestine, where some specimens such as those at Megiddo have been found. Lapis lazuli was probably the ancient sapphire or firestone. *See also* LAPIS LAZULI; SAPPHIRE.

On "ligure," *see* "jacinth" *above.*

Limestone in some varieties is hard enough for engraving and polishing. A readily available material in Palestine, limestone is known to have been frequently used for seals bearing Hebrew writing, for beads, and probably for other kinds of ornamentation, possibly more generally among the common people. A number of Egyptian scarabs made of limestone have been found dating to the OT period.

Malachite is a brilliant green copper carbonate, occasionally used in Egypt for worked objects or as inlay in jewelry but mainly as eye paint. Sinai offered an ancient source of malachite with turquoise deposits nearby.

"Marble" (*šēš;* I Chr. 29:2; Esth. 1:6; Song of S. 5:14), a crystallized limestone capable of high polish, is used in the Bible only of building material but was found in bead form at Megiddo. *See also* MARBLE.

"Mother-of-pearl" is a possible alternative to the translation "coral" in Ezek. 27:16. This material was used in Egypt from predynastic times.

Nephrite ("kidney" stone), a low-grade jade, sometimes appears among Palestinian beads.

Obsidian, a kind of dark, glassy volcanic rock, was used in ancient Egypt in small amounts and was obtained from Abyssinia.

"Onyx" (*šōham* in Gen. 2:12; Exod. 25:7; 28:9, 20; etc.; σαρδονυξ in Rev. 21:20) is a chalcedony of banded structure, often with milky-white bands alternating with black. *See also* SARDONYX; ONYX.

Opal in hyalite form (translucent, colorless), not native to the Near East, is found only in sufficient numbers to indicate that it was anciently known.

"Pearl" (*p*[e]*nînîm* in Job 28:18; μαργαρίτης in Matt. 7:6; 13:46; I Tim. 2:9; etc.), not a precious stone but always associated with gems, is among the materials used after the Ptolemaic period by the Egyptians for jewelry. A pink variety (cf. "coral" in Lam. 4:7) comes from the Red Sea. *See also* PEARL.

Peridot is a pale green chrysolite variety of olivine used as a gem stone. Although it is to be found on islands in the Red Sea, it was but rarely used in ancient Egypt. If the identification of peridot as the OT "topaz" is accurate, Palestine must have used the stone more extensively. For references, *see* TOPAZ.

Rock crystal is colorless, crystallized quartz, harder than glass or steel (*see* "adamant" *above*). Frequently rock crystal appears in Hebrew seals; in Palestinian beads; and as amulet, bead, inlay, and even vase material in Egypt. It was widely used for engraved gems only in the late Roman period.

"Ruby" in the modern sense appears not to have been known in the ancient Near East before the third century B.C., and not at all by the Greeks and Romans. *P*[e]*nînîm,* sometimes translated "ruby" in the KJV (Job 28:18; Prov. 3:15; 8:11; etc.), is better understood as "coral" or "pearl."

"Sapphire" (*sappîr* in Exod. 24:10; 28:18; 39:11; Job 28:16; etc.; σάπφειρος in Rev. 9:17; 21:19). is likely not the modern transparent blue stone, which was too hard for the ancients with their tools to use for the stylish engraved gems, but rather, as Pliny's description indicates it was for his day, lapis lazuli, which is frequent in jewelry and scarabs in Egypt and Babylonian seals and is fairly well known in Palestinian excavations. *See also* SAPPHIRE.

Sardius is suggested by the name *'ōdhem,* "red," and is transparent (Ezek. 28:13). "Sardius" may be an alternative to "carnelian," and both are included in the same grouping with red jasper; all three are frequently found in excavations in Egypt, Assyria, and Palestine. In the NT, σάρδιον is translated "carnelian" in Rev. 4:3; 21:20.

"Sardonyx" is not used in the OT but is a possible alternative translation of *šōham,* "onyx." It was popular with the Romans for cameos and signets. It is in the NT in Rev. 21:20 (σαρδόνυξ, "onyx"). *See also* SARDONYX.

Steatite, a gray-green or brown talc, also called soapstone, is frequent in Palestinian excavations. Quantities of steatite beads were found at Megiddo and elsewhere. Because it was soft, steatite was a favorite material with engravers of the early periods in Egypt, Assyria, Babylonia, Phoenicia, and Greece, but in late times it seems not to have been used.

"Topaz" in the OT *(piṭedhâ;* Exod. 28:17; 39:10; Job 28:19; Ezek. 28:13) is probably, as Pliny's account suggests, modern peridot or olivine, a green gem stone found on islands of the Red Sea. Cf. the Greek τοπάξιον (Rev. 21:20), which, if we follow Strabo, may have been used for any of a group of bright yellow transparent stones. We do not know whether Ethiopia in Job 28:19, mentioned in connection with topaz, is the jewel's point of origin (which, even when topaz is considered as peridot, seems unlikely) or the nearest known country to the Red Sea islands producing peridot, or possibly the identification name of some singularly large and fine peridot jewel. *See also* TOPAZ.

"Turquoise," though not used in English versions, is a possible alternative translation of *nōphekh.* Abundant in Egypt, where it is found frequently in jewelry combined with lapis lazuli, the material is also known in Palestinian excavation finds. The delicate sky-blue to green turquoise must have been well known to OT peoples. There are ancient turquoise workings in the Sinai Peninsula near mines which were worked from early times for malachite and copper ore. *See also* TURQUOISE.

3. Noteworthy jewel passages. Certain remarkable OT passages cite the names of specific gem stones. In the order of their canonical appearance, though possibly not in the order of their date of composition, these include:

a. Exod. 28:17-21; 39:10-14. The BREASTPIECE OF THE HIGH PRIEST is described, following directions discussed above for the engraving of the two onyx stones of remembrance for the sons of Israel. Upon the gold, blue, purple, and scarlet fine linen of which the breastpiece was made, there were to be mounted twelve precious stones, cut and polished as signets, each engraved in the same manner as the onyx stones with the name of one of the tribes of Israel. In view of the widespread ancient beliefs in the amuletic powers of gem stones, some connection might be expected between the particular stones specified and particular names of the tribes. Unless some traditional ordering of the tribe names is assumed in the Exodus passages, no evidence is offered here or elsewhere in the OT as to the assignment of special jewels to each of the twelve tribes. One may use in an attempt to link stones with tribes, as some do, a list of the tribes arranged by the age relation of the tribal heads, but this is still uncertain. Arranging the stones in rows from left to right, and identifying the stones (*a*) by the RSV translation and (*b*) by the Hebrew term in each case, one may find, within the limits of probability of the separate articles and the list above (*c*) an identification and (*d*) a general impression of the colors of stones employed.

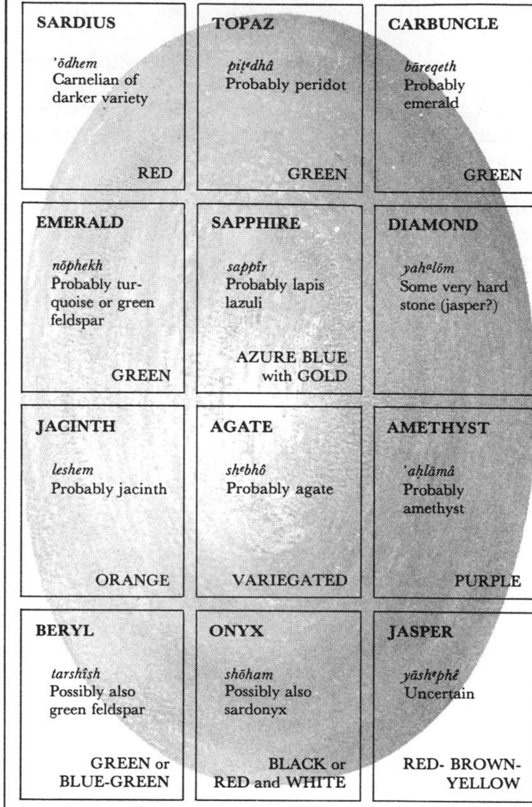

SARDIUS
'ōdhem
Carnelian of darker variety
RED
TOPAZ
piṭedhâ
Probably peridot
GREEN
CARBUNCLE
bāreqeth
Probably emerald
GREEN
EMERALD
nōphekh
Probably turquoise or green feldspar
GREEN
SAPPHIRE
sappîr
Probably lapis lazuli
AZURE BLUE with GOLD
DIAMOND
yahalōm
Some very hard stone (jasper?)
JACINTH
leshem
Probably jacinth
ORANGE
AGATE
shebhô
Probably agate
VARIEGATED
AMETHYST
'aḥlāmâ
Probably amethyst
PURPLE
BERYL
tarshîsh
Possibly also green feldspar
GREEN or BLUE-GREEN
ONYX
shōham
Possibly also sardonyx
BLACK or RED and WHITE
JASPER
yāshephê
Uncertain
RED- BROWN- YELLOW

b. Job 28:12-19. In a chapter where in some detail the technological achievements of man in mining and metallurgy are contrasted with the impotence of his crafts to secure for himself wisdom, a connection is made between treasures of earth such as gold, silver, onyx, sapphire, coral, crystal, pearls, and topaz, apparently offered as sacrifices, and the erroneous and superstitious worship of Tehom (*see* DEEP, THE) and Yam (*see* SEA). Jewels are among the gifts which, according to Job, man is prepared extravagantly but uselessly to offer for the gift of wisdom. The allusion of the passage is clearly to a false and pagan association of the wealth of the earth with the spirits of the underworld.

c. Ezek. 28:12-19. The final oracle in the book of Ezekiel dealing with Tyre depicts the king of that city as a man (*see* ADAM 1) who once lived in a veritable paradise (*see* EDEN, GARDEN OF) but who through proudness of heart and inordinate concern for splendor (vs. 17) had suffered a disastrous fall, described in terms of expulsion from Eden. There is in the Genesis account of Eden only one brief allusion to precious stones (Gen. 2:12; bdellium and onyx). The Gilgamesh Epic is a long and ancient Mesopotamian literary production which in the extent of its influence in that area of the ancient world has been compared to the *Iliad* and the *Odyssey.* It is quite possible, if not probable, that Ezekiel in his residence in Babylonia could have known of the work. In any case, it is interesting to note these lines (Tablet IX.48-51) from the Gilgamesh Epic found in a description of a mythological park called the "grove of stones."

> The carnelian bears its fruit;
> It is hung with vines good to look at.
> The lapis bears foliage;
> It, too, bears fruit lush to behold.[1]

Ezekiel 28:13 lists as ornaments of the Tyrian king's "covering" (possibly "shield") nine stones, in three groups of three: carnelian, topaz, jasper; chrysolite, beryl, onyx; sapphire (meaning lapis lazuli), carbuncle, emerald. It is frequently asserted that, in view of Ezekiel's priestly interests, there is in his listing a reflection of the stones of the Exodus high-priest's-breastpiece passage. This is conceivable, yet the smaller total number of stones and the inexact correspondence of the order in which the stones are named raise a question as to any kind of literal or mechanical interdependence of the passages. *See further below.*

d. Isa. 54:12. This is a message of comfort which the prophet directs to Jerusalem: "O afflicted one!" He casts hope in terms of a projected future for the city, when its foundations shall be sapphires, its pinnacles of agate, its gates of carbuncles, and all its walls of precious stones. The connection of jewels with the anticipation of a Jerusalem in colorful, radiant splendor is also made in Tob. 13:16-17; Rev. 21:19-21. *See further below.*

e. Lists of precious stones. The precious stones which adorn (or constitute?) the twelve foundations of the New Jerusalem (Rev. 21:19-20) are reminiscent of the twelve stones on the BREASTPIECE OF THE HIGH PRIEST in the dual lists of Exod. 28:17-20; 39:10-13 (cf. Ecclus. 45:11); the adornment of the king of Tyre, moreover, consists of nine (Hebrew; LXX twelve) precious stones (Ezek. 28:13). The problem of the interrelationship of the four biblical lists has evoked much discussion, the results of which have not been conclusive.

The identification and order of the stones in the four lists are separate problems, as the confusion arising from their conflation demonstrates. Regarding the former, certain results are impossible, given the inadequacy of ancient classification and the dissimilarity of modern terminology (*see* § 1*c above*), and pointless in view of the wide divergence of the tradition (*see further below*). The problem of order is best approached apart from the question of identification. With reference to the Hebrew text, the two lists in Exodus are identical, but the number and order in Ezekiel differ. It has been noted that the third row of stones in the breastpiece is missing in the Ezekiel list; the order of the remaining nine, moreover, is altered (*see* Table 1). On the other hand, the number and order in the LXX are constant in all three cases. That the LXX list was known in the first century A.D. is confirmed by the two accounts found in Josephus (War V.v.7; Antiq. III.vii.5). In the earlier of the two (*Jewish Wars*), given the equation ὄνυξ=ὀνύχιον, the same twelve stones appear but with variation in order within rows 2-4 of Table 2.

[1] Trans. E. A. Speiser, in J. B. Pritchard, ed., *Ancient Near Eastern Texts* (Princeton University Press; rev. ed., 1955).

Table 1

	Exod. 28:17-20; 39:10-13	Ezek. 28:13
1.	אדם	אדם
2.	פטדה	פטדה
3.	ברקת	יהלם
4.	נפך	תרשיש
5.	ספיר	שהם
6.	יהלם	ישפה
7.	לשם	
8.	שבו	
9.	אחלמה	
10.	תרשיש	ספיר
11.	שהם	נפך
12.	ישפה	ברקת

In the *Antiquities*, Josephus makes a point of correcting the order of the last two rows, but introduces still another sequence within rows 3-4 which is at variance with both the LXX and his previous list; he also substitutes σαρδόνυξ for σάρδιον, perhaps inadvertently repeating the former from the two jewels on the high priest's shoulders, just previously mentioned.

The striking feature of these five lists is the uniformity in Greek, apart from the small discrepancies mentioned; the fact that Josephus takes pains to correct his own order suggests that it held some significance for him, but which, unfortunately, he nowhere discloses. The inference appears to be that the LXX list was compiled under the impact of tradition current in Alexandria 300-100 B.C., without reference to the Hebrew counterpart, a tradition which Josephus knew late in the first century A.D. but desired to modify. The attempt, therefore, to establish equivalences between the Hebrew and Greek terms on the basis of parallel lists in Exodus and Ezekiel is at best precarious, perhaps even futile.

Table 2

	Exod. 28; Exod. 39; Ezek. 28	Jos. War V.v.7	Jos. Antiq. III.vii.5	Rev. 21
1.	σάρδιον	σάρδιον	σαρδόνυξ	ἴασπις
2.	τοπάζιον	τόπαζος	τόπαζος	σάπφιρος
3.	σμάραγδος	σμάραγδος	σμάραγδος	χαλκηδών
4.	ἄνθραξ	ἄνθραξ	ἄνθρακα	σμάραγδος
5.	σάπφειρος	ἴασπις	ἴασπιν	σαρδόνυξ
6.	ἴασπις	σάπφειρος	σάπφειρον	σάρδιον
7.	λιγύριον	ἀχάτης	λίγυρος	χρυσόλιθος
8.	ἀχάτης	ἀμέθυστος	ἀμέθυσος	βήρυλλος
9.	ἀμέθυστος	λιγύριον	ἀχάτης	τοπάζιον
10.	χρυσόλιθος	ὄνυξ	χρυσόλιθος	χρυσόπρασος
11.	βηρύλλιον	βήρυλλος	ὄνυξ	ὑάκινθος
12.	ὀνύχιον	χρυσόλιθος	βήρυλλος	ἀμέθυστος

The list in Revelation differs with regard to the names of the stones and to their order. Four new names appear along with eight known from the LXX (*see* Table 2). Were it not for the problem of order, it might be conjectured that the author has made a fresh translation of the list from Hebrew, but in view of several rather well-established correlations (e.g., ישפה=ἴασπις; ספיר=σάπφειρος), this is improbable. On the assumption that there is a literary dependence of the Revelation list on the OT lists, several solutions to the problem of terminology and order have been proposed. One proposal is that the author of Revelation read the Exodus list in a different order, with regard both to rows and to sequence within rows: row 2 in reverse; row 1 in reverse; row 4; row 3. The obvious difficulty here is that four substitutions and one exchange are necessary, and an explanation for either the peculiar method of reading or the variation is not forthcoming. Another view is that the Revelation list reverses the order established by pagan astrological speculation, in which each stone represents a sign of the zodiac; the reversal was deliberate, in order to negate pagan associations of the twelve constellations with the twelve stones. Dependence on the Exodus list is here denied, but the proposal rests for other reasons on tenuous grounds. An even more elaborate proposal has been to read the stones counterclockwise, the signs of the zodiac clockwise (along with the names of the tribes), in order to get a particular color associated with the proper tribe. This view raises the double difficulty of establishing the color-tribal equation (known from medieval texts) and of showing that the author had the twelve tribes in mind (in 21:14 the names of the twelve apostles are inscribed on the foundations). The weight of the evidence, therefore, favors the view that the content and order of the Revelation list was derived from a tradition independent of other biblical lists as well as that of Josephus.

Other references to the tradition (e.g., Isa. 54:11-12; Tob. 13:16-17; II Bar. 6:7) are of little help regarding either identification or order.

4. Rev. 21:19-20 and the symbolism of precious stones. Jewels and precious stones with pagan mythological or magical connotations play very little role in the Bible. There are, nevertheless, notable passages in which the symbolism of jewels is a significant feature; these involve the garments of the high priest, the visions of Ezekiel and the author of Revelation, and occasional allusions elsewhere. The primary passages, together with the concepts which are suggested, will be discussed.

a. Precious stones and theophany. The connection of precious stones with theophanies has some support in the Bible. In the vision of Ezekiel, upon which the author of Revelation may be dependent, certain stones are utilized in the description of the glory (or brightness) of the theophany (Ezek. 1:16, 22, 26; 10:1, 9). Likewise in Rev. 4:3 the one sitting on the throne has the appearance of jasper and carnelian, and around the throne is a rainbow which gives the appearance of an emerald (cf. 9:17). Light and related figures which are often used to express the immanence of God (e.g., Ezek. 43:2) are, of course, ultimately derived from the heavenly bodies—the sun, moon, and stars. The original connection is suggested in many texts (Ps. 104:2; Enoch 14:18; Sibylline Oracles V.420-26; Jas. 1:17; cf. the representation of the Shekinah under the figure of light in the rabbinic literature). The ability of the polished stone to reflect brilliant light is doubtless the source of the idea that the jewel was the microcosmic counterpart of the heavenly bodies and hence an apt figure for divine glory—i.e., divine immanence; from this may have developed the notion of oracular and amuletic power often associated with jewels (cf. Prov. 17:8). Josephus interprets the two jewels on the high priest's shoulders in this fashion, noting that when God wanted to indicate his presence at the sacred ceremonies, he caused the stone on the right shoulder to shine (Antiq. III.viii.214-15); the twelve stones on the breastpiece functioned in the same fashion, indicating by flashing or sparkling that God was present when the Israelites went into battle (Antiq. III.viii.216). The oracular qualities of the breastpiece stones were considerably elaborated in later times by the rabbis, and the medieval astrologists developed this theme in great detail.

There seems to be little doubt that behind the precious-stone symbolism in general floats the astral imagery which was well known in the first century A.D. and probably much earlier, so that it becomes necessary to examine the motifs which underlie this symbolism.

b. Interpretation of the twelve stones in Philo and Josephus. Philo provides an extensive interpretation of the temple and the high priest's garments along the lines of the "lesser" mystery of Aaron (the "greater" being that of Moses). Included in his triple account (*Life of Moses* II.23-24; *Questions and Answers on Exodus* II.112-14; *On the Special Laws* I.82-97) of the mystery of Aaron is an explanation of the two stones on the shoulders of the priest and the twelve stones of the breastpiece (he does not list them). The two emeralds (or sardonyxes) represent either the sun and the moon (also Josephus and Clement of Alexandria) or the two celestial hemispheres, and the six tribal names on either stone the signs of the zodiac belonging to either sphere. The twelve stones on the breastpiece are a more detailed representation of the same symbolism: the division into four rows represents the four seasons. The breastpiece as a whole stands for the immutable divine Logos, the "law of nature." In another place Philo points out the virtues of this symbolism: by constant association with this symbolism, the high priest makes his own life worthy of the universal nature; his robe signifies that the whole cosmos worships with him; the Jewish high priest, as opposed to other priests, is the mediator for all mankind. All this sets forth the cosmic significance of Jewish worship.

Josephus agrees with the major lines of this interpretation, but differs in details (War V.v.231-37; Antiq. III.vii.162-71; vii.185-87; viii.214-18). He adds in particular a note about the oracular power of the twelve stones (*see* § 4*a above*), but which, he says, ceased to function two hundred years earlier (i.e., *ca.* the time of John Hyrcanus, 135-105 B.C.). Each of the patriarchs is associated with a stone, having his name engraved on it, and the order is that in which they were born (Antiq. III.vii.169). Philo indicates that the stones were distinguished from one another by color (*Moses* II.126; *On the Special Laws* I.87), each color corresponding to a sign of the zodiac, for each "produces its own particular coloring in the air and earth and water and their phases, and also in the different kinds of animals and plants" (*Moses* II.126).

That this tradition was widely known is indicated by the reference to the same line of interpretation in the Wisdom of Solomon (18:24). Cosmic symbolism also penetrated Jewish worship in Palestine and elsewhere to an amazing degree in the third-sixth centuries A.D., as the synagogues which date to this period show. The zodiac, the four seasons, and Helios often occupy a central position in floor mosaics and appear in other ways in synagogue decoration. The details of this symbolism seem to have been only sketchily known, since the signs of the zodiac are represented in both clockwise and counterclockwise patterns, and the seasons are not always associated with the correct signs. A specific connection with jewels is, of course, lacking, but the mythology which supports both the twelve jewels and the mosaics is identical. That this imagery was known to the author of Revelation is not improbable. The fact that he connects the names of the twelve apostles with the foundation jewels is strong evidence that he was aware of the tradition, though other motifs appear to have dictated the architecture of the holy city, New Jerusalem.

c. The heavenly city, New Jerusalem, and paradise. In apocalyptic literature the myths of the heavenly city, New Jerusalem, and paradise flow together to form a composite picture in which now one element, now another, is uppermost. It is generally agreed that the three motifs were originally distinct, the first and third going back to remote antiquity. The concept of the heavenly city is found in Babylonian mythology, where its architecture has been influenced by cosmic symbols. The myth probably rests on primitive concepts of the vault of heaven: as the handiwork of the gods, it rests on four pillars, is bedecked with glittering jewels (stars), and is transversed by a golden street (Milky Way; cf. II Enoch Proem, chs. 24–30). The twelve portals, or gates, and the twelve foundations derive ultimately from the zodiacal divisions of the heavens (Ezek. 48:30-35; Enoch 72; 75:6; 76; 82:4 ff; II Enoch 13–14; 30:6; cf. Josephus and Philo, in § 4*b above*).

This mythology is in part taken over and adapted to the idea of the renewal of Jerusalem. The development is away from the idea of a simple restoration of the earthly Jerusalem in the direction of a transformation of the city or the radical substitution of a heavenly archetype for the earthly model (cf. Isa. 60:10-14; Hag. 2:7-9; Zech. 2:1-5; Pss. Sol. 17:25 with Enoch 90:28-29; II Bar. 4:2-7; Rev. 21). In the process of transition, some of the features of the heavenly city are incorporated in the picture of the New Jerusalem. E.g., the precious stones as building materials (Isa. 54:11-12; Tob. 13:16-18; Rev. 21:10-21) and the twelve portals (Ezek. 48:30-35; Rev. 21:12-14) are derived from the heavenly archetype. Paul may have had this imagery in mind in I Cor. 3:12.

A third strand is the myth of the garden of God, or paradise. It is noteworthy that precious stones are also connected with the garden in Gen. 2:12 and the Gilgamesh Epic (*see* § 3*c above*). Of greater interest is the oracle in Ezek. 28:11-19 against the king of Tyre. The setting is Eden, the garden of God, where the king has as a covering (breastpiece; or "is enclosed, hedged about"?) every precious stone; he walks, moreover, among stones of fire (stars?). The location of the tree of life in the garden had long since been established in Near Eastern mythology, and its transfer to the New Jerusalem indicates the confluence of the two concepts (Enoch 25:4-5; Rev. 22:2; cf. Test. Dan. 5:12). Thus it is clear that the picture of the New Jerusalem in Revelation is a composite drawn from several strands of mythological tradition which had been partially fused.

While the list of foundation stones of the New Jerusalem in Revelation is not directly dependent on the breastpiece tradition, the two have a single root—namely, the ancient mythological view of the heavens. Twelve in either case corresponds to the twelve zones into which the heavens had been divided already in Babylonian astrology. The author of Revelation may not have been fully aware of the implications of his symbolism, but he knew that the twelve jewels were properly associated with the divine city and stood, as in earlier tradition, for the twelve heroes of the church upon which the city rests.

Bibliography. R. H. Charles, *The Revelation of St. John,* vols. I-II, ICC (1920); W. Bousset, *Die Religion des Judentums* (3rd ed., ed. H. Gressmann, 1926), pp. 282-85; A. Jeremias, *Handbuch der Altorientalischen Geisteskultur* (1929), pp. 108-14; E. R. Goodenough, *By Light, Light* (1935), pp. 95-120; A. Rowe, *A Catalogue of Egyptian Seals in the Palestine Archaeological Museum* (1936), pp. 328-29; L. Ginzberg, *The Legends of the Jews,* vols. I-VI (1913-38), Index; R. J. Forbes, *Bibliographia Antiqua* (1940), Part C: "Precious and Semiprecious Stones"; A. Lucas, *Ancient Egyptian Materials and Industries* (3rd rev. ed., 1948), pp. 52, 442 (a list of precious stones used in ancient Egypt); A. Farrer, *A Rebirth of Images* (1949); E. Lohmeyer, *Die Offenbarung des Johannes* (1953); E. R. Goodenough, *Jewish Symbols in the Greco-Roman Period,* vols. I-IV (1953-54; see the Index to the individual volumes); J. B. Pritchard, ed., *ANET* (2nd ed., 1955), p. 89.

P. L. GARBER AND R. W. FUNK

JEWRY jo͞o'rĭ. KJV translation of יהודה (RSV JUDAH) in Dan. 5:13 and of Ἰουδαία (RSV JUDEA) in Luke 23:5; John 7:1.

JEZANIAH jĕz'ə nī'ə [יזניהו (*properly* Jezaniahu), KJV יזניה (Jer. 42:1; RSV AZARIAH), *contractions of* יאזניהו (Jaazaniah), Yahu hears] (Jer. 40:8). One of the Judean captains who remained with Gedaliah at Mizpah after the Babylonian deportation. The name occurs on a sixth-century-B.C. seal inscription from the region of Mizpah and in the first Lachish Letter (*see* LACHISH). These may refer to the biblical Jezaniah; identification is impossible. J. M. WARD

JEZEBEL jĕz'ə bəl [איזבל, *from* Phoen. זבל, prince, exalted, *plus some other element*]. Probably the deliberate Hebrew distortion of a Phoenician name honoring Baal (cf. the name Baal'zebel [בעלאזבל] from a Phoenician inscription [CIS, I, 158]). The LXX seems to understand the name in this way (cf. the LXX, reading: "If you are Elijah ['My God is Yahu'], I am Jezebel," in I Kings 19:2). *Zbl* appears as a title for Baal in Ugaritic texts (49, I.14; III.3, 9, 21; IV.29, 40; 67, VI.10, where "Prince (*zbl*), Lord of Earth," occurs in parallelism with "Aliyn Baal").

1. The wife of Ahab, king of Israel. She was a Phoenician, daughter of Ethbaal, "king of the Sidonians" (I Kings 16:31) and, according to Menan-

der's account, priest in the Phoenician cult of Baal and Astarte (cf. Jos. Antiq. VIII.xiii.2). According to the Bible, Jezebel made every effort to remain a true daughter of her father in both these respects. A ruthless devotion to the absolute rights of oriental monarchy and to the worship of the Phoenician Baal are characteristic marks of her behavior, not only during the reign of Ahab, but also during the reigns of her two sons, Ahaziah and Jehoram. Even her daughter, Athaliah, who became queen of Judah, was regarded as carrying on Jezebel's influence (II Kings 8:18). Jezebel, like any foreign queen, seems to have demanded the right to her own practice of worship from the beginning (I Kings 16:31-33; cf. 11:8). Her own unusual initiative and resolution were shown, however, when she pressed her cult on Israel, supporting hundreds of prophets of Baal and Asherah (I Kings 18:19), carried her attack against the prophets of Yahweh (vs. 4), and even succeeded in driving out the by no means irresolute Elijah (19:1-3). The "harlotries and the sorceries" ascribed to Jezebel in II Kings 9:22 are almost certainly to be taken in reference to this attack against the worship of Yahweh (cf. Hos. 4:12).

The contrast between the Israelite and the usual oriental monarch is seen in the incident of Naboth's vineyard. When Ahab accepted the right of the private citizen to refuse to sell or exchange his property, Jezebel made the taunting response: "Do you now govern Israel?" (I Kings 21:7.) She was the one who stopped only long enough to cover her action with a pretense of legal form, and had Naboth stoned so that the king could take possession. The account of the death of Jezebel, when she "painted her eyes, and adorned her head" and defied Jehu with a final magnificent insult, is a fitting climax to the biblical picture of this remorseless, "cursed," but royal woman (II Kings 9:30-37), whose strength of character was with her to the end.

2. In Rev. 2:20 the name used symbolically for the false "prophetess" who beguiles the Christians of Thyatira into idolatrous practices. D. HARVEY

JEZELUS. KJV Apoc. form of JAHAZIEL 5; JEHIEL 7.

JEZER jē'zər [יצר] (Gen. 46:24; Num. 26:49; I Chr. 7:13); JEZERITES —zə rīts. Third son of Naphtali; ancestral head of the Jezerites.

JEZIAH. KJV form of IZZIAH.

JEZIEL jē'zĭ əl [*Qere* יזיאל, *Kethibh* יזואל] (I Chr. 12:3). Son of Azmaveth; one of the disaffected Benjaminite warriors who joined the proscribed band of David at Ziklag.

JEZLIAH. KJV form of IZLIAH.

JEZOAR. KJV form of IZHAR. *See also* ZOHAR.

JEZRAHEL jĕz'rə hĕl. Douay Version form of JEZREEL.

JEZRAHIAH jĕz'rə hī'ə [יזרחיה, Yahu will arise *or* shine] (Neh. 12:42). A leader of temple singers; same as Izrahiah (I Chr. 7:3).

JEZREEL jĕz'rĭ əl [יזרעאל, God sows, *or* may God make fruitful]; JEZREELITE —ə līt; JEZREELITESS jĕz'rĭ ə lī'tĭs. **1.** A descendant of Judah (I Chr. 4:3), and related to the town in Judah of this name (locality uncertain; cf. Josh. 15:56). Whether the person is the eponymous ancestor of the town or the name represents a personification of the town is unknown.

2. A son of the prophet Hosea; his first child by his wife Gomer. The boy's name was a symbol at once recalling the bloodshed at Jezreel by which Jehu came into power (cf. II Kings 9:17-26; 10:1-11), as well as anticipating now the divine vengeance on the house of Jehu for that slaughter (Hos. 1:4-5).

Bibliography. H. G. May, "An Interpretation of the Names of Hosea's Children," *JBL*, LV (1936), 285-91.

B. T. DAHLBERG

3. A border town in Issachar (Josh. 19:18). It is identified with modern Zer'in, a village at the foot of Mount Gilboa, located approximately seven miles N of Jenin. The site commands a view of the entire Plain of Jezreel (*see* 4 *below*), and is strategically located on the routes from the Mediterranean Coast to the Jordan Valley, and from S to N Palestine. It has not been excavated. Jezreel is first mentioned as one of the towns in Solomon's fifth administrative district under Baana (I Kings 4:12), but it was not until after the division of the kingdom that the town played a prominent role in biblical history. During the reign of Ahab, it became a royal residence (I Kings 18:45-46), and was the scene of the incident involving the vineyard of Naboth the Jezreelite (ch. 21), which evoked a strong denunciation from Elijah. It was to Jezreel that Joram, Ahab's son and successor, came to recover from wounds incurred in battle with Hazael of Syria (II Kings 8:29; II Chr. 22:6). This town witnessed more of the bloodshed that accompanied Jehu's revolution than any other town in Israel, with the exception of Samaria. Here Joram, Jezebel, and the resident officialdom of Israel were murdered; Ahaziah of Judah was wounded; and it was to Jezreel that the heads of Ahab's sons were sent from Samaria (II Kings 9:1–10:11).

4. The OT name of the entire valley which separates Galilee from Samaria. The W portion of this valley is now referred to as ESDRAELON ('Εσδρηλών) by some authors, while the name Jezreel is restricted to the E part of the valley.* That the valley is divided into two parts is clear from a study of a map of Palestine. The W section is roughly shaped like a right triangle, with the base running N and S along the W

Courtesy of the Israel Office of Information, New York

22. Road at the right leading from Nazareth into the Valley of Jezreel (the Plain of Esdraelon)

slopes of the Hill of Moreh and Mount Gilboa, the apex touching the Plain of Acco, and the hypotenuse stretching along the N slopes of the Carmel Range. This area included the Valley of Megiddon (*see* MEGIDDON, VALLEY OF). It slopes gently from SE to NW; a slight rise, which runs from E to W through the center of the valley, forces the River Kishon (*see* KISHON) to the N part of this plain. The smaller E section of the valley begins at the pass between Moreh and Gilboa, and terminates abruptly at the Jordan Rift. It slopes from NW to SE and is drained by the River Jalud, which flows eastward along the narrow valley floor. Fig. JEZ 22.

The Valley of Jezreel is a geological fault basin. It is covered with alluvium and receives an abundance of water, which makes it one of the most fertile areas of Palestine. A probable allusion to its fertility is contained in Hos. 2:22—H 2:24. It is also the major corridor through the rugged hills of Palestine and, as a result, is interlaced with routes from the Mediterranean on the W, to Beth-shan, the Jordan Valley, and the Transjordanian Plateau on the E; and from the hill country and Egypt on the S, to Galilee, Syria, and Phoenicia on the N.

From early times, the Valley of Jezreel was inhabited by Canaanites. At the time of the Conquest the Canaanites in the valley were militarily strong—their equipment included iron chariots—with the result that Ephraim and Manasseh were unable to dispossess them (Josh. 17:16). Like the Plain of Megiddo, it was the scene of many battles. During the period of the judges, Gideon and the N tribes defeated a coalition of Midianites, Amalekites, and *Bne Qedem* ("people of the East") who were encamped in the valley (Judg. 6:33–7:23). From here was issued the news of the death of Saul and his sons, including Jonathan, in battle with the Philistines on neighboring Mount Gilboa (II Sam. 4:4). In the ensuing struggle for the throne between Saul's son Ish-bosheth and David, Jezreel was among the areas of Israel which were briefly ruled by Ish-bosheth (II Sam. 2:9). According to Hos. 1:5, the valley was to be the place where Yahweh would break Israel's might, as fitting punishment for the murders which had been committed nearby in the town of Jezreel, during the revolution of Jehu.

5. A town in the territory of Judah (Josh. 15:56); the home of Ahinoam the Jezreelitess, one of David's wives (I Sam. 25:43; 27:3; 30:5; II Sam. 2:2; 3:2). Josh. 15:56 indicates that the town was located in the general vicinity of Ziph, Carmel, and Juttah. Khirbet Tarrama, a site situated *ca.* six miles SW of Hebron on the Plain of Dilbeh, has been suggested as a possible location, but no certain identification has been made.

Bibliography. G. A. Smith, *The Historical Geography of the Holy Land* (1894), pp. 379-410. W. F. Albright, "The Topography of the Tribe of Issachar," *ZAW* (1926), p. 226. F.-M. Abel, *Géographie de la Palestine,* I (1933), 399, 411-13; II (1938), 364-65. G. W. VAN BEEK

JIBSAM. KJV form of IBSAM.

JIDLAPH jĭd'lăf [ידלף, he weeps, *or perhaps* he is sleepless] (Gen. 22:22). Seventh son born to Nahor and Milcah.

JIMNA; JIMNAH. KJV forms of IMNAH.

JIPHTAH. KJV form of IPHTAH.

JIPHTHAH-EL. KJV form of IPHTAH-EL.

JOAB jō'ăb [יואב, Yahu is father]. **1.** The eldest son of Zeruiah, the sister of David; brother to Abishai and Asahel (II Sam. 2:18; I Chr. 2:16). His perspicuity and military adroitness as commander of the army of David and royal confidant earned for Joab an importance among his contemporaries second only to David.

The military record of Joab commences with the defeat of Abner at Gibeon. After the death of Saul, his son Ish-baal was placed upon the throne of Israel by Abner, the commander of the army; the tribe of Judah, however, anointed David as its own king (II Sam. 2:4, 8 ff; I Chr. 11:1-3). When Abner set out from Mahanaim, the Transjordanian capital, for W Palestine with a considerable detail of soldiers, he was met at the pool of Gibeon by the men of Joab, who no doubt had this movement under careful surveillance. As they confronted each other on the opposite sides of the pool, Abner challenged Joab to choose twelve warriors from his ranks to champion the cause of Judah against an equal number who would represent Israel. In the ensuing combat, after all the participants had fallen, the opposing forces joined the melee, with the result that Israel was routed. As Abner fled from the skirmish, he was doggedly pursued by the fleet Asahel, who refused to heed Abner's warning to desist and was slain. Joab and Abishai continued the obstinate pursuit until evening and were dissuaded from further bloodshed only by the urgent pleading of Abner and the regrouping of his forces. With Abner's admission of defeat, Joab halted the conflict and marched homeward to Hebron, interring on the way the body of his brother Asahel in the family sepulchre at Bethlehem (II Sam. 2:32).

The dissolution of amicable relations between Ish-baal and Abner, which was climaxed in their altercation over Rizpah, prompted the commander of Israel's forces to open negotiations with David with a view to effecting a united monarchy under his rule. Abner and his diplomatic corps then proceeded to Hebron, where they were feted by David, and after a satisfactory plan for the unification of the kingdom was formulated, they departed to accomplish its realization. Shortly thereafter Joab, who was ignorant of what had happened, returned to Hebron from a predatory foray and learned to his amazement that David had quite forgotten the unrequited blood of his nephew Asahel by sending Abner away in peace. Without the knowledge of David, the turbulent soldier sent messengers to recall Abner, and when he returned, Joab and Abishai treacherously slew him in the gate of Hebron. This wanton murder of Abner was decried by David with a harsh invective and fierce imprecation upon Joab, who was commanded to observe the passing of his enemy with sackcloth and mourning. The motive of Joab in the assassination of Abner was hardly to dispose of a spy (II Sam. 3:25); the deed was dictated as much by jealousy lest Abner assume command of the army as by desire for blood revenge for his brother Asahel (II Sam. 3:6-39).

The military service of Joab seems to have been commensurate with all the important conquests of David. The capture of the Jebusite stronghold of Zion by the daring assault of Joab through the water shaft won for him the permanent command of the army in accordance with the promise of David, who subsequently entrusted him with the repair of the city (II Sam. 5:6 ff; 8:16; 20:23; I Chr. 11:4 ff; 18:15; 27:34). Joab participated in the campaign of David against the Edomites, who had their country occupied and their male population exterminated by the forces of Joab (II Sam. 8:13-14; I Kings 11:15; Ps. 60). He was in charge of the Israelite campaign against the Syro-Ammonite axis and threw the Syrians (Arameans) into confusion by his attack while his brother Abishai routed the Ammonites, forcing them to return to Rabbah (II Sam. 10:6-14; I Chr. 19:6-15). Later Joab was in charge of the military operations when the land of Ammon was ravaged and its capital, Rabbah, was placed under siege. It was during this siege that Joab became a party to the nefarious plot of the king against Uriah (II Sam. 11; I Chr. 20:1-3). When the fall of Rabbah was imminent, Joab displayed a kindlier aspect of his nature by inviting the king, who had remained in Jerusalem, to assume command of the troops and be given the honor of the actual capture of the city (II Sam. 12:26-28).

Although Joab is not particularly mentioned in the other conquests of David, it is most probable that he played an important role in the subjugation of the Philistines (II Sam. 5:17-25; 8:1; I Chr. 14:10-16; 18:1), the Moabites (II Sam. 8:2; I Chr. 18:2), and the Arameans (II Sam. 8:3-8; 10:6-19; I Kings 11: 23-24; I Chr. 18:3-8; *cf. above*).

As a confidant of David, Joab was successful in obtaining the recall of Absalom from Geshur, where he had fled after the slaying of Amnon. Through a clever stratagem carefully concocted by Joab and skilfully executed by a wise woman of Tekoa, the king was made aware of his inconsistent attitude toward Absalom; and he then permitted his son to return to Jerusalem, although he was debarred from the court. After two years of this unbearable situation Joab was summoned by Absalom to intercede for him again with the king, but Joab refused twice to see the prince. It was only after Absalom resorted to the desperate expedient of firing the barley field of Joab that the commander pleaded the inequitable case of Absalom and obtained from David his son's reinstatement at court (II Sam. 14).

In the rebellion of Absalom, Joab maintained his loyalty to David and marshaled a third of the royal forces against the rebel. When the plight of Absalom, who had become ensnared in the branches of an oak by his hair, was communicated to Joab, he slew the prince forthwith, in direct violation of the express orders of David, and raised a cairn over the corpse. Joab then dispatched messengers to bring David the tidings of the battle (II Sam. 18). When David learned of the death of his son, he broke out in unrestrained grief and cast such a pall over the brilliant victory of his followers that Joab had to rebuke the king for the incongruity of his behavior. For his insubordination in the death of Absalom Joab appears to have been relieved of his command, for in his preparation to assume the monarchy again, David shrewdly obviated most of the remaining difficulty by appointing Amasa, the leader of the rebel forces of Absalom, as the successor to Joab in the command of David's army (II Sam. 19:1-13).

The rebellion of Sheba, which took place immediately upon the reinstatement of David, threatened the very existence of the united kingdom and evoked from the king the urgent order for Amasa, the new commander of the army, to gather within three days the Judean forces. Amasa failed to return within the appointed time; consequently, David placed Abishai in command of the royal guards and ordered him to quell the uprising. When Amasa joined his command at Gibeon, Joab, who accompanied the expedition, perfidiously murdered him and, by an appeal to his loyal followers and by a speedy suppression of the revolt, regained incontestably his former position (II Sam. 20).

The census of the people which David ordered evoked from Joab the strongest protests, but to no avail, and occupied the commander for more than nine months (II Sam. 24:1-8; I Chr. 21:1-5; 27:24).

It was the dispute of Adonijah and Solomon over dynastic succession that ultimately led to the downfall of Joab. With Abiathar the priest, Joab supported the regal claims of Adonijah and was at the supposed coronation feast when the ominous news came that David had nominated Solomon as his successor. The proponents of Adonijah melted quickly away; Joab himself rushed for sanctuary to the horns of the altar, but even this plea for asylum did not mollify the implacable anger of Solomon toward this aged soldier, whose bloody deeds had irritated and embarrassed the house of David sufficiently long to warrant his summary dispatch by Benaiah (I Kings 1:7, 41; 2:28-35).

Joab possessed all the virtues and the vices of an ancient warrior. He was devotedly loyal to the king, utterly fearless (II Sam. 10:12; I Chr. 11:6), and a shrewd tactician (II Sam. 10:9 ff; 18:22); but he was also irrepressibly self-willed (II Sam. 18:5, 14), summarily truculent (II Sam. 3:27; 18:14; 20:10 ff), and untrustworthy toward his inferiors (II Sam. 11:14 ff; 18:12 ff). Although he was not without religious feeling, it was devoid of any real ethical content (II Sam. 10:12; 24:3; I Chr. 26:28). No small share of the military successes of David is attributable to Joab, who, with his retinue of ten armor-bearers (II Sam. 18:15; 23:37) and his renowned heroism, must have been an imposing personage in Israel, commanding the respect of his followers and inspiring fear in his enemies (I Kings 11:21).

2. Son of the Judahite Seraiah, a descendant of Kenaz, who was the father—i.e., ancestor—of the Geharashim—i.e., (the dwellers in) the valley of smiths, which may be identified with the Wadi Arabah (I Chr. 4:14; *see bibliography*).

3. The eponym of a Judean family which was represented in the return from the Babylonian captivity to Judah in the days of Zerubbabel (Ezra 2:6; Neh. 7:11; *see* PAHATH-MOAB) and in the days of Ezra, when Obadiah the son of Jehiel was head of the family (Ezra 8:9; I Esd. 8:35).

Bibliography. N. Glueck, *The Other Side of the Jordan* (1940), p. 83. E. R. DALGLISH

JOACHAZ [Ιωαχαζ, LXX A I Esd. 1:34—G 1:32; *other texts read* Ιεχονιας (JECONIAH)]. Apoc. alternate form of JEHOAHAZ.

JOACHIM. *See* JEHOIAKIM.

JOADANUS. KJV form of JODAN.

JOAH jō'ə [יואח, Yahu is brother]. **1.** A Levite; son of Obed-edom (I Chr. 26:4).

2. A Levite; son of Zimnah (I Chr. 6:21—H 6:6); perhaps the same as the Joah who assisted in the reforms of King Hezekiah (II Chr. 29:12).

3. A court official, and a member of the deputation from King Hezekiah to the Assyrian armies (II Kings 18:18, 26, 37; cf. Isa. 36:3, 11, 22).

4. Recorder under King Josiah; one of those deputized to see to the repair of the temple (II Chr. 34:8).

Bibliography. M. Noth, *Die israelitischen Personennamen* (1928), pp. 69, 141. B. T. DAHLBERG

JOAHAZ. Alternate form of JEHOAHAZ.

JOAKIM jō'ə kĭm ['Ιωακίμ]; KJV JOACIM. **1.** A son of Zerubbabel who returned from the Babylonian exile as the leader of a group (I Esd. 5:5).

2. The high priest at Jerusalem in the story of Judith (Jth. 4:6-7, 14-15; 15:8).

3. The husband of Susanna (Sus. 63).

N. TURNER

JOANAN jō ā'nən ['Ιωανάν=יוחנן] (Luke 3:27); KJV JOANNA jō ăn'ə. An ancestor of Jesus.

JOANNA jō ăn'ə ['Ιωάν(ν)α, *probably feminine of* 'Ιωάννης, John]. The "wife of Herod's [Antipas'] steward"; one, among others, who was healed and who provided for Jesus and the Twelve "out of [her] means" (Luke 8:3). In Luke 24:10 Joanna, with Mary Magdalene (as in 8:2-3), Mary the mother of James, and "the other women," is said to have been at the empty tomb. B. H. THROCKMORTON, JR.

JOANNAN. KJV Apoc. alternate form of JOHN 1.

JOARIB jō'ə rĭb ['Ιωαρ(ε)ίβ=יויריב, may Yahu contend]. The head of the priestly family from whom the Maccabees traced their descent (I Macc. 2:1; 14:29; cf. Jos. Antiq. XII.vi.1). The family first appears in the time of David (I Chr. 24:7), when it is called Jehoiarib. M. NEWMAN

JOASH jō'ăsh [יואש, Y gives, *or* has given, *from* Arab. *'wš*, to give, bestow]. Alternately: JEHOASH jĭ hō'ăsh [יהואש]. **1.** A man of Manasseh, of the clan of Abiezer; father of Gideon (Judg. 6:11-15). He lived at Ophrah, whose location has not been established with certainty. Here was a sacred oak where oracles were given. In Judg. 6:11-32 two traditions appear to have been combined, and the details are difficult to fit together. Joash had apparently built an altar to Baal, and had also made an Asherah (vs. 25). These Gideon was commanded to destroy. Joash took his son's part when the men of the town remonstrated with him (vss. 28-32).

2. A man of Judah; one of the sons of Shelah (I Chr. 4:22; LXX B reads 'Ιωαδα).

3. A Benjaminite of the clan of Becher (I Chr. 7:8).

4. A Benjaminite, son of Shemaah of Gibeah; a Mighty Man, ambidextrous in shooting arrows and slinging stones. He came to David at Ziklag, while David was held there by Saul and his men. Joash was second in command to Ahiezer (I Chr. 12:1-3).

5. One of David's officers in charge of the stores of oil (I Chr. 27:28).

6. A son of Ahab, associated with Amon the governor of Samaria. To their care Micaiah son of Imlah was entrusted after he had uttered a prophecy of doom against King Ahab as he went to campaign against Ramoth-gilead (I Kings 22:26; II Chr. 18:25).

7. King of Judah *ca.* 837-800 B.C.; son of Ahaziah.

With the murder of King Ahaziah of Judah by Jehu in his bloody revolution in the N, the throne of Judah was seized by the queen mother, Athaliah. Her first act was to destroy the royal family (II Kings 11:1), presumably to rid herself of anyone who could challenge her position. But one of Ahaziah's sons, Joash, escaped through the intervention of his aunt Jehosheba, the wife of Jehoiada the high priest of Yahweh, and was kept hidden in the temple precincts for six years along with his nurse. During this period Athaliah reigned as queen over the land.

In the seventh year, however, a revolution similar to that which had occurred in the N under Jehu, but on a much smaller scale, broke out in Judah. It is interesting to note that in the revolutions in both the N and S kingdoms religion played a prominent part. No details are given of the situation in Judah during the six/seven years of Athaliah's rule. One can imagine, however, on the basis of her former background and her initial act as queen, that she ruled as a despot and alienated the people. Further, the Davidic dynasty was imperiled and was in danger of being blotted out. It is clear, too, that the religion of Yahweh was endangered, for Athaliah was a devotee of Baal, and under her royal patronage Baalism flourished in the land. The high priest of Baal at the time, Mattan (II Kings 11:18), had a Phoenician name. It is probable that the Baal was the Tyrian Baal-Melcarth, and that the worship of this god had gained a stronghold in both the N and the S. The Judean revolt is, therefore, from the historical point of view a sequel to the Israelite revolt.

The leader of the revolution was Jehoiada, the high priest of Yahweh. When the opportune time arrived, he organized the mercenaries, the temple guards, and the people. The day chosen was the sabbath, which was a holiday. Jehoiada so arranged the guards that all three companies were present at the same time in the temple. Then he brought in the young king, crowned him, and anointed him, and those present shouted: "Long live the king!" (II Kings 11:4-12).

On hearing the shouting, Athaliah came to the temple. Apparently she realized at a glance what the situation meant. On Jehoiada's orders she was taken outside the temple to one of the palace gates and there slain (II Kings 11:13-16). It is possible that this section (vss. 13-18*a*) is secondary.

There followed a covenant-making ceremony in which king and people alike pledged themselves to be the people of Yahweh. The second covenant, "between the king and the people," is omitted by many scholars, and is absent from Chronicles. But there is point in its inclusion on this occasion. The people pledged anew their loyalty to the Davidic dynasty. The phrase "the people of the land" used here means more than "the populace." It probably means "full citizens." The people were not organized but acted in times of political crisis (cf. II Kings 21:24; 23:30*b*).

After the queen's death the people destroyed the house of Baal, with its altars and images, and murdered Mattan the Baal priest. There is no mention of further bloodshed, though the fact that special guards were placed over the temple suggests the possibility of such further acts. These, however, did not occur. "The city was quiet," and the people rejoiced (II Kings 11:17-20). The Chronicler's representation of these events (II Chr. 22:10–23:21), while based essentially on II Kings 11, differs from it in several points, particularly in its emphasis on the part played by the priests and the Levites and the sacredness of the temple. From the historical point of view Kings gives a more accurate picture of what actually happened.

Joash was seven years old when he began to reign, and he reigned for forty years. His mother was Zibiah of Beer-sheba (II Kings 12:1). It is probable that the figure of forty years is a round number, and perhaps it includes the period of Athaliah's reign. Theoretically, Joash became king at his father's death in 842. The discrepancy of twenty-two years between the regnal totals given for Israel and Judah for the period 842-721 can in large measure be corrected by relying on the synchronistic data. It is clear that Jehoiada acted as regent of the kingdom and as tutor to the boy king (II Kings 12:2). Chronicles adds the further information that "Jehoiada got for him two wives, and he had sons and daughters" (II Chr. 24:3). This item is important, as Joash represented the last member of the Davidic line.

During the reign of Joash, who proved to be a good king, repairs were made to the temple, and the system of temple revenue was improved (II Kings 12:5-17). By this time the temple was, no doubt, in need of extensive repairs. The story gives a picture of the dishonesty practiced by the temple priests, and how they misappropriated temple funds for their own use. It tells further how the king put a stop to these practices by having a collection box placed at the entrance of the temple. Into this box the "priests who guarded the threshold" had to put the money as it was handed to them in the presence of the givers. When the box wás full, the king's secretary and the high priest came and counted the money, which was then given to the overseers. They in their turn paid the workmen. The story is an interesting commentary on priestly practices, which necessitated a royal rebuke. It is noteworthy that in the account of Josiah's reformation (II Kings 22) details are taken from this narrative.

The Chronicler's account of this incident (II Chr. 24:4-14*a*) differs considerably from Kings. Presumably his source was the "Commentary [midrash] on the Book of the Kings" (vs. 27). It presents a picture which cannot be regarded as historical.

The Chronicler has a further story about a break between the king and the priesthood after the death of Jehoiada. This culminated in the murder of Jehoiada's son Zechariah, who was stoned to death by the people (II Chr. 24:15-22). That this tradition is historically reliable seems to be borne out by the reminiscence in Matt. 23:35 (cf. Luke 11:51).

In the reign of Joash, Judah suffered a bitter humiliation at the hands of Hazael of Aram (II Kings 12:17-18; cf. II Chr. 24:23-24). Hazael captured Gath, probably the modern Araq el-Menshiyeh, on the way to Gaza. This may indicate a conquest of Philistia, which would have given him control of the caravan routes from Egypt. He then planned to attack Jerusalem, but Joash bought him off by paying a heavy tribute. The details the Chronicler gives of this event are not reliable.

Joash was assassinated in a palace conspiracy led by some of his servants. The leaders are named (II Kings 12:20-21; II Chr. 24:25-26). The Chronicler here relied on a different tradition from the writer of Kings. The motive he alleges for the murder was the death of Zechariah. It seems better, however, with Kings to leave unanswered the question of motive. The general historical background was clearly one of disorder in both kingdoms.

Bibliography. W. F. Albright, "Contributions to the Historical Geography of Palestine," *AASOR,* II-III (1923), 11 ff; C. C. Torrey, "The Foundry of the Second Temple at Jerusalem," *JBL,* 55 (1936), 247 ff; H. G. May, "A Key to the Interpretation of Zechariah's Visions," *JBL,* 57 (1938), 181; R. B. Y. Scott, "The Pillars Jachin and Boaz," *JBL,* LVIII (1939), 143 ff; C. C. Torrey, "A Hebrew Seal from the Reign of Ahaz," *BASOR,* 79 (1940), 28, note 1 by W. F. Albright; J. A. Thomson, "On Some Stamps and a Seal from Lachish," *BASOR,* 86 (1942), 24 ff; W. Eichrodt, *Theologie des Alten Testaments,* I (3rd ed., 1948), 221-31; J. A. Montgomery, *The Books of Kings,* ICC (1951), p. 431; G. von Rad, *Studies in Deuteronomy* (1953), pp. 60 ff.

8. King of Israel *ca.* 801-786 B.C.; son and successor of Jehoahaz.

Joash reigned for sixteen years (II Kings 13:10). II Kings 13:12-13 is parallel to 14:15-16, and is out of place here.

During the last illness of ELISHA, King Joash went to see him. In a series of symbolic acts, reminiscent of sympathetic magic, Elisha promised him victory three times over Syria (II Kings 13:14-19). The specific mention of a victory at Aphek (vs. 17) is highly unlikely, and is probably a reference to I Kings 20:26 ff. The datum of an annual invasion of Israel by the Moabites each spring (II Kings 13:20) may be historical, in the sense of limited forays.

The background of II Kings 13:24-25 can now be filled out from Assyrian records and the Aramaic inscription of Zakir. In 805 Adad-nirari III, the Assyrian king, led an expedition to Palestine. He claims to have subjected "the country of the Hittites, Amurru-country in its full extent, Tyre, Sidon, Israel (mat Ḫu-um-ri), Edom, Palestine (Pa-la-as-tu) as far as the shore of the Great Sea of the Setting Sun," and imposed tribute upon them. Then he marched against Damascus, where he "shut up Mari, king of Damascus, in Damascus, his royal residence." Damascus had to pay a very heavy tribute—a hundred talents of gold, a thousand talents of silver, and much else in the way of spoil. Aram was left prostrate, and there seems to have been a general uprising of the neighboring states against her. The Zakir Inscription, the date of which is open to question but is in all probability after 805 B.C., tells of an unsuccessful expedition led by "Bar-hadad bar Hazael king of Aram" against Zakir, "king of Hamath and La'ash."

This is the background against which Joash' successful campaign against Ben-hadad of Syria, who had succeeded his father, Hazael, as king, is to be set. Joash took the opportunity to recover for Israel the territory previously lost to Aram in the reign of Jehoahaz.

Not only was Joash successful against Aram; he was also victorious against Judah. Amaziah king of Judah, flushed with pride as the result of his victory over Edom, challenged Joash to battle. Amaziah's army was routed at Beth-shemesh of Judah, and he himself was captured. Joash came to Jerusalem, broke down part of the wall, despoiled the temple and the royal treasuries, and took hostages back to Samaria (II Kings 14:8-14). It is clear that, for all practical purposes, Judah was reduced to the status of a vassal. Israel had recovered her position, and under Joash' son Jeroboam II she reached her greatest heights.

Bibliography. J. B. Bury *et al.*, eds., *Cambridge Ancient History,* III (1925), 375-76; F.-M. Abel, *Géographie de la Palestine,* II (1938), 282; A. Guillaume, *Prophecy and Divination* (1938), especially pp. 173-74; J. Simons, *Jerusalem in the OT* (1952), pp. 233 ff, 300 (note 3), 301 (note 2); J. B. Pritchard, ed., *ANET* (2nd ed., 1955), pp. 281-82.

H. B. MacLean

JOATHAM. KJV NT form of Jotham 2.

JOAZABDUS. KJV Apoc. alternate form of Jozabad.

JOB. KJV form of Iob.

JOB, BOOK OF. The eighteenth book in the OT canon in the English versions. The book of Job takes its title from the central figure of the story; other biblical documents—Joshua, Samuel, Ruth, Jonah, Esther, Ezra, Nehemiah, Daniel, and the various prophetic books—are named after a hero or heroine or a pre-eminent figure appearing in them.

1. Name. The English form of the hero's name, based on the Greek and Latin transcriptions, Ἰώβ and Iob, gives a rather inaccurate rendering of the Hebrew form of the name, איוב, *'iyyôbh.* The German form, Hiob, is somewhat closer to the Hebrew, but still not exact. The derivation and meaning of the name are uncertain. The apparent root of the name, איב, *'yb,* is perhaps to be connected with the idea of "enmity, hostility." The common word for "enemy" is the simple active participle of this root, אויב, *'ôyēbh* (*nomen agentis*). The form of the name (the nominal pattern *qaṭṭâl* > *qiṭṭôl*) is that usually designating a profession (*nomen professionis*), or habitual or characteristic activity, such as *gannâbh,* "thief" (professional or habitual), or *gibbôr* (< *gabbâr*), "powerful man." Accordingly, the name would mean something like "inveterate foe." This form of the root איב, however, is not otherwise attested. If the name does mean "enemy, foe," it may have been intended as symbolic of the hero's attitude toward God, of his adverse reaction to the seemingly senseless suffering inflicted on him. The opposite sense has also been suggested for the name. There is an adjective or noun of this pattern, ילוד, *yillôdh,* which has apparent passival sense, "(one) born," and accordingly the name has been interpreted as designating one who is the object of enmity or persecution; this sense is quite appropriate for the name of one who is the victim of a cruel wager and experiment on the part of the Lord and "the" Satan and the target of criticism by his fair-weather friends. The passival sense of this nominal pattern, however, is not otherwise attested and is far from certain.

The name has also been related to the Arabic root *'wb,* "return, repent," and thus *'awwâb* > *'ayyâb* > *'iyyôbh* would mean "the penitent one," or the like.

The notion that the name may have been artificially constructed, *ad hoc,* to characterize the hero of the story, is now seen to be without basis. In the Execration Texts from Egypt (*ca.* 2000 B.C.) a Palestinian chief bears the name *'ybm* (i.e., *'Ayyâbum*). The name also occurs in Akkadian documents of the second millennium B.C. from Mari, Alalakh, and Amarna. In the Amarna Letter no. 256 the prince of Ashtaroth in Bashan is one *Ay(y)âb* (*a-ya-bu*). The name has been explained by W. F. Albright as meaning "Where is (my) Father?" similar to the names *Ayaḫammu/ḫalu,* "Where is the Paternal/Maternal Clan?" The name is perhaps contracted from a longer form such as *Ayabi-sharri,* "Where is my Father, O King?" or *Ayabi-ilu,* "Where is my Father, O God?" The authenticity and the antiquity of the name *'Ayyâb*>*'Iyyôb* is thus well attested, as borne by a number of Western Semites in the second millennium B.C. It is an ordinary name and may have been chosen for this reason, or it may be that some ancient worthy bearing it actually experienced a fate such as described in the biblical story and became the type and model of the righteous sufferer.

2. Text and versions. The text of the book of Job leaves much to be desired, and resources for its restitution and reconstitution are meager. Comparison of the MT with the LXX in a few cases leads to the correction of the Hebrew, but for the most part the Hebrew has to be relied on rather than the Greek.

Many verses of the received Hebrew text were missing from the oldest form of the Greek text. In Origen's time the current Greek version was shorter than the Hebrew by some four hundred lines. Origen supplied the missing lines from Theodotion, who gave a full translation rather than the abridged form of the original LXX. The lines supplied from Theodotion were marked by Origen with asterisks. A Coptic translation of the LXX of Job, published in 1899, agrees substantially with the pre-Origen text in the omission of the passages Origen marked with asterisks. The situation with the text of Job is similar to that of Jeremiah, where the Greek is also considerably shorter than the Hebrew. Some scholars have supposed that the shorter Greek text of Job represents the more primitive form of the book and that the Hebrew was later expanded. The weight of the evidence, however, is against this view. The omissions of the Greek do not improve matters, and in many cases the difficulty of the extant material is increased by the lack of coherent context. It appears that the Greek translator did what the modern translator is tempted to do with some of the more difficult passages of the Hebrew, simply to give up the attempt to translate as futile. In many cases the LXX must be regarded as more of a paraphrase than a translation, and in some instances the sense of the Greek is so far removed from the Hebrew as to constitute a radical reinterpretation. Theological bias is apparent in many instances in the LXX and especially in passages where the sense of the Hebrew is obscured or even radically altered. A flagrant example is the famous text 13:15, where the Masoretes resorted to a simple and convenient device to change the shocking sense of the verse, but the LXX translator completely revamped the verse so as to alter entirely the sense and the tone of Job's bitter outcry.

The other versions are no more helpful than the LXX. The Peshitta is occasionally useful, as it was made from the Hebrew and clarifies some of the obscure words. The Targ. presents many curiosities, but does not contribute substantially to the restitution or understanding of the text. A portion of a Targ. of Job has been found at Qumran, but its textual value remains to be assessed. The Vulg., according to Jerome, was translated directly from the Hebrew text current in his day, at the end of the fourth century. But Jerome, as he admits, in the face of many difficulties, translated sometimes literally and sometimes freely, according to the sense. Jerome was assisted in his task by a rabbi of Lydda, who apparently influenced him along the line of traditional rabbinic exegesis. Jerome was also inevitably influenced by the LXX hexapla, which he had himself translated into Latin. The Vulg. thus must be employed with considerable discretion, but so used, it is a valuable help in the study of the text of Job. The MT, although manifestly corrupt and needing emendation in many places, remains our primary source. Conjectural emendation is often necessary, and all translators are forced to take some liberties with the text to avoid rendering nonsense. Modern research in Semitic philology and linguistics, and especially the recovery of the Ugaritic mythological texts, has shown some words and forms previously suspect to be quite correctly preserved. At the same time, while some words have been authenticated, others have been rendered suspect by new data. With the possible exception of Hosea, Job remains textually the most difficult book of the OT.

3. Place in the canon. The book belongs to the last of the three divisions of the Hebrew scriptures, the *Kᵉthûbhîm,* Hagiographa, or Writings. Except by Theodore of Mopsuestia, the canonicity of the book has not been questioned. Its position among the Writings varies somewhat. The oldest tradition (Talmud, B.B. 14*b*) gives the order as Ruth, Psalms, Job, Proverbs, Ecclesiastes, Song of Songs, Lamentations, Daniel, Esther, Ezra, Chronicles. The order Psalms, Job, Proverbs, is found in Codex Alexandrinus; but the order Job, Psalms, Proverbs, is attested by Cyril of Jerusalem, Epiphanius, Jerome, Rufinus, and the Apostolic Canons. The order Job, Proverbs, Psalms, is indicated by the Hebrew initials which designated the poetic trilogy, having a special system of accents, אמת, *'iyyôbh, mišlê, tᵉhillîm;* while the order Psalms, Job, Proverbs, is indicated by the alternative designation, תאם. Other orders are mentioned by the Latin fathers, but the order favored by Jerome, with Job as the first of the great poetic trilogy, was fixed by the Council of Trent as the order of the Vulg. and this has been generally followed in modern versions in the West.

4. Original language. The language of Job, while ostensibly Hebrew, presents many difficulties to the philologist, translator, and interpreter. In view of the Edomite connections of the characters and setting of the story, it has been suggested (Voltaire, J. G. von Herder, E. Renan) that the poem is an echo of the famed wisdom of Edom. It has even been concluded that the author was an Edomite and not a Jew. For the Edomite language, unfortunately, we have very meager linguistic data. It is known to be a dialect of Canaanite, and must have been quite similar to the neighboring dialects Hebrew, Ammonite, and Moabite. We will have to know more of the dialect of Edom before we can judge its influence on the language of the book of Job.

The suggestion was first made by Ibn Ezra that the difficulties of the book of Job derive from the fact that it is a translation. This view has been echoed by a number of modern scholars. Arabic has been suggested as the original language. A considerable number of words found in Job and not otherwise known in Hebrew have been explained from Arabic. This, however, is also true of many other OT words outside the book of Job. The explanation of this fact is quite simple—Arabic is the best known and has the richest vocabulary of any of the Semitic languages. Many obscurities in the Ugaritic texts have also been clarified by recourse to Arabic. The idea that Job is translated from an Arabic dialect is, on the face of it, improbable, and the linguistic evidence for it is insufficient to warrant a review of the case.

The most striking linguistic feature of Job is its strong Aramaic coloring. Aramaic elements in the book are universally admitted. Often in the poetic parallelism Hebrew and Aramaic words are juxtaposed as synonyms. There are also phonological and morphological features that are characteristically Aramaic. Now it is recognized that even classical Hebrew has some features and inconsistencies that seem best explained as due to Aramaic influence, so much so that some Semitists have classified Hebrew as a hybrid speech (*Mischsprache*). The admixture of Aramaic elements in Job, however, exceeds that of any other biblical book. It has been argued that the explanation of the mixture in Job is that we have, not a hybrid language, but rather a halfway translation from an Aramaic original. The incomplete translator wished to make the Aramaic poetry accessible to Hebrew-speaking readers and made only such alterations as he deemed necessary. Since much of the alleged original Aramaic would be intelligible without change, it was left unaltered. Thus in large part the supposed Aramaic original remains, in hundreds of words, grammatical forms, idioms, and phonetic traits. The Hebrew translator, it is alleged, in many cases failed to recognize the proper sense of Aramaic words and phrases and thus mistranslated. The Masoretes, quite naturally, had their troubles with this Aramaic-Hebrew mixture and vocalized many of the words incorrectly.

According to Tur Sinai, the alleged original Aramaic of Job is Babylonian and not later than the sixth century. The author was supposedly a Jew who in the early days of the Babylonian exile composed the poem on the basis of an ancient legend. Some generations later in Palestine the "translator" performed the incomplete operation on the poem.

The testing of this theory of linguistic mixture and halfway translation from Aramaic yields little by way of assured improvement in the sense. The presence of numerous Aramaic elements in the book of Job cannot be denied, but a satisfactory explanation of this fact has not been given. It seems best to operate with the Hebrew(?) text as we have it, with a minimum of alteration. It may be that no small part of our difficulty with the language of Job is due to our lack of knowledge. The Ugaritic texts have contributed a great deal to the improvement of our knowledge of ancient Northwest Semitic poetry, and it may be that future discoveries and studies will further improve our understanding.

5. Date. The patriarchal background of the prose narrative gave rise to an ancient view that the author was Moses himself (Talmud, B.B. 14*b*). The apocryphal appendix at the end of the LXX goes even deeper into antiquity, identifying Job with Jobab, king of Edom (Gen. 36:33), grandson of Esau, and great-great-grandson of Abraham. The patriarchal coloring appears to be quite authentic in detail. The religion depicted is primitive. There is no priesthood or central shrine. Divine anger is assuaged by sacrifice offered by the patriarch (Job 1:5; 42:8), as in the Balaam story (Num. 23:1, 14, 24). Wealth consists of cattle and slaves (Job 1:3; 42:12), as in the patriarchal narratives (Gen. 12:16; 32:5). The Sabeans and Chaldeans are represented still as marauding nomads (Job 1:15, 17). The unit of money mentioned in 42:11 (the קשיטה) is referred to elsewhere only in Gen. 33:19; Josh. 24:32. Job's exceptional longevity (Job 42:17) is matched or surpassed only in the patriarchal period (cf. Gen. 35:28-29) or earlier. Moreover, the style of the Prologue and the Epilogue exhibits a number of literary features which are characteristic of Semitic epic and have their most striking parallels in the Ugaritic literature. These features comprise a sort of epic substratum, as it has been termed. This epic substratum may very well derive from an older Job epic which served as the basis of the present Prologue and Epilogue. That there was an ancient Job legend, and perhaps an epic, is indicated by the allusion to Job in Ezek. 14:14, 20, in association with Noah and Danel. The antiquity of the Noah legend is patent, and we now know that the Danel here mentioned was also a relatively ancient worthy. This Danel, in all probability the prototype of the biblical hero Daniel, we meet in an Ugaritic epic which dates from the middle of the second millennium B.C. The Keret epic, also from the same time and place, has some marked affinities with Job, for it tells of a king who lost his entire family, but who by divine favor and assistance got a new wife and other children. He was also smitten with a seemingly fatal illness and yet was restored to health. Some of the Mesopotamian parallels to Job are also quite ancient. The so-called Babylonian Job, the text entitled "I Will Praise the Lord of Wisdom," long known from copies of the seventh century B.C., is now attested in a copy *ca.* a thousand years older. A Sumerian version of the Job motif, dating from *ca.* 1700 B.C. and probably derived from an original composition at least as early as the third dynasty of Ur, *ca.* 2000, has now been recovered. Thus the parallels to the Job story go back at least to the second millennium B.C. and enhance the probability that a very ancient legend and epic lies behind the prose narrative which serves as the framework of the poetic dialogue. Some scholars have dated the prose narrative in the Persian period because of the appearance of "the" Satan (with the definite article as in Zech. 3:1 ff). The Satan, however, is missing from the Epilogue, and it may be that the episodes involving the Satan are a later graft on the original prose tale. The Epilogue places the responsibility for Job's misfortunes solely on the Lord (Job. 42:11). The divine assembly of 1:6-12; 2:1-7, apart from the problem of the Satan, is a reflex of early Near Eastern mythology which we meet in Mesopotamian literature and in the Ugaritic texts and is echoed in some of the biblical Psalms and in Second Isaiah. The celestial court scene in Job has more in common with the vision of Micaiah ben Imlah (I Kings 22:19-23), in the ninth century, than with the vision of the high priest's trial in Zech. 3, in spite of the use of the definite article with the word "Satan" in both passages.

While the introduction of the Satan into the narrative may be as late as the sixth or fifth century, the core of the story featuring an Edomite hero and an Edomite supporting cast would hardly have come into existence in the exilic or early postexilic period, when the Edomites had incurred the lasting enmity of the Judeans (cf. Pss. 83:4-6; 137:7; Isa. 34:5-6; Jer. 49:7-22; Lam. 4:21; Ezek. 25:12-14; 35:2; Obad. 10-14). There is nothing to indicate that the choice of an Edomite hero was motivated by a desire to prick the consciences of particularist bigots, as may be the case with the choice of a Moabitess as the heroine of the book of Ruth.

While it is impossible to fix the date of the prose narrative exactly, there is no reason, apart from the references to the Satan, to place it later than the seventh century B.C., and its antecedents may go back a millennium or more. The author of the poetic dialogues and the latest editors of the completed book may have made considerable alterations and adaptations in the old Job legend, but there seems little ground for doubt that they made use of a narrative featuring many genuinely archaic elements.

The opinions of the rabbis as to the date of the book of Job varied from pre-Mosaic times to the time of Cyrus and Ahasuerus. Eusebius advocated a pre-Mosaic date, and a few scholars in modern times have argued for the same. Gregory of Nazianzus, in the fourth century A.D., placed the book in the time of Solomon, and this view also found favor with a small number of modern scholars. The seventh century B.C., early, middle, and late, has been proposed by a number of critics, mostly German, of the late nineteenth century. In more recent times the tendency has been to date the book between the sixth and fourth centuries. Opinion is divided as to whether Job is earlier or later than the Second Isaiah, with eminent scholars on both sides. The theme of innocent suffering is common to Job and Isa. 52:13-53:12, but, while Job is concerned with the individual, the Second Isaiah deals with the nation. It has been argued that since the nation's interest was recognized before that of the individual, the Suffering Servant passage must be earlier than Job. This argument has little cogency, since the theme of individual suffering was current in the literature of Egypt and Mesopotamia centuries earlier and is given eloquent expression by Jeremiah. It occurs also in a number of psalms, but these cannot be dated with any degree of exactness. In relation to the problem of suffering, individual or national, there is no firm basis for dating Job later than the Second Isaiah. A date between Jeremiah and the Second Isaiah has been suggested. This would place the book in the first generation of the Exile and relate it inescapably to the suffering of the nation. This view has some intriguing implications, but there is no hint in the book that the poet has any thought of the fate or destiny of any nation. The allusion to the deportation of dignitaries (Job 12:17-19) is too general to be taken as a reference to the exile of Judah. The entire history of Israel is completely ignored. If the author was a Jew of the first generation of the Exile, the shock of the experience seems to have destroyed all concern and hope for the nation. The choice of an Edomite, of all people, as the hero of the story would indicate complete rejection of nationalist aspirations. The destruction of the nation is a *fait accompli*. God has acted in history, and the act was one of destruction. Where now was there ground for hope? The rejection of nationalism by the author of Job would thus anticipate the similar development in the rise of Christianity. The implications of such speculation could be developed further, but it is only speculation, since there is nothing in the book itself to suggest an exilic setting.

The majority of critics, in the absence of any indication of exilic setting, assign the book to the post-exilic period. Within this period, however, there is no firm consensus, and the suggestions range from the fifth to the third century. The book certainly reached its final form by 200 B.C., since it was known to Ben Sirach (Ecclus. 49:9), and no critic has suggested a date later than *ca.* 250 B.C.

The reason for the considerable spread in the dating of the book is simply that the evidence is inconclusive. For almost every argument for a given century, counterarguments can be given. It does not serve the cause of truth to pretend that any great degree of certainty attaches to any of the various dates that have been proposed.

6. Author. Despite the evidences that the book is a composite, as were most literary productions of the ancient Near East, still there must have been a single personality who gave to the work the high literary quality which characterizes it. This person will doubtless remain anonymous, like the author of the poems of the latter half of the book of Isaiah, and we can know him only through his work. That he was a poet of rare genius cannot be doubted, for the book has been hailed by men of letters as the greatest, or one of the greatest, of the masterpieces of world literature. The author of the Dialogue was a deeply religious soul, sensitive to the suffering of humanity at large and especially to that of particular and exceptional individuals. He himself must have suffered greatly—if not in his own flesh, at least in his mind—out of empathy and sympathy for others. Some have felt that he could not have written as he did without having himself experienced intense and prolonged suffering. The depth and the earnestness of the author's thought and feeling, the keenness of his insight into human nature, the vivid beauty of his expression, as well as the universal human concern with the problem of pain, gives the work a quality of realism and a power to stir the human soul in all times and places. The influence of the biblical book on modern literature has been profound, as seen pre-eminently in Goethe's *Faust* and Byron's *Manfred*.

That the author was an Israelite is not entirely certain. Parts of the book may indicate familiarity with the prophetic and wisdom literature of the OT. Job's complaint recalls some of the psalms of lamentation, such as 38; 88; 102, but this type of lamentation literature was common in the ancient Near East. Some of the figures and metaphors comport with a Palestinian background, but there is little that is definite or distinctive to fix the locale. The author may have traveled widely. He appears to have been especially familiar with Egypt. The many allusions to mythological motifs now partially known from Mesopotamian and Syrian (Ugaritic) sources show that he was well versed in the lore of the ancient Near East. It is certain that he belonged to the intellectual elite of his time. Then, as now, ideas were not confined by geographical and political boundaries. "Wisdom," accordingly, had a cosmopolitan, international flavor.

7. Background and parallels. The recovery of the literatures of the ancient Near East, of Egypt, Mesopotamia, Syria, and Anatolia, has shed much light on the OT. It is no longer possible to study the OT in isolation from the larger world in which it originated. Wisdom literature of the OT in particular has so much in common with similar literatures of Egypt and Mesopotamia that international influence appears likely.

The problem faced by the book of Job especially exercised the Egyptian and Mesopotamian sages and scribes. From the early second millennium B.C. there is an Egyptian text in which a man debates with his soul the expedient of suicide when life has become unbearable. Like Job, the weary sufferer welcomes death as release from life's miseries. There are a number of ideological and phraseological parallels with Job, but hardly enough to indicate direct connection.

Another Egyptian text from the early second millennium, "The Tale of the Eloquent Peasant," has a literary form similar to that of Job. A prose prologue and epilogue introduce and conclude the text, while the central portion consists of nine semipoetic appeals for justice by the peasant. The wronged peasant appeals to the chief steward for redress, and the chief steward answers him. At first the peasant is polite, but as his appeals for justice are denied, he becomes more vehement and accuses the chief steward of injustice. He even threatens to appeal to Anubis, the god of the dead. When it looks as if the peasant will suffer death for his boldness in insisting on justice, he welcomes the prospect, as a thirsty man goes for water, or a nursing child for milk. But justice triumphs, and the persistent peasant is rewarded with the property of the one who has robbed him. While the issue here is social justice, and the peasant's complaint is against his fellow man, the plaintiff's attitude resembles that of Job.

From Mesopotamia we have numerous psalms and lamentations which deal with the problem of suffering. The best known is the text "I Will Praise the Lord of Wisdom," sometimes called the Poem of the Righteous Sufferer, or the Babylonian Job. It is, as the title suggests, a psalm of thanksgiving. The hero of the poem, stricken by disease, seeks to know the cause of his misfortune. He consults the gods, but receives no answer. He cannot believe that his distress is the result of sin, for he has been punctilious in the cult observances, and he recounts his pious acts. He concludes that the way of the gods is inscrutable, never to be understood by mortal man. He gives a long and gruesome description of the symptoms of his disease, which leaves him prostrate and wallowing in his own excrement. All attempts to compass and exorcise the disease fail. Death is expected momentarily. But the god Marduk brings about his healing, and the poem concludes with a hymn of thanksgiving and praise to Marduk.

This poem has many contacts with Job. In both, a man of high position, who has had a long and prosperous life, is suddenly reduced to misery. Both victims protest their innocence and impugn divine justice. Both give long descriptions of their afflictions and contrast their lot with their deserts. Both are finally restored to health. There are, however, marked dissimilarities. The settings and personal names are entirely different. The literary forms differ. The Akkadian poem, as much as is preserved, is entirely poetic monologue, without prose prologue or epilogue. The attitudes of the sufferers also differ somewhat. Job stresses his ethical probity, and Yahweh vouches for his innocence. The Babylonian sufferer emphasizes his ritual acts, but is prepared to entertain the idea that he may have committed some sin unwittingly. While the author of Job may have been familiar with the Akkadian poem, there is no evidence of direct literary dependence.

Another Akkadian text, which has been called the Babylonian Ecclesiastes, also has affinities with Job. It is a dialogue about human misery and divine justice, between a victim of suffering and a group of friends. The poem consisted originally of twenty-seven stanzas of eleven lines each. The lines of each stanza begin with the same syllable, and the acrostic of the twenty-seven syllables spells out the sentence "I, *Shagil-kinam-ubbib,* the conjurer, worship god and king." The very name of the sufferer, *Shagil-kinam-ubbib,* "O E sagil [i.e., Marduk's temple], declare the righteous one pure," expresses the hope for vindication. The pious sentiment of the acrostic, however, hardly agrees with the attitude of the sufferer in the dialogue. Perhaps the author wished to affirm his orthodoxy, in spite of the seeming skepticism. The sufferer begins the dialogue and answers each of his friends in turn—i.e., the sufferer speaks in the odd-numbered stanzas and the interlocutors in the even-numbered ones.

The sufferer appeals to his learned friends to hear and consider his tale of woe. Trouble began with his birth. Both his parents were snatched away, leaving him without a guardian. A friend agrees that this is a sad story, but the sufferer's attitude is self-conceited and impious. Whoever reveres the gods prospers. The sufferer responds with a description of his condition which belies the doctrine of retribution. The reply (stanza 4) is poorly preserved, but the recommended remedy is prayer, which will bring pardon. The sufferer protests that he has prayed and fulfilled all ritual requirements. The friend answers with sarcastic praise of the sufferer's great wisdom. He appeals to the world of nature, where the violent and predatory, the wild ass and the lion, eventually get their due, the arrow and the pit. The rich young upstart, too, the ruler burns along with his wealth. Why follow their path? Instead, seek divine favor. The sufferer characterizes such talk as mere wind (cf. Job 12:2). From childhood he has sought the will of the gods and has received only misfortune as his reward. The friend charges that the sufferer has rejected the truth and despised the divine ordinances. Thus the argument goes back and forth with no progress toward agreement, as with Job and his friends. In the last stanza the sufferer pleads for the mercy and understanding of his friends. He cites his humble conduct in the past. Finally he addresses a plea for mercy to the god Ninurta, the goddess Ishtar, and the king. The conclusion of the poem is not known, but we may assume that the appeal to the gods brought a change in the sufferer's lot.

The parallels between this document and the biblical books of Job and Ecclesiastes are numerous. In some cases the similarity is phraseological as well as ideological. The differences also are notable. The eleven-line stanzas of the Akkadian poem stand in sharp contrast with the long speeches of the book of Job. It is possible that the author of Job was familiar with this Akkadian poem. The extant tablets date from the seventh century B.C., but the original composition was probably some centuries earlier. Still there is no evidence of direct influence.

Another Akkadian poem, called "A Pessimistic Dialogue Between Master and Servant," relates to a concern of the book of Job, the seeming meaninglessness of life. The master summons the slave and proposes to engage in various endeavors. For each proposal the slave expresses enthusiastic approval and lauds the activity as pleasurable or profitable. Each time the master rejects the idea of pursuing the projected activity, and the obliging servant agrees and shows that it is, after all, a bootless endeavor. All aspects of human activity—the pursuit of pleasure, political power, wealth, the love of women, worship of the gods, charity, service to one's country—are shown to be futile and void of satisfaction. What then is good? The servant suggests that to break one's neck and plunge into the river is (the only) good. The master proposes to kill the servant and send him on ahead. The servant replies: "Would/could my lord live three days after me?" Whether the servant means that the master could not survive without someone to look after him, or that he would not care to prolong a life void of purpose, the pessimism, cynicism, and skepticism current in effete Mesopotamian society are vividly illustrated. While this document has more affinities with Ecclesiastes than with Job, since the victim suffers from ennui rather than physical pain, they all have in common a spirit of rebellion at the seeming futility of human existence.

A Sumerian poem which bears closer relation to the Job motif than any of the Mesopotamian documents previously known has been recovered from fragments excavated at Nippur. The original composition probably dates from the beginning of the second millennium B.C. The poem deals with the case of an unnamed man who had been healthy, wealthy, and wise, but suddenly was seized with severe illness and pain. The sufferer laments his bitter fate, but instead of railing against his god, he confesses his guilt, and the god answers the man's prayer and delivers him from affliction.

The similarities and the differences between the Sumerian poem and the book of Job are very considerable. In the Sumerian world view, evil was integral to the cosmic order. Basic to their theology and ethics was the doctrine that man's afflictions result from sin. The problem of justice was thus not so acute for them, since all men are sinful. In all cases of human suffering, it is man who is to blame and never the gods. When adversity strikes, there is nothing a man can do but praise his god and lament and plead until the god relents and hearkens to his prayer. This view is virtually identical with that espoused by Job's friends. For the Sumerians, the god with whom the man must remonstrate is his own personal god, who acts as intermediary with the major gods on behalf of his client and intercedes for him in the assembly of the gods, where men are judged and their fates decided. The Sumerian concept of a personal god may be behind Job's appeals to or for an umpire, witness, vindicator (9:33; 16:19, 21; 19:25-27), who will plead his case in the celestial court. A notable difference between the Sumerian poem and the book of Job is that the Sumerian sufferer assumes and admits his guilt all the way, while Job is declared guiltless from the beginning and protests his innocence throughout the Dialogue. In the end, however, Job is brought to the attitude with which the Sumerian sufferer began, to acquiescence before the overwhelming power and inscrutable will of the gods.

As early as the second millennium, both in Egypt and in Mesopotamia, there were literary compositions which dealt with the same concern as the book of Job and in form and content exhibited features characteristic of the biblical book. That these works, directly or indirectly, contributed to the biblical masterpiece, appears ever more probable as new materials such as the Sumerian Job are added. Even if the author of Job did not know these works at first hand, they created a literary, poetic, and religious background to his work.

In the lore of India the story of Hariscandra is parallel to the theme of Job. The story is first told in the Mārkandeya Purāna. At an assembly of the god Indra there arose a discussion as to whether a perfectly righteous man existed on earth. Most of the gods thought not. The god Vasishta nominated a certain king, Hariscandra, for this distinction, but the god Shiva expressed doubt that this person would bear testing. A wager on this issue was made between Vasishta and Shiva, and the latter then brought a series of misfortunes on Hariscandra. The monarch was deprived of his wealth, his kingdom, his wife, and his only son, but through it all he preserved his rectitude and in the end was restored to his former estate and rewarded. The possibility of direct interdependence between the Hebrew and Indian stories is remote.

In Greek literature the mystery of suffering is a prominent theme. The concept of fate, Moira, apparently came down to the Greeks from the warring Myceneans. Fatalism seems to develop inevitably among peoples inured to war. Man's share in life is like his ration of food or booty. He must take what he gets, without grumbling. To demand or take more than one's due is insubordination, or *hubris*. The belief in gods who interfere in the life of men eventually came into conflict with the idea of fatalism. Good fortune a man does not question, but misfortune sets one to thinking. When a righteous man is struck down by calamity, the problem is inescapable. The Greeks, however, had little to offer by way of a solution. Their fatalistic response is summed up in the maxim of the Delphic Apollo, "Know thyself"—i.e., be mindful of the insurmountable barrier between man and the gods. Another famous maxim, "Nothing in excess," reflects the same attitude, that a man must not attempt to arrogate to himself more than his share in life. To do so is *hubris,* the froward attempt to emulate the gods. This is certain to incite nemesis, the revenge of the jealous gods. The safest thing for man is to keep his place in all humility and never risk the ire of the gods. Man's *hubris,* overweening transgression of the bounds, and the consequent retaliation by the gods, nemesis, is the common theme of the Greek tragedies. The divine order always prevails over man's self-destructive heroism.

The tragedies of Aeschylus, Sophocles, and Euripides have much in common with the Dialogue of the book of Job, for the tragedy is above all a lament. Of all the Greek tragedies, Aeschylus' *Prometheus Bound* bears closest resemblance to Job.

Chained to a rock by Zeus as punishment for having brought mortals the gift of fire, he protests the injustice in terms reminiscent of Job. His sympathizers, the nymphs and Oceanus, beg him to confess his error and submit, much as Job's friends counseled. But Prometheus refuses; it is Zeus who must relent. When the earth opens and he plunges into fresh tortures in the nether world, Prometheus disappears with a cry: "See the injustice of my fate." Prometheus makes the same sort of accusation as Job, expresses the same wistful longing, asserts his righteousness, but there are important differences. Prometheus is an immortal Titan. There is no mystery in his suffering, for he knows Zeus to be unjust, vengeful, savage, relentless, and unpredictable. Prometheus receives sympathy from his friends, while Job is condemned by his. But Job at last, though rebuked by God for what the Greeks would have considered *hubris,* is vindicated also by God, whom he finds to be, not the tyrant his tortures had led him to think, but the source of all power and wisdom, and even justice.

Though the major Greek tragedies bear evident similarities to Job, not only in literary form but also in content, and above all in depth of sorrow for the human predicament, there is no indication of direct interdependence.

The Greeks' logic and sense of justice forced them ultimately to the conclusion that since wrongs are not always righted in this life, they must be in the afterlife. To Plato, in particular, we are indebted for the refinement of this idea, which has had a tremendous influence on the thought of later ages. The punishments of the afterlife are not entirely for retaliation or revenge, but for the purpose of purifying the sinner. Job's questioning led him to the very brink of this solution, but he withdrew without making the leap. Elihu suggested that the sufferings of this life may be intended for discipline. Neither of these "answers" is wholly satisfying to the one who has to endure suffering here and now.

The author of Job could have derived much of his material and literary forms from other portions of the OT, or from the sources on which these other portions were based. The various literary genres found in Job—narrative, dialogue, hymn, lament, proverb, oracle—are well represented in the OT.

Although the narrative portion of Job has a patriarchal setting, it bears little resemblance to the patriarchal narratives of Genesis, which are rather epic saga. The folk tale of Job has more affinity with some of the stories of the book of Judges, and is perhaps closer to the book of Ruth than to any other OT narrative.

About half the book consists of poetry which belongs to the genre of hymns and individual lamentations. Several beautiful hymns are components of the speeches of Job (e.g., 9:4-12; 12:13-25; 26:5-14), and a few bits and pieces in the speeches of the friends (e.g., 5:9-16; 11:7-11; 25:2-6; 34:18-30). Among the hymns in the Psalter, Ps. 104 has many striking contacts with Job (cf., e.g., Ps. 104:6-9 with Job 38: 8-11; Ps. 104:21, 27, with Job 38:39-41; Ps. 104:30 with Job 12:10; Ps. 104:32 with Job 9:5; 26: 11). Ps. 104 appears to have been strongly influenced by Akh-en-Aton's Hymn to the Aton, the sun disk. This beautiful Egyptian hymn of the fourteenth century B.C. may have been known internationally among scribes and sages.

A considerable part of Job's discourses are to be classed as laments (3:3-26; 6:2–7:21; 9:25–10:22; 13: 23–14:22; 16:6–17:9; 19:7-20; 23; 29:1–31:37). This literary genre had its prototype in Mesopotamia in the elegiac complaint of the sick or the persecuted. The lament is not a mere rhetorical exercise. The sufferer's woes are described with stark realism and in gruesome detail to excite divine pity and to attain healing or deliverance. The victim pins his hopes on the discourse, by which he expects to convince the offended god or gods of his innocence or penitence. The lament is thus a sort of liturgy of healing and exorcism, a purgation by poetry or catharsis by canticle. The author of Job exploited this literary genre to the full. He may have been familiar with it either from Mesopotamian sources or from Hebrew literature, since some of the biblical psalms, or parts of psalms (e.g., 22:2-19; 38; 88) belong to this genre.

There are a number of dialogues in the OT. Abraham's negotiations with Ephron the Hittite (Gen. 23: 3-16) are a model of tactful bargaining. His intercession with Yahweh (Gen. 18:22-32) resembles the prophetic intercessions of Amos (7:1-9; 8:1-3). The divine call of the lawgiver and the prophets is in the form of a dialogue (Exod. 3:2–4:17; Isa. 6; Jer. 1:1-10). The author of Job had these and many other dialogues to serve as models, but he went far beyond anything else in the OT in developing and expanding the poetic dialogue around a single theme.

Scattered in the book of Job are bits and pieces of proverbial wisdom of the sort found also in other OT wisdom literature, both canonical and apocryphal (e.g., 4:8-11; 5:1-7; 8:11-19; 12:11-12; 14:1-2). The latter part of Eliphaz' second speech (15:17-35) is largely made up of proverbial utterances. Here and there in the book are obscure sayings which seem to have little or no connection with the context and may be misplaced or mangled proverbs. In Job 11:12, e.g., is a delightfully intriguing saying:

> A stupid man will get understanding,
> when a wild ass's colt is born a man.

The sense of the Hebrew, however, is obscure, and many critics emend the text. The RSV rendering is perhaps the best sense that can be read into the text without emendation. Proverbs are often very difficult to interpret. Although there are many proverbs and wise sayings in Job, the work as a whole can scarcely be classed as wisdom literature. Most of the contacts with wisdom-type literature occur in the speeches of the friends. Job's vehement protest against their point of view makes the book, as it were, anti-wisdom literature.

8. Content. The book of Job consists of five parts: (*a*) a prologue in prose (chs. 1–2); (*b*) the Dialogue, or Symposium (chs. 3–31); (*c*) the Elihu speeches (chs. 32–37); (*d*) the theophany and speeches of Yahweh (38–42:6); (*e*) an epilogue in prose (42:7-17).

a. The Prologue. The Prologue presents a man named Job, famous for his rectitude and piety, wealthy, with a large and happy family, solicitous for the propriety of his children's conduct (1:1-5). At a meeting of the celestial court, Yahweh asks the Satan specifically about his observation of Job, and the

Satan questions whether Job's piety and rectitude are purely disinterested. He suggests that if Job were bereft of his possessions, he would curse Yahweh to his face. Yahweh accepts the wager and gives the Satan leave to test Job (vss. 6-12). The Satan proceeds to have Job robbed of all his wealth, even his children, but Job accepts the blow with resignation and blesses the name of Yahweh (vss. 13-22). The Satan, chided by Yahweh, proposes more drastic measures and is given permission to do anything short of taking Job's life (2:1-6). Job, stricken with a loathsome and painful skin disease, sits among the ashes and scrapes his sores with a potsherd. His wife urges him to curse God and die, but he rebukes her and accepts his evil state as also coming from God, whom he refuses to criticize (vss. 7-10). Three friends hear of his misfortunes and come to condole him. Appalled at his condition, they sit with him seven days in silent grief (vss. 11-13).

b. The Dialogue. Job speaks out in bitter complaint, curses his life, wishes he had died at birth, wonders why life is given to the wretched when death would be welcome release (ch. 3).

Now begins the Dialogue, which consists of three cycles of six speeches, a speech by each of the three "comforters" and a direct reply by Job to each in turn. (The third cycle, however, is incomplete and garbled.)

Eliphaz leads off cautiously and apologetically, but quickly turns to criticism of Job for faltering in the face of adversity (4:1-6). He affirms divine justice (vss. 7-11), relates a vision in which it was revealed that mortal man cannot be just before God (4:12–5:7), and advises Job to turn to God who is powerful and just and who will, after chastening Job, deliver him from adversity and restore him to a rich and full life (5:8-27).

Job replies that the intensity of his suffering is ample justification for the bitterness of his complaint (6:1-7), and he pleads again for death as release from pain (vss. 8-13). He charges that his friends have disappointed him and failed to give him moral support (vss. 14-23). He challenges them to prove that he has merited such misfortune (vss. 24-30). Human life is hard at best, and in his case sheer agony, with no hope but the grave. So he will speak out in bitter complaint (7:1-11). Why will not God simply leave him alone, give him a moment's respite before he lies down in the dust (vss. 12-21)?

Bildad characterizes Job's speech as so much wind. He asserts God's justice, hints that Job's children merely got what they deserved, and suggests that if Job would only turn to God, he might be restored (8:1-8). He appeals to history to prove that the wicked get short shrift, that God always rewards and punishes (vss. 9-20), and that hence Job may be assured of justice (vss. 21-22).

In reply Job admits that man cannot be just before God (9:1-4), for God puts the issue on the basis of power rather than justice, and man cannot argue with him (vss. 5-21). God destroys the innocent and guilty alike, mocks at the innocent, gives control of the world to the wicked (vss. 22-24). Life is short and painful. Why struggle in vain, when one can hope only for condemnation (vss. 27-31)? He asks for an arbiter to ensure fairness and allow him to speak without fear (vss. 32-35). Since he is tired of life, he will speak out and ask God why he oppresses. Can God see with man's eyes and share man's limitations? Why does he persecute (10:1-7)? Man is only clay, flesh and bone (vss. 8-12). Why pursue him like a hunted beast (vss. 13-17)? Why give him life at all? Why not leave him to live out his brief span in peace before he descends to the dismal nether world (vss. 18-22)?

Zophar accuses Job of boasting of his innocence to silence men, but God could show him his guilt (11:1-5). God's wisdom and power are beyond human comprehension (vss. 6-12). Job ought to change his attitude and appeal to God, who will restore him (vss. 13-19). The wicked will receive their due (vs. 20).

Job answers with sarcastic praise of his friends' wisdom. He is not inferior to them (12:1-3). He points to his own misery and to the prosperity of the wicked (vss. 4-6). Even the beasts, the birds, the earth, and fishes know that God is in control, with all his wisdom and power (vss. 7-25). All this Job knows as well as they (13:1-2). They are lying to defend God (vss. 3-12). He is willing to stake his life on a direct argument with God. He asks only that God give him a hearing and not resort to force and terror; that he make specific indictment of his transgressions (vss. 13-23). God, instead, persecutes him (vss. 24-28). Man's life is short and troublesome. Why does not God let him have some rest (14:1-6)? There is no hope of afterlife (vss. 7-12). If only there were, he would be content to wait (vss. 13-15). There is nothing to look for but extinction (vss. 18-22).

Eliphaz begins the second cycle by characterizing Job's speech as hot air, vain and impious talk (15:1-5). Job's own mouth convicts him (vs. 6). Does he think he is the first man ever born? Does he eavesdrop on the divine council, or have a monopoly on wisdom (vss. 7-8)? Does he know any more than they (vss. 9-10)? What right has he to berate God (vss. 11-13)? No man is clean before God (vss. 14-16). The wisdom of the ages is that the wicked always suffer (vss. 17-35).

Job answers that he has heard all this flatulent nonsense before (16:1-3). If the tables were turned, he could serve them the same verbiage (vss. 4-5). He turns again to God with bitter complaint for the vicious and unwarranted assault on him (vss. 6-17). He cries out for vindication. There must be a witness in heaven who will serve as an arbiter for him with God, as a man mediates between friends (vss. 18-22). His life is coming to an end in mockery, with no support from God (17:1-3) or his friends (vss. 4-12). His only hope is the maggot in the grave (vss. 13-16).

Bildad objects to being called stupid, and deprecates Job's histrionic agonizing (18:1-4). He paints a dark picture of the woes of the wicked (vss. 5-21).

Job rebukes his "friends" for their harsh judgment of him (19:1-6). It is God who has afflicted him unjustly (vss. 6-12). His family, friends, servants, wife, are all alienated; urchins and friends alike abhor him (vss. 13-19). His body is emaciated (vs. 20). He cries out for pity from "friends" who persecute him like God (vss. 21-22). He appeals to the future and asserts faith in ultimate vindication before God, even though he himself die (vss. 23-27). His friends had best be warned against persecuting him (vss. 28-29).

Zophar is deeply agitated (20:1-3). The seeming triumph of the wicked, he declares, is only momentary. No matter how high they rise, they become like dung, they pass away like a dream, etc., etc. (vss. 4-29).

Job requests close attention to his words. He feels he has some ground for impatience. He invites them just to look at him and be horrified, as he is horrified (21:1-6). He refutes the claim of the friends by pointing to the continued prosperity of the wicked (vss. 7-18). The reply that God takes it out on the wicked man's children is unacceptable (vss. 19-21). Death comes to all men alike, without regard to the life they lead. The wicked escape calamity and go peacefully to the grave (vss. 22-33). The "comfort" of the friends is vain and their arguments groundless (vs. 34).

Eliphaz, in his third speech, asserts that God receives no benefit from human virtue (22:1-3). It could hardly be for piety that Job is being judged (vs. 4). Hence it must be that Job's wickedness is very great. He proceeds then to charge Job with oppression of the poor, the widow, and the orphan. This is the cause of his calamity. He thought God would not see his misdeeds, and disaster inevitably followed (vss. 5-20). Return to God, however, will bring restoration of good fortune (vss. 21-30).

Job continues in his extremity to search for God, so that he may come into court with him (23:1-7). But he cannot find him (vss. 8-9). God knows Job is innocent (vss. 10-12), but he does as he pleases and uses terror against him (vss. 13-17). God's purposes are hidden and even the pious cannot know them. Violence and oppression are rampant (24:1-17). (Vss. 18-24 are corrupt and probably belong in the mouth of one of the friends rather than of Job.) No one could deny these facts (vs. 25).

Chs. 24–27 are thoroughly scrambled. Bildad's third speech is short and out of keeping with his previous utterances. Job's reply consists of the very ideas he has been so vigorously opposing. Zophar's third speech is missing altogether. The following rearrangement makes tolerably consistent sense:

Bildad's third speech (25:1; 27:7-10, 16-23), as reconstituted, declares that wealth will not save the wicked from punishment.

Job's reply (26:1-4; 27:11-12; 25:2-6; 26:5-14) consists mainly of description of God's power.

Zophar's missing speech (27:13; 24:21-24, 18-20; 27:14-15) reaffirms the certainty of the punishment of the wicked.

Ch. 28 is an entirely extraneous poem on the value of wisdom and its complete inaccessibility to man, except through piety.

Job's final speech in the Dialogue reaffirms his innocence (27:1-6) and gives a nostalgic review of his former blessed estate when he was under divine favor, happy, prosperous, respected, praised as a benefactor of the poor, a champion of justice, who confidently looked forward to a long and happy life (ch. 29), as contrasted with his present misery, derided by young upstarts, spit on by the dregs of society, racked by a painful and loathsome disease (ch. 30). Job now makes a series of negative confessions with horrible self-imprecations if ever he committed such wrongs as to lust after a maiden; attain wealth by injustice; commit adultery; mistreat his slaves, withhold charity from the poor, the widow, the orphan; put his trust in riches; worship the sun and moon; rejoice at his enemies' misfortune; put a stranger into the street; or abuse his land and tenants. Here Job rests his case, affixes his signature (31:35-37 should be transposed after vs. 40*a*), and challenges God to answer him (ch. 31).

c. The Elihu speeches. A young man named Elihu, having listened to the argument, angry because of Job's self-righteousness and the failure of the three friends to confute him, intervenes (32:1-5).

First Elihu makes a long apology for his intervention, for his youth and seeming brashness in venturing to lecture his elders, but since wisdom is a divine gift and not necessarily a concomitant of old age, and since his elders have failed to answer Job, he will now speak his piece. He is bursting with words and must give them outlet. He will speak frankly and without flattery (32:6-22). He now turns to Job and assures him that he, Elihu, is only a man, and not God, and the two of them can argue on equal terms (33:1-7). He summarizes Job's argument: that he is innocent and yet God persecutes him and refuses to answer his complaint (vss. 8-13). But, argues Elihu, God does answer man in various ways, by dreams, or illness, to warn or chasten him (vss. 14-22). When some angel intervenes, man is restored to health and repents and is redeemed from death. Thus God redeems a man time and again (vss. 23-30). Unless Job has something to answer, he should keep quiet, and let Elihu lecture him further (vss. 31-33).

Elihu launches into a second discourse, in which he charges Job with blasphemy for questioning God's justice and maintaining that piety is of no consequence. God is just and rewards and punishes. Job in denying this adds rebellion to his sin (ch. 34).

Elihu goes on to a third speech. As for Job's assertion that sin or piety does not seem to matter either to man or to God, Elihu answers that God is too high to be affected by what a man does, but the man himself is affected for good or ill. If God ignores a plea, it is because he recognizes insincerity, and this is the case with Job (ch. 35).

In a final speech Elihu continues to defend God's justice. Even kings are not immune to divine reward and punishment. The sinner who repents prospers; otherwise he dies. Affliction may be the means of deliverance, and this could be so in Job's case. God is supreme and eternal, and his ways are beyond human comprehension. He makes the rain, the storms, thunder, lightning, snow. Can Job understand or do such things? The thunderstorm shows God's power, yet he is also just (chs. 36–37).

d. The speeches of Yahweh. Yahweh himself now answers from the whirlwind. Why does Job speak in ignorance? What does he know of the founding of the earth, the binding of the sea, the dawn of day, the depths of the nether world, the breadth of the earth, the abodes of light and darkness, the stores of snow and hail, the mystery of storms, the control of the constellations, the rain (38:1-38)? Can he provide food for the lion, the raven? Does he know the gestation period of wild goats or hinds, the habits of the wild ass? Can he domesticate the wild ox? What of the swift but stupid ostrich, the war horse, the hawk, the vulture (38:39–39:30)? Yahweh challenges Job to reply, but Job confesses his inadequacy and promises to say no more (40:1-6).

Again Yahweh challenges Job to show that he has power like his, and he, Yahweh, will admit that Job's own hand can save him (40:7-14). There follow two long poems describing Behemoth, the hippopotamus (vss. 15-24), and Leviathan, the crocodile (41—H 40: 26–41:34). Job acknowledges God's omnipotence and his own ignorance. Now that he has seen God for himself, he repents in dust and ashes (42:1-6, omitting vss. 3*a*, 4, as mistakenly copied from 38:2, 3*b;* 40:7*b*).

e. The Epilogue. In the Epilogue, Yahweh rebukes Eliphaz and his two friends for not having spoken rightly of him, as Job has done. He orders them to offer sacrifice and have Job pray for them, lest he, Yahweh, take reprisals against them for not having spoken rightly of him. Yahweh now restores Job's fortunes, giving him twice as much property as he had lost. His relatives all come to visit him and eat with him and give him condolences and gifts. Job has seven sons and three exceptionally beautiful daughters. After this he lives 140 years and sees grandchildren to the fourth generation. He dies in contented old age.

9. Literary form. The precise literary classification of the book of Job has been the subject of considerable discussion, more or less unprofitable. Until modern times, it was commonly taken as sober history, although Rabbi Resh Lakish opined that Job never existed and the story is simply a parable (Talmud, B.B. 15*a*). It cannot be taken as history, but there may have been a historical personage behind the story. It is, in a sense, a parable of any and every man who suffers without cause or without knowing the cause. Job is thus a type of the righteous in affliction. It has been suggested that Job really represents the nation Israel, like the Suffering Servant of the Lord. If the work was composed in the exilic or postexilic period, by a Jew, as many scholars believe, then it would be virtually impossible for the author to be unmindful of the parallel between the afflictions of the man and the nation. Yet there is not the slightest hint of national concern in the work. It is hardly likely that the narrator would have chosen a descendant of Esau as the symbol of Jacob!

Already in the fourth century Theodore of Mopsuestia held that Job was modeled on the Greek dramas. Theodore Beza regarded the book as a tragedy, Milton as an epic. It has been compared with the Homeric epics, with which it has very little in common, and with the tragic dramas of Aeschylus, Sophocles, and Euripides. It has been argued that the book has the form of a Greek tragedy, including the chorus and the denouement by the *deus ex machina.* The dialogues of Plato have been compared, but there is no similarity whatever between these brief prose conversations, with their precise, analytical argument, and the long poetic speeches of the Job Dialogue. "Dialogue," indeed, is not a very apt term for lengthy speeches of the book of Job. Actually no general classification suits the book. It has features that partake of all the various literary forms that have been ascribed to it, but it is not to be classed with any one of them, for it is neither exclusively lyric, epic, dramatic, or didactic. The book is *sui generis,* and no single term or combination of terms that has been proposed does justice to the scope of the work.

10. Unity and integrity. A mere summary of the book's contents inevitably raises the question of its unity and integrity, for its parts are seemingly inconsistent and incongruous, and the plan and structure of the whole seems illogical and haphazard.

The major problem is posed by the incongruities between the prose introduction and conclusion and the poetic Dialogue. The Prologue presents the traditional pious and patient Job, who through all the misfortune visited on him maintains his integrity and continues to bless Yahweh. The Epilogue brings divine rebuke on the friends for having spoken falsely, and commendation of Job for having spoken the truth about Yahweh. The Dialogue, however, confronts us with an altogether different Job, whose bitter complaints and accusations against God shock the pious friends, who steadfastly defend divine justice in the world. The Prologue has a detached and impersonal, almost ironical attitude toward the ghastly experiment to see just how much Job will endure. The Dialogue, on the other hand, is charged with the anguish of the tormented victim. The Epilogue presents a patently artificial vindication of divine retribution, with a hundred per cent bonus for Job's pains, although the Job of the Dialogue has shown that one cannot count on treatment of this sort in real life. In the prose narrative Job is scrupulous in observance of the sacrificial cultus, while in the Dialogue there is no mention of such concerns, and in his final apology for his life (ch. 31) he makes no plea on this score. Even the designations of deity differ in the prose and the poetic portions; the prose uses the name Yahweh, and the poetry uses El, Eloah, Elohim, and Shaddai. For these and other reasons, critics very early cast suspicion on the Prologue and the Epilogue as editorial additions and rejected one or the other or both. The originality of the episodes featuring the Satan (1:6-12; 2:1-7*a*) has been particularly suspect, because the Satan is absent in the rest of the book, even in the Epilogue. Some critics have maintained that the author of the poetic Dialogue also composed the prose setting for his work. The view now generally held, however, is that the poet adopted and adapted an ancient folk tale as the frame for his work. Whether the folk tale was transmitted orally, or whether it had long been committed to writing, it had apparently achieved a relatively fixed form and content, which the poet could alter but little. The legendary Job had become a type of the ideal righteous man, like Noah and Daniel (Ezek. 14:14, 20). Job may also have been the type of the innocent sufferer, like the anonymous victim of the Sumerian poetic essay of *ca.* 2000 B.C. recovered among the fragments from Nippur (*see above*). What modifications were made in the ancient story we do not know. Perhaps the poet introduced the visit of the three friends to connect the Dialogue with the prose story. The divine censure of the friends' views and the praise of Job's in the Epilogue (42:7-8) is hardly compatible with the blasphemous tirades of the Job of the Dialogue and the rigidly righteous views of the friends. It may be that the older prose tale, which now has the middle cut out, included an episode in which the friends urged Job, as his wife had done, to curse God and die. It may also be that the censure of the friends and praise of Job was added in a futile attempt to harmonize the Job of the Prologue with the Job of the Dialogue.

In spite of the modifications to which the folk tale may have been subjected, it preserves the flavor and the charm of an oft-told classic.

Few critics have questioned the basic unity of the Dialogue (chs. 3–31). In spite of textual and exegetical problems, there is an organic cohesion, a unity of style and language, and a consistency in the opposing viewpoints which bears the mark of a single mind. This is not to say that the Dialogue has not been subjected to alterations by well-meaning meddlers. In the speeches of Job especially, there appear to have been attempts to tone down the shocking charges against God or to alter or deliberately obscure the sense. The Masoretes on occasion contributed to this end by imposing a vocalization which changes the sense indicated by the context. The most serious tampering with the text has been in chs. 24–27, where the order is clearly disturbed and the text of some passages has apparently been doctored (*see* § 8*b above*). Bildad's third speech is quite short (ch. 25), and Zophar's is entirely missing, while Job, surprisingly, expresses the very views hitherto espoused by the friends and vehemently denied by him. Some critics have regarded this as merely an accident in the transmission of the MS, but others have considered it a deliberate juggling of the text to bring Job around to acceptance of the "orthodox" view of retribution. Few scholars have accepted the present order and state of the text of chs. 24–27 as original. The various combinations of transpositions that have been proposed are too numerous to mention. The rearrangement suggested above in the summary of the book's content seems simplest and most satisfactory.

The poem on wisdom (ch. 28) is recognized as out of place by nearly all critics. The case for its logical connection with its surroundings is difficult to support. The admission that wisdom, the secrets of the universe and of divine providence, are inaccessible to man is hardly compatible with Job's desire to cross-examine God. The poem has marked affinities with the speeches of Yahweh (chs. 38–40), and it seems quite improper for the divine argument to be thus anticipated and pre-empted. The language and style of the poem, however, exhibit marked similarity to that of the rest of the Dialogue, and some scholars regard it as an independent composition of the author of the Dialogue, though not as an integral part of the book.

A small minority of interpreters have accepted the Elihu speeches (chs. 32–37) as authentic. Some have even held that here is found the climax of the work and the author's solution to the problem of suffering. Most critics, however, have regarded Elihu's diatribes as interpolated and of scant value either as literature or as a contribution to the argument. They could very well be dropped from the book without loss either to the content or to the literary structure. Their style is diffuse and prolix, even pompous. Almost half the volume of the four speeches is taken up with pretentious and irksome introduction. Resemblances in style and phraseology have been noted in the Elihu speeches and the Dialogue, but these are easily explained as imitation. The argument itself, for the most part, merely echoes what has already been said repeatedly by the three "friends." If Elihu has anything new to offer, it is the suggestion that suffering is disciplinary (33:14-33), but this has already been hinted by Eliphaz in his first speech (5:17). It seems likely that the author of the Elihu speeches, shocked, as he says, at Job's blasphemy and rebellion against God, disappointed at the inability of the friends to refute Job's arguments, but also, perhaps, chagrined at Yahweh's failure to speak directly to Job's challenge, ventured to inject himself into the dispute. He could not very well speak after Yahweh had spoken and silenced Job. He had to butt in before the theophany. His profuse apologies to the three friends may reflect more his qualms at presuming to speak before Yahweh than his deference to his elders. He anticipates the divine discourse (*ex eventu*) and supplements the weakness of its argument. He even sets the stage for the theophany by describing God's power in the storm (ch. 37). Perhaps the most telling reason for regarding the Elihu speeches as interpolations is the fact that they are not integrated into the work as a whole. In the distribution of praise and blame in the Epilogue, Elihu is completely ignored. It may be argued that the Satan is also ignored. But if Elihu's speeches were an original part of the Dialogue, and if the author put as much confidence in them as Elihu clearly does, they would surely have been acknowledged in the Epilogue.

Some scholars have rejected the speeches of Yahweh *in toto*. It is argued that they could not have been known to the author of the Elihu speeches, for he would not then have inserted his contribution. This argument has little force, as noted above, for it seems even less likely that the author of the Elihu speeches would have ventured to append his speech to that of Yahweh. Job's challenge: "Here is my signature! let the Almighty answer me!" (31:35*b*), calls for something more dramatic than the secondhand and third-rate tirades of Elihu. The situation demands some response from Yahweh. The first speech of Yahweh is widely hailed as a composition unsurpassed in world literature, an effort of the highest genius, transcending all other descriptions of the greatness of the Creator and the wonders of his creation. Scholars who reject the speech take a somewhat less appreciative view and see therein a brutal irony and diabolical contempt for man's predicament. While the authenticity of the first speech is generally accepted, that of the second is not. Still at least one eminent theologian regards the second speech of Yahweh as the high point of the book and perhaps a more original form of the divine reply than the first. After Job has been humbled and silenced (40:3-5), a second speech by Yahweh seems quite unnecessary and might well be considered nagging. The second speech, especially the long descriptions of the hippopotamus and the crocodile, is commonly considered spurious and inferior. (The description of the ostrich in the first speech [39:13-18] is missing in the LXX.) These nature poems, while very interesting, do seem a bit incongruous in the mouth of Yahweh, and many scholars reject them. Against the argument that a second speech by Yahweh, very much like the first, seems like nagging, it may be held that this is only pressing home the point. At the end of the first speech, Job is merely silenced (40:3-5), but with the second speech he becomes submissive and repentant (42:2, 3*b-c*, 6).

The Epilogue has been rejected by some critics, who point to the inconsistency and artificiality of Job's reward, which seems to prove the very doctrine he had refuted and to give the friends the last word. The fact, also, that Job is condemned in the divine speech and praised and rewarded in the Epilogue is often adduced as evidence of diverse authorship. This is admittedly a cogent objection. It must be considered, however, that the author was working here with prefabricated materials which he could not radically alter. It is certain that in the traditional tale the hero was in the end rewarded, as in the Sumerian and Akkadian prototypes. The author could not very well edit a well-known ending to suit his purposes, as might a modern scenario writer. Moreover, the contradiction is not explicit. While the doctrine of exact retribution may seem to be upheld by the reward, with a bonus, it is not defended as an unfailing principle. Yahweh's condemnation of Job in the speeches from the whirlwind was for presumption in passing judgment on matters beyond his comprehension. It was not on the grounds which the friends and Elihu had asserted. The condemnation of the friends in the Epilogue may indicate that in the ancient folk tale they, like Job's wife, urged him to curse God and die. It involves no contradiction to leave the rebuke of the friends in the Epilogue, for after the Dialogue it could be argued that they merited divine rebuke for asserting a lie in order to defend God. Thus the seeming contradictions may be reconciled. As for Job's restoration and reward, it would make little sense to leave him in his misery after he had been vindicated.

Except for the Elihu speeches, the book of Job has an over-all organic unity. Even the Elihu speeches, while not adding a great deal, do not seriously disturb the integrity of the book; if they are interpolated, the process was performed with considerable skill.

11. Purpose and teaching. The purpose of the book of Job has commonly been supposed to give an answer to the problem of evil, especially of undeserved suffering. The case of our hero, a man of exemplary piety, suddenly overwhelmed with misfortune and disease, poses the problem in the most acute fashion: How can these and like injustices be reconciled with divine justice? If the purpose of the book is to "solve" this problem, it must be admitted to be a conspicuous failure. The problem remains the most difficult and crucial for theology, and all attempts at a rational solution have fallen short of satisfaction, as Immanuel Kant demonstrated in his monograph *On the Failure of All Philosophical Attempts in Theodicy*. This problem is certainly the focal point of discussion in the book, especially in the Dialogue and the Elihu speeches. Several answers or attitudes are suggested. The question is which, if any, of the various answers was intended as definitive.

The explanation offered in the Prologue is that Job's sufferings were imposed, at the behest of the Satan, to test the genuineness of Job's piety. The three friends in the Dialogue argue that God is just, in spite of any and all appearances to the contrary, and that he rewards and punishes: therefore, Job must have sinned and merited his misery. This Job strenuously denies, arguing that justice is frequently abortive in the world and that God alone must be responsible: hence God is unjust. Elihu holds, with the friends, that God is just, and he suggests that suffering may be to warn and to discipline a man. Yahweh from the whirlwind ignores the question entirely (but see 40:8), points to his power in nature, and brings home to Job his ignorance and insignificance. None of these answers or attitudes can be deemed adequate, if the purpose is to justify the ways of God to man.

The intent of the book has been taken by a number of scholars to be the refutation of the doctrine expounded by the friends, that righteousness brings prosperity and wickedness misfortune in this life—the doctrine of exact retribution or terrestrial eschatology, as it has been called. This doctrine is often taught in the OT, especially with regard to the nations (e.g., Exod. 23:20 ff; Lev. 26; Deut. 28; Jer. 7:5-7), and is also applied to the individual (e.g., in the book of Proverbs, and in Pss. 1; 37; 49; 73; Isa. 58:6-14; Jer. 17:5-8). The doctrine may be quite comforting as long as one is healthy and prosperous. The three friends in the Dialogue stoutly and smugly maintain it. The pernicious aspect of the doctrine is that it carries the corollary that prosperity is a sure token of divine favor and suffering always a punishment for sin. This view has often been termed "orthodox," with the implication that it is the accepted, normative, and time-honored view of the OT. That the view was "orthodox" in some circles is quite clear, but to take it as normative for the OT is to ignore a great deal that contradicts it, apart from the book of Job. The stories of Abel, Uriah the Hittite, and Naboth were certainly not recounted to support the conclusion that they got what they deserved. The case of Jeremiah himself, who is credited, with Ezekiel, as responsible for the development of the doctrine of individual retribution (Jer. 31:30), shows that it does not hold true in every case (cf. 11:19; 12:1). That there is a measure of truth in the doctrine is obvious. Righteousness ought to be, and frequently is, rewarded with success and favor of man and God, and wickedness often overreaches itself and brings about its own merited destruction, but the attempt to make this an absolute rule goes against the hard facts of life. It ought to be so, but it certainly is not, as Job well argues and exemplifies. This view is thoroughly refuted by Job, but the Prologue of the book had already taken the ground from under the friends by assuring us that Job was quite innocent.

The mode of thought of the friends, though discredited, persisted even in later times and was confuted again by Jesus (Luke 13:1-5; John 9:2). It persists even today, because it answers the urgent need to reduce the complexities of life to a simple formula. It was hardly the whole purpose of the author of Job merely to refute a manifestly fallacious view, although it must be admitted that a large part of the book is spent in doing just this.

Some scholars have found the problem of theodicy

resolved in advance in the Prologue. Here the reader is taken behind the scenes into the celestial council and made privy to the plot. It is Yahweh himself who initiates the action by calling attention to Job. The Satan is a mere agent of Yahweh, and it is Yahweh's will that is carried out. He gives the Satan permission to work on Job and sets the limits of the experiment. The purpose is to prove to angels and men that disinterested piety is possible, that Job can and does revere God for no hope of reward, but for himself. The victory is seen in Job's confession of unshakable trust: "The LORD gave, and the LORD has taken away; blessed be the name of the LORD" (1: 21); and: "Shall we receive good at the hand of God, and shall we not receive evil?" (2:10). This is viewed as moving toward the profoundest insight of the NT, the doctrine of the Cross, that innocent suffering serves some larger purpose of God. Helpful as this understanding may be, it derives more from the hindsight of Christian faith and experience than from internal evidences of the purpose of the author. Still, in the assurance that Job's suffering was innocent, the author makes an important contribution to the problem. Job, of course, did not know that God reckoned him as righteous. Only his conscience and common sense told him there was nothing in his conduct to merit such punishment. Had he known the reason for his suffering, it would have been no test of his faith and would have no meaning for the man who must suffer without knowing why. In Job's case the issue at stake was more than the winning of an idle wager; it was the vindication of God's faith in man, as well as man's faith in God.

The Dialogue (chs. 3–31) offers no answer to the question of theodicy, except the negative result of the debate, which could have been decided after the first round. The friends assert God's justice, and Job shows that it does not hold in his and many other cases. It has been quite properly pointed out that the speeches are not really a dialogue in the sense of disputations designed to arrive at the truth, but they are like the speeches in a legal proceeding, in which each side has a predetermined point of view, which is asserted back and forth till one side gives up. This is seen as the explanation of Zophar's failure to take his last turn. This view also accords with the fact that there is no real progress in the argumentation, despite labored efforts to find some. The friends do grow more vehement and more outspoken in their indictment of Job, but their basic position remains unchanged. Job, however, appears to grow more calm toward the end. He has been groping toward some answer. He wants to argue the case with God rather than man, but he cannot find God or bring him into court. His vain appeal (9:33) for an umpire has been seen as a sort of prophetic witness to the necessity of a Christ, a being, at once man and God, who could effect reconciliation. This is an intriguing thought, but certainly oversteps the bounds of sober exegesis, since there is no hint that this umpire is, in any sense, conceived as a messianic figure. It is, however, quite possible that behind Job's appeal for a mediator lies the ancient Sumerian idea of a personal god, which each man relied on to present his cause to the greater gods in the divine assembly. Job also grasps at the hope of an afterlife, especially in ch. 14; but the idea is broached only to be rejected, and Job lapses into the standard attitude of resignation to the finality of death. It is often assumed that this, the hope of recompense in a future life, would be the answer to the problem. But this is not so. The prospect of future bliss may be of some consolation to one in agony, but it does not help to understand or bear the suffering of the present. Paul's belief in resurrection, which he held as a Pharisee and retained as a Christian, did not solve the problem of his suffering. He received the strength to endure, not from contemplating the consolation of the life beyond, but from his fellowship with Christ.

Job returns to the theme of the mediator as he appeals to a heavenly witness who would argue his case with God (16:19, 21). This witness is manifestly the person previously referred to as an umpire, for the verb which describes his action is a form of the same that designates the actor, the umpire (9:33). Job is using the terminology of the law court, and all he asks for is a fair trial, for the right to have a friendly witness or defense counsel.

The climax of Job's questing is commonly seen in the famous passage 19:25-27. Unfortunately, this is one of the most difficult passages in the book, for the ambiguities are compounded by a hopelessly corrupted text. Two interpretations are possible: either Job counts on vindication before his death, or hopes for it after death. Some scholars emend or interpret the text to remove all suggestion of an afterlife, and others emend or torture the passage to make the suggestion of afterlife more explicit. The latter interpretation has to lean on the Vulg. rather than the Hebrew. Jerome thought that Job here clearly prophesied the resurrection of the body, and he made this explicit in his translation, which has long dominated traditional Christian exegesis. Many critics, however, both ancient and modern, have thought that Job speaks of vindication before his death, as in other places he hopes for the visible triumph of his cause (13:15-16; 23:2-10) and the return to divine favor (ch. 29).

The immediate context of 19:25-27 has to be taken into account. Stricken by God, denied even the pity and support of his friends, Job wishes to leave for posterity a lasting memorial and protestation of his innocence, a document or an inscribed stela (vss. 20-24). From this thought he comes again to an appeal for personal help, for a living vindicator or redeemer who would defend his case, acquit him of guilt, and win God over to his side. The idea here is the same as that expressed previously in the appeal to an arbiter or umpire (9:33), or to a witness to testify on his behalf (16:19, 21). To see here a messianic figure is to press the metaphor too hard. There is also nothing to support the view that Job here surrenders all claim on God and places his trust in a sort of heavenly high priest. On the contrary, he is still protesting his innocence and calling for vindication. His acquittal must come, whether during his life or after he has turned to dust. Even if he dies without seeing it in the flesh, he sees it now in his mind's eye, or hopes to be conscious of it when it comes, even though it be too late.

While the solution to the problem has been seen in one or the other of the several parts of the book, the view of the majority of interpreters is that it is to be found, if anywhere, in the theophany, in the speeches of Yahweh from the whirlwind (chs. 38–42). There are, however, difficulties in this view. Job has refuted and repudiated the dogma espoused by his friends in the Dialogue and has challenged God to come forth and answer his charges. The challenge brings a direct response (if we may pass over Elihu's interruption), but Yahweh ignores the issue as Job had posed it. No explanation is given of Job's suffering. A series of ironic questions convince Job of his ignorance and insignificance, and he confesses his error and recants. In the Epilogue, paradoxically, Job is commended for having spoken correctly about Yahweh, and the friends are sharply rebuked. Job is then restored to health and prosperity, and the doctrine he had refuted is seemingly upheld. The variety of attempts to reconcile or remove the inconsistencies involved here points up the very real difficulties. The resort to surgery to remove the difficulties requires more and more of the same, till scarcely a torso is left. If the speech(es) of Yahweh are removed, the Epilogue must go too, for it presupposes the divine speech (42:7). Dissatisfaction with the content of the divine speeches is hardly warrant for rejecting them. By its position in the book, as well as by its literary power, it is obvious that the theophany was intended as the climax. Here we have to look for the best word the poet has to offer on the subject, since it is not likely that he would give less than his noblest effort to the divine utterances.

The seemingly magnificent irrelevance of Yahweh's speech(es) presumably veils the poet's meaning. Yahweh answers Job's challenge to appear, but he declines to submit to cross-examination. Instead he asks the questions, with more than a touch of irony. Here it may be that the poet reveals his purpose: to put man in his proper place in relation to God. Yahweh's evasion of the question of Job's innocence may be the poet's oblique way of saying that no answer is available to man. God cannot be hauled into court or compelled to testify against himself. Ignorant and impotent man cannot presume to tell God how to order the universe. No amount or degree of suffering could give a mere man, with his finite intelligence, license to question God's justice as Job has done. It is exactly on this point that Job confesses and repents of his error; he has spoken without knowledge or understanding (42:3*b-c*). Job makes no concession, either explicit or implicit, in regard to his innocence and integrity, and Yahweh says nothing to imply that Job has merited his misery. This is an ethical triumph for Job over the friends, who had maintained that he must be guilty and would be proved so if God were to speak. But God brings no bill of indictment against Job; this fact accords with both Prologue and Epilogue, which tell us Job was innocent. Job gets no apology and no explanation from God for having wrongfully afflicted him, but the absence of any charge of guilt is tantamount to vindication. The assurance that his suffering is not punishment for sin is a part, at least, of what Job has demanded. The further question—if not for sin, why then?—is rejected as presumptuous. Job is rebuked for speaking out of ignorance. The rebuke must have reference to Job's charges of injustice against God.

Accordingly, Job's confession does not refer only to God's power, which he has never questioned. Throughout the Dialogue, Job has complained of the hopelessness of his case in the face of God's arbitrary omnipotence. Now that he actually gets a glimpse of God, he realizes that he has spoken rashly, for God moves on a level beyond human comprehension. The last vestige of Job's rebellious attitude disappears (42:3, 5).

If the poet's best word is not here, it is hard to say where else in the book it may be found. The answer which God gives from the whirlwind, passing over the details of the zoological marvels, is as much of an answer as man has ever received, apart from a beatific vision (42:5).

Bibliography. Books: K. Kautzsch, *Das sogenannte Volksbuch von Hiob* (1900). K. Fries, *Das philosophische Gespräch von Hiob bis Plato* (1904). J. Strahan, *The Book of Job* (1913). R. H. Pfeiffer, *Le problème du livre de Job* (1915). H. M. Kallen, *The Book of Job as a Greek Tragedy Restored* (1918). S. R. Driver and G. B. Gray, *A Critical and Exegetical Commentary on the Book of Job* (1921). P. Volz, *Hiob und Weisheit* (1921). M. Buttenwieser, *The Book of Job* (1922). P. Dhorme, *Le livre de Job* (1926). P. Humbert, *Recherches sur les sources égyptiennes de la littérature sapientiale d'Israël* (1929). E. König, *Das Buch Hiob* (1929). H. Ranston, *The OT Wisdom Books, and Their Teaching* (1930). F. Baumgärtel, *Der Hiobdialog* (1933). O. S. Rankin, *Israel's Wisdom Literature: Its Bearing on Theology and the History of Religion* (1936). B. D. Eerdmans, *Studies in Job* (1939). E. J. Kissane, *The Book of Job* (1939). E. Kraeling, *The Book of the Ways of God* (1939). F. Wutz, *Das Buch Hiob* (1939). R. H. Pfeiffer, *Introduction to the OT* (1941). J. Lindblom, *La composition du livre de Job* (1945). N. H. Snaith, *The Book of Job* (Study Notes; 1945). A. M. Dubarle, *Les Sages d'Israël* (1946). V. E. Reichert, *Job* (Soncino Books of the Bible; 1946). J. J. Stamm, *Das Leiden des Unschuldigen in Babylon und Israel* (1946). M. Susman, *Das Buch Hiob und das Schicksal des jüdischen Volkes* (1946). W. B. Stevenson, *The Poem of Job* (1947). J. J. Weber, *Le livre de Job, l'Ecclésiastique* (1947). R. R. Schärf, *Die Gestalt des Satans im AT* (1948). C. Larcher, *Le livre de Job* (1950). I. J. Gerber, *The Psychology of the Suffering Mind* (1951). H. Lamparter, *Das Buch der Anfechtung* (1951). H. H. Rowley, *Submission in Suffering and Other Essays* (1951). A. Weiser, *Das Buch Hiob* (1951). D. H. Gard, *The Exegetical Method of the Greek Translator of the Book of Job* (1952). G. Hölscher, *Das Buch Hiob* (1952). C. G. Jung, *Antwort auf Hiob* (1952; trans., *Answer to Job*, 1954). H. Richter, *Studien zu Hiob, Der Aufbau des Hiobbuches, dargestellt an den Gattungen des Rechtslebens* (1954). T. H. Robinson, *Job and His Friends* (1954). F. Stier, *Das Buch Ijjob* (1954). H. Möller, *Sinn und Aufbau des Buches Hiob* (1955). H. W. Robinson, *The Cross of Job* (1955). J. Scharbert, *Der Schmerz im AT* (1955). J. Steinmann, *Le livre de Job* (1955). E. F. Sutcliffe, *Providence and Suffering in the Old and New Testaments* (1955). C. Westermann, *Der Aufbau des Buches Hiob* (1956). O. Eissfeldt, *Einleitung in das AT* (1957). S. Terrien, *Job: Poet of Existence* (1957). N. H. Tur Sinai, *The Book of Job* (1957). G. von Rad, *Theologie des Alten Testaments*, Band I: *Die Theologie der geschichtlichen Überlieferungen Israels* (1957). H. Gese, *Lehre und Wirklichkeit in der alten Weisheit* (1958).

Articles: W. E. Staples, "The Speeches of Elihu," *University of Toronto Studies*, Philological Series 8 (1925). R. H. Pfeiffer, "Edomitic Wisdom," *ZAW*, 44 (1926), 13-25. M. Burrows, "The Voice from the Whirlwind," *JBL*, 47 (1928), 117-32. F. H. Foster, "Is the Book of Job a Translation from an Arabic Original?" *AJSL*, 49 (1932-33), 21-45. W. A. Irwin, "An Examination of the Progress of Thought in the Dialogue of Job," *JR*, 13 (1933), 150-64. A. Lods, "Recherches récentes sur le livre de Job," *RHPR*, 14 (1934), 501-19. R. H. Pfeiffer, "Wisdom and Vision in the OT," *ZAW*, 52 (1934), 93-101. B. Landsberger, "Die babylonische Theodizee," *Zeitschrift für Assyriologie und verwandte Gebiete*, vol. 48 (1936). A. Alt, "Zur

Vorgeschichte des Buches Hiob," *ZAW*, 55 (1937), 265-68. W. A. Irwin, "The Elihu Speeches in the Criticism of the Book of Job," *JR*, 17 (1937), 37-47. J. Lindblom, "Job and Prometheus, a Comparative Study," *Dragma Martino P. Nilsson* (1939), pp. 280-87. A. Lods, "Les origines de la figure de Satan, ses fonctions à la cour céleste," *Mélanges Syriens Dussaud,* II (1939), 649-60. R. Gordis, "Corporate Personality in Job: A Note on 22:29-30," *JNES*, 4 (1945), 54 ff. S. Spiegel, "Noah, Danel, and Job," *Louis Ginzberg Jubilee Volume* (1945), pp. 305-55. C. L. Feinberg, "The Poetic Structure of the Book of Job and the Ugaritic Literature," *Bibliotheca Sacra,* 103 (1946), 283-92. R. Gordis, "All Men's Book: A New Introduction to Job," *Menorah,* 37 (1948), 329-58. R. Marcus, "Job and God," *RR,* 14 (1949), 27 ff. W. A. Irwin, "Prometheus and Job," *JR*, 30 (1950), 90-108. O. J. Baab, "The Book of Job," *Interpretation,* 5 (1951), 329-43. H. G. May, "Prometheus and Job," *ATR,* 34 (1952), 240-46. J. Nougayrol, "Une version ancienne du 'Juste souffrant,' " *RB* (1952), pp. 239-50. K. Kuhl, "Neuere Literaturkritik des Buches Hiob," *Theol. Rundschau,* 21 (1953), 163-205, 257-317. M. P. Nilsson, "Religion as Man's Protest Against the Meaninglessness of Events," *Bulletin de la société royale des lettres de Lund,* II (1953-54), 25-92. E. A. Speiser, "The Case of the Obliging Servant," *JCS*, 8 (1954), 98-105. S. Terrien, Introduction and Exegesis of Job, *IB,* III (1954), 877-1198. H. A. Fine, "The Tradition of a Patient Job," *JBL,* 74 (1955), 28-32. B. Gemser, "The Rib —or Controversy—Pattern in Hebrew Mentality," *Vetus Testamentum,* Supplement III (1955). P. Humbert, "Le modernisme de Job," *Vetus Testamentum,* Supplement III (1955), pp. 150-61. S. N. Kramer, "Man and His God," *Vetus Testamentum,* Supplement III (1955), pp. 170-82. G. von Rad, "Hiob XXXIII und die altägyptische Weisheit," *Vetus Testamentum,* Supplement III (1955), pp. 293-301. H. Knight, "Job (Considered as a Contribution to Hebrew Theology)," *Scottish Journal of Theology*, 9 (1956), 63-76. R. J. Williams, "Theodicy in the Ancient Near East," *Canadian Journal of Theology,* 2 (1956), 14-26. J. Daniélou, "Job," *Holy Pagans of the OT* (1957), pp. 86-102. N. M. Sarna, "Epic Substratum in the Prose of Job," *JBL,* 76 (1957), 13-25. H. H. Rowley, "The Book of Job and Its Meaning," *Bulletin of the John Rylands Library,* 41 (1958), 167-207. M. H. Pope

JOBAB jō'băb [יוֹבָב; *cf.* Akkad. *Iabibi*]. **1.** The youngest son of Joktan, and hence the name of an Arabian group (Gen. 10:29; I Chr. 1:23). It was probably connected with the town of Juhaibab, which is mentioned in a Sabean inscription and which was located in the neighborhood of Mecca.

2. The second king of Edom, who came from the N capital, Bozrah (Gen. 36:33). The LXX appendix to the book of Job confounds the latter's hero with this king.

3. A king of the town of Madon, located somewhere in the N of Palestine. He was defeated by Joshua (Josh. 11:1; 12:19).

4. A Benjaminite; son of Shaharaim (I Chr. 8:9).

5. A Benjaminite; son of Elpaal (I Chr. 8:18).

S. Cohen

JOCHEBED jŏk'ə bĕd [יוֹכֶבֶד, *see below*]. A daughter of Levi; the wife of Amram; and the mother of Aaron, Moses, and Miriam (Exod. 6:20; Num. 26:59). Only the P document has the name; the E document calls her merely a "daughter of Levi" (Exod. 2:1). The etymology of the name is uncertain. The most natural suggestion would be that it signifies "Yahweh is glory"; this would mean, however, that the name Yahweh was known prior to the time of Moses (*see* God, Names of, § B2). Thus the Priestly writer probably did not understand it in this sense. Another possibility is that the syllable יו stands for a Canaanite god *yw;* the existence of such a god has been generally denied, however.

Bibliography. G. B. Gray, *Studies in Hebrew Proper Names* (1896), pp. 156, 257; M. Noth, *Die israelitischen Personennamen* (1928), p. 111; H. Bauer, "Die Gottheiten von Ras Schamra," *ZAW*, LI (1933), 92-93; T. J. Meek, *Hebrew Origins* (rev. ed., 1950), p. 97. J. F. Ross

JOD jŏd, jōd [י, *y* (*yôdh*)]. The tenth letter of the Hebrew Alphabet as it is placed in the KJV at the head of the tenth section of the acrostic psalm, Ps. 119, where each verse of this section of the psalm begins with this letter.

JODA jō'də ['Ιωδά, 'Ιούδας]. **1.** Son of Iliadun; head of a family of Levites appointed to help repair the temple after the return from the Exile (I Esd. 5:58).

2. An ancestor of Jesus (Luke 3:26).

JODAN jō'dən [Ιώδαν, Ιώαδαν] (I Esd. 9:19). Probably same as Gedaliah.

JOED jō'ĕd [יוֹעֵד, Yahu is witness] (Neh. 11:7). A Benjaminite listed as resident in Jerusalem under Nehemiah. The name is absent from the parallel I Chr. 9:7.

JOEL jō'əl [יוֹאֵל, Yahu is God; *cf.* אליה, Elijah; 'Ιωήλ, 'Ιουήλ]; KJV Apoc. JUEL jo͞o'əl ['Ιουήλ (A)]. The comparatively wide distribution of the name Joel among the different tribes is theologically significant in view of its etymology.

1. A prince (*nāsî*) in the tribe of Simeon (I Chr. 4:35).

2. A man of the tribe of Reuben (I Chr. 5:4, 8).

3. A chief of the tribe of Gad in Bashan (I Chr. 5:12).

4. A Kohathite Levite; and, according to the Chronicler, an ancestor of Elkanah the father of the prophet Samuel (I Chr. 6:36; cf. vss. 34-35 with I Sam. 1:1).

5. The elder son of Samuel the prophet (I Sam. 8:2); and, according to the Chronicler, a Kohathite Levite and father or ancestor of Heman the singer (I Chr. 6:33). In I Chr. 6:28 the name Joel has dropped out of a corrupted Hebrew text but can be restored on the basis of vs. 33, I Sam. 8:2, and the Syr., as in the RSV. The KJV reads "Vashni," merely transliterating the Hebrew phrase "and the second," which precedes the name of the second son.

6. A man of the tribe of Issachar (I Chr. 7:3).

7. One of David's "Mighty Men" (I Chr. 11:38). In a related list Igal (יגאל) stands for possibly this name (II Sam. 23:36).

8. A chief of the Levite "sons of Gershom," who with 130 of his brethren took part in the ceremonies connected with bringing the ark of the Lord up to Jerusalem in the reign of David (I Chr. 15:7, 11). He is apparently the same as the Joel, son of Laadan, in I Chr. 23:8, who shared responsibility with his brothers for the temple treasuries (I Chr. 26:22).

9. Son of Pedaiah; chief officer over the half-tribe of Manasseh in the reign of David (I Chr. 27:20).

10. A Kohathite Levite who took part in the cleansing and reconsecration of the temple during the reign of King Hezekiah (II Chr. 29:12).

11. The prophet Joel, son of Pethuel. *See* JOEL, BOOK OF.

12. One of the postexilic Jews among Ezra's contemporaries who are listed as having married foreign wives (Ezra 10:43; I Esd. 9:35).

13. An overseer, or chief representative (*pāqîdh*) of the laity (not merely of the Benjaminites), in postexilic Jerusalem (Neh. 11:9).

Bibliography. R. A. Bowman, Exegesis of Nehemiah, *IB,* III (1954), 774.

14. In the pseudepigraphical literature, the archangel Joel, the same as Jaoel or Jahoel or Jehoel (יהואל; Apocalypse of Moses 29:4; 43:5; Apocalypse of Abraham 10:20; 17:22; etc.; *see bibliography*).

Bibliography. L. S. A. Wells in R. H. Charles, ed., *Apoc. and Pseudep. of the OT* (1913), II, 148, 154; G. H. Box, ed., *The Apocalypse of Abraham* (1918), pp. xxv-xxvi, 46n.; M. Noth, *Die israelitischen Personennamen* (1928), pp. 16, 70, 77, 107, 140.

B. T. DAHLBERG

JOEL, BOOK OF [יואל; Ἰωήλ]. The second of the twelve short prophetic books which together make up the concluding section of the OT. In the versions the book consists of three chapters; the MT has four. The versions have combined two of the Hebrew chapters into one. In the case of the English versions, following the LXX and the Vulg., chs. 2–3 of the Hebrew have been thus amalgamated into 2:1-27, 28-32.

Nothing is known of the author apart from his name. The oracles suggest Jerusalem as their place of origin, and the date has been variously given as pre-exilic or postexilic. Majority opinion now favors a date *ca.* 400 B.C. The occasion of the prophecies appears to have been an unusually severe plague of locusts, which suggested to the author the imminence of the Day of Yahweh (*see* DAY OF THE LORD). These are the two main topics of his short work, although it has frequently been argued that the apocalyptic sections are not original. The main interest of the oracles as they stand, apart from their literary qualities and the impressive conception of the Day of Yahweh, lies in the connection between the prophecy of the outpouring of the Spirit (2:28-32) and the pentecostal experience of the early church (Acts 2:14-21).

See map "Palestine: Joel, Obadiah, Jonah," under OBADIAH, BOOK OF.

A. *THE AUTHOR.* The prophet is described as the son of Pethuel or Bethuel (LXX), but nothing is known apart from this of either father or son. His name, which means "Yahweh is God," was not an uncommon one (*see* JOEL). From his interest in the temple ritual it has been inferred that he was a cultic prophet.

B. *THE BOOK.* 1. The prophecies. *a. The locusts.* The prophet describes a swarm of locusts of unprecedented intensity, which have apparently devastated the land (1:2-4). With the ferocity of lions the creatures have stripped trees and vines and left them bare (vss. 5-7). Even the holy offerings to Yahweh cannot be made in the temple for sheer lack of corn, wine, and oil. The priests are in despair (vss. 8-10), as are the farmers (vss. 11-12). Joel calls upon the priesthood to summon the people to fasting and penitential prayer that the plague might cease (vss. 13-14).

b. The meaning of the visitation. The prophet sees this calamity as more than a natural phenomenon. It is a warning of the approaching judgment, a sign of the impending Day of Yahweh (1:15). In graphic detail he depicts the catastrophic plight of man and beast. Not only locusts but also forest fires and lack of vital rainfall have emptied the granaries and turned the lush pastures into a barren waste (vss. 16-20).

Now let the alarm ring out from Jerusalem through the land, that all may take heed of the clear warning which Yahweh has given. Let them see in this onslaught of destruction a presage of the coming judgment. The black clouds of insects that darken the sky are a foretaste of the darkness and gloom of the Day of the Lord. They sweep through the land like a consuming fire, like an invading army (2:1-5). Men cringe in terror before this irresistible onset. Stout city walls cannot hold them back. They swarm into the dwelling houses of Jerusalem (vss. 6-9). The very earth and heavens seem to shudder, and light itself is blotted out, as it will be on that dread day (vss. 10-11).

c. Repentance and its sequel. Yet there is still hope. If only the people will repent and turn to Yahweh in sincerity of heart, they will find him ready to forgive their past offenses and to rid them of this plague. The land will again yield its fruit, and the sacred offerings may be made once more (2:12-14). So the prophet calls anew (cf. 1:14) for national repentance. Let the priests intercede with Yahweh that this disaster may be averted and that the world may thus see that Israel does not worship him in vain (2:15-17).

From the next words it appears that Joel's appeal has been heeded and that the people have repented. Now the prophet predicts the sequel. The land will once again yield its proper fruits. The swarms of locusts will be swept away and destroyed (2:18-20). The rains will fall once more in their due season. Grain, wine, and oil in plenty will gladden men's hearts. The protracted losses due to the visitation of locusts will be made up. Israel will know that Yahweh alone is her true God, and never again will the heathen have cause to doubt his power (vss. 21-27).

d. The coming of the Spirit. After this prospect of material abundance has been confidently predicted, the prophet goes on to envisage even greater blessings. Yahweh will send down his Spirit upon all Israel. From the oldest to the youngest, from the highest to the lowest, his people will no longer depend on the voice of a few prophets to communicate divine truth, but each and every one will be a prophet in his own right, with the prophet's insight through vision and ecstasy into the nature and purpose of God (2:28-29).

Then convulsions on earth and portents in the heavens will herald the approach of the Day of the Lord, with all its terrors. But true worshipers of Yahweh need have no fear. For not all in Israel are doomed to destruction. Those whom Yahweh has called to be his faithful servants will survive the horrors that mark the coming of the judgment (vss. 30-32).

e. Judgment upon the world. These will be the days when the Lord will summon the heathen nations to meet him in the Vale of Judgment (*see* JEHOSHAPHAT, VALLEY OF) and to stand their assize. He will charge them with scattering his people in exile, with despoiling their lands and selling even their children into slavery (3:1-3). He will call to account the Phoenicians and the Philistines for plundering the territories of his people and for selling them to the Greeks as slaves. But the tables will be turned, for the scattered people of Yahweh will be brought back from their places of exile to take vengeance on these foes. They in their turn will become slaves of the Jews, who will sell them to the traders of distant Sheba (vss. 4-8).

The nations of the earth rally for a final battle against Jerusalem, in preparation for which they forge every peaceful tool into a weapon of war, and even their weaklings become warriors (vss. 9-10). There in the Vale of Judgment the angelic host of heaven will carry out the sentence which the Lord has passed upon his enemies. Cut down like grain at harvesttime, crushed like grapes in a winepress, the heathen will perish in the Valley of Decision (*see* DECISION, VALLEY OF) while heaven and earth tremble and Yahweh roars from Zion (vss. 11-16*a*).

f. The golden age. But in the midst of this terrible judgment Israel will be protected by her God. Hence she will know for certain that Yahweh will never be absent from his people. Never again will Jerusalem, his holy city, be violated by the heathen. Hitherto unimagined fertility will bless the land, and a miraculous life-giving spring will flow from the temple (3: 16*b*-18). While Egypt and Edom, the ancient enemies of Israel, become a wilderness, Judah will be inhabited forever, and Yahweh will live eternally in Jerusalem (vss. 19-21).

2. Interpretation. The book of Joel is generally recognized as falling naturally into two distinct parts, as indicated more clearly by the Hebrew division, into chs. 1–2; 3–4, or, in the English versions, into 1:1–2:27; 2:28–3:21. The problem of its interpretation arises from the fact that the first part (1:1–2:27) appears to deal with a recent historical event—namely, a plague of locusts which so devastated the land that the prophet, regarding this affliction as a clear indication of Yahweh's displeasure, called the people to repentance. The people responded to his call, whereupon he predicted the destruction of the locusts and the restoration of fertility to the land.

The second part (2:28–3:21), on the other hand, appears to be wholly eschatological in character. The prophet speaks of a future time when a supernatural visitation of the spirit of Yahweh will bestow upon all his people the gift of prophecy. He further depicts in apocalyptic terms the final conflict between the hosts of Yahweh and the armies of the heathen nations, ending in the annihilation of the latter and the ultimate vindication of Israel.

Yet while the first part is predominantly historical and the second part mostly apocalyptic, the division is not so radical as is at first apparent. The Day of Yahweh occurs in both sections (cf. 1:15; 2:1-2, 10-11), and elements in the description of the invading army of locusts seem to have already a kinship with the supernatural character of the events described in the second half of the book (e.g., 2:2-11, 20). The question has therefore been raised as to whether the locusts are, in fact, real locusts, or whether they are merely symbols of the heathen armies whose destruction is described in ch. 3. If they are symbolic, either they may represent hostile attacks in the course of the past history of Israel, or they may be wholly apocalyptic in character as in Rev. 9:1-11.

The fathers favored an allegorical interpretation. The locusts of chs. 1–2 are the powers of darkness which threaten the church. But in the end God's judgment will fall upon the world. Later explanations identify the four types of locust (1:4) with four great world empires which harried Israel—Egyptian, Assyrian, Babylonian, and Greek; or Babylonian, Persian, Greek, and Roman—or with four separate assaults on the country during the Persian period. None of these allegorical interpretations is satisfactory. As has been pointed out many times, if the locusts are armed warriors, they cannot be said to be like themselves (cf. 2:4-7).

The view generally held now is that the locusts are real and not symbolic. Close observers of the habits of these creatures, and spectators who have witnessed the devastation they have caused, recognize in the prophet's description an accurate picture of such a fearful onslaught as must have given rise to this book. Their behavior suggests nothing more vividly than the terrible havoc wrought by invading armies, and might well be described in the highly colored terms of ch. 2. In the normal manner of apocalyptic thought, as in Ezekiel, Daniel, and Revelation, this would lead the prophet, in the second part of the book, to regard such a disaster as a warning of the judgment to come (cf. Isa. 13). The association of the two elements would readily account for the apocalyptic coloring and eschatological references of the first part. *See* ESCHATOLOGY OF THE OT.

3. Integrity. On this view there is no reason to suppose that Joel was not responsible for the whole work. Many other suggestions have, however, been advanced. It has been conjectured that 1:1–2:27 forms the original work and that 2:28–3:21 is by the hand of a later apocalyptist. In this case references to the Day of Yahweh in 1:15; 2:1-2, 10-11, have to be eliminated. More recently 1:1–2:27 has been held to contain liturgical poems which formed part of the New Year Festival ritual, and to which have been added at subsequent dates fragments of an apocalyptic character. None of these suggestions appears to be based on incontrovertible evidence, and there would seem to be no advantage to be gained from treating the book as composite. There is also the fact that nothing suggests conclusively that its various parts come from different periods.

4. Date. Critics have ranged from the ninth century to the second century B.C. in seeking to determine a date for the prophecies, either as a whole or in part. The modern consensus, however, regards them as postexilic and narrows the range of time to the period *ca.* 400.

The grounds for postulating a date about this time are well-nigh conclusive. Israel and Judah have ceased to exist as separate nations, and the names appear to be used synonymously (2:27; 3:2, 16). The monarchy has disappeared, and many of the people are scattered in exile (3:2-3). But the temple is standing and is in full operation (1:13-14; 2:15-17). The walls of Jerusalem are intact (2:9), and the community is small enough to be gathered within the temple courts (2:16). Its leaders are priests and elders (2:16-17). The priesthood and the ritual figure prominently (1:13-14; 2:12-17), in particular the meal offering and drink offering (1:9, 13; 2:14). Greeks have replaced Assyrians and Babylonians as masters of the dispersed slaves, though not yet as rulers of the world (3:6). Despite the possible qualification in 2:32, it would seem that the prophet drew a sharp distinction between Israel and the rest of the world in his view of the Day of the Lord. Whereas earlier prophets (cf. Amos 5:18-20) had thought in terms of judgment upon Israel for its sins, Joel thinks rather of the punishment of Israel's enemies and the triumph of the Jews (ch. 3).

All this points to the period after the Exile, when the worship of the restored TEMPLE had become the lifeblood of the people, when formalism in ritual had taken the place of moral issues as the main concern of a prophet (2:12-14). Disappointment and disillusionment over the failure of earlier prophetic promises to materialize had led to a growth of nationalism and exclusiveness (2:28-32; 3:18-20), which saw the Jews as the victims of a world too corrupt to be redeemed, and which placed its only hope in their vindication by the total and supernatural annihilation of their enemies. This attitude was encouraged by the legislation of Nehemiah and the promulgation of the law. The affinities of the book of Joel are with the oracles of Zech. 9–14 rather than with Malachi, and the above considerations appear to point to conditions in Jerusalem at the end of the fifth or the beginning of the fourth century.

C. *THE SIGNIFICANCE OF JOEL.* This fascinating little book has many intriguing features, and these not only theological. Naturalists commend the accuracy of the description of the ravages of the locusts, and littérateurs are impressed by the vividness of the imagery and the poetic quality of the style. It would appear from the number of phrases which can be paralleled in other OT books that the author had modeled himself on earlier masters like Amos and Zephaniah, Ezekiel and Second Isaiah. Indeed, he acknowledges a quotation (from Obad. 17) in 2:32, but he in his turn probably influenced the imagery of the second part of Zechariah.

His artistic skill in weaving backward and forward between the historical phenomenon of the locusts and the suprahistorical events of the Day of Yahweh is considerable. Each of these themes takes on something of the coloring of the other—a fact which, as we have seen, gave rise to the suggestion that the locusts themselves must be as supernatural as the judgment.

But it is in his role as a harbinger of the apocalyptic school that Joel's importance lies for biblical theology. In other respects he shares the older prophetic ideas. The plague of locusts is a certain sign of Yahweh's wrath. Repentance is therefore incumbent on the whole community for their unspecified sins. The most tragic aspect of the rift between Yahweh and his people is seen as the cessation of the daily offerings, now, in the postexilic theocracy, the guarantee of the covenant relationship (*see* WORSHIP IN THE OT). But given repentance, divine favor will be manifested, not only in terms of material prosperity for the community, but also, and more important, in the restoration of the means of preserving the covenant relationship. By this both Israel and the world will know that Yahweh is I ord and that his own people are his peculiar care.

It is on this conventional basis of rewards and punishments that Joel builds his apocalyptic structure (*see* APOCALYPTICISM). The events of history are projected onto a cosmic canvas and become prefigurations of what lies beyond the natural sequence of occurrences within the time process. The plague of locusts becomes a type of the powers of evil that oppress Yahweh's people. Their rout and the subsequent restoration of prosperity are transposed into the final judgment upon the world and its sequel in a golden age for the people of the promise.

There are three main aspects of apocalyptic eschatology which are expressed more fully in the later writings of the intertestamental period, but it is remarkable to find them all side by side within the compass of this short book. The first is the pastoral motif, more familiar in the context of Isa. 2:2-4, where the eschatological hope revolves round the conception of paradise regained, the reversal of the Fall, and the idyllic prospect of a transformed natural world and its denizens existing together in a state of peace and bliss, while man lives in the midst of it in harmony with the Creator.

That this aspect, expressed in an apocalyptic context in Joel 3:17-18, was no longer conceived of as a state of purely material well-being can be seen from the reference to the miraculous fountain which comes from the dwelling place of God and which is regarded as the water of life (cf. John 4:14; Rev. 22:1-2). Nor does the fact that national exclusiveness is featured side by side with this vision of the golden age vitiate its value. Whatever the failure of Israel may have been to fulfil the vocation of a people of God, the mission and the historical concept were not invalidated. The Zion of the age to come in 3:17 is an eternal reality, even if the prophet saw it with the limited vision of Jewish nationalism, and the essence of the hope which is here expressed is part of the Christian heritage.

The second main type of apocalyptic expectation is one which springs from the increasingly nationalistic outlook of the Jews in the period after the return from exile. When a people had seen their children sold for a song into slavery, they looked to a supernatural intervention for redress, of which they saw no prospect in the normal way. Joel in his oracle against the Phoenicians and the Philistines has worked this out on the strictest basis of retributive justice (3:4-8).

In his vision of the cosmic battle between the nations of the world and the hosts of heaven (cf. Ezek. 38–39; Zephaniah), in which Isa. 2:2-4 is parodied, he assumes the total extermination of the heathen and the preservation of Israel alone (3:9-17). It should be remembered, however, that in apocalyptic thought the "nations" ceased to consist of men, women, and children, and became the incarnation of the evil that warred unceasingly against the good purposes of God. That these good purposes were thought of as canalized in his peculiar people led inevitably to an identification of the harrying of Israel with a frontal assault on God himself.

Yet once again it was basically a true insight that led the apocalyptic seers of Israel to regard every attack on the people of the law and the promises as a violation of the law and promises themselves. The human fallibility of old and new Israel alike cannot obliterate the truth that, however imperfect be the fulfilment, the basic aspiration of both has been to serve God, and the initial stand has been taken on the side of what has been accepted as the direct revelation of God's will. It should be noted that in his picture of the annihilation of the forces of evil (3:13; cf. Rev. 14:14-20) Joel refrains from the lurid descriptions of later apocalyptic (e.g., Zech. 9:15; 14:12).

The third main tendency of apocalyptic thought, the mystical or spiritual emphasis, is expressed by Joel (2:28-29) in a passage which was regarded as deeply significant by the early church. Again its form has the limitations common to all Jewish apocalyptic ideas. It rests upon the words of Num. 11:29, where Moses reproves Joshua for seeking to confine the onset of prophetic ecstasy within approved channels. Moses utters the wish that all the people of Yahweh might be similarly endowed with a visitation of his *rûaḥ*.

It is this apparently miraculous possession by the spirit of Yahweh that is foreseen by Joel as one of the supernatural manifestations of the end, doubtless influenced by the decline in prophecy which eventually led to the situation described in Zech. 13:1-6. It is in terms of dream, vision, and ecstasy that the prophet thinks, rather than in terms of spiritual insight and communion with God in the Christian sense. Moreover, in his thought the gift is limited to Israel. Yet once more the prophet—or the apocalyptist—speaks more truly than he knows, and the fulfilment in the experience of the church is richer than the prophecy.

In his sermon on the day of Pentecost, when prophetic ecstasy of the OT type fell upon all present so that they seemed to the bystanders to be behaving like drunk men, Peter quoted in full these words of Joel in explanation of the miracle (Acts 2:14-18). Yet just as the early church spiritualized and reinterpreted the other elements of Joel's vision (Acts 2:19-21), so, from the beginning, the presence of the Spirit was held to be evidenced, not only by ecstatic frenzy, but also by the witness of lives lived in a new dimension through the coming of the Messiah and the realization of the *eschaton* in history (Acts 11:24; Gal. 5:22). Nor did the gift of the Spirit remain for very long the sole prerogative of the Jews, for it was soon seen to be available for all within the new Israel, both Jew and Gentile (Acts 2:21, 39; 10:45; Rom. 10:12-13). *See* HOLY SPIRIT; PENTECOST.

Bibliography. Commentaries: J. A. Bewer, ICC (1912); G. W. Wade, WC (1925); G. A. Smith, EB (1928); R. F. Horton, Century Bible; E. Sellin, KAT (1929); S. R. Driver, Cambridge Bible (1934); T. H. Robinson, HAT (1938); J. A. Thompson, *IB* (1956). See also Introductions to the literature of the OT by Driver, Pfeiffer, Bentzen, *et al.*

For background: H. H. Rowley, *The Relevance of Apocalyptic* (1944); S. B. Frost, *OT Apocalyptic* (1952).

Special studies: L. Dennefeld, *Les problèmes du livre de Joël*, RSR, XV (1925), 35-57, 591-608; A. S. Kapelrud, *Joel Studies* (1948). W. NEIL

JOELAH jō ē′lə [יועאלה] (I Chr. 12:7—H 12:8). One of the sons of Jeroham of Gedor who are named among the famed Benjaminite warriors that joined the proscribed band of David at Ziklag.

JOEZER jō ē′zər [יועזר, Yahu is help] (I Chr. 12:6—H 12:7). One of the famed warriors of the tribe of Benjamin who joined the followers of the proscribed David at Ziklag. It seems best to interpret his gentilic name, Kohathite, as referring to his place of origin.

JOGBEHAH jŏg′bə hə [יגבהה, height]. A fortified city of Gad, mentioned next to Jazer (Num. 32:35). When Gideon was pursuing the Midianites, he made a circuit about Nobah and Jogbehah in order to attack his enemies from the rear (Judg. 8:11). The site is Khirbet el-Ajbeihat, seven miles NW of 'Amman.

S. COHEN

JOGLI jŏg′lī [יגלי; LXX Εγλι, may (God) reveal(?)] (Num. 34:22). The father of the Danite leader Bukki, who was selected to help superintend the distribution of W Jordanian Canaan among the tribes to occupy that territory.

Bibliography. M. Noth, *Die israelitischen Personennamen* (1928), p. 244. R. F. JOHNSON

JOHA jō′ə [יוחא]. **1.** A Tizite who, with his brother Jediael, is mentioned among the Mighty Men of David known as the "Thirty" (I Chr. 11:45).

2. One of the sons of Beriah included in the genealogies of the tribe of Benjamin (I Chr. 8:16).

JOHANAN jō hā′nən [יוחנן, Yahu has been gracious (*cf.* JEHOHANAN); Apoc. ['Ιωάννης (A)]; KJV Apoc. JOHANNES jō hăn′ĭz. **1.** One of the Benjaminites who joined David's forces at Ziklag (I Chr. 12:4).

2. One of the Gadites who joined David at Ziklag; an officer (I Chr. 12:12, 14).

3. A priest, and a son or more distant descendant of the priest Azariah, who was a contemporary of King Solomon (I Chr. 6:9-10—H 5:35-36; cf. I Kings 4:2; the reference to service in Solomon's temple in 6:10 correctly belongs with the first "Azariah" in vs. 9).

4. An Ephraimite (II Chr. 28:12). The Hebrew name here (יהוחנן) requires transliteration as "Jehohanan," not "Johanan" as in the KJV-RSV.

5. A son of King Josiah (*ca.* 640-609 B.C.). Although the eldest, for some reason he did not succeed to the throne (I Chr. 3:15).

6. Son of Kareah, and a contemporary of the prophet Jeremiah. He was one of the Jewish military leaders in Judah who, after the fall of Jerusalem to Babylon in 586 B.C., gave his allegiance to Gedaliah, the governor of Judah appointed by the Babylonian king Nebuchadnezzar (Jer. 40:8; cf. II Kings 25:23). He warned Gedaliah of a plot to assassinate him, but the latter disbelieved him (Jer. 40:13-16); and when the deed was actually accomplished, Johanan led a force to avenge his death. He then, with the other leaders, prepared to take the company into Egypt to escape the feared reprisals from Babylon for the death of Gedaliah (41:11-18). Jeremiah the prophet counseled him and the others to remain in Judah, trusting in God for their safety, but they distrusted his advice and migrated to Egypt, taking the prophet with them (42:1–43:7).

7. Son of a certain Elioenai, a descendant of David (I Chr. 3:24).

8. One of those who returned from Babylon with Ezra (Ezra 8:12; I Esd. 8:38). For "Johanan the son of Hakkatan" (הקטן; lit., "the little one"), read probably "Johanan the Younger."

9. Grandson of the high priest Eliashib, and himself a high priest (Neh. 12:22-23, where "son," as in many other passages, can mean "grandson" or an even more distant heir). In Neh. 12:11 he is called JONATHAN (יונתן), but this is probably an error for "Johanan"; the difference in Hebrew is slight. If he is identical (as seems probable) with the Jehohanan (יוחנן=יהוחנן) into whose chamber Ezra retired to fast (Ezra 10:6), the relationship is significant, for Eliashib was Nehemiah's contemporary (e.g., Neh. 3:1; *and see* ELIASHIB 2); and the contemporaneity of his grandson with Ezra, if granted, requires the dating of Ezra's advent in Jerusalem sometime after that of Nehemiah.

This Johanan is the high priest referred to by this name in the Elephantine Papyri (*see bibliography*), which place him, moreover, as a contemporary of the Persian king Darius II (423-404 B.C.). The Jewish historian Josephus (*ca.* A.D. 100), calling him by the Greek form of his name, John (Ἰωάννης), writes that while the latter was high priest, he murdered his brother Jesus (Jeshua) in the temple, believing the latter about to usurp his office. *See bibliography*.

10. KJV form of JEHOHANAN 4, 6.

Bibliography. M. Noth, *Die israelitischen Personennamen* (1928), pp. 21, 62, 187. On 9 *above,* see: Josephus *Antiquities* XI.vii.1; A. Cowley, ed., *Aramaic Papyri* (1923), p. 114, no. 30, line 18; H. H. Rowley, "The Chronological Order of Ezra and Nehemiah," *The Servant of the Lord* (1952), pp. 145-51; R. A. Bowman, Exegesis of Ezra and Nehemiah, *IB,* III (1954), 654, 787, 789.

B. T. DAHLBERG

JOHANNES. KJV Apoc. form of JOHANAN; JEHOHANAN.

JOHN jŏn [יוחנן; Ἰωάννης]. A name once common among Jews.

1. The father of MATTATHIAS 1, and grandfather of JUDAS MACCABEUS (I Macc. 2:1; 14:20). The text speaks of the family as "sons of JOARIB"; the latter is probably the Joarib mentioned in I Chr. 24:7 as the forebear of the first of the twenty-four families of priests.

2. The oldest of the five sons of Mattathias, and the grandson of 1 *above* (I Macc. 2:2). He was called Gaddi (in some texts Caddi), possibly the same name borne by an earlier person, of some eminence in the tribe of Manasseh (Num. 13:11). That Judah, John's brother, led the Hasmoneans initially, and was replaced after his death by Jonathan Maccabeus, suggests that John, though the oldest son, was not the leader. Virtually nothing is related of him except for the incident of his death (I Macc. 9:35-42): John was sent by his brother Jonathan to carry the property of the Maccabeans into Nabatea for safekeeping. He was slain (probably in 161 B.C.) by a marauding tribe, the Jambri, from Medeba.

The mention of a Joseph (II Macc. 8:22; 10:19) is often regarded as a false reading for "John."

3. An envoy from the Jews to Lysias, a general of Antiochus Epiphanes (*see* ANTIOCHUS 4). The text (II Macc. 11:17) does not further identify him.

4. The son of Accos (I Macc. 8:17), and the father of EUPOLEMUS. Nothing is known of him except his name.

5. The father of PETER (John 1:42; 21:15-17). Matt. 16:17 reads *bariona* or *bar Iona,* which is Aramaic for "son of Jonah," not "John." Perhaps Ἰῶνα is to be regarded as a diminutive of Ἰωάνης; but the Hebrew יונה, Jonah, is quite distinct from יוחנן, John, and the former would not be a diminutive of the latter; or, perhaps, two different traditions existed about the name of Peter's father.

Various ingenious emendations or explanations have been proposed for *bariona*—e.g., that it is an Aramaic word meaning "swordsman" (*see bibliography*). Two harmonizing efforts merit outright rejection; one attributes to Peter's father the double name of Jonah-Johanan; the other makes Jonah the father and Johanna (Ἰωάννα) the mother (Paris Mss. Reg. 1789, 1026).

Bibliography. On *bariona,* see H. Hirschberg, "Simon Bariona and the Ebionites," *JBL,* LXI (1942), 171-91, and R. Marcus' rejection on pp. 281 ff.

6. *See* JOHN THE BAPTIST.

7. *See* JOHN THE APOSTLE.

8. *See* MARK, JOHN.

9. A member of a priestly family, mentioned in Acts 4:6 and otherwise unknown. A far-fetched view identifies him with a prominent rabbi, Johanan ben Zakkal. Codex Bezae (D) reads "JONATHAN," often identified as the son of ANNAS, who in A.D. 36 succeeded CAIAPHAS as high priest (Jos. Antiq. XVIII. iv.3; v.3; XIX.vi.4; War II.xii.5-6). Jonathan was assassinated at the behest of FELIX (Antiq. XX.viii.5; War II.xiii.3). While a few commentators have proposed to regard "Jonathan" as correct and to regard John as an error, the majority do not find the reading of D significant. S. SANDMEL

JOHN, ACTS OF. Commonly regarded the earliest of the apocryphal Acts (*see* ACTS, APOCRYPHAL), this work contains a series of wonder stories, miracles, and discourses of the apostle John in Asia Minor; all are of a strongly Docetic nature.

The work purports to be an eyewitness account of the events and scenes described, and from the fifth century has been ascribed to a shadowy Leucius, who eventually came to be regarded as the author of the whole series of five Acts which the Manichaeans substituted for the canonical Acts (*see* APOCRYPHA, NT). It is commonly dated in the second half of the second century, in part because of probable reference to it by both Clement of Alexandria and Tertullian, in part because of the nature of its teaching.

In the Stichometry of Nicephorus it is listed as containing 2,500 lines, substantially less than the Acts of Paul (*see* PAUL, ACTS OF) and slightly less than the canonical Acts. About two thirds of it is still extant, large portions being preserved in Greek, and there is a Latin version of some parts not found in Greek. The beginning is now lost, but a late Greek text tells of John's return from Patmos, his shipwreck, and his swimming to Miletus on a piece of cork. The first long episode recounts many romantic and not uninteresting happenings in Ephesus: the healing of Cleopatra and the raising to life of her husband Lycomedes; the portrait of John, surreptitiously acquired and reverenced; the destruction of the temple of Artemis; the swarm of bedbugs in the deserted inn, halted by the indignant prayer of the weary apostle; the lurid tale of Drusiana and the attempt in the tomb after her death to ravish her corpse. In all the stories a very strong ascetic tone of hostility to marriage and everything sexual is ever present.

The Docetic emphasis is most clearly revealed in the long discourse in which John tells of his early contacts with Jesus, whose appearance and form were always changing—to James he appeared a child, to John a full-grown man. In the account of the Transfiguration a most belabored attempt is made to dwell on this evanescence, strangely interrupted by the detail that Jesus, to teach him to "be not faithless, but believing," had tweaked John's beard so vigorously that John had suffered pain for thirty days. The account proceeds: "Sometimes when I would lay hold on him, I met with a material and solid body, and at other times, again, when I felt him, the substance was immaterial and as if it existed not at all." Then follows the account of how Jesus had led the disciples onto a mountain on the night of his arrest, and of the antiphonal hymn with its many curious paradoxes:

> I would be wounded, and I would wound. Amen.
> I would be born, and I would bear. Amen.
> I would eat, and I would be eaten. Amen.
> I would be thought, being wholly thought. Amen.

Then there is an account of the dance which Jesus had at that occasion taught them. Again and again, the dominant note is struck: "What now I am seen to be, that am I not." At the Crucifixion, John fled to the Mount of Olives in tears. Suddenly Jesus appears to him with the word: "John, unto the multitude below in Jerusalem, I am being crucified and pierced with lances and reeds, and gall and vinegar is being given to me to drink. But unto thee I speak, and what I speak hear thou." This sermon to Drusiana and his other hearers concludes: "Having therefore beheld, brethren, the grace of the Lord and his kindly affection toward us, let us worship him as those unto whom he has shown mercy, not with our fingers, nor our mouths, nor our tongues, nor with any part whatsoever of our body, but with the disposition of our soul" (cf. I John 1:1).

The remaining section in Greek tells of John's peaceful death. A trench is dug at his command; he places his garments in it and lies down upon them, following a lengthy prayer in which, among other things, he thanks God for having kept him "untouched by union with a woman" even until this hour, despite his own earlier inclinations. With the single word: "Peace be with you, brethren," he "gave up his spirit rejoicing." Of course, this was later heightened with additions to the effect that on the next day the grave was found empty, for he had been translated, or was empty save for his sandals. Augustine reports that in his day it was commonly believed that the earth over the grave was seen to move as if stirred by his breathing.

In the Latin version other stories are given—carefully purged of their heretical (Gnostic) notes, but with a very strong condemnation of wealth and of the folly of those who prized it. Notable among these is the story of Craton the philosopher and the two youths, Atticus and Eugenius, who gave up their wealth, only later to repent it, and of its miraculous return to them and the subsequent discovery of their folly and their second relinquishing of it. Tertullian knows a story of John's having been "plunged, unhurt, into boiling oil" (Presc. Her. 36). This story, while well known in the Latin West, is never referred to by any of the Greek fathers. That it was a part of the earliest version of these Acts is most uncertain, although often assumed.

The famous story told by Clement of Alexandria about John and the robber chief does not occur in any version of the Acts and apparently, although this has been questioned, was never a part of this cycle of romances. On the other hand, the story of John and the partridge, told by John Cassian (*Collationes Patrium* XXIV.12), is paralleled by another, quite different story on the same theme in an eleventh-century Greek MS of the Acts. All this illustrates the uncertain content of the original "Leucian" Acts. That all that now purports to be a part of this ancient work was in its first draft is quite unlikely.

Despite its obvious unorthodox representation of the physical nature of Jesus and the heated criticism it received from many fathers and by the Second Council of Nicea, this writing has exerted a real influence upon both Christian literature and art. It is also of great value to the historian, not only for its firsthand view of certain Gnostic teachings, not burlesqued as at the hands of unsympathetic critics like Irenaeus, but also for the light it throws upon the early practice of a "eucharist for the dead" and upon the sort of prayer felt appropriate for such an occasion. Any attempt to see it in whole or in part as reflecting actual tradition about the historical John —e.g., his perpetual virginity—is utterly unwarranted. John is simply the vehicle chosen for the expression of the writer's views. On the other hand, it is far from impossible that it was just because of the distinctly anti-Docetic polemic in I John that the later writer chose John to be the mouthpiece of the particular views that apostle had traditionally attacked, precisely as the author of the Acts of Paul had chosen Paul as the sponsor for women as preachers, in contradiction of the opposite teaching of the Pastoral letters.

Bibliography. The not uninteresting stories, together with the turgid and often very slow-moving preachments, of this curious book are conveniently available in M. R. James, *The Apocryphal NT* (1924), pp. 228-70. For further bibliography, *see* APOCRYPHA, NT. M. S. ENSLIN

JOHN, ACTS OF, BY PROCHORUS prŏk'ə rəs [Πρόχορος]. A Greek fifth-century romance, originally quite distinct from the "Leucian" Acts of John (*see* JOHN, ACTS OF); it recounts the wondrous deeds of John during his fifteen years on Patmos. Besides the Greek text of this very popular writing, versions in Latin, Sahidic, Ethiopic, Armenian, Arabic, and Old Slavonic are extant. Many of the Latin MSS contain large sections of the Leucian Acts—the tale of Lycomedes, the temple of Artemis, Drusiana, and the death of John—but never those sections reporting the Lord's life and passion. Prochorus, the alleged author and amanuensis, to whom John is represented (in Byzantine art) as dictating his gospel, is surely a reflection of the Jerusalem deacon (Acts 6:5) whom tradition made one of the Seventy and subsequently bishop of Nicomedia.

See also APOCRYPHA, NT.

Bibliography. The complete text of Prochorus may be found in T. Zahn, *Acta Ioannis* (1880). M. S. ENSLIN

JOHN, APOCRYPHON OR SECRET BOOK OF. A second-century Gnostic work, long unknown, refuted by Irenaeus (Her. I.29-31). Coptic translations of this work are now available in the fifth-century Codex Berolinensis and also in the great collection of Gnostic texts discovered in Upper Egypt at the ancient site Chenoboskion in 1946. *See* APOCRYPHA, NT. M. S. ENSLIN

JOHN, GOSPEL OF. Written, according to tradition, by John the son of Zebedee, this gospel stands as the last of the four canonical gospels in the NT, consistently with its traditional date of composition; though some early MSS—notably Codex Bezae (D) and the Washington Codex (W)—put first the two gospels considered of apostolic authorship, Matthew and John, with Luke and Mark in third and fourth place respectively.

John was highly valued in ancient times as the "spiritual gospel," first so called by Clement of Alexandria, and was perhaps the single most influential book of the NT in the fashioning of early Christian dogma.

Since the beginning of the period of modern critical study, however, there has been much controversy about its authorship, place of origin, theological affiliations and background, and historical value. Already in the late second century certain conservative and otherwise orthodox Christians, the so-called "Alogi," denied its apostolic authorship. This was, however, on the grounds of its teaching, which they judged unorthodox, and not because of any authentic alternative tradition. In the modern period too, dogmatic presuppositions have played a considerable part, if not always consciously, in the controversy about this gospel. Conservative scholars have been at pains to uphold its apostolic authorship, and others to deny it, both sides tacitly agreeing that it constituted a bulwark of orthodoxy. It has not always been sufficiently realized by both parties to the controversy that to settle the question of its authorship would not necessarily decide that of its value. Even if it could

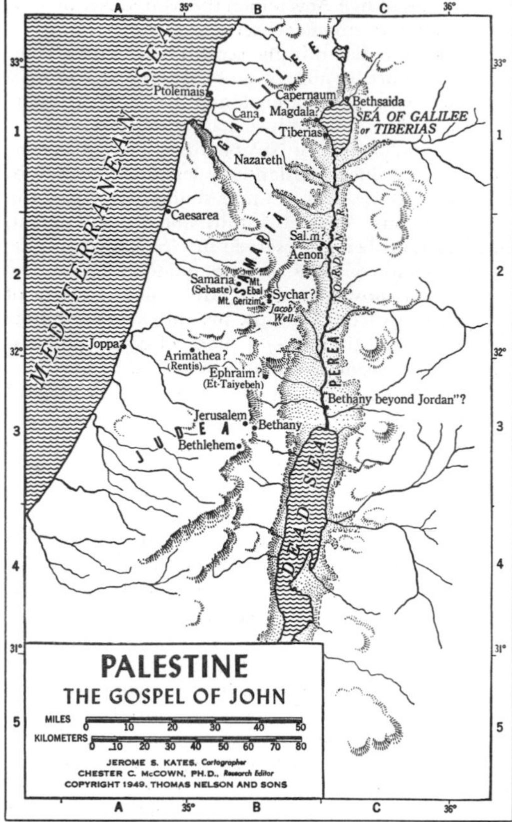

be proved that it was not the work of an apostle and eyewitness of the events it purports to describe, it would not follow necessarily that its testimony is intrinsically inferior to that of the other gospels, and vice versa.

The real focal point of the controversy about John is therefore not the problem of authorship, but the question why it differs as it does from the other gospels. Only if the latter question is satisfactorily answered can there be any hope of understanding the origin, purpose, and value of John.

Accordingly, this article aims at giving as fairly and fully as possible the data of which any hypothesis about John must take account, rather than at tracing the course of the long and so far inconclusive controversy about it. These data, and the theories based on them, can be most conveniently considered under the following heads, the order of which is designed in general to allow the objective data to be presented before the theories:

A. Contents and structure
   1. Summary of contents
   2. Dislocations of the text
B. Text and canonicity
   1. The MS evidence
   2. Place in the NT canon
C. Relationship to other NT writings
   1. The other gospels
   2. The letters of John
   3. Revelation
D. Teaching
   1. The theology of John

2. Theological affiliations of John with other religious literature
    a. The teaching of Jesus in the other gospels
    b. Paul
    c. Jewish literature
    d. Pagan literature

E. Evidence of use and authorship from early Christian literature
F. Internal evidence of purpose and authorship
G. The origin and purpose of John
H. Historical and religious value
Bibliography

A. *CONTENTS AND STRUCTURE.* John falls into four main sections of unequal length:

I. Prologue, 1:1-18
II. Testimony that Jesus is the Christ, furnished by John the Baptist and other witnesses, and by his own acts—the "signs"—and words, 1:19–11:57 (omitting, however, 7:53–8:11 [*see* § B1 *below*])
III. Passion and Resurrection, chs. 12–20
IV. Postscript, ch. 21

1. Summary of contents. The Prologue (1:1-18) deals with the nature and incarnation of the divine WORD, or Logos, the agent of God in creation and revelation.

The second section (1:19–11:57) may be outlined as follows:

1:19-36, the testimony of John the Baptist that Jesus is the Lamb of God (vss. 29, 36) and Son of God (vs. 34).

1:37-51, the testimony of Andrew that Jesus is the Messiah (vs. 41), and of Nathanael that he is Son of God and King of Israel (vs. 49). Jesus claims to be, as Son of man, a new Jacob (vs. 51).

2:1-11 (the first sign), Jesus changes water into wine. His disciples believe in him.

2:12-25, Jesus cleanses the temple, and gives the first hint of his death and resurrection (vss. 19-22). Many, seeing his signs, believe in him (vs. 23).

3:1-21, Jesus expounds to Nicodemus the new birth by water and the Spirit, and claims, as Son of man, to fulfil the OT type of the serpent which Moses set up as a means of salvation in the wilderness (vs. 14), thus also obliquely hinting at his crucifixion. At vs. 16 Nicodemus disappears from view, and there begins what is probably a meditation by the evangelist, rather than a continuation of Jesus' discourse, on the purpose of Christ's coming, interrupted by 3:22-30, and resumed at 3:31.

3:22-24, Jesus exercises a ministry of baptism in Judea parallel with John's.

3:25-30, final testimony of John the Baptist.

3:31-36, conclusion of the evangelist's meditation on the coming of Christ.

4:1-42, Jesus leaves Judea for Galilee, and goes through Samaria. His conversation with a Samaritan woman (vss. 7-26) culminates in his claiming to be Messiah. The woman bears witness to Christ (vss. 27-30). Jesus predicts to his disciples a harvest of fruit for eternal life (vss. 31-38). Many Samaritans believe because of the woman's testimony, many more because of Jesus' own word; they recognize him as Savior of the world (vss. 39-42).

4:43-45, Jesus is welcomed in Galilee.

4:46-54 (the second sign), Jesus saves from imminent death the son of an official, who believes.

5:1-9 (the third sign), Jesus heals a man who has been ill for thirty-eight years, at the pool Beth-zatha in Jerusalem on the sabbath.

5:10-47, the Jews object to his action, which Jesus defends.

6:1-15 (the fourth sign), Jesus feeds five thousand men with five loaves and two fish. He is acclaimed as the prophet who is to come into the world, and he avoids an attempt to make him king, by withdrawing to the hills.

6:16-21, as the disciples are crossing the sea, they see Jesus "walking on the sea" (vs. 19). It is not clear whether this should be classed as a "sign" or as a nonmiraculous action like the cleansing of the temple. "On the sea," ἐπὶ τῆς θαλάσσης, could be translated "by the sea" (cf. ἐπὶ τῆς γῆς, "at the land," in vs. 21). The miracle, if it is meant as such, is not so much emphasized as in Matt. 14:22-33, and it is perhaps better not to regard this as a "sign."

6:22-25, the people look for Jesus, and at last find him.

6:26-59, a discourse of Jesus in which he contrasts the bread he will give with the manna which Moses gave, speaks of himself as the bread of life, and describes his flesh as real food and his blood as real drink.

6:60-71, a discourse which offends many of his disciples. In spite of further explanation that the flesh by itself is of no avail, since it is the spirit which gives life, all except the Twelve leave Jesus. Simon Peter affirms their faith (vss. 68-69), but Jesus hints at a further defection.

Ch. 7; 8:12-59, Jesus at the Feast of Tabernacles (in vss. 1-9 Jesus at first remains in Galilee, but in vss. 10-13 he goes up to the feast in private). In 7:14-36 Jesus preaches in the temple, challenging the Jews' unbelief, against a background of mounting hostility. In 7:37-44, on the last day of the feast, Jesus invites anyone who thirsts to come to him and drink; the evangelist explains this offer as of the Spirit which he was to give (vs. 39). An attempt is made to arrest Jesus. In 7:45-52 the officers are unable to effect his arrest. Nicodemus speaks on his behalf, but to no avail. 8:12-59 is a continuation of Jesus' dispute with the Jews. He proclaims himself the light of the world (vs. 12), gives a further hint of his passion (vs. 28, echoing 3:14, and looking forward to 12:32 ff), and denies that the Jews are true sons of Abraham (vss. 39 ff). When he claims: "Before Abraham was, I am" (vs. 58), there is an abortive attempt to stone him.

9:1-12 (the fifth sign), Jesus heals a man blind from birth.

9:13-41, the man is persecuted by the Jews for his faith in Jesus, who condemns them for thinking they see when in fact they are blind.

10:1-18, parables of the sheepfold, the sheep, and the shepherds. Jesus likens himself to the door by which the sheep enter the fold, and contrasts himself, the good shepherd who lays down his life for the sheep (vs. 11), with the thieves and hirelings.

10:19-21, there is a division of opinion among his hearers.

10:22-42, Jesus at the Feast of the Dedication is

challenged to say plainly if he is the Christ. His claims that he and the Father are one (vs. 30), and that he is the Son of God (vs. 36), provoke further attempts against him (vss. 31, 39). He withdraws from Jerusalem, and it is noted that many believed in him (vs. 42).

11:1-44 (the sixth sign), Jesus raises from the dead his friend LAZARUS OF BETHANY.

11:45-53, this action calls forth both faith and opposition. The chief priests and Pharisees determine to put Jesus to death.

11:54-57, Jesus remains in retirement, the Passover is at hand, and the stage is set for the Passion.

The third section (chs.12–20) may be outlined as follows:

12:1-11, Jesus, among his friends at Bethany, is anointed by Mary, sister of Lazarus. The chief priests plan to put Lazarus also to death.

12:12-19, Jesus rides into Jerusalem on an ass, and is hailed as King of Israel.

12:20-36, some Greeks attending the feast wish to see Jesus, and are brought to him. Jesus accepts this as a sign that the time has come for the Son of man to be glorified (vs. 23). This is the time of judgment for the world (vs. 31), when he will be lifted up and will draw all men to himself (vs. 32; cf. 3:14; 8:28).

12:37-43, the evangelist's reflections on the unbelief of the Jews.

12:44-50, Jesus proclaims that he has come as light into the world, and points out the consequences of belief and unbelief.

13:1-30, the Last Supper (in 13:1-11 Jesus washes the disciples' feet, and in 13:12-20 he explains the significance of his action).

13:21-30, he predicts his betrayal, and points out the betrayer to the disciple whom he loved. Judas goes out into the night.

13:31–16:33, the conversation of Jesus with the remaining disciples. The salient features of this conversation are: the new commandment to love one another (13:34; cf. 15:12-17); the prediction of Peter's denial (13:38); the sayings "I am the way, and the truth, and the life" (14:6), "He who has seen me has seen the Father" (14:9), "If you ask anything in my name, I will do it" (14:14; cf. 16:23-24); the promise of "another Counselor, . . . even the Spirit of truth" (14:16-17; cf. 14:26; 15:26; 16:7-15); the parable of the vine and branches (15:1-11). A spirit of calm confidence in victory pervades the whole.

Ch. 17, the prayer of Jesus for the disciples, and for those who are to believe in him through their word, "that they may be one; even as thou, Father, art in me, and I in thee" (vs. 21).

18:1-11, Jesus is arrested in Gethsemane. Peter resists, wounds Malchus, and is rebuked by Jesus.

18:12-14, Jesus is bound and taken to Annas.

18:15-18, Peter and another disciple, known to the high priest, follow into the house.

18:19-24, Jesus is questioned by Annas and sent to Caiaphas.

18:25-27, Peter denies that he is a disciple of Jesus.

18:28–19:16, Jesus is brought before Pilate. The Jews refuse Pilate's offer to try Jesus themselves; they want him crucified (18:31-32). Pilate questions Jesus about his kingship, and is told that it is not of this world (18:36). Pilate attempts to release Jesus, but the crowds demand Barabbas (18:40). Pilate has Jesus scourged (19:1), and the soldiers put on him a crown of thorns and a purple robe (19:2), and mock him (19:3). Pilate continues his efforts to save Jesus; but when the Jews say that if he releases him, he is not Caesar's friend (19:12), he hands Jesus over to be crucified (19:16).

19:17-37, the Crucifixion. Jesus is crucified between two others (vs. 18), and Pilate has the title "the King of the Jews" put over him (vs. 19). The guard cast lots for his clothes (23-24). Jesus gives his mother into the keeping of the disciple whom he loved (vss. 25-27). Jesus says: "I thirst," is given vinegar, says: "It is finished," and dies (vss. 28-30). The Jews ask Pilate to remove the bodies. The other two are killed, but Jesus is found to be dead already. One of the soldiers pierces his side with a spear, and blood and water flow out (vss. 31-37).

19:38-42, the burial of Jesus. Joseph of Arimathea asks for Jesus' body, and, helped by Nicodemus, buries him in a new tomb in a garden.

20:1-29, appearances of the risen Jesus. In vss. 1-10 Mary Magdalene finds the stone taken from the tomb. She tells Peter and the other disciple whom Jesus loved. Peter goes into the tomb, and sees the empty gravecloths, and so does the other disciple. In vss. 11-18 Jesus makes himself known to Mary Magdalene and tells her to tell the disciples that he is ascending to his and their Father and God. This she does. In vss. 19-25 Jesus appears to the disciples, gives them the Holy Spirit, and the power to forgive and retain sins. Thomas is not with them and refuses to believe them. In vss. 26-29 Jesus appears to the disciples a week later, and overcomes Thomas' disbelief. Thomas confesses him "my Lord and my God." Jesus blesses those who have not seen and yet have believed.

20:30-31, the purpose of the gospel: "that you may believe that Jesus is the Christ, the Son of God, and that believing you may have life in his name."

In the Postscript (ch. 21) Jesus appears to some of his disciples by the sea of Tiberias. They have had an unsuccessful night's fishing, but following Jesus' instructions, they catch 153 fish (vss. 1-11). Jesus gives the disciples a meal, and then commissions Peter to feed his sheep and prophesies Peter's death (vss. 12-19). His words about the disciple whom he loved are recorded with the comment that they have been misunderstood in the church (vss. 20-23). In a footnote (vss. 24-25) the author is identified as the disciple whom Jesus loved.

Running through the whole gospel and bringing it into a unity are a number of themes, the most important of which are stated in the Prologue. Thus the gospel is not unlike a sonata in form. Examples of these recurrent themes are:

a) Christ as the Logos. Though "Logos" is not used again as a title in the gospel, references to Christ's or God's "word" are particularly important (e.g., 2:22; 4:41, 50; 5:24, 38; 6:63, 68; 8:31, 47; 12:48; 15:3; 17:17). The words disclose the Word.

b) Christ as the source of life (1:4; cf. 3:15-16; 5:24, 26, 29, 39-40; 6:35, 63, 68; 8:12; 10:10, 28; 11:25; 14:6; 17:2-3; 20:31). The signs, particularly the raising of Lazarus, show the Christ as giver of life.

c) Christ as the source of light (1:4-5 etc.; cf. 3:19-

21; 8:12; 9:5; 12:35-36, 46). This is particularly illustrated by the healing of the blind man.

d) Witness to, and faith in, Christ (though John does not use the noun "faith"; cf. [for "witness"] 1:7, 15, 19; 4:39; 5:36; 8:18; 19:35; [for "belief"] 2:11, 22-23; 3:15-16, 18, 36; 4:39, 41, 53; 5:46-47; 6:35, 40, 69; 7:31, 38; 8:24, 30; 9:38; 10:42; 11:25-27, 45; 12:11, 42, 44, 46; 14:1, 11-12; 16:30; 19:35; 20:8, 25, 29, 31).

e) Christ as the source of truth (1:14, 17; cf. 4:23-24; 5:33; 8:32, 40, 44-46; 14:6, 17; 15:26; 16:13; 17:17, 19; 18:37-38 [significantly the last occurrence of the word in John]).

The recurrence of these (and other) themes imparts to John a peculiar richness and closeness of texture to which no summary can do justice.

2. Dislocations of the text. Many critics, impressed both by the occasional abruptness of transitions in John's text and by the difference in the order of events between John and the other gospels (*see* § C1 *below*), infer that the text of John has been dislocated, either by accident or by design. By restoring the supposedly original order, they claim to improve the flow of the narrative, avoid abrupt transitions, and make harmonization with the other gospels easier. Some or all of the following changes have been recommended by various critics:

a) Remove 3:22-30 and place it after either 2:12 or 3:36, thus avoiding the interruption of the passage 3:16-21, 31-36, which reads as a continuous whole.

b) Transpose chs. 5 and 6, since 6:1 follows more naturally on 4:54 than on 5:47.

c) Rearrange chs. 7 and 8 thus: 7:15-24; 8:12-20; 7:1-14; 7:25-52; 8:21-59.

d) Put 10:1-18 after 10:29, thus avoiding the abrupt opening of ch. 10.

e) Put 12:36-43 (from "When Jesus had said this") after 12:50, thus bringing together the speech of Jesus at present divided by the evangelist's reflections.

f) Put 13:31–14:31 (from "Now is the Son of man glorified") after ch. 16, so that "Rise, let us go hence," does not break into Jesus' discourse.

The preferred opinion today is that, if dislocation has occurred, it was not accidental. The order of the gospel as it stands is plainly intentional, but it may not correspond to the intention of the original author. The gospel as it stands may reflect the activity of more than one mind. *See* § G *below*.

B. *TEXT AND CANONICITY.* 1. The MS evidence. John is not only found in all the most important uncial codices of the NT—Sinaiticus (א), Vaticanus (B), Ephraemi (C), Bezae (D), Alexandrinus (A), and the Washington (W) and Koridethi (Θ) codices—and in all the early versions, but is also particularly well represented among the earliest papyrus fragments that have come to light. Of the sixty-eight fragments listed to date, fifteen are of John, and these include the earliest of all NT MS fragments—the Rylands Papyrus 457 (Papyrus 52), a few lines from John 18 dating from the first half of the second century—as well as the Chester Beatty Papyrus (Papyrus 45), which includes parts of John 10 and 11 and of the other gospels, and the Bodmer Papyrus II (Papyrus 66), which contains nearly all of John 1–14. These latter papyri are of approximately the same date, probably very early in the third century. This is striking evidence of the early popularity of John, at least in Egypt.

The text is not only well represented, but on the whole also very well preserved. The following variants are worthy of notice:

1:3-4. The punctuation, "without him was not anything made. That which has been made was life in him" (RSV mg.), is to be preferred. Not only is it found in the earliest extant quotation of John (by Tatian *ca.* 170), as well as in nearly all pre-Nicene quotations, but the alternative is probably a deliberate alteration, to exclude the interpretation which would count the Holy Spirit among the things made.

1:18. "Only Son" has the inferior MS attestation to the alternative "God only-begotten," found in אBCWΘ and other authorities. There is some slight evidence in favor of "the only-begotten," a reading which would account for both the other alternatives.

4:9. "For Jews have no dealings with Samaritans" is omitted by אD and some Latin MSS.

7:39. "For as yet the Spirit had not been given" is the reading of the Latin and Syriac versions. Several Greek MSS, headed by א, read: "For as yet the Spirit was not"; W and the majority add "Holy," while B has: "For as yet the Holy Spirit had not been given." The reading of א is to be preferred, the others being expansions of it.

7:53–8:11. This whole passage, though found in D and most later Greek MSS, is omitted by papyrus 66, אBWΘ, and by most of the early versions and fathers. One group of Greek MSS puts it at the end of John, another after Luke 21:38. It is clearly no part of John, but was perhaps put in here to illustrate John 8:16.

8:57. א has the curious variant: "Has Abraham seen you?"

13:10. "Except for his feet," is omitted by א and some Latin MSS—probably correctly, in spite of the relatively weak attestation.

2. Place in the NT canon. It is not known when the four gospels as we now have them were collected into one and accepted as alone authoritative, but it was probably sometime between Marcion's choice of a revised edition of Luke as the sole authoritative gospel (*ca.* 140) and the publication by Tatian *ca.* 170 of his *Diatessaron,* a continuous narrative made out of our four gospels. The choice of the four may well have been meant as a counterblast to Marcion, and Tatian's use of them testifies to the esteem in which they were then held. John was one of them, and since the time of Tatian its place in the canon has been challenged only by a group of ultraconservative but otherwise orthodox Roman Christians who apparently thought it countenanced certain heretical views. But by the end of the second century the place of John as part of the NT canon was assured. *See* CANON OF THE NT.

C. *RELATIONSHIP TO OTHER NT WRITINGS.* 1. The other gospels. The differences between John and the other three gospels are sufficiently obvious, in subject matter, arrangement of material, and style.

John contains many incidents to which the others have no parallel—e.g., the "beginning of signs" at Cana, baptism by Jesus and his disciples, Jesus' conversations with Nicodemus and the Samaritan woman, his frequent visits to Jerusalem and his preaching and miracles there, and, not least, the raising of Lazarus. The author's point of view is Judean rather than Galilean: Judea is Jesus' "own country" in John (cf. 4:43-45, contrasted with Mark 6:4 [cf. Matt. 13: 57; Luke 4:24]).

John puts what are apparently the same events at different places in his narrative—e.g., the cleansing of the temple and the anointing at Bethany.

He also has alternative versions of what look like the same events—e.g., the first encounters of Jesus with John the Baptist and with Simon Peter (John 1:29 ff [cf. Mark 1:9-11]; John 1:42 [cf. Mark 1:16-17]); the Last Supper; the arrest, trials, and crucifixion of Jesus; the Resurrection; the draught of fishes (John 21:4-8; cf. Luke 5:1-11).

He also does not mention events to which some or all of the other evangelists appear to attach considerable importance. He omits the birth and baptism of Jesus, his temptations, his exorcisms, his transfiguration, and his blessing and distribution of bread and wine at the Last Supper.

There are also differences in the form and content of Jesus' teaching in John. In the other gospels it is given mainly in parables and epigrams, in forms which often resemble those of Hebrew prophecy. In John it is given mainly in long meditative discourses and dialogues more like those of the *Corpus Hermeticum* (*see* § D2*d below*) than of the other gospels. In John much of Jesus' teaching is about himself and his relationship to the Father—sayings beginning "I am" are characteristic of John but absent from the others. The "theme words" of John (*see* § A1 *above*) are more characteristic of Hellenistic mysticism and of the Dead Sea Scrolls than of the teaching of Jesus in the other gospels.

These differences would be even more remarkable if we could be sure that the author of John knew one or more of the other gospels. On this subject scholars are divided. It is generally agreed that points of contact between John and Matthew are too slight to suggest that John knew Matthew, but the case is different with Mark and Luke.

a. John and Mark. If, as is probable, the author of Matthew in Syria and Luke in Macedonia or Achaia both knew of Mark toward the end of the first century, it appears more likely than not that John in Ephesus also knew of it at much the same period—i.e., if we may provisionally accept the traditional date and place for the composition of John. Moreover, to prove a negative is notoriously difficult. So it may well seem antecedently more probable that John knew Mark. It does not follow, however, that if John knew Mark, he must necessarily have used Mark as a source.

The following are the main passages which must be taken into consideration:

1:1. "In the beginning" may be read as a tacit correction of Mark 1:1: "The beginning of the gospel of Jesus Christ," suggesting that the gospel's beginning is the Creation. But the allusion to Gen. 1:1 is obvious, and may well be thought a sufficient reason for the form of words in John.

1:19-34. Though most of the material in this passage is unlike anything in Mark, there are close parallels between John 1:23 and Mark 1:3; John 1:26 and Mark 1:8; John 1:27 and Mark 1:7; John 1:32 and Mark 1:11. It may be that John took these from Mark, but he might well have got them from a common tradition.

2:13-22. The cleansing of the temple, both here and in Mark 11:15-17, occurs at Passover, but at different periods in the ministry of Jesus. The allusion to the Passion in John 2:19 recalls the accusations made against Jesus at his trial in Mark 14:58 and when he was on the cross (Mark 15:29-30), and tells in favor of Mark's date for the cleansing against John's (if we are to assume that Jesus cleansed the temple only once). It is conceivable that John has taken the incident from Mark, but it may also be felt, in view of the differences in detail between the stories, that John was using an independent tradition.

3:24. "John had not yet been put in prison" may be meant as a cross reference to Mark 1:14: "After John was arrested, Jesus came into Galilee," but can equally well be taken as an independent note of time.

4:44. "Jesus himself testified that a prophet has no honor in his own country" recalls Mark 6:4: "A prophet is not without honor, except in his own country," but the difference in setting may argue for independence.

5:1-18. The healing of a paralyzed man here recalls a similar incident in Mark 2:1-12. In spite of some obvious differences (in John it takes place in Jerusalem, in Mark in Capernaum, etc.), the essentials of the two stories are the same. In both John 5:8; Mark 2:9 occur the words: "Rise, take up your pallet, and walk"; and John 5:14: "Sin no more," recalls the forgiveness of the man's sins in Mark 2:5. Unless these parallels are fortuitous, there is a case for supposing that John has added to his tradition material taken from Mark.

6:1-21. Both here and in Mark 6:34-52, Jesus feeds five thousand men, then sends his disciples across the lake, and appears to them walking on the sea. Here, if anywhere, there is a case for John's dependence upon Mark. Both mention two hundred denarii as the probable cost of bread (John 6:7; Mark 6:37), five loaves and two fish (John 6:9; Mark 6:38), the men sitting on grass (John 6:10; Mark 6:39), Jesus' blessing the bread (John 6:11; Mark 6:41), the twelve baskets of fragments (John 6:13; Mark 6:43), and the five thousand men (John 6:10; Mark 6:44), often in the same words: in the second incident the words of Jesus to the disciples are in part identical in the Greek, though the RSV translates John 6:20: "It is I; do not be afraid," and Mark 6:50: "It is I; have no fear." But if John is borrowing from Mark, where did he get his independent features—e.g., the parts played by Philip and Andrew, the boy who provided the food, and, above all, the attempt to make Jesus king (John 6:15)? Unless these come from John's own imagination, he must have had an independent source for them, and if for them, why not for the rest?

6:42. The description of Jesus as "son of Joseph" may be taken as a correction of his description in Mark 6:3 as "son of Mary," similar to, and for the same reason as, those in Matt. 13:55: "Is not this the carpenter's son?" and Luke 4:22: "Is not this Joseph's son?"—i.e., to avoid the implication of illegitimacy involved in calling a man the son of his mother, as if his father were unknown.

6:66-71. In Mark 8:29, Peter's confession that Jesus is the Christ closely follows Mark's account of the second feeding of the multitude (Mark 8:1-10). Similarly here Peter makes a confession of faith in Christ (John 6:68-69). That John had the passage from Mark in mind may be suggested by the fact that in 6:70-71 Judas is identified as "a devil." Is this a tacit correction of Mark 8:33, where it is Peter who is called Satan?

12:1-8. The anointing of Jesus at Bethany shortly before the Passover recalls Mark 14:3-9, the anointing of Jesus at Bethany two days before the Passover. Points of similarity are: the rare Greek word translated "pure nard" (John 12:3; Mark 14:3); the objection to the waste of the ointment, worth "more than three hundred denarii" (Mark 14:5), or "three hundred denarii" (John 12:5); and Jesus' saying about the disciples' always having the poor with them (Mark 14:7; John 12:8). But again John has details not derived from Mark, and this fact weakens the case for his dependence.

12:12-19. The description of Jesus' entry into Jerusalem is, in detail, so different from that in Mark 11:1-10 that it can hardly be dependent upon it.

12:27. Jesus' refusal to pray to be saved from "this hour" may be meant as a correction of Mark 14:35, where he in fact does so pray. This may appear more plausible if it is also supposed that John 18:11: "Shall I not drink the cup which the Father has given me?" is a similar correction of Mark 14:36: "Remove this cup from me."

13–21. From the Last Supper to the end of the gospel John is so clearly following an independent tradition, though covering the same ground as Mark, that it is unnecessary to consider their resemblances and differences in detail any further.

The examination of John 1–12 suggests that Mark can hardly have been a source of John, though John may occasionally have expected his readers to compare his own account with Mark's. If it appears plausible to distinguish between an author and an editor of John, the occasional cross references to Mark will most plausibly be attributed to the editor. If John and Mark are substantially independent, this adds considerably to the force of their testimony where their traditions overlap (e.g., in the feeding of the multitude).

b. John and Luke. Such points of contact as there are between John and Luke all occur in material peculiar to Luke—i.e., in parts of his gospel which he did not get from Mark or from the hypothetical source which he shared with Matthew. This suggests that Luke's tradition was in part dependent on that used by John rather than that John utilized Luke. The chief points of contact are: the use of "the Lord" instead of "Jesus" in the body of the narrative (Luke 7:13; 10:1; 11:39; 12:42; 13:15; 18:6; 19:8; 22:61; John 4:1; 6:23; 11:2; 20:20), which by itself only shows that both share a common environment, that of the Gentile church; the absence of exorcisms; the disciple Judas (not Iscariot; Luke 6:16; John 14:22); Martha and her sister Mary (Luke 10:38-42; John 11:1 ff; 12:1-3); LAZARUS (Luke 16:19-31; John 11:1 ff); the location of Jesus' resurrection appearances in Jerusalem (Luke 24:36-43; John 20:19-29); the draught of fishes (Luke 5:1-11; John 21:1-14). It is not easy to estimate the precise significance of all this. It is hardly enough to prove that John knew Luke, unless one is to suppose that John's only sources were the other gospels and his own imagination. It is, e.g., hard to see why he put Martha and Mary down as sisters of Lazarus, unless he had information on this point.

c. Conclusion. The independence of John is sufficiently obvious. We should not, however, make the mistake of ascribing the difference between John and the other gospels to the fact that the others are historical and John is theological. The fact that all are gospels goes far to outweigh the differences. All are theological in the sense that they presuppose their authors' faith that Jesus is the Christ, and are written to foster this faith in others. And John is concerned to stress that the events which he narrates really happened, and is, so far, historical, at least in intention. *See* § H *below.*

Furthermore, the fact that John gained acceptance as canonical, though so obviously unlike the other gospels, is a fact to be taken into consideration when estimating the value of the tradition of its authorship. *See* § E *below.*

2. The letters of John. The similarity of thought and language between the gospel and the letters of John (*see* JOHN, LETTERS OF) is at first sight so close that the traditional ascription of them to the same author is often taken as self-evident, even by scholars who do not also accept their traditional ascription to John the son of Zebedee. Nevertheless, there are some slight differences which some scholars have thought to raise a doubt about their identity of authorship.

Thus, e.g., the thought of the letters, particularly their eschatology, is more conventional than that of the gospel. The chief concern of the letters, theologically, is to stress the reality of Christ's flesh; while this interest is not, of course, absent from the gospel, it is by no means so prominent in it. On the other hand, the concern of the gospel for the apostasy of Israel finds no echo in the letters.

There are also differences in matter of detail: e.g., in I John 2:18 the time of writing is for the author the "last hour," while for the gospel the eschatologically decisive "hour" is that of the Crucifixion (cf. John 12:23, etc.); the "last day," on the other hand, is mentioned six times in John (6:39, etc.), but never in the letters; eschatological technical terms found in the letters and not in the gospel are "the coming," παρουσία (I John 2:28), and "antichrist" (five times; I John 2:18, etc.); the term "Paraclete," παράκλητος, is used of the Holy Spirit in John 14:16, 26; 15:26; 16:7 (translated "Counselor" in the RSV), but of Christ in I John 2:1 (where the RSV translates it "advocate"); "the word" has not the particular personal sense in I John 1:1 that it has in John 1:1 (and also in the interpolation in I John 5:7 KJV); the same idea, "the lust of the flesh," is expressed by θέλημα σαρκός (John 1:13) and ἐπιθυμία σαρκός (I John 2:16); words important in the gospel, like "Lord," "glory," "scripture," "save," are not in the letters, while "faith," absent from the gospel (carefully avoided by it, we may say), is found in I John 5:4; and the common conjunction οὖν, "therefore," found some two hundred times in John, occurs only once in the letters—III John 8.

What weight should be attached to these facts, in view of the close similarity that otherwise exists between the gospel and the letters, is hard to estimate. The evidence of Revelation has also to be considered. It will be suggested (*see* § G *below*) that the facts may perhaps best be accounted for on the hypothesis that the author of the letters edited the gospel (but *see also* JOHN, LETTERS OF).

3. Revelation. Tradition eventually ascribed Revelation as well as the letters of John to the author of the gospel, but few scholars today would maintain this view, for in spite of some resemblances between John and Revelation, the differences between them are much greater than between the gospel and the letters. John and Revelation are the only books of the NT to use Logos and Lamb as titles of Christ, but the Logos of Rev. 19:13 is more akin to the warrior of Wisd. Sol. 18:15 ff than to the Logos of John 1:1 ff, while the word used for "lamb" in John 1:29, 36, is ἀμνός, and in Rev. 5:6, etc. (twenty-nine examples in all), ἀρνίον. Their theology also is different, at least in emphasis. The eschatology of Revelation is predominantly futurist, unlike that of the gospel, and its conception of the Holy Spirit is impersonal, while that of the gospel is clearly personal. There are, however, some resemblances in theology, for both appear to see a symbolical significance in numbers, and (more important) both in their different ways emphasize the true humanity of Christ—Revelation uses the human name Jesus even in the most exalted contexts. They also resemble one another in the simplicity of their syntax, though in the Greek this resemblance is made much less obvious by the bizarre grammatical and syntactical usages of Revelation. The language of Revelation is not simply bad Greek, but a deliberately constructed language, defying the ordinary rules, yet fully self-consistent and most effective in conveying an unearthly atmosphere. So one cannot really argue from differences of language; the other differences, however, are generally felt to rule out the possibility that John and Revelation are by the same author. Nevertheless, there is some interrelation among the gospel, the letters, and the Revelation of John—theologically the letters are midway between the gospel and Revelation—and it is not beyond the bounds of possibility that Revelation is the work of the author of the letters (the editor, perhaps, of the gospel), or is a pseudepigraph meant to be taken as his and perhaps incorporating some of his work. *See* REVELATION, BOOK OF.

D. *TEACHING.* 1. The theology of John. The theological ideas which underlie and pervade the gospel impart to it a distinctive quality and flavor, and even influence the form of the narrative, which is dictated rather by the necessity of an orderly development of doctrine than by the observance of a strictly chronological sequence of events.

John's thought, like that of the NT as a whole, is eschatological, but whereas elsewhere in the NT the predominant eschatological contrast is that between the present age and the age to come—a temporal contrast—in John it is between two orders of existence, the temporal and the eternal. This fact may be illustrated by John's interpretation of the concepts of life, judgment, and glory. In John life, or eternal life, ζωὴ αἰώνιος, is often spoken of as a present possession of the believer (cf. 3:36; 5:24; 6:47, 54; 17:3), while elsewhere it is not so much "eternal" life as the life "of the [coming] age" (cf. Matt. 19:16, 29 [and parallels, Mark 10:17, 30; Luke 18:18, 30]; 25:46; Luke 10:25; Rom. 2:7; 6:22; Gal. 6:8). There is perhaps no ultimate difference here, but there are certainly two different points of view. Similarly, while judgment is elsewhere thought of as future, as in Matt. 10:15; 11:22 (=Luke 10:14), 24; 12:36; Heb. 9:27; 10:27; and (significantly) I John 4:17, in John, apart from the isolated instance of John 5:29, which speaks of those who have done evil coming to the resurrection of judgment, the peculiar and characteristic conception is that judgment is in the present (cf. 3:19: "This is the judgment, that the light has come into the world, and men loved darkness rather than light"; 5:24; 12:31; 16:11). In the same way the glory of Christ is elsewhere thought of as subsequent to his humiliation and suffering, as in Matt. 24:30 (=Mark 13:26; Luke 21:27); 25:31; Phil. 2:5-11; Heb. 2:9; and particularly clearly in I Pet. 1:11, but in John the Crucifixion is consistently regarded as the glorification of Christ (7:39; 12:23; 17:1), and as his "lifting up" (3:14; 8:28; 12:32), which, as I Tim. 3:16 suggests, implies glorification.

Consistently with his peculiar eschatology, John's theology tends to deal in contrasts—light and darkness, life and death, spirit and flesh, God and the world. But though it sounds dualistic, it has nothing more than its language in common with the ontological dualism characteristic of Gnosticism. Light and darkness are not two equal and opposed powers with the same metaphysical status. The world, though under the usurped power of a ruler who is opposed to God (cf. 12:31; 16:11), and so unable to recognize and obey the Christ (1:10) or God (17:25), and hating Christ and his disciples (15:18-19; 17:14, 16), is yet the creation of God (1:10), the object of his love (3:16), and destined to be saved (3:17; 12:47), and to come to belief and knowledge (17:21, 23). It is not simply a matter of certain elect souls' being saved from the world; Christ is the Savior of the world (4:42). It is true that there are occasional passages like 17:9: "I am praying for them; I am not praying for the world," which are susceptible of a dualist interpretation, but these should not count against the general tenor of John's thought, for his cardinal principle of incarnation is quite incompatible with ontological dualism.

For John, God is unknowable and unknown unless and until he reveals himself through his Logos or Son (1:18; 5:37; 6:46; 7:28-29; 8:19, 54-55; 14:6-7; 15:21; 16:3; 17:25). But this revelation, when made, is the fullest possible, so that to see the Son is to see the Father (14:9). God is then known as Father, primarily as the Father of Jesus Christ, but also of those who are Christ's, in virtue of their union with Christ (17:21; cf. 1:12-13). "God is spirit" (4:24), and we may infer from 3:8 (where "wind" is the same word as "spirit") that it is because he is spirit that the Father is unknowable. The reason for God's revelation of himself through his Son is his love for the world, of which, again through his Son, he is the creator (3:16 ff).

The agent of God in all his dealings with the world, both in creation and in salvation, is his Logos.

John introduces the term quite without explanation at the beginning of his gospel, as if he fully expected his readers to understand its meaning, but he does not use it after 1:14: "The Word became flesh," in which verse he speaks for the first time of Son and Father, the terms which he uses henceforward. The Logos is himself God (1:1, where there is a sublety in the Greek which no English translation can reproduce—"the Word was with God," where the article is used, πρὸς τὸν θεόν, making "God" a substantive, while in "the Word was God" "God" has no article, θεὸς ἦν ὁ Λόγος, and is thus adjectival). The climax of the gospel is Thomas' confession of the risen Christ as Lord and God (20:28). Being himself divine, the Son can reveal the Father. He is in perfect union with the Father—this thought is most emphatically expressed in 10:30: "I and the Father are one"; he is the object of the Father's love (3:35, etc.), and invested with his authority to execute judgment (5: 27) and to grant eternal life (17:2). The Son, for his part, imitates his Father, and does nothing by himself (5:19; 8:28-29), but simply carries out his Father's will in perfect filial obedience (4:34; 5:30; 6:38). It is noteworthy that this gospel, which is most emphatic in maintaining the full divinity of Christ, also lays such stress on his obedience—and, indeed, subjection—to the Father's will.

If the Son is to reveal the Father, he must share, not only his divine nature (only as God can he reveal *God* to man), but also our human nature (only as man can he reveal God to *man*). Hence John's affirmation that "the Word became flesh" (1:14). John offers no explanation of this paradox, such as the church fathers hammered out in the ensuing centuries of christological controversy, for he does not share their metaphysical interests. His affirmation is as much religious as theological. He is concerned to maintain the reality of Jesus' humanity, and introduces his human name at the first opportunity (1:17), as if to point this out. He can make this affirmation because the experience of Christians was that if they would know what God is like, all they had to do was to study Jesus. This intuition is independent of, and prior to, christological speculation. Hence "we have beheld his glory, glory as of the only Son from the Father" (John 1:14).

The incarnate Christ is given the title SON OF GOD far more freely in John than in the other gospels. In Mark, e.g., apart from the evangelist's own words in 1:1 and the centurion's confession at 15:39, this title is used only by supernatural speakers, divine or diabolical. In John, however, the Baptist uses it at 1:34 and Nathanael at 1:49. Similarly "Messiah" is used by Andrew at 1:41. It is noteworthy that the untranslated Μεσσίας is used by John alone of the evangelists (here and at 4:25). John also has the title "Lamb of God" in the Baptist's testimony to Jesus at 1:29, 36. "The Lamb of God who takes away the sin of the world" is a complex concept, weaving together various allusions to OT types—the Passover lamb (cf. the fulfilment of the scripture referring originally to the Passover lamb in the fact that no bone of Jesus' body was broken on the cross [19:36]); the scapegoat (the Passover lamb did not "take away sin," but the scapegoat did); the lamb led to the slaughter, of Isa. 53:7 (ἀμνός in the LXX of Isaiah, as in John, whereas in Exod. 12:3 LXX the word is πρόβατον); the lamb which God provided as a substitute for Isaac, in Gen. 22:8 (hence the lamb of *God*); and finally, perhaps, if the Baptist may be supposed to have spoken in Aramaic, an allusion to the two senses of the Aramaic טליא, "lamb" and "servant."

John also uses the title SON OF MAN, found in the other gospels. It is as if, having emphasized Jesus' divinity by the title "Son of God," he would redress the balance by using one that emphasizes his humanity. But he tends to use it in a way which suggests that its implication for him is that of the "heavenly man" familiar in the Christology of Paul. In 1:51 it occurs in a context in which Jesus claims to fulfil the type of Jacob; in 3:13-14 he is clearly the man from heaven; in 5:27 he has authority to execute judgment, as Son of man (cf. Matt. 25:31 ff); in 6:27, 53, the Son of man gives food and drink that convey eternal life—his flesh and blood; in 13:31 Jesus speaks of the Son of man being glorified (in his crucifixion).

John also stresses that Jesus is King, much more explicitly than do the other evangelists, though he does not give Jesus the title "Son of David" (cf. Nathanael's confession [1:49]; the words of the crowd at his entry into Jerusalem [12:13; contrast Matt. 21:9; Mark 11:9-10; but cf. Luke 19:38]; and Jesus' conversation with Pilate [John 18:33 ff], in which he does not disclaim the title, but explains the nature of his kingship).

According to John, the purpose of Jesus' ministry is to reveal the Father by his words and actions. The actions which he narrates are "signs" revealing Jesus as the agent of the Father. The meaning of the signs is made explicit in the discourses which accompany them (*see* §G *below*). An important feature of Jesus' ministry is his bringing of the Spirit. He himself, in virtue, presumably, of his divinity, is endowed with the Spirit (cf. 1:33; 3:34) and finally bestows it upon his disciples (20:22), in order to fulfil the promise he had made to them that they would have the Spirit after his departure (14:16-17, 26; 15:26; 16:7 ff). Jesus had united "flesh" and "Spirit" in himself, and so had brought within man's reach the possibility of union with, and knowledge of, God, which is the supreme object of man's existence.

Because he had already united flesh and Spirit in himself, Jesus was able to devise a means whereby Spirit could be communicated to men and enable them to share the divine life. He indicated what this means was to be when he gave the bread to the multitude which he fed. This bread was a symbol of his flesh, which was to be given for the life of the world (6:51). By eating the bread, men would participate in the spirit-bearing flesh of the incarnate Son, himself the living bread, the real manna (6:32-33). But to guard against any magical conception of the sacrament (if we may use a term which John does not), he emphasizes elsewhere that the flesh, apart from the spirit, is valueless; it is the spirit which is the life-giving principle (6:63).

John thus attaches to the feeding of the multitude the significance of Jesus' action in giving bread to the faithful which the other evangelists associate with the Last Supper. That the latter is the proper context is suggested by the fact that John also makes Jesus speak of drinking his blood, as well as eating his flesh (6:

53-56), though we are not told that Jesus gave anything to drink at the feeding of the multitude.

John again offers no explanation of the way in which the bread of the Eucharist is, represents, or symbolizes the flesh of Christ. He accepts and adapts the words which the faithful believed to be those of Christ, sharing their conviction that the Eucharist is a means of imparting the life-giving Spirit to believers.

He likewise interprets the water of baptism as a vehicle of the Spirit (cf. 3:5 ff). The mention of Jesus' baptizing at the outset of his ministry (3:22)—after he has told Nicodemus that he must be "born of water and spirit" (3:5, where "spirit" has no article in the Greek—the RSV "the Spirit" may be misleading), and of the washing of the disciples' feet at the Last Supper (13:5 ff), is meant presumably to indicate water as the future vehicle of Spirit, as is also the bread given at the feeding of the multitude. During Jesus' actual ministry they could not convey the Spirit, as is clear from 7:39: "As yet the Spirit had not been given, because Jesus was not yet glorified." Only after his death does he breathe on his disciples, as a sign that the Spirit can now be received (20:22). It may also be noted that the emphatic way in which John draws attention to the blood and water which flowed from Jesus' side after his death (19:34) suggests that John sees in them a sacramental significance.

John also stresses the necessity of faith if men are to receive the Spirit. Already in 1:12-13 he makes it clear that the new birth as children of God depends on faith, and repeats the thought (3:15-16, 36; 5:24; 6:35, 40, 47; 7:38-39; etc.). He avoids using the noun πίστις, "faith," perhaps because it had lost in some circles what John judged to be its full and proper meaning; instead he uses the verb πιστεύω, "believe."

The result of Jesus' ministry was to call into being a body of believers, whose destiny it was to be united through the Son to the Father (17:21 ff). They are likened to a flock of which Jesus is the shepherd (10:11 ff), and to the branches of a vine, the vine being Jesus (15:1 ff). Both "flock" and "vine" are symbols of Israel in the OT (cf. Ps. 80, which uses both [vss. 1, 8 ff]; Isa. 40:11; 5:1-7; etc.). They are to come both from Israel and from the Gentiles, being the "children of God who are scattered abroad" (John 11:52; cf. 10:16). They are those who are to come to the light (3:21), and worship the Father in spirit and truth (4:23); who, though in the world, are not on the world's side ("of the world"; 17:14; etc.), since they belong to God (17:6 ff). The bond which unites them to one another and to Christ and the Father is love—the Father's love for the Son and for those who belong to him, and their love responding to it (14:21; 15:10; 17:23, 26). Love is, indeed, the motive behind the whole ministry of Christ (3:16 ff), and, supremely, this love is shown by his death (15:13). Both as the supreme evidence of love for man, and as the means whereby the Spirit is to be made available for men, Christ's death is the efficient cause of man's salvation. By his lifting up on the cross, which for John is Christ's glorification, he draws all men to himself (cf. 3:14-15; 8:28; 12:23-25, 32). His death is his victory over the world (16:33), of which his resurrection is the evidence. It is the conclusive sign of his divine commission and nature.

Those who respond in love and faith to the love of Christ shown in his death will, as the fruit of his death and resurrection, enjoy the gift of the Spirit—not as an impersonal power, which is what one might infer from the references to spirit early in the gospel (e.g., 3:5; 7:39), but as a personal presence. John tells us nothing about the precise relationship of the Spirit to the Son, or about his metaphysical status, except that he "proceeds from the Father" (15:26), which the later church took as justifying the equal metaphysical status of the Spirit with the Son. But here again John's interest is not speculative, but religious. He is concerned to establish that the withdrawal of Christ's visible presence does not leave the faithful destitute of his help, for they have the Spirit, who is, as it were, Christ's second self. This comes out clearly in 14:16-18, where Jesus says first that the Spirit will be with and in his disciples, and then continues: "I will not leave you desolate; I will come to you" (vs. 18)—i.e., the presence of the Spirit is that of Christ.

This indwelling Spirit is called παράκλητος (RSV "Counselor," KJV "Comforter"; 14:16, 26; 15:26; 16:7). This word is used elsewhere in the NT only in I John 2:1, where it is a title or description of Christ himself, and is translated "advocate" by both the KJV and the RSV. This is etymologically closest to its root meaning, "one called to the side of another," *advocatus*. "Advocate" is a possible translation in the gospel passages; the Spirit is a kind of counsel for the defense of the disciples, as also in Mark 13:11, and in John 16:8-11 he also appears as counsel for the prosecution of the world. But his functions are wider than the purely forensic term allows, so that "Counselor" is preferable. "Comforter," now archaic, is misleading; it meant "Strengthener." The Counselor, then, "the Spirit of truth" (14:17; 16:13), will teach the disciples and remind them of Christ's words (14:26; 16:13-15), bearing a testimony to Christ concurrent with that of his disciples (15:26-27). The Spirit is, in fact, to inspire Christian prophecy, and it may well be that the evangelist himself was a prophet, and would have claimed for his work the inspiration of the Spirit. *See* § G *below*. *See also* PARACLETE.

One further feature of John's thought calls for comment—his ideas on predestination. Here again his interest is practical rather than speculative, and he does not have a rigidly consistent theory. While on the one hand he stresses the importance of belief, on the other he makes salvation depend wholly on the divine initiative: "You did not choose me, but I chose you" (15:16). The faithful are already God's, even (it seems) before they are conscious of the fact: "Thine they were, and thou gavest them to me" (17:6). Conversely, Judas appears doomed from the start (cf. 6:70-71; 12:4; 13:21-30).

2. Theological affiliations of John with other religious literature. The question of the origin of John's distinctive teaching receives a bewildering variety of answers. To the traditionalist all the teaching which John puts into the mouth of Jesus is to be accepted as his and to be harmonized as nearly as possible with the evidence of the other gospels. To many, however, this appears a task impossible of achievement, and it is widely recognized that the teaching attributed by John to Jesus contains elements which do not, in fact, come from him. But, when this has been recognized, the questions still remain, how much of John's teaching goes back to Jesus, and what are the sources of that which does not come from him? Some would limit the part played by Jesus virtually to giving the initial impulse, the teaching material in John being provided almost entirely from elsewhere. Others would see a considerable substratum of Jesus' own teaching embodied in the discourses and dialogues in John. If, as appears likely, John was himself a prophet, and if much of his material is, in fact, Christian prophecy, he would no doubt reject as mere pedantry the modern critic's distinction between the words spoken by Jesus in the days of his flesh and those spoken by his Spirit through his prophets. But the distinction is to us a valid one, and poses a question which we must try to answer.

The other question, of John's other sources, has also received a variety of answers. Paul; the Jewish philosopher Philo of Alexandria, an approximate contemporary of Paul; the *Corpus Hermeticum,* portions of which may be as early as the middle of the first century A.D.; the early Gnostics, particularly the Mandeans, who originated in Transjordan possibly in the first century A.D.; and, most recently, the sect which produced the DEAD SEA SCROLLS have all in their turn been regarded by competent scholars as having had a contributory, or even principal, influence in molding the thought of John.

It can hardly be disputed that the period from the conquests of Alexander to the early Christian centuries was one of great importance in the history of religion. Greek philosophy and religion were brought into contact with the ancient cults of the East, with momentous effects on both sides. In the ensuing ferment of ideas Judaism was involved as much as the religions of Asia Minor, Egypt, and Mesopotamia. It had, moreover, already undergone the influence of Iranian religion. Out of the cross-fertilization of Greek and oriental religions arose a great variety of syncretistic cults and theologies. It was in this environment that Christianity arose, and it would be idle to deny that it shared certain common features with contemporary religious movements. But it does not follow that it was wholly a product of the same forces which produced, e.g., the Hermetic and Mandean literature. Yet if it was to secure a hearing in the Hellenistic world, it had to put its message into language which its contemporaries could understand, and it may well be that John only did this more thoroughly than other Christian writers. Certainly his fundamental proposition, that the Word became flesh, is something unparalleled in any literature that can conceivably have influenced him, and this should put us on our guard against reducing his thought entirely to the product of contemporary influences in Judaism or outside it.

After these preliminary observations, it may be convenient to consider the possible sources of John's theology in the following order:

a. The teaching of Jesus in the other gospels. To determine what is original in the TEACHING OF JESUS in the other gospels is a problem in itself, but one which need not be considered here. For the present purpose the other gospels can be taken as they stand, as affording evidence of what may be presumed to have been in the tradition accessible to John.

It is clear that John stands within the Christian tradition. He presupposes the church, the leadership within it of the Twelve, the sacraments of baptism and the Eucharist, and the tradition of Jesus' teaching. He shares with the other evangelists a belief in the importance of Jesus' acts of healing, etc., as more than marvelous displays of power; if for him they are signs of Jesus' messianic authority, so too for Matthew and Luke his exorcisms show that the "kingdom of God has come upon" his hearers (Matt. 12:28=Luke 11:20). His death has in John a meaning found also in the other gospels. Jesus lays down his life for his friends (15:13); he gives his life a ransom for many (Mark 10:45=Matt. 20:28). The words of Jesus in John 6:53 about eating his flesh and drinking his blood recall his words at the Last Supper in Matt. 26:26-29; Mark 14:22-24; Luke 22:17-19. Jesus' saying that "no one comes to the Father, but by me" (John 14:6), recalls Matt. 11:27: "No one knows the Father except the Son and any one to whom the Son chooses to reveal him," and its parallel in Luke 10:22.

But even if all such parallels are adduced, and full weight given to them, there remains much, both in form and in substance, peculiar to John. Even when the same phrase is used in John as in the other gospels, it may have a different nuance, as, e.g., "Son of man," or again the command to love. It is difficult to resist the impression that in John love is something which operates within the Christian community—Christians are to "love one another" (15:12); contrast the command to love "your neighbor as yourself" (Mark 12:31), which looks outward to those not in the community. John says, it is true, that God loved the world, but he does not record any command to Christians to do so.

The feature of John most difficult to reconcile with the teaching of Jesus in the other gospels is the large amount of controversy about Jesus' own status and function, and, in the course of this, the explicit claims made by Jesus on his own behalf, in particular the "I am" sayings (6:35 [cf. vss. 41, 48, 51]; 8:12; 10:7 [cf. vs. 9], 11 [cf. vs. 14], 25; 14:6; 15:1 [cf. vs. 5]). Though it may be argued that these only make explicit what is implicit in the other gospels, it cannot be denied that the total impression made by John is different from that of the other gospels. It would, indeed, appear that a considerable amount of material in John represents the results of meditation upon the life and teaching of Jesus by the evangelist, based, indeed, upon actions and sayings of Jesus, but modifying them considerably in the process.

b. Paul. The thought of John is closest to that of Paul in the Letter to the Colossians (*see* COLOSSIANS, LETTER TO THE). In Col. 1:15-19, Paul makes a series of affirmations about Christ very similar to ideas of John. Paul's description of Christ as the "image of the invisible God" recalls John 1:18; his claim that "all things were created through him and for him" likewise recalls John 1:3; and the statement that "in him all the fullness of God was pleased to dwell," though it has no exact verbal parallel in John, is fully in accord with his ideas, and moreover has in common with John 1:16 the word "fulness," πλήρωμα, a technical term of Hellenistic theology for the sum total of the divine attributes (*see* PLEROMA).

Now if Colossians is indeed the work of Paul, it is by common consent one of the latest, if not the very latest, of his extant letters. He wrote it to refute certain heretical notions which had gained currency at Colossae, a city in the province of Asia, of which Ephesus, the traditional place of origin of John's Gospel, was the capital. When it was customary to date John's Gospel much later than now seems possible (*see* § G *below*), it was easy to find in Colossians a source of John's theology, even allowing for the late date of Colossians. Indeed, this was possible even if Colossians was not ascribed to Paul. But if John is to be dated in the first century, it is perhaps more reasonable to see Colossians and John as similar responses to the same challenge, rather than Colossians as an actual source of John's Christology. The point of contact between Paul and John may well lie in the thought of the "Hellenists," the associates of Stephen, who had first faced the problem of presenting Christianity to the pagan world.

This suggestion may be reinforced by the consideration that the Letter to the Hebrews, which is not, of course, by Paul, has in its opening verses resemblances to John quite as close as any in Colossians; cf. Heb. 1:1-3: "God . . . has spoken to us by a Son, whom he appointed heir of all things, through whom also he created the world. He reflects the glory of God and bears the very stamp of his nature." Hebrews may, of course, be the work of a disciple of Paul, but it could equally well be the work of one of the early "Hellenists," and so, like John, an example of a similar reaction to the same situation rather than of dependence upon Paul.

c. Jewish literature. In order to assess the value of the material found in John, it is very important to have as accurate a knowledge as possible of the author's background. Is it primarily Jewish, or primarily Hellenistic? This contrast can easily be overstressed, for there had been a certain amount of assimilation—in both directions—between Jewish and Hellenistic religion and culture. Books like Ecclesiastes and Wisdom of Solomon testify to the influence of Greek philosophy within Judaism, while Philo is an example of a man writing in the interests of the Jewish religion whose ideas are nevertheless profoundly influenced by Greek philosophy. And the influence of Judaism and its sacred literature upon the syncretistic religions of the period cannot be ignored. Nevertheless, the distinction of Jewish and Hellenistic is, within limits, a valid one. Now if the author of John can be shown to be primarily Jewish in his ideas and background, it is open to the critic to admit the possibility that the tradition which he preserves is primitive more easily than if he is primarily Hellenistic. And conversely, if he appears to be primarily Hellenistic, then it is easier to regard his gospel as a work of imagination, a theological romance of a type not unparalleled in Hellenistic literature.

The fact that both views of John are maintained should induce caution. It is easy when arguing for one side to ignore or minimize what tells in favor of the other. Those scholars who regard John as primarily a work of imagination stress its Hellenistic features, while the more conservative maintain its essentially Jewish character. The view which best accounts for all the evidence is perhaps that John was written by a man of Jewish origin, familiar with the Palestinian background of the story which he had to tell, who was also anxious to make his message intelligible to a predominantly Gentile audience. In this case he would resemble Philo in his objective, if not necessarily in his ideas and method. There is a somewhat similar controversy over Paul, and in his case also the most satisfactory solution to the problem may well be that he was a man of primarily Jewish origin addressing a primarily Gentile audience.

The familiarity of John with the Jewish scriptures, both canonical and apocryphal, is sufficiently obvious, but does not of itself decide the issue. The Jewish scriptures were studied and valued by Gentile as well as by Jewish Christians, and familiarity with them does not necessarily argue a Jewish origin. Features of John which suggest more convincingly a Jewish and even Palestinian background are its language, its echoes of rabbinic ideas and methods of argument, and its parallels in thought and language with the recently discovered documents of the Qumran community, though it must be remembered that all these are more or less matters of dispute.

That the language of John has a Semitic flavor, particularly in the simplicity of its syntactical structure, is fairly generally recognized, but the precise implication of this is disputed. Some scholars have gone so far as to maintain that John is the translation of an Aramaic original, but this view has not met with wide acceptance. John's Semitic characteristics are rather attributed to the use of originally Aramaic sources, or to the fact that its author was bilingual, writing in Greek but thinking in Aramaic (or, as some scholars infer, in rabbinic Hebrew). Nevertheless, though its precise explanation may be in dispute, the Semitic character of the language of John tells in favor of a Jewish background.

Apparent parallels to rabbinic ideas, phraseology, and methods of argument have also been found in John, particularly in passages of controversy between Jesus and the Jews. These, by themselves, would, if substantiated, only suggest the faithful reproduction of primitive sources. But they are not confined to such passages, being found also in those which are clearly the author's own composition. Thus in 1:14: "The Word became flesh and dwelt among us, full of grace and truth; we have beheld his glory," and in vs. 17: "The law was given through Moses; grace and truth came through Jesus Christ," the evangelist appears to be claiming for the incarnate Word the functions of mediation and revelation which the rabbis attributed to the Torah. The use of the verb ἐσκήνωσεν, "dwelt," may be a kind of bilingual pun, since it contains the same root consonants as the rabbinic technical term *Shekinah,* the manifestation of the divine presence. Grace and truth, the divine attributes, to be seen according to the rabbis through the Torah, came in fact through Jesus Christ. This contrast between the Torah and the Christ is a recurrent theme in John, and gives a point to many incidents narrated in it. In rabbinic literature the Torah is frequently likened to water, wine, bread, and light. Such symbolism is readily understandable. And it is not difficult to see it underlying those narratives in John in which reference is made to these substances. Thus in the miracle at Cana (2:1-11) there is the contrast between the "good wine" given by Jesus and the inferior wine that had been used up, as well as the water in the jars "for the Jewish rites of purification" (2:6); in 4:12-14 there is the contrast between the water that Jesus gives and that of Jacob's well; in 6:32 the bread which Moses gave is contrasted with the true bread from heaven; in 8:12 Jesus proclaims himself the light of the world, which, according to the rabbis, it is the function of the Torah to be (cf. 1:5, 9).

In John the word νόμος, "law," is used only in the same senses as the Hebrew Torah, in contrast to Paul, who occasionally gives it a Greek meaning, alien to that of the Hebrew Torah. This is in itself noteworthy. Moreover, in the allusions to the law in John there are many indications of the author's acquaintance with rabbinic usage. Thus 7:22-24 shows familiarity with the rabbinic ruling that the need to circumcise a child on the eighth day suspends the law of the Sabbath rest, and employs the familiar rabbinic argument "from light to heavy" in the plea that if one may circumcise on the Sabbath, one can also heal; 7:51 quotes the rule that a man must not be condemned unheard, and 8:17 the rule that two witnesses are necessary.

These are only a few examples of the many that could be cited to show the familiarity of the author of John with rabbinic ideas.

The documents of the Qumran community, the DEAD SEA SCROLLS, show, along with many differences that must not be ignored, some striking affinities in outlook and terminology to John. They share the same ethical dualism, both stopping short of the full ontological dualism taught by some later Gnostics; and they use the same terminology to express it. For both this world, though the creation of God, lies in the power of a rebellious spirit, created, indeed, but hostile to the creator. There is an irreconcilable opposition between the two powers of light and darkness, truth and falsehood, life and death. These pairs of opposites, found in John, occur also in the Scrolls, as do also phrases characteristic of John like "do the truth" (3:21), "the works of God" (6:28), "walk in darkness" (8:12; 12:35), "the light of life" (8:12), "sons of light" (12:36), "the spirit of truth" (14:17; 15:26; 16:13). These affinities are the more remarkable inasmuch as they occur precisely with those aspects of the thought and language of John which, before the discovery of the Scrolls, seemed to bring John into contact with the thought-world of Hellenistic Gnosticism, and so to preclude a date in the first century for the composition of the gospel. But now it is no longer necessary to look beyond Palestine and the first century A.D. for the environment in which these ideas, so characteristic of John, could have originated. John can no longer be regarded as a Hellenistic document pure and simple, as was often done in the past. Much still remains in dispute with regard to the precise relationship between the first Christians and the Qumran community and between their respective literatures, but this much at least seems beyond reasonable doubt: whether it was that the early Christians borrowed from the ideas of the Qumran community or reacted against them, the Qumran documents provide valuable evidence for the moral and religious climate in which early Christianity developed and the tradition found in John was formulated.

Philo of Alexandria, an approximate contemporary of Paul, has, both in his general outlook and in particular in his doctrine of the Logos (*see* WORD, THE, § 4), obvious points of resemblance to John. Philo was entirely loyal to Judaism, but his philosophy was so thoroughly Hellenized as to have little distinctively Jewish about it. He used the technique of allegorical exegesis (which the Stoics had elaborated) in order to extract from the OT a variant of the popular Stoicism of his period, and, apparently in all sincerity, presented this as the true meaning of the sacred text. At the time when it was easy to regard John as both later in date and more definitely Hellenized in character than now seems probable, it was natural that Philo should have been regarded as a major influence upon John. Critics could point to the fact that, for both Philo and John, to know God is the principal aim of human existence, and that God can be known only through his Logos, his agent both in creation and in revelation. Some even went so far as to suggest that John was designed to be interpreted allegorically on the lines of Philo's exegesis of the OT. But to compose a narrative and deliberately to adapt it to allegorical interpretation is something very different from so interpreting a given text; and, though John is undoubtedly interested in symbolism, symbolism is not the same thing as allegory, while the manifest conviction of the evangelist that the events which he describes really did happen is hard to reconcile with the suggestion that he could consciously have adapted them to allegorical interpretation. John is also less philosophical and more obviously religious in his interests than Philo, and while for Philo the Logos is a personified attribute of God, John's affirmation is that the Logos "became flesh," which goes far beyond anything in Philo. It is therefore probable that we should regard Philo, not as a major influence on John, but as evidence for the beliefs of some, at least, of the readers to whom John was designed to appeal.

d. Pagan literature. The conclusion suggested above about Philo and John is probably also that most appropriate to the non-Jewish literature which now has to be considered, the *Corpus Hermeticum*, and the Mandean and Gnostic writings. The *Corpus Hermeticum* is a collection of tracts, Egyptian in origin and written in Greek, mainly in the second and third centuries A.D., containing what purport to be the revelations of "Hermes Trismegistus," a deified Egyptian sage. The chief sacred books of the Mandeans, a somewhat bizarre community still surviving in Iraq, are the Ginza (i.e., "Treasure"), and the Book of John, written in Aramaic and put into their present form not earlier than 700 A.D. The Gnostics, properly speaking, were Christian heretics, whose writings survive mainly in fragments, but the term "Gnosticism" is also used to describe a system or systems of belief thought to antedate the origin of Christianity, and to be presupposed by the various Gnostic systems known today.

Though none of this literature can certainly be

dated earlier than John in its present form, it is argued, with some show of probability, that it is dependent upon earlier writings, which it is claimed (particularly in the case of the Mandean literature) can be reconstructed from that now extant. Then it can be argued that this earlier literature could have influenced John.

These various writings (like some of the OT wisdom literature and the works of Philo himself) all appear to owe their ultimate origin to the ferment of religious and philosophical ideas which marked the Hellenistic age, when Greek popular philosophy encountered and came to terms with the native religions of Egypt, Syria, and Mesopotamia; syncretized, rationalized, and allegorized their mythologies; and discovered in them its own teaching, revealed as the esoteric wisdom of the East.

The resultant systems of belief all have a strong family likeness. They are concerned primarily with the salvation of the individual, and pessimistic about the world as it is. They are ethically and sometimes also ontologically dualist; they preach a supreme deity unknowable except insofar as he wills to reveal himself, which he does by means of some divine or semidivine emissary and agent (Hermes in the *Corpus Hermeticum*, John the Baptist in the Mandean books, Jesus in the Gnostic systems), who preaches the knowledge (γνωσις) which saves mankind. They all use more or less the same basic terminology, found also in John—"light," "life," "truth," "Logos," "knowing," and "believing"—and this is used as an argument for their influence upon John. But if John's use of this terminology can be adequately explained otherwise, from literature that can be dated with much greater probability to his period, then Hermetic, Mandean, or Gnostic influence is much less likely, and, insofar as this literature preserves more ancient elements, these are to be used to illustrate the beliefs of the Hellenistic world to which John was addressed rather than those which actually influenced its thought. John is basically Jewish Christian, though designed (as were Paul's letters) to be understood by men brought up in a different tradition. *See* GNOSTICISM.

E. *EVIDENCE OF USE AND AUTHORSHIP FROM EARLY CHRISTIAN LITERATURE.* There are possible echoes of John in isolated passages of I Clement and Barnabas, but the first clear traces of fairly systematic use of John are in the epistles of Ignatius of Antioch (*ca.* A.D. 110) and in the writings of Justin Martyr, a generation later. Neither actually mentions John. Indeed, when Ignatius wrote to Ephesus (the traditional place of writing of John), he called the Christians there "Paul's fellow initiates," but said nothing of John. Justin knew of more than one gospel, for he speaks of the "memoirs of the apostles which are called gospels," and he attributes Revelation to the apostle John, but does not attribute any gospel to him.

The earliest mentions of John of Ephesus are in connection with Polycarp and Papias, both bishops in Asia Minor younger than Ignatius and older than Justin. Eusebius (Hist. III.39) calls Papias, on the authority of Irenaeus (who lived toward the end of the second century), a "hearer of John, and a companion of Polycarp." He also quotes a letter of Irenaeus to Florinus (Hist. V.20), in which Irenaeus speaks of having heard, when he was very young, Polycarp telling of "his association with John and with the others who had seen the Lord." Eusebius (Hist. III.39) quotes a passage from Papias' own book in which he speaks of inquiring "about the sayings of the elders—what Andrew or Peter said, or what Philip, or Thomas, or James, or John, or Matthew, or any other of the Lord's disciples, and what Aristion and the elder John, the disciples of the Lord, say." Though some scholars deny it, saying that Papias has only expressed his meaning clumsily, it is natural to suppose from this that he distinguished John the apostle, who was presumably dead when he wrote, from John the elder, who was still alive. Thus the John whom Papias and Polycarp knew was presumably the elder, which is borne out by the fact that, according to Eusebius, Papias quoted I John, while Polycarp's extant Epistle to the Philippians shows clearly that he knew I John—the author of II and III John, who must also have written I John, calls himself "the elder."

About the time of Justin the Leucian Acts of John, a historically valueless and heretical romance, identifies the BELOVED DISCIPLE with John the son of Zebedee, but denies that he wrote a gospel. This at least shows that by this time the belief (whether well founded or not) was current that John of Ephesus was the Beloved Disciple and son of Zebedee, and the denial that he wrote a gospel looks like an attempt to discredit John in the interests of the heretical work of "Leucius."

Ca. A.D. 160 the Valentinian Gnostic Heracleon wrote a commentary on John, considerable fragments of which remain in the homilies of Origen on John. These contain no mention of the authorship of John, and it may perhaps be inferred from the fact that Origen usually quotes Heracleon only when he disagrees with him, that they held the same view on authorship—i.e., that John was the work of the son of Zebedee. A little later than Heracleon, Tatian, a pupil of Justin, not only used John in his Diatessaron, a harmony of the four gospels, but also made the earliest known formal quotations of John—of John 1:5 in his *Oratio* XIII.1 and of John 1:3 in XIX.4.

Ca. A.D. 180, Theophilus of Antioch (*Apology* II.22) quotes John 1:1 as scripture and ascribes it to John; Irenaeus (Her. III.1) identifies the author as the Beloved Disciple, and adds that he published the gospel at Ephesus, being apparently unaware of the fact that this contradicts the obvious inference from John 21:20-23 that this disciple was dead when the gospel was published; and the Muratorian Canon (*see* CANON OF THE NT § C6) says that John, "one of the disciples," wrote the gospel after it had been revealed to Andrew, "one of the apostles," that he should do so. This sounds like an attempt to provide apostolic authority for a work not actually of apostolic authorship, in the face of the attacks being made at this time, particularly in Rome, against John by the Alogi. *See* § B2 *above*.

Polycrates, bishop of Ephesus at the end of the second century, in his letter to Pope Victor (Euseb. Hist. V.24), describes the Ephesian John (whom he identifies with the Beloved Disciple) as having been a "priest who wore the πέταλον" (i.e., the gold plate attached to the high priest's turban; Exod. 28:36-38). None of these actually says that John of Ephesus was the son of Zebedee, and it is difficult to see how Polycrates' description of him can ever have been thought to apply to a former Galilean fisherman.

Nevertheless, the view that John was the work of the son of Zebedee was firmly established in the following century, and it remains to be seen how this accords with the evidence of the gospel itself.

F. ***INTERNAL EVIDENCE OF PURPOSE AND AUTHORSHIP.*** John 21:20-24 identifies the author as the disciple next to Jesus at supper (13:23; 21:20). It had been expected that he would not die, but presumably he had done so, and ch. 21 was added to the gospel (which clearly is meant to end at 20:31) in order to explain the misunderstanding of Jesus' words that was responsible for this belief. If so, the man who published the gospel (John of Ephesus?) cannot have been the BELOVED DISCIPLE. Was the Beloved Disciple then John the son of Zebedee? The sons of Zebedee were present at the events described in ch. 21 (vs. 2), and so the identification is possible if the rest of the gospel bears it out.

The Beloved Disciple is the "witness" of 19:35, and from his association with Peter in 20:2 ff and at the Last Supper it follows that he is also the disciple "known to the high priest" (18:15-16). As it is unlikely that a son of Zebedee would be known to the high priest, the suggestion has been made that the disciple of 18:15; 20:2 is not the same as the Beloved Disciple. He may, indeed, be the John of Ephesus. But there are other difficulties in the way of the identification of the son of Zebedee with the Beloved Disciple, the chief one being that the standpoint from which the gospel is written is Judean rather than Galilean. On the other hand, the presence of the Beloved Disciple at the Last Supper suggests that he was one of the Twelve, unless others besides the Twelve were present.

Some scholars, impressed by the difficulty of identifying the Beloved Disciple, dismiss him as an "ideal figure." But to do this makes nonsense of the whole tenor of the gospel; no reliance can be placed upon the author's assurance that the events which he describes really happened. There is, however, a great air of verisimilitude about John which induces many to accept the traditional view of its authorship (in spite of its difficulties), or else to dismiss the problem of authorship as insoluble. Admittedly it is not of primary importance, though it would be very desirable to have the solution to it.

There are two alternative possibilities: either (*a*) that the Beloved Disciple is the John whose mother's house in Jerusalem was a meeting place for the church there (cf. Acts 12:12)—if the Last Supper was held there, it would account for the presence at it of the son of the house; or (*b*) that he is Lazarus (for details *see* LAZARUS OF BETHANY), and that John of Ephesus (who in this case may still be the son of Mary of Jerusalem) published his gospel, and added to it ch. 21. If the disciple known to the high priest (or, as the Greek may also mean, related to him) is other than the Beloved Disciple, then he may be John of Ephesus, and Lazarus the Beloved Disciple. If John were of high-priestly family, this might account for Polycrates' description of him as a high priest himself. It would then have to be assumed that in the course of the second century the local patriotism of the Ephesians led them to identify their elder John with the Beloved Disciple of the gospel which he published, and to claim him as John son of Zebedee, which is not, indeed, incompatible with the evidence of the gospel.

G. ***THE ORIGIN AND PURPOSE OF JOHN.*** Whoever it was who put John in its present form and published it, whether he was its author or its editor, the Beloved Disciple or another, he offered it to the church and to the world as evidence for the claim that Jesus is the Christ, the Son of God (20:31), furnished by a selection of Jesus' own acts—the "signs"—expounded in the discourses, and by the testimony of individuals, primarily of the Beloved Disciple.

There are six signs, one less than the perfect number seven, and, both by this fact and by their content, they lead up to the final and perfect sign, the death and resurrection of Christ. The first sign, the changing of water into wine, symbolizes Christ's ministry as the substitution of the wine of the gospel for the water of the law; the second and third, two miracles of healing, show Christ as the bringer of life and forgiveness—the paralyzed man by the pool represents the sinner whom the law cannot save; the fourth shows him as the bringer of the real manna; the fifth illustrates that "in him was life, and the life was the light of men," by the curing of the blind man; the sixth, the raising of Lazarus, shows Christ as victor over death and prepares immediately for his own resurrection. The inner meaning of these events is expounded in the discourses, which are held together by the themes which run through them and give the gospel its unity. The fact that the main themes are stated in the Prologue suggests that the Prologue is integral to the gospel, which is, in fact, an exposition of its meaning. It is difficult to imagine the Prologue as an originally independent hymn to the Logos, subsequently attached to the gospel, though this has been suggested.

The discourses may well have originated in sermons expounding the "signs": the feeding of the multitude and the discourse associated with it would be an appropriate Easter sermon, and, indeed, it may be that the association of the signs with feasts gives a clue to the occasions on which these sermons were preached. They were then formed into the gospel, and may have undergone a certain amount of rearrangement by the editor, thus giving rise to the phenomena explained by some critics as due to dislocation of the text (*see* § A2 *above*). The present order, however, is clearly intentional, even if it is not according to the author's intention.

It is not easy to date the gospel at all precisely. Much of its material, even in the discourses, may be primitive, but it may have been gradually brought into shape during a lifetime of preaching, and the traditional date for its publication, late in the first century, fits the evidence of its early use by Ignatius. A man who was a youth at the time of the Crucifixion could well have published the gospel in the nineties when he was himself, as the tradition asserts, an old man, perhaps the last survivor of those who had seen the Lord.

Published at Ephesus at that time, the gospel must have been designed not only to remind the church of vital truths about its Lord, but also to win from the mystery cults and Gnosticism those pagans who sought salvation.

H. *HISTORICAL AND RELIGIOUS VALUE.* There is no reason to doubt that the author believed that the events he narrates actually happened. The fact that he finds them full of symbolical significance is no argument to the contrary. He chose those which best suited his purpose. And they contain many details, particularly topographical, from which no symbolical significance can be extracted, and which may stand as evidence for the historicity of the narratives in which they are found. John's dating of the Crucifixion at the time when the Passover lambs were being slaughtered for the coming feast has been widely suspected as unhistorical, but the alternative dating, on the actual day of the feast, is not without difficulty, and John may after all be correct.

It is, however, probably too much to expect that the events are in the actual order of occurrence. The order of the gospel is theological rather than chronological. But, even so, it must not be too readily assumed that where John and the other gospels disagree, John is necessarily wrong.

Nor can it be expected that the discourses were uttered by Jesus precisely as we have them in John. Its author was a prophet, and his own inspired utterances were "words of the Lord" as truly as any spoken by Jesus in his earthly ministry. They take up and expound many actual words of Jesus (in our sense), but their final form and emphasis is the evangelist's. John 16:14 suggests the process by which this happened. But, no doubt, the fact that the author had known Jesus and had grown up in Judea put limits to his freedom. John is not the first apocryphal gospel.

Its religious value can be considered even more briefly. If it is indeed wholly or mainly the work of a disciple, matured through years of preaching and meditation, it fully merits the description which Clement of Alexandria gave it of the "spiritual gospel." Its author possessed the "mind of Christ" (I Cor. 2:16) as truly as Paul, and generations of Christians have found in his work an insight into the life of their Lord given nowhere else. It may not be legitimate to press this consideration in a strictly critical study, but it cannot be wholly ignored.

Bibliography. Of the innumerable books on John the following list aims at giving a selection representing different points of view:

Commentaries: B. F. Westcott (1882). A. Loisy (1903). M. J. Lagrange (1924). J. H. Bernard, ICC (1928). W. Bauer (1933). R. Bultmann (1937-41; supplement, 1950). E. C. Hoskyns (ed. F. N. Davey; 1940). C. K. Barrett (1955). R. H. Lightfoot (ed. C. F. Evans; 1956).

Other books and articles: E. F. Scott, *The Fourth Gospel, Its Purpose and Theology* (1906). J. Rendel Harris, *The Origin of the Prologue to St. John's Gospel* (1917). C. F. Burney, *The Aramaic Origin of the Fourth Gospel* (1922). H. Odeberg, *The Fourth Gospel Interpreted in Its Relation to Contemporaneous Religious Currents in Palestine and the Hellenistic-Oriental World* (1929). R. Eisler, *The Enigma of the Fourth Gospel* (1938). P. Gardner-Smith, *Saint John and the Synoptic Gospels* (1938). E. Percy, *Untersuchungen über den Ursprung der johanneischen Theologie* (1939). W. F. Howard, *Christianity According to St. John* (1943). J. N. Sanders, *The Fourth Gospel in the Early Church* (1943). P. H. Menoud, *L'évangile de Jean d'après les recherches récentes* (1947). E. K. Lee, *The Religious Thought of St. John* (1950). W. F. Albright, "Recent Discoveries in Palestine and the Gospel of St. John," *The Background of the NT and Its Eschatology* (ed. W. D. Davies and D. Daube; 1953), pp. 153-71. C. H. Dodd, *The Interpretation of the Fourth Gospel* (1953). F. M. Braun, "L'arrière-fond judaïque du quatrième évangile et la communauté de l'alliance," *RB,* LXX (1955), 5-44. W. F. Howard, *The Fourth Gospel in Recent Criticism and Interpretation* (4th ed., rev. C. K. Barrett, 1955). K. Aland, "Das Johannes-evangelium auf Papyrus," *Forschungen und Fortschritte,* XXI (1957), 50-55.

J. N. Sanders

JOHN, LETTERS OF. These three letters, together with the Gospel of John (*see* John, Gospel of) and the Revelation (*see* Revelation, Book of), constitute a corpus of writings which have been traditionally associated with the name John. Early patristic citations indicate that all five books were written in the province of Asia during the last decade of the first century or the first decade of the second century. Internal evidence, supplemented by information from other sources, enables us to give a more or less detailed description of the circumstances which called forth each of the five books. But whether the churches of Asia numbered among their leaders one John or more than one, and whether the Johannine writings come from one hand or from a Johannine school, are questions to which there is still no generally accepted answer.

The value of the letters, however, does not entirely depend on the solution of such historical problems as these. For, whoever may have written them, these short writings raise in striking form questions which are of permanent interest and importance for Christian faith and practice: the validity of religious experience, the relation of inspiration to authority, the meaning of love, the nature of Christian assurance, and the proper attitude toward those whose convictions are radically different from our own.

1. Purpose. Each of the three letters was written to deal with a challenge to the teaching or authority of the writer which had arisen within the churches of Asia. They cannot properly be called polemical writings, for they are not addressed to those who have caused the trouble. Rather, they are pastoral letters, directed to those Christians who have remained faithful, in order to undergird their faith and reinforce their loyalty during the period of crisis. But, reading between the lines, we can gain a reasonably clear picture of the opposition.

a. The nature of the opposition. Throughout the first letter we find a series of warnings against those who make claims which are not justified by the facts:

"if we say we have fellowship with him while we walk in darkness" (1:6); "if we say we have no sin" (1:8); "he who says 'I know him' but disobeys his commandments" (2:4); "he who says he abides in him" (2:6); "if any one says, 'I love God,' and hates his brother" (4:20). It is obvious that these denunciations are not made without good reason and that someone has actually been making such professions. The opposition has been laying claim to a special knowledge and love of God and to a peculiarly intimate relationship with him which has set them above the common distinctions between good and evil and therefore above the demands of Christian ethics. It is probable, too, that the initial message of the letter: "God is light and in him is no darkness at all," is directed against a theology which held that God comprehended in himself both light and darkness.

These heretical teachers have also been denying that Jesus was the Christ (2:22). We are not to conclude from this that they were Jews or Judaizers who denied his Messiahship, but rather that they were Christians who denied his Incarnation. For their error is more particularly defined later in the letter as a denial "that Jesus Christ has come in the flesh" (4:2). In this connection the writer warns his readers to test the spirits to see whether they are of divine origin, which suggests that his opponents have been basing their teaching on what they claimed to be the divinely inspired utterances of a prophet or prophets. It is a reasonable conjecture, therefore, that the strange word "chrism" or "unction," which is twice used to describe the gift of the Spirit in which all Christians participate (2:20, 27), has found its way into the vocabulary of the letter because the heretics had first used it to describe what they believed to be their own unique spiritual endowment.

The opponents were Christians and had formerly been members of the church. But they had recently withdrawn from the Christian fellowship to start a new movement of their own (2:19), which had met with a readier acceptance in the pagan world than the church had been accustomed to find (4:5).

Into this picture we may readily fit the evidence of the second letter, which was written by one who calls himself "the presbyter" (RSV "elder") to inform a particular church of the existence of a heretical missionary movement, which was denying the reality of the Incarnation, and to caution them against encouraging such missionaries by offering them hospitality.

The opposition in the third letter comes from a certain Diotrephes, who has refused to acknowledge the authority of the presbyter who writes the letter, and has managed to win so much support in the church to which he belongs that the presbyter's emissaries have been excluded from its meetings and even denied hospitality by its members. But there is no reason to connect him in any way with the heretical party of which we hear in the other two letters, unless it was that he took advantage of the confusion which their schism created to assert his own independence.

b. The identity of the opponents. An aberrant Christianity, which teaches salvation by esoteric knowledge, excites an enthusiasm devoid of moral concern, and nourishes a spirituality contemptuous of all things material, can be identified unmistakably as an early form of the movement which came to be known as Gnosis or GNOSTICISM. At this stage, however, there is no sign of the gross sensuality which was countenanced by some of the later developments of the Gnostic heresy; the moral laxity here stigmatized consists solely in an indifference to the practical demands of the law of love.

We can be equally sure that the denial that Jesus has come in the flesh was a form of the Docetic heresy, which is so strongly denounced in the letters of Ignatius. Docetism consisted either in a general denial of the reality of Christ's human nature or in a more precise theory that the Christ had adopted only the outward appearance of human form, a shallow disguise used to accommodate his divine nature to the feeble capacities of human comprehension. This idea was a natural concomitant of Gnosticism, which, by its depreciation of all matter and of the physical body in particular, seemed to rule out the possibility that flesh and blood could be a genuine medium of divine revelation. The belief that there is a fundamental antagonism between spirit and matter was ultimately of oriental origin, but it had long since made a deep penetration of Hellenistic thought. It need not surprise us, then, to find that the other factor which contributed to the growth of Docetism was the purely Greek, philosophic conception of the impassibility of God, since, if God cannot be said in any sense to suffer, the divine nature of Christ cannot have been involved in the Crucifixion.

Among the early Gnostics there is one, CERINTHUS, who is known to have been active in Asia in the closing years of the first century, and his teaching shows certain points of similarity with that which is attacked in I John. He taught that Jesus was merely human "and that after his baptism there descended into him from the Supreme Power Christ in the form of a dove, and that he then proclaimed the unknown father and performed miracles, but that finally Christ withdrew again from Jesus, so that it was Jesus who suffered and rose again, while Christ remained impassible, being pure spirit" (Iren. Her. I.26.1). In other words, Cerinthus denied that Jesus Christ had come in the flesh, because he denied that the human Jesus could in any real way be identified with the divine Christ. Whether the opponents of John were actually associates or disciples of Cerinthus, it is perhaps too much to say, but they certainly moved in the same universe of discourse.

c. The author's own background. Though the author of I John deals firmly with his Gnostic opponents, his theology has nevertheless much in common with theirs. He does not repudiate the OT as they tended to do, but he is the only NT writer who never quotes from it. He protests against allowing Hellenistic notions to distort the facts of the apostolic tradition, yet he is himself the most thoroughly Hellenized of all the NT writers and the only one to equate God with an abstraction: "God is light" (1:5); "God is love" (4:8). To expound his own doctrinal beliefs, he takes over from his opponents the idea that the Christian life consists in the outpouring of a divine unction (2:20, 27) or the implanting of a divine seed (3:9). He does not believe in salvation through esoteric knowledge, but he does lay emphasis on the cognitive side of faith. Above all, when he is combatting the absolute dualism of the Gnostics, he expresses himself in dualistic terms; he sees everything black and white, without halftones in between: light and darkness, truth and untruth, love and hate, life and death, God and the world. This propensity for thinking in extremes was characteristic of the Semitic mind (see especially the Manual of Discipline among the DEAD SEA SCROLLS), and could be illustrated abundantly from the traditions of primitive Christianity. But the dominant place which these stark contrasts occupy in the thought of I John suggests that the author was not merely drawing on the common Semitic background of early Christian theology but was at home in the religious atmosphere in which Gnosticism also flourished.

2. Contents. ***a. The first letter.*** This document defies precise analysis, because its thought moves, not forward in a logical progression, but spirally, with the same few ideas constantly recurring for new consideration and new development. For the sake of convenience, however, the letter may be summarized as follows:

I. Apostolic Christianity, 1:1-4
II. The tests of true Christianity, 1:5–2:27
  A. The test of obedience, 1:5–2:17
  B. The test of truth, 2:18-27
III. The new life of the children of God, 2:28–4:12
  A. The life free from sin, 2:28–3:10
  B. The life that is love, 3:11-18
  C. The life of assurance, 3:19-24
  D. The life in God's family, 4:1-12
IV. Christian certainty, 4:13–5:12
  A. Love excludes fear, 4:13-21
  B. Love is founded on truth, 5:1-12
V. Postscript, 5:13-21

The letter opens abruptly without the usual epistolary introduction, which would have given us information about its author and destination; and for this reason it has sometimes been treated as a tract rather than as a letter. On the other hand, it is clearly addressed to a particular situation and to a particular people, whom the author knows and loves with a warm personal affection. In his first paragraph, whatever else he may have omitted to tell us, he does make one thing abundantly plain: that even in controversy his purpose is not primarily polemic but pastoral, and that he means to combat the errors of his opponents by positive action, by calling his flock back to the gospel of the primitive church, which rested ultimately on the testimony of the eyewitnesses to the ministry of Jesus. He thus firmly lays down the one paramount criterion for distinguishing between genuine and spurious Christianity: that Christian teaching must preserve, undiminished and uncorrupted, the apostolic witness to Christ. In his own day it was enough to appeal to the living tradition, handed down from the earliest period of Christian history. Before long, however, the church was to discover in its fight against Gnosticism the need for a further criterion to distinguish the authentic tradition from accretions of legend, myth, and fantasy, and the answer to this need which began to emerge in the second century was the CANON OF THE NT, the purpose of which was to distinguish decisively between that which is apostolic, and therefore authoritative, and that which is not. Thus the prescription of I John leads directly to the guiding principle of Protestantism, that to be apostolic the church must be controlled by the NT scriptures.

The main argument of the letter begins with the provision of two tests whereby we may tell whether a man's faith is really the apostolic faith and whether the religious experience he claims to have had is really an experience of the one true God. The first test is an ethical one: a Christian is one who believes that God is utter goodness, that he himself is under an obligation to be like God, and that the road to goodness lies, not through his own moral effort, but through acceptance of the means which God has provided in Christ for dealing effectively with sin; and this belief will show itself outwardly in love and by an inner conviction of forgiveness, knowledge, and victory. The second test is a theological one: a Christian is one who believes that Jesus is the Christ, that the human Jesus is the incarnate Son of God, who perfectly reveals the Father. The two tests belong inseparably together, because it is through the human life of Jesus that our ideas of union with God and eternal life are filled with ethical content and the goodness and love of God are spelled out in human form. This insistence on the constant interplay of the intellectual and the moral elements in faith finds expression in other parts of the NT (e.g., John 7:17; Heb. 5:11-14), but nowhere more emphatically than in I John.

We are now told that those who have passed these tests have the right to call themselves children of God, since they have already entered upon a life which has its source in God. This life has certain distinctive qualities, which have already been touched on, but which require further elaboration. In the first place, the Christian life is a life free from sin, and the author is at pains to make clear that by sin he means, not a subjective state or a psychological disorder, but a definite violation of the moral law. This is one occasion when his black-and-white thinking is in evidence, for he has already warned his readers against the self-deception of thinking that they are without sin. Here he is concerned to say in the strongest possible fashion that there can be no salvation, no eternal life, no union with God, which does not involve a thorough moral purification. Christ came, not merely to give men the assurance that their sins no longer stood between them and the God of mercy, but actually to destroy their sins along with the devil from whom those sins took their origin. The Gnostic who denied that he was sinful was quite right in his belief that a Christian should be without sin, but wrong in claiming that he personally had reached the point where he could dispense with the sin-destroying power made available to all through the victory of Christ.

The epitome of all sin is hatred, which leads on to murder and death. By the same token the opposite of sin is love, which is almost synonymous with life. Love, indeed, is the one clear indication that a man has broken with the old order and entered the new. From the cross of Christ we can see that love means a willingness to serve the needs of others at whatever cost to ourselves. In time of crisis we may be called upon to make the ultimate sacrifice, but at other times the same law of love operates at a lower level, even in the smallest expenditure for the benefit of others of money, time, or effort which might have been spent on ourselves.

The Christian, then, because love has become the dominant principle of his life, constantly has free access to God. His conscience, it is true, may sometimes trouble him, but these occurrences should never be allowed to interrupt his normal state of calm assurance, based as it is, not on his own achievement, but on God's knowledge of him. This state can also be described as keeping Christ's commandments, abiding in him, or having the gift of the Spirit.

Love, moreover, provides every Christian with a standard for discriminating between true and false inspiration. The gift of the Spirit of God is inseparable from the gift of love, and Christian love will always recognize its source in Jesus, the incarnate Son of God. Those who claim to speak as inspired prophets but deny the reality of the Incarnation, and thus deny that the love displayed in the ministry of Jesus was God's love, show that they are controlled by a spirit antagonistic to God. The actual source of their doctrine is paganism, and this is why the pagan world finds that teaching congenial. By contrast, those who have a personal acquaintance with love are able to recognize God in Christ: for God is love. Once again we are made to see that the intellectual and the moral, belief in the Incarnation and obedience to the commandment of love, are obverse and reverse of one coin. To know God is to know love, and to know love is to express it in all the concrete duties and relationships of God's family.

We are now in a position to place over against the ill-founded confidence of the heretics, who claimed to know God and to abide in him, a Christian assurance, based on the inner witness of the Holy Spirit, that the love which moves in our hearts is the love of God, or rather the love which is God, and confirmed by the witness of the apostolic tradition that God was in Christ. Thus the historic act of God's love in Christ and the continuing and growing action of that love in the heart produce in the believer a conviction which enables him to live now in tranquil communion with God and to face the Last Judgment without trepidation. In other words, Christian assurance is based, not on human effort or achievement, but on God's love for us and God's love in us—always remembering that love is not love unless it finds active expression.

One final problem remains to be faced. The Christian who tries to live the life of love as a member of the family of God has also to live in a world which is hostile to God and which is constantly undermining his good intentions with evil suggestion or flattening them with social pressures. The life of love, therefore, becomes possible only through the victory of faith. This victory, we are now told in cryptic terms, consists in a belief that Christ came by water, blood, and spirit. These words have been carefully chosen so as to have a double reference to the historic life of Christ and to the continuing life of the church. The victory of God over the world was wrought out in the first instance by the operation of the Holy Spirit in the complete ministry of Jesus from his baptism with water to the shedding of his blood on the cross, but the same Spirit, made available to believers in the sacraments of Baptism and the Lord's Supper, operates in their lives with the same victorious results. We thus arrive at a final definition of Christianity: the Christian is one who believes that God's decisive victory over the world in the life and death of Jesus Christ is being reproduced in his own life, so that he is being set free from the trammels of worldliness to live the life of love, which is life eternal.

Almost as an afterthought, the writer now turns briefly to the subject of prayer as an expression of Christian confidence. The Christian prays for the fulfilment of God's will and can expect an answer to his prayers, especially when he prays for the restoration of those who through sin have fallen away from God (though he has to allow for the possibility that some sinners have deliberately put themselves beyond the scope of God's mercy). The letter then ends with a reiteration of the three great certainties: that those who belong to God do not sin, that we belong to God, that our God was revealed in Jesus Christ.

b. The second letter. This is written by one who calls himself "presbyter," or "elder," and is addressed "to the elect lady." This lady has a large family, some of whom live with her and are said to be beloved not only by the presbyter but also by all true Christians. Others of her children the presbyter has met elsewhere, and he declares that some of them are faithful Christians (is it implied that others are not?). She has a sister who lives in the same locality as the presbyter and whose children join their greetings to his. He addresses her sometimes in the singular and sometimes in the plural. The only reasonable explanation of all this is that the two ladies are not individuals but churches, and this has become the almost universally accepted interpretation.

The presbyter writes to warn the church against a vigorous missionary campaign launched by heretics who have denied the reality of the Incarnation, and presumably they are representatives of the same heresy as that denounced in the first letter. These heretics apparently claimed to be "progressive" or "advanced"; to this claim the presbyter retorts that they have advanced right out of the limits of true Christian doctrine. He urges the church not to offer hospitality to these missionaries, since this would be tantamount to supporting their mission and endorsing their doctrine.

If we entitle I John "The Letter of Love," then to II John we must give the title "The Letter of Love's Limitation." It challenges the Christian to decide in what circumstances he would be justified in withholding from his neighbor the ministrations of love. In particular, it raises the question of the limits of toleration. Is the Christian at all times bound to uphold liberty of conscience for those who disagree with him, or does the point come where it is a Christian obligation to boycott or otherwise to restrain those whose beliefs constitute a threat to the faith or freedom of others? Whenever the church has been engaged in a struggle for its very life, its leaders have usually agreed with the presbyter that toleration lies too near compromise to be always a safe policy and that, above all, it is wrong to tolerate those who do not believe in toleration and who, given the opportunity, would rob others of their religious liberty. But is this the teaching of the Sermon on the Mount?

c. The third letter. This letter is also written by a presbyter to one Gaius (*see* GAIUS 3), whom he describes as his "child"—certainly his faithful adherent, probably one of his own converts. This Gaius, it seems, has opened his home to some itinerant Christians, who have subsequently visited the presbyter and at a meeting of the church have testified to Gaius' loyalty and hospitality. They are proposing to set out on another missionary journey, and the presbyter has written to "the church"—Gaius would know which one he meant, since it must be a church with which he had some connection, though he can scarcely have been a member of it—asking that they be given a welcome. But his letter has provoked a crisis. A certain DIOTREPHES, who refused to recognize the presbyter's authority, has secured the support of a majority of the members and has persuaded them not to receive anyone who came with the presbyter's recommendation and to eject from the church anyone who proposed to carry out the presbyter's instructions. The presbyter is confident that he can deal with this crisis by a personal visit. In the meantime he is concerned to provide for the missionaries by asking Gaius to repeat his offer of hospitality and to help his guests further with a contribution toward the expenses of their journey.

Diotrephes is important because he represents a stage in the transition from the church order of the first century to that of the Ignatian letters. In the later NT writings each congregation is governed by a board of presbyters, who are also called bishops, but the independence of the local church is qualified by the paternal oversight of men like the Presbyter, who exercise authority over a wide area in virtue of their age, experience, and intimate connection with the apostolic origins of the Christian movement. By the time of Ignatius the local church in Asia is governed by a bishop presiding over the board of presbyters, and congregational independence is complete. The episode of Diotrephes belongs to the growing pains of this period of development. He is in revolt against the paternalism of the presbyter. We may regard him either as the prototype of the Ignatian bishop or as the kind of upstart whose ambition made the emergence of the Ignatian bishop inevitable. In either case he is the champion of the autonomy of the younger churches as they emerge from their missionary period. It would be interesting to know the outcome of the presbyter's visit.

3. I John and the Fourth Gospel. Any careful reader of the NT is bound to notice a close resemblance of vocabulary, style, and thought between I John and the Fourth Gospel. Both works employ a small vocabulary to express a small number of ideas which are constantly repeated in new forms, and most of the words and ideas that are characteristic of the letter are found also in the gospel—e.g., "love," "life," "truth," "light," "Son," "Spirit," "advocate," "manifest," "sin," "world," "flesh," "lie," "abide," "know," "walk," "witness," "commandments." Still more striking are the many phrases which the two books have in common—e.g., "Spirit of truth," "do the truth," "born of God," "children of God," "walk in darkness," "have sin," "cross out of death into life," "overcome the world," "take away sin," "Savior of the world." Both books share certain points of style, such as asyndeton and the use of a demonstrative pronoun to introduce a subordinate clause. Both books teach union with God, made possible through the Incarnation and interpreted in ethical terms as a union of obedience and love.

These similarities are obvious and undeniable and have usually been taken as a clear indication of common authorship. Indeed, when A. E. Brooke wrote his commentary, he apologized for raising afresh the question of common authorship, which seemed to him to have become long since a closed question. On the other hand, the evidence so far considered does not exclude the possibility that the letter was written by one who had been deeply influenced either by personal contact with the evangelist and his teaching or by reading his gospel. There are significant differences between the two writings which lend substance to this second hypothesis.

The letter makes no use of some thirty of the words which are characteristic of the gospel, including the very important word "glory," and uses about forty words which do not occur in the gospel, including "fellowship," "expiation," and "antichrist." Of the words which are common to both works, some—e.g., "Paraclete" or "Advocate"—are used in quite different senses. The style of the letter is much less varied than that of the gospel, and is distinguished by the monotonous repetition of a few favorite syntactical devices: in its 105 verses there are twenty conditional sentences, forty-four substantival uses of article + participle, thirty-two sentences introduced by a demonstrative (eight of them beginning "By this we know"), fourteen pairs of antithetical sentences, and four rhetorical questions. There is also the marked absence from the letter of the Semitic idiom and coloring and of the OT references which are so much in evidence in the gospel. There are, moreover, several points at which the thought of the letter comes closer to that of the primitive church than to the highly developed theology of the gospel: the death of Christ as an expiation, the Spirit as the Spirit of prophecy, the imminence of the Parousia.

4. Patristic references. The first writer to show any acquaintance with the Johannine letters is Polycarp of Smyrna (*see* POLYCARP, EPISTLE OF), who quotes from I John without acknowledgment (Phil. 7). The date of this letter is still in dispute, and the part in which the quotation occurs may have been written at any time from 115 to 140. We have it on the authority of Eusebius (Hist. III.39.17) that I John was also known to Papias of Hierapolis (*ca.* 140), who quoted from it a number of times. Toward the end of the second century Irenaeus of Lyons, another native of the province of Asia, quotes from both I and II John as though they were a single letter and ascribes them, along with the Fourth Gospel, to John the apostle (Her. III.15.5, 8). Clement of Alexandria makes frequent use of I John, which he describes as John's "larger epistle" (Strom. II.15.66), thereby implying that he knew of at least two letters. The Muratorian Fragment (*ca.* 200) also mentions two letters of John among the writings generally accepted as canonical, and one of them was certainly I John, since it is quoted earlier in the document. There is thus no evidence for the circulation of III John during the second century.

Origen (*In Joann.* V.3) attributed to John the apostle the gospel, the Revelation, and one short letter, adding that he may also have written a second and third, but that not everyone admitted them to be genuine; and it is possible that Origen himself shared these doubts, since elsewhere he frequently makes use of I John but never of the other two letters. Eusebius also places II and III John among the disputed books (Hist. III.25.3) and makes the suggestion that they may have been written, not by John the evangelist, but "by another man with the same name." This was the theory favored by Jerome, who ascribed the gospel and the first letter to John the apostle and II and III John to John the presbyter; and through his influence all three letters found a place in the Roman list of 382 (*Iohannis apostoli epistula una alterius Iohannis presbyteri epistulae duae*). During the fourth century, however, the Eastern churches, led by Cyril and Athanasius, came out strongly in favor of the apostolic authorship of all three letters, and this was the opinion which ultimately prevailed.

5. Authorship. The one fact that emerges from this survey of the early patristic citations is that they provide no compelling reason for regarding the three letters as an inseparable triad. There are those who regard the first two letters as a pair and make no mention of the third; there are those who treat all three, together with the gospel, as the work of the one John, the apostle; and there are those who link the first letter with the gospel and attribute the other two to a different hand. For convenience we may call these theories the Muratorian, the traditional, and the Hieronymian; and we shall find that none of them is thoroughly satisfactory.

The Muratorian theory is that the first and second letters are by one author and the third by another. It rests chiefly on the negative evidence of Irenaeus and the Muratorian Fragment, but gains some support from the intensely personal character of the third letter, which differentiates it in a striking fashion from the other two; but this theory is open to one damaging criticism. Both II and III John claim to be written by the presbyter, a man so important and well known that he needs no further designation. If they did not in fact come from a single writer, one must be an imitation of the other. Now it is prima facie credible that II John was written by an imitative writer who modeled his work on III John, though we should then have to explain how the imitation came to be accepted as canonical while the original remained unknown or unregarded. On the other hand, it is quite impossible to believe that III John is an imitation. It bears the stamp of originality in every line. It is written by one in authority, who expects his authority to be recognized and who has therefore no need to father his correspondence on another and more impressive figure. To this it may be added that the failure of the second-century sources to mention the letter or to quote from it is hardly surprising. It is not a document that would be useful in controversy, and it must have been preserved solely because it was believed to have come from the hand of a well-known leader. The obvious and simple conclusion is that the one presbyter wrote both the letters which bear his name.

The traditional theory is that the gospel and all three letters are the work of John the apostle. To attack this hypothesis at its weakest point, we may ask whether it is possible to identify John the apostle with the presbyter of II and III John. There is ample evidence that in the subapostolic age in the province of Asia there was a small group of men called presbyters and regarded as the sole remaining link with the apostolic past. Irenaeus mentions them several times and calls them "disciples of the apostles" (Her. V.36.2). Papias in one place refers to a nameless presbyter (Euseb. Hist. III.39.15) and in another place distinguishes between John the apostle and John the presbyter (Euseb. Hist. III.39.4). It is surely easier to envisage Diotrephes defying the authority of such a presbyter than asserting himself against one of the closest friends of Jesus; and if the presbyter had been the apostle, could he have refrained from crushing his troublesome opponent by an appeal to his apostolic dignity?

These considerations lead directly to the Hieronymian theory that the gospel and the first letter were written by John the apostle and the other two letters by John the presbyter. There is one small piece of internal evidence which has been thought by some scholars to bear out Jerome's suggestion. The second letter, like the first, attacks the Docetists, who deny the reality of the Incarnation, but with a significant modification of syntax. I John uses a perfect tense ("every spirit which does not confess that Jesus Christ has come in the flesh"); II John uses a present ("men who will not acknowledge the coming of Jesus Christ in the flesh"). A single instance of this kind cannot be a decisive argument against common authorship, though it would be strange to find an author using an expression in a precise fashion on one occasion and in a slovenly fashion on another. It is, however, hardly likely that Jerome's judgment was based on such calculations. He simply could not believe that the apostle would have referred to himself merely as presbyter, and we have already seen that his doubts in this respect were justified. Jerome's theory of dual authorship, then, depends on his major premise that John the apostle wrote the gospel and I John; if we are satisfied with this assumption, we shall be satisfied also with Jerome's theory as a whole. If we abandon the idea of apostolic authorship for either or both of the larger works, then we must reconsider the possibility that they were written by the presbyter who wrote II and III John. For the presbyter claims to possess such authority that he can hardly have been a subordinate member of the Johannine school, and on this ground alone we should suspect that he was the author of one or both of the other Johannine works.

Apart from its traditional association with the gospel, the case for the apostolic authorship of I John rests wholly on its opening sentence. Indeed, the author of the Muratorian Fragment was so convinced by this sentence that he believed he had only to quote it in order to silence those critics who questioned the apostolic authorship of the Fourth Gospel itself. But will the sentence bear this much weight? The author states that he is going to build his argument on eyewitness evidence, but the apostles were not the only eyewitnesses to the ministry of Jesus. John the presbyter, according to Papias, was a disciple of the Lord. Moreover, it is quite reasonable to suppose that the author is referring, not to his individual experience, but to the corporate experience of the church, considered as a close-knit fellowship throughout the world and throughout the years. It remains, then, to examine the evidence for the apostolic authorship of the gospel. *See* JOHN, GOSPEL OF.

Jerome's theory still has its advocates among modern scholars, but others prefer to ascribe the gospel and all three letters to the presbyter of II and III John, who may or may not be identified with Papias' presbyter John. In support of this theory it may be urged that Irenaeus, our earliest witness, certainly confused James the apostle with James the Just (Her. III.12.14), and, though we might have expected him to be better informed about the Christian history of his own native province, he nevertheless erroneously supposed Papias to have been a disciple of John the apostle (Euseb. Hist. III.39.1), so that he could unquestionably have confused John the apostle with John the presbyter, who was also a disciple of the Lord.

Another theory, which has grown in favor, is that the presbyter wrote all three letters but not the gospel; this is the theory to be adopted if we are convinced that the differences between the gospel and I John are so impressive as to outweigh the uniform testimony of antiquity to their common authorship.

Amid this welter of conflicting theories it is possible to make one statement that will command universal agreement—that the authorship of the Johannine letters is still very much an open question.

6. Text. The text of the Johannine letters is well preserved, and the few points where there is room for dispute over divergent readings involve only minor details and not serious matters of interpretation. There are, however, a number of passages where our modern critical texts differ from the Textus Receptus, so that there is a corresponding difference between the RSV and the KJV; and of these, five are for various reasons worthy of mention, all in the first letter:

In the KJV the second half of I John 2:23 ("He that acknowledgeth the Son hath the Father also") is printed in italics. The half verse had for some reason been omitted from the majority of the Greek MSS on which this version was based, the one notable exception being Codex Alexandrinus. The translators apparently felt too much respect for A to ignore its testimony altogether, but not enough to accept its reading as an authentic part of the text. Nowadays the A reading has the confirmation of א, B, C, P, and a number of less important authorities, and is generally accepted.

In I John 2:20 the KJV reading ("Ye know all things"), which had the support of A, C, and a majority of Greek MSS, has rightly been supplanted in the RSV by the reading of א and B ("You all know"). Here is a textual variant which makes a real difference to our understanding of the letter. The argument is directed against the arrogance of the Gnostics, who claim special, esoteric knowledge, and the point is not that the Holy Spirit confers complete knowledge on anybody but that he confers the knowledge of God upon all.

Another point of theological importance turns upon the reading of I John 4:19. Here the KJV follows the majority of MSS in reading: "We love him, because he first loved us." א reads: "We love God . . . ." But the RSV rightly adopts the reading of A and B: "We love, because he first loved us." For the point of the paragraph is not that God's love calls forth a responsive love from us, but that God's love, once perfectly active in Christ, becomes active in us also through our love of the brethren.

One of the greatest textual curiosities in the NT is the passage about the three heavenly witnesses in I John 5:7-8 (KJV): "There are three that bear record [in heaven, the Father, the Word, and the Holy Ghost: and these three are one. And there are three that bear witness in earth], the spirit, and the water, and the blood: and these three agree in one." There is not the slightest doubt that the words enclosed in brackets are an interpolation. They occur in only two late Greek MSS, and in each case the lack of articles betrays the Latin origin of the text. They are not found in any ancient version except the Latin. They were absent from the Old Latin text used by Tertullian, Cyprian, and Augustine, and from Jerome's Vulg. They were first quoted as part of I John by the Spanish heretic Priscillian, who died in 385. At a later date they were accepted into the Vulg. and thus eventually into the Complutensian Polyglot of 1514. Erasmus excluded them from his 1516 edition but promised to restore them if one Greek MS could be found to support them. The late Codex Britannicus was produced, and he reluctantly admitted the disputed verse into his edition of 1522. It was accepted by Stephanus and so found its way into the Textus Receptus and the KJV. In 1897, Leo XIII, acting on the advice of a committee of cardinals, declared that no Roman Catholic might deny or even call in question the authenticity of this *comma Johanneum*. This is, therefore, one of the places where there is a textual difference between the official Roman Catholic Bible and modern Protestant texts and translations of the Bible. But it must be added that since 1927 Roman Catholic scholars have been free, and have even been encouraged, to use their own judgment, and that their judgment has usually brought them into agreement at this point with Protestant scholarship. It should be noted that the RSV has not only eliminated the old vs. 7, but has renumbered the verses of the passage so as to leave no gap in the numbering.

In I John 5:18 a difference of one letter produces a very striking alteration in meaning. The KJV reads: "He that is begotten of God keepeth himself"—a reading which in 1611 had almost unqualified MS support and has since acquired the additional testimony of א. There can be little doubt, however, that the true reading is that of B and the first hand of A: "He who was born of God keeps him" (i.e., Christ keeps the Christian).

Bibliography. B. F. Westcott (3rd ed., 1892). A. E. Brooke, ICC (1912), is the fullest treatment and indispensable for scholarly study. H. Windisch, *Handbuch zum NT* (2nd ed., 1930). C. H. Dodd, Moffatt NT Commentary (1946), is the most illuminating. J. Bonsirven, *Verbum Salutus*, IX (3rd ed., 1956). A. N. Wilder, *IB*, vol. XII (1957). G. B. CAIRD

JOHN, REVELATION TO. *See* REVELATION, BOOK OF.

JOHN MARK. *See* MARK.

JOHN SON OF ZEBEDEE. *See* JOHN THE APOSTLE.

JOHN THE APOSTLE. Son of Zebedee and brother of James. The clearest information concerning the apostle John is found in the Synoptic gospels and in Acts and Galatians. Disputed data are derived from the Gospel and Letters of John and the book of Revelation, and also from later church tradition.

1. The Synoptic gospels. Here it is clear that John, like his father, Zebedee, and his brother James, was a fisherman on the Sea of Galilee (Matt. 4:21-22; Mark 1:19-20; Luke 5:10 adds that James and John "were partners with Simon" Peter). A comparison of Matt. 27:56 with Mark 15:40 suggests that their mother's name was Salome. Mark's reference to "hired servants" implies that the family was well-to-do, and Mark 1:21 implies that the family residence was in or near Capernaum. When the sons of Zebedee are mentioned by name, John is usually named second; from this it would seem that he was younger than James. These two brothers Jesus called early in his ministry in Galilee; only Peter and Andrew were called earlier, and the calls were almost simultaneous.

John was chosen by Jesus as one of the Twelve (Matt. 10:2; Mark 3:17; Luke 6:14), and he was one of the three apostles who were closest to Jesus. These three, Peter and the two sons of Zebedee, were present when Jesus raised the daughter of Jairus from the dead (Mark 5:37; Luke 8:51), when Jesus was transfigured (Matt. 17:1; Mark 9:2; Luke 9:28), and when Jesus went apart to pray in Gethsemane (Matt. 26:37; Mark 14:33).

Luke 9:54 tells that when Jesus and his disciples left Galilee for Jerusalem and a Samaritan village refused to welcome them, James and John wished to "bid fire come down from heaven and consume them," but were rebuked by Jesus. On another occasion John told Jesus that he and the other disciples had rebuked a man who, though not a member of Jesus' group, was casting out demons in the name of Jesus (Mark 9:38; Luke 9:49); Jesus, however, condemned John's narrow zeal. The sons of Zebedee, according to Mark 10:35-41 (Matt. 20:20-24 ascribes the request to their mother), asked Jesus for the highest rank among his followers in the final kingdom, and in response to a question by Jesus, declared their readiness to "drink the cup" and "be baptized with the baptism" of martyrdom, which martyrdom Jesus then predicted they would suffer. Such events throw light upon the statement of Mark 3:17 that Jesus gave to the sons of Zebedee the surname BOANERGES—i.e., "sons of thunder." They had a tendency to be severe and aggressive. Perhaps they did not relish being second to Peter, but this suggestion should not be pushed too far, for in Luke 22:8 Jesus sends Peter and John together to prepare the Passover, and these two appear together in the apostolic age.

2. Acts and Galatians. The apostle John is mentioned in three passages in Acts, and in all three he is associated with Peter. The list of the Eleven in the upper room at Jerusalem names John second, immediately after Peter (1:13). Peter and John went up together to the temple at the hour of prayer, and met the lame beggar, who was healed at the word of Peter; after a crowd had gathered and Peter had preached to them, Peter and John were arrested, imprisoned overnight, examined and threatened by the Jewish leaders, and released (chs. 3–4). Peter and John were sent to Samaria to see whether the conversions under the ministry of Philip, one of the Seven, were genuine; from Samaria they returned to Jerusalem (8:14-25). In both stories Peter is the spokesman and leader of the two; no word or act of John alone is mentioned. After the visit to Samaria there is no suggestion that Peter and John worked again as a team of two.

James the brother of John was executed by Herod Agrippa I (12:2), but Acts gives no indication that this persecution affected John directly, and John is assumed to have been present at the council in ch. 15.

Paul mentions the apostle John but once (Gal. 2:9). In telling of his conference with the Christian leaders at Jerusalem, he names as the outstanding three "who were reputed to be pillars" James (the brother of the Lord), Cephas (Peter), and John. Here again John is associated with Peter; he is an outstanding leader at Jerusalem but apparently not so influential as James or Cephas; and he is prominent in the Christian mission to Jews rather than in the Gentile mission. Thus the explicit NT references to John end with this glimpse of him residing at Jerusalem, active in the church there, and concerned with the preaching of the gospel to his fellow Jews.

3. The "Johannine" writings. According to church tradition, the apostle John wrote the Gospel of John; I, II, and III John; and Revelation. The book of Revelation is the only one of these five writings which names its author (the titles of the books in English Bibles were added later). Its author calls himself Christ's "servant John" (1:1), gives his name as John when he addresses his letters to the seven churches (1:4), calls himself the brother of Christians suffering for their faith and states that he was on the island of PATMOS when he saw the vision he records (1:9), and speaks of his role as that of prophet and of his writing as a book of prophecy (10:11; 22:6-10, 18-19). He does not call himself an apostle or give any clear statement concerning his exact identity.

In the opening words of II and III John the writer calls himself "the elder." He speaks with a note of authority, but does not give his name or call himself an apostle. The completely anonymous I John implies in 1:1-4 that its author had been a personal companion of Jesus during Jesus' earthly ministry. It may be possible to understand that "we" in these verses is a reference to all Christians, as some scholars have claimed, but by far the more natural interpretation of these verses is that which takes the "we" to refer to all the actual eyewitnesses of Jesus' ministry or to the apostolic circle of the Twelve or simply to the writer, who in this case uses the editorial "we" to refer solely to himself. One thing is clear: the writer does not identify himself by name.

The Gospel of John likewise refrains from naming its author. Moreover, it never mentions the apostle John by name, although the Appendix (ch. 21) states that the "sons of Zebedee" were among seven disciples to whom the risen Jesus appeared by the Sea of Tiberias (vs. 2). That the gospel rests on the witness of a Palestinian Jew, whose Greek reflects an Aramaic background, is widely recognized. The claim to be an eyewitness appears to be made in 1:14; 19:35, and is made in behalf of the witness in 21:24. If the original Greek for "first" in 1:41 were πρῶτος, this verse would imply that Andrew was the first of the two hearers of Jesus to bring his own brother (Peter) to Jesus, and then the other hearer brought *his* brother; since James and John the sons of Zebedee were the only other pair of brothers among the Twelve, this could mean that John was the unnamed other hearer of Jesus and at once brought his brother James to Jesus. But the better Greek text for "first" in 1:41 seems to be πρῶτον, which means that the first thing Andrew did was to bring his brother to Jesus; this verse then says nothing of the identity or action of the unnamed other hearer of Jesus.

Whether the apostle John appears in this gospel or was the witness and writer depends mainly upon the identity of the BELOVED DISCIPLE. He appears only at the Last Supper, where he "was lying close to the breast of Jesus" and at a signal from Peter asked who would betray him (13:23-26); at the Cross, where Jesus committed his mother to the Beloved Disciple, who "from that hour . . . took her to his own home" (19:26-27); at the resurrection site, to which he and Peter ran on hearing the tomb was empty, and where he "saw and believed" (20:2-10); and by the Sea of Tiberias, where he first recognized the risen Jesus standing on the beach (21:7), and Jesus said of him that it was no concern of Peter's whether this Beloved Disciple survived until the Lord's return—a saying that apparently caused perplexity in the church when the Beloved Disciple died (21:20-23). The group of disciples responsible for adding the Appendix (ch. 21) to the gospel credit the testimony and writing of the gospel to the Beloved Disciple (21:24).

If we assume that the Gospel of John was written to be intelligible when read as an independent document, we can only conclude that the Beloved Disciple was Lazarus of Bethany. Jesus' love for Lazarus is emphasized in 11:3, 5, 11, 36; Lazarus appears with Jesus at a supper in 12:2; the Beloved Disciple appears at the Last Supper with Jesus a few days later (13:23); and Lazarus is the only man named in this gospel who is thus described as loved by Jesus. Moreover, Lazarus of Bethany would fit well as the source for this Judea-centered gospel; his resurrection in ch. 11 is the climax of Jesus' ministry and embodies the theme of life, which dominates the gospel; it is fitting that he, having been raised from the dead, should first realize that Jesus was risen (20:8) and first recognize the risen Jesus by the Sea of Tiberias (21:7); and Lazarus, who had died and been raised, is the one disciple concerning whom the report might most easily have found credence that he was not to die (21:22-23). The Appendix may be a stage in a process by which the Beloved Disciple was identified with the apostle John, but even the Appendix, read in connection with the gospel, still points to Lazarus as the Beloved Disciple.

The challenge to this conclusion comes, not from this gospel, but from other writings. In the Synoptic gospels and Acts, where the Twelve play a more prominent role than they do in the Gospel of John, Peter and John appear closely related, and this is especially true in Luke and Acts. This recalls that Peter and the Beloved Disciple are related in a similar way in the Gospel of John, a parallel which suggests that John is the Beloved Disciple. The apostle John is one of the three most closely associated with Jesus in the Synoptic gospels, and is the only one of these three who could be identified with the Beloved Disciple. It seems a bit strange to identify the Beloved Disciple and author of the Gospel of John as one of the aggressive "sons of thunder" of the Synoptic gospels; this makes the "son of thunder" an advocate of love as the keynote of Christian living; but it has been argued that John was transformed by his association with Christ, and that traces of his thunderlike temperament survive in the Gospel and Letters of John, as well as in the book of Revelation.

4. Later tradition. The dominant church tradition states that the apostle John moved to Ephesus after years of leadership at Jerusalem, and there wrote the five writings known as Johannine. He is said to have lived to old age and to have died a natural death at Ephesus. However, there is a strong and early tradition that he once was banished to the island of PATMOS, although Eusebius states that he returned to Ephesus and lived until the time of Trajan (Hist. III.18.1; 20.9; 23.4). A number of stories tell of his life in Asia Minor; according to Apollonius, he raised a dead man at Ephesus (Euseb. Hist. V.18.14); Clement of Alexandria tells how in the region near Ephesus he reclaimed a robber for Christ (*What Rich Man Can Be Saved?* 42); Irenaeus tells that he opposed the heretic Cerinthus (Her. III.3.4); and in his old age, when too weak to speak with his former vigor, he is said to have been carried to meetings of Christians and to have said repeatedly, "Little children, love one another" (Jerome *Commentary on Galatians* 6.10).

The key witness for the Ephesian residence of John is Irenaeus. He claims explicitly (Her. III.3.4; V.33. 4) that through Polycarp and Papias he has direct reports of the presence and work of John in the Ephesian region. He goes into detail concerning his hearing of these things from Polycarp when he (Irenaeus) was "still a boy" (Euseb. Hist. V.20.5). The testimony of Irenaeus became the accepted tradition of the church.

The ancient tradition, however, is more complex than this might suggest. Other reports, not all of them in conflict with the tradition of a long residence in Ephesus, must be taken into account. Tertullian says that John went to Rome, "was plunged, unhurt, into boiling oil, and then exiled on an island" (Presc. Her. 36). Polycrates of Ephesus, who confirms John's Ephesian residence, adds that John was a "priest, wearing the sacerdotal plate" (see Euseb. Hist. V.24. 3); this would suggest priestly origin for this John. The Muratorian Fragment (ll. 9-23) states that John was with the rest of the apostles when he was led to write his gospel; this, if true, would suggest a date while the other apostles were alive and would favor Palestine as the place of writing.

A more serious challenge to the Irenaeus tradition is the statement found in a medieval copy of the writing of the ninth-century George the Sinner and in an eighth-century fragment of an epitome of the Chronicle by the fifth-century Philip of Side; the statement is that both sons of Zebedee were martyred. This report, which would imply that John was martyred instead of going to Ephesus and living to old age, recalls Mark 10:39, and has some support in church calendars which list John among Christian martyrs. But the balance of evidence is against this tradition, which may be due to a confusion of the apostle John with John the Baptist, who was martyred.

It is puzzling that Polycarp and especially Ignatius in his Letter to the Ephesians, ch. 12, do not refer to John as a leader at Ephesus. Ignatius speaks of Paul but not of John.

An added difficulty is that all five Johannine books are ascribed to one John, and such common authorship is highly improbable. But unless this common authorship is accepted, there is something radically wrong with the ancient tradition. This does not exclude Ephesian residence for John, but the earliest explicit testimony as to authorship is the statement by Justin Martyr (Dial. 81) that the apostle John wrote the book of Revelation. This would raise a question as to whether John could have written the gospel and the letters.

There was dispute about the authorship of the Gospel of John in the second century. It is reported that Gaius of Rome and a group called the Alogi denied its apostolic authorship, and Hippolytus, at the end of the second century, wrote at Rome a work called *In Defense of the Gospel and Revelation of John.* This defense implies that the Johannine authorship had been questioned.

The testimony of Papias is much debated. While Irenaeus claims that Papias "was a hearer of John," Eusebius states flatly that "Papias himself, in the preface to his discourses, makes it plain that he was in no sense a hearer and eye-witness of the holy apostles" (Hist. III.39.2). Eusebius goes on to quote Papias, who distinguishes between (the apostle) John and "John the Elder" (Hist. III.39.4). Some have denied that Papias speaks of two Johns, but his words as quoted, and certainly as understood by Eusebius, seem to refer to two Johns. In that case, II John 1 and III John 1 could favor the Elder as author of the gospel and the Johannine letters. In any event, if Irenaeus was wrong, as appears to be the case, in reporting that Papias heard the apostle John, the force of his testimony is considerably weakened. He appears to confuse James the Lord's brother with James the son of Zebedee (Iren. Her. III.12.15), and Polycrates of Ephesus seems to have confused Philip the apostle and Philip one of the Seven (Euseb. Hist. III.39.9). In other words, we note a tendency to identify as one of the apostles another person of the same name.

Such data do not disprove the Ephesian residence of the apostle John. There is considerable strength to the tradition for that residence. But a number of opposing items clearly exist, and the ancient advocates of the tradition tended to claim too much. If the Ephesian residence is accepted, this does not necessarily carry with it authorship by John of any particular Johannine writing. The tradition for apostolic authorship of the book of Revelation is earliest, and the author of this book, whether an apostle or not, was certainly named John. The author of II and III John, who probably wrote the Gospel of John and I John, calls himself "the elder," which could mean the elder John mentioned by Papias or some other prominent elder. The apostle John could have been the source of the witness recorded in the Gospel of John, or his connection with the gospel could have been a confusion in developing church tradition. The Ephesian residence of the apostle John and the apostolic authorship of part of the five Johannine writings are traditions with strength, but are confronted by opposing traditions which cannot be ignored, and no final conclusion on these questions is now attainable.

See also JOHN, LETTERS OF; JOHN, GOSPEL OF; REVELATION, BOOK OF.

Bibliography. I. T. Beckwith, *The Apocalypse of John* (1919), pp. 343-94; C. F. Nolloth, *The Fourth Evangelist* (1925); J. H. Bernard, *The Gospel According to St. John* (1929), I, xxxiv-lxxviii; B. H. Streeter, *The Four Gospels* (4th ed., 1930), chs. 15-16; B. W. Bacon, *The Gospel of the Hellenists* (1933), pp. 3-132; W. Michaelis, *Einleitung in das Neue Testament* (1946), pp. 89-117, 298-300, 303-4, 315-19; F. C. Grant, *The Gospels: Their Origin and Growth* (1957), ch. 12.

F. V. FILSON

JOHN THE BAPTIST [Ἰωάννης ὁ βαπτίζων]. A prophet of priestly descent, whose mother, Elizabeth, was related to Mary the mother of Jesus. John lived in Judea and had close contacts with the wilderness, where he began his public ministry by proclaiming a baptism of repentance for the forgiveness of sins. Multitudes came to be baptized by John in the River Jordan, among them Jesus himself. Later John was arrested, imprisoned, and finally executed by Herod Antipas. The disciples of John formed a "Baptist" community, which continued to exist long after his death. (The term "Baptist" will be used in this special sense throughout this article.) Apparently the community produced a literature of its own. Fragments of Baptist literature are preserved in the Synoptic gospel tradition.

The historical reconstruction of what can be known about John the Baptist will be preceded by a literary and historical analysis of our sources of information.

A. *LITERARY-HISTORICAL ANALYSIS OF SOURCES.* John the Baptist is mentioned by Josephus and certain NT writers. Most of our information about John in the NT is derived from tradition preserved in the Synoptic gospels. However, there are important references to the Baptist in the Fourth Gospel, and he is also mentioned in Acts.

1. The Synoptic gospels. Information about John the Baptist contained in the Synoptic gospels has come from two different kinds of sources, which should be distinguished: Baptist and Christian.

a. Baptist sources. Paul Winter has shown that Luke 1:5-80 was originally a Baptist document. It was an infancy narrative concerning John. It has been adopted as an introduction to the birth narrative of Jesus, which begins at 2:1. Luke 1:26-46*a* constitutes the single major interpolation in this Baptist document. 1:25 is followed very well by 1:46*b*, and except for vs. 56 the narrative is uninterrupted by further Christian interpolation. It is quite possible, however, that vs. 25 is also secondary, in which case we should proceed directly from vs. 24 to vs. 46*b*. The question is unsettled as to whether vss. 26-46*a* contain material originally found in the Baptist document but now modified by the Christian interpolater, or whether they are wholly secondary.

This Baptist document can be reconstructed as follows: Luke 1:5-24 or 25, 46*b*-55, 57-80. From this source, which contains a great deal of legendary material about John, we may glean the following historically reliable information: John was of priestly descent. His father, a priest of the division of Abijah, was named Zechariah, and his mother Elizabeth (vs. 5). John was born in Judea (vs. 65), and as a youth he had close contacts with the wilderness (vs. 80). We may further infer from the document itself that John's influence did not perish with his death, but rather that he was remembered and honored by a community which regarded him as a messianic forerunner, if not the Messiah. This Baptist community probably produced other literature in which further traditions concerning John were incorporated.

Whatever were the intermediate stages in the development of the Baptist tradition as it has come to us through the gospels, it may be doubted whether these writings contain any reliable information concerning John in the period prior to his baptism of Jesus that has not come originally from Baptist sources. It follows that a comparative study of the relevant passages in Matthew, Mark, and Luke should enable us to reconstruct the most probable form of this Baptist tradition. Such a study produces the following information: John began his ministry in the wilderness (Matt. 3:1; Mark 1:4; Luke 3:2). He proclaimed the judgment of God and called for Israel to repent of its sins. Great numbers of people came to him from Jerusalem and the country of Judea, as well as all the region about the Jordan (Matt. 3:5; Mark 1:5*a;* Luke 3:3, 7). Many of these responded to his message and were baptized by John in the Jordan River, confessing their sins (Matt. 3:6; Mark 1:5*b*). The judgment of God was imminent, and the need for repentance was urgent, for the wrath of God was about to be poured out upon all the unrighteous (Matt. 3:7-10, 11*b*-12; Luke 3:7-9, 16*b*-17).

John's baptism was accompanied by ethical exhortation. "He who has two coats, let him share with him who has none; and he who has food, let him do likewise" (Luke 3:10). Specific instructions were given to meet the exigencies of the moment. Tax collectors were to collect no more than was appointed to them (3:12-13). Soldiers were to be content with their army rations and to refrain from improving their lot at the expense of helpless civilians (3:14). In their present form these ethical teachings no doubt reflect the needs of the primitive Baptist community, which faced the problems which confronted the early Christian church—namely, the delayed consummation of the *eschaton* and the consequent necessity of giving advice to those who, while awaiting the consummation of the *eschaton,* still had to face the stern realities of finding daily food and other necessities of life. It is not possible to say to what extent these teachings are from John. They underline John's acknowledged concern for righteousness (cf. Matt. 21:32; Mark 6:20; Jos. Antiq. XVIII.v.2). Perhaps these teachings reflect the kind of charges which John leveled against the people: "You brood of vipers, who warned you to flee from the wrath to come?" You who have two coats do not share with your brothers who have none! You who collect taxes, collect more than is appointed to you! You men under arms are not content with your rations, so you fall upon helpless people! Or perhaps John's teachings reflect his picture of a corrupt society which would soon be swept away—a society characterized by inequality of wealth, oppressive taxation, and abuse of power.

John promised that he would be followed in time by one "mightier" than he, whose sandals he was "not worthy to stoop down and untie" (Mark 1:7; cf. Matt. 3:11; Luke 3:16). It has been assumed that these words were early Christian polemic designed to show the superiority of Jesus over John. But it is possible that this passage belonged originally to a Baptist document in which the coming One referred to was an eschatological figure like the apocalyptic Son of man. Or possibly it referred to the Lord (God) himself, whose way was being prepared in the wilderness through the work of John in accordance with the words of Isaiah (Isa. 40:3; cf. Matt. 3:3; Mark 1:3; Luke 3:4; John 1:23, 27).

In Mark 6:17-29 we may be once again in touch with material which originated in Baptist circles. This passage refers to the circumstances surrounding the arrest, imprisonment, and execution of John. According to this source of information, John had charged that it was unlawful for Herod to live with the wife of his brother Philip (vs. 18). This woman (Herodias) had a grudge against John and wanted to kill him (vs. 19). But Herod feared John, knowing that he was a righteous man and holy, so he kept John safe (vs. 20). Then follows a legendary account of how Herod could have pronounced the death sentence upon John, since he did not want to execute him (vss. 21-26). This account does not exonerate Herod, for he still bears the responsibility for having issued the order of execution (vs. 27). Furthermore, to picture this oriental monarch allowing his stepdaughter to dance before his guests (vs. 22) was not calculated to improve Herod's reputation. Therefore, this source is definitely not pro-Herodian. Why then would it picture Herod as reluctant to execute John? The answer is probably the same as the answer to the question of why the gospel tradition represents Pilate as being reluctant to execute Jesus. There was, apparently, among the disciples of John as well as among the disciples of Jesus, a reluctance to acknowledge the fact that their teachers had been executed because they were believed by the authorities to constitute a threat to the state as potential leaders of insurrection. The passage closes with an account of the execution—John was beheaded in prison by a soldier (vs. 27), and when John's disciples heard of the execution, "they came and took his body, and laid it in a tomb" (vs. 29).

We may glean from this passage the following information as historically reliable: (*a*) John was arrested, imprisoned for a period, and finally executed by Herod Antipas; (*b*) John's disciples were allowed to take his body and give it proper burial; (*c*) these disciples remembered and passed on to others what they had seen and what they had done, thus accounting for the origin of the authentic tradition about John which has been preserved in this account; (*d*) it most likely would have been within the Baptist community that these traditions were woven together with other traditions about Herod Antipas' family and court life to form this legendary story.

It should be noted that Matthew parallels Mark, including the story in his gospel (Matt. 14:3-12). But Luke does not include it. Instead, he preserves only a very brief statement which eliminates most of the legendary material, but adds nothing new (Luke 3:19-20). Possibly Luke did not include the passage as a whole because he recognized some of the difficulties entailed in accommodating certain details in this story with information provided in the histories of Josephus.

b. Christian sources. Traditions about John the Baptist originating in Christian circles (including disciples of John who later became disciples of Jesus) are found in all three Synoptic gospels.

i. Q. Q stands for a hypothetical source of Christian tradition about Jesus which is found in both Matthew and Luke. This source included at least one rather extended passage containing valuable information about John and Jesus' attitude toward him. This passage, preserved in Matt. 11:2-19; Luke 7:18-35, is itself a compilation of heterogeneous literary units which have been placed together because they all contain some reference to John. Three of these literary units are clearly discernible: (*a*) Matt. 11:2-6 (Luke 7:18-23); (*b*) Matt. 11:7-11 (Luke 7:24-28); (*c*) Matt. 11:16-19 (Luke 7:31-35).

Matt. 11:2-6 (Luke 7:18-23): John, who is in prison, sends his disciples to Jesus to inquire: "Are you he who is to come, or shall we look for another?" The reply of Jesus, a paraphrase of Isa. 29:18-19, reflects the christological concern of the primitive church and may be late. But the saying with which the pericope ends: "Blessed is he who takes no offense at me," may well be an authentic logion of Jesus. If an actual incident in the ministry of Jesus is reflected here, we may observe the following: (*a*) While in prison, John continued to exert his influence in national affairs through his disciples; (*b*) these disciples are distinguishable from the disciples of Jesus, though not hostile to them or to Jesus; (*c*) there was a continuing relationship between Jesus and John. John was concerned about the intent and purpose of Jesus, and Jesus was mindful of John's interest in him.

Matt. 11:7-11 (Luke 7:24-28): This literary unit may be analyzed in four parts:

a) Matt. 11:7-9 (Luke 7:24-26): "What did you go out into the wilderness to behold? A reed shaken by the wind? . . . to see a man clothed in soft raiment? . . . Why then did you go out? To see a prophet? Yes, I tell you, and more than a prophet." This saying may be regarded as an authentic utterance of Jesus, since it is opposed to a later Christian tendency to depreciate John. To refer to John as Jesus does here indicates that those who had been to the wilderness to see John held a continuing interest in, and regard for, the Baptist. That they are no longer in the wilderness may mean that John has been arrested. Jesus withdrew when John was arrested (Matt. 4:12; Mark 1:14). Because the first two questions are ironical, we may surmise the following: (*a*) John was not the kind of man to break under pressure—not a "reed shaken by the wind" (probably a reference to his spirited resistance to Herod even while in prison); (*b*) John was a man of austere dress (in contrast to those who lived in luxury in Herod's household?).

b) Matt. 11:10 (Luke 7:27): This is a loose quotation of Mal. 3:1 and is generally regarded as a later insert into Q.

c) Matt. 11:11*a* (Luke 7:28*a*): "I say to you, among those born of women there has risen no one greater than John the Baptist." Taken with the first two verses of this pericope, this saying constitutes the strongest kind of endorsement of John. Jesus speaks of John as of one with whom he was closely allied and with whom he seems to feel a strong sense of solidarity.

d) Matt. 11:11*b* (Luke 7:28*b*): "Yet he who is least in the kingdom of heaven is greater than he." This is commonly regarded as a later addition. But it may form, with the saying which precedes it, a single depreciatory unit. It does not depreciate John in particular. Rather, it depreciates all men in general (of whom John represents the best) in relation to those men in particular who enter the kingdom.

Matt. 11:16-19 (Luke 7:31-35): John is mentioned only in the second half of this pericope: "John came neither eating nor drinking, and they say, 'He has a demon'; the Son of man came eating and drinking, and they say, 'Behold, a glutton and a drunkard, a friend of tax collectors and sinners!' " (Matt. 11:18-19*b*). These verses reflect a situation in the primitive Palestinian church when Christians could protest against the fickleness and inconsistency of the nation in its refusal to accept either John or Jesus. The charge that John had a demon is, no doubt, an authentic tradition. The same charge was leveled against Jesus by those who rejected him (John 7:20; 8:48; 10:20). The charge that Jesus was a glutton (φάγος) and a drunkard (οἰνοπότης) refers, not to excessive eating and drinking, but to his unlawful eating with tax collectors and sinners who did not observe all the dietary regulations. Translated literally, ἄνθρωπος φάγος καὶ οἰνοπότης means a "man who eats and drinks"—i.e., one who eats and drinks with those who do not keep the law, the tax collectors and sinners. "John came neither eating nor drinking" means that, unlike Jesus, John did not eat with tax collectors and sinners.

The expanded version in Luke 7:33: "John the Baptist has come eating no bread and drinking no wine," is later. It represents an early attempt to interpret the words "neither eating nor drinking" (which, taken literally, are nonsensical) in the light of other traditions about John—i.e., that he had been dedicated as a Nazarite, to whom wine was forbidden (Luke 1:15), and that he lived on an austere diet of locusts and wild honey (Mark 1:6). However, neither these traditions nor Jewish practice in general can be cited to support a prohibition against eating bread.

A comparison of Matthew and Luke indicates that in Q, located between the above-mentioned second and third literary units, there was an additional pericope. Matt. 11:12-14 reads: "From the days of John the Baptist until now the kingdom of heaven has suffered violence, and men of violence take it by force. For all the prophets and the law prophesied until John; and if you are willing to accept it, he is Elijah who is to come." It is clear that John marked the end of one era and the beginning of a new one. But in what way the kingdom has suffered violence, and who the men of violence are who take the kingdom by force, is one of the unsolved mysteries of gospel criticism. The parallel passage in Luke 16:16 only makes the exegetical problem more difficult.

ii. Mark. Mark 1:6 preserves the tradition that John was clothed with camel's hair and wore a leather girdle around his waist, and that he ate locusts and wild honey. John's mode of existence was not primarily that of an ascetic, but that of a legal purist. The food he ate was both ceremonially clean (Lev. 11:21-22) and available in the wilderness, where life was uncontaminated by the legal impurity of life in the towns and cities. This passage is preserved also in Matt. 3:4, but not in the same order as in Mark. There is no reason to doubt its historical authenticity.

Mark 1:14 suggests that the arrest of John was the occasion for Jesus to go to Galilee. The parallel passage in Matthew explicitly says that "when he [Jesus] heard that John had been arrested, he withdrew into Galilee" (Matt. 4:12). It is possible that the imprisonment of John and his subsequent execution had a more determinative effect upon the course of Jesus' ministry than is suggested by the surface impression given in the gospels.

In Mark 2:18 (Matt. 9:14; Luke 5:33) Jesus is asked: "Why do John's disciples and the disciples of the Pharisees fast, but your disciples do not fast?" Luke's fuller version of the question: ". . . fast often and offer prayers," is probably a Lukan expansion made in the light of the tradition that John taught his disciples to pray (Luke 11:1). The question as found in Mark is probably historically genuine, and is important because it informs us, not only that John's disciples fasted, but also that their religious practice paralleled, in this respect, that of the Pharisees.

Mark preserves the tradition that some believed Jesus was John the Baptist raised from the dead (Mark 6:14; 8:28; cf. Matt. 14:1-2; 16:14; Luke 9:7, 19), and that Jesus believed John to be Elijah (Mark 9:12-13; cf. Matt. 17:12-13).

Mark 11:30-32 (Matt. 21:23-27; Luke 20:1-8) records that when Jesus asked the chief priests and elders whether John's baptism was from heaven or from men, they hesitated to answer, because they were afraid of the people, who all held that John was a true prophet. If this is an authentic tradition, as it seems to be, then "the people" were probably mostly former supporters of John now looking to Jesus for leadership. Jesus' act of cleansing the temple would have appeared as a bold messianic act, in complete accord with the priestly concern of John for righteousness.

iii. M. In M, source material peculiar to Matthew, the following logion of Jesus is found: "Truly I say to you, the tax collectors and the harlots go into the kingdom of God before you. For John came to you in the way of righteousness, and you did not believe him, but the tax collectors and the harlots believed him; and even when you saw it, you did not afterward repent and believe him" (Matt. 21:31-32). A parallel passage in Luke 7:29-30 reads "all the people" instead of "harlots." This is more in accord with the usual expression "tax collectors and sinners" (Mark 2:15-16 [Matt. 9:10-11; Luke 5:29-30]; Q: Matt. 11:19; Luke 7:34; L: Luke 15:1), and indicates that "harlots" may have been used metaphorically. In the OT, "harlotry" is used figuratively of improper intercourse with foreign nations (Isa. 23:17; Ezek. 16:26-28; 23:30, 43; Nah. 3:4).

iv. L. In material found only in Luke, sometimes designated L, there are three passages which refer to John:

a) Luke 3:19-20 may be dependent on Mark 6:17-18. It adds nothing new.

b) Luke 7:29-30 preserves a tradition that all the people and the tax collectors justified God when they heard Jesus speak about John, because they had been baptized by John. This implies that many of Jesus' hearers were previously disciples of John.

c) In Luke 11:1 we read that the disciples of Jesus made the following request: "Lord, teach us to pray, as John taught his disciples." This request not only indicates that John taught his disciples to pray, but it also suggests the possibility that in Jesus' response to this request we may be in touch with tradition which preserves in outline a Baptist catechesis on prayer.

2. John. In the first chapter of the Fourth Gospel, John the Baptist is mentioned several times. By a literary device he is made to function as a christological spokesman for the early church: "I am not the Christ" (vs. 20); "I came baptizing with water, that he might be revealed to Israel" (vs. 31); "I have seen and have borne witness that this is the Son of God" (vs. 34; cf. 5:33-36).

John baptized at Bethany E of the Jordan (1:28; cf. 10:40), and at Aenon near Salim (3:23). Bethany has been identified with a site in Perea not far from where a main highway leading from Jerusalem to Transjordan crosses the river. Aenon, meaning "springs," is probably to be located near the headwaters of Wadi Far'ah, where there are numerous springs providing an abundant supply of water. This site is only a few miles from Jacob's well in the direction of the Jordan Valley.

John 10:40-41 represents Jesus returning to the place E of the Jordan where John first baptized. There he remained and was accepted by many as a successor of the Baptist. If historical, this incident probably took place after John's arrest. It may reflect an early Christian attempt to woo into the church disciples of John still living near John's first headquarters.

3. Acts. Acts 11:16 may preserve an original logion of Jesus: "John baptized with water, but you shall be baptized with the Holy Spirit" (cf. 1:5).

Acts 1:22; 10:36-37; 13:24 mention John but add nothing to our knowledge about him.

Acts 19:1-7 gives an account of an incident in Ephesus when Paul found twelve men who had received only the baptism of John. Their rebaptism is evidence that the church faced aggressively the problem of a competing messianic community which had sprung from the ministry and martyrdom of John. It is this situation of rivalry in the early church which accounts for the rigorous subordination of John to Jesus in certain NT passages: "After me comes he . . . whose sandals I am not worthy to stoop down and untie" (Matt. 3:11; Mark 1:7; Luke 3:16; John 1:27; Acts 13:25); "he who comes after me ranks before me" (John 1:15); "he must increase, but I must decrease" (John 3:30; cf. 5:36).

To what extent this rivalry can be traced back to a rivalry between Jesus and John or to their first disciples is difficult to decide. The fact that Jesus had been a disciple of John was an embarrassment to the early church, but there is no evidence that it was an embarrassment to Jesus or to his first disciples. Rather, it seems to have worked in Jesus' favor when he dealt with crowds peopled by the disciples of John. But after the death of Jesus the disciples of John could no longer regard Jesus as the historical bearer of John's message and work. This placed Jesus and John on equal footing as martyred teachers. Those disciples of John who became Christians confessed Jesus to be the Messiah and adopted the view that John was the forerunner. Those disciples of John who did not become Christians resented this relegation of their founder to a secondary role. This resentment aggravated the delicate relationship between the two rival communities and eventually led to the polemical situation reflected in the secondary material in the gospel tradition.

4. Josephus. The single passage from Antiq. XVIII.v.2 is here given in full: "But some of the Jews believed that Herod's army was destroyed by God, God punishing him very justly for John called the Baptist, whom Herod had put to death. For John was a pious man, and he was bidding the Jews who practiced virtue and exercised righteousness toward each other and piety toward God, to come together for baptism. For thus, it seemed to him, would baptismal ablution be acceptable, if it were used not to beg off from sins committed, but for the purification of the body when the soul had previously been cleansed by righteous conduct. And when everybody turned to John—for they were profoundly stirred by what he said—Herod feared that John's so extensive influence over the people might lead to an uprising (for the people seemed likely to do everything he might counsel). He thought it much better, under the circumstances, to get John out of the way in advance, before any insurrection might develop, than for himself to get into trouble and be sorry not to have acted, once an insurrection had begun. So because of Herod's suspicion, John was sent as a prisoner to Macherus, the fortress already mentioned, and there put to death. But the Jews believed that the destruction which overtook the army came as a punishment for Herod, God wishing to do him harm." [1]

In the light of this passage three points may be made: (*a*) John's imprisonment and execution took place in the Maccabean-Herodian mountain fortress Macherus, near the Dead Sea on the S border of Perea. (*b*) John was arrested because Herod feared the political consequences of his popularity. This does not preclude the factor of personal resentment against John on the part of members of Herod's family. Any charges he may have made against immorality or riotous living in court circles were subject to being interpreted as incitement to insurrection, since such charges would have tended to undermine confidence in Herod's right to rule. (*c*) John's memory was honored by some Jews long after his death, for some believed that Herod's defeat was a sign of divine retribution for his unjust execution of John.

Although not a direct source for John the Baptist, another passage in Josephus (Life 2), is so pertinent as to merit quotation: "On hearing of one named Bannus, who dwelt in the wilderness, wearing only such clothing as trees provided, feeding on such things as grew of themselves, and using frequent ablutions of cold water, by day and night, for purity's sake, I became a zealous disciple of him."

This passage is of primary importance in considering the peculiarities of John's dress, diet, and practice of water baptism. They are perfectly explicable in terms of a wilderness sojourn for one concerned with strict obedience to the purity laws of Moses as interpreted in first-century Judaism.

B. *HISTORICAL RECONSTRUCTION.* 1. Historical background. John the Baptist steps forth on the scene of history as a prophet proclaiming the eschatological day of the Lord. In obedience to the words of Isaiah, John was in the wilderness crying: "Prepare the way of the LORD, make straight in the desert a highway for our God." Of priestly origins, he stands in the prophetic tradition of Elijah, who was expected by the Jews to return and play an important role in the ushering in of the messianic age. John's simple dress and ritually pure diet bespoke his rejection of the corrupt society of his time and his strict adherence to the laws of Moses.

The "sons of Abraham" had been disinherited. The Promised Land was occupied by the legions of Rome, and the chief priests in the temple had "no king but Caesar" (John 19:15). The chief priests, like Herod Antipas, held their offices at the pleasure of their Roman masters.

God had promised Israel the land and political sovereignty (Deut. 15:6). The prophets and seers of Israel had written of a day of judgment when God's wrath would be poured out upon the wicked and his promises fulfilled to the righteous. These divine promises and sacred writings constituted the basis upon which were raised the peoples' hopes for the coming of the kingdom of God.

This would mean deliverance from the clutches of the Gentiles. From the point of view of the righteous, who were zealous for the covenant, those apostate

[1] Reprinted by permission of the publishers and The Loeb Classical Library from Loeb Classical Library Volume: Josephus *Antiquities* (Cambridge, Mass.: Harvard University Press, 1930, 1957).

Jews who had gone over to the side of the Gentiles, such as the chief priests and the supporters of Herod Antipas, had sold their inheritance for a "mess of pottage." They were like a "brood of vipers." In the Day of Wrath they would be baptized with a baptism of fire and be utterly destroyed. Their laxness in observing the laws of Moses, as well as the presence of the Gentiles in the land, rendered life in the cities and towns unclean.

The alternatives for the righteous were limited. Some escaped the unclean and corrupt life of the cities and towns by withdrawing into the wilderness and separating themselves from all impurity. Others banded together and remained in the towns and cities, maintaining their purity by complicated and highly refined systems of ritual washing. However, the vast majority of Jews, either voluntarily or by virtue of their occupations, were inexorably entangled in the web of impurity which was woven into the fabric of political, economic, and social life under the conditions of Gentile occupation. The importance of this fact will be more fully developed in connection with the meaning of John's baptism.

2. The wilderness of Judea. The wilderness of Judea was the center of religious hope as well as a place of refuge. It was the symbol of the wilderness in which God had tabernacled with his people for forty years before bringing them into the Promised Land. In the wilderness the way of the Lord was to be made straight, and some believed the Messiah would first appear here (Matt. 24:23-26).

The DSS community was living in the heart of this wilderness. There they were preparing the way for the Lord's coming through the study of the law and strict obedience to all that had been revealed to the prophets. United by a priestly discipline, the community constituted a "holy of holies" in which, through sacrifices of praise and perfect obedience, atonement was made for the guilt of transgressions, and for the purification of the land. Set apart in this way, the community served as a house of holiness for the priests and a house of community for the Israelites who were obedient to the law until the coming of the Day of the Lord. This day would be marked by the appearance of two messianic figures, an anointed priest and an anointed king for Israel (1QS 8.15; 9.11). *See* DEAD SEA SCROLLS.

Thus the stage is set, and one can understand the excitement which swept through the towns and cities of Judea with the advent of the news that a young priest, an Elijah, was baptizing in the wilderness. The King Messiah would soon appear, and the Day of Judgment was about to be ushered in.

3. John's teaching. As the multitudes from Jerusalem and the country around Judea flocked to him in the wilderness, John cried out: "You brood of vipers! Who warned you to flee from the wrath to come? Bear fruit that befits repentance."

The radical character of John's ethical teaching is often not fully appreciated. His injunction to share clothing and food strikes at the very heart of an acquisitive society and indicates that John advocated a kind of eschatological brotherhood, perhaps similar to that practiced in Essene communities.

John had been in the wilderness since childhood and no doubt was acquainted with Essene thought and practice. It is known that some Essene communities adopted boys, and it is quite likely that John's childhood in the wilderness was spent with some such religious community.

A strict legalist, John, like the Essenes and Pharisees, refused to eat with those who failed to observe the Mosaic purity laws. The chief offenders in this regard were the tax collectors, whose unrighteous mammon made their well-laden tables doubly offensive. Nonetheless, these people went to hear John. They repented and were baptized by him.

a. Tax collectors. The tax collector was the most obvious agent of collaboration at the local level. He was not a despised social outcast, as is sometimes believed. He could be one of the leading laymen of a synagogue, and could render his fellow Jews important services by virtue of his influence with the Roman officials (Jos. War II.xiv.2-5). But the prevailing system of tax collection encouraged greed and unfairness on the part of the collectors.

The requirement that tax collectors refrain from collecting more than was appointed to them would have set them at odds with the social and economic structures of which they were a part. It would have resulted in a radical reduction in their standard of living and necessitated serious economic and social readjustments on the part of their families. Furthermore, it would have required a complete reorientation of their motivation in accepting the responsibilities of their office. Because, once the prospect of becoming rich has been removed, few would want to continue the onerous duties of collecting unpopular taxes from a resentful people. Especially so when the money directly or indirectly supported the occupation forces and the concomitant collaborating bureaucracy.

b. Soldiers. At the opposite extreme from the tax collectors were the fiery patriots known as Zealots. Because of their refusal to render taxes unto Caesar, these men were forced to hide in caves in the mountains and in the wilderness in order to save their lives. The soldiers who came to hear John are usually assumed to have been under Herod's command, but they may have been part of an organized Jewish resistance to Rome, active ever since the Roman census for taxation was made in A.D. 6. Josephus writes that the seditious ferment which was set in motion in those early years of Roman occupation, when Judea was first made a province of the Empire, increased till at last the entire nation was caught up in the fever of rebellion in A.D. 66.

Jesus numbered among his closest disciples both a tax collector and a Zealot, and there is no reason to think that the response to John's preaching was less inclusive of the social, economic, and political extremes within Israel. These zealous patriot groups sustained themselves in part by forcibly expropriating the property of Gentiles and collaborating Jews. Their abuse of this practice was so widespread that Jesus could take for granted that his hearers would immediately feel themselves involved when he told his parable concerning the good Samaritan. To travel from Jerusalem to Jericho carried one through the very heart of the Judean wilderness. Only a few miles from this road lived the militant but well-disciplined DSS community, which was constrained to include the following restrictive order for its zealous members: "Let no man put forth his hand to shed the blood of a man of the Gentiles for the sake of property and gain; also let him not carry off anything of their property" (Zadokite Document 12.6-7). John's exhortation to the soldiers who came to him is in the same vein: "Rob no one by violence or by false accusation, and be content with your wages." The DSS community qualified their restrictive order by adding "except by the decision of an Israelite court." What is prohibited is unwarranted, privately initiated pillaging. Neither the DSS community nor John forbade organized military efforts to obtain food and supplies. Nevertheless, in an occupation situation, to require that a member of a resistance force voluntarily be content with his military rations, when it was within his power to ameliorate his austere life by forcibly expropriating food and property from the more comfortable, collaborating elements in the population, was to make a very radical ethical demand. It is safe to assume that the cutting edge of Jesus' social teaching was not blunted by his association with John in the wilderness.

4. John's baptism. In addition to the background depicted in § A2 *above,* the baptism of John is to be seen more particularly in the light of contemporary Jewish ritual bathing. These baths were for the purpose of cleansing the believer from ritual defilement.

Ceremonial washing was widespread in the ancient world, but it is probable that Jewish ritual bathing in the first century was primarily a development of more ancient Jewish practice in the postexilic period. E.g., in Lev. 15 several different forms of bodily discharge (some quite normal), which render the person temporarily unclean, are dealt with. Bathing in water is prescribed to effect ritual purity. Since they were not members of the Mosaic covenant, Gentiles were not bound by such laws. Nonetheless, from the point of view of the strict Jew, Gentiles were virtually in a continuous state of uncleanness. Any contact with a Gentile was as defiling as contact with an unclean Israelite. The dwellings of Gentiles, their lands, and, for some scrupulous Jews, even the air above their lands constituted threatening sources of defilement.

Under the early Maccabees, Judea and its temple had been established as an island of purity in a sea of Gentile uncleanness. But by the beginning of the first century the waters of this sea had gradually encroached on this island until only the forbidding wastelands of the Judean wilderness were left untouched.

The Dead Sea Scroll entitled "The War of the Sons of Light and the Sons of Darkness" reflects the kind of militant eschatological thinking current in the wilderness of Judea in the days of John. According to this document, men are involved in a great cosmic struggle between Light and Darkness. The Children of Light are those obedient to Mosaic law. The Children of Darkness, under the command of Belial, are the Romans and those apostate Jews who do not observe the laws of Moses. Victory was assured to the Children of Light because the God of the Covenant was the Lord of the heavenly hosts.

However, those angelic warriors of the Lord would not abide in the camps of the Children of Light unless these camps were free from all impurity. Therefore, ritual purity baths for all recruits were essential to ensure the assistance of those heavenly battalions so necessary to gain the victory over the otherwise overwhelmingly more powerful armies of Rome.

Within this context, John may be seen as a prophet declaring the advent of this great eschatological conflict. Every son of Abraham was called forth to be a volunteer for the Lord. He must not complacently say, "I have Abraham for my father." He must renounce all uncleanness and unrighteousness and henceforth, in perfect obedience to God, stand ready to march against the forces of Darkness.

John's baptism thus may be seen as an eschatological plenary cleansing of the individual from all ritual defilement; a rite of purification which made it possible for the baptized to take his place within the ranks of the Children of Light. From this point of view, John's baptism would have been a part of, and possibly the high moment in, a ceremony of initiation into a "new covenant" community—an eschatological community which awaited expectantly the advent of the One to Come whom God would quickly send to lead the Children of Light to victory over Belial and his forces of Darkness. Possibly, as seems to have been the case in the DSS "new covenant" community, the effectiveness of John's baptism was conditional upon repentance. It certainly was accompanied by repentance and confession of sins, and was undertaken in a context of ethical exhortation.

5. John's death. It need not be supposed that Herod Antipas and the authorities in Judea were unaware of the danger to their own security which such messianic eschatological belief and activity represented. The beliefs themselves could not be stamped out. But any individual in whom these beliefs were popularly centered could be arrested and imprisoned, and, if need be, put to death. Those who rejected John's message with the charge "He has a demon" could be counted on to give tacit approval to John's arrest and imprisonment, if not his capital punishment. And John's indictment of Herod for his illicit marriage to Herodias would have weighed against him, as his fate was being decided in the court of Herod.

John's execution as recorded in the gospels and by Josephus is perfectly intelligible in the light of our knowledge about conditions in Palestine at that time. And a consideration of John's treatment at the hands of the authorities throws light on otherwise obscure aspects of Jesus' ministry and passion.

6. John the Baptist and Jesus. Jesus had been baptized by John in the Jordan River. Following his baptism, Jesus remained in the wilderness. The forty-day period of the gospels is to be taken figuratively to represent a period of waiting upon the Lord, a period of temptation and discipline corresponding to the forty-year period of preparation Israel spent in the wilderness before entering the Promised Land.

John had been active in widely separated parts of the wilderness. At one time he was E of the Jordan near the main highway running from Jericho to Transjordan. At another time he penetrated northwestward into Samaria and baptized within a few miles of its well-populated towns. Furthermore, some who had been baptized by John were contemporaneously active in other parts of the wilderness. Jesus was preaching and his disciples were baptizing in Judea while John was in Samaria. John had initiated a movement, therefore, which, from the point of view of the authorities, was widespread and growing at an alarming rate.

Consequently, his incarceration in the remote military stronghold of Macherus in the extreme S of Perea may be viewed as a prudent step to stop a menacing messianic movement by removing its instigator as far as possible from the multitudes which flocked to hear him.

The arrest of John must have had a profound effect upon those who had been baptized by him. No doubt, many returned to their homes to await developments. Some stationed themselves near Macherus and kept in touch with their leader. Jesus returned to Galilee and began immediately to preach in its synagogues. This constituted a defiant answer to the repressive measures of the "fox" Herod Antipas. Many who had been baptized by John heard Jesus gladly, and some saw in him the one who was to come to lead Israel into the kingdom.

Through his disciples, John maintained contact with Jesus and followed his activities carefully. His question to Jesus: "Are you he who is to come, or shall we look for another?" indicates that, though in prison, John had not relinquished his role as a guiding hand in Israel's preparation for the eschatological struggle.

John was no "reed shaken by the wind," and his imprisonment failed to thwart his exercising continuing influence in the affairs of the nation. From the point of view of the authorities, it was more expedient for one to die than for the whole nation to perish in some uprising which the Romans were certain to crush (cf. John 11:48-50). But the execution, which was designed to achieve John's political end, turned into a martyrdom, which only stimulated the expectant imagination of the Jewish populace. After his disciples laid his body in a tomb, they continued to wait for the consummation of God's purpose, and while they waited, they fasted and prayed as John had taught them.

Jesus' decision that he too must suffer and die at the hands of wicked men and his determination to set his face steadfast toward Jerusalem may have been in part a response to the news of John's death. Certainly his forthright act in cleansing the temple was in accord with John's priestly concerns. So closely were their ministries associated in popular thinking that some had thought Jesus to be John the Baptist raised from the dead. When the chief priests and elders challenged his authority, Jesus confounded them by asking where John's authority had come from. Thus, at the end as well as at the beginning of his ministry, Jesus publicly identified himself with John. A sufficient number of those gathered in Jerusalem that Passover believed John to have been a true prophet, that the chief priests and elders maintained a discreet silence, rather than risk the wrath of the pilgrims by denying that John's authority was from God.

Clearly, the influence of John did not cease with his death. Six years later the army of Herod Antipas suffered defeat at the hands of the Nabateans. Josephus writes that this defeat was regarded by some Jews as a sign of divine punishment for Herod's unjust treatment of John. There are many indications that disciples of the Baptist continued to exist during the early centuries of this era. John's denial that he is the Messiah, in the gospel tradition, is too strong to permit any doubt that some of his disciples claimed for him messianic rank. In the *Clementine Recognitions* the statement is found that "one of John's disciples declared *John* to be the Messiah and not Jesus" (I.60). There is a small Baptist sect alive in Mesopotamia today known as the Mandeans, which claims to perpetuate the movement begun by John the Baptist.

Within the Christian church, John's role, from the earliest times, has been recognized as that of "forerunner." In a quite literal sense, John was the historical figure who ran "before" Jesus. In spite of the later rivalry between their disciples, the memory of the historical solidarity between John and Jesus was never lost. With the passing of time, the polemical need for Christians to minimize the significance of this solidarity has gone. Quite to the contrary, with the rise of modern historical research, a firm grasp of the significance of this solidarity has become an essential first step toward an understanding of the mission and message of Jesus.

Bibliography. For a comprehensive critical study with exhaustive bibliographical references, see C. H. Kraeling, *John the Baptist* (1951). But see also R. J. Hutcheon, ed., *Studies in the NT: Collected Papers of Clayton R. Bowen* (1936), pp. 30-76.

On light shed on John the Baptist by the Dead Sea Scrolls, see B. Reicke, "Nytt ljus över Johannes döparens förkunnelse," *Religion och Bibel,* XI (1952), 5-18. W. H. Brownlee, "John the Baptist in the New Light of Ancient Scrolls," *The Scrolls and the NT* (1957), pp. 33-53.

On Luke 1:1-80 being based on a Baptist source, see Kraeling, p. 16. P. Winter, "The Proto-Source of Luke I," *Novum Testamentum,* vol. I, fasc. 3 (1956).

On the topographical identification of "Aenon near Salim" (John 3:23), see W. F. Albright, "Recent Discoveries in Palestine and the Gospel of St. John," *The Background of the NT and Its Eschatology* (1956), p. 159.

On the background of John's diet of locusts and wild honey (Mark 1:6), see Elijah of Wilna's compilation of "The Rules of Uncleanness," found in H. Danby's translation of the *Mishnah* (1933), p. 802, 14*c* and 16*e*. And on the uncleanness of Gentiles, see p. 801, 10; p. 803, 19*b*, 19*d*, and 20*b*.

W. R. Farmer

JOHN THE DIVINE, DISCOURSE OF SAINT. A Greek version of the Assumption of the Virgin.

JOHN THE EVANGELIST, BOOK OF. A writing used by the Albigenses and commonly regarded as stemming from the Bogomiles. It is in the form of a series of questions and answers propounded to Jesus by "John your brother and partaker in tribulation . . . while I lay on the breast of our Lord Jesus Christ." This pattern—questions propounded by a disciple or disciples to the Lord in the interim after the Resurrection—is very common. Not only is it to be found in the Gospel (Questions) of Bartholomew (*see* Bartholomew, Gospel of), but also in many very early Gnostic writings, in part preserved in the Coptic Berlin Papyrus (Codex Berolinensis) and in the many Gnostic texts discovered in 1946 at Chenoboskion in Egypt (*see* Apocrypha, NT).

This present writing is not only of the same general pattern but evidences the same dualism characteristic of both the Gnostics and Marcion. The world was created, not by God, but by Satan, who had fallen from his place of glory and had seduced many other angels. Christ was not born of Mary, who was an angel sent to earth "to receive him." Rather, he "entered in by the ear and came forth by the ear" of Mary. John the Baptist was sent by Satan; his disciples (catholic Christians) are not disciples of Christ. Baptism and apparently—the text at this point is defective—the Lord's Supper are valueless. True disciples of Christ, unlike those of John the Baptist, do not marry.

This curious little late edition of standard Gnostic theology ends with an account of the Last Judgment so conventional and free from heresy as to suggest it has been severely tampered with.

The writing is preserved only in Latin, and in its present form is not earlier than the twelfth century, although its original may well be as early as the seventh century.

Bibliography. The Latin text is to be found in J. C. Thilo, *Codex Apocryphus NT* (1832). A convenient English translation is available in M. R. James, *The Apocryphal NT* (1924), pp. 187-93. M. S. ENSLIN

JOHOJANAN. KJV Apoc. alternate form of JEHOHANAN.

JOIADA joi'ə də [יוידע, Yahu knows, *abbreviation of* יהוידע, Jehoiada]. Alternately: JEHOIADA jĭ hoi'ə də (Neh. 13:28; Neh. 3:6 KJV). **1.** Son of Paseah, and a builder of the wall of Jerusalem under Nehemiah (Neh. 3:6).

2. A postexilic high priest; son of Eliashib, and contemporary of Nehemiah (Neh. 12:10-11, 22; 13: 28). Some scholars find in Neh. 12:23 an indication that Johanan was Joiada's brother, not his son; but this is doubtful, since "son of Eliashib" could apply to the grandson—i.e., Johanan. *See* PRIESTS AND LEVITES. J. M. WARD

JOIAKIM joi'ə kĭm [יויקים, Yahu raises up, *abbreviation of* יהויקים, Jehoiakim] (Neh. 12:10, 12, 26). A high priest, son of Jeshua. *See* PRIESTS AND LEVITES.

JOIARIB joi'ə rĭb [יהויריב, may Yahu contend]. Alternately: JEHOIARIB jĭ hoi'— [יויריב] (I Chr. 9: 10; 24:7). **1.** A priest in the time of David (I Chr. 24:7).

2. One of those who assisted Ezra in securing temple servants before the return to Palestine (Ezra 8:16); perhaps to be identified with Jarib in the same verse.

3. The name of a priestly house (undoubtedly related to 1 *above*) that lived in Jerusalem after the Exile (I Chr. 9:10). It is specifically mentioned during the time of Zerubbabel (Neh. 12:6), the high priest Joiakim (12:19), and Nehemiah (11:10).

4. A Judahite ancestor of Maaseiah who lived in Jerusalem after the Exile (Neh. 11:5).

M. NEWMAN

JOKDEAM jŏk'dĭ əm [יקדעם] (Josh. 15:56). A village of Judah in the hill-country district of Maon; possibly identifiable with Khirbet Raqa', near Ziph. The LXX B reads JORKEAM, which may be the more original, and which appears in I Chr. 2:44.

JOKIM jō'kĭm [יוקים, *probably for* יויקים, may Yahu establish; *see* JOIAKIM] (I Chr. 4:22). A descendant of Judah.

JOKMEAM jŏk'mĭ əm [יקמעם]. **1.** A Levitical city in Ephraim (I Chr. 6:68—H 6:53). A parallel passage in Josh. 21:22 has KIBZAIM, and both cities may have originally been at this point in the list.

2. A city of Zebulun (I Kings 4:12); identical with JOKNEAM. W. L. REED

JOKNEAM jŏk'nĭ əm [יקנעם]. Alternately: JOKMEAM jŏk'mĭ əm [יקמעם] (I Kings 4:12). A Levitical town near the border in Zebulun (Josh. 19:11; 21:34). Jokneam is identified with Tell Qeimun (Fig. JOK 23), a mound situated on the N slopes of the Carmel Range approximately seven miles NW of Megiddo, overlooking the Valley of Jezreel. The site is strategically located at the junction of two important routes. One is the chief route through the Valley of Jezreel from Acco to Megiddo, Taanach, and Jenin; the other is the first and lowest pass E of Mount Carmel through the Carmel Range, connecting the Plain of Sharon and the Valley of Jezreel.

Courtesy of Herbert G. May

23. Jokneam (modern Tell Qeimun)

Jokneam is number 113 in the list of towns taken by Thutmose III; it is spelled *'nqn'm* in Egyptian; the *'n* at the beginning, which means "spring," perhaps refers to the good springs located just E of the mound. According to Josh. 12:22, the town fell to Joshua during the Conquest. Jokneam, corruptly spelled "Jokmeam," was later included in Solomon's fifth administrative district (I Kings 4:12).

Bibliography. C. R. Conder and H. H. Kitchener, *SWP,* II (1882), 169-70; W. F. Albright, "Contributions to the Historical Geography of Palestine," *AASOR,* 2-3 (1923), 24, note 10; W. F. Albright, "Review of Abel *Géographie* . . . II," *JBL,* 58 (1939), 184; D. Baly, *The Geography of the Bible* (1956), pp. 115, 151, 153. G. W. VAN BEEK

JOKSHAN jŏk'shăn [יקשן] (Gen. 25:2-3; I Chr. 1: 32). A son of Abraham and Keturah, and the father of Sheba and Dedan. It has been suggested that this name is merely the Hebrew equivalent of Joktan in another genealogy (Gen. 10:25), but the equation is phonologically difficult. S. COHEN

JOKTAN jŏk'tăn [יקטן, younger son(?); *cf.* Arab. *Yaqṭân, from* be watchful]. The younger son of Eber, and the brother of Peleg. His descendants represent a number of Arabian groups (Gen. 10:25-29; I Chr.

1:19-23). These comprise the aboriginal inhabitants of the country, in contrast to the later immigrants, the children of Abraham by Hagar and Keturah. Arabic historians of the Islamic period have tried to identify Joktan with Kahtan, a character of Arab legend, but the consonants are not the same in the Semitic alphabet.

The thirteen peoples enumerated as descendants of Joktan are reported to have lived in the territory which extended from the district of Mesha, in the N part of Arabia, to the mountain of the East, in the S part. The first four names, which include Hazarmaweth (Hadramaut), were evidently located along the coast that faces the Indian Ocean; others may have been in Yemen, while the remainder occupied the area farther N. S. COHEN

JOKTHEEL jŏk'thĭ əl [יקתאל]. **1.** A village of Judah in the S Shephelah district of Lachish (Josh. 15:38). Some commentators would read "Joktheel" for "Eshtaol" in vs. 33 also. The site is unknown.

2. When Amaziah of Judah (*ca.* 800-783) completed his Edomite campaign by storming SELA (Umm el-Bayyarah), the ancient Edomite stronghold, he changed its name to Joktheel (II Kings 14:7). It is of interest to note that when he fled from a conspiracy against him, Amaziah went to Lachish, near which the Joktheel of Josh. 15:38 was located. V. R. GOLD

JONA. KJV form of JOHN (5) in John 1:42.

JONADAB jō'nə dăb [יונדב, Yahu is liberal, *or* Yahu is noble, *or* Yahu has impelled]. Alternately: JEHONADAB jĭ hō'nə dăb [יהונדב] (II Sam. 13:5; II Kings 10:15, 23; Jer. 35:8, 14, 16, 18). **1.** A nephew of David; son of Shimeah. He was the shrewd friend of David's son Amnon who devised the plan whereby the latter tragically seduced his half sister Tamar (II Sam. 13:3, 5). When Tamar's brother Absalom avenged her defilement by killing Amnon, Jonadab corrected a false report brought to David to the effect that Absalom had slain all David's other sons (vss. 32-36). He may have been the man, called Jonathan son of Shimei, who slew one of the Gittite "giants" (II Sam. 21:21; I Chr. 20:7).

2. Son of Rechab, and first of the ultraconservative Rechabites who advocated and maintained an austere antiagriculturalist tradition during the period of the monarchy (II Kings 10:15, 23; Jer. 35:6-19). He was a sympathizer with the bloody reform of Jehu and accompanied him in the final purge of the syncretistic house of Ahab. This group was descended from the Kenites and the Calebites (I Chr. 2:55; 4:11-12), and some of its prohibitions resembled those of the NAZIRITE.

Bibliography. J. A. Montgomery, *The Books of Kings,* ICC (1951), pp. 409-10. J. M. WARD

JONAH jō'nə [יונה, dove; Ἰωνάς]; KJV Apoc. and NT JONAS —nəs. **1.** Son of Amittai (II Kings 14:25), from Gath-hepher of Zebulun. He was a prophet, but the dates of his activity cannot be ascertained. He foretold the restoration of the territory of the N kingdom, from the entrance of Hamath to the Sea of the Arabah (*see* DEAD SEA)—which, incidentally, were the ideal boundaries for Israel (cf. Amos 6:14). Jeroboam II of Israel successfully recovered these territories and thus fulfilled Jonah's prediction. Later, a prophetic mission to Nineveh was also attributed to this prophet, and on this account he became the central figure of the book of Jonah. *See* JONAH, BOOK OF. S. SZIKSZAI

2. One of the Levites who were found by Ezra to have foreign wives at the return from the Exile (I Esd. 9:23). In the canonical list at Ezra 10:23 he is called Eliezer.

JONAH, BOOK OF [יונה; Ἰωνᾶς]. The fifth in the collection of short books which form the concluding section of the OT and which are generally known as the Twelve Prophets. It differs from the other eleven in being a story about a prophet rather than a book of prophetic utterances, and its contents, or part of them, are probably more familiar to the world at large than most other OT writings. Unfortunately this notoriety is not based on the intrinsic merit of the book itself, and it is a sad reflection of our misunderstanding of its purpose that a story which has so much of the spirit of the gospel in it should be generally thought of as a story about "a whale" (the text has: "a great fish"), either to be dismissed as ridiculous or to be defended as a proof of our orthodoxy.

The book is now mostly held to have been written *ca.* the fourth century B.C. by an unknown writer who shared the view of Second Isaiah that God's concern for man was not confined to the Jews but was as wide as the world itself. About that time in Jerusalem, Nehemiah and Ezra (*see* EZRA AND NEHEMIAH, BOOKS OF) had been pursuing their policy of racial exclusiveness, narrow nationalism, and religious intolerance in a misguided attempt to preserve the unique heritage of the Jewish faith. The book of Jonah, like the book of RUTH, is designed as a counterblast to that policy. Its message is that the real vocation of Israel as the people of God is to spread the good news of God's love among the Gentiles, and not to hoard its religious legacy. The book of Jonah is thus to be reckoned among those OT writings which come closest to the spirit of the Christian gospel.

See map "Palestine: Joel, Obadiah, Jonah," under OBADIAH, BOOK OF.

1. The reluctant prophet. The chief character of the book is JONAH the son of Amittai, who is further described in II Kings 14:25 as a prophet from Gath-hepher, near Nazareth, who correctly predicted that Jeroboam II would reconquer from Syria large tracts of territory previously held by Israel. This prophet is summoned by Yahweh to set out for NINEVEH, the capital of Assyria, which not only represented the oppressive power of the war lords of the Near East, but, like Babylon and Rome in later years, was also regarded by Jews of the stricter sort as a synonym for the worst infamies, vicious practices, blasphemy, and irreligion of the Gentile world (cf. Nah. 3).

Jonah's mission to Nineveh is to proclaim the judgment of Yahweh upon it, but the prophet, for reasons which are not disclosed until later in the story, is unwilling to fulfil his assignment. At Joppa he boards a ship bound for TARSHISH, which lay in precisely the opposite direction at the other end of the Mediterranean, hoping thus to escape from Yahweh. Yahweh, however, causes a great storm to arise which threatens to wreck the ship. The pagan sailors invoke the aid of their various gods and throw tackle and cargo overboard. Meantime Jonah, asleep in the hold, is discovered by the captain, who is shocked to find that he is not saying his prayers like the rest, and orders him forthwith to beseech whatever god he believes in to save them all from their peril.

The crew now proceed to draw lots to discover which of them has provoked the gods to such wrath, and Jonah is revealed as the culprit. He discloses his identity and declares himself to be a worshiper of Yahweh, albeit a disobedient one. He admits that it is because of his attempt to escape the obligation laid upon him by Yahweh that the tempest has come upon them all and adds that their only hope lies in throwing him overboard, whereupon the storm will cease. Pagans though they are, the sailors shrink from such a deed and try their hardest to row the ship back to land. But the storm intensifies until at length, with a prayer to Yahweh to save them and to hold them guiltless of the death of his prophet, they throw Jonah into the sea. At once the storm subsides, and the grateful sailors offer an appropriate sacrifice.

Jonah is not to be allowed to escape his mission by death. Yahweh has arranged that a great fish should swallow him and convey him safely to land. After a sojourn of three days and three nights in the belly of the fish, during which time he composes a hymn of thanksgiving for deliverance, Jonah is spewed out on the seashore. Tradition identifies the spot as the "Gate of Jonah" near Alexandretta. For the second time Yahweh commands him to fulfil his mission to denounce the people of Nineveh for their sinful ways, and this time Jonah obeys. He enters this vast city, which takes three days to cross, and at the end of the first day he publicly pronounces Nineveh's impending doom. The effect is instantaneous. The whole city turns to Yahweh and dons the garments of penitence. Even the king of Nineveh joins in this act of devotion and issues a proclamation declaring a general fast for man and beast, and enjoining the wearing of sackcloth for all inhabitants and their cattle (cf. Jth. 4:10), in the hope that Yahweh's wrath may yet be averted.

Moved by this mass conversion, Yahweh stays his hand, and thereby arouses the bitter anger of his prophet, who now discloses the reason why he has sought to evade his original mission. He admits that it was because he knew that Yahweh is a gracious and compassionate God who would be ready to forgive the Ninevites if they turned from their evil ways. His real fear was that the hated Gentiles would not be destroyed after all. Now that his worst premonitions have been realized, Jonah prays for death rather than live to see the Gentiles admitted to Yahweh's favor. Twitted by Yahweh for his petulance, the prophet leaves the city and takes up a position outside it, building himself a flimsy shelter and sulkily hoping against hope for Nineveh's destruction. Then Yahweh causes a large plant, perhaps a castor-oil plant, to spring up overnight; the prophet welcomes it as a shelter from the burning heat of the sun. But no sooner is the plant ready to serve its purpose than Yahweh causes it to be destroyed by a grub. When the sun beats down upon him next morning, assisted by a sirocco—likewise part of Yahweh's plan—the unhappy prophet faints with sunstroke and again asks Yahweh to put him out of his misery.

Yahweh now sees that Jonah is ripe for his final lesson. The apparently senseless destruction of the young plant, to whose creation and growth he contributed nothing, has angered and saddened him, awakening the first symptoms of human sympathy so far displayed in his unattractive nature. Yahweh therefore poses his last question: If you can find it in your heart to have pity on this hapless plant, ought not I to take pity on this great pagan city with its teeming thousands of little children and its helpless dumb creatures as well?

There, abruptly but perfectly, the story ends. The unlovely character of the dour, recalcitrant Hebrew prophet is finely contrasted with the humane and charitable Gentile sailors, and the readiness of the pagan city to respond to the proclamation of the truth about God and his will for man. Yahweh, having issued his initial command to the prophet to pronounce his judgment upon Nineveh, assumes the role of a *deus ex machina* until the final denouement, when he emerges as the merciful Creator and Father of all men, a conception as lofty as any in the OT.

2. The book as a historical narrative. The story of Jonah may be regarded as history, allegory, or parable, and all three views have found support. It will be most convenient to examine these in turn and then to consider the psalm (2:2-9) separately.

There are various arguments for accepting the book as a historical narrative: (*a*) Jonah the son of Amittai (II Kings 14:25) was clearly a historical figure in the reign of Jeroboam II (*ca.* 786-746 B.C.), and the author appears to recount these events as biographical. (*b*) Jesus (Matt. 12:39-41) speaks of Jonah's sojourn for three days and three nights in the "belly of the whale" as a prefiguring of his own state between the Crucifixion and the Resurrection. He seems to regard the mass repentance of the people of Nineveh as a historical fact. (*c*) The mission of Jonah to pagan Nineveh is paralleled by similar missions to Sidon and Syria by his immediate predecessors, Elijah and Elisha, and the miraculous features largely in the lives of all three prophets (I Kings 17–19; II Kings 2–9). (*d*) It is only relatively recently that there has been any suggestion that the book is other than historical narrative, and solutions which differ from the traditional explanation appear to have originated in an attempt to placate incredulous scientists who refused to swallow the whale.

If the narrative is regarded as historical, we should assume a date somewhere between the reign of Jeroboam II and the fall of Nineveh in 612, presumably earlier rather than later—i.e., eighth century B.C.—and an author who, although not necessarily the prophet himself, derived his information from the prophet. This would account for such details as would be known only to Jonah, including his dialogue with Yahweh. The sailors, whose ship presumably returned to port, might perhaps have supplied the account of what happened when the prophet was asleep (1:5) and after he had been thrown overboard (1:16).

3. Some difficulties. ***a. The problem of the miraculous.*** The chief difficulty in accepting the story as historical is not that of believing that Jonah reached the belly of "the whale" intact, which appeared to be the main stumbling block in the science-versus-religion controversies. It is known that there are sperm whales in the Mediterranean which have gullets large enough to swallow a man whole. But we should have to believe also that the tempest subsided immediately, that the prophet emerged unscathed from the inside of the monster seventy-two hours later, and that at some point during this time he composed and uttered a psalm of thanksgiving. We have further to believe that he made his way to the center of a foreign and, no doubt, hostile city and denounced its inhabitants, somehow mysteriously knowing their language, and that, far from finding himself clapped in irons, he brought about an instantaneous mass conversion of the whole population from the king downward—of which conversion Assyria's record bears little evidence. The magic plant and the worm which destroyed it suggest the story of "Jack and the Beanstalk" or some such fairy tale rather than history. In short, it is not one miracle but a whole series of miracles that have to be accounted for.

b. The problem of Nineveh. There is further the problem of Nineveh itself, not to speak of the problem of identifying the personage called the "king of Nineveh," which is like talking of the "king of London." The phrase could hardly have been used if the Assyrian Empire had still been in existence. We are told (3:3) that it "*was* an exceedingly great city," which suggests that at the time of writing it was no longer in existence—i.e., that the book was written after, and not before, 612. This difficulty may be explained away by saying that the whole narrative is cast in the past tense or that this phrase is a later gloss. A more awkward problem is that of the size of the city. We are told that it was "three days' journey in breadth." But we know from archaeological excavations that the circumference of the walls of the ancient city of Nineveh was approximately eight miles. This could certainly not contain a population with 120,000 children, in those days implying probably a total of 1,000,000 inhabitants. Even if we include the neighboring cities of CALAH, REHOBOTH-IR, and RESEN (Gen. 10:11-12) as constituting an urban conglomeration, a traveler would surely have had to walk up and down every street and alley to fill up three days.

c. The problem of language and form. Apart from the Aramaisms in the language and other linguistic features which mostly suggest a postexilic date, and the almost certain dependence on Jeremiah and Joel, which would confirm it (cf. 3:10 with Jer. 18:7-8; 3:5 with Joel 1:13-14; 3:9 with Joel 2:14; 4:2 with Joel 2:13), we may well question the historical view on other grounds. Does it detract from the theological value of the book if it is not regarded as unvarnished history? Does not the OT elsewhere use the imagery and symbolism of myth, legend, allegory, and parable to convey religious truth as freely as it uses the facts of history? Does it deepen our conception of God to think of him as one who on occasion behaves rather like a music-hall magician with an inexhaustible bag of tricks? Should we not rather see this book as an imaginative fantasy, like the stories of DANIEL and Tobias (*see* TOBIT), which does not ask us to treat it as historical fact at all?

d. The problem of Jesus' use of Jonah. There is no real reason why Jonah the son of Amittai of II Kings should not have been a historical personage, but equally no real reason why this book should be regarded as an excerpt from his biography. Jonah was no doubt chosen by the author as a suitable peg on which to hang his tale, since what little we know of Jonah suggests that he was concerned about the prestige and expansion of Israel at the expense of the Gentiles. As for Jesus' apparent support of the historicity of the book of Jonah in Matt. 12:39-41, his comparison of Jonah's period in the belly of the whale with his own entombment is highly suspect as a Matthean interpolation. It does not occur in the Lukan parallel passage (11:29-32) and is in keeping with the First Evangelist's mechanical use of OT texts to prove that the Scriptures had been fulfilled. In refusing to perform some spectacular "sign" of his messiahship, Jesus compares his own proclamation of the kingdom with the traditional story of how Jonah proclaimed God's judgment at Nineveh, and contrasts the response of Israel to his own preaching with that of the Gentiles to Jonah. It is an illustration based on a popular story, as was his reference to the visit of the Queen of Sheba to Solomon. It is not a pronouncement on the historicity of either event.

e. The problem of the date. If, then, the story is not directly dependent on Jonah the son of Amittai, but is didactic in character, there is no obvious reason why it should date from the time of the monarchy at all. As we have seen, everything appears to point to a much later date, when the prophet of Gath-hepher and the Assyrian Empire alike were but dim memories. Accordingly the great majority of scholars regard the book as postexilic, and find its *raison d'être,* like that of the book of Ruth, in the situation which obtained in Palestine after the return from exile. The worthy motive of the school of Nehemiah and Ezra to protect the religious heritage of the people of God from syncretism and the infiltration of pagan standards, by attempting to reproduce in Palestine the splendid isolationism of Jewry, which had developed during the Exile, had borne bitter fruit.

When this rigid policy was developed to its logical conclusion, it meant that no member of the Jewish community might have any contact whatever with any person outside the covenant. Mixed marriages were forbidden, and marriages already contracted must be dissolved. The Jews were the people of God;

all Gentiles were to be hated and shunned. The book of Jonah therefore finds its place in the OT as the work of an unknown writer of the fourth century B.C. who, in a little tale of the lesson which Yahweh taught to a harsh and intolerant Jew, protested against this travesty of the message of Second Isaiah, and sought to persuade his countrymen that God's love is wide enough and deep enough to include the hated Gentile. Israel, like Jonah, must learn by bitter experience that Jewry has no prescriptive right to be called God's people. Several centuries later the rigorists in the Jewish-Christian section of the church had likewise to be taught that "to the Gentiles also God has granted repentance unto life" (Acts 11:18).

4. The book as an allegory. It is possible to regard the tale as a complete allegory, with each feature representing an element in Israel's experience. This is perhaps suggested by the fact that "Jonah" means a "dove," a traditional symbol of Israel (Ps. 74:19; Hos. 11:11). If this is taken as the clue, the experiences of the prophet represent the mission and failure of Israel to be the people of God. It was to be its task to bring the pagan world to the knowledge of God. Its stubborn refusal to do so, and its tendency to apply the revelation of God's love jealously to itself, was its traditional failing.

We may see in Jonah's flight to Tarshish Israel's avoidance of its mission before the Exile, turning its back upon God, embarking upon the sea of world politics in the ship of diplomatic intrigue. The storm which broke upon it and upon the Gentile world (the sailors), when the center of power moved from Assyria to Babylon, was followed, for Israel, by the exile in Babylon (the whale; cf. Jer. 51:34). Delivered from this chastening experience, Israel, having turned to God in captivity like Jonah, has the task of proclaiming its faith to its pagan neighbors in Palestine (Nineveh).

It is at this point of history that the author stands. In depicting the instantaneous conversion of the Ninevites, he suggests the readiness of Israel's neighbors to respond to the message, and in the picture of the prophet sulking in his flimsy shelter he depicts the Nehemiahs, Ezras, Joels, and Obadiahs of his day, sheltering under the precarious protection of their recently rebuilt temple, uncompromising in their hatred of the Gentiles, hoping for the apocalyptic judgment of God to fall upon them, and still unwilling to recognize the purpose of God to save the whole world and not only the Jews (cf. Ezek. 38–39, etc.).

5. The book as a parable. It is equally possible to regard the story of Jonah as simply a parable of the same type as that of the ewe lamb (II Sam. 12:1-4) or the good Samaritan (Luke 10:30-37). We should then not expect to find any precise parallelism between Israel's history and the experiences of the prophet. Many may feel that an allegorical interpretation of the story, however plausible, depends too much upon the imaginative fancies of the interpreter. But if Jonah is intended to be no more specific a character than the "certain man" of Jesus' parable, he still remains unmistakably a portrait of the narrow and intolerant Hebrew of Ezra's day, or the narrow, intolerant Christian of our own day, who refuses to face the universalistic implications of the divine revelation and its call to world mission.

Moved neither by the words nor by the works of God, he peers out upon the world from his tiny sanctuary, a forlorn, self-centered figure, clutching his faith to his bosom, while ordinary humanity, with its many likable qualities, waits ready to respond to the message of God's salvation, which his religious dogmatism makes him unwilling to share. The author ends his book with a question mark, because he does not know whether the Jewish church of his day will respond to his challenge. The question mark still stands after two thousand years of Christian history and challenges all branches of the church alike.

6. The psalm (2:2-9). The psalm, which is reminiscent of many others (cf. Pss. 5:7; 18:6; 31:22; 42:7; 120:1; 142:3; 143:4), seems to be unsuited to its present position. It is ostensibly not a prayer for deliverance, as might have been expected, but one of thanksgiving for escape from death by drowning. It would have come more appropriately, therefore, after 2:10 than after 2:1. Possibly not an original part of the book, it may have been inserted later because of the affinity of the idea of SHEOL with that of the whale's belly (2:2) and the similarity of its theme to the experience of Jonah. Most probably it was first intended to be understood figuratively as the thanksgiving of one who has been rescued from the spiritual death of estrangement from God into the living worship and fellowship of his people. Its inclusion or omission makes no difference to the point of the narrative, and most commentators would date it somewhere in the third century B.C.

Bibliography. Commentaries: J. A. Bewer, ICC (1912); R. F. Horton, *Cambridge Bible;* H. C. O. Lanchester, *Cambridge Bible* (1915); G. A. Smith, *EB* (1928); E. Sellin, *KAT* (1929); G. A. F. Knight, *Torch Bible* (1952); J. D. Smart, *IB* (1956). See also Introductions to literature of the OT by Driver, Pfeiffer, Bentzen, etc.

Special studies: H. Schmidt, *Jona* (1907); A. R. Johnson on Jonah 2:3-10 in H. H. Rowley, ed., *Studies in OT Prophecy* (1950).

W. NEIL

JONAM jō′nəm [Ἰωνάμ] (Luke 3:30); KJV JONAN —nən. An ancestor of Jesus.

JONAS. KJV Apoc. and NT form of JONAH; KJV form of JOHN (5) in John 21:15-17.

JONATH 'ELEM REHOQIM. *See* MUSIC.

JONATHAN jŏn′ə thən [יונתן; יהונתן, Yahu has given]. **1.** A Levite of the tribe of Judah who served as house priest in the sanctuary which the Ephraimite Micah had established, and who later founded the priesthood which ministered to the tribe of Dan (Judg. 17–18). Jonathan, a native of Bethlehem in Judah, was invested as the resident priest of the house of Micah in the hill country of Ephraim and was supplied by his benefactor with images, ephod, teraphim, and shrine as his priestly accouterment. When a party of spies from the neighboring tribe of Dan arrived at the home of Micah on their way northward to locate a more suitable homestead, they received a favorable oracle from Jonathan regarding the success of their mission. Encouraged by the report of the spies, the Danites dispatched a vanguard of six hundred men, who on their way to Laish seized the religious paraphernalia of Micah and persuaded the rather forward Jonathan to assume the more honorable office of priest to the tribe of Dan. The sanctuary at Dan (Laish) was thus provided with a priesthood, whose founder was the son of Gershom, son of Moses (MT Manasseh, written with a suspended *nun*, which is generally agreed to be a Masoretic insertion in deference to Moses; *see bibliography*).

Bibliography. C. D. Ginsburg, *Introduction to the Massoretico-critical Edition of the Hebrew Bible* (1897), pp. 334 ff.

2. *See* JONATHAN SON OF SAUL.

3. Son of Abiathar the priest, who rendered important service to David during the rebellion of Absalom by conveying the secret plans of the enemy, but whose career appears to have been later eclipsed by his complicity with the regal ambitions of Adonijah. Jonathan was in the priestly company that brought the ark to David when he had abandoned Jerusalem. At the instance of the king, Zadok and Abiathar returned to the capital to secure information from the spy Hushai, while Jonathan and Ahimaaz, the sons of Abiathar, were stationed as couriers at En-rogel, whence they kept the king informed (II Sam. 15:24 ff). When this espionage was discovered, Jonathan and Ahimaaz fled for their lives to the camp of David at Mahanaim (II Sam. 17:17, 20).

In the closing days of David, when Adonijah invited the sons of the king and the royal officers of Judah to En-rogel to a sacrificial feast, which was certainly planned as the occasion when he would be proclaimed king, Jonathan brought back to the festal gathering the disconcerting news that Solomon had secured the succession and had been anointed in Gihon by the order of the king. Apparently Jonathan was implicated with his father in this attempt of Adonijah to secure the throne and no doubt shared the banishment of Abiathar, who was dismissed from his priestly office by Solomon (I Kings 1:42-43; 2: 26-27).

4. An uncle of David. He was a sagacious counselor on the personal staff of the king, as well as the royal scribe. Since he is nowhere else mentioned, he has been identified at times with his namesake, the son of Shimei (*see* 5 *below*), and has been represented as sharing with Jehiel, son of Hachmoni, in the tutelage of the royal princes (so RSV), but in each case without sufficient warrant (I Chr. 27:32).

5. Son of Shimea or Shimei, David's brother. He slew a Philistine giant who taunted Israel at Gath (II Sam. 21:21; I Chr. 20:7).

6. Son of Shammah—or, less likely, Shagee—the Hararite; a member of the company of the Mighty Men of David known as the "Thirty" (II Sam. 23: 32; I Chr. 11:34).

7. Son of Uzziah. He was in charge of the royal treasuries of David in the cities, villages, and towers outside the capital (I Chr. 27:25; KJV JEHONATHAN).

8. The scribe or secretary whose house was converted into a prison in which Jeremiah was incarcerated many days after his apprehension on the alleged charge of desertion (Jer. 37:15, 20; 38:26).

9. KJV form (following MT) of the name of one of the two sons of Kareah; a captain of a Judean military contingent, stationed in the open country, when the Babylonians captured Judah (Jer. 40:8; RSV Johanan). The name appears to be a dittography of JOHANAN, since it is omitted in the LXX and in the parallel passage of II Kings 25:23.

10. The father of Ebed, who was head of the family of Adin and joined Ezra in his journey to Jerusalem with fifty of his clansmen (Ezra 8:6; I Esd. 8:32).

11. A priest who was the head of the priestly family of Malluchi in the days of the high priesthood of Joiakim (Neh. 12:14).

12. One of the high priests of the postexilic period, whose father was Joiada and whose son was Jaddua (Neh. 12:11). However, in this text the name Jonathan appears to be a corruption of JOHANAN, by which appellation he is called in Ezra 10:6; Neh. 12:22-23; I Esd. 9:1. In these last references he is referred to as the son of Eliashib; however, it appears best to interpret this relationship as meaning generally the descendant of Eliashib, who was actually his grandfather. Johanan is reported to have killed his brother Jesus in the temple because he feared that he might displace him in the high-priestly office with the support of the governor Bagoas (Jos. Antiq. XI.vii.1). While the tenure of his high priesthood cannot be precisely defined, it is certain that it included the years 411-408 B.C. *See bibliography*.

Ezra betook himself to the chamber of Johanan, where with fasting he mourned over the iniquities of the returned exiles (Ezra 10:6; I Esd. 9:1).

Bibliography. A. E. Cowley, *The Aramaic Papyri of the Fifth Century B.C.* (1923), nos. 30-31.

13. Son of Shemaiah and father of Zechariah, who participated with other priestly personnel as a trumpeter in the thanksgiving procession when the walls of Jerusalem were rededicated in the days of Nehemiah (Neh. 12:35).

14. Son of Asahel. He opposed the formation of the Jerusalem commission to consider the cases of the Jews who had married foreign wives in the days of Ezra (Ezra 10:15; I Esd. 9:14).

15. A descendant of the family of Jerahmeel of the tribe of Judah; a son of Jada and the father of Peleth and Zaza (I Chr. 2:32-33). E. R. DALGLISH

16. Son of MATTATHIAS 1, and one of the remarkable family under whose leadership the Jewish nation achieved independence from Syria in 166-142 B.C. Mattathias, who initiated the revolt, was succeeded by his third son, Judas Maccabeus, who was followed in turn by Jonathan (I Macc. 9:23–12:53). Upon the latter's death, yet another son of Mattathias, Simon, assumed the leader's role; and it was under his rule that the nation's freedom was finally won. *See* MACCABEES.

17. Son of ABSALOM 2. He was sent by Simon Maccabeus on an important errand described in I Macc. 13:11. J. KNOX

JONATHAN SON OF SAUL. King Saul's eldest son, whose filial piety and altruistic friendship with David have secured for him the admiration of posterity.

1. His military exploits at Michmash. Jonathan no doubt proved his military prowess in the liberation of Jabesh-gilead from the ultimatum of the Ammonites (I Sam. 11), for in the subsequent Philistine campaign he was placed in charge of one thousand troops, stationed at Geba (cf. I Sam. 13:2 with vs. 16), while Saul commanded two thousand men at Michmash. Jonathan initiated the war with the Philistines by liquidating the prefect (נציב) or garrison of Geba, whereupon Saul dispatched a general summons to all Israel to muster at Gilgal. The Philistines assembled meanwhile their superior forces and occupied the strategic heights of Michmash, while the intimidated Israelites failed to respond to the call to arms, and even the regular soldiers deserted the ranks, reducing the army of Saul from three thousand to six hundred men. At Michmash the Philistines posted a garrison to maintain their position and then dispersed three raiding bands to devastate the surrounding country (I Sam. 13).

It was in this dark hour that Jonathan and his armor-bearer left Geba without the knowledge of Saul and struck a telling blow against the enemy. Discovering themselves to the guard detail the Philistines had stationed above the rocky crag of Bozez, the two followed the omen which the accost of the guard furnished, and routed the garrison when they had climbed the heights. The suddenness of the onslaught combined with an earthquake (?) to throw the entire camp of the Philistines into utter confusion (I Sam. 14:1-15). When Saul saw the wild retreat of the enemy, he pursued them with his forces, now augmented by former deserters and captives, and chased the disorganized foe down to Aijalon before nightfall.

The precipitate king, however—motivated, no doubt, by religious devotion—laid an oath upon the people to abstain from food that day. Being absent from the camp, Jonathan did not hear the oath and refreshed himself with some wild honey as he pursued the enemy. When the abstinent troops informed him of the king's oath, Jonathan replied that his father had troubled Israel, in that, if they had eaten of the food spoils of the enemy, they would have had the strength to enhance the victory. The wisdom of his words was palpably demonstrated at sundown when the famished soldiers violated a religious taboo by eating cattle with their blood. That evening the oracle of Yahweh was silent when the king inquired whether he should continue to pursue the enemy during the night. The divine displeasure, adduced from the silence, was interpreted on the morrow to have been caused by Jonathan's violation of the oath. Saul would have slain his son for his unwitting error had he not been ransomed by the appreciative Israelites (I Sam. 14).

It is fair to assume that Jonathan also participated in the other campaigns of Saul, including the Moabite, Ammonite, Edomite, Amalekite, Philistine, and that against the kings of Zobah (I Sam. 14:47-48).

2. His friendship with David. After David had finished recounting to Saul the exploit of the dispatch of the Philistine giant, Jonathan loved David as his own soul and made a covenant with him, bestowing upon him his own robe and armor (I Sam. 18:1-4). The meteoric success of David in the military service of Saul ultimately proved too much for the mentally disturbed king. No longer did he conceal his intention of slaying David, but he encouraged Jonathan and the courtiers to do away with this potential supplanter. At this juncture Jonathan expostulated with his father concerning the loyal service of David and gained for him a temporary reinstatement at court (I Sam. 19:1-7). The respite was terminated suddenly when the king suffered a mental relapse, and David fled for his life to Naioth in Ramah.

When Jonathan and David next met, they formulated a plan whereby the king's attitude toward David could be ascertained. The foreboding prospect that open hostilities might jeopardize their covenant of friendship prompted Jonathan to exact an oath from David that when Yahweh would cut off all his enemies, David would show kindness to Jonathan and his posterity. At the feast of the New Moon, when Jonathan explained the disconcerting absence of David, he discovered that the hatred of his father toward David was irreparable and conveyed on the morrow this sad information to David at the appointed rendezvous (I Sam. 20).

The final meeting of the two friends was in the Wilderness of Ziph when Jonathan strengthened David's hand in God and made a covenant to the effect that David was to be the next king and Jonathan was to be his first minister (I Sam. 23:16-18).

3. His death at Mount Gilboa. Jonathan was slain in the battle at Mount Gilboa against the Philistines, where his father and his brothers, Abinadab and Malchishua, also fell. Their corpses were despoiled on the day following the battle and were exposed by the Philistines on the wall ("public square" in II Sam. 21:12) of Beth-shan. From this ignominy the royal dead were rescued by the men of Jabesh-gilead, who repaid the kindness of Saul by retrieving the bodies and burying them in Jabesh (I Sam. 31; II Sam. 2:5-7; 21:12; I Chr. 10:1-12). When the news of the Israelite debacle at Mount Gilboa reached the camp of David, it evinced the deepest expressions of grief and a moving elegy, in which David lamented the bitter irony of the fate of the king and the loss of his beloved friend Jonathan (II Sam. 1). Some years later, David reinterred the remains of Saul and his sons in the tomb of Kish in Zela of the land of Benjamin (II Sam. 21:13-14).

4. His family relations. Jonathan had one son, named Meribbaal, or Mephibosheth (*see* MEPHIBOSHETH 1), who was five years old when the tragedy on Mount Gilboa occurred (II Sam. 4:4). The brotherly covenant between Jonathan and David not only secured for this lame prince the lands of Saul and membership at the royal court but ultimately spared him from the doom which befell the other sons of Saul in the Gibeonite exaction (II Sam. 9; 21:7). In addition to Abinadab and Malchishua, Jonathan had a brother named ISH-BAAL (alternately called Ish-bosheth and Ishvi, a corruption of Ishyahu —I Sam. 14:49) and two sisters, Merab and Michal (I Chr. 8:33; 9:39). The name of his mother was Ahimoan; she was the daughter of Ahimaaz, and was described by Saul in an unguarded moment of furious anger as a "perverse, rebellious woman" (I Sam. 20:30).

5. His character. Swift as an eagle and strong as a lion, this crown prince of the house of Saul, a worthy son of the famed Benjaminite archers, possessed intrepidity that knew no retreat and provided inspiration for his followers. With considerable self-effacement and amid adverse tension he proved his love for David continually. While the impetuosity and unreasonableness of Saul might furnish a foil for the gentleness and discernment of his son, Jonathan was united with his father in life, and in death they were not divided (II Sam. 1:23). E. R. DALGLISH

JONATHAS. KJV Apoc. form of JATHAN.

JOPPA jŏp′ə [יפוא, יפו, *Yāphô,* beauty *or* beautiful, *cf.* Egyp. *and* cuneiform *Iapu;* Phoen. יפו, יפי; Ἰόππη, *from* Jope, *daughter* of *Aeolus, god of the winds*]; KJV once JAPHO jā′fō (Josh. 19:46). A city thirty-five miles from Jerusalem built on a rock hill 116 feet high which projects beyond the coast line to form a small cape. Its small harbor is formed by a natural breakwater of rocks parallel to the coast line, 300-400 feet offshore. Access from the S is blocked by rocks; the narrow N entrance is shallow and treacherous. A rock *ca.* 10 feet high at this entrance was said to have been the one to which Andromeda was chained to be devoured by a sea monster, to appease the wrath of Poseidon, only to be rescued in the nick of time by Perseus.

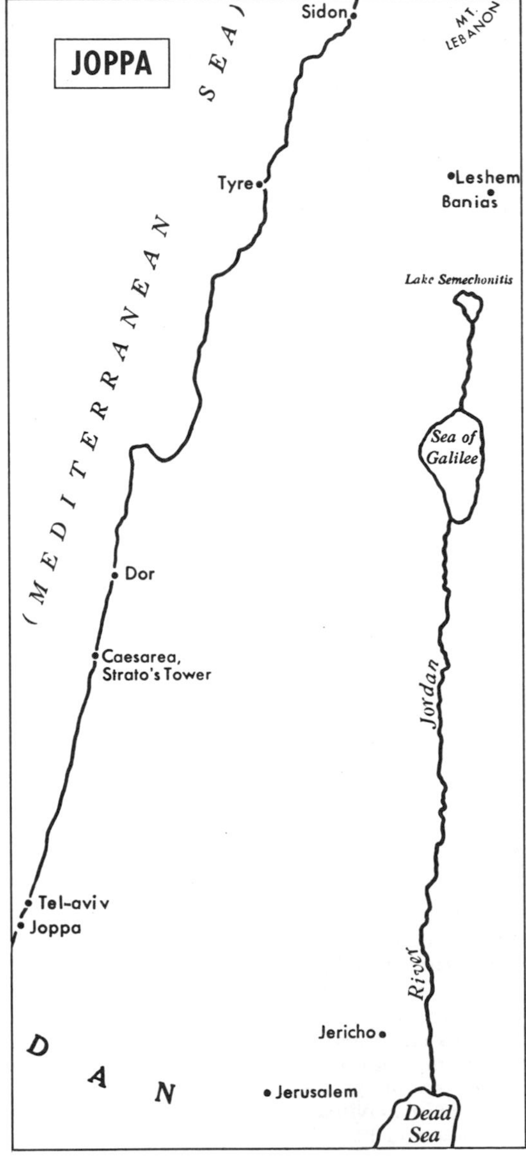

It is possible that in biblical times the harbor was somewhat larger and better protected by the natural breakwater, then in better repair. While the port facilities have recently been somewhat improved, the chief port of modern Israel is Haifa on the Carmel promontory *ca.* fifty-five miles to the N. Modern Jaffa's (Joppa's) sister city to the N, Tell Aviv, is the cultural, social, and commercial center of modern Israel. Since Jaffa is built on the ruins of its predecessors, little excavation has been possible, and our information is based largely on literary sources.

Joppa first appears in ancient sources in the list of Palestinian cities captured by Thut-mose III (*ca.* 1490-1436 B.C.) and in the account of its capture at the time by Thut-mose' commander, Thoth, told in the fourteenth-century Papyrus Harris 500. During the Amarna period (mid-fourteenth century), Joppa was ruled by a native prince who needed military support from Abdu-heba, prince of Jerusalem. An Egyptian letter from the same period from a royal official, Hori, to a scribe, Amen-em-Opet, tells of the beauties of Joppa's gardens and the skill of her workers in leather, wood, and metal (*ANET* 475-79).

Joppa was on the N border of Dan (Josh. 19:46) until the Philistine invasion, when it became the major N city of the Philistine Plain. The Danites then migrated northward to Leshem (LAISH; Josh. 19:46 ff). Solomon apparently developed its facilities so that it became a major port serving Jerusalem. Rafts of cedar logs from Lebanon were floated to Joppa and then shipped to Jerusalem for use in the temple (II Chr. 2:16). Sennacherib listed Joppa as one of the cities he occupied in the course of his campaign of 701 (cf. II Kings 18:13 ff; II Chr. 32:1 ff; Isa. 36:1 ff; *ANET* 287). Jonah attempted to flee from his responsibility by embarking on a ship sailing from Joppa to Sardinia (Jonah 1:3).

Early in the Persian period, as in Solomon's day, cedar logs from Lebanon were floated to Joppa from Tyre and Sidon and then shipped to Jerusalem for use in rebuilding the temple (Ezra 3:7; I Esd. 5:55). The early-fourth-century Eshmunazar and Ben Abdas inscriptions inform us that Joppa and Dor were dependencies of Sidon and that the cult of Eshmun (=Osiris=Adonis) and Baal Gad had been established there. The cities were probably given to Eshmunazar by Artaxerxes II (*ca.* 404-358).

At the destruction of Sidon by Artaxerxes III (*ca.* 358-338), Joppa became an independent city. Alexander the Great established an important mint in Joppa, as well as changed the name of the city from Yapho to Joppa. Joppa suffered during the wars of the Diadochi following Alexander's death. After changing hands three times, it finally returned to Ptolemy I (*ca.* 323-283) after the Battle of Ipsus in 301 and remained in Egyptian hands until 197, when it was annexed to the Seleucid kingdom by Antiochus III, the Great, after the Battle of Paneion (Banias).

Antiochus IV Epiphanes landed at Joppa in 168 en route to Jerusalem to plunder the temple and enforce his program of Hellenization. In 164, as a result of Judas' successes against the Seleucids, the Jewish minority in Joppa suffered an atrocity at the hands of a spiteful non-Jewish citizenry. Two hundred Jews were drowned after having been induced, for reasons unknown, to board ships in the harbor. Judas avenged the act by burning the harbor installations and the boats moored there, but he was unable to enter Joppa, since he was unable to breach the wall which protected the city on the E (II Macc. 12: 3-9). In 147 the high priest Jonathan and his brother Simon defeated the Syrian general Apollonius Taos and occupied Joppa, a prize promised him by Alexander Balas, a contender for the Syrian throne against Demetrius II Nicator. Demetrius was trying to prevent Jonathan's occupation of the maritime plain (I Macc. 10:69-85; Jos. Antiq. XIII.iv.4). In 145, Jonathan paid a state visit to Ptolemy VI at Joppa (I Macc. 11:1-6; Jos. Antiq. VIII.iv.5). After the death of Ptolemy and Alexander Balas, Trypho, acting as regent for Antiochus VI, minor son of Alexander, extended the grant of the coastal plain to Jonathan, but some leaders in Joppa conspired to turn the city over to the generals of Demetrius II. So in 143, Jonathan sent Simon to place a strong Jewish garrison in the city (I Macc. 12:33-34). The next year, after Trypho had treacherously captured (and later killed) Jonathan, Simon renounced his loyalty to Trypho, strengthened Joppa's fortifications, and forced the Greek inhabitants to leave, lest they again try to betray the city into his enemy's hands. This provided the new Jewish state with a reliable seaport (I Macc. 13:11; 14:5; Jos. Antiq. XIII.vi.4). Joppa thus became a Jewish city and remained so for the next two centuries.

Antiochus VII tried to regain control, but Simon routed his troops under Cendebeus in 138 (I Macc. 15:25-31, 35; 16:1-10). Joppa continued to change hands until the Roman occupation under Pompey in 66, when it again became an autonomous city in the subprovince of Phoenicia, the province of Syria, and minted its own coins. In 47 B.C., Julius Caesar returned it to the Jews for services rendered by Antipater, but it retained its autonomous status (Jos. Antiq. XIV.x.6). Herod captured Joppa in 37 (Jos. Antiq. XIV.xv.1), but because of Joppa's opposition to him, he then established a rival port at Straton's Tower, which he renamed Caesarea. After Augustus' banishment of Herod Archelaus to Gaul in A.D. 6, Joppa came under the jurisdiction of Caesarea, the province of Syria (Jos. Antiq. XVII.xiii.2-4).

An early Christian community arose in Joppa, one beloved member of which, Tabitha, or Dorcas, was raised from the dead by Peter (Acts 9:36-42). Peter

Courtesy of Harriet-Louise H. Patterson

24. Joppa (modern city of Jaffa) on the Mediterranean

stayed there for a few days in the house of Simon the tanner, and then went to Caesarea at the invitation of the Roman centurion Cornelius (9:43-10:23). It was a principal center of the First Revolt and was destroyed by Vespasian in 68. Joppa was rebuilt and through the centuries has enjoyed roles of varying importance in the history of Palestine; today it has been annexed to the city of Tel Aviv.

Fig. JOP 24.

Bibliography. S. Tolkowsky, *The Gateway of Palestine: A History of Jaffa* (1924); S. Tolkowsky, "New Light on the History of Jaffa," *JPOS*, 5 (1925), 82-85; F.-M. Abel, *Géographie de la Palestine*, vol. II (1938), *ad loc.;* R. North, "Leeds Excavations at Jaffa," *Bibl.*, 34 (1953), 121; J. Pritchard, ed., *ANET* (2nd ed., 1955); S. Yeivin, "Archaeology in Israel, Nov. 1951–Jan. 1953," *AJA*, 59 (1955), 163; J. Kaplan, "Notes and News," *IEJ*, 6 (1956), 259-60.

V. R. GOLD

JORAH jôr'ə [יוֹרָה, autumn rain] (Ezra 2:18). The head of a family which returned to Palestine after the Exile. *See* HARIPH.

JORAI jôr'ī [יוֹרַי, *possibly hypocoristic for* Yahu has seen] (I Chr. 5:13). A Gadite.

JORAM jôr'əm [יוֹרָם *or* יֹרָם, Yahu is high]. Alternately: JEHORAM jĭ hôr'əm [יְהוֹרָם]. **1.** Son of Toi, king of Hamath. He was sent by Toi to bring his congratulations to King David on the occasion of David's victory over Hadadezer king of Zobah (II Sam. 8:9-12). He also brought with him gifts of silver, gold, and bronze.

In I Chr. 18:10 he is called Hadoram. In all probability this represents the true form of the name of the prince. It is a shortened form of "Hadad-ram," "Hadad is exalted." Hadad was the Syrian storm-god. Cf. also the combinations Hadadezer and Ben-hadad.

2. King of Judah *ca.* 849-842 B.C.; son and successor of Jehoshaphat.

Jehoram became king at the age of thirty-two and reigned for eight years (II Kings 8:17; II Chr. 21:5). His wife was Athaliah, daughter of Ahab. No mention is made of his mother's name.

The Chronicler records that when he became king, Jehoram put to death six of his brothers, all of whom are mentioned by name. There is no reason to deny the historicity of this event. No motive is given, but the words "who were better than yourself" (II Chr. 21:13) at least hint that in the eyes of the Chronicler his brothers disapproved of the new king's religious attitude. In view of the fact, however, that Jehoram put to death some of the princes of Judah as well, it seems possible that Jehoram had to face a rebellion stirred up by his brothers and their partisans.

With the death of Ahab in Israel and Jehoshaphat in Judah, a change came over the political climate in both kingdoms. This was doubtless due in large measure to the reappearance of Assyria in the West (*ca.* 848). Edom seized the opportunity to revolt and succeeded in regaining her independence from Judah. The details of what happened in the ensuing war are obscure (II Kings 8:21; II Chr. 21:9), and the location of Zair (II Kings 8:21) is uncertain; but it is clear that the revolt was completely successful. Libnah also rebelled against Judah at the same time. Thus Jehoram had to face revolt both in the East and in the West. Libnah was presumably on the Philistine border.

Chronicles reports an invasion of Judah during Jehoram's reign by Philistines and Arabs (II Chr. 21:16-17). The whole section (vss. 11-19) raises many questions regarding its historicity.

In all probability the Chronicler has based his account on certain historical data: (*a*) the sharp contrast between the characters of Jehoram and his father, Jehoshaphat—this manifested itself particularly in their differing attitudes toward the worship of Yahweh; (*b*) an attack on Judah by the Philistines and the Arabs; (*c*) the severe sickness of Jehoram which brought about his death. The Chronicler has woven around these data his own viewpoint.

As against II Kings 8:24, which declares that Joram "was buried with his fathers in the city of David," the Chronicler records that "he departed with no one's regret. They buried him in the city of David, but not in the tombs of the kings" (II Chr. 21:20*b*). The Chronicler adds, further, that "his people made no fire in his honor, like the fires made for his fathers" (vs. 19*b*). The additions of the Chronicler here are of doubtful historical value. They give the impression of being assumptions.

Bibliography. F.-M. Abel, *Géographie de la Palestine,* II (1938), 369-70; N. Glueck, "The Third Season of Excavation at Tel el-Kheleifeh," *BASOR,* 79 (1940), 2-18; E. R. Thiele, *The Mysterious Numbers of the Hebrew Kings* (1951), pp. 61-62, 258-59.

3. King of Israel *ca.* 849-842 B.C.; brother and successor of Ahaziah, murdered by Jehu.

Conflicting data are given in Kings regarding both Jehoram's relationship to Ahaziah and the year of his accession. The MT states that Ahaziah died and "Jehoram . . . became king in his stead" (II Kings 1:17). In the light, however, of the following phrase, "because Ahaziah had no son," אחיו is added with the LXX after "Jehoram." The word may have dropped out because of its similarity to תחתיו ("in his stead").

For the date of his accession II Kings 1:17 gives the "second year of Jehoram the son of Jehoshaphat." II Kings 3:1, however, gives the "eighteenth year of Jehoshaphat king of Judah" and states that "he reigned twelve years." Both dates are difficult to reconcile with other given data. Ahab of Israel and Ben-hadad of Syria were allies at the Battle of Qarqar in 853. Jehu of Israel paid tribute to Shalmaneser III in 841 and, therefore, must have begun his reign in 842. Further, according to II Kings 3:7 ff, Jehoram was reigning in Israel before the death of Jehoshaphat. The probable solution to the difficulty is to ascribe to Jehoram a reign of *ca.* eight years, and to regard II Kings 1:17 as an interpolation in the text.

It is noteworthy that the writer of Kings does not make an outright condemnation of Jehoram, as is his usual custom. "He did what was evil in the eyes of the LORD, only not like his father and mother, for he put away the pillar of Baal which his father had made" (II Kings 3:2). It is probable that the reference here is to an "image" of Baal.

In Jehoram's reign occurred the revolt of Moab from Israel (II Kings 3:4-27). Verification of this revolt is to be found in the evidence of the Moabite Stone, which is perhaps to be dated *ca.* 830. It is to be noted, however, that the reference here is to a revolt in the time of Omri's "son." But "son" may be used in the sense of "descendant." On the evidence of I Kings 22:47; II Kings 8:20, Edom had no king at this time. Presumably the reference is to the ruler of Edom, who acted on orders from Judah. Jehoram appealed to Jehoshaphat, king of Judah, for assistance. Together with the king of Edom, the allies marched against Mesha king of Moab. The story has come down to us in Kings in the form of a "prophetic" narrative, but the main events are clear. A successful war was waged in S Moab. The Moabite cities were destroyed until only Kirhareseth remained, and it was besieged and surrounded. This fortress is usually identified with Kerak, in the very S of the country. At the height of the siege, when the king of Moab saw that the battle was going against him, he attempted a break-through with seven hundred swordsmen (II Kings 3:26). The purpose of this sortie has been variously interpreted. It may have been made "against" the king of Edom, on the assumption that Edom was an unwilling ally of Israel and Judah. It may have been made "opposite" the king of Edom, on the assumption that this was the weak link in the allied attackers. Or perhaps ארם ("Aram") should be read instead of אדום ("Edom"), through confusion of ד and ר, as often happened. The king of Moab tried to break through to Aram. This last seems to be the best interpretation. The sally was unsuccessful. As a last desperate resort the king of Moab "offered up his eldest son as a burnt offering" on the city wall in full view of the attackers. The effect was such that the allies lost heart and withdrew. Presumably the defenders staged a successful rally and drove off the besiegers.

It is clear that intermittent warfare continued between Israel and Aram, but the details are obscure. The story of the healing of Naaman the Syrian by Elisha (II Kings 5) cannot be dated with accuracy in the reign of Jehoram. The name of the king of Israel is not given (vss. 4 ff). The incident, if historical, may have occurred at any time of peace during this period.

The same judgment holds for the incidents reported in II Kings 6:8-23, dealing with Elisha's ability to foretell the military movements of the king of Aram's army. The historical background of these verses cannot be stated. The reference is to Syrian raids against Israelite territory (vs. 23*b;* cf. 5:2).

II Kings 6:24–7:20 describes a siege of Samaria by Ben-hadad king of Syria. The defenders were reduced to such dire straits by the resultant famine in the city that mothers ate their own children. It is not possible to date this event precisely, but it doubtless contains historical reminiscences (cf. also the mention of Hittites and Musrites in 7:6). It is scarcely possible that the latter reference is to the "kings of Egypt" (מצרים). Rather, it refers to Musur in Anatolia. That Ben-hadad of Syria was murdered by Hazael, who became king in his stead, is certainly historical (8:7-15). The date of Hazael's accession can be fixed within fairly narrow limits from the Assyrian inscriptions of Shalmaneser III—i.e., between 846 and 842. The historicity of Elisha's part in Ben-hadad's murder is open to question.

Jehoram was wounded in battle against Hazael, king of Syria, at Ramoth-gilead (II Kings 8:28), and returned to Jezreel to recover from his wounds. In the meantime a revolt against the Omride Dynasty, inspired by Elisha, had broken out, and Jehu, one of the army commanders, was proclaimed king at Ramoth-gilead. From there he came to Jezreel. As he approached the city, Jehoram and Ahaziah king of Judah, who had come to visit him, went to meet Jehu. Jehoram was killed by an arrow from Jehu's bow, and his body was thrown on the plot of ground that belonged to Naboth the Jezreelite.

Bibliography. N. Glueck, "The Boundaries of Edom," *HUCA,* XI (1936), 148 ff; F.-M. Abel, *Géographie de la Palestine,* II (1938), 418-19; F. M. Cross, Jr., and D. N. Freedman, *Early Hebrew Orthography* (1952), pp. 39 ff; J. B. Pritchard, ed., *ANET* (rev. ed., 1955), pp. 320-21.

4. A Levite; descendant of Eliezer, son of Moses (I Chr. 26:25; cf. 23:15, 17).

5. One of the two priests sent out by Jehoshaphat, along with princes and Levites, to instruct the people of Judah in the law of the Lord (II Chr. 17:8).

H. B. MacLean

JORDAN jôr′dən [ילדן, הילדן]. The longest and most important river of Palestine, traversing the entire country from its sources at the N border to its outlet in the Dead Sea. It is remarkable not only because of its unique natural character but also because of the part that it played in the history of Palestine and the religions that evolved on its soil.

1. Name
2. Geological features
3. Description
   a. Sources
   b. From the sources through the Sea of Galilee
   c. From the Sea of Galilee to the Dead Sea
4. Biblical terms relating to the Jordan
5. History
   a. In the prebiblical period
   b. In OT times
   c. In NT times

Bibliography

1. Name. The oldest form of the name Jordan is found in Egyptian records of the Nineteenth Dynasty, which give it as *ya-ar-du-na,* the equivalent of a Canaanite *yardôn* (ירדון). The form which is used throughout the OT, *yardēn,* is the Aramaic form of the word, which apparently had replaced the former by the time of the patriarchs. The LXX, Apoc., and NT use the Greek form Ιορδάνης, with characteristic modifications of the vowels and addition of a final syllable to make the word more pronounceable to Greek-speakers; it is from this that the modern form, "Jordan," is derived.

The etymology of the word "Jordan" has been much in dispute between those who consider it to be of Indo-Aryan origin and those who regard it as a Semitic word. According to the former, the components of the word are *yor,* the same root as "year," and *don,* meaning "river," which is found in such names of rivers in SE Europe as the Danube (German Donau), Don, Dniester, and Dnieper. Jordan would thus mean "perennial river," a term which is the exact equivalent of the Sumerian name Idigna for the Tigris. This derivation has been contested on historical and geographical grounds, but is by no means impossible, as it is known that Palestine was invaded by groups that spoke Indo-Aryan languages and who penetrated the entire country, such as Shuwardata of Keilah, whose name appears in the Amarna Letters.

According to the greater number of scholars who consider the word Semitic, the name Jordan is derived from the root ירד, "to descend," and means "the stream that descends rapidly," a name that is aptly descriptive of the Jordan, especially in the part above the Sea of Galilee.

2. Geological features. The valley of the Jordan lies in a deep rift in the earth, the N part of the same line of weakness in the earth's crust that has produced the Wadi el-ʿArabah, the Red Sea, and the Great African Rift.* It resulted from the sinking of a stretch from N to S between two parallel faults and apparently occurred, not all at once, but in successive stages. As early as the Eocene period of the Tertiary era this depression was in existence, but it was for a time covered by an inland sea that extended for a short time into the Transjordan region. During the Miocene and Pliocene periods the mountains to the E and the W began to rise, and the rift between sank lower, so that the inland lake began to be confined to the Jordan Valley, while further crosswise faulting produced the four great river valleys of the Transjordan: the Yarmuk, the Jabbok, the Arnon, and the Zered. Fig. JOR 25.

From *Atlas of the Bible* (Thomas Nelson & Sons Limited)

25. The Jordan Valley, near the Dead Sea, S of Jericho, looking W

During the Pleistocene period there was considerable volcanic activity in the Jordan Valley, and one of the results was the formation of ridges of basalt above and below the Sea of Galilee. While such activity apparently ceased before historic times, its aftereffects are noticeable in the earthquakes and landslides which occur now and then in the Jordan Valley, as well as the numerous hot springs that are to be found along its course. During the earlier part of this period there were three seas: one in the region of the Dead Sea, one that lay in the area between Tiberias and Beisan, and that in the Huleh basin. In the middle of the Pleistocene period came a period of very heavy rain (the Pluvial period) as a result of which the whole valley filled up, the lakes joined, and there was a single salt sea. Masses of gravel were washed down from the hills and choked up the mouths of all the streams that had been emptying into the rift.

After the rains of the Pluvial period ceased, there

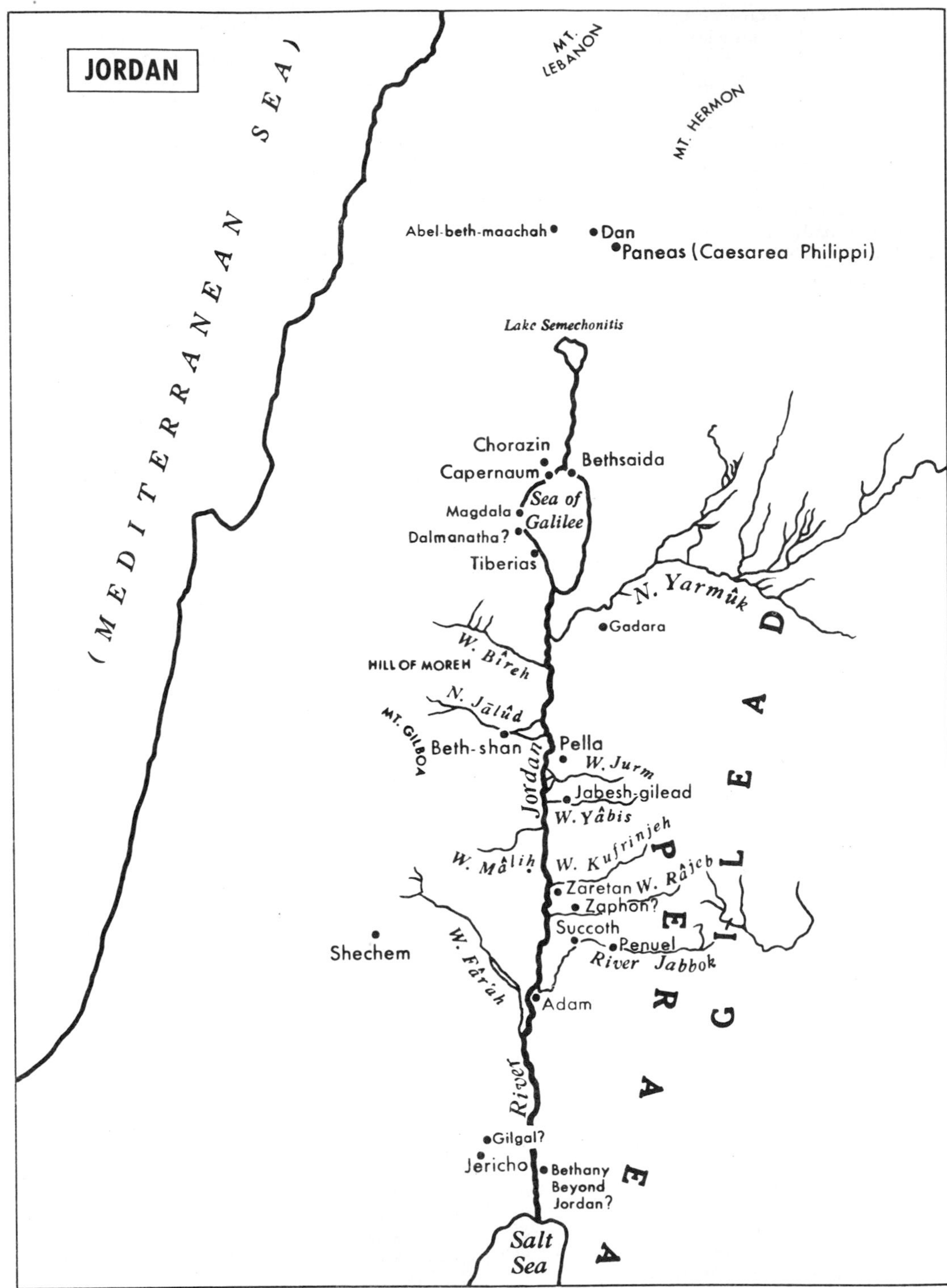

followed a drier time, which has lasted till the present. The salt sea gradually shrank into the fresh-water lakes of Huleh and Galilee, and the salt-water lake of the Dead Sea, and the Jordan began to flow in its present course. The lowering of the level which the tributaries had to reach resulted in renewed activity on their part and increased erosion. The Jordan had to carve its way through the basalt dam, and farther S, in the alluvium left by the lake and its streams, it digs its winding way. The tributary valleys, especially to the E, have cut canyons through the rocks or have leaped down from them in great waterfalls. One river, the Zerqa Maʿin, which was unable to make its way along its original course because of the gravel that had choked it, made a new path for itself by cutting through the softer sandstone.

Since the Pleistocene period there have been no essential changes in the climate of the Jordan Valley. The varying nature of its settlement, at times very thin and at others considerably dense, are due solely to such human factors as skill in utilizing the water supply and to the devastations caused by war and neglect.

3. Description. The air-line length from the source of the Jordan to the Dead Sea is *ca.* eighty miles, but the full length of the river is more than two hundred, on account of the twists and turns of its lower course. Its width below the Sea of Galilee is normally *ca.* ninety to a hundred feet, its depth from three to ten; in the spring, when it floods, it is naturally wider. No parts of it are navigable, except the lakes; there are numerous fords—at least sixty have been counted —where it can be waded. As there were no bridges in Bible times, the Jordan formed a great military obstacle, and the possession of the fords became an important factor in the warfare of that age.

a. Sources. The four sources that unite to form the Jordan all arise in the parting of the watersheds near Mount Hermon.* From this area the Abana and the Pharpar flow to the E, the Litani to the W, and the Jordan streams to the S. The most eastern source of the latter, the Nahr Banias, six miles in length, bursts forth from the base of Mount Hermon out of a large cave, which from the earliest times was regarded as the home of a god, whom the Greeks identified with Pan and gave the name Paneion, which has survived in the modern Banias. It was here that Philip, the son of Herod the Great, built the city of Caesarea Philippi. Fig. JOR 26.

Courtesy of the Israel Office of Information, New York

26. The Jordan River in upper Galilee, showing Mount Hermon in the background

The second source, *ca.* two miles farther W, is the Nahr el-Leddan, which arises from the strong springs of 'Ain Leddan, located W and SW of the site of the biblical city of Dan (Tell el-Qadi), which marked the N boundary of Israel. It flows *ca.* four miles before uniting with the Nahr Banias. The third source is the Nahr Hasbani, *ca.* twenty-four miles long, which joins the other streams a little below their junction; it arises on the Mount Hermon side of the valley between Hermon and Lebanon, down which it flows. The fourth and most western source, the Nahr Bareighit, is a short stream which comes from the W part of the same valley and empties into the Nahr Hasbani near its end. With the junction of these four sources, the River Jordan begins its flow southward.

b. From the sources through the Sea of Galilee. The Jordan flows *ca.* seven miles before it enters Lake Huleh (the Semachonitis of Josephus). In this area the water table is very near the surface, and the entire area is rather swampy. The vegetation consists of reeds, bulrushes, and high grass, while the papyrus plant flourishes so abundantly that it must have been a good source for the papyrus which was manufactured at Gebal and other places of Phoenicia and was the chief writing material for centuries. The climate is rather warm, and the animals there include hyenas, jackals, and wild boars. Nearby to the NW is the elevated site of Abel-beth-maacah (Tell Abil), besieged by Joab in the time of David (II Sam. 20).

Lake Huleh, some 230 feet above sea level, is a small body of water, shaped in the form of a triangle with its base at the N. Its broadest width is *ca.* two miles and its length *ca.* three; it varies from *ca.* nine to sixteen feet in depth.

On leaving Lake Huleh, the Jordan flows for *ca.* ten miles to the Sea of Galilee (*see* GALILEE, SEA OF), and in this short stretch descends to 696 feet below sea level. It flows fairly steadily for *ca.* two miles until it reaches the crossing of the highroad between Galilee and Damascus, now the site of the "Bridge of the Daughters of Jacob" (Jisr Banat Yaqub). For the next seven miles it cuts its way through a gorge in the black basalt rock, tumbling and cascading continually, and changing its color from a clear to a muddy stream. It emerges into a plain and in another mile flows through a delta into the waters of the lake.

The Sea of Galilee (Chinnereth) is a heart-shaped body of water, *ca.* twelve miles long and five miles wide at its broadest part. It is closely shut in by hills around its entire circumference, with only occasional stretches of plain. The warm winters, the long summers, and the abundance of water make the region one where almost any sort of crop can be raised, and it is regarded as one of the most favored areas in the whole of Palestine. It is reasonable to suppose that it was well populated in OT times, though there are comparatively few references to it in the contemporary narratives. Later on, after Galilee had acquired a large Jewish population and the Greek cities of the

Courtesy of the Israel Office of Information, New York

27. The S part of the Jordan River

Decapolis arose to the E, it became a frequently mentioned region. Among the cities that surrounded it were Capernaum, Chorazin, Julias (Beth-saida), Magdala, Tiberias, and Dalmanutha, and the Greek cities of Gerasa (Gergesa) and Gadara (many of these are mentioned in the NT).

c. From the Sea of Galilee to the Dead Sea. This stretch of the Jordan is the one that appears most frequently in the narratives of the OT. The length of the valley is *ca.* sixty-five miles, but the river curves and twists for three times this distance; the breadth of the valley is from three to fourteen miles. The current is still swift, for the drop from the Sea of Galilee to the Dead Sea is 590 feet, an average of about 9 to the mile; every now and then the river has rapids and whirlpools. Like all alluvial rivers, it meanders in contorted loops and is constantly shifting its banks. It is a dirty brown color and not at all a beautiful stream. Fig. JOR 27.

The closer the river approaches the Dead Sea, the more the Jordan Valley becomes divided into several levels. The lowest, which the Arabs call the Zor, is a trench cut in the soft alluvium which can be as much as 150 feet below the upper level. On both sides of the river there are dense thickets of tamarisks, oleanders, willows, poplars, bushes, and vines, as well as thorns and thistles. This part is utterly desolate, a veritably impenetrable jungle, inhabited by wild beasts, with rare habitable areas. On either side of the Zor are the *qattarah* hills, desolate badlands of ash-gray marl in all sorts of shapes and forms, completely unsuitable for cultivation. These lead up on both sides to the Ghor, the highest part of the valley.

The Ghor on both sides of the valley is a fertile area that slopes steadily downward from the cliffs that hem in the valley to the edge of the *qattarah* hills. Here there are plantations and pasturage, especially in the twenty-five-mile stretch from the Sea of Galilee to the point where the valley is narrowed for five miles by the approach of the hills on either side. Most of the wider Ghor below this area is uncultivated at the present time, but was more fruitful in ancient times as the result of irrigation. It is only in the last few miles, when the valley narrows again and the Dead Sea is near, that there is a barren saline stretch, at the end of which the Jordan flows to its outlet through a curving delta.

The stretch below the Sea of Galilee is also notable as the only part of its course in which the Jordan has any tributaries. Not far below the lake the River Yarmuk comes in from the E, bringing down almost as great an amount of water as the Jordan itself. The Jalud, flowing down from the NW past Beth-shan, arrives *ca.* eight miles farther on. Still lower the Jurm, Yabis, Kufrinjeh, Rajib, and Jabbok enter from the E, the latter also bringing a good volume of water; from the W the Far'ah, after paralleling the Jordan for some distance, makes its junction a few miles below the Jabbok. There are about a dozen other, smaller water courses. The deltas of these streams are always fertile areas which widen the extent of cultivable land in the valley. Many cities of antiquity were built close to the point of junction of the tributaries and the main river, such as Adam, Succoth, Zaphon, Zarethan, Jabesh-gilead, and Pella on the E side, and Jericho, Gilgal and Beth-shan on the W. These, however, were but a fraction of the sites occupied in biblical times. N. Glueck, in his explorations of the region, found at least seventy places where people lived and worked, but the ancient names of which have never been recorded.

4. Biblical terms relating to the Jordan. The River Jordan in the OT is almost always used with the article, הירדן. The expression על ירדן ירחו, usually rendered as "by the Jordan at Jericho" (Num. 26:3, 63; 31:12; 33:48, 50; 35:1; 36:13), really means "by the Jordan of Jericho," the part of the river near that city. See also מעבר לירדן ירחו (Num. 22:1; 34:15; Josh. 13:32; 20:8; I Chr. 6:78—H 6:63), "beyond the Jordan at Jericho," which must mean "beyond the Jordan of Jericho"—i.e., E of the Jordan and across the Jordan from Jericho, as the contexts show; in Josh. 13:32; 20:8 the RSV renders "beyond the Jordan east of Jericho." The other exceptions, ארץ ירדן and ירדן, occur in poetic passages (Ps. 42:6—H 42:7; Job 40:23). In the former case the "land of the Jordan" means the birthplace of the Jordan, using a poetic figure by which the Jordan, like Abraham of old (Gen. 12:1), leaves the place of its origin to travel to distant regions.

הערבה is a term used to denote the Jordan Valley from the Sea of Galilee to the Dead Sea and either the E or the W part of it, but also includes the Dead Sea and the Wadi el-'Arabah that reaches to the Gulf of Aqabah. The plural of the word indicates specific stretches, such as those in Moab or near Jericho. For details, *see* ARABAH.

גאון הירדן, correctly rendered by the RSV as "jungle of the Jordan," refers to the thicket on either side of the lower river. Jeremiah is asked the pointed question as to how he is to survive in the terrible calamity of which this is a figure (Jer. 12:5); it is also spoken of as a place where lions lurk (Jer. 49:19; 50:44; Zech. 11:3).

ככר הירדן, properly the "round district of the Jordan," is used in general for the broader parts of the Jordan Valley. In the story of Lot, it probably indicates the region of the Dead Sea, regarded as a fruitful plain before the destruction that befell the wicked cities (Gen. 13:10); in the account of the casting of the copper vessels for the temple of Solomon (I Kings 7:46) it is in the neighborhood of Succoth and Zarethan. The shorter form הככר, the "round district," is used with the same meaning (Gen. 19:17, 25; Deut. 34:3). It should be noted, however, that the expression דרך הככר (II Sam. 18:23), used to describe the course taken by Ahimaaz in conveying news of the defeat of Absalom to David, does not refer to a specific district, but is an adverbial expression meaning "by a short cut" (lit., "through the circle, diametrically").

גלילות הירדן, to be translated "districts of the Jordan" (Josh. 22:10-11; RSV "region about the Jordan"; KJV "borders of the Jordan"), indicates separate parts of the Jordan Valley that have names of their own, as is still the practice among the Arabs today.

עמק סכות, the "Vale of Succoth" (Pss. 60:6—H 60:8; 108:7—H 108:8), refers to the lower course of the Jabbok and the regions nearby; בקעת ירחו, the "valley of Jericho" (Deut. 34:3), is a general term for the lower part of the Jordan Valley.

5. History. ***a. In the prebiblical period.*** The earliest inhabitants of the Jordan Valley existed at an age when the climate was still a tropical one, and such animals as the elephant and the rhinoceros were plentiful in the land, for their skeletons, together with flint and basalt axes, have been found on the W bank of the Jordan near the "Bridge of the Daughters of Jacob." These men, who were hunters, belonged to the human species known as *Paleoanthropus Palestinensis,* skeletons of whom have been found at Mount Carmel and who lived perhaps a hundred thousand years ago. As the climate gradually changed to the dry, warm climate that still prevails in modern times, these men wandered off or disappeared before the Natufian civilization of the Mesolithic age and the Ghassulian civilization of the Neolithic age (seventh to fifth millennium B.C.). Agriculture began to flourish, animals were tamed, houses took the place of caves as dwellings, and dolmens were erected for the dead.

The pattern of life in the Jordan Valley now became one of periods of intense development, then of depopulation until a new resettlement, which has continued down to the present day. There were settlements throughout the Chalcolithic period (late fifth millennium to thirty-second century B.C.); and in the latter part of this time, from the thirty-fifth century on, there was a great increase in population, which disappeared toward the end of it. During the Early Bronze Age (thirty-second to twenty-first century B.C.) the greatest development was in the first half of the period. There seems to have been a gradual decline in the latter half of the period, which became very rapid in the latter quarter. When new settlements began in the Middle Bronze Age (twenty-first to sixteenth century B.C.), there had been so little sedentary settlement for so long a period that most of the villages and towns of this period were located on virgin soil. From the nineteenth century to the fourteenth the population seems to have decreased again, but not to the extent of the practical disappearance of permanent settlements that appears in the Transjordan region. This was the condition of agricultural civilization in the Jordan Valley during the age of the patriarchs.

b. In OT times. The first mention of the Jordan in the Bible occurs in the story of Abram and Lot. When the two decided to separate, Lot chose to travel to the "round district of the Jordan" (Gen. 13:10-11) and settled there near Sodom. A short time afterward the cities of the district were taken and plundered and Lot was taken captive, but Abram, hearing of the disaster, summoned his servants and the followers of his friends as far as the region of Dan, at the sources of the Jordan, routed them in a night attack, and rescued both captives and booty (Gen. 14). Since it is unlikely that he could have overcome the massed forces of the eastern kings, it is probable that he attacked the slow-moving and heavily burdened rear division as it was preparing to cross the river—precisely the same sort of stroke that was made by Odenathus of Palmyra against the army of the Persian king Sapor as it was returning across the Euphrates in A.D. 260. Jacob crossed the river twice, on his journey to and his return from Aram; on his richly rewarded way back he relates that he had crossed it with only his staff, perhaps indicating that he used the latter to help him through the ford (Gen. 32:10—H 32:11).

In the account of the conquest of Canaan, the Jordan was the last obstacle to be surmounted before the promise made by God to the Israelites could be fulfilled. The last wish of Moses was to be permitted to pass across the river (Deut. 3:23-25); when this was denied him, he entrusted the task to Joshua, who at the very beginning of his leadership received the command to "go over this Jordan" (Josh. 1:2). The place where the Israelites crossed over was not far below Adam (Tell ed-Damieh), for the biblical account declares that the waters ceased flowing and backed up

Courtesy of Denis Baly

28. The River Jordan near Adam, showing the grayish-marl hills (*qattaras*) which separate the lower from the upper Jordan Valley

as far as Zarethan (Josh. 3:16, where the verse should be rendered: "as far as the side of Zarethan").* This favorable circumstance was probably due to a heavy landslide, as the Jordan has been dammed and its flow curtailed on more than one occasion (as in 1927); but later tradition magnified it into a miracle, and a poet later sang of how the Jordan had "turned back" at the approach of Israel (Ps. 114:3). The consequence of this unexpected breaching of the river barrier was the rapid conquest of Jericho and the central part of W Palestine, which led, in successive stages, to the complete subjugation of the Canaanites. Fig. JOR 28.

During the period of the judges and the early kingdom, the possession of the fords of the Jordan more than once meant the difference between defeat and victory. When the Moabites spread across the river and enslaved the tribe of Benjamin, Eglon's assassination of the king was followed up by the seizing of the fords and the annihilation of the enemy (Judg. 3:28-29). Similarly, when Gideon defeated the Midianites near the hill Moreh in the Valley of Jezreel, the host of the enemy split in two; one half succeeded in getting across the river and attaining the hills, but the others, fleeing southward, were trapped by the Ephraimite militia at the fords and slain or captured (Judg. 7:24-25). When the Ephraimites challenged Jephthah and confidently crossed the river to meet him in battle, he completed their discomfiture by seizing the crossings and dooming them to death by the test of the word "Shibboleth" (Judg. 12:5-6).

From these and other narratives it is apparent that the Jordan was a strong line of defense, not to be easily forced. When Saul marched to the rescue of the city of Jabesh-gilead and when, in gratitude, the men of that city rescued the bodies of Saul and his sons from the walls of Beth-shan, the crossing had to be made at night (I Sam. 11:11; 31:12). Abner and Ishbosheth escaped to safety across the river after the Philistines had won all the W country by their victory at Gilboa (II Sam. 2:8). David sent his father and mother across the river to live in Moab and thus escape the wrath of Saul (I Sam. 22:3-4); later in his life he was to cross the Jordan in haste and at night (II Sam. 17:22). As in the case of Jacob, the ignominy of his flight across the river is contrasted with the splendor of his return (II Sam. 19).

In the remaining historical narratives of the Bible, the scene of the action shifts away from the Jordan, and it is but seldom mentioned. There is no doubt, however, that there was a large settlement in the valley all during the period of the kings, and that at that time it was one of the richest parts of Palestine.

The Jordan is featured, however, in the miracles that are reported of Elijah and Elisha. Jericho is especially mentioned as the place where they and their disciples gathered; it was near there that Elijah, just before his ascension to heaven, took off his cloak, and struck the water, which divided to let him and Elisha pass on dry ground; Elisha, on his return, performed the same feat, to show that he had received a double portion of his master's spirit (II Kings 2). It was in the same neighborhood that Elisha healed the spring of bitter waters (II Kings 2:19-22); according to tradition, this was 'Ain es-Sultan, near Jericho. When Naaman, the commander of the army of Syria, came to Elisha to be cured of his leprosy, the prophet told him to go and bathe seven times in the Jordan. Naaman at first scornfully rejected the prescription, contrasting the dirty, turbid waters of the Jordan with the clear, sparkling streams of his native Damascus; but eventually he took the advice of his servants, obeyed the prophet's command, and was cured (II Kings 5:1-14). It was also in the waters of the Jordan that Elisha brought about the miraculous floating of the iron axe head which one of his disciples had dropped into the river (II Kings 6:1-7).

c. In NT times. The essential story of the gospels begins at the Jordan River. It was there that John the Baptist came out of the wilderness like Elijah to preach the coming of the kingdom of heaven, followed the prescription of Elisha to cure a moral instead of a physical illness, and bade the people to bathe in the Jordan and repent of their sins. It was from John that Jesus, through baptism, received his first mission to go forth to teach and perform miracles (Matt. 3; Mark 1:4-9; Luke 3; John 1:29-34). The traditional site of the baptism of Jesus is below Jericho; but the gospel accounts are not uniform, and it is very possible that this event took place not far below the Sea of Galilee, close to the home of Jesus, as well as to that of John in Peraea, where he was arrested shortly after this event (Luke 3:18-20; cf. Matt. 14:3-12; Mark 6: 14-17).

The first part of the ministry of Jesus was in the cities about the Sea of Galilee. The decisive moment of his career took place at Caesarea Philippi, on the site of the ancient Paneion, the most eastern source of the Jordan, where gods had been worshiped for centuries. There he put to his disciples the question: "Who do men say that I am?" and accepted the answer of Peter: "You are the Christ [Messiah]" (Mark 8:27-30; Luke 9:18-20; with a slightly different version in Matt. 16:13-20). One of the mountains nearby was the site of the Transfiguration, which followed this event (Mark 9:2-8). The second part of his ministry followed as he pursued his course down the E side of the Jordan Valley, performing new miracles, and speaking to the multitudes in parables, especially those of the magnificent collection in Luke 12–18. He crossed the Jordan for the last time at Jericho, and thence set forth for the final part of his ministry in Jerusalem.

Bibliography. G. A. Smith, *Historical Geography of the Holy Land* (1903; 2nd ed., 1906). F.-M. Abel, *Géographie de la Palestine,* I (1933), pp. 161-78, for hydrography. N. Glueck, *The River Jordan* (1946), is the most modern account, with fine illustrations; "The Geography of the Jordan," *National Geographic Magazine,* LXXXVI (1944-45), 719-44, is the same thing in briefer form. D. Baly, *Geography of the Bible* (1957), pp. 16-26, for geology; pp. 193-202, for description.

S. COHEN

JORIBAS. KJV Apoc. form of JARIB.

JORIM jôr'ĭm ['Ιωρίμ] (Luke 3:29). An ancestor of Jesus.

JORKEAM jôr'kĭ əm [ירקעם] (I Chr. 2:44). A place in Judah occupied by the Calebite family of Hebron. With the LXX B, Jorkeam should perhaps be read for JOKDEAM in Josh. 15:56.

JOSABAD. KJV alternate form of JOZABAD.

JOSAPHAT. KJV NT form of JEHOSHAPHAT.

JOSAPHIAS. KJV Apoc. form of JOSIPHIAH.

JOSE. KJV form of JOSHUA 4.

JOSECH jō′zĭk [Ἰωσήχ] (Luke 3:26); KJV JOSEPH jō′zəf. An ancestor of Jesus.

JOSEDECH; Apoc. JOSEDEC. KJV alternate forms of JOZADAK.

JOSEPH jō′zəf [יוֹסֵף, may (God) add (posterity); יְהוֹסֵף (Ps. 81:5—H 81:6), *see* JOSEPH SON OF JACOB; Ἰωσήφ]. Alternately: JOSEPHUS jō sē′fəs (I Esd. 9:34 KJV); JOSES jō′zĭz [Ἰωσῆς] (Mark 15:40; KJV also Matt. 13:15; 27:56; Acts 4:36). **1.** *See* JOSEPH SON OF JACOB.

2. The father of Igal, the spy from the tribe of Issachar among the twelve sent by Moses to reconnoiter the land of Canaan (Num. 13:7).

3. A Levite of the "sons of Asaph" (I Chr. 25:2, 9).

4. One of Ezra's contemporaries listed among those who married foreign wives (Ezra 10:42; cf. I Esd. 9:34).

5. A priest, contemporary with the postexilic high priest Joiakim (Neh. 12:14).

6. Son of a certain Zechariah; a military commander under Judas Maccabeus (*ca.* 163 B.C.). Judas left him and Azariah in charge of a force to guard Judah while Judas went off to battle in Gilead. Joseph and Azariah were ordered not to initiate any military action, but they did so and were routed in defeat (I Macc. 5:18, 55-62). *See* JUDAS 10.

7. An ancestor of Judith (Jth. 8:1).

8. An ancestor of Jesus Christ (Luke 3:24).

9. An ancestor of Jesus Christ who lived between the time of King David and Zerubbabel the postexilic governor of Judah (Luke 3:30; cf. vss. 27, 31).

10. *See* JOSEPH HUSBAND OF MARY.

11. A brother of Jesus Christ, according to Matt. 13:55.

12. A brother of James the younger (Mark 15:40; cf. Matt. 27:56). *See bibliography.*

13. *See* JOSEPH OF ARIMATHEA.

14. A Christian in the early church, also called Barsabbas and Justus (not the Barsabbas of Acts 15:22), who was considered as a candidate to fill the place vacated by Judas Iscariot among the remaining eleven apostles; but the choice fell to another—namely, Matthias (Acts 1:23; cf. vss. 15-26).

15. The given name of BARNABAS (Acts 4:36).

16. KJV form of JOSECH.

Bibliography. M. Noth, *Die israelitischen Personennamen* (1928), pp. 28, 60, 64, 107, 212; V. Taylor, *The Gospel According to Mark* (1952), p. 598. B. T. DAHLBERG

JOSEPH, DEATH OF. *See* JOSEPH THE CARPENTER, HISTORY OF.

JOSEPH, PRAYER OF. A Jewish apocalypse, no longer extant except in fragments preserved in Greek quotations by Origen. (For a discussion of this type of literature, *see* APOCALYPSES, APOCRYPHAL.) From ancient lists we learn that it was about as long as the Wisdom of Solomon. Jacob is represented as preexisting in the form of an angel, Israel. In our fragments he alone is the speaker, and he foretells mankind's fate and makes huge claims for himself: he is the first-born of all living beings.

The work seems to represent a tendency among Jews in the early Christian centuries to exalt Abraham, Isaac, and Jacob above all angels, almost to the extent of deification. This was true of the book of Asenath, e.g. It has been thought that the Prayer of Joseph was decidedly anti-Christian, but this seems improbable to many because of the respect in which Origen held it ("a writing not to be despised"). An extreme view holds it to be pro-Christian, since Israel and Jacob may be names for Jesus Christ, whose angel-appearance (Jacob) is shown to surpass that of the great archangel URIEL. The riddle of the book is not yet solved, but it must have been anti-Christian to some extent at least.

Bibliography. Fabricius, *Codex pseudepigrapha V. T.,* I, 761-71; E. Schürer, *History of the Jewish People,* vol. II, pt. iii, p. 128 (English trans.; 1891); V. Burch, *JTS,* XX (1918), 20; M. R. James, *Lost Apoc.* (1920), pp. 21-31. N. TURNER

JOSEPH HUSBAND OF MARY. The husband of the mother of Jesus.

This Joseph is mentioned only a few times in the NT and almost exclusively in the birth and childhood stories of Matthew and Luke. Mark nowhere refers to him, directly or indirectly (unless we should read in 6:3 "son of the carpenter," as in P45 and a few other MSS). In the Fourth Gospel, Jesus is twice said to be the "son of Joseph" (1:45; 6:42). Since Joseph appears uniformly as the father or foster father of Jesus and the references to him drop out early in the gospel narratives, it is a likely inference that he died before Jesus' ministry began. Otherwise he probably would have left a deeper imprint on the tradition.

The birth and infancy stories of Matthew and Luke express more or less poetically and symbolically the church's faith in Jesus as God's unique act in history for the salvation of all mankind. They are not primarily historical records, though they contain valuable historical data. To insist too narrowly on the accuracy of the stories is to misunderstand their nature and purpose. No fully historical account of Joseph's career or any part of it is possible.

The two genealogies of Joseph (Matt. 1:2-16; Luke 3:23-38), though discrepant, trace his descent through David. Their aim is to show that Jesus belonged to the Davidic line. Matthew and Luke (at least according to the present text of these gospels) wish to affirm, not that Joseph was Jesus' actual father, but that he was his legal (foster) father. Both present the doctrine of the virgin birth.

From Matthew one would conclude that Joseph was a resident of Bethlehem, who settled in Nazareth because conditions were not propitious in Judea under Archelaus (2:22-23). Luke states that he lived in Nazareth prior to the birth of Jesus and journeyed to Bethlehem to meet the requirement of the enrollment (2:1 ff, 39). But both agree that his family's historic connections were with Bethlehem. It has been suggested in the interest of harmonization that his trade (carpentry; Matt. 13:55) took him temporarily to Nazareth before the birth of Jesus.

At the time when Joseph discovered Mary's condition, he was legally betrothed to her. According to Jewish custom betrothal was almost tantamount to marriage. In some cases betrothal was officially entered into through sexual intercourse, though usually —and apparently more honorably—it came about through a declaration made to the prospective bride, accompanied by a small gift, in the presence of two witnesses, or through the delivery to her of a written declaration. The woman henceforth was called "wife." If her betrothed should die before the consummation of the marriage (betrothal in the case of a virgin lasted about a year and in the case of a widow one month), she became a widow. She was subject to the law of Levirate marriage. She could be dismissed from the relationship of betrothal only by a letter of divorce. She was subject to the penalty concerning adultery. From the Matthean account it appears that Joseph suspected her of adultery, though some interpreters (chiefly Roman Catholic) prefer to think that he suspended judgment or feared to consummate marriage with one in whom God had worked so great a miracle. The assurance of the angel that the pregnancy was "of the Holy Spirit" (Matt. 1:20) seems to confirm the first alternative.

Joseph is described as a just (δίκαιος) man (Matt. 1:19), by which is meant that he was a devout servant of God and regulated his life by the standards of the law. He was also kind and wise. Joseph's deep piety is indicated by his glad response to the revelation which came to him through a dream: Mary was quite innocent of wrongdoing; she was to become the mother of the Savior of Israel, through the instrumentality of the Holy Spirit (Matt. 1:20-21); he should have no fear of proceeding with his plans with respect to her.

In Luke 2:1-7 we are told that Joseph and Mary journeyed to Bethlehem to be enrolled for taxation and that the child was born there. Luke further reports the visit of the shepherds to the manger, where they found Mary and Joseph and the babe (vs. 16); the circumcision and naming of the child on the eighth day (vs. 21); the purificatory rites and presentation of the boy in the temple (vss. 22-24); the marveling of the parents over the blessing and prophecy of Simeon (vs. 33); the return to Nazareth (vs. 39); and the yearly journeys of the parents to Jerusalem for the Passover (vs. 41). Joseph is pictured as sharing with Mary the anxiety of the search for Jesus, the astonishment over his association with rabbis in the temple, and the perplexity concerning his statement about belonging in his Father's house (vs. 49). Apparently Joseph's authority in the home at Nazareth was respected by Mary's son (vs. 51). Luke represents Joseph as a faithful and affectionate father to Jesus.

Matthew pictures Joseph as frequently receiving guidance from angels in dreams: to flee into the land of Egypt because of the hostility of Herod, to return from Egypt after his death, and to settle in Galilee rather than Judea (2:13-23). Opinions differ concerning the historical value of these stories, but they at least agree with Luke's in presenting Joseph as a man of deep piety and fine character.

The second-century Book of James (Protevangelium) and the fourth-century History of Joseph the Carpenter (Death of Joseph) present Joseph as a widower with children at the time he espoused Mary, a girl of twelve years. The latter book describes in great detail his death at the age of 111. The Gospel of Thomas (second century) also presents fanciful incidents concerning Jesus and Joseph. In the Middle Ages a cult of Saint Joseph grew up. Today he is honored in the Roman Catholic Church on special festival days.

Bibliography. M. R. James, *The Apocryphal NT* (1924), pp. 38-70; U. Holzmeister, *De sancto Ioseph quaestiones biblicae* (1945); R. Bulbeck, "The Doubt of St. Joseph," *The Catholic Biblical Quarterly,* X (1948), 296-309; D. Buzy, *Saint Joseph* (1951); S. Morenz, *Die Geschichte von Joseph dem Zimmermann* (1951); H. Rondet, "Saint Joseph," *Nouvelle Revue Theologique,* LXXV (1953), 113-40. E. P. BLAIR

JOSEPH OF ARIMATHEA ăr′ə mə thē′ə. A member of the Jewish Sanhedrin, who buried the body of Jesus in a tomb on his own property.

Although he had come from a tiny village in the NW corner of the central hill country of Judea (ARIMATHEA in Greek, probably the same as Ramathaim in Hebrew), Joseph became a "respected member" of the council—either his village council or the Sanhedrin in Jerusalem (Mark 15:43). Matthew (27:57) adds the information that he was rich, an estimate that is supported by the claim that he owned a tomb of his own, rock-hewn and unused. A further detail from John's account (19:41) is that the tomb was located in a garden, not far from the site of the Crucifixion. Perhaps it may be conjectured that Joseph rose to wealth and power in Jerusalem, after moving there from his native village of Arimathea. This conjecture would fit with the report that the tomb was new, since there would probably have been a family tomb for one of the old aristocratic families of Jerusalem. On the other hand, it may have been necessary to use a special tomb, since Jewish law prohibited burying executed criminals in family tombs. Even so, for Joseph to have possessed an extra tomb is a sign of affluence.

The question of the motive for Joseph's request for the body of Jesus is not easily decided. It has been suggested that he made the request of Pilate as a favor to the disciples. But we are then led to ask why a leading Jew, probably a member of the Sanhedrin, would risk his reputation to do a favor for some frightened, despairing Galilean followers of a man condemned by Roman and Jewish authorities alike. One possible answer is implied in Mark 15:42-43: Joseph took seriously the rabbinic tradition that a dead body should not be allowed to remain unburied beyond the day of death. Besides, the explicit command of Deut. 21:23 required immediate burial of any criminal on the day of his execution. Since death by crucifixion did not occur until after the victim had been on the cross for two days or more, the Romans usually left the body of a crucified criminal exposed indefinitely, until vultures destroyed the corpse. But in Jewish lands the Romans bowed to the religious regulation, hastening the death of the victim in order to have the body buried by nightfall. Joseph, therefore, was performing an act of piety—actually preventing the defilement of the land, according to Deut. 21:23—by removing the body of Jesus and burying it.

But the gospels suggest a further, and more urgent, motive for Joseph's action. Although Mark's account of the burial makes no explicit claim for sympathy on the part of Joseph toward Jesus and his followers, it does state that Joseph was "looking for the kingdom of God." In itself, this could mean nothing more than that he was a good Pharisee. But the added information: "[He] took courage and went to Pilate, and asked for the body of Jesus" (Mark 15:43), clearly suggests that he had responded to Jesus' announcement of the dawning of the kingdom, at least to the extent of willingness to risk official disapproval, by performing this last gracious act toward the departed Herald of the kingdom. Luke goes beyond this hint to affirm that Joseph was unsympathetic with the intent of the council and refused to give his consent to the action of the Sanhedrin in condemning Jesus (Luke 23:51). In Matthew's version there is an unequivocal claim that Joseph was one of the circle of Jesus' disciples (Matt. 27:57).

The other gospel accounts agree with Mark (15:46) in his description of Joseph as having bought a linen shroud, and as having laid the body of Jesus in a tomb and rolled a stone against the door. The faithful women, Mary Magdalene and Mary the mother of Joses, saw where he was laid. The Gospel of John adds the information that Nicodemus assisted Joseph in the burial, providing at his own considerable expense the spices for the preparation of the body (John 19:39).

Among the late legends usually included in the NT Apoc. is a narrative of the ASSUMPTION OF THE VIRGIN, ascribed to Joseph of Arimathea, who reports that he cared for Mary during the years between Christ's ascension and her death.

Bibliography. H. L. Strack and P. Billerbeck, *Kommentar zum NT,* I (1922), 1047-51; J. Klausner, *Jesus of Nazareth* (1925), p. 355; F.-M. Abel, *Géographie de la Palestine,* II (1938), 428-29.

H. C. KEE

JOSEPH OF ARIMATHEA, NARRATIVE BY. A Latin version of the ASSUMPTION OF THE VIRGIN. This is a totally different work from the Story of Joseph of Arimathea, which latter is an appendix (in Greek) to the Acts of Pilate. *See* PILATE, ACTS OF.

M. S. ENSLIN

JOSEPH SON OF JACOB. The name יוסף is "hypocoristic," being the first element of a much longer name. The full form would be composed of: (*a*) the verb יוסף; (*b*) the name of a god who is considered to be subject of the verb. The name for God which is supplied in Gen. 30:24 is Yahweh (*see* GOD, OT), but this is too early for such a formation. We know from ancient extrabiblical examples like Jacob-El and Jacob-Har or Yashub-Dagan and Yashub-El that the divine element used with these hypocoristic forms varied. Unfortunately, we have no such examples of the name Joseph. The supposed town name of Joseph-El in the List of Thut-mose III is a misreading based on ignorance of comparative linguistics. The Egyptian *sh* was never used to transcribe Hebrew *samekh.*

The form יהוסף, "May (God) add (yet another son)," which occurs once in the Bible but more frequently on ossuaries and graffiti of the first century A.D., is to be explained as a hypercorrection. The first syllable of this name was improperly expanded from יו to יהו by analogy with the vast number of personal names that contain the divine element in the first syllable. After the time of the Exile it was considered more proper to write these names with the longer form of the theophorous element—namely, יהו. In any case, we must remember that in the name Joseph this variation was purely graphic, and the pronunciation remained the same.

1. The birth of Joseph
   a. The nature of his birth
   b. The date of his birth
   c. The culture of his birthplace
2. Joseph in Hebron
   a. The life of a shepherd boy
   b. Joseph the favored son
   c. The master of dreams
   d. The conspiracy at Dothan
3. Joseph in Potiphar's house
   a. The rise to power
   b. The seduction
   c. The prison
4. Joseph as lord over Egypt
   a. The dreams of Pharaoh
   b. The investiture of Joseph
   c. Joseph as an administrator
5. The descent into Egypt
   a. The famine in Canaan
   b. The reconciliation
   c. The settlement in Goshen
   d. The passing of the patriarchs

Bibliography

1. The birth of Joseph. Joseph is described as the eleventh son of Jacob and the first-born of Rachel, the favorite wife of Jacob.

a. The nature of his birth. Like his father, Jacob, and his grandfather, Isaac, Joseph was born to a woman who had previously been barren. This often-repeated pattern—cf. the birth of Samuel and of John the Baptist—tends to impress the reader with divine activity in connection with childbirth. It also tends to single out the child thus born as one especially favored by God. The origin of this motif is, of course, uncertain, but it is interesting to compare the biblical accounts with the background of the Ugaritic "Legend of Aqhat." In this Ugaritic tale the hero's father, Danel, is without an heir, and the birth of his son, Aqhat, requires a special sort of divine permission, which is obtained by persistent prayer before the deity. This procedure has been called "incubation." After his unusual birth, the child Aqhat is singled out as the hero of the tale which follows. He is described by one of the gods as *n'mn 'mq nšm,* "the charming one, strongest of men." We can safely assume that the Joseph story was intent upon enhancing our appreciation of the divine favoritism evident throughout. The story does this by supplying a detail of Joseph's birth which is considered most significant—i.e., the fact that Joseph was the first-born of the favorite, but originally barren, wife.

b. The date of his birth. The cautious student will avoid attempts to date precisely happenings in the "patriarchal age." Before we can fix a date for such an event as the birth of Joseph, we must consider the type of "history" reported in early biblical narratives.

Scholars have offered answers from every conceivable point of view. At one end of the scale there are those who view the Joseph story as a historicized myth; at the other end come those who treat it as a matter-of-fact account such as one might write today. The rapidly accumulating evidence from archaeological sources seems to be tipping the balance strongly in favor of the basic historicity of these accounts, but no serious student of antiquity can fail to perceive that dramatic patterns and didactic applications bring flesh to the dry bones of history. Within the great national saga that lies behind these stories, Joseph was born three generations after Abraham but before the small family of Jacob entered Egypt. Translating this into the frame of secular history, archaeological evidence puts the age of Abraham in the Middle Bronze Age, somewhere in the first half of the second millennium, and the entry into Egypt during the second "intermediate" period (*see* HYKSOS), which covers a period of over two hundred years. Our only hope for dating Joseph more exactly lies within the realm of archaeology—i.e., the possibility of establishing a convincing synchronism for Gen. 14, or the recovery of more Hyksos documents.

c. The culture of his birthplace. Although we are unable to date the birth of Joseph, we can describe, to some extent, the type of culture into which he was born. An abundance of information concerning the social background of his parents' life and activity in his birthplace, Haran, is offered by the recently discovered Nuzi and Mari documents (*see* HORITES). These Hurrian documents contain close parallels to the patriarchal life at Haran (*see* JACOB; ISAAC; ABRAHAM). A further source for our understanding of this culture is the Autobiography of Idri-mi, king of Alalakh (*ca.* 1480-1450 B.C.). Although the Nuzi and Idri-mi materials come from a period somewhat later than Joseph in the Hyksos period (the seventeenth and first half of the sixteenth centuries), they reflect the customs and practices of an earlier period. The agreement between biblical and extrabiblical mores and practices proves the essential historicity of the biblical account.

2. Joseph in Hebron. Immediately after the birth of Joseph the family left Haran and returned to the land of Canaan. After a series of adventures the small group arrived at Kiriath-arba (Hebron). It is here that Esau and Jacob are said to have buried their father, Isaac, and it was from this area that Joseph was sent forth to seek his brothers. In Num. 13:22 we are offered a very precise basis for dating the foundation of HEBRON. The city of Zoan (Tanis), which was built seven years after Hebron, is generally identified with the Hyksos capital city, and its foundation is dated at the very beginning of the Hyksos period. If we are to believe that Gen. 37:14 reflects the contemporary name of the city, this would indicate that the Hyksos invasion of Egypt was already in the past—contrast, however, 35:27.

a. The life of a shepherd boy. In connecting the family of Jacob with the region of Hebron the biblical writer does not mean to imply that they are to be considered as "city dwellers." The Bible accurately portrays the life of the patriarchs as being "seminomadic." The expression "seminomadic" is purposely intended to contrast, on the one hand, with the true "Bedouin" (camel) culture of a later time; and, on the other hand, with the "sedentary" (farming) culture which existed in the more fertile plains or around some dependable source of water. The shepherd life of Joseph's time was not sedentary, because of the constant need for seeking areas in which to graze flocks. As flocks were moved from pasture to pasture, most, if not all, of the shepherd community moved with them, living in tents. The series of towns by which Jacob's family passed on their way S from Succoth (Gen. 33:17–35:27) is probably typical of the movement of such a shepherd community. The towns listed are within reasonable walking distance of one another. The sheep or goats are in constant need of water, thus limiting the distance that such communities might wander from sedentary (watered) areas. Although shepherds moved from place to place, the life Joseph knew was not strictly nomadic. Jacob built himself a house in Succoth, in contrast to tents for his livestock, and he stayed behind in Hebron with Joseph when the rest of the family followed the flocks in Shechem. It is also significant that the dream of Joseph concerning "sheaves" further betrays close contact with sedentary (farming) life.

b. Joseph the favored son. Gen. 37:3 explains that Joseph was favored by his father, "because he was the son of his old age." This psychological explanation can still be easily understood today. In the world of the seventeenth and eighteenth centuries B.C. it was more normal to favor the legitimate heir, who was usually the oldest son; but Jacob, who had purloined his older brother's birthright, seemed determined to by-pass convention by favoring first Joseph, then Benjamin, and finally by setting Ephraim before Manasseh. This pattern of favoring the younger over the older seems to appear quite frequently in the biblical account (*cf.* ABEL; DAVID; SOLOMON; etc.). Although this type of favoritism is more difficult to find in extrabiblical sources, it is not entirely lacking. It was not unheard of among the Hittites. From the middle of the sixteenth century we have the very famous case of Hattusilis I, who passed the throne to Mursilis I instead of to his oldest son, Labarnas. The exaltation of a younger brother over an older one is also found in the Tale of Two Brothers, which is very close to the Joseph story in some ways (*see* § 3*b below*). Idri-mi, king of Alalakh, was also younger than the brothers who acted against him. In the Keret Epic from Ugarit we also read: "The youngest [feminine] of them [feminine] I will make the first-born."

The preference of Jacob for Joseph expresses itself in the making of a "long robe with sleeves." The name used for this robe, פסים, has been the occasion of much discussion. Later Jewish tradition supposes that the robe reached to the hands and feet. This word is used only one other place in the Bible, to describe the robe worn by Tamar (II Sam. 13:18-19). The passage in II Samuel states specifically: "Thus were the virgin daughters of the king clad." The question which arises is, What is the significance of making a woman's garment for Joseph? The answers have been given range everywhere, from a mythical interpretation, which views this as the garment of a "hierodule" placed upon a depotentized god, to the view that Joseph was dressed as a girl to protect him from hard work. Actually there is no a priori reason for holding that this robe was distinctively feminine. As a matter of fact, the distinction between masculine and feminine dress was not at all clearly defined. If one will observe the famous painting of the party of Asiatics depicted on a tomb at Beni-hasan (nineteenth century),* he will notice that there is little difference between the covering worn by the women and that of the more important males in the caravan. Another analogy may be drawn from the annals of the Assyrian kings of a much later date. One of the most famous articles of

29. A wall painting from the tomb of an Egyptian noble at Beni-hasan, showing Asiatics bringing him eye paint

clothing to come from the area of Syria and Palestine was the colorful garment decorated with *birmu,* which is a narrow band woven from wool threads of assorted colors. Garments decorated with these narrow, bright strips are described in the Annals of Ashurnasirpal II as the garb of two hundred females. In the Annals of Ashurbanipal, however, a garment decorated with *birmu* is given to Necho, a puppet ruler of Egypt, as a part of his royal garb. Thus it would seem that the robe Joseph wore could very well have had the significance the Bible attributes to it—namely, that it marked the wearer as a favorite. *See* CLOTH § 6. Fig. JOS 29.

c. The master of dreams. DREAMS were very important in the ancient world. In this respect the OT is no exception. Joseph's dreams cannot be separated from those which he interpreted in Egypt. They belong to the same genre: they come in pairs; they require a man of special skill to interpret them; but, once interpreted, their meaning is quite obvious. It is impossible to say where this type of material originates, because of its universal popularity. Since the dreams recorded in the Joseph story are all of the same type, and since the majority of them are said to have been dreamed in Egypt, one may suspect that this was their proper provenience. Indeed, a recently discovered Egyptian papyrus from Thebes gives rules for the interpretation of dreams about such varied subjects as receiving white bread or looking down a well. One of the dreams interpreted is about a man who sees a large cat; the interpretation is that he will have a large harvest, which immediately reminds us of one of the dreams in the Joseph story.

One of the expressions used to describe Joseph is בעל החלמות, "The lord [*ba'al*] of dreams." It is needless to say that this has been used to support the thesis that Joseph was really a deity, one of the Baals that the prophetic movement was to have so much trouble with later. The word in this context does not require such an interpretation. To be "lord" of something means simply to possess it, to be in charge of it, or to master it. In this context the translation "dreamer" (Gen. 37:19) might not be quite strong enough, for the expression implies one who is able to possess, originate, master (interpret), dreams. We can be quite sure that the older brothers had no idea of flattering Joseph when they used this expression, but what could better describe the peculiar talent that was to bring Joseph both fame and power than to call him the "master of dreams"?

d. The conspiracy at Dothan. Joseph was sent after his brothers at Shechem. Not finding his brothers in Shechem, he follows the directions of a stranger, who was passing by, and went on to Dothan. It was at Dothan that the brothers threw Joseph into a pit and sold him to the Ishmaelites (Midianites). Even the casual reader is aware that there are difficulties in this chapter. The Hebrew text does not state clearly whether Joseph was sold to the Midianites or to the Ishmaelites. It appears at one point that Reuben was the only brother who wished to spare Joseph's life, but in another section it was Judah who spoke out against the murder. Gen. 37 is one of the most convincing illustrations of the "documentary hypothesis" (*see* PENTATEUCH). Scholars have generally attributed to E the section dealing with Joseph's being cast into a pit, his being drawn out by the Midianites, and his sale in Egypt by them. To J has been attributed the brothers' plan to kill Joseph, the passing of an Ishmaelite caravan, and the report of the brothers to Jacob. Some sort of division along these lines seems quite possible. One ought to be warned, however, of the constant need for reappraisal of this kind of approach. An excellent example of its shortcomings is the case of the double allusion to Midianites and Ishmaelites which may have its origin in poetic parallelism.

3. Joseph in Potiphar's house. After his betrayal Joseph was brought to Egypt, where he was sold to an Egyptian named POTIPHAR. The practice of bringing slaves to Egypt from Canaan is no novelty. The normal means of obtaining slaves was, of course, warfare, but there is no reason to exclude trading expeditions as a second source. We now possess an Egyptian slave list from the eighteenth century B.C. which contains a number of persons bearing Northwest Semitic names—that is to say, names of persons linguistically akin to Joseph.

a. The rise to power. The biblical account implies that Joseph was not long in Potiphar's household before he was promoted to the highest position in the house. G. von Rad in *Josephsgeschichte und aeltere Chokma* attempted to show that Joseph is the idealized portrait of an official during the time of David and Solomon: he was the "type" of the civil employee, as seen by the earliest wisdom writers. Although the views of von Rad are only conjectural, it must be agreed that Joseph was the very model of an administrator. He is pictured as modest—at least in his Egyptian career—hard-working, honest, wise, and devoted to his superior. All these qualities contributed to the rapid rise of Joseph.

The story of Joseph in the house of Potiphar gives the reader his first hint of the theology presupposed by the Joseph story. It is said that Joseph became a successful man because his master noticed "that the LORD was with him, and that the LORD caused all that he did to prosper in his hands." In the mind of the writer this was the reason Joseph was able to prosper. All other factors are of secondary importance. For the man who is favored by God, there is nothing that cannot be overcome. The most complete expression of this is found at the end of the Joseph story (Gen. 50:20): "As for you, you meant evil against me; but God meant it for good." Thus Joseph, who was favored by a God who could convert the evil directed against him to good, could not be kept down, even in slavery.

b. The seduction. It has long been observed that there are strong affinities between the Joseph story and the famous Egyptian myth of Bata and Anubis, the so-called Tale of Two Brothers. The similarities are most striking in connection with the seduction of the younger brother, Bata.

The relationship between this Egyptian myth and the Joseph story is so remarkable that there are scarcely any scholars who deny it. The only question is, How are the two stories related? There are many answers to this question. The present MS of the Tale of Two Brothers can be dated on the basis of language and orthography to *ca.* 1225 B.C. Some of the more conservative scholars of the nineteenth century were inclined to take this date at face value, and they considered the Egyptian story to be a pale recollection of the history of Joseph. The nature of the Egyptian story, however, leads one to suspect that it had a long prehistory before it was finally written down in its present form. It is for this reason that many, perhaps most, scholars feel that the Joseph story is dependent upon its Egyptian counterpart. This does not mean that the Joseph story is fiction. There are many ways to account for the similarity. Presupposing a current and extremely popular Egyptian myth about the shepherd deities Bata and Anubis, it is not difficult to see how an incident in the life of a human shepherd would become more and more like that of the deity. Moreover, one can imagine that, once the story was told and a precedent was established, every attempted rape or seduction that ended in failure was explained along the lines of such an illustrious predecessor. Finally, one might even imagine that Potiphar's wife, who would be familiar with the Egyptian story, was pulling an old trick on this "bumpkin" from Hebron.

This incident is not, however, a really vital part of the Joseph story—contrast this with the story of Eve, where her seduction is used to explain the subsequent status of women in society; likewise, consider Tamar, whose seduction is used to explain a complex genealogical relationship. The story of Joseph could have developed quite normally without this rather detailed episode. It would be much easier to understand its retention if there were important literary precedents.

c. The prison. One of the most difficult things to explain about the Joseph story is, Why did Potiphar react by simply imprisoning Joseph? One might suspect that the violent urge to kill, shown by Anubis in the Tale of Two Brothers, would be more characteristic of the times. Unfortunately, no good parallel can be found anywhere. We are in the dark about the legal aspects of the situation. In the first place, we have scarcely any knowledge of Egyptian law. Egypt has bequeathed no great legal corpus such as the ones known from Mesopotamia, nor is there any literary evidence leading us to suspect that such a code ever existed. The king of Egypt was considered a god, and the law of Egypt was the will of this god-king. To codify the demands of one pharaoh might impinge dangerously upon the divine prerogative of the next. This difficulty is further complicated by the fact that if we did have a code of normative Egyptian legal practice, it would be practically useless in dealing with the Hyksos period. Hat-shepsut's charge that the Hyksos ruled without Re, together with what we know of the Hyksos from other sources, indicates that from the Egyptian point of view Hyksos practice was considered anomalous. Finally, the discovery of a legal code might prove disappointing, for there would be little chance that it would mention the case of an attempted seduction of a noble woman by a slave without legal rights.

While in prison Joseph met the royal butler (cupbearer) and baker. The dreams of both were interpreted by Joseph, and the predicted outcome was brought to pass. The baker was executed and the butler restored to his former position. The office of BUTLER was very important in the court of the Pharaoh. In addition to the fact that "he placed the cup in Pharaoh's hand," we know that the butler acted in the capacity of a trusted adviser. That the Egyptian butler might be employed in a variety of official capacities is verified by the report of a trial which resulted from a harem conspiracy in the reign of Ramses III. In this famous trial the king's butlers served with several other officials as judges in the case. It is not surprising, therefore, that when the king sought help in interpreting his dream, the butler was present with the "magicians" (this may be an Egyptian word, although no satisfactory etymology has yet been offered) and "wise men" whom the Pharaoh summoned. It is thus quite understandable that the king would take a butler's advice when he recommended Joseph as an interpreter.

4. Joseph as lord over Egypt. In response to Joseph's suggestion that the Pharaoh "select a man discreet and wise" comes Pharaoh's answer: "Since God has shown you all this, there is none so discreet and wise as you are." Each time that Joseph's social status is improved, we are reminded that it is under the auspices of God.

a. The dreams of Pharaoh. The nature of the dreams of the Pharaoh is quite Egyptian. They sparkle with the color of the time and country to which they were ascribed. It is appropriate that the Pharaoh should dream of cows, since there are a great many paintings from Egypt which depict caring for cattle. This contrasts with the situation in the hill country of Palestine, where the family of Joseph raised sheep. The available pasture in the hill country from Hebron N to Shechem made it impossible to raise cattle to any extent. We are told that shepherds were an abomination in Egypt. This statement about shepherds is subject to a variety of interpretations, but the simplest explanation is to suppose that it is the result of the well-known, natural enmity for sheep on the part of cattle raisers, whose cattle have nothing to eat after the sheep have grazed on their pastures.

A second Egyptianism in the first dream is the use of a word which is translated as "the reed grass." This word, which appears in Hebrew as *'aḥū,* is simply the Hebrew transcription of the Egyptian *'ꜣḫ(w).* In Egyptian the word is related to the term for "inundation"; hence it is properly the pasture that has been produced in the wake of the annual flood. It is extended from this meaning to include pasture land in general. The word occurs only one other time in the Bible, and then it is found in the book of Job, where it is asked: "Can *'aḥū* grow without water?" What could be more appropriate than this to describe the nature of the Egyptian pasture in its dependence upon the flood waters? The same word appears in Ugaritic, where it is employed to describe the alluvial plain of *Šmk.*

The seven years of famine that are predicted in the dreams of the Pharaoh are the common property of the ancient Near Eastern countries. The Egyptian version is found in an inscription from the Ptolemaic period which purports to tell of a famine during the reign of Djoser in the early Third Dynasty. Although it is conceded that this inscription may be intended to support the territorial claims of a later age, it does clearly show that the Egyptians themselves preserved the tradition of a seven-year famine. The cycle of seven years of "husks" is to be found in the sixth Tablet of the Gilgamesh Epic. There are also seven unfavorable years mentioned in the Autobiography of Idri-mi. The texts from Ugarit also inform us that "Baal will be lacking seven years, eight (years) the Rider of the Clouds: Without rain (and) without dew." The fact that the oldest references to such cycles are poetic, the frequent use of the number seven in other contexts, and the Ugaritic device of matching seven with eight in parallelism leads one to suspect that the number seven in such a context is not to be considered too literally, but is simply a round number which was applied to any short series of years.

b. The investiture of Joseph. Another section of the Joseph story reminiscent of Egypt is the account of Joseph's promotion. There are three words in this brief section that have an Egyptian origin—the word for "signet ring," the word for "fine linen" (lit., "linen of the king"), and the word usually translated "bow the knee." The last word, אברך, appears to be Egyptian, although the exact equivalent has been a matter of speculation.

There are also a number of historical parallels to be drawn from this episode. The "gold of honor," which may well correspond to the golden chain which was put upon Joseph, is a much-mentioned item in Egyptian biography. The chariot in which Joseph was to ride reminds us that it was during the Hyksos period that the horse and chariot were introduced in Egypt. The fact that a foreigner could hold such a high office in the Egyptian government also suggests the rule of the Hyksos, who were themselves foreigners. In fact, one of their rulers bore the name Jacob-Har.

This basic mode of investiture appears to have been familiar in other areas of the Near East. Very similar procedure was followed when Ashurbanipal (seventh century) invested an underling named Necho: "I clothed him with a garment of brightly colored material; a golden chain (*allu*), the symbol of his kingship, I put upon him. I bound upon his wrists golden bracelets. I wrote my name on the pommel of an iron dagger inlaid in gold, and I gave it to him. I gave him chariots, horses, and mules for his royal riding." The number of items has grown since the time of Joseph, but the symbols are remarkably similar.

The office into which Joseph was being inducted was apparently that of vizier. The Pharaoh's statement concerning the wide powers to be exercised by Joseph corresponds well with what we learn from the Autobiography of Rekh-mi-Re, who was vizier of Egypt during the reign of Thut-mose III (1490-1435).

As a final gesture Joseph was given a new name, ZAPHENATH-PANEAH. He also received a wife, who is called ASENATH and is described as the daughter of POTIPHERA. These names, together with the name of Ramses and the mention of camels, which the Ishmaelites were supposed to possess, form the most striking anachronisms to be found in the Joseph story.

The significance of the fact that Asenath was a daughter of a priest of On (Heliopolis) eludes us. We know far too little about the status of Egyptian shrines during the Hyksos period even to hazard a guess.

c. Joseph as an administrator. The greatness of Joseph's administrative ability is judged in terms of his results in acquiring all the land in Egypt for the king. Although we have no contemporary documents to explain how it was done, we do know from extra-biblical sources that there was just such a shift of land tenure during the Hyksos period.

The report in Gen. 47:22 that the priests were not forced to sell their land is in strict accord with an Egyptian practice that was current as early as the Fifth Dynasty, according to a stele of Nefer-iri-ka-Re which was found at Abydos. This stele was written to exempt the priests of a certain district from the normal labor conscription raised within the district. Just how privileged the priesthood was to become is reflected in the successful resistance to Akh-en-aton and his reforms on the part of the offended priests.

5. The descent into Egypt. The story of Joseph continues with an account of the famine in Canaan and the journey to Egypt to buy grain. From this point on, Joseph is no longer the unique concern of the narrative. The action is now concerned with the whole family of Jacob—with their coming to Egypt, the reconciliation of the brothers, and the settlement in Goshen.

a. The famine in Canaan. The famous Egyptian inscription of Hor-em-heb describes foreigners from famine-stricken lands descending upon Egypt in the manner of their fathers and grandfathers before them. The biblical witness is in full agreement with this testimony from secular history. The Bible relates that Abraham and Isaac and finally the family of

Jacob were forced to turn to the land of the Nile in search of grain, which seems constantly in danger of failure in Canaan. It is perhaps just such a reason that brought to Egypt the well-known band of Asiatics depicted on the walls of a Beni-hasan tomb. Although they date from the early nineteenth century, they probably reflect in many ways the type of persons who made up the small caravan of Jacob's family. There may have been a similarity in dress, in the fashion of beards, in weapons, in footwear, and in their use of the dependable little beast of burden, the ass. We must remember, however, that there is a basic difference in the occupation of the two groups, for the caravan depicted on the tomb was probably a roving band of smiths and tinkers, who carried their bellows with them.

b. The reconciliation. The Autobiography of Idri-mi, which has many parallels to the Joseph story, reaches one of its climactic stages when it pauses to tell of the reconciliation which takes place between the hero and his brothers. Like Joseph, Idri-mi generously restores his older brothers to their former brotherly status. We can imply from this parallel that in the world of Joseph and Idri-mi there was probably a well-established set of mores that judged such an action as proper. In the case of Joseph, however, it was exercised within the theological framework of what God had planned in contrast to the brothers' design.

It is easy for us to understand the first approach Joseph used in dealing with his brothers. There is perhaps a natural urge in every man to do a bit of testing before restoring an offender. So it was that Joseph devised a series of tricks to worry his brothers. He accused his brothers of being spies and kept Simeon as a hostage until Benjamin was brought to him. On their second trip to Egypt, Joseph terrified the brothers by planting a silver cup in the baggage of Benjamin and then accusing him of theft. This action brought forth a burst of eloquent pleading from Judah (Gen. 44:16 ff). There is an Egyptian parallel in the story of the Eloquent Peasant, who is detained by officials when he comes to complain about an injustice, in order that they may listen to his eloquence. There is one major difference between the two accounts, because Joseph was not entertained as the officials were. Joseph wept freely because of what he was told, and we are led to suppose that the testing of the brothers had a serious purpose.

c. Settlement in Goshen. We know from Egyptian documents that it was customary for the Egyptians to allow Asiatics to graze their animals in the Delta. It was in accord with this custom that the family of Jacob was allowed to settle there. The number of persons coming to Egypt is listed as seventy (seventy-two is the figure given by the LXX and one Hebrew MS discovered in Qumran). This may be a round number, just as in Ugaritic, where it is listed as the number of sons of Asherah.

d. The passing of the patriarchs. The final days of Jacob in Egypt form an interesting contrast to the old age of an Egyptian named Sinuhe, who found himself far from home, wandering in the land of Canaan. Just as Sinuhe longed to be buried in his homeland, so Jacob requested that Joseph should swear to bury him in the land of his birth. Just as Sinuhe longed to be properly embalmed, so was Jacob embalmed. The forty-day period given for the embalming process is confirmed by our knowledge of the practice from other sources. The same procedure of embalming and removal to Canaan is followed in the case of Joseph. One wonders, however, why Joseph was taken back to Shechem for burial rather than to the traditional burial place at Mamre.

Before the death of Jacob, he had a chance to see his children and grandchildren and bless them. In the first blessing of Jacob, Joseph was replaced by his two sons, Ephraim and Manasseh, thereby doubling Joseph's portion. The name is thus connected with the two strongest of the N tribes. In consequence of this, the name of Joseph is later used to define: (*a*) the tribe of Ephraim alone (Num. 1:32), (*b*) the tribe of Manasseh alone (Num. 36:1), (*c*) the tribe of Ephraim and Manasseh together, (*d*) the whole N kingdom, and (*e*) the people as a whole (Ps. 80:1). In both the blessing of Jacob (Gen. 49) and the blessing of Moses (Deut. 33) Joseph is praised far out of proportion to the other tribes, in accordance with the early importance of the Joseph tribes.

The final chapter of the Joseph story is written with the death of Joseph himself; he ended his life in the role of a prophet: "I am about to die; but God will visit you, and bring you up out of this land to the land which he swore to Abraham, to Isaac, and to Jacob." Then after insisting that his "bones" be taken from Egypt, he died at the age of 110, which, as we gather from the Instruction of the Vizier Ptah-Hotep, was an ideal age for any good vizier.

Bibliography. For general information see the Commentaries on Genesis, particularly those by Gunkel, Driver, de Vaux, and von Rad. Other sources of interest are: W. F. Albright, "Historical and Mythical Elements in the Story of Joseph," *JBL*, XXXVII (1918), 111-43; K. Sethe, "Der Denkstein mit dem Datum des Jahres 400 der Aera von Tanis," *ZA*, 65 (1930), 85-89; H. G. May, "The Evolution of the Joseph Story," *AJSL*, XLVII (1931), 83-93; W. F. Albright, *The Archaeology of Palestine and the Bible* (1932), pp. 143, 148 ff; S. Smith, *The Statue of Idri-Mi* (1949); O. Eissfeldt, *Die ältesten Traditionen Israels* (1950); G. von Rad, "Josephsgeschichte und ältere Chokma," *Supplements to Vetus Testamentum*, vol. I (1953); M. Noth, *Geschichte Israels* (1954), *passim;* J. B. Pritchard, ed., *ANET* (2nd ed., 1955), *passim;* W. F. Albright, *From the Stone Age to Christianity* (2nd ed., 1957), pp. 241-48.

O. S. WINTERMUTE

JOSEPH THE CARPENTER, HISTORY OF. An Egyptian glorification of Joseph, not earlier than the fourth century and heavily indebted to the Protevangelium of James (*see* JAMES, PROTEVANGELIUM OF). It purports to relate the life and death of Joseph and the eulogy spoken over him by Jesus, who is represented as later recounting the incidents to his disciples on the Mount of Olives. The complete text is preserved in Bohairic and Arabic (of which latter a Latin version was made in the fourteenth century). In addition there are fragments in Sahidic. The statement: "Even thou, O my virgin Mother, must look for the same end of life as other mortals" (ch. 18), suggests that this writing is anterior to the fifth century, when the doctrine of the Assumption began to prevail.

See also APOCRYPHA, NT.

Bibliography. For the full text, see: F. Robinson, *Coptic Apocryphal Gospels* (1896); P. Peeters, *Évangiles apocryphes* (1914). A brief summary of the book is given by M. R. James, *The Apocryphal NT* (1924), pp. 84-86. M. S. ENSLIN

JOSEPHUS, FLAVIUS. A historian (Hebrew name, Joseph ben Mattathias), and a commanding officer of the Galilean Jewish forces in the war against Rome, A.D. 66-70. He was born A.D. 37/38 and died sometime after 100.

Despite certain inconsistencies between the account in his *Vita,* written toward the end of his life, and various autobiographical statements scattered through his earlier *History of the Jewish War Against Rome,* the general outline of his life is more or less clear. He was of a priestly family and, on his mother's side, a descendant of the Hasmoneans. He reports that already by the age of sixteen he began a study of the chief Jewish sects: PHARISEES; SADDUCEES; and ESSENES. He then attached himself as disciple to a hermit, Bannus, with whom he lived in the wilderness for *ca.* three years. At the age of nineteen he joined the Pharisees. His writings later reflect an admiration for the Essenes and their way of life; on the other hand, though he reports on the popularity enjoyed by the Pharisees, his language at times reveals a critical, unfavorable estimate of them.

In 64 he journeyed to Rome to plead for the liberation of some priests whom the procurator FELIX had sent to be tried by Nero. As it turned out, this visit to the great city was important, not so much because Josephus succeeded in his mission (with the help of Poppea, Nero's wife, whom Josephus met through one of her favorites, a Jewish actor), but because the splendor and might of Rome impressed him profoundly. On his return to Judea, he found his countrymen dominated by those who pressed for revolt against Rome. Unable to restrain the war party, he reluctantly joined it, hoping that in short time the governor of Syria, Cestius Gallus, would crush the rebellion. But Cestius failed, and his army was thoroughly routed.

Josephus contradicts himself on a number of details regarding his commission and conduct at this point; as a result, his motives and his behavior as commander of the Galilean forces are not clear. Apparently, however, he spent the half year between Cestius' defeat and Vespasian's arrival in reorganizing and administration of Galilee, fortifying a number of cities, storing up provisions, and training his army —though it is unknown where he learned military discipline and tactics.

Before long his enemies began to accuse him of various treacheries, and on several occasions both his commission and his life were in danger. His bitterest enemy was John of Gischala, whom Josephus always speaks of in most abusive terms.

By the spring of 67 Josephus, deserted by most of his army, was driven to the fortified town of Jotapata. The town fell after a siege of forty-seven days. He hid for some time in a cave with a number of survivors, who vowed that they would take their own lives rather than surrender. Either through trickery or by coincidence, Josephus and one companion were the last to remain after the others had killed themselves. With his companion, Josephus emerged from the cave and gave himself up. He was brought before Vespasian as a prisoner. He now predicted to Vespasian that he, Vespasian, would shortly become emperor. When this prediction was fulfilled in 69, Vespasian made Josephus a free man.

From the time of his surrender to the end of his life Josephus remained a client of the Flavian emperors (hence the adoption of the name Flavius). So long as the Great War lasted, he served the Roman forces as interpreter and mediator. After the war he not only received gifts from Titus (*see* TITUS 3), but also accompanied the Roman commander to Rome, settled there on an imperial pension with the rights of a Roman citizen in a former palace of Vespasian, and devoted himself to a literary career.

His domestic life was not a happy one. He was married four times; his second wife deserted him; his third wife he divorced. By his third wife he had three sons and by his last wife, two.

Josephus' words have survived because of the church's interest in them, most likely because of a debatable passage on the Founder of Christianity in the *Antiquities.* These works are the principal source for the history of the Jews from Hasmonean times to the fall of Masada in 73. They are also an apologia, at times in behalf of Rome, at times in behalf of the Jews and Judaism, always in his own behalf.

His earliest work was the *War*—i.e., the history of the Jewish war against Rome—which he wrote shortly after the fall of the Jewish state. It is a revision or new edition in Greek of a work he originally composed in Aramaic. The work is divided into seven books, the first of which is a rapid survey of Jewish history in the Hellenistic-Roman period; a primary source for him was the life of Herod written by Nicholas of Damascus. In the remaining books Josephus takes up the story of the revolt against Rome and its aftermath. Here he had not only his own limited experience to draw on, but also the records kept by the Roman commanders which were at his disposal, as well as information from those who fled Jerusalem and took refuge with the Roman forces. The history is written with dramatic effect. Thucydidean speeches in the mouths of leading persons, echoes of the idiom of Sophocles, descriptive passages (of geographical locations, of particular scenes of suffering or heroism, of fighting stratagems), give the work rhetorical vigor. As in the composition of all his subsequent works, Josephus had the assistance of Greek collaborators, since his own knowledge of Greek was probably never more than mediocre, especially when he was preparing his first work. What stands out above all in the *War* is its pro-Roman tone: the work was not only produced under Flavian auspices but was also supposed to impress all readers with the futility of rising against the Empire.

There is a Slavonic version of the *War,* but it is doubtful if this version was based directly on the Aramaic original. Most scholars are still of the opinion that the Slavonic is a secondary translation of the Greek.

Ca. twenty years after the publication of the *War, ca.* 93-94, during the reign of Domitian, Josephus put out his second great work, the *Jewish Antiquities.* It is a history of the Jews, in twenty books, modeled after the *Roman Antiquities* by Dionysius of Halicarnassus, from patriarchal times up to the outbreak of the war with Rome. The first ten books, which bring the story down to the Babylonian captivity, are essentially a paraphrase of the LXX version supplemented by homiletic and haggadic material. The latter ten volumes take up the story from the return to Judea under Cyrus. In these books Josephus drew on biblical and apocryphal sources, haggadic traditions, handbooks of Greek historians, and the writings of Nicholas of Damascus, Strabo, and other Roman historians. The work was designed to portray to the cultivated Greco-Roman world the high antiquity and splendid achievements of the Jews.

It is instructive to compare what Josephus says in the *Antiquities* with what he says in the *War,* where subject matter overlaps. In the *Antiquities* the account is often more ample, the tone less decidedly pro-Roman, and altogether the mood less enthusiastic toward his earlier political attitude and appraisals. Careful analysis of the Greek idiom reveals also where Josephus turned from one of his Greek assistants to another, a slavish imitator of Thucydidean mannerisms. Of special interest also are the documents and edicts incorporated by Josephus in this work.

It was to the *Antiquities* that Josephus attached his *Vita* as an appendix. This little work was written as a self-defense against the accusations of a rival historian, Justus of Tiberias, who charged that Josephus was responsible for the outbreak of the war, at least for the revolt of Tiberias against Rome. The autobiography is chiefly an account of Josephus' life during the six months when he "commanded" the forces in Galilee before the arrival of Vespasian.

Finally, he wrote an eloquent apology for Judaism in two books, *Against Apion.* The work is more than a defense of Judaism against the slanders of Apion; it is a defense against all sorts of Egyptian and Greek calumnies of Jewish morality and culture. In making this defense Josephus also takes an aggressive position, criticizing Gentile morality and teachings as he compares them with "Mosaic law." *Against Apion* remains one of the classic and most vigorous apologies for Judaism.

In his writings Josephus refers to other works which he planned: a treatise on Jerusalem and the temple, a work on the Mosaic code and the nature of God; but apparently he never produced these. Several works were at one time ascribed to Josephus by the church fathers, of which he is not the author.

Bibliography. The principal edition of the Greek text of Josephus' works is that by B. Niesen (Berlin, 1885-95). Other editions are: N. Bentwich, *Josephus* (1914); H. St. John Thackeray and R. Marcus, eds., *Josephus,* Loeb Classical Library, vols. I-VIII (1926); H. St. John Thackeray, *Josephus, the Man and the Historian* (1929); W. R. Farmer, *Maccabees, Zealots, and Josephus* (1956). J. GOLDIN

JOSES jō'zĭz [Ἰωσῆς]. **1.** A brother of Jesus (Mark 6:3).

2. A brother of James the Less, whose mother, Mary, stood by the cross of Jesus and came to his grave (Mark 15:40, 47).

3. KJV form of JOSEPH 15.

JOSHAH jŏsh'ə [יושה] (I Chr. 4:34). A Simeonite.

JOSHAPHAT jŏsh'ə făt [יושפט, Yahu hath judged]; KJV JEHOSHAPHAT jĭ hŏsh'ə făt in I Chr. 15:24. **1.** A Mithnite included by the Chronicler among the Mighty Men of David known as the "Thirty" (I Chr. 11:43).

2. One of the priests who were charged with the responsibility of blowing the trumpet before the ark of God, particularly in the procession that accompanied the ark as it was being conveyed into Jerusalem by David (I Chr. 15:24). E. R. DALGLISH

JOSHAVIAH jŏsh'ə vī'ə [יושויה] (I Chr. 11:46). One of the sons of Elnaam who is included by the Chronicler among the Mighty Men of David known as the "Thirty."

JOSHBEKASHAH jŏsh'bĭ kā'shə [ישבקשה]. According to I Chr. 25:4 (cf. vs. 24), one of the singers appointed by David; yet the names in this verse form a liturgical prayer, and may not refer to real persons. *See* GIDDALTI.

JOSHEB-BASSHEBETH jō'shĭb bă shē'bĭth. *See* JASHOBEAM.

JOSHIBIAH jŏsh'ə bī'ə [יושביה, may Yahu cause to dwell (safely)] (I Chr. 4:35); KJV JOSIBIAH jŏs'ĭ bī'ə. A Simeonite.

Bibliography. M. Noth, *Die israelitischen Personennamen* (1928), pp. 28, 202.

JOSHUA jŏsh'ōō ə [יהושע, יהושוע, Yahu is salvation]. **1.** *See* JOSHUA SON OF NUN.

2. The man of Beth-shemesh in whose field the ark, drawn in a cart by two milch cows, came to a halt after it was sent away by the Philistines (I Sam. 6:14). *See* ARK OF THE COVENANT.

3. A governor of the city of Jerusalem during the reign of King Josiah (II Kings 23:8).

4. Alternate form of JESHUA.

Bibliography. M. Noth, *Die israelitischen Personennamen* (1928), pp. 16, 18, 70, 106-7, 110, 154. B. T. DAHLBERG

JOSHUA, BOOK OF. The sixth book in the OT, and in the Hebrew Bible the first of the Former Prophets (*see* CANON OF THE OT). It describes the invasion of Canaan after the Exodus and wilderness wandering and the division and allotment of the land to the tribes of Israel. The central figure in the book is JOSHUA SON OF NUN, from whose name the title (LXX, Ἰησοῦς; Vulg. *Iosue*) comes.

- A. Outline of contents
- B. Composition
  1. Pentateuchal documents in Joshua
  2. Sanctuary and tribal traditions
     - *a.* Gilgal traditions
     - *b.* Traditions of the tribe of Benjamin
     - *c.* S traditions
     - *d.* N traditions
  3. Border and town lists
  4. The Deuteronomic compilation
  5. Successive editions
- C. Joshua in the Deuteronomic history
- D. Historical significance
  1. Narratives of conquest
  2. Division of the land

3. Amphictyonic covenant traditions
E. Theology
Bibliography

A. *OUTLINE OF CONTENTS.*

I. The conquest of Canaan, 1:1–12:24
 A. Crossing the Jordan, 1:1–5:12
  1. Preparation for the crossing, ch. 1
  2. Spies in Jericho, ch. 2
  3. Miraculous crossing, 3:1–5:1
  4. Ceremonies at Gilgal, 5:2-12
 B. First conquests, 5:13–8:35
  1. Appearance of Yahweh's angel, 5:13-15
  2. Capture of Jericho, ch. 6
  3. Campaign to Ai, 7:1–8:29
   a. Failure at Ai, 7:1-5
   b. Punishment of Achan, 7:6-26
   c. Success at Ai, 8:1-29
  4. Covenant ceremony at Shechem, 8:30-35
 C. Success in S-central Canaan, 9:1–10:27
  1. Preparation of kings for war, 9:1-2
  2. Covenant with Gibeonites, 9:3-27
  3. Battle at Gibeon, 10:1-15
  4. Capture of five kings at Makkedah, 10:16-27
 D. S campaign, 10:28-43
  1. Capture of Makkedah, vs. 28
  2. Capture of Libnah, vss. 29-30
  3. Capture of Lachish, vss. 31-32
  4. Defeat of king of Gezer, vs. 33
  5. Capture of Eglon, vss. 34-35
  6. Capture of Hebron, vss. 36-37
  7. Capture of Debir, vss. 38-39
  8. Summary of S success, vss. 40-43
 E. N campaign, 11:1-15
  1. Preparation of Canaanites for war, vss. 1-5
  2. Battle at Waters of Merom, vss. 6-9
  3. Destruction of Hazor, vss. 10-15
 F. Summary of conquest, 11:16–12:24
  1. Summary of land conquered, 11:16-20
  2. Decimation of the Anakim, 11:21-23
  3. Summary of kings conquered, ch. 12
   a. Transjordanian kings, vss. 1-6
   b. Canaanite kings, vss. 7-24
II. Allotment of the land, chs. 13–21
 A. Land still unconquered, 13:1-7
 B. Inheritance of Transjordanian tribes, 13:8-33
  1. Transjordanian territory, vss. 8-14
  2. Borders of Reuben, vss. 15-23
  3. Cities of Gad, vss. 24-28
  4. Region of Transjordanian Manasseh, vss. 29-31
  5. Summary, vss. 32-33
 C. Allotment of Canaan, chs. 14–19
  1. Introduction, 14:1-5
  2. Allotment to Judah, 14:6–15:63
   a. Claim of Caleb, 14:6-15
   b. Borders of Judah, 15:1-12
   c. Conquests of Caleb and Othniel, 15:13-19
   d. Cities of Judah, 15:20-63
  3. Allotment to Joseph tribes, chs. 16–17
   a. S boundary, 16:1-4
   b. Borders of Ephraim, 16:5-10
   c. Allotment to Manasseh, 17:1-13
   d. Complaint of Joseph tribes, 17:14-18
  4. Allotment to other tribes, chs. 18–19
   a. Survey of remaining territory, 18:1-10
   b. Borders and cities of Benjamin, 18:11-28
   c. Cities of Simeon, 19:1-9
   d. Borders of Zebulun, 19:10-16
   e. Cities of Issachar, 19:17-23
   f. Borders of Asher, 19:24-31
   g. Borders and cities of Naphtali, 19:32-39
   h. Cities of Dan, 19:40-48
   i. Joshua's city, 19:49-50
   j. Completion of allotment, 19:51
 D. Cities of refuge, ch. 20
 E. Levitical cities, ch. 21
III. Departure of Transjordanian tribes, ch. 22
IV. Joshua's last days, chs. 23–24
 A. Joshua's farewell address, ch. 23
 B. Covenant at Shechem, 24:1-28
 C. Death and burial of Joshua, 24:29-31
 D. Two burial traditions, 24:32-33
  1. Burial of Joseph's bones at Shechem, vs. 32
  2. Burial of Eleazar at Gibeah in Ephraim, vs. 33

B. *COMPOSITION.* The problems of the book of Joshua are numerous and complicated. Not least among them is the problem of composition. Contemporary scholarship dismisses the tradition that Joshua was the author. The book has received its title from the fact that Joshua is the principal actor in it. Most scholars find in the book a multiplicity of authors, though a few students of the problem (notably Yehezkel Kaufmann; *see bibliography*) conclude that with some additions and subtractions the book was composed by a single author soon after the events which it relates. Inner contradictions in the book and the witness of archaeology sufficiently disprove this view. But among those who assert that the book was compiled, composed, and edited much later, there is by no means unanimity on the process and steps through which it went.

1. Pentateuchal documents in Joshua. A number of scholars discover the documents of the Pentateuch in Joshua, thus giving rise to the term HEXATEUCH. The argument is twofold: (*a*) the narratives of Joshua provide the climax to the Pentateuchal promise that Israel will possess the land (cf. Gen. 13:14-17; 15:7, 18; 17:8; etc.); (*b*) the documentary components of Joshua show literary affinities with the Pentateuchal documents.

The kinds of inconsistencies to be observed in the Pentateuch are also visible here: (*a*) According to Josh. 4:8, twelve stones were carried out of the Jordan and set up at Gilgal. According to vs. 9, the stones were set up in the middle of the Jordan. (*b*) In 6:5 the order was given to shout at the blast of the trumpet, whereas in vs. 10 the people were not to shout until Joshua gave the command. (*c*) On the eve of the second attack upon Ai (8:3), Joshua sent thirty thousand men to lie in ambush behind the city. The next morning he sent five thousand to the same place (vs. 12). Such contradictions provide some ground for separation of the sources.

This hypothesis finds the bulk of the conquest narrative (chs. 1–12) to be E and D, with a very few traces of J (e.g., 5:13-14; 9:6-7; 10:12-13*a;* and a few other doubtful places). The editing done by the Deuteronomist has been so thorough that J has virtually been suppressed. It is almost as difficult to discover original remains of E (cf. a substratum in 2:1-9, 12-23; an incomplete stratum of the crossing of the Jordan in chs. 3–4; 5:2-3, 8-9, 13-14; one of the strands of the Jericho story in ch. 6; part of the narrative of the compact with the Gibeonites in 9:3, 6*a,* 8-11[?], 14-15*a;* some of the details of chs. 10–11, perhaps 10:6, 16-24; 11:1-9; etc.). The Deuteronomic editor has so covered up the original JE (or J and E) reports that they are scarcely recoverable.

The P document does not appear, save for some glosses, until the division of the land (chs. 13–21), and most of this section is usually ascribed to P, some of it to an even later time. Most of ch. 22 is also ascribed to P. Ch. 23 is a farewell address composed by the Deuteronomist, while ch. 24 is substantially E with Deuteronomic editing.

Scholars who presuppose the existence of the Pentateuchal documents in Joshua are hard pressed to explain their absence! Analysis is complicated by the complete Deuteronomic rewriting, which obliterated them, and the conclusion is that much of the J and E material has been suppressed. Those who attempt documentary analysis come to radically different conclusions.

The results are so inconclusive that it seems justifiable to doubt that the Pentateuchal documents continue into Joshua. The argument from the promise of the land cannot stand apart from the demonstration of literary contacts. The only literary contact on which everyone agrees is with Deuteronomy and the rest of the Deuteronomic history (Judges–Kings). In its present form Joshua is thoroughly Deuteronomic. As will be seen below, even the ascription to P of the allotment of the land has been undercut by the most recent work.

2. Sanctuary and tribal traditions. Within this category is the pre-Deuteronomic material now contained in chs. 1–12. The Deuteronomic editor has so totally recast the material that it is only with the greatest difficulty and diffidence that one can identify any fragment as unchanged from its original form. The most we can say is that much of Josh. 1–12 originated as tribal and sanctuary traditions. The precise form in which the traditions existed before their recasting by the Deuteronomic editor can no longer be ascertained. But the editor was certainly not creating the narratives from his imagination.

a. Gilgal traditions. After the crossing of the Jordan (chs. 3–4), the center of Israelite activity was the sanctuary of Gilgal. Here the twelve stones from the Jordan were set up as a memorial of the miraculous crossing (4:20-24). Here the circumcision of the nation took place (5:2-9), and the Passover which marked the end of the manna was celebrated (5:10-12). From this point until the survey of the land (18:1), Israel had its permanent camp at Gilgal, and Joshua brought the army back there after each campaign into the hills (cf. 9:6; 10:6, 15, 43; 14:6). Gilgal was apparently the principal Benjaminite sanctuary, for here the Benjaminite Saul was crowned, according to one of the strands of the Saul narrative (I Sam. 11:12-15; cf. 13:2-15*a*). Independent evidence, therefore, shows that for a time, at least, Gilgal took a leading part in the religious and military life of the Israelite confederacy. The material which may most probably be assigned to the Gilgal sanctuary is the substratum underlying the Jericho traditions (Josh. 2; 6), the kernel of the story of crossing the Jordan (3:1–5:12), and perhaps the tradition of the naming of the Valley of Achor (7:1, 6-26; this may possibly be a Judahite story).

b. Traditions of the tribe of Benjamin. The separation of the traditions of Gilgal, the Benjaminite sanctuary, from those of the tribe of Benjamin is somewhat arbitrary, and the distinction must be regarded as tentative at best. The remainder of chs. 2–9 is included in this category—i.e., the traditions of the capture of Ai (7:2-5; 8:1-29) and of the covenant with the Gibeonites (9:3-27). Both these stories take place in the hill country of Benjamin, and they may be regarded as general traditions of the tribe. The story of the covenant with the Gibeonites has been well worked over, and the words "for the house of my God" (9:23*b*) and "for the altar of the LORD" (vs. 27*b*) probably represent Deuteronomic expansion. The Ai tradition is best explained as a folk legend from the Benjaminite area around Ai, connected with the name of the site, which means "ruin."

Whether the battle at Gibeon and in the Valley of Aijalon (10:1-15) belongs with the Benjaminite traditions is uncertain. The close connection of the story with the following narrative of the kings in the cave at Makkedah (vss. 16-27) suggests to some that the two were originally one story, broken now by vs. 15, which is probably an addition (cf. vs. 43). On the other hand, the important part played by Gibeon (Benjaminite) and the Valley of Aijalon (probably Danite) in the fragment from the Book of Jashar (vss. 12*b*-13*a; see* JASHAR, BOOK OF) may indicate that the story of the battle (vss. 1-14) has been arbitrarily connected with that of the five kings. The battle, indeed, may have been concocted to explain the poetic fragment.

c. S traditions. If the two portions of 10:1-27 are originally separate, vss. 16-27 must come from the Shephelah of Judah in the neighborhood of MAKKEDAH, the location of which is uncertain. The introduction of the five kings in 10:3, 5, is the secondary effort to combine the two stories.

From the S comes also the catalogue of S fortresses conquered by Joshua (10:28-43). This campaign is not described with the narrative detail of the other traditions and may come from an ancient annal.

d. N traditions. Josh. 11:1-15 presents the narrative of a N campaign, in which the only details are that the major battle took place at the Waters of Merom (vs. 7) and that Joshua burned only Hazor of all the N fortified cities (vss. 11-13). Again the impression is of annals rather than of folk traditions. The substratum of the whole section, 10:28–11:15 (discounting such a clearly Deuteronomic addition as 10:40-43), may belong to an early catalogue of victories in Joshua's campaign.

3. Border and town lists. Chs. 13–19 present the border and town lists of the twelve tribes, to which are appended the lists of the cities of refuge in ch. 20 (cf. Num. 35:9-28; Deut. 19:1-13) and the Levitical cities in ch. 21 (cf. Num. 35:1-8; I Chr. 6:54-81). A few narrative fragments have also found their way into this section. Most of these are paralleled by other OT narratives (Josh. 14:6-12 [cf. Num. 13–14]; Josh. 15:14-19 [cf. Judg. 1:10-15, 20]; Josh. 17:3-4 [cf. Num. 27:1-7, greatly expanded by priestly editors]). The priority is very hard to determine. The traditions probably go back to early times, when the independent origin of Calebite and Kenizzite clans was still acknowledged in Judah, and when the clans of Manasseh were still known. They probably belong, therefore, to tribal traditions and have been inserted into the boundary lists by the editor.

The lists themselves are of diverse character. In some particulars, border and city lists differ from one another. Kiriath-jearim is on the Benjaminite side of the Judah-Benjamin border (18:28), yet it is mentioned as a Judahite city (15:60). Beth-arabah is listed in both Judah (15:61) and Benjamin (18:22). Benjamin likewise has some towns which are N of the border delineated in 18:11-20—e.g., Zemaraim (vs. 22) and Ophrah (vs. 23). The city list of Judah includes most of the cities of Simeon (cf. 15:26-32; 19:2-7), as well as several of the tribe of Dan (e.g., Eshtaol, Zorah, and Ekron). We do not have border accounts for the tribes of Dan, Issachar, Transjordanian Manasseh, and Simeon (explained in 19: 9). The border accounts of Ephraim, Manasseh, Asher, Naphtali, Reuben, and Gad are sketchy in the extreme. We are not given city lists for Ephraim, Manasseh, or Transjordanian Manasseh, and we have brief and obviously incomplete city lists for Zebulun, Asher, and Reuben. The list of Levitical cities in ch. 21 (cf. I Chr. 6:54-81, which differs in some details) contradicts border accounts in four cases: Shechem is placed in Ephraim instead of in Manasseh, Daberath is placed in Issachar instead of in Zebulun (Josh. 19:13), Jokneam is placed in Zebulun instead of in Asher(?), and Heshbon is placed in Gad instead of in Reuben (13:17). These divergences and omissions make the tribal claims of Josh. 13–19 uncertain, at best. Tribal boundaries probably shifted more than once, and the lists of chs. 13–21 represent a multiplicity of sources and ages.

It has been suggested, most persuasively by Alt and Noth (*see bibliography*), that the lists of chs. 13–19 come from a document which set out tribal boundaries in the premonarchic period. This is true not only of the lists which purport to present boundaries but also of some of the Galilean city lists, which were actually, as Noth says, *Grenzfixpunkte,* points which lay on the boundary but without the designation of lines between them. These lists have been expanded, in some cases by the addition of lines along the fixed points of the borders and in some cases by the addition of other material such as the city lists of Judah and Benjamin. It has been suggested (by Cross and Wright; *see bibliography*) that the city list of Benjamin (18:21-28) belongs with that of Judah (15:21-62) as the official description of administrative districts in the time of Jehoshaphat. Alt, on the other hand, feels that these lists are from the time of Josiah, and Kallai-Kleinmann (*see bibliography*) dates the town list of Judah to the time of Hezekiah and that of Benjamin to the conquests of Abijah (cf. II Chr. 13).

The chief difficulty with Noth's hypothesis lies in the N tribes. It is all but impossible to determine the borders of Ephraim and Manasseh, and Manasseh is said to have possessed towns in Issachar and Asher (17:11; En-dor is in the very center of Issachar). The borders of Dan (19:40-48) are not given, and the list of cities is extremely difficult to analyze as a series of boundary points. Noth explains the Dan list as an extract from the province list of 15:21-62, but Cross and Wright think that it is a mixed list in which are both a boundary description and a town list, with no stylistic distinction between them. With the tribes of the far N, the situation is quite difficult. The Zebulun list (19:10-16) purports to give the boundary, which is most difficult to fix, together with a list of only five towns. That of Issachar (19:17-23) is a city list, of which, in its present order, no sense can be made as a series of boundary points. The same seems to be true of Asher (19:24-31), which appears to have been worked into a border account by someone unfamiliar with the territory (cf., e.g., vs. 27, where the boundary goes N from Beth-emek to Kabul, which is actually S of Beth-emek!). The difficulty with Naphtali (19:32-39) is the uncertainty of the boundary on the S and the W, particularly at Hukkok (vs. 34), which is too far E to touch Asher. The analysis of these Galilean lists as official documents seems hazardous and tenuous, and it is tempting to suggest that they are the work of someone who has listed cities of the N tribes from memory. They have subsequently been worked into boundary descriptions by an editor who had no firsthand knowledge of Galilee.

The boundary and town lists, therefore, partake of a double character. Those of Judah and Benjamin are precise, and the town lists reflect administrative districts of monarchic times. The other boundaries are extremely vague. The accounts of Judah and Benjamin, with the city list of Simeon, probably came from Jerusalem archives. The city lists of the N tribes may be from memory, having been worked later into border descriptions. The very sketchy description of the N territory may reflect the period after the destruction of Israel in 721 B.C., when the details were not remembered and the sense of Yahweh's judgment on Israel contributed to the hazy recollection.

4. The Deuteronomic compilation. As we have seen, Joshua is a Deuteronomic book. Probably during the Babylonian exile the work of compiling Israel's history was undertaken. Available to the compiler were a series of Benjaminite traditions, perhaps already in collected form, which may or may not have been attached to Joshua's name, and some annals of the Conquest. He was able to use administrative documents from the government archives in Jerusalem. He rewrote the Benjaminite traditions to a considerable degree, and he placed the boundary descriptions in order, beginning with the Transjordanian territories promised by Moses according to other traditions then extant, and moving on to Judah, Ephraim, and Manasseh, the most influential tribes. Recalling that the sanctuary had at one time been at Shiloh, he placed the report of the survey there (18:1) and put down, in the order in which they occurred to him, the territories of the remaining tribes.

He then appended the lists of cities of refuge (ch. 20), which had probably been traditional for some time, and of the Levitical cities (ch. 21), which may have been drawn up under Josiah (though Albright dates this list in the time of Solomon, on the ground that none of the cities was founded after 950 B.C.). The editor inserted connecting and summarizing links in the recast material, and he wrote the introduction to the book (ch. 1) and Joshua's farewell address (ch. 23).

The narrative of the ceremony at Shechem (ch. 24) is a difficult problem. Most scholars agree that it did not form a part of the Deuteronomic Joshua, at least in its present position. Yet the style is strongly Deuteronomic, and the historical recapitulation (vss. 2-13) is of the same cult-lyric genre as, e.g., Deut. 26:5-11. Placing the ceremony at Shechem reflects the importance of the Shechem sanctuary in the premonarchic period, though Shechem had its importance at later times as well (cf. I Kings 12:1-25). The relation of Josh. 24 to 8:30-35 might shed light on the problem. The latter tradition is purely Deuteronomic in style, and it closely parallels the procedure outlined in ch. 24, but without any ceremonial details. Perhaps ch. 24 stood in the place of 8:30-35 in the original Deuteronomic edition, later being removed to its present position and replaced by the précis of 8:30-35. This, at least, would remove the necessity of postulating a second Deuteronomic hand in ch. 24.

Thus the shape of the book of Joshua comes from the work of a Deuteronomist, who reworked the narrative traditions from Benjamin and some local traditions from Judah and the N, inserted from annalistic sources the outline of the Shephelah and N campaigns (10:28–11:15), wrote campaign summaries (11:16-23), and inserted lists of conquered kings (ch. 12), which may also have come from ancient annals. He organized the division of the land into its present form, recasting some lists and inserting a few narrative traditions and the official town lists of Judah and Benjamin. The whole was concluded with Joshua's farewell address (ch. 23), perhaps also including the tradition of Joshua's burial (24:29-31).

5. Successive editions. Of what remains, we have mostly glosses. It is possible that an editor with a dramatic sense moved the Shechem covenant account (ch. 24) from its original place to its present location. A local tradition of the altar built by the Transjordanian tribes may have been added after the main Deuteronomic compilation (ch. 22). Some see in this tradition the hand of P. It certainly reflects a pan-Israelitism. At the same time, the ascription of this chapter to P is difficult to uphold purely on the basis of style, though there may be some priestly glosses in it (e.g., the "whole assembly of the people of Israel" [vs. 12]; "Phinehas the son of Eleazar the priest" [vss. 13, 30-32]). There are doubtless priestly glosses elsewhere in the book (e.g., 3:4*b*, 12; 4:19; 5:10-11; 9:17-21[?]; 13:21*b*-22; 14:1-5[?]; 19:51 ["Eleazar the priest . . . and the heads of the fathers' houses of the tribes of the people of Israel"]). Certain portions of ch. 21 may also bear the priestly imprint (cf. the lists of Levitical families in 21:4-7; the "descendants of Aaron" in vs. 10*a;* vss. 10*b*-13*a* [to "Aaron the priest"]). To priestly glossators may likewise be assigned the two burial traditions closing the book (24: 32-33). But these successive editions scarcely deserve the name. They are little more than occasional glosses, and they are not sufficient to assign to any individual, such as a P author. The book of Joshua had substantially its present form following the work of the Deuteronomic compiler and editor during the period of exile.

C. *JOSHUA IN THE DEUTERONOMIC HISTORY.* To Martin Noth we owe what has become a commonplace of OT scholarship: the recognition that Deuteronomy–Kings forms a separate historical work. The book of Joshua takes its place as the first stage of the Deuteronomic history of Israel. The Deuteronomist is not interested in the patriarchs at all, save for a somewhat hazy interest in Jacob. Moses forms the beginning of Israel with his giving of the covenantal law. But the conquest of Canaan is the point at which, for the Deuteronomic history, Israel's story really begins. Here the covenant is put to work, renewed, and spread to cover the covenantal people in the Land of Promise. The historian looks back on the Conquest with nostalgia (24:31). Some of its monuments remain "to this day." At the time he is writing his historical work, the nostalgia is the greater, for Israel does not, in fact, possess the land. The story of its conquest with the help of Yahweh is told with the greater zeal, and it betrays a certain eschatological fervor on the part of the historian. For this historian, indeed, the situation worsened after the glorious days of Joshua. The period of the judges, for all its transitory victories, was a period of anarchy (cf. Judg. 21:25), which was removed only by the power of Davidic royalty. Indeed, Joshua foreshadows the monarchy in the Deuteronomist's account (*see* JOSHUA SON OF NUN; priestly glossators have highlighted this motif by coupling him with Eleazar the priest, as Moses, the royal prototype, had his priestly colleague in Aaron, Zerubbabel his in Jeshua [cf. Ezra 3:2, 8; 5:2; Zech. 4], and Nehemiah, according to the present form of EZRA AND NEHEMIAH, in Ezra).

The book of Joshua, therefore, presents the historian's view of the possession of the land. He knew that Israel had more battles to fight before the land was entirely won (cf. 13:1-6; 15:63; 16:10; 17:12-13, 16-18; Judg. 4–5; 13:2–16:31; II Sam. 5:6-9). Nevertheless, Joshua's conquest is presented as complete (cf. Josh. 11:23), and the parceling out of the land includes territory which never belonged to Israel (e.g., in the far N of Asher) or which belonged to the nation only much later (e.g., the Philistine territory on the S ranges of the Coastal Plain in the town lists of Judah and Dan). There is a visionary character to this stage of the Deuteronomist's history which must not be forgotten. His dream, set down during the dark days of the Babylonian overlordship, is the full possession of the whole land, and he expresses Israel's claim to the land by his ordering of the materials regarding Joshua's conquest.

D. *HISTORICAL SIGNIFICANCE.* We have seen that the Deuteronomic editor reworked the original materials into his own coherent account of Joshua's achievements. We may now assess these traditions for their historical worth.

1. Narratives of conquest. The greatest controversy has centered around the narratives of chs. 1–12. Alt and Noth (*see bibliography*) have concluded that the detailed narratives (2:1–10:27) represent local traditions of an etiological character. Albright and his followers (*see bibliography*) have objected to this rather high-handed treatment of historical documents. They accuse Alt and Noth of dispensing with archaeological information altogether.

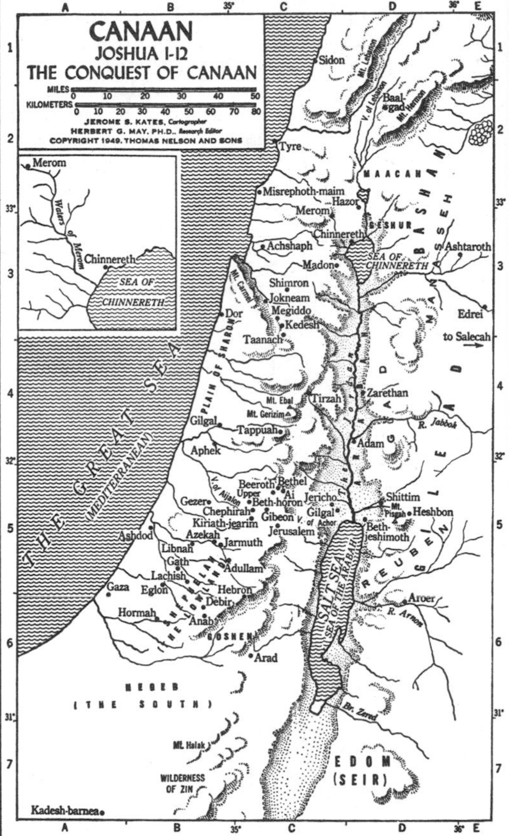

When the detailed narratives are examined in the light of the history of traditions and of archaeology, we may only conclude that 2:1–10:27 presents etiological traditions which have no bearing on the history of the Conquest. The tale of the spies, of course (ch. 2), cannot be checked. That it has undergone extensive rewriting is evident in the narrative style. It belongs with the Jericho narrative (ch. 6). The story of the crossing of the Jordan (3:1–5:9) is a complex of traditions involving two versions of the crossing and one circumcision tradition, if not two. The two versions of the crossing cannot be separated into complete strands, as the editing has been very heavy (*see* § B1 *above*). Interwoven with them is an interpretation, probably the work of the editor, which makes the story virtually a doublet of the crossing of the sea under Moses (Exod. 14). The circumcision traditions involve both the name of a hill near Gilgal, Gibeath-haaraloth (the "hill of the foreskins"; 5:3), and the name of Gilgal itself (5:9). The interest of these stories lies in these phenomena, though the Deuteronomist has made them more edifying. Archaeology has not yet cast much light on the GILGAL story.

Archaeological evidence at JERICHO is ambiguous. Late Bronze remains are very scarce, and the usual dating of them is during the fourteenth century B.C. At the time usually given for Joshua's invasion (last half of the thirteenth century B.C.) the city could hardly have been more than a hilltop fortification, if it was that much. The great victory of Josh. 6 is highly imaginative. Is it etiological? Noth is reluctant to specify the etiological basis of the story. It probably explains the ruins of the great city in the midst of Benjamin, for Jericho was not rebuilt until the ninth century B.C. Local legend probably dwelt on the city's former glories, and a fall at the hands of Joshua explained their loss.

The story of the treachery and execution of Achan (7:1, 6-26) turns around the naming of the Valley of Achor. No archaeological check can be made on the story, but mention of the heap of stones which "remains to this day" (vs. 26*a*), together with the name of the valley, places the tradition in the realm of etiology. As for Ai, excavations at et-Tell, the undoubted site of Ai, show that, except for a few houses *ca.* 1000 B.C., Ai had been uninhabited since *ca.* 2200 B.C. Hence the story cannot be historical, unless we accept the attractive theory of Albright, that the tradition of the capture of Bethel, only *ca.* 1½ miles distant, has been transferred to the ruin of Ai. But this hypothesis, ingenious as it is, cannot be treated as established fact.

The remaining Benjaminite tradition is that of the covenant with the Gibeonites (ch. 9), which tells how the Gibeonites became servants of Israel (cf. vss. 21, 27). Once again archaeology casts a shadow on the story. Recent campaigns at el-Jib, which hardly anyone doubts is ancient Gibeon, have failed to unearth any remains of the Late Bronze Age or of the first two centuries of the Early Iron Age. The town is mentioned in the campaign report of Sheshonk I, which comes from the second half of the tenth century B.C. (cf. I Kings 14:25-28; *see* SHISHAK). Thus far, at least, we have no evidence that Gibeon existed at the time of Joshua's campaign. The etiological element of the story becomes, therefore, its literary *raison d'être*.

It would seem natural to suppose that if these Benjaminite traditions do not reflect the invasion under Joshua, they bear on the entry of Benjamin into Canaan. Yet the archaeological evidence suggests that, save for the narratives of a camp at Gilgal and perhaps the fall of Jericho, the stories are of no more value for a hypothetical Benjaminite invasion than for that under Joshua. The actual course of Israel's conquest of Canaan is shrouded by time and obscurity.

We are still in the realm of legend with the battle at Gibeon (10:1-15) and the five kings in the cave at Makkedah (vss. 16-27). If Gibeon was not in existence, a battle could hardly have been fought over it. The story, indeed, probably took its rise from the quotation of the Book of Jashar, which can only refer to a later battle at Gibeon, possibly aided by dense clouds which obscured the light. Such, at least, is the most probable meaning of the sun and moon "standing still" (עמד; vss. 12*b*-13*a;* cf. Hab. 3:11). The reference to hailstones (vs. 11) points to this interpretation, though a later glossator, perhaps the

Deuteronomist, has given a more miraculous cast to the tale by explaining that the sun stayed in the sky for a whole day (vs. 13).

The story of the capture of five kings in the cave at Makkedah (vss. 16-27) rings much truer, and several scholars have severely criticized Noth for his insistence on its etiological character. At the same time, lacking any external check on the story, to say that it is the report of an actual happening is no less hypothetical than to explain it as etiological. The etiological factor is there: the sealed cave with five trees standing near by (vss. 26-27). If we could be certain of the location of Makkedah, some minimal archaeological check might be available.

Criticisms of Alt and Noth, principally from Albright and his followers, lean heavily on archaeological data, which provide strong support for the remainder of Josh. 10-11. Excavations at Lachish (10:31-32; modern Tell ed-Duweir), Eglon (vss. 34-35; modern Tell el-Hesi), and Debir (vss. 38-39; modern Tell Beit Mirsim) have shown evidence of violent conflagrations in the last half of the thirteenth century B.C. Recent work at Hazor (11:1-11; modern Tell el-Qedah) and Bethel (12:16) yields approximately the same result.

The evidence is clearly not all available. But a campaign in the Shephelah probably took place as reported in Josh. 10:28-39; and a N campaign, as related in 11:1-15, probably occurred at about the same time. But the substantial accuracy of these annalistic narratives cannot be used to uphold the historical accuracy of 2:1–10:27.

2. Division of the land. We have seen above that the documents underlying chs. 13–21 are of little use in reconstructing the history of Joshua's time. Some are official records from a later date; others may be lists of sites set down and put in order from memory. That the territories of the tribes were carefully defined in this early period is most improbable. Border cities move from tribe to tribe in various passages of the OT (cf., e.g., the location of Kiriath-jearim in Benjamin in 18:28, but in Judah in 15:60; Judg. 18:12). At the same time, the care with which the borders of Judah and Benjamin are drawn in Josh. 15:1-12; 18:11-20 suggests that some effort was made —perhaps in the premonarchic period—to establish and maintain the proper boundaries (cf. the injunctions against removing landmarks in Deut. 19:14; 27:17; Job 24:2; Prov. 22:28; 23:10). That the borders of the N tribes are so doubtful may be due to the fact that the Deuteronomic history is a product of Judah, and the details of these N territories may have been forgotten.

3. Amphictyonic covenant traditions. A great deal of emphasis has been placed in recent study on the so-called amphictyonic relationship of the Israelite tribes after the Conquest (*see* JUDGES, BOOK OF; ISRAEL, HISTORY OF, § 3). The term is taken from the twelve-clan leagues of ancient Greece, and it denotes a confederacy of independent tribes centered around a sanctuary. In a number of passages, evidence is to be found that SHECHEM was that sanctuary (cf., e.g., Deut. 11:26-32; 27). Josh. 24 is extremely important in this regard, for it presents

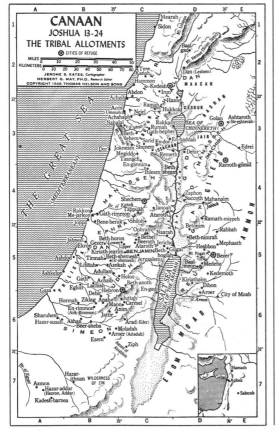

CANAAN
JOSHUA 13-24
THE TRIBAL ALLOTMENTS
CITIES OF REFUGE
JEROME S. KATES, Cartographer
HERBERT G. MAY, PH.D., Research Editor
COPYRIGHT 1949. THOMAS NELSON AND SONS

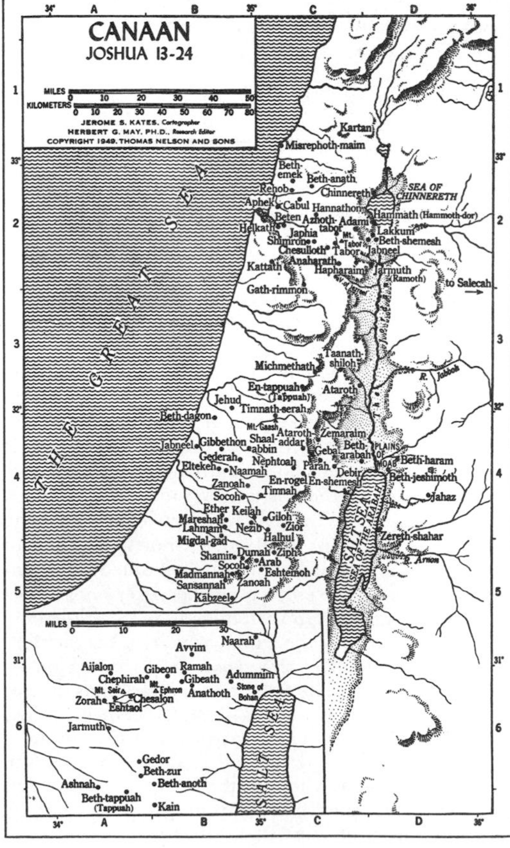

evidence to suggest that the tribes held a covenant renewal ceremony at Shechem, perhaps yearly.

Before coming directly to Josh. 24, some other factors in the structure of Joshua may be noted. Three main shrines figure in the book as centers of national activity. Gilgal is the base of operations from 4:19 to 17:18, save for the side trip to Shechem in 8:30-35. Gilgal is associated, therefore, with the Conquest and with the allotment of land to the Transjordanian tribes and to Judah, Ephraim, and Manasseh. In chs. 18–23 we may presume the center to be Shiloh (cf. 18:1, 8-10; 22:12). Shiloh, therefore, is associated with land allotment to the remaining seven tribes, with the designation of cities of refuge and Levitical cities, and with the misunderstanding over the altar built by the Transjordanian tribes (ch. 22). In ch. 24 we come to Shechem for the second time. It has been suggested above that perhaps ch. 24 stood in the place of 8:30-35 in the first Deuteronomic edition and that it was subsequently moved to its present position. This would put the Shechem covenant account after the first phase of the Conquest, the capture of Jericho and of Ai. (The fact that in the LXX 8:30-35 follows 9:2 is of no importance. In either position the renewal of the covenant represents a consolidation by the conquering tribes.)

It has often been noted that Joshua relates no conquest of the central portion of Palestine, the territory of Ephraim and most of Manasseh. In this connection the covenant at Shechem is most interesting, for it may represent what was in the first instance the coalition of only a few tribes. Which ones they were is a matter of conjecture. Josh. 19:50; 24:30 make Joshua an Ephraimite. Perhaps the Shechem covenant was the alignment of Ephraim and Manasseh, the latter having been resident in central Palestine since before the descent into Egypt of the tribes involved in the Exodus. Whether other tribes were at first included in the Shechem covenant must remain doubtful. Shechem later became the central sanctuary of the twelve-tribe amphictyony for a time, but the sanctuary was moved, probably to Bethel (cf. Judg. 20:18) and still later to Shiloh (cf. I Sam. 1). The latter situation may be mirrored in Josh. 18–23. But the complexities of location of the Israelite amphictyonic sanctuary have not yet been elucidated.

E. *THEOLOGY.* Since the book of Joshua in its present form is Deuteronomic, it is informed throughout by the Deuteronomic viewpoint. No other theology can now be discerned beneath the Deuteronomic overlay, if any other was ever there.

This viewpoint sees the keystone to Joshua's work as the gracious act of God in giving Israel the land of Canaan. Though there is much glorification of Joshua, the glory for the Conquest goes to God alone (cf. 1:9*b;* 3:10; 4:23-24; 6:16; 8:1*b;* 10:14; 11:6-8; 13:6*b;* 18:3; 21:43-45; 23:2*b*-16; 24:2-13, 17-18). God has given Israel the land. He has fought for and with the armies, and at his command Israel has taken and divided the territory. The Conquest is not Israel's but Yahweh's. No battles could have been won unless God had fought them; indeed, one was lost because Achan disobeyed God's command (7:1-5). Obedience is demanded because of God's gracious leading (23:5-6; 24:13-14, 16-18), and this obedience is the service of Yahweh "with all your heart and with all your soul" (22:5). With the possession of the Promised Land goes the vast obligation to responsibility (23:14-16; 24:19-20). The allotment of the land is undertaken under the direction of Yahweh (cf. 19:51). At the same time, we do not hear in Joshua, as we do elsewhere (e.g., I Kings 8:36; Ps. 85:1—H 85:2; Isa. 14:25; Jer. 2:7; 16:18; Ezek. 38:16; Joel 2:18; 3:2—H 4:2), that the land belongs in the first instance to Yahweh. Yahweh takes it from the Canaanites in order that Israel may "inherit" it, but "inherit" means "take possession of it and pass it on to your heirs" (*see* INHERITANCE). The marvel of the Conquest is not that Israel is given that which belongs to no one else, but that Israel is made to displace the previous owners.

This has raised acute questions for the religious conscience. Can a God of justice and mercy condone the arbitrary ascription to his will of bloody conquest? No easy answer is possible. For the editors of the book of Joshua, the holy war was the means by which Israel actualized God's promise (*see* WAR, IDEAS OF). That Israel ascribed glory to God for it does not mean that she sought to escape moral responsibility. It means only that Israel was well aware that her history did not consist solely of the machinations of men. She recognized and acknowledged with joy and fear that Yahweh directed the course of history for his own inscrutable plans. The glorious conquest of the past meant the possibility in the future of Yahweh's re-establishing Israel in her land. In the meantime, Israel's business was to give him unwavering devotion, trust, and obedience.

Bibliography. Commentaries: J. Garstang (1931); F.-M. Abel, *La Sainte Bible* (1950); F. Nötscher, *Echter-Bibel* (1951); J. Bright, *IB* (1953): the best in English; M. Noth, *HAT* (2nd ed., 1953): now the standard work; H. W. Hertzberg, *ATD* (1953). See also Introductions to the OT by Pfeiffer, Bentzen, Weiser, Eissfeldt.

Special studies: A. Alt, "Eine galiläische Ortslist in Josua 19," *ZAW,* XLV (1927), 59-81. A. Saarisalo, *The Boundary Between Issachar and Naphtali* (1927). M. Noth, "Studien zu den historisch-geographischen Dokumenten des Josuabuches," *ZDPV,* LVIII (1935), 185-255. W. F. Albright, "The Israelite Conquest of Canaan," *BASOR,* 74 (April, 1939), 11-23; "The List of Levitical Cities," *Louis Ginzburg Jubilee Volume* (1945), pp. 49-73. S. Mowinckel, *Zur Frage nach dokumentarischen Quellen in Josua 13–19* (1946). G. E. Wright, "The Literary and Historical Problem of Joshua 10 and Judges 1," *JNES,* V (1946), 105-14. M. Noth, "Überlieferungsgeschichtliches zur zweiten Hälfte des Josuabuches," *Alttestamentliche Studien* (Nötscher Festschrift; 1950). H. H. Rowley, *From Joseph to Joshua* (1950). A. Alt, "Josua," *Kleine Schriften,* I (1953), 176-92; "Das System der Stammesgrenzen im Buche Josua," *Kleine Schriften,* I (1953), 193-202; "Judas Gaue unter Josia," *Kleine Schriften,* II (1953), 276-88. Y. Kaufmann, *The Biblical Account of the Conquest of Palestine* (1953). A. D. Tushingham, "Excavations at OT Jericho," *BA,* XVII (1954), 98-104. E. Nielsen, *Shechem, a Traditio-Historical Investigation* (1955). J. Bright, *Early Israel in Recent History Writing,* Studies in Biblical Theology (1956): a telling criticism of Alt and Noth from the standpoint of W. F. Albright. F. M. Cross, Jr., and G. E. Wright, "The Boundary and Province Lists of the Kingdom of Judah," *JBL,* LXXV (1956), 202-26. Z. Kallai-Kleinmann, "The Town Lists of Judah, Simeon, Benjamin, and Dan," *Vetus Testamentum,* VIII (1958), 135-60.

E. M. GOOD

JOSHUA SON OF NUN. Alternately: HOSHEA hō shē′ə [הוֹשֵׁעַ, salvation] (Num. 13:8, 16; Deut. 32:

44 RSV mg.); JEHOSHUA jĭ hŏsh'ōō ə (Num. 13:16 KJV); JEHOSHUAH (I Chr. 7:27 KJV); OSHEA ō shē'ə [הושע, salvation] (Num. 13:8, 16, KJV); JESUS jē'zəs ['Ιησοῦς, *also the* LXX *form, perhaps presupposing* ישוע] (Acts 7:45 KJV; Heb. 4:8 KJV). The major figure in the OT account of the conquest of Canaan. *See* JOSHUA, BOOK OF.

Joshua first appears as the Israelite general in the battle against Amalek (Exod. 17:8-16), and then as Moses' "servant" (or "lieutenant," משרת; 24:13; 32:17), who serves in the tent of meeting with him (33:11; here described as a "youth," נער). Joshua's main exploit before the Conquest was his participation as the representative of the tribe of Ephraim in the spying out of Canaan (Num. 13:8). With Caleb, he argued that the land could be taken (14:6), and with Caleb he was rewarded by being permitted to enter Canaan (14:30, 38; 26:65; 32:12).

Before Moses' death, Joshua was commissioned as his successor (cf. Num. 27:18-23; Deut. 31:7-29). When Moses died, Israel obeyed Joshua as they had obeyed Moses, because he "was full of the spirit of wisdom" (Deut. 34:9). He then led the Conquest, narrated in the book of Joshua. It has been suggested (*see* JOSHUA, BOOK OF, § D) that the traditions bearing on Joshua's work are the annalistic accounts of Josh. 10:28–11:15 (now expanded by the Deuteronomist) and perhaps the covenant tradition lying behind 24:1-28. The archaeological data point strongly to the latter half of the thirteenth century B.C. for Joshua's conquest. This rules out the identification of Joshua with the Yashuya of Tell el-Amarna Letter no. 256, which most scholars have denied on linguistic grounds as well. The argument which places Joshua prior to Moses, in the Amarna age, is highly dubious.

Joshua's work in Canaan, therefore, seems to have comprised an alliance with a tribe or tribes of central Canaan at Shechem (perhaps Manasseh, already resident around Shechem, and Ephraim, which was in the Exodus), the conquest of a circle of fortress cities in the Shephelah (Josh. 10:28-43), and at least one foray into N territory (11:1-15). Following this, he settled down in TIMNATH-HERES (Judg. 2:9; Timnath-serah in Josh. 19:50; 24:30), where he died and was buried at the reported age of 110 years (Josh. 24:29; Judg. 2:8).

It has been argued (by Möhlenbrink; *see bibliography*) that the presence of Joshua in Pentateuchal narratives is secondary. Certainly this is true of some of Joshua's appearances (e.g., Exod. 24:13; 32:17; Num. 14:30). The priestly editors have inserted Joshua at several points (e.g., the change of his name in Num. 13:16 [*see below*]; the commissioning before Eleazar the priest in 27:18-23; the command to divide the land with Eleazar in 34:17). At the same time, other narratives have a truer ring—e.g., his very general identification in Num. 11:28; the spy narrative of Num. 14 (though it is not impossible that only Caleb is original here); and perhaps the tradition associating Joshua with the tent of meeting (Exod. 33:11). Joshua probably was Moses' successor.

The tradition has, however, been expanded considerably. In some of the notices in the book of Joshua, he is almost a second Moses. He has the presence of Yahweh, as Moses did (1:5); he is obeyed, as Moses was (1:17); he sanctifies Israel before Yahweh's wonders, as Moses did (3:5; cf. Exod. 19:14); he is exalted before Israel as Moses was (Josh. 3:7; 4:14). The miraculous crossing of the Jordan (3:7–4:24) has many reminiscences of the crossing of the Red Sea (cf. the explicit connection in 4:23). When the angel accosted Joshua before Jericho, he spoke to him precisely as Yahweh addressed Moses at the burning bush (5:15). Joshua, like Moses, wrote the law on stones (8:32; cf. 24:26). Yahweh "hearkened to the voice" of Joshua (10:14), as he had to Moses (Deut. 9:19; 10:10). Finally, when Joshua brought the tribes to Shechem for the covenant ceremony, he gave them a summary of Israel's history (24:2-13), perhaps parallel to the summary of Deut. 1:6–3:29, though Josh. 24:2-7 begins farther back than does Deut. 1:6.

The figure of Joshua has also been invested with a certain royal aura. He is described as having the "spirit" (Num. 27:18; Deut. 34:9; cf. I Sam. 10:10; 16:13; Isa. 11:2). He is called the "servant of Yahweh" (Josh. 24:29). He calls the people together for the making of a covenant (Josh. 24:1; cf. II Sam. 5:3). His name is said to have been changed from Hoshea to Joshua (Num. 13:16), recalling the common royal practice of assuming a regnal name (*see* KING). His division of the land is parallel to the king's erection of administrative districts (I Kings 4:7-19). Likewise, Joshua is called upon to decide claims (cf. Josh. 14:6-15; 17:4, 14-18), a function of the judge which also fell to the king (cf. Isa. 11:3*b*-4). The priestly glossators have heightened this atmosphere by providing Joshua with a priestly associate, Eleazar. Cf. JOSHUA, BOOK OF, § C.

Later legends have somewhat lengthened Joshua's shadow. He is called the "successor of Moses in the prophetic office" (Ecclus. 46:1 LXX [διάδοχος; so also Vulg.]; Hebrew שרת, "minister"). His piety in fulfilling the word (the Torah?) made him a "judge in Israel" (I Macc. 2:55), and he was known as an intercessor for the people (II Esd. 7:107). Joshua received the Torah from Moses and passed it on to the elders (Pirke Aboth 1:1), though another tradition reports that the Torah was sealed in the ark of the covenant from the death of Joshua and Eleazar until it was opened by Zadok (Zadokite Fragment 7:5). In Heb. 4:8, Joshua's invasion is represented as a type of the rest into which the faithful in Christ would enter.

Bibliography. K. Möhlenbrink, "Josua im Pentateuch (Die Josuaüberlieferung ausserhalb des Josuabuches)," *ZAW*, LIX (1943), 14-58; T. J. Meek, *Hebrew Origins* (2nd ed., 1950), pp. 1-48. See also histories of Israel by Kittel, Noth, and Oesterley and Robinson. For full bibliography, *see* JOSHUA, BOOK OF.

E. M. GOOD

JOSIAH jō sī'ə [יאשיה(ו), let (or may) Yahweh give; 'Ιωσίας (Matt. 1:10-11; KJV JOSIAS)]. King of Judah *ca.* 640-609 B.C.; son and successor of Amon.

The root of the name is the Arabic *'wš,* "to give." Cf. also Joash and *Yā'ōš* of the Lachish Letters (from *Yā'oš-yahu*—i.e., Josiah). Alternately, the root may be the Arabic *'asā,* "to nurse, cure."

Josiah was made king by the "people of the land" (II Kings 21:24; II Chr. 33:25) after his father, Amon, had been murdered. He came to the throne at the age of eight, and reigned for thirty-one years (II Kings 22:1; II Chr. 34:1). His mother was Jedidah, daughter of Adaiah of Bozkath (cf. Josh. 15:39).

The pictures of the early years of Josiah's reign vary considerably in our sources. The Chronicler presents us with a sequence: (*a*) In the eighth year of his reign (*ca.* 632) he began to seek the God of David his father (II Chr. 34:3*a*). This indicates his rejection of the gods of his Assyrian overlord, and may point to a weakening of Assyrian control over the provinces in the W. (*b*) In the twelfth year of his reign (*ca.* 628) he began to purge Judah and Jerusalem (vss. 3*b*-5), and then extended his efforts to Manasseh, Ephraim, and as far as Naphtali (vss. 6-7). Such action could have been possible only if Josiah were in effective control of these former Assyrian provinces. But no mention is made in any of the sources that he had already won this control. It may indicate, however, that while still nominally a vassal of Assyria, in reality Josiah had taken advantage of Assyria's clear weakness to establish his claim to the old Davidic empire. Assyria was apparently powerless to intervene. (*c*) In the eighteenth year of his reign (*ca.* 622) with the finding of the "book of the law" in the temple, Josiah carried out a great reform program which clearly had political as well as religious overtones (II Chr. 34:8–35:19).

But the author of Kings knows only of the reformation in the eighteenth year of the king (II Kings 22: 3). It is noteworthy, however, that this reformation, too, extended beyond the borders of Judah, and included also the "cities of Samaria" (II Kings 23:19).

There is also a difference in the biblical sources at another point. According to II Kings 23, Josiah removed not only the Assyrian cult, but the Canaanite cult as well. According to the Chronicler only the Canaanite cult was removed. Manasseh had already removed the foreign emblems of worship (II Chr. 33:15). Essentially, however, the Chronicler's picture in 34:3*b*-7 is dependent on II Kings 23.

But is it possible, historically, that as early as *ca.* 628 Josiah exercised control over the Assyrian province of Samaria? The answer to this question depends to a large extent on the date of Ashurbanipal's death, for with his death Assyrian power in the W began to wane. The most likely date appears to be *ca.* 630. This would have provided an opportunity for the subject nations to revolt. The Babylonian Chronicle gives an exact date for the successful revolt of Babylon against Assyria with the accession of Nabopolassar to the throne of Babylon on November 22/23, 626. For a year previously "there was no king in the land." It is clear that from at least *ca.* 627 Assyria was fully occupied in the E. In the circumstances it is quite possible that *ca.* 628, when Josiah came of age, he asserted his independence from Assyria and began a reformation in the land. In the course of time he extended his reform measures to the former N kingdom, as far N as Galilee. Such a course of action would have been impossible unless he also controlled the country politically. It is questionable if he openly broke with Assyria. Rather the picture would appear to be that while still professing loyalty to his Assyrian overlord, he quietly took over the N territory. That an independent Judah should cast longing eyes on the former N kingdom of Israel is altogether understandable. But this shows Josiah in a new light. His goal was a reunited Israel, the restoration of the old Davidic empire.

Josiah's reign was rendered notable, not only because of his reform measures, but also by reason of the discovery of the "book of the law" in the temple. The details of the actual discovery are uncertain and pose many questions. Where was the book found? We are not told either the circumstances of the finding or the place. The most probable explanation seems to be that it was written early in Manasseh's reign. Its author drew upon the lessons of Hezekiah's reformation and prepared a plan over against the time when a suitable occasion should arise to put it into effect. When it was found by Hilkiah some fifty years later, no one knew either its age or its source.

Who was Huldah the prophetess, to whom the deputation went for advice (II Kings 22:14 ff; II Chr. 34:22 ff)? We do not know. Why could not Hilkiah the high priest decide this matter himself? Why did Josiah not go to the temple, as his predecessor Hezekiah had done? Where was Jeremiah at the time? Why was he not consulted? Zephaniah may also have been prophesying at this time. To none of these questions can we give an answer, because of lack of evidence.

The code now forms the kernel of our present book of Deuteronomy. Josiah was also responsible for the collection of the old traditions of Israel from the time of the Conquest to his own day. The whole work of the Deuteronomist was a review of Israel's past history in the light of the great prophetic principle of exclusive loyalty to Yahweh. At the same time it recalled the nation to the great traditions of its classic past, and demonstrated the inevitable sequence of evil-doing and divine punishment. Begun in 622, it was probably not completed for several years. It was revised *ca.* 560, when additions were made to bring it up to date.

The major interest of the Deuteronomist was in the covenant entered into by king and people alike (II Kings 23:1-3). This was followed by a general cleansing of the land from idolatrous worship—a cleansing which included Bethel as well. But in this connection vs. 19 is to be noted, with its statement that "all the shrines also of the high places that were in the cities of Samaria . . . Josiah removed." On his return to Jerusalem a great Passover feast was held (vss. 21-23). II Chr. 35, on the other hand, enters into a minute and detailed description of the Passover feast (vss. 1-19), with special emphasis on the role of the priests, Levites, and singers.

The events of the intervening years till 609 are completely ignored in the biblical record. But great changes had taken place meantime in the world outside Judah. The Babylonian Chronicle gives us information about the beginning of that kingdom during the years 626-623. A break follows in the record till 616.* Then we find that the Medes have emerged as the leaders against the Assyrians, while Egypt has allied itself to Assyria. In 614 Assur fell to Cyaxares, the Median king. The city had fallen before the arrival of Nabopolassar, but a treaty was made between the Medes and the Babylonians. In 612 Nineveh fell

Courtesy of the Trustees of the British Museum

30. A chronicle of the years 616-609 B.C., from the chronicles of the Chaldean kings

to a combined assault, and the Assyrians withdrew to Harran, where Ashuruballit II tried to restore the Assyrian Empire. But he was compelled to withdraw from Harran in 610 despite Egyptian reinforcements, and the Babylonians and Medes captured the city, which they held in face of a strong Assyrian-Egyptian attack in 609. Fig. JOS 30.

What was Josiah's part in the events of the year 609? Details are almost completely lacking, but it is clear that Josiah met his death at Megiddo in a vain attempt to preserve his newly won independence by preventing Pharaoh Neco and the Assyrians from joining forces. In all probability he was acting in conjunction with the Babylonians. Neco had urgent business with the Assyrians, but he found his way barred at Megiddo by Josiah. In the ensuing battle Josiah was killed (II Kings 23:29). His servants brought him back to Jerusalem, where he was buried. The Chronicler has a different account of Josiah's death. In the battle he was seriously wounded, but his servants brought him back to Jerusalem, where he died. "All Judah and Jerusalem mourned for Josiah" (II Chr. 35:24*c*).

Josiah was remembered by later generations as one of Judah's greatest kings. "Before him there was no king like him, who turned to the LORD with all his heart and with all his soul and with all his might, according to all the law of Moses; nor did any like him arise after him" (II Kings 23:25). But why then did Jeremiah take so little notice of him? His verdict is given in the sharp contrast which the prophet draws between Jehoiakim and his father (Jer. 22:15-16). Josiah did "justice and righteousness," and "judged the cause of the poor and needy." But perhaps Jeremiah looked beneath the surface and saw that Josiah's real goal was the establishment of a political kingdom.

Bibliography. W. F. Albright, "The Oldest Hebrew Letters: The Lachish Ostraca," *BASOR,* 70 (1938), 11-17, especially 12-13, note 6; C. C. Torrey, "A Hebrew Seal from the Reign of Ahaz," *BASOR,* 79 (1940), 27-28, note 1 on 28-29 by W. F. Albright; M. Noth, *Überlieferungsgeschichtliche Studien* (1943), pp. 3-110; A. Poebel, "The Assyrian King List from Khorsabad," *Journal of Near Eastern Studies,* II (1943), 56-90, especially 88 ff; H. H. Rowley, ed., *Studies in OT Prophecy* (1950), pp. 164 ff; J. A. Montgomery, *The Book of Kings,* ICC (1951), pp. 523-49; M. B. Rowton, "Jeremiah and the Death of Josiah," *Journal of Near Eastern Studies,* X (1951), 128-30; A. Alt, *Kleine Schriften zur Geschichte des Volkes Israel,* II (1953), 250-75, 276-88; F. M. Cross, Jr., and D. N. Freedman, "Josiah's Revolt Against Assyria," *Journal of Near Eastern Studies,* XII (1953), 56-58; W. Rudolph, *Chronikbücher* (1955), pp. 318-33; D. N. Freedman, "The Babylonian Chronicle," *BA,* XIX (1956), 50-60; M. Noth, *Geschichte Israels* (3rd ed., 1956), pp. 246 ff; D. J. Wiseman, *Chronicles of Chaldean Kings* (1956), pp. 5-20, 51-65; G. E. Wright, *Biblical Archaeology* (1957), pp. 172-74.

H. B. MacLean

JOSIAS. KJV Apoc. form of Jeshaiah.

JOSIBIAH. KJV form of Joshibiah.

JOSIPHIAH jŏs′ə fī′ə [יוספיה, may Yahu increase] (Ezra 8:10; I Esd. 8:36); KJV Apoc. **JOSAPHIAS** jō′sə fī′əs. The father of Shelomith, who returned to Palestine with Ezra.

JOSUE jŏs′o͞o ē. Douay Version form of Joshua.

JOT. *See* Iota.

JOTBAH jŏt′bə [יטבה, pleasantness] (II Kings 21:19). A city mentioned only as the residence of Meshullemeth, the mother of King Amon of Judah. It was probably in Judah, but its site is unknown.

JOTBATHAH jŏt′bə thə [יטבתה, goodness *or* pleasantness(?)]; KJV **JOTBATH** jŏt′băth in Deut. 10:7. A stopping place of the Israelites in the wilderness (Num. 33:33-34), where they found a "land of brooks of water" (Deut. 10:7). It may have been in the Arabah, N of Ezion-geber.

J. L. Mihelic

JOTHAM jō′thəm [יותם, may Y complete; Ἰωάθαμ]; KJV NT **JOATHAM** jō′ə thəm. **1.** A Judahite, son of Jahdai, descendant of Jerahmeel (I Chr. 2:47).

2. Youngest of the seventy sons of Gideon (Judg. 9:5; cf. 8:30).

In the massacre of the sons of Gideon by their half brother Abimelech, Jotham escaped by hiding himself. Thereafter Abimelech was made king at Shechem.

When Jotham heard what had happened, he went to the top of Mount Gerizim, S of Shechem, and addressed to the men of Shechem a fable on the trees' anointing a king (Judg. 9:7-15), together with its interpretation (vss. 16-21). The kingship was first offered to the olive, then to the fig tree, then to the vine. All in turn refused the offer on the ground that they had other, more important tasks to perform. This shows the unimportant character of kingship at the time in Israel. Finally the bramble was approached, and accepted. Abimelech is clearly represented under the figure of the bramble. The application follows. Jotham accuses the men of Shechem of having acted in bad faith toward Jerubbaal (Gideon). He had fought for them and risked his life for them. In return they had slain his sons and given the reward to one who was an upstart, because he was their kinsman. Jotham ends his speech with a curse, which turns out to be prophetic. The reaction of the Shechemites is clear from vs. 21. Jotham was compelled to flee for his life.

3. Regent of Judah *ca.* 750-742 B.C.; king of Judah *ca.* 742-735; son and successor of Uzziah (Azariah). His mother was Jerusha the daughter of Zadok.

The name is probably a contraction from Yahuyatom, with omission of the divine name. The root is תמם. It may, however, be derived from יתום, meaning "orphan."

Jotham became king at the age of twenty-five and is said to have reigned sixteen years (II Kings 15:33; II Chr. 27:1). The figure of sixteen years may very well be correct if we include the eight-year period when he acted as regent for his father (II Kings 15:5; II Chr. 26:21). *Ca.* 750 Uzziah was smitten with leprosy. This rendered him unfit to perform his royal duties, and Jotham became regent of Judah (*see* Uzziah 3). The approximate date when this occurred is indicated by I Chr. 5:17, where Jotham and Jeroboam II (who died *ca.* 746) are named as contemporaries. Jotham himself reigned as king for *ca.* eight years.

A curious synchronism occurs in II Kings 15:30, where we are told that Hoshea of Israel became king "in the twentieth year of Jotham the son of Uzziah." This is all the more surprising as the writer of Kings has as yet not dealt with the reign of Jotham. Besides, it contradicts the statement in vs. 33 that Jotham reigned sixteen years, unless to the sixteen years of his own reign is meant to be added the period of his regency. Further, it contradicts II Kings 17:1, where it is said that Hoshea became king in the twelfth year of Ahaz. No adequate explanation of this strange datum has yet been forthcoming.

Of Jotham's building operations the writer of Kings mentions only that "he built the upper gate of the house of the Lord" (II Kings 15:35*b;* cf. II Chr. 27:3*a*). This was in line with the main concern of the Deuteronomist. This upper gate appears to have faced N (cf. Jer. 20:2; Ezek. 8:3; 9:2). The Chronicler tells in addition of extensive building on the wall of Ophel (II Chr. 27:3*b*). This was presumably to strengthen the work on the defense of Jerusalem begun by Uzziah. It is possible that there is here a hint that Jotham extended the city walls—a task which was continued by Hezekiah (II Chr. 32:5) and Manasseh (33:14). Further building also took place in Judah itself. Cities were built in the hill country of Judah, and forts and towers were established on the wooded hills. As in the case of Uzziah, archaeology seems to support this general picture of intense building activity during the eighth century B.C. Jotham's reign was marked by continued prosperity in the land. This view is confirmed in the contemporary prophetic writings of Hosea and Isaiah.

In the military sphere too, Jotham continued to win victories. The Chronicler reports a successful campaign against the Ammonites, who for three years were forced to pay Jotham a very heavy tribute (II Chr. 27:5). This tradition has every appearance of being historical, and may have been at least a partial reason for the Syro-Ephraimitic War. The actual attack on Jerusalem by Rezin the king of Syria and Pekah the son of Remaliah came in the reign of Ahaz, Jotham's son (II Kings 16:5), but already in Jotham's time attacks against Judah by the N allies had begun with the object of forcing Judah to join the anti-Assyrian coalition (II Kings 15:37). Faced by the threat of an Assyrian invasion under Tiglath-pileser III, Aram and Israel forgot their differences and closed their ranks to meet the common foe. Both militarily and economically Judah was perhaps the strongest state in Syria-Palestine at the time, and without her support resistance to Assyria stood little chance of success. But Judah was apparently unwilling to join the alliance.

At Ezion-geber (Elath) was found a signet ring with a seal bearing the letters "ltym" in Hebrew characters—i.e., "belonging to Jotham."* The Jotham in question is almost certainly the son of Uzziah. The omission of any further title, such as "son of the king" or "servant of the king," would be explained if the seal belonged to Jotham, either in his capacity as regent or as king. Archaeology thus confirms the fact that at this time, during the reigns of Uzziah, Jotham, and Ahaz (at the beginning of his reign), Judah exercised control over Elath. Fig. JOT 31.

Courtesy of Nelson Glueck

31. Impression of the seal of Jotham, from Ezion-geber (Tell el-Kheleifeh)

The Chronicler makes no mention of this incident, but it is noteworthy that in the summary of Jotham's reign he tells that Jotham became mighty and speaks of "all his wars" (II Chr. 27:7). This may be a reference to the struggle with Aram and Israel.

Bibliography. N. Glueck, "The Third Season of Excavation at Tell el-Kheleifeh, *BASOR,* 79 (1940), 13 ff, with a note by W. F. Albright, p. 15; M. Noth, *Die israelitischen Personennamen* (1928), pp. 189 ff; G. E. Wright, *Biblical Archaeology* (1957), p. 160; J. Simons, *Jerusalem in the OT* (1952), p. 330.

H. B. MacLean

JOURNEY, DAY'S. *See* Day's Journey.

JOY. The experience of joy, as related to praise and thanksgiving in public worship, or to the quiet confidence of the individual in God, or to the proclamation of God's saving power, is one of the characteristic elements in religious faith as this is described in the Bible.

In the OT thirteen Hebrew roots, found in twenty-seven words, are used primarily for some aspect of joy or joyful participation in the cult. The root which appears most frequently is שמח, the most general term for "joy," either cultic or secular, individual or connected with tumultuous group expression (Exod. 4:14; Ps. 97:1, 12). Other roots are גיל, the usual literary parallel for שמח, and probably connected originally with cultic dance (Ps. 96:11); שיש and אשרי, associated especially with the blessings of prosperity (Ps. 1:1; Isa. 60:15); and רוע, רנן, and הלל, all suggesting shouting or singing in praise of God's power in creation and victory or as part of the more formal pattern of public worship (Ezra 3:10-11; Ps. 100:1-2, 4). Physical expression of joy is often mentioned. Expressions which occur most frequently in connection with the terms for rejoicing are the sounds of singing, shouting, noise, uproar, a loud voice, singing praise; words for musical instruments—the pipe, harp, trumpet, flute, or stringed instruments; or words describing motion—dancing, clapping, leaping, or stamping the feet. The most frequent occasions for joy are feasting and offering sacrifice (Deut. 12:12; Isa. 56:7), celebrating harvest or victory (I Sam. 18:6; Joel 1:16), enjoying prosperity or personal triumph as seen especially in the recovery of health (Ps. 31:7; Isa. 61:3-7); or rejoicing in God as part of public worship (Pss. 33:1-3; 95:1-2).

In the LXX the most common Hebrew term (שמח) is usually translated by εὐφραίνω or εὐφροσύνη, words referring to personal emotion as well as to the occasions for it, especially the joy of feasts or festivals. גיל is usually rendered by ἀγαλλιάω and its derivatives.

In the NT both these terms appear often in connection with joy in God's salvation (I Pet. 1:6) or the joy of eating and drinking or holding festival (Luke 12:19; Acts 7:41), much as they are used in the LXX. The words which appear most frequently in the NT, however, are χαίρω and χαρά, the most common Greek words for joy of all kinds, and καυχάομαι ("to boast, take pride, or rejoice in"). The latter is Paul's favorite term, with which he contrasts man's inclination to boast in himself (Rom. 3:27) with his right to boast in Christ or in his cross (Gal. 6:14; Phil. 3:3). The one real difference between OT and NT attitudes toward joy is that the NT writers go on to the bold statement of joy in suffering as well as in salvation. The OT makes clear that man's cause for rejoicing is in God and not in himself (Jer. 9:23-24). Joy is, however, related primarily to God's triumph over evil, as demonstrated in recovery of health, or in some other victory of national or personal existence. It is in the NT that we find the statement of joy in suffering itself, or in weakness seen in terms of a power of God "made perfect in weakness" (Matt. 5:12; II Cor. 12:9).

Bibliography. A. Wünsche, *Die Freude in den Schriften des alten Bundes* (1896); P. Humbert, "'Laetari et exultare' dans le vocabulaire religieux de l'AT," *RHPR*, XXII (1942), 185-214.
D. Harvey

JOZABAD jō'zə băd [יוזבד, Yahu has bestowed, *same as* יהוזבד, Jehozabad; Ἰώζαβδος; Apoc. Ἰώσαβδος]; KJV JOSABAD in I Chr. 12:4; I Esd. 8:63; JOAZABDUS jō'ə zăb'dəs in I Esd. 9:48. **1.** A Benjaminite from Gederah who joined David's forces at Ziklag (I Chr. 12:4).

2. A military leader of the tribe of Manasseh who deserted Saul to join forces with David (I Chr. 12:20).

3. Another military leader mentioned with 2 *above* (I Chr. 12:20).

4. A Levite who shared responsibility for the temple treasury during the reign of King Hezekiah (II Chr. 31:13).

5. A chief of the Levites during the reign of King Josiah (II Chr. 35:9). The parallel I Esd. 1:9 gives Joram (Ἰωράμ).

6. One of the chiefs of the Levites having charge of the "outside work" of the temple (Neh. 11:16; *see* Temple, Jerusalem), and presumably the same individual mentioned in Ezra 8:33 (cf. I Esd. 8:63) as being in attendance when Ezra delivered the temple treasures from Babylon to the Jerusalem temple. He is perhaps the same Jozabad listed as having married a foreign wife (Ezra 10:23; cf. I Esd. 9:23), and perhaps also the Levite of this name who with others assisted Ezra at the public reading of the law (Neh. 8:7; cf. I Esd. 9:48).

Bibliography. R. A. Bowman, Exegesis of Nehemiah, *IB*, III (1954), 736-37, 777.

7. One of the priests who had married foreign wives in the time of Ezra (Ezra 10:22). In I Esd. 9:22, "Gedaliah" stands apparently for this name (KJV "Ocidelus"; Ὠκίδηλος).

Bibliography. M. Noth, *Die israelitischen Personennamen* (1928), pp. 21, 47, 77.
B. T. Dahlberg

JOZACAR jō'zə kär [יוזכר] (II Kings 12:21). Son of Shimeath, and one of the servants of King Joash who were responsible for his murder. Some Hebrew MSS and the Syr. read "Jozabad" (cf. "Zabad" in the parallel II Chr. 24:26), but "Jozacar" is preferable.

JOZADAK jō'zə dăk [יוצדק, Yahu has been just]. Alternately: JEHOZADAK jĭ hō'zə dăk [יהוצדק] (I Chr. 6:14-15—H 6:40-41; Hag. 1:1, 12, 14; 2:2, 4; Zech. 6:11); KJV JOSEDECH jō'zə dĕk in Hag. 1:1, 12, 14; 2:2, 4; Zech. 6:11; KJV JOSEDEC in I Esd. 5:5, 48, 56; 6:2; 9:19; Ecclus. 49:12. The father of Jeshua the high priest (Zerubbabel's contemporary), and among those carried into Babylonian exile by Nebuchadnezzar (in the above and Ezra 3:2, 8; 5:2; 10:18; Neh. 12:26).

Bibliography. M. Noth, *Die israelitischen Personennamen* (1928), pp. 161-62, 189.
B. T. Dahlberg

JUBAL jōō'bəl [יובל; Ἰωβαλ, Ἰουβαλ] (Gen. 4:21). Son of Lamech; credited by the J tradition with the invention of musical instruments. *See* Music.

JUBILEE, YEAR OF. The final year in a cycle of fifty years, consisting of seven Sabbatical Year periods, or forty-nine years, plus this fiftieth year. The manifestly basic role of the number seven in this reckoning of years and also the perfect parallelism between this fifty-year time unit and the pentecontad, consisting of seven weeks, or forty-nine days, plus an extra day—fifty days in all—suggest strongly that the Jubilee Year had its origin in the pentecontad calendar (*see* Sabbath). Hence, the fifty-year Jubilee period was the ultimate unit of time reckoning of this primitive, agricultural calendar. If so, it would be a reasonable inference that, just as each fiftieth day was celebrated as a sacred day, the עצרת, the "concluding festival," of its pentecontad, so correspondingly the Jubilee Year was also originally of sacred character and marked, in fitting, festal manner, the close of the fifty-year time unit.

While all this is distinctly probable, it cannot be proved; for, although the pentecontad calendar itself is well attested, the Jubilee Year and the fifty-year Jubilee time unit are mentioned, in all Semitic literature, only in the Bible, and there only infrequently and only in postexilic—i.e., relatively late—writings.

The specific name, "Jubilee Year" (שנת היובל; lit., the "Year of the Ram's Horn"; Lev. 25; 27:18, 23-24) or simply "Jubilee" (היובל; Lev. 25; Num. 36:4), unquestionably derives from the word יובל, "a ram's horn" (Exod. 19:13; Josh. 6:5). The narrative in Josh. 6 distinguishes sharply between the יובל and the שופר, the ordinary trumpet, and ascribes to the former greater sanctity and supernatural effect, in that it was carried and blown only by priests and that it was the blast from it, rather than that from the שופר, carried and blown upon by the people at large, which caused the walls of Jericho to fall. In all likelihood the "great trumpet" (Isa. 27:13), a blast from which would inaugurate a new and happier era for conquered and dispersed Israel, was a יובל. All this suggests cogently that the ram's-horn trumpet was of unusual character, used only upon extraordinary occasions and for some particular purpose (cf. Exod. 19:13*b*). Accordingly it is a very probable inference that the "loud trumpet," which was blown upon the tenth day of the seventh month—the New Year's Day of the solar calendar, the official calendar still in the early postexilic period (*see* Calendar)—and thus heralded the commencement of the Jubilee Year (Lev. 25:9-10) and proclaimed "liberty throughout the land to all its inhabitants," was, as is, even though not specifically so stated, clearly implied in vs. 10*b*, likewise a יובל. This year acquired its name just because this unique, fiftieth year was ushered in by this blast upon the יובל, whereas the commencement of ordinary years was signalized by a blast upon only a שופר (II Sam. 15:10; cf. Lev. 23:24; *see* New Year).

The Jubilee Year in principle discharged two primary functions. It effected the automatic release or emancipation of a Jew who, for one reason or another, had at some moment within the preceding forty-nine years become enslaved to a fellow Jew, and likewise the automatic release or return to the original owner or his family of property, whether fields or houses in unwalled—i.e., country—towns, which had been sold to a fellow Jew during the course of a similar forty-nine-year period. Very significantly, the primary legislation for the Jubilee Year is found in the Holiness Code (*see* PENTATEUCH), the earliest stratum of which must be dated to 516 B.C. Furthermore, the original H legislation for the Jubilee Year was extensively reworked and expanded by priestly legislators from the final quarter of the fifth century B.C. onward.

It is readily apparent that this H legislation for the automatic liberation in the Jubilee Year of Jews enslaved to fellow Jews contradicts absolutely the earlier, pre-exilic legislation (Exod. 21:2-6 [C]; Deut. 15:12-18 [D]) for such liberation at the close of six years of servitude. Furthermore, no pre-exilic, Pentateuchal legislation makes any provision whatsoever for automatic restoration to the original owner of property sold to a fellow Jew. Manifestly this H legislation for the Jubilee Year represents an attempt by early postexilic legislators to solve in an altogether unprecedented manner a problem, or even two problems, of distinctly social character, which had found no effective solution throughout the entire pre-exilic period, and which had presumably become acute once again. It may well be that their appreciation of the complete impracticability of the relatively brief, six-year period of enslavement of one Jew to another, which the pre-exilic legislation sanctioned, induced them to provide for a potentially much longer period of such servitude, and so to link this with the Jubilee Year of their ancient, pentecontad calendar, which they still employed extensively for the regulation of agricultural activities and related matters. But certainly, whatever may have been its specific import previously, the Jubilee Year had never before discharged either of the two functions now assigned to it. And, despite the amplification of the original H legislation for the Jubilee Year by later priestly legislators, abundant evidence indicates unmistakably that this legislation never became effective in any manner. The references to it in Num. 36:4 (P) and in Ezek. 46:17 (from *ca.* 450 B.C.), where it is called שנת הדרור, the "Year of Liberty," are entirely theoretical and unrealistic. (Undoubtedly upon the basis of this byname, the "Year of Liberty," for the Jubilee Year, Jos. Antiq. III.xii.3 mistakenly interpreted יובל as meaning "Liberty.") And certainly Neh. 5:1-13 proves definitively that in the third quarter of the fifth century B.C. the automatic emancipation in the Jubilee Year of Jews enslaved to fellow Jews, if it had ever been actually practiced, had already fallen into desuetude.

Under any condition the Jubilee Year period persisted in Jewish usage only as the largest unit of time reckoning and nothing more. Such is its only function in the book of JUBILEES, certainly a Jewish sectarian work, and apparently also in the writings of the so-called Qumran sectaries (Zadokite Document XX.1; 1QS X.8; *see* DEAD SEA SCROLLS). Moreover, in the book of Jubilees a Jubilee period consists of only forty-nine years—i.e., seven sabbatical periods of years. Presumably the forty-ninth year, the final Sabbatical Year of this larger, Jubilee period, functions as the concluding year thereof, while the fiftieth year, the original and true Jubilee Year, is completely disregarded. Furthermore, in the official count of Sabbatical Years in the Maccabean and post-Maccabean periods the Jubilee Year was omitted entirely and the Sabbatical Years followed each other in uninterrupted succession every seven years. Moreover, certain later, rabbinic authorities likewise reckoned a Jubilee period as of only forty-nine years, although the majority adhered, quite naturally, to the biblical reckoning of the period as of fifty years. In rabbinic Judaism and its literature the Jubilee Year had only antiquarian character and import and nothing more. Eventually, as might readily be anticipated, the Jubilee Year became completely obsolete.

Bibliography. F. K. Ginzel, *Handbuch der mathematischen u. technischen Chronologie* (1911), II, 29-32; A. Jirku, *Das israelitische Jobeljahr* (1929).

See also bibliography under SABBATH.

J. MORGENSTERN

JUBILEES, BOOK OF [τὰ Ἰωβηλαῖα *or* οἱ Ἰωβηλαῖοι]. One of the most important books of the PSEUDEPIGRAPHA. It gives a graphic picture of Judaism in the two pre-Christian centuries. Its purpose was to show that Judaism, as it then was, had been the same from the very beginning of known history. It was also concerned to demonstrate that the sacred number seven played a more important part in history than had been before recognized. The whole history of the world is divided into jubilee periods—a plan given to Moses on Mount Sinai. The book is valuable as showing the development of angelology and demonology. Emphasis is also placed on Jewish tenets and customs, and the importance of preserving the difference between Jews and Gentiles is stressed.

1. Title and text. The book was known by various titles: Jubilees; the Little Genesis; the Apocalypse of Moses; the Testament of Moses; the Book of Adam's Daughters; the Life of Adam.

The existing MSS are in Ethiopic, Greek, Latin, and Syriac (*see bibliography*). There are four Ethiopic MSS; the first (fifteenth century) and the second (sixteenth century) are the most trustworthy. The book is completely preserved only in the Ethiopic version. The Greek version, with the exception of a few fragments, is lost. One fragment, which consists of 11:2-21, can be found in Charles's edition of the Ethiopic text. About one fourth is preserved in the Latin version. It is almost of equal value with the Ethiopic, but it has suffered at the hands of correctors. The evidence of a Syriac version is very slight and rests on a Syriac fragment entitled "Names of the Wives of the Patriarchs According to the Hebrew Book Called Jubilees."

2. Date and authorship. Jubilees was written between 153 and 105 B.C. Its historical background reflects the period of the Maccabean hegemony, as under Simon and Hyrcanus. The book is generally regarded as the work of one author. He was probably a Pharisee of the strictest sect or a Levite priest, since he held the strictest views on circumcision, the sabbath, and the validity of the law, and believed in angels, demons, and immortality. He also was a supporter of the Maccabean pontificate. He draws freely upon earlier books and traditions, especially the book of Noah, which he uses in a modified form, and also on the book of Enoch, thus helping us place the dates of certain parts of the book.

3. Purpose and contents. The purpose of the author was to do for Genesis what the Chronicler did for Samuel and Kings—to rewrite the facts in such a way that it would appear that the law was rigorously observed by the patriarchs. He attempts to prove that his own book was a revelation of God to Moses, a supplement to the Pentateuch, which he calls the "first law" (vss. 1-22). His desire was to save Judaism from the demoralizing effects of Hellenism by glorifying the law and picturing the patriarchs as irreproachable; by glorifying Israel and urging her to preserve the separateness from the Gentiles; and by denouncing the Gentiles and also Israel's national enemies. The "Angel of the Presence" reveals to Moses on Sinai the history and religious laws of Gen. 1-Exod. 3 in the form of sermonized translations, or midrashic Targums, which show only favorable practices and omit anything derogatory.

The whole history of the world is divided into "jubilee" periods, cycles of seven times seven (see Lev. 25:8-12). From 2:1-2 the book runs parallel to Gen. 1:1-Exod. 14:31, with midrashic expansion. Jewish tenets are emphasized, and great importance is attached to the observance of feasts. The contrast between Jews and Gentiles is sharply drawn, and Israel is warned to keep separate. The development of angelology and demonology has progressed further than in Enoch. Mention is made of Beliar (1:20; 15: 33) and Mastema (10:8). Much legendary matter is introduced, and anything is omitted that would put the patriarchs in an unfavorable light.

The writer of Jubilees had deep veneration for the Torah; nevertheless, he brings to the interpretation of it the method of apocalyptic, used in Daniel and Enoch. Thus Moses receives revelation from an angel. This was a new way of presenting this material, and it makes Jubilees an original and unique book.

4. Language. Charles believes that the book was written in Hebrew, for the following reasons: (*a*) a book supposed to be written by Moses would naturally be in Hebrew, as it was the sacred and national language; (*b*) the revival of the national spirit is accompanied by a revival of the national language; (*c*) the existing text must often be retranslated into Hebrew in order to explain unintelligible expressions.

Charles C. Torrey believes, on the other hand, that the original language was Aramaic.

Bibliography. R. H. Charles, *The Ethiopic Version of the Hebrew Book of Jubilees* (1895), for a full description of the existing MSS; *The Book of Jubilees* (1902). C. C. Torrey, *The Apocryphal Literature* (1945). *See also* the bibliographies under APOCRYPHA; PSEUDEPIGRAPHA. S. TEDESCHE

JUCAL. Alternate form of JEHUCAL.

JUDA. KJV alternate form of JUDAH; JUDAS; JODA.

JUDAEA. *See* JUDEA.

JUDAH jōō′də [יהודה, *presumably originally a name of a place or a region which has become a tribal name and finally the name of a person* (*cf.* Jehud; *also* Baal-jehud, *which probably was called by the full name* Beth-baal-jehud = house of the local numen of Jehud)]. **1.** The fourth son of Jacob, and the *heros eponymos* of the tribe of Judah. Born to Leah (Gen. 29:35; Matt. 1: 2 ff; Luke 3:33; the folk etymology given in Gen. 29 derives the name from ידה, "to praise"). In all lists of the sons of Jacob, Judah is given fourth position (Gen. 35:23; 46:12; Exod. 1:2; I Chr. 2:1). In the Joseph story Judah plays a special role along with Reuben and Benjamin as the spokesman for the brothers (Gen. 37:26; 43:3, 8; 44:14, 16, 18; 46:28). What the Yahwist narrates in Gen. 38 concerning the experiences of the son of Jacob (alluded to in Ruth 4:12) is, in reality, disguised tribal history.

Judah belongs to that first great wave of Israelite tribes of the so-called Leah group which gradually succeeded in occupying (probably from the S upward) the whole Palestinian hill country, so that finally in the N, Issachar and Zebulun dwelt along with Asher; in the middle, Simeon and Levi; in the S, Judah, with Reuben and Gad. The last two of these traveled farther into the land E of the Jordan. The group, which was consolidated to the S of that strong crossbar of Canaanite cities which extended from Jerusalem through Kirjath-jearim, Aijalon, and others toward Gezer, took over, as did Ephraim later, its name (Judah) from a given geographical location. The actual territory in which it settled was not large. It was the mountain ridge between Jerusalem and Hebron, exclusive of the two cities, a territory *ca.* 15-20 miles in length, still less in breadth, in which, apparently, there were no old cities and which was being cleared of forest to make it usable for agriculture. Genuinely Judean villages in the list of places in Josh. 15, which originates in the time of Josiah, are those of the district of Beth-zur (vss. 58-59) and of Bethlehem (vs. 59 LXX). To the E a natural boundary was set by the E slope of the mountains, the Wilderness of Judah, which was not well suited for settlement. To the N was a political boundary. Jerusalem was first conquered, contrary to Judg. 1:8 (cf. Josh. 15:63; Judg. 1:21), by David and with the mercenaries without the Judeans (II Sam. 5:6 ff). The description of the Judean N boundary, which is derived basically from the period before the kings (Josh. 15:8), is a further unmistakable proof. Furthermore, it is apparent from this that the Judeans, at least in the NE, participated in the settlement of the valley of the Jordan to the S of Jericho (vss. 6 ff). The attempt to expand toward the W led to the downfall of several Judean tribes; this is the sense of the tradition in Gen. 38 which took place in the region of the Canaanite cities Adullam (Khirbet esh-Sheikh Madhkur) and Timnah (Tibnah). Judah certainly did not get down into the coastal plain (Judg. 1:18-19). Judah's expansion had to be toward the S.

But this expansion toward the S signified a new stage in development; Judah became Great Judah, at first a loose alliance of tribes, then a state; for this "drive toward the S" led to a mingling, not only in settlement but also in blood, of the Judean hill clans with other, related clans—from the desert, but, nevertheless, not "Israelite." Above all, it brought to the Judean element the political leadership in an area which exceeded the bounds of its own former territory considerably. Here, where, in the SW, Simeon had found refuge after the catastrophe at Shechem, at the edge of the cultivated land (as the Edomites, the Moabites, and the Ammonites, who also belonged to an earlier wave, had done in the E) several smaller tribes had established themselves, apparently even before the Israelites, who were therefore compelled to take up land farther inland. No one of them possessed much more than the territory of an old city-state: Caleb, the territory around Hebron (Josh. 14:5 ff; 15:13-14; Judg. 1:20); Kenaz, SW of it, the territory around Debir (Khirbet er-Rabud; Josh. 15: 15-19 =Judg. 1:11-15); Cain, SE of it, the territory around Arad (Tell 'Arad; Judg. 1:16). The position of Jerahmeel's property cannot be determined, but the remnant of Simeon in the neighborhood of Zephath-hormah (Tell es-Seba'; Judg. 1:17) completes the survey. The old notices in Judg. 1 are all already colored by the fact of Great Judah, but they still give evidence of the way in which the tribe of Judah, at least politically, developed toward the S beyond its area proper. The Chronicler in I Chr. 2:4 made use of materials concerning these relationships which have been investigated but slightly up to this time. That the S expansion was successful for Judah is not only based on the gradually developing political superiority of the larger group, but it also has a very real presupposition in the common property which still bound all these groups from the time of the period in the wilderness. Even in David's time there was on the steppe S of Beer-sheba a Negeb of Judah in addition to a Negeb of the Jerahmeelites, of the Kenites, and of the Calebites (I Sam. 27:10; 30: 14). Similar economic interests created a feeling of solidarity which ultimately became very active politically in the establishment of the Judean state. This community of interest may have appeared first in the religious sphere in the formation of an amphictyony of six groups. Two famous ancient places presented themselves immediately as common shrines—Mamre, on the border between Judah and Caleb; and Beer-sheba, centrally located between Cain, Kenaz, Simeon, and Jerahmeel.

From the beginning of the occupation of land, the tribe of Judah went through a special development. Because the way to the N was blocked, it oriented itself toward the S. It is not surprising, therefore, that Judah is not mentioned in the Song of Deborah. The rest of the oldest poetry shows Judah in various stages of its development. The item on Judah in the Blessing of Moses sees Judah from the point of view of the N as an insignificant tribe, for whom a double favor from Yahweh is solicited (Deut. 33:7):

> Hear, O LORD, the voice of Judah,
> and bring him to his people.
> With thy hands contend for him,
> and be a help against his adversaries.

This sounds as though it were about to succumb and is a request for assistance to the tribe and for union with its brothers in the N. The statement stems from a relatively early period (Minor Judah). Very different is the Blessing of Jacob, in which, apparently, several Judean sayings are combined (Gen. 49:8-12). The first (vs. 8) lauds Judah's authority in the circle of the brothers—i.e., Caleb, Cain, etc.; the second (vs. 9), his lion's strength. The third, which extols Judah's economic wealth (vss. 11-12; Judah, not the ruler proclaimed in vs. 10, is the subject), compares the tribe in vs. 10 to one who wields the scepter, and holds out the prospect of the kingdom. Here Great Judah finds itself close to that political consolidation with which the name Judah acquired a new political significance.

As a tribe Judah appears later only occasionally in literature, as in the lists of the Priestly Code, and, in accordance with its importance, often in the first position (Num. 2:3, 9; 7:12; 10:14; 34:19; in the traditional spot after Reuben and Simeon in 1:7; 13:6; also 1:26-27; 26:19-22 [cf. vss. 15-18, where Gad is inserted in order at least to give Judah the leadership of the S camp]). P's skilled craftsman Bezalel was a Judean (Exod. 31:2; 35:30; 38:22). In the list of the Levite cities Judah takes the lead (Josh. 21:4, 9 or 11; I Chr. 6:65 or 55—H 6:50 or 40), but it is Great Judah which is meant, as also, for the most part, in the sections of the Deuteronomic historical work which treat of the time before the kings, where one might still mention the border description of the "tribe of the people of Judah" (Josh. 15:1 ff) and the list of cities appended to it (vss. 21 ff), and also in passages like Deut. 34:2; Josh. 18:5, 11, 14; 19:1, 9; Judg. 1:4, 8-10; 15:10-11; 17:7; I Sam. 11:8; 15:4; 22:5; 23:23; 30:16-26 (cf. vss. 27 ff); II Sam. 1:18; 2:1, 4. The tribe of Judah in the narrower sense may be thought of, in addition to Deut. 27:12, in the tradition of Achan's theft (Josh. 7:1, 16-18) and perhaps in Judg. 1:2 ff, where Judah, as in 20:18, appears as the foremost champion; but it is surely not meant in I Kings 12:20; II Kings 17:18, although the expression "tribe of Judah" occurs there once more. The Chronicler naturally knows the tribe of Judah in lists (I Chr. 12:24—H 12:25; 27:18) and likes to designate the inhabitants of the S as "Judah and Benjamin" (I Chr. 9:3-4, 7; 12:16—H 12:17; II Chr. 11:1, 3, 10, 12, 23; 14:7; 15:2, 8-9; 17:14, 17; 31:1; 34:9; Ezra 1:5; 4:1; 10:9; Neh. 11:4, 25, 31, 36). But it is clear that he is always thinking of Great Judah, a fact which is most clearly evident in the genealogies of I Chr. 2:4. The same is true of the prophets, although Mic. 5:1 may constitute an exception. In Ezek. 48:7, Judah in the N, like Benjamin in the S, acquires the position of honor as the immediate neighbor of the sanctuary. The middle one of the gates of the N is named for Judah as the middle gate in the E is named for Benjamin (vs. 31). In the Psalms the tribe of Judah appears in 60:7—H 60:9 (=108:8—H 108:9); 68:27—H 68:28; 78:68; the actual tribe is no longer intended anywhere in the Psalms.

In the NT, Judah ranks at the head of the list of the sealed (Rev. 7:5). Elsewhere the tribe is mentioned in Heb. 7:14; 8:8; Rev. 5:5.

For the territory of Judah, *see* TRIBES, TERRITORIES OF, § D1. *See* bibliography under ASHER.

K. ELLIGER

2. A Levite (Ezra 3:9); same as HODAVIAH in Ezra 2:40 and JODA in I Esd. 5:58.

3. A Levite (Ezra 10:23 [LXX B Ιοδομ; LXX A Ιεδομ]; I Esd. 9:23).

4. A Benjaminite (Neh. 11:9); son of Hassenuah.

5. A Levite (Neh. 12:8).

6. A prince of Judah (Neh. 12:34).

7. A priest and musician (Neh. 12:36; lacking in the LXX).

8. An ancestor of Jesus (Luke 3:30). L. HICKS

JUDAH, HILL COUNTRY OF [הר יהודה]; KJV MOUNTAIN OF JUDAH. A district in Palestine which included the central ridge of hills S of the hill country of Ephraim between the Shephelah on the W and the wilderness of Judah on the E. The KJV rendering "the mountain of Judah" is misleading. In view of the fact that the territory included a ridge of hills, most modern English translations use "hill country of Judah" (see Josh. 11:21; 20:7; 21:11; II Chr. 21:11; 27:4). The extent of the district is not defined in the OT. Hebron was located in it (Josh. 20:7; 21:11); and although it is called merely "hill country" in Josh. 15:48; Jer. 32:44; 33:13, these passages make it clear that the district included a number of cities.

Probably the same area is referred to in Luke 1:65, where the "hill country of Judea" (ὀρινός τῆς 'Ιουδαίας) is mentioned.

See also PALESTINE, GEOGRAPHY OF.

W. L. REED

JUDAH, KINGDOM OF. *See* ISRAEL, HISTORY OF.

JUDAH, WILDERNESS OF [מדבר יהודה] (Judg. 1:16; Ps. 63); JUDEA, WILDERNESS OF [ἡ ἔρημος τῆς 'Ιουδαίας] (Matt. 3:1). On the basis of the OT passages, the wilderness of Judah is usually located in the desolate area in the Negeb of S Palestine, extending to the W shore of the Dead Sea.*

Copyright: The Matson Photo Service

32. The Wilderness of Judah: in the background are the mountains of Moab and the Dead Sea; in the foreground are Bethphage and Bethany.

In Matt. 3:1 the wilderness of Judea is identified only as the place where John the Baptist started his preaching. Parallel passages in Mark 1:4; Luke 3:2 refer to the area merely as "the wilderness." The context of these passages suggests that the district was in the Jordan Valley at the N end of the Dead Sea. Fig. JUD 32.

See also PALESTINE, GEOGRAPHY OF.

W. L. REED

JUDAISM jōō′də ĭz′m ['Ιουδαϊσμός]; KJV THE JEWS' RELIGION. The belief and life of the Jews. The word does not refer to dogma, but to the total way of life of the Jewish community, elected by God and in covenant relationship with him. The beliefs and practices of the Judaism of Jesus' day differed in various Jewish sects and parties—among them PHARISEES; SADDUCEES; ZEALOTS; ESSENES. But all Jews believed in the one God of Israel and acknowledged the LAW.

The Greek word 'Ιουδαϊσμός occurs only in Gal. 1:13-14. The RSV adds "to Judaism" after "converts" in Acts 13:43, and this surely represents the meaning of the verse.

B. H. THROCKMORTON, JR.

JUDAIZING jōō′dĭ īz′ĭng. The Greek word meaning "to Judaize," ἰουδαΐζειν, occurs in the Bible only in Gal. 2:14, where Paul tells of his rebuking Peter for refusing to eat with the Gentile members of the church at Antioch. It is implied that the food being eaten did not conform to Jewish food laws, and that if the Gentiles had accepted these Jewish laws and practices, Peter would have eaten with them. Peter's action, Paul declares, was, in effect, an attempt to "compel the Gentiles to Judaize"—i.e., "live like Jews" (so RSV).

This is the meaning of the word in the few other cases where the Greek word occurs. The LXX of Esth. 8:17 says that "many of the Gentiles had themselves circumcised, and Judaized [lived as Jews] for fear of the Jews." Plutarch (*Cicero* 7.6) tells of a freed slave Caecilius, who was said to be "guilty of Judaizing"—i.e., living as a Jew. Josephus tells of a Metilius who saved his life by promising "that he would Judaize even to circumcision," and he also tells of a time in Syria when the Syrians, though they thought they had rid themselves of the Jews, "had under suspicion those who were Judaizing"—i.e., Gentiles following Jewish ways (War II.xvii.10; xviii.2). Ignatius condemns professing Christians "living until now according to Judaism" and says "it is wrong to talk of Jesus Christ and yet to Judaize"—i.e., live as a Jew (Magn. 8:1; 10:3). In the Acts of Pilate 2:1, Pilate tells the Jews that "you know that my wife is god-fearing and more than ever Judaizes with you."

Thus every use of the Greek word applies to Gentiles who live in the Jewish way. It is not enough to say that they "sympathize with" the Jews, or "imitate" the Jews. They "live as Jews"; this is what the word means. As applied to Gentile Christians, it means that they accept the Mosaic law as binding and observe Jewish customs. (The modern use of the word to mean "inculcate or impose Judaism," which *Webster's New International Dictionary* gives as one meaning, has no basis in the Greek usage.)

Paul maintained that to compel Gentile Christians to "live as Jews" was to lead them to abandon the gospel. The demand that the Gentiles "Judaize" was made in Antioch and Jerusalem (Acts 15:1, 5), as well as in Galatia and probably in other churches founded by Paul. The claim was that the law was of permanent validity; it prescribed these Jewish practices; and no one could be a member of God's people and be saved without observing them. Paul argued that no one can keep the law; a totally new way of salvation is needed; and God's free grace in Christ provides it. Gentiles must not be asked to "live as Jews" as a condition of salvation. The issue is treated in Paul's letters to the GALATIANS and the ROMANS and at the COUNCIL OF JERUSALEM.

F. V. FILSON

JUDAS jōō′dəs [Ἰούδας=יהודה, Judah]. **1.** See JUDAS MACCABEUS.

2. Son of Chalphi, and one of the commanders of Jonathan's army (I Macc. 11:70). When the troops all fled in battle at Hazor, Mattathias and Judas stood with Jonathan.

3. Son of Simon, and nephew of Judas Maccabeus. Following the death of Judas Maccabeus, the younger brother Jonathan was placed in command. After Jonathan's imprisonment (I Macc. 12:29-53), Simon, second eldest of the "glorious brothers," having been military governor of the coastal district, was elected leader (13:1-11); upon him and his descendants was conferred permanent authority as high priests. When, however, troops under Cendebeus invaded Judea, Simon called in his two older sons, Judas and John, and said: "I have grown old, and you by His mercy are mature in years. Take my place and my brother's, and go out and fight for our nation" (16:3). Though they defeated Cendebeus, Judas was wounded in the battle. Invited to a banquet at Jericho, Judas and another brother, Mattathias, together with their father, Simon, were treacherously killed by their brother-in-law and host, Ptolemy, the son of Abubus (16:11, 15-17).

4. An otherwise unidentified Jew (considered by some to be JUDAS MACCABEUS); one of the senders of a letter addressed to Aristobulus and the Jews in Egypt (II Macc. 1:10).

J. C. SWAIM

5. Judas of Galilee, a Jewish leader who, with a Pharisee named Zadok, promoted a rebellion against Roman authority in A.D. 6 or 7, when ARCHELAUS was deposed and the legate P. Sulpicius Quirinius (*see* QUIRINIUS) ordered a census taken, thus outraging the religious sensibilities of many Jews. He is mentioned with THEUDAS in Acts 5:37 as an example of futile rebellion against Rome. Josephus speaks of him, his sons, and descendants, in Antiq. XVIII.i.1-6; XX.v.2; War II.viii.1; xvii.8-9; VII.viii.1. Acts calls him a Galilean, and Josephus does the same in several passages, but in Antiq. XVIII.i.1 the latter says that he was from Gamala in Gaulanitis, across Lake Tiberias from Galilee proper; "Galilee" may be used in a broad sense, or that province may have been the seat of his rebellion. Josephus credits Judas with having founded the "fourth sect" of the Jews in his day (in addition to Pharisees, Sadducees, and Essenes), composed of violent revolutionaries and assassins with religious motivation, later known as Zealots (*see* ZEALOT) and Sicarii. Josephus (unlike Acts) says nothing about the death of Judas, but he records the violent end which befell his sons Jacob, Simon, and Menahem, and his grandson Eleazar. Josephus also mentions a Judas, son of Hezekiah, who revolted against Rome in 4 B.C. (War II.iv.1). It is impossible to say with certainty whether he was the same man as Judas of Galilee.

Bibliography. J. S. Kennard, Jr., "Judas of Galilee and his Clan," *JQR,* 36 (1945-46), 281-86; W. R. Farmer, *Maccabees, Zealots and Josephus* (1956).

6. A person mentioned in Matt. 13:55; Mark 6:3 as one of Jesus' brothers, in whatever sense that term is to be understood (*see* BROTHERS OF THE LORD). His name is given as Judas in the passages cited above, but in the shortened form JUDE in Jude 1, where the man in question has traditionally been taken to be the Lord's brother. He could not have been the same man as Judas the son (or brother) of James, who is one of the Twelve in Luke 6:16; Acts 1:13 (cf. John 14:22), since he was not a follower of Jesus during his earthly ministry.

In the absence of more exact information, we may assume that Judas' attitude toward Jesus was like that of James and the other brothers. They were critical or indifferent at first (Matt. 12:46-50 and parallels; Mark 3:21, where "relatives" is better than the RSV "friends"; John 7:5 says explicitly that his brothers did not believe in him). After the Resurrection and the appearance to James (I Cor. 15:7) the brothers became ardent Christians and leaders in the early church (Acts 1:14; I Cor. 9:5).

There is an interesting tradition concerning the grandson of this Judas, preserved by Hegesippus and quoted by Eusebius in Hist. III.19-20 (1-6), 32 (6). According to it the Roman emperor Domitian (A.D. 81-96) became afraid of a messianic uprising among the Jews, and ordered that the descendants of David be put to death. Some heretics reported two grandsons of Judas, and they were brought into the emperor's presence. They admitted Davidic descent, but explained that Christ's kingdom was heavenly and angelic, not of this world. When Domitian learned that they were small landowners and saw that they bore every evidence of hard work, he dismissed them and brought the persecution to an end. Later they became "rulers of churches."

F. W. GINGRICH

7. Judas Iscariot, one of the twelve apostles; the betrayer of Jesus.

This apostle is certainly the most enigmatic person in the gospel story. The meaning of his name (or designation), his background, his character, his motive in betraying Jesus, the manner of his death—all are riddles now quite insolvable.

The most diverse explanations have been offered for the name Iscariot: "man from Kerioth"; "the assassin" (from σικάριος); "man from Sychar" (i.e., "a Samaritan"); "man of Issachar"; "man from Jericho"; "carrier of the leather bag" (*scortea*); "false one, liar, hypocrite." By far the commonest interpretation is the first—"man from Kerioth"—in part because of the D reading in John 12:4; 13:2, 26; 14:22 (ἀπὸ Καρυώτου), seemingly comparable names in Josephus (Ἴστοβος—איש טוב) and the Talmud, and the Johannine reference to Judas' father as Simon Iscariot (6:71; 13:26). The uncertainty concerning the location of Kerioth (see Josh. 15:25; Jer. 48:24; Amos 2:2)—usually identified with modern Qaryatein in S Palestine—the strangeness in Greek texts of the untranslated word for "man" (איש), if the designation means "man of Kerioth," and the fact that the popular language was Aramaic, not Hebrew (hence why איש?), have been adduced as arguments against this understanding of the designation. Quite plausible is the suggestion that the term is Aramaic, from a root meaning "false one, liar, hypocrite" (שקר), an apt epithet on the lips of Aramaic-speaking Christians for the betrayer of Jesus. If the name, in spite of difficulties, is taken to mean "man from Kerioth," it may be held that this apostle was thus designated because he was the only Judean among the Twelve.

That Jesus chose Judas because he saw possibilities of nobility and great usefulness in him may be assumed. One scholar hazards the suggestion that he was the brother of Mary, Martha, and Lazarus, whose complaint at the waste of ointment was motivated by a purely selfish interest (John 12:4-6). But whether Judas belonged to this family beloved by Jesus or to some other, the love that knew no bounds reached out to him for good. At the beginning Judas must have responded with enthusiasm to Jesus and his proclamation.

It is probable that Judas was an important member of the apostolic circle. The lists (Mark 3:16-19; Matt. 10:2-4; Luke 6:14-16; Acts 1:13) put his name last, undoubtedly because of the betrayal, but the fact that he was treasurer of the group (John 12:6; 13:29) and may even have been reclining alongside Jesus at the Last Supper (13:21-26), contradicts the lowly listing. Eastern church tradition held that his name once stood higher in the apostolic list (third or sixth).

The motives behind Judas' betrayal of Jesus are unascertainable. So obscure or so obviously slanted are the accounts of Judas' treachery and death that some scholars have doubted the historicity of the betrayal. But the primitive church would hardly have invented an episode so infamous and derogatory to one of the apostles. With the passing of time Judas' name became more and more blackened (the Fourth Gospel practically identifies him with Satan and the Antichrist: John 6:70; 17:12), but the crescendo in hostility should not undermine belief in the historicity of the event itself.

Did Judas' enthusiasm for Jesus gradually cool? Was he disappointed because Jesus failed to strike decisively at his enemies and the enemies of the nation—in fact, even on occasions ran away from them? Did he stumble over Jesus' indifference to many points of the law and perhaps resent his association with the wrong people—tax collectors and sinners? Was the supreme disappointment the failure of Jesus to manifest his power in the Holy City, after he had doggedly journeyed there for a showdown appearance? Did Judas at the last sincerely believe Jesus a false messiah, a deceiver of the people, who according to the law (Deut. 13:1-11) should be done away with?

Or was Judas by the betrayal attempting to force Jesus into a display of power so that the religious and political authorities would be convinced of his messiahship? If he was the Messiah, could he not call on a legion of angels to deliver him? Thus all doubt would be cleared away, and the nation would be won to him.

Perhaps Judas was simply avaricious and dishonest, a man who could not resist an opportunity for personal gain (John 12:4-6; cf. Matt. 26:14-16). But the sum of money appears trivial for a treachery so heinous, and the motive superficial. Nothing short of disillusionment over Jesus, from whom he had hoped so much, and a corresponding zeal to uphold the law and institutions of Judaism against the attacks of false prophets and messiahs would seem to explain a deed so radical.

Exactly what information Judas delivered to the religious authorities is unclear. Was it that Jesus had accepted anointing at Bethany and thus openly claimed messiahship (Mark 14:3-11)? Or was it simply the place of his nocturnal retreat, so that he could be apprehended quietly, without exciting his many sympathizers and supporters (vss. 1-2)? The latter supposition better accords with the gospel representation.

Whether Judas partook of the bread and wine at the Last Supper has been much debated. From Luke one would conclude that he did (Luke 22:14-23). The other gospels leave the matter in doubt. Judas' participation in the covenant fellowship would, of course, raise theological problems. In view of the tendency in the tradition concerning Judas to reduce him to the status of a devil, Luke's more theologically difficult and less tendentious account of the Supper may contain historic fact. If Judas participated in this holy sacrament, his subsequent deed appears the more reprehensible.

Judas' end is shrouded in the same obscurity as the events leading up to it. According to Mark and Luke, Judas offered to betray Jesus to the chief priests and received from them a promise of money. Matthew has them pay Judas on the spot—thirty pieces of silver—a detail derived from Zech. 11:12. Matthew later pictures Judas as repenting and offering to return the money to the priests. On their refusal to accept it, Judas throws down the money in the temple and proceeds to hang himself. The priests, unwilling to put "blood money" in the temple treasury, purchase with it a potter's field, which becomes known as the "Field of Blood." A widely divergent story is told in Acts (1:18-19), according to which Judas himself buys the field and through a headlong fall (or swelling up?) is disemboweled.

The manner of the death of Judas was much commented on by early Christian preachers and writers, who introduced all sorts of gruesome details to make the death more horrible.

Both biblical and postbiblical accounts of the death appear to have been influenced by OT and apocryphal stories of the demise of evil men (cf. the LXX account of the death of Ahithophel [II Sam. 17:23]; Antiochus Epiphanes [II Macc. 9:7-18]; Nadan [the Story of Ahikar]; etc.), or at least by a loose tradition concerning the way traitors and villains should die. The two NT accounts agree only that Judas died violently as a consequence of his perfidy and that a plot of ground in Jerusalem was purchased and became known as the "Field of Blood" as a result of his acts.

Tradition has located this field at the confluence of the Kidron, Tyropoeon, and Hinnom valleys.

Bibliography. J. R. Harris, "Did Judas Really Commit Suicide?" *AJT*, IV (1900), 490-513. D. Haugg, *Judas Iskarioth in den neutestamentlichen Berichten* (1930). K. Lake, "The Death of Judas," in F. J. Foakes-Jackson and K. Lake, eds., *The Beginnings of Christianity*, V (1933), 22-30. C. C. Torrey, "The Name 'Iscariot,'" *HTR*, XXXVI (1943), 51-62. R. B. Halas, *Judas Iscariot* (1946). P. Benoit, "La mort de Judas," *Synoptische Studien* (*A. Wikenhauser Festschrift;* 1953), pp. 1-19.

K. Lüthi, *Judas Iskarioth in der Geschichte der Auslegung von der Reformation bis zur Gegenwart* (1955); "Das Problem des Judas Iskariot—neu untersucht," *Evangelische Theologie*, 16 (1956), 98-144. B. Gärtner, *Die Ratselhaften Termini Nazoräer und Iskariot* (Horae Soederblomianae, IV; 1957).

8. According to Luke 6:16; Acts 1:13, the son or brother of James, and one of the twelve apostles.

Matt. 10:3; Mark 3:18 have "Thaddaeus" (Western texts have "Lebbaeus") instead of this name. The Textus Receptus in Matthew has "Lebbaeus called Thaddaeus."

Luke probably supplies the true name of this apostle. Thaddaeus (from a root meaning "breast nipple"?) and LEBBAEUS (from a word meaning "heart"?) may be descriptive designations of the apostle, introduced to avoid confusion with the traitor and because of the odium attached to his name. The "Judas (not Iscariot)" of John 14:22 is possibly this apostle.

Bibliography. J. R. Harris, *The Twelve Apostles* (1927), pp. 28-44; V. Taylor, *The Gospel According to St. Mark* (1952), pp. 233-34; R. Bultmann, *Das Evangelium des Johannes* (14 *Aufl.*, 1956), p. 481. E. P. BLAIR

9. The man to whose house (on the street called "Straight") in Damascus Paul was brought in his blinded condition after his conversion experience (Acts 9:11). It was here that Ananias found him and restored his sight. Judas may have been a Christian; if not, he was not hostile to Christianity.

10. Judas Barsabbas, one of two leading members of the Jewish Christian church in Jerusalem who were commissioned by that church to carry a message to the churches in Antioch, Syria, and Cilicia, acquainting the Christians there with the decision of the COUNCIL OF JERUSALEM that there should be no strife between Jewish and Gentile Christians (Acts 15:22, 27). In 15:32, Judas and Silas are called prophets (*see* PROPHET IN THE NT); they not only brought the news of the decision to Antioch, but preached to the church as well. The name of Judas Barsabbas is also to be found in the spurious vs. 34.

It is not impossible that Judas Barsabbas and the Joseph Barsabbas of Acts 1:23 were brothers; this is especially probable if Barsabbas means "son of Sabbas" or some such name; further, they were both members of the Jewish Christian group at Jerusalem. If the name means "son of the sabbath," the two men may simply have been born on the sabbath.

Bibliography. H. J. Cadbury, *The Book of Acts in History* (1955), pp. 97-98, 119 and references there.

F. W. GINGRICH

11. KJV form of JUDAH 1 in Matt. 1:2-3; KJV Apoc. form of JUDAH 3.

JUDAS MACCABEUS măk'ə bē'əs. Leader of the Jewish revolt against Antiochus, and most renowned of intertestamental heroes.

1. Background
2. Campaigns
3. Characteristics
4. Significance

1. Background. Judas was the heir of a family tradition which regarded piety and patriotism as identical. He was the third son of Mattathias, a priest who, having "moved from Jerusalem and settled in Modein" (I Macc. 2:1), watched with horror the encroachments of Antiochus: the plundering of the temple, the introduction of foreign customs (symbolized by wearing the "Greek hat"; II Macc. 4:12), the defiling of the altar, the peaceful words designed to smooth the way for innovation and invasion, and outrage committed upon women and children (Jos. Antiq. XII.v.4). When the invaders offered Mattathias and his sons a supposedly flattering opportunity to become "friends of the king," Mattathias replied that even if everyone else departed from the religion of the fathers, he and his family would not "desert the law and the ordinances" (I Macc. 2:21).

When a collaborationist offered sacrifice according to the king's command, Mattathias slew him on the altar, and the revolt was on. Mattathias and his sons withdrew to the hills and rallied an army. When some in hiding were slain by the invader because of their refusal to fight on the sabbath, the decision was made to do battle whenever the enemy invoked it. In a farewell address, the aging Mattathias recounted the frequent deliverances God had wrought in history for his faithful people, then committed the leadership to his third son: "Judas Maccabeus has been a mighty warrior from his youth; he shall command the army for you and fight the battle against the peoples" (I Macc. 2:66).

2. Campaigns. Those who gathered round Judas "gladly fought for Israel" (I Macc. 3:2), but he who had taken command of the armies found himself beset from every quarter. When Apollonius came with a "large force from Samaria to fight against Israel," Judas not only roundly defeated him but also "took the sword of Apollonius, and used it in battle the rest of his life" (vs. 12). At Beth-horon, Judas with a small force put to rout a large Syrian army under Seron. Antiochus, seeking needed revenues in Persia, entrusted half his army to Lysias and commanded him "to wipe out and destroy the strength of Israel and the remnant of Jerusalem" (I Macc. 3:35). Entrusting command to Ptolemy, Nicanor, and Gorgias, Lysias sent forty thousand infantry and seven thousand calvary against Judah; these troops were reinforced by men from Syria and the land of the Philistines. At Emmaus, Judas routed picked troops under Gorgias, and at Beth-zur he defeated mercenaries and chosen men under Lysias.

The way was now cleared for cleansing the temple of its defilement. Taking Mount Zion, Judas replaced the desecrated altar with one made of unhewn stones; "rebuilt the sanctuary and the interior of the temple, and consecrated the courts" (I Macc. 4:48); and completely refurnished the sanctuary, providing it with curtains, lamps, and holy vessels. The rededication ceremony took place "on the twenty-fifth day of the ninth month." Thus the "reproach of the Gentiles was removed" (vs. 58).

But other Gentile groups still harassed, and Judas fought with the sons of Esau, the sons of Baean, the sons of Ammon, and the Nabateans. He campaigned against Timothy in Gilead, and fought also at Hebron and Ashdod. After battles at Beth-zechariah and the citadel, Lysias agreed to make peace, but his successors conspired with Jewish rebels under Alcimus to carry on the conflict. Judas defeated

Nicanor, but lost his own life at Elasa in an engagement with reinforced armies under Bacchides.

3. Characteristics. II Maccabees emphasizes the warrior's resourcefulness. Forced into hiding, Judas "kept himself and his companions alive in the mountains as wild animals do" (II Macc. 5:27). In his military campaigns he would set fire to ships and harbors, make surprise appearances, and attack under cover of night. The words he addressed to his troops "filled them with good courage and made them ready to die for their laws and their country" (8:21; cf. 15:11, 17). Judas, however, never boasted in his own achievements, but believed himself to be an agent of God's deliverance.

Before battle at Mizpah he and his men fasted and "put on sackcloth and sprinkled ashes on their heads, and rent their clothes" (I Macc. 3:47), and his prayers before battle are sometimes reported (I Macc. 4:30-33; II Macc. 15:22-24). At battle's end he and his men "blessed the Lord who shows great kindness to Israel and gives them the victory" (II Macc. 10:38). His rallying cry was: "It is better for us to die in battle than to see the misfortunes of our nation and of the sanctuary. But as his will in heaven may be, so he will do" (I Macc. 3:59-60). II Maccabees represents him as miraculously aided in his exploits by "appearances which came from heaven to those who strove zealously on behalf of Judaism" (2:21).

4. Significance. Judas was careful to observe the provisions of the law regarding classes exempt from military service (I Macc. 3:56) and exemplary in carrying out all the duties of piety, remembering even on his expeditions to send sin offerings to Jerusalem (II Macc. 12:43). One of the enemy generals observed of him and his men "how ready they were either to live or to die nobly" (I Macc. 4:35). In words not unlike those of John 21:25, the author of I Maccabees says of Judas: "The brave deeds that he did, and his greatness, have not been recorded, for they were very many" (I Macc. 9:22). He bequeathed to his people a legacy of courage and devotion to the nation which is not only among the most illustrious in Hebrew annals, but is of significance also for NT study.

The cleansing of the temple from the defilement wrought by Antiochus Epiphanes, carried out at the winter solstice, gave the nation a new festival, that of חנוכה, "Renewal." John 10:22 thus dates one incident in the life of Jesus: "It was the feast of Dedication at Jerusalem." Not alone does the achievement of Maccabeus explain this reference, but it is possible that the spirit of Judas and his brothers lies back of much that takes place in the gospels. Among the followers of Jesus were fierce patriots who longed for a new deliverance from foreign rule. Even after the Resurrection the question still was asked: "Will you at this time restore the kingdom to Israel?" (Acts 1:6). Jesus' driving the money-changers from the temple must have brought to some minds thoughts of an earlier cleansing. Judas' treatment of enemies (e.g., II Macc. 15:28-33), however, is very unlike that enjoined in Matt. 5:44.

When Judas died in battle, the people said:

> How is the mighty fallen,
> the savior of Israel!
> (I Macc. 9:21).

A more sober appraisal is given in 3:3-9:

> He extended the glory of his people.
> . . . .
> all the evildoers were confounded.
> . . . .
> He made Jacob glad by his deeds,
> and his memory is blessed forever.

J. C. Swaim

JUDE, LETTER OF ['Ιούδας, *see* Judas]. A letter claimed to have been written by Jude, brother of James, to the church at large. It belongs to the "Catholic letters," among which it occupies the last place in our canon. The letter itself is an appeal to uphold the faith against heretical dangers and devotes itself mainly to a polemical characterization of the heretics. Although closely related to II Peter, which makes wide use of it in ch. 2, it did not obtain early recognition and had a disputed place in the canon. This may well be due to its negative character, its use of apocryphal literature, and to the general difficulty of identifying its author, the church(es) to which it is addressed, and the heretics under consideration.

The importance of the letter lies in the contribution it makes to the complex story of heresy within the church. It documents the early struggle of "orthodoxy" versus "heresy," which subsequently forced the church to establish the "apostolic" norms of canon, tradition, and authoritative interpretation.

1. Content and purpose
2. Authorship, date, and destination
3. The heretics
4. Canonicity

1. Content and purpose. The author addresses himself to Christendom at large, "to those who are called, beloved in God the Father and kept for[?] Jesus Christ." It seems that the author intended to write about "our common salvation," but he was interrupted by the urgency of the new heretical threat invading the churches. He therefore changes his plans and directs an urgent appeal to "contend for the faith which was once for all delivered to the saints" (vs. 3). The author himself conceives this fight as a sharp attack on the moral and religious character of the heretics. Their moral turpitude (ἀσελγεια) stands under a sure judgment, as is documented by three OT examples (vss. 4-7). Making use of apocryphal citations from the Assumption of Moses and the book of Enoch and employing symbolic language derived from the OT, the author elaborates the judgment theme (vss. 9-12, 14-15). The heretics reject ethical norms and established order. Apart from their sexual misbehavior (vss. 7-8, 16, 18), they scorn angelic powers (κυριότης, δόξαι; vs. 8), they undermine the ordered life of the church (vs. 16), and they undercut the unity of the church by their religious pride (vs. 19). They boast of visions (vs. 8) and want to be counted as pneumatics (vs. 19), but in reality they are the "hidden rocks" in the love feasts of the faithful (vs. 12). In order to counteract them, the faithful are reminded of the apostolic faith: "You must remember, beloved, the predictions of the apostles of our Lord Jesus Christ" (vs. 17). The apostles predicted that these heresies would come. In fact, they are part of the plan of salvation; for they manifest the tribulations at the close of the eschatological timetable (vs. 18). Sticking faithfully to their confession, the Christians must expect the parousia of Christ (vs. 21; cf. vs. 1). Textual confusion makes it difficult to determine precisely the attitude the faithful must take with respect to the heretics and those influenced by them (vss. 22-23). With Jude's preference for triads (vss. 2, 4, 5-7, 8, 11-12, 19), we may assume a threefold reference and read with the RSV (versus the KJV): "And convince [ἐλέγχετε A.C.] some, who doubt; save some [σώζετε], by snatching them out of the fire; on some have mercy with fear, hating even the garment spotted by the flesh." Since the last clause makes no sense, some critics have made the conjecture to read (for ἐλεᾶτε) ἐλάσατε or ἐκβάλετε, clearly pointing to excommunication (cf. I Cor. 5:5; Tit. 3: 10; I Tim. 1:20). An elaborate liturgical doxology forms the end of the letter. The purpose of the letter, then, is twofold: negatively, it wants to indict the heretics for their moral and religious apostasy from the Christian faith; positively, it contends for the trustworthiness of the apostolic faith and tradition, and for the unity of the church with its established order and authority.

2. Authorship, date, and destination. The questions of authorship, date, and destination are interwoven. The letter claims to have been written by "Jude, a servant of Jesus Christ and brother of James." This is not the apostle Judas, referred to in Luke 6:16; John 14:22; Acts 1:13, who is said to be the son of James; but it must refer to Judas the brother of James and Jesus (Matt. 13:55; Mark 6:3; possibly I Cor. 9:5). This Jude is virtually unknown in the history of early Christianity, except for a story attributed by Eusebius to Hegesippus, who relates that there survived of the family of the Lord grandsons of Judas, who were accused before Domitian, but released by him because of their simple way of life (Euseb. Hist. III.20). Scholarship is divided on the issue of whether to acknowledge the letter as a product of the brother of James and Jesus or to view it as the work of an unknown author who assumed the pseudonym Jude. Some even regard "a brother of James" as a later interpolation—to enhance the authority of his letter. The issue cannot conclusively be solved, since destination and date are obscure. Yet internal evidence militates against an early date and against the ascription of the letter to the brother of Jesus. Although the author employs much OT imagery, apocryphal tradition, and Septuagintal terminology, still an early and/or Palestinian origin of the author seems impossible, because:

a) His language is decidedly Hellenistic, and he abounds in *hapax legomena*—some twenty-two, if we include II Peter's borrowings from Jude.

b) His salutation diverges from the common one in apostolic times: "Grace and peace" in Paul (cf. also I Peter and Revelation), and is close to the one used by I Timothy, II Timothy, and II John: "Grace, mercy, and peace," but in this form: "May mercy, peace, and love be multiplied"—a form found in the Martyrdom of Polycarp: "May mercy, peace, and love of God the Father and our Lord Jesus Christ be multiplied."

c) The author speaks of faith as a deposit "once for all delivered to the saints" (cf. also vs. 20: "your most holy faith"), which undoubtedly refers to the apostolic tradition or Christian confession.

d) The author speaks from the standpoint of post-apostolic times: "You must remember . . . the predictions of the apostles of our Lord Jesus Christ; they said to you, 'In the last time . . .' " (vss. 17-18). Now the last time has arrived, which the apostles long ago prophesied, the time of scoffers in the history of salvation. And (vs. 5) he does not include himself within the apostolate, which we might have expected of a brother of the Lord (vs. 17).

On these grounds we have reason to believe that the letter was composed sometime in the beginning of the second century; and that the author was not a Palestinian Jew or a brother of the Lord, but either an unknown person named Jude—through interpolation identified as the brother of James—or a person who adopted a pseudonym to give his letter enhanced authority. In this last case it must remain a riddle why he would have chosen the—at least for us—obscure authority of Jude. The destination of the letter cannot be established, although the description of the heretics makes Asia Minor a likely choice.

3. The heretics. It has been a constant problem for scholarship to identify the heretics alluded to in Jude. An exact identification will probably be forever an impossibility, because of the nebulous way in which Jude describes them. The author is not interested in a description of—or, for that matter, in a debate with—the heretics. His work is an invective characterizing and indicting them in blunt but general ways. Two extremes must be avoided. The first is to see the heretics as early Palestinian Christians who have relapsed into moral laxity. The second is to identify the heretics with the fully developed Gnostic systems of the second century. The first extreme denies the fact that we have to do here with an outspoken heretical scheme of definite Gnostic color; the second extreme reads into Jude too much of an elaborate system based on the Gnostic systems described by Irenaeus, Hippolytus, and Epiphanius. In this way the heretics have been identified in the past with the Carpocratians, the Marcosians, or with unknown groups like the Balaamites or Nikolaites.

The important thing is not to associate the heretics with the name of a well-known heresiarch, but to determine, if possible, what stage of the early Christian movement they may illuminate for us. In this way the place of Jude in the history of the struggle of "orthodoxy" against "heresy" can be evaluated. Since II Peter, which was probably written not too long afterward, appropriates much of Jude, most scholars understand II Pet. 2 as being directed to a similar heresy, although probably somewhat more developed (*see* PETER, SECOND LETTER OF). It is of central importance to recognize with recent scholarship that Gnosticism is not a late offshoot of the Christian gospel, but that a Gnostic climate surrounds the NT from its beginning (*see* GNOSTICISM), and that already Paul had to struggle with Gnostic tendencies in some of his churches (*see* COLOSSIANS). It is probable that we witness in Jude that moment of transition in the struggle of orthodoxy versus heresy in which the church rallies its forces and attempts to drive heretics out of its midst.

The relation of the heretics to the church is not clear. The author describes them in vs. 4 as having "slipped into" the church from the outside; but vs. 12 portrays them as belonging to the church, "hidden rocks" at the love feasts of the Christians. Yet again the reference to "shepherding themselves" (vs. 12) suggests that the heretics are "separatists" who do not submit themselves to apostolic authority. The ambiguous vs. 23 (see the conjecture) may mean that the church is ready to excommunicate them. Notwithstanding their "illegal entrance" (vs. 4), they have gained quite a hearing for their Gnosticizing teachings. The author characterizes their Gnosticism as licentiousness (ἀσέλγεια), which was probably based on their gospel of freedom (ἐλευθερία; II Pet. 2:19; cf. ἑαυτοὺς ποιμαίνοντες in vs. 12). They feel themselves as "spirituals" elevated in a spiritual realm, in which they are free from the moral norms and authorities of this world (vss. 8, 12, 16). As such (vs. 19) they claim special visions (vs. 8) and know themselves separated from the body of believers (vs. 19). This knowledge is based on their claim to be victorious over angelic powers which dominate this created world. At least vs. 8 seems to imply a certain cosmology in which the angels are characterized as the evil(?) powers. The emphasis in Jude on the Judgment and the Parousia (vs. 21[24]) may indicate a teaching of a spiritual resurrection (II Tim. 2:18) and a denial of the Christian judgment and parousia (cf. also ἀφόβως in Jude 12 versus the φόβος of the Christian in vs. 23). It is difficult to determine whether the heretics had a Gnostic Christology. The denial (ἀρνούμενοι) of our only Master and Lord Jesus Christ in vs. 4 may be only a consequence of their perversion of the "grace of our God" into licentiousness. The μόνος reference in vs. 4 (and vs. 25, where it is liturgical) is not strong enough evidence of a Gnostic separation between Christ and the historical Jesus.

On the basis of the otherwise established post-apostolic date of Jude, we should see here, probably, a reflection of the inner-Christian struggle around heresy which with different emphases we see as well in II Peter, the Johannine letters, the Pastorals, Revelation, and Ignatius of Antioch. Since no direct appeal to an established clergy is found in Jude, we surmise it to form a chapter of the struggle with heresy in Asia Minor just prior to the Ignatian epistles. *See* IGNATIUS, EPISTLES OF.

4. Canonicity. Jude, notwithstanding its brevity and its apocryphal references has, in contrast to II Peter, enjoyed a relatively strong position in the regard of the church. The earliest evidence of its existence and authority is in II Peter, where it largely constitutes the second chapter. Although doubts about its authenticity are voiced later by Eusebius and Origen, it is accepted at the end of the second century in three important church centers: Alexandria, Carthage, and Rome. In Alexandria, Clement of Alexandria (190-202) quotes it as a work of Jude (Paed. III.8), and so does Origen (*ca.* 230). In Africa, Tertullian mentions it, but Cyprian omits any reference to it. In Rome it received a place in the Muratorian Canon (*ca.* 190). Eusebius (*ca.* 324) lists the letter as "spurious" and elsewhere as "disputed" (Euseb. Hist. II.23.24-25; III.25.3; VI.13.6; VI.14.1), but Athanasius (367) ends the ambiguity by including Jude as the last one among the seven Catholic letters.

For bibliography, *see* PETER, SECOND LETTER OF.

J. C. BEKER

JUDE THE LORD'S BROTHER. *See* JUDAS 6; BROTHERS OF THE LORD.

JUDEA jōō dē'ə ['Ιουδαία=יהודה]; KJV JUDAEA except in Ezra 5:8. The S part of W Palestine, formerly called JUDAH (1) after the tribe of Judah, which settled there. It lay between Samaria and the Nabatean-Arabian Negeb.

1. The region. The name Judea appears first in Greek, in Ezra-Nehemiah and Maccabees, where it denotes the Jewish state after the Exile. In the Persian period it was a very small area around Jerusalem governed by Nehemiah, extending no farther S than Beth-zur (note the districts named in Neh. 3). Under the Maccabees, Judea achieved its first independence and then adopted an expansionist policy. The Maccabean kingdom of Judea assimilated Galilee, Samaria, and Idumea, and the entire coast except Ashkelon, and the whole length of Transjordan to the borders of Arabia. However, this was not considered an enlargement of Judea, but rather the

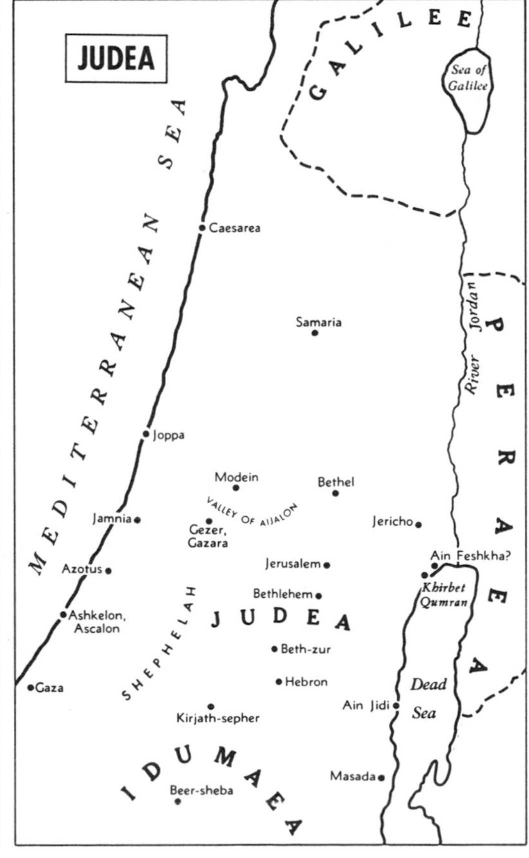

creation of a small empire with Judea ruling over the subject lands. But when the Romans established Herod the Great over much the same territory, he was designated king of Judea, the title referring to the entire realm which he managed to control. But again, when his kingdom was divided, his son Archelaus became the ethnarch of Judea, including only Idumea and Samaria and not the cities of the maritime plain or Galilee or Perea. After Archelaus was removed in A.D. 6, each procurator of Judea controlled the same territory—though no longer from Jerusalem, but from the new capital at Caesarea on the Samaritan coast. It is therefore evident that political circumstances at times extended the area to which the name Judea was applied, although Judea proper was a limited region around Jerusalem. It may be simply described as one of the three main divisions of Palestine: Judea; SAMARIA; GALILEE.

Judea proper was almost a square, *ca.* forty-five miles on a side. It extended from the Jordan and Dead Sea westward to the coast, excluding ASHKELON and at times the other independent coastal cities of Jamnia, Azotus, and Gaza. Along the coast it reached from below Gaza northward to Joppa, and along the Dead Sea from the fortress of Masada (fifteen miles from the S end) northward beyond Jerusalem. It never extended far N of Jerusalem, this boundary remaining stable in contact with the N kingdom of Israel and later with the district of Samaria. There is a natural demarcation along the Valley of Ajalon, N of the rocky outpost of Gazara (Gezer) where the Valley of Ajalon cuts eastward into the mountains, the line of the wadies continuing S of Bethel and N of Jericho to the Jordan. Judea is chiefly "hill country," a mountainous fortress of limestone ranging between 2,000 and 3,346 feet (N of Hebron). This is the traditional "wilderness" or "DESERT," where the population has always been sparse because the springs are few. But where the mountains fall off to the W, there are the broken foothills of the Shephelah "lowland" (I Macc. 12:38), pierced by intermittent valleys which have been the gates to Judea for both friend and foe.

The highways of commerce have always passed around Judea, and only the deliberate visitor has sought access to her mountain trails, along the wadies that break out into the open, both to the W and to the E. Judea's E gates are three oases: 'Ain Jidi (Engedi) on the W-central shore of the Dead Sea, opposite Hebron; 'Ain Feshkha, ten miles S of Jericho, on the Dead Sea (made famous by the sensational DEAD SEA SCROLLS discoveries in caves near QUMRAN), from which the traveler may reach Bethlehem; and Jericho, with its "fountain of Elisha," the direct approach to Jerusalem. There is only one N-S road over the tableland, which passes from Bethel and Jerusalem to Hebron, to Kirjath-Sepher, and to Beer-sheba.

2. Its life. Judea's livelihood was pastoral and self-contained. The shallow and stony soil yielded olives and grapes, figs and citrus, and some grain in the valleys. The Dead Sea yielded common salt, and in later times other minerals such as potash became profitable. But the greatest wealth of Judea was the annual half-shekel temple tax laid upon all male adult Jews by the Torah, which brought large and regular contributions from the Diaspora. The wealth of Judea, as well as its population, was concentrated about JERUSALEM, which alone held the status of a πόλις. The rest of Judea was organized into ten administrative toparchies (Jos. War III.iii.5). During the Greco-Roman period the Sanhedrin sat in Jerusalem, with autonomous power under the Maccabees and delegated power under the Romans. This governing body ruled directly over all Judea, while its prestige reached also to Jewish towns lying outside. The Jewish population of Judea proper has been estimated to be *ca.* 200,000, half of whom resided in Jerusalem. Perhaps a fifth of the Jerusalem residents were priests. Pilgrims in great numbers converged upon Jerusalem, especially for the great feasts. In Roman times a small military guard was assigned to Judea, chiefly in Caesarea and Jerusalem. *See* ARMY.

The town of MODEIN on the N border of Judea proper was where the Maccabean Revolt first flared in 168 B.C. In the Judean hills the war for Jewish independence was fought and won. From this mountain fortress of Judea a small empire was governed by Hyrcanus and Janneus. In Judea also the Herods of conquered Idumea rose to power, with the support of Rome, and ruled when the Christian era began. Jerusalem, ancient fortress and holy city, was the setting for the crucifixion of Jesus of Nazareth—an administrative incident which became central to the Christian faith (I Cor. 2:2). Once again revolt arose in Judea in A.D. 66 and 135, which resulted in the downfall of Jerusalem and the Jewish state. In 451 the Council of Chalcedon created the Patriarchate of Jerusalem, in which Judea became Diocese I. The Muslims seized Judea in 637 and, except for the Crusader kingdom (1099-1187), held it until it was made a British mandate after World War I. In 1948, Palestine was partitioned by the United Nations, and the Shephelah and the Maritime Plain, and a wedge whose point encloses Jerusalem's "new city" on the W, were assigned to the new state of Israel. The remainder of Judea was subsequently incorporated within an expanded Kingdom of Jordan.

Bibliography. E. Huntington, *Palestine and Its Transformation* (1911), pp. 66-103; G. A. Smith, *Historical Geography of the Holy Land* (1931), pp. 243-319. K. W. CLARK

JUDGE [דין (RSV PROTECTOR), פלילי, שפט; KJV אלהים (RSV God); δικαστής, κριτής]. An official with authority to administer justice by trying cases in law; also, one who usurps this authority outside court; in a special sense, the war leader in Israel, having temporal authority and the grace of God to deliver his people in the period between Joshua and David. The patriarchs were judges in their own families (Gen. 21–22; 27; etc.).

Men who served as magistrates were called judges. They served God in their judgment (II Chr. 19:6). Moses appointed judges upon the advice of Jethro (Exod. 18:15). Subordinate judges are also known in the Pentateuch (Num. 11:16-17; Deut. 1:9 ff). During the monarchy the king was the supreme judge (II Sam. 15:2-3). There are a few references to royally appointed judges (I Chr. 23:4; II Chr. 19:5), but even in the monarchy they had only local authority (Deut. 16:18; 17:8-9). The priests also were the judges, and so the sanctuary became a place of judgment (Exod. 33:8 ff; Deut. 17:12). The elders of the city could serve as judges at the gate (Judg. 8: 16; Ruth 4:2; Job 29:7-8). A judge might go from town to town, as did Samuel (I Sam. 7:15). Ezra appointed magistrates and judges. In Hellenistic times the high priest was the supreme judge in place of the king (cf. II Chr. 19:8). Christians and Jews were to avoid taking their quarrels before Gentile judges. In NT times the Sanhedrin was the supreme court for the Jews. As in all places and times, bribing a judge was not unknown (Mic. 7:3; etc.). The parable of an unjust judge is given in Luke 18.

Some men judged their neighbors outside the courts of law. They were condemned for so doing (Gen. 19:9; Exod. 2:14; Lev. 19:15; Acts 7:27). Jesus declared that no one except God should judge (Luke 6:37; cf. Jas. 4:12). Paul, however, requests his hearers to judge his message whether it be true or not (I Cor. 10:15).

The judges (שפטים) were military leaders endowed by the grace of God to deliver and govern his people in time of oppression. In Ps. 2:10 they have parallel authority to kings (cf. Hos. 7:7). These men were not connected with a normal tribal or city government. Perhaps, like the American Indian war chief, their authority was limited to the duration of the crisis. They usually claimed loyalty from the tribes transcending tribal divisions (Judg. 5). Yet their authority could be confined to one tribe, such as that of Samson (Judg. 15). Some of these judges were probably contemporaries of one another. In a way Moses could be called the first judge and Samuel the last. For a list of the judges and the chronological problem, *see* JUDGES, BOOK OF.

God is a judge. He is called a judge because he is the supreme arbiter pronouncing sentences on man (Gen. 18:25; Isa. 33:22; Jas. 4:12). He is the judge of all the earth (Ps. 94:2; Acts 10:42; Rom. 3:6). He judges between the nations (Isa. 2:4). The sinner seeks to avoid God's judgment by loyalty to the covenant (Pss. 7:8; 50:4-5; 82:8; 96:10; Ezekiel *passim;* Heb. 10:30; 12:23; etc.). Jesus is called a judge (Jas. 5:9; I Pet. 4:5). He set a new standard of judgment which, if enforced, would allow no one to be guiltless (John 7:24; *see* SERMON ON THE MOUNT). Jesus claimed during his lifetime to judge for the Father (John 8:16). He judges the whole world (II Tim. 4: 1). At the end of the world (*see* ESCHATOLOGY) he will be assisted by his saints (I Cor. 6:2-3).

C. U. WOLF

JUDGES, BOOK OF. A history of the period between Joshua and Samuel; now found as the seventh book in the OT canon. In the Hebrew Bible it is the second book in the second division, which is known as the Former Prophets, and it is preceded by the book of Joshua and followed by Samuel. In the English Bible, as in the LXX and the Vulg., it is classed among the historical books, and it occupies the same position following the book of Joshua, but is followed immediately by Ruth rather than Samuel.

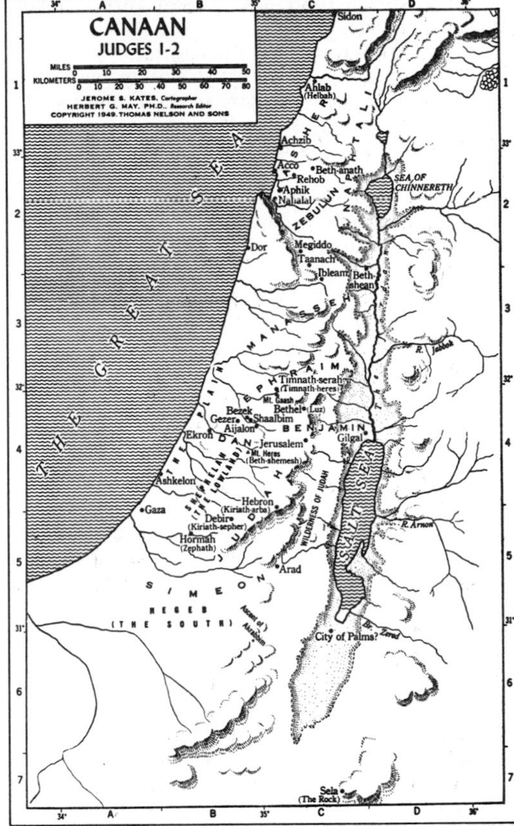

As the only biblical narrative of the Israelites' adventures between their entrance into Canaan and the rise of the monarchy, the book is a valuable historical source for understanding the last stages of the Conquest, the social conditions of the period, intertribal relations and relations with non-Israelites, and the heroes of the era. As essentially religious literature rather than a historical document, the book emphasizes the Spirit of Yahweh as moving through the history of the period and especially in the careers of his chosen heroes or "judges," for whom the book is named.

See map "Canaan: Judges 3–21, Ruth," under RUTH, BOOK OF.

A. Title
B. Text and versions
C. Contents
 1. Preface: Summary of the Conquest
  a. The southern tribes
  b. The central and northern tribes
  c. Religious implications
 2. The careers of the judges
  a. Introduction: The role of the judges
  b. Othniel and Cushan-rishathaim
  c. Ehud and the Moabites
  d. Shamgar and the Philistines
  e. Deborah and the Canaanites
  f. Gideon and the Midianites
  g. Supplement: Abimelech's kingship
  h. Tola and Jair, two "minor" judges
  i. Recapitulation and further introduction
  j. Jephthah and the Ammonites

- *k.* Ibzan, Elon, and Abdon, three "minor" judges
- *l.* Samson and the Philistines
3. Supplement: Two tribal movements
   - *a.* The new sanctuary of the Danites
   - *b.* War against the Benjaminites

D. Composition and literary structure
1. Sources
2. Pre-Deuteronomic editions
3. Deuteronomic edition
4. Final edition

E. Historical value
1. History of the period
2. Literature of the period
3. Social and cultural conditions

F. Religious significance
1. Religion of the period
2. Prophetic criticism of culture

Bibliography

A. *TITLE.* The title "Judges" (שפטים; LXX Κριταί; Vulg. *Judicum*) was given to the book as early as Origen and the Talmud. This name was used because the bulk of the book tells the stories of the chief Israelite leaders who are called "judges" both in the book itself (Judg. 2:16-18) and elsewhere (Ruth 1:1; II Sam. 7:7, 11; II Kings 23:22; I Chr. 17:6, 10; Ecclus. 46:11).

The noun "judge" or "judges" designating an office is used at only two points in the book. It is used once of Yahweh as "the Judge" who should "judge" or "decide" in a territorial dispute between the Israelites and the Ammonites in the days of Jephthah (Judg. 11:27). Six times it is used in an introductory description of these persons as deliverers whom Yahweh would raise up to save the people from their oppressors, during whose lifetime faithful Israel prospered, but at whose death faithless Israel again suffered (2:16-19).

While no person in the book is specifically called a judge, eight are said to have "judged" Israel: Othniel (3:10), Tola (10:2), Jair (10:3), Jephthah (12:7), Ibzan (12:8-9), Elon (12:11), Abdon (12:13-14), and Samson (15:20; 16:31). In each of these cases the connotation of the term, if given at all, is not that of "rendering decisions," but rather that of "delivering Israel from an enemy," usually by war. Thus the judges were not so much legal consultants as champions or heroes vindicating Israel in war and impelled by Yahweh's Spirit. Only in the case of Deborah do both the connotation of the verb form used (שפטה; 4:4) and the statement that "the people of Israel came up to her for judgment" (למשפט; 4:5) indicate that the function was that of judicial decision or arbitration.

However, while the language used emphasizes the savior character of these judges, they usually are said to have "judged" for so many years—from six to forty—most of which time was after the hero's war of deliverance. Of only Jephthah is another term used—viz., "ruler" (קצין; 11:6, 11; RSV "leader")—because he was promised continued rule if successful in driving out the enemy. It is implied that each judge had his period of virtual dictatorship. It is obvious further that the judges were regarded as a series of successive rulers, not a hereditary succession, but each separately appointed by God. Thus in the sense of "ruler" the Hebrew term "judge" (שופט) has been compared to the Akkadian office of a *shapitu,* the Phoenician *shuphetim* or "regents," the Carthaginian *sufetes* or "chief magistrates," and by Livy with the consuls of Rome. *See* JUDGE.

B. *TEXT AND VERSIONS.* The Hebrew text of the book of Judges has been unusually well preserved. Except for the Song of Deborah (ch. 5), its oldest portion, its preservation has been perhaps better than that of any other OT book outside the Pentateuch. The relatively few textual corruptions which are evident are those usual in the centuries-long transmission of the text, caused by confusion or transposition of letters, dittography of words, or omission of words or parts of words, etc.

The Greek translation of the book is unique among all OT books, for the wide divergence between the two oldest and best LXX MSS, Codex Alexandrinus and Codex Vaticanus, is so great that many scholars have regarded them as two distinct and almost, if not wholly, independent translations from the Hebrew. Therefore, since 1882 the standard editions of the LXX, except Swete's, have printed both texts side by side. Most scholars have regarded the Alexandrine text as perhaps more nearly the original, but studies showing that this text was influenced by Theod. render this judgment not conclusive. Some scholars lay stress on the preferred readings of Origen's M, N, L, y, b^2, in his Hexapla, especially as over against the Lucianic recensions.

The Vulg., Syr., and Targums, all representing texts closely akin to the Hebrew consonantal text of the MT, are regarded as being more valuable for their interpretations than for their evidence of the original text.

To date, the MT of the book of Judges is considered to be, on the whole, the best evidence for the original text, unrivaled by any version, although obviously individual passages must be judged on their own merits.

C. *CONTENTS.* The present book of Judges is clearly composed of three parts: (*a*) a preface summarizing the Conquest and the final settlement of the Israelites in Canaan (1:1–2:5); (*b*) the stories of the careers of the judges (2:6–16:31); and (*c*) a supplement recounting two tribal movements—viz., that of the Danites to their new N sanctuary and that of the intertribal war against the Benjaminites (chs. 17–21).

1. Preface: Summary of the Conquest. The prefatory summary of the Conquest and final settlement in Canaan (1:1–2:5) provides a very fitting introduction to the present book of Judges. This is so because it shows how the old Canaanite inhabitants were left in possession of the chief cities. Their religion of Baalism was thus the occasion for the apostasy of Israelites from Yahweh. The failure of the invaders to exterminate both the inhabitants and their gods was the cause of the evils which came upon Israel in subsequent generations.

This section, while fragmentary and possibly a condensation of a longer account, proceeds in fairly orderly fashion. Although many passages are parallel to material found in the book of Joshua, as a whole this record presents a very different picture of the Conquest from that in Joshua. Here the separate tribes conquer territory which has been previously allotted to them, while in Joshua the whole of Israel carries on a united campaign under Joshua's leadership which ends in his parceling out the land to each of the tribes.

The opening words of the book: "After the death of Joshua," indicate that the account is to be understood as a sequel to Joshua's accomplishments. This phrase is obviously an editorial attempt to link the book of Judges with the end of the book of Joshua. The facts that (*a*) at the opening of the second section of the book of Judges (2:6-10) Joshua's concluding act and death are mentioned as though no previous reference had been made to them in the book, and that (*b*) this entire first section has many points in common with scattered references in Joshua, show that here is a condensed, parallel account of the invasion. Much of what is ascribed to Joshua in the previous book is here more accurately stated as accomplished by the respective tribes.

The section is composed of three parts: (*a*) a description of the Conquest by the S tribes (1:1-21); (*b*) an outline of the accomplishments of the central and N tribes (1:22-36); and (*c*) the religious implications of the Israelites' failure to exterminate the Canaanites (2:1-5).

a. The southern tribes. The S invasion (1:1-21) was accomplished by (*a*) the tribe of Judah, together with its clans Caleb and Othniel and friendly non-Israelites, and (*b*) the lesser tribe of Simeon. The first event of the Conquest was Judah's volunteering to fight against the Canaanites and taking Simeon with him (vss. 1-3). The first city conquered was Jerusalem (vss. 4-9). This was done after their defeating ten thousand Canaanites at Bezek and capturing and mutilating Canaanite king Adoni-bezek (cf. Adoni-zedek, king of Jerusalem, in Josh. 10:1-3; LXX "Adoni-bezek" in both references; cf. Melchizedek, in Gen. 14:18). Later in the account it is stated that "the people of Benjamin did not drive out the Jebusites" from Jerusalem (vs. 21; according to the parallel in Josh. 15:63, "the people of Judah could not drive" them out). Although there might have been two destructions of Jerusalem, the city was not conclusively captured for Israel until the days of David (II Sam. 5:6-9).

In the campaign farther S (Judg. 1:9) the two Judean clans of Caleb and Othniel played the chief roles against, respectively, Hebron and Debir (although both were originally captured by Joshua in Josh. 10:36-39). The city Hebron, assaulted by Judah (Judg. 1:10; by Caleb in vs. 20; Josh. 15:13-14), was given to Caleb. Nearby Debir was taken by Caleb's nephew OTHNIEL, who by this exploit became also Caleb's son-in-law (Judg. 1:11-15; paralleled in Josh. 15:15-19). The points farthest S in the campaign were settled by friendly Kenites and by the weaker tribe Simeon (Judg. 1:16-17; no parallel in Joshua).

Contradictory statements are made concerning the Philistine Plain. The first, perhaps a late editorial gloss, inaccurately states that Judah took three of the five Philistine cities, Gaza, Ashkelon, and Ekron (1:18; but they remained unconquered in Josh. 13:3, as part of Yahweh's design to "test Israel," according to Judg. 3:1-4). The second statement correctly points out that the Judeans were confined to the hill country because they could not compete with the superior Philistine iron chariots (1:19; cf. Joshua's advice to the Joseph tribe in Josh. 17:16-18).

b. The central and northern tribes. The story of the settlement of the central and N tribes (Judg. 1:22-36) deals with (*a*) the conquest of Bethel (vss. 22-26); (*b*) the Canaanite strongholds not captured by the Israelites (vss. 27-33); and (*c*) the struggles on the S border of the central territory (vss. 34-36).

The conquest of Bethel, formerly Luz, by the central tribes, the "house of Joseph," followed the reconnoitering of spies and the escape to a northern Luz of a friendly citizen who helped the invaders (vss. 22-26; cf. Rahab and the spies, in Josh. 2; 6:22-25; and Joshua's capture of Ai, possibly really Bethel, in Josh. 8:1-29).

The Joseph tribe of Manasseh did not ("could not" in parallel Josh. 17:11-13) drive out, but eventually made slaves of, the inhabitants of the strong Canaanite fortresses in their area (Judg. 1:27-28). Such was also the action of the Joseph tribe of Ephraim (vs. 29; parallel in Josh. 16:10) and the N tribes of Zebulun, Asher, and Naphtali (vss. 30-33; no parallel in Joshua).

On the S border of the central tribes' territory it was especially the Danites who had difficulty with the local inhabitants, here called Amorites, a synonym for Canaanites (vss. 34-36; cf. Josh. 19:40-48). Although no mention is made of it here, this presages the migration of the tribe of Dan to its N home described in the final section of the book (Judg. 17–18).

c. Religious implications. The final portion of the preface to the book of Judges is a statement of the religious implications drawn from the factual account of Israel's conquest and settlement (2:1-5). The statement is in the form of a declaration by the angel of Yahweh when he moved on from Gilgal, the first camp of the Israelites after they had crossed the Jordan (Josh. 4:19). In their settlements the Israelites had failed to obey Yahweh's command to make no covenant with the inhabitants of Canaan; therefore, these inhabitants would now become adversaries and their gods snares to Israel. The response of the people gave the name to the new location of the sanctuary as Bochim, "Weepers," possibly really Bethel. Thus by this preface, with its tragic conclusion, the groundwork is laid for the role to be played by the "judges" in the body of the book.

2. The careers of the judges. The stories of the careers of the judges which form the body of the book (2:6–16:31) are organized into the following sections: (*a*) an introduction defining the role of the judges (2:6–3:6); (*b*) Othniel and deliverance from Cushan-rishathaim (3:7-11); (*c*) Ehud and deliverance from the Moabites (3:12-30); (*d*) Shamgar and the Philistines (3:31); (*e*) Deborah and deliverance from the Canaanites (chs. 4–5); (*f*) Gideon and deliverance from the Midianites (chs. 6–8); (*g*) a supplement to the Gideon story describing Abimelech's abortive kingship (ch. 9); (*h*) Tola and Jair, two "minor" judges (10:1-5); (*i*) recapitulation and introduction to the last judges (10:6-16); (*j*) Jephthah and deliverance from the Ammonites (10:17–12:7); (*k*) Ibzan, Elon, and Abdon, three "minor" judges (12:8-15); and (*l*) the adventures of Samson and the beginning of deliverance from the Philistines (chs. 13–16).

Of the thirteen persons included, six whose careers are related in some detail and whose role as deliverers is emphasized—Othniel, Ehud, Deborah, Gideon, Jephthah, and Samson—are usually classified as the "major" judges. Six who are little more than mentioned—Shamgar, Tola, Jair, Ibzan, Elon, and Abdon—are called the "minor" judges. The thirteenth, Abimelech, is recognized as supplemental to the story of Gideon.

However, this customary classification is not that suggested by the order of the judges' appearance in the book itself. Provided with the framework of a traditional chronology and apparently numbering exactly twelve, one from each tribe, these heroes were understood to be a succession of inspired leaders, all God-appointed except for self-appointed Abimelech. Perhaps the shadowy figure of SHAMGAR is really a replacement for Abimelech, whose conduct was unworthy of a judge. *See* § E1 *below*.

a. Introduction: The role of the judges. The general theme of the stories of the judges is that Israel's historical experience, from the beginning of Joshua's leadership to the end of Samson's days, was a series of cycles of successive stages: Israel's faithfulness to Yahweh during the days of the leader; their apostasy to the Baals after his death; Yahweh's punishment of permitting oppression by an enemy; the people's cry for deliverance; Yahweh's answer of sending a judge as deliverer; Israel's faithfulness during the days of the judge; their apostasy after his death; Yahweh's punishment; etc. The principles of this theme, which are to be illustrated in the successive stories of the judges, are stated and elaborated in the introduction (2:6–3:6).

This introduction opens with almost exact repetition of the conclusion of the story of Joshua as told in the previous book (2:6-9; cf. Josh. 24:28-31). Then when, after Joshua's death, the new generation arose which had not experienced Yahweh's deeds for Israel—obviously the crossing of the Jordan and the conquest under Joshua—the trouble began (Judg. 2:10). The faithfulness known under Joshua disappeared, and the cycle of apostasy, oppression, prayer, and deliverance was begun.

In addition and in some contradiction to this main theme are the following subsidiary themes: Because of the Israelites' persistent failure to keep their covenant with Yahweh after Joshua's death, Yahweh deliberately left the Canaanite nations in the land instead of driving them out. Thus subsequently these nations could become the means by which Israel might learn the power of Yahweh through their experience of victory in war. On the other hand, these peoples were definitely the means by which Yahweh tested his people's faithfulness to him. Since they intermarried with the peoples, who are enumerated in this introduction, and they served their gods, the Israelites failed the test. Hence the need of judges.

In accord with this introductory explanation there appears at the beginning of the account of each major judge, at least in some form, this characteristic formula: "The people of Israel did what was evil in the sight of the LORD, forgetting the LORD their God, and serving the Baals and the Asheroth. Therefore the anger of the LORD was kindled against Israel, and he sold them into the hand of . . . ; and the people of Israel served . . . [so many] years. But when the people of Israel cried to the LORD, the LORD raised up a deliverer" (3:7-9, 12, 14-15; 4:1-3; 6:1, 7; 13:1). Before the story of Jephthah this formula is enlarged. *See* § C2*i below*.

The career of each of the major judges except Samson was distinguished by successful deliverance of Israel from an enemy: Othniel from Cushan-rishathaim, Ehud from the Moabites, Deborah from the Canaanites, Gideon from the Midianites, and Jephthah from the Ammonites. Although the life story of each was very different, each was a military leader whose army achieved victory, except for the woman Deborah, whose military leadership was that of being the power behind the action. Only Samson was unique, as a one-man army who succeeded only in beginning deliverance from his foe, the Philistines. The notable features of the account of each of these heroes may be briefly summarized. For detailed discussion, consult the separate articles on each of the judges.

b. Othniel and Cushan-rishathaim. The first-mentioned judge, Othniel (3:7-11), appears as prime example of the philosophy of history just concluded in the introduction to all the judges (2:6–3:6). Because of Yahweh's anger at his people's apostasy, they suffered under Cushan-rishathaim. Then in response to their cry, Yahweh specially raised up this charismatic leader; and, as he was empowered by the Spirit of Yahweh, Othniel's "hand prevailed over" the enemy, and "so the land had rest forty years."

Earlier in the book of Judges, Othniel had been introduced—the only judge, be it noted, to be mentioned prior to this main body of the book—in the story of his capture of Debir and his thus winning his Judean uncle Caleb's daughter as bride (Judg. 1:11-15; *see* § C1*a above*). As he is the only judge clearly from a S tribe, and as his story is told in the typical formula with no peculiar, authenticating details, some think him to have been a fiction in order to place a Judean hero at the first of the list of judges. On the other hand, he may well have been a historical figure, the head of a Judean clan comparable to the Calebites, who saved S Judean clans from the invasion of a powerful foreign ruler sweeping down from the Upper Euphrates region. *See also* CUSHAN-RISHATHAIM.

c. Ehud and the Moabites. The story of the second judge, Ehud (3:12-30), has the ring of an old and authentic tradition. This left-handed Benjaminite delivered his people from an eighteen-year oppression of the Moabites by treacherously assassinating their king, Eglon, and cutting off the escape across the Jordan of the Moabite army of occupation. Although he is not called a judge, the God-inspired nature of Ehud's career is probably indicated by his association with the "sculptured stones" near Gilgal (vss. 19, 26; cf. 2:1).

d. Shamgar and the Philistines. Of the six very brief accounts of the so-called minor judges, the one about Shamgar is unique in that he is the only one mentioned twice (3:31; 5:6), and the only one described as delivering Israel by an exploit—viz., killing six hundred Philistines with an oxgoad. Also the reference to Shamgar in 3:31 is awkward, for the immediately following beginning of the Deborah account (4:1) clearly implies that there was no deliverer between Ehud and Deborah. Apparently for this reason some Greek MSS omit the reference to Ehud in 4:1 and repeat this reference to Shamgar after the similar anti-Philistine exploits of Samson (i.e., after 16:31). Because of these uncertainties some scholars consider Shamgar to be an editor's invention, replacing dishonorable Abimelech in order to keep the number of judges at twelve. On the other hand, Shamgar may have been a local twelfth-century-B.C. Galilean hero victorious over some now unknown foe.

e. Deborah and the Canaanites. Unique in the book of Judges is the fact that the story of the third major judge, Deborah, appears in two forms. The first is prose (ch. 4), and the second, poetry (ch. 5). The latter, commonly called the Song of Deborah, is an ode of victory perhaps contemporary with the events. The prose and the poetry both purport to tell essentially the same story of two Israelite heroines: Deborah, prophetess, judge, "mother in Israel," who spurred the military leader Barak on to victory; and Jael, the "wife of Heber the Kenite," who assassinated the fleeing enemy general. However, the differences between the two stories are as instructive as their similarities.

In the prose narrative the enemy is Jabin, "king of Canaan," the commander of whose army is Sisera; in the poem Sisera is not a general but leader of a confederation of Canaanite kings, and Jabin is not mentioned. In the prose account some ten thousand foot soldiers from Zebulun and Barak's tribe of Naphtali are involved, but according to the Song six tribes bordering on the Plain of Esdraelon, where the conflict took place, put forty thousand men into the fray. The prose narrative speaks of Deborah as a prophetess carrying on the judicatory activity of a judge under her sacred palm tree, then summoning Barak to his task, and finally accompanying him in the battle when he has refused to do his duty otherwise; while Deborah and Barak are together the singers of the Song, in which she, "mother in Israel," is summoned to sing, and he to lead away captives. In the prose Barak's troops charge down from Mount Tabor; the Song speaks only of Taanach, the waters of Megiddo, and the Kishon—a torrent sweeping away the enemy chariots.

Most scholars regard the two accounts as differing sharply concerning the fate of fleeing Sisera; the prose narrative tells of his treacherous murder at the hands of Jael while in exhausted sleep, and the poetry vividly pictures his being struck down by the woman while unguardedly drinking the curds she has brought. The prose account ends with the eventual destruction of Jabin; the remarkably authentic poem, which begins with a vivid portrayal of the difficult social situation preceding the struggle and appropriate praise or blame to the various tribes for their participation or nonparticipation in the battle, concludes with an unforgettable picture of Sisera's queen mother consoling herself at her son's delay, and a prayer.

Deborah, then, is the only one of the judges clearly cast in more than one role as judge (*see* § A *above*). In the prose account she is judge in the sense of making judicial decisions at a sacred location. While not herself a "deliverer," as were the other major judges, according to both accounts she is the constant inspiration behind and with the military leader Barak. Both her functions are obviously God-inspired. The result is not deliverance from an invader, as in the case of the other major judges, but stopping the last full-scale native Canaanite uprising against the Israelites and winning the all-important Plain of Esdraelon.

f. Gideon and the Midianites. The story of the fourth major judge, Gideon, is probably composite, the longest narrative of those judges who were military leaders (chs. 6–8). It opens with an account of annual Midianite raids and the warning of a nameless prophet who implied that these raids were permitted by Yahweh because of ungrateful Israel's apostasy from him. The call of Gideon is related, first, in the appearance to him of an angel of Yahweh, and, second, in Gideon's breaking down his father's Baal altar and receiving the name Jerubbaal, and then having his call verified by a sign of wet and dry fleece. His rout of the camp of supposedly 135,000 Midianites was accomplished through divinely suggested strategy with an unbelievably small force of 300 men. His pursuit of the Midianite fugitives resulted, first, in capturing and beheading Midianite princes Oreb and Zeeb by jealous Ephraimites, and, second, in Gideon's blood-revenge slaughter of Midianite kings Zebah and Zalmunna and construction of an ephod for permanent memorial. Although a wealthy local potentate of central Palestine, Gideon modestly refused the offer to inaugurate a hereditary monarchy, for Yahweh alone should be ruler (but for the sequel story of Abimelech, *see* § C2*g below*). Gideon was the true charismatic leader, peculiarly favored with special revelations and unusual power. He succeeded in completely delivering Israel from the annual Midianite raids. Thus he was doubtless the ideal judge.

g. Supplement: Abimelech's kingship. The story of Abimelech (ch. 9) is a supplement to the narratives of Gideon, in this section called only Jerubbaal. Abimelech, son of Gideon by his concubine in Shechem (8:31), persuaded fellow Shechemites to finance the murder of his seventy half brothers from the Baal-berith temple treasury and make himself king. Jotham, the one son of Jerubbaal who escaped being murdered, recited an old fable of the trees' election of a bramble bush and applied it with devastating effect to Abimelech. True to Jotham's interpretation of the fable, "God sent an evil spirit between Abimelech and the men of Shechem," so that the latter deprived their abortive king of his revenue. Abimelech was subsequently able to put down a revolt engineered by Gaal, to destroy Shechem, and to burn its tower, but in an immediately following campaign against Thebez, twelve miles away, Abimelech's three-year reign ended with his ignominious death. His tragic story is concluded with the moral that his fate and that of Shechem were retribution for the crime of murdering the seventy sons of Jerubbaal-Gideon.

That this turbulent period in Israel's life contained such a three-year abortive attempt at local kingship as that of Abimelech is historically probable. Since, however, Abimelech's rule was in no way divinely inspired and his character was unsavory, he was never regarded as a judge. Thus his possible place in the roll of judges was perhaps taken by Shamgar. *See* § C2*d above*.

h. Tola and Jair, two "minor" judges. Of the five minor judges other than Shamgar, two, Tola and Jair, are mentioned (10:1-5) as having "judged Israel" successively over a forty-five-year period between Abimelech and Jephthah, the fifth major judge. The typical brief formula describing the judge's career mentions only his name, his genealogy or location, his length of service, and the place of his burial. The additional detail about Jair's "thirty sons who rode on thirty asses" and their "thirty cities" probably is a note to point out the judge's wealth and wide influence beyond his clan. On these minor judges, *see also* § C2*k below*.

i. Recapitulation and further introduction. Before the Jephthah story the characteristic formula introducing each major judge (*see* § C2*a above*) is enlarged to a recapitulation of the preceding history and a lengthy introduction to the last five judges (10:6-16). This passage restates the theme of the introduction (2:6–3:6). It lists seven foreign gods into whose worship the Israelites have successively fallen and, therefore, seven foreign nations into the hands of whom Yahweh has sold his people until they have cried for deliverance. As special attention is given in this passage to oppression by the Ammonites and the Philistines (vss. 7-9), the section seems to have been intended to introduce the subsequent stories of both Jephthah and Samson.

j. Jephthah and the Ammonites. The story of the only major judge from the E Jordan territory, Jephthah of Gilead, who as fifth major judge delivered Israel from the Ammonites (10:17–12:7), is not only preceded by the long introduction just described. It also contains a long interpolation (11:12-28) which purports to be Jephthah's diplomatic negotiations with the enemy Ammonites, but is actually an account concerning the Moabites, based on Num. 20–22. Unlike the other judges, Jephthah, a man exiled because of illegitimate birth and for years leader of an outlaw band, was called in crisis because of popular demand and was promised permanent position as "chief" or "ruler" if successful in completing his mission (Judg. 10:17–11:11). Upon his consecration in a solemn ceremony (11:11), "the Spirit of Yahweh came upon Jephthah" (vs. 29). When his work was crowned with success, he, in faithful fulfilment of a vow to Yahweh, sacrificed his only child, a virgin daughter, after she had been given time to bewail her virginity and thus establish an Israelite custom (vss. 29-40). Unlike Gideon, who appeased jealous Ephraimites with flattery, Jephthah had them massacred, when at the fords of the Jordan their dialect mispronunciation of the password SHIBBOLETH betrayed them (12:1-7).

k. Ibzan, Elon, and Abdon, three "minor" judges. The brief accounts of the last three minor judges, Ibzan, Elon, and Abdon (12:8-15), like those of Tola and Jair (*see* § C2*h above*), are given with the simple formula: "After him [so and so] of [such and such] judged Israel; and he judged Israel [so many] years. Then [so and so] died, and was buried at [such and such]." As in the case of Jair (10:3-5), Ibzan and Abdon were evidently men of peculiar prestige, as indicated by their large families and notable possessions.

While some interpreters consider these minor judges to be unhistorical inventions to fill chronological space, others regard this uniquely brief information as based on official records about the office of judge in premonarchical Israel.

l. Samson and the Philistines. The account of the last major judge, Samson the Danite, is most unique in all the Bible (chs. 13–16). It is a cycle of folk tales about a superhumanly strong hero who as a one-man army persistently pestered the nearby Philistines. These stories were adapted to religious motivation by understanding Samson's strength to have been the result of a prenatal Nazirite vow and his exploits and heroically tragic end to have been the beginning of Yahweh's plan for delivering Israel from Philistine oppression.

According to the stories Samson was born as the child promised by an angel to a long-time barren woman who kept the vows of a Nazirite (ch. 13). In connection with his intended marriage to a Philistine woman, Samson, moved by sudden power from Yahweh, tore a lion apart, propounded a riddle about the experience, and took personal revenge by igniting Philistine crops with live-fox-tail torches (14:1–15:8). His exploits provided two place names, the "Hill of the Jawbone" and the "Spring of Him Who Called" (15:9-20). He interrupted a night with a Philistine harlot to pull up and carry away the gates of Gaza nearly forty miles (16:1-3). In illicit love with Delilah he toyed with his sacred vow and lost his hair, his power, his eyes, and his freedom (16:4-22). In a final act of heroism he pulled the temple of Dagon down on his own head and so killed more Philistines in his death than in his whole life (16:23-31).

Unlike the stories of the other judges, the Samson cycle includes riddles, poetic fragments, and folk tales. The characteristic formula of introduction appears only in very brief form (13:1). The typical concluding formula: "And he judged Israel . . . years," appears twice (15:20; 16:31*b*), thus possibly indicating that the cycle originally concluded with ch. 15.

The cycle of adventure stories of this folklore hero, whose exploits merely began Israel's deliverance from the Philistines, closes the stories of the judges and opens the way for the subsequent careers of Samuel, Saul, and David in I–II Samuel.

3. Supplement: Two tribal movements. The concluding section of the book of Judges is the account of two tribal movements, the migration of the Danites and their setting up of a sanctuary in a new N home, and a bitter intertribal war against the Benjaminites (chs. 17–21).

It is notable that this section, which follows immediately after the Samson stories, contains no introductory statements to tie it in with the rest of the book. It simply begins with the story: "There was a man of the hill country of Ephraim." The only expression common to the section is the notation: "In those days there was no king in Israel; every man did what was right in his own eyes." This observation appears four times: soon after the opening of the story (17:6); in briefer form when the tribe of Dan is introduced (18:1*a*); at the transition to the story of the Benjaminites (19:1*a*); and finally in full at the conclusion of the section, which is also the end of the present book of Judges (21:25).

Apparently this concluding section of the book is a supplement to illustrate the tragic results of the relative anarchy which existed when there was only tribal authority and custom—a situation corrected by the subsequent rise of the monarchy. A secondary motif in the section is the significant role of the Levites, as a Levite plays the chief role in each of these tribal affairs. In the first story a certain Levite was raised from private priesthood to become first tribal priest of the Danite sanctuary. In the second, another Levite, his honor injured by the Benjaminites, was vindicated by "all Israel."

a. The new sanctuary of the Danites. The story of the Danites' move to the N and the founding of their sanctuary (chs. 17–18) begins with the simple account of Micah's household shrine with its cultic objects and his replacement of his son as priest with a Levite who would know better how to win Yahweh's favor by performing the proper religious rites (ch. 17). Five Danite spies, originally assured of success in their reconnoitering of land to the N by the Levite's consultation of his oracle, led six hundred warriors to Micah's home, where they stole both his cult objects and his Levite and took them to their new sanctuary at Laish (ch. 18).

The priest's pleasure at his being promoted from his position as priest to a family to that of the officiant for a whole tribe provides significant insight into the development of Israelite priesthood. Thus the tribe of Dan, or a substantial portion of the tribe, even though by thievery, established in its new location a sanctuary whose cult equipment had proven efficacy and whose trained priesthood traced its ancestry back to Moses.

b. War against the Benjaminites. The account of the bitter war against the Benjaminites (chs. 19–21) begins with the reason for the struggle: A certain Levite traveler, on his way home with his repossessed and reconciled concubine, passed up Jerusalem, city of foreigners, to stay in friendly Ephraimite territory; but the Benjaminites of Gibeah not only failed to give him the proper hospitality; instead, like the Sodomites (Gen. 19), they abused his concubine until she was dead; whereupon the Levite sent the twelve pieces into which he had ritually divided her body (cf. Saul in I Sam. 11) throughout all Israel (Judg. 19). Aroused to revenge by the Levite's appeal and the Benjaminites' refusal of their ultimatum that the culprits of Gibeah be handed over, the Israelites, although surprisingly defeated in the first two encounters, finally burned Gibeah and ravaged much Benjaminite territory (ch. 20). When, however, it was understood that the great slaughter of the tribe of Benjamin and the irrevocable oath against intermarriage with Benjaminite women made possible the extinction of the tribe, the Israelites found a way to repopulate Benjamin by seizing virgins from Jabesh-gilead, which naturally had not participated in the struggle against its relative, Benjamin, and by permitting Benjaminites to capture other maidens at the annual festival at Shiloh (ch. 21).

With such obviously rugged primitivity in both these supplemental narratives of tribal adventures, it is small wonder that the book of Judges ends, not with any summary, but with only the cogent comment: "In those days there was no king in Israel; every man did what was right in his own eyes" (21:25).

D. *COMPOSITION AND LITERARY STRUCTURE.* The present book of Judges is chiefly the product of the Deuteronomic historians of the exile period. However, the strikingly different literary features of each of the three parts of the book, as discussed in the previous section, demonstrate the composite nature of the book. It has no clear unity, nor is there scholarly agreement as to the successive phases of its composition. The following may be a relatively accurate account of its origin and composition.

1. Sources. Back of the present narratives in the book lie, first of all, various oral hero stories. These may have circulated at local centers. Such were the stories of tribal warrior heroes, Benjaminite Ehud of Gilgal, Manassite Gideon of Ophrah, and Gileadite Jephthah of Mizpah, and the tales of the folkloristic Danite hero Samson of Zorah. The story of the migration of the Danites (chs. 17–18) probably originated from traditions at their N sanctuary.

The Song of Deborah (ch. 5) was probably first sung not long after the events it memorializes, in the twelfth century B.C. The recognized antiquity of this masterpiece suggests that other traditions may have received their first written form as narrative poems, transcriptions of a poetic oral tradition, perhaps composed and written down by the tenth century B.C. Jotham's fable (9:7-15) and Samson's riddles (14:14, 18; 15:16) have long been regarded as early poetic fragments used by later prose narrators. Other examples may be: 6:17-18, 30-31; 14:3, 16; 16:6, 15, 17, 23-24. Besides these written poetic traditions there may have been such prose compositions as the earliest form of the summary of the conquest of Canaan, now found in 1:1–2:5.

2. Pre-Deuteronomic editions. It seems likely that at least some of the above-named sources were combined into a single book, possibly in editions with varying contents, sometime between the tenth and seventh centuries B.C. The exact contents of this pre-Deuteronomic book it is impossible to determine, and the question as to whether it is continuous with the J and E sources of the Hexateuch is an unsolved problem. Some scholars have attempted detailed analysis into the strands of material of the Pentateuchal J and E documents and their redactors. Others have seen only general division of the stories of such heroes as Gideon and Jephthah into earlier and later narratives such as the sources of the books of Samuel.

The pre-Deuteronomic book of Judges must have contained in some form the stories of Ehud, Deborah, Gideon, Abimelech, Jephthah, and Samson (i.e., most of 3:12-30; chs. 4–5; 6:11–8:28; 8:29–9:57; 10:17–12:7; chs. 13–16, omitting the Deuteronomic formulas; *see* § D3 *below*), as well as brief references to Shamgar, Tola, Jair, Ibzan, Elon, and Abdon (3:31; 10:1-5; 12:8-15). A summary of the Conquest and settlement (1:1–2:5) and narratives of the migration of the Danites and the war against the Benjaminites (chs. 17–21) in some form must also have been in the pre-Deuteronomic book, for these introductory and concluding sections of our present book of Judges contain evidences of early composition.

3. Deuteronomic edition. It is generally agreed that the central core of our present book of Judges (2:6–16:31) was given its form by the Deuteronomic editors of the seventh and sixth centuries B.C. The philosophy of these editors is most clearly seen in the introduction provided for the stories of the judges' careers (2:6–3:6; *see* § C2*a above*). The binding framework upon which the respective stories were hung was a characteristic formula detailing the usual cycle of apostasy, oppression, prayer, and deliverance (3:7-9, 12, 14-15; 4:1-3; 6:1, 7; 8:28, 33-35; 13: 1), which was enlarged into a long recapitulation and further introduction at the opening of the story of Jephthah (10:6-16; *see* §§ C2*a, i, above*). The account of the peculiarly southern hero Othniel may be the addition of these editors, as his story is told only in the typical language of the formula (3:7-11). *See* § C2*b above*.

That this edition of the book deliberately omitted the old summary account of the Conquest (1:1–2:5) seems clear from the fact that the Deuteronomists' introduction (2:6-9) connects directly with the end of the book of Joshua (Josh. 24:28-31). It may also be that the Song of Deborah (Judg. 5), the summary references to the minor judges (3:31; 10:1-5; 12:8-15), the last section of the Samson cycle (ch. 16), and the stories of the Danite migration and the Benjaminite war (chs. 17–21) were intentionally omitted, for there is no mark of the Deuteronomic formulas in these sections.

4. Final edition. Our present book of Judges may be the product of possibly late-sixth-century-B.C. restoration of sections of the pre-Deuteronomic book rejected by the Deuteronomists, as suggested above, with a few editorial changes. Thus the core of the book (2:6–16:31) is probably essentially as it left the hands of the Deuteronomic editors.

According to most scholars, the introductory summary of the Conquest providing the preface to the book (1:1–2:5) bears no marks of the restoring priestly editors' redaction. The concluding supplement (chs. 17–21), however, may have been added by postexilic priestly redactors from ancient tribal traditions which the Deuteronomic editors had deliberately omitted. Possibly Deuteronomic loyalty had forbidden even the mention of the N sanctuary of Dan, apostate though it was, or such an unsavory episode as the Benjaminite war. Probably the early postexilic editors restored the rejected material, including the Danite claim to a priesthood of Mosaic origin which had lasted until the Exile (18:30). The mark of these priestly editors' hands may be such touches as: "The congregation assembled as one man to the LORD" (20:1); "So the congregation sent thither" (21:10); and "Then the whole congregation sent word to the Benjaminites" (21:13). Perhaps to these editors the whole final section was important as demonstrating what had happened when "there was no king in Israel; every man did what was right in his own eyes"—viz., a degeneration which required both the subsequent monarchy and the later formation of official, priestly Judaism.

E. *HISTORICAL VALUE.* The historical value of the book of Judges lies in three areas: (*a*) its source material for determining the historical events of the period which it describes; (*b*) its preservation of fragments of literature of great antiquity; and (*c*) its insight into the social and cultural conditions of the period following the entrance into Canaan and just prior to the rise of the monarchy.

1. History of the period. At least two aspects of the stories of the judges at once raise questions concerning the historical accuracy of these accounts. One is the obviously artificial nature of the chronological scheme. This is seen both in the frequent use of forty, eighty, and twenty years—perhaps respectively indicating in round numbers one generation, two generations, or half a generation—and in the impossibility of correlating the sum total of the chronology with the other biblical or historical evidence concerning the length of the judges period.

After deliverance respectively by Othniel (3:11), Deborah (5:31), and Gideon (8:28), the land rested each time forty years; and the Philistine oppression before Samson's judgeship lasted the same number of years (13:1). For only twenty years the oppression which occasioned Deborah's exploits lasted (4:3), and Samson's judgeship was for a similar brief time (15:20; 16:31); whereas Ehud's deliverance resulted in eighty years of freedom (3:30). The other figures for periods of oppression, judgeship, or deliverance are more realistic: eight (3:8; 12:14), eighteen (3:14; 10:8), seven (6:1; 12:9), three (9:22), twenty-three (10:2), twenty-two (10:3), six (12:7), and ten (12:11).

The sum of these figures, from the second generation after Joshua (2:10; 3:8) through the career of Samson (16:31), is 410 years. This figure is far too large to square with the statement in I Kings 6:1 that Solomon began to build the temple in the 480th year after the Exodus. It seems obvious that the careers of various judges overlapped one another. *See also* CHRONOLOGY OF THE OT.

The second aspect of the stories of the judges which raises the problem of historical accuracy is the apparent schematization of the tribal origins of the various judges. Each seems to be the representative of a tribe to the total number of twelve. Thus Othniel was from Judah (1:8-15; 3:9), Ehud from Benjamin (3:15), Deborah's general Barak from Naphtali (4:4-6), Gideon from W Manasseh (6:11, 24, 34-35), Tola from Issachar (10:1), Elon from Zebulun (12:11), Abdon from Ephraim (12:13-15), and Samson from Dan (13:2, 24-25). IBZAN was probably the representative of Asher (12:8). Jair (10:3) and Jephthah (11:1) were both Gileadites, but it is possible that Jair represented N Gilead or E Manasseh (Deut. 3:13-14; Josh. 13:29-31), and that Jephthah was originally from S Gilead or Gad (Deut. 3:16; Josh. 13:24-28). Reuben or Simeon, the two remaining unrepresented tribes, might have laid claim to Shamgar, for the brief notation concerning him (Judg. 3:31) appears in the narrative immediately after the story of the conflict with Moab, whose territory was adjacent to Reuben, and Shamgar's anti-Philistine exploits could have located him geographically in the territory of Simeon.

The judges were doubtless tribal heroes portrayed as national champions delivering "all Israel." But that there was exactly one such hero from each of the tribes smacks of artificiality.

Despite these questions, however, the book of Judges is a most valuable source for reconstructing the history of the settlement of Canaan. The essential reliability of the Judges summary of the original conquest by the Israelites (ch. 1), as compared with the Joshua account, has long been maintained. Nevertheless, some recent scholarship has questioned the customary critical disparagement of Josh. 10 and pointed out that Judg. 1 is a collection of fragments rather than a unified document. Even so, the essential accuracy of the Judges picture of the Conquest as accomplished by separate tribes rather than by united Israel is unquestioned, and many of its details may be correct. *See* § C1 *above*. *See also* ISRAEL, HISTORY OF, § 3; JOSHUA, BOOK OF, § 4*a*.

As for the judges themselves, while some may be purely legendary figures, the accomplishments of such heroic persons as Deborah, Othniel, Ehud, Jephthah, and Gideon may be historical. Also there is some ground for regarding the brief fragments of information about the minor judges—Tola, Jair, Ibzan, Elon, and Abdon (10:1-5; 12:8-15)—as based upon official records concerning the office of judge in premonarchical Israel. Biblical and archaeological evidence combine to suggest the following historical reconstruction of the whole turbulent period following the initial conquest.

Perhaps early in the twelfth century B.C. the pressure of invading Philistines upon local Canaanites (1:34) caused the Danites, originally on the seacoast (5:17), to migrate to an inland N home (chs. 17–18). Except for this initial displacement, however, the Philistine occupation of the coastal plain by the mid-twelfth century seems, according to the Samson legends (chs. 13–16), at first to have resulted in free communication, trade, and even intermarriage with the Israelites, including, perhaps, remaining Danites. Such conflicts as occurred during this century were only local disputes. Samson was only to "begin to deliver Israel from the hand of the Philistines" (13:5). It was Samuel and Saul, probably spurred on by Philistine expansion activities, making use of their superior, iron-using culture, who later attempted to confine these foreigners (I Sam. 4–6; 13).

An invasion of S Judah by a foreign ruler from the Upper Euphrates, given the opprobrious Hebrew name CUSHAN-RISHATHAIM, may have taken place early in the twelfth century and been repelled by OTHNIEL (3:8-10). At about the same time a Moabite foothold farther N in W Jordan Benjaminite and Ephraimite territory was lost when Ehud treacherously assassinated the obese Moabite king Eglon (3:12-30).

Perhaps in the last quarter of the twelfth century the crucial battle celebrated in the contemporary Song of Deborah, in which native Canaanite defenders in league with invading sea peoples took their last stand against encroaching Israelites, won for the latter the coveted Plain of Esdraelon (ch. 5).

In perhaps the early eleventh century B.C. the first real defense by the Israelites of Transjordan territory was achieved by Jephthah (11:1–12:7). His repulse of invading Ammonites seems to have been effective until the days of Saul (I Sam. 11). By the middle of the eleventh century the first known raids by camel riders who penetrated from distant Midian through Israelite territory even to Philistine Gaza were an annual menace. Gideon's deliverance may be associated with a Midianite war conducted also by the Edomite king Hadad (Gen. 36:35; Judg. 6:11–8:35). So important was Gideon's success that the phrase "the day of Midian" became an idiom meaning "victory."

2. Literature of the period. One of the greatest historical contributions of the book of Judges is its preservation of fragments of literature of antiquity. Such was the memorable Song of Deborah, doubtless contemporaneous with the events, and such were Jotham's fable, Samson's riddles, and other poetic and prose fragments. *See* § D1 *above*.

3. Social and cultural conditions. The frank and colorful picture of Israel's life, when in the twelfth and eleventh centuries the Israelites were on the frontier of agricultural versus nomadic economy, appears in the book of Judges. In fact, it has been suggested that the cycle of Samson stories (chs. 13–16) provides instructive sociological material of more value to the historian than a list of conquered cities on such a significant monument as the Moabite Stone. Here was the ideal rugged folklore hero of the frontier: humorous trickster; conqueror of women, wild beasts, and warriors; possessor of enormous muscular strength, but given to selfish passion and feats of vengeance to restore injured honor. Here were local marriage customs: procurement of the bride; riddles and jesting of the bridegroom's friends during the long wedding festivities; the quick marriage of a forsaken bride to another to save face. Here were the events of a pagan religious festival: the grim sport of watching the antics of a blinded foreign slave.

The essential dangers of the era when only a loose tribal confederacy is in control are obvious: "In those days there was no king in Israel; every man did what was right in his own eyes" (17:6; 21:25). "In the days of Shamgar . . . caravans ceased and travelers kept to the byways" because of marauding bands (5:6). Harassed Israelite farmers fled into caves and mountain hideouts for fear of Midianite camel raiders (6:2-6, 11; 7:12). Blood revenge was a solemn duty (8:7-21).

Devastating tribal feuds took place, as nowhere better illustrated than in the bitter war against the Benjaminites (chs. 19–21). Tribal jealousies flared, as when the proud Ephraimites were incensed at Gideon and at Jephthah (7:24–8:3; 12:1-6). Differences of dialect between tribes were effectively used in intertribal conflict (*see* SHIBBOLETH) when Jephthah massacred Ephraimites, and Danites recognized Micah's Levite by his accent (18:3). At no time was there complete tribal unity, for even when the coalition joined Deborah and Barak against the common Canaanite enemy, a number of tribes remained aloof (5:13-18, 23).

In times of extreme crisis an outlawed harlot's son,

banished to prevent his sharing any family inheritance, could be recalled and as "ruler" be made practical dictator by popular acclaim (10:17–11:11). But neither Jephthah's nor Gideon's popularity in their hours of triumph led to any permanent common rule. In fact, the refusal of such a wealthy local potentate as Gideon to take advantage of popular appeal to inaugurate a hereditary monarchy (8:22-23) shows the true Hebrew tradition of primitive popular democracy. Its tenacity was proved by the abortive attempt at kingship on the part of Abimelech, as roundly criticized in Jotham's fable (ch. 9).

The low level of the morals of the period, even according to ancient standards, is illustrated, not only by the cruel atrocities of war, but also by the stealing of Micah's household gods (18:14-17) and the treatment of the Levite's concubine (19:22-30). Since the capture of defenseless maidens at the Shiloh festival was apparently legitimate (21:16-23), the rape of the concubine was less a sexual offense than a violation of the Bedouin law of hospitality. Similar violation of hospitality in the death of Sisera, while lauded for its patriotic motivation, was nevertheless a serious offense (4:17-22; 5:24-27).

E. *RELIGIOUS SIGNIFICANCE.* The religious significance of any such quasi-historical OT book as this one is twofold. In revealing something of the state of religious life in Israel in the period of which it speaks, it provides valuable information for a stage in the history of the religion of Israel. By its underlying presuppositions, its selection of facts, its peculiar emphases, its editorial comments, it reveals its theology, its understanding of the total revelation of God to Israel and through Israel to all mankind.

1. Religion of the period. The cultural and moral aspects of the life of Israel, described above, can only artificially be separated from the religious. But one may note the specifically cultic affairs in twelfth- and eleventh-century Israel. While certain place names were explained by etiological legends (15:9-20), other sacred spots marked the presence of deity: Deborah's palm tree (4:5); "sculptured stones" near Gilgal where God inspired Ehud (3:19, 26); the commemorative altar where the angelic messenger appeared to Gideon (6:24). The cultic center of the tribal federation probably moved from Gilgal (2:1) to Shiloh (21:12; note the annual festival in 21:19; cf. I Sam. 1:3; 2:19), but an individual tribe such as the Danites could found their own sanctuary (chs. 17–18).

The simplicity of cultic equipment and organization seems evident in Gideon's ready establishment of a Yahweh altar (6:24), his making a perhaps gold-overlaid ephod as a Yahweh symbol to memorialize his victory (8:24-27), and in Micah's use of various cult objects in his household shrine and his installing one of his sons as priest (17:1-5). The semihumorous elevation of the Levite from family to clan priesthood is an instructive chapter in the history of the slowly emerging priestly organization prior to the monarchy (17:7–18:20; *see* PRIESTS AND LEVITES).

At the simple family or local level the rarified Yahwism of the fathers was syncretistically Baalized by unconscious or semiconscious indigenous customs. Jephthah's deliberate, hardly rash, sacrifice of his virgin only child, explained as the origin of a four-day customary annual feast of lamentation (11:30-31, 34-40), was doubtless related to the prevalent Near Eastern FERTILITY CULTS.

Occasionally, however, with frenzied zeal a champion of Yahweh would arise to strike out against Baalism. Thus Gideon broke down his family's and community's Baal altar and received the name JERUBBAAL, whereas his son by a Shechemite concubine financed revolt from the Baal-berith temple treasury (6:25-32; 9:4).

It was at the seminational level that the zeal for Yahweh really counted. Thus the tribal coalition joined in Yahweh's holy war against paganism, celebrated in the Song of Deborah (ch. 5). It was not the human troops of Deborah and Barak which brought victory. Rather,

> From heaven fought the stars,
> from their courses they fought against Sisera (5:20).

It was the awful judgment of God.

Indeed, the power and the intervention in Israel's life by Yahweh were most clearly seen in the essentially charismatic nature of judgeship. While charism was evident in the account of Othniel (3:9-10), it was nowhere more clearly seen than in the story of Gideon. His call was accompanied by or verified by unusual signs—a divine messenger bringing forth divine fire, miraculously wet or dry fleece (6:11-24, 36-40). Literally, "the Spirit of the LORD clothed itself with Gideon" (vs. 34). Therefore, he could be successful against impossible odds—300 against 135,000 (8:4-10). Jephthah's charismatic leadership began with consecration in a solemn ceremony (11:10-11, 29).

Strikingly enough, Samson, a onetime folklore hero raised to religious savior, proved what God's charismatic individual should not do. The Lord's Spirit, given because of his mother's Nazirite vows and evident even in his childhood (13:2-14, 24), showed itself in mighty feats of strength (14:6, 19; 15:14). But when his uncontrolled passion made him forgetful of sacred vows, although the Lord's Spirit came surging back again in response to prayer, Samson's life story ended in grim tragedy (16:20, 28-30).

2. Prophetic criticism of culture. As it left the final editors' hands, the book of Judges was a document of prophetic protest and pride—protest against the repeated disloyalty of God's people in their frequent yielding to the temptations of Canaanite culture, pride in their God's power in his repeated victory over enemies and in his patient providence in disciplining but sustaining his own chosen children.

The basic religious concern and chief motivation of this book is the activity of Yahweh and his people in the struggle with Baalism. The problem of the settling Israelites was Canaanite culture's corrosive effect upon inherited Hebrew faith, the danger of Israel's losing the consciousness of her unique relationship to her God.

The incoming Israelites failed to obey Yahweh's command to make no covenants with local inhabitants. Hence local gods were continual snares to Israel (2:1-5). Israel repeatedly failed the test of faithfulness. Yet in crises her God heeded her prayers and raised up a succession of deliverers (2:6–3:6; 10:

6-16). But despite these lessons of history, despite continued divine patience and providence, popular degeneration sank to the depths of Benjaminite civil war when "there was no king in Israel; every man did what was right in his own eyes" (chs. 19–21).

Therefore, Israel could be saved subsequently from the corrosion of Canaanite culture only by God's anointed monarchy and especially his spokesmen the prophets (cf. 6:7-10).

The great judges were great heroes of faith (cf. their evaluation in I Sam. 12:11; Heb. 11:32), but their role in the developing life of God's people was only temporary. The period between Joshua and Samuel was seen as taking its proper place in the continuing drama of God's revelation and his people's history. Thus the book of Judges took its place in the true succession of the Former Prophets. The Latter Prophets—and the New Covenant—were yet to come.

Bibliography. Commentaries: G. F. Moore, ICC (1895), is still the most useful. C. F. Burney (2nd ed., 1930) is perhaps the most adequate. G. W. Thatcher, New Century Bible (1904). G. A. Cooke, Cambridge Bible (1913). R. Kittel, Heilige Schrift des AT (1922). V. Zapletal (1923). A. Schulz (1926). A. Cohen, Soncino Books of the Bible (1950). J. M. Myers, *IB,* vol. II (1953). See also Introductions to the literature of the OT by: S. R. Driver, W. O. E. Oesterley and T. R. Robinson, R. Pfeiffer, A. Bentzen, O. Eissfeldt, etc.

General studies: G. F. Moore in P. Haupt, ed., *The Sacred Books of the Old and New Testaments* (1898); *The Sacred Books of the OT* (1900). O. Eissfeldt, *Die Quellen des Richterbuches* (1925). H. M. Wiener, *The Composition of Judg. 2:11 to I Kings 2:46* (1929). J. Garstang, *The Foundations of Bible History: Joshua, Judges* (1931). H. Cazelles in L. Pirot and A. Robert, *Supplément au Dictionnaire de la Bible* (1949), IV, 1394-1414. N. H. Snaith in H. H. Rowley, ed., *The OT and Modern Study* (1951), pp. 90-95. Y. Kaufmann, *The Biblical Account of the Conquest of Palestine* (1953). C. A. Simpson, *Composition of the Book of Judges* (1957). For historical or cultural aspects, consult the histories by Oesterley and Robinson, Noth, and Bright, and the relevant pages in the following: J. Pedersen, *Israel: Its Life and Culture* (1926, 1940). W. F. Albright, *Archaeology and the Religion of Israel* (3rd ed., 1953); *From the Stone Age to Christianity* (2nd ed., 1957).

Special studies: O. Pretzl, "Septuaginta Problem im Buch Richter," *Biblica* (1926), pp. 233 ff, 353 ff. K. Wiese, *Zur Literarkritik des Buches der Richter,* BWANT, vol. 3 (1926). E. Robertson, "The Period of the Judges: A Mystery Period in the History of Israel," *Bulletin of the John Rylands Library,* XXX (1946), 91-114. G. E. Wright, "The Literary and Historical Problem of Joshua 10 and Judges 1," *JNES,* V (1946), 105-14. C. M. Cooper, "Theodotion's Influence on the Alexandrian Text of Judges," *JBL,* LXVII (1948), 63-68. J. Schreiner, *Septuaginta-Massora des Buches der Richter* (1957). E. Täubler, *Biblische Studien: Die Epoche der Richter* (1958).

C. F. Kraft

JUDGMENT. *See* Eschatology of the OT § 1*b;* Law in the OT.

JUDGMENT, HALL OF [אלם המשפט] (I Kings 7:7). One of Solomon's buildings. *See* Hall. For KJV "judgment hall" in John 18:28 ff, *see* Praetorium.

JUDGMENT SEAT [βῆμα, *from* βαίνω; KJV κριτήριον (Jas. 2:6; RSV COURT); *see* Court of Law)]. Alternately: THRONE (Acts 12:21); TRIBUNAL (Acts 18:12, 16-17; 25:6, 10, 17; KJV "judgment seat"); PLATFORM (I Esd. 9:42 [KJV PULPIT]; II Macc. 13:26 [KJV "judgment seat"]). Excavation has identified the βῆμα in Corinth where Paul confronted Gallio as a large, richly decorated rostrum, centrally located in the market place for hearing cases and addressing the populace (*see* Agora). For βῆμα as Pilate's seat, *see* Praetorium; as the seat of final judgment, *see* Eschatology of the NT.

Bibliography. O. Broneer, "Corinth: Center of St. Paul's Missionary Work in Greece," *BA,* XIV (1951), 91-92.

I. W. Batdorf

JUDITH jo͞o'dĭth. **1.** יהודית, a foreign wife of Esau (Gen. 26:34).

2. Ἰουδίθ, a wealthy widow whose charms brought deliverance to the Hebrew people, according to the apocryphal book (found in the Alexandrian, but not in the Jerusalem, canon) which bears her name. When drunken Holofernes, general of the invading army, invited her to his tent, she cut off his head. *See* Judith, Book of.

Judith was descended from Merari, one of the sons of Levi (Gen. 46:11; Exod. 6:16, 19). Legend tells that in the wilderness wanderings the sons of Merari carried the heavy portions of the tabernacle. In the War of the Children of Light and the Children of Darkness, the "standard of Merari" bears the legend: "Offering unto God." The name Judith (="Jewess") suggests the personification of that pious devotion to Israel which leads one to offer all to the nation.

J. C. Swaim

JUDITH, BOOK OF [Ἰουδ(ε)ίθ]. The fourth book in the OT Apoc. It tells how a small Jewish town, inspired by the example of a devout woman, resisted the overwhelming might of a heathen army.

1. Contents. Nebuchadnezzar, "king of the Assyrians, the Great King, the lord of the whole earth," decides to punish the vassal states that have disregarded his order to supply auxiliary troops to assist him in his war against the Medes. Commanded by Holofernes, the punitive expeditionary force subdues various insubordinate nations, but one people—the Jews—remains stubborn in its recalcitrance. Having encamped in the Plain of Esdraelon (*see* Jezreel), at the foot of mountainous central Palestine, Holofernes finds his advance barred by the inhabitants of Bethulia, a town commanding access to the road to Jerusalem. Surprised by this unexpected resistance of a nation of whom he has never heard, Holofernes calls the chieftains of the Moabites and the Ammonites and asks them for information about this strange people that acts unlike others. Achior, the leader of the Ammonites, tells Holofernes in a long speech the whole history of the Jews: Descended from the Chaldeans, they had turned to worship the "God of heaven [cf. Ezra 1:2; 5:12; 6:9-10; 7:21, 23; Neh. 1:4-5; 2:4; Dan. 2:19, 44], the God they had come to know," and, "as long as they did not sin against their God they prospered, for the God who hates iniquity is with them." But when they defected from God's commandments, they were destroyed and carried off as captives to a country not their own. Having repented and returned to the worship of God, they had recently been brought back to their homeland, and had rebuilt Jerusalem. (1:1–5:19.)

Having narrated this history, Achior bids Holofernes to find out "if there is any unwitting error in this people and they sin against their God"; if it is so, he will overcome them easily. But if there is no disobedience to law in their nation, Holofernes should refrain from attacking the Jews, "for their Lord will defend them, and their God will protect them, and we shall be put to shame before the whole world." Enraged by Achior's advice, Holofernes exclaims: "Who is God except Nebuchadnezzar?" He orders Achior to be bound and delivered at the foot of the steep hill on which Bethulia stands, to share the fate of the city's inhabitants when they will be destroyed by his victorious army. The Jews find Achior, and take him to Bethulia. In the meantime, the Assyrian army, 120,000 infantry and 12,000 cavalry troops, augmented by 50,000 auxiliaries from tributary Palestinian tribes, encircle the little town. The chieftains of the pagan neighbors of the Jews advise Holofernes not to risk a frontal attack on the mount on which Bethulia is built, but to seize the spring at the foot of the mountain so as to deprive the inhabitants of their water supply and force the town's capitulation through hunger and thirst. Holofernes does as he is advised. When Bethulia has been under siege for thirty-four days, the cisterns in the city are empty, and the citizens begin to lose heart. They demand of their rulers to parley for terms of surrender, for it seems better to them that they should live as slaves than die with their families in vain. Ozias (Uzziah), the town's headman, is persuaded to agree with their demand provided no relief arrives within five days. (5:20–7:32.)

Judith, a noble widow in Bethulia, as beautiful as she is pious, is perturbed by this decision. Surrender of the town would open up the way to Jerusalem; the sanctuary would thus be exposed to attack and the very existence of the nation imperiled. In an address to the rulers and citizens of Bethulia, she entreats them to persevere, and to "give thanks to the Lord our God, who is putting us to the test as he did our forefathers." Ozias commends Judith for her devotion and bids her to pray for rain so that the cisterns may be filled and the people cease to languish for lack of water. Judith has other plans. She declares that she will leave the town with her maid, and hints that God will through her accomplish Bethulia's delivery. In sackcloth and ashes she offers her prayer to God, and then she anoints herself and puts on festival garments in order to entice any man she might meet. She collects food, and calls her maid to carry it for her in a bag. Thus equipped, she asks that the gate of the city be opened, and she proceeds with her maid to the camp of the heathen enemies. (8:1–10:5.)

The Assyrian guards, entranced by her appearance, escort her upon her request to Holofernes. In the general's presence, Judith assures him that Achior has spoken the truth: the Jews will come to no harm unless they sin against God. Holofernes, however, need not be downcast, because sin has already overtaken them; they intend to appropriate consecrated food to assuage their hunger. Once they have acted on their impious intention, they will be immediately destroyed, and all their resistance will collapse. Pleased by Judith's words no less than by her appearance, Holofernes asks her to stay as his guest. Judith accepts, yet professes that she "serves the God of heaven day and night"; she will eat only of the food she has brought with her; also she must say her prayers and do her ritual washings at the appointed time. For three days she stays in the camp, leaving each night to bathe in the fountain near Bethulia. On the fourth day, Holofernes invites Judith to a banquet in his tent. Her beauty, her finery, her wit, make her the center of attraction. When the subaltern officers have left Holofernes alone with Judith, the general, the worse for drink, falls asleep. Fortified by a prayer, Judith seizes his scimitar, smites his neck twice, and severs his head from his body. She gives the head to her maid to put it in her bag for victuals. Both women leave tent and camp without arousing suspicion. This time, Judith passes the spring and returns to Bethulia. There she shows her trophy to the elders. With newly found courage, the citizens of Bethulia make a sortie at daybreak. The beleaguering army, leaderless, is put to flight, and falls an easy prey to the Jews, who pursue them beyond Damascus. A great thanksgiving takes place, and Judith sings a song of praises to the Lord. (10:6–16:24.)

"And no one ever again spread terror among the people of Israel in the days of Judith, or for a long time after her death" (16:25).

2. Literary character. The narrative is slightly disproportionate in its parts—chs. 1–3 record "Nebuchadnezzar's" wars against non-Jewish nations; chs. 4–7 describe the general situation in Judea and that in Bethulia in particular; only in ch. 8 does Judith, the heroine, enter the story—but the story is nevertheless held together by its central theme and moves swiftly forward to its climax. Strongly Jewish as the writer is in his tendency and thought, his presentation is markedly affected by Hellenistic style and motifs. Extensive speeches, or prayers, a vehicle for conveying religious lessons and exhortation, alternate with narrative sections. This stylistic device, common in Hellenistic literature, is elsewhere in the Bible employed most effectively in the Acts of the Apostles. The book of Judith has been called a "typical Hellenistic novel," which "could have found its place in a collection of novels such as that made by Parthenius." Novelistic traits are reflected in descriptive details, frequently repeated, as to the effect of Judith's beauty. The Assyrian soldiers, under her spell, lead her immediately to the general, and Holofernes, on seeing Judith, loses his head before it has been cut off. There appears to be a nucleus of fact behind the report in chs. 1–3; Holofernes (Orophernes) and Bagoas are names of Persian origin; bearers of these names are known to have taken part in a punitive expedition against Egypt under Artaxerxes III Ochus (359-338 B.C.). The rest of the story is invention. The author thought up the central figure of his story, to whom he attributed all characteristics of piety expected in his own age, and to whom he ascribed the deed of Jael (Judg. 4:21) from Israel's ancient past. Josephus, prone as he is to record Jewish deeds of bravery, never mentions Judith's heroic exploits anywhere. It seems that the writer did not intend his book to be taken as an account of actual happenings; the numerous anachronisms appear to have been intentionally introduced so as to warn readers of the fictional character of the story. As a novel the book has certain literary merits. Composed with a view to encouraging the people to offer resistance to the enemies of their religious and political liberty, it is both entertaining and edifying. The high lights of the story—namely, the speeches by Achior and Judith's prayers and speeches—are well written and express not unworthy sentiments.

3. Original language, date of composition, and purpose. Modern scholarship is agreed that the book was originally composed in Hebrew. The quotations from the OT conform, however, to LXX readings.

Though the scene is set in a time shortly after the return from the Babylonian exile, the period to which the story refers is evidently of a later date. Apparently free from foreign suzerainty, the Jews are governed by a high priest who is assisted by a senate (*see* SANHEDRIN); little towns have local councils of elders. Galilee and the coastal plain appear not yet to be settled by a Jewish population. A puzzle concerns the locating of Bethulia in what the OT called the "hill country of Ephraim." This region, at the time when the book was written, was inhabited by the SAMARITANS, who are, however, nowhere mentioned in Judith. Moabites, Ammonites, Edomites, and the inhabitants of the seacoast are named as the local enemies of the Jews—they are the same nations who figure as Israel's enemies in the Scroll of War from Qumran—but not the Samaritans. This omission is hardly fortuitous. Bethulia itself is identified by most authors with SHECHEM, which was captured in 128 B.C. by John Hyrcanus I. If the book was composed before the city was conquered, one of the aims of the writer may have been to plead with the Samaritans to make common cause with the Jews against pagan enemies. If a later date of composition is preferred, it could be argued that the omission of the Samaritans was due to the writer's conviction that the Samaritans were no longer of any consequence.

Most modern scholars have placed the origin of the book in the period of success of the Maccabean revolt, somewhere between the years 150 and 125 B.C. This view has been challenged; Grintz assigns the story to Persian times, in the reign of Artaxerxes Ochus. Yet, though recollections of this monarch's campaign in the W provinces of his empire may have furnished the author of Judith with materials for chs. 1-3, the rest of the story can hardly be fitted within that period. No Persian king of the Achaemenian (*Hakhāmanishya*) dynasty could have served as a model for "Nebuchadnezzar," who is said to have wanted "to destroy all the gods of the land, so that all nations should worship Nebuchadnezzar alone" (3:8). This description appears rather to suit Antiochus IV Epiphanes. A Hebrew midrash, reflecting the story of Judith but much abridged and told with more realism (*see bibliography*), designates Judith's victim by the title *hēgemōn* and assigns the story to the time of Seleucid oppression. This setting may well be indicated both by the book's spirited determination to resist a numerically superior foe and by the description of the leading persons among Israel's enemies. "Holofernes" possibly stands for NICANOR 1 (cf. II Macc. 15:30), the "Assyrians" for Seleucid Syrians, while "Nineveh" might represent Antioch. The plot as a whole portrays a time of national distress for the Jews ("a people with no strength or power for making war" [5:23]), when partisan resistance—even isolated action by women—would have appeared a justifiable means in the struggle for self-preservation. Although the main elements of his story are fictional, the intention of the writer was to celebrate recent victories, to entertain as well as to inspire resistance.

4. Theology. Judith exemplifies a type of piety which lays great stress on rigorous compliance with ritual requirements. The heroine prepares for her action by fasting and prayer; she religiously observes the sabbaths, the festivals, and the days of the new moon; she eats only food that has been ritually prepared. She says her prayers at the appointed time of day and does her washings regularly. This emphasis on ritual should not, however, be allowed to obscure the genuine spiritual sentiment that comes to the fore in Judith's prayer (9:11-14 orig. tr.):

> Your strength is not in numbers
>   nor your might in stout men;
> You are the God of the lowly,
>   a helper of the oppressed . . . ,
> Protector of the neglected,
>   the savior of those without hope.
> Yes—God of my father,
>   and God of the inheritance of Israel,
> Lord of the heavens and of the earth,
>   creator of the waters,
> King of all your creation,
>
> . . . .
>
> Make every nation and every tribe of yours realize
>   that you are God,
> The God of all power and might,
>   and that the people of Israel have none to protect
>   them but you.

There is a keen awareness of God's interest in human affairs. Men's deeds reap their reward. Man is free in his decisions, and accountable for his actions.

The modern reader may feel repelled by the writer's immoderate praise of a woman who resorts to such doubtful means as Judith is reported to have used; he extols the virtue of a woman who first excites the passion of a man and then kills him in his sleep. The story has to be understood against the background of the time which it describes—a period of history in which the Jewish nation depended for its survival upon the resourcefulness and even ruthlessness of individuals.

The work contains no explicit mention of the resurrection faith, but in the triumphal ode at the conclusion a Day of Judgment is mentioned. The Almighty will avenge every evil deed, will put "fire and worms" in the flesh of sinners, and "they shall weep in pain for ever"—an idea elaborated in certain NT descriptions of hell.

Judith's punctilious observance of ritual laws mirrors a type of Pharisaic piety. This does not mean that the Pharisees were on the whole narrow-minded and bloodthirsty. It was also a Pharisee of whom the Talmud records the saying: "The descendants of Haman learned Torah; the Holy One, blessed be He, decided to take them under the wings of the Shechinah" (T.B. Sanh. 96*b*).

5. Canonicity. The Hebrew original of Judith is lost, though later midrashim, based on the story, are extant. No fragments from the book have come to light among the DEAD SEA SCROLLS. One naturally wonders why ESTHER came to enjoy canonical status in the Hebrew canon in preference to Judith. From an aesthetic and literary viewpoint, the story of Judith is of better quality, is told with more verve, and in places rises to true poetry. Both books are similar in aim and spirit. The eclipse of Judith may be due partly to the fact that the story is localized in a small place, in Samaritan territory, while Esther has its setting at the center of the known world, at the court of a Persian king. Of greater importance may be the consideration that the story of Esther is associated with an annual feast in the Jewish calendar. The book of Judith, having no such connection with practical life, soon fell into neglect.

Of the Greek translation, which was made at an early date, there exist three recensions that differ in minor details. There is also a Syr. version and an OL version, both of which are based on the text of one of the three Greek recensions. The Vulg. text differs from all these versions and offers a considerably abridged text with numerous transpositions.

Jerome, in the Vulg. preface to Judith, stated that the Council of Nicea had included the book among holy scriptures. The Forty-seventh Canon of the Third Council of Carthage lists the book among canonical writings. The Council of Trent re-emphasized its inspired character.

The book now enjoys canonical status in the Roman Catholic and the Greek Orthodox churches.

Bibliography. O. F. Fritzsche, *Kurzgefasstes exegetisches Handbuch*, pt. 2 (1853). For the Hebrew midrash reflecting the story of Judith, see A. Jellinek, *Beth Ha-Midrasch* (1853-78); German trans. in A. Wünsche, *Aus Israels Lehrhallen*, vol. II (1908). E. Schürer, *A History of the Jewish People*, div. 2, vol. III (1886), pp. 32-37. A. V. Scholz, *Kommentar zum Buche Judith* (1887). C. J. Ball in H. Wace, *The Holy Bible, Apoc.* (1888). M. Löhr in E. F. Kautzsch, *Die Apokryphen und Pseudepigraphen des AT* (1900). C. Steuernagel, *Lehrbuch* (1912). A. E. Cowley in R. H. Charles, *The Apoc. and Pseudep. of the OT* (1913). O. Eissfeldt, *Einleitung in das AT* (1st ed., 1934; 2nd ed., 1956). E. J. Goodspeed, *The Story of the Apoc.* (1939). C. C. Torrey, *The Apocryphal Literature* (1945). F. Stummer, *Geographie des Buches Judith* (1947). R. H. Pfeiffer, *History of NT Times* (1949). J. Klausner, *Historiyah shel habayith hasheni*, III (1951-52), 184-88. J. M. Grintz, *Sefer Yehudith* (1957).

P. WINTER

JUEL. KJV Apoc. form of JOEL.

JULIA jōōl'yə [Ἰουλία; Lat. *Julia*] (Rom. 16:15). A Christian woman, recipient of a greeting. Cf. vs. 7, where this name is a variant reading for Ἰουνιᾶν.

F. W. GINGRICH

JULIUS jōōl'yəs [Ἰούλιος]. A Roman centurion, assigned the task of escorting Paul from Palestine to Rome. Julius is a common Roman name, made famous by the Julian family, of which Julius Caesar (*see* CAESAR, JULIUS) was the most distinguished member. The Julius mentioned by name in Acts 27:1, 3, 11, and referred to in vs. 43 and (according to some late MSS) in 28:16, was a CENTURION of the AUGUSTAN COHORT stationed at Caesarea on the coast of Palestine. Centurions were advanced in the Roman army by being transferred from cohort to cohort and from legion to legion, in order to allow a centurion to move from commanding troops at the rear of a legion to the highest ranking post open to a centurion: officer of the first *centuria* (one hundred men) in the first cohort (six hundred men) at the front of a legion (six thousand men). Therefore, even if we knew whether his *centuria* from the Augustan Cohort was composed of Syrian troops or men from Samaria, we should still be unable to determine the land of origin of Julius the centurion.

Paul had been accused by some of the Jewish leaders of being a disturber of the peace and of having attempted to profane the temple of Jerusalem (Acts 24:1-9). Hearings before the Roman governors had been inconclusive, and Paul had exercised his right as a Roman citizen to appeal to Caesar himself (25:8-12).

The governor, Festus, and the puppet king, Agrippa, agreed that Paul should be sent to Rome for a hearing before Nero (Acts 26:30-32). It was in the custody of Julius that Paul was placed for the trip to Rome (27:1). The journey was made in a merchant ship, rather than a military vessel, so that some of Paul's companions were able to accompany him (vs. 2). Furthermore, Julius' kindness and sympathy for Paul were so great that he allowed the prisoner to go ashore at Sidon, where he visited friends and received from them certain kindnesses, before resuming the journey westward toward Rome.

Bad weather delayed the travelers beyond the time of year when it was safe to travel in the open Mediterranean. Paul's advice to winter in the harbor of Fair Havens in Crete was ignored by the centurion, who seems to have been eager to get his prisoners to their destination in Rome (Acts 27:9-11). Later, after a storm had driven the ship on rocks off Malta, Julius restrained the soldiers aboard from killing Paul and the other prisoners in order to prevent their escape. Acts tells us nothing further about Julius, except in the MSS of the Western text type (*see* TEXT, NT), where Julius is reported to have turned Paul over to an officer charged with responsibility for prisoners from the provinces (28:16).

Bibliography. T. R. S. Broughton in F. J. Foakes-Jackson and K. Lake, eds., *Beginnings of Christianity*, V (1933), 427-45; vol. IV gives a full statement about the allusions in Acts to the Roman army.

H. C. KEE

JUNGLE OF THE JORDAN [גאון ירדן, pride of the Jordan]; KJV SWELLING OF JORDAN in Jer. 12:5; 49:19; 50:44; PRIDE OF JORDAN in Zech. 11:3. Through the centuries the Jordan has eroded a narrow, winding bed, where the tropical heat and seasonal flooding combine to produce a tangled thicket of tamarisk, willows, and other shrubs. It was a haunt of wild beasts (Jer. 49:19; 50:44; Zech. 11:3) and a place of danger (Jer. 12:5). *See also* JORDAN.

L. E. TOOMBS

JUNIAS jōō'nĭ əs [Ἰουνιᾶς] (Rom. 16:7); KJV JUNIA —ə [Ἰουνία]. A Jewish Christian, fellow prisoner of Paul. If the name is masculine (so RSV), it is found nowhere else than in this passage, and must be a short form of Junianus. Grammatically it might be a feminine (so KJV), though this seems inherently less probable, partly because the person is referred to as an apostle. F. W. GINGRICH

JUNIPER. KJV translation of רתם, *rōthem* (RSV BROOM), in I Kings 19:4-5; Job 30:4; Ps. 120:4. This is a mistaken translation, but the ערער, *'ar'ār,* of Jer. 17:6 (SHRUB; KJV HEATH) and probably the ערוער, *'arô'ēr,* of Jer. 48:6 (emended to WILD ASS, reading עריד, *'ārôd;* KJV HEATH) refer to the *Juniperus phoenicia* L., as is evident from the plant's wilderness associations in Jer. 17:6. The Arabs call this shrub *'ar'ar.* The RSV emendation in Jer. 48:6 (with the LXX and Aq.) to "wild ass" seems unnecessary. The city AROER was perhaps named after this shrub.

The juniper of the Lebanons is a large, timber-producing tree (*Juniperus excelsa* Bilb.), which some scholars would identify with the Hebrew *berôš* (*see* FLORA § A9*g*), but *see* PINE.

See also FLORA §§ A9*h, k.*

Bibliography. I. Löw, *Die Flora der Juden,* III (1924), 33-38.

J. C. TREVER

JUPITER jōō'pə tər. The great sky-god of the Latin peoples, worshiped on every hilltop in ancient Italy. Identified with Zeus, he took on many of the anthropomorphic traits of the Greek deity, together

Courtesy of the Arab Information Center, New York

33. Ruins of the temple of Jupiter at Baalbek

with his myths. The Latin god is not mentioned in the Bible, but through the influence of the Vulg. and also of the classical practice of the period, the KJV uses his name to render that of ZEUS (Acts 14:12-13; II Macc. 6:2).

Fig. JUP 33. F. W. BEARE

JUSHAB-HESED jōō'shĭb hē'sĕd [יושב־חסד, may covenant love be returned] (I Chr. 3:20). A son of Zerubbabel.

JUSTICE. *See* LAW; RIGHTEOUSNESS; PEACE IN THE OT.

JUSTICE (OFFICER). The translation of πράκτωρ in Luke 12:58 (KJV OFFICER). The Greek word is generally used for an OFFICER of the court who executes sentences, collects fines and revenue, and arraigns prisoners. He is always under a judge's authority. He may be best considered a bailiff.

C. U. WOLF

JUSTIFICATION, JUSTIFY. In biblical thought, the fundamental moral need of man. When rightly understood, the terminology of "justification," though forensic, is seen to describe the basic diagnosis of the human problem and the divinely provided solution of it.

The clearest formulation of the biblical doctrine of justification comes from Paul, whose distinctive thought it expresses.

1. Terminology. The Hebrew root צדק, "just," is used with reference to rulers and judges and pre-eminently to Yahweh, in the sense of seeing that men get their right, and this can refer to both accuser and accused. The prominent sense, however, is seeing that justice is done to the accused (e.g., Pss. 35:24-28; 40:9-17). As a divine activity this takes the form of punishment for sin (Isa. 5:13-16; 10:22; cf. 42:24; Dan. 9:7), but it may also be seen as the vindication of God's oppressed people (Isa. 42:6; 46:13; 62:1-2). The word may be rendered "deliverance" (as in Isa. 51:1, 5, 8; cf. 41:10, where "victorious right hand" is literally "right hand of my צדק"). In later writers the meaning tends to rise above strict justice into something like benevolence, and it is often in the same context as faithfulness, mercy, etc. (e.g., Ps. 40:9-10).

The sense of vindication is clearest in the causative form of the verb, which means "put in the right, give verdict in favor of." It is a bad judge who will pronounce in favor of a wicked man (Exod. 23:7; Prov. 17:15; Isa. 5:23). But the distinctive teaching of the OT comes out in reference to Yahweh's dealing with refractory Israel. God's problem, if we may so put it, is that his people are often guilty, and he must give a verdict against them, because he is just. But equally because he is just, and because the Hebrew conception of justice was a redeeming and not merely a punishing activity, God's punitive judgments are not final, but the means to ultimate redemption. Thus, in a certain sense, he does "justify the ungodly" (Rom. 4:5), though to say no more than this would be to caricature the OT doctrine.

The Greek δικαιόω means "treat rightly" (persons), "regard as right" (things). Its cognate words, particularly the noun δικαιοσύνη, express "justice" or "rightness" more or less in the modern English sense. NT usage is not that of secular Greek, but is strongly influenced by the fact that the LXX used these Greek terms to translate the above Hebrew terms, and thus carried over their connotation into the NT (and incidentally made it difficult for Greek Christians to understand Paul's teaching on justification). The LXX used δικαιόω to translate the causative Hebrew verb הצדיק, and δικαιοσύνη to translate the two cognate nouns צדק, צדקה. This is the background of Paul's usage. The meaning "declare innocent, regard as in the right," for δικαιόω is found in Matt. 12:37; Luke 18:14; I Cor. 4:4—a less theological sense than is characteristic of Paul. *See* RIGHTEOUSNESS.

2. Biblical usage in general. The dominant biblical thought forming the background for the language of justification may be summarized as follows: God is righteous: "Shall not the Judge of all the earth do right?" (Gen. 18:25). The main contribution of the prophets was their moralizing of the primitive conception of divine holiness (especially in the pre-exilic period; but cf. also Deut. 32:4; Job 8:3; 37:23; Pss. 50:6; 89:14; 143:1-2; Isa. 45:18-24). This divine justice involved obligations upon man, at least upon Israel, who were in covenant with Yahweh. Israel's failure to rise to these obligations caused Yahweh to punish them, precisely because he was God, and a righteous God at that (cf. Gen. 3; Jer. 7; Ezek. 5; and frequently). After this lesson had been learned through the calamity of 586 B.C. (cf. Isa. 42:24; Ezek. 39:21-24), further reflection raised doubts whether man could achieve the right living God required. God was not insensitive to man's efforts after righteousness, but these efforts fell short. Right relationship with God is not attainable by observing statutes and judgments—Israel does not even keep the first commandment, but goes "a-whoring" after other gods (cf. Hosea, Jeremiah, and Ezekiel)—nor does the elaborate postexilic system of sacrifice really avail (cf. Ps. 143:2; Isa. 64:6).

Thus there is need for divine intervention and help if man is to attain righteousness. Biblical faith holds on to this possibility. God will vindicate his people (Isa. 50:7-9). He will perform an act of deliverance or justification (the meaning of the key verb הצדיק, as explained in § 1 *above*). Second Isaiah is very significant on this point (cf. Isa. 46:13; 51:4-8). God is Savior (Isa. 43:11), and has not forgotten Israel involved in the consequences of her sins. The book of Job, too, has special significance. It is concerned, not only with the problem of suffering, but even more with the problem of righteousness: How can a man be just before God? (9:2; 25:4). Job is too involved in the difficulties, too aware of the complexities that life's conditions present to the idealist, to be satisfied with the orthodoxy created by the prophetic doctrine that sin is always punished. This orthodoxy, as voiced by his "comforters," who argue that Job's sufferings must be the consequence of his sins, was too easy a dogma, supported perhaps by superficial evidence but not by the deeper realities of man's exposure to the slings and arrows of outrageous fortune.

3. Pauline usage. The chief NT spokesman of salvation in terms of justification is Paul. Presupposing universal sinfulness (Rom. 3:23), he teaches that a right relationship with God must precede right treatment of one's fellow man; and he proclaims as his gospel a divine offer of righteousness for all who take God seriously and give up the assumption that moral effort alone can achieve righteousness. Paul's teaching may be considered under four headings:

a. Sin. In Paul's usage sin is the objective power which impedes man's endeavors to obey the will of God. It is not synonymous with guilt or with the individual's consciousness of sin. It is not individual and subjective, but corporate and objective, a condition of human existence as such (Rom. 3:23; 5:12; cf. Ps. 51:1-5). Humanity as a whole, and without exception, is involved in sin, precisely as it is liable to death. The classic statement of this view is Rom. 5:12-21, which takes it as axiomatic that sin and death mutually imply each other.

Paul is not concerned primarily with sinfulness or remorse. If he wants to deal with these, he speaks of sin's being "imputed" (RSV "counted"—i.e., entered to someone's debit account; Rom. 5:13), or "coming alive" (7:9), or being "shown up" (7:13). In these contexts law—i.e., moral obligation—is the causative factor which awakens the sense of guilt.

If man then is to be "justified," he must be delivered, not merely from a bad conscience, but from the whole nexus of involvement in imperfection, finitude, and death; from what Paul in one place (Rom. 8:21) calls the bondage of corruption, and what he describes more objectively as experience of a strangling power which frustrates his very determination to do good (Rom. 7:15-20). God has provided this deliverance through Christ as his agent and through Christ's death as the means (Rom. 3:24-25; 5:6-9). *See* SIN.

b. Law. Law, meaning predominantly the Mosaic legislation, but also any moral code and the sense of obligation in whatsoever form apprehended, is not in Pauline teaching a means by which man either (ethically speaking) attains goodness or (religiously speaking) secures right relationship with his Maker (cf. Heb. 7:19).

Simply to know what ought to be done does not automatically convey the will and power to do it. In Pauline thought on this problem law was never intended to produce goodness (Rom. 3:21, 28; 4:14; Gal. 3:21). Its function was a more subsidiary one. This was a dangerous admission to make for a Hebrew whose whole religion was based on the axiom that God's holiness was a moral holiness. Nevertheless, this is Paul's interpretation of how the moral struggle had been resolved for him by his experience of divine grace (Rom. 3:20; Gal. 2:21; 3:11-13, 21-24).

The law brings wrath (Rom. 4:15). Wrath means the consequences of sin, considered not simply as objective penalties such as moral degradation (e.g., Rom. 1:21-32) or ultimately death (Rom. 6:23), but as the divine reaction to sin (Rom. 1:18; 5:9; *see* WRATH). The law actually causes sins (Rom. 5:20 ["Law came in, to increase the trespass"]; cf. Gal. 3:19). The meaning of these provocative statements must be that simultaneously with the awareness of goodness, which a moral code brings, there comes also knowledge of badness; and moral awareness—not the actual code, but the faculty within man—

inevitably carries with it exposure to temptation, so that in practice knowledge of law has as its consequence temptation and submission to temptation—viz., transgression (Rom. 7:7-11). This sequence is familiar to psychology, and daily experience provides abundant confirmation of the truth of Paul's argument. Law imposes a kind of tyranny on mankind, who feel the obligation to obey, but are impotent to fulfil it regularly (Rom. 6:16-23; 8:1-4, 15; Gal. 4:1-9; 4:21–5:1).

Nevertheless, law is not satanic. It is part of God's providential ordering of human affairs (Rom. 7:12-16, 22). The effects of law's domination are intended to bring man to the point where he will have no illusions about his capabilities, but will resign himself (Rom. 7:13*b*, 24) and accept God's offer of superhuman power, by which alone the requirements of righteousness can be met and the limitations arising from the weakness of human nature overcome (Rom. 7:25–8:4). Thus law has a definite function—not, indeed, of bestowing the salvation man needs, but of preparing man for it, of leading him, as it were, to where it can happen, of being "our custodian until Christ came" (Gal. 3:23-25). It is a witness laying out evidence that God's full redemption or gift of righteousness is on the way (Gal. 3:21-22). *See* LAW.

c. Faith. Faith for Paul was the primary move on man's part toward acceptance of the righteousness which God freely offers. The possibility of righteousness (justification) for man depends, objectively, on God's gracious initiative; and, subjectively, on man's response to that initiative. This response is what Paul means by FAITH. Thus he can write that we are justified by grace (Rom. 3:24), and also that we are justified by faith (vss. 26-28; 5:1; Gal. 2:16; 3:24). Faith means taking God's promise of salvation with simple seriousness, believing that he was savingly operating in the ministry, death, and resurrection of Christ. Faith is centered on Christ (Gal. 2:16), more particularly on his self-sacrifice at Calvary, which Paul conceives as provision of atoning blood (Rom. 3:25). Such faith results in salvation and justification (Rom. 10:9-10). The divine righteousness which is revealed to men is communicated "through faith for faith" (Rom. 1:17). Faith can be said to take the place of the righteousness supposedly attained by "works of law," in the sense that God can do something with a man who trusts him, but can do nothing with one who submits his own moral performance as the basis of acceptance with God, because that performance is nonexistent in God's judgment, and the merit imaginary.

d. Variation of meaning. The actual word δικαιοσύνη in Paul's usage, especially in Romans, is not free from ambiguity. Strictly speaking, three senses can be distinguished—the theological, the forensic, and the ethical. But the way Paul's mind moves from one to the other is often confusing, and the precise meaning of a particular passage may be difficult to determine. Paul is not a precise writer, even when handling terms which are fundamental to his argument.

The variation of meaning in Romans may be indicated as follows: The argument opens at 1:17 with the grand affirmation that a righteousness which is divine in origin is being revealed. The present tense is to be noted, as implying that this revelation is a continuous process. Elsewhere we learn that the point of origin is the cross and resurrection of Christ (Rom. 3:24; 10:9). Comparison with the Synoptic gospels shows that Paul's doctrine of divine righteousness revealed or communicated to man is his restatement of what Christ himself proclaimed as a "coming" of God's kingdom.

This righteousness of God is an activity, not an attitude or quality. It means God's dealing with the human situation where righteousness has proved unattainable. The best human ethics has assumed that the good life consists of doing (Rom. 2:13); but man has to learn that it is possible only on the basis of God's gift (3:24; 5:17), the essential contribution on man's side being, not works, but faith—i.e., a basic attitude of gratitude and receptiveness which recognizes that God has taken the initiative in providing moral incentive. This is the divine GRACE (χάρις; Rom. 5:15).

This is the main presupposition of Paul's thought. But Paul is not insensitive to the ordinary ethical connotation of δικαιοσύνη, and he sometimes uses the word with this meaning in reference to men—viz., of moral goodness, though not perfection. He is not limited to the sense of δικαιοσύνη as a mere status divinely imposed, but unrelated to man's moral experience, which is what scholastic subtlety has sometimes made of Paul's doctrine. He can use it of real moral achievement (e.g., Rom. 5:15-21, where the parallelism between goodness and life and sin and death is very marked; 6:11-19, where justification is tending to be identified with SANCTIFICATION; 8:4*a* ["just requirement," δικαίωμα]; 8:10 [here clarity is sacrificed for the sake of neat antithesis]). The nonmoral, purely theological sense is dominant in 3:21-26; 5:1, 9. The Greek aorist tense in 5:1 ("since we are justified") implies that the justification is past; it has already secured a standing in God's grace (vs. 2); what is still future is "sharing the glory of God," which unredeemed mankind fall short of (3:23)—viz., that divine image in man which sin effaces. The recovery of this image is "our hope" (5:2) and the ultimate outcome of our justification (notice the future tenses in 5:9-10, 17, 19). In Rom. 9:30 we see how Paul can pass from the moral to the theological sense of righteousness within a single verse. But whatever sense is uppermost in his mind, Paul always implies that the righteousness which is part of the believer's experience is due to God's gift rather than his own endeavors. There is no room for self-congratulation (Rom. 3:27), which is encouraged by moralistic religions like Judaism. By Jewish standards Paul had himself claimed perfection (Phil. 3:6: "as to righteousness under the law blameless"), but he gave up this claim in the light of his experience as a Christian (vs. 12).

4. Summary. The forensic metaphor is dropped, and even strict morality transcended, in what the Bible says about God's dealing with sinful man. The comparison of God to a judge carries us part way, but the divine צדק, or righteousness or justification, means much more than punishment of sin. It means that activity wherein God restores the sinner to goodness. This is the deepest insight of the OT and the real truth underlying the logic of the Letter to the Romans. God puts in the way of righteousness men who can claim no actual righteousness but who offer a simple coin stamped on one side PENITENCE and on the other FAITH. Man's ultimate perfection is the gift of God.

Bibliography. E. D. Burton, *Galatians* (1921), pp. 460-74; C. H. Dodd, *The Bible and the Greeks* (1935), pp. 42-59; V. Taylor, *Forgiveness and Reconciliation* (1941), pp. 34-82; N. H. Snaith, *Distinctive Ideas of the OT* (1944), pp. 51-78, 161-73; R. Bultmann, *Theologie des neuen Testaments* (1948), pp. 270-80 (trans. K. Grobel; 1952). E. C. BLACKMAN

JUSTUS jŭs'təs [Ἰοῦστος; Lat. *Justus*]. **1.** A surname of Joseph Barsabbas (Acts 1:23; *see* BARSABBAS), a candidate (with Matthias) for the place of Judas Iscariot among the Twelve.

2. Titius Justus (Acts 18:7), a "worshiper of God" who invited the Christians of Corinth to meet in his house when they could no longer meet in the synagogue. His name is given in the KJV simply as Justus, and in some MSS as Titus Justus. Goodspeed (*see below*) would identify him with the Gaius of Rom. 16:23, in whose house the Corinthian church met. In this case Gaius would be his praenomen, Titius his nomen, and Justus his cognomen.

3. A surname of Jesus, who is mentioned by Paul in Col. 4:11 as one of the few Jewish Christians who worked with him and were a comfort to him.

Bibliography. E. J. Goodspeed, "Gaius Titius Justus," *JBL*, 69 (1950), 382-83. F. W. GINGRICH

JUTTAH jŭt'ə [יוטה, extended, inclined] (Josh. 15:55; 21:16). A city of Judah in the SE hill-country district of Maon; identified with Yatta, *ca.* 5½ miles SW of Hebron. Its assignment to the family of Aaron made it one of the Levitical cities (Josh. 21:16; it is omitted in the parallel I Chr. 6:59).

Eusebius says that Jettan (Ἰέτταν=Juttah) was a very large Jewish village eighteen (Roman) miles from Eleutheropolis (Beit Jibrin) in the middle of the Darome (the Negeb).

A pious tradition once associated Juttah with the city of Judah in the hill country in which Mary visited Elizabeth (Luke 1:39 ff), but most scholars feel there is little substance to this tradition.

V. R. GOLD